Y0-CCI-334

THE PHILO INDEX

THE PHILO INDEX

A Complete Greek Word Index to the Writings of Philo of Alexandria

Peder Borgen
Kåre Fuglseth
Roald Skarsten

William B. Eerdmans Publishing Company
Grand Rapids, Michigan / Cambridge, U.K.

BRILL
Leiden / Boston / Köln

Published jointly 2000 by
Wm. B. Eerdmans Publishing Company
255 Jefferson Ave. S.E., Grand Rapids, Michigan 49503
and by
Koninklijke Brill NV
Leiden, the Netherlands

Printed in the United States of America

05 04 03 02 01 00 5 4 3 2 1

Library of Congress Cataloging-in-Publication Data

Eerdmans ISBN 0-8028-3883-9
Brill ISBN 90 04 11477 7

CONTENTS

Introduction VI

Abbreviations XI

Α 1

Β 62

Γ 68

Δ 80

Ε 100

Ζ 160

Η 162

Θ 168

Ι 175

Κ 181

Λ 203

Μ 210

Ν 231

Ξ 236

Ο 237

Π 264

Ρ 305

Σ 307

Τ 327

Υ 341

Φ 349

Χ 359

Ψ 366

Ω 368

Introduction

1. General description

This word index contains all the Greek words in the writings of Philo of Alexandria (20 BCE?–40 CE?), main fragments included. It is a product of the Norwegian 'Philo Concordance Project', a project headed by Peder Borgen (University of Trondheim). Other participants in the project have been Roald Skarsten (University of Bergen) and Kåre Fuglseth (University of Trondheim).

The text base is established on four text editions:

1. Leopold Cohn and Paul Wendland (eds.), 1896–1915, *Philonis Alexandrini opera quae supersunt.* G. Reimer, Berlin.
2. F. H. Colson, 1941, *Hypothetica* and *De Providentia* in the Philo–edition of the Loeb Classical Library (volume IX), Harvard University Press, Cambridge, Massachusetts and William Heinemann, London.
3. Françoise Petit, 1978, *Quaestiones in Genesim et in Exodum. Fragmenta Graeca.* Éditions du Cerf, Paris.
   These fragments and the fragments in the Loeb edition (volume IX) were copied from the *Thesaurus Linguae Graecae* (TLG) compact disk (CD disk #D) published by the University of California, Irvine, 1992, with permission.
4. Joseph Paramelle, 1984, *Philon d'Alexandrie Quaestiones in Genesim. Liber 2, 1–7. Polyglot.* P. Cramer. Genève.

2. History of the Project

The Philo Concordance Project was initiated by Peder Borgen and Roald Skarsten already in the late 1960s at the University of Bergen when the use of computers in the Humanities was still in its infancy. The project has been funded by the Norwegian Council for Research in the Humanities and it has developed in three stages:

1) 1970–73

A machine–readable text of Philo's writings was assembled based on the text in the Cohn–Wendland edition of Philo manuscripts, and a Key–Word–In–Context (KWIC) concordance was produced by Roald Skarsten. In this concordance the words were organised mechanically, on the basis of the Greek alphabetic order of the text–forms ('tokens'). Two copies were printed in 1974, typed with Greek letters.[1]

Later, some words were completely lemmatised and tagged in context and all words were automatically organised based upon this initial lemmatisation and tagging by Roald Skarsten.

2) 1990–93

On the initiative of Peder Borgen, the Norwegian Council for Research in the Humanities, decided in 1989 to fund the completion of the project. Kåre Fuglseth, Roald Skarsten and Richard Holton Pierce co–operated in developing new programs, the words not lemmatised initially were lemmatised, and Kåre Fuglseth checked all the words. The texts of *Hypothetica*, *De Providentia* and the *Quaestiones* fragments including the unidentified fragments were added, lemmatised and tagged.[2]

3) After 1993

The database was further checked and corrected and a preliminary printout with vocabulary and references was produced from the database in 1997 by Kåre Fuglseth and published by the Department of Religious Studies at the University of Trondheim (NTNU).[3] The text from Paramelle *Quaestiones in Genesim* was included into the database and lemmatised.

3. Explanations

From database to print

We have lemmatised the words with computer based searching in mind, and the transformation of the electronic database to a printed edition has resulted in solutions related to that fact. The database contains much information that is not easily represented in a printed edition like this index. In our electronic database each entry has several 'fields' containing the necessary information, *e.g.* one field for the text form or token and one for the main chosen lexicon form of that token, the 'lemma'. In addition, there are also fields

[1] See Roberto Radice and David T. Runia (eds.), 1988, *Philo of Alexandria. An Annotated Bibliography 1936–1986*. Leiden, Supplements to Vigiliae Christianae. Klijn and Brill, p. 49.

[2] QE, QG, QE isf, QG isf (isf = Incertae sedis fragmenta, 'unidentified fragments'), cf. Petit *Quaestiones*.

[3] See the book review of the index in David T. Runia, 1998, '*A New Philo Word Index*'. Studia Philonica Annual 10, pp. 131–134.

containing supplementary information, *e.g.* one field for alternative lemmas. In this way the electronic search–possibilities have been increased.

- In this printed edition a supplementary lemma is put in brackets behind the main lemma entry, *e.g.* ἀγήραος (ἀγήρως) ('undying').
- The Philo manuscripts may use different spellings for the same word. For instance, both ἀκράχολος and ἀκρόχολος ('passionate') are found. Electronic searches for every occurrence of such words are difficult. In our electronic database each variant is located under the respective lemma, and the alternative spelling of the word is displayed in a supplementary field. In this printed edition such variants of a lemma have been put between brackets behind the main lemma form.
- Contracted words have been kept separate in the database, but have only one entry in this edition. When words are contracted with καί and ὁ, the καί and ὁ are placed in the supplementary field of the database, *e.g.* τἀγαθά has both ἀγαθός and ὁ, while κἀγαθία has both ἀγαθία and καί. In this printed edition καί and ὁ in contracted forms are put in brackets behind the main lemma of that token. Thus the entry ἀγαθός (ὁ) in this printed edition means that at least one of the references in the list has ὁ in a supplementary field in the electronic database.
- Lemmas with several meanings (homographs) have not been differentiated, *e.g.* εἰμί or εἶμι in compound verbs. The meanings of these forms are found by seeing the word in context.
- Several textforms or tokens that can be searched in the electronic version are not found in this printed edition, *e.g.* verbal adjectives and forms of ἀγαθός (see below).
- The references to the high–frequency words δέ, καί and ὁ are omitted in this printed edition.

Main lemmatising principles

- The lemma forms are mostly in accordance with the dictionary forms of the *Greek–English Lexicon*, H.G. Liddell, R. Scott and H. Jones, 1940, 9. edition, The Clarendon Press, Oxford (= LSJ). This means that we do not use Attic forms, *e.g.* διαταράξῃ (token form in *Legatio ad Gaium* § 337) becomes διαταράσσω (lemma–form) and not διαταράττω ('confound').
- Verbs, which in Philo only occur in middle form, are lemmatised in accordance with their respective active forms and entries of LSJ.

- When LSJ employs a middle form only, and Philo clearly employs an active form, *e.g.* χαρίζω in stead of χαρίζομαι ('to show favour'), we follow the use in the Philo text.
- Verbal adjectives are normally lemmatised under their verbal origin, not as adjectives (in accordance with the practice of LSJ).
- All forms of ἀγαθός (comparative and superlative) are lemmatised under ἀγαθός (contrary to LSJ).
- Forms of *εἴδω are lemmatised both as εἶδον and as οἶδα, also in compound verbs of these forms, *e.g.* you will find both συνεῖδον and συνοράω.
- Similarly, the reader will find both λέγω and εἶπον, ἐσθίω and φαγεῖν.
- Compound adverbs and particles are not split up here, *e.g.* μεντοί (contrary to LSJ).

Technical matters

- The abbreviations and their full Latin titles are listed below.
- The paragraphs are normally denoted by numbers. However, in the fragments of the *Quaestiones* (QG, QE, QG isf and QE isf) there may also be a letter *(e.g.* 1:1b) in the reference, agreeing with the practice in Petit *Fragmenta Graeca* (based again on the order of the Armenian version of QE and QG). The references with asterisks, QG 4:7*, 8* and 9*, refer to Greek fragments of *lacunae* in the Armenian version (see Petit *Fragmenta Graeca*, p. 199).
- The *Quaestiones* text published by Paramelle containing QG 2, 1–7, are denoted with 'Par' in brackets behind the reference to QG, *e.g.* QG (Par) 2:1.
- The frequency numbers of words occurring more than 5 times are marked and placed in brackets behind the main entry.

Please also notice that there are Greek words in the Loeb edition of 'Questions and Answers on Genesis and Exodus' that are not included in our database.[4]

---

4 Some of these Greeks words in the footnotes in Loeb are reconstructed by the translator, Ralph Marcus, from the Armenian versions, cf. Ralph Marcus, 1953, *Questions and Answers on Genesis and Exodus. Translated from the Ancient Armenian Version of the Original Greek.* Supplement volumes I and II. The Loeb Classical Library. Harvard University Press, Cambridge, Massachusetts and William Heinemann, London. See p. viii, supplement volume I.

4. Acknowledgements

We should like to thank the following institutions and persons who have assisted us in producing this index and also the electronic database:

The Computing Section, Faculty of Arts, University of Bergen, Norway
The Computing Section, Faculty of Arts, University of Trondheim (NTNU), Norway
The Department of Religious Studies, University of Trondheim (NTNU), Norway
The Norwegian Council for Research in the Humanities
Richard Holton Pierce, Bergen
Bjørn Kristian Indergård, Trondheim
Jarl Henning Ulrichsen, Trondheim
David Runia, Leiden, and other Philo scholars

Abbreviations

The main abbreviations are in accordance with the 'instructions to contributors' in ***The Studia Philonica Annual***, (ed. D.T. Runia), cf. the 1998 edition pp. 207–208. In the index the sequence of Philo's writings follows the traditional sequence found in Cohn/Wendland *Philonis Alexandrini opera*, below listed in Latin alphabetic order.

Abr = De Abrahamo
Aet = De aeternitate mundi
Agr = De agricultura
Cher = De Cherubim
Conf = De confusione linguarum
Congr = De congressu eruditionis gratia
Contempl = De vita contemplativa
Decal = De Decalogo
Det = Quod deterius potiori insidiari soleat
Deus = Quod Deus sit immutabilis
Ebr = De ebrietate
Flacc = In Flaccum
Fug = De fuga et inventione
Gig = De gigantibus
Her = Quis rerum divinarum heres sit
Hypoth = Hypothetica
Ios = De Iosepho
Leg 1 = Legum allegoriae I
Leg 2 = Legum allegoriae II
Leg 3 = Legum allegoriae III
Legat = Legatio ad Gaium
Migr = De migratione Abrahami
Mos 1 = De vita Moysis I
Mos 2 = De vita Moysis II
Mut = De mutatione nominum
Opif = De opificio mundi
Plant = De plantatione
Post = De posteritate Caini
Praem = De praemiis et poenis, De exsecrationibus
Prob = Quod omnis probus liber sit
Prov = De Providentia (I, II)
QE = Quaestiones et solutiones in Exodum (I, II) (Petit)
QE isf = Quaestiones et solutiones in Exodum incertae sedis fragmenta (Petit)
QG = Quaestiones et solutiones in Genesim (I, II, III, IV) (Petit)
QG isf = Quaestiones et solutiones in Genesim incertae sedis fragmenta (Petit)
QG (Par) = Quaestiones et solutiones in Genesim (Paramelle)
Sacr = De sacrificiis Abelis et Caini
Sobr = De sobrietate
Somn 1 = De somniis I
Somn 2 = De somniis II
Spec 1 = De specialibus legibus I
Spec 2 = De specialibus legibus II
Spec 3 = De specialibus legibus III
Spec 4 = De specialibus legibus IV
Virt = De virtutibus

*** (70) (lacunae) Opif 101 Leg 3:92, 144, 171, 245 Sacr 8 Det 138 Post 14, 56, 59, 109, 115, 153, 183 Deus 108 Agr 101, 145, 166 Plant 32 Conf 9, 57, 136, 137, 138, 141 Migr 19 Congr 144 Fug 45, 95, 145 Mut 61, 133, 140, 218 Somn 2:6, 12, 15, 52, 69, 144, 162, 247, 264, 282, 282, 290, 300, 302 Ios 67, 67 Mos 1:146 Spec 1:172 Spec 2:155, 212, 214, 241 Spec 3:83, 166 Spec 4:101 Virt 188 Praem 78, 79 Prob 96 Contempl 53, 55 Aet 27, 103, 131 Legat 180, 291

A

α QG 2:5a, QG (Par) 2:5

Ἀαρών (32) Leg 1:76 Leg 3:45, 45, 103, 118, 123, 125, 128, 132, 133, 135 Det 39, 126, 132, 132, 135 Post 75, 76, 76 Ebr 127, 128 Migr 78, 78, 84, 84, 85, 168, 169 Her 195 Mut 207, 208 Somn 2:235

Ἄβαι Prov 2:33

ἀβαρής Mos 1:218

ἀβασίλευτος Somn 2:286

ἀβάσκανος Post 138

ἄβατος (23) Agr 104 Plant 61 Her 38 Congr 28 Fug 162 Mut 152 Abr 204 Ios 82 Mos 1:172, 194, 238 Mos 2:70, 95 Spec 1:105, 188, 270 Spec 3:89 Spec 4:126 Virt 107, 189 Prob 3 Legat 308 QE 2:45b

ἀβέβαιος (50) Opif 156 Leg 3:164, 228 Cher 69 Sacr 13, 32 Det 136 Post 13, 114 Gig 39 Deus 172 Ebr 188, 205 Conf 31, 140, 159 Her 23, 98 Mut 151 Somn 1:12 Somn 2:162 Abr 60, 84, 212, 269 Ios 130, 142 Mos 1:183, 197, 285 Mos 2:248, 269 Spec 1:27, 29, 62 Spec 4:50, 88, 139, 153 Virt 10, 56, 204 Prob 11 Flacc 109 Legat 1, 1 Hypoth 11:3 QG 2:54a QE 2:107 QE isf 16

ἀβεβαιότης Deus 27 Somn 1:202

Ἄβελ (40) Cher 40 Sacr 1, 1, 2, 3, 5, 10, 11, 11, 14, 51, 88, 89 Det 1, 1, 1, 32, 32, 37, 42, 45, 47, 47, 48, 57, 68, 78, 103 Post 10, 38, 124, 124, 170, 172, 172, 173 Migr 74 QG 1:60:2, 62:1, 3:11a

Ἀβιμέλεχ Plant 169 QG 4:7

ἄβιος Contempl 17

Ἀβιούδ (6) Leg 2:57, 58 Migr 168, 169 Her 309 Fug 59

ἀβίωτος (13) Ebr 219 Her 45 Fug 123 Somn 2:150 Ios 20 Spec 3:154 Virt 210 Prob 14, 114 Aet 84 Flacc 41 Legat 89, 236

ἀβλαβής Gig 10 Spec 1:191 Legat 127

ἀβουλεί Leg 3:187

ἀβουλέω Mut 241 Ios 227

ἀβούλητος (45) Cher 29, 34 Sacr 28, 70, 129 Fug 102, 115 Somn 1:7, 111, 221 Abr 184, 186, 202, 230 Ios 26, 30, 115, 179, 182, 183, 246, 267, 270 Mos 2:13, 227, 233 Spec 1:224, 259 Spec 2:39, 46, 67, 112 Spec 3:104, 135 Virt 100, 116, 123, 127 Praem 138 Prob 18, 97 Legat 109, 145, 237 QG 4:204

ἀβουλία Ios 173 Spec 2:15

ἄβουλος Ebr 204 Decal 61 QG 4:191a

Ἀβραάμ (161) Leg 2:59 Leg 3:9, 24, 27, 85, 177, 197, 203, 217, 217, 228, 244 Cher 7, 10, 18, 31, 40, 45, 106 Sacr 5, 43, 59, 122 Det 59, 124, 159 Post 17, 27, 62, 75, 76, 76, 76, 173, 173, 174 Gig 62, 64 Deus 4, 161 Plant 73 Ebr 24, 94, 105 Sobr 8, 17, 17, 17, 56, 56, 65 Conf 26, 79 Migr 1, 44, 94, 122, 125, 127, 130, 132, 140, 173, 176, 177 Her 8, 8, 30, 90, 249, 258, 266, 277, 286, 313 Congr 1, 1, 12, 23, 35, 43, 48, 63, 71, 71, 71, 73, 92, 109, 119 Fug 200 Mut 1, 1, 12, 13, 15, 39, 54, 60, 66, 69, 71, 83, 87, 88, 130, 152, 177, 186, 190, 228, 253, 270 Somn 1:3, 14, 47, 47, 52, 60, 64, 70, 70, 70, 159, 160, 160, 166, 168, 170, 171, 172, 173, 173, 194, 195, 195, 195, 195, 195, 214 Somn 2:89, 226, 244, 255 Abr 51, 52, 77, 81, 82, 92 Mos 1:76 QG 2:26b, 3:11a, 18, 23, 24, 4:30, 81, 86a, 144 QG isf 17

Ἀβράμ (12) Leg 3:83, 83 Cher 4, 7 Gig 62, 62 Mut 60, 61, 66, 69 Abr 81, 82

ἀβροδίαιτος (33) Opif 153 Leg 2:29 Det 34 Agr 154 Ebr 22, 131, 219 Fug 3 Somn 1:121 Somn 2:211 Mos 1:29, 160, 209 Mos 2:58, 184 Spec 1:134, 153 Spec 2:18, 101, 173, 214 Spec 4:102, 122, 228 Virt 149, 149 Praem 100, 107, 146 Contempl 37, 73 Flacc 91 Legat 15

ἀβρύνω Prob 157

ἄβρωτος Spec 3:144

ἄβυσσος Opif 29, 32 Fug 192 QG 2:64a

ἀγαθός (ὁ) (1465) Opif 8, 8, 8, 8, 18, 21, 21, 21, 22, 22, 23, 27, 36, 45, 53, 53, 53, 54, 65, 67, 67, 68, 68, 71, 73, 74, 77, 81, 82, 88, 90, 104, 104, 115, 120, 126, 136, 136, 137, 138, 139, 139, 140, 140, 140, 156, 167, 170 Leg 1:14, 14, 34, 34, 35, 41, 47, 47, 57, 58, 66, 72, 72, 72, 80, 99, 99, 102, 106 Leg 2:2, 3, 3, 6, 15, 16, 17, 17, 17, 50, 50, 53, 53, 60, 65, 95, 95 Leg 3:12, 20, 47, 48, 52, 62, 72, 73, 78, 80, 83, 84, 85, 86, 86, 86, 86, 86, 87, 89, 91, 92, 97, 105, 105, 105, 105, 105, 115, 128, 131, 135, 146, 157, 163, 163, 164, 166, 168, 177, 178, 196, 203, 203, 203, 222, 222, 228, 236, 246 Cher 4, 4, 27, 29, 29, 34, 36, 37, 49, 73, 84, 98 Sacr 4, 4, 5, 7, 10, 10, 22, 23, 25, 28, 30, 33, 34, 35, 35, 36, 37, 37, 37, 40, 40, 40, 40, 41, 41, 41, 51, 53, 53, 54, 56, 57, 59, 76, 82, 82, 83, 87, 92, 92, 99, 99, 100, 100, 101, 106, 109, 114, 115, 117, 122, 123, 123, 124, 124, 126, 129, 131, 135 Det 4, 4, 7, 7, 7, 7, 9, 9, 10, 11, 17, 35, 37, 43, 44, 52, 52, 55, 56, 62, 68, 69, 74, 74, 83, 93, 101, 105, 120, 129, 134, 137, 138, 140, 142, 145, 145, 145, 156, 156, 157, 157, 157, 176 Post 11, 15, 26, 26, 30, 32, 32, 37, 41, 51, 61, 75, 78, 79, 80, 82, 84, 85, 86, 87, 88, 94, 94, 95, 112, 112, 114, 118, 118, 120, 125, 133, 133, 141, 143, 159, 159, 160, 160, 162, 163, 164, 173, 173, 181 Gig 2, 15, 16, 20, 25, 37, 37, 40, 40, 42, 43, 45, 65, 65 Deus 5, 13, 16, 22, 24, 25, 40, 46, 49, 49, 50, 50, 50, 61, 67, 70, 80, 85, 87, 87, 94, 107, 108, 118, 119, 121, 148, 148, 149, 150, 151, 152, 153, 155, 155, 156, 165, 176 Agr 18, 29, 40, 42, 44, 45, 49, 50, 53, 81, 83, 97, 97, 99, 100, 100, 122, 129, 133, 133, 145, 145, 157, 168, 172, 173 Plant 14, 31, 39, 45, 52, 53, 53, 64, 68, 72, 81, 88, 88, 91, 91, 98, 100, 104, 106, 106, 110, 114, 118, 131, 135, 147, 161, 168, 171, 171, 172, 176 Ebr 20, 21, 26, 37, 52, 52, 56, 70, 80, 83, 84, 87, 115, 118, 136, 148, 187, 200, 200, 201, 204 Sobr 2, 5, 5, 13, 14, 15, 15, 20, 29, 39, 52, 52, 53, 55, 56, 58, 60, 62, 64, 67, 67, 67, 67, 68, 68, 68, 69, 69 Conf 7, 7, 34, 34, 48, 50, 54, 60, 60, 69, 72, 73, 73, 91, 91, 103, 108, 108, 112, 116, 121, 133, 141, 145, 161, 164, 170, 178, 180, 180, 180, 180, 181, 188, 195, 196 Migr 10, 11, 19, 19, 23, 28, 30, 30, 32, 33, 36, 37, 44, 47, 53, 59, 59, 61, 67, 72, 73, 86, 86, 86, 88, 94, 100, 100, 101, 105, 106, 108, 108, 110, 116, 120, 121, 123, 128, 133, 140, 146, 148, 148, 149,

156, 157, 171, 172, 179, 185, 193, 195, 196, 209 Her 5, 15, 26, 31, 34, 46, 46, 48, 69, 73, 76, 76, 77, 89, 89, 95, 97, 97, 98, 98, 103, 112, 174, 178, 178, 202, 224, 240, 241, 249, 279, 283, 290, 294, 299, 302, 314, 315 Congr 3, 7, 32, 32, 33, 36, 45, 45, 45, 50, 51, 51, 52, 52, 53, 58, 67, 81, 84, 84, 97, 98, 112, 112, 130, 143, 145, 156, 157, 157, 160, 162, 162, 171, 171, 175, 175 Fug 10, 17, 20, 24, 24, 26, 26, 30, 30, 36, 40, 42, 42, 43, 47, 58, 58, 62, 62, 63, 66, 66, 67, 70, 70, 73, 73, 74, 79, 91, 91, 93, 94, 96, 97, 99, 126, 129, 129, 136, 141, 148, 148, 148, 152, 152, 153, 156, 168, 172, 172, 174, 175, 176, 195, 197, 205, 213 Mut 1, 7, 8, 12, 13, 19, 31, 32, 35, 37, 46, 50, 65, 69, 98, 102, 102, 112, 115, 121, 122, 122, 123, 128, 131, 140, 141, 142, 149, 149, 150, 153, 155, 155, 161, 163, 164, 166, 171, 173, 174, 174, 185, 188, 188, 203, 208, 216, 217, 219, 221, 222, 225, 227, 231, 236, 238, 240, 240, 246, 247, 247, 253, 260, 268 Somn 1:7, 10, 23, 42, 57, 68, 68, 95, 97, 104, 124, 132, 137, 137, 140, 149, 152, 152, 162, 163, 171, 176, 177, 183, 185, 191 Somn 2:8, 8, 9, 9, 76, 90, 100, 105, 107, 120, 140, 164, 167, 170, 170, 175, 176, 179, 180, 188, 202, 211, 223, 227, 228, 229, 240, 240, 255, 268, 269, 270, 270, 282, 282, 288, 289, 291, 296 Abr 7, 8, 10, 14, 17, 18, 19, 21, 23, 26, 27, 35, 36, 37, 41, 45, 47, 52, 61, 83, 86, 88, 89, 93, 101, 110, 116, 124, 125, 128, 129, 129, 134, 143, 143, 145, 159, 164, 168, 198, 199, 205, 207, 215, 216, 221, 222, 228, 235, 242, 245, 246, 256, 261, 264, 268, 268, 268 Ios 1, 2, 12, 21, 39, 56, 57, 67, 69, 71, 83, 87, 95, 100, 101, 112, 113, 137, 137, 143, 145, 148, 165, 177, 191, 192, 196, 208, 212, 254, 259, 264, 266, 270 Mos 1:3, 3, 6, 7, 26, 26, 32, 42, 48, 62, 62, 63, 86, 95, 146, 149, 149, 150, 154, 161, 181, 183, 187, 188, 189, 224, 226, 234, 235, 245, 247, 248, 257, 262, 285, 293, 301, 304, 317, 319, 323, 332 Mos 2:2, 5, 8, 12, 13, 16, 24, 29, 49, 51, 53, 65, 65, 66, 67, 69, 115, 134, 153, 171, 183, 184, 187, 196, 200, 249, 249, 276, 277 Decal 9, 12, 35, 50, 51, 52, 61, 69, 72, 73, 74, 81, 81, 81, 91, 91, 92, 101, 109, 109, 110, 113, 134, 134, 143, 144, 146, 150, 166, 176, 176, 177, 178 Spec 1:6, 10, 22, 23, 24, 33, 35, 36, 48, 51, 51, 57, 62, 67, 72, 90, 114, 115, 133, 144, 149, 157, 186, 188, 195, 196, 198, 198, 201, 203, 203, 209, 216, 224, 227, 229, 238, 244, 246, 258, 265, 269, 270, 272, 275, 275, 277, 283, 284, 300, 311, 312, 320, 323, 335, 336, 340, 341 Spec 2:10, 12, 13, 14, 22, 28, 29, 29, 30, 35, 35, 42, 45, 48, 53, 53, 53, 57, 57, 61, 62, 62, 64, 67, 73, 83, 84, 84, 96, 139, 141, 141, 151, 156, 168, 169, 169, 171, 173, 177, 178, 178, 179, 181, 181, 181, 184, 184, 184, 184, 187, 192, 199, 201, 201, 203, 203, 204, 209, 209, 219, 227, 231, 235, 239, 240, 249, 256, 258, 260 Spec 3:7, 16, 29, 33, 41, 44, 99, 112, 125, 131, 167, 171, 172, 185, 186, 186, 192, 195, 209 Spec 4:13, 15, 40, 54, 58, 64, 71, 71, 71, 73, 73, 77, 80, 89, 95, 106, 109, 109, 116, 123, 129, 131, 134, 137, 147, 147, 151, 152, 158, 165, 165, 171, 173, 182, 182, 184, 186, 186, 187, 187, 188, 218, 218, 230, 230, 237, 238 Virt 3, 3, 19, 30, 38, 45, 47, 49, 53, 56, 61, 67, 67, 69, 70, 71, 78, 79, 80, 83, 109, 110, 116, 133, 140, 155, 161, 165, 167, 167, 170, 175, 176, 176, 178, 179, 182, 183, 187, 187, 187, 188, 188, 189, 194, 197, 198, 205, 205, 207, 209, 211, 211, 213, 217, 218, 222, 223, 226, 227, 227 Praem 3, 11, 15, 32, 40, 40, 40, 47, 48, 51, 59, 62, 63, 63, 64, 64, 65, 67, 68, 70, 71, 71, 80, 87, 88, 88, 102, 105, 115, 117, 118, 118, 125, 126, 127, 130, 135, 139, 160, 161, 161, 164, 168, 170 Prob 9, 31, 39, 56, 57, 64, 74, 83, 84, 84, 91, 92, 101, 102, 103, 120, 121, 131, 136, 139 Contempl 2, 2, 2, 14, 14, 16, 21, 22, 39, 62, 82, 82, 90 Aet 1, 15, 32, 32, 38, 41, 41, 42, 42, 43, 43, 43, 56, 65, 68, 75, 106, 130 Flacc 7, 23, 40, 127, 151, 162, 187 Legat 5, 5, 5, 7, 8, 9, 11, 16, 18, 22, 27, 41, 47, 47, 47, 51, 51, 68, 76, 76, 82, 83, 84, 89, 90, 95, 95, 99, 109, 118, 137, 141, 147, 149, 168, 195, 203, 220, 242, 245, 245, 265, 278, 281, 287, 287, 289, 306, 309, 318, 342 Prov 1, 2:1, 9, 9, 10, 10, 12, 16, 16, 20, 21, 21, 37, 54, 67 QG 1:3, 21, 51, 65, 79, 89, 100:1b, 2:34a, 41, 41, 41, 62, 62, 3:3, 23, 30a, 4:20, 76b, 102b, 191b, 191d, 198, 200c QG isf 1, 5, 5, 8, 9 QG (Par) 2:4 QE 1:21, 2:6b, 17, 25d, 38a, 46 QE isf 5, 11, 19, 25

ἀγαθότης (26) Leg 1:34, 59, 63, 65 Leg 3:73, 73, 73, 73, 78, 105 Cher 27, 27, 28, 29, 29, 127 Sacr 27, 59, 59 Deus 73, 108, 108 Migr 37, 183 Mos 2:132 QG 2:13b

Ἀγάθων Contempl 57

ἀγάλλω (7) Leg 1:64 Conf 19 Her 206 Somn 2:203, 211 Prov 2:15 QG 1:65

ἄγαλμα (29) Opif 55, 137 Cher 93 Ebr 109 Sobr 3, 38 Somn 2:223 Abr 159, 267 Mos 1:66, 298 Mos 2:205 Decal 7, 51, 60, 66, 76, 156 Spec 1:23, 56 Spec 4:76, 238 Virt 5, 221 Contempl 7 Legat 98, 148, 292 QE isf 14

ἀγαλματοφορέω (16) Opif 18, 69, 82, 137 Conf 49 Mut 21 Somn 1:32, 208 Mos 1:27 Mos 2:11, 113, 135, 209 Virt 165, 188 Legat 210

ἄγαμαι (26) Sacr 50 Det 60 Conf 149 Migr 95, 208 Congr 75, 78, 108 Mut 57, 105 Somn 2:21 Abr 93, 273 Mos 1:47, 147, 317 Spec 3:189 Virt 90, 145 Prob 142 Contempl 14 Legat 11, 295 Hypoth 11:18 QG 4:81, 166

ἄγαν (46) Opif 156 Leg 3:206 Sacr 21 Post 70, 148, 152 Migr 48, 89, 104, 210 Fug 156 Mut 212, 212, 250 Somn 2:3 Abr 199 Ios 9, 53, 179, 204 Mos 1:51, 237, 312 Spec 1:306 Spec 2:8, 83, 95, 146, 208 Spec 3:56, 175 Spec 4:122, 129 Virt 152, 165 Praem 106 Prob 101 Flacc 130 Legat 48, 332 Prov 2:65 QG 4:202a QG (Par) 2:3, 2:5, 2:5 QE 1:6

ἀγανακτέω (19) Leg 3:20 Agr 117 Plant 160 Somn 2:99, 117 Mos 1:45, 236, 292, 328 Decal 75, 112 Spec 2:11, 80 Spec 3:119 Praem 77 Flacc 35, 141 Legat 361 QG 3:52

ἀγανάκτησις Det 69, 69 Deus 68 Mos 1:244 Spec 3:42

ἀγαπάω (65) Leg 2:48, 48, 48, 56 Leg 3:129, 176, 193, 198 Cher 72, 73 Sacr 19, 19, 19, 20 Post 12, 69, 69 Deus 69, 69 Plant 105 Ebr 84 Sobr 6, 21, 21, 21, 22, 23 Conf 41, 109 Migr 21, 60 Her 42, 44, 47, 49, 49, 127, 186 Congr 31, 177 Fug 58, 114, 154 Mut 225, 227 Somn 1:195 Abr 22, 50, 87, 221 Spec 1:17, 300 Spec 4:5, 23 Virt 103, 104 Aet 2 Prov 2:54, 57 QG 3:26, 4:166, 166, 167, 167 QE 2:21

ἀγάπη Deus 69 QE 2:21, 21

ἀγαπητικός Migr 169 Somn 1:163 Spec 1:31

ἀγαπητός (26) Leg 1:86 Leg 3:10, 143, 203, 207, 209 Sacr 37 Post 171 Deus 4 Ebr 30 Migr 140, 222 Mut 50, 118, 128, 183, 219 Somn 1:194, 195, 237 Somn 2:88 Abr 168, 196 Mos 1:13 Legat 71, 182

Ἄγαρ (27) Leg 3:244 Cher 3, 6, 8 Sacr 43, 43 Post 130, 130, 137 Sobr 8 Congr 1, 11, 20, 23, 23, 24, 71, 88, 121, 122, 139, 180 Fug 2, 5, 202 Mut 255 Somn 1:240

ἀγαυός Contempl 17

ἀγγεῖον (37) Leg 2:37 Leg 3:138, 149 Det 170 Post 137, 137, 146, 163 Migr 193, 197 Her 311 Congr 21, 21 Fug 194 Somn 1:26 Ios 178, 180, 181, 197, 198, 207, 215,

217 Mos 1:203 Mos 2:97 Spec 1:215, 218, 262 Spec 2:216 Spec 3:58, 58, 60, 62 Prob 15 QG (Par) 2:7, 2:7, 2:7

ἀγγέλλω Mos 2:264 Legat 288

ἄγγελος (77) Leg 3:177, 177, 177, 178 Cher 3, 35 Sacr 5, 5 Post 89, 91, 92 Gig 6, 6, 16, 16, 17, 17 Deus 1, 2, 158, 181, 182 Agr 51 Plant 14, 59 Sobr 65 Conf 28, 116, 146, 174, 181, 181 Migr 173, 174 Fug 1, 1, 1, 1, 5, 67, 119, 177, 203, 212 Mut 87, 162 Somn 1:3, 27, 115, 133, 141, 148, 157, 189, 190, 195, 196, 232, 238, 238, 239, 240 Abr 113, 115 Ios 94 Mos 1:66, 67, 166, 273 Decal 145 Spec 1:66 Virt 74 QG 1:92, 3:11a, 4:52a QE 2:16, 16

ἄγγος Sacr 64 Post 130

ἀγείρω Post 66 Somn 2:127 Spec 1:336 Spec 4:47

ἀγελαῖος (14) Cher 58 Her 76, 127, 211, 303 Congr 27, 174 Mut 93, 213 Somn 2:230 Praem 89 Prob 3 Flacc 177 QG isf 10

ἀγελαρχέω Somn 1:255 Somn 2:153 Legat 76

ἀγελάρχης (19) Post 68 Agr 29, 66 Mut 105, 221 Somn 1:198 Somn 2:152, 153, 288 Mos 1:63 Mos 2:61 Decal 114 Spec 2:142 Spec 4:22 Virt 58 Prob 30 Legat 20, 76 Hypoth 11:8

ἀγελαστικός Decal 132 Spec 1:162

ἀγέλη (49) Opif 85 Agr 29, 32, 39, 51, 66, 90 Fug 10 Mut 105, 112, 114, 117 Somn 1:189, 198, 255 Somn 2:152, 153, 288 Abr 45, 209, 220 Ios 2, 11, 257 Mos 1:60, 60, 63, 145 Mos 2:22 Spec 1:136, 141, 163 Spec 4:11, 13, 25, 104, 117 Virt 95, 126, 141, 142, 144 Praem 141 Prob 30 Legat 20, 44, 76 Prov 2:14, 57

ἀγεληδόν (6) Mos 1:133 Mos 2:64 Spec 4:152 Prob 63, 89 Prov 2:65

ἀγενής Conf 43 Prob 155

ἀγένητος (101) Opif 7, 9, 12, 54, 171 Leg 1:51 Leg 3:31, 100, 101, 208 Cher 44, 52, 86 Sacr 57, 60, 63, 66, 66, 98, 100, 101 Det 124, 158 Post 63, 172 Gig 14, 42 Deus 56, 60, 78, 160 Plant 22, 31, 50, 64, 66 Ebr 84, 94, 152, 199, 208 Conf 98 Migr 91, 157, 192 Her 14, 98, 206, 246 Congr 48, 107, 134 Fug 59 Mut 12, 22, 45, 181 Somn 1:77, 94, 184, 249 Somn 2:231, 234, 253, 283 Abr 162, 257 Ios 167, 265 Mos 2:171 Decal 41, 60, 64, 120 Spec 2:166 Spec 3:45 Spec 4:48 Virt 180, 213, 218 Praem 46, 87 Aet 7, 10, 12, 20, 27, 27, 52, 52, 55, 69, 75, 93 Flacc 139 Legat 5, 118 QG 1:64c, 2:16 QE isf 6, 10

ἀγεννής (9) Cher 50, 78 Fug 5 Mut 138 Abr 136 Ios 143 Virt 25 Praem 5 Legat 90

ἀγέραστος Mos 2:242

ἄγευστος (9) Sacr 111 Ebr 148 Congr 174 Fug 199 Spec 1:304 Spec 2:11 Spec 3:163 Virt 39 Prob 4

ἀγεώργητος Fug 124

ἀγήραος (ἀγήρως) (16) Sacr 76, 100, 124 Agr 171 Sobr 24 Ios 264 Spec 2:5 Virt 37 Aet 21, 21, 26, 26, 36, 60, 61, 74

ἀγήρως ἀγήραος

ἁγιάζω (8) Leg 1:17, 18 Sacr 118, 134 Post 64 Her 117 Fug 59 Spec 1:167

ἁγίασμα Plant 47, 50 Migr 103

ἅγιος (135) Opif 89 Leg 1:16, 17, 17, 17, 17, 17, 18, 55 Leg 2:56, 56 Leg 3:8, 118, 125, 125, 135 Cher 94 Sacr 101, 109, 134, 134 Det 62, 64, 65, 133, 133 Post 95, 95, 95, 95, 96, 96, 96, 173 Gig 23, 52 Deus 88 Plant 50, 53, 53, 95, 117, 125, 126, 126, 135 Ebr 127, 143 Migr 104, 104, 169, 202 Her 75, 84, 84, 110, 186, 196, 199, 226 Congr 94, 95, 95, 169 Fug 93, 100, 163, 196, 196, 196, 213, 213 Mut 192, 192 Somn 1:33, 34, 81, 82, 149, 207, 216, 234, 253, 253, 254 Somn 2:34, 123, 189, 189, 231, 231, 246, 251, 272 Abr 13, 14, 56 Mos 2:80, 87, 89, 114, 155, 158, 208 Decal 133 Spec 1:66, 100, 115, 124, 151, 234, 238, 238, 238, 245, 275, 296 Spec 2:157, 194, 194 Spec 4:105 Praem 77, 123, 123 Contempl 65, 81 Flacc 46 Legat 278 QG 4:59 QG isf 17 QG (Par) 2:4, 2:4, 2:4 QE isf 9, 9

ἁγιστεία (17) Sacr 27 Deus 17, 132 Plant 107 Ebr 66 Sobr 40 Migr 92 Her 82 Somn 1:226 Spec 1:21, 74, 100, 109, 131 Spec 4:98 Legat 295 Hypoth 6:6

ἁγιστεύω Spec 1:125

ἀγκαλίς Spec 2:251

ἀγκιστρεύω (12) Opif 166 Sacr 21 Deus 115 Agr 24 Plant 102 Mut 172 Somn 2:51 Mos 1:296 Spec 3:101 Spec 4:67 Virt 40 Prov 2:31

ἄγκος Somn 1:22

ἄγκυρα Post 142, 163

ἀγκών Contempl 45, 69 Legat 272

ἁγνεία (11) Cher 94 Det 170 Somn 2:25 Abr 98 Mos 2:137, 152 Spec 2:56 Spec 3:81 Virt 37 Prob 84 Contempl 68

ἁγνευτικός (6) Deus 8 Mos 2:149 Decal 158 Spec 2:148, 163 QE isf 14

ἁγνεύω (11) Cher 50 Her 185 Mut 44 Somn 1:81 Mos 2:68, 231 Decal 45, 128 Spec 1:107, 193, 274

ἀγνοέω (119) Opif 51, 87, 166 Leg 1:92 Leg 3:18, 69, 145, 173, 243 Cher 54 Sacr 23, 79, 100 Det 57, 59, 151 Deus 27 Agr 179 Ebr 19, 88, 186 Sobr 17 Conf 142, 144 Migr 35, 42, 170, 177 Her 24, 301 Congr 146, 157 Fug 138, 168, 203 Mut 27, 88 Somn 1:26, 183 Somn 2:1, 100, 103, 164 Abr 26, 32, 53, 56, 65, 129 Ios 56, 66, 67, 81, 120, 139, 163, 189, 193, 217, 250 Mos 1:1, 74, 84, 110, 137, 160, 162, 172, 185, 310 Mos 2:8, 188, 263 Decal 90, 91, 111, 132, 151, 154 Spec 1:70, 302, 332 Spec 2:9, 171 Spec 3:61, 104, 159, 180, 203 Spec 4:31, 32, 133, 169, 188, 188, 232 Virt 177 Prob 136 Aet 59, 72, 134, 139 Flacc 76 Legat 40, 59, 155, 174, 178, 182, 190, 264, 303, 348 Hypoth 7:12 Prov 2:1 QG 1:74, 77, 4:206b QG isf 5

ἄγνοια (64) Leg 1:35 Leg 3:91, 121 Sacr 28 Post 52 Gig 30 Deus 46, 135 Agr 161, 162 Plant 98, 108 Ebr 6, 6, 154, 154, 155, 157, 158, 160, 161, 162, 203 Migr 140 Her 240 Fug 8, 82 Mut 183 Somn 1:114 Somn 2:150 Ios 183, 194 Mos 1:12, 182, 222, 227, 273 Decal 8, 129 Spec 1:15, 53, 223 Spec 2:194 Spec 3:15, 35, 117 Spec 4:18, 49, 70, 198 Virt 172, 180 Praem 55 Flacc 7 Legat 20, 31, 69, 127, 208 Hypoth 6:2, 6:3, 7:14 QG 1:77, 4:64

ἁγνός (7) Ios 43, 43 Spec 1:107 Spec 2:30, 145 Praem 159 Contempl 65

ἀγνωμοσύνη Leg 3:2 Flacc 141

ἀγνώμων (11) Det 50 Conf 153 Mut 244 Somn 1:91 Somn 2:292 Mos 2:107 Decal 61 Spec 1:79, 241 Spec 2:137 QE 2:11b

ἄγνωστος Opif 149 Mut 10 Spec 1:89 Spec 4:192

ἀγονέω Spec 2:154 Virt 157 Praem 159

ἀγονία (15) Opif 38, 80 Migr 123 Fug 124 Abr 140, 249 Ios 30 Spec 1:92 Spec 3:35, 39, 62 Praem 130, 141 Contempl 62 QE 2:19

ἄγονος (43) Opif 38 Leg 1:9, 34, 34, 49 Leg 3:236 Gig 11 Deus 13 Agr 8 Plant 97 Ebr 211, 212, 213, 220, 224 Migr 34, 69 Her 204, 211 Congr 13 Mut 68, 68, 143 Somn 1:11, 17, 106 Somn 2:141, 192 Abr 247 Ios 59, 153 Mos 1:192 Mos 2:258 Decal 15 Spec 1:11, 330 Spec 2:199 Spec 3:36 Spec 4:229 Praem 108 Prob 75 Prov 2:66 QE isf 5

ἀγορά (35) Opif 17 Sacr 21 Gig 39 Plant 102 Somn 1:96 Somn 2:62, 91 Abr 20 Ios 50 Mos 1:103, 144 Mos 2:172, 212 Spec 1:320, 321 Spec 2:44 Spec 3:40, 51, 105, 160, 169, 171, 174 Spec 4:126 Praem 157 Prob 34 Flacc 56, 64, 74, 95, 138, 166, 174 Legat 122, 131

ἀγοραῖος Spec 4:193

ἀγορανομία Prob 6

ἀγορανόμος Spec 3:74 Spec 4:193

ἄγος (19) Det 96 Post 49 Agr 21 Ebr 66 Conf 161 Fug 113 Abr 181 Ios 13 Mos 1:314 Spec 3:18, 42, 89, 92, 112, 127 Virt 199 Legat 30, 66 QG 1:77

ἄγρα Opif 147 Sacr 29 Plant 103 Spec 4:120, 121

ἀγραμματία Her 210

ἀγράμματος Det 18 Prob 51

ἄγραφος (14) Her 295 Abr 5, 16, 275, 276 Decal 1 Spec 4:149, 150, 150 Virt 194 Praem 150 Prob 104 Legat 115 Hypoth 7:6

ἀγριαίνω Plant 103 Decal 89

ἄγριος (48) Opif 40, 83 Leg 1:49 Leg 3:76 Det 105, 111 Agr 6, 19 Plant 41, 97, 98 Ebr 224 Her 137, 137, 211 Mut 117 Somn 2:67, 87, 89 Abr 45, 266 Ios 171 Mos 1:61, 127, 192 Decal 78, 78, 78 Spec 1:74, 80 Spec 2:146, 205 Spec 3:145 Spec 4:103, 209, 229 Virt 2, 155 Praem 59, 91, 143, 149 Contempl 8 Aet 64, 96 Flacc 36 Legat 131 QG 1:76b

ἀγριότης (13) Ios 81 Mos 1:43 Decal 110 Spec 2:16, 94 Spec 3:103 Virt 87, 134 Praem 88 Prob 89 Flacc 66 Legat 22 Prov 2:69

ἀγριόω Spec 3:138

Ἀγρίππας (13) Flacc 25, 39, 103 Legat 179, 261, 263, 268, 269, 291, 294, 325, 331, 333

ἀγρόθεν Congr 123 Flacc 185 Legat 127

ἀγροικία Leg 3:2 Somn 2:165

ἄγροικος Leg 3:2 Fug 1, 204, 209

ἀγροικόσοφος Migr 75 Fug 209

ἀγρονόμος Spec 4:21, 21

ἀγρός (45) Opif 129, 129, 129 Leg 1:21, 21, 22, 23, 23, 24, 24, 24 Leg 2:9, 10, 10 Leg 3:251 Det 114, 114, 114 Deus 145, 154 Agr 14, 15, 152 Migr 55 Fug 3 Mut 74 Somn 1:7 Somn 2:257 Abr 138 Mos 1:262, 312 Spec 2:19, 115, 116, 119, 119, 216 Spec 4:20, 22 Virt 95 Praem 107 Prob 102 Flacc 177 Prov 2:62 QG 4:81

ἀγρυπνέω Aet 70

ἄγρυπνος Aet 70

ἀγύμναστος Ebr 198

ἀγύρτης Sacr 32

ἀγχέμαχος Contempl 17

ἀγχιβαθής Mos 2:35

ἀγχίθυρος Agr 161 Ebr 71

ἀγχίνοια (13) Opif 153 Agr 135 Ebr 129 Migr 19 Congr 98, 121 Fug 125 Mut 193 Mos 1:154 Mos 2:185 Legat 142 QG 1:31 QE isf 16

ἀγχίνοος Mut 220 Virt 167

ἀγχίσπορος Opif 144 Mos 1:279 Spec 4:14, 236 Virt 80

ἀγχιστεύς Spec 2:114 Spec 3:129, 131, 133

ἄγχιστος Fug 107

ἀγχόνη (8) Post 27 Her 269 Mut 62 Somn 2:44 Ios 150 Spec 3:161 Praem 151 Aet 20

ἄγχω Somn 2:168 Spec 2:49 Spec 4:122, 217

ἄγω (307) Opif 44, 46, 49, 84, 85, 86, 88, 128, 149 Leg 1:18, 29, 50 Leg 2:9, 28, 29, 38, 40, 40, 84, 85, 104, 104 Leg 3:7, 74, 84, 109, 119, 130, 151, 156, 223, 223 Cher 58, 72, 86, 117 Sacr 16, 32, 50, 50, 90, 101, 104, 106, 113 Det 1, 7, 24, 173 Post 31, 79, 92, 101, 102, 108, 127, 153, 154 Gig 44, 51 Deus 56, 142, 176 Agr 51, 69, 69, 69, 91, 113, 152, 157, 158, 166 Plant 3, 21, 37, 86, 145, 157, 162 Ebr 6, 48, 50, 76, 125, 143, 148, 150, 164, 177, 195 Sobr 35, 41, 61 Conf 3, 150, 165, 194, 195 Migr 10, 39, 76, 108, 171, 183, 204, 219 Her 6, 13, 46, 47, 70, 207, 241, 286, 288, 290 Congr 16, 24, 50, 78, 88, 114, 170 Fug 10, 21, 112, 118, 144, 173, 184 Mut 56, 112, 118, 120, 217, 239, 243 Somn 1:76, 88, 104, 168, 179, 209, 226, 241, 246 Somn 2:12, 170, 203, 282 Abr 4, 94, 96, 108, 229, 249, 251, 251, 253, 269 Ios 37, 44, 50, 98, 204, 209, 210, 221, 224, 233, 251 Mos 1:15, 52, 57, 58, 65, 119, 164, 164, 195, 196, 210, 237, 246, 290, 295 Mos 2:22, 23, 41, 100, 147, 189, 211, 214, 224 Decal 51, 81, 90, 96 Spec 1:55, 68, 102, 107, 108, 109, 132, 163, 181, 183, 186, 189, 215, 268, 315, 328, 336, 344 Spec 2:23, 36, 40, 42, 46, 52, 56, 95, 109, 149, 156, 158, 193, 196, 197, 200, 251, 251 Spec 3:13, 20, 22, 23, 27, 35, 52, 69, 70, 80, 101, 121, 121, 143, 162 Spec 4:2, 7, 72, 108, 112, 112, 167, 204, 213 Virt 6, 31, 48, 51, 61, 118, 125, 130, 171 Praem 117, 139, 140, 148, 167, 171 Prob 31, 48, 53 Contempl 11, 19, 61, 83, 83 Aet 22, 22, 36 Flacc 4, 93, 161 Legat 25, 47, 82, 116, 147, 155, 207, 216, 300 Hypoth 6:4, 11:3, 11:14 QG 1:21, 2:13b, 3:23, 4:145, 173 QE 2:26

ἀγωγή (10) Det 16, 118 Post 181 Deus 61, 119 Plant 177 Ebr 193, 195 Congr 158 Mut 114

ἀγώγιμος Deus 115 Her 109 Mut 113 Prob 151

ἀγωγός (7) Somn 2:181 Abr 67 Ios 4 Spec 4:18, 97 Virt 15, 36

ἀγών (82) Opif 33, 78, 125 Leg 2:108 Cher 73 Sacr 17 Det 2, 23, 36, 42, 45, 141 Deus 147 Agr 59, 91, 110, 112, 113, 113, 116, 119, 119, 149, 151, 152, 160, 165 Plant 146, 160 Migr 82, 85, 200 Congr 165 Fug 36, 39 Mut 81, 106 Somn 1:132 Somn 2:145, 168 Abr 40, 48, 105, 235, 267 Ios 138 Mos 1:106, 215, 218, 222, 307, 309 Spec 1:57, 79 Spec 2:183, 246 Spec 3:127, 176 Spec 4:74 Virt 45 Praem 4, 6, 11, 13, 15, 22, 52, 93 Prob 21, 26, 112, 132 Contempl 41 Flacc 48, 85, 93 Legat 12, 29, 45, 349 Hypoth 11:6 Prov 2:56

ἀγωνία (8) Mut 81 Decal 145 Spec 4:214 Virt 24 Praem 148 Legat 243, 266, 366

ἀγωνιάω Legat 190, 330

ἀγωνίζομαι (16) Leg 3:242 Cher 74, 80 Agr 154 Plant 76, 175, 175 Ebr 177 Migr 75 Mos 1:318 Praem 15, 137 Prob 131, 133 Legat 194, 349

ἀγώνισμα (12) Leg 3:48 Agr 115 Plant 71 Ebr 207 Somn 2:90 Mos 1:61 Mos 2:136, 236 Spec 2:259 Spec 3:18 Virt 39 QG 4:228

ἀγωνιστής (12) Opif 78 Det 29, 41 Migr 26 Her 125 Mut 106 Somn 1:59 Abr 35 Mos 1:260, 315 Mos 2:242 Prob 113

ἀγωνοθετέω Migr 27

ἀγωνοθέτης Somn 1:130, 165

'Αδά Post 75, 79, 83, 112

ἀδακρυτί Her 310 Ios 182 Mos 1:182

'Αδάμ (51) Opif 149 Leg 1:90, 90, 90, 90, 92 Leg 2:9, 9, 13, 19, 31, 40, 40, 53, 64 Leg 3:1, 49, 49, 50, 54, 55, 66, 185, 222, 246 Cher 1, 10, 40, 54, 57 Post 10, 34, 89, 91, 124 Plant 34, 46, 59, 60 Conf 169 Her 52, 53, 257 Congr 58, 171 Mut 63 Somn 1:192 Somn 2:70 QG 1:21, 28, 2:17c

ἀδάμας Abr 193 Mos 1:43

ἀδεής (16) Cher 99 Agr 47 Conf 13, 25 Mos 1:130 Spec 1:192, 261, 320 Spec 2:105 Spec 4:100, 117 Virt 97, 115 Praem 103 Prov 2:58, 70

ἄδεια (45) Leg 2:91 Cher 74, 92 Sacr 23 Post 98 Gig 52 Conf 163 Congr 158, 173 Somn 2:167 Ios 43, 85 Mos 1:193, 301 Decal 150 Spec 1:55, 108 Spec 2:42, 66, 68, 97, 109, 109, 122, 145, 216 Spec 3:11, 23, 140 Virt 28, 111, 123 Prob 17, 57, 87, 148, 148, 149 Flacc 40, 55, 67 Legat 28, 192 Hypoth 7:19 Prov 2:64

ἄδεικτος (6) Det 31 Conf 81 Migr 183 Her 130 Mut 58, 264

ἀδέκαστος (25) Cher 17 Det 21 Post 59 Deus 18 Plant 106, 108 Ebr 169 Conf 25, 121 Migr 95, 115 Her 143 Mut 194 Somn 2:39, 138, 243, 292 Abr 128 Mos 1:33, 150 Spec 1:30, 259 Spec 4:64, 169 QE 2:10b

ἄδεκτος Her 98 Aet 23

ἀδελφιδέος (ἀδελφιδοῦς) (17) Abr 212, 214, 215, 229, 231, 234 Mos 2:143, 153, 244, 278 Spec 2:132 Virt 53, 59, 59, 66 Praem 78, 109

ἀδελφιδοῦς ἀδελφιδέος

ἀδελφοκτονία (7) Det 96 Post 49 Agr 21 Ios 13 Spec 3:16, 18 Virt 199

ἀδελφοκτόνος (7) Cher 52 Ebr 66 Fug 60 Praem 68, 72, 74 Legat 234

ἀδελφός (ὁ) (300) Opif 12, 63, 151 Leg 1:30 Leg 2:8, 20, 24, 51 Leg 3:26, 71, 90, 180, 193, 242 Cher 40 Sacr 1, 15, 129 Det 1, 1, 5, 5, 5, 9, 16, 25, 39, 40, 46, 47, 57, 57, 62, 63, 66, 66, 66, 69, 79, 100, 110, 122, 126, 126, 132, 135, 165 Post 30, 34, 52, 61, 61, 76, 76, 100, 100, 109, 120, 180, 183 Deus 119, 121 Agr 21, 84, 154 Plant 110 Ebr 9, 61, 67, 67, 70, 70, 71, 72, 74, 76, 90, 95 Sobr 12, 14, 32, 34, 51 Conf 37, 90, 124 Migr 3, 22, 60, 66, 78, 78, 84, 159, 203, 208, 208 Her 62, 291 Congr 18, 43, 176 Fug 4, 23, 23, 23, 36, 39, 44, 44, 45, 48, 49, 88, 89, 90, 90, 91, 127, 127, 211 Mut 92, 170, 171 Somn 1:46, 91, 109, 251 Somn 2:7, 33, 33, 41, 108, 111, 111, 111, 134, 142, 266 Ios 5, 6, 8, 9, 9, 10, 11, 12, 15, 163, 164, 168, 170, 171, 173, 175, 175, 178, 179, 180, 184, 185, 187, 188, 188, 200, 209, 210, 216, 217, 217, 218, 223, 223, 224, 225, 232, 233, 234, 235, 236, 237, 238, 247, 250, 251, 252, 261, 267 Mos 1:12, 16, 84, 85, 91, 97, 99, 103, 113, 126, 129, 180, 240, 242 Mos 2:9, 40, 142, 143, 153, 176, 176, 178, 179, 220, 244, 244, 256, 278 Decal 64, 64 Spec 1:112, 112, 114, 250, 253, 297, 316 Spec 2:73, 73, 79, 80, 127, 127, 132, 132, 136 Spec 3:14, 14, 18, 22, 23, 24, 26, 27, 27, 28, 65, 67, 131, 149 Spec 4:88, 135, 157 Virt 51, 82, 82, 91, 116, 140, 176, 208, 209, 222, 225 Praem 36, 57, 62, 78, 109, 134, 134, 148, 148, 155 Prob 1, 57, 57, 79, 142 Contempl 7, 18 Aet 61 Legat 26, 38, 54, 84, 85, 85, 87, 87, 92, 234, 234 QG 1:69, 70:1, 2:71a, 71b, 4:172, 173, 227, 228 QG isf 10

ἄδεσμος Deus 114

ἀδέσποτος Somn 2:295 Virt 98

ἀδηλέω (15) Opif 61, 114 Ebr 36 Conf 119 Congr 136 Somn 1:173 Somn 2:4, 17 Ios 7 Mos 2:263 Spec 3:61, 121 Aet 102, 121 Prov 2:24

ἄδηλος (69) Opif 43, 69 Leg 1:20 Leg 3:47 Cher 16 Sacr 91 Det 1 Deus 29 Agr 141 Ebr 167 Conf 119 Migr 19, 80 Her 179, 303 Congr 135, 138, 138, 152, 164 Fug 204, 205, 206, 206 Mut 65 Somn 1:23, 25, 91, 91, 156 Somn 2:2, 105 Abr 52, 86, 200 Ios 113, 115, 116, 140, 191 Mos 1:198, 280 Mos 2:6, 145, 164, 269 Decal 43, 128 Spec 1:27, 200 Spec 3:52 Spec 4:18, 201 Virt 29, 124, 124 Praem 55, 165 Aet 1, 1 Flacc 24, 45, 129 Legat 38, 109, 173 Prov 2:33 QG 2:54a, 4:52b

ἀδηλότης (6) Deus 29 Mut 10 Virt 152 Legat 51, 322 QG 2:54a

ἀδημονέω QE isf 17

ἀδημονία Det 98 Ios 90 Mos 1:120 Praem 151 Flacc 167

ἄδην Plant 162

ᾅδης Post 31 Mos 1:195 Mos 2:281 Legat 235

ἀδηφαγέω Agr 66

ἀδιάγωγος Leg 3:156 Sacr 32

ἀδιαίρετος (12) Gig 27, 52 Agr 128 Her 132, 233, 237, 308 Spec 1:137, 169, 180, 287 QG 2:14

ἀδιάκοπος Leg 2:81 Det 115

ἀδιακόσμητος Aet 4, 89

ἀδιάκριτος Opif 38 Det 118 Spec 3:57

ἀδιάλυτος (11) Conf 103 Congr 89 Fug 112 Mut 135 Somn 1:17, 22 Spec 4:168 Virt 35 Prov 2:3 QG 4:200b QG (Par) 2:4

ἀδιάστατος (44) Opif 153 Leg 3:92 Det 118 Post 12 Plant 53, 89 Sobr 28 Conf 115 Migr 32, 56 Her 16, 76, 200 Congr 4, 134 Mut 86 Somn 1:147 Somn 2:290 Abr 138, 154 Ios 146 Mos 1:123 Mos 2:54, 184 Decal 24, 24, 26 Spec 1:285, 338 Spec 2:20, 42, 56, 210, 220 Spec 4:161 Virt 6, 52 Praem 72, 102, 154 Aet 62, 75 Prov 2:12 QG 4:169

ἀδιάστροφος Abr 37 Spec 1:105 Spec 2:160 QG 1:51

ἀδιατύπωτος Leg 1:32 Sacr 32 Somn 1:29 Spec 3:108

ἀδιάφθαρτος Conf 25

ἀδιάφθορος (12) Opif 153 Post 134 Migr 17, 31 Congr 165 Fug 114 Abr 157 Ios 112 Spec 1:191 Spec 2:30 Praem 13 QG (Par) 2:4

ἀδιαφορέω (19) Deus 83 Agr 27 Plant 136 Conf 62, 81 Migr 39, 47, 80, 129 Her 83 Fug 19, 173 Somn 1:182 Somn 2:224 Mos 1:123 Spec 1:212 Spec 2:13 Flacc 60 QG 4:180

ἀδιάφορος (12) Opif 74 Leg 2:17 Sacr 99 Her 253 Fug 152 Spec 2:46 Praem 70 Prob 60, 61, 83 QG 4:64 QG isf 5 ἀδίδακτος Cher 71 Ebr 13 Decal 59 QG isf 16

ἀδιεξήγητος Conf 15

ἀδιεξίτητος Post 36 Fug 57 Decal 149

ἀδιερεύνητος (7) Agr 23 Ebr 195, 198 Migr 216 Congr 125 Spec 2:164 Aet 134

ἀδικέω (ὁ) (139) Opif 81, 128 Leg 1:51 Leg 2:68, 100, 100, 107 Leg 3:165 Cher 80 Sacr 50 Det 73 Post 82, 82 Gig 46, 47 Deus 47, 68, 181 Agr 91, 92, 123 Ebr 25, 26 Sobr 32, 69 Conf 24, 25, 27, 69, 119, 120, 153, 161 Migr 219, 225, 225 Her 6 Congr 151, 153, 163 Fug 25, 25, 78, 105, 158, 159, 160 Mut 47, 129, 195, 217, 217, 229, 242, 244 Somn 1:91, 103 Somn 2:137, 266 Abr 96, 213 Ios 20, 20, 52, 156, 228 Mos 1:40, 40, 54, 56, 67, 67, 67, 106, 111, 308, 308 Mos 2:204, 232 Decal 66, 123, 130, 139, 140 Spec 1:237, 279 Spec 2:11, 13, 26, 26, 44, 138, 218, 241, 247 Spec 3:75, 122, 140, 142, 158, 195, 201 Spec 4:5, 7, 9, 10, 17, 34, 34, 142, 142, 185, 197 Virt 84, 124, 147 Praem 137 Prob 128 Aet 75 Flacc 1, 7, 52, 82, 96, 104, 105, 107, 115, 124 Legat 112, 123, 199, 206, 220 Prov 2:24 QG 3:23, 52 QG isf 13 QE 2:3a

ἀδίκημα (ὁ) (110) Opif 152 Leg 1:35, 66 Leg 2:61, 107 Leg 3:77 Det 146, 170 Post 48 Deus 7, 128, 138, 138 Agr 89, 178, 180 Ebr 73, 163 Sobr 5, 31 Conf 15, 30, 60, 114, 116, 116, 160, 177 Her 109, 172, 186, 289 Congr 57, 172 Fug 79, 108, 192 Somn 1:90, 122, 175, 199 Somn 2:170, 279 Abr 40, 97, 133 Ios 44, 170, 176, 212, 216, 220 Mos 1:102, 149, 303 Mos 2:59, 213, 227 Decal 2, 13, 91, 95, 121, 127, 130, 131, 173 Spec 1:102, 103, 127, 193, 229, 235, 243, 330 Spec 2:38, 49, 170, 232, 243 Spec 3:31, 65, 65, 72, 73, 74, 87, 90, 90, 102, 134, 143, 149, 156, 167, 181 Spec 4:17, 32, 84, 196, 198 Praem 157 Flacc 73, 80, 130, 146 Prov 2:55 QG 1:66, 68, 4:172

ἀδικία (70) Opif 73, 79 Leg 1:73 Leg 3:211, 211 Cher 71 Sacr 15, 22 Det 72 Post 52, 93 Gig 5 Deus 112, 122 Agr 17, 44, 83, 112, 113 Sobr 46 Conf 21, 90, 108, 117, 130, 150, 152, 163 Migr 60, 124 Her 161, 162, 163, 209, 243, 245, 284 Mut 182, 189, 197 Somn 1:40, 233 Abr 242 Ios 70 Mos 2:53 Spec 1:214, 215, 270 Spec 2:204 Spec 3:128 Spec 4:141 Virt 180 Praem 15, 23, 52, 105, 159 Prob 56 Contempl 2, 17, 70 Aet 2 Legat 85 Prov 2:8, 39 QG 1:100:1a, 100:2a, 100:2a, 4:204 QE 1:6

ἀδικοπραγέω Decal 89, 177 Spec 2:15 Spec 3:182 Spec 4:199

ἄδικος (110) Leg 1:35 Leg 2:18 Cher 15, 32 Sacr 32 Det 71, 134, 143 Post 32 Gig 2, 3, 4 Deus 49, 85, 126, 170 Agr 20, 95, 118 Ebr 187, 194 Sobr 42, 46 Conf 27, 83, 121, 129 Migr 61, 61 Her 77, 90, 162, 162 Congr 57, 101 Fug 82, 145 Mut 50, 153, 238, 243 Somn 1:236 Somn 2:182, 194 Abr 33, 103, 104, 211 Ios 143 Mos 1:45, 58, 95, 140, 142, 281, 311 Mos 2:107, 156 Decal 61, 140 Spec 1:204, 277, 295 Spec 2:14, 253 Spec 3:85, 164, 209 Spec 4:2, 14, 36, 39, 42, 44, 44, 54, 63, 66, 76, 77, 121, 143, 158, 194, 204, 215, 217, 218, 224 Virt 98, 174, 182, 194 Praem 154, 154 Prob 79 Aet 112, 112 Flacc 132, 141, 173 Legat 105 Hypoth 7:8, 7:8 Prov 2:22 QG 1:70:2, 74, 4:64, 64 QG isf 10

ἀδιοίκητος Sacr 32

ἀδιόρθωτος Sacr 32

ἀδόκητος QG 2:72

ἀδόκιμος (7) Leg 3:119 Det 162 Conf 34, 198 Somn 1:227 Somn 2:284 QG isf 7

ἀδολεσχέω Leg 3:43, 43

ἀδολέσχης Sacr 32

ἀδόλεσχος Det 130

ἄδολος (25) Opif 136 Leg 1:77 Post 133 Deus 22 Ebr 49 Her 95, 110, 129 Fug 78 Somn 1:218 Somn 2:133 Ios 67, 72, 148 Mos 1:63, 150 Decal 58, 65 Spec 2:258 Spec 4:161, 194 Virt 62, 124 Prob 109 QG 4:228

ἀδοξέω Det 41 Prob 23 Flacc 31

ἀδοξία (17) Gig 29 Sobr 38 Conf 16, 18, 112 Her 212, 284 Abr 106 Ios 131 Spec 2:208 Virt 5, 10, 37, 166 Prob 34, 151 QE isf 26

ἄδοξος (18) Det 34 Deus 111 Agr 61 Ebr 195 Fug 16 Somn 1:155 Mos 1:51 Decal 42, 71 Spec 4:74, 172 Virt 32, 174 Prob 120 Legat 13 Prov 2:1 QG 3:22 QG isf 5

ἀδούλωτος (16) Plant 68 Her 275 Somn 1:114 Somn 2:79, 122 Mos 1:39 Spec 3:91 Prob 23, 23, 40, 88, 95, 102, 111, 114, 159

ἄδραστος Somn 2:141

ἀδρομερής Her 142

ἀδρός Agr 115 Mut 269 Abr 26

ἀδυναμία Her 212 Virt 167 QE isf 3

ἀδυνατέω (79) Leg 1:86 Leg 3:1, 39, 54, 92, 132, 147, 202 Cher 129 Sacr 36, 61 Det 6, 127, 149 Post 22, 145 Gig 20, 31 Deus 28, 56, 63, 111, 116 Agr 33, 48, 74 Plant 80 Ebr 32, 64, 185 Sobr 42, 58 Conf 155 Migr 148 Her 12, 72, 142, 238, 269 Congr 60 Fug 38, 43 Mut 56, 56, 173, 209 Somn 1:44 Abr 112, 135 Mos 2:145 Decal 116, 146 Spec 1:40, 72 Spec 2:247 Spec 3:35, 78 Spec 4:3, 81, 111, 199 Virt 12, 24, 31, 88, 183 Praem 29, 121, 130 Prob 63, 87 Contempl 76 Legat 6 Prov 2:19, 52 QG isf 2, 13 QE 2:26 QE isf 6

ἀδύνατος (50) Leg 1:34, 91 Leg 2:4, 93 Leg 3:4, 10 Cher 58, 59 Sacr 123 Det 154, 155 Post 5, 7 Gig 9, 28 Deus 180 Agr 141 Plant 81, 96 Ebr 155 Sobr 30 Migr 46 Her 132 Congr 67 Mut 34, 36, 49, 50, 210, 236 Somn 1:155 Somn 2:120, 122 Abr 80 Mos 1:174 Mos 2:261 Spec 1:32, 282, 341 Spec 2:136 Praem 49 Aet 21, 23, 46, 82, 89, 104 Legat 68 Prov 2:11 QE 2:28

ἀδυσώπητος Spec 1:152 Flacc 177

ἄδυτος (28) Leg 1:62 Cher 95 Det 40 Post 14, 173 Deus 9 Ebr 135 Her 82 Congr 168 Fug 162 Somn 2:232 Mos 2:82, 87, 95, 152, 154, 174, 178 Spec 1:23, 84, 231, 274, 275, 297 Praem 75 Legat 188, 306, 308

ᾄδω ἀείδω

ἀδωροδόκητος Deus 50 Prov 2:61

ἄδωρος Somn 2:44

ἀεί (αἰεί) (434) Opif 33, 43, 92, 94, 100, 140, 140, 141, 168, 171, 172 Leg 1:29, 46, 72, 89 Leg 2:12, 59, 83 Leg 3:11, 25, 25, 27, 27, 47, 53, 68, 69, 125, 131, 139, 149, 164, 216, 219, 222, 252 Cher 33, 51, 66, 70 Sacr 32, 38, 42, 44, 63, 66, 76, 79, 92, 116, 127, 127, 134, 137 Det 74, 113, 133, 178 Post 11, 18, 18, 19, 22, 24, 25, 30, 45, 94, 116, 119, 134, 134, 143, 145, 145, 163, 165 Gig 1, 33, 42, 49, 52, 55 Deus 34, 111, 119, 137, 166, 176 Agr 13, 23, 34, 35, 36, 45, 56, 56, 78, 90, 97, 121, 122, 159 Plant 7, 25, 31, 58, 81, 89, 113, 127, 131, 159, 161, 162 Ebr 5, 13, 24, 27, 49, 53, 61, 145, 159, 169, 174, 182, 211, 224 Sobr 12, 24, 56 Conf 2, 7,

14, 21, 30, 43, 52, 69, 85, 101, 112, 115, 122, 130, 148, 161 Migr 11, 26, 67, 85, 111, 128, 162 Her 17, 32, 35, 48, 71, 109, 128, 161, 205, 206, 227, 234, 241, 252, 269, 292, 295 Congr 4, 33, 47, 58, 103 Fug 27, 51, 57, 63, 64, 114, 114, 146, 186, 200 Mut 2, 60, 60, 88, 126, 151, 167, 196, 198, 217 Somn 1:9, 33, 35, 44, 45, 110, 117, 126, 151, 155, 192, 211, 223, 234 Somn 2:6, 10, 47, 74, 100, 104, 112, 114, 115, 133, 184, 186, 220, 225, 237, 278, 282, 288 Abr 28, 47, 141, 213, 215, 222, 246, 253 Ios 5, 7, 41, 41, 65, 141, 159, 162, 213, 264, 265 Mos 1:4, 8, 10, 14, 31, 46, 48, 148, 149, 168, 181, 190, 204, 231, 257, 265, 295, 328 Mos 2:18, 41, 69, 169, 215, 222, 245, 262, 279 Decal 49, 50, 53, 57, 67, 74, 82, 83, 87, 95, 96, 100, 101, 113, 149, 152, 178 Spec 1:27, 33, 64, 76, 113, 115, 127, 133, 148, 178, 224, 229, 243, 250, 252, 285, 288, 288, 296, 301, 342 Spec 2:19, 27, 46, 60, 71, 83, 116, 129, 168, 173, 187, 195, 200, 228 Spec 3:1, 1, 4, 17, 29, 40, 123, 151, 172, 181, 195, 197 Spec 4:24, 51, 60, 68, 105, 139, 161, 165, 169, 173, 180, 187 Virt 6, 9, 18, 20, 22, 55, 94, 107, 114, 130, 131 Praem 15, 24, 26, 27, 34, 70, 72, 84, 88, 98, 102, 104, 104, 134, 154, 166, 169 Prob 11, 13, 138, 155 Contempl 11, 26, 69 Aet 1, 17, 61, 64, 69, 73, 109, 112, 128, 138, 147 Flacc 4, 35, 44, 87, 133, 143, 147, 153, 166, 180 Legat 18, 44, 63, 85, 85, 165, 178, 186, 198, 200, 211, 310, 325, 366 Hypoth 7:5, 7:10, 7:13, 7:16 Prov 2:9, 25, 30, 64, 67 QG 1:89, 2:10, 4:166 QE isf 9

ἀειδής (18) Det 31, 86, 87 Post 14, 15 Gig 54 Plant 21, 126 Conf 100, 147 Migr 5 Fug 72 Mut 7 Somn 1:188 Abr 75, 79 Mos 1:158 Spec 1:20

ἀείδω (ᾄδω) (74) Leg 2:21, 103 Leg 3:221 Sacr 131 Post 106, 114, 163 Deus 74, 150 Agr 79, 81, 81, 82, 82, 94 Plant 63, 126, 127, 131 Ebr 79, 94, 95, 121 Sobr 13, 36 Conf 35, 49 Migr 60, 108, 113, 128 Her 21, 262 Congr 15, 115 Fug 50, 59, 178 Mut 20, 115, 143, 169 Somn 1:37, 75, 233, 233, 256 Somn 2:38, 242, 269, 269, 270, 271 Mos 1:180, 255, 284 Mos 2:29, 162, 239, 256 Spec 1:342 Spec 2:220 Prob 91, 114 Contempl 14, 80, 80, 84, 87 Aet 57, 139 Legat 96, 204, 284

ἀειθαλής (6) Opif 153 Sacr 25 Agr 171 Mut 140 Spec 4:181 Prob 69

ἀεικίνητος Leg 3:234 Sacr 127 Abr 155, 162 Aet 84

ἀειπάρθενος (8) Leg 1:15 Her 170 Congr 7 Fug 50 Mut 194, 196 Mos 2:210 Contempl 65

ἀέναος (ἀέννaος) (30) Opif 168 Cher 123 Sacr 66 Post 129, 151 Agr 105 Plant 91, 121 Sobr 53 Conf 182 Congr 120 Fug 137, 198 Somn 2:183, 245 Abr 42, 157 Mos 1:189, 212 Spec 1:277, 285, 303 Spec 2:20, 180 Virt 6, 10, 79 Praem 168 Legat 9, 101

ἀέννaος ἀέναος

ἀέξω Opif 104

ἀεροβατέω Det 152

ἀερομυθέω Migr 138

ἀερόμυθος Sacr 32

ἀεροπορέω Mos 1:218 Spec 3:5

ἀεροπόρος (11) Opif 63, 65, 84, 147 Cher 111 Her 238 Decal 115 Spec 1:162 Contempl 8, 54 Aet 45

ἀερώδης Somn 1:145

ἀετός Post 161 Her 154 Abr 266

ἀζήμιος (9) Sobr 5, 42 Conf 153 Mos 1:67 Decal 114 Spec 1:224 Virt 93 Prob 59 Legat 287

ἀζήτητος Leg 3:47

ἄζυγος Spec 1:268

ἄζυμος (14) Sacr 62 Congr 161, 162, 168, 168 Spec 1:181 Spec 2:41, 150, 158, 158, 158, 159, 161 Contempl 81

ἄζυξ Her 125

ἄζωστος Contempl 72

ἀηδής (8) Det 99 Mos 1:108 Spec 1:301 Spec 2:55 Spec 3:49, 82 Flacc 177 Legat 165

ἀηδία (15) Det 131 Agr 41 Ebr 176, 177 Conf 7, 44, 49 Congr 162 Fug 32 Abr 192 Ios 202 Mos 1:105 Spec 1:343 Virt 126 Legat 89

ἀηδών Leg 2:75 Post 105

ἀήθεια Legat 31

ἀήθης (8) Opif 59 Mos 1:119, 200 Spec 2:67 Praem 68 Prob 58 Flacc 120 Legat 223

ἀήρ (241) Opif 29, 29, 32, 64, 70, 78, 80, 84, 113, 146, 161 Leg 1:8, 46, 91 Leg 3:5, 99, 101, 171 Cher 4, 62, 88, 111 Det 62, 83, 85, 87, 88, 89, 154 Gig 6, 8, 9, 10, 10, 11, 22, 22 Deus 79, 83, 84, 87, 107 Agr 24, 51, 53 Plant 3, 3, 4, 6, 10, 10, 12, 13, 14, 24, 120, 127 Ebr 91, 101, 106, 190, 190, 191 Conf 136, 154, 157, 174, 176 Migr 47, 52, 184 Her 14, 134, 135, 136, 146, 146, 197, 197, 197, 198, 208, 224, 226, 238, 240, 247, 281, 282, 307 Congr 104, 117, 133 Fug 110 Mut 59, 158, 179 Somn 1:16, 20, 31, 33, 39, 134, 134, 135, 136, 137, 144, 144, 145, 157 Somn 2:116, 166 Abr 1, 43, 44, 138, 159, 160, 176, 205 Mos 1:41, 96, 97, 113, 114, 118, 119, 120, 121, 127, 129, 129, 143, 202, 212 Mos 2:37, 88, 88, 118, 118, 121, 121, 121, 126, 133, 148, 148, 154, 238, 264, 266, 267, 268 Decal 16, 31, 33, 33, 35, 53, 54, 77 Spec 1:13, 34, 62, 85, 85, 94, 97, 210, 210, 322, 338 Spec 2:45, 143, 153, 172, 255 Spec 3:8, 111, 152, 188 Spec 4:116, 118, 235, 235 Virt 6, 93, 135, 154 Praem 2, 36, 41, 144, 148 Prob 8, 76 Contempl 3, 3, 22, 23, 24, 35, 54 Aet 25, 29, 33, 33, 45, 61, 67, 83, 87, 103, 103, 107, 107, 110, 110, 110, 110, 111, 115, 115, 115, 115, 123, 126, 126, 131 Flacc 123 Legat 125, 127 Hypoth 11:6 Prov 2:23, 45, 55, 66, 68 QG 2:64c, 64c

ἀήσσητος (23) Plant 9 Sobr 38 Congr 165 Mut 203 Abr 106 Mos 1:111, 130, 259, 309 Mos 2:252 Decal 53 Spec 1:38 Spec 2:42 Spec 4:29, 51, 111, 222 Virt 45 Praem 89 Prob 97, 133 Aet 37, 80

ἀθανασία (23) Plant 36, 37, 45 Conf 7 Migr 37, 189 Her 239 Fug 199 Mut 210 Somn 2:184 Abr 183 Mos 1:183 Spec 2:262 Virt 9 Praem 110 Prob 117 Aet 46, 112 Legat 84, 85, 91, 117, 369

ἀθανατίζω (17) Opif 135, 154 Mos 2:108 Decal 58 Spec 1:289, 303 Spec 2:124, 225 Spec 4:112 Virt 67 Prob 109 Aet 9, 35, 109, 144 Legat 91 QG 4:166

ἀθάνατος (116) Opif 119, 119, 135, 135, 135, 152, 155, 156, 165 Leg 2:57, 96 Leg 3:99 Cher 2, 52 Sacr 8, 100, 129 Det 75, 75, 87, 95, 178, 178 Post 32, 39, 43, 68 Agr 167 Plant 44 Ebr 107, 141, 150 Sobr 12 Conf 41, 176, 176 Migr 53, 74, 76, 141, 185 Her 34, 77, 172, 209, 265, 276 Congr 57, 97, 108 Fug 55, 58, 61, 61 Mut 38, 79, 85, 85, 104, 181, 213, 270 Somn 1:115, 127, 137 Somn 2:14, 67, 72, 100, 228, 231 Abr 11 Ios 264 Mos 2:14, 291 Decal 64, 101, 107, 107 Spec 1:31, 81, 345 Spec 3:51, 84 Spec 4:169, 181 Virt 9, 73, 76, 205 Praem 1, 13, 44, 70 Prob 20, 46, 46, 69, 105, 137

Contempl 6, 13, 68 Aet 13, 19, 44, 46, 60, 69 Flacc 123 Legat 84, 85, 91 QG 4:169 QE 2:19 QE isf 3

ἀθέατος (8) Ebr 135, 136 Sobr 6 Migr 115 Somn 1:157 Mos 1:158 Spec 1:72 Legat 224

ἄθεος (30) Opif 170 Leg 1:49, 51 Leg 2:57 Leg 3:13, 108, 212 Det 103, 114, 119 Post 42 Migr 69, 69, 69 Her 203 Congr 57, 87 Fug 114, 180 Mut 61 Mos 2:273 Decal 91, 91 Spec 1:344, 345 Spec 3:179 Prob 127 Legat 77 QG 1:69 QE isf 30

ἀθεότης (24) Leg 3:33 Sacr 69 Post 2, 52 Deus 21 Ebr 18, 78, 110 Conf 2, 114, 121, 162, 196 Congr 159 Somn 2:122 Mos 2:193, 196 Decal 91 Spec 1:32, 330 Praem 162 Prob 127 Aet 10 Legat 163

ἀθεράπευτος (13) Opif 155 Leg 2:63 Cher 68 Somn 2:197 Ios 19 Decal 88 Spec 2:136 Spec 3:98 Virt 171 Contempl 10 Aet 72 Prov 2:30 QG 4:51a

ἄθεσμος Mos 2:198 Spec 2:50 Praem 126

ἀθεώρητος Congr 87

Ἀθηνᾶ QG 2:12a

Ἀθῆναι Prob 47, 127, 130, 140

Ἀθηναῖος (6) Opif 104 Mos 2:19, 19 Spec 3:22 Prob 132, 140

Ἀθήνησιν Abr 10 Prob 128

ἀθήρ Sacr 109 Ios 113

ἀθήρατος Spec 3:44 Virt 39

ἀθησαύριστος Mos 1:204 Mos 2:259 Praem 103

ἀθλέω Ebr 22 Migr 26, 200 Congr 108 Spec 2:183

ἄθλησις (7) Sacr 86 Congr 46, 162 Mut 84 Somn 1:170 Spec 2:98 Hypoth 11:7

ἀθλητής (50) Leg 1:98, 98, 98, 98 Leg 2:21 Leg 3:14, 70, 72, 72, 201, 201, 202 Cher 80 Sacr 116 Det 49 Post 161 Deus 38 Agr 91, 120 Plant 145 Ebr 207 Sobr 65 Migr 27, 221 Congr 164 Mut 33 Somn 1:59, 126, 129 Abr 256 Ios 26, 138, 223 Mos 1:106, 259 Spec 2:60, 91, 98, 246 Spec 4:214 Virt 6 Praem 5, 6, 29, 157 Prob 88, 112 Contempl 41 Flacc 26 QG 4:228

ἀθλητικός (6) Plant 157 Somn 2:9 Abr 48 Ios 82 Virt 193 Prob 26

ἄθλιος (41) Leg 2:102 Leg 3:230 Det 62, 113 Deus 97 Agr 36 Conf 106, 153 Migr 99, 161 Her 113 Congr 174 Fug 30 Mut 193 Ios 154 Mos 1:291, 299 Mos 2:199 Decal 68, 80, 87, 130 Spec 1:176 Spec 4:91, 200 Virt 86 Prob 8, 41 Contempl 41 Flacc 30, 37, 41, 132, 159, 173, 179 Legat 31, 130, 208, 224, 343

ἀθλοθετέω Spec 2:235

ἀθλοθέτης Opif 78 Agr 112 Mut 106 Spec 3:176

ἆθλον (88) Leg 3:74, 242 Post 183 Deus 96 Agr 113 Plant 139, 161 Ebr 35, 35, 74, 74, 76, 109 Migr 27, 44, 109, 133, 134, 163, 167 Her 253 Congr 22, 159 Fug 40, 40, 47, 47, 97, 187 Mut 22, 48, 82, 88 Somn 1:132 Somn 2:154 Abr 38, 47, 110, 128, 129, 254 Ios 18, 138 Mos 1:222, 259, 322 Mos 2:57, 65, 160, 236, 242 Spec 1:118, 123, 125, 125, 132, 153 Spec 2:257, 259, 259, 261 Spec 3:40, 51, 62, 124 Spec 4:72, 169, 195 Virt 175, 201 Praem 3, 13, 14, 16, 16, 22, 27, 31, 37, 47, 49, 53, 57, 65, 67 Contempl 82 Prov 2:9 QE 2:19

ἆθλος (24) Det 2 Deus 13, 38 Agr 121 Ebr 22, 82 Migr 26 Congr 24, 108, 180 Mut 81 Somn 1:131 Ios 177, 230 Mos 1:48 Spec 1:38, 330 Virt 210 Prob 21, 135 Legat 32, 74, 81 QE isf 7

ἀθρέω Cher 58 Somn 1:188

ἀθροίζω (14) Somn 2:187 Ios 158, 258 Mos 2:163, 278 Decal 32, 36 Spec 1:56 Spec 3:80 Virt 67 Prob 138 Contempl 65 Legat 199, 216

ἄθροισμα Det 8 Virt 73

ἀθρόος (115) Opif 34, 41, 57, 71, 80, 130, 158 Leg 3:163, 163, 164 Cher 61, 62, 76 Sacr 40, 41 Det 7, 117 Post 53, 138 Deus 18, 41, 113 Agr 39, 126, 129 Plant 31, 160 Ebr 44, 148, 221 Sobr 58 Conf 17, 30, 48 Migr 9, 31, 121, 144, 156 Her 204, 279 Fug 186, 200 Mut 115, 150, 225 Somn 2:13, 84 Abr 42, 110, 138, 199 Ios 217, 219, 246 Mos 1:18, 100, 118, 136, 180, 211, 233 Mos 2:10, 30, 154, 282, 283, 288 Decal 39, 169 Spec 1:182, 224 Spec 2:191, 220 Spec 3:160 Spec 4:45, 85, 140, 222 Virt 33 Praem 106, 159, 164 Prob 102 Contempl 83 Aet 82, 89, 91, 92, 92, 143, 146 Flacc 1, 114, 137, 153, 165 Legat 9, 67, 73, 80, 124, 134, 186, 190, 221, 223, 225, 267, 342, 348 Hypoth 11:4 Prov 2:34 QE 2:25b, 25d

ἀθυμέω (7) Conf 104 Ios 181 Mos 1:40, 184, 192 Spec 2:87 Legat 184

ἀθυμία Ios 247 Mos 1:181 Praem 151

ἄθυμος Deus 65

ἄθυρμα Spec 2:193 Contempl 52 Flacc 36, 85 Legat 168

ἄθυρος Fug 85 Somn 2:147, 165

ἀθύρω Aet 42

ἄθυτος (9) Cher 94 Plant 108 Mos 2:107, 162 Spec 1:56, 223 Spec 3:125 Spec 4:122 Virt 40

ἀθῷος Leg 3:150 Spec 1:204 Spec 3:61, 196

Ἄθως Somn 2:118

Αἰγαῖος Flacc 151

αἴγειος Migr 97

Αἴγειρα Aet 140

αἴγειρος Aet 64

αἰγιαλῖτις Mos 2:42

αἰγιαλός (9) Opif 113 Mos 1:176 Mos 2:42, 255 Aet 42, 122 Flacc 56, 122 Legat 127

Αἰγυπτιακός (21) Leg 3:212 Agr 62 Migr 160 Her 203 Congr 163 Fug 90 Somn 2:281 Mos 1:284 Mos 2:161, 169, 193, 196, 270 Spec 1:2, 79 Spec 3:125 Flacc 17, 29 Legat 163, 166, 205

Αἰγύπτιος (78) Leg 2:103 Leg 3:13, 37, 38, 242 Sacr 48, 51, 130 Det 93, 95 Post 2, 96, 158 Ebr 36, 95, 208 Conf 36, 70, 70 Migr 14, 141 Congr 1, 20, 20, 71, 84 Fug 18, 19, 148, 179, 180 Mut 117, 118, 170 Somn 2:88, 106, 109, 259, 277, 280 Abr 93, 107, 251 Ios 201, 203, 237, 250 Mos 1:17, 23, 24, 91, 98, 101, 109, 134, 145, 147, 172, 178 Mos 2:19, 19, 193, 194, 195, 248 Decal 76 Spec 3:23 Virt 106, 107 Praem 90 Prob 125 Contempl 8, 8 Flacc 78, 80, 92 Legat 80, 166

Αἴγυπτος (186) Leg 2:59, 77, 84, 87 Leg 3:38, 81, 94, 175, 212, 212 Sacr 51, 62, 118, 134, 134 Det 38, 39, 46, 94, 94, 177 Post 29, 60, 62, 62, 96, 155, 156, 165 Deus 174 Agr 64, 84, 88, 88, 89 Ebr 111, 210 Sobr 13 Conf 29, 72, 81, 88, 92 Migr 18, 20, 21, 23, 29, 54, 76, 77, 151, 154, 159, 160, 162, 201, 202, 204 Her 79, 80, 251, 255, 255, 315, 316, 316 Congr 21, 83, 83, 85, 86, 118, 164 Fug 18, 180 Mut 20, 90, 97, 97, 125, 173, 174, 207 Somn 1:114, 220, 240 Somn 2:5, 43, 109, 123, 189, 216, 255, 255, 258, 266, 300 Abr 92, 103 Ios

15, 27, 37, 117, 121, 135, 151, 157, 159, 161, 164, 184, 186, 188, 195, 238, 242, 248, 251, 254, 255, 259 Mos 1:5, 5, 21, 34, 36, 81, 85, 86, 99, 107, 112, 113, 114, 116, 118, 120, 122, 143, 149, 163, 164, 167, 171, 179, 193, 202, 210, 216, 237, 240, 247, 290 Mos 2:1, 29, 246 Decal 80 Spec 1:5 Spec 2:146, 217, 250 Virt 106 Prob 125 Contempl 21 Aet 62 Flacc 2, 3, 43, 45, 45, 93, 152, 158, 163 Legat 139, 148, 250, 281, 338 Hypoth 0:1, 6:1, 6:1 Prov 2:65 QE 2:2, 2

αἰδέομαι (33) Leg 2:65, 65, 65 Cher 95 Gig 47 Agr 61 Plant 162 Conf 173 Fug 6 Somn 1:99, 107 Somn 2:208, 292 Abr 135 Ios 48 Mos 1:36 Spec 1:115 Spec 2:11, 193, 234, 237, 238 Spec 3:21, 32 Spec 4:119, 188, 201 Praem 116, 164 Aet 108, 134 Flacc 81, 181

αἴδεσις Hypoth 6:6, 6:8

αἰδήμων Virt 182

Ἅιδης Her 45, 78 Congr 57, 57 Somn 1:151

ἀΐδιος (62) Opif 7, 67, 171 Leg 3:101, 148 Cher 2, 4, 9, 25 Det 143 Post 39 Deus 92, 108 Plant 8, 18 Ebr 224 Conf 41 Her 169 Fug 97, 173 Mut 122, 140 Somn 2:14 Abr 55, 76 Ios 265 Mos 2:52, 65 Decal 41, 60, 64, 134 Spec 1:20, 28, 47 Spec 2:166 Spec 4:73, 141 Virt 204, 214 Aet 7, 9, 9, 53, 53, 55, 55, 62, 69, 69, 70, 70, 75, 113, 116, 118, 119, 130, 130, 131, 132 QG 2:10

ἀϊδιότης (11) Opif 12, 44 Congr 56 Mut 122 Abr 55 Virt 65 Aet 36, 52, 55, 75, 105

αἰδοῖος Spec 1:83

αἰδώς (70) Opif 152 Leg 2:65, 65 Sacr 26, 27 Post 147, 181 Conf 37, 116 Her 128 Congr 13, 124 Fug 3, 3, 3, 5, 5, 6, 119 Mut 201, 217 Somn 1:97, 124 Somn 2:62, 80 Abr 94, 153 Ios 107, 153, 222, 246, 257 Mos 1:20, 84, 161 Mos 2:234 Spec 2:26 Spec 3:14, 25, 51, 54, 56, 176, 209 Spec 4:2, 140 Virt 122, 195 Praem 64, 97, 97, 106 Prob 87 Contempl 33, 81 Aet 16, 20 Flacc 28, 89 Legat 5, 36, 142, 204, 276, 293, 352 Hypoth 7:12 QG 2:71a, 3:29, 58

αἰεί ἀεί

αἰθέριος (21) Leg 3:161, 161 Gig 62 Deus 78 Plant 3, 18 Conf 4, 5, 95 Her 87 Fug 138 Somn 2:67 Mos 2:158, 258 Decal 44 Spec 4:123, 123 Praem 84 Aet 30, 119, 147

αἰθεροβατέω Migr 184 Her 238 Spec 1:37, 207 Spec 2:45

αἰθερώδης Somn 1:145

αἰθήρ (38) Opif 70 Leg 3:161, 202 Gig 62 Plant 14, 18, 21, 22 Conf 156 Her 79, 87, 88, 240, 283 Mut 72, 179 Somn 1:22, 54, 139, 145 Ios 78 Mos 1:217 Mos 2:154, 194, 285 Spec 3:2, 185, 187 Spec 4:115, 236 Virt 75, 183 Praem 36, 36, 37 Prob 99 Aet 102 Legat 347

Αἰθιοπία (6) Leg 1:63, 68, 68, 85 Mos 1:99 Flacc 43

Αἰθιόπισσα Leg 2:67, 67, 67

Αἰθίοψ Deus 174

αἰθρία (12) Opif 58, 113 Sacr 90 Her 208 Somn 1:202 Somn 2:166 Abr 79 Mos 1:41, 125 Spec 2:143 Spec 4:52 QG 2:64c

αἴθυια Leg 3:155 Det 101 Spec 4:113 Contempl 55

αἴθω Conf 156

αἰκία (21) Leg 3:201 Det 51 Agr 116 Mos 1:44 Decal 170 Spec 2:94, 95 Spec 3:159, 181 Spec 4:84 Praem 140 Prob 25, 106 Contempl 42 Flacc 59, 71, 72, 96, 117 Legat 128, 302

αἰκίζω (15) Leg 3:33, 38 Det 99 Post 184 Agr 117 Conf 47 Fug 121 Abr 104 Mos 1:44 Spec 3:159 Flacc 75, 84, 173, 173 Legat 128

Αἰλίμ Fug 183, 183, 183 Mos 1:188

αἴλουρος Decal 79

αἷμα (123) Leg 1:91 Leg 2:56 Leg 3:202 Det 69, 79, 79, 80, 80, 81, 83, 84, 91, 92, 100, 177 Agr 21, 154 Ebr 87 Migr 83 Her 54, 54, 55, 56, 56, 57, 58, 64, 182, 182, 185, 277 Fug 188, 190 Somn 1:30, 74, 74, 221 Somn 2:259 Abr 67, 198 Ios 14, 22, 53, 78, 240 Mos 1:81, 99, 99, 101, 130, 144, 284, 303 Mos 2:150, 152, 152, 230 Spec 1:62, 110, 137, 160, 199, 204, 205, 205, 218, 231, 231, 233, 254, 268, 268, 317 Spec 2:128 Spec 3:25, 91, 91, 150, 150, 155 Spec 4:19, 119, 122, 123, 123, 123, 125, 178 Virt 2, 79, 102, 195, 199 Praem 68, 109, 144 Prob 25, 99 Contempl 15, 72 Aet 128 Flacc 190 Legat 54, 75, 97, 235, 356 QG 1:62:1, 62:2, 70:1, 2:59, 59, 59, 59, 59, 59, 59, 59, 59 QG (Par) 2:3, 2:3 QE 2:14

αἱμασιά Mut 74 Mos 1:271

αἱμοειδής Spec 1:216

αἱμορραγία Mos 1:99

αἱμωπός Legat 266

Αἰνάν Fug 149

αἴνεσις Leg 3:26 Spec 1:224, 224

αἰνετός (7) Plant 95, 117, 126, 135 Somn 1:33, 35 Abr 13

αἰνέω Fug 59

αἴνιγμα (8) Leg 3:103, 226, 226, 231, 233 Her 262 Somn 2:3, 4

αἰνιγματιστής Leg 3:225

αἰνιγματώδης Her 63 Somn 2:3 Spec 1:200 Prov 2:24

αἰνίσσομαι (80) Opif 154 Cher 21, 60 Det 155, 178 Post 18 Gig 58 Deus 21 Agr 95, 110 Plant 48 Ebr 96, 100, 223 Sobr 49, 58 Conf 96, 158 Migr 7, 65, 223 Her 54, 116, 128, 243, 290 Fug 157 Mut 7 Somn 1:218 Somn 2:14, 74, 222 Abr 83, 166 Mos 2:102, 106, 128, 131, 147, 150, 180, 186, 207, 244 Spec 1:9, 23, 89, 173, 206, 260, 269, 289 Spec 2:89, 147 Spec 4:66, 109, 113, 137, 144 Praem 17, 63, 113, 131 Prob 2, 29, 68, 153 Contempl 17 Aet 4, 111, 121 Legat 181 Prov 2:50 QG 3:11a, 11a, 4:86b, 228 QG (Par) 2:7 QE 2:14, 18

αἴξ (16) Opif 85 Agr 61 Her 106, 126 Somn 1:189, 197, 198, 199 Somn 2:19 Spec 1:135, 163, 165 Spec 2:35 Virt 95 Prob 30 Legat 76

αἰπόλιον (10) Somn 1:198 Somn 2:152 Ios 257 Mos 1:133 Spec 1:136, 141, 163 Virt 126 Praem 107 Aet 79

αἰπόλος (8) Opif 85 Sacr 104 Agr 48 Somn 2:152 Spec 4:22 Virt 144 Prob 30 Legat 76

αἱρεσιόμαχος Mos 1:24 QE isf 4

αἵρεσις (32) Cher 30 Post 78 Gig 18 Deus 49 Plant 45, 147, 151 Ebr 171 Her 241 Congr 110, 130 Mut 153 Abr 215 Mos 2:160, 176, 177, 278 Spec 1:340 Spec 2:228, 228 Spec 4:108, 157, 157 Virt 60, 185, 205 Praem 16, 54, 78 Prob 83 Contempl 29 QE isf 4

αἱρετέος Leg 1:65 QG 1:55c

αἱρετός (10) Cher 6 Post 39 Deus 163 Ebr 155 Congr 80 Mut 197 Somn 2:20 Spec 3:98 Praem 138 Prob 61 αἱρέω (125) Opif 9, 156 Leg 1:86 Leg 2:51 Leg 3:16, 52, 156 Cher 41, 76 Sacr 31, 37, 46, 47, 81 Det 1, 175 Post 67, 75, 75, 119 Gig 21 Deus 27, 50 Agr 48, 59 Plant 81, 147 Ebr 123, 150, 160, 166, 169, 169, 178 Conf 39, 112, 133, 178 Migr 189 Her 77, 178, 206 Congr 82, 84, 176 Fug 3 Mut 51, 151, 227 Somn 1:7, 174 Somn 2:32, 122, 144 Abr 86, 221, 257 Ios 77, 161 Mos 1:37, 83, 111, 161, 216, 221, 222, 243, 253, 254, 259, 306, 332 Mos 2:3, 31, 88, 141, 142, 176 Decal 175, 177 Spec 1:54, 162, 219, 280, 303 Spec 2:15, 31, 44, 93, 166, 173 Spec 3:30 Spec 4:9, 21, 158, 170, 173, 174, 175 Virt 25, 57, 63, 66, 68, 184, 184, 185, 205, 206 Praem 11 Prob 120 Contempl 83 Aet 41, 81, 104, 128 Flacc 74, 140 Legat 215, 239, 301, 343, 369 Hypoth 6:6 QE 2:46

αἴρω (81) Opif 41, 70, 163 Leg 2:58 Post 110, 136 Gig 66 Deus 137 Agr 154 Conf 4, 18, 57, 74, 90 Migr 184 Her 20, 241, 305 Congr 159 Fug 40 Mut 22, 67, 81, 154, 265 Somn 1:107, 115, 131, 154, 211 Somn 2:98, 171, 207, 245 Abr 42, 43 Ios 102, 138, 149, 181, 187, 195 Mos 1:85, 115, 180, 181, 185, 217, 218, 218, 233, 250, 290 Mos 2:54, 90, 96, 136, 173 Spec 1:37, 44, 57, 300, 330 Spec 2:230 Spec 3:105, 127 Spec 4:74, 128 Virt 45, 135, 201 Praem 8, 27, 80, 152 Contempl 3 Aet 63, 86, 135 Flacc 144 Legat 227

αἰσθάνομαι (68) Leg 1:22 Leg 2:64, 64, 68, 69, 69, 70, 71 Leg 3:198, 216, 216, 216 Cher 73 Sacr 2, 20, 106, 125 Post 36, 42 Deus 16 Agr 167 Plant 80, 83 Sobr 30 Conf 53, 125, 165 Migr 8 Her 29, 73, 107 Congr 99, 101, 127 Fug 134, 135 Mut 56 Somn 1:21 Somn 2:83, 162, 293 Abr 126 Ios 48, 244 Mos 1:56, 243 Mos 2:252 Spec 1:62 Spec 3:35, 115 Spec 4:81, 233 Virt 39 Praem 72, 93, 94, 129, 171 Prob 31, 58 Flacc 2, 98, 121, 124, 141 Legat 174, 300 Prov 2:39

αἴσθησις (567) Opif 31, 53, 62, 62, 112, 117, 120, 130, 130, 139, 139, 147, 162, 165, 165, 165, 166, 166 Leg 1:1, 1, 1, 1, 1, 1, 11, 19, 21, 22, 22, 22, 22, 25, 25, 26, 26, 26, 26, 27, 27, 27, 28, 28, 28, 28, 29, 29, 29, 29, 30, 30, 39, 39, 103, 104 Leg 2:4, 5, 6, 8, 9, 14, 24, 24, 24, 25, 25, 25, 26, 30, 30, 30, 36, 37, 38, 38, 38, 39, 40, 41, 42, 43, 44, 44, 44, 45, 46, 49, 49, 49, 50, 50, 50, 50, 64, 67, 69, 69, 70, 70, 70, 71, 71, 71, 73, 76 Leg 3:17, 20, 21, 22, 41, 41, 44, 44, 49, 50, 50, 50, 56, 57, 57, 57, 58, 58, 59, 60, 61, 61, 64, 64, 67, 81, 81, 103, 108, 108, 108, 109, 109, 111, 111, 112, 112, 115, 182, 182, 183, 183, 184, 184, 185, 185, 185, 188, 198, 198, 199, 200, 200, 200, 200, 202, 203, 211, 216, 216, 219, 220, 220, 220, 221, 222, 222, 222, 224, 224, 225, 234, 234, 235, 243, 251, 251 Cher 41, 41, 41, 52, 57, 58, 58, 58, 59, 60, 65, 65, 70, 70, 70, 71, 73, 97, 113, 117, 124 Sacr 31, 49, 78, 97, 104, 105, 106 Det 17, 25, 33, 34, 52, 53, 54, 54, 85, 99, 100, 109, 110, 159, 171 Post 36, 55, 56, 56, 98, 126, 127, 135, 137, 159, 177 Gig 8, 17 Deus 41, 41, 42, 43, 62, 150 Agr 30, 34, 58, 80, 80, 89, 97, 97 Plant 14, 28, 50, 83, 133, 133, 159 Ebr 8, 46, 58, 63, 70, 71, 108, 133, 161, 169 Sobr 2, 12 Conf 19, 52, 53, 90, 105, 106, 110, 123, 125, 126, 127, 133, 133, 194, 194 Migr 2, 2, 3, 5, 7, 10, 50, 77, 99, 100, 100, 104, 137, 187, 188, 190, 190, 191, 191, 192, 195, 195, 197, 197, 199, 200, 201, 203, 203, 203, 204, 204, 205, 206, 209, 212, 213, 213, 214, 214, 219 Her 15, 42, 52, 52, 53, 63, 66, 69, 71, 73, 85, 89, 89, 98, 106, 107, 108, 108, 109, 110, 111, 111, 118, 119, 126, 129, 132, 142, 184, 186, 246, 257, 257, 315 Congr 20, 21, 21, 21, 27, 27, 81, 92, 96, 97, 99, 100, 100, 143, 143, 143, 144, 144, 144 Fug 22, 45, 45, 46, 71, 91, 92, 101, 109, 134, 135, 182, 188, 189, 189, 189, 190, 192, 192, 193 Mut 7, 56, 56, 110, 118, 157, 164, 205, 223 Somn 1:20, 25, 27, 32, 33, 41, 42, 42, 42, 43, 44, 44, 46, 49, 53, 55, 55, 59, 59, 68, 69, 70, 77, 79, 79, 81, 84, 88, 89, 118, 119, 135, 146, 174, 177, 180, 246 Somn 2:13, 16, 51, 65, 109, 165, 267, 292 Abr 29, 57, 60, 64, 72, 74, 118, 147, 149, 154, 156, 159, 164, 165, 236, 238, 239, 240, 243, 244 Ios 49, 114, 130, 142 Mos 1:11, 105, 124, 125 Mos 2:27, 81, 81, 82, 148, 199, 201, 211, 227 Decal 35, 147 Spec 1:17, 19, 26, 27, 29, 46, 99, 100, 174, 193, 201, 201, 211, 219, 293, 298, 321, 333, 337, 339, 344, 344 Spec 2:89, 163 Spec 3:111, 161, 182, 184, 192, 195 Spec 4:25, 92, 100, 123, 188, 192, 197, 200 Virt 11, 12, 200 Praem 26, 28, 29, 143 Prob 11, 66 Contempl 10, 27, 45 Aet 1, 15, 77 Flacc 159 Legat 2, 12, 21, 43, 168 Prov 2:36 QG 1:24, 24, 32, 76a, 2:34a, 34a, 59, 4:8a, 43 QG (Par) 2:6 QE 2:3b, 9a QE isf 20, 21, 33

αἰσθητήριον (8) Leg 1:104 Leg 3:183, 235 Det 15 Post 112 Ebr 155, 201 Conf 20

αἰσθητικός (29) Opif 65, 66, 67 Leg 2:24, 35, 37, 45 Leg 3:21, 26, 41, 111, 172, 183, 185 Cher 59, 59, 64 Sacr 75 Post 127 Deus 42 Ebr 105, 171 Migr 119 Spec 1:18 Spec 4:123 QG 1:29, 2:59, 59, 59

αἰσθητός (263) Opif 12, 12, 12, 16, 16, 19, 25, 27, 31, 31, 34, 36, 36, 37, 41, 49, 53, 55, 70, 71, 82, 101, 101, 129, 134, 135 Leg 1:1, 22, 22, 22, 24, 24, 24, 24, 24, 26, 26, 26, 27, 27, 27, 28, 28, 29, 29, 29 Leg 2:36, 70, 71 Leg 3:11, 15, 16, 17, 18, 44, 58, 60, 109, 109, 179, 184, 198, 200, 220, 224, 251 Cher 57, 65, 97, 97 Sacr 105, 106 Det 4, 4, 15, 25, 53, 100, 109, 110 Post 5, 98, 99 Gig 61 Deus 31, 32, 58, 58 Agr 34, 42, 58, 80 Plant 14, 50, 118 Ebr 30, 54, 61, 63, 70, 132, 133, 134 Sobr 3, 4, 55 Conf 72, 78, 81, 81, 96, 97, 98, 99, 104, 133 Migr 13, 13, 20, 28, 95, 100, 101, 101, 102, 103, 104, 105, 141, 190, 191, 195, 198, 199, 207, 209, 214 Her 14, 51, 60, 71, 75, 75, 88, 89, 109, 110, 111, 126, 131, 134, 134, 185, 209, 242, 263, 280, 289 Congr 20, 21, 21, 25, 31, 50, 51, 52, 100, 103, 106, 117 Fug 134, 189, 190 Mut 3, 3, 6, 7, 44, 65, 92, 93, 93, 96, 111, 116, 117, 117, 118, 118, 118, 180, 180, 267, 267 Somn 1:43, 44, 72, 79, 82, 84, 119, 157, 185, 186, 188, 215 Somn 2:107, 283 Abr 29, 52, 77, 79, 84, 88, 119, 200, 243 Mos 2:74, 82, 82, 82, 127, 263, 271 Decal 59 Spec 1:6, 17, 20, 279, 288, 302 Spec 2:56, 57, 141, 185 Spec 3:111, 191 Virt 212, 214 Praem 36, 45 Prob 111 Contempl 11, 27 Aet 1, 1, 15, 15, 46, 112, 133 Legat 290, 319, 320 QG 1:24, 24, 2:34a, 54a, 3:12, 49a, 4:8b QE isf 20, 21

αἴσιος (17) Cher 33 Agr 169 Plant 161 Her 9 Somn 2:142 Ios 6, 210 Mos 1:282, 329 Mos 2:24 Decal 158 Spec 3:98 Virt 75 Prob 160 Flacc 22, 177 QE 2:18

ἀΐσσω (ᾄσσω) (7) Her 126 Mut 62 Somn 1:198 Mos 2:273 Spec 4:26, 83 Praem 94

αἶσχος (13) Leg 3:62 Sobr 42 Migr 98, 161 Mut 199 Somn 1:109, 109, 224 Mos 2:139 Spec 1:219, 326 Prob 4, 137

αἰσχροκερδής Sacr 32

αἰσχροπαθής Sacr 32

αἰσχρός (91) Opif 73, 153 Leg 1:61 Leg 2:32, 66, 68, 68, 70 Leg 3:63, 158 Cher 92 Sacr 138, 138 Det 74, 97, 101, 133 Post 81, 86 Gig 21, 39 Deus 49, 105, 123 Agr 123, 144 Plant 158 Ebr 16, 187, 194, 212, 222 Migr 153 Her 36, 77, 242 Fug 34, 84 Mut 30, 193, 193, 197, 198,

199, 206 Somn 2:148, 202, 216, 216, 217, 217 Abr 106 Ios 143, 216 Decal 93, 115, 115, 123 Spec 1:280 Spec 2:135 Spec 3:24, 49, 51, 64, 65 Spec 4:6, 6, 95, 95, 146 Virt 10, 24, 180, 205, 205 Praem 16, 18, 92, 96, 116 Prob 115, 136, 136 Aet 41, 76 Flacc 34 Legat 42, 103 Hypoth 7:1 QG 4:99 QG (Par) 2:6

αἰσχρουργία Somn 2:168

αἰσχρουργός Sacr 32

Αἰσχύλος Prob 143

αἰσχύνη (28) Leg 2:70 Det 51, 134 Deus 98, 100 Her 109, 291 Fug 144, 158 Somn 1:104, 113 Ios 19, 50 Mos 1:3, 293 Spec 1:281 Spec 3:54, 64, 160, 173 Spec 4:6, 182 Virt 37, 40, 202 Praem 5 Flacc 75, 166

αἰσχύνω (21) Leg 2:53, 65, 68 Cher 51 Det 133 Conf 27, 47, 49 Migr 34, 225, 225 Fug 31 Abr 94 Ios 87, 172 Spec 1:321 Spec 3:25, 51 Spec 4:6, 64 Legat 105

αἰτέω (46) Cher 72 Det 60 Post 147, 147, 179 Plant 90 Conf 7, 74 Migr 121 Congr 127 Mut 253 Somn 1:126 Mos 1:182, 331 Mos 2:5, 24, 36 Spec 1:24, 67, 144, 193, 193, 229, 235, 237, 283, 284, 299 Spec 2:196 Spec 3:67, 131, 204 Prob 39 Contempl 19, 27 Flacc 64, 97, 98, 105 Legat 232, 239, 247, 287, 287 QG 1:68, 4:81

αἴτημα Spec 1:43

αἴτησις Sacr 53 Deus 87 Agr 99 Virt 77, 78

αἰτία (244) Opif 21, 45, 47, 54, 72, 77, 79, 80, 82, 83, 84, 100, 131, 132, 133 Leg 1:8, 18, 34, 59, 99, 99, 99 Leg 2:50, 68, 69, 94, 96 Leg 3:35, 65, 69, 75, 77, 77, 246 Cher 4, 37, 38, 55, 55, 59, 125, 127 Sacr 52, 72, 126 Det 35, 43, 77, 86, 106, 141, 142, 150 Post 111, 153 Gig 1, 62 Deus 21, 87, 108 Agr 131, 179 Plant 155, 165 Ebr 9, 11, 15, 73, 140, 160, 180, 211 Sobr 18, 32 Conf 112, 114, 124, 142, 144, 156, 158, 165 Migr 47, 65, 136, 194 Her 59, 115, 124, 249, 300, 301, 301 Congr 163, 179 Fug 3, 4, 8, 15, 64, 94, 161, 162, 206 Mut 13, 16, 126, 136 Somn 1:33, 40, 72, 167, 172 Somn 2:54, 76, 289 Abr 13, 27, 84, 91, 206 Ios 32, 80, 89, 115, 148, 156, 165, 184, 212, 235 Mos 1:8, 94, 157, 281 Mos 2:5, 81, 158, 159, 174, 182, 211, 229, 272 Decal 14, 15, 18, 97, 118, 176 Spec 1:3, 13, 14, 111, 113, 124, 147, 154, 172, 191, 195, 214, 263, 283, 289, 317, 340 Spec 2:11, 51, 134, 210, 221, 243, 251, 253 Spec 3:58, 80, 82, 97, 103, 107, 124, 129, 131, 134, 178, 180, 190, 199 Spec 4:9, 11, 25, 92, 120, 123, 125, 147, 158 Virt 23, 27, 100, 134, 165 Praem 6, 12 Prob 127 Aet 4, 20, 22, 22, 23, 24, 26, 27, 74, 75, 78, 106, 146 Flacc 9, 46, 140 Legat 38, 39, 57, 69, 171, 177, 190, 198, 199, 206, 293, 373 Prov 2:64 QG 1:77, 93, 2:11, 22, 54a, 4:52d QG (Par) 2:6 QE 2:18, 21

αἰτιάομαι (52) Leg 2:78 Leg 3:179 Cher 33, 34, 36, 37, 128 Agr 33, 64, 175 Ebr 25 Conf 155, 161, 190 Migr 75 Her 91, 105 Fug 20, 80 Somn 1:226 Somn 2:132, 182 Abr 130, 181 Ios 30, 182, 215, 225, 233 Mos 1:90, 170, 183 Decal 87 Spec 1:40, 154 Spec 2:231 Spec 3:55 Spec 4:64 Virt 141, 147, 152 Prob 91 Flacc 181 Legat 229, 248, 257, 332, 358, 360 Prov 2:22, 54, 58

αἰτιατός Plant 33

αἰτιολογία Fug 163

αἰτιολογικός Fug 163

αἴτιος (328) Opif 8, 30, 38, 52, 53, 115, 164 Leg 1:20, 25, 35, 82, 99, 101, 105 Leg 2:19, 46, 69 Leg 3:6, 7, 7, 29, 35, 54, 73, 73, 76, 97, 100, 102, 206, 215, 243, 247 Cher 28, 29, 34, 36, 46, 48, 87, 88, 90, 125, 125, 125, 126, 127, 127, 127, 128, 130 Sacr 3, 8, 54, 54, 54, 56, 92, 94, 96 Det 16, 58, 89, 95, 98, 103, 122 Post 14, 19, 38, 168, 177, 179 Gig 10, 29 Deus 53, 56, 60, 68, 87, 105, 116, 125 Agr 31, 49, 91, 96, 129, 172, 173 Plant 20, 27, 33, 35, 48, 60, 61, 64, 72, 91, 93, 109, 131, 139, 147, 148, 171 Ebr 6, 12, 61, 73, 75, 105, 107, 107, 108, 126, 138, 141, 163, 166, 171 Conf 10, 13, 98, 123, 124, 161, 167, 180, 181, 189, 196 Migr 30, 131, 172, 179, 181 Her 22, 74, 143, 169, 171, 236, 289 Congr 42, 66, 79, 117, 127, 166, 171, 173 Fug 8, 12, 23, 25, 80, 133, 137, 140, 141, 171, 198, 213 Mut 15, 46, 87, 104, 117, 122, 155, 205, 221, 221 Somn 1:27, 67, 92, 147, 161, 190, 240 Somn 2:41, 41, 288, 291 Abr 78, 134, 143, 244, 261, 268 Ios 30, 33, 170, 183, 241, 244 Mos 1:11, 26, 138, 237, 308 Mos 2:219 Decal 12, 59, 64, 107, 151, 155, 176 Spec 1:10, 23, 25, 31, 62, 62, 99, 200, 215, 252, 337, 343 Spec 2:5, 7, 7, 21, 48, 65, 106, 114, 118, 137, 146, 151, 163, 171, 197, 198, 204, 228, 228, 228, 243, 245, 246, 248, 254 Spec 3:40, 41, 97, 117, 117, 145, 178, 180 Spec 4:34, 68, 95, 110, 181, 237 Virt 34, 35, 45, 65, 94, 143, 150, 165, 166, 178, 187, 202, 210, 212, 216, 221 Praem 13 Prob 84, 90, 133, 150 Contempl 1, 86 Aet 8, 34, 52, 70, 70, 70, 70, 78, 89, 89, 106, 116, 128 Flacc 50, 142, 143, 189 Legat 2, 3, 39, 83, 141, 149, 161 Hypoth 7:9 Prov 2:40, 45, 53, 66, 68 QG 1:58, 100:1b, 100:1b, 100:2a, 2:13b, 34a, 4:51b QG isf 8, 13 QE 2:25c, 26, 64 QE isf 3

Αἰτωλία Legat 281

αἰφνίδιος (32) Leg 1:17 Cher 38 Sacr 78 Gig 20 Deus 26, 89 Agr 174, 175, 176 Migr 156, 184 Fug 115 Somn 2:125, 137 Ios 6, 211 Mos 1:127, 133, 179 Mos 2:154, 254, 283 Spec 1:75 Spec 3:126 Spec 4:201 Praem 146 Aet 129 Flacc 128, 140, 154 Legat 221 Prov 2:29

αἰχμαλωσία Leg 2:35

αἰχμαλωτίς Leg 3:21

αἰχμάλωτος (25) Leg 3:225, 232 Sacr 26 Det 14 Migr 150 Abr 229 Ios 47, 47 Mos 1:36, 142, 250, 311 Virt 110, 114, 115 Praem 164 Prob 19, 37, 114, 122 Flacc 60, 87, 95 Legat 155 Hypoth 7:8

αἰών (76) Leg 3:25, 198, 199 Cher 2, 71, 90 Sacr 47, 76 Det 149, 178 Post 119 Gig 19 Deus 2, 32, 32, 115 Plant 47, 47, 51, 51, 53, 114, 116, 169 Ebr 31, 195 Sobr 24, 67 Migr 8, 125 Her 165, 165, 165 Fug 46, 52, 57, 57, 57, 96, 107, 115 Mut 12, 12, 80, 185, 267, 267 Somn 1:19, 46, 114, 139 Somn 2:31, 36, 101, 199, 212, 248 Abr 271 Ios 24 Mos 1:206 Mos 2:14, 212 Decal 67, 104 Spec 1:170, 172, 282, 282 Praem 37, 85 Legat 85, 300 Prov 2:19 QG 3:11b QE 1:1, 2:20

αἰώνιος (29) Leg 3:85, 199 Sacr 127 Post 121, 123 Deus 142 Plant 8, 73, 74, 85, 89 Ebr 76, 127, 141, 142, 155 Her 290 Congr 105 Fug 78, 211 Mut 12 Somn 2:285 Abr 51, 54 Ios 146 Virt 129 Prob 24, 117 Aet 75

αἰώρα Deus 172 Somn 2:46, 61

αἰωρέω Ebr 36 Somn 2:16, 62

ἀκαθαίρετος (20) Opif 164 Ebr 99 Migr 215 Her 284 Somn 1:103, 131 Somn 2:285, 290 Mos 1:50, 260 Spec 4:169 Virt 6, 186 Praem 97, 169 Prob 151 Legat 22, 41, 196, 240

ἀκαθαρσία (6) Leg 1:52 Leg 2:29 Plant 95, 99, 109 Her 113

ἀκάθαρτος (40) Leg 1:52 Leg 3:8, 139, 139, 147 Det 103, 169 Deus 8, 127, 127, 128, 131, 132, 132 Agr 131, 145 Plant 103 Ebr 127, 143 Sobr 49 Conf 167 Migr 65, 69 Fug 81 Mut 200 Somn 1:202 Decal 94, 95 Spec 1:100, 119, 150, 223 Spec 3:50, 206, 208, 208, 209 Spec 4:106, 109 Virt 147

ἀκάθεκτος (11) Agr 84 Migr 132 Somn 1:36, 122 Ios 40, 153 Spec 2:9, 193 Spec 4:82 Praem 94 Legat 190

ἀκαιρεύω Mos 2:208 Spec 2:49

ἀκαιρία (6) Plant 103 Sobr 42, 43 Migr 126 Mut 185 Ios 42

ἀκαιρολόγος Sacr 32

ἄκαιρος (12) Ebr 97 Fug 191 Somn 2:83, 85 Mos 1:139 Mos 2:206 Spec 1:120 Spec 3:32 Prob 84 Aet 26 Flacc 101 Legat 14

ἀκακία (6) Opif 156, 170 Leg 3:110 Ebr 6 Her 38 Virt 195

ἄκακος (8) Agr 96 Ios 6 Spec 1:105 Spec 3:101, 119 Virt 43 Flacc 68 Legat 234

ἀκάκωτος Her 125

ἀκαλλώπιστος Opif 1 Cher 42 Contempl 38

ἀκάματος Sacr 40 Fug 41 Aet 8, 64 Legat 90

ἀκαμπής (8) Migr 175, 223 Congr 61 Spec 1:306 Virt 3 Praem 27 Flacc 60 Legat 301

ἄκανθα Leg 3:248, 248, 248, 249 Somn 1:89

ἀκανθώδης Mos 1:65 Spec 4:29

ἀκαρής (9) Post 25 Plant 53 Her 83, 143 Mut 186 Abr 161 Ios 141 Mos 1:180 QG (Par) 2:7

ἀκαρπία Somn 2:199

ἄκαρπος Leg 1:50, 52

ἀκατακάλυπτος Leg 2:29 Spec 3:60

ἀκατάληπτος (23) Leg 1:20 Leg 2:65 Cher 97 Det 89 Post 15, 169, 169 Ebr 187 Conf 138 Her 132, 132, 209, 246 Mut 10, 15 Somn 1:15, 21, 23, 25, 33, 67 Spec 1:47 QG 2:54a

ἀκαταληψία Ebr 175

ἀκατάλλακτος (11) Migr 150 Her 43, 244, 245 Mut 95 Somn 2:98 Abr 14, 105, 213 Ios 156 Legat 205

ἀκατάπληκτος (7) Migr 61 Mos 1:233, 251 Virt 27, 32, 71 Praem 95

ἀκατασκεύαστος Aet 19

ἀκατάσχετος (7) Sacr 61 Det 110 Deus 138 Mut 239 Somn 1:107 Somn 2:275 Prov 2:12

ἀκατονόμαστος Somn 1:67 Legat 353

ἄκενος (διάκενος) QG 4:30

ἄκεντρος Mos 1:68

ἀκέομαι (8) Leg 1:70 Post 138 Congr 18 Mos 1:187 Spec 1:249 Aet 63 Legat 274 QG isf 13

ἀκέραιος Legat 334

ἄκεσις Migr 124 Spec 1:77

ἀκέφαλος Somn 2:213

ἀκηλίδωτος (7) Cher 95 Sacr 139 Det 171 Spec 1:150, 167 Virt 205, 222

ἀκήρατος (10) Cher 50 Det 77 Gig 8, 22 Conf 177 Her 34 Congr 25 Mut 219 Ios 146 Virt 55

ἀκήρυκτος (14) Sacr 17, 35, 130 Deus 166 Conf 42 Fug 114 Mut 60 Somn 1:106 Somn 2:166 Spec 4:202 Praem 87 Legat 100, 119 QE isf 30

ἀκιβδήλευτος (6) Cher 29 Sacr 26 Det 137 Plant 106 Her 105 Fug 130

ἀκίβδηλος Migr 116

ἀκίνδυνος (13) Det 42 Sobr 37 Somn 1:124 Somn 2:86, 143 Ios 139 Mos 1:85, 285 Mos 2:254 Spec 2:52 Spec 3:132 Virt 176 Legat 47

ἀκίνητος (32) Opif 9, 61, 100, 100, 101 Leg 3:45 Post 28 Gig 65 Agr 43 Sobr 41 Migr 167 Congr 45 Somn 1:69, 136, 249 Somn 2:119, 136 Mos 2:7 Spec 2:58 Spec 3:172 Spec 4:143, 232 Praem 76 Contempl 4 Aet 59, 59, 121, 125 Legat 68, 300 Prov 2:3 QG 1:24

ἀκκισμός Mos 1:297

ἀκλεής Sacr 122 Ebr 198

ἄκλειστος Fug 85 Mut 5 Somn 2:165

ἄκληρος Her 187

ἀκλινής (39) Opif 97 Leg 2:83 Sacr 63 Det 12, 148 Post 23 Gig 49, 49, 54 Deus 22, 23 Conf 30, 87, 96 Her 87, 95, 298 Fug 47, 150 Mut 87, 176 Somn 2:219, 220, 278 Abr 63, 170, 273 Mos 1:30 Spec 1:64, 191 Spec 2:2 Virt 158, 216 Praem 30, 169 Prob 28 Aet 116 Legat 1 QE isf 12

ἀκμάζω (23) Opif 42, 140 Det 113 Deus 173 Plant 161 Conf 149 Fug 146, 180 Somn 2:85 Abr 67 Ios 135 Mos 1:6, 226, 265 Mos 2:30 Spec 2:153, 228 Prob 73 Aet 63, 73 Legat 142 Prov 2:23 QE isf 4

ἀκμή (43) Opif 103, 140 Leg 1:10 Leg 3:179 Sacr 15, 25, 80, 80, 87 Det 98 Post 71 Agr 85, 153 Ebr 146 Sobr 16 Conf 7 Migr 126, 141 Her 130, 299 Fug 125 Somn 1:11, 199 Ios 91, 166 Mos 2:43, 140 Spec 1:282 Spec 3:39, 81 Virt 26 Praem 141 Prob 15, 132 Aet 58, 62, 64, 71 Legat 87, 203, 249 Hypoth 11:7 Prov 2:15

ἀκμής Cher 86, 90 Ebr 21 Mos 1:215 Spec 2:102

ἄκμων Post 116 Decal 72

ἀκοή (174) Opif 4, 62, 62, 119, 165, 172 Leg 1:25, 83 Leg 2:7, 26, 39, 74, 75 Leg 3:44, 50, 56, 57, 58, 216, 220 Cher 42, 72 Sacr 7, 61, 73, 78, 78, 131 Det 125, 157, 168, 171 Post 86, 104, 106, 106, 143, 161, 161, 165, 165, 166, 166 Gig 18 Deus 42, 111, 120 Agr 34, 132 Plant 29, 62, 127, 159 Ebr 82, 82, 82, 94, 103, 156, 158, 159 Conf 19, 52, 57, 72, 72, 72, 90, 110, 140, 141, 141, 141, 141, 148 Migr 38, 47, 48, 48, 49, 52, 103, 119, 137, 188 Her 10, 12, 14, 14, 185, 232 Congr 27, 66, 113, 143, 143 Fug 191, 200, 208, 208, 208, 208 Mut 102, 102, 111, 202, 247 Somn 1:20, 27, 36, 45, 55, 80, 140, 248 Somn 2:160, 259, 263 Abr 60, 127, 150, 150, 160, 167, 236, 266 Ios 20, 61 Mos 1:3, 220, 235 Mos 2:150, 211 Decal 35, 44, 55, 148 Spec 1:8, 29, 193, 211, 272, 337, 342 Spec 2:202, 232 Spec 3:134 Spec 4:59, 60, 60, 61, 137, 140 Praem 79 Contempl 31 Flacc 124 Legat 18, 175, 216, 227, 237, 255, 268, 310 Hypoth 11:15 QG 1:32 QG (Par) 2:3 QE 2:9:1, 9a, 9b, 9b, 16, 118 QE isf 21

ἀκοίμητος (11) Mut 5, 40 Abr 162 Ios 147 Mos 1:185, 289 Spec 1:49, 330 Spec 4:139, 201 QE 2:15b

ἀκοινώνητος (20) Cher 86 Sacr 32 Sobr 67 Fug 35 Mut 104 Ios 30 Decal 123, 171 Spec 2:16, 73, 75 Spec 3:23 Spec 4:187, 204, 207 Virt 141 Praem 92 Legat 34, 68 QG isf 10 ἀκολάκευτος (7) Det 21 Ebr 107 Sobr 13 Migr 86 Somn 1:54 Somn 2:292 Ios 63

ἀκολασία (37) Opif 73 Leg 2:18 Sacr 15, 22 Det 72 Deus 112 Agr 17, 98, 101, 112 Conf 21, 90 Her 209, 245, 254 Mut 197 Somn 2:181, 210 Ios 70 Mos 1:295, 305, 311 Mos 2:55 Spec 1:173, 282 Spec 3:23, 51, 62, 64, 65 Spec 4:89 Praem 159 Prob 56, 159 Prov 2:8 QG 4:204 QE 2:4

ἀκολασταίνω (6) Det 73 Post 82 Migr 219 Somn 2:266 Abr 134 QG 4:173

ἀκόλαστος (33) Leg 2:18 Cher 51 Sacr 32 Det 133, 143 Post 52, 156, 181 Deus 126, 170 Ebr 210 Sobr 42 Fug 28, 153 Mut 50, 153 Somn 1:88 Abr 103, 107 Ios 40, 50, 64 Decal 168 Spec 1:148, 323, 325 Spec 4:94 Virt 40, 182, 194 Praem 100 Prob 57 QG 4:168

ἀκολουθέω (30) Leg 1:108 Leg 2:50 Leg 3:67, 109, 197, 236 Cher 117 Sacr 51 Post 4, 6, 120 Agr 37 Ebr 34, 38 Sobr 12 Conf 32 Migr 151, 207, 211 Her 185 Mut 37 Somn 2:103 Abr 70 Mos 1:268 Decal 113 Spec 1:25 Praem 58 Contempl 67 Aet 84, 145

ἀκολουθία (43) Opif 28, 65, 131 Leg 3:110 Sacr 125 Post 23 Agr 106 Plant 49 Ebr 24 Sobr 26 Conf 14 Migr 84, 110, 131 Her 301 Fug 119, 150, 152 Mut 47, 135 Somn 2:44 Abr 6 Mos 2:48, 130, 263, 266 Decal 83 Spec 1:1, 195 Spec 2:52, 129, 150, 223 Spec 3:180 Spec 4:39, 46 Contempl 1 Aet 27, 27, 103, 112 Flacc 6 Legat 34

ἀκόλουθος (ό) (80) Leg 3:150, 204, 223 Sacr 112, 128 Det 52, 61, 81, 91, 95, 119, 150 Post 4, 66, 139, 169 Gig 67, 67 Deus 20, 33, 59, 69, 77, 141 Agr 125 Plant 20, 32, 93 Ebr 206 Sobr 1, 30 Conf 127, 171 Migr 128, 173 Her 50, 95, 266, 283 Congr 63, 122 Fug 165, 177 Mut 11, 178, 195 Somn 1:61, 82, 173, 191 Somn 2:169, 215 Abr 3, 118 Ios 58 Mos 1:29, 113, 156 Mos 2:1 Decal 1, 32 Spec 3:48, 136 Virt 19, 129 Praem 3, 11, 42, 52, 82 Prob 22, 96, 160 Aet 53 Flacc 112 Legat 77, 94, 365 QG 2:48 QE 2:16

ἀκονάω (25) Gig 60 Agr 114, 135 Sobr 2 Conf 43, 131 Migr 124, 210 Her 109, 123, 130, 140 Congr 17 Fug 125 Mut 108 Somn 1:49, 199 Somn 2:39, 280 Mos 2:279 Decal 63 Spec 4:191 Prob 7 Prov 2:29, 66

ἀκόνη Congr 25

ἀκονιτί (8) Leg 3:15 Deus 147 Agr 150 Her 7, 47 Mut 81 Virt 38 Praem 31

ἀκοντίζω Mos 1:99 Prob 108

ἀκοντιστής Mos 1:168

ἀκόρεστος (22) Leg 3:148 Det 113 Post 174 Deus 154 Plant 25 Ebr 4, 220 Her 109 Somn 1:50 Mos 2:23 Spec 1:192 Spec 3:1, 9 Spec 4:20, 91, 113 Virt 9 Praem 135, 154 Flacc 180 Legat 89 QG (Par) 2:7

ἄκος Her 10 Somn 1:51 Somn 2:60 Mos 1:211 Flacc 118

ἀκοσμέω Migr 60

ἀκοσμία (13) Opif 33 Conf 109 Her 206 Somn 1:241 Somn 2:152 Ios 87 Mos 1:302 Aet 54, 54, 85, 105, 106 Legat 204

ἄκοσμος Sacr 32 Fug 31 Somn 2:260 Spec 4:210 Praem 20

ἀκούσιος (85) Opif 128 Leg 1:35 Leg 3:141 Cher 22, 66, 75, 96 Sacr 48, 128, 129, 130, 132, 133 Det 97 Post 10, 10, 11, 11, 48, 87 Deus 48, 75, 89, 113, 128, 130, 130 Agr 175, 176, 176, 178, 178, 179, 179, 180 Ebr 66, 95, 123, 125, 163, 163 Conf 179 Migr 225 Fug 53, 65, 65, 75, 76, 76, 77, 86, 93, 94, 96, 102, 105, 107, 108, 115, 115, 117 Mut 241, 243 Somn 1:71 Decal 68, 142 Spec 1:158, 227, 234, 235, 238 Spec 2:52, 87, 196 Spec 3:123, 128, 128, 129, 132, 134, 136 Prob 109 QG 3:52, 52, 4:64

ἄκουσμα (17) Opif 78, 162 Leg 3:156 Gig 31 Agr 35 Migr 216 Congr 113 Mut 138, 209, 211, 212 Somn 1:165 Ios 142 Mos 1:10, 20 Spec 1:174 Legat 43

ἀκουστής Migr 224

ἀκουστικός Fug 182 Somn 1:170 QG 1:32

ἀκουστός Migr 48, 48, 51, 104 Decal 47

ἀκούω (268) Leg 1:54, 83, 90 Leg 2:16, 35, 59, 69, 69, 82, 82, 82 Leg 3:41, 51, 54, 54, 54, 56, 84, 103, 111, 142, 183, 183, 216, 216, 219, 222, 222, 243, 245, 245 Cher 27, 57, 62, 73 Sacr 24, 26, 29, 45, 98, 106, 125 Det 5, 28, 61, 99, 123, 124, 131, 134, 175 Post 1, 36, 37, 87, 126, 179 Gig 45 Deus 52, 82, 84 Agr 13, 57, 59 Plant 29, 72, 83, 129 Ebr 96, 96, 98, 106, 123, 155, 157, 158, 160, 160, 219 Sobr 21 Conf 1, 3, 52, 58, 59, 59, 59, 62, 72, 117, 123, 134, 148, 189, 194, 195 Migr 38, 47, 47, 48, 69, 137, 197, 197, 208, 218 Her 2, 10, 10, 11, 11, 71, 267, 292 Congr 20, 66, 68, 96, 143, 180 Fug 23, 85, 122, 123, 127, 147, 153, 154, 159, 198, 208 Mut 6, 61, 99, 119, 138, 138, 143, 157, 170, 171, 200, 202, 202, 204 Somn 1:27, 37, 55, 55, 140, 158, 193, 193 Somn 2:8, 21, 114, 160, 263, 264 Abr 99, 112, 148, 214, 238, 239 Ios 22, 26, 92, 105, 116, 125, 126, 126, 151, 167, 175, 179, 183, 226, 256 Mos 1:45, 76, 83, 85, 125, 173, 227, 233, 233, 275, 280, 281, 283 Mos 2:114, 165, 200, 201, 201, 217, 228, 257, 260 Decal 46, 74, 75, 88, 88, 89, 90, 139 Spec 1:45, 50, 279, 321 Spec 2:11, 41, 94, 216, 256, 256 Spec 3:178 Spec 4:40, 61, 107, 202 Virt 39, 59, 173, 217 Praem 163 Prob 118 Contempl 45, 73 Aet 11, 142 Flacc 10, 32, 40, 40, 40, 88, 103, 114, 114 Legat 132, 181, 182, 186, 201, 206, 224, 241, 243, 255, 349, 350, 353, 357, 370 Hypoth 6:9, 7:20 Prov 2:60 QG 2:71b, 4:110a QG isf 2 QE 2:6a, 16 QE isf 26

ἄκρα (6) Opif 63 Leg 3:115 Cher 86 Spec 3:138, 184 Flacc 156

ἀκράδαντος (7) Post 25, 122 Plant 153 Conf 87 Mut 135 Abr 269 Mos 2:14

ἀκραιφνής (25) Opif 8, 45, 150 Leg 3:64 Sacr 12 Post 20 Gig 8 Deus 79 Plant 58 Migr 52 Her 184, 294 Spec 1:46, 51, 66, 106 Spec 2:55 Spec 3:121 Spec 4:56, 236 Aet 77 Legat 40, 165 QG 1:93, 3:58

ἀκρασία (29) Opif 158, 164 Cher 92 Det 113 Post 93 Agr 101 Somn 2:202, 204, 210 Abr 94 Ios 56, 57 Mos 2:164 Decal 123, 169 Spec 2:19, 135 Spec 3:23, 34, 40, 49, 137 Spec 4:122 Virt 36, 143 Praem 116 Contempl 6 Legat 14 Prov 2:69

ἀκρατεία Virt 180

ἀκρατής (16) Leg 3:62, 109 Det 174 Migr 52 Mut 170, 215 Somn 2:182, 201, 202, 205 Abr 90, 95, 103 Virt 208 QG 2:68a, 3:21

ἀκρατίζομαι (6) Leg 3:82 Ebr 148 Somn 2:248 Mos 1:187 Mos 2:204 Prob 102

ἄκρατος (120) Opif 20, 71, 144, 150 Leg 3:62, 149, 155 Cher 2, 29, 86 Sacr 32 Det 68 Post 32, 37, 137, 142, 176 Deus 77, 77, 77, 78, 78, 81, 82, 82, 82, 83, 158 Agr 37, 157 Plant 39, 143, 144, 147, 154, 160, 162, 163, 171, 171 Ebr 2, 4, 5, 11, 29, 78, 95, 123, 128, 152, 161, 220, 221 Conf 73 Her 94, 183, 183, 184, 236, 289 Congr 22, 36 Fug 31, 72, 166, 176, 202 Mut 102, 154,

184 Somn 1:117, 122, 143, 145, 163 Somn 2:8, 149, 183, 190, 205, 249 Abr 135, 205, 205 Ios 91, 155 Mos 1:255 Mos 2:23, 152, 162 Decal 108 Spec 1:37, 99, 192, 249 Spec 2:50, 193 Spec 3:186 Spec 4:91, 113 Virt 162, 182 Praem 38, 71, 122 Prob 5, 13, 31, 117, 156 Contempl 40, 45, 85 Aet 87 Flacc 136 Legat 2, 14, 83, 320 QG 2:68a

ἀκράτωρ (19) Opif 80 Leg 3:149, 156 Sacr 61 Det 25 Plant 145 Ebr 210, 223 Her 109 Fug 31 Somn 2:147, 184, 203, 215 Mos 1:161 Mos 2:196 Spec 3:34 Spec 4:127 Virt 163

ἀκράχολος (ἀκρόχολος) Sacr 32 Ebr 223 Somn 2:192

ἀκρεμών Mos 1:65, 189

ἀκρίβεια (23) Cher 128 Sacr 85 Post 112, 133, 159 Deus 150 Agr 135 Plant 141 Ebr 201 Her 1 Ios 130, 140 Mos 1:279 Decal 52, 71 Spec 1:213 Spec 4:1 Contempl 31 Flacc 3, 112 Legat 351 Prov 1 QG 2:54d

ἀκριβής (105) Opif 52, 56, 65, 66, 71 Leg 1:99 Leg 2:25, 61 Leg 3:115, 183 Cher 11, 17, 129 Sacr 137 Det 11, 47 Gig 57 Deus 93, 121, 123 Agr 18 Conf 57, 97 Migr 34, 89, 189, 191, 195, 222 Her 63, 74, 142, 152 Congr 143 Fug 7, 34, 53 Mut 60 Somn 1:11, 58, 59, 60, 204, 228 Somn 2:99, 103, 107 Abr 49, 84, 157, 266 Ios 7, 49, 162, 165, 205 Mos 1:24, 49, 68, 122, 230 Mos 2:51, 52, 129, 145, 167 Decal 147 Spec 1:27, 61, 75, 154, 160, 167, 195 Spec 2:253 Spec 3:53, 141 Spec 4:105, 132, 154, 156, 171, 190 Virt 56, 57, 165 Praem 28 Prob 75 Contempl 75 Aet 1, 86 Flacc 77, 90, 96 Legat 154, 208, 220, 259, 269, 372 Hypoth 6:9 Prov 2:54 QG 1:32, 3:3 QG isf 5

ἀκριβοδίκαιος Her 143 Somn 2:101 Ios 65

ἀκριβολογέομαι Agr 136 Her 256

ἀκριβολογία Agr 143 Spec 1:260

ἀκριβόω (73) Opif 28, 77 Leg 1:91 Leg 3:95, 206 Cher 66, 91 Sacr 1, 70 Agr 1, 28, 95, 124 Plant 74 Ebr 3 Sobr 33 Migr 89, 176, 184, 189 Her 125, 215 Congr 21, 81, 89 Fug 38, 47, 87 Mut 69, 130, 153, 266 Somn 1:4, 133, 172, 197 Somn 2:8, 17, 155, 206 Abr 2, 167, 240 Ios 125, 151 Mos 1:4 Mos 2:46, 115 Decal 1, 18, 48, 82 Spec 1:1, 105, 110, 189, 269 Spec 2:1, 200 Spec 3:117 Spec 4:231 Virt 12, 24, 166 Prob 16, 20 Contempl 14, 49, 51 Aet 39, 130 Prov 2:17, 66

ἀκρίς (8) Opif 163 Leg 2:105 Mos 1:121, 122, 126, 145 Spec 4:114 Praem 128

ἀκριτόμυθος Leg 3:119 Somn 2:275

ἄκριτος (24) Leg 3:66, 119, 128, 131 Deus 171, 182 Somn 2:115 Abr 20, 264 Ios 44, 52 Mos 2:214 Spec 2:163 Spec 4:88 Prob 157 Flacc 54, 105, 106, 126, 140 Legat 241, 302, 344 QE isf 18

ἀκροάομαι (14) Ebr 25 Conf 9 Her 12, 13 Congr 69 Ios 65 Decal 33, 46 Contempl 31, 76, 77, 80 Flacc 106 Hypoth 7:12

ἀκρόασις (13) Sacr 31 Ebr 213 Her 12, 253 Mut 203, 210 Somn 2:37 Mos 2:214 Praem 7 Contempl 79 Legat 169, 175 QE 2:13b

ἀκροατήριον Congr 64

ἀκροατής (13) Leg 3:121 Sacr 78 Det 134 Her 14, 15 Congr 70 Mut 18, 270 Somn 1:36 Spec 4:43 Flacc 24 Legat 168, 183

ἀκροατικός Det 124, 125 Prob 81

ἀκροβατέω Somn 1:131 Mos 1:169 Decal 45 Virt 173

ἀκροβολίζομαι Leg 3:238

ἀκροβολισμός Sacr 4

ἀκροβυστία QE 2:2

ἀκρόδρυα (16) Opif 116 Somn 2:49 Mos 1:230 Mos 2:186, 223 Spec 1:134, 248 Spec 2:216, 221 Spec 4:208, 214 Virt 95, 149 Praem 101, 107 Contempl 54

ἀκροθίνιον QG 1:60:2

ἀκροθώραξ Ebr 221 Contempl 46

ἀκροκιόνιον Mos 2:77

ἀκρόπολις (10) Leg 2:91 Agr 46 Sobr 57 Conf 83, 113, 144 Somn 1:32 Abr 150 Spec 4:49 QG (Par) 2:5

ἀκροποσθία Spec 1:4

ἄκρος (124) Opif 33, 68, 71, 110, 137 Leg 1:10, 28 Leg 2:86 Leg 3:88, 104 Cher 6, 81, 111, 111 Sacr 4, 21, 37 Det 28, 39, 54, 81, 129, 131 Post 104, 157, 174 Deus 35, 40, 43, 55, 110, 118, 127, 168 Agr 98, 121, 161, 162, 162, 181 Plant 9, 16, 111, 160 Ebr 20, 150, 216, 217 Sobr 2 Conf 55, 150, 197, 197 Migr 135, 163, 175 Her 67, 139, 141, 143, 181, 206, 218, 218, 229, 276 Fug 132, 172 Mut 88, 123, 212, 227 Somn 1:37, 40, 60, 148, 152, 169, 219 Somn 2:70, 144, 189, 213, 221, 230, 235, 289 Abr 58, 122, 257 Ios 268 Mos 2:58, 150, 150, 150, 151, 151 Decal 21 Spec 1:37, 166 Spec 2:98, 157 Spec 4:83, 92, 92, 102, 179 Virt 42, 50, 99, 188 Prob 141 Contempl 31, 51, 72, 77 Aet 2, 143 Legat 195, 267, 310 Prov 2:65 QG 4:43, 9*

ἀκροτελεύτιον Her 8 Contempl 80

ἀκρότης (18) Opif 8 Cher 6 Det 65 Deus 81 Her 29, 121, 156 Congr 107 Mut 2, 122 Somn 2:60 Abr 153 Spec 3:33 Spec 4:144 Virt 203, 226 Contempl 90 Aet 54

ἀκρότομος (6) Leg 2:84, 86, 86 Somn 2:222 Mos 1:210 Decal 16

ἀκρόχολος ἀκράχολος

ἀκρώμιον Mos 2:112, 122, 133 Spec 1:86

ἀκρώρεια Mos 2:163

ἀκρωτηριάζω (18) Cher 96 Sacr 110, 115 Deus 66 Agr 86 Somn 2:84, 95, 168 Abr 44 Spec 1:3, 9, 47, 80 Spec 2:244 Spec 3:179 Contempl 44 Aet 49 Legat 135

ἀκτέον Spec 4:9

ἀκτή Mos 2:42

ἀκτήμων Plant 69 Virt 98 Praem 54 Prob 77

ἀκτινοβολέω Somn 1:114

ἀκτινοειδής Legat 95

ἀκτινωτός Legat 103

ἀκτίς (22) Cher 97 Deus 78, 79 Plant 40 Conf 60, 157 Her 222 Fug 165 Mut 6 Somn 1:23, 77, 90, 115, 202 Abr 76 Mos 1:123 Mos 2:262 Spec 1:40 Spec 4:52 Prob 5 Contempl 68 Legat 103

ἀκυβέρνητος Det 144 Somn 2:283

ἀκύμων Somn 2:166

ἀκυρολογέω Det 131

ἄκυρος (9) Leg 3:164 Sacr 71 Her 23 Mos 2:272 Spec 2:137 Prob 41, 104 QG 3:22 QE isf 16

ἀκυρόω Ebr 197 Conf 193 Spec 2:115

ἀκώλυτος (7) Deus 160 Sobr 40 Fug 191 Spec 1:113 Praem 119 Prov 2:1, 45 ἄκων (36) Leg 3:16, 60, 90, 164 Sacr 71 Det 92 Gig 20 Deus 64 Ebr 63, 122, 177 Conf 37, 121 Migr 222 Fug 14 Mut 56 Somn 1:7 Somn 2:126, 137 Mos 1:69, 142 Decal 144, 177 Spec 1:156, 230 Spec 3:77, 141 Virt 94, 94, 118 Prob 60, 61, 78, 97, 108 QG 1:68

ἀλαζονεία (33) Ebr 192 Migr 136, 147, 171 Fug 194 Somn 2:296 Ios 70, 249 Decal 5, 40 Spec 1:10, 265, 293 Spec 2:18, 19, 83 Spec 3:8, 137, 201 Spec 4:146, 165, 170 Virt 161, 162, 165, 171, 172 Praem 47 Prob 126 Legat 178, 218 QG 4:100 QE 2:37

ἀλαζονεύομαι Fug 33

ἀλαζών (6) Sacr 32 Congr 41 Mos 2:240 Spec 4:72, 88 Virt 172

ἄλαλος Conf 39

ἀλάομαι Migr 154 Her 287 Mut 152 Ios 26 Spec 2:168

ἀλάστωρ Sacr 32 Congr 57 Flacc 175

ἀλγεινός Leg 3:202, 203 Deus 66

ἀλγέω (10) Opif 161 Leg 3:200, 200, 200, 211 Det 131 Her 43 Somn 2:122 Prob 23 QG 1:29

ἀλγηδών (28) Opif 161, 161 Leg 3:200, 202, 202, 216 Cher 62 Ebr 8 Her 154 Congr 81, 84 Somn 2:122 Abr 64, 96, 192 Mos 1:11, 128, 183 Spec 1:3, 254, 292 Spec 2:89 Virt 128 Praem 72, 145 Prob 30, 146 QG (Par) 2:3

ἄλγημα Somn 2:259

ἀλεαίνω (7) Cher 88 Conf 157, 157 Mos 1:114 Spec 4:56 Prov 2:23, 48

ἀλεγίζω Prob 125

ἀλεεινός Spec 2:221

ἄλειμμα Det 19 Somn 2:58, 59 Legat 273 Prov 2:44

ἀλείπτης (10) Leg 1:98 Sobr 65 Migr 166 Somn 1:69, 129 Mos 1:22, 48 Spec 2:98 Praem 5 Prob 80

ἀλειπτικός Somn 1:250, 251 Spec 2:230 Virt 155

ἀλειφόβιος Flacc 138

ἀλείφω (39) Conf 91 Her 123 Congr 31 Fug 25, 96 Mut 84 Somn 1:189, 249, 249, 250, 251 Abr 48 Ios 5, 176 Mos 1:60, 298 Mos 2:146, 189 Spec 1:314 Spec 2:46, 60, 99 Spec 3:24, 39, 51 Spec 4:101, 134, 179 Virt 51, 70 Prob 111 Flacc 5 Legat 39, 161, 178 Hypoth 11:1 Prov 2:24, 44 QG 2:15b

ἄλεκτος (29) Opif 54 Leg 3:84 Post 52 Gig 51 Agr 91 Plant 105 Migr 217 Mut 179 Somn 1:188 Somn 2:60, 106 Abr 170 Ios 157 Mos 2:56, 291 Decal 63 Spec 1:36, 248 Spec 2:146 Spec 4:235 Virt 67, 224 Praem 26, 103 Prob 90 Aet 146 Flacc 10 Legat 133, 338

ἀλεκτρυών Prob 131

Ἀλεξάνδρεια (17) Mos 2:35 Prob 125 Contempl 21 Flacc 2, 26, 28, 43, 45, 74, 110, 163 Legat 150, 165, 172, 250, 338, 346

Ἀλεξανδρεύς (12) Flacc 23, 78, 78, 80 Legat 120, 162, 164, 170, 172, 183, 194, 350

Ἀλεξανδρίς Flacc 27

Ἀλέξανδρος Cher 63 Mos 2:29 Prob 94, 95, 96

ἀλεξάνεμος Somn 2:52

ἀλέξημα Contempl 38

ἀλεξίκακος (8) Agr 98 Ebr 172 Mut 251 Somn 1:110 Ios 80 Virt 11 Legat 112, 144

ἀλεξιφάρμακος Leg 3:124, 200 Prov 2:60

ἀλέπιδος (ἀλεπίδωτος) Spec 4:101

ἀλεπίδωτος ἀλέπιδος

ἀλετρίς Mos 1:134

ἄλευρον Spec 3:55, 57, 60

ἀλέω Sacr 86 Mos 1:208

ἄλη Praem 117

ἀλήθεια (406) Opif 1, 21, 45, 132, 136, 145, 170, 171 Leg 2:10, 20, 56 Leg 3:36, 36, 45, 45, 45, 61, 63, 118, 124, 128, 132, 140, 174, 175, 178, 191, 228, 229, 229, 231, 232, 233, 233 Cher 50, 83, 86, 94, 121, 122 Sacr 12, 13, 27, 28, 91, 91, 99 Det 7, 9, 21, 22, 26, 28, 125, 138, 160, 161, 162, 162 Post 12, 42, 51, 52, 52, 88, 95, 101, 119, 134, 136, 147, 160, 162, 164, 165, 166, 167, 177 Gig 15, 24, 33, 41, 45, 58 Deus 30, 54, 61, 64, 96, 102, 159, 172 Agr 3, 41, 43, 69, 81, 116 Plant 42, 111, 112, 128, 135, 164 Ebr 6, 34, 34, 39, 43, 45, 70, 73, 75, 76, 86, 142, 164, 167 Sobr 11, 57 Conf 2, 48, 105, 126, 138, 141, 159, 190 Migr 12, 76, 86, 86, 88, 90, 107, 110, 146, 153, 158, 172, 183, 184, 190, 225 Her 15, 43, 53, 70, 71, 71, 93, 95, 109, 143, 169, 201, 231, 248, 260, 266, 291, 303, 305 Congr 57, 61, 80, 87, 132 Fug 33, 71, 128, 139, 156 Mut 7, 11, 22, 57, 94, 170, 171 Somn 1:9, 23, 60, 73, 107, 121, 124, 179, 181, 186, 215, 218, 220, 229, 229, 235, 245 Somn 2:97, 106, 115, 133, 138, 147, 249, 253, 264, 280, 296 Abr 6, 7, 8, 11, 64, 80, 121, 123, 143, 159, 179, 222, 271 Ios 38, 58, 59, 65, 68, 77, 90, 106, 112, 116, 126, 145 Mos 1:2, 24, 48, 62, 213, 235 Mos 2:48, 67, 100, 113, 122, 128, 128, 129, 135, 140, 167, 177, 237, 253, 265, 270, 271, 273, 284 Decal 6, 15, 32, 57, 65, 67, 81, 91, 128, 138 Spec 1:28, 51, 59, 63, 66, 74, 88, 89, 97, 138, 191, 207, 230, 287, 303, 309, 313, 313, 319, 323, 344 Spec 2:2, 49, 52, 164, 164, 171, 194, 227, 236, 244, 258, 259 Spec 3:53, 58, 141, 155, 164, 181, 186 Spec 4:5, 33, 43, 43, 44, 50, 52, 69, 69, 69, 71, 75, 80, 156, 156, 178, 189, 192 Virt 6, 17, 20, 56, 65, 102, 178, 182, 187, 195, 195, 214, 219, 221 Praem 4, 8, 25, 25, 27, 28, 36, 46, 58, 110, 123, 148, 162 Prob 12, 27, 37, 41, 42, 74, 83, 158 Contempl 1, 27, 39, 39, 63, 89 Aet 1, 2, 56, 68, 69, 76, 90, 138 Flacc 96, 99, 106, 119, 164 Legat 20, 30, 60, 77, 248, 277, 279, 359 Prov 2:7, 9, 11, 16, 20, 36, 53, 54 QG 1:1, 97, 2:54a, 54a, 3:29, 30b, 4:69 QG isf 5 QE 2:2 QE isf 7

ἀληθεύω (13) Leg 3:124 Cher 15, 15 Ebr 40 Abr 107 Ios 95 Mos 2:177 Decal 84 Spec 4:60 Aet 48 QG 4:69, 69 QE isf 17

ἀληθής (ὁ) (317) Opif 56, 72, 78, 82, 139 Leg 1:7, 17, 45, 65, 85 Leg 2:46, 68, 81, 93, 93 Leg 3:7, 51, 58, 120, 122, 157, 224, 229, 229 Cher 9, 23, 42, 76, 87, 93, 108, 119, 124, 127 Sacr 14, 26, 35, 65, 74, 108, 109 Det 10, 19, 38, 43, 74, 138, 157 Post 1, 27, 45, 102, 115, 185 Gig 59 Deus 65, 105, 107, 125, 128, 146, 182 Agr 69, 97, 119, 141, 159, 159, 164, 164 Plant 40, 80, 133, 162 Ebr 12, 36, 38, 45, 47, 55, 61, 79, 88, 92, 95, 111, 139, 155, 166, 166, 205, 211, 223, 224 Sobr 67 Conf 9, 72, 98, 116, 144, 190 Migr 19, 21, 66, 69, 76, 95, 95, 99, 152, 171, 202, 213 Her 19, 62, 75, 111, 115, 132, 132, 199, 243, 256, 268, 279, 285, 303, 305, 306, 315 Congr 6, 13, 18, 19, 22, 44, 51, 93 Fug 11, 19, 27, 82, 126, 154, 160, 208, 212 Mut 33, 45, 128, 140, 175, 213, 248, 248, 264 Somn 1:84, 128, 166, 185, 226, 233, 237, 238 Somn 2:47, 64, 72, 128, 162, 181, 188, 194 Abr 20, 25, 50, 60, 68, 94, 120, 158, 203, 219, 261 Ios 22, 30, 52, 104, 119, 165, 200, 254, 258 Mos 1:182, 183, 190, 255, 274, 286 Mos 2:12, 75,

103, 108, 128, 171, 185, 235 Decal 3, 8, 18, 40, 47, 124, 136 Spec 1:10, 30, 30, 34, 36, 38, 53, 116, 137, 154, 168, 176, 245, 314, 326, 327, 332 Spec 2:10, 22, 23, 53, 59, 91, 95, 163, 173, 176, 203, 224, 248, 252, 262 Spec 3:65, 83, 100, 115, 121, 129, 149, 156 Spec 4:48, 51, 73, 84, 184, 185, 231 Virt 4, 4, 8, 33, 44, 64, 185, 193, 205, 205 Praem 30, 43 Prob 1, 113 Contempl 10, 40, 52 Aet 10, 15, 37, 47, 69, 76, 83, 106, 106, 126 Flacc 72, 140 Legat 5, 110, 125, 215, 237, 260, 265, 290, 299, 347, 357 Hypoth 6:4, 7:19 Prov 2:8, 42, 62 QG 1:55a, 70:1, 70:2, 100:1b, 4:67, 88 QE 2:9b, 16, 47, 50b QE isf 13, 16

ἀληθινός (18) Leg 1:32, 35 Leg 3:52 Det 10 Gig 33 Her 162 Congr 101, 159 Fug 17, 82, 131 Somn 2:193 Mos 1:289 Spec 1:332 Virt 78 Praem 41, 104 Legat 366

ἀληθόμαντις Mos 2:269

ἀληθότης Leg 3:120, 122, 124, 124, 127

ἄληκτος (10) Sacr 66 Agr 36 Plant 39 Ebr 95, 159 Congr 6 Spec 4:142 Praem 73 Legat 35 QG 2:29

ἄληστος (15) Agr 133 Plant 31 Sobr 28 Migr 205 Mut 84, 270 Somn 1:193 Ios 27 Mos 1:48 Spec 1:133 Virt 165, 176 Prob 90 Contempl 26 Legat 177

ἀλητεύω Migr 171

ἀλήτης Sacr 32

ἀλιεύω Agr 24 Plant 102

ἀλίζω Mos 2:257

ἅλις (12) Deus 20 Somn 1:14, 189 Somn 2:261 Decal 154 Spec 2:38, 139, 203 Spec 4:133 Praem 57 Prob 16 Hypoth 7:20

ἁλίσκομαι (59) Leg 3:17 Cher 124 Det 74, 178 Deus 103, 153 Agr 93, 116, 150, 160 Ebr 5, 64, 68, 74, 79 Conf 111, 126, 174, 177 Migr 219 Fug 47, 107 Mut 62, 215 Somn 2:94 Abr 64, 258 Ios 44, 215, 216, 221 Mos 1:251, 252 Decal 111 Spec 3:94, 121, 123 Spec 4:7, 57, 120, 121 Virt 23, 46, 186 Praem 18, 29, 149 Prob 31, 115, 121, 152 Aet 49 Flacc 59, 147, 150 Legat 163 Prov 2:34 QG 4:198 QE 2:21

ἀλκή (22) Opif 85 Post 161 Agr 95, 146 Ebr 174 Conf 49 Somn 2:10, 170 Mos 1:70, 111, 132, 259 Spec 3:39 Virt 45 Praem 89 Prob 40, 112, 134, 147 Contempl 60 Legat 111 Prov 2:61

ἄλκιμος Agr 83 Spec 2:56 Prov 2:56

ἀλλά (3263) Opif 5, 12, 13, 13, 20, 20, 23, 26, 26, 28, 33, 34, 35, 38, 41, 41, 42, 43, 43, 45, 45, 51, 57, 58, 67, 72, 77, 84, 89, 90, 97, 107, 113, 122, 126, 130, 133, 135, 137, 142, 145, 145, 149, 149, 151, 153, 154, 156, 157, 158, 161 Leg 1:1, 2, 4, 5, 17, 18, 18, 20, 24, 29, 31, 32, 33, 33, 35, 41, 42, 46, 49, 54, 54, 55, 58, 59, 60, 65, 67, 74, 77, 77, 80, 82, 85, 85, 85, 87, 89, 90, 93, 95, 97, 98, 98, 98, 99, 99, 103, 103, 105, 106, 106 Leg 2:2, 4, 5, 10, 13, 15, 17, 18, 20, 27, 29, 31, 33, 34, 35, 40, 43, 44, 45, 46, 50, 50, 53, 56, 57, 58, 60, 62, 63, 63, 64, 68, 70, 73, 75, 77, 78, 78, 79, 82, 84, 85, 85, 85, 85, 91, 92, 93, 100, 100, 104 Leg 3:6, 9, 10, 10, 11, 14, 15, 17, 20, 20, 20, 22, 23, 23, 24, 25, 26, 26, 26, 27, 31, 32, 33, 35, 36, 40, 40, 42, 46, 47, 49, 50, 51, 51, 51, 55, 55, 56, 56, 57, 59, 61, 61, 61, 64, 66, 66, 67, 67, 68, 70, 71, 73, 73, 73, 78, 79, 82, 82, 83, 84, 84, 85, 86, 86, 87, 87, 87, 89, 90, 90, 99, 100, 102, 102, 105, 106, 106, 111, 117, 119, 122, 123, 125, 125, 126, 126, 126, 126, 126, 128, 129, 129, 130, 130, 131, 132, 134, 134, 134, 136, 136, 136, 137, 138, 140, 141, 142, 142, 144, 146, 148, 149, 149, 151, 153, 157, 160, 160, 162, 162, 163, 163, 164, 166, 167, 168, 170, 174, 175, 175, 176, 177, 179, 180, 180, 181, 181, 182, 183, 184, 185, 188, 190, 190, 191, 192, 193, 193, 195, 199, 199, 200, 202, 203, 206, 206, 207, 209, 210, 210, 210, 211, 213, 214, 216, 217, 217, 222, 226, 227, 227, 233, 234, 234, 236, 238, 239, 242, 242, 244, 246, 247, 248, 249, 252, 252, 253 Cher 1, 4, 6, 8, 12, 14, 16, 20, 33, 36, 37, 45, 46, 48, 49, 51, 51, 53, 58, 60, 65, 65, 70, 71, 78, 82, 84, 87, 96, 99, 100, 104, 107, 114, 114, 114, 115, 116, 117, 119, 130 Sacr 4, 8, 9, 12, 19, 25, 30, 33, 34, 37, 37, 37, 38, 39, 42, 43, 46, 47, 48, 52, 52, 54, 56, 57, 58, 62, 68, 68, 68, 69, 71, 71, 72, 72, 76, 76, 77, 78, 78, 79, 80, 82, 88, 90, 90, 92, 92, 93, 95, 95, 97, 99, 100, 104, 107, 107, 111, 113, 115, 116, 127, 133, 134, 135, 136, 137 Det 8, 10, 12, 14, 15, 17, 18, 18, 24, 24, 24, 24, 25, 28, 31, 33, 33, 35, 35, 38, 38, 41, 43, 46, 47, 49, 50, 51, 52, 53, 54, 57, 58, 58, 59, 62, 63, 68, 73, 83, 83, 84, 85, 87, 89, 90, 92, 94, 96, 101, 101, 101, 101, 102, 102, 107, 112, 114, 116, 120, 122, 132, 133, 134, 141, 149, 152, 152, 152, 152, 153, 157, 162, 163, 165, 166 Post 6, 9, 10, 13, 13, 14, 18, 19, 19, 22, 25, 30, 39, 42, 50, 50, 53, 54, 72, 77, 80, 81, 85, 89, 90, 94, 95, 95, 95, 101, 110, 113, 119, 120, 126, 126, 126, 129, 132, 134, 139, 141, 141, 141, 142, 142, 144, 144, 147, 148, 152, 158, 160, 160, 163, 166, 166, 167, 168, 169, 171, 172, 173, 173, 184 Gig 1, 4, 5, 9, 18, 20, 25, 25, 30, 33, 33, 33, 37, 42, 45, 48, 51, 52, 54, 56, 66 Deus 3, 8, 11, 13, 16, 21, 22, 24, 25, 32, 32, 49, 54, 54, 55, 60, 62, 69, 72, 75, 76, 76, 77, 79, 80, 83, 85, 89, 90, 100, 100, 104, 104, 108, 112, 114, 118, 121, 121, 122, 124, 130, 133, 136, 138, 142, 145, 148, 148, 150, 152, 162, 165, 167, 169, 172, 173, 173, 174, 174, 177, 179, 181, 182 Agr 3, 4, 5, 13, 17, 19, 22, 22, 24, 29, 35, 45, 46, 47, 50, 50, 53, 60, 64, 67, 73, 81, 85, 86, 88, 88, 91, 91, 91, 92, 95, 99, 103, 104, 107, 110, 111, 112, 115, 118, 119, 120, 125, 126, 129, 130, 133, 134, 142, 150, 150, 151, 152, 153, 154, 154, 155, 156, 157, 157, 161, 161, 162, 167, 169, 172, 174, 179, 179, 180 Plant 1, 17, 18, 18, 27, 27, 31, 36, 44, 49, 51, 55, 57, 62, 63, 69, 70, 71, 71, 72, 72, 73, 74, 74, 79, 81, 84, 88, 90, 92, 101, 105, 107, 108, 108, 110, 115, 125, 126, 126, 128, 130, 134, 135, 138, 145, 147, 153, 155, 156, 159, 162, 162, 165, 167, 168, 168, 168, 168, 173, 173, 174, 176 Ebr 4, 6, 7, 13, 19, 25, 26, 27, 27, 28, 32, 32, 40, 40, 45, 50, 52, 53, 56, 58, 58, 61, 61, 66, 69, 70, 70, 72, 74, 75, 76, 78, 82, 84, 85, 88, 89, 95, 96, 100, 101, 103, 104, 104, 106, 110, 112, 113, 122, 123, 128, 131, 131, 132, 134, 135, 135, 144, 146, 147, 154, 162, 163, 167, 169, 170, 171, 175, 176, 186, 189, 191, 191, 191, 193, 195, 196, 198, 198, 204, 211, 214, 215, 217, 217, 220, 222, 223, 223 Sobr 2, 2, 7, 9, 11, 14, 16, 16, 18, 20, 21, 22, 24, 27, 31, 33, 42, 45, 45, 46, 52, 56, 57, 57, 63 Conf 3, 9, 10, 11, 14, 14, 15, 19, 22, 25, 25, 29, 36, 36, 37, 41, 43, 45, 45, 46, 46, 49, 50, 51, 52, 55, 55, 59, 59, 61, 67, 67, 70, 71, 72, 72, 74, 75, 75, 76, 82, 87, 91, 98, 98, 98, 107, 115, 116, 118, 119, 119, 121, 122, 126, 127, 130, 132, 140, 140, 141, 142, 143, 143, 147, 152, 154, 155, 158, 160, 160, 161, 162, 162, 167, 169, 170, 173, 182, 184, 185, 187, 188, 191, 193, 194, 195 Migr 5, 5, 7, 8, 9, 11, 12, 20, 21, 25, 27, 28, 37, 40, 41, 42, 42, 43, 43, 43, 46, 46, 47, 48, 48, 49, 51, 51, 52, 55, 58, 60, 64, 64, 65, 66, 76, 81, 82, 88, 93, 95, 96, 97, 99, 100, 101, 103, 105, 106, 110, 111, 115, 115, 126, 131, 134, 136, 140, 144, 146, 148, 149, 149, 155, 156, 162, 166, 170, 171, 173, 175, 179, 181, 182, 186, 189,

192, 193, 194, 195, 196, 200, 201, 206, 206, 206, 209, 216, 220, 222, 225 Her 3, 10, 11, 11, 12, 12, 13, 14, 14, 16, 17, 17, 19, 21, 22, 22, 23, 23, 27, 28, 28, 32, 32, 42, 42, 43, 44, 44, 49, 51, 56, 61, 62, 62, 64, 67, 67, 68, 69, 70, 78, 81, 83, 84, 84, 86, 86, 96, 97, 100, 100, 103, 103, 105, 108, 109, 110, 114, 121, 121, 123, 124, 133, 137, 141, 142, 142, 145, 149, 150, 156, 160, 164, 170, 171, 171, 174, 184, 190, 200, 201, 206, 213, 223, 226, 226, 228, 231, 234, 241, 242, 246, 252, 252, 253, 254, 255, 256, 258, 258, 258, 267, 273, 276, 280, 284, 287, 289, 290, 291, 293, 304, 308, 308, 309, 316 Congr 5, 7, 9, 11, 12, 13, 25, 33, 34, 44, 44, 50, 53, 53, 56, 57, 58, 64, 65, 66, 68, 69, 69, 69, 73, 75, 81, 81, 85, 90, 95, 95, 97, 97, 106, 110, 112, 119, 121, 121, 125, 138, 138, 139, 140, 140, 152, 153, 161, 162, 166, 170, 172, 172, 174, 178, 179, 180 Fug 5, 6, 6, 16, 16, 19, 19, 21, 22, 32, 39, 39, 44, 46, 49, 53, 54, 60, 61, 62, 63, 65, 65, 70, 73, 75, 76, 78, 79, 80, 82, 84, 87, 93, 99, 101, 102, 102, 105, 108, 108, 116, 117, 121, 123, 124, 128, 131, 134, 141, 144, 145, 146, 149, 151, 155, 155, 156, 158, 162, 162, 165, 167, 168, 181, 186, 187, 190, 193, 199, 200, 204, 204, 211, 213 Mut 3, 3, 8, 13, 15, 17, 17, 18, 18, 19, 21, 26, 27, 32, 39, 45, 54, 56, 60, 64, 65, 68, 70, 79, 81, 81, 81, 87, 88, 89, 104, 109, 114, 117, 117, 118, 119, 120, 121, 124, 127, 131, 138, 141, 144, 147, 147, 148, 151, 152, 152, 160, 165, 166, 168, 170, 172, 174, 175, 177, 177, 177, 178, 181, 186, 186, 187, 188, 190, 192, 199, 200, 203, 209, 213, 218, 222, 229, 230, 231, 232, 237, 240, 241, 244, 249, 254, 255, 258, 260, 266, 267, 269, 269, 270 Somn 1:6, 6, 6, 6, 7, 8, 8, 10, 16, 18, 19, 19, 25, 26, 26, 27, 28, 29, 30, 36, 37, 39, 45, 46, 48, 48, 52, 54, 58, 64, 65, 66, 66, 67, 68, 70, 71, 72, 75, 76, 76, 79, 90, 91, 93, 98, 100, 105, 110, 111, 112, 117, 120, 122, 124, 125, 135, 137, 142, 143, 147, 154, 156, 158, 162, 163, 164, 171, 172, 172, 174, 176, 179, 181, 184, 185, 188, 190, 192, 192, 199, 200, 202, 203, 209, 210, 220, 227, 228, 228, 229, 230, 230, 232, 232, 235, 244, 246, 246, 250, 250, 250, 252, 254, 255, 256, 256 Somn 2:10, 15, 19, 19, 23, 24, 30, 44, 46, 50, 54, 57, 59, 60, 61, 62, 66, 67, 67, 67, 70, 72, 75, 77, 78, 81, 83, 85, 90, 91, 93, 93, 96, 97, 98, 98, 99, 100, 107, 112, 114, 115, 116, 120, 124, 128, 129, 135, 136, 136, 136, 138, 138, 140, 141, 141, 144, 150, 153, 155, 156, 161, 163, 164, 176, 178, 180, 182, 182, 185, 185, 187, 189, 193, 196, 200, 202, 202, 203, 210, 211, 215, 223, 224, 229, 230, 231, 234, 235, 236, 243, 243, 245, 249, 250, 254, 260, 261, 269, 270, 270, 270, 277, 278, 280, 281, 282, 288, 298, 298, 301 Abr 2, 4, 8, 9, 11, 14, 22, 25, 26, 28, 31, 34, 36, 37, 37, 38, 41, 43, 44, 47, 53, 58, 60, 62, 69, 73, 75, 75, 78, 78, 80, 85, 86, 88, 89, 97, 98, 107, 109, 111, 113, 115, 118, 121, 122, 122, 123, 127, 128, 131, 131, 131, 135, 136, 138, 142, 142, 145, 146, 147, 154, 154, 155, 160, 162, 168, 177, 178, 180, 190, 190, 195, 196, 198, 199, 200, 201, 205, 209, 214, 214, 216, 219, 221, 222, 223, 224, 225, 225, 232, 237, 243, 246, 248, 258, 259, 260, 263, 265, 266, 269, 270, 270, 271, 273, 275 Ios 4, 5, 12, 12, 13, 21, 23, 24, 26, 27, 30, 33, 33, 36, 43, 43, 43, 45, 46, 46, 50, 52, 63, 67, 67, 68, 69, 71, 72, 73, 74, 81, 85, 85, 86, 93, 95, 101, 101, 106, 107, 107, 111, 113, 115, 122, 124, 125, 125, 128, 133, 134, 135, 135, 141, 144, 144, 147, 148, 149, 150, 154, 157, 165, 166, 166, 168, 174, 179, 181, 185, 187, 192, 198, 200, 204, 210, 210, 211, 213, 215, 218, 225, 228, 229, 230, 233, 238, 241, 242, 244, 244, 244, 248, 248, 248, 248, 252, 255, 257, 258, 259, 263, 264 Mos 1:4, 19, 20, 25, 27, 36, 38, 39, 39, 40, 45, 45, 46, 48, 51, 51, 51, 55, 58, 59, 61, 62, 63, 65, 67, 68, 69, 71, 76, 82, 87, 89, 92, 94, 103, 108, 110, 111, 112, 119, 119, 121, 123, 125, 125, 132, 134, 134, 141, 141, 144, 144, 146, 148, 153, 157, 157, 160, 161, 164, 166, 170, 172, 175, 176, 183, 187, 189, 192, 200, 201, 204, 207, 207, 209, 211, 213, 216, 220, 230, 232, 233, 233, 234, 236, 240, 241, 243, 245, 245, 251, 255, 256, 256, 258, 259, 261, 266, 268, 272, 273, 273, 278, 281, 281, 284, 286, 288, 302, 303, 305, 307, 309, 313, 314, 323 Mos 2:1, 2, 5, 6, 13, 15, 17, 17, 17, 19, 19, 20, 21, 22, 25, 28, 29, 33, 34, 40, 41, 48, 50, 53, 53, 58, 60, 61, 65, 68, 69, 78, 87, 97, 106, 107, 119, 129, 131, 135, 137, 138, 140, 142, 152, 155, 156, 156, 160, 166, 167, 168, 171, 174, 177, 181, 185, 187, 192, 195, 196, 198, 203, 205, 205, 206, 207, 210, 211, 212, 217, 219, 221, 224, 229, 231, 232, 232, 233, 234, 235, 242, 242, 243, 245, 245, 248, 250, 252, 255, 255, 258, 260, 261, 262, 263, 266, 268, 273, 274, 275, 279, 279, 280, 288, 291 Decal 2, 11, 12, 14, 14, 15, 15, 15, 31, 33, 33, 33, 36, 40, 41, 43, 43, 44, 47, 59, 59, 61, 61, 62, 62, 64, 66, 68, 71, 72, 74, 75, 75, 76, 86, 87, 94, 99, 101, 104, 113, 115, 120, 123, 123, 124, 141, 150, 151, 158, 169, 173, 177 Spec 1:9, 14, 20, 28, 28, 29, 30, 32, 32, 37, 38, 44, 46, 46, 47, 49, 50, 52, 52, 55, 57, 58, 58, 63, 63, 65, 66, 68, 68, 74, 76, 89, 97, 100, 103, 104, 106, 107, 108, 108, 110, 112, 120, 122, 125, 131, 134, 137, 138, 138, 139, 144, 151, 152, 153, 154, 159, 163, 164, 166, 167, 186, 193, 202, 204, 207, 209, 211, 211, 215, 221, 224, 228, 230, 230, 236, 240, 241, 245, 252, 252, 252, 253, 255, 260, 260, 261, 265, 266, 267, 273, 276, 277, 283, 290, 293, 294, 294, 298, 299, 300, 300, 303, 304, 306, 307, 307, 308, 308, 313, 314, 315, 322, 324, 326, 327, 329, 338, 341, 345 Spec 2:4, 5, 5, 6, 8, 11, 18, 19, 21, 27, 32, 32, 35, 37, 42, 46, 49, 50, 52, 55, 60, 60, 64, 66, 66, 67, 67, 69, 69, 69, 72, 74, 77, 83, 83, 84, 85, 87, 87, 88, 89, 91, 91, 94, 95, 95, 98, 99, 104, 104, 105, 107, 113, 113, 119, 121, 122, 122, 133, 135, 141, 144, 146, 148, 149, 154, 155, 161, 164, 164, 165, 169, 169, 170, 170, 170, 173, 175, 182, 186, 191, 196, 198, 199, 201, 205, 207, 210, 211, 218, 220, 226, 228, 229, 232, 232, 233, 233, 233, 237, 238, 239, 241, 244, 245, 245, 247, 252, 254, 255, 256, 257, 259, 261 Spec 3:1, 4, 5, 6, 6, 6, 9, 12, 16, 17, 19, 23, 26, 28, 29, 30, 32, 33, 34, 37, 38, 43, 43, 45, 50, 52, 53, 55, 56, 59, 65, 65, 67, 68, 80, 81, 81, 86, 87, 87, 92, 94, 94, 96, 100, 104, 106, 107, 113, 118, 121, 122, 128, 128, 128, 130, 136, 137, 137, 138, 141, 142, 142, 143, 146, 151, 152, 153, 155, 157, 158, 163, 163, 166, 171, 174, 174, 176, 179, 182, 184, 189, 189, 195, 197, 208 Spec 4:4, 4, 10, 11, 11, 13, 16, 20, 20, 23, 26, 31, 35, 37, 48, 48, 49, 50, 51, 52, 63, 66, 71, 72, 74, 74, 76, 77, 80, 82, 85, 85, 92, 93, 96, 97, 99, 100, 102, 102, 103, 108, 113, 115, 120, 121, 123, 126, 137, 138, 139, 140, 140, 141, 143, 146, 148, 149, 149, 151, 153, 153, 154, 157, 159, 161, 162, 163, 169, 170, 172, 173, 177, 180, 181, 184, 185, 186, 193, 194, 195, 195, 200, 202, 205, 206, 206, 207, 208, 215, 219, 228 Virt 1, 5, 6, 6, 8, 9, 14, 17, 23, 25, 27, 29, 31, 32, 38, 44, 53, 53, 54, 55, 56, 60, 60, 61, 62, 62, 63, 64, 65, 67, 67, 67, 69, 70, 78, 79, 81, 82, 83, 88, 89, 90, 91, 91, 91, 95, 96, 98, 99, 103, 107, 108, 110, 112, 113, 113, 115, 116, 120, 123, 130, 134, 135, 136, 137, 137, 140, 140, 146, 146, 147, 149, 151, 151, 154, 155, 156, 159, 162, 169, 170, 171, 172, 176, 179, 180, 183, 187, 187, 191, 195, 198, 199, 200, 202, 203, 206, 206, 207, 207, 215, 216, 217, 218, 220, 221, 222, 222, 222, 224, 225 Praem 2, 6, 9, 25, 26, 28, 34, 39, 40, 42, 43, 44, 44, 52, 54, 57, 78,

78, 79, 83, 85, 85, 93, 97, 101, 103, 105, 105, 106, 107, 108, 110, 112, 112, 112, 117, 123, 124, 124, 125, 130, 132, 134, 136, 138, 140, 145, 156, 157, 160, 161, 170, 171 Prob 2, 4, 6, 7, 9, 10, 12, 18, 20, 23, 24, 27, 29, 32, 35, 42, 43, 44, 46, 50, 59, 61, 62, 68, 69, 69, 71, 75, 76, 78, 79, 79, 79, 86, 91, 92, 93, 95, 96, 100, 101, 101, 104, 105, 106, 113, 115, 118, 118, 120, 122, 124, 128, 134, 140, 140, 141, 147, 149, 155, 156, 157, 158 Contempl 1, 4, 5, 5, 5, 6, 7, 8, 9, 10, 10, 10, 12, 14, 14, 15, 16, 20, 20, 25, 29, 30, 31, 31, 37, 37, 40, 43, 53, 56, 58, 59, 64, 65, 67, 67, 68, 69, 71, 72, 73, 75, 89 Aet 3, 3, 6, 8, 12, 12, 14, 16, 37, 49, 51, 54, 56, 58, 60, 61, 63, 63, 66, 66, 70, 71, 73, 77, 77, 80, 81, 81, 82, 85, 87, 88, 91, 91, 92, 92, 94, 95, 98, 100, 101, 106, 107, 107, 111, 112, 114, 114, 115, 115, 125, 126, 130, 130, 132, 134, 138, 138, 141, 142, 143, 146, 146, 147, 149 Flacc 1, 3, 4, 7, 24, 24, 28, 35, 35, 36, 40, 41, 41, 48, 49, 51, 54, 58, 59, 60, 60, 60, 78, 81, 82, 89, 90, 92, 95, 95, 97, 101, 103, 106, 107, 121, 124, 126, 126, 128, 128, 130, 133, 136, 139, 141, 143, 146, 147, 163, 164, 165, 166, 170, 173, 174, 177, 178, 180, 181, 186, 187 Legat 6, 6, 7, 10, 11, 25, 27, 28, 32, 39, 42, 43, 43, 44, 45, 48, 48, 58, 59, 63, 75, 76, 80, 90, 91, 99, 103, 106, 109, 114, 114, 118, 119, 119, 122, 125, 132, 133, 137, 142, 142, 142, 142, 143, 149, 153, 154, 157, 157, 158, 158, 161, 161, 162, 164, 169, 170, 171, 172, 183, 184, 192, 193, 204, 206, 206, 207, 207, 208, 209, 213, 214, 215, 216, 218, 227, 232, 239, 242, 245, 246, 248, 249, 251, 252, 253, 253, 257, 258, 264, 268, 272, 275, 280, 280, 281, 282, 283, 293, 294, 297, 299, 307, 307, 310, 310, 312, 318, 322, 324, 329, 330, 330, 334, 337, 341, 342, 343, 343, 345, 347, 349, 352, 353, 356, 357, 359, 366, 368, 369, 372 Hypoth 6:2, 6:3, 6:4, 6:8, 6:9, 7:1, 7:1, 7:2, 7:2, 7:2, 7:3, 7:4, 7:6, 7:7, 7:9, 7:10, 7:10, 7:11, 7:11, 7:14, 7:15, 7:17, 7:18, 7:19, 11:3, 11:6, 11:12, 11:13, 11:17, 11:18 Prov 1, 2:2, 4, 20, 21, 25, 26, 27, 28, 32, 33, 34, 35, 37, 39, 43, 45, 46, 47, 49, 53, 53, 57, 58, 59, 61, 62, 63, 64, 69 QG 1:3, 20, 21, 24, 28, 32, 51, 51, 55b, 60:1, 60:1, 60:2, 60:2, 66, 93, 94, 96:1, 100:1b, 100:1b, 2:11, 13b, 15a, 15a, 26a, 34c, 39, 41, 41, 54a, 54a, 54c, 54d, 59, 59, 62, 62, 64a, 64a, 64b, 64b, 68a, 71a, 71a, 71a, 71b, 72, 74, 3:3, 8, 11a, 11c, 18, 18, 20a, 22, 23, 24, 26, 29, 29, 38b, 58, 4:33b, 43, 51b, 51b, 52b, 64, 86b, 88, 110a, 145, 145, 172, 172, 173, 191c, 193, 8*, 9*, 198, 200c, 202a, 211, 228, 228, 228 QG isf 3, 3, 10, 10, 11, 16, 16 QG (Par) 2:3, 2:7 QE 2:2, 4, 6a, 17, 18, 25c, 25d, 44, 45a, 47, 47, 50b, 55b, 71 QE isf 2, 7, 8, 15, 16, 29

ἀλλαγή Mut 70, 130 Mos 1:81 Virt 124

ἄλλαγμα Post 95

ἀλλάσσω (27) Opif 41, 97 Leg 3:110, 110 Sacr 89, 89, 112, 114, 114 Post 13, 95, 95 Deus 176 Ebr 172, 173 Conf 74 Fug 57 Mut 89, 123 Ios 36, 165 Mos 1:156, 282 Spec 1:47 Spec 4:146 Flacc 18 QG 4:51c

ἀλλαχόθεν (6) Ios 182 Mos 1:21, 203 Spec 3:5 Spec 4:170 Praem 165

ἀλλαχόθι Sacr 67 Post 29 Ebr 99 Mut 168 Somn 1:62

ἀλλαχόσε Abr 91 Flacc 71

ἀλλαχοῦ QG 1:100:2b

ἀλλεπάλληλος Prov 2:28

ἀλληγορέω (25) Leg 2:5, 10 Leg 3:4, 60, 238 Cher 25 Post 51 Agr 27, 157 Ebr 99 Migr 131, 205 Mut 67 Somn 1:67 Somn 2:31, 207 Abr 99 Ios 28 Decal 101 Spec 1:269 Spec 2:29 Praem 125, 158 Contempl 28, 29

ἀλληγορία (16) Opif 157 Leg 3:236 Post 7 Plant 36 Fug 179 Somn 1:73, 102 Somn 2:8 Abr 68, 131 Decal 1 Spec 1:287, 327 Spec 2:147 Praem 65 Contempl 78

ἀλληγορικός Somn 2:142

ἀλληλοκτονέω Abr 261

ἀλληλοκτονία Legat 144

ἀλληλοτυπία Aet 8

ἀλληλουχέω Migr 180 Praem 56

ἀλληλοφαγία Praem 134

ἀλλήλων (114) Opif 33, 67, 83 Leg 1:17, 28 Leg 3:21, 115, 173 Cher 20, 21, 22, 25, 54, 109, 111, 113, 120 Sacr 2, 4, 20, 75 Det 2, 7, 88 Post 184, 185 Gig 56 Deus 107 Agr 27, 120 Plant 89, 160 Ebr 24, 175, 196 Sobr 34 Conf 7, 8, 9, 9, 21, 26, 153, 176, 185, 195 Migr 178 Her 44, 126, 132, 147, 207, 218 Congr 81 Fug 112 Mut 66, 104 Somn 1:53 Somn 2:302 Abr 42, 100, 215, 248, 254 Ios 30, 256 Mos 1:178 Mos 2:7, 8, 89 Decal 2, 6, 64, 153 Spec 1:138, 208 Spec 2:43, 64, 68, 151, 155, 190, 210, 243 Spec 3:28, 51 Spec 4:210 Virt 18, 35, 116, 140, 184, 225 Praem 81, 148 Prob 48, 79 Contempl 24, 40, 63 Aet 57, 109, 109 Flacc 185 Legat 47, 217, 351 Hypoth 6:2, 7:10, 7:12, 7:13 Prov 2:45 QG 1:69 QE isf 18

ἀλλογενής Somn 1:161 Spec 1:124 Spec 4:16 Virt 147

ἀλλόγλωσσος Post 91

ἀλλοδαπός (11) Det 151 Conf 76 Her 267 Congr 23 Abr 65, 245 Ios 225 Mos 1:49 Spec 2:164 Spec 4:16 Praem 20

ἀλλοεθνής Spec 3:29 Legat 183

ἄλλοθεν Agr 35 Fug 52 Spec 4:84

ἀλλοῖος (7) Cher 88 Post 25, 110 Gig 28 Mut 55 Spec 1:143 Legat 79

ἀλλοίωσις Leg 1:74, 74 Aet 113, 113, 116

ἀλλόκοτος (6) Mos 1:11 Spec 3:4 Virt 219 Prob 63 Flacc 167 Legat 34

ἄλλος (ὁ) (1301) Opif 1, 15, 17, 20, 31, 34, 46, 49, 51, 52, 53, 56, 57, 58, 59, 60, 61, 63, 63, 68, 69, 69, 72, 77, 77, 79, 83, 95, 100, 100, 116, 116, 126, 128, 130, 130, 131, 138, 140, 147, 147, 148, 162, 163, 164, 167, 170 Leg 1:5, 7, 7, 7, 19, 22, 22, 25, 34, 39, 44, 44, 47, 62, 75, 91, 91, 91, 91, 92 Leg 2:2, 2, 4, 4, 6, 8, 12, 15, 15, 15, 17, 18, 20, 22, 24, 24, 30, 39, 70, 75, 75, 75, 79, 86, 89, 97, 102, 108 Leg 3:14, 38, 40, 50, 57, 57, 59, 59, 69, 82, 86, 86, 87, 96, 98, 101, 106, 113, 121, 124, 131, 138, 145, 145, 145, 149, 167, 171, 181, 181, 183, 204, 205, 206, 207, 220, 220, 230, 236, 236 Cher 33, 34, 35, 42, 56, 58, 64, 65, 68, 68, 69, 74, 75, 91, 91, 96, 104, 109, 117 Sacr 15, 18, 20, 21, 29, 29, 31, 49, 70, 71, 74, 91, 91, 98, 109, 109, 111, 113, 115, 115, 118, 131, 136, 139 Det 13, 18, 19, 33, 33, 46, 51, 72, 72, 85, 88, 91, 98, 102, 108, 114, 127, 136, 157, 165, 173 Post 3, 3, 13, 18, 19, 19, 28, 32, 33, 36, 36, 38, 40, 42, 50, 50, 52, 90, 93, 105, 106, 119, 144, 147, 151, 165, 174, 179 Gig 6, 11, 11, 15, 15, 18, 18, 18, 26, 28, 29, 55, 60, 62 Deus 7, 7, 11, 19, 19, 29, 42, 44, 46, 47, 48, 56, 59, 71, 74, 79, 83, 100, 112, 133, 133, 150, 152, 152, 163, 169, 176, 176 Agr 8, 22, 22, 25, 26, 30, 35, 36, 44, 51, 54, 54, 71, 78, 87, 101, 101, 103, 104, 104, 113, 114, 115, 117, 138, 140, 141, 149,

151, 151, 152, 152, 166, 166, 167, 171 Plant 7, 14, 17, 18, 27, 29, 30, 33, 35, 42, 48, 55, 57, 63, 64, 64, 83, 118, 122, 126, 130, 141, 151, 152, 153, 159, 170, 171, 176 Ebr 1, 4, 13, 18, 25, 29, 35, 35, 42, 43, 64, 64, 75, 79, 89, 92, 102, 106, 106, 109, 119, 136, 156, 173, 176, 176, 183, 184, 187, 194, 195, 196, 196, 202, 217, 219, 219 Sobr 35, 36, 36, 36, 38, 58, 61, 62 Conf 3, 9, 11, 16, 21, 24, 25, 36, 42, 42, 59, 90, 95, 97, 98, 110, 123, 179, 185, 187 Migr 3, 10, 18, 23, 50, 51, 59, 91, 92, 102, 109, 122, 123, 124, 137, 138, 138, 140, 160, 172, 178, 179, 184, 190, 191, 191, 202, 217, 217, 217, 219 Her 74, 79, 86, 92, 110, 115, 116, 121, 136, 139, 139, 144, 144, 148, 151, 153, 161, 183, 185, 188, 209, 217, 217, 223, 224, 234, 245, 249, 256, 261, 280, 284, 295, 301, 315 Congr 2, 11, 17, 20, 22, 27, 46, 58, 65, 77, 89, 98, 112, 115, 133, 142, 143, 146, 165, 178 Fug 20, 38, 51, 51, 55, 56, 66, 68, 82, 87, 95, 122, 136, 154, 180, 182 Mut 4, 4, 8, 21, 59, 67, 89, 111, 138, 157, 186, 192, 230, 230, 230, 239, 239, 256, 258 Somn 1:16, 18, 20, 27, 28, 35, 45, 49, 53, 55, 62, 75, 76, 79, 103, 105, 109, 110, 115, 122, 124, 137, 140, 141, 143, 145, 145, 179, 184, 184, 185, 186, 187, 205, 233, 236 Somn 2:8, 14, 49, 61, 62, 62, 74, 80, 83, 88, 123, 123, 124, 125, 128, 131, 132, 136, 161, 182, 187, 188, 215, 218, 224, 232, 252, 284, 284, 288, 291, 300 Abr 1, 5, 10, 13, 14, 14, 20, 22, 31, 56, 57, 58, 69, 74, 84, 91, 110, 119, 125, 133, 138, 150, 154, 154, 158, 159, 162, 163, 165, 173, 179, 197, 197, 208, 219, 226, 227, 228, 229, 234, 240, 247, 260, 261, 263 Ios 4, 12, 12, 29, 29, 34, 34, 43, 44, 44, 69, 70, 88, 94, 105, 119, 126, 130, 143, 153, 153, 157, 158, 166, 169, 176, 176, 178, 182, 201, 204, 225, 233, 238, 242, 246, 246, 249, 270 Mos 1:6, 21, 23, 26, 27, 32, 37, 37, 39, 39, 52, 52, 64, 74, 87, 97, 109, 124, 133, 134, 137, 139, 139, 145, 146, 147, 149, 152, 153, 155, 168, 178, 189, 201, 203, 203, 207, 212, 216, 228, 232, 232, 237, 237, 243, 250, 251, 251, 265, 275, 278, 285, 287, 291, 303, 317, 323, 324, 327, 331, 333 Mos 2:13, 13, 16, 17, 19, 25, 26, 30, 37, 37, 38, 44, 49, 53, 53, 63, 67, 73, 78, 78, 93, 102, 112, 114, 115, 127, 146, 153, 164, 169, 174, 177, 178, 179, 180, 185, 191, 195, 212, 214, 218, 219, 223, 225, 227, 229 Decal 5, 9, 9, 9, 18, 22, 29, 36, 44, 53, 55, 66, 66, 69, 71, 72, 74, 79, 98, 107, 108, 113, 118, 127, 127, 133, 142, 151, 162, 162, 167, 177 Spec 1:9, 11, 13, 16, 20, 21, 27, 34, 59, 61, 64, 80, 83, 90, 92, 97, 98, 102, 107, 108, 109, 109, 111, 111, 113, 114, 117, 122, 125, 134, 134, 135, 136, 141, 141, 145, 151, 153, 157, 158, 164, 172, 172, 180, 184, 186, 193, 197, 204, 207, 208, 210, 212, 214, 214, 224, 231, 232, 233, 233, 240, 247, 249, 252, 255, 262, 269, 274, 281, 295, 300, 300, 303, 317, 327, 336, 339, 340, 340, 340 Spec 2:8, 8, 10, 36, 40, 45, 48, 57, 62, 66, 70, 71, 73, 83, 105, 108, 113, 121, 127, 143, 145, 148, 151, 157, 165, 166, 167, 177, 181, 183, 184, 192, 193, 203, 215, 218, 220, 221, 233, 239, 248, 256, 259 Spec 3:5, 11, 12, 25, 26, 30, 34, 43, 45, 50, 51, 56, 64, 67, 68, 70, 70, 72, 74, 78, 90, 95, 110, 115, 116, 128, 130, 134, 139, 151, 159, 167, 168, 175, 175, 183, 183, 184, 188, 191, 192, 198, 199, 206, 208 Spec 4:11, 39, 42, 48, 55, 55, 56, 68, 72, 78, 78, 82, 88, 96, 98, 100, 101, 104, 116, 134, 136, 142, 144, 148, 159, 163, 164, 168, 170, 170, 171, 193, 194, 223, 230 Virt 5, 15, 19, 21, 22, 23, 29, 29, 29, 32, 39, 39, 41, 47, 53, 55, 55, 62, 63, 63, 64, 74, 95, 101, 104, 111, 122, 124, 127, 134, 142, 162, 166, 168, 168, 174, 178, 180, 181, 203, 207, 213, 216 Praem 2, 6, 8, 15, 28, 43, 45, 45, 52, 52, 53, 61, 65, 66, 89, 90, 107, 107, 125, 130, 131, 135, 143, 160, 165, 172 Prob 2, 3, 6, 9, 20, 21, 21, 23, 33, 45, 47, 53, 63, 64, 65, 73, 81, 81, 96, 107, 123, 124, 131, 150, 151, 152, 154, 156 Contempl 2, 5, 7, 13, 15, 25, 25, 31, 34, 40, 52, 58, 61, 62, 75, 80, 82 Aet 2, 5, 5, 10, 21, 26, 30, 30, 34, 36, 37, 38, 49, 63, 64, 70, 83, 83, 87, 93, 96, 98, 106, 107, 130, 131, 132, 140, 144, 144, 149 Flacc 24, 37, 52, 55, 63, 66, 71, 76, 85, 115, 123, 139, 139, 144, 148, 154, 156, 163, 167, 171, 181 Legat 6, 14, 43, 43, 51, 51, 68, 74, 76, 89, 90, 108, 108, 116, 118, 127, 133, 139, 164, 165, 175, 177, 177, 182, 182, 183, 186, 194, 206, 214, 216, 223, 225, 231, 232, 249, 268, 281, 282, 283, 284, 292, 299, 300, 302, 307, 316, 319, 320, 327, 338, 339, 346, 353, 355, 370 Hypoth 6:6, 6:8, 7:3, 7:5, 7:6, 7:7, 7:8, 7:9, 7:11, 7:19, 11:4, 11:9, 11:10, 11:15, 11:17 Prov 1, 1, 2:2, 15, 17, 21, 23, 27, 39, 41, 41, 46, 51, 55, 61, 71 QG 1:31, 55a, 58, 96:1, 2:15a, 29, 4:51a, 51b, 51b, 69, 153, 189, 204 QG isf 10, 16, 16 QG (Par) 2:3, 2:3 QE 1:1, 1, 19, 2:2, 3a, 9a, 11a, 13b, 25d, 105 QE isf 3, 16, 16, 16, 21, 21

ἄλλοτε (17) Opif 147 Post 25, 110 Gig 28 Agr 166 Ebr 176 Mut 55 Somn 1:150, 150, 233 Mos 2:38 Spec 1:61, 143 Spec 2:220 Legat 79 QG (Par) 2:3 QE 2:25d

ἀλλότριος (ὁ) (112) Opif 12, 74 Leg 1:26, 50, 61 Leg 2:40 Leg 3:22, 23, 32, 160, 239, 241 Cher 9, 78, 117 Sacr 29, 97 Det 134, 165 Post 109, 172 Agr 6, 84 Plant 143, 165 Ebr 176 Sobr 3 Conf 74, 82, 115, 186 Migr 10 Her 44, 105, 259 Fug 15 Mut 197 Somn 1:23, 100 Somn 2:47, 67 Abr 95, 129, 135, 211, 258 Ios 18, 44, 66, 144, 164, 216 Mos 1:17, 53, 141, 235 Mos 2:273 Decal 128, 135, 137, 171 Spec 1:340 Spec 2:50, 73, 76, 106, 123, 168, 236 Spec 3:9, 12, 21, 24, 51, 113, 116, 116, 146, 183 Spec 4:5, 7, 20, 26, 33, 38, 54, 67, 70, 157, 158, 185, 203 Virt 89, 91, 100, 105, 125, 167, 173, 226 Praem 139 Prob 19, 106 Aet 40 Flacc 56, 74, 77, 132 Legat 72, 201 QG 1:21 QE 2:6b

ἀλλοτριότης (7) Det 164 Her 270 Spec 2:73 Praem 85 Prob 79 Legat 72, 112

ἀλλοτριόω (33) Leg 1:103 Cher 18 Post 156 Ebr 69, 161, 177 Conf 150 Migr 7, 11 Her 26, 278 Fug 154 Somn 2:107 Abr 211 Ios 230 Mos 1:13, 49, 234, 307 Mos 2:19, 172, 243, 245 Decal 152 Spec 1:114 Spec 2:111, 126 Spec 3:155 Virt 40, 146, 207 Praem 134 Legat 57

ἀλλοτρίωσις (21) Cher 41, 74 Sacr 96 Post 135 Gig 33 Plant 25 Ebr 6 Conf 82 Migr 19 Her 154 Congr 152 Ios 166, 232 Mos 1:280 Decal 124 Virt 190, 196 Aet 105 Flacc 180 Legat 178 QE 2:2

ἀλλόφυλος (8) Her 42 Somn 1:161 Spec 1:56 Virt 160, 222 Prob 93 Legat 200, 211

ἅλμα Prov 2:26

ἁλμυρόγεως Mos 1:192

ἁλμυρός (9) Opif 38 Leg 2:32 Cher 70 Ebr 12 Conf 26, 26 Somn 1:18 Somn 2:281 Praem 145

ἀλοάω (6) Ios 112, 112 Decal 77 Spec 1:165 Virt 145, 146

ἀλογέω (77) Leg 3:72, 243 Det 37, 45, 65, 114 Gig 15 Agr 78, 93, 104 Plant 14 Ebr 16, 35, 40, 110 Conf 48 Her 64, 71, 109 Congr 27, 151 Fug 25, 35, 115 Somn 2:11 Abr 192 Ios 62, 153 Mos 1:9, 270, 284 Mos 2:69, 193, 205, 213 Decal 110, 136 Spec 1:51, 56, 62, 143, 150, 176 Spec 2:11, 18, 46, 174, 195 Spec 3:62, 166, 176 Spec 4:16, 26 Virt 115, 205 Praem 78, 106, 138 Prob 22, 106, 116, 133, 151 Contempl 68 Aet 68, 131 Flacc 52, 67 Legat 128, 132, 256 Prov 2:17, 21, 22, 29, 56 QG 1:51

ἀλογία Leg 3:123 Ebr 157 Her 71

ἀλογιστία Prov 2:58

ἀλόγιστος Leg 1:17 Leg 3:202 Sobr 11 Ios 143 Prob 150

ἄλογος (241) Opif 73, 79, 148 Leg 1:11, 17, 24, 24, 24, 40, 40, 40, 41 Leg 2:2, 6, 6, 23, 23, 58, 64, 75, 75, 97, 100 Leg 3:24, 30, 50, 89, 108, 111, 115, 116, 127, 185, 220, 224, 229, 229, 246, 248, 249, 251, 251, 251, 251 Cher 12, 32, 36, 39, 58, 64, 70, 111 Sacr 45, 46, 46, 47, 47, 47, 80, 104, 105, 106 Det 3, 5, 6, 9, 25, 38, 38, 46, 53, 82, 83, 91, 168, 170 Post 26, 46, 66, 68, 69, 69, 73, 74, 98, 161, 162 Gig 20, 40, 41 Deus 52, 90 Agr 31, 41, 56, 56, 63, 63, 68, 88, 90, 94, 139, 175, 179, 179 Plant 16, 43, 49 Ebr 98, 110, 111, 199 Sobr 14 Conf 9, 24, 90, 111, 126, 176, 177 Migr 3, 26, 66, 66, 152, 185, 200, 206, 206, 210, 212, 213, 224 Her 16, 61, 64, 109, 132, 132, 138, 138, 167, 185, 192, 209, 232, 245 Congr 26, 26, 27, 55, 56, 96, 97 Fug 22, 72, 90, 91, 126, 152, 158, 207 Mut 110, 246 Somn 1:109, 199, 255 Somn 2:16, 115, 151, 153, 245, 276, 278 Abr 249, 266, 267 Mos 1:60, 127, 133, 272 Mos 2:96, 139, 156 Decal 76 Spec 1:66, 66, 74, 79, 88, 148, 201, 201, 209, 260, 333, 333 Spec 2:69, 83, 89, 146, 163 Spec 3:43, 57, 99, 129, 189 Spec 4:24, 55, 79, 121, 123, 203 Virt 81, 117, 125, 133, 140, 148, 148, 160, 172 Praem 26, 59, 74, 91, 91 Prob 131, 133, 157 Contempl 8, 9 Aet 73, 77 Prov 2:63, 68 QG 1:76b, 94, 94, 2:65

ἀλοητός Spec 2:70 Spec 4:12

ἀλουργής Contempl 49

ἀλουργίς Somn 2:53 Decal 4 Spec 2:20 Spec 3:41

ἅλς (22) Opif 66 Conf 26 Somn 1:247, 248 Somn 2:210 Ios 196, 210 Mos 2:104 Spec 1:175, 175, 289, 289, 289 Spec 3:96 Praem 154 Contempl 37, 41, 73, 81, 81, 81 QG 4:8*

ἄλσος (7) Leg 1:48, 48, 49, 49 Abr 138 Spec 1:74 Legat 151

ἀλυκός Conf 26

ἄλυπος Cher 86 Abr 202 Spec 1:115 Praem 35 Legat 13

ἄλυρος Fug 22 Mut 229

ἀλυσείδιον ἀλυσίδιον

ἀλυσίδιον (ἀλυσείδιον) Mos 2:113

ἄλυσις Leg 1:28 Flacc 74

ἀλυσιτελής (19) Leg 3:61, 222 Agr 39, 47 Ebr 16, 20 Somn 2:275 Abr 18 Spec 1:100 Spec 4:151 Praem 20 Contempl 20 Flacc 19, 137 Legat 218 Prov 2:37, 37 QG isf 14 QE isf 25

ἄλυτος (10) Conf 166 Her 23 Somn 1:111 Mos 1:207 Spec 1:52, 137, 317 Praem 81 Aet 13, 13

ἄλφα Leg 3:121 Mut 61 Abr 81

ἀλώβητος Migr 95

Ἀλωεῖδαι Conf 4

ἅλων (ἅλως) (11) Leg 3:248, 249 Sacr 107, 109, 109 Her 296 Somn 1:239 Spec 1:134 Spec 4:29 Hypoth 7:6 Prov 2:47

ἅλως ἅλων

ἅλωσις (6) Mos 1:295 Praem 148 Flacc 9, 54 Legat 122, 292

ἁλωτός (7) Det 46 Spec 4:200 Virt 36 Contempl 9 Aet 21, 24, 74

ἅμα (201) Opif 13, 17, 26, 28, 40, 41, 67, 79, 150, 168 Leg 1:34 Leg 2:73 Leg 3:57, 57, 179 Cher 22, 67, 84, 99, 121 Sacr 40, 42, 65, 94, 98 Det 87 Post 38, 40, 71, 142, 150, 152 Agr 31 Plant 2, 73 Ebr 7 Sobr 36 Conf 5, 22, 28, 142 Migr 170 Her 14 Congr 66, 84, 100 Mut 32, 53, 61, 139, 167 Somn 1:234 Somn 2:195 Abr 65, 66, 77, 95, 176, 228 Ios 11, 11, 23, 103, 197, 207, 217, 255 Mos 1:18, 47, 57, 77, 83, 91, 117, 120, 121, 136, 164, 164, 204, 207, 208, 209, 230, 236, 252, 260, 276, 286, 286, 306 Mos 2:36, 59, 66, 94, 166, 196, 202, 232, 233, 264 Decal 63 Spec 1:68, 77, 80, 132, 138, 169, 193, 194, 203, 222, 279, 330, 341 Spec 2:88, 92, 130, 130, 157, 160, 188, 203, 203, 230 Spec 3:18, 23, 32, 36, 55, 94, 112, 197 Spec 4:57, 99, 163, 174, 213, 221 Virt 12, 43, 74, 90, 90, 92, 99, 115, 181, 215 Praem 9, 63, 89, 111, 146, 149 Prob 24, 118, 127, 128, 149 Aet 96, 141, 143 Flacc 12, 18, 26, 29, 48, 70, 83, 114, 122, 140, 167 Legat 42, 42, 178, 194, 197, 197, 222, 222, 245, 250, 290, 303, 331, 331, 352, 353, 358 Hypoth 6:1 Prov 2:6, 6 QG 2:12c, 41 QG (Par) 2:7, 2:7 QE 2:105 QE isf 7, 9

ἀμαθαίνω Her 180

ἀμαθής (11) Cher 129 Sacr 32 Det 143 Her 14 Fug 9 Mut 17, 56 Somn 2:259 Ios 204 Praem 111 Hypoth 6:4

ἀμαθία (45) Opif 45 Leg 3:20, 33, 36, 52, 193, 195 Sacr 47, 48, 86 Det 3 Post 52 Gig 30 Deus 134 Agr 74 Plant 80, 144 Ebr 137 Migr 18, 149, 170 Her 10, 48, 77 Congr 88 Fug 8, 39, 42, 82 Somn 1:109 Abr 24 Ios 106 Spec 1:306 Spec 4:47, 146 Virt 4, 180, 220 Praem 61, 61, 61 Prob 12, 159 Legat 2 QE 2:25b

Ἀμαλήκ (8) Leg 3:186, 186, 187, 187 Ebr 24 Migr 143 Congr 54, 55

ἀμαξήλατος Agr 102

ἁμαρτάνω (112) Opif 78 Leg 1:35, 35, 93 Leg 2:60, 63, 68, 78, 78, 78, 78 Leg 3:34, 105, 106, 212, 237 Cher 65, 94 Sacr 131 Det 145 Post 58 Gig 16 Deus 74, 134, 141, 142 Agr 1, 179 Ebr 11 Sobr 10, 31, 33, 42, 47, 50, 50 Conf 10, 22, 40, 110, 119, 163 Fug 76, 99, 105, 157 Mut 48, 79, 195, 217, 233, 238, 251 Somn 1:91, 236 Abr 17 Ios 52, 104, 156, 176, 220, 254 Mos 1:96, 154, 273, 326 Mos 2:147, 166, 167 Decal 139, 141, 177 Spec 1:67, 79, 187, 193, 193, 227, 230, 230, 233, 241, 243, 244, 279 Spec 2:11 Spec 3:89, 90, 140, 182 Spec 4:42, 156, 225 Virt 177, 177 Praem 117, 163 Prob 132 Flacc 44, 81, 105 Legat 7, 242 Prov 2:61 QG 1:65, 65, 65, 77, 3:11a, 4:64 QG isf 13, 13

ἁμάρτημα (114) Leg 1:93 Leg 2:61, 63 Leg 3:77, 241, 241 Sacr 54, 132 Det 146 Post 11, 98 Deus 21, 72, 73, 113, 126, 134, 138, 138 Agr 10, 123, 142, 146, 176 Plant 143, 143, 166 Ebr 12, 95, 95, 160, 163 Conf 9, 11, 25, 71, 76, 116, 171, 178 Her 7, 173, 295, 297, 299, 304, 306, 307 Fug 65, 65, 67, 80, 105, 117, 158, 158, 193, 194 Mut 47, 196, 233, 236, 241, 243, 250 Somn 1:87, 175, 198 Somn 2:174, 196, 299 Mos 1:58 Mos 2:24, 107, 134, 147, 203, 220 Decal 6 Spec 1:187, 190, 191, 192, 215, 215, 228, 230, 234, 238, 242, 245, 259 Spec 2:31, 196 Spec 3:54, 64, 136, 167, 168 Spec 4:2, 55, 68 Virt 75, 124, 163 Praem 74, 112 Prob 60 Flacc 35 QG 2:13a, 68b, 4:64, 172 QE isf 26

ἁμαρτία (29) Plant 108 Conf 179 Migr 206 Her 20, 305 Fug 157, 159 Mut 233, 233, 234, 248 Somn 1:104 Somn 2:296 Mos 2:203, 235 Decal 83 Spec 1:190, 193, 194, 196, 197, 226, 239, 243, 247, 251, 252 QG 1:41, 2:65

ἀμάρτυρος Sacr 34

ἀμαυρός (7) Opif 140 Mos 2:56 Decal 149 Spec 2:46 Spec 4:190 Prob 146 Legat 269

ἀμαυρόω (24) Opif 31, 57 Mos 1:124 Mos 2:44 Decal 11, 34, 68, 147 Spec 1:30, 58, 100, 288 Spec 2:247 Spec 4:52, 191, 200 Virt 162 Prob 11, 126 Flacc 153, 182 Legat 2, 63 Prov 2:15

ἀμαχεί (ἀμαχί) (13) Det 29 Legat 233

ἀμαχί ἀμαχεί

ἄμαχος (11) Agr 78 Conf 118 Her 288 Abr 231 Mos 1:70, 111, 225, 263 Virt 33 Praem 137 Legat 215

ἀμάω (7) Fug 170, 171, 171 Somn 2:24, 77 Virt 90 Praem 127

ἀμβατός ἀναβατός

ἀμβλίσκω (ἀμβλόω) (8) Congr 129, 138 Somn 1:107 Spec 3:108, 108 Virt 157 Praem 130 Hypoth 7:7

ἀμβλόω ἀμβλίσκω

ἀμβλύνω Fug 125

ἀμβλύς (12) Opif 97, 97 Det 98 Deus 63 Agr 13 Her 89 Somn 1:27, 236 Abr 188, 240 Flacc 67, 124

ἀμβλυωπής Post 161

ἀμβλυωπία Prob 47

ἀμβλωθρίδιον Leg 1:76 Deus 14 Migr 33

ἄμβλωσις Spec 3:117

ἀμβροσία Deus 155

ἀμβρόσιος Somn 2:249

ἀμέθεκτος Praem 121

ἀμέθελκτος Fug 92

ἀμείβω (25) Opif 104, 147 Leg 3:10 Sacr 72 Det 151, 154 Agr 166 Sobr 58 Her 104 Abr 90 Ios 46, 212, 215, 258 Mos 1:33, 33, 149 Spec 1:46, 172, 224 Spec 2:64, 78 Aet 109, 109 Legat 185

ἀμείλικτος (21) Migr 225 Somn 2:293 Ios 15, 82, 170 Mos 1:49 Spec 2:129, 253 Spec 3:5, 84, 113, 203 Spec 4:14, 82, 89 Virt 124 Prob 120 Flacc 182 Legat 301, 350 Prov 2:25

ἀμείωτος Ios 178

ἀμέλγω Virt 144

ἀμέλεια Agr 39 Somn 1:8 Contempl 61

ἀμελετησία Sacr 23, 86 Her 213 Fug 14, 121

ἀμελέτητος Mos 1:92, 259

ἀμελέω (39) Leg 3:76, 152 Sacr 41 Det 19, 43, 50, 55, 157 Deus 171 Agr 47, 143 Plant 39 Conf 191 Migr 92 Her 303 Somn 1:52, 155, 203 Ios 77, 131, 248 Mos 1:51, 109 Decal 118 Spec 2:27, 108, 250 Spec 3:130 Spec 4:41, 175 Virt 162, 202 Praem 156, 171 Prob 87 Contempl 36 Flacc 43 Prov 2:54 QE isf 26

ἀμελής (13) Agr 67 Migr 88 Congr 81 Mut 147, 153 Somn 1:217 Somn 2:114 Spec 2:132 Spec 4:102 Praem 12 Prob 44 Flacc 170 Prov 2:60

ἀμελλητί Sacr 53, 68

ἄμεμπτος (14) Leg 3:63 Post 181 Gig 63 Agr 127 Plant 58 Migr 129 Mut 47, 48, 51 Spec 1:138 Virt 60 Prob 59 QG 1:63, 3:23

ἀμενηνός Spec 1:28 Legat 130

ἀμερής (10) Opif 41 Sacr 137 Agr 134 Her 131, 142, 143, 236, 236 Congr 4 Mut 180

ἀμέριστος Sacr 110 Her 308 Decal 103, 103, 104

ἀμετάβλητος (11) Leg 2:67, 86 Cher 90 Conf 104 Mut 28, 54 Somn 2:237 Mos 2:39 Spec 1:312 Spec 3:178 Praem 15

ἀμετάβολος QG 4:8b

ἀμετάπτωτος Congr 140, 141

ἀμεταστρεπτί (11) Deus 116 Sobr 13 Conf 40 Migr 25 Her 305 Virt 30, 181 Praem 17, 62, 117 Contempl 18

ἀμέτοχος (55) Opif 73, 149 Leg 1:31, 88 Leg 2:53 Leg 3:169, 229 Cher 17, 90 Sacr 98, 111 Deus 41, 90 Plant 13, 42, 44 Ebr 61, 76, 115 Conf 177, 177 Migr 29, 118 Her 48, 61 Fug 20, 108, 117 Somn 1:22 Somn 2:230 Abr 202 Ios 146 Mos 2:210 Decal 31, 177 Spec 1:166, 230, 259, 296, 311, 327 Spec 2:11, 48, 53, 56, 214 Spec 3:136 Spec 4:55, 111 Praem 35 Contempl 6 Aet 32, 73 Flacc 73 QG 1:100:1c

ἀμέτρητος Agr 101

ἀμετρία (15) Opif 159 Leg 2:77 Post 52, 115 Ebr 22, 131 Migr 18, 21 Congr 60 Mut 143 Abr 134 Spec 3:209 Virt 195 Prov 2:70 QG (Par) 2:2

ἀμετροεπής Mut 251 Somn 2:260

ἄμετρος (45) Opif 81 Leg 2:16 Leg 3:111, 149, 155, 165, 183, 195 Cher 105 Sacr 32 Det 98 Agr 32, 88 Plant 105 Ebr 214 Sobr 2 Conf 117, 162 Her 32, 105, 297 Congr 55 Fug 42 Mut 214 Somn 1:122 Abr 20, 45, 91 Decal 77 Spec 1:305, 343 Spec 2:50 Spec 3:9, 151 Spec 4:79 Virt 163 Praem 47, 48, 135 Flacc 107, 167 Legat 162, 368 Hypoth 7:8 QE isf 24

ἀμῇ Somn 1:15

ἄμης Ebr 217 Somn 2:48

ἄμητος (12) Opif 115 Fug 171 Somn 2:6, 24 Ios 6 Spec 1:183 Spec 2:158, 186 Spec 4:208 Virt 90 Praem 101 Legat 257

ἀμήτωρ (11) Opif 100 Leg 1:15 Ebr 61 Her 62, 170, 216 Mos 2:210, 210 Decal 102 Spec 2:56 QG 2:12a

ἀμηχανέω QE isf 4

ἀμηχανία Sacr 71 Aet 128

ἀμήχανος (94) Opif 15, 79, 102 Leg 3:235 Cher 66, 96, 102 Sacr 3, 36, 79 Det 155 Post 5, 97, 163, 168 Gig 5, 19 Deus 29, 77 Agr 49, 53, 118, 161, 178 Plant 21 Ebr 138, 145, 192 Conf 156, 187 Migr 13, 195 Her 60, 72, 88, 202, 242, 306 Congr 36, 138, 152 Fug 117, 141 Mut 89, 185 Somn 1:9, 91, 236 Somn 2:89, 262 Abr 105, 175, 224 Mos 1:47, 62, 121, 143, 173 Mos 2:163, 247 Decal 11, 120, 123 Spec 4:127, 175 Virt 54, 215 Praem 40, 44 Prob 30, 80 Aet 5, 21, 48, 52, 81, 90, 93, 104, 114, 129 Flacc 18, 133 Legat 178, 196, 209, 303, 363 Prov 2:64 QG 2:34b, 4:174, 9* QE 2:2 QE isf 3

ἀμίαντος (15) Leg 1:50 Cher 50 Det 169 Post 133 Migr 31 Congr 124 Fug 50, 114, 118, 144 Somn 2:185 Spec 1:113, 250 Spec 4:40 QE 2:1

ἀμιγής (45) Opif 31, 71, 136 Leg 2:2 Cher 86 Sacr 110 Det 68 Post 32, 133 Deus 56, 77, 81 Ebr 44 Conf 73, 182 Migr 52, 153 Her 94, 183, 183, 184, 236 Congr 36 Fug 174 Mut 102 Somn 1:163 Somn 2:9 Abr 122, 205, 205 Mos 2:110, 204 Decal 177 Spec 1:224, 262 Spec 2:55, 59, 161 Spec 3:4 Praem 71 Contempl 81 QG 1:32, 2:12a, 3:58 QE 2:3b

ἄμικτος (16) Leg 1:50 Leg 2:15 Sacr 32 Her 28 Fug 35 Ios 30 Spec 2:16 Spec 4:204 Virt 135, 141 Praem 92 Legat 34, 147 QG 2:12c QG isf 10 QE 2:14

ἅμιλλα (17) Leg 3:233 Det 1, 28, 32, 36, 39, 41 Agr 110, 111, 162 Migr 75 Somn 1:152 Abr 105, 210, 244 Mos 1:232 Praem 94

ἁμιλλάομαι (18) Sacr 100 Det 29 Post 161 Agr 115 Migr 167 Somn 2:114 Abr 40, 209, 242 Ios 18 Mos 1:8 Mos 2:136, 171 Spec 1:186 Spec 4:205 Virt 186 Prob 105 Legat 144

Ἀμιναδάμ Post 76

ἀμισής Ebr 215 Ios 114, 206

ἅμμα Aet 88

Ἀμμανῖται Leg 3:81, 81 Post 177

ἄμμος (7) Leg 3:37, 203 Fug 148 Somn 1:3, 175, 175 Spec 3:160

ἀμνάς Spec 1:226, 233, 251, 253 Spec 3:46

ἀμνημονέω Migr 191

ἀμνήμων Ios 99 Mos 1:140

ἀμνησίκακος Ios 246

ἀμνηστία (21) Conf 160 Congr 109 Fug 89, 99 Somn 2:292, 299 Ios 92, 212, 239, 262 Mos 1:311 Mos 2:24, 134 Spec 1:161, 187, 193, 229, 236, 242 Spec 3:128 Flacc 84

ἀμνός (10) Her 174 Mut 159 Spec 1:169, 170, 177, 178, 184, 184, 198 Spec 4:105

ἀμοιβή (24) Leg 3:7 Cher 122, 123 Det 108 Plant 130 Somn 2:279 Ios 267 Mos 1:58 Mos 2:256 Decal 112, 115, 167 Spec 1:123 Spec 2:97, 171, 234 Spec 4:166, 195, 196 Aet 108 Flacc 50 Legat 59 QG 1:64a QE 2:11b

ἀμοιρέω (32) Opif 74, 158 Cher 35 Det 86 Post 145 Gig 11 Conf 177 Mut 8, 12 Somn 1:137 Abr 51, 74 Mos 1:135 Mos 2:27, 60, 73, 235 Spec 1:40, 44, 52, 64, 111, 310 Spec 2:149 Spec 3:17 Virt 120, 123, 206 Praem 15 Flacc 61 QG 4:76b QE 2:13a

ἄμοιρος Leg 3:55 Somn 2:184 Praem 110

Ἀμορραῖος (9) Leg 3:225, 232, 232 Deus 99 Her 300, 302, 304, 308 Mos 1:258

ἄμορφος (9) Opif 38 Conf 87 Her 140 Spec 1:47, 328, 328 Contempl 7 Aet 41, 56

ἀμουσία Her 81, 210

ἄμουσος (21) Leg 3:36 Det 18 Post 107 Plant 167 Ebr 33 Conf 15, 55, 150 Migr 72 Fug 22 Mut 229 Ios 206 Spec 1:174, 321 Spec 3:32 Spec 4:145, 233 Prob 51 Aet 74 QG 4:8* QG (Par) 2:7

ἀμοχθί Leg 3:69

ἀμπέλιος Somn 2:164

ἄμπελος (31) Opif 116 Det 106 Plant 32, 71 Ebr 2, 222, 222, 222, 223, 224 Mut 162 Somn 2:158, 159, 159, 162, 163, 169, 171, 190, 191, 191, 195, 199 Ios 91, 92 Mos 1:228, 231 Aet 63 Legat 82 QG 1:28, 28

ἀμπελουργικός Plant 1, 140

ἀμπελουργός Plant 1

ἀμπελόφυτος Spec 4:215

ἀμπελών (25) Deus 94, 96, 145, 154, 154 Agr 1, 148, 149, 157, 157, 166 Plant 1, 140 Fug 175, 176 Somn 2:172, 173 Spec 2:105 Spec 4:203, 208, 213 Virt 28, 91, 92 Praem 128

ἀμπεχόνη (12) Somn 1:93, 102, 187 Somn 2:52, 53, 126 Ios 41, 52 Virt 18, 19 Praem 99 Aet 67

ἀμπέχω (9) Leg 2:53 Cher 95 Sacr 21 Somn 1:96, 101 Spec 3:41 Spec 4:93, 203 Virt 18

ἀμπίσχω Spec 3:206

ἀμπωτίζω Deus 177 Somn 2:121 Mos 1:176 Spec 2:143

ἄμπωτις Opif 113

ἀμυγδαλέα Mos 2:186

ἀμυδρός (22) Opif 65, 141, 145 Leg 3:111 Sacr 30 Post 118 Deus 43 Plant 27 Migr 38, 79 Congr 135, 140 Mut 162 Somn 1:116, 171, 202 Somn 2:17, 138 Abr 240 Spec 1:37 Spec 3:4 Virt 56

ἀμυδρότης Praem 143

ἀμυδρόω Deus 3, 78 Praem 38

ἀμύητος (15) Leg 1:60 Cher 48, 94, 121 Det 77, 79 Agr 25 Ebr 37, 51 Conf 116 Fug 179 Somn 2:30 QG 4:8c QG isf 2 QE isf 13

ἀμύθητος (69) Opif 43 Leg 1:61 Leg 3:148 Sacr 29, 122 Det 170 Post 108, 110, 141, 167 Deus 112 Agr 35 Plant 103 Ebr 171, 171, 202, 217 Sobr 42 Conf 10, 15, 171 Her 33, 131, 284 Fug 54 Mut 146, 239 Somn 1:6 Somn 2:48 Abr 159, 261 Ios 57, 269 Mos 1:145, 212, 323 Mos 2:62, 115, 289 Decal 2, 156 Spec 1:90, 151, 163, 184, 192, 322, 339 Spec 2:63, 169, 205 Spec 3:2, 28, 178, 194 Spec 4:82, 85 Virt 149 Praem 107, 132 Prob 9, 64 Contempl 19 Aet 64 Legat 101, 226 Hypoth 6:1 Prov 2:14, 28

ἄμυνα (23) Leg 1:68 Leg 3:115 Deus 60 Agr 147 Plant 41 Conf 45 Mut 159, 200 Abr 213 Ios 166, 263 Mos 1:170, 244, 304 Mos 2:273 Decal 75, 177 Spec 3:129 Spec 4:224 Virt 109 Praem 140 Legat 68, 215

ἀμυντήριος (16) Opif 84 Leg 2:8 Leg 3:26, 155 Sacr 130 Deus 68 Her 203 Mut 159 Somn 1:103, 235 Mos 1:170 Decal 178 Virt 3 Aet 148 Flacc 90 Legat 229

ἀμύνω (33) Opif 85 Leg 2:79 Leg 3:200 Sacr 135 Det 36 Agr 95 Ebr 71 Migr 26 Fug 210 Abr 211 Ios 50 Mos 1:40, 46, 111, 142, 173, 215, 249, 314 Mos 2:252 Spec 3:17, 19, 85, 195 Spec 4:7, 121, 185, 197, 222 Contempl 41 Legat 100 QG 1:74 QE 2:6a

ἀμύστις Ebr 221

ἀμφημερινός Conf 151

ἀμφήριστος Mos 1:218 Spec 3:55

ἀμφί Somn 1:14 Mos 1:90, 101 Spec 1:152

Ἀμφιάραος Legat 78

ἀμφίβιος Det 154

ἀμφίβολος (10) Post 46 Agr 16, 136 Plant 113 Somn 2:184 Ios 183, 191 Spec 1:63 Legat 218 QG 3:58

ἀμφίδοξος Decal 128

ἀμφιθαλής Congr 132 Prob 10 Legat 93

ἀμφικλινής Mos 2:237 Legat 15 QG 1:55c

Ἀμφίλοχος Legat 78

ἀμφισβητέω (8) Leg 3:205 Sacr 91, 91 Plant 82 Decal 86, 92 Spec 2:10 Spec 3:131

ἀμφισβήτημα Aet 142

ἀμφισβήτησις Leg 3:233 Decal 140 Spec 4:173 Flacc 24

ἀμφότερος (137) Opif 38, 92, 99, 104, 106, 116, 136, 156 Leg 1:1, 21, 21, 86, 89, 95, 96 Leg 2:50 Leg 3:83, 109, 122 Cher 109 Sacr 3, 138 Det 35, 54, 108 Post 37, 95 Deus 50 Agr 29, 75, 82, 145, 176 Plant 172 Ebr 35, 77, 83, 84, 85, 94, 115, 130 Sobr 24 Conf 72 Migr 54,

67, 69, 73, 82, 88, 89, 165, 166, 175 Her 11, 15, 49, 126, 206, 310 Congr 84, 154 Fug 70, 73, 148, 188 Mut 19, 23, 41, 118, 155, 201 Somn 1:41, 111, 159 Somn 2:8, 42, 139, 147, 156, 156, 157 Abr 6, 157, 246 Mos 1:24, 47, 78, 97, 240, 302 Mos 2:40, 142, 154, 180, 182, 245, 266 Decal 50, 51, 110, 156 Spec 1:333 Spec 2:66, 139, 191 Spec 3:21, 58, 73, 134 Spec 4:1, 37, 69, 106, 129, 198, 208, 215, 234 Virt 22, 208, 222 Praem 137 Prob 118 Contempl 53 Aet 121 Flacc 132 Legat 79, 142, 195, 228, 236, 305 Prov 2:42, 43 QG 2:71a, 4:202a

ἄμφω (78) Opif 13, 65, 99, 103, 106 Leg 1:106 Leg 2:71, 72 Leg 3:184, 217 Cher 27, 48, 73, 112 Sacr 14, 36, 65, 138 Deus 179 Agr 118, 145, 161 Plant 44, 87 Sobr 54 Conf 89 Migr 3, 73, 78, 86, 147, 148, 207 Her 45, 139, 213 Congr 22, 82 Fug 145, 156 Mut 43 Somn 1:23 Somn 2:12, 227, 263 Abr 88, 205 Ios 148, 205 Mos 1:27, 301 Mos 2:98, 119, 221 Decal 31 Spec 1:6, 116, 233 Spec 2:225, 232, 233 Spec 3:14, 23, 24 Spec 4:11, 31, 102, 111, 186 Virt 54, 116, 225 Praem 95 Prob 57 Contempl 85 Legat 111 Prov 2:71 QG 4:64

ἀμώμητος Aet 41 QG isf 2

ἄμωμος (17) Leg 1:50, 50 Cher 85 Sacr 51 Agr 130 Her 114 Congr 106 Fug 18, 80 Mut 60, 233 Somn 1:62 Somn 2:72, 185 Spec 1:201, 268, 283

ἄν (καί) (1660) Opif 4, 12, 16, 20, 20, 20, 23, 24, 25, 26, 27, 31, 31, 38, 41, 44, 44, 46, 47, 59, 61, 69, 72, 72, 73, 75, 77, 78, 81, 83, 86, 87, 88, 90, 97, 98, 100, 102, 104, 109, 112, 115, 131, 131, 135, 136, 143, 144, 147, 168, 168, 171 Leg 1:2, 22, 27, 29, 29, 33, 34, 35, 38, 38, 42, 42, 42, 43, 44, 48, 52, 59, 62, 76, 84, 90, 91, 92, 93, 101, 105, 107, 108 Leg 2:1, 3, 8, 9, 14, 15, 18, 19, 32, 39, 57, 60, 63, 69, 78, 81, 82, 85, 86, 89, 90, 103, 104, 104, 105 Leg 3:1, 4, 5, 6, 14, 14, 21, 21, 21, 21, 21, 45, 47, 47, 53, 54, 56, 56, 70, 72, 78, 83, 89, 89, 95, 100, 101, 110, 112, 113, 115, 121, 148, 155, 162, 171, 176, 182, 184, 185, 189, 202, 204, 204, 205, 206, 206, 207, 207, 210, 214, 214, 215, 219, 236, 240, 241, 244, 245, 245 Cher 6, 32, 36, 36, 37, 46, 48, 53, 55, 56, 66, 66, 74, 75, 77, 78, 81, 83, 86, 90, 90, 91, 96, 98, 100, 109, 115, 117, 120, 122, 128 Sacr 1, 4, 10, 15, 19, 19, 23, 23, 24, 24, 29, 31, 33, 34, 37, 40, 48, 49, 64, 66, 70, 70, 70, 75, 77, 87, 89, 89, 97, 97, 99, 100, 101, 104, 106, 106, 115, 121, 122, 123, 124, 135 Det 2, 4, 10, 13, 14, 14, 22, 25, 26, 36, 44, 45, 55, 60, 62, 68, 74, 75, 77, 79, 81, 87, 103, 104, 113, 123, 124, 127, 128, 128, 130, 138, 143, 144, 147, 148, 151, 152, 153, 154, 154, 160, 175, 176 Post 4, 5, 7, 9, 9, 9, 19, 19, 21, 21, 38, 39, 40, 49, 49, 50, 50, 53, 58, 71, 71, 72, 75, 80, 81, 81, 82, 83, 88, 95, 99, 109, 109, 109, 110, 116, 116, 117, 126, 126, 128, 131, 132, 133, 138, 143, 144, 145, 148, 159, 161, 161, 161, 163, 169, 179, 181, 185 Gig 10, 21, 25, 25, 26, 32, 38, 43, 43, 44, 53, 67 Deus 1, 8, 22, 35, 40, 43, 48, 50, 50, 59, 66, 66, 66, 73, 76, 79, 81, 99, 101, 106, 107, 115, 116, 120, 122, 127, 128, 128, 132, 145, 157, 158, 170, 170 Agr 3, 5, 9, 9, 11, 17, 19, 22, 36, 37, 41, 56, 57, 60, 61, 68, 70, 73, 78, 83, 84, 85, 85, 86, 98, 110, 115, 116, 118, 118, 118, 119, 121, 125, 129, 142, 147, 147, 149, 152, 154, 162, 167, 167, 173, 175 Plant 1, 6, 7, 11, 27, 27, 33, 33, 33, 37, 54, 68, 71, 81, 84, 88, 91, 96, 100, 101, 102, 102, 107, 108, 108, 108, 114, 126, 130, 132, 146, 147, 147, 155, 160, 160, 163, 164, 166, 174, 175, 176, 177, 177 Ebr 13, 14, 19, 25, 33, 43, 45, 53, 64, 65, 74, 76, 76, 83, 84, 93, 93, 96, 103, 104, 106, 111, 116, 119, 126, 127, 130, 133, 138, 146, 146, 156, 158, 164, 167, 168, 170, 172, 174, 177, 182, 183, 187, 192, 195, 197, 198, 199, 206, 207, 221 Sobr 6, 13, 15, 20, 20, 21, 22, 22, 24, 35, 35, 36, 46, 48, 62 Conf 1, 2, 6, 11, 13, 14, 29, 38, 38, 40, 41, 74, 76, 81, 91, 93, 96, 98, 104, 106, 108, 112, 113, 114, 117, 119, 126, 128, 129, 139, 142, 146, 146, 153, 160, 162, 162, 163, 164, 167, 168, 170, 171, 183, 185, 190, 190, 191, 192, 194, 194, 194, 194, 194, 194 Migr 4, 6, 10, 14, 19, 24, 26, 31, 33, 33, 35, 49, 55, 56, 60, 89, 106, 108, 110, 112, 112, 121, 122, 137, 143, 144, 150, 162, 162, 165, 167, 167, 182, 183, 183, 191, 193, 210, 211, 212, 218, 222, 224, 225 Her 3, 5, 9, 13, 20, 21, 33, 78, 81, 82, 83, 83, 84, 84, 90, 90, 90, 101, 101, 103, 104, 109, 113, 121, 141, 142, 144, 145, 149, 154, 154, 154, 158, 189, 235, 246, 247, 255, 256, 266, 270, 270, 271, 272, 277, 278, 296, 316 Congr 23, 24, 31, 32, 33, 42, 46, 50, 51, 52, 62, 74, 79, 80, 87, 89, 95, 99, 106, 113, 127, 137, 153, 153, 170, 176 Fug 16, 20, 22, 25, 31, 33, 51, 51, 51, 55, 62, 68, 71, 71, 76, 77, 80, 80, 82, 84, 91, 95, 96, 99, 99, 114, 122, 129, 146, 152, 153, 160, 167, 170, 171, 171, 188, 191, 194, 200, 209 Mut 2, 12, 12, 13, 18, 22, 26, 35, 38, 48, 50, 62, 63, 71, 71, 72, 79, 82, 85, 91, 111, 120, 124, 128, 129, 131, 138, 148, 157, 161, 169, 170, 178, 181, 188, 192, 211, 211, 215, 217, 227, 231, 239, 243, 243, 252, 256, 261, 262, 262, 262, 264 Somn 1:1, 3, 7, 7, 12, 14, 16, 21, 23, 24, 27, 27, 36, 44, 62, 68, 79, 95, 95, 97, 98, 101, 101, 105, 112, 120, 122, 129, 143, 146, 152, 158, 163, 164, 168, 179, 183, 192, 200, 202, 209, 211, 220, 228, 230, 245 Somn 2:1, 6, 48, 58, 83, 97, 99, 101, 102, 104, 115, 116, 116, 127, 131, 134, 140, 159, 168, 169, 176, 177, 182, 187, 189, 189, 200, 223, 231, 232, 236, 251, 253, 253, 261, 264, 276, 281, 295, 300 Abr 3, 3, 5, 17, 33, 35, 46, 73, 76, 82, 86, 86, 115, 115, 116, 116, 119, 121, 136, 150, 151, 174, 183, 187, 192, 193, 197, 197, 198, 199, 204, 208, 211, 215, 216, 216, 217, 238, 249, 252, 259, 264, 271 Ios 2, 24, 25, 25, 27, 39, 47, 48, 62, 66, 68, 68, 71, 73, 76, 77, 96, 111, 114, 122, 123, 144, 147, 153, 156, 156, 166, 167, 169, 176, 178, 185, 216, 226, 227, 231, 231, 245, 252 Mos 1:19, 24, 30, 33, 49, 55, 62, 66, 81, 109, 110, 112, 127, 128, 130, 130, 130, 139, 141, 146, 156, 157, 160, 161, 201, 212, 213, 213, 213, 226, 247, 254, 278, 281, 291, 294, 294, 298, 298, 300, 310, 325, 329, 329 Mos 2:2, 7, 11, 14, 17, 27, 44, 61, 62, 97, 99, 100, 108, 108, 122, 142, 145, 147, 186, 191, 197, 203, 203, 203, 204, 214, 214, 217, 227, 239, 244, 265, 266, 270, 271 Decal 6, 11, 13, 20, 24, 35, 36, 39, 42, 43, 47, 58, 60, 61, 61, 75, 75, 77, 79, 87, 87, 88, 110, 110, 112, 113, 122, 125, 127, 130, 137 Spec 1:17, 26, 36, 42, 43, 45, 46, 65, 67, 68, 75, 84, 89, 90, 90, 102, 104, 107, 108, 113, 118, 119, 124, 127, 127, 141, 147, 153, 153, 154, 155, 155, 160, 175, 192, 210, 211, 211, 211, 220, 242, 242, 246, 263, 263, 271, 271, 272, 275, 277, 278, 281, 282, 286, 293, 302, 315, 316, 329, 335, 338 Spec 2:2, 8, 11, 11, 17, 18, 19, 31, 41, 42, 42, 48, 48, 59, 73, 74, 75, 81, 96, 122, 135, 174, 178, 187, 191, 193, 194, 195, 198, 199, 207, 213, 214, 216, 228, 229, 232, 233, 237, 246, 248, 248, 252, 253, 258 Spec 3:8, 9, 14, 27, 30, 34, 42, 50, 50, 53, 53, 54, 68, 70, 71, 75, 77, 78, 78, 78, 78, 79, 86, 86, 87, 87, 88, 89, 89, 90, 94, 98, 99, 101, 103, 106, 107, 111, 113, 113, 119, 119, 121, 122, 122, 133, 133, 136, 141, 141, 146, 149, 151, 158, 165, 166, 166, 175, 175, 180, 181, 182, 185, 191, 191, 193, 195, 198, 202, 202, 205, 206, 208, 209 Spec 4:2, 7, 10, 17, 17, 18, 19, 21, 26, 26, 37, 46, 52, 56, 58, 71, 73, 75, 83,

85, 86, 99, 103, 107, 112, 120, 140, 140, 145, 147, 148, 150, 151, 152, 154, 156, 160, 169, 170, 170, 171, 171, 171, 181, 186, 188, 190, 202, 202, 213, 215, 216, 221, 222, 225, 229, 230, 230, 230, 235 Virt 4, 16, 27, 41, 48, 55, 57, 59, 66, 82, 86, 89, 90, 92, 96, 96, 99, 104, 108, 109, 109, 114, 114, 116, 116, 117, 124, 127, 128, 132, 133, 135, 135, 136, 136, 137, 139, 145, 157, 160, 160, 160, 171, 174, 179, 179, 185, 186, 188, 189, 190, 193, 195, 198, 199, 210, 213, 218, 226, 226, 227 Praem 14, 20, 25, 27, 31, 32, 67, 69, 69, 83, 84, 84, 90, 94, 97, 100, 105, 108, 110, 117, 117, 117, 117, 119, 135, 136, 137, 148, 149, 164 Prob 5, 19, 25, 31, 36, 41, 42, 47, 47, 59, 60, 61, 61, 78, 86, 86, 97, 101, 101, 104, 109, 112, 131, 131, 136, 136, 140, 141, 149, 152, 156, 156 Contempl 6, 9, 12, 19, 34, 48, 56, 75, 79 Aet 2, 2, 14, 16, 18, 20, 21, 21, 26, 33, 33, 34, 36, 44, 46, 46, 46, 54, 60, 65, 67, 75, 75, 78, 84, 85, 87, 88, 88, 90, 91, 104, 105, 107, 107, 118, 119, 126, 128, 130, 130, 134, 135, 135, 138, 139 Flacc 6, 12, 14, 14, 35, 35, 40, 48, 48, 50, 54, 58, 59, 59, 59, 60, 81, 94, 97, 111, 127, 129, 140, 159, 159 Legat 3, 6, 10, 24, 27, 36, 38, 56, 58, 68, 91, 107, 108, 111, 118, 119, 140, 152, 154, 195, 198, 209, 211, 211, 215, 218, 218, 220, 220, 227, 236, 238, 242, 246, 258, 274, 287, 287, 307, 307, 308, 315, 323, 327, 327, 337, 357, 368, 369, 369, 370 Hypoth 6:4, 6:9, 7:1, 7:8, 7:8, 7:9, 7:10, 7:16, 7:17, 7:17, 7:17, 7:20, 11:7, 11:12, 11:13 Prov 1, 1, 1, 1, 2:7, 8, 8, 11, 12, 15, 17, 22, 39, 44, 46, 52, 60, 67 QG 1:17a, 51, 65, 70:1, 70:1, 70:2, 2:28, 41, 65, 66, 68a, 71a, 3:3, 8, 30b, 49a, 4:51b, 74, 76a, 76b, 76b, 86a, 88, 166, 166, 180, 180, 191c, 198, 200a, 202b, 228 QG isf 2, 5, 11, 13, 13, 16 QG (Par) 2:4 QE 2:11a, 12, 25c, 25d, 50b QE isf 10, 29

ἀνά (79) Opif 45 Leg 3:65, 65, 65, 156, 182, 182, 184, 185, 246 Cher 75 Sacr 9 Det 1 Post 37 Gig 52 Deus 116, 147 Agr 5, 35, 59, 88, 143, 147 Plant 61, 133, 164 Ebr 111, 127, 127, 139 Sobr 58 Conf 39, 133 Migr 22, 204 Her 163, 163, 166, 186, 206 Congr 113, 153 Fug 101 Mut 52, 52, 217 Somn 1:76, 76 Somn 2:144, 229, 235 Abr 44, 134, 170, 244 Ios 109, 158 Mos 1:6, 243, 253 Mos 2:41, 195 Decal 159 Spec 1:77, 78, 172, 172, 223 Spec 2:160 Spec 3:2, 24, 47 Spec 4:100, 104 Virt 18, 47 Contempl 69 Flacc 147 Legat 214

ἀναβαθμός Post 113 Somn 2:67 Praem 110 Legat 77

ἀναβαίνω (50) Opif 131 Leg 1:28 Leg 2:91 Leg 3:179, 214, 214 Det 93 Post 127, 132, 136, 136, 136 Deus 99 Agr 93 Conf 74, 95, 158 Migr 18, 168, 169, 170 Her 45, 45, 251 Fug 170, 170, 178, 181, 194, 195 Mut 270 Somn 1:3, 57, 62, 133, 189, 197, 199 Somn 2:16, 19, 119, 216, 216, 218 Ios 35, 148 Mos 2:161 Aet 58, 58 Legat 294

ἀναβάλλω Agr 85 Spec 3:102 Hypoth 11:9

ἀνάβασις Aet 147 QG 4:100

ἀναβαστάζω Opif 86

ἀναβάτης (17) Leg 2:102, 103, 103, 104 Agr 67, 68, 72, 73, 73, 78, 82, 92, 94, 124 Ebr 111 Migr 62 Somn 2:269

ἀναβατός (ἀμβατός) Conf 4

ἀναβιβάζω (8) Leg 3:214 Det 114, 118 Post 29, 31 Somn 2:170 Ios 120 Flacc 142

ἀναβλαστάνω (18) Opif 77 Sacr 125 Post 163, 172 Agr 10, 30 Plant 2, 48 Ebr 9, 61 Migr 123, 125 Her 279 Congr 146 Somn 1:220 Somn 2:14 Aet 100 Legat 321

ἀναβλέπω (17) Leg 3:39 Cher 62 Post 17 Deus 181 Her 76, 76, 86 Somn 1:64, 67, 164, 189, 197, 199 Abr 78 Spec 3:187 Virt 179 Prob 56

ἀναβλύζω Ebr 32 Somn 1:97

ἀναβοάω (7) Mos 1:235 Flacc 41, 122, 144, 169 Legat 301, 356

ἀναβολή Mos 1:46 Spec 3:94 Flacc 129 Legat 248 Hypoth 7:1

ἀναγγέλλω (19) Leg 3:16, 16, 16, 17, 17, 21, 174, 176 Det 5, 5, 12 Post 89 Deus 131 Plant 59 Migr 140 Congr 170 Fug 20, 127 Mut 14

ἀνάγειον Contempl 33

ἀναγέννησις Aet 8

ἀναγιγνώσκω (20) Leg 1:83 Det 47 Agr 18 Congr 20, 74, 148 Mut 66 Somn 1:205 Somn 2:127 Abr 177 Mos 1:4 Spec 4:160, 161, 163 Virt 131 Prob 82 Flacc 98 Legat 254 Hypoth 7:13, 7:13

ἀναγκάζω (77) Leg 3:110, 120, 155 Cher 81 Det 13, 131, 134 Post 54, 165 Deus 102, 164 Agr 47, 49, 101, 111 Ebr 22, 159 Conf 38 Migr 114 Her 270, 310 Congr 6 Fug 145 Mut 241, 262 Somn 1:77, 99, 129, 204, 246 Somn 2:123, 133, 196, 280 Ios 26, 142, 147 Mos 1:38, 95, 112, 268 Mos 2:166 Decal 114, 129 Spec 1:99, 165 Spec 2:85, 90, 107, 112 Spec 3:197 Spec 4:112, 158 Virt 84, 127 Prob 27, 30, 34, 36, 60, 60, 60, 60, 61, 61, 94, 95, 96, 96 Aet 136 Flacc 31, 130, 153, 155 Legat 61, 141, 293

ἀναγκαῖος (ὁ) (491) Opif 2, 8, 9, 12, 26, 26, 35, 53, 61, 67, 78, 79, 80, 82, 83, 97, 111, 115, 119, 133, 135, 143, 145, 151, 153, 153, 162, 164, 167, 167, 171 Leg 2:16, 17, 17, 33 Leg 3:22, 45, 51, 91, 140, 141, 147, 147, 151, 154, 157, 159, 194, 227 Cher 78, 85, 87 Sacr 98, 115, 121, 125 Det 12, 34, 44, 81, 104, 130, 141, 157, 160, 161 Post 91, 91, 108, 112 Gig 8, 9, 29, 34 Deus 4, 30, 71, 153, 170 Agr 19, 39, 58, 68, 88, 98, 106, 131, 141, 141, 149 Plant 15, 37, 51, 54, 65, 75, 100, 104, 141, 164 Ebr 15, 28, 31, 112, 131, 169, 192, 195, 214 Sobr 20, 33, 36, 54, 61, 63 Conf 38, 135, 158, 170, 176 Migr 82, 173, 223 Her 14, 35, 63, 90, 102, 133, 139, 141, 145 Congr 24, 29, 29, 30, 63, 100, 165 Fug 8, 38, 70, 87, 98, 154, 161, 206 Mut 96, 100, 103, 150, 166, 184, 197, 213, 219 Somn 1:4, 36, 42, 42, 55, 64, 68, 97, 104, 124, 242 Somn 2:22, 28, 33, 49, 64, 82, 116, 155, 180, 180, 215, 240, 261, 262 Abr 3, 49, 60, 65, 78, 91, 156, 237, 249, 259 Ios 3, 34, 95, 109, 115, 118, 124, 153, 154, 155, 163, 165, 183, 190, 195, 225, 241, 243, 243, 253, 263 Mos 1:5, 28, 111, 124, 124, 141, 151, 160, 191, 195, 201, 206, 209, 223, 224, 231, 237, 251, 316, 324, 333 Mos 2:3, 6, 48, 51, 63, 66, 70, 72, 88, 123, 134, 141, 142, 146, 147, 151, 159, 177, 183, 205, 222, 222, 222, 223, 223, 226, 228, 230, 233, 241, 246, 251, 255, 258, 270 Decal 10, 16, 18, 32, 45, 50, 52, 67, 97, 99, 113, 117, 118, 164, 165, 170 Spec 1:7, 8, 31, 34, 54, 68, 70, 97, 98, 131, 133, 133, 134, 153, 158, 165, 179, 195, 211, 224, 227, 267, 269, 298, 323, 327, 332, 340, 342, 343, 345 Spec 2:3, 6, 17, 23, 25, 34, 34, 39, 53, 65, 68, 70, 81, 85, 91, 113, 123, 130, 133, 141, 159, 160, 161, 166, 172, 173, 175, 177, 180, 185, 195, 199, 203, 205, 207, 228, 233, 241, 245, 247, 248, 260 Spec 3:4, 25, 59, 61, 81, 90, 95, 152, 179, 201 Spec 4:36, 55, 63, 68, 171, 175, 178, 206, 211, 217, 228 Virt 6, 27, 56, 65, 75, 79, 87, 93, 100, 104, 118, 122, 133, 144, 145, 149, 149, 152, 154, 178, 180, 180, 181, 190 Praem 10, 42, 98, 105, 106, 107,

120, 127, 134, 138 Prob 8, 32, 34, 76, 80, 115, 121, 142 Contempl 10, 15, 24, 25, 29, 35, 53, 61 Aet 1, 5, 16, 36, 37, 49, 65, 67, 82, 90, 112, 130, 132, 134, 136, 144 Flacc 4, 51, 62, 64, 134, 143 Legat 10, 51, 74, 81, 124, 128, 147, 178, 193, 248, 252, 253, 274, 299, 318, 326 Hypoth 7:14, 11:9 Prov 2:5, 11, 12, 23, 45, 47, 49, 53, 55, 69, 69, 72 QG 4:102b, 172 QG (Par) 2:7, 2:7 QE 2:3a, 14, 18, 71 QE isf 14, 25, 25

ἀνάγκη (236) Opif 72, 132, 139 Leg 1:2, 73, 86 Leg 2:16, 28, 57, 71 Leg 3:5, 41, 60, 77, 117, 121, 151, 151, 189, 200, 218 Cher 2, 13, 56, 66, 74, 82, 83, 109, 115 Sacr 3, 13, 31, 39, 69, 71, 104, 106 Det 11, 50, 54, 104, 119, 124, 125, 141, 153, 167, 171 Post 3, 4, 9, 19, 53, 61, 67, 69, 98, 135, 184 Gig 4, 7, 18, 43, 49, 64 Deus 12, 27, 28, 47, 48, 66, 100, 117, 119 Agr 1, 31, 49, 70, 77, 88, 116, 118, 150 Plant 7, 19, 35, 43, 122, 172, 175 Ebr 7, 48, 129, 170, 196, 214 Sobr 36 Conf 17, 41, 91, 127 Migr 3, 30, 169, 179 Her 41, 45, 142, 181, 187, 226, 272, 274, 300 Congr 20, 40, 73 Fug 32, 32, 63, 98 Mut 49, 149, 270 Somn 1:46, 110, 114, 132, 177 Somn 2:20, 34, 44, 81, 129, 136, 150, 154, 253, 253, 293 Abr 184, 186 Ios 71, 186, 192, 264, 269 Mos 1:10, 39, 58, 89, 184, 247 Mos 2:53, 201, 224, 250 Decal 39, 57, 85, 140, 150 Spec 1:30, 101, 103, 126, 127, 127, 130, 143, 292, 338 Spec 2:74, 124, 137, 209 Spec 3:34, 97 Spec 4:70, 119, 136, 150, 179, 193, 198 Virt 7, 25, 30, 67, 83, 122, 128 Praem 19, 20, 121, 124, 156 Prob 41, 58, 96 Contempl 34, 61, 68 Aet 18, 21, 32, 45, 51, 51, 52, 53, 55, 71, 85, 92, 104, 115, 149 Flacc 17, 186 Legat 126, 327, 360 Hypoth 6:7, 7:7, 11:13, 11:17 Prov 2:23, 32 QG 1:21, 2:34c QE 2:2, 16, 16 QE isf 16

ἀναγκοφαγέω Legat 275

ἄναγνος (6) Opif 7 Cher 94 Sacr 138 Post 177 Abr 14 Spec 4:217

ἀναγνώρισις Ios 237

ἀνάγνωσις Leg 3:18 Her 253

ἀνάγνωσμα Legat 165

ἀνάγραπτος (8) Abr 11, 177, 262 Mos 2:108 Spec 4:175, 238 Virt 95, 201

ἀναγραφή (9) Congr 175 Fug 137 Mut 189 Somn 1:33, 48 Somn 2:265, 301 Praem 2 Hypoth 6:5

ἀναγράφω (123) Opif 6, 12, 25, 104, 128 Cher 124 Sacr 19, 54 Det 15, 20 Deus 50, 127, 137, 181 Agr 50, 140, 145, 172 Plant 175 Ebr 37 Sobr 6, 12, 17, 48, 49, 69 Conf 6, 23, 128, 141, 143, 149, 168 Migr 14, 20, 69, 204 Her 165, 227, 260, 291 Congr 30, 37, 44, 56, 99, 120 Fug 2, 142, 178, 180, 185 Mut 12, 53, 132, 267 Somn 1:134, 167, 172, 190, 219 Somn 2:1, 4, 10, 157, 234, 277, 290, 300 Abr 1, 5, 17 Ios 1, 1, 228 Mos 1:1, 299 Mos 2:188, 222 Decal 1, 97, 121, 131, 154, 165, 169 Spec 1:20, 31, 56, 92, 112, 129, 170, 280 Spec 2:3, 41, 42, 79, 140, 150, 152, 223 Spec 3:155 Spec 4:2, 114, 140, 150, 206 Virt 52 Praem 43, 54, 67, 127, 150 Contempl 57 Aet 31, 120 Flacc 164 Legat 13, 56 Prov 2:33 QG 4:168 QG isf 13

ἀνάγω (61) Leg 2:93 Leg 3:7 Sacr 8, 110 Det 20 Deus 4 Agr 127 Plant 108, 162, 164 Ebr 129 Migr 171, 202 Her 226 Somn 1:62 Somn 2:72, 74 Abr 234 Ios 139 Mos 1:276, 284 Mos 2:73, 141, 153, 159, 162, 270 Spec 1:38, 145, 152, 166, 168, 169, 183, 184, 185, 185, 188, 228, 257, 271, 272, 283 Spec 2:188 Spec 3:125 Spec 4:174 Praem 82 Flacc 63, 125, 155 Legat 151, 156, 157, 280, 312, 317, 326, 334, 355 Hypoth 6:9 QE isf 13

ἀναγωγή Flacc 27

ἀνάγωγος (8) Sacr 47 Deus 64 Ebr 13, 33 Fug 201 Mut 229 Somn 1:255 Somn 2:259

ἀναδείκνυμι (14) Opif 114 Sacr 30, 35 Det 39, 44 Agr 8 Plant 110, 118 Conf 103, 179 Congr 93 Fug 96 Spec 1:90 Praem 153

ἀνάδελφος Spec 2:127

ἀναδέμω Agr 113, 157

ἀναδεύω Opif 38 Her 58 Spec 1:179

ἀναδέχομαι (30) Cher 46, 78 Sacr 114, 132 Deus 16, 16, 115 Agr 151, 152 Ebr 35, 218 Conf 163 Migr 144 Her 272, 286 Congr 46, 92, 165 Somn 2:122 Abr 246 Spec 3:90 Praem 128, 139 Legat 61, 85, 117, 118 QG 1:77, 4:169 QE isf 29

ἀναδέω (6) Agr 112, 113 Mut 44, 109 Spec 2:235 Legat 95

ἀναδιδάσκω (95) Opif 8, 160, 170 Cher 29, 42, 48, 129 Det 10, 43, 44, 135 Post 16 Deus 148 Agr 93 Ebr 37 Conf 142 Migr 179 Her 97, 182, 203, 213 Congr 15, 15, 28, 80, 122, 163 Fug 74 Mut 80, 104, 167 Somn 1:68, 159 Somn 2:1, 252 Abr 6, 61, 75, 258, 275 Ios 2, 129, 143 Mos 1:76, 102, 146, 207, 207 Mos 2:9, 40, 67, 74, 128, 141, 153, 177, 183 Decal 37, 115, 137 Spec 1:22, 25, 41, 72, 161, 167, 205, 230, 332 Spec 2:21, 55, 66, 88, 112, 142, 170, 197, 228 Spec 4:169 Virt 116, 133, 160, 165, 168 Praem 77 Prob 2, 81, 82, 145 Aet 134 Legat 31, 58, 170, 223 QE 2:18

ἀναδίδωμι (44) Opif 42, 56, 133, 133, 158 Leg 3:13, 161 Agr 112 Ebr 85, 112, 218 Migr 31 Congr 114, 118, 173 Fug 200 Mut 43, 159 Somn 1:49, 49, 97, 144, 152 Somn 2:62, 74 Abr 38, 141 Ios 92 Mos 1:65 Mos 2:56, 143 Spec 3:184 Spec 4:104 Praem 27 Contempl 23, 53 Aet 62, 63 Flacc 37, 97 Legat 178, 254 QG (Par) 2:7, 2:7

ἀναδικάζω Deus 183

ἀναδίπλωσις Ios 107

ἀναδονέω Somn 2:1

ἀναδύομαι (8) Post 18 Somn 1:13 Mos 1:58 Spec 3:70 Virt 63, 83, 89 Aet 68

ἀναζάω ἀναζωόω

ἀναζεύγνυμι Ios 208 Mos 1:177, 187

ἀναζέω Congr 55, 162 Mos 1:127

ἀναζητέω (26) Opif 166 Leg 3:47 Sacr 64 Post 21, 182 Deus 155 Agr 23, 26 Plant 79 Ebr 73, 113 Sobr 27 Conf 75 Her 247 Fug 143 Mut 105, 108 Somn 2:50, 61, 271 Ios 117 Spec 1:3 Spec 2:165 Prob 19, 65 Legat 202

ἀναζωγραφέω Migr 214 Ios 126 Spec 1:27 Legat 306

ἀναζώννυμι Leg 2:28 Leg 3:153

ἀναζωόω (ἀναζάω) Somn 1:147

ἀνάθεμα Mos 1:253

ἀναθερίζω Virt 92

ἀνάθεσις (19) Her 75 Mut 93 Somn 1:242, 242, 252, 252 Flacc 43, 51 Legat 138, 207, 207, 217, 233, 248, 299, 306, 333 Hypoth 7:4, 7:5

ἀνάθημα (26) Det 20 Plant 126 Migr 98, 98 Her 200 Fug 42, 42 Mut 220 Somn 1:243, 243, 251, 253 Decal 133 Spec 1:66 Spec 2:32, 37, 115, 115, 115 Spec 4:69 Legat 151, 157, 280, 297, 319, 335

ἀναθλίβω Spec 1:218 Spec 3:114, 193

ἀναθυμίασις Leg 1:42 Somn 1:144 Mos 2:105 Prov 2:68

ἀναθυμιάω Opif 165

ἀναιδής Mos 1:130 QG 4:99

ἄναιμος Ebr 87 Somn 2:259

ἀναιμωτί (6) Agr 150 Mos 1:180 Virt 33, 38 Praem 97 Legat 233

ἀναίρεσις (21) Leg 3:189 Agr 88 Conf 34 Migr 92 Fug 93 Somn 2:213 Abr 180, 189 Spec 2:232 Spec 3:88, 121 Aet 5, 79, 79, 81, 111, 114 Flacc 53, 105, 162 Legat 335

ἀναιρετικός Leg 3:76

ἀναιρέω (188) Opif 81, 157 Leg 1:20 Leg 2:99 Leg 3:35, 35, 73, 189 Cher 50, 55, 74, 75, 75 Sacr 55, 58, 121, 133 Det 16, 47, 48, 48, 48, 50, 50, 51, 51, 69, 75, 78, 78, 78, 122, 165, 166, 168, 177, 178, 178 Post 38, 85, 182, 185 Gig 32 Deus 18 Agr 16, 18, 105 Plant 90, 110 Ebr 67, 69, 95 Conf 72, 160, 160, 166, 193 Migr 92 Her 244 Congr 119 Fug 60, 107, 147 Mut 49 Somn 1:174 Somn 2:24, 67, 123, 267 Abr 176, 197, 233, 234 Ios 10, 12, 25, 233 Mos 1:17, 44, 45, 109, 135, 145, 218, 258, 300, 302, 303, 304, 308 Mos 2:156, 172, 186, 214 Decal 81 Spec 1:56, 108, 120, 160, 262, 319, 327, 328, 329, 344 Spec 2:83, 85, 134, 192 Spec 3:42, 84, 85, 86, 87, 92, 95, 116, 118, 119, 120, 120, 120, 121, 126, 126, 127, 128, 132, 132, 136, 136, 141, 142, 142, 145, 146, 151, 153, 165, 168 Spec 4:7, 95, 204, 222 Virt 43, 46, 90, 129, 139, 143, 200, 224 Praem 69, 72, 95, 150 Prob 19, 79, 158 Aet 23, 78, 82, 84, 84, 85, 85, 92 Flacc 9, 10, 49, 67, 132, 174, 174, 185, 189 Legat 30, 30, 81, 117, 146, 206, 316, 342 Hypoth 7:6, 7:9 Prov 2:55 QG isf 13

ἀναισθησία (8) Ebr 4, 5, 154, 162, 166 Mos 1:272 Legat 1, 70

ἀναισθητέω Ebr 6, 154

ἀναίσθητος Sacr 32 Det 85 Somn 1:248 Spec 2:95 Virt 200

ἀναισχυντέω Leg 2:65, 65, 65 Spec 3:54 Hypoth 11:16

ἀναισχυντία (10) Leg 2:65, 65, 66 Sacr 21 Conf 116, 117 Migr 224 Ios 222 Prob 8 Legat 204

ἀναίσχυντος (16) Opif 45 Leg 2:67 Abr 213 Mos 1:302 Decal 171 Spec 1:270, 278 Spec 3:66, 172 Spec 4:2, 127 Virt 91, 182, 195 Legat 56, 132

ἀναίτιος (8) Opif 75 Ios 30 Spec 3:56, 121 Spec 4:5 Virt 147 Aet 78 QG 1:100:1c

ἀνακαθαίρω Leg 2:29

ἀνακαίω (8) Ebr 27 Sobr 43 Her 37 Fug 81 Somn 2:186 Mos 1:65, 68 Spec 1:288

ἀνακαλέω (29) Opif 149 Leg 3:95, 101, 102 Gig 23 Plant 23, 26, 26, 26, 26, 45 Sobr 2, 53 Her 308 Mut 126 Somn 1:193, 194, 196, 197 Ios 105, 219 Mos 2:207, 269 Decal 45 Spec 2:133 Spec 3:125 Flacc 126 Legat 97 QE 2:46

ἀνακαλυπτήρια Ebr 6

ἀνακαλύπτω (7) Ebr 139 Congr 124 Somn 1:87, 99 Ios 90, 238 Mos 1:249

ἀνακάμπτω (16) Opif 44, 47, 101 Leg 2:40 Deus 35 Her 149, 150 Mos 1:178, 274 Mos 2:81 Spec 1:178 Spec 2:122 Praem 170 Aet 31, 58 QG (Par) 2:4

ἀνάκειμαι (21) Opif 49 Plant 118 Her 119 Congr 147, 151 Fug 93 Somn 1:77, 248 Somn 2:268, 291, 297 Abr 164, 186 Spec 2:27, 166, 196 Praem 79 Contempl 81 Legat 28 QG 4:9* QE 2:17

ἀνακεράννυμι (28) Opif 74 Sacr 108 Deus 74, 79 Ebr 116 Conf 16, 89, 90 Migr 24, 104 Her 22, 28 Fug 174 Somn 1:202 Mos 2:228 Spec 1:188 Spec 2:55, 55 Spec 3:91 Virt 75, 113 Praem 97 Prob 105 Aet 29 Legat 85, 176, 235 QE isf 33

ἀνακηρύσσω Somn 2:43 Prob 157

ἀνακινέω (6) Opif 18, 149 Somn 2:51 Spec 4:29 Praem 18 Legat 182

ἀνακίρναμαι Cher 79 Deus 76 Contempl 88 QE isf 21

ἀνακλαίω Opif 161 Ios 200

ἀνάκλησις Plant 27 Spec 2:190 QE 2:46

ἀνακλητικός Spec 2:101

ἀνακόλουθος Fug 152 Aet 47

ἀνακομίζω Her 44 Spec 2:37

ἀνακοπή (8) Mos 1:115 Mos 2:203 Spec 1:72 Spec 2:201 Spec 3:42 Spec 4:203 Virt 128 Contempl 86

ἀνακόπτω (9) Somn 2:236 Mos 1:123 Mos 2:254 Spec 1:67, 343 Spec 2:147, 163 Spec 4:218 Praem 48

ἀνακουφίζω Deus 85 Agr 76 Spec 3:4

ἀνακράζω Mut 134 Somn 1:185

ἀνακρεμάννυμι Abr 59 Ios 156

ἀνακρούω Somn 1:175 Mos 1:178

ἀνακτάομαι (7) Mut 84 Somn 2:107 Spec 2:60, 98 Spec 4:216 Aet 62 Legat 273

ἀνακυκάω Somn 2:239 Flacc 180 QE isf 31

ἀνακυκλέω Post 83 Plant 89 Spec 1:219

ἀνακύκλησις Mut 67 Spec 2:57

ἀνακύπτω (11) Leg 2:34 Cher 78 Post 74 Ebr 70 Conf 66 Migr 64 Her 41 Praem 153 Aet 129 Flacc 160 Legat 370

ἀνακωχή Leg 3:14

ἀναλαμβάνω (45) Opif 160 Leg 2:58, 60, 81 Sacr 7 Deus 90 Agr 5 Plant 86 Ebr 7, 86, 154 Sobr 35 Conf 186, 186 Migr 212 Congr 39 Somn 1:216, 255 Somn 2:67, 280 Abr 243 Ios 32 Mos 1:24, 333 Mos 2:171, 273, 291 Spec 1:16, 82, 84 Spec 2:114 Spec 4:57, 183, 185 Virt 18, 21 Praem 21 Flacc 38, 67 Legat 79, 96, 100, 101, 359, 364

ἀναλάμπω (10) Deus 32 Agr 162 Plant 40 Migr 123 Somn 1:11 Mos 2:27 Spec 1:90 Spec 2:140 Spec 4:52, 52

ἀνάλαμψις Opif 33 Mos 1:212

ἀναλγησία Agr 152 Spec 3:114

ἀναλέγω Conf 3 Her 212

ἀνάληψις (20) Leg 1:97, 103, 104, 105 Cher 101 Sacr 80 Post 137 Deus 100 Plant 31 Her 298 Congr 79 Somn 1:51, 60, 205 Ios 92, 206 Mos 2:141 Spec 4:162 Virt 100, 176

ἀναλίσκω (ἀναλόω) (32) Cher 100 Sacr 24 Det 154 Ebr 133, 134 Congr 55 Mut 144 Somn 2:90 Abr 44 Ios 93, 109 Mos 2:55, 63, 264, 287 Spec 1:223, 225, 243, 245, 290 Spec 2:183 Spec 4:149 Prob 87 Contempl 16 Aet 123 Flacc 133 Legat 144, 344 Prov 2:40 QE 2:15a, 28, 47

ἀναλλοίωτος Somn 1:188

ἀναλογέω (15) Opif 91, 92, 126 Leg 2:23 Leg 3:149 Cher 23 Sacr 25 Det 120 Post 143 Deus 39 Her 177 Somn 1:199 Somn 2:183, 197 Spec 4:232

ἀναλογία (37) Opif 78, 94, 96, 107, 108, 109, 110 Leg 3:63 Cher 22, 105 Sacr 75 Her 145, 145, 152, 152, 152, 153, 153, 154, 154, 160, 191, 192 Congr 16, 75 Mut 135 Somn 1:204, 205 Abr 69 Decal 21, 23 Spec 1:88 Spec 2:40, 200 Aet 116 QG 2:34b, 4:102b

ἀνάλογος (9) Leg 2:43 Mut 232, 235 Somn 1:188 Spec 3:48 Spec 4:11 Virt 95 Aet 46 QE 2:25c

ἀναλόω ἀναλίσκω

ἀναλύζω Legat 188

ἀνάλυσις Aet 94, 96 Flacc 115, 187 QG 2:29

ἀναλύω (27) Leg 2:49, 50 Post 164 Migr 3 Her 190, 226, 281, 282 Fug 91 Mut 33 Somn 2:67 Mos 2:154, 239 Spec 1:266 Aet 6, 8, 85, 87, 87, 99, 102, 102, 102, 105, 107, 125 QG 2:64c

ἀνάλωμα Somn 2:176 Spec 2:106, 125 Contempl 61 Flacc 130

ἀνάλωσις Ios 113 Virt 143

ἀναλωτικός Somn 2:67 Mos 2:106

ἀναμανθάνω Post 90 Conf 13

ἀναμάρτητος Mut 51 Prob 59

ἀναμάσσω Migr 26 Her 181 Virt 24 Aet 2 Legat 166

ἀναμείγνυμι (18) Leg 1:50 Sacr 108 Deus 83, 84 Conf 23 Migr 163 Somn 1:145, 202 Abr 20 Mos 2:152, 155 Spec 2:159 Spec 3:95 Virt 136 Contempl 81, 85 Legat 334 Prov 2:71

ἀναμέλπω Agr 79 Plant 126

ἀναμένω (15) Plant 161 Somn 1:119 Somn 2:86 Abr 150 Mos 1:322, 325 Decal 159 Spec 2:67, 146 Spec 4:99 Virt 89 Contempl 71 Flacc 26, 175 QG 2:48

ἀνάμεστος Mut 3 Somn 2:25

ἀναμετρέω (6) Leg 3:39 Mut 267 Somn 2:36 Ios 247 Mos 1:238 Mos 2:91

ἀναμέτρησις Mut 190

ἀναμιμνήσκω (11) Leg 3:92, 92, 93 Deus 90, 138 Plant 108 Congr 39, 42 Mut 100, 102 Somn 2:294

ἀναμίξ Flacc 68

ἀνάμνησις (29) Leg 3:91, 91, 91, 92, 92, 93, 93 Agr 132 Sobr 28, 28, 28, 29 Migr 205, 205, 206 Congr 39, 40, 41, 41, 42, 111 Mut 99, 100, 100, 101, 101 Mos 1:21 Virt 176 Praem 9

ἀναμφίβολος Prob 41

ἀνανδρία (12) Leg 3:54 Fug 82 Somn 1:10 Ios 70 Spec 3:31, 39, 156 Spec 4:224 Virt 6, 20, 24, 25

ἄνανδρος (15) Leg 2:18 Cher 50, 78 Post 82 Gig 4, 43 Agr 35 Ebr 63 Sobr 42 Fug 128 Mut 138 Mos 1:233 Spec 3:156 Praem 5 Hypoth 6:6

ἀνανεύω Cher 41 Mut 254, 254 Spec 3:70

ἀνανήφω Leg 2:60

ἀνανήχομαι (6) Det 100 Post 178 Gig 13 Conf 66 Mut 107 Spec 3:3

ἀνανταγώνιστος (22) Deus 150 Ebr 112 Sobr 57 Conf 34, 100 Migr 120 Somn 1:69, 129, 169, 250 Somn 2:38, 279 Abr 37, 243 Ios 82 Mos 1:218 Decal 146 Spec 1:207 Spec 4:164 Virt 33 Praem 93, 97

ἀνάντης Abr 59 Spec 4:109, 112

Ἀναξαγόρας Contempl 14 Aet 4

Ἀνάξαρχος Prob 106, 109, 109

ἀναξηραίνω Mos 1:177 Mos 2:254 Aet 122

ἀνάξιος (27) Opif 168 Leg 3:195 Sacr 124 Det 13, 62, 142 Gig 16 Deus 76 Her 91 Fug 151, 155 Abr 146 Ios 75 Mos 1:3 Spec 1:211, 314, 325 Spec 3:67 Spec 4:151, 152 Virt 122, 210 Praem 96 Aet 85 QG 3:29, 4:206a QG isf 9

ἀνάπαιστος Flacc 139

ἀνάπαυλα (19) Leg 1:43 Cher 87 Det 122 Ios 179 Mos 1:38 Spec 2:39, 64, 69, 89, 96, 101, 207, 260 Spec 4:8, 173 Praem 153 Legat 171 Hypoth 7:15, 7:16

ἀνάπαυσις (15) Leg 3:77 Cher 87 Post 24 Congr 45, 48 Fug 174 Somn 1:174 Abr 27, 27, 28 QG 2:39, 39, 4:93 QG (Par) 2:4 QE isf 11

ἀναπαύω (15) Leg 3:77 Cher 87, 90, 90 Post 24 Deus 12 Congr 45, 48 Fug 173 Somn 1:113, 128, 174 Mos 1:291 Praem 157 QG 4:33b

ἀναπείθω (25) Leg 3:110, 212 Post 185 Agr 48 Plant 105 Ebr 38 Conf 131 Her 29, 92, 97 Congr 126 Fug 97 Somn 2:76, 89, 162, 192 Mos 2:175 Decal 123, 141 Spec 3:5, 166 Virt 15, 208 Prob 13 Legat 246

ἀναπείρω Mut 160 Spec 3:144, 145, 146 Virt 136

ἀναπέμπω Sacr 74 Deus 84 Somn 1:29 Spec 4:190

ἀναπετάννυμι (18) Leg 3:43, 219 Sacr 22 Agr 34 Plant 58 Conf 19 Mut 138 Abr 154 Mos 1:46 Spec 1:75 Spec 2:62, 105 Spec 4:9, 43 Prob 13, 85 Flacc 88 Legat 169

ἀναπέτομαι Cher 31 Post 84 Gig 13 Mut 237

ἀναπηδάω Mut 179

ἀναπίμπλημι (46) Leg 1:36, 51 Cher 106 Sacr 20 Det 123 Gig 39 Agr 45 Ebr 87 Sobr 15, 42 Migr 59 Her 67, 240, 307 Somn 1:178 Somn 2:2, 147, 162 Abr 16, 40, 96, 119 Mos 1:100 Decal 126, 144, 175 Spec 1:50, 153, 331 Spec 2:22, 50 Spec 3:51, 102 Spec 4:95 Praem 157 Prob 62 Contempl 10, 27 Aet 56 Flacc 5, 41, 125 Legat 90, 102, 354 Prov 2:71

ἀναπίνω Opif 38

ἀναπίπτω (13) Plant 145 Ebr 122, 167 Congr 164 Ios 114 Mos 1:69, 173, 182, 233 Spec 1:313 Virt 25, 71, 88

ἀνάπλασις Opif 124

ἀναπλάσσω Gig 15 Ios 137 Spec 1:332 Prob 62

ἀναπλέκω Sacr 21 Spec 3:37

ἀνάπλεος (16) Migr 212 Congr 61 Fug 80 Ios 53 Decal 33 Spec 1:209, 327 Spec 2:155 Spec 3:79 Spec 4:56 Virt 32, 211 Praem 41, 159 Contempl 6 QE isf 26

ἀναπλέω Det 151

ἀναπληρόω (15) Opif 126 Leg 2:20, 38 Plant 40 Ebr 53 Her 300, 304 Mut 168 Somn 1:135 Ios 206 Spec 1:294 Praem 111 Legat 257 QE 2:3a, 20

ἀναπλήρωμα Mos 2:208

ἀναπλήρωσις Virt 43

ἀναπλόω Conf 186

ἀναπνέω Decal 74 Virt 6 Contempl 75 Flacc 88 Legat 369

ἀναπνοή (9) Ebr 106 Somn 1:20 Mos 2:148 Spec 1:338 Praem 143 Aet 135 Legat 125, 126, 270

ἀναπόδεικτος Plant 115 Spec 4:31

ἀναποδήμητος Abr 65

ἀναπολέω (9) Leg 3:17, 17 Agr 132 Conf 159 Ios 211 Spec 4:107 Flacc 180 Legat 17, 310

ἀναπομπή Spec 2:117

ἀναπράσσω (14) Migr 91 Somn 1:95 Mos 2:197 Decal 95 Spec 1:55 Spec 2:75, 94, 247 Spec 3:102, 163 Spec 4:214, 218 Virt 42 Legat 343

ἀνάπτυξις Leg 1:99 Cher 128 Congr 44, 148

ἀναπτύσσω Leg 1:99 Gig 36 Agr 136 Congr 20 Somn 1:91

ἀνάπτω (55) Opif 79, 148, 160 Leg 3:44 Cher 63, 113 Sacr 9, 99 Det 105 Post 37, 114 Deus 2, 26 Plant 67 Sobr 63 Migr 3, 186 Her 7, 23, 301 Fug 163 Mut 22, 90 Somn 1:77, 78, 224 Abr 237 Ios 28, 135, 151, 166 Mos 2:58 Decal 42 Spec 1:14, 252, 307, 334 Spec 2:30, 165 Spec 3:184 Spec 4:176, 177 Praem 29, 56 Contempl 70 Aet 33, 127 Flacc 104 Legat 130, 141, 190, 347 Prov 2:2 QG 4:76a QE 2:40

ἀναπυνθάνομαι Gig 50

ἄναρθρος Fug 22 Mos 2:164

ἀναρίθμητος Leg 1:102

ἀνάριθμος Post 3

ἀναρμοστία (6) Opif 22 Conf 150 Spec 2:191 Virt 183 QG 2:64a, 4:174

ἀνάρμοστος (19) Opif 149 Sacr 32 Post 107, 107 Gig 41 Deus 4, 105 Conf 15 Congr 16 Fug 22 Somn 1:28 Ios 145, 269 Spec 2:130, 154 Spec 3:19, 23 Spec 4:187 Aet 75

ἀναρπάζω (6) Plant 24 Mut 214 Prob 132 Aet 49 Legat 58, 160

ἀναρρήγνυμι (6) Opif 158 Leg 3:156 Ebr 208, 214 Aet 139 Flacc 56

ἀναρριπίζω (12) Opif 158 Leg 3:187 Gig 51 Plant 144 Her 296 Congr 92 Somn 2:147 Spec 4:27, 113 Virt 9 Praem 171 Flacc 44

ἀναρρίπτω Agr 152 Aet 33

ἀναρτάω Her 43 Somn 1:157 Mos 2:113 Spec 3:160

ἀναρχία (14) Opif 11 Sacr 106 Det 141 Agr 46 Somn 2:154, 286, 289, 290, 295 Mos 1:26 Mos 2:161, 163 Spec 3:125 Legat 17

ἄναρχος Aet 53, 75

ἀνασείω (6) Cher 38 Agr 174 Conf 35 Mut 215 Somn 2:132 Legat 177

ἀνασκεδάννυμι Plant 60 Congr 56 Abr 79, 229 Mos 1:123

ἀνασκευάζω QE isf 4, 4

ἀνασκευή Prov 2:2

ἀνάσκητος Mos 1:259

ἀνασκίδνημι Det 95 Gig 3 Deus 46 Virt 164

ἀνασκιρτάω (7) Leg 3:128 Sacr 4 Agr 93 Plant 38 Spec 2:135, 142 Aet 128

ἀνασκολοπίζω (8) Post 61 Somn 2:213 Ios 96, 98 Spec 3:151, 152 Flacc 83, 84

ἀνασκοπέω Legat 261

ἀνασπάω (10) Leg 1:38, 38 Agr 7 Plant 24 Congr 127 Mut 224 Somn 1:102 Mos 2:240 Spec 4:227 Virt 154

ἀνάσσω Prob 125

ἀνάστασις (7) Post 185 Agr 151 Mos 1:164 Legat 330 QG 2:15a, 15c, 15c

ἀνάστατος Decal 126

ἀναστέλλω (16) Leg 3:153 Post 50, 127 Deus 39, 79, 182 Conf 14 Her 70 Fug 34 Mos 1:99 Decal 50 Spec 2:172 Spec 3:147 Spec 4:111 Prob 65 Prov 2:17

ἀναστενάζω Ios 187

ἀναστέφω Spec 1:57, 115

ἀναστοιχειόω (7) Post 5 Her 29, 184, 200 Abr 43 Mos 2:288 Aet 94

ἀναστομόω Mos 1:211 Contempl 23

ἀναστράπτω Decal 143

ἀναστρέφω (8) Leg 3:48 Gig 53 Deus 35 Sobr 12, 15, 68 Fug 196 Flacc 180

ἀναστροφή Deus 72

ἀνασῴζω (6) Leg 2:33, 34 Migr 16, 63 Somn 2:109 Praem 165

ἀνατείνω (20) Sacr 25 Plant 20 Ebr 102 Conf 157 Her 79 Abr 164, 235 Mos 1:192 Mos 2:36, 154 Decal 44 Spec 1:185 Spec 4:34 Virt 57 Contempl 66, 77, 89 Flacc 169 Legat 353 Prov 2:29

ἀνατέλλω (44) Opif 57, 129, 129 Leg 1:18, 21, 24, 24, 46, 46, 46 Leg 2:30 Leg 3:32, 35, 171, 242, 248 Sacr 79 Post 57, 58 Deus 123, 123 Plant 40 Ebr 44 Conf 61, 63 Migr 68 Her 50, 264 Mut 246, 260 Somn 1:72, 76, 79, 80, 83, 84, 116 Abr 156 Mos 2:44, 222, 266 Virt 164 Prob 3 QG 4:51a

ἀνατέμνω (30) Opif 69, 80, 85, 114, 115, 144 Post 31 Agr 142 Plant 80 Ebr 73 Sobr 36 Conf 57 Migr 195 Her 125 Abr 7 Mos 1:99, 201, 256 Mos 2:189 Decal 77 Spec 1:91, 192, 335 Spec 2:199 Spec 4:102, 155 Virt 145 Prob 33 Contempl 86 Legat 348

ἀνατίθημι (97) Opif 37, 45, 72 Sacr 106, 109 Post 113 Agr 20, 43, 50 Plant 119, 133 Migr 98 Her 73, 74, 108, 110, 114, 117, 165, 179, 187, 200 Congr 74, 89, 93, 98, 105, 114, 155 Fug 67, 73, 206 Mut 220, 221 Somn 1:203, 241, 244, 247, 251 Somn 2:69, 75, 76, 241 Abr 2, 47, 69, 84, 267 Ios 234, 235, 240 Mos 1:97, 102, 252, 254, 259, 317 Mos 2:28, 190, 216, 222 Decal 108, 161 Spec 1:13, 69, 248 Spec 2:24, 51, 58, 134, 175, 195 Spec 3:180 Praem 12, 13 Prob 15 Contempl 64 Aet 8, 146 Flacc 41 Legat 135, 136, 136, 188, 260, 265, 299, 299, 303, 305, 305, 335, 346, 365, 367 Hypoth 7:4 QG 2:12a

ἀνατολή (36) Opif 58 Leg 1:43, 46, 61 Leg 2:10 Cher 22 Deus 88 Plant 32, 40, 118 Conf 1, 60, 60, 61, 62, 62, 64, 64, 65, 66, 67 Migr 140 Mut 190, 264 Somn 1:3, 175 Abr 161, 226 Ios 134, 166 Mos 1:278 Mos 2:92 Spec 1:69 Spec 3:187 Flacc 45 Legat 191

ἀνατολικός Legat 289

ἀνατομή Agr 1 Congr 54 Mos 1:38 Mos 2:253 Spec 3:117

ἀνατρέπω (48) Opif 80 Cher 38 Det 73, 144 Post 55, 72, 181 Deus 98 Agr 35, 75, 106, 120, 164 Ebr 79 Sobr 42 Conf 17, 35, 43, 132 Migr 63, 171 Fug 24, 27 Mut 81, 239 Somn 1:222 Somn 2:145, 214, 278 Abr 240 Ios 26, 97, 130, 139 Mos 1:261 Mos 2:255 Decal 132 Spec 2:14 Spec 3:79 Spec 4:50, 212 Virt 49, 132 Praem 6 Aet 11, 21 Legat 371, 371

ἀνατρέφω (12) Sacr 15, 104 Agr 91 Ebr 164, 211 Somn 2:9 Abr 92 Ios 162 Mos 1:11 Spec 3:47 Legat 310 Prov 2:39

ἀνατρέχω (34) Opif 46 Leg 1:38 Leg 2:34 Leg 3:94, 126, 213, 238, 239 Cher 41, 50 Det 159 Deus 37 Agr 10 Plant

22 Ebr 8, 40, 51 Sobr 65, 67 Her 125 Congr 77 Mut 247 Somn 2:285 Abr 88 Mos 1:58, 106, 115, 216, 228 Spec 2:6 Spec 3:152 Aet 33, 49, 51

ἀνατρίβω Sacr 86 Det 49

ἀνατροπή (12) Post 22, 184 Deus 166 Conf 101, 122, 145 Migr 184 Mut 50, 72 Praem 143 Prob 38 Legat 134

ἀνατυπόω Plant 27

ἄναυδος Spec 4:198 Praem 54

ἀναφαίνω (48) Opif 38, 100 Det 134 Gig 5 Agr 33 Plant 129 Migr 183 Her 306, 306 Congr 124, 153 Fug 28 Somn 1:84 Somn 2:51 Ios 165, 255 Mos 1:79, 82, 155, 194, 214 Mos 2:26, 64, 228, 263, 267 Spec 1:296 Spec 2:59, 141, 152 Spec 3:6, 61, 200 Spec 4:51, 52 Virt 85 Praem 4, 37, 44 Prob 149 Contempl 58 Aet 121 Flacc 27 Legat 22, 89, 90, 120 QE isf 26

ἀναφαίρετος (10) Leg 2:63 Ebr 74 Her 27 Somn 2:212, 248 Mos 1:235, 304 Spec 1:207 Spec 2:259 Spec 4:194

ἀναφανδόν Spec 2:28 Spec 3:66

ἀναφέρω (72) Leg 1:50, 61, 82 Leg 2:102 Leg 3:72, 136, 168 Sacr 2, 51, 116, 132, 136 Det 12, 32, 134 Post 65, 123, 123, 168 Gig 15 Deus 69 Ebr 18, 37, 187, 202, 216 Sobr 67 Conf 7, 149, 179, 181 Migr 117 Her 173, 174, 199 Congr 98 Mut 75, 249 Somn 1:191, 195, 195, 235 Somn 2:97, 159, 199 Ios 8, 171, 180, 246 Mos 1:79, 105, 248 Mos 2:151, 177, 237 Decal 19 Spec 1:232, 233, 291 Spec 2:182, 223 Spec 3:44, 77, 134 Spec 4:132, 230 Virt 221 Prob 15 Aet 64 Flacc 111 Legat 184 QG 1:55c

'Ανάφη Aet 121

ἀναφής Somn 2:232 Legat 6

ἀναφθέγγομαι (12) Leg 2:40 Det 92 Post 143 Plant 39 Conf 44 Somn 2:107 Mos 1:288 Mos 2:268, 275 Spec 2:4 Spec 4:90 Prob 19

ἀνάφθεγμα Somn 2:17

ἀνάφθεγξις Mut 262 Legat 354

ἀναφλέγω (14) Plant 10 Ebr 27 Sobr 43 Her 37, 64 Somn 2:212 Ios 41 Mos 1:297 Spec 1:150 Spec 4:26, 29, 83 Virt 9, 163

ἀναφορά (14) Leg 1:50 Det 81 Deus 1 Migr 131 Her 171, 314 Spec 1:131, 336 Spec 2:242 Legat 369 QG 1:1, 55a, 55b, 66

ἀναφορικός QG 3:52

ἀναφράσσω Cher 78

ἀναφύω Opif 40 Somn 2:218 Ios 102

ἀναχαιτίζω (14) Opif 79, 88 Leg 1:73 Sacr 49 Agr 70 Somn 2:83 Mos 1:25, 177, 270 Spec 2:18, 147, 163 Spec 4:99 Virt 41

ἀναχαλάω Praem 161

ἀναχέω (47) Opif 38, 38, 113 Leg 1:34 Leg 3:87 Cher 123 Det 40 Deus 128, 177 Plant 15, 171 Ebr 147, 152, 193 Sobr 53 Conf 23 Migr 121 Her 32, 264 Fug 179 Somn 2:245, 247 Abr 42 Ios 109, 159, 235 Mos 1:6, 123, 145, 179 Mos 2:63 Decal 35 Spec 1:303 Spec 2:143, 214 Virt 81, 160 Praem 41, 99 Contempl 86 Aet 33, 96, 126, 147 Legat 82 Prov 2:12, 41

ἀνάχυσις (12) Opif 57 Ebr 133 Somn 1:19 Somn 2:249, 278 Abr 159 Mos 1:212 Decal 41 Spec 1:34 Aet 62, 102, 110

ἀναχωρέω (16) Opif 35 Leg 2:85 Leg 3:12, 13, 13, 14, 213 Det 45 Ebr 40 Migr 190 Abr 30 Mos 1:105 Spec 1:219, 298 Contempl 89 QG 4:204

ἀναχώρησις (15) Ios 13 Mos 2:253, 267 Spec 1:16, 58 Spec 2:83 Spec 3:93 Aet 117 Flacc 93, 155 Legat 220, 239 QG 1:24, 2:13a, 41

ἀναψάω QG 3:30b

ἀνάψυξις Abr 152

ἀνδραγαθία Mos 1:318 Spec 1:79 Spec 3:127 Legat 90

ἀνδραγαθίζομαι (7) Mos 1:217, 259, 325 Mos 2:242, 274 Spec 2:245 Virt 69

ἀνδραποδίζω (8) Opif 158 Leg 2:70 Sacr 26 Conf 47 Mos 1:36 Spec 4:17, 19, 19

ἀνδραποδισμός (6) Post 185 Agr 151 Somn 2:124 Mos 1:164 Spec 4:16 Legat 330

ἀνδραποδιστής Ios 18 Spec 4:13, 14

ἀνδραποδοκάπηλος Spec 4:17 Prob 37

ἀνδράποδον (13) Leg 3:202 Ios 35 Spec 1:58 Spec 2:34 Spec 3:101 Spec 4:31, 68 Contempl 50, 70 Flacc 113 Legat 166, 205 Hypoth 11:4

ἀνδραποδώδης Sacr 32 Abr 149 Spec 1:174 Spec 4:100 Contempl 45

ἀνδρεία (55) Opif 73 Leg 1:63, 65, 68, 68, 68, 70, 70, 71, 86 Cher 5 Sacr 27, 37, 84 Det 18, 24, 51 Post 128 Deus 13, 164 Agr 18 Ebr 23, 115, 116, 116 Her 209 Mut 197, 225 Abr 24, 219 Mos 2:185, 216 Spec 1:145 Spec 2:62 Spec 4:45, 57, 145, 146 Virt 1, 4, 17, 18, 22, 50 Praem 52, 160 Prob 67, 70, 107, 146, 159 Contempl 60 Legat 112 QG 4:204 QE isf 24

ἀνδρεῖος (23) Leg 1:86 Leg 2:18, 63 Leg 3:11 Sacr 54 Det 75 Sobr 38 Conf 43 Migr 95, 219 Mut 146, 146, 153, 214 Abr 225 Ios 143 Mos 2:184 Spec 2:56 Spec 4:120 Virt 167 Legat 64 Prov 2:7 QG 4:204

ἀνδριαντοποιία Gig 59

ἀνδριαντοποιός Ebr 89 Ios 39 Decal 70 Spec 1:21, 33

ἀνδριάς (35) Opif 137 Leg 3:70, 70 Cher 11 Agr 25, 168 Plant 5 Ebr 89 Her 12 Congr 48, 65 Mut 93 Spec 1:33 Spec 3:109, 184 Virt 203 Legat 134, 138, 151, 188, 203, 207, 207, 220, 238, 246, 260, 265, 306, 308, 334, 335, 337, 346 Prov 2:15

"Ανδριος Flacc 156, 161

ἀνδρόγυνος (8) Sacr 100 Her 274 Somn 1:126 Spec 1:325 Spec 3:38, 40 Virt 21 Contempl 60

"Ανδρος Flacc 151, 157, 173, 185

ἀνδροφονέω (7) Post 82 Conf 163 Decal 132, 170 Spec 2:245 Spec 3:88, 104

ἀνδροφονία (16) Post 49 Conf 117 Her 173 Spec 3:83, 85, 90, 112, 114, 124, 128, 181, 204 Spec 4:1, 7, 84 Legat 68

ἀνδροφόνος (24) Ebr 66, 74 Conf 160 Fug 53, 64 Somn 1:74 Ios 84, 226 Spec 3:84, 85, 86, 87, 88, 90, 91, 91, 91, 118, 120, 150 Prob 118 Legat 31, 97 Prov 2:39

ἀνδρόω Post 131 Agr 18 Sobr 29 Conf 102 Prob 160

ἀνδρών (8) Leg 3:40, 98 Cher 100 Somn 2:55 Contempl 32 Legat 151, 358 Prov 2:17

"Ανδρων Flacc 76

ἀνδρωνῖτις Sacr 103 Agr 79 Ebr 59 Migr 96 Somn 2:184

ἀνεγείρω (25) Leg 3:172 Agr 97 Plant 20 Ebr 98, 159, 177 Conf 5 Her 34 Fug 91 Mut 56, 173, 176 Somn 1:80 Somn 2:165, 279 Mos 1:132, 251 Decal 148 Spec 3:4 Spec 4:29, 139, 218 Virt 49 Praem 6 Legat 325

ἀνέδην Opif 80 Mos 1:300 Virt 153 Legat 132

ἀνείδεος Conf 85 Congr 61 Fug 8 Mut 135

ἀνειδωλοποιέω Ios 126

ἀνειμένως Agr 66 Ebr 27

ἄνειμι (13) Leg 3:202 Post 127 Agr 71, 73 Somn 1:115 Somn 2:46 Ios 78 Mos 2:19, 70 Praem 130 Prob 25, 99 Legat 10

ἀνείμων Somn 1:99 Spec 1:83 Prov 2:26

ἀνεῖπον (ἀνερῶ) Sobr 55 Congr 90 Somn 1:207 Mos 1:156 Spec 2:194

ἀνείργω (15) Opif 33, 34 Agr 15 Mut 246 Mos 1:130, 178, 215 Decal 173 Spec 1:56 Spec 2:123 Spec 3:63, 115, 176 Spec 4:104 Virt 25

ἀνερῶ ἀνεῖπον

ἀνέκδοτος Spec 2:125

ἀνέκπλυτος Spec 3:89 Spec 4:163

ἀνελεύθερος (20) Leg 3:195 Sacr 32 Det 18 Deus 163, 164 Agr 34, 73 Ebr 214 Her 186 Fug 28 Somn 1:107 Ios 77 Spec 1:221 Spec 2:92 Spec 4:183 Virt 87, 92 Prob 154 Flacc 64, 130

ἀνελίσσω Mos 1:48

ἀνέλκω (7) Deus 151 Plant 3, 16 Migr 83 Somn 1:152 Ios 15 Virt 14

ἀνελλιπής (8) Post 136 Plant 91 Congr 4 Mos 1:189 Spec 1:285 Spec 4:144 Praem 102 Aet 75

ἀνέλπιστος Deus 91 Migr 157 Mos 1:168 QE 2:24b

ἀνεμιαῖος Leg 3:45

ἄνεμος (16) Cher 38 Plant 24 Mos 1:115, 118, 120, 122 Spec 1:322 Spec 3:160 Spec 4:50 Virt 49 Aet 125, 132 Legat 364 Prov 2:43 QG 2:28, 28

ἀνεμόφθορος Somn 2:218 Praem 141

ἀνεμπόδιστος Post 141 Mos 2:144

ἀνενδεής Det 54 QG isf 16

ἀνένδετος Leg 2:22

ἀνενδοίαστος (17) Det 148 Deus 4 Agr 16 Plant 88, 111, 147 Migr 25, 44 Abr 245 Ios 138 Mos 1:85, 159 Spec 1:63, 160 Spec 3:118, 196 QG 3:58

ἀνένδοτος (13) Cher 86 Migr 146, 223 Congr 24, 61 Fug 47 Abr 170 Ios 177 Spec 4:57 Virt 3, 69 Prob 97 Aet 64

ἀνεξάλειπτος Her 181 Spec 1:58 Prob 15

ἀνεξαπάτητος Her 74 Somn 1:205 Spec 1:336 Contempl 63

ἀνεξέλεγκτος Her 304 Aet 39, 41

ἀνεξέταστος (17) Opif 156 Sacr 23 Det 155 Deus 21 Ebr 198 Her 91 Fug 33 Somn 2:103 Abr 264 Ios 50 Decal 92 Spec 2:231, 244 Spec 4:88 Virt 10 Legat 70 Prov 2:31

ἀνέορτος Spec 3:125

ἀνεπαίσθητος QG isf 12

ἀνεπάνακτος Cher 3 Spec 4:17

ἀνεπανόρθωτος Aet 41, 54 Legat 72

ἀνέπαφος Ios 114

ἀνεπαχθής Ebr 215

ἀνεπιβούλευτος Spec 3:74 Spec 4:166 Virt 138 Praem 90 Prov 2:57

ἀνεπιδεής (10) Deus 57 Plant 35 Spec 1:294 Spec 2:38, 174, 180 Spec 4:146 Virt 9 Praem 102 Aet 74

ἀνεπίδεκτος Opif 73 Aet 53

ἀνεπικέλευστος Leg 3:144 Decal 163

ἀνεπίληπτος (34) Opif 67, 75, 142 Agr 135 Plant 132 Migr 74, 89, 207 Congr 4, 69, 138 Fug 52 Abr 4 Ios 88 Mos 1:327 Mos 2:1 Decal 71 Spec 1:124 Spec 2:42, 44, 48 Spec 3:24, 135 Spec 4:102, 134, 157, 164 Virt 190, 226 Praem 158 Prob 59, 140 Flacc 94 QG 4:86b

ἀνεπίπληκτος Congr 159

ἀνεπίσκεπτος Spec 2:231

ἀνεπίστατος Spec 3:57

ἀνεπιστημοσύνη (8) Gig 29 Ebr 6, 45, 162 Migr 170 Somn 1:225 Spec 4:154 Virt 213

ἀνεπιστήμων (16) Opif 171 Leg 3:87 Det 18 Post 90 Gig 2 Agr 165 Somn 2:30, 252 Spec 1:209, 263, 279 Virt 174 Contempl 42, 62 Legat 56 QG 4:76b

ἀνεπίστρεπτος Leg 3:14

ἀνεπίσχετος (9) Leg 2:11 Sacr 32, 121 Det 174 Deus 155 Agr 37 Ebr 95 Migr 204 QE 2:13a

ἀνεπιτήδειος Agr 84 Mut 106 Spec 4:25 Virt 60 Legat 34

ἀνεπιτηδειότης Det 2 Congr 13

ἀνεπιτίμητος Det 145

ἀνεπιτρόπευτος (6) Sacr 45 Det 145 Agr 44, 49 Somn 2:283 Legat 20

ἀνεπίφαντος Ios 249 Flacc 110

ἀνεπίφατος Flacc 27

ἀνέραστος Her 42

ἀνερεθίζω (13) Gig 35 Ebr 18 Migr 210 Congr 74 Fug 25 Mut 173 Somn 1:226 Somn 2:87 Praem 21, 89 Flacc 17, 30 Prov 2:61

ἀνερείπομαι Prov 2:7

ἀνερευνάω Leg 3:232 Abr 217

ἀνερίθευτος Flacc 145 Legat 68

ἀνερμάτιστος (7) Det 144 Mos 2:260 Decal 67 Spec 4:50 Virt 40 Prob 38 Prov 2:8

ἀνέρομαι Cher 126

ἀνέρπω (7) Opif 63 Ios 101 Mos 1:103, 104, 144 Spec 1:62 Aet 128

ἀνέρχομαι (14) Leg 3:45 Agr 69 Conf 4, 134 Migr 160, 166 Mut 179 Somn 1:138, 142, 147, 236 Ios 101 Mos 2:70, 144

ἀνερωτάω Det 59 Legat 365

ἄνεσις (38) Cher 38, 92, 105 Sacr 23 Deus 162 Plant 56, 166, 170 Ebr 21 Her 156 Congr 160 Mut 87 Somn 2:184 Abr 152 Ios 33 Mos 1:20, 89, 89, 191 Mos 2:21 Decal 163 Spec 1:192 Spec 2:60, 67, 83, 96, 98, 99, 104 Spec 3:109 Praem 155 Contempl 58 Aet 43 Legat 12, 168 Hypoth 7:17 QG 2:64a, 64a

ἀνέστιος Contempl 47 Flacc 115, 123 Legat 123

ἄνετος Leg 3:56 Virt 78

ἄνευ (174) Opif 23, 81, 86, 100, 130, 132, 132, 139, 144, 168 Leg 1:92 Leg 2:41, 56, 107 Leg 3:49, 75, 77, 98, 99, 135, 144, 146, 178, 216, 226, 235, 240, 251 Cher 8, 24, 59, 71, 87, 102 Sacr 36, 37, 40, 80, 84 Det

61, 104 Post 87, 97, 111 Gig 52 Deus 9, 55, 58, 93, 109 Agr 4, 20, 61, 68, 77, 92, 129, 134, 145 Plant 11, 168 Ebr 145 Sobr 37, 41 Migr 31, 58, 70, 80, 116, 142, 171 Her 29, 60, 295, 315 Congr 21, 28, 33, 46, 107, 129, 171 Fug 32, 66, 72, 102, 158, 175 Mut 4, 31, 142, 157, 166, 219, 249, 270 Somn 1:42, 174, 188, 188, 236 Somn 2:25, 200, 288 Abr 6, 16, 18, 53, 87, 122, 125, 192, 235 Ios 37, 65, 67, 117, 127, 222 Mos 1:38, 133, 266, 274 Mos 2:5, 32, 50, 76, 119, 132, 154, 210, 210, 213, 219, 223 Decal 30, 159 Spec 1:40, 191, 195, 272, 340 Spec 2:39, 65, 198, 230, 246, 262 Spec 3:7, 53, 111, 127, 161 Spec 4:9, 30, 75, 228 Virt 83 Praem 32, 34, 85 Prob 80 Contempl 37, 81 Aet 89, 130 Flacc 86, 140 Legat 365 Prov 2:11 QG 3:11a QE 2:18, 46 QE isf 27

ἀνεύρεσις Deus 86

ἀνεύρετος Fug 153 Somn 1:8, 16

ἀνευρίσκω (61) Opif 114 Leg 1:26 Leg 3:36, 55 Cher 121 Sacr 120 Post 182 Plant 78, 79 Conf 75, 88 Migr 220 Her 16 Congr 67, 127 Fug 126, 131, 140, 149, 153, 158 Mut 168 Somn 1:6, 49 Somn 2:51, 213, 271 Abr 87, 164 Ios 197, 210, 217 Mos 1:204, 237, 255, 255, 317 Mos 2:273 Decal 16, 17, 78 Spec 1:41, 64, 191 Spec 3:68, 80, 93, 141 Spec 4:69, 75, 127 Praem 5, 36, 170 Prob 66 Aet 2 Flacc 118 Legat 5, 89, 178 Prov 1

ἀνευρύνω Det 100 Post 50, 126

ἀνέφικτος Leg 1:75 Post 13 Conf 7 Spec 1:44

ἀνέχω (64) Opif 128 Leg 1:93 Leg 3:193 Sacr 9, 34, 79 Det 107 Post 135 Deus 32, 72, 126 Ebr 166 Conf 60, 60, 92 Migr 23 Her 238 Congr 5 Mut 107 Somn 1:125 Abr 176 Ios 65, 79, 118 Mos 1:205, 239, 240, 255 Mos 2:39, 205, 211 Decal 98 Spec 1:117, 330 Spec 2:60, 66, 252 Spec 3:32, 48, 200 Spec 4:7, 43, 103 Virt 150, 164, 196 Prob 36, 56, 81 Aet 138 Legat 133, 201, 208, 222, 268, 275, 335, 357 Hypoth 7:5, 7:6, 7:11, 7:17, 7:19 QG 3:48

ἀνεψιαδοῦς Praem 109

ἀνεψιός (9) Post 109 Praem 109 Flacc 12 Legat 23, 26, 36, 54, 67, 75

ἀνηβάω (11) Sacr 76 Det 51, 106 Post 151 Conf 7 Migr 141 Somn 2:10 Spec 2:91 Praem 157 Aet 132, 149

ἄνηβος Opif 104

ἀνηγεμόνευτος Plant 53 Somn 2:286

ἀνήκεστος (34) Leg 3:216 Cher 68 Det 176 Post 81 Plant 157 Conf 13, 154 Migr 172 Mut 144 Somn 1:27 Ios 26, 193, 248 Mos 1:139 Decal 152 Spec 3:101, 104, 159, 166 Spec 4:172 Virt 115 Flacc 1, 96, 105, 117, 139, 179 Legat 17, 24, 109, 237, 293 Prov 2:30 QE 2:6a

ἀνήκοος Conf 116 Somn 2:63

ἀνηλεής (18) Leg 3:199 Det 146 Agr 114 Migr 14 Somn 1:107 Somn 2:84, 87 Ios 81, 171 Mos 1:37, 172 Spec 2:93 Spec 3:119 Spec 4:202 Praem 138 Flacc 68 Legat 87 Prov 2:40

ἀνήλιος Somn 2:133

ἀνήμερος (13) Leg 2:11 Sacr 20, 117 Plant 43 Ios 82, 177 Decal 78 Spec 3:146, 152 Spec 4:225 Virt 132 Contempl 9 Prov 2:2

ἀνήνυστος Aet 5

ἀνήνυτος (33) Opif 81 Leg 2:102 Cher 78 Sacr 39, 114 Det 19 Post 74 Gig 35 Ebr 5 Conf 177 Migr 100 Congr 53 Fug 91, 162 Mut 171, 173 Somn 1:256 Abr 96 Ios 61 Mos 1:194, 216, 237 Decal 149 Spec 1:16 Spec 4:80, 158 Virt 178, 214 Contempl 2 Legat 216, 302 Prov 2:26 QE isf 14

ἀνήρ (511) Opif 3, 17, 84, 104, 104, 104, 105, 105, 105, 132, 134, 153, 156, 156, 165, 165, 167, 167, 168 Leg 1:80 Leg 2:19, 19, 38, 44, 45, 47, 50, 50, 59, 59, 59, 63, 73 Leg 3:24, 59, 60, 60, 61, 148, 150, 181, 181, 220, 220, 220, 221 Cher 43, 43, 46, 49, 49, 51, 114, 121 Sacr 49, 79, 100, 100, 100, 101, 101, 126 Det 9, 50, 75, 134, 147, 149 Post 7, 50, 53, 66, 80, 109, 117, 132, 134, 165, 166 Gig 51 Deus 121, 132, 136, 148, 170 Agr 9, 50, 57, 80, 81, 158 Plant 29, 36, 163 Ebr 14, 14, 40, 41, 54, 55, 67, 76, 114, 114, 118, 193, 211, 211 Sobr 9, 11, 19, 46 Conf 13, 15, 55, 130, 145 Migr 3, 90, 97, 100, 120, 164, 196, 221 Her 62, 139, 164, 247, 274, 290, 301 Congr 19, 34, 37, 41, 71, 72, 80, 137, 137 Fug 3, 3, 27, 28, 40, 40, 51, 63, 82, 114, 114, 128, 146, 149, 154, 188, 189 Mut 61, 64, 132, 132, 140, 149, 152, 205 Somn 1:124, 125, 222 Somn 2:4, 9, 9, 50, 98, 114, 123, 182, 185, 185, 185, 273 Abr 1, 4, 5, 26, 31, 38, 46, 47, 48, 52, 54, 68, 88, 88, 90, 95, 98, 99, 99, 101, 107, 109, 114, 114, 135, 136, 137, 142, 182, 191, 208, 247, 248, 260, 260, 267, 273, 275 Ios 31, 50, 60, 66, 77, 79, 104, 106, 114, 116, 127, 128, 128, 129, 134, 191, 196, 204, 207, 230, 259, 264, 268 Mos 1:1, 3, 4, 40, 51, 54, 76, 122, 134, 147, 147, 180, 180, 221, 227, 242, 244, 253, 262, 264, 284, 296, 301, 305, 311, 317, 325 Mos 2:58, 65, 103, 136, 142, 171, 193, 202, 234, 236, 242, 247, 256, 256, 256, 283 Decal 1, 32, 38, 65, 89, 124, 126, 151 Spec 1:8, 9, 11, 42, 57, 92, 101, 105, 106, 107, 108, 108, 109, 124, 129, 129, 138, 144, 163, 201, 204, 211, 211, 271, 275, 277, 310, 314, 316, 323 Spec 2:24, 24, 25, 29, 29, 30, 30, 31, 32, 33, 43, 55, 124, 125, 133, 146, 200 Spec 3:14, 30, 30, 31, 32, 36, 45, 48, 49, 51, 53, 55, 61, 61, 62, 63, 64, 72, 89, 117, 169, 170, 171, 172, 173, 173, 174, 175, 176, 176, 178, 178, 186 Spec 4:20, 42, 120, 128, 131, 140, 142, 149, 151, 152, 171, 178, 178, 218, 225 Virt 8, 18, 19, 20, 21, 38, 41, 42, 43, 71, 112, 172, 177, 185, 190, 199, 201, 220, 223 Praem 7, 23, 52, 52, 57, 109, 113, 114, 125 Prob 10, 12, 47, 62, 62, 74, 91, 92, 124, 139, 140, 144 Contempl 1, 14, 14, 29, 49, 57, 59, 59, 59, 69, 78, 83, 87, 87, 88 Aet 60, 60, 69, 76, 134 Flacc 15, 68, 76, 89, 157 Legat 32, 39, 39, 48, 58, 62, 66, 99, 104, 116, 124, 136, 144, 161, 170, 195, 208, 254, 312, 338, 338 Hypoth 0:1, 6:2, 6:8, 7:3, 7:5, 7:7, 7:8, 7:14, 11:3, 11:14, 11:18 Prov 2:20, 26, 39, 40, 66 QG 1:20, 27, 27, 27, 2:11, 11, 26a, 71b, 3:18, 20a, 20b, 21, 4:81, 145 QG isf 12, 12 QE 1:7a, 21, 2:3a, 3b, 6b

ἀνθέλκω (8) Post 156 Ebr 53 Somn 2:11, 227 Abr 73 Mos 2:165 Legat 218 QG 4:202a

ἀνθέμιον Her 218, 218, 219, 220

ἀνθέω (27) Leg 1:23 Leg 2:75 Post 112, 121, 164 Gig 29 Deus 173 Agr 153 Plant 85, 159 Her 208 Somn 1:11, 37 Somn 2:109, 199, 272 Ios 130 Mos 2:119, 186, 186 Spec 1:93, 311 Spec 2:152 Spec 4:209 Prob 73 Contempl 52 Prov 2:15

ἀνθήλιος Somn 1:239

ἀνθηροποικίλος Somn 2:57

ἀνθηρός Somn 1:225

ἄνθησις Spec 4:210

ἄνθιμος Ebr 218

ἄνθινος (11) Migr 103, 103 Mos 2:110, 119, 119, 120, 121, 133 Spec 1:93, 93, 94 ἀνθίστημι (10) Cher 35 Gig 66 Deus 181 Conf 32, 43 Migr 61 Somn 2:88, 93 Mos 1:273 Spec 4:111

ἀνθοβαφής Spec 2:20 Contempl 49

ἀνθογραφέω Opif 138

ἀνθολκή Mut 184

ἄνθος (11) Opif 104 Fug 153 Somn 1:199 Somn 2:62 Spec 1:282, 325 Spec 3:39 Virt 112 Aet 64 Prov 2:13, 71

ἀνθράκινος Leg 1:82

ἀνθρακοειδής Ebr 173

ἀνθρακόομαι Legat 130

ἄνθραξ (16) Leg 1:63, 66, 67, 79, 81, 81, 84 Spec 1:4, 72 Aet 86, 86, 86, 86, 87, 88, 90

ἀνθρώπεια (ὁ) Somn 1:192 Mos 2:5, 187

ἀνθρώπειος (62) Opif 69, 160 Leg 3:38, 126 Cher 96 Sacr 22, 71, 100, 111 Det 73, 156 Post 175 Ebr 37, 86 Conf 114 Migr 3, 19 Congr 53 Fug 38 Mut 15, 39, 104 Somn 1:156, 218 Somn 2:63, 68, 81, 136, 184, 230, 291 Ios 136, 140, 170 Mos 1:27, 31, 41, 109 Mos 2:6, 16, 158, 216 Decal 91, 95 Spec 1:334 Spec 2:67, 224 Spec 3:19 Spec 4:32 Virt 2, 22 Praem 68, 125 Prob 89 Flacc 102, 146 Legat 97 Hypoth 7:20 QG 1:20 QG isf 1 QG (Par) 2:1, 2:2

ἀνθρωπικός Contempl 58

ἀνθρώπινος (160) Opif 5, 25, 54, 69, 105, 114, 135, 150, 163 Leg 1:38, 38, 43, 69 Leg 3:29, 30 Cher 127 Det 90 Post 35, 79, 115, 173 Gig 28 Deus 52, 120, 137, 177 Plant 39 Ebr 76, 91, 166 Sobr 38, 56 Conf 115 Migr 158, 179 Her 35, 84, 84, 126, 128, 129, 179, 182, 183, 264, 283 Congr 79 Fug 62, 162, 167, 168, 170, 204 Mut 18, 219, 225, 237 Somn 1:57, 66, 77, 94, 112, 118, 212, 219, 245 Somn 2:193, 194, 233, 277, 288 Abr 8, 124, 202 Mos 1:5, 32, 83, 133, 238, 279 Mos 2:255 Decal 60, 66, 122, 177 Spec 1:27, 36, 197, 238, 254, 255, 336 Spec 2:21, 51, 71, 225, 225, 231 Spec 3:115, 118, 119, 129, 185, 207, 209 Spec 4:11, 41, 71, 82, 103, 138, 175, 188, 202 Virt 5, 56, 64, 79, 171, 172, 199, 200, 213 Praem 36, 81, 145, 163, 165 Prob 24, 80, 80, 105, 131 Contempl 39 Flacc 121, 126, 176 Legat 21, 46, 75, 143, 162, 190, 355 Hypoth 11:10 Prov 2:1, 9, 22, 54, 72 QG 4:52b, 9* QG isf 5 QG (Par) 2:3, 2:6 QE isf 2, 3, 4, 9, 29

ἀνθρωποβόρος Praem 90, 92 Contempl 9 Prov 2:65

ἀνθρωπογονέω Aet 66 Prov 2:66

ἀνθρωποειδής Opif 137 Abr 8 Mos 1:43 Decal 80 Spec 2:255

ἀνθρωποθυτέω Abr 193

ἀνθρωπολογέω Sacr 94 Deus 60 Conf 135

ἀνθρωπόμορφος (15) Opif 69 Leg 1:36 Sacr 95 Post 4 Deus 59 Plant 35 Conf 135 Congr 115 Mut 54 Somn 1:15 Abr 33, 113 Spec 1:266 Spec 3:99 Virt 195

ἀνθρωποπαθέω Leg 3:237 Decal 43 Flacc 121

ἀνθρωποπαθής Sacr 95 Post 4 Deus 59 Plant 35

ἀνθρωποπλάστης Somn 1:210

ἄνθρωπος (ὁ) (1172) Opif 25, 40, 45, 53, 58, 64, 65, 65, 66, 68, 68, 69, 69, 69, 72, 72, 72, 73, 75, 75, 76, 77, 77, 77, 78, 78, 79, 79, 80, 82, 82, 83, 83, 85, 87, 87, 88, 103, 105, 114, 134, 134, 135, 135, 136, 138, 139, 140, 140, 140, 141, 142, 143, 145, 146, 147, 148, 151, 153, 156, 162, 162, 169, 170 Leg 1:8, 10, 10, 21, 25, 27, 31, 31, 31, 31, 32, 32, 43, 47, 53, 53, 53, 53, 88, 88, 90, 97, 105, 105 Leg 2:1, 1, 1, 4, 4, 4, 5, 11, 13, 13, 19, 21, 23, 48, 49, 73, 85, 108 Leg 3:2, 30, 38, 70, 76, 96, 96, 126, 161, 174, 176, 201, 201, 237 Cher 39, 40, 43, 43, 50, 53, 54, 56, 79, 87, 90, 91, 111, 111, 124 Sacr 7, 19, 35, 79, 93, 94, 98, 101, 124 Det 5, 5, 5, 10, 13, 17, 22, 22, 22, 23, 27, 30, 76, 80, 80, 82, 83, 84, 84, 85, 85, 86, 102, 113, 122, 127, 135, 138, 138, 138, 139, 139, 139, 139, 151, 152, 153, 160, 162, 162, 174 Post 36, 37, 49, 58, 67, 77, 79, 101, 105, 106, 113, 119, 157, 160, 161, 161, 162, 168, 173, 185 Gig 1, 5, 6, 15, 16, 16, 17, 19, 32, 32, 33, 33, 33, 33, 51, 53, 60, 61, 62, 63 Deus 1, 2, 3, 19, 20, 20, 20, 21, 22, 26, 27, 29, 33, 36, 44, 47, 47, 48, 49, 50, 51, 51, 53, 53, 54, 55, 62, 69, 69, 69, 71, 73, 75, 81, 117, 117, 117, 118, 124, 138, 139, 150, 156, 173, 176 Agr 1, 1, 6, 8, 9, 20, 22, 23, 24, 37, 41, 44, 46, 62, 67, 84, 90, 96, 97, 102, 103, 107, 107, 108, 113, 116, 125, 139, 143, 148, 148, 148, 148, 166, 166 Plant 1, 17, 17, 18, 19, 20, 28, 32, 34, 38, 41, 41, 42, 44, 70, 102, 137, 140, 151, 156, 177 Ebr 13, 26, 30, 36, 47, 62, 68, 69, 70, 70, 73, 73, 75, 78, 82, 83, 84, 91, 101, 119, 120, 144, 156, 160, 175, 214, 220 Sobr 3, 21, 23, 25 Conf 1, 1, 5, 6, 9, 11, 13, 15, 24, 24, 41, 41, 44, 44, 46, 49, 62, 65, 93, 98, 107, 116, 121, 140, 142, 142, 146, 147, 150, 158, 168, 169, 170, 176, 178, 179, 179, 182 Migr 2, 4, 19, 22, 40, 42, 59, 61, 66, 81, 87, 90, 108, 113, 121, 124, 124, 126, 131, 140, 142, 171, 178, 181, 192, 194, 218, 219, 220 Her 7, 12, 49, 56, 57, 76, 84, 95, 109, 115, 117, 118, 121, 127, 137, 142, 151, 155, 155, 155, 164, 164, 168, 171, 191, 224, 231, 231, 233, 233, 246, 258, 261, 284, 296, 302, 303 Congr 11, 17, 27, 50, 54, 84, 97, 97, 122, 131, 170, 173 Fug 1, 9, 10, 21, 38, 57, 64, 68, 68, 70, 71, 71, 71, 72, 72, 72, 91, 104, 108, 127, 127, 131, 149, 149, 163, 167, 169, 184 Mut 6, 7, 10, 12, 24, 25, 26, 26, 26, 26, 31, 36, 40, 44, 50, 52, 63, 64, 104, 117, 118, 119, 125, 127, 131, 151, 181, 182, 183, 184, 186, 197, 198, 205, 210, 213, 218, 246, 256, 258, 259, 263 Somn 1:29, 33, 34, 34, 35, 52, 55, 58, 74, 74, 74, 103, 103, 104, 105, 107, 108, 108, 110, 113, 146, 153, 170, 170, 172, 174, 194, 205, 215, 215, 215, 231, 233, 234, 236, 237, 237, 238, 254, 256 Somn 2:49, 54, 66, 89, 98, 114, 115, 116, 132, 174, 188, 188, 188, 189, 189, 189, 229, 230, 231, 231, 233, 234, 243, 262, 267, 267 Abr 7, 8, 8, 8, 9, 10, 11, 12, 20, 23, 31, 32, 33, 33, 33, 36, 45, 46, 51, 54, 54, 55, 56, 56, 94, 98, 115, 118, 126, 136, 175, 186, 189, 207, 208, 208, 217, 223, 247, 261, 264, 266, 272, 273, 275 Ios 2, 24, 25, 35, 44, 52, 59, 71, 80, 99, 116, 126, 144, 155, 172, 174, 193, 194, 203, 210, 241, 244 Mos 1:11, 44, 60, 72, 76, 84, 87, 94, 100, 102, 111, 127, 130, 133, 145, 149, 155, 157, 169, 173, 184, 192, 193, 197, 200, 213, 216, 222, 272, 283, 283, 285, 289, 290, 304, 314 Mos 2:9, 22, 26, 27, 36, 53, 59, 60, 65, 81, 84, 127, 127, 128, 135, 155, 156, 186, 189, 191, 193, 197, 197, 199, 206, 217, 222, 223, 238, 248, 251, 263, 281, 291 Decal 4, 10, 15, 31, 32, 34, 41, 43, 47, 52, 75, 78, 81, 83, 91, 91, 99, 104, 106, 107, 109, 109, 110, 110, 111, 113, 114, 115, 118, 121, 132, 133, 134, 153, 155, 160 Spec 1:10, 30, 43, 44, 64, 67, 74, 76, 89, 97, 100, 116, 116, 116, 135, 152, 159, 168, 169, 172, 179, 184, 190, 195, 196, 206, 211, 234, 234, 252, 265, 268, 272, 276, 277, 277, 285, 294, 295, 303, 303, 307, 310, 318, 320, 322, 330, 331 Spec 2:11, 17, 27, 28, 35, 38, 42, 44, 54, 63, 68, 69, 69, 78, 82, 82, 84, 89, 89, 96, 103, 133, 141, 156, 158, 159, 162, 164, 165, 165, 167, 167, 171, 172, 173, 174, 179, 185, 188, 189, 190, 196, 213,

217, 251, 252, 253 Spec 3:5, 11, 25, 38, 43, 45, 46, 48, 49, 52, 52, 57, 57, 83, 83, 99, 103, 108, 109, 111, 117, 121, 144, 144, 146, 166, 192, 207 Spec 4:14, 44, 48, 63, 73, 103, 116, 119, 123, 157, 161, 179, 180, 200, 201, 202, 218, 223, 227, 228 Virt 10, 36, 52, 54, 54, 58, 63, 74, 74, 81, 81, 84, 86, 96, 119, 125, 131, 140, 143, 148, 149, 149, 150, 154, 160, 162, 185, 204, 206, 217 Praem 1, 8, 9, 13, 14, 14, 17, 23, 62, 63, 68, 69, 69, 72, 85, 85, 86, 87, 89, 91, 92, 95, 96, 110, 117, 126, 130, 132, 149, 149, 152, 153, 154, 155, 163, 172 Prob 7, 11, 12, 17, 17, 18, 43, 43, 45, 63, 71, 77, 111, 121, 123, 139, 156, 158 Contempl 14, 17, 40, 62, 69 Aet 23, 29, 43, 46, 46, 55, 55, 57, 58, 60, 61, 65, 65, 66, 68, 69, 69, 69, 73, 75, 97, 130, 130, 131, 145, 146, 149 Flacc 2, 4, 6, 13, 48, 101, 104, 109, 115, 123, 130, 135, 170, 187 Legat 3, 33, 43, 50, 68, 76, 76, 76, 81, 83, 98, 106, 109, 118, 118, 118, 139, 141, 144, 174, 190, 190, 194, 196, 198, 210, 211, 218, 242, 249, 263, 265, 277, 278, 278, 303, 306, 326, 327, 332, 347, 348, 355, 367 Hypoth 6:4 Prov 1, 2:8, 14, 16, 21, 35, 44, 57, 60, 62, 69 QG 1:21, 21, 21, 29, 31, 51, 55a, 55a, 55a, 55b, 69, 92, 93, 94, 94, 96:1, 96:1, 100:2a, 2:5b, 10, 11, 11, 13a, 15b, 17c, 54a, 54a, 54a, 54a, 54a, 54a, 54c, 62, 62, 66, 72, 4:47b, 51b, 52d, 69, 76b, 179, 180, 9* QG isf 3, 5, 10, 10, 16, 16 QG (Par) 2:5, 2:5 QE 2:12, 21, 25a, 55b QE isf 3, 3, 16, 26, 29

ἀνθρωπότης Det 76 Post 115 Somn 2:230 Spec 2:21

ἀνθυπαλλάσσω Spec 4:88 Virt 205 Flacc 151, 157

ἀνθύπατος Legat 315

ἀνθυποβάλλω Hypoth 7:8

ἀνθυπουργέω Prob 79

ἀνία (23) Opif 167 Leg 3:216 Cher 118 Ios 27, 97, 201, 233 Mos 1:11, 128, 198, 247 Mos 2:230 Spec 2:138 Praem 72, 72, 105, 135, 139 Flacc 146, 153, 159 Legat 184, 339

ἀνιαρός (8) Leg 3:211 Somn 2:151 Ios 183, 183, 186 Spec 3:115 Praem 73 Flacc 118

ἀνίατος (61) Cher 2, 10, 42 Sacr 48 Det 148, 174 Post 11, 71, 74 Gig 35 Deus 182 Agr 40 Ebr 18, 28, 140, 222, 223 Conf 22, 24, 163 Migr 210 Fug 80 Somn 1:86, 87 Somn 2:85, 191, 196, 205 Abr 115, 182, 207 Ios 87, 191 Mos 2:167 Decal 87 Spec 1:174, 230, 237, 314, 324 Spec 2:232 Spec 3:11, 28, 34, 88, 88, 88, 122, 173 Spec 4:152, 181, 200 Praem 72, 135, 145, 149 Prob 76, 90 Legat 190 QG 1:65, 4:51a

ἀνιάω (14) Her 310 Abr 29, 202, 204, 214, 230 Ios 71, 227 Mos 1:247 Mos 2:177, 279 Spec 1:314 QG isf 9, 9

ἀνίδρυτος (30) Opif 156 Sacr 32 Det 12 Post 22 Gig 67 Deus 4 Ebr 170, 170 Her 288 Congr 58 Mut 156 Somn 1:156, 192, 192, 192 Abr 84, 85 Mos 1:196 Spec 1:29 Spec 2:168, 213 Spec 4:88, 139, 153 Virt 40 Praem 29, 151 Prob 38 Legat 67 QE isf 18

ἀνίερος (30) Cher 94 Sacr 32, 128, 138 Gig 16 Deus 128 Agr 113 Plant 108 Conf 160, 161 Congr 169 Fug 83, 114 Mut 107 Somn 1:253 Somn 2:168 Mos 2:107 Spec 1:102, 150, 223, 270, 281, 292 Spec 3:40, 88 Spec 4:40, 217 Virt 135 Praem 52 QE 2:14

ἀνιερόω (8) Sacr 103, 108 Ebr 152 Her 179 Mut 220 Somn 1:32, 243 Mos 1:253

ἀνίημι (80) Opif 40, 64, 141 Leg 2:28 Leg 3:153, 190 Cher 128 Sacr 37, 128, 137 Det 45 Post 13, 13 Gig 53 Deus 24, 47, 79, 81, 163 Agr 59 Plant 162 Ebr 116, 218 Conf 166 Migr 181 Fug 130 Mut 215, 240 Somn 1:19, 123, 181 Somn 2:104 Abr 20, 73, 233, 234 Ios 23, 238 Mos 1:39, 155, 168, 201, 281 Mos 2:66, 144 Spec 1:75, 92, 99, 159, 237 Spec 3:111, 159 Spec 4:97, 102, 216 Virt 79, 83, 97, 111, 215 Praem 9, 48, 68, 144 Contempl 14, 33, 36 Flacc 36, 112 Legat 39, 83, 146, 162, 267 Hypoth 7:3, 7:19 Prov 2:10, 46 QG 2:64c QE 1:19

ἀνίκητος Sacr 80, 87 Gig 47 Fug 149 Somn 2:141

ἀνιμάω Plant 24 Spec 4:107

ἀνίπταμαι Det 88

ἄνιπτος Spec 2:6

ἀνισόδρομος Cher 22

ἄνισος (34) Opif 97 Cher 22 Sacr 32 Det 36 Post 5, 52 Conf 48, 108 Her 150, 160, 164 Fug 106 Mut 103 Somn 2:80, 112 Ios 140 Decal 41, 61, 167 Spec 1:121, 121, 295 Spec 2:21, 190 Spec 3:181 Spec 4:89, 166, 205, 237 Virt 146 Prob 24 Contempl 17 Aet 112 QG (Par) 2:2

ἀνισοταχής Prov 2:18

ἀνισότης (19) Her 161, 162 Ios 142 Decal 5 Spec 1:121 Spec 2:34, 204 Spec 4:166, 187, 231, 237 Contempl 70 Legat 85 QG 2:12b, 12b, 14 QE 1:6, 6, 2:64

ἀνίστημι (57) Leg 2:25, 101 Leg 3:229 Det 1, 47, 47, 134 Post 76 Ebr 54, 156, 203 Conf 72, 74, 79 Migr 80, 177, 208 Her 262 Congr 83 Fug 23, 48 Mut 113, 156 Somn 1:46, 100, 189, 249, 249 Somn 2:6, 78 Mos 1:215, 283, 284 Spec 1:68 Spec 2:62, 119 Spec 4:141, 158 Praem 165 Prob 130, 132, 141 Contempl 80, 83 Aet 42 Flacc 114, 115 Legat 144, 173, 201, 203, 228, 228, 252, 350 Hypoth 6:1 QE 2:17

ἀνίσχω (17) Opif 34 Plant 40 Migr 68 Her 264 Mut 6, 162 Somn 1:11, 72, 83 Somn 2:34 Spec 1:171 Spec 4:7, 147 Contempl 27, 89 Aet 120 Hypoth 11:6

Ἄννα Deus 5 Ebr 145 Mut 143 Somn 1:254

ἀνοδία (20) Det 18 Agr 101 Ebr 51 Somn 2:161 Abr 86 Mos 1:167, 237 Mos 2:138 Decal 81 Spec 1:60, 215, 301 Spec 2:23 Spec 3:29 Spec 4:109, 155 Praem 117, 167 QE 2:13a, 26

ἄνοδος Det 114 Fug 194 QG 4:100

ἀνόητος (8) Fug 14, 123 Somn 2:163, 181, 208 Mos 1:293 Spec 2:254 Legat 367

ἀνόθευτος Sacr 26 Det 137

ἄνοθος (11) Gig 14 Agr 104 Plant 24 Migr 86, 116 Mos 2:139 Decal 58 Spec 1:32 Virt 185 Prob 99 Prov 2:16

ἄνοια (15) Leg 3:164, 211 Ebr 93 Sobr 11 Conf 5, 54, 65 Congr 61 Mut 193, 193 Somn 2:115, 169, 191, 200 Prov 2:58

ἀνοίγνυμι (23) Leg 2:47, 47 Leg 3:104, 105, 180, 180, 181, 181 Cher 46, 46 Deus 156, 156 Migr 34, 121 Her 25, 51, 76 Congr 7 Fug 192 Mut 132, 133 Abr 7 Ios 162

ἀνοίκειος (17) Opif 74, 74, 149 Leg 3:204 Sacr 91, 96 Deus 141 Plant 144 Her 261 Congr 138 Spec 2:154 Spec 4:50, 208 Virt 2, 146 Legat 102 QG 2:54a

ἀνοικισμός Flacc 62

ἀνοικοδομέω Conf 142 Migr 63

ἄνοικος Legat 123

ἀνοιμώζω Ios 217 Flacc 157

ἀνομβρέω (12) Leg 1:34 Leg 3:12 Det 44 Plant 81 Her 31 Fug 182, 192 Somn 1:19 Mos 1:65, 212 Decal 16 QG 1:3

ἀνομβρία Virt 49

ἀνομία (17) Leg 3:79 Sacr 57 Det 141 Post 52 Ebr 143 Sobr 25, 48 Conf 108 Her 212, 300 Mut 150 Mos 2:165 Spec 1:188, 279, 321 Prob 76 Legat 30

ἀνομοιογενής Spec 3:47 Virt 140

ἀνόμοιος (17) Opif 22, 54, 71 Cher 110 Sacr 100 Det 164, 164, 164 Plant 151 Sobr 60 Conf 185 Mos 2:193 Spec 1:121 Spec 3:181 Spec 4:187 Virt 19 Contempl 20

ἀνομολογέομαι (21) Leg 1:2, 67 Cher 124 Sacr 7, 136 Plant 174 Ebr 16, 83, 142 Sobr 2 Conf 5, 115 Migr 42 Her 118 Congr 178 Mut 152 Spec 4:101 Aet 106 Flacc 18 Legat 353 Hypoth 6:7

ἄνομος Somn 2:296

ἀνόνητος Sacr 117 Agr 171

ἄνοος Leg 2:69 Leg 3:164 Cher 116 Conf 65

ἀνοργίαστος Cher 94 Sacr 32 Ebr 146 QG isf 2 QE isf 14

ἀνορθιάζω (7) Ebr 156 Mut 138 Somn 1:193 Decal 45 Spec 2:62 Contempl 77 Legat 169

ἀνορθόω Plant 17 Virt 3

ἀνόρθωσις QE 2:17

ἀνορχέομαι Ebr 146 Prob 39 Legat 354

ἀνόσιος (30) Post 34 Ebr 42, 194 Conf 36, 123 Her 201 Congr 171 Mut 153, 197 Somn 2:120, 290 Ios 143, 216 Mos 2:199, 203, 279 Decal 63, 86 Spec 1:279, 316, 327 Spec 2:10 Spec 3:91, 141 Virt 43, 138 Aet 106 Flacc 104 Legat 160 QG isf 14

ἀνοσιουργέω Mos 1:301

ἀνοσιούργημα (11) Ios 47, 173 Mos 1:46 Mos 2:201 Decal 2 Spec 1:56, 319 Spec 3:13, 14, 19, 84

ἀνοσιουργία Legat 30

ἀνοσιουργός (6) Conf 116, 161 Congr 87 Mos 1:8 Mos 2:273 Spec 3:84

ἄνοσος (23) Opif 153 Gig 34 Agr 123 Conf 25 Migr 119 Her 184 Mut 213 Somn 2:73 Abr 26, 267, 275 Mos 2:185 Spec 1:173, 224 Virt 176 Praem 119 Aet 21, 25, 26, 26, 70, 74 Flacc 144

ἀνουθέτητος Sacr 23, 32

ἄνους (ἄνοος)

ἀνοχή Legat 100

ἀνταγαπάω Abr 50

ἀνταγωνιστής Leg 3:190, 190 Det 29 Agr 112

ἀνταδικέω Spec 2:44

ἀντακολουθέω Praem 81

ἀνταλλάσσω Spec 3:96

ἀνταμελέω Spec 2:27

ἀνταναιρέω Spec 3:128

ἀνταπειλέω Prob 153

ἀνταποδίδωμι Deus 5 Sobr 10 Her 184 Decal 117

ἀνταποθνήσκω Leg 3:32, 35

ἀνταποτίνω Spec 2:78

ἀνταρκτικός Opif 112

ἀνταυγάζω Spec 1:321

ἀντεῖπον Mos 1:299

ἀντεισάγω Cher 50 Det 16

ἀντεκτίνω (9) Her 104 Somn 2:183 Ios 267 Mos 2:7 Decal 117 Spec 2:68, 97 Spec 4:166 Legat 47

ἀντέκτισις Cher 110 Aet 108, 116

ἀντεξελαύνω Flacc 120

ἀντεξετάζω Cher 121 Post 19 Sobr 9 Abr 37 Ios 24

ἀντεπίθεσις Opif 33 Somn 1:222 Somn 2:35 Spec 2:43, 52

ἀντεπισπάω Post 116

ἀντεπιτίθημι (6) Migr 82 Somn 2:12 Mos 1:191, 215 Spec 2:190 QE 1:7b

ἀντεπιτρέχω Spec 4:111

ἀντεπιφέρω Det 2 Post 185 Conf 15 Abr 261 Legat 144

ἀντερείδω Cher 78

ἀντέρεισις Cher 79

ἀντεφεστιάω Mos 2:33

ἀντεφήδομαι Spec 3:85

ἀντεφορμάω Mos 1:260

ἀντεφόρμησις Abr 214

ἀντέχω (18) Leg 3:201 Gig 13 Ebr 58 Migr 26 Mut 214 Abr 182 Mos 1:233 Mos 2:70 Spec 3:4, 29 Spec 4:111 Praem 38 Prob 118 Contempl 35 Aet 128, 137 Flacc 10, 179

ἄντηχος Agr 79 Contempl 88

ἀντί (237) Opif 5, 33, 94, 152, 165, 165, 165, 165, 170 Leg 1:89, 89 Leg 2:10, 16, 16, 21, 21, 32, 35, 35, 38, 44, 46, 90, 92, 92 Leg 3:52, 82, 87, 107, 156, 180 Cher 7, 7, 7, 65, 75, 75, 75, 91, 122 Sacr 78, 88, 88, 88, 118, 118, 125, 129, 135 Det 21, 105, 106, 106, 122, 131 Post 10, 124, 145, 145, 145, 156, 158, 167, 170, 179 Gig 21, 45 Deus 171 Agr 11, 168 Plant 38, 98, 98, 98, 98, 114, 147, 157, 158 Ebr 109, 223, 224 Conf 5, 38, 38, 78, 159, 191 Migr 69, 119, 173 Her 8, 32, 77, 77, 77, 77, 77, 124, 206 Congr 65, 67, 93, 93, 93, 137, 176 Fug 86, 97, 145 Mut 79, 130, 150 Somn 1:74, 171 Somn 2:14, 39, 51, 140, 292, 295 Abr 51, 64, 70, 242, 242, 242 Ios 35, 46, 86, 105, 123, 123, 123, 123, 201, 221 Mos 1:33, 125, 125, 202, 218 Mos 2:78, 116, 131, 158, 167, 242, 253, 267 Decal 140 Spec 1:111, 111, 113, 125, 127, 180, 240 Spec 2:11, 35, 35, 36, 95, 106, 170, 207, 222 Spec 3:32, 82, 96, 106, 125, 150, 156, 158, 168, 168, 168, 182, 197, 197 Spec 4:12, 17, 26, 125, 146, 159, 159, 195, 227 Virt 72, 84, 98, 179, 223 Praem 8, 22, 52, 58, 110, 155, 162 Prob 38, 64, 79, 79, 160 Contempl 41, 62 Aet 37, 37, 41, 66, 68, 74 Flacc 3, 37, 37, 37, 38, 69, 93, 96, 175 Legat 60, 149, 183, 203, 209, 232, 276, 368 Hypoth 11:17 Prov 2:46 QG 2:68a, 3:23 QE 2:50a

ἀντιβαίνω (10) Leg 1:86 Leg 3:156, 202 Post 72 Deus 183 Ebr 58 Mut 159 Virt 170 Legat 160, 233

ἀντιβιάζομαι (7) Deus 149 Mut 185 Somn 2:12 Spec 4:115 Praem 5, 94 Aet 33

ἀντιβλάπτω Spec 4:211

ἀντιβλέπω Leg 3:202

ἀντιβολία Legat 248

ἀντιβρίθω Mos 2:228

Ἀντιγενίδας Prob 144

ἀντιγεννάω Leg 3:10 Decal 112

Ἀντίγονος Prob 114

ἀντίγραφος Legat 315

ἀντιδιατίθημι Spec 3:85 Spec 4:103

ἀντιδίδωμι (16) Leg 3:24, 110 Cher 123 Ebr 82 Migr 38 Congr 134 Fug 132 Mut 25 Somn 2:118 Abr 273 Ios 105 Mos 1:155, 251 Spec 1:208 Spec 2:83 Legat 89

ἀντίδικος (8) Leg 1:87 Leg 2:92 Virt 174 Aet 142 Flacc 126 Legat 350, 361, 362

ἀντιδοξέω Her 125 Aet 76, 84

ἀντίδοσις (15) Leg 1:29 Leg 3:24, 110 Cher 110, 122 Det 108 Migr 173 Mut 25 Decal 112 Spec 2:97 Virt 185, 225 Aet 116 Legat 47, 85

ἀντιδράω Leg 3:201 Cher 81 Plant 160 Prob 112

ἀντιδωρέομαι Spec 3:127

ἀντίθεος (6) Post 37, 123 Conf 88 Congr 118 Fug 140 Somn 2:183

ἀντιθεραπεύω Spec 3:27 Legat 39

ἀντίθεσις Ebr 187 Prov 2:2

ἀντίθετος Det 38 Praem 52

ἀντικαθήμαι Conf 20, 43 Mut 113 Virt 11

ἀντικαταλαμβάνω Post 167

ἀντικαταλλάσσομαι (15) Sacr 38, 112 Post 26, 94, 95 Deus 18, 150, 169 Migr 97 Her 239 Congr 98 Fug 59, 152 Prob 135 Prov 2:11

ἀντικατηγορέω Decal 75

ἀντικηρύσσω Prob 25

ἀντικινέω Abr 150

ἀντικοπή Aet 8

ἀντικρύ (18) Cher 11, 11, 20, 25 Mos 1:170, 257 Mos 2:78, 80, 94 Spec 1:231, 268 Spec 2:216 Spec 3:55, 60, 60 Spec 4:80 Flacc 75 Legat 151

ἄντικρυς (53) Opif 79 Leg 1:85 Leg 3:8 Cher 9 Sacr 18 Det 52, 80 Post 32, 169 Deus 133 Ebr 101, 141 Sobr 27 Conf 47 Migr 5, 13 Her 56 Congr 154 Fug 211 Mut 204, 265 Somn 1:245 Somn 2:65, 139, 184, 226, 272 Abr 31, 127 Ios 67 Mos 1:263 Spec 1:22, 41, 230, 235, 266 Spec 2:11, 198 Spec 3:86, 94, 168 Spec 4:120, 138, 199 Virt 106, 147, 149 Praem 40 Flacc 1, 32 Legat 52, 164, 171

ἀντιλαμβάνω (25) Leg 1:38 Leg 2:36, 43 Leg 3:56, 56, 60 Sacr 36 Det 101 Gig 18 Plant 132 Ebr 190, 191 Congr 143 Mos 1:11, 262 Mos 2:7 Spec 1:272, 317, 334 Aet 29 Flacc 16 Legat 59, 62 QG 1:27 QE isf 3

ἀντιλέγω (9) Plant 176 Conf 54 Ios 225 Mos 1:85 Prob 53, 63, 125 Legat 301 QG 1:66

ἀντίληψις (32) Opif 53, 139 Leg 1:25, 29 Leg 2:24, 36, 40, 70, 71 Leg 3:58, 97, 109, 112 Sacr 36 Deus 79 Plant 84 Conf 105, 127 Mut 56 Abr 72, 157 Mos 2:148, 227 Decal 34 Spec 2:46 Spec 4:190 Virt 24, 200 Contempl 33 Aet 86 Flacc 10, 66

ἀντιλογία Leg 3:65 Ebr 37 Conf 52

ἀντιλογικός Conf 52 QE isf 4

ἀντιλοχέω Somn 2:40

ἀντιλυπέω Mos 1:141, 270 Virt 140

ἀντιμαρτυρέω Det 166

ἀντιμεθέλκω Post 25

ἀντιμεθίστημι Decal 57

ἀντιμετακλίνω Somn 2:145

ἀντιμεταλαμβάνω Aet 31

ἀντίμιμος (7) Her 88 Fug 179 Somn 1:215 Mos 2:62, 65, 195 QG 2:13a

ἀντίος Prov 1

ἀντιπαθής Agr 98

ἀντίπαις Cher 114

ἀντίπαλος (71) Opif 33 Leg 1:86 Leg 3:7 Cher 15, 81 Sacr 17 Det 29, 35, 164 Deus 43, 137, 143 Agr 79, 114, 120, 163 Ebr 35, 122 Conf 179 Migr 26, 69, 85 Congr 164 Fug 25 Mut 81, 185 Somn 1:86, 174 Somn 2:146, 277 Abr 48, 225, 234, 240, 256 Ios 5 Mos 1:169, 217, 252, 261, 282, 294, 296, 309 Mos 2:13, 185, 252 Spec 1:149 Spec 3:36 Spec 4:46, 111 Virt 2, 38, 116, 116, 153 Praem 25, 59, 93, 95, 169 Prob 26 Contempl 15 Aet 136, 138 Flacc 172 Legat 183, 359 QG 2:15c, 4:228 QE 2:21

ἀντιπαραδέχομαι Aet 109

ἀντιπαραχωρέω Spec 2:64, 155

ἀντιπαρέκτασις Conf 185

ἀντιπαρεκτείνομαι Conf 187 Mos 1:231

ἀντιπαρέχω Plant 130 Sobr 58 Ios 46 Spec 4:195

ἀντιπάσχω (6) Leg 3:201 Cher 79, 82 Spec 3:195 Prob 112 QE 2:24b

ἀντιπαταγέω Mos 1:118

ἀντιπέμπω Legat 47, 89

ἀντιπέραν Mos 2:255 Contempl 86 Flacc 155

ἀντιπέρας Mos 1:319

ἀντιπεριάγω Gig 44 Agr 70

ἀντιπεριΐστημι Somn 1:20

ἀντιπηρόομαι Spec 3:195

ἀντιπνέω Leg 3:202 Mut 95 Somn 2:13 Ios 149 Spec 4:50

ἀντίπνοια Plant 152

ἀντιπολεμέω Mos 1:217

ἀντιπράσσω Legat 117

ἀντιπροεῖδον Flacc 185

ἀντιπροσαγορεύω Legat 181, 352

ἀντιπροσφθέγγομαι Opif 152

ἀντιπρόσωπος (6) Cher 25 Her 132, 207, 213 Fug 211 Mos 2:98

ἀντιρρέπω (13) Leg 2:83 Sacr 122 Post 22, 100 Gig 28 Agr 89 Plant 111 Migr 148 Mut 124, 185 Abr 212 Mos 2:228 Spec 4:167

ἀντίρρησις Aet 132

ἀντίρροπος Opif 113 Leg 1:8 Virt 186 Flacc 174

Ἀντισθένης Prob 28

ἀντισοφίζομαι Ebr 50 Conf 14

ἀντισοφιστεύω Migr 83

ἀντίσπασμα Migr 149 Fug 22

ἀντισπάω (18) Sacr 49 Post 25 Agr 70 Ebr 53 Migr 67 Her 46, 241 Mut 173 Somn 1:57, 152, 243 Somn 2:11 Abr 73, 176 Mos 2:165, 237 Spec 2:21 QG 1:55c

ἀντίστασις Fug 211

ἀντιστατέω (16) Leg 1:69, 87 Leg 2:91 Leg 3:201 Cher 11, 13, 20 Det 72 Post 71 Agr 3 Plant 144 Ebr 57, 196 Conf 17 Mut 10 Ios 149

ἀντιστροφή Contempl 84 QG isf 3

ἀντίστροφος Ios 80

ἀντίταξις Det 9 Her 306 Congr 32

ἀντιτάσσω (22) Leg 2:108 Cher 12, 78 Sacr 55, 121 Deus 124 Ebr 115 Congr 31 Mut 160, 265 Abr 233 Mos 1:175 Spec 4:222 Virt 5, 10, 43, 43 Praem 96 Prob 126 Contempl 40, 64 Legat 349

ἀντιτείνω Sacr 117 Aet 136

ἀντιτειχίζω Conf 145

ἀντιτεχνάομαι Det 176

ἀντίτεχνος Prob 144

ἀντιτίθημι (8) Opif 36 Det 16 Gig 40 Deus 85 Mos 1:193 Virt 37 Prob 55 Legat 110

ἀντιτιμάω Abr 177 Mos 2:67 Spec 4:184 Prob 42 Legat 272

ἀντιτυπής Mos 2:183

ἀντίτυπος Plant 133 Conf 102 Her 181

ἀντίφθογγος Mos 2:256

ἀντιφιλέω Virt 225

ἀντιφιλονεικέω (9) Leg 2:32 Leg 3:156 Deus 97 Conf 52 Mos 1:130 Spec 2:19 Spec 4:25 Virt 5 Legat 144

ἀντίφωνος Agr 79 Plant 167 Contempl 84, 88

ἀντιχαρίζομαι (6) Det 108 Plant 130 Abr 177, 203 Ios 258 Decal 112

ἀντλέω Post 151 Mut 111

ἄντρον Post 49

ἀντρώδης QG 4:80

ἀντωθέω Somn 2:145 Spec 4:111

ἀντωφελέω Decal 114 QG 1:17a

ἀνύβριστος Abr 98 Ios 210 Spec 2:95 Flacc 79

ἀνυδρία Hypoth 6:2

ἄνυδρος Somn 1:40

ἀνυπαίτιος (41) Opif 16, 136 Det 78 Gig 16 Deus 61, 128, 134 Agr 49 Plant 108 Sobr 50 Conf 125, 149 Migr 6 Congr 101 Mut 36, 51 Somn 2:73 Mos 2:138 Spec 1:102, 117, 127, 153, 167, 202, 227, 259, 300 Spec 2:35, 44, 48, 175 Spec 3:59, 61, 154, 166 Spec 4:121 Virt 58, 177 Praem 23 Aet 83 Hypoth 11:9

ἀνύπαρκτος Mut 36 Spec 3:45 Prob 72 Aet 5, 105

ἀνυπέρβλητος Mos 2:207 Spec 2:158 Aet 22

ἀνυπέρθετος (28) Opif 42 Sacr 53, 68 Deus 159 Agr 80, 85 Conf 110 Mut 142 Abr 108 Ios 118 Mos 1:109, 184 Spec 1:55, 83, 225, 316 Spec 2:13, 60, 182 Spec 3:8 Spec 4:138 Virt 41, 88, 126, 185 Praem 136 Flacc 100 Legat 99

ἀνυπεύθυνος (9) Sacr 23 Agr 56 Somn 2:244 Spec 3:137 Prob 59, 124 Legat 28, 134, 190

ἀνύποιστος Conf 110 Mos 1:39, 105

ἀνυπόκριτος QG 3:29

ἀνύποπτος Abr 251 Ios 185

ἀνυπόστατος Praem 95

ἀνυπότακτος Her 4

ἀνύπουλος Praem 163 Prob 155 Legat 41

ἀνύσιμος (9) Det 131 Agr 86 Migr 154 Ios 86 Spec 1:52 Spec 4:109 Aet 97 Flacc 67 Legat 251

ἀνύω (12) Opif 86 Det 70 Conf 153 Migr 133 Abr 62 Ios 181, 185 Mos 2:247 Spec 2:142 Praem 78 Prob 111 QE 2:26

ἄνω (198) Opif 41, 54, 70, 122, 128, 137, 163 Leg 1:4, 71 Leg 3:4, 82, 120 Cher 27 Sacr 6, 8, 59, 60, 77, 108 Det 85, 176 Post 170 Gig 22, 31 Deus 53, 175 Agr 136 Plant 14, 23, 25, 64 Ebr 75 Conf 139 Migr 168, 172, 182 Her 34, 70, 115, 126, 143, 217, 234, 238, 239, 239, 241 Congr 8 Fug 97, 180, 197 Mut 72, 107, 146 Somn 1:21, 25, 26, 54, 119, 128, 139, 147, 151, 152, 154, 156, 235 Abr 46, 58, 60 Ios 16, 93, 131, 136, 169, 176, 244 Mos 1:31, 34, 111, 118, 190, 198, 238, 314, 322 Mos 2:71, 99, 204 Decal 6, 53, 57, 57, 57, 65, 74, 103 Spec 1:3, 32, 37, 54, 66, 94, 94, 131, 164, 185, 194, 195, 207, 263, 301, 301, 328 Spec 2:5, 27, 63, 65, 82, 165, 231, 233, 234 Spec 3:1, 15, 29, 46, 62, 184, 192, 207 Spec 4:115, 159, 159, 170, 176, 236 Virt 34, 35, 53, 65, 77, 119, 176, 183, 209, 216 Praem 41, 43, 52, 109, 124, 135, 151, 152, 162 Prob 148 Contempl 33, 66 Aet 29, 33, 33, 58, 109, 113, 115, 135, 135, 136 Flacc 14, 46, 50, 73, 120, 126, 131, 162 Legat 46, 50, 59, 77, 86, 90, 118, 121, 198, 204, 333, 341, 359 Prov 2:27 QG 1:55a, 2:15a, 34a, 62, 4:51c QE 2:3b, 65

ἄνω ἀνώτατος

ἄνω ἀνώτερος

ἀνώδυνος Cher 86 Agr 97

ἄνωθεν (41) Opif 117 Det 86 Deus 155 Agr 134 Sobr 57 Migr 35 Her 64, 166, 184, 218, 274 Congr 36 Fug 49, 101, 138, 166, 180, 192 Mut 260 Somn 1:162 Somn 2:86, 142, 198 Abr 43, 157 Mos 1:115, 117 Mos 2:48, 69, 118, 144 Spec 1:85 Spec 3:2 Virt 42, 217 Praem 73, 133 Aet 147 QG 4:51c QG (Par) 2:5, 2:5

ἀνωθέω (ὠθέω) (9) Opif 63 Det 100 Post 175 Agr 174 Fug 191 Mut 214 Mos 1:270 Spec 4:50 Prov 2:58

ἀνώλεθρος Mut 80 Somn 1:158 Aet 7

ἀνωμαλία (18) Abr 212 Ios 36, 142, 247, 269 Spec 1:106 Spec 2:52 Spec 4:88 Virt 10 Aet 43, 117, 119, 132, 137 Flacc 71 Legat 34, 346 Prov 2:44

ἀνώμαλος (8) Opif 97 Her 160 Congr 28 Somn 1:115, 150, 153, 156 Spec 3:181

ἀνώμοτος Somn 1:13 Decal 84, 141, 157 Prob 84

ἀνώνυμος Sobr 52 QG 1:20

ἀνώτατος (ἄνω) Mut 58

ἀνώτερος (ἄνω) Leg 2:105 Somn 1:75

ἀνωφελής (14) Opif 11 Sacr 36, 115 Post 164 Ebr 168 Mut 211 Somn 2:22 Ios 143, 173 Mos 1:67 Mos 2:48 Decal 12 Spec 2:95 Virt 129

ἀνώφοιτος (6) Opif 147 Fug 62 Mos 1:189, 218 Aet 29, 136

ἄξενος Abr 107

ἀξία (14) Leg 1:87, 87 Leg 3:10, 126 Sobr 40 Mos 2:9, 51 Spec 1:121, 135, 248 Spec 2:36, 37, 233 Spec 4:57

ἀξιέραστος (13) Post 12 Migr 36, 163 Mut 143 Somn 2:109 Abr 88, 191 Mos 1:59 Mos 2:205 Spec 4:161 Virt 66, 164 Praem 36

ἀξιοθέατος Migr 36

ἀξιόλογος Spec 2:5

ἀξιόμαχος Spec 4:221

ἀξιομνημόνευτος Migr 17, 18 Somn 2:109 Contempl 57

ἀξιόνικος Sacr 92 Migr 186 Ios 123 Mos 2:205 Spec 4:54

ἀξιόπιστος Mut 258 Ios 252 QE isf 14

ἀξιοπρεπής Sobr 62 Virt 188

ἀξιόρατος Migr 36

ἄξιος (307) Opif 4, 6, 89, 155, 156, 170 Leg 1:44, 70, 85 Leg 2:14, 42, 85 Leg 3:10, 15, 79, 83, 106, 141, 164, 171, 209 Cher 42, 80, 112 Sacr 29, 33, 54, 61, 77, 94, 118, 124, 128 Det 57, 70, 101, 118, 137 Post 22, 91, 96, 105, 135, 139 Gig 1, 16, 36 Deus 1, 76, 90, 104, 105, 106, 108, 171 Agr 45, 60, 120 Plant 158 Ebr 111, 158, 192, 194, 223 Sobr 5, 16, 31, 52 Conf 53, 82, 140, 168, 178 Migr 21, 57, 108, 170, 203 Her 7, 10, 14, 32, 33, 90, 109, 123, 128, 215, 226, 227, 247, 252, 277, 293 Congr 5, 13, 27, 73, 98, 173 Fug 20, 24, 29, 30, 40, 73, 74, 79, 84, 87, 93, 96, 118, 129 Mut 52, 58, 64, 82, 83, 91, 104, 145, 186, 197, 224, 236 Somn 1:5, 93, 95, 147, 153, 167, 207, 212, 212, 246, 246, 248 Somn 2:66, 93, 122, 160, 177, 179, 227, 258, 263, 282 Abr 10, 11, 22, 107, 167, 204, 204, 255, 266, 271 Ios 2, 28, 42, 44, 46, 58, 153, 170, 171, 206, 216, 220, 249 Mos 1:1, 47, 148, 212, 273, 291 Mos 2:9, 11, 59, 135, 143, 162, 171, 191, 217, 285 Decal 20, 67, 73, 94, 117, 118, 141 Spec 1:43, 57, 96, 234, 258, 264, 284, 297, 309, 314, 314, 315, 319, 323 Spec 2:4, 14, 23, 36, 107, 115, 129, 141, 149, 149, 173, 185, 202, 226, 232, 234, 253, 255 Spec 3:38, 89, 90, 103, 143, 148, 153, 155, 176, 195 Spec 4:6, 15, 59, 59, 65, 77, 150, 182, 218, 230 Virt 52, 89, 117, 139, 155, 176, 202, 223 Praem 13, 23, 44, 69, 87, 113, 162 Prob 15, 42, 44, 61, 95, 97, 141, 143, 145, 156 Contempl 3, 6, 34, 66, 73 Aet 1, 3, 41, 71, 73, 80 Flacc 80, 93, 109 Legat 38, 51, 71, 103, 110, 144, 187, 245, 288, 341, 349 Hypoth 7:2, 7:9 QG 2:71a, 3:29, 4:102a, 180, 200c, 202a, 202b QE 2:15b, 118

ἀξιοσπούδαστος Mos 2:194

ἀξιοτίμητος Migr 163

ἀξιόχρεως (14) Cher 45, 98, 100 Sacr 57 Det 62 Post 143 Plant 33, 69, 126 Conf 146 Migr 197 Fug 110 Mut 26 Legat 37

ἀξιόω (316) Opif 30, 45, 53, 142, 148 Leg 1:33, 39, 55, 95 Leg 3:14, 27, 74, 87, 93, 94, 106, 192, 197 Cher 34, 84, 99 Sacr 6, 28, 42, 47, 100, 119, 128, 130 Det 7, 14, 52, 54, 102, 116, 134, 134, 145, 160 Post 54, 71, 78, 83, 90, 130 Gig 12, 36, 58, 61 Deus 4, 22, 31, 47, 104, 110, 157, 158, 180 Agr 121, 149 Plant 26, 44, 62, 63, 72, 146, 151, 156 Ebr 25, 65, 72, 74, 75, 94, 95, 216 Sobr 20, 22, 29, 53, 58, 69 Conf 76, 79, 110, 116, 133, 161, 182 Migr 27, 94, 145, 158, 191 Her 13, 18, 28, 43, 49, 49, 64, 105, 185, 194, 223, 247, 270, 303 Congr 13, 125, 130 Fug 38, 114, 160, 209 Mut 18, 25, 59, 64, 83, 114, 195, 216, 227, 245, 255 Somn 1:16, 21, 45, 69, 121, 190, 196, 205, 228, 244 Somn 2:62, 115, 124, 134, 192 Abr 22, 37, 41, 46, 50, 76, 98, 115, 127, 165, 243, 256, 270 Ios 12, 25, 86, 152, 154, 154, 192, 205, 241 Mos 1:2, 8, 20, 98, 142, 155, 158, 243, 321, 323, 324, 331 Mos 2:5, 53, 58, 67, 96, 142, 173, 194, 200, 203, 208, 242, 274 Decal 12, 14, 18, 36, 41, 49, 50, 68, 95, 102, 109, 163, 177 Spec 1:24, 31, 42, 42, 51, 63, 161, 168, 177, 229, 283, 291, 303, 308, 318, 319 Spec 2:23, 66, 71, 78, 104, 106, 133, 139, 219, 229, 234, 238, 246, 255 Spec 3:13, 39, 62, 116, 192, 198 Spec 4:11, 55, 63, 72, 126, 170, 202, 213 Virt 20, 54, 60, 84, 102, 105, 109, 112, 115, 144, 151, 165, 172, 179, 201, 203, 209, 210, 225 Praem 23, 61, 74, 75 Prob 44, 75 Contempl 36, 57 Aet 89 Flacc 40, 44, 61, 83, 106 Legat 53, 69, 75, 80, 84, 86, 98, 106, 141, 178, 191, 250, 285, 294, 333, 346, 347 Hypoth 7:12, 7:19, 11:1, 11:13, 11:13 Prov 2:10, 12, 16, 21, 40 QG 1:20, 60:2, 76b, 96:1, 2:11, 65, 4:40, 88, 193, 227, 228

ἀξίωμα (ὁ) (42) Leg 3:191 Cher 29, 99 Sacr 14, 16, 73, 119 Post 62, 63, 110 Deus 116, 150 Agr 140 Her 3, 223 Congr 137, 149 Fug 50 Mut 217 Somn 1:132 Ios 72, 107, 216 Mos 1:168, 268 Mos 2:234 Spec 1:139, 159, 187 Spec 2:34, 145, 215 Virt 186, 191, 223 Praem 157 Prob 126 Flacc 78 Legat 140, 276, 286, 300

ἀξίωσις (6) Opif 37 Ebr 131 Ios 164 Spec 1:242, 245, 324

ἀοίδιμος (18) Opif 82 Cher 91 Ebr 152 Migr 184 Her 27, 76, 214 Congr 160 Somn 1:166 Somn 2:24 Abr 167 Spec 1:50, 322 Virt 207 Prob 137 Contempl 26 Prov 2:17, 30

ἀοίκητος Her 147 Mos 1:195

ἄοικος (8) Leg 3:2, 3 Sacr 32 Gig 67 Congr 58, 62 Virt 190 Contempl 47

ἄοκνος (13) Det 56, 62 Post 13 Ebr 159 Sobr 38 Migr 97, 216 Her 9 Somn 2:38 Spec 2:83 Virt 215 Prob 34 Hypoth 11:6

ἄοπλος Mos 1:172 Legat 229 Prov 2:58

ἀορασία Her 250 Somn 1:114 QG 4:40

ἀόρατος (113) Opif 12, 29, 31, 69, 135 Leg 3:206 Cher 98, 101, 101 Sacr 133, 133 Det 31, 31, 40, 86, 86, 89, 128 Post 15, 15 Gig 8 Deus 29 Plant 18 Ebr 86, 129, 132, 192 Conf 136, 138, 172 Migr 5, 51, 181, 183, 220 Her 75, 115, 115, 119, 170, 180, 259, 266, 280 Congr 25, 144 Fug 46, 46 Mut 7, 14, 139, 139 Somn 1:71, 72, 73, 73, 90, 111, 135, 148, 157, 164, 199, 210 Somn 2:2, 213, 252, 282, 291 Abr 69, 73, 74 Ios 255 Mos 1:158 Mos 2:37, 65, 76, 217, 217 Decal 33, 44, 59, 60, 120 Spec 1:18, 20, 46, 46, 50, 72, 137, 279, 302 Spec 2:165, 185 Spec 4:31, 31, 192 Virt 47, 57, 172 Prob 111 Contempl 78 Aet 19, 69 Legat 2, 290, 310, 318 QG 2:11, 28, 64c QE 2:37

ἀόργητος Praem 77

ἀόριστος (10) Post 116 Conf 117 Spec 1:48 Spec 2:221 Spec 4:122 Praem 36, 36, 85 Aet 103 QG 1:1

ἀόρμητος Deus 41

'Αουίλλιος Flacc 1

ἀπαγγέλλω (15) Leg 2:62 Leg 3:120 Plant 78 Migr 78 Her 261 Fug 7 Mos 1:3, 84, 179, 232, 250 Flacc 119 Legat 186, 197, 226

ἀπαγόρευσις (22) Leg 1:93, 93, 94, 94 Deus 53 Ebr 91 Her 173 Congr 120 Fug 100, 105 Mos 2:4, 46, 47, 51 Decal 51, 121, 170, 176 Spec 1:23, 299 Spec 4:39, 183

ἀπαγορευτικός Conf 141 Fug 104 Ios 29

ἀπαγορεύω (55) Leg 1:48, 93, 94, 101 Leg 3:22, 56 Ebr 138, 138 Migr 130 Fug 95, 98, 193 Ios 190 Mos 1:14, 37, 38, 112 Mos 2:4, 187, 219 Decal 39, 138, 142 Spec 1:38, 64, 223 Spec 2:67, 90 Spec 3:9, 110, 160, 174, 204 Spec 4:104, 183, 196, 203, 214 Virt 82, 134, 146 Praem 29, 55, 55, 55, 139, 155 Prob 47, 110 Contempl 1, 55 Flacc 181 Legat 299 Prov 2:63 QE 2:4

ἀπάγω (50) Leg 3:21 Cher 100 Sacr 26 Det 14, 54 Deus 112 Ebr 66 Conf 160, 161 Fug 83, 84, 102 Somn 1:174 Somn 2:84 Ios 35, 52, 80, 85, 104, 154, 220, 247 Mos 1:49, 243, 282, 285, 311 Mos 2:199, 201, 217 Decal 13, 15, 32 Spec 1:301 Spec 3:26, 90, 141, 159 Virt 96,

117 Praem 164 Prob 37, 114 Aet 82 Flacc 35, 72, 85, 115 Legat 186 Hypoth 7:2

ἀπαγωγή Flacc 121 Legat 17

ἀπᾴδω (9) Opif 133 Post 1, 51 Deus 90 Plant 35 Ebr 196 Conf 150 Abr 5, 222

ἀπαθανατίζω (10) Opif 44, 77 Det 111 Post 123 Conf 149 Somn 1:36 Mos 2:288 Spec 4:14 Virt 14 QG 1:51

ἀπάθεια (6) Leg 2:100, 102 Leg 3:129, 131 Plant 98 Abr 257

ἀπαθής (19) Opif 101 Det 46 Conf 12 Her 184, 204, 312, 314 Abr 145 Ios 13 Mos 1:65 Mos 2:59 Decal 150 Spec 4:83, 93 Aet 21 Legat 328, 371 QG 2:15a, 64b

ἀπαιδαγώγητος Cher 71 Sacr 23 Det 145 Fug 9

ἀπαιδευσία (33) Leg 3:2, 20, 33, 121, 148, 193 Post 52 Ebr 6, 11, 12, 27, 125, 137, 138, 140, 141, 143, 153, 154 Migr 136 Her 210 Congr 88 Fug 14, 121, 152 Somn 1:225 Somn 2:213, 259 Ios 53, 79, 249 Prob 12 QE 2:25c

ἀπαίδευτος Det 143, 175 Ebr 13 Somn 2:260

ἀπαιδία Ios 187 Spec 1:11 QG 3:20b

ἀπαίρω (14) Det 5, 27 Fug 21, 127, 131 Somn 1:172, 188 Abr 62, 92 Ios 169, 233 Mos 1:286 Flacc 26 Legat 179

ἄπαις Spec 1:129

ἀπαιτέω (7) Migr 91 Ios 227 Spec 3:140 Spec 4:31 Legat 28, 275 Hypoth 7:20

ἀπαιωρέω (10) Post 26 Agr 75 Conf 38 Fug 152 Mos 1:231 Mos 2:121 Spec 1:93 Spec 3:114 Prob 158 Contempl 51

ἀπακριβόομαι Opif 138 Legat 274

ἀπάλαμνος Opif 104

ἀπαλγέω Praem 135

ἀπαλείφω (10) Leg 1:100 Leg 3:187 Deus 20, 51 Somn 1:244 Abr 19 Spec 3:62 Flacc 131 QG 1:94, 2:15b

ἀπαλλαγή (16) Leg 3:87, 177, 178 Her 275 Abr 96, 128 Ios 263 Mos 1:314 Spec 1:4, 77, 195 Spec 2:95 Spec 3:80 Virt 115 Aet 129 QG 4:67

ἀπαλλάσσω (46) Leg 1:108 Leg 3:128 Sacr 117, 130 Post 23 Plant 14 Ebr 71 Migr 34 Congr 65, 66 Fug 5, 37, 55 Mut 80, 219, 243, 261 Somn 1:70 Somn 2:229 Abr 30 Ios 25, 170, 184, 224, 233 Mos 1:22, 191 Spec 1:105 Spec 2:85, 106, 139, 253 Spec 3:27, 30, 62, 63, 82, 107 Spec 4:4, 15, 196 Virt 68 Prob 156 Legat 337, 367 QG 2:68a

ἀπαλόνυχος Virt 130

ἀπαλός (13) Post 165 Her 38, 125 Mut 212 Somn 1:199 Somn 2:10 Abr 108 Spec 1:313 Spec 4:25 Virt 178 Prob 160 QG 4:200a QE 2:4

ἀπαμπίσχω (10) Ebr 6 Fug 158 Somn 1:98, 216 Ios 14, 185, 238 Spec 3:121 Spec 4:185 Prov 2:35

ἀπαμφιάζω (14) Leg 2:53, 54 Cher 17 Sacr 30 Gig 53 Deus 56, 103 Ebr 34 Mut 199 Somn 2:170 Abr 102 Spec 3:61 Virt 111 Prov 2:17

ἀπαμφιέννυμι Leg 3:153

ἀπαναγκάζω Abr 213

ἀπανθρακίζω Somn 2:50

ἀπανθρωπία (9) Ios 81 Mos 1:95 Spec 2:75, 93, 146, 167 Spec 3:110, 167 Spec 4:4

ἀπανίστημι Abr 86, 258

ἀπανταχοῦ Spec 4:179 Virt 64 Hypoth 7:9

ἀπαντάω (36) Opif 80 Leg 3:202 Cher 33 Det 36, 120 Deus 38 Conf 6, 59, 116 Migr 82, 84 Her 261 Somn 1:4, 61, 71, 71, 116, 118 Somn 2:142 Abr 250 Ios 78, 256 Mos 1:214, 285 Spec 2:109 Virt 88 Praem 107 Prob 25, 99 Contempl 66, 79 Aet 132 Legat 122, 322, 336 Prov 2:24

ἀπάντησις Deus 166

ἀπαντλέω Gig 25 Her 31

ἀπάντλησις Post 164

ἅπαξ (63) Opif 168 Leg 2:54 Leg 3:51 Cher 3 Sacr 127 Det 41, 149, 178 Post 163 Gig 33, 52, 60 Deus 4, 82, 82 Agr 8, 104, 105 Ebr 42, 136, 169, 198 Migr 40, 137 Congr 4 Fug 101 Mut 119, 247 Somn 1:62, 77 Somn 2:88 Ios 179 Mos 1:46, 183, 283, 326 Mos 2:65, 258 Decal 96, 99 Spec 1:59, 72, 261 Spec 2:146, 183 Spec 4:26, 85 Praem 6, 72 Contempl 19 Aet 42, 59, 68, 91 Flacc 180 Legat 58, 77, 218, 303, 306, 356 Prov 2:70 QE 2:17

ἁπαξάπας Aet 37, 144

ἀπαξιόω (6) Post 96, 164 Somn 2:174 Mos 2:238 Spec 1:308 Aet 2

ἀπαράβατος Aet 112

ἀπαράδεκτος Agr 71 Fug 117

ἀπαραίτητος (32) Det 136 Post 9 Gig 47 Deus 48, 68 Agr 98, 117 Ebr 135 Conf 116 Migr 225 Fug 99 Somn 1:236 Somn 2:88, 293 Ios 21, 170 Mos 1:45, 89, 303 Spec 1:55, 338 Spec 3:42, 76 Spec 4:19 Praem 149 Legat 192, 212, 218, 244, 307, 336 QG 3:52

ἀπαράλλακτος Ebr 90, 169

ἀπαράσκευος Sacr 32 Prov 2:58

ἀπαρέσκω QG 4:88

ἀπαρηγόρητος (8) Mos 2:245 Decal 63, 95 Spec 2:134 Spec 3:129 Spec 4:3, 82 Praem 94

ἀπαρνέομαι Hypoth 7:4

ἀπαρρησίαστος Her 29 Praem 124

ἀπαρτάω (8) Opif 141 Leg 2:78 Gig 56 Agr 3 Mut 53 Spec 1:68 Spec 3:182 Aet 105

ἀπάρτησις Det 90 Conf 67

ἀπαρχή (95) Sacr 72, 72, 74, 107, 108, 109, 117, 136 Conf 124 Her 113, 113, 253 Congr 7, 89, 98 Mut 2, 191, 191, 192 Somn 2:75, 77, 272 Abr 196 Ios 194 Mos 1:252, 254, 316, 316, 317, 318 Mos 2:137 Decal 160 Spec 1:77, 77, 78, 78, 117, 120, 126, 128, 129, 132, 133, 138, 139, 147, 151, 152, 152, 153, 183, 213, 216, 252, 255, 279 Spec 2:41, 120, 134, 162, 162, 167, 168, 171, 171, 175, 175, 179, 179, 184, 186, 216, 219, 221, 222 Spec 4:98, 99, 99, 125, 180 Virt 95, 159 Prob 15 Legat 156, 157, 216, 291, 311, 312, 316 QG isf 17, 17, 17 QE 2:50b, 50b

ἀπάρχομαι (30) Sacr 74 Post 97 Congr 95, 96, 96, 101 Mut 2, 191 Somn 2:6, 76, 148 Mos 1:254, 254 Mos 2:137 Spec 1:78, 133, 134, 137, 141, 157, 248, 255 Spec 2:175, 175, 180 Spec 4:98 Virt 95 Legat 157 QG 1:64b QE 2:50b

ἅπας (πᾶς) (749) Opif 17, 38, 38, 39, 40, 42, 45, 48, 69, 69, 77, 78, 78, 79, 79, 84, 88, 99, 100, 111, 121, 126, 128, 137, 140, 146, 148, 150, 171 Leg 1:5, 23, 28, 61, 104, 106 Leg 2:13, 15, 39, 63, 93, 108 Leg 3:21, 25, 29, 29, 35, 57, 86, 138, 140, 183, 229 Cher

24, 32, 39, 46, 56, 57, 66, 70, 76, 86, 91, 96, 97, 105, 113, 117, 119, 119, 121, 122, 123 Sacr 29, 35, 38, 41, 46, 47, 49, 59, 70, 75, 82, 92, 97, 98, 99, 118, 132 Det 15, 29, 34, 39, 42, 55, 63, 68, 87, 99, 116, 125, 131, 145, 147, 150, 151, 157, 164, 173, 176 Post 7, 42, 72, 74, 80, 80, 93, 99, 99, 139, 143, 150, 158, 162, 163, 166, 170, 181, 185 Gig 18, 60 Deus 3, 17, 22, 36, 45, 69, 80, 107, 116, 118, 125, 126, 127, 132, 135, 148, 150, 153, 179 Agr 8, 9, 18, 22, 24, 24, 41, 44, 52, 53, 60, 78, 88, 104, 120, 139, 143, 147 Plant 6, 14, 30, 31, 33, 48, 55, 56, 58, 77, 79, 93, 108, 132, 134, 135 Ebr 37, 42, 71, 87, 89, 90, 92, 110, 136, 156, 175, 195, 202, 220, 224 Sobr 10, 13, 20, 57 Conf 11, 23, 25, 46, 48, 54, 58, 91, 98, 112, 126, 161 Migr 3, 10, 13, 40, 46, 50, 88, 119, 121, 122, 125, 137, 151, 180, 201, 217, 218, 219 Her 23, 97, 110, 110, 130, 151, 152, 152, 174, 199, 223, 225, 226, 236, 244, 274, 277, 280, 291, 298, 300, 311 Congr 58, 107, 121, 156, 172 Fug 29, 30, 46, 51, 101, 112, 147, 164, 174, 191, 210 Mut 26, 40, 90, 164, 178, 185, 254, 263, 264 Somn 1:11, 53, 83, 91, 130, 149, 157, 158, 159, 176, 176, 192, 205 Somn 2:13, 24, 32, 41, 66, 153, 164, 170, 248, 270, 293 Abr 6, 14, 20, 23, 25, 28, 40, 44, 52, 57, 74, 83, 86, 96, 103, 116, 127, 138, 140, 147, 150, 162, 199, 230, 234, 242, 268 Ios 20, 28, 33, 49, 55, 60, 65, 85, 106, 122, 135, 147, 147, 153, 157, 162, 165, 172, 175, 177, 178, 208, 213, 216, 229, 236, 238, 239, 240, 246, 250, 258, 263, 267 Mos 1:32, 39, 67, 69, 71, 74, 84, 85, 100, 107, 110, 111, 127, 134, 136, 139, 148, 148, 149, 168, 176, 193, 196, 198, 201, 209, 228, 233, 239, 246, 250, 263, 264, 308, 325, 327, 329, 332 Mos 2:9, 17, 17, 20, 22, 27, 36, 50, 54, 62, 62, 65, 90, 121, 131, 142, 143, 151, 152, 153, 159, 165, 167, 170, 179, 179, 189, 194, 225, 241, 247, 255, 291 Decal 7, 41, 60, 64, 76, 88, 127, 132, 134, 161, 172 Spec 1:9, 13, 52, 55, 56, 59, 77, 79, 89, 97, 100, 109, 111, 112, 134, 142, 147, 151, 151, 152, 152, 154, 154, 154, 156, 162, 168, 168, 189, 229, 259, 262, 269, 283, 289, 300, 303, 304, 320, 332, 336, 340, 345 Spec 2:42, 42, 46, 62, 95, 101, 104, 111, 117, 121, 125, 138, 139, 142, 143, 144, 145, 153, 156, 157, 162, 163, 163, 164, 173, 186, 188, 195, 203, 204, 236, 239, 248, 250 Spec 3:2, 11, 23, 33, 36, 37, 41, 47, 56, 58, 69, 108, 128, 138, 152, 179, 184, 192 Spec 4:4, 23, 55, 66, 84, 87, 98, 132, 138, 157, 160, 161, 174, 175, 176, 186, 191, 219, 222 Virt 23, 27, 42, 47, 48, 51, 66, 70, 77, 100, 122, 122, 123, 153, 171, 173, 177, 179, 186, 206, 209, 216, 219, 222 Praem 3, 8, 9, 26, 26, 34, 58, 60, 60, 76, 78, 90, 119, 119, 121, 125, 135, 170 Prob 4, 30, 32, 38, 41, 49, 50, 77, 93, 104, 113, 119, 132, 141, 154 Contempl 1, 1, 4, 47, 54, 70, 75, 78, 79 Aet 11, 20, 26, 31, 45, 60, 62, 65, 69, 70, 75, 99, 102, 111, 123, 128, 146, 147 Flacc 23, 27, 28, 43, 44, 65, 84, 112, 117, 130, 132, 133, 137, 142, 144, 148, 151, 151, 167, 172, 190 Legat 11, 33, 33, 43, 67, 73, 74, 75, 81, 90, 101, 108, 124, 134, 143, 147, 147, 151, 157, 164, 174, 184, 190, 190, 196, 201, 207, 210, 211, 212, 213, 214, 223, 231, 232, 243, 252, 265, 279, 279, 295, 297, 306, 327, 335, 346, 352, 354, 355, 358, 373 Hypoth 6:2, 6:4, 6:9, 7:3, 7:3, 11:4, 11:12, 11:13 Prov 1, 2:1, 6, 12, 18, 37, 40, 40, 43, 69, 70 QG 2:13a, 15c, 34a, 64b, 71a, 4:51b, 67 QG (Par) 2:3 QE 2:17, 38a, 64 QE isf 16

ἀπαστράπτω (8) Cher 62 Det 118 Deus 78, 96 Fug 139 Mos 1:66 Mos 2:70, 254

ἀπατάω (69) Leg 3:59, 61, 61, 61, 63, 66, 66, 121, 190, 230 Sacr 28, 77, 85 Det 61 Gig 17, 41 Deus 113 Agr 42, 164 Ebr 65, 147, 183 Conf 65, 126 Migr 12, 83, 83 Her 71, 303 Fug 34 Mut 198, 201, 208, 240 Somn 1:224 Somn 2:39, 101, 133 Abr 88 Ios 93, 142 Mos 1:182, 195, 282, 301 Decal 141, 172 Spec 1:26, 315 Spec 2:112 Spec 3:72, 81, 101 Spec 4:53, 57, 188 Virt 180 Aet 117 Flacc 13, 172 Legat 28, 40, 62, 111, 163, 180 Prov 1, 2:31 QG isf 2

ἀπατεών (6) Sacr 32 Conf 140 Her 85, 185 Mos 1:90 QG 4:206a

ἀπάτη (53) Opif 155, 165 Leg 3:64, 66 Sacr 22, 26, 76 Det 27, 38, 61 Gig 15, 59 Deus 66 Agr 13, 16, 43, 96 Plant 104 Ebr 46, 217 Sobr 15 Conf 54 Congr 18 Somn 2:40 Abr 101 Ios 56 Mos 1:43, 94, 235, 280 Decal 3, 55, 125 Spec 1:10, 29 Spec 4:50, 89, 109 Virt 196, 214, 214 Praem 24, 129, 147 Prob 56, 66, 151 Aet 132 Flacc 109 QG 4:228, 228 QE 2:9a, 14

ἀπατηλός (6) Fug 22, 208 Prob 155 Aet 77 Prov 2:15, 36

ἀπαύγαζω Abr 119

ἀπαύγασμα Opif 146 Plant 50 Spec 4:123

ἀπαυθαδίζομαι Virt 210

ἄπαυστος (29) Opif 33 Sacr 39 Det 55, 89, 174 Post 13, 167 Plant 89, 93, 135 Her 16 Somn 1:36 Somn 2:200 Abr 29, 43, 138 Ios 246 Mos 1:121 Decal 57 Spec 1:27, 169 Spec 3:10 Spec 4:113 Praem 135 Prob 56 Flacc 9 Legat 13, 198, 243

ἀπαυτοματίζω (18) Opif 149 Leg 3:30 Ebr 199 Fug 171 Mut 166, 219, 257 Mos 1:320 Decal 16 Spec 1:35 Spec 2:105, 107 Spec 3:189 Virt 97 Praem 42 Aet 63 QG 2:34a, 2:34b

ἀπαυχενίζω (13) Agr 34 Ebr 93 Conf 54 Her 245 Abr 135, 212, 228 Spec 1:304 Spec 2:232 Spec 4:220 Virt 113 Aet 30 QG 2:64c

ἀπεῖδον (ἀφοράω) (30) Opif 55 Deus 108, 146 Plant 65 Ebr 150 Sobr 11 Mut 164 Somn 1:203 Abr 71, 173 Ios 117 Mos 1:212 Mos 2:51 Decal 9 Spec 1:41, 139, 294 Spec 2:32, 56, 104, 244 Spec 3:102, 164 Spec 4:95 Virt 32 Prob 28 Aet 4 Prov 2:14 QG 2:26b QG (Par) 2:4

ἀπείθεια Ebr 15, 15

ἀπειθέω (11) Leg 1:96 Deus 50 Agr 70, 166 Ebr 14, 16, 18, 18 Migr 174 Mut 206 QG 4:88

ἀπειθής (20) Sacr 32 Agr 88 Ebr 14, 16, 17, 17, 29, 93, 95 Congr 61 Fug 39 Mos 1:43 Mos 2:261 Spec 1:106 Spec 2:66 Spec 4:24 Virt 15, 109, 141, 208

ἀπεικάζω (30) Leg 1:15, 22, 24, 83 Leg 2:11, 81, 99 Leg 3:46, 76 Sacr 104 Det 114 Agr 14, 31, 89, 175 Ebr 87, 112, 155, 222 Conf 30 Migr 104 Her 47, 127, 197, 307 Mut 74 Somn 1:238 Somn 2:255 Decal 8 Spec 2:30

ἀπεικονίζω (14) Opif 16, 69 Leg 3:96 Cher 86 Det 78 Deus 110 Plant 19, 20 Fug 5, 100 Mos 2:74 Spec 4:164 Contempl 88 QG 2:62

ἀπεικόνισμα (24) Opif 16, 139 Leg 1:45 Leg 3:96 Det 83, 160 Post 105 Ebr 90 Her 112, 231 Somn 1:214 Mos 2:11, 117, 127 Decal 134 Spec 1:47, 84 Spec 2:2, 151, 224 Virt 12 Praem 65 Prob 94 Legat 318

ἀπεικός ἀπέοικα

ἀπειλέω (23) Leg 3:84 Det 45 Deus 144, 166 Ebr 102 Conf 188 Fug 23, 39 Ios 68, 170, 224 Mos 1:46, 242, 243 Spec 1:301 Spec 2:81 Prob 125, 144, 145, 153 Legat 304 QG 1:94 QE isf 30

ἀπειλή (21) Opif 128, 128 Det 46 Deus 64, 68 Plant 10 Ebr 32, 102 Conf 116 Somn 2:96 Ios 222 Spec 2:83, 232

Spec 4:72 Virt 5, 124 Prob 25, 144 Legat 262, 276 QG 2:17b

ἄπειμι (25) Cher 72 Sacr 124 Deus 177 Agr 36, 147 Ebr 183 Conf 134 Her 186, 269 Abr 258 Ios 169, 187, 190, 193 Mos 1:10, 12 Decal 149 Spec 1:295 Spec 4:80 Virt 9 Praem 6 Prob 138 Aet 38 Flacc 162 QG 3:11c

ἀπεῖπον (26) Opif 23 Leg 3:190 Cher 15 Sacr 17 Det 29, 32 Mut 204, 231 Somn 1:164 Mos 1:263 Decal 138, 141 Spec 2:182 Spec 3:13, 22, 24, 47, 117, 168 Spec 4:95, 100, 205 Virt 18 Prob 27, 112 Prov 2:64

ἀπειράκις Her 190, 235

ἀπείργω Leg 3:246

ἀπειρία (13) Opif 47 Leg 1:35, 73 Cher 55 Det 41 Deus 134, 152 Conf 12, 144 Fug 27 Decal 27 QG 2:12b, 12b

ἀπειροκαλία Ios 205 Contempl 52

ἀπειρόκαλος Sacr 32 Prov 2:46

ἀπειρομεγέθης Her 227 Mut 179 Somn 1:42 Aet 103

ἄπειρος (52) Opif 60, 60, 171, 171 Leg 1:35 Leg 2:19 Leg 3:105, 170, 171, 202 Cher 66 Det 76 Post 18, 108 Gig 2 Deus 122, 129 Agr 31, 92, 160 Plant 53, 67, 144 Ebr 199 Her 154, 190, 228, 235 Congr 111, 120 Mut 49 Abr 162 Ios 195, 225 Mos 1:229 Decal 29 Spec 1:48, 329 Spec 3:189 Spec 4:80 Prob 51, 52 Aet 102, 119, 132 Legat 30, 85, 163, 164, 198, 215 QG 4:76b

ἀπελαύνω (23) Leg 3:1, 1, 171 Cher 96 Det 163 Post 20 Agr 161 Ebr 104 Conf 144 Migr 69, 183 Her 26, 87, 179 Congr 171 Fug 74 Abr 32, 210 Decal 119 Spec 1:344 Praem 153 Flacc 15 Prov 2:57

ἀπελέγχω (8) Det 10, 71 Migr 225 Spec 2:26 Virt 213 Aet 107 Flacc 141, 141

ἀπελευθεριάζω (12) Opif 87 Sacr 104 Deus 29 Ebr 101 Conf 98 Abr 213 Ios 66 Decal 163 Spec 2:97 Spec 3:177 Prob 104 Aet 74

ἀπελεύθερος Deus 48 Prob 157 Flacc 112 Legat 272

ἀπελευθερόω Legat 155

Ἀπελλῆς Legat 203, 204, 205

ἀπελπίζω Praem 88

ἀπεμπολέω Spec 4:17 Prob 122

ἀπέναντι Cher 1 Post 24, 32 Somn 1:89

ἀπέοικα (ἀπεικός) Somn 2:211

ἀπεραντολόγος Det 130

ἀπέραντος Congr 53 Abr 20, 110 Aet 102

ἀπέρατος Migr 100 Her 212 Fug 57 Ios 137

ἀπεργάζομαι (97) Opif 16, 33 Leg 2:13 Leg 3:19, 70, 109, 156, 251 Cher 94, 103 Sacr 80, 108 Det 15, 60, 98, 113, 146, 154 Post 4, 85 Deus 25 Agr 16, 66, 142 Plant 16, 28, 40, 171 Ebr 89, 98 Conf 89 Migr 116 Somn 1:29, 106, 200 Abr 136, 150 Ios 47, 88, 112, 142 Mos 1:200 Mos 2:93, 211 Decal 131, 151 Spec 1:29, 54, 99, 123, 146, 192, 217, 254, 335 Spec 2:39, 48, 75, 192 Spec 3:11, 25, 28, 194 Spec 4:5, 10, 82, 86, 112, 118, 146, 166, 190, 207, 237 Virt 14, 39, 44, 70, 90, 103, 116, 155, 170, 178 Praem 97, 121, 138 Prob 79, 88, 159 Contempl 23 Aet 67 Flacc 132 Legat 91, 100, 237, 246

ἀπερίγραφος (23) Opif 23 Leg 1:20 Sacr 59, 59, 124 Post 19, 151, 174 Conf 162 Her 31, 131, 190, 212 Somn 1:12, 175 Abr 71 Ios 29, 113 Spec 2:164, 221 Spec 3:151 Spec 4:96 Praem 85

ἀπερικάθαρτος (6) Plant 95, 113, 113, 113, 114, 115

ἀπερίληπτος (6) Plant 151 Her 229 Abr 159 Mos 1:311 Spec 2:164 Virt 35

ἀπεριμάχητος Opif 11

ἀπερινόητος Fug 141 Mut 15

ἀπεριόριστος Sacr 124

ἀπερίσκεπτος (15) Sacr 32 Agr 176 Ebr 85, 108, 195 Migr 45 Fug 125 Mut 147 Somn 2:103 Ios 51 Spec 3:79 Spec 4:26 Contempl 14 Aet 146 QG 2:72

ἀπερίτμητος Migr 224 Spec 1:304

ἀπερυγγάνω Somn 1:122

ἀπέρχομαι (16) Leg 3:253 Migr 1, 3, 7, 9, 10 Her 275, 276, 277, 277 Somn 1:70, 189 Ios 17, 126 Legat 367 QG 3:11a

ἀπερῶ (28) Leg 3:8, 110 Deus 66 Ebr 2 Conf 37 Congr 164, 169 Somn 2:67 Mos 1:170 Spec 1:249 Spec 2:9, 65 Spec 4:74, 120, 170 Virt 6, 34 Prob 26 Contempl 55 Flacc 10, 128 Legat 209, 362, 366, 372 Prov 2:27 QE 2:3a, 9b

ἀπεσθίω Plant 160

ἀπευθύνω Opif 3 Mos 2:138 Spec 1:188

ἀπευκταῖος Ios 187 Contempl 56

ἀπευκτός (6) Det 148 Agr 40 Ios 9, 21 Mos 2:245 Spec 2:131

ἀπεύχομαι Decal 75 Legat 345

ἀπεχθάνομαι Ebr 87 Mut 170 Flacc 146 Legat 346

ἀπέχθεια Flacc 29, 128 Legat 373

ἀπεχθής Mut 168

ἀπέχθομαι Ios 167 Contempl 69 Legat 211, 293

ἀπέχω (31) Opif 170 Leg 1:102 Leg 2:88 Leg 3:154 Post 71 Agr 91, 113 Mut 47 Somn 1:36 Somn 2:257 Abr 28, 253 Ios 256 Mos 1:308 Decal 45 Spec 2:15, 94, 198 Spec 3:12, 21, 21 Spec 4:129, 202 Virt 126, 140, 163 Contempl 82 Legat 131, 361 Prov 2:63, 70

ἀπήμων (9) Gig 10 Sobr 5 Conf 153 Migr 119 Her 35, 184 Fug 112 Somn 1:149 Spec 1:224

ἀπήνη Ios 251

ἀπηχέω Somn 2:259 Ios 21

ἀπιστέω (21) Sacr 93 Migr 140 Her 93, 251 Mut 188 Abr 269, 269 Ios 17 Mos 1:74, 76, 212, 236 Mos 2:69, 177, 261 Virt 153, 188 Praem 49, 150 Prob 5 Legat 67

ἀπιστία (21) Leg 3:164 Sacr 22 Deus 101 Ebr 40 Conf 57 Her 95 Fug 152 Mut 181, 201 Ios 19, 30 Mos 1:90 Mos 2:269, 280 Decal 84, 172 Spec 1:273 Spec 2:8 Spec 4:32 Praem 28 Legat 118

ἄπιστος (29) Opif 114 Leg 3:164 Sacr 32, 32 Ebr 78, 205 Conf 48 Her 93, 302 Somn 1:12 Somn 2:44 Abr 60, 111 Ios 252 Mos 1:200, 231, 264 Mos 2:166, 253, 280 Spec 2:252 Spec 4:60, 137, 155 Virt 223 Prob 27 Legat 3, 73, 339

ἀπλανής (55) Opif 28, 31, 54, 70, 113, 147 Leg 3:99 Cher 21, 22, 22, 23 Det 84 Agr 43 Plant 12 Conf 140 Her 208, 233 Congr 104, 108 Fug 119 Mut 67, 179 Somn 1:21 Abr 69, 158 Ios 142, 147 Mos 1:166, 212 Mos 2:237 Decal 52, 53, 81, 102, 103, 104 Spec 1:13, 17, 34, 210 Spec 2:45, 151, 255, 259 Spec 3:187, 189 Spec 4:155 Praem 41 Contempl 5 Aet 10, 46, 83 Flacc 26 Legat 2 QG 2:34a ἄπλαστος (17) Leg 3:2 Sacr 26, 45 Det 93 Plant 44, 44 Migr 106 Congr 61, 62 Somn 2:140 Spec 2:235 Spec 3:101, 108 Spec 4:71 Praem 162, 166 Prob 155

ἀπλατής Opif 49 Her 131 Congr 147

ἄπλετος Det 173 Prov 2:71

ἀπλήρωτος Leg 3:148 Sacr 23 Ebr 220 Mos 2:185 Legat 14

ἀπληστία (18) Opif 54, 159 Det 103 Post 98 Agr 58 Ebr 4, 6, 22 Somn 2:211 Abr 104 Spec 1:150 Spec 2:197 Spec 4:100, 100 Contempl 55 Aet 74 QG (Par) 2:7, 2:7

ἄπληστος (43) Leg 2:87 Leg 3:39, 148, 184 Cher 92 Sacr 32 Det 25, 101 Post 174 Gig 31 Deus 154 Agr 34, 36, 101 Plant 23, 148 Ebr 122, 222 Conf 154 Her 29, 100, 136 Fug 31 Somn 1:50 Somn 2:147 Abr 149 Ios 93, 256 Spec 3:1, 9 Spec 4:94, 113, 129 Virt 9 Praem 135, 156 Prob 71 Contempl 9, 74 Aet 128 Legat 89 Prov 2:18 QG 4:200a

ἁπλότης Opif 156, 170 Mos 1:172

ἁπλοῦς (53) Leg 2:2 Leg 3:101, 140, 178, 236 Cher 121 Post 114 Deus 56, 82, 104 Agr 140, 140, 141 Plant 44, 65, 111 Ebr 76, 78, 135, 162, 174, 189, 190, 192, 211 Sobr 58 Conf 192 Migr 153 Her 21 Congr 36, 143 Fug 164 Mut 184 Somn 1:8, 45, 63, 79 Somn 2:156 Abr 77 Spec 1:299 Contempl 65, 82 Flacc 12, 90, 128 Legat 36, 207, 261 Hypoth 7:1, 7:6 QG 1:77, 77, 4:8a

ἄπλωτος Somn 2:143, 180 Mos 1:172 Spec 1:301 Prob 67

ἀπνευστί (18) Agr 115, 177 Plant 160 Her 201 Congr 64 Fug 97 Mut 61, 117 Somn 2:81, 180 Abr 183 Ios 181 Mos 1:44 Mos 2:251, 254 Contempl 76 Flacc 188 QE isf 26

ἀπό (1298) Opif 12, 13, 17, 31, 31, 32, 33, 41, 47, 52, 62, 67, 68, 72, 72, 77, 78, 79, 91, 92, 93, 93, 94, 96, 96, 101, 101, 101, 101, 101, 102, 102, 102, 106, 106, 127, 127, 128, 131, 134, 135, 135, 141, 147, 148, 156, 158, 163, 167, 171 Leg 1:3, 9, 15, 16, 18, 31, 37, 42, 59, 64, 64, 66, 90, 90, 90, 90, 97, 97, 97, 97, 100, 100, 100, 100, 101, 101, 105, 105, 107 Leg 2:18, 18, 54, 55, 77, 78, 86, 87, 88, 90, 90, 96, 105 Leg 3:1, 8, 12, 13, 14, 16, 19, 19, 20, 23, 24, 24, 27, 27, 29, 39, 47, 56, 58, 60, 61, 62, 65, 65, 94, 97, 100, 100, 100, 102, 102, 107, 107, 111, 129, 130, 130, 133, 136, 137, 145, 145, 147, 165, 172, 183, 183, 185, 186, 188, 193, 200, 210, 210, 210, 210, 212, 222, 222, 229, 235, 240, 241, 246, 252, 252, 253 Cher 2, 3, 10, 12, 13, 14, 15, 16, 22, 22, 22, 31, 33, 33, 41, 76, 99, 106, 127 Sacr 4, 8, 12, 19, 25, 33, 37, 47, 47, 50, 52, 52, 52, 70, 71, 72, 72, 74, 77, 77, 88, 88, 98, 101, 107, 107, 107, 107, 108, 110, 131, 136, 136, 136, 138 Det 1, 9, 10, 12, 40, 53, 54, 63, 63, 88, 92, 96, 98, 98, 98, 100, 107, 114, 118, 121, 121, 121, 122, 127, 141, 150, 150, 152, 152, 154, 156, 156, 163, 163, 163, 170, 174 Post 1, 4, 6, 9, 27, 44, 44, 45, 46, 48, 52, 64, 64, 69, 91, 97, 102, 102, 102, 111, 122, 122, 126, 127, 130, 133, 136, 136, 138, 140, 146, 153, 153, 159, 170, 173, 173, 173, 182 Gig 6, 22, 24, 25, 39 Deus 20, 35, 35, 40, 49, 51, 51, 51, 75, 79, 79, 84, 87, 93, 99, 120, 121, 121, 127, 132, 147 Agr 9, 10, 21, 25, 25, 30, 44, 72, 103, 138, 154, 167, 167, 169, 170, 180 Plant 3, 3, 9, 9, 16, 22, 56, 57, 71, 74, 76, 76, 76, 77, 103, 111, 111, 125, 145, 151, 154, 161, 163, 165 Ebr 8, 11, 12, 12, 15, 15, 24, 42, 51, 51, 72, 72, 72, 76, 89, 94, 100, 100, 100, 105, 105, 114, 131, 133, 148, 165, 166, 169, 170, 176, 188, 190, 191, 198, 221 Sobr 1, 19, 21, 23, 53, 53, 56, 57, 64, 65 Conf 1, 13, 23, 23, 27, 36, 42, 44, 51, 60, 65, 67, 70, 79, 93, 98, 106, 112, 118, 129, 157, 160, 161, 162, 175, 183, 197 Migr 3, 12, 13, 14, 15, 20, 25, 26, 30, 56, 62, 67, 76, 93, 101, 101, 115, 117, 117, 125, 130, 137, 156, 158, 165, 181, 183, 184, 185, 187, 195, 208, 225 Her 4, 19, 20, 23, 44, 61, 61, 84, 97, 98, 98, 98, 98, 102, 112, 117, 118, 119, 131, 134, 145, 149, 149, 156, 163, 184, 189, 190, 195, 198, 201, 202, 207, 231, 239, 239, 241, 251, 251, 252, 253, 255, 269, 271, 274, 277, 279, 279, 282, 284, 284, 284, 289, 289, 315, 315, 316, 316, 316 Congr 22, 22, 25, 30, 36, 48, 48, 50, 56, 57, 60, 65, 69, 83, 90, 90, 95, 95, 95, 96, 96, 99, 99, 99, 99, 101, 106, 106, 109, 110, 111, 122, 135, 150, 152, 173 Fug 1, 1, 2, 7, 13, 53, 59, 64, 78, 83, 88, 116, 137, 140, 154, 156, 166, 176, 176, 182, 186, 192, 192, 194, 202, 210 Mut 2, 2, 5, 8, 16, 22, 33, 36, 38, 48, 62, 65, 67, 69, 69, 72, 76, 76, 81, 83, 92, 105, 117, 117, 146, 150, 164, 171, 175, 175, 175, 179, 179, 191, 200, 201, 211, 228, 234, 246, 256, 258, 258, 259, 259, 259, 259, 265, 270 Somn 1:4, 4, 5, 29, 35, 41, 42, 42, 42, 49, 57, 57, 70, 70, 81, 89, 96, 102, 103, 117, 120, 134, 151, 167, 176, 178, 187, 187, 188, 188, 192, 201, 202, 204, 205, 205, 208, 220, 240 Somn 2:6, 6, 6, 9, 27, 42, 42, 52, 58, 71, 73, 74, 75, 79, 88, 91, 91, 110, 112, 119, 133, 142, 150, 198, 204, 210, 210, 221, 233, 242, 255, 257, 257, 257, 257, 257, 258, 267, 272 Abr 1, 10, 11, 12, 17, 26, 36, 53, 60, 62, 62, 67, 67, 67, 71, 72, 76, 76, 77, 99, 113, 119, 130, 134, 156, 157, 157, 157, 161, 164, 171, 176, 186, 189, 203, 205, 217, 218, 223, 251, 258 Ios 6, 15, 32, 44, 71, 71, 84, 93, 121, 161, 189, 217, 218, 224, 228, 240 Mos 1:4, 5, 7, 8, 15, 16, 21, 21, 34, 37, 51, 59, 59, 65, 77, 83, 84, 84, 98, 99, 106, 112, 115, 120, 127, 128, 129, 129, 131, 133, 134, 135, 136, 144, 149, 163, 164, 181, 181, 187, 219, 237, 240, 244, 244, 253, 254, 259, 260, 266, 276, 278, 278, 285, 290, 293, 300, 302, 303, 310, 313 Mos 2:2, 14, 19, 20, 29, 29, 48, 60, 63, 68, 69, 69, 74, 77, 79, 85, 101, 117, 118, 118, 121, 127, 127, 138, 148, 150, 154, 158, 170, 171, 172, 180, 183, 196, 196, 202, 216, 230, 231, 246, 263, 264, 266, 266 Decal 14, 16, 31, 46, 58, 60, 74, 77, 77, 78, 81, 89, 96, 121, 153, 160, 173 Spec 1:1, 4, 12, 28, 37, 48, 51, 54, 61, 68, 69, 74, 77, 85, 102, 103, 103, 111, 115, 131, 132, 134, 134, 136, 137, 137, 141, 142, 144, 145, 145, 145, 145, 145, 147, 147, 157, 160, 166, 178, 183, 198, 207, 218, 232, 232, 235, 248, 255, 255, 257, 257, 262, 263, 268, 286, 294, 296, 298, 298, 303, 309, 317, 318, 325, 333, 337, 344 Spec 2:21, 25, 28, 30, 33, 33, 33, 40, 40, 41, 42, 55, 56, 58, 60, 67, 72, 78, 82, 85, 121, 122, 128, 134, 140, 142, 145, 146, 147, 150, 152, 152, 153, 155, 162, 165, 168, 172, 176, 177, 182, 188, 189, 191, 200, 202, 207, 212, 213, 213, 215, 216, 219, 220, 220, 243, 253 Spec 3:2, 2, 5, 25, 48, 55, 57, 59, 59, 59, 73, 73, 91, 107, 123, 126, 126, 160, 162, 184, 188, 188 Spec 4:16, 19, 21, 53, 55, 56, 60, 73, 75, 83, 85, 98, 105, 110, 114, 115, 125, 128, 130, 140, 159, 160, 176, 178, 178, 194, 206, 233, 234, 234, 236 Virt 10, 34, 35, 54, 63, 72, 79, 79, 81, 82, 95, 95, 102, 102, 103, 120, 125, 132, 145, 147, 148, 148, 151, 187, 193, 203, 221 Praem 1, 7, 9, 28, 43, 46, 46, 46, 67, 84, 88, 91, 99, 117, 144, 163, 164, 168, 171, 172 Prob 10, 17, 17, 24, 24, 29, 51, 57, 59, 60, 60, 60, 61, 61, 62, 63, 76, 86, 94, 119, 125, 139, 157 Contempl 15, 23, 24, 24, 38, 39, 39, 68, 72 Aet 8, 15, 27, 29, 30, 33, 50, 50, 60, 63, 64, 64, 67, 67, 88, 88, 88, 89, 91, 106, 110, 110, 119, 119, 125, 132, 138, 143, 145 Flacc 9, 18, 22, 22, 26, 35, 41, 43, 44, 45, 45,

45, 50, 64, 74, 76, 92, 92, 104, 109, 115, 120, 137, 139, 144, 152, 155, 157 Legat 10, 15, 22, 37, 44, 48, 49, 54, 75, 89, 89, 89, 89, 99, 108, 108, 108, 123, 138, 144, 145, 156, 161, 165, 165, 173, 182, 185, 186, 200, 205, 219, 220, 222, 223, 225, 231, 245, 252, 252, 267, 288, 294, 310, 321, 346, 349, 364 Hypoth 0:1, 0:1, 6:1, 6:1, 6:1, 7:11, 7:16, 7:19, 11:16 Prov 2:23, 47, 48, 54, 59, 67 QG 1:1, 3, 27, 28, 60:1, 60:1, 74, 74, 97, 100:2b, 2:5a, 5a, 12c, 15a, 15a, 15a, 31, 3:11a, 23, 4:211 QG isf 17 QG (Par) 2:3, 2:3, 2:4, 2:4, 2:5, 2:5, 2:5, 2:7 QE 1:19, 2:18, 21, 24b QE isf 9

ἀποβαίνω (27) Opif 58 Leg 2:104 Sacr 125 Agr 76 Plant 161 Somn 2:2, 131, 141 Ios 210 Mos 1:12, 199 Mos 2:63, 178, 253, 269, 287, 288 Virt 212 Aet 139 Flacc 27, 111, 154, 160 Legat 208, 218, 251 Prov 2:34

ἀποβάλλω (40) Leg 2:54 Leg 3:193, 193 Cher 68 Sacr 125 Det 51 Deus 86, 89, 90, 90 Plant 172 Ebr 39 Sobr 4 Conf 70, 73, 163 Migr 10, 67 Congr 41 Fug 91 Somn 2:287 Abr 235, 256 Mos 1:68 Decal 42, 68 Spec 1:295 Spec 2:217 Spec 3:202, 203 Virt 44 Praem 37, 144, 158, 159 Prob 18 Aet 46 Flacc 60 QG (Par) 2:7 QE 2:3b

ἀποβιάζομαι Spec 3:177

ἀποβλέπω (15) Opif 18 Det 153 Mut 160 Abr 61 Ios 166, 182, 234 Spec 1:219, 293 Spec 2:237 Virt 69, 70, 133 Legat 191, 359

ἀπόβλητος Spec 2:169

ἀποβολή Praem 33

ἀποβράσσω Mos 2:255 Spec 4:112 Aet 122

ἀπόγαιος Her 305

ἀπογαλακτίζω Somn 2:10

ἀπογεννάω (7) Opif 48, 50 Cher 29 Deus 120 Ebr 116 Spec 2:177 Spec 4:227

ἀπογεόομαι Aet 107

ἀπογεύω (7) Spec 4:17 Virt 99 Contempl 35 Flacc 96 Legat 166, 275, 364

ἀπογιγνώσκω (36) Leg 2:51 Cher 29 Sacr 71 Deus 180 Plant 64, 66 Ebr 46, 72, 72 Migr 124 Fug 89 Mut 8, 218 Somn 1:60, 60, 60, 119 Abr 111, 175, 254 Ios 138, 231 Mos 2:249 Spec 2:67 Spec 3:99, 128 Virt 34, 152 Praem 115 Prob 114 Flacc 11, 16, 17 Legat 352 QG 2:11, 41

ἀπόγνωσις (9) Mut 222 Abr 268 Mos 1:104, 192, 210 Spec 3:6, 44 Flacc 75 Legat 249

ἀπόγονος (16) Opif 145 Post 40, 40 Gig 17 Conf 122 Congr 54 Ios 42 Mos 1:240 Mos 2:55 Spec 2:214, 217 Spec 4:181 Virt 195, 210 Legat 30, 300

ἀπογυμνόω (11) Ios 185, 247 Mos 2:145 Spec 3:53, 61, 67 Virt 10, 69, 76, 152, 202

ἀποδακρύω Virt 111

ἀποδείκνυμι (45) Opif 96 Leg 1:7, 55 Leg 3:54, 95 Cher 39, 50 Post 31, 52, 154, 161 Deus 112 Agr 43 Plant 93 Sobr 40 Conf 18, 55 Her 298, 313 Mut 62, 71 Somn 1:11 Abr 252 Ios 177 Mos 2:262 Decal 126 Spec 2:215 Spec 3:39, 75 Spec 4:82, 132 Virt 207 Praem 165 Prob 53 Contempl 40 Aet 5, 30, 112, 116, 144 Flacc 9 Legat 24, 32, 299 QE 2:3b

ἀποδεικτικός Prob 62 Aet 39

ἀποδειλιάω Mos 1:234

ἀπόδειξις (26) Opif 99 Sacr 83, 85, 130 Post 131, 167 Agr 16 Plant 156, 173 Ebr 11 Conf 102 Congr 17 Abr 61 Mos 1:95, 196, 274 Mos 2:177, 262 Decal 140 Prob 16, 58 Aet 12, 24, 56, 78 Legat 37

ἀποδεκατόω Congr 99

ἀποδέρω Spec 1:199

ἀποδέχομαι (66) Leg 2:17, 18, 101 Leg 3:62 Cher 34 Sacr 77 Det 95 Post 71, 154 Gig 37 Deus 116 Agr 35, 43 Plant 108 Migr 164 Her 48, 77, 123, 163, 239, 291 Congr 91 Fug 207 Mut 40, 42 Somn 1:82, 91, 129, 174, 207 Somn 2:98, 106, 162 Abr 38, 90, 200 Ios 59, 93 Mos 1:15, 84, 98, 153 Mos 2:9, 173 Spec 1:43, 51 Spec 2:132, 234, 261 Spec 3:64, 122, 127, 180 Spec 4:102 Praem 152 Contempl 48 Flacc 98 Legat 154, 155, 211, 253, 254 Prov 2:39 QG 3:29, 4:102a, 8*

ἀποδέω (15) Opif 141 Agr 85 Plant 81 Ebr 174 Mos 2:180 Spec 1:73 Spec 3:25 Virt 66 Prob 34 Flacc 43, 135 Legat 252, 300, 317 Prov 2:37

ἀποδηλόω Mut 41

ἀποδημέω (7) Det 87 Conf 77, 78 Fug 44 Somn 1:180 Ios 210 QG 4:20

ἀποδημία (14) Her 82, 276 Congr 48 Somn 1:42 Ios 167, 255 Mos 1:278 Mos 2:232 Praem 19, 80 Flacc 184, 184 Legat 338, 344

ἀποδιδράσκω (104) Leg 1:55 Leg 2:25, 90, 93 Leg 3:8, 9, 14, 15, 16, 16, 16, 17, 18, 20, 22, 28, 29, 48, 125, 195, 242 Cher 3, 6 Sacr 77, 95 Det 154, 155 Post 43, 76 Deus 163 Agr 111, 167 Plant 8 Sobr 48 Conf 27, 161 Migr 26, 93, 154, 208, 208 Her 69, 77, 238, 248, 305 Fug 1, 1, 2, 2, 4, 6, 7, 7, 7, 20, 23, 36, 39, 43, 48, 49, 106, 108, 128, 199, 205, 213 Mut 38, 57, 217, 265 Somn 1:28, 43, 46, 225 Somn 2:70, 122, 225 Abr 241, 246 Ios 49, 51 Mos 1:49, 73, 326 Spec 2:167 Spec 4:166 Praem 16, 100, 148 Prob 63, 120, 138 Aet 21, 37 Flacc 145, 166 Legat 25, 341 Prov 2:28, 28 QG 3:26, 29

ἀποδίδωμι (90) Opif 85 Leg 3:10, 51, 225 Cher 122, 122, 122 Sacr 18, 53, 112 Det 43, 91 Post 5 Gig 1 Deus 4, 33, 101, 101, 142 Agr 179 Plant 1, 101, 101, 113 Ebr 210 Sobr 48 Migr 139, 139, 142, 202 Her 104, 258, 271, 282 Congr 7 Fug 168 Somn 1:92, 93, 100, 101, 112, 113, 114, 252 Somn 2:34 Abr 228, 240 Ios 15, 167, 178, 180, 188, 194, 194, 195, 201, 209, 215, 227, 227, 238, 249, 255 Mos 1:101, 142, 219, 242, 242 Mos 2:242 Decal 62, 118 Spec 1:267 Spec 2:111, 116, 121 Spec 4:13, 31, 67, 196 Virt 72, 83, 88, 96, 96, 117 Aet 52, 54, 58 Flacc 83 QG isf 17

ἀποδιοπομπέομαι Post 72 Prob 78 Prov 2:41

ἀποδοκιμάζω (11) Leg 3:31 Cher 41, 73 Sobr 20 Congr 24 Mos 1:161 Spec 4:116, 151, 175, 175 Virt 59

ἀπόδομα Mos 2:242

ἀπόδοσις (36) Opif 83, 157 Leg 1:16, 99 Leg 2:14 Cher 14 Agr 28, 97 Plant 87, 101, 101, 103 Sobr 18, 33, 33 Conf 14, 190 Her 50, 106, 289 Fug 108, 181 Somn 1:100 Abr 88, 119, 147, 200 Ios 125, 197, 213 Decal 167 Spec 1:236 Spec 2:77 Spec 4:67 Virt 89 QE 2:38a

ἀποδοχή (25) Deus 171 Her 51 Fug 129 Mut 255 Abr 37 Ios 118, 230 Mos 1:23, 31 Mos 2:17, 19, 200 Decal 38, 167 Spec 1:15 Spec 2:164, 237 Spec 4:179 Praem 13, 82 Legat 236, 277 Hypoth 11:18 Prov 2:13 QG 4:166

ἀποδρέπω Agr 157

ἀποδρύπτω Mos 1:271

ἀποδύρομαι Ios 27 Flacc 160

ἀποδύω (11) Leg 2:56, 58 Det 106 Post 137 Agr 119 Ebr 7 Conf 7, 31 Migr 192 Somn 1:225 Somn 2:128

ἀποζάω Fug 33 Spec 1:134 Prob 8 Prov 2:57

ἀποζεύγνυμι (7) Agr 13 Fug 160 Abr 224 Mos 2:130 Spec 1:111 Spec 3:118 Virt 111

ἀποθαρσέω Legat 52

ἄποθεν Mos 1:12 Flacc 112

ἀπόθεσις Post 48

ἀποθλίβω Agr 157 Ios 91 Virt 157

ἀποθνήσκω (109) Leg 1:90, 101, 101, 105, 105, 106, 106, 107, 108 Leg 2:27, 77, 78, 82 Leg 3:32, 34, 35, 212, 212 Cher 8 Det 34, 94, 178 Post 39, 45, 73, 143 Gig 14 Agr 95, 148, 148, 148, 156, 164, 175 Plant 147, 177, 177, 177 Ebr 86, 127, 140 Conf 122 Migr 206, 206 Her 19, 276, 292 Fug 53, 55, 59, 60, 62, 64, 115, 117 Mut 96, 96, 210 Somn 1:48, 143, 151, 217 Somn 2:282 Ios 23, 24, 223 Mos 1:141, 171, 183, 183, 279, 309 Mos 2:225, 227, 227 Spec 1:84, 108, 115 Spec 2:130 Spec 3:26, 64, 133, 133, 148, 149, 153, 157 Spec 4:15, 37 Praem 70, 70, 72, 72, 137, 158 Prob 111, 118, 133 Aet 126 Flacc 11, 132, 187 Legat 29, 62, 65, 236 Hypoth 6:9 QG 4:173 QE isf 3

ἀποθραύω Agr 114 Aet 132

ἀποικία (44) Opif 135 Conf 77, 78 Migr 176 Her 98 Congr 84 Fug 36, 95 Abr 66, 68, 72, 77, 85 Mos 1:71, 103, 163, 170, 195, 222, 233, 236, 239, 254, 255 Mos 2:232, 246, 288 Spec 2:25, 146, 150, 158 Spec 3:111 Spec 4:178 Virt 77, 102, 219 Praem 16, 17, 80 Contempl 22 Flacc 46 Legat 281, 282 QG 1:27

ἀποικίζω (8) Post 68 Mos 1:220, 237 Spec 1:59 Praem 84, 117 Prob 130 QE 2:49a

ἀποίκιλος Sacr 26 Plant 111 Ebr 86, 215 Congr 19

ἄποιος (18) Opif 22 Leg 1:36, 51 Leg 2:80 Leg 3:36, 206 Cher 67 Conf 85 Her 140 Congr 61 Fug 8, 9 Mut 135 Somn 2:45 Spec 1:47, 328 Spec 4:187 Praem 130

ἀποκάθημαι Fug 188, 189

ἀποκαλέω Mos 1:10, 30 Flacc 39, 54

ἀποκαλύπτω (13) Leg 2:66 Cher 14 Gig 32, 35, 39 Conf 71 Migr 126 Fug 188, 188, 189, 190, 192, 193

ἀποκάλυφος Cher 17

ἀποκάμνω Mos 1:251 Mos 2:252

ἀποκατάστασις Her 293 Decal 164

ἀποκαταστατικός Opif 101

ἀπόκειμαι Det 128 Mut 199

ἀποκείρω (8) Opif 85 Somn 1:106 Ios 105, 179 Spec 1:250, 254, 305 Virt 111

ἀποκήρυκτος Her 26 Somn 2:148

ἀποκηρύσσω Praem 61 QG 1:76b

ἀποκλείω Spec 3:90 Virt 107 Hypoth 7:3, 7:6

ἀποκληρόω (12) Det 82, 119 Post 92 Agr 116 Plant 131 Her 136, 191 Fug 118 Spec 1:158 Spec 2:120 Aet 107 Legat 214

ἀποκλήρωσις Mos 1:278

ἀποκλίνω (25) Post 22, 100, 101, 102 Gig 64 Deus 150, 162 Ebr 18, 131 Conf 131 Migr 145, 148 Somn 1:86, 246 Abr 198 Ios 142 Mos 1:160 Mos 2:58, 139, 193 Aet 64 Flacc 24 Legat 32 Hypoth 11:3 QG 4:52a

ἀπόκλισις Migr 148

ἀποκλύζω Post 163

ἀποκναίω Det 72 Post 86 Agr 136 Migr 111 Mut 197

ἀποκνέω (11) Her 144 Mut 222 Mos 1:63, 239, 321 Spec 1:32 Spec 2:4 Virt 17 Aet 95 Legat 217 Prov 2:51

ἀποκομίζω QG 1:62:2

ἀποκοπή (7) Gig 25 Decal 92 Spec 1:338 Spec 2:4, 244 Spec 3:175 Spec 4:149

ἀπόκοπος Spec 1:330, 344

ἀποκόπτω (30) Leg 3:8, 127, 129, 130, 134, 140, 147 Agr 39, 86 Plant 104, 109 Ebr 23, 28, 39, 69, 213 Migr 69 Mut 205 Somn 2:64, 68, 69, 184 Spec 1:325 Spec 3:179, 180 Aet 49, 51, 143 Flacc 53 Legat 242

ἀπόκρατος Det 95

ἀποκρίνω (78) Opif 39 Leg 2:46, 89, 90 Leg 3:59, 60, 77, 78, 88 Cher 72 Sacr 64 Det 27, 57, 59 Post 5, 90, 139 Deus 60, 92, 108, 145, 167 Agr 57, 59 Plant 128 Ebr 120, 149 Migr 196, 213 Her 17, 17, 138, 140 Congr 94 Fug 86, 87, 132, 133, 135, 206 Mut 11, 91, 230 Somn 1:192, 210 Somn 2:15 Abr 175 Ios 90, 199, 223 Mos 1:88, 128, 244, 258, 281, 321 Mos 2:180, 190 Spec 1:216, 218 Virt 149 Praem 84, 130 Prob 62, 101, 129 Contempl 32 Aet 4, 78, 95, 123, 147 Legat 271, 360, 362 QG 4:191c QG (Par) 2:7 QE 1:19

ἀπόκρισις (23) Leg 1:13 Leg 3:53, 54 Det 57, 58, 58, 59, 61 Post 62 Her 18 Fug 169 Mut 91, 106, 253 Mos 1:244 Mos 2:188, 192, 192, 221, 233 Legat 259, 333 QG 4:208

ἀπόκροτος Mos 2:202 Spec 2:169 Praem 114 Prob 65 Contempl 62

ἀποκρούω Somn 1:103

ἀποκρύπτω (34) Opif 72 Leg 3:1, 1, 4, 4, 5, 6, 6, 7, 9, 27, 27, 27, 28, 28, 39, 48, 54 Sacr 33 Det 163 Ebr 44 Conf 143 Congr 76 Mut 38 Somn 1:83, 119 Somn 2:3 Mos 2:80 Spec 1:166, 221, 322 Virt 169 Contempl 28 Legat 147

ἀπόκρυφος Leg 3:36 Sacr 26, 62 Abr 147 Mos 2:37

ἀπόκρυψις Opif 58, 115 Spec 4:185

ἀποκτείνω (40) Leg 3:69, 70, 73, 74, 75 Det 1, 45, 46, 47, 47, 50, 164, 167 Post 10, 124, 170 Agr 97 Ebr 67, 70, 70, 70 Conf 160 Fug 23, 53, 77 Somn 2:297 Ios 188, 249 Mos 1:167, 171 Mos 2:171 Spec 3:86, 128, 129, 136, 141, 144, 159 Spec 4:38 Legat 229

ἀποκυέω (28) Opif 161 Leg 1:15 Cher 54 Sacr 3, 103 Det 114, 116, 121 Post 63, 112, 114 Deus 5 Plant 135, 136 Ebr 30 Conf 144 Her 294 Congr 6, 129 Fug 208 Mut 137 Decal 128 Spec 3:111, 118 Virt 131, 137 Aet 66 QG 3:18

ἀποκύησις Virt 128

ἀποκυΐσκω Cher 102 Plant 15 Virt 126

ἀπολαγχάνω Post 72

ἀπολαμβάνω (19) Opif 64 Congr 136 Fug 151 Abr 257, 259 Ios 24, 188, 193, 209 Mos 1:79 Mos 2:63, 86, 91 Spec 3:108 Spec 4:195 Virt 83, 88 Praem 18 Flacc 162

ἀπόλαυσις (106) Opif 42, 77, 78, 153 Leg 1:103 Leg 3:20, 52, 80, 112, 151, 155, 227, 227 Cher 113 Sacr 22, 57, 124, 125 Det 33, 60, 98, 114, 156 Post 144, 148, 185 Gig 60 Deus 147, 156 Agr 24, 36, 108, 157 Plant 34, 52, 132, 162, 166 Ebr 214 Sobr 61 Conf 25, 85, 93 Migr 11, 35, 217, 218 Her 137, 255, 285 Congr 32, 56, 65, 164 Fug 32, 176 Mut 165, 215 Somn 1:48 Somn 2:48, 209, 212, 214 Ios 57 Mos 1:187 Mos 2:24, 70,

212 Decal 161 Spec 1:165, 303, 322 Spec 2:19, 186, 205 Spec 3:113 Spec 4:82, 103, 120 Virt 30, 30, 126, 127, 133, 135, 156, 159, 169, 175, 182, 207 Praem 87, 103, 135, 139 Aet 63 Legat 8, 16, 318 Prov 2:1, 30, 57, 63, 69, 70 QE 2:71

ἀπόλαυσμα Deus 120 Plant 38

ἀπολαυστός Fug 174

ἀπολαύω (46) Opif 151, 156 Leg 1:57 Leg 3:68, 237, 247 Gig 31 Deus 81 Agr 150, 150, 155 Migr 19, 120 Her 31, 254 Somn 1:51 Somn 2:106, 211 Abr 65 Ios 139 Mos 1:158, 209, 298, 332 Spec 1:127, 157 Spec 2:91, 106, 175, 180 Spec 4:122 Virt 98, 165 Praem 139, 170 Flacc 77, 83, 95, 125, 184 Legat 127, 137, 187, 285, 299 Prov 2:29

ἀπολέγω Deus 15

ἀπολείπω (133) Opif 131 Leg 2:20 Leg 3:4, 29, 31, 43, 148 Cher 31 Sacr 7, 68, 125 Det 141, 141, 142 Post 6, 7, 19, 73, 105, 173, 173 Deus 150, 151 Agr 123, 123, 150 Plant 5, 174 Ebr 99, 177 Conf 5, 135, 136 Migr 25, 118, 151, 155, 197, 198, 214, 216 Her 31, 83, 132 Fug 3, 33, 88, 92, 92, 189 Mut 49, 51, 192 Somn 1:9, 61, 116, 161, 181 Somn 2:34 Abr 23, 190, 246, 247 Ios 16, 19, 19, 52, 185, 189, 223, 254 Mos 1:2, 4, 36, 204, 328 Mos 2:6, 29, 80, 136, 194, 198, 288 Decal 91, 122 Spec 1:40, 52, 58, 68, 205, 220, 223, 310 Spec 2:125, 125, 128, 129, 136, 146, 156, 240 Spec 3:16, 207 Spec 4:81, 108, 169 Virt 43, 53, 102, 181 Praem 8, 61, 83, 101, 108, 169 Prob 80, 90 Contempl 13, 29, 54, 76 Aet 7, 8, 21, 134 Flacc 11, 49 Legat 23, 33, 225, 246 QG 4:191a

ἀπόλειψις (13) Cher 115 Det 28, 143 Deus 12 Migr 53, 151, 177, 192 Her 287 Abr 245 Mos 2:184 Praem 16, 142

ἀπολέμητος Her 275

ἀπόλεμος (11) Opif 142 Ebr 100 Conf 46 Fug 174 Somn 2:250 Abr 28 Spec 1:57, 224 Spec 2:45 Virt 47 Hypoth 6:6

ἀπολήγω Spec 1:178

ἀπόλιπος QE isf 20

ἄπολις (8) Leg 3:2, 3 Sacr 32 Gig 67 Migr 99 Congr 58 Virt 190 Flacc 123

ἀπόλλυμι (44) Leg 3:22, 23, 25, 27, 225, 225, 226, 231, 231, 233 Cher 130 Conf 35 Migr 68 Fug 27, 63, 161 Mut 203 Somn 2:290 Mos 1:44, 69, 101, 122, 227, 291, 305, 325 Mos 2:53, 249, 281 Spec 1:235 Spec 4:129 Praem 22, 147 Prob 104 Aet 45, 148 Flacc 57 Legat 41, 207 Prov 2:33, 41 QG 1:96:1, 2:15c QE 2:49b

'Απόλλων (6) Decal 54 Legat 93, 95, 106, 109, 110

'Απολλωνιακός Legat 103

ἀπολογέομαι (17) Leg 1:87 Post 38 Congr 153 Ios 167, 185, 197, 215 Mos 2:274 Spec 3:54, 77, 80, 120 Spec 4:64 Flacc 103, 106, 141 Legat 360

ἀπολογία (23) Leg 3:65, 66, 66, 68, 75 Agr 92 Ios 52, 80, 222 Mos 1:286, 303 Spec 2:95 Spec 3:142 Spec 4:24 Virt 197 Flacc 7, 126 Legat 38, 67, 350 Prov 2:56 QG 1:77, 4:191c

ἀπόλογος Mut 243

ἀπολούω (14) Leg 3:141 Det 170 Her 113 Mut 49, 229 Somn 1:82, 148 Somn 2:25 Mos 2:64 Spec 1:207, 261 Spec 3:89, 205, 206

ἀπόλυσις Mut 228 Spec 1:215

ἀπολυτρόω Leg 3:21

ἀπολύτρωσις Congr 109 Prob 114

ἀπολύω (6) Her 2, 34 Flacc 96, 96 Hypoth 7:13 QG 3:11c

ἀπομανθάνω (12) Leg 3:236 Migr 149, 151 Her 192 Congr 162 Decal 40 Spec 1:56 Spec 2:135 Spec 3:29 Spec 4:218 Virt 220 Prob 12

ἀπομαραίνω Spec 1:282

ἀπομάσσω (12) Migr 190 Fug 14 Ios 83, 175 Spec 1:259 Spec 3:31 Spec 4:55, 182 Virt 197, 207 Aet 49 Legat 103

ἀπομάχομαι Leg 3:238 Det 36 Post 52, 72 Prob 118

ἀπομειλίσσομαι Contempl 37

ἀπομηκύνω (6) Opif 87 Det 35 Post 86 Somn 1:115 Spec 4:136 Virt 16

ἀπομιμέομαι (7) Det 152 Deus 36 Plant 49 Conf 90 Mut 129 Spec 2:135 Prob 120

ἀπομιτρόω Fug 111

ἀπομνημονεύω Cher 27 Ebr 173 Spec 1:99 Flacc 146

ἀπονεμητικός Leg 1:87

ἀπονέμω (96) Opif 15, 143, 153, 171 Leg 1:28, 65, 87 Cher 120 Sacr 103, 138 Deus 12, 19, 37 Plant 107 Sobr 40 Migr 109, 179 Her 49, 116, 152, 177, 224 Fug 62, 70, 88, 148 Mut 58, 153 Somn 1:184 Somn 2:9, 28 Abr 253 Ios 98 Mos 1:318 Mos 2:1, 9, 82, 128, 129, 158, 194, 242, 244 Decal 7, 61, 160, 161 Spec 1:25, 65, 121, 131, 131, 146, 148, 158, 190, 196, 196, 222, 233, 240, 256, 258 Spec 2:35, 64, 95, 103, 113, 118, 120, 131, 170, 235 Spec 3:99, 123, 184 Spec 4:92, 105, 180, 208 Virt 19, 105, 219 Praem 3, 49, 67 Contempl 82 Aet 33 Flacc 187 Legat 310, 318 QG 1:60:2, 3:8, 4:51a QE 2:46, 46

ἀπονεύω Plant 21 Sobr 3 Her 78, 246 Somn 1:237

ἀπόνηρος Flacc 12

ἀπονητί Agr 155

ἀπονία Migr 30 Her 212

ἀπονίζω (ἀπονίπτω) Migr 98 Ios 201 Mos 2:138 Spec 1:198 Spec 3:89

ἀπονίναμαι (10) Agr 156, 173 Plant 45 Ebr 48 Migr 27 Congr 14, 46 Somn 1:50, 113 Virt 29

ἀπονίπτω ἀπονίζω

ἀπονοέομαι Decal 73 Virt 41

ἀπόνοια (13) Det 44 Post 35, 52 Conf 117, 173 Somn 2:277 Abr 213 Decal 59 Spec 1:79, 270 Spec 4:222 Flacc 25, 101

ἀπονομή Spec 4:57

ἄπονος (16) Opif 79 Leg 3:135, 135, 135 Cher 12, 87 Sacr 7 Deus 97 Congr 37, 173 Mut 258 Abr 171 Mos 1:183 Mos 2:267 Spec 1:132 Praem 50

ἀποξέω Det 107, 107

ἀποπάλλω Mut 211

ἀποπατέω Deus 59

ἀπόπειρα (7) Congr 164 Somn 1:194 Ios 232 Flacc 119, 130 Legat 196 QG isf 5

ἀποπειράομαι (6) Opif 149 Congr 124 Abr 105 Ios 41, 220 Mos 2:33

ἀποπεμπτόω Migr 204

ἀποπέμπω (6) Leg 1:96 Leg 3:197 Sacr 98 Plant 35 Spec 3:35 QG (Par) 2:6

ἀποπέτομαι Ios 126

ἀποπηδάω (8) Fug 41 Mut 211 Ios 126 Mos 2:166 Decal 89 Spec 1:26 Praem 105 QG 2:39

ἀποπίμπλημι Decal 129

ἀποπίπτω (8) Leg 2:99, 101 Agr 93, 110, 122, 171 Virt 90, 91

ἀποπιστεύω Leg 3:228

ἀποπληρόω (8) Sacr 64 Agr 36 Ebr 32, 206, 221 Ios 253 Spec 4:163 Virt 115

ἀποπλύνω Decal 45 Spec 1:199, 206

ἀποπνέω Sacr 21

ἀποπνίγω Spec 4:122

ἀποπομπαῖος Leg 2:52 Post 72 Plant 61 Her 179, 187

ἀποπομπή Post 70

ἀποπόμπιμος Leg 2:52

ἀποπρεσβεύω QG 4:144

ἄποπτος (6) Ebr 131 Fug 81 Mos 2:87 Prob 7 Contempl 30 Legat 228

ἀποπτύω Opif 123

ἀπόρευτος Deus 144 Mos 1:194, 214 Prob 67

ἀπορέω (44) Opif 72, 77 Leg 1:70 Leg 3:60, 114, 236 Det 86 Deus 70 Agr 13 Plant 43, 123 Her 31, 101, 101 Fug 54, 131, 133, 140 Mut 83, 157 Abr 95, 231 Mos 1:58 Mos 2:165, 217 Decal 2, 36 Spec 1:153 Spec 2:96, 119 Spec 4:40, 179 Virt 48, 53, 90 Praem 50 Aet 6, 102 Flacc 59, 68 Legat 263, 263, 370 Prov 2:5

ἀπορία (24) Det 131 Agr 39 Conf 164 Abr 86 Ios 183 Mos 1:34, 99, 191 Mos 2:247, 251 Spec 2:87, 203 Spec 4:213 Virt 85, 91, 127 Praem 127, 130, 136 Flacc 62 Legat 263 Hypoth 6:2 Prov 2:31 QG 4:200c

ἄπορος (43) Cher 68 Agr 141 Fug 29, 108 Somn 1:97 Somn 2:213 Abr 175, 232 Mos 1:174 Mos 2:250 Decal 16, 42, 71 Spec 1:24, 133, 139, 308 Spec 2:71, 74, 106, 115, 122, 164 Spec 3:159 Spec 4:3, 74, 76, 77, 127, 172, 195 Virt 6, 84, 85 Prob 8 Contempl 14 Aet 129 Flacc 18 Legat 123, 178, 196 Hypoth 6:6 QE 2:2

ἀπορράπτω Cher 116 Det 134 Her 25 Legat 360

ἀπορρέω Det 83 Agr 74 Mut 100 Ios 131 Decal 11

ἀπορρήγνυμι ἀπορρήσσω

ἀπορρήγνυμι (7) Mut 84 Decal 87 Spec 3:195 Aet 118 Flacc 159, 179 Legat 31

ἀπόρρησις Virt 192

ἀπορρήσσω (ἀπορρήγνυμι) Fug 146 Spec 3:28

ἀπόρρητος (18) Leg 2:57 Leg 3:27 Sacr 60, 131 Plant 176, 177 Fug 191 Mut 199, 246 Somn 1:97, 102, 226 Ios 60, 247 Mos 1:86 Spec 2:50 Flacc 111 Hypoth 7:8

ἀπορρίπτω (17) Leg 2:90, 90 Det 95 Post 79 Ebr 7 Conf 69, 73 Migr 144, 158 Her 247 Fug 205 Abr 187 Mos 1:39, 204 Spec 1:317 Virt 31 Legat 108

ἀπορροή Migr 71, 71 Congr 33 Mut 100

ἀπόρροια Leg 1:63, 63 Spec 1:27, 40

ἀπορρύπτω (7) Leg 2:32 Leg 3:140, 141 Cher 95 Migr 190 Decal 10 Aet 2

ἀπορρώξ Mos 1:192 Prov 2:27

ἀπορφανίζω Somn 2:273 Spec 2:31

ἀποσβέννυμι Deus 173 Spec 1:268 Aet 85, 88

ἀποσείω (7) Leg 3:140, 201 Cher 81 Plant 106 Her 181 Congr 108 Somn 2:128

ἀποσεμνύνω (11) Opif 7 Post 115 Plant 61, 117 Congr 118 Mut 205 Abr 31 Decal 66, 120 Virt 179 Legat 116

ἀποσιωπάω Opif 6

ἀποσκάπτω Agr 114

ἀποσκεδάννυμι (7) Cher 61 Her 244 Somn 1:165 Ios 106 Mos 1:216, 284 Spec 1:185

ἀποσκευάζω Deus 131, 135

ἀποσκευή Her 272, 273, 274

ἀποσκήπτω Virt 150

ἀποσκίδνημι Mos 1:122

ἀποσκοπέω Somn 2:142

ἀπόσπασμα (7) Opif 146 Leg 3:161 Det 90 Her 283 Mut 223 Somn 1:34 Mos 2:154

ἀποσπάω Deus 35 Virt 128, 138, 142

ἀποστάζω Migr 157 Prov 2:46

ἀπόστασις Abr 226 Flacc 94

ἀποστατέω Cher 52 Congr 53 Aet 21

ἀποστέλλω (33) Leg 2:77 Cher 2 Det 3, 5, 5, 10 Post 44, 44, 45, 57, 116 Agr 51 Migr 22, 174 Her 20, 222 Congr 8, 65 Fug 23, 149, 149, 151, 180, 182 Somn 1:21, 69, 112, 116 Mos 2:32 Spec 4:236 Aet 86 QE 2:21, 24:1

ἀποστερέω (7) Mos 1:142 Spec 1:278 Spec 3:112 Virt 100, 152 Flacc 48, 191

ἀποστολή Post 73 Gig 17

ἀποστρέφω (97) Leg 3:175, 220, 221, 252, 252, 252 Cher 41, 62 Sacr 23, 33, 45 Det 21, 93, 142 Post 101, 135, 183 Gig 21, 45 Deus 27, 138, 150 Agr 84, 88, 148, 148, 148 Plant 108, 155 Ebr 160, 166, 169, 178 Conf 48, 131, 131 Migr 20, 27, 122, 148, 208 Her 293, 298, 298, 299, 304, 306 Congr 127, 143, 152, 167, 179 Fug 1, 23, 28, 30, 35, 141, 149, 207 Mut 134, 254 Somn 1:3, 70, 89, 180 Somn 2:106 Abr 79, 126, 197 Ios 175, 205 Mos 2:139, 279 Decal 124 Spec 1:167, 265, 277, 310 Spec 3:13, 50, 66, 167, 200 Spec 4:108, 111, 179 Flacc 24 Legat 229 QG 1:70:1, 70:2, 2:12d, 3:26 QG (Par) 2:6 QE 2:18, 18, 99

ἀποστροφή (6) Leg 3:220 Sacr 96 Conf 129 Migr 219 Prob 61 QG 1:66

ἀποσυλάω Deus 135 Hypoth 7:4

ἀποσφάζω Legat 87, 308

ἀποσχίζω Fug 112

ἀποσχοινίζω (8) Det 70, 143 Post 69, 177 Deus 111 Her 278 Somn 2:184 Virt 192

ἀποτάσσω (10) Leg 2:25 Leg 3:41, 142, 145, 238 Deus 151 Sobr 5 Migr 92 Mos 1:38 Legat 325

ἀποτείνω (26) Opif 39, 41, 85 Plant 152 Ebr 200 Migr 181 Her 13, 34 Congr 56 Mos 1:115, 160 Mos 2:84, 85, 139, 186 Decal 34, 43, 44 Spec 3:98, 178 Spec 4:122, 222 Virt 140 Flacc 61 Legat 261 QG (Par) 2:5

ἀποτέλεσμα (22) Opif 28, 129 Leg 1:100 Leg 2:40, 62, 63 Leg 3:34, 204, 250 Plant 125 Sobr 48 Migr 43 Her 209, 226, 226, 227 Fug 133 Mos 2:76 Spec 2:189 Spec 3:191 Contempl 5 Aet 101

ἀποτελευτάω Aet 135

ἀποτελέω (88) Opif 17, 19, 35, 92, 92, 95, 96, 97, 102, 116, 126, 126, 136 Leg 1:2, 7, 8, 23 Leg 2:13, 37, 37,

37, 74 Leg 3:98 Sacr 69, 74, 108, 109 Det 54, 87, 120 Post 169 Deus 46, 84, 88 Ebr 116 Conf 186, 186, 187 Migr 6, 136, 180 Her 141, 149, 149, 150, 160, 197, 214, 233, 266 Congr 142 Fug 26 Somn 1:35 Somn 2:165 Ios 84 Mos 1:71, 96, 97, 207, 210 Mos 2:34, 74, 88, 124, 126, 127, 256, 282 Decal 26, 31 Spec 1:87 Spec 2:40, 57 Spec 4:87, 91, 161 Praem 97, 102 Contempl 88 Aet 41, 79, 88, 94, 98, 99 Flacc 117 Prov 1 QG (Par) 2:2

ἀποτέμνω (17) Opif 112 Leg 1:52 Cher 4 Sacr 97 Fug 112 Somn 2:24, 64, 153, 213 Ios 96, 98 Spec 1:3 Spec 2:172 Virt 156 Aet 48 Legat 10 QG 1:24

ἀπότεξις Prob 130

ἀποτίθημι (24) Opif 115 Post 48 Gig 16 Deus 26, 116 Agr 25, 47 Plant 56 Ebr 86 Migr 30, 211 Fug 111, 173 Spec 1:102, 268, 306 Spec 2:102, 251 Spec 3:176 Flacc 66 Legat 95, 102 Hypoth 7:19 QE isf 26

ἀποτίκτω (27) Opif 41 Leg 1:15 Cher 52 Sacr 102 Det 60, 127 Post 35, 56, 83, 135 Deus 39, 137, 154 Ebr 60, 163 Migr 219 Congr 3, 160 Mut 151 Spec 3:44, 47 Virt 137, 138, 139 Aet 60, 65 Prov 2:66

ἀποτινάσσω Conf 69, 73

ἀποτιννύω ἀποτίνυμι

ἀποτίνυμι (ἀποτιννύω) Spec 2:78 Spec 4:29, 37 Legat 343

ἀποτίνω (12) Leg 3:248 Abr 259 Mos 1:333 Spec 1:234 Spec 3:64, 145, 146, 146, 148 Spec 4:12, 22 QG 2:54a

ἀπότιτθος Mos 1:18 Spec 3:200 Virt 142

ἀποτολμάω (6) Leg 1:38 Post 42 Ios 50 Prob 43 Legat 77, 287

ἀποτομή (13) Somn 2:255 Ios 257 Mos 1:278 Spec 1:76, 131 Spec 2:120, 168, 222 Prob 76 Aet 138 Flacc 39 Legat 48, 155

ἀποτομία Spec 2:94 Flacc 95

ἀπότομος Sacr 32

ἀποτορνεύω Her 229

ἀποτρέπω Gig 33 Ebr 79

ἀποτρέχω Leg 3:198 Spec 3:174 QG 4:131

ἀποτρόπαιος Praem 151

ἀποτροπή (12) Sacr 48, 70 Det 123 Ebr 224 Her 15, 172 Fug 99 Abr 129 Mos 1:149 Mos 2:5 Spec 1:283 Spec 3:171

ἀποτρύχω Spec 1:125 Spec 2:101 Spec 4:215

ἀποτρύω Spec 4:38

ἀποτρώγω Det 176 Prob 108 Contempl 40

ἀποτυγχάνω (10) Deus 93, 98 Agr 85 Conf 167 Ios 41, 150 Decal 149 Spec 3:44 Prob 60 Contempl 61

ἄπους Opif 157 Migr 65, 69 Mos 1:77 Spec 4:113

ἀπουσία (9) Leg 3:113 Cher 118 Det 141, 141 Sobr 43 Migr 155 Somn 2:288 Mos 2:161 Prov 2:9

ἀποφαίνω (116) Opif 7, 26, 53 Leg 1:17, 87 Leg 3:166, 206 Cher 50 Sacr 9, 91 Det 7, 58, 72, 80, 148 Post 88, 153 Gig 2, 25, 33, 38 Deus 31 Agr 31, 92, 129, 173 Plant 144 Ebr 111, 138, 138, 141, 199 Migr 83, 137, 180, 186 Her 20, 46, 88, 155, 276 Congr 3 Fug 133, 171, 171 Mut 59, 141, 181, 221 Somn 1:81, 95, 98, 175 Somn 2:29, 243, 277 Abr 88, 150, 270 Mos 1:1, 36, 150, 235 Mos 2:218, 284 Decal 35, 140, 176 Spec 1:125, 181, 182, 188, 221, 223, 238, 322 Spec 2:24, 38, 110, 137, 142, 157, 192, 249 Spec 3:52, 82, 119, 173 Spec 4:32, 49, 63, 153, 159, 189, 217 Virt 61, 79 Praem 40 Prob 37, 104, 107, 130, 142 Contempl 14 Aet 12, 47, 142, 145 Legat 36, 121, 350, 370 Hypoth 7:5 Prov 2:8 QG 3:20a, 52

αποφαντικός Leg 3:51

ἀπόφαντος Congr 149

ἀπόφασις Migr 162 Spec 3:208 Prob 97

ἀποφέρω Leg 3:74

ἀποφεύγω (6) Fug 27, 42 Mos 1:91 Praem 62 Flacc 129 Legat 341

ἀπόφημι Hypoth 7:5

ἀποφθέγγομαι (7) Conf 62 Her 259 Ios 117 Mos 1:176 Mos 2:33, 253, 263

ἀπόφθεγμα Ios 95

ἀποφορά Leg 1:42 Det 157

ἀποφορτίζομαι Mut 168 Spec 2:15 Praem 33, 157

ἀπόφραξις Praem 143

ἀποφράς Decal 145 Spec 3:183 Praem 171

ἀποφράσσω Spec 3:78

ἀποχέτευσις Opif 123

ἀποχετεύω Agr 37 Spec 3:10 Prov 2:38 QG (Par) 2:3, 2:7

ἀποχέω Ios 200

ἀποχή Decal 159 Spec 2:203

ἀποχράω (18) Opif 52, 163 Cher 121 Post 148 Deus 81 Migr 76 Mut 14 Abr 15, 255 Mos 2:45 Spec 1:212 Spec 4:126, 212 Virt 105 Prob 58 Prov 2:33, 59 QG 4:52d

ἀποχρώντως (13) Sacr 72 Post 98 Deus 51 Fug 143 Mut 130 Ios 80 Decal 32, 175 Spec 2:262 Spec 3:104 Spec 4:132 Virt 50, 101

ἀποχωρέω Mos 1:77

ἀποψύχω Aet 128

ἀπραγμοσύνη Sacr 27 Flacc 184 QG 4:47a

ἀπράγμων Abr 22 Mos 2:235 Flacc 183

ἄπρακτος (14) Leg 1:25 Leg 2:26, 26, 70 Leg 3:14, 34, 35 Migr 34 Mos 1:67, 267 Mos 2:269 Spec 2:64 Praem 90 Flacc 110

ἀπραξία (11) Opif 7 Leg 2:30 Cher 87 Ebr 161 Migr 91 Her 170, 257 Abr 154 Aet 84, 85 Flacc 57

ἀπρεπής Cher 92 Ebr 194 Fug 66 Spec 1:148

ἀπρίξ Cher 33 Mut 84

ἀπροαίρετος Post 71 Deus 48

ἀπρονόητος Sacr 32 Praem 23 Hypoth 6:4

ἀπροόρατος (11) Opif 128 Sacr 32 Deus 130 Somn 1:110 Somn 2:214 Mos 2:162 Spec 3:79 Spec 4:26 Praem 20 Legat 2, 109

ἀπροσδεής Deus 56 Agr 54 Abr 30

ἀπροσδόκητος (19) Ebr 111 Her 249 Somn 1:71 Somn 2:145, 268 Ios 211, 214 Mos 1:136, 170, 257 Mos 2:203 Spec 2:219 Spec 3:5 Praem 165 Legat 184, 197, 342 Prov 2:60 QG isf 5

ἀπρόσιτος Ios 82 Mos 2:70

ἀπροσπέλαστος QE 2:45b

ἀπροστασίαστος Sacr 32, 45 Post 68 Somn 2:283

ἀπροφάσιστος Post 13 Abr 226 Virt 31 Legat 257

ἄπταιστος (27) Cher 70 Sacr 63, 123 Det 131 Post 22, 80 Deus 75, 141, 182 Agr 177 Plant 49 Ebr 199 Conf 14 Migr 73, 79, 133 Mut 122, 149 Abr 269 Ios 142, 147 Decal 50 Spec 1:224 Spec 2:202 Spec 4:167 Praem 55 Flacc 149

ἀπτός Abr 239

ἅπτω (46) Leg 1:30, 38 Leg 3:111 Cher 57, 62, 73, 87 Sacr 85 Post 20 Gig 33 Agr 53, 161 Ebr 51, 152, 168 Sobr 6 Conf 133, 156 Congr 96 Mut 256 Somn 1:9, 54, 55 Somn 2:70, 93 Abr 238 Ios 126, 126 Mos 1:109, 143 Mos 2:156 Decal 127 Spec 3:115, 175, 206 Spec 4:91, 103 Praem 134 Prob 116, 136 Aet 148 Legat 208 Prov 2:17, 18, 18, 18

ἄπτωτος Somn 2:145

ἄπυρος Plant 108

ἄπυστος Aet 5

ἀπῳδός (9) Ebr 116 Conf 55, 150 Her 81 Congr 16 Somn 1:28 Mos 2:228 Decal 15 Spec 4:24

ἀπωθέω (28) Opif 165 Sacr 28 Det 95, 143 Post 67 Ebr 84 Sobr 2 Conf 12 Migr 13, 22 Her 181, 202 Fug 49 Somn 1:102, 103, 110 Decal 64, 85 Spec 1:10 Spec 2:209 Spec 3:27 Virt 65 Prob 12, 139 Aet 74 Flacc 24 Legat 325 QE isf 14

ἀπώλεια (19) Agr 94 Conf 22, 196 Congr 119 Mut 228 Somn 2:281 Ios 191 Mos 1:10, 96, 133, 138, 145, 307 Spec 2:251 Virt 132 Praem 133 Aet 20, 74 Legat 233

ἀπωτάτω Fug 189

ἄρα (111) Opif 19, 25, 26 Leg 3:1, 211 Cher 48, 66, 90, 99 Sacr 70, 77, 114 Det 87, 157 Post 38, 54 Deus 18, 62, 78, 110, 115, 116, 149 Plant 5, 176, 177 Ebr 42, 177, 214 Conf 6, 67 Migr 75, 130 Her 19, 21, 73 Congr 100, 177 Fug 164 Mut 57, 138, 163 Somn 1:185 Somn 2:72, 117, 136, 141, 259 Abr 17, 131, 206 Ios 20, 45, 87, 167, 187, 229 Mos 1:27, 85, 161, 204, 207, 274, 280, 294 Mos 2:167, 200, 235 Decal 37, 70, 120 Spec 1:154, 211, 238, 277 Spec 2:54, 70, 253 Spec 3:3, 46, 67, 141 Spec 4:84 Virt 96 Praem 42, 83 Prob 50, 52, 53, 59, 60, 145 Aet 21, 28, 55, 70, 124 Flacc 6, 165, 170, 187 Legat 62, 128, 180, 183, 307 Hypoth 6:5, 7:20 Prov 2:27 QG 2:29 QE 2:49b

ἆρα (103) Opif 129 Leg 2:20, 76 Leg 3:74, 151 Cher 35, 108, 126 Det 13, 24, 141, 143 Post 17, 33, 90, 172 Gig 11 Deus 104, 157 Agr 118 Ebr 74, 190, 200 Sobr 37 Conf 117 Migr 61, 112 Her 6, 51, 65, 115, 186, 260 Congr 170, 173, 178 Fug 90 Mut 54, 72, 101, 136, 194, 205, 210, 232, 252, 256 Somn 1:30, 32, 46, 93, 164, 172 Somn 2:7, 50, 55, 72, 83, 111, 130, 139, 189 Abr 263 Ios 9, 116 Mos 1:74, 84 Decal 32, 100, 118, 119, 151 Spec 1:31 Spec 2:107 Spec 3:116 Spec 4:163, 196, 218, 234 Virt 97, 203, 218 Praem 45 Prob 44, 95, 97, 124, 135 Contempl 3 Aet 125 Flacc 51 Legat 99, 110, 114, 215, 316 Hypoth 7:1, 7:11, 7:14 Prov 2:30 QG 1:17b, 32, 2:30

ἀρά (36) Leg 3:107, 112 Det 71, 96 Post 24, 81 Agr 107 Sobr 30, 32, 47, 51 Conf 51 Migr 114 Her 177, 250 Congr 57 Fug 73 Somn 2:237 Mos 1:263, 278, 285, 292, 305 Mos 2:199 Spec 1:188 Spec 2:129 Spec 3:61 Praem 72, 126, 126, 127, 157, 162, 169 Hypoth 7:9 QG 4:51c

'Αραβία Ios 15 Mos 1:47

ἀραιός Congr 169 Mos 1:118

ἀραίωμα Opif 38, 131

ἀράομαι Conf 65, 65, 72 Mos 1:278

ἀράσσω Contempl 40

ἀρατικός Agr 140 Congr 149

ἀραχνοϋφής Somn 2:53 Contempl 51 Prov 2:17

Ἄραψ Mos 1:51 Virt 34

'Αρβόχ QG 4:72

ἀργαλέος (65) Opif 81 Sacr 32, 35 Det 140, 176 Deus 48, 66, 97, 114 Agr 37, 120, 163, 171 Ebr 6, 150 Sobr 57 Conf 20, 90, 92 Mut 150, 244 Somn 1:184 Somn 2:147 Abr 64, 104, 230 Ios 5, 68, 77, 214 Mos 1:11, 42, 108, 145, 164, 168, 183 Mos 2:177 Decal 140, 156 Spec 1:100, 301 Spec 3:3, 28, 54, 154, 197 Spec 4:80, 91 Virt 35, 161 Praem 6, 72, 73, 90, 128 Flacc 21, 95, 182 Legat 190, 302, 334 Prov 2:65 QG isf 12 QG (Par) 2:7

ἀργαλεότης Plant 115

ἀργέω Spec 1:125 Spec 2:60 Flacc 33 Legat 128 Hypoth 7:14

ἀργία (11) Opif 169 Cher 111 Her 77, 213 Fug 36 Somn 2:301 Mos 1:322 Spec 3:106 Prob 69 Aet 84 Flacc 41

'Αργοναυτής Prob 128, 142

ἀργός (17) Opif 65 Leg 1:32 Conf 43 Somn 1:29, 107 Mos 1:54 Mos 2:136 Decal 162 Spec 1:21 Spec 2:86, 88, 101 Virt 25, 97 Flacc 148 Hypoth 7:15 QG 1:24

Ἄργος Legat 281

ἀργυραμοιβός Sobr 20 Spec 4:77

ἀργύρεος (ἀργυροῦς) Leg 1:51 Somn 2:61 Ios 207 Mos 2:77 Spec 1:22

ἀργύριον (20) Sacr 55 Gig 37 Deus 169 Her 44 Fug 15 Ios 180, 193, 194, 197, 209, 213, 215 Spec 1:23, 139, 323 Spec 4:158 Virt 86 Flacc 142 Legat 158, 343

ἀργυρισμός (7) Cher 34 Post 150 Conf 93 Fug 35 Ios 125, 258 Virt 92

ἀργυρολογέω Spec 2:94 Spec 4:215 Flacc 131

ἄργυρος (34) Leg 2:107 Cher 48, 80 Det 20, 157 Plant 57 Sobr 41 Congr 112 Fug 26 Mut 89 Abr 220 Ios 243, 258 Mos 1:152 Mos 2:90 Decal 66, 133 Spec 1:21, 22, 25 Spec 4:74, 223 Virt 188 Prob 9, 31, 65, 76 Legat 9, 108, 151, 216 Prov 2:10, 12, 17

ἀργυροῦς ἀργύρεος

ἀργυρώνητος (12) Her 42 Abr 232 Ios 219 Spec 1:126 Spec 2:122, 233 Spec 4:15, 152 Virt 189 Prob 19, 158 Flacc 127

'Αργώ Prob 143, 143

ἄρδην Abr 233 Prob 104 Flacc 116

ἄρδω (36) Opif 41, 133 Leg 1:26, 28, 34, 64, 65 Sacr 61 Post 125, 153 Deus 37 Plant 15 Sobr 36 Migr 33, 101 Her 32, 174 Congr 130 Fug 180, 187 Mut 260 Somn 1:38, 122 Somn 2:239, 242, 271 Mos 1:202 Decal 81 Spec 1:148, 216 Spec 2:180 Spec 3:199 Virt 130 Aet 91, 98 QG (Par) 2:3

ἀρειμάνιος Ebr 115 Virt 1

ἀρέσκεια (24) Opif 144 Sacr 37, 53 Det 64 Her 123 Congr 78, 78, 80 Fug 88 Somn 1:66 Abr 130 Ios 66, 67, 193 Decal 64 Spec 1:176, 205, 297, 300, 317 Spec 2:93 Flacc 82 Legat 332 QE 2:3b

ἀρέσκω (6) Leg 3:177, 188, 194 Deus 23 Fug 159 Aet 87

ἀρεστός Congr 153 Spec 1:318 Spec 4:131

ἀρετάω (18) Opif 39 Migr 140 Her 204 Mut 265 Somn 2:139 Ios 257 Mos 1:224 Spec 1:246, 335 Spec 2:54, 88 Spec 3:59 Spec 4:212, 217, 226 Praem 10, 41 Legat 282

ἀρετή (ὁ) (955) Opif 8, 73, 73, 73, 73, 81, 81, 82, 104, 104, 144, 153, 154, 156, 168, 170 Leg 1:18, 34, 35, 45, 45, 45, 45, 46, 47, 47, 48, 49, 52, 54, 54, 54, 56, 56, 57, 57, 58, 59, 59, 59, 61, 61, 62, 63, 63, 63, 64, 65, 65, 65, 65, 65, 66, 66, 69, 70, 70, 71, 72, 73, 79, 89, 89, 89, 92, 97, 97, 102, 103, 104, 105, 107 Leg 2:18, 47, 48, 49, 53, 55, 60, 60, 64, 78, 79, 80, 80, 82, 98, 98 Leg 3:1, 1, 2, 2, 3, 3, 10, 14, 14, 15, 18, 19, 22, 22, 24, 39, 48, 52, 54, 55, 68, 74, 89, 93, 107, 110, 120, 122, 123, 124, 126, 126, 128, 132, 135, 136, 140, 144, 150, 151, 152, 167, 175, 180, 181, 181, 181, 186, 192, 199, 205, 209, 217, 218, 219, 242, 244, 244, 244, 244, 245, 245, 245, 246, 247, 249, 249, 249 Cher 2, 3, 5, 7, 9, 10, 12, 29, 40, 41, 42, 43, 46, 47, 48, 49, 50, 52, 78, 84, 93, 96, 101, 103 Sacr 9, 14, 16, 16, 18, 20, 26, 27, 33, 35, 36, 37, 39, 43, 45, 46, 51, 57, 57, 59, 63, 65, 73, 73, 78, 80, 84, 86, 90, 100, 101, 101, 103, 109, 111, 115, 115, 120, 135, 135 Det 18, 18, 26, 27, 28, 32, 35, 42, 45, 45, 46, 48, 53, 59, 59, 60, 60, 61, 66, 70, 72, 74, 75, 77, 95, 111, 114, 114, 116, 120, 122, 137, 141, 148, 156, 160, 160, 165, 166 Post 31, 32, 45, 46, 60, 62, 62, 62, 63, 89, 91, 91, 91, 92, 93, 99, 118, 127, 128, 129, 130, 133, 134, 136, 139, 150, 151, 154, 170, 172, 173, 182, 185 Gig 4, 17, 33, 35, 44, 48, 48 Deus 4, 19, 24, 26, 29, 49, 79, 88, 95, 96, 103, 111, 118, 122, 137, 140, 154, 180 Agr 6, 9, 18, 25, 44, 77, 79, 81, 91, 101, 104, 109, 119, 121, 125, 142, 157, 160, 168 Plant 31, 35, 37, 37, 38, 40, 41, 42, 43, 43, 46, 60, 108, 121, 122, 122, 126, 134, 145, 159, 171, 172 Ebr 2, 6, 6, 8, 16, 21, 23, 29, 42, 80, 82, 83, 85, 94, 94, 95, 116, 119, 128, 133, 134, 137, 138, 139, 139, 148, 150, 150, 187, 211, 224, 224 Sobr 8, 9, 15, 20, 25, 29, 38, 41, 41, 43, 61, 65, 69 Conf 43, 52, 57, 60, 61, 67, 67, 68, 69, 70, 81, 86, 91, 103, 147, 149, 161, 167, 198 Migr 18, 26, 27, 37, 45, 47, 53, 70, 86, 99, 104, 122, 123, 126, 128, 132, 144, 145, 147, 151, 154, 156, 158, 163, 163, 167, 167, 200, 219, 225 Her 5, 35, 37, 38, 44, 48, 62, 88, 91, 110, 110, 112, 128, 175, 179, 194, 209, 241, 241, 243, 256, 258, 274, 285, 290, 292, 298, 307, 307, 307, 309, 310, 311, 316 Congr 2, 3, 4, 6, 7, 9, 10, 11, 12, 18, 19, 22, 22, 23, 23, 24, 26, 35, 37, 53, 56, 63, 64, 71, 82, 82, 111, 113, 114, 123, 123, 128, 129, 138, 142, 178, 179, 180 Fug 6, 18, 18, 18, 21, 25, 36, 38, 43, 51, 55, 58, 82, 110, 112, 114, 126, 128, 139, 149, 154, 176, 183, 183, 187, 187, 194, 209 Mut 14, 50, 71, 73, 75, 78, 80, 81, 83, 88, 133, 142, 148, 148, 149, 149, 149, 149, 150, 150, 167, 167, 171, 183, 184, 187, 196, 196, 199, 213, 220, 224, 225, 229, 254, 255, 258, 260, 261, 263, 265, 269 Somn 1:37, 48, 49, 51, 84, 86, 94, 117, 121, 124, 131, 167, 174, 174, 177, 179, 179, 200, 220, 225, 246, 248, 248, 251, 256 Somn 2:11, 22, 74, 76, 90, 98, 107, 133, 170, 173, 176, 178, 182, 190, 225, 230, 232, 235, 243, 243, 244, 256, 258, 277, 279, 281 Abr 1, 4, 15, 16, 19, 23, 25, 26, 27, 31, 31, 31, 34, 36, 37, 41, 47, 48, 50, 52, 54, 55, 60, 89, 99, 99, 100, 101, 101, 102, 103, 103, 104, 105, 105, 106, 114, 114, 116, 146, 168, 191, 204, 206, 219, 219, 220, 224, 227, 243, 244, 261, 269, 270 Ios 59, 80, 87, 153, 153, 172, 230 Mos 1:48, 48, 76, 148, 159, 226, 259, 318, 329, 329 Mos 2:7, 8, 8, 9, 10, 11, 17, 29, 45, 53, 57, 66, 113, 115, 128, 129, 134, 138, 140, 180, 181, 183, 184, 189, 200, 216, 239 Decal 29, 52, 100, 110, 119 Spec 1:19, 52, 55, 105, 150, 150, 173, 186, 201, 209, 215, 221, 245, 269, 269, 277, 287, 287, 290, 295, 303, 304, 308, 314, 320, 324 Spec 2:11, 13, 23, 23, 29, 30, 39, 42, 45, 46, 47, 61, 62, 68, 73, 73, 147, 170, 187, 209, 226, 228, 235, 236, 259, 262, 262, 262 Spec 3:51, 128, 155, 186, 191, 209 Spec 4:14, 58, 101, 108, 124, 134, 134, 135, 144, 145, 147, 148, 150, 151, 177, 179, 181, 192, 206 Virt 8, 10, 15, 22, 47, 53, 55, 60, 67, 85, 85, 94, 95, 120, 127, 142, 164, 170, 181, 181, 188, 190, 194, 198, 205, 206, 210, 211, 216, 226, 227 Praem 3, 5, 11, 15, 20, 27, 27, 31, 50, 52, 53, 62, 64, 65, 66, 90, 93, 112, 115, 119, 152, 160, 164, 172 Prob 8, 27, 53, 57, 60, 60, 61, 62, 63, 68, 69, 74, 74, 80, 88, 92, 105, 107, 109, 111, 114, 117, 135, 146, 150, 151, 152, 154 Contempl 1, 26, 34, 60, 72, 90 Aet 2, 75 Legat 5, 81, 91, 98, 143, 196, 309, 312 Hypoth 11:2 Prov 2:1, 6, 14, 19, 21, 38, 41 QG 1:51, 96:1, 97, 97, 100:1b, 2:11, 38, 39, 3:8, 29, 29, 4:153, 169, 173, 180, 204, 206a QE 1:7b, 2:20 QE isf 7, 26

ἀρήγω Somn 1:86 Abr 95 Legat 113

ἀρήν (12) Spec 1:188, 189, 251, 253 Spec 4:12 Virt 133, 142, 142, 144 Praem 87 Legat 76, 317

Ἄρης (6) Legat 93, 97, 97, 111, 112, 113

ἀρθριτικός Praem 145

ἄρθρον Fug 72 Somn 1:229, 229 Legat 238

ἀρθρόω (9) Det 22 Post 106 Her 4, 25 Mut 56 Somn 1:29 Mos 1:84 Decal 46 QG (Par) 2:3

ἄρθρωσις Praem 2

ἀρίγνωτος Aet 37

ἀρίδακρυς Sacr 32

ἀρίδηλος (26) Deus 29 Agr 97 Plant 12, 27 Migr 35, 39, 93 Her 303 Somn 1:201 Somn 2:3, 241 Ios 145 Mos 1:59, 269, 298 Mos 2:248 Decal 34 Spec 4:139 Virt 53, 63 Prob 95 Flacc 7, 144 Prov 2:24, 27, 71

ἀριθμέω (8) Leg 3:39 Post 96, 96 Her 86, 97 Somn 2:192 Ios 158 Mos 1:147

ἀριθμητικός (7) Opif 107, 108 Sacr 1 Somn 1:205 Decal 21 Spec 2:200 Spec 4:105

ἀριθμός (267) Opif 13, 13, 13, 14, 14, 27, 47, 47, 47, 49, 49, 50, 51, 51, 52, 53, 55, 60, 60, 78, 89, 91, 91, 92, 93, 96, 96, 97, 98, 99, 99, 100, 101, 101, 101, 102, 102, 106, 107, 109, 120, 123, 127, 138 Leg 1:3, 4, 14, 15, 15, 63 Leg 2:3 Cher 68 Sacr 7, 122 Det 63, 82, 88 Post 36, 48, 64, 89, 95, 96, 96, 96, 96, 96, 173 Gig 55, 56 Deus 11, 85, 90 Agr 104 Plant 59, 75, 76, 76, 94, 117, 118, 121, 122, 123, 124, 125, 125, 132, 133, 151 Ebr 15, 115 Sobr 19 Migr 152, 154, 169, 176, 198, 201, 202, 203, 207 Her 88, 107, 108, 126, 144, 145, 146, 156, 175, 189, 190, 190, 190, 193, 195, 298, 299 Congr 4, 88, 90, 91, 94, 95, 102, 109, 113, 116, 117 Fug 57, 73, 87, 87, 94, 184, 185, 186 Mut 1, 88, 143, 183, 188, 188, 189, 192, 192, 200 Somn 1:30, 138 Somn 2:112, 193, 194 Abr 13, 13, 28, 28, 69, 69, 98, 122, 244 Ios 29, 101, 113, 182 Mos 1:23, 96, 188, 311, 315 Mos 2:28, 79, 80, 81, 84, 102, 115, 115, 124, 174, 266 Decal 20, 20, 20, 23, 23, 26, 27, 28, 102, 168 Spec 1:91, 163, 170, 177, 178, 181, 336 Spec 2:32, 40, 40, 41, 41, 47, 56, 58, 84, 86, 108, 113, 140, 150, 156, 176, 177, 179, 201, 215, 217, 230 Spec 4:41, 54, 105, 105, 105, 113 Virt 10, 43, 46, 77, 158, 185 Praem 26, 65, 110, 111, 111, 111, 125 Prob 72 Contempl 65 Aet 58, 145 Flacc 163 Prov 1, 2:22 QG 1:1, 76b, 77, 77, 2:5a, 12a, 12a, 12b, 13b, 14, 3:38a, 49b, 61, 61, 4:8a, 8b QG isf 17 QG (Par) 2:5 QE 2:46, 46 ἀριστάω Prob 122

ἀριστεία Mos 2:173 Spec 1:57 Spec 3:124 Virt 2, 38

ἀριστεῖα Mos 1:327 Mos 2:65, 160 Spec 1:132 QG isf 17

ἀριστεῖος Somn 1:130

ἀριστερός Post 101, 102 Deus 163

ἀριστεύς Mos 1:304 Mos 2:274

ἀριστεύω Gig 43 Spec 2:245

ἀριστίνδην (33) Migr 201 Congr 114 Somn 1:128 Somn 2:54, 272 Abr 83 Ios 260 Mos 1:221, 306 Mos 2:31, 88, 142, 160 Decal 18, 175 Spec 1:78, 79, 101, 163, 166, 198, 259, 303 Spec 2:125, 173 Spec 4:170 Virt 10, 42, 57, 66 Contempl 72 Flacc 149 Legat 350

Ἀρίστιππος Plant 151

ἀριστοκρατία QE 1:7b

ἀριστοποιέω Mos 1:169

Ἀριστοτέλης Aet 10, 12, 16, 18

ἀρκεόντως Det 141 Gig 67 Ebr 11

ἀρκέω (24) Opif 87 Leg 2:12 Leg 3:165, 227 Sacr 71 Gig 56 Conf 1, 75, 110 Migr 216 Her 20, 133, 193 Ios 30, 258 Spec 4:5, 129, 148, 238 Virt 101 Prob 145 Legat 311, 347 Prov 2:9

ἀρκτέον (9) Cher 43 Her 207 Fug 7 Abr 119 Mos 2:117, 192 Spec 2:41, 243 Aet 132

ἀρκτικός Opif 112 Legat 8

ἄρκτος (11) Opif 114 Leg 1:8 Somn 2:87 Abr 161 Mos 1:109 Decal 113 Spec 1:69 Spec 2:57 Praem 89 Legat 89, 145

ἄρκυς Sacr 31 Agr 24 Mos 1:172 Flacc 121

ἅρμα (17) Leg 3:223 Ebr 111 Migr 160, 161 Her 301 Mut 93, 149 Somn 1:157 Somn 2:16, 46, 201, 294 Ios 120, 148 Mos 1:168, 179 Spec 4:79

ἁρμάμαξα Ios 251 Flacc 92

ἁρμάτειος Ios 149

ἁρματροχία Agr 75

ἁρμόδιος Sacr 40

ἁρμόζω (216) Opif 13, 78, 82, 117, 137, 152, 169 Leg 1:45 Leg 2:67, 91 Leg 3:104, 131, 195 Cher 11, 18, 23, 32, 110 Sacr 24, 36, 45, 74, 75, 85, 86, 99, 100 Det 88 Post 30, 60, 66, 88, 157 Gig 41 Deus 4, 19, 22, 24, 25, 70, 84 Agr 76, 79, 159 Plant 6, 15, 16, 73, 86, 150, 159, 163, 167, 169 Ebr 36, 58, 71, 111, 116, 203 Sobr 36, 36, 58 Conf 25, 55, 67, 83, 85, 85, 150, 171, 174, 175, 198 Migr 55, 132, 164, 178, 192, 193 Her 40, 130, 144, 153, 185, 247 Congr 122, 136 Fug 61, 66, 88, 112, 114, 119, 146 Mut 51, 56, 62, 94, 104, 111, 147, 184, 211, 232 Somn 1:37, 52, 102, 111, 161, 200, 205 Somn 2:18, 28, 92, 159, 180, 262, 263, 290 Abr 100, 117, 143, 155, 165, 191, 217, 246, 248 Ios 204 Mos 1:155, 241, 245, 255, 324, 334 Mos 2:67, 73, 75, 90, 103, 129, 149, 158, 212, 217, 234, 289, 289 Decal 18, 33, 43, 84, 175 Spec 1:5, 103, 137, 152, 194, 222, 286, 294, 309, 329, 340 Spec 2:1, 30, 34, 42, 125, 148, 175, 184, 199, 203, 239, 244 Spec 3:28, 39, 51, 131 Spec 4:36, 64, 68, 103, 119, 142, 168 Virt 21, 32, 72, 74, 89, 103, 114 Praem 22, 41, 95, 97, 100, 154 Prob 24, 99 Aet 11, 13, 47, 60 Flacc 135 Legat 8, 147, 284, 323 Prov 2:3 QG 3:21 QE 2:17, 20

ἁρμονία (72) Opif 96, 96, 96, 107, 107, 126 Sacr 37 Post 12, 14, 103 Deus 11, 24 Agr 79 Plant 60 Conf 56, 58, 67, 150 Migr 220 Her 15, 242 Congr 16 Fug 112 Mut 87 Somn 1:22, 30, 35 Somn 2:270 Mos 1:29 Mos 2:48, 52, 119, 120, 132, 140, 243, 256 Decal 23, 33, 132 Spec 1:93, 110, 342 Spec 2:52, 99, 130, 150, 191, 200 Spec 3:23, 28, 184 Spec 4:39, 102, 187, 203 Virt 73, 184, 225 Praem 56, 81, 145 Contempl 63, 84 Aet 75 QG 2:34a, 34b, 3:3, 38a, 49b, 4:174, 200b

ἁρμονικός (9) Opif 95, 107, 107, 108, 109, 110 Mos 1:23 Decal 21 Spec 2:200

ἁρμόνιος Sacr 83 Deus 84

ἀρνέομαι (20) Cher 41 Sacr 23, 79 Plant 107 Ebr 188, 192 Somn 1:49 Abr 112, 206 Spec 1:235, 278 Spec 2:54, 255 Spec 3:71 Spec 4:32, 32, 40, 40 Legat 247 QG 1:68

ἄρνησις (6) Cher 14 Ebr 198 Somn 2:202 Mos 2:228 Spec 4:87 QG 3:58

ἀρνίον Legat 362

Ἀρνών Leg 3:225, 230

ἀροτήρ Decal 77

ἄροτος Opif 85 Spec 2:70 Spec 4:12, 205 Virt 146

ἀροτριάω Spec 4:205

ἄροτρον Post 142

ἄρουρα (29) Plant 73, 74, 75 Ebr 211 Conf 38 Her 32 Fug 180 Mut 190 Somn 2:239, 271 Ios 109, 260 Mos 1:6, 116, 202 Mos 2:66 Spec 1:105 Spec 2:29 Spec 3:32, 33, 39 Spec 4:23 Virt 145 Praem 154 Contempl 62 Aet 69, 98 Flacc 63 Legat 249

ἀρόω Mos 1:201 Decal 162 Spec 1:165 Spec 3:34 Virt 146

ἁρπαγή (20) Agr 83 Conf 117 Ios 213 Decal 171 Spec 1:204, 235 Spec 3:158 Spec 4:84, 196 Flacc 5, 56, 57, 57, 62, 69, 105 Legat 105, 122, 129, 302

ἁρπάζω (24) Cher 93 Gig 13 Agr 151 Plant 107 Conf 47 Her 71 Somn 2:65, 67 Ios 93 Spec 1:236, 278 Spec 3:69, 104 Praem 140 Prob 133 Contempl 12 Flacc 53, 60, 77, 94, 94, 171 Legat 169 Hypoth 7:4

ἅρπυιαι Plant 24

ἀρραβών Fug 149, 150, 151, 151, 151

ἀρραγής (7) Migr 223 Her 217 Congr 113 Somn 1:217 Spec 1:146 Spec 2:20 QG (Par) 2:4

ἀρρενικός (ἀρσενικός) (10) Leg 3:8, 11 Sacr 89, 89, 102, 103, 104 Deus 141 Spec 1:135, 248

ἀρρενογονέω Gig 5 Migr 126, 206

ἀρρενόομαι Ios 79 Spec 3:173 Virt 20 Legat 320

ἀρρεπής (12) Gig 50 Deus 23 Conf 30, 32 Mut 87, 153, 183 Somn 2:220, 227 Abr 170 Prob 29 QE isf 12

ἄρρηκτος (11) Det 103, 158 Agr 112 Plant 9 Ebr 102 Conf 166 Migr 181 Her 67 Fug 112 Mut 240 Aet 125

ἄρρην ἄρσην

ἄρρητος (13) Opif 126 Det 102, 175, 176 Her 170 Mut 14, 15, 15 Somn 1:67, 191 Abr 20 Spec 3:178 Prob 108

ἀρρηφορέω Ebr 129

ἄρρυθμος Cher 105 Congr 16 Spec 1:343

ἀρρώστημα (28) Opif 150 Sacr 48, 70, 121 Det 43 Post 46, 72, 74, 74 Deus 65, 67, 182 Sobr 45 Conf 16 Her 284 Congr 53 Somn 1:69 Mos 1:133 Spec 1:167, 253, 257 Spec 2:17 Spec 3:98 Spec 4:100 Virt 162 Prov 2:18, 32 QG isf 13

ἀρρωστία Cher 68

ἀρσενικός ἀρρενικός

ἄρσην (ἄρρην) (103) Opif 13, 13, 14, 76, 134, 161 Leg 2:13, 97, 97 Leg 3:3, 188, 202, 243 Cher 43, 54, 111, 111 Sacr 103, 103, 106, 112, 112 Det 28, 121, 170, 172, 172 Post 10, 177 Gig 4, 5 Deus 111 Agr 73, 73, 139 Plant 158 Ebr 33, 55, 164, 211, 212, 224 Migr 95, 140 Her 61, 139, 164 Congr 131 Fug 51, 51, 51, 52, 204, 208 Mut 261 Somn 1:200 Somn 2:15, 184 Abr 101, 101, 102, 135 Mos 1:8, 13 Mos 2:60, 234, 235 Decal 54 Spec 1:138, 198, 200, 201, 212, 228, 228, 233, 240, 325, 331 Spec 2:33, 33, 34, 50, 56, 58, 125, 164 Spec 3:37, 37, 43, 178, 178 Virt 18 Prob 124 Contempl 59 Hypoth 7:1 Prov 2:71 QG 2:14 QE 1:7a, 2:3a, 3b QE isf 22, 22

ἄρσις Her 241

ἀρτάω (19) Opif 117 Leg 3:16 Cher 67, 104 Sacr 13 Post 26 Gig 39, 45 Plant 165 Conf 57 Migr 44 Her 56, 97 Somn 1:45 Mos 1:184 Mos 2:121, 130 Spec 1:26 Prob 19

Ἄρτεμις Decal 54

ἀρτηρία (6) Post 104 Deus 84 Mos 1:84 Decal 32 Praem 144 QG (Par) 2:3

ἄρτι (30) Opif 136 Leg 1:94 Leg 3:159 Cher 114 Det 12 Post 131, 152, 172 Agr 161 Plant 52, 99, 151, 161 Migr 150 Fug 146 Mut 172 Somn 1:9, 199 Abr 231 Ios 250 Mos 1:49, 215, 230, 251 Mos 2:222 Spec 3:119 Contempl 52 Legat 23 QE 1:7b, 2:25b

ἀρτίγονος Virt 130 Aet 67

ἀρτιοπέρισσος (6) Opif 14 Decal 20, 20 Spec 2:58 QG 3:38a, 49b

ἄρτιος (35) Opif 13, 13 Det 7 Post 32, 80 Gig 41 Deus 179 Plant 38, 125 Ebr 135 Mut 70, 88, 182 Somn 1:131 Somn 2:163 Mos 2:84 Decal 20, 20, 164 Spec 2:58 Spec 3:106 Spec 4:167 Virt 98, 101 Aet 104 Flacc 50 Legat 58, 351 QG 2:14, 3:38a, 49a, 49b, 61, 61 QE 2:26

ἀρτιότης QE isf 16

ἀρτίπους Mut 187

ἄρτος (55) Leg 3:81, 81, 142, 162, 169, 173, 173, 174, 176, 251, 251 Sacr 107, 107 Sobr 8 Migr 157, 157 Her 175, 226 Congr 161, 167, 168, 170 Fug 137, 139, 139, 185 Mut 259 Somn 1:36, 126 Somn 2:158 Mos 2:104 Decal 160 Spec 1:132, 172, 172, 173, 175, 185 Spec 2:20, 158, 161, 179, 182, 185, 186 Praem 99 Contempl 37, 73, 81, 81, 81 QE 2:18, 18, 18, 18

ἀρτύω Ebr 219

ἀρύτω ἀρύω

ἀρύω (ἀρύτω) (19) Opif 31 Post 130 Plant 168 Fug 97, 202 Mut 165 Somn 2:190 Mos 1:81, 144, 182 Spec 1:262 Spec 3:58, 186 Spec 4:75, 81, 140 Virt 79, 125 Prob 57

Ἀρφαξάτ Mut 189

ἀρχάγγελος Conf 146 Her 205 Somn 1:157

ἀρχαιολογέω Sacr 79 Abr 5 Mos 2:48 Spec 1:8

ἀρχαιολογία Her 279 Spec 2:146

ἀρχαῖος (65) Opif 21 Sacr 78 Det 63, 149 Post 90, 98, 101, 110 Deus 138, 178 Plant 161 Ebr 164 Migr 150 Her 181, 278, 283 Congr 89 Mut 85, 171 Somn 1:205 Abr 19, 67, 81 Ios 262 Mos 1:3, 31, 93, 101, 164, 186, 241, 262 Decal 11 Spec 1:2, 102, 103 Spec 2:13, 35, 74, 78, 85, 115, 122, 160 Spec 3:30, 35 Spec 4:47, 149 Virt 67, 83, 84 Praem 170 Prob 15 Contempl 80 Flacc 153 Legat 135, 301, 305, 315 Hypoth 6:1 QG 3:38a, 48, 49b, 61 QE 2:19

ἀρχαιότροπος Plant 158 Migr 201 Prob 82

ἀρχέγονος Post 63 Contempl 2 Aet 57

ἀρχέκακος Ebr 12 Spec 4:85 Contempl 70

ἀρχέτυπος (79) Opif 16, 25, 25, 69, 71, 78, 141 Leg 1:22, 43, 45 Leg 2:4 Leg 3:96, 102 Cher 11, 86, 97 Det 78, 83, 87 Post 105, 185 Deus 25, 32 Plant 20, 27, 50 Ebr 133, 133 Conf 63, 108, 172 Migr 12, 12, 40 Her 126, 225, 230, 280 Congr 8 Mut 135, 146, 183, 267 Somn 1:37, 75, 75, 115, 126, 173, 188, 206, 232 Somn 2:147 Abr 3 Ios 87 Mos 2:74 Decal 26, 101 Spec 1:171, 279, 327 Spec 2:152, 237 Spec 3:83, 207 Spec 4:55, 164 Virt 51, 70, 197 Praem 29, 163 Prob 62, 94 Contempl 29 Aet 15 Legat 246, 365 QG 4:110b

ἀρχή (523) Opif 2, 3, 13, 26, 26, 27, 27, 44, 44, 44, 44, 45, 52, 54, 57, 62, 67, 79, 82, 82, 82, 82, 84, 91, 94, 97, 97, 98, 127, 141, 141, 148, 148, 151, 152, 170 Leg 1:5, 6, 6, 9, 19, 43, 63, 64, 65 Leg 2:15, 15, 107 Leg 3:8, 70, 78, 84, 89, 92, 113, 167, 185, 185, 187, 188, 188, 205, 253 Cher 5, 5, 7, 28, 29, 29, 36, 54, 107, 117 Sacr 19, 35, 49, 59, 120 Det 33, 44, 56, 64, 81, 88, 118, 122, 142, 145, 153, 154, 157 Post 7, 65, 112, 113, 117, 127, 128, 129, 170, 174, 174, 181 Gig 14, 15, 47, 66 Deus 26, 28, 70 Agr 31, 47, 49, 56, 60, 85, 125, 125, 157, 158, 169, 173, 173, 180, 181 Plant 53, 76, 77, 88, 90, 92, 93, 150 Ebr 15, 42, 57, 75, 126 Sobr 21, 23, 25, 40, 57, 69 Conf 42, 42, 55, 68, 106, 114, 144, 146, 153, 177, 187, 193 Migr 42, 56, 172, 186 Her 62, 92, 114, 114, 116, 116, 116, 117, 120, 121, 121, 121, 122, 122, 125, 126, 163, 172, 190, 198, 209, 273, 281, 315 Congr 2, 2, 81, 89, 92, 120, 146 Fug 10, 12, 20, 26, 88, 107, 148, 171, 171, 172, 172, 178, 183, 186 Mut 15, 16, 17, 17, 20, 22, 36, 58, 65, 77, 79, 79, 79, 79, 88, 100, 102, 258 Somn 1:5, 142, 151, 162, 162, 187, 211, 211 Somn 2:29, 99, 123, 154, 217, 221, 241, 243, 243, 244, 284, 287, 289, 290 Abr 1, 5, 7, 19, 25, 37, 46, 46, 47, 60, 64, 91, 105, 112, 116, 134, 162, 164, 219, 242, 263 Ios 12, 37, 70, 85, 87, 92, 92, 98, 119, 131, 133, 137, 148, 159, 166, 173, 217, 225, 246 Mos 1:8, 22, 32, 46, 48, 60, 81, 96, 98, 138, 139, 148, 150, 163, 186, 226, 231, 251, 256, 300, 307, 311, 327, 328 Mos 2:1, 34, 37, 39, 49, 51, 60, 64, 80, 93, 181, 181, 181, 181, 220, 222, 241, 246, 246, 258, 285 Decal 5, 35, 51, 52, 53, 58, 89, 102, 117, 136, 142, 164 Spec 1:51, 55, 102, 172, 180, 182, 186, 188, 188, 198, 266, 300, 325 Spec 2:38, 40, 40, 56, 65, 110, 111, 119, 122, 125, 126, 133, 140, 140, 142, 142, 151, 152, 155, 156, 157, 157, 157, 177, 204, 210, 212, 231, 233 Spec 3:16, 29, 121, 184 Spec 4:12, 25, 89, 97, 100, 143, 147, 151, 157, 158, 160, 170, 176, 186, 209, 214, 231 Virt 22, 53, 54, 59, 61, 63, 70, 79, 81, 107, 179, 188, 202, 218 Praem 1, 7, 9, 23, 46, 63, 68, 69, 97, 98, 102, 105, 107, 118, 130 Prob 20, 42, 107, 117, 139 Contempl 6, 17, 39, 63, 65 Aet 14, 19, 20, 42, 53, 59, 59, 71, 73, 89, 98, 98, 99, 118, 143 Flacc 2, 10, 11, 12, 18, 18, 20, 23, 45, 45, 91, 103, 105, 107, 138, 146 Legat 10, 15, 19, 23, 24, 28, 32, 34, 36, 68, 71, 76, 85, 87, 143, 144, 149, 190, 213, 230, 232, 255, 279, 290, 293, 335, 347 Hypoth 7:17 Prov 2:2, 25 QG 1:20, 96:1, 2:12b, 17c, 31, 31, 31, 41, 54a, 4:51a, 153, 189, 204, 206b QE 1:1, 1, 1 QE isf 16

ἀρχηγέτης (33) Opif 79, 136, 142 Post 42 Ebr 42 Fug 73, 89 Mut 64, 88 Abr 9, 46, 276 Mos 1:7, 34, 242 Mos 2:65, 274 Decal 1 Spec 2:3, 217 Spec 4:123, 181 Virt

193, 199, 206 Praem 57, 60, 166 Prob 10 Contempl 29 Legat 54 QG 2:17c QG isf 17

ἀρχηγικός Mos 2:219

ἀρχηγός Leg 3:175 Somn 1:89

ἀρχιδεσμοφύλαξ Deus 111, 116 Ebr 210

ἀρχιερεύς (68) Leg 2:56 Sacr 130 Gig 52 Ebr 85 Migr 102 Her 82, 182, 303 Fug 87, 106, 106, 108, 115, 116, 118, 118 Somn 1:214, 215, 216, 219 Somn 2:183, 185, 189 Mos 1:301, 304 Mos 2:3, 6, 31, 66, 75, 109, 117, 133, 142, 146, 153, 176, 178, 187, 292 Spec 1:72, 84, 96, 97, 105, 107, 109, 110, 113, 113, 226, 228, 229, 230, 230, 244, 244, 268 Spec 2:164 Spec 3:123, 131, 134 Spec 4:69 Praem 78 Legat 278, 296, 307 QE 2:105

ἀρχιερωσύνη (7) Fug 42 Mos 1:334 Mos 2:2, 275 Praem 53, 56 Legat 278

ἀρχικός (7) Abr 99, 124 Ios 189 Spec 4:147 Prob 159 Legat 53 Prov 2:38

ἀρχιμάγειρος (15) Leg 3:236, 236 Deus 111 Ebr 210, 210, 210, 210, 216 Mut 173 Somn 2:16 Ios 27, 61, 104, 152, 154

ἀρχιοινοχόος (18) Ebr 208, 210, 210, 216, 218 Somn 2:5, 16, 155, 158, 181, 195 Ios 88, 90, 99, 104, 152, 154, 156

ἀρχιπροφήτης Mut 103, 125 Somn 2:189

ἀρχισιτοποιός (14) Ebr 210, 210, 214, 216 Somn 2:5, 16, 155, 158 Ios 88, 93, 104, 152, 154, 156

ἀρχιστράτηγος Congr 125

ἀρχισωματοφύλαξ Legat 175

ἀρχιτεκτονέω Somn 1:206

ἀρχιτεκτονικός Opif 17, 20

ἀρχιτέκτων Opif 24 Leg 3:95 Mut 30 Somn 2:8

ἄρχω (ἄρχων) (447) Opif 18, 31, 40, 57, 67, 68, 100, 100, 101, 117, 168 Leg 1:5, 6, 16, 18, 18, 26, 41, 72, 72 Leg 2:70, 72, 78, 78, 82, 96 Leg 3:73, 81, 84, 87, 88, 159, 163, 187, 191, 214, 222, 222, 223, 224, 228, 231, 244, 253 Cher 3, 7, 27, 27, 29, 31, 41, 50, 53, 83, 115, 115 Sacr 9, 12, 16, 28, 31, 44, 66, 104 Det 9, 12, 23, 25, 26, 82, 134, 141, 141, 159 Post 16, 64, 98, 109, 128, 134, 138, 152, 172, 174 Gig 1, 45, 54, 65, 66 Deus 35, 110, 112, 170 Agr 1, 8, 20, 31, 33, 41, 47, 47, 48, 56, 58, 84, 86, 88, 95, 118, 125, 125, 134, 159, 160, 165, 177, 181 Plant 1, 3, 52, 55, 57, 76, 86, 87, 98, 140 Ebr 3, 9, 11, 15, 98, 109, 131, 165, 221 Sobr 1, 14, 22 Conf 1, 33, 54, 83, 108, 112, 152, 154, 155, 170, 173 Migr 8, 8, 13, 20, 76, 116, 149, 150, 169, 184, 190, 202 Her 4, 30, 51, 102, 131, 134, 149, 163, 166, 189, 190, 195, 251, 256, 256, 258, 269, 271, 295 Congr 6, 109, 114 Fug 95, 95, 98 Mut 18, 23, 77, 80, 112, 128, 228 Somn 1:9, 124, 155, 155, 163, 182, 193, 194, 195, 240 Somn 2:2, 68, 91, 91, 119, 136, 136, 198, 244, 290, 299 Abr 10, 10, 70, 84, 99, 121, 122, 182, 193, 211, 223, 226, 237, 272 Ios 2, 44, 63, 76, 79, 79, 269 Mos 1:5, 5, 71, 90, 98, 114, 115, 134, 142, 151, 153, 160, 165, 170, 176, 181, 187, 311, 324 Mos 2:1, 5, 28, 34, 47, 48, 69, 99, 100, 184, 214, 214, 226, 235, 260, 266, 266 Decal 13, 14, 53, 66, 97, 119, 121, 165, 167, 167 Spec 1:1, 12, 13, 13, 14, 33, 77, 121, 172, 194, 219, 226, 228, 229, 229, 233, 300, 307, 307 Spec 2:3, 48, 78, 133, 141, 142, 145, 166, 166, 181, 226, 227, 234, 241, 251 Spec 3:74, 85, 105, 126, 146, 183, 184 Spec 4:7, 8, 8, 21, 85, 96, 110, 116, 127, 152, 157, 157, 162, 163, 169, 169, 175, 184, 184, 184, 188, 193, 224 Virt 63, 64, 66, 72, 76, 132, 151, 217 Praem 21, 28, 37, 54, 89, 97, 123, 123, 129, 153, 164, 166, 171 Prob 19, 22, 30, 35, 47, 96, 115, 123, 152 Contempl 9, 78 Aet 19, 62, 68, 110, 125, 149, 149 Flacc 4, 9, 15, 17, 19, 33, 43, 50, 76, 80, 81, 104, 115, 117, 123, 124, 125, 127, 147 Legat 5, 18, 20, 22, 48, 51, 57, 69, 70, 78, 87, 108, 119, 119, 140, 140, 180, 187, 222, 256, 273, 315, 346, 364, 365 Hypoth 7:3, 7:5 Prov 1 QG 1:66, 66, 2:66, 3:30b, 30b, 30b, 30b, 4:130 QG isf 5, 8, 17 QE 2:6a, 6a QE isf 9, 22

ἄρχων ἄρχω

ἀρωγός Leg 1:45 Conf 171 Migr 57, 225

ἄρωμα Leg 1:42 Somn 1:178 Somn 2:59

ἀσάλευτος Somn 1:158 Mos 2:14, 124 Prob 28 Aet 116

ἀσαπής QG (Par) 2:4

ἄσαρκος Gig 31 Ebr 87 Fug 58 Ios 101

ἀσάφεια (16) Leg 3:123, 226, 226 Sacr 85 Her 63, 302, 302 Somn 2:102, 106 Ios 106, 131, 140, 143 Spec 1:64 Spec 4:190 Prob 16

ἀσαφής (6) Leg 3:127, 228 Migr 19 Congr 136 Decal 148 Legat 38

ἀσάω QE isf 17

ἄσβεστος (19) Plant 4 Ebr 134, 212, 223 Conf 61, 156 Her 36, 276 Fug 81 Somn 2:67, 248 Abr 157 Ios 146 Decal 122 Spec 1:285, 285, 288 Spec 2:183, 215

ἀσέβεια (93) Leg 1:43 Cher 65 Sacr 15, 22, 71, 95 Det 50, 72 Post 2, 38, 52, 54 Deus 21, 112, 163, 164 Ebr 18, 41, 78, 109, 111 Conf 114, 117, 132, 134, 152, 155, 196 Migr 179 Congr 159, 160 Fug 61 Mut 19 Somn 2:119, 182 Abr 24 Ios 174 Mos 1:6, 90, 95, 237, 295, 301, 305, 311 Mos 2:161, 193, 196, 197, 274 Decal 62, 63, 75, 91, 92, 94, 111, 141 Spec 1:20, 62, 120, 215, 312, 330 Spec 2:8, 191, 249 Spec 3:90, 125, 126 Spec 4:147 Virt 34, 94, 144 Praem 105, 129, 142 Prob 90 Flacc 128 Legat 163, 193, 206, 355 Hypoth 7:2 Prov 2:39 QG 1:66, 2:13a, 13b, 15b, 17b QG isf 13 QE 2:45a, 47

ἀσεβέω (17) Leg 1:49 Det 73 Conf 15, 153 Her 250 Mut 125, 226 Somn 1:95 Decal 120 Spec 2:27, 170 Spec 3:19, 19 Virt 92 Hypoth 7:2 Prov 2:24 QG 1:66

ἀσέβημα (16) Deus 22 Mos 1:33, 294 Mos 2:200, 201, 204, 217 Spec 2:251, 254 Spec 3:84, 110, 180 Aet 85 Flacc 125 Legat 118 QG 1:66

ἀσεβής (69) Opif 80 Leg 3:9, 9, 10, 10, 207 Cher 2 Sacr 32 Det 103, 122, 143 Post 12, 34, 35, 39, 42, 53, 177 Deus 59 Ebr 223 Sobr 42 Conf 121, 125, 131, 182, 188 Migr 92, 113 Her 90 Congr 57, 87 Fug 144, 199 Mut 61, 136, 169, 197, 265 Somn 1:22 Somn 2:133 Ios 143, 198 Mos 1:39, 96, 96 Mos 2:47, 56, 57, 221, 279, 282, 285 Spec 1:55, 327 Spec 2:11, 253 Spec 3:36, 84, 209 Praem 69, 157 Prob 79 Aet 73 Legat 293 Prov 2:33 QG 1:60:2, 60:2 QG isf 10 QE 2:26

ἀσέλγεια Mos 1:3, 305 Spec 3:23

ἀσελγής Det 95 Post 156 Ios 51

ἀσέληνος Aet 88

ἄσεμνος Decal 80 Virt 182

Ἀσενέθ Somn 1:78

ἄση Det 98, 131 Ios 90 Mos 1:120

ἀσημείωτος Mos 1:255

ἄσημος (13) Migr 79 Her 180, 180, 180 Fug 9, 9, 11 Mut 140 Somn 1:255 Mos 2:164, 234 Virt 222 Prov 2:17

ἄσηπτος Mos 2:77 QG (Par) 2:4

᾿Ασήρ Migr 95 Somn 2:35

ἀσθένεια (61) Leg 1:69 Cher 89, 90 Sacr 17, 94, 96, 101, 139 Det 16, 35, 102, 113, 168 Post 4, 47, 120, 162, 175 Deus 15, 52, 80 Plant 145 Ebr 121, 185 Conf 164 Migr 144 Her 212, 284 Congr 164 Fug 96 Mut 100 Somn 1:119, 218 Somn 2:154, 170 Abr 26, 76 Ios 110, 130 Mos 1:8, 37, 53, 111, 184 Spec 1:293, 294 Spec 4:201, 223 Virt 25, 147, 157, 165, 167 Praem 119, 160 Prob 5 Aet 74, 125 Legat 14, 19 QG 4:180

ἀσθενέω (16) Sacr 88 Det 106 Deus 10, 14, 85, 173 Agr 181 Mut 143 Somn 2:94, 95, 170 Ios 111 Decal 147 Praem 159 Hypoth 11:13 QG 4:7*

ἀσθενής (44) Opif 23 Leg 1:86 Leg 3:48, 111 Agr 119, 146 Ebr 55, 186 Conf 103 Her 300 Mut 263 Somn 1:116, 155 Somn 2:152 Abr 105, 216, 240 Ios 41, 102 Mos 1:50, 65, 68, 69, 76 Decal 135 Spec 2:141 Spec 4:74, 89, 176, 205, 206 Virt 31, 146, 146 Praem 86, 134, 154 Prob 44, 91 Contempl 70 Aet 58, 106 Legat 319 QG 2:54a

ἆσθμα Ios 212 Flacc 176 Legat 125, 186, 243

᾿Ασία (19) Cher 63 Deus 175 Somn 2:54 Ios 134 Mos 2:19, 20 Prob 94, 132 Aet 141 Flacc 46 Legat 22, 48, 88, 144, 144, 245, 250, 281, 311

᾿Ασιανός (6) Mos 1:263 Mos 2:19 Legat 10, 144, 280, 283

ἀσινής (13) Det 125 Agr 16, 130 Her 105, 114 Congr 106 Fug 80 Abr 98 Spec 1:166, 191 Praem 13, 60, 65

ἀσιτία Leg 3:147 Det 34 Agr 152 Prob 121

ἄσιτος Virt 136

῎Ασκαλων Prov 2:64

᾿Ασκάλων Legat 205

᾿Ασκαλωνίτης Legat 205

ἄσκεπτος Opif 2 Congr 125

ἀσκέω (40) Leg 1:47, 54 Leg 3:128, 132, 190 Cher 42 Sacr 116 Det 39 Ebr 220 Fug 35, 156 Mut 39, 81 Abr 53, 129 Mos 2:66, 146 Spec 1:71, 83 Spec 2:228 Spec 3:37 Virt 21, 39, 94, 140, 178 Praem 100, 104 Contempl 39, 52 Flacc 112 Legat 30, 79, 79, 81, 151, 185, 296 Hypoth 11:14 QE isf 26

ἄσκηπτος Flacc 36

ἄσκησις (60) Leg 1:84 Leg 3:18, 135 Cher 41, 92 Sacr 17, 63, 85, 86, 116 Det 10, 46, 51, 51, 65 Post 174 Gig 26 Agr 42, 91 Plant 42 Ebr 21 Conf 110, 181 Migr 31, 46, 166, 214 Her 253 Congr 24, 35, 35, 36, 69 Mut 12, 84, 88 Somn 1:150, 167, 169 Somn 2:275 Abr 52, 53, 53, 54 Ios 1, 82, 82 Mos 1:60 Mos 2:27 Spec 1:259 Spec 2:209 Spec 4:99, 101 Praem 51, 65 Contempl 28, 41 Hypoth 7:11 Prov 2:16, 56

ἀσκητέος Spec 1:149

ἀσκητής (102) Leg 1:80, 83, 89 Leg 2:87, 89 Leg 3:11, 18, 18, 22, 36, 93, 144, 168, 196 Sacr 5, 38, 46, 47, 64, 81 Det 3, 12, 12, 17, 26, 35, 43, 45, 64 Post 59, 78, 101, 154 Deus 92 Plant 44, 90, 110 Ebr 24, 48, 48, 82, 124 Sobr 40 Conf 74, 80 Migr 5, 28, 38, 153, 199, 213 Her 253 Congr 31, 33, 61, 70, 70, 123 Fug 4, 49, 52, 67, 143 Mut 14, 41, 84, 85, 210 Somn 1:46, 68, 118, 150, 150, 152, 163, 166, 171, 174, 196, 208, 213, 249, 255 Somn 2:19, 65, 133, 134 Abr 37 Mos 1:29 Mos 2:185 Spec 1:271 Spec 2:44 Spec 4:121 Virt 4 Praem 11, 27, 36, 47 Prob 43, 111 Contempl 69 Prov 2:1

ἀσκητικός (28) Leg 1:98 Post 158 Deus 120 Ebr 111 Her 38, 43 Congr 99, 162 Fug 15, 38, 40, 43 Mut 82, 83, 88, 214 Somn 1:115, 119, 126, 159, 168, 170, 182 Somn 2:134 Abr 52 Ios 1 Mos 1:76 Mos 2:183

ἀσκητός Det 65

ἄσκιος (13) Her 87, 308 Mut 6 Somn 1:202, 218 Abr 119 Decal 49 Spec 2:155, 204 Spec 4:52, 192, 231 QG 4:30

ἀσκός (6) Post 130, 137, 137 Sobr 8 Prob 97, 109

ᾆσμα (21) Leg 2:102, 102 Gig 17 Deus 10 Agr 51, 54 Plant 48 Ebr 111, 115 Conf 35 Migr 113, 157 Mut 115, 143 Somn 2:246, 271 Mos 1:255 Spec 2:216, 217, 220 Contempl 29

ἀσμενίζω (7) Opif 151 Sacr 23 Her 127 Abr 259 Ios 235 Spec 3:8 Hypoth 11:11

ἀσμενισμός Migr 88

ἄσμενος (25) Opif 115 Sacr 123 Deus 66 Agr 152 Her 295 Somn 1:129 Abr 127, 215 Ios 228 Mos 1:17 Mos 2:32 Spec 1:271 Spec 2:122, 198 Spec 3:154, 157 Spec 4:221 Virt 210 Praem 100 Prob 114, 135 Contempl 72 Legat 233, 369 Prov 2:11

ἀσπάζομαι (56) Opif 151, 164 Leg 2:16, 18 Cher 52, 107 Sacr 12, 58, 76 Det 21 Gig 35 Deus 79 Agr 43, 167 Plant 64 Ebr 34, 70, 165 Sobr 5 Migr 203 Her 44, 44, 274 Congr 154 Fug 92 Somn 2:9 Abr 6, 13, 22, 30, 30, 65 Ios 11, 14 Mos 2:48, 58 Decal 109 Spec 2:19 Virt 179 Praem 12, 20, 54, 87, 100, 152 Prob 3, 142 Contempl 1, 24, 58, 90 Flacc 38 Legat 261 Prov 2:13 QG 4:8* QE 2:99

ἀσπαίρω Legat 63

ἄσπασμα Abr 212 Ios 256

ἀσπασμός Ios 23

ἀσπαστός Flacc 162 Legat 103

ἀσπίς (19) Leg 3:115 Agr 151 Ebr 222, 223 Somn 2:88, 89, 191 Mos 1:109 Decal 78 Prob 78 Flacc 90 Legat 97, 133, 163, 166, 299, 300, 305, 306

ἀσπονδεί Decal 87 Praem 92

ἄσπονδος (35) Opif 164 Sacr 17, 32 Det 72, 149, 165 Gig 35 Ebr 97 Conf 45 Her 44, 245 Fug 114 Somn 1:106 Somn 2:98, 166, 210 Ios 263 Mos 1:242 Spec 2:134 Spec 3:96, 155, 195 Spec 4:16, 23 Virt 131 Praem 87 Contempl 41 Flacc 13, 59, 126 Legat 180, 292 Prov 2:4 QG 2:54a QE isf 30

᾿Ασσύριος (6) Leg 1:63, 69, 69, 85, 86 Mos 1:23

ᾄσσω ἀΐσσω

ἀστάθμητος Mos 1:31, 41 Legat 1

ἀστασίαστος (8) Abr 28, 216, 226 Spec 4:166 Flacc 145 Legat 8 Hypoth 6:2 QG 3:8

ἄστατος (18) Leg 3:53 Sacr 32, 90 Det 12, 148 Post 22 Gig 15 Deus 4 Ebr 180, 181 Conf 114 Mut 91 Somn 1:156, 202 Spec 1:26 Spec 2:71 Spec 4:156 Prov 2:34

ἄσταχυς (6) Sacr 80 Her 296 Decal 160 Spec 2:41 Spec 4:29 Virt 49

ἄστεγος Fug 189, 191, 191, 191, 191

ἀστεΐζομαι Mos 1:266

ἀστεῖος (119) Leg 1:93 Leg 3:23, 53, 67, 77, 77, 89, 167, 190, 191 Cher 105 Det 4, 52, 66, 68, 71, 72, 75, 112, 140, 170 Post 32, 81, 101, 160 Gig 27 Deus 107, 154 Plant 114, 131, 139, 172, 172, 176, 176 Conf 73, 106, 109 Migr 24, 99, 118, 130, 142 Her 19, 42, 50, 78,

243, 259, 276, 292 Congr 4, 131, 132 Fug 18, 55, 154 Mut 45, 147, 168, 175, 180, 193, 193, 204, 252 Somn 1:171, 176, 200 Somn 2:24, 26, 81, 134, 227, 230, 244 Abr 22, 52, 83, 85, 90, 99, 103, 118, 214, 225, 242, 274 Mos 1:9, 18, 48 Mos 2:33 Spec 1:275, 277, 284 Spec 2:30 Virt 167 Prob 1, 18, 21, 27, 28, 30, 53, 59, 61, 72 Contempl 69, 72 QG 2:72, 4:51a, 67, 76a, 174, 193, 204, 204, 211 QE 2:17

ἀστεϊσμός Contempl 59

ἀστεροειδής Opif 82 Her 87, 88 Somn 1:84

ἀστεφάνωτος Post 78 Mut 81 Praem 6 Prob 26

ἀστή ἀστός

ἀστήρ (108) Opif 31, 31, 45, 54, 55, 56, 57, 59, 61, 73, 114, 114, 115, 144, 147 Leg 2:30 Leg 3:39, 40, 99, 203 Cher 22, 24 Sacr 97 Post 19, 19 Gig 7 Deus 107 Agr 51 Plant 12, 118, 151 Ebr 44, 106 Migr 179, 181, 184, 194 Her 86, 88, 97, 280, 283 Congr 51, 133 Mut 67, 72 Somn 1:22, 53, 83, 135, 145, 214 Somn 2:6, 111, 113, 114, 131, 132 Abr 69, 77, 157, 158 Ios 8, 9 Mos 1:120, 176, 212 Mos 2:44, 102, 122, 239, 271 Decal 49, 53, 55 Spec 1:13, 13, 15, 16, 39, 66, 90, 91, 207, 210, 296, 300, 322, 339 Spec 2:5, 45, 151, 155, 255 Spec 3:187 Spec 4:155 Virt 12, 74, 212 Praem 41 Contempl 5 Aet 4, 46, 47 Flacc 169 QG 2:34a, 4:51b QE 2:55a

ἀστοιχείωτος Plant 52

ἀστός (ἀστή) (42) Leg 2:97, 97 Sacr 26 Migr 99 Congr 6, 22, 23, 23, 24, 24, 25, 31, 32, 34, 36, 41, 43, 43, 51, 59, 59, 63, 75, 76, 77 Fug 76, 154, 212 Mut 147 Ios 47 Mos 1:35 Spec 3:66, 80, 136, 171 Spec 4:142 Virt 82, 173 Prob 158 QG 3:20a, 21, 21

ἀστραπή Abr 43 Mos 1:118 Decal 44 Prov 2:45

ἀστράπτω Spec 4:52 Aet 86

ἀστρατεία Spec 4:223 Virt 23

ἀστράτευτος Cher 32 Agr 150, 156

ἀστρολογικός Abr 82

ἄστρον (16) Opif 29, 53 Leg 1:8, 8 Leg 3:202 Her 86 Fug 184 Somn 1:137 Ios 78 Praem 45, 45 Prob 25, 99 Aet 4, 121 Prov 2:51

ἀστρονομέω Congr 50 Somn 1:53, 54

ἀστρονομία (8) Leg 1:57 Migr 178 Her 98 Congr 11, 49 Somn 1:161 Abr 69, 77

ἀστρονομικός Virt 212

ἄστυ (12) Conf 106 Her 127 Mos 1:312 Spec 3:74, 78, 170 Spec 4:20, 237 Contempl 24 Flacc 185 Prov 2:57, 62

ἀστυγείτων Mos 1:239, 263

ἀστυνόμος Spec 3:74 Spec 4:21

ἀσυγκατάθετος Leg 2:65 Deus 100

ἀσύγκριτος (7) Det 29 Gig 41 Deus 56 Ebr 43 Fug 141 Mut 3 Somn 2:227

ἀσύγχυτος Opif 28 Conf 195 Spec 4:106, 132 Virt 52

ἀσυλία (10) Mos 2:236 Decal 177 Spec 1:159, 255 Spec 3:88, 88 Virt 124 Prob 148, 149 Legat 346

ἄσυλος (6) Gig 16 Sobr 66 Her 108 Mos 1:34 Praem 90 Prob 151

ἀσύμβατος (23) Sacr 32 Det 166 Abr 14, 105 Ios 156 Mos 1:242 Spec 1:295, 313 Spec 2:16 Spec 3:16 Spec 4:28, 32, 89, 178, 184, 202 Virt 40, 108, 191 Praem 137 Flacc 19 Legat 205 QG 2:54a

ἀσύμμετρος Sacr 32

ἀσύμπλοκος Abr 122

ἀσύμφορος Mut 197 Ios 143

ἀσυμφωνία Opif 22

ἀσύμφωνος (12) Sacr 32 Ebr 116, 180, 198 Conf 67, 150 Congr 16 Somn 2:284 Ios 145, 269 Spec 2:130 Aet 75

ἀσύνδετος Her 198

ἀσυνήθης Opif 161 Sacr 1 Flacc 89

ἀσύντακτος Mos 1:250 Flacc 35, 135, 172

ἀσύστατος Leg 3:252

ἀσφαγής Spec 3:144

ἀσφάλεια (43) Opif 142 Leg 3:164 Cher 126 Det 36, 37, 42 Agr 149, 167 Plant 92, 146 Conf 103 Her 125 Fug 30, 80 Mut 111 Ios 63, 251 Mos 1:36 Mos 2:58 Decal 178 Spec 1:75, 159 Spec 2:52 Spec 3:128, 130, 132, 166 Spec 4:21, 58, 166 Virt 24, 152 Prob 151 Contempl 22, 23 Flacc 41, 53 Legat 42, 128, 195, 207 QG 3:20b QG (Par) 2:4

ἀσφαλής (52) Cher 103 Det 33 Gig 46 Agr 93, 162, 168 Plant 70 Ebr 185, 205 Conf 104, 106, 106 Migr 217, 224 Her 314 Congr 141 Fug 6, 136, 206 Mut 242 Somn 1:124, 158, 181 Somn 2:92, 127 Abr 269 Ios 255 Mos 1:15, 47, 85, 178, 333 Mos 2:247 Spec 1:69, 154 Spec 3:166 Spec 4:50, 159 Praem 58, 147, 153 Aet 17, 74 Flacc 31, 52, 115, 177 Legat 184, 247, 361 Prov 2:28 QG (Par) 2:2

ἀσφαλτοπίσσα Conf 106

ἄσφαλτος (8) Conf 1, 102, 102, 104, 104, 105 QG (Par) 2:4, 2:4

ἀσφαλτόω QG (Par) 2:4, 2:4

ἀσχαλάω (ἀσχάλλω) Flacc 29

ἀσχάλλω ἀσχαλάω

ἄσχετος Mos 1:198

ἀσχημάτιστος Her 181 Fug 8 Somn 2:45 Spec 1:48

ασχημονέω Cher 94 Det 130 Somn 1:99

ἀσχημοσύνη (11) Leg 2:27, 66 Leg 3:158, 158 Gig 32, 35, 39 Fug 193 Somn 1:92, 101, 109

ἀσχήμων Decal 169

ἄσχιστος Her 232

ἀσώματος (113) Opif 16, 18, 29, 29, 29, 34, 34, 36, 36, 49, 49, 53, 55, 92, 92, 98, 111, 129, 130, 134, 144 Leg 1:1, 82, 91 Leg 2:59, 80 Leg 3:186, 206 Cher 49, 49, 60, 114 Sacr 5, 59, 69 Det 159 Post 20, 99, 137 Gig 14, 31, 61 Deus 55, 83 Agr 139, 140 Plant 14 Ebr 87, 99, 124, 133, 134, 136 Conf 61, 62, 81, 105, 106, 172, 174, 176 Migr 13, 90, 103 Her 63, 66, 131, 132, 209 Fug 58, 164 Mut 7, 33, 56, 59, 267 Somn 1:30, 36, 62, 79, 113, 115, 127, 131, 135, 187, 232 Somn 2:72, 73 Abr 13, 118, 236 Mos 1:158 Mos 2:74, 127, 271 Decal 102 Spec 1:66, 288, 302, 327, 329 Spec 2:176, 212 Spec 3:190 Virt 12 Praem 26, 30, 37 QG 1:70:1, 4:8b QG isf 2 QG (Par) 2:4

ἀσωματότης Leg 1:3 Leg 2:57

ἀσωτία Sobr 40 Praem 52

ἄσωτος (8) Plant 101 Ebr 131 Fug 28 Somn 2:148 Spec 4:91 Contempl 47 Prov 2:4 QE isf 14 ἄτακτος (14) Opif 22, 97 Sacr 32, 45, 85 Det 141 Agr 74 Plant 3 Abr 151 Spec 1:48 Praem 20 Aet 75 Legat 344 Prov 2:17

ἀταλαίπωρος (9) Opif 2, 79 Cher 12 Congr 37, 173 Mut 258 Mos 2:267 Spec 1:132 Virt 29

ἀταμίευτος (12) Opif 23 Mos 1:204 Mos 2:9, 259 Spec 1:221 Spec 2:22, 199 Praem 103 Legat 51, 147, 163 Prov 2:18

ἀταξία (26) Opif 28 Sacr 82 Plant 3 Ebr 144 Fug 10 Somn 1:241 Somn 2:152 Abr 151 Ios 143, 145 Decal 155 Spec 1:329 Spec 4:187, 210, 210, 235 Praem 76 Aet 31, 32, 40, 40, 106 Legat 94, 147 Prov 2:1 QG 1:64d

ἄταφος Somn 2:269 Ios 25 Mos 1:39

ἅτε (177) Opif 16, 36, 81, 84, 88, 127, 141, 142, 144, 159, 169 Leg 1:18, 23, 27, 31, 44 Leg 3:1, 72, 108, 124, 149 Cher 44, 49, 49, 88, 89 Sacr 10, 34, 48, 64, 70, 71, 104 Det 37, 55, 89, 93, 106, 114, 146, 172, 172 Post 7, 7, 10, 11, 23, 67, 75, 96, 101, 157, 173, 184 Deus 31, 40, 56, 76, 82 Agr 149 Ebr 124, 170, 215, 223 Sobr 56, 60 Conf 106, 108 Migr 14, 140, 184, 206 Her 100, 301 Congr 50, 138, 145 Fug 6, 12, 13, 66, 66, 66, 101, 115, 187, 191 Mut 88, 128, 219, 246, 266 Somn 1:213 Somn 2:3, 10, 81, 97, 97, 152, 230 Abr 20, 95, 127, 137, 155, 162, 231 Ios 4, 53, 145, 146, 191, 205, 217 Mos 1:38, 89, 95, 100, 137, 169, 250, 286, 299, 318 Mos 2:34, 159, 163, 231 Decal 99, 177 Spec 1:53, 106, 127, 152, 269 Spec 2:5, 91, 109, 118, 247 Spec 3:36, 78, 79, 85, 102, 121, 130, 189, 202 Spec 4:20, 25, 123, 179, 188 Virt 39 Praem 76, 93 Prob 30, 43, 61, 146 Aet 26, 30, 59, 76, 102, 116, 148 Flacc 119, 176 Legat 133 Hypoth 7:19 Prov 1, 2:19, 67 QG 1:32, 4:172

ἀτείχιστος Fug 189, 190 Mos 1:330

ἀτέκμαρτος (11) Leg 1:20 Cher 33 Her 179 Somn 1:11, 54 Somn 2:105, 145, 212 Spec 4:18, 201 Virt 122

ἀτεκνία Det 51 QG 3:20a

ἄτεκνος Her 2, 34, 36 Hypoth 11:13

ἀτέλεστος Somn 1:164, 191 QE isf 14

ἀτελεύτητος (17) Opif 23 Ebr 52 Fug 61 Somn 1:12, 24 Somn 2:44, 133 Spec 4:122 Virt 37 Praem 70 Aet 53, 75, 116 Flacc 71, 167, 180 Legat 100

ἀτελής (86) Opif 42, 63 Leg 1:23, 80 Leg 2:97 Leg 3:47, 135, 135, 207, 213, 249 Cher 94 Sacr 29, 43, 57, 65, 113, 114, 129 Det 46 Post 85, 95, 171 Gig 45 Deus 93 Agr 54, 140, 141, 145, 160, 169 Sobr 12, 24 Conf 158 Migr 55, 73 Her 19, 116, 242, 269, 275 Congr 48, 137, 148 Fug 13, 141, 162, 207 Mut 122, 122, 230 Somn 1:213 Somn 2:213 Abr 135 Spec 1:11, 200 Spec 2:158, 158, 158 Spec 3:11, 32, 34, 85 Spec 4:32, 158 Virt 29, 156, 156, 184, 209 Praem 56, 110, 127, 142, 149, 166 Aet 43, 48, 49, 71, 99 Hypoth 11:3 QG 4:104 QG isf 16 QE 1:7a QE isf 27

ἀτενής Decal 147

ἀτέραμνος Spec 1:218

ἀτερπής Sobr 23 Legat 168

ἀτεχνής Contempl 1

ἀτεχνία Her 210 Fug 27 Somn 1:225

ἄτεχνος (11) Leg 3:36 Det 18, 109, 143 Post 109 Gig 2 Plant 141, 173 Spec 4:40 Prob 51 QG 4:228

ἀτημέλητος Post 68

ἀτίθασος (45) Opif 83 Leg 1:69 Leg 2:11, 92 Leg 3:17, 156 Cher 111 Sacr 20, 62, 105, 105 Post 160 Gig 35 Agr 154 Plant 43 Conf 24, 110, 165 Migr 210 Her 138 Somn 2:192 Abr 32 Ios 25, 36, 82 Mos 1:43, 109 Decal 78 Spec 1:295 Spec 2:9 Spec 3:103, 145, 158 Spec 4:16, 119, 225 Virt 132 Praem 59, 88 Prob 89 Contempl 9, 40 Legat 22, 131 Prov 2:14

ἀτιμάζω (10) Ebr 17 Congr 128, 139 Mos 2:9, 19, 58 Decal 119 QG 3:22, 22, 22

ἀτιμία (23) Deus 111, 171 Agr 61 Conf 18 Fug 30 Somn 2:43 Ios 123 Mos 1:273 Decal 126 Spec 2:248, 253 Spec 3:168, 181 Virt 166 Prob 7, 55 Contempl 42 Flacc 77, 79, 152, 172 Legat 110, 301

ἄτιμος (15) Cher 93 Det 34 Deus 150 Her 26, 172 Somn 2:148 Mos 2:241 Decal 6 Virt 174, 195 Prob 156 Contempl 7 Aet 46 Legat 119 QG 4:47b

ἀτιμόω Spec 2:132, 253 Flacc 144, 172 QG 4:200c

ἀτιμώρητος Mos 1:308 Prov 2:35

Ἀτλαντικός Ebr 133

Ἀτλαντίς Aet 141

ἄτμητος (11) Gig 27 Agr 30 Her 232, 233, 234, 234, 236, 237 Spec 1:274, 287 Virt 90

ἀτμίς Her 251 Spec 1:72

ἀτμός (27) Opif 62, 139, 165 Leg 2:7, 39 Leg 3:44, 56, 58, 173, 235 Cher 57 Sacr 31, 98 Det 157, 173 Plant 159 Conf 52 Migr 50, 51, 51 Her 226 Mut 111 Somn 1:27 Abr 148, 239 Ios 142 QE isf 21

ἀτοκέω Her 36, 51

ἀτόκιος Hypoth 7:7

ἀτολμία Mos 1:234 Virt 5, 180

ἄτολμος Spec 4:140 Virt 25

ἄτομος (8) Leg 1:1, 22 Agr 134 Her 131, 142 Fug 148 Mut 180 Aet 8

ἀτοπία Leg 1:36 Cher 91 Sacr 95 Agr 145 Aet 145

ἄτοπος (53) Opif 56 Leg 2:61 Leg 3:53, 53, 205, 234 Sacr 5 Post 87 Agr 130, 151 Conf 7 Migr 12, 17, 25, 217 Mut 132, 240 Somn 1:95, 137 Somn 2:32 Abr 208 Mos 1:308 Decal 29, 76 Spec 1:125, 127, 191, 329 Spec 2:38 Spec 3:90 Spec 4:34, 55, 195 Virt 64, 143, 150 Prob 121, 135 Aet 22, 53, 78, 84, 99 Flacc 39, 184 Legat 44, 125 Hypoth 6:4 Prov 1, 2:14 QG 1:20, 3:3 QE isf 13

ἀτραγῴδητος Ios 249

ἀτραπός (19) Post 18, 102, 155 Gig 64 Deus 143 Migr 128, 129, 146 Somn 2:134 Mos 1:50, 165, 179 Mos 2:254 Spec 2:202 Spec 4:102, 109, 154 Prob 3 QE 2:13a

ἀτρεμίζω Decal 35 Spec 2:103

ἄτρεπτος (42) Leg 1:51, 51 Leg 2:32, 33, 54, 67, 89 Leg 3:94, 125 Cher 19, 19, 52, 90 Sacr 101 Post 27, 27, 28 Deus 22 Ebr 88 Conf 96, 106 Mut 24, 28, 54, 87, 135, 175 Somn 1:232, 249 Somn 2:221, 228, 237 Abr 63 Mos 1:45 Decal 43, 95 Spec 1:312 Spec 2:230 Praem 15 Aet 59 QG 1:93, 4:8b

ἀτριβής (12) Deus 144 Her 287 Somn 2:180 Mos 1:167, 170 Mos 2:247 Spec 1:188, 301 Spec 2:199, 250 Spec 4:126 Legat 216

ἄτριβος Agr 160

ἄτριπτος Leg 2:98 Agr 104

ἀτροφέω Aet 88, 127

ἄτροφος Leg 2:105

ἄτρυτος (12) Opif 80, 167 Det 19 Ebr 21 Conf 92 Fug 173 Spec 2:60, 260 Praem 27, 128, 156 Legat 90

ἄτρωτος (6) Det 46 Ebr 177 Mut 109 Somn 2:144 Virt 44 Prob 40

ἄττα (9) Cher 68 Conf 185 Congr 144 Fug 34 Spec 4:198 Contempl 7, 40 Aet 122 QG 2:64a

ἀττακός Leg 2:105

Ἀττικός Post 94 Flacc 156, 173 Legat 281

ἀτύπωτος Sacr 85 Her 180, 299 Somn 2:45

ἀτυφία (20) Cher 42 Ebr 124 Congr 138 Fug 25, 35 Somn 2:40, 63, 140 Abr 24, 104 Mos 2:96 Decal 162 Spec 1:309 Virt 16, 17, 178, 195 Praem 59 Contempl 39, 39

ἄτυφος Somn 2:64 Spec 2:235 Prob 84

ἀτυχέω (14) Opif 167 Leg 3:47 Det 114 Post 21 Migr 134, 155 Her 112 Decal 69 Spec 3:27 Spec 4:200 Flacc 159, 183 Legat 190 QG isf 9

ἀτύχημα (8) Ios 99 Mos 2:227 Spec 1:81 Spec 2:208 Spec 3:70 Spec 4:24, 72, 76

ἀτυχής (6) Mos 2:241 Spec 2:87 Spec 3:16, 57 Spec 4:76 Contempl 19

ἀτυχία (14) Congr 13 Ios 72, 205, 247 Decal 71 Spec 1:103 Spec 2:76, 78, 85 Praem 129 Legat 197, 342 Prov 2:4 QG 4:52b

αὖ (115) Opif 73, 88, 91, 99, 103, 113, 119, 124, 139, 156 Leg 1:4, 7, 12 Leg 2:7 Leg 3:99, 113 Sacr 59 Det 9, 105, 117, 125 Post 3, 41, 108, 109, 116, 126, 141, 145, 155 Gig 18, 27 Deus 37, 49, 164 Agr 11, 14, 27, 51, 51, 63, 112, 129, 140 Plant 2, 45, 121, 133 Ebr 75, 91, 142, 173, 180, 183, 185, 185, 194 Sobr 24, 24, 36, 36 Conf 89, 176, 194 Migr 148 Her 114, 135, 140, 152, 153, 177, 184, 190, 191, 247 Congr 84 Fug 82, 111, 161, 182 Mut 63, 78, 147, 157, 173, 221 Somn 1:205 Abr 21, 75, 121, 147 Ios 12, 60 Mos 1:3, 150, 248 Mos 2:47, 264 Decal 23 Spec 1:184, 281, 331 Spec 3:26 Spec 4:147, 237 Virt 9, 19, 126, 214 Praem 44 Aet 36, 42, 98 Legat 261 Hypoth 7:3

αὐαίνω Spec 4:209

αὐγάζω (12) Ebr 189 Conf 140 Migr 189 Fug 136 Mut 199 Somn 2:1, 133 Ios 68 Mos 2:139 Spec 3:100 Spec 4:60 Prov 2:35

αὐγή (61) Opif 31, 71 Cher 97 Deus 3, 29, 46, 135 Plant 40 Ebr 44, 173 Her 87, 88, 263, 308, 310 Congr 8, 47 Mut 6, 162, 162 Somn 1:84, 112, 116, 117, 202, 239 Somn 2:67 Abr 70, 76, 119, 157, 158 Mos 1:68, 145 Mos 2:148, 254, 271 Spec 1:40, 297 Spec 2:210 Spec 4:192, 236 Virt 221 Praem 25, 37 Prob 5 Aet 86, 86, 86, 88, 88, 88, 90, 90, 92, 92, 92, 92 Prov 2:47, 49 QG 2:14

αὐγοειδής (13) Opif 30 Post 159 Deus 79 Her 222 Fug 110 Somn 1:217 Mos 1:66 Decal 44 Spec 1:54 Virt 164, 179, 188 Aet 2

αὐδάω Prob 143

αὐθάδεια (13) Leg 2:99 Det 44 Post 52 Agr 47, 163 Her 21 Abr 213 Ios 66, 73, 174 Mos 1:139 Spec 4:9 Prob 54

αὐθάδης (10) Leg 3:231 Sacr 32 Det 23 Her 21 Somn 2:80 Spec 1:304, 306 Virt 89 Flacc 35 Legat 301

αὐθαίρετος Prob 118

αὐθέκαστος Ios 65 Flacc 15

αὐθέντης Det 78

αὐθημερόν Virt 88 QE 2:15a

αὐθιγενής (17) Cher 50 Congr 22 Somn 1:160 Abr 42, 159 Mos 1:6, 192, 212 Mos 2:54 Spec 1:34, 210 Spec 2:172 Virt 6 Praem 41 Aet 147 Legat 200, 214

αὖθις (122) Opif 45, 46, 47, 67, 154, 170 Leg 3:22, 88, 92, 102, 164 Cher 3, 4, 49, 50 Sacr 11, 134 Det 11, 64, 75, 81, 106, 118, 138, 147, 163 Post 10, 40, 75, 117, 154 Deus 30, 86, 90, 103, 183 Agr 59, 76, 132, 181 Plant 50, 141 Ebr 48, 48, 50 Conf 10, 76, 124, 158 Migr 44, 84, 150, 176 Her 123, 226, 260 Congr 14, 84 Fug 99, 181 Mut 83, 166 Somn 1:139 Somn 2:271, 283 Abr 49, 56, 71, 140 Ios 127 Mos 1:42, 58, 150, 162, 167, 181, 332 Mos 2:27, 60, 62, 152, 229, 288 Decal 98 Spec 1:154, 217, 262, 292 Spec 2:115, 122, 133, 229 Spec 3:31, 106, 154, 175 Spec 4:173, 223 Virt 22, 86, 138, 197 Prob 15, 73, 160 Contempl 63 Aet 71, 100, 138, 147 Flacc 24, 58, 82, 138 Legat 144, 326, 329 Hypoth 7:15, 7:17 QG 2:11, 15b QE 2:17

αὐλαία (6) Congr 116, 117 Mos 2:84, 85, 86, 87

αὖλαξ (7) Opif 85, 115 Sobr 36 Mos 1:201 Decal 77 Spec 2:172 Virt 145

αὔλειος (6) Leg 3:40 Congr 10 Spec 3:169 Contempl 30 Flacc 89, 166

αὐλέω Sobr 36 Congr 46 Prob 144

αὐλή (12) Leg 3:40 Plant 44 Congr 116 Fug 41 Mut 190 Mos 2:80, 82, 90, 91, 91, 93 Legat 12

αὐλητής Congr 46 Prob 144 Flacc 85

αὐλητρίς Contempl 58

ἄϋλος (ἄυλος) Leg 1:82, 82, 88 Leg 2:80

αὐλός (11) Opif 119 Leg 2:75 Leg 3:221 Sacr 18 Post 105 Sobr 36 Mos 1:99 Spec 1:217 Spec 2:193, 246 QG 4:76b

αὐλών Leg 3:40

Αὐνάν Post 180 Deus 16, 18 Migr 164, 165

αὐξάνω (αὔξω) (38) Opif 101, 113 Leg 3:214 Sacr 55 Det 105 Post 125 Deus 37 Agr 158 Plant 114 Sobr 12 Fug 30 Mut 23, 192, 229, 263 Somn 2:76 Abr 71, 137 Ios 102 Mos 1:8, 63, 150 Mos 2:270 Spec 1:178 Spec 2:57, 143, 217 Spec 3:74 Spec 4:215 Virt 158 Praem 131 Aet 48, 58, 71, 72 Legat 321 Prov 2:43 QG 2:71a

αὔξησις (40) Opif 41, 59, 101, 103, 105 Leg 1:10 Leg 3:172, 227 Sacr 73, 98 Det 14 Gig 30 Ebr 53 Sobr 15 Conf 196 Migr 53 Congr 96 Fug 176 Mut 67 Mos 2:277 Spec 1:178 Spec 2:125, 143, 154 Spec 3:58, 188 Virt 156 Aet 43, 58, 60, 60, 98, 101 Prov 2:45 QG 2:17b, 29, 3:12, 4:8a, 51b QG (Par) 2:7

αὐξητικός Deus 37 Her 137

αὔξω αὐξάνω

ἄϋπνος (ἄυπνος) Fug 41 Ios 103

αὔρα (28) Opif 41 Leg 1:42, 42 Leg 3:89 Sacr 31 Gig 10 Deus 26, 177 Agr 62 Ebr 58 Congr 114 Mut 181, 215 Somn 1:49, 51, 178 Somn 2:74 Abr 116 Mos 1:30 Spec 2:143, 172 Spec 3:5 Virt 93 Prob 8 Contempl 23 Aet 64 Flacc 11 Legat 126

αὔριον Sacr 69, 70

αὐστηρός (29) Cher 6 Det 6, 157 Post 72, 101 Deus 170 Plant 167 Ebr 149 Sobr 23 Her 48 Fug 3, 25, 33, 41 Ios 65, 204 Mos 1:161 Mos 2:23, 185 Spec 1:71, 74, 155 Spec 2:19, 159, 160 Spec 4:124, 179 Praem 35 Legat 167 αὔτανδρος Mos 2:281

αὐτάρ Conf 4 Aet 17

αὐτάρκης (46) Opif 146 Leg 3:163, 165, 198 Cher 46 Post 49 Deus 183 Plant 33, 128, 136 Ebr 58 Fug 29, 165 Mut 8, 172 Somn 1:117 Somn 2:47, 50, 56 Abr 30, 155 Ios 111, 194 Mos 1:204, 205 Mos 2:119 Decal 29, 31, 81, 100 Spec 1:277 Spec 2:84, 120, 178, 234 Spec 4:122, 230 Virt 9 Prob 47 Aet 38, 74 Flacc 90, 99 Prov 1, 1 QE 1:6

αὐτεξούσιος (14) Leg 3:73 Cher 88 Post 115 Plant 46 Ebr 43 Her 85, 301 Ios 148 Spec 1:14 Spec 2:81 Virt 209 Prob 57 Legat 183 QG 4:51b

αὐτεπάγγελτος Mos 2:252

αὐτήκοος (8) Plant 168 Ebr 94 Sobr 65 Somn 1:160, 168 Abr 6 Praem 27 Legat 245

αὐτίκα (72) Opif 42, 51, 64, 93, 95, 112, 117, 165 Leg 1:54 Leg 3:186 Cher 13 Det 152 Agr 27, 29, 158 Plant 28 Ebr 190 Her 50 Congr 25, 90 Fug 4, 126 Mut 19, 179 Somn 1:6, 44, 216 Somn 2:157, 215, 223 Abr 21, 90, 147 Mos 1:48, 77, 91, 126, 258, 261, 277, 331 Mos 2:171, 191, 203 Spec 1:114, 160, 262 Spec 3:129, 145 Virt 23, 135, 148, 151, 199 Praem 57, 61 Prob 40 Contempl 1 Aet 58, 68, 78, 88, 91, 127, 143 Flacc 75 Legat 130, 305, 329 Hypoth 11:10 Prov 2:46 QE 2:40

αὐτοβοεί (8) Abr 180, 229 Mos 1:169, 233, 243 Mos 2:274 Virt 43 Prob 132

αὐτογενής Mut 260

αὐτοδίδακτος (19) Opif 148 Sacr 79 Post 78 Plant 110 Conf 81 Migr 29, 140, 167 Her 65 Congr 36, 99 Fug 166 Mut 88 Somn 1:160 Somn 2:10 Decal 117 Spec 2:240 Praem 27, 59

αὐτοκέλευστος (28) Sacr 130 Det 11, 120 Deus 47 Agr 147 Conf 59 Mut 104, 108, 270 Somn 1:111 Somn 2:267 Ios 240 Mos 1:21, 50, 63 Mos 2:137 Spec 1:57, 79, 144 Spec 2:146, 239 Spec 3:75, 127 Spec 4:9, 75, 193 Prob 22 Legat 245

αὐτοκίνητος Opif 149

αὐτοκρατής (14) Opif 17, 46 Decal 58 Spec 1:19 Spec 2:1, 24 Virt 218 Prob 19 Aet 112 Legat 26, 54, 143, 190 QG 4:51b

αὐτοκρατορικός Legat 157, 166, 328

αὐτοκράτωρ (55) Leg 3:198 Plant 90 Sobr 69 Conf 125, 125, 175, 181 Migr 186 Her 85, 301 Congr 49, 49, 116 Fug 111 Abr 78 Spec 1:13 Flacc 9, 15, 83, 97, 105, 150 Legat 11, 28, 29, 30, 53, 56, 69, 73, 119, 121, 133, 136, 140, 142, 160, 175, 236, 255, 277, 288, 289, 298, 300, 301, 305, 309, 316, 322, 322, 324, 325, 361, 368

Αὐτοκράτωρ Legat 352

αὐτολεξεί Legat 353

Αὐτόλυκος Contempl 57

αὐτομαθής (44) Opif 148 Leg 1:92 Leg 3:135 Sacr 6, 78 Det 30 Post 78 Deus 4 Plant 168 Ebr 60, 94 Sobr 65 Conf 74 Migr 29, 101, 140 Her 295 Congr 36, 36, 99, 111 Fug 43, 166, 168, 168, 170 Mut 1, 88, 137, 255, 263 Somn 1:68, 160, 168, 194 Somn 2:10 Abr 6, 16 Ios 1 Spec 2:240 Praem 27, 36, 59 Legat 245

αὐτοματίζω Migr 32

αὐτόματος (ὁ) (13) Opif 81, 167 Fug 170, 170, 170, 170, 171, 172, 199 Mut 260 Somn 1:11 Spec 3:92 Hypoth 7:19

αὐτομολέω (16) Det 173 Post 172 Gig 43, 65, 66 Ebr 58 Somn 2:253 Ios 177 Spec 1:52 Virt 181, 221 Praem 16, 152 Aet 76 QG 4:206a QE 2:2

αὐτομόλησις Gig 66

αὐτομολία Gig 66 Abr 232 Mos 1:305

αὐτόμολος Leg 2:10 Gig 67

αὐτόνομος Somn 2:100, 293 Ios 136, 242 Prob 91

αὐτοπραγία Ios 66 Prob 21

αὐτόπρεμνος Agr 7 Plant 24 Mut 224

αὐτοπρόσωπος Leg 3:177 Decal 19, 39, 175

αὐτός (ὁ) (4617) Opif 1, 8, 8, 8, 12, 12, 13, 15, 15, 15, 19, 20, 20, 23, 25, 26, 26, 26, 27, 31, 33, 33, 36, 37, 37, 38, 38, 39, 40, 44, 46, 49, 51, 52, 53, 54, 54, 58, 58, 60, 63, 66, 66, 67, 68, 69, 69, 71, 72, 73, 74, 74, 77, 77, 77, 78, 80, 81, 84, 84, 84, 88, 88, 88, 90, 94, 94, 100, 101, 104, 111, 119, 126, 127, 128, 129, 131, 131, 133, 134, 135, 139, 139, 139, 141, 141, 142, 144, 144, 146, 149, 150, 150, 151, 152, 156, 160, 165, 166, 168, 170, 170, 171, 171 Leg 1:1, 2, 6, 6, 8, 8, 14, 14, 15, 15, 15, 16, 17, 18, 18, 22, 22, 23, 24, 25, 26, 28, 29, 30, 30, 31, 32, 34, 34, 35, 35, 37, 38, 38, 38, 41, 41, 41, 42, 44, 44, 44, 44, 44, 46, 50, 51, 52, 53, 53, 54, 56, 57, 57, 57, 59, 60, 60, 61, 61, 61, 62, 64, 65, 72, 74, 75, 76, 76, 77, 78, 79, 79, 81, 82, 82, 82, 82, 83, 86, 88, 88, 89, 89, 90, 90, 90, 90, 90, 93, 96, 96, 99, 100, 100, 103, 104, 104, 105, 106 Leg 2:1, 1, 1, 2, 3, 3, 3, 3, 5, 5, 6, 8, 8, 9, 9, 9, 9, 9, 15, 15, 15, 16, 17, 18, 18, 19, 19, 20, 24, 25, 27, 28, 30, 31, 31, 32, 33, 35, 36, 37, 38, 38, 39, 40, 40, 41, 44, 44, 45, 45, 47, 47, 48, 48, 48, 49, 49, 51, 51, 53, 57, 57, 57, 59, 59, 60, 61, 62, 63, 63, 63, 64, 66, 66, 66, 67, 67, 69, 72, 73, 79, 80, 81, 81, 87, 88, 88, 88, 88, 88, 89, 89, 90, 91, 91, 92, 95, 96, 98, 99, 101, 102, 104, 105, 107 Leg 3:1, 1, 2, 4, 6, 7, 13, 13, 13, 15, 15, 16, 16, 16, 16, 16, 16, 16, 17, 17, 17, 18, 18, 19, 20, 20, 21, 23, 23, 23, 26, 27, 28, 32, 32, 33, 35, 35, 38, 39, 40, 40, 41, 46, 49, 49, 49, 49, 50, 50, 50, 51, 56, 56, 56, 57, 57, 57, 59, 60, 60, 60, 61, 61, 62, 62, 65, 65, 65, 66, 68, 68, 69, 70, 72, 72, 73, 74, 74, 74, 77, 78, 78, 79, 81, 82, 82, 82, 83, 83, 84, 84, 85, 85, 88, 88, 89, 90, 90, 90, 92, 94, 94, 95, 95, 95, 96, 97, 98, 99, 100, 100, 100, 101, 102, 102, 103, 105, 106, 107, 109, 109, 110, 111, 112, 112, 112, 113, 113, 114, 116, 116, 118, 120, 122, 124, 126, 127, 128, 129, 129, 130, 131, 132, 133, 133, 134, 134, 135, 135, 136, 140, 140, 141, 141, 141, 142, 142, 142, 143, 147, 147, 147, 151, 151, 153, 153, 153, 154, 154, 154, 156, 160, 161, 162, 164, 165, 167, 167, 169, 169, 172, 173, 176, 176, 176, 177, 177, 177, 177, 178, 178, 179, 179, 180, 180, 180, 180, 180, 180, 181, 182, 183, 183, 183, 185, 186, 188, 188, 188, 188, 188, 188, 188, 188, 189, 189, 189, 190, 190, 190, 191, 192, 194, 194, 194, 195, 197, 200, 200, 202, 202, 202, 203, 204, 205, 205, 206, 206, 207, 207, 207, 208, 208, 209, 210, 214, 215, 216, 217, 217, 217, 217, 218, 219, 220, 222, 222, 225, 225, 225, 229, 230, 230, 233, 234, 234, 234, 235, 235, 235, 238, 240, 240, 242, 243, 244, 244, 245, 245, 245, 247, 247, 248, 248, 250, 251, 252, 252, 253 Cher 1, 5, 5, 5, 6, 8, 9, 10, 10, 12, 14, 15, 20, 21, 22, 22, 23, 23, 23, 25, 28, 32, 35, 36, 37, 39, 40, 40, 40, 44, 45, 46, 48, 49, 49, 50, 51, 53, 53, 54, 54, 54, 56, 56, 60, 62, 63, 64, 67, 68, 71, 72, 73, 74, 76, 83, 86, 89, 90, 97, 97, 98, 99, 100, 101, 103, 106, 106, 106, 113, 113, 114, 115, 117, 123, 127, 128, 130 Sacr 1, 2, 3, 3, 4, 4, 4, 4, 5, 5, 6, 6, 8, 8, 9, 9, 9, 9, 10, 12,

17, 17, 19, 19, 19, 19, 19, 19, 19, 22, 25, 25, 27, 28, 29, 30, 33, 33, 34, 34, 36, 36, 37, 39, 39, 40, 41, 41, 45, 45, 47, 47, 48, 48, 50, 53, 54, 57, 57, 57, 59, 59, 59, 60, 60, 60, 60, 60, 62, 62, 64, 65, 65, 65, 67, 68, 72, 73, 74, 75, 76, 79, 80, 81, 81, 82, 82, 85, 85, 86, 87, 88, 88, 88, 88, 89, 89, 90, 91, 91, 92, 93, 93, 93, 94, 95, 97, 97, 98, 100, 105, 107, 108, 112, 114, 115, 117, 118, 119, 120, 121, 121, 122, 123, 123, 124, 125, 125, 128, 130, 130, 131, 133, 133, 137 Det 1, 1, 1, 1, 4, 5, 5, 5, 5, 5, 5, 5, 6, 6, 6, 7, 8, 8, 9, 9, 10, 11, 12, 13, 13, 14, 15, 15, 16, 17, 17, 18, 19, 22, 22, 22, 24, 25, 26, 28, 29, 29, 35, 39, 40, 41, 43, 43, 44, 45, 47, 47, 47, 49, 49, 52, 52, 54, 55, 56, 59, 59, 60, 60, 61, 62, 63, 66, 66, 68, 76, 78, 80, 85, 86, 87, 88, 89, 90, 93, 95, 96, 98, 98, 99, 100, 100, 102, 103, 105, 107, 109, 112, 112, 112, 114, 114, 114, 119, 122, 124, 125, 125, 126, 126, 126, 128, 128, 129, 131, 133, 134, 137, 137, 142, 143, 143, 143, 144, 146, 147, 147, 151, 154, 154, 157, 159, 160, 160, 160, 163, 165, 177, 178, 178, 178 Post 2, 7, 8, 8, 9, 11, 12, 12, 13, 13, 15, 15, 16, 16, 17, 19, 20, 25, 25, 25, 28, 29, 30, 33, 33, 34, 35, 36, 38, 40, 43, 49, 49, 50, 50, 52, 53, 54, 64, 64, 64, 64, 64, 67, 67, 68, 69, 70, 70, 70, 71, 72, 72, 72, 73, 74, 79, 80, 81, 83, 83, 85, 89, 89, 90, 91, 92, 95, 98, 99, 101, 102, 103, 106, 107, 107, 110, 110, 112, 115, 118, 121, 121, 122, 123, 124, 124, 127, 128, 132, 132, 132, 132, 132, 135, 137, 140, 140, 142, 144, 145, 145, 147, 147, 148, 153, 156, 157, 160, 160, 163, 164, 165, 166, 168, 169, 169, 169, 173, 176, 177, 179, 180, 181, 181, 182, 184, 185, 185 Gig 1, 1, 3, 5, 5, 8, 8, 9, 16, 16, 17, 17, 19, 19, 20, 23, 26, 27, 29, 29, 30, 31, 32, 33, 34, 35, 35, 37, 37, 38, 41, 43, 47, 49, 50, 51, 52, 55, 57, 58, 60, 63, 64, 64, 66 Deus 3, 5, 6, 7, 7, 9, 11, 14, 15, 16, 16, 18, 21, 21, 24, 26, 26, 27, 27, 28, 28, 29, 31, 31, 32, 35, 37, 38, 40, 42, 44, 45, 46, 47, 47, 47, 48, 49, 49, 51, 54, 54, 55, 55, 55, 61, 62, 64, 67, 69, 69, 70, 72, 72, 74, 76, 78, 79, 79, 79, 79, 81, 83, 84, 87, 88, 89, 89, 92, 93, 93, 98, 99, 99, 100, 103, 104, 109, 110, 113, 116, 116, 117, 117, 119, 120, 121, 124, 125, 126, 127, 132, 134, 134, 135, 135, 138, 140, 141, 144, 145, 147, 147, 148, 150, 156, 162, 166, 167, 167, 167, 173, 174, 174, 176, 179, 183 Agr 1, 3, 3, 6, 7, 11, 14, 15, 17, 18, 21, 21, 23, 24, 25, 28, 32, 39, 40, 41, 43, 43, 44, 47, 49, 53, 56, 58, 60, 60, 62, 64, 66, 69, 69, 70, 72, 72, 75, 77, 77, 81, 82, 83, 85, 86, 86, 88, 88, 88, 89, 89, 90, 91, 93, 93, 94, 95, 99, 99, 101, 103, 104, 107, 107, 110, 112, 112, 113, 117, 117, 120, 123, 125, 125, 130, 132, 134, 145, 148, 148, 148, 148, 148, 148, 148, 148, 148, 152, 154, 156, 157, 158, 159, 161, 161, 161, 164, 164, 165, 166, 167, 167, 167, 168, 168, 170, 171, 171, 174, 175, 175, 175, 175, 179, 181, 181 Plant 2, 3, 5, 9, 10, 11, 14, 14, 14, 15, 16, 18, 19, 21, 21, 22, 23, 27, 28, 29, 35, 36, 37, 37, 40, 45, 46, 47, 48, 48, 49, 49, 50, 53, 54, 55, 56, 56, 59, 60, 61, 62, 62, 63, 63, 63, 64, 64, 64, 64, 67, 69, 71, 73, 74, 78, 78, 80, 83, 84, 85, 85, 88, 93, 95, 95, 95, 95, 99, 106, 107, 108, 110, 113, 113, 113, 114, 115, 117, 118, 119, 123, 123, 123, 125, 128, 129, 130, 132, 134, 135, 135, 135, 136, 137, 138, 141, 141, 144, 144, 145, 145, 148, 149, 151, 151, 151, 152, 155, 158, 159, 160, 161, 164, 166, 168, 169, 174 Ebr 1, 2, 2, 3, 5, 6, 8, 8, 9, 10, 13, 14, 14, 14, 14, 14, 14, 14, 14, 14, 16, 17, 23, 23, 23, 23, 24, 25, 28, 28, 29, 33, 35, 35, 37, 37, 40, 42, 42, 45, 46, 51, 51, 51, 53, 53, 56, 58, 61, 65, 67, 67, 67, 70, 71, 79, 80, 82, 84, 88, 89, 90, 90, 90, 91, 91, 91, 92, 99, 101, 103, 106, 106, 107, 107, 108, 109, 111, 112, 113, 113, 114, 116, 116, 116, 117, 118, 119, 122, 122, 124, 129, 134, 135, 137, 140, 143, 146, 148, 149, 150, 152, 154, 156, 156, 157, 164, 164, 165, 169, 169, 169, 170, 170, 171, 172, 176, 176, 178, 178, 179, 187, 189, 190, 190, 190, 193, 198, 199, 200, 202, 203, 207, 209, 210, 210, 211, 218, 222, 222, 222, 222, 222, 222, 222 Sobr 1, 1, 1, 3, 8, 10, 12, 13, 15, 18, 19, 21, 21, 21, 21, 26, 30, 30, 30, 32, 34, 37, 38, 45, 47, 48, 49, 50, 51, 51, 52, 53, 54, 55, 56, 58, 59, 60, 68 Conf 1, 1, 1, 1, 1, 1, 1, 1, 1, 2, 2, 7, 9, 17, 18, 22, 23, 23, 24, 25, 27, 29, 29, 30, 38, 38, 39, 40, 41, 41, 44, 46, 46, 48, 50, 50, 50, 54, 55, 55, 55, 62, 64, 65, 66, 69, 75, 76, 76, 78, 84, 85, 93, 96, 97, 98, 98, 100, 100, 101, 102, 102, 103, 105, 106, 108, 110, 115, 116, 119, 121, 122, 124, 124, 126, 127, 130, 131, 134, 136, 140, 141, 144, 145, 146, 147, 150, 150, 151, 151, 153, 154, 155, 155, 156, 157, 157, 157, 158, 160, 160, 161, 162, 163, 168, 168, 168, 173, 178, 179, 179, 179, 180, 180, 181, 182, 182, 182, 183, 183, 183, 185, 186, 187, 188, 189, 190, 191, 191, 192, 192, 193, 196 Migr 2, 3, 3, 7, 9, 11, 14, 15, 18, 25, 26, 26, 31, 36, 36, 37, 40, 41, 42, 46, 47, 55, 56, 56, 57, 58, 60, 62, 62, 66, 68, 68, 68, 73, 76, 76, 76, 76, 78, 78, 78, 79, 79, 80, 80, 80, 81, 81, 81, 86, 90, 91, 101, 102, 104, 105, 111, 114, 115, 118, 119, 121, 122, 127, 127, 128, 129, 130, 132, 132, 132, 135, 138, 139, 140, 147, 148, 148, 149, 150, 150, 151, 152, 155, 155, 155, 157, 158, 159, 159, 159, 159, 162, 162, 164, 164, 167, 170, 171, 171, 171, 172, 173, 173, 173, 174, 174, 174, 174, 177, 179, 180, 181, 182, 183, 185, 185, 186, 189, 191, 191, 194, 195, 196, 196, 197, 197, 202, 203, 204, 206, 207, 208, 208, 209, 210, 210, 211, 211, 212, 214, 214, 215, 219, 219, 219, 221 Her 4, 8, 11, 17, 20, 20, 20, 21, 23, 23, 36, 36, 40, 40, 42, 44, 44, 44, 51, 53, 55, 56, 66, 67, 68, 70, 71, 71, 74, 76, 76, 81, 84, 84, 85, 85, 86, 86, 86, 87, 94, 95, 96, 98, 100, 100, 101, 101, 106, 108, 110, 110, 110, 112, 114, 119, 124, 129, 130, 134, 137, 140, 146, 149, 149, 150, 150, 156, 159, 159, 160, 161, 164, 164, 164, 165, 166, 166, 168, 169, 170, 170, 178, 186, 188, 193, 194, 194, 196, 205, 206, 214, 214, 215, 216, 218, 218, 218, 218, 218, 219, 220, 220, 221, 221, 223, 224, 224, 224, 224, 225, 226, 226, 226, 228, 228, 228, 229, 238, 238, 239, 241, 242, 243, 245, 246, 247, 247, 248, 249, 251, 251, 251, 256, 258, 258, 259, 262, 262, 263, 265, 265, 266, 268, 270, 273, 278, 278, 282, 289, 291, 291, 293, 295, 300, 304, 305, 306, 307, 307, 308, 310 Congr 1, 1, 1, 3, 5, 5, 6, 7, 7, 8, 9, 9, 12, 12, 12, 13, 14, 15, 19, 19, 23, 25, 33, 38, 41, 42, 42, 42, 43, 44, 48, 49, 50, 50, 51, 53, 53, 54, 55, 56, 57, 62, 66, 70, 71, 71, 71, 72, 72, 73, 74, 74, 76, 76, 78, 78, 78, 80, 81, 85, 86, 86, 86, 86, 86, 86, 86, 89, 93, 96, 96, 98, 98, 99, 100, 102, 103, 104, 105, 105, 105, 108, 109, 114, 118, 119, 119, 119, 125, 131, 131, 131, 133, 133, 134, 134, 134, 134, 135, 137, 138, 139, 139, 142, 142, 143, 144, 145, 147, 152, 152, 153, 153, 158, 160, 163, 163, 163, 163, 170, 175, 177, 177, 178 Fug 1, 1, 1, 1, 1, 1, 1, 1, 1, 1, 3, 5, 7, 7, 7, 9, 12, 13, 15, 16, 19, 20, 23, 23, 25, 26, 30, 30, 40, 40, 41, 41, 42, 46, 53, 53, 53, 53, 57, 60, 60, 62, 63, 65, 66, 69, 73, 73, 75, 77, 79, 79, 82, 82, 86, 87, 91, 91, 91, 93, 94, 96, 97, 100, 100, 101, 102, 102, 103, 106, 107, 109, 112, 112, 112, 114, 114, 114, 115, 117, 117, 119, 124, 124, 125, 126, 127, 127, 127, 127, 127, 131, 131, 135, 139, 140, 142, 142, 146, 147, 148, 148, 148, 149, 149, 149, 153, 156, 156, 159, 159, 164, 164, 167, 170, 170, 173, 177, 177, 187, 187, 188, 188, 188, 189, 190, 196, 198, 202, 203, 203, 204, 206, 207, 207, 209, 209, 210, 211 Mut 1, 4, 4, 5, 5, 7, 8, 11, 13, 13, 13, 13, 13, 15, 15, 16, 18, 18, 19, 20, 26, 26, 26,

27, 27, 28, 28, 30, 32, 37, 38, 41, 41, 41, 44, 46, 46, 48, 54, 55, 55, 56, 57, 58, 58, 62, 64, 67, 72, 73, 73, 77, 79, 79, 79, 80, 80, 81, 81, 83, 84, 84, 85, 87, 88, 92, 94, 96, 105, 106, 111, 112, 113, 116, 116, 117, 117, 119, 120, 120, 122, 123, 123, 126, 128, 129, 130, 130, 131, 132, 133, 136, 136, 137, 137, 139, 141, 141, 142, 144, 144, 145, 146, 146, 148, 151, 151, 155, 156, 157, 161, 164, 164, 166, 167, 168, 168, 168, 168, 168, 171, 171, 174, 177, 179, 179, 180, 182, 183, 186, 189, 191, 193, 194, 195, 196, 199, 199, 200, 200, 208, 209, 211, 212, 217, 224, 230, 233, 234, 234, 234, 234, 234, 237, 238, 239, 249, 255, 261, 261, 263, 263, 264, 265, 267, 270, 270, 270 Somn 1:3, 3, 3, 4, 5, 5, 6, 10, 10, 10, 15, 17, 18, 21, 22, 22, 22, 25, 29, 30, 30, 32, 32, 32, 34, 37, 41, 43, 46, 46, 46, 47, 47, 47, 48, 49, 49, 50, 53, 55, 56, 58, 59, 61, 62, 63, 63, 63, 64, 64, 65, 66, 66, 66, 66, 67, 68, 70, 70, 71, 71, 74, 74, 75, 75, 76, 78, 79, 81, 82, 83, 84, 86, 86, 87, 91, 92, 92, 92, 92, 95, 96, 101, 101, 103, 106, 107, 107, 108, 109, 109, 117, 118, 120, 120, 123, 124, 126, 129, 129, 129, 130, 131, 133, 133, 133, 136, 139, 142, 142, 143, 145, 147, 147, 148, 153, 158, 159, 159, 159, 159, 159, 160, 163, 164, 167, 167, 168, 172, 172, 172, 172, 174, 177, 178, 178, 179, 181, 182, 183, 184, 188, 188, 188, 189, 190, 192, 192, 193, 194, 195, 195, 195, 196, 203, 203, 204, 205, 205, 206, 209, 211, 213, 214, 215, 216, 222, 222, 224, 228, 229, 230, 231, 232, 232, 232, 237, 239, 239, 239, 239, 241, 246, 246 Somn 2:4, 5, 9, 9, 9, 10, 13, 19, 23, 24, 25, 27, 33, 34, 39, 42, 44, 46, 50, 54, 60, 63, 64, 66, 74, 75, 77, 78, 86, 88, 90, 91, 91, 92, 93, 95, 96, 96, 96, 98, 99, 100, 101, 104, 106, 106, 109, 111, 111, 111, 112, 116, 117, 120, 121, 123, 129, 130, 133, 133, 137, 141, 142, 143, 147, 149, 153, 154, 156, 157, 159, 159, 174, 175, 176, 181, 190, 190, 191, 191, 191, 191, 191, 196, 198, 199, 203, 205, 206, 206, 206, 207, 209, 211, 213, 214, 216, 217, 217, 217, 219, 220, 220, 224, 227, 228, 230, 233, 236, 237, 243, 244, 249, 249, 254, 255, 255, 255, 257, 259, 260, 260, 270, 272, 275, 277, 277, 278, 280, 285, 295, 297, 300 Abr 2, 4, 6, 7, 10, 10, 17, 28, 28, 31, 31, 34, 35, 36, 37, 37, 37, 38, 39, 41, 46, 46, 47, 47, 49, 50, 50, 57, 57, 60, 60, 69, 70, 71, 79, 85, 87, 87, 89, 90, 93, 94, 96, 97, 98, 102, 103, 108, 110, 110, 116, 116, 122, 123, 126, 126, 127, 128, 130, 132, 136, 136, 138, 140, 145, 158, 162, 162, 163, 164, 168, 171, 181, 181, 181, 182, 183, 189, 193, 194, 195, 198, 206, 208, 208, 208, 212, 213, 215, 215, 216, 220, 222, 222, 225, 227, 230, 230, 232, 234, 235, 235, 237, 243, 243, 245, 245, 248, 249, 253, 259, 260, 261, 262, 269, 270, 270, 270, 273, 273, 276 Ios 3, 4, 11, 11, 12, 12, 13, 15, 18, 21, 22, 22, 26, 29, 36, 38, 39, 39, 39, 45, 46, 47, 48, 49, 50, 50, 50, 50, 51, 59, 60, 61, 61, 63, 64, 76, 80, 82, 87, 92, 93, 100, 105, 105, 112, 117, 119, 120, 121, 121, 123, 125, 136, 145, 145, 145, 150, 152, 156, 158, 164, 164, 165, 167, 168, 175, 179, 179, 179, 184, 185, 185, 186, 186, 191, 193, 193, 198, 203, 205, 207, 209, 212, 217, 218, 219, 220, 226, 227, 229, 233, 234, 236, 238, 238, 239, 241, 245, 246, 248, 249, 249, 251, 255, 257, 257, 257, 258, 259, 269 Mos 1:1, 2, 2, 4, 5, 8, 10, 14, 15, 15, 17, 20, 21, 22, 24, 24, 25, 27, 30, 32, 38, 38, 38, 45, 45, 45, 46, 47, 47, 48, 51, 51, 55, 56, 58, 58, 59, 59, 65, 68, 71, 72, 74, 75, 76, 78, 79, 84, 84, 86, 86, 87, 95, 96, 98, 99, 102, 105, 107, 111, 111, 113, 118, 120, 120, 121, 126, 128, 132, 137, 139, 141, 143, 143, 143, 148, 149, 150, 151, 153, 155, 156, 158, 161, 162, 162, 164, 164, 164, 173, 175, 175, 179, 196, 196, 202, 205, 206, 211, 214, 216, 217, 220, 222, 231, 232, 235, 235, 239, 242, 243, 245, 248, 249, 253, 254, 258, 260, 262, 262, 262, 266, 267, 269, 269, 277, 278, 279, 281, 283, 284, 285, 287, 287, 287, 291, 291, 295, 295, 297, 298, 301, 301, 303, 304, 309, 310, 311, 318, 320, 321, 324, 324, 325, 325, 328, 331, 334 Mos 2:2, 3, 3, 5, 12, 14, 14, 15, 17, 31, 34, 36, 37, 38, 38, 39, 40, 45, 48, 51, 56, 58, 58, 60, 61, 64, 65, 67, 71, 72, 81, 81, 82, 84, 87, 87, 88, 89, 93, 99, 103, 113, 115, 116, 117, 119, 128, 132, 133, 135, 138, 139, 141, 142, 143, 146, 148, 150, 151, 152, 152, 153, 154, 159, 161, 165, 173, 174, 177, 180, 181, 181, 183, 188, 189, 190, 191, 196, 199, 199, 206, 207, 209, 209, 210, 210, 211, 214, 214, 221, 225, 229, 231, 232, 236, 241, 244, 245, 246, 247, 252, 252, 254, 256, 256, 257, 257, 257, 259, 259, 263, 265, 267, 272, 274, 275, 277, 278, 279, 279, 285, 286, 287, 288, 291, 291 Decal 7, 14, 18, 18, 19, 23, 27, 32, 38, 38, 43, 45, 46, 49, 50, 52, 54, 56, 57, 59, 61, 61, 66, 70, 81, 86, 87, 92, 95, 100, 101, 102, 105, 106, 115, 117, 117, 134, 138, 142, 142, 143, 144, 146, 146, 159, 159, 159, 169, 174, 175, 175 Spec 1:11, 15, 17, 29, 30, 32, 36, 37, 40, 40, 40, 42, 46, 48, 49, 50, 52, 53, 55, 56, 57, 58, 58, 59, 60, 60, 61, 62, 64, 65, 66, 67, 68, 71, 72, 94, 95, 96, 97, 97, 101, 102, 102, 105, 105, 108, 110, 112, 116, 131, 135, 146, 146, 151, 154, 156, 157, 158, 164, 164, 167, 180, 182, 186, 193, 193, 195, 196, 196, 197, 201, 209, 209, 210, 210, 210, 210, 214, 215, 216, 216, 217, 218, 218, 223, 223, 225, 229, 233, 235, 237, 239, 242, 243, 246, 247, 248, 252, 252, 252, 253, 256, 256, 257, 259, 264, 265, 266, 267, 269, 270, 271, 277, 279, 283, 286, 289, 290, 291, 293, 294, 297, 300, 300, 300, 300, 300, 302, 309, 310, 312, 316, 316, 316, 316, 317, 323, 324, 326, 329, 332, 332, 333, 333, 334, 336, 337, 337, 344, 345 Spec 2:6, 13, 15, 15, 19, 20, 21, 24, 26, 30, 32, 38, 40, 41, 45, 45, 46, 46, 48, 51, 52, 53, 54, 54, 55, 56, 56, 56, 56, 58, 60, 64, 65, 70, 71, 71, 78, 78, 81, 82, 82, 92, 92, 93, 96, 96, 98, 101, 104, 106, 106, 108, 110, 118, 119, 121, 121, 129, 131, 132, 133, 136, 137, 138, 140, 142, 143, 146, 150, 155, 164, 169, 170, 173, 177, 180, 181, 181, 183, 187, 194, 195, 200, 205, 211, 217, 220, 220, 222, 223, 224, 228, 230, 234, 235, 240, 240, 243, 246, 249, 253, 256, 257, 258, 259, 260, 261 Spec 3:1, 4, 5, 7, 8, 8, 9, 14, 14, 14, 14, 14, 27, 27, 27, 29, 34, 35, 36, 39, 39, 39, 41, 44, 47, 49, 50, 58, 64, 67, 70, 70, 71, 73, 73, 77, 79, 84, 85, 86, 87, 90, 91, 95, 96, 96, 98, 100, 102, 103, 103, 105, 115, 127, 128, 131, 134, 135, 137, 139, 140, 140, 142, 146, 148, 149, 151, 152, 153, 161, 162, 164, 167, 172, 175, 183, 184, 189, 190, 191, 195, 201, 203, 208 Spec 4:6, 7, 8, 10, 12, 14, 14, 16, 18, 21, 23, 23, 25, 26, 28, 31, 43, 50, 50, 56, 57, 58, 60, 68, 68, 69, 82, 82, 83, 83, 83, 83, 88, 92, 92, 93, 94, 94, 97, 103, 105, 106, 107, 109, 112, 113, 116, 121, 122, 126, 130, 140, 141, 142, 144, 147, 149, 149, 150, 150, 155, 159, 161, 162, 163, 167, 169, 171, 173, 173, 174, 176, 180, 181, 184, 186, 187, 187, 188, 189, 193, 195, 196, 197, 200, 201, 204, 204, 205, 208, 209, 209, 212, 213, 214, 214, 216, 216, 217, 219, 223, 223, 226, 227, 229, 230, 230, 235, 235 Virt 1, 3, 5, 9, 12, 14, 18, 19, 21, 27, 28, 30, 31, 34, 35, 38, 43, 51, 52, 53, 54, 54, 55, 55, 56, 61, 62, 63, 64, 64, 65, 66, 66, 67, 70, 70, 72, 74, 78, 79, 79, 81, 81, 82, 85, 90, 91, 91, 93, 94, 96, 103, 103, 105, 106, 108, 109, 109, 111, 113, 113, 115, 115, 116, 120, 127, 129, 130, 134, 135, 136, 142, 142, 143, 146, 146, 148, 154, 154, 155, 157, 159, 160, 161, 164, 169, 173, 175, 184, 185, 185, 186, 191, 192, 194, 194, 195, 195, 202, 208, 210, 215, 216, 217, 217, 217, 218, 222, 223, 224, 226, 227 Praem 4, 5, 13, 13, 15, 16, 23, 24, 26,

28, 28, 29, 34, 35, 36, 38, 40, 41, 43, 44, 45, 45, 45, 53, 55, 56, 62, 62, 64, 70, 71, 71, 72, 72, 73, 78, 90, 93, 98, 107, 125, 129, 129, 131, 137, 144, 146, 148, 150, 152, 157, 157, 159, 163, 164, 164, 166, 169, 171, 172 Prob 3, 4, 9, 10, 12, 15, 17, 23, 30, 31, 39, 47, 50, 51, 54, 61, 62, 69, 75, 78, 79, 80, 82, 86, 89, 91, 92, 93, 96, 98, 100, 101, 105, 106, 110, 112, 114, 118, 118, 121, 127, 141, 143, 146, 154, 157 Contempl 1, 6, 7, 14, 15, 27, 28, 29, 31, 32, 32, 34, 37, 37, 38, 40, 41, 43, 43, 51, 59, 60, 64, 65, 68, 75, 77, 77, 80, 82, 90, 90, 90 Aet 1, 4, 4, 6, 7, 8, 17, 21, 21, 21, 22, 22, 24, 25, 26, 37, 38, 38, 38, 43, 48, 48, 49, 49, 50, 51, 51, 53, 54, 58, 61, 63, 65, 68, 72, 72, 74, 74, 78, 80, 84, 89, 93, 94, 95, 96, 97, 98, 99, 102, 106, 109, 109, 114, 118, 120, 129, 132, 133, 134, 136, 137, 138, 143, 143, 144 Flacc 3, 5, 7, 8, 10, 11, 12, 14, 14, 15, 19, 20, 23, 25, 25, 27, 28, 29, 30, 32, 33, 35, 37, 47, 53, 54, 64, 72, 76, 79, 79, 82, 82, 87, 89, 92, 96, 97, 99, 102, 104, 105, 108, 110, 112, 113, 114, 124, 125, 125, 126, 126, 128, 129, 134, 138, 139, 139, 141, 142, 143, 145, 146, 146, 148, 148, 149, 151, 152, 153, 158, 159, 161, 167, 168, 170, 170, 172, 174, 177, 177, 180, 181, 181, 186, 187 Legat 3, 3, 5, 6, 16, 16, 18, 23, 26, 31, 31, 32, 33, 34, 39, 41, 41, 46, 48, 55, 57, 58, 58, 59, 61, 61, 62, 65, 76, 76, 78, 80, 82, 85, 86, 93, 95, 96, 98, 99, 103, 105, 106, 108, 109, 109, 112, 114, 115, 116, 121, 125, 129, 131, 132, 133, 134, 140, 142, 143, 148, 149, 153, 156, 157, 159, 163, 163, 163, 165, 165, 166, 169, 170, 171, 172, 172, 173, 173, 176, 178, 179, 181, 188, 189, 197, 199, 200, 211, 211, 212, 214, 214, 216, 219, 219, 223, 223, 227, 234, 238, 238, 240, 243, 245, 248, 248, 252, 253, 255, 256, 257, 259, 262, 262, 263, 266, 267, 267, 268, 271, 274, 277, 281, 287, 289, 295, 295, 298, 298, 299, 300, 301, 302, 302, 306, 307, 307, 308, 308, 310, 314, 316, 322, 323, 324, 332, 334, 334, 338, 343, 345, 346, 347, 352, 354, 355, 358, 361, 367, 371 Hypoth 0:1, 6:1, 6:1, 6:1, 6:1, 6:2, 6:2, 6:4, 6:4, 6:4, 6:5, 6:6, 6:7, 6:8, 6:8, 6:8, 6:9, 6:9, 6:9, 6:9, 7:2, 7:2, 7:3, 7:3, 7:4, 7:5, 7:5, 7:6, 7:6, 7:7, 7:9, 7:9, 7:11, 7:11, 7:12, 7:12, 7:13, 7:14, 7:14, 7:15, 7:15, 7:15, 7:16, 7:17, 7:17, 7:17, 7:17, 7:18, 7:19, 7:19, 7:19, 7:19, 7:20, 11:2, 11:4, 11:5, 11:8, 11:11, 11:12, 11:13, 11:17, 11:18, 11:18 Prov 2:6, 6, 6, 7, 7, 12, 13, 14, 15, 17, 17, 18, 20, 23, 26, 28, 29, 31, 32, 33, 33, 36, 39, 41, 49, 51, 55, 60, 66, 69 QG 1:20, 21, 21, 21, 24, 29, 29, 32, 66, 66, 70:1, 70:1, 70:2, 74, 77, 85, 89, 97, 100:2b, 100:2b, 2:10, 12a, 13b, 15a, 16, 17c, 34a, 39, 54a, 54a, 54a, 54d, 59, 64a, 3:8, 11a, 18, 20a, 20a, 22, 22, 23, 24, 29, 29, 38a, 49a, 49b, 4:8a, 20, 33b, 51a, 88, 88, 153, 153, 153, 167, 167, 180, 191c, 194, 194, 7*, 7*, 8*, 8*, 200b, 211, 211, 227 QG isf 8, 13 QG (Par) 2:2, 2:3, 2:4 QE 1:6, 2:2, 3b, 16, 17, 24a, 25a, 45a, 45a, 46, 46, 55a, 105 QE isf 8, 8, 21, 21, 26, 31

αὐτοστατέω Somn 2:228

αὐτοσχεδιάζω Flacc 101

αὐτοσχέδιος Somn 2:50 Contempl 38 Legat 201, 246

αὐτοτελής Congr 149 Mut 260

αὐτοῦ Gig 54 Deus 23 Conf 31 Mut 178 Somn 2:227

αὐτουργέω Mos 1:130 Spec 2:67

αὐτουργία Ios 34 Decal 159 Spec 2:67 Prob 142

αὐτουργός Plant 168 Mut 259 Somn 2:202 Spec 1:14 Prob 32

αὐτοφυής QG isf 16

αὐτόφωρος Spec 3:52 Spec 4:7

αὐτόχειρ (7) Ebr 66 Mos 1:10, 303, 308 Spec 3:96, 114 Virt 132

αὐτοχειρία (8) Mos 2:197 Spec 3:85, 91 Spec 4:7, 10, 160 Legat 30, 61

αὐτόχθων (17) Cher 120 Sacr 44 Conf 12, 79 Congr 22 Fug 76 Somn 1:160 Abr 209, 252 Mos 1:8, 35 Mos 2:58 Spec 1:52, 124 Spec 2:170 Virt 104, 108

αὐχενίζω Somn 1:222 Somn 2:134 Spec 4:114, 217

αὐχέω (21) Leg 3:12, 42 Cher 63 Sacr 49 Deus 146, 148, 168 Agr 60, 63 Migr 20 Her 214 Congr 127 Somn 2:30, 202 Mos 1:272 Spec 1:10, 150 Spec 4:74 Virt 187 Praem 94 QE 2:37

αὔχημα (13) Leg 3:193 Cher 63, 107 Sacr 49, 62 Conf 131 Congr 134 Mut 26 Somn 1:228 Spec 1:311 Spec 3:37 Virt 197 Praem 94

αὐχήν (καί) (34) Cher 81 Sacr 21 Post 3 Gig 31 Agr 70, 75 Plant 16, 16, 145 Ebr 131, 173 Fug 107 Mut 160 Somn 2:78, 83, 213 Abr 164 Ios 256 Mos 1:228 Mos 2:35, 240, 252 Decal 4 Spec 3:160, 184 Virt 173 Prob 155 Contempl 45, 53 Flacc 160 Legat 30 Prov 2:27, 29 QG 4:99

αὐχμηρός (6) Fug 33 Spec 1:134 Praem 35, 121, 161 Legat 83

αὐχμός (7) Abr 91, 179 Mos 1:265 Spec 1:92, 184 Spec 2:191 Virt 49

αὐχμώδης Spec 2:153

ἀφαγνίζω Somn 2:25 Spec 3:205

ἀφαίρεμα Leg 3:133, 136 Sacr 107, 107, 107

ἀφαίρεσις (24) Opif 167 Leg 2:60, 60 Leg 3:113 Cher 118 Sacr 1, 8, 98 Gig 25 Her 149, 187 Fug 128 Mos 1:46 Spec 4:143, 144, 146, 147, 158 Aet 113, 113 Flacc 151 Legat 28, 87 QE 2:25b

ἀφαιρέω (125) Leg 2:35, 69, 78 Leg 3:32, 112, 129, 130, 130, 131, 136, 147, 147, 183 Cher 58, 69, 74 Sacr 1, 5, 89, 97, 98, 101, 107, 107, 107, 107, 110, 111, 115 Det 105, 158, 158 Gig 24, 43, 43 Deus 173 Conf 195 Migr 67, 105 Her 49, 91, 120 Fug 15, 16, 16, 19, 55 Mut 32, 56, 192 Somn 1:98, 105, 114, 137 Somn 2:162 Abr 8 Ios 52, 58 Mos 1:8, 55, 55, 137, 181, 293 Mos 2:34, 244 Spec 1:115, 132, 132, 254, 310, 328 Spec 2:24, 87, 139 Spec 3:56, 197, 204 Spec 4:5, 15, 101, 143, 146, 147, 159, 178 Virt 30, 65 Praem 33, 99, 139, 172 Prob 36, 55, 57, 117 Contempl 60 Aet 42, 50, 51, 51, 86, 114, 114, 125 Flacc 5, 29, 49, 77, 94, 103, 122, 171 Legat 157, 232, 276, 326, 347 Hypoth 6:7 Prov 1 QG 1:28, 2:65, 4:172 QE 2:3a, 25c

ἀφάνεια Her 157

ἀφανής (105) Opif 39, 43 Leg 2:30 Leg 3:3 Cher 16, 96, 128 Det 23 Post 50, 59 Deus 39 Plant 20, 79, 128 Ebr 65, 193 Sobr 41 Conf 196 Migr 35, 89, 105, 147, 186, 214 Fug 160 Mut 222, 232 Somn 1:6, 7, 68, 119, 203, 222, 224 Somn 2:43, 120, 214, 252 Ios 131, 248 Mos 1:30, 32, 49, 56, 109, 114, 127, 134, 160, 166, 173, 177, 211, 280 Mos 2:76, 79, 164, 241, 252 Decal 1, 40, 70 Spec 1:6, 140, 200 Spec 2:68, 108, 250 Spec 3:80, 117, 121, 121, 125, 130, 136, 147, 178, 194 Spec 4:50, 69 Virt 18, 162 Praem 31, 61, 129, 171 Prob 66, 133 Contempl 78 Aet 121 Flacc 80 Legat 33, 146, 172, 191, 220, 263, 280, 317, 337 Prov 2:1, 26, 54 QG 4:99 QE 2:24a ἀφανίζω (63) Opif 57, 169 Leg 3:23, 27, 27 Sacr 69 Post 93, 113 Deus 43, 73, 123 Agr 11, 167, 169 Ebr 111 Conf 13, 187, 188, 193 Migr 24, 85, 122 Mut 186 Somn 1:194 Somn 2:13, 109, 128 Abr 19, 41, 43, 45, 142 Mos 1:3, 102, 110, 175, 261, 311 Decal 11 Spec 2:47, 170 Spec 4:52, 81, 147, 202 Virt 164, 201 Prob 73 Aet 20, 79, 88, 120, 127, 140, 141, 144 Flacc 116 Legat 134, 144, 202 Hypoth 7:7 QG 2:15b QE 2:17

ἀφάντατος (8) Opif 73 Post 8, 21 Deus 41 Plant 13 Her 137 Somn 1:136 Virt 160

ἀφαυαίνω (16) Opif 38, 113, 131 Det 108 Post 112, 125 Deus 37 Ebr 9 Migr 101, 123 Her 270 Fug 124 Spec 2:153 Spec 4:209 Prob 69 Aet 96

ἀφεγγής Legat 103

ἀφειδέω Leg 3:209 Agr 168

ἀφειδής Spec 2:22 Spec 4:222 Praem 128 Legat 198

ἀφέλεια Ebr 6 Abr 117 Prob 84

ἀφέλκω Abr 88 Spec 4:70 Virt 30

ἀφελληνίζω Legat 147

ἀφενάκιστος Fug 125

ἄφεσις (20) Sacr 122 Det 63, 144 Migr 32 Her 273 Congr 89, 108, 109 Mut 228 Mos 1:123 Mos 2:147 Spec 1:190, 215, 237 Spec 2:39, 67, 122, 176 Flacc 84 Legat 287

ἄφετος (21) Leg 3:17, 244 Sacr 104 Deus 47, 49 Agr 36, 73 Ebr 71, 101, 151 Sobr 39 Conf 98 Somn 2:196 Abr 67 Mos 2:161 Spec 1:100 Spec 3:145 Spec 4:122 Virt 31 Praem 62 Flacc 182

ἁφή (26) Opif 62, 62 Leg 2:7, 39, 74 Leg 3:58 Cher 57 Sacr 31, 73 Det 168 Deus 131, 131 Plant 133 Conf 52, 90 Migr 137, 188 Her 48, 232 Fug 182 Somn 1:55, 80 Abr 148, 149, 236, 241

ἀφηβάω Her 299

ἀφηγέομαι (20) Sacr 49, 50 Gig 55 Agr 66, 81 Ebr 115, 125 Migr 60, 143, 172 Her 241 Congr 50 Mut 114 Spec 2:181 Virt 58 Prob 30 Flacc 8, 109, 116 QG 1:76b

ἀφηδύνω Plant 159

ἀφηνιάζω (34) Opif 86 Leg 1:73, 95 Leg 2:104 Leg 3:128, 193, 223 Sacr 105, 106 Agr 32, 74 Ebr 15 Migr 62 Her 206 Congr 118 Mut 115 Abr 212 Mos 1:88, 167 Mos 2:53, 169 Spec 1:343 Spec 2:142, 232 Spec 4:96 Prob 40, 104 Flacc 4, 17, 188 Legat 265, 332 Prov 2:33 QE 2:25c

ἀφηνιασμός (7) Sacr 49 Det 23 Agr 71 Decal 39 Spec 2:18 Spec 4:79, 99

ἀφηνιαστής (17) Leg 3:136 Sacr 32, 45 Agr 84 Plant 49 Ebr 111 Congr 158 Somn 2:293 Mos 1:26 Decal 49, 174 Spec 1:304 Spec 2:39 Spec 4:79, 127 Virt 13, 195

ἀφησυχάζω Abr 10

ἀφθαρσία (25) Opif 153 Sacr 5 Agr 100 Ebr 140, 212 Her 35 Fug 56, 59 Mut 210 Somn 1:181, 217, 218 Somn 2:258 Abr 55 Mos 2:61, 194 Aet 1, 27, 27, 46, 47, 76, 150 QG 3:11a QE isf 15

ἄφθαρτος (120) Opif 82, 82, 119, 134 Leg 1:4, 51, 51, 78, 78 Leg 3:31, 36 Cher 5, 6, 7, 51, 86 Sacr 7, 63, 95, 97, 101 Det 49, 75, 77, 78, 85, 85, 115 Post 105, 135 Gig 14, 14, 45, 61 Deus 26, 36, 46, 123, 142, 151, 180 Agr 141 Plant 44, 114 Ebr 110, 136, 145, 208, 209, 212 Conf 41 Migr 13, 18, 18, 19, 132, 198, 199 Her 14, 79, 118, 118, 138, 205, 311, 314, 316 Congr 108 Fug 59, 109 Mut 3, 14, 78, 80, 122, 181, 195 Somn 1:31, 34, 94, 137, 243 Somn 2:230, 253, 258, 283 Abr 55, 55, 165, 243 Ios 265 Mos 2:158, 171 Decal 41 Virt 67 Praem 1 Prob 46, 105 Aet 3, 7, 7, 10, 12, 13, 17, 17, 19, 19, 20, 34, 44, 51, 51, 69, 75, 88, 93, 129 Legat 85, 118

ἀφθονία (51) Opif 77, 168 Leg 1:54 Sacr 76 Det 21, 113, 137 Agr 34, 39, 58, 101 Sobr 13 Conf 7 Migr 30 Her 286 Fug 96, 176 Abr 134, 208 Mos 1:6, 152, 193, 201, 210, 211 Decal 16, 17, 117 Spec 1:141 Spec 2:19, 158, 169, 180, 185, 192, 203 Spec 3:203 Spec 4:228 Virt 127, 144 Praem 106 Prob 9, 64, 87 Flacc 130, 143 Legat 90 Prov 2:12, 38, 46 QG 1:89

ἄφθονος (122) Opif 39, 79, 113, 133 Leg 1:45, 80 Leg 3:164, 203 Cher 99 Sacr 10, 22, 48 Det 14, 20 Post 98, 115, 145, 147, 151 Gig 36 Deus 108, 153 Agr 25, 32, 48, 149 Plant 65, 91, 102 Ebr 32 Sobr 39, 53, 56 Conf 25 Migr 15, 121, 204 Her 31, 213 Fug 35, 102, 129 Mut 32, 89, 215 Somn 2:61, 93, 181, 252 Abr 92, 234, 252 Ios 55, 109, 161, 210, 253 Mos 1:25, 55, 164, 209, 228, 255, 320 Mos 2:6, 9, 13, 23, 53, 58, 134 Decal 178 Spec 1:71, 78, 133, 134, 154, 286 Spec 2:20, 199, 205 Spec 3:111 Spec 4:28, 74, 83, 126, 140, 195 Virt 6, 48, 133, 149, 161, 163, 187 Praem 103, 107, 129, 168 Prob 13, 87 Contempl 16, 35, 56 Aet 62, 148 Flacc 63, 184 Legat 107, 118, 141, 252, 311 Hypoth 11:10 Prov 2:1, 5, 29, 57 QG 4:43, 81, 172 QE 2:25b

ἀφίδρυμα (19) Post 158, 165 Ebr 109 Somn 1:208 Mos 1:298 Mos 2:205 Decal 7, 51, 74, 74, 156 Virt 102, 221 Legat 81, 208, 310, 317, 319 QE isf 14

ἀφιερόω Gig 12 Plant 132 Spec 2:115

ἀφίημι (63) Leg 2:34 Leg 3:41, 56, 128 Cher 91 Sacr 34, 82 Det 53, 141, 142, 144, 150 Post 78, 131 Agr 36, 44, 49, 76 Plant 152 Sobr 26, 57 Conf 48, 165, 189 Migr 32 Her 20, 20 Fug 15, 173 Mut 107, 162, 257 Somn 1:105 Somn 2:139 Ios 71 Spec 1:266, 298 Spec 2:79 Spec 3:64, 114, 175, 184, 196 Spec 4:3 Virt 28, 97, 203 Praem 103, 140, 166 Prob 96, 156 Legat 190, 205, 228, 304, 323, 325 Hypoth 7:15 Prov 2:32 QG 1:73, 2:64b QE 2:3a

ἀφικνέομαι (117) Opif 86 Leg 3:156 Cher 106, 120, 120 Sacr 42, 90, 128 Det 39, 158, 158 Post 8, 53, 84, 152, 176 Gig 53 Deus 35, 131, 134, 143 Agr 160 Plant 162 Ebr 49, 158, 213, 218 Sobr 24 Conf 29, 175 Migr 175, 194 Her 150, 238, 283 Congr 81, 155 Fug 41, 44, 44, 98, 107 Mut 114, 116, 163, 168, 199 Somn 1:3, 66, 86, 112, 122, 131, 133, 236 Somn 2:19, 139, 147, 264 Abr 79, 161, 172, 240, 241 Ios 6, 12, 168, 168, 187, 188, 196, 226, 240, 251 Mos 1:49, 188, 194, 310 Mos 2:167, 217, 247 Decal 44, 80, 88, 145 Spec 1:24, 34, 68, 316 Spec 2:238 Spec 3:16 Spec 4:173 Virt 30, 132 Praem 110 Prob 81, 85, 103, 160 Contempl 50 Flacc 15, 27, 28, 122 Legat 52, 172, 180, 182, 185, 199, 252, 338, 349 Prov 2:17, 19 QG 4:43 QG isf 6

ἀφιλήδονος Prob 84

ἀφιλόδοξος Prob 84

ἀφιλόνεικος Agr 159 Conf 14 Abr 28 Mos 1:24 Legat 68

ἄφιλος Sacr 32 QG isf 10

ἀφιλόσοφος Opif 2, 26 Abr 110 Spec 1:174 QG 4:69 QG (Par) 2:7

ἀφιλοχρήματος Prob 84

ἄφιξις (17) Det 37 Agr 161, 161, 179 Her 265 Congr 121 Mut 171 Ios 185, 255 Mos 1:280 Mos 2:171 Flacc 28, 31, 161 Legat 257 Prov 2:26 QE 2:45a

ἀφίστημι (72) Opif 141 Leg 1:82, 89 Leg 2:28 Leg 3:71, 84, 239, 242 Cher 18, 33 Sacr 38, 47 Det 15, 63, 85 Post 18, 120, 122, 152 Gig 38 Deus 9, 14, 134 Agr 125, 155, 174 Plant 22, 99 Ebr 38 Conf 76, 140, 157, 157 Migr 194 Her 206 Congr 54, 157 Fug 103 Mut 226, 265, 265 Somn 1:68, 119 Somn 2:198 Abr 169, 197 Ios 45, 117, 177 Mos 1:250 Mos 2:89, 91, 94, 102 Decal 34, 87, 147 Spec 4:82, 128, 219 Virt 34, 96, 182, 183 Praem 80 Prob 107 Flacc 27, 93 Legat 171 Hypoth 7:15 QG 1:100:2b QE 2:28

ἄφοβος (10) Cher 86 Migr 169 Abr 202 Ios 266 Spec 1:55 Spec 3:128, 166 Praem 35 Legat 13, 322

ἀφοράω (22) Opif 114 Post 141 Agr 5, 49 Plant 69 Ebr 37 Sobr 7, 16, 43 Migr 153, 190 Her 79 Fug 129 Ios 259 Spec 3:8 Virt 63, 122, 197 Prob 23 Contempl 64 Legat 213 QG 1:21

ἀφοράω ἀπεῖδον

ἀφορέω Somn 1:115 Somn 2:238 Spec 1:246 Spec 4:211

ἀφόρητος (22) Leg 3:194, 202 Det 46 Agr 40 Mut 129 Ios 26, 262 Mos 1:191 Spec 1:100 Spec 2:201 Spec 3:99, 195 Spec 4:113 Praem 132, 137, 137, 153 Flacc 58, 95, 117 Legat 209, 345

ἀφορία (11) Opif 58 Conf 167 Abr 1, 91, 268 Mos 1:265 Spec 1:92, 246 Spec 2:213 Praem 132 Legat 257

ἀφορίζω (9) Leg 1:63, 65 Post 128, 129 Somn 1:101 Somn 2:241, 243, 243 Spec 2:35

ἀφόρισμα Sacr 107

ἀφορισμός Somn 1:101

ἀφορμή (39) Opif 47 Leg 3:66 Plant 36, 141 Conf 68, 68, 191 Migr 2 Her 300 Mut 229 Abr 162, 218, 220 Ios 258 Mos 1:46 Mos 2:44 Decal 17 Spec 1:156, 286 Spec 2:85, 93, 118 Virt 222 Prob 51, 71, 78 Flacc 1, 34, 35, 40, 47, 102 Legat 63, 152, 200, 248, 259 Prov 2:5 QG 1:55c

ἄφορος Plant 97 Mut 225

ἀφοσιόω Legat 102, 154

ἀφραίνω (6) Det 73 Agr 40 Ebr 5 Migr 219 Somn 1:155 Somn 2:266

Ἀφροδίτη Decal 54 Contempl 59

ἄφροντις Prob 22, 23

ἀφρόντιστος Sacr 23

ἀφρός Opif 67

ἀφροσύνη (94) Opif 73, 79 Leg 1:75, 75, 86 Leg 3:193, 211, 242 Cher 10, 32, 71, 92 Sacr 15, 17 Det 178 Post 93, 176 Deus 112, 181 Agr 17, 44, 73, 77, 112 Plant 40 Ebr 10, 20, 27, 95, 125, 128, 140 Sobr 26, 38 Conf 21, 66, 68, 75, 90, 91, 197 Migr 60, 124, 134, 169, 224 Her 209, 245, 284 Congr 61, 179 Fug 113, 188 Mut 197 Somn 2:160, 162, 181, 192, 192, 192, 195, 196, 198, 200, 203, 234 Abr 24 Mos 2:162, 198 Spec 1:98, 99, 214, 288, 305, 343 Spec 2:49, 214, 239 Virt 180 Praem 59, 159 Prob 28, 56, 63 Contempl 2, 74 Aet 2 Prov 2:8, 20, 38 QG 3:22, 4:179, 204 QE 2:4

ἀφρούρητος Ebr 160 Mos 1:330 Legat 226

ἄφρων (94) Leg 1:75, 86 Leg 2:18 Leg 3:67, 67, 189, 189, 189, 200, 216, 229, 248, 251, 252 Cher 32, 41, 121 Sacr 46, 51, 51 Det 48, 123, 143, 162, 162, 169 Post 22, 24, 32, 32, 100, 179 Deus 64, 68, 126 Agr 42, 74 Plant 141, 166, 171 Ebr 11, 110, 147, 150 Sobr 10, 15, 23, 42, 68, 69 Conf 49, 75, 110, 119, 162, 165, 198 Migr 38, 67, 100, 156 Her 73, 83 Congr 175 Fug 16, 19 Mut 23, 50, 91, 128, 153, 170, 175, 195, 254 Somn 1:234 Somn 2:116 Abr 274 Mos 1:95 Decal 177 Spec 2:239 Virt 174 Prob 30, 51, 57, 136 Aet 56 QG 2:12c, 3:11b, 22, 4:33a, 76a QG isf 11 QE isf 26

ἀφυής Deus 100 Mut 68, 211 QG 4:102b

ἀφυΐα Gig 2 Her 212

ἄφυκτος Somn 1:81 Mos 1:172

ἀφύλακτος (6) Ebr 160 Fug 190, 191 Spec 4:27 Flacc 113 QE 2:13a

ἀφωνία Cher 93 Ios 214 Mos 1:83 Decal 92 Contempl 1

ἄφωνος (13) Opif 126 Det 91, 91 Agr 136 Plant 10 Ebr 195 Conf 55 Her 3, 210 Congr 150 Mut 63, 64 Ios 239

ἀφώρατος Flacc 27

ἀφώτιστος Somn 1:117 Spec 2:140

ἀχάλινος (14) Det 44, 174 Her 110 Somn 2:132 Abr 29, 191 Ios 246 Mos 2:198 Spec 1:53, 241 Virt 113 Praem 154 Flacc 14 Legat 162

ἀχαλίνωτος (8) Agr 84 Conf 165 Somn 2:165, 275 Mos 1:25 Spec 2:6 Spec 3:45, 79

ἀχανής (20) Opif 29, 32 Cher 116 Det 100 Her 3 Ios 22, 214, 239 Mos 1:194 Mos 2:251 Spec 3:147, 149 Contempl 33 Aet 147 Flacc 10, 87, 114 Legat 189, 223 Prov 2:33

ἀχαριστέω Spec 1:284

ἀχαριστία (7) Opif 169 Sacr 58 Her 226 Mos 1:58 Virt 165 Legat 118 QG 1:96:1

ἀχάριστος (6) Deus 48, 74 Her 302 Ios 99 Legat 60 QE 2:49a

ἄχει Somn 2:216

Ἀχειμάν Post 60, 61

ἀχειραγώγητος Somn 2:161

ἀχείρωτος Prob 149

ἄχθομαι (11) Leg 3:211 Sacr 125 Post 84 Conf 49 Migr 191 Abr 86, 259 Ios 189 Virt 88 Praem 72 Prob 55

ἄχθος (42) Cher 78 Det 9 Post 74, 149 Gig 16 Deus 2, 15 Agr 20, 25, 49 Plant 56 Migr 14, 144 Her 46 Congr 171 Mut 185 Somn 1:110, 128 Somn 2:62, 171, 208 Abr 207 Ios 179, 217 Mos 1:30, 231 Spec 1:74 Spec 2:83, 89 Spec 3:50, 114, 160, 160, 193, 199 Spec 4:212, 216 Praem 157 Aet 65 Flacc 14, 119, 160

ἀχθοφορέω (9) Gig 31 Plant 8 Migr 91, 144, 221 Decal 4 Spec 2:69 Virt 116 Prob 34

ἀχθοφόρος Virt 88 Flacc 92

ἀχλύς (9) Leg 1:46 Leg 3:171 Cher 61 Deus 130 Migr 197 Somn 1:165 Abr 79 Spec 3:4 Praem 37

ἀχλυώδης Legat 269

ἀχόρευτος Migr 72 Mos 2:162 Spec 3:125 Spec 4:145 Legat 168

ἀχορήγητος Mos 1:243

ἄχραντος Sacr 139

ἀχρεῖος Spec 1:287

ἀχρηματία Gig 29 Fug 25 Spec 4:3, 77

ἀχρήματος Plant 69 Virt 98 Praem 54 Prob 77

ἄχρι (235) Opif 47, 94, 101, 103, 105, 105, 105, 105, 105, 105 Leg 1:10, 11, 13, 29, 37 Leg 2:33, 38, 60, 63 Leg 3:47, 183 Cher 95 Sacr 3, 15, 83 Det 10, 87, 89, 107, 153 Post 14, 33, 61, 130, 173, 184 Gig 14, 44, 62 Deus 29, 35, 75, 102, 127, 143 Agr 17, 17, 23, 25, 101, 103, 138, 161, 165, 180, 181 Plant 123, 160 Ebr 143, 158, 200, 202 Sobr 23, 42 Conf 42, 140, 157 Migr 181, 218 Her 39, 149, 149, 222, 271, 294, 300, 310 Congr 34, 53 Fug 37, 55, 182 Mut 36, 102, 237 Somn 1:54, 95, 97, 119, 134, 145, 151, 175, 181, 192 Somn 2:67, 81, 102, 232, 257, 257 Abr 56, 150, 182, 214, 223, 241, 253, 253 Ios 10, 26, 41, 66, 96, 139, 156, 159, 169, 187, 256, 270 Mos 1:2, 15, 44, 99, 104, 128, 130, 165, 218, 228, 287, 291, 325, 327, 329 Mos 2:19, 79, 118, 118, 163, 174, 178, 223, 259, 271 Decal 114 Spec 1:45, 85, 102, 166, 178, 178, 232, 335 Spec 2:33, 33, 42, 116, 145, 155, 189, 196, 213 Spec 3:163, 182, 184 Spec 4:48, 82, 83, 99, 107, 140, 222 Virt 18, 26, 52, 72, 96, 109, 120, 133, 137, 140, 145 Praem 25, 82, 120 Prob 66, 89, 92, 110, 130, 131, 133 Contempl 33, 55, 86, 89 Aet 4, 60, 60, 86, 96, 97, 100 Flacc 27, 37, 48, 81, 85, 112, 152, 154, 155, 156, 173, 173 Legat 1, 10, 127, 141, 252, 255, 260, 267, 281, 309 Prov 2:17, 19, 27, 35 QG 2:64a QG isf 2 QG (Par) 2:5

ἄχρονος (15) Sacr 53, 64, 69, 69, 76, 76 Det 89 Agr 176 Ebr 48, 119 Migr 126, 139 Fug 167, 169 Mut 180

ἀχρώματος Sacr 32 Spec 3:25

ἄχυρον Sacr 109 Ios 113 Mos 1:38, 38

ἀχώριστος Gig 48

ἄψαυστος (13) Cher 50 Congr 124 Fug 50 Abr 90 Spec 3:14, 74 Spec 4:33, 119 Legat 6, 308, 328, 346 QE 2:3b

ἀψεύδεια Virt 178

ἀψευδέω (11) Det 37 Her 302 Ios 95, 171, 263 Mos 1:196, 221, 331 Mos 2:135 Spec 2:10 Prob 137

ἀψευδής (108) Opif 59, 81, 142 Leg 3:128, 206 Cher 86, 129 Sacr 26 Det 93, 124, 138 Post 13, 59, 143 Deus 14, 61 Agr 146 Plant 128 Ebr 45, 56, 76, 98, 139, 169, 198 Sobr 67 Conf 34, 125 Migr 106, 108, 115, 138, 183, 190 Her 4, 5, 42, 121, 186, 201 Congr 74, 103, 153, 163 Fug 17, 27, 57, 89, 101, 208 Mut 22, 65, 103, 131, 206, 213, 221 Somn 1:10, 156 Somn 2:140, 160, 220, 243, 253, 291 Abr 243, 268, 269 Ios 126, 185, 265 Mos 1:82, 303 Mos 2:100, 128, 237, 280 Spec 1:191, 273, 341 Spec 2:2, 49, 150 Spec 4:32, 85 Virt 120 Praem 17, 28, 81, 155, 163 Prob 19, 46, 54, 84, 111 Aet 28 Flacc 191 Legat 59, 77 Hypoth 11:3 Prov 2:32, 36, 66 QG 2:34a, 59, 3:29 QE 2:15b

ἀψίκορος (10) Sacr 32 Det 118 Deus 28 Ios 36 Spec 3:79 Virt 113 Aet 16 Legat 61 QG 1:85 QE 2:40

ἀψίς Opif 71 Cher 23 Det 84 Mut 179

ἀψοφητί Somn 1:148 Spec 3:101 Prov 2:35

ἄψυχος (82) Opif 9, 22, 62, 66, 73, 153 Leg 1:36 Leg 2:22, 97, 97 Leg 3:35, 73, 160 Cher 80, 111 Sacr 46, 69, 88 Det 130, 136 Post 61, 99 Gig 15, 20, 37, 41, 65 Deus 8, 8, 8, 8 Agr 56, 139, 152 Plant 177 Ebr 132, 164, 177, 183, 183 Migr 167, 185 Her 12, 137, 137, 138, 160, 209 Congr 48 Fug 19, 61, 122, 126, 148 Mut 173 Somn 1:248 Somn 2:259, 259 Abr 148, 267 Decal 7, 33, 76, 133, 133 Spec 1:29 Spec 2:97, 199, 245, 256 Spec 4:13, 35, 35, 227 Virt 85, 219 Praem 25 Prob 46, 46, 156 Contempl 4 Prov 2:15

ἄωρος Opif 104

B

Βαβυλών (9) Gig 66, 66 Somn 2:59 Abr 188 Mos 1:5, 34 Virt 223 Legat 216, 282

βαδίζω (39) Leg 3:139, 159 Cher 95 Det 39 Post 18, 31, 102, 136 Deus 8, 57, 159 Agr 88, 104 Conf 75 Migr 143, 146, 216 Congr 10, 122, 124 Somn 1:152 Somn 2:79 Abr 172, 269 Ios 190 Mos 1:55, 85, 167, 266, 274 Mos 2:165 Decal 74, 127 Spec 1:17 Spec 3:106, 141, 171 Prob 2 Flacc 178

βάδισμα Sacr 21, 26 QG 4:99

βαθμός Conf 38 Aet 58, 58

βάθος (20) Opif 49, 98 Det 107 Post 130 Her 144 Congr 147 Somn 1:21, 21, 26 Mos 2:96, 253 Decal 25 Virt 12 Prov 2:26 QG (Par) 2:2, 2:2, 2:5, 2:5, 2:5 QE isf 21

Βαθουήλ (6) Post 76 Fug 48, 50, 51 QG 4:97:1, 97:2

βάθρον Ebr 177

βαθύγειος (21) Opif 39 Plant 16, 28 Somn 1:17, 107 Abr 134 Ios 251 Mos 1:201, 224 Spec 1:335 Spec 2:39, 199 Spec 3:39 Spec 4:29 Virt 145 Praem 128, 141, 156 Contempl 62 Aet 64 Prov 2:66

βαθύνω Post 118 Spec 2:172 Spec 3:147 Virt 158

βαθύπλουτος Somn 1:98

βαθύς (116) Opif 38, 63, 63, 85, 85, 102, 113, 113, 168 Leg 3:13 Cher 62 Post 185 Gig 3 Deus 39, 46, 97, 130 Agr 6, 68, 76 Plant 144 Ebr 97, 112, 133, 157, 161, 209, 221 Conf 116 Migr 190 Her 92, 181, 250, 302 Congr 81 Fug 200 Mut 162 Somn 1:6, 165, 200 Somn 2:4, 18, 106, 118, 133, 140, 147, 162, 170, 229, 271, 282 Abr 43, 70, 70, 138, 241 Ios 12, 14, 105, 140, 145, 166, 168 Mos 1:5, 54, 124, 145, 170, 179, 192, 192, 194, 200, 225, 228, 319 Mos 2:77, 91, 180 Decal 2, 15, 44, 139 Spec 1:30, 75, 246, 276, 320, 321 Spec 2:102, 151, 169, 207 Virt 145, 179, 221 Praem 82, 152, 168 Prob 115, 144 Contempl 45 Aet 64, 88, 122 Flacc 27, 167, 167 Legat 33, 47, 90, 269, 326 Prov 2:20 QG 2:15a

βαθυχαίτης Contempl 51

Βαιθήλ Conf 74

βαίνω (38) Opif 147 Leg 1:89 Leg 2:98 Cher 19 Det 24 Post 80 Gig 39 Deus 4, 29, 172, 182 Agr 101 Conf 99, 113 Migr 64, 80, 128, 166, 183 Her 35, 70 Congr 28 Fug 30, 81, 130 Somn 1:54, 131 Somn 2:70 Abr 241 Mos 2:128 Spec 1:207 Spec 2:249 Spec 4:62 Virt 172 Praem 19 Flacc 164 QG (Par) 2:2 QE 2:26

βαιός Deus 103, 103 Aet 30

βακτηρία (16) Opif 84 Leg 2:89 Plant 153 Migr 83 Mos 1:78, 80, 82, 91, 92, 93, 99, 107, 177, 210 Spec 3:106 Spec 4:164

βάκτρον Cher 59 Somn 2:102 Spec 4:70 Aet 99

βακχεία Contempl 85

βακχεύω Ebr 123, 146 Her 69 Somn 2:205 Contempl 12

βάκχη Plant 148

Βάκχος Legat 96

Βαλαάμ (8) Cher 32, 33 Det 71 Deus 181 Conf 159 Migr 113, 115 Mut 202

Βαλάκ Conf 65, 65

Βαλάκης Mos 1:263, 276, 278, 280, 305

βαλανηφαγία Praem 8

βαλάντιον βαλλάντιον

βαλαντιοτόμος Spec 4:33, 87

βαλβίς Plant 76, 76 Mos 2:171, 291 Flacc 175

Βάλλα (9) Leg 2:94, 96 Leg 3:146, 146 Deus 119, 121 Congr 30, 30, 33

βαλλάντιον (βαλάντιον) Ios 144, 180, 207

βάλλω (27) Leg 1:86 Leg 3:40, 227 Sacr 25 Agr 11 Conf 103 Migr 125 Her 34 Congr 129, 129 Fug 210, 210 Somn 1:211, 221 Somn 2:95 Abr 199 Mos 2:157 Spec 2:110 Spec 3:166 Spec 4:28, 120, 220, 222 Prob 68, 151 Legat 104, 174

βάναυσος (8) Leg 1:57 Sacr 32 Fug 82 Somn 1:107 Mos 2:219 Spec 1:335 Spec 2:65 Prob 34

βαπτίζω (6) Leg 3:18 Det 176 Migr 204 Prob 97 Contempl 46 Prov 2:67

βάπτω Somn 2:53 Spec 1:262

Βαράδ Fug 213, 213

βάραθρον (6) Leg 1:73 Agr 101 Plant 61 Somn 2:103, 276 Spec 4:79

βαραθρώδης Aet 141

βαρβαρικός (11) Cher 91 Plant 67 Abr 181 Ios 56 Mos 2:27 Spec 3:17 Legat 8, 8, 83, 116, 215

βαρβαρισμός Leg 3:188

βάρβαρος (41) Opif 128 Ebr 193 Conf 6, 6, 190 Mut 35 Abr 136, 184, 267 Ios 30, 30, 134 Mos 2:12, 18, 19, 20 Decal 153 Spec 1:211, 313 Spec 2:44, 165 Spec 3:163 Spec 4:120 Praem 165 Prob 73, 74, 94, 98, 138 Contempl 21, 48 Legat 102, 141, 145, 147, 162, 292 Prov 2:15, 66, 68 QE isf 4

βαρέω Ebr 104, 131 Legat 269

βάρος (14) Opif 80 Det 154 Her 46, 146, 198, 198 Abr 171 Mos 2:249 Spec 2:102 Virt 70 Prob 28 Aet 29, 129 Legat 27

βαρυδαιμονία (13) Cher 2 Sacr 32 Her 109, 240 Fug 85 Mut 169 Spec 3:15, 29 Praem 133, 135 Legat 90 Prov 2:24, 32

βαρυδαίμων (9) Leg 3:211 Conf 90 Congr 159 Fug 28 Somn 2:130 Decal 62 Praem 135 Prob 115 Legat 274

βαρυήκοος Mos 1:120

βαρύθυμος Sacr 32

βαρύμηνις (7) Sacr 32 Mos 1:89, 172 Virt 116 Prob 90 Legat 260, 303

βαρύνω (21) Opif 158 Det 16, 99 Gig 31 Deus 14 Ebr 125, 214 Sobr 2 Migr 204 Somn 2:208 Mos 2:286 Spec 1:100 Spec 2:89, 134, 232 Spec 4:216 Virt 156 Praem 105, 154, 154, 155

βαρυπενθής Sacr 32

βαρύποτμος Somn 1:110

βαρύς (150) Opif 81, 96, 121, 125 Leg 1:14 Leg 2:2 Leg 3:45, 45, 90 Cher 78 Sacr 16, 54 Det 123 Post 148 Gig 16, 51 Deus 2, 15, 24, 84, 128 Agr 20, 49, 120, 149 Plant 7, 56, 147 Ebr 54, 116, 186 Conf 16, 22, 54, 92 Migr 14, 144, 145 Her 134, 135, 135, 146, 208, 210, 271, 284, 286, 287 Congr 60, 164 Fug 25, 190 Mut 238, 241, 243 Somn 1:17, 28, 110, 148, 223 Somn 2:46, 62, 85, 124, 131, 144 Abr 46, 210, 211 Ios 5, 71, 110, 113, 140, 170, 179, 187, 220, 233 Mos 1:14, 37, 39, 42, 90, 118, 119, 136, 137, 191, 217, 231, 233 Mos 2:185, 204, 256 Spec 1:10, 299 Spec 2:46, 83, 134, 138 Spec 3:114, 160, 195 Spec 4:82, 113, 173, 212 Virt 26, 116, 117, 128, 182 Praem 70, 77, 80, 133, 136, 143 Prob 29, 45, 139 Contempl 52, 88 Aet 65, 90, 105, 115, 136 Flacc 9, 57, 71, 119, 153, 160, 181, 189 Legat 14, 16, 62, 119, 144, 171, 184, 325, 340, 356 Prov 2:36 QG 4:51c QG (Par) 2:7

βαρύσπλαγχνος Sacr 32

βαρύτης Mos 2:256 Legat 178

βαρυτονέω Leg 3:51

βασανίζω (8) Sacr 80, 80 Deus 102 Fug 151 Decal 48 Spec 1:61 Virt 113 Flacc 84

βασανιστής Det 176 Spec 4:82 Prob 108 Flacc 96

βάσανος (30) Opif 110 Det 176 Fug 151, 155 Mut 208, 209 Abr 96, 104, 104, 104, 104, 251 Ios 86 Mos 2:167 Decal 16 Spec 1:61, 68 Spec 2:94 Spec 3:159, 161 Spec 4:106, 156, 156 Virt 56, 60 Prob 25 Flacc 140 Legat 368 Prov 2:11 QG isf 5

βασιλεία (56) Opif 148 Sacr 49 Gig 66 Deus 6, 174 Plant 56, 67 Ebr 216 Migr 196, 197, 197 Her 301 Congr 118 Fug 10 Mut 15, 135 Somn 2:243, 244, 285 Abr 24, 242, 261, 261 Ios 119 Mos 1:25, 46, 60, 148, 149, 253, 254, 290, 334, 334 Mos 2:30, 66, 241 Spec 1:57, 207, 334 Spec 3:13, 100 Spec 4:164 Virt 54 Praem 53 Prob 117, 125 Flacc 25, 29, 38 Legat 179, 278, 278, 326 Prov 2:54 QE 2:105

βασίλειον (21) Post 5 Sobr 66, 66 Conf 113 Congr 116 Abr 56 Ios 123, 256 Mos 1:15, 91, 118, 138, 312 Mos 2:42, 194, 194 Spec 4:94 Praem 123, 123 Flacc 92 Legat 299

βασίλειος (6) Deus 136 Fug 74, 111 Mut 128 Ios 97 Mos 2:187

βασιλεύς (344) Opif 17, 56, 71, 84, 85, 88, 139, 144, 148 Leg 1:59 Leg 3:13, 24, 38, 79, 79, 79, 79, 80, 81, 115, 115, 197, 212, 212, 212, 225, 232 Cher 29, 63, 99, 99, 99 Sacr 9, 48 Det 13, 14, 23, 26, 94, 94 Post 8, 54, 101, 101, 128 Gig 45, 64 Deus 148, 159, 160, 174 Agr 41, 41, 50, 51, 51, 57, 59, 60, 61, 66, 78, 85 Plant 14, 33, 51, 51, 55, 57, 68, 88, 92, 169 Ebr 24, 105, 111, 113, 113, 143, 208, 220 Sobr 57, 66 Conf 29, 29, 72, 88, 170, 170, 173, 175 Migr 8, 54, 146, 161, 170, 197, 204 Her 20, 288 Congr 50, 92, 116, 125 Fug 16, 66, 118, 124, 145 Mut 17, 20, 28, 56, 89, 112, 116, 151, 152, 152, 173, 207 Somn 1:32, 140, 191 Somn 2:5, 42, 43, 44, 83, 99, 100, 116, 117, 154, 211, 243, 244, 244, 277, 290 Abr 74, 74, 93, 96, 103, 144, 180, 183, 226, 226, 227, 231, 232, 234, 236, 240, 241, 261 Ios 2, 2, 7, 27, 76, 88, 91, 92, 93, 96, 97, 100, 105, 105, 107, 107, 116, 119, 123, 131, 133, 133, 148, 148, 148, 148, 149, 149, 151, 151, 157, 163, 166, 166, 222, 242, 248, 248, 250, 251, 257, 258 Mos 1:8, 10, 13, 15, 32, 32, 33, 34, 45, 49, 61, 62, 73, 87, 91, 105, 120, 122, 123, 134, 138, 158, 166, 167, 215, 250, 252, 256, 258, 263, 267, 275, 277, 282, 283, 287, 292, 296, 321 Mos 2:2, 3, 4, 4, 4, 5, 5, 6, 16, 28, 28, 30, 31, 32, 100, 116, 131, 187, 248, 292 Decal 40, 41, 41, 61, 155, 178 Spec 1:18, 18, 31, 142, 308 Spec 3:18, 43, 100, 100, 111, 184 Spec 4:92, 123, 164, 168, 176, 186, 191, 212, 213, 218 Virt 53, 85, 85, 154, 216, 218 Praem 54, 54, 55 Prob 20, 31, 42, 42, 42, 43, 93, 96, 96, 132, 136 Flacc 25, 29, 33, 34, 35, 38, 40, 103, 123, 170 Legat 3, 138, 142, 179, 207, 261, 278, 292, 300, 300, 300

Hypoth 11:18 Prov 2:2, 3, 3, 17, 17, 19, 21, 24, 50 QG 1:3, 20, 4:76a, 76b, 206b QE 2:45a, 105

βασιλεύω (30) Leg 1:41 Plant 47, 51, 53 Conf 54, 91 Migr 160, 170 Her 7 Fug 140 Mut 28, 125 Somn 2:7, 7, 93, 93, 94, 95, 100, 100, 100, 215, 289 Abr 237 Ios 149 Mos 1:149, 217 Mos 2:2 Flacc 39 Legat 294

βασιλικός (61) Cher 63 Post 101, 101, 102, 102, 102 Gig 64 Deus 144, 145, 159, 159, 160, 162, 180 Plant 56, 68 Ebr 91, 92 Conf 149 Migr 146 Fug 95, 98, 100, 103 Mut 15, 28, 152, 221 Somn 1:126, 163 Somn 2:44, 211 Abr 121, 121, 125 Ios 91, 93, 120, 148 Mos 1:8, 20, 61, 153, 256, 275 Mos 2:2, 99, 99 Spec 4:147, 168 Virt 216 Prob 123, 126, 154 Flacc 4 Legat 6, 54 QG 3:29, 4:76b QG (Par) 2:5 QE 2:50b

βασιλίς (20) Leg 1:65 Sacr 44 Post 128 Agr 25 Ebr 201 Congr 2, 18, 37, 50, 50 Mut 80 Somn 2:243 Abr 15, 150, 270 Mos 2:211 Spec 1:269 Spec 4:147 Virt 188 Prov 2:18

βασίλισσα Congr 45

βάσιμος Deus 165 Prob 67

βάσις (41) Opif 118 Leg 3:106 Cher 100 Sacr 42 Det 85 Post 3, 25 Gig 22 Deus 57, 60 Agr 75 Plant 5, 7 Ebr 156 Migr 102 Congr 46 Mut 81 Somn 1:134, 144, 146, 235 Somn 2:189, 223 Mos 2:77, 78, 78, 82, 82, 90, 97, 113 Decal 44 Spec 1:117, 231, 340 Spec 3:184 Spec 4:167, 198 Flacc 189 Legat 135 QG 2:39

βασκαίνω Agr 112 Flacc 143

βασκανία (10) Cher 33 Mut 95, 112 Somn 1:107 Abr 184 Mos 1:4, 246 Spec 2:141 Virt 170 QG 4:191b

βάσκανος (11) Sacr 32 Agr 64 Congr 71 Abr 21, 199 Ios 144 Spec 1:241 Praem 83 Flacc 29 QG 4:191c, 227

Βάσσος (6) Flacc 92, 109, 111, 112, 114, 115

βαστάζω (6) Det 9 Migr 144 Mut 224 Somn 1:174 Somn 2:171, 210

βάτος (9) Leg 3:253 Fug 161 Somn 1:194, 194 Somn 2:161 Mos 1:65, 67, 68 QG 3:49a

βάτραχος (6) Sacr 69, 69 Migr 83 Somn 2:259 Mos 1:103, 144

βαφή Congr 117 Somn 2:53

βαφικός Plant 159

βδέλυγμα Sacr 51, 51 Migr 64 Her 162 Fug 18

βδελυκτός Spec 1:323

βδελυρία Somn 2:211 Spec 3:45 QG (Par) 2:6

βδελυρός Det 95

βδελύσσομαι (6) Sacr 51, 51 Migr 63 Her 163 Fug 18 Virt 106

βέβαιος (156) Opif 151 Leg 1:89 Leg 3:53, 92, 101, 199, 206, 208 Cher 26, 65, 72, 83, 101, 103, 109, 109 Sacr 86, 90, 93, 124, 126 Post 13, 28, 100, 119, 122 Gig 28, 52, 67 Deus 34, 49, 54 Agr 121, 160 Plant 8, 70, 82, 84, 88 Ebr 48, 50, 170, 183, 205 Conf 31, 65, 76, 87, 87, 94, 104, 106 Migr 41, 105, 148 Her 23, 95, 101, 224, 275, 298, 314 Congr 121, 140, 141 Fug 151 Mut 55, 84, 164, 182, 270 Somn 1:124, 159, 241, 248 Somn 2:101, 170, 212, 220, 223, 278, 298 Abr 111, 182, 220, 225, 268, 275 Ios 100, 107, 122, 126, 147 Mos 1:30, 95, 220, 266, 283, 298, 331 Mos 2:14, 17, 99, 108, 124, 161 Decal 43, 67 Spec 1:26, 30, 70, 77, 110, 124, 191, 242, 290, 311 Spec 2:2, 13, 118, 232 Spec 3:70, 130 Spec 4:16, 50, 61, 70, 107, 108, 158, 160, 161, 220 Virt 41, 216, 216, 226 Praem 30, 97, 152, 169 Prob 37, 95 Contempl 31 Legat 61 QG 1:17b, 2:54a, 54a, 3:21, 4:148, 180 QE 2:16, 17, 45a QE isf 16

βεβαιότης (20) Leg 3:164 Cher 13 Sacr 16, 93 Gig 48 Deus 4, 17, 22 Plant 31 Ebr 126, 139 Migr 44 Fug 150, 154 Mut 87 Somn 1:158 Somn 2:227 Spec 1:283 Aet 59, 116

βεβαιόω (63) Opif 99 Leg 3:46, 93, 203, 204 Cher 9 Sacr 34, 37, 64, 85, 127 Det 12 Plant 112, 149 Ebr 75, 77 Sobr 57 Conf 40, 105, 112, 131, 153, 180, 197 Migr 70, 128 Her 25, 98, 260, 307 Congr 107, 113 Fug 74 Somn 1:12, 12, 181 Abr 71, 110, 144, 262, 263, 263 Ios 267 Mos 2:173, 221 Spec 1:138, 284, 318 Spec 2:9, 12, 25, 28, 117, 121 Spec 3:114, 182 Spec 4:77 Virt 209 Prob 86, 88, 160 Flacc 50 QE isf 19

βεβαίωσις (21) Leg 2:55 Cher 108 Post 181, 184 Her 96, 306 Congr 151 Mut 155 Somn 2:29 Abr 273 Ios 92, 164 Mos 2:199 Decal 123 Spec 2:13, 24 Spec 3:82 Praem 118 Prob 138 Legat 153, 162

βεβαιωτής Leg 3:207 Spec 4:157 Flacc 20

βέβηλος (46) Leg 1:62, 62 Cher 94 Sacr 32, 101, 138, 138 Post 96, 110 Plant 53, 61 Ebr 127, 143 Migr 69 Congr 25, 25, 169 Fug 19, 114, 114, 213 Mut 104, 136, 200 Somn 1:253 Somn 2:292 Abr 20 Mos 2:158, 199 Decal 94, 173 Spec 1:100, 102, 104, 123, 150, 223 Spec 2:6, 249, 249 Spec 3:130, 183 Spec 4:40, 84 Hypoth 7:2, 7:10

βεβηλόω Somn 1:89 Spec 4:39

βεβήλωσις Congr 25

Βεελφεγώρ Conf 55 Mut 107, 107

βέλος (19) Sacr 82, 82 Det 99 Deus 60 Plant 152 Sobr 26 Conf 48 Mut 247 Somn 1:236 Somn 2:120 Mos 1:131 Spec 3:92 Prob 78 Flacc 90 Legat 95, 104 QG 2:64b, 64b, 64b

βελτιόω (43) Opif 101 Leg 3:84 Cher 4 Sacr 42 Det 56, 88 Post 78 Gig 24, 63 Deus 132 Agr 6, 169 Migr 71, 149 Congr 110 Fug 30, 166 Mut 23, 75, 84 Somn 1:104, 162, 170, 178, 240 Abr 23 Ios 83, 88 Mos 1:22, 64, 328 Mos 2:66, 69, 215 Decal 17 Spec 2:61 Spec 3:209 Prob 57, 98 Contempl 1 Legat 7, 52 QE isf 7

βελτίωσις (40) Opif 103, 128 Cher 86 Sacr 10, 62, 113, 114 Post 174 Agr 166 Her 316 Congr 37 Mut 19, 65, 88, 120 Somn 1:60 Somn 2:107, 301 Abr 17, 26, 268 Ios 74 Mos 2:59 Decal 113 Spec 1:197, 260, 300 Virt 115, 193 Praem 65, 119, 163, 167 Prob 64, 133 Aet 43 Legat 44, 63 QG 3:48, 4:172

Βενιαμίν Fug 73 Mut 92, 92 Somn 2:36

Βεσελεήλ (10) Leg 3:95, 96, 102, 102, 102, 102 Gig 23 Plant 26, 27 Somn 1:206

βῆμα Ios 35

βία (61) Opif 58, 63, 80, 113 Leg 1:73 Post 116 Deus 177 Agr 70, 76, 89 Conf 117, 117, 157 Her 241 Congr 73 Mut 186 Somn 2:81, 92, 294 Abr 44, 73, 160 Ios 41, 52, 209 Mos 1:25, 41, 49, 115, 118, 211, 270 Mos 2:139 Spec 1:92, 99, 204, 301 Spec 2:191 Spec 3:3, 64, 69, 76, 153, 159 Spec 4:2, 111 Virt 89, 146 Praem 52, 73, 153 Prob 63 Contempl 71 Aet 30, 33, 119, 129, 147 Flacc 188 Prov 2:2, 39

βιάζω (90) Opif 142 Leg 2:34 Leg 3:147 Cher 19, 22, 94, 115 Sacr 121 Det 32 Gig 35 Deus 100, 100, 101, 166 Agr 110, 111 Plant 147, 152 Ebr 116, 123, 143, 167, 185, 200 Sobr 6 Conf 91, 133 Migr 26 Her 241, 310 Fug 32

Mut 173, 262 Somn 1:7 Somn 2:124, 133, 145, 299 Abr 59, 184 Ios 42, 51, 52, 52, 83, 118 Mos 1:108, 215, 292, 308, 314 Mos 2:51 Decal 85 Spec 1:127, 159 Spec 2:2, 4, 50, 90 Spec 3:64, 70, 72, 77, 77, 160, 173 Spec 4:70, 136, 205 Praem 130 Prob 27, 34, 61, 97, 108 Aet 28, 56, 74, 135, 136, 139 Flacc 143 Legat 31, 155 Hypoth 7:1, 11:9, 11:16 QG 4:51c QG (Par) 2:2, 2:4

βίαιος (48) Opif 141 Leg 3:17, 80 Cher 13, 37, 92 Det 100 Post 163 Gig 13, 31, 51 Deus 103 Agr 46 Conf 17 Migr 217 Fug 49 Mut 239 Somn 1:222 Somn 2:166 Abr 65, 135 Ios 25, 81, 84, 223, 239 Mos 1:44, 93, 120, 123, 131, 176 Decal 147, 170 Spec 3:79, 136, 168 Praem 69 Contempl 9, 75, 86 Aet 11, 20, 128, 139 Flacc 62, 162 Prov 2:35

Βίας Prob 153

βιαστικός Abr 195 Spec 1:9 Spec 3:35 Virt 122

βιβλιοθήκη Legat 151

βιβλίον (6) Leg 1:19 Sacr 51 Plant 1 Somn 2:175 Spec 4:163, 163

βίβλος (50) Opif 129 Leg 1:19, 21 Cher 124 Det 139, 139, 161 Post 1, 65, 158 Plant 26 Ebr 1, 208 Sobr 17 Conf 3, 128, 149 Migr 14 Her 20, 258 Somn 2:127 Abr 1, 2, 9, 11, 156, 177, 258 Mos 1:4 Mos 2:11, 36, 45, 59, 95, 188 Decal 1, 154 Spec 2:150 Spec 4:164, 175 Virt 17, 34, 95, 201 Prob 82 Aet 19 QG 1:1, 1, 76b, 2:15b

βιβρώσκω (6) Leg 3:230 Plant 95, 113, 113, 113, 114

Βιθυνία Legat 281

βίος (611) Opif 54, 78, 79, 103, 105, 119, 128, 152, 153, 153, 156, 156, 164, 167, 167, 170 Leg 1:57, 107, 108, 108 Leg 2:21, 57, 70, 89, 93, 98, 98, 107 Leg 3:80, 224, 237, 247, 251, 253 Cher 6, 32, 33, 37, 91, 95, 120 Sacr 11, 13, 23, 26, 38, 63, 109, 123, 125 Det 23, 33, 34, 48, 49, 60, 68, 74, 95, 95, 103, 119, 157 Post 2, 22, 34, 43, 45, 56, 70, 73, 86, 113, 121, 122, 156, 165, 185 Gig 14, 51, 53, 55, 56, 57, 64 Deus 7, 25, 32, 61, 75, 102, 114, 129, 182 Agr 25, 35, 43, 60, 62, 98, 135, 143, 144, 157, 164, 180 Plant 49, 147 Ebr 12, 36, 58, 73, 75, 86, 87, 95, 99, 100, 101, 131, 139, 149, 151, 152, 155, 195, 202, 212, 215, 219 Sobr 11, 38, 69 Conf 42, 43, 48, 69, 71, 79, 105 Migr 11, 19, 47, 54, 56, 59, 70, 88, 100, 105, 129, 133, 145, 153, 158, 165, 171, 179 Her 41, 43, 45, 48, 53, 82, 111, 113, 200, 238, 285, 290, 307, 315 Congr 11, 52, 53, 53, 57, 61, 67, 69, 70, 90, 165 Fug 3, 22, 25, 33, 35, 36, 36, 36, 37, 37, 41, 44, 45, 45, 47, 49, 55, 58, 59, 61, 62, 113, 122, 123, 128, 129, 145, 150, 150, 153, 154, 154, 158, 159, 176, 191, 204 Mut 36, 38, 44, 50, 51, 55, 80, 103, 103, 169, 185, 213, 214, 215, 267 Somn 1:10, 46, 82, 104, 109, 113, 121, 121, 124, 124, 125, 128, 139, 150, 150, 150, 174, 177, 179, 202, 205, 221, 234, 243 Somn 2:11, 25, 44, 47, 47, 63, 64, 66, 70, 74, 81, 97, 105, 107, 133, 134, 142, 145, 147, 148, 150, 161, 168, 200, 202, 235, 250, 265, 302, 302 Abr 5, 6, 17, 19, 22, 27, 30, 37, 40, 47, 54, 61, 84, 87, 155, 163, 207, 216, 222, 230, 246, 246, 256, 256, 260, 268, 271, 276 Ios 1, 20, 55, 87, 126, 141, 143, 230, 269 Mos 1:1, 3, 4, 29, 29, 29, 29, 48, 89, 111, 158, 160, 183, 195, 209, 213, 214, 238, 279 Mos 2:36, 66, 138, 150, 150, 151, 181, 185, 186, 211, 215, 219, 235, 281, 288, 289, 292 Decal 1, 49, 60, 66, 77, 99, 99, 101, 108, 117, 122, 138, 150, 174 Spec 1:31, 57, 60, 62, 69, 96, 100, 108, 110, 120, 134, 152, 154, 161, 186, 202, 203, 206, 224, 224, 259, 280, 320, 321, 336, 342, 345 Spec 2:10, 18, 19, 19, 42, 45, 46, 48, 52, 62, 64, 65, 68, 70, 71, 91, 92, 101, 101, 123, 130, 142, 157, 160, 170, 173, 195, 199, 214, 240, 262, 262 Spec 3:2, 6, 50, 50, 54, 57, 59, 117, 119, 122, 123, 135, 161, 166, 169, 173, 192 Spec 4:11, 13, 41, 66, 69, 69, 71, 82, 91, 95, 102, 108, 109, 124, 134, 138, 166, 167, 169, 182, 186, 194, 201, 225, 228 Virt 5, 17, 19, 29, 39, 47, 51, 52, 67, 72, 76, 78, 149, 149, 180, 183, 184, 190, 194, 205, 210, 211, 222, 226 Praem 2, 6, 10, 11, 24, 27, 35, 36, 51, 51, 53, 79, 81, 82, 88, 98, 107, 112, 116, 119, 120, 121, 135, 142 Prob 14, 49, 50, 51, 63, 64, 74, 76, 84, 91, 92, 110, 114, 115, 120, 140, 143, 154 Contempl 1, 13, 16, 17, 25, 47, 58, 64 Aet 56, 74, 84, 142 Flacc 41, 53, 91, 159, 176, 183, 184, 187 Legat 5, 13, 15, 20, 43, 46, 63, 83, 89, 92, 141, 147, 158, 224, 236, 325, 343 Hypoth 11:4, 11:10, 11:13, 11:18 Prov 2:1, 12, 24, 25, 29, 30 QG 1:64a, 70:1, 76a, 100:1b, 2:11, 12d, 3:22, 4:69, 169, 173, 189, 204 QG isf 6, 15 QE 2:20, 55b QE isf 3, 9, 15, 26, 33

βιοτή Prob 145

βιόω (40) Opif 172 Det 62, 75, 78, 134, 154 Post 69 Agr 144, 159 Sobr 8 Conf 149 Her 57, 277, 290 Somn 1:47 Somn 2:31 Abr 4, 191, 270 Ios 31, 71, 268 Mos 2:48, 223 Decal 49, 94, 168 Spec 2:33, 164 Spec 3:142, 142, 154, 202 Virt 4, 15, 47, 127 Contempl 74, 90 Legat 85

βιωτικός Mos 2:158 Prob 49, 51, 52

βιωφελής (19) Ebr 213 Somn 1:52 Somn 2:42, 256 Abr 101 Ios 79 Decal 50, 84 Spec 1:165, 179, 210, 335 Spec 2:7 Spec 3:31 Spec 4:99, 146 Contempl 60 Hypoth 11:7 QG 4:102c

βλαβερός (56) Opif 10 Leg 2:105 Leg 3:27, 76, 80, 104, 110, 131 Cher 93 Sacr 71 Det 72, 105, 134, 175 Agr 11, 41, 47, 133 Plant 100, 116, 161 Ebr 39, 185, 187 Conf 12 Her 109 Congr 88, 179 Fug 14, 43 Mut 170, 197, 243 Somn 1:27 Somn 2:64, 150 Ios 143 Mos 1:108, 222 Decal 13, 156 Spec 1:120, 173, 206, 306, 321, 340 Spec 2:195 Spec 4:119, 194 Virt 227 Prob 69 Contempl 20 Legat 49, 81, 89

βλάβη (40) Leg 3:184 Cher 14 Det 2, 99 Deus 98 Plant 92, 103, 110 Ebr 18, 166, 184, 185 Conf 162, 189 Migr 172 Her 252 Congr 167 Mut 202, 246 Somn 1:102 Somn 2:52, 163 Abr 127 Mos 1:246 Spec 2:87, 206, 207 Spec 4:2, 34, 194 Praem 88, 91, 100, 140 Prob 55, 103 Legat 339 Prov 2:54 QG 4:172 QE 2:25d

βλάβος Conf 50 Spec 1:100 Spec 4:23, 29

βλαπτικός Opif 64

βλάπτω (74) Opif 80 Leg 1:51 Leg 3:16, 62, 123 Det 52, 71, 76, 104, 109, 109, 143 Post 67, 144, 184 Gig 27, 43, 43 Deus 113 Agr 39, 125 Plant 89, 144, 144 Ebr 155, 168, 185, 206 Conf 48, 159 Migr 210 Mut 243 Somn 2:54, 239, 240 Ios 139, 216 Mos 1:145, 278 Decal 66, 68 Spec 1:252 Spec 2:74, 117, 197 Spec 3:104, 143 Spec 4:2, 26, 41, 65, 186, 189, 198, 198, 211 Virt 13, 25, 93, 156, 211 Aet 37, 80 Legat 176, 297, 344 Hypoth 7:16 Prov 2:44 QG 2:15a, 4:191b, 193 QE 2:11a, 11a, 18

βλαστάνω (43) Opif 47, 132, 153 Leg 1:23, 89 Leg 2:75 Leg 3:170, 248 Sacr 25, 40 Post 125, 125, 133, 163, 164, 182 Agr 7 Plant 74 Ebr 8 Congr 95 Mut 260 Somn 2:22, 199, 272 Mos 1:121 Mos 2:119, 186 Spec 1:93, 138 Spec 2:152 Spec 4:209, 209 Virt 199 Praem 68, 128, 172 Prob 70 Contempl 62 Aet 30, 61, 69, 98, 149

βλάστη (8) Leg 2:10 Sacr 79 Gig 4 Deus 67 Agr 10 Somn 1:106 Somn 2:64 Prob 69

βλάστημα (15) Leg 1:23, 24 Det 132 Post 151 Deus 181 Plant 42, 107 Migr 140 Congr 57 Somn 2:77, 171, 173, 242 Spec 3:39 Prov 2:66

βλαστόν Det 111

βλαστός (8) Opif 41 Plant 4 Her 218, 220 Somn 2:159, 199 Mos 2:179 Spec 4:25

βλασφημέω (10) Conf 154 Migr 115 Fug 84, 84 Somn 2:131 Mos 2:206 Decal 63 Spec 1:53 Spec 4:197 Legat 169

βλασφημία (11) Migr 117 Ios 74 Mos 2:205 Decal 86, 93 Flacc 33, 35, 35, 142 Legat 368 QE 2:6b

βλάσφημος Ios 247 Legat 141

βλέμμα (14) Conf 11 Abr 153, 175 Ios 48, 166 Mos 1:331 Spec 3:8 Virt 40 Prob 39 Contempl 31, 77 Legat 180, 349 QG 4:99

βλέπω (85) Opif 53 Leg 2:46, 67, 93 Leg 3:81, 109, 110, 172 Post 21, 36 Gig 31 Agr 54 Plant 38, 58 Ebr 157, 160 Sobr 4, 40 Conf 63, 123 Migr 38, 52, 191, 222, 224 Her 48, 55, 76, 78 Congr 81 Fug 123 Mut 40, 143, 157 Somn 1:114 Abr 25, 65, 70, 79, 164 Ios 58, 66, 126, 126, 147, 258, 265 Mos 1:55, 153, 188, 190 Mos 2:162, 162, 201, 252 Decal 74, 101 Spec 1:14, 18, 18, 279 Spec 2:23, 77 Spec 4:62, 189, 202 Virt 7, 85, 151, 172, 193 Praem 45, 54, 69 Prob 101 Contempl 11, 13 Legat 5, 109 Prov 2:12 QG isf 2, 15 QE isf 4, 6, 31

βλῆμα Mos 2:202 Praem 140 Prob 151 QE 2:24b

βοάω (17) Opif 79 Det 48, 69, 79, 91 Her 14, 15, 19 Congr 163 Fug 84, 196 Mos 1:69 Spec 2:11 Spec 3:77, 77 Legat 323 QG 1:70:1

βοή Leg 3:214 Flacc 39 Legat 227

βοηδρομέω Ios 211 Legat 101, 226

βοήθεια (19) Sacr 70 Ebr 185 Migr 57 Her 58, 60 Somn 2:128 Ios 33 Mos 1:49, 72, 184 Mos 2:252 Spec 1:309 Spec 2:217 Spec 3:172 Spec 4:8 Contempl 44 Flacc 11 Legat 39, 274

βοηθέω (24) Leg 2:5, 5, 7, 8, 8 Leg 3:31 Migr 225 Somn 1:86, 111 Abr 95 Ios 20 Mos 1:24, 40 Spec 1:216 Spec 3:77, 78, 173, 175 Spec 4:9, 42, 199 Legat 113 QG 1:17a QE 2:16

βοήθημα Sacr 70 Ebr 160 Somn 1:112 Aet 89

βοηθός (37) Leg 2:1, 5, 5, 5, 5, 6, 7, 7, 7, 8, 8, 9, 9, 9, 9, 10, 14, 24 Leg 3:48 Ebr 111 Conf 39 Her 58, 59 Somn 2:265 Ios 51 Mos 1:56, 58, 174, 306 Spec 3:74, 140 Spec 4:171, 178, 179 Prob 104 Legat 112 QE 2:3a

Βοηθός Aet 76, 78

βόθρος Leg 3:223 Agr 68 Ios 14 Flacc 188, 190

Βοιωτία Legat 281

βολή Praem 95 Legat 229 Prov 2:53

βόλος Mos 1:93 Mos 2:250

βομβυσμός QG 2:12d

βόρβορος Spec 1:148

βορβορώδης Agr 144

βορέας Somn 1:3, 175 Prov 2:23

βόρειος (9) Cher 88 Gig 10 Her 147 Mos 1:179 Mos 2:102, 104, 104 Spec 3:188, 188

βόσκημα (7) Mos 1:133, 330, 331 Spec 4:26 Legat 124 Hypoth 11:4 QE 2:12

βόσκω Det 5, 25, 25 Fug 127 Spec 4:22

βοτάνη Opif 40 Sacr 70 Somn 1:125

βοτρυηφορέω (βοτρυοφορέω) Ios 91

βοτρυηφόρος Somn 2:171

βοτρυοφορέω βοτρυηφορέω

βότρυς (8) Ebr 222 Mut 224 Somn 2:159, 171, 191, 199 Ios 91 Mos 1:231

βούβαλος Spec 4:105

Βουζύγιος Hypoth 7:8

βουθυτέω Det 20 Agr 127 Plant 107 Fug 186

βουκόλιον (13) Sacr 89, 104, 104 Somn 2:152 Abr 108 Ios 257 Mos 1:133 Spec 1:136, 141, 163 Virt 126 Praem 107 Aet 79

βουκόλος (10) Opif 85 Sacr 104, 104, 105 Agr 48 Somn 2:152 Spec 4:22 Virt 144 Prob 30 Legat 76

βούλευμα (30) Deus 135 Migr 24 Mut 195 Ios 266 Mos 1:260, 311 Mos 2:140, 212, 289 Spec 1:205, 333, 344 Spec 3:73 Spec 4:47 Virt 3, 70, 80, 183, 184 Praem 81 Prob 155, 155 Flacc 21 Legat 25, 56, 280 QG 4:174 QG isf 8, 8 QE isf 11

βούλευσις Fug 53, 77

βουλευτήριον (14) Det 40 Mut 198 Somn 1:122 Somn 2:188 Abr 20 Decal 98 Spec 1:55 Spec 2:44 Spec 3:74, 169 Spec 4:9 Contempl 27 Flacc 102 QE isf 20

βουλευτής Conf 86 Ios 63 Spec 1:55, 121 Legat 75

βουλευτικός Legat 74

βουλεύω (51) Cher 73 Sacr 62 Det 40, 69, 96, 97, 97 Post 53, 59, 156 Deus 26 Agr 176 Ebr 165, 165, 166, 169, 204 Conf 125, 158, 160, 161 Migr 72 Fug 14, 22, 125 Mut 197, 238, 238, 244 Ios 12, 73, 176 Mos 1:15, 89, 305, 305 Decal 60 Spec 3:21, 70, 86 Prob 6 Flacc 2, 20, 21, 110, 140, 178 Legat 51, 204, 244, 350

βουλή (35) Opif 75 Leg 3:205 Det 134 Post 11, 36, 80, 85, 86, 175 Plant 168 Ebr 165, 165, 203 Conf 153, 198 Migr 201 Her 244 Congr 4 Mut 237 Somn 2:187 Abr 101 Mos 1:242, 294 Spec 2:29 Spec 4:134 Virt 45, 183 Prob 68, 138 Flacc 40 Legat 51, 55, 67, 160 QE isf 20

βούλημα (29) Opif 3 Leg 2:62 Leg 3:239 Det 72 Post 73 Her 272 Fug 209, 211 Somn 2:117 Abr 204 Mos 1:59, 95, 287 Mos 2:31 Spec 1:323 Spec 2:132 Spec 3:85, 121, 136, 176 Virt 185 Legat 33, 263, 311, 331 Prov 2:35 QG 3:3 QE 2:20 QE isf 19

βούλησις (7) Plant 106 Her 246 Ios 192 Decal 135 Aet 13 Legat 317, 322

βούλομαι (275) Opif 16, 44, 77, 87, 138, 149 Leg 1:4, 35, 63, 90 Leg 2:17, 25, 32, 32, 36, 37 Leg 3:39, 45, 55, 56, 69, 134, 153, 210, 213, 223, 245 Cher 14, 60, 95 Sacr 23 Det 1, 29, 71, 127, 154, 168 Post 2, 5, 71, 83, 144, 145 Gig 60 Deus 21, 70, 75, 80, 121, 144, 153, 164 Agr 5, 15, 73 Plant 8, 14, 87, 94 Ebr 41, 50, 82, 85, 110, 195 Conf 4, 57, 64, 83, 91, 115, 166, 196 Migr 2, 34, 46, 60, 66, 75, 99, 162 Her 44, 44, 86, 88, 92, 112, 158, 225, 243, 290 Congr 38, 90, 127 Fug 30, 74, 148, 155, 165, 191 Mut 26, 53, 79, 129, 144, 181, 210, 227, 242, 258, 270 Somn 1:15, 90, 163, 188, 202, 202, 210 Somn 2:24, 48, 86, 92, 117, 154, 176, 229, 246, 258 Abr 5, 9, 102, 129, 142, 207, 216, 251, 268 Ios 55, 90, 90, 94, 99, 146, 165, 181, 217, 241 Mos 1:16, 17, 49, 62, 96, 110, 110, 111, 144, 164, 168, 198, 209, 213, 220, 221, 248 Mos 2:80, 152, 167, 202 Decal 9, 37, 72, 81, 86 Spec 1:36, 67, 68, 96, 111, 116, 138, 167, 195, 203, 210, 241, 253, 257, 263, 286 Spec 2:5, 48, 118,

123, 157, 160, 214 Spec 3:71, 77, 129, 130, 134, 148, 173, 177, 184 Spec 4:69, 81, 104, 105, 117, 160, 186, 187 Virt 18, 83, 119, 134, 188 Praem 103, 121 Prob 59, 94, 95, 96, 101, 138 Contempl 40 Aet 94, 130 Flacc 28, 51, 82, 86, 111, 114, 114, 129, 137, 189 Legat 26, 41, 73, 132, 134, 182, 198, 200, 218, 247, 303, 303, 308, 316, 351, 363 Hypoth 6:2, 6:4, 6:6, 7:19, 11:12 Prov 1, 2:9, 28, 30 QG 4:20, 51a, 200c QG isf 13 QE 2:3a, 16, 17, 20, 46, 47 QE isf 5

βουνός Post 57, 59

βούπαις Contempl 50

Βοῦρα Aet 140

βοῦς (47) Opif 85 Sacr 55 Deus 117 Plant 108, 164 Ebr 174 Migr 152 Her 16, 20 Congr 95, 154 Mut 56, 159 Somn 1:108 Somn 2:144, 216, 216, 217, 217 Abr 31 Ios 16, 101, 108, 108 Decal 77 Spec 1:135, 163, 165, 291 Spec 2:35, 70 Spec 3:44, 46 Spec 4:11, 12, 12, 13 Virt 95, 145, 145, 146, 146, 146, 147 Prob 30 Aet 23 Legat 76

βραβεῖον (16) Leg 3:74 Sacr 17 Deus 137 Agr 112, 114 Migr 27 Congr 159 Mut 81 Somn 1:130, 152 Praem 6, 11, 27, 47, 47 QG 4:228

βραβευτής (15) Opif 11 Det 23 Agr 112 Ebr 111 Migr 67 Her 271 Somn 1:152 Somn 2:138 Ios 270 Spec 1:180 Spec 2:139 Spec 4:64, 66 Contempl 43 QE 2:10a

βραβεύω (13) Leg 1:87 Leg 3:35 Ebr 77 Her 95 Ios 72 Mos 1:163 Spec 3:133 Spec 4:55, 173 Flacc 106 Legat 2 Prov 2:2, 36

βραδύγλωσσος Her 4, 16 Mos 1:83

βραδύνω (10) Sacr 87, 87 Migr 25 Her 255 Mos 1:102 Spec 1:243 Spec 2:4 Spec 4:140 Contempl 76 Flacc 69

βραδύς (25) Sacr 78 Deus 93 Plant 161 Ebr 120 Conf 48 Her 149, 254 Congr 13 Fug 159, 159 Somn 1:101, 165 Abr 59, 109, 150, 150 Mos 1:183 Decal 35, 85 Spec 2:221 Aet 71, 133, 135 Flacc 34 Legat 213

βραδυτής (9) Opif 156 Sacr 53 Agr 175 Plant 161 Migr 151 Ios 182 Mos 1:275 Spec 2:38 Legat 248

βρασμός Post 71 Agr 37

βραχίων (16) Leg 3:133, 134, 134, 135, 135, 135, 136, 137 Post 132, 140, 140, 146 Mos 1:54 Spec 1:145, 147, 147

βραχυλογία Opif 130

βραχύς (208) Opif 6, 6, 72, 82, 113, 121 Leg 1:14 Leg 3:25, 70, 134, 134, 135, 135, 171, 196, 197 Det 89, 90, 90, 91, 153 Post 58, 112 Deus 27, 30, 103, 127, 146, 155, 178 Agr 10, 53, 115, 130, 169 Plant 6, 11, 28, 81, 128, 156 Ebr 32, 58, 154, 168, 183, 196, 221 Sobr 7, 64 Conf 5, 13 Migr 65, 122, 123, 123, 137, 194 Her 89, 102, 142, 145, 148, 148, 149, 150, 154, 155, 155, 290 Congr 11, 150, 150 Fug 176 Mut 65, 78, 180, 186, 223 Somn 1:10, 46, 125, 220 Somn 2:289 Abr 44, 71, 71, 86, 94, 122, 166, 199, 199, 258, 262 Ios 27, 38, 39, 101, 130, 131, 147, 168, 170, 230 Mos 1:22, 30, 38, 108, 200, 275 Mos 2:135, 140, 168, 173, 192, 204, 268 Decal 135, 137 Spec 1:18, 69, 71, 141, 151, 166, 242, 275, 338 Spec 2:49, 55, 131, 170, 180, 201 Spec 3:5, 25, 42, 50, 121, 126, 170, 170, 170 Spec 4:52, 83, 85, 136, 145, 171, 173, 213 Virt 26, 135, 221 Praem 82, 131, 138, 168, 172, 172 Prob 55, 84, 96, 130, 136 Contempl 16, 34 Aet 29, 41, 69, 100, 100, 101, 104, 114, 135, 149 Flacc 17, 37, 55, 58, 79, 124, 155, 165, 168 Legat 18, 24, 48, 117, 128, 193, 269, 282, 330, 341, 347 Hypoth 6:2, 7:10 Prov 2:11, 15, 44 QG (Par) 2:2, 2:5, 2:7 QE isf 2, 4

βραχύτης Opif 41 Det 105 Deus 37

Βρεντέσιον Flacc 26, 152, 173

βρέφος (31) Opif 103, 124, 132, 161 Leg 1:9 Cher 114 Her 294 Congr 4 Somn 1:192 Somn 2:10, 204 Ios 127, 128, 129 Mos 1:12, 17 Spec 2:33 Spec 3:110, 114, 115, 117, 118, 119, 199, 200 Virt 131 Praem 110 Aet 60, 67 QG 3:52, 52

βρεφώδης Sobr 11 Congr 19

βρέχω (6) Leg 1:21, 25, 26, 29 Somn 1:85 QG 4:51a

βρίθω (16) Opif 40, 85 Deus 85 Plant 7, 24, 25, 144 Her 46, 295 Mut 165 Mos 1:217 Mos 2:179 Spec 1:34 Spec 4:114 Praem 128 Aet 136

βριμόομαι Somn 2:168

βροντή Abr 43, 160 Mos 1:118 Decal 44 Prov 2:45

βροτός Aet 121

βροῦκος βροῦχος

Βροῦτος Prob 118

βροῦχος (βροῦκος) Leg 2:105

βροχή Leg 1:26

βρόχος Mos 2:252 Spec 3:160 Legat 131

βρύον Aet 140

βρῶμα Fug 174

βρώσιμος Leg 1:52 Plant 96

βρῶσις (23) Opif 38, 38 Leg 1:56, 58, 90, 97, 98, 98, 99, 99, 99 Plant 95 Congr 29 Somn 2:155, 215 Ios 154 Mos 1:184 Spec 1:150, 184, 222, 256 Prob 153 QG 4:167

βύβλος Flacc 37

βύζην Virt 43

βύθιος (10) Det 15, 100 Post 153 Deus 76 Somn 1:122 Mos 1:175 Spec 3:6 Legat 357 Prov 2:65 QG 2:15a

βυθός (14) Leg 2:34, 102 Agr 89, 169 Plant 144 Ebr 22 Conf 66 Mut 107 Mos 2:249, 252 Spec 3:114 Prob 66 Legat 371 Prov 2:33

βύσσος (8) Migr 97 Congr 117, 117 Somn 1:216 Mos 2:84, 87, 88, 111

βῶλος Opif 157 Spec 3:58

βωμολοχία Deus 102 Spec 1:319

βωμολόχος Cher 94 Sacr 32 Ios 125 Spec 3:101 Spec 4:50

βωμός (82) Cher 96 Sacr 137, 138 Agr 130 Plant 107, 108, 164 Ebr 85, 87, 129, 131, 134, 134 Conf 161 Congr 102, 169 Fug 80 Somn 1:195 Somn 2:67, 299 Abr 173, 176, 197 Mos 1:219, 277, 277, 282, 287, 287 Mos 2:94, 94, 106, 144, 146, 150, 152, 154, 155, 158, 224, 270 Decal 7 Spec 1:21, 98, 125, 147, 150, 167, 185, 199, 199, 205, 212, 215, 221, 231, 232, 233, 239, 254, 254, 255, 273, 276 Spec 2:162, 182, 183, 215, 216 Spec 3:55, 91 Spec 4:125 Virt 135 Praem 154 Legat 12, 139, 201, 203, 317, 334, 356 QG 1:62:1

Γ

Γάδ Somn 2:35

γαῖα Aet 17, 30, 30

Γαϊδάδ Post 66, 69

Γάιος (95) Flacc 9, 9, 10, 11, 12, 12, 14, 22, 25, 26, 31, 97, 98, 100, 108, 109, 114, 180 Legat 8, 14, 16, 17, 19, 24, 25, 32, 33, 36, 36, 38, 38, 52, 58, 60, 62, 67, 69, 69, 73, 81, 86, 91, 101, 110, 114, 119, 133, 134, 137, 141, 162, 164, 168, 171, 172, 173, 175, 178, 185, 188, 197, 201, 202, 204, 206, 218, 219, 222, 230, 231, 232, 248, 248, 253, 255, 257, 261, 261, 263, 265, 268, 271, 271, 275, 290, 314, 315, 330, 335, 335, 337, 346, 354, 356, 373

γάλα (19) Agr 9 Plant 15 Sobr 8 Somn 2:204 Spec 3:199, 200 Spec 4:12, 12 Virt 128, 130, 130, 142, 143, 144, 144, 144 Prob 160 Aet 66 Prov 2:51

Γαλαάδ Leg 3:16, 19 Congr 43

γαλακτοτροφέω (6) Mos 1:9, 16 Spec 3:199 Virt 129, 133 Aet 67

γαλακτοτροφία Mos 1:18

γαλακτώδης Agr 9 Migr 29 Congr 19 Somn 2:10

γαλαξίας Opif 112

γαλήνη (15) Opif 63 Sacr 16, 90 Post 22 Gig 51 Deus 129 Congr 93 Fug 191 Somn 2:166, 229 Mos 1:41 Spec 1:224 Spec 3:5 Spec 4:154 Praem 116

γαληνιάζω Cher 38 Deus 26 Conf 32 Abr 207 Spec 2:54

γαληνίζω Plant 167

γαληνός (7) Conf 43 Her 285 Fug 50 Abr 30, 153 Mos 1:214 Legat 197

Γαλιλαία Legat 326

γαμβρός Her 44 Spec 1:111, 111 Legat 62, 71

γαμετή (14) Congr 152 Abr 168, 246, 253 Spec 3:27, 80 Virt 111, 223 QG 3:20a, 21, 21, 23, 24, 24

γαμέω (13) Agr 152 Mos 1:13 Decal 130 Spec 1:105, 110, 111, 129 Spec 3:30, 62 Virt 28, 29, 222, 223

γαμικός QG 4:86a

γάμμα Leg 3:121

γάμος (61) Opif 103, 104 Cher 92 Post 79 Gig 29 Deus 87 Congr 5, 5, 70 Fug 52 Somn 1:200 Abr 90, 94, 98, 100, 100, 135 Ios 43, 44, 45, 121 Mos 1:60 Mos 2:137 Decal 126 Spec 1:101, 105, 107, 108, 109, 112, 138 Spec 2:25, 50, 125, 133, 135 Spec 3:11, 15, 22, 29, 61, 63, 63, 67, 70, 72, 72, 80, 82 Spec 4:203 Virt 112 Legat 40, 72 Hypoth 11:14 QG 3:21, 38a, 49b, 4:86a, 86b, 88, 145

γαμψός Spec 1:164

γανόω (11) Leg 3:173, 173 Sacr 24 Det 157 Agr 157 Plant 170 Ebr 5, 62 Somn 2:248 Spec 3:193 Flacc 98

γάνυμαι Opif 152 Leg 1:64 Mos 2:210 Legat 355

Γανυμήδης Prov 2:7

γάνωμα Plant 39 Somn 1:49 Somn 2:249

γάρ (5948) Opif 4, 6, 7, 9, 10, 12, 13, 13, 13, 14, 15, 16, 21, 22, 23, 23, 23, 24, 26, 26, 27, 28, 28, 28, 29, 30, 30, 31, 32, 33, 34, 36, 38, 40, 41, 41, 41, 44, 44, 45, 46, 46, 47, 49, 49, 52, 53, 53, 54, 54, 57, 58, 59, 60, 60, 61, 62, 63, 63, 63, 63, 65, 65, 66, 66, 67, 68, 69, 69, 69, 69, 69, 72, 72, 73, 75, 77, 80, 80, 80, 80, 81, 82, 83, 84, 85, 88, 89, 92, 95, 96, 97, 97, 97, 99, 99, 100, 100, 100, 101, 102, 103, 108, 108, 109, 109, 110, 110, 110, 111, 112, 113, 113, 114, 114, 115, 116, 119, 120, 122, 123, 124, 125, 126, 126, 129, 130, 131, 132, 133, 134, 135, 135, 136, 137, 139, 140, 140, 141, 141, 141, 142, 146, 147, 148, 149, 150, 151, 153, 154, 156, 158, 158, 159, 161, 162, 164, 164, 165, 165, 166, 166, 168, 171, 171, 171 Leg 1:1, 2, 4, 5, 6, 6, 6, 8, 9, 10, 10, 17, 17, 18, 20, 21, 21, 22, 23, 23, 24, 25, 25, 25, 26, 27, 27, 28, 30, 31, 32, 32, 34, 35, 36, 36, 37, 38, 39, 39, 40, 40, 41, 42, 42, 42, 43, 43, 43, 44, 45, 46, 47, 48, 49, 50, 50, 51, 51, 51, 51, 52, 57, 57, 57, 58, 61, 61, 62, 65, 65, 68, 68, 68, 69, 70, 70, 72, 73, 74, 74, 76, 77, 78, 78, 78, 79, 79, 80, 80, 81, 82, 82, 82, 84, 84, 84, 86, 86, 86, 88, 89, 90, 90, 90, 91, 91, 91, 91, 92, 93, 93, 94, 95, 96, 96, 97, 98, 98, 98, 99, 100, 100, 100, 101, 102, 103, 104, 104, 104, 106, 108 Leg 2:1, 2, 3, 3, 4, 4, 4, 4, 5, 5, 5, 8, 8, 8, 9, 9, 10, 11, 13, 13, 15, 15, 16, 17, 18, 19, 19, 20, 21, 22, 24, 24, 25, 25, 31, 32, 33, 34, 36, 36, 37, 37, 38, 41, 41, 41, 41, 42, 42, 42, 44, 45, 45, 46, 48, 50, 51, 52, 53, 55, 57, 57, 58, 59, 59, 59, 60, 60, 60, 63, 63, 63, 65, 67, 67, 67, 69, 70, 70, 71, 73, 73, 74, 74, 76, 77, 77, 78, 78, 79, 79, 81, 82, 84, 84, 85, 86, 86, 87, 88, 89, 89, 89, 90, 90, 90, 91, 92, 95, 96, 96, 96, 97, 98, 99, 100, 100, 101, 102, 105, 106, 106 Leg 3:1, 1, 2, 3, 4, 4, 5, 5, 5, 7, 9, 9, 10, 10, 10, 10, 11, 12, 14, 14, 15, 15, 15, 15, 16, 17, 18, 19, 20, 21, 21, 21, 21, 22, 22, 22, 23, 24, 25, 25, 25, 26, 27, 28, 29, 29, 31, 32, 33, 33, 33, 34, 34, 36, 36, 38, 40, 40, 41, 41, 42, 43, 43, 44, 45, 45, 45, 46, 46, 47, 47, 47, 49, 50, 50, 51, 51, 51, 53, 54, 56, 57, 58, 58, 59, 60, 60, 60, 61, 61, 64, 69, 69, 69, 70, 71, 71, 72, 73, 73, 73, 74, 74, 74, 75, 75, 76, 77, 77, 78, 79, 79, 81, 81, 82, 82, 82, 83, 83, 84, 86, 86, 86, 86, 87, 88, 88, 89, 89, 91, 92, 92, 93, 93, 94, 96, 98, 98, 101, 101, 102, 102, 103, 105, 105, 105, 106, 107, 108, 108, 110, 110, 111, 113, 113, 114, 114, 115, 116, 116, 116, 117, 119, 120, 121, 121, 121, 123, 124, 124, 125, 127, 128, 128, 129, 130, 131, 132, 133, 135, 137, 138, 138, 139, 140, 141, 141, 143, 143, 144, 144, 145, 146, 147, 147, 147, 149, 150, 151, 152, 152, 153, 154, 155, 156, 157, 158, 158, 160, 160, 160, 160, 161, 161, 161, 161, 163, 164, 165, 165, 166, 167, 169, 171, 171, 172, 172, 172, 173, 173, 174, 174, 175, 175, 176, 177, 179, 179, 180, 180, 180, 181, 181, 181, 182, 182, 183, 183, 185, 185, 186, 188, 189, 191, 191, 192, 192, 192, 193, 193, 194, 195, 195, 196, 198, 198, 200, 200, 201, 201, 202, 203, 203, 204, 205, 205, 206, 207, 207, 208, 209, 210, 210, 211, 212, 212, 213, 214, 215, 216, 218, 219, 219, 219, 220, 220, 222, 224, 225, 225, 228, 229, 229, 230, 231, 231, 232, 233, 236, 236, 237, 239, 240, 242, 244, 244, 245, 246, 247, 247, 248, 249, 249, 251, 252, 253 Cher 2, 5, 5, 7, 9, 14, 18, 18, 21, 22, 22, 24, 25, 26, 27, 28, 29, 32, 36, 36, 37, 38, 41, 41, 42, 44, 45, 46, 49, 50, 50, 51, 51, 52, 53, 57, 58, 58, 59, 63, 65, 66, 67, 69, 70, 72, 73, 74, 74, 75, 76, 77, 78, 79, 79, 80, 85, 86, 86, 87, 88, 88, 89, 91, 91, 97, 97, 99, 100, 102, 104, 107, 108, 109, 109, 110, 113, 114, 115, 115, 118, 120, 120, 122, 122, 123, 124, 125, 126, 127, 128, 128 Sacr 2, 3, 4, 5, 5, 6, 7, 9, 10, 10, 11, 12, 13, 15, 17, 18, 20, 22, 24, 25, 26, 26, 28, 29, 29, 30, 31, 34, 35, 35, 36, 36, 36, 37, 40, 40, 40, 41, 41, 42, 43, 44, 47, 49, 50, 50, 51, 54, 54, 55, 59, 59, 60, 61, 62, 63, 63, 63, 64, 64, 65, 65, 67, 68, 70, 71, 72, 72, 74, 75, 77, 77, 79, 80, 81, 82, 82, 83, 84, 86, 86, 87,

88, 89, 91, 91, 92, 93, 94, 97, 97, 98, 102, 104, 106, 108, 111, 111, 112, 112, 112, 113, 114, 114, 116, 118, 118, 118, 120, 122, 123, 125, 127, 129, 131, 131, 132, 135, 135, 138, 139 Det 1, 2, 2, 3, 4, 4, 5, 5, 6, 7, 8, 8, 9, 9, 10, 11, 11, 12, 13, 15, 17, 18, 18, 19, 21, 22, 25, 25, 26, 28, 30, 30, 31, 32, 32, 33, 34, 35, 36, 37, 38, 40, 40, 41, 41, 43, 44, 46, 46, 48, 48, 49, 49, 49, 50, 51, 52, 52, 54, 55, 55, 56, 57, 57, 60, 61, 62, 63, 64, 64, 65, 66, 68, 70, 71, 75, 80, 80, 85, 85, 86, 86, 87, 89, 90, 90, 91, 93, 94, 94, 95, 96, 97, 97, 97, 98, 99, 99, 100, 100, 101, 101, 101, 102, 103, 104, 106, 108, 108, 109, 112, 113, 114, 116, 116, 119, 120, 122, 122, 123, 123, 124, 124, 126, 126, 127, 128, 129, 129, 131, 133, 133, 135, 136, 137, 138, 138, 139, 142, 143, 144, 146, 147, 148, 151, 152, 154, 157, 158, 159, 160, 161, 163, 163, 164, 165, 166, 167, 168, 171, 172, 173, 178 Post 2, 3, 5, 5, 9, 10, 11, 12, 14, 14, 14, 16, 18, 21, 23, 24, 26, 27, 27, 28, 30, 30, 30, 30, 32, 33, 34, 36, 39, 40, 43, 45, 46, 47, 48, 49, 49, 50, 53, 54, 55, 56, 56, 57, 57, 60, 60, 61, 62, 62, 66, 66, 68, 69, 69, 70, 71, 72, 72, 74, 74, 75, 76, 78, 79, 80, 80, 81, 83, 84, 84, 85, 85, 86, 86, 87, 90, 91, 92, 93, 94, 95, 96, 96, 97, 98, 98, 99, 100, 100, 100, 101, 101, 102, 103, 104, 104, 105, 106, 107, 109, 109, 110, 110, 114, 116, 117, 118, 118, 119, 119, 119, 120, 120, 121, 122, 123, 124, 127, 127, 128, 129, 130, 131, 132, 134, 134, 135, 136, 136, 137, 137, 137, 139, 140, 141, 141, 141, 142, 142, 143, 144, 145, 147, 147, 147, 148, 150, 151, 152, 153, 155, 157, 158, 159, 161, 161, 161, 162, 163, 163, 163, 164, 165, 166, 168, 168, 168, 169, 169, 169, 170, 170, 171, 172, 172, 173, 174, 175, 175, 176, 177, 179, 180, 181, 182, 183, 184, 185, 185 Gig 1, 3, 5, 5, 7, 8, 8, 16, 18, 19, 20, 20, 20, 21, 24, 25, 25, 26, 28, 30, 31, 33, 34, 35, 35, 37, 37, 39, 40, 43, 43, 46, 47, 48, 48, 49, 51, 52, 55, 60, 62, 64, 64, 65, 66, 66, 66 Deus 3, 4, 5, 5, 6, 7, 7, 7, 8, 9, 9, 11, 13, 14, 15, 17, 18, 22, 22, 23, 24, 25, 29, 29, 29, 31, 31, 31, 32, 35, 35, 37, 37, 38, 39, 41, 42, 43, 45, 46, 47, 47, 48, 48, 49, 52, 53, 55, 55, 57, 57, 59, 60, 62, 62, 64, 65, 66, 66, 68, 69, 70, 72, 75, 76, 77, 77, 78, 79, 79, 81, 82, 82, 82, 83, 84, 84, 88, 90, 92, 93, 95, 98, 98, 100, 103, 104, 106, 106, 107, 109, 112, 115, 116, 117, 117, 117, 120, 121, 123, 124, 125, 129, 131, 134, 134, 134, 137, 137, 138, 139, 141, 143, 143, 144, 148, 151, 152, 153, 154, 154, 154, 156, 160, 161, 162, 162, 166, 166, 167, 168, 168, 169, 170, 171, 171, 176, 177, 177, 179, 180, 181, 182 Agr 1, 3, 4, 5, 5, 6, 8, 9, 12, 15, 16, 21, 22, 24, 25, 27, 29, 29, 32, 32, 35, 37, 40, 41, 42, 42, 43, 43, 43, 44, 46, 47, 48, 49, 50, 51, 51, 53, 54, 56, 57, 58, 61, 65, 67, 69, 71, 72, 73, 77, 78, 80, 82, 83, 83, 84, 87, 88, 89, 90, 90, 91, 91, 93, 94, 98, 99, 99, 101, 103, 103, 104, 106, 107, 108, 108, 110, 112, 113, 115, 116, 118, 118, 120, 121, 123, 123, 125, 126, 127, 129, 130, 132, 134, 135, 145, 145, 149, 149, 150, 150, 151, 158, 158, 160, 161, 161, 162, 164, 164, 165, 167, 167, 170, 171, 171, 171, 175, 175, 176, 177, 179, 181 Plant 1, 3, 4, 6, 9, 12, 14, 15, 17, 19, 21, 22, 23, 24, 25, 26, 26, 27, 27, 32, 33, 33, 34, 35, 36, 36, 40, 41, 43, 44, 44, 44, 44, 47, 49, 52, 53, 53, 53, 60, 60, 61, 62, 63, 63, 64, 64, 64, 68, 68, 71, 71, 72, 76, 78, 79, 80, 80, 81, 82, 83, 84, 85, 86, 86, 90, 95, 96, 97, 100, 101, 101, 105, 106, 107, 108, 108, 108, 110, 112, 113, 114, 118, 120, 124, 124, 125, 126, 128, 130, 132, 134, 134, 135, 136, 136, 137, 138, 140, 141, 143, 144, 147, 151, 152, 152, 157, 160, 161, 161, 162, 164, 164, 165, 166, 170, 171, 174, 177 Ebr 2, 7, 8, 9, 9, 10, 12, 13, 14, 15, 16, 19, 22, 24, 26, 27, 28, 28, 31, 32, 35, 37, 37, 39, 39, 40, 40, 41, 42, 42, 43, 44, 44, 48, 48, 49, 51, 54, 55, 55, 58, 59, 60, 61, 61, 61, 66, 67, 69, 70, 71, 75, 77, 78, 79, 82, 82, 84, 84, 85, 86, 86, 86, 87, 90, 91, 92, 93, 94, 94, 96, 98, 98, 99, 100, 103, 104, 105, 105, 106, 107, 110, 112, 113, 115, 115, 116, 118, 120, 123, 123, 124, 125, 126, 127, 129, 130, 133, 134, 136, 138, 140, 140, 141, 142, 143, 144, 145, 146, 147, 150, 151, 152, 156, 156, 158, 158, 159, 160, 163, 163, 164, 165, 167, 168, 168, 170, 172, 176, 176, 179, 180, 183, 184, 185, 185, 187, 189, 192, 197, 199, 201, 203, 204, 208, 209, 210, 213, 213, 217, 220, 220, 221, 222 Sobr 2, 3, 3, 4, 8, 9, 9, 10, 12, 12, 13, 18, 19, 20, 21, 22, 23, 28, 28, 30, 31, 32, 32, 33, 34, 37, 43, 44, 45, 46, 47, 47, 48, 49, 49, 50, 53, 54, 54, 55, 55, 56, 60, 62, 62, 63, 63, 65, 66, 67, 67 Conf 1, 3, 5, 5, 6, 7, 7, 8, 10, 10, 11, 17, 17, 19, 22, 22, 24, 25, 25, 25, 26, 26, 28, 29, 31, 31, 32, 36, 37, 38, 38, 38, 42, 43, 46, 47, 48, 50, 52, 53, 54, 56, 59, 59, 60, 63, 64, 65, 65, 68, 69, 69, 69, 70, 72, 72, 74, 75, 76, 76, 76, 77, 78, 84, 87, 88, 89, 89, 92, 93, 96, 97, 97, 98, 99, 100, 102, 103, 104, 104, 106, 114, 115, 116, 118, 120, 123, 124, 125, 129, 130, 131, 132, 134, 137, 139, 140, 142, 142, 146, 147, 147, 149, 150, 151, 153, 153, 154, 156, 157, 158, 159, 160, 161, 162, 163, 163, 165, 166, 168, 169, 169, 170, 170, 174, 175, 179, 179, 181, 182, 182, 186, 186, 187, 190, 191, 191, 192, 195, 196, 197 Migr 2, 3, 3, 4, 8, 10, 12, 13, 14, 15, 20, 20, 21, 24, 25, 26, 26, 30, 33, 35, 36, 37, 37, 38, 39, 39, 40, 40, 42, 44, 44, 45, 46, 47, 47, 48, 48, 49, 50, 51, 52, 52, 53, 54, 55, 55, 55, 56, 58, 59, 60, 60, 61, 61, 62, 62, 63, 64, 65, 66, 66, 68, 68, 68, 69, 70, 70, 72, 72, 73, 75, 76, 78, 78, 78, 79, 80, 81, 83, 84, 84, 85, 85, 86, 86, 87, 89, 89, 91, 93, 95, 97, 98, 99, 100, 101, 104, 105, 106, 107, 107, 108, 108, 110, 114, 114, 114, 115, 116, 118, 119, 121, 122, 123, 124, 126, 126, 129, 131, 132, 132, 132, 134, 135, 138, 138, 139, 140, 140, 140, 141, 142, 142, 143, 145, 146, 148, 148, 149, 150, 151, 152, 152, 153, 155, 155, 156, 157, 157, 160, 161, 164, 165, 165, 167, 169, 170, 171, 172, 172, 174, 174, 174, 174, 175, 176, 180, 181, 181, 182, 183, 184, 185, 186, 188, 188, 190, 191, 191, 193, 195, 196, 197, 199, 199, 200, 200, 201, 201, 202, 202, 202, 203, 203, 204, 204, 205, 206, 206, 208, 209, 210, 210, 211, 212, 212, 213, 213, 214, 215, 215, 216, 220, 222, 223, 224, 224, 224, 225, 225, 225 Her 2, 3, 4, 10, 11, 12, 12, 15, 15, 17, 20, 20, 21, 22, 23, 25, 26, 29, 30, 31, 32, 33, 35, 36, 36, 39, 40, 41, 43, 44, 44, 48, 49, 49, 51, 53, 55, 56, 59, 59, 62, 62, 63, 66, 66, 68, 70, 72, 75, 76, 77, 79, 80, 81, 81, 83, 83, 84, 86, 87, 88, 89, 89, 89, 89, 92, 94, 97, 99, 101, 101, 102, 105, 107, 108, 111, 113, 114, 118, 119, 121, 124, 124, 125, 127, 128, 131, 132, 133, 134, 136, 138, 141, 144, 144, 149, 151, 152, 154, 154, 157, 163, 163, 164, 165, 166, 167, 170, 170, 171, 172, 174, 178, 179, 179, 180, 181, 182, 183, 184, 187, 188, 188, 190, 191, 193, 194, 194, 195, 196, 196, 197, 197, 197, 198, 200, 201, 202, 203, 204, 206, 207, 208, 213, 214, 215, 216, 216, 216, 219, 222, 225, 226, 226, 227, 228, 231, 232, 233, 233, 234, 235, 236, 237, 238, 241, 241, 242, 243, 244, 244, 246, 248, 250, 251, 251, 251, 251, 251, 251, 253, 253, 254, 255, 257, 257, 257, 258, 259, 261, 261, 261, 262, 263, 264, 265, 265, 266, 267, 268, 269, 269, 270, 270, 272, 272, 277, 277, 278, 278, 279, 279, 280, 281, 282, 283, 286, 286, 287, 288, 289, 290, 290, 291, 294, 295, 296, 298, 299, 300, 301, 301, 306, 307, 308, 310, 310, 312, 312, 313, 315, 316, 316, 316 Congr 2, 3, 3, 5, 6, 6, 7, 8, 8, 9, 10, 10, 11, 12, 12, 13, 14, 15, 18, 20, 21, 22, 22, 23, 24, 26, 27, 30, 31, 32, 33, 35, 36, 37, 37, 38, 39, 39,

41, 41, 42, 43, 45, 46, 46, 46, 47, 48, 49, 50, 51, 53, 53, 55, 55, 56, 56, 57, 58, 59, 59, 60, 63, 65, 67, 68, 69, 69, 70, 70, 70, 72, 73, 75, 77, 78, 79, 84, 91, 95, 95, 96, 96, 97, 98, 99, 100, 101, 103, 103, 104, 104, 105, 106, 107, 108, 111, 112, 113, 113, 114, 115, 116, 117, 117, 117, 117, 117, 120, 121, 122, 123, 125, 126, 129, 130, 130, 131, 133, 137, 138, 138, 139, 140, 141, 142, 142, 143, 143, 144, 144, 144, 146, 147, 147, 149, 149, 152, 154, 154, 155, 155, 158, 159, 162, 163, 163, 163, 164, 164, 164, 166, 166, 167, 169, 171, 171, 174, 176, 177, 177, 178, 178, 179, 180 Fug 2, 5, 6, 6, 6, 7, 8, 9, 12, 13, 13, 14, 14, 15, 16, 16, 17, 18, 19, 20, 22, 23, 24, 25, 25, 27, 28, 30, 31, 31, 33, 34, 35, 35, 35, 36, 38, 39, 40, 42, 43, 43, 44, 44, 45, 45, 47, 48, 50, 51, 51, 52, 55, 55, 56, 57, 57, 59, 59, 62, 63, 65, 66, 66, 67, 68, 71, 72, 72, 74, 75, 76, 77, 79, 80, 82, 84, 84, 88, 91, 91, 92, 97, 98, 99, 101, 103, 104, 105, 106, 106, 108, 109, 110, 112, 114, 114, 115, 115, 117, 117, 117, 118, 119, 120, 122, 123, 124, 127, 127, 128, 130, 131, 132, 135, 135, 136, 136, 137, 138, 140, 141, 141, 141, 142, 143, 145, 146, 148, 148, 149, 151, 153, 153, 154, 155, 156, 156, 157, 158, 159, 159, 160, 160, 160, 161, 162, 162, 163, 164, 165, 165, 166, 167, 167, 168, 170, 170, 171, 171, 172, 173, 174, 174, 176, 180, 180, 181, 183, 183, 184, 186, 186, 189, 190, 192, 194, 195, 196, 197, 198, 198, 198, 202, 203, 204, 206, 207, 208, 208, 208, 208, 209, 212, 213 Mut 1, 2, 2, 3, 4, 4, 5, 6, 7, 7, 7, 9, 10, 12, 13, 13, 14, 15, 15, 18, 19, 19, 21, 22, 24, 24, 25, 26, 27, 27, 27, 28, 28, 29, 30, 30, 33, 35, 36, 36, 37, 40, 40, 41, 44, 44, 45, 45, 46, 47, 48, 49, 50, 52, 54, 55, 58, 59, 60, 61, 62, 63, 63, 66, 68, 69, 69, 69, 71, 72, 73, 73, 77, 78, 79, 84, 84, 86, 86, 88, 89, 91, 91, 92, 93, 94, 95, 96, 97, 98, 98, 99, 99, 100, 102, 102, 103, 105, 106, 106, 106, 107, 111, 112, 114, 114, 116, 118, 120, 121, 122, 122, 123, 123, 124, 125, 126, 128, 129, 130, 132, 133, 134, 137, 138, 140, 142, 143, 144, 146, 147, 149, 149, 151, 152, 153, 156, 156, 157, 157, 161, 161, 162, 163, 163, 163, 164, 166, 168, 168, 169, 170, 170, 170, 173, 173, 174, 175, 178, 179, 180, 182, 182, 183, 184, 185, 186, 187, 187, 191, 192, 193, 194, 194, 195, 196, 196, 196, 199, 201, 205, 206, 206, 208, 209, 210, 211, 211, 213, 213, 215, 217, 217, 218, 219, 219, 225, 227, 230, 230, 233, 235, 237, 238, 238, 239, 239, 241, 243, 244, 246, 247, 247, 249, 251, 253, 253, 254, 255, 260, 264, 265, 266, 269, 269, 270, 270 Somn 1:4, 6, 8, 9, 10, 11, 17, 18, 19, 21, 22, 23, 30, 32, 34, 35, 35, 37, 40, 41, 42, 42, 43, 44, 45, 47, 48, 49, 49, 51, 56, 58, 59, 60, 61, 62, 62, 64, 68, 69, 70, 71, 71, 72, 73, 75, 75, 75, 76, 77, 78, 79, 82, 83, 86, 87, 89, 89, 90, 91, 92, 92, 95, 97, 98, 100, 101, 101, 101, 102, 103, 104, 104, 105, 107, 107, 108, 108, 109, 109, 110, 111, 112, 112, 113, 114, 116, 116, 116, 117, 119, 121, 125, 128, 130, 130, 131, 132, 134, 135, 135, 136, 137, 141, 143, 144, 147, 148, 149, 150, 150, 151, 152, 154, 157, 157, 158, 160, 161, 162, 163, 166, 166, 168, 169, 169, 172, 172, 173, 173, 175, 176, 176, 177, 178, 179, 179, 180, 181, 181, 182, 183, 184, 185, 187, 187, 188, 189, 192, 194, 195, 196, 197, 200, 200, 203, 204, 205, 206, 208, 209, 210, 211, 211, 214, 215, 217, 220, 225, 226, 227, 227, 228, 230, 230, 232, 236, 237, 239, 240, 242, 245, 246, 246, 247, 248, 248, 249, 251, 253, 254, 255, 256 Somn 2:2, 3, 10, 11, 12, 12, 14, 14, 15, 18, 20, 22, 24, 27, 28, 30, 33, 33, 33, 35, 36, 36, 42, 44, 45, 47, 57, 58, 59, 63, 64, 67, 67, 69, 71, 72, 74, 75, 78, 80, 81, 82, 86, 88, 90, 91, 93, 94, 94, 95, 100, 100, 101, 102, 108, 118, 120, 128, 134, 134, 137, 138, 141, 143, 145, 148, 149, 152, 152, 154, 156, 157, 160, 162, 163, 165, 173, 175, 176, 177, 180, 181, 184, 186, 189, 189, 191, 192, 195, 199, 200, 200, 201, 201, 204, 206, 207, 207, 209, 211, 214, 216, 221, 222, 223, 224, 224, 226, 227, 228, 230, 231, 235, 235, 235, 236, 238, 241, 243, 244, 246, 247, 248, 248, 250, 252, 253, 255, 257, 258, 259, 260, 260, 262, 262, 262, 264, 265, 267, 269, 270, 271, 274, 275, 277, 278, 278, 282, 282, 284, 286, 288, 290, 294, 295, 296, 298, 300, 301, 302, 302 Abr 5, 6, 8, 10, 14, 14, 18, 18, 19, 21, 21, 22, 25, 27, 29, 31, 35, 37, 40, 40, 42, 43, 44, 44, 45, 45, 46, 46, 47, 48, 50, 51, 51, 51, 52, 52, 53, 53, 55, 57, 58, 59, 61, 65, 69, 74, 74, 76, 76, 77, 79, 80, 81, 82, 83, 83, 83, 87, 93, 95, 101, 104, 104, 105, 106, 109, 110, 111, 111, 112, 116, 118, 119, 121, 121, 128, 129, 129, 130, 131, 131, 134, 135, 138, 140, 141, 142, 145, 148, 149, 150, 151, 154, 154, 154, 156, 157, 158, 166, 167, 168, 171, 179, 181, 185, 186, 189, 193, 195, 197, 199, 200, 202, 204, 207, 208, 212, 215, 215, 224, 225, 227, 227, 230, 232, 232, 232, 232, 235, 235, 237, 237, 238, 239, 239, 241, 243, 243, 246, 246, 247, 249, 252, 256, 261, 261, 263, 266, 266, 269, 269, 271, 272, 273 Ios 2, 5, 6, 7, 8, 9, 9, 10, 12, 15, 16, 17, 19, 20, 21, 22, 24, 27, 28, 28, 29, 29, 31, 32, 33, 35, 36, 37, 38, 38, 39, 40, 44, 46, 47, 49, 50, 51, 51, 52, 56, 56, 58, 59, 60, 61, 63, 65, 66, 68, 68, 69, 70, 71, 75, 76, 78, 81, 82, 83, 83, 86, 87, 87, 90, 92, 94, 95, 100, 101, 102, 103, 105, 106, 106, 108, 112, 113, 114, 117, 118, 122, 123, 126, 134, 139, 140, 144, 144, 144, 145, 147, 148, 150, 150, 152, 153, 155, 156, 156, 159, 160, 161, 167, 167, 168, 170, 171, 171, 175, 176, 179, 182, 183, 184, 187, 190, 190, 192, 193, 198, 200, 204, 209, 210, 211, 211, 212, 214, 215, 216, 219, 220, 225, 227, 229, 231, 232, 235, 242, 244, 245, 249, 252, 254, 256, 260, 262, 263, 263, 266 Mos 1:2, 4, 6, 8, 11, 15, 17, 22, 26, 28, 29, 31, 32, 34, 35, 37, 38, 41, 43, 46, 54, 56, 58, 58, 59, 60, 60, 61, 62, 67, 72, 72, 73, 83, 84, 85, 87, 89, 96, 98, 101, 102, 103, 103, 104, 108, 110, 111, 112, 112, 114, 115, 115, 116, 118, 119, 120, 121, 123, 123, 124, 125, 128, 130, 130, 131, 133, 133, 134, 135, 137, 139, 141, 141, 142, 144, 145, 146, 149, 150, 150, 151, 155, 156, 157, 157, 158, 159, 166, 168, 170, 170, 175, 178, 179, 180, 181, 182, 183, 189, 190, 191, 192, 192, 194, 196, 200, 202, 203, 204, 205, 206, 207, 207, 209, 209, 211, 212, 215, 216, 217, 224, 225, 226, 230, 231, 231, 233, 233, 234, 236, 237, 240, 242, 244, 247, 248, 249, 251, 254, 254, 256, 265, 269, 271, 272, 274, 274, 274, 277, 280, 281, 285, 294, 295, 296, 297, 301, 302, 306, 312, 314, 315, 315, 320, 323, 325, 325, 326, 328, 333, 334 Mos 2:2, 3, 5, 5, 6, 6, 7, 9, 17, 20, 21, 22, 22, 23, 27, 30, 31, 33, 34, 37, 39, 44, 48, 51, 60, 61, 63, 63, 63, 70, 75, 78, 82, 82, 84, 85, 86, 88, 88, 88, 90, 91, 92, 97, 98, 100, 101, 102, 103, 107, 107, 108, 110, 110, 111, 116, 118, 119, 119, 120, 121, 121, 122, 122, 123, 124, 125, 126, 127, 128, 129, 130, 132, 134, 137, 137, 140, 142, 145, 150, 153, 154, 155, 156, 158, 164, 166, 168, 168, 169, 173, 176, 177, 179, 180, 180, 181, 181, 184, 184, 191, 192, 194, 194, 195, 197, 204, 205, 205, 207, 210, 214, 215, 216, 217, 222, 222, 227, 228, 232, 235, 238, 239, 242, 243, 244, 246, 247, 248, 250, 253, 254, 256, 256, 258, 261, 262, 263, 265, 266, 267, 269, 271, 274, 281, 282, 285, 287, 289, 291 Decal 3, 6, 7, 8, 12, 12, 15, 17, 18, 23, 25, 25, 27, 27, 30, 31, 32, 34, 35, 41, 43, 44, 45, 47, 48, 53, 54, 57, 57, 58, 59, 60, 62, 63, 66, 67, 68, 69, 69, 71, 72, 74, 76, 76, 77, 77, 78, 81, 82, 83, 84, 85, 86, 86, 86, 87, 88, 89, 92, 93, 94, 97, 102, 102, 105, 106, 108, 110, 112, 112, 113, 118, 119, 122, 123, 124, 125, 126, 128,

132, 133, 135, 138, 140, 140, 141, 142, 147, 149, 149, 150, 153, 153, 163, 166, 173, 175, 178, 178 Spec 1:5, 6, 6, 7, 9, 10, 11, 16, 18, 22, 25, 26, 27, 33, 35, 36, 37, 42, 43, 44, 47, 52, 53, 56, 58, 61, 63, 65, 65, 67, 68, 69, 72, 72, 76, 77, 78, 79, 81, 83, 85, 86, 87, 88, 92, 95, 96, 97, 99, 100, 102, 102, 102, 103, 103, 105, 108, 111, 113, 114, 116, 120, 120, 121, 121, 122, 123, 125, 128, 129, 130, 132, 133, 135, 136, 137, 140, 143, 145, 146, 147, 152, 152, 153, 154, 155, 156, 157, 159, 160, 163, 164, 167, 168, 172, 173, 175, 177, 180, 181, 182, 184, 186, 188, 188, 189, 191, 192, 193, 195, 200, 203, 205, 206, 207, 209, 210, 211, 215, 216, 216, 217, 221, 221, 222, 228, 228, 228, 229, 231, 233, 238, 239, 242, 242, 242, 244, 246, 246, 248, 249, 252, 252, 252, 253, 254, 256, 256, 258, 259, 260, 260, 263, 265, 265, 266, 267, 268, 269, 270, 271, 272, 274, 275, 276, 282, 283, 284, 284, 285, 287, 288, 289, 289, 294, 295, 296, 297, 298, 299, 313, 314, 315, 317, 317, 318, 319, 320, 320, 321, 325, 327, 327, 328, 329, 329, 329, 332, 332, 333, 335, 338, 341, 342, 343, 344, 345 Spec 2:2, 2, 4, 5, 8, 10, 10, 11, 11, 11, 13, 14, 15, 23, 24, 25, 26, 27, 27, 33, 34, 35, 38, 44, 46, 49, 50, 52, 53, 55, 56, 57, 58, 59, 60, 60, 61, 69, 69, 70, 73, 73, 74, 78, 81, 83, 84, 85, 86, 87, 89, 91, 93, 95, 97, 98, 101, 101, 104, 105, 112, 113, 113, 116, 118, 119, 122, 123, 124, 127, 128, 129, 129, 134, 137, 138, 140, 141, 142, 143, 145, 147, 149, 151, 154, 157, 158, 159, 161, 162, 163, 169, 172, 172, 174, 175, 175, 176, 177, 178, 180, 180, 181, 181, 183, 186, 189, 194, 195, 197, 197, 202, 204, 205, 207, 208, 209, 211, 213, 215, 216, 219, 221, 225, 225, 226, 227, 227, 232, 233, 236, 236, 237, 239, 239, 240, 241, 243, 245, 246, 247, 248, 249, 251, 252, 253, 256, 258, 258, 259, 260, 261, 262 Spec 3:4, 6, 8, 12, 13, 16, 16, 17, 21, 23, 25, 25, 26, 27, 28, 28, 29, 31, 32, 32, 33, 34, 36, 37, 42, 43, 43, 44, 44, 54, 58, 62, 68, 72, 73, 74, 74, 75, 77, 78, 78, 81, 82, 86, 87, 88, 91, 94, 95, 97, 98, 98, 99, 102, 105, 107, 109, 111, 113, 115, 115, 119, 121, 121, 122, 123, 125, 129, 130, 130, 135, 137, 138, 139, 140, 144, 149, 150, 152, 154, 155, 165, 165, 166, 168, 170, 173, 174, 175, 176, 177, 179, 180, 181, 182, 183, 184, 185, 186, 191, 191, 192, 193, 194, 197, 203, 204, 207, 209, 209 Spec 4:3, 4, 6, 6, 8, 9, 10, 12, 15, 17, 18, 19, 21, 24, 25, 26, 28, 30, 31, 34, 40, 40, 42, 42, 44, 46, 46, 47, 49, 50, 52, 52, 53, 54, 55, 56, 62, 63, 64, 64, 67, 69, 70, 72, 73, 75, 76, 79, 80, 81, 81, 82, 83, 84, 85, 90, 94, 98, 99, 100, 101, 103, 105, 106, 107, 109, 110, 112, 114, 122, 123, 128, 129, 130, 131, 132, 134, 137, 138, 139, 141, 143, 143, 144, 146, 147, 149, 150, 150, 151, 152, 153, 155, 159, 160, 161, 162, 165, 170, 171, 173, 174, 175, 177, 178, 179, 182, 183, 184, 186, 187, 187, 187, 189, 191, 193, 195, 196, 197, 198, 202, 203, 204, 207, 208, 209, 210, 212, 214, 216, 218, 218, 220, 221, 225, 227, 227, 228, 229, 231, 232, 234, 235, 235, 237, 237 Virt 2, 6, 6, 9, 10, 10, 12, 12, 14, 18, 19, 19, 20, 21, 24, 24, 26, 26, 28, 29, 30, 30, 31, 33, 34, 38, 38, 39, 44, 49, 50, 51, 52, 53, 59, 61, 65, 65, 66, 67, 71, 77, 79, 80, 81, 84, 84, 85, 87, 90, 90, 93, 98, 100, 100, 104, 105, 109, 112, 113, 113, 114, 115, 117, 118, 123, 124, 124, 126, 126, 127, 128, 130, 130, 132, 134, 134, 135, 135, 136, 138, 138, 142, 143, 145, 146, 147, 149, 152, 156, 156, 157, 160, 162, 162, 163, 164, 165, 165, 166, 167, 169, 171, 173, 176, 177, 181, 182, 183, 183, 184, 186, 188, 188, 188, 190, 191, 193, 194, 195, 196, 197, 197, 201, 204, 206, 208, 215, 216, 217, 223, 224, 224 Praem 1, 4, 6, 9, 9, 11, 16, 17, 18, 19, 20, 20, 21, 23, 24, 25, 26, 28, 29, 29, 31, 33, 36, 36, 37, 40, 41, 42, 44, 46, 47, 49, 49, 50, 50, 51, 51, 52, 54, 54, 55, 55, 55, 57, 61, 63, 69, 70, 72, 73, 77, 80, 81, 81, 83, 85, 87, 88, 92, 93, 94, 95, 97, 97, 100, 101, 103, 104, 106, 107, 109, 111, 112, 114, 115, 120, 121, 123, 125, 127, 127, 128, 129, 130, 131, 131, 132, 132, 134, 135, 135, 136, 138, 139, 139, 140, 141, 141, 142, 142, 149, 153, 154, 155, 158, 159, 164, 164, 169, 172 Prob 2, 6, 7, 8, 12, 15, 17, 18, 19, 20, 22, 22, 24, 25, 27, 27, 28, 30, 31, 32, 33, 35, 36, 37, 38, 41, 44, 48, 51, 53, 55, 58, 60, 61, 63, 63, 70, 71, 73, 77, 78, 81, 82, 85, 86, 86, 89, 91, 95, 96, 97, 99, 99, 101, 102, 105, 107, 109, 113, 114, 116, 118, 118, 118, 120, 122, 124, 125, 126, 128, 130, 133, 133, 138, 140, 141, 143, 144, 146, 149, 155, 156, 156, 157, 159 Contempl 1, 2, 2, 6, 8, 13, 14, 16, 19, 21, 24, 28, 32, 37, 39, 39, 40, 41, 41, 42, 43, 47, 49, 51, 56, 57, 59, 59, 60, 61, 62, 63, 65, 66, 69, 69, 70, 72, 74, 74, 75, 76, 78, 80, 81, 81, 82, 86, 86 Aet 1, 5, 5, 8, 21, 21, 22, 23, 25, 27, 29, 30, 30, 32, 33, 36, 37, 38, 38, 38, 38, 39, 39, 40, 40, 41, 41, 41, 42, 43, 44, 46, 46, 47, 49, 49, 49, 50, 51, 52, 53, 53, 54, 57, 58, 59, 60, 60, 62, 63, 66, 66, 67, 68, 68, 69, 71, 72, 73, 74, 75, 76, 77, 78, 79, 80, 81, 82, 83, 84, 85, 86, 88, 88, 88, 88, 89, 89, 91, 92, 97, 97, 98, 98, 101, 104, 104, 105, 106, 106, 107, 107, 107, 108, 109, 110, 111, 114, 115, 115, 116, 118, 119, 119, 120, 121, 121, 126, 127, 128, 129, 130, 132, 136, 137, 138, 139, 139, 142, 143, 145, 148, 149 Flacc 1, 1, 2, 7, 8, 9, 11, 12, 14, 15, 18, 19, 20, 21, 26, 27, 28, 29, 31, 31, 33, 35, 35, 36, 39, 42, 44, 45, 45, 48, 50, 52, 54, 58, 60, 62, 63, 65, 66, 74, 76, 78, 79, 81, 83, 85, 86, 87, 93, 94, 95, 96, 97, 99, 100, 103, 104, 105, 106, 109, 109, 111, 113, 113, 114, 115, 115, 116, 118, 120, 122, 125, 125, 128, 129, 130, 131, 133, 144, 146, 148, 148, 149, 151, 154, 159, 159, 165, 167, 170, 181, 182, 184, 186, 186, 189 Legat 1, 2, 5, 6, 6, 7, 7, 8, 11, 14, 15, 16, 16, 17, 18, 19, 20, 21, 23, 23, 23, 28, 28, 29, 30, 30, 32, 33, 34, 36, 38, 39, 41, 42, 44, 48, 49, 51, 54, 55, 56, 57, 59, 59, 60, 61, 63, 63, 67, 70, 72, 73, 75, 75, 76, 78, 81, 83, 84, 85, 91, 99, 100, 101, 104, 105, 106, 108, 110, 113, 115, 116, 118, 119, 119, 121, 123, 124, 126, 129, 130, 131, 132, 134, 136, 140, 144, 149, 151, 155, 160, 162, 165, 166, 169, 171, 173, 175, 176, 178, 179, 180, 181, 182, 182, 184, 185, 186, 186, 187, 189, 190, 190, 191, 192, 193, 194, 194, 199, 201, 202, 205, 207, 208, 209, 209, 210, 210, 212, 214, 216, 216, 220, 221, 222, 223, 223, 225, 227, 227, 234, 235, 242, 243, 243, 247, 247, 249, 250, 251, 252, 256, 257, 259, 260, 263, 268, 273, 274, 274, 277, 278, 280, 282, 287, 289, 290, 293, 293, 301, 305, 310, 311, 312, 313, 317, 318, 319, 322, 324, 325, 327, 327, 328, 328, 329, 330, 334, 335, 337, 337, 338, 338, 343, 344, 346, 349, 350, 351, 351, 351, 353, 355, 356, 357, 359, 360, 362, 368, 368, 369, 370, 371, 372 Hypoth 6:4, 6:4, 6:6, 6:7, 6:7, 7:5, 7:15, 7:15, 7:16, 7:16, 7:17, 7:17, 7:19, 7:20, 11:2, 11:7, 11:8, 11:12, 11:14, 11:15, 11:17 Prov 1, 1, 1, 2:1, 3, 9, 11, 11, 13, 14, 16, 17, 20, 20, 23, 23, 24, 25, 27, 28, 28, 29, 30, 32, 33, 33, 34, 34, 35, 36, 36, 37, 37, 39, 40, 41, 42, 43, 44, 47, 50, 51, 53, 54, 56, 56, 59, 61, 62, 62, 63, 64, 65, 65, 66, 66, 69, 71, 71 QG 1:17b, 20, 20, 21, 21, 24, 27, 41, 51, 51, 55a, 55b, 55c, 62:2, 63, 64c, 65, 66, 66, 68, 70:1, 70:2, 70:2, 72, 76a, 89, 93, 96:1, 96:1, 96:1, 97, 100:1b, 100:1c, 100:2a, 2:5a, 11, 12a, 12c, 12d, 14, 14, 15a, 15b, 16, 22, 28, 28, 29, 31, 34a, 34a, 39, 39, 39, 48, 54a, 54a, 54a, 54a, 54a, 54d, 59, 59, 59, 62, 62, 64a, 64b, 64c, 65, 66, 66, 66, 68b, 72, 74, 3:3, 3, 11a, 11a, 11b, 12, 18, 20b, 21, 21, 22, 22, 22, 23, 23, 29, 30b, 38a, 48, 49a, 49a, 49a, 49b, 58, 61, 4:8a, 47b,

51c, 52a, 52b, 52d, 64, 69, 74, 76b, 88, 102a, 110a, 110b, 130, 144, 145, 148, 153, 166, 166, 167, 168, 169, 173, 173, 174, 174, 180, 184, 191c, 8*, 9*, 200a, 200b, 200c, 202a, 202a, 202b, 204, 204, 211, 227, 227, 228 QG isf 2, 5, 5, 5, 5, 8, 10, 10, 13, 16, 16, 17 QG (Par) 2:2, 2:2, 2:3, 2:3, 2:4, 2:5, 2:5, 2:5, 2:5, 2:6, 2:7, 2:7, 2:7, 2:7, 2:7, 2:7, 2:7 QE 1:19, 19, 2:1, 1, 2, 2, 2, 3a, 4, 6a, 6b, 9a, 10b, 11a, 11b, 14, 14, 16, 16, 16, 19, 20, 25a, 25b, 25d, 26, 45a, 49b, 49b, 50b, 55b QE isf 1, 3, 5, 8, 14, 16, 20, 21, 22, 22, 22, 26, 29, 32

γαργαλίζω Spec 4:100

γαργαλισμός Leg 3:160 Sacr 26 Det 110 Spec 3:10

γαστήρ (127) Opif 118, 124, 157, 158 Leg 1:9, 83, 86, 104 Leg 2:26, 76 Leg 3:62, 88, 88, 114, 114, 138, 138, 139, 141, 142, 144, 145, 145, 145, 146, 148, 148, 149, 150, 157, 159 Cher 93, 93 Sacr 4, 33, 49, 49 Det 113, 157, 157 Post 3, 155, 155 Gig 18, 18 Deus 15 Agr 36 Ebr 22, 220 Migr 65 Her 20 Congr 80, 80, 128, 129, 130, 131, 135, 136, 137, 138, 138, 139, 139, 139 Fug 1, 31, 35, 35, 204, 204 Mut 134 Somn 1:122 Somn 2:51, 147, 208 Ios 61, 101, 154 Mos 1:19, 28, 160, 160, 195 Mos 2:23, 156 Spec 1:150, 166, 174, 192, 192 Spec 2:49, 148, 163, 195, 195 Spec 3:43, 43, 62, 108, 117 Spec 4:82, 91, 96, 113, 113, 127 Virt 86, 126, 135, 137, 139, 163, 182, 182, 208, 208 Prob 130, 156 Contempl 55 Legat 56, 275 Prov 2:17, 18 QG 4:168 QG (Par) 2:2, 2:7

γαστριμαργία (10) Opif 79, 158 Agr 37 Ebr 206 Somn 2:155, 181, 201 Abr 133 Virt 136 Legat 14

γαστρίμαργος Somn 2:50 Abr 149 Spec 1:223 Spec 4:91, 126

γάστρις Post 181

γάστρων Somn 2:205

γαυριάω Cher 70 Agr 73 Somn 1:224 Somn 2:267 Legat 86

γαῦρος Conf 18 Somn 2:78 Ios 150

γαυρόω Mos 1:284

γέ (467) Opif 12, 23, 29, 86, 113, 114 Leg 1:5, 9, 11, 12, 13, 21, 35, 36, 50, 50, 57, 78, 85, 87, 91, 105 Leg 2:3, 9, 10, 20, 20, 20, 39, 74, 91 Leg 3:2, 5, 9, 22, 48, 56, 66, 74, 77, 78, 109, 132, 165, 166, 167, 180, 180, 183, 198, 205, 206, 207, 212, 214, 216, 221, 221, 228, 230, 244, 246 Cher 32, 35, 57, 100, 112 Sacr 12, 49, 52, 71, 78, 81, 85, 91, 93, 101, 115, 122, 130, 136 Det 10, 11, 24, 62, 70, 74, 79, 110, 111, 119, 120, 127, 129, 138, 176, 177 Post 6, 28, 34, 37, 46, 85, 85, 87, 94, 94, 95, 108, 116, 141, 159, 160, 161, 169, 169, 169, 172 Gig 41, 42, 67 Deus 10, 25, 30, 58, 62, 62, 63, 77, 106, 114, 163, 166, 167 Agr 11, 26, 28, 28, 29, 49, 60, 61, 102, 131, 133, 149, 150, 153, 156, 157 Plant 35, 50, 65, 101, 102, 106, 107, 113, 126, 163, 172, 172 Ebr 3, 18, 20, 74, 106, 134, 138, 148, 149, 150, 172, 183, 220 Sobr 31, 51, 68 Conf 9, 9, 29, 33, 46, 49, 62, 62, 67, 87, 100, 118, 127, 130, 142, 144, 164, 183, 191 Migr 38, 54, 86, 162, 167, 180, 183, 225 Her 29, 43, 56, 65, 99, 101, 165, 165, 180, 186, 270, 286, 289 Congr 3, 39, 118, 146, 148, 151, 173 Fug 30, 50, 51, 55, 61, 62, 73, 93, 93, 96, 105, 106, 115, 125, 144, 155, 157 Mut 19, 47, 82, 103, 127, 128, 132, 160, 181, 189, 210, 253, 256 Somn 1:27, 67, 93, 101, 112, 136, 145, 167, 228, 247 Somn 2:7, 46, 52, 56, 60, 70, 76, 78, 85, 90, 104, 109, 111, 130, 160, 189, 200, 223, 266, 280 Abr 64, 64, 83, 118, 120, 136, 143, 180, 199, 216, 248, 250, 252, 263, 267, 269 Ios 71, 142, 252 Mos 1:51, 84, 143, 191, 243, 314 Mos 2:7, 58, 58, 135, 197, 204, 227, 262 Decal 20, 32, 33, 84, 88, 119, 126, 128, 151 Spec 1:10, 65, 104, 104, 261, 339, 345 Spec 2:2, 19, 36, 42, 46, 134, 151, 232, 249, 260 Spec 3:6, 26, 39, 68, 73, 114, 116, 121, 149 Spec 4:1, 3, 19, 52, 56, 138, 185, 188, 206, 235 Virt 11, 13, 16, 20, 60, 61, 84, 86, 89, 90, 106, 120, 132, 134, 137, 167, 185, 210, 222 Praem 43, 52, 56, 62, 85, 91, 153 Prob 31, 36, 41, 62, 95, 115, 124, 134, 134, 143, 156 Contempl 3, 6, 35, 72 Aet 6, 13, 13, 13, 13, 37, 39, 47, 65, 70, 74, 81, 84, 90, 91, 120, 126, 130, 132, 134, 145 Flacc 4, 36, 40, 44, 51, 92, 94, 124, 157 Legat 24, 111, 114, 137, 138, 139, 182, 218, 242, 293, 320, 322, 362, 362 Hypoth 6:2, 6:2, 6:9, 7:3, 7:7, 7:9, 7:9, 7:15, 11:3 Prov 2:13, 24, 42, 50 QG 1:62:1, 4:102c, 208, 228 QE 2:49b QE isf 2

γέγωνα Leg 3:119, 183, 232

γεγωνός (12) Leg 3:41 Cher 7 Sacr 98 Det 38 Post 103 Deus 83 Plant 126 Ebr 94 Migr 169 Fug 92 Abr 83 Mos 2:127

Γεδεών Conf 130, 130

γεηπόνος γεωπόνος

γείνομαι Mos 2:236

γειτνίασις Contempl 24

γειτνιάω (8) Opif 33 Mos 1:35 Spec 1:122 Spec 3:162 Spec 4:19 Praem 110 Aet 100 Legat 14

γείτων (15) Conf 52, 52, 54 Her 193, 224, 307 Mut 1 Somn 1:178 Abr 122 Spec 1:120, 216 Spec 4:93, 235 Aet 144, 148

γειώρας Conf 82

γελάω (49) Leg 3:85, 217, 218, 218, 218 Cher 93 Sacr 70 Agr 55, 115 Sobr 6, 32 Conf 3, 55 Migr 156 Her 81, 295 Fug 35, 107, 155 Mut 154, 155, 156, 157, 157, 166, 166, 166, 168, 175, 176, 209 Somn 1:218 Abr 112, 206, 206 Ios 125 Mos 1:62, 293 Spec 1:1, 2 Spec 2:23, 55 Praem 24, 171 Contempl 73, 73 Flacc 147 Legat 362 Prov 2:9

γελοῖος Abr 20 Contempl 58 Flacc 34

Γελῷοι Ebr 174

γέλως (63) Leg 1:82 Leg 3:87, 217, 217, 218, 219, 219 Cher 67 Det 123, 124, 124, 124 Post 179 Agr 62, 93 Plant 168, 168, 168, 169 Ebr 62, 149 Migr 157 Her 48 Congr 61 Fug 31 Mut 103, 131, 137, 137, 154, 157, 157, 157, 166, 261 Somn 2:167 Abr 112, 201, 201, 206 Mos 1:20, 164 Mos 2:211, 240, 249 Decal 129 Spec 1:176 Spec 2:18, 54, 164, 246 Spec 4:200 Virt 5, 202 Praem 5, 31, 31 Prob 54, 104 Contempl 58 Legat 169, 361 QG 4:43

γεμίζω (10) Opif 71 Abr 133 Ios 170, 207 Decal 40 Spec 1:70 Spec 4:129, 140 Prob 14, 56

γέμω (58) Leg 2:99 Leg 3:123, 160, 226 Deus 112 Conf 57, 141 Migr 36, 79, 115, 136, 147 Her 87, 113, 266, 291 Congr 53 Mut 189 Somn 1:121 Somn 2:85, 97, 117, 286, 296 Abr 151, 151 Ios 81, 89, 143, 145, 250 Mos 2:273 Spec 1:64, 309 Spec 2:46, 93, 107, 146, 187 Spec 3:193 Virt 3, 221 Praem 59 Prob 8, 26, 95, 101, 109, 123 Contempl 19, 54 Flacc 92 Legat 135, 218 Prov 2:1, 22, 32 QG 2:54a

γενάρχης (6) Her 279 Congr 61, 133 Somn 1:167 Mos 1:189 Flacc 74 γενεά (78) Opif 104, 140, 141, 148 Leg 3:83 Sacr 112 Det 121 Post 60 Gig 4 Deus 117 Ebr 40, 61, 127 Sobr 10 Conf 149 Migr 27 Her 61, 260, 293, 293, 295, 296, 297, 298, 298 Fug 126, 129, 208 Mut 12 Somn 1:200 Somn 2:15 Abr 31, 36, 38, 247 Ios 251, 261 Mos 1:7, 13, 238, 242 Mos 2:29, 210, 235 Decal 128 Spec 1:3, 111, 201 Spec 2:31, 56, 127, 133, 138, 199 Spec 3:37, 159 Spec 4:175 Virt 18, 102, 108, 214, 222 Praem 2, 23, 158, 169 Flacc 68 Legat 196, 230, 308 QG 2:5a, 11, 11, 15b, 65 QG (Par) 2:5 QE 2:49a QE isf 22

γενεαλογέω Abr 31 QG 1:97

γενεαλογία Congr 44

γενεαλογικός Mos 2:47, 47

γενεθλιακός Flacc 83

γενεθλιαλογικός Migr 178, 194

γενέθλιος (8) Opif 89 Ios 97 Mos 1:207 Mos 2:210 Spec 1:170 Spec 2:59, 70 Flacc 81

γένειον (7) Opif 103, 104, 105 Ios 23, 105 Contempl 30 Legat 223

γένεσις (438) Opif 12, 12, 12, 14, 25, 27, 31, 34, 37, 40, 42, 43, 46, 52, 52, 54, 58, 59, 64, 67, 67, 68, 72, 75, 77, 79, 100, 129, 133, 139, 140, 151, 152, 161, 168, 171 Leg 1:1, 7, 18, 18, 19, 19, 21 Leg 2:2, 6, 11, 15, 24, 74, 83, 83 Leg 3:7, 73, 77, 78, 78, 85, 86, 89, 101, 185 Cher 16, 19, 43, 50, 51, 54, 62, 75, 97, 108, 109, 114, 114, 120, 125 Sacr 4, 10, 14, 17, 42, 58, 64, 66, 66, 70, 70, 72, 72, 73, 98, 102, 102, 120 Det 46, 80, 114, 121, 124, 138, 139, 146, 147, 148 Post 5, 23, 23, 29, 30, 33, 42, 65, 89, 125, 133, 168, 171, 172, 177, 182 Gig 1, 3, 42, 53 Deus 4, 21, 31, 56, 58, 61, 75, 77, 87, 108, 117, 119, 119, 123, 157, 179 Agr 6, 25, 103 Plant 12, 53, 61, 61, 64, 66, 86, 93, 117, 130 Ebr 30, 31, 42, 69, 73, 77, 171, 208, 208, 211 Sobr 4, 8, 22, 22, 23, 26, 28, 60, 62 Conf 42, 57, 98, 106, 114, 144, 149, 175, 186, 187, 190, 191, 192, 196 Migr 6, 22, 95, 115, 136, 183, 207 Her 30, 38, 45, 45, 50, 93, 97, 103, 115, 121, 122, 146, 163, 164, 170, 170, 171, 171, 172, 179, 206, 209, 246, 247, 257, 280, 314 Congr 13, 14, 59, 81, 84, 91, 130, 134 Fug 70, 84, 109, 136, 160, 161, 173, 176, 204 Mut 10, 13, 18, 27, 27, 28, 36, 46, 46, 48, 74, 127, 130, 156, 157, 166, 177, 188, 195, 218, 223, 228, 255, 264, 268 Somn 1:37, 37, 38, 66, 77, 184, 189, 197, 211, 244, 249 Somn 2:28, 59, 67, 68, 100, 107, 131, 221, 221, 231, 253, 273, 290 Abr 1, 1, 9, 11, 31, 110, 162, 195, 248, 254 Mos 1:96, 98, 116, 212, 279 Mos 2:1, 37, 47, 48, 51, 60, 64, 80, 111, 119, 147, 260, 263, 266 Decal 58, 117, 163 Spec 1:6, 10, 16, 27, 43, 80, 102, 112, 112, 114, 140, 210, 277, 295, 326 Spec 2:5, 6, 42, 58, 58, 133, 152, 154, 160, 166, 233, 248 Spec 3:23, 36, 47, 58, 62, 112, 178, 178, 179, 179, 188, 199 Spec 4:68, 187, 208, 209 Virt 62, 72, 93, 112, 130, 132, 134, 203, 218 Praem 1, 1, 9, 13, 22, 63, 68, 132, 145, 149, 160, 160 Prob 80, 105 Contempl 6, 65 Aet 8, 8, 8, 14, 14, 27, 53, 57, 62, 65, 66, 73, 78, 79, 89, 94, 95, 99, 100, 100, 111, 111, 117, 118, 134, 137 Flacc 187 Legat 56 Prov 1, 2:10, 59, 71 QG 1:1, 1, 64c, 2:13b, 15a, 17b, 31, 34a, 66, 3:12, 21, 4:8a, 8b, 8b, 51b QE 1:1, 2:19, 46, 46 QE isf 10

Γένεσις Post 127 Abr 1 Aet 19

γενητός (97) Opif 12, 45, 67, 135, 171 Leg 2:5, 6, 12, 33, 34, 99 Leg 3:4, 31, 100, 101, 180, 180, 208, 209 Cher 16, 31, 77, 77, 99, 109, 119, 121 Sacr 94, 100, 101, 139 Post 20, 135, 145 Gig 26 Deus 58 Plant 66 Ebr 84, 199, 209 Conf 122 Migr 91, 134, 157, 180, 183 Her 56, 143, 206 Congr 107 Fug 141 Mut 14, 22, 85, 142, 201 Somn 1:60 Somn 2:253 Abr 206 Ios 254, 265 Mos 1:174 Mos 2:6, 65, 147, 168, 171 Spec 1:13, 20, 252, 293 Spec 2:55, 166 Spec 4:73 Virt 65, 65, 180, 213 Praem 28, 39 Aet 7, 7, 7, 13, 14, 17, 17, 18, 19, 55, 73, 78 Legat 5, 118 QG 2:16, 62 QE isf 3

γενικός (39) Leg 1:22, 22, 23, 23, 24, 59, 59, 63, 64, 64, 65, 65, 65 Leg 2:13, 86, 86 Leg 3:175, 175, 175 Cher 5, 6, 7 Det 118 Post 128 Deus 95 Agr 138 Plant 1 Ebr 138 Her 167, 173 Congr 120 Fug 176 Mut 78, 79, 80, 148 Spec 2:189 Praem 67 Aet 79

γενναῖος (37) Leg 3:75 Det 150 Gig 4, 40 Agr 86, 167 Ebr 224 Conf 41 Her 91, 105 Mut 177, 187, 261 Somn 1:93 Somn 2:10, 253 Abr 192 Mos 1:40, 234 Mos 2:274 Decal 73 Spec 1:271 Spec 2:84, 129, 247 Spec 4:45 Virt 17, 71, 127, 133, 167 Prob 24 Aet 54, 132 Flacc 52 Legat 215 Prov 2:37

γενναιότης Sacr 27 Mos 1:309 Virt 5

γεννάω (304) Opif 42, 47, 50, 51, 51, 55, 66, 84, 94, 99, 99, 99, 99, 99, 99, 99, 99, 99, 99, 99, 99, 100, 100, 100, 100, 100, 100, 100, 100, 101, 101, 113, 133, 144, 152, 161, 167 Leg 1:7, 10, 15, 15, 15, 15, 99 Leg 2:9, 12, 25, 37, 37, 45, 45, 46, 47 Leg 3:83, 87, 113, 146, 217, 217, 218, 219, 219, 219, 219, 234, 244, 247 Cher 23, 27, 27, 44, 44, 49, 53, 119, 124 Sacr 3, 24, 65, 87, 101 Det 54, 116, 119, 145 Post 40, 66, 90, 98, 135, 170, 177 Gig 1, 5 Deus 1, 3, 4, 15, 19, 30, 40, 47, 117 Plant 9, 15, 15, 31, 97, 110, 124, 125 Ebr 2, 73, 86, 94, 98 Conf 63, 122, 132, 145, 187 Migr 31, 33, 92, 142, 183, 193 Her 36, 54, 60, 62, 157, 171, 171, 172, 172, 200, 205, 216, 248, 265, 295 Congr 4, 23, 43, 56, 74, 76 Fug 50, 52, 161, 167, 209 Mut 10, 29, 63, 68, 137, 138, 163, 188, 189, 193, 263, 267, 267 Somn 1:20, 31, 35, 76, 166, 171, 173, 181, 190 Somn 2:24, 26, 141 Abr 98, 136, 180, 195, 228, 250 Ios 58, 188, 254 Mos 1:5, 8, 9, 11, 33, 147, 204 Mos 2:164, 185, 210, 222, 235 Decal 9, 25, 27, 27, 42, 51, 107, 112, 120, 132 Spec 1:6, 84, 96, 121, 130, 139, 172, 209, 291, 294, 313, 314, 329, 330, 336, 339 Spec 2:29, 29, 40, 52, 52, 59, 129, 137, 172, 173, 186, 205, 225, 228, 228, 231, 233, 240, 260 Spec 3:14, 23, 43, 49, 113, 116, 154, 189 Spec 4:15, 147, 166, 182, 182, 210, 238 Virt 93, 126, 128, 192, 202, 205, 207, 208, 223, 224 Praem 65, 121 Prob 79 Contempl 9, 17, 18, 70 Aet 58, 59, 67, 92, 100 Flacc 46, 91, 158 Legat 58, 89, 278, 338 Prov 2:53, 65, 66, 68 QG 1:74, 2:5b, 12a, 12a, 34c, 34c, 65, 3:11a QG (Par) 2:5 QE 1:6 QE isf 3, 22

γέννημα (49) Leg 1:31 Leg 2:8, 48 Leg 3:85, 89, 131, 150, 209, 217, 218 Cher 44, 48, 52 Sacr 104 Det 114, 114, 114 Post 10, 63, 172 Deus 4, 56, 117 Plant 95, 135, 136, 137, 137, 137 Sobr 22 Migr 78, 140, 142, 200 Her 48, 247 Congr 6, 7 Somn 1:201, 202 Decal 160 Spec 1:183 Spec 2:179, 181 Spec 4:12, 217 Hypoth 7:7 QG 1:60:2, 60:2

γέννησις Mut 96 QG 1:28, 3:18, 52

γεννητής (13) Conf 149 Somn 2:178 Mos 2:205, 209 Decal 53, 107 Spec 1:209 Spec 2:30, 31, 198 Virt 85 Praem 46 Aet 1

γεννητικός (25) Opif 13, 123, 162 Leg 3:8, 150 Sacr 58 Post 3 Deus 111 Mut 173, 205 Somn 2:68, 158, 184, 195 Ios 58 Mos 1:302 Spec 1:2, 216, 325 Spec 2:49 Spec 3:10, 41, 175 QG 3:38a, 49b γεννητός QG 4:8a

γένος (535) Opif 16, 44, 54, 61, 62, 63, 63, 64, 64, 65, 76, 76, 77, 79, 81, 114, 117, 120, 133, 134, 135, 136, 140, 141, 148, 157, 163, 169, 169 Leg 1:4, 14, 16, 20, 31, 45, 45, 47, 78, 86 Leg 2:4, 8, 11, 12, 12, 13, 13, 13, 13, 17, 22, 47, 50, 86, 95, 96, 96 Leg 3:42, 78, 166, 206 Cher 5, 8, 49, 66, 96, 99, 106, 106, 107 Sacr 6, 6, 7, 8, 35, 64, 65, 70, 78, 84, 92, 98, 105, 109, 111 Det 7, 25, 46, 60, 76, 77, 78, 99, 102, 122, 151, 152, 174 Post 42, 43, 43, 92, 103, 104, 105, 109, 109, 134, 173, 185 Gig 1, 56 Deus 7, 16, 19, 21, 73, 75, 76, 81, 95, 119, 121, 144 Agr 41, 83, 100, 133, 144, 154 Plant 13, 129 Ebr 13, 60, 78, 111, 122, 162, 214, 217, 220 Sobr 52, 65 Conf 1, 42, 43, 50, 56, 70, 74, 90, 91, 95, 117, 150, 182, 192 Migr 18, 20, 29, 46, 54, 54, 63, 66, 69, 84, 114, 121, 124, 125, 140, 155, 155, 158, 171, 218 Her 7, 36, 45, 47, 52, 58, 61, 76, 82, 112, 118, 126, 164, 172, 177, 182, 183, 184, 186, 187, 203, 249, 265, 272, 275, 276, 278, 278, 283, 284 Congr 20, 20, 22, 22, 36, 41, 51, 85, 94, 108, 132 Fug 9, 42, 62, 64, 73, 103, 104, 105, 107, 114, 140, 147, 168 Mut 1, 8, 12, 34, 54, 58, 64, 78, 78, 85, 88, 88, 109, 110, 117, 120, 133, 137, 166, 189, 213, 246, 256, 263 Somn 1:12, 28, 45, 68, 110, 112, 147, 159, 166, 175, 194, 209, 240, 256 Somn 2:14, 16, 48, 90, 149, 174, 186, 188, 210, 210, 228, 230, 276, 279 Abr 7, 9, 23, 30, 45, 46, 50, 51, 54, 56, 98, 115, 136, 202, 204, 207, 211, 251, 272 Ios 2, 30, 42, 56, 93, 233, 241 Mos 1:5, 7, 69, 100, 103, 109, 147, 149, 226, 302, 304, 324 Mos 2:8, 9, 27, 36, 55, 59, 60, 61, 62, 64, 65, 65, 84, 87, 121, 126, 142, 186, 189, 196, 245, 289 Decal 23, 52, 71, 81, 130, 153 Spec 1:1, 30, 76, 97, 110, 118, 122, 160, 168, 169, 172, 190, 194, 201, 211, 243, 253, 298, 303, 329, 342 Spec 2:35, 47, 52, 95, 100, 111, 114, 129, 133, 158, 162, 164, 167, 167, 171, 217, 225, 237, 239 Spec 3:7, 11, 11, 21, 25, 27, 38, 46, 99, 100, 113, 113, 118, 125, 157, 162, 165, 176, 185, 192 Spec 4:14, 18, 101, 101, 105, 113, 114, 116, 118, 123, 132, 132, 133, 157, 180, 192, 206, 208 Virt 10, 38, 60, 119, 122, 123, 131, 132, 149, 191, 193, 197, 199, 206, 206, 207, 212, 225 Praem 8, 9, 14, 26, 36, 58, 68, 68, 72, 83, 84, 85, 90, 107, 110, 125, 141, 163 Prob 18, 35, 63, 71, 93, 114, 158 Contempl 11, 21, 35, 37, 62 Aet 12, 45, 55, 55, 69, 97, 117, 130, 145, 146, 149 Flacc 13, 39, 96 Legat 3, 4, 8, 10, 26, 33, 48, 54, 62, 68, 76, 98, 142, 143, 144, 149, 178, 201, 265, 320, 346, 348 Hypoth 11:2, 11:2 Prov 2:8, 38, 43, 44, 66, 69 QG 1:76b, 96:1, 97, 2:13a, 15b, 17c, 54a, 3:12, 4:153, 179 QG isf 1, 17 QE 2:2, 19, 46, 46 QE isf 22

γεραίρω (23) Sacr 117 Plant 131 Her 110 Abr 235 Mos 1:23, 155 Mos 2:256 Decal 61, 78 Spec 1:21, 52, 272 Spec 2:132, 134, 164, 199, 209 Spec 3:184 Virt 77, 218 Praem 121, 126 Legat 96

γεράνδρυον Praem 172

γέρανος Spec 4:117

γέρας (72) Sacr 77 Det 42, 92 Post 105 Deus 45, 168, 169 Plant 42, 63 Ebr 65 Sobr 16, 37 Conf 30, 57 Migr 141 Her 291 Congr 37, 108 Fug 37, 118 Somn 1:35, 169 Abr 98, 165 Mos 1:148, 205, 236, 304, 321, 327 Mos 2:17, 58, 67, 142, 173, 194, 236, 242, 274 Decal 161 Spec 1:57, 79, 117, 122, 123, 135 Spec 2:183, 235, 258, 258, 259, 261 Spec 3:128 Spec 4:121 Virt 53, 102 Praem 2, 22, 36, 52, 74, 90, 120, 152, 166 Contempl 36, 90 Aet 68 Legat 46 QG 1:20, 3:8, 4:202a

Γερμανία Legat 10

Γερμανικός Legat 10, 206, 356

γερμανός Somn 2:121

γερουσία (10) Ebr 14 Sobr 24 Migr 168 Mos 1:73 Mos 2:153 Spec 3:80 Flacc 74, 76, 80 Legat 229

γέρων (11) Opif 105, 105, 105 Sacr 76 Sobr 20 Somn 2:36, 36 Ios 127, 128 Legat 1 Hypoth 7:13

γεῦμα Congr 174

γεῦσις (52) Opif 62, 62, 162, 165 Leg 1:25 Leg 2:7, 26, 39, 74, 96 Leg 3:58, 156, 216, 220, 220 Cher 57 Sacr 44, 73 Det 99, 101, 168, 173 Gig 18 Agr 36 Ebr 217 Conf 19, 52, 90 Migr 51, 137, 188 Her 48, 232 Fug 182 Mut 111, 164 Somn 1:55, 80 Somn 2:51, 215 Abr 148, 149, 236, 241 Spec 1:174, 337, 338 Spec 4:100 Contempl 45, 53 QG (Par) 2:3 QE isf 21

γευστός Ebr 191

γεύω (35) Leg 3:111, 216, 216 Cher 57, 62, 73 Sacr 85 Ebr 106 Conf 194 Congr 96 Fug 138 Somn 1:48, 55, 165 Somn 2:149 Abr 89, 238 Ios 25, 126, 126 Mos 1:182, 190 Mos 2:192 Decal 74, 80 Spec 1:37, 176, 223 Spec 4:92, 99 Virt 136, 188 Prob 114 Legat 310 QG 1:85

γέφυρα Somn 2:118

γεώδης (39) Opif 135 Leg 1:1, 31, 32, 88 Leg 3:172, 252, 252 Cher 89 Det 85, 98, 109, 112, 114, 163 Post 89 Plant 44 Conf 92, 95, 104 Migr 9, 63 Her 197 Congr 20, 96 Mut 21, 34 Somn 1:86, 146, 177 Mos 2:119 Aet 29, 29, 33, 86, 87, 90, 135 QG 2:12d

γεώλοφος (7) Det 2 Somn 1:125 Mos 1:276 Contempl 22 Aet 42, 118, 148

γεωμέτρης Agr 138 Mut 80 Prob 49, 157

γεωμετρία (18) Opif 49, 98 Leg 1:57 Cher 105 Agr 13, 18 Plant 121 Ebr 49 Congr 11, 16, 75, 144, 146, 146 Somn 1:205 Mos 1:23 Mos 2:39 Spec 2:230

γεωμετρικός (9) Opif 107, 108 Mut 146, 146 Somn 1:9 Mos 2:96 Decal 21 Spec 2:200 Prob 49

γεωπονέω (9) Leg 1:43 Det 112 Conf 124 Migr 91 Her 121 Spec 2:207 Virt 98 Prob 34, 76

γεωπόνος (γεηπόνος) (26) Opif 80, 85, 115, 168 Leg 3:170, 227 Sacr 38 Det 104, 112 Post 142 Deus 38, 91 Plant 136 Conf 38 Mut 149, 221, 259 Spec 2:104, 213 Spec 3:32 Virt 145, 157 Praem 128 Hypoth 11:8 Prov 2:44, 66

γεωργέω (16) Det 104 Agr 5 Plant 42, 96, 98, 112 Sobr 36 Congr 123 Somn 2:64, 163 Spec 4:75 Prob 69 Contempl 89 Legat 47 Hypoth 7:15 Prov 2:43

γεωργία (27) Cher 34 Sacr 11 Det 104, 108 Deus 87 Agr 3, 25, 26 Plant 2, 139 Her 115, 121, 137 Congr 65 Somn 2:21 Mos 1:201 Decal 162 Spec 1:335 Spec 2:206 Spec 4:215 Virt 93, 98, 98 Contempl 62 Hypoth 7:17 QG 2:66, 4:189

γεωργικός (26) Opif 81, 167 Cher 33 Det 105, 109, 111 Agr 4, 7, 10, 17, 20, 125, 181 Plant 1, 94, 94, 140 Sobr 36 Migr 55 Fug 170 Somn 2:61 Spec 2:172 Virt 155 Praem 12 Prob 68 Prov 2:26

γεωργός (38) Leg 1:47, 80 Det 104, 104, 105, 108, 112 Agr 1, 2, 4, 5, 20, 22, 26, 27, 67, 124, 125, 158, 181 Plant 1, 1, 140 Sobr 35, 36, 36 Migr 221 Somn 2:64 Ios 260 Mos 1:22 Spec 1:305 Spec 3:33, 39 Praem 60 Aet 63, 98 Flacc 57 QE isf 25 γῆ (849) Opif 26, 29, 38, 38, 39, 40, 42, 42, 45, 45, 45, 46, 47, 58, 59, 62, 63, 63, 64, 64, 69, 72, 78, 84, 85, 111, 113, 114, 116, 129, 129, 129, 131, 131, 131, 132, 133, 133, 133, 133, 133, 134, 136, 137, 146, 147, 147, 154, 157, 158, 163, 167, 168, 171 Leg 1:1, 1, 2, 2, 19, 21, 21, 21, 21, 21, 21, 25, 25, 26, 26, 27, 28, 28, 28, 31, 32, 34, 56, 63, 63, 63, 66, 66, 66, 68, 78, 90, 96 Leg 2:4, 9, 11, 13, 19, 53, 59, 71, 88, 88, 106 Leg 3:4, 5, 12, 42, 65, 65, 82, 83, 99, 101, 107, 161, 161, 161, 161, 169, 172, 202, 202, 222, 246, 247, 247, 252, 253, 253, 253 Cher 12, 25, 41, 49, 53, 62, 99, 100, 108, 108, 111, 111, 119, 121 Sacr 11, 25, 25, 51, 51, 52, 57, 72, 89, 90, 97, 107, 118, 134 Det 8, 62, 69, 79, 80, 85, 85, 85, 87, 88, 89, 96, 98, 99, 100, 104, 106, 107, 108, 114, 118, 119, 119, 121, 122, 150, 150, 151, 152, 152, 154, 156, 156, 159, 163, 163, 163, 163, 170, 174 Post 1, 50, 65, 65, 91, 116, 125, 127, 127, 144, 163, 180 Gig 1, 3, 7, 12, 22, 31, 58, 60, 60, 62, 65, 66 Deus 19, 20, 20, 20, 33, 51, 79, 87, 107, 122, 140, 140, 145, 149, 149, 153, 155, 157, 161, 181 Agr 1, 3, 4, 5, 6, 7, 17, 20, 21, 21, 21, 22, 22, 23, 24, 25, 26, 26, 27, 51, 65, 67, 68, 76, 97, 113, 124, 181 Plant 1, 3, 3, 4, 6, 10, 12, 13, 14, 14, 15, 16, 16, 22, 24, 25, 34, 60, 67, 74, 95, 96, 120, 127, 135, 140, 145 Ebr 40, 75, 105, 106, 106, 110, 113, 158 Sobr 36, 41, 42, 64 Conf 1, 1, 1, 1, 1, 1, 5, 5, 10, 15, 23, 24, 44, 60, 81, 81, 82, 89, 107, 113, 136, 154, 156, 157 Migr 1, 1, 1, 2, 3, 3, 3, 3, 7, 27, 28, 44, 64, 64, 65, 83, 101, 118, 120, 122, 131, 163, 174, 177, 178, 181, 182, 184, 185, 187, 216, 218 Her 7, 8, 8, 29, 30, 32, 35, 57, 69, 78, 83, 84, 96, 110, 112, 122, 134, 135, 136, 146, 146, 147, 162, 197, 198, 208, 222, 226, 226, 238, 239, 239, 240, 247, 251, 267, 267, 268, 277, 277, 280, 281, 282, 287, 293, 313, 314 Congr 71, 81, 83, 86, 86, 90, 95, 95, 104, 109, 117, 121, 133, 171, 173 Fug 57, 57, 87, 110, 163, 174, 175, 178, 178, 180, 180, 181, 182, 192 Mut 21, 59, 67, 72, 152, 174, 179, 179, 237, 256, 258, 259, 264 Somn 1:3, 3, 3, 3, 3, 16, 17, 18, 19, 22, 33, 39, 45, 52, 52, 53, 54, 83, 85, 97, 107, 116, 133, 134, 134, 135, 136, 144, 144, 144, 157, 174, 175, 180, 189, 189, 203, 208, 210, 214 Somn 2:6, 6, 7, 22, 75, 75, 77, 110, 111, 116, 118, 180, 239, 245, 250, 255, 284, 287 Abr 1, 29, 44, 67, 67, 72, 95, 133, 140, 140, 141, 141, 145, 159, 161, 205, 227 Ios 12, 17, 23, 24, 56, 78, 78, 109, 136, 168, 194, 239, 257 Mos 1:2, 5, 30, 81, 96, 97, 107, 113, 117, 129, 143, 155, 175, 202, 212, 214, 217, 217, 237, 254, 319 Mos 2:37, 51, 62, 62, 63, 63, 64, 88, 88, 98, 98, 101, 104, 105, 118, 119, 119, 120, 121, 121, 122, 122, 126, 133, 148, 194, 194, 196, 210, 210, 212, 238, 241, 251, 258, 267, 268, 281, 282, 285, 285, 287 Decal 5, 14, 31, 42, 44, 53, 54, 56, 56, 78, 116, 134, 152 Spec 1:37, 40, 68, 69, 74, 76, 85, 86, 86, 92, 93, 93, 94, 97, 131, 165, 184, 207, 207, 210, 264, 266, 300, 302, 321, 335, 339 Spec 2:5, 45, 53, 70, 89, 96, 118, 120, 143, 144, 151, 162, 168, 169, 171, 173, 197, 205, 208, 222, 255 Spec 3:2, 8, 34, 50, 58, 58, 59, 60, 111, 147, 152, 152, 152, 188 Spec 4:10, 12, 13, 66, 85, 104, 114, 115, 118, 128, 149, 154, 177, 205, 212, 215, 216, 217, 226, 232, 236 Virt 28, 73, 85, 92, 146, 146, 146, 183, 188, 199 Praem 7, 8, 9, 26, 36, 41, 44, 68, 80, 101, 104, 105, 130, 131, 133, 153, 164, 168 Prob 25, 25, 65, 67, 70, 72, 76, 99, 99, 145 Contempl 3, 3, 54 Aet 4, 4, 19, 19, 25, 29, 33, 33, 33, 45, 55, 55, 57, 57, 61, 62, 64, 66, 66, 66, 68, 87, 88, 90, 96, 98, 103, 107, 107, 110, 110, 111, 111, 115, 115, 115, 117, 118, 119, 123, 125, 131, 132, 135, 136, 136, 137, 139, 146 Flacc 104, 123, 187, 187 Legat 8, 44, 49, 81, 116, 141, 144, 144, 182, 190, 251, 252, 282, 309, 347 Hypoth 6:1, 6:1, 6:5, 6:6, 6:6, 6:7, 7:7, 7:15, 7:17, 7:19 Prov 2:10, 12, 43, 44, 45, 67, 68 QG 1:1, 3, 3, 51, 51, 51, 51, 70:1, 72, 93, 100:2a, 2:13a, 13a, 15a, 15a, 15a, 15a, 28, 64c, 65, 66, 3:30b, 4:51a, 51b, 76a, 88 QE 2:46

γηγενής (25) Opif 69, 82, 132, 136, 156 Leg 1:33, 79 Leg 2:16 Somn 1:68 Abr 12, 56 Spec 2:124, 160, 160 Virt 199, 203 Praem 9 Aet 67 QG 1:20, 20, 21, 2:17c, 54a QE 2:46, 55b

γήδιον Flacc 168

γηθέω (γήθω) (58) Leg 3:87, 212, 218 Cher 33, 37, 86 Sacr 33, 136 Det 94, 124, 125, 129, 131 Post 149 Deus 9, 113, 170 Agr 83 Plant 108, 162 Ebr 10, 146 Migr 79 Fug 154 Mut 167 Somn 2:100 Abr 22, 151, 182, 207, 235 Ios 92, 210, 255, 267 Mos 1:58, 177, 257 Mos 2:166, 225, 257 Decal 87 Spec 1:77, 144 Spec 2:84, 185, 216 Spec 3:141 Spec 4:75 Virt 67, 88 Praem 32, 32 Prob 39 Flacc 100 Legat 10, 20 QG isf 9

γηθοσύνη Plant 167

γήθω γηθέω

γήινος (33) Leg 1:31, 31, 31, 90, 90, 95 Leg 2:89 Leg 3:161, 162, 162, 168, 214 Det 163 Post 101 Deus 144, 148, 148, 159, 166, 180 Agr 22 Plant 46, 71 Migr 101, 146 Her 52, 78, 239 Congr 58, 97 Fug 196 Somn 2:70 QG 4:171

γηραιός Mos 1:257 Decal 116 Contempl 68

γῆρας (62) Opif 103, 103 Cher 68, 75, 116 Det 106 Post 71, 112, 164 Agr 56, 103, 151 Sobr 16, 23 Conf 7, 7, 16 Migr 217 Her 212, 249, 275, 290, 291, 291 Congr 53 Fug 55 Somn 1:151, 192 Somn 2:147, 148 Abr 111, 182, 195, 240 Ios 128, 129, 230 Mos 2:223 Decal 117, 167 Spec 1:282 Spec 2:238 Spec 3:14 Virt 3, 26, 52, 72 Praem 25, 51 Aet 21, 26, 58, 60, 74, 77 Flacc 68, 80 Hypoth 11:3, 11:13 QG 3:11c, 11c, 4:200a

γηράσκω (7) Agr 153 Ebr 179 Sobr 7 Fug 146 Somn 1:26 Ios 223 Aet 61

γηροτροφέω Decal 117 Prob 87

Γηρυόνης Legat 80

γῆρυς Ebr 102

γήτειον Somn 2:49

Γηών Leg 1:63, 68, 68, 85

γιγαντώδης Mos 1:229

γίγας (6) Gig 58, 58, 60, 66, 67 Mos 1:229

γίγνομαι (γίνομαι) (1786) Opif 9, 10, 13, 14, 16, 20, 21, 23, 26, 26, 26, 27, 28, 31, 33, 35, 37, 38, 41, 41, 42, 43, 45, 45, 49, 49, 52, 53, 55, 58, 59, 60, 67, 69, 77, 79, 82, 83, 83, 86, 87, 97, 97, 99, 101, 104, 110, 115, 116, 119, 124, 126, 129, 129, 130, 134, 135, 135, 136, 136, 139, 140, 140, 141, 146, 148, 151, 159, 164, 164, 165, 167, 171, 172 Leg 1:2, 2, 2, 7, 8, 8, 10, 18, 18, 19, 20, 20, 20, 20, 21, 22, 22, 22, 23, 24, 26, 29, 31, 31, 32, 32, 33, 37, 41, 41, 41, 41, 42, 42, 42, 53, 54, 61, 61, 61, 63, 66, 72, 72, 76, 76, 80, 89, 92, 93, 95, 99, 107 Leg 2:2, 2, 4, 6, 14, 15, 17, 17, 18, 19, 20, 25, 26, 40, 44, 45, 45, 48, 48, 49, 52, 60, 61, 61, 63, 69, 70, 73, 74, 75, 79, 87, 88, 88, 90, 90, 92, 93, 94, 94, 96, 96, 97, 98, 105 Leg 3:5, 5, 7, 11, 27, 29, 35, 35, 45, 51, 52, 53, 54, 67, 67, 74, 74, 82, 85, 85, 86, 86, 86, 89, 96, 100, 102, 103, 104, 109, 113, 117, 129, 131, 138, 142, 143, 156, 156, 161, 164, 169, 175, 178, 184, 189, 193, 200, 204, 204, 205, 205, 211, 211, 212,

217, 218, 218, 225, 236, 237, 239, 244 Cher 5, 7, 7, 7, 14, 19, 23, 24, 26, 26, 47, 57, 61, 75, 77, 83, 84, 86, 97, 98, 99, 100, 100, 106, 119, 120, 121, 123, 125, 125, 127 Sacr 4, 5, 7, 10, 11, 15, 19, 19, 29, 32, 45, 49, 52, 60, 62, 63, 64, 64, 65, 67, 70, 76, 89, 100, 104, 118, 119, 120, 124, 127, 130, 132, 134, 134 Det 1, 2, 12, 16, 25, 28, 33, 33, 35, 52, 62, 63, 64, 65, 66, 69, 74, 75, 75, 76, 77, 78, 80, 82, 89, 94, 95, 97, 100, 106, 106, 106, 108, 110, 113, 114, 116, 117, 118, 129, 131, 133, 134, 138, 141, 142, 142, 153, 153, 161, 165, 172 Post 7, 8, 11, 14, 16, 16, 19, 19, 22, 24, 25, 34, 47, 47, 53, 65, 65, 68, 74, 82, 89, 90, 95, 107, 108, 111, 111, 113, 115, 117, 119, 131, 131, 134, 136, 138, 144, 149, 152, 165, 174, 185 Gig 1, 1, 4, 5, 7, 10, 24, 25, 25, 36, 42, 54, 56, 57, 60, 61, 63, 63, 64, 65 Deus 5, 5, 14, 22, 37, 39, 39, 50, 55, 55, 56, 58, 65, 67, 70, 80, 106, 107, 113, 115, 115, 116, 120, 125, 131, 131, 131, 132, 135, 136, 138, 153, 153, 160, 182, 183 Agr 24, 31, 49, 58, 89, 91, 94, 96, 99, 100, 128, 134, 148, 156, 156, 158, 158, 162, 171, 173, 175, 177, 179 Plant 18, 19, 19, 46, 48, 49, 51, 59, 60, 61, 68, 81, 88, 109, 126, 127, 127, 131, 132, 145, 148, 165, 166, 168, 175 Ebr 9, 13, 25, 30, 35, 36, 37, 51, 61, 69, 72, 73, 76, 84, 90, 93, 94, 99, 104, 106, 107, 108, 111, 118, 125, 144, 145, 152, 160, 174, 174, 180, 181, 191, 201, 202, 207, 221, 222, 223, 224 Sobr 2, 8, 17, 21, 21, 25, 35, 38, 47, 54, 56, 59 Conf 1, 1, 7, 8, 14, 16, 38, 39, 39, 52, 61, 68, 80, 89, 98, 102, 104, 106, 106, 110, 114, 114, 116, 124, 126, 127, 127, 129, 136, 138, 140, 140, 144, 147, 149, 158, 160, 169, 171, 175, 183, 185, 189, 191, 195 Migr 10, 21, 26, 26, 27, 28, 35, 35, 36, 39, 41, 47, 63, 72, 76, 81, 83, 85, 90, 98, 105, 109, 110, 110, 114, 123, 126, 127, 128, 131, 135, 136, 138, 148, 156, 157, 167, 172, 175, 180, 193, 198, 205, 205, 206, 207, 209, 210, 219, 221, 224 Her 3, 4, 7, 14, 26, 29, 33, 37, 37, 39, 49, 49, 56, 63, 66, 67, 68, 98, 101, 101, 105, 109, 124, 143, 161, 162, 165, 166, 168, 180, 185, 205, 206, 215, 217, 225, 225, 232, 234, 236, 246, 248, 259, 262, 264, 269, 272, 273, 280, 281, 283, 289, 293, 300, 301, 307, 307, 310, 316 Congr 3, 23, 31, 34, 41, 43, 48, 49, 50, 57, 59, 74, 76, 79, 88, 94, 96, 105, 106, 107, 121, 121, 127, 138, 166, 176, 177, 180 Fug 12, 12, 12, 13, 18, 23, 25, 27, 31, 35, 35, 36, 46, 47, 59, 63, 68, 76, 79, 82, 82, 84, 91, 95, 95, 96, 97, 97, 102, 105, 114, 119, 121, 141, 145, 149, 151, 151, 152, 159, 162, 162, 166, 166, 186, 191, 200, 204 Mut 1, 1, 3, 6, 16, 26, 26, 26, 33, 34, 42, 45, 45, 47, 51, 72, 73, 81, 97, 105, 114, 117, 123, 131, 134, 141, 143, 150, 157, 158, 160, 166, 176, 177, 180, 181, 184, 186, 186, 205, 219, 222, 225, 227, 270 Somn 1:5, 9, 13, 27, 27, 34, 34, 36, 36, 38, 42, 45, 52, 55, 66, 75, 75, 81, 84, 84, 90, 90, 100, 116, 135, 149, 155, 162, 163, 177, 179, 181, 182, 202, 217, 247, 256 Somn 2:24, 26, 40, 69, 70, 74, 86, 116, 116, 125, 136, 140, 140, 151, 152, 154, 188, 207, 217, 231, 233, 268, 274, 276, 282, 283, 292, 293, 298, 299 Abr 5, 6, 9, 16, 18, 19, 22, 30, 34, 35, 36, 37, 37, 38, 45, 46, 60, 63, 68, 69, 84, 91, 111, 117, 119, 121, 129, 134, 137, 139, 145, 158, 163, 163, 168, 174, 179, 189, 194, 209, 210, 214, 215, 222, 223, 240, 242, 247, 248, 249, 253, 253, 254, 254, 260, 261 Ios 2, 8, 12, 25, 25, 35, 37, 42, 48, 51, 56, 66, 75, 80, 82, 94, 99, 112, 114, 114, 115, 121, 121, 124, 124, 127, 132, 138, 152, 156, 158, 167, 167, 175, 178, 185, 200, 202, 206, 208, 215, 216, 223, 231, 232, 235, 241, 241, 244, 247, 258, 266 Mos 1:7, 8, 18, 29, 31, 31, 32, 54, 57, 62, 63, 65, 66, 67, 71, 77, 81, 84, 87, 91, 91, 94, 95, 116, 122, 123, 126, 128, 130, 133, 136, 139, 145, 146, 147, 149, 153, 162, 164, 164, 165, 175, 177, 177, 180, 186, 186, 189, 200, 201, 206, 217, 217, 218, 223, 228, 232, 232, 236, 236, 237, 243, 251, 258, 261, 262, 266, 269, 275, 277, 279, 280, 287, 288, 298, 301, 307, 308, 311, 314, 325, 332 Mos 2:3, 8, 10, 11, 12, 22, 27, 29, 30, 44, 44, 55, 59, 60, 60, 65, 65, 67, 91, 99, 100, 101, 107, 117, 136, 145, 160, 161, 161, 167, 172, 174, 187, 192, 193, 195, 196, 205, 213, 217, 224, 225, 228, 229, 231, 234, 235, 239, 244, 246, 246, 249, 255, 256, 263, 264, 271, 274, 274, 278, 288 Decal 6, 8, 12, 16, 27, 31, 34, 57, 58, 58, 61, 64, 64, 72, 75, 79, 91, 93, 97, 101, 114, 130, 130, 151, 158 Spec 1:13, 14, 14, 17, 19, 30, 41, 51, 55, 56, 57, 69, 97, 99, 102, 108, 114, 115, 118, 121, 125, 127, 131, 154, 154, 159, 165, 165, 167, 182, 195, 196, 199, 204, 210, 211, 215, 218, 234, 234, 235, 238, 241, 242, 244, 245, 254, 266, 274, 274, 282, 284, 286, 293, 296, 308, 309, 325, 329, 340, 343 Spec 2:4, 12, 12, 14, 16, 27, 34, 37, 39, 45, 48, 48, 54, 69, 70, 71, 74, 87, 102, 106, 109, 114, 118, 125, 133, 133, 133, 135, 142, 155, 166, 170, 171, 174, 175, 179, 186, 191, 195, 197, 201, 203, 209, 217, 225, 228, 231, 241, 248, 250, 254, 255, 256, 261, 261 Spec 3:5, 11, 14, 14, 16, 18, 21, 24, 26, 28, 30, 32, 32, 34, 39, 44, 45, 49, 61, 68, 71, 77, 78, 78, 85, 86, 91, 91, 96, 104, 105, 106, 107, 108, 110, 113, 114, 117, 117, 118, 124, 127, 136, 144, 162, 164, 165, 166, 189, 190, 191, 199, 200, 202, 205, 209 Spec 4:34, 34, 37, 44, 49, 60, 67, 87, 89, 121, 126, 131, 136, 138, 143, 144, 148, 152, 160, 171, 171, 189, 196, 213, 218, 229, 230 Virt 2, 22, 25, 38, 40, 53, 54, 55, 55, 58, 64, 70, 78, 84, 92, 98, 105, 106, 115, 116, 120, 122, 132, 133, 133, 138, 142, 143, 149, 151, 163, 166, 172, 182, 184, 184, 185, 187, 189, 189, 190, 193, 193, 198, 199, 201, 202, 202, 205, 210, 211, 218, 222, 225, 227 Praem 1, 1, 5, 22, 23, 23, 24, 32, 42, 42, 44, 46, 54, 55, 57, 58, 59, 63, 65, 68, 74, 75, 78, 79, 85, 88, 90, 91, 92, 97, 103, 108, 110, 116, 119, 119, 119, 121, 131, 135, 136, 137, 139, 141, 146, 147, 158, 159, 163, 168 Prob 3, 10, 12, 27, 37, 38, 42, 62, 66, 75, 77, 90, 91, 96, 105, 121, 125, 128, 151 Contempl 1, 5, 7, 14, 14, 24, 27, 29, 46, 52, 53, 66, 75, 78, 79, 83, 85, 86, 87 Aet 5, 5, 5, 7, 8, 13, 13, 14, 17, 21, 26, 27, 27, 30, 38, 40, 41, 42, 43, 44, 46, 52, 55, 55, 58, 60, 68, 71, 71, 74, 78, 78, 82, 84, 87, 88, 88, 89, 90, 91, 91, 92, 95, 97, 101, 102, 104, 111, 111, 114, 115, 118, 119, 121, 122, 125, 127, 136, 139, 140, 141, 141, 142, 144, 149 Flacc 3, 3, 9, 12, 18, 19, 20, 29, 29, 35, 54, 57, 62, 76, 89, 90, 94, 96, 103, 104, 108, 110, 111, 114, 114, 119, 121, 123, 124, 127, 128, 135, 140, 142, 145, 146, 147, 148, 148, 150, 154, 158, 159, 167, 169, 181, 189, 191 Legat 3, 6, 11, 13, 15, 15, 19, 24, 31, 38, 39, 54, 58, 59, 61, 62, 65, 66, 68, 71, 75, 88, 88, 91, 92, 99, 106, 110, 116, 123, 128, 136, 138, 141, 143, 149, 158, 165, 183, 187, 192, 192, 199, 201, 203, 206, 208, 215, 217, 219, 223, 232, 236, 236, 237, 238, 250, 266, 285, 285, 287, 294, 298, 306, 309, 315, 320, 323, 327, 329, 333, 336, 338, 369, 370, 372 Hypoth 6:1, 7:2, 7:19, 11:16, 11:17 Prov 1, 1, 2:6, 23, 46, 46, 50, 52, 56, 59, 60, 64, 64, 69, 71 QG 1:1, 1, 1, 1, 20, 28, 51, 74, 94, 94, 96:1, 2:5b, 5b, 13a, 16, 17c, 17c, 22, 28, 31, 34a, 34b, 64a, 64b, 64c, 65, 3:11a, 38b, 38b, 58, 58, 61, 4:51a, 51b, 153, 153, 153, 174, 180, 189, 7* QG isf 5, 10 QG (Par) 2:2, 2:3, 2:3, 2:3, 2:5, 2:5, 2:7, 2:7, 2:7, 2:7, 2:7 QE 2:3b, 4, 15a, 25b, 25c, 105 QE isf 3, 4, 21, 22, 24

γιγνώσκω (γινώσκω) (166) Opif 8, 23 Leg 1:60, 90, 100 Leg 2:79 Leg 3:103, 157 Cher 29, 40, 49, 54, 103, 118

Sacr 33, 33, 86 Det 22, 27, 56, 57 Post 13, 18, 33, 33, 37, 51, 82, 119, 124, 132, 134, 134, 143, 180 Gig 32 Deus 4, 161, 183 Plant 138, 138, 153 Ebr 19, 25, 41, 42, 42, 42, 43, 45, 78, 103, 160 Sobr 1, 5, 30 Conf 24, 27, 119, 169, 195 Migr 8, 138, 140, 195, 213 Her 18, 25, 30, 92, 100, 100, 115, 156, 206, 262, 262, 267, 267, 312 Congr 2, 24, 152, 164 Fug 46, 89, 151, 164, 165, 204 Mut 16, 21, 41, 54, 139, 140, 186, 201 Somn 1:57, 57, 58, 58, 60, 60, 212, 220, 230 Somn 2:99, 101, 134, 228 Abr 78, 222 Ios 12, 233, 251 Mos 1:15, 137, 204, 212, 212, 216, 220, 224, 259 Mos 2:164, 176, 280 Decal 45, 58, 69, 113 Spec 1:10, 17, 44, 176, 263, 264 Spec 2:9, 31, 93 Spec 4:213 Virt 53, 69, 121, 140, 215 Praem 17 Prob 21 Aet 59, 64 Flacc 6, 16, 113, 114 Legat 69, 160, 160, 218, 240, 258, 309, 349, 355, 370 QG 4:52d

γλακτοφάγος Contempl 17

γλαφυρός Gig 59 Fug 141 Spec 1:335

γλαφυρότης Sacr 44 Congr 16, 78

γλισχρολογέομαι Congr 52

γλισχρολογία Somn 1:107 Somn 2:301

γλίσχρος Migr 217 Prob 121 Flacc 130

γλισχρότης Cher 42

γλίχομαι (39) Opif 71, 166 Leg 1:30 Leg 3:9, 171 Cher 31, 45, 109 Sacr 41, 65 Det 89 Post 18 Agr 97 Ebr 124 Conf 117, 128 Her 76, 243 Fug 141 Somn 1:234 Somn 2:204 Abr 21, 103, 150, 166 Mos 1:69, 286 Mos 2:234 Decal 146 Spec 1:37, 207 Spec 2:165 Spec 3:4 Virt 30 Prob 39 Aet 37 Legat 127 Prov 2:38 QE 2:65

γλυκαίνω (13) Leg 3:173 Det 117 Post 156 Gig 25 Migr 36, 36 Congr 163, 166, 166 Fug 139 Mos 1:186 Decal 16 Spec 1:292

γλύκιος Mos 1:211

γλυκύπικρος Somn 2:150

γλυκύς (17) Opif 38, 38, 131, 131 Leg 2:32 Cher 70, 70 Ebr 112, 190 Her 208 Congr 166, 166 Fug 138, 139 Somn 1:18 Spec 4:56 Aet 104

γλυκύτης Det 118 Post 154 Congr 169

γλυπτός Leg 3:36, 36

γλυφή Fug 185 Somn 2:55 Mos 2:114, 132, 133

γλῶσσα (102) Opif 104, 104, 159 Leg 1:69 Cher 35, 105, 116 Sacr 49, 61 Det 23, 44, 92, 102, 127, 174, 175, 176 Post 93 Deus 84 Agr 53, 95 Ebr 103, 106 Sobr 28, 45 Conf 1, 9, 11, 27, 33, 36, 68, 156, 168, 189 Migr 47, 71, 81, 114 Her 11, 14, 25, 266 Congr 80, 177 Fug 85, 86 Mut 56, 178, 240, 244 Somn 1:29, 161 Somn 2:51, 132, 147, 165, 267, 267, 278, 302 Abr 20, 27, 57 Ios 121 Mos 1:84, 274 Mos 2:26, 31, 40, 97, 114, 127, 196, 200, 208, 239 Decal 32, 63, 91, 93, 159 Spec 1:53, 147, 272 Spec 2:6, 41, 49, 145, 194, 195 Spec 4:90 Virt 193 Praem 14, 143, 163 Prob 108 Legat 113, 280, 360 Prov 2:18 QG (Par) 2:3

γλωσσαλγία Mos 2:198 Spec 3:174 Flacc 33 QE 2:118

γλώσσαργος Legat 170

γνάμπτω Abr 170 Ios 26 Mos 1:182, 251 Prob 121

γνήσιος (129) Leg 2:94, 97 Sacr 21, 29, 43, 45, 58 Det 21, 21, 62, 135, 157 Post 102, 163 Gig 17, 44 Deus 4, 116, 121, 151 Agr 32 Plant 60, 71, 126 Sobr 8, 14, 14, 56 Conf 48, 69, 72, 181 Migr 86, 94 Her 19, 44, 51, 123 Congr 6, 14, 23, 35, 112 Fug 50, 152, 152, 189, 208 Mut 5, 147, 204 Somn 1:23, 53 Somn 2:22, 47, 64, 266, 272, 273 Abr 25, 110, 132, 168, 194, 194, 221, 221, 250, 254, 264 Ios 43, 59, 74, 210, 218, 258 Mos 1:15, 17, 19, 28, 32, 72, 147, 328 Mos 2:5, 139 Decal 3, 126, 128 Spec 1:309, 316 Spec 2:88 Spec 3:29 Spec 4:51, 184, 191, 203 Virt 59, 62, 75, 79, 145, 185, 224 Praem 39, 43, 57, 108, 139 Prob 3, 79, 87, 99 Contempl 72, 90 Aet 56, 83 Flacc 9, 19 Legat 24, 38, 62, 71, 195 Prov 2:22, 31 QG 4:86b QG isf 7 QE isf 7

γνόφος Post 14, 14 Gig 54 Mut 7 Mos 1:158

γνοφώδης Mos 1:176

γνώμη (233) Opif 45, 156 Leg 1:87 Leg 2:67, 108 Leg 3:53, 125, 144, 205, 232 Cher 14, 15, 16, 17, 78, 96 Sacr 26, 79, 93, 123 Det 10, 12, 50, 56, 62, 69, 96, 134, 134 Post 9, 10, 75, 80, 140, 176 Gig 37, 54, 66 Deus 22, 23, 26, 28, 29, 47, 66, 100, 120, 147, 182 Agr 178 Plant 108 Ebr 115, 123, 123, 124, 138, 138 Sobr 15, 18, 68 Conf 32, 52, 65, 150, 160 Migr 7, 25, 120, 148, 172, 184, 201, 225 Her 9, 68, 85, 99, 243 Congr 73, 121 Fug 52, 65, 86, 114, 115, 118, 119, 171, 205 Mut 10, 91, 200, 203, 243, 244 Somn 1:81, 91, 132, 191, 202 Somn 2:26, 29, 73, 91, 99, 104, 174, 185, 278, 292 Abr 6, 6, 110, 141, 168, 170, 211 Ios 15, 73, 240, 246 Mos 1:86, 150, 196, 199, 214, 235, 244, 273, 282, 285, 294 Mos 2:9, 53, 143, 154, 172, 175, 228, 231 Decal 68, 141, 177 Spec 1:30, 38, 79, 103, 203, 241, 246, 248, 259, 271, 300 Spec 2:5, 87, 88, 137, 165, 231 Spec 3:15, 19, 34, 55, 73, 86, 93, 120, 129, 141 Spec 4:34, 43, 76, 193 Virt 19, 27, 43, 56, 61, 64, 69, 71, 83, 94, 184, 202, 207, 208 Praem 54, 138 Prob 24, 27, 97, 98, 99, 132, 141 Contempl 13, 68, 71 Aet 59, 142 Flacc 16, 19, 50, 51, 134, 145 Legat 26, 39, 51, 141, 213, 219, 223, 241, 245, 246, 258, 319, 350 Hypoth 11:13 Prov 2:39, 48 QG 2:54a, 54a, 4:200b QG isf 8 QE 2:2 QE isf 5, 5, 18, 26

γνωρίζω (71) Opif 53, 153, 156 Leg 1:91 Leg 2:69 Leg 3:57, 58, 61, 100, 183 Cher 40, 59, 115, 115, 115 Sacr 20, 132 Det 56, 131, 142 Post 35, 167 Gig 3 Deus 126, 135, 161, 167 Plant 64, 66 Ebr 72, 89, 187, 187 Conf 183 Migr 13, 22, 93, 137, 213 Her 54, 246 Congr 18 Fug 38 Mut 17, 91 Somn 1:29 Somn 2:42 Abr 71, 125, 200 Ios 157, 165, 165, 193 Mos 1:59 Mos 2:124 Spec 1:42, 335 Spec 4:69 Contempl 10 Flacc 3, 96, 111, 111, 142, 144 Legat 255, 269, 269, 272 QE isf 3

γνώριμος (87) Opif 61, 149 Leg 3:9, 120 Cher 16, 16, 16, 46 Sacr 79 Det 49, 57, 79, 86 Post 12, 13, 90, 141, 148, 150, 151 Gig 25, 26 Deus 146, 148 Plant 115 Ebr 33, 42, 72, 114 Sobr 20, 35, 68 Conf 39, 119 Migr 201, 203, 224 Her 15, 81, 122, 213 Congr 122, 127 Fug 136, 160 Somn 1:87, 91, 111, 124, 173, 191 Somn 2:2 Abr 6, 19, 123, 273 Ios 90 Mos 1:1, 80 Mos 2:153, 205 Decal 82, 88, 123 Spec 1:50, 59, 319, 345 Spec 2:132, 132, 226 Spec 3:6 Spec 4:140, 162 Virt 55, 74, 218 Prob 36, 82 Contempl 63 Aet 16, 133 Flacc 3 Hypoth 11:1 QG 1:21, 4:104 QE 2:16

γνώρισμα (8) Sacr 91 Plant 118 Conf 13 Mut 91 Somn 1:21 Mos 1:59 Spec 1:33, 42

γνωριστικός Opif 154

γνωσιμαχέω Congr 53 Somn 1:32 Abr 215 Mos 1:220, 232

γνωσιμαχία Somn 2:264

γνῶσις (16) Leg 3:126 Deus 143 Migr 42 Her 91 Fug 82 Somn 1:60 Abr 268 Mos 2:218 Decal 147, 149 Spec 4:63, 64, 70, 189 Virt 178 QG 4:9* γνωστός Leg 1:56, 60, 61 Leg 3:101 Mut 8

γόης (6) Sacr 32 Her 302 Spec 1:315 Praem 25 Hypoth 6:2, 6:3

γοητεία (13) Opif 2, 165 Post 101 Plant 104, 106 Ebr 71 Somn 2:40 Mos 1:301 Decal 125 Praem 8 Legat 162 Hypoth 6:2, 11:14

γοητεύω Somn 1:220

γομόρ Congr 100

Γόμορρα Ebr 222 Somn 1:85 Somn 2:191, 192

γονάτιον Contempl 51

γονεύς (161) Opif 99, 171 Leg 1:99 Leg 3:10 Sacr 129 Det 145 Post 49, 90, 109, 181 Deus 17 Plant 146 Ebr 17, 32, 33, 35, 42, 72, 77, 80, 83, 93, 95, 131 Sobr 23 Migr 69, 116 Her 170, 172, 295 Fug 3, 29, 43, 47, 84, 88, 109 Mut 40, 147, 206, 206, 226 Somn 2:83, 128, 178 Ios 74, 187 Mos 1:9, 32 Mos 2:198, 207, 245 Decal 42, 51, 51, 106, 107, 110, 112, 116, 117, 118, 118, 119, 120, 121, 165, 166 Spec 1:101, 114, 137, 139, 139, 250, 310 Spec 2:3, 124, 125, 129, 129, 130, 131, 223, 224, 225, 225, 227, 229, 232, 233, 234, 237, 239, 240, 243, 244, 248, 254, 261 Spec 3:21, 23, 29, 67, 80, 116, 116, 131, 153, 154, 159, 168, 168 Spec 4:150, 178, 178, 178, 184 Virt 82, 114, 131, 178, 193, 194, 198, 202, 208, 208, 226 Praem 109, 134, 148, 148 Prob 10, 87, 119, 143 Contempl 18, 47, 72 Flacc 68, 148 Legat 5, 58, 115, 142, 289, 343 Hypoth 7:3, 7:8 Prov 2:3, 5 QG 1:27, 27, 74, 74, 3:52, 4:88, 88, 200b, 202a QE 2:3a

γονή (25) Opif 14, 105, 124 Leg 3:180 Cher 43 Det 102, 147 Post 176 Deus 5, 137 Ebr 211 Congr 9, 130 Mut 110, 142, 255 Somn 1:37 Abr 101, 135 Spec 1:105 Spec 3:32, 34, 39 Aet 30 Hypoth 7:7

γόνιμος (25) Opif 103, 117, 124, 133 Leg 1:9, 11, 39, 76 Leg 3:150 Det 168 Agr 30 Her 208, 211, 232 Mut 144 Somn 1:17 Mos 1:5 Decal 159 Spec 1:6 Spec 2:172, 177 Spec 3:33 Aet 97, 97 Prov 2:68

γονορρυής Leg 3:7, 7, 8 Spec 1:118

γόνυ Agr 75 Ios 219 Mos 1:271 Contempl 51

Γοργών Legat 237

γοῦν (268) Opif 25, 47, 51, 85, 85, 90, 94, 135 Leg 1:14, 41 Leg 2:32, 107 Leg 3:2, 30, 56, 63, 71, 78, 86, 118, 123, 124, 145, 149, 150, 156, 157, 186, 186, 187, 203 Cher 50, 54, 113, 130 Sacr 8, 41, 46, 86, 100, 101, 130, 135 Det 49, 59, 72, 98, 130, 145, 151, 170, 176 Post 14, 19, 25, 81, 96, 102, 105, 115, 121, 126, 166 Gig 47, 62 Deus 16, 26, 27, 92, 144 Agr 14, 23, 41, 59, 81, 123, 126, 136 Plant 80, 120, 127, 147, 154, 168 Ebr 13, 30, 31, 82, 131, 160, 177, 177, 194, 208 Sobr 4, 8, 17 Conf 70, 74, 97, 116, 159 Migr 4, 13, 17, 80, 130, 173, 206, 213, 217 Her 14, 56, 65, 239, 242, 260 Congr 54, 72, 74, 123 Fug 4, 43, 89, 143, 191 Mut 13, 14, 194, 195, 213, 215, 224, 229, 254 Somn 1:7, 19, 46, 48, 145 Somn 2:4, 23, 37, 56, 167, 212, 229, 291 Abr 136, 213 Ios 47, 86, 94, 146, 160, 249, 260 Mos 1:9, 32, 39, 49, 56, 58, 109, 159, 160, 231, 238, 239, 268, 273, 315 Mos 2:15, 52, 157, 203 Decal 72, 91, 104 Spec 1:45, 52, 60, 78, 127, 142, 157, 163, 166, 186, 254, 298, 300, 325 Spec 2:60, 62, 71, 106, 126, 199 Spec 3:4, 17, 40, 74, 96, 128, 184 Spec 4:23, 28, 67, 151, 157, 209, 215, 230 Virt 53, 59, 63, 80, 83, 106, 106, 124, 129, 133, 157, 186, 217 Praem 19 Prob 94, 99, 101, 121, 124, 131, 133, 153, 157 Contempl 1, 26, 54, 75 Aet 20, 48, 63, 76, 100, 125 Flacc 94, 129 Legat 7, 12, 18, 22, 50, 60, 131, 287, 289, 296, 298, 313, 372 Hypoth 11:3, 11:18 Prov 2:8, 49, 58 QE 2:47

γράμμα (55) Sacr 79 Deus 6 Plant 131, 173 Conf 50 Migr 85, 139, 195 Her 176, 258 Congr 58 Mut 63, 64 Somn 1:57, 202 Abr 60, 275 Ios 168 Mos 1:23, 23 Mos 2:132, 290, 292 Decal 140 Spec 1:31, 58, 336 Spec 2:159, 230, 238 Spec 3:8 Spec 4:30, 142, 161, 162 Praem 79 Prob 95, 104, 158 Contempl 28, 75, 78 Flacc 55, 108, 131 Legat 69, 195, 231, 253, 260 QG 2:15b, 15b QE 1:6, 2:19 QE isf 8

γραμματεῖος Legat 178

γραμματεύς Agr 148 Flacc 3

γραμματικός (29) Opif 126, 126 Leg 1:14, 94 Cher 105 Sacr 74 Det 18, 75, 75, 75 Ebr 49 Her 210, 282 Congr 11, 15, 74, 142, 142, 148 Mut 80, 146, 146 Somn 1:9, 205 Prob 49, 49, 51, 51, 157

γραμματιστής Ios 132

γραμματιστική Congr 148

γραμματοκύφων Flacc 20, 131

γραμμή (19) Opif 49, 49, 49, 98, 102 Agr 138 Her 131, 210 Congr 77, 144, 146, 147 Somn 1:187 Mos 2:115 Decal 24, 25, 25, 26 Contempl 51

γραφεύς (7) Leg 2:26 Cher 11 Post 141 Ebr 109 Her 169 Mos 2:205 Legat 290

γραφή (58) Opif 77 Cher 11, 104 Sacr 71 Post 38, 113 Agr 168 Ebr 11 Conf 14 Migr 34 Her 106, 159, 167, 167, 266, 286 Congr 34, 90 Fug 4 Somn 1:1 Abr 4, 11, 23, 61, 68, 121, 131, 236 Ios 87 Mos 1:158, 287 Mos 2:40, 51, 74, 84, 203 Decal 8, 37, 51 Spec 1:1, 33, 214 Spec 2:104, 134 Spec 4:55 Virt 51 Praem 65 Prob 62, 94 Flacc 185 Legat 148, 151, 276, 365 Prov 2:17 QG 2:68a, 3:3 QE 2:50a

γραφικός Opif 41 Leg 2:75 Abr 267 Decal 7, 156

γραφίς Decal 72

γράφω (108) Opif 78, 141, 163 Leg 3:198 Sacr 60 Det 141 Post 24, 80, 102, 104, 176, 179 Agr 18 Ebr 64 Sobr 68 Conf 112, 160, 197 Migr 35, 85, 110, 167 Her 20, 102, 172, 245, 250, 277, 294, 295 Congr 74, 126, 137, 148, 178 Mut 23, 48, 52, 93 Somn 1:13, 92, 95, 205, 244, 244 Somn 2:43, 49, 133, 175, 197, 205 Abr 10, 186 Mos 1:35, 300 Mos 2:14, 26, 203, 230 Decal 47, 132, 140 Spec 2:132 Spec 3:53, 62, 166 Spec 4:2, 63, 142, 160, 160, 161, 162, 163, 163, 163 Virt 193 Praem 53 Prob 19, 37, 104 Flacc 132, 134 Legat 27, 53, 92, 119, 138, 202, 207, 207, 218, 254, 260, 303, 314, 315, 315, 330, 333 Hypoth 6:9, 6:10, 11:2 Prov 2:17, 37, 37 QG 2:15b, 4:144

γρύζω Somn 2:267 Contempl 75

Γύαρα Flacc 151, 151

γυῖον Opif 104

γυμνάζω (33) Opif 63 Sacr 78, 85 Det 41, 49, 66 Gig 60 Ebr 22 Sobr 65 Conf 39 Migr 74, 199 Congr 17, 27, 180 Fug 125 Mut 81, 84, 85 Somn 1:250 Somn 2:263 Abr 96 Ios 26, 223 Mos 1:48 Spec 4:101, 111, 163 Virt 18 Praem 153 Prob 111 Aet 129 Flacc 5

γυμνασία Spec 2:98

γυμνασιαρχέω Flacc 130

γυμνασιαρχία Prob 6

γυμνασίαρχος Prov 2:44, 46, 46

γυμνάσιον (10) Opif 17 Mut 172 Somn 1:69, 129 Flacc 34, 37, 138 Legat 135 Prov 2:44, 56

γύμνασμα (9) Agr 160 Conf 75 Mut 81, 230 Abr 48 Mos 1:61, 310 Prob 88 Hypoth 11:7

γυμναστικός Spec 2:230

γυμνικός (11) Opif 78 Det 2 Plant 160 Spec 2:246 Spec 3:176 Spec 4:74 Praem 6, 11 Contempl 41 Legat 45 Hypoth 11:6

γυμνός (55) Opif 1, 24 Leg 2:22, 53, 53, 56, 57, 59, 64, 64, 70, 71 Leg 3:49, 54, 54, 55, 55 Cher 17, 31 Sacr 30, 84 Det 36 Gig 53 Deus 83, 103 Ebr 34 Sobr 32 Migr 90, 192 Fug 158 Mut 199 Somn 1:43, 98, 99 Somn 2:121, 170 Abr 102, 117, 236 Decal 77 Spec 1:63, 295, 295 Spec 2:131 Spec 4:71, 185 Praem 4, 166 Prob 43, 160 Contempl 78 Aet 67 Flacc 36 Prov 2:26, 35

γυμνοσοφισταί Abr 182 Prob 74, 93

Γυμνοσοφισταί Somn 2:56

γυμνότης Leg 2:59 Leg 3:55 Ebr 4, 6 Sobr 1

γυμνόω (15) Leg 2:53, 53, 54, 57, 59, 59, 60, 60 Leg 3:157 Cher 17 Ebr 5 Spec 1:83 Spec 3:56, 176, 176

γύμνωσις (7) Leg 2:57, 58, 59, 60, 60, 61, 64

γυναικεῖος (14) Leg 3:218 Cher 8, 50 Sacr 21 Det 28 Post 134, 166 Ebr 60 Congr 180 Fug 128, 167 Somn 2:185 Spec 1:108 Contempl 33

γυναικοκτόνος Legat 234

γυναικομανής Spec 3:79

γυναικόμορφος Spec 2:50

γυναικόω Somn 2:185 Abr 136

γυναικώδης Gig 4 Ebr 63 QE 2:3b

γυναικωνῖτις (11) Leg 3:98 Sacr 103 Agr 79 Migr 96 Somn 2:9, 9, 55, 184 Contempl 32 Legat 358 Prov 2:17

γύναιον (14) Leg 3:63 Agr 149 Somn 2:83 Abr 182 Mos 1:16, 257 Spec 3:101, 159 Virt 221 Prob 117, 119 Flacc 62, 87, 89

γύνανδρος Sacr 100 Her 274 Virt 21

γυνή (440) Opif 124, 132, 133, 133, 134, 151, 151, 153, 156, 165, 165, 167 Leg 1:13 Leg 2:14, 19, 19, 20, 38, 38, 38, 38, 44, 44, 48, 49, 50, 50, 53, 64, 73, 74 Leg 3:1, 49, 49, 50, 56, 56, 59, 60, 61, 61, 65, 66, 66, 74, 74, 85, 182, 184, 184, 185, 188, 188, 188, 198, 200, 200, 213, 217, 222, 225, 225, 234, 236, 236, 243, 244 Cher 14, 40, 40, 41, 41, 43, 50, 50, 52, 54, 60, 72 Sacr 19, 20, 28, 100, 100, 100, 101, 101, 102 Det 50 Post 33, 33, 33, 34, 35, 75, 75, 76, 76, 76, 76, 79, 109, 112, 117, 124, 124, 134, 166, 180, 181, 183 Gig 6 Deus 19, 39, 119, 121, 121, 136 Agr 80, 81, 96, 97, 148, 157, 158, 166 Plant 15, 65, 169 Ebr 54, 54, 55, 59, 73, 74, 149, 164, 193, 211, 211 Sobr 21, 23 Migr 95, 97, 99, 99, 100, 126, 141, 217 Her 47, 49, 53, 61, 139, 164, 186, 257, 258 Congr 1, 23, 23, 34, 34, 38, 41, 43, 50, 51, 71, 71, 72, 73, 73, 76, 78, 80, 137, 137, 180 Fug 3, 3, 48, 51, 55, 121, 128, 149, 151, 188, 188 Mut 61, 77, 143, 166, 226, 253 Somn 1:123, 246, 247 Somn 2:106 Abr 31, 93, 98, 99, 101, 108, 109, 112, 132, 136, 137, 245, 248, 253, 255, 255, 260, 267 Ios 40, 43, 45, 46, 52, 52, 56, 60, 60, 64, 66, 80, 232, 261, 269 Mos 1:8, 51, 59, 85, 134, 147, 147, 179, 180, 180, 296, 296, 300, 305, 311, 330, 330, 331 Mos 2:64, 64, 68, 136, 236, 240, 247, 256, 256, 256 Decal 32, 42, 45, 124, 126, 128, 151 Spec 1:9, 11, 56, 56, 104, 109, 124, 138, 144, 201, 201, 211, 281, 316, 323, 325 Spec 2:24, 24, 30, 30, 32, 33, 43, 56, 124, 133, 135, 139, 139, 146, 207 Spec 3:9, 11, 12, 14, 21, 26, 26, 26, 30, 31, 31, 32, 34, 41, 43, 45, 48, 49, 51, 53, 54, 55, 56, 59, 59, 62, 63, 72, 80, 82, 108, 113, 169, 170, 171, 172, 173, 174, 174, 175, 176, 176, 178 Spec 4:142, 178, 203, 218, 223, 225 Virt 18, 19, 21, 30, 35, 36, 38, 39, 42, 43, 110, 115, 139, 199, 207, 220 Praem 109, 139, 146 Prob 10, 35, 115, 140, 151 Contempl 6, 18, 32, 47, 59, 59, 68, 69, 83, 87, 87, 88 Aet 41, 65, 66, 69 Flacc 14, 68, 95 Legat 14, 39, 39, 59, 61, 65, 104, 116, 121, 124, 135, 136, 208, 227, 230, 234, 308, 319 Hypoth 7:3, 7:5, 7:7, 7:8, 7:14, 11:14, 11:14, 11:17 Prov 2:26, 27 QG 1:27, 27, 27, 28, 28, 29, 2:26a, 26a, 48, 71b, 3:18, 21, 24, 58, 4:145, 145 QG isf 10 QE 2:3b, 3b QE isf 22

γυρόω Spec 2:172 Virt 156

γωνία (7) Opif 97, 97 Plant 121 Mos 2:78, 79, 80 QG (Par) 2:2

Δ

δ QG 2:5a QG (Par) 2:5

Δαβίδ Conf 149

δᾳδουχέω Ebr 168 Her 311

δᾳδοῦχος Her 311

δαιδαλεύομαι Somn 2:53

Δαιδάλος Spec 3:44

δαιμονάω Det 46

δαιμόνιον Mos 1:276

δαιμόνιος Prob 112 Aet 47, 64, 76

δαίμων (15) Gig 6, 16, 16 Somn 1:141 Decal 54 Virt 172 Prob 39, 130 Flacc 168, 179 Legat 65, 112 Hypoth 6:1, 6:9 Prov 2:8

δαΐς Gig 25 Aet 33

δακετόν Sobr 46

δάκνω (28) Opif 157 Leg 2:8, 77, 81, 81, 84, 84, 85, 85, 87, 93, 94, 99, 99 Gig 35 Agr 94, 95, 98, 106, 107, 109, 109 Ebr 223 Sobr 46 Migr 210 Somn 2:88 Spec 3:103 Contempl 40

δάκρυ Ios 256 Flacc 87

δακρυόεις Migr 156

δάκρυον (19) Opif 123 Leg 1:13 Migr 157, 157, 157, 157 Abr 174 Ios 23, 175, 200, 238 Prob 153 Flacc 9, 157 Legat 186, 187, 223, 228, 243

δακρυρροέω Ios 219 Mos 2:291

δακρύω (11) Migr 155, 156 Her 310 Somn 1:10 Ios 175 Mos 1:10, 15, 39, 138 Mos 2:225 Legat 275

δακτύλιος (7) Opif 141 Deus 43 Migr 97 Fug 150 Mut 135 Somn 2:44 Ios 149

δακτυλοδεικτέω Flacc 153

δάκτυλος (13) Cher 81 Deus 168 Plant 160 Migr 85, 85 Somn 2:70 Mos 1:112, 218 Spec 1:231 Contempl 40, 77 Aet 143 Prov 2:65

δαμάζω (6) Opif 111 Leg 2:104, 104 Ebr 221 Congr 158 Abr 170

δάμαλις Her 106, 125 Spec 1:268

Δαμασκός Her 2, 54, 58, 61

Δάν (14) Leg 2:94, 94, 94, 94, 94, 96, 97 Agr 94, 95, 99, 100, 107, 109 Somn 2:35

δανείζω (24) Post 5, 142 Migr 10 Her 282 Somn 1:92, 95, 98, 100, 100 Decal 31, 95 Spec 2:74, 74, 77, 168, 183 Virt 82, 86, 89 Praem 106, 107 Prob 35 Aet 29 Legat 344

δάνειον (15) Post 142 Migr 11, 91 Her 104, 282 Mos 2:63 Decal 167 Spec 2:39 Spec 4:30, 30 Virt 83, 89, 122 Legat 275, 343

δάνεισμα Post 5

δανειστής (15) Plant 101 Somn 1:93, 95, 96, 98, 100 Spec 2:72, 75, 122, 122 Spec 3:204 Virt 89, 123 Praem 106 Legat 13

δαπανάω (17) Ios 14, 27 Mos 2:106, 108, 157 Decal 173 Spec 1:267 Spec 4:26 Praem 153 Prob 119 Aet 91, 93, 123, 125 Flacc 71, 174 Prov 2:40

δαπάνη (8) Det 20 Deus 163 Praem 128 Prob 86 Flacc 61, 130 Legat 198 Prov 2:46

δαπάνημα Somn 2:57

δαπανηρός Mos 1:68

Δαρδανίς Prob 115

δᾴς δαΐς

δασμός (25) Opif 85 Migr 204 Somn 2:116, 132 Abr 226, 237 Ios 135 Mos 1:28, 152 Decal 163 Spec 1:143 Spec 2:92, 205, 247 Spec 3:163 Spec 4:12, 113, 212, 213, 214, 218, 228 Virt 154 Praem 156 Flacc 133

δασύς (10) Opif 121 Leg 1:14 Leg 2:59 Leg 3:2 Migr 153, 153, 154, 158 Abr 138 Mos 1:14

δατέομαι Migr 164 Abr 227 QG 4:8a

δάφνη Somn 2:62

δαψίλεια Legat 253

δαψιλής Mos 1:11 QE 2:71

δέ (11509) passim

Δεβών Leg 3:225, 233

δέησις (8) Cher 47 Post 169 Spec 3:68 Legat 227, 239, 276, 290, 331

δεητικός Spec 2:196 Legat 303

δεῖ δέω

δεῖγμα (60) Opif 87, 130, 157, 161, 163 Sacr 120, 139 Deus 10 Agr 135, 152 Plant 40, 61, 121 Migr 190 Her 129, 195, 289 Fug 206 Mut 224 Somn 1:25 Somn 2:32, 98, 171, 265 Abr 114, 141, 245, 255 Ios 51, 106, 149, 170 Mos 1:188, 226 Mos 2:29, 124, 189 Decal 29, 63 Spec 1:86, 154, 202, 279 Spec 2:161 Spec 3:61, 137 Spec 4:196 Virt 52, 66, 80, 101 Prob 84, 91 Flacc 2, 4, 78 Legat 100, 317, 332 QE 2:14

δείδω (65) Leg 3:15, 128 Cher 15, 24, 130 Sacr 26, 28 Deus 64, 166 Ebr 179 Her 20, 24, 28 Fug 14, 24 Mut 22, 217 Somn 1:107 Somn 2:90, 122 Abr 95, 126, 228, 232, 247 Ios 15, 48, 129, 225, 232, 261 Mos 1:8, 26, 36, 84, 227, 291 Mos 2:169, 197 Spec 2:213, 240, 241 Spec 3:33 Spec 4:40 Virt 37, 48, 56, 63, 114 Praem 86 Prob 101, 118, 121, 154 Aet 11, 108 Flacc 12, 181 Legat 33, 133, 249, 256, 262, 293 QG 1:74

δείκνυμι (89) Opif 49, 60 Leg 1:2 Leg 3:60, 102, 106, 121, 121, 206 Cher 90 Det 19, 27, 31, 128, 163, 177 Post 65 Deus 1, 81, 109 Agr 108 Plant 165 Ebr 93, 106, 110, 157, 220 Conf 81, 81, 138 Migr 1, 36, 36, 40, 42, 43, 43, 44, 183 Her 72, 121, 214, 225, 225, 226, 277, 298 Congr 163 Mut 58, 58, 207, 237, 264 Somn 1:79, 168, 185 Abr 79, 256, 276 Ios 17 Mos 1:71, 90, 185, 285 Mos 2:56, 105, 121, 246 Spec 2:176, 224 Prob 147 Aet 19, 24, 49, 52, 53, 88, 90, 105 Flacc 111 Legat 31, 194 QG 1:41, 68, 69, 100:2b, 4:100 QG (Par) 2:4 QE 2:47

δεικτικός QG 1:1

δείλαιος Sacr 71 Agr 75 Flacc 68, 167 Legat 61

δείλη (7) Leg 3:43 Spec 1:169, 256 Flacc 27, 110 Legat 269 Hypoth 7:13

δειλία (41) Opif 73, 79 Leg 1:68, 68, 86 Leg 2:18 Leg 3:54 Sacr 15 Det 37, 51 Deus 112, 163, 164 Agr 17, 154 Ebr 115, 116 Conf 21, 52, 90 Her 209, 245 Mut 197 Abr 24 Mos 1:233, 325 Spec 1:214 Spec 3:88 Spec 4:146 Virt 24, 25, 26 Praem 52, 148 Prob 21, 56, 159 Legat 90 Prov 2:8 QG 4:204 QE isf 32

δειλινός Her 174, 199

δειλός (8) Leg 1:86 Leg 2:18 Sacr 32 Deus 170 Mut 153 Mos 1:236 Virt 23 Prov 2:65

δειματόω Decal 145 Flacc 176

δεῖνα (11) Deus 170 Mut 79 Ios 77, 77 Spec 2:16, 16, 16 Prob 46, 46 Prov 2:21, 21

Δεῖνα Migr 223 Mut 194, 194

δεινός (114) Leg 1:74 Leg 3:224, 232 Cher 2, 15, 78, 82, 116 Det 43, 99, 113, 131 Post 137 Agr 46 Plant 24, 80 Ebr 16, 219 Sobr 40 Conf 5, 29, 48, 65, 76, 193 Migr 74, 125 Her 60, 251, 268, 297 Congr 165 Mut 172 Somn 1:104, 220 Somn 2:82, 88 Abr 188, 193 Ios 7, 49, 83, 137, 140, 214 Mos 1:45, 101, 122, 138, 181, 210, 263, 301, 325, 329, 330 Mos 2:27, 164 Decal 72, 72, 109, 125 Spec 2:27, 75 Spec 3:44, 62, 111, 114, 137, 147, 158 Spec 4:39, 120, 145 Virt 31, 141 Praem 76, 78, 78, 88, 97, 143, 143, 146 Prob 34, 156 Contempl 1 Aet 10, 66, 84, 149 Flacc 62, 96, 114, 135, 143, 146 Legat 33, 39, 57, 123, 162, 196, 217, 222, 263 Hypoth 11:14 Prov 2:8, 24, 38, 56, 69 QG isf 12 QG (Par) 2:7

δεινότης (9) Cher 105 Agr 143 Fug 82, 82 Somn 2:283 Praem 97 Contempl 31, 75 Hypoth 6:4

δεῖξις (6) Det 31 Ebr 94 Conf 138 Migr 5, 35 Her 66

δειπνοθήρας Somn 2:51

δεῖπνον (6) Opif 78 Leg 3:156 Contempl 83 Legat 310, 344 Prov 2:29

δειπνοποιέω Abr 233

δειρή (δέρη) Prob 116

δεισιδαιμονέω Somn 1:230

δεισιδαιμονία (10) Sacr 15 Det 24 Gig 16 Deus 103, 163, 164 Plant 107 Mut 138 Spec 4:147 Praem 40

δεισιδαίμων Cher 42 Det 18

δέκα (58) Opif 104, 105 Deus 119 Plant 124 Sobr 19 Her 167, 168 Congr 71, 111, 113, 113, 114, 116, 118, 119, 120 Mut 23 Somn 2:33 Ios 163, 167, 268 Mos 1:96, 234, 236 Mos 2:83, 84, 85, 86, 91 Decal 27, 30, 32, 36, 50, 154, 175, 176 Spec 1:1, 177, 181, 184, 189 Spec 2:1, 41 Spec 3:7 Spec 4:41, 78, 105, 106, 132, 133, 133, 134 Praem 2 Aet 65 Flacc 92, 113 Legat 138

δεκάδαρχος Congr 110

δεκαετία Congr 81, 88, 121

δεκάζω (9) Conf 126, 141 Her 71 Congr 27, 27 Ios 142 Spec 1:277 Prob 11 Prov 2:8

δεκαπλασιάζω Migr 169

δεκαπλάσιος QG (Par) 2:5, 2:5, 2:5

δεκάς (63) Opif 47, 47, 47, 91, 91, 95, 99, 99, 102 Leg 1:15, 15, 15 Sacr 122 Post 48, 97, 173, 173, 173 Plant 123, 123, 124, 125, 125, 125 Congr 88, 89, 90, 91, 94, 109, 109, 111, 116, 119 Fug 186 Mut 2, 228, 228 Abr 244 Mos 1:97 Mos 2:79, 84, 84 Decal 20, 22, 23, 24, 26, 27, 27, 27, 29 Spec 1:178 Spec 2:40, 40, 40, 41, 201 Spec 4:105 QG 1:77, 2:5a, 12a QG (Par) 2:5

δέκατος (51) Opif 103, 104 Leg 2:52 Leg 3:174 Post 48, 95, 96 Congr 90, 92, 93, 94, 95, 95, 95, 95, 98, 99, 99, 100, 101, 102, 102, 103, 103, 105, 105, 105, 106, 106, 106, 106, 107, 107 Mut 2, 191, 191, 192, 192, 234, 245 Mos 1:134 Spec 1:156, 157, 186, 256 Spec 2:41, 200, 200 Virt 95 QG isf 17, 17

δεκατρεῖς QG 3:61

δεκτικός Det 99 Mut 211 Aet 22

δελεάζω (31) Opif 165, 166 Agr 103 Ebr 50 Migr 29, 150 Her 71, 93, 274, 304 Congr 77 Fug 189 Mut 116 Somn 1:218 Somn 2:101 Mos 1:171, 268 Spec 1:29, 155 Spec 3:29 Spec 4:81, 100 Virt 40 Praem 25 Prob 31, 159 Contempl 18, 18, 63 Legat 180 Hypoth 11:15

δέλεαρ (23) Post 72 Deus 168 Agr 16 Plant 102, 103 Ebr 70, 165 Sobr 23 Fug 33, 39, 151, 155 Mut 172 Somn 2:51 Ios 213 Mos 1:295 Spec 1:314 Spec 2:74 Spec 4:43, 67 Aet 56 Legat 28, 345

δέλτος (7) Spec 2:242, 262 Spec 3:7, 7, 8 Legat 276 QG 2:15b

δελφάκιον Prob 121

Δελφικός Legat 69

Δελφοί Post 113 Prov 2:33

δέμω (6) Abr 173 Mos 1:277 Mos 2:72 Spec 1:21 Spec 2:119 Virt 28

δενδρῖτις Spec 4:215

δένδρον (106) Opif 38, 40, 41, 43, 153, 154, 154 Leg 1:49, 56 Cher 102, 111 Sacr 125 Det 107, 108 Gig 4 Deus 91 Agr 6, 8, 10, 11, 12, 14, 17, 158 Plant 3, 24, 28, 32, 33, 44, 46, 74, 74, 74, 85, 96, 103, 106, 119, 135, 136, 137 Ebr 106, 174, 224 Sobr 36, 65 Her 270 Mut 73, 140, 162, 165 Somn 1:58 Somn 2:64 Abr 45 Mos 1:22, 119, 189, 192, 224, 226, 228 Mos 2:22, 186, 222 Decal 161, 162 Spec 1:74, 172, 172, 254 Spec 2:105, 143, 153, 205, 207 Spec 4:22, 81, 208, 208, 209, 209, 209, 227 Virt 6, 81, 156, 157, 160 Praem 41, 129, 141 Prob 70, 70 Aet 35, 35, 57, 63, 75, 96, 100, 132, 133 Prov 2:70 QG 4:51b QE 1:1

δενδροτομέω Spec 4:226 Virt 149 Contempl 15 Legat 132

δενδροτομία Spec 2:191 Virt 150 Legat 17

δενδροφόρος Abr 138 Legat 249

δενδρόω Somn 2:170

δεξιόομαι (17) Leg 2:18 Leg 3:93 Plant 45 Ebr 176, 209 Sobr 29, 68 Her 41 Mut 242 Somn 1:119 Somn 2:69 Ios 182, 257 Spec 3:178, 180 Legat 181, 352

δεξιός (49) Opif 122 Leg 1:4 Leg 2:20 Leg 3:90 Cher 21, 37 Post 101, 102 Deus 73, 145, 162, 162, 163, 163, 163, 175 Sobr 27 Conf 139 Migr 146 Her 151, 176, 209 Somn 1:26 Somn 2:67, 126 Abr 124, 176, 224, 224 Ios 229, 238 Mos 1:270, 294 Mos 2:78, 150, 151, 291 Decal 31 Spec 1:145 Spec 4:32 Virt 67 Contempl 30, 69, 77 Legat 95, 95, 104, 177, 181

δεξιότης Fug 31 Somn 1:110 Abr 208 Ios 249 Mos 2:151

δεξίωσις Deus 79 Her 40 Mos 1:275

δέον δέω

δεόντως (56) Opif 98 Leg 1:104 Leg 2:76, 105 Leg 3:77, 131 Cher 14, 14, 15, 128 Sacr 68 Det 103 Post 100 Deus 48 Agr 118 Ebr 14, 106 Sobr 32, 49 Conf 145 Migr 48 Her 281, 313 Congr 56, 179 Fug 33, 135 Mut 204 Somn 1:70 Abr 5, 202 Ios 58 Mos 1:129, 157 Mos 2:7, 17, 125 Decal 36, 76, 113 Spec 1:150, 192, 197 Spec 2:59 Spec 3:119, 155, 181 Spec 4:150 Aet 44, 49, 54, 138 Flacc 40 Legat 103, 149 QG 4:76b

δέος (42) Leg 1:84 Sacr 33 Plant 3 Migr 170 Her 3, 23, 23 Abr 186, 188 Ios 9, 189 Mos 1:46, 77, 91, 178, 263 Mos 2:251 Spec 1:120 Spec 2:4, 55 Spec 3:29, 102, 126, 159, 166 Spec 4:6 Virt 23 Praem 18, 21 Prob 22, 128 Flacc 47, 89, 115 Legat 66, 74, 128, 194, 325, 334 Prov 2:26, 29 δέρη δειρή

δέρμα Cher 79 Sacr 139 Sobr 49 Mut 107

δερμάτινος Leg 3:69, 69 Post 137, 180 Conf 55

δέρω Sacr 84

δεσμεύω Somn 2:6, 17, 33

δέσμιος Flacc 74

δεσμός (61) Opif 131 Leg 2:57, 72 Sacr 36, 81 Det 103, 103, 158 Deus 35, 47 Agr 36 Plant 9 Ebr 152 Conf 136, 166, 166, 167 Migr 181, 220 Her 23, 23, 68, 137, 188, 242, 246, 273 Fug 112 Mut 240 Somn 1:181 Ios 179, 179, 187, 188, 193, 195 Mos 1:38 Mos 2:86 Spec 1:52, 137, 317 Spec 3:181 Spec 4:168 Virt 78 Praem 56, 81 Prob 18 Aet 13, 30, 36, 75, 125, 129, 137 Legat 14, 72, 146, 324 Hypoth 7:2, 7:7 QG (Par) 2:4

δεσμωτήριον (19) Leg 3:21, 42 Deus 111, 113 Ebr 101, 208 Migr 9 Her 85, 109 Mut 173 Somn 1:22, 139 Ios 80, 98, 104, 154, 270 Aet 47 Legat 368

δεσμώτης (8) Deus 112 Ebr 101 Ios 85, 89, 123, 244, 247 Legat 340

δεσμῶτις Deus 115

δεσπόζω (12) Opif 148 Leg 2:107 Plant 55, 72 Sobr 63 Conf 91, 133 Migr 185 Mut 24 Somn 2:100 Abr 84 QE 2:105

δέσποινα (37) Leg 3:146, 202 Cher 71, 115 Sacr 72 Deus 48 Agr 58 Sobr 57 Migr 18 Her 42 Congr 14, 23, 37, 73, 74, 77, 154 Fug 5, 206 Somn 1:27 Ios 45, 51, 52, 71 Mos 1:184, 191 Spec 2:16 Spec 4:82, 82 Virt 130, 181, 223 Praem 117 Contempl 37 Prov 2:17 QG 3:29 QG (Par) 2:7

δεσποτεία (15) Opif 167 Leg 3:192 Cher 69, 75 Deus 114 Agr 47 Migr 186 Her 186 Ios 70 Mos 1:39 Spec 2:81, 233 Spec 4:113 Praem 137 QE isf 30

δεσπότης (220) Opif 83, 85, 142, 165, 165 Leg 1:95, 96 Leg 2:63, 83, 104 Leg 3:9, 84, 88, 156, 156, 194, 194, 194, 195, 199, 213, 224 Cher 61, 83, 107, 118, 119 Sacr 58, 117 Det 56, 56 Post 68, 109, 109, 138, 184 Gig 45, 46 Deus 47, 64, 159 Plant 53, 56, 90, 91, 101 Ebr 122, 122, 131, 198 Sobr 55, 55, 69 Conf 170 Migr 169 Her 2, 6, 7, 9, 22, 22, 22, 23, 23, 24, 27, 100, 273 Fug 3, 20 Mut 19, 21, 46 Somn 1:7 Somn 2:108, 133, 295 Abr 116, 213, 213, 228 Ios 35, 36, 37, 40, 45, 46, 47, 47, 52, 66, 66, 69, 71, 76, 79, 80, 92, 104, 123, 150, 199, 213, 219, 222 Mos 1:36, 156, 201, 271, 324 Mos 2:22, 239 Decal 61, 114, 165, 166, 167 Spec 1:24, 126, 126, 126, 127 Spec 2:67, 83, 90, 106, 109, 113, 122, 122, 219, 226, 227, 233, 234, 241 Spec 3:5, 137, 141, 142, 145, 146, 148, 195, 197, 203 Spec 4:7, 15, 17, 89, 152, 153, 186 Virt 59, 96, 115, 124, 124 Praem 86, 89, 137, 138, 164 Prob 17, 19, 35, 38, 40, 45, 79, 100, 101, 104, 136, 159 Contempl 9, 19 Flacc 23, 26, 69, 96, 121, 126, 127 Legat 13, 105, 119, 119, 121, 122, 166, 168, 169, 173, 178, 183, 208, 218, 222, 233, 237, 239, 247, 271, 276, 285, 286, 290, 301, 314, 321, 326, 355 Hypoth 7:8, 7:14 Prov 2:2, 8, 62 QG 2:16, 4:206b

δεσποτικός (20) Cher 3 Det 56 Plant 90 Mut 24 Somn 2:294 Abr 45, 129 Ios 67 Mos 2:50 Spec 1:127, 128 Spec 2:93 Spec 3:163 Virt 114, 124 Praem 130, 137 Prob 156, 158 Legat 350

δεσπότις Spec 1:269

Δευκαλίων Praem 23

δεῦρο Det 5, 10 Conf 65, 72, 72

δεῦτε (6) Conf 1, 1, 1, 107, 168, 182

δευτερεῖος (46) Opif 45, 148 Leg 3:93, 94 Sacr 72, 88 Deus 12 Agr 121 Plant 26, 27, 132 Ebr 35, 35, 87 Conf 148 Migr 160, 161, 205 Congr 39, 51 Fug 208 Mut 195 Somn 1:116, 132 Somn 2:43, 46 Abr 26, 38, 39 Ios 120, 138, 148, 148, 187 Decal 50 Spec 1:17, 38, 289 Spec 2:175, 235 Virt 176, 210 Prob 135 Legat 71 Prov 2:9 QG 1:60:2

δευτερεύω Leg 2:81 Leg 3:197 Abr 64, 64, 150

Δευτερονόμιον Leg 3:174 Deus 50

δεύτερος (235) Opif 37, 41, 79, 82, 92, 102, 102, 103, 137, 141, 157, 171 Leg 1:10, 33, 39, 63, 68, 70, 71, 71, 71, 71, 81, 103 Leg 2:5, 24, 36, 45, 80, 86 Leg 3:26, 52, 80, 94, 94, 115, 128, 132, 177, 177, 191 Sacr 132 Det 145 Post 75, 94, 142, 145, 173 Deus 110 Agr 178 Plant 156, 165 Ebr 107, 163, 201, 201 Conf 124, 148, 156 Migr 26, 53, 101 Her 10, 59, 59, 104, 169, 251, 295, 299 Congr 22, 51, 106 Fug 51, 73, 87, 95, 206 Mut 48, 78, 102, 240 Somn 1:1, 2, 5, 44, 44, 51, 62, 72, 79, 104, 116, 180 Somn 2:2, 3, 69 Abr 5, 17, 85, 123, 128 Ios 112, 175, 175, 185, 187, 216 Mos 1:36, 58, 102, 188, 220, 237, 261 Mos 2:46, 47, 60, 65, 190, 191, 222, 222, 231, 231, 243, 263 Decal 10, 21, 21, 39, 82, 82, 84, 103, 106, 132, 135, 139, 156, 170, 175 Spec 1:5, 32, 38, 45, 74, 94, 108, 109, 111, 127, 134, 156, 159, 178, 217, 242, 250 Spec 2:34, 41, 56, 87, 135, 138, 169, 181, 196, 239, 262 Spec 3:8, 30, 129, 130, 162 Spec 4:1, 5, 35, 41, 54, 62, 138, 175, 176, 211, 236 Virt 113, 129, 130, 149, 176, 213 Praem 15, 22, 98, 166 Aet 33, 41, 65 Flacc 1, 86, 149 Legat 32, 75, 187, 278, 286, 318, 356 Hypoth 6:8 Prov 2:54 QG 1:55a, 60:2, 64c, 77, 2:11, 13a, 16, 17c, 31, 31, 39, 62, 71a, 3:8, 12, 18, 4:8b QG isf 5 QG (Par) 2:2, 2:7 QE 2:2, 18, 46 QE isf 14

δεχάς Decal 23

δέχομαι (178) Opif 6, 18, 20, 22, 23, 86, 123, 151, 165, 166 Leg 1:37, 37, 61, 61, 61, 79 Leg 2:83 Leg 3:183 Cher 5, 29, 43, 46, 72, 75, 82 Sacr 60, 61, 69, 83, 84, 101, 127, 137, 138 Det 10, 15, 15, 46, 87, 92, 96, 100, 103, 127, 127, 136, 156 Post 26, 45, 104, 142, 146, 148, 151, 176, 178 Gig 38 Deus 43, 47, 48, 79, 88, 96 Agr 16, 21, 36, 113, 132 Plant 19, 28, 111, 114 Ebr 32, 32, 111, 137, 148, 178, 206, 214 Conf 23, 87, 106 Migr 121, 130 Her 75, 123, 125, 136, 139, 149, 156, 181, 185, 187, 242, 295, 309 Congr 9, 42, 104, 135 Fug 91, 201 Mut 3, 30, 31, 55, 88, 111, 141, 150, 181, 203, 218 Somn 1:124, 129, 177 Somn 2:176, 200, 203, 248 Abr 129 Ios 12, 20, 179 Mos 1:52, 57 Mos 2:150, 196, 241 Decal 23, 39 Spec 1:43, 45, 199, 214, 216, 217, 271 Spec 2:201, 240 Spec 3:89 Spec 4:107, 140, 221 Virt 107, 143, 203 Praem 163 Prob 4, 13, 130 Aet 6, 6, 18, 24, 37, 40, 43, 82, 102, 106, 131 Legat 153, 212, 214, 232, 237 Hypoth 7:5, 7:5, 7:17 Prov 2:7 QG 2:74, 3:26 QG (Par) 2:3, 2:3 QE 1:1

δέω (δεῖ) (591) Opif 7, 13, 14, 23, 49, 72, 75, 82, 83, 88, 105, 113, 114, 139, 143, 146, 169 Leg 1:26, 26, 37, 51, 70, 76, 83, 94, 94, 94, 103, 103, 104 Leg 2:17, 24, 40, 66, 72, 76 Leg 3:73, 120, 129, 136, 136, 144, 145, 165, 175, 183, 205, 222, 224, 241, 244 Cher 14, 44, 52, 55, 78, 87, 97, 109, 119, 125, 126 Sacr 35, 44, 49, 53, 60, 69, 77, 79, 89, 91, 92, 92, 98, 99, 123 Det 11, 54, 55, 59, 99, 138, 154 Post 26, 49, 50, 65, 84, 94, 101, 110, 137, 141, 142, 142, 142, 142, 142, 162, 185 Gig 4 Deus 19, 30, 40, 56, 56, 58, 59, 59, 61, 63, 100,

107, 154 Agr 31, 69, 85, 123, 129, 130, 151, 157, 160, 176 Plant 35, 51, 66, 83, 101, 115, 128, 133, 162 Ebr 12, 18, 38, 48, 86, 86, 111, 129, 158, 180, 195, 215 Sobr 6, 39 Conf 3, 13, 54, 103, 144, 164, 175, 179, 182 Migr 3, 25, 75, 77, 89, 102, 105, 105, 105, 105, 130, 140, 152, 154, 169, 181, 184, 197 Her 5, 14, 25, 32, 101, 188, 196, 199, 212, 226, 253, 287 Congr 3, 35, 36, 70, 80, 93, 96, 157 Fug 27, 62, 64, 98, 98, 123, 168, 169, 170, 172, 189 Mut 8, 13, 33, 45, 75, 91, 140, 153, 182, 201, 235, 237, 238, 248, 248, 258 Somn 1:54, 105, 112, 142, 143, 238 Somn 2:4, 27, 42, 54, 58, 60, 61, 61, 63, 85, 87, 102, 109, 128, 150, 188, 206, 265, 275, 288, 301 Abr 26, 32, 41, 51, 51, 167, 189, 259 Ios 25, 38, 45, 59, 72, 76, 115, 117, 143, 171, 171, 173, 175, 177, 179, 184, 193, 205, 210, 222, 227, 239, 243, 244, 261, 263, 265 Mos 1:3, 5, 6, 18, 58, 59, 63, 87, 95, 117, 157, 160, 208, 220, 261, 273, 274, 274, 274, 286, 314, 322, 325, 325, 331 Mos 2:5, 59, 66, 68, 74, 141, 150, 159, 166, 173, 183, 185, 187, 187, 187, 194, 200, 201, 227, 231, 243, 259, 274 Decal 6, 15, 17, 29, 32, 37, 44, 70, 77, 94, 100, 101, 113, 116, 123, 124, 157 Spec 1:27, 34, 42, 67, 108, 116, 123, 125, 131, 137, 154, 158, 163, 168, 177, 188, 189, 220, 221, 229, 229, 243, 254, 255, 262, 266, 271, 277, 279, 283, 301, 302 Spec 2:6, 14, 23, 36, 70, 91, 111, 112, 114, 121, 134, 154, 163, 165, 174, 176, 181, 190, 204, 240, 246, 247, 248, 262 Spec 3:7, 25, 59, 79, 119, 147, 149, 149, 150, 156, 171, 178, 200, 205 Spec 4:2, 33, 37, 38, 43, 48, 50, 55, 61, 64, 66, 69, 84, 94, 108, 119, 132, 132, 133, 137, 158, 159, 184, 186, 196, 201, 203, 207, 229, 231 Virt 12, 17, 23, 29, 31, 33, 50, 61, 69, 83, 97, 98, 102, 106, 122, 127, 133, 154, 155, 205, 223 Praem 14, 46, 47, 49, 54, 55, 55, 55, 70, 80, 81, 112, 162 Prob 23, 30, 33, 64, 68, 113 Contempl 1, 13, 21, 44, 80 Aet 13, 30, 40, 40, 47, 56, 56, 58, 71, 82, 83, 90, 107 Flacc 22, 31, 44, 71, 74, 83, 92, 93, 94, 97, 111, 115, 125, 156, 182 Legat 5, 38, 43, 81, 95, 101, 101, 102, 103, 114, 116, 125, 149, 154, 197, 206, 214, 234, 239, 248, 253, 275, 279, 290, 301, 324, 329, 329, 340 Hypoth 7:2, 7:6, 7:11, 7:11, 7:17, 7:19, 7:19 Prov 1, 2:1, 18, 22, 58, 60 QG 1:3, 20, 64a, 64c, 96:1, 2:26b, 62, 65, 3:23, 52, 4:69, 81, 110a, 130, 191c QG isf 10 QG (Par) 2:7 QE 1:19, 2:1, 14 QE isf 3, 4, 5, 8, 14, 16, 19

δή (476) Opif 8, 19, 36, 42, 54, 55, 55, 56, 68, 69, 74, 88, 92, 97, 104, 113, 117, 141, 144 Leg 1:1, 11, 14, 23, 24, 26, 27, 45, 63, 71, 71, 72, 82, 90 Leg 2:30, 50, 52, 57, 69, 93, 93, 98, 106 Leg 3:3, 4, 13, 76, 99, 99, 104, 111, 113, 178, 202, 205, 211, 218, 240 Cher 25, 29, 58, 77, 85, 91, 121 Sacr 1, 16, 34, 38, 60, 88, 90, 125, 128 Det 33, 49, 50, 68, 73, 78, 85, 91, 95, 99, 109, 111, 137, 165, 168, 176 Post 13, 45, 71, 85, 132, 160 Gig 1, 19, 28, 37 Deus 2, 15, 19, 20, 34, 35, 36, 44, 53, 57, 68, 81, 129, 154, 168 Agr 18, 34, 51, 67, 76, 77, 116, 159 Plant 7, 7, 11, 12, 39, 46, 53, 89, 94, 103, 104, 105, 129, 160, 163, 165, 177 Ebr 16, 23, 33, 33, 39, 83, 104, 108, 110, 125, 142, 150, 156, 175, 191, 192, 206, 211, 212, 218 Sobr 6, 24, 44, 46, 58, 59, 62, 64 Conf 1, 14, 16, 38, 52, 73, 156, 171, 180 Migr 12, 17, 21, 51, 59, 118, 139, 187 Her 15, 23, 24, 74, 76, 111, 231, 232, 249, 268, 306 Congr 19, 23, 63, 68, 100, 101, 106, 112, 117, 146 Fug 8, 11, 18, 23, 33, 71, 81, 97, 129, 154, 169 Mut 26, 39, 61, 69, 73, 88, 105, 110, 145, 156, 161, 203, 208, 243 Somn 1:14, 21, 25, 29, 33, 39, 66, 102, 115, 128, 133, 148, 162, 165, 189, 196, 198, 204, 207, 219, 225 Somn 2:8, 8, 10, 14, 17, 32, 70, 145, 155, 182, 219, 253, 256, 261, 274, 300 Abr 45, 46, 163, 197, 199, 203, 224, 249 Ios 6, 17, 25, 43, 44, 80, 117, 173, 183 Mos 1:40, 46, 52, 73, 79, 95, 124, 142, 143, 143, 147, 172, 202, 212, 223, 234, 239, 263, 266, 292, 300, 324, 334 Mos 2:31, 39, 71, 82, 117, 121, 127, 167, 196, 198, 213, 224, 249, 288 Decal 2, 28, 36, 58, 80, 84, 105, 111, 132, 141, 154 Spec 1:12, 42, 44, 112, 198, 224, 243, 283, 301, 311, 312, 323, 330, 333 Spec 2:6, 14, 19, 19, 22, 38, 85, 121, 132, 139, 144, 146, 158, 176, 203, 219, 242 Spec 3:2, 47, 61, 91, 132, 136, 192, 203 Spec 4:54, 59, 123, 133, 141, 146, 176, 202 Virt 8, 60, 66, 79, 103, 129, 135, 144, 154, 194, 196, 200 Praem 41, 45, 57, 70, 72, 98, 106, 138, 147 Prob 16, 21, 27, 29, 68, 93, 97 Contempl 16, 64, 67, 71, 90 Aet 13, 21, 25, 27, 28, 29, 31, 34, 37, 40, 46, 48, 67, 80, 99, 112, 112, 123, 129, 136, 146, 149 Flacc 22, 28, 104, 126, 135 Legat 5, 10, 22, 29, 80, 86, 102, 115, 177, 183, 213, 218, 250, 274, 279, 340, 369, 370 Hypoth 6:1, 6:1, 6:5, 7:8, 7:13, 7:16, 7:20, 11:10, 11:13 Prov 1, 1, 2:7, 49, 51 QG 1:55c, 2:28, 34a, 4:227 QG (Par) 2:2

δῆγμα Agr 97 Mos 1:109

δηγμός Leg 2:84 Det 110

δηϊόω (6) Somn 1:105 Spec 1:184 Spec 4:23, 226 Praem 127 Legat 249

δηκτικός Somn 2:192 Mos 1:131

δηλονότι (10) Leg 1:40, 47 Leg 3:123 Congr 8 Mos 1:247 Mos 2:69, 236, 291 Spec 1:318 Spec 2:74

δῆλος (79) Opif 25, 25, 43, 56, 81, 98, 132 Leg 1:100 Leg 3:1, 113, 120 Sacr 119 Det 6, 32, 51 Post 50 Deus 30 Plant 123, 170 Conf 96, 183 Migr 57, 110 Congr 112, 161 Fug 156, 163, 172 Somn 1:91, 149, 201 Somn 2:5, 231, 246 Abr 8, 77, 89, 164 Ios 51, 57, 71 Mos 1:280 Mos 2:25, 199 Decal 89 Spec 1:142, 151, 275 Spec 2:64, 215, 225, 227, 260 Spec 3:21 Spec 4:123, 224 Virt 50, 198 Praem 29 Prob 60, 60, 61 Aet 35, 45, 72, 75, 78, 93, 121, 126, 129, 131 Flacc 9, 35 Legat 136, 191 Hypoth 7:1 QG 2:29 QG (Par) 2:5

Δῆλος Aet 120, 121, 121, 121, 121

δηλόω (243) Opif 65, 67, 90, 97, 150 Leg 1:18, 43, 57, 60, 60, 70, 81, 106 Leg 2:6, 11, 20, 45, 71 Leg 3:28, 64, 96, 115, 138, 169, 189, 196, 225, 253 Cher 25, 39, 53, 53, 54, 117 Sacr 8, 51, 67, 112 Det 6, 17, 22, 27, 32, 46, 67, 68, 83, 96, 114, 129, 131, 135, 159, 167, 177, 178 Post 10, 13, 22, 28, 32, 53, 55, 59, 89, 95, 112, 124, 128, 172 Gig 19, 23, 33 Deus 42, 51, 103, 104, 128 Plant 73, 113, 121 Ebr 154, 206 Sobr 16, 21, 22, 31 Conf 15, 128, 156, 160, 191, 197 Migr 7, 12, 57, 85, 92, 127, 166, 172 Her 161, 227, 241, 306, 307, 314, 315 Congr 155 Fug 64, 68, 157, 178 Mut 13, 13, 13, 13, 25, 34, 66, 70, 90, 106, 110, 114, 148, 177, 179, 270 Somn 1:1, 4, 27, 33, 40, 41, 48, 61, 67, 74, 82, 158, 242 Somn 2:48, 190, 193, 199, 215, 229, 257 Abr 36, 47, 47, 48, 50, 54, 60, 68, 120, 123, 133, 142, 167, 230, 258 Ios 11, 28, 108, 120, 224, 256 Mos 1:59, 76, 95, 130, 266 Mos 2:3, 11, 31, 38, 39, 81, 99, 120, 151, 168, 187, 191, 201, 215, 228, 246, 266, 268 Decal 1, 102, 155 Spec 1:27, 89, 208, 209, 262 Spec 2:134, 171, 205, 242, 250, 257 Spec 3:55, 143, 208 Spec 4:4, 60, 83, 157, 221 Virt 52, 55, 166 Praem 162 Contempl 28, 75 Aet 3, 13, 150 Flacc 4, 76 Legat 112, 222, 248, 314 Hypoth 6:1, 6:5, 6:7 Prov 2:29 QG 1:96:1, 2:13b, 26b, 59, 3:22, 4:51b QE 2:18, 44, 105 δήλωσις (26) Leg 3:73, 118, 132 Cher 54 Sacr 4 Det 126 Post 64 Deus 71 Ebr 23 Migr 78 Her 165, 303 Mut 194 Mos 2:113, 128, 129, 129, 154 Spec 1:65, 88, 89 Spec 4:49, 69, 69 Legat 6 QE isf 3

δηλωτικός Mos 2:128 QG 1:93

δημαγωγέω Ebr 37

δημαγωγία Somn 2:79

δημαγωγός Ebr 68

δημαρχία Somn 2:79 QG 4:47b

δημηγορέω Flacc 108

δημηγόρος Ios 35

Δημήτηρ Spec 3:40

Δημήτρα Opif 133 Decal 54 Contempl 3

δήμιος Spec 1:316 Spec 2:248 Prov 2:39, 39

δημιουργέω (144) Opif 10, 13, 16, 21, 52, 55, 63, 76, 88, 131, 140, 142 Leg 1:6, 20, 34, 39 Leg 2:19, 19, 24, 26, 73 Leg 3:22, 91, 98, 99, 146, 161 Cher 39, 98 Sacr 8, 21, 44, 75 Det 8, 16, 33, 68, 80, 86, 88 Post 14, 26, 103 Deus 25, 30, 46 Agr 38, 95 Plant 11, 27, 28, 118 Ebr 85, 89, 90, 132 Conf 42, 107, 132, 175, 179, 180 Migr 41, 98, 167, 193 Her 53, 133, 156, 156, 158, 160, 184, 199, 216, 225 Congr 117 Fug 69, 95 Mut 74, 137, 149, 157 Somn 1:27, 206 Somn 2:116, 203, 213, 250 Abr 153, 159 Ios 87 Mos 1:158 Mos 2:60, 74, 75, 76, 84, 88, 94, 114, 136, 141, 171, 205, 263, 266 Decal 33, 69, 70, 100 Spec 1:10, 29, 33, 35, 81, 88, 96 Spec 2:151, 224 Spec 3:108, 199 Spec 4:113, 195 Praem 149 Prob 149, 156 Aet 41, 43, 44, 66, 89 Flacc 123 Legat 195, 337 Prov 1, 1, 2:31 QG 1:64a, 4:8b QG (Par) 2:2, 2:3, 2:6 QE 2:46

δημιούργημα (7) Leg 2:24, 75 Leg 3:88 Det 84, 86 Migr 194 Mut 31

δημιουργία Sacr 2 Agr 158 Ebr 85

δημιουργός (113) Opif 10, 18, 36, 68, 72, 138, 139, 146, 171 Leg 1:77 Leg 2:3 Leg 3:76, 95, 98, 99, 209 Cher 100, 112, 126, 126, 127, 127 Det 62, 124, 126, 154, 170 Post 53, 117, 119, 157, 175 Gig 11, 12, 23 Deus 21, 31, 80, 84 Plant 6 Ebr 30, 89, 154, 154, 212 Sobr 2 Conf 88, 144 Migr 136, 181 Her 77, 111, 161, 232 Congr 105 Fug 26, 47, 70, 71, 212 Mut 18, 29, 32 Somn 1:76, 204, 206 Somn 2:27, 57, 66, 187, 204, 214, 220 Abr 163 Mos 1:38, 92 Mos 2:155 Decal 5, 66, 156 Spec 1:20, 33, 71, 265 Spec 2:165, 228, 255 Spec 3:44 Spec 4:195, 196 Praem 42, 43, 130 Prob 55, 78, 160 Contempl 5 Aet 13, 15, 41, 43, 116 Flacc 143 Legat 41, 90, 113, 202, 222, 246 Hypoth 11:9 Prov 2:13, 16 QG (Par) 2:6

δημοβόρος Legat 108

δημογέρων Mos 1:86

δημοθοινία Somn 2:211 Ios 98 Spec 2:193 Virt 169

δημόκοινος Legat 97

δημοκοπέω Ios 67

δημοκοπία QG 4:47b

δημοκόπος Sacr 32 Ios 35 Flacc 20, 135

δημοκρατία (6) Deus 176 Agr 45 Conf 108 Abr 242 Spec 4:237 Virt 180

δημοκρατικός Spec 4:9

Δημόκριτος Contempl 14, 15 Aet 8

δημόπρατος Flacc 150

δῆμος (28) Det 134 Conf 111 Migr 205 Somn 2:188 Ios 28, 63, 67, 69, 75, 79, 148, 149, 149 Decal 14 Spec 1:55 Spec 3:40, 74 Prob 47, 118 Flacc 132, 141, 161 Legat 10, 158, 338 Prov 2:35, 37 QE 1:21

δημοσιεύω Mos 1:296

δημόσιος (19) Opif 17 Post 50, 110 Gig 36 Agr 117 Her 12 Abr 139 Ios 158 Mos 1:103 Spec 1:56, 73 Spec 2:28 Spec 4:84, 141, 156 Prob 143 Flacc 123, 133 Legat 156

δημοτελής (6) Opif 116 Somn 2:144 Spec 1:183 Spec 3:183 Praem 171 Legat 280

δημότης (7) Abr 67 Spec 2:82, 126, 129 Spec 4:16 Prob 9 QG isf 10

δημοτικός Agr 62 Ebr 215 Somn 1:222 Flacc 41

δημοφανής Mos 2:224

δημώδης Prob 2

δημωφελής Mos 2:277

δήποτε (13) Opif 72 Cher 125 Sacr 11, 72 Plant 43 Fug 87 Mut 236 Spec 1:119, 213 Aet 75, 90 Flacc 95 Hypoth 6:8

δήπου (37) Leg 1:6 Leg 2:20 Leg 3:99 Det 68, 141 Post 36 Gig 64 Plant 33, 113 Ebr 190 Sobr 18, 25 Conf 78, 158 Migr 67, 78, 103, 132, 140, 191 Her 53, 145, 290 Mut 38, 210, 235, 242 Somn 1:30 Somn 2:142, 257 Spec 2:99, 205 Aet 44, 69, 106 Hypoth 6:3 QG 3:11a

δήπουθεν (6) Plant 172 Ebr 193 Sobr 66 Her 253 Somn 1:227 Aet 143

δῆτα Sacr 39 Spec 4:130 Virt 217 Hypoth 7:11, 7:13

δήωσις Spec 2:191 Virt 150 Legat 17

διά (2414) Opif 5, 35, 37, 38, 45, 45, 45, 47, 48, 48, 48, 48, 48, 48, 48, 48, 54, 66, 67, 67, 69, 73, 74, 75, 77, 79, 80, 80, 83, 84, 85, 87, 90, 95, 95, 96, 96, 100, 102, 106, 106, 107, 107, 107, 107, 107, 107, 119, 119, 120, 123, 123, 123, 123, 123, 123, 128, 128, 131, 131, 134, 139, 141, 147, 148, 152, 154, 154, 154, 154, 157, 158, 159, 161, 162, 162, 164, 165, 165, 166, 166, 166, 169, 170, 170, 171, 171 Leg 1:2, 2, 13, 17, 18, 21, 24, 27, 27, 30, 30, 33, 33, 33, 34, 37, 41, 41, 41, 41, 41, 43, 48, 51, 55, 57, 63, 70, 74, 81, 82, 83, 84, 84, 85, 87, 91, 95, 96, 96, 99, 102, 104 Leg 2:1, 7, 7, 11, 11, 16, 16, 16, 16, 16, 20, 29, 36, 38, 42, 44, 44, 54, 62, 63, 63, 68, 74, 74, 74, 74, 74, 74, 74, 75, 75, 77, 80, 80, 81, 84, 95, 98, 102, 107, 107, 107 Leg 3:3, 4, 12, 14, 15, 18, 20, 21, 24, 40, 44, 45, 49, 50, 54, 55, 57, 65, 68, 69, 72, 77, 80, 83, 84, 93, 99, 99, 101, 101, 102, 103, 108, 111, 112, 113, 113, 113, 120, 133, 134, 134, 135, 136, 136, 139, 141, 146, 147, 148, 148, 152, 152, 156, 162, 167, 167, 169, 170, 170, 174, 176, 176, 176, 178, 178, 178, 178, 178, 178, 178, 183, 184, 187, 189, 200, 200, 202, 203, 213, 225, 240, 242, 244, 245, 246, 247, 248, 251 Cher 9, 12, 14, 21, 21, 29, 29, 33, 35, 35, 39, 40, 57, 57, 57, 57, 57, 61, 61, 64, 68, 68, 68, 68, 71, 77, 80, 84, 87, 90, 99, 105, 110, 117, 124, 125, 125, 125, 125, 125, 126, 126, 127, 127, 128, 128, 130 Sacr 4, 8, 8, 26, 29, 30, 34, 36, 51, 54, 54, 57, 57, 57, 59, 61, 61, 63, 66, 67, 69, 69, 70, 72, 75, 76, 77, 78, 93, 93, 96, 102, 109, 110, 111, 116, 124, 125, 126, 127, 127, 127, 129, 129, 130, 132, 132, 132, 133 Det 4, 4, 12, 14, 15, 16, 16, 21, 22, 25, 29, 33, 34, 38, 39, 40, 43, 52, 53, 53, 54, 58, 59, 62, 64, 68, 69, 74, 77, 80, 84, 88, 92, 92, 96, 103, 104, 120, 125, 127, 129, 134, 138, 146, 147, 151, 154, 155, 156, 157, 157, 157, 162, 164, 164, 166, 167, 177, 178 Post 6, 7, 14, 16,

17, 18, 23, 24, 29, 31, 38, 54, 64, 67, 77, 78, 87, 87, 96, 100, 113, 115, 117, 126, 126, 126, 127, 129, 136, 140, 140, 142, 142, 144, 151, 152, 153, 153, 155, 161, 165, 167, 169, 173, 183 Gig 1, 7, 8, 9, 11, 16, 17, 17, 18, 18, 18, 19, 23, 27, 29, 50, 50, 52, 59 Deus 3, 7, 7, 7, 13, 15, 15, 21, 24, 27, 27, 37, 39, 42, 46, 50, 64, 64, 69, 69, 71, 73, 77, 79, 84, 103, 110, 110, 121, 123, 127, 128, 130, 134, 137, 143, 145, 145, 145, 145, 145, 146, 149, 152, 153, 154, 154, 158, 158, 160, 160, 166, 167, 182, 183 Agr 6, 9, 10, 13, 13, 16, 16, 19, 20, 23, 24, 26, 28, 30, 35, 42, 53, 54, 58, 73, 78, 91, 93, 95, 97, 127, 131, 132, 133, 137, 137, 137, 145, 147, 148, 149, 152, 154, 157, 167, 169, 173, 176, 181 Plant 5, 12, 23, 35, 38, 48, 52, 59, 63, 64, 66, 79, 79, 82, 86, 111, 114, 125, 125, 126, 126, 128, 131, 131, 133, 133, 133, 133, 133, 133, 144, 147, 148, 151, 152, 157, 159, 173 Ebr 5, 9, 10, 15, 19, 19, 22, 27, 52, 54, 60, 70, 71, 73, 77, 84, 84, 84, 85, 85, 94, 94, 95, 96, 100, 102, 106, 107, 117, 119, 120, 120, 128, 128, 133, 135, 136, 143, 144, 152, 160, 160, 169, 174, 185, 185, 187, 191, 191, 192, 209, 210, 212 Sobr 3, 15, 18, 23, 36, 38, 40, 42, 47, 49, 49, 55, 58, 65, 68 Conf 1, 4, 7, 11, 12, 12, 19, 33, 36, 37, 38, 39, 46, 49, 53, 57, 59, 66, 72, 72, 75, 77, 78, 90, 96, 98, 102, 105, 124, 127, 129, 133, 135, 136, 136, 137, 141, 143, 150, 155, 156, 158, 158, 159, 159, 161, 164, 172, 179, 180, 182, 185 Migr 3, 16, 19, 19, 24, 32, 33, 35, 36, 38, 39, 39, 39, 39, 44, 47, 47, 47, 52, 52, 53, 53, 65, 65, 67, 69, 71, 72, 73, 76, 81, 92, 92, 101, 109, 110, 110, 114, 118, 122, 127, 131, 136, 154, 155, 156, 156, 157, 164, 169, 169, 170, 178, 190, 195, 206, 212, 219 Her 3, 11, 12, 14, 15, 15, 20, 27, 28, 48, 48, 48, 51, 66, 67, 72, 72, 92, 95, 98, 100, 111, 111, 111, 111, 111, 112, 118, 119, 123, 124, 127, 140, 145, 147, 147, 153, 157, 157, 191, 199, 217, 219, 227, 227, 228, 236, 238, 238, 241, 246, 251, 261, 261, 262, 263, 263, 265, 277, 280, 284, 289, 297, 304, 311, 311, 312 Congr 4, 6, 9, 9, 10, 13, 13, 15, 18, 20, 21, 27, 28, 29, 35, 35, 35, 37, 44, 59, 60, 66, 68, 71, 71, 73, 76, 76, 76, 80, 81, 84, 89, 98, 105, 106, 110, 110, 128, 138, 139, 140, 141, 142, 143, 143, 143, 153, 159, 163, 170, 172, 176, 177 Fug 3, 3, 5, 5, 5, 6, 6, 6, 22, 22, 31, 36, 50, 50, 54, 56, 61, 64, 66, 66, 66, 68, 68, 70, 74, 75, 87, 87, 87, 89, 90, 90, 91, 94, 95, 95, 96, 97, 99, 105, 108, 109, 122, 125, 131, 141, 150, 154, 156, 162, 164, 174, 175, 181, 182, 187, 197, 209, 209, 209, 212, 213 Mut 4, 7, 13, 29, 30, 34, 38, 46, 54, 57, 58, 59, 59, 63, 70, 81, 82, 83, 84, 84, 87, 88, 91, 94, 100, 108, 111, 116, 118, 118, 124, 126, 126, 126, 128, 128, 132, 144, 145, 155, 155, 158, 170, 171, 177, 177, 179, 195, 200, 203, 204, 206, 208, 220, 228, 232, 236, 241, 243, 243, 246, 247, 248, 249, 250, 251, 251, 254, 270 Somn 1:5, 5, 5, 9, 10, 10, 12, 14, 15, 24, 28, 28, 28, 36, 36, 37, 40, 41, 41, 46, 51, 61, 62, 70, 72, 74, 82, 82, 87, 90, 91, 95, 99, 100, 103, 111, 112, 116, 135, 135, 137, 142, 143, 144, 147, 147, 153, 162, 172, 174, 175, 181, 181, 188, 188, 190, 201, 202, 206, 212, 218, 229, 235, 237, 237 Somn 2:3, 4, 13, 16, 17, 20, 24, 27, 51, 53, 54, 55, 61, 62, 67, 75, 91, 106, 109, 109, 117, 120, 120, 122, 127, 142, 147, 147, 147, 150, 157, 160, 160, 169, 170, 170, 170, 179, 182, 184, 191, 193, 222, 227, 237, 245, 245, 246, 247, 255, 256, 262, 281, 289, 294 Abr 1, 2, 6, 13, 13, 20, 22, 22, 23, 23, 24, 28, 34, 42, 50, 57, 57, 57, 58, 60, 60, 65, 71, 72, 72, 76, 80, 83, 83, 85, 88, 91, 91, 99, 101, 104, 104, 106, 110, 111, 115, 118, 119, 119, 122, 125, 125, 128, 128, 129, 129, 132, 133, 143, 144, 144, 145, 145, 147, 149, 153, 157, 175, 180, 184, 194, 198, 202, 212, 213, 230, 238, 239, 239, 239, 239, 239, 240, 243, 249, 253, 262, 269, 269, 269, 269, 273 Ios 1, 7, 7, 9, 9, 9, 22, 22, 27, 30, 34, 35, 36, 37, 39, 40, 51, 53, 56, 58, 58, 60, 61, 62, 64, 66, 72, 72, 79, 85, 99, 99, 100, 130, 134, 136, 142, 147, 147, 148, 150, 153, 154, 156, 158, 160, 162, 165, 171, 172, 177, 179, 185, 186, 204, 205, 216, 217, 225, 233, 242, 250, 256, 258, 262, 269 Mos 1:2, 2, 3, 4, 5, 6, 8, 14, 17, 22, 23, 23, 23, 25, 26, 26, 29, 31, 34, 40, 48, 59, 64, 66, 71, 73, 77, 82, 82, 87, 91, 95, 95, 100, 105, 108, 109, 111, 113, 114, 115, 117, 118, 120, 126, 126, 126, 126, 129, 129, 130, 136, 141, 149, 164, 164, 167, 170, 171, 173, 179, 182, 183, 184, 186, 198, 200, 210, 212, 215, 217, 221, 225, 240, 243, 243, 245, 246, 252, 257, 259, 260, 263, 265, 274, 280, 285, 294, 295, 303, 305, 305, 314, 316, 316, 324, 334 Mos 2:3, 5, 13, 13, 23, 23, 24, 34, 49, 58, 59, 65, 66, 69, 69, 84, 93, 99, 102, 115, 115, 115, 115, 125, 131, 133, 138, 145, 148, 149, 155, 159, 176, 177, 177, 185, 187, 187, 187, 188, 188, 189, 189, 191, 192, 196, 201, 201, 202, 202, 207, 207, 211, 213, 213, 219, 219, 219, 221, 225, 226, 232, 232, 234, 238, 242, 244, 247, 253, 254, 255, 256, 263, 263, 270, 272, 273, 278, 287, 288, 292 Decal 4, 4, 7, 18, 18, 19, 19, 22, 22, 22, 22, 24, 33, 35, 43, 43, 43, 47, 48, 63, 72, 77, 77, 89, 93, 93, 101, 105, 105, 105, 107, 107, 109, 112, 113, 113, 123, 127, 136, 140, 140, 141, 150, 152, 160, 167, 169, 175, 176 Spec 1:1, 5, 6, 9, 17, 25, 26, 27, 30, 32, 38, 40, 52, 61, 62, 64, 64, 66, 69, 69, 72, 74, 81, 84, 85, 89, 89, 94, 102, 103, 104, 107, 111, 116, 117, 117, 121, 121, 124, 128, 147, 159, 160, 166, 167, 167, 172, 173, 184, 191, 193, 193, 195, 195, 196, 197, 197, 197, 200, 201, 205, 206, 207, 207, 209, 213, 215, 216, 216, 216, 216, 218, 219, 219, 229, 230, 230, 242, 248, 252, 252, 253, 258, 258, 260, 264, 269, 269, 269, 272, 273, 275, 275, 285, 286, 289, 293, 298, 298, 300, 304, 309, 310, 313, 313, 314, 321, 321, 322, 322, 323, 325, 326, 329, 330, 336, 336, 336, 336, 338, 338, 339, 339, 340, 342, 342 Spec 2:12, 16, 24, 29, 39, 40, 41, 46, 48, 50, 51, 56, 57, 61, 63, 63, 65, 66, 66, 67, 70, 80, 85, 86, 88, 91, 91, 94, 96, 103, 104, 107, 112, 113, 129, 132, 132, 132, 133, 134, 136, 137, 139, 139, 140, 144, 146, 148, 154, 155, 156, 158, 168, 169, 170, 171, 177, 177, 180, 181, 182, 185, 186, 189, 189, 192, 193, 194, 194, 195, 195, 196, 196, 197, 197, 198, 200, 200, 200, 200, 200, 201, 205, 206, 206, 207, 207, 210, 212, 213, 214, 220, 221, 221, 226, 226, 230, 230, 232, 232, 232, 236, 240, 243, 245, 245, 246, 248, 250, 251, 257, 261, 262 Spec 3:4, 8, 10, 16, 16, 17, 19, 20, 21, 34, 34, 36, 40, 44, 45, 56, 58, 58, 58, 70, 70, 82, 84, 85, 91, 95, 97, 97, 98, 99, 101, 103, 103, 108, 110, 111, 117, 126, 128, 129, 136, 144, 153, 154, 159, 161, 161, 165, 165, 166, 169, 184, 189, 189, 190, 194, 198, 198, 200, 204, 209 Spec 4:2, 3, 10, 18, 24, 28, 30, 35, 35, 38, 40, 40, 42, 42, 60, 60, 62, 66, 69, 75, 79, 83, 85, 88, 89, 95, 101, 107, 109, 113, 113, 114, 120, 121, 121, 121, 123, 125, 134, 137, 138, 138, 139, 141, 144, 146, 154, 155, 167, 169, 179, 179, 182, 191, 198, 200, 200, 202, 205, 211 Virt 8, 9, 9, 12, 12, 16, 17, 18, 24, 25, 30, 32, 37, 38, 38, 38, 40, 42, 47, 53, 65, 67, 67, 67, 73, 75, 77, 80, 83, 100, 112, 112, 119, 123, 127, 128, 130, 132, 132, 133, 133, 135, 136, 138, 143, 144, 145, 152, 154, 156, 162, 165, 172, 183, 187, 188, 193, 193, 196, 207, 207, 208, 213, 213, 213, 213, 226 Praem 1, 2, 2, 6, 11, 17, 17, 27, 32, 35, 41, 43, 44, 45, 47, 47, 51, 53, 56, 61, 62, 65, 69, 79, 82, 93, 97, 99, 104, 105, 107, 107, 108, 110, 118, 118, 118, 120, 120, 121, 124, 126, 129, 130, 133, 136, 142, 143, 146, 148, 151, 154, 155, 155,

156, 167, 168, 170, 170, 172 Prob 1, 2, 5, 7, 8, 22, 26, 29, 42, 44, 55, 55, 56, 56, 58, 63, 68, 70, 72, 73, 76, 76, 82, 107, 111, 114, 116, 128, 132, 134, 140, 143, 150, 160, 160 Contempl 2, 3, 13, 17, 17, 20, 24, 25, 26, 29, 31, 35, 35, 37, 55, 65, 68, 73, 78, 78, 78, 81, 86 Aet 2, 2, 2, 2, 12, 13, 13, 14, 15, 16, 20, 21, 24, 26, 30, 33, 37, 51, 52, 58, 59, 61, 67, 67, 74, 78, 86, 92, 92, 97, 107, 112, 118, 121, 132 Flacc 1, 9, 9, 9, 12, 17, 26, 29, 32, 33, 33, 35, 41, 45, 52, 54, 55, 56, 56, 56, 59, 59, 65, 71, 74, 74, 76, 76, 85, 87, 89, 94, 97, 97, 97, 100, 122, 124, 124, 128, 139, 140, 142, 151, 160, 166, 167, 171, 172, 173, 173, 173, 174, 179, 186, 190 Legat 2, 9, 12, 13, 14, 14, 18, 18, 24, 29, 30, 34, 35, 39, 47, 58, 61, 61, 66, 66, 68, 70, 75, 75, 75, 77, 86, 89, 98, 99, 99, 100, 106, 108, 110, 112, 117, 119, 122, 124, 125, 125, 128, 130, 131, 133, 134, 141, 142, 143, 144, 144, 146, 152, 153, 156, 165, 168, 171, 172, 178, 179, 182, 182, 187, 195, 204, 208, 209, 213, 213, 223, 230, 230, 245, 250, 250, 250, 250, 251, 252, 252, 261, 273, 274, 281, 284, 284, 285, 287, 287, 288, 290, 291, 291, 309, 324, 339, 341, 343, 354, 360, 361, 368, 368, 372 Hypoth 6:1, 11:2 Prov 2:1, 1, 2, 14, 15, 24, 24, 26, 27, 29, 29, 32, 33, 41, 41, 41, 42, 44, 50, 63, 71 QG 1:1, 21, 21, 51, 58, 58, 60:2, 68, 76b, 77, 77, 93, 94, 94, 94, 96:1, 2:11, 11, 12b, 12b, 13a, 14, 15b, 26a, 34a, 34a, 34a, 54a, 54d, 59, 62, 64b, 64c, 64c, 65, 68a, 68a, 3:3, 8, 20a, 21, 23, 58, 4:8b, 43, 51a, 51c, 74, 74, 76b, 86b, 88, 88, 100, 102b, 130, 144, 144, 145, 145, 153, 167, 180, 8*, 198, 203, 204, 227, 228, 228 QG isf 3, 3, 5, 7, 13, 13, 13, 17 QG (Par) 2:2, 2:3, 2:4, 2:4, 2:5, 2:5, 2:6, 2:6, 2:7 QE 2:2, 2, 6a, 14, 18, 18, 20, 20, 26, 49a QE isf 6, 9, 14, 21

διαβαίνω (19) Leg 2:89, 89, 89 Leg 3:16, 18, 18, 94, 172 Agr 25 Migr 217 Mut 160 Abr 159 Mos 1:319, 330, 331 Spec 3:139, 162 Prob 9, 132

διαβάλλω (10) Conf 48 Fug 20 Mut 35 Somn 2:143 Abr 178 Ios 80 Virt 141 Flacc 141 Legat 215, 241

διάβασις (12) Leg 3:94, 154, 165 Sacr 63, 63 Migr 25, 25 Her 255 Congr 106 Spec 2:147 Legat 207 Prov 2:26

διαβατήρια (9) Mos 2:224, 226, 228, 233 Spec 2:41, 145, 147, 150 QE 1:4

διαβεβαιόω Det 38 Decal 139

διαβοάω Praem 124

διαβολή (19) Cher 17 Det 74 Conf 3 Mut 60 Ios 19, 66, 184 Mos 1:46 Mos 2:176 Spec 1:241 Flacc 33, 89 Legat 25, 160, 170, 171, 199, 241 QG 4:228

διάβολος Sacr 32

διαγανάκτησις Mos 2:280

διαγγέλλω (14) Opif 166 Det 13 Plant 14 Her 110 Somn 1:27, 141 Abr 115 Ios 161 Mos 1:66 Spec 1:316 Legat 15, 99 QG 2:34a, 71a

διαγίγνομαι (διαγίνομαι) QG 2:13a

διαγιγνώσκω (διαγινώσκω) (27) Leg 2:93 Leg 3:6, 207 Cher 15 Sacr 17 Det 155 Post 8 Agr 116 Ebr 17 Migr 164 Her 252 Congr 164, 170 Mos 1:48, 186 Mos 2:167 Spec 1:39, 41, 326 Spec 3:145 Virt 193 Praem 87, 117 Aet 3 Flacc 116 Legat 250 Prov 2:35

διαγνωρίζω Det 97

διάγνωσις Det 12 Fug 156 Spec 1:45 Flacc 100

διαγογγύζω Congr 163

διαγορεύω (11) Migr 7, 85 Spec 1:249 Spec 2:130 Spec 3:150 Spec 4:143, 219 Virt 145 Praem 79 Legat 211 QG 2:54d

διάγραμμα Opif 107, 111

διαγράφω Opif 17 Sobr 36 Spec 4:110

διαγρυπνέω Flacc 101, 183

διάγω (16) Opif 79 Leg 3:125 Her 310, 311 Congr 174 Mos 1:145 Mos 2:211, 225 Spec 1:69 Spec 2:187, 206 Spec 3:166 Prob 5 Flacc 116 Prov 2:23 QG 4:33a

διαγωγή Abr 163 Contempl 40, 57

διαγωνίζομαι (7) Agr 59, 111, 111 Migr 75 Mut 109 Mos 1:315 Contempl 1

διαδείκνυμι Gig 2 Ebr 85 Abr 75 Spec 1:91 Prob 102

διαδέχομαι (17) Agr 51 Migr 154 Mos 1:13, 52, 113, 207 Mos 2:263 Decal 128 Spec 2:124, 127, 129 Spec 4:178 Flacc 1 Legat 60, 168, 231, 356

διάδηλος Somn 1:201 Somn 2:217

διάδημα Congr 118 Fug 111 Mos 2:116, 131 Flacc 37

διαδιδράσκω Mut 195 Mos 1:263 Spec 2:253 Spec 3:121

διαδίδωμι (7) Opif 148 Leg 3:183 Ebr 147 Her 67 Spec 1:135 Contempl 64 Flacc 45

διαδοχή (26) Det 75 Plant 127 Her 37, 100 Mut 95 Somn 2:184 Ios 36, 246 Mos 1:38, 191, 231 Mos 2:221, 233, 243, 244 Spec 1:296 Spec 2:127, 129 Spec 3:16 Praem 151, 169 Prob 148 Aet 69, 74 Legat 143, 288

διάδοχος (21) Deus 5, 113 Agr 156 Abr 252 Ios 119, 136, 166 Mos 1:32, 150 Spec 1:16 Spec 4:170, 173 Virt 56, 64, 68, 70, 70 Praem 108 Prob 20 Flacc 9 Legat 23

διαδράσσομαι Spec 3:175

διαδύνω Abr 140 Spec 4:186

διάδυσις Conf 116

διαζάω Somn 2:150 Contempl 47

διαζεύγνυμι (58) Opif 33 Leg 3:121 Cher 18 Det 149 Post 104 Gig 55, 56 Deus 40 Agr 13, 137, 141 Ebr 70 Conf 9 Migr 7, 11, 12, 58, 150, 178, 220 Her 202 Congr 49, 76 Fug 55, 91, 92, 117, 196 Mut 270 Somn 1:28, 147, 205 Somn 2:28, 28 Abr 213, 215, 223 Ios 225 Mos 1:241 Mos 2:7, 282 Spec 1:139 Spec 2:25, 256 Spec 3:23, 64, 70, 105 Spec 4:210 Virt 133, 161, 190 Contempl 63 Aet 139 Flacc 15 QG 1:24, 4:20, 74

διάζευξις (10) Gig 25 Plant 25 Conf 67 Abr 258 Ios 169 Spec 3:80 Virt 76, 126, 128 Praem 19

διαζωγραφέω Mos 2:76

διαζώννυμι Opif 112 Conf 109 Mos 1:228, 246 Spec 2:169

διαθεάομαι Migr 185

διάθεσις (29) Leg 3:210 Cher 62, 104 Det 3, 139, 157 Post 36, 170 Agr 97 Plant 31, 44, 60 Ebr 120 Sobr 6 Conf 31, 31 Fug 17, 177 Mos 2:207, 248 Spec 1:253 Spec 2:35 Spec 3:191 Virt 74, 83 Contempl 48, 61 Legat 103 QE 2:50b

διαθέω Flacc 120, 162

διαθήκη (23) Leg 3:85, 85 Sacr 57, 57 Det 67, 68 Her 313 Mut 51, 52, 52, 52, 53, 57, 58, 58, 58, 263 Somn 2:223, 223, 224, 224, 237 Spec 2:16

διαθλέω (24) Leg 2:108 Det 2, 27 Post 101 Deus 13 Ebr 82 Congr 70, 165, 180 Fug 36, 43, 162 Mut 81 Somn 1:179

Ios 177 Mos 1:48 Mos 2:236 Spec 1:79 Praem 11, 52 Prob 110 Contempl 1 Hypoth 11:6 QE isf 7

διαθρέω Mut 134

διαίρεσις (23) Opif 95 Sacr 84, 85, 86, 87 Post 159 Agr 129, 141, 145 Ebr 93 Her 168, 236 Fug 186 Spec 1:195, 196, 209 Spec 4:108 Aet 79, 79, 80 QG 1:64a, 64d, 4:30

διαιρετός (8) Leg 1:3 Det 90 Agr 134 Spec 1:137, 180 Spec 3:28, 180 Virt 103

διαιρέω (63) Opif 95 Leg 1:3 Leg 3:32, 32, 170 Cher 31, 80 Sacr 76, 82, 97, 110 Post 85, 162 Deus 173 Agr 127 Ebr 23 Conf 111 Migr 124 Her 130, 130, 131, 132, 133, 134, 134, 136, 138, 140, 141, 141, 141, 142, 143, 146, 146, 164, 164, 165, 174, 176, 180, 215, 216, 219, 220, 230, 232, 233, 235, 235, 236, 242, 242, 312 Congr 8 Mut 173 Somn 1:17 Somn 2:215 Spec 1:194, 196 Spec 4:77 Aet 128 QG 2:14

διαίρω (12) Det 23 Ios 214 Mos 2:285 Spec 3:151 Spec 4:48, 235, 236 Virt 71, 163 Aet 118 Legat 191, 202

διαΐσσω Mut 247

δίαιτα (35) Leg 3:226 Sacr 70 Det 77, 95, 115 Post 71 Plant 55, 102, 162 Ebr 171 Her 127 Congr 53 Fug 41, 92 Mut 230 Somn 1:123 Somn 2:9 Ios 53, 93, 204 Mos 1:64, 153 Spec 2:19, 85, 125, 160, 187, 207 Virt 19, 104 Prob 98 Flacc 90 Legat 14, 83, 274

διαιτάω (12) Opif 63 Sacr 3, 124 Deus 151 Plant 10 Migr 3 Abr 215 Mos 2:125 Spec 1:148 Spec 2:5, 56, 206

διαίτημα Cher 116

διαιτητής Somn 1:142

διαιωνίζω (9) Gig 19 Plant 93 Congr 38 Mut 209 Somn 1:45 Somn 2:149 Decal 58 Spec 3:113 Praem 72

διαιώνιος Legat 157

διακαθαίρω Decal 162

διακαθιζάνω Leg 2:27, 28

διακαίω Her 147 Mos 1:114

διακαλύπτω Ios 106 Spec 4:51 Contempl 78

διάκειμαι (22) Leg 3:126, 127, 141 Post 27, 61 Ebr 128 Conf 44 Her 308 Congr 152 Somn 2:158 Abr 169 Ios 211, 226, 255 Mos 1:118, 298 Mos 2:248 Legat 159, 169, 201, 279 QG isf 12

διακελεύομαι Leg 3:56 Prob 36

διάκενος ἄκενος

διακινέω (14) Ebr 165 Migr 189 Somn 1:182 Mos 1:26, 114, 120, 197 Mos 2:147 Decal 35, 87 Spec 1:53 Spec 3:75, 92 Spec 4:238

διακλάω Deus 153

διακληρόω (11) Plant 61 Abr 124 Mos 1:191, 321 Mos 2:285 Spec 1:156, 188, 298, 333 Spec 2:121 Aet 34

διακναίω Flacc 167

διακομίζω (7) Opif 86 Migr 18 Ios 27 Mos 1:141, 226 Spec 4:31 Legat 254

διακονέω Contempl 70

διακονία Ios 167 Spec 2:91 Virt 122 Flacc 162 QG 4:88

διακονικός Contempl 50, 71 Flacc 113

διάκονος Post 165 Gig 12 Ios 241 Mos 2:199 Contempl 75

διακόπτω (12) Leg 3:32 Conf 104 Her 242 Fug 91 Mos 1:211 Mos 2:254 Spec 2:43 Prob 113 Contempl 7 Flacc 189, 190 Prov 2:26

διακορής Det 106 Ebr 207 Fug 31 Virt 115 Contempl 53

διακόσιοι Mos 2:283 Spec 2:33, 146

διακοσμέω (41) Opif 20, 40, 45, 47, 53, 54, 62, 113 Cher 105 Plant 5, 14, 86 Conf 174, 174 Migr 4, 60, 182 Her 87, 303 Fug 10, 97 Somn 2:54, 57 Abr 121 Mos 2:99, 133, 137, 243 Spec 1:33, 270, 307 Spec 2:151, 151 Spec 3:37 Virt 39 Aet 4, 54, 54 Flacc 30, 38 Legat 79

διακόσμησις (7) Spec 1:208, 208 Aet 6, 9, 81, 85, 94

διακρατέω Conf 69, 166 Fug 190 Mos 2:238 Aet 75

διακρίνω (86) Opif 76, 125, 131, 137, 154 Leg 1:7, 50 Leg 2:96 Leg 3:115, 119, 157 Cher 25 Sacr 3, 101 Agr 95, 130, 136, 142, 163 Plant 147 Ebr 37, 193, 198 Conf 87, 185, 187, 191 Migr 18, 19, 24, 48 Her 134, 177, 201, 205, 216, 236, 271 Congr 18, 129, 129 Fug 57 Mut 43, 192, 208, 249 Somn 1:12, 18, 76, 138 Somn 2:4, 22, 24, 24, 28 Ios 90, 104, 113, 143, 203, 248 Mos 1:78, 144 Spec 1:227, 227, 326, 342 Spec 2:32, 151, 190, 210 Spec 4:77, 99, 104, 106, 116, 224, 235 Praem 37 Aet 5, 30, 144, 147 Flacc 78 Legat 190 QG 2:12c

διάκρισις (27) Opif 136 Leg 1:106 Leg 3:119 Cher 127 Deus 82 Plant 3, 45 Conf 36, 191, 192, 192 Somn 2:7, 24, 35, 39, 110, 152 Ios 93, 98, 110, 116, 125, 269 Mos 1:212 Spec 1:100, 340 Virt 145

διακριτικός Leg 3:50 Spec 1:218, 218

διακρούω Conf 120 Legat 199

διακύπτω (21) Sacr 85 Det 12 Plant 169 Ebr 167 Conf 57, 140 Migr 216, 222 Her 111 Fug 34 Abr 72, 115 Ios 16, 146 Decal 86 Spec 3:2, 6 Praem 28 Prob 21, 54 Flacc 144

διακωλύω (6) Abr 176 Mos 1:286 Spec 1:22 Spec 4:7, 50 Legat 207

διαλαγχάνω Spec 3:40, 170

διαλαλέω Ios 12, 175 Prob 90 Legat 52

διαλαμβάνω Contempl 60

διαλανθάνω Agr 161 Mut 37 Ios 250 Spec 1:166 Praem 149

διαλέγω (46) Leg 1:101, 104 Leg 2:15, 16, 23 Leg 3:118 Cher 50, 50, 58 Sacr 12 Det 48 Post 109, 136 Deus 33 Plant 85 Ebr 93, 101, 206 Conf 6, 168 Her 4, 218 Fug 69, 76, 166 Mut 207 Somn 1:232 Abr 131, 223, 273 Ios 80, 107 Mos 1:87 Mos 2:163, 187, 233 Decal 39, 82 Spec 1:194, 234 Spec 2:1 Virt 72 Contempl 1, 31, 33, 79

διάλειμμα Hypoth 7:10, 7:16

διαλείπω Migr 67 Congr 4, 4 Decal 96

διαλεκτικός Agr 13, 140 Plant 115 Congr 18 Mos 2:39

διάλεκτος (17) Leg 2:15 Conf 1, 8, 9, 10, 12, 12, 13, 190, 191, 192 Congr 44 Abr 12 Mos 2:26, 38 Decal 46 Prob 75

διαλελυμένως Her 198

διάλεξις Contempl 79

διάλευκος (9) Somn 1:189, 200, 201, 202, 208, 213, 216, 219 Somn 2:19

διαλλακτής Mos 2:166

διαλλάσσω (9) Sacr 137 Det 164 Deus 41 Ebr 8 Ios 39 Mos 2:126 Spec 3:85 Contempl 54 QG 1:32

διαλογίζομαι Spec 1:213 QG isf 3

διάλογος Ebr 56 Spec 1:342

διάλυσις (16) Leg 3:22 Plant 60 Ebr 140 Conf 167 Her 276 Virt 118 Aet 17, 27, 28, 28, 78, 106, 117, 129 Legat 100, 128

διαλυτός Her 23, 58, 160

διαλύω (33) Opif 33, 131 Leg 3:22, 101 Cher 115 Agr 32 Plant 3, 10, 147 Conf 89, 103, 193, 198 Fug 112 Somn 1:26 Abr 23, 210 Mos 2:33, 262 Praem 91 Contempl 43 Aet 20, 22, 31, 36, 80, 90, 125, 137 Flacc 4, 190 Legat 41 Hypoth 11:14

διαμαρτάνω (59) Opif 21, 47 Leg 3:90, 91 Cher 70, 124 Sacr 128 Det 97, 141 Post 86, 182 Agr 92 Plant 145, 162, 166, 174 Ebr 25, 131 Sobr 37, 67 Conf 115, 165 Migr 133 Her 298 Fug 104, 131, 145 Mut 48, 240, 248 Somn 1:91 Somn 2:195 Abr 40 Ios 9, 229 Mos 1:222 Mos 2:36, 62, 204, 279 Decal 66 Spec 1:252 Spec 2:54, 164 Spec 3:29, 122 Spec 4:120, 159, 181, 198 Praem 56 Prob 37 Aet 47 Flacc 7, 170 Legat 223 Prov 2:18 QG isf 3 QE 2:13a

διαμαρτία Plant 108

διαμάχη (10) Opif 33 Det 1, 32 Her 237 Fug 211 Somn 1:152 Abr 222 Spec 2:182 Aet 136 QE isf 4

διαμάχομαι (8) Leg 2:91, 105 Cher 20 Deus 144 Agr 3 Ebr 196 Prob 99 QG 4:200b

διαμέλλω Sacr 58 Plant 160 Contempl 76

διαμένω (40) Opif 131, 169 Leg 1:78 Post 171 Gig 28 Migr 124 Her 35, 152, 181, 217 Fug 161 Mut 24, 102 Abr 165, 170, 226 Ios 112 Mos 1:30, 65, 68, 119, 205, 218 Mos 2:14, 26, 61, 70, 264, 266 Spec 1:76, 76 Spec 2:67 Spec 4:181 Legat 41 Hypoth 6:1 QG 1:51, 2:15b, 54a, 64b, 3:8

διαμερίζω Post 89 Plant 59 Congr 58

διαμετρέω Opif 23 Mut 232 Spec 1:327 Contempl 80 QE 2:25d

διαμιμνήσκομαι (7) Det 81 Ebr 2 Migr 128 Her 250 Congr 65, 66 Somn 1:45

διαμισέω Sobr 23 Migr 20 Abr 137 Spec 3:167 Legat 167

διαμονή (33) Opif 10, 38, 61, 66, 133 Leg 2:8, 96 Sacr 121, 126 Det 102, 151 Gig 10 Ebr 13, 211 Congr 96 Spec 1:16, 216, 289 Spec 2:133, 195, 198 Virt 143 Praem 32 Aet 37, 61, 74, 83 QG 2:29 QG (Par) 2:7, 2:7, 2:7 QE 2:19, 64

διαμορφόω Spec 4:196

διαναγιγνώσκω Legat 69, 203, 209, 304, 331

διαναπαύω (6) Det 121, 122 Somn 1:110 Decal 99 Spec 2:64 Aet 62

διανέμησις Conf 192

διανέμω (62) Opif 52, 56, 67 Sacr 84, 111 Det 106, 168 Post 90, 91 Gig 26 Agr 87 Conf 111 Migr 3, 45, 60 Her 49, 175, 182, 186, 191, 194, 195, 235 Mut 67 Abr 229, 232 Ios 18, 243, 259 Mos 1:97, 173, 254, 257, 315, 332 Mos 2:89, 124, 124, 236, 256 Decal 50, 56, 103 Spec 1:178, 199, 279, 333, 337 Spec 2:100, 119 Spec 4:98, 120 Praem 57 Contempl 69 Aet 147 Flacc 56, 85, 135 Legat 122, 158, 227 Prov 2:33

διανθίζω Plant 111

διανίστημι (20) Post 149 Deus 97 Ebr 159 Migr 206 Somn 1:122, 165, 182 Somn 2:18, 79, 276 Abr 155 Ios 122, 147, 170 Mos 1:93 Decal 143 Spec 2:101 Aet 113, 137 QE 2:15b

διανοέω (81) Opif 13, 19, 24, 82 Leg 1:51 Cher 73, 81 Det 170 Post 82, 86, 87, 152 Gig 16, 23, 47 Deus 20, 20, 28, 31, 33, 49, 56, 93 Agr 64 Plant 81 Ebr 51, 124 Sobr 36 Conf 4, 24, 25, 154, 155 Migr 14 Her 74, 110 Congr 98, 99 Fug 194 Somn 1:32, 112 Somn 2:123, 130 Abr 41, 94, 163 Ios 13, 245 Mos 1:1, 46, 103, 169, 313 Mos 2:31, 55, 136, 174, 249 Spec 1:170 Spec 2:8, 156 Spec 3:141, 157, 172, 199, 204 Spec 4:7, 157 Virt 197 Prob 130 Aet 25 Flacc 12, 82, 101 Legat 198, 242, 262, 347 QG 2:54a, 4:206b QE 2:25b

διανόησις (8) Leg 3:44 Cher 71 Post 36, 80 Deus 34 Ebr 101 Conf 123 Her 108

διανοητικός Leg 2:22, 23 QG 1:55a

διάνοια (492) Opif 2, 5, 46, 46, 71, 79, 90, 128, 135, 146, 172 Leg 1:49, 62, 72 Leg 2:11, 55, 85, 91, 106 Leg 3:16, 17, 21, 35, 36, 44, 47, 56, 58, 61, 116, 123, 125, 168, 187, 210, 215, 218 Cher 9, 13, 16, 19, 29, 31, 82, 85, 95, 102, 107 Sacr 10, 26, 33, 36, 36, 64, 66, 74, 78, 86, 102, 113, 135 Det 10, 13, 15, 20, 22, 29, 35, 37, 38, 40, 40, 48, 97, 122, 125, 126, 127, 128, 137, 146, 147, 168 Post 18, 20, 22, 26, 80, 83, 87, 88, 88, 100, 102, 113, 118, 118, 123, 136, 151, 164, 165, 167, 184 Gig 17, 53 Deus 3, 4, 8, 9, 45, 46, 67, 118, 136, 138 Agr 9, 27, 43, 49, 53, 81, 108, 126 Plant 7, 21, 40, 42, 58, 74, 103, 111, 138, 159, 169 Ebr 23, 28, 39, 59, 69, 70, 82, 94, 108, 126, 140, 159 Sobr 3, 11, 38, 42 Conf 20, 27, 44, 49, 59, 66, 74, 100, 105, 123, 129, 131, 132, 133, 159, 177, 191 Migr 3, 14, 34, 50, 71, 71, 72, 74, 77, 78, 81, 81, 84, 111, 114, 115, 117, 132, 155, 157, 169, 187, 204, 213, 214, 219, 222, 224 Her 4, 12, 15, 70, 71, 89, 93, 110, 124, 204, 242, 245, 246, 249, 250, 251, 257, 268, 280, 296, 307 Congr 33, 45, 47, 56, 65, 121, 129, 137, 143, 156, 162, 180 Fug 10, 92, 110, 118, 138, 144, 148, 150, 154, 156 Mut 26, 33, 45, 69, 114, 118, 132, 144, 152, 154, 165, 168, 176, 177, 178, 178, 179, 193, 194, 194, 201, 205, 216, 236, 245, 245, 247, 250 Somn 1:11, 27, 29, 44, 66, 72, 79, 81, 90, 91, 115, 128, 148, 164, 184, 199, 250 Somn 2:2, 22, 65, 74, 76, 95, 137, 162, 171, 173, 176, 179, 180, 226, 229, 251, 272 Abr 57, 71, 77, 78, 107, 119, 122, 152, 161, 172, 175, 177, 201, 226, 251, 273 Ios 8, 11, 61, 71, 97, 106, 113, 126, 165, 179, 192, 235, 254, 265 Mos 1:24, 159, 188, 190, 223, 244, 259, 274, 278, 286, 301 Mos 2:24, 51, 69, 76, 96, 129, 129, 135, 140, 141, 167, 171, 237, 252, 272, 273 Decal 1, 13, 15, 35, 43, 52, 64, 80, 82, 86, 101 Spec 1:9, 11, 20, 30, 32, 49, 54, 59, 61, 105, 176, 191, 205, 210, 214, 259, 269, 283, 287, 288, 290, 299, 321, 331 Spec 2:9, 9, 30, 30, 36, 45, 46, 54, 64, 185, 197 Spec 3:2, 51, 92, 121, 135, 189, 192 Spec 4:20, 62, 75, 160, 163, 191, 191, 192 Virt 11, 30, 45, 57, 92, 103, 118, 127, 134, 161, 189, 214 Praem 28, 31, 50, 61, 80, 88, 104, 123, 153, 163 Prob 11, 17, 20, 22, 29, 46, 55, 61, 75, 87, 128, 140 Contempl 13, 27 Aet 43, 78 Flacc 10, 19, 102 Legat 2, 35, 52, 77, 109, 177, 274, 310, 329 Prov 2:12, 18, 20, 28, 35, 66 QG 2:16, 54a, 54a, 54d, 3:29, 4:33a, 211 QE 2:2, 21, 28, 38a, 38b, 45a, 45b, 47 QE isf 7, 8

διανοίγω (18) Sacr 89, 89, 89, 89, 102, 103, 104, 112, 118 Migr 222 Her 117, 124 Mut 56 Somn 2:36, 36, 275 Mos 2:281 QE isf 22

διανομεύς Legat 147 QG 1:62:1

διανομή (19) Her 179, 182 Mos 1:206, 318, 321, 324 Mos 2:85, 289 Decal 14 Spec 1:175, 204, 208 Spec 2:116, 136, 139 Flacc 140 Legat 158, 158 QG 3:12

διαντλέω Cher 120

διανυκτερεύω Aet 4 Flacc 36

διαπαλαίω Flacc 188

διαπάσσω Mos 1:127

διαπατάω Mos 1:74 Flacc 165 Hypoth 11:15

διαπέμπω (11) Fug 149, 154, 155 Ios 14 Mos 2:232 Spec 4:107 Flacc 97, 103 Legat 165, 220, 313

διαπεραίνω Contempl 81

διαπεράω QG isf 6

διαπέτομαι Flacc 165

διαπίπτω Leg 3:150, 150 Sacr 32

διαπιστέω Virt 74

διαπλάσσω (45) Opif 63, 68, 134, 135, 140, 148, 153 Leg 2:96 Leg 3:85, 161 Post 33, 104 Deus 46 Plant 6, 34 Ebr 110 Conf 90, 95, 175 Migr 3 Her 52 Congr 90, 136 Fug 68, 69 Mut 30, 137, 146 Somn 1:15 Mos 1:279 Mos 2:84 Spec 1:28, 105, 266 Spec 4:196, 218 Praem 160 Aet 66, 69, 98 Legat 56, 290 QG 1:51, 2:17c, 66

διαπλέκω Contempl 50

διαπλέω Mos 2:41 Legat 47, 190

διαπνέω (15) Leg 3:14 Deus 38 Ebr 207 Mut 84 Somn 2:146 Ios 5 Mos 1:42, 106 Decal 163 Spec 1:69 Spec 2:60 Spec 4:214, 223 Praem 153 Prob 110

διαποζεύγνυμαι Post 156

διαπολεμέω Mos 1:319

διαπονέω (21) Opif 128 Agr 64 Plant 25, 94 Congr 24, 142 Abr 69 Ios 152, 230 Spec 1:149 Spec 2:61, 64 Spec 3:100, 117 Virt 4, 94 Praem 119 Prob 74, 80, 146 Contempl 1

διαπόνητος Abr 133

διαπονητότατα (διαπόνητος)

διαπορέω (19) Leg 1:43, 85, 90, 101 Det 32, 57 Post 1, 33 Gig 1 Deus 104 Plant 8 Congr 73 Mut 15 Somn 1:5 Mos 1:16 Decal 18 Spec 2:129 Aet 85 Prov 2:72

διαπόρησις Mos 2:237 Contempl 77

διάπραξις Conf 158

διαπράσσω (10) Conf 55, 155 Abr 196 Mos 1:83, 327 Mos 2:30, 217 Spec 3:76 Virt 41 Flacc 137

διαπρεπής Migr 203 Mos 2:140 Spec 4:69 Virt 36

διαπρέπω Migr 161 Fug 154

διαπτοέω (6) Ios 183, 197, 239 Mos 2:250 Flacc 176 Legat 370

διαπτύσσω Her 63 Somn 2:127 Spec 3:6 Contempl 78

διαπυνθάνομαι Fug 153 Hypoth 7:14

διάπυρος (6) Mut 139, 180 Somn 1:22 Somn 2:67 Abr 79 Aet 47

διαριθμέω Ios 158, 180 Decal 96 Spec 2:140 Spec 4:11

διαρκής Opif 80 Spec 1:173 Prob 122

διαρπάζω Flacc 76

διαρρέω (17) Sacr 32, 80 Post 113, 119, 122 Ebr 131 Conf 38, 102 Fug 201 Mut 33 Mos 2:184 Spec 2:19, 240 Spec 3:37 Spec 4:91 Flacc 16 QG 2:12d

διαρρήγνυμι Leg 2:57 Fug 111 Somn 1:245 Ios 217

διαρρήδην Opif 25

διαρρύομαι Leg 3:42

διαρτάω (10) Det 7 Fug 112 Ios 187 Mos 2:197 Spec 3:23 Spec 4:210 Aet 114 Legat 131, 366 QG 3:3

διάρτησις Plant 60

διασείω Leg 2:99 Agr 106 Mut 158 Prob 79 Aet 36

διασημαίνω Opif 84 Contempl 77 Legat 264 Prov 2:48 QG 3:20a

διάσημος Somn 1:201, 226 Mos 2:284

διασκεδάννυμι Agr 40

διασκεδαστής Leg 3:12

διάσκεψις Fug 162 Legat 221

διασκοπέω Conf 86 Migr 189, 220 Mut 145

διασμύχομαι Mos 2:56

διασπάω Agr 40 QG 2:14

διασπείρω (16) Post 89 Plant 59 Conf 1, 1, 1, 118, 121, 196, 196, 196 Congr 56, 56, 57, 58 Mos 1:128 Flacc 71

διασπορά Conf 197 Praem 115

διάστασις (13) Opif 102, 102, 102, 102, 120 Post 129 Her 144 Congr 147 Somn 1:26 Decal 25 Aet 79 QG (Par) 2:2, 2:2

διαστατός Opif 36, 49 Somn 1:26 Decal 25

διαστέλλω (24) Leg 3:88, 157, 168 Cher 129 Sacr 4, 4 Post 44, 60 Agr 133, 142 Ebr 127, 143 Migr 19 Her 139, 166, 215, 312 Congr 129, 129 Mut 192 Somn 2:24, 110, 296 Mos 2:237

διάστημα (50) Opif 26, 33, 35, 37, 96 Sacr 137 Det 107 Post 18, 19 Deus 30 Agr 115 Plant 81 Ebr 181 Conf 5 Migr 139 Her 148, 149, 150, 150 Fug 101 Mut 142, 179, 190, 267 Somn 1:28 Mos 2:35, 78, 89, 91, 91, 91, 94, 163 Decal 148 Spec 1:178 Spec 2:142 Spec 4:81, 128, 232, 234 Praem 112 Contempl 28, 86 Aet 4, 52, 53, 54 Flacc 92 QG 2:64b QE 2:28

διαστηματικός Decal 24, 24

διαστολή (6) Agr 13, 129 Mut 252 Mos 2:158 Spec 1:100 Spec 4:108

διαστρέφω Sobr 10

διασυνιστάνω Mut 164

διασυνίστημι (27) Leg 1:1 Leg 2:83 Sacr 132 Post 63 Gig 3 Deus 130 Ebr 77, 124, 185 Conf 119 Migr 41, 54 Her 8, 54, 61, 162, 237, 258, 291 Somn 2:245 Abr 166 Ios 1 Mos 1:198 Mos 2:262, 282, 286 QE isf 18

διασυρμός Legat 176, 176

διασύρω Det 12 Migr 83 Prov 2:56

διασύστασις Opif 106 Prob 58

διασῴζω (33) Leg 1:73 Leg 3:189 Sacr 123 Plant 144 Ebr 68, 111 Migr 122, 125 Her 247 Congr 58 Mut 60 Abr 46, 98, 164, 177, 180, 230 Ios 205 Mos 1:69 Mos 2:234, 255 Spec 1:159, 184, 334, 338 Spec 3:129 Virt 201 Aet 35 Legat 41, 328 Hypoth 6:2 QG 1:96:1, 4:69

διάταγμα (25) Sacr 88 Post 95, 146 Deus 131 Sobr 21 Migr 162 Congr 120 Somn 1:101 Abr 5 Mos 2:36, 203, 213, 233 Decal 17, 168 Spec 1:1 Spec 2:42 Spec 4:4, 72, 97, 161, 207 Virt 90, 134 Legat 301

διάταξις (7) Sacr 136 Fug 96 Mos 2:48 Spec 1:230, 232 Contempl 78 QG 3:52

διαταράσσω Legat 337

διάτασις Leg 3:229

διατάσσω (56) Opif 1, 39, 54 Deus 87, 133 Conf 2, 137 Migr 182 Abr 2 Mos 1:2 Mos 2:10, 15, 49, 52, 78, 138 Decal 158, 174 Spec 1:108, 177, 179, 233, 235, 247 Spec 2:1, 34, 79, 116, 250 Spec 3:12, 23, 153 Spec 4:10, 61, 102, 160, 167, 215, 232 Virt 18, 19, 80, 88, 91, 99, 101, 105, 113, 143, 201 Aet 34, 54 Legat 210, 317, 361 Prov 2:1

διατείνω Opif 61, 111 Leg 2:22 Ebr 182 QG 3:22

διατειχίζω (8) Opif 33 Post 45, 91 Migr 158, 164 Her 201 Somn 1:76 Abr 223

διατελέω (50) Leg 2:32, 54 Leg 3:34, 94, 101 Agr 45, 123, 152 Plant 23, 162 Ebr 148 Conf 12, 167 Migr 119 Fug 166, 199 Mut 17, 80 Somn 2:106, 144 Abr 34, 85, 155, 209 Ios 103, 223 Mos 1:40, 148 Decal 49, 117 Spec 1:113, 115, 304 Spec 2:168, 207 Virt 136, 217 Prob 4 Contempl 10, 47, 63 Aet 19, 61, 93 Flacc 122 Legat 123 Hypoth 11:5 Prov 2:19, 21, 35

διατέμνω Spec 3:198 Spec 4:107 Flacc 189

διατηρέω (34) Opif 131, 168 Leg 3:189, 196 Cher 84, 85 Sacr 111 Det 67, 68 Deus 6 Migr 142 Congr 106 Somn 2:111, 141 Abr 37, 90, 106, 243 Mos 1:118 Decal 114 Spec 1:3, 175, 290, 324 Spec 3:46, 62, 74 Contempl 33 Aet 35 Flacc 79 Legat 308, 321, 325 QE 2:38a

διατήρησις Leg 1:55 Det 62 Congr 89, 98

διατίθημι (39) Leg 2:39 Leg 3:76, 85, 235 Cher 75, 81 Deus 44 Plant 155 Sobr 18 Conf 53, 145, 154 Migr 4 Her 313 Fug 138, 191 Somn 1:198 Somn 2:51, 83, 164, 279 Abr 102 Ios 156, 199 Mos 1:218 Spec 1:248 Spec 2:137 Spec 3:79, 84, 106 Spec 4:103, 103, 222, 227, 227 Virt 168 Contempl 43 Legat 245 QE 2:24b

διατονικός Leg 3:121 Post 104 Agr 137 Congr 76 Somn 1:205

διατορεύω Leg 3:88

διατρέφω Leg 3:175 Spec 1:338 Spec 2:199

διατριβή (12) Sacr 24 Post 173 Sobr 67 Congr 81 Fug 202 Somn 1:68 Abr 23 Ios 118 Spec 2:44, 119 Contempl 20 Flacc 177

διατρίβω (40) Opif 144 Leg 1:68, 71 Leg 3:152 Gig 62 Plant 96 Migr 189, 191, 196 Her 82 Fug 129 Mut 116 Somn 1:45 Somn 2:91, 125, 244 Abr 119 Ios 168, 185, 270 Mos 1:47, 137 Mos 2:71 Decal 29, 102 Spec 1:165, 261 Spec 2:165, 250 Spec 3:78 Spec 4:8 Virt 3, 212 Prob 6 Flacc 168 Legat 185, 231, 271, 296, 351

διάτριτος Conf 151

διατυπόω Opif 25 Leg 1:99 Congr 136 Ios 54 QG 1:21

διατύπωσις Leg 1:5

διαυγής (8) Leg 3:170 Agr 144 Plant 116 Conf 92 Her 311 Mos 1:99 Spec 2:202 Contempl 73

διαυλοδρομέω (7) Opif 101 Spec 1:178 Spec 2:122 Spec 4:85, 234 Praem 170 Aet 58

δίαυλος Deus 36 Mut 117 Spec 1:338 Spec 2:246

διαφαίνω (10) Opif 57, 76 Deus 140 Spec 1:90 Prob 15, 120 Aet 120 Flacc 91 Legat 277 QG 1:96:1

διαφανής (7) Her 196, 197, 197, 198 Somn 2:53 Legat 364 Hypoth 0:1

διαφερόντως (64) Opif 53, 164 Leg 2:106 Post 61 Deus 116 Agr 51, 62 Plant 7, 31, 55, 74, 119 Ebr 220 Sobr 63 Conf 82 Migr 178 Her 118, 191, 222 Congr 50, 156 Fug 198 Mut 39, 60 Somn 1:25, 49 Somn 2:123 Abr 214, 222, 256 Ios 55, 97, 240 Mos 1:29, 98, 228, 263 Mos 2:9, 30, 38, 67, 159 Decal 100 Spec 1:179, 240 Spec 2:110, 195 Spec 4:55, 235 Virt 2, 55, 61, 154, 163, 175 Praem 53 Prob 81 Contempl 78 Flacc 23, 180 Legat 136, 210, 346 Hypoth 11:14

διαφέρω (187) Opif 41, 62, 63, 64, 136, 140, 150 Leg 1:88, 93 Leg 3:53, 72, 196, 234 Cher 56, 56 Sacr 93, 129 Det 6, 16, 56, 81, 105, 127, 151 Post 22, 34, 62, 64, 112, 141, 145, 162, 172 Gig 16, 24, 39 Deus 84, 101, 172 Agr 26, 28, 48, 67, 67, 120, 121, 143 Plant 44, 146, 154, 165 Ebr 177, 196 Sobr 34 Conf 144, 185, 187 Migr 104, 108, 138, 148, 180 Her 23, 40, 89, 126, 126, 150, 240, 244, 250, 283 Congr 35, 65, 81 Fug 62, 62, 152 Mut 4, 66, 78, 83, 146, 182, 211 Somn 1:28, 38, 64, 65, 79, 205, 205 Somn 2:24, 28, 28, 132, 224, 249, 254 Abr 38, 49, 130, 213 Ios 29, 44, 142, 147 Mos 1:24, 35, 43, 183, 221, 245, 296 Mos 2:50, 57, 78, 82, 112, 162, 180, 180, 191, 196, 221, 289 Decal 67 Spec 1:87, 253, 273, 293, 318, 318, 327, 344 Spec 2:26 Spec 3:27, 57, 78, 175 Spec 4:172, 186 Virt 11, 16, 127, 130, 134, 224 Praem 43 Prob 5, 19, 24, 62, 89, 126, 149 Contempl 1, 59 Aet 10, 42, 132 Flacc 149, 162 Legat 33, 43, 76, 80, 278, 320 Hypoth 7:15, 11:10 Prov 1, 2:34, 66 QG 1:20, 31, 62:1, 4:110b, 110b, 180, 184, 200b QE 2:46, 55b QE isf 8, 21, 26

διαφεύγω (10) Det 153 Mos 1:87 Mos 2:255 Decal 150, 173 Spec 1:36, 45 Spec 2:253 Virt 46 Praem 149

διαφθείρω (111) Leg 3:22, 25, 27, 113, 227, 228, 228, 229, 229, 233, 243, 248 Sacr 123, 134 Det 32, 38, 99, 116, 141, 165, 174 Post 82, 94, 145 Deus 16, 21, 105 Agr 77, 101, 126 Plant 144 Ebr 28 Sobr 13 Conf 25, 27, 193 Migr 66, 200 Her 302 Congr 55, 137 Fug 117 Mut 144, 189, 195 Somn 2:161, 288 Abr 11, 98, 135, 136, 180, 229 Ios 36, 45, 50 Mos 1:8, 11, 39, 100, 105, 110, 133, 143, 236, 305 Mos 2:235, 286, 287 Decal 16, 64, 77, 122, 124 Spec 1:289, 313 Spec 3:11, 34, 39, 51, 96, 107 Spec 4:23 Virt 42, 149, 186 Praem 12 Prob 71, 104 Contempl 9, 16, 86 Aet 21, 47, 49, 49, 67 Flacc 66, 67, 68 Legat 107, 123, 124, 128, 130, 230 QG 1:94, 2:13b, 54a QE 2:47 QE isf 26

διαφθορά (8) Leg 3:234 Ebr 211 Somn 2:63 Virt 17 Prob 127 Legat 40 QG 2:13a QE isf 23

διαφθορεύς Legat 92

διαφίημι Mos 2:22, 211 Prob 18 Legat 175

διαφορά (74) Opif 58, 134 Leg 1:42 Leg 2:75, 76, 85, 87, 97 Leg 3:99, 133, 140 Cher 37, 114, 129 Sacr 23, 77, 84, 98, 100 Det 77, 108 Post 40, 78, 109, 117 Agr 26, 59, 124, 140 Ebr 171, 202, 217 Conf 8, 173 Congr 70, 130 Fug 52, 86, 96, 174 Mut 30, 41 Somn 1:203, 209 Somn 2:32, 183 Abr 159, 210, 214 Ios 32, 62, 155 Mos 1:75 Mos 2:237, 289 Decal 9, 20, 28 Spec 1:53, 240, 339 Spec 2:123, 178, 221 Spec 3:74, 76, 105, 119 Spec 4:20 Virt 117 Flacc 78 QG 1:60:1, 4:30, 148

διάφορος (25) Opif 41 Leg 1:83 Leg 2:73 Post 81 Plant 152, 153 Ebr 30, 88, 89, 90, 109, 170 Her 244 Congr 25 Fug 26 Somn 1:202 Ios 155 Mos 2:179 Decal 50 Spec 2:28, 29, 150, 243 Hypoth 6:2 Prov 2:17

διαφορότης Spec 4:207

διάφραγμα Spec 4:93

διαφυλάσσω (41) Leg 3:168, 189 Cher 85 Sacr 69 Deus 28 Ebr 224 Conf 102 Migr 55 Her 108, 114, 181, 184, 184, 314 Fug 112 Somn 1:3, 149, 179 Somn 2:9 Mos 1:241 Mos 2:34 Spec 2:16, 30, 111, 198 Spec 4:119, 143 Virt

37, 96, 222 Praem 13 Contempl 68 Aet 36, 59, 74 Flacc 5, 8 Legat 300, 328 Hypoth 6:2 QG 2:15b

διαφύομαι Spec 1:217

διάφυσις Opif 39 Mos 1:228

διαφωνέω (7) Plant 156 Ebr 114, 116 Conf 55, 56 Mut 109 QE 2:38a

διαφωνία Her 248 QE isf 4

διάφωνος Leg 2:15

διαχαράσσω Somn 1:188

διαχειμάζω Legat 15

διαχειρίζω Spec 4:193

διαχέω Post 104 Sobr 49, 49 Legat 309

διαχλευάζω QG 2:71a

διαχράομαι Spec 3:109, 162 Prob 114

διαχωρίζω Sacr 139 Migr 13 Her 163, 198 Somn 1:76

διαψεύδω Mos 1:283

δίγλωσσος Sacr 32

δίδαγμα Leg 3:194 Det 135 Post 147 Deus 183 Migr 91

διδακτικός Congr 35 Mut 83, 88, 255 Praem 27

διδακτός Leg 3:50 Sacr 113 Mut 263 Mos 1:76 QG isf 16

διδασκαλεῖον Mos 2:216 Decal 40 Spec 2:62 Praem 66 Legat 312

διδασκαλία (68) Opif 79 Leg 1:92, 94, 94 Cher 10, 101, 102 Sacr 7, 48, 79 Det 66, 143 Post 91, 131, 141, 146 Deus 54 Conf 59, 72, 98, 140 Migr 39, 184 Her 66 Congr 24, 36, 69, 112, 127 Fug 146, 200 Mut 8, 12, 84, 99, 257, 257 Somn 1:168, 170 Somn 2:6 Abr 52, 53, 53 Ios 1 Spec 1:105, 132 Spec 2:80, 141, 164 Spec 4:96, 97, 106, 124, 175 Virt 15, 74 Praem 49, 58, 162 Prob 13 Contempl 76 Aet 3 Legat 277 QG 2:54a, 54a, 4:102b QE 2:25b QE isf 25

διδασκαλικός Agr 122 Abr 52

διδάσκαλος (54) Sacr 51, 65, 65 Det 17, 49, 66, 145 Post 38, 54, 80, 141 Gig 54 Deus 134 Agr 66 Migr 116 Her 19, 102, 182, 295 Congr 114, 122, 122 Mut 86, 270 Somn 1:191 Somn 2:202 Abr 6 Ios 74, 254 Mos 1:21, 80 Spec 1:41, 56, 59 Spec 2:99, 226, 233 Spec 3:11, 39 Spec 4:140 Flacc 3, 34, 124 Legat 26, 27, 31, 53, 54, 227 Prov 2:70 QG 2:41, 4:104 QE 2:4, 16

διδάσκω (131) Opif 142, 167 Leg 1:93 Leg 2:76, 85 Leg 3:1, 36, 50, 55, 173, 179 Cher 68, 85 Sacr 104 Det 66, 78, 132, 134 Post 90, 120, 132, 138, 139, 140, 140, 141, 142, 148, 150, 159, 166, 185 Deus 125 Plant 110 Ebr 11, 81, 84, 157 Sobr 44 Conf 148 Migr 8, 42, 90, 140 Her 17, 39, 61, 71, 121, 156, 169, 207, 243, 291, 295 Congr 12, 69, 70, 90, 94, 97, 107, 126 Fug 6, 11, 55, 116, 122, 139, 140, 169, 172, 172, 207 Mut 5, 18, 32, 76, 85, 88, 138, 220, 236, 256, 263, 270 Somn 1:115, 160, 173 Somn 2:45, 68, 124 Ios 86 Mos 1:22, 23, 308 Mos 2:141, 190, 215 Decal 84, 87, 123, 124 Spec 1:42, 319 Spec 2:96, 107, 160, 239 Spec 3:21 Spec 4:107, 115, 130, 154, 161, 223 Virt 63, 183 Praem 23, 49, 61 Prob 61, 144 Flacc 52, 121 Legat 56, 64, 115, 364 QG 4:104 QE 2:12

διδαχή Spec 2:3

δίδραχμος Her 186, 187, 189

δίδυμος (20) Gig 56 Ebr 90, 90 Her 162 Congr 18, 82 Mut 248 Somn 2:69, 70, 72 Mos 1:240 Spec 3:23, 179, 179 Virt 51, 208 Praem 63, 63 Prob 1 Prov 2:8

διδυμοτοκέω QG 2:12c

δίδωμι (358) Opif 45, 46 Leg 1:89 Leg 2:46, 59 Leg 3:23, 26, 43, 56, 56, 56, 56, 57, 58, 58, 58, 58, 59, 60, 61, 61, 61, 61, 64, 66, 68, 83, 84, 106, 133, 169, 173, 173, 177, 180, 182, 217 Cher 2, 20, 122 Sacr 9, 19, 43, 56, 64, 72, 89, 97, 97, 98, 98, 98, 102 Det 21, 112, 126, 161, 161, 161, 161 Post 9, 63, 145, 147 Gig 43 Deus 5, 6, 6, 7, 50, 57, 57, 94, 145, 156, 158, 158, 169 Agr 21, 168, 172 Plant 95, 96, 107 Ebr 47, 67, 106, 119, 212 Sobr 8, 21 Conf 8, 57, 160, 175, 191 Migr 2, 80, 84, 101, 115, 120, 121, 142, 173, 191 Her 2, 2, 8, 20, 22, 24, 25, 31, 31, 33, 33, 36, 38, 49, 65, 96, 99, 103, 104, 114, 114, 123, 123, 123, 124, 124, 162, 187, 205, 267, 273, 300, 302, 313 Congr 56, 71, 72, 81, 99, 99, 108, 119, 130, 137, 137 Fug 53, 58, 69, 75, 76, 117, 139, 150, 151, 154, 175 Mut 2, 12, 19, 51, 62, 130, 131, 131, 131, 134, 136, 141, 145, 147, 174, 191, 208, 218, 231, 253, 270 Somn 1:3, 78, 100, 103, 103, 174, 194, 252, 254 Somn 2:44, 45, 75, 92, 159, 176, 177, 255, 290, 290 Abr 155, 171, 196, 215 Ios 37, 120, 149, 188, 198, 228, 229, 249, 251, 257, 260 Mos 1:17, 18, 59, 84, 168, 241, 266, 301, 306, 315, 316, 322, 327 Mos 2:21, 142, 234, 242, 245, 266 Decal 17, 61, 74, 78, 106, 118, 132, 177 Spec 1:43, 52, 104, 122, 142, 142, 144, 145, 145, 147, 151, 152, 157, 187, 278, 284, 340 Spec 2:26, 27, 69, 72, 75, 78, 83, 83, 84, 113, 135, 157, 180, 182, 182, 183, 216, 218, 219, 245, 262 Spec 3:46, 90, 128 Spec 4:7, 11, 30, 31, 31, 77, 173 Virt 60, 79, 86, 96, 100, 104, 122, 165, 169, 223, 226 Praem 6, 39, 69 Prob 51, 52 Aet 91 Flacc 7, 14, 24, 25, 40, 61, 84, 96, 113, 113, 140, 140, 171, 178, 185 Legat 13, 37, 72, 73, 158, 179, 183, 200, 222, 225, 232, 248, 287, 334, 334, 343, 343, 345 Hypoth 11:10 Prov 2:6, 33, 37, 38 QG 1:21, 27, 27, 77, 2:13a, 41, 3:23, 4:206a QG isf 17 QE 2:49b

διεγείρω Decal 143 Spec 1:266 Contempl 89

διεῖδον διοράω

διεῖδον Somn 1:188 Aet 77

δίειμι Virt 146

διεῖπον Ios 98

διεκδύομαι (6) Det 153 Post 178 Agr 103 Migr 219 Somn 1:220 Somn 2:89

διεκπαίω Mos 2:154

διελέγχω (22) Cher 17 Sacr 94, 94 Gig 21 Ebr 58 Conf 14, 53, 141 Her 305, 306 Fug 28 Mos 1:70, 94 Spec 1:23, 64 Spec 2:38 Spec 3:139 Spec 4:52, 60 Aet 143 Flacc 89 Prov 2:26

διενοχλέω Legat 301

διεξαρκέω Mut 192 Spec 2:199

διεξαρτάομαι Migr 68

διέξειμι (50) Leg 3:63, 145, 148 Cher 89 Det 66, 72, 102, 164 Post 162 Agr 139 Plant 2 Conf 3, 114 Migr 138 Her 246 Fug 22 Mut 61, 197 Somn 1:13 Somn 2:63, 180 Abr 208, 247 Ios 167, 185, 246 Mos 1:47, 57, 175, 233, 234, 306 Mos 2:278 Spec 2:143, 144, 199, 216 Spec 4:54, 136, 238 Prob 141 Aet 10 Flacc 15 Legat 37, 38, 63, 190, 197, 243 QE isf 26

διεξέρχομαι (45) Opif 130 Leg 3:222 Cher 84 Sacr 29 Deus 60 Plant 28 Ebr 138 Sobr 1 Conf 52 Migr 113 Her 1, 12, 21, 24, 109, 131 Congr 64, 113, 148 Somn 1:40, 122 Somn 2:112, 161 Abr 84, 142, 255 Ios 159, 244 Mos 1:214 Mos 2:66, 238, 246, 257, 275 Decal 52 Spec

2:211, 223, 242 Virt 16 Praem 3, 26 Flacc 6, 81 Legat 240, 302

διεξοδικός Congr 30, 33

διέξοδος (18) Det 130 Post 53, 79 Deus 34 Agr 135, 145 Plant 49 Conf 14 Migr 72, 100, 117 Mos 1:23, 167 Mos 2:150 Spec 1:272, 342 Spec 4:111 Praem 145

διέπω Ebr 79 Mos 2:187 Flacc 105

διερεθίζω Deus 138 Mut 159 Praem 19 Contempl 74

διερείδω Det 41, 42 Post 71 Somn 1:129

διερευνάω (40) Opif 21, 69 Plant 79 Ebr 165 Conf 57 Congr 63 Somn 2:215 Abr 3, 3, 52, 69, 163, 208 Ios 181 Mos 1:10, 27, 190 Decal 78 Spec 1:8, 36, 213, 283 Spec 2:45 Spec 3:117, 183 Spec 4:92, 114 Virt 27 Praem 26, 66 Prob 66, 74 Contempl 31 Aet 86 Legat 67, 174, 213, 261 Prov 1, 2:18

διερμήνευσις Det 167 Migr 79

διερμηνεύω (19) Opif 31 Leg 3:87 Post 1 Deus 144 Sobr 33 Conf 53 Migr 12, 73, 81 Her 63 Ios 95, 189 Mos 1:286 Mos 2:31, 34 Spec 2:256 Spec 4:132 Contempl 31 Legat 353

διέρπω Spec 4:83

διέρχομαι (20) Leg 1:14 Leg 3:4 Det 1 Deus 145, 145, 145, 166, 166 Ebr 65 Conf 137 Her 312 Congr 95 Ios 89, 97 Mos 1:191 Spec 1:65 Praem 93 Flacc 155 Legat 342 Hypoth 6:9

διερῶ (45) Opif 116 Sacr 98 Det 16, 52 Deus 123 Plant 61, 109, 111 Ebr 25 Conf 197 Migr 78, 202 Her 170, 174, 193, 279 Congr 95, 96, 103, 134, 162 Fug 37, 88 Mut 191 Somn 1:62 Somn 2:184 Mos 1:205 Decal 159, 162 Spec 1:84, 104, 169, 180, 206, 216, 232, 238 Spec 2:60, 238 Spec 3:46, 179 Spec 4:138, 197 Virt 149 Flacc 185

διερωτάω Hypoth 7:14

διεσθίω (8) Leg 3:186 Post 56 Somn 1:77 Mos 1:121 Spec 4:83 Praem 143 Aet 20 Flacc 167

διετής Ios 100

διετία Flacc 128

διευθύνω Agr 177

διηγέομαι (25) Det 134 Migr 34, 140 Somn 1:189 Somn 2:21, 32, 111, 137 Abr 253 Ios 6, 90, 94, 103, 104, 107, 252 Mos 1:213, 268 Mos 2:226, 239 Prob 5 Flacc 103 Legat 226, 304 QG 4:144

διήγημα Ios 183 Decal 56 Legat 295 QE 2:38a

διήγησις (11) Sacr 79 Det 133 Plant 128 Abr 20 Ios 28, 94 Spec 2:39 Spec 3:49 Praem 61 Legat 223 QG 4:168

διηθέω Opif 137 Abr 9 Spec 1:218

διηκριβωμένως Leg 3:23

διήκω Leg 1:11 Plant 30 Spec 1:137 Aet 4 QG (Par) 2:3

διημερεύω Gig 31 Flacc 34, 36, 167

διηνεκής Sacr 94 Abr 26 Mos 2:135

διίπταμαι Mos 2:291

διΐστημι (34) Opif 33, 36, 38, 96, 152 Cher 9, 58, 103 Det 49, 50, 107 Post 91, 98, 162 Gig 58 Agr 27 Ebr 196 Her 244, 270 Fug 98 Somn 2:262 Ios 5, 230 Mos 1:163, 177, 216 Mos 2:254 Virt 135 Aet 75, 79, 80, 139 Flacc 71 QG (Par) 2:4

δικάζω (53) Opif 62, 125, 130, 159 Leg 3:13 Cher 15 Deus 75, 76, 76 Agr 95 Ebr 41, 223 Sobr 4, 22 Conf 125 Migr 91 Congr 143 Mut 134 Somn 1:9 Somn 2:43 Abr 64, 141, 240 Ios 72, 72 Mos 1:47, 48 Mos 2:150 Decal 47, 141 Spec 1:175 Spec 2:49, 164, 232 Spec 3:127, 136 Spec 4:55, 57, 70, 77, 176 Virt 6 Prob 6, 42 Aet 77 Flacc 4, 38, 131, 133 Legat 183 Prov 2:32, 34, 35

δικαιάδικος Spec 4:63

Δικαιάρχεια Flacc 27 Legat 185

δικαιολογέομαι Legat 290

δικαιολογία Mos 2:228 Legat 331, 364

δικαιονομέω Leg 3:197

δικαιονομία Spec 4:176

δικαιοπραγέω Agr 123 Ebr 26 Congr 6, 163 Fug 35

δίκαιος (281) Opif 1 Leg 1:35, 72, 87 Leg 2:18 Leg 3:9, 9, 9, 10, 10, 10, 30, 77, 78, 79, 165, 191, 228 Cher 15, 15 Sacr 54, 72, 74 Det 18, 18, 75, 88, 105, 121, 121, 123, 130, 170 Post 32, 48, 59, 88, 173, 174 Gig 3, 5 Deus 49, 85, 117, 118, 140 Agr 2, 13, 20, 43, 50, 80, 181 Plant 1, 140, 141, 171, 175 Ebr 17, 29, 34, 58, 64, 81, 107, 111, 187, 194, 197 Sobr 10, 30, 38, 40, 47 Conf 35, 105, 152 Migr 61, 121, 124, 125, 196, 219 Her 36, 77, 94, 95, 104, 118, 162, 162, 162, 162, 162, 168, 169, 223, 260, 260 Congr 90, 90, 101 Fug 38, 62, 63, 82, 82, 90 Mut 40, 50, 62, 104, 146, 146, 153, 189, 196 Somn 1:91, 184 Somn 2:7, 116, 193, 194, 194, 223, 224, 296 Abr 27, 27, 31, 33, 33, 38, 46, 232, 232, 242 Ios 9, 72, 143 Mos 1:24, 31, 45, 50, 55, 102, 142, 244, 260, 274, 279, 302, 314, 315, 323 Mos 2:4, 47, 100, 108, 214, 228, 279, 279 Decal 14, 38, 69, 106, 140, 178 Spec 1:102, 160, 300 Spec 2:14, 27, 139, 171, 180, 236, 243 Spec 3:27, 61, 82, 122, 129, 131, 137, 153, 164 Spec 4:2, 10, 40, 46, 55, 56, 62, 63, 64, 64, 65, 66, 66, 66, 67, 67, 67, 67, 70, 77, 103, 137, 137, 138, 139, 141, 141, 143, 166, 169, 169, 183, 189, 193, 194, 204, 205, 206, 222 Virt 50, 88, 91, 109, 124, 167, 167, 174, 182, 189, 194, 226 Praem 93 Prob 44, 72, 149 Contempl 17 Flacc 50, 53, 106, 121, 126, 134, 173 Legat 25, 28, 63, 64, 180, 213, 239, 243, 289, 350, 363, 366, 371, 371 QG 1:70:2, 97, 2:11, 11, 11, 11, 16, 3:8, 4:52b, 64, 64, 172, 184, 204 QG isf 12 QE 2:19

δικαιοσύνη (123) Opif 51, 73, 81 Leg 1:63, 65, 72, 72, 87, 87, 87 Leg 3:77, 150, 247 Cher 5, 96 Sacr 27, 37, 57, 84 Det 18, 72, 73, 121, 122, 123, 143, 157 Post 93, 128 Deus 79 Agr 18 Plant 122, 122 Ebr 23 Conf 86, 112 Her 94, 95, 161, 162, 163, 209, 243 Congr 2, 16, 31, 109, 179 Mut 177, 197, 225, 240 Somn 1:49, 80, 179, 198 Somn 2:74, 174 Abr 27, 33, 56, 103, 104, 208, 219 Ios 153 Mos 1:154, 328 Mos 2:9, 185, 216, 237 Decal 164 Spec 1:277, 304 Spec 2:12, 13, 62, 63, 204, 259 Spec 3:155 Spec 4:56, 57, 134, 135, 136, 141, 143, 170, 181, 194, 204, 218, 226, 230, 230, 231, 238 Virt 1, 47, 175, 180 Praem 15, 22, 23, 66, 157, 160, 162 Prob 67, 70, 83, 159 Contempl 17 Aet 108 Legat 85, 312 Hypoth 6:8 Prov 2:2 QG 4:64 QE 1:6, 2:10b

δικαιότης Prov 2:36

δικαιόω (66) Cher 33 Det 38, 81, 170 Deus 9, 159 Ebr 48, 51, 95, 131 Migr 73, 95, 144, 155, 216 Her 194 Congr 119 Fug 69 Mut 19, 24, 136 Somn 1:59, 212, 214 Somn 2:10, 107, 114, 132 Abr 142, 171, 207, 246 Ios 237 Mos 1:44, 96, 243, 311 Mos 2:130, 131, 211 Decal 43 Spec 1:6, 67, 109, 140, 180, 215, 298 Spec 2:18, 72, 113, 158 Spec 3:52, 168, 172, 180 Spec 4:23, 215 Virt 16, 82 Praem 120 Contempl 1 Legat 84 Hypoth 6:5 QG 3:20b QG isf 13 δικαίωμα (7) Det 67, 68 Her 8 Congr 163 Somn 2:175 Decal 109 QG 4:184

δικανικός Spec 1:342

δικασμός Leg 3:233

δικαστήριον (40) Deus 112 Plant 108, 173 Ebr 139 Conf 126, 141 Migr 223 Congr 27, 143 Fug 118 Mut 198 Somn 1:122 Somn 2:188 Abr 20 Mos 2:217 Decal 111 Spec 1:55 Spec 2:44 Spec 3:52, 64, 74, 121, 141, 145, 148, 169 Spec 4:9, 19, 34, 66, 136 Virt 171, 206 Praem 28, 69, 69 Flacc 7 Legat 368 Prov 2:36, 61

δικαστής (70) Opif 11, 128, 155 Leg 1:87, 87 Leg 3:205 Cher 11, 72 Det 23 Deus 50, 112, 128, 183 Agr 116 Conf 25, 126 Her 271 Fug 118 Mut 112 Somn 2:99 Abr 133, 168 Ios 63, 215 Mos 2:217, 228, 238 Decal 87, 87, 140, 140 Spec 1:55, 121, 277 Spec 3:53, 69, 71, 77, 82, 143 Spec 4:7, 8, 43, 56, 59, 64, 70, 71, 71, 78, 136, 172, 174, 188, 190, 206 Contempl 44 Aet 142 Flacc 54, 106, 126, 129, 134 Legat 183, 341, 349, 350, 359, 359, 360

δικαστικός Her 247 Mut 110

δίκη (145) Opif 46, 80, 80, 169 Leg 1:64 Leg 3:106, 202, 233 Det 100, 169, 176 Post 9, 12 Gig 21, 31 Deus 34, 48, 74, 76, 76, 76 Agr 36, 51, 117 Plant 107 Ebr 28, 30, 111, 135, 223 Sobr 6 Conf 8, 108, 116, 118, 120, 121, 128, 160, 162, 170, 174, 182 Migr 186, 225 Her 226 Mut 62, 106, 110, 125, 194, 194 Somn 1:94 Somn 2:154, 290 Abr 41, 141 Ios 43, 48, 71, 170, 228 Mos 1:46, 55, 134, 218, 237, 245, 326 Mos 2:53, 99, 162, 200, 202, 206 Decal 95, 122, 150, 177 Spec 1:14 Spec 2:27, 28, 28, 78, 231, 234, 243, 252 Spec 3:19, 31, 39, 46, 58, 76, 90, 102, 129, 131, 140, 168, 175, 175 Spec 4:7, 10, 11, 19, 20, 77, 90, 173, 176, 201 Virt 42, 76, 100, 147, 227 Praem 69, 136, 147, 149, 157 Prob 79, 89 Flacc 14, 104, 107, 115, 115, 128, 131, 146, 181, 189 Legat 107, 336 Hypoth 7:1 Prov 2:33, 40 QG 1:77, 89, 2:15b, 72, 4:51a QE 2:6a

δίκτυον (11) Cher 57 Sacr 29 Det 65 Post 116 Deus 153 Agr 24, 44, 103 Conf 92 Praem 20 QG 2:54c

διμερής Congr 26

διμοιρία Her 49 Spec 2:139

δίμοιρος ἐπιδίμοιρος

δίνη Gig 13 Plant 24 Conf 23 Somn 2:237

διό (234) Opif 38, 66, 83, 127, 135, 139, 163 Leg 1:6, 31, 58, 76, 86 Leg 2:8, 12, 18, 27, 34, 38, 46, 47, 55, 58, 60, 89, 90, 92, 101 Leg 3:8, 20, 26, 34, 39, 42, 45, 78, 139, 142, 154, 160, 167, 172, 180, 196, 207, 213, 214, 229, 237, 253 Sacr 53, 66, 79, 103, 109, 114 Det 27, 47, 67, 78, 90, 103, 119, 139, 144, 160 Post 69, 73, 75, 96, 122, 123, 127, 135, 142, 145, 145, 152, 163, 177 Gig 28 Deus 74, 127 Agr 55, 100, 110, 144 Plant 17, 19, 42 Ebr 23, 120, 122, 138, 146, 166 Conf 102, 147, 154, 161, 182 Migr 27, 73, 75, 76, 97, 135, 145, 147, 153, 168, 182, 193 Her 4, 19, 33, 58, 81, 100, 159, 198, 233, 252, 256 Congr 57, 122 Fug 40, 63, 71, 86, 128, 138, 159, 203 Mut 17, 68, 74, 138, 176, 180, 200, 229, 249, 254, 263 Somn 1:10, 40, 109, 116, 137, 167, 221, 229, 241, 245, 252 Somn 2:3, 42, 80, 93, 100, 135, 149, 236, 280, 296 Abr 19, 80, 103, 159, 166 Mos 1:50, 61, 279 Mos 2:41, 53, 82, 197 Decal 93, 142 Spec 1:42, 42, 77, 248, 290, 310, 344 Spec 2:49, 115, 142, 150, 167, 240 Spec 3:77, 96, 119, 137 Spec 4:14, 43, 44, 61, 66, 131, 184, 191, 194, 213 Virt 163, 187, 192, 216 Prob 47, 139, 140 Aet 33, 38, 89, 91, 121, 127, 132, 133 Prov 2:67, 68, 70 QG 1:27, 29, 97, 97, 2:15c, 3:29 QG (Par) 2:4 QE 2:9b, 46 QE isf 25

Διογένης Plant 151 Prob 121, 157 Aet 77

διοδεύω Migr 216, 216, 219, 220

διοίγνυμι (23) Sacr 78 Det 100, 103 Post 18 Deus 39 Plant 169 Sobr 3 Migr 39, 165 Her 25, 50, 78, 118, 119 Fug 31 Mut 255 Abr 70 Mos 1:93, 185 Spec 3:6 Praem 37 Legat 269 QE isf 22

διοιδέω Legat 254 Prov 2:18

διοικέω (7) Opif 3, 73 Plant 13, 49 Conf 170 Mos 2:133 Spec 2:130

διοίκησις (10) Deus 163 Abr 241 Mos 2:148 Spec 3:203 Spec 4:187 Praem 81 Aet 83 Flacc 4 Prov 2:54 QG (Par) 2:7

διοικίζω (33) Det 149, 160 Post 91 Gig 18, 56 Ebr 124 Conf 10 Migr 12, 138, 150, 175, 178, 216 Her 83, 179, 258, 270, 277 Fug 43, 62, 92 Somn 1:66 Somn 2:180, 198, 258 Decal 11 Spec 1:320 Spec 4:94, 210 Virt 207 Flacc 79 Legat 281 Hypoth 7:8

διοικισμός Migr 150

διόλλυμι Sacr 106 Post 68 Ebr 224

διόμνυμι Decal 94

διομολογέω Spec 3:71 Spec 4:195 Flacc 140

διονομάζω Virt 203 Contempl 64 Legat 246

Διονυσιακός Legat 96

Διονύσιος Ios 132 Flacc 20 Prov 2:29, 30

Διόνυσος (7) Prob 130 Legat 78, 79, 82, 88, 89, 92

διόπερ (34) Leg 1:96 Leg 3:120 Cher 51 Sacr 76 Det 131, 175 Post 58, 123, 135, 148, 167, 185 Agr 171 Sobr 61 Conf 166 Migr 60, 85, 163, 171 Her 190 Congr 153, 158, 179 Fug 44, 118 Mut 31 Somn 1:185 Abr 206 Mos 2:256 Decal 38 Spec 2:24, 152 Spec 3:168 QG 3:21

δίοπος Cher 36 Post 182 Spec 4:200

διορατικός Her 36

διοράω διεῖδον

διοράω Leg 3:35 Det 61 Ebr 88 Somn 1:248

διόρθωσις Sacr 27

διορίζω Leg 1:20 Spec 2:125

διορύγμα Leg 3:32, 32 Spec 4:7

διορύσσω Leg 3:157 Flacc 73

διορυχή Somn 1:39

Διόσκοροι Διόσκουροι

Διόσκουροι (Διόσκοροι) (6) Decal 56 Legat 78, 79, 84, 87, 92

διότι (110) Opif 27, 30, 37, 37, 49, 144, 156, 160 Leg 1:14 Leg 3:130 Cher 30, 108 Deus 72, 90 Agr 84, 101, 109, 165, 165 Ebr 23, 111 Sobr 28 Conf 152, 161 Migr 79, 124, 166, 171, 197 Her 21 Fug 51, 109, 110, 176 Mut 203 Somn 1:31, 117, 136, 175, 210 Somn 2:242 Abr 11, 18, 102, 129, 145, 150, 154, 166, 166 Ios 176, 254 Mos 1:302 Mos 2:58, 88, 100, 104, 123, 241, 288 Decal 27, 111, 137 Spec 1:94, 94, 162, 179, 205, 229, 252, 326 Spec 2:133, 173, 179, 181, 187, 214 Spec 3:20, 83, 146 Spec 4:124, 180, 217 Virt 114, 146, 156, 196 Praem 16, 40, 113, 171 Prob 21, 109 Aet 1, 16, 23, 50, 61, 87, 133 Flacc 181 Hypoth 11:14 Prov 2:10, 35, 58, 68 QG 4:76b QG isf 3, 3 QG (Par) 2:7

διοχλέω Plant 176

δίπηχυς Spec 4:128

διπλασιάζω (11) Opif 106 Abr 81 Mos 1:47, 132 Mos 2:220, 266 Spec 1:170, 180 Spec 2:177 Spec 4:212 Flacc 118

διπλάσιος (27) Opif 48, 48, 91, 91, 92, 95, 109, 109, 109 Somn 1:26 Mos 1:187, 207 Mos 2:90, 115, 264 Decal 21, 22 Spec 2:15, 75, 97, 133, 136, 138, 200 Spec 4:17, 214 Virt 225

διπλασίων (7) Opif 93, 94, 106, 107 Virt 44, 88 Contempl 35

διπλόος (διπλοῦς) (35) Sacr 19 Post 41, 62, 63 Agr 16, 136 Plant 124, 149 Ebr 162 Sobr 21 Her 49 Mut 196 Somn 2:26, 26, 90 Mos 1:137, 205 Mos 2:113, 127, 162, 180, 225 Spec 1:71 Spec 3:156, 197 Spec 4:2, 5, 11, 13, 33 Contempl 32 Aet 85 Flacc 147 QG 1:77, 4:80

διπλοῦς διπλόος

δίς (27) Opif 48, 48, 51, 95, 99, 99, 99, 105 Leg 1:3 Leg 3:190 Cher 3 Gig 33 Deus 82 Her 15, 255 Congr 4 Mut 61 Somn 2:25, 27 Abr 176 Mos 2:115 Decal 22 Spec 1:171, 261 Spec 2:58, 200 Contempl 27

δισμύριοι Mos 1:304

δισσός (102) Opif 54, 109, 116, 118, 118, 123, 152 Leg 1:13, 31, 78, 105 Leg 2:9, 23 Leg 3:211, 242 Cher 22, 79 Sacr 46 Post 60 Agr 26, 30, 133 Plant 13, 61, 142 Ebr 8, 85, 162, 169 Conf 60, 108 Her 22, 55, 57, 182 Congr 32, 129 Mut 43, 106 Somn 2:6, 240 Abr 119, 157 Ios 100, 107, 107, 194, 213 Mos 2:92, 109, 127 Spec 1:57, 88, 172, 180, 180, 187, 195, 218, 232, 233, 342 Spec 2:37, 150, 188 Spec 3:106, 126, 170, 197 Spec 4:17, 21, 32, 35, 106, 108, 110, 158, 215, 216, 218, 218 Praem 16, 16, 22, 65, 70, 85, 99, 127 Contempl 38 Aet 20, 22, 98 Flacc 43, 77, 77 Prov 2:33, 60 QG 1:55a, 2:54a, 68b QE 2:45a

δισχίλιοι Spec 1:158 Spec 2:120 Hypoth 6:9

δισώματος Contempl 63

διυφίημι Spec 3:118

διφθέρα Opif 84

δίφορος Spec 4:203, 208

δίφρος Agr 75 Ios 149

διφυής Leg 1:49 Det 83 Deus 129 Prob 134

δίχα (93) Opif 16, 72, 103, 117, 167 Leg 1:83, 92 Leg 2:29, 71, 71 Sacr 40, 45, 112 Det 87, 135 Post 157 Gig 38 Deus 93, 109 Agr 133 Ebr 190 Sobr 36 Conf 105 Migr 179, 192, 193 Her 161, 215, 225, 242 Congr 7, 8, 21, 173, 178, 178 Fug 6, 89 Mut 81, 157, 157 Somn 2:257 Abr 16, 46, 53, 271 Ios 46, 155, 190, 225, 226 Mos 1:130, 142, 238 Mos 2:79, 80, 123, 223 Decal 28 Spec 1:23, 147, 180, 181, 291 Spec 2:115, 233 Spec 3:42 Spec 4:70, 150 Virt 38, 135, 206, 226 Praem 130 Prob 88, 124 Contempl 6, 54 Aet 52, 74, 98, 104, 149, 149 Flacc 150 Legat 28, 118, 215, 275 Prov 2:39, 55, 62, 66

διχῇ Sacr 131 Decal 56

διχηλέω (8) Agr 131, 133, 134, 142, 145, 145 Spec 4:106, 108

διχόθεν (6) Congr 33 Somn 2:227 Ios 82 Mos 1:229 Contempl 61 Flacc 57

διχόμηνος Spec 2:155

διχόνοια Decal 9

διχόνους Sacr 32 Prob 154 QG 2:12c

διχοτόμημα Her 215, 237, 311, 312, 312

διχότομος Opif 101, 101 Spec 1:178, 178

διχῶς Opif 91 Leg 2:36 Plant 115 Her 55

δίψα (16) Leg 2:84, 86 Post 138, 172 Ebr 159 Somn 1:124 Somn 2:60, 150 Mos 1:191 Spec 1:249 Spec 4:82, 82 Virt 130 Contempl 37, 56 QG (Par) 2:7

διψαλέος Leg 3:149

διψάω (30) Leg 3:12 Det 113 Post 86, 136, 142 Agr 34 Ebr 5, 112, 221 Her 100, 269 Congr 127 Fug 139, 187 Mut 165 Somn 1:38, 50 Decal 149 Spec 2:62 Spec 4:56 Virt 2, 9, 30, 79 Prob 13 Contempl 37 Legat 18, 97 QG (Par) 2:7 QE 2:13b

δίψος (10) Congr 165 Mos 1:100, 181, 183, 187, 191, 211 Decal 16 Praem 136 Hypoth 6:3

διωθέω (9) Opif 10 Leg 3:143 Det 123 Agr 178 Her 299 Congr 130 Virt 165 Flacc 18 QE isf 4

διώκω (40) Leg 3:20 Cher 15, 74, 75, 75, 75, 77, 130 Det 18 Post 18 Deus 99, 100 Agr 93 Conf 48 Her 203, 270 Mut 113 Somn 1:199 Somn 2:279 Abr 231 Mos 1:140, 167, 176, 178, 178 Mos 2:248, 251, 254 Decal 146 Spec 3:39 Spec 4:80, 111 Virt 7, 30 Praem 95, 147, 148 Flacc 151, 178, 188

διωλύγιος Post 116 Somn 2:162

Δίων (8) Aet 48, 48, 49, 49, 49, 50, 50, 51

δίωξις Ios 181

διῶρυξ Mos 1:38, 99, 103

διώροφος QG (Par) 2:7, 2:7

δόγμα (161) Opif 11, 25, 158, 172 Leg 1:54, 55, 108 Leg 2:55 Leg 3:1, 20, 35, 35, 35, 84, 188, 194, 229 Cher 9, 17, 85, 86, 121 Sacr 3, 5, 19, 50, 65, 77, 121, 130 Det 6, 28, 32, 41, 48, 50, 66, 66, 103, 133, 135 Post 24, 34, 38, 51, 66, 129, 130, 133, 175, 180 Gig 52 Deus 18, 72, 88, 166 Agr 44 Plant 52, 62, 70, 77, 77, 98 Ebr 198, 212, 213 Conf 34, 35, 36, 51 Migr 22, 34, 53, 131, 152, 159, 197 Congr 35, 36, 54, 111, 142, 167 Fug 45, 57, 148, 173, 200, 210 Mut 5, 16, 32, 65, 168, 202, 210 Somn 1:50, 148, 181, 199, 250 Somn 2:74, 170, 244, 256, 284, 285 Abr 79, 81, 82, 101, 112, 220, 243 Ios 86 Mos 1:24, 29, 48 Mos 2:66, 140, 212 Decal 30 Spec 1:37, 50, 106, 269, 345 Spec 2:29, 61, 63, 147 Spec 3:1, 46 Spec 4:75, 92, 107, 140, 141, 149 Virt 8, 42, 99 Praem 122 Prob 3, 97 Contempl 26, 31, 35, 68 Aet 2, 17, 55, 76, 76, 77 QG 2:41, 4:33b QE 2:16, 17, 17 QE isf 7

δογματικός (13) Leg 2:100 Leg 3:215 Cher 121 Sacr 42, 64 Post 59, 138 Migr 119 Her 114, 246, 276, 292 QG 1:70:1

δοκέω (565) Opif 21, 46, 68, 71, 72, 79, 127, 128, 133, 136, 140, 154, 163, 163, 164 Leg 1:6, 16, 49, 52, 69, 76 Leg 2:6, 69 Leg 3:6, 27, 34, 35, 97, 112, 113, 164, 167, 174, 178, 182, 190, 202, 210, 236, 245 Cher 57, 63, 67, 75, 94, 98, 113, 114 Sacr 2, 30, 35, 35, 41, 48, 62, 91, 94, 123, 128 Det 10, 35, 41, 46, 49, 50, 50, 55, 57, 61, 69, 70, 78, 89, 95, 102, 109, 144, 175 Post 16, 95, 114, 136, 143, 152, 161 Gig 50 Deus 46, 69, 87, 93, 121, 141, 142, 148, 157, 170 Agr 3, 27, 40, 43, 54, 60, 69, 69, 127, 136, 169, 169 Plant 3, 7, 12, 33, 56, 65, 100, 128, 141, 147, 175, 176 Ebr 1, 23, 35, 37, 44, 54, 64, 73, 84, 87, 88, 106, 146, 164, 166, 187, 204, 205, 208 Sobr 18, 27, 31, 47, 47 Conf 52, 57, 59, 69, 91, 99, 100, 103, 106, 125, 138, 179 Migr 12, 40, 83, 86, 87,

88, 90, 96, 110, 115, 140, 156, 160, 163, 167, 178, 186, 201, 211, 222, 225, 225 Her 5, 16, 18, 21, 29, 55, 76, 85, 113, 116, 121, 128, 130, 145, 148, 150, 171, 180, 216, 224, 266, 276, 283, 294, 299 Congr 5, 13, 38, 100, 110, 115, 128, 146, 163, 177, 178 Fug 41, 65, 75, 76, 82, 92, 140, 155, 156, 173, 175, 179 Mut 60, 61, 104, 113, 166, 170, 179, 181, 206, 211, 222, 231, 232, 233, 248, 252 Somn 1:2, 6, 9, 31, 35, 37, 47, 87, 114, 131, 135, 163, 185, 238 Somn 2:24, 107, 113, 119, 132, 138, 154, 166, 181, 214, 215 Abr 41, 44, 52, 64, 84, 98, 101, 103, 113, 123, 144, 167, 178, 188, 190, 193, 206, 216, 267 Ios 6, 15, 27, 30, 35, 38, 51, 58, 59, 66, 70, 87, 91, 93, 101, 116, 117, 124, 126, 143, 170, 176, 177, 189, 190, 204, 215, 228, 235, 238, 248, 253 Mos 1:3, 4, 12, 21, 48, 51, 62, 64, 74, 90, 122, 146, 149, 160, 191, 202, 265, 305, 314, 316 Mos 2:10, 49, 74, 90, 107, 138, 158, 162, 175, 186, 204, 214, 221, 227, 235, 241, 245, 270 Decal 23, 33, 33, 39, 43, 46, 55, 57, 61, 68, 80, 89, 108, 110, 113, 128, 136, 141, 142 Spec 1:2, 7, 9, 13, 21, 23, 79, 79, 80, 84, 133, 152, 195, 209, 215, 227, 235, 312, 315, 316, 330 Spec 2:11, 11, 68, 75, 89, 97, 106, 131, 169, 191, 235, 239, 252 Spec 3:1, 18, 19, 21, 70, 75, 77, 80, 100, 119, 120, 121, 136, 159, 166, 175, 192, 194 Spec 4:3, 9, 14, 40, 46, 61, 80, 82, 95, 103, 138, 138, 202, 206, 238 Virt 16, 18, 29, 37, 63, 85, 91, 103, 136, 139, 192, 225 Praem 9, 12, 40, 78, 89, 91, 136, 136, 149 Prob 27, 57, 100, 124, 140 Contempl 3, 17, 45, 59, 78, 79 Aet 4, 27, 31, 61, 63, 75, 75, 78, 102, 106, 109 Flacc 1, 2, 11, 19, 26, 52, 53, 59, 59, 76, 80, 106, 116, 119, 125, 126, 130, 138, 140, 141, 153, 162 Legat 4, 35, 73, 91, 93, 95, 113, 117, 118, 176, 178, 180, 182, 192, 214, 216, 220, 243, 255, 259, 265, 303, 308, 325, 333, 335, 361, 367, 372 Hypoth 6:1, 6:4, 6:8, 7:1, 7:1, 7:14, 7:14, 7:18, 11:1 Prov 2:18, 24 QG 2:11, 3:20b, 52, 4:145, 172, 172, 202a, 203, 206a, 228 QG isf 5 QE 2:16, 17, 47, 105 QE isf 2, 7, 26

δόκησις (10) Det 162 Ebr 34, 39 Sobr 14 Migr 108, 158 Congr 103 Mos 1:43 QE 2:45a, 107

δοκησίσοφος (9) Leg 3:179 Sacr 3, 32 Post 52 Ebr 37 Migr 136 Mut 105, 176 Somn 2:298

δοκιμάζω (40) Leg 1:77 Leg 2:7 Leg 3:168 Sacr 77, 80 Det 142 Post 62, 96 Deus 128 Ebr 186, 190 Conf 184 Migr 48, 51, 117 Her 308 Abr 253 Ios 118, 138 Mos 1:164, 226, 263, 306, 327 Mos 2:34, 177 Spec 4:153 Virt 32, 54, 54, 60, 63, 66, 208, 227 Prob 23 Legat 220 Prov 2:11 QG 2:11, 3:3

δοκιμασία (7) Congr 164 Fug 149, 155 Spec 4:106, 157 Virt 68 Flacc 130

δοκιμαστής Her 252 Virt 64

δοκιμεῖον Somn 1:226

δόκιμος (73) Opif 128 Leg 1:66, 66 Leg 2:67 Leg 3:95, 104, 119, 120, 168 Sacr 137 Post 96, 162 Deus 65 Agr 16, 66 Plant 18, 81 Sobr 20 Conf 4, 159 Her 158, 180, 216, 252 Fug 19, 63 Mut 124, 179, 208, 208 Somn 1:202, 255 Somn 2:20 Abr 180, 189 Ios 114, 161, 201 Mos 1:24, 221, 267 Mos 2:28, 32, 187, 234 Spec 1:61, 78, 104, 166, 214 Spec 2:36, 125 Spec 3:117, 176 Spec 4:47, 77, 137, 174, 196 Virt 65, 201 Praem 111 Prob 98, 140 Contempl 41 Aet 48 Flacc 163 Legat 107, 144, 173, 282 Prov 2:35 QG isf 7

δοκίς Mos 1:231

δολερός Fug 79 Spec 3:86 Spec 4:185 Prob 91, 154

δόλιος Sacr 32 Conf 39

δολιχεύω (8) Opif 44, 113 Plant 9 Mos 1:118 Decal 104 Spec 1:172 Aet 109 QE 1:1

δόλιχος Opif 85 Det 35 Somn 1:115 Spec 2:103, 246

δόλος (11) Leg 3:108 Conf 160 Fug 53, 77, 78 Spec 4:183 Legat 62 QG 4:228, 228, 228, 228

δολοφονέω (15) Det 61, 69, 96 Post 49, 124, 172 Conf 47 Ios 15 Spec 3:90, 131, 131 Virt 199 Flacc 65, 179 Legat 65

δολόω Hypoth 7:7

δόμα (10) Leg 3:196, 196 Cher 84 Sacr 111 Deus 6 Migr 94, 142 Mos 2:242 QG 4:148, 148

δόξα (256) Opif 79, 154, 171 Leg 1:51, 59, 75 Leg 2:56, 56, 57, 107 Leg 3:7, 7, 13, 20, 31, 36, 86, 126, 230 Cher 9, 66, 71, 83, 117 Sacr 2, 3, 5, 69, 78 Det 6, 9, 17, 32, 33, 71, 78, 95, 122, 136, 157, 160, 161 Post 13, 19, 34, 35, 38, 38, 42, 52, 65, 117, 122 Gig 15, 15, 36, 37, 37, 39, 53, 62 Deus 120, 150, 172 Agr 56, 129, 130 Plant 171 Ebr 36, 36, 38, 45, 52, 57, 57, 70, 73, 75, 76, 79, 144, 162 Sobr 3, 15, 57, 61, 67 Conf 48, 93, 106, 112, 118, 118 Migr 19, 21, 69, 86, 87, 92, 107, 152, 154, 172, 180, 183, 184, 187, 192 Her 48, 71, 92, 169, 212, 289 Congr 6, 15, 27, 54, 124 Fug 15, 16, 16, 19, 25, 33, 35, 39, 47, 128, 128, 151 Mut 92, 93, 94, 96, 214 Somn 1:73, 82, 124, 126, 218, 232, 237, 248, 255 Somn 2:12, 15, 16, 42, 47, 48, 50, 53, 55, 57, 59, 61, 62, 78, 93, 93, 95, 115, 133, 155 Abr 70, 77, 123, 123, 123, 184, 187, 219, 223, 263, 264 Ios 59, 147, 254 Mos 1:62, 293 Mos 2:53, 177 Decal 4, 65, 72, 125, 151, 153 Spec 1:11, 27, 28, 28, 45, 45, 59, 196, 311, 313, 328 Spec 2:11, 164, 208, 244 Spec 3:1, 31, 164 Spec 4:53, 71, 82, 88, 188 Virt 7, 35, 65, 161, 162, 166, 214, 214 Praem 11, 24, 27, 28, 29, 100, 162 Prob 3, 11, 19, 66, 75, 158 Contempl 17, 64 Aet 7, 7, 12, 47 Flacc 170 Legat 279, 328 Prov 2:8, 13, 18, 19 QG 4:43 QE 2:2, 45a, 45a, 45a, 45a, 45a, 47, 107 QE isf 16

δοξάζω (12) Opif 19 Leg 3:35 Cher 37, 69 Sacr 95 Post 25 Deus 21 Agr 82 Migr 108 Somn 1:91 Somn 2:269 Aet 106

δοξοκόπος Sacr 32

δοξομανέω Fug 30 Somn 2:114

δοξομανής Fug 126 Somn 2:98 Flacc 41

δορά (10) Ebr 87 Mos 1:127 Spec 1:151, 165, 232, 268 Praem 143, 146 Contempl 38 Flacc 71

δοράτιον Spec 3:92 Spec 4:222

δορκάς Agr 115 Spec 4:105

δόρυ Flacc 92

δορυάλωτος Leg 3:117 Flacc 60

δορυφορέω (21) Opif 139 Leg 1:59 Sacr 28, 59 Deus 109, 113 Conf 17 Migr 37 Her 223, 286 Congr 8 Mut 21 Somn 2:114, 232 Abr 122 Mos 1:189 Spec 1:30, 45, 173 Spec 3:41 Spec 4:168

δορυφόρος (26) Leg 3:115, 115 Det 33, 85 Ebr 201 Sobr 62 Conf 17, 18, 19, 20, 55, 101 Migr 170 Her 286 Somn 1:27, 32, 103 Somn 2:96 Mos 1:275 Spec 3:111 Spec 4:92, 123 Virt 8 Flacc 30, 38 Legat 6

δόσις Leg 3:26, 64 Cher 84 Spec 4:195

δοτός Deus 6, 6

δουλαγωγέω Prob 63

δουλεία (53) Leg 3:17, 192, 198, 199 Cher 75 Sacr 122 Deus 114 Plant 53 Her 268, 269, 271 Congr 175 Fug

207, 212 Abr 241 Ios 15, 20, 136, 219, 221 Mos 1:171, 247 Spec 1:58, 77 Spec 2:122, 122 Spec 4:14, 15, 17 Virt 111, 210 Praem 124, 137 Prob 10, 17, 32, 36, 42, 45, 57, 64, 105, 115, 118, 124, 135, 136, 137, 138, 139, 155, 158 Legat 17

δουλεύω (33) Leg 3:88, 193, 195, 199, 221, 240 Cher 71, 107 Her 272, 275 Congr 176, 176 Somn 2:100, 100, 136 Abr 164 Ios 247, 270 Spec 1:57 Spec 2:79, 85 Spec 4:17, 152 Virt 209 Praem 139, 164 Prob 57, 114, 115 Hypoth 7:3 QE 2:105, 105 QE isf 29

δούλη (12) Her 53 Congr 31, 33, 36, 79, 154, 154, 155 Abr 251 Ios 135 Mos 2:211 Virt 115

δουλικός Prob 36, 114

δουλοπρεπής (16) Leg 3:195 Agr 73 Her 186 Fug 28 Ios 77 Spec 2:28 Spec 4:183 Virt 87, 92 Prob 24, 24, 34, 99, 154 Contempl 72 Flacc 64

δοῦλος (157) Opif 85, 165, 167 Leg 2:97, 97, 107 Leg 3:88, 89, 156, 156, 193, 194, 198, 198, 201, 224 Cher 83, 117 Sacr 9, 72 Det 34, 56, 146 Post 109 Gig 46 Agr 58 Plant 101 Ebr 198 Sobr 32, 32, 51, 55, 59, 69 Conf 48, 91, 133, 133 Migr 26, 45 Her 5, 7, 273 Fug 20, 212, 212 Mut 33, 46 Somn 2:30, 51, 62, 136, 136, 294 Abr 45, 109, 228 Ios 35, 47, 66, 67, 69, 76, 123, 228, 244, 248 Mos 1:36, 201, 299, 324 Mos 2:21, 22, 50 Decal 61, 165, 166 Spec 1:126, 176 Spec 2:48, 68, 69, 69, 81, 82, 84, 90, 122, 123, 226, 227 Spec 3:145, 195 Spec 4:3, 4, 91, 113 Virt 121, 122, 123, 124, 124, 125, 162 Prob 1, 11, 22, 23, 24, 35, 35, 36, 37, 37, 38, 40, 41, 44, 45, 48, 48, 50, 51, 52, 60, 60, 61, 79, 101, 104, 136, 140, 142, 156, 159 Contempl 9, 71 Legat 13, 119, 119, 119, 119, 203, 233, 285 Hypoth 7:2, 7:14, 11:17 Prov 2:8, 17 QG 2:16, 16, 3:22, 4:168, 206b QG isf 5 QE isf 29

δουλοσύνη Prob 134

δουλόω (15) Leg 2:29, 49 Leg 3:17, 89, 220 Agr 42 Congr 165 Somn 1:114 Somn 2:279 Mos 1:167 Virt 118 Prob 22, 149, 159 Prov 2:35

δούρειος Spec 3:44

δράγμα (32) Somn 2:6, 6, 17, 17, 21, 30, 31, 32, 32, 33, 41, 75, 75, 78, 80, 80, 110 Ios 6, 112, 113, 158 Decal 160 Spec 1:158 Spec 2:41, 70, 162, 171, 175, 176 Spec 4:29 Virt 90, 145

δράκων (12) Agr 95, 96 Ebr 222 Migr 83 Somn 2:191 Mos 1:77, 91, 92 Praem 8 Aet 128, 128, 129

δρᾶμα Migr 112 Legat 202

δραματοποιΐα Legat 351

δράξ Mut 234, 249, 249 Somn 2:71, 73

δραπετεύω Migr 209 Spec 3:5 Virt 210

δραπέτης Migr 209

δρασμός (12) Leg 2:91 Leg 3:194 Cher 4 Sacr 129 Migr 26, 209 Her 270 Fug 14, 23, 78, 206 Prob 127

δράσσομαι Mut 234, 249 Somn 2:71, 73

δραστήριος (9) Opif 8, 8 Leg 3:86 Cher 87 Det 161 Fug 11 Mut 16 Prob 101 QG 3:61

δραστικός Congr 156 Mos 2:53 Spec 1:200 QG 3:38a, 49b

δραχμή (11) Her 145, 186, 187, 189 Congr 113, 113 Ios 258 Spec 2:33, 33, 33, 33

δράω (191) Opif 13, 85 Leg 1:5 Leg 2:38, 38 Leg 3:7, 33, 210, 210, 247 Cher 14, 75, 81, 122 Sacr 54, 68, 128, 130, 132 Det 12, 57, 64, 69, 104, 161, 172 Agr 25, 119, 123, 150, 153, 163 Plant 87 Ebr 73, 78, 122 Sobr 37 Conf 6, 47 Migr 129 Her 170 Fug 65, 74, 93, 94, 106, 133, 156 Mut 122, 243 Somn 1:7, 111 Somn 2:89, 196 Abr 122, 135, 174, 183, 184, 185, 188, 263 Ios 47, 66, 81, 166, 263 Mos 1:24, 38, 44, 46, 79, 94, 95, 201, 205, 297, 303, 305, 305, 308 Mos 2:30, 73, 144, 165, 213, 217, 220 Decal 60, 69, 74, 98, 105, 141 Spec 1:16, 57, 113, 127, 186, 234, 246, 284, 313, 314, 318, 321 Spec 2:13, 14, 52, 91, 98, 146, 234, 245, 248, 253 Spec 3:19, 19, 37, 64, 69, 74, 84, 87, 88, 88, 92, 95, 128, 149, 149, 153, 155, 156, 158, 180, 182, 197, 204, 209, 209 Spec 4:17, 32, 73, 77, 142, 184, 187, 193, 197, 198, 202 Virt 34, 127, 139, 166, 172 Praem 11, 32, 46, 72, 106, 135 Prob 27, 59, 61, 97 Contempl 1, 15, 42, 73 Aet 21, 38 Flacc 72, 137 Legat 92, 98, 102, 209, 233, 239, 261, 348 Hypoth 7:11, 7:11, 7:11 QG 3:3, 52, 4:69, 206b QE 2:19

δρεπανηφόρος Mos 1:168

δρέπανον Ios 6

δρέπω (15) Opif 156 Deus 40, 154 Agr 25, 152 Mut 165 Somn 1:58 Ios 91 Mos 1:230 Mos 2:22 Spec 4:81 Virt 91, 97, 156, 159

δρομαῖος Legat 364

δρομεύς Post 161 Deus 36 Agr 115, 177 Migr 133

δρόμος (20) Opif 86, 88 Leg 3:48 Det 23, 89, 141 Agr 68, 74, 177 Plant 9, 22, 76 Conf 115 Her 245 Somn 2:201 Abr 160 Mos 2:291 Spec 1:340 Aet 88 Flacc 26

δρόσος (9) Leg 3:169, 169 Migr 101, 101 Mos 1:200, 204 Mos 2:258 Virt 93 Praem 131

Δρουσίλλα Flacc 56

δρύϊνος Congr 61 Fug 39, 42 QG 4:161

δρυμός Abr 138 Spec 1:75

δρυοτόμος Contempl 7

δρῦς (7) Migr 216, 223 Congr 61, 61 Mut 211 Aet 64 Legat 127

δυάς (25) Opif 13, 13, 49, 95, 98 Leg 1:3 Gig 52 Deus 84, 84, 84 Mut 200 Somn 2:70 Abr 122 Mos 2:115, 288 Spec 1:180 Spec 3:180, 180 Praem 46, 46 Aet 113, 113 QG 2:12b, 3:61, 4:30

δύναμαι (644) Opif 4, 21, 23, 63, 76, 90, 103, 104, 124, 141, 156, 156, 162, 166 Leg 1:10, 62, 62, 86, 91 Leg 2:26, 48, 57, 65, 71, 73, 80 Leg 3:1, 4, 5, 5, 6, 15, 32, 40, 40, 50, 50, 52, 84, 109, 111, 116, 118, 120, 131, 140, 145, 146, 151, 152, 170, 180, 180, 202, 206, 206, 207, 207, 236, 240, 240, 244, 245 Cher 6, 17, 27, 36, 39, 39, 59, 65, 65, 78, 84, 85, 109 Sacr 19, 33, 37, 37, 49, 94, 95, 101, 114, 116, 116, 122, 124, 125, 135 Det 22, 31, 36, 43, 60, 78, 87, 89, 91, 96, 97, 100, 101, 101, 101, 105, 149, 151, 152, 152, 153, 161, 165, 176 Post 2, 20, 21, 50, 66, 67, 71, 74, 96, 134, 139, 142, 163, 175, 184 Gig 13, 29, 34, 38, 51, 52, 56 Deus 12, 47, 52, 55, 64, 68, 78, 78, 79, 80, 81, 129, 147, 149 Agr 4, 19, 22, 33, 37, 37, 47, 56, 56, 63, 76, 84, 93, 93, 94, 97, 113, 121, 142, 146, 147, 150, 151, 164, 179 Plant 21, 31, 60, 87, 89, 96, 130, 152 Ebr 27, 44, 48, 54, 56, 58, 59, 63, 71, 73, 75, 101, 103, 122, 126, 155, 156, 160, 164, 168, 169, 198, 199, 211, 213, 221, 224, 224 Sobr 6, 14, 21, 36, 42, 58, 61, 62 Conf 8, 11, 22, 25, 32, 39, 46, 66, 97, 98, 102, 105, 112, 112, 160, 161, 185, 194 Migr 26, 26, 27, 55, 64, 74, 78, 80, 85, 95, 144, 150, 154, 155, 167, 175, 192, 199, 207 Her

13, 34, 43, 44, 49, 58, 63, 82, 86, 109, 111, 125, 142, 143, 154, 194, 236, 237, 239, 240, 244, 246, 256, 274, 287, 304, 308, 308, 310 Congr 6, 8, 12, 14, 44, 52, 58, 72, 77, 81, 88, 106, 110, 121, 158, 163, 171 Fug 27, 30, 34, 61, 62, 96, 96, 109, 121, 159, 164, 187, 197, 201 Mut 7, 11, 68, 82, 100, 107, 117, 126, 158, 165, 183, 183, 196, 203, 209, 214, 224, 227, 231, 242, 252 Somn 1:4, 35, 37, 44, 49, 51, 54, 56, 57, 79, 81, 82, 91, 103, 117, 131, 136, 143, 164, 204, 220, 236, 237, 238, 239, 256 Somn 2:3, 11, 22, 24, 94, 101, 103, 122, 123, 171, 172, 176, 184, 226, 237, 241, 259, 276, 278 Abr 47, 47, 71, 122, 140, 162, 182, 184, 200, 211, 216, 216, 224, 236, 240, 243, 249, 252, 267, 268 Ios 9, 22, 27, 47, 58, 104, 140, 147, 158, 188, 214, 226, 227, 231, 238, 242, 249, 258 Mos 1:3, 11, 24, 78, 83, 104, 115, 124, 152, 170, 186, 188, 205, 207, 237, 243, 263, 278, 283, 295, 305, 328 Mos 2:6, 10, 13, 34, 70, 87, 175, 226, 229, 239, 247, 263 Decal 31, 64, 67, 87, 112, 112, 117, 130, 140 Spec 1:10, 10, 39, 42, 44, 49, 54, 65, 99, 113, 147, 176, 203, 263, 292, 298, 326, 332, 340, 341 Spec 2:15, 52, 105, 114, 121, 122, 189, 202, 207, 220, 231, 258 Spec 3:3, 25, 77, 78, 92, 94, 100, 103, 106, 159, 175, 175, 197, 198, 200 Spec 4:7, 29, 41, 105, 114, 186, 197, 204, 204, 223, 230, 235 Virt 5, 11, 29, 42, 54, 71, 74, 89, 105, 153, 158, 170, 203, 203, 213, 221 Praem 6, 11, 19, 26, 36, 43, 45, 67, 72, 80, 88, 94, 131, 133, 137, 140, 149, 156, 167 Prob 5, 7, 56, 109, 114, 128, 130, 146 Contempl 63, 68, 78 Aet 9, 49, 51, 82, 103, 128, 129 Flacc 1, 6, 11, 17, 31, 35, 43, 57, 64, 65, 72, 118, 118, 132, 143, 159, 176, 184 Legat 21, 27, 28, 39, 71, 111, 130, 131, 132, 134, 168, 171, 174, 189, 209, 223, 229, 238, 251, 260, 269, 311, 360, 368, 370 Prov 1, 2:8, 19, 27, 72 QG 1:3, 17a, 77, 2:12c, 15a, 62, 74, 3:26, 4:69, 76b, 104, 168, 184, 198, 206b QG isf 5 QG (Par) 2:5 QE 2:45b QE isf 4, 4

δύναμις (701) Opif 5, 7, 13, 13, 20, 21, 23, 23, 31, 46, 47, 49, 51, 51, 52, 57, 64, 67, 81, 85, 96, 101, 103, 125, 126, 126, 131, 140, 141, 141, 145, 148 Leg 1:10, 14, 14, 28, 30, 32, 37, 38, 38, 39, 42, 60, 61, 62, 62, 96, 98, 100, 100, 100 Leg 2:21, 21, 21, 22, 23, 24, 24, 35, 37, 40, 41, 41, 41, 45, 73, 86 Leg 3:14, 33, 35, 49, 49, 49, 73, 88, 96, 97, 115, 124, 136, 145, 185, 191, 202, 231, 232 Cher 19, 20, 27, 28, 29, 32, 51, 59, 59, 62, 63, 64, 70, 82, 96, 106, 128 Sacr 14, 18, 31, 36, 38, 39, 39, 41, 45, 47, 56, 56, 59, 59, 59, 60, 60, 69, 72, 73, 75, 76, 102, 108, 110, 119, 128, 131 Det 3, 6, 25, 29, 41, 53, 66, 72, 82, 83, 83, 89, 90, 92, 95, 102, 102, 112, 159 Post 5, 9, 14, 20, 27, 36, 64, 66, 120, 122, 126, 127, 141, 141, 143, 151, 161, 163, 167, 168, 169 Gig 37, 47, 56 Deus 3, 19, 34, 37, 56, 77, 78, 79, 80, 81, 85, 88, 109, 109, 110, 116, 167 Agr 12, 22, 22, 59, 63, 78, 85, 86, 86, 88, 94, 95, 111, 119, 157, 162, 166, 167, 172 Plant 14, 30, 45, 46, 50, 78, 83, 86, 86, 89, 90, 123, 125, 129, 133, 141, 144, 157 Ebr 6, 15, 22, 30, 32, 65, 82, 83, 91, 92, 105, 106, 113, 115, 121, 156, 185, 190, 192 Sobr 7, 13, 26, 43, 43, 47, 61 Conf 19, 30, 37, 49, 51, 52, 55, 104, 111, 115, 136, 137, 137, 166, 171, 172, 175, 175, 182, 187, 187, 188, 190, 192, 193, 195 Migr 3, 9, 40, 55, 57, 61, 76, 77, 82, 91, 102, 110, 119, 120, 124, 144, 170, 181, 181, 182, 202, 205, 213, 220 Her 4, 9, 24, 43, 73, 99, 102, 110, 118, 144, 151, 153, 160, 166, 166, 170, 172, 185, 212, 269, 270, 281, 288, 298, 304, 312 Congr 29, 30, 31, 55, 63, 78, 98, 125, 143, 155 Fug 15, 51, 69, 70, 81, 95, 97, 98, 100, 101, 103, 112, 122, 141, 146, 151, 162, 179, 182, 182, 191, 204 Mut 14, 15, 16, 28, 29, 29, 33, 59, 65, 65, 84, 84, 110, 111, 122, 129, 145, 220, 222, 232, 235, 250 Somn 1:45, 62, 69, 70, 77, 112, 131, 157, 162, 163, 170, 170, 185, 201, 240 Somn 2:1, 68, 69, 71, 95, 129, 145, 151, 200, 201, 212, 215, 220, 221, 254, 265, 291, 292, 297 Abr 26, 29, 30, 53, 54, 54, 57, 57, 59, 65, 67, 69, 73, 81, 99, 105, 105, 121, 122, 125, 129, 131, 140, 143, 145, 146, 180, 203, 214, 220, 228, 231, 235, 236, 239, 240, 243, 244, 261 Ios 58, 76, 82, 118, 138, 268, 269 Mos 1:3, 8, 21, 37, 50, 50, 69, 70, 81, 94, 100, 106, 111, 111, 148, 150, 156, 168, 169, 185, 185, 189, 224, 224, 225, 233, 261, 305, 334 Mos 2:1, 2, 7, 52, 65, 80, 96, 99, 99, 120, 132, 136, 181, 190, 192, 238, 248, 253, 255, 291 Decal 35, 44, 64, 69, 103, 109, 135, 147 Spec 1:30, 36, 44, 45, 46, 47, 49, 66, 99, 129, 159, 190, 209, 218, 229, 252, 252, 263, 265, 279, 294, 307, 308, 329, 341, 342 Spec 2:2, 15, 24, 29, 42, 45, 46, 60, 83, 99, 99, 132, 150, 157, 177, 177, 212, 224, 225, 240, 240 Spec 3:16, 26, 178, 180, 190, 195 Spec 4:26, 28, 29, 51, 56, 69, 74, 83, 115, 116, 132, 170, 178, 187, 187, 205, 214, 221 Virt 13, 26, 27, 33, 46, 49, 54, 155, 165, 166, 167, 185, 186, 203, 218 Praem 25, 26, 54, 64, 80, 89, 122, 125, 156, 157, 163 Prob 26, 61, 96, 104, 117, 131, 152 Contempl 6, 26, 63, 65, 65 Aet 8, 21, 21, 25, 26, 62, 74, 76, 79, 86, 107, 108, 116, 135, 137, 137, 148, 150 Flacc 1, 5, 163 Legat 6, 9, 54, 58, 78, 112, 118, 126, 216, 222, 233, 237, 256, 268, 346 Hypoth 7:20 Prov 2:40, 52, 62, 71, 71 QG 1:3, 21, 100:1a, 2:15a, 26a, 28, 54a, 64a, 64c, 3:18, 4:8a, 8b, 51b, 51b, 102a, 104, 145 QG isf 1, 8 QE 1:7b, 2:2, 18, 21, 24b, 28, 45a, 45a, 65

δυναστεία (32) Opif 33, 148 Leg 3:73 Sacr 49 Sobr 3 Her 24, 60, 270, 284 Fug 82 Somn 2:81 Abr 24, 221, 242, 244, 244, 261 Mos 1:148 Decal 136 Spec 1:208, 308 Spec 2:81 Spec 3:8, 69, 137 Spec 4:184 Praem 121 Prob 17 Flacc 105 Prov 2:40 QG 4:76b QE 2:6a

δυναστεύω (7) Opif 79 Leg 2:72 Somn 2:94, 291 Prob 45 Aet 80 QG 4:69

δυνάστης Abr 95 Spec 1:142 Prob 89

δυνατός (121) Opif 46, 151 Leg 1:29 Leg 2:81 Leg 3:42, 207, 214 Cher 34, 39, 78 Sacr 80, 80, 125 Det 30, 48, 49, 130 Gig 28 Deus 7, 134 Agr 95, 141 Plant 24, 176 Ebr 7, 82 Sobr 40, 53 Conf 47, 91, 102, 111 Migr 72, 73 Her 11, 33, 54, 202 Congr 5, 67, 156 Fug 40, 63, 63, 70 Mut 44, 218 Somn 1:87, 155, 187, 222, 231 Somn 2:14, 32, 122, 136 Abr 30, 53, 59, 90, 95, 112, 175, 184, 211, 223, 228, 229 Ios 42, 189, 244, 255 Mos 1:8, 39, 49, 91, 111, 174, 294 Mos 2:135 Decal 77 Spec 1:43, 68, 139, 140, 282 Spec 2:141 Spec 3:52, 85, 92 Spec 4:89, 127, 172 Virt 26, 62, 146, 168 Praem 5, 29, 86, 87, 134, 148, 154 Prob 17, 71, 108, 118, 132 Contempl 18, 70 Aet 136 Flacc 22, 105, 126 Legat 74, 110, 209 QG 2:5b, 4:7* QG (Par) 2:5

δύο (374) Opif 48, 48, 48, 49, 51, 51, 51, 51, 56, 60, 60, 95, 95, 96, 99, 102, 102, 102, 109, 109, 110, 118, 119, 119, 169 Leg 1:12, 12, 12, 22, 30, 53, 67, 72, 79, 79, 85 Leg 2:4, 20, 44, 48, 49, 49, 52, 53, 64, 71, 94, 95 Leg 3:7, 29, 53, 65, 81, 88, 88, 90, 91, 104, 120, 122, 140, 161, 189, 220 Cher 27, 28 Sacr 2, 4, 4, 4, 19, 20, 52, 59, 108, 133, 133 Det 31, 50, 82, 118, 118, 164 Post 28, 44, 75, 175, 183 Gig 65 Deus 53, 69, 69, 82, 129, 142 Agr 15, 30, 71, 79, 118, 138 Plant 14, 61, 123, 124, 124, 124, 172 Ebr 85, 115, 164, 195, 203, 210 Sobr 21, 34 Migr 51, 70, 177 Her 47, 49, 75, 134, 139, 144, 144, 146, 146, 147, 147, 164, 166, 167, 174, 176, 177, 177, 179, 179, 217, 219, 230, 233, 234

Congr 20, 24, 30, 43, 106, 113, 137 Fug 101, 147 Mut 43, 53, 97, 97, 97, 97, 200, 200, 233, 233, 234, 253 Somn 1:65, 73, 162, 198, 205, 215, 216, 228, 237 Somn 2:6, 10, 27, 112, 155, 167, 169, 224, 257, 262 Abr 5, 46, 105, 119, 142, 145, 150, 170, 190, 208, 218, 241 Ios 20, 52, 88, 154, 188, 188, 189, 223, 235, 240 Mos 1:150, 180, 205, 227, 231, 234, 235, 236, 240, 249, 287, 320, 325 Mos 2:48, 66, 77, 78, 78, 79, 91, 97, 99, 101, 112, 113, 122, 128, 129, 129, 133, 142, 147, 221, 256, 257, 262, 276, 277 Decal 20, 21, 21, 22, 22, 22, 25, 25, 26, 26, 27, 28, 50, 50, 106, 111, 123, 126, 161, 161 Spec 1:8, 32, 86, 131, 145, 145, 162, 169, 172, 172, 177, 178, 178, 180, 184, 184, 188, 189, 195, 201, 212, 217, 220, 222, 225, 240, 273, 278, 337, 337 Spec 2:1, 35, 63, 113, 149, 157, 179, 184, 187, 187, 204, 220, 260, 261 Spec 3:27, 31, 54, 142 Spec 4:12, 17, 64, 65, 97, 125, 127, 133, 165, 203 Virt 22, 28, 52, 52, 53, 199, 208, 222 Praem 59, 63, 71, 71, 152 Prob 38, 57, 112 Contempl 24, 33, 57, 83 Aet 48, 49, 51, 65, 146 Flacc 54, 55, 125, 186 Legat 7, 10, 74, 299, 307, 311, 317, 327, 351 Prov 2:3 QG 1:29, 29, 2:12b, 3:61, 4:30, 80, 80, 198, 200a, 200a QG (Par) 2:3 QE 2:14, 21

δυοκαίδεκα Somn 2:112

δυσαιτιολόγητος Prov 2:51

δυσαλγής Mos 1:127

δυσάλωτος (10) Post 18 Ebr 75 Somn 2:14, 90 Mos 1:8, 333 Spec 1:146 Spec 4:93 Praem 25 Prob 147

δυσανάλωτος Aet 90

δυσαναπόρευτος Somn 2:103 Mos 1:237 Spec 4:79, 112

δυσανασχετέω Mos 1:199 Mos 2:214 Prob 103 Legat 202 QG 4:52c

δυσανάσχετος Mos 1:72

δυσάντης Post 154

δυσαπάλλακτος Agr 55

δυσαπολόγητος Fug 108

δυσαπόσπαστος Abr 67, 88 QG 4:20

δυσαπότριπτος Migr 151 Mut 239 Somn 1:223

δυσαρεστέω Ebr 176 Abr 35, 85 QG 3:38b

δυσάρεστος Ebr 4, 177 Abr 153 Contempl 24

δυσαυλία Det 19

δυσβάστακτος Prob 28

δύσβατος Ebr 150 Abr 86 Legat 216 QE 2:13a

δυσγένεια (10) Her 212, 284 Congr 54, 54 Virt 190, 197, 200, 213, 219 Praem 152

δυσγενής Spec 4:206 QG 2:65

δυσδιάλυτος Aet 125

δυσέκλυτος Det 6

δυσέκπλυτος Fug 85 Decal 10 Aet 2

δύσελπις Leg 3:164 Sacr 32 Det 139 Abr 8, 14

δυσελπιστία (6) Leg 3:164 Deus 156 Ios 114 Mos 1:194, 197 Legat 340

δυσέντευκτος Flacc 24

δυσεξάλειπτος Spec 1:106

δύσεργος Sacr 48 Deus 2 Spec 1:299

δύσερις (7) Sacr 32 Agr 159 Ebr 17 Congr 129 Abr 213, 225 Legat 198

δυσερμηνεύτος Somn 1:188

δυσεύρετος (11) Sacr 32 Post 43 Her 248 Fug 153, 157 Somn 1:8, 8, 16, 24 Abr 19, 24

δυσέφικτος Sacr 32 Migr 134

δυσήκοος Abr 240

δυσθανατάω Virt 92

δυσθανατέω Mos 1:123 Mos 2:211, 250

δυσθεράπευτος Deus 182 Plant 32 Ebr 115 Spec 3:23 Virt 4

δύσθετος Leg 3:53

δυσθεώρητος Migr 222 Mos 1:21

δυσθήρατος (10) Post 13 Ebr 174 Migr 150 Her 248 Fug 164 Mut 236 Abr 24 Decal 125 Spec 1:36 Spec 4:185

δυσθυμία Mos 1:119 Spec 2:83

δυσίατος (20) Opif 155, 167 Leg 3:33 Deus 67 Agr 93 Fug 80 Abr 96 Ios 10, 118 Spec 1:4, 292 Spec 2:15, 23 Spec 3:28, 98 Spec 4:5, 79, 100 Contempl 2 QG 1:65

δύσις (14) Opif 58 Cher 22 Plant 118 Her 265 Mut 190 Abr 161 Ios 134, 166 Spec 1:69 Spec 3:152, 187 Contempl 34 Legat 145, 191

δυσκαθαίρετος Leg 1:86 Mos 1:8

δυσκάθαρτος (14) Det 144 Post 75 Deus 9, 183 Plant 107 Conf 153 Fug 85 Mut 62 Somn 1:227 Spec 2:23, 27, 253 Legat 66 Prov 2:40

δυσκαρτέρητος Somn 1:124 Abr 96, 185 Ios 223 Mos 2:184

δυσκατάληπτος Spec 1:32, 36

δυσκατέργαστος Spec 1:218

δυσκατόρθωτος Mos 1:19

δυσκίνητος Spec 1:99

δύσκλεια Sacr 100 Deus 171 Her 113 Somn 2:120 Legat 369

δυσκολία Sacr 30, 35 Fug 106 Abr 192 Hypoth 6:4

δύσκολος (7) Post 156 Plant 115 Ebr 177 Somn 1:7 Spec 1:306 Praem 49 Hypoth 6:4

δυσκρασία Opif 125

δύσληπτος Spec 4:185

δύσλυτος Sacr 32

δυσμαθής Mos 2:261

δύσμαχος Abr 136 Legat 190

δυσμεναίνω Cher 37

δυσμένεια (9) Mut 95 Ios 176 Spec 4:185, 227 Praem 137 Flacc 24 Legat 171, 205 QE 2:11b

δυσμενής (33) Leg 3:1, 71 Cher 77 Sacr 20 Det 37, 37, 165 Post 24 Agr 88, 146, 159 Ebr 10, 69, 70, 176 Her 245 Somn 2:89 Ios 167 Mos 1:291 Mos 2:9 Spec 3:113 Virt 151, 195 Praem 61, 85, 118, 127, 170 Flacc 62, 126, 146, 147 Legat 293

δυσμή (13) Her 249, 258, 263, 264, 307, 307 Somn 1:84, 92, 112 Somn 2:147 Ios 159 Mos 2:92 Flacc 45

δυσμορφία Prov 2:31

δύσνοια Ios 5

δυσοδέω Legat 126

δυσοδία Ios 183 Mos 1:194 Spec 4:111

δυσοδμία Her 79 Mos 2:260

δυσοιώνιστος Flacc 177

δυσόρατος Fug 164 Praem 38

δυσόργητος Sacr 32

δυσπαρηγόρητος Spec 3:28

δυσπεριγένητος Somn 1:8

δυσπερινόητος Fug 164

δυσπεψία Spec 4:100

δυσπλοΐα Mut 150 Somn 1:150

δυσπόρευτος Abr 86

δυσπόριστος Opif 80

δυσπραγία Ios 244

δυσπραξία Prov 2:25

δυσσεβής Conf 2 Spec 2:135 Spec 3:14

δυστέκμαρτος Migr 195

δύστηνος Somn 2:119 Prob 40 Legat 23, 29, 31

δυστοκέω Mut 96

δυστόπαστος (7) Post 13 Migr 195 Fug 164 Somn 1:182 Spec 1:32 Spec 2:165 Praem 38

δύστροπος Somn 1:7 Spec 1:306

δυστυχής (9) Agr 35 Mut 55, 231 Somn 1:122 Somn 2:298 Flacc 64, 172 Legat 52, 367

δυστυχία Ios 223 Praem 169

δύσυδρος Aet 148

δυσυπομόνητος Sacr 30 Abr 185 Spec 2:90 Virt 5 Praem 145

δυσυπονόητος Sacr 32 Decal 125

δύσφημα Legat 101

δυσφροσύνη Ios 245

δυσχείμερος Mos 1:118

δυσχεραίνω (43) Opif 161, 161 Deus 166 Agr 54, 57 Plant 39 Ebr 9, 208 Conf 2, 41 Her 43 Somn 1:95, 222, 236 Somn 2:160 Abr 41, 97, 257 Ios 50, 166, 171, 246 Mos 1:40, 90, 196, 321 Mos 2:167 Spec 2:19, 87, 245 Spec 3:50, 118, 166 Prob 61, 125 Flacc 24, 89, 107, 138 Legat 154, 253 QG 2:39, 4:227

δύσχρηστος Sacr 32

δυσχωρία Legat 127

δυσώδης Leg 2:7 Post 112 Mos 1:204 Aet 125

δυσωδία Mos 1:100 Mos 2:262

δυσώνυμος (6) Leg 3:44 Sacr 32 Sobr 52 Conf 115 Somn 2:166 Legat 101

δυσωπέω (18) Opif 128 Det 146 Post 97 Deus 126 Conf 52 Fug 118, 203 Somn 1:124 Decal 87, 169 Spec 2:36 Spec 4:127 Praem 91 Prob 124 Legat 52 QG 1:1, 21 QE 2:45a

δυσωπία Plant 8

δύω (31) Opif 115, 147 Leg 1:46 Leg 3:171 Det 151 Plant 40, 144 Ebr 22 Her 264, 264 Somn 1:4, 5, 72, 72, 81, 83, 83, 114, 116, 117, 118 Abr 44 Ios 54 Mos 2:19 Spec 1:171, 296 Contempl 27 Aet 120, 141 Legat 10 Hypoth 11:6

δώδεκα (46) Opif 60, 107, 107, 108, 108, 108, 109, 109, 110 Sobr 66 Her 175, 176, 195 Congr 168 Fug 73, 183, 184, 184, 185, 185, 185 Mut 263 Somn 2:257 Ios 167 Mos 1:188, 189, 221, 306 Mos 2:112, 112, 124, 126, 133, 160, 175, 178 Spec 1:79, 87, 87, 172 Spec 2:33, 161, 177 Virt 77 Praem 57 Prob 122

δωδεκάς Spec 2:177

δωδεκατημόριος Somn 2:112

δωδέκατος Somn 2:113

Δωθαείμ Det 5, 28

Δωθαΐν Fug 127, 127, 128

δῶμα Agr 170

δωμάτιον Prov 2:26

δωρεά (109) Opif 23, 77 Leg 3:78, 87, 147, 166 Cher 84, 121, 122, 122, 123 Sacr 26, 57 Post 36, 42, 80, 144 Deus 57, 105 Agr 90 Plant 89 Ebr 32, 94, 119 Sobr 55 Conf 7, 127 Migr 46, 53, 70, 86, 106, 127 Her 26, 80, 205, 206 Congr 96 Fug 29, 66 Mut 8, 30, 52, 58, 61, 64, 126, 142, 218, 269 Somn 1:113, 117, 162, 163 Abr 46, 90, 155, 159, 273 Ios 46, 231, 241, 249, 258 Mos 1:21, 184, 204, 266, 267, 293, 333 Mos 2:155 Decal 112, 167 Spec 1:43, 57, 151, 152, 172, 277 Spec 2:55, 97, 108, 111, 138, 158, 160, 180, 180, 187, 219 Spec 3:99, 111 Spec 4:217 Virt 105, 130, 133, 165, 169, 202 Praem 79, 163 Flacc 23, 171 Legat 88, 335, 343 Prov 2:21 QG 2:16

δωρέω (62) Opif 66 Leg 1:80 Leg 3:95, 105, 166, 179, 203 Cher 44, 106, 119, 122 Sacr 24, 40, 98, 124 Det 124, 151 Post 142, 174 Deus 47, 104, 108 Agr 168, 180 Ebr 119, 172 Migr 70, 88, 109, 122, 172, 203 Her 97, 302 Congr 17, 75, 146 Fug 76, 155 Somn 1:227 Somn 2:76, 224, 224 Abr 7, 39, 54 Ios 150, 251 Mos 1:304 Decal 17 Spec 1:224 Spec 2:6, 115 Virt 83, 94 Aet 63, 68, 69 Legat 166, 333 QG 1:62:1, 62:2

δώρημα Deus 5 Somn 1:103 Abr 54 Spec 2:159 Virt 97

δωρητικός Cher 123 Post 151 Her 166 QG 1:62:1

Δώριος Somn 2:55

δωροδοκέω Spec 4:63

δωροδοκία Spec 1:277 Spec 4:87 Flacc 105, 140 Legat 302

δῶρον (51) Opif 165 Leg 3:83, 196, 196 Cher 84 Sacr 89, 111 Det 21 Deus 6 Ebr 114, 117, 117, 118, 118 Migr 142 Her 195, 195 Congr 38, 89 Mut 234 Somn 1:252, 254 Somn 2:44, 45, 62, 71, 71 Abr 177, 203 Ios 70, 193, 199 Spec 1:180, 204, 277, 281, 289 Spec 4:62, 62, 64, 66, 177 Virt 8, 165 Praem 50, 100 Prob 151 QG 1:62:1, 62:1, 62:2, 4:130

E

ἐάν ἤν

ἐάν (322) Opif 79 Leg 1:17, 25, 29, 29, 49, 50, 51 Leg 2:29, 48, 61, 81, 88, 89, 90, 100, 100, 102 Leg 3:16, 32, 32, 32, 35, 35, 56, 74, 95, 103, 116, 143, 150, 150, 194, 194, 207, 212, 215, 228, 248 Cher 27, 37, 37, 48, 71, 71, 118 Sacr 19, 24, 42, 53, 58, 76, 89, 97, 114, 114, 114, 115, 115, 115, 117 Det 13, 19, 25, 51, 52, 52, 54, 54, 150, 158 Post 72, 90, 95, 95, 95, 96, 134, 135, 147, 178, 181 Gig 35, 44 Deus 116, 123, 131, 145, 169, 171, 171 Agr 26, 64, 70, 78, 93, 111, 111, 127, 170, 170, 175 Plant 7, 103 Ebr 14 Sobr 21, 21, 22, 49, 49, Conf 62, 62, 160, 197 Migr 11, 62, 102, 119, 133, 210, 220 Her 13, 49, 86, 193, 254, 262, 305 Congr 5, 54, 109, 137, 137, 178 Fug 28, 32, 47, 53, 53, 77, 115, 117 Mut 118, 192, 233, 234, 250, 250 Somn 1:81, 91, 92, 92, 101, 171, 177, 177, 237 Somn 2:71, 175, 266, 292, 293, 299 Abr 29 Ios 39, 39, 72, 73, 73, 115, 169, 187, 188, 228, 229 Mos 1:74, 76, 76, 111, 161, 257, 257, 296, 330 Mos 2:2, 40, 40 Decal 16 Spec 1:20, 64, 117, 118, 129, 153, 212, 212, 214, 230, 233, 235, 259, 268 Spec 2:9, 13, 26, 34, 34, 35, 35, 36, 79, 125, 127, 142, 243 Spec 3:27, 27, 30, 49, 49, 55, 64, 67, 69, 70, 70, 71, 71, 71, 73, 80, 82, 82, 86, 88, 106, 108, 108, 142, 143, 144, 145, 146, 148, 148, 173, 182, 182, 184, 195, 201 Spec 4:2, 2, 3, 7, 10, 22, 29, 33, 36, 37, 47, 57, 59, 146, 162, 193, 214, 220, 221, 222 Virt 47, 48, 48, 48, 96, 115, 139, 166, 193 Praem 79, 81, 114, 114, 114, 163 Prob 53 Contempl 67 Aet 83, 84 Legat 169, 183, 236, 242, 253, 283, 323, 328, 334, 355 Hypoth 7:1, 7:1, 7:1, 7:1, 7:1, 7:2, 7:2, 7:2, 7:2, 7:2, 7:2, 7:2, 7:2, 7:5, 7:5, 7:5 QG 2:12d, 4:204 QE 2:18, 25b QE isf 3, 5

ἔαρ (31) Opif 45, 52, 58, 85, 116, 116 Cher 112, 112 Plant 120 Her 146, 165, 208 Somn 2:131 Mos 1:226, 226 Mos 2:124, 186 Decal 161 Spec 1:183, 210 Spec 2:152, 153 Spec 4:208, 209, 214, 235 Virt 93, 157 Praem 130 Aet 63, 132

ἐαρίζω Opif 58 Mos 1:118 Spec 1:92 Prov 2:44

ἐαρινός (21) Opif 116, 153 Deus 39 Her 147, 149, 150 Somn 1:20 Mos 2:186, 222 Decal 161 Spec 1:172, 172, 181 Spec 2:151, 158, 160, 210 Spec 4:233 QG 2:17c, 17c, 31

ἑαυτοῦ (1468) Opif 9, 13, 14, 17, 18, 21, 21, 22, 23, 23, 23, 23, 44, 57, 72, 74, 77, 78, 82, 88, 93, 93, 97, 100, 101, 126, 128, 138, 139, 139, 148, 152, 158, 165, 166, 171, 172, 172 Leg 1:3, 18, 21, 25, 29, 33, 34, 34, 37, 38, 43, 44, 44, 44, 51, 51, 51, 51, 82, 82, 82, 82, 89, 91, 91, 91, 91, 92, 92 Leg 2:1, 29, 31, 32, 40, 46, 54, 69, 69, 73, 79, 80, 83, 83, 86, 86, 87, 93, 94 Leg 3:2, 4, 15, 20, 26, 27, 28, 29, 29, 31, 33, 33, 33, 33, 33, 35, 35, 37, 39, 39, 41, 43, 44, 44, 44, 47, 48, 49, 50, 55, 59, 67, 68, 69, 70, 71, 72, 75, 76, 79, 79, 88, 104, 104, 109, 109, 123, 128, 136, 136, 144, 164, 166, 167, 169, 172, 173, 173, 175, 178, 178, 181, 186, 186, 186, 198, 198, 198, 199, 201, 203, 205, 205, 205, 206, 206, 206, 207, 207, 207, 207, 208, 212, 214, 220, 234, 238, 238, 239, 246, 247, 247 Cher 5, 17, 23, 24, 31, 36, 37, 38, 42, 43, 44, 46, 46, 48, 48, 57, 57, 58, 58, 59, 61, 63, 64, 65, 65, 66, 67, 69, 73, 75, 76, 77, 78, 79, 79, 81, 85, 86, 96, 111, 113, 113, 113, 118, 118, 123 Sacr 8, 8, 9, 10, 20, 21, 28, 28, 29, 29, 30, 31, 34, 39, 41, 41, 43, 50, 51, 53, 54, 56, 57, 58, 59, 60, 67, 71, 71, 72, 74, 74, 78, 79, 87, 94, 95, 95, 95, 103, 106, 109, 115, 119, 124 Det 8, 16, 17, 20, 25, 32, 33, 34, 40, 41, 47, 47, 48, 49, 49, 49, 50, 50, 51, 51, 52, 52, 54, 56, 57, 58, 61, 66, 69, 71, 72, 74, 74, 76, 77, 86, 86, 95, 98, 106, 109, 111, 116, 126, 127, 134, 135, 135, 136, 137, 137, 142, 146, 146, 148, 148, 148, 163, 176 Post 5, 5, 6, 6, 10, 12, 13, 13, 14, 14, 16, 16, 20, 21, 21, 22, 26, 28, 32, 37, 42, 42, 46, 49, 51, 53, 54, 55, 61, 66, 67, 75, 75, 75, 75, 76, 76, 77, 78, 79, 91, 110, 115, 115, 116, 119, 129, 130, 141, 143, 143, 144, 150, 169, 175, 175, 175, 183 Gig 6, 14, 15, 18, 18, 20, 38, 46, 54, 59, 60 Deus 1, 3, 4, 5, 7, 7, 8, 8, 15, 17, 19, 19, 19, 19, 29, 31, 34, 35, 43, 50, 56, 56, 58, 59, 73, 73, 75, 77, 80, 87, 100, 102, 103, 105, 107, 107, 108, 108, 109, 110, 117, 119, 120, 126, 129, 129, 141, 142, 157, 158, 161, 165, 166, 182 Agr 19, 31, 33, 35, 37, 47, 48, 51, 60, 68, 84, 88, 116, 132, 134, 134, 142, 152, 161, 162, 167, 168, 168, 171, 171, 172 Plant 2, 3, 3, 10, 12, 80, 91, 105, 106, 115, 118, 145, 166, 175 Ebr 25, 31, 31, 41, 44, 44, 48, 49, 54, 56, 56, 69, 88, 95, 100, 102, 106, 108, 118, 119, 122, 130, 142, 150, 160, 161, 165, 165, 166, 166, 176, 178, 186, 186, 187, 188, 189, 195, 221 Sobr 4, 17, 23, 29, 31, 33, 68 Conf 1, 1, 15, 20, 21, 29, 42, 49, 50, 51, 54, 61, 69, 75, 75, 91, 98, 106, 107, 107, 108, 110, 111, 116, 116, 123, 123, 124, 136, 161, 161, 164, 165, 166, 171, 175, 175, 177, 179, 180, 183, 188, 195 Migr 3, 4, 4, 10, 13, 33, 40, 41, 55, 70, 87, 90, 90, 92, 97, 98, 98, 99, 121, 122, 123, 124, 125, 134, 137, 138, 158, 158, 163, 170, 171, 179, 183, 185, 185, 185, 186, 187, 189, 190, 195, 195, 195, 195, 206, 206, 209, 215, 215 Her 6, 7, 12, 12, 13, 21, 23, 30, 43, 49, 52, 58, 58, 68, 70, 71, 85, 88, 93, 107, 107, 108, 109, 109, 110, 111, 111, 114, 123, 123, 129, 130, 140, 160, 160, 169, 174, 186, 188, 188, 191, 198, 200, 200, 214, 216, 264, 273, 274, 295, 314 Congr 52, 56, 57, 71, 72, 73, 80, 85, 91, 107, 122, 126, 127, 128, 130, 130, 134, 139, 139, 140, 143, 145, 150, 159, 169 Fug 6, 20, 50, 52, 56, 66, 66, 69, 70, 70, 76, 76, 80, 85, 94, 103, 104, 118, 122, 123, 132, 135, 136, 141, 141, 146, 154, 155, 171, 176, 184, 189, 189, 197, 199, 200, 206 Mut 4, 4, 5, 7, 19, 25, 27, 27, 30, 32, 40, 46, 46, 52, 54, 54, 56, 57, 58, 59, 59, 67, 86, 91, 105, 111, 117, 119, 127, 131, 134, 141, 156, 166, 175, 199, 201, 202, 203, 222, 232, 241, 246, 257, 270 Somn 1:2, 21, 23, 25, 35, 43, 51, 58, 58, 60, 60, 60, 63, 63, 63, 64, 69, 70, 70, 77, 91, 91, 91, 93, 95, 107, 119, 119, 122, 128, 128, 131, 143, 150, 157, 176, 177, 180, 180, 188, 191, 200, 211, 212, 214, 214, 220, 232, 237, 243, 243, 244, 248, 249, 252, 252 Somn 2:1, 1, 2, 16, 20, 25, 30, 40, 45, 77, 78, 80, 87, 94, 95, 103, 107, 107, 113, 116, 116, 119, 128, 130, 132, 140, 147, 158, 161, 163, 164, 165, 183, 187, 192, 200, 212, 223, 224, 224, 227, 227, 229, 232, 232, 245, 249, 274, 277, 283, 290, 292, 292, 293, 296, 298, 299 Abr 28, 30, 30, 30, 31, 38, 47, 51, 54, 54, 59, 59, 73, 75, 75, 79, 79, 80, 80, 84, 93, 103, 106, 107, 122, 125, 128, 131, 143, 144, 152, 153, 175, 179, 182, 184, 191, 197, 203, 213, 214, 223, 228, 229, 238, 239, 240, 243, 261 Ios 5, 8, 23, 29, 53, 67, 79, 87, 87, 87, 88, 99, 116, 118, 119, 127, 129, 137, 142, 157, 166, 167, 170, 170, 173, 176, 180, 199, 205, 212, 217, 219, 219, 230, 236, 257, 269 Mos 1:4, 7, 10, 11, 11, 17, 22, 22, 26, 26, 30, 48, 57, 59, 63, 80, 83, 83, 97, 120, 125, 137, 140, 155, 157, 158, 158, 159, 160, 182, 185, 196, 214, 234, 252, 273, 274, 280, 287, 294, 303, 306, 317 Mos 2:5, 17, 18, 21, 26, 29, 32, 34, 62, 69, 84, 96,

125, 153, 176, 177, 177, 181, 188, 194, 196, 207, 224, 238, 249, 250, 269, 291 Decal 13, 18, 28, 29, 37, 43, 65, 72, 81, 81, 89, 93, 98, 101, 108, 117, 118, 147, 153, 177, 177 Spec 1:3, 10, 10, 36, 40, 42, 47, 58, 64, 89, 96, 97, 104, 106, 115, 163, 177, 188, 192, 204, 209, 211, 214, 219, 219, 227, 229, 230, 235, 235, 248, 248, 252, 252, 254, 263, 263, 264, 270, 272, 277, 278, 281, 284, 294, 294, 298, 298, 303, 312, 314, 317, 320, 321, 322, 335 Spec 2:6, 13, 30, 31, 32, 38, 40, 40, 43, 54, 61, 71, 96, 122, 123, 135, 135, 137, 139, 151, 157, 167, 174, 190, 196, 200, 239, 259, 259 Spec 3:9, 13, 38, 51, 51, 54, 85, 92, 93, 96, 102, 112, 118, 127, 136, 139, 143, 143, 152, 154, 156, 162, 172, 173, 178, 178, 186, 186, 189, 190 Spec 4:6, 9, 16, 26, 34, 36, 42, 42, 54, 56, 65, 70, 74, 74, 81, 122, 126, 131, 131, 142, 144, 160, 173, 176, 178, 189, 192, 193, 199, 201, 217, 220, 235, 235, 236 Virt 9, 33, 54, 57, 67, 87, 92, 103, 104, 105, 122, 135, 138, 142, 149, 152, 152, 163, 172, 190, 210, 222, 227 Praem 4, 12, 39, 40, 43, 45, 52, 61, 62, 65, 88, 93, 110, 112, 121, 126, 126, 138, 148, 149, 153, 163, 163, 170 Prob 7, 12, 13, 14, 19, 24, 36, 41, 44, 62, 71, 75, 76, 90, 101, 109, 111, 114, 117, 119, 124, 125, 128, 159 Contempl 4, 5, 16, 16, 19, 27, 30, 47, 59, 64, 64, 68, 72, 85, 89 Aet 2, 8, 15, 20, 20, 33, 36, 38, 38, 38, 38, 40, 43, 47, 49, 53, 70, 70, 70, 70, 74, 80, 88, 94, 95, 97, 98, 120, 127, 129, 143, 149 Flacc 4, 10, 13, 24, 30, 33, 41, 44, 49, 64, 79, 81, 86, 89, 94, 97, 97, 101, 106, 109, 113, 135, 141, 162, 181, 189 Legat 18, 30, 31, 44, 53, 61, 65, 69, 71, 77, 77, 78, 85, 87, 118, 119, 123, 136, 136, 147, 149, 153, 154, 162, 165, 171, 180, 189, 197, 198, 211, 218, 229, 233, 235, 261, 267, 304, 307, 308, 318, 332, 335, 341, 343, 351, 366, 368 Hypoth 6:2, 7:3, 7:14 Prov 2:8, 10, 24, 30, 32, 35, 40, 41, 51, 58, 61, 71, 71 QG 1:51, 60:2, 60:2, 60:2, 64b, 64c, 94, 2:5b, 11, 59, 62, 65, 3:29, 4:180, 191b, 7*, 198, 200c QG isf 10, 10, 12, 13, 13, 13 QG (Par) 2:5 QE 2:10a, 11a, 18, 18, 26 QE isf 16, 18

ἐάω (151) Opif 131, 169 Leg 1:89 Leg 2:28, 34, 34, 63 Leg 3:128, 160, 169 Cher 71, 96 Sacr 9, 13, 34, 45, 92 Det 23, 105, 107, 143, 157 Post 58, 68, 94 Deus 29, 47, 73, 178 Agr 10, 11, 13, 23, 30, 35, 45 Plant 52, 53 Ebr 71, 128, 157, 160, 167, 198 Sobr 2, 3, 42 Conf 14, 165 Migr 26, 168 Her 67, 203, 232 Congr 125 Fug 112, 124, 126 Mut 180 Somn 2:8, 67, 109, 109, 196, 275, 286 Abr 160, 207, 214 Ios 47, 48, 142, 228, 233 Mos 1:25, 38, 39, 50, 139, 246 Mos 2:265 Decal 5, 70, 142, 150, 156, 162 Spec 1:60, 100, 102, 109, 157, 157, 241, 261 Spec 2:27, 64, 73, 86, 88, 105, 138, 192, 240, 254 Spec 3:18, 37, 38, 39, 45, 46, 46, 63, 79, 102, 142, 145, 147 Spec 4:4, 27, 62, 83, 122, 136, 196, 214 Virt 14, 98, 113, 113, 122, 150, 156 Praem 112, 152 Contempl 14, 55 Aet 42, 67, 125 Flacc 57, 79, 81, 144 Legat 141, 178 Prov 2:17 QG 2:15a, 64c, 4:33a, 191c

ἑβδομάς (93) Opif 90, 91, 94, 95, 95, 97, 97, 97, 98, 99, 99, 100, 101, 102, 102, 102, 102, 103, 104, 104, 105, 105, 106, 106, 111, 111, 115, 117, 124, 128 Leg 1:4, 8, 8, 8, 9, 13, 13, 15, 16, 16, 19 Post 173 Deus 11, 12, 13 Plant 124 Sobr 19 Migr 169 Her 170, 216 Congr 106 Fug 173, 186 Mos 1:205 Mos 2:210 Decal 99, 102, 102, 103, 105, 158, 160, 161 Spec 1:178, 178, 188, 188 Spec 2:41, 57, 58, 59, 59, 64, 86, 110, 149, 149, 156, 176, 194, 194, 214, 223, 223, 260 Praem 153, 153, 154, 154, 157 Contempl 65, 65 QE 2:46

ἑβδοματικός Decal 162

ἑβδομήκοντα (24) Gig 24, 24 Sobr 19 Migr 168, 176, 176, 198, 199, 199, 201, 201, 202, 202, 202 Fug 183, 186, 186, 186, 186 Somn 1:47 Mos 1:188, 189 Spec 1:181, 189

ἑβδομηκοντάκις QG 1:77

ἑβδομηκοστός Migr 201, 202, 202, 207

ἕβδομος (146) Opif 29, 89, 92, 93, 93, 94, 94, 103, 106, 106, 106, 116, 116, 119, 121, 123, 125, 128 Leg 1:5, 12, 12, 16, 17, 17, 18, 18 Leg 2:52, 94 Cher 90 Post 64, 64, 64, 65, 173 Ebr 52 Migr 91 Her 215, 216, 218, 219, 220, 220, 220, 225 Congr 8 Fug 186 Mut 144, 260 Somn 2:123, 123 Abr 28, 28, 30 Ios 260 Mos 1:7, 97, 207 Mos 2:21, 102, 209, 213, 215, 216, 218, 219, 263, 264, 266, 268 Decal 51, 96, 97, 98, 100, 106, 159 Spec 1:168, 170, 170, 170, 172, 177, 182, 186, 261 Spec 2:39, 39, 39, 40, 41, 41, 56, 61, 62, 66, 69, 69, 71, 71, 79, 84, 86, 86, 86, 86, 97, 105, 108, 122, 150, 157, 214, 224, 249, 250, 251, 260, 260 Spec 3:205 Spec 4:4, 215, 216 Virt 97, 98, 100, 122 Prob 81, 81 Contempl 30, 32, 36 Legat 156, 158 Hypoth 7:12, 7:15, 7:15, 7:17, 7:20, 7:20 QG 2:17c, 31, 31, 31, 31 QE 2:46, 46

Ἑβραϊκός Mos 1:16, 240, 285

Ἑβραῖος (60) Plant 169 Sobr 45 Conf 68, 129, 130 Migr 13, 20, 20 Her 128 Congr 37, 40, 42 Fug 168 Mut 71, 117, 117 Somn 1:58 Somn 2:250 Abr 17, 27, 28, 57, 251 Ios 28, 42, 50, 104, 203 Mos 1:15, 105, 143, 144, 144, 145, 146, 147, 179, 180, 216, 218, 243, 252, 263, 276, 278, 284, 288, 289, 295, 305, 311 Mos 2:32 Decal 159 Spec 2:41, 86, 145 Virt 34, 35 QG 1:3 QE 2:2

ἔγγαιος ἔγγειος

ἐγγαστρίμυθος Somn 1:220

ἔγγειος (ἔγγαιος) Her 208

ἐγγηράσκω Ebr 51 Somn 1:58 Prob 15

ἐγγίγνομαι (ἐγγίνομαι) (35) Leg 3:120, 235 Sacr 127 Det 9 Post 46 Gig 28 Agr 123 Ebr 137 Conf 72 Migr 218 Her 119, 269 Mut 111 Somn 1:113 Somn 2:52, 102, 255, 260 Abr 151, 201 Decal 15 Spec 1:4, 117, 337 Spec 2:68, 209 Spec 3:94 Spec 4:161 Praem 18 Prob 76, 150 Aet 67 Legat 106 QG 1:63 QE 2:40

ἐγγίζω (13) Leg 2:57 Leg 3:9 Cher 18 Det 46 Post 27 Deus 161 Ebr 96 Migr 56, 132 Her 30 Fug 59, 162 QE 2:28

ἐγγλύφω Leg 1:81 Her 176 Mos 2:123

ἔγγονος (48) Leg 2:34 Sacr 103 Post 112, 177 Deus 4, 15, 116, 118, 138 Agr 32 Sobr 47, 48 Her 65, 186 Congr 75, 119, 152 Mut 68, 147, 189, 193, 255 Somn 1:141, 141, 169 Somn 2:96, 134, 139, 184, 266 Abr 82 Spec 2:101, 259 Spec 4:85 Virt 82, 126, 128, 129, 133, 134, 136, 138, 142 Aet 15, 112 QG 1:21, 3:18 QE 2:3b

ἐγγράμματος Agr 136 Plant 10 Flacc 55

ἐγγραφή Ios 69

ἐγγράφω (20) Opif 143 Leg 1:19 Leg 3:244 Det 139 Gig 61 Deus 121 Agr 81, 119 Conf 109 Somn 1:39 Mos 1:157 Mos 2:211, 274 Spec 1:63, 106 Spec 2:45 Spec 3:36, 72 Prob 7 QG 4:99

ἐγγυάω (19) Post 78 Agr 157 Congr 12, 38, 72, 73, 134 Somn 1:254 Ios 121, 132 Decal 47 Spec 1:109 Spec 3:22, 26, 34, 81 Virt 28, 114 Legat 37

ἐγγύη Spec 3:70

ἐγγυητής Cher 45 Agr 50

ἐγγύθεν Abr 75

ἐγγυμνάζω Fug 36 Ios 38 Spec 2:91

ἐγγύς (78) Cher 19, 19 Det 25 Post 20, 27, 84, 84, 109, 152 Gig 41, 44, 46, 47 Agr 25, 148, 161 Ebr 67, 70, 70, 71, 174 Conf 9, 124, 157 Migr 57 Her 83, 202 Fug 90, 90, 92, 101 Mut 217, 237, 237 Somn 1:32, 54 Somn 2:129, 180 Abr 26, 121, 121 Ios 116, 117, 238 Mos 1:198, 263, 275 Mos 2:8, 122, 169, 245, 249, 251 Decal 15, 33, 59, 120, 148 Spec 1:116 Spec 2:114, 127, 216 Spec 3:157, 164, 192 Spec 4:139 Virt 80, 132, 183 Praem 80 Contempl 23, 24 Flacc 124, 151 Legat 29, 183, 228 QG 2:64b

ἐγείρω (53) Opif 115 Leg 2:25, 30 Leg 3:14, 69, 224 Cher 38 Sacr 103 Post 54, 148 Deus 26 Agr 77, 122 Plant 159 Ebr 147, 156, 179 Sobr 5 Conf 133 Migr 122 Fug 189 Mut 56, 209 Somn 1:80, 99, 150, 174 Somn 2:18, 50, 106 Abr 215 Ios 103, 125, 126, 142, 143, 147 Mos 1:284, 291 Decal 35 Spec 1:192, 298, 338 Spec 2:101, 193 Spec 3:28 Spec 4:129, 139, 141, 223 Virt 5, 71 Praem 151

ἐγκαθέζομαι Prov 2:58

ἐγκάθημαι Leg 2:94 Agr 94, 105 Spec 1:270

ἐγκαθίζω Leg 2:98, 98

ἐγκαίνια Congr 114

ἐγκαινίζω Agr 148, 148

ἐγκαλέω Deus 27 Migr 91 Flacc 146

ἐγκαλλωπίζομαι Abr 190

ἐγκαλύπτω (11) Sacr 21 Conf 118 Congr 124, 125, 125 Mut 134 Somn 2:203 Decal 118 Spec 1:270, 279 Virt 131

ἐγκάρδιος Spec 1:6

ἐγκάρσιος (6) Ebr 131 Conf 157 Mos 1:165 Contempl 45 Aet 113 Flacc 189

ἐγκαρτερέω Det 149 Prob 24, 110

ἐγκαταγηράσκω Agr 143

ἐγκατακλείω Mos 2:182 Praem 145

ἐγκαταλαμβάνω (7) Det 90 Migr 190 Mos 1:166 Aet 21, 87 Legat 63 Prov 2:35

ἐγκαταλείπω Post 121 Conf 166 Congr 160 Fug 197 Somn 1:3

ἐγκαταμείγνυμι Somn 1:220 Legat 169 QE isf 21

ἐγκαταμένω Virt 214

ἐγκαταπίνομαι (7) Det 100 Ebr 79 Migr 85, 125 Fug 49 Somn 2:86 Spec 3:6

ἐγκατάποσις Leg 3:146

ἐγκατασκευάζω Leg 3:137 Somn 1:129, 135 Mos 1:111 Spec 4:82

ἐγκατασκήπτω Det 178 Ebr 140 Contempl 2

ἐγκατασπείρω Virt 134

ἐγκατατρίβω Agr 143

ἐγκατορύσσω QG 1:70:1

ἔγκειμαι (7) Cher 48 Sacr 46 Sobr 33 Her 296 Flacc 175 QG 2:54a, 4:202a

ἐγκεράννυμι ἐγκιρνάω

ἐγκέφαλος Sacr 136 Spec 1:213, 214, 215 QG (Par) 2:3

ἐγκιρνάω (ἐγκεράννυμι) Prov 2:47

ἐγκισσάω Somn 2:19

ἔγκλημα (25) Sacr 52, 72, 88 Det 142 Ebr 27 Sobr 48 Conf 161 Mut 243 Somn 2:137 Decal 76 Spec 1:127 Spec 3:57, 63, 80 Spec 4:5, 40 Virt 147 Flacc 6, 129, 139 Legat 23, 169, 177 Prov 2:69 QG 2:71a

ἐγκοίλιος Leg 3:143, 143, 144

ἐγκολάπτω Somn 1:202, 241

ἐγκολλάω QG 2:54d

ἔγκολλος Mut 211 Spec 4:160 Praem 64

ἐγκολπίζω Plant 7 Conf 137 Congr 152 Aet 66

ἔγκοτος (6) Fug 39 Praem 86 Flacc 19 Legat 199, 260, 303

ἐγκράτεια (62) Opif 164 Leg 3:18 Sacr 27 Det 19, 19, 72, 95, 103 Agr 98 Her 48, 253, 254, 274 Congr 31, 80, 80, 80 Mut 229 Somn 1:124 Somn 2:15, 40, 106, 211 Abr 24, 103, 104, 253 Ios 55, 153 Mos 1:154, 161, 303 Mos 2:185 Spec 1:149, 150, 173, 175, 186, 193 Spec 2:195 Spec 3:22 Spec 4:97, 99, 101, 112, 112, 124 Virt 127, 180 Praem 100, 116 Contempl 34 Legat 14 Hypoth 7:11, 11:14 Prov 2:70 QG 2:22, 68a, 4:168, 172 QE 2:2, 18

ἐγκρατής (13) Leg 1:86 Leg 3:237, 239, 240, 241 Her 203 Ios 54, 166 Virt 167, 182 Prob 84 Flacc 96 QG 4:200a

ἐγκρίνω Post 96

ἐγκρίς Det 118

ἐγκρύπτω Post 118

ἐγκρυφίας Sacr 59, 60, 62, 86 Abr 108

ἐγκύκλιος (45) Leg 3:167, 244, 244 Cher 3, 6, 101, 104, 105 Sacr 38, 43, 44 Post 137 Gig 60 Agr 9, 18 Ebr 33, 49, 51 Sobr 9 Migr 72 Her 274 Congr 9, 10, 14, 19, 20, 23, 35, 72, 73, 79, 79, 121, 154, 155, 156 Fug 183, 213 Mut 229 Somn 1:240 Mos 1:23 Spec 1:336 Prob 160 Legat 166, 168

ἐγκύμων (15) Leg 3:104, 180 Cher 57 Det 60 Deus 5, 15, 39 Congr 140, 145 Mut 134, 144 Somn 1:200 Abr 253 Spec 2:54 Spec 3:44

ἔγκυος Cher 47 Spec 3:108 Virt 139

ἐγκωμιάζω Her 217 Abr 158 Mos 2:191 Flacc 7

ἐγκωμιαστικός Plant 131 Abr 217 Spec 1:342

ἐγκωμιαστός Migr 110

ἐγκώμιον (26) Leg 2:67 Plant 128 Ebr 74 Migr 112, 113 Her 9, 91, 110, 162 Fug 73 Mut 220 Somn 2:38, 272 Abr 247, 255, 265 Ios 205 Mos 2:240 Spec 1:336 Spec 2:85 Spec 4:150, 230 Praem 118 Flacc 108 Legat 38 QG 4:228

ἐγό Leg 2:85

ἐγρήγορσις (21) Leg 2:25, 30, 30 Leg 3:183 Cher 92 Det 172 Ebr 159, 204 Sobr 5 Migr 190, 222 Her 257, 257 Somn 2:39, 160 Abr 154 Ios 147 Spec 1:298 Spec 2:100, 103 Flacc 177

ἐγχαλινόω Leg 3:155, 195 Cher 19 Det 53 Deus 47

ἐγχαράσσω (20) Opif 128 Leg 1:19 Leg 3:16, 230 Agr 167 Fug 26 Mut 200, 270 Somn 1:256 Mos 2:112 Decal 50, 101 Spec 1:30, 59, 313 Spec 4:149 Virt 178 Praem 114 Contempl 76 QG 2:54d

ἐγχειρέω (19) Opif 62 Deus 22, 135 Ebr 16 Sobr 36, 36 Conf 9, 158 Migr 83 Her 299 Mut 47 Somn 2:120, 122 Spec 1:265 Spec 4:220 Virt 171 Prob 24, 34 Legat 209

ἐγχείρημα Det 122 Migr 98 Congr 113 Mut 249 QE 2:1

ἐγχείρησις Somn 2:200 QG isf 3

ἐγχειρητής Somn 2:37 Abr 183 Legat 213

ἐγχειρίδιον Flacc 90 QE 2:1

ἐγχειρίζω (12) Plant 56 Ebr 66 Ios 67, 188, 227, 257 Spec 4:156 Praem 51, 78 Legat 37, 50 QG 1:27

ἐγχέω Ebr 221 Her 182 Spec 3:58 Prob 15

ἐγχορεύω (8) Sacr 33 Post 137 Plant 38 Ebr 138 Congr 20 Fug 187 Mut 225, 229

ἐγχρίμπτω Mos 1:131

ἐγχρίω Congr 47 Somn 1:164

ἐγχρονίζω Abr 185 Mos 2:140 Decal 137

ἐγχωρέω Fug 141

ἐγχώριος (28) Abr 209 Ios 44, 113, 121, 157, 167, 195, 230, 242 Mos 1:132, 276, 296, 319 Mos 2:58 Decal 80 Spec 1:79 Spec 2:217 Spec 3:16 Prob 93 Contempl 8, 69 Flacc 37, 136 Legat 163, 166, 199, 295 QE 2:2

ἐγώ (καί) (1613) Opif 17, 21, 32, 49, 61, 61, 81, 100, 117, 125, 127, 131, 135, 136, 136, 140, 140, 153, 154, 163, 164, 165, 170 Leg 1:45, 47, 48, 49, 51, 52, 59, 61, 61, 62, 70, 78, 78, 91, 98, 98, 99 Leg 2:2, 2, 7, 8, 9, 9, 20, 22, 22, 32, 32, 36, 40, 40, 41, 42, 46, 46, 46, 77, 78, 78, 82, 85, 88, 88, 89, 97, 101 Leg 3:20, 20, 21, 21, 27, 27, 27, 35, 42, 42, 56, 56, 56, 56, 56, 58, 58, 59, 60, 66, 69, 69, 81, 85, 101, 101, 104, 105, 105, 115, 117, 119, 119, 120, 129, 131, 151, 153, 156, 162, 162, 166, 166, 167, 167, 169, 173, 174, 175, 175, 176, 177, 177, 177, 179, 179, 179, 180, 180, 181, 181, 183, 191, 191, 191, 196, 196, 196, 198, 198, 198, 198, 202, 202, 202, 203, 207, 211, 212, 214, 218, 218, 219, 219, 225, 236, 237, 239, 245 Cher 5, 5, 5, 7, 27, 35, 36, 36, 37, 37, 37, 49, 49, 50, 55, 57, 65, 66, 66, 66, 66, 66, 67, 67, 67, 67, 67, 68, 70, 72, 72, 74, 74, 74, 74, 75, 84, 84, 91, 92, 94, 99, 105, 108, 113, 113, 114, 114, 114, 115, 115, 119, 120, 128 Sacr 8, 20, 22, 22, 23, 24, 27, 30, 30, 30, 33, 35, 41, 42, 42, 56, 56, 56, 57, 62, 64, 66, 66, 67, 68, 69, 75, 85, 87, 87, 87, 87, 98, 99, 106, 108, 108, 109, 111, 111, 111, 111, 111, 118, 118, 118, 118, 124, 126, 134, 136 Det 4, 4, 4, 5, 5, 5, 5, 10, 10, 15, 23, 29, 30, 31, 46, 46, 50, 50, 52, 53, 54, 57, 57, 62, 62, 69, 72, 79, 82, 84, 85, 86, 89, 95, 95, 98, 102, 121, 121, 121, 122, 123, 123, 126, 127, 139, 141, 144, 146, 150, 150, 156, 156, 157, 158, 160, 163, 175 Post 10, 16, 16, 19, 23, 26, 28, 29, 29, 30, 30, 30, 30, 30, 30, 30, 31, 39, 41, 49, 55, 58, 61, 61, 68, 68, 72, 80, 82, 89, 89, 89, 90, 90, 90, 90, 90, 91, 102, 104, 118, 120, 122, 124, 132, 136, 139, 143, 143, 145, 155, 164, 166, 167, 168, 168, 170, 175, 178, 179, 179, 184 Gig 1, 8, 15, 15, 17, 19, 20, 32, 40, 45, 45, 45, 47, 49, 50, 60, 63, 63 Deus 6, 6, 6, 6, 7, 23, 28, 45, 46, 57, 69, 84, 92, 106, 108, 109, 111, 121, 128, 131, 133, 134, 135, 135, 136, 138, 138, 138, 145, 145, 145, 149, 155, 156, 157, 166, 167, 168, 169, 169 Agr 9, 22, 30, 45, 50, 50, 51, 51, 52, 52, 59, 108, 112, 112 Plant 12, 29, 36, 36, 42, 44, 49, 52, 62, 63, 64, 64, 83, 90, 90, 94, 95, 100, 110, 130, 131, 132, 133, 133, 137, 138, 147, 147, 159 Ebr 14, 14, 23, 28, 31, 31, 37, 39, 39, 40, 40, 47, 50, 54, 54, 57, 59, 61, 63, 64, 84, 84, 85, 93, 96, 97, 98, 105, 106, 114, 118, 123, 140, 149, 149, 152, 164, 169, 189, 190, 193, 193, 194, 198, 224 Sobr 4, 12, 15, 18, 19, 26, 33, 56, 56, 60, 68 Conf 15, 21, 31, 44, 44, 44, 44, 49, 50, 50, 51, 51, 52, 52, 55, 55, 65, 65, 69, 72, 72, 79, 80, 80, 84, 94, 98, 98, 121, 127, 127, 127, 129, 130, 133, 135, 138, 142, 165, 169, 169, 181, 181, 181, 183, 190 Migr 3, 13, 21, 21, 50, 51, 56, 68, 80, 86, 89, 90, 95, 95, 104, 130, 138, 142, 142, 142, 142, 142, 151, 156, 157, 157, 164, 169, 171, 172, 174, 174, 183, 206, 206, 208, 208, 212, 214 Her 2, 2, 2, 2, 2, 2, 8, 8, 8, 8, 14, 15, 19, 19, 20, 20, 20, 20, 20, 20, 20, 22, 24, 25, 25, 25, 26, 27, 28, 28, 29, 30, 30, 31, 31, 32, 32, 33, 34, 39, 39, 39, 42, 43, 45, 52, 58, 58, 58, 59, 59, 59, 62, 65, 65, 65, 71, 72, 76, 80, 80, 81, 92, 93, 95, 96, 102, 107, 112, 112, 113, 113, 113, 113, 116, 117, 117, 121, 123, 125, 125, 126, 128, 133, 153, 153, 179, 183, 185, 186, 186, 186, 206, 206, 207, 213, 216, 224, 225, 230, 230, 231, 231, 231, 234, 234, 234, 236, 236, 251, 251, 263, 263, 264, 265, 272, 272, 273, 282, 291, 304 Congr 1, 1, 2, 2, 2, 2, 2, 2, 5, 6, 6, 6, 7, 12, 12, 13, 13, 13, 14, 19, 26, 27, 30, 30, 38, 56, 72, 74, 76, 80, 81, 85, 86, 86, 86, 86, 86, 86, 86, 86, 90, 94, 96, 96, 98, 99, 100, 101, 102, 110, 123, 125, 133, 134, 152, 152, 152, 153, 156, 163, 177 Fug 1, 1, 3, 15, 15, 15, 15, 15, 15, 15, 20, 21, 21, 22, 22, 22, 23, 23, 41, 55, 59, 61, 62, 67, 67, 67, 69, 69, 74, 75, 79, 79, 82, 84, 91, 103, 104, 104, 106, 116, 117, 118, 127, 127, 127, 137, 148, 149, 154, 155, 156, 165, 175, 182, 197, 203, 211 Mut 1, 8, 9, 9, 10, 11, 12, 12, 13, 13, 14, 14, 14, 15, 16, 18, 18, 20, 20, 23, 23, 23, 27, 29, 29, 31, 37, 38, 39, 39, 39, 41, 47, 50, 52, 52, 57, 57, 58, 58, 58, 58, 62, 77, 79, 79, 97, 97, 97, 115, 115, 120, 136, 137, 138, 138, 139, 152, 154, 157, 166, 166, 173, 173, 179, 181, 184, 206, 206, 218, 230, 231, 233, 243, 246, 248, 254, 257, 263, 265 Somn 1:3, 3, 3, 6, 7, 15, 21, 25, 25, 30, 31, 32, 35, 41, 42, 43, 46, 47, 59, 64, 64, 65, 75, 75, 77, 84, 86, 92, 97, 102, 110, 110, 111, 112, 118, 134, 142, 143, 143, 147, 154, 159, 163, 164, 164, 166, 173, 173, 177, 177, 179, 183, 189, 189, 189, 189, 189, 195, 195, 196, 196, 198, 203, 204, 219, 225, 226, 227, 227, 228, 229, 231, 238, 240, 241, 241, 241, 241, 249, 252, 254 Somn 2:1, 2, 6, 6, 7, 7, 7, 9, 17, 33, 54, 63, 69, 75, 91, 91, 93, 94, 94, 95, 95, 100, 100, 102, 104, 104, 108, 111, 111, 115, 123, 129, 133, 137, 137, 139, 139, 142, 149, 153, 159, 159, 159, 160, 163, 164, 170, 172, 182, 182, 182, 184, 200, 205, 207, 207, 216, 218, 221, 221, 222, 223, 224, 224, 224, 227, 229, 244, 252, 255, 258, 267, 267, 269, 272, 272, 291, 291, 291, 291, 291, 297, 297, 301 Abr 28, 29, 42, 46, 51, 64, 98, 113, 115, 115, 128, 128, 129, 129, 129, 130, 142, 144, 147, 157, 160, 164, 166, 167, 178, 184, 193, 204, 204, 206, 236, 237, 243, 248, 249, 249, 250, 252, 261, 267, 276 Ios 6, 7, 9, 9, 15, 17, 17, 18, 19, 19, 20, 20, 20, 23, 25, 26, 27, 27, 27, 42, 43, 45, 46, 47, 47, 47, 50, 50, 51, 64, 64, 64, 66, 66, 68, 69, 71, 71, 75, 77, 78, 78, 93, 104, 104, 104, 104, 106, 106, 110, 117, 118, 125, 126, 127, 129, 132, 147, 167, 170, 171, 177, 184, 184, 187, 188, 192, 215, 216, 221, 222, 224, 225, 226, 227, 228, 238, 239, 241, 242, 243, 245, 262, 263, 264, 266, 266 Mos 1:4, 11, 12, 35, 56, 58, 62, 72, 73, 75, 75, 84, 84, 88, 92, 146, 171, 194, 195, 201, 225, 226, 235, 245, 245, 274, 274, 277, 278, 278, 279, 280, 281, 283, 298, 298, 329, 330, 330 Mos 2:31, 82, 99, 129, 155, 158, 168, 168, 171, 185, 235, 235, 252, 272, 281 Decal 23, 31, 31, 33, 38, 41, 43, 47, 68, 75, 88, 88, 89, 91, 91, 113, 141, 142 Spec 1:8, 18, 22, 23, 41, 41, 41, 43, 43, 45, 46, 47, 49, 80, 89, 95, 100, 171, 171, 197, 209, 214, 214, 214, 215, 222, 253, 258, 264, 266, 266, 266, 266, 281, 282, 314, 317, 318, 323, 340, 343, 345 Spec 2:11, 11, 11, 20, 34, 47, 55, 89, 100, 104, 142, 160, 167, 191, 201, 217, 219, 239, 252 Spec 3:3, 3, 4, 5, 5, 19, 72, 119, 159, 166, 176, 185, 192, 194 Spec 4:39, 69, 69, 95, 123, 123, 138, 163, 164, 202,

231, 237, 238 Virt 11, 14, 68, 136, 139, 183, 188, 192, 195, 195, 195 Praem 54, 80, 89, 91 Prob 1, 25, 25, 27, 38, 58, 62, 64, 95, 96, 96, 96, 99, 99, 103, 116, 124, 124, 125, 128, 130, 140, 144, 145, 145, 146, 146, 152 Contempl 17 Aet 12, 13, 13, 29, 44, 63, 69, 71, 91, 95, 102, 106, 134, 137 Flacc 22, 23, 43, 49, 51, 54, 59, 86, 94, 97, 101, 102, 103, 116, 121, 124, 125, 143, 157, 159, 163, 170, 173, 175, 178, 178, 178, 179, 179 Legat 1, 4, 27, 49, 53, 54, 56, 58, 76, 86, 89, 91, 91, 113, 114, 119, 120, 134, 152, 157, 174, 176, 181, 182, 182, 183, 184, 186, 187, 188, 193, 197, 218, 220, 224, 230, 231, 233, 236, 253, 255, 256, 258, 264, 265, 265, 274, 274, 274, 275, 276, 276, 278, 281, 286, 287, 294, 308, 315, 323, 324, 326, 326, 327, 329, 334, 347, 351, 352, 353, 356, 357, 357, 357, 359, 362, 362, 367, 367, 367, 370, 370, 372 Hypoth 6:5, 7:2, 7:4, 7:8, 7:18, 7:20, 11:1 Prov 2:9, 30, 35, 38, 43, 52, 54, 63, 63, 64, 69 QG 1:17b, 21, 68, 70:1, 100:2a, 100:2b, 2:11, 11, 54a, 3:23, 23, 58, 4:173, 173, 173, 180, 202a, 202a, 202b, 206a, 227 QG (Par) 2:4 QE 1:19, 2:15:1, 18, 21, 105 QE isf 26

ἔδαφος (ὁ) (33) Cher 104 Deus 38 Ebr 172 Somn 1:125 Somn 2:54, 56, 140 Abr 65 Mos 1:77, 91, 107, 302 Mos 2:85, 254 Spec 2:172 Spec 3:58, 59 Spec 4:17, 214 Virt 105, 158 Prob 7, 133 Contempl 33, 86 Aet 129 Flacc 71, 160, 162 Legat 228, 352 Prov 2:26, 46

Ἐδέμ (19) Leg 1:43, 45, 63, 64, 65, 65 Cher 12, 12, 13 Post 1, 32, 32, 32, 128 Plant 32, 38 Conf 61 Somn 2:241, 242

ἔδεσμα Spec 2:50, 148 Spec 4:91, 113

ἕδος Spec 3:89 Aet 17 Legat 290

ἕδρα Sacr 42 Aet 136 QG (Par) 2:6, 2:7

ἐδωδή (30) Opif 159 Ebr 220 Fug 31 Mut 164 Somn 2:49, 155, 157, 205 Abr 148 Ios 152, 206 Mos 2:23 Spec 1:135, 190, 233, 240, 244, 256 Spec 2:98, 175 Spec 3:9, 97 Spec 4:97, 110, 113 Virt 6, 126 Contempl 9, 55 Aet 63

ἐδώδιμος (17) Leg 1:99, 99 Leg 3:184 Cher 84 Agr 19, 19 Plant 96, 97, 109 Sobr 28 Her 253 Mos 2:180, 180, 180 Spec 3:95, 198, 202

Ἐδώμ (8) Post 101 Deus 144, 145, 148, 166, 180 Migr 146 QG 4:171

ἐθάς (8) Deus 38 Agr 105 Somn 1:151 Somn 2:63 Flacc 3 Legat 53, 187, 254

ἐθέλεχθρος Sacr 32 Mos 1:248 Flacc 40

ἐθελόδουλος Sacr 32 Ebr 122

ἐθελοκακέω (7) Sacr 29 Ios 226 Mos 1:94 Flacc 40, 129, 154 Legat 32

ἐθελοντής Post 10 Ios 228, 240 Virt 63, 94

ἐθελουργός (9) Det 11 Deus 47 Conf 59 Mut 270 Mos 1:63 Spec 1:57 Spec 2:146 Spec 3:127 Prob 22

ἐθελούσιος Cher 22 Deus 100 Spec 4:157 Contempl 71 QE 2:2

ἐθέλω (θέλω) (140) Opif 21, 24, 46, 88, 104, 137 Leg 3:36, 81, 243 Cher 91, 115, 118 Sacr 22, 24, 37, 40, 115 Det 152 Post 95, 156, 175 Gig 39, 43 Deus 4, 173 Agr 5, 6, 72, 112, 152 Plant 81, 130 Ebr 167 Sobr 20, 32, 46 Conf 5, 11, 38, 153, 161, 175 Migr 11, 118, 211, 219 Her 115, 158, 194, 266 Congr 53, 71 Fug 28, 35, 145 Mut 37, 60, 241, 242, 265 Somn 1:7, 98, 158, 188 Somn 2:49, 83, 86 Abr 5, 115 Ios 228 Mos 1:2, 19, 141, 158, 201, 249, 297, 298, 300, 317 Mos 2:52 Decal 43, 63, 112 Spec 1:65, 75, 127 Spec 2:60, 236 Spec 3:31, 78, 82, 154, 175, 202 Spec 4:32, 81, 124, 140, 229, 238 Virt 27, 108, 136 Praem 44, 99, 115, 117, 135, 140 Prob 21, 54, 69, 86, 101, 111 Contempl 64 Aet 13, 13 Flacc 12, 50, 51, 54 Legat 36, 154, 160, 209, 229, 301, 315, 334 Hypoth 11:12 QG 1:17a, 2:16, 3:22, 4:191b QG (Par) 2:1, 2:5 QE 2:11a, 25d

ἐθίζω (21) Opif 85 Her 234 Congr 47 Abr 136, 178, 269 Mos 2:205 Decal 43, 124 Spec 1:133 Spec 2:46, 60, 67, 88, 101 Spec 3:37 Spec 4:65 Prob 107, 110 Contempl 35 Prov 2:56

ἐθισμός Ebr 54 Legat 315

ἐθνάρχης Her 279

ἐθνική Mos 1:69, 188

ἔθνος (287) Leg 3:88, 187 Cher 91 Sacr 4, 57 Post 89, 89, 90, 91, 91 Gig 51 Deus 148, 173, 176, 178 Plant 59, 59, 67, 67 Ebr 28, 34, 193, 195 Conf 10, 11, 15, 15, 46 Migr 1, 53, 53, 56, 56, 60, 60, 60, 68, 120 Her 8, 174, 272, 272, 277, 278, 278 Congr 3, 58, 119, 129 Fug 185 Mut 148, 148, 148, 150, 151, 191, 263 Somn 1:167, 177, 177 Somn 2:133, 287 Abr 40, 56, 57, 98, 98, 181, 183, 188, 226, 276 Ios 38, 56, 134, 135, 136, 242, 259 Mos 1:4, 7, 8, 34, 71, 73, 73, 86, 88, 123, 139, 149, 158, 189, 189, 217, 220, 222, 240, 240, 242, 242, 245, 247, 254, 263, 278, 290, 291, 303 Mos 2:15, 19, 19, 20, 43, 44, 143, 153, 154, 159, 166, 179, 194, 202, 224, 229, 232, 232, 246, 250, 254, 256, 257, 271, 288, 291 Decal 1, 15, 32, 37, 37, 96, 159 Spec 1:2, 3, 7, 54, 78, 79, 111, 111, 113, 133, 136, 141, 144, 162, 168, 190, 226, 228, 229, 229, 229, 230, 233, 244, 244 Spec 2:82, 121, 123, 134, 145, 150, 162, 162, 163, 166, 167, 170, 170, 171, 188, 190, 215, 217, 222 Spec 3:110, 131, 131, 139 Spec 4:16, 153, 158, 159, 179, 179, 181, 183, 184, 219, 224 Virt 34, 42, 56, 58, 60, 64, 67, 70, 75, 77, 79, 103, 107, 119, 141, 141, 185, 186, 212, 226 Praem 7, 57, 57, 65, 77, 77, 84, 85, 95, 107, 114, 114, 166, 169, 172 Prob 75, 137, 138 Flacc 1, 45, 45, 117, 124, 170, 191 Legat 10, 10, 19, 48, 116, 117, 119, 133, 137, 144, 147, 160, 161, 171, 178, 184, 194, 196, 207, 210, 214, 226, 240, 256, 256, 268, 274, 279, 279, 301, 347, 351, 373 Hypoth 6:1, 6:2, 6:10 Prov 2:23, 41 QG 3:18, 43 QE 2:6a

ἔθος (195) Leg 1:99 Leg 3:30, 43 Cher 42, 122 Sacr 15 Det 2, 87, 87, 134 Post 9, 50, 181 Deus 17, 88, 133, 167, 169, 179 Agr 29, 43, 56, 95, 140 Plant 74, 133, 163 Ebr 54, 55, 55, 59, 68, 74, 80, 124, 193, 195, 198 Sobr 19, 33, 35 Conf 28, 154 Migr 20, 90, 116, 142, 156, 157, 159, 173, 203, 214, 221 Her 142, 279, 311 Congr 85, 173 Fug 73 Mut 104, 160, 269 Somn 1:98, 115, 201 Somn 2:9, 56, 78, 90, 123 Abr 31, 67, 137, 170, 184, 185, 185, 188, 188, 193, 260 Ios 15, 29, 42, 83, 93, 164, 207, 230, 247, 257 Mos 1:14, 24, 31, 49, 87, 96, 123, 196, 213, 275, 278, 310, 324 Mos 2:19, 33, 53, 193, 215, 266, 268 Decal 1, 85, 92, 137, 141, 160, 176 Spec 1:3, 58, 78, 113, 257, 313 Spec 2:91, 109, 147, 148, 179, 188 Spec 3:13, 29, 29, 56 Spec 4:16, 23, 149, 149, 150, 218, 218 Virt 65, 72, 88, 102, 218, 219 Praem 40, 54, 106, 135 Prob 58, 114, 154 Contempl 1, 12, 32, 66 Flacc 41, 43, 48, 50, 50, 52, 53, 75, 79, 81, 116, 154 Legat 81, 89, 115, 116, 134, 161, 164, 170, 201, 210, 240, 268, 300, 356, 360 Hypoth 6:9, 7:6, 7:10, 7:11 Prov 2:44 QG 4:51b, 191a QE 2:2 QE isf 17 ἔθω (165) Opif 50, 102, 131, 133 Leg 3:239, 246 Cher 27, 70 Sacr 10, 77 Det 35, 39, 81, 145, 177 Post 53 Gig 6, 10, 12 Deus 45, 86, 132, 182 Agr 2, 9, 39, 41, 53, 56, 66, 139 Plant 27, 55, 62, 113, 115, 174 Ebr 18, 99, 102, 119, 155, 172, 183, 205 Sobr 16 Conf 3, 49, 77, 93, 114, 174 Migr 75, 122, 127, 219 Her 22, 81, 145, 245, 249, 295 Congr 7, 150, 162, 165, 180 Mut 42, 59, 106, 116, 154 Somn 1:55, 102, 141 Somn 2:81, 91, 101, 127, 132, 214, 252, 291 Abr 89, 163, 193 Ios 2, 41, 44, 60, 125 Mos 1:64, 102, 175, 176, 204, 216, 266, 326 Mos 2:7, 24, 58, 106, 116, 137, 160, 186, 195, 268 Decal 57, 65, 87 Spec 1:97, 97, 140, 184, 311, 321 Spec 2:4, 206, 240 Spec 3:65, 89, 147, 178, 199 Spec 4:53, 96, 136, 148, 168 Virt 10, 17, 24, 39, 55, 137, 163 Praem 8, 79, 166 Prob 31, 62, 69, 131 Contempl 27 Aet 36, 43, 52, 122 Flacc 17, 33, 41, 64, 138 Legat 117, 128, 140, 261 Hypoth 11:13 Prov 2:44, 51 QG 3:11a QG isf 5 QE isf 25

εἰ (1351) Opif 21, 23, 24, 25, 25, 27, 28, 28, 33, 47, 54, 81, 82, 84, 88, 90, 90, 97, 102, 104, 106, 110, 118, 130, 130, 135, 139, 145, 145, 153, 169, 171 Leg 1:19, 21, 27, 32, 35, 38, 38, 60, 60, 79, 95, 95, 100, 108 Leg 2:3, 3, 6, 7, 7, 7, 7, 7, 18, 18, 18, 18, 20, 32, 46, 57, 63, 66, 73, 91, 93, 93, 105 Leg 3:1, 1, 4, 5, 10, 13, 13, 17, 21, 21, 21, 22, 27, 47, 47, 57, 66, 69, 71, 77, 85, 86, 98, 109, 110, 113, 128, 162, 164, 164, 164, 167, 176, 193, 204, 205, 214, 215, 217, 224, 231, 236, 237, 240, 240, 245 Cher 10, 19, 32, 36, 37, 40, 54, 65, 72, 87, 91, 98, 99, 100, 126 Sacr 1, 35, 37, 48, 53, 65, 66, 67, 70, 78, 85, 91, 100, 100, 100, 108, 109, 116, 121, 121, 122, 123, 125, 130, 136, 139 Det 5, 10, 12, 13, 20, 20, 22, 42, 49, 51, 51, 57, 60, 62, 63, 68, 70, 76, 81, 86, 90, 95, 110, 124, 124, 132, 138, 141, 141, 142, 145, 150, 152, 153, 154, 154, 154, 156, 156, 156, 156, 157, 163, 163, 165, 168 Post 1, 2, 4, 7, 8, 34, 36, 36, 37, 71, 80, 81, 82, 82, 82, 83, 83, 88, 95, 95, 99, 108, 108, 115, 142, 144, 144, 148, 156, 157, 160, 160, 163, 163, 164, 171, 176, 181, 185 Gig 11, 21, 26, 41, 42, 47, 51, 62, 64 Deus 4, 11, 17, 18, 19, 25, 40, 57, 59, 64, 66, 68, 75, 80, 81, 100, 108, 133, 135, 145, 166, 166, 168, 170, 173, 183 Agr 11, 29, 33, 57, 61, 69, 72, 98, 104, 112, 122, 149, 152, 156, 160, 168, 176, 180 Plant 6, 7, 8, 24, 45, 45, 48, 58, 68, 81, 81, 127, 132, 133, 142, 146, 147, 147, 147, 154, 155, 159, 161, 169, 172, 173, 175, 176 Ebr 12, 17, 19, 19, 32, 42, 43, 79, 103, 105, 110, 132, 135, 155, 158, 165, 168, 169, 192, 195, 198, 198, 220 Sobr 4, 6, 13, 28, 48 Conf 5, 6, 13, 14, 40, 59, 67, 67, 97, 100, 104, 116, 144, 147, 158, 164, 175, 185, 191, 192 Migr 4, 16, 21, 21, 26, 26, 51, 55, 60, 75, 87, 92, 130, 131, 144, 152, 167, 171, 172, 192, 196, 207, 210, 213, 218, 219, 224 Her 3, 7, 20, 20, 23, 29, 32, 39, 49, 49, 63, 68, 69, 81, 88, 88, 90, 92, 100, 111, 115, 116, 118, 142, 144, 161, 177, 188, 244, 249, 252, 255, 256, 278, 282, 282, 282, 282, 306, 310, 314 Congr 3, 9, 12, 24, 42, 46, 51, 66, 80, 93, 110, 140, 145, 152, 157, 157, 160, 170, 178 Fug 6, 19, 20, 20, 32, 34, 34, 51, 62, 70, 78, 84, 91, 93, 98, 99, 106, 107, 115, 117, 129, 151, 151, 151, 153, 154, 160, 172, 189 Mut 9, 10, 13, 15, 15, 26, 31, 31, 33, 37, 45, 47, 56, 56, 56, 73, 73, 79, 81, 120, 124, 128, 128, 131, 140, 140, 143, 146, 157, 171, 172, 176, 177, 179, 181, 186, 186, 188, 213, 214, 217, 219, 222, 225, 225, 226, 226, 226, 226, 227, 227, 228, 229, 231, 242, 252, 256, 258, 258 Somn 1:27, 36, 44, 53, 53, 53, 53, 53, 73, 82, 91, 93, 131, 135, 184, 204, 207, 228, 230, 231, 237, 238, 248, 253, 256 Somn 2:49, 49, 56, 58, 61, 61, 76, 88, 99, 103, 109, 109, 117, 123, 125, 127, 128, 130, 136, 152, 170, 170, 177, 188, 189, 219, 231, 297, 301 Abr 12, 19, 22, 25, 35, 41, 53, 58, 64, 73, 74, 102, 105, 105, 115, 115, 116, 116, 128, 130, 131, 136, 152, 153, 163, 177, 179, 187, 188, 193, 204, 208, 210, 211, 230, 238, 250, 251, 263, 264, 265 Ios 13, 17, 17, 23, 24, 25, 25, 27, 44, 45, 48, 57, 66, 69, 69, 74, 94, 94, 109, 119, 127, 146, 147, 168, 168, 176, 179, 192, 199, 203, 210, 216, 216, 224, 225, 227, 233, 234, 264 Mos 1:6, 16, 24, 26, 28, 32, 32, 33, 45, 45, 49, 51, 56, 68, 84, 108, 108, 109, 110, 139, 147, 153, 156, 159, 160, 172, 186, 191, 199, 202, 212, 213, 215, 221, 224, 224, 239, 242, 243, 243, 245, 245, 250, 258, 274, 274, 286, 294, 300, 301, 311, 314, 314, 315, 328 Mos 2:6, 10, 11, 13, 19, 27, 44, 52, 61, 62, 72, 80, 107, 108, 108, 135, 135, 139, 142, 145, 167, 168, 168, 171, 177, 185, 200, 206, 227, 229, 233, 235, 243, 261, 264, 265, 271, 271, 281, 281 Decal 1, 16, 37, 41, 60, 61, 61, 64, 71, 71, 72, 85, 85, 85, 86, 89, 91, 91, 91, 93, 93, 93, 93, 98, 112, 115, 124, 125, 130, 148, 150, 150 Spec 1:17, 17, 32, 36, 40, 42, 46, 54, 65, 81, 90, 91, 91, 104, 116, 120, 121, 137, 153, 154, 159, 168, 195, 214, 214, 223, 230, 233, 238, 241, 242, 277, 281, 283, 283, 294, 300, 317, 320, 327, 335, 338, 344 Spec 2:2, 4, 5, 6, 6, 6, 6, 6, 11, 19, 27, 35, 36, 37, 37, 37, 42, 48, 49, 52, 53, 59, 67, 67, 71, 73, 85, 87, 87, 89, 91, 95, 96, 124, 126, 127, 128, 132, 135, 147, 163, 165, 176, 178, 202, 216, 219, 232, 245, 248, 253, 255, 257, 262 Spec 3:5, 8, 9, 20, 21, 28, 28, 31, 32, 33, 42, 46, 50, 54, 61, 61, 62, 62, 65, 67, 74, 74, 77, 78, 84, 85, 85, 86, 86, 90, 98, 100, 106, 108, 111, 113, 113, 116, 117, 119, 128, 128, 132, 134, 136, 139, 142, 145, 149, 163, 165, 165, 173, 175, 190, 193, 193, 196, 198, 202, 203 Spec 4:7, 7, 11, 15, 21, 31, 34, 36, 37, 39, 41, 48, 56, 68, 74, 79, 81, 82, 84, 87, 88, 89, 89, 93, 101, 103, 103, 108, 121, 123, 131, 132, 136, 144, 170, 184, 185, 188, 194, 202, 204, 215, 218, 231, 235, 238 Virt 7, 16, 19, 22, 26, 28, 32, 32, 32, 32, 32, 32, 33, 33, 41, 44, 51, 53, 59, 60, 60, 74, 80, 83, 88, 88, 89, 105, 106, 108, 109, 109, 114, 114, 124, 129, 133, 134, 135, 136, 136, 138, 144, 154, 157, 179, 179, 184, 186, 187, 190, 195, 202, 206, 210, 214, 221, 222, 224, 227, 227 Praem 17, 34, 34, 36, 41, 43, 54, 56, 78, 84, 86, 86, 88, 91, 95, 99, 119, 136, 136, 137, 138, 148, 150, 161 Prob 7, 21, 31, 36, 37, 39, 40, 40, 40, 42, 44, 53, 56, 60, 63, 63, 63, 64, 72, 95, 101, 103, 104, 104, 105, 113, 138, 143, 150, 157, 159, 159 Contempl 6, 24, 40, 43, 59, 61, 64, 69, 72, 75 Aet 2, 3, 6, 6, 21, 21, 34, 35, 36, 37, 41, 41, 42, 43, 46, 46, 52, 54, 55, 55, 56, 63, 65, 69, 70, 70, 71, 72, 75, 75, 78, 78, 82, 83, 84, 87, 88, 90, 91, 92, 118, 123, 125, 129, 130, 131, 137, 138, 143, 144, 144, 146 Flacc 4, 11, 28, 29, 31, 35, 35, 50, 50, 50, 58, 69, 78, 80, 81, 94, 94, 96, 124, 127, 167 Legat 3, 5, 5, 5, 7, 7, 24, 38, 46, 48, 58, 65, 67, 73, 89, 91, 91, 99, 103, 107, 108, 117, 119, 122, 125, 127, 136, 136, 136, 144, 149, 154, 158, 159, 174, 178, 187, 192, 192, 196, 207, 223, 233, 233, 238, 257, 267, 268, 274, 277, 287, 289, 293, 301, 308, 313, 322, 322, 328, 329, 335, 339, 343, 369, 371 Hypoth 6:2, 7:3, 7:9, 7:10, 7:11, 7:13, 7:17, 7:17, 11:13, 11:13, 11:16 Prov 1, 1, 2:5, 9, 13, 16, 17, 17, 17, 17, 18, 18, 18, 18, 18, 21, 22, 23, 23, 28, 30, 34, 35, 41, 42, 44, 44, 54, 54, 56, 58, 62, 63, 66 QG 1:51, 2:39, 54a, 65, 71a, 3:11a, 30b, 30b, 52, 4:52b, 69, 88, 88, 88, 88, 144, 180, 7*, 7*, 198, 200b, 206b, 228 QG isf 16 QG (Par) 2:1, 2:2, 2:2, 2:5, 2:7 QE isf 16, 17

εἴγε Post 102 QG isf 10

εἰδέχθεια Opif 158

εἰδεχθής Leg 3:62 Ios 101, 108 Aet 56 Prov 2:31

εἴδησις Plant 36 Migr 42

εἰδικός Cher 7 Deus 76, 95, 110 Mut 78

εἰδοποιέω Opif 130 Spec 1:48, 327

εἶδον εἴδω ὁράω

εἶδον (εἴδω) (463) Opif 71, 71, 83, 85, 141, 149, 155 Leg 1:20, 28, 65, 74 Leg 2:7, 9, 16, 17, 26, 47, 65, 81, 81, 82, 87, 93, 97 Leg 3:4, 16, 38, 54, 56, 57, 62, 63, 73, 85, 98, 101, 105, 111, 115, 140, 162, 169, 169, 180, 214, 221, 222, 226, 234, 240, 245 Cher 17, 35, 49, 57, 61, 127 Sacr 4, 24, 28, 36, 38, 38, 81, 98, 106, 118, 125 Det 5, 5, 9, 10, 11, 24, 27, 30, 31, 59, 59, 86, 99, 106, 126, 126, 126, 129, 130, 132, 135 Post 15, 18, 116, 137, 138, 150, 167, 167, 168, 168 Gig 6, 51, Deus 20, 44, 50, 51, 56, 131, 135, 146, 150, 170, 181 Agr 5, 43, 51, 78, 79, 128 Plant 21, 28, 60, 65, 105, 123, 169, 169 Ebr 5, 15, 22, 72, 82, 83, 108, 111, 134, 135, 155, 155, 158, 160, 167, 172, 177, 192, 206, 219 Sobr 8, 13, 32, 32, 42, 51 Conf 1, 1, 3, 24, 25, 29, 36, 52, 62, 72, 92, 93, 97, 97, 134, 140, 150, 150, 151, 155, 167, 169 Migr 38, 42, 46, 48, 49, 49, 54, 56, 62, 78, 79, 79, 109, 115, 135, 135, 174, 196, 218 Her 51, 52, 113, 124, 146, 159, 159, 249, 251, 291, 308 Congr 1, 12, 20, 58, 123, 131, 139, 139, 150, 153 Fug 1, 23, 25, 39, 58, 131, 132, 132, 133, 133, 133, 134, 134, 134, 134, 134, 137, 138, 141, 156, 165, 165, 204, 212, 213 Mut 5, 7, 8, 10, 19, 42, 57, 58, 132, 134, 134, 159, 162, 165, 168, 168, 174, 189, 212, 241, 253, 259 Somn 1:3, 3, 25, 27, 56, 62, 64, 65, 67, 117, 133, 171, 172, 179, 189, 194, 194, 195, 195, 197, 199, 200, 204, 208, 219, 238, 239, 240 Somn 2:5, 19, 19, 19, 111, 113, 133, 133, 136, 137, 137, 216, 216, 218, 222, 265, 266, 268, 277, 280, 282 Abr 65, 78, 79, 80, 84, 93, 102, 104, 171, 173, 191, 238, 260 Ios 6, 8, 12, 17, 26, 80, 87, 90, 93, 103, 162, 183, 196, 200, 217, 233, 249, 253, 255 Mos 1:19, 54, 70, 76, 177, 200, 233, 246, 272, 273, 277, 289, 302, 310 Mos 2:69, 165, 171, 172, 209, 214, 259, 261, 291 Decal 60, 88, 88, 139 Spec 1:15, 16, 32, 33, 37, 40, 99, 167, 259, 321 Spec 2:51, 98, 194, 199 Spec 3:6, 40, 47, 172, 189 Spec 4:61, 75 Virt 22, 96, 116, 117, 179, 182, 188, 200, 221 Praem 11, 33, 39, 44, 88, 129 Prob 5, 26, 32, 37, 99, 101, 141, 148,157 Contempl 12, 45, 87 Aet 131, 149 Flacc 6, 15, 27, 37, 92, 114, 114, 157, 164, 169 Legat 8, 12, 30, 224, 226, 262, 315, 351 Hypoth 7:16, 11:14 Prov 1, 2:19, 29, 58, 60, 65 QG 1:20, 21, 2:11, 11, 34a, 41, 3:24, 58, 4:52a, 131, 173 QG (Par) 2:1 QE 2:25d, 37, 45a, QE isf 3, 4, 6

εἶδος (250) Opif 25, 38, 51, 76, 76, 78, 82, 91, 92, 95, 130, 151, 172 Leg 1:22, 64, 66 Leg 2:8, 9, 9, 12, 13, 13, 13, 14, 22 Leg 3:103, 131 Cher 4, 5, 6 Sacr 8, 27, 84, 100, 104, 133 Det 46, 46, 77, 78, 83 Post 10, 32, 47, 60, 81, 91, 92, 99, 105, 118 Gig 53 Deus 46, 62, 95, 113, 119, 123, 130 Agr 13, 90, 98, 133, 137, 140, 167, 171 Plant 1, 18, 110, 140, 167, 172, 172, 174 Ebr 36, 85, 88, 92, 138, 157 Sobr 18, 34, 52 Conf 60, 63, 64, 84, 85, 90, 96, 99, 99, 108, 117, 176, 185, 188, 191, 192 Migr 13, 17, 54, 66, 67, 71, 98, 105, 110, 117, 137, 155, 155, 155, 207 Her 57, 57, 126, 138, 138, 164, 172, 173, 181, 209, 209, 262 Congr 73, 100 Fug 10, 12, 26, 53, 176 Mut 33, 58, 78, 78, 80, 80, 110, 119, 148, 148, 192, 212, 220, 270 Somn 1:1, 2, 2, 15, 30, 45, 79, 188, 189, 232 Somn 2:1, 1, 4, 15, 155, 163, 181, 190, 201, 210, 215, 216, 216 Abr 41, 56 Ios 165 Mos 1:79, 159, 159, 264 Mos 2:29, 61, 62, 76, 133, 191, 212, 223, 272 Decal 154, 168, 175 Spec 1:1, 45, 60, 64, 137, 151, 194, 211, 224, 226, 228, 254, 328 Spec 2:1, 39, 40, 140, 175, 182, 189, 193, 216, 224 Spec 3:7, 55, 72, 99, 125, 170, 182 Spec 4:92, 113, 132, 147, 186, 196, 211 Virt 19, 67, 73, 164 Praem 2, 70, 85, 99, 150 Prob 15, 90, 101, 111 Contempl 38, 49, 54 Aet 69, 86 QG 2:13a, 34a, 3:29, 61 QE 2:47

εἴδω (819) εἶδον οἶδα

εἴδωλον (23) Opif 18 Leg 2:46 Plant 21 Conf 69, 71, 74 Congr 65 Fug 14, 143 Somn 1:153 Somn 2:133, 162 Abr 153 Spec 1:25, 26, 26, 28, 219 Praem 19, 116 Prob 146 Contempl 72 Flacc 164

εἰδωλοποιέω Somn 2:97

εἴθε Leg 3:34 Det 112, 178 Conf 76 Somn 2:199

εἰκάζω (27) Opif 69 Leg 1:69, 77 Leg 2:74 Leg 3:188 Post 129 Deus 127 Agr 12 Plant 76 Ebr 167 Her 234 Congr 137 Fug 176, 179 Mut 161 Somn 1:204, 232, 233, 234 Somn 2:240, 245, 259, 302 Mos 2:63, 82 Flacc 109 QG 1:92

εἰκαιολογία Somn 2:115

εἰκαῖος (15) Sacr 32, 61 Abr 83 Ios 125 Mos 2:175 Decal 104 Spec 1:275 Spec 2:44, 244 Praem 21 Prob 63 Contempl 69 Flacc 69 Legat 201 QG 4:74

εἰκαιότης Det 10

εἰκάς QG 2:31, 31

εἰκασία (14) Leg 3:228 Cher 69 Post 80 Conf 140, 159 Her 98 Somn 1:23 Mos 1:68, 294 Mos 2:265 Spec 1:38, 63 Spec 4:50 Legat 21

εἰκαστικός Cher 116 Sacr 13 Det 38

εἰκῇ Mut 266 Ios 26

εἰκονογραφέω Legat 290

εἰκός (188) Opif 5, 13, 27, 45, 72, 148, 154, 155, 157, 161 Leg 1:17 Leg 3:65, 137, 231, 233 Cher 89 Sacr 11, 12, 13, 81, 136 Det 1, 13, 31, 43, 90, 94 Post 23, 33, 49, 136 Gig 11, 56 Deus 13, 14, 104, 106, 124, 132, 160 Agr 13, 57, 89, 112, 117 Plant 5, 7, 45, 75, 149 Ebr 14, 70, 154 Sobr 6 Conf 27, 38, 108, 118, 126 Migr 177 Her 4, 12, 264 Fug 6, 155 Mut 6, 49, 154, 157, 173 Somn 1:32, 136, 164, 220, 232 Somn 2:148, 203, 211, 226 Abr 45, 63, 117, 145, 235 Ios 7, 97, 104, 143, 179, 236 Mos 1:11, 13, 27, 50, 115, 128, 136, 140, 145, 204, 275, 287 Mos 2:32, 44, 64, 91, 122, 141, 155, 219, 247 Decal 3, 18, 40, 44, 52, 60, 80 Spec 1:3, 39, 61, 72, 78, 106, 293, 314, 332, 334 Spec 2:73, 119, 129, 138, 146, 157, 189, 189, 232 Spec 3:45, 49, 74, 189 Spec 4:18, 25, 31, 113, 129, 159, 178, 214 Virt 54, 64, 151 Praem 29, 43, 76, 92, 128, 129 Prob 1, 61, 71, 73 Aet 2, 44, 46, 107, 112, 118, 130, 137 Flacc 100, 141, 181 Legat 37, 55, 136, 208, 217, 223, 262 Hypoth 6:3, 6:5, 7:10 Prov 2:34 QG 1:63, 69, 4:69, 88

εἰκοσαετία Sobr 8 Spec 1:77 Spec 2:33, 33

εἴκοσι (24) Opif 93, 101 Leg 1:10 Det 63, 64 Gig 55, 55, 57 Mos 2:78, 80, 84, 84, 85, 89, 91, 91 Decal 27 Spec 2:33, 33, 40 Spec 3:126 Virt 41 Legat 141, 298

εἰκοσιεννέα Opif 91, 93

εἰκοτολογέω Her 224 Legat 57

εἰκότως (181) Opif 36, 59, 63, 97, 133, 136, 144 Leg 1:24, 79, 92, 95, 102 Leg 2:6, 17, 90 Leg 3:67, 87, 103, 112, 139, 161, 207, 207, 247 Cher 41 Sacr 51, 54, 128,

130 Det 48, 176 Post 74, 99, 101, 162 Gig 3, 22, 51 Deus 46, 47, 142, 151 Agr 54, 63, 66, 68, 71, 85, 94, 118, 145 Plant 10, 80, 96, 99, 136, 147, 175 Ebr 28, 58, 95, 130, 149, 155, 203, 214 Sobr 26, 47, 69 Conf 25, 49, 79, 80, 92 Migr 48, 58, 197, 205, 213 Her 43, 108, 117, 189, 217, 225, 236, 256 Congr 11, 23, 48, 78, 83, 102, 121, 130, 145, 170 Fug 14, 64, 74, 80, 159, 198, 210, 211 Mut 34, 93, 116, 128, 157, 166, 170, 183, 201, 205, 252 Somn 1:95, 98, 170, 196, 247, 251 Somn 2:1, 11, 80, 182, 300 Abr 14, 27, 41, 51, 183, 240, 271 Ios 5, 31, 154, 156 Mos 1:157, 328 Mos 2:177, 237, 256, 261 Decal 13, 23, 24, 131, 161 Spec 1:34, 52, 100, 113, 179, 185, 245, 285, 309, 344 Spec 2:24, 46, 52, 86, 221 Spec 3:179 Spec 4:58, 120, 199, 210 Virt 174, 205 Prob 86, 105 Aet 59, 83 Legat 163 Prov 2:59 QG 1:77, 94, 2:65, 65

εἴκω (22) Leg 3:128, 186 Ebr 16 Conf 48 Her 41 Somn 1:20 Somn 2:10, 124 Abr 213 Ios 65, 153, 173, 192 Mos 1:139, 225 Spec 3:201 Spec 4:146 Prob 131 Legat 218, 218 Prov 2:58 QE 2:37

εἰκών (120) Opif 17, 25, 25, 25, 25, 31, 69, 69, 71, 71, 72, 78, 100, 134, 134, 146 Leg 1:3, 31, 31, 33, 42, 43, 53, 53, 90, 92, 94 Leg 2:4, 4, 4, 4 Leg 3:96, 96, 96, 96, 96, 176 Det 83, 86, 87, 163 Deus 4 Agr 109 Plant 19, 19, 44, 44, 50 Ebr 110, 132, 133, 134 Conf 62, 97, 146, 147, 147, 169 Migr 40 Her 56, 57, 112, 164, 187, 231, 231, 231, 231 Fug 12, 68, 101 Mut 31, 93, 183, 212, 223 Somn 1:74, 74, 79, 115, 232, 239, 241 Somn 2:15, 45, 206 Abr 3, 153 Mos 1:66 Mos 2:51, 65, 267 Decal 101 Spec 1:81, 81, 96, 171 Spec 2:176, 178, 237 Spec 3:83, 180, 207 Spec 4:69, 146 Virt 4, 205, 205 Praem 29, 44, 114 Prob 62 Flacc 41 Legat 134, 138, 210, 334, 346 QG 2:62, 4:110b

εἰλέω εἴλω

εἰλικρινής (εἱλικρινής) (30) Opif 8, 31 Leg 1:88 Leg 2:82 Leg 3:111 Post 134 Ebr 101, 189, 190 Migr 222 Her 98, 308 Congr 143, 143 Somn 2:20, 74, 134 Abr 129 Ios 145 Mos 2:40 Spec 1:39, 99, 219 Praem 40, 45 Prob 5 Contempl 2, 82 QE 2:47 QE isf 3

εἴλω (εἰλέω) (15) Opif 47 Leg 2:74, 75 Cher 22 Sacr 95 Post 173 Sobr 34 Somn 2:14, 112 Abr 128, 165 Mos 1:92, 115 Spec 1:218 QE 2:55a

εἱμαρμένη μείρομαι

εἶμι (61) Opif 71 Leg 1:2 Leg 3:202 Cher 22, 91 Sacr 113 Deus 116, 160 Plant 36 Ebr 39 Conf 84 Migr 146 Her 312 Fug 31, 31, 57, 141 Somn 1:55, 210, 214 Abr 105, 224, 229 Ios 12, 78, 78, 117 Mos 1:58, 73 Mos 2:168, 174, 194, 231 Decal 86 Spec 1:20, 237, 243, 263, 270, 300, 321 Spec 3:53, 55, 61, 61, 67, 97 Spec 4:78, 140, 141, 224 Virt 25, 123, 185, 213, 215 Prob 25 Contempl 12 Aet 88 Legat 290 QE 2:10a

εἰμί (6961) Opif 1, 2, 3, 3, 4, 8, 8, 8, 8, 9, 12, 12, 12, 13, 13, 13, 14, 15, 17, 20, 21, 22, 23, 23, 24, 24, 25, 25, 25, 25, 26, 26, 27, 27, 27, 27, 27, 28, 28, 29, 31, 32, 32, 34, 36, 38, 38, 38, 40, 41, 41, 43, 43, 45, 47, 47, 47, 49, 49, 49, 51, 53, 53, 54, 57, 59, 59, 63, 63, 65, 66, 67, 67, 67, 67, 67, 67, 68, 69, 69, 71, 72, 72, 72, 72, 73, 73, 73, 73, 73, 74, 75, 77, 77, 77, 78, 80, 80, 81, 81, 81, 81, 81, 82, 84, 85, 88, 89, 90, 90, 92, 93, 96, 96, 97, 97, 97, 97, 98, 98, 99, 100, 100, 101, 102, 103, 104, 104, 104, 104, 105, 105, 105, 106, 106, 107, 107, 110, 110, 112, 112, 113, 113, 114, 118, 120, 121, 122, 123, 123, 126, 126, 129, 129, 129, 130, 131, 131, 132, 132, 132, 132, 133, 134, 135, 135, 135, 135, 135, 136, 136, 136, 136, 138, 139, 139, 139, 139, 140, 140, 142, 142, 143, 143, 143, 144, 144, 144, 145, 147, 147, 147, 147, 148, 148, 149, 151, 152, 153, 153, 154, 155, 157, 157, 157, 159, 163, 163, 164, 166, 170, 170, 171, 171, 171, 171, 171, 171, 171, 172, 172, 172 Leg 1:2, 3, 3, 4, 5, 6, 7, 8, 10, 10, 10, 10, 11, 14, 14, 14, 15, 16, 16, 17, 21, 21, 22, 22, 22, 23, 23, 23, 24, 24, 25, 26, 26, 27, 27, 27, 28, 28, 29, 31, 31, 32, 32, 32, 33, 34, 34, 35, 36, 37, 37, 39, 39, 39, 40, 41, 42, 42, 43, 43, 44, 44, 44, 45, 45, 45, 46, 48, 49, 49, 49, 50, 50, 51, 52, 53, 53, 53, 53, 54, 54, 54, 55, 55, 55, 55, 55, 56, 56, 57, 57, 57, 57, 58, 58, 58, 59, 59, 60, 60, 60, 60, 60, 61, 61, 61, 61, 61, 61, 62, 62, 62, 62, 62, 62, 63, 63, 63, 63, 65, 65, 65, 65, 66, 66, 66, 66, 66, 67, 67, 67, 67, 67, 68, 68, 68, 68, 69, 70, 70, 70, 71, 71, 71, 72, 72, 72, 74, 75, 75, 77, 77, 77, 77, 77, 77, 77, 78, 78, 79, 79, 79, 80, 80, 80, 81, 81, 82, 82, 82, 85, 85, 86, 86, 87, 87, 88, 88, 88, 90, 90, 91, 91, 91, 95, 97, 97, 98, 98, 99, 99, 99, 100, 100, 100, 100, 100, 102, 103, 104, 105, 105, 105, 106, 106, 107, 107 Leg 2:1, 1, 1, 1, 1, 1, 1, 1, 1, 1, 2, 2, 2, 2, 2, 3, 3, 3, 4, 4, 4, 4, 4, 4, 4, 4, 5, 5, 6, 6, 6, 7, 8, 8, 8, 8, 8, 9, 9, 9, 10, 11, 12, 13, 13, 14, 14, 15, 15, 15, 15, 15, 16, 19, 19, 20, 20, 21, 22, 22, 22, 22, 23, 23, 23, 23, 24, 24, 25, 26, 27, 27, 30, 31, 31, 32, 33, 33, 34, 36, 36, 38, 40, 41, 41, 42, 44, 44, 45, 46, 46, 46, 47, 47, 48, 49, 50, 51, 52, 53, 53, 53, 53, 53, 55, 55, 58, 59, 59, 59, 59, 60, 60, 60, 64, 64, 64, 64, 64, 64, 65, 65, 67, 67, 68, 69, 69, 70, 71, 73, 75, 76, 78, 79, 80, 81, 81, 82, 84, 84, 85, 86, 86, 86, 86, 86, 88, 89, 89, 89, 92, 93, 93, 94, 94, 96, 97, 97, 97, 97, 98, 99, 100, 102, 103, 103, 103, 105, 105, 106, 106, 107 Leg 3:1, 1, 1, 2, 2, 2, 3, 3, 3, 4, 4, 4, 6, 6, 7, 7, 7, 7, 7, 9, 9, 10, 13, 15, 16, 18, 21, 22, 22, 23, 23, 25, 28, 28, 29, 29, 29, 29, 32, 32, 32, 33, 34, 35, 35, 35, 36, 36, 37, 37, 38, 39, 39, 40, 40, 40, 41, 42, 43, 45, 45, 45, 45, 45, 49, 49, 49, 49, 50, 50, 51, 51, 51, 52, 53, 53, 53, 53, 53, 54, 54, 55, 57, 60, 60, 61, 61, 62, 63, 63, 64, 64, 65, 67, 68, 70, 71, 72, 73, 73, 74, 75, 75, 76, 78, 78, 78, 78, 79, 80, 81, 82, 82, 82, 82, 82, 82, 83, 85, 86, 86, 86, 86, 87, 88, 88, 88, 90, 90, 92, 93, 95, 96, 96, 99, 99, 100, 100, 101, 105, 105, 105, 106, 107, 107, 107, 108, 109, 110, 111, 111, 111, 111, 112, 113, 113, 113, 115, 115, 115, 118, 119, 119, 119, 120, 120, 120, 121, 121, 121, 122, 123, 123, 124, 124, 125, 126, 128, 128, 130, 130, 130, 131, 131, 132, 132, 134, 134, 135, 135, 135, 138, 139, 139, 141, 142, 143, 143, 146, 148, 148, 148, 149, 150, 150, 151, 153, 155, 157, 160, 160, 160, 161, 161, 161, 161, 163, 164, 164, 167, 167, 169, 169, 169, 170, 170, 171, 171, 171, 171, 171, 171, 172, 173, 173, 173, 173, 174, 174, 175, 175, 175, 177, 177, 177, 180, 180, 181, 181, 182, 182, 183, 184, 184, 185, 185, 186, 186, 188, 188, 188, 189, 191, 194, 194, 195, 197, 198, 198, 200, 200, 203, 204, 204, 204, 204, 204, 205, 205, 205, 205, 205, 206, 207, 207, 207, 208, 209, 210, 210, 211, 211, 211, 214, 215, 215, 217, 217, 217, 218, 218, 219, 219, 219, 220, 221, 222, 223, 225, 226, 227, 227, 228, 229, 229, 229, 230, 232, 232, 234, 234, 236, 236, 236, 236, 237, 239, 239, 239, 239, 241, 242, 243, 244, 245, 245, 246, 246, 246, 246, 246, 247, 247, 247, 247, 249, 249, 250, 251, 251, 252, 252, 253, 253, 253 Cher 3, 4, 4, 5, 7, 7, 13, 13, 14, 17, 18, 18, 19, 19, 21, 22, 25, 25, 26, 26, 27, 27, 27, 27, 28, 32, 35, 35, 36, 37, 41, 41, 42, 42, 43, 44, 44, 48, 49, 49, 50, 54, 55, 55, 56, 56, 56, 57, 58, 58, 59, 59, 62, 63, 65, 65, 65, 67, 68, 68, 69, 69, 70, 70, 70, 73, 73, 76, 78, 78, 83, 83, 83, 84, 84, 84, 86, 86, 87, 87, 87, 88, 89, 90, 97, 97, 97, 101,

101, 108, 108, 108, 108, 109, 112, 114, 114, 114, 114, 116, 119, 119, 119, 121, 122, 124, 125, 126, 126, 128 Sacr 1, 1, 2, 2, 2, 4, 4, 5, 7, 8, 9, 10, 10, 10, 11, 11, 12, 14, 18, 19, 19, 20, 20, 21, 22, 23, 25, 28, 29, 30, 30, 32, 33, 34, 35, 35, 36, 40, 41, 42, 42, 46, 46, 47, 48, 48, 49, 49, 51, 51, 53, 54, 54, 55, 57, 57, 59, 59, 60, 60, 63, 63, 65, 67, 68, 69, 69, 71, 72, 72, 72, 73, 74, 77, 77, 77, 77, 79, 80, 82, 82, 83, 85, 87, 87, 87, 88, 89, 89, 89, 91, 91, 91, 92, 93, 96, 98, 98, 100, 100, 101, 101, 103, 103, 105, 106, 106, 107, 107, 108, 109, 109, 110, 112, 114, 115, 117, 118, 118, 118, 119, 119, 120, 121, 121, 126, 127, 128, 128, 128, 129, 131, 132, 133, 136, 139 Det 1, 1, 1, 2, 3, 4, 4, 4, 6, 6, 6, 7, 8, 9, 9, 10, 13, 13, 21, 22, 23, 29, 30, 30, 31, 32, 38, 38, 38, 39, 40, 40, 43, 45, 46, 48, 49, 49, 50, 54, 55, 55, 56, 56, 57, 57, 58, 59, 61, 61, 62, 63, 66, 66, 68, 70, 70, 70, 71, 75, 75, 76, 78, 79, 80, 80, 82, 83, 85, 87, 89, 89, 90, 90, 91, 92, 92, 93, 94, 96, 97, 98, 99, 102, 103, 104, 105, 108, 109, 112, 113, 115, 116, 118, 123, 124, 124, 124, 125, 126, 128, 130, 132, 134, 135, 136, 136, 137, 138, 139, 139, 140, 140, 141, 146, 148, 149, 151, 152, 153, 153, 154, 154, 156, 156, 159, 160, 160, 160, 160, 160, 160, 160, 160, 160, 160, 161, 161, 162, 162, 162, 162, 163, 164, 167, 168, 170, 177, 178, 178 Post 2, 2, 3, 4, 5, 5, 7, 7, 8, 8, 9, 12, 13, 13, 14, 14, 14, 15, 15, 15, 15, 16, 16, 17, 18, 20, 20, 20, 21, 21, 21, 22, 22, 23, 24, 24, 25, 25, 26, 26, 27, 27, 28, 28, 32, 32, 32, 33, 35, 35, 36, 36, 39, 40, 40, 40, 41, 42, 42, 43, 44, 45, 46, 46, 47, 48, 48, 49, 49, 49, 50, 51, 52, 53, 53, 54, 55, 55, 57, 58, 58, 59, 60, 62, 63, 63, 63, 64, 66, 67, 67, 69, 69, 69, 72, 73, 73, 73, 75, 79, 80, 81, 82, 85, 87, 88, 95, 95, 95, 95, 95, 96, 98, 99, 100, 100, 101, 101, 102, 102, 102, 103, 103, 104, 109, 109, 112, 112, 113, 114, 116, 117, 117, 117, 118, 120, 120, 126, 128, 128, 130, 132, 132, 133, 134, 134, 136, 137, 137, 138, 139, 142, 146, 147, 147, 148, 152, 154, 155, 157, 157, 159, 159, 159, 160, 160, 161, 162, 164, 165, 165, 166, 166, 167, 167, 167, 168, 168, 168, 168, 168, 168, 169, 169, 171, 173, 173, 174, 175, 175, 176, 177, 179, 180, 180, 182, 183, 184, 184, 185 Gig 2, 3, 6, 6, 7, 8, 8, 9, 10, 11, 11, 14, 17, 19, 20, 20, 22, 23, 24, 25, 27, 29, 33, 33, 36, 37, 38, 39, 39, 40, 41, 42, 46, 47, 47, 49, 52, 55, 56, 56, 58, 62, 62, 62, 62, 63, 64, 64, 66, 67, 67 Deus 1, 2, 4, 4, 5, 6, 6, 7, 8, 8, 9, 10, 10, 11, 12, 13, 14, 14, 15, 16, 16, 16, 19, 24, 28, 29, 29, 30, 30, 31, 32, 33, 33, 34, 35, 37, 39, 40, 42, 42, 43, 44, 45, 46, 47, 48, 50, 51, 52, 52, 52, 53, 54, 55, 55, 55, 56, 57, 60, 60, 61, 62, 62, 66, 69, 69, 70, 70, 71, 71, 72, 76, 78, 78, 79, 81, 81, 82, 83, 86, 87, 88, 88, 89, 89, 90, 95, 103, 104, 104, 104, 106, 107, 107, 108, 108, 108, 109, 109, 110, 110, 110, 112, 113, 117, 117, 118, 118, 118, 118, 119, 119, 119, 119, 119, 119, 120, 121, 123, 125, 125, 127, 127, 127, 128, 131, 132, 134, 136, 140, 141, 142, 143, 144, 145, 149, 157, 159, 160, 161, 165, 167, 167, 170, 170, 171, 171, 172, 174, 177, 178, 179, 182 Agr 1, 3, 3, 4, 4, 7, 9, 9, 9, 11, 11, 12, 13, 14, 15, 15, 18, 19, 20, 21, 22, 24, 26, 26, 26, 28, 28, 29, 31, 34, 36, 40, 41, 41, 43, 43, 44, 44, 45, 47, 50, 50, 51, 52, 53, 53, 54, 54, 56, 57, 57, 59, 59, 61, 62, 65, 67, 71, 71, 73, 73, 73, 82, 84, 84, 85, 88, 89, 92, 93, 95, 97, 99, 99, 99, 101, 102, 103, 103, 103, 104, 107, 108, 109, 110, 110, 110, 111, 112, 112, 114, 117, 124, 125, 126, 127, 128, 129, 130, 131, 133, 135, 139, 139, 142, 145, 148, 149, 152, 152, 154, 157, 161, 161, 163, 166, 167, 168, 171, 173, 174, 175, 179, 181 Plant 1, 1, 1, 2, 3, 3, 3, 4, 5, 6, 7, 7, 7, 8, 12, 14, 14, 14, 14, 18, 18, 18, 20, 21, 21, 22, 24, 26, 30, 31, 32, 33, 35, 35, 36, 37, 39, 40, 40, 41, 43, 43, 44, 45, 48, 50, 50, 51, 52, 53, 54, 56, 57, 58, 60, 61, 62, 63, 64, 64, 64, 69, 70, 70, 70, 72, 74, 75, 76, 76, 77, 78, 79, 79, 82, 84, 86, 87, 88, 89, 89, 90, 91, 92, 93, 93, 95, 95, 95, 97, 97, 99, 101, 104, 105, 105, 106, 106, 107, 107, 108, 111, 113, 113, 113, 113, 113, 114, 114, 116, 116, 117, 120, 121, 121, 122, 122, 124, 125, 125, 126, 126, 127, 128, 128, 130, 133, 134, 135, 137, 137, 138, 139, 140, 140, 142, 143, 144, 146, 147, 147, 149, 149, 150, 152, 154, 156, 158, 161, 163, 163, 165, 168, 168, 169, 170, 172, 173, 174, 174, 176, 177, 177 Ebr 1, 2, 2, 3, 4, 5, 5, 11, 13, 13, 14, 14, 16, 17, 18, 19, 19, 19, 19, 22, 26, 27, 27, 29, 30, 31, 31, 33, 35, 35, 37, 42, 43, 43, 43, 44, 44, 45, 46, 47, 52, 53, 54, 55, 61, 62, 64, 65, 66, 69, 70, 70, 71, 72, 73, 73, 74, 77, 78, 80, 81, 82, 83, 83, 86, 86, 86, 88, 90, 91, 94, 96, 96, 97, 99, 100, 101, 104, 104, 105, 105, 107, 107, 108, 108, 114, 115, 116, 117, 117, 117, 119, 119, 119, 121, 122, 124, 128, 129, 130, 133, 134, 135, 138, 138, 139, 140, 141, 142, 142, 144, 145, 147, 149, 150, 150, 151, 152, 153, 154, 156, 157, 158, 158, 166, 166, 166, 167, 168, 169, 170, 170, 174, 175, 178, 182, 183, 183, 183, 186, 190, 192, 193, 193, 197, 197, 198, 199, 199, 200, 201, 201, 204, 205, 206, 206, 208, 210, 210, 211, 212, 212, 212, 214, 215, 216, 219, 220, 223 Sobr 4, 4, 5, 6, 6, 9, 12, 13, 14, 14, 17, 18, 18, 19, 20, 21, 22, 23, 24, 24, 25, 25, 26, 27, 28, 28, 30, 31, 32, 32, 32, 34, 39, 40, 40, 41, 42, 44, 45, 45, 49, 50, 50, 51, 51, 52, 54, 57, 58, 60, 65, 65, 66, 66, 67, 67, 68 Conf 1, 1, 1, 4, 4, 4, 4, 5, 6, 7, 9, 12, 13, 13, 14, 15, 15, 17, 23, 23, 25, 26, 26, 27, 27, 33, 37, 37, 38, 41, 41, 41, 41, 43, 45, 46, 47, 48, 48, 56, 65, 66, 71, 75, 76, 76, 79, 82, 84, 87, 88, 91, 95, 96, 97, 97, 98, 100, 102, 105, 107, 107, 107, 108, 108, 113, 114, 114, 114, 115, 117, 117, 117, 118, 119, 122, 122, 123, 125, 127, 129, 132, 133, 134, 136, 137, 137, 138, 138, 139, 142, 144, 144, 144, 145, 145, 146, 147, 149, 149, 150, 151, 154, 154, 154, 156, 156, 157, 157, 158, 159, 161, 162, 163, 165, 165, 166, 167, 170, 170, 170, 170, 171, 171, 171, 171, 171, 174, 174, 175, 175, 176, 177, 179, 180, 180, 180, 182, 183, 184, 185, 186, 187, 189, 190, 191, 191, 192, 192, 193, 195, 195, 197 Migr 1, 2, 3, 3, 5, 5, 5, 6, 7, 7, 8, 8, 12, 12, 14, 16, 18, 18, 19, 19, 20, 21, 21, 22, 23, 25, 26, 27, 28, 28, 28, 29, 30, 30, 33, 34, 34, 35, 36, 38, 39, 40, 40, 40, 46, 46, 46, 47, 48, 49, 50, 50, 51, 51, 51, 51, 52, 54, 56, 57, 58, 58, 59, 60, 61, 61, 61, 62, 64, 64, 65, 66, 67, 69, 70, 70, 74, 77, 78, 79, 79, 79, 80, 81, 81, 81, 81, 82, 84, 84, 85, 86, 86, 86, 87, 88, 88, 88, 89, 91, 92, 92, 93, 93, 95, 96, 96, 96, 103, 103, 104, 105, 106, 106, 106, 106, 107, 108, 108, 108, 112, 114, 114, 115, 116, 116, 116, 119, 121, 121, 122, 126, 126, 128, 129, 130, 130, 131, 134, 134, 134, 136, 137, 137, 137, 137, 138, 139, 139, 140, 141, 143, 144, 144, 144, 145, 146, 147, 148, 148, 149, 149, 151, 151, 152, 152, 154, 155, 157, 157, 159, 160, 161, 162, 162, 165, 167, 169, 169, 170, 170, 170, 171, 172, 174, 174, 176, 176, 179, 179, 179, 179, 179, 180, 181, 182, 182, 183, 183, 183, 183, 183, 184, 186, 186, 186, 187, 188, 188, 192, 193, 194, 195, 197, 197, 197, 198, 199, 199, 200, 201, 201, 201, 202, 203, 204, 205, 205, 205, 205, 206, 207, 209, 212, 213, 213, 214, 215, 216, 216, 216, 216, 217, 218, 220, 222, 222, 223, 224, 224, 224, 225, 225, 225 Her 1, 2, 4, 5, 10, 10, 12, 12, 16, 18, 21, 22, 23, 23, 23, 23, 23, 26, 30, 31, 32, 33, 33, 36, 36, 39, 41, 41, 42, 44, 46, 49, 51, 52, 54, 55, 55, 56, 57, 58, 58, 58, 61, 62, 63, 63, 66, 70, 70, 71, 72, 73, 74, 75, 76, 76, 78, 81, 82, 82, 83, 83, 84, 84, 86, 86, 87, 90, 93, 95, 95, 97, 97,

97, 101, 101, 107, 107, 108, 108, 111, 114, 114, 115, 117, 119, 121, 123, 124, 127, 129, 133, 133, 136, 137, 137, 143, 144, 144, 144, 145, 147, 148, 150, 151, 152, 152, 153, 154, 155, 156, 158, 158, 159, 162, 162, 162, 162, 163, 165, 166, 166, 167, 167, 168, 169, 170, 171, 172, 173, 173, 177, 180, 181, 182, 183, 184, 184, 186, 187, 188, 189, 191, 192, 192, 193, 193, 193, 194, 195, 195, 196, 197, 199, 202, 202, 205, 206, 207, 207, 212, 214, 214, 215, 216, 217, 218, 218, 218, 219, 221, 221, 222, 223, 224, 225, 225, 226, 227, 227, 228, 229, 229, 231, 231, 233, 234, 234, 234, 236, 237, 239, 242, 243, 243, 244, 246, 246, 246, 246, 246, 246, 246, 246, 249, 251, 252, 257, 258, 259, 261, 264, 265, 267, 267, 268, 272, 274, 278, 278, 279, 282, 283, 284, 286, 287, 288, 289, 291, 295, 296, 298, 299, 302, 303, 307, 309, 311, 311, 314 Congr 1, 2, 2, 2, 3, 5, 6, 8, 8, 9, 10, 11, 11, 12, 20, 20, 20, 22, 22, 22, 25, 25, 29, 32, 36, 36, 42, 42, 42, 44, 48, 50, 51, 51, 52, 53, 55, 57, 58, 58, 60, 61, 61, 62, 62, 63, 67, 67, 67, 68, 68, 70, 74, 76, 78, 79, 80, 80, 81, 83, 87, 87, 87, 89, 90, 95, 95, 96, 96, 97, 98, 98, 100, 100, 101, 103, 106, 106, 107, 108, 112, 113, 113, 114, 115, 116, 117, 117, 120, 122, 123, 124, 125, 125, 126, 128, 128, 130, 131, 131, 132, 132, 133, 133, 137, 137, 140, 140, 142, 143, 144, 144, 144, 144, 144, 146, 147, 149, 153, 154, 155, 156, 156, 157, 159, 159, 162, 163, 163, 164, 166, 168, 171, 172, 172, 174, 175, 178, 178, 178, 179, 180 Fug 1, 3, 4, 6, 6, 6, 8, 8, 9, 10, 10, 10, 12, 12, 13, 14, 15, 15, 16, 18, 19, 19, 19, 19, 20, 20, 22, 27, 27, 30, 34, 34, 34, 35, 40, 40, 40, 42, 43, 44, 44, 45, 45, 45, 46, 47, 51, 51, 51, 52, 55, 57, 57, 57, 58, 59, 60, 61, 61, 62, 63, 65, 65, 66, 66, 71, 73, 75, 76, 78, 78, 79, 80, 80, 80, 81, 82, 84, 87, 88, 89, 89, 91, 92, 92, 93, 94, 94, 94, 95, 97, 99, 99, 100, 100, 101, 101, 101, 101, 103, 104, 106, 106, 108, 109, 110, 112, 112, 112, 113, 114, 115, 116, 117, 122, 124, 128, 129, 133, 133, 136, 137, 137, 137, 138, 138, 138, 139, 140, 140, 140, 141, 141, 143, 143, 146, 146, 148, 148, 149, 149, 149, 153, 153, 153, 153, 154, 154, 154, 155, 156, 156, 163, 163, 164, 164, 164, 164, 165, 165, 165, 167, 167, 169, 170, 172, 172, 174, 174, 178, 180, 181, 182, 183, 183, 186, 188, 189, 189, 189, 192, 193, 194, 195, 196, 196, 198, 198, 201, 202, 202, 203, 204, 208, 208, 209, 209, 211, 213 Mut 1, 1, 2, 3, 4, 6, 7, 7, 7, 7, 8, 9, 10, 11, 11, 11, 11, 11, 12, 13, 13, 14, 14, 15, 15, 15, 16, 17, 17, 17, 18, 18, 21, 21, 23, 24, 27, 27, 27, 27, 28, 29, 29, 29, 29, 31, 31, 32, 36, 36, 36, 37, 37, 38, 38, 39, 39, 44, 44, 45, 45, 46, 46, 46, 48, 49, 51, 52, 53, 53, 55, 56, 57, 57, 58, 58, 58, 60, 63, 64, 65, 68, 69, 69, 69, 73, 78, 79, 79, 79, 80, 82, 83, 87, 87, 88, 89, 91, 91, 92, 96, 96, 97, 97, 98, 98, 99, 101, 101, 103, 104, 104, 108, 108, 110, 114, 117, 118, 119, 123, 124, 125, 126, 127, 128, 128, 131, 132, 134, 135, 137, 138, 138, 140, 140, 140, 141, 142, 142, 142, 144, 145, 146, 148, 148, 151, 151, 152, 152, 152, 153, 154, 156, 156, 157, 157, 163, 165, 166, 167, 167, 168, 169, 169, 169, 170, 172, 173, 173, 176, 178, 182, 182, 182, 184, 184, 185, 187, 188, 189, 191, 192, 193, 193, 193, 194, 196, 199, 200, 202, 202, 206, 207, 207, 208, 209, 210, 212, 213, 213, 216, 217, 219, 220, 221, 222, 230, 231, 232, 232, 234, 236, 237, 238, 238, 238, 239, 240, 240, 240, 241, 243, 246, 247, 247, 248, 248, 250, 254, 255, 257, 258, 260, 264, 266, 266, 269, 270, 270 Somn 1:1, 2, 2, 3, 3, 4, 4, 6, 6, 8, 9, 11, 11, 12, 14, 15, 15, 16, 17, 19, 20, 21, 21, 22, 22, 22, 22, 23, 25, 25, 25, 26, 26, 27, 27, 27, 29, 30, 30, 30, 31, 32, 34, 34, 35, 35, 39, 39, 39, 41, 47, 48, 48, 49, 53, 53, 58, 60, 60, 60, 61, 63, 63, 64, 64, 64, 65, 65, 66, 66, 66, 67, 67, 68, 73, 75, 75, 76, 76, 79, 82, 89, 90, 91, 91, 92, 93, 93, 94, 95, 98, 100, 101, 101, 102, 102, 104, 105, 105, 106, 107, 107, 111, 112, 114, 117, 118, 121, 123, 125, 125, 126, 127, 127, 128, 129, 134, 135, 135, 135, 140, 144, 145, 145, 145, 146, 146, 148, 148, 149, 151, 152, 156, 157, 158, 158, 159, 159, 160, 160, 162, 164, 166, 166, 167, 168, 172, 172, 173, 176, 176, 179, 179, 179, 180, 182, 182, 182, 183, 183, 183, 184, 185, 185, 185, 185, 185, 186, 187, 188, 189, 189, 189, 192, 192, 194, 196, 196, 197, 198, 201, 201, 202, 203, 205, 206, 209, 209, 209, 211, 211, 212, 215, 215, 217, 218, 218, 218, 219, 223, 225, 227, 228, 228, 228, 229, 229, 230, 230, 230, 230, 231, 231, 231, 231, 232, 232, 234, 236, 237, 238, 240, 240, 241, 244, 244, 246, 248, 252, 253, 256 Somn 2:2, 3, 5, 6, 6, 9, 12, 15, 15, 17, 20, 22, 24, 24, 25, 25, 26, 29, 29, 30, 31, 33, 33, 34, 36, 36, 40, 42, 45, 46, 48, 48, 50, 56, 58, 59, 60, 61, 62, 62, 63, 66, 67, 71, 71, 72, 74, 76, 78, 78, 81, 83, 85, 89, 94, 98, 100, 100, 101, 104, 104, 107, 109, 112, 112, 115, 116, 118, 120, 123, 127, 129, 130, 132, 134, 136, 138, 138, 141, 141, 145, 147, 147, 148, 148, 150, 152, 153, 153, 154, 154, 157, 159, 159, 160, 160, 161, 163, 169, 169, 170, 173, 173, 176, 177, 178, 179, 180, 184, 185, 187, 189, 189, 192, 192, 193, 193, 193, 193, 200, 200, 201, 201, 202, 202, 203, 203, 205, 206, 207, 208, 211, 212, 213, 219, 219, 221, 221, 221, 221, 221, 222, 223, 223, 223, 224, 224, 226, 226, 227, 228, 228, 229, 230, 231, 231, 237, 237, 238, 239, 242, 243, 244, 246, 246, 246, 246, 247, 248, 249, 250, 250, 251, 252, 253, 253, 254, 254, 257, 259, 260, 260, 261, 265, 268, 273, 275, 276, 278, 278, 279, 282, 283, 283, 284, 284, 289, 289, 292, 293, 296, 299, 299, 302 Abr 2, 2, 4, 5, 6, 6, 7, 8, 9, 9, 10, 10, 10, 11, 13, 15, 19, 24, 25, 26, 27, 28, 28, 30, 31, 31, 33, 33, 36, 36, 41, 41, 43, 45, 48, 50, 50, 51, 52, 52, 53, 57, 57, 57, 57, 60, 61, 62, 67, 69, 73, 74, 74, 75, 75, 76, 76, 76, 77, 79, 80, 80, 82, 83, 84, 88, 91, 93, 99, 99, 99, 100, 102, 102, 103, 104, 105, 107, 110, 114, 114, 115, 115, 115, 118, 118, 119, 119, 120, 121, 121, 121, 122, 123, 124, 124, 125, 126, 129, 130, 131, 134, 135, 135, 141, 143, 143, 143, 145, 146, 147, 147, 149, 150, 150, 154, 155, 156, 156, 156, 157, 159, 162, 162, 162, 162, 164, 165, 166, 166, 167, 170, 178, 179, 189, 191, 191, 192, 192, 193, 193, 195, 201, 202, 203, 204, 204, 204, 205, 206, 208, 208, 208, 208, 209, 211, 212, 213, 214, 215, 216, 216, 217, 218, 219, 221, 222, 224, 224, 225, 225, 227, 227, 228, 231, 232, 235, 235, 236, 237, 239, 243, 247, 248, 249, 250, 252, 252, 255, 257, 261, 261, 262, 262, 265, 267, 270, 271, 272, 273, 274, 276, 276 Ios 1, 2, 3, 4, 4, 4, 7, 8, 10, 12, 17, 17, 21, 25, 26, 27, 28, 29, 29, 29, 30, 31, 34, 34, 38, 38, 39, 39, 47, 47, 51, 52, 52, 52, 58, 58, 59, 64, 73, 74, 76, 78, 80, 81, 87, 88, 90, 90, 93, 93, 93, 93, 94, 96, 99, 104, 104, 105, 107, 107, 109, 110, 111, 111, 115, 115, 117, 117, 123, 125, 126, 126, 126, 126, 127, 129, 132, 135, 137, 142, 144, 145, 147, 148, 148, 149, 150, 150, 151, 151, 153, 153, 154, 154, 154, 156, 163, 165, 167, 168, 170, 173, 174, 175, 176, 179, 183, 185, 188, 189, 189, 191, 192, 195, 198, 198, 200, 203, 204, 209, 215, 216, 222, 223, 223, 223, 225, 229, 232, 236, 238, 242, 242, 244, 244, 247, 248, 248, 251, 254, 254, 257, 260, 263, 266 Mos 1:2, 5, 7, 7, 7, 9, 10, 13, 15, 15, 21, 26, 27, 31, 32, 34, 36, 36, 38, 40, 40, 40, 42, 43, 44, 44, 47, 48, 50, 54, 54, 54, 55, 55, 56, 58, 59, 61, 64, 65, 65, 66, 66, 66, 68, 69, 69, 72, 75, 75, 75, 75, 75, 76, 76, 76, 77, 81, 81, 81, 83, 83, 83, 84, 85, 86, 88, 89, 92, 94, 96, 98, 104, 105, 105, 108, 111, 111, 111, 112, 114, 116, 119, 120,

120, 123, 124, 130, 130, 130, 131, 132, 133, 137, 138, 140, 141, 143, 143, 145, 147, 147, 149, 150, 153, 153, 153, 154, 155, 157, 157, 158, 158, 160, 161, 162, 166, 170, 171, 174, 176, 178, 181, 182, 183, 183, 188, 189, 189, 191, 192, 192, 194, 197, 198, 200, 200, 202, 204, 205, 207, 208, 211, 212, 212, 213, 213, 213, 217, 218, 222, 222, 224, 224, 225, 226, 226, 227, 228, 231, 231, 233, 234, 240, 241, 245, 245, 247, 249, 250, 251, 254, 255, 259, 259, 260, 264, 265, 269, 271, 272, 273, 275, 275, 277, 279, 283, 284, 292, 293, 294, 294, 296, 300, 305, 305, 306, 306, 307, 308, 308, 310, 312, 314, 315, 315, 316, 317, 320, 320, 323, 324, 333 Mos 2:1, 4, 6, 8, 9, 14, 18, 28, 29, 31, 34, 34, 36, 37, 45, 45, 46, 47, 49, 49, 50, 51, 51, 60, 62, 64, 65, 67, 67, 67, 68, 70, 72, 75, 77, 78, 79, 80, 80, 81, 81, 82, 82, 82, 85, 86, 86, 87, 88, 89, 90, 90, 91, 94, 96, 97, 97, 98, 99, 100, 100, 100, 100, 101, 106, 108, 109, 115, 116, 117, 118, 119, 120, 120, 121, 121, 124, 126, 127, 127, 127, 128, 131, 132, 132, 132, 132, 132, 134, 135, 135, 136, 139, 142, 144, 147, 147, 152, 153, 155, 161, 161, 161, 162, 162, 163, 164, 164, 166, 167, 168, 171, 174, 174, 176, 177, 180, 180, 181, 181, 182, 182, 188, 189, 191, 192, 192, 196, 197, 203, 205, 212, 214, 214, 215, 216, 219, 220, 221, 222, 223, 225, 227, 230, 231, 231, 233, 234, 240, 241, 241, 241, 243, 245, 245, 246, 247, 249, 249, 250, 251, 253, 253, 253, 254, 256, 258, 258, 259, 260, 260, 264, 265, 265, 267, 267, 267, 270, 270, 271, 272, 276, 276, 277, 279, 282, 288, 290 Decal 2, 3, 5, 5, 8, 10, 13, 14, 15, 16, 18, 19, 23, 23, 25, 27, 28, 29, 30, 31, 31, 31, 31, 32, 35, 37, 37, 38, 38, 43, 45, 47, 47, 49, 50, 50, 50, 51, 51, 52, 52, 58, 58, 58, 58, 59, 59, 60, 60, 60, 61, 61, 62, 62, 63, 64, 67, 72, 72, 73, 75, 76, 80, 81, 81, 81, 81, 82, 82, 84, 85, 86, 87, 89, 91, 92, 92, 95, 95, 96, 97, 99, 100, 102, 102, 106, 107, 109, 110, 111, 111, 111, 115, 118, 118, 120, 120, 120, 121, 125, 125, 125, 128, 133, 133, 135, 136, 136, 137, 137, 138, 140, 140, 140, 142, 142, 143, 150, 151, 154, 156, 160, 162, 164, 166, 168, 170, 175, 176, 178, 178 Spec 1:2, 3, 3, 7, 8, 10, 11, 13, 13, 16, 18, 18, 18, 20, 21, 23, 25, 26, 26, 26, 27, 27, 27, 28, 30, 31, 31, 32, 32, 32, 33, 36, 38, 39, 40, 40, 41, 41, 42, 43, 43, 45, 46, 46, 48, 49, 50, 52, 53, 55, 59, 62, 62, 63, 65, 65, 66, 66, 66, 67, 67, 71, 71, 72, 72, 73, 73, 74, 74, 75, 78, 78, 78, 79, 80, 80, 80, 81, 81, 83, 84, 85, 85, 86, 86, 89, 93, 94, 95, 97, 97, 97, 100, 101, 103, 103, 107, 110, 111, 113, 122, 123, 124, 124, 127, 127, 129, 129, 130, 130, 131, 132, 133, 133, 133, 135, 135, 136, 137, 138, 138, 141, 142, 145, 148, 148, 150, 151, 151, 155, 156, 159, 159, 161, 161, 162, 164, 165, 166, 168, 168, 171, 172, 172, 175, 176, 178, 178, 189, 191, 191, 193, 195, 197, 198, 198, 200, 201, 201, 201, 201, 202, 205, 209, 209, 209, 212, 214, 214, 215, 216, 216, 219, 221, 221, 221, 221, 221, 221, 223, 224, 227, 228, 229, 229, 230, 231, 238, 238, 239, 240, 241, 241, 242, 244, 245, 246, 247, 248, 252, 252, 253, 253, 256, 256, 256, 256, 257, 259, 260, 263, 264, 264, 266, 266, 267, 269, 270, 273, 274, 275, 275, 277, 277, 277, 277, 279, 279, 279, 284, 285, 286, 287, 288, 290, 290, 291, 292, 295, 299, 300, 300, 300, 301, 302, 304, 305, 306, 307, 307, 307, 307, 307, 309, 309, 311, 311, 313, 313, 313, 314, 314, 315, 316, 316, 317, 317, 318, 318, 320, 321, 323, 324, 327, 327, 327, 327, 328, 329, 330, 330, 331, 331, 332, 332, 332, 332, 333, 333, 334, 335, 337, 338, 339, 343, 344, 344, 345, 345, 345 Spec 2:2, 2, 2, 2, 2, 8, 8, 13, 13, 14, 16, 16, 18, 18, 19, 19, 20, 20, 20, 26, 28, 29, 31, 31, 33, 34, 34, 35, 36, 38, 39, 40, 41, 41, 41, 42, 42, 44, 45, 45, 47, 48, 48, 49, 51, 52, 52, 52, 53, 53, 54, 55, 58, 61, 63, 64, 65, 68, 72, 74, 75, 75, 76, 80, 81, 81, 82, 82, 84, 85, 87, 97, 97, 98, 99, 102, 105, 106, 107, 107, 113, 113, 116, 117, 119, 120, 122, 123, 123, 124, 124, 126, 127, 127, 127, 127, 128, 128, 129, 129, 132, 132, 135, 135, 138, 139, 140, 141, 145, 146, 150, 150, 151, 152, 153, 154, 154, 155, 156, 157, 158, 158, 159, 160, 160, 160, 161, 162, 162, 164, 164, 164, 165, 165, 167, 168, 169, 169, 169, 170, 171, 171, 173, 174, 175, 175, 176, 176, 177, 177, 177, 177, 177, 178, 178, 181, 181, 181, 181, 182, 182, 184, 184, 185, 185, 186, 187, 187, 188, 189, 190, 190, 190, 193, 197, 200, 203, 204, 204, 205, 206, 207, 207, 207, 208, 210, 211, 212, 213, 214, 215, 215, 217, 217, 219, 220, 221, 221, 222, 224, 225, 225, 225, 225, 226, 227, 228, 228, 228, 229, 229, 233, 235, 235, 236, 239, 239, 243, 244, 245, 246, 247, 247, 248, 249, 253, 254, 255, 258, 258, 259, 259, 261 Spec 3:1, 4, 8, 10, 11, 17, 21, 21, 22, 29, 29, 31, 33, 34, 35, 36, 36, 36, 37, 37, 38, 39, 40, 42, 44, 44, 45, 45, 46, 50, 55, 57, 57, 57, 60, 62, 70, 72, 72, 74, 74, 75, 75, 77, 78, 79, 79, 81, 83, 83, 84, 85, 85, 85, 86, 87, 89, 92, 93, 96, 97, 98, 100, 100, 101, 102, 105, 109, 109, 113, 113, 116, 117, 118, 118, 119, 121, 122, 122, 125, 125, 126, 127, 127, 128, 130, 130, 131, 131, 134, 134, 135, 137, 137, 138, 141, 142, 142, 142, 144, 145, 145, 145, 151, 152, 156, 158, 162, 162, 165, 166, 168, 171, 172, 175, 178, 178, 178, 179, 180, 180, 182, 185, 189, 189, 191, 195, 195, 198, 200, 202, 203, 205, 206, 208, 209 Spec 4:1, 2, 3, 3, 5, 5, 6, 8, 10, 10, 12, 13, 13, 14, 14, 14, 15, 16, 19, 19, 20, 21, 21, 24, 25, 28, 30, 35, 36, 39, 40, 40, 40, 41, 42, 45, 46, 46, 48, 49, 51, 55, 55, 56, 59, 59, 63, 63, 64, 65, 65, 65, 67, 68, 68, 71, 71, 73, 73, 74, 75, 78, 79, 79, 80, 80, 82, 84, 85, 87, 93, 94, 96, 97, 100, 100, 101, 103, 104, 105, 105, 106, 107, 107, 112, 112, 113, 113, 114, 119, 121, 122, 123, 123, 126, 127, 130, 131, 133, 134, 136, 137, 138, 139, 139, 141, 143, 144, 145, 145, 147, 148, 152, 152, 152, 154, 155, 156, 157, 159, 163, 163, 163, 164, 165, 168, 169, 170, 171, 173, 173, 174, 176, 177, 179, 182, 182, 184, 184, 185, 185, 186, 186, 187, 187, 187, 187, 187, 188, 190, 192, 192, 193, 196, 198, 201, 202, 204, 206, 206, 207, 208, 208, 209, 212, 217, 218, 219, 221, 224, 228, 229, 231, 236, 237, 238 Virt 3, 4, 6, 8, 9, 9, 10, 10, 12, 13, 14, 15, 17, 17, 18, 18, 19, 19, 22, 23, 26, 26, 29, 33, 34, 34, 34, 35, 35, 36, 38, 39, 40, 41, 43, 45, 47, 52, 52, 53, 54, 55, 55, 55, 56, 56, 59, 59, 60, 60, 62, 63, 64, 64, 64, 64, 68, 70, 74, 75, 78, 79, 79, 82, 83, 85, 86, 88, 88, 92, 98, 101, 102, 103, 105, 109, 113, 114, 114, 120, 121, 124, 126, 127, 127, 128, 130, 130, 130, 142, 143, 144, 144, 145, 145, 145, 146, 146, 146, 147, 150, 151, 152, 154, 155, 156, 160, 162, 166, 172, 173, 174, 175, 175, 176, 179, 179, 179, 180, 181, 182, 182, 183, 183, 183, 184, 185, 185, 185, 188, 189, 190, 190, 194, 201, 201, 202, 205, 206, 206, 207, 208, 209, 209, 211, 212, 212, 213, 214, 215, 216, 216, 216, 217, 218, 219, 219, 221, 223 Praem 1, 2, 2, 5, 6, 8, 9, 10, 11, 11, 12, 13, 14, 15, 17, 18, 18, 20, 21, 21, 23, 25, 26, 27, 27, 29, 31, 32, 32, 33, 35, 38, 39, 39, 39, 40, 40, 40, 40, 42, 44, 44, 44, 45, 55, 55, 55, 56, 56, 57, 60, 63, 64, 65, 68, 69, 69, 70, 70, 71, 74, 74, 77, 78, 80, 80, 81, 83, 84, 85, 88, 93, 95, 95, 96, 99, 101, 103, 105, 107, 109, 109, 109, 111, 111, 112, 113, 113, 114, 115, 119, 121, 122, 123, 123, 124, 125, 126, 127, 128, 133, 136, 137, 138, 141, 142, 143, 144, 145, 149, 150, 152, 159, 161, 164, 167, 168, 169 Prob 1, 1, 6, 10, 11, 11, 12, 18, 20, 22, 22, 23, 23, 24, 24, 28, 30, 32, 32, 34, 35, 35, 35, 36, 37, 37, 40, 40, 41, 41, 41, 41, 42, 42, 43, 43, 44, 44, 45, 45, 47,

47, 47, 50, 50, 51, 52, 52, 53, 53, 55, 57, 57, 58, 59, 59, 60, 60, 61, 61, 61, 61, 62, 62, 62, 64, 67, 68, 69, 70, 71, 71, 73, 74, 75, 77, 79, 79, 84, 85, 85, 86, 87, 91, 91, 92, 92, 93, 93, 96, 98, 99, 99, 100, 100, 100, 101, 101, 103, 104, 105, 105, 111, 117, 118, 118, 128, 130, 132, 136, 136, 139, 139, 140, 143, 143, 146, 147, 148, 149, 149, 150, 150, 150, 156, 156, 157, 157, 160 Contempl 2, 2, 3, 4, 6, 6, 11, 13, 21, 22, 23, 24, 25, 28, 29, 32, 34, 36, 37, 37, 38, 41, 45, 46, 50, 51, 53, 57, 58, 58, 59, 64, 65, 65, 66, 67, 68, 69, 70, 72, 73, 75, 81, 82, 87 Aet 1, 3, 4, 4, 5, 5, 5, 5, 5, 5, 6, 6, 7, 7, 8, 10, 11, 12, 13, 18, 18, 19, 19, 21, 21, 21, 21, 21, 22, 22, 22, 22, 23, 25, 26, 26, 28, 28, 29, 32, 33, 35, 35, 37, 37, 37, 38, 38, 38, 39, 41, 43, 43, 46, 46, 47, 47, 48, 48, 48, 49, 51, 51, 52, 53, 53, 53, 53, 53, 57, 58, 59, 59, 60, 61, 61, 66, 66, 68, 68, 70, 70, 70, 70, 71, 71, 72, 73, 74, 75, 75, 76, 77, 78, 78, 78, 78, 78, 78, 79, 80, 82, 85, 85, 86, 86, 88, 88, 88, 89, 89, 89, 90, 91, 93, 93, 94, 94, 95, 98, 99, 100, 100, 101, 103, 104, 104, 104, 105, 106, 107, 107, 107, 111, 112, 113, 113, 114, 114, 118, 119, 119, 121, 124, 124, 124, 125, 126, 129, 130, 130, 130, 131, 131, 132, 132, 133, 134, 135, 137, 137, 139, 139, 143, 144, 149 Flacc 2, 3, 3, 4, 6, 9, 9, 14, 15, 16, 22, 23, 25, 26, 26, 28, 29, 30, 33, 34, 35, 35, 35, 36, 42, 43, 45, 45, 47, 49, 50, 51, 52, 54, 55, 56, 57, 58, 59, 60, 63, 72, 78, 78, 79, 79, 80, 81, 81, 85, 86, 92, 93, 93, 95, 96, 97, 100, 101, 106, 108, 108, 109, 112, 115, 116, 119, 120, 120, 126, 128, 130, 130, 131, 133, 135, 135, 136, 138, 139, 139, 142, 143, 144, 144, 145, 146, 147, 147, 148, 149, 150, 151, 159, 163, 164, 164, 165, 167, 167, 172, 174, 180, 182, 184, 184, 186 Legat 1, 1, 2, 4, 6, 7, 12, 14, 15, 15, 15, 16, 17, 18, 22, 23, 26, 26, 27, 28, 28, 29, 30, 32, 33, 36, 37, 37, 38, 40, 42, 42, 43, 47, 52, 52, 53, 54, 58, 58, 59, 60, 61, 64, 65, 67, 68, 68, 69, 71, 73, 75, 76, 76, 79, 80, 84, 85, 89, 93, 93, 98, 98, 99, 103, 103, 108, 109, 112, 113, 113, 117, 117, 118, 118, 118, 119, 125, 127, 129, 130, 130, 132, 135, 135, 136, 138, 138, 139, 140, 142, 142, 142, 145, 146, 149, 151, 155, 160, 161, 162, 162, 163, 164, 164, 165, 166, 166, 168, 168, 171, 173, 173, 176, 176, 176, 177, 178, 178, 179, 180, 182, 182, 182, 183, 184, 186, 187, 190, 192, 192, 192, 194, 195, 196, 198, 198, 199, 200, 200, 202, 204, 205, 205, 205, 207, 208, 209, 209, 210, 210, 212, 213, 214, 215, 216, 217, 218, 218, 220, 222, 225, 226, 229, 230, 233, 237, 241, 242, 242, 242, 243, 244, 245, 246, 246, 247, 249, 251, 254, 257, 259, 260, 262, 262, 263, 269, 271, 272, 277, 277, 278, 278, 280, 280, 281, 282, 286, 288, 289, 290, 290, 292, 293, 295, 299, 300, 301, 301, 301, 302, 303, 303, 304, 304, 306, 306, 308, 310, 312, 315, 315, 316, 317, 317, 317, 318, 319, 319, 320, 322, 322, 323, 324, 327, 329, 332, 335, 335, 338, 339, 341, 344, 345, 346, 346, 347, 347, 350, 351, 353, 353, 355, 357, 359, 360, 362, 363, 364, 367, 372 Hypoth 6:1, 6:1, 6:3, 6:4, 6:4, 6:4, 6:6, 6:7, 6:8, 6:9, 7:1, 7:1, 7:3, 7:3, 7:5, 7:8, 7:9, 7:9, 7:9, 7:11, 7:11, 7:14, 7:14, 7:17, 11:2, 11:7, 11:8, 11:9, 11:11, 11:12, 11:17, 11:18 Prov 1, 1, 2:1, 1, 3, 4, 6, 7, 7, 8, 10, 11, 11, 12, 13, 13, 14, 14, 17, 17, 23, 23, 25, 27, 28, 29, 30, 33, 34, 36, 37, 42, 44, 47, 48, 49, 50, 51, 53, 53, 54, 55, 55, 56, 60, 60, 61, 62, 62, 64, 64, 65, 65, 66, 66, 67, 69, 69, 70 QG 1:1, 1, 17b, 20, 21, 21, 24, 29, 32, 51, 55a, 55a, 55b, 64a, 64b, 64d, 65, 66, 66, 68, 69, 69, 70:1, 70:1, 70:2, 72, 72, 72, 73, 74, 76b, 77, 79, 79, 93, 94, 97, 97, 100:1a, 100:1b, 100:1b, 100:1b, 2:5a, 10, 10, 12a, 12b, 13b, 13b, 13b, 13b, 13b, 15a, 15a, 16, 26a, 28, 29, 34a, 34a, 34b, 34c, 39, 48, 54a, 54a, 54b, 54c, 54d, 59, 59, 59, 59, 59, 59, 62, 6[illegible] [illegible]2, 64b, 64c, 68b, 71a, 71a, 74, 3:3, 7, 12, 12, 18, 18, 20a, 20b, 21, 23, 30b, 38a, 48, 49a, 49b, 52, 58, 4:8b, 8c, 40, 51c, 51c, 52d, 64, 69, 69, 76b, 80, 88, 88, 99, 100, 102b, 102c, 104, 153, 166, 169, 172, 173, 174, 179, 189, 191a, 193, 198, 198, 200a, 200a, 200c, 200c, 203, 204, 206a, 206a, 227, 228, 228, 228 QG isf 4, 5, 9, 10, 10, 11, 17, 17 QG (Par) 2:2, 2:2, 2:3, 2:3, 2:3, 2:4, 2:4, 2:4, 2:4, 2:5, 2:5, 2:7, 2:7, 2:7 QE 1:6, 7a, 21, 2:1, 2, 2, 2, 10b, 12, 13a, 14, 15b, 16, 17, 17, 18, 19, 20, 20, 21, 21, 24b, 26, 26, 38a, 45a, 45a, 45b, 46, 47, 47, 47, 47, 47, 49a, 49b, 64, 107 QE isf 1, 2, 3, 3, 3, 3, 9, 11, 11, 13, 14, 15, 16, 16, 16, 17, 17, 25, 26, 26, 29, 30

εἰνοσίφυλλος Conf 4

εἴπερ (25) Det 26, 152 Post 17, 82, 159 Plant 84 Ebr 45 Sobr 5, 36 Ios 250 Mos 1:58 Decal 70 Spec 1:127 Spec 3:67, 151, 166 Prob 12, 61 Aet 14, 60, 132 Flacc 60, 82 Legat 209 Prov 2:51

εἶπον (λέγω) (662) Opif 13, 21, 24, 58, 67, 71, 72, 75, 76, 80, 82, 88, 107, 133, 135, 139, 139, 166 Leg 1:1, 19, 35, 40, 60, 88, 91 Leg 2:1, 8, 9, 11, 15, 40, 44, 68, 88, 88, 88, 88 Leg 3:9, 24, 39, 49, 59, 59, 63, 65, 66, 71, 85, 86, 96, 107, 115, 138, 169, 169, 173, 173, 179, 179, 182, 184, 200, 204, 206, 217, 217, 218, 222, 224, 245 Cher 1, 18, 40, 42, 51, 63, 65, 68, 70, 72, 75, 77, 87, 88, 91, 100, 112, 114, 124, 128, 128 Sacr 31, 33, 35, 42, 56, 69, 69, 70, 99, 104, 108, 121, 126 Det 1, 4, 5, 5, 5, 5, 50, 54, 55, 59, 62, 69, 73, 74, 130, 138, 141, 142, 143, 165, 169 Post 12, 17, 25, 27, 33, 41, 42, 49, 58, 80, 120, 126, 126, 132, 132, 132, 133, 172, 181, 185 Gig 19, 28, 56 Deus 2, 14, 18, 20, 31, 59, 66, 72, 74, 101, 104, 140, 145, 146, 149, 157, 160 Agr 69, 86, 101, 149, 171, 176, 176, 179, 179 Plant 1, 18, 18, 33, 48, 49, 64, 65, 68, 71, 78, 90, 101, 108, 108, 125, 133, 137, 139, 141, 153, 158, 175 Ebr 12, 13, 40, 51, 61, 79, 84, 84, 93, 96, 106, 133, 138, 150, 150, 155, 170 Sobr 21, 44, 47 Conf 1, 1, 1, 29, 39, 55, 58, 81, 119, 134, 135, 136, 142, 144, 144, 150, 165, 169, 169, 192 Migr 1, 43, 48, 50, 55, 58, 112, 115, 135, 137, 139, 147, 152, 163, 166, 187, 225 Her 12, 14, 20, 25, 30, 38, 55, 66, 67, 68, 76, 82, 86, 88, 90, 96, 98, 101, 113, 116, 117, 122, 124, 164, 177, 181, 189, 230, 251, 275, 277, 290 Congr 1, 12, 13, 18, 50, 67, 73, 86, 93, 97, 99, 106, 125, 143, 154, 161, 176 Fug 1, 1, 1, 1, 11, 16, 23, 32, 49, 51, 54, 59, 61, 68, 68, 82, 127, 127, 139, 149, 149, 149, 171, 172, 177, 194, 197, 198, 202 Mut 1, 14, 18, 33, 45, 47, 64, 68, 71, 98, 140, 169, 170, 176, 177, 177, 178, 181, 181, 188, 194, 207, 218, 223, 227, 250, 251, 253, 265 Somn 1:3, 21, 22, 22, 27, 64, 65, 74, 75, 87, 96, 97, 101, 106, 163, 166, 173, 183, 183, 184, 189, 189, 189, 194, 195, 195, 195, 195, 195, 196, 196, 209, 214, 229, 230, 252 Somn 2:9, 30, 32, 72, 86, 111, 111, 128, 172, 182, 182, 188, 189, 217, 230, 245, 245, 259, 260 Abr 15, 17, 24, 25, 33, 33, 44, 46, 54, 67, 73, 112, 114, 121, 134, 193, 199 Ios 17, 18, 18, 24, 48, 92, 94, 106, 116, 117, 119, 166, 173, 187, 189, 212, 219, 239, 247 Mos 1:54, 73, 74, 84, 88, 92, 141, 244, 274, 280, 281, 281, 283, 285, 285, 285, 292, 294, 294, 296, 311, 333 Mos 2:7, 18, 62, 97, 99, 101, 122, 135, 138, 171, 185, 188, 270 Decal 18, 37, 73, 88, 98, 110, 113, 124, 124, 151 Spec 1:15, 49, 117, 137, 154, 168, 190, 203, 205, 233, 261, 271, 278, 289, 302, 328 Spec 2:53, 53, 59, 63, 75, 80, 91, 96, 104, 119, 157, 163, 176, 193, 194, 213, 219, 248, 251, 261, 262 Spec 3:50, 59, 149, 183, 200, 202, 206 Spec 4:20, 48, 84, 123, 133, 156, 184, 225, 231 Virt 1, 33, 44, 57,

59, 88, 99, 104, 146, 195, 199, 211, 218 Praem 31, 40, 54, 65, 69, 72, 83, 108, 111, 152, 153 Prob 28, 42, 43, 84, 95, 109, 112, 113, 123, 143, 144, 152, 157 Contempl 1, 1, 14, 40, 75 Aet 66, 74, 83, 97, 107, 107, 126 Flacc 2, 6, 48, 59, 101, 134, 157 Legat 5, 10, 10, 38, 86, 91, 102, 125, 140, 141, 152, 168, 178, 182, 195, 197, 215, 242, 261, 263, 274, 275, 304, 337, 351, 353, 362, 367 Hypoth 6:10, 7:2, 7:4, 7:9, 7:14 Prov 2:2, 42, 46, 56, 59 QG 1:65, 2:26a, 48, 54a, 65, 68a, 71a, 3:22, 24, 4:88, 144, 191c, 228 QG (Par) 2:6, 2:7 QE 1:21, 2:6a QE isf 16

Εἴρ (8) Leg 3:69, 69, 71, 73, 74, 74, 74, 75

εἴργω (9) Leg 3:81 Deus 3, 144 Migr 69 Mos 2:101 Spec 1:103, 120 Legat 334, 364

εἰρεσία Plant 152 Ebr 182

εἰρηναῖος (12) Leg 3:79, 117, 140 Post 118 Ebr 100 Conf 43, 70 Her 206 Somn 2:250 Spec 2:45 Spec 4:221 Legat 102

εἰρηνεύω Legat 204

εἰρήνη (146) Opif 33, 81, 142 Leg 1:45 Leg 3:46, 79, 81, 130, 187, 242 Cher 37, 86 Det 2, 2, 174 Post 183, 183, 185 Gig 51 Agr 25, 146, 153, 159 Ebr 62, 74, 75, 76, 97, 100, 104 Conf 41, 46, 47, 49, 49, 57, 130, 132 Migr 63 Her 162, 212, 275, 275, 284, 285, 286, 288, 289, 290 Congr 32, 176 Fug 173, 173, 174 Mut 150, 240 Somn 2:12, 36, 36, 40, 147, 147, 149, 229, 250, 253, 253, 254, 254 Abr 1, 215, 225, 226, 242, 261 Ios 34, 57, 115, 204 Mos 1:60, 142, 304, 304, 310, 323, 323, 332 Decal 178, 178 Spec 1:57, 313 Spec 2:22, 208 Spec 3:17, 69, 131, 169 Spec 4:95, 221 Virt 22, 22, 61, 109, 153, 153 Praem 3, 92, 98, 116, 118, 118, 157 Prob 9, 34, 64, 76, 78 Contempl 60 Aet 68 Flacc 5, 8, 48, 62, 135, 184 Legat 8, 16, 68, 68, 90, 100, 108, 113, 132, 141, 141, 301, 306, 309, 312 Prov 2:12 QG 4:7*, 206b, 206b QE 2:11b, 64

εἰρηνικός (33) Cher 49 Gig 48 Ebr 76 Conf 41, 49 Congr 25, 177 Mut 108, 131, 144 Somn 1:174 Somn 2:166 Abr 27, 28, 61, 105, 225 Ios 166, 167, 213 Mos 1:243 Spec 1:224 Spec 3:125, 137 Spec 4:224, 225 Virt 47 Praem 87 Flacc 94 Legat 161, 230 Prov 2:1, 57

εἰρηνοποιός Spec 2:192

εἰρηνοφυλακέω Decal 178

εἰρηνοφύλαξ Her 206 Spec 2:192 Legat 147

εἱρκτή (15) Her 68, 273 Somn 1:139 Ios 52, 80, 86, 123, 247 Mos 2:201, 217 Decal 74 Spec 2:251 Prob 18 Flacc 173 Legat 368

εἱρκτοφυλακέω Deus 115

εἱρκτοφύλαξ (7) Deus 115 Migr 9 Mut 173 Ios 81, 84, 85, 123

εἱρμός (21) Opif 28, 65, 131 Post 23 Conf 14 Migr 55 Her 301 Congr 63 Fug 119, 150, 152, 154 Mut 47, 135 Somn 2:44 Mos 2:263 Decal 83 Spec 1:195 Spec 2:223 Spec 4:39 Aet 112

εἴρω Her 188 Aet 75

εἴρων Sacr 32

εἰρωνεία Cher 17 Plant 106 Her 43 Mos 1:274 Hypoth 11:16

εἷς (871) Opif 15, 20, 35, 38, 41, 48, 48, 49, 49, 49, 50, 55, 57, 60, 60, 69, 72, 84, 89, 95, 96, 98, 99, 100, 102, 102, 105, 109, 128, 131, 132, 141, 151, 152, 171, 171, 171, 172, 172 Leg 1:3, 10, 44, 51, 51, 61, 63, 66, 81, 97, 97, 98, 100, 101, 102, 102, 103, 104 Leg 2:1, 2, 3, 3, 8, 15, 19, 35, 35, 48, 48, 49, 49, 49, 51, 52, 52, 60, 68, 94 Leg 3:7, 7, 8, 48, 49, 53, 78, 82, 105, 105, 105, 115, 124, 126, 139, 145, 189, 211, 236, 253 Cher 22, 25, 26, 27, 58, 83, 87, 109, 119 Sacr 3, 6, 10, 19, 19, 25, 40, 41, 52, 59, 108, 111, 131 Det 30, 30, 31, 51, 53, 76, 107, 108, 134, 148, 153, 154 Post 16, 28, 44, 49, 50, 75, 85, 95, 95, 129 Gig 2, 3, 16, 22, 34, 51, 53, 64, 65 Deus 10, 11, 14, 14, 18, 53, 55, 61, 67, 78, 85, 113, 130, 148, 153, 159, 174, 176, 181 Agr 5, 30, 49, 49, 54, 54, 71, 73, 90, 103, 118, 178 Plant 2, 31, 38, 64, 67, 67, 103, 113, 113, 123, 124, 124, 124, 127, 128, 129, 131, 137, 142, 150, 150, 152, 153, 154, 154, 156, 164, 167, 173 Ebr 4, 8, 8, 45, 57, 89, 92, 114, 115, 116, 116, 116, 146, 165, 171, 177, 178, 189, 193, 195, 198 Sobr 8, 12, 17, 18, 21, 31, 42, 47, 60 Conf 1, 1, 1, 1, 4, 5, 7, 7, 8, 10, 11, 15, 15, 15, 17, 17, 17, 25, 25, 29, 41, 41, 43, 43, 46, 55, 56, 100, 117, 117, 144, 145, 147, 150, 150, 150, 157, 165, 169, 169, 169, 170, 170, 170, 170, 170, 171, 187, 187, 192, 192, 192, 197 Migr 3, 14, 58, 60, 60, 61, 61, 62, 62, 64, 69, 73, 78, 104, 120, 134, 137, 148, 148, 152, 153, 155, 173, 180, 180, 206, 207 Her 14, 15, 20, 23, 66, 110, 121, 138, 138, 144, 144, 146, 146, 160, 213, 216, 216, 217, 230, 234, 246, 268, 288, 290 Congr 8, 22, 51, 74, 82, 104, 113, 113, 113, 142 Fug 56, 71, 71, 87, 114, 132, 154, 154, 168, 177, 186 Mut 15, 33, 48, 57, 61, 77, 110, 145, 146, 147, 200, 200, 200, 200, 200, 205, 224, 225, 225, 230, 233, 233, 253 Somn 1:5, 41, 96, 128, 149, 154, 166, 179, 185, 196, 205, 215, 229, 230, 237 Somn 2:14, 15, 33, 72, 96, 156, 171, 210, 218, 224, 248, 257, 262, 264, 270, 281, 284 Abr 5, 34, 43, 46, 46, 49, 50, 50, 56, 64, 81, 105, 110, 110, 116, 119, 122, 122, 124, 125, 130, 130, 131, 131, 131, 132, 139, 141, 145, 162, 165, 196, 199, 199, 229, 235, 247 Ios 1, 5, 13, 29, 29, 31, 33, 33, 33, 36, 52, 76, 77, 84, 91, 102, 107, 112, 123, 131, 167, 169, 180, 185, 188, 191, 220, 233, 259 Mos 1:10, 31, 44, 48, 59, 86, 92, 97, 102, 103, 114, 123, 126, 128, 128, 130, 133, 133, 136, 139, 151, 201, 205, 213, 216, 221, 231, 235, 242, 242, 254, 263, 284, 284, 286, 290, 295, 301, 304, 324, 324 Mos 2:7, 10, 30, 40, 48, 58, 59, 78, 78, 83, 91, 121, 121, 152, 160, 168, 170, 170, 174, 179, 180, 180, 182, 212, 232, 239, 273, 291 Decal 8, 21, 21, 22, 26, 26, 27, 28, 29, 36, 36, 37, 37, 39, 39, 41, 43, 50, 51, 64, 65, 74, 91, 100, 123, 153, 155, 155, 159, 161 Spec 1:4, 9, 9, 9, 14, 30, 32, 52, 54, 56, 65, 67, 67, 72, 79, 86, 110, 126, 127, 151, 163, 177, 178, 178, 180, 184, 195, 199, 199, 208, 208, 208, 211, 220, 222, 224, 225, 240, 243, 272, 296, 313, 317, 317, 327, 331, 332, 344 Spec 2:34, 35, 42, 65, 113, 122, 134, 165, 182, 184, 232, 234, 250, 258, 262 Spec 3:28, 29, 65, 65, 73, 74, 84, 90, 90, 95, 126, 126, 131, 131, 131, 142, 165, 168, 185, 189 Spec 4:12, 17, 27, 45, 47, 53, 53, 54, 54, 54, 83, 85, 96, 109, 113, 113, 133, 136, 138, 159, 159, 165, 170, 172, 176, 178, 212, 212, 213, 219, 230 Virt 6, 15, 21, 29, 34, 35, 40, 52, 52, 53, 85, 88, 98, 102, 103, 130, 134, 138, 138, 163, 185, 202, 207, 213, 214, 215, 216, 221 Praem 7, 23, 24, 40, 52, 56, 57, 58, 61, 63, 69, 85, 85, 87, 94, 112, 114, 117, 123, 155, 162, 164, 164, 165, 165, 166 Prob 18, 79, 82, 86, 118, 122 Contempl 2, 45, 77, 85, 87 Aet 4, 6, 8, 21, 21, 25, 26, 56, 65, 79, 123, 141, 144 Flacc 41, 45, 55, 57, 76, 92, 112, 137, 144, 173, 173, 175, 189 Legat 17, 19, 19, 27, 27, 48, 48, 48, 49, 58, 80, 115, 117, 117, 132, 144, 149, 170, 184, 209, 214, 225, 225, 232, 257, 281, 283, 284, 297, 314, 322, 326, 327, 329, 334, 336, 338, 344 Hypoth

7:3, 7:10, 7:13, 11:10, 11:12, 11:12 Prov 2:5, 7, 11, 33, 34, 54 QG 1:29, 29, 2:11, 14, 14, 14, 26a, 54a, 65, 66, 68b, 71a, 3:3, 8, 8, 4:8b, 110b, 110b, 145, 198 QE 2:2, 14, 14, 20, 25a, 25b, 25d QE isf 5, 11, 14, 16

εἰς (2432) Opif 9, 9, 18, 22, 27, 34, 38, 38, 38, 39, 41, 41, 42, 45, 49, 52, 53, 53, 54, 56, 59, 59, 61, 61, 62, 62, 62, 62, 62, 64, 67, 67, 67, 67, 67, 68, 71, 78, 78, 78, 78, 79, 79, 80, 80, 81, 83, 86, 87, 95, 95, 95, 101, 105, 105, 105, 105, 105, 113, 114, 117, 124, 128, 134, 139, 144, 144, 152, 152, 156, 161, 167, 171, 171 Leg 1:10, 31, 31, 32, 32, 32, 33, 34, 39, 43, 50, 52, 53, 54, 56, 56, 58, 58, 63, 80, 94, 103, 103 Leg 2:25, 34, 34, 38, 38, 49, 49, 50, 56, 59, 61, 62, 66, 77, 85, 85, 93, 94, 99, 100, 100, 102, 102, 103, 103 Leg 3:7, 7, 8, 13, 15, 16, 18, 19, 19, 28, 36, 37, 39, 39, 40, 40, 41, 43, 45, 45, 52, 56, 61, 66, 73, 77, 81, 85, 88, 90, 92, 92, 99, 106, 118, 119, 125, 126, 155, 156, 161, 161, 162, 163, 165, 166, 167, 167, 170, 175, 195, 196, 202, 213, 213, 215, 215, 223, 225, 227, 237, 238, 238, 238, 239, 241, 252, 253, 253 Cher 2, 2, 3, 11, 14, 18, 18, 20, 23, 41, 49, 50, 52, 53, 61, 95, 98, 99, 108, 110, 114, 119, 120, 121 Sacr 7, 9, 13, 25, 29, 33, 33, 48, 50, 63, 64, 69, 70, 72, 82, 82, 83, 84, 85, 85, 85, 85, 89, 90, 90, 95, 98, 100, 101, 117, 126, 126, 131, 131, 133, 137 Det 1, 1, 3, 5, 5, 7, 8, 10, 17, 28, 29, 30, 32, 37, 39, 39, 40, 42, 43, 45, 46, 50, 50, 63, 66, 71, 80, 80, 84, 85, 88, 98, 105, 105, 106, 114, 119, 126, 127, 146, 149, 151, 152, 153, 154, 157, 158, 159, 163, 168, 170, 177, 177, 177 Post 5, 8, 11, 13, 14, 14, 15, 17, 17, 22, 29, 29, 31, 32, 43, 53, 60, 65, 66, 70, 76, 76, 77, 79, 84, 101, 101, 101, 104, 113, 128, 129, 130, 132, 132, 134, 136, 136, 141, 150, 150, 151, 154, 156, 156, 161, 162, 163, 164, 170, 173, 176, 177 Gig 1, 13, 15, 17, 19, 26, 31, 54, 56, 57, 60, 61, 65, 65, 67 Deus 8, 27, 38, 47, 55, 56, 62, 69, 71, 79, 87, 89, 93, 93, 108, 111, 112, 113, 119, 119, 120, 130, 130, 131, 134, 135, 138, 145, 147, 149, 156, 162, 166, 173 Agr 6, 7, 10, 11, 13, 30, 44, 47, 51, 54, 55, 58, 78, 80, 82, 84, 86, 88, 88, 89, 89, 90, 90, 94, 110, 111, 119, 132, 134, 135, 136, 136, 137, 137, 137, 137, 138, 138, 141, 142, 145, 148, 148, 148, 149, 152, 160, 162, 165, 168, 169, 176 Plant 3, 3, 19, 29, 29, 29, 29, 36, 41, 43, 43, 44, 47, 47, 54, 56, 61, 69, 74, 75, 86, 90, 96, 97, 98, 114, 116, 128, 129, 130, 135, 135, 144, 145, 145, 146, 157, 157, 166, 166, 167 Ebr 8, 14, 14, 22, 25, 29, 31, 39, 40, 48, 67, 73, 78, 78, 94, 111, 125, 127, 127, 129, 133, 138, 143, 147, 150, 150, 172, 185, 188, 205, 208, 210, 211, 213, 213, 218, 219, 224 Sobr 6, 7, 7, 11, 11, 13, 16, 16, 24, 28, 28, 31, 39, 40, 42, 60, 61, 64 Conf 1, 4, 7, 8, 9, 13, 15, 15, 18, 23, 25, 40, 52, 74, 75, 77, 78, 80, 81, 85, 86, 90, 90, 90, 90, 93, 102, 102, 103, 104, 104, 121, 133, 133, 140, 144, 151, 153, 163, 165, 173, 175, 176, 176, 179, 181, 185, 185, 186, 187, 192, 192, 192, 194, 195 Migr 1, 1, 2, 3, 3, 3, 3, 3, 3, 5, 9, 11, 18, 22, 25, 26, 26, 27, 27, 28, 29, 36, 39, 43, 48, 49, 53, 53, 55, 62, 64, 68, 68, 75, 76, 79, 80, 83, 83, 98, 104, 108, 113, 113, 115, 117, 117, 119, 121, 123, 124, 124, 126, 128, 157, 174, 177, 183, 184, 187, 195, 195, 201, 207, 208, 208, 218, 219, 221, 225 Her 18, 20, 29, 29, 40, 45, 47, 56, 56, 66, 67, 76, 76, 79, 80, 84, 86, 86, 94, 103, 110, 111, 121, 124, 130, 131, 131, 132, 132, 132, 132, 133, 134, 134, 135, 135, 136, 136, 136, 136, 136, 136, 138, 138, 139, 142, 152, 161, 164, 168, 170, 170, 174, 175, 180, 182, 184, 190, 190, 191, 193, 194, 207, 217, 217, 219, 226, 226, 226, 226, 229, 229, 235, 254, 255, 261, 264, 271, 274, 277, 277, 281, 282, 309, 316 Congr 8, 16, 16, 37, 44, 57, 58, 70, 70, 81, 83, 86, 88, 89, 109, 121, 122, 152, 153, 155, 155, 163, 163, 164 Fug 5, 10, 23, 29, 32, 32, 35, 36, 39, 44, 48, 48, 49, 49, 53, 59, 82, 84, 86, 88, 91, 93, 94, 101, 109, 114, 117, 118, 118, 119, 121, 122, 124, 127, 131, 132, 132, 144, 160, 175, 176, 182, 182, 182, 182, 182, 183, 187, 193, 194 Mut 7, 9, 13, 18, 28, 33, 38, 42, 54, 62, 67, 77, 81, 88, 88, 97, 104, 107, 121, 121, 148, 148, 150, 151, 155, 155, 157, 164, 168, 177, 178, 179, 188, 194, 200, 204, 215, 226, 228, 228, 233, 233, 237, 239, 243, 250, 264, 269 Somn 1:3, 3, 4, 5, 9, 10, 13, 15, 17, 26, 34, 34, 36, 40, 41, 42, 42, 45, 45, 46, 51, 52, 55, 57, 60, 61, 62, 64, 65, 67, 67, 68, 69, 70, 70, 71, 71, 76, 77, 80, 85, 89, 91, 91, 96, 103, 107, 112, 129, 133, 150, 151, 163, 180, 181, 188, 189, 193, 200, 203, 205, 210, 211, 214, 216, 226, 226, 241, 247, 256 Somn 2:13, 19, 34, 51, 59, 60, 67, 75, 76, 91, 100, 106, 107, 108, 108, 113, 116, 118, 119, 126, 133, 140, 145, 147, 159, 159, 163, 175, 184, 189, 198, 203, 203, 213, 217, 217, 221, 227, 231, 232, 237, 241, 243, 243, 243, 245, 248, 259, 264, 269, 272, 282, 284, 285, 292, 295, 301 Abr 24, 24, 24, 24, 24, 24, 37, 43, 47, 61, 62, 62, 67, 67, 72, 85, 85, 86, 101, 105, 105, 108, 108, 110, 113, 118, 129, 129, 132, 140, 142, 157, 158, 161, 162, 173, 184, 199, 209, 213, 229, 229, 232, 235, 241, 251, 253 Ios 4, 6, 7, 7, 9, 12, 13, 14, 15, 21, 27, 37, 44, 45, 52, 58, 59, 64, 66, 78, 80, 82, 91, 104, 106, 113, 115, 117, 118, 118, 122, 123, 132, 138, 142, 148, 149, 154, 154, 161, 161, 164, 165, 166, 179, 183, 185, 187, 188, 188, 194, 195, 197, 201, 205, 206, 206, 207, 213, 213, 215, 218, 220, 224, 227, 230, 234, 238, 239, 243, 243, 244, 247, 248, 250, 250, 254, 255, 258, 259, 260, 260, 263, 266, 267 Mos 1:3, 5, 8, 8, 15, 22, 22, 22, 25, 26, 29, 34, 35, 36, 38, 41, 41, 41, 43, 43, 47, 47, 47, 48, 49, 49, 57, 59, 60, 63, 64, 64, 65, 65, 71, 77, 78, 79, 79, 79, 81, 85, 86, 86, 90, 91, 91, 93, 97, 98, 99, 100, 101, 103, 105, 106, 108, 110, 111, 116, 119, 119, 120, 122, 127, 128, 130, 134, 138, 140, 144, 144, 145, 151, 152, 158, 158, 158, 162, 163, 164, 166, 170, 172, 176, 176, 177, 180, 185, 185, 186, 188, 194, 195, 195, 196, 197, 197, 201, 201, 204, 205, 209, 209, 209, 211, 212, 214, 215, 217, 220, 222, 230, 237, 237, 240, 240, 240, 249, 250, 254, 255, 257, 258, 263, 272, 278, 282, 285, 287, 293, 302, 312, 313, 333 Mos 2:9, 18, 26, 27, 31, 36, 36, 38, 41, 45, 55, 60, 63, 67, 70, 70, 70, 72, 78, 78, 84, 84, 89, 93, 97, 100, 102, 111, 119, 124, 129, 138, 147, 148, 149, 153, 154, 156, 157, 159, 161, 167, 170, 172, 178, 180, 185, 194, 196, 199, 201, 203, 206, 211, 212, 214, 215, 217, 218, 223, 239, 242, 249, 249, 251, 252, 255, 255, 256, 256, 257, 260, 260, 263, 264, 267, 280, 281, 285, 288, 288, 288, 291 Decal 9, 13, 15, 32, 32, 36, 40, 46, 50, 56, 63, 67, 76, 78, 80, 80, 81, 84, 86, 98, 100, 101, 110, 111, 112, 117, 120, 124, 132, 135, 140, 147, 149, 158, 159, 162, 163, 164, 167, 167, 167, 167, 167, 167, 167, 167 Spec 1:7, 8, 15, 24, 24, 33, 34, 38, 41, 43, 48, 55, 55, 58, 60, 67, 68, 69, 70, 71, 76, 77, 78, 80, 83, 83, 84, 87, 89, 100, 101, 103, 104, 104, 105, 105, 106, 111, 115, 120, 130, 132, 132, 137, 146, 150, 152, 154, 158, 158, 159, 160, 162, 163, 163, 165, 165, 165, 166, 178, 178, 178, 179, 184, 185, 186, 188, 190, 190, 193, 194, 199, 202, 208, 208, 211, 211, 211, 216, 217, 218, 218, 218, 219, 220, 221, 222, 223, 234, 234, 234, 236, 237, 251, 251, 253, 256, 256, 259, 261, 262, 266, 266, 266, 268, 269, 270, 279, 280, 289, 293, 294, 298, 300, 303, 304, 316, 322, 322, 322, 325, 325, 333, 335, 340, 342 Spec 2:2, 4, 9, 18, 19, 19, 23, 23, 24, 27, 28, 29, 33, 35, 40, 41, 42, 50, 56, 63,

65, 65, 67, 70, 70, 82, 83, 85, 85, 91, 95, 96, 98, 98, 100, 102, 109, 111, 117, 120, 121, 122, 125, 135, 135, 138, 141, 146, 148, 155, 156, 158, 165, 166, 175, 179, 186, 187, 187, 189, 191, 199, 199, 201, 202, 203, 203, 205, 209, 216, 217, 217, 218, 223, 225, 230, 233, 233, 234, 237, 238, 242, 248, 249, 250, 251, 251, 252, 255, 256 Spec 3:3, 6, 7, 10, 15, 17, 20, 21, 22, 23, 23, 25, 25, 32, 32, 33, 37, 37, 39, 41, 41, 50, 52, 53, 55, 55, 56, 63, 65, 65, 72, 81, 82, 84, 87, 87, 88, 90, 94, 99, 101, 101, 102, 102, 102, 105, 106, 107, 109, 111, 114, 116, 119, 121, 123, 125, 127, 128, 128, 130, 130, 130, 131, 132, 139, 140, 141, 141, 142, 152, 152, 166, 171, 171, 181, 182, 182, 183, 183, 186, 186, 187, 188, 195, 198, 205, 206 Spec 4:4, 12, 16, 18, 25, 26, 28, 29, 31, 34, 34, 34, 38, 43, 45, 49, 57, 57, 57, 69, 70, 72, 72, 74, 75, 79, 80, 85, 85, 89, 98, 104, 104, 107, 108, 112, 112, 115, 123, 124, 130, 132, 137, 141, 142, 153, 158, 163, 163, 168, 173, 173, 175, 178, 178, 178, 182, 185, 187, 192, 200, 204, 204, 208, 208, 208, 210, 213, 214, 220, 221, 229, 229, 230, 235, 235, 235 Virt 6, 16, 25, 25, 28, 30, 31, 32, 36, 37, 38, 39, 44, 47, 50, 52, 57, 57, 58, 61, 61, 63, 63, 67, 67, 71, 76, 87, 88, 90, 91, 91, 93, 93, 95, 100, 100, 107, 108, 110, 116, 119, 121, 122, 122, 122, 123, 123, 124, 124, 126, 127, 131, 133, 137, 140, 144, 149, 150, 152, 153, 159, 160, 168, 169, 171, 171, 177, 179, 179, 180, 180, 180, 180, 180, 180, 180, 182, 183, 183, 193, 195, 197, 197, 199, 200, 203, 203, 203, 205, 205, 213, 214, 223, 223, 224, 225, 225 Praem 1, 4, 4, 4, 8, 14, 22, 26, 28, 28, 38, 41, 42, 55, 56, 57, 65, 66, 71, 77, 80, 82, 87, 87, 88, 95, 112, 116, 117, 117, 119, 119, 119, 120, 124, 128, 129, 130, 130, 133, 135, 138, 139, 140, 140, 140, 145, 147, 154, 156, 163, 167, 167, 170, 171, 171, 172 Prob 4, 4, 15, 20, 23, 23, 25, 26, 28, 35, 38, 70, 78, 78, 80, 81, 86, 89, 90, 96, 96, 99, 101, 102, 104, 105, 108, 110, 115, 119, 121, 130, 133, 142, 151, 151, 151 Contempl 8, 19, 22, 23, 29, 30, 32, 32, 32, 33, 37, 44, 46, 46, 51, 54, 61, 61, 66, 66, 68, 73, 77, 78, 79, 80, 84, 86, 86, 87, 89, 89, 89 Aet 4, 5, 6, 6, 8, 16, 21, 21, 28, 28, 30, 30, 52, 56, 66, 68, 69, 69, 69, 74, 78, 79, 82, 82, 85, 86, 86, 87, 90, 90, 90, 90, 94, 94, 95, 96, 98, 98, 99, 101, 102, 102, 103, 103, 103, 103, 104, 105, 107, 107, 109, 109, 110, 110, 110, 110, 110, 110, 111, 111, 113, 113, 113, 113, 123, 123, 125, 129, 134, 142, 147, 147, 147 Flacc 1, 27, 30, 30, 31, 31, 35, 38, 40, 41, 45, 46, 47, 48, 49, 50, 51, 53, 55, 56, 58, 59, 64, 66, 66, 74, 75, 77, 79, 79, 82, 84, 92, 92, 93, 94, 99, 99, 102, 103, 105, 105, 112, 112, 114, 120, 121, 121, 123, 125, 128, 130, 130, 135, 138, 142, 143, 146, 151, 155, 155, 159, 160, 161, 162, 163, 166, 166, 169, 173, 173, 182, 183, 185, 185, 190 Legat 6, 8, 8, 14, 15, 22, 23, 32, 32, 38, 49, 51, 52, 56, 58, 60, 62, 63, 63, 69, 69, 72, 72, 77, 77, 79, 79, 79, 80, 80, 80, 87, 90, 90, 91, 95, 96, 98, 101, 103, 103, 105, 113, 116, 118, 118, 118, 119, 121, 124, 127, 128, 132, 134, 137, 144, 147, 147, 147, 151, 155, 156, 156, 157, 157, 158, 161, 162, 163, 165, 166, 168, 172, 172, 175, 179, 185, 190, 191, 198, 200, 201, 201, 204, 205, 207, 212, 212, 213, 216, 220, 221, 224, 225, 227, 228, 228, 233, 235, 238, 238, 246, 248, 249, 250, 255, 257, 257, 259, 268, 270, 272, 274, 274, 281, 281, 281, 284, 292, 294, 296, 300, 301, 305, 305, 306, 311, 312, 313, 315, 316, 323, 326, 326, 332, 334, 338, 338, 344, 344, 344, 346, 347, 352, 353, 355, 356, 364, 365, 368, 368 Hypoth 6:1, 6:1, 6:1, 6:1, 6:2, 6:2, 6:5, 6:6, 6:6, 6:6, 6:6, 6:9, 7:2, 7:2, 7:2, 7:2, 7:7, 7:12, 7:15, 7:15, 7:16, 7:17, 11:4, 11:9 Prov 1, 2:2, 5, 6, 14, 18, 19, 21, 26, 26, 33, 42, 45, 46, 57, 60, 64, 69, 69, 71 QG 1:17b, 28, 29, 29, 51, 77, 85, 2:11, 13a, 13b, 15c, 17b, 26b, 26b, 28, 34a, 34a, 41, 48, 54d, 59, 64a, 64b, 64c, 65, 65, 66, 68b, 3:12, 22, 4:33b, 51a, 51a, 51a, 51b, 88, 145, 145, 172, 191a, 202a, 211 QG isf 3 QG (Par) 2:3, 2:3, 2:3, 2:5, 2:5, 2:6, 2:7, 2:7, 2:7, 2:7, 2:7, 2:7 QE 1:19, 2:6a, 6b, 10a, 10a, 13a, 17, 21, 40, 45a, 64, 118 QE isf 3, 11, 13, 21, 26

εἰσάγω (124) Opif 72 Leg 1:35, 52, 52, 53, 54 Leg 3:7, 92, 121 Cher 21, 32, 40, 45, 95 Sacr 11, 14, 17, 64, 65, 89, 90 Det 20, 170 Post 34, 49, 67, 130, 135 Gig 56 Deus 43, 54, 59, 60, 68, 111, 121 Agr 2, 41, 44, 97, 107, 125 Plant 1, 34, 35, 43, 44, 44, 47, 52, 99 Ebr 31, 60, 77, 105, 198, 203, 208 Sobr 17, 26 Conf 5, 58, 64, 70, 77, 88, 98, 101, 122 Migr 13, 48, 135, 153, 174, 202, 212 Her 16, 56, 243, 260, 276, 291, 300 Congr 57, 68, 83, 86, 90, 122 Fug 89, 120, 126, 175, 202 Mut 143, 152, 202, 254 Somn 1:126, 142, 221 Somn 2:10, 23, 156, 301 Abr 56 Ios 36, 88, 105, 196, 197 Mos 2:60 Spec 1:28 Prob 29, 116 Flacc 74, 131 Legat 80, 208, 350, 352 QG 3:18, 21 QE 2:25b

εἰσαγωγή Deus 52 Her 102 Hypoth 7:1 QG 1:55a

εἰσαεί (7) Sacr 22, 40 Det 75, 77 Conf 61 Fug 55 Somn 1:149

εἰσακοή Mut 99 Somn 2:33

εἰσακοντίζω Mos 1:131

εἰσακούω (8) Leg 2:88 Post 12 Ebr 14, 14 Migr 174 Congr 70 Somn 1:92 Somn 2:175

εἰσάπαν (30) Leg 3:189 Cher 10, 66 Det 143 Gig 20 Deus 73, 120, 144 Agr 85 Ebr 13, 51, 156 Conf 76, 120, 175 Congr 5 Mut 17, 24, 36, 49, 186 Somn 1:16, 17, 28, 44, 82, 117, 152 QG 2:12d, 4:194

εἰσαῦθις (6) Opif 155 Post 145, 150 Her 44, 221 Abr 248

εἰσβιάζομαι Spec 1:325

εἰσβολή Mos 1:239, 251

εἰσδύνω (εἰσδύομαι) (8) Cher 98 Sacr 95 Det 17 Conf 185 Decal 63 Prov 2:35, 62 QE isf 21

εἰσδύομαι εἰσδύνω

εἴσειμι (35) Leg 3:126 Deus 2 Plant 35 Ebr 129, 136 Migr 104, 104 Her 84 Somn 1:10, 188, 216 Somn 2:184, 189, 231 Mos 1:302 Mos 2:90, 91, 133, 138 Spec 1:72, 75, 84 Spec 3:205, 206 Spec 4:57, 77, 142 Virt 90 Praem 113 Contempl 72 Flacc 167, 181 Legat 214, 293 QG 4:33b

εἰσελαύνω Somn 2:133

εἰσέρπω Legat 48

εἰσέρχομαι (77) Opif 78 Leg 2:34, 34, 56, 56 Leg 3:81, 99, 118, 238, 241 Sacr 39 Det 63 Post 14, 67, 77, 177, 180 Gig 31, 54 Deus 131, 131, 132, 132, 133, 135, 138, 138 Agr 105 Plant 95, 96 Ebr 73, 213 Conf 144 Migr 44, 142 Her 69, 81, 81, 203 Congr 1, 12, 14, 122, 123, 123, 125, 126 Fug 113, 124, 168 Mut 7 Somn 1:85 Somn 2:75, 76, 106, 217, 217 Abr 107, 116 Ios 230 Mos 1:158 Mos 2:9, 153, 153, 179 Spec 1:242 Spec 2:101 Spec 3:209 Spec 4:14 Aet 67 Legat 306, 349 QG 2:11, 13a, 48, 4:51a, 145

εἰσέτι Mos 2:216

εἰσηγέομαι (55) Leg 3:1 Cher 9, 33, 121 Sacr 121 Det 134 Post 34, 42, 53, 175 Gig 60 Deus 72, 125 Agr 43 Ebr 25, 25, 80, 199 Conf 144 Her 243, 246, 246 Mut 10, 91, 106, 150, 170 Somn 1:191 Ios 73 Mos 2:51 Spec 1:329, 331 Spec 2:71, 73, 104, 129, 201, 246 Spec 4:72, 102,

151, 157, 210 Virt 69, 139 Praem 23 Aet 47, 75, 75 Flacc 19, 41 Legat 51 QG 1:64d, 4:30 QE 2:18

εἰσήγησις (8) Sacr 15 Deus 18 Conf 34 Abr 101 Spec 1:3 Spec 4:215 Virt 3, 227

εἰσηγητής (13) Opif 171 Leg 3:35, 79 Det 6, 28 Post 38 Ebr 18 Spec 1:324, 344 Spec 2:60 Spec 4:120 Praem 75 QG 1:20

εἴσθεσις Deus 42

εἰσκομίζω (11) Ios 205 Spec 1:72, 74, 104 Spec 2:207 Contempl 25, 54, 54, 73, 81 Legat 308

εἰσκρίνω Leg 1:32, 32 Plant 14 Somn 1:31

εἴσκρισις Contempl 67

εἴσοδος (23) Opif 119 Sacr 96, 135 Deus 60, 132 Ebr 9 Fug 183 Somn 1:235 Abr 116 Ios 182 Mos 1:302 Mos 2:62, 78, 91, 92, 93, 94, 136 Spec 1:156, 261 Flacc 113, 115 Prov 2:26

εἰσοικίζω (17) Her 265 Congr 53 Fug 117 Mut 154 Somn 1:149 Decal 14, 80, 145 Spec 1:89 Spec 2:170, 230 Virt 28, 217, 223 Praem 25 Legat 20 QE 2:25b

εἴσοπτρον Migr 98

εἰσοράω Prob 101

εἰσπέμπω Ios 27 Legat 125

εἰσπέτομαι Mos 1:108

εἰσπηδάω Legat 364

εἰσπίπτω Spec 4:85

εἰσπνοή Spec 3:114

εἰσποιέω Mos 1:32, 33 Spec 2:165

εἰσποιητός Sobr 56

εἰσπορεύω Leg 3:125 Sacr 57 Deus 1 Ebr 127, 138

εἰσπράσσω Spec 2:73

εἰσρέω Abr 42

εἰστρέχω Flacc 113 Legat 365

εἰσφέρω (36) Opif 146 Sacr 72 Agr 5 Ebr 22, 22, 23, 95 Conf 185 Migr 97 Her 113, 145, 145, 145 Somn 1:122 Somn 2:176 Abr 226 Ios 135, 176 Mos 1:316 Mos 2:136, 178 Spec 1:77, 139, 139, 139, 142, 294 Spec 2:72, 205 Spec 3:51 Spec 4:113 Virt 84 Flacc 11 Legat 51, 224, 232

εἰσφοιτάω Legat 307

εἰσφορά (6) Ebr 15 Congr 114 Spec 1:77, 140, 144 Spec 2:233

εἴσω (ἔσω) (55) Opif 166 Leg 3:40, 239 Post 104, 118 Gig 53 Deus 38, 132 Ebr 135 Migr 222 Her 81, 81, 82, 83 Congr 10 Fug 34, 98 Mut 43, 44, 112 Somn 1:216 Somn 2:126 Ios 146 Mos 1:321 Mos 2:87, 93, 95, 152, 153, 180, 182 Spec 1:71, 156, 159, 171, 231, 261, 274, 296 Spec 2:121 Spec 3:10, 132, 169 Spec 4:220 Virt 128 Praem 28, 145 Prob 21 Contempl 30 Aet 21, 78 Legat 188, 306 Prov 2:18 QG 4:80

εἶτα (251) Opif 37, 40, 41, 54, 55, 101, 101, 167 Leg 1:91 Leg 2:73, 73 Leg 3:6, 18, 97, 115, 123, 152, 179, 212, 217, 227, 235 Cher 54, 68, 106 Sacr 76, 84 Det 11, 19, 67, 77, 134 Post 60, 65, 116, 159 Gig 13 Deus 26, 39, 103, 131, 176 Agr 44, 60, 75, 114, 119, 150, 157, 175 Plant 81, 113 Ebr 151 Conf 59 Migr 79, 137 Her 130, 134, 161, 198, 224, 274, 315 Congr 159 Fug 91, 92 Mut 46, 64, 85, 165, 177, 199, 237 Somn 1:57, 95, 129, 131, 166 Somn 2:12, 13, 43, 44, 51, 65, 69, 71, 76, 79, 89, 140, 147, 220, 284, 289, 296, 299 Abr 136, 228, 261 Ios 23, 30, 90, 101, 102, 119, 127, 127, 127, 166, 182, 196, 197, 201, 218, 226, 237 Mos 1:11, 15, 17, 37, 89, 92, 139, 141, 164, 168, 169, 182, 193, 195, 208, 217, 246, 270, 275, 277, 282 Mos 2:154, 162, 166, 178, 210, 227, 247, 260, 278 Decal 9, 66, 90, 95, 115, 128 Spec 1:34, 68, 86, 87, 105, 152, 188, 193, 193, 194, 199, 210, 210, 211, 262, 268, 268, 323 Spec 2:96, 127 Spec 3:43, 70, 80, 82, 101, 147, 177, 187, 188, 190 Spec 4:64, 127, 129, 222 Virt 77, 160, 163, 174 Praem 5, 158 Prob 32, 63, 82, 86, 101, 111, 117, 123, 160 Contempl 13, 53, 55, 84, 85 Aet 19, 40, 62, 125, 128 Flacc 5, 38, 39, 51, 54, 96, 130, 131, 137, 148, 152, 185 Legat 44, 56, 79, 95, 98, 141, 162, 165, 199, 211, 229, 235, 256, 257, 260, 313, 359, 363, 365 Hypoth 6:6, 7:15 Prov 2:21, 26 QG 1:74, 2:68a, 71a, 4:110a, 130

εἴτε (98) Opif 18, 29, 140, 140, 140, 140 Leg 2:17, 17 Cher 16, 16 Det 76, 76, 76, 76 Post 137, 137 Agr 118, 118 Plant 144, 144, 171, 171 Her 158, 158 Fug 46, 46 Somn 1:91, 91 Somn 2:147, 147, 147, 170, 170 Abr 21, 21, 47, 47 Ios 184, 184 Mos 1:142, 142, 211, 211 Mos 2:154, 154 Spec 1:51, 51, 284, 284, 284 Spec 3:24, 24, 27, 43, 43, 71, 71, 167, 167, 168, 168, 168 Praem 40, 40, 125, 125 Contempl 13 Aet 95, 95 Flacc 9, 9, 9, 33, 33 Legat 211, 211, 245, 245, 245, 260, 260, 338, 338 Hypoth 6:1, 6:1, 6:9, 6:9, 7:7, 7:7 QG 1:55c, 55c QG isf 8, 8 QG (Par) 2:6, 2:6 QE 2:45a, 45a QE isf 22

ἐκ (καί) (2152) Opif 9, 13, 13, 14, 17, 18, 19, 20, 21, 22, 23, 27, 31, 33, 38, 41, 41, 41, 42, 43, 44, 44, 44, 44, 45, 48, 49, 50, 51, 51, 51, 51, 52, 54, 54, 56, 59, 60, 60, 60, 60, 60, 60, 60, 67, 81, 81, 85, 91, 95, 97, 97, 98, 100, 101, 102, 102, 103, 106, 106, 106, 107, 108, 108, 108, 109, 114, 116, 117, 123, 125, 126, 127, 128, 131, 131, 132, 134, 135, 135, 135, 136, 136, 137, 137, 137, 140, 142, 146, 155, 155, 156, 158, 158, 161, 169, 171 Leg 1:2, 2, 15, 20, 25, 28, 28, 31, 32, 37, 42, 45, 55, 56, 63, 65, 65, 76, 78, 83, 86, 96, 96 Leg 2:2, 4, 9, 13, 16, 19, 19, 19, 20, 20, 34, 39, 40, 40, 41, 41, 41, 41, 42, 44, 44, 45, 45, 45, 45, 46, 46, 46, 59, 59, 60, 60, 84, 86, 87, 94, 94, 94, 96 Leg 3:7, 8, 10, 42, 42, 50, 67, 68, 69, 70, 75, 76, 81, 81, 81, 84, 88, 92, 93, 94, 95, 102, 104, 134, 144, 146, 161, 161, 161, 162, 162, 175, 177, 177, 179, 180, 181, 185, 185, 187, 197, 200, 202, 210, 212, 217, 225, 225, 225, 229, 229, 234, 235, 235, 241, 244, 244, 246, 247, 250, 252 Cher 10, 11, 15, 20, 29, 36, 38, 43, 47, 47, 49, 53, 53, 54, 55, 56, 56, 62, 62, 69, 73, 79, 88, 91, 96, 102, 102, 103, 104, 109, 110, 113, 115, 121, 125, 125, 126, 127 Sacr 4, 7, 15, 24, 29, 30, 31, 33, 34, 35, 38, 39, 39, 40, 40, 44, 47, 62, 62, 63, 71, 74, 79, 79, 79, 83, 85, 86, 89, 101, 104, 104, 106, 108, 114, 114, 115, 118, 119, 126, 137 Det 1, 2, 5, 6, 6, 7, 7, 8, 8, 10, 15, 19, 33, 36, 40, 43, 44, 48, 48, 56, 57, 59, 59, 60, 61, 64, 69, 77, 78, 79, 81, 83, 86, 87, 104, 106, 108, 110, 110, 114, 114, 114, 115, 115, 116, 118, 118, 118, 122, 124, 125, 127, 130, 131, 134, 134, 136, 150, 154, 163, 171, 174 Post 4, 5, 5, 7, 8, 9, 9, 11, 12, 15, 16, 16, 19, 21, 22, 26, 26, 28, 31, 33, 42, 42, 43, 44, 46, 52, 63, 67, 71, 76, 81, 85, 103, 114, 115, 119, 127, 128, 129, 132, 134, 135, 137, 137, 139, 141, 149, 153, 155, 164, 164, 166, 166, 167, 167, 167, 169, 169, 169, 175, 177, 178, 181, 182 Gig 4, 4, 14, 18, 18, 33, 35, 46, 59, 64 Deus 12, 22, 23, 26, 28, 28, 37, 38, 39, 46, 46, 46, 47, 56, 65, 65, 66, 66, 70, 73, 75, 79, 84, 88, 96, 97, 109, 110, 117, 119, 119, 119, 127, 132, 138, 155, 156, 157, 158 Agr 1, 1, 4, 5, 7, 7, 7, 9, 21, 31, 33, 36, 37, 39, 42, 46,

47, 47, 49, 62, 70, 90, 93, 95, 105, 105, 110, 112, 118, 134, 142, 146, 147, 148, 148, 174 Plant 2, 3, 3, 3, 3, 6, 7, 12, 22, 24, 34, 43, 44, 46, 63, 68, 88, 101, 107, 115, 115, 115, 120, 123, 124, 124, 124, 124, 124, 124, 129, 138, 147, 148, 155, 155, 170, 172, 172, 175 Ebr 7, 14, 14, 19, 28, 28, 31, 44, 61, 61, 61, 61, 61, 66, 67, 69, 86, 87, 115, 121, 131, 132, 136, 142, 152, 160, 160, 163, 164, 166, 186, 187, 187, 190, 191, 191, 192, 193, 193, 197, 206, 208, 211, 214, 219, 222, 222, 222 Sobr 2, 20, 22, 23, 24, 26, 27, 27, 28, 29, 32, 36, 65 Conf 1, 7, 7, 8, 13, 14, 15, 20, 20, 41, 51, 57, 61, 62, 65, 65, 74, 75, 77, 88, 91, 103, 108, 110, 116, 118, 119, 119, 144, 144, 160, 160, 163, 165, 168, 177, 177, 178, 178, 181, 181, 181, 183, 186, 186, 186, 187, 187, 188, 196 Migr 1, 1, 1, 2, 3, 7, 9, 10, 12, 30, 35, 38, 41, 41, 43, 43, 47, 69, 69, 86, 94, 98, 102, 104, 125, 136, 142, 150, 152, 154, 157, 162, 168, 170, 176, 176, 177, 177, 190, 191, 199, 201, 205, 205, 211, 213, 213, 213, 216 Her 7, 19, 20, 23, 40, 42, 42, 49, 51, 54, 54, 56, 58, 58, 58, 59, 62, 62, 62, 68, 71, 76, 76, 85, 93, 96, 103, 112, 125, 140, 142, 155, 159, 160, 181, 187, 188, 191, 197, 197, 213, 214, 216, 216, 218, 218, 245, 247, 258, 273, 274, 277, 277, 277, 279, 281, 282, 282, 283, 284, 295, 296, 306, 311 Congr 1, 2, 3, 8, 12, 12, 14, 24, 30, 32, 33, 33, 39, 40, 52, 53, 54, 59, 59, 60, 72, 74, 76, 82, 87, 90, 94, 95, 105, 106, 113, 117, 117, 117, 117, 128, 130, 131, 141, 146, 152, 163, 163, 169, 171, 173, 178 Fug 10, 12, 24, 24, 48, 52, 62, 67, 67, 67, 72, 73, 78, 79, 81, 87, 87, 90, 102, 110, 114, 117, 118, 137, 137, 142, 142, 149, 149, 162, 171, 178, 195, 199, 200, 200 Mut 13, 17, 39, 49, 56, 63, 72, 76, 81, 84, 86, 88, 91, 99, 100, 100, 102, 106, 110, 111, 115, 124, 130, 132, 134, 139, 141, 142, 144, 145, 149, 151, 156, 159, 177, 180, 184, 186, 199, 203, 203, 205, 207, 209, 219, 219, 229, 237, 237, 242, 246, 256, 258, 260 Somn 1:2, 11, 12, 15, 15, 19, 20, 23, 23, 29, 37, 38, 47, 49, 75, 89, 91, 108, 137, 139, 144, 145, 151, 151, 155, 155, 155, 155, 155, 155, 155, 155, 155, 155, 162, 163, 165, 169, 176, 179, 186, 189, 191, 191, 192, 194, 194, 195, 205, 205, 211, 212, 217, 220, 249, 254 Somn 2:1, 10, 18, 20, 24, 28, 29, 34, 40, 41, 41, 51, 56, 56, 72, 82, 90, 99, 106, 109, 137, 144, 147, 152, 152, 152, 152, 169, 180, 186, 190, 190, 191, 191, 200, 209, 209, 209, 214, 216, 216, 221, 222, 227, 227, 232, 241, 250, 263, 276, 282, 292 Abr 6, 6, 8, 24, 24, 24, 24, 24, 24, 26, 40, 47, 51, 52, 52, 52, 56, 59, 70, 75, 83, 85, 86, 88, 95, 95, 99, 107, 112, 122, 131, 133, 136, 139, 151, 153, 164, 164, 164, 165, 168, 170, 171, 174, 183, 191, 196, 205, 210, 220, 226, 229, 230, 232, 238, 245, 246, 248, 251, 254, 254 Ios 1, 1, 6, 10, 25, 36, 40, 40, 50, 52, 56, 57, 57, 60, 70, 78, 79, 81, 82, 84, 89, 98, 101, 106, 110, 111, 113, 113, 130, 167, 172, 177, 184, 186, 198, 215, 232, 232, 233, 234, 236, 238, 242, 254, 255, 258, 269 Mos 1:4, 13, 17, 19, 23, 26, 27, 34, 39, 40, 42, 42, 47, 56, 63, 64, 64, 65, 67, 72, 72, 88, 90, 93, 97, 97, 97, 102, 105, 107, 107, 113, 115, 117, 117, 117, 117, 119, 122, 122, 128, 130, 132, 132, 134, 139, 139, 144, 147, 149, 164, 173, 184, 185, 191, 195, 196, 207, 209, 211, 215, 216, 216, 221, 221, 225, 228, 229, 231, 231, 233, 236, 243, 251, 251, 253, 254, 255, 256, 259, 263, 265, 265, 270, 272, 274, 274, 278, 279, 279, 282, 290, 306, 312, 312, 317, 323, 327, 327, 330 Mos 2:1, 2, 5, 17, 24, 25, 25, 27, 34, 35, 36, 39, 43, 55, 56, 58, 64, 69, 75, 78, 80, 84, 86, 87, 87, 88, 88, 88, 88, 90, 91, 91, 93, 104, 105, 112, 113, 119, 119, 121, 121, 124, 124, 127, 127, 130, 132, 133, 135, 139, 142, 148, 152, 152, 154, 156, 162, 163, 164, 169, 169, 170, 180, 181, 181, 183, 188, 188, 188, 188, 193, 207, 210, 210, 210, 210, 212, 225, 233, 238, 251, 252, 256, 260, 266, 266, 266, 267 Decal 8, 13, 16, 16, 18, 27, 27, 27, 31, 33, 34, 39, 45, 46, 48, 81, 92, 102, 103, 109, 111, 129, 137, 140, 141, 142, 148, 150, 155, 155, 164 Spec 1:10, 22, 22, 30, 51, 51, 53, 55, 64, 66, 69, 69, 72, 75, 75, 78, 79, 80, 82, 84, 87, 87, 92, 93, 96, 101, 101, 103, 108, 108, 110, 110, 113, 115, 126, 126, 127, 134, 134, 138, 141, 142, 143, 146, 151, 151, 158, 159, 162, 173, 184, 193, 193, 198, 199, 199, 201, 203, 203, 204, 208, 211, 239, 246, 248, 248, 249, 253, 259, 262, 262, 262, 264, 266, 266, 274, 275, 278, 279, 287, 290, 291, 291, 293, 296, 300, 300, 303, 310, 313, 314, 317, 318, 319, 326, 327, 329, 331, 332, 332, 333, 338, 344, 344 Spec 2:13, 20, 21, 23, 35, 40, 47, 56, 58, 58, 59, 64, 64, 68, 69, 73, 74, 77, 78, 80, 83, 88, 88, 89, 93, 94, 94, 107, 109, 109, 111, 119, 121, 123, 123, 123, 126, 135, 136, 136, 139, 139, 139, 149, 160, 168, 172, 175, 177, 177, 179, 187, 196, 199, 204, 206, 209, 215, 217, 217, 227, 227, 228, 232, 233, 237, 237, 239, 250, 254, 260, 260 Spec 3:4, 5, 13, 18, 23, 24, 26, 28, 29, 34, 35, 39, 45, 48, 49, 58, 58, 65, 69, 76, 78, 86, 92, 92, 92, 98, 106, 111, 111, 113, 117, 122, 125, 128, 128, 135, 139, 142, 163, 163, 182, 182, 187, 190, 193, 201 Spec 4:5, 16, 18, 24, 29, 39, 40, 56, 60, 61, 68, 68, 74, 79, 82, 91, 107, 127, 132, 143, 144, 150, 154, 154, 157, 158, 158, 166, 174, 178, 179, 182, 187, 187, 187, 187, 187, 187, 187, 195, 202, 203, 210, 212, 212, 214, 223, 224 Virt 2, 7, 8, 26, 33, 34, 37, 39, 42, 42, 44, 46, 49, 50, 52, 55, 55, 56, 65, 67, 67, 67, 76, 76, 76, 79, 79, 80, 82, 90, 90, 98, 110, 115, 115, 116, 119, 122, 122, 122, 124, 128, 129, 133, 135, 135, 140, 141, 145, 156, 176, 176, 178, 179, 179, 180, 180, 180, 180, 180, 180, 183, 187, 189, 189, 190, 192, 193, 197, 198, 199, 199, 204, 206, 207, 207, 208, 208, 211, 211, 219, 221, 222, 223, 224, 225, 227, 227 Praem 9, 9, 13, 21, 21, 22, 24, 25, 27, 31, 43, 49, 58, 58, 64, 64, 64, 66, 71, 73, 73, 82, 85, 86, 89, 89, 91, 97, 104, 105, 109, 110, 115, 116, 117, 117, 120, 128, 133, 135, 137, 137, 138, 145, 146, 148, 148, 148, 149, 150, 151, 151, 152, 154, 154, 159, 162, 167 Prob 7, 10, 18, 18, 23, 25, 35, 41, 41, 52, 56, 57, 61, 70, 76, 77, 87, 87, 88, 91, 96, 98, 98, 99, 99, 106, 107, 111, 114, 118, 124, 126, 129, 136, 148, 149, 149, 149, 149, 151, 151, 160 Contempl 2, 4, 5, 8, 12, 12, 13, 14, 15, 20, 23, 23, 28, 30, 32, 33, 46, 51, 51, 61, 63, 63, 65, 67, 78, 79, 85, 86 Aet 2, 4, 4, 5, 5, 5, 6, 7, 8, 20, 20, 21, 25, 26, 26, 26, 28, 30, 38, 42, 47, 52, 53, 55, 57, 58, 59, 59, 59, 62, 69, 69, 71, 74, 74, 78, 78, 79, 79, 80, 80, 80, 86, 86, 89, 91, 92, 93, 94, 94, 98, 98, 98, 98, 99, 100, 100, 100, 101, 101, 101, 103, 105, 107, 112, 115, 116, 118, 123, 127, 129, 131, 139, 143, 149, 149 Flacc 3, 7, 9, 15, 17, 18, 23, 24, 25, 32, 35, 39, 41, 41, 46, 55, 56, 57, 57, 57, 59, 62, 69, 75, 85, 89, 91, 94, 101, 103, 103, 106, 108, 115, 120, 123, 126, 128, 130, 135, 146, 146, 151, 151, 169, 170, 172, 176, 179, 185, 187, 191 Legat 7, 9, 9, 12, 17, 18, 19, 20, 20, 20, 23, 25, 38, 54, 57, 67, 68, 68, 74, 74, 77, 80, 82, 83, 88, 95, 101, 106, 108, 114, 115, 120, 123, 123, 124, 126, 133, 135, 137, 146, 157, 161, 167, 169, 170, 174, 179, 181, 192, 196, 196, 198, 199, 199, 202, 206, 210, 213, 213, 216, 218, 228, 230, 258, 263, 265, 270, 270, 279, 280, 282, 290, 293, 293, 298, 304, 305, 308, 312, 312, 317, 322, 323, 325, 326, 340, 351, 361 Hypoth 0:1, 6:1, 6:2, 6:4, 6:7, 6:10, 7:6, 7:6, 7:6, 7:10, 7:11, 7:13, 7:19, 11:10, 11:13 Prov 1, 2:12, 25, 29, 32, 40, 45, 55, 59, 63, 64, 66, 67, 68 QG 1:28, 28, 28, 51, 51, 55c, 58, 58, 58, 64b, 70:1, 74, 76b, 76b, 77, 96:1,

100:1b, 2:5a, 11, 11, 14, 15b, 54a, 54a, 54d, 54d, 64b, 68a, 68a, 71a, 71a, 3:3, 3, 23, 23, 24, 61, 4:8b, 51b, 51b, 145, 167, 169, 174, 189, 200a, 200c, 204 QG isf 5, 5, 5, 5 QG (Par) 2:1, 2:2, 2:2, 2:2, 2:2, 2:2, 2:3, 2:4, 2:5, 2:5, 2:6, 2:6, 2:7 QE 1:7b, 2:2, 3b, 16, 24a, 46, 46, 50b QE isf 22, 32

ἑκασταχοῦ Virt 61 Legat 119, 215

ἕκαστος (747) Opif 15, 18, 18, 23, 31, 46, 54, 56, 62, 64, 69, 73, 82, 103, 113, 113, 115, 116, 117, 130, 138, 141, 143, 146, 147, 148, 149, 165, 166 Leg 1:28, 64, 65, 70, 87, 89, 91 Leg 2:2, 16, 17, 39, 75 Leg 3:21, 43, 69, 111, 157, 165, 170, 184, 202, 216, 220, 220, 230, 245, 247, 250 Cher 22, 23, 33, 33, 61, 66, 67, 75, 76, 78, 91, 105, 112, 112, 120, 129 Sacr 15, 20, 30, 55, 59, 74, 75, 75, 82, 84, 85, 85, 103, 104, 106, 108, 126 Det 7, 7, 8, 18, 23, 74, 82, 98, 99, 101, 103, 111, 114, 129, 131, 142, 148, 151, 172, 173, 177 Post 5, 14, 14, 20, 36, 41, 53, 53, 56, 59, 74, 82, 83, 83, 84, 89, 99, 110, 115, 126, 127, 128, 162, 168, 171, 175, 185 Gig 7, 8, 10, 30, 37, 51, 60, 60 Deus 19, 41, 43, 56, 79, 126, 148, 153, 167, 176 Agr 9, 13, 13, 22, 30, 45, 46, 53, 58, 78, 95, 97, 108, 116, 124, 130, 132, 136, 138, 142 Plant 21, 29, 31, 75, 79, 84, 92, 102, 105, 108, 126, 176 Ebr 11, 15, 22, 37, 56, 67, 67, 67, 67, 102, 103, 106, 106, 118, 165, 167, 178, 181, 187, 192, 193, 195, 216 Sobr 29, 35, 36, 40, 42, 61 Conf 1, 12, 21, 23, 44, 46, 48, 49, 53, 87, 89, 110, 111, 123, 140, 155, 162, 164, 174, 187, 188, 189, 189, 195 Migr 3, 10, 26, 39, 40, 42, 42, 55, 58, 100, 105, 111, 116, 129, 136, 136, 137, 179, 186, 189, 189, 189, 202, 204, 219, 219 Her 18, 52, 73, 93, 108, 110, 115, 116, 116, 119, 121, 132, 136, 145, 152, 154, 156, 157, 173, 188, 191, 191, 193, 195, 196, 196, 212, 213, 221, 222, 225, 231, 236, 247, 281, 282, 282, 286, 289, 312 Congr 2, 4, 19, 20, 25, 44, 64, 65, 78, 101, 106, 113, 136, 143, 144, 150 Fug 12, 13, 25, 37, 46, 88, 90, 189, 210 Mut 10, 63, 108, 111, 130, 184, 195, 197, 201, 232, 232 Somn 1:27, 40, 42, 42, 55, 64, 103, 104, 133, 135, 145, 193, 201, 222 Somn 2:1, 11, 31, 33, 37, 78, 82, 98, 112, 116, 187, 210, 224, 243 Abr 34, 40, 40, 49, 53, 60, 63, 67, 72, 74, 124, 157, 220, 239, 240, 240 Ios 21, 37, 60, 81, 84, 99, 112, 127, 129, 136, 142, 143, 149, 151, 157, 161, 179, 182, 202, 217, 221, 226, 234, 235, 243 Mos 1:26, 29, 64, 72, 83, 92, 94, 130, 136, 137, 156, 189, 194, 202, 204, 206, 209, 213, 221, 227, 233, 252, 254, 265, 274, 277, 287, 290, 306, 317, 324 Mos 2:3, 9, 9, 27, 33, 37, 44, 60, 63, 63, 63, 67, 76, 77, 84, 94, 117, 124, 126, 129, 146, 148, 151, 151, 159, 159, 167, 171, 181, 184, 224, 225, 238, 258, 273, 288, 291 Decal 14, 14, 31, 35, 36, 37, 39, 52, 52, 55, 59, 66, 76, 84, 85, 87, 99, 142, 151, 158, 159, 161 Spec 1:3, 14, 39, 48, 69, 71, 77, 78, 78, 87, 89, 100, 134, 134, 137, 141, 144, 145, 158, 168, 168, 169, 171, 181, 182, 190, 191, 194, 198, 207, 209, 209, 211, 219, 247, 256, 276, 300, 327, 329, 336, 340, 343, 344 Spec 2:21, 34, 40, 42, 60, 85, 102, 113, 120, 143, 145, 146, 147, 148, 152, 199, 207, 215, 216, 216, 239, 242, 259 Spec 3:6, 7, 25, 33, 33, 51, 75, 131, 131, 153, 190, 191, 195, 199 Spec 4:50, 57, 69, 78, 107, 118, 131, 132, 133, 134, 142, 144, 148, 160, 161, 162, 170, 175, 194, 215, 219, 233, 235 Virt 3, 12, 16, 30, 32, 32, 33, 42, 43, 52, 81, 113, 144, 152, 162, 212, 227 Praem 2, 7, 22, 28, 49, 57, 61, 80, 98, 109, 110, 112, 119, 143, 148, 168 Prob 67, 119, 138, 140 Contempl 8, 21, 25, 27, 30, 49, 54, 81, 89 Aet 16, 25, 28, 32, 32, 34, 35, 35, 35, 41, 56, 69, 69, 75, 82, 83, 96, 117, 118, 129, 131, 144, 150 Flacc 5, 29, 44, 46, 94, 98, 115, 117, 131, 149, 163, 175, 186 Legat 22, 39, 43, 80, 83, 98, 107, 132, 147, 152, 153, 157, 206, 211, 213, 214, 216, 229, 238, 245, 251, 254, 264, 269, 273, 277, 280, 283, 310, 317, 321, 331, 351, 371 Hypoth 7:3, 7:13, 11:10, 11:11, 11:16 Prov 1, 2:15, 18, 36, 41, 52, 60, 64, 69 QG 1:17b, 2:12a, 4:173 QG (Par) 2:2, 23, 2:7 QE 2:20 QE isf 4, 8, 9, 26

ἑκάστοτε Leg 1:75 Her 213

ἑκάτερος (283) Opif 2, 13, 33, 38, 53, 63, 69, 78, 82, 91, 103, 116, 118, 135, 136, 145, 151, 152 Leg 1:28, 58, 68, 73 Leg 2:53, 53 Leg 3:67, 89, 118, 118, 229, 249 Cher 25, 26, 29, 81 Sacr 4, 28, 36, 36, 52, 109, 112, 137, 138 Det 54, 57, 82, 88, 102, 108 Post 10, 22, 32, 95, 100, 106, 172 Gig 28, 48 Deus 48, 80, 162, 165 Agr 46, 47, 80, 89, 99, 114, 145, 180 Plant 88, 100, 131, 143, 155, 158, 172 Ebr 8, 9, 35, 35, 85, 177, 185 Sobr 9, 21 Conf 173 Migr 54, 71, 105, 110, 117, 133, 148, 158 Her 121, 134, 138, 155, 177, 263, 311 Congr 26, 129, 154 Fug 120, 146 Mut 45, 66, 118, 189, 194, 263 Somn 1:18, 35, 38, 119, 159 Somn 2:8, 17, 134, 156, 158, 163, 169, 189, 215, 235, 238, 241, 263, 274 Abr 14, 88, 121, 122, 145, 157, 208, 220, 221, 267 Ios 12, 30, 104, 140, 205, 270 Mos 1:60, 115, 131, 142, 170, 233, 240, 257, 271 Mos 2:50, 69, 78, 80, 88, 89, 101, 112, 122, 123, 123, 133, 140, 165, 186, 253, 284, 286 Decal 20, 42, 51, 57, 72, 78, 110, 126, 159, 161, 161 Spec 1:33, 56, 92, 169, 172, 222, 228, 253, 258, 319, 324, 342 Spec 2:1, 63, 157, 207, 232, 256 Spec 3:16, 23, 31, 59, 87, 135, 170, 176, 176, 197, 202 Spec 4:1, 11, 31, 79, 88, 97, 102, 111, 142, 147, 168, 170, 173, 187, 211 Virt 13, 19, 27, 116, 130 Praem 2, 28, 33, 55, 63, 85, 99, 161 Prob 112, 146 Contempl 39, 51, 58, 83, 85 Aet 3, 7, 21, 43, 53, 113, 123, 136, 139, 146 Flacc 92, 147, 160 Legat 14, 54, 81, 97, 104, 111, 247, 288 Prov 2:71 QG 2:12d, 64a, 66, 66, 4:7*, 202a QG isf 5 QG (Par) 2:3 QE 2:2, 14, 25c

ἑκατέρωθεν (16) Leg 1:59 Plant 152 Her 216, 218, 223 Congr 8 Fug 49 Mos 1:179 Mos 2:78, 85, 102 Spec 1:86, 158 Contempl 86 Flacc 38 Legat 350

ἑκατόμβη Det 20 Spec 1:271 Legat 356

ἑκατόν (17) Gig 55, 55, 57 Plant 75, 108 Her 145 Mut 188, 189, 190, 192 Ios 268 Mos 2:89, 91 Decal 27 Spec 1:189 Spec 2:33 Flacc 43

ἑκατονταέτης Leg 3:85, 217 Mut 1, 176, 177

ἑκατονταετία Leg 3:70

ἑκατοντάρχης Congr 110 Mos 1:317 Flacc 86, 109 Legat 30

ἑκατονταρχία Abr 232

ἑκατοντάς (7) Mut 1, 2 Decal 27, 27, 27 Praem 94, 94

ἑκατοστεύω Mut 190, 268

ἑκατοστός Mut 2, 190, 191

ἐκβαίνω (7) Leg 1:3, 82 Leg 3:117 Sacr 95 Post 7 Conf 98 Congr 82

ἐκβάλλω (31) Opif 104 Leg 1:55, 55, 96 Leg 2:63, 63 Leg 3:149 Cher 1, 1, 2, 3, 8, 8, 9, 10, 97 Det 147, 147, 149, 149, 150, 150, 152, 156, 163, 163 Post 10 Fug 114, 114, 145 QE 2:25a

ἐκβιάζω Decal 144 Spec 2:9, 16 QE isf 31

ἐκβιβάζω Gig 65 Deus 55

ἐκβιβρώσκω Post 56

ἐκβλάστημα Leg 1:24 Post 48

ἔκβλητος Her 29 Fug 61

ἐκβοάω (12) Leg 3:213 Det 93 Conf 93 Her 14 Fug 161 Somn 2:65 Mos 1:112, 136 Spec 1:41, 272 Spec 2:198 QG 4:227

ἐκβόησις Det 92 Ebr 97, 102 Mos 2:163 Prob 141

ἐκβολή Opif 105

ἐκγίγνομαι (ἐκγίνομαι) (20) Det 35, 63 Post 88 Agr 87 Mut 108, 128, 185, 213, 225 Somn 1:50, 51 Abr 58 Mos 2:40, 225, 255 Spec 4:115, 140 Virt 176 Praem 30, 83

ἔκγονος (42) Opif 10, 38, 46, 75, 99 Leg 2:6 Leg 3:198 Sacr 134 Det 50, 51, 106, 116 Post 35, 40, 48, 74, 91, 124, 179 Ebr 33, 42, 93 Conf 55, 124 Migr 203 Her 261 Fug 98, 210, 211 Somn 1:122 Decal 117, 129 Spec 1:135, 137 Spec 3:16 Praem 61, 169 Contempl 68 Flacc 91, 136 Legat 322 QE 2:14

ἐκδακρύω Conf 92 Migr 15 Ios 217 Spec 3:193

ἐκδέχομαι (24) Opif 34, 80 Leg 2:2, 89 Leg 3:7, 12, 33, 206 Post 12, 39, 136 Deus 107 Agr 99 Plant 114 Fug 172 Mut 22 Somn 1:9, 118 Decal 177 Flacc 125, 147, 159 Hypoth 7:18 QG 4:202a

ἐκδέω Somn 2:83 Mos 1:52 Spec 3:160 Praem 58 Flacc 70

ἔκδηλος (9) Leg 1:100 Leg 2:30 Leg 3:120 Cher 61, 84 Sacr 30 Deus 121 Plant 20 Ebr 54

ἐκδημέω Abr 65, 65 Spec 4:142

ἔκδημος Spec 4:36

ἐκδιαιτάω (8) Gig 21 Ios 44 Mos 1:26, 31, 241, 298 Praem 98 Flacc 14

ἐκδιαίτησις (8) Ebr 21 Somn 2:123 Ios 254 Mos 1:278 Mos 2:167, 270 Spec 3:126 Flacc 50

ἐκδιδάσκω (9) Cher 46, 130 Sacr 76, 76, 112 Det 105 Post 130 Agr 84 Plant 66

ἐκδίδωμι (27) Leg 3:117, 194 Det 46 Post 77 Gig 15, 37 Deus 129 Agr 68 Ebr 12 Fug 74, 83 Somn 1:19 Somn 2:109 Ios 44, 219 Spec 1:241 Spec 2:251 Spec 3:88, 91, 121, 130, 167 Virt 124 Praem 138 Flacc 23 Legat 118, 121

ἐκδιηγέομαι Her 206 Mos 1:58, 235

ἐκδικέω Det 167, 167, 169, 173 Praem 147

ἐκδίκησις Leg 3:105, 106

ἐκδοχή Leg 2:2 Cher 25 Sacr 47 Det 155 QE 2:45a

ἐκδύνω ἐκδύω

ἐκδύω (ἐκδύνω) (10) Leg 2:55, 80 Cher 66, 76 Det 41 Plant 110 Mut 233 Somn 1:43 Spec 4:95 QE isf 21

ἐκεῖ (ὁ) (68) Leg 1:43, 47, 63, 63, 66, 66, 67, 67, 67, 77, 77, 77, 77, 77, 79, 79, 101 Leg 3:115, 115, 152, 179, 179 Cher 41 Sacr 67, 67, 68, 68 Post 60 Gig 61 Plant 32, 41 Conf 1, 1, 1, 60, 168, 189 Migr 44 Her 18, 35 Congr 81, 86, 163, 163 Fug 77, 183 Mut 72 Somn 1:57, 57, 62 Somn 2:120, 121, 133, 221, 221 Ios 80, 247 Mos 1:193, 220, 223 Spec 1:37, 88 Spec 2:45 Virt 30 Praem 6 Prob 102 Contempl 85 Legat 225

ἐκεῖθεν (19) Leg 1:63 Post 76, 128 Conf 1, 1, 196, 197 Migr 196, 197 Her 255 Fug 23, 47, 48 Somn 2:241 Mos 1:114 Virt 10 Flacc 26, 47 Legat 205

ἐκεῖθι Plant 46 Migr 177 Fug 153 Legat 351

ἐκεῖνος (καί) (693) Opif 6, 16, 19, 26, 31, 31, 51, 52, 55, 65, 69, 71, 83, 86, 87, 98, 99, 101, 106, 131, 135, 136, 139, 142, 145, 148, 148, 152, 165 Leg 1:3, 35, 55, 63, 66, 78, 92, 101, 106, 106, 108, 108 Leg 2:4, 12, 14, 22, 24, 32, 84, 87, 93, 103 Leg 3:6, 24, 24, 60, 63, 64, 113, 145, 185, 192, 195, 212, 223, 243, 245, 253 Cher 22, 35, 37, 42, 50, 59, 63, 82, 98, 109, 122 Sacr 10, 25, 31, 31, 43, 121, 124, 129, 129, 134 Det 12, 26, 41, 44, 45, 52, 52, 55, 56, 69, 84, 85, 90, 94, 134, 141, 160 Post 39, 44, 48, 49, 90, 90, 126, 139, 145, 146, 147, 175 Gig 13, 24, 25, 58, 60 Deus 1, 1, 2, 21, 31, 31, 66, 72, 78, 86, 93, 99, 128, 138, 152, 161, 180, 182 Agr 5, 15, 48, 68, 69, 85, 99, 122, 123, 126, 152, 156, 168, 171, 173 Plant 18, 27, 68, 79, 81, 98, 105, 106, 128, 159, 167 Ebr 10, 37, 50, 67, 77, 87, 89, 93, 103, 107, 123, 131, 137, 148, 186, 193 Sobr 8, 17, 31, 33, 47, 48, 63 Conf 8, 50, 62, 63, 64, 99, 108, 145, 170, 180, 181 Migr 12, 26, 26, 46, 85, 93, 93, 94, 103, 106, 110, 118, 122, 149, 149, 173, 183, 183, 211 Her 12, 25, 39, 42, 50, 52, 57, 65, 71, 108, 189, 202, 215, 226, 227, 231, 240, 264, 280, 282, 313 Congr 10, 50, 69, 70, 70, 73, 78, 80, 111, 112, 123, 143, 144, 145, 145, 163 Fug 14, 16, 18, 27, 56, 72, 90, 93, 132, 151, 169, 172, 176, 190 Mut 7, 9, 24, 27, 31, 44, 80, 86, 128, 134, 143, 146, 159, 171, 174, 231, 255 Somn 1:4, 12, 15, 49, 58, 66, 98, 100, 115, 116, 117, 120, 128, 136, 158, 177, 188, 218, 232, 239 Somn 2:14, 21, 46, 70, 98, 104, 104, 108, 116, 161, 182, 206, 224, 229, 245, 257, 258, 279 Abr 4, 5, 6, 36, 38, 38, 40, 44, 45, 46, 48, 51, 56, 60, 67, 67, 69, 80, 95, 118, 124, 142, 146, 150, 151, 155, 165, 182, 184, 188, 197, 224, 224, 239, 241, 269, 269 Ios 5, 15, 17, 18, 37, 52, 54, 66, 76, 79, 83, 104, 111, 119, 128, 143, 143, 145, 170, 174, 176, 185, 189, 200, 219, 219, 220, 238, 258 Mos 1:10, 14, 51, 69, 84, 111, 135, 146, 160, 160, 165, 190, 210, 234, 245, 249, 264, 280, 280, 286, 292, 308, 309, 325 Mos 2:17, 21, 22, 29, 30, 40, 70, 127, 127, 128, 136, 142, 174, 188, 196, 207, 216, 225, 231, 242, 257, 276, 285 Decal 10, 18, 19, 33, 51, 53, 68, 70, 72, 80, 113, 114, 149, 154 Spec 1:53, 65, 87, 119, 128, 153, 154, 192, 213, 219, 234, 249, 280, 281, 291, 312, 313, 323, 328, 329, 344 Spec 2:16, 23, 34, 35, 35, 55, 82, 83, 87, 89, 93, 122, 132, 135, 137, 139, 141, 142, 145, 148, 151, 152, 153, 155, 158, 159, 164, 164, 176, 190, 210, 211, 218, 225, 225, 236, 237, 237, 239, 250, 256 Spec 3:21, 27, 32, 50, 55, 64, 75, 82, 102, 105, 122, 123, 125, 153, 156, 159, 173, 175, 180 Spec 4:34, 37, 53, 75, 81, 82, 123, 136, 143, 187, 194, 197, 200, 238 Virt 4, 22, 48, 49, 80, 88, 94, 117, 145, 152, 169, 179, 184, 192, 223 Praem 8, 40, 74, 78, 88, 103, 135, 138, 171 Prob 1, 12, 19, 22, 27, 31, 48, 60, 120, 125, 128, 136, 141, 144, 155 Contempl 2, 14, 40, 42, 73 Aet 13, 15, 15, 17, 27, 35, 39, 45, 46, 68, 71, 83, 85, 88, 104, 106, 107, 124, 128, 132, 138, 143 Flacc 1, 14, 22, 51, 56, 60, 117, 125, 143, 165, 181 Legat 16, 27, 52, 58, 65, 68, 80, 80, 81, 85, 88, 92, 103, 137, 141, 142, 149, 157, 160, 173, 190, 245, 307, 320, 321, 327, 356 Hypoth 6:1, 6:1, 6:3, 6:4, 6:6, 6:8, 6:8, 6:9, 7:1, 7:8, 7:15, 7:18, 7:19, 11:10 Prov 1, 2:5, 9, 10, 17, 60 QG 1:28, 55b, 65, 77, 77, 94, 2:54a, 62, 3:11c, 20b, 52, 4:191b, 198, 202a, 203, 227 QG (Par) 2:4, 2:6 QE 1:19, 2:2, 46 QE isf 23

ἐκεῖσε (καί) (22) Leg 3:38 Cher 13, 63, 81 Sacr 90 Post 22, 113 Gig 13 Agr 68, 75 Conf 78 Her 287 Fug 63 Abr 212 Mos 1:270 Mos 2:165 Decal 67 Spec 1:62 Spec 4:158 Legat 291 QG (Par) 2:4 QE 2:55b

ἐκεχειρία (31) Cher 92 Sacr 23 Conf 165 Migr 220 Congr 158 Ios 85, 254 Mos 2:22, 211 Decal 150, 161 Spec 1:192 Spec 2:42, 69, 93, 109, 117, 160 Spec 3:183 Virt

122, 226 Praem 155 Prob 17, 123, 148 Flacc 40, 67, 83, 171 Legat 12 Prov 2:64

ἐκζητέω Fug 142, 158

ἐκζωπυρέω Migr 66 Somn 2:299

ἐκηβολία Mos 1:291

ἐκήβολος Flacc 90

ἐκθαυμάζω Somn 2:70

ἐκθειάζω Leg 3:44

ἐκθειόω (8) Post 115 Conf 173 Decal 8, 53, 70, 79 Spec 1:10, 344

ἐκθερίζω Somn 2:23 Praem 128

ἔκθεσις Spec 3:110, 117 Virt 131

ἔκθεσμος (14) Sacr 32 Det 61, 72 Gig 32 Plant 35 Abr 135, 137 Mos 1:302 Spec 3:46, 77 Spec 4:204 Virt 219 Aet 51, 85

ἐκθέω Mos 1:333

ἐκθέωσις (6) Decal 81 Legat 77, 201, 332, 338, 368

ἐκθηεριόω (καί) Conf 164

ἐκθηλύνω (10) Cher 52 Sacr 103 Post 166 Agr 35 Plant 158 Somn 1:126 Somn 2:9 Mos 2:184 Spec 2:193 Spec 3:39

ἐκθηριόω Migr 210 Prob 106

ἐκθλίβω (9) Post 55 Somn 1:106 Somn 2:58, 159, 203, 204, 204 Mos 1:115, 211

ἔκθλιψις Praem 151

ἐκθνήσκω Mos 1:39 Decal 80

ἐκθυμιάω (7) Leg 1:42 Leg 3:11 Her 196, 199, 200 Somn 1:178 Somn 2:232

ἔκθυμος (7) Agr 151 Fug 144 Ios 182 Mos 1:33, 236 Legat 277, 277

ἐκκαθαίρω (7) Plant 64 Ebr 28 Somn 2:73, 158, 272 Mos 1:303 Decal 10

ἑκκαίδεκα Opif 94

ἐκκαίω Leg 3:248

ἐκκαλέω Spec 4:139 Legat 247

ἐκκαλύπτω Det 128

ἔκκαυμα Spec 2:251

ἔκκειμαι Mos 1:14

ἐκκενόω Post 132, 150

ἐκκεντέω Leg 3:242 Cher 32 Post 183

ἐκκηρύσσω Flacc 132

ἐκκλησία (23) Leg 3:8, 81, 81 Post 143, 177 Deus 111 Ebr 213, 213 Conf 144, 144 Migr 69 Her 251 Mut 204 Somn 2:184, 187 Abr 20 Decal 32, 45 Spec 1:325 Spec 2:44 Virt 108 Prob 138 Aet 13

ἐκκλησιάζω Migr 69 Ios 73 Decal 39 Prob 6

ἐκκλησιαστής Spec 1:55

ἐκκλίνω (6) Sacr 77 Post 102 Deus 145 Congr 125 Mut 160 Prob 159

ἐκκομίζω (7) Mos 1:100 Mos 2:179 Spec 1:127, 156, 232 Contempl 55 Flacc 75

ἐκκοπή QG 3:48

ἐκκόπτω (16) Leg 3:242 Det 105 Deus 68 Agr 11, 12, 17 Mut 62 Abr 96 Decal 67 Spec 3:184, 195, 196, 198, 201, 202 Legat 224

ἐκκρέμαμαι (11) Opif 141 Post 26, 27, 61 Deus 15 Agr 54 Mos 2:121 Spec 1:319 Spec 3:160, 178 Praem 77

ἐκκρεμάννυμι (6) Sacr 41 Agr 97 Conf 106 Migr 44, 168 Abr 170

ἐκκρίνω Leg 3:242 Cher 73 Mut 106

ἔκκρισις Opif 123 Mut 106

ἐκκύπτω Somn 2:233 QG 2:34a

ἐκλαλέω (29) Leg 1:104 Cher 48 Sacr 60, 62 Det 102, 175 Plant 134 Sobr 6, 32 Her 38 Fug 85, 191 Mut 244 Abr 29 Ios 5, 110, 168, 200, 247 Mos 1:283 Spec 2:50 Prob 108 Contempl 26 Flacc 32 Hypoth 11:16 Prov 2:32 QG 2:71a, 4:8c QG isf 2

ἐκλαμβάνω Leg 3:120, 240 Aet 7

ἐκλάμπω (13) Leg 2:30 Post 58 Agr 168 Mut 5 Somn 2:186 Abr 157 Ios 4, 124, 136 Mos 1:69, 166 Mos 2:41 Praem 171

ἐκλανθάνω (22) Leg 3:92 Cher 68 Post 115, 115 Agr 173 Congr 40, 73, 78, 159 Ios 64, 99, 109 Mos 1:106, 285 Mos 2:161, 165, 270 Spec 1:344 Spec 3:30 Spec 4:215 Virt 163, 179

ἐκλατομέω Deus 94 Fug 175

ἐκλέγω (17) Det 5 Gig 6, 64 Deus 50 Agr 153 Plant 56 Migr 60 Somn 1:62 Mos 1:152 Spec 2:109, 115, 122 Spec 4:212, 213 Virt 82 Prob 35 Hypoth 7:18

ἐκλείπω (32) Leg 3:218 Cher 8, 50 Sacr 3, 5, 5, 6, 8, 81 Det 28 Post 81, 82, 134 Plant 24 Ebr 58, 60 Conf 1, 44, 51, 162 Congr 60 Fug 128, 128, 131, 167 Somn 2:185 Ios 253 Mos 2:163, 271 Spec 3:155 QG 4:169, 169

ἐκλείχω Leg 3:186 Migr 143 Congr 55

ἔκλειψις (15) Opif 58 Det 28, 28, 28 Congr 60 Fug 128 Mos 1:123 Spec 3:187 Spec 4:52 Flacc 159 Prov 2:50, 50, 50 QG 4:169, 169

ἐκλεκτός (11) Cher 7 Gig 64 Mut 66, 69, 69, 71 Somn 2:216, 217 Abr 82, 83 QG 3:43

ἔκλευκος Contempl 51

ἐκλιπαρέω Flacc 31

ἐκλιχμάομαι Leg 3:186

ἐκλογεύς (6) Abr 228 Ios 135 Spec 1:143 Spec 2:93 Spec 3:159 Legat 199

ἐκλογή Spec 4:157 QE 2:46

ἐκλογίζομαι Mos 1:220 Spec 3:167 Virt 165 Aet 103

ἐκλογιστής Plant 57

ἔκλογος Contempl 54 Flacc 148

ἔκλυσις (6) Cher 82 Det 168 Conf 7 Legat 268 Hypoth 7:5 QG 2:64a

ἐκλυσσάω Conf 164

ἐκλύω (18) Leg 3:193 Sacr 80, 81, 86 Det 167 Post 112 Ebr 50 Her 25, 186 Congr 177 Abr 193 Ios 61 Mos 1:325 Decal 122 Spec 3:33 Virt 88 Aet 129 Flacc 78

ἐκμαγεῖον (14) Opif 71, 146 Deus 43 Her 57, 181, 231 Fug 12 Mut 223 Somn 2:206 Mos 2:118 Spec 1:47 Spec 2:152 Spec 3:83 Aet 15

ἐκμαίνω Her 70 Ios 269 Spec 2:9

ἐκμανής Conf 21 Praem 19 Legat 42, 121

ἐκμανθάνω Ebr 198 Congr 46 Mut 153

ἐκμαρτυρέω Sacr 92

ἐκμασάομαι Plant 35

ἐκμάσσω Fug 13

ἐκμελής (11) Leg 2:7 Leg 3:57 Cher 105 Ebr 116 Conf 15, 55, 150 Congr 16 Fug 42 Spec 1:343 Virt 74

ἐκμετρέω Mut 190

ἐκμιμέομαι Somn 1:123

ἐκμυσάσσομαι Spec 3:24

ἐκνέμω Spec 1:136 Spec 3:145 Flacc 46

ἐκνεοττεύω QG (Par) 2:3, 2:3, 2:3

ἐκνευρίζω Post 166 Spec 2:240 Praem 140, 157 Legat 189

ἐκνεύω Cher 41 Deus 170 Abr 152 Mos 2:82, 251

ἐκνήφω Sobr 1

ἐκνίζω (21) Cher 17, 95 Det 170 Deus 7, 9 Ebr 59 Migr 67 Her 93, 113 Fug 41 Mut 49, 124 Somn 1:82, 148, 211 Somn 2:25 Mos 2:199 Spec 1:188, 206, 259, 281

ἐκνικάω (7) Conf 103, 104 Somn 2:12 Abr 35 Ios 230 Spec 2:109 Prob 89

ἔκνομος (18) Det 171, 176 Gig 32 Ios 41 Mos 2:198, 214 Decal 131, 168 Spec 2:50 Spec 3:48 Spec 4:17, 197, 215 Praem 111, 126 Flacc 102, 189 Legat 103

ἐκνοσηλεύω Somn 1:69 Spec 1:343 Spec 2:102

ἑκούσιος (133) Leg 1:99 Leg 3:141, 144 Cher 75, 96 Sacr 48, 84, 129 Det 10, 97, 122, 147 Post 9, 10, 11, 11, 21, 48, 72, 75, 78 Deus 47, 48, 49, 75, 100, 113, 128, 129 Agr 173, 176, 180 Ebr 66, 94, 95, 123 Sobr 4 Conf 21, 177, 179 Migr 32, 169, 169, 206 Her 68, 123, 192, 240 Fug 53, 54, 65, 76, 78, 86, 102, 105, 108, 115, 115, 117 Mut 26, 57, 85, 270, 270 Somn 1:71, 131 Somn 2:174, 253, 253 Abr 6, 6, 40, 186 Ios 219, 240 Mos 1:224, 273 Mos 2:53, 59, 173, 231 Decal 62, 68, 142, 177 Spec 1:30, 103, 227, 235, 238, 259 Spec 2:52, 88, 196 Spec 3:15, 19, 34, 120, 128, 134, 134, 181 Spec 4:34, 76, 115, 150, 193 Virt 83, 94, 202 Praem 34, 54, 54, 138 Prob 24, 109 Contempl 13, 68 Flacc 50, 145 Legat 117, 308 Hypoth 11:2, 11:13 Prov 2:57 QG 1:21, 55a, 66, 66, 4:64 QG isf 13 QE isf 29

ἔκπαλαι Agr 152

ἐκπειράζω Congr 170

ἐκπέμπω (23) Opif 58 Det 13, 15, 146 Plant 19 Sobr 8 Conf 78 Her 263 Ios 10, 11, 161, 163, 166 Mos 1:87, 103, 258, 266, 282, 306 Mos 2:31 Spec 1:188 Flacc 112 Legat 281

ἐκπετάννυμι Leg 3:43 Ebr 101 Mut 21

ἐκπίμπλημι (10) Det 145 Abr 249 Mos 1:111, 184, 251 Mos 2:233 Prob 119 Flacc 98, 162 Prov 2:24

ἐκπίνω Spec 3:61 QG 2:68a

ἐκπίπτω (12) Leg 3:183 Cher 2 Post 169 Agr 127 Conf 69 Ios 132 Spec 2:251 Prob 127, 127, 127, 129 Prov 2:48

ἐκπληκτικός Mos 1:65

ἔκπληξις Mos 2:250 Prob 141 Flacc 87, 114 Legat 189

ἐκπληρόω (19) Opif 32 Cher 60 Post 6 Gig 27 Her 188 Fug 38, 75, 186 Somn 1:62, 68, 68 Somn 2:210 Abr 250 Mos 2:91 Spec 2:124, 148 Spec 3:85 Spec 4:235 Praem 108

ἐκπλήρωσις (12) Opif 146 Leg 1:104 Leg 3:34, 145, 145 Cher 110 Congr 91 Fug 144 Somn 2:201 Ios 243 Decal 175 Flacc 174

ἐκπληρωτικός Somn 2:203

ἐκπλήσσω Ios 218 Mos 1:81 Spec 1:73, 253 Prob 124

ἐκπλύνω Leg 3:141, 159 Migr 67

ἐκπνέω Post 113 Legat 125

ἐκποδών (21) Cher 50 Sacr 53 Det 178 Post 38 Deus 18 Agr 97 Ebr 192 Conf 112 Somn 2:67 Ios 17, 167, 245 Spec 2:95 Spec 3:85 Prob 19 Flacc 12, 145 Legat 24, 59, 68, 329

ἐκπολιορκέω Leg 2:91

ἐκπονέω (13) Cher 9 Det 165 Agr 55 Ebr 216 Migr 72, 178 Fug 8 Somn 1:57, 208, 251 Spec 2:206 Spec 4:48 Legat 46

ἐκπορεύω (11) Leg 1:63, 65, 65, 76 Leg 3:46, 174, 176 Post 128 Congr 170 Somn 2:277 QG 4:7*

ἐκπόρθησις Mos 1:263

ἐκπορίζω (12) Opif 10 Mos 1:11, 195, 201 Decal 99, 116 Spec 1:23, 283 Spec 2:240 Prob 8, 76 Contempl 19

ἐκπορνεύω Somn 1:89

ἐκπρεπής Post 92 Plant 65 Congr 124 Abr 94 Mos 2:111

ἐκπρόθεσμος Mos 2:225, 231 Spec 2:38 Spec 4:196

ἐκπυρόω (6) Leg 2:58 Aet 83, 88, 88, 90, 107

ἐκπύρωσις (19) Her 228 Spec 1:208, 208 Aet 4, 9, 47, 54, 76, 77, 81, 87, 88, 89, 90, 95, 99, 104, 105, 107

ἔκπωμα (13) Somn 2:60, 60, 249 Ios 91, 92, 207, 213, 216, 235 Contempl 49 Flacc 148 Legat 9 Prov 2:17

ἐκρέω Praem 129

ἐκρήγνυμι Post 122

ἐκρίπτω QE isf 13

ἐκρύπτω Mut 229

ἐκσοῦ QG 3:23

ἐκσπερματίζω Leg 3:150

ἔκσπονδος Spec 3:113

ἔκστασις (22) Leg 2:19, 31, 31 Cher 69, 116 Plant 147 Ebr 15 Her 249, 249, 250, 251, 251, 257, 257, 258, 263, 264, 265 Spec 3:99 Contempl 40 QG 1:24, 4:79b

ἐκστρατεύω Congr 92

ἔκτασις Post 116 Agr 6 Mos 1:103

ἐκτάσσω Mos 1:169, 331 Contempl 49 Flacc 5

ἐκτείνω (16) Leg 2:88, 88, 93 Leg 3:24, 33, 33 Det 90 Ebr 105 Mos 1:103, 120 Mos 2:285 Decal 135, 146 Spec 2:221 Spec 3:25 Flacc 1

ἐκτέμνω (45) Opif 73 Leg 3:128, 129, 130, 131, 131, 132, 140, 147, 251 Cher 96 Sacr 115 Det 124, 175 Deus 67, 130 Agr 17 Plant 107 Ebr 123, 139, 213 Conf 11 Migr 67, 143, 200, 201 Somn 2:14, 184 Mos 1:231 Spec 1:11, 66, 330, 331 Spec 2:96 Spec 3:31, 179 Spec 4:68 Praem 71, 72, 140 Aet 49 Legat 119 Hypoth 7:7 QE 2:25b, 25c

ἐκτενής Legat 60

ἐκτήκω Praem 146

ἐκτίθημι (7) Leg 1:59 Mos 1:10, 11, 12 Spec 3:115, 116 Prob 128

ἐκτικός Leg 2:22

ἐκτιμάω (20) Opif 128 Sacr 130 Plant 119 Ebr 80 Congr 152, 154, 156 Fug 57 Mut 173, 205 Mos 1:98, 153 Mos 2:15, 21 Spec 2:86 Spec 4:178 Virt 144, 225 Praem 117 Prob 66

ἐκτιναγμός Conf 68

ἐκτινάσσω Conf 69, 70

ἐκτίνω (6) Her 282 Mut 125 Spec 3:106 Spec 4:3, 5, 33

ἔκτισις Spec 4:11

ἐκτομή (6) Sacr 46 Migr 92 Mut 72 Spec 1:9, 9, 191

ἐκτοξεύω Det 149 Post 91, 140 Ebr 10 Congr 61

ἐκτόπιος Somn 2:130 Prob 6

ἔκτοπος (16) Agr 37 Plant 3 Ebr 29 Sobr 23 Migr 216 Mut 267 Somn 1:130 Abr 137 Ios 223 Mos 2:201 Spec 2:170 Virt 126, 136 Praem 38 Aet 76 Flacc 73

ἕκτος (13) Opif 13, 103, 104, 121, 123 Leg 1:2, 3, 3 Leg 2:11 Mos 1:320 Mos 2:266 Decal 21 Spec 2:41

ἐκτός (146) Opif 20, 91, 118, 142, 166 Leg 1:29, 30, 60, 60, 60, 82, 89 Leg 2:56, 60, 61, 62, 63 Leg 3:20, 40, 40, 40, 40, 64, 109, 120, 168, 183, 183, 239 Cher 57, 58, 65, 66, 96 Sacr 22, 49, 97, 105, 106, 115, 115 Det 4, 4, 7, 8, 9, 9, 15, 21, 53, 88, 103, 109, 110, 127, 136, 137, 154, 158 Post 3, 61, 61, 98, 112, 112, 115, 116, 117, 118, 119, 123, 135 Deus 27, 167 Agr 72, 101 Plant 7, 30, 69 Ebr 46, 190, 200 Sobr 13, 60, 61, 67, 68 Conf 17 Migr 15, 22, 203 Her 284, 285 Congr 136 Fug 148, 153, 190 Mut 32, 91, 111, 112, 221 Somn 1:184, 192, 192 Somn 2:9, 11, 70 Abr 154, 220, 221, 223, 226, 269 Ios 79, 131 Mos 2:53, 81, 82, 101 Decal 173 Spec 1:158, 224, 275 Spec 2:46 Spec 4:21 Virt 15, 187 Praem 88, 118, 129 Prob 55 Aet 20, 20, 20, 21, 21, 21, 22, 24, 78, 78, 102, 114 QG 4:43, 80

ἐκτραγῳδέω Mut 196 Somn 1:35

ἐκτραχηλίζω (14) Opif 158 Leg 3:109 Det 19 Fug 122 Somn 2:134 Abr 96 Ios 22 Spec 2:92 Spec 4:214, 218 Praem 29, 156 Flacc 118, 166

ἐκτραχύνω Mos 1:44 Legat 268, 302

ἐκτρέπω (40) Opif 63 Det 163 Gig 64 Deus 164 Migr 133 Congr 28 Fug 3, 32 Somn 1:246, 246 Somn 2:174, 295 Mos 1:165, 237, 246, 277 Decal 72 Spec 1:215, 239 Spec 2:23, 44 Spec 3:29, 176 Spec 4:167, 170 Virt 87 Praem 20, 148 Prob 63, 76 Contempl 37 Flacc 36, 64, 89, 167, 186 Legat 276, 332 Hypoth 11:11 QE 2:13a

ἐκτρέφω Leg 3:179, 179 Spec 2:29

ἐκτροπή Deus 162, 165

ἐκτρυχόω (ἐκτρύχω) Mos 1:128

ἐκτρύχω (ἐκτρυχόω) Virt 157

ἔκτρωμα Leg 1:76, 76

ἐκτυπόω Somn 2:191

ἐκτύπωμα Migr 103

ἐκτύπωσις Sacr 2

ἐκτυφόω Opif 1 Spec 1:28 Legat 162

ἐκφαγεῖν (ἐξεσθίω) Ios 110

ἐκφαίνω Opif 104 Abr 168

ἐκφέρω (21) Opif 164 Leg 3:128 Sacr 62, 79 Det 110 Post 151 Agr 70, 152, 163 Her 198, 279 Fug 205, 206 Somn 2:98 Spec 3:31 Spec 4:79 Praem 125 Flacc 2 Legat 77, 262, 328

ἐκφεύγω (40) Leg 3:5, 35, 93, 236 Det 155 Agr 121, 145 Ebr 111 Conf 158 Migr 9, 82 Her 60, 142 Fug 25 Mut 26, 114 Somn 1:223, 256 Abr 86 Ios 71, 205, 210 Mos 1:143 Mos 2:65 Spec 1:235, 252 Spec 2:207 Spec 3:2, 8, 105, 197 Spec 4:201 Virt 130 Praem 88, 91 Legat 356, 368 Prov 1 QG (Par) 2:7 QE isf 2

ἐκφθείρω Spec 3:16, 101

ἐκφοιτάω Leg 3:89 Agr 34

ἐκφορέω Mos 1:141 Prob 102 Flacc 56 Legat 122, 129

ἔκφρων Ebr 197 Conf 16 Legat 132

ἔκφυλος Det 61 Deus 18 Fug 144 Abr 137

ἐκφυσάω Mut 154 Prob 71

ἔκφυσις (10) Opif 41, 103, 105 Deus 38 Agr 7 Spec 1:80, 148, 164 Spec 3:200 Aet 133

ἐκφύω (14) Sacr 25, 40 Post 129 Her 220, 268 Mut 159 Ios 91, 102 Mos 2:102, 179 Spec 1:217 Aet 57, 68 Flacc 17

ἐκφωνέω (6) Ebr 177 Mut 215 Somn 2:207 Abr 261 Ios 51 Flacc 162

ἐκφώνησις Mut 262

ἐκχέω (31) Opif 71, 80, 158 Sacr 32, 61, 66 Post 181 Deus 164 Ebr 149, 152 Somn 1:74, 74 Somn 2:281 Abr 76, 157 Mos 1:81, 115, 121, 169, 211 Spec 1:37 Spec 2:251 Spec 4:128 Aet 147 Flacc 9, 56, 122, 157, 190 Legat 127, 223

ἑκών (38) Sacr 23, 33, 133 Det 92 Gig 20, 33 Deus 47 Plant 146 Ebr 63, 122, 125, 128 Migr 222 Fug 53, 65 Mut 32, 53, 56, 242 Somn 1:7 Somn 2:137 Abr 211 Ios 269 Mos 1:163 Spec 1:127, 156, 160 Spec 2:87 Spec 3:77, 78, 141 Prob 36, 61, 116 Flacc 131 Legat 232 Hypoth 6:6 QG 1:68

ἐλαία (7) Plant 32, 71 Somn 2:58 Mos 2:180 Spec 1:134 Spec 2:20 Aet 63

ἐλαιολογέω Virt 91

ἔλαιον (27) Det 115, 117, 118 Fug 110, 176 Mut 84, 234 Somn 1:250 Somn 2:71, 74 Mos 2:152, 152, 223 Spec 1:134, 141, 179, 179, 248, 256 Spec 3:56 Spec 4:98, 125 Virt 95 Praem 107, 129 Aet 91 Prov 2:46

ἐλαιόω Conf 186

ἐλαιών (7) Deus 94, 96 Fug 175, 176 Spec 2:105 Virt 92 Praem 129

ἔλασις (6) Cher 9 Spec 3:181 Aet 103 Flacc 62, 105, 184

ἐλασσονέω Her 191

ἐλασσόω (26) Opif 87 Leg 2:3 Gig 25, 25, 27 Her 189, 194 Mut 183 Abr 211 Ios 179 Mos 1:315 Spec 2:138 Spec 4:206 Virt 46 Prob 12, 135 Contempl 61 Aet 65, 120, 123 Legat 158, 182, 214 Prov 2:66 QG 2:30, 3:22

ἐλάτη Sobr 8 Aet 64

ἐλάττωσις Mos 1:64

ἐλαύνω (55) Cher 10, 75, 80 Sacr 15, 129 Det 95 Post 116 Agr 161 Plant 61 Ebr 10, 109 Conf 196 Her 217 Congr 58 Fug 85, 85 Mut 112, 149, 205 Somn 2:83, 277 Abr 86, 203 Mos 1:50, 53, 140, 169, 277 Mos 2:158, 231 Decal 146 Spec 1:60, 150, 325, 326, 333 Spec 2:141, 157 Spec 3:49 Spec 4:25, 75 Virt 137, 146, 190 Praem 52 Prob 7, 7, 159 Aet 135 Flacc 123, 151, 172 Legat 49, 121, 359

ἔλαφος Agr 115 Ebr 174 Spec 4:105

ἐλαφρός Leg 1:42 Ebr 32

ἐλαχύς (107) Opif 45, 95, 112, 145 Leg 2:3, 3 Leg 3:88, 98, 135, 165, 200, 241 Post 71, 104 Deus 85, 119 Agr 87, 141 Ebr 51, 163, 184, 185 Migr 59 Her 143, 191, 194, 194, 194 Congr 35, 119 Fug 38, 87, 106, 159 Mut 78, 253 Somn 1:28, 98 Somn 2:114, 188, 198, 229 Ios 2, 148, 156, 250 Mos 1:62, 81, 137, 141, 221, 228, 312, 316 Mos 2:227, 264, 276, 277 Decal 146 Spec

1:228 Spec 2:28, 141, 142, 178, 199, 227, 254, 261 Spec 3:74, 79, 137, 138, 195 Spec 4:7, 74, 171, 225 Virt 44 Praem 138 Prob 125, 146 Contempl 16, 43 Aet 50, 51, 81, 88, 95, 101, 101, 119, 125 Flacc 1, 58, 80, 127 Legat 124, 142, 191, 240 Prov 1, 1 QG 2:14, 14, 4:102b QG (Par) 2:2 QE isf 25

Ἐλεάζαρ Somn 2:186

Ἐλεάτης Prob 106

ἐλεγεῖον Opif 104

ἔλεγχος (58) Opif 128 Leg 3:49, 50 Det 24, 146 Post 59 Deus 125, 135, 135, 182, 183 Ebr 125, 185 Her 76, 77 Congr 157 Fug 6, 27, 118, 118, 131, 203, 207, 211 Mut 65, 154, 170, 195 Somn 1:91 Abr 35, 135, 141 Ios 107, 127, 235 Mos 1:272 Mos 2:177, 200 Decal 87, 140, 151 Spec 1:235, 237 Spec 2:163 Spec 3:52, 61 Spec 4:40 Virt 75, 210 Praem 4 Prob 149 Contempl 64 Aet 89 QG 1:1, 2:17b, 65, 3:26, 4:168

ἐλέγχω (40) Leg 3:77 Cher 88 Det 23, 58, 146 Deus 28, 126, 128 Ebr 43, 188 Conf 52, 52, 52, 121, 126, 126 Her 95, 254 Congr 18, 151, 177, 177, 179 Mut 198 Somn 1:156 Abr 104, 135 Ios 48, 215, 262 Spec 1:235 Spec 3:54 Spec 4:6, 30, 40 Virt 92, 206 Aet 99 Flacc 142 QG 1:60:2

ἐλεέω (25) Leg 1:45 Sacr 42 Deus 76, 76 Ebr 38 Her 38 Fug 95 Mut 40 Somn 1:95 Ios 25, 144 Mos 1:15, 45, 72, 95, 198 Spec 4:72, 76 Virt 91, 100, 114 Praem 39, 117 Legat 257 QE 2:10:1

ἐλεήμων Somn 1:92, 93

Ἑλένη Flacc 156

ἔλεος (48) Sacr 42, 121 Det 145 Post 9 Deus 74, 74, 75, 76, 76, 115 Her 112 Fug 162 Mut 133 Somn 1:96, 112, 147 Somn 2:149 Ios 20, 72, 230, 255 Mos 1:34, 86, 303 Mos 2:227, 228 Decal 69 Spec 1:308 Spec 2:96, 115, 138 Spec 3:4, 76, 116 Spec 4:72, 76, 77, 180 Virt 141, 144, 209 Praem 154 Flacc 60, 121 Legat 244, 367 QG 4:200c QE 2:10a

ἑλέπολις (7) Mos 1:224 Decal 63 Spec 3:87 Spec 4:95, 222 Virt 109 Prob 38

ἐλευθερία (97) Opif 167 Leg 3:17, 41, 86, 89, 194 Cher 72, 74, 107 Sacr 117, 121, 122, 127, 127 Det 63 Deus 47, 47 Plant 53 Conf 93, 94 Migr 25 Her 124, 271, 273, 275 Congr 108 Fug 20 Mut 228 Somn 2:100 Ios 136 Mos 1:71, 86, 141, 171, 193, 247 Mos 2:22 Spec 1:57, 77, 176 Spec 2:66, 67, 84, 122, 218 Spec 3:172, 196, 198 Spec 4:3, 15 Virt 115, 122, 182 Praem 124, 165 Prob 10, 17, 18, 20, 21, 22, 36, 41, 42, 47, 47, 48, 63, 64, 88, 92, 95, 96, 98, 111, 113, 116, 117, 118, 124, 125, 131, 136, 137, 138, 138, 139, 141, 142, 158, 160 Contempl 19 Legat 116, 147, 287 Hypoth 11:3, 11:4

ἐλευθεριάζω Ebr 151

ἐλευθέριος (6) Ios 42 Mos 1:36 Contempl 69 Flacc 80 Legat 215, 332

ἐλευθεροποιός Sobr 57 Her 186 Fug 212

ἐλεύθερος (ὁ) (137) Leg 2:97, 97 Leg 3:21, 56, 89, 194, 198, 202 Cher 72, 80 Sacr 26 Det 17 Post 138 Deus 49, 114 Agr 59, 73 Plant 68 Ebr 58, 71, 101, 122, 195 Sobr 39, 57 Migr 67 Her 186, 186 Congr 31 Fug 16, 212, 212 Mut 173 Somn 1:7, 181 Somn 2:51, 62, 79, 136, 196, 243, 293 Abr 16, 38, 67, 109, 251 Ios 35, 47, 66, 67, 106, 206 Mos 1:36, 39, 140, 263 Mos 2:21, 50 Decal 71 Spec 1:100 Spec 2:39, 66, 68, 69, 79, 84, 84 Spec 3:67, 69, 136, 171, 184, 195 Spec 4:14, 18, 43, 68, 122, 194 Virt 31, 121, 122, 123, 125, 162, 173, 222, 222 Praem 137 Prob 1, 19, 20, 24, 35, 37, 40, 41, 42, 44, 45, 45, 50, 50, 52, 52, 52, 59, 59, 61, 62, 62, 79, 91, 100, 114, 115, 116, 116, 117, 119, 119, 123, 133, 136, 140, 141, 142, 149, 157 Contempl 70, 71, 72 Flacc 183 Hypoth 7:2, 11:17 QG isf 5

ἐλευθεροστομέω Migr 116 Her 7 Somn 2:95 Prob 99, 148

ἐλευθερόω (14) Leg 3:21 Sacr 114, 127 Deus 48, 48 Migr 32 Her 68 Somn 2:154 Spec 2:80 Spec 3:197, 201 Praem 164 Prob 156 Legat 155

ἐλεφάντινος Spec 2:20

ἐλεφαντόπους Somn 2:57

ἐλέφας (7) Post 161 Ebr 89 Her 154 Praem 89 Contempl 49 Aet 128, 129

ἐλιγμός QG (Par) 2:7

Ἐλιέζερ Her 2, 58, 58, 59, 60

Ἑλίκεια Aet 140

Ἑλικών (6) Legat 166, 168, 178, 203, 205, 206

ἕλιξ Deus 39 Conf 38 Mut 162

Ἐλισάβετ Post 76

Ἐλιφάς Congr 54, 54, 56

ἕλκος Mos 1:128 Praem 143

ἑλκόω Ios 160 Legat 35

ἑλκυσμός Cher 69

ἕλκω (18) Post 116 Gig 31 Agr 103 Ebr 63 Her 70 Abr 65, 161 Ios 150 Mos 2:139, 236, 252 Praem 58, 58 Flacc 70, 188 Legat 44, 262 QG 4:202a

ἕλκωσις Mos 1:127, 128, 145

ἐλλαμβάνω (20) Opif 46, 88 Cher 33 Sacr 13 Det 23, 118 Agr 69, 75 Plant 110 Conf 38, 51 Migr 6, 151, 221 Somn 1:103 Ios 47 Spec 1:26 Aet 137 Flacc 189 QE isf 16

ἐλλάμπω Deus 3

ἑλλάς Post 93

Ἑλλάς (29) Leg 1:69 Deus 173 Sobr 28 Abr 12 Ios 134 Mos 1:21 Mos 2:18, 31 Spec 3:16, 16 Praem 14, 165 Prob 73, 94, 132, 138, 140 Contempl 14, 21, 57 Legat 102, 141, 147, 147, 237 Prov 2:15, 66, 66 QE isf 4

ἐλλείπω (6) Opif 127 Migr 166 Mos 2:233 Spec 2:48 Spec 3:15 Praem 109

ἔλλειψις (7) Sacr 9, 24 Deus 162 Migr 146 Spec 4:168 QE 1:6, 6

Ἕλλην (51) Opif 127, 128 Leg 2:15 Plant 14 Ebr 193 Conf 6, 6, 68 Her 214 Congr 37, 42 Mut 35, 71, 179 Somn 1:58 Abr 17, 27, 136, 180, 267 Ios 28, 30, 30 Mos 1:2, 23 Mos 2:12, 20, 40, 97 Decal 153 Spec 1:211 Spec 2:44, 165, 194 Spec 3:15 Spec 4:61, 120 Praem 8, 23, 31 Prob 95, 96, 98, 140 Contempl 14, 48, 68 Aet 57 Legat 145, 162, 292

ἑλληνικός Cher 91

Ἑλληνικός (14) Plant 67 Conf 190 Ios 56 Mos 2:27, 32, 38, 38, 40 Spec 3:16 Prob 75, 88 Legat 8, 8, 83

Ἑλληνιστί Abr 72, 99, 201 Praem 44 Legat 4

Ἑλλήσποντος Somn 2:118

ἐλλιπής Congr 149 Abr 47 Ios 206 Legat 358

ἐλλόγιμος Opif 126 Mos 1:266 Praem 111

ἐλλοχάω Spec 1:270 Aet 86, 90

ἔλμινς Prov 2:59

ἕλος Abr 138 Mos 1:14, 103

ἐλπίζω (72) Opif 46 Leg 3:85, 86, 87, 87, 164 Cher 75 Sacr 53, 78 Det 138, 138, 138, 139, 139, 160 Post 97 Gig 36 Deus 68 Agr 158 Conf 4, 65 Migr 195, 224 Her 39, 39, 100, 310 Congr 137 Fug 145, 164 Mut 8, 161, 163, 172 Somn 1:91 Somn 2:31, 131, 167, 212, 276, 285 Abr 9, 47, 128, 169, 195, 248 Ios 9, 133, 138, 144 Mos 1:72, 180, 214, 305 Mos 2:174 Decal 16 Spec 1:49, 138 Spec 2:196, 219 Spec 3:62 Virt 42 Praem 14, 102, 169 Legat 11, 28, 29, 73, 111, 137

ἐλπίς (177) Opif 81, 155 Leg 2:43 Leg 3:194 Cher 29, 106 Sacr 123 Det 120, 138, 138, 140 Post 26, 26 Gig 39 Agr 162 Plant 88 Ebr 25, 58, 58 Conf 104, 104, 166 Migr 44, 70, 123, 124, 154 Her 269, 311 Congr 5 Fug 99 Mut 155, 158, 163, 163, 163, 164, 165, 219, 222, 269 Somn 1:71, 204, 227 Somn 2:94, 142, 209, 279 Abr 7, 7, 8, 8, 10, 14, 14, 15, 16, 17, 51, 86, 110, 254, 268 Ios 3, 12, 20, 45, 93, 104, 113, 162, 208, 239, 252, 260 Mos 1:32, 58, 67, 137, 149, 171, 182, 187, 193, 195, 222, 250, 268, 285 Mos 2:14, 253, 259, 269 Decal 91, 113, 126 Spec 1:70, 78, 78, 310 Spec 2:67, 158, 187, 199, 238 Spec 3:6, 11, 34, 115 Spec 4:17, 28, 32, 81, 158, 172, 203 Virt 29, 30, 67, 75, 88, 109, 123, 138, 154, 159, 163, 207 Praem 5, 10, 11, 11, 11, 11, 11, 12, 13, 15, 72, 77, 129, 142, 147, 149, 160, 161 Prob 111, 133 Contempl 46, 87 Flacc 11, 16, 22, 100, 102, 109, 124, 124, 176 Legat 16, 82, 151, 172, 195, 195, 196, 197, 242, 318, 329, 329, 348, 356 Prov 2:5 QG 1:79, 85, 4:198

ἐμαυτοῦ (καί) (32) Leg 3:203, 206 Sacr 87 Det 59 Post 30 Agr 102 Migr 34, 35, 214 Her 29, 29, 36 Fug 54 Abr 273 Ios 48, 71 Mos 1:280 Decal 42, 43 Spec 1:213 Spec 3:2 Spec 4:1 Virt 63, 120 Prob 152 Flacc 159 Legat 27, 182, 323 Prov 2:24 QG 4:202a, 202a

ἐμβαθύνω Opif 77 Plant 80 Fug 213 Somn 1:10 Praem 28

ἐμβαίνω Plant 98

ἐμβάλλω (14) Cher 37 Post 156 Agr 94 Migr 36 Congr 16, 163 Somn 2:294 Mos 1:258 Spec 1:262, 268 Spec 2:135 Spec 4:29, 29 Legat 132

ἐμβιβάζω Leg 3:61 Deus 27

ἐμβλέπω (9) Sacr 21 Det 34 Sobr 3 Congr 47 Somn 2:18, 142 Ios 236 Spec 3:91, 193

ἐμβοάω Her 67

ἐμβολή Prob 101

ἐμβόσκομαι Mos 1:320 Spec 2:109 Spec 4:94 Contempl 14

ἐμβριθής (10) Abr 214 Ios 9 Mos 1:26, 95 Spec 2:163, 232, 241 Virt 15 Praem 4 Flacc 4

ἔμβρυον Congr 136

ἔμετος Leg 3:149 Legat 14

ἐμμανής Ios 16

ἐμμέθοδος Aet 130

ἐμμειδιάω Spec 2:54

ἐμμέλεια Opif 165 Leg 2:26 Spec 4:134 Legat 42

ἐμμελετάω Ebr 138 Congr 113 Spec 4:141, 169

ἐμμελής (28) Opif 54 Leg 2:75 Leg 3:57, 99 Cher 26 Sacr 23, 84 Post 107 Deus 24, 25 Agr 80 Plant 131, 159 Conf 35 Migr 104, 178, 184 Her 88, 199 Congr 76 Somn 1:28 Abr 73, 148 Mos 2:50 Spec 3:187 Contempl 57, 83 QE 2:38b

ἐμμένω (8) Migr 160 Congr 78, 125 Somn 2:101 Ios 85 Mos 1:283 Spec 4:150 QG isf 3

ἔμμισθος Agr 5, 13 Mut 151 Abr 128 Spec 4:63

ἐμός (ὁ) (90) Opif 25 Leg 1:27 Leg 2:41, 41, 41, 69 Leg 3:56, 125, 192, 192, 195, 195, 195, 198, 198, 198 Cher 5, 27, 63, 67, 67, 84, 108, 116, 116, 119, 119 Post 39, 168 Conf 50 Her 8, 30 Congr 152, 156 Fug 211 Mut 14, 39, 97, 152 Somn 1:172, 228 Somn 2:6, 80, 200, 200 Abr 143, 204, 249, 250, 251, 251, 252 Ios 6, 25, 66, 66, 94, 117, 150, 168, 192, 245 Mos 1:280, 294, 298 Mos 2:280 Decal 31 Spec 1:44, 49, 190, 273 Spec 4:39 Virt 62 Prob 19, 20, 75, 116, 128 Aet 13 Flacc 159, 159, 173, 174 Legat 58, 58, 281, 283, 294, 334 QG 2:13b, 3:58

ἐμπαθής Plant 171

ἐμπαίζω Migr 21 Fug 153

ἔμπαλιν (ὁ) (100) Opif 7 Leg 1:62, 73 Leg 2:25, 32, 50, 97 Leg 3:48, 89, 186, 189, 213, 217 Cher 70, 81, 105 Det 43, 130, 133, 154 Post 75, 110 Gig 16 Deus 124, 180 Agr 39, 123, 129 Plant 10, 17, 53, 167 Ebr 5, 16, 24, 35, 111, 130, 143, 169, 176, 179 Sobr 2, 7, 37, 52 Conf 12, 73, 82, 102, 191, 194 Migr 26, 72, 110, 162, 189, 204 Her 81, 82, 162, 255, 270, 316 Fug 28, 30, 78, 146, 152 Mut 91 Somn 1:83 Somn 2:165, 176, 185, 256, 301 Abr 14, 22, 101, 151 Ios 62, 136, 139 Mos 1:224, 234, 242, 265 Mos 2:139 Decal 6 Spec 3:22 Spec 4:159, 172, 237 Praem 46 Aet 101, 148 Legat 107 Hypoth 7:7, 11:12 QE 1:6

ἐμπαρέχω (11) Opif 54, 85 Cher 115 Deus 98 Somn 2:134 Abr 73 Mos 1:297 Mos 2:69 Virt 49 Praem 48 Flacc 102

ἐμπαροινέω Ios 45 Virt 162 Contempl 42 Flacc 4 QE isf 14

ἐμπεδόω Migr 18

ἐμπειρία (12) Leg 1:73 Det 104 Agr 147 Sobr 35 Conf 85 Fug 27 Somn 1:205 Mos 1:225 Spec 1:71 Virt 43, 74 Flacc 3

ἐμπειροπόλεμος Agr 160 Conf 145

ἔμπειρος (16) Sacr 64 Det 109 Gig 25 Agr 4 Migr 76 Somn 2:21 Spec 2:62 Prob 49, 50, 51, 52, 82 Contempl 31 Flacc 26 Hypoth 7:11, 7:13

ἐμπεριέρχομαι Ios 140

ἐμπεριέχω Opif 15 Ebr 181

ἐμπεριπατέω (14) Det 4 Post 122 Deus 9, 165 Agr 103 Ebr 10 Conf 19 Migr 77 Mut 265 Somn 1:148 Somn 2:248 Abr 204 Praem 123 Prov 2:48

ἐμπηδάω Leg 2:6

ἐμπίμπλημι (24) Leg 1:46 Leg 2:26, 86 Leg 3:202 Cher 74 Sacr 34, 55 Det 98, 113 Gig 23 Deus 94, 151 Migr 204 Her 109 Fug 175 Somn 1:48, 58 Ios 78 Mos 1:136 Mos 2:163 Prob 25, 99 Flacc 105 Prov 2:67

ἐμπίμπρημι (26) Leg 3:224, 249 Ebr 27, 223 Conf 158 Migr 100 Her 307 Congr 109 Fug 157 Abr 138, 145, 182 Mos 1:311 Mos 2:58 Spec 1:313 Spec 4:27, 223 Praem 12 Aet 20, 20 Flacc 68, 69, 174 Legat 129, 132, 249

ἐμπίνω Post 138 Deus 81 Agr 157 Ebr 2 Aet 128

ἐμπίπτω (6) Sacr 82 Deus 130 Agr 101 Plant 61 Abr 241 Hypoth 6:1

ἐμπλέκω (6) Her 243 Fug 189 Somn 1:122 Mos 2:7 Flacc 87, 189 ἔμπλεος Sacr 111

ἐμπλέω (7) Opif 88, 113 Leg 3:179 Her 301 Praem 33 Prob 67 Aet 138

ἐμπλόκιον Migr 97

ἐμπνέω (22) Opif 126, 139 Leg 1:32, 33, 35, 35, 36, 37, 37, 37, 37, 38, 39, 39, 39, 40 Det 86 Plant 19 Migr 104 Somn 2:94 Mos 1:252 Virt 203

ἐμποδίζω (10) Migr 191 Mos 1:84 Mos 2:24, 129 Spec 1:75, 216 Virt 133 Praem 104 Contempl 33 Legat 364

ἐμπόδιος (6) Gig 30 Ebr 121 Ios 142 Spec 1:100 Virt 25 QE 2:26

ἐμποδοστατέω Sacr 117

ἐμποδών (13) Agr 177 Conf 14, 163 Migr 217 Mos 1:258 Spec 1:55, 219 Spec 2:9 Spec 3:108 Prob 21 Aet 61 Legat 242, 313

ἐμποιέω (40) Opif 83, 85, 113 Leg 3:20 Cher 62 Det 110, 118 Post 26 Gig 26 Deus 93 Ebr 18, 161 Sobr 5 Migr 151 Her 23, 123, 128, 249, 251, 270 Congr 16 Fug 172 Somn 2:58 Ios 142, 214 Mos 1:46, 77, 108, 120, 161 Decal 125 Spec 2:4, 38 Spec 3:10 Spec 4:6, 147, 198 Virt 23 Praem 151 QE 2:25d

ἐμπορεύομαι Sacr 28 Congr 112 Contempl 89 Flacc 134 Legat 204

ἐμπορία (6) Cher 34 Congr 65 Abr 65 Ios 18 Prob 78 Legat 129

ἐμπορικός Cher 33

ἐμπόριον Mos 1:194 Spec 4:154 Legat 15

ἔμπορος (10) Opif 147 Sacr 116 Migr 217 Somn 2:170 Ios 15, 27, 139 Spec 4:193, 194 Flacc 57

ἐμπρεπής (24) Opif 148 Det 36 Deus 139 Agr 9, 51 Plant 170 Ebr 119 Conf 175, 179, 180, 198 Her 10, 200 Congr 113, 138 Mut 79, 253 Somn 1:165 Somn 2:76, 274 Abr 110 Decal 178 Spec 3:176 Aet 41

ἔμπρησις Leg 3:225 Spec 2:191 Aet 147 Legat 134

ἐμπρόθεσμος Mos 2:231 Flacc 107

ἐμπρομελετάω Congr 18 Mos 1:60

ἔμπροσθεν (ὁ) Opif 123 Leg 2:100 Conf 156 Praem 37 QG 2:72

ἐμπρόσθιος Plant 16 Contempl 51

ἐμπτύω Leg 2:66

ἐμπύρευμα (11) Sacr 123 Migr 122 Her 37 Somn 2:299 Ios 124 Mos 2:65 Spec 2:47, 67, 160, 192 Spec 3:37

ἐμφαγεῖν (ἐνεσθίω) Opif 156 Fug 159

ἐμφαίνω (88) Opif 66, 75, 97, 149 Leg 1:37, 74, 82, 104 Leg 2:20 Leg 3:89 Cher 29, 29 Sacr 1, 60, 123, 136 Det 69, 79, 115, 135, 156 Post 129, 140 Deus 129 Plant 86, 115, 155 Ebr 4, 88, 94 Sobr 6, 45 Conf 69, 169, 190 Migr 92 Her 11, 22, 40, 96, 102 Fug 68, 72 Mut 54, 232, 249 Somn 1:38, 145, 153 Somn 2:15, 16, 16, 16, 229, 301 Abr 18, 82, 153, 199 Ios 58 Mos 1:9 Mos 2:11, 191 Decal 22, 28, 105 Spec 1:93, 155, 279 Spec 2:249, 257 Spec 3:191 Spec 4:109, 151 Praem 39, 47 Contempl 2, 78 QG 1:1, 93, 2:54a, 71b, 4:20, 172, 227 QG (Par) 2:6 QE 1:19, 2:45a

ἐμφανής (ὁ) (69) Opif 27, 57, 92, 129 Leg 3:1, 9, 9, 11, 12 Cher 96 Det 40, 163 Post 57, 102, 141 Deus 37 Sobr 6 Conf 142, 143, 190 Migr 157 Fug 34 Somn 1:45, 76, 90, 90, 173 Somn 2:129, 221 Abr 27, 77 Mos 1:70, 95, 146, 274, 280 Mos 2:65, 79, 177, 214 Decal 1, 7, 120, 120, 125, 151, 169 Spec 1:6, 96, 166 Spec 2:43, 143 Spec 3:52, 95, 121, 152, 194 Virt 39, 63 Praem 151, 165 Aet 56, 102 Flacc 89, 142 Legat 59 QE 2:2, 21, 45a

ἐμφανίζω (6) Leg 3:27, 101, 101 Post 16 Mut 8 Spec 1:41

ἐμφαντικός (14) Leg 1:34 Cher 49, 56 Det 131 Post 12 Agr 2, 16 Plant 42 Sobr 25 Migr 81 Somn 2:192 Mos 2:39, 182 Decal 47

ἔμφασις (22) Opif 6, 71, 127 Leg 3:82, 100, 101, 102, 196 Migr 79 Her 72, 197 Mut 147 Somn 2:206 Abr 120, 174 Mos 1:199 Mos 2:168 Spec 2:4 Spec 4:203 Prob 62, 74 QG 2:65

ἐμφέρεια (7) Opif 69 Conf 183 Her 225, 236 Somn 1:74 Virt 4 Legat 55

ἐμφερής (21) Opif 69, 71, 152 Agr 103 Plant 72 Ebr 133, 174 Her 57, 131, 294 Congr 117 Fug 101 Mut 8, 223 Somn 2:206 Mos 1:66 Mos 2:51, 90 Spec 4:207 Legat 103 QE 2:47

ἐμφέρω (31) Cher 129 Agr 103, 144 Plant 151, 154 Conf 171 Migr 155, 183, 193 Mut 192, 201 Somn 1:63, 133 Abr 1, 207 Ios 145 Mos 2:218 Decal 39, 85, 162, 172 Spec 1:252 Spec 2:12, 39, 40 Spec 4:136 Virt 22 Aet 33 Prov 2:55 QG 2:59 QG (Par) 2:5

ἐμφιλόσοφος Abr 150

ἐμφορέω (38) Opif 158 Leg 3:52, 155, 184 Sacr 32 Det 68, 101 Deus 154 Agr 32, 34, 39 Plant 148 Ebr 122, 152, 207 Her 109, 243 Fug 22, 31 Somn 2:150 Abr 149 Ios 93, 101, 256 Mos 2:162 Decal 108 Spec 2:197 Spec 3:108, 183, 186 Spec 4:25, 113, 129 Virt 136, 162 Contempl 40, 55 Legat 137

ἐμφράσσω Post 112 QG 4:193

ἔμφρων Plant 166 Decal 177

ἐμφύλιος (26) Sacr 25 Post 118 Agr 45, 171 Ebr 75, 98 Conf 42 Migr 56 Her 162, 244, 244, 246, 284 Congr 92 Fug 174 Somn 2:147 Ios 57 Mos 1:305 Decal 5, 152 Spec 3:16 Flacc 44 Legat 68, 102, 335 QG 3:7

ἐμφυσάω (13) Opif 134, 135 Leg 1:31, 33, 36, 36 Leg 3:161 Det 80 Her 56 Somn 1:34 Spec 4:123, 123 QG 2:59

ἐμφυτεύω (6) Agr 168 Plant 37, 46 Ebr 224 Sobr 36 Praem 71

ἔμφυτος (6) Deus 101 Fug 122 Spec 3:138 Virt 23 Praem 5 QG isf 16

ἐμφύω (7) Agr 121 Ebr 223 Her 243 Somn 1:69 Somn 2:176 Aet 1 Legat 277

ἐμφωλεύω (10) Agr 97, 154 Ebr 28 Migr 146 Somn 1:32, 222 Legat 174 QG (Par) 2:3, 2:3, 2:3

ἐμψυχία Opif 22

ἔμψυχος (26) Opif 62, 66, 153 Leg 2:97, 97 Leg 3:35, 35, 73 Cher 57, 111 Sacr 88 Gig 41 Plant 27 Ebr 183 Migr 167, 185 Her 137, 209 Somn 1:22 Abr 5 Mos 1:105, 162 Mos 2:4 Virt 160, 219 Aet 94

Ἐμώρ Migr 224, 224 Mut 193

ἐν (καί) (4000) Opif 6, 8, 11, 12, 13, 14, 16, 17, 17, 18, 20, 25, 26, 27, 28, 31, 33, 33, 34, 34, 35, 36, 37, 41, 41, 41, 42, 43, 44, 45, 45, 47, 48, 48, 48, 48, 49, 50, 50, 50, 50, 52, 52, 53, 53, 53, 55, 61, 63, 65, 65, 66, 67, 67, 69, 69, 69, 69, 71, 76, 76, 77, 78, 78, 78, 79, 81, 82, 82, 84, 84, 88, 88, 92, 93, 93, 94, 95, 96, 96, 96, 96, 97, 97, 99, 99, 99, 99, 100, 100, 101, 101, 103, 104, 104, 104, 105, 106, 106, 107, 107, 107, 111, 111, 113, 114, 116, 116, 117, 118, 119, 122, 122, 123, 124,

125, 126, 128, 128, 129, 129, 130, 136, 139, 139, 140, 142, 142, 142, 144, 149, 150, 150, 151, 155, 158, 159, 163, 165, 165, 165, 167, 167, 170, 172 Leg 1:1, 1, 2, 13, 14, 18, 18, 20, 21, 22, 22, 23, 27, 34, 34, 39, 41, 43, 45, 46, 47, 48, 49, 49, 49, 49, 49, 51, 53, 53, 54, 55, 55, 55, 56, 56, 57, 58, 60, 60, 60, 61, 61, 61, 61, 62, 62, 62, 62, 62, 62, 62, 64, 66, 71, 74, 74, 74, 75, 76, 76, 77, 78, 78, 79, 80, 81, 84, 84, 88, 89, 90, 91, 97, 100, 100, 100, 100, 100, 100, 108 Leg 2:6, 9, 9, 10, 11, 12, 12, 12, 13, 13, 17, 21, 22, 22, 23, 24, 27, 27, 29, 35, 38, 38, 38, 38, 45, 48, 55, 56, 57, 60, 60, 61, 61, 63, 67, 67, 69, 69, 69, 70, 70, 70, 73, 77, 77, 78, 81, 81, 84, 84, 84, 85, 85, 86, 87, 87, 88, 88, 89, 89, 89, 92, 93, 93, 94, 97, 97, 98, 98, 102, 104, 105, 105 Leg 3:1, 4, 4, 4, 5, 6, 7, 8, 12, 17, 21, 22, 23, 23, 23, 25, 26, 26, 28, 30, 32, 32, 32, 34, 34, 34, 35, 36, 36, 37, 38, 40, 40, 40, 41, 42, 42, 46, 46, 47, 51, 51, 51, 54, 54, 65, 67, 67, 68, 72, 75, 75, 78, 82, 88, 89, 91, 96, 99, 99, 101, 101, 101, 101, 101, 102, 103, 103, 103, 103, 105, 105, 105, 105, 106, 106, 107, 108, 112, 115, 116, 116, 116, 117, 119, 122, 129, 131, 131, 131, 139, 142, 142, 145, 151, 152, 152, 153, 155, 157, 159, 160, 160, 167, 168, 172, 174, 178, 180, 181, 181, 181, 183, 184, 186, 186, 190, 190, 191, 194, 194, 200, 201, 204, 212, 214, 216, 219, 222, 225, 228, 230, 230, 230, 239, 240, 241, 244, 246, 247, 247, 248, 249, 251, 252 Cher 3, 5, 5, 6, 6, 12, 23, 23, 24, 24, 29, 29, 29, 29, 37, 44, 48, 51, 52, 53, 57, 63, 65, 66, 66, 71, 75, 76, 76, 80, 83, 84, 85, 85, 86, 86, 87, 88, 92, 94, 94, 105, 105, 106, 109, 116, 119, 121, 124, 127 Sacr 2, 3, 4, 14, 17, 19, 22, 22, 25, 25, 25, 26, 26, 30, 30, 37, 37, 39, 40, 41, 42, 54, 57, 58, 60, 60, 60, 62, 63, 66, 67, 69, 70, 71, 74, 74, 75, 78, 79, 80, 82, 82, 84, 89, 94, 95, 98, 102, 104, 104, 109, 111, 111, 112, 118, 118, 118, 120, 123, 131, 134, 134, 134, 136, 136 Det 1, 1, 2, 2, 2, 3, 3, 4, 4, 5, 5, 5, 6, 6, 8, 8, 8, 9, 9, 10, 16, 16, 16, 17, 19, 22, 23, 26, 26, 28, 28, 29, 29, 33, 35, 38, 40, 43, 43, 43, 46, 48, 48, 49, 49, 51, 53, 55, 59, 60, 63, 65, 67, 72, 74, 75, 75, 75, 76, 76, 77, 85, 88, 89, 90, 91, 95, 95, 103, 104, 108, 110, 110, 114, 116, 120, 125, 126, 126, 128, 128, 130, 131, 134, 135, 135, 137, 137, 137, 137, 140, 140, 141, 141, 142, 145, 145, 145, 160, 161, 163, 164, 166, 169, 169, 172, 172, 173, 173, 177 Post 1, 1, 1, 6, 6, 7, 11, 14, 14, 24, 25, 26, 26, 36, 41, 42, 42, 50, 53, 58, 59, 59, 64, 64, 64, 68, 69, 72, 72, 80, 80, 80, 81, 83, 85, 85, 85, 85, 85, 85, 86, 89, 89, 92, 95, 96, 96, 98, 104, 104, 107, 118, 118, 121, 122, 127, 133, 141, 142, 142, 144, 155, 158, 161, 161, 162, 163, 167, 171, 173, 176, 181, 183, 184, 185 Gig 3, 4, 9, 10, 15, 17, 18, 19, 19, 22, 25, 28, 31, 39, 43, 45, 47, 49, 51, 51, 51, 51, 53, 53, 55, 58, 60, 60, 62 Deus 2, 5, 6, 6, 7, 9, 10, 10, 11, 11, 11, 12, 14, 20, 25, 25, 27, 28, 29, 30, 32, 36, 38, 38, 39, 43, 45, 45, 45, 46, 47, 50, 50, 53, 61, 62, 63, 65, 75, 77, 77, 79, 79, 80, 84, 88, 95, 99, 102, 105, 107, 111, 112, 116, 117, 122, 123, 123, 123, 125, 125, 127, 129, 129, 130, 131, 131, 131, 131, 132, 134, 135, 136, 137, 145, 147, 150, 153, 154, 154, 157, 163, 166, 174, 176, 177, 182 Agr 1, 2, 2, 6, 7, 9, 9, 11, 13, 18, 23, 24, 26, 26, 27, 28, 48, 51, 51, 53, 63, 68, 72, 72, 75, 75, 78, 84, 85, 87, 95, 97, 97, 101, 107, 110, 111, 113, 113, 117, 128, 130, 140, 147, 148, 148, 148, 151, 152, 153, 157, 167, 168, 170, 172 Plant 1, 1, 2, 2, 3, 8, 8, 11, 13, 14, 16, 23, 26, 27, 27, 27, 28, 28, 29, 32, 33, 36, 37, 39, 39, 42, 42, 43, 44, 45, 46, 49, 52, 56, 57, 59, 63, 66, 71, 74, 76, 77, 78, 79, 83, 83, 83, 83, 83, 83, 84, 85, 91, 93, 93, 94, 100, 101, 101, 104, 109, 110, 111, 113, 117, 119, 121, 123, 125, 128, 131, 132, 132, 142, 144, 147, 156, 156, 159, 159, 160, 162, 162, 167, 173, 174, 174 Ebr 1, 6, 8, 8, 13, 23, 26, 30, 36, 47, 48, 56, 57, 62, 67, 67, 73, 75, 75, 76, 83, 83, 84, 84, 85, 86, 86, 89, 91, 91, 91, 92, 93, 95, 96, 98, 98, 99, 99, 101, 101, 104, 108, 110, 119, 119, 130, 131, 133, 135, 135, 139, 140, 140, 141, 143, 155, 155, 157, 160, 164, 164, 165, 166, 167, 169, 171, 173, 174, 177, 184, 185, 187, 198, 198, 200, 203, 208, 208, 208, 210, 215, 222 Sobr 1, 8, 8, 8, 9, 9, 10, 11, 11, 11, 22, 24, 24, 28, 28, 30, 33, 35, 38, 40, 41, 42, 45, 45, 47, 47, 49, 49, 50, 53, 56, 59, 62, 62, 63, 63, 67, 68, 68, 68 Conf 1, 1, 3, 8, 12, 13, 21, 22, 22, 24, 27, 29, 31, 37, 38, 39, 39, 46, 46, 47, 52, 52, 55, 60, 61, 66, 67, 69, 74, 74, 75, 76, 78, 78, 80, 81, 81, 81, 81, 82, 82, 83, 83, 92, 93, 94, 97, 98, 98, 99, 99, 102, 104, 105, 106, 108, 108, 111, 126, 128, 130, 135, 136, 139, 141, 143, 149, 154, 154, 159, 164, 170, 173, 174, 179, 184, 184, 185, 187, 196, 196, 197 Migr 1, 3, 4, 4, 12, 21, 29, 37, 37, 39, 46, 49, 50, 50, 51, 52, 54, 54, 55, 56, 59, 60, 64, 65, 66, 68, 68, 69, 69, 71, 76, 78, 79, 85, 85, 90, 90, 91, 98, 100, 108, 110, 110, 113, 114, 115, 117, 118, 122, 122, 124, 124, 124, 126, 126, 131, 144, 147, 150, 154, 155, 157, 160, 161, 161, 166, 169, 169, 172, 174, 179, 179, 180, 182, 183, 185, 186, 189, 190, 190, 190, 190, 191, 193, 193, 195, 195, 196, 196, 201, 205, 210, 212, 214, 217, 222, 223, 224 Her 1, 5, 8, 12, 12, 12, 12, 14, 15, 20, 20, 21, 28, 29, 30, 41, 41, 41, 41, 44, 45, 50, 50, 60, 68, 70, 70, 78, 80, 81, 82, 82, 88, 88, 102, 106, 109, 109, 112, 113, 117, 117, 120, 121, 121, 122, 123, 137, 144, 144, 144, 145, 146, 147, 150, 150, 151, 151, 151, 152, 156, 158, 158, 159, 159, 162, 162, 162, 162, 162, 162, 162, 162, 167, 168, 173, 180, 186, 189, 193, 197, 207, 208, 210, 211, 215, 218, 226, 226, 228, 233, 233, 233, 233, 233, 234, 234, 235, 236, 239, 240, 246, 250, 250, 250, 250, 251, 251, 251, 256, 257, 258, 262, 262, 263, 263, 264, 265, 267, 267, 267, 267, 273, 275, 277, 280, 286, 289, 290, 293, 294, 298, 299, 299, 302, 313, 315 Congr 2, 2, 10, 10, 16, 19, 21, 28, 31, 31, 32, 32, 36, 38, 51, 52, 53, 53, 53, 55, 57, 61, 65, 69, 71, 75, 77, 77, 77, 77, 81, 81, 85, 86, 86, 86, 87, 88, 90, 90, 95, 96, 97, 97, 97, 98, 100, 100, 100, 104, 104, 106, 107, 108, 109, 112, 128, 129, 130, 131, 133, 134, 134, 135, 137, 138, 138, 139, 139, 139, 142, 142, 143, 144, 149, 153, 155, 158, 160, 163, 164, 166, 168, 170, 170, 170, 174, 175, 176, 176, 179, 180, 180 Fug 1, 1, 1, 2, 4, 9, 9, 10, 10, 10, 15, 20, 28, 33, 34, 35, 35, 37, 39, 40, 42, 45, 46, 47, 50, 52, 52, 53, 56, 56, 58, 59, 59, 61, 61, 63, 63, 64, 67, 69, 69, 73, 74, 76, 79, 82, 82, 87, 91, 96, 100, 100, 102, 106, 107, 117, 117, 118, 120, 122, 127, 127, 129, 130, 132, 136, 137, 142, 143, 144, 145, 145, 146, 148, 149, 149, 153, 158, 159, 159, 161, 161, 163, 166, 169, 169, 170, 172, 173, 174, 176, 178, 183, 184, 185, 185, 186, 186, 186, 191, 192, 203, 204, 204, 212, 213, 213, 213 Mut 7, 10, 12, 12, 13, 17, 19, 20, 23, 27, 37, 39, 42, 44, 50, 53, 55, 60, 65, 65, 65, 68, 69, 74, 75, 79, 79, 80, 80, 80, 81, 87, 87, 91, 91, 91, 93, 93, 93, 93, 93, 94, 96, 97, 98, 109, 111, 114, 115, 119, 123, 130, 134, 140, 143, 145, 149, 150, 152, 152, 152, 153, 153, 160, 165, 166, 166, 168, 169, 173, 179, 182, 182, 187, 192, 196, 199, 199, 200, 200, 201, 203, 214, 215, 220, 227, 227, 228, 231, 236, 236, 237, 237, 237, 238, 246, 246, 256, 260, 265, 266, 267, 267, 268 Somn 1:1, 1, 2, 3, 3, 3, 3, 4, 5, 6, 6, 7, 7, 8, 13, 15, 15, 16, 19, 19, 22, 23, 24, 25, 25, 27, 29, 30, 31, 31, 32, 33, 33, 33, 34, 34, 34, 35, 38, 40, 40, 42, 45, 45, 46, 46, 47, 48, 48, 49, 54, 54, 57, 60, 62, 64, 66, 74, 74, 74, 75, 77, 81,

84, 89, 90, 91, 92, 92, 96, 101, 106, 110, 110, 112, 113, 114, 116, 117, 117, 120, 120, 122, 126, 126, 130, 131, 132, 132, 133, 134, 135, 136, 144, 146, 146, 147, 148, 148, 148, 151, 154, 168, 172, 174, 176, 177, 179, 182, 183, 183, 183, 184, 184, 184, 184, 185, 186, 188, 189, 192, 198, 202, 203, 205, 205, 206, 207, 215, 227, 228, 228, 229, 229, 229, 229, 230, 232, 233, 238, 250 Somn 2:1, 6, 9, 9, 12, 19, 20, 22, 26, 27, 31, 37, 44, 50, 51, 53, 57, 62, 81, 91, 91, 93, 94, 95, 98, 100, 109, 112, 112, 127, 133, 134, 139, 141, 143, 144, 147, 147, 150, 153, 159, 159, 159, 160, 168, 175, 189, 191, 192, 193, 193, 195, 200, 200, 201, 201, 201, 203, 206, 211, 211, 212, 215, 216, 216, 216, 218, 218, 221, 221, 222, 225, 233, 234, 235, 235, 237, 237, 242, 244, 245, 246, 247, 248, 248, 248, 250, 250, 251, 255, 258, 260, 260, 260, 263, 265, 265, 267, 271, 272, 272, 275, 284, 292, 293, 297, 300, 302, 302 Abr 1, 1, 4, 5, 11, 11, 13, 19, 20, 23, 26, 27, 27, 28, 28, 29, 29, 30, 31, 35, 36, 40, 40, 41, 41, 41, 48, 48, 52, 54, 57, 58, 60, 61, 65, 68, 69, 69, 69, 70, 71, 74, 74, 79, 85, 92, 92, 93, 93, 95, 99, 101, 101, 102, 103, 109, 110, 112, 115, 115, 117, 119, 119, 119, 119, 121, 122, 127, 131, 137, 139, 140, 141, 145, 147, 147, 147, 148, 148, 148, 148, 152, 152, 154, 156, 158, 159, 159, 161, 162, 164, 164, 166, 167, 170, 175, 175, 177, 177, 177, 180, 180, 183, 184, 186, 188, 190, 191, 192, 193, 195, 202, 205, 205, 209, 209, 211, 213, 214, 215, 216, 216, 218, 222, 223, 232, 233, 236, 239, 239, 240, 242, 243, 244, 245, 246, 252, 258, 258, 260, 260, 261, 261, 263, 264, 266, 266, 267, 267, 267, 268, 271, 271, 271, 272, 272, 272, 272, 272, 272, 272, 274 Ios 2, 5, 17, 21, 25, 27, 28, 34, 40, 46, 49, 53, 56, 63, 63, 64, 68, 69, 71, 75, 76, 80, 85, 87, 88, 91, 94, 97, 98, 98, 104, 107, 110, 111, 111, 111, 113, 113, 113, 114, 115, 115, 115, 116, 119, 126, 128, 128, 128, 128, 128, 128, 131, 132, 134, 140, 141, 141, 141, 142, 144, 144, 145, 147, 147, 149, 155, 159, 159, 163, 173, 175, 175, 179, 179, 184, 188, 193, 195, 197, 198, 199, 200, 202, 203, 204, 205, 207, 213, 215, 217, 223, 241, 247, 250, 253, 254, 257, 257, 258, 265, 267, 269, 269, 270, 270, 270, 270 Mos 1:2, 3, 5, 10, 10, 11, 11, 14, 21, 23, 23, 24, 24, 29, 30, 30, 33, 36, 38, 41, 46, 48, 48, 52, 55, 59, 62, 64, 64, 69, 71, 81, 86, 87, 89, 89, 91, 91, 93, 94, 96, 99, 104, 104, 106, 114, 114, 115, 116, 118, 118, 120, 121, 122, 123, 124, 130, 133, 137, 138, 139, 141, 142, 142, 142, 142, 143, 145, 150, 153, 153, 153, 164, 168, 169, 171, 179, 180, 181, 183, 183, 187, 189, 189, 189, 191, 193, 197, 198, 198, 198, 200, 202, 205, 206, 206, 207, 207, 209, 209, 212, 213, 216, 217, 217, 218, 218, 221, 224, 224, 224, 225, 225, 225, 226, 229, 232, 237, 244, 247, 249, 251, 252, 255, 255, 257, 262, 264, 265, 270, 279, 280, 280, 284, 291, 309, 310, 310, 310, 312, 312, 313, 315, 316, 317, 319, 322, 324, 324, 327, 329, 330, 330, 333 Mos 2:1, 2, 3, 8, 10, 11, 17, 19, 23, 24, 26, 29, 29, 30, 30, 33, 36, 37, 39, 40, 41, 42, 42, 43, 47, 50, 51, 52, 53, 54, 57, 58, 58, 61, 62, 66, 67, 71, 72, 73, 73, 75, 78, 78, 79, 80, 80, 81, 82, 84, 84, 89, 93, 94, 95, 95, 101, 102, 103, 106, 109, 114, 115, 115, 115, 115, 115, 115, 120, 120, 120, 121, 124, 126, 127, 127, 127, 138, 140, 140, 146, 150, 151, 151, 152, 152, 155, 159, 163, 163, 167, 172, 174, 177, 181, 185, 186, 188, 191, 194, 198, 205, 210, 211, 213, 214, 219, 222, 222, 224, 227, 228, 230, 231, 235, 235, 241, 241, 247, 250, 254, 257, 258, 259, 263, 263, 263, 264, 267, 274, 277, 289, 290, 291 Decal 1, 2, 2, 4, 14, 16, 18, 19, 20, 21, 21, 22, 22, 22, 22, 30, 31, 31, 31, 33, 38, 43, 44, 45, 47, 49, 49, 50, 57, 63, 65, 66, 74, 81, 89, 92, 94, 94, 97, 97, 98, 98, 98, 98, 100, 101, 101, 102, 102, 104, 106, 110, 111, 111, 111, 111, 114, 115, 116, 117, 117, 117, 117, 120, 123, 125, 127, 134, 138, 150, 154, 154, 159, 159, 160, 160, 164, 166, 166, 166, 166, 167, 168, 168, 173, 175, 175 Spec 1:1, 1, 5, 9, 11, 13, 13, 14, 16, 18, 22, 23, 25, 31, 32, 33, 38, 41, 47, 49, 56, 57, 58, 58, 62, 63, 63, 67, 68, 69, 72, 73, 73, 74, 78, 80, 82, 83, 88, 91, 92, 94, 96, 98, 100, 103, 103, 104, 109, 109, 113, 114, 120, 121, 121, 121, 121, 124, 136, 138, 140, 145, 148, 151, 152, 154, 156, 156, 156, 156, 158, 163, 165, 165, 171, 172, 173, 177, 180, 181, 181, 186, 186, 187, 189, 189, 193, 193, 199, 200, 205, 205, 210, 210, 211, 213, 214, 215, 217, 219, 222, 224, 224, 224, 226, 226, 226, 229, 229, 229, 229, 231, 232, 233, 238, 239, 240, 241, 247, 248, 256, 257, 258, 259, 262, 266, 268, 269, 269, 270, 274, 274, 275, 277, 280, 286, 290, 295, 296, 297, 300, 301, 302, 302, 308, 308, 308, 312, 313, 313, 314, 319, 320, 320, 323, 324, 325, 330, 335, 339, 342, 342, 342, 343 Spec 2:1, 1, 3, 6, 14, 16, 20, 23, 28, 32, 37, 37, 40, 40, 42, 44, 45, 45, 52, 52, 55, 57, 60, 62, 62, 70, 73, 75, 77, 78, 84, 91, 98, 101, 103, 103, 108, 112, 115, 116, 116, 118, 119, 119, 119, 119, 120, 121, 123, 124, 124, 125, 126, 127, 129, 130, 134, 137, 140, 140, 141, 142, 142, 144, 145, 150, 152, 152, 153, 156, 157, 158, 158, 162, 169, 170, 170, 170, 175, 175, 177, 178, 178, 178, 179, 181, 181, 181, 182, 184, 184, 187, 187, 188, 189, 189, 190, 192, 192, 193, 193, 194, 195, 197, 198, 199, 200, 200, 200, 201, 203, 203, 205, 206, 206, 207, 208, 208, 208, 208, 208, 208, 208, 214, 223, 223, 224, 227, 227, 230, 231, 236, 238, 245, 246, 250, 259, 261, 262 Spec 3:1, 2, 3, 3, 4, 5, 7, 7, 7, 8, 8, 11, 13, 14, 15, 16, 17, 17, 17, 17, 17, 26, 27, 27, 33, 36, 37, 37, 40, 43, 46, 47, 60, 62, 69, 74, 75, 77, 78, 78, 78, 79, 80, 83, 91, 96, 99, 99, 103, 104, 104, 109, 109, 117, 121, 125, 142, 149, 155, 155, 155, 155, 160, 161, 161, 162, 166, 166, 169, 171, 171, 172, 173, 174, 177, 178, 178, 178, 183, 183, 183, 191, 192, 194, 197, 202, 203, 206 Spec 4:1, 4, 6, 7, 10, 10, 10, 11, 12, 13, 14, 15, 18, 20, 20, 21, 27, 28, 30, 30, 31, 35, 36, 41, 42, 49, 52, 52, 57, 66, 66, 67, 67, 68, 69, 69, 69, 72, 72, 74, 83, 85, 88, 93, 94, 95, 102, 105, 109, 111, 112, 114, 116, 117, 121, 123, 123, 126, 126, 126, 126, 126, 128, 129, 130, 131, 138, 140, 140, 140, 141, 141, 141, 142, 143, 151, 153, 154, 154, 155, 157, 159, 163, 168, 173, 173, 179, 183, 185, 191, 192, 195, 196, 197, 197, 197, 198, 200, 201, 201, 201, 202, 203, 203, 204, 205, 206, 206, 206, 206, 207, 208, 209, 211, 212, 215, 217, 218, 220, 231, 233, 235, 235, 235, 235, 235, 237, 237, 237, 237, 238 Virt 2, 3, 4, 10, 11, 14, 16, 16, 19, 20, 20, 21, 21, 22, 22, 24, 43, 45, 47, 52, 56, 61, 68, 69, 72, 73, 75, 75, 78, 81, 81, 83, 84, 85, 85, 85, 86, 88, 89, 90, 91, 91, 95, 95, 96, 101, 101, 103, 105, 109, 111, 117, 124, 126, 129, 133, 133, 134, 136, 137, 140, 140, 141, 142, 142, 144, 145, 146, 146, 147, 149, 151, 152, 152, 153, 153, 160, 162, 162, 169, 176, 176, 176, 176, 176, 180, 181, 183, 183, 184, 186, 186, 188, 190, 191, 192, 192, 193, 193, 196, 198, 200, 200, 201, 201, 205, 210, 211, 213, 216, 218, 218, 221, 222, 223 Praem 1, 2, 2, 3, 6, 7, 10, 12, 15, 18, 22, 23, 28, 28, 33, 34, 38, 41, 41, 43, 50, 51, 51, 53, 53, 55, 58, 59, 60, 62, 62, 65, 65, 65, 66, 67, 69, 71, 72, 72, 73, 79, 80, 82, 85, 88, 88, 88, 97, 97, 104, 111, 111, 113, 114, 114, 117, 119, 125, 125, 132, 135, 141, 141, 143, 144, 144, 144, 147, 150, 152, 157, 164, 165, 166, 168, 169, 172, 172 Prob 5, 5, 5, 6, 8, 12, 14, 14, 21, 26, 33, 34, 34, 41, 46, 46, 49, 49, 50, 57, 60, 68, 68, 68, 70, 71, 73, 74, 74, 74, 75, 81, 81, 87, 87, 92, 94, 94, 95, 96, 98, 99, 103, 108,

109, 109, 111, 111, 111, 112, 117, 122, 125, 127, 131, 131, 132, 133, 133, 135, 137, 139, 139, 140, 140, 140, 142, 146, 148, 156 Contempl 1, 1, 7, 7, 16, 16, 17, 17, 18, 20, 21, 23, 24, 25, 25, 26, 27, 28, 29, 30, 31, 33, 36, 40, 41, 41, 42, 42, 43, 46, 53, 54, 56, 57, 57, 57, 57, 58, 64, 66, 66, 71, 72, 75, 75, 75, 78, 78, 80, 81, 84, 85, 90 Aet 1, 1, 4, 6, 8, 12, 13, 13, 14, 15, 15, 19, 19, 19, 19, 21, 24, 25, 29, 31, 32, 34, 35, 35, 38, 46, 48, 58, 61, 64, 65, 66, 69, 71, 73, 73, 74, 76, 82, 85, 86, 98, 100, 101, 102, 104, 104, 107, 111, 115, 119, 121, 129, 135, 138, 141, 142, 143, 143, 146, 146, 148, 148, 148, 150 Flacc 2, 2, 4, 5, 7, 17, 18, 19, 24, 28, 32, 34, 34, 36, 38, 39, 41, 45, 46, 46, 52, 54, 55, 55, 61, 62, 62, 62, 62, 72, 74, 76, 77, 77, 79, 79, 82, 84, 86, 88, 90, 92, 92, 93, 95, 95, 98, 102, 108, 111, 114, 114, 116, 116, 116, 117, 118, 119, 122, 122, 123, 124, 124, 125, 130, 134, 134, 137, 140, 141, 148, 149, 151, 153, 154, 158, 159, 162, 162, 163, 163, 165, 167, 168, 169, 171, 173, 180, 182, 183, 186, 186, 187, 187 Legat 1, 2, 2, 5, 7, 14, 18, 26, 29, 29, 30, 30, 32, 34, 34, 35, 38, 39, 42, 43, 43, 43, 43, 45, 49, 54, 55, 55, 56, 56, 61, 67, 71, 73, 75, 75, 76, 77, 79, 87, 92, 94, 94, 94, 104, 107, 108, 108, 109, 110, 112, 112, 119, 122, 122, 125, 127, 128, 129, 130, 134, 134, 135, 138, 138, 143, 144, 147, 147, 148, 148, 151, 151, 158, 158, 159, 165, 166, 173, 178, 178, 181, 181, 193, 196, 200, 203, 203, 206, 209, 210, 213, 214, 218, 221, 222, 222, 222, 227, 227, 231, 232, 233, 235, 238, 240, 241, 245, 249, 252, 252, 252, 259, 259, 259, 261, 265, 266, 269, 278, 278, 280, 280, 280, 280, 283, 283, 286, 288, 289, 294, 294, 296, 298, 299, 300, 303, 303, 303, 305, 306, 310, 310, 312, 318, 320, 320, 322, 326, 328, 332, 334, 335, 335, 337, 337, 337, 338, 338, 342, 342, 346, 346, 347, 350, 350, 350, 351, 358, 359, 363, 364, 365, 366, 368, 368, 370 Hypoth 6:2, 6:2, 6:3, 6:5, 6:6, 6:6, 7:3, 7:6, 7:7, 7:8, 11:5, 11:6, 11:7, 11:13 Prov 1, 1, 1, 1, 1, 2:1, 3, 15, 15, 15, 17, 20, 21, 23, 23, 23, 27, 33, 33, 33, 33, 34, 34, 35, 36, 36, 37, 37, 37, 39, 41, 44, 44, 44, 49, 52, 54, 54, 55, 55, 55, 58, 58, 60, 61, 62, 62, 62, 63, 64, 65, 65, 66, 69, 71 QG 1:17b, 28, 29, 41, 64a, 76a, 76a, 76b, 77, 77, 100:1b, 100:2b, 2:5a, 5a, 5b, 5b, 11, 11, 12a, 12c, 12c, 12c, 15a, 16, 17b, 22, 30, 31, 34a, 39, 41, 54a, 54a, 59, 59, 59, 62, 62, 62, 66, 3:11c, 11c, 11c, 12, 20a, 20b, 22, 38b, 49a, 4:8b, 8b, 30, 30, 33a, 33b, 43, 43, 47a, 51a, 51a, 69, 102b, 172, 193, 200a, 200a, 204, 204 QG isf 16, 16 QG (Par) 2:3, 2:4, 2:4, 2:4, 2:4, 2:5, 2:5, 2:5, 2:5, 2:5, 2:5, 2:7, 2:7 QE 1:6, 7b, 19, 2:2, 2, 3a, 3b, 4, 10:1, 10b, 19, 20, 24a, 25a, 38a, 38b, 44, 44, 49b, 49b, 50b, 50b QE isf 4, 12, 13, 18, 20, 20, 22, 25

ἐναβρύνομαι Ios 244 Spec 2:219 Spec 3:27

ἐναγής (10) Sacr 32 Det 96 Fug 60 Mos 2:196 Spec 1:89 Spec 3:86, 93, 136 Praem 68 Legat 208

ἔναγχος Mos 2:225

ἐνάγω Spec 1:316 Flacc 30, 33

ἐναγώνιος Somn 1:168 Prob 134 QE isf 7

ἐναδολεσχέω Ios 125

ἐναθλέω Mos 1:323

ἔναθλος Somn 1:168

ἔναιμος (12) Her 54, 58, 60, 61, 63, 65 Spec 1:171, 171, 255, 274, 275 Contempl 73

ἐνακμάζω Contempl 67

ἐνάλιος Decal 54

ἐναλλαγή Cher 92

ἐνάλλαξις Post 30

ἐναλλάσσω (14) Leg 3:90 Cher 88, 129 Post 30 Plant 12 Ebr 88 Sobr 27 Conf 139 Her 155 Aet 115 Legat 111, 266 Prov 2:23 QG 4:204

ἐναλλοιόω QE isf 14

ἐνάλλομαι Flacc 70 Legat 131

ἐναλύω Spec 4:202, 217

ἐνάμιλλος Opif 96

ἔναντι Leg 3:74 Post 27

ἐναντιόομαι (42) Leg 1:87 Leg 3:115, 237 Sacr 114, 114, 130 Det 41 Agr 146 Plant 177 Ebr 18, 77 Conf 27 Migr 211 Her 169, 288 Fug 210 Somn 2:44, 95, 263, 302 Abr 231 Ios 40, 173 Mos 1:243, 259 Spec 3:68, 77, 140 Spec 4:185 Virt 109 Prob 114 Flacc 48, 52, 167 Legat 157, 209, 218, 218, 223, 233, 244, 247

ἐναντίος (ὁ) (371) Opif 2, 22, 40, 73, 74, 75, 82, 112, 113, 154, 161, 163 Leg 1:18, 86, 106 Leg 2:7, 51, 60, 79, 79, 83, 85 Leg 3:9, 11, 39, 63, 71, 77, 118, 126, 129, 192, 223 Cher 13, 14, 14, 17, 18, 18, 21, 30, 38, 50, 108, 119 Sacr 2, 30, 64, 108, 135 Det 3, 18, 32, 36, 51, 55, 71, 73, 74, 114, 139, 154, 163, 173, 178 Post 22, 25, 38, 52, 70, 70, 81, 93, 122 Gig 1, 3, 3, 5, 5, 11, 41, 41, 63, 65 Deus 24, 49, 50, 50, 65, 66, 79, 85, 86, 88, 92, 98, 122, 124, 127, 132, 175 Agr 86, 93, 97, 101, 118, 118, 126, 128, 145, 174 Plant 10, 45, 60, 114, 149, 150, 161, 171, 172, 172, 172, 175 Ebr 2, 6, 7, 8, 9, 16, 18, 21, 24, 35, 37, 78, 95, 97, 109, 142, 152, 158, 160, 176, 179, 183, 185, 186, 194, 197, 198, 205, 218 Sobr 27, 42 Conf 18, 35, 37, 104, 125, 134, 167, 176, 191 Migr 24, 61, 67, 69, 85, 101, 115, 148, 172, 179, 194, 209, 217, 219, 223 Her 34, 46, 48, 136, 187, 207, 207, 208, 209, 213, 213, 214, 239, 246 Congr 25, 62, 82, 84, 152, 154, 160, 173 Fug 25, 65, 177 Mut 10, 113, 150, 150, 163, 167, 194, 237 Somn 1:83, 115, 124, 150, 152, 192, 227 Somn 2:83, 85, 91, 122, 136, 145, 159, 163, 164, 170, 183, 274, 282, 286, 291 Abr 1, 14, 27, 87, 96, 100, 143, 223, 224 Ios 59, 74, 109, 137, 143, 144 Mos 1:26, 41, 50, 68, 103, 103, 115, 144, 224, 234, 248, 270, 294, 323 Mos 2:15, 167, 177, 180, 248, 251 Decal 43, 57, 110, 114, 125, 144, 157 Spec 1:92, 142, 219, 286, 288, 301, 331, 344 Spec 2:12, 24, 34, 55, 71, 129, 209, 245, 249 Spec 3:35, 209 Spec 4:41, 56, 90, 102, 106, 108, 144, 147, 204, 209, 224, 228, 231 Virt 30, 61, 165, 166, 167, 182, 195, 205, 211 Praem 7, 33, 62, 106, 121, 131 Prob 36, 38, 83, 101 Contempl 17, 86 Aet 7, 10, 28, 31, 43, 81, 94, 101, 104, 105, 138, 139, 139, 148 Flacc 34, 82, 155 Legat 52, 73, 91, 98, 115, 218, 265, 268, 279, 354 Hypoth 6:9 QG 1:100:1a, 100:1b, 100:2a, 100:2a, 2:11, 3:3, 22, 4:51c QG isf 5 QE 2:4, 16, 17, 25b, 55b QE isf 8

ἐναντιότης (10) Opif 33 Conf 64 Her 23, 132, 133, 241, 311 Fug 196 Mos 1:117 Aet 21

ἐναντίωσις Conf 33 Abr 38 Mos 1:2 Aet 150 QG 1:100:2a

ἐναπεργάζομαι Contempl 60

ἐναπερείδω Spec 4:107

ἐναπερεύγω Decal 129 Virt 110

ἐναποθησαυρίζω Deus 42

ἐναποθλίβω Congr 150

ἐναποθνήσκω Mos 1:100 Decal 71 Spec 4:119 Aet 65

ἐναπόκειμαι (7) Deus 34, 135 Fug 34 Spec 2:206 Prob 66 Contempl 78 Flacc 86

ἐναπολαμβάνω Mos 2:123 Legat 217

ἐναπολείπω Opif 38 Aet 122

ἐναπομάσσω (13) Opif 151 Leg 1:79 Post 165 Deus 43 Mut 212 Mos 1:159, 159 Mos 2:76 Spec 1:47 Spec 2:228 Spec 4:163 Praem 116 Prob 15

ἐναποσημαίνω Deus 124

ἐναποτίθεμαι Ios 8 Spec 4:129

ἐνάργεια (22) Opif 56 Leg 2:39 Cher 56 Post 167 Plant 115 Conf 72, 156 Migr 35, 76, 154 Mut 164 Somn 2:42, 97, 106 Mos 1:95 Spec 1:273 Spec 2:227 Spec 4:86 Virt 102 Aet 99 Flacc 165, 165

ἐναργής (135) Opif 45, 84, 103, 109, 116, 134, 161 Leg 1:100 Leg 3:45, 91, 100, 103, 145, 183, 183 Cher 29, 35, 88, 108 Sacr 4, 34, 91, 110, 120 Det 3, 15, 22, 30, 68, 112, 131, 159 Post 16, 28 Gig 39 Deus 1, 4, 10, 14, 87 Agr 135 Plant 21, 36, 112, 137 Ebr 23, 36, 82, 93, 175, 185 Sobr 11, 21 Conf 84, 85, 148, 198 Migr 125 Her 129, 162, 195, 214, 237 Congr 136, 140, 143, 178 Fug 82, 175 Mut 164, 212 Somn 1:24 Somn 2:93 Abr 35, 61, 77, 120, 141, 153 Ios 51, 149, 179, 242 Mos 1:71, 188, 196, 268, 289, 303 Mos 2:12, 120, 200, 242, 262, 263 Decal 16, 46, 101, 151 Spec 1:26, 40, 45, 90, 250 Spec 2:141 Spec 3:52, 52, 114 Spec 4:49, 192, 196 Virt 63, 66 Praem 4, 17 Prob 32, 48, 136 Aet 18, 62 Flacc 35, 116, 150, 162 Legat 138, 154, 211, 316 Prov 2:11 QG 2:11, 13a, 13b, 3:11a QE 2:45a, 47

ἐνάρετος Deus 11

ἔναρθρος (8) Opif 126 Det 126 Post 105 Somn 1:29, 29 Decal 33 Legat 6 QG (Par) 2:3

ἐνάριθμος Leg 3:166

ἐναρμόζω (12) Opif 4 Det 107 Agr 6 Congr 4 Somn 1:27 Abr 51 Mos 1:117 Mos 2:38, 112, 112, 125 Spec 1:28

ἐναρμόνιος (34) Opif 54 Leg 1:14 Leg 3:57, 99, 121 Cher 24 Sacr 83 Post 104 Agr 11, 20, 51, 137 Migr 84, 104, 206 Congr 51, 76, 133 Fug 186 Somn 1:28, 205 Abr 47 Ios 145 Spec 1:90 Spec 2:57, 151, 230 Spec 3:137 Virt 77 Praem 7, 41 Contempl 88 Aet 32 Prov 2:7

ἐνάρχομαι Leg 3:96

ἐνασκέω (12) Migr 75 Congr 113 Mut 252 Ios 38 Decal 14 Spec 1:176, 203 Spec 2:88 Spec 3:43, 174 Aet 2 Legat 195

ἐναστράπτω Ebr 44 Migr 76

ἔνατος (8) Opif 103, 104 Congr 91, 102, 103, 104 Spec 2:41 Spec 4:41

ἐναυγάζω (8) Leg 1:46 Det 95, 128, 129 Conf 116 Migr 86, 222 Spec 3:6

ἐναύγασμα Leg 3:7

ἔναυλος (9) Leg 3:91 Post 155 Ebr 177 Congr 67 Mut 85 Mos 2:213 Spec 2:243 Praem 18 Flacc 167

ἔναυσμα Praem 171 Legat 245

ἐναυχέω Conf 118

ἐναύω Migr 91 Mos 2:219 Spec 2:65, 251

ἐναφανίζω Mos 1:124, 234 Legat 85

Ἐνάχ Post 60

ἐνδεής (16) Leg 3:149 Cher 59 Sacr 32 Det 34, 55, 56 Post 147 Plant 92 Somn 2:178, 178 Decal 99 Spec 2:107, 174 Virt 6 Praem 161 Prob 8

ἔνδεια (70) Cher 118 Det 113, 141 Post 82, 85, 144 Agr 39, 53, 90 Plant 69, 157 Migr 146, 155 Her 212, 289 Congr 172 Abr 45, 245 Ios 109, 113, 115, 161, 191, 242, 243, 260 Mos 1:184, 193, 197, 215, 251 Spec 1:80, 286, 294, 308 Spec 2:82, 85, 88, 187, 201, 203 Spec 3:17 Spec 4:72, 195, 211 Virt 86, 91, 130, 149, 156 Praem 103, 127, 130, 136 Prob 71, 77, 121 Contempl 14, 15, 35 Aet 36, 74, 93 Flacc 64 Legat 58, 257 Prov 2:38 QG (Par) 2:7 QE 2:3a, 10a

ἐνδείκνυμι (6) Leg 2:34 Det 108 Conf 91 Somn 1:88 Abr 81 Praem 166

ἔνδειξις (11) Opif 45, 87 Conf 173 Her 197, 200 Mut 54 Mos 1:96 Mos 2:45 Spec 1:286 Spec 3:55, 139

ἕνδεκα (8) Plant 63 Somn 2:6, 111, 113 Ios 8, 9, 9 Mos 2:178

ἐνδελέχεια Somn 1:30 Spec 1:170

ἐνδελεχής (7) Plant 164 Her 174 Congr 89, 103, 105 Somn 2:109 Spec 1:256

ἔνδεσις Conf 106

ἐνδέχομαι (75) Opif 159, 167 Leg 2:78 Leg 3:10, 234 Cher 51, 51, 89, 96 Sacr 7, 31, 125 Det 51, 57, 178 Post 10, 11, 97 Gig 28, 42 Deus 55, 183 Agr 163 Ebr 29, 123 Her 202, 297 Congr 60 Mut 57, 157 Somn 1:20 Somn 2:197 Abr 151, 157, 162, 175 Ios 32 Mos 1:246 Mos 2:107, 264, 281 Decal 85, 104, 112, 174 Spec 1:26, 36, 38, 117, 223, 230 Spec 2:143 Spec 3:119, 151, 197, 205 Spec 4:38, 53, 200, 211 Virt 168, 193 Praem 6 Prob 60 Aet 20, 59, 144 Flacc 59, 115, 181 Legat 67, 73, 80, 257, 325

ἐνδέω (36) Opif 126 Leg 2:22 Leg 3:151, 165 Det 85 Post 95, 152 Deus 35 Conf 92, 106, 177 Her 142, 158, 274 Fug 51 Mut 36, 88 Somn 1:111, 138 Somn 2:57, 235 Abr 250 Ios 264 Mos 1:25 Spec 2:186 Spec 4:54, 188 Virt 27, 74, 109 Contempl 15 Legat 47, 268 Hypoth 11:17 Prov 1, 1

ἐνδημέω Spec 4:142

ἐνδιάθετος (8) Opif 149 Migr 157 Mut 131 Abr 83 Mos 2:127, 129 Spec 4:69, 69

ἐνδιαιτάομαι (18) Opif 73, 142, 147, 161 Leg 1:9 Ebr 136 Conf 19 Somn 1:68 Mos 2:184 Spec 1:213 Spec 2:21, 207 Virt 183, 187 Praem 122 Flacc 123 Legat 338 Prov 2:58

ἐνδιαίτημα (19) Leg 1:44, 70 Cher 98 Post 49 Plant 33, 53 Migr 3, 28, 146 Her 238 Congr 116 Fug 162 Somn 1:149 Somn 2:90, 253 Spec 1:75, 270 Spec 4:92 QG 4:33b

ἐνδιαίτησις Plant 33 Spec 1:146

ἐνδιατίθημαι Flacc 48

ἐνδιατρίβω (18) Sacr 86 Gig 52 Agr 93, 103, 178 Conf 76, 78 Migr 28, 168, 197 Congr 23 Somn 1:47 Abr 115 Decal 30 Spec 1:75 Spec 3:89, 90 Praem 122

ἐνδίδωμι (33) Leg 2:28 Leg 3:201 Cher 32, 69 Sacr 26, 30 Post 72, 156 Ebr 58, 165 Sobr 23 Migr 26 Abr 94, 187 Ios 114 Mos 1:44, 89, 213, 268 Decal 174 Spec 2:93, 240 Spec 3:29, 61, 77, 79, 93 Spec 4:224 Prob 26, 61 Aet 132 Flacc 155 Legat 257

ἔνδικος (19) Opif 143, 147 Cher 101 Det 147 Agr 119 Fug 51 Mut 259 Somn 2:153, 177, 253 Abr 25, 74, 271 Mos 2:273 Decal 110 Spec 1:207 Spec 4:171 Aet 34 QE isf 29 ἔνδοθεν (14) Det 23, 127 Ebr 85 Conf 105, 121 Mut 43 Somn 2:233 Abr 73 Mos 2:95 Praem 50, 55 Prob 123 Aet 23 QG (Par) 2:4

ἐνδοιάζω (22) Opif 149, 170 Leg 3:89 Deus 26 Plant 88 Ebr 139, 169 Her 101 Congr 153 Fug 203 Mut 177, 178 Somn 1:12 Somn 2:17 Abr 107 Mos 2:261 Spec 2:84 Praem 40 Aet 77 QG 1:21, 21, 55a

ἐνδοιασμός (11) Post 13 Conf 31 Congr 153 Mut 178 Ios 183 Mos 1:16 Spec 2:213 Spec 3:55 Prov 2:42 QG 1:55a, 55c

ἐνδοιαστής Migr 148 Legat 244

ἐνδοιαστικός QG 1:55a

ἔνδον (40) Leg 3:40, 241 Deus 132, 183 Ebr 85, 86, 86, 87, 147 Her 13, 82, 82, 84 Fug 34 Mut 43 Abr 15, 115, 116, 170 Ios 51, 71 Mos 1:104, 316 Mos 2:60, 101, 152 Decal 49 Spec 1:72, 235, 276 Spec 3:138, 169, 206 Praem 113, 113 Legat 174, 319, 372 QG 2:71a QG (Par) 2:7

ἔνδοξος (24) Det 34 Post 109, 113 Agr 82 Ebr 195 Sobr 57 Migr 161 Fug 16, 25 Mut 232 Somn 1:155 Somn 2:269 Ios 76 Mos 1:160 Spec 4:74, 172, 172 Virt 170, 170 Prob 72 Legat 13, 173 QG 3:22 QG isf 5

ἐνδόσιμος Migr 104

ἔνδροσος Spec 2:143

ἔνδυμα Fug 185 Spec 1:85

ἐνδύνω ἐνδύω

ἐνδύω (ἐνδύνω) (11) Cher 9 Deus 102 Ebr 86 Conf 31 Fug 110, 110 Somn 1:214, 215, 225 Mos 2:135 Legat 97

ἐνέδρα (25) Cher 14 Det 78 Agr 105 Plant 103 Conf 160 Migr 144, 150 Fug 24 Somn 1:225 Ios 166, 181, 213 Spec 1:75, 314 Spec 3:66, 86, 97 Spec 4:67 Virt 42, 124 Praem 86, 147 Aet 56 Legat 345 Prov 2:31

ἐνεδρευτικός Sacr 32

ἐνεδρεύω Leg 2:98 Somn 2:40 Flacc 119, 178 QG 4:228

ἐνεῖδον ἐνοράω

ἐνεῖδον Opif 15 Agr 91 Spec 4:92

ἐνειλέω QG isf 6 QE isf 15

ἔνειμι (49) Opif 77, 138 Leg 1:38 Leg 3:151 Cher 15, 98 Sacr 22, 65, 98, 124 Det 136, 138, 153 Post 157 Gig 24 Plant 126, 153 Sobr 62 Migr 46, 84, 189 Her 1, 12, 315 Congr 10, 21 Fug 181, 208 Mut 49, 58 Somn 1:186 Somn 2:90 Abr 137, 267 Ios 193 Decal 101, 124 Spec 1:21, 191 Spec 4:66, 78, 116, 137, 185 Virt 167 Prob 63 Flacc 82 Legat 270 Prov 2:9

ἐνεῖπον QE 2:18

ἕνεκα (309) Opif 5, 21, 74, 74, 74, 84, 85, 87, 128, 163, 167 Leg 1:37, 43, 79, 98, 98 Leg 2:16, 16, 49, 49, 103 Leg 3:43, 126, 167, 167, 167, 167, 181, 203, 204, 209, 209 Cher 55, 126 Sacr 25, 86, 93, 116 Det 58, 59, 102, 104, 132 Post 49, 91, 117, 119, 136, 144 Deus 17, 34, 54, 57, 60, 122 Agr 14, 114, 133, 143 Plant 33, 56, 88, 104, 106, 115, 155 Ebr 20, 155 Sobr 29, 44 Conf 77, 98, 116, 129, 140, 196 Migr 76, 149, 154, 164, 209, 217 Her 34, 111, 123, 183, 223, 237 Congr 65, 80, 163 Fug 5, 22, 88, 94 Mut 72, 74, 136, 147 Somn 1:33, 69, 147, 165, 238 Somn 2:32, 96, 96, 116, 116, 262, 301 Abr 20, 23, 41, 56, 65, 79, 89, 97, 111, 118, 137, 142, 170, 186, 206, 225, 249, 273 Ios 59, 85, 94, 100, 112, 169, 170, 193, 230, 237, 254, 264 Mos 1:104, 148, 149, 245, 266, 323 Mos 2:41, 58, 61, 81, 91, 101, 145, 158, 169, 211, 248, 282, 291 Decal 1, 29, 59, 113 Spec 1:19, 28, 32, 39, 56, 56, 83, 95, 98, 122, 131, 133, 147, 159, 167, 195, 243, 244, 280, 283 Spec 2:12, 18, 34, 47, 50, 62, 104, 108, 150, 191, 195, 240, 251, 254 Spec 3:21, 44, 70, 78, 90, 105, 110, 113, 121, 128, 131, 141, 158, 163, 186, 203 Spec 4:14, 15, 31, 37, 43, 58, 92, 98, 98, 124, 127, 136, 158, 200, 213, 215, 223, 223 Virt 18, 28, 34, 96, 100, 101, 122, 126, 135, 203, 208 Praem 58, 138 Prob 22, 34, 65, 67 Contempl 1, 17, 22, 33, 42, 50, 72, 85 Aet 4, 20, 21, 39, 48, 56, 61, 107, 107 Flacc 20, 46, 82, 110, 116, 126, 145 Legat 36, 39, 81, 91, 105, 137, 137, 178, 187, 245, 253, 274, 286, 299, 309, 316, 361 Prov 2:7, 21, 22, 44, 56 QG 1:29, 93, 2:13a, 54a, 3:8, 21, 21, 4:168, 204, 206b QG isf 5, 10 QE 2:21

ἐνενήκοντα (7) Leg 3:85, 217 Mut 1, 1, 176, 188, 192

ἐνενηκονταέξ Opif 94

ἐνεπιδείκνυμαι Sobr 40 Abr 190

ἐνεργάζομαι (19) Opif 166 Cher 32 Sacr 26, 59 Ebr 8 Ios 157 Mos 1:58, 233, 263, 291 Spec 1:45 Spec 2:230 Spec 3:97 Spec 4:226 Praem 18, 54 Legat 74, 82 QE 2:45a

ἐνέργεια (61) Opif 75, 81 Leg 1:28, 56 Leg 2:24, 24, 36, 36, 37, 37, 37, 38, 40, 40, 44, 45, 45, 101 Leg 3:18, 22, 144, 183 Cher 62, 70, 71, 87, 128 Sacr 73, 97 Det 122, 172 Deus 47, 49 Agr 38 Ebr 101, 106, 106, 119, 171 Sobr 2, 34 Conf 68, 105 Migr 3, 32 Her 108, 110, 119 Mut 257 Somn 2:34 Abr 154, 155, 158 Ios 58, 147 Mos 2:130 Spec 1:47 Spec 2:60, 228 Spec 4:140 QG 1:24

ἐνεργέω (44) Leg 1:6, 29 Leg 2:31 Leg 3:20, 32, 86, 86, 234 Cher 14, 15, 79 Sacr 77, 133 Det 63, 64, 104, 114, 172 Agr 22 Ebr 185 Sobr 35, 37, 50 Migr 137 Congr 46 Fug 46, 173 Mut 122, 270 Abr 155 Decal 74 Spec 1:16, 145, 340 Spec 2:60, 67, 103 Spec 3:209 Contempl 42 QG 2:29, 4:204, 211 QE 2:16 QE isf 33

ἐνέργημα Det 114

ἐνερεύγομαι Contempl 45

ἐνερευθής Ebr 147

ἐνεσθίω ἐμφαγεῖν

ἐνευκαιρέω (7) Agr 56 Ebr 195 Conf 3 Somn 2:127 Spec 3:102 Spec 4:160 Flacc 33

ἐνευλογέομαι (6) Migr 1, 118, 122 Her 8 Somn 1:3, 176

ἐνευφραίνομαι (11) Post 32 Plant 39 Somn 1:50 Mos 2:210 Spec 1:304 Spec 2:46, 52, 219 Spec 3:1 Spec 4:141 Contempl 35

ἐνεχυράζω Somn 1:92, 101, 105, 113

ἐνεχύρασμα Somn 1:92

ἐνεχυριάζω Spec 3:204

ἐνέχυρον (10) Agr 149 Fug 150 Somn 1:92, 95, 98, 100 Ios 185 Virt 89, 89 QE isf 14

ἐνηβάω Prob 15 Contempl 67

ἐνηδυπαθέω Spec 3:165

ἐνήλατον Somn 2:57

ἐνηρεμέω Migr 189 Ios 53 Mos 2:36

ἐνησυχάζω Mos 2:36

ἐνηχέω (6) Her 67, 71 Mut 57 Mos 2:37 Spec 1:65 Spec 4:49

ἔνθα (20) Opif 139 Ios 202 Mos 1:14, 47, 65, 158, 276 Mos 2:92, 92 Decal 94 Spec 1:232 Spec 3:162 Spec 4:54, 69, 92, 123 Aet 33 Legat 229 Hypoth 0:1 Prov 2:23

ἐνθάδε Opif 135 Migr 196 Ios 224 Mos 1:280 Flacc 31

ἐνθαλασσεύω Deus 98

ἐνθάπτω Migr 16, 23 Mos 1:171

ἔνθεν (13) Sacr 36, 36 Migr 149 Mos 1:46, 46, 231, 231 Spec 1:86, 86 Contempl 86, 86 Legat 217, 217

ἐνθένδε (32) Sacr 119 Post 7, 35 Plant 34, 115, 150 Migr 189 Her 97, 99, 116, 276 Congr 99, 161, 177 Fug 21, 52, 63 Ios 92 Mos 1:71, 86, 276 Mos 2:47, 49, 165, 288 Spec 1:152 Virt 22, 53, 76, 139 Praem 29, 80

ἔνθεος (ἔνθους) (18) Deus 138 Conf 59 Migr 35, 84 Her 249, 264 Fug 168 Mut 39 Somn 1:36 Mos 1:175, 201, 277, 288 Decal 35, 175 Spec 4:48 Prob 80 Flacc 169

ἔνθερμος (10) Cher 30 Migr 165 Her 282, 309 Fug 134 Mut 180 Somn 1:31 Somn 2:67 Abr 79 Mos 2:172

ἔνθεσις Agr 6

ἐνθήκη Flacc 57

ἔνθους ἔνθεος

ἐνθουσίασις Spec 4:52

ἐνθουσιασμός Conf 159 Congr 112 Fug 90 Mos 2:246, 258

ἐνθουσιάζω ἐνθουσιάω

ἐνθουσιάω (ἐνθουσιάζω) (26) Opif 71 Cher 49 Sobr 27 Conf 44 Migr 190 Her 70, 258, 259, 261, 263 Congr 132 Somn 1:254 Somn 2:1 Mos 1:57, 286 Mos 2:37, 192, 280 Spec 1:56, 65, 315 Spec 3:91, 126 Spec 4:49 Contempl 12, 87

ἐνθουσιώδης Somn 2:233 Mos 2:191

ἐνθυμέομαι (8) Deus 20, 33, 49 Migr 73 Mut 240, 241 QG 1:93 QG isf 3

ἐνθύμημα (21) Leg 3:230 Cher 16 Det 40, 72, 125, 127, 128, 130, 132, 132 Migr 4, 35, 73, 79, 79, 80, 81 Fug 16 Somn 2:260 Mos 2:38, 199

ἐνθύμιος Sacr 76 Mut 239 Spec 4:69 Contempl 78

ἐνιαύσιος Spec 2:204

ἐνιαυτός (77) Opif 52, 55, 60, 60, 104, 116 Leg 1:6 Leg 3:11 Gig 52 Plant 118, 119, 136 Ebr 195 Congr 4, 90 Fug 57, 184 Mut 267, 267, 268 Somn 1:20 Ios 108, 112, 260, 270 Mos 1:202, 238 Mos 2:222 Decal 163 Spec 1:90, 172, 180 Spec 2:39, 48, 71, 86, 86, 97, 113, 117, 117, 121, 122, 146, 152, 211, 213, 220, 223 Spec 4:215, 233, 235, 235 Virt 98, 99, 122 Praem 112, 153, 153, 155 Aet 19, 52, 71, 109, 118, 123, 145, 145, 146 Flacc 133 Legat 148, 216, 306 QG 2:5b QG (Par) 2:5 QE 2:20, 25a

ἐνιδρύω (24) Opif 128, 139, 152 Det 123 Conf 107 Migr 98 Decal 52, 63 Spec 1:64, 191 Spec 2:232, 239 Spec 3:4, 68 Spec 4:20, 160 Praem 25, 80, 135, 148 Prob 113 Contempl 35 Legat 73 Prov 2:63

ἐνίημι Prob 119 Legat 197

ἔνικμος Opif 39

ἑνικός Decal 43

ἔνιοι (146) Opif 15 Leg 1:34, 57, 57 Leg 3:85, 86, 86, 115, 160, 182, 210, 215 Sacr 101 Det 36, 101, 122 Post 41, 97 Gig 18, 18, 34 Deus 16, 113, 152 Agr 130, 134, 136 Plant 80, 107, 110 Ebr 104, 122, 172, 176, 177 Conf 43, 118 Migr 45, 66, 158, 158 Her 155, 280 Congr 78 Fug 55, 120 Mut 28, 60, 71, 164, 227 Somn 1:106, 118 Somn 2:277 Abr 65, 184, 193, 246, 255, 267, 276 Ios 137, 139 Mos 1:10, 25, 119, 148, 150, 183, 265 Mos 2:8, 174, 211, 222, 260 Decal 59, 63, 96, 112, 114 Spec 1:5, 10, 58, 79 Spec 2:56, 72, 129, 244 Spec 3:43, 47, 65, 128, 161 Spec 4:46, 61, 90, 122, 133, 151 Virt 139, 169, 218 Praem 12, 89, 95, 96, 146 Prob 58 Contempl 35, 68 Aet 12, 16, 17, 18, 47, 76 Flacc 46, 105, 141, 148, 173, 180 Legat 116, 153, 165, 215, 285, 340, 356, 358, 361, 362, 370 Hypoth 11:8 Prov 2:44, 59, 71 QG 1:93, 3:29, 52, 52 QE 1:7b, 2:2, 9b, 17, 40

ἐνίστημι (28) Leg 1:6 Leg 2:42 Sacr 47 Agr 59 Plant 114 Migr 43 Mut 109 Somn 2:209, 210 Ios 158, 260 Mos 1:115, 220 Spec 1:183, 186 Spec 2:84, 179, 210, 220 Virt 47 Praem 71 Aet 10 Flacc 83 Legat 30, 158, 275 QG 2:72, 72

ἐνλαλέω Fug 203

ἐννάκις Opif 93

ἐννέα (23) Opif 51, 93, 107, 107, 108, 108 Det 14 Plant 124 Ebr 105 Congr 92, 94, 104, 105, 105 Mut 1, 1 Abr 10, 236, 242, 244 Mos 2:85, 86 QG 3:61

ἐννεάζω Somn 1:11

ἐννέμω Mos 1:237, 320

ἐννήχομαι Ebr 182 Somn 2:260

ἐννοέω (24) Opif 19 Leg 2:61 Cher 75 Det 90, 97 Plant 71 Ebr 134 Migr 114 Her 130 Mut 139 Somn 1:91, 100, 187 Somn 2:116 Abr 235 Mos 1:287 Mos 2:219 Decal 10, 69 Spec 1:33 Spec 2:11 Virt 54 Prov 2:10 QG 1:93

ἐννόημα (7) Cher 69 Sacr 103 Det 76 Post 36 Deus 120 Her 242 Somn 1:45

ἔννοια (68) Opif 36, 49, 59 Leg 1:35, 37, 91 Leg 2:32, 32 Leg 3:81, 98, 119, 215, 234 Sacr 91, 101 Det 68, 86, 86, 87, 91 Post 14, 80, 115, 135 Gig 20 Deus 7, 34, 49 Agr 126 Ebr 101 Conf 120, 127 Her 240, 241, 299 Fug 70, 99 Mut 241 Somn 1:68, 143, 234 Abr 69, 102, 143 Ios 227 Mos 1:122, 140, 197 Decal 60, 146 Spec 1:33, 34, 35, 65 Spec 2:30, 208 Spec 4:71, 138 Virt 214 Praem 40, 42 Contempl 87 Aet 103 Flacc 183 Legat 214 Hypoth 7:2 QG 2:34a QE 2:47

ἔννομος Post 176 Migr 22 Abr 242

ἐνοικέω (13) Leg 3:3, 46, 223 Cher 104 Post 122 Plant 169 Sobr 66 Mos 1:27 Spec 1:146 Spec 4:49 Virt 29 Praem 87 Prov 2:23

ἔνοικος QG 4:97:1, 97:2

ἐνομιλέω (20) Opif 165 Sacr 9 Det 154 Deus 55, 167 Agr 93, 166 Ebr 37 Migr 13 Congr 18, 31 Somn 1:228 Somn 2:252 Abr 157 Mos 1:49 Spec 1:298 Spec 4:161 Virt 10 Praem 36 Flacc 165

ἐνομματόω (6) Ebr 82 Congr 145 Mut 56, 82 Somn 1:164 Virt 11

ἐνοπλίζω Cher 35

ἔνοπλος Aet 57, 68

ἐνοπτρίζω Migr 98

ἐνοράω ἐνεῖδον

ἐνοράω (8) Fug 115 Abr 115 Ios 4 Mos 1:99 Mos 2:142

ἐνορθιάζω Sacr 21

ἐνορμέω Congr 30 Flacc 92

ἐνορμίζω (13) Agr 174 Plant 152 Her 305 Congr 113 Fug 50 Somn 1:124 Somn 2:85, 225 Abr 47 Decal 67 Spec 2:52 Virt 105 Praem 58

ἐνοχλέω Ebr 180 Mos 2:24 Spec 1:336

ἔνοχος (33) Leg 3:32, 35 Sacr 71 Sobr 50 Congr 57 Fug 78 Somn 2:237 Ios 80, 216, 219 Mos 2:203 Decal 133, 138 Spec 1:20, 104, 223, 277 Spec 2:26, 31 Spec 3:61, 62, 77, 86, 89, 119, 120, 129, 154 Spec 4:10, 55, 87 Flacc 80 QG 3:52

ἑνόω (41) Opif 131 Leg 2:49, 50 Leg 3:139 Det 49, 50, 108 Conf 67 Migr 132, 180, 220 Her 130, 198 Mut 200 Somn 1:111, 128, 169 Abr 51, 63 Mos 1:179 Mos 2:254, 287 Spec 1:68, 286 Spec 2:239 Spec 3:27, 28, 113 Spec 4:68 Virt 26, 138 Praem 56, 64 Prob 113 Aet 80, 139, 139 Flacc 71 QG 2:54d, 3:3 QG (Par) 2:4

ἐνσημαίνω Det 77 Post 93 Ebr 89, 133 Her 181

ἐνσκευάζω Sacr 28 Ebr 7 Somn 2:182 Flacc 40 Legat 94

ἐνσοφιστεύω Agr 96 Ebr 71 Ios 125

ἐνσπαθάω Spec 4:217

ἔνσπονδος (19) Conf 26, 40 Migr 202 Her 246 Somn 2:12, 104 Ios 263 Mos 1:243 Spec 3:30, 113 Spec 4:224 Virt 50, 107, 118, 151, 153, 154 Praem 92 QG 4:7*

ἐνστάζω Prob 160

ἔνστασις Leg 3:189 Ios 130, 246 Spec 4:29

ἐνστόμιος Ebr 106, 190 Conf 194

ἐνσφραγίζω (27) Opif 18, 20, 166 Sacr 135 Det 38, 86 Ebr 88, 90 Conf 102 Somn 1:29, 158 Somn 2:16 Mos 1:230 Mos 2:76, 132, 209 Decal 11 Spec 1:30, 59 Spec 2:104 Spec 3:35 Spec 4:16, 107, 160, 218 Virt 52 Legat 77

ἐνσχολάζω Sacr 86 Gig 52 Ebr 10 Somn 2:127 Praem 122

ἐνσώματος Leg 1:1

ἐνταῦθα (καί) (27) Opif 70, 71 Leg 1:101 Leg 3:115, 249 Sacr 67 Det 87, 89 Deus 162 Migr 20 Her 114 Congr 70 Fug 19, 149 Somn 2:221 Abr 195 Ios 167 Mos 1:171, 193, 202 Mos 2:174 Spec 2:118 Spec 3:74 Praem 6, 65 Legat 347 QG 4:88

ἐνταυθοῖ (8) Migr 28, 171 Fug 62 Ios 168 Mos 1:320, 322 Mos 2:36 Flacc 172

ἐντείνω Spec 3:141

ἐντελέχεια Opif 47 Leg 1:100 Leg 2:73

ἐντελεχής Legat 157, 280, 291, 317

ἐντελής Mut 50 Spec 2:184 Spec 4:144

ἐντέλλω (11) Leg 1:90, 90, 92, 95, 95, 96 Leg 3:222, 246 Post 102 QG 2:16, 16

ἐντέμνω Det 107 Plant 152

ἐντεριώνη Det 107

ἔντερον QG (Par) 2:7, 2:7

ἐντεῦθεν (9) Opif 105 Det 5, 27 Migr 171 Fug 127, 131 Mut 43 Legat 87 QG 4:200a

ἔντευξις Sacr 35 Det 92 Mos 2:242 Legat 276

ἔντεχνος Det 41 Plant 173 Migr 85 Mut 87 Mos 1:277

ἐντήκω (8) Post 165 Gig 44 Ebr 159 Migr 157 Her 310 Congr 64 Mut 174 Prob 117

ἐντίθημι (14) Deus 42 Agr 69 Plant 29 Ebr 70, 139 Somn 1:232 Somn 2:58 Decal 35 Spec 3:44 Spec 4:79, 137 Virt 45, 71 QG 1:100:2b

ἐντίκτω Sobr 2 Conf 85 Spec 4:80 Virt 8

ἔντιμος Fug 30 Spec 3:130 Virt 174 Contempl 83

ἐντολή (10) Leg 1:93 Post 62 Her 8 Congr 170 Somn 2:175 Spec 1:300 Praem 2, 79, 101 Flacc 74

ἔντονος Sacr 37

ἐντός (ὁ) (64) Opif 91, 118, 118 Leg 1:15, 15, 15, 60 Leg 3:40, 40, 99, 239 Cher 22, 23 Sacr 31 Post 3, 5 Gig 38 Agr 24 Plant 3, 30 Ebr 185 Her 233 Congr 136 Fug 104, 153 Somn 1:184 Abr 128, 226 Ios 168 Mos 1:108, 115 Mos 2:34, 80, 82, 90, 180 Decal 43, 119 Spec 1:158, 160, 241 Spec 2:113, 114, 116, 117, 121, 213 Spec 3:205 Spec 4:4, 21 Aet 20, 22, 22, 78 Flacc 121 Legat 10, 126, 212, 253, 330 Prov 2:57 QG 2:5b QG (Par) 2:5 QE isf 32

ἐντοσθίδια Spec 1:213, 232

ἐντόσθιος Praem 143

ἐντρέπω Leg 2:66 QG 1:65

ἐντρέφω (19) Leg 1:102 Sacr 33, 63, 76, 78 Her 274, 275 Fug 173 Mut 252 Somn 2:26 Spec 1:309, 314 Spec 4:16, 150 Prob 98, 114 Legat 170, 195 Hypoth 6:1

ἐντρέχω Spec 4:99

ἐντρίβω Contempl 50

ἐντροπή QG 3:58

ἐντρυφάω (10) Post 32 Somn 2:55 Ios 205 Spec 1:304 Spec 2:52 Spec 3:27 Virt 67, 99 Prov 2:12, 64

ἐντρύφημα Somn 2:242

ἐντυγχάνω (84) Opif 6, 165 Leg 3:248 Cher 32, 48, 57, 62 Sacr 48, 58, 79 Det 159, 165 Deus 61, 91, 93, 93, 120, 136, 160 Ebr 48, 49, 52, 79, 124, 174 Sobr 3, 17 Migr 29, 177 Her 24, 29, 30, 109, 286 Congr 9, 143 Fug 26, 130 Mut 116, 119, 126, 129, 225 Somn 1:49, 70, 71, 214 Somn 2:233, 301 Abr 4, 15 Ios 137, 164, 210, 256 Mos 1:139, 173, 275 Mos 2:11, 40, 229, 243 Decal 37 Spec 1:28, 214, 321 Spec 2:104 Spec 3:6, 105 Spec 4:56, 60, 60, 142, 161, 162 Virt 17, 170 Contempl 28 Aet 12 Flacc 38 Legat 195, 239 QG 4:144 QE isf 8

ἐντυμβεύω Leg 1:106, 108 Spec 4:188

ἐντυπόω Leg 3:95 Spec 2:89 Spec 4:137 Praem 64 Legat 177

ἐντύφω (10) Ebr 27 Migr 123 Her 296 Somn 2:93 Abr 140 Ios 4, 124 Spec 1:4 Spec 4:27 Aet 93

ἐνυβρίζω Spec 4:202

ἔνυδρος (30) Opif 62, 84, 147, 147 Cher 111, 111 Det 151, 151, 152 Gig 7, 10, 11 Conf 6 Her 139, 139 Somn 1:135 Somn 2:288 Mos 1:103 Decal 78 Spec 3:8 Spec 4:100, 101, 110, 116, 118 Praem 87 Contempl 8, 54 Aet 45 Legat 139

ἐνυπάρχω (13) Opif 64, 76 Leg 3:97 Cher 91 Ebr 28 Migr 55 Abr 140 Ios 40 Spec 3:103 Aet 108 Legat 63 Prov 2:59 QG 2:64c

ἐνυπνιάζω Somn 1:3, 133 Somn 2:105, 111, 135

ἐνυπνιαστής Somn 2:42, 104 Ios 12

ἐνύπνιον (19) Leg 3:226, 229, 229, 229 Cher 128 Migr 19 Somn 1:121 Somn 2:78, 96, 97, 111, 111, 135, 136, 138 Ios 126, 130, 134, 143

ἔνυστρον Spec 1:147, 148

ἐνυφαίνω Somn 1:225 Contempl 49

ἐνώμοτος Conf 26 Somn 1:13 Somn 2:298 Spec 2:14

ἐνώπιος (22) Leg 3:9 Ebr 54, 84, 149 Congr 139 Fug 59, 141, 212 Mut 39, 40, 41, 41, 42, 47, 201, 201, 216 Somn 2:226 Spec 4:131 QG 2:11, 4:131 QE 2:47

Ἐνώς (6) Det 138, 139 Abr 8, 12 Praem 14 QG 3:11a

ἕνωσις (22) Leg 1:8, 37 Leg 3:38 Det 107 Post 12 Agr 6 Plant 60 Conf 69 Migr 220 Her 40, 242 Fug 112 Mos 2:243 Spec 4:168, 207 Virt 135 Aet 75, 147 Prov 2:3 QG 3:3, 21 QG (Par) 2:4

ἑνωτικός (7) Opif 131 Plant 89 Spec 1:52, 137, 317 Virt 35 Contempl 63

ἐνώτιον Leg 3:23 Post 166 Migr 97 Congr 113

Ἐνώχ (17) Post 33, 33, 35, 35, 40, 40, 40, 41, 44, 66 Conf 122, 123 Mut 34, 34 Abr 17, 17 QG 3:11a

ἕξ (73) Opif 13, 13, 14, 51, 96, 105, 107, 107, 107, 107, 108, 108, 108, 109, 109, 110, 128 Leg 1:3, 12 Plant 123 Ebr 111 Her 175, 177, 215, 216, 219, 220, 220, 225 Congr 8 Fug 73, 87, 94, 100 Somn 1:26 Abr 28, 29, 30 Mos 2:78, 80, 102, 103, 112, 123, 123, 133 Decal 28, 96, 97, 98, 99, 101, 163 Spec 1:158, 172, 172 Spec 2:41, 56, 60, 66, 67, 79 Spec 3:123 Praem 155, 155 Prob 122, 122 Contempl 30, 35 Legat 227 QG 3:38a, 49b QE 2:46

ἐξαγγέλλω Plant 128 Migr 73 QE isf 13

ἐξάγιστος Post 159 Gig 20 Legat 166

ἐξαγκωνίζω Congr 46 Mos 1:299 Flacc 74 Legat 129, 228

ἐξαγορεύω Somn 2:296, 299 Praem 163

ἐξαγριαίνω Sacr 104 Somn 2:87

ἐξαγριόω (καί) (15) Sacr 20 Det 25 Plant 43 Migr 210 Mut 39 Somn 2:66, 165 Mos 2:61 Spec 1:313 Spec 2:136 Spec 4:82 Praem 146 Aet 68 Legat 10, 163

ἐξάγω (25) Opif 64 Leg 2:11, 13, 84, 87 Leg 3:39, 40, 40, 40, 41, 41 Post 67, 155 Agr 44 Ebr 14 Her 76, 81, 81, 85, 96 Mut 207, 209 Somn 1:71 Somn 2:222 Mos 1:171

Ἐξαγωγή Migr 14 Her 14, 251 Somn 1:117

ἐξαγώνιος Ios 138

ἐξαδιαφορέω Leg 3:202 Det 122 Post 81 Spec 2:46

ἐξαδιαφόρησις Her 253

ἐξαερόω Somn 1:144 Aet 107

ἑξαετία (8) Spec 2:39, 84, 104 Spec 4:215 Virt 98, 123 Flacc 8, 158

ἑξαήμερος Leg 2:12 Decal 100

ἐξαιματόω Spec 1:216

ἐξαιμάτωσις Spec 1:218

ἐξαιρετός (93) Opif 15, 62, 66, 99 Leg 3:26, 86, 139 Det 92 Post 105, 127 Gig 11, 64 Deus 45 Plant 17, 21, 42, 55, 58, 63 Sobr 53 Conf 187 Her 36, 205 Congr 17, 108 Fug 118 Mut 40 Somn 1:18, 25, 35 Somn 2:75 Abr 7, 150, 162, 165, 197, 199, 261 Ios 4, 42, 157, 178, 257 Mos 1:87, 205, 236, 278, 317 Mos 2:17, 155, 194, 291 Decal 76, 112, 159, 161 Spec 1:52, 102, 145, 290 Spec 2:55, 89, 110, 164, 190, 195 Spec 3:134 Spec 4:12, 35, 125, 179 Virt 199, 206, 217 Praem 14, 36, 53, 123, 163 Prob 8 Contempl 36 Aet 79 Flacc 117 Legat 117, 149, 212, 318, 371 QG 1:20, 2:62, 4:173 QE 2:3a, 55a

ἐξαιρέω (13) Sacr 117 Det 16 Deus 47 Conf 93 Migr 14, 25 Her 59, 124, 271 Spec 2:218 Praem 124 Legat 147 QG 2:54c

ἐξαίρω (34) Opif 147 Leg 3:186 Cher 81 Det 152 Gig 22 Agr 10, 89, 169 Plant 24, 152 Ebr 14, 28, 39, 128 Sobr 2, 64 Migr 65, 168, 171, 172 Her 269 Fug 45, 194 Somn 1:139 Somn 2:78, 139, 284 Mos 1:27, 31, 177 Decal 143 Virt 14, 173 Aet 136

ἐξαίσιος (8) Opif 113 Abr 43 Mos 1:119 Mos 2:209 Spec 1:92 Contempl 78 Aet 11, 141

ἐξαιτέω Spec 2:239

ἐξαίφνης (38) Opif 113 Leg 3:227 Cher 62, 100 Sacr 26 Post 113 Deus 37, 92, 97 Agr 176 Migr 35 Mut 165 Somn 2:143 Abr 138 Ios 23, 214, 238 Mos 1:65, 118, 283 Mos 2:271 Spec 1:57 Spec 3:96, 107 Virt 49 Praem 15, 37, 80, 127, 128 Aet 141 Flacc 113, 124 Legat 123, 217, 337 Hypoth 6:7 QG isf 5

ἑξακόσιοι Ebr 111 Mos 1:168

ἐξαλείφω Her 20 QG 2:15a, 15a, 15b

ἐξαλλάσσω Cher 53 Mos 2:272 Spec 1:62

ἐξαλλοιόω Somn 2:118

ἐξάλλομαι Agr 76, 115 Prov 2:65

ἔξαλλος Migr 203

ἐξαμαρτάνω (19) Plant 107 Ebr 18 Her 271 Somn 2:292 Ios 156, 171 Decal 70, 98, 172 Spec 1:53, 100, 237 Spec 3:175, 182 Spec 4:200 Virt 160 Praem 88, 171 Flacc 51

ἐξαμαυρόω Mos 1:287 Virt 191 Prob 73 Prov 2:49

ἐξαμβλόω Det 147

ἐξανάγω Her 305 Somn 1:42 Somn 2:85 Decal 14

ἐξαναλίσκω (ἐξαναλόω) (25) Ios 22, 56, 96 Mos 1:68, 69, 119 Mos 2:154, 157, 262, 283 Spec 3:10 Spec 4:26, 28, 83 Praem 129 Aet 21, 85, 125, 127, 128, 137 Flacc 65 Legat 131, 344 QG 2:28

ἐξαναλόω ἐξαναλίσκω

ἐξανατέλλω Leg 1:56

ἐξαναχωρέω (16) Opif 113 Post 18 Deus 177 Agr 93 Ebr 106, 183 Mut 67 Somn 1:236 Mos 1:91, 144, 176 Decal 146 Spec 2:143 Spec 3:188 Spec 4:81 Aet 142

ἐξανεμόω Somn 2:298

ἐξανθέω Deus 129 Spec 1:118

ἐξάνθημα Spec 1:80

ἐξάνθησις Mos 1:127

ἐξανίημι Spec 4:215

ἐξανιμάω Deus 156

ἐξανίστημι (15) Leg 2:26 Sacr 77 Det 41, 127 Post 10, 124, 170, 170, 175, 182 Deus 73 Agr 31 Mos 1:124 Spec 3:106 Prov 2:29

ἐξαπατάω Leg 3:109 Hypoth 6:3 QG 1:31

ἐξαπάτη Prov 2:36

ἐξάπινα Fug 115

ἐξαπιναῖος (34) Opif 83, 156, 161 Her 249, 279 Somn 1:71 Somn 2:214 Abr 169, 242 Ios 101 Mos 1:79, 123, 135, 168, 218, 269 Mos 2:167, 251 Decal 16, 114 Spec 1:26, 65 Spec 2:108, 143 Spec 3:3, 104 Praem 133, 150, 169 Legat 124, 184, 226, 344 Prov 2:56

ἑξαπλάσιος Opif 96, 96 QG (Par) 2:5, 2:5, 2:5

ἐξαπλόω Leg 3:43, 43, 44 Agr 16 Spec 4:79

ἐξάπλωσις Ebr 185

ἐξαπόλλυμι Aet 5

ἐξαποστέλλω (15) Leg 1:96 Leg 3:8, 21, 21, 21, 21, 21 Cher 1 Post 70 Gig 17 Ebr 77 Conf 94 Fug 20, 22 Mos 1:88

ἐξαποστολή Post 41, 44

ἐξάπτω (23) Cher 64 Det 84 Gig 25, 34 Agr 75 Plant 144 Ebr 199 Migr 100, 123 Her 89, 226 Congr 30 Fug 61 Somn 1:157, 222 Somn 2:181, 291 Spec 1:62 Spec 4:83, 137, 138 Legat 130, 220

ἐξαριθμέω Her 86

ἐξαρκέω (19) Leg 1:34 Leg 3:47, 211, 234 Cher 91 Sacr 121 Post 168 Gig 66 Ebr 110 Conf 152 Her 100 Mut 232 Ios 51 Spec 4:170 Virt 123, 188 Praem 103 Legat 274, 343

ἔξαρνος Her 105 Decal 171

ἐξαρπάζω Deus 89 Migr 224 Somn 2:146, 233 Abr 176

ἐξαρτάω (8) Cher 24 Sacr 41 Gig 44 Deus 14 Ebr 82 Somn 2:232 Spec 1:338 Spec 4:138

ἔξαρχος (13) Plant 122 Ebr 94, 121, 125, 153 Migr 28 Somn 2:254, 277 Mos 2:256 Spec 1:56 Spec 4:190 Contempl 83 QG 1:66

ἐξάρχω (18) Agr 81 Ebr 95, 96, 96, 96, 105, 105, 110, 111, 112, 115, 123, 209 Conf 59 Mos 1:180 Mos 2:256 Contempl 87 Flacc 121

ἑξάς (25) Opif 13, 89, 95 Leg 1:4, 16 Post 64 Deus 12 Plant 124 Her 165, 175, 176, 219 Mos 2:266 Decal 159, 159 Spec 1:172 Spec 2:58, 58, 59, 59, 64, 177 Praem 65 QE 2:46, 46

ἐξασθενέω (17) Leg 3:186 Cher 15, 82, 103 Deus 14 Conf 37 Abr 240 Decal 34 Spec 4:211 Virt 156, 157 Praem 29, 48 Aet 36, 128, 129 Flacc 16

ἐξατμίζω Aet 110

ἐξαύγεια QE isf 6

ἑξαχῆ (7) Leg 1:4 Cher 23 Agr 30 Her 232, 233 Somn 1:26 Decal 103

ἔξαψις Spec 1:298 Contempl 3

ἐξεγείρω Post 71 Somn 1:183 Somn 2:218

ἐξεθίζομαι Spec 2:174 Spec 4:161 Virt 95

ἐξεικονίζω Congr 137, 137 Somn 2:16

ἔξειμι (55) Opif 119 Leg 3:81, 163 Cher 3 Post 6, 179 Deus 8, 148 Plant 64, 169 Conf 30, 92 Migr 115, 135 Her 299 Somn 1:10 Somn 2:83, 86, 278 Abr 104, 170 Ios 43, 157 Mos 1:147, 170, 227, 275 Mos 2:24, 213 Spec 1:115, 163, 242, 254, 320 Spec 2:183, 183, 232, 250 Spec 3:150 Spec 4:129, 142 Virt 57 Praem 113 Prob 32, 59 Contempl 44 Flacc 50 Legat 30, 128, 181, 191, 280, 297 Hypoth 11:12 Prov 2:57

ἐξεῖπον Cher 49 Congr 91 Abr 170

ἐξείργω Hypoth 7:7

ἐξελαύνω (6) Gig 59 Her 169 Mos 1:139 Decal 155 Spec 3:90 Spec 4:25

ἐξελέγχω (6) Sacr 30 Post 119 Aet 69 Flacc 76 Legat 302 QG 1:60:2

ἐξέλκω Migr 196, 197 Prob 130

ἐξεναντίας Cher 35

ἐξεπίσταμαι Prov 2:25

ἐξεργάζομαι (8) Plant 85, 141 Fug 123 Spec 1:204, 339 Spec 4:7 Virt 113 Hypoth 7:17

ἐξερεθίζω Spec 4:139

ἐξερευνάω Plant 141

ἐξέρχομαι (72) Leg 2:59 Leg 3:43, 43, 43, 44, 47, 152, 152, 162, 225, 229, 229, 240, 240, 241, 241, 248, 249 Cher 12, 13 Sacr 135 Det 29, 126, 129, 163 Post 1, 5, 10, 67 Deus 99, 145, 166 Agr 78 Ebr 9, 101, 101 Conf 105 Migr 62, 79, 176, 216 Her 68, 81, 84, 84, 251, 272 Congr 137, 163 Mut 21, 81, 177, 243 Somn 1:4, 5, 41, 47, 85, 189 Somn 2:231, 232 Mos 1:139, 290 Mos 2:154 Praem 95 Prob 26 Legat 225 QG 2:39, 48, 66, 4:51a, 88

ἐξεσθίω ἐκφαγεῖν

ἐξετάζω (116) Opif 88, 118 Leg 1:49, 54 Leg 2:35, 38 Leg 3:13, 119, 182, 201, 241, 246, 252 Cher 5, 58, 105 Sacr 14, 99 Det 8, 68, 88, 120, 171 Deus 90, 95, 173 Agr 95 Plant 94, 121, 132 Migr 51, 102, 102, 185, 199 Her 114, 114, 152 Congr 101, 149 Fug 47, 125 Mut 12, 65, 145, 152, 215, 236, 267 Somn 1:56, 228, 233 Somn 2:103, 159, 164, 188, 235 Abr 102, 160, 218 Ios 68, 125, 173 Mos 1:24, 29, 111, 229, 245, 295, 329 Mos 2:27, 52, 210 Decal 31, 71, 93, 110 Spec 1:154, 189, 195, 200, 209, 224 Spec 2:170 Spec 3:52, 66, 68, 129, 141, 166, 171, 172 Spec 4:70, 140, 151, 154, 197 Virt 22, 22, 32 Praem 34, 56, 91 Prob 24 Aet 145 Flacc 79, 148 Legat 49, 112, 350 Hypoth 11:6 Prov 2:17, 39 QG (Par) 2:1, 2:2, 2:3

ἐξέτασις (9) Opif 77 Det 47 Gig 57 Ebr 218 Congr 143 Mut 68 Spec 1:167 Spec 4:206 Flacc 133

ἐξεταστής Ios 47 Spec 3:53 Spec 4:171

ἐξεταστικός Congr 125 Abr 253

ἐξέτι Deus 49

ἐξευδιάζω Spec 4:58

ἐξευμαρίζω (9) Opif 81 Abr 185 Ios 10 Mos 1:19, 67 Spec 4:99 Praem 93, 115 Contempl 35

ἐξευμενίζω (18) Sacr 37 Migr 100, 211 Fug 6 Somn 2:292 Abr 6 Ios 227 Mos 1:49, 105 Mos 2:147, 166 Spec 1:97 Spec 2:17, 196, 209 Flacc 22, 108 Legat 178

ἐξευνουχίζω Det 176 Deus 111 Ebr 211

ἐξευρίσκω Leg 2:94 Somn 2:25 Abr 232 Mos 2:39 Virt 96

ἐξέχω Post 180 Her 218

ἐξηγέομαι Leg 3:21 Hypoth 7:13

ἐξήγησις Contempl 78

ἐξηγητής Spec 2:159

ἑξήκοντα (6) Opif 93, 106 Mos 1:147 Mos 2:89 Spec 2:33, 33

ἑξηκονταετία Spec 2:33

ἑξηκοντατέσσαρες Opif 91, 94, 94

ἐξήκω Leg 1:6

ἐξημερόω (καί) Mos 1:26 Virt 161 Prob 64

ἑξῆς (121) Opif 47, 99, 101, 105, 131 Leg 1:101 Leg 2:19, 73 Leg 3:4, 179, 214, 222 Sacr 112 Det 32, 38, 57, 67, 141, 177 Post 33, 44 Gig 57 Deus 51, 70, 150 Plant 73, 176 Ebr 80 Sobr 1 Conf 1, 54, 57 Migr 109, 118, 127 Her 12, 130, 237, 256, 293, 307 Congr 173 Fug 2, 7, 77, 83, 92, 119, 143, 177 Mut 13, 54, 130, 151 Somn 1:120 Somn 2:13, 44, 300 Abr 3, 17, 27, 60, 133, 136 Ios 1, 80, 159, 203, 217, 268 Mos 1:334 Mos 2:69, 78, 109, 246, 258, 270 Decal 1, 18, 82, 138 Spec 1:65, 117, 129, 161, 212, 226, 235, 256 Spec 2:1, 39, 40, 79, 86, 188, 223 Spec 3:22, 136 Spec 4:39, 203 Virt 1, 51, 146, 156 Praem 52, 67, 110 Contempl 30, 66

Flacc 156, 156 Legat 138, 252 Prov 2:2 QG 1:76b, 2:5a, 48, 3:23, 4:51a QG (Par) 2:5 QE 2:1

ἐξησσάομαι Sacr 81

ἐξητασμένως (8) Post 70, 170 Migr 104 Fug 202 Mut 177, 194, 250 Somn 2:156

ἐξηχέω (8) Her 15 Abr 160 Mos 1:169 Decal 33, 46 Spec 2:189 Contempl 81 Flacc 39

ἐξιάομαι Congr 153 Spec 4:2 Legat 35

ἐξικμάζω Opif 159 Sacr 98

ἐξικνέομαι Post 161 Agr 53 Conf 80

ἐξιλάσκομαι Post 70, 72

ἕξις (47) Opif 149 Leg 1:10 Leg 2:18, 22, 22, 36, 36, 37, 37, 37, 38, 40, 44, 45, 45, 45 Leg 3:210, 210, 210 Cher 9, 62 Det 172 Post 141, 141 Deus 35, 35, 36 Agr 101 Plant 31 Sobr 34 Her 137 Fug 177 Mut 121, 121, 122, 122, 150, 152 Somn 1:136 Mos 2:8, 187 Spec 4:144 Aet 75, 86, 125 QG (Par) 2:4, 2:4

ἐξισόω (7) Post 161 Her 218 Abr 185 Decal 167 Spec 1:300 Spec 2:177 Aet 116

ἐξίστημι (31) Leg 2:31, 31 Ebr 146 Sobr 26 Conf 142, 154 Her 69, 251, 251, 251, 251 Somn 1:132 Somn 2:89, 90, 91, 91 Ios 34, 119 Mos 1:242 Spec 1:248 Spec 2:37, 238 Spec 3:28 Virt 208, 208 Contempl 18 Flacc 148 Legat 232, 327 QG 1:24, 4:168

ἐξίτηλος (6) Opif 148 Sacr 32 Det 76, 77 Post 113 Mos 1:287

ἐξιχνεύω Decal 102

ἐξογκέω QG (Par) 2:6

ἐξόδιος Spec 2:211

ἔξοδος (20) Opif 119 Sacr 96, 135 Post 9 Deus 60 Ebr 9 Migr 15, 151 Her 97, 273 Somn 1:235 Mos 1:105, 122, 268 Mos 2:248 Virt 77 Flacc 163 Hypoth 6:1, 6:2, 6:5

ἐξοικειόω Virt 185 Flacc 82

ἐξοικίζω (10) Det 85, 121 Her 265 Congr 122 Fug 117 Mut 124 Somn 1:149 Spec 2:42 Flacc 55 Legat 157

ἔξοινος Ebr 95, 166

ἐξοιστράω Ebr 147

ἐξοκέλλω (9) Leg 2:60 Agr 34 Conf 7 Mut 215 Somn 1:246 Somn 2:147, 211 Spec 2:135 Praem 170

ἐξολιγωρέω Decal 6

ἐξολοθρεύω Fug 188

ἐξομματόω Leg 3:108 Migr 123

ἐξομοιόω (39) Opif 18, 100, 171, 172 Migr 123 Her 240, 311 Mut 74, 92, 97, 248 Somn 1:73, 153, 175 Somn 2:130, 172, 210 Abr 69, 87 Ios 83 Mos 2:186 Decal 74, 101 Spec 1:6, 118, 170 Spec 2:158, 160, 176, 256 Spec 3:209 Prob 96 Aet 44 Legat 78, 111, 114 QG 2:17c, 62, 66

ἐξομοίωσις (7) Opif 144 Abr 61 Decal 73, 107 Spec 4:188 Virt 8, 168

ἐξομολογέομαι (7) Leg 1:80, 80, 82, 82 Leg 2:95, 96 Leg 3:26

ἐξομολόγησις Leg 1:82 Leg 3:146 Plant 134 Somn 1:37

ἐξομολογητικός Leg 1:82, 84 Leg 2:95 Mut 136

ἐξοπίσω Opif 104

ἐξοπλίζω Cher 32

ἐξορθόω Praem 113 Prov 2:36

ἐξορίζω Det 142 QG 1:76b

ἐξορκίζω QG 4:86a

ἐξορμάω Mos 1:14 Spec 3:173 Praem 21

ἐξορμίζω Somn 2:85

ἐξορύσσω Leg 2:27 Leg 3:153 Somn 1:42

ἐξοτρύνω Legat 132

ἐξουθενέω Leg 2:67 Mos 2:241

ἐξουσία (32) Opif 17 Leg 1:95 Leg 2:91 Leg 3:73 Cher 27, 27 Sacr 59, 60 Conf 181 Somn 2:294 Abr 129 Ios 67, 166 Mos 1:328 Spec 1:294 Spec 2:24 Spec 3:70, 137 Virt 218 Praem 124, 137 Prob 59 Contempl 43 Flacc 44, 57 Legat 26, 28, 54, 71, 114, 190 QG 1:55a

ἐξουσιαστικός QG 3:29

ἐξούσιος Flacc 76

ἐξοχή (8) Leg 1:106 Fug 72 Abr 10, 10, 32, 93 Spec 2:181 QG 2:59

ἐξυβρίζω (11) Leg 2:29 Det 110 Post 145, 182 Agr 32, 32, 48 Mos 2:13 Spec 3:43 QG 2:64c QG isf 5

ἐξυδατόω Aet 107

ἐξυμνέω Ios 246

ἔξω (168) Leg 2:54, 55, 62 Leg 3:5, 39, 40, 40, 46, 151, 152, 159, 240, 240 Cher 22, 23, 96 Sacr 61, 139 Det 17, 56, 119, 154, 160 Post 7, 14, 104, 173 Gig 54 Deus 3, 29, 84 Plant 5, 6, 65, 96, 130, 156 Ebr 85, 86, 100, 134, 147, 152, 201 Sobr 28 Conf 154 Migr 23, 95, 183, 192 Her 12, 68, 76, 78, 81, 81, 81, 82, 82, 82, 83, 85, 86, 233 Congr 41 Fug 11, 81 Mut 43, 43, 44, 100, 113, 116, 141, 173, 180, 199, 247 Somn 1:21, 58, 187 Somn 2:180, 238 Abr 23, 44, 65, 77, 128, 241 Mos 1:28, 39, 73, 88, 160, 277, 313, 325 Mos 2:34, 78, 87, 110, 136, 152, 180, 214, 231 Decal 9, 45, 59, 104, 109 Spec 1:71, 147, 147, 160, 165, 232, 241, 261, 268, 268, 276 Spec 2:116, 170, 206, 249 Spec 3:74, 77, 109, 132, 171, 189 Spec 4:20 Virt 83, 89, 105, 137, 146, 147, 212 Praem 113, 113, 140 Prob 9, 13 Contempl 20 Aet 24, 36, 114, 135 Flacc 5, 27, 110, 141, 167, 169 Legat 174, 175, 212, 282, 299, 319, 334, 366 Prov 2:19, 62 QG 2:71a, 71b

ἔξωθεν (39) Leg 2:39 Agr 39 Plant 128 Ebr 85, 160 Conf 105 Migr 206 Her 13 Congr 130 Fug 115, 200 Mut 43, 90, 107, 141, 243 Somn 1:27, 31, 110, 119 Somn 2:137, 212, 267 Ios 183 Mos 2:95, 243 Decal 142 Spec 1:338 Virt 12, 128 Praem 144 Aet 21, 23, 25, 26, 74, 98 QG (Par) 2:4, 2:4

ἐξωθέω Post 55 Agr 164 Aet 119 Legat 123

ἐξώλεια Spec 4:34 Hypoth 7:9

ἐξώλης Sacr 32

ἐξωμίς Contempl 38 Hypoth 11:12

ἔξωρος Spec 1:282 Legat 203

ἐξώτατος Leg 3:41

ἔοικα (181) Opif 38, 41, 47, 67, 69, 126, 133, 137, 139, 140, 154, 166 Leg 1:61 Leg 2:22, 22, 81 Leg 3:94, 169 Cher 58, 69 Sacr 82, 110 Det 135 Post 119 Deus 43, 82, 95 Agr 38, 77, 96 Plant 7, 36, 48, 117, 161, 171 Ebr 77, 115, 204 Sobr 58, 65 Conf 4, 13, 85, 158 Migr 12, 71, 73, 93, 94, 116, 122, 131, 180 Her 40, 75, 89, 143, 288 Congr 25, 39, 136, 143 Fug 22, 56, 128, 160, 182 Mut 102, 177, 230 Somn 1:21, 101, 150, 202, 215 Somn 2:3, 138, 163, 166, 243, 245, 252, 260 Abr 47, 48, 52, 131, 185, 200, 240, 258 Ios 9, 30, 46, 63, 126, 140,

150, 213 Mos 1:82, 272, 293 Mos 2:10, 15, 17, 39, 50, 96, 112, 123, 202, 205, 248, 270, 288 Decal 95, 107, 147, 149 Spec 1:26, 59, 68, 229, 290 Spec 2:19, 66, 141, 177, 194, 211, 213, 237 Spec 3:109, 186, 208 Spec 4:6, 14, 31, 54, 99, 108, 143, 149, 203, 215 Virt 79, 121, 167, 188 Prob 5, 30, 57, 123 Contempl 78 Aet 28, 56, 95, 98, 134 Flacc 102, 128, 178 Legat 114, 183, 208, 237, 245, 245 Hypoth 6:7, 7:16 Prov 2:27, 61 QG 1:1, 62:1, 62:2, 2:34a, 59, 3:11a, 4:228 QE 2:6a

ἑορτάζω (13) Opif 116 Cher 86, 90 Sacr 111 Mos 2:24, 210, 210 Decal 96 Spec 1:193 Spec 2:49, 70, 215 Flacc 118

ἑορτή (110) Opif 89, 116 Cher 84, 85, 85, 90, 92, 94 Sacr 111, 111, 111 Ebr 95 Migr 92, 202 Congr 161, 161, 162, 162, 167 Fug 186 Somn 2:75, 144 Mos 1:88, 89 Mos 2:41, 159, 224 Decal 158, 159, 161 Spec 1:69, 168, 181, 182, 183, 187, 188, 189, 189, 190, 191, 192 Spec 2:39, 40, 41, 41, 42, 42, 46, 48, 51, 52, 52, 53, 56, 86, 140, 140, 142, 144, 145, 146, 150, 155, 156, 157, 157, 157, 157, 158, 160, 162, 162, 167, 176, 179, 188, 192, 193, 193, 194, 194, 204, 206, 210, 211, 212, 213, 214, 215, 215, 215, 223 Spec 3:40, 125, 183 Praem 153, 171 Prob 140 Contempl 65 Flacc 116, 117, 118 Legat 12, 83, 280 QG 3:61 QE 2:15:1, 15b, 15b

ἑορτώδης Migr 91 Decal 161 Spec 1:192 Spec 2:216 Praem 157

ἐπαγγελία Mut 201

ἐπαγγέλλω (15) Leg 1:52 Post 139 Agr 17, 64 Migr 37 Her 124 Congr 138 Somn 2:167 Spec 1:57 Spec 2:30 Virt 54, 64 Contempl 2, 3 Hypoth 7:17

ἐπάγγελμα (9) Post 139 Deus 146 Plant 81 Congr 133, 148 Mut 128 Spec 2:99 Virt 64 Flacc 54

ἐπάγω (65) Opif 165 Leg 2:27, 77, 77 Leg 3:105, 158, 158 Sacr 57 Det 168 Post 106, 113, 130, 135, 156 Ebr 193 Conf 25 Migr 78 Her 268, 271, 274, 276, 284, 304 Congr 171 Somn 1:52, 96 Somn 2:88, 137 Abr 64, 92, 96, 190 Ios 211, 261 Mos 1:96, 251, 301 Mos 2:20, 153 Decal 76 Spec 1:96, 237, 243 Spec 3:28 Spec 4:14 Virt 42 Praem 26, 136 Prob 58, 104 Aet 26 Legat 184, 230, 251, 340 Prov 2:41 QG 1:76a, 76a, 100:2a, 2:17b, 28, 3:52, 4:51a, 174, 202a

ἐπαγωγός Sacr 30 Sobr 23 Spec 4:139 Contempl 49

ἐπαγωνίζομαι Post 13 Virt 142 Aet 70

ἐπαείδω Migr 112 Spec 1:30, 60

ἐπαίνεσις Plant 158

ἐπαινέτης Plant 128 Her 161

ἐπαινετός Deus 154

ἐπαινετός (71) Leg 3:75, 77, 83, 104 Cher 24 Sacr 83, 116 Det 35, 59 Post 75, 87 Deus 48, 71 Agr 9, 66, 129, 129, 157 Ebr 20, 194 Migr 20, 70, 108, 115, 129 Her 158 Congr 4, 5, 67 Fug 26, 52, 86 Mut 47, 124, 197, 208 Somn 2:162, 177, 259 Abr 14, 191, 271 Ios 19 Mos 1:48 Mos 2:1, 30, 50, 138 Spec 1:43, 102, 138, 209, 269 Spec 2:63 Spec 3:128, 186, 209 Spec 4:15 Virt 172, 184, 208 Praem 83, 113 Prob 88, 93 Prov 1, 2:36 QG 3:11a, 29, 4:102a, 228

ἐπαινέω (73) Opif 89, 163 Leg 2:62, 67, 91 Leg 3:10, 86, 87, 94, 95 Cher 129 Det 34 Post 146 Deus 34 Agr 70, 118 Plant 128, 129 Ebr 67 Sobr 58 Conf 64, 147 Migr 95, 96, 108, 110, 110, 112, 148 Her 102, 159, 160 Congr 97 Fug 25, 206 Mut 178, 206, 224 Somn 2:40, 93, 108, 140 Abr 104, 183, 187, 209 Mos 1:313 Mos 2:191, 242 Decal 38 Spec 1:57 Spec 2:4, 173 Spec 3:155, 176 Spec 4:88, 120, 150 Virt 27, 227 Praem 118 Prob 22 Contempl 53 Flacc 7, 12 Legat 46, 137, 259, 331, 332 Prov 2:37 QG 2:11, 4:180

ἔπαινος (80) Opif 163 Leg 3:15, 77 Cher 122 Det 59, 61 Post 71, 71, 72, 141 Gig 36 Deus 47 Plant 126, 128 Ebr 74, 177 Sobr 37, 37, 57 Migr 110, 118 Her 90, 90, 129, 159, 178, 217 Congr 119 Fug 27, 30, 73 Mut 93, 192 Somn 1:35, 127, 244 Somn 2:38 Abr 4, 158, 178, 186, 186, 190, 190, 262, 275 Ios 154, 205, 246, 249 Mos 1:154, 303 Mos 2:45, 238 Spec 1:337 Spec 2:144, 234, 235 Spec 4:230, 230, 238 Virt 10 Praem 33 Prob 141, 141 Contempl 31, 77 Flacc 6, 99 Legat 38, 38, 284, 295 Hypoth 6:4 Prov 2:13 QG 2:16, 3:24, 4:8* QE 2:6b QE isf 26

ἐπαίρω (33) Opif 158 Leg 3:186 Sacr 21, 31, 62 Deus 97 Plant 92, 157 Ebr 18, 162 Sobr 40 Conf 110 Migr 170 Fug 107 Abr 42 Ios 22, 166 Mos 1:70 Mos 2:139, 240 Spec 1:293, 311 Spec 2:185 Spec 3:4, 165 Spec 4:88 Virt 2, 173 Praem 11 Legat 171, 269 Hypoth 6:3 QE 2:14

ἐπαισθάνομαι (11) Cher 74 Det 35 Post 22 Deus 120 Somn 2:147, 147 Mos 1:145 Spec 1:223 Prob 157 Prov 2:65 QG isf 12

ἐπαίτιος Flacc 42

ἐπαιωρέω Somn 1:192

ἐπακμάζω (8) Opif 113, 140 Sacr 76 Post 151 Agr 171 Somn 2:10 Praem 103, 157

ἐπακολουθέω (33) Cher 43 Det 173 Ebr 73 Conf 190 Migr 164 Fug 130 Abr 177, 275 Ios 217 Mos 1:168, 169, 286 Mos 2:61, 175 Spec 1:25, 64, 79, 338 Spec 4:155 Virt 64, 75, 205, 227 Praem 145 Contempl 86 Flacc 113 Legat 185, 252 Prov 2:45, 50, 53 QE 2:9a QE isf 10

ἐπακολούθημα Prov 2:45, 47, 49

ἐπακολούθησις Prov 2:59

ἐπακούω (15) Det 93 Post 137 Conf 8 Fug 1, 5 Somn 1:129, 191 Ios 238, 265 Mos 1:47 Mos 2:170, 229 Spec 4:32 Legat 132 QG 1:70:2

ἐπαλείφω Conf 106 Her 294 Somn 2:165 Spec 1:231

ἐπαληθεύω (6) Agr 2 Sobr 48 Abr 32 Spec 1:236, 341 Spec 3:68

ἐπαλλάσσω Cher 110 Spec 4:147

ἐπάλληλος (55) Opif 54, 80, 167 Sacr 16, 21, 25, 116, 127 Det 113 Post 12, 106 Deus 130, 153 Agr 160 Plant 89 Sobr 29 Conf 23, 46, 105 Her 4, 37 Somn 1:122 Somn 2:237, 245 Abr 42, 134, 245 Ios 175, 223 Mos 1:118, 147, 200 Mos 2:263, 284 Decal 71 Spec 1:148 Spec 2:8, 98, 202 Spec 3:16 Spec 4:39, 212 Virt 200 Praem 101, 155 Prob 58, 84, 141 Flacc 121 Legat 66, 83, 255, 302 Prov 2:30, 68

ἐπαμάομαι Ios 25 Mos 1:39

ἐπαμπίσχω (7) Ebr 7 Fug 110 Mut 209 Somn 1:43, 220 Spec 1:216 Virt 24

ἐπαμφοτερίζω (15) Opif 170 Leg 3:67 Det 131 Post 100 Deus 22 Plant 70, 111 Ebr 139 Migr 162 Mut 124 Mos 2:228 Spec 1:63 Praem 40, 63 Legat 244

ἐπαμφοτερισμός Conf 31 Decal 128 QG 1:55b

ἐπαμφοτεριστής Sacr 70 Migr 148 QG 1:55b, 2:12c

ἐπάν Agr 114, 158 Virt 78 Contempl 89

ἐπαναγκάζω Spec 2:74

ἐπανάγκης Hypoth 7:5

ἐπαναδίδωμι QE isf 21

ἐπαναζώννυμαι Contempl 51

ἐπαναιρέω Sacr 95 Conf 70 Spec 4:194

ἐπανάληψις Contempl 76

ἐπαναπλέω Mos 2:255

ἐπαναπόλησις Post 149

ἐπανάστασις (6) Agr 46 Her 284 Fug 77 Mos 2:16, 169 Praem 73

ἐπαναστρέφω Migr 126 QG 1:85

ἐπανασῴζω Her 255

ἐπανάτασις (12) Deus 64, 167 Conf 165 Somn 2:7, 96 Ios 225 Mos 1:95 Spec 2:83 Virt 5 Praem 4 Prob 144 Legat 368

ἐπανατείνω (25) Det 46 Agr 40, 98 Migr 9 Fug 6 Mut 23 Somn 2:121 Ios 68 Decal 33, 149 Spec 2:163 Spec 3:86, 158 Spec 4:72, 199 Virt 114 Praem 137 Prob 25, 40, 136, 144, 145 Flacc 89 Legat 350, 368

ἐπανατέλλω Spec 2:210

ἐπανατίθημι Somn 1:128 Somn 2:155, 202

ἐπανατρυγάω Virt 91, 92

ἐπάνειμι (28) Leg 3:84 Sacr 49 Deus 70 Congr 108, 123 Fug 7, 181 Mut 85, 116 Somn 2:107 Abr 43, 62, 132, 235 Ios 108 Mos 1:58, 240, 267, 310 Mos 2:166, 269 Spec 3:30, 133 Virt 44 Praem 110 Legat 15, 93 Hypoth 11:6

ἐπανέρχομαι (24) Det 149 Ebr 24 Sobr 68 Conf 78, 78 Migr 211 Fug 6 Mut 109 Somn 1:256 Ios 169, 184, 195, 224, 226 Mos 1:293, 309, 332 Spec 1:129 Spec 2:102, 190 Spec 3:171 Virt 96 Flacc 105, 112

ἐπανέχω Sacr 44 Mut 118 Decal 140 Spec 1:60 Prob 11

ἐπανήκω Mut 116 Somn 2:165 Mos 1:232 Spec 4:36

ἐπανθέω Opif 113 Sacr 25 Migr 126, 140

ἐπανθίζω Sacr 21 Somn 1:224 Somn 2:53

ἐπανισόω Her 158 Spec 2:139

ἐπανίστημι (10) Leg 3:103 Post 71 Agr 146 Spec 3:17, 17 Praem 74 Prob 21, 89 Contempl 40 Prov 2:35

ἐπανίσωσις Migr 173 Contempl 51

ἐπάνοδος (13) Opif 155 Cher 2 Det 63 Congr 89 Fug 5, 119 Somn 1:45, 45 Ios 178 Mos 1:232 Praem 115 Aet 28 Legat 195

ἐπανορθόω (19) Leg 3:123 Det 74, 144, 146 Agr 47 Plant 92 Spec 1:10, 238 Spec 2:166 Spec 3:145, 148 Spec 4:23, 146 Praem 113 Prob 63 Contempl 14 Flacc 103 QG 3:20a, 4:200c

ἐπανόρθωμα Praem 158

ἐπανόρθωσις (29) Leg 1:85 Leg 3:106 Gig 38 Deus 17, 182 Agr 13, 35, 90 Plant 146 Ebr 91 Conf 171, 182 Mut 70, 248 Mos 2:36 Decal 174 Spec 1:336 Spec 2:12, 107 Spec 3:76, 106 Spec 4:72 Virt 91, 176 Flacc 124 Legat 300, 369 Prov 2:6 QE 2:10a

ἐπαντλέω (19) Leg 2:32 Leg 3:202 Sacr 61 Det 15 Post 104 Fug 191, 200 Mut 229 Mos 1:46, 55 Decal 169 Spec 1:191, 217 Spec 4:59, 75, 140 Virt 42, 116 Prob 13

ἐπανύω Leg 2:61

ἐπάνω (13) Opif 32 Leg 1:21, 33 Leg 2:11 Gig 22 Her 166 Somn 2:78 Abr 150 Spec 1:150 Spec 2:46 Virt 71 Praem 17 Prob 146

ἐπάξιος (31) Leg 3:107 Sacr 77 Det 116, 169, 169 Conf 26, 182 Migr 57, 64, 106, 133, 141 Her 99, 193 Mut 42, 62, 268 Somn 1:22 Somn 2:97, 138, 202 Abr 24, 70 Mos 1:245, 304 Mos 2:57, 239 Spec 1:284 Spec 3:35, 84 Prov 2:6

ἐπαοιδός (ἐπῳδός) Migr 83

ἐπαπειλέω Mos 1:39

ἐπαποδύω (20) Opif 33 Det 32 Agr 159 Ebr 22, 207 Somn 2:71, 276 Abr 256 Decal 64 Spec 3:119 Spec 4:75 Virt 5, 31, 142 Praem 11 Flacc 128 Legat 62, 93 Hypoth 11:6 Prov 2:12

ἐπαπορέω Somn 2:300 Spec 1:32, 213

ἐπαράομαι Praem 72

ἐπάρατος (28) Leg 3:111 Cher 52 Det 96 Post 88, 159, 176 Sobr 67 Conf 196 Migr 113 Her 296 Abr 40 Mos 2:196 Decal 87 Spec 2:50 Spec 4:91 Virt 202 Praem 134, 141, 141, 141, 141, 141, 141 Prob 137 Flacc 134 Legat 89, 166, 171

ἐπάργυρος Flacc 30

ἐπάρδω Spec 4:56

ἔπαρσις Leg 3:246 Congr 169 Spec 1:293 Spec 2:185

ἐπαρτάω Cher 82

ἐπασπιδόομαι Somn 2:82

ἐπαυγάζω Praem 28

ἔπαυλις (18) Abr 139 Mos 1:103, 144, 262, 312, 330 Spec 2:116, 116, 119, 121, 121 Spec 4:27 Praem 141 Contempl 23 Flacc 169 Legat 185, 351, 358

ἐπαυχέω Leg 2:66 Ebr 151 Abr 159

ἐπαφάω Mos 1:124

ἐπαφή Mos 1:78 Spec 1:216

ἐπαχθής Leg 3:251 Sacr 30 Deus 114 Migr 145 Virt 161

ἐπαχθίζομαι (11) Abr 171 Ios 251 Mos 1:141, 203, 312 Mos 2:249 Spec 2:102 Spec 4:171 Virt 157 Prob 32 Legat 27

ἐπεγείρω Mos 1:297 Mos 2:213 Legat 168

ἐπεί (285) Opif 12, 20, 23, 26, 35, 67, 71, 89, 100, 106, 117, 143, 151, 151, 155, 156 Leg 1:18, 24, 38, 43, 44, 83, 96, 104 Leg 2:1 Leg 3:105, 108, 116, 206, 210, 212, 230, 236, 243, 249 Cher 3, 88, 122 Sacr 40, 60, 63, 91, 97, 115 Det 6, 59, 132, 137, 160 Post 4, 40, 69, 94, 127, 143, 145, 152 Gig 5, 9, 47, 56 Deus 57, 64, 123 Agr 9, 35, 49, 133, 149 Plant 34, 42, 50, 70, 99, 135, 144, 148, 171, 175 Ebr 57, 124, 142, 154 Sobr 6, 35 Conf 12, 41, 104, 115, 120, 135 Migr 7, 92, 115, 183, 197 Her 21, 36, 41, 141, 158, 178, 223, 226, 229, 259, 279, 286, 307 Congr 64, 84, 117, 138, 158 Fug 61, 141 Mut 8, 90, 150, 178, 185, 224, 270 Somn 1:132, 159, 193 Somn 2:56, 66, 137, 140, 242, 251, 261 Abr 2, 3, 18, 27, 40, 45, 55, 57, 78, 120, 140, 228 Ios 20, 41, 125, 158, 175, 220 Mos 1:8, 10, 18, 57, 95, 114, 116, 129, 162, 202, 283, 305, 311 Mos 2:8, 27, 28, 58, 73, 82, 151, 163, 174, 198, 223, 280, 282 Decal 6, 64, 89, 102 Spec 1:40, 64, 101, 112, 131, 168, 180, 223, 229, 234, 254, 288 Spec 2:13, 72, 116, 135, 136, 160, 166, 222, 234, 248 Spec 3:7, 21, 34, 59, 88, 151, 151, 155 Spec 4:44, 79, 104, 108, 119, 176, 187, 188, 195, 202, 204 Virt 165, 182 Praem 55, 67, 70, 78, 85 Prob 37, 58, 62, 102, 121, 140, 153, 157 Contempl 34, 38 Aet 2, 27, 32, 52, 53, 61, 66, 72, 75, 112, 114, 126, 134, 140, 142, 143, 145 Flacc 16, 38, 143, 185 Legat

27, 32, 168, 174, 220, 228, 300, 361 Hypoth 7:18, 7:19, 11:3 Prov 1, 2:24, 29 QG 1:21, 58, 96:1, 100:2b, 2:5a, 17c, 34a, 4:228 QG (Par) 2:5 QE 2:45a QE isf 32

ἐπείγω (35) Opif 86 Deus 40, 93, 98 Agr 37, 69, 115, 175 Plant 22 Ebr 152 Her 305 Somn 1:165, 167 Somn 2:103, 186, 251 Abr 40, 49, 65, 122 Ios 118, 169 Mos 1:178, 216, 251, 328 Decal 147 Spec 1:317, 333, 344 Spec 2:97 Spec 3:105 Contempl 72 Aet 136 QE 2:13b

ἐπειδάν (120) Opif 6, 17, 165 Leg 2:18, 61, 69, 70 Leg 3:152, 186, 186, 224 Cher 34, 94 Sacr 64, 70 Det 49, 127, 134, 143 Post 130 Gig 1 Deus 123, 130 Agr 31, 34, 66, 79, 132, 167 Plant 132, 172 Ebr 7, 10, 37, 58, 101, 101, 111, 221 Sobr 9, 36, 42 Conf 21, 59, 70, 78, 89, 114, 155 Migr 13, 68, 80, 144, 157, 166, 175, 189, 196, 208, 209, 214 Her 29, 131, 194, 203, 264, 274 Congr 115, 121, 148 Fug 20, 25, 31, 41, 47 Mut 66, 81, 84, 171 Somn 1:81, 83, 119, 193 Somn 2:68, 71, 95, 105, 151, 152, 196, 223, 233 Abr 105, 119, 126, 182, 243 Ios 150 Mos 1:160 Decal 146 Spec 1:219, 323 Spec 2:9 Spec 3:68 Spec 4:26, 64, 75 Praem 62 Prob 104, 156 Contempl 46, 66, 79 Aet 89, 91, 129, 149 Legat 172 Prov 2:17, 38

ἐπειδή (384) Opif 2, 13, 13, 15, 29, 32, 38, 45, 74, 76, 82, 98, 102, 116, 126, 133, 171 Leg 1:1, 3, 59 Leg 2:72 Leg 3:2, 15, 45, 51, 67, 87, 88, 104, 185, 195, 250 Cher 16, 19, 25, 41, 50, 55, 82, 83, 87, 90, 98, 121 Sacr 65, 124 Det 154, 172 Post 27, 51, 52, 55, 96, 101 Gig 22 Deus 5, 29, 42, 118 Agr 63, 88, 122, 131, 159, 177, 179 Plant 3, 21, 48, 132, 165 Ebr 40, 84, 98, 133, 136, 170, 214 Sobr 31, 58 Conf 148, 155, 167, 180, 186 Migr 3, 32, 47, 54, 58, 77, 79, 93, 147, 163, 165, 202, 206, 215, 221 Her 2, 2, 23, 30, 55, 58, 65, 76, 118, 172, 179, 234, 244, 263, 311 Congr 25, 33, 73, 88, 162 Fug 51, 73, 75, 97, 140, 146, 156 Mut 30, 36, 38, 87, 96, 98, 137, 178, 184, 184, 201, 208, 218, 248 Somn 1:8, 38, 63, 75, 77, 79, 117, 126, 135, 142, 221, 226 Somn 2:28, 34, 35, 123, 134, 180, 192, 238 Abr 7, 76, 101, 145, 146, 217, 242 Ios 4, 95, 99, 129, 153, 154, 223, 234 Mos 1:44, 98, 149, 163, 187, 205, 246, 273 Mos 2:6, 55, 59, 100, 104, 115, 121, 148, 149, 152, 187, 218, 245, 279, 288 Decal 15, 34, 49, 104, 141, 160 Spec 1:9, 30, 36, 38, 48, 56, 67, 85, 88, 94, 103, 120, 135, 140, 146, 159, 177, 178, 178, 183, 196, 200, 238, 252, 282, 285, 291, 298, 307, 310, 315 Spec 2:6, 19, 25, 29, 60, 64, 65, 95, 112, 118, 121, 133, 152, 158, 175, 177, 196, 202, 221, 225, 240, 243, 249, 261 Spec 3:39, 47, 52, 57, 58, 84, 99, 107, 159, 192, 207, 209 Spec 4:10, 12, 20, 40, 54, 127, 147, 168, 171, 178, 192, 199, 223, 231 Virt 17, 19, 29, 34, 53, 56, 63, 66, 90, 94, 107, 117, 127, 128, 137, 146, 146, 148, 155, 156, 168, 187, 189, 216, 221 Praem 7, 36, 49 Prob 13, 63, 75, 92, 114, 118, 122, 127, 144 Contempl 10, 16, 18, 28, 64, 66 Aet 3, 21, 22, 24, 37, 57, 68, 89, 102, 121 Flacc 5, 7, 14, 32, 53, 96, 97, 100, 125, 187 Legat 7, 62, 77, 84, 99, 103, 149, 164, 167, 178, 246, 289, 341, 369 Hypoth 6:5, 11:12 Prov 2:30, 54, 57, 66 QG 1:21, 51, 51, 77, 2:62, 3:20b, 4:69, 76b, 81, 104, 198 QG isf 15 QE 2:3a, 6a QE isf 3

ἐπεῖδον (ἐφοράω) (12) Leg 3:14 Post 82 Fug 211 Somn 1:240 Somn 2:290 Mos 1:47 Mos 2:255 Decal 100 Spec 3:154 Praem 60 Prob 111 Legat 233

ἔπειμι (27) Opif 89 Sacr 66 Agr 23 Plant 41 Ebr 195 Migr 62 Her 154, 256 Mut 160 Somn 1:27 Somn 2:87, 122 Abr 232 Ios 89, 157, 162 Mos 1:175, 257 Mos 2:13, 275 Spec 4:220 Virt 88, 109 Prob 118 Flacc 1 Legat 358 Prov 2:67

ἐπείπερ Aet 13

ἐπεῖπον (ἐπιλέγω) Abr 36 Spec 3:204 Virt 68

ἐπεισάγω Agr 43

ἐπεισβαίνω Legat 129

ἐπείσειμι (10) Opif 67, 159 Post 56 Abr 104 Decal 142 Spec 1:250 Virt 89 Flacc 86 QG (Par) 2:7, 2:7

ἐπεισέρχομαι Opif 119 Sacr 135 Deus 3 Virt 115 QG 2:34a

ἐπεισκωμάζω Spec 3:37

ἐπεισοδιάζω Leg 3:235 Mut 90

ἐπείσοδος Leg 2:57

ἐπεισρέω Prob 15 Flacc 133 Legat 126 QE isf 6

ἐπειστρέχω Mos 1:302

ἐπεισφέρω Deus 42 Virt 84

ἐπεισφοιτάω Mut 243

ἐπεισφορέω Migr 204

ἐπεισχέω (8) Leg 2:32 Cher 61 Sacr 61 Det 15 Ebr 221 Migr 100 Spec 3:5 Spec 4:222

ἔπειτα (καί) (121) Opif 25, 41, 79, 95, 136, 140, 159 Leg 2:5, 15 Leg 3:80, 120, 128, 163, 205, 207, 245 Cher 100 Sacr 57, 76, 78, 128 Det 38, 122 Deus 14 Agr 69, 152, 157, 174 Plant 29, 35, 113 Ebr 19, 51, 73, 150, 175 Conf 31, 44, 98 Migr 46, 195, 195 Fug 200 Mut 242 Somn 1:4, 55, 76, 214, 218 Somn 2:237 Abr 67, 173, 193 Ios 162 Mos 1:14, 115, 120, 127 Mos 2:14, 48, 69, 77, 124, 143, 146, 210, 263, 271 Decal 123 Spec 1:96, 178, 198, 203, 210, 231, 248, 311 Spec 2:3, 82, 123, 140, 166, 171 Spec 4:37, 79, 175, 189 Virt 6, 6, 70, 80, 151, 172, 199 Praem 163, 169 Contempl 57, 80 Aet 17, 19, 22, 42, 48, 62, 94, 114, 150 Flacc 89, 140 Legat 60, 67, 143, 190, 213, 227 Hypoth 6:6 Prov 2:17, 37 QG (Par) 2:7, 2:7 QE isf 5

ἐπεκθέω Mos 1:168, 250 Mos 2:248 Spec 3:172

ἐπέκτασις Decal 34

ἐπεκτρέχω Leg 2:100

ἐπελαύνω Mos 1:178 Spec 4:80 Virt 105

ἐπελαφρίζω (17) Cher 82 Deus 21 Plant 24, 144 Abr 185, 257 Mos 1:217 Decal 117 Spec 1:99 Spec 2:138 Spec 4:24, 171 Praem 72, 157 Aet 29 Legat 27 Prov 2:4

ἐπελπίζω Leg 2:43 Ebr 106 Her 60 Prov 2:12

ἐπεμβαίνω Spec 4:200, 201 Prov 2:4

ἐπεμπίπτω Mos 1:131, 178 Spec 3:79 Legat 109

ἐπεντρώγω Contempl 55

ἐπεντρώματα Leg 3:143

ἐπεντρώσεις Leg 3:140

ἐπεξαμαρτάνω Spec 4:65

ἐπεξανίστημι Legat 244

ἐπέξειμι Leg 3:106 Conf 164, 167 Mut 244

ἐπεξέλευσις Legat 161

ἐπεξεργάζομαι Leg 2:62 Deus 9

ἐπεξέρχομαι (9) Leg 2:61 Sacr 72 Conf 163 Migr 192, 224 Fug 53 Somn 1:112 Flacc 174 Hypoth 6:5

ἐπέξοδος Deus 68 Agr 85 Mos 1:303 Spec 3:85 Flacc 124

ἐπέραστος Somn 2:97

ἐπερείδω (18) Leg 2:41, 90 Leg 3:145 Cher 13 Sacr 81 Agr 122 Plant 7, 153 Fug 150 Somn 1:158, 241 Abr 268 Spec 4:70, 160, 165 Virt 158 Praem 30 Contempl 69

ἐπέρχομαι (8) Det 87 Migr 218 Somn 2:54 Mos 1:49 Spec 2:167 Spec 4:116 Praem 94, 127

ἐπερωτάω Post 89 Plant 59 Fug 149

ἐπεσθίω Prob 153 Contempl 40

ἐπέτειος Mos 2:186 Spec 2:179

ἐπευφημέω Abr 190

ἐπεύχομαι Contempl 89

ἐπευωνίζω (8) Cher 123 Gig 39 Fug 153 Spec 2:34 Virt 10 Prob 37, 121 Flacc 132

ἐπέχω (97) Opif 81, 168 Leg 1:16, 18 Leg 3:4, 112 Det 23, 44 Post 18, 28, 145 Deus 149, 181 Ebr 101, 169, 192, 200, 205 Conf 29, 105 Migr 191 Her 4, 223, 243, 245 Fug 135, 193, 206 Mut 239, 250 Somn 1:37, 37, 68, 182, 238 Somn 2:83, 133, 262, 295 Abr 43, 44 Ios 5, 92, 96, 176 Mos 1:69, 90, 107, 107, 175, 176 Mos 2:63, 214, 236 Decal 150 Spec 1:118, 270, 338, 343 Spec 2:87, 104, 202 Spec 3:25, 33, 33, 175 Spec 4:54 Virt 113, 137 Praem 68, 76, 134 Aet 29, 77, 79, 79, 91, 101, 115 Flacc 35, 40, 119, 159 Legat 42, 65, 186, 187, 197, 226, 257, 259, 262, 275, 360, 366 Prov 2:55 QG 2:59

ἐπήκοος (7) Sacr 26 Deus 157 Mos 1:244 Decal 158 Praem 84, 166 Contempl 33

ἔπηλυς (6) Cher 121 Praem 152 Flacc 54 QE 2:2, 2, 2

ἐπηλύτης (10) Mos 1:7, 147 Spec 1:52, 53 Spec 2:118, 119 Virt 102, 103, 182, 219

ἐπήλυτος (9) Cher 120, 121, 121 Somn 1:160 Spec 1:309 Spec 4:176, 177 Virt 104, 104

ἐπήν Ebr 150

ἐπηρεάζω (9) Ios 71 Mos 2:199 Spec 2:218 Flacc 47, 52, 52, 52, 130 Legat 213

ἐπήρεια (10) Mos 1:47 Spec 3:55, 146 Prob 56 Flacc 103, 179 Legat 134, 203, 301, 302

ἐπηχέω Plant 126 Ebr 82

ἐπί (καί) (2326) Opif 5, 8, 29, 41, 44, 46, 55, 58, 63, 64, 66, 68, 71, 75, 77, 77, 78, 78, 79, 79, 83, 88, 93, 93, 93, 95, 96, 101, 101, 102, 102, 102, 103, 111, 117, 122, 122, 129, 135, 135, 140, 140, 141, 147, 147, 150, 154, 155, 156, 157, 157, 158, 162, 165, 165, 167 Leg 1:4, 14, 17, 21, 21, 22, 22, 25, 26, 26, 27, 34, 35, 47, 50, 53, 57, 61, 61, 64, 78, 80, 80, 81, 86, 89, 107, 107 Leg 2:6, 13, 18, 19, 19, 22, 27, 28, 29, 31, 40, 41, 43, 46, 47, 53, 66, 66, 67, 69, 71, 79, 88, 88, 94, 94, 95, 97, 98, 98, 100, 101, 102, 105, 106 Leg 3:2, 4, 12, 13, 17, 29, 31, 32, 39, 40, 41, 44, 44, 47, 48, 53, 57, 62, 63, 65, 71, 72, 75, 77, 82, 84, 84, 85, 86, 86, 86, 86, 87, 87, 94, 94, 98, 109, 109, 114, 118, 118, 120, 123, 123, 124, 126, 126, 126, 130, 132, 132, 134, 134, 138, 139, 139, 139, 139, 139, 141, 144, 144, 146, 148, 149, 152, 153, 153, 154, 158, 159, 160, 160, 166, 166, 168, 169, 169, 170, 172, 174, 174, 176, 176, 178, 179, 188, 188, 194, 198, 203, 210, 211, 212, 217, 225, 227, 234, 238 Cher 1, 9, 12, 14, 14, 15, 15, 18, 22, 22, 22, 25, 28, 37, 41, 43, 46, 50, 53, 54, 54, 55, 56, 67, 73, 73, 80, 89, 91, 99, 107, 118, 122 Sacr 2, 11, 11, 26, 29, 36, 37, 49, 49, 51, 51, 65, 66, 70, 70, 71, 71, 71, 75, 75, 76, 76, 82, 93, 101, 103, 113, 113, 115, 119, 122, 124, 124, 134, 135 Det 1, 1, 10, 11, 13, 14, 24, 24, 31, 32, 32, 34, 45, 46, 47, 49, 49, 58, 69, 69, 69, 85, 93, 103, 111, 114, 118, 119, 121, 122, 130, 136, 136, 136, 136, 137, 137, 138, 139, 139, 140, 140, 143, 145, 151, 152, 174, 177 Post 12, 18, 24, 26, 33, 44, 54, 57, 67, 70, 72, 72, 76, 76, 76, 80, 90, 100, 102, 113, 116, 116, 118, 122, 123, 123, 127, 131, 132, 132, 132, 136, 140, 140, 146, 151, 151, 151, 154, 158, 161, 162, 163, 168, 180, 185 Gig 1, 15, 15, 23, 23, 24, 24, 27, 58, 64, 66, 67 Deus 4, 13, 20, 20, 21, 26, 33, 35, 35, 35, 39, 47, 47, 48, 54, 70, 71, 71, 85, 88, 98, 99, 101, 102, 102, 118, 125, 128, 132, 140, 160, 162, 162, 162, 166, 166, 172, 174, 182 Agr 6, 12, 15, 21, 24, 24, 35, 44, 46, 47, 56, 60, 60, 69, 75, 76, 78, 80, 84, 85, 88, 91, 93, 94, 94, 94, 97, 100, 102, 110, 113, 116, 117, 117, 121, 123, 123, 127, 130, 133, 143, 148, 150, 151, 155, 159, 168, 169, 171, 171, 175, 178 Plant 3, 4, 4, 5, 9, 9, 10, 16, 35, 36, 41, 45, 47, 51, 55, 58, 73, 73, 80, 80, 82, 82, 83, 84, 90, 90, 90, 93, 101, 102, 103, 105, 107, 134, 141, 144, 145, 152, 159, 159, 176 Ebr 2, 14, 15, 20, 22, 22, 23, 24, 25, 29, 45, 49, 50, 51, 65, 67, 70, 70, 90, 95, 112, 112, 112, 121, 134, 150, 156, 168, 169, 169, 170, 177, 177, 178, 178, 184, 187, 205, 206, 208, 210, 210, 210, 218 Sobr 6, 8, 13, 25, 26, 27, 29, 32, 33, 36, 48, 48, 48, 48, 49, 56, 57, 67, 68 Conf 1, 1, 1, 3, 4, 4, 4, 6, 9, 10, 15, 22, 22, 24, 24, 26, 26, 29, 29, 30, 38, 38, 39, 48, 49, 60, 64, 67, 69, 72, 75, 76, 91, 92, 103, 107, 113, 114, 114, 116, 118, 118, 122, 126, 133, 139, 139, 149, 150, 150, 151, 154, 157, 161, 162, 168, 169, 169, 170, 170, 178, 179, 179, 179, 181, 185, 187, 188, 190, 190, 191, 192 Migr 20, 20, 22, 45, 57, 61, 62, 64, 64, 65, 65, 65, 66, 66, 66, 70, 75, 83, 83, 83, 87, 90, 91, 92, 95, 99, 99, 103, 103, 103, 106, 110, 111, 114, 117, 121, 139, 142, 148, 148, 148, 150, 154, 160, 166, 168, 174, 178, 180, 182, 184, 184, 194, 209, 216, 217, 221 Her 1, 7, 10, 12, 20, 20, 21, 22, 25, 31, 35, 46, 50, 84, 85, 89, 89, 95, 98, 98, 107, 109, 112, 122, 125, 126, 128, 145, 147, 150, 151, 162, 169, 170, 171, 171, 173, 175, 176, 177, 192, 206, 214, 216, 218, 218, 218, 218, 218, 221, 226, 237, 239, 240, 249, 251, 251, 251, 251, 252, 252, 252, 256, 257, 260, 261, 274, 284, 291, 296, 314, 314, 315 Congr 2, 10, 14, 53, 70, 77, 81, 86, 91, 97, 97, 97, 102, 102, 108, 110, 113, 115, 120, 124, 125, 127, 137, 138, 138, 151, 159, 160, 162, 164, 167, 168, 170, 173, 176 Fug 1, 1, 1, 1, 2, 7, 21, 29, 30, 31, 31, 39, 41, 53, 59, 60, 61, 63, 65, 71, 71, 73, 73, 73, 74, 77, 83, 84, 93, 93, 94, 97, 98, 107, 109, 109, 110, 112, 112, 113, 115, 124, 124, 131, 141, 143, 149, 149, 149, 151, 166, 172, 176, 177, 177, 180, 181, 185, 195, 196, 202, 206, 209, 209 Mut 8, 22, 25, 28, 34, 44, 52, 54, 56, 56, 56, 56, 60, 62, 64, 71, 75, 81, 83, 111, 117, 126, 130, 150, 154, 162, 163, 173, 177, 179, 179, 199, 202, 202, 206, 209, 217, 228, 230, 232, 233, 234, 234, 234, 237, 239, 240, 243, 244, 250, 250, 256, 261, 268 Somn 1:1, 2, 3, 3, 3, 3, 6, 6, 11, 19, 22, 26, 26, 37, 37, 43, 54, 56, 59, 64, 67, 68, 69, 77, 85, 85, 85, 86, 91, 92, 92, 93, 95, 95, 100, 104, 107, 112, 116, 124, 124, 128, 131, 133, 133, 133, 152, 157, 157, 157, 157, 157, 157, 157, 157, 157, 157, 157, 161, 164, 172, 174, 175, 178, 180, 180, 189, 194, 194, 195, 195, 197, 199, 201, 208, 210, 214, 234, 237, 246, 256 Somn 2:3, 7, 7, 8, 14, 16, 16, 16, 19, 34, 46, 49, 50, 61, 67, 71, 79, 84, 90, 93, 94, 95, 96, 97, 100, 100, 104, 107, 110, 111, 123, 124, 144, 148, 158, 163, 170, 175, 175, 179, 180, 182, 187, 190, 202, 203, 203, 203, 207, 207, 207, 210, 211, 221, 221, 223, 226, 229, 231, 235, 236, 236, 238, 245, 248, 271, 271, 271, 274, 276, 277, 277, 278, 278, 278, 284, 284, 285, 291, 292 Abr

1, 3, 4, 9, 15, 17, 17, 19, 21, 22, 22, 31, 41, 48, 49, 52, 53, 54, 54, 58, 64, 65, 65, 66, 84, 88, 88, 88, 91, 94, 95, 96, 97, 114, 120, 124, 124, 126, 136, 137, 142, 150, 150, 159, 160, 161, 161, 169, 172, 183, 188, 190, 192, 194, 195, 196, 196, 198, 200, 202, 202, 205, 214, 216, 217, 217, 221, 231, 235, 245, 257, 258, 260, 266, 269, 275 Ios 6, 9, 12, 12, 15, 22, 23, 24, 26, 35, 37, 39, 43, 44, 47, 57, 72, 85, 87, 93, 95, 95, 119, 120, 123, 125, 129, 135, 137, 139, 140, 141, 148, 149, 163, 166, 167, 167, 173, 174, 176, 178, 179, 184, 184, 197, 197, 200, 207, 208, 209, 210, 213, 216, 219, 222, 225, 226, 229, 233, 234, 235, 237, 239, 246, 250, 256, 265, 267, 268, 268, 269 Mos 1:2, 9, 11, 14, 15, 17, 21, 24, 27, 32, 34, 37, 39, 40, 43, 44, 46, 50, 52, 53, 57, 58, 71, 72, 74, 75, 81, 82, 85, 88, 90, 90, 96, 99, 100, 100, 101, 102, 105, 106, 112, 113, 119, 136, 137, 137, 144, 148, 150, 164, 164, 165, 167, 167, 169, 170, 170, 180, 181, 182, 182, 183, 193, 196, 196, 203, 206, 216, 219, 227, 228, 236, 237, 238, 238, 245, 247, 247, 248, 248, 250, 251, 255, 257, 258, 263, 264, 265, 266, 267, 268, 269, 269, 270, 274, 274, 276, 277, 279, 280, 280, 282, 283, 285, 287, 289, 292, 292, 293, 298, 300, 301, 302, 304, 305, 306, 309, 313, 322, 325, 327, 328 Mos 2:1, 5, 7, 7, 20, 27, 33, 38, 42, 42, 44, 51, 58, 69, 70, 74, 78, 78, 80, 86, 103, 104, 112, 122, 133, 133, 133, 138, 139, 140, 144, 151, 153, 154, 154, 166, 167, 172, 177, 177, 179, 180, 181, 183, 192, 207, 212, 213, 214, 227, 228, 233, 235, 236, 240, 243, 245, 247, 248, 254, 254, 256, 257, 258, 261, 264, 268, 269, 271, 277, 277, 279, 281, 285, 291, 291 Decal 4, 14, 19, 21, 21, 21, 25, 25, 25, 25, 44, 50, 51, 51, 61, 61, 62, 75, 75, 76, 80, 81, 81, 82, 84, 86, 86, 90, 92, 95, 95, 98, 105, 110, 110, 113, 117, 118, 126, 126, 134, 135, 135, 140, 141, 146, 146, 157, 157, 161, 161, 161, 165, 165, 165, 165, 171, 172, 178 Spec 1:12, 16, 20, 30, 37, 40, 42, 45, 49, 50, 55, 56, 57, 58, 59, 64, 67, 67, 70, 76, 79, 86, 86, 88, 92, 104, 107, 112, 112, 112, 115, 129, 131, 151, 154, 156, 160, 172, 172, 183, 187, 188, 189, 193, 193, 193, 193, 195, 195, 195, 197, 197, 197, 204, 206, 207, 210, 212, 215, 215, 219, 226, 227, 232, 232, 233, 234, 235, 238, 239, 241, 242, 244, 245, 249, 251, 255, 263, 269, 279, 281, 283, 283, 284, 285, 288, 289, 289, 291, 296, 298, 300, 300, 300, 301, 301, 303, 309, 311, 311, 314, 314, 316, 323, 323, 324, 330, 336, 340, 341, 343, 344 Spec 2:2, 3, 6, 8, 10, 15, 20, 23, 34, 34, 35, 35, 38, 46, 55, 71, 71, 72, 74, 83, 87, 90, 94, 98, 106, 109, 110, 112, 113, 116, 116, 117, 122, 127, 131, 132, 132, 135, 137, 140, 142, 143, 144, 148, 156, 161, 161, 164, 165, 168, 170, 171, 176, 182, 185, 185, 192, 202, 202, 203, 208, 209, 210, 214, 215, 217, 221, 224, 231, 232, 233, 233, 235, 240, 242, 248, 249, 250, 252, 253, 253, 253, 253, 254, 258 Spec 3:2, 6, 11, 11, 11, 15, 21, 21, 22, 27, 39, 39, 44, 51, 51, 53, 56, 56, 61, 61, 62, 63, 63, 63, 64, 65, 66, 71, 72, 77, 80, 80, 88, 93, 96, 97, 100, 104, 107, 111, 115, 118, 118, 119, 121, 128, 130, 136, 139, 139, 146, 147, 149, 150, 152, 156, 157, 158, 162, 162, 167, 168, 173, 181, 181, 181, 181, 184, 185, 188, 189, 204, 208 Spec 4:1, 1, 5, 7, 9, 11, 13, 16, 17, 18, 21, 28, 30, 39, 40, 43, 43, 44, 45, 62, 63, 63, 63, 64, 66, 67, 67, 69, 76, 76, 77, 77, 78, 80, 81, 83, 90, 92, 94, 102, 104, 107, 108, 108, 110, 112, 113, 118, 120, 127, 128, 129, 129, 133, 134, 136, 137, 145, 154, 157, 160, 160, 167, 167, 174, 175, 176, 184, 192, 194, 202, 203, 207, 218, 221, 226, 232, 234, 234, 236 Virt 1, 9, 17, 18, 19, 34, 37, 40, 51, 52, 58, 64, 64, 65, 66, 82, 86, 88, 88, 88, 89, 89, 91, 99, 109, 112, 116, 116, 116, 121, 123, 125, 126, 131, 132, 135, 139, 140, 141, 146, 146, 148, 148, 149, 152, 156, 156, 160, 162, 166, 169, 180, 185, 188, 188, 199, 202, 205, 206, 206, 208, 215, 218, 221, 225, 226, 227 Praem 3, 5, 7, 8, 9, 14, 16, 16, 20, 23, 24, 31, 32, 32, 32, 41, 41, 47, 50, 51, 52, 63, 70, 72, 74, 75, 77, 96, 97, 100, 104, 105, 105, 106, 108, 110, 124, 133, 134, 136, 139, 148, 148, 152, 158, 163, 169, 170 Prob 4, 22, 27, 32, 38, 54, 55, 56, 57, 61, 62, 70, 70, 86, 97, 103, 105, 106, 112, 117, 118, 118, 123, 124, 127, 132, 136, 140, 141, 143 Contempl 12, 14, 22, 31, 33, 40, 40, 41, 42, 42, 43, 43, 58, 69, 69, 69, 70, 73, 75, 77, 81, 81, 90 Aet 1, 4, 33, 33, 36, 36, 37, 39, 43, 48, 49, 51, 81, 88, 94, 101, 105, 119, 121, 126, 128 Flacc 1, 4, 9, 9, 9, 12, 14, 20, 24, 24, 26, 28, 29, 38, 44, 53, 56, 56, 64, 66, 69, 69, 75, 76, 79, 79, 83, 84, 84, 85, 87, 89, 95, 95, 100, 102, 104, 105, 105, 114, 117, 119, 122, 124, 125, 126, 128, 134, 138, 139, 140, 141, 141, 144, 145, 146, 149, 150, 156, 158, 160, 161, 167, 173, 175, 178, 180, 186 Legat 6, 10, 11, 14, 15, 18, 19, 19, 25, 28, 30, 32, 33, 33, 35, 42, 43, 43, 44, 50, 50, 52, 58, 60, 67, 68, 69, 71, 72, 79, 85, 86, 91, 91, 95, 95, 98, 101, 104, 111, 116, 117, 119, 129, 137, 143, 153, 159, 159, 161, 171, 172, 177, 181, 182, 185, 190, 196, 202, 202, 203, 206, 206, 206, 207, 219, 244, 247, 248, 254, 260, 262, 264, 269, 269, 281, 288, 290, 293, 293, 297, 299, 303, 305, 308, 310, 331, 333, 335, 337, 340, 350, 351, 357, 361, 361, 369, 369, 370 Hypoth 6:1, 6:3, 6:7, 7:3, 7:4, 7:5, 7:6, 7:6, 7:9, 7:14, 7:16, 7:18, 11:1, 11:2, 11:6, 11:15 Prov 2:12, 13, 14, 14, 15, 15, 19, 24, 25, 27, 27, 29, 31, 32, 32, 36, 39, 40, 40, 43, 43, 44, 44, 50, 50, 54, 54, 54, 60, 60, 61, 64, 64, 69, 69 QG 1:1, 20, 20, 21, 55a, 65, 65, 72, 74, 74, 76b, 93, 2:15b, 54a, 54a, 72, 3:12, 12, 38b, 52, 4:51a, 51a, 51b, 51b, 52b, 69, 86a, 99, 144, 145, 169, 173, 180, 180, 180, 202a, 202a, 227, 227, 228 QG isf 9, 9, 13 QG (Par) 2:3, 2:7, 2:7 QE 1:7b, 2:2, 11a, 19, 26, 45a, 49a QE isf 5, 8, 9, 14, 21, 26, 26

ἐπιβάθρα Agr 106 Conf 2 Somn 2:51 Spec 3:179 Legat 6

ἐπιβαίνω (63) Opif 32 Leg 2:99 Leg 3:53 Cher 32, 33, 35, 81 Post 14, 14, 54 Gig 58 Agr 68, 75, 89, 103, 110 Plant 22 Ebr 111 Conf 11, 38, 38, 98, 113, 116, 152 Congr 91 Fug 22 Somn 1:159, 200 Somn 2:278, 294 Abr 42, 135 Ios 159 Mos 1:6, 115, 115, 243, 251, 255, 265, 290 Decal 14 Spec 1:14, 89, 156 Spec 3:27, 44, 46, 47, 148 Virt 105, 112, 143 Praem 114 Prob 7, 21, 111, 143 Aet 71 Flacc 27, 110, 155

ἐπιβάλλω (38) Opif 23, 138, 143, 146 Leg 2:19, 31, 31, 31 Leg 3:57, 60, 192 Cher 90 Sacr 91, 98 Deus 49, 108 Agr 20, 53, 91 Plant 131 Ebr 71 Her 191, 257 Congr 137 Somn 1:195 Somn 2:107 Abr 34, 246 Mos 1:206, 332 Mos 2:148 Decal 14 Spec 2:64, 183 Spec 4:57, 142 Virt 32 Legat 147

ἐπίβασις (8) Leg 3:142, 142, 188, 189 Plant 16 Mos 1:202 Aet 147 Prov 2:26

ἐπιβατεύω Virt 97

ἐπιβατήριος Legat 151

ἐπιβάτης Leg 2:104 Agr 77, 83 Conf 22 Spec 4:28

ἐπιβατικός Mos 2:157 Spec 1:121 Spec 4:186

ἐπιβιόω (7) Agr 95 Somn 1:31 Abr 188 Spec 2:130 Spec 3:94 Flacc 159 Legat 24

ἐπιβλέπω Plant 29

ἐπιβοήθεια Praem 148

ἐπιβοηθέω Contempl 24

ἐπιβολή (16) Leg 3:117, 231 Post 20, 79, 83 Sobr 18 Migr 32 Congr 143 Somn 1:1 Somn 2:200 Mos 1:26 Spec 3:180 Praem 50, 104 Contempl 79 QG 2:17c

ἐπιβουλεύω (31) Det 45, 69, 69 Ebr 160 Conf 22 Migr 86, 209 Somn 2:133, 144 Abr 90 Ios 26, 40, 236, 270 Mos 1:46, 140 Decal 68 Spec 3:85, 94, 99, 141, 150, 182, 195, 196, 203, 204 Flacc 52 Legat 28, 201 Prov 2:22

ἐπιβουλή (40) Migr 150 Somn 2:24 Ios 25, 40, 170, 173, 174, 218, 233, 236, 248, 250 Mos 1:67, 73, 132 Mos 2:156 Spec 1:185 Spec 2:218 Spec 3:95, 111, 119 Spec 4:104, 201 Contempl 15 Flacc 1, 1, 1, 24, 73, 76, 95, 101, 103, 123 Legat 23, 132 Prov 2:26, 57, 63 QG 1:74

ἐπίβουλος (43) Leg 3:69, 71 Sacr 32 Post 43 Ebr 6 Migr 223 Her 109, 169 Somn 1:220, 224, 226 Somn 2:89, 89, 154, 192 Mos 1:131, 160 Mos 2:186 Decal 4, 142, 155 Spec 1:265, 293 Spec 2:30, 83 Spec 3:104 Spec 4:5, 16, 100, 116, 183, 224 Virt 100, 181 Prob 45, 79, 117 Contempl 37, 47 Flacc 41, 79 Prov 2:36 QE isf 32

ἐπιβρίθω Aet 149

ἐπιγαμία (11) Fug 49 Mut 110 Decal 127 Spec 1:111, 317 Spec 2:31, 126 Spec 3:25 Legat 63, 71, 72

ἐπίγειος (ὁ) (28) Opif 101, 113, 117 Leg 1:8, 43, 45, 45 Cher 101, 106 Det 87 Plant 17, 63 Migr 178 Her 88, 223, 225 Somn 1:53 Somn 2:132 Abr 69 Ios 145, 147 Mos 1:190 Spec 1:16 Spec 2:191 Spec 3:111 Spec 4:236 Praem 51 QG 2:64a

ἐπιγέννημα Det 124 Post 64

ἐπιγίγνομαι (ἐπιγίνομαι) (40) Opif 34, 152 Leg 1:16 Leg 3:86, 97 Cher 38 Sacr 16 Post 164 Agr 39, 56, 142 Conf 158 Migr 206 Somn 2:154 Ios 10 Mos 1:123, 134, 178, 191, 210 Spec 1:103, 119 Spec 2:122 Praem 33, 64, 128, 131, 161 Aet 20, 60, 132, 135 Flacc 27 Prov 2:48 QG 1:51, 55c, 4:189 QG (Par) 2:7, 2:7 QE isf 22

ἐπιγιγνώσκω (ἐπιγινώσκω) (8) Leg 2:51 Sacr 19, 20 Det 176 Sobr 21 Somn 1:231 Mos 1:221 Spec 1:265

ἐπιγνώμων Opif 124 Spec 2:24 Spec 3:52

ἐπίγνωσις Leg 3:48, 77 Mos 2:97 Spec 1:64 Prob 74

ἐπιγονή Spec 1:141

ἐπίγραμμα (6) Somn 1:241, 241, 242, 242, 244, 246

ἐπιγραφή Legat 133, 299

ἐπιγράφω (43) Opif 75 Leg 3:31, 33, 35, 178 Cher 36, 77 Sacr 2, 72 Det 148 Post 42 Plant 174 Sobr 56 Conf 41, 144 Migr 67, 69 Her 109 Congr 130 Fug 114 Somn 1:78, 159, 171 Somn 2:76, 273 Abr 1 Ios 71 Mos 2:178, 179 Decal 8, 41, 178 Spec 1:252, 332 Spec 2:113, 198 Spec 3:148 Aet 12, 19 Flacc 20 Legat 171 Hypoth 0:1 Prov 2:59

ἐπιδακρύω Abr 258 Ios 17, 23, 262

ἐπιδαψιλεύω (12) Opif 81 Sobr 55 Ios 45 Mos 2:229 Spec 2:37, 139 Spec 3:23 Virt 81, 142, 148 Prov 2:5 QG 4:81

ἐπιδεής (12) Leg 1:44 Leg 3:161 Cher 112, 123 Somn 2:210 Abr 122 Decal 41 Spec 1:152 Spec 3:118 Virt 9 Praem 132 QG isf 16

ἐπιδείκνυμι (193) Opif 51, 83, 95, 96, 97, 101, 111, 113, 122, 141, 166 Leg 1:4, 34 Leg 2:75 Leg 3:3, 27, 120 Cher 41, 63, 69, 74, 83 Sacr 30, 91 Det 21, 41, 44, 52, 62, 64, 102, 112, 134, 138, 138 Post 38, 57, 102, 111, 139, 141, 144, 148, 162, 163 Deus 36, 102, 103 Agr 22, 29, 59, 67 Plant 27, 90, 94, 115, 122, 156, 160, 160 Ebr 91 Sobr 9, 16, 38, 42 Conf 83, 98 Migr 4, 43, 44, 46, 178 Her 110, 166, 177 Congr 11, 65 Fug 47, 141, 155, 179, 211 Mut 23, 199, 269, 270 Somn 1:76, 91, 147, 164, 216 Somn 2:83, 168, 169, 171, 203, 208, 243, 272 Abr 5, 80, 98, 117 Ios 5, 18, 39, 51, 80, 170, 197, 217, 218 Mos 1:20, 23, 29, 183, 230, 249, 259, 264, 276, 282, 302, 318 Mos 2:2, 43, 48, 120, 125, 170, 177, 187, 291 Decal 125 Spec 1:110, 205, 247, 248, 270 Spec 2:19, 40, 59, 75, 176, 195, 214, 230, 246 Spec 3:137, 152, 188 Spec 4:36, 52, 127, 150, 184, 202, 227, 235 Virt 27, 33, 144, 160, 200 Prob 1, 36, 51, 90, 94, 95, 132, 141 Aet 55, 105 Flacc 4, 24, 34, 76, 88, 126, 126, 152, 161 Legat 84, 122, 170, 301 QG 4:51a, 51b QE 2:38b, 44, 46, 49a

ἐπιδεικτικός Mos 1:91

ἐπίδειξις (31) Opif 149 Post 141, 142 Ebr 41 Sobr 39 Conf 163 Migr 53 Somn 1:166 Somn 2:42, 57, 117 Ios 206 Mos 1:91, 310 Mos 2:211, 237, 255 Spec 2:19, 250 Praem 4 Prob 74 Contempl 48, 52, 75 Flacc 75, 85, 103 Legat 9, 103, 168 QG 1:21

ἐπιδειπνίς Contempl 54

ἐπιδεύομαι Aet 41

ἐπιδέχομαι (13) Opif 73, 97 Sacr 98 Deus 82 Abr 127 Spec 1:178, 196, 209, 327 Spec 2:55 Praem 144 QG 2:54a, 4:8b

ἐπίδηλος Flacc 49

ἐπιδημέω Flacc 28, 28, 103 Legat 179

ἐπιδημία Ios 223 Flacc 30

ἐπιδιαιρέω QG 1:62:1, 62:2

ἐπιδιανέμω Spec 1:185 QE 2:25d

ἐπιδιαφθείρω Prov 2:40

ἐπιδίδωμι (53) Opif 41 Leg 1:10, 98 Sacr 114 Post 125, 141, 145 Gig 1, 10, 25 Deus 147 Agr 86, 146 Plant 110 Migr 68 Her 145 Congr 84 Fug 29, 39 Somn 2:170 Abr 116, 179, 184, 186, 197, 213 Ios 41, 101, 212 Mos 1:8, 240, 275, 301 Mos 2:2, 55, 69, 185, 215 Decal 118, 137, 149 Spec 2:62, 68 Spec 3:154 Praem 66, 172 Prob 122 Aet 91, 101, 103 Hypoth 7:13 QG 4:8a, 81

ἐπιδικασία Spec 3:162 Virt 222

ἐπιδίμοιρος (δίμοιρος) QG (Par) 2:5, 2:5, 2:5

ἐπιδίπλωσις Contempl 51

ἐπίδοσις (19) Opif 103 Sacr 117 Post 174 Agr 158 Sobr 15 Conf 196 Migr 53, 70 Somn 1:60 Mos 1:18, 64 Mos 2:44, 151 Spec 2:119 Virt 157 Prob 92 Contempl 46 Aet 72, 133

ἐπιδράσσομαι (9) Somn 2:31, 32, 37, 37, 42, 71, 74 Ios 140 Mos 1:77

ἐπιδρομή (9) Ebr 111 Her 202, 243 Fug 90 Somn 1:175 Somn 2:82, 121 Mos 1:243, 330

ἐπιδύω Spec 3:152

ἐπιείκεια (10) Opif 103 Mos 1:198 Spec 2:93, 110 Virt 106, 134, 160 Praem 166 Legat 119 QG 2:13a

ἐπιεικής (27) Cher 37 Sacr 49 Det 146 Agr 47 Ebr 131 Conf 37, 116 Migr 95, 147 Mut 242 Somn 1:191 Somn 2:165, 295 Ios 221 Mos 2:204 Spec 1:97 Spec 3:96 Spec 4:23, 32 Virt 81, 125, 140, 148 Flacc 14, 61, 79 Legat 352

ἐπιζεύγνυμι Det 95 Aet 113

ἐπιζήμιος (13) Opif 10 Agr 16, 133 Ebr 6 Conf 171 Migr 171 Congr 137 Mut 149 Abr 126 Decal 12 Spec 1:155 Spec 4:221 Legat 89 ἐπιζητέω (22) Opif 77 Her 33 Somn 2:268 Abr 26 Ios 115, 204 Mos 1:76, 109 Mos 2:190, 203 Spec 1:46, 74, 102, 214, 321 Spec 2:235 Spec 3:10, 109 Flacc 118 Legat 246, 253, 360

ἐπιθαρσέω Spec 3:132, 158

ἐπιθειάζω (15) Sacr 10 Deus 4 Migr 84 Mut 113 Somn 2:172 Mos 2:188, 259, 263, 263, 272, 291 Virt 55, 214, 217 Contempl 84

ἐπιθειασμός Deus 139 Her 69 Spec 3:1

ἐπίθεμα (6) Leg 3:129, 133, 136, 136 Mos 2:95, 97

ἐπίθεσις (23) Leg 3:90 Migr 191 Fug 53 Mut 114 Somn 2:35 Abr 91 Ios 254 Mos 1:67, 110 Spec 1:75, 203 Spec 2:46 Spec 3:18, 93, 94 Spec 4:89 Praem 138 Flacc 73 Legat 37, 146, 159, 201 QG 1:74

ἐπιθέω Decal 150

ἐπιθεωρέω Decal 100

ἐπίθημα Fug 100

ἐπιθυμέω (15) Leg 3:211, 250 Sacr 24 Migr 155 Somn 2:266 Ios 144, 216 Mos 1:13 Decal 136, 142 Spec 3:66 Spec 4:78, 90 Praem 71 QG 4:173

ἐπιθύμημα Conf 50

ἐπιθυμητικός (10) Leg 1:70, 70, 70, 71, 71, 72, 72 Leg 2:18 Leg 3:115, 115

ἐπιθυμητός Leg 3:250

ἐπιθυμία (218) Opif 79, 158 Leg 1:69, 70, 73, 86, 86, 103 Leg 2:8, 18, 72 Leg 3:113, 115, 116, 118, 148, 149, 149, 149, 154, 156, 250 Cher 33, 50, 71, 92 Det 16, 25, 110, 113, 174 Post 26, 26, 27, 52, 71, 116 Gig 18, 34 Deus 15 Agr 17, 36, 73, 78, 83, 84, 112 Plant 105 Ebr 4, 6, 75, 102, 206, 208, 215, 223 Conf 21, 21, 50, 52, 90, 117 Migr 9, 14, 21, 60, 66, 66, 67, 67, 67, 68, 119, 155, 155, 219 Her 64, 109, 173, 245, 269, 270 Congr 57, 59, 65, 81, 88, 162, 172 Fug 31, 91, 144 Mut 72, 171, 172, 215 Somn 2:276, 278 Abr 135, 160, 236, 238, 249 Ios 41, 49, 60, 64, 66, 70, 77, 79, 153 Mos 1:25, 141, 160, 297 Mos 2:23, 58, 139, 185 Decal 49, 51, 129, 142, 142, 142, 149, 149, 150, 153, 173, 173 Spec 1:44, 50, 148, 149, 150, 150, 174, 192, 206, 270 Spec 2:9, 18, 30, 37, 37, 46, 135, 157, 193, 240 Spec 3:43, 49, 61, 69, 85 Spec 4:10, 80, 81, 82, 83, 84, 85, 86, 89, 92, 93, 95, 96, 113, 113, 118, 129, 130, 131, 132, 215, 217 Virt 9, 13, 100, 110, 113, 113, 115 Praem 17, 59, 71, 94, 117, 124, 124, 154, 159 Prob 18, 31, 45, 76, 159 Contempl 2, 55, 56, 59, 61, 74 Legat 14, 65, 89, 114, 162, 337, 368 Prov 2:8, 18, 70 QE 1:19, 2:2

ἐπιθυμιάω (9) Ebr 85, 87, 190 Her 226 Spec 1:84, 171, 275, 276 Legat 306

ἐπίκαιρος Cher 63 Prov 2:37 QG 4:43

ἐπικαίω Agr 17

ἐπικαλέω (20) Opif 113, 163 Det 138, 139 Plant 73, 85 Migr 56 Mut 89 Somn 1:159 Abr 82 Ios 51 Mos 2:29 Decal 103 Spec 1:146, 181, 184, 189 Spec 3:44 Prob 127 Contempl 21

ἐπικαλύπτω Leg 2:58 Sobr 56 Fug 190 QG 2:29

ἐπικαρπία Virt 28

ἐπικαταλαμβάνω Sacr 66, 66 Ios 159

ἐπικαταράομαι Conf 72

ἐπικατάρατος (13) Leg 3:65, 107, 107, 108, 111, 113, 222, 246 Det 96 Post 84 Agr 21 Sobr 32, 51

ἐπικατασφάζω Prob 119 Legat 105, 235

ἐπίκειμαι Leg 3:136 Somn 2:207

ἐπικέλευσις (8) Cher 106 Sacr 4, 106 Ebr 101 Fug 66 Somn 1:141 Spec 2:83 Contempl 71

ἐπικελεύω Congr 176 Fug 101 Spec 4:7

ἐπικέρδεια Abr 65

ἐπίκηρος (13) Opif 72 Leg 3:38 Ebr 121 Fug 104 Somn 1:142 Somn 2:149 Decal 107 Spec 1:252 Spec 4:200 Virt 204 Praem 132, 159 Aet 80

ἐπικηρυκεύομαι Cher 37 Her 206 Virt 109, 151

ἐπικίχρημι Spec 4:235

ἐπικλάω Legat 331

ἐπίκλην Plant 110

ἐπίκλησις (13) Cher 8, 22 Det 30, 78 Gig 50 Deus 4, 18 Ebr 60 Migr 29, 84 Somn 1:194 Abr 52 Legat 188

ἐπικλινής Opif 155 Cher 62 Post 140 Fug 105 Legat 167

ἐπικλίνω Somn 2:174 Legat 43

ἐπικλύζω (25) Leg 3:13, 18, 163 Post 113 Deus 178, 181 Agr 126 Plant 144 Ebr 22 Migr 101 Fug 49 Mut 138 Somn 1:19, 107 Somn 2:13, 239 Abr 42 Mos 2:54 Spec 2:147 Spec 3:33 Praem 73 Aet 120, 139, 140, 142

ἐπικοινωνέω Fug 103

ἐπικομπάζω Fug 30 Mut 196 Somn 1:131 Somn 2:291

ἐπικοσμέω (9) Abr 37 Spec 1:194, 242 Spec 3:59, 65 Spec 4:69 Virt 95 Aet 63 Prov 2:16

Ἐπικούρειος Post 2

ἐπικουρέω Spec 2:71

ἐπικουρία (11) Somn 1:69, 147, 238 Ios 144 Spec 1:298 Spec 2:217 Virt 45, 124 Aet 65 Flacc 191 QG 1:3

ἐπικουρικός Mos 1:111 Praem 95

ἐπίκουρος Leg 1:45 Sacr 96 Post 4

Ἐπίκουρος Aet 8

ἐπικουφίζω (καί) (34) Leg 3:110 Cher 82, 118 Post 71 Deus 21 Plant 144 Sobr 2 Conf 93 Her 201, 272 Fug 162 Somn 1:110 Ios 99, 113, 140, 175, 179, 221, 229 Mos 1:42, 72, 218 Mos 2:204 Decal 109 Spec 1:298 Spec 2:46, 55 Virt 110, 111 Contempl 27 Aet 33, 136 Flacc 121 QG 2:54b

ἐπίκρανον (ὁ) Spec 3:56

ἐπικράτεια (8) Leg 3:186 Abr 53 Spec 4:207 Flacc 8, 31, 105 Legat 252, 311

ἐπικρατέω (22) Opif 33 Leg 3:221 Deus 174 Plant 56, 68 Her 308 Somn 1:114 Somn 2:94 Abr 227, 233, 242, 256 Ios 136, 201 Mos 1:290 Mos 2:99 Spec 1:208 Virt 13 Aet 37, 59 Legat 148 Hypoth 6:4

ἐπικρατής Ios 192

ἐπικρεμάννυμι (18) Agr 151 Plant 88 Conf 12, 119 Her 275 Mut 24 Somn 1:237 Abr 95 Mos 1:171, 216 Virt 200 Aet 11 Flacc 129 Legat 194, 213, 218, 325 Prov 2:28

ἐπικρίνω (32) Cher 17 Sacr 98 Conf 59 Congr 114, 114 Fug 126 Somn 2:98 Abr 83, 218 Ios 28, 58 Mos 2:88, 142, 160, 281 Decal 175 Spec 1:78, 79, 101, 163, 166, 198, 214, 259, 342 Spec 2:24, 125 Spec 3:56 Virt 32 Contempl 72 Aet 142 Flacc 149

ἐπίκρισις (12) Opif 159 Cher 11, 14, 18 Sacr 139 Post 161 Ebr 187 Migr 219 Her 47, 151, 179 Fug 122 ἐπικρύπτω (20) Opif 1 Leg 3:27, 62 Cher 48 Sacr 29 Agr 26 Fug 193 Ios 77 Mos 1:79 Mos 2:87, 282, 287 Decal 136 Spec 1:321 Spec 3:152 Legat 63, 103, 332 Prov 2:26, 60

ἐπικυδής (9) Post 136 Abr 30, 214 Mos 1:217 Decal 69, 136 Spec 4:201 Virt 25, 38

ἐπικυλινδέω (ἐπικυλίω) Mos 1:179

ἐπικυλίω ἐπικυλινδέω

ἐπικυματίζω Migr 125 Fug 49 Spec 3:5

ἐπικυρόω Spec 2:12

ἐπικωμάζω Prov 2:1

ἐπιλαγχάνω (26) Opif 23, 84 Leg 1:92 Cher 43 Sacr 112 Det 145 Post 115 Deus 40 Her 64 Fug 50, 55 Mut 219 Somn 1:57, 140 Somn 2:248, 299 Abr 10, 162 Spec 3:103 Virt 222 Praem 64, 122 Prob 105 Legat 76, 131 Prov 1

ἐπιλαμβάνω (10) Leg 2:88, 88 Cher 7 Sacr 68 Conf 135 Mut 84 Somn 2:68 Ios 49 Mos 1:95 Flacc 53

ἐπιλάμπω (23) Cher 8 Sacr 78 Det 128 Gig 3 Deus 123 Ebr 44 Her 264 Mut 1, 15, 149 Somn 1:23, 72, 82 Somn 2:140 Ios 87 Mos 1:145 Spec 1:288 Spec 2:155 Spec 4:147 Virt 164 Praem 25, 37, 88

ἐπίλαμψις Opif 101 Sacr 34 Abr 43 Spec 3:187

ἐπιλανθάνω ἐπιλήθω

ἐπιλεαίνω (7) Leg 1:98 Sacr 86 Post 148, 159 Agr 132 Spec 1:30 Spec 4:107

ἐπιλέανσις Leg 3:143 Post 149

ἐπιλέγω ἐπεῖπον

ἐπιλέγω (44) Leg 3:74, 217 Cher 18 Det 79 Post 65 Gig 18 Agr 36 Conf 102 Migr 79, 201 Her 90, 130, 230, 275, 315 Congr 173 Mut 58 Somn 1:128 Somn 2:54, 223, 236, 272 Abr 9, 33, 215 Ios 23, 150, 260 Mos 1:306 Decal 18 Spec 1:303 Spec 2:82 Spec 3:60, 88 Spec 4:170, 177 Virt 10, 42, 165 Prob 101, 127 Legat 223, 350 QG 4:227

ἐπιλείπω (24) Sacr 27 Post 82, 82 Agr 166 Plant 131 Ebr 53 Conf 163 Migr 31 Somn 1:256 Somn 2:63, 108 Abr 154 Ios 190, 210, 243 Mos 1:181, 210, 213 Spec 1:80, 164, 178 Spec 4:238 Aet 149 Legat 323

ἐπίλεκτος Post 92 Conf 56 Abr 56, 83

ἐπιλήθω (ἐπιλανθάνω) (26) Leg 2:29 Leg 3:94 Sacr 55, 55, 55 Post 121 Deus 90 Sobr 28 Migr 206, 208 Congr 41 Fug 23 Somn 1:211, 246 Somn 2:232, 232, 294 Decal 43, 62 Spec 4:201 Virt 184 Praem 18 Prob 134 Flacc 9, 186 QG 2:15a

ἐπιλήνιος (ὁ) Agr 152

ἐπίληπτος (31) Opif 155 Leg 3:68, 75, 104, 247 Post 75 Deus 71, 135 Ebr 28 Sobr 48 Conf 126 Congr 59 Somn 2:274 Abr 19, 40 Ios 177 Decal 129 Spec 3:88, 128, 172, 177, 209 Spec 4:79, 182 Virt 173, 206, 211 Contempl 6 Aet 41 QG 1:64d QE 2:17

ἐπιλήσμων Mos 1:58

ἐπιλιχμάω Agr 36 Congr 55 Fug 31

ἐπιλιχνεύω Opif 158 Leg 3:251

ἐπιλογίζομαι (7) Opif 129 Leg 1:62 Leg 3:16, 99 Conf 153 Abr 75 QG 1:1

ἐπιλογισμός Leg 3:102, 226 Sacr 35 Plant 123 Somn 1:75

ἐπίλογος Post 64 Mos 2:51

ἐπίλυπος (7) Leg 3:216, 247 Mut 156, 169 Abr 202 Spec 2:52 QE isf 33

ἐπιλύω Leg 2:63 Agr 16 Contempl 75 Prov 2:2 QG 2:13a

ἐπιμαίνω (14) Leg 3:63 Plant 65 Abr 195 Ios 40 Spec 2:50, 135 Spec 3:9, 11, 43, 45 Spec 4:7 Contempl 6, 59 QG 3:21

ἐπιμανής Sacr 32 Virt 113 Legat 34

ἐπίμαχος Somn 2:1 Virt 48

ἐπιμείγνυμι Cher 110

ἐπιμέλεια (110) Opif 88, 160 Sacr 11, 37, 47, 112, 115, 123 Det 11, 43, 111 Post 181 Agr 4, 6, 51, 60, 61, 64, 171 Plant 26, 55, 73, 101, 162 Ebr 33, 91, 199 Sobr 40, 63 Migr 3, 193, 203, 211, 212 Her 105, 137 Congr 6 Mut 18, 105 Somn 2:38, 123, 147 Abr 70 Ios 2, 4, 25, 37, 67, 88, 117, 154, 157, 217, 248, 267 Mos 1:20, 22, 61, 71, 129 Mos 2:174 Decal 167 Spec 1:16, 71, 310, 318 Spec 2:14, 30, 83, 101, 233 Spec 3:36, 106, 116, 117 Spec 4:153, 156, 178, 183 Virt 39, 47, 52, 54, 58, 63, 70, 133 Praem 9, 11, 56, 104 Prob 69 Contempl 16, 36, 72 Aet 11 Flacc 105 Legat 143, 153, 240, 250, 278, 336 Hypoth 7:9, 7:17, 11:13 Prov 2:32, 44 QG 2:12d, 54d

ἐπιμελέομαι (41) Opif 9, 171 Cher 118 Det 33, 34, 105 Agr 153 Plant 97 Migr 82, 89, 93 Congr 17 Mut 40, 115, 149 Somn 1:121, 149, 162 Abr 82, 82, 221 Ios 196 Mos 1:149 Decal 91 Spec 1:156, 295, 318 Spec 2:125, 260 Spec 3:68, 189 Spec 4:58 Virt 57, 143, 160 Praem 12, 42 Flacc 74 Prov 2:17, 44, 72

ἐπιμελής (30) Leg 3:98 Deus 20 Agr 158 Plant 152 Conf 24, 140 Her 190, 296 Congr 89 Fug 125 Somn 1:57 Abr 105 Ios 158 Mos 2:136 Decal 93, 102 Spec 1:21 Spec 3:11, 46 Spec 4:154, 154, 187, 191 Prob 24, 121 Legat 249, 274 QG 2:54a, 54d, 4:227

ἐπιμελητής (14) Plant 56 Congr 123 Mut 90 Ios 114, 152, 197, 211, 257 Spec 1:131 Spec 2:207 Spec 3:81 Spec 4:21 Praem 77 Prob 45

ἐπίμεμπτος Post 176 Virt 172

ἐπιμέμφομαι Leg 3:179 QG 4:202b

ἐπιμένω (19) Leg 3:94 Cher 115 Sacr 85 Det 30 Gig 44 Deus 28 Agr 70 Sobr 69 Migr 220 Congr 38 Fug 45 Abr 26 Ios 33 Mos 1:226, 230 Spec 4:48 Contempl 31, 77 QG 4:145

ἐπιμερής Decal 20

ἐπιμήκης Deus 128 Flacc 68

ἐπίμικτος (7) Migr 152, 152, 152, 153, 154, 155, 163

ἐπιμιμνήσκομαι (9) Somn 2:32 Abr 37, 208 Decal 29 Spec 2:129 Virt 52, 101 Legat 193, 349

ἐπιμιξία Leg 1:8 Decal 127 Spec 3:25 Spec 4:179 Contempl 20

ἐπιμοιράομαι Mos 2:283

ἐπιμονή (11) Leg 1:55, 55 Cher 41, 47, 102 Det 118 Congr 38, 111 Fug 24, 45 Somn 2:37

ἐπίμονος Sacr 83 Ebr 21

ἐπιμορφάζω (17) Leg 3:47 Det 10, 19 Deus 102 Plant 70 Ebr 43, 198 Her 258 Fug 20, 35, 209 Mut 170, 199 Somn 2:295 Abr 103 Ios 166 Flacc 19

ἐπιμύλιος Spec 3:204

ἐπινεανιεύομαι (6) Det 62 Post 170 Deus 170 Spec 4:215 Prob 123 Flacc 67 ἐπίνειον Flacc 155

ἐπινείφω (ἐπινίφω) (7) Deus 155 Migr 33, 35, 121 Mos 1:200, 202 Virt 49

ἐπινέμω (13) Det 110 Deus 176 Fug 158, 186 Ios 160, 263 Decal 150 Spec 1:128, 141, 145 Spec 2:212 Flacc 141 Prov 2:40

ἐπινεύω (12) Leg 3:85 Ebr 165 Migr 111 Mut 253, 254 Abr 107 Mos 1:84, 105, 163, 252 Mos 2:36 Spec 1:302

ἐπινήχομαι (6) Opif 63 Sacr 13, 61 Migr 125, 184 Mut 158

ἐπινίκιος (9) Ebr 110, 115, 121 Conf 35 Congr 99 Abr 235 Mos 1:219, 284 Contempl 57

ἐπινίφω ἐπινείφω

ἐπινοέω (40) Leg 2:26 Sacr 86, 87, 92, 95 Det 88, 134, 172 Post 9 Deus 63 Ebr 219 Conf 137, 139 Fug 22 Somn 1:62, 204, 236 Somn 2:32 Ios 235 Mos 2:173, 197 Spec 1:214, 258, 336 Spec 4:40, 122, 215 Virt 34 Praem 27, 145 Prob 80 Aet 48, 56 Flacc 70, 73, 86, 97 Legat 199, 358 QE 2:45a

ἐπίνοια (27) Opif 28 Conf 158 Migr 142, 184, 192 Her 23, 229 Fug 168, 170 Mut 219, 249 Somn 1:40 Somn 2:119, 200, 212, 285 Mos 1:8, 17 Spec 1:335 Spec 2:29 Spec 3:44 Virt 107 Praem 145 Contempl 63 Flacc 87 Legat 254 QG 4:200b

Ἐπινομίς Her 162, 250 Spec 4:160, 164

ἐπίνοσος Her 297

ἐπιορκέω Spec 1:235 Spec 2:26 QG isf 14

ἐπίορκος Decal 88 Spec 2:27 Spec 4:40

ἔπιπαν Opif 124 Leg 3:84 Agr 5 QG (Par) 2:2

ἐπίπεδος (11) Opif 50, 50, 92, 98, 98, 98, 106 Plant 75 Somn 1:21 Mos 2:60 Legat 358

ἐπίπεμπτος Spec 1:236

ἐπιπέμπω (20) Leg 1:28 Leg 2:31, 86 Sacr 44 Post 37, 44, 44, 73 Plant 114 Conf 21, 157 Migr 73 Mut 260 Somn 1:1, 86 Somn 2:213, 268 Praem 95 Legat 342 QE 2:2

ἐπιπηδάω Praem 100

ἐπιπίπτω (12) Her 249, 249, 258, 263, 264 Abr 233 Ios 214, 256 Mos 1:119 Spec 3:3 Spec 4:85 Virt 49

ἔπιπλα Mut 89 Spec 3:206 Flacc 148 Legat 122, 232

ἐπίπληξις (6) Congr 177, 179 Fug 205 Mos 1:26, 98, 126

ἐπιπλήσσω (11) Opif 128 Leg 2:46 Det 145 Post 93, 97 Deus 126 Mos 1:102 Flacc 35, 35, 40 Legat 305

ἐπιπλοκή Her 301 Aet 8

ἐπιπνέω Congr 38 Abr 116 Decal 35 Spec 1:224 Spec 2:172

ἐπίπνοια Somn 1:129

ἐπιποθέω (6) Opif 10 Abr 48, 87, 195 Mos 1:184 Legat 360

ἐπιπολάζω (10) Ebr 59 Mos 1:6 Mos 2:174 Decal 75 Spec 2:191 Prob 73 Contempl 48 Aet 115 Prov 2:38 QG 2:15b

ἐπιπόλαιος (10) Post 119 Ebr 112 Her 40, 92 Congr 121 Somn 1:6 Somn 2:298 Spec 3:68 Prob 29 Legat 181

ἐπιπολή Praem 64

ἐπίπονος (16) Det 46, 157 Post 56, 94, 95 Deus 93 Congr 163 Mos 1:329 Mos 2:211 Spec 1:301 Spec 2:100 Spec 4:112 Virt 3, 205 Flacc 177 Legat 83

ἐπιποτάομαι (6) Leg 2:11 Gig 20 Her 242 Somn 2:212 Decal 116 Praem 125

ἐπιπροσθέω Agr 162 Decal 159 Spec 4:52

ἐπιρραίνω (6) Mos 2:146, 152 Spec 1:199, 231, 262, 268

ἐπιρράσσω Her 244 Abr 46 Mos 2:248

ἐπιρρέπω Mos 1:218 Legat 244

ἐπιρρέω (7) Leg 3:148 Det 40 Ebr 32, 70 Somn 2:237 Aet 147 Prov 2:28

ἐπιρριπτέω Legat 130

ἐπιρρίπτω Spec 4:201 Legat 330

ἐπιρροή (7) Post 125 Her 32, 56 Fug 200, 201 Spec 2:201 Hypoth 11:3

ἐπίρροια Leg 2:32 Mos 2:104 Virt 128, 130, 154

ἐπισαρκάζω Mut 61

ἐπισείω Det 95

ἐπισεμνύνομαι Ebr 84 Conf 118 Congr 170 Mut 137 Spec 1:279

ἐπίσημος (10) Migr 79 Her 180, 180, 180 Fug 10, 10, 11 Somn 1:201 Legat 325 Prov 2:17

ἐπισκάζω Mut 187

ἐπισκέπτομαι (ἐπισκοπέω) (44) Opif 91, 101 Leg 3:236 Cher 21 Det 79 Post 67 Agr 7, 44 Plant 140 Ebr 1, 33 Migr 18 Her 40 Congr 22, 54, 81 Fug 178, 188 Somn 1:55, 56 Somn 2:205 Mos 1:68, 113 Decal 52 Spec 1:1, 33, 81, 212, 213, 214, 226, 262, 287 Spec 2:40, 150, 223, 262 Virt 51, 58 Praem 10, 61, 67, 126 Aet 125

ἐπίσκεψις (11) Cher 45, 99 Agr 49, 131, 157 Migr 76, 195, 195 Spec 1:166, 259 Praem 28

ἐπισκήπτω Opif 125 Post 89 Legat 161

ἐπίσκηψις Ebr 35 Ios 12

ἐπισκιάζω (39) Opif 6, 170 Leg 2:30, 58 Leg 3:7 Gig 2 Deus 3, 103 Conf 60 Migr 126, 191 Mut 246 Somn 1:72, 102 Somn 2:196 Abr 102 Ios 49, 106, 238 Mos 1:209 Mos 2:27, 43, 200, 271 Decal 138 Spec 1:72, 321 Spec 3:4, 121 Spec 4:36, 51, 52, 70 Praem 37 Prob 5 Legat 109, 260 Prov 2:31 QG 4:204

ἐπισκοπέω ἐπισκέπτομαι

ἐπισκοπέω (7) Cher 45 Ebr 136 Mut 67 Decal 98, 103 Spec 1:19 Virt 12

ἐπίσκοπος (11) Leg 3:43 Ebr 98 Migr 81, 115, 135 Her 30 Mut 39, 216 Somn 1:91 Somn 2:186 Virt 219

ἐπισκοτέω Sacr 1 Ebr 44 Ios 147

ἐπισπάω (15) Leg 3:31 Sacr 36 Post 116 Gig 44 Ebr 176 Conf 121 Congr 122 Fug 31 Mut 113 Abr 59 Ios 41 Mos 1:93 Virt 41 Aet 104, 128

ἐπισπεύδω (11) Opif 44 Plant 161 Her 66, 255, 310 Abr 62 Ios 255 Mos 2:171 Spec 1:243 Flacc 86 Legat 101

ἐπίσταμαι (54) Leg 3:51, 88, 221, 244 Sacr 64 Det 53, 126, 126 Post 151 Deus 49 Agr 56, 162 Plant 44 Ebr 41, 42, 107 Sobr 21 Conf 13 Migr 40, 78 Her 18, 24 Congr 85 Mut 21, 202 Somn 2:53, 103, 141 Ios 203 Mos 1:49, 144, 184 Mos 2:217 Decal 90, 129 Spec 1:30, 60, 325 Spec 2:100 Spec 4:18, 27, 120, 154 Virt 51 Prob 152 Flacc 43 Legat 133, 156, 156, 163, 317, 372 QG 2:54a, 4:172

ἐπιστασία (19) Cher 24 Det 6, 142, 145 Gig 12 Agr 49 Plant 141 Ebr 91 Sobr 69 Migr 22 Her 125 Fug 14, 207 Mut 105, 258 Somn 2:152 Ios 3 Spec 1:14 Virt 210 ἐπίστασις Leg 3:49

ἐπιστατέω (13) Sacr 50 Agr 53, 56, 58 Sobr 54 Her 166 Congr 2 Fug 10 Somn 1:164 Somn 2:152 Mos 1:60 Spec 1:33 Hypoth 6:4

ἐπιστάτης (15) Sacr 45, 104, 104 Det 104 Post 54, 54 Agr 45 Plant 2 Ebr 199 Sobr 12 Mut 14 Mos 1:37 Prob 30 Aet 1 Legat 44

ἐπιστέλλω (9) Mos 1:83 Legat 209, 248, 261, 276, 305, 311, 313, 314

ἐπιστένω (6) Leg 3:211 Sobr 6 Conf 164 Ios 217 Spec 1:143 Flacc 168

ἐπιστεφανόω Abr 35

ἐπιστήμη (318) Opif 8, 41, 53, 69, 77, 82, 126, 128, 138, 167, 171 Leg 1:6, 60, 68, 70, 89 Leg 2:70 Leg 3:84, 95, 126, 152, 161, 163, 168, 178, 179, 205, 233 Cher 9, 19, 32, 41, 48, 52, 68, 71, 105, 121, 127 Sacr 6, 7, 13, 44, 64, 78, 85, 86, 126, 130 Det 3, 6, 18, 25, 54, 55, 65, 88, 104, 110, 114, 118, 143, 149 Post 18, 36, 62, 78, 130, 137, 138, 141, 150, 151, 152, 153, 174 Gig 17, 22, 23, 25, 27 Deus 19, 22, 24, 26, 71, 79, 92, 93, 143, 143 Agr 2, 4, 20, 42, 55, 87, 92, 93, 125, 137, 138, 161, 162, 163, 164, 181 Plant 23, 31, 80, 82, 98, 168 Ebr 5, 30, 39, 40, 44, 137, 154, 158, 159, 160, 161, 184, 203, 209, 219 Sobr 9, 35, 36 Conf 12, 40, 52, 55, 97, 145, 159, 175, 178 Migr 39, 41, 42, 50, 55, 57, 76, 83, 134, 142, 175, 185, 197 Her 14, 18, 53, 100, 115, 116, 121, 128, 129, 132, 160, 160, 194, 204, 207, 286, 308, 313 Congr 14, 22, 23, 36, 46, 47, 48, 50, 50, 64, 79, 122, 123, 127, 128, 129, 140, 140, 141, 142, 142, 143, 144, 154, 155, 156 Fug 8, 19, 37, 52, 76, 97, 164, 168, 176, 187, 195, 200, 200, 213, 213 Mut 5, 8, 63, 76, 88, 150, 202, 203, 220 Somn 1:6, 8, 9, 11, 11, 42, 47, 49, 50, 60, 80, 84, 160, 204, 207, 207, 250 Somn 2:4, 271, 297 Abr 58, 71, 73 Ios 106, 142 Mos 1:22, 23, 62, 154, 220, 222, 227, 293 Mos 2:5, 96, 97, 111, 216 Decal 1, 81, 141 Spec 1:15, 35, 64, 209, 288, 336, 339, 345 Spec 2:64, 228 Spec 3:5, 100 Spec 4:70, 75, 145, 147, 156, 156 Virt 1, 61, 65, 155, 172, 180, 213, 220 Praem 41, 61 Prob 12, 83, 107 Contempl 5, 25, 35, 64 Aet 1, 2, 41, 134, 145, 149 Flacc 7 Legat 21, 53, 69, 89, 149, 246 Prov 1, 1, 2:66 QG 4:9* QG isf 4 QE 2:13b, 25b QE isf 7

ἐπιστημονικός (16) Gig 2 Her 48, 158 Mos 1:22, 117 Mos 2:196 Spec 1:35 Spec 4:106 Virt 174 Praem 51, 56, 83 Contempl 49 QG 1:20, 21 QG isf 16

ἐπιστήμων (29) Leg 3:87, 202 Post 90 Gig 60 Deus 30, 50 Agr 71 Plant 141, 144 Ebr 89, 195 Sobr 37 Migr 40, 40, 42, 56, 58 Congr 46, 142 Mut 220 Virt 170, 170 Praem 100 Prob 157 Legat 46, 56 Hypoth 11:8 Prov 2:60 QG 4:76b

ἐπιστηρίζω Somn 1:3, 133, 158

ἐπιστολή (12) Prob 96 Legat 199, 207, 207, 254, 254, 259, 291, 301, 303, 314, 315

ἐπιστολιμαῖος Ios 168 Flacc 108

ἐπιστομίζω (17) Leg 2:104 Leg 3:118, 128, 134, 155, 159 Det 23 Agr 58, 88, 94 Conf 40 Her 3 Decal 63 Spec 1:128, 193, 343 Spec 4:97

ἐπιστρέφω (33) Leg 2:8 Cher 37 Post 106, 135 Deus 17 Agr 143 Conf 130, 131 Migr 195 Her 46 Fug 124, 142 Mut 209 Somn 1:247 Somn 2:144, 174, 175 Abr 176 Ios 87, 175, 200, 230 Mos 2:247 Spec 2:11, 189, 256 Spec 3:41 Praem 95 Contempl 45 Flacc 30, 163 Legat 272 QG 1:51

ἐπιστροφάδην Abr 229 Mos 2:273 Spec 3:126 Spec 4:222

ἐπιστύλις Somn 2:54

ἐπισυμβαίνω Prov 2:47

ἐπισυμπίπτω Spec 1:62

ἐπισυνάγω Opif 38 Plant 60 QG (Par) 2:5

ἐπισυνίστημι Ios 34 Mos 2:278 Aet 36 Flacc 4 Legat 312

ἐπισυρμός Mos 2:208

ἐπισυρρέω Spec 4:173

ἐπισύρω Mos 2:85

ἐπισφάζω Spec 4:202

ἐπισφαλής Deus 65 Praem 33 Prov 2:60

ἐπισφίγγω (7) Leg 3:104, 105 Somn 2:165, 294 Prob 18 Legat 131, 324

ἐπισφραγίζω (16) Det 31 Migr 30 Ios 98, 212 Spec 2:14, 19, 176, 211, 227 Spec 4:105, 157 Virt 37 Praem 108 Flacc 19 Legat 240 QG 3:21

ἐπίσχεσις QG 2:29

ἐπίταγμα (33) Opif 167 Leg 3:56, 80 Cher 115 Ebr 64 Conf 92 Migr 14 Congr 176 Mut 206, 226, 254, 256 Somn 1:56, 191 Somn 2:124 Abr 226 Ios 186 Mos 1:37, 40 Spec 2:67, 90, 93 Spec 3:8, 163, 177, 195 Praem 139, 154 Prob 22, 36, 104, 120 Legat 236

ἐπίτασις (14) Deus 162 Her 156 Fug 146 Mut 87, 179 Somn 1:9 Ios 33 Spec 2:99 Virt 171, 201 Aet 43 QG 2:64a, 64a, 64a

ἐπιτάσσω (17) Leg 3:80, 80 Cher 115 Migr 8 Mut 226, 254 Somn 1:56 Abr 74, 228 Ios 135, 152 Mos 1:37 Prob 22, 30, 101, 104 Legat 259

ἐπιτείνω (21) Leg 3:106, 183, 211 Cher 128 Post 13 Deus 24 Plant 171 Ebr 116, 185 Migr 132 Mut 267 Somn 2:184 Mos 1:25 Spec 3:44, 151 Spec 4:80, 102 Virt 105 Legat 268 QG 2:64a, 64c

ἐπιτειχίζω (24) Opif 79 Agr 46 Plant 159 Conf 54, 128 Fug 148 Mut 33 Somn 2:59, 276 Abr 133, 261 Mos 2:65, 194 Spec 1:28 Spec 3:138 Spec 4:5, 17 Virt 132 Praem 59, 68 Aet 69 Flacc 65, 86 QG isf 13

ἐπιτείχισμα Mos 1:8 Virt 35

ἐπιτειχισμός (9) Conf 90 Somn 2:46 Abr 223 Mos 2:176, 185 Spec 1:173 Spec 2:46 Praem 25 Prov 2:36

ἐπιτελέω (55) Opif 61 Cher 14 Plant 165 Ebr 129 Migr 97 Her 82 Fug 37, 161 Somn 1:90, 214, 215 Somn 2:153 Ios 208 Mos 1:87, 253, 287, 298, 304 Mos 2:94, 147, 154, 221 Decal 162, 164 Spec 1:3, 56, 97, 98, 113, 217, 221, 297 Spec 2:61, 145, 167 Spec 3:56, 72, 125, 171 Spec 4:67 Virt 98, 100 Praem 79, 126, 131 Prob 36, 140 Contempl 71 Flacc 97 Legat 157, 157, 218, 317 QG 2:16 QE 2:16

ἐπιτέλλω Opif 115, 115 Plant 151

ἐπιτέμνω (10) Her 133 Ios 181 Spec 1:144 Spec 2:38 Spec 4:96, 148 Praem 135 Prob 115 Legat 246 Hypoth 6:10

ἐπιτέχνησις Deus 156 Conf 185

ἐπιτήδειος (ὁ) (71) Opif 80 Leg 1:28 Cher 79, 100 Sacr 87, 90 Det 5, 113 Gig 34 Agr 32, 39, 152 Plant 53 Ebr 218 Conf 75, 110 Migr 212 Her 247 Fug 155 Mut 82, 89 Somn 1:170, 236 Ios 186, 210, 248, 249, 251 Mos 1:192, 203, 205, 245, 305, 320 Mos 2:36, 60, 141, 161, 267 Decal 16, 18, 94, 99, 116 Spec 1:161, 267,

297 Spec 2:6, 109, 158, 175 Spec 3:91, 122, 200 Spec 4:126, 171 Virt 57, 63, 133 Praem 9, 100 Prob 20 Contempl 22 Flacc 184 Legat 120, 124, 162, 201, 257 Hypoth 11:10 QG isf 9

ἐπιτηδειότης Somn 1:129

ἐπίτηδες Abr 190 Spec 2:93 QG 2:65

ἐπιτήδευμα (54) Opif 80 Leg 3:30, 211 Sacr 100, 103, 113 Det 111 Deus 105, 111, 123 Agr 41, 56 Ebr 51, 218 Her 50, 109, 121 Congr 85, 86, 86, 87 Fug 26, 128 Mut 195, 249, 255 Somn 1:106, 126, 251 Somn 2:21, 211 Abr 37, 40 Ios 50, 64 Mos 2:55, 289 Spec 1:343 Spec 3:11, 24, 42 Virt 87 Praem 18, 82, 142 Contempl 1, 60 Flacc 3, 57, 94 Legat 45, 45, 91, 230

ἐπιτήδευσις (23) Cher 34, 92 Sacr 14, 38, 101 Agr 18, 28 Ebr 13 Congr 65, 79 Fug 167 Mut 88 Spec 2:159, 170 Spec 3:37, 103 Spec 4:68 Praem 85, 85, 91 Prob 77 Legat 106 QE isf 31

ἐπιτηδεύω (102) Cher 33, 36, 95 Sacr 116 Det 11, 18, 19, 28, 35, 74 Post 157 Gig 36, 60, 60, 62 Deus 102, 126 Agr 8, 115 Plant 139, 151 Ebr 53, 54, 216 Conf 121 Migr 224 Her 302 Congr 53, 73, 80 Fug 25, 160 Somn 1:7, 112, 151, 205 Somn 2:40, 76, 160, 179, 181, 182, 211 Abr 41, 61, 192 Ios 59, 59, 61, 67, 73, 75, 222 Mos 1:24, 153 Mos 2:48, 53, 67 Decal 62 Spec 1:32, 273, 306, 330 Spec 2:146, 147, 258 Spec 3:17, 116, 138 Spec 4:5, 16, 48, 135 Virt 47, 114, 190, 195 Praem 8, 97, 100 Prob 34, 49, 78, 90 Contempl 20, 69 Flacc 24, 25, 33, 66, 149 Legat 98, 110, 169, 312, 361 Hypoth 11:7 Prov 2:2, 18, 21 QG 4:204 QG isf 10

ἐπιτηρέω (8) Leg 3:189 Ios 33 Mos 1:26 Spec 3:33 Virt 157 Legat 122, 128, 128

ἐπιτήρησις QG 3:61

ἐπιτίθημι (92) Opif 50, 79, 114 Leg 1:91, 91, 92 Leg 2:62, 63 Leg 3:13, 14, 38, 90, 118, 189, 200, 224 Sacr 100 Det 11, 12 Post 81, 81, 94 Gig 24 Agr 105, 108 Sobr 8, 27 Conf 1, 12, 17, 86, 160, 160, 162, 162, 163, 167 Her 60, 226 Fug 53, 77, 78 Mut 234, 234, 251 Somn 1:110, 130 Somn 2:71, 92, 151, 269, 279 Abr 176, 191, 228, 242, 275 Ios 5, 254 Mos 1:42, 46, 46, 67, 96, 141, 143, 231 Mos 2:53, 131, 147, 169, 174, 251, 277 Decal 121, 139 Spec 1:202 Spec 2:137, 218 Spec 3:73, 107 Virt 25 Praem 121 Prob 118 Aet 21 Flacc 1, 37, 128 Legat 120, 371 Prov 2:22, 25

ἐπιτιμάω (9) Ebr 110 Mut 195 Somn 2:111, 135, 137 Ios 73, 74 Spec 2:23 Virt 187

ἐπιτιμία Her 27 Spec 1:102 Spec 3:78 Flacc 79

ἐπιτίμιον (11) Sobr 46 Congr 138 Mut 243 Decal 176 Spec 2:26 Spec 3:181 Spec 4:3, 11, 33 Praem 2, 3

ἐπίτιμος Cher 93 Congr 128 Flacc 172

ἐπιτοκία Spec 2:78 Legat 343

ἐπιτολή Opif 58, 115

ἐπιτολμάω (7) Opif 5, 90 Post 115 Deus 148 Mut 104 Somn 2:98 Prov 2:65

ἐπιτομή Legat 179, 254

ἐπίτομος (6) Abr 172 Mos 1:164, 237, 246 Flacc 26, 28

ἐπιτραγῳδέω Somn 2:291 Mos 1:153 Aet 131

ἐπιτρέπω (109) Leg 2:57 Leg 3:197, 213 Cher 10 Sacr 77 Det 62, 62, 64 Post 94 Agr 29, 39, 85, 101, 112 Ebr 2, 136, 211, 213 Conf 179, 181 Migr 97, 124 Her 172, 267 Fug 159, 181 Mut 64 Somn 1:123, 215 Somn 2:92 Abr 143 Ios 46, 50, 75, 88, 92, 162, 165, 217, 224, 242, 252 Mos 1:20, 73, 97, 105, 122, 126, 129, 266, 296, 300, 320, 330 Mos 2:33, 75, 174, 232, 248 Spec 1:55, 72, 111, 124, 125, 220, 324 Spec 2:16, 116, 123, 142, 222, 232, 251 Spec 3:22, 27, 96, 123, 130 Spec 4:32, 32, 36, 58, 171, 205 Virt 61, 111, 137 Prob 12, 20, 35, 120, 143 Flacc 2, 31, 33, 35, 43, 97, 97, 134, 158, 179 Legat 49, 99, 241, 247, 311 Prov 2:70 QE isf 17

ἐπιτρέχω (38) Cher 78 Sacr 25 Det 129 Post 138 Agr 33, 93, 123 Plant 152 Migr 175, 197 Mut 239 Somn 2:54, 150, 212 Abr 26, 266 Ios 6, 102 Mos 1:102, 130, 179, 182, 235, 313 Spec 1:316 Spec 2:143 Spec 4:81 Virt 30, 43, 48 Contempl 86 Aet 20, 139, 147 Flacc 188 Legat 109, 121 Prov 2:33

ἐπίτριτος (9) Opif 48, 48, 96, 107, 108 Mos 2:115 Decal 21, 22 Spec 2:200

ἐπιτροπεύω (15) Deus 30 Sobr 14, 54 Abr 74 Ios 3, 259 Decal 103, 105 Virt 54 Aet 83 Flacc 74, 128, 133 Legat 245 Hypoth 11:8

ἐπιτροπή (7) Post 181 Migr 3 Ios 117 Virt 68 Flacc 128 Legat 231, 302

ἐπίτροπος (41) Det 145 Post 68 Deus 30, 30, 113, 134 Plant 56 Congr 118 Somn 1:107 Somn 2:43 Ios 38, 67, 74, 178, 184, 190, 196, 207, 210, 218, 232 Mos 1:113 Spec 1:221 Spec 3:67 Spec 4:71, 71 Virt 67 Prob 35 Flacc 2, 43, 152, 163 Legat 20, 26, 27, 132, 299, 306, 311, 333, 351

ἐπιτυγχάνω (17) Det 62 Post 70, 80 Ebr 63, 160, 165 Conf 21 Fug 171 Somn 1:122 Somn 2:230 Spec 1:125, 225 Spec 2:169 Spec 3:51, 178 Prob 113 QG 4:47a

ἐπιτυχία Spec 3:161

ἐπιφαίνω (17) Opif 83 Sacr 26 Plant 171 Congr 92 Mut 6, 15 Somn 1:71, 228, 232 Abr 142, 145, 167 Ios 106, 255 Spec 1:65 Virt 164 Prov 2:9

ἐπιφάνεια (31) Opif 49, 49, 102 Leg 2:38 Post 118 Deus 35 Congr 146, 147 Fug 182 Somn 1:21, 187 Somn 2:144 Ios 136 Mos 1:3, 108 Mos 2:90, 96, 115, 255 Decal 24, 25, 26 Spec 2:149 Virt 12 Legat 328, 357 QG 2:15a, 15a QG (Par) 2:4, 2:4 QE isf 21

ἐπιφανής (21) Plant 171 Migr 161 Fug 30 Somn 1:112, 155, 226 Somn 2:44, 61 Abr 234, 267 Ios 121, 172 Mos 1:51 Spec 2:175 Spec 3:124 Prob 10 Flacc 81, 81, 185 Legat 151, 191

Ἐπιφανής Legat 346

ἐπιφάσκω Migr 136 Flacc 130 Prov 2:17

ἐπιφέρω (162) Opif 50, 80, 84, 157, 159 Leg 1:6, 20, 24, 33, 51 Leg 2:9, 31, 38, 46, 73, 87, 101 Leg 3:20, 21, 159, 167, 201, 247, 253 Cher 81, 106 Sacr 29 Det 47, 51, 67, 106, 139 Post 38, 60, 74, 96, 137, 142, 171 Gig 17, 22, 40 Deus 124, 131, 137, 141 Agr 37, 44, 100, 175 Plant 137 Ebr 32, 140, 160 Sobr 27 Conf 13, 154 Migr 49, 104 Her 59, 109, 164, 181, 204, 242 Congr 158 Fug 71, 187, 196 Somn 1:23, 50, 72, 103, 109, 173 Somn 2:71, 88, 161, 181 Abr 176 Ios 109, 184, 195, 199, 207, 210 Mos 1:81, 98, 103, 105, 107, 119, 121, 127, 129, 203, 209, 267, 270, 286 Mos 2:70, 133, 255 Decal 144, 149 Spec 1:150, 167, 196, 198, 202, 239, 254, 262, 292, 326 Spec 2:8, 158, 248 Spec 3:58, 163, 174 Spec 4:6, 7, 26, 81, 125, 182 Virt 20, 37, 128, 208 Praem 73, 133 Prob 26, 41, 106, 111, 139 Contempl 37, 72 Aet 47, 89, 129 Flacc 71, 189 Legat 31, 37, 100, 107, 125, 133, 136, 237, 364 QG 2:12c, 41, 65, 4:40 QG isf 13 QE 2:24b, 25d, 47 ἐπιφημίζω (47) Opif 12, 15, 29, 127 Cher 65 Post 101 Deus 5 Agr 29, 30, 66 Conf 62, 191 Her 135, 139, 170, 291 Congr 112 Mut 11, 64, 71 Somn 1:40, 166 Abr 51, 55 Ios 12, 30, 74 Mos 2:171, 272 Decal 53, 104 Spec 2:154 Spec 3:83 Praem 109 Prob 10, 31, 42, 124, 158 Contempl 41 Legat 136, 164, 353, 354 Hypoth 7:3, 7:5, 7:5

ἐπιφθέγγομαι Ios 87 QG 1:17b

ἐπίφθονος Ios 205

ἐπιφοιτάω (30) Opif 38, 117, 126, 131, 147 Gig 24 Agr 166 Her 13, 240, 242, 242 Somn 1:119 Somn 2:214 Abr 23 Ios 160 Mos 1:53, 130, 175, 272, 277 Spec 1:73 Spec 2:107 Spec 3:89, 115 Spec 4:49 Legat 18, 201, 217 Prov 2:65 QE 2:47

ἐπιφοίτησις Spec 3:91

ἐπιφορέω Post 149, 176 Conf 4

ἐπιφόρος Spec 4:27

ἐπιφράσσω (10) Leg 2:25 Cher 42 Sacr 131 Deus 180 Agr 105 Migr 191 Somn 1:107 Mos 2:200 Spec 3:174 Virt 100

ἐπιφροσύνη (22) Det 61 Agr 169 Sobr 18 Migr 123, 171 Her 278 Fug 135 Somn 2:25 Abr 18, 235 Ios 37 Mos 1:85, 132, 211 Mos 2:5, 32, 58, 154, 261, 278 QG 3:18 QE 2:18

ἐπίφυσις Agr 6 Somn 1:106 Somn 2:64 Spec 2:172 Virt 156

ἐπιφύω Plant 100, 106 Somn 1:223 Somn 2:64

ἐπιφωνέω Leg 3:202 Sacr 70 Plant 51 Prob 97, 115

ἐπιχαίνω Det 103 Plant 105 Decal 135 Spec 4:5

ἐπιχαιρεκακέω Agr 93

ἐπιχαιρεκακία Virt 116

ἐπιχαιρέκακος Sacr 32

ἐπιχαλάω Abr 73 Spec 1:99 Spec 2:240 Aet 63 Legat 168

ἐπιχαράσσω Leg 1:100

ἐπιχειλής Her 305

ἐπίχειρα (ὁ) (12) Opif 167 Her 271 Somn 2:85 Ios 174 Mos 1:139 Praem 142, 171 Legat 14, 60, 206, 258 Prov 2:58

ἐπιχειρέω (49) Opif 118 Leg 2:14 Leg 3:189 Det 134 Post 141, 141 Deus 8, 142, 143 Plant 143, 144 Conf 43, 160 Migr 224 Her 258 Fug 147 Mut 195, 203, 224 Somn 1:103, 105 Somn 2:140 Abr 158 Ios 51, 216 Mos 1:53, 167 Mos 2:177 Decal 63 Spec 1:184 Spec 2:3, 246 Spec 3:11, 86, 105, 142 Spec 4:2, 2, 7, 25, 212 Virt 160, 166 Aet 37, 129, 138 Legat 77, 338 Prov 2:60

ἐπιχείρημα Ebr 23 Somn 2:284

ἐπιχειρονομέω Deus 170 Spec 4:215 Contempl 84 Legat 354

ἐπιχέω (10) Det 100 Her 185 Mut 84, 107, 234 Somn 2:60, 86, 183, 249 Spec 4:170

ἐπιχλευάζω (καί) (6) Det 12, 78 Conf 142 Somn 2:301 Praem 169 Legat 122

ἐπίχρυσος (6) Flacc 30 Legat 79, 133, 203, 299, 337

ἐπιχώννυμι Conf 4

ἐπιχώριος Migr 216 Mos 1:49

ἐπιψάλλω Deus 24 Somn 1:37

ἐπιψαύω Det 89 Plant 80 Mos 1:68 Mos 2:22 QE 2:45b

ἐπιψεκάζω Leg 1:25 Her 204 Fug 138 Virt 49

ἐπιψεύδομαι (6) Leg 3:61 Mos 2:176, 278 Spec 3:119 Spec 4:52 Flacc 170

ἐπιψύχω Spec 4:56

ἐπόγδοος Spec 2:200

ἐποικέω Spec 2:168

ἐποικοδομέω (8) Cher 101 Gig 30 Conf 5, 87 Her 116 Mut 211 Somn 2:8 Contempl 34

ἔποικος Mos 1:8

ἐπομβρέω (7) Leg 1:25 Post 135 Deus 155 Conf 23, 127 Migr 32 Legat 22

ἐπομβρία (8) Leg 3:227 Abr 91, 179 Mos 1:265 Spec 1:92, 184 Spec 2:191 Aet 119

ἑπομένως Fug 94 Decal 83

ἐπονείδιστος Spec 1:280 Praem 6, 117

ἐπονομάζω Cher 54 Post 33, 124 Congr 163 Praem 23

ἐπόπτης Hypoth 7:9

ἐπορχέομαι Contempl 84

ἔπος (25) Opif 13, 88, 107 Cher 112 Det 73, 165 Post 25 Deus 104 Plant 158 Ebr 51 Conf 4, 134 Her 12, 66 Fug 16 Somn 1:96, 106 Somn 2:259 Mos 2:18 Decal 151 Spec 2:63 Spec 3:206 Spec 4:133 Contempl 17, 80

ἐπουράνιος Leg 3:168 Gig 62 Virt 12

ἐπουρίζω Somn 2:67 Abr 20 Mos 1:283 Decal 148

ἐποχέομαι (19) Leg 2:102 Cher 33 Gig 22 Agr 67, 67, 71, 72, 77, 78, 110 Ebr 111 Migr 62, 161 Her 301 Mos 1:269, 270 Aet 115, 115 Legat 134

ἐποχετεύω (7) Opif 41, 80 Sobr 36 Spec 1:216, 218, 338 Spec 4:140

ἐποχή Fug 136

ἔποχος (7) Opif 86 Cher 24, 24 Agr 92 Her 99 Fug 101 Somn 2:83

ἑπτά (124) Opif 91, 93, 95, 100, 101, 101, 101, 104, 104, 104, 105, 105, 105, 105, 105, 105, 105, 112, 113, 114, 118, 119, 120, 121, 122, 124, 124, 126, 127 Leg 1:8, 8, 12, 12, 13, 14, 14 Leg 2:66 Cher 22, 22, 23 Det 167, 167, 168, 168, 169, 170, 172, 173 Post 60 Deus 10, 11, 119 Agr 30 Her 218, 219, 219, 219, 221, 221, 222, 232, 233 Congr 104 Fug 186 Mut 110, 111, 116, 143, 143 Somn 2:216, 216, 217, 218, 218, 218 Ios 101, 102, 102, 108, 108, 108, 108, 108, 108, 111, 159 Mos 1:52, 101, 277, 282, 287 Mos 2:103, 153 Decal 28, 103, 160, 161, 161, 161 Spec 1:177, 178, 181, 182, 182, 184, 188, 189, 261 Spec 2:57, 110, 156, 157, 176, 211 Spec 3:205 Virt 129 Prob 73 Contempl 54, 65 Legat 13 Hypoth 7:10 QG 1:77, 2:13a, 13b

ἑπταετία (9) Opif 103 Leg 1:10, 10, 10 Her 294 Ios 109, 109, 158 Spec 4:4

ἑπταέτις Sobr 8

ἑπτακαίδεκα Ios 2, 270

ἑπτάκις (6) Opif 91, 105, 105 Mos 2:146 Spec 1:231, 268

ἑπτακόσιοι Opif 91, 93

ἑπταμερής Leg 1:11

ἑπτάμηνος Opif 124 Leg 1:9

ἑπτάς QG 2:12a

ἑπταφεγγής Her 225

ἐπταχῆ Opif 117 Leg 1:12

ἑπτάχορδος Opif 126 Leg 1:14

ἕπω (122) Opif 28, 70, 131, 144, 157 Leg 3:110, 154 Sacr 2, 106 Det 161 Post 32, 48, 49, 71, 73, 78, 146, 169 Deus 138, 181 Agr 1, 38, 90 Plant 49, 94, 109, 130, 139 Ebr 28, 34, 40, 55, 137, 165 Sobr 1, 5, 26 Conf 14, 145, 174 Migr 104, 128, 131, 143, 146, 173, 191 Congr 35 Fug 73, 143, 165 Mut 46, 130, 170 Somn 1:14, 41, 102 Somn 2:8, 117, 174 Abr 28, 60, 74, 89, 204 Ios 128, 156 Mos 1:37, 50, 85, 102, 133, 166 Mos 2:1, 58, 198, 211 Decal 69, 81, 82, 98, 100, 156 Spec 1:112, 155, 323 Spec 2:42, 140, 223, 223 Spec 3:76, 176, 180 Spec 4:1, 7, 39, 46, 90, 187 Virt 18, 104, 118, 181, 190, 227 Praem 33, 82, 98, 98, 105, 119 Contempl 1, 79 Aet 27, 60, 88 Legat 26, 153, 361 Prov 2:53 QG 1:66, 89

ἐπῳδή Migr 83 Spec 3:101

ἐπῳδός ἐπαοιδός

ἐπῳδός Agr 82

ἐπώδυνος Leg 3:247 Abr 240 Legat 224

ἐπωθέω Praem 73

ἐπωμίς (7) Mos 2:109, 111, 113, 122, 130, 133, 143

ἐπωνυμία (6) Somn 2:112 Decal 55 Spec 4:130 Contempl 3 Legat 143, 354

ἐπωνυμιός QG 1:20

ἐπώνυμος (19) Cher 8 Sacr 17, 17 Post 173 Sobr 52 Migr 39, 205, 224 Fug 42 Abr 10, 206 Ios 1, 1 Mos 1:76 Spec 2:192 Aet 139 Flacc 55, 80 Legat 305

ἐρανίζω Det 74 Somn 1:95 Ios 66 Hypoth 7:6

ἔρανος (11) Agr 90 Ebr 20, 23, 23, 29 Fug 29 Spec 2:78 Virt 86 Flacc 64 Legat 51, 51

ἐραστής (59) Opif 166 Leg 2:96 Leg 3:72, 182, 243 Cher 41, 46 Sacr 18, 126 Det 114 Plant 104, 105, 106 Ebr 49 Conf 166 Migr 57, 101, 149, 164 Her 100, 180 Congr 176 Fug 33, 45 Mut 37, 205 Somn 1:49, 124, 177, 205 Somn 2:80, 115 Abr 7, 220, 224, 227 Mos 1:298, 302 Decal 8 Spec 1:59, 103, 173, 309, 316, 332 Spec 2:48, 147 Spec 3:51 Virt 182, 218 Praem 59 Contempl 61 Aet 55 Legat 204 Hypoth 11:11 Prov 2:1 QG 1:51, 3:11b, 4:74

ἐράω (46) Opif 166 Leg 1:75, 75 Leg 2:55, 59, 80, 83 Leg 3:15, 63, 213 Cher 111 Sacr 77 Det 118 Post 13, 137, 165 Plant 25, 158 Her 241, 243 Congr 61 Fug 97, 146, 153 Somn 2:40, 120 Abr 271 Ios 64, 80 Mos 1:46 Spec 1:193 Spec 2:107, 258 Spec 3:44, 61, 61 Spec 4:218 Virt 51, 62, 79 Prob 158 Contempl 61, 61, 63, 67 Prov 2:28

ἐργάζομαι (247) Opif 77, 113 Leg 1:8, 21, 25, 25, 27, 27, 27, 27, 27, 27, 29, 51, 53, 54, 55, 55, 80, 80, 88, 89, 89, 89, 96 Leg 2:12, 61, 85 Leg 3:46, 50, 50, 77, 79, 80, 83, 108, 122, 184, 238 Cher 23, 35, 62, 81, 109, 122, 128 Sacr 8, 11, 21, 36, 40, 48, 51, 78, 85, 86, 130, 135, 135 Det 16, 46, 63, 63, 74, 76, 85, 86, 103, 104, 104, 109 Post 48, 49, 50, 53, 62, 103, 117, 135, 156 Gig 26 Deus 35, 43, 49, 49, 57, 79, 138 Agr 5, 21, 21, 21, 25, 88, 124, 133, 142, 171 Plant 3, 5, 68, 158, 170 Ebr 4, 30, 45, 133, 157, 157, 159, 177 Sobr 5, 30, 36 Conf 59, 92, 189 Migr 20, 87 Her 121, 139, 158, 183, 232, 273 Congr 15, 31, 58, 119, 172 Fug 25, 89, 93, 155 Mut 174, 194, 200 Somn 1:83, 123, 198, 202, 218 Somn 2:60, 192, 213, 291 Abr 6, 176 Ios 13, 52, 171, 220, 262, 269 Mos 1:38, 40, 125, 127, 197, 292, 305 Mos 2:107, 171, 204, 218, 227 Decal 100, 103, 136 Spec 1:36, 79, 295 Spec 2:13, 65, 78, 106, 134, 172, 229, 251 Spec 3:36, 42, 84, 87, 90, 113, 152, 181, 183, 199 Spec 4:23, 40, 100, 154, 178, 187, 203, 235 Virt 88, 129, 199 Praem 1, 106, 115, 127, 136, 140, 148, 151, 164 Prob 17, 79, 86, 96, 107 Contempl 15, 38, 41 Flacc 80, 84, 87, 110, 115, 174, 189 Legat 87, 146, 217, 222, 226, 229, 265, 303, 339, 351 Hypoth 7:18 Prov 2:40, 41, 43, 72 QG 1:72, 4:110a, 202b QG (Par) 2:7, 2:7 QE 2:25d QE isf 23

ἐργαλεῖον Cher 125 Somn 1:207 Decal 72

ἐργασία (7) Agr 3, 20, 26 Plant 148 Spec 1:102, 282 Hypoth 7:15

ἐργαστήριον (7) Somn 2:215 Mos 2:84 Spec 3:33, 109 Aet 66 Flacc 56 Legat 56

ἐργάτης (13) Leg 1:26, 54, 55 Sacr 51 Det 108 Agr 5, 22, 26, 27, 67 Spec 3:202 Spec 4:199 Prov 2:44

ἐργοδιώκτης Her 255 Mos 1:37

ἔργον (458) Opif 9, 79, 84, 104, 128, 148, 149, 171 Leg 1:2, 3, 16, 18, 47, 48, 50, 74, 82, 102, 103 Leg 2:26, 61, 62, 68, 84, 86, 104, 104 Leg 3:21, 27, 27, 36, 44, 77, 79, 88, 95, 95, 99, 130, 140, 186, 204, 207, 212, 222, 231, 237, 238, 238, 239, 246, 247 Cher 14, 15, 41, 92, 92, 112, 119, 119, 122 Sacr 23, 30, 41, 46, 49, 50, 53, 53, 65, 68, 75, 78, 95, 129 Det 18, 35, 43, 52, 63, 64, 93, 108, 120, 121, 124, 125, 129, 155 Post 38, 54, 64, 64, 87, 87, 88, 101, 141, 166, 167, 175, 181, 183 Gig 23, 23, 65, 66, 66 Deus 7, 12, 28, 34, 36, 59, 67, 78, 86, 106, 134, 156, 177 Agr 13, 25, 57, 59, 119, 130, 153, 162 Plant 6, 26, 81, 128, 130, 131, 156, 158, 162, 163, 170 Ebr 31, 75, 82, 99, 126, 151, 156 Sobr 46 Conf 39, 55, 59, 59, 83, 90, 93, 93, 95, 96, 97, 103, 153, 191, 191 Migr 15, 24, 46, 66, 97, 116, 128, 129, 163, 167, 185, 193, 225, 225 Her 18, 50, 93, 95, 97, 101, 110, 115, 121, 160, 167, 196, 196, 199, 199, 206, 216, 225, 254, 260, 291 Congr 49, 105, 109, 137, 172, 173, 178, 178, 179 Fug 26, 37, 59, 65, 89, 95, 135, 152, 162, 172, 205 Mut 39, 64, 76, 79, 81, 138, 160, 223, 237, 237, 243, 243, 244, 244 Somn 1:112, 181, 182, 204, 205, 210, 220, 248 Somn 2:21, 27, 34, 34, 76, 120, 141, 302 Abr 5, 28, 37, 54, 70, 74, 75, 176, 178, 181, 193, 196, 199, 232, 255, 262, 267 Ios 38, 50, 52, 64, 85, 119, 216, 230, 230, 267 Mos 1:29, 37, 44, 59, 89, 117, 151, 153, 158, 180, 193, 202, 205, 249, 256, 283, 318, 329 Mos 2:28, 32, 48, 48, 60, 74, 111, 130, 140, 140, 141, 150, 150, 160, 161, 177, 211, 219, 241, 253, 267, 269, 273, 280 Decal 6, 29, 47, 76, 88, 97, 98, 136, 177 Spec 1:35, 41, 57, 71, 79, 95, 121, 138, 188, 205, 236, 265, 322 Spec 2:22, 52, 52, 59, 60, 64, 66, 75, 96, 159, 170, 170, 178, 188, 197, 250, 261 Spec 3:83, 100, 116 Spec 4:7, 55, 63, 68, 183, 203, 212, 215 Virt 19, 22, 24, 56, 88, 120, 152, 190, 196 Praem 9, 23, 43, 70, 82, 83, 119, 126, 131, 142 Prob 2, 74, 74, 81, 86, 93, 96, 96, 96, 102, 111, 141 Contempl 14, 87 Aet 13, 15, 40, 44, 57, 69 Flacc 3, 19, 40, 92, 97, 104, 126, 140 Legat 34, 41, 58, 103, 150, 176, 176, 233, 290, 323, 350 Hypoth 7:2, 7:11, 7:11, 7:14, 7:15, 7:16, 7:16, 7:19 Prov 1, 1, 2:2, 4, 15, 24, 29, 33, 45, 47, 47, 49, 53 QG 1:20, 66, 89, 3:18, 4:64 QG isf 8 QE 2:1, 11b, 16, 16, 105 QE isf 9

ἔρδω (ἔρδω) Opif 104

ἐρεθίζω Ebr 14, 16 Somn 2:90 Spec 4:100

ἐρεθισμός Ebr 15

ἐρεθιστής Ebr 14, 95

ἐρείδω (14) Post 24 Plant 5 Conf 19, 87 Mut 135 Somn 1:246 Somn 2:229 Abr 273 Ios 256 Decal 44 Spec 2:2 Prob 28, 29 QE 2:17

ἐρείπιον Mos 2:56

ἐρείπιος Det 33 Praem 168

ἐρείπω Aet 42

ἔρεισμα (9) Plant 8 Conf 104 Migr 121 Congr 30 Mut 156 Somn 1:158, 159 Decal 67 Spec 4:74

ἐρέτης Spec 1:121

ἐρεύγομαι Ebr 131

ἔρευθος Sacr 21

ἔρευνα (17) Leg 3:71 Cher 129 Sacr 85 Agr 18 Sobr 31 Conf 74 Her 92, 247 Congr 52 Mut 60 Spec 3:58, 191 Spec 4:5 Prob 68 Aet 41 Flacc 90, 96

ἐρευνάω (63) Opif 66 Leg 1:99 Leg 3:84 Cher 14, 105 Sacr 52, 89 Det 13, 57, 141 Post 40, 153 Gig 62 Deus 167 Agr 72 Plant 74 Conf 53, 183, 183 Migr 90, 138, 176, 185 Her 81, 115 Congr 44 Fug 165, 194 Mut 7, 67, 72, 86, 236 Somn 1:41, 54, 54, 127, 167, 201, 222 Somn 2:17, 54 Abr 147, 188 Ios 127, 217 Mos 1:62 Decal 50, 94 Spec 1:166 Praem 7, 46 Prob 54, 65, 158 Aet 3, 130 Flacc 86, 88, 93, 94 Prov 2:35, 51

ἐρημία (42) Leg 2:25, 85 Sacr 45, 50, 104 Ebr 160 Migr 90, 191, 225 Her 297 Abr 175, 190 Mos 1:13, 54, 172, 194, 209, 238, 251, 255 Mos 2:214, 240 Spec 1:188 Spec 2:25, 208 Spec 3:74, 77, 78, 115 Spec 4:126, 180 Virt 96 Contempl 20, 24, 62 Flacc 162, 167, 177 Legat 20, 127, 171 Prov 2:62

ἐρῆμος (87) Opif 32 Leg 1:34, 44 Leg 2:64, 84, 84, 84, 85, 86, 87 Leg 3:4, 169, 170 Cher 115 Sacr 50, 67, 69, 125 Det 153 Post 6, 155 Gig 11 Deus 136, 138 Plant 175 Conf 136 Her 26, 67, 287 Congr 165, 170 Fug 1, 92, 92, 92, 131, 190 Mut 149, 152 Somn 1:21, 71, 137 Somn 2:170, 245 Abr 85, 211, 247 Ios 189, 254 Mos 1:55, 87, 164, 167, 170, 192, 225, 288 Mos 2:1, 73, 247, 267 Decal 2, 13, 15, 42 Spec 1:129, 205, 310, 310 Spec 2:31, 127, 133, 170, 199, 207, 250 Spec 3:39, 78, 162 Spec 4:141 Virt 218 Praem 83, 112, 158, 168 Flacc 56 QE 2:25a

ἐρημόω (16) Leg 2:54, 83 Deus 137 Abr 136 Mos 1:134, 262, 327 Decal 152 Spec 3:99 Spec 4:178 Virt 43, 132 Praem 133, 153 Hypoth 7:9 Prov 2:41

ἐρικτός Sacr 76, 86, 87

ἔριον Opif 85 Spec 1:84 Spec 4:12, 207 Virt 95

ἔρις (13) Leg 3:131 Deus 97 Ebr 15, 18, 99 Her 246, 247 Mut 10, 95 Mos 1:24 Spec 1:108 Virt 115 QE isf 4

ἐριστικός (12) Leg 3:131, 131, 140, 233 Cher 129 Det 36, 41, 45 Conf 35 Fug 209 Somn 2:264, 276

ἔριφος (10) Fug 149, 149, 151 Ios 14 Spec 1:198 Virt 133, 142, 144 QG 4:200a, 200a

ἕρκος (6) Opif 104 Plant 92 Somn 1:103 Mos 2:180, 182 Spec 1:146

ἕρμα Prob 41, 128 Legat 5

Ἑρμᾶ Deus 99

ἕρμαιον Legat 202, 341

ἑρματίζω Spec 3:29

ἑρμηνεία (31) Leg 3:95, 121 Cher 53, 105 Det 39, 68, 79 Post 32, 55, 74, 120 Migr 12 Her 108, 110 Congr 17, 33 Mut 126 Somn 1:101 Somn 2:242, 262, 274 Mos 2:27, 39, 41, 129, 191 Spec 1:336 Virt 193 Contempl 28, 76 QG 3:52

ἑρμήνευμα Spec 3:6

ἑρμηνεύς (38) Leg 1:10 Leg 3:207 Sacr 34 Det 39, 40, 43, 44, 68, 74, 129, 133 Post 108 Deus 138 Migr 72, 78, 81, 84, 219 Her 213, 259 Somn 1:29, 33 Ios 175 Mos 1:1, 84, 277 Mos 2:40, 188, 191 Decal 175 Spec 1:65 Spec 2:189 Spec 3:7 Spec 4:49, 60 Praem 2, 55 Legat 99

ἑρμηνευτικός Leg 1:74 Congr 29, 30

ἑρμηνεύω (158) Leg 1:68, 68, 74, 74, 90 Leg 2:89, 96, 96 Leg 3:18, 19, 25, 69, 74, 77, 79, 83, 93, 96, 175, 186, 218, 225, 226, 228, 230, 231, 232 Cher 7, 12, 65, 87 Sacr 2, 30 Det 9, 28, 32, 121, 124, 127, 138 Post 35, 41, 41, 60, 61, 62, 66, 73, 79, 83, 100, 110, 112, 114, 124, 182 Gig 62, 64, 66 Deus 5, 5, 137 Agr 42, 43, 95 Plant 27, 38, 64, 134, 169 Ebr 94, 128, 144, 222 Sobr 28, 44 Conf 65, 79, 123, 130, 159 Migr 20, 25, 35, 72, 84, 143, 145, 148, 165, 169, 188, 223 Her 40, 58, 128, 302 Congr 20, 25, 40, 41, 45, 48, 51, 56, 61 Fug 44, 128, 183, 203, 208, 213 Mut 56, 66, 77, 89, 91, 98, 99, 105, 107, 121, 123, 125, 189, 193, 193, 194, 202, 208, 254 Somn 1:41, 47, 77, 89, 89, 206, 254 Somn 2:32, 33, 35, 36, 47, 89, 173, 192, 211 Abr 57, 82, 99 Mos 2:40 Legat 4 QG 4:23, 79a, 97:2, 161, 163:2 QE 1:4

Ἑρμῆς (7) Decal 54 Prob 101 Legat 93, 94, 99, 99, 102

ἐρνόομαι Virt 156

ἔρνος (20) Sacr 25 Det 105, 107 Post 163 Deus 37 Agr 30 Plant 4 Ebr 8, 61 Migr 55 Her 279 Fug 187 Somn 2:192 Mos 2:22 Praem 152, 172 Prob 69, 70 Aet 121 Prov 2:68

ἔρομαι Leg 3:77 Deus 108 Her 222 Legat 262

ἑρπήν ἕρπης

ἑρπετόν (25) Opif 64, 156, 163 Leg 2:11, 105 Deus 51 Conf 7, 24 Migr 64, 65, 69 Her 238, 239, 239, 239 Mos 1:192 Decal 78 Spec 1:62 Spec 4:113, 113, 114 Praem 90 Legat 48 Prov 2:59 QG 1:74

ἑρπηνώδης (6) Det 110 Decal 150 Spec 4:83 Praem 143 Aet 20 Prov 2:30

ἕρπης (ἑρπήν) Ios 160

ἕρπω Leg 3:139 Agr 97 Ebr 172 Migr 64 Mos 1:77

ἔρρω Flacc 22, 22 Legat 193, 196, 196

ἐρρωμένος ῥώννυμι

ἐρρωμένος (41) Opif 85 Leg 3:14, 70 Sacr 49 Det 34 Agr 109, 111, 119 Plant 157 Ebr 55, 122 Conf 51 Migr 25, 82, 125, 144, 144 Her 236, 274 Congr 165 Mut 199, 263 Somn 2:94 Abr 233, 243, 244 Ios 40 Mos 1:106, 111, 135 Decal 64 Spec 1:334 Spec 4:170, 205, 206 Virt 5, 27, 31, 69, 146 Flacc 8

Ἐρυθρά Mos 2:247

ἐρυθριάω (21) Opif 171 Cher 70 Her 128 Congr 53, 150 Fug 31 Somn 1:99 Mos 1:54, 280 Mos 2:212 Decal 90, 169 Spec 2:8, 240 Spec 3:25, 37, 65 Virt 10 Prob 71 Aet 47 QG 4:99

ἐρυθρός Ebr 173 Her 128 Mos 1:165 Mos 2:1 Contempl 85

ἔρυμα Somn 1:103, 108 Somn 2:262 Mos 1:333

ἐρυμνός Mos 1:229 Virt 48 Prob 151

ἐρυμνότης Mos 1:224

ἐρυσίβη Praem 129

ἐρύω (ῥύομαι) (19) Leg 3:177 Det 93 Conf 161, 181 Migr 15 Her 20 Fug 67, 140 Mut 113, 117 Abr 231 Mos 1:47,

173, 216 Spec 1:237 Spec 2:218 Spec 3:156 Spec 4:36 QE 2:2

ἔρχομαι (208) Opif 27, 54, 69 Leg 1:43 Leg 2:85 Leg 3:45, 120, 130, 155, 156, 215, 225 Cher 110, 114 Sacr 11, 43, 59 Det 5, 10, 32, 41, 89, 130, 151 Post 15, 17, 17, 30, 60, 95, 96, 130, 151, 161 Deus 62, 93, 177 Agr 55, 64, 91, 132, 152, 155, 156, 156, 181 Plant 135, 146 Ebr 15, 31, 37, 51, 133, 156 Sobr 28 Conf 72, 75, 140, 155 Migr 5, 22, 34, 35, 76, 128, 133, 195, 195, 196, 218 Her 12, 45, 66, 121, 149, 170, 170, 251, 254, 254 Congr 52, 81, 88, 94, 152, 155, 163 Fug 1, 10, 11, 32, 59, 62, 101, 109, 183, 196, 203, 205 Mut 9, 13, 18, 35, 97, 108, 157, 188, 237, 247 Somn 1:5, 41, 45, 60, 61, 64, 65, 66, 67, 67, 68, 69, 70, 71, 71, 71, 96, 172, 181, 193 Somn 2:7, 67, 90, 111, 111, 139, 221, 227, 292 Abr 53, 142, 162, 209, 214, 244, 258, 258 Ios 9, 113, 126, 164, 215, 224, 227, 268 Mos 1:122, 140, 146, 197, 238, 249, 263, 325 Mos 2:58, 147, 163, 187 Decal 32, 112, 147 Spec 1:8, 45, 195, 295, 335 Spec 2:166, 179, 189, 203, 248 Spec 3:72, 90, 104 Virt 110, 124, 203 Praem 42, 167 Prob 127 Contempl 31 Aet 30 Flacc 46, 64, 75, 125, 130, 156, 183 Legat 41, 187, 215, 291 Hypoth 6:5, 6:7, 7:14 QG 2:34a, 4:169, 228 QG isf 8

ἐρῶ (λέγω) (301) Opif 56, 65, 87, 98, 103, 105, 114, 115, 126, 130, 133, 142, 145, 157, 163 Leg 1:19, 21, 23, 24, 26, 26, 28, 41, 42, 45, 59, 59, 70, 82 Leg 2:14, 31, 88, 88 Leg 3:54, 55, 58, 122, 140, 159, 161, 173, 180, 185, 225, 250 Cher 12, 27, 53, 69, 71, 119 Sacr 63, 108 Det 6, 8, 57, 91, 103, 129, 150, 160 Post 30, 89, 111, 170 Gig 7, 17, 30, 37, 40, 41, 67 Deus 3, 23, 41, 52, 66, 71, 77, 82, 103, 118, 122, 153 Agr 26, 26, 51, 67, 122, 124, 181, 181 Plant 4, 32, 42, 59, 60, 61, 73, 134, 141, 165, 165 Ebr 1, 4, 14, 40, 58, 84, 116 Sobr 1, 25, 35 Conf 1, 17, 31, 55, 79, 94, 144, 156, 168, 181 Migr 45, 51, 62, 66, 80, 84, 105, 156, 157, 166, 176, 209 Her 5, 14, 23, 50, 85, 91, 144, 189, 266, 267, 281, 313 Congr 31, 54, 63, 66, 86, 116, 153, 170, 178 Fug 2, 25, 26, 65, 75, 93, 102, 112, 179 Mut 13, 77, 106, 126, 130, 139, 147, 147, 174, 175, 192, 207, 235, 245 Somn 1:18, 40, 77, 102, 118, 127, 180, 215, 219, 228, 230 Somn 2:17, 19, 100, 110, 137, 222, 301 Abr 13, 19, 47, 49, 52, 54, 81, 90, 107, 114, 124, 199, 241, 244, 255, 275 Ios 54, 67, 125, 226 Mos 1:206, 243 Mos 2:10, 25, 57, 89, 128, 221 Decal 24, 28, 48, 59, 89, 166 Spec 1:8, 15, 147, 159, 190, 219, 256, 258, 265 Spec 2:1, 40, 215, 234, 237 Spec 3:7 Spec 4:11, 120, 132, 135, 148, 148, 173, 230 Virt 15, 16, 101, 152, 180, 184, 226 Praem 47, 115, 118, 130, 138 Prob 48, 48 Contempl 38 Aet 14, 54, 100, 104, 106, 107, 121, 132, 150 Flacc 97, 125 Legat 5, 30, 74, 81, 112, 361, 373 Prov 2:10, 50, 70 QG 1:1, 77, 2:26a, 59, 4:8a, 173, 204 QG (Par) 2:3, 2:4 QE 2:10b, 16

ἔρως (93) Opif 5, 70, 77, 111, 152 Leg 2:72 Leg 3:39, 84, 113, 136, 183 Cher 19, 20 Sacr 23, 129 Det 99 Post 157 Gig 31 Deus 138 Agr 55, 84, 91 Plant 39, 144 Ebr 84, 136, 159 Conf 7, 21, 106 Migr 13 Her 14, 70, 269 Congr 64, 112, 166 Fug 58, 195 Somn 1:36, 107, 165 Somn 2:150, 165, 232 Abr 65, 66, 170, 194 Ios 40, 56, 70, 269 Mos 1:297 Mos 2:67, 96 Decal 151 Spec 1:44, 64, 64 Spec 2:9, 136 Spec 3:44, 65, 70 Spec 4:7, 80, 85, 161, 226 Virt 8, 55, 112, 113 Praem 15, 19, 38, 84, 135 Prob 21, 43, 107, 117, 151 Contempl 12, 59, 59, 60 Legat 61, 277, 338 Prov 2:8 QG 3:21

ἐρωτάω (14) Det 5, 57, 57, 58, 59 Her 18, 18 Fug 127 Mut 14 Spec 3:71 Prob 54, 62 Aet 143 Legat 361

ἐρώτημα Det 58 Agr 140 Congr 149 Legat 361

ἐρώτησις Her 18

ἐρωτικός Agr 37 Congr 65, 126 Fug 189

Ἐσεβών (6) Leg 3:225, 225, 225, 226, 229, 233

ἔσθημα (6) Leg 2:53 Leg 3:239 Sacr 83 Virt 18, 20 Prov 2:17

ἐσθής (57) Cher 95 Sacr 21, 26 Migr 102 Fug 110, 185 Mut 246 Somn 1:97, 98, 102, 216, 220, 224 Abr 220 Ios 14, 16, 23, 27, 51, 52, 105, 120, 217, 256 Mos 1:138, 153 Mos 2:109, 117, 131, 143, 146, 152 Decal 45, 77 Spec 1:33, 82, 83, 84, 95, 97, 165 Spec 2:20, 83, 233 Spec 3:176, 206 Virt 21, 39, 104, 111 Prob 86 Contempl 38, 38 Flacc 148 Hypoth 11:12 Prov 2:13, 31

ἐσθίω φαγεῖν

ἐσθίω (18) Leg 1:99, 99, 100, 101 Leg 2:29 Sacr 107 Det 113 Her 80, 255 Congr 162 Somn 1:81 Somn 2:163 Abr 118, 118 Mos 1:291 Contempl 37, 53 QG (Par) 2:7

ἐσθλός Aet 41

ἑσμός Mos 1:95

ἑσπέρα (30) Opif 34, 34, 34, 35 Somn 1:81, 101 Somn 2:257 Ios 179 Mos 1:136, 209 Spec 1:119, 169, 296 Spec 2:102, 145, 155, 155, 196 Spec 4:196 Praem 151, 151 Contempl 27, 28 Flacc 27, 110, 111, 167, 167 Legat 269 QG 4:30

ἑσπερινός Spec 1:171 QG 4:30

ἑσπέριος (7) Cher 22, 22 Somn 1:175 Mos 2:20 Flacc 45 Legat 8, 89

Ἐσσαῖος (6) Prob 75, 91 Contempl 1 Hypoth 11:1, 11:3, 11:14

ἑστία (13) Cher 104 Sacr 103 Deus 134 Agr 79 Ebr 59 Migr 3, 96 Her 27 Spec 2:173 Virt 73, 124 Praem 154 Flacc 115

Ἑστία Cher 26

ἑστίασις Mos 1:275 Legat 344

ἑστιάτωρ (15) Opif 78, 78 Post 98 Ebr 214 Abr 116, 117 Ios 205 Mos 2:33 Spec 1:221, 221, 242 Spec 2:173, 193 Contempl 52, 53

ἑστιάω (36) Opif 54 Agr 153 Her 35 Fug 166 Mut 165, 165 Somn 1:50 Abr 110, 116, 117, 167, 167, 235 Ios 25, 98, 201, 234 Mos 1:187 Mos 2:42 Decal 41 Spec 1:37, 221, 242, 321 Spec 2:193 Spec 3:80 Spec 4:92 Virt 99 Praem 122 Contempl 35, 57, 85 Flacc 4, 112 Legat 310, 310

ἑστιοῦχος Ebr 210

ἐσχατιά (25) Migr 144 Somn 2:195, 198 Abr 218, 274 Mos 1:217 Mos 2:82, 110, 194, 194, 241 Spec 2:189 Spec 4:94, 112 Virt 183, 223 Praem 75, 80, 117, 164 Legat 49, 103, 128, 240 QE 2:40

ἔσχατος (43) Opif 88, 109, 109 Leg 2:48, 107 Cher 23, 99 Deus 127 Agr 134, 169 Plant 22, 111, 127, 144 Conf 85 Migr 181 Her 172, 261, 282 Congr 53 Mut 19, 107, 179 Somn 1:134, 134 Somn 2:195 Abr 274 Ios 123, 244 Mos 1:104 Mos 2:120 Spec 1:40, 94, 211, 281 Spec 4:213 Virt 18, 50, 91 Flacc 53, 173 Legat 144, 193

Ἐσχώλ Migr 164, 165

ἔσω εἴσω

ἔσωθεν QG (Par) 2:4

ἐσώτατος Mos 2:78

ἑταίρα (6) Leg 3:182 Ios 43 Mos 1:302 Spec 3:80 Virt 112 Aet 56

ἑταιρεία Conf 97 Abr 126 Spec 3:96 Contempl 18 Flacc 4

ἑταιρεῖος Prob 44

ἑταιρέω Ios 43 Spec 1:281

ἑταίρησις Virt 37

ἑταιρία (8) Det 15 Agr 104 Migr 158 Decal 89, 89 Spec 2:95 Hypoth 11:5 QG 4:72

ἑταιρικός Virt 40

ἑταιρίς Opif 166 Prov 2:31

ἑταῖρος (57) Leg 2:10 Leg 3:7, 22, 53, 62, 182 Post 52, 91 Deus 3, 55, 143, 146 Plant 65, 104 Ebr 10, 58, 78 Sobr 13 Conf 40, 48, 62 Migr 197 Her 60 Congr 20, 62 Fug 3, 11, 19, 28 Mut 39, 112 Somn 1:111 Somn 2:63, 83, 205, 245 Abr 67 Ios 65 Mos 1:266 Spec 1:282 Spec 2:132, 132 Virt 182 Praem 139 Prob 42, 44 Contempl 13, 40 Flacc 2, 22, 32 Legat 113, 286, 295, 328, 328 QG 4:172

ἑτερήμερος Somn 1:150 Decal 56

ἑτερογενής Spec 1:253 Spec 3:46 Spec 4:203, 204

ἑτερόγλωσσος Conf 8

ἑτεροδοξέω Her 247

ἑτεροδοξία QE isf 4

ἑτερόδοξος Sobr 68 Migr 175 Spec 2:193 QE 2:47

ἑτεροεθνής Spec 4:19 Virt 147

ἑτεροειδής Spec 4:207 Aet 79 QG 3:3

ἑτερόζυγος Spec 4:203

ἑτεροιότης Opif 22 Spec 4:187

ἑτεροιόω Mos 1:81 Spec 1:62 QG (Par) 2:7

ἑτερομήκης Leg 1:3 QG 2:12b, 14, 14

ἑτερόμορφος Somn 1:232 QG 3:3

ἕτερος (ὁ) (955) Opif 2, 20, 23, 24, 24, 36, 38, 51, 54, 54, 55, 57, 62, 62, 68, 71, 72, 75, 75, 86, 87, 95, 97, 97, 97, 97, 100, 101, 104, 110, 120, 132, 135, 139, 141, 141, 152, 168 Leg 1:5, 6, 7, 7, 18, 34, 35, 51, 53, 60, 70, 78, 81, 91, 98, 99, 100, 105 Leg 2:8, 14, 20, 26, 27, 35, 44, 48, 51, 60, 69, 79, 93 Leg 3:4, 33, 33, 40, 42, 54, 65, 65, 96, 142, 169, 169, 169, 186, 189, 201, 201, 201, 202, 203, 205, 211, 241, 244 Cher 21, 23, 23, 25, 43, 56, 56, 60, 68, 69, 79, 86, 97, 98 Sacr 1, 2, 8, 20, 20, 26, 47, 52, 67, 72, 74, 74, 77, 100, 111, 125, 133, 136 Det 16, 47, 49, 49, 49, 49, 49, 49, 57, 58, 66, 77, 103, 107, 107, 108, 138, 153, 165 Post 6, 10, 26, 28, 29, 37, 40, 44, 48, 50, 89, 109, 112, 124, 142, 142, 145, 170, 172, 172, 172, 173, 174, 179 Gig 18, 22, 24, 26, 27, 36, 49 Deus 29, 44, 52, 53, 60, 66, 69, 69, 77, 87, 109, 111, 119, 142, 162 Agr 6, 43, 43, 90, 96, 118, 148, 148, 148, 149, 151, 155, 167 Plant 62, 62, 87, 113, 115, 115, 116, 119, 142, 172, 172, 172 Ebr 7, 8, 9, 9, 13, 13, 25, 44, 80, 86, 94, 94, 94, 115, 121, 176, 176, 176, 179, 187, 188, 194, 195, 197 Sobr 6, 28, 32, 36, 39, 68 Conf 6, 55, 72, 75, 109, 112, 117, 129, 135, 142, 175, 182, 189, 194, 196 Migr 16, 26, 46, 46, 77, 118, 127, 131, 138, 162, 173, 173, 193, 210 Her 11, 13, 50, 64, 92, 103, 117, 123, 127, 135, 142, 144, 168, 173, 174, 175, 186, 188, 198, 209, 209, 215, 217, 230, 243, 243, 259, 266, 268, 278 Congr 13, 65, 65, 71, 75, 82, 152, 155, 157, 166 Fug 10, 20, 30, 34, 36, 37, 58, 58, 66, 68, 70, 70, 73, 74, 74, 76, 76, 87, 98, 120, 148, 164, 167, 167, 168, 169, 177, 186 Mut 2, 28, 28, 31, 31, 39, 41, 59, 59, 61, 62, 86, 98, 98, 98, 110, 123, 128, 132, 132, 160, 181, 186, 188, 192, 202, 206, 230, 230, 259, 267, 267, 267, 269 Somn 1:9, 9, 9, 17, 18, 18, 18, 18, 18, 37, 59, 65, 65, 74, 75, 97, 98, 101, 111, 132, 162, 168, 177, 177, 189, 198, 198, 215, 216, 228, 230, 236, 237 Somn 2:9, 12, 14, 30, 58, 60, 61, 89, 95, 100, 110, 111, 120, 126, 136, 150, 157, 157, 181, 190, 191, 201, 216, 222, 224, 224, 246, 246, 248, 257, 262, 274, 280, 281, 281, 293 Abr 21, 30, 31, 37, 38, 46, 48, 54, 63, 67, 86, 88, 122, 124, 125, 144, 164, 164, 174, 184, 186, 195, 199, 204, 210, 216, 249, 266 Ios 8, 34, 34, 34, 36, 36, 43, 48, 52, 61, 73, 93, 101, 102, 102, 108, 112, 139, 151, 185, 188, 194, 205, 215, 232, 239, 259, 262 Mos 1:4, 29, 46, 49, 53, 59, 73, 79, 79, 83, 124, 137, 146, 153, 191, 191, 193, 193, 202, 204, 239, 246, 267, 277, 278, 282, 286, 296, 307, 315, 322, 325 Mos 2:2, 17, 18, 27, 41, 45, 48, 124, 136, 138, 148, 149, 181, 182, 199, 216, 218, 221, 225, 236, 262, 262, 270 Decal 11, 26, 28, 31, 35, 38, 39, 50, 51, 53, 53, 76, 81, 91, 101, 108, 108, 112, 121, 121, 126, 140, 164, 168 Spec 1:2, 10, 22, 23, 25, 32, 33, 42, 52, 53, 65, 76, 84, 102, 104, 105, 106, 106, 107, 109, 113, 113, 127, 129, 131, 156, 188, 193, 195, 195, 197, 199, 200, 213, 214, 218, 221, 235, 245, 252, 269, 272, 277, 278, 293, 297, 307, 316, 328, 330 Spec 2:1, 13, 18, 37, 64, 64, 76, 96, 113, 116, 123, 131, 132, 132, 135, 147, 157, 164, 164, 165, 168, 170, 176, 177, 185, 190, 196, 220, 220, 226, 248, 256, 258, 258, 262 Spec 3:7, 10, 11, 17, 23, 24, 27, 30, 36, 37, 42, 44, 61, 72, 81, 93, 95, 96, 107, 110, 142, 145, 158, 158, 161, 163, 163, 166, 166, 167, 168, 168, 171, 174, 176, 178, 182, 182, 190, 190 Spec 4:2, 7, 22, 34, 34, 36, 40, 42, 49, 54, 60, 65, 67, 79, 106, 110, 111, 123, 129, 133, 160, 162, 163, 167, 167, 197, 197, 198, 201, 207, 208, 211, 211, 214, 219, 223, 235 Virt 24, 29, 30, 34, 45, 51, 66, 66, 67, 98, 98, 100, 109, 114, 115, 116, 116, 123, 124, 128, 144, 145, 166, 169, 193, 206, 206, 208, 211, 221 Praem 2, 13, 24, 40, 43, 44, 45, 55, 63, 74, 95, 102, 102, 113, 165, 167, 170, 171 Prob 35, 36, 41, 82, 86, 90, 122 Contempl 3, 3, 16, 19, 26, 40, 45, 49, 49 Aet 4, 5, 14, 21, 22, 22, 24, 24, 28, 39, 41, 46, 48, 48, 82, 88, 104, 104, 106, 111, 132, 142, 144 Flacc 24, 29, 31, 35, 35, 38, 49, 50, 53, 64, 70, 76, 78, 78, 96, 128, 154, 171, 174, 174, 178, 186 Legat 7, 9, 12, 30, 30, 41, 43, 80, 89, 106, 113, 119, 129, 134, 135, 136, 163, 168, 184, 189, 200, 206, 262, 262, 266, 285, 295, 298, 317, 323, 326, 327, 335, 337, 341, 344, 346, 357, 358, 362, 362, 365, 366, 368, 371 Hypoth 7:4, 7:17, 11:6, 11:6, 11:17 Prov 2:7, 34, 34, 35, 43, 48, 60, 61 QG 1:17b, 28, 64a, 66, 2:11, 11, 17c, 17c, 30, 54a, 59, 59, 59, 62, 64a, 68b, 3:11a, 11a, 21, 4:52b, 69, 144, 144, 167, 173, 191c, 202a, 204, 206b QG isf 8, 13, 16, 16 QG (Par) 2:3, 2:3, 2:3, 2:3, 2:3, 2:3, 2:6 QE 1:7a, 2:10b, 14 QE isf 8, 8, 26

ἑτερότης QG 2:12b

ἑτέρωθεν Agr 5 Prob 85

ἑτέρωθι (28) Leg 3:139 Det 87, 118 Deus 82 Agr 100 Ebr 101, 210 Sobr 48 Conf 36, 63, 167 Migr 47, 122, 130, 185, 221 Her 16 Congr 58 Fug 18, 77 Mut 23 Somn 1:92, 193 Somn 2:191 Mos 2:232 Spec 3:204 Legat 151 QG 3:11a

ἑτέρωσε (8) Sacr 109 Post 2 Deus 178 Agr 64 Congr 65 Somn 1:72, 79, 107

ἐτησίαι Mos 1:115 Flacc 26

ἐτήσιος (81) Opif 52, 55, 58, 59, 85, 113, 158, 168 Cher 88 Det 87 Post 163 Agr 8 Plant 33, 56, 120 Ebr 91, 106 Migr 92 Her 165 Congr 4 Mut 67, 246 Somn 1:97 Somn 2:62, 131 Abr 1, 69, 226 Ios 135 Mos 1:114, 116, 201, 212, 254 Mos 2:124, 125, 148 Decal 163 Spec 1:16, 34, 87, 144, 179, 210, 322 Spec 2:41, 57, 96, 158, 172, 191, 205, 211, 214, 247 Spec 3:163, 188 Spec 4:12, 208, 212, 213, 215, 228, 235, 235 Virt 6, 93, 120, 145, 154 Praem 41, 130, 132, 156 Aet 62, 109 Legat 190, 312 Prov 2:23 QG 4:51b, 51b

ἔτι (462) Opif 18, 43, 103, 104, 104, 104, 104, 107, 111, 127, 128, 136, 145, 148, 150, 153 Leg 1:15, 28, 74, 84, 99 Leg 2:6, 9, 11, 12 Leg 3:4, 9, 82, 84, 88, 94, 99, 115, 132, 194, 195, 210, 225, 225, 234, 244, 252 Cher 4, 6, 10, 18, 65, 76, 95 Sacr 15, 26, 78, 79, 130 Det 28, 40, 62, 63, 74, 106, 113, 113, 130, 131, 150, 174 Post 3, 32, 37, 50, 90, 95, 112, 155, 165, 185 Gig 60, 62 Deus 8, 12, 13, 60, 68, 98, 107, 120, 156 Agr 13, 35, 36, 51, 83, 124, 141, 142, 153, 155, 157, 162, 173, 175 Plant 35, 47, 51, 94, 118, 135, 160 Ebr 17, 23, 51, 57, 59, 63, 76, 78, 91, 126, 155, 165, 173, 177, 179, 183, 194, 198, 206, 221, 222 Sobr 3, 14, 24, 61 Conf 2, 19, 37, 52, 90, 123, 164, 185, 187 Migr 21, 28, 67, 99, 163, 168, 175, 184, 189, 195, 196, 196, 198, 199, 200, 211, 214, 224 Her 23, 31, 44, 60, 63, 77, 84, 125, 160, 191, 195, 202, 203, 247, 256, 262, 264, 270, 279, 304, 308 Congr 36, 81, 96, 121 Fug 14, 15, 39, 43, 45, 129, 160, 187, 212 Mut 18, 108, 146, 159, 167, 173, 200, 215, 222, 258 Somn 1:50, 80, 81, 82, 114, 147, 148, 153, 173, 179, 199, 217, 218, 232, 235, 238, 246, 253, 255 Somn 2:18, 49, 49, 66, 66, 93, 95, 98, 101, 103, 107, 136, 152, 189, 235, 276, 276 Abr 27, 112, 116, 122, 148, 158, 182, 223, 253, 273 Ios 7, 11, 21, 70, 86, 129, 143, 144, 167, 172, 183, 185, 212, 217, 220, 224, 249, 266 Mos 1:12, 16, 19, 21, 31, 44, 76, 78, 84, 88, 115, 121, 138, 175, 175, 179, 187, 196, 198, 204, 206, 212, 241, 251, 302, 305, 312, 321, 327 Mos 2:1, 56, 71, 73, 126, 140, 148, 154, 167, 172, 208, 213, 213, 227, 252, 257, 273, 280, 291 Decal 14, 21, 45, 76, 105, 149, 149, 160 Spec 1:50, 62, 104, 105, 129, 141, 282, 300, 313, 313, 319, 322, 342, 342 Spec 2:30, 30, 46, 74, 125, 139, 163, 180, 186, 217, 227 Spec 3:27, 33, 43, 82, 90, 99, 117, 206 Spec 4:17, 135, 149, 153 Virt 11, 22, 85, 89, 100, 105, 115, 138, 140, 141, 165, 178, 191, 203 Praem 41, 52, 107, 158 Prob 9, 45, 62, 73, 84, 89, 106, 110, 118, 160 Contempl 13, 18, 50, 67, 75, 79 Aet 13, 26, 35, 64, 75, 83, 83, 90, 100, 103, 106, 118 Flacc 10, 11, 14, 32, 46, 96, 117, 119, 125, 162, 167, 182 Legat 1, 15, 26, 28, 32, 38, 54, 56, 62, 63, 64, 71, 86, 115, 117, 131, 132, 142, 169, 170, 178, 180, 189, 226, 227, 254, 268, 328, 333, 355, 366 Hypoth 6:1, 6:6, 7:11, 11:14, 11:18 Prov 2:17, 27, 42 QG 1:69 QG isf 10 QE 2:11a, 11b

ἑτοιμάζω (10) Plant 47, 50 Migr 84, 174 Mut 269 Mos 2:60 Decal 14, 17 Virt 77, 129

ἕτοιμος (61) Opif 42, 81, 169 Sacr 58, 63 Det 10, 36 Agr 16, 95, 168 Plant 47, 50, 53 Conf 25 Migr 14, 30, 173 Congr 38 Fug 28, 98, 176, 191, 199 Mut 115, 219, 263 Somn 1:124, 169, 170, 176 Somn 2:154 Ios 198, 254 Mos 1:17, 85, 139, 275, 286 Mos 2:69, 144 Spec 1:49, 105, 113, 132, 225, 225, 302 Spec 2:103 Spec 4:12, 162 Virt 79, 83 Praem 139 Prob 87 Contempl 13, 75 Legat 9, 95, 135, 233, 259

ἑτοιμότης (6) Det 10, 120 Agr 147 Sobr 2 Mos 2:172 Spec 1:144

ἔτος (113) Opif 45, 80, 104, 104, 105, 105 Leg 1:10 Leg 3:85, 179, 217 Det 63, 63 Post 60 Gig 55, 55, 56, 57 Deus 119 Agr 5 Plant 61, 95, 95, 95, 113, 113, 113, 114, 116, 117, 125, 132, 132, 136 Ebr 136 Sobr 8 Conf 80 Migr 126, 154, 176, 176, 198, 204 Her 150, 269, 290 Congr 71 Fug 179 Mut 1, 176, 189, 266 Somn 1:33, 47 Abr 134, 270 Ios 2, 109, 111, 121, 158, 159, 268 Mos 1:6, 206, 220, 237, 238 Mos 2:23, 41, 195 Decal 159, 161, 164 Spec 1:72, 77, 172 Spec 2:33, 39, 39, 79, 84, 86, 86, 97, 105, 110, 116, 117, 160, 197, 199 Spec 3:17 Spec 4:99, 215, 216 Virt 97, 158 Prob 67 Aet 63 Flacc 8, 152 Legat 138, 141, 298, 307, 350 Hypoth 6:9, 7:15, 7:17, 7:18, 7:18, 7:19 QG 1:1

ἐτυμολογία Plant 165

ἔτυμος (20) Opif 36, 126, 127, 133 Conf 137 Somn 2:174 Mos 1:17, 130 Mos 2:105, 149 Decal 160 Spec 1:88, 93, 147, 183, 329 Spec 2:188 Prob 73 Contempl 2 Aet 54

εὖ (202) Opif 23, 23, 32, 33, 54, 77, 86, 131, 149, 150, 164 Leg 1:6, 108 Leg 2:26, 31, 78, 85, 100 Leg 3:27, 51, 56, 67, 160, 198, 203, 210, 243, 246 Cher 29, 35 Sacr 10, 26, 29, 54, 106, 137 Det 13, 52, 52, 54, 57, 58, 104 Post 19, 71, 126 Deus 66, 173 Agr 112, 115, 118, 173 Plant 87, 89 Ebr 39, 84, 120, 142, 183 Sobr 7, 18 Conf 33, 93 Migr 60, 70, 112, 189 Her 56, 87, 94, 97, 178, 302 Congr 33, 44, 99, 99, 127 Mut 160, 197, 199 Somn 1:209 Somn 2:10, 60, 71, 85, 104, 174, 291 Abr 11, 19, 116, 153, 191, 192, 256 Ios 20, 35, 87, 245, 267 Mos 1:30, 33, 78, 131, 158, 181, 183 Mos 2:10, 38, 57, 126, 182, 204 Decal 17, 17, 43, 55, 94, 112, 147, 165, 166, 167 Spec 1:29, 94, 104, 146, 178, 298, 337, 339, 343 Spec 2:8, 56, 137, 140, 202, 209, 226, 227, 229, 261, 262 Spec 3:12, 147 Spec 4:15, 29, 46, 61, 186, 197, 232 Virt 24, 32, 54, 61, 105, 118, 166, 170, 184, 212 Praem 118, 120 Prob 27, 59, 59, 80, 102, 155 Contempl 50, 72, 80 Aet 13, 38, 43, 69, 111, 132 Flacc 48, 60, 139, 143, 147 Legat 103, 106, 133, 152, 172, 246, 255, 362 Prov 1, 2:15, 46, 56 QG 1:3, 93, 4:193 QE 2:10b, 20

Εὔα (11) Leg 2:79, 81 Cher 54, 57, 60 Post 33, 124 Agr 95, 99, 107, 108

εὐαγγελίζομαι (11) Opif 115 Somn 2:281 Ios 245, 250 Mos 2:186 Virt 41 Praem 161 Legat 18, 99, 231 QG 4:144

εὐαγής (39) Cher 42, 94, 100 Sacr 98, 138 Det 69, 102 Deus 135 Agr 126 Plant 33, 68 Conf 142 Congr 25 Somn 1:82 Somn 2:67 Abr 69 Mos 1:44, 44 Mos 2:34, 147, 214, 273 Decal 96 Spec 1:68, 79, 159, 186, 194, 201, 224, 229, 316 Spec 2:12, 175 Spec 3:96, 124 Contempl 6 Aet 32 Hypoth 7:6

εὐάγωγος Plant 33 Mut 56 Spec 1:105 QE 2:6b

εὐαισθησία (7) Leg 3:86 Sobr 61 Abr 263 Praem 119 Prov 2:1 QG 4:43 QE isf 16

εὐάλωτος (9) Leg 1:86 Leg 3:210 Migr 144 Fug 155, 156 Ios 130 Mos 1:296, 325 Praem 21

εὐανδρέω (7) Somn 1:137 Abr 139 Mos 1:8 Spec 2:170 Spec 3:16 Praem 172 Legat 104

εὐανθής Mut 82 Somn 1:123, 205

εὐαρεστέω (37) Leg 2:96 Leg 3:78, 177 Post 43 Gig 63 Deus 109, 113, 116, 117, 118 Mut 34, 34, 38, 39, 40,

40, 41, 41, 47, 47 Abr 17, 31, 35, 35, 235, 248 Ios 66 Decal 38 Spec 1:219, 265 Spec 4:131 Virt 184 Praem 24, 34, 167 QG 3:38b QG isf 3

εὐαρέστησις Deus 116 QG isf 3

εὐάρεστος (10) Congr 156, 157 Mut 42, 48 Ios 195, 255 Spec 1:201 Virt 67, 208 QG 1:63

εὐαρμοστία Det 125 Ebr 117 Ios 269

εὐάρμοστος (15) Opif 22, 23, 138 Post 88, 107 Ebr 116 Conf 41, 43 Migr 110, 169 Her 15, 217 Congr 76 Abr 77 Spec 4:134

εὐαφής QG 1:29

εὔβλαστος Ios 108 Mos 1:22 Spec 4:75

Εὐβοία Legat 282

εὔβοτος Somn 2:76

εὐβουλία (10) Sacr 27 Det 35 Sobr 40 Her 291 Mut 237, 262 Somn 2:180, 190 Virt 69 Praem 107

εὔβουλος Migr 219 Prov 2:36

εὔγειος Somn 1:200 Somn 2:76, 170

εὐγένεια (42) Deus 150 Her 212 Abr 219, 229, 263, 265 Ios 37, 216, 248 Mos 1:140, 149 Mos 2:270 Spec 1:51, 82, 101, 117, 123 Spec 4:182, 230 Virt 186, 187, 189, 189, 190, 191, 195, 200, 202, 203, 203, 207, 210, 210, 219, 220, 222, 226 Praem 152, 171 Prob 109 Legat 63 QG 4:180

εὐγενής (52) Det 107, 107 Post 42 Agr 6, 59, 158 Plant 30 Ebr 58 Sobr 56 Migr 67 Congr 56 Abr 38, 251 Ios 4, 76, 106 Mos 1:18, 22, 266 Mos 2:179, 197 Spec 1:221 Spec 2:22 Spec 3:13 Spec 4:75, 211 Virt 32, 77, 187, 189, 191, 198, 198, 218 Prob 69, 95, 99, 119, 123, 126, 149, 155 Contempl 69, 72 Flacc 64 Legat 116, 142, 195, 195, 215, 332, 342

εὐγηρία Sacr 100 Mos 2:186

εὐγήρως (6) Her 291, 292 Ios 268 Praem 110 Legat 142, 224

εὐγνώμων Mut 238 Ios 230 QG 4:191c

εὐγονία (8) Decal 160 Spec 1:92, 138 Spec 2:169 Spec 4:98 Virt 93 Praem 168 Flacc 63

εὐδαιμονέω (22) Leg 2:101, 102 Leg 3:209, 218, 218, 219, 219, 245 Det 59 Gig 38 Agr 157 Plant 91 Congr 7 Fug 99 Mut 36, 94 Virt 183, 187 Praem 171 Prob 44 Hypoth 6:1 Prov 2:42

εὐδαιμονία (81) Opif 144, 150 Leg 2:82 Leg 3:52, 205 Cher 8, 19, 49, 86, 86 Det 60, 60, 86 Post 185 Deus 26, 55, 92, 118 Plant 35, 37, 49, 66 Ebr 224 Sobr 56 Migr 120, 194 Her 86 Congr 53 Mut 216, 237 Somn 1:57, 94 Somn 2:235, 287, 289 Abr 58, 115, 141, 202, 268 Mos 2:151, 189, 212 Decal 73, 74, 100 Spec 1:23, 25, 209, 345 Spec 2:38, 48, 236, 259 Spec 3:128 Spec 4:69, 201 Virt 61, 119, 178, 205 Praem 11, 81 Prob 24, 69, 69, 117, 139 Contempl 11, 90 Legat 5, 11, 22, 69, 90, 211 QG 2:34b, 4:43, 173 QG isf 6 QE isf 12

εὐδαιμονίζω (7) Sacr 40, 75, 124 Migr 74 Somn 1:256 Somn 2:27 Spec 3:2

εὐδαιμονικός Spec 4:89, 126

εὐδαιμονισμός (7) Agr 80 Her 110 Somn 1:35 Somn 2:38 Spec 1:224 Spec 2:7, 199

εὐδαίμων (90) Opif 135, 152, 156, 172 Leg 1:4 Leg 2:10 Leg 3:83 Cher 29, 39, 41, 94, 106 Sacr 5, 99, 125 Det 8, 33, 48, 49, 60, 90, 140 Post 72, 80, 104, 113, 134 Deus 97, 108 Agr 25 Plant 25 Ebr 73, 100 Conf 177 Migr 11, 86, 88, 184 Her 111, 285 Mut 51, 185 Somn 1:107, 121, 190 Somn 2:146, 147, 230, 249 Abr 35, 67, 87, 115, 227 Mos 1:13, 159, 193, 209, 226, 319 Decal 4, 104, 134 Spec 1:329 Spec 2:53, 141, 230 Spec 4:48, 95 Virt 50 Praem 11, 30, 60, 63, 122 Prob 41, 41, 91 Aet 46, 140 Flacc 46, 151, 157, 163 Legat 5, 5, 257 Prov 2:7, 8 QE 2:40

εὔδενδρος Abr 227 Mos 1:188, 228

εὔδηλος QG 2:30

εὐδία (11) Opif 63 Gig 51 Deus 26, 129 Spec 1:69, 224 Spec 2:42 Spec 3:5 Spec 4:154 Praem 116 Prov 2:47

εὐδιάγωγος Leg 1:43 Spec 1:74

εὐδιάζω Abr 207 Legat 145

εὐδιάλυτος Ebr 142

εὐδικία Somn 2:40 Praem 107 Legat 90

εὔδιος (9) Conf 43 Her 285 Fug 50 Somn 2:86, 225 Abr 26, 30, 153 Mos 1:214

εὐδοκιμέω (10) Det 41 Migr 96 Mut 45 Decal 91, 110 Spec 2:244 Flacc 108, 124 Legat 344 Prov 2:15

εὐδόκιμος (9) Gig 59 Deus 170 Plant 173 Ebr 83, 95 Conf 13 Somn 2:50 Ios 40 Aet 120

εὐδοξέω Ios 144

εὐδοξία (12) Conf 18 Her 285, 286 Fug 17 Ios 150 Praem 107, 114 Prob 140 Flacc 30 Legat 75 Prov 2:1 QG 4:191a

εὔεδρος Opif 86

εὐεκτέω Mut 215 Prob 160

εὐέκτης Mut 33 Virt 170, 170

εὐεκτικός Mos 1:22

εὔελπις Det 139 Abr 9, 11, 14, 16

εὐελπιστία Plant 161 Her 206 Fug 96 Ios 255 Mos 1:233

εὐένδοτος Cher 78 Sacr 32 Plant 133 Migr 144 Somn 2:10

εὐέντευκτος Decal 42

εὐεξία (25) Opif 85 Leg 3:72 Det 29 Plant 157 Migr 167 Abr 48 Ios 82, 138 Mos 1:15, 225 Mos 2:53, 69, 185 Spec 1:139 Spec 2:34, 230 Virt 32, 188 Praem 64, 146 Prob 146 Flacc 149 QG 1:70:1, 4:43, 200a

εὐέπεια Ios 269

εὐεπίβατος Migr 147

εὐεπιβούλευτος Fug 189 Legat 42

εὐεπιχείρητος Sacr 32 Mos 1:168

εὐεργεσία (51) Leg 1:95 Leg 3:78, 215 Cher 99 Sacr 10, 60, 131, 133 Deus 7, 76 Agr 178 Ebr 32 Migr 30, 118 Her 29, 32, 33 Congr 173 Fug 66 Mut 28, 53, 59, 61, 64, 232, 269 Somn 1:143, 162, 163, 179 Ios 47 Mos 1:183, 199 Mos 2:41, 207, 259 Spec 1:169, 225, 283 Spec 2:231 Virt 94 Praem 97, 101, 108, 124 Legat 86, 268, 284, 287, 323 QG 2:16

εὐεργετέω (33) Opif 23, 23, 23 Det 54 Post 140 Deus 80, 108 Plant 86, 87, 89, 130 Migr 73 Fug 96 Mut 18, 24, 24, 28, 40, 129 Abr 146 Spec 1:152 Spec 2:84, 85 Spec 3:197 Virt 72 Legat 50, 60, 283, 297 QG 1:89, 2:13b, 4:191b QE 2:49a

εὐεργέτης (52) Opif 169 Leg 1:96 Leg 2:56 Leg 3:137 Cher 73 Sacr 127 Post 154 Deus 110 Plant 87, 90 Sobr 55, 55, 58 Congr 38, 97, 171 Mut 28 Somn 1:163 Ios 46, 99 Mos 2:198, 256 Decal 41, 165, 166 Spec 1:152, 209, 221, 272, 300 Spec 2:3, 174, 219, 226, 227, 229,

234 Spec 4:58 Virt 41 Prob 118, 118 Flacc 48, 74, 81, 103, 126 Legat 22, 118, 148, 149 Hypoth 7:2 QG 2:13a

εὐεργετικός Plant 90 Mut 28 Praem 97

εὐεργέτις (16) Conf 182 Abr 124, 125, 129, 145, 145 Mos 2:189, 238 Spec 1:307, 307 Spec 4:187 Virt 133 Praem 122 Legat 6, 7 QE 2:2

εὐεργός Opif 136

εὐερκής (6) Conf 19 Migr 215 Fug 96, 203 Somn 1:149 Somn 2:170

εὐερνής Somn 1:58 Ios 91 Mos 1:188 Mos 2:77

εὐετηρία (23) Plant 102 Congr 173 Mut 260 Abr 92 Ios 108, 109, 267 Mos 1:193, 225, 251, 265 Spec 2:2, 171, 187, 192, 203 Spec 3:203 Spec 4:126 Virt 86 Flacc 63 Legat 13, 90, 306

εὔζωνος Sacr 63 Spec 4:128 Legat 254

εὐήθεια (15) Leg 2:70 Cher 65 Det 155, 166 Deus 154 Plant 32 Ebr 192 Fug 38, 146 Mut 118 Somn 2:85, 116 Abr 86 Aet 66, 145

εὐήθης (22) Leg 1:2, 91 Cher 89 Post 94, 141, 152 Deus 8 Agr 155 Conf 141 Migr 45 Mos 2:244 Decal 151 Spec 1:103, 215 Spec 2:8, 245 Spec 3:21, 194 Praem 88 Aet 6, 97 Legat 141

εὐηθικός Deus 163

Εὐήιος Legat 96

εὐημερέω Mut 103 Abr 104 Legat 49

εὐημέρημα Mos 1:250

εὐημερία Contempl 27, 27, 89

εὐήμερος Post 12 Her 290

εὐήνιος Agr 70

εὔηχος Her 266

εὐθαλής Her 270 Ios 108

εὐθανασία Sacr 100

εὐθαρσής Mut 188 Virt 70 Prob 122

εὐθηνέω Det 106 Praem 129

εὐθηνία (28) Migr 15 Congr 173 Mut 260 Abr 1, 92 Ios 108, 109, 112, 158, 250, 260, 267, 270 Mos 1:193 Mos 2:267 Spec 2:22, 171, 192, 203 Spec 3:203 Virt 86 Prob 8 Flacc 63 Legat 13, 90 Hypoth 6:2, 6:3, 7:15

εὔθηρος Mos 1:209 Spec 4:120

εὔθικτος (6) Leg 1:55 Post 79, 80 Deus 93 Legat 57, 168

εὐθιξία (6) Leg 1:55, 55 Cher 102 Mut 98 Somn 2:37 Praem 50

εὐθυβολέω Mos 2:265

εὐθυβόλος (51) Opif 15, 37, 150, 165 Leg 2:8, 38 Leg 3:60 Cher 1, 26 Det 22, 65, 131 Post 80 Deus 71, 93 Agr 2, 134 Plant 14 Ebr 120, 164 Conf 62, 65, 191 Migr 79, 145, 152 Her 54, 124 Congr 68 Mut 90, 94, 164, 253, 262 Ios 28, 104, 116 Mos 1:287 Mos 2:33, 119 Decal 8 Spec 1:15, 209, 330 Spec 2:73 Spec 4:51 Prob 95, 124 Aet 52 Flacc 132 Legat 6

εὐθυδρομέω Leg 3:223 Agr 174

εὐθυμία (27) Leg 3:217 Sacr 27 Deus 4 Plant 56, 92, 166 Migr 165 Congr 161 Mut 131 Somn 2:144, 167, 249 Ios 113, 245 Mos 1:333 Mos 2:211 Decal 161 Spec 1:69 Spec 2:43, 98, 156 Virt 67 Praem 32, 71 Flacc 118, 164 Legat 82

εὔθυμος Ios 162, 198 Virt 90

εὔθυνα (7) Mut 243, 244 Mos 1:327 Decal 98 Spec 1:19 Spec 3:140 Flacc 105

εὐθύνω (18) Leg 1:69 Leg 2:104 Leg 3:136, 224 Post 22, 28 Gig 49, 64 Deus 164 Conf 115 Migr 129 Somn 2:134 Abr 70, 269 Ios 33 Mos 2:291 Spec 1:224 Praem 121

εὐθύς (300) Opif 2, 3, 35, 37, 40, 60, 63, 67, 78, 83, 167 Leg 1:17, 43, 60 Leg 2:24, 33, 75, 82 Leg 3:1, 57, 57, 60, 74, 74, 92, 106, 184, 212, 215 Cher 29, 56, 57, 61, 94, 118 Sacr 15, 20, 52, 64, 69, 73, 79, 81 Det 59, 116 Post 98, 102, 103, 104, 128, 138, 171 Gig 21, 43 Deus 61, 120, 122, 123, 143, 161 Agr 36, 74, 138, 150 Plant 73, 134, 141 Ebr 30, 58, 101, 118, 137, 142, 146, 209 Sobr 22, 27, 30, 54 Conf 8, 13, 157 Migr 68, 146, 154, 185, 219 Her 14, 49, 66, 106, 132, 201, 210, 245, 251, 260 Congr 12, 56, 81, 82, 88, 107, 121, 154 Fug 25, 97, 117, 141, 166, 178 Mut 59, 91, 130, 142, 154, 160, 176, 177, 189, 247 Somn 1:4, 5, 31, 42, 72, 119, 185, 204, 208, 244 Somn 2:17, 51, 118, 146, 157, 243 Abr 25, 45, 77, 194, 219, 229, 240, 254 Ios 165, 249, 254 Mos 1:9, 11, 15, 21, 58, 59, 78, 99, 105, 127, 137, 139, 165, 176, 199, 212, 235, 254, 267, 269, 297, 304 Mos 2:4, 31, 34, 49, 135, 139, 166, 207, 262, 275 Decal 11, 14, 20, 39, 63, 83, 144, 176 Spec 1:17, 33, 62, 103, 117, 200, 223, 261, 265, 300 Spec 2:5, 122, 162, 164, 182, 197 Spec 3:13, 18, 35, 50, 79, 84, 106, 139, 141, 142, 199, 205 Spec 4:40, 62, 107, 154, 163, 192, 195, 221 Virt 68, 88, 157, 163, 182, 200, 208 Praem 11, 26, 68 Prob 4, 24, 37, 42, 103, 117, 155, 155 Contempl 2 Aet 60, 67, 88, 143 Flacc 17, 19, 26, 45, 46, 65, 66, 74, 91, 114, 125, 148, 155, 188 Legat 14, 22, 32, 58, 96, 128, 143, 160, 171, 180, 202, 207, 209, 223, 237, 294, 305, 307, 335, 339, 349, 354, 357 Hypoth 6:6, 7:3, 7:10 Prov 2:35 QG 1:55c, 60:1, 60:2, 2:34a, 41, 72, 3:30b, 4:51a, 64 QG (Par) 2:7 QE isf 9, 22

εὐθυσμός Fug 203 QG 3:27, 4:59

εὐθυτενής (7) Agr 101 Plant 58 Ebr 182 Migr 133 Ios 147 Mos 2:253 Praem 148

εὐθυωρία Post 169

Εὐιλάτ (6) Leg 1:63, 66, 66, 74, 75, 85

εὐκαιρέω Legat 175

εὐκαιρία (7) Opif 17 Post 122 Migr 126 Mut 264 Mos 1:224, 229 Virt 48

εὔκαιρος Somn 2:252 Contempl 22

εὐκάρδιος Prob 116

εὐκαρπία (10) Det 108 Agr 7 Somn 2:131 Ios 109 Spec 2:171, 216 Spec 3:32 Virt 159 Praem 152 Prov 2:66

εὔκαρπος Agr 6 Somn 1:174 Ios 257 Spec 3:39

εὐκάτακτος Spec 3:58

εὐκαταφρόνητος (7) Det 34 Agr 47 Abr 89 Mos 2:248 Spec 4:224 Prob 147 Legat 364

εὐκίνητος Mos 1:22 Spec 1:99 Spec 2:67, 103 Legat 82

εὐκλεής (14) Leg 2:108 Sacr 113, 125 Deus 18 Agr 110, 118 Plant 171 Sobr 57 Mut 206 Somn 2:24 Spec 2:253 Virt 2 Prob 113 Legat 192

εὔκλεια (22) Sacr 16 Post 136 Agr 167 Plant 45 Sobr 52 Her 48 Fug 18, 30 Abr 106, 184 Ios 268 Mos 1:69, 265 Virt 10, 32, 37, 84 Praem 82, 171 Prob 120 Contempl 75 QG 1:20

εὐκληματέω Somn 2:171

εὐκολία (9) Sacr 27 Mos 1:153 Spec 1:173 Spec 4:101 Virt 8 Prob 77, 84 Contempl 69 Flacc 91 εὔκολος Spec 1:4, 306 Legat 14

εὔκομος Prob 122

εὐκοσμία (11) Deus 17 Conf 109 Her 125 Mut 246 Somn 2:152 Spec 1:282 Spec 3:22, 37 Spec 4:21 Aet 106 Legat 5

εὐκρασία (15) Opif 17, 41 Her 147 Abr 1, 92 Spec 1:34, 322 Spec 2:172 Virt 13, 93, 154 Praem 41 Contempl 22, 23 Legat 126

εὐκταῖος (7) Opif 103 Spec 2:154 Spec 4:147 Virt 114, 176 Praem 136 Legat 288

εὐκτικός Congr 149

εὐκτός Mut 225 Mos 2:249

εὐλάβεια (20) Opif 156 Leg 3:113 Cher 29 Det 45 Her 22, 22, 29 Mut 201 Somn 2:82, 82, 141 Spec 1:270, 330 Spec 3:23 Virt 24 Legat 236, 352 Prov 2:26 QG 2:71a, 4:52d

εὐλαβέομαι (33) Gig 47 Sobr 6 Her 29 Fug 131, 141 Mut 24, 134 Somn 1:163 Abr 206 Ios 10, 144, 189, 255 Mos 1:73, 164, 215, 236 Spec 1:30, 56 Spec 2:3, 54, 234, 241 Spec 3:132 Spec 4:6 Virt 67 Aet 89 Flacc 145 Legat 136, 199, 259, 293 QG 2:13a

εὐλαβής (11) Leg 3:15 Her 22 Somn 2:80 Ios 245 Mos 1:83 Praem 89 Legat 159, 182 QG 2:48, 4:202a QG isf 9

εὔληπτος Leg 1:86 Mos 2:182 Legat 304

εὐλογέω (43) Leg 1:17, 17, 18 Leg 3:177, 203, 203, 210, 210, 215, 217 Post 64 Plant 135 Sobr 17, 58, 58 Migr 1, 1, 1, 70, 107, 108, 109, 109, 113, 115 Her 177, 251, 251 Fug 73, 73 Mut 25, 125, 127, 148, 230, 263 Mos 1:291 Mos 2:196 QG 4:198, 227, 228 QE 2:18, 18

εὐλογητός Sobr 51 Migr 1, 107, 107, 108

εὐλογία (28) Leg 3:191, 192, 195, 210 Det 67, 71 Ebr 67 Sobr 66 Migr 70, 73, 106, 108, 108, 115, 117 Her 177 Fug 73 Mut 25, 200, 230, 237 Somn 2:180 Mos 1:283 Praem 78, 79, 113 QG 4:180, 227

εὐλογιστέω Leg 3:190, 192, 215 Sobr 18

εὐλογιστία Conf 66 Migr 71 Mut 128

εὐλόγιστος (8) Leg 1:17, 17, 18 Leg 3:210, 210, 210 Mut 91 Somn 1:155

εὔλογος (47) Opif 27, 45, 72 Leg 3:161 Sacr 12, 12, 13 Det 38, 38, 38, 95 Deus 127 Agr 156 Plant 54, 176, 177, 177 Ebr 70 Migr 76, 180 Her 192, 278 Fug 167 Mut 51 Somn 1:220 Abr 55 Ios 143 Mos 1:83, 174, 196, 244 Mos 2:261 Spec 1:38 Spec 2:185 Spec 3:18, 55, 119 Spec 4:40 Virt 23 Aet 44, 46, 60 Legat 248 Prov 2:34 QG 2:17c, 28, 4:88

εὐμάθεια (εὐμαθία) (6) Cher 102 Agr 168 Plant 110 Congr 127 Somn 1:205 Spec 1:56

εὐμαθής Somn 2:37 Mos 2:153

εὐμαθία εὐμάθεια

εὐμάρεια (8) Cher 12, 87 Sacr 40 Sobr 69 Somn 2:83 Spec 4:38 Praem 95, 122

εὐμαρής (34) Opif 81 Leg 3:135 Det 41, 68 Post 79 Conf 4, 19, 111, 167 Migr 219 Her 125 Mut 65, 218, 231 Somn 1:4, 58 Abr 191 Ios 129 Mos 1:83, 94 Mos 2:174, 261 Spec 2:88, 207, 216, 230 Spec 4:111, 128 Virt 133 Praem 67, 145 Contempl 33 Legat 209 Hypoth 11:12

εὐμεγέθης Mos 1:166 Decal 93

εὐμένεια (11) Cher 37 Somn 1:110 Mos 2:27 Praem 163, 167 Prob 39 Legat 12, 181, 283, 287 QE 2:18

εὐμενής (19) Leg 1:66 Det 95 Deus 183 Plant 171 Congr 71 Fug 99 Abr 96 Ios 104 Mos 1:160 Mos 2:5, 238 Spec 2:218, 248 Spec 3:193 Virt 125 Legat 159, 243, 329 QG 4:193

εὐμετάβολος Deus 27

εὐμήχανος Sacr 44 Spec 3:121 QG (Par) 2:7

εὐμοιρία (16) Post 71, 154 Deus 93 Sobr 38 Migr 75 Congr 37 Mut 2 Somn 2:147 Mos 1:21, 160 Mos 2:66 Virt 80 Praem 27, 50 Prob 35 Prov 2:1

εὔμοιρος (6) Deus 61 Mut 84 Abr 37 Spec 2:21 Praem 63 Prov 2:16

εὐμορφία (29) Opif 136 Leg 2:75 Leg 3:63 Sacr 29 Post 117 Gig 17 Agr 168 Sobr 12 Fug 153 Mut 199 Somn 1:248 Abr 93, 267 Ios 40, 268 Mos 1:15, 296 Mos 2:137 Spec 1:29, 311 Spec 2:34 Spec 3:51 Spec 4:11, 82 Virt 182, 188 Prob 31 Flacc 149 Prov 2:15

εὔμορφος Virt 39, 110 Prob 38 Contempl 50

εὐνή (10) Abr 233 Ios 41 Mos 1:124, 302 Spec 3:14, 63 Virt 112, 223 Flacc 167 Prov 2:17

εὔνοια (74) Cher 33 Plant 90, 106 Conf 48 Migr 116 Her 40 Fug 6, 40, 98, 112 Somn 2:108 Abr 153, 168, 194, 249 Ios 4, 5, 74, 218, 232, 263 Mos 1:19, 33, 148, 324 Mos 2:176, 236, 291 Decal 152 Spec 1:52, 52, 114, 137, 250, 317 Spec 2:80, 167, 232, 239, 239, 240 Spec 3:101, 116, 154, 155, 156 Spec 4:16, 70, 166, 184 Virt 53, 56, 75, 104, 132, 192, 224, 225 Praem 97, 97, 118 Prob 42, 84 Flacc 14 Legat 26, 40, 59, 62, 84, 277, 286 QG 1:27, 4:202a QE 2:6b

εὐνοϊκός Spec 2:132

εὐνομέομαι Abr 6

εὐνομία (18) Opif 81 Post 118, 184 Her 289 Congr 173 Mut 240 Somn 2:40 Abr 261 Spec 1:188 Spec 2:22 Spec 3:131 Spec 4:56, 95 Virt 61 Flacc 5, 94 Legat 90 Hypoth 6:8

εὔνομος (16) Opif 143 Det 134 Abr 25, 61 Spec 1:33 Spec 2:190 Spec 4:21, 237 Virt 180 Praem 34, 41, 66 Contempl 19 Flacc 143 Legat 8 QE 2:64

εὔνους (10) Leg 3:182 Ios 6, 67, 79 Mos 1:46, 328 Spec 1:316 Flacc 18 Legat 36 Prov 2:25

εὐνοῦχος (23) Leg 3:236, 236, 236, 236, 236 Ebr 210, 210, 210, 220, 224 Somn 2:184, 195 Ios 27, 37, 58, 58, 59, 60, 88, 89, 98, 153, 248

εὔογκος Prob 101

εὐοδέω (19) Cher 36 Post 80, 81 Conf 163 Her 285, 285, 285 Somn 2:200, 214 Ios 150, 213 Mos 2:279 Spec 1:7, 216 Praem 105, 142, 143 Flacc 53 Legat 126

Εὔοδος Flacc 76

εὐοδόω QG 4:189

εὐόλισθος Ios 254 Virt 36 Prob 78, 117

εὐοπλέω (6) Opif 85 Mos 1:175, 250 Spec 4:220 Virt 48 Praem 149

εὐορκέω Plant 82 Decal 84 Spec 2:13, 14

εὐορκία Sacr 27

εὔορκος Somn 1:13 Decal 157

εὔορμος Legat 151

εὐπαγής Conf 89 Ios 82

εὐπάθεια (37) Opif 142 Leg 1:45 Leg 3:22, 86, 107 Cher 12 Sacr 103 Det 28, 120, 137 Post 120 Plant 171 Conf

91 Migr 119, 157, 219 Her 77, 192 Congr 36, 174 Mut 1, 131, 167, 188 Abr 201, 204 Mos 1:89 Spec 1:176, 224 Spec 2:48, 54, 98, 185 Spec 3:1 Virt 67 Praem 32, 160

εὐπαίδευτος Fug 10, 47

εὐπαιδία Mut 133 Ios 179

εὔπαις (7) Deus 13 Somn 1:200 Ios 187 Spec 2:133 Praem 109, 110 Hypoth 11:13

εὐπαράγωγος (10) Gig 39, 59 Agr 16, 96 Ebr 46 Fug 22 Spec 1:28 Praem 29 Contempl 63 Legat 57

εὐπαράδεκτος Leg 3:249 Post 150 Her 38 Fug 172, 176

εὐπάρυφος Spec 2:244 Spec 4:63 Legat 344

εὐπατρίδης (17) Cher 120 Ios 69, 172, 248 Decal 71 Spec 1:52, 82, 124 Virt 77, 108, 199, 199 Praem 152, 171 Prob 10, 149 Legat 203

εὐπείθεια Flacc 99 Hypoth 6:8, 7:3

εὐπειθής Decal 39 Spec 2:39 Virt 15 Hypoth 6:2, 6:4

εὐπετής Conf 164 Abr 5 Spec 4:7 Praem 117

εὔπλευρος Leg 2:21

εὐπλοέω Somn 1:44

εὔπλοια (14) Leg 3:80 Cher 37 Agr 174 Mut 221 Somn 1:150 Ios 33, 139, 149 Spec 4:154, 201 Virt 61, 176 Praem 11 Flacc 27

εὐποιία Mut 24

εὐπορέω (15) Post 71, 128 Deus 7, 122 Migr 79 Mos 1:209, 312 Spec 1:131, 134, 153 Spec 2:85, 249 Prob 8 Legat 6 Prov 2:60

εὐπορία (13) Opif 79 Post 142 Sobr 43 Her 285 Somn 2:11 Ios 115 Mos 1:172 Spec 2:22, 185 Spec 4:76 Contempl 52 Prov 2:5, 11

εὐπόριστος Somn 1:124 Praem 99

εὔπορος (12) Det 88 Agr 141 Spec 1:133, 163 Spec 2:72, 107 Spec 4:195 Virt 85, 90 Contempl 14 Legat 123 Prov 2:22

εὐπραγία (38) Cher 105 Gig 38 Deus 174, 178 Agr 62, 173 Ebr 9, 201 Migr 155 Fug 44, 47, 145 Somn 1:223 Somn 2:81 Ios 5, 99, 270 Mos 1:30 Mos 2:6, 15, 240, 246 Spec 1:224, 284, 314 Spec 2:122, 208, 259 Spec 3:18, 135 Virt 91, 193, 204 Legat 8, 32, 140 QG 4:191b QE 2:55b

εὐπραξία Mut 237, 264 Somn 2:180

εὐπρέπεια Mut 195 Aet 126

εὐπρεπής (13) Opif 139 Cher 122 Ebr 69 Conf 97 Migr 42 Mut 60 Somn 1:224 Spec 2:175 Spec 3:65 Spec 4:52 Virt 24, 196 QG (Par) 2:6

εὐπρόσιτος Decal 42

εὐπρόσωπος Virt 196

εὐπροφάσιστος Aet 75

εὕρεμα Her 214

εὑρεσιλογέω (εὑρησιλογία) (6) Agr 92, 157 Ios 50 Aet 54, 90 Prov 1

εὑρεσιλογία (εὑρησιλογία) Somn 1:54 Somn 2:301 Prob 19 Aet 132

εὕρεσις (35) Sacr 64 Det 79, 134 Post 52 Deus 86 Agr 13, 143 Ebr 119 Conf 39 Migr 35, 171 Her 214 Congr 29 Fug 120, 121, 126, 166, 175, 177 Mut 269 Somn 1:107, 205 Somn 2:212, 270 Ios 245 Mos 1:256 Spec 1:36, 40, 235 Spec 2:165 Virt 214 Praem 50 Aet 16 Flacc 86 Prov 2:51

εὑρετής (16) Leg 1:74 Cher 57 Plant 148 Her 302 Somn 1:204 Somn 2:202 Mos 2:201 Spec 1:335 Spec 3:49 Aet 12, 145 Flacc 20, 73 Legat 88, 106 QG 1:20

εὕρημα (8) Leg 3:78 Plant 35 Congr 148 Decal 15 Spec 4:51 Virt 8, 19 Contempl 4

εὑρησιλογέω εὑρεσιλογέω

εὑρησιλογία εὑρεσιλογία

Εὐριπίδης Prob 99, 116, 141

εὑρίσκω (382) Opif 78, 79, 94, 106, 118, 167 Leg 1:76, 102 Leg 2:10, 13, 69, 70, 107 Leg 3:4, 10, 32, 32, 35, 47, 49, 57, 68, 74, 75, 77, 77, 78, 78, 87, 92, 102, 104, 116, 116, 135, 140, 140, 147, 148, 180, 181, 182, 217, 226, 229, 229, 231, 248, 249, 249, 249 Cher 47, 68, 96, 113, 116, 117, 122, 127, 128, 129 Sacr 19, 22, 24, 35, 37, 64, 71, 81, 92, 97, 101, 111, 113, 122, 129 Det 4, 5, 10, 17, 17, 22, 23, 28, 29, 41, 42, 48, 49, 56, 57, 70, 73, 95, 98, 100, 116, 119, 123, 125, 137, 149, 162, 164, 164, 164, 166, 169, 177 Post 9, 9, 21, 43, 53, 86, 107, 117, 132 Gig 1 Deus 22, 61, 70, 74, 86, 86, 86, 90, 92, 92, 93, 104, 107, 109, 111, 115, 120 Agr 2, 4, 26, 27, 72, 83, 87, 90, 97, 147, 164 Plant 45, 78, 80, 81, 82, 83, 93, 123, 127, 130, 138 Ebr 65, 83, 114, 118, 118, 120, 166, 170, 187, 204 Sobr 13, 13, 21, 28, 29, 62 Conf 1, 7, 37, 60, 68, 74, 75, 76, 153, 163, 197 Migr 14, 28, 34, 44, 60, 102, 121, 144 Her 88, 107, 111, 143, 154, 192, 193, 274, 275 Congr 37, 68, 109 Fug 1, 4, 50, 52, 60, 60, 97, 99, 119, 120, 120, 120, 127, 127, 132, 133, 135, 137, 142, 143, 143, 144, 147, 149, 149, 149, 157, 158, 166, 168, 169, 171, 177, 202, 203 Mut 8, 34, 34, 35, 38, 50, 139, 190, 192, 219, 228, 234, 250, 251, 258, 262, 268, 269 Somn 1:8, 8, 37, 38, 40, 40, 40, 44, 66, 146, 204, 204, 222 Somn 2:27, 64, 92, 180, 251, 259, 260, 270, 279, 292 Abr 12, 17, 19, 19, 24, 128, 131, 175, 232 Ios 80, 104, 116, 137, 146, 180, 183, 215 Mos 1:165, 174, 191, 204, 207, 279 Mos 2:6, 13, 52, 210, 266, 273, 289 Decal 81 Spec 1:69, 77, 133, 163, 195, 214, 236, 255, 260, 309, 335 Spec 2:17, 69, 171, 172, 184, 260, 261 Spec 3:76, 88, 202 Spec 4:24, 33, 50, 165, 173 Virt 11, 28, 109, 188, 196, 201 Praem 16, 17, 50, 70, 88 Prob 78, 86, 131 Aet 20, 23, 46, 78 Flacc 22, 56, 74, 79, 90, 111, 165 Legat 60, 67, 108, 162, 202, 206, 213, 262 Prov 2:22, 58 QG 1:62:1, 96:1, 2:39, 4:191c, 9* QG (Par) 2:1, 2:2, 2:3, 2:5

εὖρος (7) Mos 2:60, 83, 84, 85, 89, 91 Prov 2:26

εὔρυθμος Leg 3:57 Congr 76 QE 2:38b

εὐρύνω (21) Deus 39 Agr 53 Sobr 60 Migr 146 Congr 159 Fug 176 Mut 22, 107 Somn 1:131, 175 Somn 2:36, 71 Mos 1:93, 115, 194 Mos 2:281 Spec 1:300 Spec 3:147 Contempl 51, 86 Flacc 37

εὐρύς (6) Opif 113 Mos 1:177 Decal 50 Spec 4:111 Aet 121 Legat 151

Εὐρυσθεύς Prob 120

εὐρύστερνος Aet 17

εὐρυχωρία Somn 1:40 Spec 1:75 Legat 125, 151 QG 4:33a

εὐρυχώρος Sacr 61

Εὐρωπαῖος Legat 10, 144, 283

Εὐρώπη (17) Cher 63 Deus 175 Somn 2:54 Ios 134 Mos 2:19, 19, 20 Prob 94, 132 Flacc 46 Legat 22, 48, 88, 144, 144, 280, 281

εὐρώς Prob 104

εὐρωστέω Virt 166

εὔρωστος Ios 102

εὐσάλευτος Leg 3:45

εὐσαρκία (8) Opif 138 Leg 3:63 Somn 1:248 Somn 2:58 Mos 1:64 Mos 2:140 Prob 121 Contempl 53

εὔσαρκος Abr 108 Ios 101 Spec 4:100 Praem 146 Contempl 54

εὔσβεστος Ios 154

εὐσέβεια (162) Opif 9, 155, 172 Leg 3:209 Cher 42, 94, 96 Sacr 15, 27, 37, 130 Det 18, 21, 24, 55, 56, 72, 73, 114, 143 Post 181 Deus 17, 69, 102, 164 Agr 174, 177 Plant 35, 70, 77, 107 Ebr 18, 37, 41, 78, 84, 91, 92 Sobr 40 Conf 132 Migr 97, 132, 194 Her 123, 172 Congr 98 Mut 39, 76, 155 Somn 1:194, 251 Somn 2:67, 106, 182, 186 Abr 24, 60, 61, 98, 129, 171, 179, 198, 199, 208, 268 Ios 240, 246 Mos 1:146, 183, 187, 189, 198, 303, 307, 317 Mos 2:66, 108, 136, 142, 165, 170, 192, 216, 260, 270, 284 Decal 52, 58, 100, 108, 110, 119 Spec 1:30, 51, 52, 54, 67, 68, 79, 132, 186, 193, 248, 250, 299, 309, 313, 316, 317 Spec 2:26, 28, 63, 183, 197, 209, 224, 237 Spec 3:29, 127 Spec 4:40, 50, 97, 129, 135, 147, 147 Virt 42, 45, 51, 95, 175, 201, 218, 221 Praem 12, 40, 53, 160, 162 Prob 83 Contempl 3, 25, 88 Flacc 48, 98 Legat 216, 242, 245, 297, 316, 319, 347 Hypoth 6:6, 6:8, 7:13 QG 4:202a QE 2:15b, 26, 38a QE isf 13, 14

εὐσεβέω (16) Det 114 Congr 6 Abr 177, 190 Mos 1:189, 254 Mos 2:159 Decal 63, 117, 120 Spec 1:64, 78, 312 Praem 40 Flacc 103 Legat 280

εὐσεβής (18) Leg 3:10, 209 Det 20 Post 39 Agr 128 Fug 131 Abr 208 Ios 122, 143 Spec 1:57 Praem 93 Aet 10 Legat 213, 279, 280, 335 QG 1:100:1b QE 2:50b

εὔσηπτος Spec 1:220

εὐσθένεια Legat 16

εὔσκοπος (18) Somn 2:172 Abr 266 Ios 104, 116 Mos 2:265 Spec 4:120 Praem 50, 95, 140 Prob 16, 26 Contempl 79 Flacc 132 Legat 6, 31, 104, 174, 229

εὐστάθεια (18) Post 28, 118, 184 Conf 132 Her 289 Somn 2:11, 152, 166 Ios 57, 167 Spec 4:166 Virt 32 Flacc 94, 135, 184 Legat 90, 113, 161

εὐσταθής (6) Conf 43, 70, 109 Congr 25 Abr 260 Prob 84

εὔσταχυς Abr 92, 141, 227 Ios 102

εὐστοχέω QE 2:24b

εὐστοχία Plant 31

εὔστοχος (11) Post 81, 131 Sobr 26 Conf 144 Her 116 Congr 29 Mut 44 Mos 2:33 Spec 4:222 Praem 40, 140

εὐσυνθεσία Sacr 27

εὐταξία Ios 204

εὐτεκνία Spec 1:138

εὔτεκνος Praem 60, 109, 158, 160

εὐτέλεια (9) Opif 164 Deus 161 Mos 1:153 Mos 2:185 Spec 1:173 Spec 2:19, 160 Virt 18 Legat 274

εὐτελής (23) Opif 68 Det 14 Migr 106 Her 158, 158 Congr 51 Somn 1:6, 93, 124 Somn 2:48, 56 Ios 204 Mos 1:111, 112 Spec 1:271 Spec 2:34 Virt 49 Praem 99 Contempl 24, 37, 38, 69 Hypoth 11:12

εὐτοκέω Post 125 Congr 7 Somn 2:259 Praem 68

εὐτοκία (16) Sacr 101 Agr 5 Migr 123 Congr 3, 5, 37, 129 Mut 133, 143, 221 Somn 2:131 Ios 109 Mos 1:64 Spec 3:35 Praem 68, 107

εὔτοκος Deus 13

εὐτολμία (17) Her 5, 21 Fug 6 Somn 2:37 Abr 150, 183 Mos 1:251, 306 Mos 2:273 Spec 4:121 Virt 3, 32, 43 Prob 109, 120, 124, 131

εὔτολμος (9) Migr 165 Ios 189 Mos 1:260 Decal 120 Virt 27 Prob 103 Flacc 86 Legat 215 Hypoth 11:16

εὐτονία (17) Leg 1:42 Leg 3:69, 87 Det 119, 136 Post 112, 148 Gig 36 Plant 157 Somn 1:217 Somn 2:58 Spec 2:230 Virt 158, 193 Prob 40, 111 Prov 2:14

εὔτονος (23) Leg 2:81 Sacr 49, 80 Post 47 Agr 66, 70 Migr 146 Her 67 Somn 1:171 Somn 2:10 Ios 34, 41, 140 Decal 64 Spec 1:64 Spec 2:163, 241 Virt 17, 155, 165 Prob 149 Flacc 4, 8

εὐτραπελία Legat 361

εὐτρεπής (17) Leg 3:184 Sacr 63 Deus 96 Agr 71 Plant 50 Ebr 219 Migr 57 Fug 66, 85 Mut 200 Abr 173 Ios 114 Mos 1:170, 204 Flacc 27 Legat 108, 222

εὐτρεπίζω (52) Opif 78, 78, 158, 158 Leg 1:68 Sacr 24 Det 26 Agr 36, 58, 66 Plant 35, 133 Conf 130 Her 71 Congr 19 Fug 166 Mut 269 Somn 1:123, 165, 226 Somn 2:87, 156, 181 Abr 110, 231 Ios 62, 93, 196, 206 Mos 1:17, 53, 55, 275 Mos 2:267 Decal 14, 41, 45 Spec 1:258 Spec 2:69, 97, 148, 158, 161, 187, 197 Virt 136 Praem 17 Contempl 69 Aet 68 Legat 233, 252 Prov 2:61

εὐτροπία Virt 142

εὐτροφία Abr 1 Prov 2:68

εὔτροχος (9) Det 131 Post 81 Agr 18 Migr 79 Her 4 Somn 1:256 Mos 1:48, 84 Contempl 76

εὐτυχέω Opif 167 Mos 2:43 Decal 43

εὐτύχημα Ios 253 Praem 150

εὐτυχής (19) Cher 59 Det 145 Mut 86 Abr 266 Ios 93 Mos 1:64 Spec 1:320 Praem 107, 129 Prob 114, 130 Flacc 157 Legat 114, 224, 326, 342 Hypoth 11:13 Prov 2:17, 32

εὐτυχία (46) Opif 17 Post 71 Deus 91, 174 Agr 61 Migr 172 Congr 159 Mut 215 Abr 246, 252 Ios 76, 92, 137, 163, 244 Mos 1:30, 32 Mos 2:44, 53 Spec 1:224, 293, 313 Spec 2:76 Spec 3:165, 172 Spec 4:18, 121, 151 Virt 204 Praem 133, 135, 152, 168, 169, 170 Prob 36, 77 Contempl 90 Flacc 29, 152 Legat 11, 33, 43, 105, 211 Hypoth 6:8

εὔυδρος (6) Abr 134 Mos 1:65, 188, 255, 320 Spec 2:172

εὐφημέω Migr 115 Spec 1:301 Spec 2:248 Legat 297, 297

εὐφημία (18) Post 181 Sobr 52 Migr 88, 115 Mut 14 Somn 2:167 Abr 103, 184, 191 Mos 1:291, 293 Spec 1:144 Spec 2:11 Virt 84, 211, 222 Praem 82 QE 2:6b

εὔφημος (7) Conf 159 Fug 86 Mut 242 Somn 1:130 Ios 12 Virt 2 Praem 47

εὐφορέω (7) Somn 1:115 Somn 2:200, 238 Ios 159, 250 Spec 3:23 Praem 158

εὐφορία (26) Opif 39 Post 141 Deus 48 Conf 167 Migr 123 Her 32, 295 Congr 56, 98 Mut 221 Somn 1:115 Somn 2:272 Abr 134 Ios 111, 260 Mos 1:240 Mos 2:179 Spec 2:97 Spec 4:81, 98 Virt 120 Praem 103, 106, 107, 128 Flacc 148

εὔφορος Conf 89 Spec 2:67, 91, 199 Spec 3:31

εὐφραίνω (29) Leg 1:72 Leg 3:86, 87 Cher 86 Sacr 33 Agr 148, 148 Ebr 5 Migr 79 Fug 141 Mut 161 Somn 2:175, 175, 176, 176, 177, 177, 178, 179, 183, 246, 247 Abr 207 Mos 1:187, 247 Spec 1:321 Spec 2:194 Spec 3:186 QG 2:10

Εὐφράτης (20) Leg 1:63, 72, 72, 85, 85, 87 Her 315, 316, 316 Somn 2:255, 255, 300 Abr 226 Virt 223 Legat 10, 10, 207, 216, 259, 282

εὐφροσύνη (51) Leg 3:81, 87 Cher 8 Sacr 111 Deus 81, 96, 96, 154 Plant 161 Ebr 4, 6, 223 Migr 92, 204 Her 76, 315 Congr 161, 162, 167, 174 Fug 22, 176 Mut 161, 168, 262 Somn 2:167, 169, 172, 174, 179, 181, 190, 248, 249, 249 Mos 1:255 Spec 1:36, 191, 191, 193 Spec 2:49, 156, 193, 194, 214 Virt 67 Contempl 46 Legat 13, 83, 88 QE 2:15b

εὐφυής (34) Leg 3:196 Sacr 7, 64, 120, 120 Det 107 Agr 158 Ebr 94 Migr 164, 165 Her 38 Congr 71, 82, 122, 127 Fug 138, 176 Mut 68, 98, 102, 212, 213 Somn 1:200 Somn 2:33, 37 Abr 26 Mos 1:22 Mos 2:141 Spec 2:39 Spec 4:75, 101 Prob 135 Legat 169 QG 4:102b

εὐφυΐα (17) Leg 1:55 Leg 3:249, 249 Cher 101, 102 Gig 2 Migr 165 Her 212 Mut 98, 98, 101, 210 Somn 2:33, 37 Praem 50 Flacc 34 QE isf 25

εὐφωνία Leg 2:75 Spec 1:29

εὔφωνος Congr 46

εὐχαριστέω (33) Sacr 52 Deus 7 Plant 126, 130, 136 Her 31, 174, 199, 200, 226 Congr 96, 114 Mut 186, 222 Somn 2:268 Mos 2:41 Spec 1:67, 167, 210, 211, 211, 283, 284 Spec 2:168, 175, 185, 203, 204 Spec 3:6 Virt 165 Flacc 100, 121 QG 1:64b

εὐχαριστήριος Mos 2:148 Contempl 87 Legat 355

εὐχαριστητικός Sacr 74 Deus 7 Ebr 94, 105

εὐχαριστία (48) Leg 1:84 Sacr 54, 63 Agr 80 Plant 126 Migr 25, 92, 142 Her 15, 226, 226 Mos 1:33, 317 Mos 2:42, 101 Spec 1:97, 131, 144, 169, 171, 195, 210, 211, 211, 224, 229, 272, 275, 276, 285, 286, 297, 297, 298 Spec 2:146, 156, 171, 175, 182, 185, 192 Spec 4:98 Virt 72 Praem 56 Flacc 98, 123 Legat 284 QG 4:130

εὐχαριστικός Leg 1:80 Ebr 121 Mos 1:180

εὐχάριστος (25) Leg 1:82 Leg 3:245 Plant 131, 135, 136, 136 Migr 43 Congr 7 Mut 220, 222 Somn 2:38, 72 Ios 213 Mos 2:108, 207, 256 Spec 1:287 Spec 2:174, 180, 209 Virt 74, 75, 165 Flacc 48 QG 1:96:1

εὐχέρεια (14) Det 10 Deus 28 Agr 33 Ebr 205 Migr 89 Ios 118 Spec 1:3, 128 Spec 2:6, 24, 37, 37 Virt 137, 152

εὐχερής (9) Sacr 29, 32 Ebr 188 Her 81, 97 Somn 1:13 Ios 50 QG 2:72 QG isf 2

εὐχή (118) Leg 1:17, 84 Leg 2:63, 63 Leg 3:104, 107, 192 Cher 94 Sacr 53, 53 Post 179 Deus 87, 87, 87, 132, 157 Agr 94, 95, 99, 175, 175, 175 Plant 90 Ebr 2, 66, 79, 126, 130 Sobr 53, 66, 67 Conf 159 Migr 114, 117, 118 Her 260 Congr 7, 99 Fug 115, 154 Somn 1:126, 163, 189, 215, 252, 252 Somn 2:299 Abr 235, 250 Ios 195, 206, 210 Mos 1:47, 149, 219, 252, 280, 285, 292 Mos 2:5, 5, 24, 36, 42, 107, 133, 147, 154, 174 Decal 73, 75, 126, 158 Spec 1:83, 97, 97, 113, 193, 224, 229, 247, 248, 249, 250, 251 Spec 2:12, 17, 24, 32, 34, 36, 38, 115, 129, 148, 167, 196 Spec 3:11, 131, 171 Virt 53, 59, 77, 120, 209 Praem 56, 78, 79, 84, 126, 166 Contempl 67, 89 Legat 280 QG 1:70:1, 70:2, 4:198 QG isf 13

εὔχομαι (113) Leg 1:17 Leg 2:63, 78, 94, 96, 96 Leg 3:104, 177, 179, 193 Sacr 53, 69, 69, 99, 124 Det 46, 103, 144, 147 Post 67, 82 Deus 8, 156, 164 Agr 39, 44, 45, 94, 99, 99, 156, 168, 175 Plant 46, 49, 52, 161, 162 Ebr 2, 125, 224 Sobr 12, 59, 61, 62, 64, 67, 68 Conf 39, 163 Migr 101, 111, 124, 171 Her 34 Congr 7, 38, 57, 99, 175 Fug 115, 118, 164 Mut 41, 125, 127, 188, 204, 209, 210, 210, 213, 216, 218, 252, 253 Somn 1:163, 189, 252, 253 Somn 2:72, 101 Abr 58 Ios 88 Mos 1:122, 252 Mos 2:154, 214 Decal 72, 74 Spec 1:167, 252, 254, 254 Spec 2:34, 35, 36, 36, 37, 37, 38, 38 Spec 3:197 Virt 77 Praem 151 Prob 57, 63 Contempl 27, 56 Flacc 167 Legat 306 Prov 2:14, 64

εὔχορτος (7) Opif 40 Abr 141 Mos 1:65, 228, 320 Spec 2:109 Aet 63

εὔχρηστος Congr 141, 141

εὔχροια Opif 138 Leg 3:63 Mos 2:140 Praem 64

εὐώδης (13) Leg 2:7 Sacr 21 Det 157 Ebr 218 Her 197 Somn 2:62, 74 Mos 2:146 Spec 1:171, 175 Spec 3:37, 37 Aet 64

εὐωδής QG 4:69

εὐωδία (7) Opif 165 Leg 1:42 Ebr 87 Congr 115 Somn 1:178 Abr 148 Prov 2:71

εὐώνυμος (26) Opif 122 Leg 1:4 Leg 2:20 Leg 3:90 Cher 21 Deus 145, 162, 163 Sobr 27, 29 Conf 139 Migr 146 Her 151, 176, 209 Somn 1:26 Abr 224 Mos 1:270 Mos 2:78 Decal 31 Contempl 30, 45, 69 Legat 95, 95, 105

εὐωχέω (14) Her 29, 255 Somn 2:66 Ios 96, 98, 234 Mos 1:284 Mos 2:33 Decal 41 Spec 1:242, 304 Spec 3:115 Praem 139 Prob 102

εὐωχία (31) Opif 78, 78 Agr 66 Plant 162 Ebr 91 Migr 204 Somn 2:87 Abr 117 Ios 25, 202, 204 Mos 1:187, 275 Spec 1:176, 185, 212, 221, 222 Spec 2:148, 149 Spec 3:96 Spec 4:103, 121 Virt 136 Contempl 48, 56, 66 Legat 83, 356 Prov 2:32 QG 4:8*

ἐφάλλομαι Agr 69

ἐφάμιλλος Gig 41 Virt 85

ἐφάπτω (33) Leg 2:42 Cher 6, 58 Det 87 Agr 178 Ebr 86, 167 Conf 38 Migr 158, 160 Congr 22, 52 Fug 104, 104, 163 Mut 208 Somn 2:189, 230, 235 Ios 13 Mos 2:202 Spec 1:122, 329 Spec 2:21, 261 Spec 3:178, 179, 209 Spec 4:60, 122 Praem 36, 142 Aet 114

ἐφαρμόζω (60) Leg 2:15, 31 Cher 105 Sacr 43, 82, 115 Det 81, 108 Post 4, 110 Plant 172, 172, 177 Sobr 38, 60 Conf 139 Her 164, 259 Congr 154 Fug 47, 148 Mut 97, 101, 175, 231 Somn 1:1, 125, 177, 189 Somn 2:9, 140, 210, 268, 296 Mos 1:48 Mos 2:3, 3, 38, 49, 77, 78, 90 Spec 1:43, 120 Spec 2:1 Spec 3:7, 57, 134, 169 Spec 4:105, 133, 176, 204 Praem 98 Prob 16 Aet 49 Flacc 140 QG 4:76b QG isf 8 QE isf 8

ἐφεδρεία Ios 36 Mos 1:306 Virt 131 Praem 149 Prob 151

ἐφεδρεύω (41) Sacr 135 Plant 101, 103 Migr 57 Mut 185 Somn 1:9, 32 Somn 2:146, 233 Abr 230, 242, 246 Mos 1:191, 198, 227, 316, 321 Mos 2:162, 249 Decal 95 Spec 1:301 Spec 2:64, 168 Spec 3:3, 62, 129, 202 Spec 4:173, 203 Virt 43, 126, 130, 131 Praem 102, 130 Contempl 52 Aet 36 Flacc 5, 174 Legat 11, 129

ἔφεδρος (22) Agr 168 Somn 1:119 Abr 263 Ios 130, 139 Mos 1:315, 327 Mos 2:251 Spec 1:52, 160 Spec 2:76, 207, 213 Spec 3:131 Spec 4:17, 33 Prob 7 Flacc 72 Legat 14, 29, 190 QG (Par) 2:7

ἐφέλκω (8) Leg 3:11 Det 27 Migr 200 Mos 1:311 Spec 2:83 Spec 4:129 Legat 215 QE 2:11b

ἐφεξῆς Mos 1:9 Hypoth 6:8, 7:10

ἐφέπω Mos 1:228

Ἐφέσιος Legat 315

ἔφεσις Conf 25

ἐφέστιος Mos 1:36

ἐφευρίσκω Legat 124

ἔφηβος Ios 127, 128, 129 Prob 140

ἐφήδομαι (7) Spec 2:76 Virt 116 Praem 169 Flacc 121, 147 QG 2:39, 4:52a

ἐφηδύνω Sacr 31 Fug 139

ἐφημερευτής Contempl 66

ἐφημερινός Virt 122

ἐφημερίς Legat 165

ἐφημερόβιος Virt 88

ἐφήμερος (ὁ) (15) Opif 156 Post 122 Deus 151 Ebr 142 Her 34 Congr 57 Ios 130 Spec 2:247 Virt 204 Praem 156 Prob 8 Flacc 143 Legat 91 QG 4:148, 166

ἐφιδρύσις Leg 3:188

ἐφιδρύω (11) Opif 86 Leg 3:136, 145 Fug 100, 101, 189 Mut 81, 128 Abr 8, 268 Aet 99

ἐφιζάνω Contempl 31

ἐφίημι (133) Opif 70, 88, 162 Leg 1:93 Leg 2:4, 77, 80, 84 Leg 3:160, 249, 251, 251, 252 Cher 123, 127 Sacr 12, 41, 121 Det 65, 115 Post 23, 23, 134 Deus 23, 116, 165 Agr 17, 125 Ebr 2, 48, 113, 115, 214 Conf 52, 97, 103, 144, 175 Migr 12, 91, 94, 216 Her 14, 36, 63, 111 Congr 5, 12, 31, 51 Fug 108, 121, 126 Mut 75, 88, 118, 169, 226 Somn 1:62, 95, 218, 219 Somn 2:11, 38, 251 Abr 47, 48, 52, 100, 166, 184, 232, 261 Ios 43, 69 Mos 1:48, 97, 122, 134, 205, 236 Mos 2:22, 52, 151, 245 Decal 50 Spec 1:68, 105, 108, 109, 113, 128, 157, 193, 276 Spec 2:37, 61, 66, 73, 106, 112, 121, 146, 183, 202 Spec 3:20, 22, 47, 82, 131, 133, 134, 183, 205 Spec 4:71, 99, 100, 226 Virt 9, 90, 100, 147 Contempl 11 Flacc 35, 50, 54 Legat 132, 158, 280, 346 QE 2:65 QE isf 14, 15

ἐφικνέομαι (19) Leg 1:30, 83 Agr 121 Migr 134 Her 100 Fug 38 Mut 24, 219 Somn 1:179 Abr 38, 47 Ios 138 Mos 2:10 Decal 146 Spec 1:17 Spec 2:77, 207 Praem 80 QE 1:7b

ἐφικτός (6) Opif 90 Leg 1:38 Det 153 Abr 167 Spec 1:44, 49

ἐφίστημι (44) Opif 85 Leg 3:118 Post 67 Deus 182 Ebr 14 Conf 96, 121 Fug 32, 123, 124 Mut 170, 270 Somn 1:91 Somn 2:272 Abr 70 Ios 6, 25, 97, 129, 204 Mos 1:40, 43, 89, 107, 168, 226, 233 Spec 1:71, 127, 153 Spec 2:163 Spec 3:87 Spec 4:222 Virt 109, 109 Praem 154 Contempl 37 Flacc 113, 135 Legat 30, 143, 226 Prov 2:39, 70

ἐφοδιάζω Congr 112 Spec 2:85

ἐφόδιον Her 273

ἔφοδος (15) Migr 26 Her 202, 243 Fug 177 Mut 130 Somn 2:96, 125 Mos 1:233 Spec 1:184, 301 Contempl 24 Flacc 76 Prov 2:49, 56 QE 2:21

ἐφοράω (14) Leg 3:171 Gig 47 Conf 121 Somn 1:140 Ios 265 Spec 4:32 Virt 133 Praem 169 Prob 44, 89 Aet 83 Legat 336 Prov 2:54 QG 1:69

ἐφορμάω Mos 1:178, 258 Spec 3:103 Spec 4:222

ἐφορμέω (9) Leg 3:113, 139 Migr 98 Somn 1:23, 164, 222, 227 Praem 29 Flacc 53

ἐφόρμησις Mos 2:254 Spec 2:190

ἔφορος (25) Opif 11 Mut 39, 216 Somn 2:101, 186 Abr 71, 104 Ios 48, 170, 260, 270 Mos 1:36 Decal 95, 177 Spec 2:253 Spec 3:19, 129 Spec 4:200 Virt 57, 74, 200, 219 Flacc 121, 146 QE isf 25

Ἐφραΐμ (13) Leg 3:90, 90, 93, 93, 94 Sobr 28, 28 Migr 205 Congr 40 Mut 97, 97, 98, 101

Ἐφρών Conf 79 QG 4:79a, 81

ἐφυβρίζω Decal 129

ἐφυμνέω Agr 82

ἐφύμνιον Congr 115 Contempl 80

ἐχεθυμία Sacr 27

ἐχεμυθέω Sacr 60 Det 102 Agr 59 Spec 4:90

ἐχθαίρω (6) Sacr 20 Somn 2:69 Spec 3:119 Flacc 180 Legat 64 Hypoth 7:6

ἐχθές Sacr 12 Det 4

ἔχθος Migr 209 Ios 11, 235 Spec 2:139 Legat 329

ἔχθρα (22) Leg 3:65, 182, 184 Sacr 96 Somn 1:40 Somn 2:98 Ios 6 Mos 1:242, 242 Decal 152 Spec 1:108 Spec 3:16, 101 Spec 4:88 Virt 118, 152, 197 Prob 79 Flacc 61, 106 Legat 359 Hypoth 7:8

ἐχθραίνω Conf 121 Spec 2:204 Virt 116

ἐχθρός (236) Opif 74 Leg 2:10 Leg 3:1, 79, 111, 182, 185, 189 Cher 11, 20, 75, 76, 77 Sacr 20, 35 Det 2, 37, 165, 166 Post 25, 172 Gig 35, 43, 66 Deus 27, 60, 98, 167 Agr 46, 78, 93, 112, 120, 147, 150, 155, 156, 168 Ebr 14, 24, 69, 80, 159, 164, 165 Conf 20, 45, 48 Migr 62, 112, 116, 150 Her 41, 48, 161, 203, 243, 244, 289 Congr 65 Fug 14, 25, 114 Mut 30, 114, 197, 269 Somn 1:8, 103, 223 Somn 2:14, 40, 63, 90, 92, 104, 117, 279 Abr 14, 55, 105, 153, 180 Ios 67, 79, 153, 166 Mos 1:45, 61, 142, 164, 164, 170, 172, 181, 183, 216, 218, 227, 257, 280, 291, 292, 307, 308, 310, 312, 314, 327, 332 Mos 2:53, 249, 249, 251, 254, 255 Decal 68, 110, 135 Spec 1:184, 306, 312, 313, 316, 340 Spec 2:129, 134, 138, 190, 191, 248, 252 Spec 3:11, 24, 27, 36, 88, 113, 129, 155, 181, 195, 197 Spec 4:23, 44, 70, 89, 121, 121, 170, 178, 184, 202, 226 Virt 25, 37, 46, 47, 50, 108, 116, 117, 125, 154, 154, 160, 195, 195, 197, 226 Praem 61, 79, 85, 95, 96, 118, 127, 128, 137, 138, 139, 147, 147, 148, 164, 169 Prob 33, 93, 106, 120, 133 Contempl 37, 41, 44, 47, 47 Flacc 7, 13, 18, 54, 58, 61, 62, 75, 89, 101, 121, 124, 125, 126, 132, 135, 146, 147, 173 Legat 40, 113, 119, 171, 180, 256, 292, 349, 371 Hypoth 6:7, 6:7, 11:16 Prov 2:4, 25, 56 QG 3:26, 4:193 QE 2:11a, 11a, 16, 21

ἐχῖνος Sacr 95

ἔχις Ebr 223 Spec 3:103

ἐχομένως Leg 2:99

ἐχυρός (20) Cher 69, 103 Sacr 13, 126 Post 163, 178 Gig 28, 39, 52 Conf 38, 102, 103 Migr 108 Fug 94, 203 Somn 1:251 Somn 2:90 Mos 1:282 Spec 1:159 Legat 364

ἐχυρότης (6) Her 34 Somn 2:223 Mos 1:224, 229, 233, 251

ἔχω (1141) Opif 11, 14, 20, 20, 21, 21, 28, 35, 36, 41, 42, 48, 54, 57, 69, 69, 71, 77, 78, 84, 85, 87, 88, 91,

92, 94, 95, 96, 99, 99, 100, 102, 104, 104, 106, 108, 108, 109, 109, 111, 112, 128, 131, 131, 133, 138, 138, 143, 153, 155, 161, 163, 165, 171 Leg 1:8, 14, 18, 22, 28, 35, 42, 51, 57, 58, 59, 70, 70, 72, 85, 91, 92, 93, 94, 95, 103, 104 Leg 2:10, 21, 21, 22, 23, 29, 32, 40, 51, 65, 70, 77, 89, 95, 96, 102, 105 Leg 3:3, 7, 18, 33, 46, 47, 47, 53, 57, 63, 64, 67, 68, 75, 82, 83, 85, 86, 91, 93, 104, 114, 115, 121, 123, 124, 129, 140, 141, 141, 148, 148, 150, 157, 161, 173, 173, 174, 178, 183, 200, 232, 233, 234, 236, 247 Cher 6, 22, 23, 32, 33, 51, 58, 58, 62, 65, 68, 72, 91, 107, 113, 113, 114, 118, 120 Sacr 15, 19, 29, 30, 35, 39, 40, 48, 61, 63, 63, 66, 97, 102, 120, 124, 129 Det 8, 13, 14, 15, 25, 52, 59, 77, 85, 88, 92, 111, 120, 120, 124, 125, 136, 140, 154, 156, 167, 171, 171 Post 2, 4, 4, 7, 12, 12, 25, 32, 37, 42, 53, 55, 61, 62, 67, 72, 72, 74, 83, 90, 105, 109, 122, 138, 143, 155, 165, 185 Gig 7, 25, 34, 36, 42, 50, 52, 56 Deus 1, 7, 25, 27, 31, 47, 50, 57, 57, 59, 77, 80, 81, 84, 86, 100, 103, 105, 128, 129, 141, 146, 146, 162, 167, 167, 183, 183 Agr 5, 12, 34, 39, 54, 54, 57, 64, 67, 78, 82, 93, 101, 101, 118, 128, 130, 131, 134, 134, 135, 139, 149, 157, 167 Plant 7, 12, 14, 33, 37, 41, 49, 54, 56, 57, 65, 71, 72, 78, 80, 89, 100, 101, 112, 120, 125, 128, 130, 132, 135, 137 Ebr 13, 17, 28, 36, 48, 50, 52, 59, 64, 68, 92, 95, 121, 131, 134, 146, 154, 156, 164, 166, 170, 174, 177, 184, 189, 192 Sobr 9, 11, 30, 32, 35, 47, 51, 51, 56, 58 Conf 19, 33, 38, 40, 48, 52, 64, 67, 99, 106, 131, 150, 158, 163, 163, 168, 171, 178, 181, 183, 192 Migr 4, 42, 47, 49, 87, 97, 103, 121, 126, 139, 148, 165, 165, 172, 176, 189, 202 Her 14, 28, 31, 53, 56, 63, 87, 87, 88, 100, 103, 103, 105, 113, 115, 126, 144, 146, 149, 171, 198, 198, 214, 216, 219, 226, 233, 239, 244, 255, 270, 280, 304, 308, 311, 315 Congr 5, 12, 15, 15, 22, 23, 23, 24, 26, 27, 35, 38, 43, 45, 61, 71, 75, 76, 78, 122, 124, 124, 126, 128, 130, 130, 130, 131, 132, 134, 134, 135, 137, 138, 138, 139, 139, 139, 142, 147, 147 Fug 1, 5, 16, 25, 27, 35, 39, 51, 51, 51, 73, 73, 102, 102, 105, 123, 141, 145, 149, 150, 154, 169, 200, 204 Mut 7, 24, 26, 54, 74, 79, 80, 85, 87, 89, 93, 101, 101, 126, 129, 134, 135, 160, 163, 167, 167, 184, 229, 230, 260, 260, 262 Somn 1:6, 10, 11, 18, 20, 21, 21, 22, 25, 26, 27, 29, 36, 49, 53, 58, 60, 60, 71, 75, 97, 98, 101, 101, 103, 105, 114, 117, 126, 130, 133, 137, 149, 159, 173, 175, 176, 179, 179, 192, 201, 210, 216, 217, 220, 222, 236 Somn 2:4, 95, 95, 100, 100, 112, 115, 121, 123, 137, 150, 160, 218, 220, 232, 235, 245, 298, 300 Abr 37, 51, 59, 65, 67, 73, 87, 101, 105, 120, 127, 132, 146, 148, 153, 154, 183, 194, 196, 196, 203, 209, 213, 220, 224, 224, 227, 247, 263, 264, 265 Ios 11, 15, 25, 39, 53, 58, 58, 67, 67, 87, 91, 107, 109, 116, 135, 144, 145, 162, 166, 167, 176, 199, 206, 207, 209, 216, 225, 232, 242, 245, 245, 248, 257, 262, 265 Mos 1:3, 14, 20, 25, 27, 38, 45, 48, 74, 77, 80, 84, 91, 92, 92, 104, 127, 141, 147, 152, 156, 164, 167, 189, 189, 190, 193, 198, 205, 207, 225, 233, 248, 251, 257, 274, 311, 322, 325 Mos 2:7, 7, 7, 20, 59, 69, 73, 78, 84, 85, 88, 89, 91, 109, 114, 115, 117, 121, 126, 136, 140, 141, 141, 167, 167, 175, 179, 180, 181, 190, 192, 202, 213, 222, 237, 243, 246, 249, 263, 275 Decal 6, 8, 16, 21, 21, 30, 31, 49, 49, 76, 77, 95, 95, 112, 119, 122, 122, 140, 157 Spec 1:4, 13, 24, 31, 53, 55, 61, 63, 66, 71, 73, 76, 80, 84, 94, 95, 96, 102, 106, 108, 129, 133, 134, 146, 150, 152, 159, 159, 164, 182, 187, 192, 195, 200, 204, 207, 210, 215, 216, 218, 219, 224, 242, 248, 260, 260, 311, 324, 336, 342 Spec 2:13, 16, 19, 20, 25, 29, 29, 31, 37, 40, 49, 58, 67, 69, 82, 107, 110, 115, 117, 118, 124, 142, 150, 158, 163, 170, 176, 188, 200, 204, 208, 214, 215, 216, 216, 223, 228, 243, 253 Spec 3:1, 4, 9, 10, 35, 63, 70, 75, 98, 104, 115, 140, 142, 143, 151, 155, 157, 159, 166, 182, 183, 192, 197 Spec 4:5, 15, 18, 25, 30, 70, 70, 81, 101, 107, 110, 113, 122, 126, 129, 133, 139, 141, 142, 144, 152, 163, 164, 166, 170, 173, 178, 179, 182, 192, 200, 222, 237 Virt 6, 9, 10, 20, 28, 32, 34, 38, 53, 58, 79, 79, 86, 89, 100, 106, 107, 111, 115, 124, 147, 147, 162, 165, 171, 172, 186, 197, 198, 200, 208, 211, 216 Praem 2, 2, 8, 15, 20, 29, 40, 58, 61, 72, 79, 89, 90, 97, 100, 112, 135, 145, 149, 149, 159, 169, 171 Prob 2, 8, 8, 28, 30, 40, 45, 59, 61, 71, 81, 87, 96, 110, 117, 123, 124, 124, 126, 127, 141, 141, 145, 155, 159 Contempl 9, 9, 26, 30, 32, 33, 39, 45, 52, 58, 64, 75, 78, 82 Aet 2, 13, 18, 26, 27, 28, 29, 34, 37, 66, 75, 76, 80, 85, 86, 88, 92, 99, 103, 129, 133, 148, 149 Flacc 1, 7, 9, 19, 24, 35, 36, 39, 40, 43, 48, 51, 76, 78, 86, 92, 93, 94, 94, 100, 111, 119, 126, 128, 128, 131, 135, 138, 163, 170, 176, 184 Legat 2, 11, 11, 17, 27, 28, 30, 34, 58, 63, 80, 84, 99, 133, 135, 144, 152, 156, 159, 161, 167, 168, 170, 175, 177, 195, 196, 199, 211, 215, 221, 237, 245, 255, 259, 282, 282, 286, 294, 299, 299, 303, 321, 361, 366, 369 Hypoth 6:4, 6:5, 6:6, 6:9, 7:1, 7:8, 7:11, 7:13, 7:14, 7:20 Prov 2:26, 42, 57, 59, 60, 62, 62, 72 QG 1:32, 64b, 65, 77, 2:14, 14, 29, 39, 54a, 3:20a, 24, 61, 4:20, 30, 43, 51a, 51a, 86b, 88, 102a, 145, 145, 168, 173, 198, 228 QG (Par) 2:2, 2:3, 2:3, 2:4 QE 2:4, 15b, 16, 17, 38a QE isf 9, 32

ἕψω (8) Sacr 81 Mos 1:208 Mos 2:148, 156 Spec 1:223, 254 Virt 142, 144

ἕωθεν Spec 1:24 Spec 2:102, 155 Spec 4:173

ἑωθινός Spec 1:171 Spec 2:196 Contempl 28 Flacc 41, 85

ἕωλος Spec 1:220 Spec 2:46

ἑῷος (13) Cher 22, 22 Somn 1:175 Abr 226 Mos 1:263 Mos 2:20, 116 Flacc 45 Legat 8, 89, 145, 207, 256

ἕως (101) Leg 1:82, 100 Leg 2:70 Leg 3:8, 24, 25, 92, 177, 195, 218, 225, 225, 230, 230, 233 Cher 33 Sacr 3 Det 97, 128 Post 132, 132, 147, 147 Deus 3, 51, 51, 99, 134, 145, 173 Plant 97, 111 Ebr 58, 98, 105, 146 Conf 1, 27, 107, 128, 197 Migr 68, 68, 174, 208, 216 Her 84, 117, 118, 149, 264, 304, 315, 316, 316 Fug 23, 117 Mut 108, 111, 166, 215 Somn 1:3, 114, 122, 164 Somn 2:95, 152, 153, 214, 231, 232, 255, 267, 279, 290 Abr 43, 213, 233, 234 Ios 150 Mos 1:101, 128, 301 Mos 2:14, 26, 231 Decal 11 Spec 1:296 Spec 2:19 Spec 3:89, 133, 133 Spec 4:26 Virt 63 Aet 91 Flacc 71, 174 Legat 18, 242 QG 1:51 QE 2:15:1

ἕως, ἡ (ἠώς)

ἑωσφόρος Cher 22 Decal 54

Z

Z Aet 113

Ζαβουλών Fug 73 Somn 2:34

ζάλη Leg 3:227 Somn 1:256 Abr 91 Mos 1:124

Ζέλφα (6) Leg 2:94 Deus 119, 121 Congr 30, 30, 33

ζέσις Leg 3:128

ζεύγνυμι Somn 2:118

ζεῦγος Mut 234, 245, 248

Ζεύς (10) Opif 100 Prob 102, 127, 130 Aet 81 Legat 188, 265, 346 Prov 2:7, 24

ζέω (7) Sacr 15 Plant 144 Migr 210 Her 64 Somn 1:19, 19 Mos 2:280

ζῆλος (44) Leg 1:34 Leg 3:242 Post 46, 183 Deus 60 Agr 91, 105 Ebr 21, 84 Sobr 26 Conf 52, 57 Migr 164 Her 38 Congr 16, 112, 162, 166 Mut 108, 199 Somn 2:106, 176, 235 Abr 4 Mos 2:9, 31 Spec 1:55, 186 Spec 2:230, 259 Spec 3:126, 128 Spec 4:14, 124 Praem 15 Prob 22, 64 Contempl 32, 68 Flacc 41 Legat 5 Hypoth 6:4, 11:2 QG 4:168

ζηλοτυπέω Cher 14 Flacc 32

ζηλοτυπία (8) Sacr 20 Congr 180 Abr 249, 251 Spec 1:108 Spec 3:28, 28 Virt 115

ζηλότυπος Hypoth 11:14 QG 3:20a

ζηλόω (55) Leg 3:242 Sacr 100 Det 165 Post 99, 183 Plant 156 Conf 164 Her 179 Congr 23 Fug 35, 122 Mut 114 Somn 1:121 Somn 2:111, 148 Abr 38, 41, 136 Ios 44 Mos 1:32, 303, 325 Mos 2:169, 185, 193, 235 Spec 1:79, 312 Spec 2:45, 240, 259 Spec 3:11, 43, 57, 61, 137, 181 Spec 4:50 Virt 15, 194, 220 Praem 100, 116 Prob 12, 140 Contempl 1, 24, 48, 70, 82 Legat 81, 90, 119, 338 QG 1:51

ζήλωσις (7) Plant 158 Ebr 36, 131 Conf 10 Migr 201 Somn 2:47 Prob 82

ζηλωτής (27) Migr 62 Mut 93 Somn 1:124 Somn 2:39, 274 Abr 22, 33, 60 Ios 203 Mos 1:153, 160, 161 Mos 2:55, 161, 196 Spec 1:30, 333 Spec 2:170, 253 Spec 3:42, 165 Spec 4:89, 91, 199 Virt 175 Praem 11 Prob 125

ζηλωτικός Leg 3:242

ζηλωτός Mos 2:43 Spec 4:82, 115 Virt 211

ζημία (50) Det 142 Post 68, 184 Deus 103, 113 Agr 7 Plant 109 Conf 154, 195 Migr 61, 172 Mut 173 Somn 1:27, 103, 124, 147 Ios 139, 215 Mos 1:120, 141 Mos 2:53 Spec 2:87, 114, 213 Spec 3:51, 82, 106, 146, 168, 181, 197, 199 Spec 4:184 Virt 156, 169, 182 Praem 91, 99, 128 Prob 55, 55, 145 Aet 67 Legat 60, 343, 345 Hypoth 7:1 QG 4:191d, 227 QE 2:9a

ζημιόω (19) Det 52 Post 87 Gig 43 Plant 100 Ebr 22, 23 Congr 137 Fug 14 Spec 2:137 Spec 3:70, 108, 143 Spec 4:34 Virt 115 Contempl 61 Prov 2:44 QG 4:172, 179 QE 2:11a

Ζήνων Prob 53, 57, 106

Ζηνώνειος Prob 97, 160

ζητέω (133) Opif 104 Leg 1:33, 48, 91 Leg 2:103 Leg 3:46, 47, 47, 47, 47, 78, 78, 84, 97, 116, 116 Cher 122 Sacr 64 Det 5, 5, 24, 25, 26, 57, 154 Post 15, 95, 168 Gig 33 Deus 81, 93, 93, 107, 122 Agr 97 Plant 7, 80, 128, 153 Conf 14, 75 Migr 189, 218, 220, 222 Her 1, 18, 45, 63, 101, 101, 190, 238 Congr 37 Fug 55, 120, 120, 120, 126, 127, 127, 129, 130, 131, 133, 137, 140, 143, 144, 147, 153, 157, 158, 161, 164 Mut 7, 8, 11, 14, 50, 86, 143, 269 Somn 1:41, 45, 53, 55, 184, 222 Somn 2:58, 250, 301, 301 Abr 68, 87 Ios 104, 115, 174, 174, 217 Mos 1:24, 178, 207, 212, 304 Mos 2:273 Decal 1, 14, 65, 167 Spec 1:36, 39, 69 Spec 3:171 Spec 4:24 Praem 50 Prob 16, 18, 58 Contempl 75 Aet 3, 7, 32, 48 Flacc 97 Legat 91, 170, 339, 347 QG 1:62:1, 94, 4:191c QE isf 4

ζήτησις (44) Opif 54, 128, 167 Det 32 Post 15, 21, 84 Deus 70, 93 Plant 54, 79 Ebr 198 Migr 76, 89 Her 246, 253 Fug 120, 121, 141, 141, 149, 166, 175 Somn 1:24, 39, 57, 182 Somn 2:301 Abr 91 Mos 1:5, 207 Mos 2:33, 211, 219 Spec 1:32, 32, 40, 62, 345 Spec 2:164 Virt 215 Prob 68 Prov 2:51 QE isf 7

ζητητικός (8) Leg 3:3, 249 Det 76 Deus 86, 107 Conf 5 Migr 214, 216

ζοφερός Plant 110 Mut 149 Abr 205

ζόφος (7) Leg 1:46 Leg 3:171 Deus 46 Virt 164 Praem 36, 82 Flacc 167

ζοφόω Spec 2:140

ζυγάδην Opif 95 Post 62 Praem 22

ζυγομαχέω Leg 3:239

ζυγόν (8) Opif 116 Leg 3:193 Her 162, 162 Ios 140 Spec 4:193, 194 Hypoth 7:8

ζύμη (6) Congr 169 Spec 1:291, 293 Spec 2:182, 184 QE 2:14

ζυμόω (6) Spec 2:159, 179, 182, 185, 185 Contempl 81

ζῶ (302) Opif 77, 77, 79, 142, 153 Leg 1:31, 32, 32, 59, 98, 105, 107, 108, 108, 108 Leg 2:9, 11, 13, 18, 81, 81, 93 Leg 3:52, 72, 146, 161, 174, 176, 212, 240 Cher 57, 115, 117 Sacr 41, 41, 41, 41, 115, 124, 125 Det 33, 33, 48, 48, 49, 49, 70, 70, 78, 80, 82, 95, 151 Post 39, 44, 69, 70, 72, 72, 73, 82, 98, 181 Gig 10, 34 Deus 18, 123, 124, 124, 125, 125, 163 Agr 98, 154, 155 Plant 49 Ebr 155, 211, 214, 215, 216 Sobr 4 Conf 43, 161 Migr 21, 90, 128 Her 53, 53, 56, 57, 61, 82, 111, 201, 201, 242, 251, 256, 258, 315 Congr 30, 33, 86, 170, 171, 174, 176 Fug 55, 55, 55, 56, 56, 56, 59, 59, 59, 64, 77, 77, 117, 118, 198 Mut 51, 173, 201, 201, 209, 210, 210, 213, 215, 216, 216, 218, 252 Somn 1:34, 117, 125, 150 Somn 2:31, 66, 66, 94, 177, 234, 234, 235, 235, 282, 297 Abr 5, 182, 196, 230, 230, 236 Ios 17, 17, 24, 43, 154, 155, 184, 184, 189, 199, 199, 217, 255, 264, 266 Mos 1:29, 44, 49, 134, 138, 171, 193 Mos 2:223, 227, 231, 252, 281, 291 Decal 17, 17, 17, 17, 60, 67, 68, 98, 169 Spec 1:31, 105, 108, 127, 129, 153, 176, 300, 337, 337, 339, 345, 345 Spec 2:2, 44, 65, 74, 125, 129, 139, 229, 229, 243, 243, 248 Spec 3:11, 11, 26, 27, 30, 38, 50, 59, 59, 67, 71, 97, 132, 133, 142, 143, 148, 202, 204 Spec 4:21, 123, 169, 193, 195, 224, 228 Virt 91, 143, 149, 219, 221, 221 Praem 23, 70, 100, 135, 158 Prob 5, 22, 45, 59, 62, 89, 96, 96, 120, 160 Contempl 37 Aet 97, 130, 143 Flacc 8, 11, 14, 70, 84, 132, 174, 184, 187 Legat 14, 107, 131, 233, 249, 299, 329, 342, 352 Prov 2:6, 11, 22, 28, 32 QG 1:70:1, 70:2, 70:2, 76a, 2:10, 3:11a QG isf 10 QE isf 3, 19

ζωγραφέω Gig 15 Plant 27 Sobr 36

ζωγράφημα Abr 267 Decal 70 Prov 2:15

ζωγραφία (8) Opif 141 Gig 59 Plant 71 Migr 167 Somn 2:53 Ios 39 Decal 66 Spec 1:29

ζωγράφος (7) Plant 71 Sobr 35, 36, 36 Ios 39 Decal 70 Spec 1:33

ζωγρέω Ios 133 Virt 43, 111 Flacc 116

ζῳδιακός (8) Opif 112 Fug 184 Somn 2:6, 112, 113 Mos 2:124 Spec 1:87 Praem 65

ζῴδιον Somn 2:112

ζῴδιον Somn 2:112 Mos 2:123, 124, 124 Spec 1:87

ζωή (149) Opif 30, 134, 151, 153, 154, 154, 155, 156, 164, 172 Leg 1:31, 32, 35, 56, 59, 59, 59, 61 Leg 3:52, 52, 65, 107, 161, 161 Cher 1, 115 Det 48, 80, 84 Post 12, 24, 25, 39, 39, 45, 68, 69, 69, 69 Gig 14 Deus 50, 50 Agr 95, 97 Plant 19, 36, 37, 44, 44 Conf 80 Migr 21, 37 Her 42, 45, 46, 46, 47, 52, 52, 53, 54, 54, 56, 60, 63, 65, 209, 290, 292 Congr 33, 87, 93, 96 Fug 39, 58, 58, 58, 59, 61, 78, 97, 197, 198, 198, 198, 198 Mut 48, 209, 213, 213, 223 Somn 1:20, 34, 148 Somn 2:47, 66, 73 Abr 6, 84, 271 Mos 2:138 Decal 56, 87 Spec 1:31, 227, 345 Spec 2:31, 197, 262 Spec 3:4, 102, 198, 198, 201 Spec 4:91, 123, 169 Virt 32, 53, 68, 76, 132, 143, 177, 205 Praem 35, 68, 116, 122, 151 Contempl 13 Aet 74, 97, 106 Flacc 129, 147, 159, 179 Legat 20, 31, 192, 224 Prov 2:45 QG 1:70:1, 70:2, 2:59, 3:11a, 4:43, 169

ζωηφορέω QG 2:12d

ζώνη (7) Leg 2:27 Leg 3:153, 171 Her 147 Mos 1:114 Mos 2:143 QE 1:19

ζώννυμι QE 1:19

ζῳογονέω (10) Opif 124 Leg 3:3, 243 Spec 3:108 Virt 14, 134 Praem 160 Aet 66, 98 Prov 2:59

ζῳογονία Opif 65

ζῳογονικός Mos 2:84

ζῷον (391) Opif 42, 43, 52, 58, 59, 62, 64, 64, 66, 66, 67, 68, 68, 72, 73, 73, 73, 77, 83, 84, 86, 88, 113, 114, 119, 132, 133, 133, 140, 147, 149, 152, 152, 157, 162, 163, 163 Leg 1:4, 12, 28, 30, 30, 69, 71 Leg 2:71, 75, 75, 76, 96, 104 Leg 3:30, 43, 57, 57, 75, 76, 76, 80, 99, 130, 130, 223, 223, 224, 239 Cher 58, 62 Sacr 15, 25, 46, 47, 48, 85, 97, 102, 103, 104, 112, 115 Det 38, 49, 55, 78, 82, 83, 139, 151, 151, 154, 154 Post 3, 103, 104, 148, 161, 171 Gig 7, 8, 11 Deus 38, 41, 44, 44, 47, 48, 107, 119 Agr 8, 51, 67, 71, 74, 76, 90, 95, 103, 115, 130, 131, 145 Plant 12, 12, 14, 15, 16, 151 Ebr 13, 69, 101, 106, 110, 144, 171, 175, 183 Conf 6, 6, 7, 134, 176, 195 Migr 47, 185 Her 110, 115, 115, 137, 137, 139, 140, 151, 154, 154, 155, 211, 215, 234 Congr 4, 17, 30, 61, 95, 96, 97, 133 Fug 13, 182 Mut 63, 69, 148, 150, 221, 246, 247, 264 Somn 1:29, 35, 103, 108, 135, 135, 135, 137, 161, 198, 203 Somn 2:122, 132, 260, 262, 288 Abr 1, 32, 41, 45, 159, 173, 266, 266, 267 Ios 2 Mos 1:23, 62, 77, 108, 109, 110, 119, 121, 127, 130, 130, 131, 132, 133, 145, 184, 192, 204, 212, 272, 272 Mos 2:30, 34, 60, 62, 64, 65, 126, 156, 162, 262, 290 Decal 33, 76, 79, 107, 115, 132, 134, 160 Spec 1:6, 10, 16, 27, 34, 74, 79, 92, 136, 161, 162, 165, 177, 189, 198, 202, 208, 210, 210, 213, 228, 233, 240, 248, 251, 253, 258, 260, 267, 291, 295, 322, 338, 339 Spec 2:35, 36, 36, 69, 74, 83, 84, 89, 144, 146, 154, 169, 173, 181, 205 Spec 3:43, 44, 47, 57, 108, 118, 191 Spec 4:11, 13, 14, 35, 37, 37, 38, 86, 105, 106, 107, 116, 118, 121, 128, 129, 203, 206 Virt 81, 103, 117, 125, 137, 138, 140, 146, 155, 156, 160, 204 Praem 9, 13, 22, 41, 68, 88, 90, 90, 91, 92, 125, 132 Prob 75, 121, 131 Contempl 3, 8, 78 Aet 4, 4, 20, 23, 26, 34, 35, 35, 45, 62, 66, 66, 68, 74, 74, 75, 95, 95, 97, 100, 117, 125, 128, 130, 131 Legat 76, 80 Hypoth 7:7, 7:9 Prov 2:14, 33, 43, 64, 68, 69, 69, 71 QG 1:20, 21, 31, 2:13a, 17b, 39, 3:3, 12, 4:51b

ζῳοπλαστέω Opif 62, 67 Decal 120 Spec 3:33

ζῳοπλάστης (8) Leg 2:73 Leg 3:88 Sacr 108 Det 80 Her 106 Mut 56 Spec 1:10 QG (Par) 2:7

ζῳοτοκέω Gig 11

ζῳοτόκος Her 211

ζῳοτροφέω Migr 210 Somn 1:136 Spec 1:136

ζῳοφόρος (6) Mos 2:123, 126, 133 Spec 2:142, 177, 178

ζῳοφυτέω Spec 2:169 Spec 4:217

ζωπυρέω (38) Opif 41 Leg 2:26 Sacr 55, 123 Det 74, 95, 178 Plant 88 Migr 16, 122, 123 Her 58, 309 Mut 209 Somn 1:51 Somn 2:184, 186 Abr 23, 213 Ios 4, 7, 15, 41, 168 Mos 1:242, 309 Decal 35 Spec 1:50, 285 Spec 2:160, 192 Virt 197 Praem 12 Prob 71 Aet 86 Flacc 153 Legat 325, 337

ζώπυρον Leg 3:186 Mos 1:186 Spec 2:67 Flacc 11

ζωτικός (17) Opif 30 Det 82, 82, 92 Deus 129 Abr 140 Mos 1:100, 189 Mos 2:143 Spec 1:218 Spec 2:172 Virt 93 Praem 144 Aet 128 Legat 125 QG 2:15a, 59

ζῳώδης Abr 149

H

H Aet 113

ἤ (2654) Opif 2, 2, 4, 7, 8, 8, 8, 11, 11, 17, 17, 20, 23, 24, 24, 26, 26, 26, 26, 26, 26, 37, 40, 45, 45, 45, 46, 48, 54, 58, 58, 58, 58, 58, 58, 58, 58, 58, 58, 62, 62, 63, 63, 64, 66, 67, 72, 78, 79, 79, 80, 80, 80, 80, 85, 89, 91, 91, 92, 92, 111, 111, 112, 113, 114, 132, 132, 134, 134, 134, 135, 137, 142, 146, 146, 150, 150, 154, 154, 161, 162, 164, 168, 172 Leg 1:2, 64 Leg 2:3, 3, 3, 6, 7, 7, 7, 15, 16, 16, 17, 18, 18, 18, 19, 20, 24, 26, 43, 46, 63, 65, 68, 68, 68, 69, 70, 71, 71, 71, 71, 79, 85 Leg 3:5, 5, 5, 5, 10, 13, 36, 47, 53, 57, 57, 57, 57, 57, 57, 57, 57, 57, 58, 69, 77, 80, 87, 87, 87, 87, 87, 91, 98, 99, 101, 101, 101, 101, 101, 119, 119, 119, 121, 121, 121, 121, 121, 121, 125, 141, 161, 162, 167, 167, 168, 171, 183, 183, 186, 189, 189, 206, 206, 206, 206, 206, 206, 206, 206, 221, 221, 224, 227, 227, 229, 229, 230, 236, 241, 242, 242, 248, 248 Cher 14, 14, 15, 15, 15, 15, 16, 17, 17, 33, 33, 36, 37, 38, 38, 41, 42, 53, 55, 62, 62, 65, 65, 68, 68, 68, 68, 69, 75, 79, 79, 80, 80, 80, 80, 81, 81, 89, 94, 100, 100, 107, 115, 115, 116, 117, 121, 121, 122, 122, 127 Sacr 2, 2, 2, 9, 9, 17, 24, 24, 24, 24, 25, 33, 34, 47, 49, 56, 66, 72, 72, 76, 79, 79, 79, 85, 90, 90, 98, 106, 106, 111, 112, 116, 121, 122, 124, 124, 125, 125, 125, 130, 132, 132, 132, 135, 136, 138 Det 7, 7, 10, 13, 16, 16, 18, 19, 19, 19, 20, 20, 20, 23, 26, 26, 28, 32, 32, 33, 39, 46, 46, 49, 49, 49, 57, 57, 58, 62, 69, 74, 75, 75, 75, 75, 75, 77, 87, 87, 87, 87, 87, 88, 90, 98, 98, 98, 99, 99, 99, 101, 105, 110, 113, 113, 119, 119, 120, 120, 127, 127, 134, 134, 134, 136, 137, 137, 140, 140, 140, 140, 141, 143, 144, 145, 146, 147, 147, 151, 153, 157, 157, 164, 164, 172, 172, 174, 175, 175, 176 Post 2, 2, 5, 9, 22, 40, 42, 42, 46, 46, 49, 50, 60, 60, 62, 68, 68, 68, 73, 82, 82, 90, 90, 90, 93, 100, 100, 105, 108, 109, 109, 109, 109, 110, 110, 110, 110, 112, 112, 115, 116, 116, 116, 117, 117, 117, 117, 117, 117, 117, 119, 119, 119, 119, 119, 126, 141, 142, 142, 142, 142, 143, 144, 159, 159, 159, 160, 161, 161, 161, 161, 163, 163, 163, 167, 168, 171, 172, 178 Gig 11, 15, 15, 15, 20, 26, 32, 48, 48, 48, 51 Deus 4, 16, 27, 27, 27, 29, 29, 39, 43, 43, 69, 69, 71, 71, 71, 71, 78, 78, 90, 90, 104, 112, 115, 134, 134, 134, 150, 150, 152, 152, 157, 157, 157, 160, 169, 169, 170, 170, 170, 170, 170, 172, 177 Agr 8, 10, 11, 11, 17, 22, 22, 22, 22, 48, 48, 48, 61, 66, 68, 76, 83, 85, 87, 87, 88, 91, 93, 97, 99, 100, 110, 113, 113, 113, 115, 115, 115, 118, 118, 121, 136, 141, 146, 146, 150, 151, 152, 152, 154, 155, 155, 157, 157, 175 Plant 7, 7, 32, 32, 32, 33, 43, 57, 62, 64, 67, 67, 69, 71, 71, 81, 84, 84, 97, 101, 101, 107, 107, 107, 107, 112, 112, 116, 119, 127, 127, 128, 133, 133, 133, 133, 133, 133, 144, 146, 146, 146, 152, 152, 159, 159, 159, 163, 170, 176, 177, 177, 177 Ebr 13, 13, 28, 28, 32, 42, 47, 49, 54, 57, 58, 62, 67, 68, 73, 75, 75, 79, 79, 83, 87, 94, 101, 101, 101, 102, 104, 104, 116, 116, 121, 127, 129, 129, 131, 131, 131, 131, 135, 137, 138, 138, 139, 145, 145, 152, 155, 158, 166, 166, 166, 167, 167, 168, 169, 169, 173, 174, 177, 182, 184, 187, 188, 190, 190, 192, 192, 192, 192, 192, 195, 197, 197, 197, 198, 199, 199, 200, 211, 218, 218, 219, 221, 221 Sobr 3, 5, 6, 6, 6, 7, 22, 36, 36, 36, 38, 38, 38, 43, 44, 55, 55, 58, 67, 67, 69, 69 Conf 6, 6, 7, 7, 12, 16, 16, 16, 27, 38, 45, 45, 45, 46, 48, 53, 53, 53, 53, 54, 55, 59, 67, 71, 83, 93, 93, 93, 95, 95, 95, 97, 106, 114, 114, 114, 114, 115, 116, 116, 117, 122, 123, 123, 126, 126, 129, 134, 134, 134, 134, 141, 157, 157, 157, 163, 163, 163, 163, 170, 192, 192, 192 Migr 5, 5, 11, 12, 12, 12, 16, 16, 38, 40, 46, 47, 48, 49, 57, 59, 60, 60, 60, 60, 64, 68, 69, 74, 74, 75, 77, 77, 83, 87, 90, 90, 91, 91, 91, 91, 91, 91, 91, 102, 112, 112, 117, 118, 118, 118, 118, 120, 130, 134, 136, 136, 137, 138, 148, 156, 156, 157, 163, 169, 171, 172, 172, 172, 172, 179, 179, 181, 184, 185, 195, 210, 217, 218, 219, 219, 219, 219, 219 Her 5, 7, 7, 13, 15, 15, 15, 20, 20, 21, 21, 31, 31, 34, 42, 44, 44, 67, 81, 81, 82, 89, 91, 91, 91, 104, 109, 110, 111, 115, 126, 142, 143, 153, 162, 162, 183, 191, 243, 249, 249, 260, 274, 274, 290, 291, 297, 301 Congr 4, 8, 13, 19, 32, 32, 46, 46, 46, 46, 46, 46, 46, 50, 54, 56, 66, 71, 71, 112, 115, 129, 129, 129, 135, 145, 150, 150, 152, 159, 167, 169, 169, 170, 172, 172, 173, 177 Fug 15, 16, 22, 22, 24, 27, 28, 28, 41, 51, 52, 55, 80, 81, 82, 83, 84, 90, 122, 128, 130, 146, 150, 151, 151, 151, 153, 153, 153, 153, 153, 153, 153, 153, 153, 162, 162, 162, 163, 164, 164, 164, 164, 164, 167, 168, 171, 172, 191, 198, 203, 203, 205 Mut 10, 35, 36, 40, 40, 40, 40, 46, 50, 50, 50, 50, 50, 50, 60, 63, 63, 64, 64, 72, 82, 88, 145, 147, 158, 159, 159, 163, 165, 165, 165, 173, 179, 181, 181, 181, 188, 194, 195, 195, 202, 205, 205, 207, 211, 215, 217, 219, 221, 221, 221, 221, 223, 225, 225, 225, 225, 227, 227, 233, 234, 235, 235, 239, 240, 240, 240, 240, 240, 243, 245, 248, 253, 256, 256, 264, 267 Somn 1:21, 21, 21, 22, 22, 22, 23, 23, 27, 29, 30, 30, 30, 30, 30, 30, 30, 30, 31, 31, 31, 31, 37, 37, 53, 53, 55, 55, 83, 95, 95, 97, 98, 98, 98, 98, 98, 99, 99, 100, 101, 110, 110, 111, 112, 112, 115, 117, 125, 132, 139, 145, 150, 152, 152, 155, 157, 163, 163, 164, 167, 167, 167, 170, 177, 177, 177, 181, 183, 184, 184, 185, 193, 222, 222, 236, 244, 244 Somn 2:5, 7, 22, 23, 36, 43, 46, 48, 53, 53, 53, 54, 56, 60, 62, 62, 62, 62, 62, 68, 68, 71, 73, 76, 86, 86, 87, 87, 89, 100, 115, 125, 125, 125, 125, 125, 125, 125, 126, 130, 130, 131, 131, 133, 133, 136, 140, 147, 147, 147, 152, 152, 152, 160, 166, 166, 166, 166, 166, 166, 170, 170, 170, 176, 180, 180, 184, 192, 193, 193, 200, 202, 202, 221, 221, 226, 228, 228, 250, 251, 251, 254, 254, 255, 257, 296, 296, 296, 296, 296, 300, 301 Abr 1, 1, 1, 1, 1, 5, 19, 23, 24, 24, 27, 31, 31, 31, 38, 53, 54, 54, 54, 59, 63, 65, 65, 66, 67, 98, 101, 104, 106, 107, 110, 113, 113, 118, 119, 119, 122, 122, 128, 128, 140, 140, 140, 148, 148, 148, 148, 148, 149, 149, 162, 162, 162, 162, 163, 164, 172, 179, 179, 179, 179, 186, 186, 186, 187, 187, 188, 188, 193, 195, 195, 197, 197, 197, 197, 202, 202, 202, 202, 208, 209, 228, 230, 233, 236, 238, 238, 238, 238, 239, 239, 239, 239, 239, 239, 239, 239, 243, 246, 259, 263, 263, 263, 263, 266, 266, 269, 273, 275 Ios 4, 17, 20, 24, 25, 27, 28, 30, 30, 30, 30, 30, 34, 39, 48, 53, 61, 67, 70, 71, 76, 76, 76, 77, 77, 81, 81, 89, 94, 94, 99, 101, 101, 126, 138, 165, 165, 174, 174, 174, 187, 187, 215, 223, 231, 236, 248, 248, 249, 250, 262, 266, 269 Mos 1:3, 7, 9, 19, 22, 22, 26, 27, 27, 32, 36, 39, 45, 45, 49, 49, 58, 58, 69, 90, 102, 102, 110, 122, 123, 124, 128, 141, 146, 159, 161, 161, 167, 167, 171, 176, 183, 183, 186, 192, 192, 192, 192, 192, 194, 202, 208, 221, 224, 224, 224, 229, 243, 251, 254, 270, 282, 282, 284, 291, 296, 305, 307, 307, 308, 308, 310, 311, 311, 321, 321, 324, 324, 333, 333 Mos 2:2, 2, 12, 13, 13, 16, 16, 16, 16, 16, 16, 16, 16, 16, 16, 19, 19, 19, 22, 34, 36, 39, 51, 51, 51, 51, 66, 70, 124, 137, 138, 138, 139, 139, 139, 139, 144, 156, 156, 169, 169,

191, 199, 200, 211, 211, 211, 216, 218, 219, 219, 222, 232, 238, 249, 264, 270, 273, 273 Decal 4, 11, 12, 31, 31, 31, 31, 31, 31, 32, 32, 39, 40, 42, 42, 44, 46, 52, 52, 59, 59, 68, 68, 77, 77, 79, 79, 90, 98, 105, 114, 118, 118, 118, 118, 118, 133, 140, 150, 151, 151, 151, 151, 153, 153, 153, 155, 158, 162, 162, 171, 176 Spec 1:25, 27, 30, 33, 33, 33, 33, 33, 47, 50, 63, 67, 67, 77, 77, 80, 80, 80, 80, 80, 106, 106, 112, 112, 114, 114, 116, 117, 117, 117, 117, 118, 119, 129, 130, 142, 156, 157, 167, 167, 167, 167, 174, 190, 191, 198, 198, 200, 208, 214, 214, 215, 223, 226, 229, 233, 235, 235, 235, 236, 236, 244, 244, 259, 261, 265, 265, 277, 277, 278, 278, 278, 278, 278, 283, 283, 283, 283, 286, 288, 292, 295, 297, 299, 300, 300, 300, 300, 301, 301, 301, 301, 302, 303, 307, 308, 308, 316, 316, 316, 316, 316, 317, 320, 322, 328, 332, 332, 332, 341 Spec 2:2, 4, 6, 9, 9, 10, 10, 12, 12, 12, 13, 13, 13, 13, 16, 16, 16, 16, 16, 19, 19, 20, 20, 20, 20, 24, 26, 26, 26, 26, 28, 30, 30, 32, 32, 32, 34, 35, 35, 44, 44, 44, 51, 72, 77, 87, 95, 95, 96, 105, 105, 114, 122, 122, 131, 132, 143, 147, 158, 172, 172, 172, 172, 172, 172, 175, 178, 179, 181, 183, 183, 183, 185, 189, 195, 196, 197, 207, 208, 215, 221, 224, 229, 231, 232, 235, 239, 240, 243, 244, 246, 246, 246, 246, 246, 246, 247, 248, 253, 255, 255, 255, 255, 255, 258, 262 Spec 3:1, 1, 1, 3, 10, 17, 23, 26, 26, 26, 26, 26, 30, 30, 32, 34, 35, 36, 47, 49, 49, 52, 52, 53, 61, 61, 62, 62, 63, 64, 64, 64, 66, 66, 67, 67, 68, 70, 70, 72, 78, 85, 85, 87, 87, 87, 88, 89, 92, 92, 92, 92, 92, 95, 103, 103, 104, 105, 105, 105, 105, 106, 109, 113, 113, 114, 141, 142, 144, 145, 145, 147, 147, 147, 147, 147, 148, 150, 153, 153, 154, 154, 156, 158, 158, 158, 158, 158, 158, 159, 159, 159, 161, 161, 164, 165, 165, 168, 172, 172, 180, 180, 181, 181, 181, 183, 183, 183, 183, 184, 190, 190, 191, 191, 195, 204 Spec 4:2, 5, 6, 11, 17, 22, 22, 22, 23, 23, 28, 28, 29, 29, 29, 29, 34, 34, 37, 37, 38, 38, 54, 54, 55, 55, 59, 59, 67, 67, 73, 73, 79, 79, 82, 84, 84, 84, 90, 90, 95, 99, 100, 100, 102, 106, 106, 109, 109, 110, 110, 111, 111, 112, 113, 113, 113, 116, 116, 121, 121, 127, 129, 133, 141, 146, 147, 147, 152, 154, 154, 160, 163, 190, 192, 206, 207, 211, 211, 225, 226, 227, 230 Virt 3, 3, 18, 26, 28, 28, 30, 30, 30, 30, 30, 31, 34, 37, 45, 47, 52, 53, 53, 54, 54, 61, 61, 61, 62, 66, 77, 88, 90, 96, 96, 111, 112, 112, 113, 115, 117, 122, 123, 124, 124, 128, 133, 135, 135, 144, 144, 154, 154, 154, 154, 157, 160, 166, 166, 169, 179, 188, 188, 189, 190, 193, 193, 193, 208, 213, 215, 217, 221, 227, 227 Praem 5, 12, 12, 27, 36, 40, 40, 40, 44, 45, 45, 45, 55, 57, 70, 71, 71, 71, 80, 80, 82, 85, 87, 87, 88, 93, 94, 97, 97, 109, 109, 110, 112, 114, 121, 121, 121, 127, 129, 129, 132, 132, 139, 139, 142, 149, 153, 159, 163, 165, 167 Prob 4, 4, 7, 7, 8, 8, 9, 15, 19, 19, 26, 27, 31, 33, 33, 33, 33, 36, 37, 37, 37, 37, 40, 41, 44, 45, 45, 45, 46, 46, 47, 47, 49, 49, 54, 54, 55, 55, 55, 55, 56, 60, 60, 60, 62, 62, 67, 67, 67, 68, 68, 69, 77, 78, 78, 78, 78, 78, 78, 78, 78, 78, 80, 86, 86, 89, 91, 96, 97, 101, 104, 104, 104, 105, 106, 106, 106, 111, 111, 112, 114, 121, 130, 130, 136, 136, 138, 140, 145, 146, 157, 157, 158, 158, 159, 159, 159, 159, 160 Contempl 1, 2, 5, 5, 5, 7, 12, 13, 14, 15, 19, 20, 26, 31, 31, 33, 34, 38, 40, 48, 49, 50, 51, 51, 52, 56, 59, 62, 68, 75, 75, 75, 80, 80, 89, 89 Aet 2, 2, 2, 2, 4, 4, 6, 11, 11, 11, 14, 14, 20, 20, 20, 20, 21, 21, 28, 36, 36, 36, 36, 38, 39, 40, 40, 41, 41, 41, 42, 46, 47, 47, 47, 48, 62, 62, 67, 67, 68, 74, 79, 79, 90, 90, 95, 95, 96, 105, 105, 105, 106, 107, 107, 107, 107, 108, 108, 125, 129, 135, 139, 144, 147, 147, 148, 148, 148 Flacc 1, 12, 12, 23, 25, 29, 30, 32, 35, 43, 43, 49, 50, 59, 60, 64, 66, 66, 68, 85, 93, 93, 98, 98, 113, 127, 130, 131, 134, 137, 149, 149, 159, 159, 159, 160, 163, 171, 173, 186 Legat 5, 5, 5, 12, 19, 21, 27, 27, 28, 38, 39, 42, 42, 42, 42, 42, 42, 42, 44, 44, 44, 45, 45, 48, 48, 48, 48, 50, 58, 62, 70, 84, 89, 89, 92, 101, 103, 105, 105, 109, 110, 111, 118, 119, 121, 122, 123, 123, 124, 125, 127, 127, 127, 127, 127, 130, 133, 138, 138, 140, 142, 142, 142, 147, 150, 150, 152, 158, 158, 160, 160, 191, 192, 192, 194, 195, 195, 198, 199, 209, 211, 211, 224, 230, 230, 232, 237, 240, 240, 240, 240, 242, 249, 249, 257, 260, 261, 261, 261, 262, 264, 275, 277, 280, 285, 287, 290, 292, 292, 293, 295, 298, 299, 301, 301, 301, 307, 307, 307, 307, 325, 327, 327, 327, 327, 334, 334, 334, 334, 334, 335, 335, 341, 343, 343, 343, 343, 351, 366, 367 Hypoth 6:4, 6:4, 6:4, 6:4, 6:5, 6:6, 6:8, 6:8, 6:9, 6:9, 7:1, 7:1, 7:1, 7:2, 7:2, 7:4, 7:6, 7:7, 7:13, 7:17, 7:19, 11:3, 11:13, 11:14, 11:14, 11:17, 11:17 Prov 1, 1, 2:1, 5, 17, 17, 17, 20, 21, 21, 21, 23, 26, 26, 33, 33, 33, 34, 34, 37, 37, 41, 41, 43, 44, 44, 50, 50, 61 QG 1:1, 3, 17b, 21, 55a, 60:2, 60:2, 64a, 73, 73, 2:15b, 16, 30, 54a, 54a, 54a, 54a, 54b, 54c, 62, 74, 3:8, 11a, 27, 43, 4:23, 59, 72, 74, 76b, 76b, 80, 97:1, 161, 163:1, 169, 171, 191b, 191b, 193, 7*, 8*, 206a, 206b, 206b QG isf 2, 5, 5, 5, 9 QG (Par) 2:2, 2:2, 2:7 QE 1:7a, 2:2, 2, 4, 6a, 18, 25d, 38b, 40, 105 QE isf 3, 3, 6, 16, 16, 16, 16, 19, 29

ἦ (7) Leg 3:203 Det 32 Post 9 Spec 2:132 Contempl 6 Aet 83 Hypoth 7:9

ἡβάω (23) Opif 153 Cher 114 Post 71 Agr 153, 171 Plant 151, 161 Ebr 179 Sobr 56 Her 296 Congr 85, 162 Fug 146 Somn 1:11, 26, 199 Mos 1:216, 306 Mos 2:222 Prob 122 Aet 97 QG 2:5b QG (Par) 2:5

ἥβη Opif 104

ἡβηδόν (16) Fug 90 Abr 229, 234 Mos 1:135, 167, 218, 261, 303 Mos 2:172 Spec 1:79 Spec 2:134 Spec 4:222 Virt 2, 186 Praem 95, 147

ἡγεμονεύω (16) Leg 3:73, 146 Sacr 9 Sobr 13 Conf 54 Congr 2, 32 Fug 69 Mut 24, 80 Abr 84 Ios 255 Mos 1:152 Mos 2:30 Spec 1:207 QG 1:3

ἡγεμονία (105) Opif 87, 142 Leg 1:72 Leg 3:89, 205 Cher 29, 108 Post 115, 129 Deus 114 Agr 46, 47, 84 Plant 67 Ebr 126, 216 Sobr 25 Migr 186 Her 271 Fug 11, 20, 73, 111, 147 Mut 17, 22, 221 Somn 1:77, 162, 163 Abr 25, 220, 263, 263 Ios 9, 38, 119, 132, 135, 166, 270 Mos 1:13, 60, 149 Mos 2:29, 65, 175 Decal 136 Spec 1:215, 311, 334 Spec 2:20, 56, 134, 208, 233 Spec 3:18, 111, 184 Spec 4:82, 147, 151, 164, 169 Virt 55, 57, 72, 161, 162, 188 Praem 9, 53, 56, 65, 97 Prob 42, 124, 154 Flacc 11, 12, 104 Legat 8, 27, 28, 30, 32, 32, 39, 44, 47, 55, 58, 60, 63, 68, 68, 141, 143, 153, 168, 231, 259, 356 Prov 2:1, 2

ἡγεμονικός (83) Opif 84, 117, 117, 119, 139, 147, 154 Leg 1:12, 39, 39, 59, 61, 61, 62, 65 Leg 2:6 Leg 3:89, 188 Sacr 104, 112, 119, 134, 136, 137, 139 Post 104, 108, 126, 127, 137 Deus 45, 84, 88 Agr 59 Plant 31, 44 Ebr 8, 115 Her 55, 55 Fug 110, 165, 182, 182, 182 Mut 123 Somn 2:123 Abr 57, 99, 129, 218, 219 Mos 1:77, 318 Mos 2:82, 127, 211, 239 Spec 1:171, 200, 213, 214, 258, 305 Spec 2:21, 173 Spec 3:195 Spec 4:69, 123, 137 Virt 85, 187 Praem 1 Flacc 4 Legat 53, 54, 56, 56, 149, 256 Prov 2:3 QG (Par) 2:3 QE 2:50a

ἡγεμονίς (23) Opif 126 Leg 1:65 Leg 3:13, 38, 191 Cher 41 Sacr 44 Post 128 Plant 122 Ebr 153 Abr 27, 150, 164

Mos 1:124, 189 Decal 119 Spec 1:29 Spec 2:154 Spec 4:96, 135, 168 Virt 95 Flacc 158

ἡγεμών (271) Opif 17, 30, 69, 69, 75, 78, 83, 100, 100, 100, 116, 135, 144, 148, 148, 165, 165 Leg 3:30, 81, 88, 110, 150, 167, 224, 232 Cher 83, 83, 99, 107, 117 Sacr 2, 9, 22, 40, 45, 54, 59, 104, 105, 106, 129, 130 Det 25, 29, 30, 34, 114, 145, 155, 168 Post 18, 92, 92 Gig 38, 46 Deus 19, 113, 174 Agr 8, 31, 33, 45, 57, 80, 87 Plant 2, 14, 60, 69, 91, 159 Ebr 113, 121, 131, 195, 199 Sobr 60, 62, 69 Conf 59, 95, 133, 149, 170, 174 Migr 8, 57, 62, 104, 171, 174, 219 Her 7, 117, 186, 205, 278 Fug 32, 69, 74, 103, 114, 124, 190 Mut 13, 16, 22, 45, 61, 63, 107, 112, 127, 129, 151, 153, 221, 240 Somn 1:30, 44, 73, 87, 93, 148, 162, 168, 198, 198, 240, 256 Somn 2:10, 21, 62, 120, 153, 207, 227, 267, 276, 288, 291, 293 Abr 30, 74, 83, 88, 227 Ios 132, 151, 177, 193, 249, 255 Mos 1:26, 36, 71, 86, 148, 160, 166, 180, 193, 198, 200, 228, 236, 243, 255, 284, 290, 318, 329 Mos 2:43, 59, 65, 67, 88, 122, 166, 168, 187, 215, 234, 238, 273, 277, 283 Decal 90, 155, 166, 167, 167, 178 Spec 1:18, 32, 34, 34, 56, 79, 97, 142 Spec 2:22, 61, 92 Spec 3:16 Spec 4:92, 153, 172, 172, 175, 176, 180, 190, 201 Virt 7, 32, 42, 61, 70, 169, 205 Praem 27, 29, 41, 57, 75, 119 Prob 20, 20, 30, 62, 118, 146 Contempl 83 Aet 1, 1, 13, 65 Flacc 5, 19, 31, 100, 131, 133, 140, 143, 163 Legat 19, 24, 32, 44, 69, 75, 144, 144, 166, 247, 250, 256, 287, 318 Hypoth 11:8, 11:15 Prov 2:12, 61 QG 1:20, 66, 2:34a QE 2:6a, 25a QE isf 11

ἡγέομαι (92) Opif 131, 144 Leg 1:51 Leg 2:18, 68 Leg 3:37, 71, 90, 177, 189, 191, 245 Cher 70, 73 Sacr 8, 20, 50, 71, 76 Det 21 Post 101 Deus 106 Agr 59, 62, 67 Plant 57, 69, 132, 161 Ebr 209 Sobr 15, 60, 62, 67 Conf 123, 160 Migr 14, 17, 175, 203 Her 42, 82, 100 Congr 8, 35, 162, 164 Fug 70 Mut 136 Somn 2:109 Abr 8, 116, 258 Ios 15, 202 Mos 1:45, 50, 255, 306 Mos 2:27, 51, 69, 247, 249 Spec 1:8, 170, 314 Spec 2:12, 48 Spec 3:206 Spec 4:191, 200 Virt 15, 197 Prob 69 Contempl 70 Aet 38, 138 Flacc 46, 185 Legat 119 Hypoth 0:1, 6:2 Prov 2:21, 70 QG 1:17a, 2:48, 4:172, 191b QG isf 8 QE 2:21, 21

ἡδέ Aet 37

ἤδη (304) Opif 24, 24, 36, 50, 57, 59, 64, 66, 134, 148, 166, 171 Leg 1:10 Leg 2:22, 43, 44, 95, 96 Leg 3:83, 87, 89, 138, 173, 191, 238, 245 Cher 7, 32, 53, 54, 84 Sacr 16, 25, 33, 66, 125, 126 Det 12, 89, 106, 135, 172, 176 Post 13, 14, 96, 115, 152, 153, 162 Deus 147, 149 Agr 18, 36, 93, 125, 126, 148, 158, 174 Plant 65, 93, 149, 168 Ebr 58, 103, 110, 133, 163, 177 Sobr 8, 9, 15, 22, 29, 36, 44 Conf 7, 13, 91, 152, 155, 176, 181, 196 Migr 26, 27, 44, 55, 98, 120, 139, 150, 177, 214 Her 19, 71, 158, 219, 255, 292 Congr 73, 84, 106, 137 Fug 3, 11, 104, 107, 145, 157, 162, 197 Mut 9, 106, 163, 222 Somn 1:10, 19, 87, 133, 136, 172, 195, 216 Somn 2:93, 110, 143, 147, 148, 152, 191 Abr 9, 37, 111, 133, 140, 156, 168, 177, 182, 213, 233, 248, 248, 252, 256 Ios 37, 46, 50, 54, 87, 121, 127, 161, 163, 164, 170, 178, 182, 189, 200, 235, 236, 260, 267 Mos 1:15, 20, 25, 35, 54, 64, 77, 82, 87, 94, 104, 169, 178, 199, 210, 214, 217, 230, 244, 266, 268, 269, 275, 292, 306, 320 Mos 2:25, 29, 45, 66, 72, 157, 252, 252, 288, 291 Decal 50, 72, 84, 108 Spec 1:12, 27, 46, 56, 137, 192, 267, 268, 336 Spec 2:55, 94, 158, 197, 205, 213 Spec 3:6, 33, 87, 96, 98, 108, 117, 164, 169, 187, 200 Spec 4:16, 19, 67, 72, 85, 90, 158 Virt 8, 49, 68, 109, 118, 130, 137 Praem 128 Prob 26, 38, 123 Contempl 13, 56 Aet 56, 85, 118, 118, 120, 129 Flacc 3, 27, 41, 61, 68, 83, 97, 100, 108, 121, 124, 126, 140, 175 Legat 10, 11, 27, 28, 66, 107, 109, 114, 181, 187, 208, 218, 243, 244, 260, 265, 267, 300, 337, 342, 345, 353, 354, 356 Hypoth 7:20, 11:3 Prov 2:30, 39, 58 QG 1:72, 85, 2:65

ἥδομαι (30) Leg 3:200, 200, 250 Sacr 24 Det 157 Fug 138 Mut 136, 171 Somn 2:266 Abr 21, 148 Ios 196 Mos 1:20, 167, 248 Mos 2:32 Spec 2:138, 258 Praem 71, 129 Flacc 88, 89, 98, 124, 172 Legat 244, 285, 361 QG 1:29, 4:173

ἡδονή (422) Opif 54, 79, 152, 153, 157, 160, 161, 161, 162, 164, 165, 165, 166, 167 Leg 1:43, 69, 75, 86, 86, 86, 104 Leg 2:8, 17, 17, 18, 26, 29, 48, 71, 72, 73, 74, 74, 74, 75, 75, 76, 76, 76, 77, 77, 79, 79, 81, 84, 84, 85, 87, 87, 88, 90, 92, 92, 93, 93, 105, 105, 106, 106, 107, 107, 107, 107, 108 Leg 3:14, 21, 25, 25, 37, 61, 61, 62, 63, 64, 66, 68, 75, 76, 76, 77, 107, 108, 111, 111, 111, 112, 112, 113, 113, 113, 114, 114, 116, 116, 116, 138, 138, 138, 138, 139, 139, 139, 140, 141, 142, 142, 143, 143, 144, 148, 156, 160, 160, 160, 161, 182, 182, 183, 184, 184, 184, 185, 185, 188, 189, 189, 236, 237, 239, 240, 242, 246, 250, 251 Cher 12, 62, 71, 92, 93, 105 Sacr 20, 28, 30, 30, 33, 33, 35, 45, 49 Det 9, 16, 26, 26, 33, 34, 46, 95, 95, 98, 110, 113, 156, 157 Post 26, 52, 56, 71, 72, 101, 116, 116, 119, 122, 135, 155, 159, 164, 179, 181, 183 Gig 17, 18, 33, 35, 40, 43, 44, 60 Deus 18, 71, 98, 111, 137, 143, 168, 170 Agr 17, 22, 23, 24, 25, 37, 41, 59, 83, 84, 91, 97, 97, 98, 100, 101, 103, 103, 105, 108, 108 Ebr 8, 71, 102, 165, 176, 209, 212, 215, 222 Sobr 23, 61 Conf 7, 48, 52, 85, 90, 93, 112, 117, 144, 145 Migr 9, 14, 18, 19, 29, 60, 65, 92, 119, 143, 217, 219 Her 38, 48, 48, 49, 57, 77, 154, 269 Congr 12, 27, 57, 59, 66, 81, 84, 169, 172 Fug 3, 25, 32, 33, 35, 39, 148, 148 Mut 72, 89, 170, 214, 226 Somn 1:124, 199 Somn 2:9, 13, 13, 16, 48, 60, 69, 106, 122, 150, 156, 182, 209, 214, 276, 278 Abr 96, 100, 133, 147, 164, 196, 236, 238 Ios 43, 61, 63, 64, 73, 77, 79, 112, 153, 154, 154, 202 Mos 1:11, 28, 154, 181, 187, 204, 235, 248, 285, 295, 301 Mos 2:23, 58, 139, 225, 257 Decal 45, 143, 151, 153 Spec 1:9, 9, 9, 36, 74, 150, 176, 193, 292 Spec 2:30, 46, 89, 135, 160, 161, 163, 175, 195, 208, 209 Spec 3:8, 9, 32, 34, 39, 43, 49, 103 Spec 4:100, 112, 122, 179 Virt 36, 116, 126, 136, 136, 182, 207, 208 Praem 17, 19, 24, 32, 34, 71, 117, 124, 159 Prob 18, 31, 72, 159 Contempl 2, 58, 68, 69 Aet 63 Flacc 77 Legat 12, 46, 171, 176, 303, 344, 354 Prov 2:1, 8, 29, 69, 71 QG 1:51, 2:22, 22, 3:26, 4:43, 86b, 168 QG (Par) 2:3 QE 1:19, 2:2, 14, 14 QE isf 23

ἡδονικός Leg 2:18

ἡδύνω (6) Leg 2:75 Sacr 29 Post 106 Ebr 219 Contempl 50, 53

ἡδύς (72) Opif 156 Leg 2:7 Leg 3:84, 173, 174, 220, 250 Cher 99 Sacr 23, 35, 44, 79 Det 34, 53, 99 Post 158 Gig 39 Deus 115 Agr 48, 91, 156 Plant 38, 166 Ebr 95, 112, 216 Her 274 Congr 157, 163, 166 Mut 254 Somn 1:49, 58, 125 Somn 2:9, 59, 204 Abr 23, 65, 87 Ios 62, 206 Mos 1:208, 209 Mos 2:162, 256 Spec 1:321 Spec 2:55, 159, 180 Spec 4:101, 103, 141 Virt 99 Praem 7, 8, 33, 71, 139 Flacc 177, 178 Legat 82, 89, 165, 362 Hypoth 11:7 Prov 2:51, 70 QG 1:41, 41 QE 2:105 QE isf 7

ἥδυσμα (19) Opif 158 Post 156 Migr 36 Her 196, 198 Somn 2:49, 155, 249, 301 Ios 152 Spec 1:174, 175, 220 Virt 143 Prob 31 Contempl 53, 73, 81 QE 2:14

ἡδυσμός Her 196, 197, 198

ἡδύτης Opif 165

ἠθικός (21) Leg 1:39, 39, 57 Leg 2:12, 16 Agr 14, 15 Plant 120 Ebr 91, 202 Mut 74, 75, 76, 220, 220 Mos 2:96 Spec 1:336 Virt 8 Prob 74, 80 QG 2:12d

ἠθοποιέω Plant 170

ἠθοποιία Agr 16 Ebr 92 Her 81 Somn 1:58 Spec 1:23

ἠθοποιός Ebr 48

ἦθος (105) Opif 128, 156 Leg 1:16, 85 Leg 3:195 Sacr 26 Det 38 Agr 13, 96 Ebr 6, 91, 223 Her 81, 183 Congr 53 Fug 47, 209 Mut 70, 75 Somn 1:178, 226 Somn 2:98, 165 Abr 104, 117, 124, 125, 168, 210, 264 Ios 6, 36, 64, 168, 206, 220 Mos 1:47, 242 Mos 2:59, 177, 215, 256, 269 Decal 132 Spec 1:70, 105, 110, 260 Spec 2:16, 39, 104, 180, 209 Spec 3:79, 101, 134, 208 Spec 4:16, 32, 50, 88, 114, 120, 152, 183, 203, 218 Virt 27, 39, 40, 54, 66, 115, 117, 119, 167, 179, 196, 225 Praem 77, 87, 119 Prob 23, 57, 90, 95, 98, 144, 149, 155 Contempl 20, 57 Legat 34, 59, 63, 332, 346 Hypoth 11:3, 11:14 QG 1:17b, 3:29, 4:20, 172 QG isf 5 QE isf 14

ἠϊών Mos 1:169, 180 Mos 2:249

ἥκω (68) Leg 3:214, 215 Det 111, 154 Gig 21 Agr 126 Plant 71 Ebr 9 Migr 75, 126 Her 12, 229 Congr 66 Mut 163, 170, 173 Somn 1:9 Somn 2:107, 267 Abr 132, 136, 142, 216, 260 Ios 8, 47, 109, 109, 167, 225, 250 Mos 1:36, 55, 59, 237, 258, 266, 267, 275, 312, 313 Mos 2:33 Spec 1:43, 251 Spec 2:249 Spec 3:39, 149 Spec 4:52, 115 Virt 107, 132, 203 Praem 94 Prob 57 Flacc 31, 44, 114, 119, 123, 141, 160, 185, 186 Legat 30, 202, 254 QG 1:100:2a QE 2:45a

ἡλιακός (20) Cher 62 Deus 79 Ebr 173 Conf 60 Mut 267 Somn 1:23, 90, 91, 202 Mos 1:212 Mos 2:262 Spec 1:40, 279 Spec 2:150, 153, 206 Spec 4:52 Prob 5 Legat 103 Prov 2:49

ἡλίβατος Mos 1:192

ἡλίθιος (8) Sacr 32 Spec 2:132 Spec 3:113, 142 Flacc 6 Legat 71, 77 QG 4:191c

ἡλιθιότης (ἡλιότης) (8) Post 168 Mos 1:224 Spec 1:79 Spec 2:164 Spec 3:194 Praem 52 Legat 163 QE 2:45a

ἡλικία (118) Opif 103, 104, 105, 105 Leg 1:10 Leg 2:73 Cher 114 Sacr 15, 98 Post 71, 90, 109, 152 Agr 9, 18 Sobr 6, 7, 8, 10, 11, 26, 29 Conf 102 Migr 201 Her 294, 295, 296, 297 Congr 5, 19, 53, 82, 85 Fug 13, 40, 146 Somn 1:192 Abr 48, 168, 195 Ios 1, 15, 43, 129, 166, 167, 175, 185, 189, 203, 217, 222, 230 Mos 1:19, 25, 134, 147, 311 Decal 117, 137 Spec 1:69, 314 Spec 2:21, 34, 88, 228, 233 Spec 3:4, 29, 118, 119, 131 Spec 4:16, 154 Virt 26, 43, 52, 55, 120, 141, 178 Praem 25, 110, 110, 146, 162 Prob 81, 114, 117 Contempl 30, 59, 61, 63, 67 Aet 58, 60, 71, 73, 77 Flacc 3, 15, 68 Legat 23, 29, 87, 142, 167, 182, 203, 210, 227, 234 Hypoth 7:1, 11:3 QG 2:5b, 74, 4:88 QG (Par) 2:5

ἡλικιώτης Post 90 Prob 34

ἡλίκος (15) Conf 44, 49 Her 100 Fug 193 Mut 61, 217 Somn 2:81, 179, 179, 228 Mos 2:240 Spec 4:234 Legat 17, 136, 259

ἧλιξ Spec 2:237

ἡλιοειδής Congr 47 Mos 1:166 Mos 2:70, 288

ἥλιος (228) Opif 29, 30, 31, 33, 34, 34, 45, 46, 56, 57, 60, 116, 147, 168 Leg 1:2, 2, 46 Leg 2:30, 30 Leg 3:32, 35, 171 Cher 22, 26, 88, 96 Sacr 34 Post 19, 57, 58 Gig 3 Deus 78, 78, 107 Agr 51 Plant 27, 40, 118 Ebr 44, 106, 110 Conf 100, 116, 157, 173 Migr 40, 40, 138, 179, 184 Her 89, 149, 165, 165, 165, 165, 222, 224, 224, 247, 249, 258, 263, 263, 263, 280, 307 Congr 133 Fug 57, 184 Mut 59, 67, 92, 149, 162, 199 Somn 1:4, 5, 53, 72, 73, 73, 74, 76, 76, 77, 77, 79, 79, 81, 83, 84, 85, 85, 87, 88, 89, 90, 92, 92, 112, 116, 116, 118, 176, 239, 239 Somn 2:6, 111, 112, 120, 131, 133, 134, 140, 282 Abr 57, 69, 76, 158 Ios 8, 9, 68, 145 Mos 1:120, 123, 176 Mos 2:14, 19, 44, 63, 102, 103, 108, 122, 124, 212, 271 Decal 53, 54, 66, 77, 138 Spec 1:13, 15, 16, 16, 16, 34, 37, 40, 90, 90, 90, 171, 207, 210, 279, 279, 296, 300, 321, 339 Spec 2:5, 45, 140, 141, 151, 153, 155, 191, 210, 255 Spec 3:1, 152, 152, 160, 187, 188 Spec 4:7, 7, 10, 52, 192, 201, 231, 232, 236 Virt 74, 164, 164, 181 Praem 41, 45, 45 Contempl 5, 11, 24, 27, 34, 89 Aet 10, 19, 46, 52, 67, 83, 88 Flacc 48, 101, 110, 123 Legat 10, 103, 123, 191, 364 Hypoth 11:6 Prov 2:24, 35, 50, 52 QG 2:34a, 54a, 4:51a, 51a, 51a, 51b

Ἥλιος Post 54, 57 Somn 1:77, 78 Ios 121

ἡλιότης ἡλιθιότης

Ἦλις Agr 119

ἡλιτόμηνος Deus 14 Migr 33 Prob 130

ἡμέρα (440) Opif 13, 15, 30, 35, 35, 37, 37, 45, 55, 56, 56, 57, 60, 60, 60, 62, 80, 85, 89, 101, 101, 115, 116, 124, 125, 128, 129 Leg 1:2, 2, 2, 3, 3, 5, 6, 16, 17, 17, 20, 21, 21, 90, 101, 105 Leg 2:11, 66 Leg 3:25, 65, 105, 106, 142, 161, 162, 162, 163, 163, 166, 166, 167, 167, 167, 167, 177, 212 Cher 22, 26, 92 Sacr 19, 27, 34, 38, 47, 52, 52, 71, 88, 118, 134 Det 4, 46, 94, 131, 173 Post 17, 64, 64, 65 Gig 41, 55, 58 Deus 20, 90, 174 Agr 35, 58, 136, 175, 179 Plant 61, 102, 105, 108, 118, 118, 164 Ebr 22, 67, 91, 134, 149, 150, 155, 195, 208, 208 Sobr 21 Conf 24, 46, 80, 80, 100, 100, 151 Migr 111, 139, 154, 157, 202, 208 Her 58, 146, 148, 148, 149, 149, 149, 149, 150, 163, 163, 165, 174, 208, 251, 261, 290, 313 Congr 64 Fug 23, 46, 57, 58, 107, 184, 186 Mut 48, 92, 92, 93, 162, 195 Somn 1:36, 46, 46, 76, 99, 99, 100, 114, 122, 154 Somn 2:20, 36, 36, 41, 42, 57, 63, 64, 106, 112, 112, 120, 257 Abr 28, 96, 139, 149, 155, 169, 251 Ios 8, 15, 37, 44, 81, 86, 92, 96, 97, 123, 131, 146, 196, 228 Mos 1:14, 29, 31, 38, 64, 73, 101, 120, 123, 123, 123, 125, 133, 139, 163, 166, 181, 194, 204, 205, 207, 207, 212, 258, 290, 304, 313 Mos 2:14, 22, 27, 54, 63, 69, 70, 94, 122, 153, 159, 161, 174, 184, 194, 214, 224, 225, 228, 231, 258, 264, 266, 271 Decal 45, 57, 74, 87, 96, 97, 98, 99, 101, 151, 159, 160, 161, 161, 161 Spec 1:16, 34, 90, 119, 125, 156, 168, 169, 169, 171, 181, 182, 182, 187, 189, 190, 220, 222, 223, 225, 240, 243, 256, 261, 276, 285, 319, 321 Spec 2:21, 41, 41, 42, 56, 60, 66, 67, 86, 86, 100, 101, 122, 142, 145, 149, 155, 156, 157, 162, 176, 184, 187, 195, 199, 200, 210, 210, 211, 215, 222, 223, 251 Spec 3:17, 38, 39, 55, 94, 125, 126, 131, 142, 183, 195, 205 Spec 4:9, 10, 160, 161, 170, 195, 232, 232, 233 Virt 6, 20, 37, 111, 113, 129, 134, 134, 138, 142, 144 Praem 111, 112, 112, 112, 151, 153, 153, 155, 164 Prob 5, 86, 138, 157 Contempl 27, 30, 34, 35, 35, 42, 73 Aet 19, 52, 64, 104, 141 Flacc 27, 54, 57, 90, 94, 110, 159, 163, 175 Legat 13, 39, 59, 122, 123, 124, 157, 171, 184, 251, 269, 280, 296, 307, 310, 317, 323, 351 Hypoth 7:10, 7:12, 7:15, 11:11 Prov 2:14, 41 QG

1:60:1, 60:2, 2:13a, 13a, 29, 29, 30, 3:52, 4:51a, 51a, 173 QE 2:13b, 20, 25d, 46, 46, 46, 49b QE isf 9

ἡμερήσιος Leg 3:25 Mos 1:145 Spec 1:170 Spec 4:128

ἡμερινός Spec 1:219

ἡμερίς Mut 162

ἥμερος (105) Opif 40, 153 Leg 1:49, 49 Leg 3:76 Cher 102, 111 Sacr 105 Det 105, 107, 111 Deus 91, 154, 154 Agr 6, 8 Plant 29, 46, 98, 98, 100, 101 Ebr 223, 224 Migr 147 Her 127, 137, 137, 211 Congr 71, 94 Fug 204 Mut 39, 165, 226, 246 Somn 2:294 Abr 45, 266 Ios 177, 221 Mos 1:11, 60, 61, 192, 241, 244 Mos 2:279 Decal 15, 77, 115, 132, 160, 160 Spec 1:74, 74, 134, 162, 163, 295 Spec 2:146, 169, 205 Spec 3:103, 116, 139, 163 Spec 4:11, 13, 23, 103, 104, 104, 117, 209, 227, 227 Virt 81, 81, 95, 110, 114, 125, 126, 146, 149, 154, 155, 182 Praem 8, 59, 60, 92, 141 Contempl 8, 9 Aet 68, 96 Flacc 59 Legat 20, 243, 321 Prov 2:2, 57, 66

ἡμερότης (23) Cher 29, 99 Sacr 27 Conf 166 Fug 99 Mos 1:43 Decal 162 Spec 1:164 Spec 2:79, 93, 107 Spec 4:18, 24 Virt 84, 109, 116, 121, 134, 188 Praem 156 Legat 106, 119 QE 2:11a

ἡμεροτοκέω Sobr 65 Migr 125

ἡμεροφύλαξ Spec 1:156

ἡμερόω (24) Opif 83, 103 Sacr 104 Det 25 Agr 6 Plant 103 Migr 36, 210 Fug 209 Somn 1:91 Ios 85 Mos 2:61 Decal 113, 113 Spec 3:152 Virt 127 Praem 88, 89, 91, 152 Legat 82, 147, 333 Prov 2:64

ἡμέρωσις Migr 211

ἡμέτερος (126) Opif 72, 90, 112, 117, 140, 140, 145 Leg 1:6, 43 Leg 2:6, 23, 80 Leg 3:57, 77, 116, 215 Cher 115 Sacr 93, 96, 101, 117 Det 91, 122, 122 Post 10, 161 Deus 28 Agr 48, 110, 155 Plant 18, 28, 127 Ebr 44 Conf 169 Migr 52, 52, 193 Her 91, 201, 229, 232, 234, 235, 263 Congr 44 Fug 65, 68, 105, 117, 131, 172, 177 Mut 31, 215 Somn 1:2, 28, 36, 210 Somn 2:2, 60, 255 Abr 54, 72, 76 Ios 151, 194, 195, 215 Mos 1:172, 307 Mos 2:20, 186 Decal 1, 32, 57 Spec 1:8, 66, 153, 201 Spec 2:5, 52, 96, 198, 199 Spec 3:20, 42, 102, 167, 177, 182 Spec 4:118 Virt 38 Prob 96 Contempl 58 Aet 59, 80 Flacc 53, 53, 59, 74, 79, 96, 124 Legat 150, 157, 181, 192, 231, 232, 238, 240, 257, 290, 301, 316, 322, 366, 371 Hypoth 11:1 Prov 2:48 QG 1:32, 2:12d, 4:180 QG (Par) 2:2, 2:6

ἡμίβρωτος Contempl 55

ἡμίεργος (6) Agr 146 Somn 1:112 Abr 47 Spec 3:23, 92 Praem 9

ἡμίθεος (7) Congr 15 Virt 172 Prob 105 Contempl 6 Legat 78, 93, 114

ἡμιμόχθηρος Spec 4:63

ἡμιόλιος (7) Opif 48, 48, 107 Mos 2:115 Decal 21, 22 Spec 2:200

ἡμίονος Spec 3:47

ἡμιπαγής Agr 146

ἥμισυς (45) Opif 13, 57 Leg 1:3, 76, 76 Cher 59 Det 64, 64, 64 Agr 125, 125 Ebr 125 Her 49, 116, 116, 174, 175, 175, 182, 182, 186, 189 Fug 6 Mut 195 Somn 2:112, 156, 163 Abr 155 Mos 1:315, 318 Mos 2:27, 78, 83, 89, 90 Spec 1:256, 256 Spec 2:15, 220 Spec 3:21, 64 Spec 4:63 Virt 225, 225 Legat 207

ἡμισφαίριον (9) Cher 25, 26 Mos 2:98, 122, 123, 133 Decal 56, 57 Spec 1:86

ἡμιτελής Ebr 35, 80 Somn 1:9 Decal 110

ἡμίφλεκτος Mos 1:119 Flacc 68 Legat 130

ἡμίφωνος Opif 126 Congr 150

ἤν (ἐάν) (13) Leg 1:26 Sacr 22, 29, 135 Det 89, 165 Conf 47 Congr 50 Somn 2:145 Mos 1:298, 331 Virt 110 Prob 54

ἡνία (16) Opif 46, 88 Leg 1:73 Leg 3:195, 223 Cher 24 Sacr 49 Det 23 Agr 35, 74, 93 Conf 165 Somn 2:201, 294 Mos 1:25, 177

ἡνίκα (89) Opif 68, 72, 115 Leg 3:20, 172, 223 Cher 31, 63, 67 Sacr 8, 59 Det 24 Gig 1 Deus 40 Agr 21, 73 Plant 127 Ebr 60, 82, 96, 127, 138, 208 Sobr 8, 27 Migr 151, 197 Her 25, 71, 71, 133, 191, 258 Congr 58, 70, 74, 92, 100, 108, 111, 114, 118, 123 Fug 35, 53, 68, 69, 152 Mut 16, 125, 134, 170, 189 Somn 1:37, 79, 194 Somn 2:19, 170 Abr 131, 132 Ios 260 Mos 1:6, 144, 247, 281 Mos 2:270 Decal 45 Spec 1:84, 129 Spec 2:158, 250 Spec 3:125, 200 Spec 4:136 Prob 130, 132 Contempl 57 Aet 43, 53, 53, 53, 66, 77 Flacc 14, 28 Legat 96, 159, 294 Prov 2:49

ἡνιοχέω (30) Opif 88 Leg 1:72 Leg 3:109, 123, 127, 137, 193 Sacr 105 Det 53 Ebr 199 Migr 71, 186 Her 301 Mut 16, 91, 105 Somn 1:157 Mos 1:26, 178, 274 Decal 60, 155 Spec 2:142 Spec 3:79 Virt 13 Praem 34, 37 Aet 83 Flacc 26 QG 2:64c

ἡνιόχησις Agr 77 Her 125 Fug 101 Mos 2:254

ἡνιοχικός Agr 93

ἡνίοχος (38) Opif 46, 88, 88 Leg 1:73, 73 Leg 3:118, 128, 132, 134, 136, 223, 223, 224 Sacr 45, 49 Det 141 Agr 72, 73, 73 Conf 115 Migr 67 Her 99, 228, 301 Fug 101, 101 Mut 149 Somn 1:157 Somn 2:83, 201, 294 Abr 70 Spec 1:14 Spec 2:163 Spec 4:79 Praem 38 Aet 83 QG 2:34c

ἧπαρ (15) Opif 118 Leg 1:12 Sacr 136 Ebr 106 Spec 1:212, 213, 216, 217, 218, 219, 219, 232, 233, 239 QG (Par) 2:7

ἤπειρος (31) Opif 114, 114 Her 136 Mut 35 Somn 2:118, 118 Abr 42 Ios 30 Mos 1:212 Spec 1:211 Spec 2:168 Spec 3:25 Spec 4:85, 154 Praem 165 Contempl 86 Aet 138, 139, 139 Flacc 46, 151, 186 Legat 18, 90, 144, 144, 214, 282, 283, 288, 347

ἠπειρόω Post 144 Deus 177 Somn 1:17 Aet 122, 138

ἠπειρώτης Ios 134 Mos 2:20 Spec 1:335

ἤπιος Mos 1:72

ἠπιότης Sacr 27 Decal 167

Ἤρ Post 180

Ἥρα Decal 54 Contempl 3

Ἡράκλειος Prob 120

Ἡρακλειτείος Leg 3:7

Ἡράκλειτος (6) Leg 1:108 Her 214 Aet 111 Prov 2:67 QG 2:5a QG (Par) 2:5

Ἡρακλῆς (7) Prob 99, 127 Legat 78, 79, 81, 90, 92

ἠρέμα (7) Opif 34 Det 117 Migr 101 Her 204 Ios 205 Aet 120 Flacc 177

ἠρεμαῖος (8) Leg 1:42 Leg 3:138 Sacr 26 Det 117 Abr 27 Prob 90 Contempl 77 Legat 66

ἠρεμέω (68) Opif 117 Leg 1:29 Leg 2:37, 39, 40, 85 Leg 3:13, 35, 160, 160 Sacr 114, 116 Det 172 Post 108 Gig 47 Agr 37, 132, 162 Ebr 97 Sobr 37, 44, 45, 46, 50 Conf

32, 46 Congr 45 Mut 113, 180 Somn 1:110, 187 Somn 2:124, 228, 265 Abr 43, 152, 153, 162, 230 Mos 1:177, 270 Mos 2:213, 220 Decal 86, 117, 143, 177 Spec 1:270 Spec 2:52 Spec 3:17, 194 Spec 4:29, 81 Praem 157 Aet 33 Legat 184, 204, 270, 272, 337, 337, 337, 371 Prov 2:61 QG 1:24, 3:8 QE 1:7b QE isf 20

ἠρεμία (34) Opif 58, 67, 85 Leg 3:160, 160 Cher 38 Det 172 Post 23, 24, 28, 29, 30, 32 Gig 49 Deus 23 Sobr 34, 48, 49 Conf 31, 132 Migr 75 Her 13, 14, 249, 257 Fug 136 Mut 239 Somn 1:20, 113 Somn 2:228 Spec 3:171 Praem 121 Aet 84 QG 4:47a

ἠρίον Flacc 159

Ἡρῴδης Flacc 25 Legat 294, 296, 297, 299

ἡρωικός Somn 2:50 Prob 109

ἥρως Plant 14 Congr 15 Prob 105, 106 QE isf 26

Ἡρώων Ios 256

Ἠσαῦ (32) Leg 2:59 Leg 3:2, 2, 88, 88 Sacr 17, 81, 120, 135 Det 45 Ebr 9, 9 Sobr 26, 26 Migr 153 Her 252 Congr 54, 61, 175 Fug 4, 23, 39, 39, 42, 43 Mut 230 QG 4:161, 163:2, 166, 169, 174, 206a

Ἡσίοδος Aet 17, 18

ἧσσα (16) Leg 3:15 Det 37 Deus 16 Ebr 35, 121 Somn 2:43 Abr 214 Mos 1:251, 295, 327 Virt 38 Praem 6, 96 Prob 111 Flacc 132, 147

ἡσσάομαι (49) Cher 75 Sacr 116, 120 Deus 15, 170 Agr 79, 83, 110, 111, 112, 112, 112 Migr 74, 85, 95 Somn 1:131, 184 Somn 2:12, 24, 161 Abr 106, 188, 216 Ios 20, 59, 138 Decal 115 Spec 1:114, 186, 313 Spec 3:35, 156, 173 Spec 4:64, 64 Virt 53, 186 Praem 78 Prob 131, 131 Flacc 12, 60, 60, 134, 134 Legat 36, 42, 268 QG 4:52c

ἥσσων μικρός

ἡσυχάζω (96) Opif 5, 90 Leg 1:60 Leg 2:63 Leg 3:145, 181 Cher 121 Sacr 30, 31, 34 Det 102 Post 147, 150 Deus 38 Agr 162 Sobr 6, 32, 43, 50, 50 Conf 40, 117 Migr 10, 31, 108, 118 Her 5, 13, 249, 266 Congr 46, 66 Fug 120, 135 Mut 195, 195, 242 Somn 1:153 Somn 2:92, 263, 266, 274 Abr 27, 29, 154, 167, 174, 216, 255 Ios 21, 30, 47, 94, 165, 170, 265 Mos 1:177, 315 Mos 2:207, 214, 219, 245, 282 Decal 5, 44 Spec 1:97, 153 Spec 2:11, 14, 50, 129 Spec 3:168 Spec 4:90, 140, 148, 230 Praem 128, 128 Prob 108 Contempl 1 Aet 89, 134 Flacc 2, 48, 51, 51, 183 Legat 99, 101, 227, 323, 350 Prov 2:52 QG 4:47b, 202b QE 2:118

ἡσυχῇ (12) Opif 81, 85 Abr 210, 257 Ios 129, 175 Mos 1:26, 200 Virt 89 Prob 90 Legat 43 QE 2:25c

ἡσυχία (56) Opif 86 Det 42, 102 Post 108 Agr 132 Ebr 71, 71, 97, 104 Sobr 35, 37, 41, 49 Conf 37 Her 10, 14, 257 Congr 45 Fug 136 Mut 195, 217, 242, 251 Somn 1:193 Somn 2:37, 125, 262, 263, 268, 274 Abr 20, 73 Mos 1:3, 41, 49, 66, 67, 125, 285 Decal 63 Spec 2:62, 102, 250 Spec 3:17 Praem 18, 93, 157 Prob 74 Contempl 31, 75, 80 Aet 125 Legat 197, 337, 360 QG 4:47a

ἥσυχος Somn 1:111 Virt 136

ἧττα Leg 3:121

ἤτοι (20) Opif 37 Leg 3:154 Gig 48 Deus 4 Plant 97 Ebr 139 Spec 1:208, 283 Spec 2:158, 206 Spec 4:121 Contempl 2 Aet 17, 21, 39, 106 Flacc 130 Legat 70 QG 1:1 QG (Par) 2:2

ἦτρον Leg 1:12, 70, 71, 71 Leg 3:115

Ἥφαιστος Decal 54 Contempl 3 Aet 68

ἠχεῖον Migr 52 Her 259 Mut 69

ἠχέω Cher 7 Mut 247

ἠχή Leg 3:183 Det 126, 127 Somn 1:36 Decal 44

ἦχος (13) Leg 2:56 Leg 3:21, 44 Sacr 69 Det 157 Post 88 Somn 1:29 Somn 2:259 Mos 2:35 Decal 33, 148 Contempl 88 QG 3:43

ἠχώ (8) Cher 7 Gig 64 Mut 66, 69, 69, 71 Abr 82, 83

ἠώς (ἕως, ἡ) (17) Ios 103, 159, 207, 255 Mos 1:136, 200, 208, 276 Mos 2:258 Spec 1:169 Spec 2:155 Spec 4:128 Contempl 27, 89 Flacc 122, 167 QE isf 9

Θ

θ QG 2:5a QG (Par) 2:5

θαλαμαῖος Spec 2:207

Θαλαμείν Post 60, 61

θαλαμεύω Agr 153 Flacc 89 Prov 2:57

θάλαμος Leg 3:40

θάλασσα (158) Opif 39, 58, 63, 69, 72, 78, 113, 114, 114, 131, 136 Leg 1:34 Leg 2:102, 104 Leg 3:171, 172, 203, 223 Cher 37, 38 Det 87, 89, 151 Post 84, 116, 144, 163 Gig 3, 7, 51 Deus 177 Agr 23, 24, 24, 82 Plant 144 Ebr 111, 113, 133, 158, 172, 182 Sobr 42 Conf 10, 26, 70, 154 Migr 185, 218 Her 7, 20, 136 Congr 117, 133 Mut 179, 237 Somn 1:3, 17, 19, 135, 175, 175 Somn 2:86, 118, 118, 121, 166, 180, 246, 269, 280, 281 Abr 29, 42 Ios 56, 136 Mos 1:41, 99, 115, 118, 122, 155, 165, 169, 177, 181, 209 Mos 2:1, 35, 63, 247, 249, 249, 251, 252, 253, 254 Decal 5, 42, 54, 116, 152 Spec 1:69, 91, 262, 300, 335, 339 Spec 2:45, 208 Spec 3:8, 114, 188 Spec 4:66, 85, 128, 154, 177 Virt 183 Praem 80 Prob 66, 72 Contempl 23, 54, 85 Aet 117, 120, 120, 123, 138, 140, 141, 142, 148 Flacc 104, 123, 125, 154, 155, 186 Legat 8, 44, 47, 49, 81, 141, 144, 146, 185, 190, 252, 294, 305, 309 Prov 2:33, 64 QG 3:30b, 4:76a

θαλασσεύω (15) Cher 13 Sacr 116 Det 141 Post 22, 100 Deus 175 Agr 175 Abr 47 Spec 1:301 Spec 4:154 Prob 68 Flacc 27, 110 Legat 15 QE 2:55b

θαλάσσιος Opif 131 Plant 151

θαλασσόω Aet 138

θαλάσσωσις Mos 2:254 Aet 122

θαλία Ebr 95 Congr 161 Legat 83

θαλλός Somn 2:62

θάλλω (9) Sacr 80 Somn 2:159, 199, 200 Ios 91, 102 Spec 2:151 Praem 68, 146

θάλπος (13) Congr 165 Mut 246 Somn 1:102, 124 Somn 2:52 Decal 77 Spec 2:207 Praem 99 Contempl 38 Aet 67, 67 Flacc 36 Hypoth 11:6

Θάμαρ (10) Leg 3:74, 74 Deus 136, 137 Congr 124 Fug 149 Mut 134 Somn 2:44, 44 Virt 221

θαμινός Sacr 28

Θαμνά Congr 54, 60

θάμνος Somn 1:125

θανάσιμος Plant 147 Spec 3:95, 98 Spec 4:86

θανατάω (7) Spec 3:102 Virt 34 Praem 159 Prob 7 Contempl 43 Aet 89 Legat 265

θάνατος (243) Opif 104, 125, 164 Leg 1:76, 76, 90, 105, 105, 105, 106, 106, 106, 107, 107, 108 Leg 2:77, 77, 78, 87 Leg 3:52, 74, 107 Cher 75, 114 Sacr 38, 125 Det 70, 76, 99, 178 Post 39, 39, 41, 44, 44, 45, 61, 73, 73, 73, 74 Deus 16, 50, 89, 123 Agr 75, 98, 100, 163 Plant 37, 45, 147, 147 Ebr 71, 71, 135, 140 Sobr 4, 8 Conf 36, 37 Migr 7, 68, 189, 206 Her 52, 209, 276, 290, 290 Congr 87, 93 Fug 53, 54, 55, 58, 58, 64, 74, 78, 84, 87, 93, 97, 106, 113, 116 Mut 62, 95, 96 Somn 1:10 Somn 2:84, 88 Abr 55, 64, 64, 64, 183, 187, 258 Ios 15, 23, 43, 44, 68, 68, 129, 156, 169, 187, 216, 216, 221, 221 Mos 1:44, 133, 134, 134, 171, 183, 242, 311 Mos 2:171, 204, 206, 217, 227, 281 Decal 114 Spec 1:295, 338 Spec 2:28, 28, 28, 95, 232, 243, 249, 252 Spec 3:11, 31, 54, 58, 64, 70, 84, 90, 96, 97, 98, 102, 107, 117, 136, 143, 150, 151, 153, 154, 159, 202, 205 Spec 4:19, 23, 35, 36, 82, 91 Virt 32, 111, 132, 139, 200, 221 Praem 68, 69, 70, 70, 71, 110, 135 Prob 22, 30, 111, 114, 116, 117, 120, 131, 134, 145 Contempl 9 Aet 13, 20, 74, 84, 97, 108, 111, 111, 111, 126, 128 Flacc 48, 70, 85, 129, 147, 159, 175, 179, 181 Legat 14, 17, 71, 107, 110, 117, 127, 192, 192, 209, 212, 233, 237, 237, 307, 308, 325, 341, 341, 366, 369 Hypoth 7:1, 7:2 Prov 2:61 QG 1:51, 74, 76a, 77, 3:52, 4:173 QG (Par) 2:7

θανατόω (11) Leg 2:77, 87, 87 Conf 160 Fug 53, 53, 54, 54, 64 Spec 1:237 QG 2:12c

θανατώδης Opif 159 Abr 46

θάπτω Ios 23 Mos 2:291 Prob 133

Θάρρα Somn 1:47, 48, 52, 58, 58

θαρσαλέος Abr 233 Ios 222 Virt 3 Legat 322

θαρσαλεότης Her 21 Somn 2:37 Virt 32, 180

θαρσέω (43) Post 38 Deus 148 Agr 127 Ebr 84, 179 Her 19, 20, 22, 24, 27, 28, 29, 71, 155 Congr 133 Fug 6, 31, 82 Mut 265 Somn 1:24 Somn 2:78, 95, 100 Abr 105 Ios 90 Mos 1:87, 251 Mos 2:169, 252 Spec 1:42 Spec 3:33, 54, 86 Flacc 126, 166, 182 Legat 133, 271, 287, 303 Prov 2:27, 29, 42

θάρσος (11) Her 21, 22, 28 Mos 1:77, 233, 234, 252 Spec 1:270 Praem 95 Prob 150 Flacc 32

θαρσύνω (8) Fug 5 Abr 206, 256 Ios 177, 267 Mos 1:173, 177, 306

θαῦμα Opif 117 Plant 3 Fug 46 Prob 5, 6

θαυμάζω (132) Opif 7, 45 Leg 1:60 Leg 2:14, 40 Leg 3:5, 208 Cher 10, 53 Sacr 99 Post 133 Gig 28, 37, 51 Agr 54, 116, 129, 143 Plant 58, 80, 80 Ebr 2, 46, 54, 120, 130, 169, 198 Sobr 3, 4 Conf 41, 43, 49, 108, 164, 167 Migr 4, 21, 26, 75 Her 52, 201, 203, 252, 256, 295 Congr 130, 179 Fug 34, 63, 132, 162 Mut 46, 105, 139, 145, 167, 214, 256, 258 Somn 1:73, 120, 205, 238 Somn 2:140, 183, 228 Abr 74, 89, 103, 107, 183, 199, 223, 253, 260 Ios 4, 8, 19, 203, 249, 258, 266 Mos 1:78, 177, 264 Mos 2:25, 167, 197, 236 Decal 16, 20, 24 Spec 1:73 Spec 2:3, 23, 41, 52, 160, 167, 173, 199, 240 Spec 4:177 Virt 180 Praem 24, 34, 42, 152 Prob 47, 93, 157 Contempl 14 Aet 107 Flacc 146 Legat 8, 46, 86, 86, 98, 189, 297, 310 Hypoth 6:8, 7:10 Prov 2:9, 16, 17, 19, 21, 41 QG 4:202a

θαυμάσιος (53) Opif 3, 49, 78, 90, 172 Leg 2:16 Det 67 Post 147 Deus 24, 147, 147 Agr 82, 121, 149 Ebr 86, 149, 174, 210 Conf 58, 58 Migr 33, 184, 210 Her 5, 100 Congr 156 Mut 264 Somn 1:49, 130, 163 Somn 2:160 Abr 38, 38, 73, 216 Mos 1:4, 206, 213 Mos 2:17, 109, 290, 290 Decal 33 Spec 1:95, 230, 295, 342 Spec 2:216 Spec 3:188 Spec 4:143 Contempl 16 Legat 149 Prov 2:65

θαυμαστικός Somn 1:126, 184, 222 Mos 1:91

θαυμαστός (46) Opif 95, 106 Cher 92 Deus 116 Agr 71 Plant 132 Ebr 75, 151, 189, 199 Her 95, 95, 182, 191 Congr 111, 145 Fug 111, 149 Mut 10, 61, 215 Abr 178, 211 Mos 1:156, 180 Mos 2:10, 17 Spec 1:168 Spec 2:177 Spec 3:33, 163 Spec 4:45 Virt 224 Praem 115, 160 Prob 36, 63 Aet 41, 137 Legat 85 Hypoth 7:11, 7:17 Prov 2:35, 44, 63 QG 2:16

θαυματοποιός Plant 3 Abr 73 Contempl 58

θαυματουργέω (13) Mut 162 Somn 2:119 Abr 118 Mos 1:71, 79, 203 Mos 2:179 Decal 33, 44 Spec 2:218 Contempl 85 QG 3:18, 4:51b

θαυματούργημα Mos 1:82

θέα (66) Opif 151 Leg 2:85 Leg 3:171 Det 12 Deus 151 Agr 91 Ebr 51, 152, 158, 168, 177, 195, 223 Sobr 3, 5 Migr 76, 169, 170, 191 Mut 56, 82 Somn 1:147, 165, 188, 248 Somn 2:160, 279, 281 Abr 65, 165 Mos 1:231, 273 Mos 2:214, 255 Decal 67 Spec 1:38, 49, 56, 75, 96, 339 Spec 2:202 Spec 3:16, 111, 176, 189 Spec 4:115, 129, 139, 154 Praem 39, 43 Contempl 11, 66 Flacc 28, 68, 74, 85, 154, 160 Legat 224, 296 QG 2:39, 4:33b QE 2:15b, 15b

Θεά Prob 140

Θεαίτητος Fug 63

θέαμα (18) Opif 54, 78, 78, 162 Leg 3:156 Gig 31 Agr 35 Migr 216 Mut 212 Somn 1:165 Ios 142 Mos 1:20, 27, 65 Spec 1:174 Praem 139 Flacc 85 Legat 43

θεάομαι (139) Opif 17, 46, 71, 83, 151, 158 Leg 2:5, 40, 61 Leg 3:97, 99, 130 Cher 58 Sacr 81, 124 Det 11, 19, 107 Post 112, 168, 169 Gig 15 Deus 78, 146 Agr 96 Plant 65, 78 Ebr 17, 131 Sobr 59 Conf 46, 74, 96, 142, 194 Her 247 Congr 145 Fug 34, 81, 161, 187 Mut 91, 97 Somn 1:188, 188, 214, 241 Somn 2:6, 87, 206 Abr 61, 70, 88, 94, 107, 197, 235 Ios 10, 25, 98, 165, 182, 226, 234, 257 Mos 1:14, 90, 128, 136, 167, 182, 223, 272, 277, 278, 303, 320 Mos 2:62, 172, 249, 252, 261 Decal 60, 86 Spec 1:33, 34, 45, 56 Spec 2:251 Spec 3:52, 103, 160 Spec 4:30, 39, 157 Virt 74 Praem 38, 41, 58, 150, 157 Prob 7, 38, 39, 56, 124, 133 Contempl 50, 75, 75, 89 Aet 4, 32, 89, 105 Flacc 62, 114, 152, 152, 162 Legat 42, 202, 224, 238, 263, 295, 308, 352, 355 Hypoth 0:1 Prov 2:31, 64 QG 1:28, 2:13a, 34a, 34a QE 2:47 QE isf 3, 6

θεατής (18) Opif 78 Sacr 78 Det 134 Deus 102 Agr 93, 112 Congr 145 Mut 7, 18 Somn 2:63 Mos 1:146 Praem 5 Prob 141 Contempl 42 Flacc 96 Legat 46, 168, 204

θεατός Somn 1:157

θεατρικός Flacc 38, 72 Legat 359

θεατρομανέω Mos 2:211

θέατρον (29) Opif 78, 78 Post 104, 104 Gig 31 Deus 36 Agr 35, 113, 117 Ebr 177 Congr 64 Mut 198 Somn 1:122 Abr 20, 103 Spec 4:185 Flacc 19, 41, 74, 84, 95, 173, 173 Legat 79, 204, 368, 368 QG 4:69, 204

θεήλατος (14) Ebr 79 Mut 108 Somn 2:125 Mos 1:110, 132, 236 Mos 2:16 Spec 2:170, 190 Spec 4:179 Praem 136 Legat 293 Prov 2:41, 53

θεία Spec 2:127

θειάζω Her 46 Mut 128

θεῖον Somn 1:85 Abr 141 Mos 2:56

θεῖος (555) Opif 20, 23, 25, 31, 36, 45, 55, 67, 84, 135, 135, 143, 144, 144, 146, 148, 153, 168, 170 Leg 1:5, 9, 16, 17, 18, 20, 33, 61, 61 Leg 2:10, 23, 78, 95 Leg 3:7, 7, 8, 14, 47, 71, 81, 82, 84, 97, 104, 141, 142, 152, 161, 161, 167, 171, 208, 217, 218, 242 Cher 3, 8, 19, 19, 23, 36, 41, 42, 46, 72, 93, 93 Sacr 22, 60, 62, 63, 66, 70, 72, 86, 95, 109, 117, 138 Det 29, 55, 61, 73, 83, 90, 90, 116, 117, 118, 133, 147, 152, 156, 160 Post 18, 27, 32, 42, 89, 101, 122, 129, 138, 139, 170, 177, 181, 184 Gig 8, 23, 23, 27, 28, 29, 31, 47, 53, 54, 55 Deus 2, 5, 5, 46, 59, 104, 105, 106, 111, 120, 134, 137, 151, 176, 180, 182 Agr 51, 79, 80, 119, 139 Plant 10, 14, 18, 23, 24, 39, 39, 162, 169, 177 Ebr 19, 31, 37, 39, 70, 72, 100, 143, 145 Conf 15, 28, 51, 59, 62, 81, 100, 108, 114, 115, 115, 120, 122, 133, 134, 138, 144, 153, 154, 174 Migr 29, 39, 46, 52, 52, 64, 66, 67, 80, 83, 85, 104, 129, 130, 130, 131, 140, 150, 157, 158, 169, 171, 174, 184 Her 1, 14, 55, 57, 57, 63, 64, 69, 76, 79, 84, 88, 101, 112, 119, 126, 127, 128, 129, 132, 176, 176, 179, 182, 183, 188, 191, 199, 216, 225, 234, 235, 236, 240, 241, 264, 265, 278, 312 Congr 57, 79, 84, 96, 96, 100, 106, 116, 120, 174 Fug 5, 13, 20, 21, 38, 62, 63, 74, 80, 83, 84, 85, 94, 97, 99, 101, 108, 137, 139, 162, 163, 168, 186, 195, 208 Mut 3, 3, 7, 13, 25, 54, 70, 104, 105, 114, 116, 126, 134, 136, 142, 169, 184, 185, 202, 209, 219, 219, 223, 223, 226, 254, 255 Somn 1:1, 34, 62, 64, 65, 66, 68, 71, 84, 85, 91, 113, 118, 118, 119, 127, 128, 129, 140, 147, 148, 165, 175, 186, 190, 190, 215, 227, 233, 256 Somn 2:25, 74, 119, 173, 190, 222, 223, 232, 233, 242, 245, 247, 248, 277, 291 Abr 18, 26, 70, 101, 107, 115, 128, 141, 144, 159, 162, 170, 235, 244, 275, 275 Ios 37, 95, 95, 110, 116, 174 Mos 1:27, 83, 84, 85, 94, 99, 119, 132, 162, 190, 211, 266, 268, 272, 279, 281, 282 Mos 2:5, 5, 6, 12, 32, 51, 58, 60, 70, 103, 124, 147, 154, 158, 187, 188, 189, 208, 216, 244, 245, 245, 253, 254, 255, 261, 265, 278 Decal 2, 6, 7, 13, 36, 63, 104, 104, 111, 121 Spec 1:23, 32, 116, 171, 209, 266, 269, 272 Spec 2:2, 127, 127, 129, 132, 158, 163, 224, 225, 225, 231, 249, 261 Spec 3:1, 26, 121, 137, 178, 207, 209 Spec 4:32, 34, 40, 49, 50, 123, 132, 163, 238 Virt 50, 52, 54, 54, 55, 66, 73, 74, 79, 95, 108, 171, 177, 203, 217 Praem 9, 26, 40, 69, 79, 83, 109, 121, 160, 165 Prob 13, 13, 24, 43, 44, 74, 84 Contempl 6, 9, 26, 39, 67 Aet 47, 69, 112 Flacc 25, 125 Legat 3, 5, 54, 76, 99, 322, 368 Prov 2:6, 28, 36, 50, 66 QG 1:21, 51, 51, 55a, 69, 70:1, 93, 93, 93, 96:1, 2:11, 28, 28, 34a, 54a, 59, 62, 3:3, 18, 4:8b, 40, 47a, 51b, 51c QG isf 1, 5 QE 2:4, 10b, 15b, 18, 18, 21, 24b, 45a, 45a, 45b, 99 QE isf 1, 9

θειότης Det 86

θειόω Ebr 110

θέλημα Leg 3:197

θέλω ἐθέλω

θέμα Spec 1:172

θεμέλιος (26) Opif 41 Leg 2:6, 41, 96 Leg 3:113, 145 Cher 101 Sacr 25, 81 Gig 30 Conf 5, 87 Her 116, 134 Congr 33, 146 Mut 211 Somn 2:8 Mos 2:157 Spec 2:110 Virt 158 Praem 120, 150 Contempl 34 Aet 115 Legat 132

θεμελιόω Opif 102 Ebr 31

θέμις (101) Opif 11, 80, 144 Leg 2:3 Cher 43, 77, 88, 124 Sacr 27, 57, 92, 110 Det 55, 173 Post 158 Deus 165 Agr 34 Plant 23, 27, 51, 164, 169 Ebr 131 Conf 126, 136, 170, 174 Migr 170, 182 Her 177, 259, 265 Fug 59, 76, 76, 85, 203 Mut 181 Somn 1:94, 191 Somn 2:2, 136 Abr 44, 121, 243, 258 Ios 47, 219 Mos 1:56, 166, 277, 298 Mos 2:114, 135, 135, 144, 196, 201, 201 Decal 41 Spec 1:53, 74, 83, 122, 156, 221, 254, 329 Spec 2:6, 175, 198, 219, 243, 256 Spec 3:12, 134, 175, 189 Spec 4:3, 201 Virt 61, 62, 79, 100, 108, 202 Praem 40, 152 Prob 3, 137 Aet 43, 84 Legat 56, 224, 348 Prov 2:26 QG 2:54a, 62 QG isf 2 QE 2:17 QE isf 14

θεμιτός (9) Opif 17 Decal 58 Spec 1:89 Spec 3:135 Spec 4:76 Flacc 42 Legat 194, 353 Prov 2:64

θεογαμία Decal 156

θεογονία Decal 156 Spec 1:344

θεόδμητος Aet 121

Θεόδοτος Prob 1

Θεόδωρος Prob 127

θεοειδής (19) Opif 16, 53, 69, 137 Det 84 Post 93 Ebr 70, 137 Her 38, 65 Somn 1:113 Somn 2:186, 223 Mos 1:66, 158 Spec 3:83, 207 Prob 150 Prov 2:10

θεοληπτέομαι Cher 27

θεόληπτος Aet 76

θεολογέω Opif 12

θεολόγος Mos 2:115 Praem 53 QG 2:59, 3:21

θεομισής Somn 1:211 Legat 353

θεομίσητος Decal 131

θεόπεμπτος Somn 1:1, 133, 190 Somn 2:1, 113

θεοπλαστέω (21) Post 165 Ebr 95, 95, 109 Migr 179 Her 169 Fug 8, 11, 90 Ios 254 Mos 2:195 Spec 1:21, 22, 344 Spec 2:1, 258 Praem 25 Prob 66 Legat 118, 139 QG 1:100:1b

θεοπλάστης Aet 15

θεοπρεπής (14) Opif 116 Leg 3:26, 203 Cher 84 Deus 69 Congr 113 Mut 208 Mos 2:15 Decal 48 Praem 1 Aet 13 QG 2:15b, 4:40, 153

θεοπρόπιον Her 287 Somn 1:148 Somn 2:227

θεοπρόπος Det 40 Ebr 85 Conf 29 Fug 139

θεόπτης Mut 7

θεός (2480) Opif 7, 13, 16, 16, 19, 23, 23, 24, 25, 25, 26, 27, 30, 30, 33, 38, 42, 44, 45, 46, 61, 69, 69, 69, 69, 72, 74, 75, 75, 77, 81, 82, 100, 104, 129, 134, 134, 137, 139, 140, 144, 148, 149, 149, 151, 153, 168, 169, 171, 171, 171, 172 Leg 1:2, 5, 5, 6, 16, 17, 17, 18, 18, 19, 21, 21, 21, 25, 25, 26, 26, 29, 31, 31, 31, 32, 33, 33, 34, 36, 36, 37, 37, 38, 38, 38, 39, 40, 40, 40, 40, 41, 41, 41, 41, 41, 41, 43, 43, 43, 44, 44, 45, 47, 48, 48, 48, 48, 49, 49, 49, 50, 50, 50, 51, 51, 51, 51, 51, 51, 53, 54, 56, 64, 64, 65, 65, 67, 77, 77, 78, 79, 80, 80, 82, 82, 82, 84, 88, 88, 89, 89, 90, 91, 91, 95, 95, 95, 96, 96 Leg 2:1, 1, 1, 2, 2, 2, 2, 3, 3, 3, 3, 3, 4, 6, 9, 17, 19, 31, 31, 32, 33, 34, 40, 46, 46, 47, 47, 49, 49, 51, 52, 53, 55, 56, 57, 57, 58, 60, 67, 67, 68, 71, 73, 78, 79, 79, 80, 81, 82, 83, 85, 85, 86, 86, 86, 86, 87, 88, 89, 89, 91, 92, 93, 95, 96, 101, 101, 102, 106 Leg 3:1, 1, 1, 2, 3, 4, 4, 4, 4, 4, 6, 6, 7, 7, 7, 8, 10, 10, 11, 11, 12, 12, 13, 19, 22, 22, 23, 23, 24, 26, 27, 27, 28, 28, 29, 29, 29, 31, 32, 32, 33, 33, 35, 35, 35, 36, 38, 38, 39, 39, 42, 42, 42, 42, 43, 43, 44, 46, 46, 47, 47, 48, 49, 51, 51, 52, 54, 54, 57, 59, 59, 65, 68, 69, 71, 71, 73, 73, 73, 74, 75, 77, 77, 77, 78, 78, 78, 78, 79, 81, 82, 82, 83, 83, 85, 88, 88, 89, 91, 95, 95, 96, 96, 96, 96, 96, 96, 99, 99, 101, 101, 102, 102, 103, 104, 104, 105, 105, 105, 106, 106, 107, 107, 126, 126, 131, 135, 135, 136, 137, 141, 142, 146, 147, 161, 162, 163, 163, 164, 164, 164, 166, 166, 169, 170, 171, 172, 173, 174, 174, 175, 176, 176, 177, 177, 177, 177, 177, 178, 179, 180, 180, 181, 181, 181, 181, 186, 187, 195, 196, 197, 197, 199, 203, 203, 204, 204, 204, 204, 204, 205, 205, 205, 206, 207, 207, 207, 208, 209, 209, 212, 213, 213, 214, 215, 215, 217, 222, 228, 228, 229, 237, 239, 242, 243, 245 Cher 2, 9, 10, 12, 13, 16, 16, 17, 17, 19, 20, 24, 24, 27, 27, 29, 29, 29, 31, 31, 35, 40, 44, 44, 45, 46, 46, 47, 49, 49, 50, 50, 51, 52, 52, 60, 65, 71, 72, 77, 77, 83, 85, 86, 86, 87, 87, 90, 90, 94, 96, 97, 98, 99, 101, 106, 107, 108, 109, 118, 120, 121, 121, 121, 123, 124, 124, 125, 127, 127, 127, 128, 130 Sacr 2, 2, 4, 5, 5, 5, 7, 8, 9, 9, 9, 10, 10, 12, 12, 13, 35, 37, 37, 40, 40, 42, 42, 51, 51, 52, 53, 53, 54, 55, 55, 55, 56, 57, 57, 59, 59, 60, 63, 64, 64, 65, 68, 70, 71, 71, 72, 72, 72, 76, 76, 79, 79, 87, 87, 89, 90, 91, 91, 91, 91, 92, 93, 93, 93, 94, 97, 97, 101, 101, 103, 106, 109, 119, 120, 124, 127, 129, 130, 130, 131, 132, 133, 134, 136, 137, 139 Det 4, 4, 4, 13, 29, 30, 32, 39, 44, 46, 48, 54, 55, 56, 56, 56, 57, 57, 61, 68, 69, 70, 71, 78, 82, 83, 85, 86, 86, 89, 91, 91, 93, 114, 115, 121, 122, 122, 124, 124, 124, 125, 125, 138, 138, 138, 139, 139, 139, 142, 146, 147, 147, 153, 155, 158, 159, 160, 160, 160, 161, 161, 161, 162, 162, 162, 162, 163, 163, 177 Post 1, 3, 5, 6, 7, 8, 10, 10, 12, 12, 14, 15, 16, 17, 19, 19, 22, 23, 23, 26, 26, 26, 27, 27, 29, 30, 32, 37, 43, 53, 63, 64, 64, 64, 65, 67, 69, 69, 69, 69, 73, 78, 80, 80, 89, 90, 91, 91, 92, 101, 102, 102, 115, 120, 121, 121, 121, 123, 124, 127, 135, 136, 143, 143, 143, 143, 145, 145, 151, 151, 154, 165, 166, 167, 168, 169, 169, 170, 171, 174, 175, 175, 179, 179, 183, 185 Gig 6, 16, 16, 19, 19, 22, 22, 23, 40, 42, 43, 47, 49, 53, 54, 60, 61, 63, 63, 64, 64, 64, 64, 64 Deus 1, 3, 3, 4, 4, 5, 5, 5, 7, 8, 11, 12, 17, 18, 20, 20, 20, 23, 28, 29, 29, 30, 31, 31, 31, 32, 33, 48, 49, 52, 53, 56, 58, 62, 69, 70, 72, 73, 75, 77, 78, 79, 83, 86, 87, 87, 88, 92, 92, 104, 106, 107, 107, 109, 109, 110, 117, 118, 122, 138, 138, 139, 142, 143, 155, 157, 158, 161, 181 Agr 44, 49, 50, 51, 52, 53, 54, 78, 78, 79, 123, 128, 128, 130, 168, 169, 171, 172, 173, 180 Plant 5, 8, 18, 19, 19, 26, 28, 32, 33, 35, 37, 39, 41, 42, 44, 46, 48, 50, 50, 52, 54, 58, 59, 60, 61, 62, 63, 64, 65, 68, 70, 71, 73, 74, 74, 77, 82, 82, 84, 85, 86, 86, 89, 90, 93, 93, 95, 95, 96, 108, 108, 119, 126, 128, 130, 131, 135, 137, 137 Ebr 8, 30, 30, 31, 32, 37, 37, 41, 42, 43, 43, 44, 45, 45, 62, 72, 73, 74, 77, 82, 82, 82, 83, 94, 94, 105, 106, 107, 110, 111, 117, 118, 119, 120, 120, 125, 126, 139, 144, 144, 149, 150, 152, 199, 213, 223, 224 Sobr 13, 18, 51, 53, 53, 55, 55, 56, 57, 58, 58, 59, 62, 63, 64, 66, 66 Conf 24, 30, 41, 52, 56, 58, 59, 61, 64, 65, 74, 81, 92, 93, 96, 98, 98, 98, 104, 106, 108, 116, 118, 119, 123, 124, 127, 129, 129, 135, 136, 137, 139, 142, 145, 145, 145, 146, 146, 147, 147, 149, 159, 161, 161, 166, 166, 168, 169, 169, 170, 170, 171, 173, 173, 175, 179, 179, 180, 181, 181, 188, 196, 197, 198 Migr 2, 3, 4, 5, 5, 15, 18, 19, 21, 22, 22, 25, 30, 31, 33, 40, 40, 40, 42, 43, 44, 45, 47, 48, 49, 53, 56, 56, 56, 57, 58, 59, 59, 61, 62, 73, 76, 76, 80, 81, 81, 81, 84, 84, 84, 85, 85, 88, 92, 101, 103, 113, 113, 114, 115, 120, 121, 122, 123, 124, 126, 127, 128, 129, 130, 131, 131, 131, 132, 132, 134, 135, 139, 139, 142, 143, 146, 146, 160, 166, 169, 171, 172, 173, 175, 179, 179, 180, 181, 182, 185, 191, 192, 192, 194, 194, 195, 196, 201, 202, 215, 215 Her 4, 7, 7, 15, 17, 17, 19, 19, 20, 21, 22, 38, 45, 45, 47, 50, 56, 58, 58, 58, 59, 60, 62, 66, 66, 67, 73, 76, 78, 78, 84, 90, 90, 92, 93, 94, 96, 97, 97, 99, 103, 108, 110, 110, 111, 111, 114, 114, 117, 118, 120, 120, 122, 122, 124, 127, 130, 140, 143, 156, 159, 159, 160, 162, 163, 163, 163, 164, 164, 166, 167, 167, 168, 169, 169, 172, 174, 179, 183, 186, 187, 200, 206, 206, 206, 228, 231, 231, 231, 234, 251, 257, 259, 259, 267, 271, 272, 273, 278, 311, 314, 315 Congr 7, 8, 36, 38, 49, 49, 49, 51, 56, 56, 80, 86, 86, 86, 87, 93, 94, 98, 98, 101, 103, 105, 107, 113, 114, 125, 133, 152, 153, 159, 160, 170, 170, 171, 177, 177 Fug 15, 18, 38, 40, 42, 50, 51, 51, 52, 53, 56, 56, 58, 58, 59, 60, 61, 63, 65, 65, 66, 67, 67, 67, 68, 68, 71, 71, 72, 75, 76, 76, 77, 79, 79, 80,

81, 82, 84, 88, 93, 97, 99, 101, 102, 109, 114, 132, 135, 135, 136, 137, 138, 140, 141, 141, 142, 157, 160, 162, 164, 164, 165, 168, 169, 169, 170, 172, 174, 175, 196, 198, 198, 198, 199, 208, 208, 211, 212, 212 Mut 1, 6, 6, 12, 13, 18, 18, 18, 19, 19, 19, 19, 23, 23, 23, 23, 23, 23, 24, 24, 24, 25, 26, 26, 26, 26, 27, 29, 29, 30, 31, 34, 34, 38, 39, 40, 41, 41, 42, 42, 44, 44, 45, 45, 46, 51, 52, 53, 54, 59, 63, 64, 79, 81, 81, 87, 87, 104, 105, 108, 114, 125, 125, 128, 128, 129, 131, 132, 134, 136, 137, 138, 140, 141, 152, 153, 155, 156, 169, 175, 177, 181, 182, 183, 184, 184, 186, 192, 194, 195, 201, 202, 202, 203, 205, 207, 213, 216, 217, 218, 218, 221, 222, 253, 253, 256, 258, 259, 265, 266, 268, 270 Somn 1:3, 3, 3, 38, 62, 62, 62, 63, 64, 65, 66, 66, 67, 68, 69, 70, 70, 70, 71, 72, 73, 74, 74, 74, 75, 75, 76, 76, 76, 79, 86, 87, 91, 94, 103, 112, 114, 115, 116, 117, 133, 142, 143, 147, 147, 148, 149, 152, 158, 158, 159, 159, 159, 160, 160, 163, 163, 166, 166, 171, 172, 173, 173, 179, 181, 183, 185, 189, 189, 189, 195, 196, 206, 207, 214, 215, 227, 227, 228, 228, 228, 228, 229, 229, 229, 229, 230, 231, 236, 236, 237, 237, 238, 238, 238, 239, 240, 241, 243, 244, 249, 250, 251, 252, 254, 256 Somn 2:2, 3, 24, 25, 28, 34, 45, 62, 67, 76, 99, 100, 100, 107, 136, 141, 149, 173, 173, 174, 175, 176, 177, 179, 179, 179, 183, 183, 186, 188, 189, 189, 190, 193, 194, 213, 219, 221, 222, 224, 224, 226, 228, 228, 229, 230, 231, 231, 234, 242, 242, 244, 245, 246, 248, 248, 248, 249, 250, 251, 253, 253, 253, 254, 265, 266, 272, 272, 273, 289, 290, 297 Abr 6, 17, 17, 18, 18, 31, 35, 35, 39, 41, 46, 50, 51, 51, 51, 51, 54, 57, 58, 59, 60, 68, 69, 75, 75, 77, 80, 80, 87, 88, 90, 95, 98, 104, 112, 112, 115, 119, 120, 121, 124, 127, 137, 150, 156, 158, 164, 175, 175, 176, 177, 181, 192, 196, 202, 202, 202, 203, 206, 208, 232, 235, 235, 244, 254, 258, 261, 261, 262, 268, 269, 269, 269, 271, 272, 273, 275 Ios 48, 90, 99, 107, 117, 124, 149, 165, 174, 195, 198, 236, 241, 244, 246, 253, 254, 266 Mos 1:6, 12, 17, 19, 23, 36, 47, 47, 67, 71, 76, 76, 76, 76, 77, 83, 85, 86, 88, 90, 95, 96, 101, 105, 107, 108, 110, 111, 112, 112, 120, 125, 127, 134, 148, 155, 156, 157, 157, 158, 158, 163, 173, 173, 174, 174, 180, 184, 198, 201, 204, 205, 209, 212, 212, 216, 217, 219, 225, 252, 255, 259, 277, 278, 279, 283, 284, 287, 289, 290, 304, 318 Mos 2:3, 5, 6, 11, 36, 41, 53, 61, 63, 65, 67, 96, 99, 108, 131, 132, 135, 149, 161, 163, 165, 165, 166, 168, 171, 173, 177, 177, 177, 186, 188, 190, 190, 194, 198, 199, 199, 201, 203, 205, 205, 206, 213, 228, 237, 238, 240, 241, 252, 259, 270, 273, 279, 284 Decal 8, 15, 16, 18, 18, 32, 35, 37, 38, 38, 41, 41, 44, 47, 47, 48, 51, 51, 52, 58, 58, 59, 59, 65, 66, 67, 70, 73, 75, 76, 78, 81, 82, 86, 86, 90, 91, 91, 94, 96, 97, 98, 99, 100, 101, 105, 107, 108, 110, 111, 119, 120, 120, 133, 160, 175, 176, 178, 178 Spec 1:10, 13, 15, 16, 19, 20, 20, 21, 22, 24, 25, 28, 28, 30, 31, 32, 35, 36, 40, 41, 52, 53, 57, 57, 63, 65, 65, 66, 67, 70, 81, 100, 114, 116, 116, 131, 131, 133, 152, 167, 169, 176, 183, 187, 188, 195, 196, 197, 201, 205, 207, 209, 210, 211, 215, 224, 229, 242, 252, 263, 265, 265, 271, 272, 275, 276, 277, 277, 279, 279, 279, 282, 285, 287, 293, 295, 297, 298, 299, 300, 302, 307, 307, 307, 307, 309, 310, 311, 312, 313, 315, 317, 317, 318, 318, 329, 330, 331, 332, 332, 344, 344, 345, 345 Spec 2:1, 2, 3, 10, 10, 10, 11, 13, 15, 17, 23, 27, 27, 34, 35, 38, 51, 53, 54, 55, 55, 63, 108, 113, 113, 134, 134, 146, 152, 156, 164, 164, 165, 167, 171, 173, 174, 176, 180, 187, 189, 192, 196, 198, 204, 209, 215, 217, 224, 225, 235, 252, 253, 254, 255, 256, 258, 258, 260 Spec 3:6, 7, 29, 36, 52, 88, 99, 120, 121, 122, 125, 127, 178, 180, 189, 191, 194 Spec 4:14, 31, 39, 40, 48, 52, 71, 73, 73, 98, 123, 127, 131, 147, 157, 159, 164, 176, 177, 187, 188, 191, 199, 200, 217 Virt 8, 9, 26, 26, 35, 40, 41, 45, 46, 47, 49, 54, 57, 58, 61, 62, 63, 64, 65, 65, 67, 68, 72, 75, 77, 79, 85, 95, 98, 102, 102, 120, 133, 135, 159, 163, 164, 165, 165, 168, 168, 171, 172, 174, 177, 179, 179, 181, 184, 184, 184, 185, 188, 195, 200, 203, 204, 208, 209, 212, 216, 218, 218 Praem 9, 13, 14, 16, 25, 27, 27, 27, 28, 30, 32, 36, 40, 44, 44, 45, 46, 46, 51, 54, 54, 55, 55, 72, 81, 84, 84, 90, 95, 98, 101, 104, 108, 110, 115, 117, 120, 121, 122, 123, 123, 123, 124, 126, 142, 149, 152, 152, 162, 163, 167, 168, 169 Prob 19, 20, 42, 42, 43, 43, 43, 43, 44, 44, 62, 75, 80, 106, 116, 130, 130, 149 Contempl 8, 26, 29, 66, 80, 84, 86, 87 Aet 1, 1, 2, 8, 8, 10, 13, 13, 13, 19, 20, 26, 39, 40, 41, 41, 43, 46, 46, 46, 46, 47, 47, 73, 78, 83, 84, 84, 85, 106, 106, 106, 108, 112, 131 Flacc 46, 102, 121, 170, 191 Legat 4, 6, 75, 91, 99, 110, 114, 115, 118, 118, 138, 154, 157, 162, 163, 163, 164, 164, 196, 198, 213, 218, 220, 236, 240, 245, 265, 278, 278, 278, 290, 290, 317, 318, 336, 347, 347, 353, 354, 366, 367, 372 Hypoth 6:1, 6:1, 6:4, 6:9, 7:2, 7:2, 7:3, 7:3, 7:4, 7:5, 7:5, 7:6, 7:7, 7:8, 7:9, 7:18, 7:19 Prov 1, 2:2, 3, 6, 7, 9, 10, 16, 16, 34, 35, 38, 41, 43, 44, 53, 54, 61, 72 QG 1:21, 21, 55a, 55a, 55a, 55b, 60:2, 60:2, 60:2, 63, 64b, 73, 89, 96:1, 96:1, 100:1a, 100:1b, 100:1b, 100:1b, 100:2a, 100:2b, 2:10, 13b, 16, 17b, 26a, 34a, 48, 48, 54a, 54a, 54a, 54a, 54a, 54b, 62, 62, 62, 62, 64c, 3:8, 18, 4:52d, 97:1, 97:1, 97:2, 130, 180, 180, 180, 9* QG isf 3, 13, 16 QG (Par) 2:4 QE 1:1, 2:2, 3b, 3b, 10b, 14, 16, 37, 45a, 45a, 45a, 47, 47, 50b, 65, 71, 105, 105 QE isf 3, 3, 3, 7, 9, 11, 12, 14, 29, 29

θεοσέβεια (9) Opif 154 Her 60 Congr 130 Fug 150 Abr 114 Mos 1:303 Spec 4:134, 170 Virt 186

θεοσεβής Mut 197 QG 1:66

θεοσύλης Prov 2:39

θεοφιλής (73) Opif 5, 114 Leg 1:76 Leg 2:79, 81, 88, 90 Leg 3:130 Cher 49 Sacr 77 Det 13, 50 Post 179 Deus 10, 157 Plant 62, 74 Sobr 19, 29, 64 Conf 95 Migr 63, 67, 114, 158 Her 82, 201, 203 Somn 1:108, 243 Somn 2:225 Abr 27, 46, 50, 89, 98, 123, 123, 167, 181, 196, 247 Ios 167, 200 Mos 1:147, 255 Mos 2:67, 108, 160, 163, 279 Spec 1:41 Spec 2:180 Spec 3:126 Spec 4:175 Virt 77, 179, 184, 220 Praem 24, 27, 43 Prob 42 Contempl 68, 85 Hypoth 6:7 Prov 2:16 QG 2:16, 65, 4:76a, 208 QG isf 1, 10

θεοφορέω (11) Ebr 99 Her 46, 69 Somn 1:2 Somn 2:232 Mos 1:210, 283 Mos 2:69, 250, 264, 273

θεοφόρητος (13) Deus 138 Ebr 147 Her 258, 265 Congr 132 Fug 90 Mut 120, 136, 203 Somn 1:254 Somn 2:2 Mos 2:246 Spec 1:65

θεοφράδμων Her 301 Mut 96 Mos 2:269

Θεόφραστος Aet 117

θεόχρηστος Legat 210

θεράπαινα (8) Her 42 Abr 251 Spec 2:66 Spec 3:69, 184 Virt 223 QG 3:20a, 22

θεραπαινίς (26) Opif 165 Post 130 Congr 9, 9, 11, 12, 22, 23, 24, 29, 30, 72, 73, 74, 77, 78, 80, 145, 152, 154, 156 Fug 73, 205 Abr 254 Mos 1:14 Virt 223

θεραπεία (99) Leg 3:18 Cher 15, 94 Sacr 37, 37, 48, 58, 87, 120, 121, 123 Det 14, 21, 43, 55, 55, 56 Gig 12 Deus 63, 66, 102, 116 Plant 38 Ebr 75, 144 Conf 9, 94

Her 8, 123, 123, 298 Fug 40, 41, 47 Mut 89, 171 Somn 1:161 Somn 2:99, 197 Abr 128, 129, 170, 189 Ios 33, 65, 98, 115, 238, 251 Mos 1:20, 49, 147, 152, 265 Mos 2:5, 67, 173 Decal 54, 64, 76, 108 Spec 1:20, 24, 31, 57, 96, 191, 197, 230, 263, 303, 312 Spec 2:17, 38, 165, 166, 258 Spec 3:117 Spec 4:142, 147, 192 Virt 40, 54, 163, 185, 221 Praem 81, 142, 166 Prob 58 Contempl 12 Flacc 149 Legat 17, 173, 278 Prov 2:17, 17 QG 2:41, 4:8*

θεραπευτής (30) Leg 3:135 Sacr 13, 118, 127 Det 160 Post 182 Plant 60 Ebr 69, 126, 210 Conf 174 Migr 124 Congr 105 Mut 106 Somn 1:78 Mos 2:135, 149, 274 Decal 66 Spec 1:309 Virt 185 Praem 43, 108 Prob 75 Contempl 2, 22, 88, 90 Legat 97 QE isf 29

θεραπευτικός (7) Sacr 120 Det 54 Agr 167 Fug 42, 91 Mos 2:189 Contempl 11

θεραπευτρίς Post 184 Somn 1:232 Somn 2:273 Contempl 2, 88

θεραπεύω (82) Leg 2:87 Leg 3:36, 118, 127, 128 Cher 105 Sacr 39, 39, 39, 44, 118 Det 43, 53, 54 Post 141 Deus 66, 66 Plant 72, 105 Ebr 76, 86, 131 Conf 94, 95 Her 223, 299 Congr 53, 53, 134 Fug 27, 89 Somn 1:35, 77, 110, 218 Somn 2:90, 183, 232 Abr 125, 128, 130 Ios 10, 23, 64, 76, 77, 242 Mos 2:5, 22, 67, 139 Decal 71, 129 Spec 1:31, 42 Spec 2:21, 167, 239, 241, 259 Spec 3:27 Spec 4:191 Virt 185, 217 Praem 19, 56, 106 Prob 35, 39, 43 Contempl 2, 2 Flacc 9, 108 Legat 32, 35, 140, 260 Hypoth 11:13, 11:13 Prov 2:17 QG 4:168

θεράπων (37) Sacr 12, 69, 133 Det 62 Post 109 Her 7 Fug 67 Mut 21 Abr 171, 210 Ios 36, 45, 50, 104, 211 Decal 4, 167 Spec 1:126, 242 Spec 2:66, 69, 69, 91, 122, 123, 233 Spec 3:137, 196, 198, 198, 201 Prob 100, 103 Contempl 70 Legat 361 QG 2:16 QE isf 26

θερίζω (16) Deus 166 Conf 21, 152 Mut 269, 269 Somn 2:21, 23, 23, 25, 30, 30, 75, 76, 77 Ios 6 Legat 293

θερινός Opif 112 Her 147, 149, 149 Mos 1:114

θερισμός (8) Somn 2:23, 23, 23, 25, 29, 75, 75, 77

θεριστής Virt 90

θέριστρον Somn 2:53

θερμαίνω Mos 2:148

θέρμη Sobr 44, 45

θερμολουσία Sacr 21 Legat 14

θερμός (33) Opif 62, 161 Leg 2:2 Leg 3:61 Cher 28 Sacr 108 Plant 3, 4, 62, 160 Ebr 186 Conf 101 Migr 50 Her 135, 135, 146, 153, 208 Somn 1:19 Abr 148, 159, 239 Ios 175 Mos 1:212 Spec 1:57, 208 Spec 4:56 Contempl 73 Aet 26, 105 Legat 125, 126 Prov 2:59

θερμότης Deus 79 Plant 133 Aet 21, 29

θέρος (39) Opif 45, 52, 58 Cher 112, 112 Deus 39 Plant 120 Migr 217 Her 136, 146, 165, 208 Fug 180 Somn 1:20 Somn 2:131 Ios 111, 139 Mos 1:6, 115, 226, 265 Mos 2:124 Spec 1:92, 183, 210 Spec 2:20, 220 Spec 3:17 Spec 4:208, 214, 235 Virt 93 Praem 130 Contempl 38 Legat 260 Hypoth 11:12 Prov 2:23, 44, 48

Θερσίτης Contempl 9

θέσις (37) Opif 148, 149 Leg 1:35, 55 Leg 2:14, 14, 15 Leg 3:126 Cher 54, 55, 56 Sacr 15 Agr 1 Ebr 34, 81, 181 Migr 94 Her 213 Mut 64, 89 Somn 1:230 Abr 250 Ios 30 Mos 1:224, 229 Mos 2:49, 91, 98 Decal 55 Spec 1:94 Aet 29, 32 Legat 23, 28 QG 1:20, 4:184, 184

θεσμοθέτης Migr 23 Her 167

θεσμός (44) Opif 61, 143, 171 Leg 3:204 Cher 106 Det 142 Ebr 84, 84 Conf 174 Her 168, 169, 172 Congr 120 Somn 2:174 Abr 6, 276 Ios 30 Mos 2:211 Decal 32, 41, 132 Spec 1:202 Spec 2:13, 13, 58, 170, 233 Spec 3:30, 61, 63, 176 Spec 4:215, 232 Virt 104, 112, 132 Prob 3, 79 Aet 31, 59 Legat 7, 68 Prov 2:3 QG 4:8c

θεσμοφύλαξ Sacr 50

θεσμῳδέω Somn 1:193

θεσμῳδός Hypoth 7:14

θεσπέσιος (8) Plant 29 Migr 90 Spec 1:8, 314 Spec 3:178 Virt 8 Praem 43 QG 4:174

θεσπίζω (51) Leg 3:86 Her 2, 25, 100, 260 Fug 197 Mut 13, 139 Somn 1:231 Somn 2:1 Abr 127, 169, 203, 262 Ios 100 Mos 1:57, 175, 201, 274, 277 Mos 2:34, 165, 187, 188, 190, 192, 213, 229, 243, 246, 250, 258, 264, 269, 270, 280, 288 Decal 18, 19, 32, 36, 43, 175, 177 Spec 1:65 Spec 2:188 Spec 3:125 Spec 4:39 Virt 63 Praem 2 Contempl 25

θεσπιῳδός Conf 174 Mut 126

Θεσσαλία Legat 281

θέσφατος Her 287 Mos 2:74, 248 Legat 347

θετικός Mos 1:130

θετός Agr 6 Congr 23 Mut 147 Flacc 9

θέω (12) Opif 86, 88 Agr 115 Somn 2:121 Abr 183 Ios 181 Mos 1:54, 102, 118 Mos 2:170 Flacc 87, 186

Θέων (7) Aet 48, 48, 49, 49, 49, 50, 51

θεωρέω (65) Opif 54, 67, 99, 131 Leg 1:14, 74, 74 Leg 2:38, 57, 70, 80 Leg 3:34, 34 Det 3 Post 118 Gig 9, 17, 52 Deus 93 Sobr 47 Conf 31 Migr 39, 148 Her 48, 151, 151 Congr 59, 151 Fug 37 Mut 4, 82, 217 Somn 1:6, 66 Somn 2:26, 258, 302 Abr 161, 162, 208, 236, 243, 271 Mos 1:121 Mos 2:74 Decal 97 Virt 57 Praem 26, 40, 45, 45, 45, 46 Contempl 29, 30, 68, 78, 78 Aet 14, 100, 142 Prov 2:24, 58, 62 QG 3:29

θεώρημα (62) Opif 82 Leg 1:94 Leg 3:84, 92, 93 Cher 71 Sacr 80 Det 38, 65, 66, 118 Post 130, 137, 147, 149, 149 Deus 92 Agr 132, 158 Plant 31, 52, 81 Ebr 132 Conf 102 Migr 13, 55, 150, 191 Her 116, 286 Congr 19, 35, 47, 142, 143, 146 Fug 172, 200 Mut 5, 100, 122, 220 Somn 1:6, 11, 50, 59, 107 Somn 2:71 Abr 207, 220, 243, 269 Ios 2 Spec 2:40, 200 Spec 4:75, 107, 141 Virt 8 Praem 64, 122 QG 4:47a

θεωρητικός (22) Leg 1:57, 57, 57, 58 Migr 47, 70, 165, 165 Her 279 Fug 36, 176 Somn 2:173, 250 Mos 1:48 Decal 101 Spec 2:64, 64 Spec 3:117 Praem 11, 51 Contempl 58, 67

θεωρητός Post 164 Migr 95, 214 Her 131 Mut 118

θεωρία (50) Opif 77, 78, 96 Leg 1:57, 58, 58 Leg 3:141 Sacr 44, 120 Agr 12 Plant 71 Ebr 94 Migr 53, 77, 150 Her 246, 274 Congr 11, 16, 17, 20, 23, 46, 49 Fug 37, 141 Mut 76 Abr 131, 164 Mos 1:23 Mos 2:66, 69, 216 Decal 98 Spec 1:176, 269, 288, 327 Spec 2:29, 52 Spec 3:1, 2 Spec 4:105 Praem 51 Prob 63 Contempl 1, 64, 90 Aet 48 QG 2:72

θεωρός Somn 2:81 Spec 2:45 Spec 3:202

Θῆβαι Spec 3:15

θήκη Hypoth 7:7

θηλάζω Det 115 Migr 140, 140 Her 20 Virt 128

θηλυγονέω Gig 4

θηλυδρίας Cher 82 Sacr 32 Post 165 Gig 4

θηλυκός Leg 3:8 Deus 141

θηλυμανέω Abr 135

θηλύμορφος Spec 1:325

θηλύνω Cher 50 Deus 3

θῆλυς (78) Opif 13, 13, 14, 76, 134, 161 Leg 2:13, 97, 97 Leg 3:11, 243 Cher 43, 111, 111 Sacr 103, 103, 112 Det 28, 170, 172, 172 Post 177 Agr 73, 73, 139 Plant 15 Ebr 55, 61, 212 Migr 95 Her 139, 164 Fug 51, 51, 51, 128 Mut 233, 261 Somn 2:184 Abr 101, 101, 102, 136, 150, 150 Mos 1:8 Mos 2:60, 210 Decal 54 Spec 1:200, 200, 212, 228, 233, 325, 331 Spec 2:33, 33, 34, 58, 164 Spec 3:37, 37, 43, 47, 169, 178, 178 Virt 18 Prob 124 Contempl 60 Aet 66 Hypoth 7:1 Prov 2:71 QG 2:14 QE 1:7a, 2:3a, 3b

θηλυτοκέω Migr 206

θηλυτόκος Gig 5

θημών Mos 1:105 Hypoth 7:6

θήρ (12) Agr 154 Plant 41, 151 Somn 2:67 Ios 25 Decal 89 Spec 3:115 Spec 4:120, 121 Praem 85, 149 Prob 147

θήρα (27) Sacr 29 Post 18, 116 Deus 101 Plant 101 Her 251, 310 Somn 1:8, 251 Somn 2:206 Abr 126 Ios 213 Mos 1:43, 60, 61, 284, 298 Spec 3:34, 51 Spec 4:43, 67 Virt 39, 195 Prov 2:56, 63 QG 4:167 QE isf 26

θηρατικός Somn 1:49

θηράω (14) Cher 122 Post 141, 179 Deus 19 Plant 145 Ebr 198 Conf 118 Abr 190 Ios 44 Mos 2:234 Spec 2:261 Spec 3:44, 113, 157

θήρειος Spec 3:99

θηρευτικός Leg 3:2 Gig 60 Abr 266

θηρεύω (8) Cher 57, 58, 64, 65 Her 251, 252, 252, 252

θηριάλωτος Ios 36 Spec 4:119, 120

θηρίκλειος Contempl 49

θηριομαχία Mut 160

θηρίον (69) Opif 64, 153 Leg 2:9, 9, 9, 9, 11, 11, 11, 12, 53, 71, 106 Leg 3:65, 107, 113 Post 160 Agr 91 Plant 43 Ebr 174 Conf 24 Her 137 Somn 1:49 Somn 2:54, 65, 66 Abr 8, 33, 149 Ios 14, 22, 36 Mos 1:43, 109 Decal 80, 110, 113, 114, 115 Spec 1:301 Spec 3:45, 57, 99, 103, 115 Spec 4:103, 119 Virt 87 Praem 85, 87, 88, 88, 91 Prob 89 Contempl 8 Flacc 66, 188 Legat 131, 139, 163 Prov 2:14, 56, 58, 65, 69 QG 1:74, 2:26a QG isf 10 QE 2:25a

θηριόω Ios 81 Spec 2:94 Spec 4:103 Prob 64

θηριώδης (14) Sacr 32 Agr 46 Somn 2:54 Abr 32 Ios 171 Decal 78 Spec 3:158 Virt 2 Flacc 36, 177 Legat 10, 20, 121, 147

θής Spec 2:81 Virt 122

θησαυρίζω (24) Leg 3:36 Sacr 31, 33, 62 Det 35, 43 Post 57 Deus 156 Ebr 73, 200 Sobr 41, 68 Conf 50, 69, 92 Her 200 Mut 90 Ios 111, 258 Mos 1:152 Spec 2:199 Spec 4:158 Flacc 179 Legat 108

θησαυρός (28) Leg 3:104, 105, 105, 105, 105, 105, 106, 106 Cher 48 Sacr 22, 22, 25 Deus 91, 92, 96, 150, 156, 156 Plant 57 Migr 121 Her 76, 76 Congr 127 Fug 79 Ios 198 Legat 9 Prov 2:11 QE 2:50b

θησαυροφυλακέω (11) Post 62 Plant 57 Migr 160, 204 Somn 2:46 Spec 1:23 Spec 2:92 Spec 4:74 Virt 90, 140 Prob 76

θητεύω Ios 26 Spec 2:39

θίασος (33) Post 101 Plant 14, 58 Ebr 70, 94 Migr 90 Fug 10, 28, 89, 126 Mut 32, 198, 205 Somn 1:196 Somn 2:10, 127, 139, 277 Abr 20 Mos 2:185 Spec 1:323 Spec 2:44, 193 Spec 3:169 Spec 4:47 Praem 20 Prob 2, 85 Flacc 136, 137 Legat 97, 166 Hypoth 11:5

θιασώτης (15) Cher 85 Sacr 7 Det 45, 140 Deus 120 Plant 39 Conf 44, 83 Migr 149 Fug 145 Somn 1:225 Somn 2:78, 209, 254 Spec 1:344

θιγγάνω Hypoth 7:3

θίξις QE 2:45b

θλαδίας (7) Leg 3:8 Ebr 213 Migr 69 Somn 2:184 Spec 1:325, 328, 344

θλάσμα Aet 6

θλάω Mut 205 Spec 1:328

θλίβω (11) Migr 157 Ios 22, 179 Mos 1:271 Decal 145 Virt 146 Praem 145, 145 Aet 129 Flacc 160 QG 4:33a

θλῖψις Gig 17

θνησιμαῖος Spec 4:119, 120

θνήσκω (97) Leg 1:7, 107, 108, 108 Leg 3:69 Sacr 115, 125 Det 33, 48, 49, 49, 70, 70, 74, 152, 178 Post 44, 45 Ebr 95 Conf 36, 122 Migr 122, 162 Her 53, 201, 201 Fug 55, 55 Somn 1:150 Somn 2:70, 84, 234, 234, 235, 235, 260, 269, 280, 280 Abr 45, 230 Ios 17, 22, 25, 77, 156, 167, 184, 185, 189, 216, 255, 264 Mos 1:45, 73, 183 Mos 2:203, 218, 227, 252, 291 Spec 1:160, 266, 345 Spec 2:94, 95, 247, 248 Spec 3:38, 49, 94, 106, 106, 108, 129, 141, 145, 146, 150 Virt 111 Praem 70 Prob 22, 23, 116, 116 Aet 5, 27, 30, 109, 144 Legat 63, 85, 192, 325 QG 1:70:1, 70:2, 70:2

θνητός (299) Opif 4, 61, 62, 77, 84, 117, 119, 134, 135, 135, 135, 135, 142, 149, 151, 151, 152, 156, 165 Leg 1:4, 4, 5, 9, 16, 16, 18, 20, 45, 86 Leg 2:16, 17, 23, 33, 47, 57, 57, 80, 96, 96, 96 Leg 3:31, 35, 42, 84, 99, 186 Cher 31, 43, 47, 49, 51, 66, 82, 83, 85, 106, 107 Sacr 5, 35, 40, 58, 63, 64, 65, 70, 76, 79, 95, 95, 101, 109, 127, 129, 132 Det 30, 87, 87, 95, 114, 139, 159, 163 Post 8, 63, 134, 135, 171, 173 Gig 12, 17, 17, 56 Deus 4, 12, 75, 77, 79, 120, 123, 137, 152, 152, 172, 180 Agr 8, 51, 139, 139 Plant 14, 31 Ebr 70, 72, 76, 86, 100, 101, 110, 145, 152 Sobr 12, 53 Conf 41, 57, 78, 79, 122 Migr 13, 18, 18, 23, 24, 47, 53, 74, 141, 168, 171, 185, 192 Her 14, 33, 52, 77, 92, 127, 138, 139, 172, 172, 172, 205, 209, 226, 227, 240, 265, 272, 316 Congr 8, 30, 84, 85, 94, 97 Fug 39, 45, 59, 61, 62, 63, 64, 69, 84, 88, 129, 158, 159 Mut 8, 13, 36, 38, 48, 49, 54, 80, 104, 122, 122, 133, 134, 136, 142, 144, 155, 166, 181, 184, 185, 186, 187, 219 Somn 1:24, 36, 68, 82, 118, 138, 139, 147, 218, 243 Somn 2:70, 72, 178, 228, 230, 231 Abr 30, 32, 55, 66, 76, 165 Ios 71, 254 Mos 1:158, 184, 201 Mos 2:6, 68, 121, 194, 207, 288, 291 Decal 41, 99, 101, 107, 107 Spec 1:21, 81, 196, 252, 298 Spec 2:124, 173, 230, 255, 261 Spec 3:2 Spec 4:14, 188 Virt 9, 9, 10, 53, 73, 76, 78, 203, 203, 204, 205 Praem 1, 1, 13, 36, 39, 44, 87, 119, 119 Prob 19, 20, 24, 46, 105, 105, 137 Contempl 6, 6, 13, 37, 68 Aet 44, 46, 59 Flacc 123 Legat 84, 85, 91 Prov 1, 2:22 QG 2:62, 3:11a, 4:169 QE isf 3, 15

Θοβέλ Post 114, 119, 120

θοίνη (9) Sacr 33 Agr 66 Somn 2:87 Ios 25 Mos 1:187 Spec 3:115 Virt 136 Legat 356 Prov 2:70

θολερός Agr 144 Somn 2:150

θόρυβος (15) Agr 45 Mut 144 Abr 27 Mos 1:178 Decal 86 Spec 1:298 Spec 3:5 Praem 157 Contempl 19 Flacc 41, 120, 135, 142 Legat 90, 175

θράσος (22) Opif 45 Sacr 21 Deus 163, 164 Conf 29, 117, 118 Migr 170 Her 10 Abr 213 Mos 1:302 Mos 2:197 Spec 1:270 Spec 3:64, 66, 88 Spec 4:2 Prob 109 Legat 56, 262 Hypoth 11:16 QG 4:52d

θρασύνω (8) Det 44 Agr 157 Mos 1:95, 120 Spec 3:173 Spec 4:222 Praem 94 Legat 77

θρασύς (17) Leg 2:67 Leg 3:15 Sacr 32 Det 18 Post 82 Ebr 116 Conf 29 Migr 224 Mos 1:130, 130 Decal 115 Spec 1:279 Spec 4:127 Virt 2 Praem 86 Legat 132 Prov 2:65

θρασύτης (13) Det 24 Post 52, 82 Ebr 115 Migr 136 Her 21 Abr 153 Spec 3:173, 175 Spec 4:146 Virt 4 Praem 52 QE isf 24

θραῦσις Her 201 Somn 2:235, 236

θραύω Fug 201

θρέμμα (85) Opif 84 Cher 96 Sacr 11, 104 Det 13, 25 Post 68, 98 Deus 181 Agr 29, 31, 34, 39, 48, 48, 66, 68, 83 Migr 212 Congr 94 Mut 105, 105, 115 Somn 1:197, 209 Somn 2:83, 152, 153, 267 Abr 135, 149, 160, 209, 213, 221 Ios 11, 113, 257 Mos 1:51, 53, 63, 133, 145, 152, 243, 320, 330, 333 Decal 114 Spec 1:141, 148, 148, 158, 275 Spec 2:109, 142, 213 Spec 3:50, 146, 148 Spec 4:24, 36, 94, 98, 158 Virt 82, 95, 141, 144, 146, 163, 173 Praem 107, 139, 141 Prob 30 Contempl 14, 36, 74 Flacc 178 Legat 124 Hypoth 11:8 Prov 2:32 QG isf 17 QE 1:19

θρεπτικός Opif 67 Post 96 Deus 37 QG 2:59

θρηνέω Leg 3:231 Ios 21 Legat 190

θρῆνος (9) Ebr 95, 121 Migr 157 Somn 2:66 Abr 260 Mos 1:136 Mos 2:162 Spec 3:125 Contempl 73

θρηνώδης Legat 228

θρησκεία Det 21 Fug 41 Spec 1:315 Legat 232, 298

θρίξ (18) Leg 2:22 Sacr 21, 83 Deus 88 Ebr 174 Migr 97 Her 131 Somn 1:253 Ios 16 Mos 2:111 Spec 1:5, 165, 250, 254 Spec 3:37 Virt 111 Contempl 50 Legat 223

θρόνος Congr 118

θρόος (θροῦς) Her 12 Mos 2:164 Decal 148

θροῦς θρόος

θρυλέω Aet 107 Legat 73

θρύπτω (11) Opif 131 Sacr 21 Det 34 Plant 159 Ebr 22, 219 Migr 111 Mut 84 Somn 2:202 Decal 122 Aet 125

θρύψις (12) Opif 164 Cher 12, 92 Post 182 Plant 39 Ebr 21 Her 77 Somn 2:47 Abr 136 Ios 61 Mos 2:184 Spec 4:102

θυγάτηρ (85) Leg 3:21, 225, 232 Cher 67, 67, 67, 68, 68 Det 106 Post 34, 76, 76, 77, 98, 175, 177 Gig 1, 5, 6, 17, 18 Deus 1, 2, 3 Ebr 164, 165, 165, 203 Migr 31, 205, 206, 206, 224 Her 43 Congr 131 Fug 29, 48, 50, 50, 51, 52 Mut 110, 116 Somn 1:78, 88, 89, 89 Abr 98, 181, 187 Ios 121 Mos 1:13, 59, 330 Mos 2:234, 239, 243, 244 Spec 1:111, 112, 129, 130, 130, 312, 316 Spec 2:124, 127, 129, 130, 227 Spec 3:26, 29, 81 Praem 134, 158, 166 Prob 122 Contempl 13 Aet 121, 121 Legat 62, 63, 71 QG 4:97:1 QE isf 22

θυγατριδῆ Spec 3:26

θυγατριδοῦς (6) Mos 1:13, 32, 45, 149 Praem 109 Flacc 158

θυγατροποιός Ebr 164

Θυέστειος Praem 134

θυΐσκη Congr 114

θῦμα (6) Migr 202 Congr 106 Mos 2:231 Spec 1:180, 228 Legat 234

θυμαρής (θυμήρης) Abr 245 Contempl 66 Prov 2:26

θυμηδία Legat 18

θυμήρης θυμαρής

θυμίαμα (9) Her 196, 197, 199 Congr 114 Spec 1:72, 171, 171, 274, 276

θυμιατήριον (9) Her 226, 226, 227, 227 Mos 2:94, 101, 105, 146 Spec 1:231

θυμιάω Leg 2:56 Sacr 43

θυμικός (11) Opif 86 Leg 1:70, 70, 70, 71, 72, 72 Leg 3:115, 115, 124, 130

θυμός (70) Leg 1:71, 73 Leg 3:114, 116, 118, 118, 123, 123, 123, 124, 124, 127, 128, 128, 129, 130, 131, 131, 131, 132, 136, 137, 140, 147 Gig 17, 17 Deus 52, 60, 70, 71, 72 Agr 17, 73, 78, 112 Ebr 222, 222, 223 Conf 21, 21 Migr 66, 66, 67, 67, 67, 68, 208, 210 Her 64 Fug 23 Somn 1:235 Somn 2:165, 191, 191 Ios 10, 21, 173, 222 Mos 1:292 Spec 1:145, 146 Spec 3:92, 193 Spec 4:10, 92, 93 Virt 13 Praem 59 Legat 166, 367

θυμόω Deus 51, 70, 72, 72

θύρα (10) Agr 148 Ebr 49 Fug 144 Abr 15, 191 Spec 1:156 Virt 109 Prov 2:19 QG (Par) 2:6, 2:6

θύραζε Plant 35 Mos 1:115 QG (Par) 2:6, 2:7

θύραθεν Opif 67 Decal 142 Legat 126

θυραυλέω Agr 37

θυραυλία Cher 92

θυρίς Plant 169 Legat 364 QG 2:34a, 34a, 34a

θύρσος Legat 79

θυρών Fug 187

θυρωρέω QE 2:13b

θυσία (175) Leg 3:133, 137 Cher 94 Sacr 52, 76, 87, 88, 88, 110, 136 Det 21 Agr 127 Plant 107, 108, 108, 126, 162, 162, 165 Ebr 66, 79, 129, 131 Migr 67, 202 Her 174, 182 Congr 102, 103 Somn 1:62, 172, 212, 215 Somn 2:67, 71, 72, 73, 299 Abr 171 Mos 1:87, 88, 89, 277, 287, 298 Mos 2:73, 94, 106, 107, 108, 133, 141, 146, 147, 153, 158, 159, 162, 174, 224, 226, 228, 270, 279 Decal 78, 158, 159 Spec 1:21, 56, 67, 70, 83, 97, 98, 113, 125, 135, 145, 151, 151, 161, 166, 168, 170, 171, 179, 184, 185, 188, 189, 190, 193, 193, 194, 195, 196, 196, 198, 201, 212, 215, 220, 221, 221, 222, 223, 224, 224, 225, 229, 239, 240, 242, 247, 251, 252, 253, 253, 253, 254, 254, 256, 256, 256, 257, 258, 269, 270, 272, 276, 283, 286, 290, 290, 291, 297, 297, 297, 316 Spec 2:17, 35, 145, 188 Spec 3:55, 56, 56, 91, 125, 131, 171, 183 Spec 4:98 Virt 40, 126, 135, 135, 135, 136, 146 Flacc 4 Legat 12, 156, 157, 208, 232, 280, 291, 296, 312, 317, 355 QG 1:62:1, 62:1 QE 2:14, 49b

θυσιαστήριον (21) Leg 1:48, 48, 50 Ebr 127, 132, 138 Conf 160 Her 182, 251 Fug 53, 80 Mut 234 Somn 2:71 Mos 2:106 Spec 1:83, 285, 287, 290, 291, 293 QG 1:62:2

θύτης Spec 1:60 Spec 4:48

θυτικός Spec 1:64

θύω (70) Leg 3:94, 94, 94, 125, 165 Sacr 51, 71 Deus 8 Plant 108, 161, 162, 163, 163 Ebr 126, 140 Migr 25 Congr 5 Fug 18, 19 Mut 248 Somn 1:62, 172 Abr 235 Mos 1:73, 219, 302 Mos 2:147, 152, 165, 224, 231, 233 Decal 72, 74, 159 Spec 1:68, 100, 147, 177, 181, 188, 191, 195, 203, 221, 221, 223, 223, 242, 256, 260, 260, 277, 283 Spec 2:145, 146 Spec 3:80 Spec 4:191 Virt 134 Contempl 74 Legat 355, 356, 356, 357, 357 Prov 2:64 QG 1:62:1, 62:2, 63, 63

θωπεία Prob 99

θωπεύω Mos 1:46

θωράκιον Spec 3:149 Contempl 33

θωρακοειδής Spec 1:86

θώραξ (9) Leg 3:115 Mos 2:143 Spec 1:146 Spec 4:93 Prob 78 Flacc 90 Legat 97 Prov 2:17 QG (Par) 2:2

θώψ (9) Leg 3:202 Ios 73, 78 Prob 25, 99 Flacc 102, 108 Legat 162 Hypoth 11:15

I

Ἰακώβ (118) Leg 1:61 Leg 2:59, 59, 89, 94, 94, 94, 103 Leg 3:2, 2, 15, 16, 18, 18, 18, 22, 23, 23, 23, 26, 26, 88, 90, 93, 177, 181, 190, 191 Cher 40, 46, 67 Sacr 5, 17, 18, 42, 64, 81, 119, 120, 120, 135 Det 3, 13, 45, 46, 67 Post 59, 62, 75, 76, 89 Deus 119 Agr 42 Plant 44, 90, 110 Ebr 9, 9, 82, 82, 82 Sobr 26, 65 Conf 72, 72, 80 Migr 39, 125, 153, 199, 200 Her 180, 251, 252, 256, 261 Congr 35, 62, 70, 70 Fug 4, 7, 10, 23, 43, 52 Mut 12, 13, 81, 81, 83, 83, 87, 88, 97, 210, 215 Somn 1:4, 45, 168, 170, 171, 172, 183, 189, 196 Somn 2:15, 19, 66, 135 Abr 51, 52 Mos 1:76 QG 4:88, 88, 163:1, 163:2, 166

Ἰάμνεια Legat 200, 203

ἰάομαι (29) Leg 1:70, 76 Leg 3:118, 124, 129, 178, 178, 215, 226, 226 Det 146 Deus 135 Conf 22 Somn 2:297 Ios 193, 197 Mos 1:198 Mos 2:139 Spec 2:17, 136 Virt 26 Prob 58 Aet 63 Legat 106, 145, 241 Prov 2:14, 17 QG 3:8

ἰάσιμος Agr 40 Somn 2:196 Mos 1:58 Spec 3:122 Spec 4:181

ἴασις (7) Leg 2:79 Leg 3:106 Sacr 4, 4, 127 Det 43 Post 10

Ἰάσων Prob 143

ἰατρεῖον Spec 3:106

ἰατρεύω Somn 1:69 Prov 2:60

ἰατρικός (20) Leg 1:59 Leg 3:178 Det 43 Deus 87 Agr 40 Ebr 184 Conf 187 Migr 219 Her 297 Mut 122 Somn 1:251 Ios 75 Decal 12 Contempl 2 Legat 106 Prov 2:18, 60, 61, 71 QG 4:76b

ἰατρολογία Agr 13

ἰατρός (56) Opif 105 Leg 2:6 Leg 3:177, 226, 226 Cher 15 Sacr 70, 70, 121, 123 Det 44 Post 141, 142 Deus 63, 65, 67 Agr 142 Plant 173 Conf 22, 151 Congr 53, 138 Mut 122, 170, 221 Somn 1:51 Ios 10, 33, 62, 63, 160 Mos 1:42 Decal 150 Spec 1:252 Spec 2:31 Spec 3:117 Spec 4:83, 153, 186 Praem 33, 33 Prob 12, 58 Contempl 16, 44 Aet 79 Legat 17, 109, 273 Hypoth 7:16, 7:20 Prov 2:17 QG 2:41, 4:76b, 204 QE 2:25d

Ἰάφεθ Leg 2:62 Sobr 59, 59, 67

Ἴβηρος Flacc 2

ἶβις Decal 79 Contempl 8 Legat 163

ἰδέα (216) Opif 14, 16, 17, 18, 20, 22, 25, 25, 29, 34, 40, 41, 43, 55, 63, 71, 74, 102, 111, 129, 134, 145 Leg 1:1, 19, 19, 21, 21, 22, 22, 22, 22, 26, 26, 26, 27, 27, 27, 27, 27, 33, 42, 53, 54, 92 Leg 2:12, 75, 80 Leg 3:101 Cher 49, 51, 52, 64 Sacr 83, 97 Det 39, 41, 75, 76, 78, 177 Post 110 Gig 61 Deus 55, 121 Agr 26, 103, 138 Plant 15, 31, 43, 81, 131 Ebr 36, 90, 91, 99, 133, 134, 137, 173 Sobr 36 Conf 9, 69, 73, 172 Migr 49, 103, 103, 185 Her 135, 144, 145, 146, 156, 280 Congr 25, 133, 136, 150 Fug 101 Mut 8, 123, 135, 146, 180, 200 Somn 1:18, 25, 45, 67, 79, 167, 186, 188, 208 Somn 2:45 Abr 113, 118, 122, 127, 159, 218 Ios 1, 151 Mos 1:126, 128, 133, 212 Mos 2:22, 34, 74, 110, 121, 127, 127, 180, 221, 289 Decal 1, 7, 24, 102, 134, 169 Spec 1:29, 38, 48, 90, 137, 171, 205, 247, 253, 266, 281, 322, 325, 327, 328, 329, 330, 342, 344 Spec 2:50,

56, 63, 151, 172, 205, 233 Spec 3:83, 159, 207 Spec 4:113, 116, 129, 161, 234 Virt 5, 6, 81, 87, 92, 113, 134, 160, 195 Praem 1, 11, 22, 56, 90, 142 Prob 3, 66, 160 Contempl 4, 29, 39 Aet 6, 62 Flacc 66, 79, 171 Legat 131, 133, 269 Prov 2:17, 69 QG 1:92, 2:54a, 62, 3:49a, 61 QG isf 15 QE isf 3

ἰδιάζω (6) Leg 3:43 Det 29 Mos 1:294 Mos 2:161, 163 Spec 1:298

ἰδιολογέω Det 29

ἴδιος (418) Opif 52, 57, 57, 62, 97, 126, 138 Leg 1:5, 28, 91, 92, 104, 105, 106, 108 Leg 2:23, 23, 33, 34, 47, 58, 65, 78, 94 Leg 3:29, 29, 30, 32, 43, 48, 50, 61, 86, 86, 105, 123, 124, 172, 186, 200, 228, 231, 234, 238, 242 Cher 44, 46, 73, 77, 77, 77, 86, 88, 99, 113, 117, 119, 124 Sacr 12, 31, 51, 55, 95, 97, 101, 125, 136 Det 8, 9, 22, 86, 109, 124, 125, 129, 129, 138, 143, 155, 174 Post 29, 30, 50, 58, 73, 110, 117, 136, 163, 171, 179, 181, 183 Gig 26, 29, 43, 64 Deus 5, 17, 19, 38, 52, 125, 161, 170 Agr 5, 33, 35, 38, 47, 65, 75, 106, 117, 137, 151, 169 Plant 1, 13, 39, 57, 113, 130, 146 Ebr 40, 55, 79, 79, 79, 109, 129, 143, 175, 192, 209 Sobr 9, 40, 53 Conf 14, 19, 21, 46, 67, 87, 95, 154, 189 Migr 10, 11, 22, 32, 46, 50, 78, 83, 185, 189, 195, 211 Her 12, 103, 105, 128, 161, 206, 258, 259, 267 Congr 17, 69, 70, 149, 149, 150 Fug 29, 36, 47, 95, 135, 157, 199, 200, 210 Mut 14, 99, 115, 129, 131, 138, 141, 175, 186, 205, 262 Somn 1:1, 23, 56, 95, 108, 108, 113, 149, 176, 181 Somn 2:24, 99, 144, 278, 280 Abr 20, 26, 40, 51, 60, 105, 214, 235 Ios 30, 52, 64, 144, 210, 247, 248, 257 Mos 1:64, 70, 72, 137, 150, 174, 177, 233, 254, 281, 286 Mos 2:4, 44, 139, 159, 175, 188, 242, 243, 249, 271, 291 Decal 5, 39, 51, 100, 104, 118, 173 Spec 1:24, 60, 96, 103, 149, 157, 209, 263, 280, 290, 296, 321 Spec 2:12, 54, 71, 73, 76, 85, 92, 106, 107, 112, 141, 141, 145, 150, 162, 168, 168, 173, 173, 177, 188, 188, 224, 236, 240 Spec 3:23, 78, 138, 146, 153, 173 Spec 4:2, 10, 35, 49, 51, 72, 74, 133, 134, 141, 158, 159, 162 Virt 3, 14, 29, 33, 44, 51, 90, 90, 91, 95, 100, 105, 132, 165, 177, 203, 226 Praem 14, 28, 34, 44, 54, 67, 72, 87, 119, 123, 127, 139, 143, 168, 170 Prob 12, 22, 85, 86, 111, 143 Contempl 43, 61, 64, 85 Aet 30, 48, 49, 51, 92, 105, 144 Flacc 11, 21, 27, 29, 32, 50, 56, 57, 69, 77, 94, 111, 112, 117 Legat 4, 11, 18, 22, 32, 37, 78, 80, 83, 123, 128, 157, 185, 190, 193, 193, 201, 210, 211, 235, 272, 315, 317, 327, 346 Hypoth 11:4 Prov 1, 2:8, 71 QG 2:15a, 68b, 3:20b, 4:33b, 179, 198, 227 QG isf 9, 13 QG (Par) 2:4, 2:6 QE 2:1, 15b, 55a QE isf 3, 26

ἰδιότης (25) Opif 66, 149 Det 87 Post 7, 110 Agr 13 Plant 73, 133 Ebr 171 Conf 52 Her 72 Congr 135 Fug 121 Somn 1:27, 202 Somn 2:51 Ios 32, 142 Mos 1:87, 278 Mos 2:164 Decal 22 Spec 1:267 Prob 47 Aet 64

ἰδιότροπος Somn 1:101

ἰδιώτης (65) Leg 1:98 Det 104 Post 109 Deus 159 Agr 4, 33, 143, 160 Plant 56, 68, 169 Ebr 89, 113, 126, 195, 215 Conf 22 Fug 27 Somn 1:155, 155 Somn 2:21 Abr 180, 183 Ios 4, 148, 148 Mos 1:9, 153, 256 Mos 2:28, 43, 131, 214, 224, 235 Decal 40 Spec 1:121, 226, 228, 229, 233, 233, 307 Spec 2:60 Spec 3:75, 100, 134, 183 Spec 4:8, 172, 218 Virt 53, 216 Prob 3 Flacc 80, 117 Legat 51, 56, 71 Hypoth 11:18 QG 4:69, 76b, 206b QG isf 5 QE 2:6a

ἰδιωτικός (11) Leg 3:241 Cher 63 Post 110 Abr 139 Mos 1:103, 312 Spec 2:208 Spec 4:84, 156 Flacc 123, 133

ἱδρόω Her 121

ἵδρυσις (9) Opif 17 Leg 2:55 Cher 103 Sacr 126 Somn 2:222, 237 Mos 1:212 Spec 2:118 QE 2:17

ἱδρύω (93) Opif 36, 55 Leg 1:59 Leg 2:90 Leg 3:46, 53, 123 Cher 26 Sacr 8, 16, 36, 90 Det 20 Post 104, 163 Gig 48, 54 Deus 23 Agr 160 Plant 4 Ebr 98, 111, 135 Conf 13, 32, 106 Migr 41, 150, 160, 214 Her 58, 113, 215 Fug 63, 187 Mut 19, 55, 56, 81, 87, 176 Somn 1:128, 241 Somn 2:78, 107, 136, 221, 223 Abr 15, 150 Mos 1:189, 219, 276, 282, 320, 333 Mos 2:49, 72, 73, 91, 92, 94, 101 Spec 1:21, 156, 231, 274, 274, 292, 300 Spec 2:45 Spec 3:184 Virt 71, 81, 188 Flacc 46 Legat 134, 139, 148, 151, 278, 283, 292, 334, 337, 346 Hypoth 6:5 QG 4:153, 180 QG (Par) 2:2, 2:4 QE 2:55b QE isf 5

ἱδρώς (10) Opif 123, 167 Leg 1:13 Leg 3:251, 251 Ebr 150 Somn 1:8 Spec 2:91 Legat 243 Prov 2:59

ἱέραξ Post 161 Abr 266 Decal 79

ἱεράομαι (37) Leg 3:125 Sacr 129 Post 184 Deus 135 Her 82, 124 Fug 42, 74, 107 Mut 117, 191 Mos 1:149 Mos 2:75, 87, 131, 131, 145, 149, 174, 224 Spec 1:5, 79, 96, 151, 154, 166, 249 Spec 2:120, 145, 163, 183 Spec 3:55, 123, 130 Spec 4:98, 191 Virt 95

ἱεράτευμα Sobr 66 Abr 56

ἱερατικός Mos 2:186 Spec 1:111, 124, 144, 243

ἱέρεια Spec 1:21, 110

ἱερεῖον (59) Cher 85, 94 Sacr 51, 97, 110, 136 Post 122 Deus 4 Agr 130 Plant 164 Ebr 85 Congr 102 Fug 18, 80, 136, 186 Mut 233 Somn 1:195 Somn 2:74 Abr 171, 173, 175 Mos 1:282, 287, 306 Mos 2:108, 152, 224 Spec 1:83, 145, 170, 179, 184, 198, 198, 199, 200, 212, 221, 226, 226, 228, 239, 243, 259, 270, 283, 290, 298 Spec 2:145, 148 Spec 3:144 Spec 4:125 Virt 135 Contempl 68 Flacc 189 Legat 12, 317, 356

Ἱερεμίας Cher 49

ἱερεύς (168) Leg 3:79, 82, 82, 144, 242 Cher 14, 17 Det 132 Post 182 Gig 61 Deus 131, 131, 131, 131, 132, 132, 133, 134, 135 Agr 43, 130 Ebr 2, 69, 76, 126, 128 Sobr 49 Her 84, 174, 195 Congr 89, 103, 105 Fug 59, 93 Mut 2, 43, 108, 110, 191, 234, 234, 249 Somn 1:78, 78, 81, 215 Somn 2:73, 74, 75, 231 Abr 198, 235 Ios 121 Mos 1:52, 313, 316, 318 Mos 2:138, 141, 142, 150, 152, 152, 153, 174, 214, 224, 276, 276, 277 Decal 71, 159 Spec 1:5, 21, 66, 80, 80, 81, 82, 97, 101, 102, 103, 104, 108, 108, 110, 111, 111, 112, 113, 117, 117, 118, 119, 120, 122, 125, 125, 126, 129, 129, 131, 132, 133, 135, 141, 142, 145, 145, 147, 151, 152, 153, 154, 156, 157, 161, 161, 166, 184, 185, 190, 199, 233, 240, 240, 242, 242, 243, 249, 255, 255, 256, 259, 274 Spec 2:36, 37, 145, 146, 163, 164, 216, 216, 222 Spec 3:56, 58, 60, 131, 133, 134 Spec 4:190, 190, 192 Praem 74, 78 Contempl 74, 82 Legat 222, 234, 295, 306, 307 Hypoth 7:5, 7:13 QG isf 17, 17

ἱερεύω (7) Abr 233 Mos 1:277, 309 Praem 139 Prob 89 Legat 62, 233

ἱερόδουλος Praem 74

ἱερομηνία (11) Mos 2:23 Decal 159 Spec 1:168, 180, 180, 180, 186, 188, 189 Spec 2:41, 188

ἱερόν (97) Opif 55 Cher 94, 95 Det 20 Post 50 Deus 8, 8 Ebr 66 Conf 160 Migr 92 Somn 1:149, 215 Mos 1:103 Mos 2:71, 73, 75, 88, 141, 174 Decal 7, 74, 78 Spec 1:24, 66, 67, 67, 69, 71, 74, 75, 76, 104, 152, 152,

159, 159, 193, 237, 240, 241, 269, 270, 280, 316 Spec 2:148, 188, 216 Spec 3:55, 58, 88, 88, 90, 91, 130, 130, 171, 205 Spec 4:98 Virt 124 Praem 76 Prob 148 Flacc 51 Legat 139, 157, 188, 194, 198, 198, 203, 208, 212, 216, 232, 232, 234, 238, 265, 279, 290, 290, 291, 295, 297, 298, 306, 310, 316, 328, 333, 334, 335, 346 Prov 2:33, 33, 33, 64 QE 2:49b

ἱερόπολις (9) Mos 2:72 Spec 3:53, 130 Flacc 46 Legat 225, 281, 288, 299, 346

ἱεροπομπός Spec 1:78 Legat 216, 312

ἱεροπρεπής (37) Opif 99 Leg 3:204 Sacr 45 Deus 102 Plant 25, 90, 162 Migr 98, 113 Her 110 Congr 114 Fug 149 Mut 25 Somn 1:82, 256 Somn 2:269 Abr 101 Mos 2:25, 85 Decal 33, 51, 60, 175 Spec 1:185, 186, 317 Spec 2:70, 251 Spec 3:83, 187 Praem 84, 101 Prob 75, 150 Flacc 83 Legat 202 QG isf 17

ἱερός (493) Opif 17, 27, 77, 78, 97, 128, 128, 137 Leg 1:62, 76 Leg 2:105 Leg 3:11, 36, 106, 110, 118, 126, 129, 152, 162, 185, 219 Cher 42, 45, 48, 73, 124 Sacr 55, 60, 76, 88, 128, 129, 130 Det 62, 63, 133, 135, 142, 161, 170 Post 110, 153, 158, 179 Gig 16, 54, 67 Deus 6, 17, 105, 111, 140 Agr 51, 85, 91, 113, 113, 116, 118, 119, 127 Plant 26, 42, 61, 86, 94, 118, 126, 139, 161, 162, 168 Ebr 37, 85, 95, 104, 131, 143, 208, 213 Sobr 17, 40, 66 Conf 3, 27, 28, 35, 59, 97, 143, 147, 156, 174 Migr 14, 17, 23, 28, 69, 76, 85, 90, 97, 102, 131, 139, 200 Her 21, 95, 105, 106, 108, 112, 129, 159, 171, 175, 182, 184, 185, 195, 201, 207, 216, 221, 225, 251, 258, 259, 286, 293, 309 Congr 34, 40, 78, 85, 89, 90, 101, 108, 120, 134, 157, 168, 171, 175 Fug 4, 19, 81, 83, 114, 117, 137, 144, 185, 196 Mut 30, 43, 60, 81, 104, 106, 114, 126, 138, 152, 187, 189, 190, 191, 192, 204, 210, 215, 228, 245, 248, 260 Somn 1:33, 48, 49, 51, 53, 69, 70, 77, 79, 81, 96, 114, 121, 124, 127, 141, 164, 164, 172, 191, 202, 206, 208, 214, 220, 225, 226, 229, 241, 245 Somn 2:23, 63, 67, 71, 75, 119, 127, 173, 184, 185, 187, 220, 232, 243, 246, 249, 249, 265, 272, 272, 290, 292, 300, 301 Abr 1, 4, 20, 47, 48, 52, 61, 71, 115, 121, 156, 177, 181, 206, 244, 258 Ios 120 Mos 1:1, 4, 23, 34, 205, 210, 217, 277 Mos 2:5, 11, 21, 36, 45, 59, 67, 70, 74, 84, 94, 95, 109, 131, 141, 143, 144, 145, 146, 158, 159, 162, 185, 188, 194, 209, 211, 213, 231, 263, 266, 290, 292 Decal 1, 8, 10, 37, 40, 41, 51, 65, 81, 93, 96, 99, 106, 133, 138, 154, 161, 173 Spec 1:15, 59, 76, 78, 82, 95, 97, 98, 103, 105, 114, 118, 123, 126, 150, 172, 182, 189, 199, 207, 214, 215, 220, 229, 231, 232, 234, 234, 241, 244, 245, 254, 254, 256, 261, 262, 269, 280, 285, 288, 296, 297, 298, 319, 325, 328, 344 Spec 2:6, 13, 23, 39, 41, 56, 64, 80, 84, 86, 104, 108, 110, 134, 150, 156, 159, 161, 176, 183, 214, 215, 224, 238, 249, 254, 256, 260 Spec 3:6, 14, 24, 29, 40, 46, 59, 119, 120, 125, 130, 183 Spec 4:30, 33, 55, 61, 69, 84, 95, 100, 105, 120, 125, 156, 161, 165, 173, 175, 205, 215, 238 Virt 34, 79, 80, 87, 94, 95, 102, 119, 127, 135, 175, 182, 201 Praem 4, 51, 52, 52, 79, 90, 111, 119, 122, 138, 157, 162 Prob 2, 13, 81, 81, 112, 143, 158 Contempl 2, 25, 26, 28, 64, 71, 75, 78, 81, 83 Aet 19, 139 Flacc 48, 93, 121 Legat 22, 108, 115, 156, 156, 158, 195, 202, 205, 296, 296, 311, 312, 318, 330, 356 Hypoth 6:5, 7:2, 7:5, 7:13, 7:13 Prov 2:65 QG 4:8c QG isf 2 QE 1:6, 2:15a, 19, 46 QE isf 8, 11, 14, 14

ἱερός Ios 229

Ἱεροσόλυμα (Ἱερουσαλήμ) (7) Somn 2:250 Legat 156, 278, 288, 312, 313, 315

ἱεροσυλέω Leg 3:241 Conf 163

ἱεροσυλία Decal 133 Spec 2:13 Spec 3:83, 83 Spec 4:87

ἱερόσυλος Ios 84 Prov 2:33

ἱερουργέω (32) Leg 3:130 Cher 96 Plant 164 Ebr 138 Conf 124 Migr 67, 98, 140, 202 Her 174 Congr 106 Somn 1:62, 194, 212 Somn 2:72 Abr 198, 202 Mos 1:87 Mos 2:106, 141, 228, 229 Spec 1:68, 168, 177, 180, 254, 275 Spec 2:36, 145 Virt 146 Legat 296

ἱερουργία (28) Deus 132 Plant 107 Ebr 18, 130 Abr 170, 173, 198 Mos 2:73, 107, 108, 133, 174, 221, 225, 228, 231, 279 Spec 1:21, 74, 96, 100, 125, 162, 181, 229, 261 Spec 4:98 Prov 2:32

Ἱερουσαλήμ Ἱεροσόλυμα

ἱεροφαντέω (16) Cher 42 Det 13 Deus 62 Conf 149 Somn 1:207 Mos 2:37, 149, 153 Decal 41 Spec 1:323 Virt 108, 163 Prob 14, 74, 74 Legat 56

ἱεροφάντης (24) Leg 3:151, 173 Cher 49 Sacr 94 Post 16, 164, 173 Gig 54 Deus 156 Sobr 20 Migr 14 Fug 85 Somn 1:164 Somn 2:3, 29, 109 Mos 2:40 Decal 18 Spec 1:41 Spec 2:201 Spec 3:135 Spec 4:177 Virt 75, 174

ἱερόω Sacr 128 Mos 2:134

ἱερωσύνη (42) Leg 3:79, 242 Sacr 132 Post 183 Plant 63 Ebr 65, 74, 75, 126 Sobr 40 Congr 99 Fug 107, 145 Abr 98 Mos 1:304 Mos 2:5, 66, 67, 71, 173, 177, 187, 187, 225, 274, 278 Decal 159 Spec 1:57, 57, 102, 103, 108, 115, 159 Spec 2:145, 164 Spec 3:127 Virt 53, 54 Praem 75, 78 Legat 278

ἵημι (15) Somn 2:275 Abr 183 Ios 237 Mos 1:50, 102, 245, 287, 309 Mos 2:197 Decal 148 Spec 1:38, 58 Spec 3:129, 204 Spec 4:129

Ἰησοῦς (7) Ebr 96 Mut 121, 121 Mos 1:216 Virt 55, 66, 69

Ἰθάμαρ Somn 2:186

ἰθυτενής QG (Par) 2:7

ἱκανός (163) Opif 20, 90 Leg 1:10, 44 Leg 3:13, 31, 126, 134, 143, 147, 164, 165, 171, 205, 208, 234 Cher 16, 39, 46, 49, 59, 65, 123 Sacr 10, 36, 115 Det 28, 30, 32, 43, 57, 61, 66, 86, 106, 115, 124, 130 Post 16, 21, 22, 42, 124, 142, 146 Gig 35, 57 Deus 33, 40, 87, 157 Agr 22, 93 Plant 31, 42, 85, 144 Ebr 32, 32, 166, 166, 169, 188, 206, 212, 224 Sobr 51 Conf 17, 112, 147 Migr 21, 92, 140, 201 Her 15, 23, 39, 125, 125, 144, 193 Congr 9 Fug 40, 96, 97, 128, 163, 172, 202, 213 Mut 15, 27, 46, 91, 91, 108, 165, 168, 174, 233, 250 Somn 1:2, 48, 66, 240 Somn 2:25, 61, 73, 153, 185, 187 Abr 53, 199, 209 Ios 10, 91, 114, 142, 147, 178, 251, 262, 270 Mos 1:40, 63, 120, 225, 304 Mos 2:94 Decal 100 Spec 1:21, 128, 175, 252, 334 Spec 2:17, 39 Spec 4:101, 146, 148, 175, 188, 218 Praem 13, 51, 93 Prob 47 Contempl 79 Flacc 130 Legat 3, 37, 38, 257, 272 Hypoth 6:1, 7:11, 7:14 Prov 1, 1, 2:42, 72 QE 2:18 QE isf 32

ἱκεσία (24) Leg 3:215 Her 15, 186 Congr 109 Abr 6, 51 Mos 1:128, 273 Mos 2:166, 166 Spec 1:42, 45, 97, 312 Spec 2:196, 203, 209, 218 Spec 4:57 Virt 64, 221 Praem 56 Hypoth 7:9 QG isf 13

ἱκέσιος Mos 1:36

ἱκετεία (6) Cher 47 Congr 107 Mos 1:72 Praem 166 Legat 179, 248

ἱκετεύω (35) Leg 3:213 Cher 47, 47 Sacr 4, 70 Det 146 Post 13, 16 Conf 39 Migr 122 Her 186 Congr 107, 109 Mut 228 Somn 2:149 Abr 107, 131 Ios 173, 219 Mos

1:101, 125, 184, 216, 320 Mos 2:177, 228, 279 Spec 1:41, 45 Virt 63, 79 Prob 39 Legat 265, 366 QE 2:49b

ἱκετηρία Legat 228, 276

ἱκέτης (46) Leg 3:214 Sacr 119 Det 62, 63, 70, 93, 160 Post 138 Ebr 94 Conf 160 Migr 122, 124 Her 37, 124, 205 Congr 105 Fug 56, 80 Mut 222 Somn 2:99, 273 Ios 229, 229 Mos 1:34, 35, 35, 36, 72, 142, 185 Spec 1:42, 159, 309 Spec 2:118, 217 Virt 79, 79, 124, 124, 185, 185 Praem 44 Prob 64, 148 QE 2:2, 20

ἱκετικός Legat 3

ἱκέτις (8) Det 95 Post 31 Deus 116, 160 Plant 53, 63 Her 273 Somn 2:299

ἰκμάς Opif 38 Spec 3:10 Prov 2:59

ἱκνέομαι Opif 104 Ebr 150

ἴκτερος Praem 143

ἴκτινος Contempl 8

ἰλαδόν Ebr 150

ἵλαος (79) Opif 169 Leg 1:66 Leg 3:128, 140, 174 Sacr 33, 39, 39 Det 93, 146 Plant 46, 90, 171 Ebr 224 Conf 103, 166, 182 Migr 15, 122, 124 Her 206 Congr 107, 107 Fug 95, 98, 100, 104, 105, 141, 154 Mut 129 Somn 1:90, 90 Somn 2:165, 265, 292 Abr 96 Ios 104, 198 Mos 1:72, 101, 160, 185, 331 Mos 2:5, 61, 96, 96, 132, 189, 238 Spec 1:97, 145, 187, 229, 242, 265, 294, 310 Spec 2:15, 23, 27, 55, 196, 253 Spec 3:121, 193 Virt 41, 160 Praem 115, 116, 163 Prob 39 Hypoth 7:2, 7:5 Prov 2:6 QG 2:13a, 3:26 QG isf 13

ἱλαρός (20) Plant 167 Congr 161 Somn 2:144 Ios 245 Mos 1:187 Mos 2:211 Spec 1:69, 134 Spec 2:43, 48, 214 Spec 4:74 Virt 67 Praem 89 Contempl 40, 58 Flacc 118 Legat 12, 83, 180

ἱλαρότης Plant 166 Somn 2:167 Ios 204 Contempl 77

ἱλάσκομαι (10) Leg 3:174 Plant 162 Mut 235 Abr 129 Mos 2:24, 201 Spec 1:116, 234, 237 Praem 56

ἱλασμός (6) Leg 3:174 Post 48 Plant 61 Her 179 Congr 89, 107

ἱλαστήριον (6) Cher 25 Her 166 Fug 100, 101 Mos 2:95, 97

Ἴλιας Contempl 17

ἰλιγγιάω Prov 2:27

ἴλιγγος Ios 142 QE isf 31

ἰλυσπάομαι (10) Post 74 Agr 97 Her 238 Somn 2:105 Mos 1:78 Decal 149 Spec 3:1 Spec 4:91, 113 Aet 129

ἱμάς Flacc 74 Legat 131

ἱμάτιον (20) Leg 3:239, 240 Fug 110, 111 Somn 1:92, 92, 93, 98, 100, 100, 101, 101, 102, 107, 109, 113, 126 Ios 49 Spec 1:115 Spec 4:203

ἱματισμός Migr 105, 105

ἱμερόεις Aet 121

ἵμερος (36) Opif 71 Post 116 Gig 44 Plant 22 Migr 157 Her 274, 310 Mut 174, 260 Somn 1:10, 36, 50 Somn 2:150, 176, 233 Abr 65, 66 Ios 70 Mos 1:58 Decal 109, 149 Spec 1:50, 322, 339 Spec 3:4 Spec 4:20 Praem 26, 39 Prob 22, 71 Contempl 13, 14, 75 Legat 47, 372 Hypoth 11:2

ἱμονιά Mos 1:52

ἵνα (713) Opif 15, 16, 33, 45, 58, 66, 75, 78, 83, 86, 88, 100, 100, 126, 131, 133, 135, 146, 149, 168, 169 Leg 1:20, 29, 47, 59, 60, 76, 89, 95, 96, 98, 98 Leg 2:15, 20, 34, 45, 49, 55, 57, 79, 85, 88, 93, 101 Leg 3:17, 20, 24, 36, 62, 72, 73, 82, 104, 109, 120, 123, 128, 130, 131, 134, 157, 165, 166, 172, 174, 199, 225, 238, 239, 242, 244 Cher 2, 15, 17, 20, 26, 29, 29, 31, 32, 42, 72, 82, 101, 109, 112, 121, 126 Sacr 1, 8, 23, 28, 31, 40, 41, 45, 57, 60, 69, 72, 72, 76, 80, 84, 90, 90, 94, 94, 108, 129, 129, 134 Det 6, 11, 18, 46, 46, 52, 58, 71, 85, 86, 114, 154, 160 Post 13, 31, 74, 78, 103, 151 Gig 9, 14, 47 Deus 38, 49, 67, 74, 76, 85, 113, 138, 138, 142, 156, 164, 176, 178, 182 Agr 11, 24, 36, 56, 77, 86, 105, 122, 123, 130, 133 Plant 10, 15, 15, 17, 20, 33, 45, 49, 49, 110, 111, 131, 145, 160, 162, 175, 176 Ebr 14, 48, 50, 50, 52, 70, 71, 82, 157, 157, 158, 224 Sobr 40, 48, 68, 69 Conf 1, 4, 22, 25, 27, 31, 56, 59, 72, 74, 87, 93, 94, 98, 103, 110, 136, 140, 163, 175, 179, 181, 188, 189, 195, 196 Migr 12, 24, 25, 27, 36, 67, 98, 104, 105, 155, 158, 160, 174, 223 Her 20, 21, 26, 26, 35, 37, 44, 61, 67, 70, 105, 110, 110, 110, 112, 113, 121, 130, 162, 166, 169, 170, 174, 177, 186, 193, 199, 201, 205, 218, 226, 244, 261, 276, 291, 293, 309, 312 Congr 1, 7, 12, 13, 14, 33, 38, 57, 70, 76, 94, 101, 106, 109, 110, 114, 122, 124, 170, 178 Fug 18, 22, 38, 47, 59, 81, 85, 92, 97 Mut 13, 14, 21, 24, 31, 47, 47, 62, 63, 72, 85, 87, 87, 108, 112, 119, 186, 188, 188, 204, 209, 228, 230, 263, 268, 270 Somn 1:37, 52, 57, 58, 60, 71, 101, 113, 147, 149, 159, 162, 163, 165, 173, 193, 215, 231, 241, 256 Somn 2:1, 77, 86, 126, 142, 146, 169, 195, 204, 233, 242, 243, 249, 280 Abr 51, 54, 105, 143, 173, 176, 190, 215 Ios 4, 13, 17, 45, 94, 110, 113, 116, 195, 238, 244, 248, 251 Mos 1:3, 8, 11, 19, 29, 47, 55, 73, 75, 84, 106, 168, 171, 173, 221, 223, 224, 245, 256, 257, 273, 278, 279, 313, 330 Mos 2:5, 6, 36, 48, 73, 75, 78, 83, 84, 85, 86, 87, 90, 113, 130, 133, 139, 147, 187, 200, 205, 214, 214, 231, 245, 245, 248, 249, 253, 256, 267, 286, 286, 291 Decal 13, 15, 40, 74, 81, 96, 138, 161, 177 Spec 1:29, 53, 55, 81, 96, 105, 110, 115, 116, 124, 127, 131, 134, 182, 193, 219, 219, 225, 242, 242, 247, 254, 260, 260, 293, 296, 320, 325, 325, 331 Spec 2:3, 15, 17, 36, 55, 60, 64, 66, 67, 71, 73, 78, 80, 85, 86, 87, 103, 105, 111, 119, 139, 141, 142, 149, 156, 157, 170, 182, 189, 199, 201, 210, 229, 247, 256, 261, 261 Spec 3:33, 47, 48, 49, 56, 70, 70, 97, 114, 117, 122, 130, 131, 135, 156, 159, 160, 176, 178 Spec 4:3, 29, 31, 31, 56, 67, 70, 74, 77, 93, 93, 134, 139, 139, 141, 142, 155, 158, 158, 163, 169, 169, 171, 173, 175, 175, 184, 191, 205, 206, 208, 211, 215 Virt 29, 30, 34, 58, 70, 74, 98, 109, 133, 133, 136, 139, 140, 145, 145, 149, 152, 156, 157, 168, 169, 169, 209 Praem 8, 48, 71, 72, 72, 80, 100, 102, 131, 133, 152, 155 Prob 2, 16, 31, 43, 57, 64, 108, 111 Contempl 14, 15, 16, 24, 69, 82 Aet 3, 26, 26, 66, 71, 79, 102, 125 Flacc 5, 5, 7, 27, 31, 37, 40, 53, 66, 77, 93, 97, 98, 101, 111, 124, 141, 142, 152, 172, 187 Legat 31, 43, 80, 87, 91, 101, 109, 123, 141, 171, 171, 176, 204, 207, 207, 208, 224, 226, 230, 232, 233, 239, 273, 279, 286, 301, 305, 310, 311, 315, 325, 337, 346, 347, 366 Prov 2:18, 26, 38, 55, 69 QG 1:20, 55a, 66, 76b, 2:11, 13a, 15a, 41, 48, 54a, 3:18, 52, 4:47a, 51b, 173, 173, 203 QG isf 10, 10 QG (Par) 2:6 QE 1:1, 6 QE isf 3, 3, 9, 14, 22

Ἰνδικός Aet 128

Ἰνδός (7) Somn 2:56, 59 Abr 182 Praem 89 Prob 74, 93, 96

ἰοβόλος (19) Opif 156, 159 Agr 95, 97 Ebr 223 Mos 1:43, 192 Decal 78 Spec 3:103 Spec 4:86, 116 Praem 92 Prob 90 Contempl 9 Legat 48, 89, 163 Prov 2:59, 60

Ἰοθόρ (9) Sacr 50 Gig 50 Agr 43, 43 Ebr 36, 37 Mut 103, 103, 114

ἴον Somn 2:62 Prov 2:71

Ἰόνιος Flacc 154

Ἰορδάνης (6) Leg 2:89, 89 Fug 87 Mos 1:319, 330 Spec 1:158

ἰός (10) Opif 157, 159 Plant 152 Her 217 Somn 2:88 Praem 90 Aet 20 Legat 135, 166, 205

Ἰουβάλ Post 100, 103, 111

Ἰουδαία (10) Mos 2:31 Legat 199, 200, 207, 215, 257, 281, 294, 299 Hypoth 11:1

Ἰουδαϊκός (11) Flacc 55, 73, 74 Legat 157, 159, 170, 184, 201, 245, 256, 282

Ἰουδαῖος (101) Mos 1:1, 7, 34 Mos 2:17, 25, 41, 193, 216 Decal 96 Spec 1:97 Spec 2:163, 166 Spec 3:46 Spec 4:179, 224 Virt 65, 108, 206, 212, 226 Prob 29, 43, 57, 68, 75 Aet 19 Flacc 1, 21, 23, 24, 29, 29, 43, 45, 47, 49, 54, 55, 55, 56, 66, 80, 85, 86, 86, 94, 96, 116, 116, 116, 170, 170, 189, 191 Legat 115, 117, 129, 133, 134, 154, 155, 158, 158, 159, 160, 170, 178, 182, 194, 198, 200, 200, 205, 205, 210, 216, 222, 226, 245, 248, 253, 278, 282, 307, 311, 313, 315, 316, 330, 333, 335, 346, 350, 355, 368, 370, 371, 373 Hypoth 0:1, 0:1, 6:10

Ἰούδας (26) Leg 1:80, 80, 81, 82, 82 Leg 2:95, 96 Leg 3:26, 74, 74, 146 Plant 134, 135, 136 Ebr 94 Her 255 Congr 125 Fug 73, 74, 149, 149, 149 Mut 136 Somn 1:37 Somn 2:34, 44

Ἰουλία Legat 319

Ἰούλιος Prob 118

ἴουλος Contempl 52

ἵππαρχος Spec 1:121

ἵππειος Leg 2:101 Spec 1:291

ἱππεύς (22) Leg 2:94, 99, 99, 103, 103, 103, 104, 104 Agr 67, 69, 70, 71, 94, 94, 109, 122, 124 Spec 1:121 Spec 4:28 Flacc 5, 120 Legat 252

ἱππήλατος Agr 102

Ἱππημολγοί Contempl 17

ἱππικός (18) Det 55 Agr 68, 71, 85, 86, 88, 92 Abr 220, 261 Mos 1:148, 168 Praem 54 Flacc 163 Legat 9, 74, 75, 233 QG 1:3

ἱπποδρομία Det 141 Mut 149 Legat 12, 45 Prov 2:58

Ἱπποκένταυρος Spec 3:45

Ἱπποκράτης Opif 105, 124 Contempl 16

ἱππομαχία Det 2

ἵππος (55) Opif 86 Leg 1:72 Leg 2:94, 99, 99, 99, 102, 103, 104 Leg 3:24, 128, 136, 197 Det 55 Deus 117, 117 Agr 70, 71, 72, 73, 77, 78, 78, 82, 84, 84, 88, 90, 91, 93, 94, 106, 107, 109 Ebr 111 Migr 62 Her 41 Congr 158 Somn 1:108 Somn 2:78, 269 Abr 234 Mos 1:22, 26, 179 Decal 4 Spec 1:135 Spec 3:46 Spec 4:79 Virt 13 Praem 90 Aet 23 Flacc 26 Prov 2:33 QG 1:3

ἱππόστασις Spec 3:47

ἱππότης Mos 2:248 Virt 48

ἱπποτοξότης Mos 1:168

ἱπποτροφία Agr 90

ἱπποτρόφος Agr 84, 85

ἱπποφόρβιον Spec 3:47

ἵπταμαι Decal 116

ἶρις Prov 2:47, 50 QG 2:64a

ἴς Praem 146 Flacc 71

ις QG 2:5a QG (Par) 2:5

Ἰσαάκ (92) Leg 1:82 Leg 2:59, 82 Leg 3:43, 43, 85, 85, 87, 177, 218, 218, 219 Cher 8, 40, 47, 106 Sacr 6, 7, 43, 110 Det 29, 30, 30, 31, 46, 60, 124, 124, 124 Post 62, 77, 77, 134 Deus 4 Plant 78, 169, 169 Ebr 60, 94 Sobr 8, 8, 9, 65 Conf 74 Migr 29, 101, 125 Her 251, 261 Congr 34, 36, 175 Fug 167, 200 Mut 1, 12, 13, 88, 130, 131, 137, 157, 177, 190, 218, 252, 263 Somn 1:3, 14, 38, 68, 159, 160, 166, 168, 171, 172, 172, 173, 173, 194, 195 Somn 2:10 Abr 51, 52, 201 Mos 1:76 Praem 31 QG 4:88, 144, 145, 193

ἰσάζω Plant 81 Her 166

ἰσάκις Opif 51 Decal 28, 28, 28

ἰσάριθμος (32) Opif 60 Leg 1:12, 63 Post 91 Agr 83 Plant 120 Migr 199 Her 86, 165, 167, 175, 177 Congr 168 Fug 184 Somn 1:15, 137 Abr 54, 236 Mos 1:123, 221 Mos 2:88, 178 Decal 21 Spec 1:172, 182, 188, 222 Spec 2:161 Spec 4:235 Praem 57 Flacc 189 QE 2:49b

ἰσηγορία (9) Prob 48, 49, 50, 51, 51, 52, 53, 53 Flacc 24

ἰσῆλιξ (6) Opif 26 Leg 2:73 Spec 3:23 Aet 52, 130, 146

ἰσημερία (23) Opif 116, 116 Her 148, 149, 150 Mos 2:222 Decal 161, 161 Spec 1:172, 181, 182, 186 Spec 2:151, 153, 204 Spec 4:233 Flacc 116 QG 2:17a, 17c, 17c, 31, 31, 31

ἰσημερινός Opif 112 Her 147

ἰσθμός Aet 147

Ἰσθμός Flacc 155

Ἰσίδωρος (7) Flacc 20, 126, 135, 137, 141, 142 Legat 355

Ἰσμαήλ (15) Cher 8 Sobr 8, 8, 9 Fug 1, 204, 208, 208 Mut 201, 202, 204, 209, 216, 218, 252

ἰσόδρομος Cher 22 Migr 207

ἰσοδυναμέω (6) Plant 152 Migr 122, 205 Spec 2:121 Spec 3:72 QG 4:228

ἰσόθεος Mos 2:194 Decal 7 Spec 1:25 Virt 219

ἰσοκρατής Det 36 Aet 116, 116

ἰσολύμπιος Decal 7 Legat 149

ἰσομεγέθης Her 228

ἰσομοιρέω Spec 2:125, 133

ἰσομοιρία Mos 1:52 Mos 2:231 Spec 2:139

ἰσονομία Spec 1:53, 208 Aet 108, 112 Legat 13

ἰσόπεδος Somn 1:125 Mos 2:287 Spec 3:149 Aet 118

ἰσόπλευρος Congr 146

ἰσορροπέω Prob 61

ἰσόρροπος (9) Ios 5 Mos 1:78, 224 Mos 2:197 Praem 63 Prob 112 Flacc 92, 126 Legat 15

ἴσος (372) Opif 27, 51, 56, 101, 110, 110, 119 Leg 1:3, 12, 36, 49, 65, 76, 76, 84 Leg 2:3, 3, 16, 21, 81, 86 Leg 3:10, 51, 52, 78, 113, 119, 122, 189, 219, 246, 247, 253 Cher 7, 22, 57, 119 Sacr 5, 9, 12, 92, 112, 138 Det 33, 38, 58, 70, 96, 169 Gig 1, 45, 50, 56, 56, 58 Deus 6, 21, 24, 70, 105, 122 Agr 61, 85, 157, 166 Plant 54, 71, 75, 89, 90, 114, 122, 142, 142, 172 Ebr 13, 27, 32, 52, 65, 105, 107, 144, 169 Sobr 15, 33, 67 Conf 72, 84, 104, 111, 117, 142, 149, 150, 160, 162, 189, 190, 196

Migr 5, 7, 27, 42, 80, 85, 101, 126, 138, 160, 166, 167, 172, 210 Her 28, 83, 99, 101, 133, 141, 141, 142, 144, 144, 144, 145, 145, 145, 146, 146, 147, 147, 148, 148, 149, 149, 151, 151, 152, 152, 152, 154, 155, 159, 160, 160, 161, 164, 168, 174, 175, 180, 182, 191, 195, 196, 196, 196, 207, 220, 222, 224 Congr 18, 18, 24, 152, 153, 158, 172 Fug 8, 35, 124, 162, 172, 211 Mut 11, 21, 29, 48, 88, 103, 137, 142, 171, 181, 188, 235, 270 Somn 1:4, 7, 36, 39, 95, 130, 149, 149, 150, 158, 181 Somn 2:94, 94, 102, 182, 200, 221, 224, 267, 301 Abr 175, 182, 193, 198, 240, 243, 246 Ios 25, 53, 99, 99, 101, 102, 111, 125, 176, 176, 176, 192, 192, 194, 209 Mos 1:2, 30, 97, 109, 123, 123, 123, 141, 156, 221, 282, 324, 327 Mos 2:62, 83, 84, 89, 90, 91, 103, 122, 135, 155, 169, 232, 242, 260 Decal 21, 27, 28, 28, 29, 33, 38, 41, 61, 62, 77, 109, 151 Spec 1:32, 108, 121, 121, 121, 139, 140, 140, 170, 170, 178, 180, 187, 277, 291 Spec 2:27, 32, 34, 34, 37, 41, 78, 165 Spec 3:18, 29, 45, 57, 70, 106, 133, 143, 149, 163, 166, 166, 197 Spec 4:11, 18, 22, 36, 54, 89, 131, 143, 184, 197 Virt 54, 54, 69, 117, 127, 137, 137, 166, 222 Praem 69 Prob 27, 42, 126, 149 Contempl 15, 48 Aet 2, 43, 46, 60, 90, 134 Flacc 6, 24, 60, 106, 164, 186 Legat 67, 183, 195, 196, 241, 248, 253, 262, 287, 289 Hypoth 7:11, 7:15, 7:20 Prov 1, 2:45, 55 QG 1:74, 2:54c, 65, 3:20a, 4:52a, 52c, 102c, 228 QG isf 8 QE 2:46, 64 QE isf 3

ἰσοστάσιος Post 9 Conf 11 Migr 166

ἰσοταχέω Migr 175

ἰσοταχής Cher 22 Mut 67 Somn 2:112 Abr 172

ἰσοτέλεια Cher 120 Spec 1:53

ἰσοτελής Prob 148

ἰσότης (79) Opif 51, 106 Cher 105 Sacr 27 Plant 122, 122 Sobr 8 Conf 48, 108 Migr 167 Her 143, 143, 145, 146, 150, 153, 153, 161, 162, 163, 163, 164, 164, 165, 176, 177, 191, 192, 195, 196 Congr 16 Mut 153, 232 Somn 2:16, 40, 80 Ios 9, 249 Mos 1:328 Mos 2:9 Decal 162 Spec 1:121, 265, 295 Spec 2:21, 34, 68, 190, 204 Spec 3:182 Spec 4:74, 165, 166, 166, 169, 187, 231, 231, 232, 232, 233, 234, 235, 236, 237, 238 Virt 114 Praem 59 Prob 79, 84 Contempl 17 Aet 108 Legat 62, 85 Prov 1 QG 2:14, 4:102b QE 1:6, 2:10a

ἰσοτιμία Cher 120 Mos 1:35 Spec 1:52, 243

ἰσότιμος (34) Leg 2:18 Sacr 8, 91, 131 Post 95 Deus 13, 57 Sobr 4, 54, 54 Conf 170 Her 159, 177 Abr 62 Ios 232 Mos 1:324 Decal 37 Spec 1:170, 181, 228, 229, 238 Spec 2:157 Spec 3:202, 202 Virt 154, 185, 223 Praem 112 Prob 130, 148 Legat 98, 341 QE 2:20

ἰσοχρόνιος Det 75 Gig 56 Her 37

ἰσόω (7) Opif 13, 101 Her 154 Congr 23 Decal 28 Spec 2:40 Prob 3

Ἰσραήλ (79) Leg 2:34, 77, 94 Leg 3:11, 15, 133, 186, 186, 212, 214 Sacr 118, 118, 118, 119, 120, 134, 134 Det 67, 94 Post 54, 63, 89, 92, 158 Deus 121, 144, 145 Plant 59, 63 Ebr 77, 82, 82 Sobr 19 Conf 36, 56, 72, 72, 92, 93, 146, 148 Migr 15, 39, 54, 113, 125, 168, 201, 224 Her 78, 113, 117, 124, 279 Congr 51, 86 Fug 208 Mut 81, 81, 83, 207 Somn 1:62, 89, 114, 117, 129, 171, 172, 172 Somn 2:44, 172, 173, 222, 271, 280 Abr 57 Praem 44 Legat 4 QE 2:47

Ἰσραηλιτικός Her 203

Ἰσσάχαρ (11) Leg 1:80, 80, 81, 83 Leg 2:94 Plant 134, 134, 136 Ebr 94 Fug 73 Somn 2:34

ἵστημι (235) Opif 50, 85 Leg 1:6, 80 Leg 2:83, 95, 95 Leg 3:4, 9, 9, 32, 38, 65, 85, 110, 126, 146, 160 Cher 14, 17, 18, 19, 19, 26, 63, 130 Sacr 8, 22, 26, 28, 57, 63, 67, 68, 68 Det 89, 114 Post 19, 19, 23, 23, 24, 27, 27, 27, 27, 28, 28, 28, 29, 30, 30, 30, 30, 70, 84, 89, 89, 89, 91 Gig 48, 49, 49, 52, 66 Deus 23, 149 Agr 70, 79, 85 Plant 11, 59, 76, 125, 134, 135, 144 Ebr 95, 111, 124, 170, 174, 179, 183, 183 Conf 19, 29, 30, 31, 31, 31, 31, 35, 38, 38, 38, 99, 100, 100, 114, 124, 138, 190 Migr 7, 22, 75, 85, 125, 147, 192 Her 82, 166, 177, 201, 205, 206 Fug 115, 163 Mut 12, 54, 54, 57, 87, 87, 91, 175, 178, 179, 263 Somn 1:38, 62, 157, 158, 241, 244, 245, 245, 246, 250 Somn 2:129, 129, 139, 170, 216, 219, 221, 221, 222, 223, 224, 226, 226, 227, 229, 233, 235, 237, 238, 261, 269, 277, 298, 300 Abr 26, 88, 119, 121, 160, 195, 200, 214 Ios 79 Mos 1:54, 78, 158, 180, 202, 244, 255, 269 Mos 2:162, 252, 270, 291 Decal 25 Spec 1:150, 219 Spec 2:46, 216, 216 Spec 3:55, 60, 139, 160, 189, 208 Spec 4:83, 149 Virt 86, 147, 195 Praem 17 Prob 13, 92, 146 Contempl 66, 75, 89 Aet 33, 128, 136 Flacc 35, 37, 38, 75, 87, 122, 175 Legat 96, 117, 189, 235, 313, 350 Hypoth 7:20 Prov 2:12, 33, 39, 58 QG 4:180, 180 QE 2:17 QE isf 5, 5, 12

ἱστίον Plant 152, 152 Mos 2:90 Decal 14 Flacc 27

ἱστορέω Mos 2:59, 143 Spec 2:146

ἱστορία (12) Cher 105 Congr 15, 74 Somn 1:205 Somn 2:302 Abr 65 Spec 1:342 Aet 120, 139, 146, 146 Hypoth 6:5

ἱστορικός (7) Sacr 78 Congr 44 Somn 1:52 Mos 2:46, 47 Praem 1, 2

ἰσχίον QG (Par) 2:6

ἰσχναίνω Her 270

ἰσχνόφωνος Her 4, 16 Mos 1:83

ἰσχυρίζομαι Leg 3:206

ἰσχυρογνωμοσύνη Somn 1:218

ἰσχυρογνώμων Praem 30 Prob 27 Legat 196 QG 2:16, 54a

ἰσχυρός (15) Leg 2:21 Leg 3:207 Ebr 186 Somn 1:155 Abr 168, 216, 266 Spec 1:26, 307 Virt 174 Aet 21, 26 Legat 68, 74 QE 2:21

ἰσχυρότης Leg 3:204

ἰσχύς (106) Opif 103, 104 Leg 1:42, 98, 98 Leg 2:41 Leg 3:136 Cher 103, 104 Sacr 56, 56, 81, 86 Det 35, 51, 112, 112, 113, 114, 114, 118 Post 38, 48, 112, 120, 143, 145, 159, 162 Gig 36, 37 Deus 38, 147, 173 Agr 21, 86, 147, 172 Plant 88 Ebr 75, 83, 94, 96, 105, 105, 121, 122, 156, 185, 201 Sobr 3 Conf 19, 37, 44, 51, 118, 164, 188 Her 285 Congr 165 Fug 96 Mut 250 Somn 1:69, 250 Somn 2:9, 90 Ios 41, 130 Mos 1:8, 106, 224 Mos 2:69 Decal 136 Spec 1:145 Spec 2:99, 99 Spec 3:78 Spec 4:74, 89, 205 Virt 2, 44, 114, 146, 147, 155, 165, 166, 168, 168 Praem 21, 48, 95, 140, 156 Prob 40, 119 Aet 37, 65, 136 Flacc 1, 126 Legat 14 Prov 2:1, 14, 38

ἰσχύω (81) Leg 2:29, 81, 82, 95 Leg 3:6, 13, 27, 70, 147, 186, 189, 206, 242, 242 Cher 82 Sacr 49, 64, 95, 135 Det 71 Post 72 Deus 153 Agr 162, 178 Plant 8, 49, 144 Ebr 51, 73, 82, 112 Sobr 3, 38 Conf 12, 120 Migr 167 Her 13, 143, 224, 239 Congr 66 Fug 14, 22, 165 Mut 44, 178, 224, 233, 250 Somn 1:19, 24 Somn 2:93, 94, 95, 116, 253 Abr 79, 105, 164 Mos 1:49, 112, 217 Mos 2:197, 271 Decal 60, 87 Spec 1:45 Spec 4:112, 155 Virt 69, 222 Praem 41 Prob 91 Aet 58, 69, 76 Legat 319 Hypoth 6:4, 6:6, 7:11 QE isf 3 ἴσχω (23) Leg 2:70 Cher 11, 20, 22, 38, 87, 93 Sacr 2 Det 172, 172 Post 122 Deus 93 Agr 35, 36 Ebr 173 Sobr 47, 50 Conf 15, 134 Mut 85 Spec 1:72, 300 Spec 2:103

Ἰταλία (12) Leg 1:62 Aet 139 Flacc 109, 125, 157, 173 Legat 10, 108, 116, 155, 159, 252

Ἰταλικός Contempl 48

ἰχθῦς (25) Opif 63, 65, 65, 66, 66, 68, 147 Det 151 Agr 24 Plant 102 Ebr 182, 219 Her 79, 80 Somn 2:49, 260 Mos 1:93, 100 Mos 2:250 Decal 79 Spec 1:176 Spec 4:91, 113, 126 Prov 2:69

ἰχνευτικός Abr 266

ἰχνεύω Her 256

ἰχνηλατέω (16) Opif 56 Conf 143 Migr 218 Her 81 Somn 1:49 Somn 2:259 Ios 7, 104 Praem 36 Prob 64, 114 Contempl 27 Aet 106, 138 Prov 2:52 QE isf 7

ἴχνος (17) Opif 144 Post 24 Gig 39, 58 Deus 178 Agr 17 Conf 69, 71 Migr 128 Fug 130 Mut 181 Mos 1:102, 186 Mos 2:157 Virt 18, 64 Legat 347

ἰχώρ Spec 4:119

Ἰώβ Mut 48

Ἰωβήλ Post 83, 93, 100

Ἴων Spec 4:102 Prob 134

Ἰωνικός Somn 2:55

Ἰωσήφ (54) Leg 3:26, 90, 90, 179, 180, 237, 238, 242 Cher 128 Det 5, 6, 17, 28 Post 80, 96 Deus 119, 120 Agr 56 Ebr 210, 210 Sobr 12, 27 Conf 71, 72 Migr 17, 21, 159, 159, 203, 205 Her 251, 256 Fug 73, 127, 127 Mut 89, 89, 90, 91, 97, 170, 171, 215 Somn 1:78, 219 Somn 2:5, 6, 10, 15, 17, 47, 65, 66 Ios 28

K

καγχάζω Legat 42

Κάδης Fug 196, 196, 213, 213 QG 4:59

καδίσκος Mos 1:52

καθά καθάπερ

καθά (23) Cher 106 Sacr 8 Det 28 Post 89, 179 Deus 160 Ebr 67, 150 Conf 39, 145 Migr 67, 129 Her 213, 243 Mut 195 Somn 1:70 Somn 2:30, 217 Mos 1:111, 330 Spec 1:238, 291, 345

καθαγιάζω Leg 3:141 Cher 106 Somn 1:243 Somn 2:232 Spec 2:215

καθαγίζω Sacr 136

καθαγνίζω Fug 81

καθαίρεσις (26) Leg 1:75 Agr 109 Plant 35 Ebr 23, 29, 105, 112 Conf 130, 132, 145, 188 Migr 45 Her 289 Fug 207 Mut 72 Somn 2:16, 285 Mos 2:277 Decal 61 Spec 1:249 Spec 2:170 Legat 37, 153, 159 QG 2:15c QE 2:17

καθαιρετικός Legat 14, 113

καθαιρέω (90) Leg 3:189 Cher 37 Det 14, 165 Post 71, 72, 132, 140, 140, 146 Deus 174 Agr 77, 86 Plant 144 Ebr 156 Sobr 57 Conf 26, 101, 128, 131, 193 Migr 63, 191, 208, 224 Her 206, 286 Fug 147 Somn 1:152, 154, 174 Somn 2:14, 119, 152, 198, 290 Abr 223, 225 Ios 26, 131, 133, 179, 216, 217 Mos 1:31, 70, 263, 305, 327, 332 Mos 2:13, 96, 139, 185, 270 Spec 1:265, 293 Spec 2:46 Spec 3:152 Virt 26, 132, 165, 191 Praem 87, 87, 157 Prob 26 Aet 11 Flacc 4, 83, 84, 124 Legat 132, 202, 211, 303, 305, 322 QG 2:13a, 15c QG isf 13 QE 1:7b, 2:11b, 16, 17, 17, 17, 17, 17, 17

καθαίρω (81) Leg 3:100, 126, 127, 147, 200 Cher 33, 48, 107 Sacr 128, 139 Det 170, 171 Gig 54, 64 Deus 90, 132 Agr 10, 80 Plant 114, 115, 162 Ebr 78 Sobr 62 Conf 51 Migr 2, 19 Her 113, 239, 276 Congr 110 Fug 41, 80, 112 Mut 235, 245, 249 Somn 1:91, 148, 177, 198, 217, 226 Somn 2:25, 64, 138 Abr 122, 223 Ios 112 Mos 2:114, 225 Decal 45, 77 Spec 1:5, 188, 191, 201, 228, 229, 261, 262 Spec 2:148, 262 Spec 3:33, 89, 101, 130, 150, 205 Spec 4:59, 59 Virt 189 Praem 120, 163 Aet 2, 62 Legat 81 Prov 2:38, 39, 43 QG isf 2 QE isf 14

καθάλλομαι Agr 110 Mos 2:249

καθαμαξεύω (καταμαξεύω) Conf 143 Her 279

καθάπαξ Somn 1:94 Abr 36, 51

καθάπερ (καθά) (496) Opif 3, 20, 41, 42, 52, 64, 66, 66, 69, 72, 78, 85, 85, 96, 117, 127, 128, 132, 133, 142, 148, 152, 155, 163, 166 Leg 1:3, 47, 66, 72 Leg 2:30, 45 Leg 3:7, 24, 76, 96, 185, 204, 224, 230 Cher 2, 24, 32, 35, 57, 61, 82, 102, 104 Sacr 6, 16, 17, 18, 22, 36, 40, 41, 42, 44, 44, 45, 49, 49, 51, 64, 66, 67, 74, 80, 83, 95, 103, 109, 120, 121 Det 8, 12, 40, 43, 50, 59, 84, 105, 117, 123, 125, 128, 142, 164 Post 11, 34, 41, 51, 52, 56, 61, 88, 100, 104, 107, 113, 116, 125, 126, 127, 129, 137, 141, 151, 156 Gig 30 Deus 38, 45, 74, 116, 134 Agr 15, 24, 51, 58, 142, 158, 168 Plant 2, 10, 15, 24, 27, 37, 40, 55, 63, 65, 106, 110, 147, 167, 171 Ebr 11, 59, 90, 94, 101, 116, 121, 133, 140, 167, 184, 207, 215 Sobr 15, 20, 23, 41, 43, 46 Conf 67, 69, 94, 114, 144, 150, 192 Migr 3, 6, 72, 100, 101, 127, 148, 164, 171, 180, 214 Her 55, 88, 133, 214, 219, 238,

250, 279, 282, 307 Congr 23, 47, 50, 55, 59, 129, 135, 142, 144, 158 Fug 2, 19, 115, 151, 153, 183, 213 Mut 73, 84, 149, 163, 169, 191, 193, 211, 246, 262 Somn 1:40, 49, 51, 77, 91, 105, 116, 150, 165, 178, 181, 239 Somn 2:64, 78, 186, 198, 275 Abr 10, 19, 27, 31, 50, 62, 73, 116, 119, 168, 193, 196, 220, 257, 259, 269 Ios 3, 16, 17, 35, 39, 48, 58, 61, 82, 115, 160, 232, 259 Mos 1:16, 22, 29, 33, 60, 65, 93, 99, 103, 107, 111, 124, 131, 133, 144, 158, 172, 176, 177, 206, 218, 254, 270, 276, 287 Mos 2:14, 22, 30, 33, 37, 40, 44, 53, 56, 65, 74, 89, 105, 121, 122, 170, 195, 218, 267, 278, 290 Decal 14, 33, 48, 61, 89, 98, 143, 167, 178 Spec 1:13, 17, 24, 26, 30, 38, 39, 65, 106, 146, 246, 254, 289, 332 Spec 2:17, 74, 99, 101, 107, 116, 119, 121, 121, 157, 160, 165, 181, 189, 192, 213, 216, 224 Spec 3:5, 9, 16, 41, 60, 65, 76, 103, 111, 162, 174, 178, 184, 192 Spec 4:4, 20, 43, 50, 55, 74, 77, 78, 83, 85, 92, 107, 109, 114, 118, 123, 130, 139, 163, 167, 181, 185, 212, 235 Virt 19, 21, 25, 31, 43, 91, 140, 145, 155, 162, 164, 173, 179, 185, 186, 221 Praem 29, 33, 50, 58, 64, 65, 73, 89, 117, 125, 153, 157, 163, 167, 168, 172 Prob 5, 8, 21, 42, 49, 61, 63, 68, 71, 91, 94, 113, 130, 143, 160 Contempl 12, 22, 29, 30, 40, 68, 72, 85 Aet 32, 47, 56, 57, 61, 66, 92, 99, 109, 129, 132 Flacc 9, 26, 62, 80, 95, 98, 135, 153, 159, 178, 182, 188 Legat 1, 29, 44, 76, 99, 109, 117, 124, 128, 181, 214, 228, 281, 289, 320, 325, 369 Hypoth 11:13 Prov 2:4, 12, 32, 35, 40, 54, 55, 66, 71 QG 1:21, 28, 77, 4:200b QG (Par) 2:3 QE 1:21, 2:3b, 13a, 20

καθαρεύω (19) Leg 3:150 Cher 16 Deus 7, 125 Agr 50 Her 7 Mut 44 Ios 44 Mos 2:68, 138, 150 Decal 93 Spec 1:102 Spec 3:54, 57, 58, 59, 134 Praem 68

καθαρίζω Leg 2:63 Sobr 49 Conf 74

καθαριότης Spec 1:5, 156 Contempl 53

κάθαρμα Mos 1:30 Virt 174

καθαρμόζω Plant 89

καθαρμός Mos 1:216

καθαρός (219) Opif 27, 31, 55, 114, 136, 137, 137 Leg 1:50, 77, 88, 89 Leg 3:125, 150, 162, 170 Cher 50 Sacr 137 Det 169, 170, 170, 173 Gig 10 Deus 3, 8, 22, 29, 46, 49, 127, 128, 132, 132, 135, 135 Agr 144, 145, 158 Plant 14, 20, 27, 40, 111, 116, 126 Ebr 44, 49, 66, 66, 71, 101, 125, 127, 143, 151 Sobr 49 Conf 92, 167 Migr 17, 17, 46, 73, 103 Her 64, 84, 87, 88, 110, 129, 196, 216, 216, 240, 283, 308 Congr 132, 135, 143 Fug 71, 92, 109, 114, 167 Mut 6, 48, 62, 65, 111, 117, 199, 208 Somn 1:21, 81, 84, 135, 140, 146, 216, 218 Somn 2:20, 74, 133 Abr 9, 70, 79, 102, 129 Ios 67, 145, 148 Mos 1:63, 84, 101, 113, 145, 150, 303, 313 Mos 2:24, 34, 40, 72, 90, 143, 154, 154, 155, 158, 214 Decal 58, 64, 65, 98, 134, 155 Spec 1:99, 100, 101, 101, 105, 135, 150, 203, 218, 219, 232, 243, 248, 248, 250, 255, 257, 268, 268, 274, 277, 291, 321 Spec 2:6, 35, 36, 36, 36, 36, 202, 202, 258 Spec 3:4, 58, 59, 62, 91, 122, 122, 127, 136, 205, 205, 208 Spec 4:52, 105, 110, 113, 114, 161, 201, 206, 206, 235 Virt 39, 57, 62, 85, 113, 146, 146, 147, 160, 164 Praem 37, 84 Prob 3, 4, 99 Contempl 66, 73 Aet 20, 77 Flacc 122, 141 Legat 127, 165 QG 1:63, 2:12b, 12b, 4:86b, 130, 204 QE 2:45b QE isf 3

καθαρπάζω Abr 44

καθάρσιος (16) Cher 95 Det 20 Deus 8 Fug 153 Mut 124, 235, 245 Somn 1:220 Mos 1:304, 314 Spec 1:111 Spec 2:163, 249 Spec 3:89 Virt 189 Prov 2:14

κάθαρσις (39) Opif 123 Leg 1:13 Det 170 Plant 101, 101, 115, 116 Mut 236, 240, 247 Somn 2:25 Abr 100 Ios 113 Mos 2:64, 149, 196 Spec 1:109, 187, 188, 201, 216, 233, 234, 241, 258, 259, 264, 264, 267 Spec 2:70, 147, 262 Spec 4:12, 130 Virt 145 Praem 120 QG isf 2 QG (Par) 2:6 QE isf 14

καθαρτής Spec 1:60

καθέζομαι (22) Leg 2:46 Gig 48 Deus 137 Agr 150 Ebr 177 Congr 66, 124 Fug 189 Somn 2:127 Ios 203 Mos 1:270, 322 Decal 31 Spec 2:62 Prob 64, 81, 148 Contempl 30, 33 Flacc 75 Legat 42 Hypoth 7:12

καθείργνυμι (7) Ebr 101 Sobr 39 Her 109 Somn 1:181 Ios 105 Flacc 40, 117

καθέλκω (7) Opif 158 Ios 140, 147 Spec 2:232 Spec 3:3, 55 Virt 86

καθεύδω Somn 1:3, 174 Spec 1:298

καθηδυπαθέω Mos 1:160 Spec 4:126

καθήκω (23) Opif 32 Leg 1:56 Leg 2:32, 32 Leg 3:18, 126, 165, 210, 210 Cher 14, 14, 14, 15 Sacr 19, 20, 43 Plant 5, 94, 100 Sobr 21, 25 Her 191 QG 4:211

κάθημαι Gig 50 Agr 102 Legat 197

καθημέραν QG isf 6

καθησυχάζω Ios 215

καθιδρύω Legat 203

καθιερεύω Prob 119 Legat 308

καθιερόω (30) Cher 106 Her 186 Congr 98, 100, 106, 169 Somn 2:67, 77 Mos 1:316, 317 Spec 1:119, 120, 127, 131, 138, 138, 183, 191, 213, 248, 248, 286 Spec 2:35, 134, 183 Virt 159 Legat 208, 347 QG 1:60:1, 60:2

καθιέρωσις Spec 1:139

καθίζω (7) Leg 3:12 Plant 152 Ebr 165 Migr 155 Mos 2:37 Prob 122 Legat 350

καθίημι (20) Leg 3:186, 186 Sacr 17 Det 60 Deus 15 Agr 24 Plant 48, 102, 145 Congr 164 Fug 151, 155 Ios 180 Mos 1:79, 185 Spec 4:67 Virt 28, 34 Contempl 72 Prov 2:65

καθικετεύω Virt 57

καθικνέομαι Aet 128 QG 2:64b

καθιμάω Ios 14

καθίστημι (74) Opif 40, 84 Leg 1:105 Leg 3:12, 68 Det 62 Deus 120 Agr 49, 84, 87 Plant 81 Ebr 84 Conf 150, 160 Migr 88 Her 155, 253 Congr 53 Fug 107 Mut 151, 173 Somn 2:55, 123, 136, 152 Abr 242, 261 Ios 38, 119, 138, 157, 257 Mos 1:175, 196, 215, 217 Mos 2:16, 109, 143, 256, 266 Spec 1:17, 283 Spec 2:3, 153 Spec 3:53, 86, 97, 192 Spec 4:8, 56, 147, 157, 174, 230 Virt 223 Praem 54, 78 Prob 35 Contempl 31, 31 Aet 133, 147 Flacc 2, 41 Legat 100, 126, 196, 229 Hypoth 6:6 QG 1:69, 2:62, 4:51b QG (Par) 2:5

καθό Leg 3:73, 73 Plant 87, 87 Decal 64

κάθοδος (16) Cher 106 Ebr 8 Conf 197 Her 274 Fug 106, 116, 117, 119, 194 Abr 59 Decal 44 Spec 3:123, 131 Spec 4:159 Praem 117 Legat 341

καθολικός (8) Abr 3 Mos 2:243 Spec 3:47, 208 Spec 4:219 Praem 2 Legat 194 QG 1:72

καθόλου Leg 1:2, 78, 78 Cher 89 Prob 62

καθοπλίζω Leg 3:115

καθοράω (κατεῖδον) (27) Opif 76 Leg 2:26, 57 Leg 3:171 Det 87 Deus 29, 63 Agr 81 Conf 92 Migr 190 Congr 145 Fug 19, 121 Somn 1:91 Somn 2:3, 33 Mos 1:276 Spec 1:54, 330 Virt 5, 54, 151 Contempl 66 Flacc 37 Legat 211, 273 QG (Par) 2:6

καθοσιόω (9) Spec 2:249 Spec 3:91 Spec 4:99, 125 Praem 77 Legat 213, 236, 347 QE 2:47

καθόσον Fug 112

καθότι Somn 2:175

καθυβρίζω Legat 191

καθυποκρίνομαι (12) Fug 160 Mut 170 Abr 103 Ios 50, 166 Spec 2:49 Spec 4:32 Virt 39, 196 Flacc 19, 32, 72

καθυφίημι Spec 1:54 Spec 3:61

καθώς Mut 23

καί (27513) passim

Κάιν (82) Cher 12, 40, 52, 52, 53, 54, 55, 65, 124 Sacr 1, 2, 3, 5, 11, 11, 14, 51, 52, 72, 88 Det 1, 1, 1, 32, 32, 47, 47, 47, 50, 61, 68, 74, 78, 96, 103, 119, 140, 141, 163, 165, 166, 167, 168, 177, 178 Post 1, 10, 10, 12, 21, 33, 33, 34, 35, 38, 40, 40, 42, 45, 48, 51, 65, 124, 170, 172, 172 Agr 21, 127 Sobr 50 Conf 122, 122 Migr 74 Congr 171 Fug 60, 60, 64 QG 1:60:2, 60:2, 62:1, 74, 76b, 77

καινός (88) Cher 48 Sacr 76 Post 9, 9, 25, 151 Gig 43 Deus 116, 125 Agr 148, 170, 171 Plant 159 Ebr 158, 195 Sobr 53 Conf 62, 142 Migr 50 Her 214, 278 Congr 47 Fug 168 Mut 267 Somn 1:96, 129 Somn 2:130, 259 Abr 56, 64, 142, 193, 232, 257 Ios 7 Mos 1:10, 27, 42, 88, 255 Mos 2:33, 53, 143, 160, 203, 203, 281, 286 Spec 1:28, 51, 188 Spec 2:46, 87, 170 Spec 3:25, 30, 61 Spec 4:122, 215 Virt 38, 72, 115, 136 Praem 70, 70 Prob 15, 24 Contempl 80 Flacc 41, 44, 73, 93, 104, 116, 133, 159, 180 Legat 88, 89, 97, 134, 135, 136, 137, 149, 186, 342 QG 1:74

καινότης Contempl 63

καινοτομέω Mos 1:22, 199 Spec 1:193 Prob 3 Aet 16

καινουργέω (30) Det 87, 154 Deus 4 Migr 50 Somn 2:25, 117, 286 Abr 137, 183 Ios 19 Mos 1:33, 119, 216 Mos 2:198 Decal 35, 152 Spec 2:94 Spec 3:28, 49, 159 Spec 4:85 Virt 107, 136 Praem 136 Prob 106 Flacc 59 Legat 217, 305, 348 QG 4:51c

καινόω (10) Agr 171 Plant 81 Sobr 56 Abr 253 Ios 262 Mos 1:242 Mos 2:140 Spec 2:60 Flacc 153, 162

καίνωσις Ios 27

καίπερ Praem 78 Hypoth 6:6

καίριος (29) Det 60 Post 171 Ebr 154 Her 106, 133 Congr 90 Somn 2:261 Abr 168 Mos 1:211 Mos 2:125 Decal 144 Spec 1:220 Spec 3:93, 106, 155 Spec 4:28 Virt 1, 93, 101, 130, 145 Praem 101, 141 Flacc 66, 103 Legat 31, 127, 273 QE 2:24a

καιρός (263) Opif 41, 43, 55, 59, 59, 59, 103 Leg 3:11, 11 Cher 91, 92, 122 Sacr 90, 99 Det 19, 87 Post 113, 121, 121, 122, 123, 144 Gig 35, 52 Agr 85, 125, 147, 152 Plant 1, 89, 101, 147, 161, 162, 174 Sobr 42, 43 Conf 37, 132 Migr 91, 102, 126, 126 Her 30, 145, 282 Congr 73 Fug 181, 202 Mut 37, 196, 264, 264, 265, 265, 266 Somn 1:68, 95, 123, 133 Somn 2:81, 89, 92, 110, 263, 268, 279 Abr 20, 46, 65, 92, 117, 132, 183, 186, 246 Ios 6, 10, 30, 32, 53, 115, 118, 131, 135, 139, 161, 166, 185, 186, 200, 206, 241, 248, 253, 258, 262, 267, 270 Mos 1:32, 46, 46, 60, 142, 146, 151, 184, 226, 301, 305, 321, 328 Mos 2:18, 27, 33, 53, 60, 120, 140, 161, 173, 221, 273 Decal 77, 94, 95, 117 Spec 1:55, 79, 113, 168, 172, 181, 181, 183, 186, 191, 193, 297, 311, 336 Spec 2:6, 23, 39, 40, 48, 49, 56, 57, 64, 67, 78, 84, 112, 114, 144, 158, 158, 160, 175, 178, 190, 197, 204, 205, 220, 239, 262 Spec 3:17, 33, 81, 95, 104, 109, 111, 155, 155, 188, 200 Spec 4:8, 31, 51, 136, 173, 210, 213 Virt 16, 22, 22, 28, 30, 68, 71, 75, 83, 91, 100, 105, 123, 128, 138, 149, 157 Praem 3, 67, 88, 134, 136, 157 Prob 18, 20, 24, 89 Aet 132, 132, 144 Flacc 15, 74, 81, 84, 93, 140, 152, 165 Legat 3, 13, 120, 168, 173, 190, 201, 221, 227, 248, 260, 281 Prov 2:6, 15, 34, 34, 44 QG 1:100:1b, 100:1b, 100:1b, 100:1b, 100:2a, 100:2b, 100:2b, 100:2b, 2:13a, 17a, 17c, 3:21, 22, 4:51b, 204, 204 QG isf 5 QE 2:15b, 25b, 25d, 49b QE isf 8

καιροφυλακέω Mut 185 Abr 233, 242 Ios 263 Praem 86

Καῖσαρ (23) Prob 118, 118 Flacc 2, 8, 25, 35, 40, 42, 105, 112, 128, 158 Legat 8, 145, 151, 152, 166, 206, 298, 314, 315, 316, 317

Καισάρεια Legat 305

Καισάρειος Legat 150

καίτοι (151) Opif 77 Leg 1:58, 85 Leg 3:55, 130, 182 Cher 35, 96 Sacr 49 Det 119, 177 Post 19, 95, 169 Gig 29, 33, 42 Deus 8, 10, 22, 77, 78, 106, 132 Agr 3, 59, 61, 85, 95, 131 Plant 65 Ebr 38, 148, 178 Sobr 8, 22 Conf 3, 15, 31, 100, 118, 119, 124, 159, 160, 191 Migr 115, 155, 163 Her 3, 22, 71, 72, 90 Congr 13, 85, 120, 146, 161 Fug 73, 144, 147, 155 Somn 1:47, 166, 182, 204, 209 Somn 2:63, 169, 206, 301 Abr 1, 9, 10, 63, 86, 105, 170, 216, 252 Ios 158, 182, 230 Mos 1:20, 25, 42, 143, 152, 241, 243, 286 Mos 2:17, 38, 58, 197, 198, 207, 270, 279 Decal 6, 59, 60, 72, 73 Spec 1:10, 73, 104, 290 Spec 2:20, 69, 97, 251 Spec 3:6, 85, 117 Spec 4:14, 206 Virt 53, 53, 56, 59, 84, 107, 146, 222 Praem 38, 143 Prob 68, 114 Aet 46 Flacc 48, 92 Legat 61, 71, 81, 98, 101, 116, 138, 159, 242, 244, 299, 304 Hypoth 6:4, 7:17 Prov 2:65 QG 1:69, 2:54a, 4:88

καίω (31) Leg 1:5 Leg 3:226 Cher 15 Deus 66, 79 Ebr 73, 133 Conf 156 Her 307 Fug 161 Abr 138, 138, 138, 140, 140 Ios 76, 168 Mos 1:67, 67, 70, 70, 120 Mos 2:220 Decal 49, 49 Spec 1:4, 285, 296 Virt 154 Prob 96 Legat 197

κακηγορέω (17) Conf 154, 154 Fug 83, 84 Ios 74 Mos 1:90 Mos 2:198, 198 Spec 2:232, 248, 254 Spec 3:105, 174, 174 Spec 4:197, 198 Flacc 33

κακηγορία Fug 84 Mos 1:196 Spec 4:200

κακήγορος (6) Fug 83, 86 Somn 2:132 Abr 191 Decal 63 Prov 2:18

κακία (312) Opif 73, 73, 73, 73, 74, 75, 75, 79, 81, 149, 168, 168, 170 Leg 1:49, 61, 61, 61, 62, 73, 86, 103, 104, 104, 105, 106, 107 Leg 2:4, 12, 16, 18, 53, 54, 60, 64, 68, 77, 89, 98, 98, 101 Leg 3:2, 2, 21, 22, 23, 27, 27, 34, 38, 43, 52, 80, 89, 107, 122, 170, 175, 190, 212, 236, 242, 246, 246, 247, 247, 247, 251 Cher 2, 12, 17, 93, 96 Sacr 14, 16, 47, 57, 58, 81, 103, 110, 111, 120, 123, 135, 135, 139 Det 45, 49, 68, 72, 105, 110, 122, 123, 165, 168 Post 9, 32, 43, 62, 93, 172 Gig 4 Deus 4, 20, 26, 49, 113, 129, 164 Agr 10, 44, 78, 83, 83, 92, 106, 109, 110, 122 Plant 37, 43, 171 Ebr 6, 8, 25, 78, 187 Sobr 30, 38, 42, 43, 44, 45, 45, 47, 49, 50 Conf 11, 23, 24, 26, 52, 57, 60, 67, 67, 68, 70, 83, 85, 90, 90, 91, 101, 104, 113, 115, 161, 167, 177, 179, 188, 189, 193, 195, 196, 198, 198 Migr 26, 61, 61,

124, 208, 219 Her 109, 209, 241, 241, 243 Congr 53, 59, 59, 71, 82, 82, 83, 84, 85, 87, 129, 171, 172, 178, 178, 179 Fug 43, 58, 61, 64, 82, 113 Mut 30, 50, 143, 167, 269 Somn 1:174 Somn 2:14, 163, 256 Abr 1, 19, 22, 32, 40, 41, 41, 47, 105, 106, 204 Ios 18, 70, 83, 213 Mos 1:106, 186 Mos 2:16, 53, 138, 196, 200 Spec 1:32, 214, 221, 257, 278, 281, 295, 330, 330, 343 Spec 2:11, 42, 77, 92, 170, 228 Spec 3:54, 103, 125, 151, 167, 191, 209 Spec 4:55, 108, 182, 206, 237 Virt 147, 147, 164, 172, 181, 195, 211, 227 Praem 12, 32, 34, 52, 62, 115, 124, 159 Prob 17, 45, 55, 55, 60, 61, 63, 63, 78, 90 Contempl 2 Aet 2, 112, 112 Legat 91, 118 Prov 2:23, 36, 38, 39, 41 QG 1:32, 96:1, 100:1c, 2:12c, 13a, 38, 39, 54a, 54c, 74, 4:51a, 172 QE isf 31, 32

κακίζω (21) Agr 33 Ebr 121 Conf 46 Migr 34 Congr 179 Somn 2:292, 299 Ios 87, 170 Mos 1:287 Mos 2:269 Decal 89, 118 Spec 1:227, 235 Spec 2:101 Praem 116, 163 Prob 14 Prov 2:22 QG 4:174

κακόβουλος Spec 2:49

κακοδαιμονέω (7) Leg 3:17 Det 25 Deus 17 Mut 94, 242 Mos 2:186 Legat 105

κακοδαιμονία (15) Opif 156 Leg 3:52 Det 103 Conf 16, 162, 165 Her 179 Mut 237 Somn 1:121 Abr 268 Virt 61, 202 Praem 171 Legat 31, 69

κακοδαιμονίζω Det 143 Post 81

κακοδαίμων (22) Opif 152 Leg 3:211 Cher 39 Det 78, 119 Agr 36 Migr 83 Abr 35 Mos 1:193 Decal 130 Spec 1:193, 278, 304, 304 Spec 4:81 Virt 50, 205 Flacc 14, 157, 159 Legat 59 QG 4:198

κακόδουλος Contempl 19

κακοήθης Congr 71 Somn 2:192 Mos 1:244 Flacc 12

κακοικονόμος Sacr 32

κακομανέω Aet 46

κακομήχανος Sacr 32

κακονοέω Migr 116

κακόνοια Mos 1:249 Flacc 78 Legat 355

κακόνομος Sacr 32

κακόνους Sacr 32 Somn 2:108 Flacc 9 Legat 33

κακοπάθεια (7) Leg 3:135 Cher 87 Ios 26, 223 Mos 1:154 Decal 117 Praem 128

κακοπαθέω (8) Cher 88 Sacr 38 Somn 2:105, 181 Spec 2:60 Virt 88, 130 QG isf 9

κακοποιέω Somn 2:296

κακοπολιτεία Opif 171 Agr 45 Mut 150 Virt 180

κακοπραγέω Virt 122

κακοπραγία (40) Opif 151 Cher 34, 35 Sacr 28, 116 Det 142 Post 67 Deus 48 Agr 75, 151 Conf 6 Migr 194 Congr 15 Somn 1:96 Abr 64, 246 Ios 137, 187, 217 Mos 2:163 Decal 43 Spec 2:131 Spec 3:161, 166 Spec 4:200 Praem 150, 169 Flacc 29, 118, 148, 153, 167, 174, 186 Legat 124, 137, 187 Prov 2:4 QG isf 5 QE 2:55b

κακός (χείρων) (595) Opif 68, 73, 73, 74, 75, 75, 79, 156, 169 Leg 1:45, 62, 72, 72, 76, 102, 106, 108 Leg 2:17, 50, 50, 50, 53, 53, 62, 62, 65, 83, 85 Leg 3:19, 34, 46, 52, 53, 67, 67, 72, 73, 91, 92, 104, 105, 105, 105, 105, 105, 106, 106, 110, 113, 117, 174, 177, 177, 177, 178, 186, 199, 222, 246, 246 Cher 34, 36, 37, 42, 57, 75, 86 Sacr 4, 4, 5, 16, 28, 30, 70, 122, 125, 135, 137 Det 48, 57, 58, 74, 93, 119, 122, 122, 123, 140, 141, 148, 174, 178 Post 9, 26, 32, 37, 54, 75, 83, 94, 94, 176, 181 Gig 16, 37, 37, 65 Deus 9, 49, 50, 50, 85, 115, 121, 132, 138, 170, 173 Agr 31, 47, 100, 105, 110, 111, 118, 122, 133 Plant 45, 53, 87, 98, 107, 155, 171, 171, 174 Ebr 20, 26, 79, 125, 163, 187 Sobr 2, 4, 7, 42, 52, 67, 67 Conf 7, 10, 12, 13, 15, 15, 21, 21, 22, 42, 48, 50, 60, 60, 64, 75, 91, 92, 105, 108, 108, 109, 154, 161, 164, 178, 180, 181, 181, 182, 196 Migr 59, 63, 72, 86, 108, 114, 114, 147, 148, 161, 172, 185, 189, 193, 195, 209, 211 Her 15, 46, 77, 89, 97, 97, 163, 178, 184, 186, 202, 204, 240, 241, 272, 274, 284, 287, 287, 294, 295, 295, 299, 314 Congr 32, 45, 81, 84, 84, 84, 97, 130, 160 Fug 24, 30, 30, 42, 42, 43, 58, 58, 61, 61, 62, 62, 63, 67, 70, 70, 74, 74, 79, 80, 84, 99, 114, 131, 152, 153, 190, 193, 213 Mut 37, 108, 138, 144, 163, 168, 189, 195, 196, 197, 227 Somn 1:57, 91, 107, 110, 149, 151, 152, 211 Somn 2:125, 130, 140, 140, 150, 151, 163, 164, 179, 200, 204, 205, 230, 240, 240, 265, 279, 282, 289, 291, 294 Abr 14, 14, 17, 21, 45, 46, 86, 96, 129, 134, 136, 143, 145, 202, 228, 230, 246, 261, 261, 263, 268 Ios 12, 13, 15, 25, 36, 57, 57, 68, 75, 84, 86, 88, 94, 100, 101, 137, 137, 143, 156, 166, 170, 172, 187, 212, 214, 214, 227 Mos 1:3, 11, 26, 42, 69, 106, 110, 120, 122, 123, 137, 146, 146, 149, 161, 164, 168, 170, 171, 172, 191, 197, 216, 236, 247, 284, 286, 286, 295, 295, 305, 305, 323 Mos 2:5, 16, 59, 162, 174, 200, 204, 227, 240, 248 Decal 2, 5, 91, 113, 123, 144, 145, 151, 155, 176 Spec 1:48, 56, 62, 62, 121, 186, 192, 195, 196, 206, 224, 283, 284, 305, 314, 333 Spec 2:13, 15, 35, 35, 37, 46, 52, 52, 53, 76, 83, 95, 95, 131, 137, 170, 187, 201, 203, 209, 209 Spec 3:3, 4, 15, 17, 23, 28, 28, 37, 39, 39, 103, 162, 171, 183 Spec 4:3, 25, 42, 47, 64, 84, 84, 86, 89, 91, 100, 109, 113, 121, 130, 170, 186, 187, 189, 206, 213 Virt 24, 26, 61, 100, 106, 107, 111, 116, 124, 131, 150, 161, 162, 200, 205, 205, 212 Praem 62, 63, 68, 70, 71, 71, 72, 73, 93, 124, 127, 127, 132, 134, 135, 136, 138 Prob 23, 23, 56, 57, 64, 83, 84, 90, 115, 139 Contempl 39, 43, 62 Aet 5, 13, 37, 41, 41, 41, 41, 42, 43, 43, 148 Flacc 1, 18, 20, 44, 57, 66, 91, 105, 124, 128, 147, 147, 153, 162, 179, 187 Legat 2, 17, 82, 97, 99, 101, 101, 108, 119, 127, 133, 149, 184, 190, 198, 200, 223, 224, 233, 233, 267, 293, 299, 327, 328, 348 Hypoth 6:4, 7:2, 7:7 Prov 2:1, 8, 9, 24, 27, 28, 39, 53 QG 1:72, 89, 2:54b, 3:7, 4:179 QG isf 5, 9, 10, 12, 13 QG (Par) 2:7 QE 2:6a

κακοτεχνέω (6) Agr 157 Conf 14, 75 Mut 199 Spec 3:53 Spec 4:194

κακοτεχνία Congr 141 Mut 150 Somn 1:107 Spec 3:101 Spec 4:48

κακότεχνος Sacr 32 Det 18 Contempl 42

κακότης Ebr 150

κακοῦργος Deus 112 Her 109 Spec 1:75 Flacc 75

κακόω (40) Leg 3:174, 174 Post 54 Gig 10 Deus 115 Conf 51 Her 20, 20, 79, 271, 271 Congr 107, 158, 170, 170, 172, 178, 178, 178, 180 Fug 1, 2 Mut 196 Mos 1:69, 72 Mos 2:184 Spec 2:135, 136, 217 Spec 3:99, 161, 197 Praem 117, 119 Flacc 97 Legat 125 Hypoth 6:6 QE 2:2, 3a, 4

κάκωσις (28) Leg 3:174 Det 19 Agr 152 Migr 9 Her 268 Congr 157, 160, 161, 161, 167, 167, 173, 175, 178, 178, 179 Fug 2 Mos 1:129, 191 Spec 3:62, 99 Praem 143, 146, 151, 157 Flacc 121 QE 2:2, 4

κακωτής Congr 171 Legat 92

κακωτικός Legat 81

καλαμίσκος Her 216, 218, 220 Congr 8

καλαμοσφάκτης Flacc 132

Κάλανος Prob 93, 94, 96

καλέω (443) Opif 15, 31, 35, 36, 39, 57, 64, 78, 78, 102, 105, 111, 127, 133 Leg 1:1, 10, 21, 23, 31, 43, 45, 55, 59, 69, 72, 90 Leg 2:9, 9, 10, 16, 16, 18, 18, 18, 18, 44, 54, 55, 55, 67, 84, 86, 89 Leg 3:43, 44, 46, 49, 49, 49, 49, 50, 52, 79, 81, 85, 96, 104, 136, 151, 154, 162, 172, 191, 200, 214, 215, 217, 220, 233, 236, 236, 247, 248, 251 Cher 5, 10, 41, 49, 55, 57, 57, 60, 84, 87, 124 Sacr 2, 20, 33, 51, 79, 120, 126 Det 3, 4, 15, 39, 65, 76, 83, 83, 84, 118, 160, 160, 172 Post 12, 22, 34, 57, 59, 63, 68, 84, 91, 93, 94, 101, 101, 102, 103, 131 Gig 62, 64, 66 Deus 5, 44, 86, 89, 103, 121, 134, 139, 144, 150 Agr 29, 41, 56, 95, 147 Plant 14, 23, 38, 56, 78, 78, 82, 123, 129, 134, 134, 134, 136, 148, 151, 154, 169 Ebr 47, 82, 99, 101, 139, 155, 155, 164, 165, 174, 174 Sobr 9, 10, 16, 22, 28, 28, 35, 45, 52 Conf 1, 9, 28, 57, 68, 89, 111, 122, 130, 137, 148, 173, 174 Migr 4, 13, 32, 38, 46, 84, 94, 152, 157, 165, 203, 205, 221, 224 Her 47, 52, 53, 127, 135, 163, 179, 191, 223, 230, 231, 263, 273, 274, 280 Congr 20, 25, 30, 37, 42, 57, 60, 76, 142, 148, 163, 166, 168, 177 Fug 1, 29, 75, 100, 100, 188, 196, 204, 212 Mut 29, 40, 60, 63, 63, 63, 71, 81, 83, 90, 94, 99, 103, 117, 120, 126, 128, 130, 144, 160, 164, 193, 260, 261 Somn 1:42, 63, 69, 79, 85, 89, 90, 93, 115, 125, 129, 129, 130, 139, 141, 145, 172, 194, 195, 200, 206, 214, 230, 254 Somn 2:1, 33, 234, 237, 242, 248, 250, 286 Abr 1, 8, 17, 27, 28, 32, 54, 56, 81, 103, 121, 124, 176, 201 Ios 28, 61, 220, 234, 250, 256, 265 Mos 1:58, 66, 98, 130 Mos 2:29, 33, 80, 101, 106, 149, 174, 199, 243, 244, 245 Decal 16, 54, 56, 81, 86, 90, 132, 143, 160 Spec 1:4, 49, 51, 88, 94, 147, 181, 190, 193, 194, 208, 226, 242, 247, 248, 290, 297, 303, 344 Spec 2:10, 41, 41, 58, 73, 86, 101, 108, 113, 131, 132, 132, 145, 173, 211, 215, 252, 259 Spec 3:23, 155, 170 Spec 4:21, 31, 36, 69, 93, 114, 130, 187, 188, 235 Virt 23, 24, 27, 40, 91, 108, 169 Praem 4, 26, 123 Prob 6, 31, 69, 81 Contempl 2, 3, 25 Aet 1, 15, 48, 54, 54, 97 Flacc 112, 151 Legat 4, 38, 70, 138, 144, 186, 211, 294, 372 Hypoth 11:1 Prov 2:29 QG 1:21, 31, 2:5a, 65, 3:11a, 22, 38a, 49a, 49a, 49b, 4:64 QG (Par) 2:5 QE 2:2, 46 QE isf 15

καλινδέομαι Mut 173

Καλλίας Contempl 57

καλλίγραφος Prov 2:15

καλλιερέω Agr 127 Somn 1:243

καλλίνικος Agr 79

καλλιστεύω (9) Cher 48 Abr 27, 57 Mos 1:59 Spec 2:178, 259 Spec 4:11, 14 Praem 53

κάλλος (99) Opif 4, 6, 71, 97, 128, 139, 139, 139, 145 Leg 2:81 Leg 3:16, 63, 220 Sacr 21, 29, 45 Det 79, 99, 133 Post 92, 93, 112, 119, 159 Gig 17, 44 Deus 150 Plant 65 Ebr 52, 75, 137 Sobr 12, 12, 38, 68 Conf 49 Migr 12, 12, 86 Her 4 Congr 75, 124 Fug 26 Mut 267 Somn 1:164, 188 Somn 2:228 Abr 154, 159, 227, 261, 263, 267 Ios 130, 144, 269 Mos 1:64, 190, 212, 235, 299 Mos 2:26, 51, 137, 139, 209 Decal 26 Spec 1:73, 139 Spec 2:32, 40, 51, 141, 176 Spec 3:25, 51 Spec 4:51, 89 Virt 36, 39, 217 Praem 42, 64, 84, 115, 160 Prob 4, 38, 137 Contempl 26, 78 Aet 41, 76 Legat 105, 150 Prov 2:1, 7, 31 QE 2:44

καλοκἀγαθία (καλός) (77) Agr 135 Plant 42 Ebr 49, 95, 112 Sobr 65 Conf 71, 149, 196 Migr 24, 120, 219 Congr 31 Fug 19, 45, 139 Somn 1:49, 125, 148, 209 Somn 2:171, 176, 178 Abr 27, 35, 56, 98, 220, 254, 271 Ios 19, 37, 85, 124, 230 Mos 1:59, 148 Mos 2:57, 189, 215 Spec 1:101, 215, 246, 272, 304 Spec 2:46, 236 Spec 3:51 Spec 4:75, 169, 182, 196, 237 Virt 10, 52, 56, 60, 79, 117, 197, 201, 206, 226 Praem 59, 112 Prob 41, 62, 71, 75, 91 Contempl 72, 90 Flacc 2 Legat 5, 143 QG 1:85, 3:8

καλός (592) Opif 8, 16, 16, 21, 28, 28, 30, 69, 73, 76, 82, 107, 136, 138, 150, 153, 154, 170, 171 Leg 1:49, 55, 55, 55, 56, 56, 57, 58, 60, 60, 61, 61, 63, 64, 66, 67, 78, 78, 78, 78, 80, 80, 90, 97, 99, 100, 101 Leg 2:1, 1, 1, 1, 1, 1, 4, 4, 4, 55, 73, 87, 90, 100, 108, 108 Leg 3:18, 27, 38, 47, 48, 58, 72, 77, 83, 85, 88, 104, 110, 130, 136, 141, 144, 150, 156, 158, 166, 167, 167, 180, 181, 215, 218, 249 Cher 9, 13, 30, 41, 44, 46, 85, 86, 86, 86, 87, 92, 96, 98, 101, 103 Sacr 5, 17, 19, 30, 35, 36, 37, 41, 48, 51, 53, 53, 54, 55, 60, 63, 68, 68, 69, 71, 78, 115, 120, 138 Det 9, 30, 35, 37, 43, 51, 65, 69, 74, 74, 95, 111, 120, 120, 134, 149 Post 12, 21, 30, 38, 42, 62, 80, 80, 84, 88, 94, 95, 95, 99, 101, 127, 132, 133, 133, 133, 135, 135, 159, 164, 170, 174, 182 Gig 2, 4, 6, 15, 20, 21, 43 Deus 24, 25, 49, 89, 94, 111, 123, 129, 137, 154 Agr 5, 9, 50, 82, 91, 99, 104, 110, 123, 128, 153, 168 Plant 36, 50, 50, 77, 107, 158, 160, 161, 170, 171 Ebr 16, 21, 29, 33, 84, 112, 139, 146, 187, 194, 197, 200, 223, 223, 224 Sobr 15, 26, 53, 60, 62, 67, 68, 68 Conf 59, 72, 103, 118, 145, 169, 173 Migr 16, 31, 36, 46, 56, 59, 67, 70, 86, 88, 114, 125, 132, 135, 144, 144, 145, 146, 149, 153, 161, 164, 181, 205, 218, 218 Her 36, 50, 77, 99, 159, 267, 275, 290, 291, 291, 299, 312 Congr 7, 36, 69, 89, 99, 107, 108, 109, 113, 137, 166, 177 Fug 8, 34, 35, 36, 52, 58, 65, 75, 128, 129, 145, 150, 151, 153, 153, 167, 175, 200, 206, 207 Mut 30, 31, 31, 47, 76, 82, 108, 119, 138, 141, 145, 173, 189, 193, 197, 198, 255 Somn 1:13, 45, 56, 103, 106, 126, 131, 135, 149, 162, 168, 180, 207, 244, 251, 251 Somn 2:9, 20, 24, 34, 74, 77, 92, 109, 180, 192, 216, 217, 218, 218, 235, 268, 270, 272, 281, 282, 282, 296, 296 Abr 4, 7, 18, 20, 22, 26, 37, 38, 47, 52, 54, 57, 61, 74, 102, 102, 156, 156, 168 Ios 2, 18, 46, 59, 79, 101, 143, 207, 213 Mos 1:3, 3, 59, 146, 153, 168, 189, 189, 249, 289, 295, 301, 306 Mos 2:7, 9, 11, 12, 27, 34, 70, 93, 126, 128, 130, 136, 199 Decal 37, 50, 58, 63, 67, 71, 77, 84, 97, 113, 132, 162 Spec 1:10, 12, 15, 33, 55, 56, 120, 174, 195, 197, 204, 248, 250, 265, 269, 280, 301, 303, 314, 318, 320, 323, 332, 337, 339 Spec 2:7, 12, 14, 18, 29, 31, 48, 48, 66, 72, 73, 88, 110, 142, 154, 166, 193, 256 Spec 3:1, 41, 64, 77, 108, 115, 125 Spec 4:15, 46, 64, 68, 69, 69, 131, 138, 146, 161, 171, 173, 178, 182 Virt 51, 53, 54, 67, 69, 84, 99, 102, 113, 118, 127, 142, 152, 174, 197, 198, 205, 205, 210, 219, 221, 221 Praem 16, 18, 27, 32, 32, 51, 104, 112, 112, 114, 126, 152, 172 Prob 2, 15, 62, 63, 66, 74, 108, 136, 136, 139 Contempl 1, 1, 8, 16, 67, 89 Aet 13, 37, 76 Flacc 34, 74, 85, 142, 157 Legat 5, 5, 5, 89, 103, 147, 198, 206, 206, 234, 265, 277, 329, 338, 348 Hypoth 6:2 Prov 2:3, 7, 10, 16, 21 QG 2:22, 34a, 41, 3:11b, 11c, 38b, 49a, 4:51a, 191a, 200a, 206a, 211 QE 2:17 QE isf 9

κάλπις Spec 1:262

κάλυμμα Leg 2:53 Mut 43 Mos 2:87, 101

καλύπτω (6) Leg 2:27 Leg 3:158, 158 Mos 2:87 QE 2:46 QE isf 31

κάλως (6) Cher 38 Agr 174 Conf 35 Mut 215 Somn 2:132 Legat 177

καματηρός (6) Post 94 Abr 59 Mos 2:211 Spec 2:100 Praem 80 Flacc 26

κάματος (24) Opif 80, 86, 158, 167 Cher 46, 88, 88, 90 Sacr 37, 113, 114 Det 122 Deus 92 Migr 144 Somn 2:58 Mos 1:237 Spec 1:125 Spec 2:69, 89, 207 Praem 155 Prob 2 Aet 62, 63

καμηλοπάρδαλις Spec 4:105

κάμηλος (8) Post 132, 132, 148, 153 Agr 131, 145 Congr 111 Spec 1:135

κάμινος Ebr 73 Her 251 Mos 1:127

καμμύω Somn 1:164 QE isf 31

κάμνω (35) Opif 84 Leg 3:70, 226 Cher 15, 88 Sacr 123 Det 43 Post 31, 141 Deus 65, 160 Agr 13, 40 Conf 22 Migr 124, 133, 144, 220 Congr 53 Fug 27 Mut 84, 85, 221 Somn 1:51, 243 Ios 33, 77 Mos 1:128, 215 Decal 12 Spec 2:98, 233 Spec 4:153 Prob 12 Legat 241

καμπτήρ Opif 47 Plant 76, 125 Fug 98

κάμπτω (7) Opif 79 Det 99 Post 74 Plant 17 Ebr 185 Conf 51 Spec 2:46

κάμψις QG (Par) 2:7

κάνεον (κανοῦν) (7) Somn 2:158, 207, 208, 210, 210 Ios 93, 96

κανηφορέω Somn 2:158, 208, 212 Ios 93

κανονικός Opif 96

κανοῦν κάνεον

κανών (27) Leg 3:233 Sacr 59 Det 125 Post 28, 104 Gig 49 Agr 130 Ebr 185 Conf 2 Her 154, 160, 173 Fug 152 Somn 1:73 Ios 145 Mos 1:76 Decal 14, 140 Spec 1:287 Spec 3:137, 164 Spec 4:115 Virt 70, 219 Prob 83 Aet 108, 116

καπηλεία Prob 78

καπηλεύω Virt 112 Legat 203

κάπηλος Migr 217 Spec 4:193, 194

Καπίτων Legat 199, 199, 202

καπνίζω Her 251, 308

καπνός (12) Her 251, 310 Somn 2:70 Abr 141 Ios 53 Mos 2:56 Decal 44, 74 Flacc 68 Legat 130 Prov 2:49, 49

καπνώδης Legat 130

κάπτω Leg 1:98

κάρα Aet 37

Καραβᾶς Flacc 36

καραδοκέω (9) Leg 3:189 Ios 9, 97 Mos 1:12 Mos 2:178 Spec 4:220 Flacc 180 Legat 128 Prov 2:29

καρδία (39) Opif 118 Leg 1:12, 59, 68 Leg 2:6 Sacr 55, 57, 136 Det 90 Post 85, 137 Deus 20 Conf 24 Her 113 Congr 170 Fug 123, 142 Mut 123, 237, 238 Somn 1:32 Somn 2:180 Mos 1:189 Spec 1:6, 213, 214, 215, 216, 218, 304 Spec 4:137 Virt 183, 183 Praem 80 Prob 68 Prov 2:17 QG (Par) 2:3, 2:3 QE 2:50a

καρηβαρέω Mos 1:270 Contempl 89

καρκίνος Decal 72

κάρος Legat 267, 269

καρπόβρωτος Agr 12

καρπός (268) Opif 39, 40, 41, 41, 41, 42, 43, 43, 44, 44, 46, 58, 59, 80, 113, 116, 140, 153, 153, 156, 156 Leg 1:22 Leg 2:46 Leg 3:93, 99, 227, 227, 249 Cher 84, 102 Sacr 25, 25, 52, 52, 52, 72, 72, 80, 125 Det 111 Post 125, 163, 171 Gig 4 Deus 39, 39, 154, 166 Agr 5, 9, 10, 11, 14, 18, 19, 25, 157 Plant 33, 74, 74, 77, 85, 85, 93, 95, 95, 95, 98, 100, 106, 112, 112, 113, 113, 113, 114, 114, 115, 116, 117, 119, 125, 126, 132, 132, 133, 135, 137, 137, 138, 138 Ebr 106, 223, 224 Sobr 28, 65 Conf 124 Migr 125, 140, 202, 205 Her 121, 137, 137, 314 Congr 4, 56, 95 Fug 125, 176, 176 Mut 2, 73, 73, 74, 74, 74, 98, 139, 140, 162, 165, 192, 221, 246, 260 Somn 1:37, 58, 97, 105 Somn 2:22, 58, 163, 171, 272 Abr 91, 134, 138, 140, 159, 227 Ios 6, 30, 111, 112, 113, 113, 158 Mos 1:5, 116, 119, 145, 189, 192, 201, 224, 226, 231, 254 Mos 2:22, 66, 179, 180, 181, 182, 222, 258 Decal 15, 77, 160, 161, 163 Spec 1:16, 74, 92, 134, 138, 165, 172, 179, 183, 246, 309, 322 Spec 2:70, 97, 105, 107, 113, 133, 143, 153, 154, 158, 158, 169, 175, 179, 179, 181, 181, 184, 192, 198, 204, 206, 207, 213, 219, 221 Spec 4:12, 22, 25, 75, 81, 181, 208, 209, 211, 212, 217, 226, 227 Virt 6, 91, 97, 120, 145, 149, 149, 154, 156, 157, 157, 159 Praem 8, 41, 101, 129, 129, 130, 131, 133, 141 Prob 69, 70, 70, 70 Aet 63, 63, 96 Flacc 63 Legat 249, 249, 253, 257, 293 Hypoth 7:17, 7:19 Prov 2:10, 66, 70 QG 1:41, 60:1, 60:2, 4:51b QG isf 17 QE 1:1

καρποτοκέω Leg 2:75 Migr 55

καρποτόκος (8) Leg 1:49, 49, 50 Det 105, 111 Deus 87 Agr 8 Somn 2:170

καρποφορέω (12) Cher 84 Plant 31, 34, 44 Ebr 8 Congr 41 Mut 161 Somn 2:173, 199, 272 Spec 4:215 QG 1:3

καρποφορία (7) Leg 1:72 Leg 3:93 Sobr 28 Migr 205 Congr 40 Mut 98 Virt 93

καρποφόρος (10) Opif 133, 168 Leg 1:72 Leg 3:93, 94, 150 Her 32 Somn 2:76 Abr 141 Praem 60

καρπόω (52) Opif 156 Leg 2:100 Leg 3:121 Cher 29, 120 Sacr 5, 41, 127 Det 140 Post 45 Deus 81 Agr 9 Ebr 205 Sobr 32, 37, 57 Conf 118 Migr 11 Congr 32 Fug 118 Somn 1:108, 117 Somn 2:66, 74 Ios 63, 174, 266 Mos 1:53, 323, 332 Mos 2:148 Decal 74 Spec 1:77, 117, 131, 229 Spec 2:27, 209 Spec 3:1 Spec 4:5, 158 Virt 2, 29, 98 Praem 35 Flacc 25, 77, 184 Legat 258 Hypoth 11:3, 11:4 QG 4:43

κάρπωμα Leg 3:196 Cher 84 Sacr 111 Deus 6 Migr 142

κάρταλος (κάρταλλος) Somn 2:272 Spec 2:215, 216

κάρταλλος κάρταλος

καρτερέω Agr 152

καρτερία (31) Leg 2:83 Leg 3:11, 156 Cher 78, 96 Det 17, 157 Post 86, 93 Deus 13 Agr 97, 98, 100, 101, 105, 106, 109 Migr 19, 98 Her 274 Fug 33 Mut 229 Somn 1:120, 124 Somn 2:38 Ios 246 Mos 1:25, 154 Mos 2:185 Spec 4:112 QE 2:2

καρτερικός Mut 206 Ios 54 Prob 26, 84, 93

καρτερός (13) Leg 3:202, 238 Cher 103 Sacr 113 Det 168 Post 48, 72 Ebr 185 Migr 85 Mut 108 Mos 1:260 Virt 5 Prov 2:56

καρυατίζω Opif 50

κάρυον Opif 50 Mos 2:180, 180, 181, 182

καρυωτός Her 218

Καρχηδών Deus 174

Κάστος Flacc 86

κατά (2841) Opif 3, 10, 12, 14, 17, 25, 26, 27, 27, 29, 31, 31, 32, 33, 35, 40, 41, 41, 45, 46, 46, 46, 48, 49, 49, 49, 53, 54, 55, 57, 59, 61, 63, 63, 63, 64, 65, 65, 67, 69, 69, 69, 69, 70, 71, 71, 72, 72, 75, 77, 77, 81, 81, 81, 82, 83, 83, 84, 85, 86, 89, 91, 91, 91, 92, 92, 94, 98, 98, 98, 98, 101, 102, 103, 103, 103, 103, 104, 105, 106, 106, 107, 107, 107, 113, 114, 115, 116, 116, 117, 118, 120, 124, 126, 128, 130, 131, 134, 134, 135, 135, 135, 135, 136, 136, 138, 140, 140, 141, 141, 143, 144, 145, 145, 146, 146, 151, 153, 155, 156, 157, 158, 161, 163, 168, 171, 171, 172 Leg 1:3, 4, 8, 8, 8, 9, 9, 10, 10, 14, 14, 15, 16, 17, 17, 18, 19, 19, 19, 20, 20, 22, 22, 22, 22, 23, 23, 24, 26, 26, 29, 30, 30, 31, 31, 33, 34, 35, 38, 38, 42, 42, 43, 46, 53, 53, 54, 56, 56, 58, 59, 59, 61, 62, 62, 62, 63, 65, 65, 67, 73, 79, 79, 84, 86, 87, 87, 87, 87, 87, 87, 90, 91, 92, 92, 93, 94, 98, 106, 107, 108 Leg 2:1, 1, 3, 3, 4, 4, 6, 8, 9, 11, 13, 13, 18, 22, 23, 23, 24, 24, 24, 36, 36, 36, 36, 37, 37, 37, 37, 38, 40, 40, 42, 43, 44, 44, 45, 45, 45, 45, 45, 60, 63, 63, 64, 65, 68, 71, 75, 78, 78, 79, 81, 81, 89, 93, 94, 108 Leg 3:6, 6, 10, 15, 15, 15, 17, 18, 19, 20, 20, 21, 28, 29, 29, 34, 35, 36, 47, 49, 55, 56, 61, 66, 68, 80, 88, 92, 96, 96, 96, 99, 102, 103, 106, 110, 110, 112, 113, 119, 126, 126, 135, 137, 139, 140, 144, 144, 146, 170, 171, 171, 176, 178, 185, 186, 188, 192, 201, 203, 203, 203, 206, 207, 207, 207, 207, 220, 230, 231, 232, 235, 236, 237, 238, 247, 247 Cher 3, 4, 4, 5, 6, 10, 17, 21, 21, 21, 22, 22, 23, 25, 25, 27, 31, 35, 38, 38, 51, 55, 56, 58, 59, 65, 69, 70, 79, 79, 81, 89, 89, 89, 91, 96, 101, 103, 105, 106, 109, 118, 124, 124, 128 Sacr 4, 9, 10, 11, 18, 27, 31, 35, 36, 45, 46, 47, 57, 68, 73, 73, 73, 74, 74, 74, 78, 81, 84, 84, 84, 84, 87, 88, 98, 99, 100, 101, 103, 104, 106, 106, 109, 109, 120, 120, 122, 122, 124, 124, 127, 130, 131, 132, 134, 134, 136, 136, 137, 139 Det 2, 2, 2, 4, 5, 8, 8, 17, 18, 23, 41, 47, 47, 49, 70, 74, 75, 75, 76, 79, 82, 82, 82, 82, 87, 88, 89, 90, 91, 95, 97, 100, 104, 105, 106, 107, 107, 108, 110, 114, 114, 118, 119, 122, 124, 131, 131, 139, 139, 143, 143, 147, 148, 148, 151, 151, 152, 154, 154, 154, 160, 160, 172, 172, 172, 173, 173, 174, 176, 178, 178 Post 5, 12, 14, 15, 15, 16, 20, 20, 23, 36, 37, 38, 44, 44, 46, 46, 47, 48, 49, 50, 52, 56, 69, 71, 71, 71, 73, 73, 79, 81, 84, 86, 89, 89, 97, 100, 101, 103, 104, 104, 107, 108, 108, 110, 111, 115, 116, 123, 123, 125, 130, 135, 136, 142, 142, 144, 155, 156, 158, 162, 163, 164, 167, 168, 169, 173, 173, 174, 178, 184, 185 Gig 3, 3, 5, 6, 7, 11, 22, 22, 25, 25, 39, 50, 51, 51, 51, 51, 52, 52, 59, 60, 63, 64, 66, 67 Deus 6, 8, 11, 12, 14, 19, 25, 34, 39, 48, 48, 55, 56, 56, 62, 68, 70, 72, 74, 93, 109, 110, 110, 126, 128, 132, 133, 137, 147, 155, 157, 171, 172, 173, 173, 176 Agr 2, 2, 6, 9, 14, 15, 22, 27, 32, 40, 40, 43, 46, 51, 57, 58, 59, 76, 83, 85, 87, 87, 88, 89, 97, 101, 107, 108, 116, 117, 118, 124, 126, 132, 134, 136, 138, 140, 142, 143, 152, 156, 157, 157, 161, 169, 178 Plant 1, 2, 11, 12, 14, 19, 19, 20, 31, 32, 37, 44, 44, 49, 55, 56, 59, 62, 68, 74, 75, 76, 81, 83, 86, 86, 86, 86, 102, 102, 105, 108, 111, 114, 114, 115, 121, 124, 127, 127, 127, 127, 131, 136, 139, 144, 147, 150, 150, 152, 152, 154, 168, 175, 176, 177 Ebr 8, 13, 13, 22, 23, 34, 35, 36, 54, 62, 62, 64, 70, 71, 71, 71, 85, 85, 86, 87, 87, 91, 91, 91, 96, 102, 103, 105, 106, 109, 111, 111, 115, 119, 121, 121, 135, 137, 138, 144, 154, 154, 171, 171, 172, 172, 176, 178, 180, 182, 182, 184, 186, 187, 187, 189, 190, 190, 190, 190, 191, 193, 193, 193, 198, 212, 223 Sobr 8, 11, 12, 12, 14, 17, 18, 18, 20, 22, 26, 27, 30, 35, 36, 38, 38, 40, 42, 46, 46, 46, 48, 49, 49, 50, 53, 54, 63, 66 Conf 5, 9, 10, 12, 17, 21, 22, 27, 28, 31, 38, 42, 43, 46, 46, 47, 49, 50, 52, 58, 60, 61, 67, 67, 67, 67, 67, 70, 77, 89, 98, 99, 100, 103, 106, 111, 121, 124, 127, 127, 130, 131, 133, 134, 137, 137, 139, 144, 146, 146, 149, 150, 156, 161, 161, 162, 169, 169, 174, 174, 176, 180, 183, 188, 192, 194, 195 Migr 2, 7, 12, 19, 19, 30, 32, 34, 34, 37, 37, 38, 39, 42, 50, 54, 55, 60, 64, 64, 77, 80, 87, 90, 90, 92, 92, 98, 100, 102, 103, 104, 104, 105, 106, 108, 108, 115, 119, 119, 120, 122, 126, 126, 126, 128, 131, 137, 137, 137, 137, 137, 137, 138, 139, 141, 142, 149, 151, 160, 160, 160, 162, 163, 164, 173, 173, 180, 182, 182, 184, 185, 187, 190, 190, 191, 191, 194, 195, 195, 202, 216, 219 Her 4, 13, 15, 15, 15, 15, 17, 17, 17, 21, 23, 52, 56, 61, 63, 68, 69, 70, 83, 84, 84, 85, 85, 85, 87, 89, 97, 100, 100, 101, 101, 108, 109, 111, 114, 116, 122, 126, 135, 136, 136, 139, 141, 144, 144, 145, 146, 149, 150, 150, 151, 156, 156, 157, 157, 158, 160, 160, 164, 166, 166, 169, 172, 175, 176, 183, 190, 192, 193, 195, 198, 208, 212, 221, 224, 225, 226, 226, 228, 230, 231, 231, 231, 232, 238, 240, 246, 247, 248, 249, 251, 251, 264, 265, 265, 268, 269, 270, 278, 280, 282, 283, 283, 284, 284, 286, 292, 295, 296, 298, 298, 299, 299, 306, 314, 314 Congr 4, 4, 19, 21, 22, 32, 32, 32, 32, 33, 35, 35, 45, 46, 48, 64, 69, 70, 70, 86, 86, 90, 99, 99, 99, 101, 101, 106, 106, 106, 113, 120, 134, 136, 136, 137, 138, 140, 143, 143, 143, 146, 155, 163, 165, 169 Fug 3, 13, 18, 22, 25, 25, 36, 38, 39, 45, 49, 51, 54, 63, 68, 72, 76, 79, 79, 86, 92, 92, 93, 95, 95, 101, 106, 119, 128, 130, 141, 146, 147, 162, 166, 172, 173, 174, 179, 182, 186, 195, 203, 203, 204, 211 Mut 12, 13, 14, 21, 30, 31, 36, 45, 46, 50, 51, 54, 70, 70, 74, 77, 78, 80, 84, 87, 90, 95, 100, 106, 110, 112, 118, 119, 122, 141, 143, 144, 149, 152, 155, 157, 157, 157, 171, 173, 173, 173, 179, 179, 184, 187, 189, 192, 192, 194, 194, 195, 201, 205, 213, 220, 220, 222, 223, 225, 225, 256 Somn 1:1, 1, 5, 19, 19, 23, 25, 25, 30, 31, 34, 34, 35, 42, 57, 58, 62, 63, 66, 67, 68, 73, 74, 74, 77, 79, 81, 82, 83, 83, 85, 85, 87, 91, 92, 96, 103, 103, 107, 118, 121, 127, 134, 138, 145, 148, 162, 168, 173, 175, 175, 177, 179, 185, 185, 186, 186, 188, 188, 189, 190, 196, 202, 208, 214, 222, 225, 236, 248, 255 Somn 2:3, 3, 4, 4, 11, 15, 16, 28, 29, 38, 40, 46, 51, 57, 107, 112, 121, 122, 122, 131, 133, 134, 137, 139, 147, 161, 163, 166, 166, 166, 184, 185, 192, 194, 195, 198, 208, 215, 219, 220, 228, 231, 231, 237, 240, 248, 248, 263, 270, 270, 276, 280, 280, 283, 283, 288, 291, 299 Abr 1, 1, 3, 5, 7, 10, 10, 27, 31, 32, 34, 36, 36, 37, 38, 38, 42, 44, 44, 46, 47, 48, 53, 59, 64, 65, 65, 65, 67, 68, 69, 69, 69, 71, 72, 78, 79, 87, 91, 91, 93, 101, 101, 116, 122, 125, 126, 127, 132, 136, 137, 143, 143, 145, 148, 148, 148, 154, 159, 159, 160, 163, 167, 175, 175, 195, 198, 201, 201, 203, 209, 215, 217, 218, 219, 220, 230, 235, 238, 244, 245, 246, 247, 256, 260, 269, 273 Ios 1, 1, 2, 4, 5, 9, 10, 15, 15, 18, 18, 20, 28, 29, 30, 30, 31, 31, 31, 31, 34, 36, 38, 40, 43, 48, 50, 58, 63, 66, 71, 71, 76, 76, 81, 97, 98, 99, 112, 115, 116, 117, 121, 125, 126, 136, 144, 145, 149, 150, 150, 151, 151, 157, 158, 169, 170, 171, 176, 178, 179, 187, 189, 189, 202, 203, 212, 217, 221, 222, 223, 225, 225, 225, 227, 230, 230, 236, 237, 246, 246, 247, 249, 256, 258, 259, 269 Mos 1:1, 1, 2, 5, 7, 8, 9, 12, 18, 21, 22, 27, 29, 31, 47, 51, 60, 61, 63, 64, 66, 67, 69, 73, 78, 83, 83, 85, 85, 87, 96, 96, 99, 102, 105, 107, 113, 120, 120, 127, 127, 128, 128, 130, 132, 136, 136, 143, 146, 149, 156, 156, 156, 157, 157, 164, 165, 166, 167, 173,

174, 177, 191, 193, 194, 199, 201, 202, 203, 204, 204, 204, 209, 210, 213, 215, 216, 232, 245, 246, 248, 261, 262, 264, 269, 273, 278, 278, 284, 285, 287, 288, 288, 289, 290, 290, 293, 300, 302, 310, 312, 314, 331, 334 Mos 2:1, 8, 9, 15, 17, 18, 19, 19, 22, 27, 29, 29, 41, 48, 49, 51, 51, 53, 54, 56, 59, 61, 63, 63, 65, 69, 70, 71, 73, 73, 77, 78, 78, 80, 85, 85, 86, 87, 87, 89, 90, 91, 91, 91, 91, 91, 92, 93, 93, 94, 98, 99, 112, 112, 115, 117, 119, 121, 123, 123, 124, 124, 126, 126, 127, 127, 128, 129, 129, 131, 133, 133, 133, 136, 141, 148, 154, 159, 159, 162, 163, 176, 176, 177, 181, 184, 186, 191, 194, 199, 200, 202, 204, 208, 211, 212, 215, 216, 219, 222, 224, 225, 226, 229, 231, 231, 233, 236, 237, 238, 246, 246, 252, 253, 256, 258, 263, 266, 266, 267, 270, 273, 276, 279, 281, 282, 285, 288 Decal 1, 1, 4, 5, 5, 8, 10, 11, 13, 18, 21, 21, 23, 24, 24, 29, 31, 33, 33, 34, 37, 60, 60, 82, 91, 96, 97, 98, 100, 101, 104, 107, 109, 111, 111, 122, 134, 141, 147, 150, 151, 157, 159, 161, 161, 162, 162, 168, 168, 168, 168, 176, 177, 177 Spec 1:1, 3, 12, 14, 16, 19, 28, 32, 36, 36, 39, 40, 40, 41, 47, 49, 53, 63, 69, 72, 75, 79, 80, 80, 81, 89, 89, 91, 100, 103, 104, 106, 108, 112, 112, 115, 116, 131, 131, 134, 134, 137, 141, 144, 147, 151, 151, 152, 154, 156, 158, 160, 164, 168, 169, 171, 172, 172, 176, 178, 178, 178, 178, 179, 181, 183, 184, 186, 186, 189, 190, 190, 193, 196, 196, 201, 208, 208, 209, 209, 210, 211, 222, 223, 224, 224, 224, 231, 232, 237, 245, 248, 254, 256, 259, 264, 269, 276, 279, 286, 292, 296, 299, 299, 300, 307, 307, 315, 316, 316, 317, 327, 335, 338, 341, 342, 342, 344 Spec 2:1, 1, 3, 19, 19, 21, 23, 23, 27, 30, 31, 31, 31, 31, 34, 39, 41, 43, 43, 46, 47, 47, 51, 51, 53, 55, 58, 59, 61, 61, 62, 63, 64, 65, 65, 67, 71, 81, 86, 86, 95, 95, 114, 115, 116, 119, 119, 119, 123, 126, 128, 130, 140, 140, 141, 142, 143, 145, 146, 146, 146, 148, 150, 150, 151, 152, 153, 153, 154, 155, 155, 158, 160, 163, 163, 164, 164, 168, 176, 179, 181, 181, 181, 183, 184, 187, 187, 188, 188, 190, 191, 191, 193, 195, 197, 200, 201, 203, 207, 208, 210, 212, 218, 220, 223, 225, 228, 229, 231, 233, 239, 240, 242, 242, 243, 244, 250, 250, 257 Spec 3:1, 7, 7, 7, 8, 8, 9, 10, 15, 16, 27, 28, 30, 38, 42, 44, 51, 51, 52, 55, 55, 55, 58, 58, 62, 62, 63, 64, 70, 74, 74, 75, 77, 78, 82, 83, 85, 91, 95, 96, 96, 101, 102, 104, 107, 108, 113, 117, 117, 118, 122, 123, 125, 128, 131, 131, 131, 134, 135, 135, 137, 137, 142, 147, 148, 151, 160, 160, 162, 169, 169, 171, 171, 172, 172, 174, 181, 182, 188, 188, 188, 190, 191, 195, 199, 199, 202, 205, 209 Spec 4:10, 14, 14, 19, 19, 19, 34, 45, 47, 49, 54, 54, 54, 54, 55, 56, 57, 57, 63, 66, 68, 69, 69, 71, 81, 82, 105, 106, 107, 116, 116, 123, 123, 124, 126, 126, 132, 132, 140, 147, 154, 154, 158, 160, 161, 170, 175, 176, 197, 203, 204, 209, 209, 213, 214, 215, 215, 215, 215, 225, 226, 228, 232, 233, 234, 234, 234, 234 Virt 1, 2, 5, 8, 10, 12, 13, 15, 21, 22, 22, 26, 27, 29, 29, 33, 37, 38, 61, 61, 67, 74, 75, 76, 76, 85, 87, 95, 95, 97, 98, 103, 103, 103, 103, 105, 106, 112, 115, 118, 126, 127, 137, 138, 139, 144, 145, 153, 153, 156, 158, 161, 168, 172, 173, 175, 176, 176, 183, 183, 190, 192, 202, 205, 205, 208, 209, 217, 222, 225 Praem 2, 2, 3, 4, 7, 7, 7, 7, 7, 15, 19, 23, 27, 29, 29, 31, 32, 34, 36, 36, 39, 44, 44, 50, 53, 57, 63, 65, 67, 68, 70, 70, 74, 78, 79, 80, 85, 88, 92, 93, 94, 98, 100, 105, 107, 107, 107, 107, 118, 118, 119, 121, 121, 122, 123, 126, 143, 155, 161, 163, 165, 165, 165, 169 Prob 1, 5, 13, 17, 20, 34, 34, 36, 37, 37, 44, 44, 50, 51, 51, 51, 62, 62, 63, 63, 67, 74, 74, 75, 78, 78, 80, 81, 81, 85, 89, 89, 90, 92, 93, 104, 104, 105, 118, 128, 130, 138, 138, 139, 148, 152, 156 Contempl 2, 9, 16, 17, 17, 21, 27, 30, 31, 48, 49, 51, 60, 60, 63, 64, 66, 66, 68, 69, 79, 80, 80, 83, 83, 85, 85 Aet 3, 4, 4, 4, 4, 4, 9, 9, 9, 14, 23, 24, 28, 28, 29, 30, 30, 31, 33, 34, 37, 42, 44, 45, 46, 53, 54, 58, 60, 60, 68, 69, 69, 73, 75, 79, 79, 79, 79, 79, 80, 81, 81, 82, 82, 83, 83, 84, 87, 88, 88, 90, 92, 95, 96, 98, 99, 99, 100, 101, 103, 103, 103, 110, 110, 113, 116, 117, 118, 120, 120, 123, 125, 127, 128, 139, 140, 141, 143, 144, 146, 147, 149, 149, 150 Flacc 1, 3, 5, 9, 10, 11, 16, 19, 21, 28, 37, 41, 43, 46, 46, 51, 53, 68, 70, 78, 80, 89, 90, 92, 93, 94, 101, 101, 104, 110, 111, 114, 115, 116, 120, 120, 131, 136, 138, 140, 145, 149, 149, 152, 154, 157, 163, 164, 171, 175, 177, 177, 178, 179, 181, 186, 187, 190 Legat 1, 3, 8, 12, 28, 33, 35, 39, 43, 45, 47, 49, 51, 51, 54, 55, 56, 57, 57, 62, 63, 71, 71, 76, 77, 78, 89, 102, 113, 123, 124, 125, 129, 131, 132, 134, 136, 136, 139, 141, 141, 142, 142, 150, 152, 157, 158, 161, 166, 170, 171, 173, 175, 177, 178, 179, 190, 190, 197, 203, 209, 209, 212, 216, 219, 220, 222, 225, 231, 233, 237, 238, 243, 245, 246, 249, 251, 254, 259, 261, 268, 268, 276, 278, 280, 280, 283, 295, 296, 298, 299, 306, 306, 307, 310, 310, 311, 313, 317, 335, 337, 338, 346, 351, 356, 368, 371, 371 Hypoth 0:1, 6:1, 6:5, 6:5, 6:6, 7:9, 7:13, 7:14, 7:18, 11:5, 11:9, 11:11, 11:16 Prov 1, 1, 2:1, 10, 12, 13, 15, 20, 26, 26, 28, 34, 41, 45, 48, 51, 54, 59, 59, 59, 61, 64, 64, 68, 70, 70, 71 QG 1:21, 21, 24, 24, 24, 32, 55a, 64a, 64a, 64b, 77, 100:1b, 2:11, 12a, 12d, 13a, 15a, 17a, 17c, 26a, 41, 54a, 54a, 54c, 59, 59, 59, 64c, 64c, 64c, 3:11a, 22, 38a, 38a, 49a, 49a, 49b, 49b, 52, 4:8a, 8a, 8b, 8b, 8b, 33b, 40, 47b, 51b, 64, 69, 86a, 144, 161, 163:2, 173, 180, 189, 200b, 200c, 204, 206a, 206b QG isf 3, 15 QG (Par) 2:1, 2:2, 2:2, 2:2, 2:5, 2:5, 2:5, 2:6, 2:7 QE 1:19, 2:3b, 10a, 18, 18, 24b, 25c, 25c, 26, 26, 45a, 55a, 55b QE isf 3, 4, 5, 8, 8, 9, 14, 16, 21, 23, 33

καταβαθμός Flacc 43

καταβαίνω (50) Opif 117 Leg 2:59 Leg 3:179 Sacr 37, 48, 92 Det 46 Post 29, 30, 30, 132, 136, 136 Gig 12, 13 Ebr 51 Conf 1, 1, 81, 134, 142, 155, 168, 182 Migr 29, 185, 185, 201 Her 45, 84, 237, 237, 238, 251, 255, 274 Fug 195 Somn 1:3, 115, 133 Abr 205 Mos 2:70, 165 Prob 66 Flacc 27, 155 Legat 145 Prov 2:27, 33 QE 2:45a

καταβάλλω (49) Opif 67, 158 Leg 1:49 Cher 49 Det 99 Post 72, 116, 149, 163, 171 Agr 7, 97, 120 Ebr 211, 211 Sobr 36 Conf 17 Her 29, 116, 242, 245 Congr 131 Fug 24 Mut 85, 150, 176 Somn 1:124, 147, 222 Somn 2:79, 140, 160, 278, 285 Ios 239 Mos 1:270 Spec 2:29 Spec 3:3, 32, 33 Virt 2, 42 Praem 141 Contempl 62 Aet 63, 98 Flacc 10, 162 Hypoth 6:10

κατάβασις Leg 2:89 QG 4:100

καταβιάζω Somn 2:198

καταβιβάζω Sacr 138 Deus 120 Plant 145 Her 316

καταβιβρώσκω Ios 101

καταβιόω Somn 1:46

καταβοάω (6) Her 19 Somn 1:92 Mos 1:138, 173 Mos 2:278 Spec 4:127

καταβόησις Flacc 138

καταβολή (8) Opif 132 Sobr 45 Her 115 Mos 1:279 Spec 3:36 Legat 54, 125 QG 3:12

καταβρέχω Prov 2:23

κατάβρωσις Fug 15

κατάγαιος (κατάγειος) QG (Par) 2:7, 2:7

καταγγέλλω (7) Opif 106 Migr 189 Abr 261 Ios 92 Prob 64, 71 Aet 68

κατάγειος κατάγαιος

καταγέλαστος (12) Det 158 Post 142 Ebr 130 Her 81 Fug 149 Mut 199 Somn 2:43, 70, 291 Mos 1:302 Decal 79 Spec 1:223

καταγελάω Fug 149 Prob 156

καταγηράσκω Congr 77 Somn 1:45 Decal 71 Spec 1:11

καταγίγνομαι (καταγίνομαι) Post 7 Congr 11 Somn 1:117

καταγιγνώσκω (καταγινώσκω) (28) Ebr 192 Conf 178 Her 71, 71, 71 Somn 1:139 Somn 2:301 Abr 133 Ios 52, 88, 118 Mos 1:58 Spec 1:3, 53 Spec 2:164 Spec 3:136 Spec 4:4 Prob 7, 79, 127 Contempl 56 Aet 10 Flacc 126, 151, 181 Legat 241, 341 Prov 2:61

κάταγμα Aet 6

κατάγνυμι (9) Gig 4 Deus 3 Agr 76 Plant 159 Her 201 Somn 2:202, 236 Legat 111, 127

κατάγνωσις Ebr 205 Mut 155

καταγοητεύω (8) Post 156 Congr 29 Mos 1:311 Spec 1:9, 26, 28, 174 Aet 56

κατάγω (11) Cher 3 Ebr 210 Somn 1:57 Abr 115, 115 Spec 4:112 Praem 133 Flacc 27, 112 Legat 49, 129

καταγωγή Cher 99, 106 Spec 1:69

καταγωνίζομαι Ebr 113 Abr 105 Prob 159

καταδαρθάνω (6) Ios 147 Mos 1:38 Spec 1:99 Spec 2:102 Flacc 167 Legat 42

καταδεής (7) Sacr 92 Abr 211 Decal 166 Spec 1:228 Legat 95, 108, 338

καταδείδω (7) Conf 116 Abr 206 Mos 1:15, 138 Mos 2:172 Virt 70 Legat 302

καταδείκνυμι Post 103 Hypoth 7:7

καταδέχομαι Praem 79

καταδέω (11) Det 103, 103 Conf 167 Somn 2:21, 30, 41 Ios 86, 270 Spec 2:232 Spec 3:78, 145

καταδικάζω (9) Leg 3:67, 199 Deus 75, 112, 112 Plant 175 Migr 115 Mut 228 Flacc 54

καταδίκη Spec 3:116 Flacc 105

καταδουλόω Mos 1:95, 141, 142 Prob 160

καταδυναστεύω Conf 108 Spec 2:42

καταδύνω καταδύω

κατάδυσις (8) Agr 97 Conf 66 Her 238 Somn 1:119 Spec 1:321 Prob 64 Flacc 110 Prov 2:58

καταδύω (καταδύνω) (14) Opif 34, 57 Leg 2:30 Leg 3:1, 37 Agr 89 Somn 1:112, 116 Somn 2:133 Ios 222 Mos 1:176 Spec 3:54 Prob 124 Prov 2:33

καταζεύγνυμι (13) Opif 85 Leg 2:16 Deus 47 Decal 4 Spec 1:69 Spec 2:70, 83 Spec 4:205 Virt 146 Prob 18, 117 Contempl 70 Legat 146

καταθαρσέω Spec 1:56

καταθαρσύνω καταθρασύνομαι

καταθεάομαι (21) Cher 96 Det 12 Deus 34 Agr 98 Plant 17 Ebr 99, 158 Her 36 Congr 124 Fug 165 Abr 159, 166 Mos 1:15, 91, 228, 229 Mos 2:87 Spec 1:219 Spec 3:2 Virt 12 QG 2:72

κατάθεος Spec 2:256

κατάθεσις Spec 1:77 Spec 4:11

καταθρασύνομαι (καταθαρσύνω) Opif 170 Spec 3:175

καταθύω (17) Agr 130 Abr 109, 184 Mos 1:282 Spec 1:167, 167, 189, 190, 199, 212, 213, 228, 277, 290 Spec 2:35 Prob 75, 102

καταιγίζω Somn 2:85

καταιγίς Deus 60

καταιδέομαι Abr 112 Mos 1:268 Spec 4:18 Praem 163

καταίθω Leg 3:202 Ios 78 Prob 25, 99

καταικίζω Ios 22 Flacc 85

καταιονέω καταιονάω

καταιονάω (καταιονέω) Prov 2:46

καταίρω Cher 38 Abr 47 Decal 67 Spec 1:69

καταισχύνω Spec 3:14

καταιτιάομαι Conf 154

κατακαίω (12) Post 158 Fug 161 Abr 181 Mos 1:65, 67 Decal 49 Spec 1:232, 244, 268, 312 Legat 130 QE 2:28

κατακαλέω Plant 86

κατάκειμαι (6) Cher 48 Somn 2:265 Abr 258 Ios 217 Spec 3:109 Praem 104

κατακεντέω Post 182 Deus 101, 183 Mut 108, 203

κατακερματίζω (9) Det 106 Gig 26 Ebr 200 Sobr 60 Fug 148 Somn 2:90 Ios 243 Spec 4:211 Virt 156

κατακερτομέω (13) Det 78 Mut 61 Somn 1:126 Spec 4:81 Virt 202 Praem 169 Prob 54 Aet 11 Flacc 40, 119 Legat 122, 359, 363

κατακλαίω Conf 106, 106 Flacc 168

κατακλάω Opif 80 Ebr 22 Somn 2:236 Spec 2:90 Legat 221

κατάκλειστος Somn 1:164 Flacc 89

κατακλείω (6) Mos 2:180 Spec 1:160 Spec 3:132, 145 Spec 4:220 Aet 135

κατάκλησις Migr 56 Mos 2:132 Spec 4:40 Virt 77 Praem 84

κατακλίνω (11) Opif 85 Somn 1:123 Mos 1:291 Mos 2:42 Decal 31 Prob 102 Contempl 67, 75, 77 Legat 42 Prov 2:29

κατάκλισις Ios 203 Contempl 66, 69

κατακλύζω (22) Det 15 Post 176 Ebr 70 Fug 192 Mut 107, 186 Somn 2:109 Abr 43 Mos 2:255 Spec 1:148 Spec 2:202 Spec 3:6 Spec 4:201 Virt 14, 41 Prob 15 Contempl 86 Aet 138, 147 Hypoth 11:3 QG 2:64b, 66

κατακλυσμός (31) Det 170 Plant 43 Conf 23, 25, 105 Migr 125 Her 204 Fug 192 Somn 2:125, 129, 237 Abr 41, 46, 46, 56 Mos 2:53, 59, 63 Virt 201 Praem 23 Aet 141, 147 QG 2:13a, 13a, 17a, 17c, 31, 54a, 64a, 64c, 66

κατακοιμιστής Legat 175

κατακοινωνέω Spec 3:165

κατακολουθέω Virt 116

κατακονδυλίζω Ebr 198

κατακόπτω Post 159 Flacc 66 QG 3:3

κατακορής Leg 2:67 Somn 2:4

κατάκορος Decal 92 Spec 3:137 Virt 67, 148 Legat 164

κατακοσμέω Legat 319

κατακούω Her 203 Ios 94, 116 Virt 74 Legat 43

κατακρατέω (12) Leg 3:220 Abr 30 Mos 1:225 Virt 192 Prob 105 Aet 74, 80, 106, 106, 114 Legat 121 Prov 2:68

κατακρημνίζω Agr 68 Spec 3:149 Prov 2:33, 33

κατακρίνω Prov 2:61 QG 2:11

κατάκριτος (6) Mos 1:303 Virt 139 Praem 23 Flacc 81, 150 QE 2:49a

κατακρύπτω Leg 3:23

κατακτείνω Fug 90 Spec 1:79

καταλαζονεύομαι (7) Plant 65 Somn 1:57 Somn 2:292 Ios 144 Mos 1:30, 328 Praem 94

καταλαλέω Leg 2:66, 67, 78, 78, 78

καταλαμβάνω (164) Opif 69, 131, 139, 166 Leg 1:91, 91, 92 Leg 2:7, 70, 71, 86 Leg 3:57, 99, 100, 108, 183, 224 Cher 2, 59, 74, 75, 75, 77 Sacr 25, 66, 69 Det 30, 31, 87, 89, 91, 98, 129, 129, 130 Post 15, 57, 66, 148 Gig 9 Deus 45, 55, 62, 78, 126 Agr 162, 162 Plant 14, 20, 83 Ebr 204 Sobr 30 Conf 100, 138, 140, 183 Migr 5, 39, 78, 220 Her 15, 18, 74, 74, 85, 98, 101, 107, 109, 111, 142, 224, 250 Congr 21, 70, 84, 101, 130, 137, 140 Fug 97, 135 Mut 4, 6, 7, 9, 157, 257 Somn 1:4, 10, 15, 17, 24, 25, 45, 56, 60, 119, 184, 186, 188, 212, 231 Abr 19, 57, 58, 60, 71, 76, 77, 80, 119, 119, 122, 182, 189 Ios 126, 145, 147, 179, 211 Mos 1:59, 102, 212, 273, 278 Mos 2:6, 187, 248 Decal 93, 114, 139, 149, 150 Spec 1:46, 46, 46, 49, 49, 65, 184, 263 Spec 2:128 Spec 3:189 Spec 4:60, 109 Virt 12 Praem 28, 40, 40, 43, 101, 101 Prob 16, 55 Contempl 77 Aet 133, 147 Flacc 188 Legat 2, 319, 320 Prov 2:38 QE isf 3

καταλάμπω Mut 92 Somn 1:218 Spec 1:296 Prov 2:49

καταλεαίνω Aet 20, 79, 129

καταλέγω (9) Sacr 122 Post 110 Abr 232 Mos 1:216 Decal 29 Virt 42 Aet 114 Legat 323 Prov 2:33

καταλείπω (101) Opif 63 Leg 2:49, 49, 51, 56, 57, 58, 85 Leg 3:20, 41, 194, 239, 240, 252 Cher 115 Sacr 67, 120, 129 Det 27, 142, 159 Post 2, 5, 6, 8, 21, 68 Deus 137 Agr 33 Plant 6 Ebr 177, 195 Conf 25, 166 Migr 18, 187, 209 Her 68, 69, 186, 304, 306 Fug 122, 190, 191 Mut 114, 119 Somn 1:52, 52, 59, 107 Somn 2:253 Abr 62, 65 Ios 49, 51, 73, 195 Mos 1:149, 308 Mos 2:44, 48, 171, 242, 264 Decal 129 Spec 1:129, 309 Spec 3:149, 149 Spec 4:146, 238 Virt 53, 56, 59, 209, 214, 219, 222 Praem 15, 62, 65, 75, 103, 110 Prob 43 Contempl 18, 80 Aet 24, 76, 88, 102 Flacc 13, 73 Legat 230, 347, 371 QG 1:20, 29, 73, 3:20b

κατάλευσις Spec 2:253

καταλεύω (14) Ebr 95 Mos 1:119, 235 Mos 2:202, 218 Spec 2:243, 251 Spec 3:73, 144 Flacc 66, 174 Legat 127 Hypoth 7:2 Prov 2:33

καταλέω Leg 1:98 Post 158, 162, 163, 164

καταληπτικός Her 132

καταληπτός (15) Post 169, 169 Deus 62 Ebr 108 Conf 138 Her 132, 209 Somn 1:30, 40, 43, 135 Spec 1:20 Spec 3:111 Spec 4:192 Praem 40

κατάληψις (61) Opif 56 Leg 2:65, 72 Leg 3:50, 91 Cher 60, 97 Sacr 65 Det 58, 131 Post 19, 36, 79 Deus 29, 58, 93, 134 Agr 161 Plant 31, 36, 42 Ebr 199 Conf 85, 98, 102, 123, 141 Migr 39, 42 Her 98, 119, 261, 263, 314 Congr 82, 98, 141, 141 Mut 9, 56, 111 Somn 1:11, 66, 116, 184 Somn 2:162 Ios 141, 142, 165 Mos 1:223, 230 Decal 147 Spec 1:44, 45, 288 Spec 4:108, 132, 192 Praem 45 Contempl 76 QG 2:34a

καταλλαγή (13) Det 149 Ios 99, 156, 237, 262, 265 Mos 2:60 Spec 3:31 Virt 118, 124, 154 Praem 166 Flacc 76

καταλλακτήριος Somn 2:108

καταλλάσσω (6) Leg 3:134 Ebr 208 Abr 214 Ios 99 Decal 87 Flacc 19

κατάλληλος Ios 175, 175

καταλοάω Flacc 70 Prov 2:58

καταλογάδην Mut 220 Somn 2:268 Abr 23 Mos 1:3

κατάλογος (8) Leg 3:41 Deus 116, 126 Agr 147 Plant 117 Abr 31 Virt 23, 31

κατάλυσις (11) Leg 3:189 Post 181 Mut 72 Praem 119 Flacc 30, 45 Legat 194, 201, 322, 335 QG 1:20

καταλύω (38) Sacr 116, 116, 130 Post 185 Gig 35 Plant 88 Ebr 75 Conf 72 Migr 27, 68 Her 36, 244 Congr 92 Fug 145 Mut 34, 250 Somn 1:88, 89 Somn 2:92, 95, 123, 148, 287 Spec 1:51, 282 Spec 3:17, 51, 112, 182 Virt 49 Praem 91, 170 Flacc 52 Legat 301, 301 Hypoth 11:13 QG 3:52, 4:8c

καταμαίνομαι Flacc 170

καταμανθάνω (11) Leg 1:62 Leg 2:17 Leg 3:180, 183 Post 168 Deus 131 Migr 162, 189 Fug 46 Somn 1:59 Mos 1:24

καταμαξεύω καθαμαξεύω

καταμαραίνω Gig 29

καταμαρτυρέω Leg 3:199 Decal 140 Spec 4:48

καταμεθύω Ebr 29, 95

καταμέμφομαι Abr 84 Mos 1:58 Spec 2:95 QG isf 12

κατάμεμψις Ebr 32 Mos 1:275

καταμένω (43) Leg 2:33 Leg 3:152 Det 45 Gig 19, 19, 20, 29, 47, 53, 54 Deus 2, 31 Agr 147, 162 Ebr 164 Conf 75, 76, 76 Migr 28, 171 Her 82, 304 Congr 78 Fug 62 Abr 23, 171, 197, 232 Ios 167, 169, 184, 185, 190, 247 Mos 1:14, 313, 313, 315, 316 Mos 2:36 Decal 116 Praem 18 Legat 330

καταμήνιος Opif 124, 132 Leg 1:13

καταμηνύω Spec 2:26

καταμύω (9) Leg 2:25 Deus 38 Sobr 3 Migr 191 Her 79 Congr 81 Somn 2:160 Praem 37 Contempl 89

καταμωκάομαι Legat 368

καταναγκάζω Conf 91 Somn 1:22 QE isf 9

καταναλίσκω Somn 2:212 Abr 140

κατανείφω (κατανίφω) Her 204

κατανέμω Spec 4:22, 26

κατανεύω Post 169

κατανίζω (κατανίπτω) Ios 23

κατανίπτω κατανίζω

κατανίφω κατανείφω

κατανοέω (51) Leg 2:81, 85, 94 Leg 3:38, 69, 99, 102 Cher 11, 41, 84 Sacr 10, 45 Det 11 Post 16, 18, 162, 167, 168 Plant 2, 81, 145 Ebr 65, 137, 173, 192 Migr 195 Her 224 Fug 35, 208 Mut 152 Somn 1:46, 54, 101, 165, 172, 224, 239 Abr 73 Ios 182 Mos 1:158 Mos 2:210, 216 Spec 4:105 Aet 26, 108 Flacc 162 Legat 358 Prov 2:27, 30 QG 4:52d QG (Par) 2:5

κατανόησις Mut 82

κατάντης Spec 4:109, 112 Aet 110

κατανύω Congr 150

καταξαίνω Praem 143 Hypoth 7:15

κατάξηρος Her 80

καταπαγκρατιάζω Somn 2:168 Spec 4:74

καταπαλαίω (6) Agr 113 Virt 6 Prob 21 Contempl 43 Flacc 166 Legat 29

κατάπαυσις QG 1:76a

καταπαύω (9) Leg 1:5, 6, 6, 16, 18 Leg 3:169 Post 64, 64, 183

καταπειθής (14) Ebr 35, 94 Abr 60 Mos 1:57, 236 Decal 37, 49 Spec 2:236 Spec 4:152 Virt 208 Praem 79, 97 Prob 3 QE 2:16

καταπέμπω Her 112 Somn 2:142

καταπεπαίνω Praem 131

καταπέτασμα (12) Gig 53 Mut 192 Mos 2:80, 86, 87, 87, 95, 101 Spec 1:171, 231, 274, 296

καταπέτομαι Ios 93, 96 Spec 3:115 Praem 128

καταπήγνυμι Legat 223

καταπίμπλημι (12) Ebr 109 Conf 42 Migr 179 Ios 268 Decal 66 Spec 3:125 Spec 4:85, 85 Praem 32 Legat 88, 335, 346

καταπίμπρημι Her 296 Ios 133 Mos 2:56 Prov 2:33

καταπίνω (15) Leg 3:225, 230 Gig 13 Deus 181 Migr 85 Her 41 Somn 2:218 Ios 102 Mos 1:93 Mos 2:281, 286, 287 Virt 201 Aet 138, 140

καταπίπτω Agr 83 Her 241 Ios 144 Virt 6 Legat 267

καταπλάσσω Migr 124

καταπλάστης Contempl 44

κατάπλαστος Somn 2:65

κατάπλεος (κατάπλεως) Opif 153, 154 Mos 1:228 Spec 3:173 Legat 151

καταπλέω Flacc 92 Legat 151

κατάπλεως κατάπλεος

καταπληκτικός (8) Opif 78, 78 Ios 8 Mos 1:78 Decal 46 Spec 1:95, 321 Legat 74

κατάπληξις (11) Opif 83, 85 Migr 58 Her 249, 251 Mos 1:176 Praem 164 Legat 98, 226 QE 2:21, 47

καταπλήσσω (65) Opif 7 Cher 116 Sacr 48 Post 23, 147 Gig 50 Ebr 56, 119, 132, 137 Conf 173 Migr 21, 34 Her 3, 28, 179 Congr 13 Fug 161, 198 Mut 22, 139, 233 Somn 1:204, 222 Somn 2:117, 266 Abr 199, 227, 235 Ios 80, 107, 164, 180, 239, 257 Mos 1:27, 59, 92, 170, 180, 200, 213, 231, 251, 288 Mos 2:70, 166, 264 Decal 80 Spec 2:218 Spec 4:129 Virt 48, 59, 217 Praem 42, 89, 146 Prob 54, 100, 130 Flacc 139 Legat 8, 276 Prov 2:10 QG 3:29

καταπλουτίζω Legat 287

καταπνέω (23) Cher 20, 37 Agr 62, 89 Plant 23 Ebr 58 Conf 44 Migr 123 Her 56, 64, 184, 184 Somn 2:74 Mos 1:175, 201 Mos 2:67, 69, 291 Spec 3:5 Virt 217 Legat 126 Prov 2:23, 48

καταποικίλλω Somn 1:226 Spec 1:88 Praem 24

καταποντιστής Spec 1:323

καταποντόω (12) Leg 2:103, 103, 104 Gig 15 Agr 89, 89 Sobr 13 Conf 66 Somn 2:279 Mos 1:179 Legat 372 Prov 2:33

καταπορνεύω Hypoth 7:1

κατάποσις (8) Leg 2:96, 96 Leg 3:146 Congr 30, 30, 33 Spec 1:217, 292

καταπτήσσω (9) Opif 85, 142 Det 29 Agr 146 Somn 1:227 Somn 2:141 Spec 1:301 Virt 23 Legat 369

κατάρα (18) Leg 3:107 Det 71 Conf 44 Migr 115, 117, 118 Her 260 Fug 73 Mos 1:280, 283, 291 Mos 2:198 Decal 75 QG 4:202a, 202a, 202a, 202b QE 2:19

καταράομαι (30) Leg 2:62 Leg 3:36, 65, 66, 68, 75, 111, 111 Det 103 Post 26, 84 Sobr 31, 47 Migr 1, 1, 109, 109, 111, 113, 115 Her 177 Fug 73 Mos 1:285, 286, 291 Mos 2:196, 199, 203, 204 QG 4:202a

καταράσσω (11) Det 121, 122 Conf 18, 64, 159 Somn 2:134 Abr 43 Mos 1:115, 120 Aet 119 Legat 145

κατάρατος (7) Leg 3:104, 246, 247, 247 Det 98, 100 Mos 1:278

κατάρδω Spec 2:172

καταριθμέω (24) Opif 105 Leg 2:35 Post 96 Deus 90 Migr 202 Mut 200 Abr 10, 12 Mos 1:279 Mos 2:227 Decal 160 Spec 1:172 Spec 2:118, 144, 176, 181, 211 Spec 3:185 Spec 4:117 Aet 3 Legat 29, 328 QE 2:20 QE isf 22

καταρράκτης Conf 23 Fug 192 QG 2:29

καταρρέω (7) Somn 1:248 Mos 1:188 Praem 93 Flacc 190 Legat 117, 189, 267

καταρρήγνυμι (12) Deus 26 Agr 126, 174 Congr 60 Fug 192 Somn 2:13, 81 Abr 43 Aet 36 Flacc 155 Legat 361 QG 4:51b

κατάρριπτω Plant 144

καταρρυπαίνω (6) Cher 95 Deus 7 Her 113 Fug 41 Mut 49, 124

καταρτύω Opif 104

κατάρχω (13) Sacr 43 Plant 161 Sobr 66 Conf 181 Abr 198 Mos 2:257 Spec 2:149, 259 Spec 3:40 Flacc 136 Legat 234, 296 QG 1:96:1

κατασβέννυμι Congr 66 Aet 91

κατασείω (6) Somn 2:81 Ios 211 Mos 1:91 Aet 128 Flacc 176 Legat 181

κατασκάπτω Conf 130 Mos 1:311 Legat 132

κατασκαφή Congr 92 Somn 2:124 Legat 134

κατασκεδάννυμι Ebr 161 Her 183

κατασκελετεύω (6) Det 34 Mut 33 Ios 101 Virt 3, 193 Prob 121

κατασκεπάζω Spec 4:32

κατασκέπτομαι (κατασκοπέω) (6) Opif 70 Ios 168 Mos 1:220, 325 Flacc 112 QG 2:54d

κατασκευάζω (156) Opif 11, 18, 72, 126, 149 Leg 2:13, 19, 37, 79, 79, 79, 80, 93 Leg 3:76, 102, 107, 128, 130, 225, 228 Cher 99, 99, 100, 106, 126, 127 Sacr 15, 121 Det 6, 44, 110 Post 50, 51, 65, 166 Deus 144 Agr 71, 97, 99 Plant 43, 149, 157, 175 Ebr 110, 169, 219 Conf 5, 83, 88, 89, 113, 115, 129, 129, 179 Migr 136, 202 Her 112, 199, 219, 289 Congr 114 Fug 189 Mut 32, 56, 74, 190 Somn 1:77, 207, 237 Somn 2:52, 55, 57, 61 Abr 48, 136, 193 Ios 39, 77, 110, 262 Mos 1:84, 185, 256, 287, 330 Mos 2:60, 87, 88, 89, 93, 109, 111, 113, 116, 138, 141, 152, 162, 165, 270 Decal 7, 14, 156 Spec 1:21, 67, 71, 174, 215, 273, 274, 335 Spec 2:45, 159, 255 Spec 3:25, 44, 98, 125, 149, 203 Spec 4:16, 68, 93, 139, 225 Virt 29, 86, 90, 119, 166, 167, 214 Praem 97 Prob 33, 38, 75 Contempl 15, 49, 60 Aet 12, 20, 39, 41, 42, 43, 56, 94, 118 Flacc 57, 58, 93, 135 Prov 2:1, 48 QG isf 10 κατασκεύασμα Leg 3:98 Mos 2:64, 180

κατασκευαστικός Post 53 Plant 77

κατασκευαστός Conf 151

κατασκευή (74) Opif 17, 64, 66, 68, 135, 137, 139, 142, 146 Cher 9, 126, 127, 127 Sacr 82, 82 Post 104 Plant 14, 17, 26, 126 Ebr 3, 95, 134, 171, 178, 217 Conf 108, 122, 156, 168, 179, 179 Migr 97, 98, 188 Her 113 Congr 89 Abr 139 Mos 1:38, 256 Mos 2:29, 42, 71, 74, 75, 77, 136 Spec 1:71, 73, 84, 84, 95, 276 Spec 3:117 Spec 4:229 Praem 1 Aet 113, 124 Legat 76, 220, 221, 248, 280, 296, 358 Prov 1, 1, 1 QG 4:200a QG (Par) 2:1, 2:1, 2:2, 2:3, 2:6

κατασκηνόω Leg 3:46

κατασκήπτω (32) Leg 1:17 Cher 38 Deus 89 Agr 39, 176 Sobr 42 Conf 119, 151 Fug 115 Somn 1:102, 110 Somn 2:86, 131, 145, 214 Ios 160 Mos 1:118, 176, 236 Mos 2:13, 283 Spec 3:99 Spec 4:179 Aet 36, 146 Legat 14, 127, 184, 267 Prov 2:14 QG 2:17a, 41

κατάσκιος Mos 1:228 Aet 63

κατασκοπέω κατασκέπτομαι

κατασκοπή Somn 1:47 Ios 193, 213 Mos 1:227

κατάσκοπος (15) Post 60 Mut 224 Somn 1:48, 53, 57, 59 Somn 2:101 Ios 166, 184, 188, 210, 233 Mos 1:236 QG 4:7*, 206a

κατασοφίζομαι Leg 3:232 Spec 3:186 Flacc 42

κατασπαργανόω Aet 67

κατασπείρω (13) Sobr 65 Spec 1:335 Spec 3:33 Spec 4:203, 208, 213, 215 Virt 145 Praem 8, 10, 72, 128 Legat 145

κατασπιλάζω QG 2:72

καταστασιάζω Ios 236

κατάστασις (12) Leg 1:66 Deus 12 Sobr 6 Conf 109 Somn 2:166 Abr 26 Spec 1:323 Contempl 23 Flacc 143 Legat 19, 270 Prov 2:23

καταστείχω Prob 7

καταστενάζω Leg 3:212 Det 94 Conf 93

καταστερίζω Fug 184 Somn 2:112

καταστέφω Post 183

καταστηλιτεύω QE 2:17

καταστηματικός Leg 3:160

καταστίζω Spec 1:58

καταστορέννυμι Abr 234 Mos 2:255 Spec 4:222 Virt 43 Legat 222

καταστρατηγέω Decal 91, 141 Flacc 102 Legat 25

καταστρέφω Leg 3:213 Somn 1:122

κατάστρωμα Legat 129

κατασύρω (19) Opif 80 Leg 1:73 Leg 3:223 Agr 75 Plant 145 Migr 26 Mut 214 Somn 1:44 Somn 2:237 Mos 2:54 Spec 3:33 Spec 4:111 Praem 73 Prob 63 Aet 147 Flacc 71, 155, 174 Legat 131

κατάσχεσις Her 194

κατάσχετος Leg 3:82 Plant 148

κατασχίζω Ios 22 Flacc 190

κατάτασις Legat 368

κατατάσσω (8) Cher 53 Deus 116, 150 Agr 11, 149 Fug 169 Somn 2:163 Virt 95

κατατείνω (10) Cher 80 Deus 102 Mos 1:165, 287 Decal 146 Spec 3:159 Spec 4:82 Virt 128 Praem 139 Prob 108

κατατέμνω Sacr 83 Mos 2:111

κατατετραίνω Leg 1:12 QG (Par) 2:3

κατατήκω Leg 3:63

κατατίθημι (27) Plant 57 Conf 93 Her 186 Ios 178, 193, 207, 231, 260 Mos 2:97 Spec 1:135, 143 Spec 2:37, 37, 95, 114, 122, 233 Spec 3:107, 145, 159 Spec 4:2, 65 Prob 37 Flacc 60, 92 Hypoth 7:6, 11:4

κατατιτρώσκω Cher 96 Deus 183 Mos 1:69 Flacc 188

κατατρέχω (8) Plant 41 Conf 29, 111 Fug 158, 191 Somn 2:96 Spec 3:17 Flacc 56

κατατρίβω Leg 2:98 Ebr 195

κατατρυφάω Plant 39 Somn 2:242

καταυγάζω Cher 62

καταφαγεῖν (κατεσθίω) (9) Leg 3:225, 230, 230 Her 44, 44, 251 Fug 15 Somn 2:65, 217

καταφαίνω (7) Cher 55 Mos 1:169, 301 Spec 1:278 Spec 3:195 Legat 34, 228

καταφανής Ios 175, 200 Mos 2:213

κατάφασις QG 3:58

καταφάσκω Leg 3:85

καταφέρω (10) Leg 3:223 Sacr 61, 66 Agr 169 Mos 1:99 Spec 3:114, 148 Aet 33, 33 Flacc 189

καταφεύγω (41) Leg 3:28, 29, 39, 41, 48, 71 Sacr 70, 70, 71, 93, 119 Det 163 Conf 39, 160, 161 Migr 52 Fug 53, 77, 80, 94, 97 Mut 8 Abr 95 Ios 132, 229 Mos 1:34, 105 Decal 140 Spec 1:42, 324 Spec 2:217 Spec 3:88, 130, 130, 132 Spec 4:40 Virt 124, 124 Praem 147 Prob 148, 151

καταφθείρω Deus 140, 140, 141, 142

καταφιλέω (7) Her 41, 42, 43, 43, 44, 44, 44

καταφλέγω (14) Leg 3:248, 249 Cher 31 Post 159, 164 Gig 34 Conf 157 Abr 226 Mos 2:53, 157, 286 Decal 122 Spec 1:313 Spec 4:28

καταφρονέω (31) Gig 32 Ebr 57, 131 Fug 33, 33, 35 Somn 1:218 Somn 2:141 Abr 48 Mos 1:102, 153, 213, 324 Mos 2:69, 277 Decal 40, 85 Spec 3:130 Spec 4:150 Virt 15, 17 Praem 17, 24 Prob 30, 30 Contempl 63 Flacc 178 Legat 236, 249 Prov 2:18 QE 2:14

καταφρόνησις Prob 103

καταφρονητής Legat 322

καταφρονητικός (19) Leg 3:141, 147 Deus 153, 167 Congr 15, 27 Abr 183, 229 Mos 1:291 Spec 1:150 Spec 3:126 Spec 4:80 Virt 25, 43 Prob 106, 110, 149, 153 Legat 361

καταφυγή (29) Sacr 129 Deus 156, 160 Fug 75, 76, 78, 80, 86, 96, 99, 102, 103 Somn 1:44, 63, 86 Abr 51 Mos 1:219 Mos 2:251 Spec 1:52, 129, 158, 159, 192, 309, 310 Spec 4:8 Flacc 159 QE 2:2 QE isf 1

καταφυτεύω (8) Plant 47, 52, 95 Congr 56, 57 Fug 175 Spec 1:335 Praem 139

καταφωράω Agr 21 Ios 12, 213

καταχαρίζομαι Spec 2:115

καταχέω (13) Cher 59 Post 58, 165 Deus 46 Ebr 44, 157, 167 Conf 144 Fug 136 Abr 79 Ios 140 Legat 228 Prov 2:20

καταχράομαι (33) Opif 171 Det 101 Post 141 Her 105, 156, 266 Congr 119, 161 Fug 30, 70 Mut 12, 266 Somn 1:230 Mos 1:3 Mos 2:84 Decal 94, 99 Spec 1:55, 65, 120, 329 Spec 2:7, 50, 109 Spec 4:26 Virt 89, 143, 169 Flacc 56 Legat 171 Prov 2:60, 60 QE 2:6a

κατάχρησις (8) Cher 121 Sacr 101 Post 168 Mut 13, 13 Somn 1:229, 229 Abr 120

καταχρηστικός Leg 2:10 Leg 3:86 Her 124 Mut 27

καταχρίω Conf 105 Mos 2:146, 152, 152

καταχρυσόω QG (Par) 2:4

καταχώννυμι Fug 148 Spec 3:152

καταψεύδομαι (19) Opif 2, 7 Cher 94 Post 122 Agr 164 Congr 61 Fug 160 Somn 2:64, 97 Abr 104 Ios 7 Mos 1:90 Mos 2:177, 271 Decal 3 Spec 2:227 Spec 3:68, 156 Spec 4:52

καταψηφίζομαι Leg 3:74 Ebr 71 Migr 134 Mos 1:134

καταψήχω Agr 70

κατάψυξις Aet 67 Prov 2:45

καταψύχω Migr 210 Her 147, 309 Spec 4:56

κατεῖδον (καθοράω) (42) Opif 45, 54 Leg 1:45 Leg 2:81 Cher 16 Post 118 Gig 44 Deus 4, 21 Agr 95 Plant 22 Ebr 44, 47, 83 Sobr 6 Conf 78, 173 Migr 115, 135, 136, 144 Her 155 Somn 1:75 Somn 2:244 Abr 70, 104, 242 Ios 16 Mos 1:33, 180, 230 Mos 2:167, 210, 241 Spec 1:259 Spec 2:216 Spec 3:185, 187 Virt 129 Contempl 78 Aet 63 QG 4:7*

κάτειμι (19) Post 30, 30, 136 Ebr 10 Conf 134, 135 Her 240, 242 Fug 194 Somn 1:115, 138, 142, 236 Somn 2:242 Mos 1:115 Mos 2:144 Spec 1:161 Aet 58 Flacc 166

κατεῖπον Ios 48

κατειρωνεύομαι Legat 30

κατεμβλέπω Fug 141

κατέναντι (6) Leg 1:63, 69, 85, 86 Cher 12 Post 1

κατεξανίσταμαι (7) Leg 3:147 Ebr 56, 63, 126 Congr 165 Ios 34 Virt 178

κατεπαγγέλλομαι Spec 3:101

κατεπᾴδω (11) Ebr 40 Her 297 Congr 16 Somn 1:220 Somn 2:88 Mos 1:42 Spec 1:343 Spec 3:29 Spec 4:93 Aet 68 Legat 52

κατεπείγω Ios 200 Mos 1:124 Mos 2:267 Flacc 82 Legat 246

κατεργάζομαι (14) Sacr 62 Plant 47, 50, 53 Ebr 109, 113 Mos 2:146 Spec 1:249 Spec 2:225 Praem 143 Flacc 66 Legat 32, 74, 121

κατερέω Ios 48

κατέρχομαι (16) Cher 2, 10, 99 Det 117 Post 136 Conf 33, 140 Fug 87, 117, 194 Somn 1:147 Mos 2:281 Aet 58 Legat 185 Hypoth 6:1 QE 2:45a

κατεσθίω καταφαγεῖν

κατεσθίω Leg 1:76, 76

κατευθύνω Leg 1:69 Decal 60

κατευνάζω Mos 2:255

κατεύχομαι Ios 200

κατευωχέομαι Agr 90 Praem 171

κατέχω (94) Opif 5, 71 Leg 1:43 Leg 2:92, 102 Leg 3:13, 21, 197 Cher 42 Sacr 113 Post 5, 118, 163 Deus 127, 138 Plant 70, 78 Ebr 5, 166 Sobr 16 Conf 22, 165 Migr 13, 191 Her 69, 260, 260, 264 Congr 41, 138 Fug 58, 132, 135, 151, 195, 200 Mut 108, 113, 136, 153, 199 Somn 1:2, 95, 254 Somn 2:56, 162, 196, 232 Abr 152 Ios 52, 147, 159, 163, 185, 200, 201, 209, 233 Mos 1:12, 124, 136, 139, 255, 286 Mos 2:164, 188, 225, 270, 275, 288 Decal 52, 63, 123 Spec 1:41, 65, 72, 118, 315 Spec 2:67, 124, 136 Spec 3:44, 91 Spec 4:15 Virt 217 Praem 15, 26 Prob 43 Legat 16, 155, 216, 267, 338, 357

κατηγορέω (38) Leg 2:67 Plant 80 Ebr 41, 93 Migr 115 Fug 206 Mut 206, 206 Somn 2:98 Ios 88, 167, 197 Mos 1:11 Decal 86, 87 Spec 2:167 Spec 3:64, 80, 80, 112 Spec 4:6, 48, 54, 127 Prob 101 Aet 85, 108, 117 Flacc 6, 127, 139, 144, 147 Legat 160, 193 Prov 2:66 QG 3:22, 23

κατηγόρημα Agr 141 Congr 149

κατηγορία (30) Deus 48 Ebr 15, 15, 32 Conf 2 Migr 93 Fug 27, 36 Somn 1:244 Ios 19, 227 Mos 1:286 Decal 30 Spec 1:202, 204 Spec 2:95, 234 Spec 3:119 Spec 4:15 Flacc 125, 126, 128, 146 Legat 38, 136, 176, 176, 199, 248, 350

κατήγορος (26) Leg 1:87 Det 23, 58 Deus 128 Ebr 14, 29, 68 Ios 215 Mos 1:141, 294 Decal 87, 87 Spec 1:55, 153, 235, 235 Spec 4:43 Virt 172 Flacc 54, 106, 135 Legat 171, 349, 359, 359 Hypoth 0:1

κατήφεια (15) Cher 37 Plant 167 Somn 2:168 Abr 151, 260 Ios 89, 170 Mos 2:166, 226 Decal 144 Spec 2:214 Spec 3:193 Praem 35 Flacc 9 Legat 15

κατηφέω (19) Sacr 125 Agr 121 Conf 93 Her 310 Somn 2:124 Ios 24, 179, 218, 224, 239 Mos 1:14 Mos 2:166 Spec 2:49, 87 Virt 66 Prob 122, 123 Flacc 15, 117

κατηχέω Legat 198

κατισχύω Leg 3:186, 186

κατίσχω Mos 2:162

κατοικέω (40) Leg 3:2, 12, 42, 115, 194, 239, 244 Sacr 44, 55 Det 23 Post 77, 98 Deus 99 Agr 64 Sobr 59, 62, 63, 68 Conf 1, 60, 76, 76, 81, 81 Her 267, 267 Congr 23, 86 Fug 102, 211 Abr 41, 105 Mos 1:240, 254, 278 Spec 2:189 Flacc 43, 55 Legat 215, 330

κατοικητήριον Plant 47

κατοικίδιος Spec 4:225 Virt 19 Hypoth 7:9

κατοικίζω Cher 1

κάτοικος Mos 1:221 Flacc 172

κατοίομαι QG 3:48

κατοίχομαι Hypoth 7:7

κατοκνέω Decal 99 Prob 12

κατοκωχή (11) Sacr 62 Conf 59 Migr 84 Her 249, 264 Fug 90 Mos 1:277, 281 Mos 2:246 Spec 4:48 Prob 80

κατολιγωρέω Deus 18 Spec 1:156 Spec 2:80

κατομβρία Aet 147

κατόπιν (19) Opif 88, 122, 123 Leg 1:4 Leg 2:100, 101 Deus 150 Agr 93, 122 Conf 139 Fug 127 Somn 1:26 Mos 1:170, 257 Mos 2:92, 251 Contempl 51 QG 2:72 QG (Par) 2:6

κατοπτρίζω Leg 3:101

κάτοπτρον (15) Opif 76 Migr 98, 190 Fug 213 Somn 2:206 Abr 153 Ios 87 Mos 2:137, 139, 139 Decal 105 Spec 1:26, 219, 219 Contempl 78 κατορθόω (71) Opif 59, 75 Leg 1:93 Cher 70 Sacr 54, 131 Det 14, 104, 145 Post 157 Deus 47, 100, 134 Plant 143 Sobr 37 Conf 86, 115, 167 Her 9 Congr 112, 153 Fug 86, 120, 140 Mut 47, 48, 48, 112, 238 Somn 2:152, 201 Abr 6, 184, 235, 267 Ios 2, 5, 147, 150, 204, 246 Mos 1:142, 154, 322, 334 Mos 2:1, 5, 173, 216 Spec 1:14, 243, 246, 314, 340 Spec 2:246 Spec 3:31 Virt 30, 38, 44, 52 Praem 33, 56, 112 Contempl 64 Flacc 1, 4 Legat 68, 331, 354 QG 4:198, 228

κατόρθωμα (27) Leg 1:56, 64, 93, 97 Leg 3:126, 188 Sacr 73 Post 11, 72 Deus 72 Plant 135 Migr 54 Her 297 Fug 193 Mut 236 Somn 1:198 Somn 2:198 Abr 186, 235 Mos 1:313 Spec 1:245 Spec 4:193 Virt 25 Praem 12, 16 Prob 60 QG 1:65

κατόρθωσις (12) Opif 59 Sacr 63 Ebr 160 Conf 87, 179 Fug 37 Mos 1:151 Decal 98 Spec 4:182 Praem 104 Prob 133 Legat 45

κατορύσσω Migr 16 Her 280 Somn 2:109 Mos 1:189 Virt 85

κατοχή Plant 39 Migr 35

κατοψοφαγέω Contempl 55

κάτω (61) Opif 41, 122 Leg 1:4 Leg 2:89 Leg 3:4, 82, 202 Sacr 25 Gig 31 Deus 175 Plant 17, 24, 25 Conf 139 Migr 168, 182 Her 238, 241, 241 Somn 1:26, 147, 152, 156, 235 Abr 59, 140 Ios 16, 78, 136, 150 Mos 1:31, 118, 217, 238 Mos 2:110, 120, 121 Decal 57, 57, 57 Spec 1:85, 93, 94, 301 Spec 2:45 Praem 109, 151, 152 Prob 25, 99 Contempl 8, 51 Aet 109, 136 Flacc 120, 131, 162 Legat 359 QG 4:51c QG (Par) 2:7, 2:7

κάτωθεν (8) Fug 180, 192 Abr 43 Mos 1:117, 202 Praem 41, 43 Prob 37

κατωθέω Aet 29

κατωκάρα Det 85 Plant 16

καῦμα Her 165

καῦσις Ios 76 Decal 150

καυστικός Mos 1:70 Aet 86

καυστός Mos 1:70

καύχημα Spec 4:164

καύχησις Congr 107

καχεξία Plant 157

καχυπόνους Sacr 32 Legat 169

Κεγχρεάς Flacc 155

κέγχρος Mos 1:200 Mos 2:258 Aet 100

κέδρινος Spec 1:268

κέδρος Mos 1:289 Mos 2:77, 90 Aet 64

κεῖμαι (38) Leg 3:184 Det 18 Her 107, 147 Congr 53 Somn 2:154 Abr 5, 128, 129, 175 Ios 17, 22, 23 Mos 1:52, 100, 120, 225, 300, 302 Mos 2:140, 172 Decal 30, 31 Spec 1:73 Spec 3:40 Spec 4:30 Virt 16 Praem 62 Contempl 22 Flacc 10, 68, 151, 156, 189 Legat 294 Hypoth 6:2 Prov 2:33 QG 2:54a

κειμήλιον (12) Det 59 Plant 57 Conf 49, 92 Mut 89 Mos 1:157, 253 Spec 3:83 Virt 5 Legat 122, 232 QG 4:148

κείρω (11) Leg 3:201, 201 Cher 79, 79 Deus 166 Decal 31, 31 Virt 90, 149 Contempl 15, 51

κελαινός Leg 3:202 Ios 78 Prob 25, 99

κέλευσμα Abr 116 Praem 117

κελεύω (167) Opif 40, 63, 85, 128, 168 Leg 1:52 Leg 2:28, 52, 79 Leg 3:65, 83, 199, 245 Cher 9 Sacr 58 Det 56 Deus 7, 135 Plant 160 Ebr 17 Conf 160, 188, 192 Migr 204 Her 145, 174 Fug 21, 185 Mut 233 Somn 2:149, 170 Abr 16, 66, 138, 171 Ios 45, 52, 96, 98, 104, 116, 120, 162, 175, 178, 186, 196, 207, 224, 238, 249 Mos 1:8, 14, 77, 79, 89, 103, 120, 127, 186, 205, 287 Mos 2:51, 147, 178, 201, 259 Decal 33, 98, 177 Spec 1:68, 98, 112, 115, 132, 135, 141, 142, 152, 153, 181, 193, 231, 236, 242, 251, 261, 268, 268, 291 Spec 2:33, 55, 86, 91, 105, 136, 195 Spec 3:12, 38, 91, 94, 102, 128, 151, 164, 182, 182, 196, 205 Spec 4:12, 53, 59, 72, 98, 119, 142, 160, 174, 195 Virt 63, 89, 90, 95, 103, 115, 126, 139, 142, 156, 159 Praem 55 Contempl 53 Flacc 10, 27, 43, 74, 86, 110, 111, 115, 137 Legat 30, 194, 203, 207, 209, 219, 228, 239, 254, 260, 265, 267, 273, 291, 305, 313, 315, 329, 333, 335, 351 Prov 2:26 QG 2:16, 16 QG (Par) 2:4 QE 2:15a

κενοδοξέω Mut 227

κενοδοξία Mut 96 Ios 36 Legat 114

κενόδοξος Somn 2:105

κενός (136) Opif 29, 29, 32, 32 Leg 1:44 Leg 2:57 Leg 3:4, 229 Cher 69, 81, 91 Sacr 69, 84 Det 113, 130 Post 6 Deus 172 Agr 36, 56 Plant 7, 7, 157 Ebr 36, 38, 39, 40, 57, 76, 128, 144, 152, 206 Sobr 57 Migr 19, 21, 35, 80, 138 Her 67, 194, 228 Congr 6, 15, 61 Fug 45, 47, 128, 128, 143 Mut 92, 93, 94, 96, 214, 270 Somn 1:49, 82, 126, 198, 248, 255, 255 Somn 2:16, 42, 46, 47, 48, 50, 53, 55, 57, 59, 61, 62, 78, 93, 95, 105, 115, 133, 155, 245 Abr 91 Ios 126 Mos 1:195, 262, 262, 325 Decal 4, 147, 149 Spec 1:27, 205, 311, 327 Spec 3:16, 39, 148, 162 Spec 4:82, 129, 200 Virt 7, 179 Praem 19, 65, 83, 94, 100, 101, 112, 129, 129, 133, 157 Prob 66, 158 Contempl 17, 55, 55 Aet 21, 78, 102, 103 Flacc 164 Legat 119, 121, 146, 225 Prov 2:8, 18, 40 QG 2:12b, 4:30 QE 2:14, 20

κενόω (13) Leg 3:138, 226 Cher 15 Abr 136 Decal 13 Spec 2:170 Virt 43 Praem 142 Aet 128 Legat 90, 117 QG (Par) 2:7, 2:7

κεντέω (9) Leg 3:248, 253 Conf 121 Somn 1:89 Somn 2:83, 122 Ios 103 Mos 1:69 Decal 87

κεντρίζω Virt 69

κέντρον (7) Det 46 Conf 5, 156 Congr 74, 158 Somn 2:294 Legat 169

κένωσις (8) Opif 58 Cher 75 Her 297, 297 Ios 33 Mos 1:265 Aet 74 QG (Par) 2:7

κεραία Flacc 131

κεραμεοῦς Spec 2:20 Spec 3:58, 58, 60

κέραμος Legat 127

κεράννυμι κίρνημι

κεράννυμι (31) Post 37 Deus 37, 77, 77, 82, 82 Ebr 190, 192 Sobr 36 Conf 90, 186 Migr 147, 207 Her 152, 153, 153, 183, 183 Fug 71 Mut 102, 184, 200, 212 Somn 1:117, 163 Somn 2:8, 15 Abr 205, 205 Spec 1:266 Spec 4:102

κέρας Fug 132 Mut 159 Mos 1:290 Spec 1:231, 233

κέρασμα Deus 77

κερατίζω Leg 1:68

κεραύνιος (6) Ebr 223 Somn 2:125 Abr 140 Mos 1:119 Mos 2:58, 287 κεραυνός (11) Deus 60 Somn 2:129 Abr 43 Mos 1:118, 121, 126, 145 Mos 2:56, 283, 287 Prov 2:53

κεραυνόω Conf 158

κερδαίνω Abr 215 Decal 92 Spec 3:141 Virt 95 Prov 2:12

κέρδος (18) Migr 217 Congr 65 Abr 215 Ios 18, 139 Spec 2:87 Spec 3:154 Spec 4:3, 14, 17, 121, 194, 218 Virt 92 Praem 11, 154 Legat 242, 242

κέρκος Leg 2:88, 88, 92 Praem 89

κέρκωψ Sacr 32 Hypoth 6:2

κεφάλαιος (49) Leg 1:99 Leg 2:35, 102 Leg 3:188 Cher 17 Sacr 82, 82, 83, 85, 94 Post 131 Deus 53, 62, 69 Agr 2 Ebr 93, 114, 115, 195 Conf 55 Her 214 Congr 120 Fug 7, 143, 166 Mut 106, 130 Somn 1:235 Decal 19, 154, 156, 158, 168, 170, 175 Spec 2:1, 39, 63, 223, 242, 261 Spec 4:41, 132 Praem 2 Aet 89, 124 QG 1:55a, 55a, 2:54a

κεφαλαιώδης (8) Opif 129 Deus 88 Decal 20, 168 Spec 4:78, 160 Legat 178, 373

κεφαλαλγής Ebr 218 Mos 1:120

κεφαλή (125) Opif 100, 118, 119, 123, 158, 158 Leg 1:12, 70, 71, 71 Leg 3:65, 115, 115, 116, 188 Cher 14, 17 Sacr 21, 115, 115 Det 85 Post 53, 53, 53 Deus 88, 127 Agr 75, 107, 114, 175, 175 Plant 16, 16, 111, 145 Ebr 131 Sobr 27 Conf 1, 107, 113 Migr 102, 103 Congr 61 Fug 110, 111, 182 Somn 1:3, 4, 32, 49, 66, 120, 125, 128, 128, 133, 144, 146, 253 Somn 2:14, 19, 62, 189, 207, 207 Abr 275 Ios 22, 93, 93, 96, 98, 105, 256 Mos 1:15, 128 Mos 2:30, 82, 116, 131, 146, 154, 290 Decal 57 Spec 1:115, 147, 166, 198, 202, 232, 250, 254 Spec 3:4, 37, 56, 60, 184 Spec 4:83, 92 Virt 111 Praem 114, 124, 125, 125, 125, 142 Prob 155 Contempl 31, 50, 77 Aet 29, 110 Flacc 37, 98, 189 Legat 79, 95, 127, 223, 237, 257, 267, 269 QG (Par) 2:5, 2:5 QE 2:24a

κεφαλίς Mos 2:77

κηδεμονία (6) Mos 2:291 Spec 1:318 Spec 4:178 Virt 52, 224 QE 2:3b

κηδεμονικός Spec 2:101 Prov 2:3

κηδεμών (10) Congr 118 Somn 2:43 Ios 74 Mos 2:166 Spec 1:310 Spec 2:132 Spec 3:115 Legat 63 Prov 2:39 QE 2:3a

κηδεστής Legat 63

κηδεύω Migr 159 Ios 23 Mos 1:171 Mos 2:291

κῆδος Fug 49

κήδω (6) Leg 3:72 Det 14 Ebr 13 Sobr 54 Spec 2:25 Prov 2:6

κηλέω Sacr 26 Post 106, 155

κηλιδόω Leg 3:168 Cher 95 Deus 8 Somn 1:148 Mos 1:304

κηλίς (6) Somn 1:82 Somn 2:25 Decal 10 Spec 1:206, 259 Aet 2

κήλων Spec 3:47

κημός Somn 2:294

κῆπος Contempl 20 Legat 181, 351

κήρ (39) Leg 2:97 Leg 3:193, 200, 234, 235 Cher 66, 76 Sacr 15, 31, 95, 111 Det 27, 44, 98 Post 11, 52 Deus 112 Plant 43, 106, 145 Ebr 79 Sobr 38 Migr 26 Her 272, 284 Congr 46 Mut 49 Somn 1:105, 222 Mos 2:155 Decal 156 Spec 1:117 Spec 2:52 Spec 3:2 Spec 4:200 Virt 193 Aet 73 Prov 2:22, 23

κηραίνω (15) Deus 52 Ebr 135, 164 Conf 21 Her 205 Somn 1:218 Mos 2:211 Decal 153 Spec 1:81, 166, 260 Virt 31 Praem 29, 121 Prov 2:8

κήρινος Her 181

κηροειδής Leg 1:100

κηρός (15) Opif 18, 166 Leg 1:61, 100 Deus 43 Agr 16, 167, 167 Conf 187 Her 294 Mut 30, 212 Spec 1:47, 106 Aet 79

κήρυγμα (17) Agr 112, 117 Conf 197, 197 Mut 44 Somn 1:130 Abr 35 Mos 1:9 Mos 2:22, 167, 170 Spec 2:246 Spec 4:4 Praem 6 Prob 157 Legat 46 QG 2:13a

κηρύκειον Aet 68 Legat 94, 100, 102

κῆρυξ Agr 112 Somn 1:29 Ios 120 Spec 4:221 Legat 100

κηρύσσω (7) Agr 112, 112 Congr 159 Fug 20 Mos 2:167 Spec 2:104 Praem 52

κῆτος Opif 63 Her 154

κηφήν Migr 164

Κία Flacc 156

κιβδηλεύω (18) Leg 2:57 Cher 94 Post 89, 98, 165 Gig 65 Sobr 20 Conf 108 Her 123 Congr 159 Mut 208 Decal 3 Spec 1:326 Spec 3:11 Spec 4:51 Prob 98 Contempl 42 Legat 104

κίβδηλος (8) Leg 3:104, 119 Cher 17 Sacr 29, 137 Conf 159 Fug 19 Spec 4:203

κιβωτός (24) Det 170 Gig 48 Plant 43, 43 Ebr 85 Conf 105 Fug 100, 100 Mut 43 Mos 2:94, 95, 97, 146 QG 2:11, 13a, 48, 66 QG (Par) 2:1, 2:2, 2:3, 2:4, 2:4, 2:4, 2:5

κίδαρις Mos 2:116, 116, 131

κιθάρα (10) Leg 2:75 Leg 3:21, 221 Post 103, 111 Sobr 36 Fug 22 Spec 2:193 Legat 12 QG 4:76b

κιθαρίζω Sobr 36 Congr 46

κιθαριστής Agr 35 Congr 46

κιθαρῳδός (6) Leg 2:7, 21, 75 Agr 35 Ebr 177 Legat 42

κικλήσκω Aet 121

Κιλικία Legat 281

κινδυνεύω (16) Congr 92 Fug 119 Abr 90, 98 Ios 187 Mos 1:13, 318 Spec 2:137, 139 Spec 3:29, 166 Virt 14, 41 Flacc 60 Legat 160 Prov 2:55

κίνδυνος (44) Post 119 Agr 149, 151, 154 Conf 12 Ios 34 Mos 1:171, 222, 224, 322 Mos 2:58, 65, 251, 255 Decal 114 Spec 1:301 Spec 2:208, 240 Spec 3:54, 80, 81, 117, 127, 163, 172 Spec 4:35, 121, 166 Virt 38, 176, 221 Praem 36 Flacc 48 Legat 184, 193, 194, 213, 218, 247, 250, 330, 341 Prov 2:28, 30

κινέω (148) Opif 9, 26, 100, 100, 117 Leg 1:4, 6, 9, 17, 19, 29, 29 Leg 2:22, 37, 37, 37, 39, 39, 40, 43, 43, 44, 76, 85, 100 Leg 3:34, 82, 99, 144, 160, 160, 173, 220, 222, 252 Cher 30, 88, 128 Sacr 2, 65, 68 Det 33, 83, 88, 127, 172, 172 Post 19, 19, 24, 28, 28, 107 Gig 8, 48 Deus 32 Agr 35 Plant 7 Ebr 98, 105, 170, 179, 183, 183 Sobr 7, 44, 45, 46, 47, 47, 50 Conf 1, 60, 67, 134 Migr 22, 88, 167, 195 Her 137, 252 Congr 66 Fug 8, 46, 144 Mut 54, 81 Somn 1:43, 136, 187, 192 Somn 2:1, 119, 123, 136, 165, 179, 284 Abr 46, 102, 102, 119, 150, 154 Mos 1:31, 326, 326 Mos 2:13, 15 Decal 142, 150 Spec 3:116 Spec 4:83, 139, 140 Praem 76 Prob 153 Aet 53 Flacc 43, 52, 120 Legat 5, 118, 161, 169, 171, 176, 178, 197, 213, 225, 238, 300, 327, 333, 337 Hypoth

6:9, 7:7, 7:14 Prov 2:18 QG 1:21, 2:15a, 22, 22, 22, 4:200b QG (Par) 2:4, 2:6

κίνημα Leg 2:46, 97 Sacr 72

κίνησις (147) Opif 26, 26, 54, 54, 58, 59, 61, 67, 67, 78, 100, 100, 117, 120, 122 Leg 1:2, 2, 4, 12 Leg 2:40, 45, 74 Leg 3:34, 160, 160, 206, 229 Cher 21, 22, 24, 25, 62, 88 Sacr 26, 68, 73, 106, 109 Det 88, 172 Post 29, 79 Gig 8 Deus 31, 44, 48, 48, 165 Agr 35, 95, 142 Plant 12, 13 Ebr 111, 120, 171, 180, 204 Sobr 34, 34, 34, 45, 47, 47, 49, 49 Conf 11, 31, 67, 98, 99, 100, 134, 139 Migr 131, 171, 184, 194 Her 81, 84, 88, 97, 110, 119, 247 Congr 25, 31, 31, 45 Mut 67, 257 Somn 1:20, 22, 26, 35, 43, 81, 115, 235 Somn 2:2 Abr 27, 69, 73, 151 Ios 126 Mos 2:102 Spec 1:147, 178 Spec 2:230 Spec 3:188 Spec 4:79, 139, 139, 141, 155 Virt 32, 40, 173, 217 Praem 89, 113 Contempl 77 Aet 4, 30, 33, 52, 52, 53, 54, 89, 89, 89, 89 Legat 55, 101, 112, 238, 261, 337, 349 QG 1:24, 2:22, 34a, 4:51c, 99 QE 2:45a, 55a

κινητικός Conf 101

κινητός (7) Opif 66 Post 23 Gig 48 Plant 11 Somn 1:26, 249 Somn 2:219

κιονόκρανον Somn 2:55

κίρνημι (κεράννυμι) Migr 52

κισσός Somn 2:62 Legat 79

κισσύβιον Somn 2:61

κιχλίζω Sacr 21

κίχρημι Virt 83

κίων (17) Conf 5 Somn 2:54 Mos 1:166 Mos 2:77, 78, 80, 83, 85, 87, 89, 90, 91, 93, 101 Decal 44 QG isf 1 QE 1:21

κλάδος (9) Sacr 25 Det 107, 108 Mos 2:22, 102 Spec 1:254, 262 Aet 63 Legat 127

κλαίω (8) Deus 138 Agr 33, 75 Migr 155 Her 20 Praem 170 Prob 153 Legat 187

κλάσις Sacr 23 Post 106 Deus 25

Κλαύδιοι Legat 33

Κλαύδιος Legat 206

κλαυθμός Contempl 73 Legat 227

κλαῦμα Opif 161

κλάω (7) Cher 82 Sacr 21 Post 47 Gig 43 Agr 35 Plant 159 Ebr 182

Κλεάνθης Aet 90

κλεισιάδες (κλισιάδες) Congr 10 Abr 23 Mos 1:14 Spec 3:169 Prov 2:57

κλείω Legat 360

Κλεοπάτρα Legat 135

κλέος (12) Fug 205 Mos 1:2 Mos 2:27, 29 Spec 1:311 Spec 4:164 Virt 38, 197, 204 Prob 94, 109 Legat 284

κλέπτης (13) Leg 3:32, 32 Her 302 Ios 84 Decal 136 Spec 4:9, 10, 12, 13, 33, 38, 40, 87

κλέπτω (22) Leg 3:20, 33, 241 Post 82 Plant 107 Conf 163 Congr 150 Ios 213, 235 Mos 1:302 Decal 36, 135, 138, 171 Spec 1:127, 278 Spec 4:1, 3, 7, 37, 39 Legat 122

κληδών Mos 1:287 Spec 1:60, 63 Flacc 177

κλῆμα Virt 28

κληματίς (14) Det 106 Deus 38, 39 Plant 2 Ebr 222 Sobr 36 Congr 56 Mut 162, 224 Somn 2:171, 191 Mos 1:231 Virt 157 QG 1:28

κληροδοσία Plant 63

κληροδοτέω Sacr 19 Plant 54 Sobr 21 Spec 2:119

κληρονομέω (31) Sacr 57, 135 Plant 54, 62 Conf 74 Migr 94 Her 2, 65, 66, 68, 69, 96, 98, 100 Congr 23 Fug 17 Mut 155, 177 Mos 2:245, 245 Spec 2:129, 129, 130, 138 Spec 4:150 Flacc 148 Legat 9, 122, 343 Prov 2:9 QG 2:10

κληρονομία (9) Post 89 Plant 47, 48, 54 Her 44 Fug 15 Ios 137 Mos 1:323 Spec 2:131

κληρονόμος (30) Sacr 120 Her 1, 33, 36, 39, 63, 66, 68, 76, 101, 298, 313 Fug 19 Somn 1:175 Abr 252 Mos 1:155 Mos 2:244 Spec 2:124, 128, 132 Spec 4:75 Virt 53, 59, 72, 79, 207, 208 Praem 108, 139 Legat 24

κλῆρος (119) Opif 64 Leg 2:51, 51, 52, 52, 52, 52, 52, 52 Leg 3:82, 85, 242 Cher 29, 51 Sacr 7, 127, 129 Det 62, 140 Post 70, 72 Deus 112 Agr 155 Plant 48, 52, 53, 58, 60, 62, 63, 63, 68, 69, 70, 71, 71, 72 Sobr 56, 58 Conf 128, 177 Migr 30, 38, 154, 165 Her 70, 99, 100, 145, 162, 179, 179, 187 Congr 108, 108, 134, 134 Fug 102 Mut 26, 26, 51, 59, 95, 151 Somn 1:159, 159 Somn 2:189, 255, 256, 258 Abr 246, 268 Mos 1:13, 157, 217, 304 Mos 2:6, 221, 233, 243, 243, 244, 245, 289 Decal 112, 128 Spec 1:126, 131, 131, 151, 156 Spec 2:126, 129, 132, 168, 170, 183, 222, 231 Spec 3:16, 162 Spec 4:14, 149, 151, 153, 153, 153, 156 Virt 90, 189 Praem 54, 105, 169 Prob 22, 117 Legat 143, 326 QG 1:51, 2:10

κληρουχία (13) Mos 1:222, 237, 320 Mos 2:1, 234, 236, 242, 246 Decal 14, 164 Spec 2:111, 116, 118

κληροῦχος (6) Mos 1:255 Spec 2:113, 121 Virt 91, 100 Aet 73

κληρόω (30) Opif 57 Leg 3:3, 116 Sacr 104, 108 Det 125, 145 Deus 34 Ebr 52, 61 Sobr 9 Conf 21 Migr 37 Her 109, 175 Fug 126, 208 Somn 1:32 Somn 2:190 Abr 162 Mos 2:101 Spec 1:94, 188, 201 Praem 53 Aet 33 Flacc 146 Legat 95, 112, 367

κληρωτός Spec 4:151, 157

κλῆσις (26) Opif 143, 150 Leg 1:95, 96 Cher 7, 56 Det 124, 160 Plant 153 Ebr 30, 173 Her 23 Mut 262, 262 Abr 51, 51, 102 Mos 2:205 Decal 83 Spec 2:8 Virt 24 Flacc 180, 184 Legat 102, 163 QE isf 7

κλίβανος Her 308, 311

κλίμα (16) Det 99 Agr 23 Plant 67 Migr 120 Her 83 Somn 2:250, 287 Ios 56 Mos 1:114, 228 Praem 7 Aet 147 Legat 89, 116, 283, 347

κλῖμαξ (15) Somn 1:2, 3, 133, 134, 144, 146, 150, 152, 153, 157, 159 Somn 2:3, 19 Spec 4:229 Praem 43

κλινάρχης Flacc 137

κλίνη (6) Somn 1:123, 125 Somn 2:56 Spec 2:20 Flacc 136 Prov 2:17

κλινήρης Spec 3:106

κλιντήρ Somn 2:57

κλίνω (13) Post 175 Agr 89, 101 Ebr 156 Migr 13, 148, 175 Somn 2:227 Abr 240 Ios 122 Mos 1:261 Praem 6 Prob 103

κλισιάδες κλεισιάδες

κλοιός Somn 2:44, 44

κλονέω (11) Leg 3:38, 53 Cher 12 Deus 175 Conf 69 Mut 72, 189 Somn 2:11 Spec 1:292, 301 Praem 151

κλόνος (6) Opif 59 Leg 2:90 Cher 13, 38 Post 22, 32

κλοπή (16) Conf 117 Her 173 Ios 197, 209, 215, 219 Decal 51, 136 Spec 1:127 Spec 2:13 Spec 3:181 Spec 4:7, 10, 34, 35, 196

κλοποφορέω Leg 3:20

κλύδων (16) Opif 58, 63 Leg 3:223 Sacr 13, 90 Det 100 Post 100, 178 Gig 51 Deus 26 Conf 32 Congr 60 Somn 2:225 Mos 1:41 Spec 1:301 Prob 24

κλύω Prob 152

κλωσμός Legat 368

κνήμη Mos 1:271

κνησμός Det 110 Mos 1:108 Spec 3:10

κνῖσα (κνίσσα) Opif 158 Somn 1:49 Contempl 53 Prov 2:62

κνισόω Somn 1:51

κνίσσα κνῖσα

κόγχη Congr 117 Aet 122

κοιλαίνω Opif 86 Somn 2:60 Aet 119

κοιλάς Det 5, 15, 15, 16

Κοίλη Legat 281

κοιλία (41) Leg 1:12 Leg 2:46 Leg 3:65, 88, 114, 115, 116, 138, 139, 139, 141, 143, 144, 145, 147, 147, 159, 159, 159, 160 Sacr 4 Migr 65, 66, 66, 67 Somn 2:217, 217 Spec 1:148, 148, 150, 199, 206, 206, 217, 217, 217, 268 Spec 4:107, 113 QG (Par) 2:3, 2:7

κοῖλος (6) Det 16 Conf 26 Mos 1:163 Spec 4:109 Contempl 51 Aet 147

κοιλότης Det 17 Mos 2:63

κοιμάω (37) Leg 2:27, 30, 31, 36 Leg 3:237, 239 Plant 177, 177, 177 Ebr 179, 203 Fug 188 Somn 1:4, 5, 80, 92, 99, 101, 110, 120, 128, 150, 174 Somn 2:160, 218 Ios 102, 125, 142, 147, 255 Spec 1:338 Spec 4:141 Praem 151 Flacc 164 Legat 42, 175 QE 2:15:1

κοινόδημος Somn 2:144

κοινοπραγέω (10) Ios 220 Decal 123 Spec 2:141 Spec 4:34, 179 Virt 103, 223 Legat 26, 92, 122

κοινοπραγία Mos 1:136 Praem 74

κοινός (210) Leg 1:106 Leg 2:22, 23, 23 Leg 3:30, 67, 86, 216 Cher 73 Sacr 9 Det 49, 83, 136, 174 Post 112, 117, 159 Gig 29 Deus 17, 36, 95 Agr 13, 35, 43, 47, 48, 151, 156 Plant 79, 146 Ebr 30, 68, 79, 109, 129, 187, 193 Sobr 40, 67 Conf 8, 9, 21, 46, 58 Her 301 Congr 149 Fug 36, 210 Mut 40 Somn 1:11, 18, 176 Abr 7, 20, 32, 60, 135, 189, 199, 235 Ios 25, 30, 38, 63, 77, 125, 160, 204 Mos 1:97, 126, 129, 137, 151, 156, 304, 314 Mos 2:9, 22, 60, 159, 291 Decal 5, 39, 39, 41, 51, 62, 76, 95, 110, 135, 173, 178 Spec 1:69, 117, 125, 125, 143, 149, 154, 168, 190, 229, 230, 247, 255, 316, 333, 340 Spec 2:12, 28, 45, 89, 145, 150, 162, 167, 188, 190, 243, 248 Spec 3:11, 42, 51, 80, 131, 133, 191 Spec 4:2, 4, 21, 23, 35, 58, 72, 106, 123, 133, 134, 159, 169, 171, 183, 184, 219 Virt 3, 63, 199, 206, 206, 224 Praem 11, 14, 22, 56, 67, 87, 119, 154, 155, 168 Prob 8, 57, 85, 86, 86, 86, 86, 87 Contempl 30, 32, 40, 60, 61, 72 Aet 103, 149 Flacc 24, 24, 38, 41, 106, 117, 124, 144, 144 Legat 4, 11, 22, 50, 89, 143, 145, 149, 149, 158, 183, 190, 193, 194, 225, 316, 371 Hypoth 7:2, 11:4, 11:12, 11:13 Prov 2:39 QG 1:96:1 QE 2:2

κοινότης Deus 95 Her 72 Mos 1:87

κοινόω Legat 84

κοινωνέω (34) Opif 73 Leg 1:42 Leg 2:64 Leg 3:87, 171, 193 Sacr 33, 47, 73 Post 158, 160 Sobr 29 Her 186 Congr 36 Mut 213 Somn 1:176 Abr 50 Ios 23 Decal 89 Spec 1:129, 320 Spec 2:89, 107, 173 Spec 3:100 Spec 4:100, 119, 204 Virt 115, 152 Aet 60 Flacc 65 Legat 80 QE isf 14

κοινωνία (107) Opif 138, 152 Leg 1:8 Cher 110 Sacr 27, 75, 101 Det 164 Post 181 Gig 42 Agr 26, 145 Ebr 48, 78, 84 Conf 12, 13, 48, 83, 193, 194, 195 Migr 178, 180 Her 183 Congr 22, 58, 121 Fug 35, 55, 112 Mut 104 Somn 2:83 Abr 41, 74, 100, 103, 224, 248 Ios 160 Mos 1:158, 324 Mos 2:190 Decal 14, 71, 109, 123, 132, 150, 162, 171 Spec 1:104, 109, 138, 235, 295, 324 Spec 2:7, 75, 108, 110, 119, 167 Spec 3:23, 25, 28, 29, 103, 131, 158, 182 Spec 4:14, 16, 30, 83, 133, 187, 204 Virt 51, 80, 81, 84, 96, 103, 119, 175, 181 Praem 87, 92 Prob 84, 91, 107, 113 Contempl 24 Aet 143 Flacc 136, 190 Legat 47, 72, 110, 238 Hypoth 11:1, 11:14, 11:16 QG 1:17b, 3:3 QE 2:3a

κοινωνικός (17) Det 72 Migr 147, 156 Congr 71 Fug 11 Mut 149, 226 Spec 2:104 Spec 4:120 Virt 27, 90 Prob 13 Flacc 12 Legat 67 QG 4:20 QG isf 10, 10

κοινωνός (15) Sacr 100 Post 83 Fug 52 Abr 246, 256 Mos 1:150, 155 Spec 1:131, 221, 278 Flacc 10 Legat 23, 25, 28, 32

κοινωφελής (18) Ebr 212 Ios 34, 73 Mos 2:9, 28 Decal 170 Spec 1:321 Spec 4:134, 149, 157, 170, 215 Virt 3, 169 Praem 100, 107 Prob 63 Hypoth 11:5

κοίρανος Conf 170

κοίτη Spec 2:20 Spec 4:141

κοῖτος Somn 1:123

κόκκινος (9) Migr 97 Congr 117, 117 Mos 2:84, 87, 88, 111, 133 Spec 1:268

κολάζω (53) Leg 1:35, 35 Det 144, 146, 146 Post 98 Deus 80 Agr 118 Ebr 131, 135 Sobr 69 Conf 181 Migr 116 Fug 66, 66, 80, 93 Mut 129 Ios 79, 220 Mos 1:108, 144, 245 Mos 2:57, 214, 255 Decal 95 Spec 1:54, 316 Spec 2:37, 137, 232, 245, 246 Spec 3:11, 149, 152, 154, 156 Spec 4:2 Virt 100, 227 Flacc 81, 82, 180 Legat 334 Prov 2:24, 34, 34 QG 1:89, 96:1, 3:52, 4:52d

κολακεία (17) Leg 3:182 Sacr 22 Sobr 57 Conf 48 Abr 126 Ios 77 Prob 99 Contempl 37 Flacc 108 Legat 32, 40, 70, 134, 162, 361 QG 4:8* QG isf 7

κολακεύω (8) Det 21 Plant 104, 106 Migr 111, 150 Spec 1:60 Flacc 172 Legat 116

κολακικός Legat 39

κόλαξ (11) Leg 2:10 Leg 3:182 Sacr 32 Agr 164 Plant 105, 106 Migr 111 Her 77, 302 Spec 4:89 Virt 173

κολάπτω Her 167 Aet 119

κόλασις (55) Opif 156 Sacr 131, 133 Det 144 Deus 76 Agr 40, 40 Conf 171, 180 Congr 119 Fug 65 Somn 1:143 Abr 129 Ios 150, 154, 155, 170, 263 Mos 1:26, 96, 96, 97, 102, 147, 154 Mos 2:47, 169, 197, 202, 285 Decal 69, 141, 174, 177 Spec 1:55, 284 Spec 2:163, 196 Spec 3:85, 122, 183 Spec 4:6, 6, 150 Virt 41 Praem 7, 67 Flacc 96 Legat 7, 7, 95 Prov 2:37, 37 QG 4:40, 51a κολαστήριος (14) Sacr 132 Post 20 Gig 47 Agr 71 Ebr 32 Conf 171 Her 166, 203 Abr 145, 145 Spec 1:307 Legat 6, 7 Prov 2:61

κολαστής (9) Gig 46 Somn 1:91 Mos 1:107 Spec 1:160 Virt 172, 174, 194 Prob 7 Flacc 54

κολαστικός Her 166

κόλλα (7) Opif 38, 131 Migr 132 Her 188 Somn 1:111 Spec 4:107 QG (Par) 2:4

κολλάω Leg 2:50 Migr 132, 132

κολλώδης QG (Par) 2:4

κολοσσιαῖος (6) Opif 6 Ios 39 Legat 188, 203, 306, 337

κολούω Post 150

κόλπος (15) Opif 113 Plant 10, 24 Her 20 Somn 2:118 Mos 1:79, 79 Mos 2:144 Spec 1:7 Spec 4:129 Virt 145 Contempl 51 Aet 122 Flacc 154 Legat 185

κολῳάω Somn 2:260

κολωνός Abr 169 Mos 1:216

κομάω Deus 88

κόμη Sacr 25 Deus 88 Somn 1:253

κομιδῇ (20) Leg 3:210 Cher 73 Post 152 Sobr 9 Congr 74 Ios 223 Mos 1:20, 179, 311, 330 Spec 1:163 Spec 3:119 Prob 160 Contempl 67 Aet 42, 71, 145 Legat 1, 26 Hypoth 11:3

κομίζω (73) Opif 166 Leg 2:57 Leg 3:70 Cher 118 Post 5 Agr 69 Plant 101, 130 Ebr 25 Migr 11, 204 Fug 149, 151 Somn 1:100 Somn 2:90 Abr 171 Ios 15, 22, 93, 190, 194, 210, 213, 215, 227, 231 Mos 1:18, 141, 231, 317 Spec 1:152, 188, 272, 278, 279, 280 Spec 2:73, 78, 121, 122, 182, 216, 219, 220 Spec 3:55, 60, 115 Spec 4:31, 196 Virt 84, 86, 88, 88, 95, 96, 123 Praem 40, 171 Prob 32 Flacc 56, 96 Legat 129, 135, 216, 231, 267, 337, 356 Prov 2:33 QG 1:62:1, 2:54c QE 2:50b, 50b

κόμμα Somn 1:123, 208

κομπαστής Spec 2:18

κόμπος Congr 61

κομψεύω (6) Migr 75 Decal 55 Spec 2:244 Virt 196 Contempl 59 Flacc 102

κονίαμα Cher 104 Agr 152, 160

κονίζω κονίω

κονιορτός Mos 1:127, 129 Praem 133

κόνις (7) Conf 79 Abr 139 Ios 25 Mos 1:39 Spec 2:95 Aet 125 Legat 228

κονίω (κονίζω) (16) Det 29, 32 Agr 119 Ebr 57 Migr 75, 200 Congr 92 Fug 24 Somn 2:146, 154 Abr 256 Mos 2:252 Spec 3:115 Flacc 104 Legat 32 Prov 2:12

κοντός Flacc 90 Legat 129

κοπάζω (6) Her 201, 201 Somn 2:235, 236 QG 2:28, 48

κοπετός Abr 260

κοπή Ebr 24

κοπιάω Cher 41 Migr 145 Mut 254

κόπος Spec 2:39

κοπρία Flacc 56

κόπριον Fug 61

κόπτω (6) Ebr 24 Migr 144 Mut 173 Mos 2:77 Legat 188, 243

κοπώδης Migr 145 Mut 254

κόραξ QG 2:38, 39

Κορέ Fug 145

κορέννυμι (12) Leg 3:111, 155, 183 Post 145 Conf 7, 154 Somn 2:149 Abr 228 Mos 1:130, 284 Spec 1:156 Spec 3:43

κόρη (19) Opif 66 Leg 3:171 Her 79 Mut 56 Mos 1:52, 54, 108 Mos 2:234, 238 Spec 1:109 Spec 2:125 Spec 3:35, 66, 70, 80, 194 Prob 134, 140 Legat 234

Κόρη Decal 54

κορικός Mos 1:54

Κορινθιακός Somn 2:55

Κορίνθιος Flacc 155

Κόρινθος Ios 132, 132 Flacc 154, 173 Legat 281

κόριον Leg 3:169, 170, 170

κορμός Agr 6

κόρος (κοῦρος) (28) Opif 158, 169 Leg 2:29, 69, 70 Leg 3:7 Sacr 23, 85 Det 157 Post 98 Agr 32, 48 Her 240 Abr 135, 228 Mos 2:13, 164, 164 Spec 1:208 Spec 3:43 Virt 162 Flacc 77, 91, 91 Legat 234 Prov 2:12 QG 2:64c QE isf 14

κορυβαντιάω (6) Opif 71 Migr 35 Her 69 Somn 2:1 Contempl 12 Flacc 169

κορυφαῖος Somn 2:133 Prov 2:40

κορυφή (7) Ebr 8 Her 218 Somn 1:134 Somn 2:107 Abr 43 Mos 1:228 Aet 135

κορυφόω Aet 135

κοσμέω (20) Opif 139 Det 5, 20, 42 Deus 11, 150 Agr 91 Ebr 86 Conf 146 Congr 70 Fug 187 Mut 13, 217 Somn 2:55 Mos 2:140 Spec 3:135 Praem 110 Legat 157, 297, 371

κοσμικός Aet 53

κόσμιος (6) Leg 3:158 Mut 226 Ios 50 Spec 1:102, 153 Spec 3:89

κοσμιότης (8) Sacr 27 Fug 33, 50, 154 Somn 1:124 Ios 40 Spec 3:51 Flacc 99

κοσμοπλαστέω Migr 6 Her 166

κοσμοπλάστης Plant 3 Congr 48

κοσμοποιέω (6) Opif 24 Leg 3:96 Decal 105 Aet 39, 40 QG 2:13b

κοσμοποιητικός Opif 21 Legat 6

κοσμοποιία (20) Opif 3, 4, 6, 129, 170 Post 64 Gig 22 Plant 86 Fug 68, 178 Abr 2, 258 Mos 2:37 Decal 97 Spec 4:123 Praem 1, 1 QG 1:1, 1, 1

κοσμοποιός (9) Opif 7 Plant 50, 131 Fug 164 Mos 1:272 Mos 2:135 Spec 2:260 Praem 42 QG 2:34a

κοσμοπολίτης (8) Opif 3, 142, 143 Gig 61 Conf 106 Migr 59 Mos 1:157 Spec 2:45

κοσμοπολῖτις Somn 1:243

κόσμος (634) Opif 3, 3, 3, 7, 9, 11, 12, 13, 14, 15, 16, 17, 19, 20, 24, 25, 25, 26, 26, 26, 33, 35, 36, 52, 53, 55, 62, 69, 77, 77, 78, 89, 89, 111, 131, 139, 142, 143, 146, 151, 171, 171, 171, 171, 172 Leg 1:1, 1, 2, 2, 2, 2, 44 Leg 2:2, 3, 3 Leg 3:5, 5, 6, 6, 7, 7, 30, 78, 78, 84, 97, 99, 100, 175 Cher 23, 26, 26, 86, 88, 99, 104, 110, 112, 119, 119, 120, 127 Sacr 8, 8, 21, 25, 26, 34, 40, 40, 65, 97 Det 8, 54, 62, 75, 89, 90, 90, 116, 154, 154 Post 5, 6, 7, 14, 58, 144, 166, 167 Gig 7, 61, 61, 64

Deus 19, 30, 31, 31, 57, 62, 79, 97, 106, 107, 107, 108 Agr 51, 52, 152 Plant 2, 4, 6, 7, 8, 22, 28, 28, 33, 45, 48, 50, 69, 120, 126, 127, 128, 131, 139, 162 Ebr 30, 32, 62, 75, 108, 118, 187, 199 Sobr 53, 54, 55 Conf 56, 96, 97, 98, 98, 99, 106, 114, 136, 170, 172, 173, 185, 196 Migr 41, 59, 97, 97, 103, 105, 131, 136, 138, 179, 180, 181, 181, 186, 194, 203, 220 Her 37, 75, 97, 98, 99, 110, 111, 111, 120, 122, 126, 133, 134, 140, 152, 152, 155, 155, 155, 169, 197, 199, 199, 200, 206, 207, 226, 233, 236, 263, 281, 301, 311 Congr 21, 48, 49, 49, 104, 105, 113, 117, 133, 144 Fug 12, 95, 103, 110, 161, 164, 198 Mut 16, 18, 27, 30, 44, 45, 46, 46, 76, 111, 135, 140, 246, 267 Somn 1:15, 16, 23, 24, 33, 34, 39, 102, 104, 109, 116, 134, 135, 146, 149, 157, 159, 175, 184, 185, 186, 186, 188, 188, 188, 203, 207, 215, 215, 241, 243 Somn 2:6, 26, 28, 44, 45, 51, 81, 116, 117, 139, 173, 220, 220, 248, 289, 291, 294 Abr 1, 2, 2, 28, 44, 46, 57, 61, 69, 69, 70, 71, 74, 75, 77, 78, 84, 88, 159, 159, 159, 162, 163, 164, 166, 207, 267, 272 Ios 29, 69, 147, 150, 150 Mos 1:41, 96, 112, 155, 157, 201, 207, 213, 272, 284, 317 Mos 2:14, 47, 48, 51, 53, 64, 88, 101, 108, 117, 120, 127, 133, 134, 135, 135, 135, 145, 191, 194, 209, 210, 238, 243, 263, 266, 266, 267 Decal 28, 31, 37, 38, 44, 51, 53, 58, 60, 66, 81, 90, 97, 99, 100, 101, 120, 133, 134, 155 Spec 1:13, 14, 15, 31, 34, 35, 41, 44, 49, 66, 76, 81, 84, 93, 96, 96, 97, 134, 163, 170, 210, 269, 294, 296, 300, 302, 331, 336 Spec 2:5, 45, 52, 58, 59, 62, 70, 130, 150, 151, 152, 156, 160, 160, 165, 198, 198, 210, 224, 225, 255 Spec 3:1, 1, 83, 152, 187, 187, 189, 190, 191, 202 Spec 4:118, 131, 187, 210, 237 Virt 21, 62, 73, 74, 212, 216, 220 Praem 1, 23, 34, 34, 37, 41, 41, 41, 76 Prob 81 Contempl 5, 66, 75, 80, 90 Aet 1, 1, 3, 3, 4, 4, 4, 6, 7, 8, 8, 8, 8, 9, 10, 11, 12, 14, 15, 17, 18, 19, 21, 21, 22, 24, 25, 25, 27, 32, 32, 34, 34, 37, 37, 39, 41, 47, 47, 49, 50, 50, 50, 51, 51, 51, 51, 52, 52, 52, 53, 53, 54, 54, 54, 55, 55, 55, 56, 69, 70, 70, 71, 72, 74, 75, 75, 75, 75, 75, 76, 78, 78, 80, 83, 84, 85, 87, 88, 89, 90, 93, 94, 94, 95, 99, 101, 102, 102, 106, 107, 107, 108, 109, 112, 113, 114, 114, 114, 116, 117, 124, 124, 129, 129, 130, 131, 132, 137, 142, 144, 145, 150 Flacc 92, 123, 148, 169, 169 Legat 115, 118, 151, 295, 309 Hypoth 7:12 Prov 1, 1, 2:2, 3, 6, 17, 39, 44, 45, 54, 58, 69 QG 1:1, 64a, 74, 2:13b, 31, 34a, 54a, 66, 3:38b, 4:8b, 33b, 51a QG isf 1, 10 QG (Par) 2:4 QE 2:46, 46

κοτέω Prob 125

κότινος Prob 113

κουρίδιος Congr 34 Virt 114, 222 Praem 139 QG 4:145

κοῦρος κόρος

κουροτροφέω Migr 31 Somn 2:9 Prob 115

κουροτρόφος Det 115

κοῦφος (73) Leg 1:42 Leg 2:2 Leg 3:13, 45, 70 Sacr 48, 54 Det 154 Post 11, 115, 148 Gig 22 Deus 28 Agr 91, 149 Plant 24, 24, 147 Ebr 125, 163, 186 Sobr 4 Conf 20, 21 Migr 144, 161 Her 46, 134, 135, 135, 146, 146, 198, 198, 208, 238, 238 Congr 121 Mut 238, 239, 247 Somn 1:128, 139 Somn 2:16, 150, 171 Abr 171 Ios 15, 25 Mos 1:137, 168, 171, 217, 232 Mos 2:197, 273 Decal 112 Spec 3:64 Virt 124 Praem 127, 136, 148 Prob 28 Aet 105, 115, 136 Flacc 5, 128, 162, 181 Legat 124 QG 4:51c, 51c

κουφότης Cher 63 Her 269 Legat 130

κόχλιας Sacr 95

κραδαίνω (7) Cher 59 Conf 87 Abr 202 Mos 2:128, 252 Praem 21 Aet 128

κράζω (13) Ebr 96, 98, 98 Fug 15, 84, 196 Mut 56 Somn 2:267 Ios 16 Virt 147 Flacc 144, 188 Prov 2:18

κραιπαλάω Post 176

κρᾶμα (12) Deus 81 Ebr 101, 191 Conf 186 Her 29 Mut 184 Somn 1:23, 145 Mos 2:152 Spec 1:66, 262 Legat 275

κράνιον ὑποκράνιον

κράνος Prob 78 Flacc 90 Legat 97

κρᾶσις (32) Cher 29 Det 8 Post 108 Deus 84 Plant 167 Ebr 189, 218 Conf 184, 184, 185, 186 Her 153, 183, 196, 199, 236 Congr 77 Mut 87 Somn 2:48 Ios 84 Mos 2:119, 256, 256 Decal 132 Spec 1:70, 105, 110 Virt 119, 225 Praem 144 Aet 31 QG 1:17b

κραταιός (54) Opif 63 Leg 3:46 Cher 2 Sacr 25 Det 118 Gig 10 Deus 28, 35 Agr 97, 114, 147 Plant 8, 24 Conf 19, 51, 87 Migr 150 Her 246 Somn 1:31, 103, 158, 241 Somn 2:204 Abr 223, 240 Ios 41 Mos 1:177, 235 Mos 2:182, 253 Decal 137 Spec 1:146, 307 Spec 2:60, 99 Spec 4:107, 115, 177 Virt 45, 155, 158 Praem 21, 25, 94, 95 Prob 40, 108, 160 Aet 22, 125, 137 Legat 82 QG (Par) 2:3, 2:3

κραταιότης Leg 3:115

κραταιόω (6) Agr 160 Conf 101, 103 Her 308 Congr 121 Prob 27

κρατερός Post 159

κρατέω (84) Opif 141 Leg 1:73, 100, 106, 106 Leg 2:29, 70, 70 Leg 3:17, 17, 92, 116, 117, 124, 146, 151, 223 Cher 75, 75, 75, 115 Post 42, 161 Deus 147 Agr 37, 63, 74, 93, 146, 150, 150, 156 Plant 11 Ebr 104, 105, 221 Her 269 Mut 100, 262 Somn 2:12, 151, 294 Abr 121, 151, 182, 188, 220, 243 Ios 190 Mos 1:101, 142, 217, 262, 332 Decal 9, 149 Spec 1:3, 24, 312, 343 Spec 2:36, 109, 190 Spec 3:193 Spec 4:26 Virt 33, 114 Praem 81 Prob 45, 47 Contempl 2 Aet 67, 72, 90, 136 Flacc 17, 21, 22, 59 Legat 48, 95, 233 Hypoth 7:10 QG (Par) 2:4

κρατήρ (7) Ebr 221 Her 182, 184, 185, 185 Somn 2:190, 248

κρατιστεύω Deus 45 Virt 11

κράτος (105) Opif 45, 56, 79, 160 Leg 2:83 Leg 3:18, 73, 156, 246 Cher 63, 74, 75, 113 Sacr 9, 56 Det 1, 114 Post 9, 28, 37, 129 Gig 47 Deus 26, 85, 116, 147 Agr 59, 60, 88, 143, 147 Plant 46, 58, 88 Ebr 111, 139 Sobr 57, 58 Conf 34, 39, 104, 133, 193 Migr 22, 26, 34 Her 7, 23, 24, 186 Mut 203, 217, 221 Somn 1:142, 162 Somn 2:90, 136, 141, 144, 266, 290 Abr 44, 170, 237, 242, 244 Ios 129, 135, 151 Mos 1:8, 96, 216, 243, 253, 307 Decal 42 Spec 1:223, 294, 307 Spec 3:2, 16, 24, 47, 111, 184 Spec 4:100, 104, 177 Virt 18, 47 Praem 39, 97, 118, 130 Contempl 69, 70 Aet 22 Flacc 147 Legat 141, 144 Hypoth 6:6 Prov 2:38 QG 3:30b, 4:76a QE 2:24b

κρατύνω Opif 124 QG 4:76b

κραυγή Leg 3:214 Her 14

κραυρόομαι Mos 2:254

κρεανομέω Legat 233

κρέας (26) Opif 66 Her 20 Somn 2:49 Mos 1:209 Mos 2:108 Spec 1:176, 185, 190, 220, 222, 223, 232, 245, 254, 268, 290 Spec 3:144 Spec 4:126 Virt 144, 144 Flacc 96 Legat 356, 361 QG 1:62:1, 62:2, 2:59

κρεμάννυμι (9) Post 24, 25, 26, 61 Her 269 Ios 156 Praem 151 Flacc 85 Prov 2:25

κρεουργέω Prob 89 Flacc 189

κρεοφαγέω Virt 136

κρεοφαγία Spec 1:147 Spec 4:129

κρημνοβατέω Prob 2 Prov 2:27

κρημνός Leg 1:73 Agr 76 Somn 2:161, 276

κρήνη Post 50 Mos 1:99

κρηπίς Congr 30 Somn 1:124 QG 1:66

Κρήτη Spec 3:43 Legat 282

κριθή (16) Sacr 109 Conf 185 Mut 190, 268 Somn 2:23 Ios 260 Mos 2:223 Spec 1:134, 248, 271 Spec 2:175 Spec 3:32, 57 Spec 4:29, 214 Aet 63

κρίθινος Spec 2:175 Spec 3:55, 57, 60

κριθοφόρος Mos 1:228 Virt 92

κρίμα Leg 3:197 Conf 128 Congr 86, 86

κρίνον Somn 2:62

κρίνω (98) Opif 120 Leg 1:99 Leg 2:16, 17, 94 Leg 3:20, 57, 71, 119, 123, 140, 209 Cher 11 Sacr 138 Det 68 Gig 37 Deus 5, 105, 106, 108, 113, 163 Ebr 87, 172, 172, 176, 193 Migr 113 Her 7, 71, 89, 89, 89, 90, 157, 272 Congr 5, 21, 21, 21, 27, 153, 176 Mut 91, 141 Somn 2:227 Ios 72 Mos 1:83, 251, 329 Mos 2:36, 217, 273 Spec 1:57, 121, 277, 316 Spec 2:76, 227 Spec 3:54, 87, 119 Spec 4:46, 57, 57, 61, 70, 71, 71, 169, 173, 189 Virt 2, 19, 62, 223 Praem 87, 112 Prob 11, 77, 108, 114 Contempl 34 Aet 40 Flacc 2, 158 Legat 3, 118, 218, 277, 286, 335, 360 QG 1:70:2, 3:3, 29, 4:211, 227

κριός (37) Opif 85, 116 Leg 3:129, 130, 130, 130 Post 165 Migr 67 Her 106, 125 Fug 132, 135 Somn 1:189, 197, 198, 199 Somn 2:19 Mos 1:277, 287 Mos 2:147, 148 Decal 76, 77 Spec 1:135, 165, 177, 178, 184, 188, 188, 189, 234, 238, 251, 251, 253 Spec 3:46

κρίσις (56) Opif 109 Leg 2:6, 96 Leg 3:12, 13, 116, 118, 119 Deus 74, 74 Agr 95 Plant 175 Ebr 170, 196 Migr 223 Her 162, 311 Congr 87, 163 Fug 118, 196, 196, 196 Mut 106, 106, 110, 194, 194 Somn 1:28 Somn 2:24, 175 Abr 222 Mos 1:146 Mos 2:228 Decal 59 Spec 1:245, 277 Spec 3:80, 121, 121 Spec 4:71, 71, 72, 76, 174, 177, 177, 190, 206 Virt 171 Praem 29 Legat 370 Prov 2:8 QE 2:10:1, 10a, 10b

κριτήριον (22) Opif 30, 62 Leg 3:198 Cher 36, 72 Sacr 34 Deus 28 Ebr 169 Conf 127 Migr 47, 49, 103, 224 Her 71, 246 Fug 134 Somn 1:118 Mos 2:237 Virt 56, 66 Prob 55 Prov 2:54

κριτής (27) Post 136 Migr 115, 138 Her 44, 109 Mut 39 Somn 1:9, 15 Somn 2:24, 85 Ios 9, 20, 95, 264 Mos 1:33, 35, 150 Mos 2:50, 279 Spec 1:308 Spec 3:72 Spec 4:62 Virt 54, 61 Prob 23 Legat 180 Prov 2:20

κριτικός Leg 1:13 Mut 110

Κριτόλαος Aet 55, 70

κριώδης Leg 3:131

Κροῖσος Ios 133 Prob 136, 153 Prov 2:7

κρόκη Sacr 83

κροκόδειλος (7) Decal 78, 78 Praem 90 Contempl 8 Legat 139, 166 Prov 2:65

κρόκος Prov 2:71

κρόμμυον Her 79, 80 Prob 153, 153

Κρονικός Legat 13

κροτέω Deus 24 Ios 16

κρότος Contempl 79

Κροτωνίατος Prov 2:7

κρουνηδόν Mos 1:99, 211 Flacc 190

κρουνός Sacr 66

κρουστικός Leg 3:130

κρούω Agr 80 Her 259, 266 Mut 139 Spec 4:49

κρυμός (14) Mut 246 Somn 1:102 Somn 2:52, 131 Spec 2:207 Virt 93 Praem 99 Contempl 24, 38 Aet 36, 67, 67 Flacc 36 Hypoth 11:6

κρυμώδης Spec 2:221

κρύος Congr 165 Somn 1:124 Decal 77

κρυπτός Cher 16

κρύπτω (43) Leg 2:27 Leg 3:1, 6, 16, 16, 18, 23, 23, 25, 27, 37, 38, 43, 54 Sacr 60, 61 Det 128, 150, 150, 153, 153, 156, 163 Post 57 Migr 196 Fug 7, 179 Mut 60 Somn 1:6, 76, 84, 84, 90, 99, 164, 224 Somn 2:203, 271 Abr 79 Mos 2:144 Spec 3:61 Spec 4:51 Virt 202

κρυσταλλόομαι Mos 2:253, 255

κρύσταλλος Somn 1:21 Mos 1:200

κρύφα Somn 1:91 Ios 208 Spec 3:94 Spec 4:2, 31

κρυφῇ Leg 3:20

κτάομαι (111) Leg 1:77 Leg 3:15, 135, 164, 167, 167, 193 Cher 10, 19, 29, 40, 114, 117, 119, 119, 124, 127 Sacr 2, 97 Post 95, 95, 114, 128 Deus 131 Agr 88, 125, 150, 150, 157, 166, 173, 181 Plant 68 Ebr 31, 39, 94, 126, 167, 210 Sobr 39 Conf 30 Migr 46, 54 Her 6, 33, 109, 110, 252, 274, 285 Congr 5, 48, 69 Mut 76, 80, 164, 183 Somn 1:250, 252 Somn 2:60, 295 Abr 34, 34, 37, 187, 204, 209, 211 Ios 37, 82, 144, 172 Mos 1:152, 157, 157, 159, 160, 307 Spec 1:271 Spec 2:19, 69, 80, 105, 123, 168 Spec 4:165, 212, 217 Virt 79, 98, 123, 166, 216 Praem 27, 59, 64, 64 Prob 38, 76, 104, 149 Contempl 19 Flacc 130, 130, 130, 148, 171 Legat 155, 343 Hypoth 11:4 QG isf 11

κτείνω (60) Leg 3:74 Det 49, 49, 51 Post 49, 172 Agr 171 Sobr 46 Conf 47, 160, 160 Fug 54, 76, 90 Mut 173 Somn 2:122 Abr 229 Ios 25 Mos 1:46, 311, 314, 314 Mos 2:172, 273, 274 Decal 132 Spec 1:160 Spec 2:254 Spec 3:17, 17, 18, 83, 85, 87, 91, 95, 103, 120, 123, 143, 144, 146, 150, 168 Spec 4:7, 10 Virt 43, 134, 138, 142 Prob 116, 118 Flacc 144, 185, 189 Legat 23, 30, 30, 61, 233

κτῆμα (120) Leg 1:67, 67, 77 Leg 2:79, 95 Leg 3:33, 56, 78, 78, 195, 209 Cher 48, 57, 64, 65, 66, 69, 71, 73, 83, 116, 117, 118, 118, 119, 123, 124, 124 Sacr 29, 43, 54, 71, 97, 97 Det 120, 136 Deus 47, 57, 120 Agr 156 Plant 41, 41, 48, 54, 56, 56, 63, 68, 68, 71, 71, 72, 74, 130 Ebr 20, 70, 107, 112 Migr 217 Her 14, 103, 107, 118, 127, 258 Fug 18, 26, 150 Mut 26, 76, 89, 119, 191 Somn 1:113, 252 Somn 2:35, 42, 90, 128, 223 Abr 204, 264 Mos 1:152, 254 Mos 2:11, 243 Decal 133, 138 Spec 1:157, 248, 271 Spec 2:107, 113, 113, 113, 116, 116, 123, 180 Spec 3:83 Spec 4:15, 22, 72, 217 Virt 90, 91, 91, 100, 154, 163 Prob 9, 12, 35, 158 Contempl 16 Aet 56 Flacc 158 Legat 232 Hypoth 7:3 QG 4:148

κτῆνος (37) Opif 40, 64 Leg 3:65, 107, 111 Cher 67, 67, 70, 70 Sacr 89, 104, 104 Det 170 Post 98 Deus 51, 145, 169 Agr 30, 31 Migr 152 Her 117, 118 Mut 235, 250

Somn 2:267 Mos 1:319 Spec 2:35, 35, 36, 69 Spec 3:46, 145, 146 Spec 4:203 Prob 32 Legat 252 QG 2:26a

κτηνοτροφέω Mos 1:51 Spec 1:136 Spec 2:109 Virt 144

κτηνοτροφία Agr 27, 55, 59

κτηνοτρόφος (14) Post 98, 98 Agr 27, 29, 29, 39, 48, 57, 66, 67, 124 Migr 212 Ios 257 Mos 1:320

κτηνώδης Leg 3:111 Cher 70 Migr 152 Somn 2:267

κτῆσις (90) Leg 1:104 Leg 2:17 Cher 52, 52, 65, 108, 109 Sacr 2, 40, 41, 57, 78 Det 27, 32, 60, 138, 157 Post 42, 94, 117 Gig 28 Deus 13 Agr 47, 119, 121, 121, 142, 149, 157, 172, 172 Plant 88 Ebr 6, 84, 94 Conf 161 Migr 11, 200 Her 95 Congr 24, 56, 79 Fug 97, 176 Mut 14, 32, 50, 73, 75, 236 Somn 1:124 Abr 24, 261 Ios 57 Mos 1:155, 156 Mos 2:24, 212 Decal 118 Spec 1:134, 137, 142, 145, 248, 283 Spec 2:85, 91, 105, 111, 118, 216, 222, 233 Spec 3:186 Spec 4:26, 124, 158 Virt 30, 85, 95, 198 Praem 105 Prob 80, 138, 156 Contempl 14, 70 Legat 11 Prov 2:12, 21

κτητός Cher 52 Migr 46 Mut 95

κτήτωρ Spec 2:108 Virt 98

κτίζω (14) Opif 17, 19, 24 Post 49 Ebr 105 Conf 122 Abr 122 Mos 2:49, 49, 64 Decal 97 Praem 66 Aet 139 Flacc 46

κτίσις Mos 2:51

κτίστης (7) Ebr 42 Somn 1:76, 93 Spec 1:30, 294 Virt 179 Flacc 46

κτύπος Fug 22 Abr 160 Decal 44 Praem 148 Prov 2:26

κύαθος Ebr 221 Somn 2:249

κυάνεος (κυανοῦς) Ebr 173 Aet 121

κυανοῦς κυάνεος

κυβερνάω (16) Opif 88, 119 Leg 3:80 Sacr 105 Det 53 Agr 69 Ebr 199 Mut 16 Abr 84 Ios 149 Decal 14, 155 Spec 4:154 Praem 34 Legat 49 QG 2:64c

κυβερνήτης (53) Opif 46, 88, 88, 88, 114 Leg 2:104 Leg 3:80, 118, 223, 224 Cher 36 Sacr 45, 51 Det 141 Post 142 Deus 129 Agr 69 Ebr 86 Conf 22, 98, 115 Migr 6, 67 Her 228, 301 Mut 149, 221 Somn 1:157 Somn 2:86, 201 Abr 70, 116, 272 Ios 33 Decal 53 Spec 1:121, 224 Spec 2:181 Spec 4:58, 95, 186 Virt 61, 186 Praem 33, 33, 51 Aet 83 Flacc 26, 27, 110 Legat 149 QG 2:34c, 4:76b

κυβερνητικός Fug 27 Spec 4:154 QG 4:76b

κύβος (16) Opif 92, 92, 93, 93, 94, 94, 94, 106, 106, 106, 106, 106 Decal 28 Spec 2:40, 212 QG 3:49a

κυέω (κύω) Leg 2:95 Cher 43 Mos 1:16 Spec 3:117 Prob 130

κύησις Cher 42 Mos 2:210 Virt 128

Κύθνος Flacc 156

κυΐσκω Mos 1:13 Spec 3:117

κυκάω (8) Conf 23, 69, 70 Mut 239 Somn 2:129, 225, 230 Legat 120

κύκλος (122) Opif 112, 122, 158 Leg 1:12, 66, 75, 86 Leg 3:25, 99, 169, 169 Cher 23, 24 Post 5, 50, 104, 104, 104, 173 Gig 8 Deus 176 Agr 11, 24 Plant 3, 40 Conf 27, 100 Migr 154, 217 Her 55, 147, 233 Congr 146 Fug 144, 176, 184, 184 Mut 74, 263 Somn 1:19, 20, 49, 134, 183, 233 Somn 2:6, 14, 44, 112, 113, 141, 170 Abr 119, 141 Ios 120, 150, 150, 159 Mos 1:91, 93, 114, 189, 200, 255 Mos 2:36, 51, 89, 124, 150, 224, 241, 260 Decal 44, 57, 127, 150 Spec 1:72, 156, 158, 177, 199, 205, 205, 205, 219 Spec 2:48, 97, 120, 142, 150, 177 Spec 3:4 Spec 4:85, 128, 220 Praem 18, 26, 38, 65, 102, 114, 157 Contempl 23, 53 Aet 109 Flacc 39, 62, 114, 162 Legat 48, 128, 151, 181, 217, 250, 269, 282, 364 Prov 2:51 QG 2:5a QG (Par) 2:5 QE 2:55a

κυκλοτερής Her 229 Contempl 51 QG (Par) 2:2

κυκλοφορητικός Her 283

κυκλοφορικός Somn 1:21

κυκλόω (9) Leg 1:63, 63, 66, 68, 85, 86 Mos 1:172 Aet 21 Flacc 113

Κύκλωψ Contempl 40 Prov 2:66

κύκνος Post 105

κύλιξ Somn 2:61 Spec 2:20 Contempl 45, 49

κυλίω Somn 2:161

κῦμα (7) Leg 3:172, 172 Agr 89 Plant 152 Somn 2:70 Mos 2:35, 253

κυμαίνω (9) Cher 38 Post 22, 178 Gig 51 Deus 26 Conf 32 Somn 2:239 QG 2:28, 39

κυματόω Somn 2:85, 121, 166

κυμάτωσις Opif 63 Mos 2:255 QE 2:55b

κύμβαλον Spec 2:193

κυνηγέσιον Ios 3 Mos 1:60 Spec 4:120

κυνηγετικός Abr 266

κυνηγέω Leg 3:2 Her 252

κυνηγός Spec 4:120

κυνίδιον Spec 4:91 Praem 89

κυνικός Plant 151 Prob 121

κυνόμυια Mos 1:130, 131, 133, 145

κυνώδης Somn 2:267

κυοφορέω (19) Opif 43 Leg 3:217 Sacr 102 Det 127 Post 74, 134, 176 Deus 137 Migr 140 Her 51 Congr 66, 129, 138 Fug 204, 211 Mut 151, 252 Virt 137 Praem 63

Κύπρος Legat 282

κύπτω Her 41 Mos 1:302

κυρεία Ios 71

κυριεύω (9) Leg 3:187, 220 Cher 74 Somn 2:7, 7, 95, 100, 100 Hypoth 7:5

κυριολογέω (10) Sacr 101 Det 58 Post 7, 168 Deus 71 Somn 2:245 Abr 120 Mos 1:75 QG 2:54a QE isf 3

κύριος (494) Opif 37, 67, 89, 90, 102, 135, 143, 147, 154 Leg 1:48, 53, 75, 88, 90, 95, 95, 95, 96, 96 Leg 2:1, 10, 47, 51, 52, 53, 71, 77, 78, 78, 88, 88, 94, 101, 106 Leg 3:1, 9, 11, 12, 42, 46, 49, 65, 71, 71, 73, 74, 77, 81, 86, 103, 107, 118, 126, 129, 169, 169, 180, 194, 194, 198, 198, 198, 203, 218, 219, 219 Cher 1, 14, 16, 18, 72, 73, 83, 83, 109, 119, 121, 122, 130 Sacr 30, 52, 55, 56, 64, 72, 87, 89, 89, 89, 102, 103, 104, 107, 108, 121 Det 22, 31, 57, 76, 83, 115, 121, 122, 123, 130, 131, 136, 138, 138, 139, 141, 177 Post 27, 67, 67, 70, 89, 95, 101, 122, 123, 132, 138, 177 Gig 19, 32, 40, 45 Deus 20, 53, 77, 82, 86, 86, 92, 104, 109, 110, 112, 139, 156 Agr 1, 44, 44, 50, 52, 78, 82, 94 Plant 39, 44, 47, 47, 47, 59, 61, 63, 73, 74, 85, 86, 89, 90, 95, 95, 95, 117, 134, 137 Ebr 19, 23, 41, 54, 67, 77, 84, 101, 114, 120, 127, 149, 152, 213 Sobr 10, 10, 17, 51, 53, 55, 55, 58 Conf 1, 1, 1, 1, 1, 24, 134, 144, 145, 150, 155, 169, 173, 173, 192, 196 Migr 1, 36, 56, 60, 60, 62, 79, 103, 127, 129, 131, 132, 139,

168, 183 Her 14, 14, 20, 22, 22, 22, 23, 23, 23, 30, 51, 55, 55, 76, 98, 113, 117, 120, 124, 162, 162, 166, 168, 170, 186, 188, 206, 231, 259, 262, 262, 277, 296, 313 Congr 1, 12, 13, 80, 86, 86, 86, 86, 95, 95, 97, 106, 111, 115, 128, 134, 139, 143, 145, 151, 154, 155, 156, 163, 163, 170, 177 Fug 1, 1, 1, 1, 1, 1, 1, 2, 5, 18, 56, 58, 59, 59, 59, 60, 119, 139, 139, 142, 169, 175, 177, 205, 207 Mut 1, 2, 11, 12, 13, 13, 13, 14, 14, 15, 15, 15, 17, 19, 19, 19, 19, 20, 20, 20, 21, 21, 21, 22, 23, 23, 23, 23, 24, 24, 27, 28, 42, 94, 115, 121, 131, 132, 137, 166, 232, 262, 265, 266, 270 Somn 1:3, 62, 70, 75, 85, 89, 89, 114, 133, 157, 159, 159, 159, 160, 163, 163, 166, 173, 183, 185, 194, 195, 230, 237, 252 Somn 2:29, 99, 100, 172, 175, 182, 226, 229, 230, 236, 242, 264, 265, 269 Abr 33, 121, 121, 124, 131, 131 Ios 7, 28, 36, 135, 145 Mos 1:88, 157 Mos 2:38, 38, 99, 101, 138, 168, 185, 191, 203, 206, 207 Decal 104, 141, 176 Spec 1:30, 147, 190, 193, 205, 216, 223, 300, 302, 307, 318, 321, 328 Spec 2:24, 52, 111, 116, 166 Spec 3:67, 82, 101, 137, 143, 145, 145, 209 Spec 4:5, 8, 13, 23, 38, 71, 188, 228, 237 Virt 4, 58, 184 Praem 111 Prob 31, 37, 40, 104 Aet 13 Flacc 39, 49, 59, 134, 147, 159 Legat 6, 10, 122, 129, 286, 356 Hypoth 7:3, 7:5, 7:5 Prov 2:20 QG 1:55a, 100:2b, 2:48, 59, 3:22, 22, 22, 22, 22, 22, 23 QE 2:16, 46, 47 QE isf 16

Κύριος QG 4:51a

κῦρος (10) Her 23, 23 Congr 151 Somn 2:29 Ios 28 Mos 2:272 Spec 1:30, 252 Prob 41 QE isf 16

κύω κυέω

κύω (6) Cher 45, 47 Virt 138 Aet 65, 98 QG 3:24

κύων (16) Post 161 Gig 35 Plant 151, 151 Somn 1:108 Somn 2:267 Abr 266, 266 Mos 1:130 Decal 79, 114, 115 Spec 4:121 Prob 90 Contempl 40 Legat 139

κῴδιον Leg 3:201 Cher 79

κώδων (8) Migr 103, 103 Mos 2:110, 119, 119, 120 Spec 1:93, 93

κωλυσιεργέω Leg 1:103 Post 79 Gig 31 Conf 163

κώλυσις Deus 103 Conf 171

κωλύω (62) Leg 2:19 Leg 3:66, 109, 117, 154, 186 Cher 2 Sacr 80, 85 Det 108, 134 Agr 151 Conf 19, 25, 158, 163 Migr 29, 69, 151 Fug 112, 202 Mut 217 Somn 1:62, 95, 194 Somn 2:133, 149 Abr 249 Mos 1:115, 249 Mos 2:232 Decal 137 Spec 1:102, 111, 119 Spec 2:65, 112 Spec 3:22, 26, 88, 202 Spec 4:205 Virt 21, 133, 156, 156 Prob 60, 60, 60, 60, 69 Aet 143 Flacc 4, 35, 56, 189 Legat 157, 315, 334 Hypoth 7:18 QG 4:191c QE 2:26

κωμάζω Agr 37 Mos 2:162

κωμαστικός Ebr 95

κωμή (11) Ebr 193 Conf 46 Migr 90 Ios 111 Mos 1:143 Spec 3:162 Spec 4:186 Praem 141 Contempl 23 Legat 225 Hypoth 11:1

κωμηδόν Prob 76

κωμικός Her 5, 5 Congr 61 Contempl 43

κῶμος Cher 92 Spec 2:193 Contempl 54 Legat 12

κωμῳδία Leg 2:75 Mos 1:3

κώπη Plant 152

κωφάω Ebr 155 Congr 65 Mut 138 Ios 49 Praem 78

κωφός (15) Leg 3:183 Post 161 Ebr 157 Conf 189 Fug 122, 123 Mut 143, 211 Somn 1:248 Mos 2:218 Spec 2:95 Spec 4:197 Praem 140 Flacc 20 Prov 2:20

κωφόω Det 175 Conf 9 Fug 14 Decal 39

κώφωσις Praem 143

Λ

λ QG (Par) 2:5, 2:5

Λάβαν (41) Leg 3:15, 16, 16, 18, 18, 19, 20, 22 Cher 67 Sacr 46, 47 Det 4, 4 Post 59, 76 Agr 42, 42 Ebr 47 Conf 74 Migr 28, 208, 213, 213 Her 43, 180 Fug 4, 7, 9, 23, 44, 44, 44, 47, 48, 49, 143 Somn 1:45, 46, 189, 225, 227

λαβή Cher 115 Conf 37 Somn 2:74

λάβρος Leg 2:26 Conf 23 Migr 101 Somn 2:13

λαβυρινθώδης Det 6

λαγνεία (13) Opif 79 Her 109 Somn 2:147 Abr 104, 133 Mos 1:295, 305 Mos 2:185 Decal 123 Spec 3:70 Spec 4:89 Legat 14 QG 2:12d

λάγνος (6) Somn 1:88 Ios 51 Decal 168 Spec 3:9, 34, 43

λαγχάνω (154) Opif 128, 143 Leg 1:1, 59, 71 Leg 2:84 Leg 3:99, 115 Cher 13, 21, 38, 51 Sacr 126, 127, 130 Det 54, 63, 66, 83, 134, 140 Post 62, 120, 145 Deus 45, 46, 47, 61, 106 Agr 65, 146, 171, 172 Plant 14, 17, 27, 58, 68 Ebr 33, 69 Sobr 4, 19, 54, 64 Conf 108, 122, 154, 177 Migr 46, 184 Her 137, 179, 241 Congr 22, 25, 37, 84, 99, 104, 108, 116 Fug 86, 87, 109 Mut 30, 30, 31, 84, 88, 105, 182, 222, 223, 267 Somn 1:29, 35, 43, 151, 169, 177 Somn 2:158, 189, 232, 256 Abr 17, 98, 100, 115, 219, 226 Ios 187 Mos 1:7, 129 Mos 2:17, 65, 120, 173 Decal 50, 64, 103, 164 Spec 1:94, 188, 201, 211, 224 Spec 2:21, 64, 86, 111, 113, 134, 140, 144, 154, 156, 157, 162, 169, 175, 179, 222, 233, 261 Spec 3:111, 123, 128, 166, 192 Spec 4:14, 55, 151, 153, 153, 154, 168 Virt 137, 199 Praem 63 Contempl 65 Aet 1, 13, 19, 32, 33, 86 Flacc 46 Legat 278, 307 Prov 2:16 QG 1:20, 51, 4:8b QE 2:55a

λαγωδάριον Post 161 Agr 115

λαγών Somn 2:126 Contempl 30

λαθραῖος Leg 3:17

λάθρῃ (13) Leg 3:23 Somn 1:27 Ios 47, 178, 217 Mos 1:90 Decal 137, 171 Spec 1:127 Spec 3:66, 87, 158 Spec 4:6

λαῖλαψ Mut 214 Somn 2:85

λαιμαργία (10) Opif 158 Agr 101 Plant 105 Ebr 222 Her 109 Somn 2:158, 205 Spec 1:150 Spec 2:50 Virt 136

λαίμαργος Somn 2:182

λαιμαργότης Somn 2:211

Λαΐος Spec 3:15

Λακεδαιμόνιος Mos 2:19, 19 Spec 3:22 Spec 4:102

Λακεδαίμων Prob 47

λάκκος (11) Deus 94, 96, 145, 155, 157, 158 Fug 175, 176, 197, 200, 201

Λακωνικός Prob 114 Contempl 69

λαλέω (60) Leg 3:101, 103, 232, 232 Det 126, 126, 127 Post 143, 143 Deus 65, 82, 83 Ebr 67, 127 Conf 81 Migr 47, 78, 78, 78, 127, 129, 129, 129 Her 17, 17, 17, 19, 19, 20, 25, 30, 66, 67, 113, 125, 166, 237, 302 Congr 86 Fug 53, 101, 101, 119, 143, 188, 211 Mut 20, 20, 20, 193, 194, 194, 201, 270 Somn 1:3, 70, 79, 143, 143 Mos 2:239

λάλος Her 10, 16 Mut 251 Legat 190 QE 2:118

λαμβάνω (665) Opif 54, 67, 76, 88, 101, 109, 134, 135, 137, 140, 141, 146, 150, 169 Leg 1:1, 31, 37, 50, 53, 55, 55, 62, 64, 65, 73, 88, 89, 89, 96 Leg 2:19, 20, 32, 35, 35, 35, 35, 44, 44, 45, 55, 65, 67, 91, 92, 92, 93, 95 Leg 3:23, 23, 24, 24, 26, 27, 27, 42, 46, 49, 50, 74, 81, 96, 98, 100, 102, 129, 130, 133, 134, 135, 135, 137, 163, 165, 166, 180, 183, 191, 191, 192, 192, 192, 192, 213, 223, 234, 239, 242, 242, 249, 252, 252 Cher 14, 31, 44, 47, 121, 122, 122, 122 Sacr 28, 31, 39, 59, 64, 76, 76, 85, 87, 87, 98, 118, 119, 137 Det 10, 12, 14, 19, 21, 23, 30, 86, 86, 90, 91, 95, 107, 127, 160, 168, 170 Post 10, 75, 75, 75, 76, 76, 76, 77, 77, 77, 78, 108, 110, 116, 145, 156, 157, 158, 163, 173, 178, 182 Gig 6, 11, 18, 20, 35 Deus 5, 12, 48, 49, 57, 57, 81, 158, 179 Agr 24, 70, 121, 126, 148, 148, 157, 158, 158, 160, 181 Plant 28, 42, 42, 63, 93, 101, 101, 136 Ebr 15, 15, 29, 39, 73, 75, 89, 100, 105, 106, 106, 107, 112, 114, 115, 119, 160, 167, 176, 179, 187, 198, 204, 212 Sobr 8, 15, 36, 37, 57 Conf 30, 50, 55, 55, 57, 74, 75, 98, 100, 114, 120, 148, 160 Migr 3, 5, 6, 101, 150, 164, 173, 185, 197, 219, 222 Her 20, 20, 34, 39, 39, 99, 102, 103, 104, 104, 105, 108, 110, 112, 113, 113, 114, 123, 123, 123, 124, 124, 124, 125, 125, 126, 129, 129, 134, 138, 170, 177, 182, 196, 198, 213, 274, 299, 302 Congr 38, 71, 72, 106, 111, 112, 113, 129, 130, 130, 131, 131, 132, 135, 138, 138, 156 Fug 21, 37, 48, 53, 70, 88, 99, 155 Mut 2, 16, 51, 52, 59, 65, 108, 126, 133, 142, 191, 215, 218, 224, 241, 258 Somn 1:4, 12, 68, 89, 95, 98, 100, 113, 120, 128, 143, 181, 187, 195, 205, 211 Somn 2:6, 50, 159, 172, 177, 183, 224, 258 Abr 1, 46, 60, 69, 73, 79, 91, 96, 113, 137, 162, 162, 164, 203, 215, 251 Ios 6, 13, 25, 35, 41, 156, 157, 159, 164, 178, 179, 193, 194, 227, 227, 228, 229, 231, 236, 242, 255, 260 Mos 1:18, 22, 31, 36, 46, 64, 72, 81, 86, 91, 101, 125, 127, 137, 139, 142, 144, 148, 157, 163, 187, 196, 210, 226, 236, 250, 291, 294, 316, 317, 320, 321, 328, 329 Mos 2:10, 31, 36, 88, 136, 138, 146, 150, 152, 178, 233, 236, 242, 249, 252 Decal 14, 16, 51, 60, 74, 82, 98, 117, 123, 123, 134, 142, 146, 150, 161 Spec 1:19, 21, 33, 34, 35, 43, 43, 61, 68, 79, 104, 105, 106, 120, 123, 127, 144, 145, 151, 152, 152, 152, 157, 191, 199, 204, 217, 222, 227, 240, 254, 268, 277, 277, 293, 295, 308, 329, 340 Spec 2:2, 16, 55, 83, 84, 97, 106, 114, 119, 121, 136, 138, 151, 170, 180, 182, 182, 183, 198, 203, 209, 213, 219, 231, 242 Spec 3:4, 14, 56, 58, 59, 81, 85, 107, 116, 124, 139, 146, 148, 150, 161, 189 Spec 4:18, 25, 26, 30, 31, 33, 34, 36, 37, 37, 62, 67, 67, 71, 71, 86, 98, 130, 138, 151, 177, 180, 197, 209, 212, 218, 223 Virt 29, 41, 56, 63, 67, 83, 84, 84, 89, 114, 122, 126, 128, 157, 162, 165, 166, 168, 169, 183, 214, 215, 218 Praem 1, 7, 13, 14, 22, 36, 47, 55, 65, 76, 105, 152 Prob 57, 82, 86, 103, 122 Contempl 13 Aet 14, 20, 25, 27, 28, 53, 58, 69, 72, 92, 93, 96, 100, 102, 118, 135 Flacc 8, 34, 35, 41, 45, 47, 55, 102, 103, 121, 133, 171 Legat 29, 31, 45, 46, 47, 64, 100, 132, 138, 143, 158, 158, 222, 232, 262, 276, 287, 331, 343, 367, 369 Hypoth 6:6, 7:15, 7:17, 11:10, 11:10, 11:12 Prov 2:4, 9, 21, 24, 40 QG 1:27, 51, 62:1, 62:2, 63, 96:1, 4:88, 131, 168, 206b, 228 QG (Par) 2:5 QE 1:1

Λάμεχ (13) Det 50 Post 40, 41, 46, 48, 74, 74, 75, 75, 79, 112, 124 QG 1:77

Λαμία Legat 351

λαμπαδεύω Her 37

λαμπάδιον (7) Opif 148 Ebr 212 Her 218, 218, 219, 220 Mos 2:103

λαμπάς Her 311, 312

λαμπρός (60) Opif 17, 30 Leg 1:18 Leg 2:10 Leg 3:35, 40, 171 Cher 99 Sacr 50 Det 20 Gig 38 Deus 36, 78, 174 Plant 40 Ebr 44, 75, 209 Conf 116 Her 222, 311 Congr 8, 54, 108, 159 Fug 47, 136 Mut 215 Somn 1:217, 226 Somn 2:42, 138, 174, 282 Abr 35, 234, 235, 252 Ios 21, 105 Mos 1:32, 123 Mos 2:44 Spec 1:140 Spec 2:68 Spec 3:25 Virt 191, 197, 202 Praem 150 Prob 101, 126 Flacc 4, 165 Legat 62, 137, 327 Prov 2:29, 31, 35

λαμπρότης (10) Det 136 Sobr 15 Her 157 Fug 44 Mut 93, 93 Somn 1:82 Ios 76 Praem 170 Prov 2:19

λάμπω Somn 2:93 Mos 1:3 Legat 191

Λάμπων Flacc 20, 126, 128, 135

λάμψις Leg 2:30 Decal 44

λανθάνω (72) Opif 9 Leg 1:59 Leg 3:6, 16, 211 Cher 19, 75, 98 Sacr 26, 28, 40, 135 Deus 9 Agr 165 Ebr 58, 174, 195 Conf 54, 120 Migr 224 Congr 174 Fug 20 Somn 1:91 Somn 2:163 Abr 22, 93, 107, 118 Ios 9, 47, 47, 166, 166, 213 Mos 1:9, 49, 280, 302 Mos 2:213 Decal 128 Spec 1:160, 278, 279, 325 Spec 3:29, 33, 149, 162 Spec 4:2, 5, 31, 36, 64, 79, 103, 188, 200, 200 Aet 47 Flacc 13, 28, 49, 109 Legat 40, 62, 128, 180, 337 Hypoth 7:4, 11:17 Prov 2:25, 26

λαός (λεώς) (90) Leg 2:77, 77, 77, 94 Leg 3:88, 88, 88, 90, 162, 163, 186, 225, 231, 231 Cher 32 Sacr 4, 5, 6, 6, 7, 87, 87 Post 89 Agr 41, 44, 78, 84, 88 Plant 59 Ebr 37, 67, 96, 98 Sobr 10, 10 Conf 27, 28, 58, 94 Migr 14, 47, 56, 58, 59, 62, 68, 81, 143 Her 20, 20, 20, 20, 20, 251, 251 Congr 55, 83, 163 Mut 125 Somn 1:71, 89, 89 Somn 2:270, 279 Ios 2 Mos 1:61, 87, 139, 278, 284, 290 Mos 2:165, 225, 271 Decal 45, 47 Spec 1:230 Spec 2:145 Virt 184, 185 Praem 123, 125 Prob 31 Contempl 86 Hypoth 6:1, 6:2, 6:3 QG 2:65, 4:153 QE 2:6a

λάρναξ Migr 16

λάσιος (6) Abr 138 Mos 1:228 Mos 2:58 Spec 1:75 Spec 2:207 Contempl 38

λατομέω Deus 94 Ebr 113 Fug 175

λατρεία (7) Sacr 84 Ebr 144 Decal 158 Spec 2:67, 167 Spec 3:201 QE isf 29

λατρεύω Migr 132 Spec 1:300 QE 2:105

Λατώ Aet 121

λάφυρα Congr 32

λαφυραγωγέω Cher 75

λαφύσσω Fug 28

λάχανον Somn 2:49 Spec 2:20 Prob 156

λαχανώδης Prov 2:70

λαχνόομαι Opif 104

λάχνωσις Opif 105

λαώδης Leg 2:77, 78

λεαίνω (14) Opif 159 Leg 1:98, 98 Post 158 Deus 43 Agr 16, 142 Mut 212 Somn 2:58 Spec 1:106, 217 Spec 3:198 Contempl 50 Aet 118

λέγω εἶπον φημί

λέγω (1518) Opif 5, 15, 17, 20, 34, 35, 40, 47, 49, 49, 50, 53, 55, 57, 59, 62, 66, 66, 69, 69, 72, 73, 77, 78, 79, 80, 82, 82, 83, 87, 90, 91, 93, 98, 100, 101, 102, 105, 106, 108, 118, 123, 126, 127, 128, 131, 131, 132, 132, 132, 133, 138, 142, 143, 144, 147, 147, 147, 150, 156, 158, 160, 163, 170, 170, 171, 172 Leg 1:2, 3, 7, 22, 33, 34, 35, 42, 48, 49, 50, 51, 56, 57, 59, 59, 59, 60, 62, 73, 77, 85, 86, 90, 91, 96, 102, 105, 105, 107 Leg 2:9, 10, 12, 16, 21, 21, 22, 36, 48, 51, 64, 66, 69, 78, 88, 100, 103 Leg 3:4, 4, 12, 21, 23, 23, 30, 37, 40, 42, 49, 52, 53, 54, 59, 61, 67, 74, 80, 85, 86, 91, 93, 93, 95, 101, 113, 121, 121, 129, 143, 144, 147, 160, 167, 167, 172, 174, 175, 177, 179, 179, 180, 181, 187, 188, 188, 188, 188, 192, 195, 195, 198, 198, 198, 203, 204, 204, 205, 210, 211, 215, 217, 218, 219, 225, 234, 237, 239, 243, 243, 244, 248, 252 Cher 4, 9, 9, 11, 16, 16, 16, 16, 18, 22, 25, 27, 32, 33, 35, 45, 46, 49, 52, 56, 58, 67, 67, 68, 70, 79, 83, 83, 91, 94, 101, 108, 121, 122 Sacr 5, 10, 25, 27, 34, 35, 38, 38, 44, 47, 57, 63, 65, 67, 69, 69, 74, 79, 82, 86, 91, 92, 93, 97, 111, 115, 128, 128, 136 Det 5, 5, 9, 10, 28, 34, 44, 51, 56, 58, 58, 59, 59, 66, 73, 78, 80, 81, 82, 84, 86, 94, 95, 100, 101, 102, 112, 121, 124, 129, 130, 131, 135, 138, 141, 150, 158, 159, 161, 162, 163, 163, 166, 166, 167, 174, 177 Post 16, 20, 27, 34, 36, 37, 41, 41, 41, 42, 51, 54, 61, 66, 69, 69, 76, 77, 80, 80, 81, 84, 86, 88, 96, 98, 100, 106, 113, 117, 121, 122, 123, 124, 127, 143, 147, 150, 151, 158, 163, 167, 175, 177, 179 Gig 5, 15, 16, 22, 23, 24, 35, 39, 39, 48, 55, 57, 66, 67 Deus 4, 6, 10, 38, 38, 52, 54, 54, 59, 82, 99, 109, 123, 131, 133, 138, 145, 145, 147, 148, 154, 169, 171, 179 Agr 12, 19, 20, 21, 26, 39, 43, 50, 52, 53, 54, 59, 64, 67, 68, 84, 94, 95, 96, 100, 107, 119, 121, 125, 129, 141, 143, 145, 149, 153, 161, 166, 175, 181, 181 Plant 8, 13, 19, 23, 26, 29, 32, 36, 39, 40, 44, 47, 48, 50, 52, 55, 57, 58, 59, 61, 70, 71, 71, 72, 73, 83, 86, 94, 113, 115, 125, 129, 130, 131, 135, 137, 140, 147, 150, 152, 154, 156, 160, 163, 167, 173, 174, 177 Ebr 3, 4, 6, 11, 17, 24, 28, 31, 40, 41, 43, 61, 67, 68, 72, 77, 80, 96, 96, 98, 101, 103, 104, 106, 114, 118, 121, 127, 131, 132, 138, 140, 146, 154, 158, 166, 198, 199, 201, 203, 208, 210, 211, 213 Sobr 1, 12, 18, 19, 32, 35, 48, 49, 50, 63, 68, 68 Conf 1, 3, 6, 9, 21, 23, 24, 26, 32, 36, 37, 37, 41, 42, 49, 52, 58, 58, 62, 64, 65, 67, 70, 72, 76, 80, 93, 105, 116, 117, 121, 123, 124, 129, 130, 139, 140, 141, 142, 151, 152, 154, 155, 158, 159, 167, 170, 170, 176, 179, 180, 182, 196 Migr 8, 13, 15, 17, 19, 35, 36, 40, 40, 42, 44, 47, 48, 53, 56, 65, 68, 69, 70, 72, 99, 106, 108, 110, 110, 111, 112, 114, 117, 118, 122, 126, 127, 132, 145, 152, 155, 160, 164, 169, 171, 172, 172, 173, 178, 182, 182, 183, 184, 197, 199, 201, 206, 208, 214, 216, 217, 221 Her 6, 10, 10, 12, 12, 13, 14, 14, 14, 16, 19, 19, 20, 22, 25, 27, 28, 50, 55, 58, 66, 71, 73, 76, 83, 90, 101, 107, 113, 117, 124, 131, 144, 144, 152, 159, 162, 174, 186, 191, 192, 196, 215, 217, 224, 233, 233, 243, 246, 246, 251, 251, 262, 266, 271, 272, 277, 293, 298, 300, 302, 307, 311, 312, 313 Congr 43, 53, 61, 65, 67, 68, 69, 69, 70, 70, 72, 73, 80, 80, 80, 86, 94, 98, 99, 100, 101, 106, 111, 115, 123, 133, 134, 139, 142, 143, 144, 146, 147, 150, 163, 166, 167, 172, 173, 178 Fug 18, 19, 23, 23, 26, 31, 33, 35, 48, 51, 51, 52, 53, 55, 59, 64, 65, 70, 71, 71, 72, 79, 80, 88, 89, 94, 95, 98, 101, 108, 110, 115, 116, 119, 127, 131, 132, 137, 149, 149, 153, 158, 159, 167, 168, 170, 174, 177, 181, 181, 186, 187, 192, 195, 197, 202, 205, 205, 209 Mut 8, 9, 11, 14, 15, 17, 18, 19, 19, 20, 20, 21, 27, 28, 31, 36, 37, 38, 38, 39, 42, 44, 54, 56, 60, 61, 62, 79, 83, 97, 99, 106, 111, 123, 134, 136, 141, 142, 143, 144, 145, 151, 152, 158, 164, 166, 166, 167, 173, 177, 182, 189, 189, 192, 194, 195, 196, 197, 202, 206, 208, 209, 210, 210, 210, 215, 227, 230, 238,

238, 241, 242, 243, 243, 247, 259, 259, 266, 269 Somn 1:1, 5, 12, 30, 34, 38, 47, 52, 61, 70, 77, 81, 85, 85, 87, 92, 93, 98, 102, 108, 121, 125, 130, 134, 135, 143, 145, 146, 148, 151, 159, 159, 160, 166, 166, 170, 172, 174, 175, 181, 181, 184, 193, 193, 194, 195, 212, 220, 223, 226, 227, 228, 229, 229, 230, 236, 237, 249, 252, 256 Somn 2:4, 8, 18, 23, 24, 29, 30, 32, 36, 38, 77, 78, 83, 85, 93, 94, 96, 115, 119, 129, 130, 134, 144, 177, 178, 180, 181, 191, 221, 223, 226, 227, 235, 243, 244, 248, 253, 257, 257, 260, 263, 263, 264, 269, 271, 272, 274, 275, 277, 280, 284, 288, 291, 296, 297 Abr 6, 10, 13, 17, 29, 46, 48, 54, 60, 61, 67, 72, 72, 77, 80, 83, 100, 101, 107, 110, 110, 114, 119, 126, 131, 147, 156, 166, 168, 174, 176, 184, 188, 200, 202, 203, 208, 217, 239, 240, 243, 255, 261, 262, 271, 271, 274 Ios 10, 16, 22, 32, 37, 37, 42, 48, 51, 58, 59, 60, 76, 81, 95, 107, 114, 125, 126, 126, 148, 151, 152, 157, 160, 170, 172, 179, 183, 189, 189, 199, 205, 217, 252, 253 Mos 1:4, 22, 23, 29, 29, 46, 51, 57, 58, 68, 74, 75, 82, 83, 88, 89, 90, 122, 125, 133, 139, 158, 173, 183, 206, 207, 240, 251, 266, 268, 274, 277, 281, 286, 294, 298, 300, 334 Mos 2:3, 7, 10, 11, 23, 25, 45, 46, 47, 50, 70, 70, 84, 87, 90, 95, 103, 114, 119, 121, 135, 152, 152, 168, 169, 170, 182, 186, 188, 188, 191, 191, 206, 215, 221, 224, 242, 257, 260, 265, 266 Decal 2, 4, 18, 20, 30, 32, 35, 36, 37, 46, 47, 57, 58, 88, 91, 95, 100, 101, 101, 114, 143, 159, 162, 164, 173, 173, 175, 176 Spec 1:7, 14, 15, 22, 25, 30, 31, 41, 46, 65, 65, 91, 93, 107, 116, 138, 168, 178, 186, 192, 193, 198, 200, 210, 212, 212, 214, 218, 224, 244, 248, 256, 263, 299, 301, 308, 317, 317, 318, 330, 335, 336, 336, 342 Spec 2:6, 9, 11, 19, 43, 52, 57, 82, 90, 132, 150, 153, 158, 159, 161, 177, 178, 181, 186, 210, 228, 256, 256, 262 Spec 3:18, 37, 37, 51, 55, 60, 66, 74, 78, 104, 117, 124, 126, 129, 133, 134, 149, 155, 158, 178, 180, 185, 187, 197 Spec 4:1, 13, 35, 39, 40, 43, 54, 72, 78, 83, 85, 87, 90, 90, 104, 110, 135, 142, 145, 148, 152, 174, 194, 202, 203, 204, 238 Virt 8, 17, 22, 22, 34, 34, 42, 50, 66, 69, 80, 81, 138, 148, 148, 170, 189, 216 Praem 2, 9, 23, 41, 47, 52, 55, 61, 67, 79, 81, 82, 85, 90, 97, 100, 117, 117, 118, 157, 167 Prob 4, 8, 17, 27, 54, 58, 59, 75, 79, 91, 104, 115, 124, 135, 144, 145, 153, 157, 158 Contempl 1, 10, 30, 54, 76, 77, 81 Aet 3, 4, 5, 5, 5, 9, 11, 12, 13, 14, 17, 32, 34, 51, 51, 54, 57, 73, 75, 77, 78, 84, 99, 102, 105, 106, 121, 121, 134, 137, 138, 145, 146, 146, 149 Flacc 2, 24, 24, 51, 51, 55, 76, 81, 121, 131, 137, 137, 144, 169, 182 Legat 6, 22, 30, 37, 59, 61, 78, 83, 109, 124, 125, 142, 149, 151, 154, 162, 189, 208, 218, 229, 243, 243, 258, 278, 280, 281, 286, 306, 307, 326, 332, 340, 355, 358, 361, 364, 365, 373 Hypoth 6:8, 6:9, 7:1, 7:2, 7:4, 7:15 Prov 1, 1, 2:1, 8, 33, 34, 42, 53, 55, 59, 72 QG 1:3, 21, 66, 96:1, 97, 100:1b, 2:13a, 17c, 22, 34a, 54a, 54a, 54a, 54c, 54d, 59, 59, 66, 3:29, 4:43, 67, 69, 74, 76b, 86a, 131, 145, 145, 153, 153, 169, 180, 206a, 206b, 228, 228 QG (Par) 2:3, 2:3, 2:6 QE 1:7a, 2:16, 16, 16, 16, 21, 45a QE isf 2, 8, 27, 29

λεηλατέω Leg 2:91 Plant 107 Conf 47 Flacc 171

λεία (17) Cher 75 Agr 168 Abr 229, 234 Mos 1:141, 243, 253, 259, 312, 313, 315, 316, 317 Spec 4:223 Flacc 56 Legat 122, 232

Λεία (34) Leg 1:80 Leg 2:47, 47, 59, 94 Leg 3:20, 146, 180, 180, 181, 181 Cher 41, 46 Det 3 Post 62, 135, 135, 135 Plant 134 Sobr 12 Migr 95, 99, 145 Her 51, 175 Congr 25, 26, 31, 32, 123 Fug 73 Mut 132, 254 Somn 1:37

λείβω Mos 2:264

λειμών Abr 138

λεῖος (17) Leg 2:59 Post 79 Agr 142 Migr 50, 153, 153 Her 294 Congr 28, 31, 159 Somn 1:17 Somn 2:86 Abr 148, 239 Mos 1:84 Spec 1:219 Spec 2:202

λειότης Opif 62 Leg 2:59 Plant 133 Ebr 185 Spec 1:219

λείπω (21) Cher 23 Gig 65 Deus 34 Ebr 143 Conf 7 Somn 1:113 Ios 103 Mos 1:322 Mos 2:260 Decal 104, 178 Spec 1:54, 296 Spec 2:137, 230 Contempl 11 Flacc 124 Legat 32, 280 Prov 2:10, 27

λειτουργέω (10) Det 63, 66, 66 Ebr 2 Her 84 Fug 93 Mos 2:152 Spec 1:82, 113, 242

λειτουργία (24) Sacr 132 Det 63 Post 185 Her 8 Congr 98 Fug 93 Somn 1:214 Somn 2:34, 71 Mos 2:67, 75, 138, 145, 153 Spec 1:82, 98, 117, 123, 255 Spec 2:222 Virt 54 Prob 6 Contempl 82 Legat 296

λειτουργός (11) Leg 3:135 Post 184 Somn 2:186, 231 Mos 2:94, 149, 276 Spec 1:152, 249 Spec 4:191 Virt 74

λειχήν Spec 1:80

λείψανον (13) Agr 10, 36 Migr 122 Congr 102 Somn 2:212 Ios 27, 109 Mos 1:175 Spec 1:127 Spec 3:115 Aet 91 Legat 63, 131

λέξις (18) Leg 1:65 Leg 2:31 Det 95 Deus 141, 142 Agr 16, 136 Plant 113 Her 102 Fug 38 Abr 217 Mos 2:38 Spec 2:51 Contempl 78, 88, 88 QE isf 8, 8

λεοντῆ λεοντέη

λεοντέη (λεοντῆ) Legat 79

Λέπιδος Flacc 151, 181

λεπίζω Plant 110

λεπίς Spec 4:110

λέπισμα Plant 110

λέπρα (18) Leg 1:49 Det 16 Post 47, 47 Deus 123, 127, 127, 129, 131, 131, 131 Plant 111 Sobr 49, 49 Somn 1:202 Spec 1:80, 118, 118

λεπρός Leg 3:7, 8 Deus 123, 127 QG 2:12c

λεπτόγεως Leg 1:34 Somn 1:17 Mos 1:224

λεπτολογία Leg 3:147

λεπτομερής Cher 115 Her 134, 134

λεπτός (26) Leg 3:57, 169, 170 Sacr 83 Post 158, 164 Agr 134, 142 Her 217 Somn 2:53, 216, 217, 218 Abr 139 Ios 102, 108 Mos 2:90, 111 Spec 1:211 Spec 2:20 Praem 131, 146 Contempl 23 Aet 102, 125 Prov 2:29

λεπτότης Migr 52 Prov 2:66

λεπτουργία Leg 3:181

λεπτύνω Somn 1:144 Aet 110

Λευί (17) Leg 1:81 Leg 2:51, 52 Sacr 119, 120, 120 Det 67 Plant 63 Ebr 67 Migr 224 Congr 131, 131 Fug 73, 74 Mut 200, 200 Somn 2:34

Λευίτης (29) Sacr 118, 118, 118, 119, 127, 128, 128, 129, 129, 130, 132, 133 Det 62, 63, 126, 132, 132, 135 Plant 64 Ebr 94 Her 124, 124, 124 Fug 37, 88, 88 Mut 191 Somn 2:273 Mos 1:316

Λευιτικός (10) Leg 2:105 Plant 26 Her 251 Congr 98, 132 Fug 87, 90, 93 Mut 2 Mos 2:170

λευκαίνω Leg 2:43

Λευκανός Λυκανός

λευκασμός Agr 42

λευκόπυρος Mut 235 Somn 2:74

λευκός (22) Leg 2:7, 39, 43 Leg 3:57, 58, 61, 169, 171 Deus 130 Plant 110, 110, 172, 172 Ebr 186 Her 209 Fug 44, 138 Abr 10 Mos 1:79, 200 Aet 104 Legat 364

λευκόω Plant 111

λευχειμονέω Cher 95 Contempl 66 Legat 12

λευχείμων Decal 45

Λέχαιον Flacc 155

λέων (20) Deus 117, 117 Somn 1:108 Somn 2:87 Abr 266 Mos 1:109, 284, 291, 291 Decal 78, 78, 113 Praem 89 Prob 40, 40, 40, 101 Contempl 8 Legat 139 Prov 2:57

λεώς λαός

λεωφόρος (34) Opif 69, 144 Leg 3:253 Det 2 Post 31, 102, 154 Deus 61, 143, 165, 182 Agr 101 Conf 19 Her 70 Congr 28 Fug 203 Abr 7, 269 Ios 142 Mos 1:177 Mos 2:138 Decal 50 Spec 1:335 Spec 2:202 Spec 3:185 Spec 4:62, 155, 167 Virt 51 Prob 2 Contempl 86 Aet 119 Legat 216 QE 2:13a

λήγω (23) Opif 67, 68 Cher 30, 90 Sacr 40 Post 151 Plant 93 Her 130, 189, 190, 235 Congr 109 Somn 2:198 Mos 1:115, 115, 134 Spec 2:220 Spec 4:208 Praem 1 Prob 69 Aet 9, 109 Flacc 156

λήθη (43) Leg 3:91, 92, 93, 93, 94 Cher 69 Sacr 54, 55, 58 Det 65 Deus 43 Agr 132 Ebr 137 Sobr 5, 28, 28, 29 Migr 16, 205, 206, 206 Congr 39, 40, 41, 42 Mut 99, 100, 100, 102, 174 Mos 1:197 Decal 62 Spec 1:28, 98, 99, 215, 223 Spec 4:70, 82 Virt 176 Praem 162 Flacc 134 Legat 82

λῆμα Ebr 94

λῆμμα (7) Gig 39 Deus 170 Plant 105 Mut 126 Spec 1:280 Virt 10 Contempl 66

ληνός Spec 1:134 Hypoth 7:6

λῆξις (14) Sacr 66 Det 63 Post 92 Plant 63 Congr 89 Mos 1:155, 328, 331 Mos 2:234 Spec 2:111, 113, 126 Aet 31 Flacc 25

ληπτός Sacr 37 Deus 52 Migr 220 Somn 1:8

ληραίνω Leg 2:60 Leg 3:155

ληρέω (13) Leg 2:29 Plant 142, 143, 144, 174 Ebr 4, 5, 6, 11, 126, 154 Congr 62 QG 2:68b

λῆρος Post 165 Agr 152

ληρώδης Legat 168

λῃστεία Decal 136 Prob 37 Flacc 5

λῃστής (7) Spec 1:301, 323 Prob 121 Contempl 24 Legat 122, 146 QG 4:228

λίαν (51) Leg 1:34 Det 143 Deus 167 Agr 3, 28, 47 Ebr 89, 193 Sobr 25 Conf 17, 43, 142 Migr 58, 135 Her 22, 81, 159 Fug 156, 209 Mut 214 Somn 1:13, 28, 60, 60, 98, 102, 222 Somn 2:3, 138 Abr 134 Ios 66, 213, 213 Mos 1:67, 83, 161 Mos 2:13, 222 Spec 1:139, 270 Spec 2:8, 240 Spec 3:157 Spec 4:16 Praem 135 Prob 63, 150 Legat 224 Prov 2:32 QG 1:69 QE 2:11b

λίβανος Her 196, 198 Mut 234 Somn 2:71

λιβανωτός (8) Ebr 87 Her 197, 197, 226 Somn 2:74 Spec 1:175, 275 Spec 3:56

λιβάς (8) Deus 155, 178 Migr 157 Her 226 Congr 150 Somn 2:204 Mos 1:99 Praem 131

Λιβύη (6) Deus 174 Somn 2:54 Aet 141 Flacc 43, 45, 152

Λιβυκός Legat 283

λιγαίνω Sacr 29

λίθινος Mos 2:202

λιθοβολέω Ebr 14

λιθοκόλλητος Somn 2:57 Contempl 49 Prov 2:17

λίθος (81) Opif 18, 141, 142 Leg 1:63, 66, 67, 79, 79, 81, 81, 81, 82, 82, 83, 84 Leg 2:22, 22, 71 Leg 3:160 Cher 80, 100, 104, 126, 126 Sacr 21 Det 16, 33 Gig 44 Deus 8, 35 Ebr 157 Conf 1, 102, 107 Her 176 Fug 122, 144, 185 Mut 211 Somn 1:4, 120, 125, 126, 250 Somn 2:54, 56, 250 Abr 139, 173 Mos 2:72, 112, 112, 122, 122, 123, 124, 126, 133, 202, 218 Decal 66, 133 Spec 1:71, 86, 87, 94, 274, 275 Spec 2:255 Spec 3:92, 105 Virt 219 Praem 58 Prob 66 Contempl 7 Aet 75, 125 Legat 178, 237, 364 Prov 2:17

λιθοτομέω Post 50

λιθοτόμος Contempl 7

λιθόω Leg 3:213 Ebr 164

λιθώδης (10) Ebr 211 Somn 1:17 Mos 1:192 Mos 2:254 Spec 2:169 Spec 3:34 Contempl 62 Aet 119, 129 Prov 2:33

λικμάω Ios 112

λιμαγχονέω Leg 3:174 Congr 170

λιμήν (33) Opif 17, 63, 131 Cher 38 Sacr 90 Agr 69, 174 Her 305 Congr 113 Fug 50 Somn 1:42 Somn 2:143, 225 Abr 47 Ios 139 Mos 1:194 Decal 14, 67 Spec 1:335 Spec 3:87 Spec 4:154, 201 Flacc 27, 92, 92, 110, 160, 166, 185 Legat 15, 129, 151, 297

λιμηρός Her 297 Somn 2:129

λιμνάζω (9) Opif 113 Deus 177 Fug 179 Abr 92 Ios 109 Mos 1:6, 116 Mos 2:195 Flacc 63

λίμνη (11) Plant 24 Mos 1:99, 103 Spec 3:32 Praem 41 Contempl 22, 23, 23 Aet 147, 147, 148

λιμνώδης Her 32

λιμοδοξέω Spec 2:18 Flacc 116

λιμοδοξία Deus 115

λιμός (69) Opif 167 Leg 3:175, 179 Det 19, 34, 113, 116 Agr 38 Ebr 79, 148 Migr 204 Her 287, 288, 289 Congr 171, 172, 173 Somn 1:124 Somn 2:125, 150 Abr 1, 91, 245 Ios 108, 110, 114, 115, 156, 159, 186, 190, 205, 250, 259, 261, 267, 270 Mos 1:5, 34, 110, 125, 195, 216, 240, 265 Mos 2:16 Decal 16 Spec 2:187, 201, 247 Spec 3:203 Spec 4:211 Virt 86 Praem 127, 138 Prob 8 Flacc 62 Legat 17, 124, 128, 274 Hypoth 6:2, 6:3 Prov 2:11, 23, 41 QG 4:169 QG (Par) 2:7, 2:7

λιμώσσω Det 106 Ebr 222 Ios 249 Mos 1:191 QG (Par) 2:7

λίνεος Ebr 86 Mut 43 Somn 1:216 Mos 2:143 Spec 1:83

λίνον Post 116 Agr 24 Spec 1:160 Spec 4:207

λίπα Spec 3:37

λιπαίνω (8) Post 121 Congr 160 Ios 109 Mos 1:118 Spec 4:74 Praem 161 Contempl 36 QE 2:15b

λιπαρέω Mos 1:58 Spec 2:209

λιπαρής (9) Cher 48 Sacr 28 Post 156 Somn 2:149 Abr 107 Ios 261 Mos 1:49 Spec 3:68 QG 4:202a

λιπαροπλόκαμος Aet 121

λιπαρός Migr 101 Hypoth 11:13 QG 4:79a

λιπάω Congr 159 Somn 2:74

λιποθυμία Somn 1:51

λίπος Mos 2:146

λιποστράτιον Mos 1:327

λιποτακτέω Gig 43 Ebr 145 Aet 37, 65

λιποτάκτης Cher 32 Det 142 Deus 34 Decal 178

λιποτάξιον Conf 174 Mos 1:327

λιτή (12) Somn 2:299 Abr 6, 51 Mos 1:72, 105, 273 Mos 2:166 Spec 1:97, 195 Spec 2:196, 203 Flacc 124

λιφαιμία Aet 128

λίχνος (11) Leg 3:109, 143, 221 Sacr 32 Plant 127 Ebr 159 Migr 143, 216 Somn 1:49 Somn 2:50 Spec 4:91

λίψ Somn 1:3, 175

λοβός (7) Sacr 136 Spec 1:212, 213, 216, 232, 233, 239

λογάς Somn 2:56 Spec 1:274

λογεῖον (9) Mos 2:112, 113, 125, 127, 128, 130, 133 Spec 1:88, 88

λογιατρεία Congr 53

λογίζομαι (67) Leg 1:32 Leg 2:26, 61 Leg 3:18, 82, 99, 227 Cher 73 Sacr 2, 49 Det 84, 86, 127 Post 7 Gig 65 Deus 56, 130, 163 Agr 5, 156, 168 Ebr 128 Conf 180 Migr 72, 186 Her 44, 94 Congr 42 Fug 15 Mut 177 Somn 1:158 Somn 2:30, 116, 169, 219 Abr 152 Ios 139, 191, 210 Mos 2:34, 266 Spec 1:3, 128, 138, 279, 311, 334 Spec 2:52, 54, 139, 189 Spec 3:92, 128, 194 Spec 4:103, 182, 194 Virt 83, 137 Prob 23 Legat 85, 184, 318, 348 Hypoth 6:9 QG 1:21, 2:34a

λογικός (172) Opif 77, 119, 137, 144, 149, 150, 153 Leg 1:10, 10, 41, 57, 70, 70, 70, 71, 71, 72, 72 Leg 2:2, 22, 23, 23, 45, 58, 75, 97 Leg 3:24, 89, 108, 210, 210, 210 Cher 39, 111 Sacr 46, 47, 75 Det 22, 38, 82, 82, 82, 83, 83, 91, 138, 139 Post 31, 66, 68, 160 Gig 41 Deus 16, 35 Agr 14, 15, 56, 63, 63, 139 Plant 18, 37, 41, 41, 46, 135 Ebr 69, 100, 202 Sobr 18 Conf 9, 111, 176, 176, 179 Migr 3, 47, 47, 67, 68, 78, 118, 169, 185, 213 Her 132, 132, 138, 138, 155, 167, 185, 209, 232, 233, 248 Congr 11, 17, 26, 26, 29, 33, 88, 121 Fug 69, 72, 90, 91, 177, 198 Mut 74, 75, 119, 213 Somn 1:106, 115, 161, 176, 179, 215, 255 Somn 2:15, 271 Abr 5, 9, 32, 54 Mos 1:84, 162 Decal 33, 84 Spec 1:66, 171, 201, 201, 277, 333, 333, 336 Spec 2:202 Spec 3:83, 103 Spec 4:114, 123 Virt 8, 13, 144, 148, 160, 168 Praem 2, 10, 59 Prob 80 Contempl 9, 78 Aet 68, 72, 73, 94, 130 Prov 2:6, 63 QG 1:31, 76b, 2:59, 59, 59, 62, 62 QG isf 10 QG (Par) 2:3

λόγιον (107) Leg 3:118, 119, 119, 126, 132 Det 48, 67 Post 28, 28 Gig 49, 63 Deus 50 Agr 127, 127 Sobr 50 Conf 62, 81, 166 Migr 27, 85, 166, 168, 196 Her 2, 8, 113, 117, 203 Congr 134 Fug 60, 144, 157, 185 Mut 13, 34, 37, 173, 202 Somn 1:64, 164, 166, 231 Somn 2:231 Abr 62, 85, 88, 142, 169, 170, 189 Ios 95 Mos 1:57, 85, 236, 294, 294 Mos 2:56, 74, 97, 143, 176, 179, 188, 229, 230, 246, 253, 262, 263, 263, 275, 281, 289 Decal 16, 36, 41, 48, 50, 52, 175 Spec 1:315 Spec 2:146, 188, 251 Spec 3:7 Spec 4:50, 78, 132, 133 Virt 53, 63, 68, 80, 153, 184, 215 Praem 1, 78, 101, 158 Contempl 25 Legat 110, 210, 347 QG 1:72, 2:13a, 4:173

λόγιος (10) Cher 116 Post 53, 162 Mut 220 Mos 1:2, 23 Virt 174 Legat 142, 237, 310

λογιότης Mos 1:83

λογισμός (248) Opif 24, 67, 139, 165 Leg 1:42, 43, 70, 73, 79, 103, 104 Leg 2:57, 63, 98 Leg 3:9, 11, 13, 16, 17, 89, 110, 117, 125, 202, 226, 226, 228, 228, 229, 229, 229, 230, 232, 239 Cher 69, 69, 71, 73 Sacr 1, 43, 71, 105 Det 85, 121, 141, 141, 170 Post 34, 137, 168, 175, 184 Gig 64 Deus 3, 50, 72, 85, 179 Agr 29, 67, 67, 78, 108 Plant 166 Ebr 28, 55, 73, 87, 94, 128, 139, 151, 166 Sobr 48 Conf 25, 45, 55, 86, 95, 177, 188 Migr 100, 144, 206 Her 57, 68, 118, 191, 201, 234, 263, 265 Congr 59, 63, 81, 84, 98, 107, 109, 155 Fug 32, 72, 92, 121, 190 Mut 21, 81, 111, 144, 157, 185, 223, 223 Somn 1:122, 180, 192, 205 Somn 2:9, 90, 151, 184, 239, 249, 272, 276 Abr 88, 100, 101, 102, 175, 256 Ios 53, 60, 75, 140, 142, 201, 236 Mos 1:26, 48, 150, 283, 299 Mos 2:6, 13, 40, 185, 187, 214 Decal 40, 177 Spec 1:20, 37, 66, 160, 173, 201, 249, 259, 283, 288, 293, 344 Spec 2:9, 42, 89, 142, 202, 228, 231 Spec 3:69, 91, 92, 99, 156, 179, 189, 194 Spec 4:10, 49, 94, 95, 163, 220 Virt 3, 24, 32, 69, 113, 113, 151, 188, 213 Praem 26, 28, 29, 30, 40, 43, 43, 59, 69 Prob 27, 55, 140, 143 Contempl 31, 40, 89 Aet 26 Flacc 4, 18, 101, 133, 166 Legat 2, 45, 76, 94, 171, 182, 196, 211, 213, 217, 221, 261, 262, 277, 320, 372 Hypoth 6:5 Prov 2:6, 9, 19, 66, 67 QG 1:24, 93, 2:11, 12c, 16, 34a, 59, 4:74, 208 QE 2:40, 47

λογιστής Spec 3:141

λογιστικός Leg 3:115, 115, 116 QG 4:179

λογογράφος Opif 4 Plant 159 Spec 4:230 Contempl 1

λογοθήρας Congr 53 Mos 2:212 Prob 80

λογοποιέω Mos 1:193

λογοπώλης Congr 53

λόγος (1413) Opif 4, 9, 15, 20, 24, 25, 31, 36, 43, 48, 48, 52, 56, 67, 69, 73, 73, 84, 90, 93, 93, 94, 95, 96, 96, 96, 99, 100, 100, 103, 106, 107, 108, 108, 109, 117, 119, 139, 139, 143, 146, 153, 158, 165 Leg 1:15, 16, 19, 19, 21, 22, 35, 39, 46, 65, 74, 74, 74, 76, 83, 85, 93, 103, 104 Leg 2:16, 22, 24, 24, 27, 29, 46, 63, 63, 64, 65, 79, 81, 86, 86, 93, 98, 99, 105 Leg 3:1, 8, 11, 14, 17, 18, 18, 26, 32, 36, 41, 43, 44, 45, 45, 45, 45, 54, 76, 80, 82, 96, 100, 103, 104, 106, 106, 110, 116, 116, 116, 118, 118, 119, 119, 120, 120, 122, 122, 123, 123, 124, 124, 124, 127, 128, 128, 128, 129, 132, 134, 136, 137, 139, 140, 140, 144, 148, 150, 150, 153, 154, 155, 155, 156, 156, 157, 158, 158, 158, 159, 162, 162, 168, 169, 170, 170, 171, 171, 172, 173, 173, 175, 175, 175, 176, 176, 176, 177, 177, 177, 177, 177, 178, 179, 188, 188, 199, 202, 204, 204, 207, 208, 214, 217, 218, 222, 232, 232, 236, 242, 251, 252 Cher 3, 7, 9, 17, 27, 27, 27, 28, 28, 30, 32, 35, 36, 39, 41, 53, 76, 113, 116, 120, 124, 127, 128 Sacr 8, 23, 26, 28, 34, 46, 46, 47, 47, 51, 51, 55, 59, 60, 62, 65, 65, 66, 66, 66, 66, 67, 73, 74, 76, 78, 80, 80, 80, 81, 82, 82, 83, 83, 85, 86, 87, 90, 93, 95, 97, 98, 112, 119, 122, 126, 129, 130, 131 Det 4, 5, 8, 11, 13, 13, 16, 25, 28, 33, 35, 35, 35, 37, 38, 39, 40, 40, 40, 41, 42, 43, 43, 43, 43, 51, 52, 52, 54, 64, 66, 66, 68, 72, 72, 74, 74, 79, 82, 83, 88, 92, 93, 102, 103, 104, 109, 110, 118, 125, 126, 127, 129, 129, 130, 131, 132, 132, 133, 133, 146, 149, 155, 159, 167, 168, 171, 175 Post 7, 14, 18, 24, 32, 32, 36, 52, 53, 53, 55, 55, 55, 57, 68, 69, 71, 78, 85, 86, 87, 87, 87, 88, 89, 91, 91, 100, 100, 101, 102, 103, 107, 108, 108, 110, 111, 111, 119, 122, 127, 129, 129, 136, 142, 143, 153, 159, 163, 164, 167, 181, 182 Gig 5, 7, 17, 17, 25, 34, 39, 48, 52, 52, 57, 67 Deus 1, 7, 11, 20, 50, 57, 59, 71, 77, 83, 90, 90, 105, 111, 120, 126, 129, 134, 138, 141, 142, 146, 147, 152, 153, 154,

167, 168, 176, 179, 180, 182 Agr 12, 14, 16, 18, 22, 40, 51, 61, 88, 107, 125, 128, 130, 131, 133, 136, 157, 179 Plant 8, 10, 12, 14, 17, 18, 20, 29, 52, 54, 55, 60, 61, 62, 65, 70, 75, 78, 80, 83, 94, 100, 112, 114, 115, 117, 120, 121, 121, 125, 127, 128, 131, 149, 156, 157, 158, 162, 165, 172, 173, 175, 176, 177, 177, 177 Ebr 8, 29, 33, 33, 34, 48, 54, 59, 65, 68, 70, 71, 71, 77, 80, 80, 81, 82, 95, 95, 104, 115, 142, 143, 156, 157, 174, 206, 213, 224 Sobr 1, 9, 9, 22, 24, 33, 38, 46, 47, 51, 58, 62, 65, 68 Conf 9, 11, 14, 21, 27, 28, 29, 33, 34, 35, 36, 37, 39, 40, 41, 43, 44, 52, 53, 57, 59, 59, 59, 81, 97, 98, 101, 102, 102, 114, 115, 121, 129, 131, 132, 141, 146, 146, 147, 147, 159, 162, 168, 174, 181, 184, 190, 191, 194, 198 Migr 2, 2, 3, 3, 3, 4, 4, 4, 6, 7, 12, 17, 23, 24, 28, 40, 47, 48, 49, 51, 52, 54, 60, 66, 67, 70, 71, 71, 72, 73, 74, 75, 76, 77, 78, 78, 79, 79, 80, 80, 80, 81, 81, 81, 82, 83, 84, 85, 85, 90, 95, 102, 102, 105, 122, 128, 128, 129, 130, 130, 130, 130, 130, 137, 143, 148, 151, 169, 171, 173, 174, 176, 178, 189, 192, 195, 199, 201, 202, 202, 214, 219 Her 4, 14, 16, 26, 56, 69, 71, 73, 77, 79, 85, 95, 106, 107, 108, 108, 109, 110, 118, 119, 119, 125, 129, 130, 131, 132, 133, 140, 143, 154, 160, 168, 179, 185, 188, 191, 199, 201, 205, 207, 214, 215, 219, 221, 225, 230, 233, 234, 234, 235, 259, 280, 282, 283, 297, 302, 302, 303, 304, 308 Congr 4, 12, 15, 17, 18, 22, 23, 23, 40, 53, 61, 63, 64, 67, 69, 70, 70, 70, 78, 85, 89, 99, 100, 100, 108, 109, 113, 120, 140, 141, 148, 149, 150, 157, 170, 174, 178, 178, 180 Fug 5, 7, 12, 12, 13, 25, 56, 67, 76, 90, 92, 92, 94, 95, 97, 101, 101, 103, 108, 110, 112, 117, 135, 137, 144, 147, 150, 150, 152, 154, 154, 158, 166, 168, 183, 191, 196, 200, 209, 211 Mut 2, 13, 15, 18, 23, 53, 56, 56, 57, 60, 69, 69, 74, 76, 87, 89, 94, 101, 101, 108, 113, 114, 116, 118, 124, 138, 141, 169, 172, 184, 190, 191, 191, 195, 199, 206, 208, 208, 210, 215, 215, 220, 228, 229, 236, 237, 240, 243, 244, 245, 245, 247, 247, 248, 248, 250, 251, 270 Somn 1:10, 23, 25, 25, 29, 33, 36, 39, 49, 53, 58, 59, 62, 65, 65, 66, 68, 69, 70, 70, 71, 72, 75, 75, 77, 77, 79, 81, 85, 86, 102, 103, 103, 104, 105, 107, 108, 108, 109, 109, 110, 110, 110, 112, 113, 115, 116, 117, 117, 118, 118, 119, 119, 124, 127, 127, 128, 128, 141, 142, 147, 147, 148, 157, 164, 172, 175, 181, 182, 185, 190, 191, 197, 198, 198, 199, 200, 206, 208, 210, 214, 215, 226, 226, 229, 230, 233, 234, 235, 239, 241, 245, 251, 254 Somn 2:23, 39, 45, 56, 63, 67, 70, 90, 95, 97, 121, 124, 134, 135, 137, 138, 139, 154, 170, 180, 185, 186, 198, 223, 237, 238, 240, 242, 243, 245, 245, 247, 249, 259, 259, 259, 260, 260, 262, 272, 275, 278, 278, 280, 281, 283, 290, 302, 302 Abr 5, 29, 37, 41, 47, 52, 54, 61, 71, 83, 94, 101, 102, 103, 158, 159, 160, 196, 199, 206, 214, 223, 243, 244, 256, 264, 273, 276 Ios 5, 25, 29, 31, 40, 64, 73, 78, 85, 86, 86, 132, 174, 198, 214, 230, 230, 259, 266, 267, 268, 269 Mos 1:18, 23, 26, 26, 29, 29, 29, 40, 48, 84, 95, 95, 114, 151, 173, 189, 195, 233, 242, 256, 274, 274, 280, 283, 285, 317 Mos 2:1, 16, 17, 33, 48, 48, 49, 52, 59, 66, 88, 105, 115, 117, 122, 124, 125, 127, 128, 128, 129, 130, 130, 140, 140, 150, 150, 177, 184, 192, 193, 195, 208, 212, 212, 255, 280 Decal 13, 20, 21, 22, 23, 32, 47, 56, 64, 77, 84, 86, 92, 97, 98, 132, 134, 140, 150, 154, 176 Spec 1:1, 37, 39, 72, 81, 88, 90, 121, 137, 138, 144, 146, 147, 172, 178, 180, 182, 187, 189, 191, 200, 205, 209, 209, 211, 211, 215, 216, 219, 224, 257, 258, 260, 265, 273, 291, 321, 331, 335, 337, 342, 343, 343 Spec 2:2, 6, 7, 13, 23, 29, 30, 30, 31, 31, 52, 52, 57, 61, 62, 63, 80, 150, 163, 163, 173, 188, 200, 200, 209, 214, 223, 224, 226, 227, 243, 256 Spec 3:1, 13, 111, 121, 121, 132, 134, 140, 169, 207 Spec 4:14, 32, 59, 60, 68, 69, 75, 81, 92, 92, 116, 130, 134, 134, 140, 148, 156, 179 Virt 13, 40, 56, 85, 108, 127, 152, 162, 183, 183, 184, 190, 193, 196, 196, 206, 217 Praem 52, 55, 62, 77, 80, 81, 83, 107, 111, 119, 122, 155, 163 Prob 1, 2, 2, 3, 13, 16, 20, 25, 38, 43, 46, 47, 48, 54, 57, 62, 62, 68, 74, 84, 91, 93, 95, 96, 96, 96, 97, 99, 99, 111, 127, 132, 155, 155 Contempl 31, 39, 57, 74, 75, 87 Aet 1, 11, 20, 39, 44, 47, 49, 68, 70, 75, 83, 85, 86, 93, 102, 103, 113, 124, 130, 140, 142, 143, 145 Flacc 11, 19, 40, 54, 102, 105, 108, 185 Legat 6, 8, 28, 34, 39, 44, 55, 63, 67, 84, 112, 162, 250, 295, 323, 327 Hypoth 0:1, 6:2, 6:4, 7:3, 7:5, 7:20, 11:15 Prov 2:1, 7, 33, 50, 60, 61, 62, 70 QG 1:32, 2:34a, 34b, 41, 54a, 62, 62, 62, 62, 3:26, 48, 4:174, 180, 180, 228 QG isf 3 QG (Par) 2:2, 2:4, 2:5, 2:5 QE 2:3b, 16, 18, 20, 44, 107 QE isf 1, 11, 14, 18, 26, 26

λογοφίλης Leg 1:74 QE isf 7

λογχοφόρος Flacc 38

λοιδορέω Spec 3:172, 174 Virt 136 Hypoth 6:2

λοιδορία Agr 110 Somn 2:168 Decal 75 Flacc 33

λοιμικός (6) Gig 10 Abr 179 Mos 1:133, 265 Prov 2:23, 23

λοιμός (7) Ebr 79 Somn 2:125 Mos 1:110 Mos 2:16 Aet 126 Prov 2:41, 53

λοιμώδης (7) Conf 22 Somn 2:129 Abr 136 Mos 1:39, 133, 236 Prov 2:55

λοιπός (40) Opif 110, 110 Leg 1:85 Leg 3:130, 163 Post 7 Ebr 192 Migr 67 Her 33, 47, 121 Fug 106 Somn 1:135 Somn 2:23, 29 Ios 41, 167 Mos 1:130, 298 Mos 2:78, 85, 86, 101, 178 Spec 3:7, 162 Spec 4:116, 238 Praem 33 Aet 46, 130 Flacc 16, 87, 156 Legat 242, 346 Hypoth 0:1 Prov 2:72 QG 1:66 QG (Par) 2:7

λοξός Prob 155

λουτήρ Migr 98, 98 Mos 2:136, 138, 146

λουτρόν (14) Cher 95 Det 19 Plant 116, 162 Fug 153 Mut 124 Mos 1:14 Mos 2:148 Decal 45 Spec 1:191, 258, 261 Spec 3:63 Legat 235

λουτροφόρος Contempl 7

λούω (10) Leg 2:16 Leg 3:143 Deus 8 Somn 1:81 Mos 2:143 Spec 1:119, 261 Contempl 50 Legat 235 Prov 2:24

λόφος Mos 1:169, 282 Prov 2:33

λοχαγός Agr 87 Mos 1:317 Spec 1:121 Virt 32 Prob 139

λοχάω Leg 2:98 Fug 24 Somn 1:32 Abr 263 Ios 36

λοχίζω Agr 87

λόχος Ebr 198 Migr 144 Mos 1:331 Legat 129

Λυαῖος Legat 96

Λυγκεύς Prov 2:7 QG 2:72

Λυδία Ios 133

Λυκανός (Λευκανός) Aet 12

λύκος Decal 79 Praem 87 Legat 139

Λυκοῦργος Prob 47, 114

λυμαίνομαι (17) Cher 9 Sacr 29 Deus 136, 142 Ebr 157 Migr 164 Mut 203 Somn 2:214 Mos 1:108 Spec 4:62, 226 Prob 79 Contempl 61 Legat 134, 198, 312 Prov 2:65

λυμαντικός Praem 131

λυμεών Spec 1:143 Flacc 144 Legat 89, 92, 191

λύμη (12) Cher 96 Ios 154 Mos 1:119 Spec 1:206 Spec 3:11, 51 Spec 4:21, 184 Virt 18, 149 Legat 108 Prov 2:43

λυπέω (20) Leg 3:216, 217, 219, 250 Ebr 179 Somn 2:266 Abr 22 Ios 23, 262 Decal 63 Spec 1:314 Spec 2:72 Spec 3:142, 193 Virt 103, 140, 208 Praem 127 Aet 26 Legat 299

λύπη (80) Opif 79, 167 Leg 2:8 Leg 3:80, 113, 200, 200, 211, 211, 211, 216, 247, 250 Det 46, 99, 110, 119, 119, 119, 121, 122, 124, 140 Deus 71, 98 Conf 90 Migr 60, 219 Her 3, 270 Congr 81, 172 Mut 72, 163, 163, 163, 163, 168, 262 Somn 1:110 Somn 2:162, 165, 191 Abr 151, 196, 205, 207, 236, 238, 256 Ios 79, 89, 214 Mos 1:247 Mos 2:139, 225 Decal 144 Spec 2:30, 48, 106, 157 Virt 88, 116, 200 Praem 71, 71, 170 Prob 18, 21, 56, 159 Contempl 2 Flacc 118 Legat 15, 89, 187 Prov 2:8 QG 1:63, 72, 76a

λυπηρός (7) Leg 3:250 Det 121 Post 56 Fug 22 Mut 167 Mos 1:248 Spec 2:55

λυπρόγεως Ios 30 Spec 1:246 Spec 2:169

λυπρός (9) Opif 80 Ebr 211 Her 204 Mos 1:224 Virt 49 Prob 8 Aet 122 Flacc 151 Prov 2:66

λύρα (13) Opif 126 Leg 1:14 Cher 110 Sacr 18, 74 Post 88, 105, 108, 142 Deus 24 Plant 167 Ebr 116 Spec 2:246

Λυσίμαχος Prob 127, 129

λύσις (7) Deus 122 Agr 164 Her 273 Mos 2:107 Spec 1:193, 251 Spec 2:24

λυσιτελέω Legat 36, 369

λυσιτελής (53) Opif 10 Leg 3:19 Det 68 Post 181 Deus 19 Agr 41, 77, 85, 88, 122 Plant 107 Ebr 22 Sobr 3 Conf 6, 12, 164, 195 Migr 86 Her 244 Congr 18, 45, 158, 176 Fug 150, 207 Mut 119, 242 Somn 1:132, 233, 235 Somn 2:88 Ios 55, 259 Mos 1:306 Spec 1:56, 120, 270 Spec 2:18, 184, 239, 256 Spec 3:50 Spec 4:221 Praem 7 Flacc 4, 43 Legat 49, 99, 109, 242 QG 3:20b QE 2:13a, 17

λύσσα (14) Opif 83 Cher 32 Det 45 Agr 37 Conf 21 Her 249 Somn 1:122 Decal 63 Spec 2:94 Spec 4:218 Virt 1 Flacc 140 Legat 93, 132

λυσσάω (18) Sacr 32 Det 176 Mut 172 Somn 1:36 Somn 2:165, 279 Abr 32 Ios 40 Mos 1:26, 43 Decal 89 Spec 2:9 Spec 3:43, 69 Praem 19 Prob 90 Contempl 40 Flacc 66

λυτήριος Somn 1:173 Abr 179

λυτικός QE 2:64

λυτός Aet 13

λύτρον (20) Sacr 117, 118, 118, 121, 121, 126, 128 Conf 93 Her 44, 124, 124, 186 Ios 193 Spec 1:77, 135 Spec 2:95, 122 Spec 3:145, 150 Flacc 60

λυτρόω (6) Sacr 89, 114, 114 Spec 2:116, 116, 121

λυτρωτός Sacr 127, 127

λυχνία (17) Her 216, 218, 219, 221, 225, 226, 226, 227, 227 Congr 8 Mos 2:94, 102, 102, 103, 105, 146 Spec 1:296

λύχνος (11) Gig 33 Her 218, 218, 219, 220, 221, 222 Mos 2:103 Spec 1:296, 298 Aet 91

λυχνοῦχος Her 89

λύω (44) Leg 3:60, 189 Det 103, 158 Post 71 Deus 114 Agr 36 Plant 4, 4 Ebr 61, 101, 152 Sobr 39 Conf 43, 131, 136 Migr 3, 3, 90, 91 Her 68, 125 Somn 1:181 Somn 2:58 Ios 180 Mos 2:16, 61 Spec 2:6 Spec 3:27, 35, 46 Contempl 63 Aet 13, 13, 79, 137 Legat 72, 72, 72, 119, 324, 324, 339, 340

λωβάομαι Leg 2:97 Plant 164 Abr 44 Virt 31 Contempl 55

λώβη (11) Cher 96 Agr 130 Plant 164 Her 284 Somn 1:105, 226 Somn 2:64 Spec 1:80, 166, 254, 260

λωποδυτέω Somn 1:98 Spec 4:121

λωποδύτης Somn 1:98 Ios 84 Spec 4:87

Λώτ (14) Leg 3:213 Post 175, 177 Ebr 164 Migr 13, 148, 148, 149, 175 Fug 121 Somn 1:85, 247 QG 4:30, 51a

λωφάω (12) Deus 65 Conf 105 Mut 49 Somn 1:122 Ios 17, 87 Mos 1:42, 120 Mos 2:63 Legat 18 Prov 2:39 QG 2:28

M

μ QG 2:29

μά Leg 2:68 Mos 1:55 Spec 2:4

μαγγανεία Sacr 26

μαγειρεῖον Ios 53

μάγειρος (9) Det 26 Ebr 215 Conf 95 Migr 19 Mut 173 Ios 61, 62 Prob 31, 89

μαγικός Mos 1:277 Spec 3:100

Μάγιος Flacc 74

μαγνῆτις Opif 141 Praem 58

μάγος Mos 1:92, 276 Spec 3:93, 100 Prob 74

Μαδιάμ (6) Leg 3:12, 13 Agr 43 Conf 55 Mut 106, 110

Μαδιανῖτις Leg 3:242

Μαδιηναῖοι Virt 34

μᾶζα Somn 2:48

μαζός (μαστός) Aet 66

μάθημα (36) Leg 3:244 Sacr 79, 116 Post 152 Plant 73 Sobr 9 Conf 142 Fug 8, 210 Mut 211 Somn 1:52, 54 Somn 2:114, 170 Abr 48, 271 Mos 1:111, 146 Mos 2:55 Decal 29, 37, 102 Spec 1:41, 332 Spec 2:66, 142, 165, 177 Spec 4:137 Virt 168, 212 Praem 58 Legat 170, 210 QG 2:74 QE 2:18

μαθηματικός Opif 128 Cher 4 Mut 71 Mos 1:24 Spec 2:140

μάθησις (36) Sacr 7 Det 143 Post 91 Ebr 25, 82, 159 Migr 39 Her 67 Fug 14, 52, 187 Mut 99, 100, 101, 101, 210, 256 Somn 1:9, 167, 169, 170 Somn 2:33 Abr 54 Ios 1, 183 Mos 1:21 Spec 1:106 Spec 4:106, 107, 206 Virt 133 Praem 9, 65 Flacc 25 Legat 31 QG 2:54a

μαθητής (13) Sacr 7, 64, 79 Det 66, 134 Post 132, 136, 146 Agr 55 Mut 270, 270 Spec 2:227 Spec 4:140

μαθητρίς Deus 5

Μαθουσάλα Post 40, 41, 44, 73, 74

μαῖα (9) Leg 3:2, 243 Det 127 Migr 214, 215 Her 128 Fug 168, 168 Aet 67

μαιευτικός Migr 142 Her 247 Congr 3

Μαιήλ Post 69, 73

Μαικήνας Legat 351

μαιμάζω Ebr 222

μαιμάω Agr 36

μαινάς Plant 148

μαινόλης Plant 148

μαίνομαι (20) Leg 3:210 Cher 32, 69 Det 12 Agr 84 Plant 101 Ebr 13 Mut 39 Somn 2:83 Mos 1:26, 161 Spec 3:69, 126 Praem 94 Flacc 6, 6, 36, 40, 162 Legat 233

μαίομαι Conf 4

μάκαρ Aet 121

μακαρίζω Migr 95 Praem 152 Prov 2:29

μακάριος (41) Opif 135, 146, 172 Leg 1:4 Cher 86 Sacr 40, 95, 101 Deus 26, 108 Conf 164 Migr 95 Her 111, 285 Somn 1:50 Somn 2:35, 130, 230 Abr 87, 115 Decal 4, 104 Spec 1:329 Spec 2:53, 141, 230 Spec 3:1, 178 Spec 4:48, 115, 123 Praem 35, 63, 122 Prob 157 Contempl 6, 13 Legat 5, 5 QG 2:54a, 3:38b

μακαριότης (15) Leg 3:205 Sacr 27 Det 86 Deus 55, 161 Plant 35 Somn 1:94 Abr 115, 202 Mos 2:184 Spec 1:209 Virt 205 Prob 96 Legat 5 QG 2:54a

μακαρισμός Somn 2:35

Μακεδονία Gig 7 Deus 173 Plant 12 Legat 281

Μακεδών (6) Cher 63 Deus 173, 174 Ios 135 Prob 94, 115

μακραίων (10) Opif 156 Post 12, 185 Congr 57 Somn 1:34 Spec 1:31, 345 Spec 2:262 Spec 4:169 Aet 75

μακρηγορέω (16) Cher 89 Post 162 Plant 176 Ebr 180, 195 Fug 181 Somn 2:63, 169 Mos 2:33 Decal 151 Spec 2:40, 144 Spec 4:78 Praem 52 Prob 33 Aet 127

μακρηγορία Somn 2:127

μακρήγορος Sacr 32

μακρόβιος (8) Sobr 17 Her 292 Fug 106 Ios 24 Mos 1:213 Spec 4:238 Praem 135 Aet 71

μακρόθεν (13) Post 17 Somn 1:64, 65, 66 Somn 2:142 Ios 12, 111 Spec 3:48 Spec 4:104, 218 Virt 129, 137, 151

μακρολογέω Plant 153

μακρολογία Congr 73

μακρός (208) Opif 85, 103, 121, 131, 136, 141, 141, 148, 168 Leg 1:14, 82 Leg 2:54, 55 Leg 3:54 Cher 116 Sacr 64, 76 Det 106, 130, 160 Post 17, 18, 20, 38, 53, 68, 71, 98, 109, 116, 141, 141, 152, 162 Gig 38, 56 Deus 30, 134 Agr 27, 67, 103, 123, 155, 161, 174 Plant 22, 99, 129 Ebr 100, 104, 150, 155, 176, 195, 208 Conf 16, 140, 141, 157 Migr 102, 111, 138 Her 179, 270 Congr 89, 153, 157 Fug 30, 74, 98, 103, 107, 160, 169 Mut 62, 116, 265 Somn 1:10, 46, 66, 67, 119, 131, 184, 256 Somn 2:13, 51, 143, 180, 198, 246 Abr 37, 67, 70, 111, 171, 182, 190, 195, 197, 208, 213, 224, 253, 254, 266 Ios 87, 89, 94, 117, 118, 137, 169, 236, 238, 256, 261 Mos 1:21, 47, 71, 79, 98, 115, 123, 164, 194, 209, 216, 237, 250, 255, 278 Mos 2:35, 63, 223, 232, 247, 263, 275 Decal 11, 14, 34, 147, 148 Spec 1:59, 121, 224 Spec 2:38, 40, 109, 119, 207, 256 Spec 3:10, 35, 35, 91, 92, 98, 185 Spec 4:59, 81, 82, 130 Virt 3, 56, 96, 183, 193 Praem 11, 21, 80, 84 Prob 68, 68 Contempl 16 Aet 8, 19, 89, 123, 133, 133, 146 Flacc 6, 26, 27, 102, 108, 114, 139, 159 Legat 22, 35, 120, 172, 179, 251, 255, 257, 342 Hypoth 6:6 Prov 2:26, 57 QG 2:64b, 3:11b, 11c QE 2:26 QE isf 10

μακρότης Fug 58

μακροχρόνιος Her 34 Spec 2:261 Spec 4:161, 169

Μάκρων (16) Flacc 11, 12, 13, 14, 22 Legat 32, 38, 39, 39, 57, 58, 60, 62, 69, 69, 75

μάλα (733) Opif 7, 12, 18, 45, 62, 63, 73, 77, 86, 122, 125, 125, 127, 131, 137, 138, 141, 149, 150, 154, 162, 163, 167, 172 Leg 1:5, 8, 14, 39, 51, 59, 100 Leg 2:3, 4, 6, 70, 92 Leg 3:74, 80, 84, 94, 100, 182, 185, 189 Cher 9, 11, 24, 28, 41, 54, 55, 65, 66, 66, 82, 86, 96, 107, 115, 115, 119, 121, 122 Sacr 35, 47, 67, 72, 74, 82, 99, 125, 125 Det 7, 10, 14, 28, 34, 35, 54, 69, 73, 93, 97, 101, 109, 114, 143, 143, 144, 145, 146, 155, 175, 175 Post 9, 13, 38, 62, 144, 160, 167 Gig 3, 7, 10, 25, 32, 47, 51 Deus 48, 95, 113, 114, 115, 127, 166 Agr 61, 85, 85, 88, 90, 95, 100, 111, 141, 149, 151 Plant 24, 57, 62, 117, 128, 152, 157, 161, 163, 171, 175 Ebr 2, 13, 25, 36, 37, 54, 73, 79, 90, 94, 95, 121, 132, 138, 164, 168, 174, 184, 193, 200, 204, 211, 220 Sobr 3, 3,

13, 55 Conf 5, 12, 12, 15, 32, 59, 83, 126, 170, 178 Migr 12, 25, 46, 47, 74, 75, 112, 112, 117, 120, 169, 185, 189, 195, 210 Her 5, 21, 21, 22, 31, 84, 88, 111, 148, 151, 191, 203, 238, 261, 274, 291, 292, 294 Congr 48, 49, 62, 66, 127, 135, 136, 145, 167, 179 Fug 22, 25, 81, 87, 96, 122, 128, 160, 167, 171, 203, 205 Mut 18, 25, 47, 60, 68, 70, 88, 140, 145, 160, 173, 188, 189, 199, 215, 243, 260 Somn 1:34, 54, 60, 60, 66, 72, 75, 95, 99, 100, 101, 111, 132, 136, 169, 170, 203, 246, 254 Somn 2:4, 22, 48, 60, 60, 71, 112, 154, 154, 154, 160, 174, 176, 188, 202, 245, 255, 262, 283, 301 Abr 13, 54, 63, 69, 71, 107, 110, 116, 123, 130, 133, 137, 149, 170, 172, 187, 192, 209, 213, 229, 230, 233, 236, 253, 256, 267, 273 Ios 4, 7, 20, 31, 39, 53, 66, 77, 89, 99, 101, 102, 113, 119, 127, 145, 149, 186, 193, 220, 223, 233, 236, 254, 262, 267, 269 Mos 1:4, 5, 7, 13, 14, 19, 22, 24, 30, 41, 44, 46, 52, 69, 69, 69, 78, 83, 91, 108, 110, 112, 120, 128, 131, 139, 159, 160, 176, 183, 184, 187, 198, 213, 215, 226, 231, 239, 251, 264, 291, 296, 297, 307, 310, 334 Mos 2:8, 10, 17, 21, 38, 39, 40, 51, 66, 96, 108, 138, 144, 182, 189, 191, 213, 219, 222, 264, 270, 273, 274, 282, 289 Decal 37, 40, 45, 46, 52, 92, 105, 118, 147, 149 Spec 1:2, 21, 23, 25, 34, 73, 79, 136, 140, 146, 151, 165, 173, 178, 200, 214, 227, 229, 259, 281, 303, 324, 337, 341 Spec 2:3, 9, 13, 19, 53, 65, 83, 89, 96, 105, 112, 126, 136, 140, 161, 164, 175, 185, 195, 202, 227, 229, 235, 244, 256, 258 Spec 3:10, 21, 30, 37, 68, 70, 98, 100, 111, 113, 119, 126, 128, 136, 147, 164, 177, 180 Spec 4:24, 27, 28, 29, 42, 54, 55, 67, 68, 82, 84, 95, 109, 112, 112, 120, 123, 126, 129, 139, 154, 188, 192, 197, 205, 207, 215 Virt 20, 24, 26, 34, 36, 38, 44, 59, 78, 83, 105, 115, 117, 119, 124, 126, 128, 138, 155, 161, 165, 167, 187, 197, 213 Praem 9, 40, 49, 110, 114, 120, 127, 129, 132, 146, 149, 158, 163, 167 Prob 3, 15, 22, 27, 40, 54, 75, 80, 86, 95, 96, 101, 102, 106, 106, 113, 122, 138, 153, 160 Contempl 7, 21, 48, 50, 56, 61, 68, 75, 88, 89 Aet 16, 23, 26, 38, 48, 65, 77, 88, 99, 103, 105, 107, 119, 129, 130, 130, 137, 144 Flacc 11, 12, 17, 18, 31, 32, 40, 58, 82, 86, 105, 110, 118, 119, 128, 131, 148, 162, 175, 182, 186 Legat 3, 15, 21, 22, 35, 39, 48, 50, 58, 62, 64, 72, 80, 84, 108, 111, 114, 127, 132, 140, 142, 150, 156, 158, 160, 163, 168, 175, 192, 199, 200, 209, 251, 252, 257, 259, 264, 268, 272, 277, 280, 285, 299, 302, 307, 320, 325, 330, 335, 349, 355, 360, 367 Hypoth 6:1, 6:2, 6:4, 6:4, 6:5, 7:5, 7:10, 7:14, 7:16, 7:17, 11:13, 11:14, 11:18 Prov 1, 2:5, 23, 42, 56, 60, 62, 65, 71 QG 1:17b, 60:2, 60:2, 64a, 65, 69, 2:16, 34a, 54a, 54a, 54b, 64c, 3:18, 26, 4:88, 169, 172, 191b, 193, 7* QG isf 8 QG (Par) 2:2 QE 2:2, 18, 21, 25d, 38b, 40, 47, 49b QE isf 3, 3, 7, 9, 14

μαλάκεια Her 211

μαλακία (8) Spec 3:31, 39, 40, 156 Virt 23 Praem 5 QE 2:18, 18

μαλακίζομαι (6) Migr 222 Mos 2:183 Virt 5, 6 Flacc 179 QG 4:52c

μαλακός (32) Opif 41, 104 Leg 2:7, 39 Leg 3:58 Sacr 23 Migr 50 Somn 1:17, 123, 125 Somn 2:9, 56 Abr 148, 239 Spec 1:343 Spec 2:28, 143, 163, 169 Virt 15, 93, 130 Praem 4 Contempl 69 Flacc 36 Legat 111, 241, 367 QG (Par) 2:3, 2:3, 2:6 QE isf 5

μαλακότης Opif 62 Plant 133 Abr 136 Spec 1:216

μαλάσσω Spec 4:218

μαλθακός Ebr 122 Fug 39 Somn 1:123

μαλθάσσω Deus 24 Legat 174

μαλλός Opif 85

Μαμβρῆ Migr 164, 165

μάμμη Spec 3:14

Μανασσῆς (14) Leg 3:90, 90, 93, 93, 94 Sobr 28, 28 Migr 205 Congr 40, 43 Mut 97, 97, 99, 101

μανδραγόρας Contempl 45

μανθάνω (151) Leg 1:94 Leg 2:39, 89 Leg 3:51, 122, 135, 194 Cher 36, 56 Sacr 7, 8, 43, 64 Det 6, 10, 10, 12, 37, 65, 86, 102, 102 Post 100, 131, 137, 138, 140, 147, 150, 152, 179 Gig 37 Deus 4, 64, 108 Agr 59, 165 Plant 48, 52, 131 Ebr 40 Conf 55 Migr 140, 192, 195 Her 5, 18, 28, 29, 33, 73, 81, 102, 121, 191, 252, 292 Congr 41, 63, 69, 70, 103, 111, 122, 126, 126 Fug 8, 8, 137, 138, 146, 164, 172, 200, 207 Mut 84, 99, 100, 102, 104, 186, 217, 255, 256, 257, 270, 270 Somn 1:52, 151, 171, 235, 249, 255, 255 Somn 2:1, 98, 99, 107, 108, 179 Abr 21, 53 Ios 55, 67, 79, 167, 183 Mos 1:4, 75, 110, 122, 190, 308 Mos 2:280 Decal 59, 115 Spec 1:36, 42, 319 Spec 2:100, 195 Spec 4:29, 96, 99, 140 Praem 44, 49, 61, 152 Prob 22, 41 Contempl 63, 75 Flacc 34, 103 Legat 53, 53, 114, 255, 363 Prov 2:14 QG 3:30b, 30b, 30b, 4:104, 110a, 110a, 200a QG (Par) 2:6 QE 2:13b, 25b

μανία (31) Deus 138 Agr 37 Plant 147, 147, 148 Ebr 123 Migr 84 Her 249, 264, 265 Fug 168 Mut 39 Somn 1:56, 254 Somn 2:2 Decal 88 Spec 1:58 Spec 2:15, 136 Spec 3:99 Spec 4:82 Prob 8 Aet 72 Flacc 36, 140 Legat 93, 132, 183, 192 Prov 2:20 QG 1:24

μανιώδης (6) Cher 74 Her 249 Somn 1:36 Ios 73 Contempl 14, 40

μάννα (14) Leg 2:84, 86, 86 Leg 3:166, 174, 175 Sacr 86 Det 118 Her 79, 80, 191 Congr 170, 173 Decal 16

μανός Conf 102 Aet 105

μανότης Ebr 185 Somn 1:20

μαντεία (7) Deus 181 Conf 159 Migr 190 Mos 1:263, 264 Spec 1:63 Legat 124

μαντεύομαι (6) Leg 3:227 Cher 27 Conf 118 Ios 106, 182 Spec 3:18

μαντικός (11) Mut 203 Mos 1:264, 277, 284, 285 Spec 1:60, 64 Spec 4:48, 50, 52 Flacc 186

μάντις (8) Cher 34 Migr 114 Mos 1:276, 282, 282, 285, 305 Legat 109

Μάξιμος Flacc 74

μαραίνω (9) Deus 38 Migr 141 Somn 1:11 Somn 2:109, 199 Ios 130 Mos 2:140 Spec 1:311, 325

Μάρεια Contempl 22 Flacc 45

Μαριάμ (6) Leg 1:76 Leg 2:66 Leg 3:103 Agr 80, 81 Contempl 87

Μάρις Flacc 39

Μάρκος Legat 62, 294

μαρμαρυγή (7) Opif 6, 71 Deus 78 Spec 1:37 Praem 38 Prob 5 QE isf 6

μάρσιππος Her 41, 162 Somn 2:193

μαρτυρέω (91) Opif 100 Leg 2:47, 55 Leg 3:2, 4, 19, 32, 37, 46, 129, 142, 162, 196, 205, 205, 205, 208, 217, 218, 228 Cher 40, 124 Sacr 67, 92, 133 Det 48, 52, 121 Post 78, 80, 83, 83, 119, 122 Gig 17 Agr 60, 116 Plant 29, 173 Ebr 150, 188 Conf 9, 44, 94, 141, 181 Migr

115, 130 Her 76, 91, 120, 191, 259, 291 Congr 62, 68, 160, 173 Fug 56, 67 Mut 90 Somn 1:64, 231 Somn 2:47, 172, 222 Abr 81, 262, 270 Ios 269 Mos 1:59 Mos 2:171, 240, 263, 281 Decal 88, 91 Spec 1:273, 273, 343 Spec 4:43, 44, 60, 61 Prob 137 Aet 16, 16, 95 Flacc 99 Legat 150 QE 2:9b

μαρτυρία (24) Leg 3:19, 205, 205, 208 Cher 124 Sacr 91 Det 124 Post 79, 83 Plant 82, 115, 173, 173 Migr 43 Her 4 Mut 258 Abr 258 Ios 235 Decal 86 Spec 2:10 Spec 4:53 Praem 79 Aet 102 QG 4:189

μαρτύριον (13) Leg 2:54, 55 Leg 3:46 Cher 88 Det 63, 160 Ebr 127, 138, 139 Mut 134 Spec 4:136 Aet 25, 27

μάρτυς (71) Opif 88 Leg 2:55 Leg 3:43, 214 Cher 17, 108 Sacr 17, 91, 92 Det 23, 34, 50, 99, 138, 138 Post 57, 59, 59, 96, 121 Plant 82 Ebr 98, 139 Conf 57, 140, 157 Migr 3, 115, 138 Her 120 Congr 74 Fug 13, 184, 184 Mut 39 Somn 2:220, 297 Abr 29, 64, 190 Ios 134, 208, 265 Mos 2:120, 284 Decal 86, 90, 140 Spec 1:37, 55, 341 Spec 2:10, 252, 259 Spec 4:30, 31, 32, 37, 42, 54, 54 Prob 73, 92, 98 Aet 120 Flacc 54, 161 Legat 187, 294 Hypoth 11:4 Prov 2:26

Μασέκ (6) Her 2, 39, 40, 40, 52, 61

μαστεύω Post 182 Ebr 73 Mut 108

μαστιγίας Prob 156

μαστιγόω Congr 177 Somn 2:84 Flacc 72, 85

μαστίζω Flacc 78

μάστιξ (8) Agr 71 Conf 165 Congr 158 Somn 2:294 Spec 2:28 Flacc 75, 78, 80

μαστός μαζός

μαστός (9) Opif 38, 133, 133 Deus 39 Somn 2:204 Spec 3:199 Virt 128, 129, 143

μαστροπεύω Opif 166 Cher 93

μαστροπός Opif 166 Fug 28

ματαιάζω Cher 33 Det 163 Conf 159 Somn 1:255

ματαιοπόνος Aet 42

μάταιος (20) Leg 2:46 Leg 3:192 Cher 32 Sacr 70, 78 Det 71 Conf 141, 159 Migr 113 Her 170 Somn 1:244 Decal 51, 82 Spec 2:2 Spec 4:59, 59, 60, 60 QE 2:9:1, 9a

ματαιότης Conf 141, 159

ματαιουργός Mos 1:117

μάτην Leg 3:227 Spec 2:224, 253

μάχαιρα (6) Leg 3:26 Cher 31, 32, 74 Congr 176 Praem 147

μαχαιρίδιον Flacc 90

Μαχείρ Congr 42, 43, 43

μάχη (21) Opif 164 Ebr 99 Conf 44, 49, 64 Her 28 Congr 176 Abr 214 Mos 1:169, 217, 220, 250, 259, 261, 322, 331 Spec 3:17 Spec 4:197 Virt 38, 44 Prob 139

μάχιμος Leg 3:117 Sobr 13 Legat 222

μαχλάς Opif 166 Fug 153 Legat 39

μάχλος Sacr 28

μάχομαι (35) Leg 1:86, 106 Leg 2:106 Leg 3:21, 116, 190 Sacr 2, 4, 138 Det 32, 71 Post 25, 32, 175 Deus 164 Agr 151 Ebr 8, 143, 180 Conf 32, 192 Migr 152 Her 101, 132 Congr 137 Somn 2:90 Abr 193 Mos 1:118 Spec 3:29, 88 Aet 148 Hypoth 6:6 QG 1:100:1a QE isf 18, 18

μεγαλαυχέω Det 137 Deus 80 Plant 67 Mut 155 Spec 4:201

μεγαλαύχημα Praem 157

μεγαλαυχία (10) Leg 3:164 Cher 77 Post 48, 52, 115 Ebr 128 Conf 5, 113 Somn 1:131, 211

μεγάλαυχος Leg 3:172 Mut 128

μεγαλεῖος (8) Det 29 Ebr 43 Sobr 3 Fug 63 Mos 1:27, 233, 275 Virt 217

μεγαλόδωρος Congr 171

μεγαλοεργέω (μεγαλουργέω) (16) Conf 158 Abr 142 Ios 19 Mos 1:66, 94 Mos 2:53, 253 Spec 2:170, 188 Spec 3:151 Spec 4:129 Praem 134 Flacc 180 Legat 85, 213, 348

μεγαλοέργημα (μεγαλούργημα) Mos 1:165 Mos 2:257

μεγαλοεργία (μεγαλουργία) Somn 2:117 Mos 2:59

μεγαλοεργός (μεγαλουργός) Flacc 73 Legat 194

μεγαλόμικρος Ios 142

μεγαλόνοια Mut 141 Mos 1:256 Virt 84 Contempl 16

μεγαλόπολις (7) Opif 19 Ios 29 Mos 2:51 Decal 53 Spec 1:34 Flacc 163 Prov 2:39

μεγαλοπολίτης Opif 143

μεγαλοπρεπής (6) Leg 3:82 Cher 84 Deus 149 Praem 66, 93 Legat 150

μεγαλουργέω μεγαλοεργέω

μεγαλούργημα μεγαλοέργημα

μεγαλουργία μεγαλοεργία

μεγαλουργός μεγαλοεργός

μεγαλοφροσύνη Sacr 27 Mos 2:29 Spec 2:72, 88

μεγαλόφρων Virt 90, 182 Legat 203

μεγαλοφυής Somn 1:107

μεγαλόφωνος Ebr 102 Her 14 Virt 193

μεγαλύνω Migr 1, 86

μεγαλώνυμος Migr 86, 88

μέγαρον Migr 195 Somn 1:57 Prob 122

μέγας (924) Opif 4, 12, 25, 49, 53, 56, 69, 71, 88, 96, 101, 104, 104, 112, 114, 115, 116, 116, 131, 131, 143, 143, 154, 160 Leg 1:17, 63 Leg 2:8, 67, 84 Leg 3:83, 87, 88, 90, 98, 99, 100, 105, 121, 134, 195, 197, 197, 221, 241 Cher 9, 14, 29, 32, 49, 53, 57, 73, 107, 127 Sacr 28, 30, 30, 33, 35, 50, 54, 62, 100, 125, 134 Det 3, 4, 9, 15, 51, 56, 68, 74, 86, 99, 114, 134, 141, 141, 142, 150, 174 Post 9, 15, 16, 25, 26, 49, 50, 53, 67, 68, 71, 75, 83, 104, 110, 114, 115, 117, 119, 121, 167, 183, 184, 185 Gig 29, 30, 36, 37, 43 Deus 22, 22, 36, 42, 87, 87, 94, 95, 98, 101, 103, 103, 106, 113, 115, 134, 138, 138, 146, 151, 174, 174, 178 Agr 7, 16, 40, 47, 51, 52, 75, 78, 85, 100, 112, 125, 175 Plant 2, 2, 6, 6, 7, 18, 33, 35, 43, 48, 53, 59, 62, 68, 72, 76, 81, 81, 88, 92, 94, 102, 103, 109, 118, 146, 160 Ebr 1, 2, 15, 27, 32, 41, 51, 65, 74, 75, 79, 79, 79, 95, 109, 113, 117, 118, 119, 121, 126, 135, 143, 151, 155, 156, 161, 163, 163, 182, 186, 198, 198, 201, 206, 214, 216, 221 Sobr 10, 22, 31, 42, 42, 49 Conf 4, 15, 23, 23, 50, 54, 105, 118, 119, 162, 163, 165, 166 Migr 1, 21, 46, 53, 53, 54, 55, 56, 56, 58, 58, 58, 59, 59, 61, 68, 71, 80, 88, 90, 94, 94, 118, 120, 123, 125, 125, 146, 155, 157, 170, 172, 184, 217, 220, 220 Her 9, 14, 27, 83, 93, 99, 142, 145, 148, 148, 149, 150, 152, 154, 155, 157, 162, 162, 194, 194, 214, 217, 249, 251, 277, 286, 302, 315,

315, 316 Congr 11, 11, 11, 11, 18, 35, 130, 133, 134, 145, 160, 162, 175 Fug 38, 42, 97, 115, 146, 148, 162, 174, 175, 176, 191, 192, 205 Mut 30, 43, 51, 55, 61, 65, 79, 104, 104, 104, 109, 126, 128, 148, 150, 155, 182, 183, 215, 218, 222, 225, 235, 235, 244, 244, 250, 250, 253, 269 Somn 1:6, 28, 32, 39, 53, 56, 56, 59, 71, 72, 94, 103, 105, 107, 112, 124, 140, 140, 142, 162, 177, 179, 191, 201, 201, 201, 214, 219, 220, 220 Somn 2:42, 59, 61, 64, 83, 90, 112, 114, 120, 138, 140, 174, 182, 183, 191, 193, 193, 200, 231, 252, 255, 279, 280, 282, 285, 286, 287, 293 Abr 1, 39, 39, 42, 44, 48, 60, 64, 65, 71, 71, 74, 75, 81, 84, 88, 90, 98, 110, 114, 122, 134, 147, 166, 166, 167, 178, 180, 184, 185, 196, 215, 226, 235, 235, 262, 266 Ios 4, 5, 12, 13, 15, 19, 20, 27, 38, 38, 44, 46, 52, 52, 56, 60, 69, 79, 91, 118, 125, 131, 131, 137, 138, 139, 149, 156, 184, 188, 204, 212, 216, 231, 231, 252 Mos 1:1, 11, 21, 22, 30, 33, 46, 56, 59, 62, 64, 83, 111, 111, 120, 123, 133, 137, 138, 145, 150, 150, 155, 155, 158, 166, 180, 197, 205, 212, 216, 240, 254, 254, 259, 263, 264, 265, 286, 287, 294, 295, 295, 304, 313, 316, 318, 324 Mos 2:10, 17, 28, 29, 53, 53, 59, 60, 65, 66, 67, 72, 91, 93, 157, 168, 176, 191, 200, 211, 240, 248, 251, 253, 255, 259, 270 Decal 29, 41, 44, 54, 59, 61, 66, 75, 95, 95, 112, 121, 126, 136, 138, 152, 161, 173, 178 Spec 1:3, 13, 18, 20, 24, 30, 32, 71, 73, 76, 108, 116, 133, 149, 154, 161, 163, 245, 247, 248, 248, 252, 298, 307, 307, 308, 310, 311, 330, 333, 336, 340, 343 Spec 2:6, 20, 27, 34, 38, 51, 55, 84, 84, 86, 92, 128, 131, 146, 170, 176, 180, 189, 189, 189, 194, 208, 254, 254 Spec 3:3, 8, 13, 13, 16, 18, 18, 25, 31, 37, 37, 39, 41, 74, 74, 83, 84, 99, 100, 101, 101, 104, 110, 111, 112, 117, 122, 124, 127, 128, 131, 133, 139, 154, 158, 161, 170, 170, 170, 173, 180, 192, 197 Spec 4:7, 11, 13, 15, 19, 27, 32, 47, 50, 65, 67, 72, 72, 89, 97, 105, 123, 129, 130, 147, 147, 156, 158, 165, 170, 170, 171, 171, 172, 173, 174, 176, 177, 182, 184, 196, 218 Virt 9, 35, 38, 54, 54, 61, 61, 64, 85, 100, 109, 117, 144, 161, 162, 166, 171, 175, 175, 179, 183, 187, 187, 197, 199, 201, 201, 206, 208, 210 Praem 7, 23, 25, 26, 28, 33, 47, 69, 84, 88, 93, 95, 97, 138, 163 Prob 9, 9, 20, 35, 47, 57, 63, 76, 80, 94, 96, 105, 133, 136, 139, 141, 141 Contempl 58, 62, 65, 87 Aet 11, 13, 22, 36, 52, 52, 64, 95, 100, 100, 101, 101, 102, 104, 117, 122, 122, 125, 128, 139, 141, 146, 147, 147 Flacc 3, 4, 4, 17, 23, 30, 39, 44, 50, 54, 80, 123, 124, 126, 128, 151, 152, 158 Legat 2, 3, 27, 32, 46, 47, 48, 48, 57, 60, 63, 71, 76, 93, 105, 114, 118, 119, 133, 134, 137, 140, 140, 144, 149, 151, 155, 172, 173, 176, 193, 198, 212, 221, 237, 241, 248, 259, 259, 261, 295, 306, 326, 326, 327, 328, 333, 335, 338, 338, 339, 342, 343, 350, 361, 364 Hypoth 6:1, 7:5, 7:6, 7:9, 7:9, 7:9, 7:11, 7:19, 11:1, 11:18 Prov 2:13, 14, 17, 21, 24, 41 QG 1:65, 73, 89, 89, 96:1, 2:14, 16, 28, 64a, 3:3, 61, 4:8a, 172, 179, 227, 227 QG isf 5, 5, 10, 13 QG (Par) 2:2, 2:2, 2:2, 2:3, 2:3 QE 1:21, 2:15b, 105 QE isf 14

μέγεθος (116) Opif 6, 23, 23, 41, 41, 57, 63, 120, 131 Leg 1:10 Leg 3:19, 57, 171, 196 Cher 29, 68 Sacr 33 Det 13, 25, 90, 105 Post 49, 110, 141, 143 Deus 116 Plant 38, 65, 67, 73, 92, 145 Ebr 42, 128, 174 Migr 53, 54, 54, 55, 55, 56, 68, 70 Her 3, 31, 99, 144, 144, 147, 148, 150, 151, 194, 223, 247 Mut 15, 67 Somn 1:10, 94, 132 Abr 40, 71, 89, 89, 133, 199, 227, 235, 261, 275 Ios 39, 39, 80, 102, 166 Mos 1:147, 149, 170, 172, 212, 229 Mos 2:51, 284 Decal 137 Spec 1:293, 300, 339 Spec 2:32, 232 Spec 4:170, 186, 233, 234 Virt 63, 213, 216, 217 Prob 121, 128 Contempl 1 Aet 112, 147 Flacc 59, 76, 78 Legat 143, 150, 153, 227, 276, 284 Prov 2:55 QG 1:77, 3:29, 4:200a QG (Par) 2:2

μεγεθύνω Aet 100

μεγίστη QE 2:9a

μεθαρμόζω (30) Post 108 Conf 133 Migr 211 Mut 64 Ios 230, 244, 266 Mos 2:18, 31, 135, 288 Decal 152 Spec 1:15, 48 Spec 2:73 Spec 4:187 Virt 34, 37, 110, 141, 183, 214, 224 Prob 90 Flacc 105 Legat 14, 62, 83, 113, 346

μεθέλκω (7) Ebr 71, 88, 195 Migr 67 Abr 125 Spec 1:74 Virt 54

μέθεσις Plant 165

μέθη (48) Opif 71 Leg 1:84 Leg 2:69 Leg 3:82, 124, 155 Cher 92 Post 175 Agr 37 Plant 141, 141, 141, 155, 163, 165, 170, 174 Ebr 1, 15, 15, 95, 122, 138, 148, 166, 208, 209 Sobr 1, 2, 5 Fug 166 Somn 2:104, 160, 168, 200, 292 Mos 1:187, 270 Mos 2:162 Spec 1:206, 249 Spec 3:32, 126 Prob 13 Contempl 46, 89 Flacc 136 Legat 312

μεθημερινός (9) Cher 92 Ebr 106 Ios 143 Spec 1:296, 297, 298 Spec 2:102 Aet 88 Prov 2:49

μεθίημι (32) Cher 33 Sacr 40, 40, 70, 114 Det 120 Post 178 Deus 79 Plant 106, 111, 166 Migr 137 Somn 1:165 Ios 66 Mos 1:58, 167 Spec 1:3, 345 Spec 2:84, 88, 96, 245 Spec 4:124, 223 Praem 26, 164 Prob 116 Flacc 10, 60, 180 Legat 15 QE 2:13b

μεθίστημι (10) Cher 42, 114 Det 163 Post 12 Deus 34 Ios 238 Mos 1:57 Praem 75 Legat 65, 273

μεθοδεύω Det 109 Agr 25 Mos 2:212 Aet 149 Prov 2:60

μέθοδος Leg 3:15 Fug 168 Spec 2:99

μεθολκή Migr 149 Fug 89

μεθόριος (54) Opif 65, 135 Leg 3:99, 184 Det 122 Agr 161 Plant 10, 76, 120 Conf 89 Migr 147, 158, 198 Her 45, 121, 147, 172, 205 Congr 22 Fug 101, 213 Mut 45, 118, 192 Somn 1:152 Somn 2:188, 230, 234 Abr 214 Ios 148, 205 Mos 1:178 Mos 2:82, 101, 253 Decal 106, 107 Spec 1:116 Spec 2:157, 210, 224 Spec 3:72, 130 Spec 4:168 Virt 9 Praem 62 Contempl 86 Aet 33, 139, 139, 147 Legat 145 QG 1:28, 4:64

μεθορμίζω (11) Congr 108 Abr 24, 78 Mos 1:214 Spec 1:51, 227 Spec 4:159 Virt 153 Praem 15, 27, 116

μέθυ Plant 154, 154

μεθύσκω (17) Leg 2:29 Agr 1 Plant 140, 142, 149, 149, 155, 156, 166, 170, 172, 174 Ebr 4, 146 Fug 32 Somn 2:86 Contempl 89

μέθυσμα (11) Deus 158 Agr 157 Ebr 143, 149, 151 Somn 2:164, 183, 190, 192 Spec 1:98, 249

μεθύω (34) Leg 1:84 Leg 3:183, 210 Post 175 Agr 153 Plant 101, 142, 154, 163, 165, 172, 172, 174, 176, 176 Ebr 27, 146, 147, 148, 148, 153, 154, 206 Sobr 30 Fug 166 Somn 2:102 Ios 45 Mos 1:187 Spec 3:126 Virt 162 Prob 13 Contempl 42 QG 2:68a, 68b

μείγνυμι Somn 1:205 Somn 2:9 QG 2:12c QE 2:14

μειδάω μειδιάω

μειδιάω (μειδάω) (7) Ebr 146 Mut 154, 169 Spec 2:49 Spec 3:193 Flacc 15 Legat 361

μείλιγμα Mut 131 Somn 2:89 Abr 196

μειόω (19) Opif 113 Det 14 Gig 26 Ebr 22 Somn 2:236 Mos 1:6 Mos 2:63, 122 Spec 1:47, 135, 178 Spec 2:57, 143 Spec 3:74 Aet 91, 120, 123, 123 QG 2:28

μειράκιον (20) Opif 105, 105, 105 Cher 114 Ios 127, 128, 128, 129, 270 Mos 1:301 Prob 117 Contempl 52 Aet 60 Flacc 11, 36 Legat 23, 28, 68 Hypoth 11:3 QE isf 14

μειρακιόομαι Congr 82

μειρακιώδης (6) Cher 63 Somn 2:148 Mos 1:25 Contempl 6 Legat 42, 167

μείρομαι (εἱμαρμένη) (8) Migr 179 Her 300 Mut 135 Somn 2:129 Prob 111 Aet 75 Flacc 180 Legat 25

μείς μήν

μείωσις (18) Opif 101 Mut 67 Somn 1:199 Spec 1:178 Spec 2:143 Spec 3:150, 183, 188 Spec 4:234 Contempl 56 Aet 58, 60, 60, 138, 142, 149 Prov 1 QG 2:31

μελαγχολάω Plant 177, 177, 177

μελαγχολία (6) Leg 2:70 Cher 69, 116 Conf 16 Her 249 Somn 2:85

μέλαν Abr 10

μέλας (20) Opif 29 Leg 2:7, 39, 67 Leg 3:57, 61 Plant 172, 172 Ebr 186 Her 209 Congr 117 Somn 1:145, 145 Abr 10 Mos 1:176 Mos 2:88, 118 Spec 1:85, 94 Aet 104

μελετάω (53) Leg 1:29 Leg 2:91 Leg 3:16, 22, 22, 36, 131, 147, 165, 172, 189, 244 Cher 122 Det 28, 34, 42, 44 Post 22, 55, 101 Gig 14, 33 Deus 7, 111 Agr 51, 56, 109, 159 Plant 131, 135, 168 Ebr 24, 197, 212, 217 Conf 2, 43, 136 Her 89, 126, 170, 192, 234, 267 Somn 2:274, 283 Spec 2:46 Virt 196 Prob 96 Flacc 135 Legat 57 Hypoth 11:15 QG 4:173

μελέτη (50) Leg 3:18, 22 Cher 9, 92, 104 Sacr 35, 85, 87, 113 Det 64 Post 101 Gig 26 Agr 18, 91, 145, 147, 160 Plant 31 Ebr 21, 212, 219 Conf 39, 110 Migr 31, 105 Congr 24 Fug 166 Mut 166, 219, 270 Somn 1:120, 168, 170, 249 Somn 2:283 Ios 3, 40, 81 Mos 1:60, 310 Mos 2:27 Spec 4:24, 107, 121 Virt 2 Legat 30, 320 Prov 2:16 QG isf 4 QE isf 9

μέλι (7) Det 115, 117, 118 Congr 169 Fug 138 Spec 1:291, 291

μελίζω Abr 198

μελίπηκτον Ebr 217 Somn 2:48 Mos 1:208 Spec 1:174 Spec 2:20

μέλισσα Deus 99 Spec 1:291 Hypoth 11:8

Μελιταῖος Praem 89

μέλλησις (6) Leg 3:215 Sacr 53, 63 Mut 142 Ios 118 Spec 2:38

μελλητής (6) Sacr 32 Conf 48 Her 254 Somn 1:165 Somn 2:67 Decal 85

μέλλω (396) Opif 14, 17, 27, 28, 29, 33, 34, 38, 38, 40, 58, 78, 83, 115, 133, 137, 156, 169 Leg 1:54 Leg 2:5, 6, 15, 42, 43, 43 Leg 3:16, 17, 41, 87, 146, 155, 159, 218, 240 Cher 20, 33, 34, 59, 99, 102, 110 Sacr 4, 8, 10, 29, 47, 85 Det 11, 45, 57, 58, 58, 61, 62, 75, 119, 119 Post 103, 144 Gig 26, 63 Deus 8, 18, 29, 29, 29, 30, 32, 32, 66, 74, 138 Agr 69, 85, 95, 111, 123, 158, 174 Plant 2, 15, 103, 114 Ebr 60, 82, 84, 131 Sobr 6, 46 Conf 12, 20, 41, 76, 89, 155 Migr 25, 43, 43, 82, 98, 154, 159, 172, 190, 197, 223 Her 25, 49, 201, 202, 261, 278 Congr 73, 80, 82, 109, 113, 125 Fug 49, 70, 105, 107, 159, 159, 162, 186, 205, 213 Mut 30, 44, 54, 73, 87, 87, 124, 129, 158, 161, 162, 162, 163, 164, 165, 188, 217, 228 Somn 1:2, 36, 71, 212, 214 Somn 2:1, 72, 143, 204, 209, 210, 264, 269 Abr 62, 86, 98, 105, 145, 174, 188, 190, 193, 201, 202, 214, 218, 225, 233, 250, 253 Ios 3, 38, 100, 107, 112, 116, 133, 162, 175, 191, 197, 210, 215, 225, 231, 235, 236, 238, 244, 259, 266 Mos 1:12, 14, 20, 46, 48, 60, 66, 71, 81, 102, 108, 133, 137, 149, 162, 169, 178, 185, 192, 197, 199, 213, 217, 248, 255, 268, 294, 321, 329 Mos 2:8, 25, 37, 39, 74, 91, 109, 138, 139, 145, 149, 152, 162, 190, 200, 202, 214, 224, 252, 261, 266, 279, 288, 288, 288 Decal 10, 14, 17, 41, 86, 92, 93, 98, 140, 145, 149 Spec 1:64, 64, 68, 77, 82, 110, 159, 219, 243, 269, 283, 283, 284, 330, 334 Spec 2:4, 80, 84, 135, 157, 157, 157, 158, 187, 202 Spec 3:56, 95, 126, 139, 199 Spec 4:39, 56, 71, 129, 131, 140, 156, 165, 213, 222 Virt 23, 37, 41, 53, 64, 67, 67, 75, 84, 112, 114, 151, 152, 156, 156, 159, 221 Praem 71, 72, 91, 103, 108, 161 Prob 121, 122, 143 Contempl 46 Aet 37, 65, 89, 94, 99, 102, 140 Flacc 26, 48, 74, 76, 78, 83, 114, 126, 129, 141, 151, 167 Legat 2, 2, 51, 68, 99, 109, 109, 124, 128, 139, 175, 179, 186, 208, 258, 259, 266, 306, 322, 324, 335, 336, 338, 351, 369 Hypoth 6:3, 6:4, 6:4, 7:1, 7:15, 11:14 Prov 1, 2:26, 26, 44 QG 1:21, 31, 60:1, 72, 72, 89, 2:72, 72, 4:52b, 88, 153 QE 2:45a, 49a

μέλος (62) Opif 67, 103 Leg 1:12 Leg 3:221 Cher 105 Sacr 84 Det 125 Post 106, 108 Deus 52 Agr 137, 137 Plant 131, 167 Ebr 95, 116, 177 Sobr 36 Migr 104 Her 15, 133 Congr 16, 76 Mut 87, 173 Somn 1:205 Somn 2:168 Abr 198 Ios 27, 187 Mos 1:128 Mos 2:106, 239, 256, 256 Spec 1:28, 99, 145, 147, 199, 208, 210, 342, 343 Spec 3:108, 182 Virt 32, 136 Praem 125, 143, 145 Prob 89 Contempl 29, 80, 84, 88 Aet 143 Flacc 176 Legat 131, 243, 267 QG (Par) 2:2

Μελχά Congr 43, 45, 50

Μελχισεδέκ Leg 3:79, 82 Congr 99

μέλω (13) Migr 191 Mut 45 Ios 9, 63 Mos 2:207 Spec 1:277 Spec 2:11 Spec 3:50, 89 Virt 155 Flacc 102 Legat 256 Prov 2:70

μελῳδέω Leg 1:14 Post 105 Conf 56 Somn 1:35

μελῳδία (7) Det 157 Post 103, 104 Agr 137 Somn 2:27, 28, 270

μεμαθημένως QG isf 16

μεμπτός Mut 105 Spec 1:237

Μέμφις Mos 1:118

μέμφομαι (12) Cher 36 Agr 5 Migr 89 Fug 33 Somn 2:104 Abr 209 Spec 3:156, 181 Spec 4:120, 126 Legat 236, 331

μεμψιμοιρέω Mos 1:181

μέμψις (9) Migr 93 Mut 47 Ios 205 Mos 1:31 Spec 3:9, 10 Virt 127 Praem 33 Legat 336

μέν (5336) Opif 1, 2, 4, 5, 7, 7, 8, 8, 9, 10, 12, 13, 13, 13, 14, 22, 23, 29, 30, 34, 35, 36, 38, 39, 40, 41, 41, 41, 41, 42, 43, 45, 46, 46, 47, 48, 48, 49, 49, 50, 50, 51, 53, 53, 53, 54, 55, 56, 56, 57, 61, 62, 62, 63, 63, 65, 65, 67, 67, 67, 68, 68, 68, 72, 72, 73, 73, 74, 74, 74, 75, 77, 78, 78, 79, 80, 81, 81, 82, 82, 82, 82, 83, 85, 88, 88, 91, 91, 92, 92, 93, 93, 94, 95, 95, 96, 97, 97, 98, 98, 99, 99, 99, 99, 99, 100, 100, 101, 101, 101, 102, 102, 102, 103, 104, 104, 105, 105, 105, 106, 106, 107, 107, 108, 109, 109, 109, 110, 111, 112, 113, 113, 114, 115, 116, 116, 117, 118, 119, 119, 123, 123, 125, 126, 126, 128, 128, 128, 131, 131, 131, 132, 134, 135, 135, 136, 139, 140, 140, 140, 141, 142, 144, 145, 146,

147, 148, 150, 151, 153, 153, 153, 154, 155, 157, 159, 161, 162, 164, 165, 165, 165, 167, 167, 169, 169, 170, 170, 170, 170, 170 Leg 1:1, 1, 1, 3, 4, 6, 6, 9, 12, 22, 22, 23, 23, 24, 25, 27, 28, 28, 29, 30, 31, 31, 31, 34, 34, 34, 35, 37, 39, 40, 41, 41, 41, 41, 42, 42, 44, 45, 48, 52, 53, 54, 55, 55, 55, 57, 57, 59, 60, 60, 61, 62, 63, 64, 65, 70, 70, 70, 70, 71, 71, 71, 71, 72, 72, 74, 74, 77, 78, 78, 79, 80, 81, 82, 82, 84, 85, 85, 85, 86, 88, 89, 91, 91, 91, 92, 93, 93, 94, 95, 98, 99, 100, 101, 101, 102, 102, 104, 105, 105, 105, 106, 106, 107, 108 Leg 2:2, 5, 5, 5, 6, 9, 12, 12, 14, 14, 15, 15, 17, 17, 17, 22, 23, 23, 25, 30, 30, 33, 33, 34, 36, 36, 38, 38, 42, 43, 44, 45, 46, 50, 52, 53, 54, 54, 57, 57, 58, 59, 60, 60, 64, 65, 66, 70, 70, 73, 80, 80, 81, 83, 85, 87, 87, 91, 93, 94, 95, 95, 98, 103, 103, 103, 104, 104 Leg 3:2, 3, 3, 7, 9, 13, 18, 21, 22, 25, 28, 29, 29, 31, 34, 36, 39, 39, 39, 40, 40, 41, 44, 48, 51, 51, 53, 59, 59, 61, 61, 64, 67, 68, 70, 71, 72, 76, 79, 80, 80, 81, 82, 86, 88, 90, 91, 91, 92, 93, 94, 94, 96, 99, 102, 102, 102, 102, 104, 104, 105, 105, 105, 109, 111, 112, 114, 115, 115, 115, 116, 120, 121, 122, 126, 126, 128, 128, 129, 134, 135, 140, 140, 140, 140, 144, 144, 144, 147, 147, 147, 148, 149, 149, 151, 159, 160, 161, 161, 163, 164, 173, 176, 176, 177, 177, 178, 178, 181, 181, 185, 186, 186, 188, 189, 189, 189, 189, 191, 192, 194, 196, 197, 198, 200, 201, 201, 201, 202, 205, 211, 216, 217, 218, 220, 220, 220, 223, 223, 224, 227, 229, 231, 232, 235, 238, 239, 241, 242, 243, 244, 246, 249, 252 Cher 1, 2, 2, 3, 3, 4, 4, 5, 7, 7, 8, 9, 11, 12, 12, 12, 14, 16, 18, 19, 21, 22, 22, 22, 22, 23, 25, 25, 25, 27, 28, 29, 30, 33, 34, 37, 38, 39, 41, 41, 43, 44, 46, 46, 50, 52, 56, 56, 57, 60, 62, 62, 68, 73, 76, 77, 78, 79, 79, 80, 81, 82, 84, 86, 88, 88, 90, 91, 93, 93, 93, 94, 95, 95, 96, 100, 101, 102, 104, 105, 108, 111, 113, 118, 120, 121, 122, 125, 125, 127, 127, 129 Sacr 2, 2, 3, 3, 4, 6, 6, 7, 7, 8, 11, 13, 14, 14, 15, 16, 17, 18, 20, 20, 21, 25, 26, 29, 29, 29, 30, 30, 34, 34, 35, 36, 40, 40, 43, 43, 45, 46, 47, 48, 49, 52, 53, 54, 54, 55, 57, 59, 59, 61, 64, 68, 72, 72, 73, 76, 77, 78, 79, 82, 82, 84, 88, 88, 90, 92, 93, 95, 99, 99, 100, 103, 103, 103, 104, 105, 105, 106, 106, 109, 110, 112, 114, 115, 119, 119, 120, 125, 125, 127, 127, 128, 129, 129, 129, 131, 132, 133, 133, 137 Det 2, 4, 6, 7, 12, 13, 17, 20, 20, 21, 23, 25, 26, 29, 30, 32, 32, 34, 35, 35, 36, 37, 37, 41, 41, 42, 43, 43, 43, 44, 47, 48, 49, 49, 49, 52, 53, 54, 54, 55, 55, 56, 56, 56, 57, 61, 64, 65, 65, 66, 68, 69, 69, 70, 74, 75, 78, 79, 80, 82, 82, 82, 83, 83, 84, 84, 85, 85, 85, 87, 91, 91, 91, 92, 95, 96, 97, 99, 99, 101, 104, 104, 105, 105, 105, 105, 107, 107, 108, 109, 109, 110, 111, 111, 112, 113, 113, 113, 114, 114, 114, 117, 117, 118, 118, 118, 119, 119, 120, 121, 122, 124, 124, 125, 131, 134, 137, 139, 140, 140, 141, 141, 144, 145, 145, 146, 147, 149, 150, 151, 151, 154, 158, 160, 161, 162, 162, 163, 164, 164, 165, 165, 166, 166, 168, 169, 172, 172, 172, 173, 174, 178 Post 2, 3, 9, 10, 10, 12, 13, 14, 18, 19, 20, 21, 23, 23, 23, 26, 27, 28, 28, 29, 29, 30, 30, 34, 36, 37, 39, 40, 41, 41, 42, 44, 44, 45, 47, 48, 48, 49, 50, 52, 55, 57, 61, 61, 61, 62, 64, 67, 68, 69, 71, 75, 76, 77, 77, 78, 80, 86, 87, 87, 88, 90, 90, 91, 92, 95, 95, 96, 98, 98, 105, 106, 106, 107, 107, 109, 110, 112, 116, 117, 118, 119, 122, 122, 123, 124, 126, 128, 134, 137, 137, 137, 137, 139, 140, 141, 142, 142, 142, 145, 145, 147, 149, 150, 153, 153, 154, 155, 156, 157, 160, 161, 161, 162, 162, 165, 169, 171, 172, 173, 173, 174, 175, 176, 183, 183, 185 Gig 7, 11, 12, 13, 13, 14, 16, 16, 17, 17, 18, 20, 22, 26, 28, 29, 31, 31, 33, 37, 38, 39, 39, 40, 42, 43, 43, 43, 43, 47, 52, 53, 55, 56, 56, 60, 60, 60, 62, 65, 67 Deus 3, 4, 8, 8, 9, 13, 15, 15, 20, 24, 27, 28, 30, 30, 31, 34, 34, 35, 35, 35, 38, 41, 42, 44, 44, 45, 47, 47, 48, 49, 53, 54, 55, 55, 56, 57, 57, 59, 59, 61, 63, 65, 69, 70, 70, 72, 72, 75, 77, 78, 79, 79, 82, 83, 84, 85, 86, 86, 87, 87, 93, 93, 93, 95, 95, 96, 97, 98, 103, 104, 105, 106, 107, 109, 110, 111, 112, 114, 115, 116, 117, 119, 121, 127, 127, 128, 129, 129, 132, 133, 134, 137, 138, 139, 141, 145, 147, 150, 151, 154, 154, 158, 159, 162, 163, 163, 163, 163, 163, 164, 167, 175, 177, 180, 180 Agr 1, 1, 2, 4, 5, 6, 6, 7, 8, 9, 9, 11, 13, 14, 18, 18, 19, 20, 25, 26, 27, 29, 30, 31, 32, 33, 38, 40, 41, 44, 46, 47, 48, 48, 51, 54, 56, 58, 59, 61, 61, 65, 65, 66, 67, 68, 68, 70, 71, 73, 73, 73, 73, 74, 76, 79, 80, 81, 90, 90, 90, 92, 93, 96, 97, 97, 98, 100, 101, 107, 108, 111, 112, 112, 113, 115, 116, 117, 120, 122, 123, 123, 124, 128, 129, 129, 130, 131, 132, 135, 136, 139, 139, 139, 139, 139, 140, 140, 140, 141, 141, 142, 144, 145, 150, 151, 152, 152, 152, 157, 157, 157, 158, 158, 158, 160, 162, 166, 166, 171, 173, 173, 176, 178, 181 Plant 1, 2, 3, 3, 4, 4, 5, 7, 11, 11, 12, 12, 12, 14, 14, 14, 16, 17, 18, 24, 25, 27, 27, 27, 29, 32, 34, 35, 37, 37, 39, 40, 41, 43, 43, 44, 45, 46, 54, 55, 58, 60, 61, 61, 61, 61, 63, 67, 67, 69, 74, 75, 76, 76, 79, 79, 86, 87, 88, 89, 90, 93, 94, 97, 100, 102, 103, 105, 106, 108, 110, 112, 113, 114, 114, 117, 123, 123, 124, 125, 126, 127, 128, 130, 130, 131, 134, 137, 139, 141, 142, 143, 143, 144, 144, 144, 149, 149, 150, 150, 156, 157, 160, 161, 162, 165, 166, 169, 171, 171, 171 Ebr 1, 2, 2, 4, 5, 6, 6, 7, 9, 10, 11, 12, 16, 17, 17, 19, 20, 21, 22, 22, 24, 25, 26, 29, 30, 33, 34, 35, 35, 35, 35, 35, 35, 35, 36, 37, 38, 39, 40, 46, 48, 53, 58, 59, 62, 63, 66, 68, 77, 78, 80, 81, 82, 83, 84, 85, 86, 86, 87, 88, 91, 94, 95, 97, 97, 98, 101, 102, 105, 107, 107, 108, 115, 116, 116, 120, 121, 123, 126, 130, 131, 133, 133, 133, 133, 133, 134, 134, 137, 138, 140, 140, 140, 141, 144, 148, 150, 152, 153, 154, 155, 156, 156, 157, 159, 160, 160, 162, 163, 165, 165, 165, 166, 166, 169, 169, 169, 171, 172, 174, 174, 177, 178, 183, 183, 185, 185, 187, 192, 193, 194, 200, 201, 201, 211, 214, 215, 217, 220, 221, 223, 224, 224 Sobr 5, 5, 6, 8, 9, 12, 14, 16, 17, 20, 22, 22, 22, 23, 23, 23, 24, 24, 26, 26, 26, 27, 28, 28, 29, 31, 32, 33, 34, 34, 34, 36, 37, 38, 39, 40, 41, 43, 43, 44, 44, 45, 45, 47, 49, 49, 50, 51, 55, 59, 62, 62 Conf 1, 2, 4, 6, 14, 16, 18, 20, 21, 21, 28, 30, 30, 31, 33, 38, 38, 38, 40, 41, 42, 44, 49, 52, 52, 52, 54, 55, 58, 60, 60, 60, 61, 63, 66, 67, 68, 68, 70, 72, 73, 77, 78, 78, 81, 89, 91, 93, 95, 96, 97, 98, 99, 103, 104, 106, 106, 108, 108, 108, 109, 110, 111, 113, 114, 115, 117, 122, 123, 125, 125, 127, 129, 133, 133, 135, 136, 137, 137, 152, 157, 157, 158, 161, 163, 167, 175, 176, 176, 176, 177, 178, 179, 180, 181, 182, 182, 184, 185, 186, 186, 186, 187, 190, 190, 192, 194, 195, 196, 196, 198 Migr 2, 3, 3, 7, 7, 10, 12, 15, 16, 18, 19, 27, 31, 33, 34, 36, 40, 46, 46, 48, 49, 50, 51, 52, 52, 53, 55, 55, 59, 59, 60, 61, 61, 65, 66, 66, 67, 67, 69, 69, 70, 71, 71, 71, 72, 72, 72, 74, 76, 77, 78, 81, 84, 86, 89, 91, 93, 94, 94, 99, 101, 102, 103, 103, 104, 105, 107, 108, 109, 110, 111, 113, 113, 114, 114, 116, 118, 121, 124, 125, 126, 127, 130, 131, 140, 141, 144, 144, 146, 148, 148, 150, 150, 150, 152, 153, 153, 158, 160, 162, 162, 163, 164, 164, 165, 167, 169, 172, 174, 176, 177, 178, 180, 181, 183, 187, 188, 189, 190, 191, 192, 193, 196, 199, 200, 203, 203, 205, 206, 207, 212, 214, 217, 218, 220 Her 1, 4, 6, 10, 10, 12, 14, 14, 16, 19, 20, 21, 22, 23, 31, 35, 39, 40, 42, 45, 45, 46, 47, 48, 48, 53, 54, 55, 57, 63, 71, 73, 75, 75, 77, 77, 77, 79, 82, 83, 84, 89, 89, 95, 97, 98,

99, 101, 101, 102, 103, 106, 107, 109, 109, 109, 109, 109, 110, 111, 111, 115, 119, 121, 121, 123, 124, 125, 126, 127, 128, 128, 132, 134, 135, 135, 135, 136, 137, 137, 137, 138, 138, 139, 139, 141, 142, 144, 144, 146, 146, 147, 147, 147, 149, 149, 150, 152, 155, 161, 164, 165, 168, 169, 172, 177, 179, 180, 180, 181, 182, 183, 184, 185, 185, 186, 189, 192, 197, 197, 198, 199, 204, 205, 206, 208, 208, 215, 217, 217, 220, 224, 224, 225, 226, 226, 227, 230, 231, 231, 232, 233, 234, 234, 237, 240, 241, 241, 242, 243, 244, 245, 246, 246, 247, 249, 250, 259, 263, 264, 264, 265, 267, 268, 269, 269, 270, 270, 271, 275, 277, 280, 282, 282, 283, 284, 284, 285, 286, 295, 296, 297, 299, 301, 304, 307, 307, 308, 310, 311, 312, 315 Congr 3, 4, 4, 5, 6, 10, 15, 16, 19, 20, 22, 22, 23, 23, 23, 23, 24, 24, 25, 26, 26, 27, 27, 29, 30, 31, 31, 31, 32, 32, 32, 33, 34, 35, 35, 37, 39, 40, 41, 41, 43, 45, 45, 48, 51, 51, 52, 53, 55, 56, 59, 59, 61, 61, 63, 65, 65, 67, 67, 67, 70, 70, 71, 73, 77, 80, 80, 80, 81, 82, 82, 83, 84, 84, 85, 85, 88, 89, 91, 99, 100, 102, 104, 105, 109, 109, 111, 113, 117, 117, 122, 124, 126, 127, 129, 130, 130, 130, 135, 135, 136, 138, 141, 142, 143, 143, 143, 143, 143, 143, 143, 144, 144, 147, 152, 152, 152, 154, 154, 155, 155, 163, 164, 172, 179, 180 Fug 3, 4, 5, 6, 7, 9, 10, 11, 13, 23, 27, 27, 28, 30, 30, 31, 32, 34, 37, 40, 42, 43, 43, 45, 51, 51, 55, 56, 57, 58, 59, 62, 62, 65, 66, 66, 67, 69, 69, 71, 72, 73, 73, 76, 76, 78, 82, 82, 85, 86, 87, 87, 90, 91, 93, 94, 94, 97, 100, 100, 101, 102, 102, 103, 106, 106, 107, 107, 107, 109, 110, 111, 114, 115, 117, 120, 120, 121, 122, 125, 126, 126, 131, 132, 133, 133, 135, 138, 139, 141, 141, 143, 148, 148, 149, 152, 155, 156, 157, 157, 159, 160, 162, 167, 168, 169, 169, 169, 171, 171, 172, 174, 176, 177, 179, 180, 182, 186, 187, 188, 190, 191, 192, 192, 198, 202, 202, 208, 212, 213, 213 Mut 2, 3, 4, 17, 17, 19, 24, 26, 28, 30, 31, 33, 37, 37, 38, 39, 40, 41, 43, 46, 47, 47, 48, 49, 49, 51, 54, 56, 56, 58, 59, 60, 62, 69, 69, 70, 71, 74, 76, 77, 77, 78, 78, 79, 80, 80, 81, 81, 83, 84, 85, 86, 86, 87, 88, 88, 88, 91, 91, 92, 94, 98, 100, 101, 102, 102, 103, 103, 103, 104, 106, 106, 106, 110, 111, 112, 114, 114, 118, 121, 122, 122, 125, 126, 132, 133, 134, 141, 141, 143, 144, 145, 146, 147, 149, 153, 154, 155, 156, 163, 163, 163, 165, 166, 170, 175, 175, 176, 177, 184, 189, 193, 195, 196, 200, 200, 202, 203, 203, 206, 208, 209, 210, 213, 215, 217, 218, 218, 221, 223, 224, 225, 230, 230, 230, 233, 240, 241, 243, 244, 244, 245, 247, 248, 248, 248, 250, 250, 255, 256, 258, 259, 263, 265, 269 Somn 1:1, 5, 5, 7, 8, 10, 11, 11, 13, 14, 15, 16, 16, 17, 17, 17, 18, 18, 18, 21, 23, 25, 26, 27, 28, 28, 28, 29, 32, 33, 34, 35, 39, 40, 41, 43, 43, 45, 49, 50, 51, 52, 53, 58, 58, 59, 61, 62, 63, 64, 65, 71, 72, 73, 73, 74, 75, 75, 77, 80, 83, 83, 84, 86, 87, 97, 97, 98, 99, 99, 101, 102, 103, 109, 115, 118, 119, 119, 121, 122, 125, 125, 127, 128, 133, 134, 134, 134, 135, 136, 138, 139, 139, 140, 141, 144, 145, 146, 146, 147, 148, 150, 150, 150, 151, 154, 155, 155, 155, 155, 160, 160, 160, 162, 162, 163, 165, 166, 166, 167, 168, 169, 172, 173, 173, 173, 174, 175, 180, 181, 182, 184, 187, 189, 191, 192, 194, 195, 198, 198, 198, 201, 203, 204, 205, 206, 213, 215, 216, 216, 218, 219, 219, 222, 229, 229, 230, 232, 233, 233, 234, 237, 242, 256 Somn 2:2, 2, 3, 3, 6, 7, 8, 8, 8, 9, 9, 9, 10, 11, 14, 17, 17, 17, 21, 26, 28, 32, 33, 33, 33, 37, 42, 47, 52, 54, 56, 63, 63, 67, 69, 70, 79, 80, 90, 91, 91, 92, 94, 95, 97, 97, 106, 106, 108, 110, 112, 115, 116, 117, 118, 118, 118, 122, 126, 130, 131, 131, 132, 133, 133, 134, 134, 139, 140, 148, 152, 152, 153, 153, 154, 155, 155, 155, 156, 158, 158, 162, 165, 166, 167, 170, 173, 174, 176, 177, 178, 179, 179, 181, 182, 184, 184, 186, 188, 188, 190, 191, 197, 198, 201, 201, 203, 205, 207, 214, 215, 219, 220, 224, 224, 227, 229, 229, 230, 230, 231, 232, 232, 234, 234, 236, 237, 238, 238, 239, 239, 240, 240, 240, 242, 248, 253, 253, 255, 257, 257, 261, 262, 262, 270, 271, 273, 274, 276, 277, 278, 281, 282, 286, 289, 289, 290, 292, 299, 300, 302 Abr 1, 2, 2, 5, 6, 9, 12, 14, 14, 15, 16, 16, 17, 19, 20, 20, 21, 22, 23, 24, 26, 27, 27, 29, 29, 33, 38, 38, 42, 43, 46, 46, 47, 47, 47, 47, 48, 48, 49, 50, 52, 52, 52, 54, 55, 55, 56, 57, 59, 60, 64, 65, 67, 68, 73, 74, 76, 81, 82, 82, 83, 83, 84, 86, 88, 91, 92, 94, 96, 98, 99, 99, 100, 101, 101, 101, 101, 102, 103, 104, 105, 106, 107, 108, 114, 119, 119, 121, 121, 121, 122, 122, 123, 124, 125, 125, 126, 128, 129, 129, 131, 135, 137, 138, 139, 141, 143, 144, 145, 145, 145, 146, 147, 149, 150, 151, 152, 153, 153, 155, 157, 159, 164, 166, 167, 171, 173, 173, 174, 175, 177, 179, 180, 180, 183, 184, 184, 184, 185, 188, 192, 196, 197, 197, 198, 201, 202, 204, 204, 204, 205, 208, 208, 208, 211, 212, 215, 218, 218, 218, 219, 220, 221, 223, 226, 227, 229, 230, 233, 234, 236, 236, 240, 240, 241, 241, 243, 244, 246, 248, 250, 251, 251, 254, 255, 257, 261, 261, 262, 263, 265, 266, 268, 268, 269, 269, 269, 271, 272, 272, 272, 274, 275, 276 Ios 1, 6, 9, 10, 11, 12, 14, 14, 17, 19, 20, 22, 26, 27, 27, 27, 28, 29, 29, 31, 33, 34, 34, 34, 35, 38, 38, 41, 47, 52, 52, 54, 55, 58, 59, 59, 62, 63, 66, 67, 78, 81, 85, 88, 92, 92, 94, 95, 97, 98, 99, 104, 105, 109, 109, 110, 112, 119, 123, 125, 128, 130, 132, 136, 140, 141, 145, 145, 147, 148, 150, 152, 154, 154, 155, 156, 162, 164, 166, 167, 168, 169, 170, 171, 174, 176, 179, 183, 183, 184, 185, 186, 188, 189, 190, 193, 199, 205, 206, 208, 209, 210, 215, 216, 221, 223, 225, 225, 228, 242, 246, 262, 263, 269, 270 Mos 1:1, 2, 5, 8, 10, 11, 12, 21, 23, 26, 29, 30, 31, 31, 32, 32, 33, 36, 38, 40, 45, 46, 47, 49, 53, 54, 58, 59, 61, 64, 67, 67, 70, 73, 75, 76, 78, 79, 80, 81, 84, 86, 90, 91, 93, 94, 97, 99, 101, 102, 105, 110, 111, 113, 113, 114, 115, 117, 118, 119, 123, 124, 124, 129, 130, 137, 141, 141, 142, 143, 143, 146, 147, 150, 153, 153, 157, 157, 159, 164, 166, 167, 169, 169, 170, 173, 173, 175, 176, 176, 177, 178, 179, 180, 180, 181, 183, 184, 185, 186, 190, 193, 194, 197, 198, 202, 203, 204, 204, 210, 211, 212, 212, 213, 215, 217, 217, 218, 218, 224, 228, 231, 232, 233, 233, 234, 234, 236, 239, 240, 241, 243, 244, 246, 248, 249, 250, 251, 257, 259, 262, 263, 263, 264, 265, 266, 267, 267, 272, 274, 275, 277, 278, 279, 280, 281, 286, 287, 291, 293, 294, 298, 300, 301, 303, 305, 305, 306, 308, 308, 309, 311, 311, 311, 313, 315, 316, 316, 316, 318, 322, 322, 323, 325, 326, 327, 328, 330, 330, 331, 333, 334 Mos 2:1, 2, 4, 5, 8, 8, 8, 9, 10, 13, 23, 24, 29, 30, 33, 38, 42, 43, 45, 46, 47, 47, 48, 49, 49, 50, 50, 53, 53, 54, 58, 58, 63, 63, 66, 69, 69, 72, 76, 78, 78, 78, 78, 80, 81, 82, 82, 82, 83, 84, 85, 85, 86, 87, 88, 88, 89, 89, 90, 91, 91, 92, 94, 96, 96, 97, 97, 98, 99, 101, 101, 102, 104, 105, 107, 109, 110, 117, 117, 119, 121, 122, 122, 127, 127, 127, 127, 129, 129, 131, 140, 142, 143, 144, 147, 148, 148, 150, 150, 152, 153, 153, 154, 162, 164, 166, 168, 169, 169, 172, 174, 174, 176, 177, 178, 179, 180, 180, 181, 181, 182, 182, 184, 187, 188, 188, 189, 189, 190, 191, 192, 193, 193, 194, 194, 194, 194, 199, 200, 201, 204, 210, 210, 211, 214, 214, 215, 215, 217, 220, 221, 221, 222, 223, 224, 225, 227, 228, 228, 230, 231, 233, 234, 235, 235, 240, 242, 242, 243, 245, 249, 250, 251, 252, 253, 256, 256, 256, 256, 258, 261, 262, 264, 264, 269, 269, 270, 271, 273, 276, 276, 277, 281, 282, 285, 286, 287, 288, 290, 292 Decal 2, 3, 4,

16, 17, 18, 19, 20, 20, 24, 25, 26, 26, 28, 29, 31, 32, 34, 35, 36, 37, 39, 41, 44, 47, 49, 49, 50, 50, 51, 51, 52, 53, 54, 56, 57, 62, 65, 66, 66, 68, 69, 70, 71, 77, 77, 82, 87, 87, 88, 91, 92, 93, 95, 96, 98, 98, 99, 103, 105, 107, 108, 110, 110, 111, 116, 117, 117, 119, 120, 122, 123, 127, 129, 133, 135, 135, 138, 139, 140, 141, 141, 142, 142, 145, 146, 146, 152, 154, 155, 159, 161, 162, 166, 167, 167, 167, 167, 168, 175, 178, 178 Spec 1:1, 4, 6, 8, 9, 11, 12, 13, 16, 18, 19, 23, 27, 29, 30, 32, 32, 32, 41, 43, 45, 51, 51, 56, 56, 57, 64, 65, 66, 66, 69, 71, 71, 73, 74, 74, 79, 83, 84, 85, 86, 86, 88, 89, 93, 94, 96, 97, 99, 100, 102, 102, 103, 105, 105, 108, 108, 110, 111, 112, 113, 116, 117, 120, 121, 121, 125, 125, 126, 132, 134, 135, 143, 145, 145, 145, 147, 150, 152, 156, 158, 162, 162, 162, 164, 165, 168, 168, 169, 169, 169, 171, 172, 174, 175, 178, 178, 178, 180, 180, 183, 184, 184, 186, 187, 188, 188, 188, 188, 189, 190, 190, 191, 193, 194, 195, 195, 196, 196, 197, 197, 198, 200, 201, 203, 206, 208, 208, 213, 214, 216, 216, 217, 218, 218, 219, 219, 220, 222, 224, 226, 226, 227, 228, 228, 229, 233, 234, 234, 235, 239, 240, 241, 242, 243, 244, 248, 249, 251, 252, 252, 255, 256, 257, 258, 259, 259, 262, 262, 268, 270, 272, 273, 274, 274, 275, 277, 279, 282, 282, 287, 291, 292, 295, 296, 298, 298, 299, 300, 300, 300, 307, 309, 310, 311, 314, 314, 321, 321, 322, 323, 323, 327, 330, 332, 333, 333, 334, 336, 337, 338, 339, 340, 340, 340, 343, 343, 344, 344, 345 Spec 2:1, 2, 12, 14, 20, 22, 22, 24, 24, 27, 27, 28, 29, 29, 30, 30, 33, 33, 33, 33, 34, 34, 35, 35, 37, 37, 38, 38, 39, 39, 40, 40, 41, 45, 45, 47, 48, 50, 52, 53, 54, 55, 55, 56, 58, 58, 58, 62, 64, 64, 67, 68, 69, 72, 73, 75, 76, 78, 81, 83, 83, 85, 86, 92, 96, 100, 103, 106, 106, 107, 111, 112, 113, 114, 116, 116, 116, 117, 121, 122, 122, 123, 126, 129, 130, 132, 133, 134, 134, 135, 136, 137, 139, 139, 139, 140, 140, 143, 144, 146, 150, 151, 154, 155, 157, 157, 157, 159, 161, 163, 165, 166, 166, 167, 168, 170, 170, 170, 171, 171, 172, 173, 176, 177, 180, 180, 181, 181, 182, 184, 188, 188, 190, 191, 195, 197, 198, 199, 200, 203, 203, 204, 204, 206, 207, 209, 212, 214, 215, 215, 218, 221, 222, 223, 225, 227, 227, 228, 228, 230, 231, 234, 235, 239, 240, 240, 242, 243, 250, 250, 251, 253, 257, 258, 260, 262, 262 Spec 3:4, 7, 9, 10, 11, 14, 14, 17, 22, 23, 26, 29, 33, 35, 36, 37, 39, 43, 47, 48, 49, 51, 51, 51, 52, 52, 54, 54, 55, 58, 59, 60, 61, 61, 62, 64, 65, 70, 70, 72, 74, 74, 76, 76, 78, 78, 80, 82, 83, 85, 85, 85, 85, 89, 91, 92, 94, 95, 100, 101, 102, 106, 106, 106, 108, 111, 111, 111, 113, 114, 115, 116, 117, 119, 120, 121, 121, 123, 124, 125, 126, 128, 129, 129, 131, 134, 134, 136, 137, 138, 145, 151, 152, 154, 156, 157, 159, 160, 164, 165, 166, 169, 170, 170, 175, 175, 177, 178, 178, 178, 180, 185, 185, 186, 186, 188, 192, 192, 193, 193, 194, 195, 197, 198, 198, 199, 202, 202, 202, 203 Spec 4:1, 1, 2, 5, 5, 6, 7, 7, 8, 9, 11, 12, 12, 12, 12, 13, 14, 18, 19, 21, 25, 25, 30, 31, 31, 32, 32, 33, 35, 35, 36, 37, 41, 42, 42, 43, 43, 45, 49, 49, 52, 53, 54, 55, 57, 60, 60, 61, 62, 63, 64, 65, 67, 69, 71, 71, 72, 75, 78, 79, 81, 82, 82, 92, 92, 93, 98, 101, 102, 103, 108, 108, 109, 111, 112, 112, 112, 112, 113, 113, 113, 114, 119, 119, 120, 123, 124, 125, 127, 128, 129, 132, 133, 134, 135, 136, 141, 142, 143, 146, 147, 147, 150, 153, 154, 157, 158, 159, 160, 163, 164, 165, 166, 166, 171, 171, 173, 175, 176, 178, 179, 182, 185, 186, 186, 186, 187, 187, 189, 192, 193, 194, 195, 197, 200, 200, 200, 201, 202, 203, 203, 206, 208, 208, 209, 209, 209, 210, 212, 214, 219, 221, 222, 224, 227, 230, 233, 236, 237, 237 Virt 2, 2, 4, 5, 5, 6, 8, 9, 9, 10, 12, 15, 15, 19, 19, 22, 22, 24, 25, 26, 29, 29, 29, 29, 32, 34, 36, 37, 38, 42, 45, 46, 50, 52, 54, 59, 59, 61, 64, 66, 68, 69, 73, 74, 76, 79, 79, 80, 83, 85, 85, 88, 89, 90, 90, 91, 92, 93, 94, 95, 95, 97, 98, 100, 100, 102, 103, 105, 109, 109, 111, 113, 114, 115, 116, 116, 117, 120, 121, 122, 123, 124, 124, 125, 130, 130, 133, 135, 136, 138, 140, 140, 141, 141, 143, 144, 145, 145, 146, 146, 148, 149, 149, 153, 158, 159, 163, 163, 164, 164, 172, 172, 173, 173, 176, 177, 179, 180, 183, 184, 185, 186, 187, 195, 195, 195, 196, 197, 203, 204, 204, 205, 206, 208, 209, 211, 211, 211, 212, 214, 214, 217, 218, 219, 220, 222, 222, 223, 223, 224, 226 Praem 1, 1, 1, 1, 1, 2, 2, 5, 6, 6, 8, 10, 11, 12, 14, 15, 15, 16, 16, 17, 22, 23, 24, 25, 26, 26, 27, 28, 28, 29, 30, 31, 32, 33, 40, 40, 41, 44, 46, 47, 47, 47, 49, 52, 53, 56, 57, 58, 58, 59, 61, 64, 64, 64, 67, 69, 70, 71, 71, 73, 73, 73, 74, 76, 77, 78, 81, 82, 85, 86, 86, 87, 87, 91, 92, 94, 97, 98, 99, 99, 99, 101, 101, 101, 102, 104, 106, 106, 107, 107, 111, 113, 113, 114, 116, 118, 118, 119, 124, 125, 125, 126, 127, 127, 128, 128, 129, 130, 131, 133, 133, 137, 139, 140, 141, 141, 144, 147, 148, 148, 149, 150, 151, 152, 152, 153, 154, 155, 156, 157, 157, 158, 159, 159, 162, 163, 165, 166, 169 Prob 1, 2, 6, 8, 10, 11, 12, 13, 16, 17, 17, 17, 18, 19, 20, 21, 24, 24, 26, 26, 30, 30, 30, 31, 36, 39, 42, 45, 45, 47, 52, 53, 57, 57, 58, 60, 61, 63, 63, 65, 65, 66, 67, 69, 69, 70, 71, 72, 73, 73, 74, 76, 76, 80, 81, 82, 84, 84, 85, 86, 89, 94, 95, 96, 99, 101, 102, 107, 107, 108, 109, 111, 111, 113, 114, 116, 117, 117, 118, 120, 121, 122, 124, 129, 136, 136, 137, 138, 138, 141, 145, 149, 150, 151, 152, 156, 159, 159, 159, 160 Contempl 2, 3, 4, 8, 8, 10, 14, 16, 16, 16, 17, 21, 23, 23, 24, 26, 27, 30, 30, 31, 32, 33, 34, 34, 37, 38, 38, 38, 39, 39, 40, 41, 44, 47, 50, 51, 53, 55, 55, 57, 58, 60, 61, 65, 66, 69, 69, 70, 71, 73, 73, 74, 75, 75, 75, 76, 77, 78, 78, 79, 80, 81, 82, 82, 83, 84, 84, 86, 86, 86, 87, 88, 90, 90 Aet 1, 2, 4, 7, 7, 8, 8, 8, 8, 9, 9, 11, 13, 13, 15, 17, 17, 18, 20, 20, 20, 21, 21, 22, 22, 26, 27, 27, 29, 30, 31, 31, 32, 33, 33, 34, 35, 40, 41, 44, 45, 46, 46, 48, 48, 49, 49, 50, 51, 51, 58, 59, 60, 63, 63, 65, 65, 69, 69, 71, 71, 73, 75, 75, 78, 79, 80, 82, 83, 85, 86, 86, 86, 87, 88, 89, 90, 90, 91, 91, 93, 94, 96, 96, 97, 97, 100, 101, 103, 103, 104, 104, 105, 105, 106, 110, 110, 111, 112, 113, 113, 114, 115, 115, 115, 118, 118, 119, 120, 123, 126, 128, 128, 132, 132, 132, 133, 135, 136, 137, 138, 139, 139, 142, 144, 147, 147, 148, 149, 150 Flacc 1, 4, 6, 7, 8, 9, 10, 10, 11, 12, 18, 19, 19, 22, 23, 24, 26, 27, 28, 32, 34, 37, 38, 45, 45, 46, 50, 51, 52, 52, 57, 58, 58, 59, 60, 61, 62, 63, 64, 67, 69, 72, 74, 74, 75, 76, 77, 78, 85, 87, 88, 89, 89, 92, 96, 96, 103, 104, 104, 108, 109, 109, 111, 113, 115, 116, 117, 126, 126, 128, 130, 131, 133, 134, 135, 135, 142, 144, 145, 151, 154, 158, 160, 162, 167, 173, 174, 176, 180, 183, 185, 188, 189, 190 Legat 1, 1, 1, 2, 2, 4, 5, 5, 7, 8, 8, 9, 10, 14, 16, 18, 23, 24, 25, 26, 26, 27, 29, 30, 31, 33, 35, 40, 42, 47, 47, 49, 51, 54, 57, 60, 63, 65, 66, 67, 68, 69, 69, 69, 74, 75, 79, 80, 82, 84, 85, 85, 87, 89, 89, 90, 95, 95, 95, 98, 103, 104, 106, 107, 113, 116, 123, 126, 130, 132, 134, 136, 138, 140, 143, 145, 146, 147, 161, 162, 163, 165, 167, 168, 174, 176, 176, 178, 183, 185, 188, 190, 196, 197, 198, 200, 203, 204, 205, 206, 206, 206, 209, 211, 211, 215, 217, 217, 218, 222, 225, 226, 227, 229, 237, 238, 244, 246, 248, 248, 249, 250, 252, 254, 254, 256, 268, 269, 275, 275, 276, 276, 277, 277, 278, 278, 279, 281, 281, 286, 286, 287, 290, 294, 303, 304, 305, 306, 306, 308, 309, 310, 311, 312, 324, 326, 328, 331, 331, 332, 335, 344, 346, 346, 347, 350, 350, 356, 356, 359, 361, 364, 368, 370, 373

Hypoth 6:1, 6:4, 6:5, 6:5, 6:6, 6:8, 6:9, 7:1, 7:2, 7:3, 7:5, 7:13, 7:13, 7:20, 11:1, 11:1, 11:8, 11:12 Prov 1, 1, 1, 1, 2:1, 1, 3, 5, 6, 6, 7, 7, 10, 12, 13, 16, 17, 18, 19, 23, 24, 24, 25, 28, 30, 33, 34, 35, 35, 35, 36, 36, 37, 38, 42, 43, 44, 48, 49, 51, 53, 54, 59, 59, 60, 62, 65, 65, 66, 67, 68, 69 QG 1:1, 20, 24, 27, 51, 55a, 55a, 58, 60:1, 60:2, 62:1, 62:1, 62:1, 62:2, 64b, 64c, 68, 70:1, 70:2, 72, 72, 76a, 76b, 77, 2:5b, 10, 11, 12b, 12d, 13a, 13b, 14, 14, 15a, 15b, 15b, 16, 16, 26a, 26a, 29, 31, 31, 54a, 54a, 54a, 54a, 59, 59, 59, 66, 68b, 71a, 3:8, 12, 12, 18, 21, 22, 26, 52, 61, 4:8b, 8b, 8b, 30, 30, 33b, 47a, 51c, 52a, 69, 76a, 76b, 80, 80, 88, 100, 102b, 104, 110b, 145, 148, 166, 166, 167, 169, 172, 184, 7*, 198, 198, 200c, 202a, 204, 211 QG isf 5, 8, 9, 13 QG (Par) 2:2, 2:2, 2:2, 2:3, 2:3, 2:3, 2:4, 2:4, 2:4, 2:5, 2:5, 2:5, 2:7, 2:7, 2:7, 2:7 QE 1:1, 4, 19, 2:2, 3a, 3a, 3b, 3b, 6b, 9b, 10a, 14, 16, 17, 18, 21, 21, 25c, 28, 38a, 45a, 46, 46, 49a, 55a QE isf 3, 13, 14, 16, 18, 21, 22, 24, 26, 31

μένος Prob 112

μέντοι (346) Opif 32, 34, 40, 59, 62, 83, 87, 121 Leg 1:3, 6, 24, 50, 57, 70, 83 Leg 2:8, 105 Leg 3:14, 34, 44, 47, 56, 94, 108, 126, 160, 163, 197, 208, 210, 225, 230, 234 Cher 74, 100, 121 Sacr 49, 84, 87, 123 Det 12, 40, 46, 49, 51, 87, 112, 122, 123, 171, 178 Post 31, 36, 74, 82, 111, 127, 134, 139, 140, 166, 178 Gig 2 Deus 10, 57, 153, 163 Agr 5, 11, 13, 19, 32, 50, 51, 64, 93, 109, 127, 139, 145, 169, 169, 172 Plant 30, 40, 56, 59, 61, 62, 63, 104, 122, 133, 146, 148, 167 Ebr 6, 22, 88, 111, 132, 150, 169, 174, 179, 179, 182, 187, 187, 195, 202, 222 Sobr 2, 7, 10, 12, 12, 21, 31, 36, 49, 61, 65, 67, 69 Conf 8, 13, 19, 33, 35, 52, 55, 62, 63, 76, 87, 100, 110, 115, 123, 141, 145, 146, 148, 154, 155, 160, 167, 180, 182, 191 Migr 45, 98, 102, 120, 133, 162, 180, 189, 192, 219, 220, 220 Her 11, 23, 84, 112, 122, 139, 151, 153, 182, 247, 287, 290, 302 Congr 43, 52, 54, 94 Fug 30, 31, 56, 186 Mut 7, 14, 32, 162, 165, 167 Somn 1:27, 33, 37, 52, 67, 92, 103, 117, 171, 191, 193, 205, 209, 234, 235, 236, 243 Somn 2:44, 155, 174, 220, 227, 239, 255, 259, 259 Abr 11, 12, 32, 36, 39, 56, 99, 116, 120, 133, 229 Ios 2, 28, 32, 35, 37, 58, 61, 107, 129, 148, 151, 157, 176, 193, 195, 204, 250, 255 Mos 1:26, 129, 166, 207, 262, 315 Mos 2:135, 139, 186 Decal 21, 24, 48, 79, 102, 133, 141 Spec 1:24, 26, 72, 118, 119, 123, 137, 151, 272, 283, 286, 315, 336 Spec 2:2, 5, 61, 84, 98, 109, 129, 149, 157, 212, 213, 229, 232, 246, 248, 261 Spec 3:12, 77, 91, 99, 104, 115, 119, 143, 145, 146, 153, 155, 173, 182, 205, 206 Spec 4:9, 53, 119, 144, 161, 182, 197 Virt 5, 17, 21, 55, 110, 117, 154, 183 Praem 20, 133, 149, 163 Prob 43 Aet 5, 45, 52, 97, 98, 108, 117, 128 Flacc 66 Legat 159, 261, 261, 323, 334, 339 Hypoth 6:2 Prov 2:9 QG 2:59 QG isf 10 QG (Par) 2:3

μένω (107) Opif 97, 100 Leg 1:6 Leg 2:60, 63, 63, 100 Leg 3:47, 84, 100, 116, 149, 179, 252 Cher 36, 37 Sacr 98 Det 75, 76, 87, 147, 148 Gig 20, 25, 28 Deus 26, 28, 132, 154 Agr 167 Plant 91, 114 Ebr 126, 178, 212 Sobr 49 Conf 78 Migr 195 Her 68, 84, 137, 156, 270, 274, 312 Congr 48 Fug 13, 13, 117, 130 Mut 46, 80, 87 Somn 1:154, 158, 180, 192 Somn 2:145, 221 Abr 240 Ios 134, 141, 145, 211 Mos 1:104, 118, 268, 331 Mos 2:14, 39, 108, 272 Decal 12, 14, 43 Spec 1:47, 103, 124, 300 Spec 2:25, 27, 42, 126 Spec 3:82, 99, 173 Virt 21, 151, 193, 214 Aet 49, 61, 69, 81, 85, 89, 90, 113, 115 Legat 58, 75, 101, 196, 241 Prov 2:28, 28 QG 4:204

μερίζω Cher 74 Post 92 Migr 49

μερίς (29) Opif 135 Leg 3:129, 131 Sacr 119 Det 140 Post 87, 89 Deus 132, 150 Plant 59, 60, 63, 63 Sobr 67 Conf 111 Migr 164 Her 44 Fug 15 Abr 180, 214, 215 Decal 108, 110 Praem 63 Prob 105 Contempl 82 Flacc 9 Legat 183, 354

μερισμός Post 90

μεριστής Deus 84

μεριστός Decal 103, 103

μέρος (699) Opif 13, 17, 25, 36, 38, 41, 64, 67, 67, 69, 76, 99, 101, 111, 117, 118, 130, 131, 132, 133, 135, 137, 138, 146, 163, 167, 171 Leg 1:1, 2, 3, 22, 22, 22, 22, 23, 23, 24, 24, 26, 26, 27, 39, 39, 40, 56, 57, 59, 63, 65, 70, 70, 71, 71, 71, 72, 78, 78 Leg 2:8, 20, 20, 58, 75, 77 Leg 3:6, 6, 18, 31, 63, 84, 97, 114, 115, 115, 115, 116, 124, 130, 141, 145, 169, 170, 170, 171, 176, 176, 176, 230, 232, 251 Cher 5, 6, 26, 51, 61, 69, 71, 86, 89, 109, 112, 127, 128 Sacr 29, 73, 73, 84, 85, 96, 102, 112, 131, 139, 139 Det 5, 7, 8, 9, 44, 64, 64, 74, 76, 77, 78, 89, 91, 102, 103, 106, 107, 108, 111, 154, 154, 170 Post 3, 4, 4, 6, 7, 7, 50, 85, 101, 111, 127, 161, 162, 163 Gig 7, 25 Deus 52, 56, 57, 69, 107, 108, 111, 127, 173 Agr 7, 15, 17, 23, 24, 32, 49, 53, 72, 134 Plant 2, 2, 6, 7, 9, 11, 16, 30, 156, 160, 175 Ebr 6, 91, 118, 119, 137, 171, 199 Sobr 2, 3, 18, 45 Conf 5, 21, 22, 25, 46, 98, 99, 127, 134, 136, 137, 156, 173, 179, 185, 187, 188, 189, 194, 195 Migr 3, 3, 11, 16, 37, 48, 64, 66, 67, 73, 100, 101, 104, 118, 125, 144, 168, 178, 180, 180, 186, 189, 206, 220, 221 Her 20, 55, 55, 67, 111, 136, 142, 151, 152, 167, 175, 183, 184, 185, 186, 196, 202, 219, 225, 226, 226, 232, 235, 246, 282, 315 Congr 2, 8, 21, 27, 61, 69, 75, 115, 120, 136, 145, 146, 147, 148, 150 Fug 24, 46, 69, 110, 112, 112, 112, 122, 141, 172, 195 Mut 21, 64, 74, 105, 119, 124, 130, 159, 173, 184, 200, 224, 225 Somn 1:39, 112, 135, 175, 179, 204, 204, 220, 234 Somn 2:6, 12, 37, 95, 107, 116, 116, 116, 122, 133, 157, 168, 180, 187, 196, 208, 210, 210, 245, 270, 284 Abr 2, 3, 5, 43, 44, 44, 46, 63, 70, 74, 104, 116, 136, 146, 155, 166, 198, 216 Ios 5, 27, 31, 47, 111, 156, 160, 187, 187, 253 Mos 1:22, 113, 127, 128, 143, 157, 177, 191, 201, 213, 215, 217, 218, 218, 276, 282, 285, 315, 323, 323 Mos 2:1, 37, 46, 52, 66, 83, 84, 89, 91, 106, 110, 117, 117, 117, 140, 148, 150, 152, 165, 219, 224, 227, 239, 241, 249, 253, 254, 259, 279, 282, 282, 283, 288 Decal 5, 19, 28, 44, 51, 58, 66, 71, 74, 79, 81, 83, 150, 175 Spec 1:1, 6, 12, 41, 47, 66, 68, 80, 91, 93, 93, 95, 97, 99, 108, 117, 121, 137, 142, 156, 166, 205, 210, 211, 213, 226, 229, 240, 247, 248, 254, 254, 254, 278, 287, 333, 336, 340 Spec 2:1, 32, 40, 53, 58, 59, 63, 65, 67, 85, 89, 103, 103, 103, 104, 140, 166, 170, 177, 183, 190, 192, 220, 240, 242, 244, 249 Spec 3:7, 8, 21, 28, 28, 33, 39, 55, 99, 117, 126, 131, 149, 152, 177, 179, 182, 189, 199, 202, 203 Spec 4:34, 68, 83, 118, 120, 132, 133, 136, 136, 186, 197, 202, 202, 222 Virt 3, 12, 26, 30, 32, 73, 81, 90, 101, 103, 132, 138, 183, 187, 222, 225 Praem 2, 2, 2, 7, 29, 33, 48, 59, 60, 62, 67, 67, 80, 85, 98, 109, 112, 119, 123, 125, 125, 128, 143, 168 Prob 43, 89, 92, 113, 139 Contempl 1, 7, 34, 40, 46, 51, 60, 63, 67 Aet 14, 16, 21, 22, 22, 25, 26, 29, 32, 32, 34, 36, 37, 49, 50, 64, 66, 69, 73, 74, 74, 80, 82, 83, 91, 91, 92, 96, 97, 103, 114, 115, 117, 118, 124, 124, 125, 129, 132, 143, 143, 143, 146, 148, 149 Flacc 1, 5, 24, 44, 51, 62, 65, 66, 71, 73, 80, 90, 108, 114, 123, 141, 144, 171, 176, 190, 190 Legat 8, 10, 16,

31, 73, 74, 101, 118, 127, 127, 128, 131, 143, 158, 170, 178, 184, 227, 229, 238, 244, 267, 269, 282, 284, 298, 324, 350, 350 Prov 1, 1, 2:26, 44, 69 QG 1:3, 51, 74, 2:13a, 34a, 54d, 59, 64b, 3:3, 3, 4:33b QG isf 10 QG (Par) 2:1, 2:2, 2:2, 2:7, 2:7 QE isf 4

Μέρρα Post 155 Congr 163, 163

μέσαυλος Spec 3:169

μεσημβρία (12) Gig 33 Her 250 Somn 1:175, 202 Abr 107, 119, 161 Spec 1:69 Spec 2:145 Legat 89 Prov 2:48 QG 4:30

μεσημβρινός Her 264 Legat 8, 103, 145 QG 4:30

μεσιτεύω Plant 10 Migr 158 Spec 4:31

μεσίτης Somn 1:142, 143 Mos 2:166

μεσόγειος Ios 30 Aet 138 Legat 283, 294

μεσολαβέω Abr 176 Mos 1:6

Μεσοποταμία (9) Post 76 Conf 65, 66 Congr 70 Fug 48, 49 Abr 188 Mos 1:264, 278

μέσος (282) Opif 33, 33, 63, 68, 108, 109, 109, 110, 110, 154 Leg 1:28, 37, 56, 59, 59, 60, 93, 95 Leg 2:64 Leg 3:1, 28, 28, 28, 36, 65, 65, 65, 67, 99, 121, 172, 182, 182, 184, 184, 184, 185, 246 Cher 3, 6, 6, 9, 25, 27, 30, 84, 111 Sacr 22, 28, 30, 36, 37, 37, 43, 59, 115, 116, 118, 119 Det 28, 31, 65, 68 Post 96, 101, 102, 130 Deus 35, 162, 164, 164, 165 Agr 121 Plant 3, 3, 9, 9, 24, 31, 44, 44, 45, 94, 100, 100, 110 Ebr 33, 64, 127, 127, 164 Conf 38, 66, 70, 74 Migr 37, 37, 121, 133, 146, 160 Her 71, 113, 130, 132, 133, 141, 141, 143, 146, 148, 148, 163, 163, 166, 166, 201, 202, 203, 206, 206, 215, 216, 219, 220, 220, 222, 223, 223, 224, 231, 311, 312, 312 Congr 8, 12, 14, 14, 20, 22, 33, 127, 128, 140, 142, 143, 145, 153 Fug 29, 49, 101, 128, 132, 188, 193, 213 Mut 2, 30, 43, 52, 52, 52, 53, 88, 192, 203, 214, 227, 228, 229, 230, 238, 255 Somn 1:19, 68, 76, 76, 91, 168, 219 Somn 2:6, 62, 229, 232, 235 Abr 50, 52, 121, 122, 124, 257 Ios 87 Mos 1:49, 66, 135, 158, 177, 189, 212, 231, 257, 265, 313 Mos 2:9, 78, 78, 78, 80, 91, 92, 101, 101, 102, 103, 167, 172, 213, 249 Decal 21, 46, 63 Spec 1:72, 116, 221, 268, 279, 301, 320, 321 Spec 2:141 Spec 3:77, 160 Spec 4:28, 74, 102, 102, 167, 168, 168, 208 Virt 73, 140, 169 Praem 87 Prob 6, 34, 60, 86 Contempl 43, 83 Aet 33, 33, 86, 115 Flacc 56, 68, 74, 84, 85, 95, 114, 162, 169, 174 Legat 49, 122, 130, 131, 147, 190, 217, 235 Hypoth 11:4 Prov 2:58 QG 2:14, 74 QG (Par) 2:2, 2:2, 2:4, 2:4 QE 1:6, 2:46

μεσότης Deus 81 Migr 147 Her 126

μεσόω Spec 1:183

μεστός (61) Opif 2, 22, 156 Leg 2:97 Leg 3:2, 253 Cher 65, 86 Det 113, 174, 174 Post 2 Plant 40, 167 Conf 166 Migr 19 Her 48, 60, 248 Mut 169, 193, 196, 201 Somn 1:8, 244 Abr 192 Mos 1:204 Mos 2:166, 172, 205, 226 Decal 2, 86, 164 Spec 1:129, 206 Spec 2:42, 48, 52, 79 Spec 4:156 Virt 3, 32, 109 Prob 72 Contempl 9, 64 Flacc 63, 92, 152 Legat 15, 62, 90, 90, 186, 254, 282 Prov 2:27 QG 3:7, 4:30 QE isf 13

μετά (762) Opif 26, 33, 37, 38, 41, 45, 57, 64, 66, 69, 77, 78, 80, 85, 131, 134, 137, 138, 142, 152 Leg 1:49, 51, 99 Leg 2:4, 6, 24 Leg 3:2, 9, 9, 10, 14, 21, 56, 56, 57, 57, 57, 78, 81, 114, 121, 124, 126, 126, 139, 141, 144, 144, 152, 156, 157, 164, 194, 202, 212, 216, 217, 226, 237, 239, 248 Cher 12, 37, 42, 53, 75, 82, 87, 93, 99, 101, 105, 114, 114, 114, 129 Sacr 8, 12, 21, 28, 35, 38, 39, 40, 49, 52, 52, 59, 59, 61, 63, 68, 71, 76, 85, 86, 86, 88, 92, 112, 113, 121, 122, 130 Det 4, 4, 17, 20, 23, 44, 51, 78, 80, 94, 101, 102, 104, 110, 113, 113, 117, 117, 152, 157, 160, 174 Post 28, 29, 29, 29, 30, 30, 30, 30, 33, 39, 39, 74, 138, 147, 148, 155, 159, 169 Gig 1, 14, 18, 29, 49, 52, 66 Deus 1, 1, 2, 4, 22, 23, 61, 71, 76, 93, 98, 116, 119, 119, 119, 121, 121, 122, 131, 144, 151, 153, 177, 183 Agr 25, 41, 64, 70, 73, 73, 76, 78, 93, 103, 129, 132, 147 Plant 8, 64, 68, 123, 136, 161, 163, 165, 169, 169 Ebr 24, 25, 26, 26, 39, 82, 82, 87, 94, 99, 105, 107, 114, 127, 134, 138, 165, 165, 218 Sobr 12, 14, 14, 69 Conf 24, 31, 46, 55, 74, 79, 92, 97, 100, 117, 117, 117, 117, 117, 117, 117, 130, 148, 151, 152, 165, 165, 179 Migr 18, 19, 25, 27, 30, 31, 53, 61, 61, 61, 62, 88, 100, 111, 120, 148, 149, 164, 183, 197, 208, 211, 218 Her 4, 13, 14, 82, 109, 127, 165, 165, 174, 198, 201, 224, 224, 255, 272, 272, 275, 277, 284, 285, 290, 290, 295, 298, 315 Congr 61, 71, 80, 81, 88, 99, 110, 121, 126, 129, 133, 137, 151, 160 Fug 14, 22, 22, 23, 27, 35, 46, 51, 55, 63, 68, 70, 71, 107, 113, 140, 164, 165, 166, 178, 188, 198 Mut 8, 9, 14, 27, 43, 44, 44, 46, 57, 57, 60, 86, 87, 116, 117, 179, 209 Somn 1:3, 6, 43, 46, 70, 91, 100, 113, 117, 122, 179, 189, 191, 198, 208, 252 Somn 2:7, 20, 57, 83, 87, 121, 125, 126, 144, 156, 168, 199, 227, 235, 247, 258 Abr 17, 33, 40, 46, 66, 96, 112, 124, 155, 219, 229, 234, 235, 246, 263, 271 Ios 6, 13, 23, 28, 34, 34, 43, 43, 86, 92, 100, 101, 109, 111, 125, 127, 129, 166, 166, 217, 222, 222, 244, 246, 251, 257, 257, 261, 267 Mos 1:14, 36, 38, 53, 56, 58, 60, 63, 85, 87, 111, 131, 133, 134, 139, 147, 160, 168, 169, 179, 183, 187, 191, 204, 216, 218, 220, 232, 233, 236, 237, 239, 250, 251, 275, 275, 302, 315, 331, 333 Mos 2:42, 42, 51, 54, 62, 64, 64, 64, 67, 78, 118, 136, 143, 144, 151, 170, 174, 203, 209, 226, 227, 229, 234, 234, 244, 245, 266, 268 Decal 39, 52, 69, 71, 74, 87, 95, 106, 141, 176, 177 Spec 1:3, 13, 16, 22, 82, 85, 94, 108, 125, 134, 141, 144, 152, 169, 171, 179, 185, 192, 199, 209, 210, 213, 232, 237, 261, 285, 289, 305, 321 Spec 2:16, 41, 41, 52, 56, 62, 67, 97, 101, 109, 117, 127, 133, 135, 145, 145, 148, 162, 193, 193, 195, 198, 204, 205, 210, 216, 222, 229, 235, 262, 262 Spec 3:17, 39, 43, 78, 117, 123, 162, 166, 188 Spec 4:1, 9, 10, 28, 81, 107, 113, 119, 169, 193, 194, 220 Virt 6, 20, 44, 72, 72, 89, 96, 111, 111, 133, 134, 145, 158, 159, 171, 176, 182, 188, 201, 201, 202, 208, 208, 222 Praem 15, 20, 22, 23, 24, 30, 31, 36, 41, 51, 53, 54, 75, 89, 135, 151 Prob 2, 45, 54, 81, 86, 87, 120, 122, 148, 152 Contempl 14, 30, 31, 36, 42, 43, 66, 67, 71, 72, 75, 80, 81, 83, 89 Aet 19, 89, 146 Flacc 1, 2, 4, 4, 22, 27, 28, 52, 62, 68, 68, 72, 74, 84, 85, 95, 100, 105, 107, 109, 111, 112, 117, 120, 134, 147, 151 Legat 8, 12, 13, 28, 46, 60, 85, 97, 114, 119, 122, 123, 134, 160, 169, 171, 184, 190, 195, 204, 204, 218, 224, 227, 228, 240, 243, 244, 261, 280, 284, 301, 307, 307, 339, 343, 344, 350, 350, 350, 351, 352, 369 Hypoth 6:2, 6:3, 7:5, 7:10, 7:12, 7:13, 7:19, 11:14 Prov 1, 2:2, 3, 16, 22, 43, 65 QG 1:41, 60:1, 60:2, 2:13a, 13a, 17c, 29, 30, 30, 31, 48, 54a, 66, 3:52, 4:180, 7*, 228, 228, 228, 228 QG (Par) 2:5 QE 1:7b, 2:6a, 13b, 46, 50b QE isf 7

μεταβαίνω (7) Opif 95 Det 153 Agr 72 Migr 139, 194 Mut 105 Praem 130

μεταβάλλω (132) Opif 9, 113, 126, 156 Leg 1:89 Leg 3:246 Cher 5, 36, 52, 71, 90, 100 Det 152, 177 Post 134, 154, 155 Deus 130 Agr 56 Plant 91 Ebr 36, 174, 178 Conf 102, 104 Migr 36, 225 Congr 44 Mut 46, 76,

105, 123, 124, 171, 230 Somn 1:20, 129, 154, 232, 238 Somn 2:105, 108, 222, 259 Abr 17, 113, 170 Ios 131, 245, 250, 263 Mos 1:41, 56, 76, 84, 90, 93, 100, 101, 129, 144, 147, 161, 186, 204, 207, 211, 298 Mos 2:26, 44, 218, 260, 264, 267, 280 Decal 33, 80, 87, 110 Spec 1:51, 80, 118, 220, 237, 282, 300, 306 Spec 2:19, 50, 71 Spec 3:37, 99, 103 Spec 4:144, 235 Virt 67, 76, 87, 177, 205, 217 Praem 77, 89, 91, 92, 152, 163, 168 Prob 70, 103 Aet 40, 42, 43, 76, 90, 92, 113, 125, 144 Flacc 144 Legat 20, 22, 80, 89, 91, 118, 126, 238, 238, 368 Prov 2:59, 69

μετάβασις (7) Post 29, 30 Plant 11, 111 Somn 1:186 Decal 60 Spec 2:212

μεταβατικός (11) Sacr 68 Post 29, 30 Plant 11, 12, 13 Sobr 34 Conf 139 Her 81, 137 QE 2:45a

μεταβιβάζω Post 43

μεταβλητικός Deus 37

μεταβλητός Cher 19 Sacr 101 Gig 48 Somn 2:219

μεταβολή (115) Opif 12, 22, 31, 41, 113, 121, 151 Leg 1:8 Cher 62, 88 Post 73, 106, 108, 111, 113 Gig 28, 48, 66 Deus 26, 38, 48, 88, 119, 173 Agr 126 Ebr 91, 111, 170, 178 Her 247, 309 Congr 104, 133 Mut 55, 57, 243 Somn 1:20 Somn 2:136 Abr 18, 18, 26, 69, 81 Ios 32, 33, 33, 134, 144, 215, 254 Mos 1:78, 200, 282, 298 Mos 2:15, 121, 125, 154, 262 Decal 43, 104 Spec 1:26, 62, 188, 210, 311, 342 Spec 2:67, 143, 209, 249 Spec 3:41, 97, 178 Spec 4:86, 235 Virt 110, 122, 151, 153, 165, 183 Praem 41, 115, 159, 164, 169 Aet 5, 6, 14, 32, 54, 59, 60, 72, 82, 103, 109, 110, 110, 111, 116 Flacc 18, 153, 154, 159 Legat 67, 73, 80, 197 Prov 2:45, 53 QG 2:41, 4:43 QG isf 5

μεταγιγνώσκω Deus 21 Mut 233 Spec 1:103 Hypoth 7:4

μεταγράφω Mut 126 Spec 4:61, 163

μεταδιδάσκω Sacr 57 Det 5, 9 Ebr 38

μεταδίδωμι (60) Opif 44, 77, 156 Leg 1:40 Cher 86 Det 101, 124, 156 Post 28 Gig 27, 43 Ebr 110 Her 5, 26, 159 Fug 30, 84 Mut 57 Somn 2:223 Ios 52, 85, 144 Mos 1:37, 315 Mos 2:190, 192, 236 Spec 1:49, 97, 120, 126, 294 Spec 2:15, 71, 89, 107, 115, 119, 141 Spec 3:112, 116, 138, 196 Spec 4:74, 74 Virt 94, 108, 121, 125, 141, 168, 226 Prob 49, 51 Flacc 54 Legat 163 QG 2:10, 65, 4:8* QE 2:3a

μεταδιώκω (33) Opif 162 Leg 3:2 Cher 8, 105 Sacr 12, 21, 78 Det 2 Post 99, 120 Deus 163 Ebr 34 Migr 65 Her 303 Fug 128, 153 Somn 1:248 Somn 2:39, 65 Abr 135 Spec 1:176, 176, 312, 319 Spec 4:66 Virt 136 Praem 154, 162 Contempl 20, 24 QG 4:47a, 47b QE 2:3b

μετάδοσις Spec 1:225 Spec 4:74

μετάθεσις (11) Gig 66, 66 Mut 60, 130 Abr 18, 81 Ios 136 Praem 17 Aet 113, 113 QG 4:67

μεταιτέω Virt 86

μεταίτης Her 103 Spec 2:106 Flacc 64

μετακαλέω (11) Det 10 Ebr 37 Migr 184 Somn 1:188 Somn 2:99 Ios 168 Mos 1:77, 280, 292 Mos 2:288 Praem 44

μετακινέω Post 89 Spec 4:149

μετακλαίω Det 95

μετακλίνω (7) Post 100, 100, 111 Gig 44 Deus 180 Conf 129 Migr 184

μετακομίζω Ios 111 Legat 220, 305

μετακόσμιος Conf 134 Somn 1:184 Somn 2:130

μεταλαγχάνω (20) Leg 2:57 Gig 14 Her 143 Congr 7 Abr 129 Ios 27, 210 Mos 1:11, 157 Mos 2:152 Spec 1:109, 243, 269, 309 Spec 3:111 Praem 111 Aet 46 Legat 91 Prov 2:14, 22

μεταλαμβάνω (46) Opif 158 Leg 3:93 Post 13, 69 Gig 24 Plant 134 Ebr 145 Sobr 28 Migr 165, 205, 221 Her 54, 97 Congr 2, 30, 55, 60 Fug 44, 45, 50, 208 Mut 92, 98, 103, 106, 126, 193, 268 Somn 1:131, 254 Somn 2:36, 192, 250 Abr 201 Decal 38 Spec 1:124, 129, 240 Spec 4:99, 149 Virt 30 Praem 6, 14 Aet 110 Legat 283 QE isf 14

μετάληψις Plant 74

μεταλλάσσω Virt 108

μεταλλεύω Agr 25 Abr 141 Prob 65, 65

μεταλλοιόω Post 83, 93, 98 Gig 65

μέταλλον Prov 2:10 QG isf 11 QE 2:50b

μεταμέλεια Ios 173 Spec 1:242 QG 1:93, 93, 2:54a

μεταμορφόω Mos 1:57 Spec 4:147 Legat 95 QG 1:92 QE 2:1

μετανάστασις (17) Leg 3:19 Sacr 10 Det 154 Migr 2, 189 Her 265, 287, 289 Somn 1:45 Somn 2:270 Abr 77 Mos 1:86, 237 Spec 2:250 Virt 53, 76 Praem 17

μετανάστατος Her 280

μετανάστης (15) Plant 46 Ebr 100 Conf 68 Migr 28 Her 26 Mut 16, 152 Somn 1:52, 160 Somn 2:184, 273 Spec 2:118 Virt 105, 218 Flacc 94

μετανάστις Cher 103 Prob 107

μετανίστημι (77) Leg 3:20 Cher 98, 115 Sacr 7, 8, 77 Det 163 Post 2, 7, 8, 173 Gig 21, 47, 56, 61 Deus 180 Plant 34, 96, 147 Ebr 10, 39, 94 Conf 76 Migr 12, 20, 177, 187, 197 Her 71, 71, 74, 98, 99, 179, 240, 274, 287, 288 Congr 49, 58 Fug 59, 117 Mut 38, 76 Somn 1:52 Abr 47, 62, 66, 67, 71, 165, 212 Ios 251 Mos 1:5, 34, 147, 193, 240, 254, 283 Mos 2:72, 184 Spec 2:25, 217 Spec 3:99, 162, 207 Spec 4:49, 158, 178 Virt 214, 214 Praem 20, 87 Prob 128 Aet 30, 31

μετανοέω (35) Leg 2:60 Leg 3:211 Cher 2 Deus 8, 72 Fug 99, 157, 160 Mut 235 Somn 1:91, 91, 182 Abr 27 Ios 87 Mos 1:167, 283 Mos 2:167 Spec 1:103, 239, 241, 253, 253 Spec 4:18, 221 Virt 152, 175, 176, 180, 208 Praem 169 Legat 303, 337, 339 QG 2:13a, 4:131

μετάνοια (30) Leg 2:78 Leg 3:106, 213 Sacr 132 Det 96 Post 178 Deus 33 Fug 158, 159, 159 Mut 124, 235 Somn 2:108, 109, 292 Abr 17, 26 Spec 1:58, 102, 187, 236 Virt 174, 180, 183 Praem 15, 22 Aet 40 Flacc 181 QG 2:13a, 4:8*

μεταξύ (20) Opif 35 Leg 3:253 Cher 111 Sacr 65 Det 80 Post 18 Deus 158 Migr 147 Her 110 Mut 264 Somn 2:228, 234 Ios 175 Mos 2:228 Spec 1:295 Spec 2:225 Contempl 30, 33 Flacc 92 Hypoth 6:2

μεταπείθω Mos 2:177

μεταπέμπω (22) Ebr 208 Conf 65 Fug 23, 47 Abr 94, 215 Ios 92, 103, 207, 260 Mos 1:21, 266, 278 Spec 4:36 Virt 35 Flacc 76, 86, 141 Legat 222, 222, 349, 351

μεταπλάσσω Det 152

μεταποιέω (43) Opif 17 Cher 74 Sacr 100 Det 68 Post 93, 99, 100 Deus 12 Agr 114 Ebr 35 Sobr 26, 69 Conf 73 Migr 11, 21, 96, 147 Her 62, 63, 150, 299 Congr 88 Fug 38 Mut 263 Somn 1:219 Somn 2:107, 163 Abr 53, 160

Ios 92 Mos 1:242 Mos 2:139 Decal 58 Spec 1:38, 57, 265 Spec 3:137 Spec 4:187 Virt 85 Praem 22, 111 Flacc 131 Legat 80

μεταποίησις Praem 66

μετάρσιος (21) Leg 1:43 Leg 3:104, 162, 252 Cher 4, 31, 47, 89 Det 87, 154 Gig 62 Plant 3, 24, 25, 68, 127 Mut 67 Abr 43 Spec 3:1 Spec 4:236 Aet 63

μετασκευάζω Migr 211 Legat 95

μετάστασις Abr 245 Mos 1:183

μεταστένω Det 95

μεταστοιχειόω Migr 83 Somn 2:118 Mos 1:78 QG 4:51b

μετασχηματίζω Aet 79 Legat 80, 346

μετατάσσω Conf 154

μετατίθημι (27) Leg 3:107, 107, 107 Sacr 11 Post 43, 83, 84, 88 Deus 26 Mut 13, 38 Abr 17, 19, 19, 24, 47 Mos 2:34 Praem 16, 58 Aet 54, 115 Flacc 131, 184 Legat 1, 69, 104 Prov 2:44

μετατρέπω (8) Sacr 114, 116 Deus 181, 183 Conf 129, 139 Migr 83 Abr 86

μετατρέχω (6) Ebr 59 Conf 114 Fug 205 Abr 20 Mos 2:185 Praem 116

μετατυπόω Somn 1:171 Spec 4:146

μεταφέρω Prob 96

μεταφορά Sacr 126

μεταφράζω Mos 2:38

μεταχαράσσω (17) Cher 4 Det 152 Post 93, 99 Conf 159 Migr 39, 119 Mut 71, 121, 123 Somn 1:129 Spec 1:325 Prob 4, 98 Legat 70, 80, 106

μεταχωρέω Somn 1:79 Abr 78 Spec 1:309

μέτειμι (51) Opif 147 Leg 3:26, 164, 251 Cher 4, 129 Det 66, 104, 114, 120 Post 44, 101, 130 Gig 5, 39 Agr 90 Plant 73, 77 Ebr 86 Sobr 68 Migr 147 Her 78 Congr 35, 50 Fug 166, 177 Somn 2:93 Abr 27, 206, 217, 274 Mos 2:148, 233 Decal 115 Spec 2:224 Spec 3:101 Spec 4:160 Virt 1, 148, 180 Praem 3, 26, 46, 61 Prob 35, 48, 48, 76 Flacc 35 Legat 23 QG 2:72

μετέπειτα Plant 127 QG 1:28

μετέρχομαι (16) Opif 96 Leg 3:52, 188 Cher 127 Det 18, 24, 102 Gig 17 Deus 34 Ebr 14, 103 Conf 37, 190 Migr 155 Prov 2:40 QG 1:27

μετέχω (81) Opif 66, 73, 120, 134, 135, 145 Leg 1:40 Leg 2:22, 23, 63, 64 Leg 3:1, 1, 196 Cher 86, 89, 120 Sacr 95 Det 82, 82, 84 Post 159, 160 Gig 22 Deus 41, 80, 144 Agr 145 Plant 168, 172 Conf 83 Her 229 Congr 48, 84 Mut 213, 266 Somn 1:21, 68 Abr 101, 107, 123, 123, 155, 202, 246 Ios 20, 196, 266 Mos 1:58, 156, 168, 298, 313 Mos 2:226 Decal 31, 31, 99, 104 Spec 2:57, 68, 71, 175, 225, 256 Spec 3:99 Spec 4:14, 94, 105, 159 Virt 87, 91, 113, 166 Prob 50, 150, 160 Contempl 21 Prov 2:51 QG 3:38a, 49b, 58

μετεωρέω Leg 3:214

μετεωρίζω (22) Leg 3:186 Det 152 Post 115 Agr 169 Ebr 93 Her 34, 71, 241, 269 Congr 127 Ios 6 Mos 1:115, 195 Mos 2:54, 139 Spec 1:44 Spec 3:152 Praem 73 Contempl 3 Aet 86 Legat 202, 272

μετεωροθήρας Somn 2:115

μετεωρολεσχέω Mut 16 Somn 1:54

μετεωρολέσχης Mut 70 Somn 1:161 Prob 80

μετεωρολογία Ebr 92 Her 97

μετεωρολογικός (7) Ebr 91, 94 Mut 67, 68 Somn 2:112 Abr 82, 84

μετεωροπολέω (11) Leg 3:71, 84 Det 27 Plant 145 Her 128, 230, 237, 239 Somn 1:139 Mos 1:190 Spec 1:207

μετεωροπόλος Mut 67

μετέωρος (58) Opif 86, 147, 163 Leg 3:18, 18, 18, 83, 244 Cher 4, 4 Det 152 Gig 62, 62 Deus 167 Ebr 128 Conf 90 Migr 168, 172, 178 Congr 41 Fug 44, 45 Mut 66, 67, 154 Somn 1:54, 134, 211 Somn 2:16, 78 Abr 42, 82 Ios 149 Mos 1:31, 169, 177, 179, 218 Mos 2:90 Decal 4, 143 Spec 1:37, 219 Spec 2:230 Spec 4:236 Virt 14, 173 Praem 8, 47, 80, 152 Contempl 86 Aet 136 Flacc 37, 142 Legat 18, 151 QG 4:99

μετοικέω Abr 229

μετοικία Leg 3:19, 84 Congr 88 Mut 38

μετοικίζω (17) Opif 171 Leg 3:19 Post 32 Migr 187 Her 71, 280 Fug 131 Abr 47, 224 Spec 1:103 Spec 2:168 Spec 3:99, 207 Praem 20 Contempl 19 Hypoth 6:1 QG 3:11a

μέτοικος (13) Ebr 100 Conf 82 Abr 209, 231, 252 Mos 1:35, 36 Mos 2:58, 58 Spec 2:170 Virt 105, 109 Legat 200

μετονομάζω (16) Leg 3:15, 244 Cher 4, 7 Gig 62, 63 Migr 201 Mut 65, 76, 77, 81, 83, 87, 88, 121 Ios 121

μετοπωρίζω Opif 58

μετοπωρινός (15) Opif 116 Her 147, 149 Somn 1:20 Decal 161, 161 Spec 1:172, 172, 186 Spec 2:153, 204, 213 Spec 4:233 Flacc 116 QG 2:31

μετόπωρον (18) Opif 45, 52, 58, 116, 116 Cher 112 Plant 120 Her 146, 208 Somn 2:131 Mos 2:124 Spec 1:210 Spec 2:205, 220 Spec 4:235 Virt 93 Praem 130 Legat 15

μετουσία (59) Opif 167 Leg 1:22, 34 Leg 3:46, 47, 52, 171 Cher 36 Sacr 33 Det 140 Ebr 20, 116 Her 15 Fug 29, 99 Mut 71 Somn 2:48, 210, 268 Abr 6, 7, 129 Ios 220 Mos 1:149, 183 Mos 2:5, 243 Spec 1:165, 193, 195, 196, 242, 269 Spec 2:118, 132, 138, 165, 173, 183, 262 Spec 3:171, 208 Spec 4:75, 100, 143, 167 Virt 91, 156 Praem 87, 127, 135 Prob 47 Flacc 53, 118 Legat 8, 16, 318 QE 2:18 QE isf 14

μετοχετεύω Somn 1:107

μετοχή Leg 1:22

μετρέω (34) Opif 38, 91, 102, 103, 105, 130 Leg 3:149, 163, 166 Cher 31 Sacr 59, 59 Post 136 Agr 115 Ebr 185 Her 29, 32, 227, 229 Somn 2:192, 194 Ios 145 Mos 1:206 Decal 27, 28 Spec 2:60, 83 Spec 4:232, 234 Virt 195 Legat 248, 350 QG 2:68a QE 2:28

μέτρησις Aet 19

μετριάζω (7) Opif 169 Fug 35 Mut 227 Abr 191, 211 Mos 1:40 Spec 3:175

μετρικός Mos 1:23

μετριοπάθεια Leg 3:129, 132, 144 Virt 195

μετριοπαθέω Leg 3:134 Abr 257 Ios 26

μετριοπαθής Spec 3:96

μέτριος (73) Opif 7, 128, 155 Leg 3:87, 155 Sacr 26 Det 41, 51 Post 23, 141 Gig 35, 37 Agr 40, 70 Plant 142, 145 Ebr 16, 32, 116 Sobr 46 Conf 150, 152 Migr 20 Her 58, 181, 239 Congr 89, 128 Fug 32, 154 Mut 129, 160, 212, 229, 244 Abr 257, 259, 260 Ios 93 Mos 1:84 Spec

1:2, 23, 60, 194 Spec 2:19, 23, 91, 252, 253 Spec 3:44, 158, 172 Virt 105, 179, 187 Prob 109, 125, 145 Contempl 45, 56 Aet 63, 69, 104 Flacc 117 Legat 69, 116, 126, 336, 361, 365 Hypoth 11:14 QG 4:52c QE 2:25c

μέτρον (72) Opif 34, 35, 37, 51, 55, 60, 104, 130 Leg 3:25, 165 Cher 33, 105 Sacr 59, 59, 59, 60 Det 125 Post 35, 36 Agr 137 Sobr 36 Migr 125 Her 144, 151, 162, 162, 162, 162, 191, 227, 227, 229, 246 Congr 100, 100, 101, 101, 102 Fug 57 Mut 232, 245 Somn 1:205 Somn 2:192, 193, 193, 193, 194 Abr 108 Mos 1:207 Mos 2:83, 115 Spec 1:28, 179, 256, 342, 343 Spec 4:79, 129, 193, 194, 217 Contempl 29, 80, 84 Aet 56, 58 Prov 1, 1 QG 2:64a, 4:8b, 8b QE isf 24

μετωπηδόν Spec 4:111

μέτωπον Aet 37

μέχρι (175) Opif 50, 151 Leg 2:37, 39, 78, 78, 86, 91 Leg 3:14, 70, 179, 215, 252, 252 Cher 2, 4, 38, 48, 71, 94, 99, 120 Sacr 43, 122 Det 44, 45, 127, 128, 149 Post 53, 72, 116, 127, 165, 168, 173 Gig 62 Deus 2, 43, 52, 79, 116 Agr 37, 134 Plant 30, 67 Ebr 10, 23, 49, 221 Sobr 67 Conf 12, 37, 85, 104, 128, 157 Migr 16, 18, 24, 26 Her 131, 149, 247, 309 Congr 106 Fug 21, 186 Mut 36, 95, 113, 178 Somn 1:47, 129, 152, 181 Somn 2:56, 64, 109, 198, 212, 283, 293, 295 Abr 88, 140, 181, 240 Ios 93, 136, 217 Mos 1:28, 30, 33, 58, 122, 125, 136, 137, 145, 181, 218, 222, 226 Mos 2:14, 26, 29, 41, 56, 157, 163, 264 Decal 35, 87, 99 Spec 1:118, 211 Spec 2:16, 20, 54, 117, 220, 230, 232, 233 Spec 3:54, 101, 162, 204, 205, 206 Spec 4:75, 80, 83, 112, 234 Virt 139 Praem 79, 94, 151 Prob 10, 26 Contempl 7, 12, 28 Aet 62, 71, 128, 135 Flacc 10, 26, 43, 110, 156, 173, 179 Legat 13, 18, 54, 145, 157, 174, 297, 317, 322, 357 Hypoth 6:1, 7:13 Prov 2:33, 60, 70 QG 1:76b, 2:54a, 4:145 QE isf 7

μέχριπερ Conf 7

μή (2443) Opif 7, 10, 10, 15, 16, 21, 23, 27, 28, 33, 33, 38, 38, 46, 50, 66, 72, 81, 86, 90, 102, 124, 130, 131, 144, 166, 167, 168, 169, 171, 172 Leg 1:17, 20, 25, 25, 29, 29, 30, 32, 34, 34, 35, 36, 38, 38, 42, 43, 49, 51, 51, 51, 51, 59, 60, 70, 74, 76, 76, 79, 84, 97, 98, 98, 98, 100, 100 Leg 2:3, 6, 7, 7, 7, 7, 7, 15, 27, 27, 28, 31, 32, 43, 43, 46, 46, 57, 57, 59, 61, 62, 63, 63, 63, 72, 82, 88, 91, 92, 93, 93, 100, 100 Leg 3:1, 4, 6, 6, 9, 9, 10, 10, 11, 12, 13, 15, 16, 16, 16, 17, 20, 24, 24, 27, 27, 35, 38, 53, 56, 56, 56, 56, 58, 61, 65, 66, 68, 69, 70, 72, 81, 81, 82, 84, 84, 86, 101, 105, 113, 116, 116, 117, 120, 123, 125, 126, 128, 128, 136, 137, 138, 145, 150, 150, 151, 153, 156, 158, 163, 164, 164, 165, 165, 166, 166, 168, 179, 194, 199, 199, 202, 202, 207, 209, 210, 211, 212, 214, 215, 222, 222, 228, 231, 236, 240, 240, 246 Cher 10, 14, 14, 15, 15, 15, 15, 19, 32, 33, 35, 35, 36, 37, 39, 43, 48, 53, 60, 65, 72, 81, 82, 84, 86, 93, 96, 98, 109, 121, 130 Sacr 1, 10, 12, 12, 23, 26, 28, 29, 33, 36, 45, 46, 47, 48, 50, 52, 53, 53, 54, 55, 55, 56, 63, 70, 70, 72, 76, 76, 78, 78, 82, 85, 85, 89, 97, 109, 113, 113, 114, 114, 115, 116, 117, 121, 121, 123, 125, 127, 128, 130 Det 12, 18, 19, 22, 22, 25, 28, 31, 33, 38, 38, 38, 38, 46, 53, 53, 54, 55, 57, 57, 58, 58, 60, 61, 62, 64, 64, 76, 79, 81, 85, 89, 90, 96, 101, 101, 102, 104, 105, 112, 114, 118, 130, 132, 133, 134, 138, 144, 145, 156, 156, 156, 157, 160, 161, 173, 175, 175, 177, 178 Post 9, 10, 24, 31, 42, 50, 53, 56, 58, 73, 78, 81, 82, 89, 94, 96, 104, 108, 108, 115, 141, 142, 142, 143, 143, 144, 144, 147, 148, 151, 156, 157, 163, 163, 164, 171, 176, 178, 179 Gig 5, 15, 21, 24, 25, 29, 33, 33, 34, 35, 35, 37, 41, 43, 46, 47, 47 Deus 4, 5, 7, 8, 8, 8, 8, 11, 12, 17, 17, 17, 17, 17, 17, 17, 17, 17, 18, 19, 22, 33, 34, 37, 52, 55, 62, 64, 67, 78, 81, 85, 86, 87, 87, 87, 87, 87, 87, 93, 93, 97, 98, 100, 100, 100, 102, 105, 119, 122, 125, 128, 145, 152, 160, 164, 166, 170, 173, 180, 183, 183, 183 Agr 4, 6, 19, 26, 28, 34, 36, 39, 40, 44, 45, 45, 49, 53, 59, 68, 84, 85, 88, 90, 97, 103, 104, 111, 112, 112, 113, 115, 121, 121, 122, 125, 126, 127, 127, 127, 129, 130, 148, 148, 148, 156, 159, 161, 161, 162, 164, 165, 167, 167, 168, 169, 171, 172 Plant 6, 15, 21, 50, 52, 60, 72, 78, 79, 83, 84, 92, 100, 107, 110, 113, 114, 115, 127, 146, 147, 152, 154, 156, 157, 169, 173, 176, 177 Ebr 2, 13, 14, 17, 18, 18, 18, 19, 25, 26, 33, 52, 54, 72, 72, 75, 75, 75, 75, 75, 75, 75, 76, 81, 84, 87, 88, 89, 101, 102, 104, 104, 122, 125, 127, 134, 135, 135, 135, 138, 157, 157, 162, 164, 170, 177, 188, 190, 190, 198, 204, 213, 214, 218 Sobr 6, 6, 6, 8, 15, 15, 18, 42, 42, 46, 49, 56, 57, 67 Conf 1, 10, 15, 38, 39, 40, 46, 46, 46, 51, 53, 59, 65, 66, 69, 74, 75, 76, 81, 87, 97, 98, 101, 102, 103, 111, 116, 120, 123, 123, 135, 136, 141, 143, 156, 160, 162, 162, 163, 163, 166, 166, 175, 175, 183, 189, 190, 191, 195 Migr 4, 8, 12, 17, 20, 21, 22, 24, 25, 26, 26, 26, 26, 27, 36, 42, 44, 45, 48, 55, 55, 58, 64, 64, 74, 75, 78, 79, 82, 84, 87, 91, 91, 95, 96, 101, 121, 130, 134, 135, 136, 138, 138, 144, 146, 155, 155, 161, 163, 167, 169, 169, 171, 171, 172, 172, 174, 174, 181, 183, 185, 185, 191, 192, 194, 197, 200, 209, 209, 210, 216, 217, 217, 217, 217, 217, 217, 217, 217, 217, 217, 217, 217, 218, 220, 220, 223, 224, 225 Her 3, 12, 14, 18, 19, 19, 20, 20, 20, 25, 36, 42, 44, 67, 69, 71, 74, 82, 83, 91, 92, 100, 104, 105, 110, 112, 114, 114, 116, 123, 129, 130, 142, 169, 169, 170, 193, 206, 215, 216, 224, 252, 255, 278, 287, 287, 291, 301, 306, 306, 309, 314 Congr 1, 5, 5, 7, 9, 9, 9, 12, 12, 13, 13, 23, 46, 46, 46, 52, 57, 69, 69, 80, 106, 107, 110, 113, 123, 125, 137, 139, 157, 162, 171, 172, 177, 177, 178 Fug 3, 6, 7, 14, 15, 24, 25, 28, 30, 34, 46, 49, 60, 62, 70, 80, 84, 85, 85, 86, 95, 97, 98, 98, 98, 98, 99, 104, 105, 105, 115, 120, 129, 131, 149, 149, 154, 155, 159, 159, 162, 162, 162, 165, 166, 170, 171, 171, 171, 181, 193, 201, 206, 206 Mut 3, 7, 9, 9, 12, 13, 14, 26, 39, 46, 46, 47, 47, 47, 48, 48, 50, 50, 50, 50, 53, 53, 53, 53, 56, 56, 56, 60, 62, 73, 73, 81, 84, 85, 100, 104, 104, 108, 115, 118, 120, 124, 124, 127, 144, 145, 153, 153, 155, 157, 171, 171, 172, 177, 186, 188, 198, 203, 204, 207, 207, 208, 210, 211, 214, 221, 225, 226, 226, 227, 228, 229, 230, 231, 232, 232, 233, 234, 238, 238, 240, 241, 242, 242, 250, 250, 252, 256, 259, 265, 266 Somn 1:3, 3, 7, 11, 13, 18, 27, 38, 44, 45, 47, 49, 51, 52, 54, 54, 71, 73, 81, 91, 93, 93, 94, 95, 98, 99, 99, 107, 111, 117, 124, 131, 135, 143, 143, 143, 159, 160, 164, 164, 164, 164, 167, 173, 180, 181, 186, 187, 188, 192, 195, 200, 211, 212, 217, 218, 219, 222, 228, 231, 236, 239, 244, 244, 248, 250, 252, 256 Somn 2:7, 11, 22, 22, 30, 39, 39, 54, 56, 61, 62, 62, 76, 76, 88, 92, 93, 93, 94, 94, 100, 100, 117, 127, 131, 131, 136, 137, 138, 140, 146, 149, 160, 164, 169, 174, 176, 177, 182, 183, 184, 189, 202, 222, 222, 227, 231, 249, 250, 262, 268, 269, 275, 280, 281, 291, 291, 301, 301 Abr 10, 15, 20, 25, 26, 29, 31, 38, 46, 47, 49, 51, 51, 53, 54, 58, 63, 70, 73, 74, 80, 85, 86, 107, 112, 116, 116, 118, 118, 120, 122, 122, 128, 129, 129, 131, 131, 142, 154, 158, 168, 176, 177, 179, 184, 190, 191, 195, 197, 199, 206, 214, 215, 216, 221, 238, 243, 247, 249, 257, 258 Ios 4, 5, 7, 9, 10, 12, 13, 13, 15, 16, 21,

24, 27, 33, 44, 45, 45, 48, 52, 59, 62, 70, 70, 70, 70, 70, 70, 70, 70, 70, 73, 74, 94, 94, 99, 106, 107, 110, 111, 113, 115, 116, 118, 126, 129, 138, 144, 144, 144, 144, 144, 150, 154, 165, 168, 168, 169, 173, 175, 178, 184, 188, 188, 190, 193, 197, 206, 209, 210, 215, 220, 222, 224, 227, 227, 229, 230, 232, 233, 236, 239, 246, 248, 249, 249, 261, 262, 262, 266 Mos 1:1, 6, 6, 8, 8, 10, 11, 13, 15, 19, 26, 28, 33, 40, 44, 45, 56, 57, 62, 64, 67, 67, 69, 70, 75, 76, 78, 87, 102, 103, 108, 109, 114, 115, 117, 124, 140, 159, 160, 164, 166, 171, 173, 184, 192, 199, 199, 208, 211, 213, 216, 220, 222, 224, 227, 230, 230, 232, 233, 236, 236, 236, 237, 242, 243, 243, 243, 247, 250, 251, 255, 258, 272, 274, 274, 275, 278, 278, 278, 283, 285, 292, 294, 297, 315, 318, 325, 327, 327, 329 Mos 2:2, 4, 5, 6, 7, 11, 16, 17, 36, 37, 43, 49, 60, 85, 87, 90, 100, 113, 116, 130, 130, 131, 135, 136, 139, 140, 145, 147, 152, 155, 155, 161, 162, 169, 171, 175, 177, 187, 187, 187, 197, 198, 198, 200, 201, 201, 213, 222, 226, 227, 228, 231, 231, 231, 232, 232, 235, 243, 245, 245, 245, 252, 252, 252, 255, 265, 267, 272, 273, 274, 278, 279, 285 Decal 3, 6, 13, 15, 34, 42, 43, 43, 51, 58, 63, 64, 64, 72, 74, 74, 74, 74, 82, 87, 91, 91, 94, 95, 98, 99, 101, 111, 111, 112, 115, 118, 128, 132, 132, 135, 137, 146, 150, 150, 167, 170, 171, 172, 172, 172, 172, 172, 177 Spec 1:3, 11, 14, 15, 26, 26, 30, 30, 31, 37, 40, 42, 44, 52, 52, 53, 53, 53, 63, 67, 68, 83, 90, 90, 91, 91, 97, 102, 103, 107, 109, 110, 111, 112, 113, 114, 114, 114, 119, 120, 120, 123, 124, 125, 127, 127, 129, 129, 134, 135, 151, 152, 156, 160, 166, 167, 191, 193, 197, 209, 211, 211, 213, 214, 215, 215, 219, 220, 221, 230, 238, 241, 242, 242, 248, 249, 250, 250, 250, 252, 254, 255, 259, 266, 273, 274, 275, 277, 277, 280, 283, 284, 284, 289, 292, 300, 300, 300, 304, 306, 306, 310, 313, 314, 317, 321, 325, 325, 326, 335 Spec 2:1, 2, 2, 3, 5, 6, 6, 6, 6, 6, 6, 9, 9, 10, 11, 11, 16, 19, 19, 19, 19, 24, 25, 26, 28, 32, 35, 36, 36, 36, 37, 38, 42, 46, 47, 52, 54, 61, 67, 67, 67, 72, 73, 73, 78, 78, 80, 80, 83, 85, 85, 87, 87, 94, 96, 97, 101, 106, 107, 108, 113, 114, 116, 118, 118, 119, 121, 122, 122, 123, 123, 124, 125, 126, 126, 127, 129, 130, 131, 132, 132, 135, 142, 147, 165, 171, 174, 175, 178, 183, 183, 189, 193, 193, 197, 197, 197, 199, 203, 207, 210, 215, 216, 220, 224, 225, 225, 229, 229, 232, 232, 233, 240, 245, 246, 248, 252, 253, 255, 255, 256, 257, 258, 261 Spec 3:6, 6, 6, 14, 17, 20, 26, 26, 26, 26, 27, 29, 30, 32, 32, 35, 46, 47, 53, 55, 56, 61, 65, 67, 67, 68, 70, 71, 73, 77, 84, 85, 86, 86, 87, 88, 90, 91, 91, 92, 92, 96, 98, 100, 106, 106, 111, 113, 113, 115, 118, 120, 121, 125, 126, 128, 128, 128, 128, 130, 132, 133, 137, 139, 140, 141, 142, 143, 146, 146, 148, 149, 150, 152, 152, 153, 154, 155, 158, 162, 168, 171, 173, 174, 175, 176, 177, 180, 183, 184, 195, 199, 203, 205, 208 Spec 4:1, 2, 7, 10, 13, 16, 16, 20, 21, 25, 29, 32, 32, 34, 36, 37, 37, 37, 38, 38, 44, 45, 45, 53, 57, 59, 59, 60, 61, 61, 62, 64, 67, 71, 72, 74, 77, 78, 79, 82, 92, 93, 99, 103, 105, 108, 112, 113, 115, 121, 136, 137, 138, 138, 140, 141, 145, 149, 150, 158, 158, 158, 160, 162, 163, 167, 170, 170, 171, 175, 175, 177, 179, 181, 182, 183, 186, 187, 189, 193, 195, 195, 202, 202, 202, 203, 203, 203, 203, 205, 206, 207, 208, 208, 211, 212, 213, 213, 216, 217, 227, 235 Virt 9, 12, 16, 17, 19, 25, 26, 27, 29, 29, 29, 29, 30, 30, 31, 37, 41, 41, 56, 58, 60, 64, 64, 66, 70, 74, 79, 80, 83, 83, 86, 88, 89, 89, 89, 90, 92, 95, 95, 98, 99, 103, 105, 106, 106, 107, 110, 112, 115, 116, 116, 120, 123, 123, 124, 124, 129, 129, 130, 130, 133, 135, 136, 137, 138, 139, 140, 142, 144, 145, 146, 147, 149, 151, 152, 152, 154, 155, 156, 156, 156, 157, 159, 160, 160, 166, 170, 172, 179, 180, 184, 188, 188, 191, 202, 202, 206, 208, 209, 221, 222, 223, 224, 226, 227 Praem 5, 9, 14, 17, 18, 21, 28, 32, 34, 40, 45, 45, 47, 52, 55, 55, 72, 72, 72, 72, 77, 79, 83, 94, 95, 100, 100, 104, 108, 114, 115, 124, 130, 130, 130, 130, 131, 135, 143, 148, 155, 163, 170, 172 Prob 2, 3, 4, 4, 6, 7, 7, 12, 16, 27, 40, 42, 47, 53, 54, 57, 57, 60, 60, 63, 63, 66, 82, 95, 96, 96, 104, 106, 111, 112, 116, 117, 128, 129, 131, 138, 139, 147, 150 Contempl 13, 14, 14, 15, 16, 25, 25, 37, 37, 51, 64, 69, 75, 75 Aet 5, 5, 6, 11, 13, 14, 25, 27, 32, 33, 40, 51, 53, 53, 60, 60, 60, 60, 60, 60, 61, 65, 72, 77, 78, 78, 78, 82, 85, 89, 90, 92, 92, 95, 98, 99, 102, 104, 104, 106, 106, 112, 114, 118, 119, 125, 126, 131, 132, 133, 137, 138, 142, 143, 149 Flacc 3, 5, 6, 6, 10, 12, 15, 27, 31, 35, 35, 40, 40, 40, 47, 50, 50, 50, 57, 57, 57, 57, 57, 61, 66, 68, 68, 68, 69, 79, 81, 86, 91, 93, 94, 96, 101, 102, 110, 115, 118, 126, 130, 130, 130, 139, 150, 151, 160, 164, 164, 170, 181, 191 Legat 7, 7, 15, 27, 30, 33, 36, 37, 42, 43, 44, 45, 58, 70, 71, 71, 73, 76, 87, 91, 99, 104, 107, 109, 109, 128, 128, 130, 132, 132, 134, 136, 144, 148, 148, 148, 154, 169, 170, 182, 183, 183, 187, 190, 194, 195, 198, 199, 209, 209, 214, 217, 219, 223, 233, 233, 239, 240, 242, 242, 246, 246, 247, 248, 249, 253, 261, 267, 271, 274, 277, 279, 280, 286, 287, 289, 293, 297, 300, 301, 301, 301, 301, 302, 303, 310, 312, 313, 316, 322, 322, 324, 325, 326, 327, 329, 331, 335, 336, 337, 341, 352, 353, 361, 367 Hypoth 7:3, 7:4, 7:6, 7:6, 7:6, 7:6, 7:6, 7:7, 7:7, 7:7, 7:7, 7:7, 7:7, 7:7, 7:7, 7:7, 7:7, 7:8, 7:8, 7:8, 7:8, 7:8, 7:8, 7:9, 7:9, 7:9, 7:11, 7:11, 7:14, 7:15, 7:19, 11:7 Prov 1, 1, 2:6, 7, 14, 16, 18, 19, 26, 26, 26, 28, 30, 34, 37, 41, 42, 44, 48, 51, 55, 58, 60, 66, 70, 71, 72 QG 1:3, 17a, 55c, 60:2, 60:2, 63, 65, 69, 77, 77, 93, 2:11, 12b, 12d, 13b, 54a, 59, 64c, 71b, 74, 3:3, 3, 8, 18, 20a, 29, 30b, 52, 4:33b, 40, 52a, 52d, 88, 88, 144, 167, 180, 180, 191c, 194, 198, 202a, 202a, 203, 204, 206a, 206a, 206b, 227 QG isf 3, 8, 10, 15 QG (Par) 2:2, 2:6 QE 2:6a, 11a, 11b, 13a, 13b, 14, 15:1, 18, 28, 28, 40, 47, 50b QE isf 3, 7, 13, 14, 15, 22

μηδαμῇ Det 72 Ebr 166 Fug 13 Spec 3:50

μηδαμόθι Congr 58

μηδαμός Det 72 Ebr 162, 166

μηδέ (314) Opif 85, 87, 90, 138, 155, 170 Leg 1:35, 43, 97 Leg 2:63, 88 Leg 3:6, 16, 17, 31, 91, 101, 213 Cher 36, 65, 65, 74, 78 Sacr 10, 78, 95, 101, 113, 121 Det 20, 20, 23, 29, 33, 61, 86, 100, 101, 102, 102, 133, 154 Post 4, 6, 20, 42, 66, 74, 78 Gig 25 Deus 22, 91, 157, 157, 178 Agr 10, 17, 39, 84, 111, 112, 112, 134, 150, 173 Plant 6, 33, 33, 53, 65, 68, 101, 101, 162 Ebr 66, 70, 75, 88, 101 Conf 71, 116, 120, 150 Migr 26, 48, 92, 92, 156, 181, 193 Her 18, 29, 44, 82, 83, 143, 226, 238 Congr 3, 152, 167 Fug 81, 105 Mut 11, 62, 107, 107, 152, 165, 226, 226, 226, 230, 240, 242 Somn 1:48, 91, 99, 124, 131, 195, 204 Somn 2:62, 70, 76, 105, 105, 126, 128, 144, 196, 212, 251, 282 Abr 19, 19, 56, 105, 140, 224, 240, 249 Ios 9, 22, 27, 40, 68, 80, 101, 113, 140, 149, 158, 167, 188, 213, 214, 219, 222, 224, 236, 238 Mos 1:14, 30, 45, 49, 74, 112, 118, 175, 179, 186, 186, 232, 249, 300, 303, 311 Mos 2:24, 70, 128, 157, 168, 227, 272 Decal 1, 32, 62, 64, 65, 67, 74, 74, 90, 92, 101, 112, 154 Spec 1:44, 104, 123, 176, 187, 209, 249, 249, 250, 252, 294, 306, 313 Spec 2:23, 52, 83, 83, 83, 93, 94, 95, 164, 248, 258, 258 Spec 3:22, 26, 26, 27, 27, 29, 38, 46, 78, 92, 94,

104, 153, 166, 171 Spec 4:3, 17, 31, 54, 79, 146, 196, 201, 202, 223 Virt 3, 5, 39, 63, 133, 135, 137, 142, 187 Praem 26, 35, 40, 71, 77, 95, 115 Prob 108, 142 Contempl 9, 25, 75 Aet 42, 53, 60, 79, 84, 88, 97, 107, 138 Flacc 53, 54, 89, 166 Legat 23, 114, 131, 131, 141, 189, 227, 238, 268, 323, 326, 347 Hypoth 6:9, 7:1, 7:3, 7:4, 7:5, 7:6, 7:6, 7:6, 7:6, 7:8, 11:3 Prov 2:21, 65 QG 1:69, 76b, 76b, 3:3, 4:88 QE 2:11a, 12

μηδείς (742) Opif 21, 45, 46, 51, 63, 69, 77, 87, 142, 150, 158, 165 Leg 1:27, 35, 47 Leg 2:8, 70, 70, 93 Leg 3:7, 7, 24, 29, 35, 37, 38, 77, 86, 95, 126, 141, 169, 186, 194, 241, 247 Cher 31, 38, 48, 56, 64, 64, 76, 81, 99, 115 Sacr 13, 28, 48, 60, 65, 71, 76, 77, 77, 79, 79, 93, 95, 110, 114, 116, 122, 139 Det 30, 76, 100, 119, 153, 155, 175 Post 6, 7, 13, 24, 25, 64, 72, 79, 128, 162, 163, 170, 181, 182, 182 Gig 7, 31, 37, 39 Deus 5, 9, 11, 12, 40, 57, 75, 87, 103, 130, 130, 147, 150, 153, 158, 167, 172, 183 Agr 5, 17, 23, 47, 101, 110, 113, 149, 151, 156, 157, 167, 178 Plant 6, 7, 7, 36, 51, 58, 64, 66, 69, 82, 89, 93, 103, 108, 130, 172 Ebr 25, 66, 75, 78, 111, 111, 116, 119, 135, 151, 160, 169, 177, 195 Sobr 3, 4, 5, 35, 42, 48, 63 Conf 13, 19, 22, 25, 27, 54, 69, 72, 84, 84, 116, 140, 144, 150, 161, 162, 163, 181 Migr 7, 9, 11, 20, 55, 67, 67, 88, 90, 95, 117, 118, 134, 144, 155, 166, 175, 182, 183, 211, 211, 216 Her 6, 9, 11, 13, 14, 18, 42, 58, 67, 105, 110, 123, 123, 143, 153, 200, 226, 246, 250, 274 Congr 17, 44, 65, 125, 130, 167, 180 Fug 11, 14, 47, 52, 101, 101, 120, 148, 157, 160, 165, 172, 191 Mut 13, 28, 36, 87, 88, 108, 141, 142, 146, 182, 215, 222, 222, 258 Somn 1:13, 21, 58, 63, 84, 91, 137, 140, 154, 158, 195, 212, 218, 243, 253 Somn 2:15, 82, 88, 91, 95, 98, 101, 134, 141, 147, 152, 176, 178, 179, 196, 214, 245, 254, 263, 282 Abr 5, 38, 40, 45, 61, 97, 99, 107, 125, 127, 143, 170, 173, 190, 192, 193, 196, 205, 206, 222, 224, 231, 233, 238, 257 Ios 11, 48, 48, 52, 65, 68, 70, 88, 90, 93, 95, 101, 104, 114, 125, 140, 147, 149, 165, 183, 193, 197, 206, 208, 210, 225, 235, 237, 239, 248, 254, 255, 260 Mos 1:20, 24, 24, 27, 43, 44, 47, 50, 54, 63, 64, 68, 73, 73, 84, 84, 88, 99, 121, 124, 146, 151, 165, 181, 196, 221, 241, 249, 266, 283, 303, 304, 325, 327, 327, 330 Mos 2:12, 17, 22, 24, 37, 59, 61, 68, 73, 78, 87, 90, 108, 126, 126, 128, 129, 129, 137, 138, 144, 168, 177, 205, 259, 259, 283, 291, 291 Decal 40, 44, 52, 58, 59, 76, 98, 104, 122, 129, 130, 137, 138, 140, 176 Spec 1:47, 47, 55, 75, 76, 80, 81, 84, 102, 105, 107, 113, 119, 123, 152, 152, 155, 164, 166, 167, 175, 192, 196, 202, 205, 216, 219, 220, 224, 253, 256, 256, 260, 260, 272, 277, 293, 294, 297, 301, 319, 321, 323 Spec 2:1, 4, 9, 13, 17, 19, 23, 36, 37, 48, 55, 73, 83, 83, 84, 89, 105, 106, 111, 115, 117, 128, 130, 149, 155, 156, 165, 168, 172, 186, 192, 196, 198, 201, 224, 240, 240, 247 Spec 3:9, 15, 17, 37, 38, 46, 49, 63, 70, 76, 78, 80, 80, 89, 90, 94, 94, 103, 112, 115, 117, 122, 128, 135, 138, 139, 141, 142, 149, 156, 157, 158, 162, 166, 171, 182, 183, 194, 205, 206 Spec 4:4, 22, 34, 43, 44, 52, 54, 59, 77, 104, 122, 131, 136, 143, 153, 172, 182, 188, 191, 194, 197, 197, 202, 206, 215, 220, 223, 225, 229 Virt 11, 18, 20, 43, 46, 46, 67, 70, 83, 98, 105, 105, 122, 124, 127, 133, 147, 150, 151, 152, 154, 156, 168, 174, 177, 197, 203, 206, 207, 208, 208, 209, 210, 218 Praem 14, 36, 43, 45, 54, 64, 95, 98, 109, 112, 121, 133, 134, 137, 140, 157 Prob 15, 24, 26, 55, 84, 103, 105, 140, 142 Contempl 1, 1, 25, 26, 33, 43, 45, 54, 62, 72 Aet 16, 21, 22, 24, 36, 42, 51, 74, 74, 75, 75, 87, 88, 91, 93, 94 Flacc 5, 27, 56, 57, 73, 81, 82, 96, 96, 105, 106, 112, 112, 118, 144, 149, 162, 162, 167, 182 Legat 28, 32, 34, 39, 46, 50, 63, 102, 109, 110, 112, 117, 119, 123, 125, 141, 147, 148, 152, 161, 175, 178, 192, 213, 224, 229, 230, 232, 248, 260, 262, 268, 313, 318, 319, 319, 322, 332, 333, 342, 347, 351, 366 Hypoth 7:6, 7:7, 7:10, 7:12, 11:9 Prov 2:21, 57 QG 1:60:1, 65, 74, 3:38b, 4:69, 76b, 99, 102a, 206b QE 1:6, 2:4, 38a

μηδέποτε (65) Leg 1:89 Leg 2:101 Leg 3:17, 242 Cher 52 Sacr 41 Det 113, 178 Post 21, 151, 165, 184 Gig 20 Agr 34, 40, 95, 111 Plant 93, 131 Ebr 5, 27, 53, 70, 73, 125, 125, 133, 161 Conf 122, 167 Migr 8, 26, 61, 222 Her 36, 109, 246 Fug 61, 118 Somn 1:68, 113 Somn 2:25, 98, 199 Abr 154, 271 Ios 160, 220, 229 Decal 67 Spec 1:288 Spec 2:52, 141 Spec 4:108, 159 Virt 163 Contempl 11 Aet 94 Legat 154, 211 Prov 2:36 QG 1:77, 2:64b QE isf 3, 18

μηδέπω (8) Leg 2:65 Sobr 7 Conf 146 Migr 21, 199 Spec 3:111 Flacc 41 Prov 2:42

μηδέτερος (14) Gig 64, 66 Plant 175 Migr 146 Mos 1:239 Decal 130 Spec 1:215, 291 Spec 3:55 Spec 4:106, 110 Praem 62, 131 Prob 160

μηκέτι (96) Opif 128, 140, 141 Leg 3:16, 183, 213 Sacr 4, 80 Det 48, 64, 86 Post 8, 95 Deus 40 Agr 56, 76, 134, 146 Plant 67, 88, 111 Ebr 10, 51, 71, 103, 156, 175 Conf 8, 9 Migr 80, 149, 157 Her 101 Congr 121 Mut 70, 83, 270 Somn 1:36, 37, 70, 79, 163 Somn 2:105, 226 Abr 19, 195, 240, 240, 243 Ios 122, 245, 246, 264 Mos 1:18, 94, 181, 268, 286 Decal 16 Spec 1:207, 243, 248 Spec 2:206, 209, 213 Spec 3:33, 43, 142 Spec 4:7, 140 Virt 115 Praem 19, 89, 144 Prob 150 Aet 8, 39, 89, 113, 128, 129 Flacc 64 Legat 13, 53, 53, 127, 327, 333, 337 Hypoth 11:3 Prov 2:12 QG 1:94, 2:10, 54a QE 2:17 QE isf 5

μήκιστος (30) Cher 89 Post 161 Gig 18 Deus 174 Agr 24, 115, 158, 169, 171, 178 Plant 24 Sobr 7, 24 Fug 115 Somn 1:107, 178 Mos 2:186, 281 Decal 34, 44, 135, 146 Spec 2:91, 221 Aet 88, 135, 147 Flacc 129 Legat 298 Prov 2:15

μῆκος (58) Opif 13, 49, 102 Cher 22 Post 62, 113 Deus 120 Agr 56 Plant 75 Migr 154 Her 131, 144, 148, 154, 229 Congr 147, 147, 147 Somn 1:11, 26 Abr 271 Mos 1:59, 78, 175, 184, 206 Mos 2:60, 78, 83, 84, 86, 89, 89, 90, 91, 92, 96, 140 Decal 25, 99 Spec 1:71, 220 Spec 2:177, 177 Spec 3:98 Spec 4:148 Praem 85 Prob 73 Aet 61, 71, 96 Legat 1, 246, 246 QG 3:49a QG (Par) 2:2, 2:2, 2:5

μηκύνω (19) Sacr 123 Det 108, 110 Post 65 Gig 62 Agr 6, 17 Her 17, 133 Congr 178 Fug 27 Mut 178 Abr 65 Spec 2:143, 214 Contempl 56 Flacc 86, 146 QE isf 3

μηλέα Plant 32

μηλόβοτος Contempl 14

μῆλον Mos 2:180

μήν (μείς) (65) Opif 55, 60, 60, 60, 116, 124 Leg 1:6, 9, 36, 46, 105 Leg 2:52 Post 48 Plant 118 Ebr 91, 195 Congr 106, 107, 131 Fug 57, 184, 184 Mos 1:9, 11 Mos 2:222, 224, 228, 231, 291 Decal 96, 161, 161 Spec 1:90, 172, 172, 177, 182, 182, 182, 186 Spec 2:86, 86, 140, 149, 150, 152, 154, 200, 210, 223 Spec 3:33 Spec 4:235 Virt 138 Praem 112 Aet 52, 65 Flacc 168 Legat 13 QG 2:5a, 5a, 17c, 31, 31 QG (Par) 2:5 QE 2:20

μήν (185) Opif 5, 46, 86, 90, 105, 113, 114 Leg 1:4, 9, 11, 12, 13 Leg 2:3, 20, 20, 26, 75 Leg 3:56, 66, 189,

203, 205 Cher 54, 57, 66, 112, 117 Sacr 9, 91, 93, 101, 130 Det 11, 68, 74, 81, 110, 136, 141, 164, 176 Post 6, 46, 87, 108, 108, 161, 172 Deus 28, 30, 58, 164 Agr 11, 22, 46, 81, 95, 156 Plant 16, 19, 35, 50, 57, 107, 113, 144, 153, 172, 172 Ebr 18, 20, 133, 183, 186 Conf 9, 43, 118, 121, 127 Migr 65, 87 Her 101, 120, 138, 165, 165, 168, 180, 307 Congr 39, 79, 118, 148 Fug 93, 181, 190 Mut 15, 17, 92, 101, 103, 132, 160, 259 Somn 1:101, 136 Somn 2:52, 54, 56, 60, 129, 266 Abr 43, 189, 252, 267 Mos 1:160 Mos 2:50, 129 Decal 126, 128 Spec 1:29, 261, 333, 339 Spec 2:164, 182, 206, 260, 261 Spec 3:17, 34, 78, 114 Spec 4:100, 185, 224, 235 Virt 11, 13, 27, 90 Praem 62 Prob 36, 59, 60, 60, 61, 136, 151 Aet 13, 13, 22, 39, 45, 47, 71, 79, 88, 102, 116, 120, 143, 145 Flacc 1, 60, 94 Legat 111, 142, 149, 158, 193 Hypoth 6:2, 6:5, 7:15, 7:15, 11:13 Prov 2:13, 47, 62 QG 1:62:1, 2:59, 3:20a QG isf 5 QG (Par) 2:3

μηναγύρτης Spec 3:101

μηνιαῖος Spec 2:142 Spec 3:32, 33 Virt 113 Legat 158

μηνιάω Abr 213 Flacc 71, 180

μῆνιγξ Det 90 Post 137 QG (Par) 2:3

μήνιμα Mos 1:119

μηνοειδής Opif 101, 101

μήνυμα (9) Abr 52 Spec 3:31, 45 Spec 4:148 Prob 32 Aet 119 Legat 157 Prov 2:50 QG 1:55b

μήνυσις Det 130 Her 266 Ios 248 Mos 2:128 Legat 136

μηνυτής Post 16 Ios 48 Legat 99

μηνυτικός Leg 1:68

μηνύω (110) Opif 6, 15, 27, 77, 132 Sacr 31 Det 10, 129, 132, 133, 176 Post 33, 78, 169 Agr 95 Ebr 82 Sobr 62 Migr 47, 47, 144 Her 148, 216, 263, 288, 293, 300 Congr 34, 73, 126, 157 Fug 7, 72, 121, 137 Mut 14, 77, 89, 118, 137, 141, 162, 206, 267 Somn 1:74, 127, 142, 157, 192, 229, 241, 242 Somn 2:3, 169 Abr 57, 60, 93, 133, 217, 230, 256, 258, 262 Mos 1:4, 86, 217, 334 Mos 2:56, 96, 122, 132, 230, 275 Decal 1, 48, 101, 169 Spec 1:200, 328 Spec 2:177, 251, 257 Spec 3:129, 159 Spec 4:176, 187, 235 Virt 8, 80 Praem 1, 53, 132 Prob 96 Aet 17, 18, 19, 120 Flacc 112 Legat 98, 187, 276, 280, 299 Prov 2:49 QG 2:59, 64a, 3:58 QG (Par) 2:4, 2:6 QE 2:16, 47

μήποτε (71) Opif 59, 63 Leg 1:53, 80, 90 Leg 2:80 Leg 3:40, 60, 161, 171, 206, 239, 252 Cher 21, 25, 41 Sacr 40, 72, 121, 137 Det 156, 168, 178 Post 18, 51, 91, 153, 172 Deus 101, 107, 142 Plant 55, 96 Ebr 58 Sobr 55 Conf 25, 119, 186 Her 63, 206, 227 Congr 130 Fug 80, 94, 198, 211 Mut 183 Somn 1:15, 33, 65, 67 Somn 2:80 Abr 14, 51, 101, 271 Mos 1:157, 280 Spec 1:52, 113 Spec 2:24 Prob 86 Aet 10, 83 Legat 215, 238 QG 1:3, 55b, 55c, 2:64a, 4:168

μήπω (63) Opif 76, 153 Leg 2:22, 73, 91 Leg 3:89 Cher 2, 6 Det 10, 149 Agr 162 Plant 94 Sobr 13, 14 Conf 102, 105, 147 Migr 19, 207 Her 294, 308, 310 Congr 72, 81, 136 Fug 41, 204, 209, 213 Mut 157, 159, 165, 166 Somn 1:48, 57, 148, 213, 238 Abr 47, 122, 223 Ios 192, 203 Mos 1:49, 319 Mos 2:26, 73, 225, 291 Decal 145 Spec 2:158, 160 Spec 3:72, 86, 87, 109, 130 Virt 28, 109 Praem 21 Prob 114 Legat 269 QG 4:153

μήρινθος Prov 2:29 QG (Par) 2:5, 2:5

μηρός Leg 3:150 Mut 187 Spec 1:166 Flacc 162 QG (Par) 2:2

μηρυκάομαι (9) Post 148 Agr 131, 132, 134, 142, 145, 145 Spec 4:106, 107

μήτε (450) Opif 2, 2, 63, 63, 79, 79, 79, 79, 79, 100, 100, 149, 149 Leg 1:93, 93, 95, 95 Leg 2:53, 53, 64, 64, 65, 65, 65, 65, 69, 69 Leg 3:141, 141, 165, 165 Cher 29, 29, 37, 37, 82, 82 Sacr 8, 8, 36, 36 Det 8, 8, 8, 8, 8, 8, 12, 12, 55, 55, 58, 58, 58, 58, 132, 132 Post 7, 7, 102, 102 Gig 20, 20 Deus 24, 24, 69, 69, 162, 162 Agr 11, 11, 35, 35, 47, 47, 113, 113, 151, 151, 151, 178, 178, 179, 179, 179, 180, 180 Plant 101, 101, 101, 131, 131, 143, 143, 162, 162 Ebr 8, 8, 78, 78, 131, 131, 132, 132, 157, 157, 160, 160, 161, 161, 211, 211, 212, 212 Conf 27, 27, 69, 69, 72, 72, 95, 95, 116, 116, 188, 188, 189, 189, 195, 195 Migr 90, 90, 90, 90, 117, 117, 133, 133, 146, 146, 166, 166, 181, 181, 216, 216, 222, 222 Her 29, 29, 157, 157, 191, 191, 194, 194 Congr 36, 36 Fug 120, 120, 121, 121 Mut 15, 212, 212 Somn 1:36, 36 Somn 2:102, 102, 124, 124, 134, 134, 230, 230 Abr 44, 44, 257, 257 Ios 72, 72, 109, 109, 112, 112, 167, 167, 215, 243, 243 Mos 1:3, 3, 40, 40, 95, 95, 104, 104, 170, 170, 285, 285, 302, 302, 302 Mos 2:34, 34, 163, 163, 198, 198, 198, 214, 214 Decal 74, 74, 74, 74, 74, 87, 87, 88, 88, 110, 110, 130, 130, 139, 139, 139, 162, 162, 162 Spec 1:7, 7, 47, 47, 49, 49, 55, 55, 55, 61, 61, 80, 80, 80, 98, 98, 115, 115, 115, 118, 118, 123, 123, 139, 139, 164, 164, 224, 224, 311, 311, 311, 311, 311, 311, 312, 313, 319, 319, 341, 341 Spec 2:35, 35, 44, 44, 89, 89, 180, 180, 199, 199, 234, 234, 234, 234, 234, 256, 256 Spec 3:11, 11, 56, 56, 66, 66, 70, 70, 77, 77, 142, 142, 145, 145, 165, 165, 165, 196, 196, 209, 209 Spec 4:22, 22, 27, 27, 34, 34, 34, 44, 44, 70, 70, 74, 74, 119, 119, 123, 123, 142, 142 Virt 46, 46, 48, 48, 48, 90, 90, 91, 91, 93, 93, 93, 115, 115, 126, 126, 142, 142, 142, 147, 147, 149, 149, 149, 153, 153, 208, 208, 218, 218, 227, 227 Praem 52, 52, 63, 63, 106, 106, 155, 155 Prob 2, 2, 60, 60, 61, 61, 103, 103, 136, 136, 158, 158, 160, 160 Contempl 45, 45 Aet 42, 42, 43, 43, 116, 116 Flacc 24, 24, 111, 111, 139, 139 Legat 29, 29, 29, 34, 34, 41, 41, 92, 92, 102, 102, 114, 114, 141, 141, 178, 178, 247, 247, 299, 299, 303, 303, 313, 313, 313, 328, 328, 348, 348, 368, 368 Prov 1, 1 QG 1:60:2, 64b, 64b, 2:11, 11, 12a, 12a, 64a, 64a, 3:24, 24, 4:191a, 191a QG (Par) 2:5, 2:5 QE 2:20, 20

μήτηρ (177) Opif 38, 133, 133, 133, 133 Leg 1:76, 76 Leg 2:49, 49, 51, 51 Leg 3:81, 131, 180 Cher 10 Det 52, 52, 54, 106, 106, 116 Post 76, 76, 77, 162, 177 Deus 10, 19, 39, 150 Plant 14, 15 Ebr 14, 14, 14, 29, 30, 30, 31, 33, 34, 35, 35, 61, 61, 61, 64, 68, 72, 77, 80, 81, 84, 84, 95, 145, 223 Conf 44, 49, 49 Migr 25, 78 Her 53, 53, 61, 62, 171 Congr 70, 132 Fug 44, 48, 48, 83, 83, 89, 109, 109, 193 Mut 92, 130, 137, 142, 143, 144, 217, 226 Somn 1:46 Somn 2:7, 111, 139, 178 Abr 67 Ios 9, 9 Mos 1:7, 17, 18, 135 Mos 2:193, 207, 210, 210, 245 Decal 8, 41, 94, 120 Spec 1:112, 130, 130, 326, 332 Spec 2:2, 101, 130, 133, 138, 139, 214, 226, 232, 235, 237, 239, 240, 243, 253, 261 Spec 3:13, 14, 14, 14, 14, 19, 20, 21, 21, 26, 65, 115 Spec 4:68, 178, 231 Virt 111, 126, 128, 129, 134, 136, 138, 138, 142, 142, 225 Praem 109, 109, 134, 155, 158 Prob 36, 79 Contempl 3, 72 Aet 57, 67 Flacc 9 Legat 289, 294 Hypoth 7:2 QG 1:29, 3:18, 4:145, 202a, 202a QG isf 10 QE 1:6, 2:14

μήτι Legat 271

μήτρα (45) Opif 67, 161 Leg 2:47, 47 Leg 3:180, 180, 181, 181, 181, 242 Cher 46, 46 Sacr 89, 89, 89, 89, 102, 102, 103, 104, 112, 118 Post 183 Ebr 73 Migr 34 Her 50, 51, 117, 118, 119, 124 Congr 7 Mut 108, 132, 255 Spec 3:33, 33, 62, 117 Aet 66, 66, 69, 98 QE isf 22, 22

μητρόπολις (10) Conf 78 Fug 94 Somn 1:41, 181 Flacc 46 Legat 203, 281, 294, 305, 334

μητρυιά (9) Post 162 Ios 232 Spec 2:135 Spec 3:12, 20, 20, 21 Virt 224, 225

μητρῷος (13) Ebr 65 Her 61 Somn 2:16 Ios 236 Mos 1:15 Mos 2:289 Spec 1:326 Virt 144 Flacc 171 Legat 33, 54, 181 QE isf 22

μηχανάομαι (8) Somn 2:79 Ios 170 Mos 1:8 Spec 2:43 Spec 3:39, 86 Spec 4:204 Virt 42

μηχανή (12) Opif 10 Det 110 Migr 150 Spec 1:28, 149 Spec 2:9, 114, 165 Spec 3:93 Virt 34, 218 Hypoth 7:7

μηχάνημα (10) Leg 3:110 Post 185 Conf 45, 101 Abr 220 Mos 1:148, 224, 225 Spec 4:28 Prob 38

μηχανοποιός Leg 3:130 Prob 78

μιαίνω (37) Leg 1:17 Leg 3:148, 150, 150 Cher 51, 52 Det 169 Post 75, 134 Deus 89, 123, 124, 133, 135 Agr 175, 175 Sobr 49 Migr 224 Fug 109, 115, 115 Mut 136 Mos 2:158, 196 Spec 1:112, 254, 257 Spec 2:50 Spec 3:152, 207, 208 Spec 4:40 Virt 135, 199 Contempl 66 QG 2:12c QE 2:1

μιαρός (7) Leg 3:68 Deus 128 Ebr 71 Fug 81 Mut 62 Decal 95 Spec 2:253

μίασμα (26) Cher 16 Det 133, 170 Deus 125, 126 Abr 181 Ios 13, 45 Mos 1:303, 304 Mos 2:214, 231 Decal 93 Spec 1:102, 206, 281 Spec 3:42, 49, 51, 89, 92, 121, 127, 135 Virt 138 Praem 68

μιγάς (20) Leg 1:49 Leg 3:187 Ebr 36, 113, 198 Migr 152, 153, 154, 158, 207 Fug 85 Mut 144 Ios 59 Mos 1:147 Decal 10 Spec 3:79 Flacc 4, 135 Legat 120, 200

μίγμα Ebr 191 Prob 105

Μίδας Prob 136

μικρολογία Somn 1:94

μικροπολίτης Somn 1:39

μικρός σμικρός

μικρός (ἥσσων) (365) Opif 28, 39, 65, 65, 113, 130, 131, 141, 148, 159, 160 Leg 1:42, 55 Leg 2:69 Leg 3:34, 56, 89, 164, 200 Cher 53, 94, 116 Sacr 43, 43, 62, 123, 138 Det 10, 43, 74, 75, 107, 163 Post 14, 24, 25, 40, 49, 109, 110, 114, 132, 139, 147 Gig 36, 39, 48 Deus 52, 98, 127, 160, 162, 174 Agr 2, 21, 35, 39, 40, 62, 141 Plant 81, 102 Ebr 16, 35, 43, 64, 77, 90, 95, 135, 155, 165, 181, 186, 195, 198, 216, 222 Sobr 31, 35, 42 Conf 10, 11, 22, 76, 80, 140, 160, 162, 186 Migr 24, 40, 71, 76, 94, 94, 122, 203, 210, 217 Her 44, 48, 72, 149, 152, 157, 162, 162, 241, 282 Congr 52, 52, 144 Fug 48, 126 Mut 45, 62, 79, 83, 104, 104, 107, 128, 154, 177, 187, 215, 231, 233, 235, 235 Somn 1:99, 125, 126, 166, 181, 182 Somn 2:30, 47, 58, 83, 104, 104, 107, 138, 144, 157, 193, 193, 293 Abr 63, 75, 123, 128, 140, 147, 166, 166, 166, 196, 204, 204, 242 Ios 4, 13, 16, 26, 46, 48, 48, 53, 54, 60, 60, 92, 94, 101, 149, 150, 179, 187, 204, 217, 234, 236, 248 Mos 1:12, 46, 51, 51, 62, 79, 95, 102, 111, 111, 128, 133, 150, 175, 191, 205, 213, 235, 242, 255, 258, 259, 270 Mos 2:6, 8, 15, 172, 198, 237, 248, 271, 273, 283 Decal 11, 52, 66, 85, 125, 137, 151, 173 Spec 1:45, 103, 111, 253, 258, 303, 319 Spec 2:66, 72, 87, 105, 135, 138, 158, 191, 199, 209, 215, 236 Spec 3:29, 101, 159, 198 Spec 4:17, 42, 52, 82, 94, 105, 120, 147, 152, 154, 171, 175, 179, 191, 191, 200 Virt 9, 13, 26, 39, 175, 193 Praem 35, 124, 127, 135, 146, 149, 165, 168, 170, 171, 172 Prob 15, 27, 62, 101, 144, 156 Contempl 7, 44, 44, 51, 52, 69, 77, 78, 81 Aet 33, 36, 75, 100, 128 Flacc 3, 11, 17, 18, 29, 50, 62, 71, 76, 78, 78, 88, 112, 126, 147, 163 Legat 10, 14, 15, 41, 56, 58, 67, 96, 109, 116, 118, 144, 168, 186, 197, 206, 211, 244, 259, 261, 264, 267, 268, 269, 285, 285, 327, 337 Hypoth 6:1, 7:6, 7:9, 7:9, 11:6 Prov 2:23, 67, 68 QG 1:74, 3:12, 4:131 QG isf 6 QG (Par) 2:2, 2:6 QE 2:16, 49b QE isf 19, 23, 26

μικροψυχία Virt 92

μικτός (20) Opif 14, 73, 74 Ebr 192 Her 45, 46, 183, 183, 184 Abr 9 Mos 1:27 Mos 2:192, 196, 233, 246 Spec 2:55 Spec 3:47 Praem 13 Prob 105 Aet 7

Μιλτιάδης Prob 132

Μίλων Prov 2:7

μιμεία Legat 359

μιμέομαι (54) Opif 79, 133 Leg 1:48 Sacr 30, 65, 68, 82, 86, 123 Det 45 Post 104, 135 Deus 136 Plant 177 Ebr 95, 122 Conf 63 Migr 133, 149 Her 172 Congr 69 Fug 69 Abr 144, 153 Mos 1:158, 303 Mos 2:7, 128 Decal 51, 111, 120 Spec 1:14 Spec 2:141, 225 Spec 4:73, 83, 121, 173, 182, 188 Virt 53, 168, 168 Praem 115 Contempl 29, 62 Aet 135 Flacc 38 Legat 87, 88, 110 Prov 2:17 QG 1:64a, 4:69

μιμηλάζω Fug 74 Mut 208

μίμημα (67) Opif 16, 25, 139, 139, 141, 141 Leg 1:43, 45, 45 Leg 2:4, 4 Leg 3:102 Cher 31 Sacr 25, 26 Det 83, 160 Post 105 Plant 50, 73 Ebr 90, 133 Conf 108 Migr 12, 12, 40 Her 112, 126, 165, 221, 225, 230 Congr 8 Fug 100 Somn 1:206, 214, 215, 232 Mos 2:11, 74, 117, 127, 133, 135, 143, 162, 270 Decal 134 Spec 1:84, 94, 95 Spec 2:2, 151, 224 Spec 3:125, 194 Virt 12 Praem 65 Prob 94 Contempl 85 Aet 2, 15 Legat 290, 306, 310 QG 4:110b QG (Par) 2:4

μίμησις (10) Post 185 Migr 164 Somn 2:53 Abr 38 Ios 112 Spec 1:245 Spec 4:55 Praem 89 Flacc 93, 165

μιμητής Migr 26 Congr 70 Decal 114 Virt 66 QG 1:77

μιμητικός Migr 167

μιμνήσκω (75) Opif 104 Leg 1:33, 90 Leg 2:42, 43, 68 Leg 3:139 Cher 76 Sacr 11, 55, 55, 56 Det 99, 108 Post 121 Deus 73, 119 Agr 27, 136, 172 Plant 160, 162 Ebr 210 Migr 221 Her 12, 80, 286 Congr 39, 40, 41, 42, 80, 89, 120, 170 Fug 2, 44 Mut 98, 200 Somn 2:29, 114, 232 Abr 181 Ios 158, 265 Mos 1:28, 89, 165, 173 Mos 2:205 Decal 6, 62, 94 Spec 2:70, 203, 208, 216 Spec 3:36, 168 Spec 4:157, 215 Virt 203 Praem 52 Prob 122, 134 Contempl 8 Flacc 5, 133 Legat 19, 30, 44 QG 2:26a, 26a, 65, 65

μιμόλογος Spec 4:59

μῖμος (8) Agr 35 Mos 2:211 Flacc 34, 38, 72, 85 Legat 42, 359

Μίνως Spec 3:43

Μινώταυρος Spec 3:44

μίξις (20) Sacr 23 Det 102, 174 Gig 32 Agr 37 Ebr 189 Conf 184, 184, 185 Her 236 Congr 12 Ios 40 Mos 2:190

Decal 131, 168 Spec 2:50, 55 Contempl 23 Prov 2:71 QG 3:21

μιξόθηρ Spec 3:44

Μισαδαί Leg 2:58, 58

μισάδελφος Somn 2:98

μισάλληλος Conf 48

μισανθρωπία (12) Post 142 Abr 22 Ios 19 Mos 1:58 Decal 111 Spec 2:16 Spec 3:112, 138 Virt 94, 141 Prob 90 Contempl 20

μισάνθρωπος Conf 48 Somn 2:98 Spec 3:113

μισάρετος (8) Post 182 Agr 83 Conf 34, 196 Migr 114, 183, 202 Her 43

μισέω (61) Leg 2:47, 47, 47, 48, 48, 48, 48 Leg 3:77, 180 Sacr 19, 19, 19, 19, 19, 20, 20 Post 63, 134, 135, 135 Deus 138, 143 Ebr 179 Sobr 21, 21, 21, 21, 21, 22, 22, 25 Migr 63, 211 Her 36, 43, 47, 48, 48, 49, 49, 50, 51, 163, 306 Congr 85 Fug 34 Mut 132, 133, 254 Somn 2:96, 122 Abr 104 Ios 5 Mos 1:45 Decal 124 Spec 1:265 Spec 3:101 Spec 4:166, 170 Legat 355 QG 3:26

μισθαρνέω Plant 105 Ios 43 Mos 1:296

μισθαρνία Post 150 Virt 112

μισθοδοτέω Leg 1:80 Flacc 138, 141

μισθός (38) Leg 1:80 Agr 5 Plant 134, 134, 136, 136, 136 Ebr 94 Migr 114 Her 1, 2, 26 Somn 2:34, 34, 38 Ios 125 Mos 1:17, 24, 141, 142 Spec 1:123, 156 Spec 2:183 Spec 4:98, 121, 163, 195, 195, 196 Virt 88, 88, 88 Prob 86 Flacc 134, 140, 141 Legat 172 Hypoth 11:10

μισθοφορά Flacc 5

μισθόω Mos 1:287 Legat 172

μίσθωμα Spec 1:104, 280 Flacc 134

μισθωτός Spec 1:120, 123 Spec 2:82, 83, 122

μισογύναιος Spec 3:79

μισόκαλος Migr 183 Abr 21, 191 Spec 3:3

μισόπολις Legat 108

μισοπονηρία Mos 2:9

μισοπόνηρος (24) Sacr 28 Conf 46, 49, 128, 131 Migr 225 Mut 108 Mos 1:47, 149, 328 Mos 2:9, 53, 167, 279 Decal 87, 177 Spec 1:55 Spec 3:31, 75, 126, 140 Spec 4:9 Flacc 107 Legat 193

μισοπονία Post 156

μῖσος (25) Post 9 Plant 105 Migr 64 Fug 3, 3, 4, 5, 7, 8, 15, 23 Somn 2:97, 98, 108 Ios 5, 7 Decal 125 Spec 4:70 Virt 224 Praem 86 Flacc 32 Legat 120, 133, 268 QG 3:29

μισοτεκνία Prob 36

μίτρα Mos 2:116

μνάομαι (14) Agr 158, 158 Ebr 49 Congr 80 Fug 52 Ios 38, 60 Mos 1:10 Spec 1:101, 110 Virt 29, 29 Aet 74 QG 4:211

μνεία Sacr 56

μνῆμα (9) Her 280 Somn 1:139 Mos 1:100, 171 Mos 2:291 Spec 4:130 Flacc 56 Legat 127 Hypoth 7:7

μνημεῖον (15) Her 30, 175 Congr 100, 109 Abr 141 Ios 19 Mos 1:4 Mos 2:29, 56 Spec 3:16 Spec 4:169 Praem 133 Prob 90 Contempl 29 QG 4:191a

μνήμη (94) Opif 18 Leg 1:55, 55, 81 Leg 2:43 Leg 3:18, 91, 91, 92, 92, 93, 93, 93 Cher 102 Sacr 55, 78 Det 65 Post 62, 148, 148, 149, 151, 153 Deus 43, 138 Agr 133, 133, 145 Plant 31, 127 Ebr 137 Sobr 5, 28, 28, 28, 29, 29 Migr 16, 56, 98, 154, 205, 205 Her 170 Congr 39, 39, 40, 41, 111 Fug 200 Mut 12, 84, 98, 98, 101, 101, 212, 270 Somn 1:193, 205 Somn 2:37, 209, 210 Abr 11 Ios 9 Mos 1:2, 31, 48, 186 Mos 2:263 Decal 62 Spec 1:133, 334 Spec 2:2, 171 Spec 3:21 Spec 4:70, 82, 107, 142, 161, 238 Virt 67, 165, 176 Praem 18 Prob 73 Contempl 26, 57 Flacc 167 Legat 177, 310 QG 1:76b QE isf 9

Μνήμη Plant 129

μνημονεύω Leg 1:55, 89 Mos 2:292 Virt 176 Aet 66

μνημονικός Agr 133 Migr 206 Congr 41, 68 Mut 102

Μνημοσύνη Plant 129

μνημόσυνον Leg 3:187 Mut 12, 234, 249 Somn 2:71

μνήμων Leg 1:54 Det 65

μνησικακέω (12) Ios 10, 17, 166 Mos 1:46, 73 Spec 3:195 Spec 4:227 Virt 106 Flacc 19, 143 Legat 368 QG 4:193

μνησικακία Ios 261

μνηστεία QG 4:86a

μνηστεύω Agr 148

μνηστήρ Cher 46 Agr 157, 158

μοῖρα (109) Opif 84, 104, 131 Leg 3:131, 161 Cher 75 Det 92, 168 Post 5, 92 Gig 26 Deus 47, 78, 173, 177 Agr 24, 53 Plant 12, 18, 20, 44, 107 Sobr 22, 29 Conf 89, 157, 176, 181, 188 Migr 46, 139, 164, 184 Her 46, 64, 89, 112, 131, 139, 161, 180, 193, 225, 226, 232 Congr 21, 104, 105, 106 Fug 10, 55, 95, 209 Mut 114, 185 Somn 1:16, 152, 190, 220 Somn 2:94, 121, 172, 187, 255, 289 Abr 133, 226, 232 Ios 176, 251 Mos 1:113, 201, 221, 234, 263, 316, 320, 332 Spec 1:94 Spec 2:116, 138, 261 Spec 3:16, 123 Virt 40 Prob 44, 75 Aet 13, 19, 61, 69, 89, 122, 138 Flacc 11, 25, 55, 55, 135 Legat 7, 76, 76, 84, 124 Prov 2:10, 10, 16, 41 QG (Par) 2:7

μοιράω (21) Cher 71, 97 Sacr 110 Det 84, 90, 102, 138 Sobr 53 Her 38, 138, 294 Congr 36 Fug 112 Spec 1:116 Virt 138, 148, 160 Prob 143 Aet 63, 126 Prov 2:6

μοιρίδιος Legat 107

μοιχεία (21) Det 102 Conf 117 Her 173 Ios 44, 56 Decal 51, 121, 131 Spec 2:13 Spec 3:31, 52, 63, 63, 64, 65, 65, 72, 72 Spec 4:1, 84 Virt 37

μοιχεύω (10) Cher 14 Post 82 Conf 163 Ios 45 Decal 36, 124 Spec 3:8, 57, 58 Hypoth 7:1

μοιχίδιος Mut 132 Decal 128

μοιχός (11) Ios 84 Mos 1:300 Decal 123, 126, 129, 130, 168 Spec 3:58 Spec 4:89, 203, 203

μόλις (74) Opif 41, 80, 158 Sacr 16, 71 Det 106 Gig 52 Deus 106, 126 Ebr 51 Conf 165 Migr 220 Her 275 Congr 68, 158 Fug 22 Mut 34, 116, 179 Somn 1:6, 7, 68 Abr 23, 79 Ios 13, 224, 225, 256 Mos 1:122, 124, 207, 230, 238, 273, 287, 326 Mos 2:18, 30, 191 Spec 1:103, 143 Spec 2:77, 241 Spec 4:79 Praem 6, 25, 37, 69, 80, 167 Prob 8, 58, 121, 135 Contempl 35 Aet 71, 133, 136, 145 Flacc 3, 113, 125, 143, 155 Legat 56, 188, 228, 269, 369 Hypoth 11:6 Prov 2:19, 27 QG 2:54d, 4:20

μόλυβδος Mos 2:252

μοναγρία Abr 23 Contempl 20

μοναδικός Opif 35 Abr 125

μοναρχέω Her 169 Decal 51 Spec 2:224 Virt 220

μοναρχία (10) Fug 11, 154 Mos 1:10 Decal 51, 155 Spec 1:12 Spec 2:224, 256 Virt 179, 220

μονάς (81) Opif 13, 13, 15, 47, 91, 91, 91, 91, 92, 93, 93, 94, 95, 98, 101, 106, 106 Leg 1:15 Leg 2:3, 3 Post 64, 65 Gig 52 Deus 11, 11, 13, 82, 82, 83, 83 Plant 76, 76, 76, 76, 125 Her 183, 187, 187, 189, 190, 190 Congr 90, 91, 113 Fug 164 Somn 2:70 Abr 122 Mos 2:79, 115, 288 Decal 27, 28, 102, 102, 102, 103, 159, 159 Spec 1:66, 180, 188, 188 Spec 2:40, 176 Spec 3:180, 180 Spec 4:105 Praem 40, 46, 46 Contempl 2 Aet 113, 113 QG 1:77, 2:5a, 5a, 4:110b, 110b, 110b QG (Par) 2:5, 2:5

μοναστήριος Contempl 25, 30

μοναυλία Spec 3:171

μονή (15) Conf 82 Mut 84 Somn 2:237 Abr 58, 65 Mos 1:64, 316, 330 Mos 2:125 Spec 1:58, 286 Spec 3:36, 169 Aet 116, 127

μονήρης Opif 153

μόνιμος Opif 100 Leg 3:101 Spec 1:290 Legat 1 QG (Par) 2:4

μονοειδής Hypoth 7:16

μονονού (15) Ebr 56 Her 200, 305 Congr 72, 154 Fug 29, 84, 119, 179, 196, 211 Mut 56, 162, 194 Somn 2:132

μονονουχί Leg 3:63 Aet 103 Legat 322 QG 2:54d

μόνος (1593) Opif 13, 23, 33, 38, 43, 51, 57, 57, 58, 66, 72, 72, 73, 74, 75, 79, 83, 84, 84, 89, 91, 99, 100, 100, 107, 126, 128, 139, 139, 142, 142, 144, 153, 162, 170 Leg 1:8, 18, 36, 39, 53, 54, 54, 55, 55, 64, 77, 98, 98, 99, 100, 102, 103, 103, 104, 106, 107 Leg 2:1, 1, 1, 1, 1, 1, 1, 1, 2, 2, 4, 4, 4, 9, 16, 17, 17, 18, 20, 27, 33, 42, 43, 57, 61, 63, 68, 68, 70, 73, 75, 79, 81, 84, 85, 86, 87, 89 Leg 3:1, 9, 10, 22, 30, 32, 35, 47, 49, 49, 50, 58, 68, 71, 72, 78, 78, 86, 86, 87, 87, 89, 106, 108, 108, 115, 122, 123, 126, 134, 138, 142, 151, 154, 157, 164, 167, 168, 174, 176, 178, 180, 195, 195, 199, 201, 204, 206, 206, 207, 209, 227, 236, 246, 246 Cher 16, 17, 26, 43, 46, 49, 60, 79, 83, 84, 84, 86, 86, 86, 86, 86, 90, 90, 96, 97, 104, 104, 107, 108, 119, 121, 121 Sacr 12, 18, 18, 20, 30, 40, 42, 43, 44, 48, 64, 69, 70, 71, 80, 97, 100, 101, 107, 111, 118, 120, 134, 136 Det 9, 9, 15, 21, 29, 29, 30, 31, 33, 35, 37, 38, 38, 46, 46, 51, 57, 60, 62, 65, 70, 78, 85, 89, 89, 89, 90, 91, 95, 97, 101, 107, 108, 132, 137, 138, 138, 139, 149, 160, 160, 160, 160, 161, 166 Post 19, 21, 27, 49, 50, 53, 54, 80, 81, 85, 101, 106, 113, 118, 133, 133, 137, 138, 147, 148, 165, 166, 167, 169, 179, 182, 183, 184 Gig 11, 17, 33, 37, 45, 50, 51, 52, 53, 54, 64, 64, 64 Deus 4, 11, 11, 16, 19, 19, 32, 46, 47, 48, 55, 56, 62, 68, 69, 76, 81, 100, 102, 102, 104, 109, 110, 134, 137, 142, 148, 159, 159, 160, 168, 176, 182 Agr 3, 24, 39, 41, 42, 46, 47, 49, 50, 54, 60, 62, 67, 80, 91, 97, 101, 103, 104, 115, 119, 125, 129, 129, 133, 150, 152, 156, 157, 178, 179 Plant 1, 21, 22, 31, 38, 39, 41, 44, 46, 53, 56, 62, 64, 64, 64, 66, 68, 69, 73, 80, 80, 87, 126, 128, 131, 137, 138, 145, 154, 157, 165, 168, 172, 173, 173, 174 Ebr 14, 16, 25, 30, 54, 58, 61, 69, 73, 75, 76, 86, 87, 89, 106, 106, 108, 112, 113, 116, 126, 134, 135, 136, 144, 147, 154, 155, 162, 163, 165, 176, 196, 200, 211, 214, 217, 217, 220 Sobr 2, 3, 12, 15, 15, 20, 37, 49, 52, 55, 56, 56, 56, 57, 57, 58, 60, 62, 66, 67, 68, 68, 68 Conf 3, 9, 11, 15, 17, 22, 25, 39, 40, 46, 46, 48, 55, 57, 72, 74, 75, 82, 91, 92, 92, 93, 94, 98, 105, 106, 107, 110, 114, 116, 117, 118, 124, 136, 137, 140, 141, 145, 150, 152, 153, 155, 157, 160, 161, 170, 173, 175, 178, 179, 180, 181, 182, 188, 190, 191, 191 Migr 5, 17, 37, 40, 40, 40, 41, 46, 50, 51, 60, 66, 77, 81, 82, 90, 92, 94, 95, 96, 97, 106, 107, 108, 110, 111, 115, 121, 134, 134, 136, 145, 146, 146, 153, 155, 158, 167, 173, 179, 185, 186, 192, 201, 216, 218, 225 Her 11, 11, 14, 14, 15, 16, 19, 23, 32, 60, 62, 62, 64, 64, 69, 78, 78, 81, 82, 83, 86, 92, 93, 93, 94, 95, 95, 96, 101, 105, 107, 110, 114, 121, 127, 129, 133, 141, 143, 143, 167, 169, 186, 187, 216, 216, 221, 223, 226, 234, 241, 242, 258, 258, 259, 259, 267, 270, 273, 277, 292, 293, 302 Congr 2, 2, 7, 7, 22, 34, 34, 36, 50, 53, 65, 66, 69, 81, 95, 97, 103, 105, 106, 112, 113, 114, 116, 119, 127, 127, 133, 134, 147, 152, 170, 178 Fug 6, 8, 37, 40, 41, 42, 47, 54, 56, 68, 70, 70, 70, 71, 79, 80, 87, 88, 90, 91, 92, 92, 94, 94, 101, 102, 104, 107, 108, 129, 136, 140, 145, 148, 160, 163, 168, 172, 174, 186, 192, 198 Mut 3, 6, 7, 9, 22, 30, 31, 31, 32, 39, 41, 59, 64, 72, 79, 82, 85, 104, 114, 117, 117, 118, 118, 118, 136, 138, 143, 145, 146, 148, 152, 155, 156, 166, 168, 168, 175, 176, 180, 203, 204, 205, 209, 213, 217, 221, 224, 231, 232, 237, 255, 258, 259, 264, 265 Somn 1:6, 8, 19, 21, 22, 29, 29, 43, 44, 45, 48, 49, 53, 62, 63, 66, 73, 75, 76, 76, 90, 90, 91, 92, 97, 98, 101, 101, 107, 107, 109, 110, 111, 120, 124, 135, 137, 147, 148, 160, 162, 164, 176, 179, 188, 190, 194, 203, 207, 219, 229, 230, 237, 241, 246, 246, 250, 252, 256 Somn 2:8, 9, 24, 24, 50, 60, 62, 72, 76, 81, 83, 100, 114, 115, 120, 130, 136, 154, 179, 185, 187, 194, 196, 201, 203, 211, 219, 224, 227, 228, 232, 233, 236, 237, 243, 244, 253, 254, 261, 277, 283, 288, 297, 299, 300 Abr 4, 8, 31, 33, 41, 43, 46, 56, 57, 58, 60, 66, 86, 87, 89, 97, 102, 103, 104, 115, 119, 120, 122, 122, 127, 131, 132, 135, 136, 142, 143, 143, 152, 154, 156, 164, 165, 168, 168, 170, 177, 180, 189, 194, 196, 197, 202, 202, 203, 206, 211, 214, 216, 225, 226, 253, 265, 268, 270, 273 Ios 4, 13, 30, 44, 45, 46, 50, 51, 62, 62, 63, 65, 76, 85, 124, 125, 126, 133, 134, 150, 153, 157, 172, 176, 177, 181, 185, 186, 188, 189, 193, 198, 204, 220, 220, 223, 225, 226, 238, 238, 242, 243, 254, 255, 255, 258, 259, 265 Mos 1:13, 26, 29, 30, 36, 38, 39, 48, 51, 51, 59, 62, 68, 69, 71, 75, 76, 80, 80, 82, 97, 103, 108, 114, 118, 119, 126, 132, 134, 134, 137, 139, 141, 144, 146, 152, 174, 174, 183, 192, 194, 207, 207, 211, 216, 225, 236, 243, 243, 245, 256, 258, 261, 272, 278, 294, 294, 307, 313, 315, 318, 322, 333 Mos 2:1, 2, 2, 5, 10, 14, 17, 21, 25, 27, 29, 36, 36, 39, 41, 44, 58, 58, 60, 65, 78, 87, 100, 114, 131, 152, 155, 156, 163, 163, 171, 171, 177, 177, 187, 194, 196, 202, 204, 210, 210, 211, 219, 229, 231, 237, 255, 261, 263, 266, 269, 273, 274, 280 Decal 15, 18, 18, 19, 24, 28, 30, 41, 41, 43, 45, 52, 53, 57, 59, 61, 62, 63, 67, 68, 71, 74, 76, 109, 111, 113, 118, 120, 123, 123, 124, 135, 140, 142, 151, 176 Spec 1:16, 20, 20, 22, 25, 28, 30, 32, 41, 42, 42, 50, 52, 57, 62, 67, 76, 83, 97, 97, 103, 107, 108, 110, 112, 125, 131, 134, 137, 138, 153, 162, 163, 166, 186, 195, 196, 197, 211, 214, 220, 223, 225, 230, 252, 265, 266, 267, 272, 272, 276, 282, 298, 302, 307, 307, 311, 320, 326, 332, 338, 341 Spec 2:4, 4, 11, 21, 21, 32, 32, 48, 50, 53, 53, 54, 56, 60, 66, 66, 69, 73, 78, 78, 88, 89, 94, 98, 104, 121, 122, 129, 146, 165, 166, 173, 189, 198, 205, 210, 211, 218, 226, 228, 229, 232, 232, 233, 233, 237, 238, 246, 255 Spec 3:5, 5, 6, 8, 12, 16, 19, 23, 24, 33, 34, 36, 37, 45, 52, 81, 81, 87, 87, 91, 96, 100, 103, 115, 121, 128, 128, 133, 134, 153, 155, 163, 165, 174, 178, 184, 189, 197, 208 Spec 4:2, 5, 11, 16, 20, 23, 26, 31, 31, 35, 48, 50, 66, 75, 76, 94, 106, 119, 120, 122, 126, 138, 141, 149, 152, 161, 170, 173, 178,

178, 186, 187, 197, 199, 199, 200, 201, 207, 219, 228 Virt 6, 18, 32, 38, 42, 54, 55, 57, 62, 64, 65, 67, 78, 79, 79, 81, 82, 84, 84, 86, 88, 91, 98, 103, 105, 116, 146, 147, 149, 151, 155, 156, 171, 180, 187, 188, 189, 195, 198, 201, 206, 207, 214, 220, 224 Praem 6, 13, 13, 26, 30, 40, 44, 45, 54, 57, 60, 71, 82, 83, 87, 93, 97, 132, 134, 136, 138, 146, 153, 156, 160, 162, 165 Prob 6, 7, 9, 10, 12, 19, 20, 20, 23, 32, 36, 39, 40, 42, 43, 44, 55, 55, 59, 62, 62, 69, 77, 79, 92, 93, 100, 104, 110, 113, 114, 124, 128, 141, 146, 147, 149, 151, 157 Contempl 2, 8, 9, 10, 10, 29, 31, 38, 43, 45, 51, 53, 59, 59, 61, 65, 68, 90 Aet 4, 12, 15, 54, 56, 63, 66, 72, 73, 85, 94, 98, 98, 98, 99, 107, 107, 112, 125, 130, 138, 138, 147, 148 Flacc 3, 12, 19, 20, 24, 40, 41, 48, 48, 53, 72, 89, 95, 97, 101, 123, 123, 124, 126, 133, 139, 141, 147, 150, 176, 187 Legat 7, 16, 24, 29, 32, 33, 36, 39, 46, 60, 63, 68, 99, 109, 115, 115, 117, 119, 132, 146, 149, 157, 160, 161, 162, 169, 172, 174, 175, 176, 182, 187, 197, 198, 201, 209, 213, 214, 216, 232, 249, 252, 253, 262, 264, 265, 280, 282, 306, 308, 310, 311, 330, 332, 352, 355, 366, 368 Hypoth 6:2, 6:9, 7:2, 7:2, 7:3, 7:11, 7:11, 7:16, 7:17, 11:3, 11:12, 11:13, 11:14, 11:18 Prov 2:1, 12, 21, 25, 26, 35, 57, 63, 64, 66 QG 1:20, 51, 96:1, 100:1b, 2:11, 14, 34a, 64b, 71a, 71b, 72, 3:8, 11a, 11b, 4:51a, 76a, 76b, 81, 145, 169, 9*, 9* QG isf 10, 10, 13, 16 QE 2:18, 45a, 45a, 45b, 71 QE isf 12, 21

μονότροπος Cher 58 Fug 35 Praem 89

μονόω (7) Cher 45 Somn 2:188 Mos 1:283 Spec 1:105 Contempl 25, 30 Flacc 168

μονώνυχος Spec 4:109

μόνωσις (16) Opif 35, 151, 171, 172 Her 127, 183 Fug 92 Abr 22, 30, 87 Spec 2:176 Virt 55 Praem 16, 17, 20 Flacc 177

μονωτικός (8) Cher 58 Her 211, 234 Fug 25, 35 Spec 1:162 Praem 89 QG isf 10

μόριον (6) Opif 110, 110 Sacr 1 Gig 12 Her 282 Decal 21

μορμολύττομαι Prob 146

μορφή (26) Opif 76, 135, 140, 151 Leg 1:7 Migr 3 Abr 147 Mos 1:43, 66 Spec 1:47, 325, 329 Aet 5, 6, 30, 79, 144 Legat 55, 80, 110, 211, 290, 299, 346 QG 4:204 QE isf 3

μορφόω (19) Deus 55 Plant 3 Conf 63, 87 Fug 12, 69 Somn 1:173, 210 Somn 2:45 Abr 118 Decal 7, 66, 72 Spec 1:21, 171 Spec 2:255 Spec 3:108, 117 Aet 41

μόσχευμα (8) Agr 18 Plant 4, 30 Sobr 36 Mut 162 Mos 1:231 Spec 4:75 Prob 69

μόσχος (29) Leg 3:130 Post 158, 158, 162, 163, 166 Ebr 96, 124 Migr 202 Fug 90, 186 Abr 108 Mos 1:277, 287 Mos 2:147 Spec 1:135, 177, 178, 180, 184, 188, 189, 198, 226, 228, 231, 232 Spec 4:105, 205

Μοῦσα Prob 62 Aet 55

μουσικός (104) Opif 48, 54, 70, 78, 96, 126, 126 Leg 1:14, 94 Leg 3:21, 121 Cher 93, 105 Sacr 18, 18, 74 Det 18, 75, 75, 75, 125 Post 103, 103, 104, 104, 105, 105, 107, 111, 142 Deus 24 Agr 9, 18, 35, 137 Plant 159 Ebr 49, 116 Sobr 35, 36, 36 Conf 55, 56 Migr 39, 39, 72, 120, 120, 178 Her 15, 210, 274 Congr 9, 11, 16, 23, 76, 79, 89, 142, 142, 144, 156 Fug 22 Mut 56, 80, 87, 122, 122, 146, 146, 184, 229 Somn 1:36, 37, 37, 202, 205, 256 Somn 2:27, 270 Mos 1:23, 29 Mos 2:103, 115 Spec 1:336, 342, 343 Spec 2:157, 193, 200, 230, 246 Spec 4:102 Prob 49, 49, 51, 157 Contempl 88 Legat 12 Prov 2:20 QG 4:76b, 76b QE 2:20

μουσόω Leg 2:75 Virt 74 Prob 51

μοχθέω Migr 223

μοχθηρία (19) Conf 122 Ios 84 Mos 1:248 Mos 2:198, 285 Spec 1:103 Spec 2:232 Spec 3:155, 209 Spec 4:16, 48, 48, 185 Virt 86, 192 Flacc 7, 42, 135 QG 2:13a

μοχθηρός (33) Leg 2:61 Leg 3:67, 68, 243 Det 77 Post 101, 160 Deus 171 Ebr 16, 28 Conf 75, 90 Her 178, 259 Congr 57 Fug 18, 30, 131 Mut 169 Abr 37 Mos 1:245 Mos 2:248 Decal 69, 91 Spec 1:277, 325 Spec 3:166 Spec 4:32, 45, 77 Virt 94 Flacc 154 QG 4:211

μόχθος Mos 1:284

μυδάω Aet 125

μύδρος Somn 1:22 Aet 47

μυελός Mut 174 Mos 1:291 QG (Par) 2:3

μυέω (8) Leg 3:71, 100 Cher 49 Sacr 62 Gig 57 Deus 61 Mos 1:264 Spec 1:323

μύησις Cher 94

μυθεύω (10) Leg 1:15 Det 178 Gig 58 Deus 155 Her 228 Congr 57 Spec 2:164 Spec 3:45 Praem 136 Legat 112

μυθικός (17) Opif 1, 170 Cher 91 Post 2, 165 Migr 76 Congr 62 Fug 42 Decal 76 Spec 1:51, 56 Spec 4:178 Virt 102, 178 Legat 77 QE 1:6 QE isf 13

μυθογράφος Decal 55 Spec 1:28 Spec 4:59

μυθολόγος Sacr 28

μυθοπλαστέω Post 52 Gig 58 Fug 121 Spec 1:79

μυθοπλάστης Conf 6 Aet 56, 68

μυθοποιία Leg 1:43 Sacr 13, 76 Deus 59

μῦθος (24) Opif 2, 157 Det 125 Gig 7, 60 Plant 130 Conf 3 Congr 61, 62 Mut 152 Somn 1:172 Abr 243 Mos 2:253, 271 Decal 156 Praem 8, 162 Contempl 40, 63 Aet 58, 131 Legat 13, 237 Prov 2:66

μυθώδης Leg 2:19 Sacr 76 Agr 97 Conf 9

μυῖα Mos 1:130

μυκάομαι Somn 1:108

μυκτήρ (30) Opif 119, 123 Leg 1:12, 36 Leg 3:156 Cher 57 Sacr 24 Det 157 Post 126, 126, 161 Plant 29, 83, 133 Ebr 106, 190 Conf 123 Her 185 Congr 115, 143 Fug 182 Mut 157, 256 Abr 266 Mos 1:108 Decal 74 Spec 1:338 Contempl 53 Legat 125 QG (Par) 2:3

μύλη Spec 3:198

μύλος Spec 3:204

μύλων Somn 1:22

μύξα Leg 1:13

μυρεψικός Plant 159 Her 199 Mos 2:146

μυρεψός Her 196 Somn 2:59 Mos 2:152

μυριαγωγός Plant 24

μυριάκις Migr 34 Spec 2:81 Legat 41 Hypoth 6:9

μυρίανδρος Leg 2:85

μυριάς (33) Agr 35, 113 Plant 76, 76, 76 Mos 1:147, 211, 223, 284 Mos 2:202, 246, 257 Decal 27, 36 Spec 1:3 Spec 2:145, 146, 199, 250 Virt 43, 43, 46, 48 Praem 23, 94 Prob 132 Flacc 43, 163 Legat 124, 215, 242, 350 Hypoth 6:1

μυρίος (265) Opif 59, 84, 113, 114, 154, 160 Leg 1:102 Leg 2:4, 10, 22, 97 Leg 3:234 Cher 68, 97, 116 Sacr 77,

83, 86, 91, 98 Det 76, 88, 101, 108, 166 Post 34, 36, 138, 169 Gig 2, 3, 18, 25, 29 Deus 14, 19, 93 Agr 7, 31, 143, 154, 167, 168, 177 Plant 33, 38, 65, 75, 164, 174 Ebr 2, 5, 11, 53, 74, 87, 92, 103, 109, 173, 178, 183, 184, 202, 219 Sobr 38, 42, 60 Conf 5, 9, 12, 117, 126, 144, 163 Migr 55, 61, 86, 92, 113, 152, 171, 172 Her 12, 12, 41, 86, 89, 105, 234, 240, 240, 290, 295, 302 Congr 76, 77, 89 Fug 20, 153, 153, 156, 191 Mut 10, 106, 209, 223 Somn 1:17, 19, 28, 166, 179 Somn 2:32, 32, 48, 133, 144, 155, 178, 275 Abr 1, 10, 29, 45, 64, 133, 218, 218, 230, 245, 263, 263 Ios 26, 32, 35, 44, 47, 66, 130, 131, 158, 216, 225, 225, 257 Mos 1:25, 46, 69, 196, 212, 232, 265, 305, 324 Mos 2:6, 13, 88, 155, 159, 171, 174, 235 Decal 7, 8, 99 Spec 1:16, 47, 57, 69, 69, 92, 136, 162, 192, 275, 281, 286 Spec 2:39, 40, 52, 52, 62, 123, 172, 174, 213, 217, 221, 253 Spec 3:84, 90, 95, 119, 151, 188 Spec 4:41, 53, 53, 90, 113, 116, 163, 188, 189 Virt 2, 6, 11, 34, 61, 101, 136, 144, 178, 200, 211, 213 Praem 29, 53, 90, 124, 142, 157 Prob 7, 18, 19, 84, 87, 136, 151, 159 Aet 36, 39, 63, 80, 140, 149 Flacc 2, 43, 48, 60, 66, 81, 115, 125, 132, 150, 155, 163 Legat 54, 209, 283, 284, 297, 299, 305 Hypoth 7:6, 11:1 Prov 2:2, 8, 12 QG 1:76a, 3:11b QE 2:49a, 49a QE isf 2

μυριοφόρος Opif 113 Aet 138

μυρμηκία Spec 1:80

μύρμηξ Her 154

μύρον Sacr 21 Her 196 Spec 3:37

μυσάττομαι Spec 3:13, 50 Spec 4:95 Praem 116 QG (Par) 2:6

Μυσός Contempl 17

μυσταγωγέω Somn 1:164 Mos 2:71 Virt 178

μυσταγωγός Somn 2:78

μυστήριον (18) Leg 1:104 Leg 3:3, 27, 71, 100 Cher 48, 49 Sacr 33, 60, 62 Deus 61 Spec 1:319 Spec 3:40 Contempl 25 QG 4:8c QG isf 2 QE isf 13, 14

μύστης (12) Leg 3:219 Cher 42, 48, 49 Sacr 60 Post 173 Gig 54 Fug 85 Somn 2:78 Spec 1:320 Praem 121 Legat 56

μυστικός Spec 1:319

μύστις Sacr 60

μυχός (26) Opif 114 Deus 9, 29 Agr 23 Sobr 41 Conf 157 Migr 218 Her 45 Mut 199 Somn 1:90, 91, 151 Ios 200, 265 Mos 1:10, 104 Spec 1:85, 321 Spec 4:201 Virt 85 Prob 65 Flacc 88 Legat 49, 281 Prov 2:35, 62

μύω (9) Sacr 78 Deus 39, 181 Plant 58 Migr 123, 222 Somn 1:199 Ios 108 Virt 49

μύωψ Agr 71

Μωάβ (9) Leg 3:225, 225, 225, 225, 230, 231 Migr 99 Somn 1:89, 89

Μωαβῖται Leg 3:81, 81 Post 177

μώλωψ Det 50

μωμάομαι Leg 3:180 QG isf 2

μωμητός Sobr 10 QG isf 13

μῶμος (10) Leg 1:50 Leg 3:141 Sobr 11 Fug 80 Mut 60 Spec 1:117, 166, 166, 242, 259

μωμοσκόπος Agr 130

μωραίνω Cher 116

μωρία Leg 2:70 Deus 164 Sobr 11

μωρός (μῶρος) Cher 75 Sobr 10

μῶυ Mos 1:17

Μωυσῆς (480) Opif 2, 8, 12, 25, 128, 131 Leg 1:40, 74, 76, 80, 108 Leg 2:15, 27, 34, 54, 66, 67, 78, 79, 79, 80, 80, 81, 87, 88, 88, 88, 88, 90, 90, 91, 102, 103 Leg 3:12, 12, 14, 15, 22, 32, 37, 43, 45, 81, 94, 101, 101, 102, 102, 102, 102, 103, 104, 106, 107, 128, 129, 129, 129, 134, 135, 135, 140, 141, 145, 147, 169, 173, 185, 186, 194, 197, 204, 208, 225, 228 Cher 15, 16, 32, 40, 41, 45, 47, 49, 56, 65, 87, 124, 130 Sacr 6, 8, 12, 50, 51, 69, 77, 97, 118, 130, 133 Det 38, 39, 67, 83, 86, 93, 103, 122, 126, 132, 135, 135, 138, 139, 160, 160, 161, 177 Post 1, 10, 12, 28, 67, 69, 77, 77, 84, 101, 122, 123, 136, 142, 143, 158, 169, 173, 174, 177 Gig 6, 24, 26, 47, 48, 54, 56, 67 Deus 6, 60, 88, 108, 109, 110, 120, 136, 140, 148, 156 Agr 2, 20, 43, 43, 78, 80, 81, 85, 94, 95, 97, 99 Plant 14, 18, 26, 26, 27, 27, 39, 46, 52, 62, 69, 86, 108, 125, 134, 137, 168 Ebr 4, 37, 67, 73, 79, 85, 94, 96, 100, 111, 210, 213, 222 Sobr 49 Conf 29, 39, 50, 57, 62, 77, 82, 88, 95, 106, 141, 145, 173 Migr 3, 8, 23, 44, 67, 76, 85, 97, 122, 131, 135, 151, 169, 171, 180, 201, 203, 207 Her 4, 13, 14, 17, 21, 30, 44, 47, 49, 59, 81, 83, 113, 117, 120, 128, 131, 157, 161, 169, 182, 189, 191, 201, 214, 228, 231, 239, 255, 262, 262, 262, 291, 296, 300, 303 Congr 3, 7, 57, 62, 86, 89, 110, 112, 115, 120, 132, 160, 163, 163, 170, 177 Fug 93, 97, 109, 113, 123, 128, 137, 141, 143, 147, 158, 159, 168, 180, 185, 193 Mut 7, 19, 20, 20, 25, 25, 30, 42, 61, 113, 117, 121, 125, 126, 132, 134, 152, 168, 182, 187, 190, 195, 200, 204, 207, 208, 209, 220, 223, 236, 243, 258, 265 Somn 1:34, 36, 71, 76, 194, 194, 194, 206, 221 Somn 2:1, 10, 24, 67, 75, 109, 142, 174, 180, 189, 193, 222, 227, 234, 241, 245, 263 Abr 13, 181, 262 Ios 1 Mos 1:1, 5, 17, 48, 54, 71, 90, 90, 91, 97, 97, 99, 101, 103, 113, 113, 113, 120, 122, 125, 126, 127, 129, 139, 148, 177, 177, 180, 184, 210, 216, 219, 243, 257, 303, 304, 313, 317, 320 Mos 2:1, 10, 40, 66, 74, 153, 161, 163, 169, 171, 173, 176, 187, 188, 192, 205, 211, 217, 222, 258, 259, 261, 264, 271, 292 Decal 1, 18, 45 Spec 1:8, 13, 41, 59, 262, 319, 345 Spec 2:51, 58, 64, 88, 194, 256 Spec 3:6, 24, 47, 51 Spec 4:55, 61, 66, 95, 103, 105, 123, 131, 132, 157, 168, 173, 175, 176, 180 Virt 52, 70, 79, 163, 175 Praem 1, 53 Prob 69 Contempl 63, 64, 87 Aet 19 Hypoth 0:1, 0:1, 6:10 QG 1:1 QG isf 13 QG (Par) 2:6 QE 2:19, 46

N

ν QG 2:29, 30 QG (Par) 2:5, 2:5

Ναασσών Post 76

Ναδάβ (7) Leg 2:57, 58 Migr 168, 169 Her 309 Fug 59 Somn 2:67

ναί (6) Leg 3:85 Her 81 Mut 253, 253 QG 3:58, 58

Ναίδ Cher 12, 12 Post 1, 32, 32

νᾶμα (29) Leg 2:32, 86 Sacr 61 Det 40, 92 Post 125, 138, 153, 155 Deus 96 Ebr 12, 112 Migr 81 Fug 97 Mut 69 Somn 2:150, 221, 245, 262 Abr 159 Mos 1:84 Spec 1:147 Spec 2:202 Spec 4:56, 59, 75, 140 Prob 13 Hypoth 7:6

ναματιαῖος Somn 2:48 Ios 155 Praem 99 Contempl 37

ναός (32) Opif 137 Cher 100 Det 20 Ebr 85 Somn 2:246 Mos 2:72, 89, 138, 178, 276 Decal 7 Spec 1:21, 66, 72, 123, 268, 270, 274 Spec 3:89 Virt 188 Flacc 46, 92 Legat 139, 150, 151, 191, 278, 292, 295, 319, 346 Hypoth 6:6

νάπη Somn 1:22 Mos 1:289

νάπος Mos 1:65

ναρκάω Mut 187 Somn 1:130, 131 Praem 48

νάρκη Mut 187 Somn 1:130 Praem 47, 47

ναστός Plant 7, 157 Prob 26 QG 2:12b

ναυαγέω Mut 215 Somn 2:143, 147 Ios 139 Legat 371

ναυάγιον Cher 37 Spec 4:154

ναυαρχέω Prob 143

ναύαρχος Spec 1:121 Spec 4:186

ναυβαρέω Prob 128

ναυκληρία Prob 78

ναύκληρος (8) Opif 147 Sacr 116 Somn 2:86 Spec 4:186 Praem 11 Prob 67 Flacc 57 Prov 2:44

ναύλοχος Sacr 90 Plant 152 Her 305 Somn 2:225

ναυμαχέω Spec 3:87

ναυμαχία Decal 152 Legat 144

ναύμαχος Spec 4:28

ναυπηγέω Spec 1:335 Prob 33

ναυπηγός Spec 1:33

ναῦς (44) Opif 88, 88, 113 Leg 2:6, 104 Leg 3:98, 223 Cher 13, 38 Det 141, 141 Post 22 Deus 98, 175 Agr 69, 89 Plant 152 Conf 22 Fug 27 Somn 1:150, 157, 247 Somn 2:86 Abr 116, 272 Decal 14 Spec 1:33, 335 Spec 2:181, 181 Spec 4:28, 85 Virt 176, 186 Aet 138 Flacc 27, 111, 154, 160 Legat 129, 251, 252, 337 Prov 2:55

ναύτης Conf 22 Mut 221 Spec 1:121 Virt 186

ναυτικός (9) Post 119 Agr 85 Abr 220, 261 Mos 1:148 Spec 4:85 Praem 54 Flacc 163 Legat 9

ναυτιλία Deus 129

ναυτίλλομαι Plant 144

Ναχώρ Post 76 Congr 43, 45, 48 QG 4:93

νεάζω (10) Abr 56, 253 Mos 2:41, 140 Spec 2:228 Virt 3 Praem 158 Prob 73 Aet 61, 64

νεαλής Spec 2:102

νεανεία (νεανιεία) Mos 1:301

νεανίας (17) Cher 114 Sobr 9 Ios 37, 80, 85, 99, 105, 106, 119, 127, 128, 128, 129, 258 Mos 1:46, 54 Flacc 38

νεανιεία νεανεία

νεανιεία Post 170 Spec 3:41

νεανιεύομαι (6) Leg 3:202 Agr 18 Mos 1:50, 54, 301 Prob 25

νεανικός Ebr 198 Prob 43, 53

νεᾶνις Spec 3:77

νεανίσκος (11) Opif 105, 105, 105 Det 50 Conf 27 Ios 40, 50, 52, 85, 161 Legat 39

νεβρίς Legat 79

Νεβρώδ Gig 65, 66, 66

Νεῖλος Fug 180 Mos 1:115 Mos 2:195 Prov 2:65

νείφω (7) Ebr 223 Mut 259 Abr 138 Mos 1:118, 204, 208 Mos 2:195

νεκρός (50) Leg 1:108 Leg 3:35, 69, 69, 70, 72, 72, 74 Gig 15 Deus 124 Conf 55, 79 Her 58, 79, 309 Fug 55, 56, 59, 59, 61, 198 Mut 173 Somn 2:66, 213 Abr 258 Ios 17, 17, 23, 25 Mos 1:105 Mos 2:252, 255 Spec 1:62, 113, 291 Spec 2:16, 94 Spec 3:148, 152, 205 Spec 4:202, 202 Flacc 61, 71, 83, 190 Legat 124, 131, 222 Hypoth 7:7

νεκροφορέω (7) Leg 3:69, 74 Agr 25 Migr 21 Somn 2:237 Flacc 159 QG 2:12d

νεκροφύλαξ Conf 79

νεκρόω Aet 125

νέκταρ Deus 155 Spec 1:303

νέμω (23) Leg 3:115, 126, 131 Cher 94, 113 Post 127 Plant 63 Somn 2:93, 216 Abr 140 Ios 101 Mos 1:51, 214 Mos 2:142, 244 Decal 62, 173 Spec 1:87 Spec 2:168 Spec 4:26 Praem 110 Prob 75 Contempl 34

νεογνός Mut 159

νεόκτιστος Opif 136

νεομηνία (νουμηνία) (17) Somn 2:257, 257 Decal 96 Spec 1:168, 177, 180, 180, 181, 182, 182 Spec 2:41, 140, 140, 140, 141, 144, 145

νεόπλουτος Spec 2:23

νέος (226) Opif 16, 26, 113 Leg 1:2 Leg 2:3, 5, 5, 5, 6, 6, 97 Leg 3:90, 90, 90, 92, 242 Sacr 11, 11, 14, 17, 21, 25, 42, 76, 76, 76, 76, 76, 79, 79, 80, 80, 87, 88, 125, 131 Det 145 Post 63, 109, 110, 145, 151, 165 Deus 31, 32, 119, 120 Agr 10, 56 Plant 161 Ebr 31, 47, 48, 48, 48, 49, 50, 51, 52, 95, 165, 165 Sobr 1, 6, 6, 7, 12, 12, 12, 12, 12, 14, 15, 16, 22, 26, 27, 28, 29, 30 Conf 28, 72 Migr 198, 199, 205 Her 49, 49, 98, 104, 125, 278, 279, 279 Congr 6, 74, 154 Fug 40, 67, 107 Mut 172, 217 Somn 1:11, 91, 163, 199 Somn 2:36, 36, 118, 141 Abr 46, 218, 218, 219, 274 Ios 63, 89, 163, 166, 167, 168, 169, 176, 185, 185, 187, 190, 193, 195, 201, 203, 207, 209, 210, 217, 223, 225, 233, 235, 235, 242 Mos 1:3, 32, 51, 164, 188, 204, 231, 292, 311 Mos 2:24, 64, 179 Decal 165, 166, 167 Spec 1:20, 286, 331 Spec 2:41, 136, 145, 166, 179, 226, 227, 238, 251 Spec 3:21, 23, 39, 51, 134 Spec 4:75, 140, 141 Virt 39, 67, 107, 157, 199, 208 Praem 25, 91, 103, 172 Prob 15, 81, 127, 135 Contempl 67, 72, 77, 81 Aet 13, 57, 77, 89, 134, 145 Flacc 35, 110, 120, 153 Legat 22, 33, 89, 97, 142, 150, 168, 183, 190, 218, 227, 232, 333 QG 1:20,

65, 96:1, 2:65, 74, 74, 4:168, 172 QG (Par) 2:7 QE 2:13a

Νέος Legat 346

νεοσσεία (10) QG (Par) 2:3, 2:3, 2:3, 2:3, 2:3, 2:3, 2:3, 2:3, 2:3, 2:3

νεοσσιά (νοσσία) Decal 116 Hypoth 7:9 QG (Par) 2:3

νεοσσός Mut 158, 233, 234

νεοσσοτροφέω Decal 117 QG (Par) 2:3, 2:3

νεότης (35) Leg 3:177, 179 Deus 157 Agr 147 Conf 7, 181 Migr 217 Her 212, 296 Fug 67 Ios 44, 56, 254 Mos 1:215, 250, 257, 296, 311 Decal 167 Spec 2:24 Spec 4:220 Virt 23, 36, 40, 43 Praem 51 Prob 15 Aet 58, 77 Flacc 68 Legat 190 Hypoth 6:1 QG 2:54a, 54d, 4:200a

νεόφυτος Virt 28, 156, 156

Νέρων Flacc 22

νεῦμα Conf 11 Spec 3:8 Contempl 31, 77

νευρά Plant 152

νεῦρον Ios 61 Spec 1:146 Praem 64, 144 Flacc 190

νευροσπαστέω Opif 117 Fug 46 QG 1:24

νευρόω (9) Ios 41, 82 Mos 1:309 Spec 3:47 Virt 17 Prob 26, 97, 146 Prov 2:56

νευστικός Aet 136

νεύω (11) Leg 3:34, 62, 67 Cher 25, 25 Plant 17 Migr 146 Mos 2:81 Flacc 160 Legat 352 Prov 2:48

νεφέλη (10) Ebr 106 Her 203, 203 Somn 1:54 Mos 1:166, 166, 178 Mos 2:254 Decal 44 QE 2:46

Νεφθαλείμ Somn 2:36

νεφόομαι Abr 138

νέφος (17) Sacr 66 Deus 174 Agr 85 Her 244 Abr 43 Mos 1:107, 118, 123, 176, 200, 209 Spec 4:128 Praem 128 Legat 226 Prov 2:45, 47 QG 2:64c

νεφρός (9) Opif 118 Leg 1:12 Sacr 136 Spec 1:212, 213, 216, 232, 233, 239

νέφωσις (7) Opif 58, 113 Her 208 Mos 1:41, 114 Spec 2:143 QG 2:64c

νέω Abr 182 Prob 119

νεωκορία Somn 2:272

νεωκόρος (17) Fug 90, 93, 94 Mos 1:316, 318, 318 Mos 2:72, 159, 174, 174, 276, 276 Spec 1:156, 156 Spec 2:120 Praem 74 QG isf 17

νεώνητος Ios 228

νεώσοικος Opif 17 Post 50

νεωστί Virt 28

νέωτα Abr 110, 132 Hypoth 7:15

νεωτερίζω (24) Opif 80 Agr 40 Ebr 146 Sobr 10, 15 Somn 1:103, 124 Somn 2:91 Mos 1:118, 119 Mos 2:175 Spec 3:63 Spec 4:47, 90, 127, 221, 223 Virt 160 Praem 77 Flacc 47 Legat 152, 157, 292, 300

νεωτέρισμα Hypoth 11:6

νεωτερισμός (6) Plant 144 Mos 1:216 Mos 2:13, 65 Flacc 93 Legat 208

νεωτεροποιία (8) Sacr 77 Sobr 6, 16 Mos 2:203 Spec 1:184 Praem 16 Legat 165, 259

νεωτεροποιός (11) Sacr 15 Ebr 149 Sobr 20, 30 Abr 274 Decal 142 Flacc 24 Legat 190, 194 QG 2:65, 74

νή Migr 162 Spec 2:4

νηδύς Aet 128

νηκτός Opif 63

νῆμα Sacr 83 Migr 97 Mos 2:111

νηνεμία (8) Opif 58, 113 Sacr 16 Post 22 Plant 152 Her 208 Spec 1:92 Prov 2:47

νήνεμος Deus 26 Somn 2:166, 229 Mos 1:41

νήπιος (39) Opif 104 Leg 1:94 Leg 2:53, 64 Leg 3:210 Cher 63, 73 Post 152 Agr 9 Plant 168 Ebr 193 Sobr 9, 10 Migr 29, 46 Her 73 Congr 154, 154 Somn 2:10 Ios 167, 225 Mos 1:20, 102, 179, 182, 330 Decal 69 Spec 1:163 Spec 2:32 Spec 3:119 Prob 160 Aet 42, 71 Flacc 36, 62, 68 Legat 1, 26 Hypoth 11:3

νηπιότης Conf 21

νηποινεί Spec 3:38

νησιάζω Somn 1:17

νησίς Flacc 159

νησιώτης Opif 114 Ios 134 Mos 2:20 Spec 1:335

νῆσος (37) Opif 63, 114 Her 136 Mut 35 Somn 2:54 Abr 42 Ios 30 Mos 1:212 Mos 2:35, 41 Spec 1:211 Spec 2:168 Spec 3:25 Spec 4:85, 154 Praem 165 Aet 120, 138, 139, 141 Flacc 46, 110, 151, 156, 157, 161, 173, 186 Legat 18, 90, 144, 144, 214, 282, 283, 342, 347

νηστεία (13) Ebr 148 Migr 98, 204 Mos 2:23 Decal 159 Spec 1:168, 186 Spec 2:41, 193, 194, 197, 200 Legat 306

νηστεύω Spec 2:197

νηφαλέος Leg 3:82

νηφάλιος (17) Opif 71 Leg 2:29 Leg 3:210 Ebr 123, 126, 140 Sobr 2, 4 Fug 32 Abr 260 Mos 1:187 Spec 1:100, 173 Spec 4:191 Prob 13 Contempl 14, 74

νήφω (33) Leg 1:84 Leg 3:210 Post 175, 176 Plant 101, 166, 172, 172 Ebr 5, 130, 131, 147, 148, 151, 153, 166 Sobr 2, 3, 3, 6, 30, 30 Conf 159 Fug 166 Somn 2:101, 292 Ios 73 Decal 89 Spec 1:99 Spec 2:9 Contempl 42 Legat 273 Prov 2:67

νήχω Opif 147 Det 152 Prov 2:65

νῆψις Leg 3:82 Ebr 129, 152

νικάω (76) Leg 1:87 Leg 2:108 Leg 3:15, 18, 48, 116, 156, 186, 190, 242 Det 35 Post 38 Deus 147 Agr 110, 112, 112, 112, 112, 147, 152, 162 Plant 24, 145, 175 Ebr 63, 104 Migr 40, 85, 200 Fug 159 Somn 2:12, 104 Abr 44, 106, 135, 170, 216, 231, 244, 267 Ios 175, 200, 237 Mos 1:150, 250, 295 Decal 140 Spec 1:27, 160, 250, 250, 313 Spec 2:232, 246 Spec 4:28, 47, 63, 63, 64, 228 Virt 44 Praem 6, 25, 94 Prob 26, 110 Aet 76 Flacc 130, 132, 134, 134 Legat 44, 181 Hypoth 6:6 QG 4:193, 194

νίκη (37) Leg 3:74, 156, 186 Cher 80 Det 35 Deus 137 Agr 83, 110, 120 Congr 93 Mut 81 Somn 2:24, 279 Abr 48, 214, 234 Ios 138 Mos 1:180, 216, 218, 309, 317 Decal 114 Spec 3:172 Virt 2, 38, 109 Praem 15, 79, 97, 118 Prob 26, 111 Contempl 42 Legat 356 QG isf 17 QE isf 23

Νίκη Opif 100

νικητήριος (9) Leg 3:74 Ebr 35 Migr 27, 199 Mut 44, 109 Somn 1:130 Spec 1:9, 330

νικηφορέω (6) Leg 3:13 Sacr 116 Agr 91, 119 Somn 1:131 Praem 31 νικηφόρος (7) Deus 137 Agr 79 Congr 93 Mut 44, 82 Somn 2:213 Virt 175

Νιόβη Prob 122

Νοεμάν Post 120

νοερός (13) Opif 73 Leg 1:32 Leg 3:40 Plant 12 Her 233, 283 Somn 1:22, 55 Spec 1:66 Spec 4:123 Praem 21 Aet 94 QG 2:59

νοέω (63) Opif 49, 97, 150 Leg 1:3, 22, 38, 38, 42, 70, 74, 82, 91 Leg 2:3, 25, 32, 42, 64, 64, 68, 69, 69, 69, 70, 73, 99 Leg 3:69, 82, 97, 170, 170, 198 Cher 28, 73 Det 4, 60, 161, 162 Post 36, 42 Deus 109 Ebr 186 Migr 73, 95 Her 74, 74, 85 Fug 134 Mut 4, 6, 6, 208, 241, 257 Somn 1:187, 188, 238 Abr 44 Spec 1:95 Spec 2:165 Virt 17 Praem 47 Flacc 2 Legat 224

νόημα (35) Opif 1, 4 Det 79, 79, 127, 127, 128, 129, 130, 131 Post 53, 106, 119 Agr 126 Migr 80, 81, 104 Her 4 Fug 42, 167 Mut 179, 179, 243 Somn 2:260 Spec 1:6, 219 Spec 4:107, 108, 160 Contempl 31, 76, 78, 88, 88 Legat 331

νόησις (10) Deus 34, 34 Plant 31, 50 Migr 55 Congr 15 Mut 12 Somn 1:43, 45 Spec 1:95

νοητός (184) Opif 12, 15, 16, 16, 16, 18, 19, 24, 24, 24, 25, 29, 30, 31, 31, 33, 34, 35, 36, 49, 53, 55, 70, 71, 101, 111, 129, 134, 144 Leg 1:1, 1, 19, 22, 22, 23, 23, 23, 23, 23, 24 Leg 2:26, 28, 31, 69, 70, 71 Leg 3:117, 186, 198, 234 Cher 97, 97, 97 Sacr 75 Det 91 Post 99 Gig 60, 61 Deus 31, 55 Agr 80 Ebr 44, 70, 71, 132 Sobr 3, 55 Conf 81, 133, 172 Migr 13, 20, 77, 89, 101, 101, 102, 103, 104, 104, 105, 105, 141, 191, 191, 195, 198, 199, 207, 209 Her 15, 15, 65, 66, 71, 75, 75, 76, 88, 89, 111, 111, 119, 209, 235, 242, 263, 280, 289 Congr 25, 52, 100, 106, 117 Fug 101, 134, 176 Mut 6, 65, 118, 180, 267, 267 Somn 1:44, 46, 119, 186, 188, 188 Somn 2:13 Abr 13, 69, 77, 84, 88, 119, 162, 200, 217 Mos 1:88 Mos 2:74, 82, 127, 271 Decal 59 Spec 1:6, 17, 20, 46, 46, 46, 219, 272, 279, 287, 288, 302 Spec 2:56, 212, 212 Spec 3:191 Spec 4:192, 231 Virt 164, 214 Praem 26, 28, 29, 37 Prob 5 Contempl 68 Aet 1, 1, 15, 15 Legat 319, 320 Prov 2:19 QG 2:54a, 3:12, 4:8b QG isf 2 QG (Par) 2:4, 2:4

νοθεία Agr 159

νοθεύω (7) Deus 103 Her 71 Ios 45 Decal 128 Spec 1:124 Spec 3:46, 61

νόθος (53) Leg 3:182 Cher 94 Sacr 21, 29, 43 Det 21, 21 Gig 17 Deus 102, 121, 151 Plant 71 Sobr 8, 12, 14 Conf 48 Migr 94, 95 Her 175, 268 Congr 6, 35, 36 Fug 73, 152, 152 Mut 5, 132, 147, 199 Somn 1:23, 53 Somn 2:22, 47 Abr 25, 221, 221 Ios 59, 258 Mos 1:32, 147 Mos 2:193 Decal 3 Spec 3:29 Spec 4:32, 51 Virt 12, 224 Aet 56 Prov 2:17, 22, 31 QG isf 7

νοθόω Sobr 57

νομάς Spec 3:171 Legat 20

νομεύς (8) Sacr 104 Agr 48 Mos 1:64 Mos 2:61 Spec 4:24 Prob 30 Legat 20, 76

νομή Spec 1:158, 163

νομίζω (486) Opif 1, 12, 62, 97, 131 Leg 1:36, 74, 90 Leg 2:15, 46, 46 Leg 3:37, 78, 81, 98, 180, 207, 209, 228 Cher 24, 64, 65, 73, 75, 78, 96, 117, 118 Sacr 1, 20, 21, 42, 47, 54, 54, 56, 99, 124 Det 9, 12, 32, 57, 62, 70, 89, 124, 134, 160, 167 Post 19, 61, 88, 112, 121, 144, 154, 165, 165, 166, 179 Gig 25 Deus 11, 19, 69, 78, 87, 104, 108, 114, 124, 134, 149, 157, 172 Agr 22, 35, 41, 42, 48, 61, 65, 78, 85, 93, 110, 113, 157, 167, 169 Plant 22, 33, 56, 66, 68, 69, 69, 107, 126, 161, 165 Ebr 4, 64, 69, 69, 74, 81, 101, 104, 108, 144, 150, 177, 194, 200, 216 Sobr 15, 20, 22, 29, 62, 67 Conf 43, 62, 76, 78, 82, 118, 119, 143, 145, 147, 161, 182, 190 Migr 19, 44, 45, 86, 93, 108, 113, 138, 145, 155, 161, 163, 192 Her 11, 36, 42, 50, 95, 103, 104, 112, 145, 160, 178, 240, 280 Congr 19, 25, 42, 49, 54, 130, 139, 156, 156, 167, 174, 175, 177 Fug 3, 11, 16, 47, 84, 110, 129, 148, 163, 212 Mut 3, 7, 8, 26, 36, 104, 141, 155, 171, 172, 177, 183, 207, 217, 254 Somn 1:9, 32, 73, 118, 124, 132, 158, 160, 203, 212, 250 Somn 2:20, 25, 35, 62, 69, 104, 116, 122, 123, 147, 177, 194, 258, 264, 291 Abr 43, 62, 87, 101, 116, 120, 129, 143, 146, 179, 192, 219, 224, 258 Ios 7, 9, 23, 44, 52, 76, 102, 142, 187, 218, 241, 255 Mos 1:11, 15, 19, 32, 54, 69, 83, 88, 90, 94, 98, 123, 138, 146, 165, 167, 169, 190, 198, 250, 250, 254, 258, 263, 282, 300, 303, 314, 321, 333 Mos 2:8, 17, 32, 42, 49, 51, 60, 161, 168, 191, 225, 227, 249, 271 Decal 6, 59, 63, 65, 70, 75, 75, 84, 89, 143, 158 Spec 1:19, 23, 25, 26, 28, 45, 53, 55, 66, 97, 135, 144, 189, 214, 221, 223, 245, 249, 255, 275, 279, 315, 345 Spec 2:1, 8, 11, 16, 18, 36, 38, 45, 74, 95, 122, 157, 164, 164, 236, 244, 258 Spec 3:13, 50, 67, 73, 87, 96, 102, 109, 116, 126, 154, 161, 172 Spec 4:6, 46, 57, 58, 72, 147, 182, 200 Virt 1, 2, 30, 56, 69, 95, 109, 138, 195, 197, 209, 212, 216, 218, 225, 226 Praem 14, 52, 69, 78, 138, 147, 162, 168 Prob 5, 23, 24, 44, 58, 77, 81, 84, 93, 125, 140, 141, 154, 156 Contempl 13, 28, 36, 67, 72 Aet 17, 18, 46, 47, 47, 57, 60, 72, 98, 116 Flacc 14, 46, 61, 82, 83, 94, 101, 117, 119, 145, 149 Legat 1, 5, 11, 13, 18, 22, 25, 36, 40, 61, 62, 67, 73, 75, 76, 91, 115, 138, 164, 165, 198, 201, 202, 216, 232, 238, 265, 278, 290, 293, 295, 315, 320, 327, 338, 341, 353, 354, 372 Hypoth 7:13 Prov 2:4, 7, 8, 37, 43, 54 QG 1:69, 70:1, 70:2, 93, 100:1b, 100:2b, 4:43, 76b, 202a, 228

νομικός Spec 4:64

νόμιμος (89) Opif 3 Leg 3:126, 148, 150, 220, 221 Sacr 15 Det 16, 149 Post 123 Agr 43 Ebr 84, 95, 127, 141, 142, 194 Sobr 38 Migr 88, 94, 143, 160 Her 8 Congr 85, 86, 88, 163 Fug 10, 14 Mut 114, 221 Somn 2:152 Abr 276 Ios 29, 42, 43, 230 Mos 1:154, 314 Mos 2:13, 18, 19, 19, 235, 280 Decal 37, 140 Spec 1:78, 100, 132, 145, 154, 204 Spec 2:1, 12, 88, 189 Spec 3:70, 85 Spec 4:1, 46, 143, 169, 169, 212 Virt 30, 141 Praem 2 Prob 84 Aet 142 Flacc 50 Legat 152, 153, 159, 161, 240, 256, 322, 360, 362, 369, 371 Hypoth 7:6 Prov 2:2, 55 QG 4:184, 184 QE 2:2, 19

νομίμως Hypoth 7:8

νόμισμα (35) Leg 3:95, 168 Cher 17 Sacr 137 Det 152 Post 89, 98 Gig 65 Deus 105 Plant 18 Sobr 20 Conf 108, 159 Migr 39 Her 180 Congr 159 Fug 19 Mut 123, 171, 208 Somn 2:90, 184 Spec 1:104, 250, 325 Spec 2:33 Spec 3:38, 176 Spec 4:47 Virt 4 Praem 152 Contempl 41 Legat 9, 110 Hypoth 7:8

νομοθεσία (44) Leg 3:96 Cher 87 Det 80, 178 Agr 2 Plant 117 Ebr 2 Sobr 7 Conf 3, 148 Migr 14, 182 Congr 120 Fug 60, 178 Somn 1:237 Abr 5 Ios 28 Mos 2:2, 25, 31, 38, 47, 51, 290 Decal 81, 154 Spec 1:319 Spec 2:104, 164 Spec 4:44, 72, 132 Virt 15, 22, 99, 119 Praem 53 Prob 57 Contempl 78 Hypoth 0:1 QG 1:68, 2:54a, 3:3

νομοθετέω (52) Leg 3:142 Det 52 Post 143 Deus 61 Agr 117 Ebr 64 Sobr 46 Migr 91 Congr 138 Fug 77, 106, 185 Somn 1:162 Mos 2:9, 192, 203, 218 Decal 9, 156 Spec

1:82, 117, 140, 161, 198, 233, 234, 235, 299 Spec 2:35, 39, 110, 120, 122, 160, 239 Spec 3:80, 136 Spec 4:11, 39, 105, 105, 149, 219 Virt 18, 81, 97, 102, 109, 121, 125 QE 2:6a, 45a

νομοθέτης (130) Opif 1, 104 Leg 2:14 Leg 3:145, 210 Cher 40, 53 Sacr 17, 72, 83, 126, 131, 131, 136, 138 Det 6, 62, 105, 115, 135, 147, 171 Post 22, 25, 47, 57, 78, 128, 133, 166 Gig 19, 32, 58, 65, 66 Deus 21, 23, 52, 67, 94, 125 Agr 22, 27, 41, 84, 86, 144 Plant 66, 141 Ebr 1, 13, 47, 109 Sobr 1 Conf 5, 23, 107, 135, 142, 191 Migr 113 Her 21, 55, 163, 292 Congr 44 Fug 66, 99, 120, 173, 188, 194 Mut 126 Somn 1:39, 93, 112, 121 Somn 2:4 Abr 16, 64 Mos 1:1, 2, 128, 162, 162 Mos 2:3, 5, 6, 8, 12, 45, 48, 49, 187, 190, 292 Decal 176 Spec 1:9, 15 Spec 2:132, 239, 244, 247 Spec 3:22, 42, 102, 151, 164, 166, 167 Spec 4:61, 102, 120, 143 Virt 80, 133, 133, 139 Praem 55 Prob 29, 43, 68 Aet 19 Legat 119, 308 Hypoth 7:7, 7:11, 11:1 Prov 2:70 QE 2:9b

νομοθετικός (16) Sacr 131, 133 Ebr 91, 92 Congr 131, 132, 179 Fug 95 Mos 1:334 Mos 2:8, 9, 66, 187, 187 Praem 1, 2

νόμος (535) Opif 2, 2, 3, 3, 6, 13, 46, 54, 61, 70, 77, 116, 119, 128, 143, 163, 171 Leg 1:94 Leg 3:30, 43, 79, 107, 162, 167, 167, 194, 204, 205, 236, 245 Cher 101, 106, 118 Sacr 19, 71, 129, 131, 139 Det 13, 16, 18, 67, 68, 87, 102, 141, 141, 155, 159 Post 52, 52, 63, 80, 89, 94, 96, 102, 121, 132, 181, 183, 185 Gig 21 Deus 4, 17, 53, 53, 69, 99, 123, 127 Agr 31, 51, 66, 116, 131, 157, 157 Plant 111, 132, 139, 162 Ebr 17, 18, 25, 37, 37, 37, 47, 80, 84, 135, 141, 142, 143, 193, 195, 198 Sobr 6, 21, 25, 33, 49 Conf 2, 14, 108, 112, 141, 144, 159, 160 Migr 69, 89, 92, 93, 105, 116, 130, 130, 130, 130, 130, 139, 142, 145, 169, 177, 186, 197, 204 Her 167, 174, 212, 295 Congr 73, 94, 120, 137, 160, 163, 169, 178 Fug 53, 53, 100, 145 Mut 26, 104, 104, 126, 126, 150, 192, 233 Somn 1:69, 74, 81, 92, 92, 95, 102, 214 Somn 2:55, 67, 78, 123, 154, 174, 175, 223, 271 Abr 1, 3, 5, 5, 5, 16, 16, 68, 94, 135, 198, 249, 275, 276 Ios 29, 29, 30, 31, 63, 63, 174, 202 Mos 1:1, 2, 31, 36, 87, 142, 154, 162, 258, 300, 324 Mos 2:4, 4, 4, 7, 11, 12, 13, 13, 17, 19, 26, 27, 31, 34, 36, 37, 43, 44, 48, 49, 51, 51, 81, 97, 203, 224, 228, 231, 243, 245 Decal 1, 1, 2, 10, 13, 14, 15, 16, 17, 18, 18, 19, 19, 32, 40, 47, 49, 98, 132, 136, 154, 159, 162, 165, 168, 170, 172, 175, 175, 176 Spec 1:1, 12, 14, 55, 56, 63, 74, 80, 108, 112, 116, 124, 129, 131, 137, 142, 155, 157, 159, 196, 202, 204, 213, 257, 260, 273, 279, 279, 280, 298, 304, 306, 314, 318, 324, 328, 330, 332, 345 Spec 2:3, 9, 13, 13, 41, 42, 60, 69, 73, 78, 79, 82, 96, 104, 107, 113, 116, 118, 118, 120, 124, 129, 132, 135, 138, 142, 145, 146, 152, 153, 163, 164, 175, 176, 182, 183, 187, 188, 189, 192, 200, 232, 242, 253, 257 Spec 3:7, 12, 20, 29, 32, 38, 46, 52, 61, 63, 69, 73, 77, 80, 82, 112, 118, 119, 120, 125, 129, 131, 137, 143, 150, 172, 178, 180, 182, 182, 189, 196 Spec 4:9, 10, 16, 23, 55, 55, 59, 62, 76, 96, 116, 123, 131, 132, 137, 149, 150, 159, 160, 161, 165, 169, 173, 179, 183, 199, 204, 205, 213, 232 Virt 18, 51, 65, 70, 94, 95, 104, 111, 131, 137, 139, 141, 141, 145, 146, 146, 171, 182, 194, 194, 201, 219, 222, 227 Praem 5, 23, 42, 55, 76, 82, 106, 108, 110, 111, 119, 126, 138, 154, 162 Prob 3, 7, 30, 37, 45, 45, 46, 47, 47, 48, 49, 49, 51, 51, 52, 62, 80, 114 Contempl 2, 21, 25, 59 Aet 1, 31, 59 Flacc 52, 53, 97, 121, 150 Legat 7, 7, 28, 30, 62, 115, 119, 119, 134, 157, 192, 195, 208, 210, 236, 277, 280, 301, 322 Hypoth 6:8, 6:9, 6:10, 7:6, 7:9, 7:11, 7:12, 7:13, 7:13, 7:14, 7:14, 7:20 Prov 2:23, 33, 34, 37, 37, 63 QG 1:27, 2:54a, 3:52, 52, 52, 4:30, 40, 184 QG isf 17 QE 2:3a, 3b, 10a, 19, 19, 49b, 49b QE isf 13, 14, 22

νομός Ios 157 Mos 1:21 Flacc 45

νομοφυλακίς Mut 43

νόος (νοῦς) (686) Opif 8, 9, 30, 53, 53, 66, 69, 69, 73, 73, 73, 77, 103, 104, 104, 165, 165, 166 Leg 1:1, 1, 1, 1, 1, 17, 19, 21, 22, 22, 22, 23, 23, 24, 25, 26, 27, 27, 27, 28, 28, 28, 28, 29, 29, 29, 30, 30, 32, 32, 33, 37, 38, 38, 39, 40, 40, 40, 40, 40, 41, 42, 43, 47, 49, 49, 55, 75, 82, 88, 89, 90, 91, 91, 92, 95, 103 Leg 2:4, 5, 7, 8, 10, 11, 16, 17, 22, 23, 23, 23, 24, 25, 25, 25, 25, 26, 26, 26, 27, 28, 29, 30, 30, 30, 31, 35, 37, 38, 40, 40, 41, 42, 43, 44, 45, 45, 45, 45, 45, 46, 46, 46, 46, 49, 50, 50, 50, 50, 51, 53, 56, 60, 64, 64, 66, 69, 69, 69, 69, 70, 70, 70, 71, 71, 71, 73, 78, 81, 85, 89, 99, 100, 102 Leg 3:15, 16, 18, 18, 20, 28, 29, 29, 29, 30, 31, 32, 35, 37, 38, 41, 41, 43, 47, 48, 49, 49, 50, 50, 55, 56, 56, 56, 57, 57, 57, 57, 58, 58, 60, 61, 64, 71, 74, 80, 81, 81, 84, 100, 109, 109, 113, 115, 117, 126, 164, 183, 185, 185, 185, 186, 186, 186, 188, 188, 188, 189, 198, 198, 199, 200, 221, 222, 222, 222, 222, 224, 224, 225, 225, 228, 229, 229, 229, 230, 230, 231, 234, 236, 246, 246, 251, 252 Cher 7, 10, 57, 58, 61, 64, 68, 73, 73, 113, 116, 124, 127 Sacr 2, 3, 8, 9, 22, 26, 45, 51, 54, 71, 73, 97, 105, 106, 106, 114, 122, 127 Det 52, 53, 53, 54, 54, 66, 68, 83, 84, 85, 89, 90, 92, 97, 98, 100, 100, 125, 127, 129, 168 Post 19, 35, 36, 37, 41, 53, 55, 56, 57, 57, 58, 59, 66, 79, 100, 106, 107, 126, 126, 170, 175, 175, 177, 179 Gig 8, 8, 9, 15, 38, 40, 60, 60, 62, 62, 65 Deus 42, 43, 45, 47, 62, 70, 89, 105, 111, 130, 143 Agr 9, 13, 16, 30, 34, 46, 48, 57, 66, 73, 80, 80, 83, 89, 89, 92, 102, 110, 142 Plant 18, 24, 39, 39, 42, 45, 46, 64, 83, 97, 114, 126, 133, 135, 147, 159, 164 Ebr 71, 98, 99, 101, 111, 111, 144, 152, 158, 165, 166, 168, 169, 183, 198, 203, 220 Sobr 5, 30, 60, 64 Conf 19, 21, 21, 24, 73, 88, 91, 106, 107, 111, 125, 126, 127, 131, 133, 161, 162, 163, 164 Migr 3, 3, 4, 4, 13, 25, 32, 36, 51, 62, 66, 67, 77, 78, 80, 80, 84, 92, 98, 99, 100, 119, 124, 128, 139, 146, 148, 154, 160, 166, 170, 186, 190, 192, 192, 193, 193, 194, 204, 209, 214, 216, 219 Her 13, 52, 56, 64, 84, 89, 90, 98, 108, 111, 119, 184, 186, 231, 232, 232, 234, 235, 236, 248, 256, 257, 257, 263, 264, 265, 274, 286, 309 Congr 12, 17, 25, 42, 65, 97, 99, 100, 100, 110, 118, 132, 143, 143, 144 Fug 10, 45, 46, 71, 90, 109, 112, 124, 134, 135, 177, 188, 189, 189, 192, 192, 193 Mut 5, 7, 10, 15, 16, 21, 34, 56, 56, 58, 69, 107, 111, 112, 113, 116, 154, 172, 205, 208, 208, 209, 246, 257 Somn 1:2, 22, 25, 29, 30, 32, 33, 34, 35, 44, 56, 77, 77, 78, 84, 88, 89, 112, 118, 119, 135, 146, 177, 211, 240, 248 Somn 2:153, 165, 173, 183, 193, 194, 207, 213, 228, 230, 232, 237, 267 Abr 30, 73, 74, 74, 83, 88, 88, 99, 101, 103, 163, 199, 272 Ios 9, 144, 149, 151, 215 Mos 1:27, 141, 173 Mos 2:6, 81, 82, 82, 139, 218, 265, 288 Decal 32, 105, 134 Spec 1:17, 18, 46, 46, 99, 200, 201, 201, 203, 211, 215, 219, 260, 306, 333, 334, 336, 344 Spec 2:61, 66, 163, 203, 230, 256 Spec 3:1, 99, 111, 166, 185, 188, 207 Spec 4:92, 93, 123, 188 Virt 205 Praem 26, 62, 117, 120, 121, 163 Prob 95, 111, 146 Contempl 61, 66, 76, 78 Aet 1, 15, 41, 72, 75, 77 Flacc 114 Legat 21, 190 Hypoth 11:15 Prov 2:8, 54, 68 QG 1:21, 2:34a, 34a, 59, 72, 4:33b, 179 QG isf 15 QG (Par) 2:5 QE 2:17, 26 QE isf 2, 4

Νορβανός Legat 314, 315

νοσερός Det 34, 72 Agr 164 Her 299 Somn 2:150

νοσέω (36) Opif 167 Leg 2:97 Leg 3:211 Cher 15, 16 Sacr 121 Deus 124 Agr 39 Plant 157 Ebr 179 Migr 87, 87 Her 202 Fug 160, 160 Mut 170, 230, 230 Abr 46, 242 Spec 1:325 Spec 3:11, 37 Spec 4:186 Virt 25 Praem 159 Prob 87 Aet 20, 126 Flacc 75 Legat 15 Prov 2:17, 23, 55 QG 3:22 QE 2:25d

νοσηλεία Prob 87

νοσηλεύω Her 297 Ios 23 Hypoth 11:13

νόσημα (33) Opif 150 Leg 3:124 Cher 96 Det 43 Post 46, 71, 72, 74 Deus 67 Ebr 214 Migr 155, 219 Her 284 Somn 2:131, 299 Abr 179, 223 Ios 10 Mos 1:265 Decal 150 Spec 1:167, 257, 281 Spec 2:157 Spec 4:100 Virt 162 Praem 145 Prob 58 Aet 2, 20, 40, 78 Prov 2:18

νόσος (153) Opif 125 Leg 1:13, 45 Leg 2:60 Leg 3:36, 76, 87, 178, 178, 182, 211, 215 Cher 2, 10, 68, 69, 75, 116 Sacr 16, 31 Det 44, 51, 98, 101, 110, 123, 178 Post 47, 71, 112, 112, 164 Deus 65, 66, 67, 97, 135 Agr 39, 151 Plant 114 Ebr 12, 79, 121, 140, 140, 141 Sobr 2, 38, 45 Conf 16, 20, 22, 163 Migr 87, 124, 150, 217 Her 202, 209 Congr 18, 39, 39, 53, 93, 138 Fug 27 Mut 150 Somn 1:222 Somn 2:129, 295 Abr 46, 136, 136, 182 Ios 77, 87, 110, 110, 113, 130, 160, 191 Mos 1:42, 128, 133, 236 Mos 2:34, 167 Decal 12, 68 Spec 1:4, 10, 24, 77, 80, 174, 237, 239, 325 Spec 2:136 Spec 3:11, 28, 37, 98, 98, 106 Spec 4:83, 200, 237 Virt 3, 4, 5, 13, 26, 176, 193 Praem 21, 33, 98, 143 Prob 12, 76, 124 Contempl 2, 9, 60 Aet 21, 23, 26, 37, 67, 74, 149 Flacc 153, 182 Legat 14, 14, 16, 18, 106, 107, 145, 206, 356 Hypoth 11:11 Prov 2:14, 30, 33, 55 QG 1:65, 85, 2:41, 3:8

νοσσία νεοσσία

νόστιμος QG (Par) 2:7

νοσφίζω (13) Leg 3:33 Plant 103 Her 106, 107 Congr 75 Somn 2:99 Ios 258, 260 Mos 1:253 Decal 171 Spec 4:34 Flacc 69 Legat 199

νοσφισμός Spec 4:5, 36

νοσώδης Leg 2:97 Spec 4:119 Prov 2:55

νοτίζω QG 1:3

νότιος (9) Cher 88 Her 147 Mos 1:114, 120 Mos 2:102, 102 Spec 2:191 Spec 3:188, 188

νοτίς Opif 38, 38, 131, 131 Mos 2:264

νότος Mos 1:120, 176

νουθεσία (37) Opif 128, 128 Leg 3:193 Post 97 Deus 54, 182 Ebr 29 Migr 14 Her 177, 185 Congr 157, 160, 177 Fug 30, 206 Mut 22, 135 Mos 1:98, 113, 119, 129, 328 Mos 2:241 Decal 174 Spec 2:18, 241 Spec 3:141 Virt 75 Praem 4, 133, 163, 170 Legat 41, 64 QG 3:26, 4:168 QG isf 5

νουθετέω (43) Det 3 Post 68 Gig 46 Deus 52, 64, 68, 134 Conf 46 Migr 14 Congr 118, 158, 167, 172 Fug 98 Somn 1:162, 236 Ios 9, 73, 86 Mos 1:95, 110, 134, 143 Mos 2:172 Decal 87 Spec 1:57, 305 Spec 2:19, 232, 239 Spec 3:42, 126 Spec 4:96, 150, 223 Virt 41, 94, 115 Praem 149 Prob 31 Flacc 14 Legat 7, 43

νουθετητής Sacr 51 Deus 63 Her 77 Flacc 15 Legat 53

νουμηνία νεομηνία

νοῦς νόος

νυκτεγερσια Cher 92

νυκτερεύω Spec 1:301

νυκτερία Somn 2:34

νυκτερινός Legat 123

νυκτιφόρος Plant 40

νυκτοφύλαξ Spec 1:156 Flacc 120 QG 4:228

νύκτωρ (46) Opif 80 Leg 3:234 Sacr 38 Ebr 134 Conf 46, 100, 151 Migr 111 Her 174 Somn 1:101, 123 Abr 96, 155 Ios 86, 255 Mos 1:38, 166, 212 Mos 2:54, 174 Decal 74, 87 Spec 1:16, 119, 125, 169, 285, 297 Spec 2:101, 210, 222 Spec 3:17, 39 Spec 4:7, 8, 10 Virt 6, 20 Praem 151 Contempl 42 Flacc 183 Legat 13, 123, 171, 184 QE 2:13b

νύμφη Leg 3:74 Spec 1:110

νυμφίος Spec 1:110 Virt 199

νυμφοστολέω Agr 153 Congr 72 Abr 250

νῦν νυνί ταννῦν

νῦν (201) Opif 134, 140, 163 Leg 1:1, 33, 56, 62, 95, 108 Leg 2:9, 12, 24, 37, 40, 40, 41, 42, 42, 42, 43, 65, 87, 96 Leg 3:18, 55, 70, 76, 140, 164, 164, 191, 193, 218, 238, 252 Cher 1, 21, 36, 53, 115 Sacr 68, 134 Det 13, 50, 75, 96, 96, 178 Post 33, 75, 101, 117, 168 Gig 27 Deus 49, 74, 86, 174 Agr 67, 88, 107, 152 Plant 48, 67, 70, 119, 156, 160, 160 Ebr 33, 41, 42, 42, 42, 49, 78 Conf 1, 2, 6, 12, 84, 191 Migr 73, 84, 136, 150, 167, 167, 208 Her 22, 30, 39, 44, 213, 243, 256, 258, 291, 311 Congr 78 Fug 2, 21, 23, 75 Mut 18, 23, 36, 77, 120, 143, 145, 166, 167 Somn 1:10, 57, 67, 101, 116, 126, 127, 189 Somn 2:56, 93, 98, 102, 104, 246, 258 Abr 32, 114, 140, 163, 182, 201 Ios 66, 135, 135, 238 Mos 1:58, 111, 202, 222, 226, 280, 281 Mos 2:14, 29, 41, 56, 205, 208, 216, 240 Spec 1:1, 129, 323 Spec 2:20 Spec 3:61 Spec 4:204 Virt 22, 197 Praem 20, 21, 106, 106 Prob 20, 62 Contempl 31 Aet 4, 21, 41, 57, 60, 61, 65, 114, 125 Flacc 15, 23, 189 Legat 20, 86, 140, 157, 168, 199, 242, 257, 271, 317, 324, 350 Prov 2:21, 60, 70 QG 2:13b, 65, 68a, 3:29, 4:67 QE isf 7

νυνί (νῦν) (94) Opif 40, 41, 80, 168 Leg 1:43, 53, 90 Leg 2:12, 32 Leg 3:21, 28, 96, 110, 194, 214, 235 Cher 118 Sacr 11, 40 Det 17 Post 1, 29, 131, 160 Gig 57 Deus 121, 132, 169 Plant 52, 141 Ebr 1 Sobr 13 Conf 76, 190 Migr 10, 90 Her 1, 80, 123, 219 Congr 72, 73, 122 Fug 44, 181, 186, 201 Mut 37, 65, 116, 147 Somn 1:97, 118, 160, 230, 240 Somn 2:162, 203 Abr 48, 218 Ios 25, 136, 177, 193, 195 Mos 1:203, 325 Mos 2:1, 3 Decal 78, 114, 125 Spec 2:1, 8, 43, 195 Spec 3:37, 174 Spec 4:17, 135 Virt 138, 210 Prob 65 Contempl 48 Aet 3, 11, 32, 47, 54, 83, 119 Flacc 126 Legat 306 Prov 2:19

νύξ (91) Opif 30, 56, 56, 57, 85 Leg 1:2, 6 Leg 3:167 Cher 62 Sacr 34 Post 57 Gig 41 Plant 118 Ebr 106, 155, 209 Conf 116 Migr 157 Her 87, 146, 148, 148, 149, 149, 149, 149, 150, 163, 163, 208 Fug 57, 184 Somn 1:36, 76, 99, 99, 117 Somn 2:34, 36, 42, 105, 106, 133, 134, 156 Abr 149, 233 Ios 103, 146 Mos 1:120, 123, 123, 123, 125, 135, 175, 176 Mos 2:122, 194, 271 Decal 139 Spec 1:34, 90, 156, 297, 319 Spec 2:100, 100, 134 Spec 4:173, 232, 232, 233 Praem 36 Prob 5 Contempl 34 Aet 19, 52, 88, 104, 141 Flacc 27, 119, 159, 167, 169 Legat 103, 122 QG 2:14 QE isf 20, 20

νύσσω Sacr 26 Somn 2:144 Legat 42

νυστάζω Congr 81

Νῶε (54) Leg 2:60 Leg 3:77, 77 Det 105, 121 Post 48, 173, 174 Gig 1, 3, 5 Deus 70, 74, 86, 104, 109, 116, 117, 117, 117, 122, 140 Agr 1, 2, 20, 125, 181 Plant 1, 140, 140 Ebr 4 Sobr 1, 32, 44 Migr 125 Her 260 Congr 90 Mut 189 Somn 2:223 Abr 27, 31, 31 Praem 23 QG 1:96:1, 97, 2:17c, 26a, 26a, 48, 48, 65, 66, 3:11a QG (Par) 2:1

νωθής (6) Sacr 32 Post 161 Deus 63, 93 Somn 1:237 Abr 266

νώτιος Somn 1:248

νῶτον Opif 86 Agr 75 Spec 4:80 Praem 95 Aet 128

Ξάνθιος Prob 118

ξανθός Mos 1:81

ξεναγέω (6) Somn 1:42, 66, 188 Spec 3:185, 187 Praem 165

ξεναγός Opif 161

ξένη Det 13

ξενηλασία Spec 2:146

ξενία Deus 103 Ios 234, 250 Mos 2:33

ξενίζω Abr 109, 116, 131, 132

ξενικός (12) Sacr 25 Post 118 Conf 42 Migr 216 Her 162, 244 Ios 230 Mos 2:19, 58 Decal 5 Spec 3:16 Legat 68

ξένιος (6) Abr 107, 115, 167 Mos 1:36, 58 QG 2:66

ξενιτεία Ios 254 Flacc 172

ξενιτεύω (6) Ios 26, 195 Mos 2:232 Spec 1:68 Aet 31 QE 2:2

ξενοδόχος (7) Abr 110, 132, 167 Ios 205, 215 Virt 106 Flacc 27

ξένος (59) Leg 2:97 Cher 120 Post 109 Agr 65 Conf 76, 78, 81, 82 Migr 50 Her 268 Congr 22 Fug 76 Mut 267 Somn 1:45, 45, 52, 130, 181, 256 Abr 62, 62, 94, 96, 114, 231 Ios 24, 47, 47, 178, 201, 210 Mos 1:34, 35, 36, 58, 142, 199, 213, 275, 293 Mos 2:201 Decal 80 Spec 1:73 Spec 2:80, 87 Spec 3:155 Spec 4:17, 70, 142, 159 Virt 173 Flacc 54, 86 Legat 15, 294 QG 3:7 QE 2:2, 2, 2

Ξενοφῶν Contempl 57, 58

ξενόω Leg 3:83 Conf 27

Ξέρξης Somn 2:117

ξηραίνω Spec 2:153

ξηρός (32) Opif 38, 39, 131 Leg 2:2 Sacr 108 Plant 3 Ebr 186 Conf 184 Her 135, 135, 146, 151, 153, 197, 208, 282 Somn 1:24, 37, 40 Abr 269 Mos 1:120, 179 Mos 2:254 Spec 2:91, 153, 202 Spec 3:32 Spec 4:193 Contempl 86 Aet 98 Prov 2:67 QE isf 5

ξιφήρης Legat 97

ξιφηφορέω Deus 60

ξιφίδιον Prob 78

ξίφος (18) Cher 32 Somn 1:236 Somn 2:121 Abr 176 Mos 2:171, 273 Spec 2:245, 245 Spec 3:86, 92, 95, 161 Spec 4:222 Flacc 67, 113, 189 Legat 31, 31

ξόανον (16) Ebr 109 Abr 267 Mos 1:298 Mos 2:205 Decal 7, 51, 66, 76, 156 Spec 1:56 Virt 221 Contempl 7 Legat 98, 148, 292 QE isf 14

ξυλίζομαι Mos 2:220

ξύλινος (11) Leg 3:58 Cher 100 Post 26 Congr 95, 96, 97 Mos 2:60, 64, 180, 182 Spec 4:229

ξύλον (89) Opif 18, 142 Leg 1:48, 52, 56, 56, 56, 59, 59, 59, 60, 60, 60, 61, 90, 90, 97, 97, 100, 100, 101 Leg 2:22, 71 Leg 3:1, 28, 52, 56, 58, 107, 107, 160, 222, 246 Cher 1, 80, 126, 126 Post 26, 156 Deus 8, 35 Plant 44, 95, 96, 96, 109, 112 Ebr 133 Sobr 36 Conf 107 Migr 36, 37, 37, 120 Her 226 Congr 163 Fug 132, 133 Somn 2:56, 70, 213, 250 Abr 139, 171, 173 Mos 1:70, 70, 185 Mos 2:214, 220 Decal 66 Spec 1:71, 267, 268 Spec

2:255 Spec 3:92 Virt 219 Prob 96, 101, 143 Contempl 7 Aet 75 Flacc 66, 68, 69 Legat 130 QG (Par) 2:2, 2:2, 2:4

ξυρέω Agr 175 Spec 1:5

O

ὁ (58225) passim

ὀβελίας Spec 2:20

ὀβελός Virt 136

ὀβολοστάτης Fug 28 Spec 2:76 Virt 85 Praem 106

ὀγδοάς Plant 124 Spec 2:212

ὀγδοήκοντα Ios 270 Spec 2:33

ὄγδοος (12) Opif 103, 110 Det 168 Her 251 Mos 2:153 Spec 1:189 Spec 2:41, 211 Spec 3:123 Spec 4:1 Aet 97 Legat 14

ὄγκος (51) Opif 1, 41 Leg 2:77 Leg 3:47, 58, 69, 146, 149 Sacr 63 Det 27, 90, 113 Post 26, 137 Agr 61 Plant 157 Ebr 88, 128, 221 Conf 55 Migr 157, 191 Her 58, 142 Congr 96, 97, 128 Somn 1:22, 43, 77 Somn 2:70, 72 Ios 65, 101, 118 Mos 1:19, 153, 233, 275 Decal 43 Spec 3:62 Praem 129 Prob 130 Aet 100, 101 Flacc 30, 152 Legat 14 Prov 2:12 QG (Par) 2:2 QE isf 15

ὀδαξάω Spec 3:199

ὀδαξησμός Spec 3:10

ὅδε (194) Opif 9, 11, 12, 21, 47, 52, 67, 72, 79, 82, 97, 104, 107, 112, 132, 136 Leg 1:34, 67, 102 Leg 2:2, 74, 80 Leg 3:20, 86, 99, 99, 100, 136, 179, 186, 195 Cher 51, 55, 63, 63, 98, 112, 120, 127, 127 Sacr 4, 22, 48, 76, 97 Det 159 Post 5, 7, 16, 174, 184, 185 Deus 49 Plant 2, 6, 48, 101, 138 Ebr 3, 30, 30, 73, 117 Sobr 1 Conf 37, 61, 87, 97, 98, 172, 181 Migr 16, 170, 181, 220 Her 295, 296 Congr 51, 143, 144, 149 Fug 18, 24, 63, 72, 100, 137, 194, 195, 198 Mut 18, 20, 34, 177 Somn 1:2, 15, 39, 64, 116, 132, 156, 207, 215 Somn 2:30, 189, 220, 294 Abr 71, 118, 127, 128, 131, 132, 147, 247 Ios 29, 69, 268 Mos 1:137, 175, 201, 207, 222, 277, 283, 288, 290, 325 Mos 2:12, 40, 99, 139, 165, 182, 203, 250, 280 Decal 14, 18, 31, 102, 107 Spec 1:26, 31, 33, 34, 35, 41, 69, 80, 95, 214, 249, 263, 286, 298, 309 Spec 2:35, 111, 120, 146, 151, 151, 177, 212 Spec 3:23, 23, 30, 48, 60, 78, 80, 124, 129, 134, 178, 188 Virt 55 Praem 41, 65, 66, 120 Prob 139, 139 Aet 25, 25, 26, 28 Legat 315 Hypoth 7:13 Prov 2:39 QG 1:64d QG (Par) 2:4 QE 2:6a

ὁδεύω Leg 2:98 Post 155

ὁδηγία QG isf 15

ὁδηγός Mos 1:178

ὀδμή Sacr 44

ὁδοιπορέω (10) Abr 107 Ios 15, 179 Mos 1:165, 181, 206, 220, 250 Spec 2:250 QE 2:13a

ὁδοιπορία (10) Opif 84 Mut 165 Mos 1:215, 216 Mos 2:1, 73, 254 Spec 2:207 Prob 68 Legat 254

ὁδοίπορος Abr 131 Spec 1:165 Hypoth 7:19

Ὀδολλάμιτης Fug 149

ὀδοντοφυέω Spec 1:164

ὁδός (211) Opif 69, 101, 114, 144 Leg 1:57 Leg 2:94, 97, 97, 97, 98 Leg 3:108, 253 Cher 1, 3 Sacr 47 Det 10, 19, 21, 22, 24, 29 Post 7, 31, 101, 101, 102, 102, 102, 154 Gig 55, 64 Deus 61, 119, 140, 141, 142, 142, 142, 143, 144, 144, 145, 159, 159, 160, 162, 164, 165, 180, 180, 182 Agr 51, 88, 94, 100, 101, 102, 103, 104, 177 Plant

37, 97, 98 Ebr 125, 150 Conf 4, 19, 63, 95, 179 Migr 133, 143, 146, 170, 171, 174, 174, 175, 195, 209 Her 70, 149, 287 Congr 10, 28, 124, 125, 170 Fug 1, 21, 25, 131, 144, 149, 203, 203 Somn 1:3, 156, 168, 179, 209, 237, 246 Somn 2:103, 161, 170, 180 Abr 7, 59, 169, 172, 204, 269, 269 Ios 12, 25, 142, 178, 179, 181, 183, 187, 189, 212, 218, 249, 255, 256 Mos 1:73, 85, 86, 163, 164, 166, 177, 194, 195, 228, 232, 237, 243, 246, 269, 274, 290, 295 Mos 2:138, 189, 247, 253, 255 Decal 50, 81 Spec 1:17, 91, 132, 192, 215, 243, 300, 301, 335 Spec 2:23 Spec 3:29, 116, 148, 171, 185 Spec 4:69, 108, 109, 109, 111, 141, 154, 155, 168, 198 Virt 7, 51, 100 Praem 40, 62, 94, 117, 148, 167 Prob 2, 115 Contempl 86 Aet 58, 109, 110 Flacc 28, 36, 37, 111, 152, 160, 186 Legat 174, 216 Hypoth 6:2 Prov 2:26 QG 2:34a, 41, 4:144 QE 2:26, 26, 26, 65

ὀδούς (19) Opif 103, 104, 105, 157, 159 Spec 1:164, 164, 217 Spec 3:198, 198, 198, 199, 200, 201, 202, 202, 202, 202 Prob 108

ὀδυνάω Det 114 Conf 92 Ios 94 Flacc 119 QE 2:25c

ὀδύνη (11) Opif 161 Leg 3:216 Mut 92, 94 Somn 2:165 Abr 207 Praem 158 Aet 63 Flacc 180 QG 1:41 QE isf 33

ὀδυνηρός (14) Leg 3:202, 251 Det 119, 140 Mut 167 Abr 257 Spec 2:89 Spec 3:56 Virt 200 Praem 73 Flacc 66, 68, 119, 129

ὀδύρομαι Migr 156

Ὀδυσσεύς Contempl 40

ὅθεν (79) Opif 12, 49, 77, 159 Leg 3:95 Det 15 Gig 13 Plant 46, 91 Ebr 51 Conf 78 Fug 180 Mut 265 Abr 9, 17, 27, 213, 227, 258 Ios 2, 5, 60 Mos 1:303 Mos 2:102, 118, 125, 130, 219, 222, 237, 286 Decal 69, 112, 117 Spec 1:7, 43, 100, 243, 276 Spec 2:53, 106, 209, 238, 253 Spec 3:59, 94 Spec 4:8, 71, 102, 123 Virt 47, 57, 178, 184, 195 Praem 88, 112, 115 Prob 25, 48, 143, 155 Contempl 34 Aet 147 Flacc 186 Legat 292 Hypoth 6:1 QG 2:5a, 12a, 12b, 3:38a, 49b, 58, 4:67, 104, 174, 202a QG (Par) 2:5 QE 2:10b

ὀθνεῖος (18) Agr 65 Plant 15 Conf 76 Migr 11 Her 12 Congr 23 Fug 76 Mut 147, 147 Somn 2:280 Ios 254 Decal 94 Spec 2:11, 168 Spec 3:25, 155 Praem 134 Legat 72

ὄθομαι Prob 125

ὀθόνη Somn 1:217 Mos 2:90 Spec 1:84 Spec 2:20 Contempl 38

οἰακονομέω Conf 98 Mut 149 Legat 149

οἰακονόμος Mut 149

οἴαξ (12) Opif 46 Leg 3:223 Cher 38 Migr 6 Somn 2:201 Decal 14 Spec 1:224 Praem 51 Legat 50, 129, 177 QG 4:76b

οἶδα (εἴδω) (357) Opif 17, 33, 41, 50, 53, 72, 90, 149 Leg 1:9, 33, 56, 60, 61, 74, 91 Leg 2:40, 69, 84 Leg 3:2, 12, 32, 69, 90, 90, 95, 118, 146, 149, 156, 157, 169, 173, 174, 175, 179, 243 Cher 1, 27, 32, 32, 37, 48, 65, 115, 122 Sacr 10, 10, 29, 30, 32, 33, 71, 71, 77, 84, 112 Det 11, 34, 37, 43, 57, 57, 61, 76, 77, 84, 131, 142, 161, 165, 166, 167 Post 41, 52, 95, 115, 134, 141, 157 Gig 17 Deus 21, 65, 76, 80, 91, 143 Agr 1, 131, 161, 163, 179 Plant 21, 64, 80, 80, 141, 141, 161, 172 Ebr 19, 43, 48, 76, 77, 162, 162, 189, 203 Sobr 19, 20 Conf 16, 26, 71, 72, 100, 120, 135, 182, 183 Migr 10, 34, 34, 51, 55, 90, 131, 134, 136, 195, 203, 213 Her 18, 36, 226, 252, 301, 302 Congr 11, 44, 46, 73, 83, 161, 170, 179 Fug 3, 8, 8, 27, 54, 56, 115, 137, 193, 204 Mut 46, 66, 116, 139, 153, 199, 205 Somn 1:13, 26, 26, 28, 39, 45, 71, 117, 127, 183, 191 Somn 2:1, 8, 15, 52, 65, 103, 103, 123, 147, 182, 253, 296 Abr 58, 75, 102, 107, 112, 115, 116, 174, 175, 189, 204, 214, 215, 230 Ios 10, 20, 43, 62, 66, 127, 131, 208, 213, 248, 249, 254 Mos 1:2, 31, 46, 72, 88, 153, 197, 212, 220, 223, 224, 248, 295, 306, 328, 329 Mos 2:38, 61, 177, 202, 213, 217, 237, 240, 280 Decal 8, 18, 59, 61, 72, 91, 94, 94, 95, 114, 133, 138, 139, 139, 141, 142, 177 Spec 1:39, 160, 176, 281, 332 Spec 2:14, 23, 24, 26, 29, 87, 93, 96, 130, 228 Spec 3:34, 39, 62, 112, 129, 140, 145, 146, 193 Spec 4:40, 100, 145 Virt 21, 25, 51, 67, 79, 94, 96, 202, 214, 227 Prob 27, 40, 54, 54, 76, 78, 110, 123 Contempl 1, 20, 39, 43, 46, 52, 65, 73 Aet 39, 69 Flacc 39, 42, 49, 50, 77, 83, 87, 139, 175, 179 Legat 41, 53, 104, 112, 153, 154, 160, 168, 169, 172, 195, 198, 198, 201, 209, 209, 216, 219, 226, 244, 261, 278, 286, 293, 324, 349, 369 Prov 2:5, 13, 24, 42, 45, QG 4:52a, 9*, 9*, 198 QE 2:2, 13b QE isf 16

οἰδέω (10) Post 46, 122 Plant 157 Congr 128, 162 Mos 2:166 Spec 3:62, 193 Flacc 32 Legat 331

Οἰδίπους Spec 3:15

οἴησις (29) Leg 1:52, 52 Leg 3:33, 33, 47, 137 Cher 57, 71 Sacr 54, 58 Post 46, 136 Migr 34 Congr 107, 138 Mut 175 Somn 1:131, 211 Mos 1:286 Mos 2:96 Decal 40 Spec 1:10, 265, 293 Praem 47 QG 3:48, 4:100 QE 2:14, 14

οἰησίσοφος Leg 3:192

οἰητικός Cher 116

οἴκαδε (19) Plant 162 Somn 1:45, 122 Somn 2:76 Abr 86 Ios 178, 224 Mos 1:58, 59, 286 Spec 2:102 Spec 3:171 Spec 4:196 Virt 90 Flacc 28 Legat 267, 356 QG 1:62:1, 62:2

οἰκεῖος (413) Opif 12, 13, 64, 74, 74, 74, 77, 147, 149, 163 Leg 1:4, 16, 25, 27, 45, 47, 49, 61, 70, 84 Leg 2:8, 26, 38, 40, 84 Leg 3:1, 64, 68, 78, 93, 117, 123, 138, 160, 204, 205 Cher 19, 20, 20, 22, 24, 54, 54, 74, 78, 84, 90, 129 Sacr 20, 29, 46, 74, 75, 82, 82, 83, 85, 102, 129 Det 22, 96, 127, 133, 135, 138, 146, 151, 152, 165 Post 4, 30, 45, 53, 57, 75, 99, 109, 139, 142 Gig 7, 32, 32, 34, 35, 37, 62, 65 Deus 4, 29, 43, 44, 46, 47, 52, 62, 63, 69, 118 Agr 91, 152 Plant 7, 27, 29, 38, 48, 78, 130, 133, 146, 163 Ebr 66, 69, 70, 106, 111, 138, 168, 176 Sobr 2, 3, 28, 35, 36, 36, 61 Conf 29, 68, 76, 89, 111, 116, 117, 118, 123, 161, 180, 183, 186, 195, 198 Migr 11, 14, 83, 165, 204, 209, 215, 217, 218, 224 Her 21, 56, 56, 61, 79, 119, 184, 238, 238, 244, 253, 267, 272, 273, 273, 286 Congr 4, 84, 111, 130, 153, 177 Fug 47, 89, 125, 210, 213 Mut 2, 23, 63, 85, 100, 111, 191, 197, 230, 257, 260 Somn 1:2, 23, 27, 103, 103, 109, 192 Somn 2:31, 37, 47, 67, 76, 79, 128, 158, 219, 232, 286, 288 Abr 8, 27, 51, 62, 62, 70, 72, 86, 106, 150, 202, 211, 235, 235, 241, 245, 257, 259 Ios 3, 9, 18, 24, 28, 46, 46, 66, 133 Mos 1:31, 32, 36, 48, 53, 79, 100, 122, 217, 250, 293, 308, 325, 332, 333 Mos 2:19, 42, 49, 63, 120, 126, 129, 130, 142, 173, 225, 227, 235, 242, 254, 273, 274, 277 Decal 42, 102, 104, 108, 129, 134, 177 Spec 1:3, 43, 52, 57, 62, 65, 97, 115, 137, 146, 148, 160, 250, 270, 313, 340, 344 Spec 2:64, 102, 109, 114, 123, 127, 141, 160, 171, 190, 240 Spec 3:11, 57, 67, 80, 101, 108, 126, 155, 165, 166, 184, 191 Spec 4:21, 32, 58, 70, 92, 105, 132, 158, 182, 210, 216 Virt 18, 22, 25, 60, 90, 96, 100, 111, 125,

140, 167, 189, 193, 195, 197, 201, 218 Praem 17, 41, 49, 55, 83, 118, 130, 131, 134, 152 Prob 8, 24, 71 Contempl 72, 72, 78, 90 Aet 20, 31, 33, 34, 48, 62, 65, 66, 98, 126, 130, 135, 136 Flacc 9, 11, 31, 56, 59, 60, 64, 89, 162, 168, 187 Legat 15, 23, 41, 51, 69, 110, 138, 277, 277, 294, 308, 310, 321, 343, 346 Hypoth 7:4, 7:19 Prov 2:3, 17, 29, 36, 59 QG 1:20, 21, 2:34a, 4:99 QE 2:6b, 46 QE isf 4, 17

οἰκειότης (31) Opif 106 Leg 3:182 Det 164 Plant 66 Conf 150 Congr 94 Mut 147 Somn 2:83 Abr 54, 196 Ios 235 Mos 1:241, 280, 324 Mos 2:176, 278 Spec 1:316, 317, 317 Spec 2:73 Spec 3:192, 194 Spec 4:159 Virt 179 Praem 57 Prob 79 Aet 68 Legat 29, 63, 71, 72

οἰκειόω (27) Opif 146, 161 Cher 11, 18, 74 Sacr 74, 138 Det 129 Post 123 Gig 18 Agr 6, 25 Conf 87, 182 Migr 47 Her 244, 278 Mut 110, 114 Somn 2:228, 231 Mos 1:7, 234 Mos 2:8 Spec 1:112 Prov 2:66 QG 3:26

οἰκείωσις (15) Opif 10 Cher 18, 18 Post 12, 135, 140, 157 Gig 29 Plant 55 Conf 82 Her 154 Mut 120 Mos 2:243 Spec 4:68 QE 2:2

οἰκέτης (51) Cher 80, 81, 115 Det 13 Post 138, 181 Deus 47, 64 Agr 58 Plant 55 Ebr 131, 195 Sobr 32, 51 Her 6, 9 Congr 76 Fug 3, 212 Mut 89, 226 Somn 1:7 Somn 2:108 Abr 108, 170, 190, 232 Ios 66 Spec 1:127, 128 Spec 2:67, 67, 68, 83, 123 Spec 3:136, 137, 143, 184, 203 Spec 4:18 Virt 173, 173 Prob 143, 148, 156, 157, 157 Flacc 112 Legat 165, 272

οἰκετικός (6) Abr 213 Ios 219 Mos 1:152 Flacc 149 Legat 252 Prov 2:17

οἰκέτις Congr 152

οἰκέω οἰκουμένη

οἰκέω (78) Opif 114, 143, 147 Leg 1:78 Leg 3:2, 2, 83, 115 Cher 12 Sacr 4, 130 Det 163, 163 Post 1, 49 Gig 61 Agr 119, 157, 166 Plant 34, 44, 44 Ebr 10, 103 Conf 64, 66, 68, 106 Migr 23, 177, 185, 187, 208, 214 Her 147, 287, 293 Congr 62, 71, 84 Fug 3, 23, 45, 46, 76 Mut 119, 120, 149, 152 Somn 1:45, 46, 52, 151 Ios 111, 123 Mos 1:36, 209, 214, 239, 264 Mos 2:19, 73, 232 Decal 14 Spec 2:162 Spec 3:17 Virt 105 Prob 76, 125 Aet 148 Flacc 46, 55 Legat 134, 155, 160, 200 Hypoth 11:1, 11:5

οἴκημα Mos 2:60 Contempl 25

οἴκησις (7) Cher 11 Post 49 Abr 215 Mos 2:148 Spec 2:120 Spec 3:184 QE 2:25a

οἰκήτωρ (54) Post 52, 52, 61, 62 Gig 21 Sobr 64 Migr 14, 212 Her 194 Fug 76 Somn 1:149 Somn 2:170 Abr 91, 134, 139, 142 Ios 110, 267 Mos 1:6, 34, 110, 119, 129, 164, 224, 224, 229, 251, 262, 319 Mos 2:58 Spec 1:159 Spec 2:119, 170 Spec 3:16, 39, 130, 130, 162 Spec 4:156, 159 Praem 90, 133, 153, 157 Flacc 43, 163 Legat 121, 205, 282, 293, 297 Prov 2:64 QG (Par) 2:5

οἰκία (236) Opif 17 Leg 2:34, 77 Leg 3:2, 2, 2, 40, 98, 98, 99, 238, 239, 241 Cher 13, 94, 99, 126, 127 Sacr 21, 55, 124, 124 Det 14, 16, 33, 33, 159 Post 50, 50, 181 Gig 51 Deus 94, 95, 95, 131, 131, 131, 131, 131, 131, 132, 133, 135 Agr 90, 148, 148, 148, 148, 149, 152, 157, 157, 158, 166, 170, 170, 171 Plant 44 Ebr 91, 193 Sobr 63 Conf 27, 28, 46 Migr 3, 90, 124, 159, 160, 160, 162, 215 Her 26, 162, 193 Congr 10, 62, 106 Fug 144, 175, 176, 183 Mut 149 Somn 1:52, 96, 149, 177, 177 Somn 2:54, 144, 193, 272, 286 Abr 31, 40, 50, 92, 115, 116, 139, 251, 260 Ios 5, 37, 38, 38, 45, 45, 50, 117, 136, 196, 197, 199, 200, 207, 211, 253, 254, 259, 270 Mos 1:38, 103, 135, 137, 143, 144, 152, 240, 312, 324, 330 Mos 2:8, 30, 59, 64, 72, 281 Spec 1:24, 33, 68, 73, 105, 110, 122, 130, 165 Spec 2:37, 42, 85, 107, 116, 118, 119, 121, 121, 121, 148, 233 Spec 3:25, 38, 65, 89, 138, 142, 149, 164, 170, 192, 206 Spec 4:7, 27, 68, 142, 142, 186 Virt 3, 28, 30, 89, 115, 119, 163, 192, 221 Praem 57, 60, 74, 99, 106, 120, 120, 141 Prob 9, 35, 85, 119 Contempl 24, 38, 38 Aet 11, 20 Flacc 35, 56, 64, 74, 76, 86, 86, 93, 94, 111, 112, 119, 120, 148 Legat 15, 40, 83, 102, 121, 123, 132, 166, 175, 225, 232, 306 Hypoth 6:3, 11:4 Prov 2:62, 64 QG 4:206b QG isf 1 QE 1:21, 2:13b

οἰκίδιον Her 268

οἰκίζω Post 90 Mos 1:311 Praem 150, 168

οἰκιστής QG 2:65

οἰκογενής (6) Her 2, 2, 39, 42, 65 Spec 1:126

οἰκοδεσπότης Somn 1:149

οἰκοδομέω (39) Leg 1:48 Leg 2:6, 38 Leg 3:3, 225, 228 Sacr 55 Post 33, 49, 50, 50, 53, 54, 59, 60 Deus 94 Agr 148, 170 Conf 1, 1, 1, 91, 107, 111, 122, 142, 155, 155, 158, 162, 196 Fug 175 Somn 1:77, 77 Somn 2:284, 285 Virt 29, 132 Hypoth 6:6

οἰκοδομή Abr 139 Legat 361

οἰκοδόμημα (13) Opif 17 Leg 3:98 Post 52, 52 Agr 171 Sobr 64 Conf 88, 144 Migr 215 Somn 1:122 Decal 133 Legat 117 QG 4:145

οἰκοδομία Mos 1:224 Spec 1:73 Virt 21

οἰκοδόμος Spec 1:33

οἴκοθεν (11) Opif 5 Agr 5 Sobr 8 Ios 127, 199 Mos 1:105 Decal 118 Contempl 1 Flacc 61, 79 QE isf 32

οἴκοι (24) Det 45 Post 141 Agr 147, 150, 162 Sobr 6 Somn 2:125 Abr 23, 197, 232 Ios 10, 163, 167, 185 Mos 1:9, 14 Spec 2:233 Spec 4:8, 74, 141 Praem 20 Flacc 166 Legat 230, 330

οἰκονομέω (7) Opif 11, 54 Abr 69 Ios 192 Decal 53 Spec 3:198 QG 4:67

οἰκονομία (12) Ebr 92 Somn 1:205 Ios 38, 38, 38 Spec 3:170, 171 Virt 208 Prob 83 QG 4:204, 206a, 206a

οἰκονομικός (8) Ebr 91 Fug 36, 36 Mut 149 Ios 39, 54 Spec 2:187 Praem 113

οἰκονόμος Praem 113

οἶκος (168) Opif 27, 73, 137, 142 Leg 1:78, 78 Leg 2:60, 60, 61, 61, 63, 67 Leg 3:3, 42, 103, 152, 152, 204, 228, 238, 238 Cher 3, 49, 49, 52, 98, 99, 100, 101, 101, 105, 106, 115 Sacr 20, 72 Det 149, 159 Post 5, 76, 77 Deus 137, 150 Agr 1, 25, 65 Plant 44, 50, 53 Sobr 59, 62, 62, 63, 66, 66, 67, 68 Conf 19, 74 Migr 1, 2, 3, 3, 4, 4, 4, 5, 5, 7, 12, 23, 68, 93, 120, 159, 160, 185, 187, 189, 195, 214, 214 Her 44, 69, 277 Congr 58, 117 Fug 5, 15, 48, 50, 52, 124, 143 Somn 1:32, 56, 122, 122, 135, 149, 185, 186, 208, 256 Somn 2:172, 173, 251, 272 Abr 46, 62, 97, 109, 115, 247 Ios 38, 191, 232, 236 Mos 1:150, 274, 289 Mos 2:59 Decal 126, 164 Spec 1:129, 214 Spec 2:133 Spec 3:11, 31 Virt 73, 197, 214 Praem 7, 17, 57, 65, 66, 109, 110, 123 Prob 101, 111 Contempl 33 Aet 56, 112, 112 Flacc 23, 49, 103, 104, 115 Legat 33, 48, 72, 72, 144, 279, 342, 364, 365 QG 2:11, 11, 26a, 3:20b, 4:33b, 145, 145, 145, 145

οἰκόσιτος Agr 73 Plant 104

οἴκοτριψ (12) Det 14 Abr 232 Ios 219 Mos 1:36 Spec 2:233, 233 Spec 4:15, 152 Virt 189 Prob 19, 158 Flacc 127

οἰκουμένη (οἰκέω) (55) Deus 175, 176 Agr 35, 143 Ebr 109, 193 Migr 217 Somn 2:180 Abr 226 Ios 19, 56, 135, 159 Mos 1:2, 112, 157, 195, 255 Mos 2:20, 205, 241 Decal 66 Spec 2:163 Spec 3:8, 25 Spec 4:85 Praem 99 Contempl 21 Aet 66, 147 Flacc 44, 49, 151, 172 Legat 10, 10, 16, 19, 48, 49, 88, 101, 108, 116, 144, 146, 149, 173, 214, 283, 284, 330, 338, 356 Prov 2:41

οἰκουρία Congr 5 Fug 154 Ios 40 Spec 1:138 Spec 3:169

οἰκουρός Her 186 Decal 114 Spec 1:316 Praem 139

οἰκοφθόρος Agr 73

οἰκτείρω (οἰκτίρω) Migr 122 Fug 95 Virt 91

οἰκτίζω (16) Plant 46 Ebr 38, 121 Conf 167 Ios 20, 179, 225 Mos 1:10, 10, 303 Mos 2:172 Decal 80 Virt 43, 110 Praem 158 Flacc 68

οἰκτίρω οἰκτείρω

οἰκτίστος οἰκτρός

οἶκτος (39) Opif 169 Det 19, 95 Post 31, 156 Her 213 Mut 133 Somn 1:181 Abr 96, 137 Ios 25, 82, 227 Mos 1:72, 86, 101, 125 Spec 1:115, 308, 341 Spec 2:95, 138 Spec 3:4, 85, 116, 129, 156 Spec 4:18, 57, 77, 180 Virt 41 Prob 57 Flacc 102, 121 Legat 29, 257, 367 Prov 2:4

οἰκτρός (οἰκτίστος) (23) Agr 75 Her 204 Congr 159, 171 Mut 22 Somn 1:256 Somn 2:90, 161 Ios 27, 226 Mos 1:12, 39 Mos 2:240, 240, 249 Spec 1:304 Spec 3:202 Aet 74 Flacc 68, 74 Legat 130, 243, 342

οἶμος Ebr 150

οἰμωγή Ios 23 Mos 1:136

οἰμώζω Prob 53, 54

οἴναρον Deus 39 Mut 162

οἰνήρυσις Ebr 221

οἶνος (84) Leg 2:60 Leg 3:81, 82, 183 Post 176 Deus 77 Agr 1 Plant 140, 142, 144, 145, 148, 148, 154, 154, 155, 162, 174, 174 Ebr 2, 2, 2, 2, 4, 95, 96, 104, 122, 123, 125, 126, 127, 130, 131, 138, 138, 143, 146, 148, 149, 151, 154, 166, 218, 222 Sobr 1, 3 Conf 185, 186, 186 Fug 176 Somn 2:48, 158, 158, 160, 191 Ios 155 Mos 1:187, 270 Mos 2:162, 223 Spec 1:98, 100, 134, 141, 179, 179, 248 Spec 2:148 Spec 3:126 Spec 4:98 Virt 95 Praem 107 Prob 102 Contempl 40, 43, 73, 74 Aet 113 Flacc 142 QG 2:68a, 68a, 68b QE 2:18

οἰνοφλυγέω Ebr 14, 27

οἰνοφλυγία (14) Opif 158 Ebr 222 Mut 206 Somn 2:158, 201, 204 Mos 2:185 Spec 1:148, 192, 281 Spec 3:43 Spec 4:91 Legat 14 QG 2:12d

οἰνοχοεύω Prov 2:7

οἰνοχοέω Deus 158 Plant 160 Somn 2:182 Ios 92 Contempl 50

οἰνοχόη Ebr 221

οἰνοχόος (11) Det 26 Ebr 208, 214, 215, 220 Conf 95 Migr 19 Somn 2:183, 183, 190, 249

οἰνόω (8) Plant 142, 144, 154, 155, 163, 166, 174 QG 2:68b

οἴνωσις Plant 155 QG 2:68a

οἴομαι (229) Opif 26, 30, 131, 168, 171 Leg 1:2, 46, 49, 51 Leg 3:6, 7, 36, 51, 90, 129, 163, 164, 178 Cher 39, 57, 122, 124 Sacr 10, 124 Det 59, 61, 69, 77, 78 Post 28, 34, 65, 79, 101, 115, 124 Gig 1, 58 Agr 65, 84, 157 Plant 32, 33, 50, 69, 71, 107, 145 Ebr 3, 38, 48, 52, 111, 162 Sobr 17, 45, 51 Conf 106, 107, 144, 187, 190 Migr 22, 45, 124, 134, 171, 184, 197, 213, 225, 225 Her 18, 23, 89, 107, 197, 199, 233, 248, 288 Congr 23, 96, 98, 130 Fug 61, 68, 109 Mut 91, 118, 163, 165, 232 Somn 1:30, 37, 93, 119, 246 Somn 2:6, 17, 17, 18, 19, 27, 30, 33, 82, 94, 109, 153, 198, 207, 216, 219, 237, 238, 242, 261, 289 Abr 28, 224, 259 Ios 2, 8, 34, 166 Mos 1:42, 167, 239 Mos 2:19, 39, 44, 122, 154, 183, 200, 202 Decal 88, 107 Spec 1:4, 18, 108, 182, 275, 277, 285, 318 Spec 2:3, 19, 21, 27, 36, 111, 121, 129, 134, 151, 225, 251, 258 Spec 3:6, 8, 40, 58, 87, 102, 130, 156, 205 Spec 4:33, 40, 50, 55, 75, 172, 201, 206 Virt 23, 25, 31, 56, 100, 102, 106, 122, 135, 174, 187, 195 Praem 29 Prob 37, 40, 92, 111, 117, 135 Contempl 3, 35 Aet 7, 10, 14, 17, 18, 59, 90, 111 Flacc 124 Legat 1, 64, 71, 124, 162, 165, 180, 183, 223, 308, 344 Hypoth 7:11, 7:17, 7:19 Prov 2:42 QG 1:60:2, 3:23, 52, 4:81, 9*, 200b QE 2:45a

οἱονεί Opif 41 Sacr 25 Mut 21 Mos 1:226 Mos 2:143

οἷος (375) Opif 15, 18, 38, 38, 45, 46, 54, 56, 56, 67, 72, 78, 88, 90, 133, 139, 145, 154, 165, 166 Leg 1:6, 19, 26, 72, 103, 105 Leg 2:2, 16, 17, 18, 43, 53 Leg 3:5, 9, 10, 16, 52, 52, 57, 61, 61, 61, 86, 87, 120, 126, 151, 167, 169, 189, 224, 234, 244, 250 Cher 14, 62, 121 Sacr 1, 25, 53, 69, 112, 122, 123 Det 79, 116, 128, 141 Post 22, 71, 104, 113, 141, 169, 173 Gig 25, 34 Deus 4, 27, 38, 39, 48, 56, 89, 130 Agr 24, 26, 51, 84, 86, 111, 124, 176 Plant 1, 29, 50, 52, 90, 127, 139, 145, 152, 172 Ebr 1, 7, 19, 29, 32, 95, 96, 172, 186, 211 Sobr 3 Conf 22, 72, 74, 159 Migr 14, 35, 81, 105, 125, 192, 219 Her 68, 243, 264, 274, 297 Congr 36, 63, 106 Fug 26, 39, 47, 82, 91, 124, 134, 141, 164, 172, 182, 191, 201 Mut 17, 42, 112, 140, 199, 199, 200 Somn 1:1, 29, 31, 32, 58, 103, 137, 168, 187, 197, 202, 206, 232 Somn 2:145, 160, 170, 226, 263, 284 Abr 2, 7, 15, 76, 79, 115, 117, 153, 170, 210, 221, 228, 256 Ios 87, 88, 106, 142, 151, 247 Mos 1:9, 10, 20, 29, 29, 29, 40, 60, 65, 70, 113, 124, 130, 150, 157, 170, 189, 208, 218, 220, 275, 279, 294, 302 Mos 2:32, 38, 48, 61, 63, 64, 78, 127, 132, 139, 153, 166, 179, 277 Decal 20, 21, 21, 31, 60, 82, 129, 139, 148, 173 Spec 1:39, 43, 44, 46, 47, 66, 69, 95, 119, 127, 210, 219, 256, 264 Spec 2:16, 19, 45, 45, 48, 52, 101, 135, 160, 215, 225 Spec 3:7, 33, 42, 49, 73, 142, 151, 171, 180, 189 Spec 4:45, 70, 79, 86, 107, 152, 155, 180, 186, 198, 211 Virt 35, 51, 57, 58, 103, 115, 143, 154, 162, 168, 169, 184, 184, 188, 205 Praem 39, 43, 44, 51, 60, 81, 81, 93, 123, 125, 148, 158, 159 Prob 20, 26, 40, 87, 99, 118, 140 Contempl 43, 63, 68, 86 Aet 22, 35, 47, 83, 125, 135 Flacc 4, 16, 28, 97 Legat 31, 75, 77, 124, 127, 151, 151, 166, 190, 207, 227, 232, 246, 303, 304, 304, 340 Hypoth 7:9, 11:15 Prov 2:7, 29, 39, 44, 46, 50 QG 1:1, 62:1, 62:1, 70:1, 2:12c, 4:9* QG (Par) 2:2, 2:3, 2:3, 2:3, 2:7 QE 2:55b QE isf 3, 3, 21, 26

οἰστέος (φέρω) Spec 2:253

οἰστικός (8) Leg 3:113 Agr 11, 100 Plant 98 Ebr 223 Her 137 Mut 73 Spec 1:74

ὀϊστός Post 131 Plant 152 Mos 2:157 Spec 4:28

οἰστός (φέρω) Sacr 113 Spec 3:175 Flacc 58

οἰστράω Agr 76, 84

οἶστρος (16) Opif 158 Det 99, 174 Post 116 Deus 138 Agr 37 Plant 39, 144 Somn 1:36, 122 Decal 123 Spec 2:50, 136 Spec 3:34, 69 Spec 4:82

οἶφι Congr 103 Mut 234

οἴχομαι (21) Sacr 115 Post 8, 68, 173 Gig 21, 47 Agr 83, 97 Ebr 177 Sobr 13 Migr 24, 148, 149, 150 Somn 1:122 Decal 129 Spec 1:160 Flacc 165 Legat 188, 193, 195

οἰωνόμαντις Conf 159 Somn 1:220

οἰωνός (6) Deus 181 Mos 1:263, 282, 284, 287 Spec 3:115

οἰωνοσκοπία Mos 1:264

οἰωνοσκόπος Mut 202 Spec 1:60 Spec 4:48

Ὄκελλος Aet 12

ὀκλάζω (9) Leg 2:99 Det 41 Post 148 Agr 109, 180 Plant 145 Migr 133, 222 Mut 231

ὀκνέω (9) Leg 1:40 Cher 49 Post 151 Conf 119 Ios 94 Mos 1:54 Spec 2:241 Spec 4:202 Aet 84

ὀκνηρός Her 254 Mos 1:8 Spec 1:99 Virt 83

ὄκνος (14) Sacr 86 Det 37, 37, 120 Deus 152 Agr 149 Ebr 17 Sobr 5 Fug 36 Somn 1:8, 165 Somn 2:67 Spec 1:98 Prob 71

ὀκτάκις Opif 93

ὀκτώ (31) Opif 93, 99, 99, 101, 104, 105, 106, 107, 107, 108, 108, 109, 109, 109, 110 Leg 1:9 Congr 104 Mos 1:238 Mos 2:77, 78, 84, 84, 85 Decal 22, 28 Spec 1:158 Spec 2:40, 120 Flacc 74 QG 3:49a, 52

ὀκτωμηνιαῖος Opif 124

ὀλάργυρος Spec 2:33

ὄλεθρος (41) Leg 2:34 Leg 3:13 Sacr 57 Det 46, 103, 136 Deus 166 Ebr 24, 70, 79 Conf 86, 118 Migr 83 Congr 171 Fug 39 Mut 22, 240 Somn 1:86 Somn 2:179, 274 Abr 142 Mos 1:44, 192 Mos 2:249, 254 Spec 1:160 Spec 3:147, 158 Spec 4:127 Praem 96, 133, 163 Flacc 68 Legat 91, 104, 130, 293 Hypoth 6:4 Prov 2:29, 30 QE isf 32

ὀλιγάκις Conf 115

ὀλιγανδρέω Somn 2:170

ὀλιγανδρία Somn 2:170

ὀλιγαρχέω Prob 45

ὀλιγαρχία Decal 155

ὀλιγαρχικός Decal 136

ὀλιγοδεής Leg 3:147 Ebr 215 Virt 9 Prov 2:67

ὀλιγόδεια (21) Opif 164 Sacr 27 Gig 35 Ebr 58 Her 48 Somn 1:124 Somn 2:40 Abr 104 Mos 1:29 Mos 2:185 Spec 1:173, 175 Spec 2:18, 160 Spec 4:101 Virt 8 Praem 100 Prob 77, 84 Hypoth 11:11 QG 4:172

ὀλιγοδρανέω Migr 155 Prob 134 Legat 189

ὀλίγος (170) Opif 5, 41, 130 Leg 2:98 Leg 3:55 Cher 91 Sacr 7, 92, 121 Post 110, 130, 147 Gig 2, 53 Agr 44, 104, 175 Plant 83, 101, 103, 158 Ebr 26, 186, 207, 218 Conf 76, 147 Migr 61, 155 Her 102, 108, 141, 145, 193 Fug 185 Mut 138, 151, 201, 213 Somn 1:40, 45, 46 Somn 2:169, 188, 198, 299 Abr 19, 66, 71, 98, 136, 147, 167, 180, 198, 255 Ios 8, 34, 34, 37, 39, 71, 85, 144, 175, 196, 211, 258 Mos 1:2, 32, 35, 59, 106, 119, 160, 164, 169, 234, 258, 315, 316 Mos 2:27, 59, 67, 257 Decal 34, 116, 135, 168 Spec 1:147, 155, 176, 214, 316, 325 Spec 2:19, 20, 47, 48, 91, 172, 217, 250 Spec 3:95, 122, 142 Spec 4:5, 40, 43, 51, 66, 67, 81, 107, 186 Virt 5, 10, 43, 46, 76, 93, 145, 221, 223 Praem 26, 75, 89, 107, 107 Prob 65, 72, 72, 75, 118 Contempl 53 Aet 100, 101, 120, 123 Flacc 3, 27, 44, 54, 55, 67, 71, 84, 93, 110, 142, 150, 152, 168 Legat 57, 77, 116, 124, 128, 135, 161, 179, 214 Hypoth 6:3, 6:6 Prov 2:1 QG 2:13a QG (Par) 2:5 QE 1:7b, 2:25c, 40

ὀλιγοστός Migr 60

ὀλιγότης Mos 2:277 Flacc 113

ὀλιγοτόκος Her 211

ὀλιγόφρων (11) Ios 206, 254 Spec 1:74 Spec 2:74 Spec 4:114, 165 Virt 5, 40, 182 Prob 117 Legat 163

ὀλιγοχρήματος Deus 101 Plant 103 Spec 4:67

ὀλιγοχρόνιος (12) Deus 103, 103 Sobr 17 Her 34, 291, 292 Fug 106 Ios 24 Spec 3:51 Aet 30 Legat 91 QG 4:166

ὀλιγωρέω (37) Opif 155 Leg 2:8 Cher 99 Sacr 41 Ebr 81 Migr 89 Her 9 Congr 6, 77, 177 Fug 122 Mut 32, 226 Ios 154 Mos 1:168 Decal 108, 112, 118 Spec 1:128, 314, 319 Spec 3:21, 61 Spec 4:3, 18, 32, 38, 182 Virt 147, 226 Prob 105 Flacc 50 Legat 311 Prov 2:58 QG 3:21, 52, 4:191b

ὀλιγωρία (12) Sacr 123 Agr 47, 47 Congr 151 Mos 1:184 Decal 7 Spec 1:154, 314 Spec 2:38 Prob 14, 73 Contempl 16

ὀλίγωρος (6) Sacr 32, 113 Plant 79 Mut 22 Mos 1:183 Decal 95

ὀλισθάνω (8) Opif 128 Agr 171, 180 Migr 80 Somn 2:102 Decal 147 Spec 1:230 Spec 2:166

ὀλίσθημα Deus 75

ὀλισθηρός Agr 101 Abr 269, 269 Mos 1:230 Prov 2:46

ὄλισθος (13) Cher 66 Deus 130 Ebr 193 Migr 149 Congr 28 Fug 118 Mut 55 Spec 2:231 Spec 4:153, 198, 200 Prob 36 Prov 2:46

ὁλκάς (8) Opif 113 Spec 1:121 Spec 4:186 Virt 49 Flacc 26, 155 Legat 47, 251

ὁλκή (13) Opif 141 Leg 3:17 Plant 21 Migr 202 Congr 113 Abr 59 Ios 239 Spec 1:68 Spec 2:232 Spec 3:199 Spec 4:114, 115 Praem 63

ὁλκός (27) Opif 136, 141 Det 90 Post 72 Plant 45 Migr 202 Her 185, 270, 304 Congr 78, 113 Fug 151 Somn 2:157 Abr 65, 67 Mos 1:93 Spec 1:105 Spec 2:240 Virt 27, 105 Praem 18 Prob 61 Contempl 18 Aet 56 Legat 268 Prov 2:62 QE isf 10

ὄλλυμι Prob 122

ὁλοάργυρος Somn 2:57

ὀλοθρεύω Leg 2:34, 34

ὁλόκαρπος Somn 2:67

ὁλοκάρπωμα Prob 69

ὁλοκάρπωσις Fug 132, 132

ὁλόκαυστος Migr 202

ὁλόκαυτος (22) Migr 67 Somn 2:67 Spec 1:177, 181, 184, 189, 190, 190, 194, 196, 197, 198, 200, 212, 247, 252, 253, 256, 276 Legat 157, 317, 356

ὁλοκαυτόω (8) Sacr 139, 139 Post 122 Her 199 Spec 1:188, 191, 245 Spec 4:125

ὁλοκαύτωμα (12) Leg 3:141 Sacr 84, 110, 132, 139 Her 251 Mut 233, 248 Somn 1:62 Abr 198 Mos 2:148 Spec 1:151

ὁλοκαύτωσις Somn 1:194 Spec 1:251

ὁλόκληρος (66) Opif 126 Leg 2:97, 97 Cher 96 Sacr 57, 57, 74, 111, 139 Post 159 Gig 26 Deus 4 Agr 130 Plant 125 Ebr 116, 135, 156, 201 Migr 33 Her 86, 114, 213, 233, 242, 286 Fug 81, 112, 148 Mut 64, 68, 258 Somn 1:112 Somn 2:144, 163, 185 Abr 6, 44, 47, 146, 177 Mos 1:318 Mos 2:8 Decal 71, 110 Spec 1:80, 166, 196, 196, 199, 242, 253, 259, 283 Spec 2:184, 220 Spec 3:21 Spec 4:143 Virt 32, 44 Praem 119 Aet 21, 48, 48, 78 Legat 107 Prov 1

ὁλολυγή Legat 228

ὅλος (575) Opif 8, 25, 30, 34, 37, 42, 43, 46, 61, 69, 72, 73, 73, 78, 105, 123, 138, 158, 170, 171, 171, 171 Leg 1:13, 33, 57, 91, 91 Leg 2:6, 6, 24, 38, 49, 56, 67, 102 Leg 3:10, 28, 29, 31, 38, 40, 89, 103, 128, 128, 129, 130, 134, 134, 140, 141, 141, 142, 143, 144, 145, 147, 159, 170, 170, 171, 176, 186, 205, 224, 228, 247 Cher 60, 84, 84, 84, 87, 109, 112 Sacr 59, 84, 84, 92, 98, 107, 110, 110 Det 7, 12, 12, 16, 17, 77, 84, 99, 106, 147, 154, 154, 155 Post 3, 41, 65, 101, 101, 111, 127, 135, 137, 147, 150, 168 Gig 7, 7, 8, 8, 27, 40, 56 Deus 34, 49, 108, 127, 127, 129, 130, 130, 148, 173, 179 Agr 30, 30, 70 Plant 2, 5, 8, 10, 12, 39, 40, 40, 63, 69, 91, 111, 111, 145, 153, 174 Ebr 27, 27, 31, 58, 81, 131, 152, 152, 193, 196, 199, 221 Sobr 2, 3, 3, 13, 45, 45, 52 Conf 38, 57, 63, 67, 74, 98, 137, 144, 150, 166, 173, 185 Migr 4, 6, 14, 46, 65, 65, 66, 67, 104, 112, 135, 155, 155, 179, 182, 192, 193, 195, 204 Her 15, 23, 45, 46, 55, 55, 56, 82, 110, 140, 171, 184, 196, 200, 205, 217, 217, 218, 236, 251, 301, 307 Congr 21, 59, 92, 105, 106, 106, 116, 118, 145, 156 Fug 9, 10, 51, 69, 75, 84, 105, 109, 118, 136, 142, 142, 143, 148, 158, 177, 194, 196, 197 Mut 2, 10, 13, 34, 34, 61, 123, 124, 124, 129, 135, 200, 215, 224, 230, 248, 248, 260, 260, 264 Somn 1:2, 37, 43, 62, 62, 63, 70, 77, 87, 90, 91, 91, 93, 99, 104, 105, 124, 135, 135, 148, 159, 184, 204, 247 Somn 2:2, 45, 71, 73, 74, 83, 116, 116, 123, 171, 173, 178, 183, 188, 188, 188, 188, 193, 194, 216, 245, 245, 248, 267, 290 Abr 2, 9, 98, 119, 119, 121, 133, 149, 183, 196, 198, 198, 204 Ios 27, 27, 40, 56, 77, 96, 142, 160, 160 Mos 1:11, 65, 96, 98, 113, 120, 125, 149, 157, 158, 158, 228, 253, 254, 323, 323 Mos 2:48, 51, 58, 80, 86, 88, 90, 110, 113, 117, 118, 148, 157, 168, 189, 189, 191, 205, 209, 238, 239, 287, 287, 288, 288, 290, 291 Decal 32, 37, 41, 63, 64, 64, 79, 94, 105, 105, 107, 108, 136, 154, 155, 174 Spec 1:5, 22, 30, 66, 66, 85, 85, 94, 94, 96, 110, 166, 166, 167, 167, 201, 201, 201, 205, 205, 209, 210, 216, 229, 268, 294, 300, 307, 333 Spec 2:6, 10, 56, 77, 110, 135, 246, 256 Spec 3:11, 115, 122, 127, 178, 189 Spec 4:34, 60, 60, 83, 134, 134, 141, 141, 144, 144, 153, 176, 180 Virt 11, 12, 12, 32, 32, 34, 64, 88, 113, 159, 162, 172, 185, 186, 213, 214 Praem 6, 9, 23, 24, 32, 32, 32, 34, 40, 46, 57, 62, 107, 143, 143, 154, 156, 156, 163 Prob 12, 26, 70, 70, 74, 84, 94, 94, 118 Contempl 59, 65, 89, 90 Aet 1, 21, 21, 22, 25, 26, 26, 26, 29, 37, 45, 50, 59, 61, 66, 74, 83, 86, 92, 92, 97, 114, 114, 117 Flacc 19, 68, 95, 174 Legat 3, 48, 48, 104, 169, 193, 202, 204, 238, 285, 293, 308, 320, 324, 324, 343, 344, 368 Hypoth 7:7, 7:10, 7:17 Prov 2:10, 69 QG 1:51, 62:1, 68, 2:15a, 34a, 62, 64c, 64c, 68a, 68a, 3:3, 3, 3, 3, 4:8b, 67 QG isf 1, 10 QG (Par) 2:4 QE 1:21, 2:2, 26, 47 QE isf 1, 5

ὁλοστός Spec 4:52

ὁλοσχερής (9) Sacr 85 Plant 12, 28 Ebr 91 Her 136, 219 Mos 1:213 Decal 66 Spec 1:210

ὀλοφύρομαι (6) Sacr 125 Conf 80 Somn 1:256 Ios 187 Legat 197, 225

ὀλόφυρσις Det 95 Somn 2:66 Abr 260 Mos 1:184 Praem 171

ὁλόχρυσος Somn 2:57 Prov 2:17

Ὀλυμπιακός Deus 147 Agr 119

Ὀλυμπιονίκης Virt 193 Contempl 42

ὀλύμπιος (18) Det 85 Post 31 Deus 138, 151, 156 Agr 119 Plant 63, 71 Conf 114, 152 Her 93, 241 Fug 180, 199 Somn 1:84, 151 Somn 2:242 Prob 42

Ὀλύμπιος Prob 105

Ὄλυμπος Conf 4, 4 Aet 121

ὅμαδος Ebr 103

ὅμαιμος Leg 2:8

ὁμαιχμία Conf 26 Abr 240

ὁμαλός Post 47 Her 97, 160

ὁμαλότης Sacr 69 Her 97 Ios 269

ὀμβρέω (29) Leg 3:162, 164 Plant 93 Sobr 64 Migr 30, 121, 156 Her 279 Congr 36 Fug 166, 198 Mut 141, 258 Somn 1:162 Somn 2:204, 221 Abr 46 Ios 198 Mos 2:158, 258, 286 Spec 1:303 Spec 2:53 Spec 3:185 Virt 129, 143 Praem 101 Aet 66 Legat 101

ὀμβρηρός Leg 3:211

ὄμβριος Ios 12 Spec 3:147

ὄμβρος (10) Opif 80 Abr 43, 138 Mos 1:116 Mos 2:54, 63 Spec 2:172 Praem 131 Aet 62, 118

ὁμηρεία Ios 188, 201

ὁμηρεύω Her 206 Ios 169, 209

Ὅμηρος Conf 4 Abr 10 Prob 31 Contempl 17 Legat 80

ὁμιλέω (19) Cher 50 Post 109 Conf 6, 175 Congr 74 Somn 1:44, 88 Ios 34 Mos 2:36, 156 Spec 1:107, 326, 332 Spec 3:9, 61, 169 Spec 4:50 Prob 12 Contempl 6

ὁμιλητής Ios 83 Spec 2:45, 88 Virt 65

ὁμιλία (54) Leg 2:74 Leg 3:131 Cher 43 Post 176 Gig 26, 32 Deus 137 Agr 152, 167 Migr 105, 105 Congr 12, 14, 152 Mut 144 Somn 1:200 Somn 2:106, 185 Abr 30, 117, 136 Ios 43, 157, 269 Mos 1:298, 300 Mos 2:68, 163 Decal 45, 109, 168 Spec 1:9, 11, 342 Spec 2:44 Spec 3:12, 19, 26, 32, 44, 46, 48, 63, 72, 77, 79, 80, 113 Spec 4:204 Virt 115, 199, 217 Praem 20 QG 4:86b

ὅμιλος (30) Cher 56 Post 101 Agr 23, 136 Sobr 23 Migr 59, 68, 124 Ios 30, 63 Mos 1:147, 257, 317 Mos 2:163 Decal 54 Spec 1:321 Spec 2:164 Spec 3:74, 101 Spec 4:47, 68, 179 Virt 43 Prob 9, 63, 91, 158 Aet 8 Hypoth 11:1 Prov 2:41

Ὅμιλος Legat 181

ὄμμα (66) Opif 71, 131 Leg 1:83 Sacr 36, 36, 69, 78 Det 12, 22 Post 8, 18, 118, 167 Deus 93, 181 Plant 21, 22, 29, 58, 169 Ebr 44 Sobr 3 Migr 39, 48, 165, 191 Her 89 Congr 47, 135 Fug 182 Mut 3, 5, 203 Somn 1:117, 129, 164, 199 Somn 2:160 Abr 58, 70, 84, 156 Ios 47, 106 Mos 1:185, 289 Mos 2:209 Decal 68 Spec 1:37, 49, 330, 341 Spec 2:194 Spec 3:2, 4 Spec 4:140, 201 Praem 37 Prob 5, 101 Legat 2, 261, 264 Prov 2:9 QG 2:34a, 3:3

ὀμματόω QG 2:72

ὄμνυμι (46) Leg 3:203, 203, 204, 205, 206, 207, 207, 207, 208 Sacr 57, 89, 90, 91, 94 Plant 82 Conf 130 Migr 162 Fug 175 Somn 1:13, 24 Abr 273 Decal 84, 86, 91,

92, 93, 157 Spec 1:235 Spec 2:2, 3, 4, 9, 13, 15, 19, 24, 24, 25, 224, 253, 255 Spec 4:34, 36, 39 QG 4:180, 180

ὁμογάστριος (6) Migr 203 Mut 92 Somn 2:33, 41 Spec 3:22 Virt 224

ὁμογενής Mut 192 Spec 1:209 Spec 4:204 Virt 140

ὁμόγλωσσος Conf 6, 12, 13, 83

ὁμόγνιος Somn 1:52

ὁμογνωμονέω (6) Her 246 Ios 44, 176 Mos 2:257 Spec 4:157 Legat 213

ὁμογνώμων Ios 30 Mos 1:248 Spec 4:224 Legat 152

ὁμοδίαιτος (12) Cher 106, 114 Conf 11, 52 Abr 215, 224 Mos 1:136 Virt 55 Prob 86 Legat 20 Hypoth 11:11 Prov 2:63

ὁμόδουλος Abr 116 Ios 37, 51 Prob 35

ὁμοεθνής (6) Spec 2:73, 73, 122 Virt 101, 102 Legat 212

ὁμόζηλος Cher 40 Deus 180 Prob 85

ὁμοθυμαδόν (7) Conf 58 Mos 1:72, 136 Flacc 122, 132, 144 Legat 356

ὁμοιοπαθής Conf 7

ὅμοιος (211) Opif 43, 97, 100, 118, 128, 140, 141, 141, 152, 153, 166, 169 Leg 1:10, 10, 12 Leg 2:1, 74, 75 Leg 3:76, 102 Cher 22, 37 Sacr 85, 98, 130 Det 141, 164, 164, 164 Post 108, 109, 144 Gig 9, 9, 16, 25, 42, 56 Deus 28, 40, 60, 82, 117, 131 Agr 99, 167 Plant 74, 91, 145, 160 Ebr 5, 78, 175, 204, 220 Conf 54, 184 Migr 7, 44, 52, 69 Her 160, 160, 164, 172, 178, 178, 220 Congr 137 Fug 48, 82, 83, 160 Mut 27, 42, 87, 161, 235 Somn 1:64, 73, 75, 99, 154, 184, 192 Somn 2:25, 39, 164, 221, 227 Abr 4, 113, 237, 240, 240 Ios 134, 145, 156 Mos 1:27, 30, 64, 92, 118, 141, 161, 173, 325 Mos 2:26, 64, 78, 88, 93, 124, 126, 233, 264, 267 Decal 27, 38, 41, 41, 75, 104, 147 Spec 1:47, 59, 112, 121, 123, 134, 233, 235, 300, 316 Spec 2:34, 34, 122, 261 Spec 3:28, 32, 42, 65, 142, 146, 146, 165, 175, 182, 183 Spec 4:7, 22, 45, 75, 96, 143, 198, 200, 229 Virt 21, 31, 74, 104, 151, 155, 193, 199, 208 Praem 20, 46, 90, 92, 109, 144 Prob 27, 79, 144, 152, 156, 157 Contempl 38, 41, 75, 82 Aet 8, 21, 41, 42, 42, 43, 61, 62, 97, 115, 115 Flacc 16, 138 Legat 43, 78, 141, 241, 327 Hypoth 7:1, 7:2 Prov 2:11, 13, 13, 35 QG 2:5b, 4:204 QG isf 13 QG (Par) 2:2, 2:5

ὁμοιότης (21) Opif 22 Post 23 Gig 41 Ebr 90, 174 Conf 183 Her 232 Fug 51, 89 Mut 208 Ios 59 Mos 2:61 Decal 113 Spec 1:6, 296 Spec 4:187 Virt 195 Praem 29, 126 Legat 55 QG 2:54a

ὁμοιοτροπία QG 2:65

ὁμοιότροπος (52) Opif 153 Gig 62 Plant 71, 103, 156 Ebr 52, 201 Sobr 67 Conf 7, 163, 192 Migr 23 Her 154, 249, 284 Fug 151 Mut 61 Somn 2:49 Ios 30 Mos 1:64 Spec 1:47, 51, 176, 317 Spec 2:13, 32, 172 Spec 3:37, 45, 66, 92, 95, 158 Spec 4:87, 117, 196, 203 Virt 19 Prob 21, 55, 84 Aet 20, 104, 122 Legat 44, 293, 301 Prov 2:45, 47, 57 QG 4:33a, 43

ὁμοιόω (14) Opif 151 Leg 3:171 Deus 48 Agr 95, 166 Plant 18 Ebr 172 Her 236 Mos 2:88, 96 Decal 159 Spec 1:66 QG 1:77 QE 2:55b

ὁμοίωμα Migr 48, 49

ὁμοίωσις (6) Opif 69, 71, 72 Conf 169 Fug 63, 63

ὁμολογέω (139) Opif 25 Leg 1:61, 82 Leg 2:78, 93 Leg 3:21, 29, 66, 67, 77, 136, 187, 190, 198 Cher 107 Sacr 18, 42, 48, 70, 72, 87, 99, 106, 118 Det 10, 60, 61, 81 Post 72, 162, 175 Gig 29 Agr 57, 61, 129, 152 Plant 150 Ebr 53, 56, 101, 107, 117, 188, 192, 193, 200 Conf 22, 62, 116, 124, 127, 145, 181 Migr 5, 19, 22, 85, 211 Her 4, 26, 28, 108, 120, 122, 123, 246, 261 Congr 3, 154, 178 Fug 205 Mut 51, 57, 87, 140, 143, 253, 265 Somn 1:119, 174, 184 Somn 2:24, 29, 202, 261 Abr 86, 203, 215, 275 Ios 67, 139, 166, 191, 225, 227, 230, 233, 251, 263 Mos 1:71, 86, 95, 122, 247, 266, 295, 309 Spec 1:58, 235 Spec 2:55, 88, 165 Spec 3:65, 70 Spec 4:40, 188 Virt 5, 38, 124 Praem 163 Prob 42 Aet 47 Flacc 101, 140, 146 Legat 64, 121, 171, 171, 218, 237, 247 Prov 2:18 QG 1:68, 3:29, 49a, 4:202a QE 2:25c QE isf 16

ὁμολογία (29) Leg 1:82, 82 Sacr 3 Deus 25 Agr 157 Ebr 39, 107 Conf 193 Congr 73, 78, 125, 151, 177 Mut 57, 220 Somn 2:202 Abr 203 Ios 185 Mos 1:242, 253 Mos 2:140 Spec 1:107 Spec 2:38 Spec 3:72, 72, 155 QG 3:49a, 49a, 58

ὁμολογουμένως Det 18 Deus 71 Spec 3:36

ὁμομήτριος (12) Ios 163, 189, 200, 223, 232, 234 Mos 1:240 Spec 3:14, 22, 22, 22 Prob 1

ὁμόνοια (13) Her 183 Mut 200 Abr 243 Decal 14, 132 Spec 1:70, 138, 295 Virt 35, 35, 119 Praem 92, 154

ὁμόνομος Conf 11

ὁμοπάτριος (6) Migr 203 Somn 2:33, 41 Mos 1:240 Praem 57 Prob 1

ὅμορος (13) Somn 1:178 Somn 2:239 Abr 141 Mos 1:47, 250, 263 Spec 4:223 Flacc 152 Legat 205, 221, 281, 334, 336

ὁμός ὁμῶς

ὁμόσπονδος Abr 224

ὁμότιμος Mut 226

ὁμοτράπεζος (8) Cher 106 Mos 1:136 Spec 1:120, 221 Spec 2:16 Prob 86 Hypoth 11:11 Prov 2:64

ὁμότροπος Conf 10

ὁμοτύραννος Her 284

ὁμοῦ (121) Opif 67, 94, 97, 98, 106, 106, 114, 133, 135 Cher 20 Deus 45 Ebr 6, 30, 35, 70, 106, 112, 160, 193 Conf 27, 144, 150 Migr 53, 77, 115 Her 7, 107, 125, 179, 247 Congr 132 Fug 6, 118, 122, 139, 153 Mut 8, 9, 19, 23, 75, 150, 179, 246, 264 Somn 2:36, 78, 139, 171, 187 Abr 45, 50, 88, 136, 161, 246, 261, 267, 267 Ios 150 Mos 1:134, 169 Mos 2:163, 247 Decal 32, 87 Spec 1:73, 77, 95, 99, 144, 148, 195, 250, 321 Spec 2:18, 29, 40, 43, 146, 165, 180 Spec 3:22, 48, 51, 79 Spec 4:8, 120, 142, 218 Virt 28, 48, 94, 116, 130, 138, 160, 162, 184 Praem 113, 137 Prob 98 Contempl 87 Flacc 77, 149 Legat 13, 70, 82, 114, 118, 124, 143, 166, 190, 208, 262, 331, 368 Hypoth 6:6 QG 2:71b, 4:47b

ὁμοφρονέω Mos 1:231

ὁμοφροσύνη Mos 1:7 Virt 119 Praem 87 Flacc 52 Hypoth 6:3

ὁμόφυλος (19) Conf 152 Her 42 Ios 30 Mos 1:74 Spec 2:39, 80, 123 Spec 4:19, 159 Virt 66, 82, 90, 226 Contempl 10 Legat 193, 327, 332, 355 QG isf 10

ὁμοφωνία Conf 6

ὁμόφωνος (6) Post 91 Conf 6, 7, 9, 11, 83

ὀμφαλός Spec 4:93

ὁμωνυμέω Conf 64 Her 59 Congr 117

ὁμωνυμία (7) Det 77 Post 60 Plant 150, 150 Her 237 Mut 201 Somn 1:65

ὁμώνυμος (9) Det 78 Post 40 Gig 56 Plant 150, 151 Conf 122 Congr 50 Spec 4:82 Flacc 180

ὁμωρόφιος Spec 2:16 Virt 55 Prob 86

ὅμως (72) Leg 2:83 Leg 3:40, 190 Cher 49, 65, 96 Sacr 37, 123 Det 73 Post 13, 71 Deus 8, 90 Agr 91 Plant 57 Ebr 174, 222 Sobr 9, 22 Conf 119 Congr 129 Fug 158, 165 Mut 8, 37 Abr 51, 65, 204 Ios 44, 85, 124, 168, 215 Mos 1:31, 58, 83, 108, 112, 270 Mos 2:242 Spec 1:36, 39, 47, 138, 271, 303, 308 Spec 2:20, 69 Spec 3:4, 15, 65 Spec 4:180, 206 Virt 94, 107, 147, 199, 222 Prob 35, 106 Contempl 1, 58 Flacc 77, 90, 181 Legat 157, 188, 334 Hypoth 6:6 Prov 2:49 QG 4:88

ὁμῶς (ὁμός) Opif 104

ὄναρ ὄνειρος

ὄναρ (34) Cher 74 Det 35 Post 22 Deus 91 Agr 43 Somn 1:2, 4, 157, 159 Somn 2:6, 21, 32, 147, 159, 199, 251 Ios 6, 8, 93 Mos 1:145 Spec 1:176, 223 Spec 2:23, 93 Spec 4:17 Virt 3, 39, 85 Praem 35 Prob 61, 78, 157 Flacc 164 Prov 2:65

ὀνειδίζω (24) Opif 156 Cher 33 Det 145, 146 Deus 126 Conf 51 Migr 116 Congr 13, 13 Fug 30, 203 Somn 1:93 Mos 1:196 Spec 1:152 Spec 2:23, 131, 168 Spec 3:34 Virt 197 Prob 127 Flacc 153, 172 Legat 305 QG 4:168

ὄνειδος (28) Gig 39 Her 291 Mut 199 Somn 1:104, 109, 124 Abr 106 Ios 19, 172, 216, 237 Mos 1:3, 61, 293, 328 Decal 126, 169 Spec 1:241, 341 Spec 2:106 Spec 3:37, 38, 49, 135, 173 Virt 210 Flacc 177 QG 4:99

ὀνειροκριτικός Somn 2:4, 110 Ios 121, 125, 143

ὀνειροπλήξ Ios 12

ὀνειροπολέω (7) Somn 1:171 Somn 2:105, 162 Contempl 26 Legat 173, 274, 338

ὀνειροπόλος Somn 2:42

ὄνειρος (ὄναρ) (47) Cher 69 Post 114 Gig 39 Deus 172 Ebr 180 Migr 190 Fug 129, 143 Somn 1:1, 189, 190 Somn 2:1, 3, 4, 5, 8, 17, 42, 133, 138, 155, 156, 206, 215 Ios 10, 90, 95, 98, 100, 104, 106, 107, 107, 116, 125, 126, 158, 164, 248, 269 Mos 1:268 Spec 1:219 Praem 151 Contempl 26 Aet 2 Flacc 165 Hypoth 6:1

ὀνείρωξις Somn 2:298 Prob 10

ὀνειρώσσω Somn 2:18, 93 Ios 147 Spec 1:119

ὄνησις (7) Post 145 Agr 134, 135, 150 Plant 101 Congr 46 Somn 1:105

ὀνίνημι (28) Leg 2:85 Leg 3:227 Det 55, 56, 86 Gig 43 Agr 5, 126 Ebr 168 Migr 101 Congr 52 Fug 14 Mut 203 Abr 65 Mos 1:151, 274 Spec 1:321 Spec 2:197 Spec 4:15, 41 Virt 117, 193, 200, 202, 206, 211 Prob 9 Legat 92

ὄνομα (ὁ) (474) Opif 12, 15, 24, 39, 102, 112, 127, 133, 148 Leg 1:10, 33, 43, 45, 63, 63, 66, 68, 68, 68, 75, 82, 90, 91, 92 Leg 2:9, 14, 14, 15, 15, 15, 18, 38, 84 Leg 3:73, 74, 83, 85, 87, 95, 95, 120, 183, 191, 207, 208, 217 Cher 1, 10, 42, 53, 54, 54, 54, 55, 55, 56, 56, 56, 56, 84, 121, 122 Sacr 1, 6, 10, 20, 27, 30, 52, 65, 70, 79, 101, 112 Det 22, 22, 76, 83, 131, 131, 138, 138, 139 Post 1, 33, 35, 41, 69, 75, 75, 76, 101, 124, 183 Gig 16, 17, 62, 66, 66 Deus 42, 60, 86, 103, 139, 141 Agr 1, 2, 4, 26, 29, 66, 136 Plant 14, 34, 73, 74, 85, 86, 129, 134, 150, 154 Ebr 23, 59, 82, 82, 82, 82, 128, 145, 164 Sobr 6, 10, 28, 28, 35, 36, 44, 52, 52 Conf 1, 1, 4, 13, 55, 62, 62, 79, 83, 92, 106, 115, 116, 117, 117, 118, 122, 128, 139, 143, 146, 156, 191, 191, 191, 192, 198 Migr 1, 12, 14, 28, 48, 48, 49, 55, 74, 79, 79, 86, 143, 145, 165, 174, 196, 197, 200, 221, 223 Her 20, 47, 52, 53, 54, 59, 60, 72, 97, 116, 161, 170, 176, 241, 279, 282 Congr 1, 2, 20, 22, 23, 30, 43, 44, 53, 60, 68, 100, 125, 149, 149, 154, 157, 161, 163, 166, 170, 177 Fug 1, 16, 39, 40, 50, 51, 52, 54, 55, 57, 149, 196, 204, 208 Mut 11, 11, 12, 12, 13, 13, 13, 13, 13, 14, 14, 14, 14, 15, 60, 60, 60, 63, 63, 63, 64, 64, 70, 77, 78, 83, 89, 90, 94, 99, 113, 114, 120, 121, 130, 201, 207, 209, 223, 261, 261, 266 Somn 1:40, 41, 47, 78, 98, 130, 141, 163, 166, 203, 219, 230, 230, 231, 254 Somn 2:33, 36, 47, 129, 189, 215, 238, 249, 250, 286 Abr 7, 32, 47, 51, 51, 51, 54, 54, 57, 81, 81, 99, 99, 101, 120, 121, 124, 170, 194, 201, 230 Ios 28, 74, 119, 213, 219 Mos 1:17, 74, 75, 130, 130, 195, 241, 250, 263, 316 Mos 2:37, 38, 38, 39, 40, 112, 114, 115, 123, 132, 178, 179, 203, 206, 207, 208, 234, 234, 242 Decal 6, 23, 55, 82, 82, 93, 94, 120, 136, 144 Spec 1:224, 290, 315, 315, 327, 329, 344 Spec 2:2, 8, 129, 131, 133, 181, 205, 253, 256 Spec 3:20, 43, 59, 65, 72, 83, 156, 170, 170, 191 Spec 4:21, 39, 39, 40, 43, 43, 51, 52, 83, 146, 235 Virt 2, 14, 34, 37, 55, 106, 122, 135, 196, 223 Praem 14, 28, 40, 109, 111 Prob 8, 16, 19, 31, 69, 75, 88, 141, 141 Contempl 4, 78 Aet 3, 18, 54, 71, 121, 126 Flacc 20, 21, 36, 42, 53, 59, 86, 141, 159, 183, 185 Legat 4, 6, 70, 112, 164, 181, 194, 206, 234, 260, 289 Prov 2:64 QG 1:20, 55a, 93, 2:26a, 3:3, 4:67, 194 QE 1:6, 2:2 QE isf 8

ὀνομάζω (163) Opif 15, 30, 37, 89, 133 Leg 1:21, 22, 63, 66, 90, 92 Leg 2:21, 72 Leg 3:24 Cher 26, 45, 83 Sacr 7, 119 Det 38, 84, 118, 172 Post 40, 73, 74, 91, 98, 100, 101, 114, 119, 130, 138 Gig 6 Deus 144, 176 Agr 29, 130, 134, 140 Plant 3, 60, 82, 133, 163 Ebr 91 Sobr 7, 8, 11, 16, 19, 45 Conf 63 Migr 12, 16, 46, 159, 173, 214 Her 26, 52, 78, 106, 124, 128, 167, 232, 241 Congr 25, 40 Fug 45, 73, 97, 167 Mut 19, 61, 71, 83, 93, 100, 106 Somn 1:5, 12, 24, 31, 58, 59, 77, 125, 172, 173, 186, 201, 216 Somn 2:34, 63, 142, 254 Abr 10, 28, 53, 133, 156 Ios 2, 86, 160 Mos 1:17, 37, 135, 158, 188, 219, 253, 258 Mos 2:72, 84, 99, 203, 204 Decal 104 Spec 1:48, 107, 196, 341 Spec 2:3, 8, 56, 73, 76, 81, 150, 162, 179, 181, 194, 200, 200 Spec 3:65, 123, 189 Spec 4:152, 168 Virt 82 Praem 31, 47, 79 Prob 8, 154 Contempl 66 Aet 54, 63, 111, 121, 139 Flacc 39 Legat 96, 99, 113, 143, 309 QG 2:74, 3:23

Ὀνόμαρχος Prov 2:33

ὀνομαστί Somn 1:193 Abr 176 Ios 12

ὀνομαστικός Cher 60

ὀνομαστός Sobr 52 Mos 1:265

ὀνοματοποιέω Mut 160, 262

ὄνος (15) Cher 32 Sacr 89, 112, 112 Post 161 Migr 224 Mut 193 Abr 266 Spec 1:135 Spec 3:47 Spec 4:205, 206 Virt 146, 146, 146

ὄντως (175) Opif 106, 136, 172 Leg 1:18, 32 Leg 2:52, 53, 67, 77, 90, 97, 101 Leg 3:21, 21, 31, 35, 72, 182, 186, 191, 195, 236 Cher 27, 39, 42, 48, 59, 73 Sacr 34, 54 Det 7, 139, 161 Post 27, 81, 121, 167 Gig 5, 33 Deus 11, 135, 148, 172 Agr 113 Plant 91, 157 Ebr 83, 151 Sobr 24, 66 Conf 74, 105 Migr 104, 152, 153, 200, 209 Her 44, 53, 70, 108, 110, 111, 216, 266, 274 Congr 17, 41, 51, 56, 58, 61, 90, 96, 124, 132, 151, 159 Fug 14, 42, 128, 168, 208, 209 Mut 21, 94, 147, 153, 160, 169,

173, 193, 267 Somn 1:125, 184, 246 Somn 2:50, 99, 183 Abr 9, 26, 48, 124, 206, 244, 246 Ios 67, 216 Mos 1:110, 189 Mos 2:124 Decal 8, 59, 81, 93 Spec 1:28, 40, 53, 65, 65, 176, 252, 270, 307, 309, 331, 332, 344, 345 Spec 2:41, 51, 52, 167, 255 Spec 3:1, 125, 127 Spec 4:192, 205 Virt 34, 40, 51, 55, 64, 102 Prob 6, 24, 26, 79 Contempl 27, 88 Flacc 81, 169, 183 Legat 21, 48, 157, 195, 202, 280, 347 Hypoth 11:3 Prov 1 QG 1:21, 100:1b, 100:2a, 2:54a, 3:24, 4:74, 173 QG isf 10 QE 2:45b QE isf 3, 14, 16

ὄνυξ (8) Leg 2:22 Her 196, 197, 197, 198, 226 Spec 1:164 Virt 111

ὄξος Aet 113

ὀξυγράφος Spec 4:163

ὀξυδερκέω (ὀξυδορκέω) Conf 27

ὀξυδερκής (20) Leg 3:171 Sacr 134 Post 18, 118, 161 Migr 35 Congr 47, 145 Fug 19, 158 Mut 56, 82 Decal 7 Spec 2:194 Spec 3:4 Prob 140 Aet 89 Legat 320 Hypoth 11:14 QG 2:34a

ὀξυδορκέω (13) Agr 54 Ebr 88 Sobr 5 Migr 197 Somn 1:11, 164 Somn 2:171, 250 Ios 106 Decal 67, 82 Contempl 61, 75

ὀξυκίνητος (8) Leg 3:60 Cher 28 Sacr 65, 66 Post 19 Agr 106 Mut 178 Somn 2:67

ὀξύνω Congr 25

ὀξύς (46) Opif 76, 86, 88, 96, 97, 97, 121 Leg 1:14 Leg 2:11 Sacr 66, 82 Det 117 Post 113 Deus 24, 63, 84 Agr 81, 135 Ebr 116, 120, 120 Her 130, 210 Congr 158 Fug 19, 121 Mut 108 Somn 1:28 Somn 2:3, 33 Abr 25, 65 Mos 1:184, 188, 292 Mos 2:141, 256 Decal 35 Spec 1:54, 311 Virt 5 Contempl 88 Aet 135 Flacc 2, 34, 42

ὀξύτης (12) Post 140 Ebr 120 Sobr 2 Migr 52 Mut 179 Ios 141 Mos 2:145, 170, 256 Spec 1:27, 83 Spec 3:8

ὀξυτονέω Post 94

ὀξυχειρία Mos 1:44

ὀξυωπέω Sobr 3

ὀξυωπής (17) Opif 131 Plant 58 Sobr 4 Conf 92 Migr 46, 77, 222 Congr 84 Abr 266 Mos 2:209, 271 Spec 1:99, 259 Spec 4:201 Legat 2 Prov 2:7 QE isf 6

ὀξυωπία (9) Opif 112 Somn 2:39 Spec 3:91 Spec 4:163 Virt 11, 12, 151, 193 Contempl 89

ὀπαδός ὀπηδός

ὄπῃ (6) Agr 34, 68 Congr 164 Spec 3:123 Flacc 66 QE 2:13a

ὀπή (7) Cher 61 Migr 188, 188 Somn 1:42, 55, 59 Abr 72

ὀπηδός (ὀπαδός) (14) Gig 64 Agr 37 Conf 118, 174 Migr 126, 175 Her 76, 234 Mut 45, 270 Somn 1:190 Somn 2:108 Mos 2:177 Prov 2:6

ὀπήτιον Cher 72

ὀπίσθιος Leg 2:103

ὀπισθόδομος Mos 2:86, 91, 91

ὀπισθοφυλακέω Mos 1:178 Mos 2:254

ὀπισθοφύλαξ Mos 1:257

ὀπίσω (ὁ) (21) Leg 2:94, 99, 100, 103 Post 169 Agr 94 Migr 131 Fug 121, 122, 165 Mut 9 Somn 1:247, 248 Somn 2:216, 294 Mos 1:177 Praem 62 Aet 30 Legat 228 QG 2:72, 4:52a

ὀπλίζω (7) Det 36 Mos 1:132, 172, 331 Decal 31 Spec 3:126 Prov 2:28

ὅπλισις Deus 60 Mos 1:168 Aet 68 Flacc 5

ὁπλίτης Mos 1:306, 330 Spec 1:121

ὁπλοθήκη Flacc 92

ὁπλολογέω Flacc 92

ὁπλομαχία Legat 30

ὅπλον (53) Leg 2:8 Leg 3:155 Sacr 130 Post 119, 184, 185 Gig 66 Deus 60, 68 Agr 151 Ebr 113 Conf 45 Her 203 Mut 159 Somn 1:103, 173, 174, 235, 255 Somn 2:122, 280 Abr 220 Mos 1:142, 148, 169, 225, 263, 333 Spec 3:95 Spec 4:7, 28, 213 Virt 3, 48, 218 Praem 54, 132 Prob 34, 133 Aet 68 Flacc 30, 67, 86, 88, 90, 92, 92, 93, 94, 94 Hypoth 6:6 QG 2:64b, 64b

ὁπλοποιός Prob 78

ὁπλοσκοπία Mos 1:310

ὁπλοφορέω Opif 84 Congr 176 Spec 3:17

ὁποῖος (27) Opif 144 Leg 1:42 Leg 3:64, 64 Sacr 37 Det 56, 113 Gig 10 Deus 49 Plant 160 Ebr 104 Sobr 59 Her 246 Fug 34 Abr 47, 119 Mos 1:24, 68, 140 Mos 2:24 Spec 3:79 Virt 18, 44 Prob 62 Flacc 62 Hypoth 7:3 QG (Par) 2:7

ὁπόσος Her 260 Spec 2:71, 176 Virt 44 Hypoth 6:9

ὁπόταν Somn 2:1 Mos 2:249 Spec 3:35 Spec 4:51 Prov 2:23

ὁπότε (137) Opif 148, 158 Leg 1:57, 62, 62 Leg 2:32, 32 Leg 3:10, 93, 106, 156, 156 Cher 10, 92 Sacr 3, 49, 92, 100 Det 36, 49, 59, 66, 80, 153, 155, 161, 170 Post 5, 91, 134, 156, 176 Gig 10, 47 Agr 62, 73, 95, 110 Plant 22, 152 Ebr 9, 28, 86, 86, 164, 182, 204, 205, 223 Sobr 3, 10 Migr 26, 155 Her 71, 82, 82, 251, 266, 299 Congr 80, 126 Fug 3, 74 Mut 10, 15, 63, 125, 125, 159, 161, 165 Somn 1:11, 11, 123, 147, 147, 194, 214, 238, 252 Somn 2:131, 174, 204, 220 Abr 5, 76, 154, 211 Ios 12 Mos 1:42, 96, 124, 145, 217, 217, 271 Mos 2:107 Decal 149, 157 Spec 1:163, 167 Spec 2:125, 190, 190 Spec 3:32, 162, 171 Spec 4:121, 179, 224, 229 Virt 55, 217 Praem 145 Prob 50, 121 Contempl 80 Aet 31, 31, 110 Flacc 15, 24, 68, 105, 131, 154, 167 Legat 37, 42, 79, 95, 132, 296 Prov 1, 1 QG 3:52 QG (Par) 2:2

ὁπότερος Post 172 Aet 18

ὅπου (39) Leg 1:60, 67, 68, 79, 107 Leg 3:28, 49, 54, 54, 54, 54, 54, 54, 114, 115, 116, 116 Det 102 Post 14 Deus 26 Agr 34 Plant 5 Migr 48, 116, 209 Her 18 Congr 138, 138 Mut 64 Somn 2:300 Ios 34, 34 Decal 157 Spec 2:44, 75 Virt 124 Legat 42 Prov 2:65, 65

ὀπτάω (6) Conf 1, 84 Somn 2:50 Mos 2:156 Virt 136 Prob 25

ὀπτήρ Somn 2:101 Ios 260 Mos 1:228

ὀπτικός Spec 3:100

ὀπώρα (9) Agr 15, 152 Plant 151 Ios 91 Spec 2:205 Spec 4:217 Virt 6, 91, 95

ὀπωρινός Plant 151

ὅπως (74) Opif 38, 58, 149 Leg 1:37, 43 Leg 3:162, 167 Sacr 85 Post 138 Deus 79, 135 Agr 157 Plant 51, 159 Ebr 25 Sobr 27, 61, 67 Conf 14, 59, 89 Migr 16, 18, 174, 204, 204 Her 182 Congr 170 Mut 24, 43, 120, 208, 230 Somn 1:131 Somn 2:54, 87, 115, 149 Abr 71 Ios 88 Mos 1:178, 199 Mos 2:24, 138, 144, 144, 155 Decal 100 Spec 1:96, 105, 113, 216 Spec 2:45, 122, 130, 241, 241 Spec 3:152, 179 Spec 4:163, 163, 197, 212, 220

Virt 25, 31, 78, 95, 200 Aet 68 Legat 284 Hypoth 6:5 Prov 2:39 QG 4:69

ὁπωσοῦν Ebr 166, 198 Spec 1:112, 159 Legat 28

ὅραμα Leg 3:103 Her 262

ὅρασις (81) Opif 53, 54, 62, 62 Leg 1:25, 43, 56, 58 Leg 2:7, 74, 75, 75 Leg 3:44, 50, 56, 57, 216, 220, 220 Sacr 73 Det 168, 171 Deus 42, 79 Ebr 82 Conf 72, 72, 72, 90, 110, 148 Migr 38, 48, 49, 103, 119, 137, 165, 188 Her 185, 232 Congr 25 Fug 134, 135, 191, 208, 208, 208 Mut 102, 102, 111 Somn 1:20, 27, 55, 80 Somn 2:250, 254, 254 Abr 57, 150, 150, 153, 156, 164, 165, 166, 236 Mos 2:211 Spec 1:337, 339, 340 Spec 3:189, 194, 195 Spec 4:139 Praem 27, 36, 51 QG 2:34a QE isf 21, 21

ὁρατικός (30) Leg 2:67 Sacr 59 Deus 144 Plant 36, 46, 60 Ebr 107, 111 Conf 91 Migr 14, 18, 54, 163 Congr 56 Fug 139, 140, 182 Mut 98, 109, 189, 209, 258 Somn 1:39 Somn 2:33, 276, 279 Abr 122 Mos 2:196 Decal 26 QE 2:46

ὁρατός (77) Opif 12, 12, 16, 30, 37, 41, 54, 111, 129, 135, 146 Leg 2:39 Leg 3:44, 57, 220, 235 Det 87 Post 168 Gig 8 Agr 34 Plant 83 Conf 138, 172 Migr 46, 48, 48, 50, 50, 50, 51, 51, 183 Her 111 Congr 25, 144 Fug 101, 191 Somn 1:73, 73, 185, 188 Abr 69, 74, 88, 88, 150, 153, 157 Ios 106 Mos 1:66, 88 Mos 2:127, 148, 213 Decal 47, 102, 147 Spec 1:6, 20, 274, 279, 302, 302 Spec 3:190, 202 Virt 12 Praem 26, 28 Aet 10, 20, 73, 86 Legat 310, 318 QE isf 3, 3, 3

ὁράω (432) Opif 69, 120, 138, 156 Leg 1:52, 57, 86, 91, 91 Leg 2:5, 9, 34, 46, 51, 52, 69, 69, 69, 79, 82, 84, 88 Leg 3:9, 11, 15, 18, 24, 27, 31, 38, 38, 38, 43, 46, 56, 57, 63, 66, 73, 75, 76, 85, 105, 111, 131, 134, 151, 162, 169, 170, 171, 172, 181, 183, 183, 186, 203, 212, 215, 216, 216, 231, 249 Cher 3, 31, 35, 62, 67, 67, 73, 96, 130 Sacr 30, 40, 60, 66, 123, 134, 136 Det 2, 4, 15, 17, 22, 30, 38, 62, 101, 101, 159, 159, 173, 175 Post 13, 13, 17, 63, 92, 92, 118, 126, 143, 169 Gig 3, 44, 52 Deus 3, 9, 58, 69, 72, 80, 97, 113, 130, 131, 139 Agr 34, 91, 131 Plant 58, 145, 168 Ebr 72, 86, 92, 96, 106, 124, 124, 132, 182, 182 Sobr 13, 54 Conf 27, 56, 105, 146, 148, 159, 175, 194 Migr 21, 38, 39, 39, 40, 40, 47, 47, 47, 48, 52, 74, 83, 94, 111, 113, 125, 137, 160, 165, 192, 201, 205, 210, 223 Her 59, 78, 78, 78, 78, 87, 174, 175, 176, 237, 280 Congr 19, 25, 45, 51, 51, 51, 52, 54, 96, 96, 96, 135, 139, 140, 140, 143, 159 Fug 14, 31, 89, 122, 132, 134, 135, 135, 136, 164, 165, 176, 208 Mut 1, 2, 3, 4, 4, 6, 9, 9, 9, 11, 13, 15, 17, 81, 81, 98, 127, 158, 198, 202, 203, 217, 256, 267 Somn 1:55, 55, 66, 66, 83, 96, 126, 129, 147, 171, 186, 189, 189, 190, 227, 227, 228, 229, 238, 239, 240 Somn 2:17, 23, 33, 44, 70, 85, 93, 124, 160, 162, 173, 183, 192, 219, 226, 226, 226, 227, 227, 241, 251, 283 Abr 57, 58, 65, 77, 80, 113, 141, 148, 158, 173, 175, 200 Ios 81, 87, 89, 101, 106, 142, 157, 162, 165, 167, 180, 235, 236, 238, 242, 255 Mos 1:15, 18, 31, 56, 64, 65, 119, 124, 166, 172, 175, 175, 178, 182, 189, 192, 229, 272, 284, 288, 289 Mos 2:70, 201, 228, 250, 252, 257, 264, 281 Decal 7, 46, 47, 90 Spec 1:29, 40, 73, 95, 193, 250, 279, 307, 321, 322, 339, 339 Spec 2:4, 23, 141, 165 Spec 3:16, 88, 121, 177, 189 Spec 4:71 Virt 19, 35, 38, 85, 94, 133, 160, 173, 191 Praem 24, 27, 44, 114, 139, 139, 139, 146, 152 Prob 96, 100, 100, 146 Contempl 9 Aet 54, 75, 96, 118 Flacc 14, 27, 30, 40, 40, 40, 62, 126 Legat 4, 5, 26, 42, 52, 80, 98, 111, 132, 132, 187, 224, 229, 243, 243, 244, 259, 295, 303, 335 Hypoth 7:8 Prov 2:15, 26, 48 QG 1:60:1, 2:54d, 66, 72, 3:20a, 4:40, 81, 204 QE 2:28, 28, 47 QE isf 3, 3, 3

ὀργανικός (11) Opif 102, 103 Leg 1:4, 4, 12 Sacr 98 Deus 57 Ebr 111 Her 315 Congr 115 QG (Par) 2:2

ὄργανον (139) Opif 4, 53, 117 Leg 1:11, 14, 36, 104 Leg 2:75 Leg 3:41, 96, 119, 130, 183 Cher 35, 57, 58, 59, 66, 105, 116, 125, 125, 126, 126, 127, 127, 127, 128 Sacr 18, 37, 74, 133 Det 38, 68, 102, 126, 127, 173 Post 71, 103, 103, 104, 107, 108, 127, 142, 143 Deus 25, 42, 59, 165 Agr 30, 38, 80 Plant 35, 83, 159 Ebr 107, 116, 116 Sobr 36, 36 Conf 36, 38, 55, 56, 123, 150 Migr 6, 40, 47, 52, 72, 120, 195 Her 4, 14, 15, 111, 171, 259, 266 Congr 29, 33, 155 Fug 22, 45, 85, 182 Mut 7, 56, 69, 87, 139, 157 Somn 1:20, 27, 37, 42, 42, 55, 236 Somn 2:278, 280 Abr 104, 147 Mos 1:23, 29, 80, 111, 274 Mos 2:103, 148 Decal 33, 34 Spec 1:6, 9, 18, 65, 272 Spec 2:7, 157, 190, 192, 246 Spec 3:122, 198, 200, 203, 204 Spec 4:102, 134 Virt 74 Legat 126 QG 1:58, 2:64b, 4:86a QG (Par) 2:3 QE 2:20

ὀργανοποιία (7) Opif 126 Mos 1:84 Mos 2:127, 196, 239 Spec 1:147 Spec 4:49

ὀργάω Abr 137 Mos 2:273

ὀργή (71) Opif 156 Leg 2:8 Leg 3:147 Sacr 96 Gig 17, 17 Deus 52, 60, 68, 71 Agr 17 Ebr 223 Conf 48 Migr 208, 210 Fug 23, 90 Somn 1:89, 91, 235, 236 Somn 2:7, 165, 179, 179 Abr 152, 213 Ios 12, 15, 21, 154, 156, 170 Mos 1:6, 49, 89, 302, 321 Mos 2:172, 196, 214, 279 Spec 2:9, 16, 28, 247 Spec 3:104, 126, 193 Spec 4:14, 77, 103, 182, 220 Virt 1, 150 Praem 77 Prob 45, 159 Flacc 182 Legat 121, 219, 237, 241, 244, 254, 261, 304, 366 Prov 2:18 QG 2:54a

ὄργια (8) Sacr 60 Det 143 Gig 54 Plant 26 Fug 85 Prob 14 Legat 78 QE 2:15b

ὀργιάζω Abr 122 Mos 2:153 Spec 1:319 Spec 3:40

ὀργίζω (8) Leg 3:114, 123, 131 Ebr 210 Somn 2:137 Mos 2:192 Prob 144 Legat 304

ὀρέγω (49) Opif 158, 158 Leg 3:211 Cher 57 Sacr 10, 36 Det 114 Post 13, 116, 120, 131, 138, 146 Deus 73 Agr 39 Sobr 15 Migr 58, 155 Her 73 Congr 36, 121 Fug 145 Mut 52, 61 Somn 1:140 Somn 2:157 Abr 39, 187, 220, 261 Mos 1:160 Decal 146, 149 Spec 1:43, 116 Spec 2:76 Spec 3:41 Spec 4:5, 24, 43, 127 Virt 218 Prob 12, 60, 60 Contempl 68, 75 Legat 95 QG 4:102a

ὀρεινός (19) Agr 22 Ebr 128 Abr 138 Mos 1:228, 235 Mos 2:54 Decal 163 Spec 1:34, 335 Spec 2:39, 151, 154 Praem 41, 101, 141 Prob 65 Aet 63 Legat 47, 249

ὄρεξις (15) Opif 80 Leg 3:115, 138 Det 113 Post 26, 71, 116 Gig 35 Ebr 214, 222 Abr 96 Decal 123, 149 Virt 136 QG (Par) 2:7

ὀρεύς Decal 4 Spec 3:47

ὄρθιος Ebr 150

ὀρθογνωμονέω Fug 11

ὀρθογνώμων Fug 24

ὀρθογώνιος (6) Opif 97, 97 Mos 2:80 Spec 2:177 Contempl 65 QG 4:8b

ὀρθός (157) Opif 97, 97, 97, 97, 97, 143 Leg 1:2, 18, 46, 93 Leg 2:31 Leg 3:1, 32, 58, 78, 80, 93, 106, 120, 148, 150, 168, 188, 222, 251, 252 Cher 9, 39, 119, 128 Sacr 47, 51, 62, 75, 109 Det 16, 22, 27, 74, 103, 124, 134, 149 Post 24, 28, 30, 32, 68, 91, 102, 139, 142, 185 Gig 5, 17, 48, 55 Deus 16, 48, 50, 90, 126, 129, 152, 179,

183 Agr 51, 87, 101, 127, 127, 128, 128, 130 Plant 60, 121, 121, 162 Ebr 33, 34, 65, 68, 77, 80, 80, 81, 95, 142, 224 Sobr 11, 22, 33 Conf 43, 52 Migr 60, 71, 128, 134, 175 Her 67, 85 Congr 111 Fug 101, 131, 150, 152, 183, 190, 191 Mut 37, 141, 206, 208 Somn 1:119, 200 Somn 2:95, 97, 134, 135, 139, 170, 198 Ios 31, 47 Mos 1:48 Mos 2:184, 239 Decal 80 Spec 1:191 Spec 2:21, 29, 31 Spec 4:92, 115, 167 Virt 39, 127 Prob 46, 47, 59, 59, 62, 97 Contempl 74 Aet 83, 113, 113 Flacc 81 Legat 51, 68, 68 Prov 2:37 QG 1:64a, 64b QG (Par) 2:2 QE 2:3b, 13a

ὀρθότης Deus 71, 153 Plant 121 Fug 166 Somn 2:160

ὀρθόω (10) Leg 2:104 Conf 18 Somn 2:78, 79 Ios 6, 122, 142 Spec 2:240 Praem 6 Aet 127

ὄρθρος Mut 162 Mos 1:179 Spec 1:276 Praem 151 Flacc 167

ὁρίζω (90) Opif 61, 156 Leg 1:20 Leg 3:171 Cher 68 Sacr 97, 102, 122 Det 148, 148, 148, 148, 171 Post 69, 99, 99 Deus 34, 44 Agr 117, 118 Plant 14 Ebr 197 Sobr 46 Conf 162, 182 Migr 90 Her 229, 282 Congr 138, 147 Fug 87 Somn 1:138 Abr 41, 64, 94, 237 Ios 43, 97, 221, 221 Mos 2:49, 51, 120, 204 Decal 171, 176 Spec 1:12, 16, 78, 143, 156, 179, 196, 222 Spec 2:32, 113, 139, 196, 242, 244, 252 Spec 3:111, 117, 123, 131, 151, 176 Spec 4:11, 23, 79, 143, 196, 208 Virt 200 Praem 2, 74, 74, 85, 110, 126 Prob 130 Contempl 17 Aet 52, 58 Flacc 105, 115, 126 Legat 10, 212 QG 2:64a

ὁρίζων Opif 112

ὁρικός Gig 23 Deus 167, 180

ὅριον (11) Leg 3:107 Post 84, 89, 89 Deus 145 Plant 59 Mut 43 Ios 256 Mos 1:39 Spec 4:149 Flacc 43

ὁρισμός Leg 2:63

ὁρκικός Agr 140

ὅρκιον Conf 43

ὅρκος (73) Leg 3:203, 203, 204, 204, 204, 204, 205 Sacr 91, 93, 93, 93, 93, 93, 93, 96 Plant 73, 74, 78, 78, 82 Conf 26 Migr 18, 162, 162 Somn 1:4, 5, 12, 12, 13, 14, 24, 40, 42, 61, 68, 172 Abr 273, 273 Decal 84, 85, 86, 91, 92, 94, 141 Spec 1:235, 238 Spec 2:2, 2, 4, 4, 8, 9, 9, 10, 12, 13, 13, 14, 14, 16, 19, 23, 24, 24, 25, 38 Spec 4:32, 40 QG 4:180, 180, 180, 180

ὁρμάω (50) Leg 2:100 Leg 3:16, 17, 18, 19, 94, 94, 134, 149, 244 Cher 114 Sacr 130 Gig 13 Deus 35 Agr 36 Plant 45, 151 Ebr 51 Conf 78 Her 116 Congr 99, 161 Fug 180 Mut 43, 159 Somn 1:107, 167, 179, 251 Somn 2:50 Abr 149, 182, 190, 213, 241 Mos 1:22, 77, 244, 304 Mos 2:161, 269 Spec 3:44, 73 Virt 139 Praem 62, 140 Prob 117, 133 Legat 132 Prov 2:69

ὁρμέω (6) Sacr 42 Post 22 Agr 151 Her 95 Somn 2:291 Spec 2:71

ὁρμή (85) Opif 79, 81 Leg 1:29, 30, 30, 73 Leg 2:11, 23 Leg 3:47, 118, 128, 185, 229, 248, 249 Sacr 80 Det 10, 100, 127, 171 Post 22, 74 Deus 41, 44, 93, 149 Agr 58, 70, 94 Ebr 97, 98, 111 Conf 19, 90 Migr 67, 191 Her 245 Congr 55, 60 Fug 158 Mut 160, 160, 173, 200, 223, 257 Somn 1:136 Somn 2:12, 232, 247, 276 Abr 38, 67, 130, 275 Ios 44 Mos 1:26, 50, 160, 297 Mos 2:139, 170 Spec 1:44, 67, 101, 193, 305, 343 Spec 2:142, 163 Spec 3:79 Spec 4:79, 79, 99, 104 Virt 31 Praem 48, 104, 154, 165 Contempl 16 Flacc 14, 52 Legat 190 QG 1:55c

ὅρμημα Somn 2:246

ὁρμητήριον (8) Abr 244 Spec 1:192 Spec 4:65 Virt 10 Prob 38 Flacc 49 QE 2:64 QE isf 4

ὁρμητικός Leg 2:99 Leg 3:130, 131

ὁρμίσκος Fug 150 Mut 135 Somn 2:44

ὅρμος Virt 39

ὄρνεον (10) Her 230, 230, 233, 237, 237, 237, 240, 243 Ios 96 Spec 1:176

ὀρνίθιον Cher 41 Her 128

ὄρνις (9) Ebr 219 Her 128 Ios 93 Spec 1:62 Prob 132, 134, 135 Flacc 177 Prov 2:69

ὄροβος Conf 185 Spec 4:29

ὅρος (105) Opif 33, 33, 35, 37, 47, 102, 155, 168 Leg 1:65, 65 Leg 3:107, 107, 107, 232 Cher 86 Det 86, 88, 89, 95, 139 Post 9, 83, 88, 89, 91, 91, 99, 180 Deus 118, 179 Agr 161, 181 Plant 3, 22, 66, 76, 135 Ebr 15, 52, 185 Sobr 6, 56 Migr 59 Her 31, 202, 228 Congr 134, 141, 147, 171 Fug 58, 98, 168, 169, 170 Mut 19, 180 Somn 1:9, 11, 131 Somn 2:180, 194, 243 Abr 195 Mos 1:25, 32, 73, 87, 163, 194, 214, 238, 243, 255 Mos 2:92, 124 Decal 27, 27, 27, 43, 119 Spec 1:150, 160, 241, 300 Spec 3:49, 151, 164, 169 Spec 4:110, 149, 209 Virt 106, 172, 206 Praem 77 Prob 7, 83 Aet 58, 59, 108 Flacc 174 Legat 75 QG 1:100:2b QE isf 24

ὄρος (45) Leg 3:16, 19, 102, 142 Deus 99, 99, 145, 145, 167, 179 Plant 47, 48, 54 Ebr 118 Conf 4, 4, 65 Her 177, 251 Somn 1:17 Somn 2:118 Abr 41, 43 Mos 1:192, 228, 228, 278, 287 Mos 2:70, 74, 161 Spec 1:73, 300 Spec 3:125 Virt 201 Aet 64, 118, 119, 132, 132, 133, 137, 148 Prov 2:27 QE 2:45a

ὄρουσις Mut 160

ὄροφος Mos 2:85, 87

ὀρρωδέω Mos 1:181, 236

ὀρτυγομήτρα Mos 1:209 Decal 16 Spec 4:128

ὄρυγμα (6) Agr 97 Ios 12, 13 Spec 3:147, 148, 149

ὀρυκτή Somn 1:41, 55

ὀρυκτήρ Spec 4:7 Aet 119

ὄρυξ Spec 4:105

ὀρύσσω (15) Leg 2:27 Leg 3:153 Det 106 Plant 78, 79 Ebr 113 Fug 197, 199, 200 Somn 1:8, 10, 14 Flacc 188, 190 QG 4:193

ὀρφανία Sacr 45 Det 145 Spec 4:180

ὀρφανός (21) Congr 178 Somn 1:107 Somn 2:273 Ios 74 Mos 2:235, 238, 240, 243 Decal 42 Spec 1:308, 310 Spec 2:108 Spec 3:71 Spec 4:176, 177, 179 Prob 35 QE 2:3a, 3a, 3a, 4

ὄρχησις Opif 122 Legat 44

ὀρχηστής Agr 35 Mos 2:211 Contempl 58 Flacc 85 Legat 42

ὀρχήστρα Flacc 85

ὅς (5942) Opif 2, 3, 5, 9, 11, 12, 15, 16, 17, 18, 19, 20, 21, 21, 25, 29, 29, 31, 31, 33, 33, 34, 35, 35, 36, 36, 38, 41, 41, 43, 44, 45, 45, 46, 46, 47, 47, 47, 47, 48, 48, 49, 49, 49, 51, 52, 52, 53, 54, 54, 55, 55, 55, 57, 61, 61, 62, 65, 65, 66, 69, 71, 71, 72, 73, 73, 77, 77, 77, 77, 78, 78, 78, 79, 80, 81, 84, 85, 86, 88, 89, 91, 92, 92, 96, 97, 98, 100, 100, 100, 101, 101, 101, 101, 102, 102, 104, 105, 107, 107, 107, 107, 108, 108, 109, 109, 109, 111, 111, 112, 113, 114, 114, 115, 116, 116, 117, 119, 119, 122, 125, 128, 128, 128, 128, 128, 128,

129, 129, 130, 130, 131, 131, 132, 133, 135, 136, 136, 136, 137, 137, 138, 139, 139, 142, 143, 143, 143, 143, 144, 144, 146, 147, 147, 147, 148, 152, 153, 153, 154, 154, 155, 155, 156, 156, 156, 157, 157, 158, 158, 158, 159, 160, 161, 161, 161, 163, 163, 163, 164, 164, 165, 166, 166, 166, 166, 167, 170, 170, 171, 171, 171, 171, 171 Leg 1:2, 6, 8, 11, 13, 14, 15, 15, 15, 16, 18, 18, 18, 19, 21, 21, 22, 22, 22, 23, 23, 24, 26, 26, 28, 30, 31, 34, 34, 34, 35, 35, 36, 36, 37, 40, 45, 45, 47, 47, 47, 51, 51, 51, 51, 53, 54, 55, 55, 56, 56, 57, 59, 59, 59, 61, 62, 62, 63, 63, 63, 66, 67, 67, 67, 68, 68, 69, 70, 70, 71, 71, 71, 76, 76, 77, 79, 79, 80, 80, 86, 87, 89, 90, 91, 91, 91, 91, 91, 91, 91, 94, 94, 94, 96, 96, 96, 97, 101, 105, 106 Leg 2:3, 6, 6, 8, 8, 9, 13, 13, 18, 19, 19, 19, 22, 23, 23, 24, 28, 30, 30, 36, 40, 41, 46, 53, 53, 53, 58, 64, 64, 64, 65, 67, 67, 67, 71, 72, 74, 81, 82, 84, 85, 86, 86, 86, 87, 89, 93, 96, 96, 98, 99, 100, 102, 103, 104, 105, 105, 105, 106, 108 Leg 3:1, 1, 3, 4, 6, 6, 7, 8, 10, 12, 14, 15, 22, 22, 22, 23, 27, 27, 27, 28, 28, 29, 32, 32, 35, 35, 36, 38, 38, 39, 40, 40, 42, 42, 43, 43, 45, 45, 45, 46, 50, 52, 53, 53, 53, 54, 55, 56, 56, 56, 63, 65, 73, 74, 76, 76, 78, 80, 81, 83, 86, 88, 95, 96, 96, 104, 104, 111, 113, 113, 120, 122, 132, 132, 135, 139, 143, 143, 144, 145, 145, 148, 151, 152, 154, 157, 158, 159, 161, 161, 161, 162, 162, 164, 166, 169, 169, 171, 171, 173, 173, 173, 174, 177, 177, 178, 179, 179, 180, 181, 183, 184, 185, 186, 187, 188, 188, 189, 190, 191, 192, 193, 194, 194, 194, 196, 196, 197, 200, 200, 200, 203, 203, 204, 205, 206, 207, 209, 210, 211, 211, 211, 212, 218, 219, 220, 222, 223, 223, 225, 225, 227, 229, 230, 232, 233, 236, 239, 240, 242, 243, 244, 244, 245, 246, 246, 246, 246, 247, 247, 248, 248, 248, 249, 252, 252 Cher 1, 2, 3, 3, 4, 6, 7, 7, 10, 13, 13, 16, 17, 18, 21, 22, 22, 23, 23, 23, 25, 27, 27, 29, 29, 29, 29, 30, 32, 32, 33, 34, 35, 35, 36, 40, 41, 44, 46, 48, 50, 53, 53, 53, 54, 55, 56, 56, 57, 57, 57, 57, 57, 58, 58, 59, 59, 59, 59, 60, 62, 62, 65, 68, 71, 72, 75, 77, 78, 80, 80, 83, 84, 84, 84, 84, 84, 88, 91, 95, 96, 97, 98, 102, 104, 109, 109, 109, 112, 115, 117, 117, 119, 120, 122, 122, 124, 124, 124, 125, 125, 125, 125, 125, 125, 125, 125, 126, 126, 126, 126, 127, 127, 127, 128, 128, 130 Sacr 5, 7, 7, 8, 8, 8, 9, 10, 10, 12, 15, 16, 19, 19, 21, 22, 22, 24, 25, 25, 29, 29, 29, 29, 31, 31, 33, 33, 33, 35, 36, 36, 39, 39, 40, 40, 41, 42, 42, 43, 43, 47, 47, 48, 50, 51, 52, 54, 54, 57, 59, 59, 60, 61, 62, 63, 64, 64, 64, 64, 64, 66, 68, 69, 71, 72, 72, 73, 74, 76, 77, 77, 77, 77, 79, 81, 82, 84, 85, 86, 87, 89, 89, 90, 90, 91, 95, 96, 97, 97, 98, 98, 98, 99, 100, 100, 100, 102, 103, 103, 104, 104, 108, 108, 109, 110, 110, 110, 115, 115, 115, 116, 117, 118, 120, 120, 120, 122, 122, 123, 125, 126, 126, 126, 127, 129, 131, 131, 132, 134, 134, 136, 139 Det 1, 1, 2, 4, 4, 4, 7, 8, 9, 10, 11, 11, 12, 13, 14, 14, 14, 15, 16, 16, 19, 21, 25, 27, 28, 28, 29, 32, 33, 36, 37, 38, 39, 40, 40, 40, 43, 44, 46, 48, 48, 49, 50, 50, 54, 54, 55, 57, 57, 57, 57, 58, 60, 61, 62, 62, 64, 65, 65, 68, 70, 74, 75, 75, 75, 76, 76, 77, 78, 78, 82, 82, 83, 83, 84, 84, 88, 89, 91, 92, 92, 92, 99, 100, 100, 101, 104, 104, 106, 107, 107, 108, 108, 109, 110, 111, 113, 114, 114, 114, 116, 118, 118, 118, 120, 120, 121, 121, 121, 121, 122, 122, 122, 123, 123, 123, 124, 126, 127, 129, 130, 130, 131, 131, 134, 136, 137, 137, 140, 142, 142, 145, 145, 145, 145, 146, 146, 148, 148, 153, 154, 160, 167, 168, 168, 170, 173, 174, 174, 176 Post 2, 5, 5, 5, 6, 10, 13, 15, 16, 17, 17, 18, 21, 21, 22, 22, 26, 26, 26, 28, 30, 31, 32, 34, 35, 36, 37, 38, 38, 42, 43, 44, 44, 44, 44, 46, 48, 48, 52, 53, 53, 53, 54, 58, 59, 62, 63, 64, 64, 65, 65, 66, 67, 68, 69, 71, 71, 73, 73, 73, 74, 75, 77, 80, 81, 83, 83, 85, 85, 87, 89, 90, 90, 91, 91, 93, 95, 96, 97, 98, 99, 101, 101, 101, 102, 102, 105, 110, 111, 111, 112, 112, 112, 112, 113, 113, 114, 115, 116, 117, 118, 118, 119, 120, 120, 120, 120, 121, 122, 122, 122, 124, 129, 129, 130, 130, 130, 131, 131, 133, 134, 135, 135, 135, 136, 136, 137, 139, 140, 140, 142, 143, 144, 146, 146, 147, 147, 148, 150, 153, 153, 154, 155, 158, 158, 159, 159, 162, 162, 164, 165, 165, 170, 173, 173, 174, 175, 179, 182, 182, 184, 184, 185 Gig 4, 4, 5, 6, 6, 11, 15, 17, 17, 21, 22, 24, 24, 25, 29, 30, 31, 33, 34, 34, 39, 39, 43, 43, 43, 43, 45, 51, 53, 54, 55, 62, 62, 64, 64, 65 Deus 2, 3, 3, 4, 4, 5, 5, 8, 10, 12, 18, 19, 20, 21, 26, 26, 29, 35, 35, 36, 38, 39, 39, 43, 44, 45, 46, 46, 46, 46, 47, 47, 47, 47, 50, 50, 51, 53, 57, 58, 61, 62, 63, 64, 70, 70, 76, 78, 81, 86, 86, 89, 90, 91, 92, 92, 93, 94, 94, 94, 94, 96, 97, 97, 98, 101, 101, 102, 103, 107, 110, 111, 112, 112, 113, 113, 115, 116, 119, 120, 121, 126, 127, 131, 132, 132, 133, 134, 134, 134, 135, 136, 137, 137, 138, 139, 142, 150, 153, 154, 155, 156, 157, 158, 158, 159, 160, 165, 166, 167, 167, 171, 176, 179, 181, 182, 183 Agr 2, 4, 9, 10, 12, 13, 13, 14, 18, 21, 21, 23, 25, 25, 26, 26, 28, 29, 30, 34, 36, 38, 39, 41, 41, 43, 44, 45, 49, 50, 51, 54, 60, 65, 67, 67, 69, 75, 79, 82, 83, 83, 84, 85, 88, 88, 89, 90, 90, 95, 95, 99, 101, 103, 103, 104, 107, 110, 110, 112, 113, 114, 115, 116, 119, 121, 121, 123, 125, 128, 129, 130, 131, 133, 133, 139, 140, 146, 148, 149, 149, 156, 157, 159, 162, 162, 163, 167, 168, 169, 174, 178, 181 Plant 3, 3, 4, 5, 7, 7, 12, 12, 12, 14, 14, 18, 21, 25, 27, 27, 27, 28, 32, 35, 35, 37, 39, 41, 41, 42, 43, 44, 47, 47, 48, 52, 53, 55, 56, 56, 57, 60, 61, 61, 64, 64, 65, 66, 66, 68, 68, 68, 70, 74, 78, 78, 78, 78, 79, 79, 81, 85, 86, 86, 86, 86, 93, 95, 105, 107, 107, 107, 108, 109, 114, 115, 115, 115, 118, 118, 120, 123, 125, 126, 126, 126, 128, 129, 130, 131, 131, 133, 134, 134, 134, 136, 136, 137, 139, 139, 139, 144, 147, 151, 151, 151, 152, 153, 155, 157, 160, 162, 163, 167, 168, 168, 169, 169, 169, 169, 169, 170, 173, 174, 177 Ebr 2, 4, 9, 10, 12, 14, 18, 18, 18, 19, 26, 26, 28, 30, 33, 34, 36, 39, 42, 47, 52, 61, 61, 65, 65, 65, 66, 72, 72, 72, 73, 76, 79, 80, 80, 82, 86, 87, 91, 93, 94, 94, 94, 95, 95, 96, 99, 101, 101, 102, 105, 105, 107, 107, 108, 108, 109, 109, 110, 111, 112, 113, 114, 115, 115, 115, 118, 119, 119, 119, 120, 120, 121, 121, 124, 126, 128, 132, 139, 142, 143, 145, 147, 149, 152, 152, 154, 154, 155, 155, 155, 156, 160, 162, 164, 172, 172, 173, 174, 174, 176, 177, 181, 183, 184, 185, 193, 193, 197, 197, 198, 202, 202, 205, 205, 206, 207, 209, 210, 211, 214, 214, 216, 219, 220, 220, 222, 223, 223, 224 Sobr 3, 3, 3, 5, 6, 9, 12, 13, 14, 15, 17, 18, 19, 20, 20, 20, 21, 21, 21, 28, 29, 29, 30, 31, 32, 32, 33, 34, 36, 39, 40, 40, 45, 47, 51, 53, 53, 57, 58, 64, 65, 65, 65, 66, 66, 67, 68, 68, 68 Conf 1, 1, 1, 3, 4, 5, 6, 7, 8, 9, 11, 13, 20, 22, 24, 26, 27, 28, 29, 33, 36, 37, 37, 38, 38, 38, 38, 38, 38, 41, 44, 46, 49, 51, 52, 52, 52, 54, 56, 57, 58, 59, 61, 62, 63, 65, 68, 72, 74, 75, 78, 78, 78, 79, 80, 80, 81, 81, 85, 88, 89, 90, 92, 92, 93, 94, 96, 96, 96, 97, 101, 106, 107, 107, 107, 108, 108, 108, 112, 112, 115, 117, 118, 118, 119, 119, 122, 122, 124, 125, 125, 126, 126, 127, 128, 128, 129, 130, 130, 132, 132, 132, 133, 136, 136, 137, 140, 141, 142, 144, 149, 149, 149, 151, 153, 154, 154, 154, 155, 155, 155, 155, 156, 157, 159, 159, 160, 161, 162, 162, 164, 164, 165, 166, 166, 166, 167, 170, 171, 173, 174, 175, 176, 176, 179, 181, 183, 183, 186, 187, 189, 190, 191, 193, 194, 197, 198 Migr 1, 3, 5, 6, 8, 8, 12, 12, 13, 13, 16, 16, 16, 19, 20, 21, 24, 25, 28, 30, 30, 30,

31, 33, 34, 34, 34, 36, 36, 38, 38, 39, 39, 40, 42, 43, 43, 43, 46, 47, 49, 50, 51, 51, 51, 51, 51, 55, 56, 56, 58, 58, 59, 60, 60, 61, 61, 63, 64, 67, 68, 70, 76, 76, 77, 78, 78, 80, 81, 84, 84, 85, 88, 89, 89, 90, 90, 92, 93, 94, 94, 95, 95, 95, 98, 98, 99, 102, 103, 103, 104, 105, 105, 105, 109, 111, 113, 115, 117, 122, 125, 125, 126, 126, 127, 130, 130, 131, 136, 136, 137, 139, 140, 140, 141, 142, 143, 146, 146, 148, 149, 151, 153, 155, 155, 156, 157, 157, 159, 159, 161, 162, 162, 163, 165, 165, 166, 166, 170, 173, 173, 173, 174, 175, 181, 182, 183, 183, 187, 189, 190, 191, 196, 202, 203, 205, 205, 205, 205, 207, 208, 210, 211, 214, 219, 219, 220, 221, 223, 225 Her 4, 5, 8, 9, 10, 10, 10, 12, 12, 14, 14, 18, 20, 20, 23, 23, 25, 27, 29, 31, 33, 36, 37, 38, 38, 38, 39, 42, 42, 46, 47, 51, 52, 52, 54, 55, 55, 55, 55, 56, 60, 61, 63, 68, 71, 76, 76, 78, 78, 80, 81, 91, 92, 95, 95, 98, 100, 101, 102, 102, 103, 103, 105, 106, 109, 113, 113, 113, 116, 116, 119, 124, 126, 127, 128, 128, 129, 130, 134, 137, 137, 137, 137, 137, 138, 139, 139, 142, 144, 145, 145, 147, 147, 149, 151, 156, 158, 161, 162, 164, 165, 165, 166, 166, 166, 166, 166, 167, 167, 168, 168, 169, 170, 171, 172, 173, 174, 174, 175, 175, 176, 178, 179, 182, 183, 183, 184, 184, 186, 186, 189, 190, 191, 191, 191, 193, 197, 197, 199, 201, 201, 202, 203, 213, 214, 217, 218, 219, 223, 226, 227, 227, 231, 232, 233, 234, 235, 235, 238, 239, 239, 240, 242, 243, 246, 246, 249, 252, 257, 258, 260, 262, 266, 267, 267, 268, 271, 272, 274, 276, 277, 277, 279, 279, 280, 280, 281, 283, 283, 283, 284, 286, 286, 291, 293, 293, 295, 295, 296, 297, 299, 299, 299, 299, 301, 303, 303, 308, 311, 311, 312, 314, 314, 314, 315 Congr 1, 2, 4, 5, 5, 6, 7, 7, 10, 11, 15, 17, 18, 21, 22, 23, 23, 23, 25, 25, 27, 27, 32, 32, 35, 35, 36, 36, 40, 41, 41, 43, 48, 48, 50, 52, 59, 60, 61, 61, 67, 68, 78, 81, 81, 84, 85, 86, 86, 87, 89, 93, 95, 96, 96, 97, 98, 99, 99, 106, 108, 108, 110, 112, 113, 113, 114, 117, 127, 128, 131, 132, 134, 134, 137, 140, 142, 144, 144, 146, 146, 147, 147, 147, 148, 151, 151, 152, 153, 157, 160, 162, 163, 170, 170, 177, 177, 177, 178 Fug 5, 5, 5, 8, 10, 10, 12, 15, 17, 18, 18, 18, 19, 19, 20, 20, 21, 22, 22, 23, 25, 37, 42, 45, 47, 50, 51, 52, 53, 55, 57, 59, 59, 64, 66, 67, 67, 69, 71, 72, 76, 77, 77, 80, 80, 82, 83, 85, 85, 87, 87, 89, 93, 94, 94, 95, 95, 95, 95, 95, 95, 96, 96, 97, 97, 98, 98, 99, 99, 99, 100, 100, 101, 103, 103, 104, 107, 109, 109, 112, 112, 112, 113, 113, 114, 118, 120, 122, 122, 123, 125, 126, 128, 128, 131, 133, 136, 136, 136, 136, 137, 137, 138, 138, 139, 139, 143, 143, 145, 148, 148, 150, 160, 161, 162, 162, 163, 163, 166, 166, 167, 167, 167, 168, 169, 169, 171, 175, 175, 175, 175, 175, 176, 179, 180, 183, 185, 186, 188, 188, 191, 191, 192, 193, 195, 195, 196, 197, 197, 200, 202, 204, 204, 205, 208, 209, 210, 212 Mut 1, 2, 4, 7, 7, 10, 12, 14, 16, 17, 18, 18, 22, 25, 27, 28, 30, 31, 36, 39, 41, 42, 49, 52, 54, 56, 57, 59, 61, 61, 63, 63, 66, 69, 71, 72, 75, 76, 81, 82, 83, 83, 84, 84, 88, 89, 90, 91, 94, 96, 101, 104, 105, 105, 106, 108, 109, 110, 111, 114, 116, 117, 118, 128, 129, 132, 135, 136, 138, 138, 138, 138, 143, 144, 145, 146, 147, 148, 149, 150, 151, 152, 153, 153, 153, 153, 154, 157, 158, 159, 160, 162, 163, 164, 166, 167, 167, 171, 172, 173, 173, 177, 177, 178, 179, 182, 187, 189, 191, 192, 192, 193, 193, 193, 194, 196, 197, 200, 202, 203, 204, 206, 207, 208, 210, 213, 215, 218, 222, 224, 228, 232, 233, 236, 238, 238, 240, 240, 241, 242, 244, 248, 251, 254, 256, 258, 260, 260, 262, 262, 265, 267, 268, 269 Somn 1:1, 2, 3, 3, 3, 4, 7, 7, 8, 10, 11, 12, 15, 15, 16, 18, 18, 19, 20, 22, 25, 26, 27, 29, 29, 32, 34, 36, 36, 38, 40, 42, 42, 45, 47, 49, 50, 51, 51, 54, 56, 59, 61, 62, 62, 62, 64, 65, 66, 67, 68, 68, 68, 70, 70, 72, 73, 76, 77, 77, 77, 77, 77, 79, 81, 82, 82, 85, 90, 91, 95, 95, 96, 97, 97, 98, 103, 103, 105, 105, 110, 111, 112, 112, 112, 112, 113, 114, 114, 115, 116, 117, 117, 121, 123, 124, 133, 134, 134, 137, 143, 143, 145, 145, 146, 147, 148, 149, 156, 158, 159, 159, 163, 168, 169, 171, 173, 174, 174, 177, 179, 184, 185, 185, 189, 190, 191, 191, 192, 195, 198, 199, 200, 201, 201, 202, 205, 205, 206, 208, 208, 211, 212, 212, 214, 214, 215, 215, 215, 215, 216, 218, 218, 218, 220, 220, 220, 220, 222, 223, 225, 225, 227, 227, 230, 231, 236, 237, 237, 241, 244, 250, 250, 254, 256 Somn 2:2, 3, 5, 5, 6, 8, 15, 16, 16, 19, 22, 24, 24, 24, 26, 26, 27, 29, 29, 30, 31, 31, 32, 33, 33, 34, 37, 42, 42, 48, 51, 57, 59, 59, 60, 62, 64, 64, 64, 66, 67, 69, 73, 74, 75, 76, 78, 82, 89, 90, 90, 96, 100, 103, 107, 107, 109, 109, 111, 112, 116, 118, 120, 122, 123, 124, 133, 133, 134, 134, 136, 138, 144, 147, 147, 150, 154, 159, 162, 163, 163, 163, 172, 172, 179, 180, 182, 183, 184, 186, 187, 190, 192, 199, 203, 204, 208, 210, 211, 211, 211, 212, 213, 216, 219, 221, 222, 225, 227, 227, 232, 237, 242, 243, 246, 248, 248, 250, 253, 257, 259, 260, 268, 270, 271, 272, 272, 272, 275, 275, 279, 279, 279, 281, 287, 288, 289, 290, 291, 292, 292, 294, 297, 298, 299 Abr 1, 2, 4, 5, 5, 6, 8, 10, 10, 10, 11, 13, 13, 15, 15, 16, 17, 17, 21, 22, 22, 22, 23, 23, 23, 24, 25, 27, 27, 27, 28, 29, 29, 30, 32, 33, 35, 35, 37, 38, 38, 39, 39, 41, 43, 44, 46, 47, 47, 48, 48, 49, 49, 50, 50, 54, 58, 59, 60, 60, 61, 61, 61, 63, 65, 65, 67, 67, 67, 69, 70, 71, 71, 72, 73, 73, 74, 74, 75, 77, 77, 79, 79, 84, 84, 85, 89, 89, 96, 98, 98, 99, 99, 100, 100, 105, 105, 106, 106, 106, 107, 114, 114, 115, 115, 115, 121, 124, 124, 124, 126, 130, 133, 135, 141, 141, 143, 147, 149, 154, 156, 156, 159, 159, 160, 164, 164, 167, 172, 174, 175, 176, 176, 177, 178, 180, 181, 183, 184, 187, 188, 189, 190, 191, 193, 193, 196, 200, 204, 211, 211, 213, 215, 218, 219, 219, 220, 223, 225, 226, 227, 228, 235, 235, 238, 239, 240, 242, 242, 243, 247, 248, 249, 250, 251, 251, 253, 255, 256, 258, 258, 261, 262, 262, 263, 266, 266, 267, 270, 273, 273, 273, 275 Ios 1, 1, 1, 2, 3, 5, 9, 13, 15, 16, 25, 26, 26, 26, 27, 27, 29, 29, 30, 35, 39, 41, 44, 45, 46, 46, 47, 49, 50, 50, 51, 52, 52, 52, 56, 60, 61, 64, 64, 66, 68, 69, 71, 71, 74, 77, 79, 79, 80, 84, 85, 86, 87, 87, 88, 88, 92, 93, 93, 97, 98, 101, 102, 104, 104, 104, 106, 106, 108, 110, 111, 111, 114, 115, 116, 117, 117, 118, 125, 129, 130, 132, 133, 142, 147, 148, 149, 149, 149, 151, 152, 153, 153, 153, 154, 156, 156, 156, 157, 158, 158, 159, 159, 160, 163, 165, 166, 166, 167, 171, 171, 173, 176, 178, 178, 178, 181, 184, 185, 185, 186, 187, 187, 187, 188, 188, 189, 191, 192, 193, 193, 194, 195, 195, 197, 197, 198, 199, 199, 204, 204, 206, 207, 209, 210, 213, 215, 215, 216, 216, 217, 217, 217, 219, 222, 223, 227, 227, 228, 229, 231, 233, 236, 238, 238, 240, 240, 241, 242, 244, 247, 248, 252, 255, 255, 258, 260, 260, 262, 265, 265, 267, 269, 269, 269 Mos 1:2, 3, 3, 3, 4, 5, 5, 6, 7, 7, 12, 13, 17, 19, 20, 21, 23, 23, 24, 24, 25, 27, 28, 31, 31, 31, 33, 36, 36, 36, 37, 39, 39, 40, 45, 45, 45, 46, 48, 48, 48, 49, 49, 50, 52, 55, 56, 64, 66, 69, 69, 73, 75, 76, 76, 77, 80, 83, 85, 88, 89, 90, 92, 94, 95, 95, 96, 96, 97, 105, 105, 106, 107, 109, 109, 111, 113, 113, 115, 115, 116, 118, 119, 120, 121, 126, 126, 127, 127, 128, 130, 130, 130, 132, 133, 134, 136, 140, 141, 141, 141, 142, 143, 143, 143, 143, 144, 145, 146, 148, 153, 156, 156, 157, 160, 163, 163, 165, 166, 171, 173, 175, 176, 177, 177, 182, 185, 185, 185, 187, 188, 189, 189, 189, 194, 197, 197, 198, 198, 200, 200, 200, 200, 201, 201, 204, 204, 205,

207, 210, 211, 212, 214, 215, 216, 216, 219, 219, 220, 222, 222, 223, 224, 225, 226, 226, 227, 227, 228, 231, 233, 234, 236, 237, 238, 239, 240, 242, 247, 247, 251, 254, 254, 255, 255, 258, 259, 259, 260, 260, 261, 264, 265, 266, 268, 269, 269, 272, 274, 274, 274, 276, 276, 277, 278, 280, 281, 283, 284, 285, 285, 291, 293, 294, 298, 300, 304, 304, 304, 305, 305, 307, 307, 308, 308, 310, 314, 314, 316, 317, 317, 318, 319, 321, 324, 325, 331, 332, 333 Mos 2:1, 1, 1, 1, 1, 2, 3, 4, 4, 5, 6, 7, 7, 7, 10, 10, 11, 11, 12, 13, 14, 16, 17, 17, 18, 23, 23, 24, 24, 28, 29, 32, 35, 37, 39, 40, 41, 41, 45, 45, 46, 47, 49, 49, 49, 53, 60, 61, 62, 65, 65, 65, 66, 66, 67, 69, 69, 71, 72, 73, 74, 74, 78, 80, 80, 81, 84, 84, 86, 88, 88, 91, 93, 95, 97, 99, 99, 101, 101, 101, 102, 104, 105, 108, 112, 114, 115, 115, 117, 120, 121, 121, 121, 124, 127, 127, 127, 127, 128, 128, 128, 130, 131, 131, 132, 132, 133, 133, 135, 136, 137, 141, 142, 144, 146, 147, 148, 149, 151, 152, 152, 153, 155, 157, 158, 162, 162, 163, 165, 165, 171, 171, 172, 174, 174, 174, 175, 177, 177, 179, 180, 180, 180, 181, 181, 182, 183, 183, 183, 185, 185, 186, 186, 187, 187, 189, 189, 190, 190, 191, 191, 192, 196, 201, 201, 201, 201, 202, 203, 203, 205, 207, 207, 210, 211, 212, 213, 213, 214, 215, 216, 216, 217, 218, 219, 220, 221, 221, 222, 223, 224, 225, 225, 226, 228, 229, 231, 234, 235, 236, 236, 237, 240, 241, 242, 242, 243, 243, 245, 248, 251, 253, 254, 254, 255, 255, 255, 255, 257, 257, 258, 259, 260, 262, 262, 263, 264, 266, 266, 267, 270, 270, 270, 270, 271, 271, 271, 272, 273, 273, 273, 273, 275, 277, 279, 282, 282, 283, 288, 288, 290, 291 Decal 1, 1, 3, 3, 4, 4, 4, 6, 8, 9, 10, 14, 14, 16, 17, 18, 18, 18, 20, 20, 21, 21, 21, 25, 26, 28, 28, 28, 29, 30, 31, 31, 31, 33, 41, 41, 42, 44, 46, 47, 49, 50, 50, 51, 51, 52, 53, 55, 60, 60, 62, 62, 63, 63, 64, 66, 67, 69, 69, 71, 72, 72, 75, 75, 78, 79, 81, 81, 82, 84, 88, 90, 92, 93, 94, 95, 98, 100, 100, 100, 101, 102, 103, 103, 104, 104, 104, 106, 110, 111, 112, 113, 115, 118, 118, 120, 122, 122, 126, 138, 139, 140, 140, 140, 141, 141, 143, 149, 149, 150, 151, 156, 157, 158, 159, 159, 159, 159, 159, 160, 160, 160, 160, 161, 162, 164, 166, 166, 167, 168, 169, 170, 171, 171, 172, 172, 173, 175, 176, 178 Spec 1:2, 3, 4, 6, 6, 8, 9, 11, 12, 13, 14, 15, 16, 16, 19, 20, 21, 22, 23, 24, 25, 25, 26, 27, 27, 28, 33, 45, 46, 49, 51, 53, 53, 56, 57, 59, 61, 62, 62, 63, 65, 65, 65, 67, 69, 73, 75, 76, 78, 79, 79, 79, 80, 81, 81, 82, 83, 86, 89, 94, 97, 98, 99, 99, 99, 100, 103, 104, 104, 106, 107, 108, 108, 111, 113, 114, 115, 118, 122, 122, 123, 124, 126, 129, 132, 133, 138, 142, 142, 146, 146, 147, 147, 149, 151, 153, 154, 156, 156, 158, 159, 160, 160, 160, 161, 161, 163, 165, 169, 170, 170, 172, 172, 172, 172, 172, 173, 175, 176, 176, 177, 178, 178, 180, 180, 182, 183, 184, 185, 186, 186, 186, 186, 187, 188, 189, 189, 189, 190, 190, 193, 193, 195, 196, 197, 197, 201, 201, 204, 206, 207, 208, 209, 209, 211, 215, 215, 216, 216, 216, 216, 216, 217, 218, 221, 221, 221, 221, 221, 222, 223, 223, 224, 226, 227, 231, 232, 234, 235, 235, 236, 237, 237, 238, 239, 240, 241, 242, 242, 244, 246, 248, 248, 250, 252, 253, 254, 254, 255, 256, 257, 258, 259, 262, 264, 266, 270, 271, 272, 274, 275, 277, 278, 279, 279, 279, 281, 282, 283, 283, 285, 286, 288, 289, 290, 292, 294, 294, 295, 295, 296, 299, 299, 300, 300, 302, 303, 304, 305, 305, 307, 307, 309, 311, 312, 312, 313, 313, 314, 316, 317, 321, 323, 325, 327, 329, 329, 329, 330, 330, 331, 332, 333, 336, 338, 338, 339, 339, 341, 341, 342, 343, 344, 344, 344, 344 Spec 2:3, 6, 7, 7, 8, 8, 9, 13, 14, 14, 15, 16, 17, 17, 18, 20, 20, 23, 23, 23, 24, 25, 25, 27, 29, 30, 31, 31, 34, 37, 37, 37, 38, 38, 39, 39, 39, 40, 40, 40, 41, 41, 41, 41, 42, 42, 43, 44, 45, 45, 50, 51, 52, 53, 55, 56, 57, 58, 59, 59, 60, 62, 62, 63, 64, 64, 72, 73, 74, 75, 77, 77, 78, 78, 80, 80, 82, 89, 89, 89, 90, 91, 91, 92, 94, 96, 96, 97, 99, 104, 104, 107, 107, 107, 107, 108, 109, 112, 112, 113, 113, 114, 114, 119, 119, 121, 121, 129, 129, 130, 133, 133, 134, 135, 137, 137, 137, 138, 138, 140, 140, 142, 143, 143, 144, 145, 145, 146, 147, 147, 148, 150, 151, 152, 154, 154, 154, 155, 156, 156, 157, 157, 157, 157, 158, 162, 163, 163, 163, 164, 164, 165, 165, 167, 167, 168, 169, 170, 171, 171, 173, 174, 175, 175, 176, 177, 178, 179, 183, 183, 183, 184, 185, 187, 188, 188, 188, 189, 189, 191, 192, 193, 194, 195, 195, 196, 197, 198, 199, 200, 204, 207, 207, 207, 210, 215, 215, 216, 219, 222, 223, 223, 224, 224, 224, 226, 229, 230, 230, 231, 231, 232, 235, 236, 239, 240, 243, 244, 245, 245, 246, 248, 248, 248, 251, 256, 259, 260, 261, 262 Spec 3:1, 3, 3, 4, 5, 6, 10, 10, 11, 12, 14, 14, 14, 14, 16, 17, 18, 23, 25, 26, 26, 27, 28, 29, 30, 30, 31, 33, 34, 37, 37, 38, 38, 39, 39, 44, 45, 45, 46, 47, 47, 47, 49, 50, 50, 51, 51, 52, 56, 57, 60, 61, 61, 62, 64, 65, 70, 71, 72, 73, 75, 76, 79, 79, 79, 80, 82, 84, 84, 85, 89, 89, 89, 90, 91, 91, 95, 97, 98, 98, 99, 99, 99, 100, 101, 101, 103, 104, 104, 104, 106, 107, 109, 110, 111, 111, 115, 117, 117, 119, 121, 121, 123, 123, 124, 126, 128, 128, 129, 132, 133, 134, 135, 136, 139, 140, 142, 143, 145, 148, 150, 155, 155, 156, 156, 157, 158, 161, 162, 166, 166, 168, 170, 170, 172, 173, 175, 175, 176, 176, 177, 177, 178, 179, 180, 180, 182, 183, 185, 186, 188, 189, 190, 190, 195, 197, 197, 197, 198, 199, 199, 199, 200, 200, 202, 205, 206, 206, 207, 209 Spec 4:1, 2, 2, 5, 6, 6, 7, 7, 7, 9, 9, 10, 11, 11, 11, 12, 13, 14, 14, 15, 15, 16, 17, 17, 18, 19, 21, 21, 21, 23, 23, 24, 28, 28, 31, 32, 35, 36, 40, 40, 40, 43, 43, 49, 49, 55, 56, 60, 61, 61, 63, 64, 64, 65, 69, 69, 69, 69, 70, 70, 73, 74, 75, 76, 78, 79, 85, 85, 85, 87, 91, 94, 95, 95, 99, 102, 103, 104, 105, 105, 106, 106, 107, 108, 108, 111, 113, 114, 115, 115, 119, 121, 121, 121, 121, 122, 123, 123, 123, 125, 126, 126, 127, 130, 132, 132, 133, 136, 138, 138, 141, 143, 145, 147, 147, 148, 149, 150, 151, 152, 156, 157, 158, 159, 160, 162, 165, 166, 168, 169, 170, 172, 172, 173, 173, 178, 178, 180, 181, 182, 186, 188, 195, 196, 197, 197, 200, 200, 201, 201, 202, 202, 204, 206, 209, 211, 212, 213, 215, 215, 215, 218, 218, 219, 221, 222, 224, 225, 227, 228, 231, 235, 238 Virt 1, 3, 4, 5, 5, 6, 6, 8, 8, 8, 9, 10, 11, 11, 12, 20, 22, 22, 23, 27, 30, 30, 31, 31, 34, 34, 35, 37, 37, 38, 39, 42, 45, 47, 48, 50, 50, 50, 51, 52, 52, 52, 53, 53, 54, 54, 55, 55, 57, 57, 58, 61, 61, 64, 64, 67, 68, 69, 69, 72, 75, 75, 76, 77, 77, 77, 77, 79, 79, 79, 79, 80, 80, 81, 82, 84, 84, 84, 85, 86, 86, 88, 88, 91, 92, 94, 94, 95, 96, 96, 96, 97, 98, 100, 100, 100, 101, 101, 104, 107, 108, 111, 111, 118, 118, 119, 120, 121, 123, 124, 127, 127, 129, 129, 130, 130, 133, 133, 136, 137, 137, 139, 143, 144, 145, 148, 154, 157, 157, 160, 160, 161, 162, 163, 165, 165, 166, 166, 167, 167, 168, 169, 171, 176, 176, 178, 179, 179, 180, 180, 182, 183, 183, 187, 190, 194, 197, 199, 200, 201, 201, 201, 202, 202, 203, 205, 205, 206, 206, 208, 208, 208, 211, 211, 212, 212, 213, 214, 214, 215, 215, 219, 219, 220, 223, 226, 227 Praem 3, 3, 4, 6, 6, 9, 10, 11, 12, 14, 15, 18, 18, 19, 20, 20, 20, 21, 21, 22, 23, 23, 24, 24, 25, 25, 25, 26, 28, 28, 29, 32, 39, 40, 47, 49, 50, 51, 52, 52, 53, 53, 54, 55, 55, 55, 55, 56, 56, 58, 58, 61, 62, 63, 64, 65, 66, 67, 68, 69, 70, 72, 72, 73, 73, 75, 77, 77, 78, 79, 83, 84, 87, 87, 88, 88, 90, 95, 96, 97, 97, 98, 99, 99, 100, 104, 105, 106, 110, 113, 113, 115, 117, 117, 119, 121, 121, 121, 123, 124, 126, 128,

130, 131, 132, 134, 135, 136, 137, 138, 139, 139, 142, 145, 145, 145, 149, 152, 153, 154, 155, 156, 157, 158, 158, 158, 160, 162, 162, 162, 162, 163, 167, 167, 167, 168, 168, 169, 170, 170, 171, 172, 172 Prob 1, 3, 5, 7, 9, 9, 10, 11, 11, 12, 13, 14, 15, 16, 18, 18, 19, 22, 34, 34, 36, 36, 36, 37, 40, 41, 41, 42, 44, 45, 47, 47, 48, 55, 55, 57, 59, 60, 60, 60, 60, 61, 61, 61, 62, 62, 63, 66, 68, 68, 69, 71, 71, 71, 71, 73, 74, 74, 74, 75, 76, 79, 79, 80, 81, 81, 83, 84, 85, 87, 88, 91, 92, 93, 95, 96, 96, 96, 97, 98, 99, 103, 104, 108, 109, 110, 111, 113, 113, 114, 115, 116, 117, 117, 120, 123, 124, 124, 126, 129, 132, 134, 134, 136, 137, 138, 139, 141, 142, 144, 147, 149, 149, 149, 149, 150, 151, 154, 154, 156, 158, 160, 160, 160 Contempl 1, 1, 1, 2, 2, 3, 3, 6, 7, 7, 7, 8, 10, 13, 14, 17, 18, 19, 23, 24, 25, 25, 25, 29, 29, 29, 32, 35, 36, 37, 37, 37, 40, 42, 43, 46, 48, 49, 50, 53, 54, 55, 56, 56, 57, 57, 57, 58, 60, 62, 62, 63, 63, 63, 65, 67, 68, 68, 68, 68, 69, 72, 72, 73, 73, 75, 78, 80, 81, 81, 86, 87 Aet 1, 3, 4, 4, 4, 4, 5, 5, 7, 8, 8, 10, 12, 13, 13, 13, 13, 16, 19, 19, 19, 21, 21, 22, 23, 24, 26, 28, 29, 29, 30, 30, 33, 35, 37, 39, 41, 42, 46, 47, 47, 47, 52, 54, 54, 56, 56, 58, 58, 60, 63, 63, 63, 63, 63, 64, 65, 66, 67, 67, 68, 73, 74, 74, 74, 78, 78, 78, 79, 80, 84, 84, 86, 86, 87, 88, 90, 92, 92, 93, 94, 94, 95, 97, 97, 98, 99, 102, 104, 106, 106, 107, 107, 111, 114, 116, 120, 121, 122, 124, 125, 126, 127, 128, 129, 131, 132, 134, 137, 139, 139, 139, 140, 141, 142, 143, 143, 145, 147, 150 Flacc 1, 2, 4, 4, 9, 9, 9, 13, 14, 17, 20, 22, 23, 25, 26, 35, 39, 40, 40, 41, 42, 45, 46, 46, 46, 46, 48, 48, 49, 50, 50, 51, 51, 51, 52, 53, 54, 54, 59, 60, 65, 68, 69, 74, 75, 76, 76, 79, 80, 82, 84, 84, 86, 87, 91, 91, 92, 92, 92, 94, 94, 95, 101, 101, 101, 102, 102, 104, 105, 107, 108, 108, 108, 109, 109, 112, 116, 116, 116, 117, 118, 118, 123, 126, 126, 128, 132, 132, 132, 133, 135, 136, 138, 139, 140, 144, 144, 144, 146, 147, 148, 148, 149, 150, 151, 152, 152, 153, 153, 154, 156, 157, 160, 162, 163, 165, 172, 174, 179, 182, 184, 185, 185, 185, 186, 186, 186, 188, 190, 190 Legat 2, 3, 4, 5, 9, 10, 10, 10, 13, 15, 17, 18, 22, 28, 30, 30, 31, 32, 35, 35, 36, 38, 39, 47, 47, 47, 48, 49, 51, 60, 62, 68, 68, 68, 72, 80, 80, 80, 81, 89, 90, 91, 92, 98, 98, 99, 103, 105, 107, 108, 110, 112, 113, 114, 118, 125, 126, 129, 131, 132, 132, 132, 132, 133, 133, 138, 139, 141, 144, 145, 146, 148, 151, 153, 154, 155, 157, 164, 165, 166, 170, 172, 173, 175, 178, 178, 178, 179, 182, 182, 183, 187, 191, 193, 194, 195, 195, 196, 197, 198, 198, 199, 199, 199, 200, 202, 203, 204, 204, 206, 207, 207, 208, 216, 218, 218, 222, 224, 224, 229, 231, 231, 237, 238, 240, 240, 242, 242, 243, 244, 245, 245, 245, 247, 248, 249, 250, 251, 253, 256, 258, 261, 261, 261, 265, 268, 274, 275, 276, 278, 278, 280, 280, 281, 285, 287, 293, 298, 299, 299, 306, 306, 310, 312, 314, 315, 316, 316, 317, 317, 320, 321, 321, 322, 322, 327, 329, 335, 336, 338, 338, 339, 343, 346, 346, 347, 348, 349, 351, 351, 353, 355, 356, 357, 360, 361, 364, 365, 368, 368, 369, 369, 370, 372 Hypoth 0:1, 0:1, 6:2, 6:7, 6:8, 7:5, 7:6, 7:6, 7:9, 11:1, 11:6, 11:9, 11:10, 11:12, 11:16 Prov 2:3, 5, 6, 7, 8, 9, 11, 11, 12, 12, 14, 14, 15, 16, 16, 20, 21, 22, 24, 26, 26, 26, 27, 27, 29, 31, 32, 33, 33, 35, 36, 36, 36, 37, 39, 41, 42, 42, 44, 45, 45, 45, 48, 50, 58, 60, 60, 61, 61, 62, 63, 64, 65, 66, 67, 70, 70 QG 1:1, 3, 21, 27, 29, 51, 51, 64a, 65, 66, 69, 70:1, 74, 77, 93, 94, 94, 96:1, 100:1b, 2:5a, 5b, 11, 13a, 13a, 15a, 15b, 28, 30, 31, 34a, 34c, 38, 54a, 54a, 54a, 62, 65, 65, 68a, 72, 3:3, 8, 11a, 11a, 11c, 20a, 21, 23, 23, 23, 29, 58, 4:8b, 8b, 8b, 51b, 52d, 69, 69, 69, 74, 76b, 76b, 81, 110b, 144, 148, 153, 180, 191b, 191c, 198, 200c, 204, 211, 228 QG isf 10, 13, 17, 17 QG (Par) 2:2, 2:3, 2:3, 2:3, 2:3, 2:4, 2:5, 2:5, 2:5, 2:6, 2:6, 2:6, 2:6, 2:7 QE 1:6, 7b, 19, 2:2, 3b, 13b, 15b, 17, 17, 18, 19, 20, 21, 21, 25b, 26, 40, 49b, 49b, 105 QE isf 3, 8, 13, 14, 26

ὁσία Hypoth 7:5, 7:7

ὅσιος (71) Leg 1:48 Leg 3:126 Cher 42 Sacr 34, 130, 137 Post 97, 170 Plant 70 Ebr 194 Sobr 10 Conf 27, 161 Her 201 Fug 63 Mut 153, 197, 208, 208, 223 Somn 2:296 Abr 52, 76, 181 Ios 74, 95, 143, 167, 171 Mos 1:254 Mos 2:108, 154, 192 Decal 58, 93, 96 Spec 1:114, 275, 277, 314 Spec 2:42, 113, 115, 168, 175, 180 Spec 3:27, 89, 144 Virt 50, 112, 124, 201 Praem 24, 43, 95, 96 Prob 91 Aet 10, 76 Flacc 134 Legat 194, 279, 290 Prov 2:36 QG 1:70:1, 100:1a, 2:11, 3:21, 4:202a QE 2:14

ὁσιότης (72) Opif 155, 172 Cher 94 Sacr 10, 27, 37, 57 Det 21 Post 37 Deus 103 Agr 54 Plant 35, 77 Ebr 91, 92, 109 Conf 131 Migr 194 Her 123 Congr 98 Somn 2:186 Abr 172, 198, 208 Mos 1:190, 198, 307 Mos 2:136, 142, 161, 167, 171, 216, 270, 274 Decal 110, 119 Spec 1:30, 52, 54, 55, 70, 154, 186, 248, 271, 304 Spec 2:12, 63, 224, 259 Spec 3:127 Spec 4:127, 135 Virt 34, 42, 47, 51, 76 Praem 66, 104, 160, 166 Prob 75, 83 Flacc 49 Legat 30, 242 Hypoth 6:8, 11:1 QE isf 13, 14

ὁσιόω Mos 2:17 Spec 1:203 Legat 157, 308

ὀσμή (22) Leg 3:235 Cher 117 Sacr 23, 44 Post 161, 161 Plant 133 Ebr 106, 190, 191 Conf 52 Migr 188 Congr 115 Fug 191 Somn 1:47, 48, 49, 51 Mos 1:105 Prob 15 Contempl 53 Prov 2:71

ὅσος (ὅσοσπερ) (937) Opif 10, 10, 15, 16, 22, 29, 30, 31, 32, 38, 40, 62, 78, 80, 83, 84, 87, 113, 116, 116, 128, 135, 140, 142, 147, 151, 154, 159, 162, 164 Leg 1:1, 5, 6, 6, 16, 57 Leg 2:2, 10, 33, 41, 63, 69, 75, 75, 76, 104 Leg 3:46, 77, 78, 118, 156, 171, 175, 177, 178, 211, 215, 221, 234, 245, 245, 251 Cher 57, 66, 67, 75, 78, 80, 81, 91, 96, 104, 107, 113, 117 Sacr 6, 7, 21, 22, 29, 30, 31, 38, 47, 49, 55, 70, 72, 84, 89, 104, 104, 106, 106, 109, 109, 111, 113, 115, 116, 123, 124, 132, 135, 139 Det 2, 5, 15, 21, 33, 64, 76, 85, 87, 88, 91, 100, 102, 102, 103, 105, 105, 107, 109, 114, 116, 122, 147, 148, 152, 157, 165 Post 4, 9, 9, 19, 32, 42, 42, 50, 50, 61, 81, 91, 105, 105, 108, 112, 112, 117, 118, 141, 141, 141, 142, 142, 142, 148, 151, 152, 152, 157, 163, 165, 169, 181 Gig 2, 9, 10, 15, 15, 18, 31, 38, 48, 48, 58, 60 Deus 4, 4, 15, 19, 42, 59, 60, 71, 71, 72, 102, 104, 131, 146, 150, 157, 163, 167, 169 Agr 6, 6, 8, 10, 13, 25, 39, 51, 60, 71, 72, 87, 101, 103, 119, 123, 123, 130, 136, 140, 141, 141, 145, 146, 156, 171 Plant 1, 30, 56, 57, 65, 66, 68, 74, 80, 83, 127, 127, 141, 159, 159, 159 Ebr 9, 18, 18, 23, 31, 33, 36, 62, 69, 69, 75, 87, 91, 99, 124, 131, 144, 155, 158, 187, 187, 190, 194, 201, 202, 218, 219 Sobr 1, 2, 3, 5, 12, 30, 30, 36, 38, 43, 61, 62, 67 Conf 1, 6, 15, 15, 21, 21, 47, 52, 58, 68, 69, 86, 90, 95, 126, 141, 157, 162, 165, 167 Migr 4, 16, 18, 33, 42, 55, 88, 91, 97, 110, 115, 119, 119, 121, 121, 123, 135, 138, 141, 160, 172, 190, 190, 191, 211, 219 Her 21, 29, 33, 51, 89, 109, 110, 136, 146, 152, 154, 158, 159, 207, 239, 239, 240, 245, 290, 294, 295, 296 Congr 15, 64, 74, 95, 98, 129, 129, 156, 165, 172 Fug 65, 67, 85, 86, 146, 152, 161, 165, 195 Mut 4, 4, 9, 18, 20, 60, 61, 78, 107, 174, 187, 199, 221, 230, 243 Somn 1:3, 6, 27, 27, 55, 68, 90, 124, 124, 132, 138, 149, 157, 165, 165, 176, 178, 179, 188, 189, 205, 218, 227, 236, 238, 243, 248 Somn 2:55, 77, 78, 79, 81, 81, 83, 84, 86, 88, 97, 97, 100, 122, 125,

132, 155, 176, 178, 192, 196, 196, 215, 266 Abr 1, 13, 31, 43, 45, 57, 58, 67, 70, 79, 98, 103, 115, 115, 131, 133, 133, 139, 147, 163, 167, 167, 170, 173, 175, 194, 199, 203, 219, 220, 221, 221, 224, 224, 236, 263, 267 Ios 5, 9, 10, 22, 30, 32, 43, 58, 64, 70, 81, 81, 104, 107, 116, 119, 130, 142, 142, 147, 158, 170, 173, 180, 185, 194, 206, 207, 234, 242, 257, 258, 258 Mos 1:9, 30, 32, 38, 41, 51, 59, 63, 81, 92, 102, 118, 121, 122, 133, 147, 155, 157, 159, 168, 168, 196, 209, 216, 225, 228, 248, 263, 275, 291, 305, 309, 317, 334 Mos 2:6, 12, 22, 23, 30, 34, 53, 60, 68, 73, 88, 94, 136, 140, 146, 165, 167, 167, 168, 185, 187, 188, 194, 196, 211, 218, 221, 223, 235, 238 Decal 7, 8, 36, 47, 49, 57, 60, 66, 80, 82, 100, 110, 118, 128, 133, 136, 156, 156, 157, 162 Spec 1:11, 13, 21, 24, 36, 38, 43, 43, 47, 52, 65, 69, 76, 83, 92, 100, 125, 135, 139, 141, 145, 150, 150, 153, 162, 164, 166, 166, 174, 181, 189, 218, 249, 259, 262, 275, 275, 286, 300, 304, 318, 323, 327, 340, 342 Spec 2:12, 44, 48, 57, 88, 102, 105, 108, 109, 117, 121, 122, 151, 153, 160, 166, 169, 170, 174, 177, 181, 183, 187, 193, 197, 205, 211, 213, 218, 225, 228, 242, 250, 255 Spec 3:3, 6, 7, 19, 35, 36, 41, 74, 95, 103, 103, 111, 111, 115, 118, 124, 130, 142, 149, 155, 168, 175, 183, 186, 198, 206, 208 Spec 4:1, 13, 26, 48, 49, 75, 80, 82, 84, 85, 86, 88, 100, 103, 109, 111, 113, 113, 116, 152, 170, 173, 186, 193, 196, 204, 209, 223, 229, 234, 237, 237 Virt 1, 2, 5, 5, 15, 16, 17, 19, 30, 37, 43, 61, 61, 91, 99, 104, 130, 130, 132, 137, 141, 147, 148, 149, 156, 160, 168, 169, 179, 180, 191, 203, 203, 205 Praem 3, 6, 9, 26, 28, 39, 44, 70, 89, 109, 116, 129, 129, 131, 141, 141, 144, 148, 150, 163 Prob 3, 4, 5, 22, 23, 31, 32, 33, 38, 45, 50, 55, 56, 76, 76, 78, 80, 82, 84, 86, 96, 98, 118, 150, 156, 160 Contempl 25, 54 Aet 3, 3, 15, 26, 28, 36, 37, 50, 58, 63, 64, 77, 83, 91, 96, 96, 99, 100, 104, 122, 126, 129, 130, 135, 138, 138 Flacc 1, 2, 4, 56, 63, 72, 76, 76, 79, 85, 90, 94, 96, 97, 99, 100, 123, 130, 148, 156, 160, 163, 163, 170, 170, 171, 171 Legat 6, 10, 14, 17, 19, 33, 38, 43, 43, 49, 51, 71, 73, 89, 118, 125, 134, 150, 153, 164, 167, 173, 175, 180, 181, 190, 193, 201, 204, 213, 214, 233, 246, 249, 259, 259, 269, 278, 296, 297, 297, 333 Hypoth 6:3, 7:6, 7:7, 11:4, 11:6, 11:16 Prov 2:2, 8, 14, 17, 18, 21, 41, 45, 47, 53, 57, 59 QG 3:3, 52, 4:51a, 51b, 148, 172, 173, 200c QG (Par) 2:4, 2:4, 2:7 QE 2:4, 4, 16, 71 QE isf 5, 16, 33

ὅσπερ (331) Opif 6, 21, 41, 53, 58, 75, 96, 97, 97, 132, 139, 141, 154, 167 Leg 1:58, 58, 74, 80 Leg 2:3, 4, 86 Leg 3:3, 24, 37, 81, 100, 119, 128, 130, 148, 185, 186, 197, 204, 205, 207, 230, 247, 253 Cher 4, 7, 13 Sacr 33, 74, 78, 104, 106, 109, 114, 136 Det 74, 78, 155, 156, 169, 170, 171 Post 18, 25, 45, 48, 53, 94, 95, 137 Gig 27 Deus 16, 25, 72, 88, 90, 118, 127, 144 Agr 4, 134 Plant 10, 13, 22, 24, 43, 56, 97, 108, 155 Ebr 19, 80, 153, 176, 191 Conf 6, 23, 30, 49, 75, 143, 145, 173, 175, 189 Migr 12, 39, 55, 108, 108, 124, 125, 130, 160, 187 Her 64, 72, 74, 92, 132, 136, 189, 222, 263, 273, 274 Congr 153, 162 Fug 47, 76, 155, 189, 204 Mut 5, 42, 49, 223, 261, 267, 270 Somn 1:45, 80, 98, 110, 153 Somn 2:25, 40, 43, 112, 168, 190, 233, 252, 258, 278 Abr 6, 9, 44, 46, 57, 78, 103, 104, 104, 205, 228, 235, 261, 262, 266 Ios 4, 49, 52, 91, 124, 142, 150, 227 Mos 1:5, 119, 138, 149, 178, 189, 191, 218, 236, 281, 298 Mos 2:38, 39, 50, 63, 70, 80, 82, 82, 96, 101, 106, 136, 141, 152, 177, 212, 212, 233, 261, 263, 275 Decal 17, 18, 47, 52, 80, 175 Spec 1:4, 41, 97, 111, 127, 138, 159, 171, 191, 193, 201, 201, 208, 253, 254, 288, 332, 333 Spec 2:11, 35, 73, 104, 144, 189, 219, 224, 225, 228, 235, 238, 255 Spec 3:7, 19, 24, 29, 58, 59, 102, 172, 189 Spec 4:16, 65, 67, 68, 68, 186, 188 Virt 32, 54, 65, 147, 154, 178, 197, 209, 217, 223 Praem 2, 43, 53, 70, 97, 111, 158 Prob 30, 77, 140, 140 Contempl 22, 43, 53, 65 Aet 22, 43, 69, 73, 78, 78, 86 Flacc 41, 82, 96, 139 Legat 10, 69, 69, 113, 118, 120, 160, 187, 200, 201, 202, 214, 245, 262, 303, 332 Hypoth 6:4, 11:14 Prov 2:16, 26, 37, 39, 71 QG 1:74, 74, 2:64b, 68b, 68b, 71b, 4:33a, 172 QE 2:16, 17, 47, 47 QE isf 3, 15

Ὄσσα Conf 4, 4, 4

ὀστέον (14) Leg 2:22, 40, 40, 41, 41, 41, 42, 42 Leg 3:115 Migr 17 Somn 2:109 Spec 1:146 Contempl 55 QG (Par) 2:3

ὅστις (ὁστισοῦν) (174) Opif 20, 47, 72, 77, 91, 96, 130, 152 Leg 1:64, 99 Leg 2:36, 69 Leg 3:17, 49, 73, 74, 100, 103, 198, 200 Cher 9, 36, 65 Det 38, 45, 147 Post 44, 66, 67, 67, 67, 67, 79, 134, 152 Gig 25, 61 Deus 25, 108, 112, 150, 167 Agr 12, 39, 54, 105 Plant 81 Ebr 46, 104, 119, 146, 188, 192, 223 Sobr 64 Conf 32, 64, 72, 91, 102, 156 Migr 14, 42, 95, 120, 137, 138, 145, 171, 194, 195, 217 Her 97, 116, 235, 240, 295 Congr 13, 24, 176 Fug 45, 194 Mut 131, 134, 185 Somn 1:44, 57, 106, 188, 244 Somn 2:83 Abr 58, 127, 216, 219 Ios 104, 172, 197 Mos 1:2, 162, 281, 289 Mos 2:9, 22, 128, 200, 246 Decal 28, 95, 103 Spec 1:119, 148, 224, 270, 277, 281, 327 Spec 2:9, 16, 21, 21, 41, 100, 123, 149, 162, 176, 177, 197, 259 Spec 3:121, 130, 187, 209 Spec 4:14, 44, 71, 100, 140, 147, 154, 177, 237 Virt 198 Praem 30, 105, 142, 169 Prob 23, 47, 97, 146 Contempl 31, 90 Aet 33, 89 Flacc 95, 155 Legat 44, 85, 135, 220, 341 Hypoth 6:8, 7:14, 7:20, 11:7 QG 1:51, 2:22, 34a, 59, 64c QG (Par) 2:3 QE 2:24b

ὀστρακόδερμος Her 211 QE isf 15

ὄστρακον Somn 2:57

ὄστρεον Opif 147 Ios 71 Virt 76 Prob 66 QE isf 15

ὀσφραίνομαι (23) Leg 3:56, 111, 173, 216 Cher 57, 62, 73 Sacr 24 Post 126 Plant 83 Conf 123, 194 Congr 96, 115, 115, 143 Mut 157, 256 Somn 1:48, 49, 55 Abr 238 Decal 74

ὄσφρησις (34) Opif 62, 62, 165 Leg 2:7, 39, 74 Leg 3:44, 56, 58 Sacr 44, 73 Det 168, 173 Plant 29 Conf 19, 90 Migr 137 Her 48, 185, 232 Fug 182 Mut 111, 164 Somn 1:27, 55, 80 Abr 148, 149, 236, 241, 266 Spec 1:337 QG (Par) 2:3 QE isf 21

ὀσφῦς Leg 3:154 Sacr 63 QE 1:19

ὅταν (476) Opif 31, 46, 67, 96, 109, 110, 125 Leg 1:3, 16, 16, 18, 26, 33, 34, 49, 61, 61, 72, 72, 73, 81, 82, 90, 99, 99, 107 Leg 2:16, 25, 25, 25, 26, 26, 26, 27, 28, 29, 31, 37, 47, 49, 50, 50, 59, 60, 60, 63, 66, 78, 79, 99 Leg 3:43, 43, 44, 44, 45, 45, 49, 54, 60, 66, 71, 71, 74, 74, 74, 84, 86, 86, 89, 105, 106, 110, 111, 112, 114, 114, 117, 118, 122, 125, 125, 125, 137, 159, 169, 172, 174, 183, 184, 186, 186, 186, 193, 195, 196, 211, 212, 224, 225, 238, 245, 249 Cher 7, 9, 13, 14, 15, 38, 38, 50, 57, 58, 115, 118 Sacr 3, 12, 14, 14, 16, 55, 66, 71, 78, 79, 81, 83, 87, 90, 91, 105, 105, 107, 124, 125, 134 Det 3, 10, 12, 16, 16, 32, 56, 73, 90, 93, 94, 95, 95, 97, 110, 110, 117, 117, 123, 129, 131, 131, 141, 143, 143, 143, 143, 159, 162, 162 Post 15, 18, 22, 30, 30, 47, 53, 68, 74, 120, 125, 148, 149, 176, 180 Gig 35, 43, 43, 46, 57, 63 Deus 3, 14, 39, 92, 119, 120, 126, 135, 136, 137, 170, 182 Agr 16, 33, 37, 59, 66,

69, 70, 70, 76, 89, 99, 147, 148, 164 Plant 95, 96, 98, 157 Ebr 41, 43, 44, 90, 99, 116, 116, 116, 137, 138, 162 Sobr 6, 12, 12, 13, 18, 30 Conf 3, 15, 16, 17, 33, 35, 38, 46, 60, 60, 90, 131, 188 Migr 3, 67, 77, 77, 79, 84, 118, 118, 123, 123, 128, 139, 150, 156, 160, 160, 172, 172, 191, 201, 202, 209 Her 6, 7, 46, 51, 84, 150, 162, 184, 192, 238, 264, 264, 269, 285, 310 Congr 56, 82, 113, 180 Fug 26, 142, 175, 181, 189, 191, 207 Mut 6, 6, 21, 34, 103, 218 Somn 1:5, 42, 68, 72, 72, 79, 84, 84, 86, 115, 115, 116, 122, 129, 203, 216, 238 Somn 2:21, 23, 62, 70, 75, 76, 91, 104, 133, 150, 154, 177, 188, 189, 231, 232, 257, 257, 265, 267, 272 Abr 30, 59, 105, 122, 122, 160, 232, 240, 240 Ios 59, 70, 82, 82, 124, 149, 227 Mos 1:26, 26, 69, 111, 202, 327, 332 Mos 2:133, 198, 256 Decal 14, 31, 37, 77, 95, 95, 114, 129, 140, 144, 145, 150 Spec 1:47, 147, 178, 186, 189, 210, 231, 237, 248, 266 Spec 2:76, 84, 98, 122, 122, 190, 207 Spec 3:9, 63, 72, 99, 114, 115, 133 Spec 4:24, 31, 81, 107, 120, 161, 172, 172, 190, 207 Virt 23, 30, 30, 158, 161, 164, 184, 184, 192 Praem 26, 29, 63, 87, 115, 129, 129, 136, 147, 157, 159, 165, 171, 172 Prob 14, 140, 148 Contempl 18, 40, 53, 55, 81, 85 Aet 20, 20, 113, 135, 147, 147 Flacc 17, 58, 79, 137 Legat 45, 72, 114, 126, 126, 221, 355, 360 Hypoth 11:15 Prov 2:12, 40, 40, 59 QG 1:55c, 89, 2:10, 26a QG isf 8, 9, 9 QE 1:1, 2:3b, 47 QE isf 7

ὅτε (222) Opif 17, 46, 63, 80, 84, 85, 104, 113, 129, 168 Leg 1:10, 19, 20, 75, 75, 75, 75, 96, 101, 101, 108 Leg 2:10, 31, 37, 45, 54, 66, 69, 70, 70, 77, 84, 85, 95 Leg 3:2, 12, 18, 18, 70, 87, 103, 142, 183, 186, 189, 210, 223, 223, 227, 244 Cher 14, 36, 45, 58, 70, 115 Sacr 5, 9, 65, 68, 81, 130 Det 23, 66, 76, 96, 96 Post 25, 65, 77, 89, 148, 155 Gig 20, 39 Deus 4, 28, 74, 89, 101, 134, 140, 178, 181 Agr 24, 47, 151 Plant 59, 93, 105 Ebr 2, 183, 190 Sobr 45, 45, 54 Conf 115, 150 Migr 6, 34, 35, 141, 154, 176 Her 30, 77, 84, 84, 186 Congr 78, 124 Fug 156 Mut 116, 185, 193, 241 Somn 1:10, 47, 60, 84, 107, 192, 214 Somn 2:12, 25, 83, 148, 154, 161, 226, 239 Abr 77, 212 Ios 74, 115, 248, 248 Mos 1:50, 178, 197 Mos 2:64, 70, 275, 275 Decal 39, 58, 117, 125 Spec 1:26, 26, 103, 123, 252, 266, 300, 323 Spec 2:16, 20, 20, 25, 97, 107, 119, 207, 220 Spec 3:1, 4, 11, 105, 158, 162, 200 Spec 4:5, 16, 80, 152, 184 Virt 10, 64, 152, 157, 162 Praem 33, 68, 91, 103 Prob 6, 35 Contempl 41, 73, 89 Aet 13, 103, 103 Flacc 15, 130, 131, 167 Legat 14, 18, 42, 52, 79, 130, 143, 156, 158, 180, 262, 299, 356, 356 Hypoth 7:9 Prov 2:44, 49 QG 1:1, 1, 3:21, 21, 22 QE 2:13a, 18

ὅτι (ὅτιπερ) (1601) Opif 8, 8, 16, 25, 25, 30, 32, 36, 41, 45, 46, 51, 51, 52, 53, 59, 65, 73, 73, 75, 77, 79, 87, 90, 98, 98, 130, 132, 134, 134, 139, 144, 149, 149, 149, 157, 157, 157, 160, 166, 168, 170, 171, 171, 171, 171, 172, 172, 172, 172 Leg 1:1, 2, 2, 3, 3, 3, 7, 9, 15, 17, 18, 18, 18, 28, 34, 34, 39, 41, 43, 45, 48, 49, 52, 53, 57, 58, 60, 60, 61, 70, 71, 71, 75, 81, 82, 82, 86, 86, 87, 91, 92, 99, 100, 102, 105, 107 Leg 2:1, 2, 5, 7, 7, 7, 11, 11, 11, 13, 15, 15, 16, 19, 22, 31, 34, 38, 38, 40, 40, 44, 44, 46, 46, 47, 47, 50, 52, 55, 60, 60, 62, 67, 68, 68, 69, 72, 75, 75, 78, 78, 78, 78, 79, 79, 82, 82, 83, 83, 84, 85, 89, 89, 89, 100, 102, 103, 103, 103, 103, 107 Leg 3:1, 2, 9, 16, 16, 18, 19, 20, 21, 27, 27, 30, 32, 36, 36, 36, 37, 38, 40, 45, 46, 47, 49, 50, 51, 51, 54, 55, 57, 57, 58, 58, 59, 59, 61, 63, 65, 66, 66, 67, 67, 73, 73, 75, 76, 77, 78, 78, 79, 82, 83, 85, 86, 88, 91, 94, 95, 97, 99, 103, 105, 105, 106, 113, 113, 121, 121, 121, 121, 121, 121, 121, 134, 134, 136, 136, 136, 145, 146, 147, 148, 152, 157, 162, 162, 174, 176, 179, 180, 183, 184, 184, 186, 186, 187, 188, 190, 193, 196, 203, 204, 206, 206, 206, 206, 207, 214, 218, 222, 225, 228, 229, 229, 229, 243, 243, 244, 247, 249, 249, 252, 253 Cher 5, 9, 9, 12, 16, 18, 28, 31, 32, 32, 36, 39, 46, 49, 49, 53, 54, 54, 63, 67, 74, 75, 83, 84, 108, 117, 118, 119, 119, 121, 125, 130 Sacr 8, 18, 19, 20, 30, 32, 34, 34, 42, 48, 60, 64, 67, 92, 95, 95, 100, 112, 119, 121, 127, 128, 128, 129, 129, 130, 134, 134, 136, 137 Det 3, 4, 4, 6, 6, 15, 15, 17, 22, 27, 28, 32, 38, 38, 40, 47, 47, 50, 51, 51, 56, 58, 59, 62, 66, 68, 68, 69, 74, 78, 80, 80, 83, 84, 89, 95, 96, 101, 102, 102, 103, 104, 105, 112, 114, 114, 126, 126, 129, 132, 138, 138, 139, 139, 142, 151, 158, 158, 159, 159, 159, 162, 165, 166, 166, 177, 178 Post 7, 13, 15, 15, 16, 18, 19, 20, 22, 24, 24, 26, 27, 28, 28, 29, 30, 32, 35, 38, 41, 51, 54, 55, 59, 63, 64, 69, 71, 71, 71, 72, 81, 90, 95, 102, 116, 119, 133, 137, 138, 142, 143, 143, 157, 158, 159, 164, 166, 167, 168, 168, 169, 176, 180, 183, 183 Gig 3, 6, 8, 23, 24, 33, 42, 48, 52, 52, 52, 56, 56, 59, 60, 66, 67 Deus 7, 16, 20, 20, 21, 21, 26, 30, 33, 48, 49, 50, 51, 51, 53, 53, 56, 62, 62, 70, 70, 71, 72, 72, 72, 95, 99, 104, 104, 107, 108, 109, 109, 122, 123, 123, 125, 128, 131, 133, 140, 141, 167 Agr 5, 19, 22, 35, 38, 43, 63, 64, 78, 84, 85, 121, 129, 129, 131, 139, 145, 145, 145, 156, 157, 157, 160, 160, 160, 168, 175, 179, 181 Plant 7, 8, 21, 42, 44, 48, 63, 67, 67, 71, 80, 91, 113, 123, 123, 123, 125, 130, 133, 134, 137, 140, 145, 149, 149, 150, 151, 154, 157, 160, 160, 162, 163, 165, 165, 166, 167, 168, 170, 172, 174, 174, 177 Ebr 9, 16, 19, 19, 25, 37, 40, 41, 42, 54, 56, 68, 73, 76, 82, 88, 94, 95, 96, 100, 101, 104, 117, 140, 141, 186, 189, 191, 197, 203, 208, 211, 212, 213 Sobr 17, 17, 19, 21, 22, 23, 25, 26, 44, 47, 49, 50, 50, 52, 62 Conf 1, 24, 25, 26, 57, 57, 62, 70, 75, 76, 81, 91, 93, 98, 98, 100, 119, 120, 127, 135, 136, 136, 141, 141, 142, 144, 147, 156, 156, 161, 161, 167, 167, 170, 180, 181, 194, 195, 196, 197 Migr 3, 3, 5, 15, 18, 20, 22, 36, 42, 42, 44, 44, 46, 46, 47, 47, 56, 57, 57, 60, 62, 64, 65, 75, 78, 81, 85, 91, 92, 92, 94, 95, 99, 104, 118, 122, 127, 130, 130, 135, 140, 144, 152, 155, 160, 173, 177, 186, 197, 199, 201, 205, 213, 223, 225 Her 20, 20, 22, 36, 50, 51, 53, 59, 61, 71, 76, 92, 95, 100, 101, 101, 101, 103, 118, 152, 155, 156, 162, 166, 169, 177, 182, 191, 207, 217, 217, 218, 219, 221, 222, 223, 226, 227, 243, 243, 251, 252, 252, 258, 267, 267, 268, 284, 286, 300, 301, 307, 312, 315 Congr 11, 13, 19, 25, 35, 42, 54, 62, 73, 78, 83, 90, 96, 96, 113, 123, 125, 133, 139, 139, 140, 146, 147, 154, 157, 161, 170, 172 Fug 1, 2, 7, 11, 14, 27, 54, 55, 59, 61, 63, 70, 74, 75, 82, 82, 84, 90, 93, 97, 99, 111, 116, 139, 140, 140, 153, 158, 161, 163, 168, 172, 187, 196, 198, 204, 204, 208 Mut 11, 11, 18, 21, 21, 27, 32, 37, 46, 46, 53, 54, 56, 57, 60, 64, 68, 80, 81, 83, 88, 90, 94, 102, 117, 118, 126, 132, 134, 137, 143, 143, 145, 147, 147, 148, 148, 151, 167, 167, 171, 171, 177, 181, 188, 194, 206, 234, 236, 246, 250, 255, 259, 270 Somn 1:3, 12, 13, 15, 17, 17, 18, 20, 21, 21, 21, 24, 26, 26, 26, 27, 27, 27, 28, 29, 29, 29, 29, 39, 46, 47, 48, 52, 61, 74, 77, 82, 83, 91, 91, 100, 115, 120, 126, 127, 130, 142, 143, 145, 158, 158, 159, 172, 175, 183, 184, 184, 185, 186, 187, 190, 194, 195, 205, 211, 218, 220, 228, 230, 231, 233, 236, 238, 240, 241, 249, 252 Somn 2:5, 15, 21, 24, 30, 45, 52, 62, 67, 69, 69, 69, 70, 78, 83, 96, 98, 99, 100, 103, 104, 107, 114, 115, 116, 122, 122, 136, 147, 162, 164, 169, 177, 183, 217, 219, 224, 224, 227, 227, 228, 229, 229, 231, 235, 244, 246, 249, 253, 254, 256, 260, 284, 291, 291 Abr

5, 5, 8, 9, 13, 17, 24, 26, 28, 28, 31, 31, 32, 35, 36, 36, 37, 37, 53, 56, 75, 77, 80, 80, 88, 118, 130, 131, 142, 158, 164, 164, 165, 181, 191, 202, 204, 215, 241, 258, 262, 269, 275 Ios 10, 18, 22, 22, 30, 48, 52, 52, 57, 59, 66, 66, 67, 71, 74, 76, 76, 125, 143, 145, 155, 189, 199, 216, 216, 216, 221, 222, 225, 244, 251, 253 Mos 1:15, 66, 75, 76, 76, 110, 112, 122, 160, 161, 192, 212, 217, 236, 245, 248, 255, 287, 311, 313, 328, 329 Mos 2:7, 8, 12, 37, 38, 58, 139, 147, 150, 154, 164, 181, 181, 183, 186, 187, 192, 199, 210, 210, 218, 219, 220, 220, 241, 244, 244, 265, 268, 279, 285 Decal 2, 10, 13, 18, 37, 39, 47, 69, 89, 90, 91, 104, 154, 155 Spec 1:17, 18, 22, 25, 30, 30, 31, 33, 41, 45, 46, 51, 51, 56, 57, 62, 64, 74, 74, 74, 89, 89, 90, 109, 111, 111, 126, 127, 128, 129, 142, 151, 176, 178, 191, 208, 216, 220, 221, 222, 230, 239, 242, 242, 245, 245, 253, 265, 274, 275, 279, 290, 302, 307, 311, 311, 313, 313, 318, 322, 337 Spec 2:11, 14, 29, 29, 34, 34, 34, 36, 55, 55, 64, 84, 113, 113, 129, 132, 133, 139, 140, 140, 141, 142, 153, 159, 163, 166, 166, 168, 169, 170, 171, 186, 189, 203, 214, 225, 225, 228, 260 Spec 3:6, 8, 21, 39, 49, 49, 49, 80, 81, 81, 104, 108, 113, 128, 144, 145, 159, 159, 165, 180, 189, 189, 193, 195, 195, 198, 199, 204 Spec 4:5, 5, 5, 25, 27, 38, 53, 54, 54, 60, 66, 71, 73, 100, 105, 109, 109, 123, 127, 133, 137, 169, 178, 178, 182, 194, 217, 224, 232 Virt 17, 27, 34, 50, 54, 61, 67, 77, 83, 88, 88, 106, 114, 116, 116, 133, 147, 152, 165, 172, 172, 172, 183, 198, 208, 214, 226, 226 Praem 23, 39, 40, 42, 42, 44, 49, 72, 83, 88, 88, 95, 101, 101, 111, 119, 119, 152, 152, 161, 161, 166, 170 Prob 1, 21, 22, 23, 24, 32, 51, 54, 54, 59, 60, 60, 61, 62, 63, 87, 97, 100, 114, 124, 127, 128, 136, 136, 152 Contempl 1, 14, 38, 66, 73 Aet 11, 15, 16, 17, 17, 18, 19, 22, 26, 35, 37, 40, 45, 48, 51, 52, 53, 57, 58, 69, 71, 75, 78, 78, 78, 79, 82, 84, 89, 90, 92, 93, 94, 94, 99, 112, 129, 130, 130, 132, 133 Flacc 5, 40, 43, 43, 45, 48, 48, 72, 81, 89, 89, 126, 138, 139, 146, 174, 175, 179, 183, 186 Legat 7, 15, 30, 58, 61, 71, 80, 85, 99, 99, 114, 133, 140, 149, 149, 149, 153, 153, 157, 160, 172, 173, 198, 216, 219, 264, 280, 286, 289, 303, 310, 317, 318, 348, 349, 353, 362, 367 Prov 1, 2:1, 10, 12, 17, 17, 17, 25, 26, 34 QG 1:17b, 31, 60:2, 62:1, 66, 73, 94, 96:1, 2:5a, 11, 11, 11, 12b, 13b, 15b, 16, 16, 34a, 34a, 54a, 54a, 59, 59, 59, 59, 65, 3:29, 52, 4:33b, 43, 51a, 51b, 52a, 52d, 86a, 88, 145, 167, 172, 180, 189, 191b, 193, 198, 211, 228 QG isf 3, 3, 5, 5, 5 QG (Par) 2:2, 2:3, 2:5, 2:6, 2:7 QE 2:2, 10b, 18, 28, 46, 46, 47, 49a, 105 QE isf 3, 16, 16, 21

οὗ (15) Opif 163 Leg 1:66, 67, 77, 77, 77 Leg 2:84, 84, 86 Det 3 Fug 53, 75 Somn 1:62, 189 Legat 315

οὐ (καί) (4780) Opif 5, 6, 11, 12, 13, 13, 16, 17, 20, 20, 21, 23, 23, 25, 26, 26, 26, 31, 33, 35, 41, 41, 41, 41, 42, 43, 45, 45, 46, 47, 54, 56, 57, 58, 61, 63, 63, 66, 71, 72, 72, 72, 72, 74, 78, 78, 79, 79, 80, 84, 87, 89, 90, 90, 91, 95, 97, 99, 99, 100, 104, 105, 107, 111, 113, 126, 128, 129, 129, 131, 131, 132, 133, 133, 137, 139, 139, 141, 142, 144, 149, 151, 153, 153, 155, 155, 156, 157, 158, 158, 159, 159, 165, 166, 171, 171 Leg 1:2, 3, 4, 6, 6, 6, 8, 9, 18, 18, 20, 21, 21, 23, 24, 25, 25, 26, 26, 26, 27, 27, 27, 31, 31, 32, 33, 33, 36, 36, 38, 39, 40, 41, 41, 42, 43, 46, 48, 48, 49, 51, 51, 51, 51, 51, 51, 51, 52, 54, 55, 57, 57, 60, 60, 61, 62, 62, 65, 67, 68, 70, 76, 77, 77, 78, 78, 80, 82, 82, 85, 86, 89, 90, 90, 90, 91, 91, 91, 91, 91, 92, 92, 92, 94, 99, 100, 100, 100, 100, 100, 101, 101, 101, 103, 103, 103, 104, 105, 105, 106, 106, 107 Leg 2:1, 1, 1, 2, 2, 10, 11, 12, 13, 15, 18, 20, 20, 26, 31, 31, 34, 34, 35, 40, 41, 44, 45, 46, 46, 48, 50, 51, 51, 52, 53, 56, 57, 57, 58, 59, 60, 60, 65, 66, 68, 68, 68, 68, 68, 69, 69, 69, 69, 70, 75, 76, 77, 78, 78, 79, 79, 80, 80, 82, 84, 84, 84, 85, 85, 86, 87, 88, 91, 96, 100, 100, 103, 104, 107 Leg 3:2, 4, 4, 4, 5, 6, 9, 9, 10, 10, 10, 14, 14, 15, 15, 15, 15, 18, 20, 21, 21, 22, 23, 25, 26, 26, 26, 27, 27, 32, 32, 33, 35, 35, 36, 36, 40, 40, 42, 43, 46, 46, 46, 47, 49, 50, 50, 50, 50, 51, 51, 51, 51, 51, 54, 55, 55, 56, 56, 57, 57, 58, 58, 58, 58, 58, 59, 59, 61, 61, 61, 64, 64, 66, 67, 67, 68, 68, 69, 70, 70, 71, 73, 73, 73, 74, 74, 76, 78, 80, 81, 81, 82, 82, 82, 84, 85, 85, 86, 86, 87, 87, 87, 89, 89, 90, 94, 98, 99, 100, 102, 103, 103, 105, 106, 109, 110, 112, 116, 116, 117, 119, 122, 123, 123, 124, 125, 128, 129, 130, 131, 134, 134, 136, 140, 140, 141, 142, 142, 142, 143, 143, 144, 145, 147, 149, 151, 152, 160, 160, 160, 160, 161, 162, 162, 162, 163, 167, 167, 167, 169, 170, 173, 173, 173, 174, 174, 175, 175, 175, 176, 177, 178, 179, 180, 181, 181, 182, 182, 183, 183, 183, 184, 185, 188, 190, 190, 191, 192, 193, 193, 194, 195, 198, 198, 203, 203, 205, 207, 208, 210, 210, 210, 210, 211, 211, 212, 213, 214, 214, 215, 216, 217, 217, 227, 227, 233, 234, 236, 238, 239, 240, 241, 241, 241, 242, 242, 242, 243, 243, 244, 246, 247, 249, 251, 252, 252, 253 Cher 1, 2, 3, 5, 8, 8, 12, 14, 14, 15, 16, 20, 23, 27, 31, 32, 33, 33, 35, 35, 36, 36, 36, 37, 40, 42, 43, 46, 48, 49, 49, 49, 50, 51, 52, 54, 55, 58, 58, 58, 58, 59, 59, 59, 63, 66, 67, 68, 69, 70, 71, 72, 77, 83, 85, 87, 87, 88, 95, 96, 96, 97, 104, 104, 107, 108, 108, 114, 114, 115, 116, 116, 116, 119, 119, 119, 120, 121, 123, 123, 124, 125, 126, 130 Sacr 3, 7, 8, 9, 9, 10, 12, 17, 19, 26, 26, 29, 30, 31, 33, 37, 37, 37, 38, 38, 38, 41, 42, 44, 44, 45, 46, 47, 47, 48, 48, 49, 52, 54, 55, 57, 60, 62, 62, 63, 64, 66, 68, 68, 69, 71, 72, 80, 80, 85, 86, 87, 88, 90, 90, 93, 94, 94, 97, 97, 97, 97, 98, 98, 98, 100, 100, 101, 101, 107, 110, 111, 112, 115, 116, 122, 124, 125, 130, 133, 134, 135, 136, 137, 138, 139 Det 2, 4, 4, 4, 4, 5, 7, 9, 10, 14, 15, 17, 20, 22, 25, 26, 28, 31, 31, 32, 33, 33, 33, 33, 33, 33, 33, 34, 35, 35, 37, 38, 38, 38, 38, 39, 40, 41, 41, 42, 46, 47, 50, 51, 51, 52, 55, 56, 57, 57, 58, 59, 60, 60, 61, 62, 62, 63, 63, 65, 65, 68, 69, 69, 73, 74, 74, 74, 77, 77, 78, 78, 78, 78, 81, 82, 83, 83, 84, 84, 87, 89, 90, 90, 92, 93, 95, 96, 97, 98, 101, 102, 102, 103, 104, 104, 105, 106, 107, 107, 109, 112, 116, 122, 124, 126, 137, 137, 138, 138, 139, 141, 141, 141, 143, 143, 143, 143, 143, 145, 145, 147, 148, 149, 151, 152, 155, 157, 158, 159, 160, 160, 161, 161, 161, 162, 162, 163, 165, 166, 166, 167, 170, 171, 176, 177, 178, 178 Post 3, 4, 7, 8, 9, 10, 13, 14, 19, 23, 24, 24, 25, 29, 30, 30, 30, 30, 33, 42, 50, 52, 54, 58, 66, 67, 67, 67, 67, 71, 72, 77, 78, 80, 81, 82, 84, 85, 87, 89, 89, 90, 93, 94, 95, 95, 95, 96, 96, 96, 101, 102, 109, 110, 111, 112, 112, 113, 113, 118, 119, 120, 126, 129, 132, 133, 134, 134, 135, 139, 141, 141, 141, 142, 143, 143, 144, 148, 149, 155, 157, 158, 163, 165, 166, 166, 167, 168, 168, 169, 169, 171, 172, 172, 176, 177, 180, 184 Gig 1, 3, 8, 9, 9, 10, 10, 10, 16, 17, 18, 19, 20, 27, 32, 33, 33, 35, 36, 36, 37, 38, 39, 45, 48, 51, 52, 53, 54, 56, 61, 66 Deus 3, 8, 11, 13, 16, 16, 16, 19, 24, 25, 26, 28, 28, 32, 39, 46, 47, 48, 49, 53, 54, 56, 57, 58, 58, 59, 62, 65, 65, 69, 72, 72, 73, 76, 76, 77, 82, 83, 90, 90, 92, 94, 94, 94, 94, 98, 102, 104, 104, 105, 105, 112, 113, 118, 121, 121, 122, 124, 128, 129, 131, 134, 135, 136, 138, 142, 145, 145, 145, 145, 145, 145, 146, 148, 152, 157, 158, 162, 165, 166, 166, 169, 170, 172, 175, 179, 181, 182 Agr 1, 1, 2, 3, 3, 3, 5, 6, 11, 12, 13,

13, 19, 21, 22, 22, 24, 25, 29, 38, 39, 43, 44, 44, 45, 46, 47, 50, 50, 54, 56, 59, 59, 60, 60, 64, 64, 67, 67, 76, 78, 81, 83, 84, 84, 84, 85, 88, 90, 90, 91, 91, 94, 95, 99, 100, 101, 103, 105, 107, 110, 115, 115, 118, 119, 120, 121, 125, 126, 127, 127, 128, 131, 131, 131, 132, 133, 136, 140, 141, 141, 142, 145, 145, 147, 148, 148, 148, 149, 150, 150, 152, 154, 154, 154, 154, 154, 157, 157, 158, 161, 162, 163, 165, 166, 169, 170, 173, 174, 175, 179, 179, 181 Plant 1, 4, 6, 7, 14, 17, 19, 22, 24, 25, 27, 27, 29, 29, 31, 33, 37, 39, 42, 43, 44, 49, 53, 54, 59, 62, 63, 63, 63, 65, 69, 70, 71, 71, 71, 73, 74, 76, 78, 80, 81, 89, 89, 95, 96, 97, 101, 101, 101, 102, 105, 108, 112, 113, 113, 113, 114, 114, 115, 119, 126, 126, 126, 128, 129, 130, 134, 135, 135, 138, 142, 145, 145, 146, 147, 147, 149, 153, 155, 159, 160, 161, 161, 164, 165, 165, 167, 167, 168, 168, 168, 168, 169, 172, 172, 173, 174, 174, 176, 176, 177, 177 Ebr 2, 4, 5, 6, 7, 8, 14, 14, 16, 19, 19, 25, 27, 28, 30, 40, 40, 42, 42, 42, 42, 45, 45, 47, 47, 49, 50, 51, 53, 54, 56, 58, 61, 61, 61, 65, 70, 70, 71, 72, 74, 76, 77, 77, 82, 84, 85, 93, 94, 95, 95, 96, 98, 100, 102, 104, 105, 106, 106, 106, 106, 106, 106, 106, 106, 106, 106, 106, 106, 106, 106, 106, 110, 112, 113, 114, 121, 122, 123, 123, 126, 127, 127, 128, 130, 131, 133, 135, 138, 138, 138, 142, 143, 144, 146, 147, 149, 151, 154, 155, 163, 166, 167, 171, 173, 173, 174, 176, 179, 181, 182, 183, 190, 190, 193, 195, 196, 198, 198, 200, 203, 203, 208, 208, 213, 215, 217, 217, 223, 223 Sobr 2, 2, 3, 6, 7, 8, 10, 10, 11, 16, 16, 20, 21, 25, 27, 31, 31, 31, 37, 38, 45, 49, 52, 54, 55, 56, 56, 57, 62, 63 Conf 1, 1, 3, 5, 10, 10, 11, 11, 12, 13, 14, 14, 16, 17, 22, 25, 25, 27, 28, 28, 32, 36, 36, 37, 38, 39, 41, 41, 43, 44, 45, 45, 46, 49, 50, 52, 55, 55, 61, 65, 67, 70, 72, 75, 75, 76, 80, 82, 82, 83, 89, 91, 93, 98, 98, 100, 102, 103, 104, 107, 110, 114, 114, 114, 114, 115, 116, 118, 119, 119, 122, 124, 126, 126, 126, 127, 132, 135, 136, 137, 140, 140, 141, 141, 142, 142, 142, 144, 145, 149, 150, 152, 152, 153, 154, 155, 155, 155, 155, 158, 158, 158, 159, 160, 161, 162, 162, 166, 166, 168, 169, 170, 170, 171, 173, 174, 177, 179, 182, 183, 185, 185, 188, 190, 191, 191, 192, 194, 194, 194, 194 Migr 5, 5, 5, 7, 11, 18, 20, 20, 23, 25, 26, 34, 37, 40, 41, 42, 42, 42, 43, 43, 43, 44, 46, 46, 47, 47, 47, 48, 49, 50, 51, 52, 55, 60, 61, 62, 64, 64, 66, 68, 70, 72, 73, 74, 76, 78, 80, 83, 83, 86, 88, 94, 97, 100, 105, 106, 107, 110, 110, 111, 111, 112, 113, 113, 115, 122, 124, 126, 131, 131, 134, 140, 140, 140, 140, 140, 141, 142, 148, 149, 155, 162, 163, 171, 172, 173, 174, 174, 178, 182, 186, 189, 192, 192, 192, 193, 193, 196, 197, 200, 201, 205, 206, 206, 206, 206, 218, 219, 220, 223, 224, 225 Her 2, 3, 4, 6, 10, 11, 12, 12, 12, 13, 14, 15, 16, 17, 17, 19, 20, 21, 23, 24, 26, 26, 26, 26, 27, 28, 28, 31, 31, 32, 32, 39, 39, 40, 41, 42, 42, 43, 43, 44, 44, 44, 45, 48, 48, 48, 48, 48, 49, 51, 51, 58, 59, 61, 62, 62, 64, 65, 66, 68, 72, 77, 78, 81, 82, 84, 84, 84, 86, 86, 88, 90, 92, 95, 95, 96, 97, 100, 101, 102, 103, 107, 107, 108, 109, 115, 116, 121, 137, 141, 144, 145, 150, 156, 160, 162, 162, 162, 163, 167, 170, 171, 171, 177, 180, 186, 186, 188, 189, 189, 191, 191, 191, 194, 201, 213, 214, 217, 223, 226, 229, 229, 230, 231, 233, 234, 239, 240, 241, 241, 242, 242, 242, 242, 246, 247, 247, 247, 251, 252, 252, 253, 254, 254, 255, 256, 256, 258, 258, 259, 260, 260, 262, 262, 262, 264, 265, 267, 267, 267, 273, 276, 276, 277, 278, 279, 280, 284, 286, 288, 290, 293, 299, 301, 302, 304, 304, 308, 308, 310, 315, 316, 316 Congr 1, 4, 6, 6, 9, 9, 11, 13, 13, 13, 19, 19, 21, 21, 23, 24, 25, 25, 34, 36, 42, 42, 44, 45, 46, 48, 49, 49, 49, 50, 50, 52, 53, 53, 53, 56, 57, 58, 58, 58, 64, 68, 69, 69, 70, 70, 73, 73, 77, 81, 81, 86, 86, 86, 89, 90, 90, 95, 97, 112, 115, 121, 124, 125, 126, 133, 133, 133, 133, 133, 133, 133, 133, 133, 133, 133, 133, 137, 138, 138, 138, 148, 150, 150, 153, 153, 157, 159, 161, 161, 162, 163, 166, 170, 170, 170, 170, 172, 173, 178, 179, 180 Fug 6, 11, 15, 16, 18, 19, 21, 22, 26, 27, 31, 33, 34, 35, 39, 41, 44, 44, 44, 49, 53, 54, 57, 59, 59, 61, 64, 64, 65, 65, 66, 66, 70, 73, 75, 75, 76, 76, 76, 78, 82, 86, 87, 89, 89, 94, 99, 101, 102, 108, 108, 111, 111, 113, 115, 116, 117, 120, 120, 121, 123, 124, 128, 130, 136, 136, 137, 141, 141, 141, 143, 143, 143, 145, 146, 149, 149, 149, 149, 151, 151, 153, 153, 154, 154, 155, 156, 156, 157, 158, 161, 162, 164, 165, 166, 167, 167, 168, 168, 170, 170, 170, 171, 171, 172, 175, 175, 175, 175, 185, 186, 187, 190, 197, 199, 200, 202, 202, 203, 203, 204, 204, 205, 213 Mut 5, 7, 9, 11, 11, 12, 12, 12, 13, 13, 14, 15, 15, 17, 17, 18, 18, 18, 21, 21, 27, 27, 30, 30, 34, 34, 36, 37, 38, 39, 45, 46, 46, 46, 47, 49, 54, 54, 54, 60, 60, 62, 63, 64, 64, 68, 68, 79, 81, 81, 89, 95, 97, 101, 105, 116, 117, 117, 117, 119, 127, 128, 131, 134, 134, 136, 138, 140, 143, 145, 147, 147, 147, 148, 149, 151, 152, 152, 153, 158, 159, 160, 165, 166, 168, 169, 170, 172, 173, 174, 175, 177, 177, 178, 178, 180, 180, 182, 184, 186, 187, 192, 194, 196, 196, 201, 201, 202, 205, 205, 209, 210, 213, 215, 215, 217, 218, 218, 224, 227, 227, 227, 228, 230, 232, 232, 233, 234, 237, 237, 241, 241, 243, 247, 249, 250, 251, 252, 254, 255, 260, 262, 265, 266, 267, 269, 270 Somn 1:3, 6, 6, 8, 8, 8, 10, 11, 16, 18, 18, 18, 19, 19, 23, 25, 26, 27, 28, 29, 30, 30, 35, 39, 45, 45, 45, 45, 45, 46, 48, 48, 49, 51, 52, 56, 64, 66, 69, 72, 75, 76, 76, 76, 81, 82, 83, 87, 90, 91, 93, 95, 95, 99, 100, 100, 100, 107, 110, 111, 112, 115, 117, 117, 120, 121, 122, 125, 126, 130, 135, 137, 137, 142, 143, 145, 147, 151, 153, 155, 156, 162, 164, 166, 166, 167, 170, 172, 172, 174, 174, 176, 179, 181, 183, 185, 185, 186, 190, 191, 192, 193, 199, 200, 202, 202, 203, 206, 207, 209, 209, 210, 223, 224, 227, 228, 229, 230, 230, 232, 232, 233, 234, 235, 237, 238, 240, 240, 245, 246, 248, 250, 254, 255, 255, 256, 256 Somn 2:1, 3, 9, 10, 11, 13, 17, 18, 19, 21, 23, 23, 24, 27, 29, 30, 32, 33, 42, 44, 44, 47, 50, 50, 51, 52, 53, 55, 57, 60, 61, 62, 63, 63, 66, 67, 67, 67, 70, 72, 72, 75, 77, 81, 83, 83, 83, 85, 89, 90, 90, 91, 91, 93, 93, 97, 98, 99, 100, 100, 101, 103, 108, 109, 112, 114, 114, 115, 116, 120, 120, 123, 129, 130, 132, 135, 136, 136, 138, 141, 146, 146, 147, 153, 155, 156, 157, 161, 162, 163, 164, 171, 177, 178, 180, 180, 182, 182, 185, 187, 187, 189, 189, 193, 193, 193, 196, 200, 202, 202, 203, 206, 208, 210, 211, 215, 216, 217, 219, 220, 224, 226, 227, 229, 231, 236, 239, 243, 243, 249, 250, 254, 255, 259, 259, 261, 265, 267, 270, 270, 272, 277, 278, 279, 286, 287, 289, 290 Abr 4, 5, 5, 8, 10, 11, 11, 15, 17, 19, 22, 24, 26, 28, 31, 31, 32, 32, 34, 36, 36, 37, 37, 37, 39, 41, 43, 43, 51, 53, 60, 62, 63, 64, 64, 67, 67, 67, 67, 67, 67, 67, 67, 67, 67, 69, 69, 74, 75, 75, 76, 76, 76, 77, 78, 78, 79, 80, 86, 86, 88, 89, 89, 97, 98, 99, 106, 107, 110, 115, 115, 118, 120, 123, 127, 127, 128, 129, 129, 130, 131, 131, 131, 134, 135, 135, 136, 137, 138, 142, 146, 147, 150, 152, 153, 154, 154, 162, 162, 165, 166, 167, 172, 177, 178, 180, 188, 193, 196, 198, 199, 199, 200, 201, 203, 204, 204, 207, 208, 213, 214, 214, 216, 219, 225, 225, 225, 227, 229, 232, 234, 235, 237, 243, 243, 246, 248, 249, 249, 250, 252, 253, 255, 258, 260, 260, 260, 260, 260, 260, 261, 264, 265, 266, 270, 271, 275 Ios 5, 6, 12, 16, 17, 17, 22, 23, 26, 27, 27, 27, 29, 29, 30, 30, 32, 33, 33, 36, 36,

37, 43, 43, 44, 44, 46, 46, 46, 47, 47, 50, 51, 52, 53, 53, 54, 58, 62, 63, 65, 67, 67, 69, 71, 71, 73, 77, 79, 79, 85, 85, 86, 89, 93, 94, 101, 106, 107, 107, 117, 117, 118, 118, 122, 125, 125, 126, 126, 126, 126, 128, 130, 130, 130, 131, 133, 134, 136, 142, 144, 150, 154, 155, 157, 159, 166, 167, 171, 171, 174, 176, 179, 181, 181, 182, 187, 187, 198, 200, 200, 204, 205, 205, 210, 211, 213, 217, 217, 217, 218, 223, 225, 226, 229, 230, 231, 236, 236, 241, 242, 244, 248, 250, 252, 252, 255, 256, 257, 259, 263, 263 Mos 1:2, 2, 2, 11, 16, 18, 20, 21, 21, 24, 25, 29, 36, 45, 46, 47, 48, 51, 51, 51, 54, 54, 54, 54, 55, 55, 55, 56, 56, 58, 59, 59, 59, 61, 65, 65, 69, 69, 71, 71, 74, 74, 79, 81, 81, 82, 83, 83, 85, 88, 88, 95, 98, 100, 102, 108, 110, 111, 114, 117, 119, 119, 122, 126, 128, 134, 141, 141, 141, 142, 144, 145, 145, 145, 145, 145, 145, 146, 146, 147, 148, 150, 152, 152, 152, 152, 152, 152, 152, 152, 152, 153, 157, 158, 160, 161, 164, 164, 166, 167, 168, 170, 171, 172, 173, 175, 180, 182, 182, 183, 183, 183, 187, 189, 191, 192, 192, 192, 192, 192, 192, 196, 200, 200, 200, 200, 201, 205, 207, 207, 207, 209, 210, 216, 220, 228, 231, 243, 245, 245, 246, 248, 250, 251, 254, 255, 256, 256, 258, 259, 261, 263, 266, 266, 268, 270, 272, 273, 273, 274, 277, 278, 278, 280, 280, 281, 283, 283, 283, 284, 284, 287, 288, 298, 300, 306, 307, 310, 312, 313, 315, 315, 322, 323, 325, 328, 328, 333 Mos 2:1, 2, 4, 5, 5, 8, 11, 13, 16, 20, 21, 21, 22, 22, 23, 24, 24, 25, 26, 28, 29, 32, 33, 33, 34, 35, 37, 38, 38, 39, 40, 41, 43, 48, 49, 50, 50, 53, 53, 53, 55, 58, 58, 62, 63, 65, 66, 67, 87, 106, 107, 117, 124, 127, 129, 130, 132, 136, 138, 142, 156, 156, 159, 160, 165, 166, 167, 169, 169, 174, 177, 181, 182, 183, 184, 188, 192, 195, 197, 203, 204, 205, 206, 210, 211, 212, 212, 218, 219, 219, 221, 222, 223, 223, 224, 228, 229, 229, 230, 231, 232, 234, 234, 236, 238, 240, 241, 242, 242, 243, 248, 255, 258, 258, 260, 261, 261, 263, 263, 263, 264, 265, 266, 267, 268, 273, 274, 275, 279, 279, 280, 280, 291 Decal 2, 5, 5, 5, 5, 8, 11, 12, 14, 14, 15, 15, 16, 17, 18, 25, 29, 30, 32, 33, 36, 36, 36, 36, 39, 43, 43, 47, 52, 58, 58, 58, 59, 59, 59, 61, 61, 66, 68, 71, 75, 76, 81, 81, 85, 85, 86, 88, 90, 91, 92, 93, 99, 100, 104, 104, 111, 112, 113, 115, 118, 118, 123, 138, 141, 141, 141, 142, 151, 152, 156, 159, 168, 169, 177, 177, 177 Spec 1:2, 8, 9, 14, 18, 18, 19, 19, 20, 22, 22, 23, 24, 25, 25, 25, 28, 29, 30, 31, 32, 32, 32, 33, 33, 34, 38, 41, 43, 44, 45, 45, 46, 46, 48, 49, 50, 51, 57, 58, 60, 62, 64, 66, 68, 68, 74, 74, 76, 89, 97, 103, 104, 106, 106, 107, 108, 108, 109, 111, 111, 120, 122, 122, 122, 128, 128, 131, 133, 137, 138, 139, 141, 144, 147, 151, 153, 154, 156, 157, 157, 159, 159, 163, 164, 166, 167, 186, 191, 191, 193, 193, 194, 204, 204, 204, 204, 204, 211, 214, 221, 221, 223, 223, 225, 228, 229, 230, 230, 230, 236, 237, 238, 240, 241, 242, 244, 245, 252, 252, 254, 260, 260, 261, 263, 265, 266, 267, 271, 272, 273, 276, 276, 277, 277, 278, 279, 281, 281, 282, 290, 291, 294, 296, 298, 301, 301, 303, 307, 307, 307, 308, 310, 313, 313, 314, 315, 315, 319, 319, 322, 323, 325, 326, 327, 329, 329, 330, 333, 335, 336, 338, 341, 341, 345 Spec 2:4, 4, 8, 8, 11, 11, 12, 13, 14, 14, 16, 19, 19, 19, 20, 21, 21, 23, 23, 23, 24, 25, 27, 28, 31, 32, 34, 35, 36, 40, 50, 55, 60, 60, 66, 66, 69, 71, 72, 72, 73, 74, 77, 78, 84, 88, 89, 89, 91, 91, 95, 96, 98, 99, 104, 105, 106, 107, 113, 113, 113, 115, 118, 119, 120, 121, 121, 130, 132, 132, 133, 135, 136, 138, 142, 143, 144, 146, 146, 148, 150, 152, 153, 154, 161, 164, 165, 168, 170, 170, 171, 173, 173, 175, 178, 182, 182, 184, 186, 187, 189, 189, 191, 195, 195, 196, 198, 203, 205, 208, 209, 210, 211, 215, 218, 219, 222, 226, 228, 230, 231, 231, 232, 232, 233, 237, 238, 239, 239, 239, 240, 240, 240, 243, 245, 245, 246, 247, 247, 250, 251, 254, 258, 259, 261, 262 Spec 3:3, 5, 5, 6, 8, 8, 8, 8, 8, 9, 10, 12, 12, 15, 16, 17, 19, 23, 25, 27, 27, 29, 33, 34, 37, 37, 42, 44, 45, 46, 51, 52, 59, 59, 61, 62, 63, 65, 73, 73, 77, 79, 81, 81, 81, 85, 86, 87, 87, 90, 91, 94, 95, 96, 97, 97, 98, 100, 102, 104, 107, 111, 116, 121, 121, 122, 123, 127, 128, 128, 129, 129, 135, 136, 136, 137, 137, 141, 144, 145, 146, 151, 151, 155, 155, 156, 158, 158, 159, 159, 163, 172, 174, 174, 175, 175, 177, 179, 180, 182, 183, 183, 189, 189, 189, 189, 193, 194, 195, 197, 199, 202, 208 Spec 4:4, 5, 5, 10, 11, 15, 16, 19, 20, 23, 24, 26, 31, 34, 35, 36, 37, 39, 39, 39, 39, 39, 46, 47, 48, 50, 51, 54, 60, 60, 60, 60, 62, 63, 66, 67, 70, 71, 72, 73, 76, 76, 77, 78, 80, 80, 82, 82, 83, 85, 94, 97, 100, 102, 103, 105, 105, 107, 109, 110, 113, 119, 119, 120, 121, 123, 126, 127, 129, 130, 130, 131, 133, 133, 136, 136, 137, 138, 139, 141, 141, 149, 149, 150, 151, 152, 153, 154, 154, 156, 157, 161, 163, 165, 165, 169, 170, 172, 175, 176, 177, 177, 179, 184, 185, 191, 192, 195, 196, 196, 198, 199, 200, 200, 201, 204, 206, 206, 207, 208, 214, 215, 216, 218, 218, 219, 224, 228, 228, 234, 235 Virt 1, 5, 5, 6, 8, 10, 10, 10, 14, 16, 19, 21, 22, 23, 25, 26, 28, 28, 29, 31, 32, 38, 39, 44, 51, 53, 54, 54, 55, 56, 57, 58, 59, 59, 59, 60, 62, 64, 64, 66, 66, 67, 69, 69, 72, 77, 78, 79, 80, 81, 82, 82, 84, 84, 86, 86, 88, 90, 91, 91, 91, 94, 96, 97, 99, 99, 100, 106, 107, 108, 113, 114, 115, 116, 117, 122, 123, 124, 127, 133, 133, 135, 135, 136, 136, 137, 138, 142, 146, 146, 146, 147, 153, 153, 155, 156, 156, 156, 162, 166, 169, 171, 176, 177, 179, 183, 187, 188, 193, 195, 196, 196, 198, 199, 200, 201, 202, 203, 206, 207, 213, 215, 215, 216, 218, 220, 222, 223, 224, 225, 227 Praem 2, 6, 16, 23, 23, 34, 35, 36, 39, 39, 40, 40, 40, 42, 44, 44, 44, 44, 44, 45, 47, 52, 54, 57, 67, 69, 78, 80, 83, 84, 85, 85, 87, 88, 88, 88, 93, 97, 100, 105, 105, 107, 112, 112, 114, 117, 117, 119, 123, 124, 125, 127, 128, 131, 131, 131, 131, 131, 131, 132, 134, 138, 143, 145, 149, 152, 156, 160, 166, 170, 170, 171 Prob 2, 2, 5, 5, 6, 7, 7, 8, 8, 9, 10, 12, 14, 23, 27, 29, 32, 32, 34, 36, 37, 40, 42, 42, 43, 44, 46, 47, 48, 48, 51, 52, 53, 53, 55, 59, 60, 60, 60, 60, 61, 62, 62, 63, 65, 68, 69, 69, 71, 72, 75, 75, 75, 75, 76, 79, 79, 80, 84, 85, 86, 86, 87, 89, 92, 93, 94, 95, 96, 96, 96, 97, 100, 100, 101, 101, 105, 109, 109, 111, 113, 113, 114, 115, 117, 118, 118, 122, 122, 124, 124, 125, 125, 126, 127, 128, 128, 129, 129, 130, 131, 132, 135, 135, 140, 141, 143, 146, 147, 149, 154, 156, 157, 157, 160 Contempl 1, 5, 6, 8, 9, 10, 10, 15, 16, 19, 19, 19, 20, 29, 30, 31, 31, 37, 40, 43, 43, 43, 50, 53, 53, 59, 65, 67, 68, 68, 69, 70, 71, 73, 75, 75, 77, 89 Aet 2, 3, 8, 12, 12, 13, 14, 15, 16, 17, 20, 26, 32, 37, 37, 40, 41, 47, 49, 49, 49, 51, 53, 53, 54, 56, 63, 63, 63, 66, 66, 66, 66, 67, 69, 71, 72, 73, 73, 75, 77, 85, 87, 88, 88, 88, 88, 89, 91, 92, 94, 95, 95, 96, 98, 98, 101, 104, 106, 107, 107, 111, 112, 115, 115, 115, 119, 122, 125, 125, 125, 125, 129, 130, 130, 137, 138, 141, 142, 143, 143, 145, 146, 146, 147, 148, 149, 149 Flacc 1, 1, 1, 6, 7, 7, 11, 12, 22, 28, 29, 32, 35, 35, 35, 35, 35, 36, 40, 40, 41, 41, 42, 43, 43, 45, 45, 48, 48, 48, 49, 49, 50, 50, 50, 52, 52, 52, 55, 60, 64, 66, 67, 76, 76, 78, 80, 84, 84, 84, 87, 89, 92, 93, 94, 94, 94, 94, 95, 97, 97, 101, 102, 103, 107, 113, 117, 119, 121, 124, 124, 126, 126, 128, 131, 133, 135, 135, 141, 142, 146, 146, 147, 148, 157, 163, 164, 165, 165, 170, 173, 174, 174, 178, 179, 180, 181, 186, 187 Legat 6, 6, 7, 8, 10, 10, 11, 13, 13, 13, 13, 22, 28, 30, 31, 32, 39, 48,

53, 58, 58, 59, 62, 63, 63, 66, 68, 69, 80, 80, 84, 88, 98, 99, 99, 99, 103, 109, 110, 112, 112, 118, 119, 123, 124, 128, 133, 135, 135, 136, 137, 139, 140, 141, 142, 143, 146, 149, 149, 151, 153, 155, 157, 158, 159, 161, 162, 164, 168, 168, 170, 171, 171, 172, 172, 173, 182, 184, 187, 191, 192, 193, 195, 195, 195, 196, 201, 204, 207, 207, 208, 208, 209, 211, 212, 213, 214, 215, 216, 218, 226, 232, 238, 239, 241, 242, 242, 247, 247, 248, 249, 250, 251, 252, 252, 253, 253, 255, 255, 256, 257, 257, 258, 261, 261, 261, 264, 264, 265, 271, 274, 277, 280, 280, 281, 282, 283, 285, 286, 290, 292, 292, 292, 292, 292, 292, 292, 292, 292, 292, 297, 298, 299, 300, 301, 303, 304, 307, 307, 310, 310, 315, 316, 317, 322, 324, 325, 327, 330, 330, 334, 341, 342, 343, 343, 345, 347, 347, 347, 349, 353, 355, 356, 356, 357, 359, 361, 362, 362, 364, 364, 366, 367, 368, 369, 370, 371, 371, 372 Hypoth 6:1, 6:2, 6:3, 6:3, 6:3, 6:3, 6:3, 6:3, 6:4, 6:4, 6:5, 6:6, 6:8, 6:9, 7:2, 7:2, 7:2, 7:3, 7:10, 7:10, 7:11, 7:11, 7:14, 7:14, 7:15, 7:15, 7:16, 7:17, 7:17, 7:19, 7:20, 11:2, 11:2, 11:4, 11:4, 11:4, 11:4, 11:4, 11:6, 11:6, 11:6, 11:6, 11:12, 11:13, 11:14, 11:18 Prov 1, 1, 2:1, 2, 3, 4, 8, 11, 12, 22, 23, 24, 25, 26, 32, 33, 35, 35, 36, 37, 39, 39, 43, 46, 47, 47, 48, 53, 53, 54, 54, 54, 56, 57, 59, 60, 60, 61, 62, 63, 64, 64, 66, 66, 67, 69, 69, 71 QG 1:17b, 20, 21, 24, 32, 51, 51, 55a, 55a, 55b, 60:1, 60:1, 64c, 66, 73, 93, 94, 96:1, 100:1b, 100:1b, 2:5a, 12b, 12b, 12b, 15a, 15a, 15c, 16, 26a, 26a, 28, 28, 30, 34a, 39, 39, 41, 41, 54a, 54a, 54a, 54d, 54d, 59, 59, 59, 59, 62, 64a, 64b, 64c, 65, 65, 66, 68a, 71a, 71a, 71a, 72, 74, 3:11a, 11a, 11a, 11c, 18, 18, 20a, 20b, 22, 22, 23, 23, 26, 29, 48, 58, 4:8a, 33a, 43, 51b, 52b, 52d, 64, 67, 86b, 88, 104, 110a, 145, 145, 166, 167, 172, 172, 173, 180, 191b, 8*, 8*, 198, 200a, 200b, 200c, 202a, 204, 204, 206a, 211, 227, 228, 228, 228, 228 QG isf 2, 3, 3, 5, 5, 5, 5, 9, 10, 13, 13, 13, 16, 16 QG (Par) 2:3, 2:5, 2:7 QE 1:19, 2:2, 2, 2, 2, 2, 4, 6a, 6a, 9:1, 10:1, 12, 14, 14, 15:1, 18, 19, 21, 24a, 25a, 25d, 28, 38b, 40, 44, 45a, 47, 47, 50b, 50b, 71, 118 QE isf 2, 3, 3, 3, 8, 14, 14, 16, 16, 16, 16, 16, 16, 16, 17, 21, 22, 23, 25, 25, 26, 29

οὐαί Leg 3:225, 231

οὐδαμά Aet 5

οὐδαμῇ (7) Post 87 Plant 14, 116 Ebr 40, 108 Fug 82 Aet 97

οὐδαμοῦ (11) Leg 3:53 Sacr 136 Conf 136, 136, 138 Migr 183 Fug 60 Somn 1:192 Ios 134 Mos 2:114 Aet 66

οὐδαμῶς (15) Leg 1:74 Leg 2:26 Leg 3:6 Sacr 59 Post 87 Plant 14, 116 Ebr 40, 108, 178 Congr 4 Fug 82 Ios 47 Aet 97 Hypoth 7:17

οὐδέ (532) Opif 15, 16, 20, 24, 51, 77, 80, 97, 104 Leg 1:25, 26, 35, 44 Leg 2:2, 3, 15, 20, 36, 43, 88 Leg 3:4, 5, 10, 45, 49, 78, 106, 113, 120, 125, 126, 131, 134, 136, 141, 182 Cher 58, 91, 100, 100, 117, 117 Sacr 9, 10, 25, 34, 57, 65, 69, 70, 88, 91, 91, 92, 92, 92, 100, 101, 111, 111 Det 13, 18, 18, 18, 18, 18, 18, 35, 39, 43, 63, 71, 89, 125, 134, 134, 136, 136, 153, 153, 156, 162, 164 Post 4, 14, 16, 22, 24, 49, 50, 84, 94, 101, 102, 109, 126, 126, 134, 144, 164, 169, 185 Gig 21, 24, 27, 27, 28, 36, 42, 52 Deus 7, 29, 62, 62, 62, 79, 90, 107, 132, 134, 145, 159, 178, 181 Agr 43, 60, 84, 86, 90, 130, 134, 152 Plant 10, 10, 63, 83, 83, 83, 83, 83, 110, 126, 127, 145, 147, 164, 166 Ebr 7, 13, 32, 32, 32, 42, 57, 69, 85, 85, 93, 96, 103, 114, 131, 140, 165, 168, 173, 179, 179, 186, 195, 195 Sobr 17, 46 Conf 25, 44, 44, 50, 51, 55, 56, 71, 72, 72, 98, 139, 149, 156, 160, 166, 175, 177, 181, 194, 194 Migr 23, 55, 65, 87, 145, 148, 196, 225 Her 14, 15, 41, 41, 41, 43, 45, 45, 45, 66, 121, 170, 190, 228 Congr 33, 70, 97, 112, 115, 137, 137, 142, 146 Fug 16, 19, 78, 111, 113, 114, 124, 144, 149, 170, 171, 204 Mut 8, 14, 27, 64, 73, 143, 143, 147, 147, 147, 157, 157, 170, 188, 200, 218, 219, 234, 237 Somn 1:6, 6, 8, 19, 66, 67, 143, 187 Somn 2:12, 103, 114, 136, 141, 147, 231, 264, 267, 276, 288, 298, 302 Abr 37, 37, 43, 74, 76, 95, 111, 115, 189, 189, 189, 248, 259, 266 Ios 12, 27, 33, 43, 81, 86, 125, 141, 179, 248, 248, 263 Mos 1:11, 28, 38, 39, 39, 68, 81, 85, 89, 92, 112, 145, 145, 157, 160, 161, 192, 193, 195, 283, 307, 309, 323 Mos 2:15, 19, 22, 28, 196, 207, 225, 242, 257, 266, 268, 291 Decal 33, 41, 62, 69, 94, 112, 124, 156 Spec 1:22, 44, 58, 58, 65, 102, 105, 122, 124, 139, 156, 163, 223, 277 Spec 2:16, 23, 49, 70, 77, 119, 121, 222, 246, 251, 252 Spec 3:1, 3, 17, 20, 46, 46, 61, 74, 89, 116, 119, 121, 123, 166, 172, 176, 183, 183, 183, 205 Spec 4:11, 83, 85, 100, 157, 177, 205, 218, 226 Virt 6, 27, 56, 85, 107, 150, 183, 187, 187, 194, 217 Praem 80, 80, 105, 107, 108, 110 Prob 7, 8, 18, 25, 51, 51, 51, 56, 61, 61, 61, 76, 78, 78, 78, 79, 96, 96, 100, 101, 125, 134, 136, 143, 146, 157, 157 Contempl 8, 30, 71, 72 Aet 5, 13, 13, 22, 24, 25, 38, 41, 43, 51, 53, 78, 88, 88, 90, 116, 129, 131, 131 Flacc 6, 40, 59, 90, 155, 160, 170 Legat 6, 30, 30, 43, 48, 71, 99, 114, 149, 184, 195, 227, 236, 255, 274, 275, 305, 336, 337, 353 Hypoth 6:3, 6:4, 7:2, 7:2, 7:10, 7:14, 7:19, 11:3 Prov 1, 2:16, 17, 22, 37, 65, 66 QG 1:24, 28, 2:39, 54a, 54a, 54a, 54a, 64b, 65, 68a, 3:8, 30b, 4:33b, 33b QG isf 5, 16 QE 2:3a, 15:1, 45b QE isf 3, 4, 16

οὐδείς (1032) Opif 4, 5, 10, 23, 23, 24, 28, 28, 31, 34, 39, 40, 62, 62, 69, 72, 99, 99, 99, 120, 130, 130, 132, 135, 135, 139, 148, 149, 151, 152, 153, 158, 160, 161, 164, 168, 171 Leg 1:7, 26, 27, 34, 42, 44, 51, 52, 76, 85, 87, 94, 94 Leg 2:1, 2, 3, 4, 17, 24, 26, 36, 43, 46, 68, 70, 77, 85, 108 Leg 3:4, 10, 23, 27, 29, 45, 53, 53, 56, 58, 77, 78, 79, 124, 134, 145, 146, 147, 149, 157, 180, 181, 200, 203, 206, 206, 207, 234, 239, 246 Cher 16, 24, 34, 42, 44, 44, 47, 53, 59, 79, 83, 83, 86, 90, 97, 97, 107, 109, 109, 109, 113, 121 Sacr 18, 20, 22, 24, 29, 35, 35, 40, 43, 57, 63, 65, 67, 91, 91 Det 11, 13, 14, 27, 29, 36, 43, 43, 44, 54, 55, 56, 56, 70, 70, 75, 86, 90, 119, 125, 163 Post 4, 7, 14, 14, 30, 33, 40, 58, 71, 90, 90, 100, 105, 112, 119, 119, 126, 134, 137, 139, 143, 152, 152, 157, 159, 159, 164, 166, 171, 179 Gig 4, 4, 5, 12, 15, 17, 25, 28, 30, 39, 60 Deus 3, 4, 7, 26, 27, 29, 29, 31, 32, 32, 52, 52, 55, 56, 57, 57, 61, 62, 66, 83, 107, 108, 121, 133, 143, 143, 145, 149, 167, 171, 177, 177, 179 Agr 5, 8, 13, 22, 40, 48, 50, 52, 71, 75, 85, 86, 103, 116, 118, 119, 126, 130, 130, 135, 142, 143, 144, 149, 150, 154 Plant 5, 8, 18, 27, 31, 31, 34, 34, 42, 43, 43, 44, 51, 65, 72, 80, 82, 91, 112, 116, 128, 144, 154, 155, 156, 157, 174, 175 Ebr 12, 12, 13, 32, 43, 43, 44, 58, 63, 64, 86, 86, 106, 107, 113, 128, 155, 158, 170, 170, 186, 189, 193, 195, 202, 211, 213, 220, 223 Sobr 3, 31, 35, 41, 46, 46, 53, 67, 68 Conf 10, 12, 25, 37, 50, 55, 97, 98, 129, 136, 136, 139, 139, 140, 144, 153, 154, 160, 170, 173, 175, 180, 186, 194, 194, 194 Migr 20, 22, 24, 61, 65, 73, 76, 77, 98, 116, 116, 130, 135, 140, 168, 177, 179, 179, 225 Her 42, 56, 80, 81, 93, 94, 103, 121, 121, 124, 142, 142, 143, 159, 227, 228, 240, 259, 259, 270, 312 Congr 37, 41, 46, 58, 58, 58, 61, 61, 66, 66, 75, 76, 113, 133, 147 Fug 6, 16, 19, 54, 79, 82, 84, 112, 118,

123, 124, 131, 163, 170, 196, 200, 203 Mut 7, 8, 22, 28, 73, 83, 98, 109, 115, 136, 163, 169, 170, 178, 181, 196, 199, 211, 211, 213, 214, 241 Somn 1:7, 12, 21, 24, 24, 37, 38, 40, 45, 64, 73, 75, 79, 81, 82, 97, 124, 145, 184, 185, 187, 191, 212, 217, 218, 230, 234, 245 Somn 2:41, 58, 64, 88, 100, 104, 104, 107, 116, 160, 178, 260, 301 Abr 6, 14, 27, 31, 33, 58, 59, 67, 77, 84, 93, 109, 122, 123, 128, 135, 164, 171, 175, 185, 186, 196, 199, 206, 209, 211, 235, 240, 246, 252, 259, 260, 261, 269, 270 Ios 4, 8, 12, 17, 23, 24, 26, 46, 48, 61, 68, 76, 81, 81, 107, 115, 118, 126, 126, 129, 134, 142, 144, 147, 150, 153, 158, 166, 166, 171, 185, 198, 199, 208, 215, 219, 237, 244, 247, 258, 264, 267, 269 Mos 1:22, 28, 29, 31, 31, 31, 37, 38, 46, 65, 66, 72, 75, 95, 111, 125, 135, 135, 139, 143, 145, 145, 152, 153, 156, 157, 157, 157, 168, 174, 176, 178, 183, 192, 192, 192, 197, 200, 204, 205, 205, 225, 233, 246, 253, 259, 274, 281, 283, 286, 291, 293, 296, 299, 303, 305, 309, 329, 330 Mos 2:6, 15, 18, 58, 70, 96, 100, 114, 130, 154, 162, 174, 179, 180, 194, 227, 234, 235, 243, 251, 264, 268 Decal 3, 5, 31, 31, 41, 57, 62, 70, 87, 92, 105, 109, 118, 128, 141, 149, 150, 150, 158, 173, 176 Spec 1:22, 26, 35, 36, 40, 41, 41, 43, 44, 56, 60, 63, 65, 73, 74, 74, 88, 95, 100, 103, 113, 129, 160, 174, 186, 204, 223, 242, 244, 246, 255, 264, 266, 271, 274, 282, 287, 299, 310, 322, 324, 328 Spec 2:10, 11, 18, 22, 26, 38, 46, 49, 64, 65, 69, 76, 80, 87, 91, 93, 109, 124, 129, 138, 139, 140, 147, 169, 180, 185, 198, 206, 217, 227, 234, 235, 236, 237, 251 Spec 3:1, 8, 21, 39, 46, 50, 57, 68, 70, 78, 83, 84, 89, 100, 109, 118, 155, 158, 163, 199 Spec 4:8, 18, 45, 49, 67, 73, 80, 83, 99, 105, 108, 133, 143, 192 Virt 6, 7, 9, 25, 31, 31, 34, 44, 45, 53, 55, 61, 65, 94, 94, 113, 117, 147, 152, 154, 160, 187, 193, 197, 203, 203, 204, 206, 211, 212, 221, 224, 224, 226 Praem 9, 26, 48, 51, 55, 55, 61, 65, 69, 78, 82, 87, 101, 103, 108, 110, 140, 142, 142, 145, 148, 162, 167, 172 Prob 3, 19, 19, 21, 21, 22, 26, 27, 30, 31, 36, 41, 50, 54, 61, 63, 78, 85, 89, 91, 101, 117, 125, 133, 154 Contempl 18, 34, 37, 37, 66, 71, 72, 75 Aet 1, 5, 5, 6, 10, 16, 21, 21, 24, 25, 25, 28, 30, 33, 38, 38, 42, 46, 49, 65, 74, 78, 78, 78, 83, 89, 95, 98, 102, 105, 106, 106, 107, 114, 114, 118, 132, 134, 134, 142, 144 Flacc 4, 6, 23, 53, 64, 65, 71, 90, 99, 104, 115, 117, 127, 136, 139, 145, 165, 177 Legat 11, 12, 17, 18, 19, 28, 43, 61, 73, 75, 114, 116, 132, 133, 133, 138, 151, 155, 162, 167, 178, 190, 198, 233, 261, 262, 267, 269, 277, 280, 286, 287, 290, 292, 292, 295, 298, 301, 306, 310, 317, 318, 335, 336, 340, 347, 360, 366, 369 Hypoth 6:1, 6:2, 7:1, 7:3, 7:9, 7:17, 7:18, 7:18, 11:3, 11:4, 11:4, 11:9, 11:14 Prov 1, 2:10, 16, 25, 30, 35, 36, 44, 45, 53, 63, 63 QG 1:64a, 74, 100:1a, 100:2a, 2:54a, 62, 62, 3:12, 52, 4:51a, 64, 74, 76a, 179, 193, 9*, 228 QG isf 5, 11 QG (Par) 2:2, 2:6, 2:7 QE 1:7a, 2:1, 3a, 6b, 9a, 24b, 37, 55b, 105 QE isf 1, 3, 3, 16, 19, 26

οὐδένεια (11) Sacr 55 Her 29, 30 Congr 107 Fug 82 Mut 54, 155 Somn 1:60, 212 Somn 2:293 Mos 1:273

οὐδέποτε (50) Opif 12 Leg 1:5, 76 Leg 3:148, 149 Cher 30, 43, 87 Sacr 40 Det 21 Post 145, 173, 176 Deus 9 Agr 166 Plant 58 Ebr 143 Sobr 22 Conf 77, 153 Migr 28, 225 Her 130, 235, 252 Congr 112 Fug 32, 111, 114, 147 Mut 19, 55 Somn 1:243 Somn 2:185 Decal 60, 104, 149 Spec 2:230, 253 Spec 3:167 Spec 4:200, 211 Prob 13, 69 Aet 9, 95, 96, 109 Legat 48, 158

οὐδέπω Sacr 135 Fug 40 Mut 21 Abr 42 Mos 1:32

οὐδέτερος (16) Leg 1:68, 85 Sacr 100 Ebr 35 Her 22 Congr 22 Somn 1:23 Somn 2:184 Ios 20 Mos 2:122, 142, 287 Decal 117 Spec 3:82, 159 Virt 53

οὐδός Somn 2:148

Οὐιτέλλιος Legat 231

οὐκέτι (73) Opif 51, 169 Leg 1:17, 32 Leg 2:50, 95 Leg 3:108, 136 Cher 45 Sacr 6, 58 Det 41, 87, 146 Post 43, 121, 132, 173 Deus 154 Agr 37 Plant 90, 137 Ebr 58, 112, 221 Conf 54, 59 Migr 85, 195 Her 70, 93, 164, 203 Congr 13, 146 Mut 79, 114 Somn 1:70, 99, 116, 171 Somn 2:300 Abr 85, 113, 230, 273 Ios 210 Mos 1:132, 175, 287 Mos 2:250, 272, 288 Spec 1:221 Spec 2:135, 232 Spec 3:50 Spec 4:96 Virt 104 Praem 19 Prob 43, 156 Aet 58, 85, 132 Flacc 16, 138 Legat 75, 122, 366 Hypoth 11:17 QG 1:24, 2:29

οὔκουν Somn 1:167

οὐκοῦν (53) Opif 68 Leg 1:78, 100 Leg 2:30 Leg 3:111, 159, 181 Cher 54 Det 28, 57, 64, 68 Post 181 Gig 40 Deus 1, 50, 132 Agr 66, 85, 169 Plant 48, 96, 135, 141 Ebr 15, 55, 155, 160, 196 Sobr 11, 20, 39 Conf 30, 119, 183 Migr 53, 57, 103 Her 114, 124, 163, 275 Congr 87 Fug 18, 58, 198 Mut 23, 235 Somn 1:5, 25 Aet 51, 73, 95

οὐλή Spec 1:103, 103

οὖλος Contempl 51

οὖν (1606) Opif 4, 12, 13, 20, 29, 33, 36, 36, 50, 53, 63, 67, 72, 77, 78, 99, 101, 103, 105, 106, 118, 132, 133, 145, 145, 145, 149, 169 Leg 1:2, 3, 4, 5, 16, 18, 23, 23, 26, 28, 30, 31, 34, 35, 37, 37, 40, 41, 42, 45, 48, 49, 51, 53, 53, 54, 55, 60, 60, 61, 61, 64, 70, 71, 72, 77, 78, 80, 82, 86, 86, 87, 89, 89, 90, 91, 92, 94, 95, 99, 102, 102, 104, 105, 105, 107 Leg 2:3, 5, 6, 12, 12, 14, 16, 17, 21, 24, 24, 25, 33, 36, 36, 37, 44, 45, 65, 66, 68, 70, 76, 78, 79, 79, 80, 81, 82, 88, 88, 89, 90, 95, 96, 96, 97, 98, 103, 104, 108 Leg 3:2, 6, 11, 17, 18, 21, 27, 28, 35, 39, 41, 45, 49, 50, 58, 60, 60, 64, 66, 67, 67, 68, 74, 77, 80, 80, 81, 86, 91, 92, 93, 93, 94, 95, 95, 96, 97, 109, 112, 113, 115, 116, 117, 119, 123, 123, 125, 128, 131, 131, 139, 140, 147, 151, 153, 154, 161, 161, 165, 166, 166, 167, 168, 173, 173, 176, 179, 180, 184, 185, 188, 188, 189, 192, 205, 206, 207, 211, 217, 219, 222, 223, 228, 231, 233, 234, 239, 240, 243, 246, 247, 248, 249, 252 Cher 2, 10, 12, 18, 19, 21, 22, 23, 28, 36, 37, 39, 43, 44, 44, 52, 52, 60, 63, 77, 81, 82, 101, 113, 119, 124, 126, 127, 129 Sacr 3, 3, 5, 7, 14, 14, 21, 24, 29, 32, 40, 41, 41, 47, 48, 48, 53, 55, 55, 58, 59, 63, 64, 66, 66, 68, 71, 73, 74, 78, 82, 86, 87, 94, 97, 99, 100, 101, 103, 105, 106, 106, 109, 110, 112, 113, 117, 120, 124, 125, 126, 128, 132, 133, 138 Det 2, 6, 9, 10, 14, 17, 19, 24, 26, 33, 33, 36, 41, 44, 45, 54, 57, 58, 58, 59, 61, 65, 69, 77, 79, 81, 82, 82, 83, 86, 90, 91, 92, 95, 103, 104, 112, 117, 118, 119, 120, 121, 124, 129, 130, 137, 138, 139, 140, 146, 150, 152, 155, 155, 156, 158, 162, 163, 164, 164, 168, 178 Post 10, 12, 15, 21, 23, 27, 29, 30, 32, 34, 35, 37, 41, 42, 44, 44, 47, 48, 51, 61, 69, 72, 83, 90, 90, 91, 92, 93, 95, 98, 99, 111, 112, 113, 122, 124, 125, 130, 135, 138, 146, 151, 153, 154, 156, 157, 162, 164, 176, 183 Gig 2, 3, 8, 11, 11, 12, 14, 16, 26, 33, 35, 44, 53, 55, 56, 56, 60, 67 Deus 11, 13, 20, 27, 30, 32, 33, 35, 42, 51, 55, 60, 61, 64, 67, 69, 70, 70, 76, 79, 83, 85, 86, 87, 88, 95, 96, 97, 99, 104, 107, 116, 123, 129, 135, 140, 145, 152, 158, 159, 164, 171, 177, 178, 180 Agr 2, 17, 22, 26, 31, 39, 48, 59, 64, 70, 73, 74, 77,

84, 90, 94, 94, 95, 97, 98, 100, 101, 105, 107, 113, 117, 118, 118, 120, 122, 124, 125, 128, 143, 150, 154, 157, 162, 165, 173, 173, 175, 178, 180, 181 Plant 5, 5, 8, 10, 12, 20, 28, 32, 34, 36, 37, 41, 42, 43, 45, 49, 58, 61, 69, 73, 74, 77, 80, 85, 85, 87, 91, 99, 101, 103, 106, 109, 112, 113, 114, 123, 130, 131, 132, 137, 139, 141, 149, 162, 171, 176 Ebr 2, 4, 6, 11, 14, 19, 21, 24, 26, 28, 29, 32, 34, 35, 36, 45, 62, 68, 71, 82, 91, 95, 107, 121, 130, 133, 134, 137, 149, 153, 155, 157, 159, 161, 163, 165, 193, 193, 203, 215 Sobr 3, 14, 17, 26, 29, 30, 34, 37, 47, 51, 53, 68 Conf 4, 13, 18, 21, 40, 58, 67, 78, 86, 94, 111, 117, 117, 119, 139, 144, 156, 164, 167, 170, 171, 173, 174, 176, 179, 183, 184, 185 Migr 6, 9, 14, 15, 19, 31, 36, 61, 61, 61, 77, 82, 86, 93, 94, 100, 105, 110, 112, 117, 123, 124, 127, 131, 132, 134, 139, 148, 158, 164, 176, 178, 185, 187, 189, 197, 197, 203, 208, 210, 211, 216 Her 6, 7, 10, 13, 14, 19, 21, 27, 29, 32, 37, 42, 44, 45, 48, 52, 63, 63, 68, 69, 71, 75, 78, 85, 87, 90, 97, 101, 102, 107, 109, 113, 115, 117, 121, 123, 125, 128, 132, 142, 143, 144, 146, 169, 189, 207, 213, 215, 217, 225, 229, 230, 233, 234, 234, 237, 238, 240, 245, 250, 251, 255, 263, 264, 280, 285, 285, 288, 292, 298, 302, 304, 313 Congr 4, 6, 7, 11, 14, 18, 24, 29, 30, 31, 32, 40, 41, 44, 45, 48, 51, 51, 59, 68, 71, 73, 78, 79, 80, 88, 100, 102, 105, 107, 109, 111, 121, 125, 129, 136, 142, 144, 145, 145, 148, 156, 167, 170, 171, 172, 180 Fug 3, 3, 7, 8, 20, 23, 25, 28, 33, 35, 36, 38, 42, 46, 49, 52, 55, 62, 64, 69, 70, 74, 76, 79, 80, 83, 85, 88, 89, 90, 94, 102, 108, 114, 119, 121, 126, 133, 133, 134, 139, 146, 151, 151, 152, 153, 158, 159, 169, 171, 174, 177, 178, 179, 182, 189, 191, 202, 203, 205, 206, 207, 211 Mut 6, 7, 11, 15, 31, 34, 44, 46, 47, 50, 51, 57, 60, 62, 69, 70, 70, 75, 77, 78, 81, 83, 91, 93, 96, 97, 100, 110, 116, 117, 130, 141, 141, 150, 158, 163, 166, 171, 175, 180, 181, 186, 193, 201, 204, 208, 209, 210, 216, 216, 222, 227, 231, 236, 240, 245, 247, 253, 255, 258, 259, 259, 261 Somn 1:4, 6, 11, 11, 13, 15, 15, 16, 30, 39, 42, 43, 44, 46, 50, 53, 54, 61, 64, 70, 74, 92, 106, 110, 110, 114, 127, 137, 146, 149, 163, 163, 166, 166, 167, 169, 179, 182, 184, 188, 189, 199, 200, 202, 211, 216, 222, 224, 229, 232, 233, 238, 242, 249, 255 Somn 2:5, 9, 15, 23, 32, 48, 50, 53, 54, 63, 68, 73, 83, 95, 98, 101, 110, 111, 113, 115, 130, 130, 132, 139, 153, 158, 169, 179, 181, 183, 189, 190, 196, 197, 206, 208, 213, 215, 234, 237, 253, 254, 268, 269, 269, 277, 290, 299 Abr 2, 16, 24, 26, 38, 48, 49, 52, 54, 60, 67, 71, 71, 84, 88, 90, 92, 103, 107, 112, 114, 119, 119, 122, 123, 125, 147, 149, 150, 159, 165, 167, 174, 185, 188, 188, 191, 196, 208, 218, 219, 220, 222, 223, 226, 233, 236, 240, 244, 254, 268, 271, 274, 275 Ios 4, 6, 38, 54, 55, 59, 63, 72, 79, 84, 98, 105, 109, 110, 111, 120, 125, 143, 154, 161, 186, 193, 194, 206, 221, 226, 230, 251, 255, 266 Mos 1:9, 20, 23, 27, 30, 36, 49, 63, 74, 80, 84, 90, 91, 94, 98, 104, 105, 113, 118, 165, 198, 199, 200, 202, 204, 209, 210, 218, 223, 232, 243, 250, 271, 274, 288, 295, 296, 306, 308, 309, 311, 316, 322, 327, 330 Mos 2:8, 10, 30, 45, 47, 49, 56, 72, 74, 76, 78, 85, 88, 94, 110, 131, 142, 152, 169, 188, 189, 191, 217, 221, 223, 225, 230, 231, 233, 290 Decal 4, 13, 17, 19, 24, 29, 32, 37, 42, 50, 51, 61, 64, 65, 74, 76, 81, 82, 83, 85, 91, 98, 101, 103, 108, 110, 111, 119, 137, 177 Spec 1:8, 11, 19, 32, 32, 34, 39, 49, 51, 57, 73, 100, 105, 107, 108, 117, 150, 153, 162, 169, 180, 185, 188, 190, 191, 196, 205, 214, 215, 218, 228, 231, 240, 241, 245, 256, 259, 264, 266, 269, 270, 279, 299, 300, 313, 319, 334, 338, 340 Spec 2:12, 15, 29, 40, 46, 47, 72, 78, 83, 83, 85, 90, 114, 121, 130, 131, 132, 139, 146, 152, 154, 160, 173, 197, 201, 215, 227, 230, 234, 235, 243, 247, 257, 258, 260, 262 Spec 3:9, 22, 28, 35, 48, 49, 50, 53, 66, 76, 84, 90, 95, 100, 103, 112, 116, 117, 123, 128, 130, 132, 133, 134, 140, 148, 149, 156, 167, 170, 171, 179, 180, 185, 187, 195, 196, 200, 201, 202 Spec 4:11, 13, 22, 25, 29, 32, 35, 36, 45, 47, 74, 78, 79, 97, 101, 113, 116, 129, 135, 157, 164, 166, 190, 201, 204, 210, 217, 221, 230 Virt 4, 22, 25, 31, 48, 52, 64, 80, 85, 87, 121, 122, 125, 127, 134, 135, 170, 174, 179, 180, 206, 211, 222 Praem 1, 1, 8, 10, 12, 13, 25, 27, 29, 35, 37, 46, 47, 53, 58, 67, 69, 70, 71, 73, 76, 82, 93, 99, 107, 114, 117, 118, 119, 138, 162, 170 Prob 2, 15, 18, 19, 30, 31, 36, 38, 40, 49, 58, 61, 62, 69, 71, 84, 95, 104, 104, 113, 121, 135, 145, 147, 158 Contempl 18, 21, 23, 26, 30, 58, 66, 69, 79, 89 Aet 2, 3, 8, 13, 37, 46, 60, 69, 79, 85, 86, 87, 92, 94, 103, 105, 110, 113, 115, 128, 131, 137, 137, 142, 144, 147, 150 Flacc 2, 3, 16, 43, 52, 55, 58, 80, 86, 94, 96, 115, 182, 183 Legat 15, 41, 42, 65, 74, 89, 92, 110, 112, 112, 119, 123, 127, 136, 142, 148, 152, 152, 155, 156, 167, 174, 195, 195, 196, 205, 209, 217, 221, 222, 246, 252, 260, 263, 268, 287, 303, 306, 308, 315, 321, 333, 346, 357, 373 Hypoth 6:8, 6:9, 6:9, 7:7, 7:12 Prov 1, 2:1, 4, 10, 16, 36, 38, 42, 44, 45, 50, 52, 59 QG 1:20, 55a, 62:1, 64b, 72, 2:10, 16, 17c, 31, 54a, 54a, 54a, 59, 64c, 72, 3:3, 52, 61, 4:8b, 30, 33b, 102b, 153, 172, 228 QG isf 3, 3 QG (Par) 2:4 QE 2:3b

οὔποτε (10) Opif 97 Cher 86, 90 Ebr 128 Conf 114, 154 Somn 1:56 Abr 169 Spec 2:253 Prob 155

οὔπω (33) Opif 45 Leg 1:32 Leg 2:6 Leg 3:210, 218, 244 Cher 4 Det 30 Agr 158, 160 Ebr 59, 78 Migr 150, 200 Her 300 Congr 5 Fug 39, 202 Mut 17, 157, 166 Somn 1:56 Somn 2:93, 290 Abr 98 Ios 109 Mos 1:119, 122 Mos 2:17 Decal 72 Virt 30 Praem 68 Legat 59

οὐρά Mos 1:77 Praem 125 Legat 135

οὐραγία Ebr 24 Migr 144

οὐραῖος Mos 1:178 Praem 124

οὐράνιος (84) Opif 117, 147, 147, 158 Leg 1:31, 31, 31, 43, 45, 45, 90 Leg 3:162, 252 Cher 20 Sacr 86 Det 85 Gig 31, 60 Deus 96, 146, 151, 180 Plant 17, 39, 52, 151 Ebr 136 Conf 61, 78, 157, 157, 174 Migr 101, 121, 178 Her 64, 70, 79, 87, 191, 241, 283 Congr 58, 100, 106 Fug 137, 199 Mut 259 Somn 1:84, 146, 151, 181 Somn 2:132, 186, 242 Abr 66, 69 Ios 147 Mos 1:23, 55 Mos 2:67, 148, 266, 270 Decal 44, 104 Spec 1:92 Spec 3:111 Spec 4:154, 236 Virt 55 Praem 43, 84, 105, 121 Prob 130 Contempl 12, 27, 59 Aet 2, 30 Prov 2:66 QG 1:51, 3:21

οὐρανόθεν Somn 1:112

οὐρανομήκης Sacr 25 Prob 69 Aet 100

οὐρανομίμητος QG 1:51

οὐρανός (432) Opif 26, 27, 29, 29, 36, 37, 37, 45, 45, 46, 47, 52, 53, 55, 59, 61, 62, 70, 72, 77, 82, 82, 82, 84, 111, 112, 114, 129, 129, 168, 171 Leg 1:1, 1, 1, 2, 2, 9, 19, 21, 21, 21, 62, 62 Leg 2:9, 10, 10 Leg 3:4, 5, 39, 40, 42, 82, 99, 101, 104, 162, 162, 171, 187, 203 Cher 4, 21, 21, 23, 25, 41, 62, 88, 88, 99, 106, 111, 111 Sacr 22, 40, 97 Det 60, 62, 80, 84, 85, 88, 88, 89, 90, 156 Post 5, 19, 19, 31, 53, 53, 65, 65, 84 Gig 7, 60, 60, 60, 62 Deus 19, 30, 51, 62, 78, 79, 79, 107, 155, 156, 157, 181 Agr 17, 51, 65 Plant 3, 12, 17, 20, 22, 40, 127, 145 Ebr 70, 75, 91, 105, 106, 128, 223 Sobr 64 Conf 1, 4, 4, 5, 23, 77, 96, 100, 100, 107, 113, 128,

133, 133, 136, 154, 156, 173, 176, 197, 197 Migr 47, 64, 101, 138, 171, 181, 182, 185, 187 Her 34, 35, 76, 76, 79, 84, 86, 87, 88, 88, 97, 99, 99, 110, 112, 122, 136, 146, 147, 163, 184, 208, 221, 224, 225, 226, 226, 227, 227, 232, 233, 239, 247, 247, 251, 274, 276, 283, 301 Congr 36, 50, 51, 104, 133, 173 Fug 62, 103, 137, 166, 179, 180, 180, 184, 192, 192 Mut 59, 71, 140, 237, 256, 258, 259, 259, 259, 264 Somn 1:2, 3, 16, 21, 23, 24, 33, 34, 35, 35, 37, 39, 40, 54, 57, 57, 83, 85, 133, 134, 134, 135, 144, 145, 157, 159, 186, 195, 203, 208, 214, 215, 243 Somn 2:3, 6, 19, 67, 81, 112, 116, 119, 142, 283, 285 Abr 43, 46, 57, 71, 157, 158, 159, 159, 161, 162, 166, 205, 205, 235, 272, 272 Ios 145, 146 Mos 1:113, 117, 129, 176, 212, 217 Mos 2:14, 36, 37, 53, 56, 69, 98, 104, 105, 105, 122, 123, 133, 158, 191, 194, 194, 195, 196, 209, 210, 238, 239, 258, 263, 285, 288, 291 Decal 16, 46, 53, 56, 57, 66, 102, 103, 104, 134, 155 Spec 1:13, 15, 19, 34, 37, 44, 66, 86, 88, 89, 89, 92, 94, 94, 94, 185, 207, 210, 300, 302, 302, 302, 302, 322, 336, 339 Spec 2:5, 45, 53, 140, 141, 142, 151, 178, 189, 199, 230, 255 Spec 3:1, 111, 152, 185, 187, 202 Spec 4:34, 48, 112, 115, 232, 235 Virt 57, 73, 74, 85, 145, 212 Praem 1, 26, 36, 41, 44, 80, 101, 104, 121, 130, 131, 133, 152 Prob 25 Contempl 5, 66, 89, 90 Aet 4, 4, 4, 19, 19, 29, 46, 47, 52 Flacc 121, 123, 169 Legat 6, 347, 353 Prov 2:2, 27, 52 QG 1:1, 2:34a, 54a, 4:8b, 51b, 51b QE 2:55a

οὐριοδρομέω Legat 177

οὔριος Cher 38 Somn 2:86, 143

οὐς (ἑαυτούς) Post 115

οὖς (135) Opif 162 Leg 1:12 Leg 2:25 Leg 3:23, 199, 219 Cher 48, 57, 72 Sacr 24, 29, 34, 78, 131 Det 33, 72, 101, 131, 173 Post 36, 86, 104, 104, 126, 126, 137, 155, 167 Gig 54 Deus 15 Agr 35, 35, 136 Plant 29, 29, 83, 133, 160 Ebr 82, 106, 155, 156, 158, 177 Conf 123, 194 Migr 10, 38, 39, 52, 111, 188, 191 Her 11, 12, 48, 185 Congr 20, 143, 143 Fug 22, 85, 123, 182, 182 Mut 138, 157, 197, 247 Somn 1:27, 36, 55, 129, 193 Somn 2:168 Abr 20, 150, 240, 241 Ios 22, 77, 94 Mos 1:46, 108, 195, 223, 274, 283 Mos 2:114, 150, 163, 199, 200, 213 Decal 35, 45, 47, 63, 65, 74, 148, 169 Spec 1:191, 272 Spec 2:62, 193 Spec 3:174 Spec 4:43, 59, 60, 75, 88, 107, 137, 198, 200, 202 Virt 42, 116, 147 Praem 143 Contempl 31, 40, 63, 77 Aet 56 Legat 43, 135, 169, 197 Prov 2:14 QG (Par) 2:3 QE 2:118 QE isf 13, 21

οὐσία (222) Opif 18, 21, 27, 29, 43, 49, 54, 55, 66, 67, 69, 70, 78, 92, 97, 97, 98, 111, 114, 132, 132, 132, 135 Leg 1:31, 60, 61, 62, 62, 62, 66, 91, 91, 100 Leg 2:81 Leg 3:206 Cher 48, 65, 89, 114 Sacr 108 Det 76, 76, 80, 80, 81, 83, 91 Post 15, 163, 168, 169 Deus 46 Agr 156, 156 Plant 3 Ebr 22, 73, 88, 191 Conf 81, 85, 89, 108, 184, 186 Migr 7, 180 Her 55, 56, 133, 140, 145, 158, 188, 247, 282, 283 Congr 144 Fug 8, 26, 148, 165, 165 Mut 7, 10, 91, 200 Somn 1:30, 145 Somn 2:28, 45, 253, 253 Abr 13, 69, 77, 88, 113, 162, 163, 252 Ios 257 Mos 1:65, 70, 99, 113, 118, 141, 158 Mos 2:76, 84, 88, 119, 155, 158, 171, 245, 254 Decal 30, 31, 64, 107, 122, 134, 155 Spec 1:20, 32, 36, 39, 41, 47, 49, 66, 179, 263, 264, 266, 300, 327, 327, 328, 333 Spec 2:32, 56, 87, 94, 124, 127, 129, 131, 177, 212 Spec 3:163, 182, 182, 190 Spec 4:23, 122, 123, 123, 150, 159, 187, 207, 215, 235, 237 Virt 85, 162, 215 Praem 54 Prob 35 Contempl 7, 13, 14, 16, 18, 61, 61 Aet 4, 20, 21, 29, 48, 49, 51, 81, 85, 86, 90, 102, 103, 123, 135 Flacc 94, 130, 130, 132, 148, 150, 151, 171 Legat 80, 105, 114, 343, 344 Prov 1, 1, 1, 2:51 QG 1:92, 2:12d, 15b, 59, 59, 59, 59, 3:38a, 49b, 4:8b, 30

οὐσιώδης Det 92 Migr 192 QE 2:45a

οὔτε (505) Opif 4, 4, 40, 40, 69, 69, 73, 73, 84, 84, 84, 100, 100, 100, 100, 134, 134, 154, 154 Leg 1:1, 1, 15, 15, 15, 15, 29, 29, 54, 54, 55, 55, 60, 60, 62, 62, 87, 87, 87, 87, 87, 87, 93, 93 Leg 2:2, 2, 3, 3, 4, 4, 29, 29, 43, 43, 64, 64, 65, 65, 71, 71 Leg 3:50, 50, 50, 67, 67, 111, 111, 111, 111, 111, 137, 137, 155, 155, 238, 238, 246, 246, 247, 247 Cher 37, 37, 95, 95, 117, 117, 117, 117, 117, 123, 123 Det 18, 18, 43, 43, 46, 46, 49, 49, 54, 54, 77, 77, 77, 88, 88, 91, 91, 136, 136, 167, 167, 167 Post 22, 22, 101, 101, 118, 118 Gig 46, 46, 48, 48 Deus 29, 29, 32, 32, 48, 48, 52, 52, 80, 80, 120, 120 Agr 85, 85, 93, 93 Plant 70, 70, 162, 162, 177, 177, 177, 177, 177, 177 Ebr 76, 76, 155, 155, 158, 158, 185, 185, 191, 191, 191, 204, 204, 204, 211, 211, 212, 212 Conf 26, 26, 50, 50, 51, 55, 55, 98, 98, 98 Migr 51, 51, 87, 87, 110, 110 Her 133, 133, 149, 149, 156, 156, 187, 187, 206, 206, 228, 228, 299, 299 Congr 5, 5, 34, 34, 53, 53, 119, 119 Fug 5, 5, 8, 8, 63, 63, 87, 87, 96, 96, 109, 109, 153, 153, 171, 171 Mut 7, 7, 157, 157, 157, 157, 235, 235, 236, 236 Somn 1:68, 68, 147, 147, 220, 220 Somn 2:3, 3, 32, 32, 95, 95, 95, 95, 160, 160, 184, 184, 184, 184, 189, 234, 234, 235, 235, 264, 264, 267, 267, 267, 283, 283 Abr 6, 6, 53, 53, 53, 170, 170, 175, 175 Ios 48, 48, 67, 67, 74, 74, 76, 76, 126, 126, 148, 148, 154, 154, 215, 247, 247, 247 Mos 1:36, 36, 68, 72, 72, 76, 76, 118, 118, 125, 125, 125, 134, 134, 212, 212 Mos 2:119, 119, 200, 200, 200, 200, 210, 210, 210, 210, 242, 242, 247, 247, 271, 271 Decal 78, 78, 94, 94 Spec 1:39, 39, 67, 67, 105, 105, 204, 204, 204, 213, 213, 252, 252, 254, 254, 279, 279, 332, 332 Spec 2:25, 25, 31, 31, 169, 175, 175, 215, 215, 215 Spec 3:27, 27, 83, 83, 85, 85, 130, 130, 135, 135 Spec 4:102, 102, 197, 197 Virt 62, 62, 63, 63, 84, 84, 100, 100, 147, 147, 172, 172, 183, 183, 194, 194, 194 Praem 13, 13, 33, 33, 111, 111 Prob 18, 18, 18, 18, 44, 44, 60, 60, 60, 60, 70, 70, 91, 91, 121, 121 Contempl 12, 12, 24, 24 Aet 1, 1, 78, 78, 80, 80, 80, 115, 115, 115, 134, 134 Flacc 36, 36, 106, 106, 115, 115, 166, 166 Legat 43, 43, 43, 76, 76, 76, 152, 157, 157, 157, 157, 157, 158, 158, 162, 162, 171, 171, 184, 184, 209, 209, 220, 220, 224, 224, 261, 261, 280, 280, 317, 317 Prov 1, 1, 2:17, 17, 17, 27, 27, 28, 28, 29, 29 QG 1:28, 28, 28, 55a, 55a, 93, 93, 4:51b, 51b, 51b, 74, 74, 74, 74 QE 2:3a, 3a, 9a, 9a, 18, 18, 25b, 25b, 99, 99, 105, 105 QE isf 14, 14, 21, 21

οὔτις Aet 13, 97

οὗτος (3535) Opif 5, 16, 20, 25, 25, 34, 34, 34, 36, 36, 38, 39, 41, 42, 45, 47, 49, 49, 51, 52, 53, 54, 54, 65, 66, 66, 67, 67, 68, 69, 70, 72, 73, 74, 75, 77, 78, 79, 80, 90, 96, 97, 100, 100, 101, 102, 103, 104, 105, 108, 108, 109, 111, 118, 120, 128, 129, 129, 131, 132, 134, 134, 136, 137, 139, 143, 143, 144, 146, 152, 153, 154, 155, 156, 157, 159, 161, 161, 162, 165, 166, 172 Leg 1:2, 10, 16, 16, 17, 18, 19, 19, 19, 21, 22, 22, 22, 23, 26, 28, 32, 34, 37, 39, 39, 40, 40, 41, 43, 45, 47, 50, 50, 50, 51, 51, 52, 53, 54, 55, 55, 56, 56, 57, 59, 59, 60, 60, 61, 62, 63, 63, 63, 63, 65, 65, 66, 66, 68, 68, 69, 74, 79, 81, 82, 83, 89, 89, 90, 90, 92, 92, 93, 94, 96, 97, 99, 100, 100, 102, 102, 103, 103, 104, 104, 106, 106, 108 Leg 2:3, 4, 4, 5, 6, 6, 7, 8, 8, 9, 10, 10, 11, 11, 12, 12, 14, 15, 16, 16, 17, 18, 19, 22, 23, 23,

24, 28, 31, 31, 31, 33, 33, 36, 38, 40, 41, 41, 42, 44, 44, 44, 44, 49, 50, 51, 53, 54, 55, 55, 55, 56, 60, 60, 60, 63, 64, 67, 71, 72, 75, 77, 78, 79, 81, 87, 88, 89, 89, 90, 92, 93, 95, 96, 96, 98, 100, 102, 102, 103, 105, 108 Leg 3:1, 3, 5, 9, 10, 12, 17, 18, 20, 20, 22, 23, 26, 27, 32, 39, 39, 43, 44, 46, 48, 51, 51, 52, 55, 56, 56, 57, 57, 58, 59, 59, 60, 62, 63, 65, 66, 66, 67, 68, 69, 71, 72, 76, 78, 79, 80, 81, 83, 83, 84, 86, 86, 86, 87, 88, 90, 90, 90, 91, 95, 96, 97, 99, 101, 101, 102, 102, 105, 105, 107, 108, 108, 111, 112, 113, 113, 114, 115, 117, 119, 120, 122, 123, 124, 124, 124, 124, 125, 125, 125, 126, 126, 126, 129, 130, 131, 133, 134, 134, 135, 136, 138, 139, 140, 146, 146, 147, 148, 157, 161, 166, 167, 167, 168, 168, 169, 169, 169, 170, 171, 172, 173, 173, 173, 174, 175, 175, 177, 177, 177, 177, 178, 178, 178, 178, 179, 179, 180, 181, 181, 184, 184, 185, 185, 185, 186, 186, 187, 187, 188, 192, 194, 198, 200, 203, 203, 207, 209, 212, 216, 216, 218, 218, 218, 220, 226, 226, 226, 227, 227, 231, 232, 232, 235, 235, 236, 237, 240, 241, 244, 246, 246, 246, 246, 247, 249, 250, 253 Cher 7, 14, 22, 25, 29, 30, 33, 33, 39, 40, 41, 42, 44, 45, 48, 49, 52, 58, 58, 65, 66, 67, 67, 68, 69, 71, 73, 74, 76, 81, 82, 84, 85, 86, 86, 87, 89, 92, 94, 95, 109, 111, 112, 124, 126 Sacr 4, 4, 4, 8, 10, 10, 12, 14, 17, 19, 19, 19, 20, 20, 20, 22, 22, 25, 25, 26, 29, 30, 32, 32, 34, 35, 37, 37, 38, 38, 40, 41, 41, 43, 44, 45, 46, 49, 54, 54, 54, 55, 56, 56, 57, 58, 60, 62, 64, 70, 70, 73, 74, 74, 77, 77, 80, 85, 86, 91, 96, 97, 99, 101, 103, 104, 107, 108, 110, 112, 115, 119, 121, 123, 124, 127, 128, 129, 129, 129, 130, 133, 133, 134, 134, 135, 136, 139, 139 Det 4, 4, 7, 9, 10, 12, 13, 13, 16, 16, 18, 19, 21, 22, 23, 24, 24, 26, 30, 31, 33, 34, 35, 36, 37, 40, 40, 41, 44, 48, 50, 54, 57, 59, 61, 63, 66, 74, 75, 77, 79, 80, 82, 84, 86, 89, 91, 94, 97, 99, 101, 104, 104, 105, 108, 108, 111, 115, 116, 118, 118, 121, 121, 122, 123, 126, 127, 128, 131, 134, 135, 138, 138, 139, 139, 141, 141, 147, 148, 149, 151, 151, 154, 154, 155, 156, 157, 160, 161, 162, 166, 167, 168, 169, 169, 171, 174, 176, 178 Post 4, 8, 9, 12, 13, 15, 16, 17, 24, 27, 27, 31, 33, 36, 40, 43, 44, 49, 50, 51, 53, 55, 57, 59, 59, 60, 61, 62, 64, 65, 65, 65, 67, 72, 73, 74, 74, 78, 80, 82, 85, 85, 86, 87, 89, 89, 91, 91, 94, 98, 100, 100, 101, 101, 102, 103, 104, 112, 114, 116, 116, 117, 118, 118, 122, 127, 128, 129, 130, 135, 137, 138, 139, 141, 147, 153, 158, 159, 160, 160, 162, 164, 169, 169, 169, 173, 173, 173, 174, 175, 177, 177, 178, 180, 180, 180, 181, 184, 185 Gig 5, 7, 8, 8, 9, 12, 15, 16, 17, 17, 30, 32, 32, 33, 36, 37, 37, 42, 43, 47, 48, 49, 50, 50, 55, 56, 66, 67 Deus 5, 6, 6, 6, 8, 9, 12, 15, 20, 21, 25, 28, 31, 32, 34, 36, 39, 42, 44, 45, 46, 46, 48, 50, 51, 51, 59, 59, 60, 60, 61, 61, 62, 62, 65, 66, 66, 68, 72, 77, 77, 79, 79, 82, 86, 88, 88, 89, 91, 92, 92, 92, 94, 96, 97, 106, 106, 107, 107, 110, 113, 114, 116, 119, 120, 121, 123, 124, 125, 126, 128, 131, 131, 133, 135, 136, 137, 138, 143, 143, 143, 144, 144, 145, 151, 153, 153, 154, 157, 160, 166, 167, 168, 171, 179, 179, 181, 183, 183 Agr 5, 5, 6, 8, 9, 10, 11, 12, 17, 18, 18, 19, 20, 22, 23, 29, 31, 34, 36, 36, 39, 41, 42, 42, 43, 44, 44, 48, 50, 51, 51, 51, 53, 55, 56, 57, 58, 59, 60, 73, 77, 78, 83, 87, 90, 92, 94, 96, 103, 103, 109, 111, 111, 112, 113, 113, 116, 116, 119, 120, 121, 121, 123, 127, 128, 130, 135, 140, 140, 141, 141, 147, 148, 149, 149, 151, 151, 154, 154, 159, 160, 161, 164, 164, 168, 169, 173, 173, 175, 175, 176, 181 Plant 1, 4, 4, 9, 12, 14, 23, 25, 26, 31, 31, 31, 35, 37, 37, 37, 38, 39, 42, 49, 53, 55, 56, 56, 59, 62, 63, 64, 68, 70, 72, 76, 77, 77, 78, 81, 81, 82, 84, 86, 90, 91, 99, 101, 101, 104, 104, 106, 108, 110, 113, 114, 125, 126, 130, 130, 131, 133, 134, 138, 138, 146, 148, 152, 152, 153, 154, 154, 160, 161, 163, 165, 166, 167, 169, 169, 174, 176, 177 Ebr 1, 2, 3, 4, 7, 14, 17, 17, 18, 25, 25, 31, 32, 35, 38, 48, 51, 52, 52, 58, 60, 62, 65, 70, 70, 71, 72, 73, 74, 77, 79, 79, 80, 80, 82, 83, 85, 87, 87, 88, 89, 90, 92, 93, 93, 94, 94, 94, 95, 96, 97, 99, 100, 101, 101, 105, 106, 110, 111, 113, 114, 115, 117, 118, 120, 129, 132, 133, 136, 138, 140, 141, 141, 143, 145, 150, 152, 153, 154, 164, 166, 169, 171, 174, 174, 175, 175, 176, 177, 178, 180, 188, 189, 191, 192, 192, 193, 194, 197, 201, 202, 206, 207, 210, 216, 220, 220, 224, 224 Sobr 9, 10, 13, 17, 18, 19, 20, 21, 21, 24, 25, 25, 26, 27, 28, 31, 33, 39, 40, 41, 44, 49, 49, 50, 51, 54, 54, 56, 58, 58, 58, 59, 61, 61, 62, 63, 64, 65, 66, 68, 68 Conf 1, 1, 1, 2, 4, 4, 5, 6, 6, 7, 7, 9, 14, 15, 16, 19, 20, 20, 22, 23, 26, 26, 26, 34, 44, 48, 49, 49, 54, 57, 59, 59, 63, 66, 66, 69, 71, 74, 75, 77, 77, 81, 87, 88, 88, 89, 90, 90, 91, 91, 92, 96, 97, 107, 111, 117, 118, 118, 122, 124, 126, 130, 130, 132, 133, 135, 137, 141, 142, 143, 144, 145, 149, 152, 154, 155, 158, 158, 159, 160, 161, 163, 163, 171, 172, 172, 174, 175, 176, 179, 179, 180, 180, 181, 187, 189, 190, 190, 191, 195, 197 Migr 3, 5, 5, 6, 7, 9, 15, 18, 23, 24, 28, 28, 29, 33, 37, 37, 38, 40, 45, 47, 47, 49, 50, 51, 51, 51, 56, 57, 58, 59, 60, 63, 67, 68, 68, 69, 72, 81, 88, 88, 93, 93, 93, 94, 95, 101, 104, 105, 109, 110, 115, 115, 116, 116, 116, 118, 119, 122, 122, 122, 124, 126, 128, 129, 134, 137, 137, 139, 139, 143, 143, 144, 144, 145, 148, 149, 151, 151, 152, 154, 155, 156, 158, 159, 160, 160, 161, 162, 164, 164, 165, 166, 169, 169, 172, 176, 177, 179, 179, 183, 184, 184, 189, 192, 192, 195, 198, 199, 201, 202, 203, 212, 219, 219, 220, 220, 221, 221, 224, 224 Her 1, 2, 8, 11, 11, 20, 20, 20, 20, 21, 22, 24, 30, 33, 42, 46, 49, 49, 50, 52, 53, 57, 58, 59, 64, 65, 66, 68, 68, 70, 73, 74, 74, 75, 76, 81, 89, 90, 91, 93, 95, 96, 96, 97, 101, 106, 107, 108, 108, 108, 109, 110, 110, 112, 118, 123, 124, 125, 126, 127, 127, 128, 129, 129, 131, 131, 136, 136, 137, 138, 140, 144, 146, 146, 147, 147, 156, 162, 171, 172, 173, 179, 185, 186, 186, 188, 190, 191, 197, 198, 198, 199, 202, 214, 215, 230, 231, 233, 233, 234, 236, 239, 239, 255, 256, 258, 259, 261, 263, 264, 265, 265, 266, 268, 272, 274, 275, 279, 280, 280, 281, 283, 285, 297, 298, 298, 301, 302, 302, 313 Congr 3, 6, 9, 10, 18, 20, 22, 23, 30, 34, 37, 38, 42, 42, 44, 44, 52, 54, 56, 57, 58, 62, 67, 69, 70, 72, 73, 74, 74, 79, 80, 80, 81, 81, 83, 90, 93, 96, 98, 101, 101, 103, 104, 105, 105, 106, 106, 107, 107, 108, 108, 109, 112, 117, 117, 117, 120, 120, 128, 131, 132, 133, 137, 137, 138, 139, 141, 144, 146, 147, 149, 150, 151, 151, 152, 154, 163, 163, 163, 168, 175 Fug 1, 4, 8, 9, 10, 11, 17, 19, 19, 20, 22, 27, 32, 34, 35, 39, 45, 46, 47, 49, 50, 58, 58, 59, 63, 68, 73, 73, 77, 78, 82, 82, 82, 89, 90, 101, 103, 105, 110, 113, 114, 115, 115, 116, 117, 124, 124, 131, 135, 136, 138, 139, 139, 139, 142, 143, 144, 149, 151, 151, 151, 154, 157, 164, 164, 164, 166, 167, 169, 169, 171, 173, 175, 177, 177, 178, 180, 181, 182, 188, 189, 192, 194, 196, 196, 198, 203, 209, 209, 210, 212 Mut 2, 6, 12, 14, 19, 24, 25, 25, 29, 29, 30, 32, 35, 37, 38, 39, 39, 39, 42, 44, 51, 53, 58, 62, 63, 64, 66, 68, 69, 69, 73, 77, 77, 79, 79, 81, 83, 84, 85, 86, 87, 89, 92, 93, 94, 101, 104, 105, 106, 107, 108, 109, 110, 111, 119, 121, 121, 121, 124, 128, 128, 128, 128, 131, 134, 134, 138, 138, 139, 142, 144, 146, 147, 152, 154, 156, 161, 163, 168, 173, 177, 180, 181, 195, 196, 197, 198, 199, 201, 201, 202, 204, 206, 206, 206, 207, 207, 207, 208, 209, 209, 213, 216, 218, 219, 222, 225, 228, 231,

231, 240, 243, 243, 249, 252, 255, 256, 257, 264 Somn 1:1, 1, 3, 5, 6, 8, 9, 11, 13, 14, 17, 21, 23, 23, 24, 24, 25, 27, 33, 35, 43, 45, 48, 49, 51, 53, 54, 57, 58, 59, 60, 68, 69, 72, 72, 75, 82, 91, 92, 92, 95, 97, 101, 101, 101, 102, 102, 103, 104, 107, 108, 109, 111, 115, 122, 125, 125, 126, 127, 128, 128, 128, 135, 135, 135, 135, 136, 137, 138, 139, 141, 151, 152, 159, 159, 162, 164, 165, 166, 167, 171, 172, 174, 175, 177, 180, 181, 182, 183, 184, 185, 185, 185, 186, 186, 189, 189, 194, 198, 200, 201, 203, 204, 205, 206, 206, 206, 209, 210, 212, 213, 216, 218, 221, 225, 235, 235, 236, 237, 248, 248 Somn 2:3, 8, 9, 11, 21, 26, 29, 41, 45, 46, 49, 50, 64, 65, 70, 74, 75, 79, 82, 85, 89, 101, 104, 108, 109, 112, 115, 117, 128, 128, 129, 130, 131, 133, 135, 135, 140, 142, 144, 145, 147, 150, 151, 154, 155, 157, 172, 173, 175, 180, 184, 185, 187, 188, 193, 194, 205, 207, 207, 208, 210, 215, 221, 224, 229, 231, 240, 243, 245, 252, 255, 260, 261, 262, 262, 263, 265, 265, 266, 271, 273, 274, 278, 280, 282, 283, 283, 291, 297, 298 Abr 2, 4, 7, 9, 9, 9, 14, 15, 16, 17, 24, 34, 38, 39, 46, 47, 48, 50, 51, 52, 57, 60, 66, 67, 70, 71, 72, 73, 73, 75, 87, 87, 89, 93, 98, 99, 102, 112, 112, 118, 118, 119, 121, 123, 131, 132, 137, 142, 144, 150, 154, 154, 162, 164, 165, 166, 176, 180, 183, 184, 184, 194, 197, 202, 203, 203, 204, 204, 206, 210, 215, 216, 217, 220, 221, 222, 223, 224, 224, 227, 228, 230, 230, 232, 236, 239, 240, 243, 257, 258, 266, 269, 270, 275, 275 Ios 1, 7, 12, 15, 21, 23, 24, 30, 30, 33, 33, 33, 37, 44, 44, 45, 47, 50, 58, 60, 64, 68, 71, 78, 80, 88, 88, 92, 96, 103, 106, 109, 114, 117, 121, 124, 126, 127, 127, 143, 143, 143, 143, 144, 144, 144, 145, 150, 150, 156, 157, 160, 163, 166, 167, 168, 172, 172, 175, 177, 177, 177, 188, 189, 190, 202, 204, 205, 209, 214, 215, 220, 225, 226, 228, 232, 233, 235, 243, 244, 244, 245, 249, 253, 259, 264, 270 Mos 1:4, 4, 6, 7, 13, 16, 24, 31, 36, 40, 44, 45, 47, 57, 65, 69, 71, 76, 79, 80, 82, 85, 87, 88, 89, 94, 98, 101, 103, 109, 111, 111, 111, 112, 117, 129, 129, 145, 145, 145, 147, 148, 151, 152, 154, 155, 160, 169, 173, 175, 176, 177, 180, 180, 180, 190, 191, 198, 198, 200, 200, 201, 204, 206, 210, 212, 212, 213, 220, 224, 225, 227, 230, 234, 235, 237, 242, 245, 245, 245, 247, 247, 250, 252, 263, 266, 271, 275, 279, 279, 280, 285, 290, 292, 303, 315, 319, 320, 328, 333, 334 Mos 2:2, 6, 6, 9, 9, 10, 14, 17, 17, 27, 30, 36, 38, 39, 43, 44, 46, 55, 57, 64, 65, 66, 67, 69, 83, 88, 94, 96, 97, 98, 101, 106, 109, 110, 112, 118, 119, 119, 121, 124, 126, 127, 133, 138, 139, 142, 147, 150, 153, 153, 158, 174, 174, 176, 183, 193, 196, 201, 210, 211, 213, 214, 218, 222, 223, 224, 226, 226, 228, 228, 230, 232, 234, 238, 240, 242, 242, 245, 246, 246, 253, 258, 260, 266, 268, 269, 269, 277, 280, 281, 290 Decal 1, 8, 11, 12, 18, 24, 26, 27, 31, 32, 36, 41, 43, 50, 50, 63, 72, 74, 75, 77, 79, 83, 88, 89, 90, 90, 91, 93, 96, 98, 98, 105, 110, 111, 116, 118, 118, 121, 124, 126, 136, 140, 141, 143, 144, 152, 153, 154, 155, 160, 162, 168, 176 Spec 1:4, 8, 12, 16, 21, 23, 26, 30, 31, 31, 32, 32, 35, 37, 38, 41, 45, 49, 50, 51, 56, 57, 57, 58, 61, 62, 62, 64, 64, 65, 65, 68, 71, 72, 75, 79, 86, 89, 93, 98, 102, 110, 111, 112, 112, 117, 125, 128, 129, 130, 132, 135, 136, 138, 141, 141, 145, 147, 151, 154, 156, 156, 158, 161, 161, 164, 165, 168, 176, 177, 179, 184, 192, 194, 199, 200, 209, 210, 211, 212, 212, 213, 213, 213, 214, 215, 225, 226, 226, 228, 230, 230, 235, 235, 237, 238, 238, 247, 247, 248, 252, 253, 255, 259, 259, 259, 261, 262, 262, 264, 265, 266, 267, 268, 269, 270, 273, 279, 287, 288, 288, 289, 296, 299, 299, 300, 301, 302, 307, 309, 311, 313, 319, 320, 323, 323, 325, 327, 328, 329, 330, 332, 335, 335, 335, 336, 336, 338, 340, 340, 342, 344, 344 Spec 2:1, 2, 5, 6, 6, 10, 11, 12, 22, 22, 25, 29, 30, 32, 35, 36, 41, 42, 47, 48, 55, 59, 66, 71, 72, 73, 78, 82, 96, 97, 97, 100, 103, 104, 106, 110, 112, 115, 116, 116, 120, 121, 126, 133, 134, 135, 137, 139, 139, 141, 142, 144, 144, 146, 146, 149, 150, 158, 161, 162, 163, 165, 165, 167, 170, 170, 172, 174, 176, 190, 191, 192, 194, 194, 197, 197, 198, 198, 198, 203, 210, 214, 215, 215, 219, 220, 222, 225, 225, 226, 227, 229, 232, 232, 238, 241, 242, 247, 252, 258, 258, 259, 260, 261, 262, 262 Spec 3:4, 6, 7, 8, 13, 15, 17, 28, 33, 34, 39, 60, 62, 66, 72, 74, 77, 86, 91, 101, 104, 104, 110, 111, 111, 112, 116, 119, 124, 127, 127, 128, 128, 132, 133, 136, 136, 136, 137, 144, 151, 152, 154, 156, 157, 158, 159, 160, 165, 167, 168, 172, 175, 180, 183, 184, 184, 185, 188, 189, 191, 191, 192, 192, 192, 198, 198, 200, 203, 203, 204, 204, 208 Spec 4:1, 2, 7, 10, 10, 19, 23, 26, 31, 34, 39, 41, 47, 48, 57, 58, 59, 59, 78, 79, 86, 88, 92, 103, 105, 106, 107, 108, 109, 110, 110, 112, 114, 117, 125, 126, 129, 132, 133, 134, 135, 137, 138, 139, 149, 149, 154, 157, 162, 163, 166, 171, 175, 176, 177, 178, 179, 186, 187, 188, 190, 195, 196, 196, 196, 197, 199, 200, 202, 202, 202, 202, 207, 207, 212, 212, 219, 222, 227, 229, 229, 232, 235 Virt 4, 6, 8, 10, 14, 15, 17, 19, 20, 31, 33, 34, 35, 38, 39, 41, 42, 45, 51, 55, 56, 59, 60, 60, 65, 66, 67, 68, 69, 83, 86, 94, 95, 104, 109, 111, 114, 118, 119, 120, 121, 121, 121, 122, 125, 125, 131, 135, 140, 140, 145, 153, 159, 162, 165, 166, 167, 176, 180, 183, 184, 184, 188, 190, 195, 197, 198, 200, 201, 202, 203, 204, 206, 208, 211, 213, 213, 215, 218, 219, 220, 222, 224 Praem 8, 10, 10, 11, 13, 13, 14, 16, 20, 23, 24, 25, 26, 30, 35, 41, 43, 44, 44, 45, 46, 47, 52, 52, 54, 56, 57, 60, 61, 63, 65, 68, 69, 69, 70, 74, 74, 78, 80, 81, 83, 84, 85, 86, 87, 88, 95, 97, 98, 98, 104, 107, 108, 108, 111, 113, 118, 122, 123, 123, 123, 124, 124, 124, 125, 132, 134, 142, 143, 146, 148, 149, 152, 154, 156, 159, 165, 167 Prob 1, 2, 5, 12, 16, 27, 28, 31, 38, 42, 50, 59, 63, 64, 72, 76, 81, 84, 86, 93, 96, 103, 104, 105, 117, 120, 125, 128, 134, 140, 143, 143, 146, 152, 157, 160 Contempl 5, 6, 6, 9, 10, 11, 14, 15, 16, 17, 17, 32, 37, 40, 41, 42, 44, 47, 50, 53, 56, 57, 58, 61, 63, 65, 71, 72, 73, 74, 78, 81, 83, 87, 88, 89 Aet 9, 15, 16, 19, 26, 27, 31, 32, 33, 37, 44, 46, 48, 52, 52, 53, 53, 53, 54, 58, 60, 66, 67, 69, 70, 74, 80, 81, 83, 88, 90, 92, 92, 94, 96, 99, 99, 103, 103, 104, 105, 107, 107, 112, 122, 125, 130, 131, 137 Flacc 1, 2, 6, 6, 16, 19, 21, 21, 24, 24, 30, 32, 35, 36, 36, 40, 42, 43, 55, 55, 56, 58, 59, 60, 62, 72, 76, 77, 79, 80, 82, 84, 85, 85, 86, 87, 90, 92, 93, 94, 100, 101, 104, 111, 115, 116, 124, 128, 128, 133, 136, 142, 144, 146, 149, 159, 164, 171, 172, 174, 175 Legat 4, 6, 14, 22, 28, 29, 32, 52, 59, 62, 65, 68, 68, 68, 76, 77, 80, 80, 86, 89, 98, 98, 108, 110, 114, 123, 124, 128, 130, 136, 142, 145, 146, 146, 146, 147, 148, 165, 165, 166, 171, 172, 178, 179, 184, 192, 196, 197, 198, 200, 201, 204, 206, 206, 210, 213, 218, 219, 223, 230, 231, 232, 236, 237, 241, 242, 242, 243, 253, 274, 276, 277, 281, 288, 289, 290, 293, 299, 299, 302, 303, 308, 309, 312, 313, 315, 315, 315, 317, 319, 320, 320, 330, 335, 338, 338, 339, 341, 350, 355, 355, 357, 357, 358, 370 Hypoth 0:1, 6:1, 6:3, 6:4, 6:4, 6:5, 6:5, 6:6, 6:7, 6:8, 6:8, 6:9, 6:10, 7:1, 7:1, 7:2, 7:2, 7:3, 7:5, 7:5, 7:6, 7:8, 7:9, 7:9, 7:10, 7:10, 7:11, 7:12, 7:14, 7:17, 7:17, 7:17, 7:19, 7:20, 7:20, 7:20, 7:20, 11:3, 11:16 Prov 1, 2:1, 2, 2, 2, 3, 5, 7, 11, 14, 15, 16, 20, 26, 27, 32, 34, 37, 40, 41, 44, 44, 45, 46, 47, 47, 48, 48, 49, 53, 54, 59, 61, 63, 64, 66, 69, 71, 72 QG 1:1, 1, 1, 20, 20, 21,

21, 29, 41, 55c, 60:2, 60:2, 64a, 66, 66, 72, 76b, 77, 94, 96:1, 100:2b, 2:5a, 11, 11, 11, 15a, 31, 31, 31, 34a, 34a, 34a, 38, 39, 39, 54a, 54a, 54d, 59, 62, 65, 3:21, 22, 58, 61, 4:8b, 51c, 52d, 52d, 76b, 86b, 88, 100, 102c, 130, 144, 145, 173, 173, 174, 180, 198, 198, 200a, 200c, 202a, 204, 227, 228 QG isf 5, 5 QG (Par) 2:1, 2:3, 2:3, 2:3, 2:4, 2:4, 2:4, 2:4, 2:5, 2:5, 2:6, 2:6, 2:7, 2:7 QE 2:2, 2, 15b, 18, 18, 46, 46, 46, 47 QE isf 9, 14, 21

οὕτως (566) Opif 6, 23, 28, 61, 62, 72, 105, 140, 150 Leg 1:5, 18, 22, 23, 24, 39, 39, 46, 51, 60, 62, 66, 71, 74, 82, 87, 91, 100 Leg 2:2, 6, 15, 18, 18, 19, 25, 29, 32, 34, 37, 38, 60, 67, 68, 74, 77, 82, 94, 97, 102 Leg 3:7, 10, 21, 23, 33, 40, 40, 41, 48, 64, 77, 96, 99, 99, 105, 107, 110, 118, 121, 127, 128, 135, 140, 141, 141, 141, 144, 144, 149, 154, 160, 170, 171, 173, 177, 182, 202, 202, 203, 217, 224, 229, 231, 239, 248, 249 Cher 24, 25, 55, 79, 83, 103, 105, 110, 113, 118 Sacr 16, 39, 41, 41, 42, 66, 66, 72, 76, 80, 83, 83, 101, 102, 107, 109, 120, 122, 122, 126, 129 Det 18, 47, 52, 52, 58, 75, 87, 90, 91, 125, 134, 160, 166, 173 Post 13, 22, 28, 39, 40, 48, 57, 71, 76, 104, 106, 108, 111, 121, 125, 127, 149, 171, 183 Gig 16, 20, 25, 30, 54, 67 Deus 18, 27, 68, 79, 110, 133, 141, 142, 143, 147, 178 Agr 27, 41, 50, 87, 93, 96, 112, 132, 144, 155, 160 Plant 8, 11, 22, 69, 80, 82, 83, 94, 113, 115, 142, 154, 161, 171 Ebr 8, 13, 44, 47, 105, 128, 177, 177, 177, 197 Sobr 10, 12, 19, 43, 45, 58 Conf 12, 55, 55, 89, 100, 116, 131, 142, 145, 153, 158, 183 Migr 8, 39, 65, 68, 69, 82, 83, 86, 93, 98, 100, 108, 110, 123, 129, 138, 175, 186, 194, 211 Her 16, 41, 83, 86, 86, 87, 87, 87, 94, 120, 124, 133, 136, 140, 150, 155, 180, 222, 229, 242, 270 Congr 10, 50, 53, 79, 79, 90, 135, 143, 152, 168, 171, 171, 175, 177 Fug 30, 36, 37, 59, 91, 97, 98, 102, 121, 146, 186, 192, 208 Mut 14, 42, 69, 75, 80, 98, 102, 119, 123, 124, 148, 157, 182, 200, 221, 262 Somn 1:5, 12, 60, 76, 76, 87, 93, 98, 98, 101, 108, 109, 110, 118, 176, 188, 203, 211, 225, 239, 256 Somn 2:64, 86, 95, 100, 104, 139, 145, 174, 178, 180, 201, 201, 204, 232, 259, 272, 282, 298 Abr 14, 31, 63, 82, 87, 169, 198, 266, 269 Ios 34, 79, 83, 104, 126, 135, 140, 141, 153, 177, 198, 211, 226, 250, 255 Mos 1:39, 109, 118, 118, 146, 182, 194, 196, 217, 234, 236, 243, 274, 293, 298 Mos 2:2, 6, 43, 91, 120, 145, 181, 241, 248, 265, 279 Decal 8, 46, 73, 84, 95, 105, 150, 151 Spec 1:42, 105, 114, 172, 193, 301, 310, 310, 313, 328 Spec 2:27, 51, 70, 87, 132, 189, 195, 202, 239, 241, 247, 251, 254 Spec 3:27, 37, 68, 87, 100, 113, 116, 131, 142, 184, 194, 197 Spec 4:9, 52, 56, 69, 80, 82, 84, 118, 133, 184, 233, 235 Virt 10, 21, 30, 34, 84, 92, 108, 135, 141, 146, 186, 208 Praem 21, 42, 48, 91, 117, 135, 146, 153 Prob 15, 21, 22, 28, 45, 47, 49, 51, 68, 130, 131, 133, 146, 150, 154, 157 Contempl 35, 55, 66 Aet 6, 21, 28, 50, 56, 61, 67, 102, 105, 118 Flacc 8, 39, 51, 124, 127, 146, 150, 162, 165 Legat 46, 55, 67, 73, 157, 163, 211, 233, 245, 257, 260, 292, 305, 315, 320, 347, 352, 366 Hypoth 6:2, 6:8, 6:10, 11:10, 11:18 Prov 2:20, 44, 52, 64 QG 1:3, 41, 55a, 60:2, 100:1a, 100:1c, 2:41, 72, 3:3, 12, 4:64, 76b, 104, 180, 204, 227 QG isf 1, 9, 13 QE 2:6b, 21, 26, 47 QE isf 1, 30

ὀφείλω (69) Leg 2:15, 67 Gig 11 Deus 50 Agr 164 Ebr 211 Sobr 6 Conf 44, 44, 50, 50, 116 Migr 155 Her 125, 238 Congr 123 Abr 187 Ios 44, 77, 215 Mos 1:26, 58, 115, 196 Mos 2:5, 128, 135, 218, 236 Decal 99 Spec 1:5, 40, 54, 101, 114, 209, 224, 283 Spec 2:69, 113, 167 Spec 3:26, 59, 115, 159 Spec 4:56, 68, 150, 186, 193 Virt 7, 20, 127 Praem 56 Prob 44 Aet 27, 61 Flacc 24, 35, 81, 134 Legat 53, 133, 140, 152 Prov 2:23, 27 QG 1:69 QE 2:118

ὄφελος (48) Leg 1:29, 79 Leg 2:36 Leg 3:41, 121 Cher 9 Det 58 Post 86, 87 Deus 152 Agr 134, 169 Ebr 213 Conf 50, 153 Migr 55, 87 Her 279 Congr 46, 65 Mut 73, 148, 199 Abr 59, 73, 135 Ios 115 Mos 1:178, 235 Mos 2:53, 130 Spec 1:74 Spec 2:209 Spec 3:78, 78, 203 Spec 4:108 Virt 31, 152, 193, 194 Praem 108, 142 Aet 89 Flacc 186 Legat 192, 337, 357

ὀφθαλμός (180) Opif 30, 53, 53, 66, 66, 66, 119, 123, 162 Leg 1:12, 91 Leg 2:43, 67 Leg 3:57, 171 Cher 57, 96, 97 Sacr 21, 24, 29, 34, 36 Det 33, 61, 173 Post 24, 36, 118, 126, 137, 155, 161 Gig 59 Deus 15, 38, 39, 58 Agr 34, 35, 35 Plant 22, 29, 83, 133 Ebr 82, 106, 131, 135, 155, 156, 158 Sobr 4, 5 Conf 52, 92, 100, 100, 123, 194 Migr 10, 35, 38, 44, 51, 77, 165, 188 Her 48, 55, 78, 80, 89, 185 Congr 20, 135, 143, 143, 143, 143, 145 Fug 123, 182 Mut 3, 4, 40, 157, 256 Somn 1:27, 55, 64, 67, 189, 197, 211 Somn 2:19, 282 Abr 57, 76, 150, 151, 153, 154, 154, 158, 158, 161, 241 Ios 22, 23, 47, 58, 58, 226 Mos 1:55, 108, 166, 223, 274, 278 Mos 2:70, 213 Decal 47, 60, 68, 74, 89, 143, 147 Spec 1:40, 49, 117, 214, 259, 288, 340 Spec 2:209 Spec 3:6, 161, 177, 184, 184, 185, 193, 194, 195, 196, 202, 202, 202 Spec 4:60, 60, 62, 137, 139, 139, 163, 191, 200, 202 Virt 11, 12 Praem 143, 143 Prob 140 Contempl 53, 77 Aet 56, 86 Flacc 62 Legat 2, 109, 222, 224, 238, 269 QG 1:69, 2:72 QG (Par) 2:3

ὀφθαλμοφανής Mut 237

ὀφιομάχης (ὀφιομάχος) Opif 163, 164 Leg 2:105, 108 Spec 4:114

ὀφιομάχος ὀφιομάχης

ὄφις (62) Opif 156, 157, 159, 160, 163 Leg 2:53, 71, 72, 74, 74, 76, 77, 78, 79, 79, 79, 79, 80, 81, 81, 81, 84, 84, 87, 87, 88, 90, 92, 93, 94, 94, 97, 98, 106 Leg 3:59, 61, 65, 65, 66, 66, 68, 75, 76, 76, 76, 107, 188, 246 Det 177 Agr 94, 95, 97, 97, 99, 100, 107 Conf 7 Migr 66 Mos 1:192 Praem 90 QG 1:31, 32

ὀφιώδης Leg 2:84, 88, 105 Leg 3:61, 66

ὄφλημα Ios 24 Mos 1:333 Decal 117

ὀφλισκάνω (6) Deus 100 Agr 93 Ebr 65, 131 Her 226 Fug 146

ὀφρῦς (7) Sacr 21 Congr 127 Somn 1:102 Mos 2:240 Decal 40 Legat 350 QG 4:99

ὀχεία (6) Somn 1:197 Abr 135, 149 Spec 3:57 Spec 4:94, 203

ὀχετός Leg 1:13 Post 50, 126 QG (Par) 2:6

ὄχευμα Aet 96

ὀχεύω (8) Somn 1:200 Spec 3:36, 46, 47, 47, 49, 49 Spec 4:203

ὀχέω Plant 3

ὄχημα (9) Leg 2:85 Leg 3:193 Cher 24 Agr 76, 77 Migr 131 Mos 2:121 Decal 4 Aet 115

ὄχθη Ios 101 Mos 1:10, 99, 115 Aet 147

ὀχληρός Leg 3:44 Contempl 24

ὀχλικός Sacr 50 Flacc 135

ὀχλοκρατία (11) Opif 171 Agr 45, 46 Conf 108 Fug 10 Somn 2:286 Decal 155 Virt 180 Flacc 65 Legat 132 QE 1:7b ὄχλος (63) Leg 2:77, 85 Leg 3:235 Det 71 Gig 35 Deus 2 Agr 44 Ebr 113, 198 Migr 60, 154, 163, 200 Her 56, 234, 303 Congr 27 Mut 93, 144 Somn 1:43 Somn 2:188 Abr 22, 229 Ios 36, 58, 59, 60, 61, 64, 64, 66, 149, 150 Mos 1:100, 147, 197 Decal 10, 39 Spec 1:298 Spec 2:163, 231 Spec 3:174 Spec 4:46, 47, 188 Virt 25 Praem 20 Contempl 27 Flacc 3, 4, 33, 35, 41, 82, 95, 135 Legat 67, 120, 226, 252 Prov 2:17 QG 4:47b QE isf 20

ὀχυρός (11) Det 105 Agr 15 Plant 8 Conf 31, 91, 113 Mut 81 Somn 1:77 Somn 2:170, 262 Spec 1:146

ὀχυρότης Somn 1:158

ὀχυρόω (11) Leg 3:115 Cher 78 Det 35 Post 151 Plant 3 Conf 111, 193 Her 42 Somn 1:103 Mos 2:180 Spec 1:71

ὀχύρωμα Conf 129, 130

ὀψαρτυτής (14) Opif 158 Leg 3:143, 221 Agr 66 Plant 159 Ebr 214, 219 Somn 2:50 Ios 63 Spec 1:174 Spec 4:113 Prob 156 Contempl 53 Flacc 90

ὀψέ (16) Sacr 16, 71 Post 34 Ebr 51 Sobr 29 Mos 2:233 Spec 1:103 Spec 2:135 Spec 4:18 Contempl 67 Aet 71, 77 Flacc 103 Legat 363 QG 2:54d QE 2:21

ὀψίγονος (10) Leg 3:92 Sobr 26 Her 307 Abr 195 Ios 4, 223 Mos 2:222 Praem 9 Aet 130 QE 2:21

ὀψιμαθής Mut 17

ὄψιος Hypoth 7:13

ὄψις (191) Opif 120, 147, 153, 165 Leg 2:25, 26, 39 Leg 3:58, 62 Cher 17, 58 Sacr 21, 26, 26, 36, 78 Det 101, 157, 158 Post 8, 47, 132, 161, 166 Gig 9, 18, 44 Deus 45, 46, 78, 79, 93, 150 Plant 17, 20, 29 Ebr 44, 82, 156, 168, 183, 190, 217 Sobr 4 Conf 19, 57, 99, 140, 141 Migr 35, 38, 42, 145, 191 Her 79 Congr 8 Fug 59, 153 Mut 198 Somn 1:45, 140, 176, 188, 224 Somn 2:3, 110, 217, 227 Abr 57, 65, 71, 76, 94, 118, 152, 157, 162, 167, 197, 240, 266 Ios 58, 103, 106, 141, 157, 165, 175, 175, 224, 234, 239, 257 Mos 1:9, 19, 59, 66, 94, 118, 124, 200, 223, 227, 272, 272, 274, 296 Mos 2:51, 70, 78, 123, 254 Decal 68, 147 Spec 1:27, 29, 72, 75, 95, 193, 259, 321, 322 Spec 3:37, 50, 117, 171, 176, 177, 185, 187, 192, 194, 202 Spec 4:139, 157, 185 Virt 67, 173, 193, 217 Praem 19, 38, 39, 58, 165 Prob 34, 38, 40, 66, 124, 132, 147 Contempl 10, 31, 49, 50, 53, 53, 66, 89 Aet 64 Flacc 77, 89, 92, 124, 162, 169, 173 Legat 2, 5, 12, 122, 129, 173, 262, 263, 269, 276, 335 Hypoth 11:15 Prov 2:27, 29, 31 QG isf 2 QG (Par) 2:3, 2:6 QE 2:9b QE isf 21, 23, 31

ὄψον (ὄψος) (13) Ebr 211, 214, 219 Her 20 Ios 152, 152 Spec 1:127, 174 Virt 182 Prob 31 Contempl 37, 53, 74

ὄψος ὄψον

ὀψοφαγία (12) Opif 158 Agr 37 Plant 105 Abr 135 Mos 2:185 Spec 1:148, 192, 281 Spec 3:43 Spec 4:91 Legat 14 QG 2:12d

Π

παγγέλοιος Spec 1:18

πάγη (7) Sacr 29 Post 116 Mos 1:299 Spec 1:160 Spec 3:66 Spec 4:5 Prob 31

πάγιος (84) Leg 3:206 Cher 26, 83 Sacr 63, 70, 80, 86 Det 12, 118, 148 Post 24, 90, 119, 151 Gig 33 Deus 22, 49 Agr 6, 160 Plant 84 Ebr 38, 111, 166, 197, 204 Sobr 29 Conf 106 Migr 22 Her 18, 58, 98, 224, 298 Congr 121 Fug 45, 112 Mut 87, 183 Somn 1:23, 119, 158, 246 Somn 2:17, 79, 129, 219, 223, 278, 298 Abr 71, 273 Ios 122, 130, 140, 147 Mos 1:212 Mos 2:14, 73, 125 Decal 93, 139 Spec 1:26, 26, 30, 61, 129, 138, 292, 312 Spec 2:13, 213, 232 Spec 3:68 Prob 26, 29, 97, 114 Aet 137 Legat 1, 117, 177 QG 3:21 QG (Par) 2:4 QE isf 5

παγίς Ebr 70

πάγκαλος (96) Opif 2, 51, 53, 65, 139, 139, 148, 156 Leg 1:58 Leg 3:46 Det 129 Post 111 Gig 16, 40 Deus 85 Agr 54, 79, 84, 144, 179 Ebr 116, 152 Conf 99, 131 Migr 14, 100, 129, 135, 152, 173, 206, 209 Her 10, 21, 38, 61, 86, 196, 213, 225, 263 Congr 100, 111 Fug 82, 96, 168 Mut 25, 193, 216 Somn 1:144, 180, 228, 249 Somn 2:45, 63, 72, 141 Abr 9, 166, 167 Mos 1:158, 318 Mos 2:36, 66, 84, 85, 109, 210 Decal 48, 100 Spec 1:104, 195, 322 Spec 2:210, 216, 239 Spec 3:83, 83, 153 Spec 4:39, 53, 131 Virt 163, 171, 181, 183, 185 Praem 1, 111 Contempl 88, 88 QG 2:11, 62, 4:33b QG (Par) 2:7 QE 2:20

παγκρατησία Mos 1:304

παγκρατιάζω Det 32 Agr 113 Congr 46

παγκρατιαστής Spec 3:174 Prob 26, 27, 110, 146

παγκράτιον Cher 80 Spec 2:246

παγκτησία Spec 2:113 Virt 100

πάγος Leg 3:169, 172

παγχάλεπος (11) Leg 3:33 Post 8 Conf 165 Her 100 Fug 157 Somn 2:109, 197 Decal 72, 128 Praem 78 Flacc 80

πάθημα (7) Opif 70 Cher 88 Gig 10 Conf 23 Abr 2 Mos 2:126 Spec 1:210

παθητός (6) Opif 8, 9 Sacr 70 Ebr 73 Spec 3:180, 180

πάθος (536) Opif 80, 81, 103, 112, 141, 150, 163, 166, 167 Leg 1:73, 106 Leg 2:4, 5, 6, 8, 8, 9, 9, 11, 12, 16, 28, 28, 29, 41, 41, 49, 50, 52, 52, 54, 57, 79, 79, 83, 84, 84, 85, 86, 89, 89, 90, 91, 98, 99, 99, 99, 99, 99, 99, 100, 100, 101, 101, 102, 103, 104, 106 Leg 3:2, 11, 13, 13, 18, 18, 19, 21, 22, 22, 25, 27, 33, 38, 38, 80, 81, 88, 93, 94, 107, 113, 113, 113, 114, 116, 116, 118, 120, 124, 129, 131, 134, 134, 139, 140, 145, 145, 148, 148, 150, 153, 153, 154, 155, 158, 159, 160, 165, 170, 172, 172, 172, 175, 175, 185, 185, 186, 186, 187, 190, 190, 193, 200, 200, 236, 240, 240, 248, 249, 250 Cher 8, 12, 51, 78, 82, 95 Sacr 4, 4, 9, 15, 16, 17, 41, 42, 48, 49, 62, 63, 80, 81, 96, 103, 110, 111, 134 Det 16, 28, 43, 46, 46, 46, 93, 95, 99, 105, 110, 119 Post 31, 43, 46, 71, 73, 74, 74, 96, 135, 155 Gig 4 Deus 3, 44, 52, 52, 63, 67, 69, 71, 71, 111, 115, 136, 183 Agr 10, 17, 37, 64, 78, 83, 83, 89, 92, 106, 109, 110, 122, 123, 143 Plant 43, 71, 98, 111, 144, 145, 157, 171 Ebr 6, 63, 98, 101, 103, 105, 111, 112, 135, 147, 151, 155, 171, 208, 215 Sobr 5, 49, 65 Conf 23, 26, 30, 52, 53,

66, 70, 70, 81, 85, 90, 90, 91, 101, 110 Migr 18, 21, 25, 26, 26, 34, 62, 66, 77, 92, 119, 143, 151, 155, 162, 206, 208, 210, 225 Her 19, 30, 44, 77, 109, 154, 186, 186, 192, 252, 254, 255, 258, 268, 269, 271, 272, 284, 289, 296, 299, 309, 316 Congr 31, 46, 55, 55, 56, 56, 59, 59, 60, 81, 83, 84, 85, 87, 92, 106, 162, 163, 164, 172 Fug 5, 91, 192 Mut 72, 81, 85, 100, 108, 143, 172, 173, 215, 261, 261, 262 Somn 1:11, 89, 112, 122, 173, 174, 255 Somn 2:50, 109, 122, 147, 165, 170, 200, 202, 203, 255, 269, 270, 276, 278, 278, 279, 281 Abr 32, 48, 102, 115, 141, 153, 153, 162, 164, 168, 194, 202, 204, 223, 236, 238, 239, 240, 240, 243, 244, 256 Ios 5, 10, 33, 40, 41, 70, 79, 82, 118, 166, 168, 175, 200, 218, 237 Mos 1:12, 15, 26, 39, 125, 136, 198, 217, 233, 280, 292, 299 Mos 2:16, 24, 55, 56, 63, 68, 139, 164, 167, 279 Decal 12, 129, 142, 143, 144, 145, 150, 174 Spec 1:55, 108, 160, 167, 191, 239, 257, 260, 281, 305, 325, 343 Spec 2:30, 36, 46, 50, 54, 80, 135, 146, 147, 157 Spec 3:20, 28, 31, 44, 45, 53, 67, 68, 75, 80, 85, 88, 91, 99, 104, 116, 126, 173, 194, 209 Spec 4:5, 9, 55, 79, 79, 79, 80, 85, 86, 95, 99, 103, 113, 130, 223 Virt 14, 31, 31, 41, 53, 69, 75, 110, 113, 116, 116, 122, 136, 144, 162, 163, 164, 195, 225 Praem 17, 19, 21, 48, 71, 78, 116, 121, 121, 145, 159 Prob 17, 17, 45, 63, 107, 151 Contempl 2, 6 Aet 2, 40, 68, 126, 139 Flacc 79, 162 Legat 61, 195, 225, 263, 277 Hypoth 11:3 Prov 2:18, 32, 36 QG 1:55b, 2:12d, 39, 54a, 59 QE 1:19, 2:2, 3b, 15b QE isf 7, 17

παιάν Flacc 121 Legat 96

Παιάν Legat 110, 110

παίγνιον Mos 1:212

παιδαγωγέω Somn 2:165 Spec 4:218

παιδαγωγός (13) Sacr 15, 51 Det 145 Migr 116 Her 295 Mut 217 Spec 2:233 Virt 178 Flacc 15 Legat 26, 27, 53, 115

παιδάριον Ebr 146, 150 Somn 1:195

παιδεία (152) Opif 17 Leg 2:89, 89, 90, 90, 92 Leg 3:167, 244 Cher 3, 6 Sacr 43, 63, 122 Det 10, 66, 77 Post 71, 96, 97, 118, 130 Deus 54, 122 Agr 18, 44, 158, 171, 171 Plant 114, 116, 126, 127, 137, 144, 162 Ebr 6, 23, 33, 34, 48, 51, 64, 77, 80, 80, 81, 95, 113, 137, 140, 141, 143, 153, 168, 224 Conf 166 Migr 71, 223 Her 25, 77, 125, 180, 210, 254, 274, 315 Congr 12, 14, 20, 22, 22, 23, 72, 73, 88, 94, 111, 121, 127, 145, 154, 156, 167, 177 Fug 14, 45, 52, 137, 150, 152, 154, 177, 183, 188, 203, 213 Mut 33, 135, 173, 206, 211, 228, 255 Somn 1:10, 49, 107, 109, 173, 175, 208, 240 Somn 2:71, 73, 90, 134, 134, 139, 198 Abr 24, 65 Mos 1:3, 23, 32 Mos 2:1, 32 Decal 80 Spec 1:336 Spec 2:21, 29, 125, 229 Spec 3:4, 163 Spec 4:115, 145 Virt 39 Praem 111 Prob 4, 15, 107, 125, 136 Aet 16 Legat 142, 182, 245, 310, 320 Prov 2:17 QG 1:55a QE 2:13a, 25c

παιδεραστέω Spec 2:50 Spec 3:37 Hypoth 7:1

παιδεραστής Decal 168 Spec 3:39 Spec 4:89 Contempl 52, 61

παίδευμα (6) Leg 3:245 Det 43 Post 137, 138 Her 268 Congr 122

παίδευσις Cher 93 Det 16 Praem 64

παιδευτής Prob 143 Legat 53

παιδευτικός (8) Sacr 42 Gig 40 Agr 122 Migr 14, 197 Spec 4:39, 66 Virt 165

παιδεύω (75) Leg 1:99 Leg 3:128, 140, 159, 210 Sacr 48 Post 38, 68, 97, 174 Deus 54 Ebr 14, 211 Conf 135 Migr 8, 116, 192 Her 42, 43, 79, 167 Congr 172, 179 Fug 86 Mut 203, 208, 229 Somn 1:234, 237, 237 Somn 2:99, 147 Abr 16, 20, 102, 271 Ios 26, 66 Mos 1:62, 80, 95, 199, 325 Mos 2:32, 71, 280 Decal 114 Spec 1:176, 314, 343 Spec 2:46, 239 Spec 4:96, 107 Virt 220 Praem 4, 49, 162 Prob 83 Contempl 2, 66 Flacc 34, 158 Legat 5, 156, 168, 196, 210, 230 QG 1:55a, 55a, 2:54a, 54a, 3:26, 4:104

παιδιά (20) Opif 50 Cher 8 Sacr 23 Plant 167, 168, 169 Sobr 8 Her 48 Somn 2:167 Abr 201 Ios 204 Mos 1:20, 190 Mos 2:211 Spec 1:314, 314 Spec 2:193 Praem 134 Legat 168 Prov 2:65

παιδικός (17) Agr 9, 18 Conf 102 Her 294, 295 Congr 19, 82, 85 Fug 146 Somn 1:205 Somn 2:10 Abr 26, 48 Mos 1:25 Spec 1:3 Contempl 61, 61

παιδίον (23) Opif 105, 105, 105 Leg 3:177, 198 Cher 72, 73 Post 130, 130, 131 Sobr 8, 8, 8, 8, 9, 9 Migr 140 Her 38, 43, 186 Congr 137 Fug 204 Ios 228

παιδισκάριον Prob 38

παιδίσκη (16) Leg 2:94 Leg 3:146, 244 Cher 9 Congr 1, 1, 12, 14, 71, 153, 154, 154 Fug 1 QG 3:23, 24, 24

παιδοκτονία Abr 181, 188

παιδοποιέω (9) Leg 1:105 Leg 3:244 Post 175 Congr 12, 72 Mut 132 Abr 253 Decal 42 Virt 207

παιδοποιία Spec 2:135 Praem 108

παιδοσπορέω Abr 135

παιδοτριβέω Spec 1:63, 282

παιδοτροφία Gig 29 Legat 230

παιδοφόντης Legat 234

παίζω Plant 167, 169, 169, 170

παῖς (230) Opif 104, 104, 105, 105, 105 Leg 2:53 Leg 3:27, 121, 194, 210 Cher 8, 43, 72, 73, 114 Sacr 51, 68 Det 13, 30, 31 Post 91, 131, 132, 150, 152, 153, 173, 181 Gig 65 Deus 17, 63, 87 Agr 6 Plant 52, 60, 78, 173 Ebr 35, 93, 114, 193, 193, 197 Sobr 11, 15, 23, 24, 31, 32, 51 Conf 55, 128, 142, 147, 151 Migr 159 Her 38, 49, 73 Congr 6, 14, 23, 36, 89, 111 Fug 3, 3, 39, 40, 146 Mut 95, 95, 97, 206, 229 Somn 1:38, 51, 107, 194 Somn 2:116, 147 Abr 111, 131, 132, 137, 170, 170, 171, 176, 179, 184, 189, 195, 198, 271 Ios 4, 9, 9, 27, 27, 43, 50, 74, 127, 128, 128, 129, 160, 163, 167, 185, 225 Mos 1:9, 10, 10, 12, 14, 15, 16, 17, 28, 102, 134, 147, 179, 182, 257, 311, 330, 331 Mos 2:142, 240, 245 Decal 69, 112, 116, 117, 118, 126, 130, 166 Spec 1:53, 112, 129, 137, 140, 163 Spec 2:108, 129, 130, 131, 133, 135, 137, 139, 140, 228, 228, 229, 232, 232, 233, 233, 236, 236, 239, 240, 241, 241, 259 Spec 3:14, 15, 16, 67, 68, 70, 74, 76, 112, 154, 164 Spec 4:150, 184 Virt 53, 59, 91, 108, 202, 224 Praem 58, 59, 134, 139, 169 Prob 35, 36, 36, 87, 114, 115, 122, 143 Contempl 50, 67 Aet 42, 57, 60, 121 Flacc 22, 68 Legat 1, 14, 23, 30, 53, 227, 289 Hypoth 7:1, 7:3, 7:8, 7:14, 11:16 QG 2:65, 3:21, 4:86a, 86b, 88, 88, 130, 144

παίω (9) Det 49, 49 Mos 1:107, 177, 210 Spec 3:105, 106, 106 Flacc 162

παιώνιος Sacr 71

πάλαι (55) Leg 1:1 Leg 2:13 Leg 3:211 Cher 53 Sacr 34, 40, 128, 134 Det 17, 64 Post 117, 162 Deus 49, 86 Agr 110 Plant 160 Sobr 52 Conf 197 Migr 167 Her 97 Fug 82

Mut 74, 143 Somn 2:172, 271 Abr 79 Ios 87, 193 Mos 1:165 Mos 2:29, 152, 157, 273, 275 Spec 2:54, 116 Spec 4:20 Virt 157 Praem 67, 103 Prob 62 Contempl 80, 85 Aet 11, 46, 119, 121, 138, 140 Flacc 104 Legat 245, 326 Hypoth 6:1 Prov 2:24 QG 2:28

παλαιένδοξος Virt 187

παλαιόδουλος Prob 10, 148

παλαιόπλουτος Virt 187

παλαιός (110) Opif 113, 156 Cher 26, 105 Sacr 76, 76, 76, 78, 79, 79, 79, 79 Det 95 Post 35, 145, 151, 151 Gig 33 Deus 9, 21, 103, 138, 146 Agr 14, 125 Plant 17, 65, 80, 127, 130, 154 Ebr 8, 95, 150, 193 Conf 6, 184 Her 78, 96, 214, 244, 278, 279, 279 Mut 81 Somn 1:11, 233 Somn 2:56, 118, 148, 287 Abr 5, 141, 240 Ios 109, 164, 202 Mos 1:242, 280 Mos 2:24, 26, 41, 48 Spec 1:3, 188, 193, 286 Spec 2:46, 109, 146, 160, 160, 208, 250 Spec 3:15, 30, 43 Spec 4:18, 79, 149 Virt 34, 75, 107, 115, 123, 152, 162 Praem 8, 103, 133 Prob 73, 137 Contempl 29 Aet 16, 65, 120, 122, 134, 139 Flacc 29, 146 Legat 135, 136, 150, 237 Hypoth 6:1 Prov 2:64 QG 2:12b QE 1:7b, 2:107

παλαιόω Sobr 56

παλαιπλούσιος Post 42

πάλαισμα (9) Det 41, 166 Agr 163 Migr 26, 75, 82 Fug 25 Somn 1:255 Somn 2:134

παλαιστής Her 144, 144 Mut 44 Prob 110

Παλαιστίνη Abr 133 Mos 1:163 Virt 221 Prob 75

παλαίω (8) Leg 3:190 Migr 74, 200 Congr 31, 46 Mut 14 Somn 1:7, 129

παλαμναῖος Sacr 32 Congr 57 Mos 2:203 Legat 89

παλεύω Somn 1:220 Hypoth 11:14 Prov 2:8

πάλη Leg 3:190, 190 Sobr 65 Mut 14

παλιγγενεσία (13) Cher 114 Post 124 Mos 2:65 Aet 9, 47, 76, 85, 85, 93, 99, 103, 107 Legat 325

παλιλλογέω Spec 4:136 Virt 16

παλίμπρατος Flacc 41

παλίμφημος (14) Ios 93 Mos 1:269 Mos 2:107, 245 Spec 2:129, 154 Spec 3:11, 45, 49 Flacc 109, 177 Legat 99, 110, 322

πάλιν (390) Opif 29, 41, 44, 51, 58, 64, 70, 93, 101, 101, 109, 113, 119, 124 Leg 1:4, 6, 10, 12, 22, 24, 51, 58, 61, 71, 91, 96, 99 Leg 2:2, 10, 17, 23, 25, 39, 65, 75, 92, 94 Leg 3:4, 13, 16, 29, 31, 57, 57, 63, 88, 92, 94, 140, 149, 161, 165, 181, 185, 227, 253 Cher 6, 37, 47, 111 Sacr 33, 49, 75, 98, 106, 125 Det 9, 20, 34, 56, 68, 72, 80, 88, 105, 106, 110 Post 5, 40, 87, 90, 109, 151 Gig 5, 13, 49 Deus 35, 52, 59, 138, 173, 177 Agr 7, 10, 69, 120, 140, 140, 141, 146, 167 Plant 14, 14, 60, 124, 152, 153, 171 Ebr 17, 19, 70, 115, 183, 207, 208, 210 Sobr 8, 42, 65 Conf 7, 16, 19, 21, 34, 78, 148, 150, 169, 170, 176, 181, 186 Migr 3, 60, 119, 126, 160, 185, 225 Her 2, 22, 24, 28, 121, 122, 131, 134, 135, 138, 146, 148, 150, 165, 167, 177, 190, 198, 208, 210, 212, 218, 246, 262, 265, 278, 282, 287 Congr 22, 61, 73, 75, 76, 96, 118 Fug 10, 49, 59, 129, 134, 172, 186 Mut 12, 56, 61, 67, 83, 84, 99, 100, 119 Somn 1:18, 20, 28, 74, 138, 166, 180 Somn 2:7, 12, 19, 29, 44, 49, 107, 122, 205, 218, 232, 234, 252, 265, 268 Abr 16, 24, 46, 73, 85, 132, 220, 272 Ios 1, 102, 109, 143, 147, 179, 207, 212 Mos 1:70, 79, 103, 105, 106, 107, 120, 122, 125, 128, 133, 135, 154, 164, 181, 184, 197, 210, 268, 270, 274, 282, 287, 317 Mos 2:55, 96, 160, 228, 231, 275, 282 Decal 21, 77, 79, 87, 148 Spec 1:157, 163, 172, 178, 266, 268, 293, 295, 296, 302 Spec 2:1, 16, 37, 60, 70, 78, 80, 85, 102, 142, 143, 156, 168, 175, 210, 249, 255, 260 Spec 3:7, 14, 27, 30, 51, 70, 146, 152, 152, 183, 184, 191 Spec 4:13, 52, 70, 85, 107, 113, 114, 124, 142, 186, 193 Virt 64, 91, 96, 121, 145, 148, 208 Praem 4, 18, 21, 59, 67, 109, 123, 143, 158, 168, 172 Prob 48, 100, 129 Contempl 89 Aet 8, 19, 30, 42, 62, 64, 79, 82, 92, 111, 114, 132, 149 Flacc 5, 5, 30, 53, 74, 152, 152, 167 Legat 14, 18, 84, 100, 187, 218, 227, 262, 270, 335, 340, 341, 361, 365 Hypoth 7:1, 7:3 Prov 2:1, 43, 45, 47 QG 1:21, 2:5b, 17c, 34a, 48, 4:52d, 193, 206a QG (Par) 2:3, 2:3, 2:5 QE 1:7b

παλινδρομέω (9) Post 156 Migr 149 Congr 164 Fug 22, 62 Somn 1:139 Somn 2:233 Abr 86 QE 2:40

παλινῳδέω Mut 53

παλινῳδία Post 179, 179 Somn 2:292 Legat 373

παλίρροια (9) Opif 113 Leg 3:213 Deus 177 Mut 100 Mos 1:179 Mos 2:254 Spec 2:143 Spec 4:85 Contempl 86

παλίρροιος Somn 2:121

παλίσσυτος Agr 76

παλλακή (16) Leg 3:197 Sacr 43 Migr 94 Her 175 Congr 23, 23, 24, 34, 36, 43, 43, 51, 54, 54, 59, 59

παλλακίς (15) Deus 121 Congr 31, 33, 34, 36, 41, 42, 43, 52, 63 Virt 223 QG 3:20a, 21, 21, 21

παλμός Abr 151 Flacc 176 Prov 2:17, 18

παλμώδης Sacr 16 Det 110 Somn 2:299

παλτός Flacc 90

παμμεγέθης Opif 134 Sacr 77 Plant 4 Congr 130

παμμήτωρ Opif 133

παμμίαρος Conf 116 Migr 9, 224 Ios 84

πάμμουσος (7) Plant 129 Conf 43 Migr 72 Her 14, 266 Congr 51 Somn 1:35

παμμύριος Plant 2

πάμπαν Aet 13

παμπληθής (17) Opif 163 Sacr 23 Det 15 Post 104 Mos 2:41, 72 Spec 1:136, 336, 342 Spec 2:20 Aet 87 Flacc 92 Legat 9, 9, 245, 252 Prov 2:30

πάμπλουτος Sobr 56 Migr 121

παμποίκιλος Somn 1:203, 220 Somn 2:48 Mos 2:143

πάμπολυς (15) Cher 9, 58 Gig 1, 47 Plant 169 Ebr 149 Her 151, 246 Congr 127 Mut 58, 146, 256 Aet 119 Legat 344, 344

παμπόνηρος Spec 4:63

παμπρύτανις Somn 1:142

παμφάγος Agr 36 Somn 2:212

πάμφορος (6) Plant 4, 11, 139 Somn 1:174 Spec 2:169, 218

Παμφυλία Legat 281

πάμφυρτος Cher 52 Ios 84

παναγής Contempl 81

πάναγρος Agr 24

παναθηναϊκος Prob 132

πανάθλιος Det 109 Post 53 Gig 66 Congr 159 QG 1:70:1

Παναίτιος Aet 76

πανάκεια Det 123

πανακής Migr 124

πανάπαλος Praem 146

πανάρετος Migr 95

παναρμόνιος (6) Her 266 Mos 2:7, 210, 256 Spec 1:207 Virt 145

πανάρχων Prob 42

πανaύγεια Opif 31

πάνδεινος Spec 3:97, 173

πανδεχής Leg 1:61 Sacr 135 Det 34 Deus 42 Ebr 191

πανδημεί Decal 159 Spec 2:145 Legat 265

πάνδημος (10) Opif 89 Conf 22 Ios 125 Spec 2:149, 156, 215 Contempl 60, 62 Flacc 116 Legat 13

πανδοχεῖον QG 4:33b

πανδώρα Opif 133

Πανδώρα Aet 63

Πανέλληνες Contempl 42

πανέορτος Contempl 36

πανηγεμών (17) Post 5, 9 Agr 50 Plant 33, 58, 137 Ebr 42, 74 Sobr 57, 64 Conf 179 Migr 77, 175 Congr 116 Mut 204, 255 Somn 1:140

πανηγυρίζω Ios 97 Mos 2:211

πανηγυρικός Spec 2:216

πανήγυρις (21) Leg 2:108 Cher 91, 92 Agr 91, 117 Migr 92 Somn 2:144 Mos 2:41, 159, 226 Decal 78 Spec 2:160, 176, 214, 215 Spec 3:183 Prob 96 Flacc 81, 83, 118 Legat 12

πάνθειος Her 75 Aet 10

πανίερος Her 75 Virt 74 Contempl 36 Legat 191

πάνλευκος Somn 1:220

παννυχίζω Mos 2:162

παννυχίς Cher 92 Contempl 83, 83 Legat 12

πάννυχος Flacc 122

πανοικί Ios 251 Mos 1:5

πανοικία Migr 159 Legat 13

πανοίκιος (6) Agr 154 Abr 56 Flacc 14 Legat 62, 128, 157

πανοπλία (6) Somn 1:103, 108 Virt 109 Prob 32 Flacc 86, 92

πανούργημα Decal 141

πανουργία (24) Opif 155, 156 Leg 1:102 Leg 2:107, 107 Sacr 22, 48 Det 24, 71 Post 82, 101 Deus 164 Agr 73, 83 Ebr 223 Conf 117 Mut 150 Somn 2:66 Mos 2:53 Spec 3:186 Praem 52 Flacc 1 Hypoth 6:2 QE isf 24

πανοῦργος (12) Leg 2:106 Sacr 32, 47 Det 18, 165 Post 43, 82 Deus 163 Plant 111 Somn 2:148 Decal 125 Legat 171

πάνσοφος (28) Cher 18, 47, 121 Sacr 43, 48 Det 126 Post 28, 169 Gig 24, 56 Agr 20, 43 Plant 27, 28 Migr 45, 76 Fug 58 Somn 1:207 Abr 13 Mos 2:204 Spec 2:100, 194 Spec 4:69, 157, 175 Virt 60, 61 Prov 1

πανστρατιᾷ Cher 130

πάντάπασι (13) Opif 38 Post 160 Plant 158 Mut 12 Somn 1:27 Mos 1:102 Spec 2:139, 154 Spec 3:65, 142 Spec 4:51 Flacc 3 Legat 244

πάνταρχος Post 92

πανταχῇ Agr 91 Migr 216 Somn 1:235

πανταχόθεν (14) Post 116 Agr 24 Congr 78 Fug 49 Somn 2:46 Mos 1:38 Mos 2:251 Decal 116 Spec 1:23 Spec 4:128 Contempl 22 Legat 15, 212, 291

πανταχόθι Flacc 49 Legat 145

πανταχόσε (13) Ebr 159 Conf 21, 116 Migr 216 Ios 19, 161, 245 Mos 1:265 Mos 2:27, 232 Spec 4:26 Legat 161, 191

πανταχοῦ (77) Opif 63 Leg 1:72 Leg 3:4, 68, 170 Sacr 38, 67 Det 154 Post 116 Deus 152 Agr 23, 35, 78, 136 Plant 110, 131 Ebr 53 Conf 136, 136, 138 Migr 128, 183 Her 161, 262 Congr 119 Mut 102, 150 Somn 1:96, 122 Somn 2:221 Abr 16, 246 Ios 19, 44 Mos 2:12, 65, 241 Decal 178 Spec 2:19, 48, 83, 167, 195 Spec 3:8, 76, 172 Spec 4:66, 85, 139, 193 Virt 6, 140, 144, 175, 226 Praem 98, 99 Prob 15 Contempl 48, 69 Aet 68 Flacc 1, 47 Legat 16, 44, 48, 89, 110, 152, 159, 171, 198, 204, 330, 370 Prov 2:11 QG isf 11

παντέλεια (12) Opif 47, 156 Abr 244 Mos 2:79, 84, 149 Decal 20 Spec 1:82 Spec 2:58, 200, 200 Spec 4:95

παντέλειος QG isf 17

παντελής (159) Leg 2:33 Leg 3:15, 99, 112, 215 Cher 3, 92, 96, 112 Sacr 57, 122 Det 32, 38, 46, 51, 54, 63, 65, 143, 168, 178 Post 42, 72, 82, 95, 156, 164, 178, 185 Deus 16, 43, 173, 182 Agr 94, 96, 101, 125, 130, 157, 160 Ebr 4, 5, 21, 23, 29, 72, 84, 111, 116, 118, 135, 154, 162, 166, 223 Conf 67, 195 Migr 2, 124 Her 86, 271, 278, 284, 299 Congr 108, 119, 150 Fug 39, 80, 81, 153, 187 Mut 36, 49, 50, 84, 228, 229, 258 Somn 1:8, 31, 86, 148 Somn 2:18, 144, 163, 292 Abr 44, 140, 146, 177, 202, 223, 247 Mos 1:81 Mos 2:8, 107, 264 Decal 68, 92 Spec 1:80, 111, 164, 178, 196, 196, 215, 237, 242, 253, 259, 283, 344 Spec 2:47, 55, 67, 123, 197 Spec 3:21, 98 Spec 4:14, 143, 145, 181, 211, 213 Virt 38 Praem 95, 119, 127 Prob 26 Contempl 27 Aet 1, 5, 6, 23, 37, 62, 71, 81, 100, 145 Flacc 10, 16, 84 Legat 18, 28, 104, 134, 144, 257, 293, 322, 330 Hypoth 6:2, 6:6 Prov 1 QG 1:77, 2:64a

παντευχία (7) Abr 243 Mos 1:330 Spec 2:245 Virt 2, 31 Aet 68 Flacc 90

πάντῃ (40) Opif 36, 61 Leg 3:23 Cher 94 Sacr 61 Det 148, 153 Gig 27, 62 Deus 23 Plant 22 Ebr 106 Her 217 Congr 58 Fug 123 Mut 232, 247 Somn 1:24, 134, 142, 175, 179, 227, 244 Mos 2:118, 128 Decal 35 Spec 1:75, 192, 330 Spec 4:83 Praem 117, 124 Legat 6, 101, 261, 309 QG 1:62:2 QG (Par) 2:2, 2:4

παντοδαπός (13) Det 157 Plant 133 Ebr 36, 173, 214 Abr 218 Mos 2:34 Spec 1:136, 184, 343 Praem 101 Legat 266 Hypoth 11:8

πάντοθεν Spec 2:240 QG 2:72

παντοῖος (35) Opif 40, 41, 46, 46, 63, 78, 153 Plant 44, 81 Congr 104 Mut 57, 165 Somn 1:20, 154 Abr 96, 134 Ios 93 Mos 1:6, 212, 224 Spec 1:26 Spec 2:143, 151 Spec 4:113, 118 Virt 6, 49 Praem 41 Contempl 9, 29, 49 Flacc 92 Legat 12, 80 QE 2:55b

παντοκράτωρ Sacr 63 Gig 64 Somn 2:172

πάντοτε Migr 27 Spec 2:107

παντρόφος Congr 174

πάντως (123) Opif 61, 91, 94 Leg 3:56, 91, 93, 120 Cher 109, 121, 125 Sacr 48, 123, 138 Det 49, 140, 148, 154, 158, 164 Post 44, 75, 95, 145 Gig 5, 56 Agr 68, 99,

104, 118, 149, 154 Plant 145, 151, 161 Ebr 71, 157 Conf 75, 134 Migr 49, 68, 70, 75, 130 Her 18, 41, 101, 142, 159, 243 Congr 82, 140, 154, 157, 179 Fug 12, 62, 78, 117, 136, 151 Mut 18, 22, 24, 28, 31, 40, 131, 255, 261 Somn 1:18, 181, 233, 253 Somn 2:14, 61 Abr 18, 35, 104, 250 Ios 125, 168 Mos 1:42 Mos 2:198 Decal 31, 123 Spec 1:35, 46, 89, 114, 127, 254 Spec 2:126, 178 Spec 3:53, 121 Spec 4:6, 31, 61, 196 Praem 9, 70 Prob 44, 45 Aet 21, 22, 24, 41, 55, 71, 84, 124 Flacc 12, 139 Legat 7, 91, 91, 218 Prov 2:10, 23 QG 1:32, 51, 3:58, 4:144

πάνυ (117) Opif 37, 50, 63, 69, 76, 80, 165 Leg 1:2, 78 Leg 2:73, 81, 107 Leg 3:58, 58, 120, 130, 141, 158, 211, 215, 233 Cher 84, 116 Sacr 19, 98, 137 Det 6, 11, 25, 62, 79, 130 Post 12, 38, 107, 133, 152, 156 Agr 6, 16 Plant 112, 147 Ebr 54 Congr 24, 137, 165 Fug 65, 75, 86, 88, 128, 132, 202 Mut 97, 124, 173, 177, 266 Somn 1:6, 167, 236 Somn 2:3 Abr 179, 227 Ios 50, 75, 87, 155, 196, 252 Mos 1:207, 208, 250, 282, 302, 321 Mos 2:35, 126, 128, 180, 244 Decal 76, 102, 147, 162 Spec 1:15, 21, 84, 206, 280, 299 Spec 2:243 Spec 3:22, 44, 126, 153 Spec 4:102 Virt 113, 143, 152, 166 Praem 114, 145 Prob 91, 95 Contempl 64, 69 Aet 39, 89, 146 Flacc 69, 130 Legat 274, 361 Prov 2:29, 65 QG (Par) 2:6

πανύστατος (8) Sobr 23 Conf 72 Somn 1:10 Spec 3:128 Virt 26, 124 Prob 115 Flacc 35

πανωλεθρία (8) Spec 3:16, 97 Virt 201 Praem 140 Prob 118 Contempl 86 Legat 230 QE 2:6a

πανώλεθρος Cher 52

πάππος (33) Sacr 43 Det 14 Somn 1:47, 70, 159, 166, 166 Abr 9, 31 Ios 172 Mos 1:46 Spec 1:101 Spec 4:178 Virt 190, 193, 226 Praem 57, 109 Prob 10 Flacc 46 Legat 29, 54, 232, 240, 278, 291, 294, 294, 298, 322 QG 2:5b, 3:11a QG (Par) 2:5

παππῷος Mos 1:32 Flacc 25 Legat 24

πάπυρος Contempl 69 Flacc 37

παρά (898) Opif 1, 17, 84, 87, 97, 99, 120, 128, 131, 153, 164, 167 Leg 1:10, 40, 48, 48, 56, 66 Leg 2:15, 31, 31, 32, 32, 47, 67 Leg 3:25, 26, 30, 46, 51, 66, 77, 81, 88, 89, 105, 105, 113, 133, 135, 147, 194, 194, 203, 222, 229 Cher 27, 35, 43, 46, 48, 49, 56, 57, 59, 68, 91, 92, 106, 106, 130, 130 Sacr 2, 22, 23, 28, 30, 33, 35, 35, 43, 46, 47, 47, 48, 53, 54, 65, 70, 76, 76, 85, 99, 109, 118, 123, 123 Det 6, 10, 12, 28, 33, 59, 61, 78, 89, 106, 114, 138, 157 Post 10, 13, 18, 19, 24, 37, 38, 39, 43, 52, 63, 77, 78, 78, 90, 114, 135, 136, 141, 143, 162 Gig 9, 11, 14, 17, 20, 20, 41, 47, 47, 48, 48, 49, 58, 61 Deus 4, 4, 4, 31, 32, 43, 48, 52, 57, 61, 74, 76, 87, 100, 103, 104, 106, 108, 109, 111, 116, 116, 126, 136, 145, 145, 148, 150, 152, 163, 163, 165, 167, 169, 176, 179 Agr 18, 43, 43, 61, 88, 90, 93, 112, 123, 161, 169 Plant 14, 14, 36, 38, 42, 42, 53, 57, 76, 82, 101, 136, 138, 142, 157, 160, 174 Ebr 2, 13, 31, 41, 41, 43, 47, 65, 72, 74, 74, 75, 81, 83, 83, 84, 90, 95, 105, 106, 106, 106, 106, 106, 106, 106, 106, 106, 106, 106, 106, 106, 106, 106, 106, 106, 106, 107, 107, 142, 148, 151, 180, 181, 181, 181, 184, 186, 186, 186, 186, 186, 186, 186, 190, 193, 194, 196, 202, 210 Sobr 3, 6, 15, 22, 25, 29, 29, 57, 62 Conf 3, 3, 7, 13, 23, 30, 33, 36, 50, 54, 61, 68, 74, 75, 106, 106, 106, 118, 126, 128, 135, 141, 151, 156, 173 Migr 13, 20, 34, 41, 57, 60, 60, 60, 61, 61, 86, 95, 96, 99, 113, 121, 128, 133, 185, 196, 202, 206 Her 23, 23, 44, 60, 93, 95, 95, 105, 113, 124, 159, 159, 171, 178, 191, 197, 206, 206, 206, 214, 225, 237, 241, 241, 295 Congr 15, 15, 25, 37, 37, 42, 44, 74, 102, 127, 131, 148 Fug 8, 19, 19, 30, 40, 51, 55, 57, 61, 64, 77, 79, 84, 84, 112, 131, 149, 151, 164, 164, 171, 183, 186, 187, 187, 187, 187, 207 Mut 14, 35, 35, 39, 54, 93, 116, 120, 126, 134, 138, 141, 142, 147, 152, 179, 191, 202, 232, 241, 255, 257 Somn 1:9, 9, 31, 33, 33, 35, 38, 52, 94, 95, 96, 103, 154, 205, 205, 205, 205, 205 Somn 2:24, 29, 30, 43, 56, 59, 69, 78, 85, 92, 121, 123, 126, 138, 142, 200, 216, 244, 261, 267, 277, 280, 280, 281, 300 Abr 6, 11, 13, 13, 17, 25, 27, 46, 64, 65, 65, 73, 89, 95, 103, 112, 121, 131, 131, 131, 133, 162, 175, 192, 193, 224, 232, 256, 258, 260, 261, 273, 276 Ios 9, 9, 12, 17, 28, 28, 29, 37, 43, 101, 106, 126, 127, 147, 167, 167, 167, 180, 184, 185, 201, 208, 217, 239, 242, 243, 264 Mos 1:2, 4, 10, 16, 24, 24, 30, 35, 36, 49, 51, 52, 58, 67, 80, 80, 99, 113, 114, 115, 141, 142, 145, 145, 155, 163, 169, 170, 170, 182, 187, 187, 188, 196, 207, 216, 218, 221, 227, 250, 257, 271, 285, 289, 312, 315, 316, 316 Mos 2:5, 12, 19, 25, 25, 27, 30, 32, 34, 78, 80, 103, 108, 119, 136, 139, 152, 155, 221, 240, 241, 249, 263, 266 Decal 9, 23, 57, 91, 98, 110, 115, 142, 150, 154, 155 Spec 1:1, 2, 8, 11, 24, 47, 48, 56, 89, 93, 95, 100, 110, 113, 152, 152, 156, 175, 204, 217, 229, 231, 252, 271, 274, 275, 277, 277, 277, 277, 277, 281, 281, 282, 290, 295, 299, 314, 345 Spec 2:8, 10, 11, 16, 23, 34, 34, 39, 44, 44, 49, 54, 71, 73, 73, 86, 100, 110, 122, 139, 153, 164, 180, 191, 215, 216, 222, 226, 235, 244, 247, 259 Spec 3:15, 16, 16, 17, 39, 40, 42, 47, 54, 72, 74, 92, 100, 110, 117, 117, 121, 127, 136, 141, 143, 145, 150, 156, 159, 167, 178, 199, 204 Spec 4:13, 61, 71, 79, 83, 101, 107, 120, 150, 152, 168, 191, 202, 237 Virt 6, 7, 55, 104, 165, 168, 188, 195, 195, 199, 212, 216, 218, 224, 224 Praem 36, 40, 44, 44, 52, 55, 89, 90, 161, 164 Prob 12, 22, 24, 27, 39, 42, 45, 71, 75, 78, 79, 81, 82, 84, 86, 96, 99, 114, 141, 154 Contempl 3, 3, 8, 19, 30, 30, 56, 68, 70 Aet 1, 1, 7, 7, 7, 18, 18, 27, 27, 28, 32, 34, 42, 48, 57, 58, 63, 79, 91, 95, 103, 106, 113, 139, 139, 139, 142, 148 Flacc 2, 11, 23, 39, 48, 88, 94, 94, 100, 101, 108, 112, 112, 113, 124, 132, 138, 148, 158, 160 Legat 13, 29, 41, 53, 71, 71, 73, 89, 97, 103, 108, 113, 122, 153, 153, 163, 164, 170, 183, 201, 207, 211, 231, 232, 251, 265, 271, 271, 273, 288, 288, 300, 318, 327, 327, 343, 343, 347, 353, 362 Hypoth 0:1, 6:6, 6:6, 6:7, 6:8, 6:9, 7:1, 7:1, 7:5, 7:10, 7:10, 7:18, 11:1 Prov 2:1, 9, 10, 12, 13, 16, 16, 16, 16, 18, 21, 21, 25, 32, 54, 63, 65, 65 QG 1:27, 27, 65, 68, 96:1, 100:1b, 100:1b, 100:2b, 2:16, 64a, 65, 68b, 3:22, 4:191c, 191c QG (Par) 2:4, 2:6 QE 1:1, 2:2, 9b, 19, 49b QE isf 21

παραβαίνω (12) Leg 1:51 Congr 151 Mos 1:31, 242 Mos 2:49 Decal 141, 176 Spec 2:257 Spec 3:30, 61 Legat 25 Hypoth 7:10

παραβάλλω (20) Leg 1:67 Leg 2:76 Leg 3:186, 249 Sacr 109 Det 162 Deus 55 Agr 14, 144 Plant 145 Ebr 131, 223 Conf 157 Her 307 Congr 55, 172 Mos 2:271 Spec 3:10 Prov 2:40 QE 2:47

παράβασις Somn 2:123 Spec 2:242 Legat 211

παραβιάζομαι Deus 99 Congr 125

παραβιβάζω Flacc 150

παραβλαστάνω Plant 104, 104 QE isf 25

παραβλέπω Virt 173

παραβολή Conf 99 QG 2:54a QE isf 3

παραβώμιος Contempl 80

παραγγελία Flacc 141

παραγγέλλω (27) Leg 1:98, 100, 102 Leg 3:80, 151 Det 45 Post 29 Ebr 221 Migr 61 Her 255 Congr 85 Mut 113 Somn 1:191 Somn 2:272 Decal 83, 106 Spec 1:221 Spec 2:195 Virt 87, 141, 150 Prob 2 Flacc 26 QG 3:21, 4:52a, 88 QE 2:3b

παράγγελμα (27) Leg 1:94 Sacr 64 Post 12 Ebr 34 Her 10, 13 Congr 63 Somn 2:8, 263 Abr 103 Decal 58, 65, 65, 96, 106, 135 Spec 2:82, 239 Spec 3:22 Spec 4:62, 70, 149, 203 Virt 88 Praem 82 QG 4:69 QE 2:16

παραγίγνομαι (32) Leg 1:86 Leg 3:155 Det 1 Post 17, 115 Gig 53 Plant 78 Migr 139 Fug 187 Mut 111, 112 Somn 1:42, 161 Ios 50, 190, 199, 224, 234, 252 Mos 1:86, 238, 287 Spec 1:78 Spec 2:148 Praem 105, 168 Contempl 89 Flacc 15, 185 Legat 127, 229, 338

παράγω (25) Opif 81 Leg 3:64 Congr 172 Fug 34 Mut 168 Mos 1:17 Decal 76, 111 Spec 2:2, 225 Spec 4:188 Virt 67, 206 Praem 28 Prob 16, 92, 105 Contempl 8 Flacc 95, 141, 173 Legat 39, 80, 181 Prov 2:8

παραγωγή Virt 196 Flacc 101

παράδειγμα (87) Opif 16, 16, 18, 19, 25, 29, 36, 71, 71, 130, 139, 139 Leg 1:22 Leg 2:66 Leg 3:96, 96, 96, 102 Cher 12, 14 Sacr 110 Det 87 Post 70, 103, 104, 104, 105 Deus 32, 87 Plant 134 Ebr 94, 95, 133 Sobr 35 Conf 61, 63, 124 Migr 125 Her 231, 234, 280 Congr 8 Mut 267 Somn 1:75, 75, 85, 126, 206 Somn 2:241 Abr 73 Mos 1:158, 303, 325 Mos 2:11, 74, 76, 135, 141 Decal 28, 100, 100, 102 Spec 1:21, 87, 279, 302, 327 Spec 2:177, 178 Spec 3:83, 191 Spec 4:173, 176, 182 Virt 51, 70, 197 Praem 114, 152 Prob 131 Contempl 57 Aet 15, 75 Legat 321, 338 Prov 2:33 QG 4:110b

παραδειγματίζω Somn 1:89

παραδειγματικός Opif 78 Mos 1:158 Mos 2:127 Spec 4:96 QG 2:34a

παράδεισος (69) Opif 153, 153, 154, 155 Leg 1:41, 43, 43, 43, 45, 45, 46, 48, 53, 53, 53, 55, 55, 55, 56, 56, 59, 60, 60, 60, 61, 61, 62, 63, 65, 65, 88, 90, 96, 96, 97, 100, 100, 100, 101 Leg 3:1, 28, 28, 51, 54 Cher 1, 11, 20 Post 128 Plant 32, 32, 34, 34, 36, 37, 38, 40, 43, 43, 44, 44, 45, 46 Conf 61 Migr 37 Congr 171 Somn 2:241, 242 Mos 1:289 QG 2:66

παραδέχομαι (60) Leg 2:19 Leg 3:4, 181, 199, 219 Cher 48 Sacr 116 Det 13, 13, 147, 147, 155 Post 135, 166 Deus 5, 111, 137, 147 Agr 34 Plant 35, 43 Ebr 30, 211 Conf 141, 141 Her 217 Congr 6, 177 Fug 19, 118 Mut 144, 212, 255 Somn 1:202 Abr 188 Ios 47, 204 Mos 1:24, 114, 126 Mos 2:129, 279 Decal 10, 87 Spec 1:106, 106, 279 Spec 2:256 Spec 3:51, 121 Spec 4:59, 60 Virt 127 Praem 160 Aet 78, 82 Legat 290 QG 4:69 QE 2:9:1, 16

παραδηλόω Opif 6 Contempl 31

παραδίδωμι (54) Opif 78, 139, 159 Leg 3:194 Sacr 64, 64, 64, 64, 76, 78, 133 Det 65 Post 107 Deus 47, 92, 92 Agr 132 Plant 127 Ebr 120, 198 Conf 144 Migr 16, 18 Fug 45, 53, 65, 93, 168, 169, 200 Mut 95, 113, 173 Abr 108 Mos 1:3, 23 Mos 2:11 Decal 55 Spec 1:21, 28, 199, 254 Spec 2:215 Spec 3:6, 120 Spec 4:231 Virt 171 Flacc 96 Legat 149, 233, 237, 298, 356 Hypoth 7:14

παραδιηγέομαι Fug 15

παραδιήγημα Congr 100

παραδιηγήσις Cher 55

παραδοξολογέω Plant 69 Aet 48

παράδοξος (34) Opif 124 Sacr 100 Det 44, 48, 94, 153 Post 19, 50 Deus 127 Plant 62 Ebr 66, 178 Conf 31, 59, 132 Her 81, 95 Congr 3 Fug 180 Somn 2:23, 136, 185 Abr 196 Mos 1:143, 202, 203, 212 Mos 2:125, 213 Prob 58, 105 Aet 109 Legat 80 QG 3:18

παράδοσις Ebr 120 Spec 4:150

παραδύομαι Opif 131 Praem 145

παραζήλωσις Praem 89

παραθεάομαι Legat 269

παράθεσις Ebr 186, 187 Conf 185, 185 Mut 208

παραθέω Sacr 66 Conf 99 Legat 267

παραθήγω (11) Gig 60 Agr 13, 106, 142 Ebr 159 Conf 110 Congr 25 Fug 125 Spec 2:251 Flacc 182 Legat 199

παραίνεσις (39) Leg 1:93, 93, 93, 94, 95, 95 Agr 54, 84 Ebr 26 Conf 59 Migr 210 Her 114 Mut 256 Somn 1:69, 101 Abr 16, 252 Ios 206 Mos 1:71, 295, 309 Mos 2:172, 260, 270 Decal 39, 82, 100 Spec 1:299, 316 Spec 2:19 Spec 4:131 Virt 69, 70, 71, 75 Praem 83, 156 Contempl 12 Legat 70

παραινέω (36) Leg 1:94, 95, 97, 101 Leg 2:98, 105 Leg 3:244, 245 Det 170 Post 13, 38 Agr 172 Conf 46 Migr 132, 208 Her 11 Fug 5, 171 Mut 42 Somn 1:101 Abr 256 Ios 13, 46, 117 Mos 1:40 Decal 87 Spec 1:52 Spec 2:17, 241 Spec 4:44, 219 Virt 69, 122, 163, 178 Legat 228

παραιρέω Opif 103

παραιτέω (29) Leg 3:140, 144, 145, 147, 240, 245 Cher 124 Sacr 63 Det 19, 37, 38, 130, 156 Post 2, 83 Deus 19 Migr 76 Abr 215 Mos 1:83 Spec 3:70 Spec 4:110, 131, 190 Virt 23 Praem 61 Flacc 26, 31 Legat 327 Hypoth 11:14

παραίτησις Post 48 Spec 1:67 Spec 2:196 Flacc 182

παραιτητής Mut 129 Mos 2:166 Spec 1:244 Spec 2:25

παραιτητός Spec 3:121

παραίτιος (7) Ebr 27 Mos 1:71, 307, 311 Spec 1:159 Spec 3:205 Flacc 181

παρακαλέω (29) Opif 157 Post 138 Ebr 193 Sobr 40 Conf 83, 110, 190 Somn 2:106 Ios 173 Mos 1:83, 139, 233, 266, 268, 285 Mos 2:9 Spec 2:19, 252 Spec 3:67 Virt 70 Praem 166 Prob 64, 94 Flacc 123 Legat 30, 52, 187, 300 Prov 2:69

παρακάλυμμα Decal 39

παρακαλύπτω (11) Ios 72 Mos 1:300 Decal 53, 91 Spec 1:10, 330 Spec 3:156 Spec 4:71 Praem 154 Legat 148 QG 1:100:1b

παρακαταθήκη (36) Cher 14 Sacr 60 Det 65 Deus 101 Plant 101, 101, 103, 103 Ebr 213 Migr 91 Her 104, 105, 129 Abr 259 Ios 195, 227 Decal 171 Spec 1:235, 236 Spec 4:30, 31, 32, 32, 33, 34, 35, 36, 37, 67, 71, 87 Virt 96 Flacc 134 Legat 161 Prov 2:7 QG 1:27

παρακατατίθημι (10) Sacr 131 Plant 176, 176, 177 Her 104, 105, 106 Fug 89 Mos 1:48 Spec 4:137

παρακατέχω Flacc 101

παράκειμαι (6) Leg 2:68 Decal 59 Spec 1:217, 218 Aet 122, 147

παρακελεύομαι Sacr 59 Somn 2:269 Flacc 138

παρακέλευσις Deus 69 Prob 132, 139

παρακινδυνεύω Her 21 Somn 2:37

παρακινέω (9) Agr 76 Plant 39 Mos 1:291 Mos 2:214 Prob 90 Legat 159, 298, 335, 336

παρακινηματικός Contempl 40

παρακλέπτω Hypoth 7:2

παράκλησις Ios 70 Mos 1:44 Contempl 12

παρακλητεύω Flacc 23 Legat 322

παράκλητος (11) Opif 23, 165 Ios 239 Mos 2:134 Spec 1:237 Praem 166 Flacc 13, 22, 23, 151, 181

παρακμάζω Post 123

παρακολουθέω (19) Opif 17 Cher 30 Sacr 70 Det 134, 171 Post 90 Sobr 37 Migr 149, 175 Fug 12 Ios 269 Decal 88 Spec 2:206 Spec 3:76 Praem 99 Flacc 166 Legat 359 Prov 2:46, 48

παράκομμα (7) Agr 45 Plant 160 Her 44 Somn 2:184 Spec 3:101 Spec 4:48 Legat 110

παράκοπος Post 182 Legat 93

παρακόπτω (14) Sacr 32, 137 Conf 108 Mut 171, 208 Spec 1:250, 325 Spec 2:50, 249 Spec 3:38, 176 Spec 4:47 Praem 152 Contempl 41

παρακούω (11) Leg 1:96 Cher 65, 70 Det 101 Plant 84 Ebr 158 Her 109 Spec 4:53 Virt 173 Legat 370 QG 4:202a

παρακρούω Leg 3:61, 110 Her 302 Spec 4:77

παρακύπτω Legat 56

παραλαμβάνω (77) Opif 26, 27 Leg 1:3, 96, 107 Leg 2:41 Leg 3:55, 204 Cher 68 Sacr 25, 133 Post 94, 95, 142 Deus 169 Agr 66 Plant 114 Ebr 82, 90, 144 Conf 85, 128 Migr 30, 53, 55, 110 Her 22, 158, 235, 257 Fug 27 Mut 61, 173, 228 Somn 1:67, 92 Somn 2:258 Abr 154, 170, 201, 261, 270 Ios 37, 77, 117, 205, 208, 248 Mos 1:20, 60, 150, 168, 228, 276, 283 Mos 2:29, 66, 72, 248 Spec 3:122 Spec 4:75 Virt 88 Praem 53 Contempl 59 Aet 145, 150 Flacc 20, 69, 86 Legat 8, 19, 231, 232 Prov 2:37 QG 2:12b, 3:11a QE 2:50a

παραλείπω (26) Agr 119 Plant 89 Congr 125 Somn 1:205 Abr 40 Ios 23, 219, 267 Mos 1:47, 151 Mos 2:12 Spec 1:297 Spec 2:93 Spec 4:136, 143, 230 Virt 107, 117, 168 Praem 67, 69, 133 Prob 26, 31, 89 Legat 152

παραληρέω Spec 4:191

παράληρος Ebr 123, 197 Somn 2:205

παράληψις Spec 3:18

παράλιος Agr 81 Ios 30 Aet 138

παραλλάσσω (14) Leg 3:31 Post 9 Sobr 53 Abr 137, 193 Mos 1:96, 200 Mos 2:53, 281 Spec 2:94 Spec 3:49 Virt 126, 136 Flacc 73

παράλληλος Her 147 Aet 113

παράλογος (13) Post 50 Deus 90 Ebr 122 Ios 60 Mos 1:10, 170, 196, 212 Spec 1:21 Prob 8 Flacc 139 Legat 98, 171

πάραλος Flacc 154 Legat 252, 283

παραλύω (10) Det 167, 168 Fug 144 Abr 226 Spec 2:193 Legat 39, 146, 200, 293, 298

παραμείβω (9) Cher 28 Sacr 65, 66 Det 89 Post 19 Plant 22 Mos 1:250 Spec 2:246 Flacc 156

παραμείγνυμι Abr 207 Flacc 79

παραμένω (14) Leg 2:91 Leg 3:20, 20 Sacr 124 Ebr 145 Congr 102 Somn 1:113 Abr 264 Mos 1:327 Decal 43, 114 Spec 1:106 Prob 131 QG (Par) 2:7

παραμετρέω Leg 1:4 Leg 3:25 Cher 42

παραμυθία Mos 1:137 Mos 2:50

παραμύθιον Abr 196 Praem 72

παραναβλαστάνω Migr 16 Fug 183 Somn 2:64 Virt 156

παραναγιγνώσκω Flacc 100

παρανάλωμα Flacc 12 Legat 369

παραναφύω Plant 107

παρανοέω Leg 2:60 Cher 116 Plant 84 Conf 126

παράνοια Cher 69 Her 249

παρανομέω (17) Conf 154 Somn 2:124 Ios 44, 52 Mos 1:301, 308 Decal 89, 129 Spec 1:155, 155 Spec 3:76, 90 Virt 194 Prob 56 Flacc 50, 82, 107

παρανόμημα (14) Opif 152 Ios 177 Mos 2:58, 172, 214, 218, 220, 277 Decal 11, 140 Spec 1:215 Spec 3:165 Spec 4:65 Flacc 41

παρανομία (21) Agr 66 Conf 117, 193 Her 60 Somn 1:233 Abr 97, 242 Mos 1:102, 295 Mos 2:166 Decal 93 Spec 1:56, 153 Spec 2:250 Spec 3:90 Spec 4:2, 45 Praem 142 Legat 119, 190, 220

παράνομος (13) Agr 46 Ebr 142, 194 Ios 216 Decal 140, 173 Spec 1:100 Spec 2:14 Spec 3:85, 90 Spec 4:3, 46 Prob 22

παραπαίω (9) Det 131 Ebr 4 Fug 160 Somn 1:155 Somn 2:83, 162 Spec 4:191 Contempl 43 Flacc 6

παράπαν (ὁ) (121) Opif 99, 135, 160, 165 Leg 1:24, 26, 35 Leg 2:2 Leg 3:53, 68, 113, 241 Cher 33, 34, 36, 47, 53, 64 Det 33 Post 4, 137, 168 Gig 4, 28, 60 Deus 11, 52, 83 Agr 17, 130 Plant 34, 42, 108, 177 Ebr 12, 57, 186 Conf 27, 69, 98, 154, 162, 180 Migr 23, 155, 179, 219 Her 188, 216 Fug 19, 124, 170 Mut 28, 181 Somn 1:36, 40, 140, 236, 244 Somn 2:10, 107, 141, 178, 187 Abr 84, 122, 127, 140 Ios 27, 46, 126, 134, 165 Mos 1:68, 73, 75, 88, 118, 139, 205, 266, 283 Mos 2:108, 114 Decal 42, 92 Spec 1:22, 88, 89, 204, 224, 293 Spec 2:89, 198, 247 Spec 3:39, 156 Spec 4:49, 52, 99 Virt 6 Praem 14, 93, 103 Prob 7, 21, 140 Contempl 51 Aet 40, 83, 106, 114 Flacc 149, 167 Legat 280 Hypoth 11:4 Prov 2:53 QG 1:65, 3:38b, 4:193 QE 2:24b

παραπάσσω Spec 1:175

παραπείθω Migr 194

παραπέμπω (39) Opif 54, 71 Agr 69 Plant 174 Ebr 168 Migr 170, 173, 173 Somn 1:181 Somn 2:67, 143 Abr 71, 241 Ios 13, 139, 178 Mos 1:222, 286 Spec 1:78, 338 Spec 2:230 Spec 3:100, 184 Spec 4:110, 154 Virt 223 Praem 51, 124 Contempl 86 Flacc 31, 161, 163 Legat 50, 58, 207, 238, 250, 297 QG 4:20

παραπέτασμα QG 4:69

παράπηγμα Sacr 59

παραπικραίνω Leg 3:114 Somn 2:177

παραπίπτω Mos 1:142 Legat 120, 201

παραπληξία Her 250 Praem 135 Legat 76

παραπλήσιος (70) Opif 19, 139, 141 Cher 81 Det 164 Post 105 Deus 97 Agr 17, 83, 99 Plant 32, 79, 83 Ebr 157, 187, 219 Sobr 36, 50 Conf 2, 117, 151 Migr 83 Her 151, 151, 192, 216 Congr 18 Mut 187, 206, 230, 252 Somn 1:103, 164 Somn 2:231 Abr 162 Mos 2:231, 258 Decal 21, 66, 78, 82 Spec 1:65, 84, 135, 161, 299, 311 Spec 2:22, 98, 144 Spec 3:17, 126, 191 Spec 4:73, 103, 148, 159 Virt 121, 168 Praem 114 Contempl 75 Aet 23, 90, 128 Legat 7, 86, 237, 364 QE 2:13a QE isf 21

παράπλοος (παράπλους) Legat 338
παράπλους παράπλοος
παραπολαύω Abr 97, 249 Ios 21
παραπόλλυμι (13) Opif 167 Sacr 45 Det 141 Agr 76 Ebr 14 Mos 1:10, 183, 236 Flacc 62 Legat 33, 128, 192 Prov 2:55
παραπομπή Mut 93 Spec 3:109 Hypoth 6:2
παραπτύω Her 109
παράπτωμα Migr 170
παραριθμέω Sobr 14 Migr 107 Mut 228 Decal 159
παραρρήγνυμι Somn 2:125 Spec 4:222 Aet 147
παραρριπτέω παραρρίπτω
παραρρίπτω (παραρριπτέω) Spec 1:281 Spec 3:51 Spec 4:38
παράρτυμα Migr 36 Somn 2:155
παράρτυσις Ebr 211 Mut 173 Ios 154 Virt 143 Contempl 54
παραρτύω (6) Somn 2:48, 301 Spec 1:220 Praem 139 Contempl 37, 73
παρασεσυρμένως Legat 363
παρασημαίνομαι Spec 2:149
παράσημος (13) Post 182 Conf 108 Congr 118 Spec 1:104, 115 Spec 4:50, 77, 164 Virt 4 Flacc 38 Legat 81, 98 Prov 2:35
παρασιωπάω (6) Opif 155 Leg 2:55 Cher 121 Abr 49 Mos 2:117 Spec 2:129
παρασκευάζω (50) Opif 77, 81, 113 Leg 3:146, 155, 156, 206 Cher 61, 98 Sacr 8, 25, 29, 58, 113, 125 Det 36, 157 Post 57, 98 Her 73 Congr 93, 125 Mut 149 Abr 65 Ios 71, 115, 162 Mos 1:250, 252, 268 Spec 1:6, 57 Spec 2:197 Spec 3:87, 104 Spec 4:7, 103, 122, 194, 227 Virt 107, 133 Praem 131 Prob 86 Flacc 93 Legat 82, 107, 162 Prov 2:29 QG 4:7*
παρασκευή (54) Opif 43, 79, 85 Leg 3:62, 147, 221 Sacr 48 Deus 144 Plant 65 Conf 45 Mut 89 Somn 1:126 Abr 220, 233, 238 Ios 115, 118, 206, 234, 253 Mos 1:25, 142, 174, 225, 260 Decal 14 Spec 1:7, 62, 159, 221 Spec 2:19, 20, 187, 193 Spec 3:138 Spec 4:28, 28, 126, 220 Virt 48, 48, 216 Contempl 48, 53, 54 Flacc 86 Legat 108, 257, 344 Hypoth 6:6, 11:4 Prov 2:1, 29 QG 4:76b
παρασπάω Congr 144, 148 Mos 2:174 Decal 128 Spec 4:211
παρασπείρω Opif 66
παρασπόνδειος Contempl 80
παρασπονδέω (6) Migr 225 Congr 151 Decal 126 Spec 3:118 Praem 76 Legat 160
παραστάτης Leg 1:11 Spec 1:216, 216 Spec 4:171
παραστάτις Flacc 104 Legat 112
παράστημα Mos 2:172, 197, 273 Spec 1:57
παρασυκοφαντέω Plant 70
παρασυνάπτομαι Agr 141
παρασύρω Det 170 Spec 1:30 Spec 4:160 Legat 142, 168
παρασφάλλω Virt 202
παράταξις Mos 1:310, 313
παράτασις Her 17
παρατάσσω Mos 1:313
παρατείνω (6) Leg 1:13 Fug 55 Ios 156 Mos 1:125, 195 Mos 2:223
παρατετηρημένως (6) Leg 3:144 Det 160 Post 137 Plant 44 Migr 43 Spec 3:77
παρατηρέω (14) Leg 1:107 Leg 2:50 Leg 3:61, 147 Sacr 98 Deus 109 Sobr 22 Conf 75 Her 67 Spec 1:92, 239 Spec 3:81 Spec 4:155 Prov 2:27
παρατίθημι Gig 49 Spec 4:50
παρατρέπω (6) Deus 178 Plant 129 Conf 65 Congr 148 Ios 165 Spec 4:64
παρατρέφω Prob 34
παρατρέχω (9) Deus 149, 150, 177 Agr 115, 154 Sobr 68 Migr 207 Mut 178 Ios 141
παράτριψις Prov 2:45
παρατυγχάνω (16) Agr 136 Ebr 177 Migr 136 Mut 197, 217 Abr 197 Mos 1:92, 146 Mos 2:213 Spec 3:78, 176, 176 Contempl 57 Flacc 112, 144 Legat 45
παραύξησις (10) Post 173 Ebr 15 Migr 54 Congr 106 Fug 13 Mut 111 Somn 1:9 Mos 1:18 Spec 2:212 Virt 162
παραύξω (10) Opif 91, 93, 93, 94, 94 Leg 3:203 Plant 76 Her 149 Virt 138 Legat 147
παραυτίκα Mut 142 Spec 1:155, 314 Praem 103 Flacc 114
παραφαίνω (9) Opif 60 Abr 80 Ios 192 Mos 1:20 Decal 26 Spec 1:47 Spec 2:179, 180 Virt 30
παραφέρω Flacc 79
παραφθείρω Ios 108
παράφορος (6) Post 22, 175 Sobr 5 Conf 21 Ios 73 Legat 93
παραφράζω Mos 2:38
παραφροσύνη Leg 2:69, 70 Plant 148 Ebr 15 Spec 3:99
παραφυάς Plant 4
παραφυλάσσω Somn 2:263 Ios 10, 260 Legat 51, 207
παραφυτεύω Agr 7
παραφύω Contempl 62
παραχαράσσω Mut 203 Spec 2:249 Legat 116, 155
παραχράομαι Ios 144
παραχρῆμα (13) Deus 89 Agr 175, 176 Fug 115, 115 Mut 142 Decal 95 Spec 3:102, 106, 142 Virt 126, 128 Legat 334
παραχωρέω (21) Leg 1:82 Leg 2:95 Leg 3:209 Sacr 17, 136 Agr 113 Somn 2:25 Abr 216 Ios 85, 129 Mos 1:303 Spec 1:248, 252 Spec 4:49 Virt 100 Prob 131 Contempl 13 Flacc 12 Legat 232 QG 1:62:1, 62:2
παραχώρησις Leg 3:137
παραψύχω Plant 160
πάρδαλις Mos 1:109 Decal 113 Praem 89
παρεγγράφω Deus 103
παρεγγυάω QG 4:88
παρεγχειρέω QE 2:1
πάρεδρος Mut 194 Ios 48 Mos 2:53 Decal 177 Spec 4:201
παρειά Ios 23
παρεῖδον παροράω
παρεῖδον Ebr 93 Ios 202 Mos 2:285 Spec 4:53
παρεικάζω Mos 1:189
παρείκω Mos 2:215 Legat 35

πάρειμι (190) Leg 2:42, 43, 43, 43, 43 Leg 3:15, 86, 86, 87, 87 Sacr 68, 70, 79, 124, 135 Det 10, 57, 108, 119, 119, 146 Post 141 Gig 46, 56, 67 Deus 63 Ebr 33, 58, 202 Sobr 31 Conf 7, 86, 92, 140 Migr 31, 35, 44, 44, 102, 136, 154 Her 12 Congr 12, 65 Fug 39, 42, 159 Mut 36, 115, 157, 192, 213, 217, 217 Somn 1:111, 172, 229 Somn 2:90, 138, 302 Abr 86, 132, 143, 184, 190, 202, 214, 243, 246 Ios 16, 25, 42, 55, 63, 162, 170, 229, 236, 237, 259 Mos 1:18, 21, 31, 40, 52, 138, 150, 181, 192, 198, 307 Mos 2:37, 139, 235, 240, 252, 291 Decal 63, 143, 146 Spec 1:26, 45, 56, 283, 283, 284, 302, 304, 320, 330, 334 Spec 2:12, 19, 74, 127, 175, 178, 189, 197, 197, 209, 238, 239 Spec 3:7, 55, 56, 60, 80, 104, 116, 148, 160 Spec 4:38, 82 Virt 16, 30, 30, 31, 50, 75, 120, 151, 223 Praem 19, 71 Prob 24, 114, 121, 122, 138 Contempl 55 Aet 3, 41 Flacc 113, 131, 157, 162 Legat 2, 3, 28, 43, 53, 109, 173, 175, 189, 208, 227, 227, 255, 256, 261, 262, 271, 271, 272, 351, 355 Hypoth 6:1, 6:4, 7:13 Prov 2:5, 21, 32, 42, 58 QG 1:72, 4:166, 203 QE 2:45a

παρεισάγω Sacr 94

παρεισδύνω (παρεισδύω) Spec 3:88

παρεισδύω παρεισδύνω

παρεισέρπω Prov 2:26

παρεισέρχομαι Opif 150 Ebr 157 Abr 96 QG 1:55a, 3:21

παρεισρέω Somn 1:27 Spec 1:325

παρεισφθείρομαι Agr 15 Spec 4:33 Legat 166, 200

παρεκλέγω Legat 199

παρέλκω Post 4 QG 4:76b

παρεμβάλλω Fug 183

παρεμβολή (14) Leg 2:54, 54 Leg 3:46, 151, 151, 169 Det 160 Gig 54 Ebr 96, 96, 98, 100, 100, 124

παρεμφαίνω (7) Ebr 142 Her 86, 112 Mut 207 Somn 2:195, 224 Abr 200

παρενθυμέομαι Leg 2:69 Spec 4:53

παρενόχλημα Mos 1:30 Flacc 14 Legat 65

παρέξειμι Ios 141

παρεξευρίσκω Ios 29

παρεπιδείκνυμι Spec 1:56 Contempl 31 Legat 94

παρεπιδημέω Agr 65 Conf 76

παρεπίδημος Conf 79

παρέπομαι (9) Conf 166 Migr 23, 151, 164 Decal 82 Spec 1:190 Virt 127 Praem 118 Legat 168

παρεργολαβέω Congr 148

πάρεργος (34) Opif 91 Leg 2:11 Leg 3:18, 40, 147 Cher 1 Sacr 128 Post 78 Conf 1, 53, 142, 168 Her 40, 247 Mut 177, 207 Somn 1:160, 167 Abr 114 Decal 29, 52, 85 Spec 1:8, 300 Spec 2:178 Spec 4:115 Virt 22 Praem 36 Aet 16 Legat 176, 176, 323 Prov 2:60 QG 2:54d

παρέρχομαι (108) Opif 17, 88, 156 Leg 2:42, 43, 43 Leg 3:130 Sacr 13, 26, 47, 76 Det 42, 57 Post 101 Deus 32, 132, 145, 145, 145, 145, 149, 149, 152, 152, 153, 154, 154, 159, 174 Agr 85, 110, 111, 112, 162, 165 Plant 114, 127 Ebr 37 Conf 128 Migr 24, 139, 154 Mut 104, 188 Somn 1:79, 200, 228 Somn 2:62, 145, 149, 209, 210 Abr 107, 131, 131 Ios 45, 64, 104, 141, 143 Mos 1:3, 49, 238, 255, 303 Decal 101 Spec 1:33, 114, 159, 162, 213, 261, 334 Spec 2:157, 157, 157, 187 Spec 3:27, 80, 119 Spec 4:141, 160, 192 Virt 116, 223, 223 Praem 4, 36, 41, 100, 151 Prob 82, 158 Contempl 31, 43, 44 Aet 132 Flacc 112, 114, 144 Legat 143, 203, 204, 212 Hypoth 7:18 Prov 2:26 QG 4:166 QG (Par) 2:7

πάρεσις Det 168 Praem 143, 145

παρέσχατος Ios 175, 187

παρευημερέω (21) Opif 80, 168 Deus 3 Fug 129, 156 Somn 1:81 Somn 2:53 Abr 66, 223 Mos 1:272 Decal 3 Spec 1:120 Spec 2:42, 160 Praem 172 Prob 79, 104 Contempl 17 Flacc 31 Legat 150 Prov 2:14

παρευτρεπίζω Ios 178 Decal 145

παρέχω (222) Opif 38, 56, 81, 97, 97, 116, 155, 161, 162, 169 Leg 1:26, 89 Leg 2:47 Leg 3:10, 52, 81, 122, 195 Cher 45, 60, 67, 79, 109, 122 Sacr 22, 40, 109, 139 Det 25, 43, 56, 147, 156 Post 98, 98, 111, 147 Deus 39, 168, 171 Agr 32, 39, 168 Plant 54, 90, 141, 173 Migr 149 Her 103, 223, 247, 273 Congr 5, 98, 124, 173, 178 Fug 29, 31, 106 Mut 61 Somn 1:173 Somn 2:126 Abr 98, 110, 116, 118, 118, 122, 174, 227, 254 Ios 20, 45, 50, 92, 157, 170, 239, 241, 249, 255, 258, 262 Mos 1:22, 26, 47, 105, 117, 118, 146, 148, 211, 243, 266, 303, 304, 304, 318, 330 Mos 2:9, 177, 236, 238, 268 Decal 12, 42, 70, 77, 109, 112, 118 Spec 1:53, 96, 123, 151, 173, 233, 236, 250, 252, 261, 273, 279, 284, 298, 323, 340, 340 Spec 2:16, 16, 83, 96, 98, 100, 106, 118, 122, 143, 144, 173, 205, 259 Spec 3:23, 88, 111, 185, 192 Spec 4:11, 13, 38, 81, 91, 117, 140, 159, 195, 228 Virt 79, 86, 88, 89, 93, 105, 120, 179, 224 Praem 36, 90, 120, 155, 155, 163, 166 Prob 84, 116, 121, 128, 148 Contempl 23, 24 Aet 38, 52, 63, 79 Flacc 23, 24, 26, 40, 50, 106, 129, 142, 173 Legat 46, 60, 83, 98, 141, 172, 200, 220, 229, 233, 249, 274, 335 Hypoth 7:19, 11:10 Prov 2:45, 47, 49, 71 QG 1:24, 27, 41, 85, 2:65 QE 2:19, 28, 71 QE isf 14

παρηβάω Opif 140 Sacr 16 Mut 172

πάρηβος Ios 128

παρηγορέω (21) Sacr 94, 101 Fug 6 Somn 2:150 Ios 17, 23, 199 Mos 1:137, 173, 209 Mos 2:51 Spec 1:243 Spec 2:54, 107, 138, 261 Spec 3:70 Flacc 14, 176 Legat 161, 197

παρηγόρημα Abr 268 Ios 80 Spec 2:131

παρηγορία (11) Leg 2:63 Cher 119 Deus 65 Somn 1:112 Ios 13, 111 Spec 1:236 Spec 3:128, 197 Prob 56 Legat 58

παρήκω Post 173

παρησυχάζω Leg 3:33 Her 215, 226 Spec 1:344

παρθενεύω Cher 52

παρθενία Cher 49, 51, 52 Spec 3:74 QE isf 22

παρθένιος Congr 124

παρθένος (81) Cher 49, 50, 50, 50, 50, 51, 51, 52 Post 32, 132, 132, 133, 133, 134, 134, 134 Agr 152, 158 Plant 129 Migr 31, 206, 224, 225 Fug 114, 141 Mut 53, 194, 194, 196 Somn 1:200 Somn 2:185, 185 Ios 43 Mos 1:12, 51, 53, 57, 311 Mos 2:7, 236, 238, 242, 243 Decal 102 Spec 1:101, 105, 107, 107, 108, 110, 112, 129, 129 Spec 2:24, 24, 30, 30, 56, 125 Spec 3:25, 26, 65, 80, 81, 169 Spec 4:178, 223 Virt 28, 37, 43, 57, 114 Praem 53, 153, 159 Contempl 68 Flacc 89 Legat 227 QE 2:3b, 3b, 3b

Παρθένος Opif 100

Παρθυαῖοι Ios 136, 136 Legat 256

Παρθυηνός Deus 174 Legat 10

παριδρύω (7) Somn 2:180 Mos 2:105 Spec 4:69, 92, 123, 221 Virt 197

παρίημι (32) Opif 40 Leg 3:120 Cher 82 Sacr 81 Det 146, 167 Deus 15 Plant 160 Ebr 130 Migr 9 Her 133 Congr 90 Mut 196 Somn 1:51, 96 Somn 2:115, 160 Ios 215 Mos 1:109, 182, 325 Mos 2:200 Decal 1 Spec 1:219, 319 Spec 2:165, 246 Spec 4:204 Virt 193 Praem 48 Prob 26 Flacc 10

παριστάνω Cher 14 Det 168 Fug 175

παρίστημι (107) Opif 96, 103, 129, 134 Leg 1:34, 34, 43, 90 Leg 2:36, 38 Leg 3:45, 54, 120, 133, 145, 186 Cher 49, 84, 108 Sacr 4 Det 3, 28, 59, 68, 71, 80, 93, 122, 131 Post 12, 16, 28, 44, 169 Gig 55, 60 Deus 23, 50, 70, 153 Agr 176 Plant 137 Ebr 9, 19, 54, 85, 96, 190 Sobr 27 Conf 98 Migr 46, 131, 138 Her 72, 293 Congr 20, 90 Fug 4 Mut 96, 118, 147, 210, 270 Somn 1:15 Somn 2:227, 246 Abr 34, 123, 142, 154, 202 Ios 39, 58, 94, 117, 168, 238 Mos 2:122, 179, 214, 242 Decal 45, 151 Spec 1:55, 253 Spec 2:171, 186, 204 Spec 3:53, 128, 173 Virt 89 Prob 62, 136 Contempl 77 Aet 83 Flacc 7 Legat 234, 267, 294 Prov 2:42 QG 1:66, 2:13a, 15b, 3:11a, 4:203 QE 2:2

παρό (95) Opif 133, 161 Leg 1:15, 40, 55, 61, 62, 76, 98, 106 Leg 2:6, 59, 62, 104 Leg 3:2, 13, 36, 45, 53, 76, 92, 108, 115, 130, 131, 150, 171, 187, 202, 209, 229, 247 Cher 15, 16, 97 Sacr 10, 51, 62 Det 6, 18, 31, 60, 85 Post 32, 63, 67, 117, 131 Gig 8, 22, 32, 59, 66 Deus 46, 50, 54, 69 Agr 97, 179 Plant 76, 111, 135 Ebr 49, 79, 109 Sobr 25, 26, 29, 48, 56 Conf 41, 196 Her 159, 160 Congr 38 Fug 12, 15 Mut 214 Somn 1:47, 88, 123, 142 Somn 2:94 Abr 192 Ios 152 Mos 2:82, 128 Decal 23 Spec 1:3, 5, 148 Spec 2:54, 59 Spec 4:208, 238

πάροδος Praem 65, 112 Legat 178

παροιδέω Deus 26

παροικέω (16) Leg 3:244 Cher 120 Sacr 44 Agr 64 Plant 169 Sobr 68 Conf 76, 77, 78, 80, 80, 81, 81 Her 267, 267 Spec 1:216

παροίκησις Leg 3:244 Sacr 43 Congr 20

παροικία Conf 80

παροικίζω Spec 4:93

πάροικος (16) Cher 108, 119, 120, 121, 121, 121 Sacr 44 Conf 79 Her 267 Congr 22, 23 Somn 1:45 Spec 1:120, 120, 122 Virt 106

παροιμία (7) Abr 235 Mos 1:22, 156 Mos 2:29 Praem 150 Legat 125 QG 2:54c

Παροιμίαι Ebr 84

παροινέω (7) Ebr 29, 95, 146, 151 Somn 2:86, 292 Prob 56

παροινία (14) Cher 92 Post 175 Plant 174 Ebr 29, 138 Somn 2:168, 191, 200, 292 Mos 2:164 Spec 1:206 Spec 3:186 Flacc 136 Legat 312

παροίνιος Plant 160 Ebr 95 Somn 2:205

παρολιγωρέω Spec 3:117

παροξύνω Migr 68 Decal 63 Spec 1:265 Virt 171

παροράω (παρεῖδον) (11) Leg 3:63 Cher 65, 70 Det 61 Agr 36 Plant 84 Ebr 158 Her 109 Decal 98 Prob 39 Legat 142

παροργίζω Somn 2:177

παρορμάω Spec 2:209 Spec 3:102

παρόσον (29) Leg 2:14, 81 Sacr 92 Deus 90 Agr 129, 150 Plant 114 Ebr 139, 139 Sobr 52 Conf 177 Congr 61, 61 Fug 170 Somn 2:153 Abr 54, 102 Mos 2:147 Spec 1:40, 53, 93, 128 Spec 3:141, 175 Spec 4:67, 150 Contempl 2, 2, 3

παρουσία Sobr 43 Mut 163 Somn 1:113 Spec 1:286 QE 2:45a

παρρησία (32) Sacr 12, 35 Agr 64 Plant 8 Ebr 149 Conf 165 Her 5, 5, 6, 14, 19, 21, 27 Congr 151 Somn 2:83, 85, 85 Ios 73, 107, 222 Spec 1:321 Spec 3:138 Spec 4:74 Prob 95, 125, 126, 150, 152 Flacc 4 Legat 63 Hypoth 11:16 Prov 1

παρρησιάζομαι (7) Sacr 66 Her 21, 29 Mut 136 Decal 73 Spec 1:203 Legat 41

παρρησιαστής Flacc 178

παρωνυμέω Her 97 Abr 271

παρώνυμος Her 291 Prob 75

πᾶς ἅπας

πᾶς (2909) Opif 10, 10, 11, 12, 13, 15, 15, 20, 21, 21, 22, 28, 29, 29, 32, 34, 36, 37, 38, 40, 40, 41, 43, 43, 45, 46, 48, 48, 48, 48, 52, 52, 54, 55, 57, 59, 61, 61, 63, 64, 65, 66, 67, 67, 67, 68, 69, 69, 70, 72, 73, 73, 74, 75, 77, 77, 78, 80, 83, 83, 83, 83, 84, 88, 89, 90, 90, 95, 95, 96, 97, 97, 99, 101, 102, 104, 104, 107, 107, 107, 107, 108, 111, 113, 115, 117, 117, 129, 129, 130, 131, 132, 133, 133, 133, 135, 136, 140, 142, 142, 143, 144, 146, 147, 147, 149, 151, 153, 153, 158, 159, 160, 162, 168, 170 Leg 1:1, 1, 2, 14, 16, 18, 20, 21, 21, 23, 23, 24, 24, 24, 28, 28, 34, 44, 48, 49, 50, 52, 56, 61, 61, 61, 63, 63, 66, 68, 90, 91, 97, 97, 99, 100, 100, 100, 101, 101, 104 Leg 2:3, 4, 9, 9, 9, 16, 18, 19, 20, 33, 41, 53, 54, 54, 57, 57, 58, 66, 71, 73, 75, 75, 75, 79, 81, 86, 89, 91, 95, 98, 102, 106, 106, 106, 107, 107 Leg 3:1, 4, 4, 4, 7, 7, 7, 8, 8, 8, 10, 11, 16, 17, 18, 22, 24, 25, 30, 32, 33, 35, 35, 41, 43, 44, 44, 44, 46, 47, 48, 49, 51, 54, 63, 64, 65, 65, 65, 71, 72, 75, 78, 78, 95, 98, 99, 99, 99, 102, 102, 107, 107, 111, 113, 113, 113, 126, 139, 139, 139, 139, 140, 143, 145, 146, 147, 156, 158, 158, 158, 160, 161, 163, 164, 164, 166, 167, 169, 170, 171, 171, 172, 174, 175, 176, 176, 177, 179, 184, 185, 186, 187, 194, 195, 198, 202, 203, 203, 204, 204, 205, 205, 206, 209, 215, 223, 226, 227, 233, 241, 245, 245, 247, 248 Cher 2, 5, 10, 16, 17, 21, 23, 24, 25, 25, 27, 28, 28, 28, 30, 31, 32, 36, 38, 38, 41, 44, 50, 57, 57, 59, 59, 62, 63, 64, 64, 65, 66, 67, 70, 71, 71, 75, 75, 78, 81, 83, 83, 88, 90, 92, 93, 94, 99, 100, 105, 106, 107, 107, 108, 108, 109, 109, 110, 110, 110, 112, 112, 118, 119, 120, 120, 124, 126, 128 Sacr 2, 2, 3, 8, 8, 9, 19, 22, 24, 26, 28, 29, 31, 32, 35, 37, 37, 38, 40, 40, 41, 42, 42, 42, 43, 51, 51, 51, 51, 55, 55, 55, 56, 57, 59, 60, 61, 61, 63, 65, 66, 66, 67, 67, 67, 68, 69, 70, 71, 71, 71, 71, 75, 76, 76, 82, 83, 85, 89, 89, 89, 94, 97, 97, 101, 102, 103, 103, 104, 106, 108, 112, 112, 113, 113, 115, 118, 118, 118, 118, 121, 123, 127, 127, 129, 130, 130, 131, 131, 134, 134, 136, 139, 139 Det 7, 7, 8, 8, 9, 14, 14, 18, 18, 20, 25, 27, 29, 31, 32, 33, 33, 34, 37, 40, 40, 43, 53, 54, 56, 57, 61, 61, 62, 64, 73, 75, 76, 77, 77, 77, 78, 79, 80, 85, 88, 89, 89, 90, 90, 94, 101, 101, 101, 102, 102, 103, 104, 104, 105, 109, 111, 121, 122, 126, 127, 128, 132, 132, 137, 147, 149, 151, 153, 154, 154, 159, 164, 165, 165, 166, 166, 167, 168, 170, 171, 171, 173, 174, 177, 178, 178 Post 5, 5, 6, 6, 13, 14, 14, 15, 18, 19, 19, 19, 25, 25, 29, 30, 31, 32, 35, 36, 36, 37, 42, 50, 52, 53, 57, 57, 59, 62, 64, 64, 64, 66, 67, 67, 75, 75, 80, 81, 85, 88, 89, 95, 96, 103, 103, 104, 111, 112, 112, 113,

114, 117, 119, 119, 119, 122, 123, 127, 132, 133, 136, 142, 142, 151, 154, 159, 162, 165, 169, 171, 173, 175, 177, 177, 181, 181, 184 Gig 3, 4, 6, 10, 11, 15, 18, 22, 23, 25, 31, 32, 34, 34, 35, 37, 40, 40, 41, 43, 47, 52, 53, 54, 55, 57, 61, 62, 64, 66 Deus 2, 4, 11, 15, 19, 19, 19, 19, 20, 20, 22, 25, 29, 38, 39, 39, 42, 45, 55, 56, 57, 61, 61, 64, 66, 71, 72, 73, 88, 89, 104, 107, 107, 109, 111, 115, 124, 130, 132, 134, 138, 140, 141, 142, 143, 144, 147, 148, 149, 150, 152, 152, 156, 157, 157, 165, 167, 167, 170, 171, 175, 176, 176, 176, 182 Agr 5, 8, 12, 17, 23, 25, 25, 31, 34, 34, 35, 35, 36, 39, 39, 43, 44, 44, 49, 51, 53, 54, 54, 55, 59, 65, 75, 76, 78, 81, 84, 99, 116, 119, 119, 120, 125, 128, 129, 132, 132, 133, 137, 147, 153, 159, 168, 168, 174, 177, 178 Plant 2, 4, 5, 6, 7, 9, 9, 10, 10, 12, 12, 15, 15, 20, 22, 24, 31, 43, 45, 51, 54, 61, 64, 64, 67, 67, 67, 68, 69, 74, 76, 86, 90, 95, 95, 96, 98, 103, 103, 109, 114, 117, 117, 120, 122, 123, 123, 124, 125, 125, 127, 128, 128, 128, 129, 130, 132, 133, 135, 138, 152, 161, 164, 168, 169 Ebr 1, 4, 10, 16, 20, 22, 28, 30, 31, 33, 35, 35, 36, 36, 41, 42, 43, 44, 46, 60, 61, 62, 63, 65, 66, 69, 69, 73, 77, 77, 81, 86, 87, 87, 92, 95, 99, 104, 105, 106, 106, 107, 108, 110, 111, 116, 116, 116, 117, 119, 124, 126, 128, 131, 131, 133, 135, 135, 141, 143, 146, 150, 151, 152, 152, 155, 158, 160, 168, 171, 174, 175, 180, 187, 188, 189, 192, 193, 193, 198, 199, 202, 206, 211, 212, 216, 220, 223, 224, 224 Sobr 2, 3, 3, 4, 5, 15, 17, 17, 18, 21, 36, 36, 36, 39, 46, 49, 53, 58, 62, 63, 63, 64, 67 Conf 1, 1, 1, 1, 1, 1, 1, 1, 5, 6, 6, 6, 7, 8, 15, 17, 19, 21, 22, 24, 24, 25, 25, 26, 27, 28, 30, 32, 35, 41, 44, 45, 45, 47, 48, 49, 52, 52, 55, 55, 55, 55, 56, 56, 58, 58, 58, 59, 69, 69, 69, 73, 75, 77, 78, 83, 84, 86, 86, 88, 91, 92, 92, 99, 104, 106, 110, 110, 118, 120, 121, 122, 125, 127, 131, 131, 132, 133, 136, 136, 136, 137, 137, 138, 140, 144, 147, 150, 150, 150, 162, 162, 163, 166, 167, 167, 171, 174, 175, 178, 179, 181, 187, 187, 188, 196, 198 Migr 1, 7, 8, 9, 9, 9, 10, 14, 18, 20, 20, 21, 22, 23, 24, 25, 26, 31, 31, 31, 33, 35, 39, 42, 44, 46, 47, 50, 56, 57, 60, 60, 62, 63, 64, 64, 65, 66, 67, 68, 71, 73, 83, 85, 87, 92, 95, 97, 97, 106, 108, 110, 115, 116, 116, 118, 120, 120, 122, 122, 126, 128, 130, 131, 134, 135, 150, 155, 159, 159, 159, 159, 163, 168, 171, 178, 180, 181, 181, 183, 186, 186, 188, 189, 190, 192, 193, 199, 201, 204, 213, 218, 218, 220 Her 5, 6, 7, 7, 8, 8, 9, 12, 13, 15, 15, 15, 20, 20, 20, 21, 26, 33, 36, 42, 44, 53, 56, 62, 67, 67, 67, 71, 73, 83, 83, 85, 90, 93, 99, 103, 105, 105, 107, 108, 109, 111, 113, 116, 116, 116, 116, 117, 117, 118, 124, 126, 129, 131, 133, 137, 146, 146, 152, 152, 154, 155, 156, 156, 159, 159, 160, 160, 162, 162, 163, 170, 172, 173, 180, 184, 188, 189, 191, 204, 207, 209, 209, 219, 226, 232, 233, 235, 240, 243, 243, 246, 246, 246, 246, 247, 249, 251, 251, 251, 251, 252, 253, 253, 253, 258, 259, 259, 260, 263, 264, 266, 267, 274, 282, 284, 286, 301, 303, 305 Congr 3, 11, 22, 22, 23, 27, 31, 31, 34, 51, 55, 57, 61, 64, 71, 74, 75, 76, 78, 86, 94, 95, 95, 95, 98, 99, 99, 106, 106, 110, 114, 144, 144, 146, 147, 150, 169, 169, 170, 170, 176, 177, 178, 179 Fug 1, 1, 7, 10, 15, 16, 19, 19, 28, 31, 47, 51, 52, 53, 56, 60, 67, 68, 77, 81, 85, 85, 88, 91, 97, 99, 101, 108, 112, 112, 113, 114, 117, 125, 135, 136, 137, 141, 144, 144, 146, 153, 162, 166, 172, 172, 175, 178, 179, 181, 182, 190, 196, 201, 203, 209, 209, 210, 210, 211 Mut 7, 7, 9, 15, 21, 27, 28, 29, 32, 40, 45, 49, 58, 60, 62, 63, 63, 80, 80, 91, 98, 104, 107, 122, 123, 127, 128, 135, 138, 138, 149, 151, 166, 169, 174, 174, 180, 182, 198, 199, 199, 211, 211, 211, 212, 215, 215, 220, 220, 221, 223, 225, 227, 229, 237, 239, 247, 251, 251, 254, 256, 257, 261, 265 Somn 1:3, 3, 3, 7, 15, 15, 16, 18, 21, 23, 25, 28, 29, 37, 38, 39, 56, 60, 66, 66, 67, 68, 72, 72, 75, 75, 76, 77, 78, 79, 87, 89, 90, 91, 91, 94, 99, 104, 107, 108, 112, 114, 114, 117, 121, 126, 135, 135, 137, 140, 147, 161, 167, 169, 172, 173, 175, 176, 179, 181, 183, 184, 188, 188, 192, 200, 200, 202, 204, 208, 215, 215, 220, 221, 237, 240, 241, 241, 243, 251 Somn 2:4, 5, 13, 27, 28, 36, 37, 43, 45, 54, 71, 74, 75, 77, 78, 83, 84, 84, 97, 100, 101, 103, 109, 109, 116, 116, 125, 128, 129, 130, 130, 132, 134, 136, 152, 156, 162, 165, 168, 168, 175, 184, 192, 194, 196, 199, 200, 203, 207, 207, 210, 210, 212, 212, 221, 225, 227, 232, 237, 247, 247, 251, 253, 260, 269, 270, 271, 276, 284, 284, 289, 291, 291, 293 Abr 10, 18, 20, 34, 40, 40, 41, 43, 43, 44, 44, 46, 46, 50, 61, 69, 71, 74, 75, 88, 89, 92, 97, 98, 106, 108, 110, 112, 112, 116, 121, 123, 134, 139, 145, 155, 159, 159, 159, 161, 167, 170, 175, 178, 192, 196, 198, 199, 199, 202, 208, 209, 210, 216, 219, 220, 233, 235, 239, 240, 245, 246, 254, 256, 261, 261, 263, 268, 268, 269, 274, 275 Ios 5, 6, 6, 9, 10, 12, 13, 24, 24, 25, 28, 44, 46, 62, 64, 74, 75, 77, 79, 86, 87, 93, 95, 97, 99, 106, 109, 114, 117, 123, 128, 129, 134, 134, 142, 144, 145, 146, 148, 149, 153, 158, 159, 160, 169, 171, 181, 185, 186, 189, 191, 194, 217, 219, 230, 232, 242, 242, 244, 248, 250, 250, 256, 257, 259, 264, 265, 265, 270 Mos 1:1, 2, 5, 6, 12, 19, 22, 26, 26, 27, 33, 38, 41, 44, 48, 59, 72, 84, 91, 93, 94, 96, 100, 100, 103, 103, 112, 114, 117, 119, 120, 121, 126, 130, 133, 134, 134, 135, 136, 136, 138, 139, 141, 150, 151, 152, 155, 157, 171, 174, 175, 178, 184, 192, 193, 193, 194, 198, 201, 205, 207, 211, 212, 213, 217, 217, 221, 225, 225, 227, 230, 233, 235, 241, 242, 243, 255, 258, 261, 262, 275, 277, 284, 290, 294, 297, 303, 304, 305, 306, 309, 312, 316, 317, 319, 322, 324, 327, 328, 333 Mos 2:1, 3, 3, 7, 8, 8, 9, 12, 14, 15, 16, 19, 20, 22, 22, 23, 24, 25, 29, 30, 37, 38, 41, 43, 48, 52, 53, 58, 58, 59, 61, 63, 64, 65, 67, 68, 71, 83, 88, 99, 103, 108, 111, 115, 115, 115, 119, 120, 121, 123, 126, 127, 127, 127, 128, 132, 133, 136, 143, 143, 144, 147, 148, 148, 150, 152, 154, 188, 195, 196, 196, 202, 211, 211, 213, 217, 218, 229, 231, 232, 238, 238, 251, 253, 253, 255, 261, 263, 271, 271, 272, 273, 285, 288 Decal 4, 8, 9, 18, 19, 20, 20, 21, 22, 22, 23, 30, 33, 37, 37, 39, 44, 44, 45, 47, 50, 51, 51, 52, 52, 60, 60, 60, 61, 62, 64, 64, 71, 81, 86, 90, 90, 91, 91, 93, 100, 104, 109, 112, 117, 122, 124, 135, 138, 142, 149, 150, 150, 150, 153, 156, 157, 159, 159, 162, 170, 173, 178, 178, 178 Spec 1:13, 14, 15, 16, 17, 18, 19, 20, 20, 27, 28, 31, 31, 37, 41, 43, 51, 55, 59, 60, 61, 62, 62, 64, 72, 72, 72, 72, 76, 77, 78, 79, 80, 88, 90, 92, 93, 94, 95, 96, 96, 96, 108, 113, 114, 120, 120, 125, 132, 135, 140, 142, 144, 145, 145, 149, 150, 150, 151, 152, 164, 166, 170, 171, 172, 172, 179, 181, 185, 186, 190, 191, 193, 204, 205, 208, 209, 215, 218, 218, 219, 220, 221, 224, 233, 248, 252, 252, 253, 256, 263, 265, 268, 270, 271, 277, 278, 278, 279, 279, 285, 286, 289, 291, 292, 294, 300, 302, 303, 307, 313, 314, 316, 317, 317, 319, 320, 323, 323, 323, 325, 327, 328, 329, 330, 330, 335, 338, 339, 339, 342, 344, 344, 344 Spec 2:6, 6, 7, 9, 9, 9, 10, 11, 12, 13, 14, 22, 41, 42, 45, 46, 48, 48, 48, 49, 51, 53, 57, 60, 62, 62, 63, 70, 72, 72, 76, 83, 86, 86, 86, 87, 87, 93, 94, 96, 96, 105, 110, 114, 119, 122, 129, 132, 134, 145, 149, 150, 151, 152, 153, 155, 155, 160, 161, 165, 165, 165, 166, 167, 172, 175, 180, 181, 185, 189, 190, 192, 193, 196, 197, 199, 200, 200, 200, 201, 204, 206, 207, 211, 213, 214, 216, 218, 218, 219, 220, 243, 255, 259 Spec 3:6, 8, 8,

16, 19, 25, 30, 36, 54, 61, 74, 77, 78, 80, 82, 87, 88, 99, 99, 102, 103, 111, 111, 119, 125, 126, 127, 128, 131, 131, 132, 133, 136, 154, 155, 159, 172, 172, 178, 179, 186, 188, 188, 190, 206, 207, 209, 209 Spec 4:1, 13, 14, 15, 21, 25, 26, 32, 32, 40, 43, 44, 49, 49, 55, 55, 60, 70, 71, 71, 72, 79, 79, 81, 83, 83, 84, 85, 91, 93, 94, 95, 95, 95, 100, 125, 126, 127, 129, 132, 133, 134, 137, 141, 141, 141, 147, 152, 155, 158, 159, 165, 170, 170, 175, 178, 179, 181, 186, 191, 197, 200, 200, 201, 211, 211, 224, 225, 230, 230, 232, 235, 237, 238 Virt 6, 8, 9, 11, 12, 15, 17, 17, 26, 28, 32, 34, 34, 38, 39, 52, 55, 58, 61, 62, 64, 65, 67, 67, 73, 73, 77, 79, 79, 80, 90, 90, 90, 92, 94, 95, 97, 99, 100, 102, 104, 105, 110, 119, 130, 133, 137, 138, 140, 147, 151, 154, 160, 160, 163, 164, 169, 172, 172, 174, 175, 179, 179, 181, 186, 186, 187, 191, 206, 207, 217, 217, 218, 218, 218, 224, 226 Praem 1, 9, 13, 25, 27, 29, 30, 30, 35, 36, 36, 36, 40, 41, 41, 53, 57, 61, 62, 62, 63, 64, 68, 72, 82, 87, 87, 95, 102, 106, 107, 108, 109, 112, 113, 113, 114, 115, 118, 140, 140, 141, 142, 143, 149, 152, 154, 156, 164, 168, 169 Prob 1, 1, 9, 15, 24, 25, 26, 33, 41, 43, 47, 48, 50, 50, 52, 52, 59, 59, 59, 59, 59, 59, 59, 61, 65, 68, 79, 79, 80, 84, 84, 85, 86, 87, 87, 91, 91, 98, 101, 101, 104, 132, 141, 145, 146, 148, 149, 152, 154, 156 Contempl 3, 6, 19, 31, 54, 60, 61, 63, 72, 80, 81, 81, 83, 86, 90 Aet 1, 2, 3, 8, 12, 13, 15, 15, 17, 19, 21, 21, 22, 25, 26, 28, 29, 32, 33, 35, 36, 37, 37, 38, 43, 49, 52, 53, 57, 59, 61, 63, 63, 68, 69, 71, 73, 74, 76, 80, 82, 83, 83, 84, 85, 85, 89, 93, 96, 101, 105, 106, 106, 107, 115, 118, 118, 118, 118, 119, 123, 124, 124, 126, 126, 129, 143, 143, 143 Flacc 1, 3, 8, 9, 13, 18, 18, 20, 21, 30, 37, 41, 43, 43, 43, 48, 48, 54, 56, 63, 67, 68, 71, 72, 73, 75, 76, 79, 88, 91, 92, 94, 97, 98, 100, 114, 114, 123, 125, 128, 141, 143, 146, 148, 148, 160, 161, 165, 173, 173, 177, 187, 190 Legat 3, 4, 5, 8, 8, 8, 10, 12, 15, 16, 16, 18, 18, 18, 22, 32, 35, 44, 47, 47, 47, 48, 48, 49, 54, 60, 64, 66, 68, 80, 83, 83, 86, 89, 89, 89, 102, 107, 111, 112, 116, 116, 118, 118, 118, 119, 120, 128, 131, 133, 136, 136, 137, 139, 141, 144, 147, 149, 152, 154, 158, 159, 161, 162, 166, 168, 168, 173, 174, 177, 178, 178, 181, 182, 190, 198, 198, 204, 212, 213, 214, 222, 226, 228, 230, 230, 232, 233, 240, 240, 247, 250, 260, 261, 267, 272, 277, 282, 284, 295, 300, 308, 321, 327, 328, 335, 336, 338, 339, 346, 351, 351, 353, 356, 370 Hypoth 6:1, 6:2, 6:3, 7:1, 7:4, 7:9, 7:14, 7:17, 11:4, 11:5, 11:12 Prov 1, 1, 2:1, 10, 11, 17, 21, 25, 25, 26, 33, 34, 37, 43, 44, 44, 44, 52, 54, 70, 70, 71 QG 1:3, 3, 3, 20, 20, 21, 21, 32, 41, 64a, 66, 69, 69, 72, 96:1, 100:1b, 100:2a, 2:11, 11, 15a, 15a, 16, 17b, 26a, 28, 34a, 54a, 54a, 54a, 54d, 59, 62, 64c, 72, 3:7, 11a, 22, 22, 23, 26, 30b, 38b, 49a, 4:8a, 33a, 33b, 43, 43, 67, 69, 69, 69, 76a, 102a, 130, 172, 191c, 198, 228 QG isf 5, 10, 10, 10, 11, 13, 17 QG (Par) 2:2, 2:4 QE 2:2, 6a, 15b, 20, 24b, 25b, 25d, 38a, 47, 47, 50b, 65 QE isf 1, 3, 4, 4, 5, 9, 11, 14, 14, 16, 22, 26

Πασιφάη Spec 3:43, 44, 45

πάσσαλος (6) Leg 2:27, 27 Leg 3:153, 154, 157, 159

Πάσχα (16) Leg 3:94, 154, 165 Sacr 63, 63 Migr 25 Her 192, 192, 255 Congr 89, 106 Mos 2:224 Decal 159 Spec 2:41, 145 QE 1:4

πάσχω (206) Opif 23, 141 Leg 1:49 Leg 2:12, 33, 38, 38, 39, 41, 43, 43, 43, 104 Leg 3:51, 90, 112, 156, 173, 180, 201 Cher 29, 58, 75, 76, 77, 79, 79, 82 Sacr 10, 12, 42, 54, 135, 139 Det 33, 48, 48, 49, 49, 50, 161, 161, 172 Deus 97, 102, 157 Agr 163, 164, 167 Plant 21, 134, 155 Ebr 73, 98, 104, 120 Conf 6, 13, 22, 194 Migr 34, 78, 219, 225 Her 11, 73, 192, 202 Congr 74 Fug 133, 138, 191 Mut 94, 94, 108, 116, 122, 122, 161, 187, 196, 201, 243, 261 Somn 2:82, 88, 107, 202, 237 Abr 87, 102, 107, 135, 263 Ios 16, 26, 86, 156, 167, 189, 193, 236, 261, 267 Mos 1:33, 58, 102, 128, 145, 191, 218, 245, 249, 297, 308, 330 Mos 2:57, 201, 217, 227, 280 Decal 30, 31, 69, 146, 165, 166, 167 Spec 1:192, 200, 298 Spec 2:52, 226, 227 Spec 3:37, 64, 67, 79, 85, 86, 88, 95, 96, 102, 103, 106, 111, 126, 140, 145, 148, 158, 166, 195, 201 Spec 4:3, 29, 103, 103, 103, 172, 197, 222 Virt 115, 118, 166, 168 Praem 69 Prob 27, 27, 40, 90, 127 Contempl 43, 87 Aet 21, 38, 51, 128 Flacc 59, 60, 72, 72, 76, 94, 109, 124, 139, 143, 170, 191 Legat 7, 68, 69, 71, 109, 178, 258, 319 Hypoth 7:1, 7:6, 11:9 Prov 2:31, 57 QG 3:29 QE 2:28

πάταγος Deus 177 Abr 43, 160 Mos 1:169 Mos 2:35

πατάσσω (10) Leg 2:34 Leg 3:37, 38 Sacr 118, 134 Migr 68 Congr 137 Fug 53, 148 Somn 2:297

πατέω Leg 3:128 Spec 4:59 Prob 2 Flacc 65 Legat 131

πατήρ (586) Opif 7, 9, 10, 21, 46, 56, 72, 74, 75, 77, 84, 89, 135, 144, 156 Leg 1:18, 64 Leg 2:49, 49, 51, 51, 63, 63, 66, 67, 84 Leg 3:42, 81, 83, 84, 85, 90, 174, 175, 177, 179, 181, 181, 193, 219, 225, 225 Cher 4, 7, 7, 23, 44, 49, 49, 106 Sacr 42, 48, 48, 57, 64, 68, 89 Det 4, 4, 5, 6, 11, 12, 46, 49, 52, 52, 54, 124, 147, 159 Post 48, 68, 76, 89, 89, 90, 91, 98, 99, 103, 103, 111, 135, 146, 175, 175, 176, 176, 177 Gig 12, 62, 62, 62, 64, 64 Deus 19, 19, 30, 31, 31, 31, 47, 92, 119, 121, 134, 137, 150 Agr 59, 60, 154 Plant 9, 59, 129, 135 Ebr 14, 14, 14, 29, 30, 30, 33, 34, 35, 35, 42, 54, 61, 61, 61, 64, 68, 72, 74, 77, 77, 80, 81, 81, 84, 84, 95, 131, 166 Sobr 12, 32, 48, 56 Conf 41, 43, 63, 63, 74, 80, 103, 128, 144, 144, 145, 149, 170, 175 Migr 1, 2, 3, 3, 7, 12, 27, 28, 31, 46, 68, 69, 135, 159, 169, 169, 177, 193, 193, 194, 195, 201, 206 Her 8, 59, 61, 62, 62, 69, 98, 110, 119, 171, 200, 205, 236, 275, 277, 277, 277, 280, 281, 283 Congr 42, 42, 56, 70, 132, 170, 175, 177, 177 Fug 3, 15, 15, 16, 48, 48, 51, 51, 52, 62, 69, 83, 83, 84, 89, 98, 109, 109, 109, 114, 175, 177, 193, 197 Mut 23, 29, 41, 45, 66, 66, 68, 69, 69, 71, 92, 94, 110, 111, 111, 113, 127, 129, 173, 193, 200, 205, 217, 226, 227, 230, 230, 230 Somn 1:3, 35, 37, 47, 73, 89, 90, 141, 141, 159, 159, 166, 166, 166, 166, 170, 171, 172, 172, 172, 173, 173, 181, 190 Somn 2:15, 26, 111, 111, 111, 135, 141, 175, 178, 185, 187, 273 Abr 9, 9, 56, 58, 67, 75, 82, 82, 82, 83, 83, 118, 121, 125, 168, 173, 173, 173, 176, 198, 204, 207, 249 Ios 4, 5, 8, 9, 10, 12, 13, 14, 19, 20, 22, 27, 67, 163, 167, 169, 172, 179, 182, 183, 185, 189, 195, 199, 199, 210, 217, 223, 223, 223, 224, 226, 227, 229, 231, 240, 242, 245, 251, 251, 256, 257, 261, 262, 262, 263, 264, 264, 265, 266 Mos 1:7, 52, 58, 59, 59, 135, 158, 207, 324, 325, 328 Mos 2:24, 48, 88, 134, 192, 193, 207, 210, 234, 234, 235, 235, 238, 244, 244, 244, 244, 244, 245, 256, 262, 288 Decal 8, 32, 51, 64, 69, 90, 94, 105, 120, 128, 134 Spec 1:14, 22, 32, 34, 41, 57, 96, 111, 112, 129, 318, 326, 332 Spec 2:2, 3, 6, 11, 24, 25, 29, 29, 30, 31, 56, 59, 127, 130, 132, 132, 132, 132, 132, 133, 135, 137, 139, 165, 198, 226, 232, 232, 235, 236, 237, 239, 240, 243, 247, 253, 256, 261 Spec 3:14, 14, 14, 16, 20, 20, 21, 26, 26, 70, 71, 71, 115, 127, 153, 178, 183, 189, 189, 199 Spec 4:18, 178, 180, 184 Virt 34, 53, 57, 64, 77, 91, 111, 179, 192, 202, 204, 211, 212, 214, 218,

224 Praem 24, 24, 32, 39, 57, 109, 109, 134, 166, 166, 167, 168 Prob 36, 37, 37, 43, 57 Contempl 68, 72, 90 Aet 13, 15, 17, 83 Flacc 25, 46, 105 Legat 3, 27, 28, 29, 54, 62, 65, 71, 71, 115, 289, 293 Hypoth 7:2, 7:5, 7:14 Prov 2:3, 6 QG 1:29, 76b, 2:26a, 26b, 34c, 62, 65, 65, 65, 3:11a, 11a, 11a, 43, 43, 4:51b, 145, 145, 180, 180, 194, 198, 202a, 202a, 227 QG isf 10, 10 QE 2:2, 3b, 26, 49b, 65

πατρικός (6) Migr 159, 160, 160, 162 Mos 1:242 Spec 2:19

πάτριος (67) Agr 95 Ebr 193 Conf 2 Migr 88 Congr 177 Somn 1:215 Somn 2:78, 123, 123, 127 Ios 202, 230, 254 Mos 1:31, 73, 87, 241, 278, 298 Mos 2:32, 44, 97, 133, 193, 216, 270 Decal 159 Spec 1:56, 309 Spec 2:13, 41, 145, 148, 194, 253 Spec 3:62 Spec 4:150 Praem 106, 162, 170 Prob 80 Contempl 28 Flacc 43, 47, 52, 53 Legat 117, 153, 155, 156, 200, 208, 215, 232, 240, 249, 277, 300, 306, 313, 327, 335, 371 Hypoth 6:1, 7:11, 7:14 QE isf 14

πατρίς (90) Opif 142 Leg 2:85 Leg 3:83 Cher 2, 13, 15 Sacr 129 Deus 17, 19 Agr 65 Plant 146, 147 Ebr 17 Conf 76, 78, 78, 81, 106 Migr 217 Her 26, 27, 82, 274 Congr 85, 85 Fug 29, 76, 76, 107 Mut 40 Somn 1:39, 45, 52 Somn 2:124 Abr 31, 62, 63, 67, 179, 197, 212 Ios 24 Mos 1:36 Mos 2:198 Spec 1:52, 68, 97 Spec 3:16, 38, 41, 42, 139, 172 Spec 4:17, 89 Virt 3, 102, 190, 190, 214 Praem 17 Prob 129, 129, 130, 133, 145 Contempl 18, 22, 47 Aet 32 Flacc 46, 159, 162 Legat 74, 108, 158, 277, 277, 278, 279, 281, 283, 285, 287, 287, 290, 328, 342 Prov 2:35 QG isf 10

πατροκτόνος Ios 226

πατροτύπτης Leg 3:241 Spec 2:244, 247

πατρῷος (34) Sacr 42 Ebr 65 Migr 28, 160 Her 26, 27, 82, 287 Mut 173 Somn 1:45, 52, 256 Somn 2:107 Abr 62, 65 Ios 254, 270 Mos 1:13, 147 Mos 2:234, 243 Decal 128 Spec 1:53, 129 Spec 2:139 Virt 202, 207, 214 Prob 7 Flacc 171 Legat 54 Prov 2:64 QG 4:180 QE isf 22

πατρωός Spec 2:135 Spec 3:26

παῦλα Cher 87

παύω (67) Leg 1:5, 6, 6, 6, 16, 18, 18, 18 Leg 3:14, 44, 44, 77, 131, 148, 206 Cher 36, 67 Sacr 38, 90 Det 20, 32, 40, 73, 106, 109 Post 132, 134, 147 Deus 16, 39, 59, 101, 126 Agr 76 Ebr 101 Sobr 8 Conf 1, 89, 158, 196 Mut 21 Somn 1:70, 256 Somn 2:236, 236, 279 Ios 256 Mos 1:54, 280 Decal 97 Spec 1:50 Spec 2:90, 92 Spec 3:3 Spec 4:127 Prob 54, 89, 122 Legat 110, 227, 227, 255, 258, 258, 263, 301 QG 2:28

παφλάζω Somn 2:299

πάχνη Prov 2:45

παχυμερής Her 134, 134 Mos 1:97

παχύνω Post 121 Congr 160 Aet 103

παχύς Contempl 23, 38 Aet 103

πεδάω Virt 113 Aet 129

πεδιάς (41) Opif 80 Agr 22 Fug 179 Somn 1:17 Abr 41, 43, 138 Ios 159, 250 Mos 1:5, 192, 201, 228, 235, 319 Mos 2:54 Decal 160, 163 Spec 1:34, 183, 246, 300, 335 Spec 2:39, 151, 154 Spec 4:29 Virt 145, 149 Praem 41, 101, 128, 141 Prob 65 Contempl 62 Aet 63, 118, 147 Flacc 63 Legat 47, 249

πέδιλον Legat 94, 99, 101

πεδίον (41) Opif 40, 113 Leg 3:43, 248, 249 Det 1, 1, 1, 2, 2, 3, 3, 3, 5, 5, 6, 17, 22, 28, 29, 32, 37 Conf 1, 60, 75, 76 Her 32, 296 Fug 127 Somn 2:6 Abr 92 Ios 6, 109 Mos 1:22 Spec 2:109, 158, 191, 207 Spec 3:32 Legat 181 QG 4:169

πεδότριψ Prob 10

πεζεύω (6) Ebr 158 Mos 1:194 Mos 2:254 Spec 1:301 Spec 2:19 Contempl 86

πεζικός Abr 220 Mos 1:148 Praem 54

πεζομαχέω Spec 3:87

πεζομαχία Det 2 Legat 144

πεζός (12) Post 119 Agr 85 Abr 261 Mos 2:248 Decal 152 Spec 4:28 Virt 48 Flacc 5, 163 Legat 9, 233, 252

πειθαρχέω (39) Opif 167 Ebr 16, 35 Congr 2, 63, 64, 68, 176 Fug 99 Mut 104, 115, 206 Somn 2:68, 152 Abr 74, 116, 226 Ios 12, 64, 169 Mos 1:26, 329 Mos 2:61 Spec 1:153, 306 Spec 2:234 Spec 3:38, 163, 177 Spec 4:95, 96, 150 Virt 63, 94 Prob 47, 54 Flacc 26 Legat 53, 69

πειθαρχία Deus 34 Fug 207 Mos 1:85, 164 Decal 167

πειθαρχικός Flacc 14 Legat 36

πειθήνιος Sacr 105 Conf 54 Her 181

πείθω (72) Leg 1:95 Leg 3:80, 144, 244, 244 Cher 9, 81 Sacr 60 Det 52, 54, 131 Post 55 Gig 42 Deus 50, 183 Agr 40, 56, 63, 102, 150 Ebr 33, 55 Sobr 33 Conf 59 Migr 211 Her 273 Congr 107 Mut 261 Somn 1:77 Somn 2:24, 108 Abr 85, 88, 192, 232, 252, 256 Ios 13, 172, 186, 189, 225 Mos 1:85 Mos 2:257 Decal 87, 117, 171 Spec 1:45, 62, 79, 230 Spec 2:170, 197, 230 Spec 3:84 Spec 4:1, 121, 174, 223 Virt 120 Prob 94, 96 Flacc 174 Legat 3, 37, 198, 233, 240, 242 Hypoth 6:9 Prov 2:42 QG 4:88

πειθώ (12) Opif 165 Agr 13, 47 Plant 10 Her 244 Fug 139 Somn 1:191 Ios 34, 269 Virt 217 Legat 314 QG 3:49a

Πειθώ Post 54, 55 Somn 1:77

πεῖνα (11) Agr 36 Congr 165 Somn 1:124 Mos 1:191, 191 Spec 4:82, 82 Virt 130 Contempl 37, 56 QG (Par) 2:7

πεινάω (9) Post 142 Migr 143 Fug 139 Mut 165 Ios 156 Virt 30 Contempl 37 QG (Par) 2:7 QE 2:13b

πεῖρα (19) Det 131 Fug 149 Somn 1:112 Abr 209, 251 Ios 37 Mos 1:306 Spec 1:106 Spec 2:203 Spec 4:121, 153 Virt 34, 114 Prob 103 Flacc 43, 53 Legat 216, 255 Prov 2:48

πειράζω Leg 3:162, 167 Congr 163 Somn 1:195

Πειραιεύς Flacc 155

πειρατήριον Conf 130

πειρατής Conf 130

πειρατικός Somn 2:35, 40 Legat 146

πειράω (43) Leg 3:129 Sacr 1, 79, 82, 123 Deus 159, 183 Agr 86 Migr 122 Her 105 Fug 63 Somn 1:197 Abr 210, 257 Ios 51, 167, 215 Mos 1:49, 139, 196, 302 Mos 2:51, 135, 191, 252, 253, 259 Spec 1:109, 167 Spec 2:38, 187, 209, 235 Spec 3:7 Spec 4:70, 101, 161, 167 Virt 16 Praem 77 Legat 42 QE 2:11a, 38b

πεῖσμα (6) Congr 30 Fug 42, 114 Spec 1:62 Praem 58 Flacc 53

πέλαγος (72) Opif 63, 63, 113, 113, 131 Post 22, 178 Deus 177 Agr 23, 25 Plant 24, 67 Ebr 133 Migr 217 Congr 113 Mut 35 Somn 1:19, 19 Somn 2:85, 118, 118,

121, 143, 166, 180, 279 Abr 42, 159 Mos 1:170, 172, 176, 179, 194, 212 Mos 2:54, 251, 254, 255, 255 Spec 1:34, 91, 210, 224, 300, 301, 322 Spec 2:52, 143 Spec 3:3 Spec 4:85, 154 Praem 11, 41, 90 Prob 67 Contempl 23, 23, 86 Aet 122, 139, 139, 140, 141, 147 Flacc 186, 187 Legat 145, 250, 251 Prov 2:33 QG 2:28 QE 2:55b

πελαργός Decal 116

πέλας Spec 1:184 Spec 4:69, 72 Virt 116 QG isf 9

πελειάς Prov 2:64

πέλεκυς Prov 2:29

πελιδνός Legat 266

Πελοπόννησος Aet 140 Flacc 154, 173 Legat 281

πέλω Ebr 150 Aet 37

πέμμα (13) Agr 9 Ebr 217 Congr 168 Somn 2:48, 210 Ios 93 Spec 2:20 Spec 4:113 Virt 182 Prob 31, 140, 156 Contempl 53

πέμπτος (37) Opif 62, 103, 104, 121, 141, 171 Leg 2:94, 94 Plant 95, 132, 132, 133, 134, 134, 136, 136, 136 Migr 106, 207 Her 170, 283 Fug 177 Somn 1:21 Ios 111, 158 Mos 1:234 Mos 2:245 Decal 106, 165, 173 Spec 1:234, 333 Spec 2:36, 37, 41, 224 QG 4:8b

πέμπω (31) Det 6, 9, 14 Deus 145 Congr 70 Mos 1:74, 221, 281 Spec 4:221 Prob 96, 102 Flacc 32, 98, 100, 103, 109 Legat 156, 179, 192, 199, 239, 291, 315, 330, 369 QG 4:20, 86a, 88, 88, 144, 144

πένης (36) Post 109 Agr 54 Congr 127 Fug 16, 29 Mut 40 Somn 1:95, 155, 155 Ios 72, 144 Spec 1:139 Spec 2:20, 71, 75, 85, 85, 105, 107 Spec 4:72, 195 Virt 84, 88, 90, 97, 174 Prob 9 Flacc 143 Legat 13, 123, 199 Prov 2:1 QG 3:22 QG isf 5, 11 QE 2:10:1

πενθερός (11) Fug 4 Mut 103 Somn 1:78 Spec 1:111, 111 Spec 4:173 Legat 62, 62, 65, 71, 71

πενθέω (13) Migr 74, 202 Somn 2:66, 67, 124 Abr 230, 258, 260 Mos 2:225, 291 Spec 1:113 Spec 2:131 Virt 111

πένθος (27) Det 46 Migr 202 Somn 2:66 Ios 10, 27 Mos 1:12, 136, 137 Mos 2:225, 226, 230, 232, 245, 291 Decal 63 Spec 1:113, 115 Spec 2:134 Spec 3:90, 129 Praem 68, 171 Flacc 9, 56 Legat 85, 342 QG 1:74

πενία (31) Leg 3:24 Sobr 38 Conf 16, 18, 112 Migr 101 Her 212, 284 Somn 1:96 Mos 1:153 Spec 1:154 Spec 2:208 Spec 3:159 Spec 4:158 Virt 5, 5, 6, 10, 100, 166 Praem 127 Prob 34 Contempl 15 Flacc 57, 58, 77, 132 Legat 110 Prov 2:21 QE 2:10a, 99

πενιχρός Somn 1:98 Somn 2:213 Spec 2:75

πένομαι Her 189 Prob 23

πενταετία Spec 2:33, 33

πένταθλος Agr 115

πεντάκις Spec 2:177

πεντακοσιοστός Mos 1:316

πενταπλάσιος Mos 1:234 Spec 4:13

πεντάπολις Abr 147, 165, 229

πεντάς (19) Opif 62, 95 Plant 124, 133 Migr 201 Her 168, 172, 173 Mos 2:81 Decal 50, 50, 51, 51, 106, 121, 135, 168, 175 Praem 94

πενταχῇ Opif 62 Leg 2:74 Fug 91 Somn 1:27

πέντε (70) Opif 48, 48, 96, 97, 107, 107, 117, 170 Leg 1:11 Leg 3:179 Det 63, 64 Agr 30, 137 Ebr 105 Migr 176, 176, 198, 199, 199, 203, 203, 204, 205 Congr 76, 92 Fug 95, 100 Mut 110 Somn 1:28, 47 Abr 1, 29, 145, 147, 149, 165, 227, 236, 237, 241, 242, 244 Mos 2:78, 79, 80, 81, 82, 87, 89, 90, 101, 115, 234 Decal 20, 22, 28 Spec 2:177, 177, 200, 242, 257 Spec 3:7, 164 Spec 4:12, 12 Aet 19 Flacc 8, 55 Legat 370

πεντεκαίδεκα Flacc 113

πεντεκαιδεκαετία QG 2:5b QG (Par) 2:5

πεντεκαιδέκατος Spec 1:189 Spec 2:155, 210

Πεντεφρῆ Leg 3:236, 238 Mut 173

πεντήκοντα (11) Opif 105, 105 Det 63 Mos 2:60, 79, 81, 89, 91, 91, 283 QG (Par) 2:5

πεντηκονταετία Congr 89 Fug 37 Spec 2:113, 114

πεντηκόνταρχος Congr 110

πεντηκοντάς (8) Congr 109 Mut 228 Mos 2:80, 92 Spec 2:176, 177, 178 Contempl 65

πεντηκοστός (16) Sacr 122 Det 63, 64 Mut 228 Mos 1:316 Decal 160, 164 Spec 2:39, 110, 116, 117, 122, 176, 177, 179 Virt 99

πεπαίνω (9) Sacr 25, 62, 125 Det 110 Deus 40 Plant 151 Spec 1:179 Spec 2:143, 221

πεπάνσις Sacr 62

πέπειρος Somn 2:159, 199

πεποίθησις Virt 226

πέπων Her 80

πέρ Ebr 150 Spec 3:79 Prob 122

πέρα Mut 12 Spec 1:150 Aet 104

περαίνω Plant 149 Ebr 199 Abr 162 Spec 3:189

περαιόω (16) Agr 23 Migr 144, 218 Somn 2:180 Mos 1:178, 179 Mos 2:247 Spec 1:301 Spec 4:154, 155 Praem 11 Prob 115 Flacc 154, 156 Legat 216, 250

περαιτέρος Post 168 Gig 62 Deus 19 Ebr 185 Decal 37

περαίωσις Mos 1:172

πέραν (14) Leg 3:155 Det 95 Post 84 Agr 70 Ebr 128 Sobr 56 Fug 87, 103 Virt 183 Praem 80 Prob 7 Legat 155, 216, 282

πέρας (94) Opif 36, 102, 102, 111, 150 Leg 1:1, 6, 10 Cher 99 Sacr 115 Det 87, 89, 90, 153, 174, 174 Post 14, 116, 152, 174 Deus 32, 35 Agr 23, 53, 133, 161, 173, 181 Plant 9, 22, 67, 77 Ebr 52, 152, 156, 158 Sobr 64 Conf 33, 133 Migr 102, 134, 134, 181 Her 21, 121 Congr 90, 90 Mut 22, 22, 179, 237, 251 Somn 1:9, 30, 96, 175, 187 Somn 2:194, 235 Abr 53, 64, 64, 161 Ios 136, 159 Mos 1:112, 112, 136, 136 Mos 2:20, 20, 118 Spec 1:68 Spec 2:189 Praem 69, 102, 117, 167 Prob 26 Aet 86, 119, 119 Flacc 180, 186 Legat 18, 49, 108, 173, 309 QG 2:31, 31 QG isf 8, 8 QE isf 12

περάτης Migr 20

περατόω (13) Leg 1:6, 65 Plant 118 Her 227 Fug 184 Somn 1:20 Decal 20, 25, 50, 168 Spec 1:48, 177 Virt 53

περί (1421) Opif 15, 19, 33, 45, 47, 52, 55, 57, 58, 81, 90, 104, 111, 116, 125, 127, 128, 128, 128, 148, 163, 165, 170 Leg 1:10, 25, 35, 62, 62, 65, 68, 69, 71, 71, 71, 71, 83, 85, 85, 91, 91, 93, 93, 94, 102, 104, 104 Leg 2:1, 14, 22, 24, 58, 58, 64, 65, 74, 75, 75, 76, 80, 94 Leg 3:2, 7, 16, 20, 25, 59, 59, 59, 62, 63, 76, 82, 82, 84, 85, 90, 114, 114, 114, 115, 115, 115, 116, 118, 126, 126, 126, 126, 145, 149, 172, 184, 188, 188, 197, 200, 200, 205, 206, 206, 206, 207, 211, 211, 221, 222, 225, 233, 234 Cher 14, 26, 27, 29, 32, 37, 48, 53, 53,

55, 58, 66, 66, 67, 70, 74, 80, 84, 89, 105, 113, 117 Sacr 9, 10, 19, 29, 31, 31, 34, 44, 55, 55, 60, 69, 70, 79, 91, 95, 95, 95, 100, 101, 104, 104, 112, 112, 115, 115, 115, 115, 120, 126, 131, 136 Det 1, 7, 8, 8, 9, 11, 12, 13, 13, 19, 19, 29, 32, 32, 35, 35, 41, 41, 43, 49, 57, 58, 59, 63, 68, 74, 79, 85, 88, 91, 95, 98, 112, 116, 119, 122, 137, 137, 141, 145, 146, 148, 150, 158, 160, 174 Post 14, 25, 25, 28, 34, 37, 44, 55, 55, 74, 86, 97, 98, 106, 112, 112, 115, 115, 116, 116, 119, 119, 124, 133, 137, 154, 161, 162, 168 Gig 2, 58, 60, 67 Deus 2, 4, 12, 21, 33, 38, 51, 53, 56, 56, 59, 60, 61, 63, 69, 72, 73, 78, 80, 81, 87, 100, 111, 113, 120, 127, 131, 142, 142, 142, 163, 166, 167, 170, 171 Agr 1, 4, 7, 12, 13, 13, 18, 22, 22, 22, 22, 26, 56, 59, 61, 62, 63, 67, 84, 88, 88, 90, 91, 107, 111, 115, 116, 119, 120, 124, 125, 130, 140, 143, 145, 149, 151, 157, 157, 157, 157, 158, 158, 158, 162, 181, 181 Plant 1, 1, 2, 28, 35, 73, 75, 78, 79, 83, 85, 85, 86, 88, 90, 107, 108, 111, 129, 139, 139, 139, 141, 141, 145, 148, 149, 156, 159, 174, 174, 174 Ebr 1, 1, 3, 18, 31, 46, 62, 63, 66, 80, 87, 87, 91, 91, 91, 91, 91, 91, 91, 91, 93, 94, 95, 97, 111, 135, 154, 164, 169, 170, 171, 171, 171, 171, 171, 171, 174, 175, 180, 180, 181, 188, 192, 198, 198, 200, 202, 206, 217, 218 Sobr 1, 8, 13, 34, 60, 60, 60, 60, 61, 62, 68 Conf 1, 1, 2, 4, 6, 6, 7, 24, 39, 52, 52, 52, 52, 52, 52, 98, 100, 115, 120, 121, 127, 135, 144, 151, 159, 160, 171 Migr 9, 15, 18, 18, 40, 54, 56, 66, 69, 74, 75, 76, 77, 91, 91, 92, 105, 115, 119, 127, 136, 138, 138, 140, 148, 151, 157, 176, 180, 186, 190, 192, 195, 195, 195, 219 Her 1, 12, 91, 101, 110, 125, 133, 133, 141, 145, 152, 153, 169, 170, 170, 170, 172, 196, 207, 218, 221, 230, 237, 240, 244, 247, 249, 256, 257, 258, 258, 263, 265, 275, 302, 306 Congr 2, 11, 33, 35, 46, 49, 50, 52, 54, 64, 89, 96, 98, 108, 121, 139, 144, 147, 148, 149, 150, 152, 180 Fug 2, 2, 2, 53, 77, 77, 82, 87, 88, 115, 119, 120, 128, 129, 132, 136, 143, 153, 157, 158, 159, 164, 165, 166, 177, 181, 182, 188, 197, 202, 206 Mut 11, 13, 15, 18, 18, 53, 54, 57, 67, 71, 76, 76, 77, 84, 93, 121, 122, 124, 130, 144, 147, 153, 153, 161, 175, 176, 177, 178, 179, 180, 182, 182, 199, 208, 229, 230, 233, 233, 234, 248, 262 Somn 1:12, 12, 13, 25, 32, 39, 39, 49, 53, 53, 53, 53, 54, 57, 58, 58, 58, 59, 79, 92, 93, 102, 161, 172, 172, 177, 181, 182, 189, 189, 209, 209, 213, 213, 230, 231, 234, 239, 248, 250, 251 Somn 2:1, 6, 6, 12, 14, 17, 26, 26, 26, 55, 67, 112, 114, 123, 123, 138, 138, 145, 147, 147, 147, 152, 156, 156, 170, 170, 186, 205, 220, 222, 223, 226, 227, 237, 237, 237, 237, 244, 255, 261, 261, 290, 298, 302, 302 Abr 6, 15, 16, 30, 40, 48, 49, 57, 60, 62, 67, 75, 89, 96, 99, 99, 111, 114, 115, 134, 141, 148, 149, 164, 165, 167, 167, 168, 208, 208, 219, 221, 222, 242, 250, 253, 255, 255, 266, 266, 266, 267, 267, 275 Ios 2, 2, 3, 12, 18, 20, 23, 37, 40, 40, 44, 54, 75, 76, 80, 97, 106, 114, 121, 125, 130, 143, 150, 151, 152, 152, 152, 154, 156, 156, 156, 157, 157, 164, 176, 185, 197, 199, 199, 199, 204, 206, 210, 214, 223, 225, 233, 236, 236, 245, 248, 252, 253, 254, 254, 255 Mos 1:4, 4, 8, 15, 19, 46, 64, 87, 89, 92, 120, 123, 135, 138, 150, 153, 171, 179, 196, 199, 200, 200, 217, 224, 228, 229, 231, 233, 235, 255, 256, 256, 269, 274, 275, 306, 307 Mos 2:1, 1, 2, 2, 2, 3, 8, 23, 32, 34, 37, 46, 47, 47, 47, 47, 53, 55, 66, 66, 70, 71, 72, 115, 118, 127, 127, 135, 137, 145, 147, 150, 151, 174, 174, 177, 177, 187, 190, 191, 195, 211, 213, 214, 216, 218, 219, 221, 221, 224, 225, 229, 229, 229, 230, 233, 233, 243, 243, 246, 253, 257, 258, 263, 270, 270, 274, 275, 276, 278, 284, 289 Decal 9, 15, 18, 18, 20, 29, 36, 44, 51, 51, 51, 51, 51, 52, 52, 55, 56, 59, 67, 67, 82, 83, 83, 83, 86, 96, 102, 106, 106, 121, 140, 147, 147, 149, 151, 153, 155, 156, 158, 162, 164, 165, 170, 171, 172, 173, 175 Spec 1:12, 12, 21, 27, 30, 32, 36, 41, 41, 42, 45, 45, 47, 65, 74, 80, 81, 82, 95, 96, 100, 100, 105, 108, 109, 112, 115, 117, 123, 125, 131, 131, 141, 145, 159, 161, 161, 166, 167, 168, 176, 177, 180, 181, 186, 186, 186, 189, 189, 190, 193, 194, 194, 196, 197, 198, 209, 210, 210, 210, 211, 211, 211, 211, 212, 218, 226, 228, 230, 233, 234, 234, 235, 235, 235, 238, 239, 243, 247, 247, 249, 251, 252, 256, 256, 258, 260, 260, 267, 276, 284, 292, 293, 307, 313, 319, 330, 332, 336, 342 Spec 2:1, 1, 1, 8, 9, 10, 12, 19, 24, 29, 38, 39, 39, 40, 40, 40, 42, 46, 49, 51, 65, 71, 85, 85, 86, 91, 120, 121, 150, 165, 166, 178, 185, 196, 200, 206, 213, 223, 223, 223, 224, 224, 224, 224, 224, 224, 228, 243, 251, 254, 256, 260, 260 Spec 3:1, 9, 12, 16, 29, 44, 50, 62, 70, 70, 77, 78, 79, 80, 80, 81, 99, 104, 115, 125, 136, 140, 182, 191, 191, 191, 203 Spec 4:1, 4, 11, 35, 35, 36, 81, 82, 91, 91, 93, 96, 98, 98, 102, 120, 121, 121, 123, 128, 130, 132, 135, 135, 145, 148, 149, 171, 173, 175, 200, 204, 215 Virt 1, 3, 15, 17, 17, 18, 18, 19, 22, 22, 30, 35, 50, 50, 52, 67, 81, 90, 92, 97, 99, 102, 104, 104, 105, 116, 121, 125, 128, 138, 146, 148, 148, 160, 174, 178, 180, 186, 187, 201, 212, 216, 217, 220, 220 Praem 1, 3, 29, 40, 49, 53, 56, 71, 71, 76, 78, 85, 118, 121, 126 Prob 1, 16, 18, 20, 20, 38, 41, 53, 80, 84, 134, 138, 149, 149 Contempl 1, 1, 9, 15, 17, 21, 23, 27, 27, 38, 46, 53, 59, 59, 61, 64, 68, 90 Aet 3, 4, 7, 11, 12, 16, 25, 47, 48, 49, 51, 55, 62, 73, 78, 120, 127, 128, 136, 137, 139, 140, 142, 145, 150 Flacc 4, 18, 27, 27, 38, 45, 48, 48, 91, 103, 108, 110, 113, 113, 113, 124, 129, 130, 135, 141, 167, 167, 169 Legat 17, 33, 38, 43, 51, 87, 93, 109, 111, 112, 142, 144, 144, 152, 157, 165, 178, 185, 189, 191, 194, 201, 204, 207, 208, 212, 213, 218, 231, 240, 240, 240, 240, 245, 248, 267, 268, 269, 270, 275, 276, 277, 281, 290, 290, 296, 296, 300, 305, 308, 308, 310, 316, 330, 341, 346, 349, 361, 363, 368, 368 Hypoth 0:1, 6:3, 6:4, 6:5, 7:2, 7:14, 7:14, 7:15, 7:16, 7:20, 7:20, 11:8 Prov 1, 1, 2:8, 12, 17, 17, 21, 28, 33, 33, 42, 45, 59, 59, 60, 72 QG 1:1, 55a, 55b, 66, 66, 93, 2:5b, 13a, 59, 62, 3:11a, 4:43, 189, 191b QG (Par) 2:4, 2:5 QE 2:2, 6a, 38a, 45a, 45a QE isf 7, 9, 16, 16, 16

περιαγγέλλω Praem 124

περιάγω (13) Opif 158 Cher 81 Det 12 Plant 17, 157 Migr 123, 154 Fug 122 Somn 1:49 Mos 2:242 Prob 38 Contempl 53 Legat 228

περιαγωγή Contempl 77

περιαθρέω (19) Leg 3:39 Cher 63, 63 Somn 2:141, 170, 282 Spec 2:45 Spec 3:188 Spec 4:175, 201 Virt 12 Prob 5 Contempl 15 Aet 64 Flacc 112 Prov 2:9, 35 QG 2:72, 3:3

περιάθρησις Cher 20 Deus 139

περιαιρέω (13) Leg 2:63 Leg 3:21, 127 Plant 99, 103, 109, 109 Ebr 146 Somn 1:100 Spec 3:56 Virt 76, 111 Praem 172

περιαλγέω Mos 2:279 Praem 170 QG 4:52c QE 2:25c

περιαμπίσχω Ebr 85 Decal 139

περιανίστημι (10) Leg 2:26 Cher 62 Deus 39 Somn 1:189 Somn 2:106 Ios 102 Flacc 165 Legat 42, 271 QE isf 9

περιανοίγω Legat 351

περίαπτος (8) Sacr 26 Deus 103 Mut 114, 199, 199 Aet 56 Legat 98 Prov 2:35

περιάπτω (12) Leg 3:164 Cher 76 Sacr 29, 50 Agr 42, 114 Ebr 73, 152 Conf 166, 179 Somn 2:290 Spec 1:142

περιαυγάζω Ebr 44 Sobr 15 Prov 2:19

περιαύγεια Legat 103

περιαυγής Plant 40 Migr 47 Fug 165 Somn 1:72, 218

περιαυχένιος Sacr 21 Agr 69 Ios 150, 150

περιβάλλω (26) Det 157, 157 Post 50 Agr 24, 61 Plant 65, 144 Conf 188 Migr 11, 186 Congr 128 Mos 2:6, 77, 84, 89, 252 Decal 31 Spec 1:146 Spec 2:148 Spec 4:184 Flacc 30, 37 Legat 131, 151, 324 QG (Par) 2:6

περίβλεπτος Plant 69 Congr 27 Somn 1:165 Spec 1:73 Praem 152

περιβλέπω (16) Leg 3:38 Cher 63 Agr 36 Ebr 158, 164 Her 29 Mut 217 Somn 1:248 Somn 2:50 Ios 200 Mos 1:169 Spec 1:219 Spec 3:4 Spec 4:31 Praem 157 Legat 174

περίβλημα Deus 56 Somn 1:104, 108 Mos 2:86

περιβόητος (9) Migr 83 Ios 19 Mos 1:3, 264 Mos 2:284 Spec 1:25 Contempl 57 Legat 66, 300

περιβόλαιον Somn 1:92, 101, 107

περίβολος (21) Opif 143 Agr 14 Mut 43, 74 Abr 128 Mos 1:229 Mos 2:92, 231, 241 Spec 1:71, 74, 261 Contempl 32 Aet 73 Flacc 48, 123 Legat 212, 214, 347, 347 QG 4:80

περιβραχιόνιος Sacr 21

περίγειος (24) Opif 88, 142 Sacr 8, 9 Det 27, 86 Post 170 Deus 151 Conf 77, 78 Migr 121 Fug 62 Somn 1:83, 137, 140 Somn 2:119, 289 Abr 160 Mos 2:65, 105 Spec 1:13, 89 Prob 20 Legat 318

περιγίγνομαι (περιγίνομαι) (40) Opif 155 Cher 103 Sacr 37 Det 33, 35 Post 15, 137, 149, 157 Deus 96 Agr 157 Ebr 84, 105 Migr 74, 76, 88, 219 Congr 24, 33, 162 Fug 38, 67, 97, 125 Somn 1:160, 167, 169 Somn 2:76 Abr 220 Ios 79 Spec 1:339 Spec 3:53, 82 Spec 4:43, 64 Virt 65, 117 Legat 74, 320 QG 4:228

περιγραφή (7) Opif 112 Leg 1:20 Deus 95 Conf 87 Spec 2:128 Spec 3:189 Spec 4:19

περιγράφω Sacr 79 Agr 128 Her 316 Somn 1:9 Somn 2:194

περιδεής (7) Somn 1:182 Abr 202 Ios 210 Spec 2:52 Flacc 177 Legat 217 QE isf 33

περιδέξιον Migr 97

περιδέραιος Ios 120

περιδινέω Cher 26 Conf 100

περιδράσσομαι (6) Det 129 Ebr 172 Conf 38 Mos 2:10 Spec 4:107, 160

περιδρύπτω Agr 75

περιδύω Flacc 75

περιεῖδον (περιοράω) (10) Her 36, 206 Spec 2:247 Spec 3:166 Virt 124 Prob 139 Flacc 171 Legat 117, 209 QG 2:71a

περίειμι (42) Leg 1:66 Det 70, 74 Post 44, 72, 161 Agr 71, 112, 120 Ebr 131 Sobr 1 Conf 149 Migr 75, 82, 217 Fug 117 Abr 183, 229 Ios 233 Mos 1:93, 169, 217, 225, 233, 234, 258, 259 Mos 2:75 Spec 1:199 Spec 2:8 Virt 33, 34, 38 Praem 119 Prob 149 Contempl 63 Aet 97 Flacc 126 Legat 13, 137 Hypoth 6:6, 7:19

περιεκτικός Congr 149 QE isf 1

περιέλκω Spec 4:60

περιέπω (17) Leg 1:47, 66 Deus 48 Agr 35 Plant 105 Mut 16 Somn 2:288 Ios 4 Mos 2:194 Decal 111 Spec 2:132, 195, 240 Spec 3:8 Legat 62, 171 Prov 2:4

περιεργάζομαι Ebr 217 Mut 72 Flacc 5, 145 QG 4:52d

περιεργία (21) Opif 164 Leg 3:143 Agr 34 Plant 159 Ebr 135, 167 Sobr 32 Migr 187 Congr 53 Fug 162 Mut 72 Abr 20 Ios 93, 158 Mos 1:208 Spec 1:174 Spec 2:20 Spec 4:113 Prob 88, 156 Legat 262

περίεργος (12) Leg 3:140 Sacr 21 Ebr 211, 215 Migr 216 Her 306 Congr 124 Mut 173 Somn 2:155 Praem 99 Contempl 52 Flacc 148

περιέρχομαι Ios 120, 187 Legat 364

περιεσκεμμένως Somn 2:103 Legat 207

περιέχω (162) Opif 3, 14, 15, 16, 43, 44, 48, 92, 95, 95, 102, 107 Leg 1:44, 44, 100 Leg 3:5, 6, 6, 40, 51, 51, 51, 51, 51, 177, 178 Cher 23, 48, 52 Sacr 13 Det 95, 126 Post 7, 7, 14, 185 Gig 7, 12, 45 Deus 10, 79 Agr 56 Plant 2, 33, 82, 105, 123 Ebr 4, 53, 65, 101, 141, 202 Sobr 50, 63, 63 Conf 2, 3, 136, 136, 136 Migr 7, 12, 14, 162, 179, 182, 182, 192, 192, 193, 193 Her 168, 172, 227, 227, 228 Congr 120, 134 Fug 75, 75, 207 Mut 2, 41, 84, 87, 119, 144 Somn 1:1, 31, 63, 63, 64, 64, 64, 183, 185, 185 Abr 1, 61, 69, 131, 236 Ios 65, 76 Mos 1:65 Mos 2:18, 45, 59, 221 Decal 20, 22, 24, 51, 97, 106, 110, 121, 168 Spec 1:51, 138, 200, 300, 312, 314 Spec 2:29, 200, 258 Spec 4:105, 160, 175, 235 Virt 34, 50, 161, 167, 178 Praem 98 Prob 107 Contempl 1 Aet 10, 15, 73, 106, 106, 106, 114 Legat 178, 178, 217, 318 Prov 2:30, 34 QG 1:1, 2:54a, 3:49a, 4:80, 80 QE 1:6 QE isf 1, 1, 1

περίζωμα Leg 3:55 Spec 1:83 Spec 2:20

περιζώννυμι Leg 3:154 Sacr 63

περιήκω Spec 2:23, 191 Virt 91

περιήχησις Mos 2:163

περιθέω Conf 27 Fug 144 Spec 4:83

περιθραύω Agr 75 Fug 125 Somn 2:236

περιθρύπτω Her 201 Flacc 71

περίθυμος Somn 2:192

περιίστημι Ebr 205 Aet 26 Flacc 39 QG 2:71b

περικαθαίρω Plant 112, 112, 113

περικαθαρίζω Leg 1:52 Plant 95

περικάθημαι Leg 1:68 Flacc 62 Legat 128

περικαθίεμαι Sacr 21

περικαλλής (12) Opif 55 Cher 101 Sacr 33 Post 118 Ebr 157 Migr 33 Abr 93 Mos 1:66, 296 Spec 1:50 Virt 35 Contempl 50

περικάλυμμα Mut 199

περικαλύπτω Leg 2:62

περικατάγνυμι Somn 1:247

περίκειμαι Agr 15 Somn 1:187 Mos 2:182

περικλείω Mos 2:35 Flacc 186

περικόπτω Cher 59 Plant 106 Decal 126 QE isf 25

περικρατέω Leg 2:92, 93 Leg 3:92 Det 130 Virt 47

περικυκλόω Leg 1:68 Conf 28

περιλαλέω Her 72

περιλαμβάνω (10) Opif 48 Leg 3:39, 169 Sacr 63 Det 88 Deus 127 Ios 182 Spec 1:224 Spec 2:177 Spec 3:189

περιλαμπής Her 88 Somn 1:112

περιλάμπω (13) Deus 46 Ebr 134 Her 264 Congr 47 Fug 110 Somn 1:83, 90, 115 Abr 119 Ios 146 Mos 2:271 Praem 38, 82

περιλιχνεύω Migr 64 Contempl 53

περιμάσσω Spec 3:101

περιμάχητος (38) Opif 172 Leg 1:58 Cher 92 Sacr 33 Gig 38 Deus 18, 36, 150 Agr 110 Plant 69 Ebr 75 Conf 49, 49 Migr 210, 218 Her 191 Congr 27 Somn 2:26, 138, 252 Abr 39, 56, 192 Mos 2:16, 43 Spec 2:177 Spec 3:100, 128 Spec 4:82, 115, 181 Virt 131 Praem 160 Aet 77 Hypoth 11:18 Prov 2:15, 28, 30

περιμένω (7) Leg 2:94, 101, 101, 104 Leg 3:18 Agr 94, 123

περιμήκης (12) Post 163 Deus 37 Ebr 183 Conf 4 Mos 1:229, 282 Spec 1:73, 300 Spec 3:125 Aet 64, 100 Prov 2:68

περινοέω Deus 78 Agr 1

περίνοια Congr 107

περινοστέω Ebr 79 Somn 1:233 Decal 80 Spec 1:156

πέριξ Spec 4:128 Legat 125

περιοδίζω Legat 206

περιοδονίκης Virt 193

περίοδος (60) Opif 43, 45, 54, 60, 70, 78, 101, 148 Leg 1:20 Cher 22, 22 Det 85 Post 144 Gig 31 Agr 51 Plant 14 Ebr 91 Conf 151 Migr 64, 179, 184 Her 79, 88, 97, 185, 282 Fug 57, 184 Mut 72, 267 Somn 2:67 Abr 69 Mos 2:53, 65, 120, 222 Spec 1:16, 91, 179 Spec 2:57, 142, 143, 151, 153, 175 Spec 3:111, 187 Spec 4:115, 234 Virt 138 Praem 110, 121 Aet 8, 9, 52, 71, 109, 123, 146 QG 2:34a

περιοδυνάω (περιωδυνάω) Her 79

περιοικοδομέω Spec 3:147

περιολισθαίνω Conf 38

περίοπτος Conf 142 Decal 125

περιοράω περιεῖδον

περιοράω Migr 98 Somn 1:181 Prov 2:4 QG 2:12d

περιορίζω Spec 1:48 Spec 4:217

περιουσία (81) Leg 3:23, 134, 135, 227 Cher 58 Sacr 115 Det 13, 20, 114, 131, 136 Post 119 Gig 36 Agr 2, 87, 90 Plant 62, 69 Conf 164 Migr 15, 146, 217 Her 212, 286 Congr 165 Fug 18, 28, 36, 129 Mut 89, 215 Somn 1:91 Abr 25, 263 Ios 72, 266 Mos 1:152, 209, 234, 309 Mos 2:13, 277 Spec 1:133, 286 Spec 2:12, 19, 74, 115, 158, 203 Spec 4:72, 99, 195, 195 Virt 6, 48, 91, 140, 149, 149, 161, 163, 187 Praem 100, 103, 107, 118, 127, 168 Prob 77 Contempl 16, 39, 56 Aet 80 Legat 47, 118, 326 Prov 2:1 QG 2:10, 4:172 QE 2:3a

περιουσιάζω (8) Somn 1:126 Abr 209 Ios 144 Spec 1:24 Spec 2:108, 108 Praem 104 Flacc 132

περιοχή Aet 4

περιωδυνάω περιοδυνάω

περιπαθέω Cher 118 Ios 51 Mos 2:271 Flacc 9

περιπάθησις Cher 105 Abr 174 Ios 22 Legat 243, 243

περιπατέω (8) Leg 2:16 Leg 3:51 Congr 87 Mut 266 Somn 1:148 Somn 2:248 Ios 126, 126

Περιπατητικός Aet 55

περίπατος Spec 1:340 Spec 3:107 Spec 4:112

περιπείρω Somn 2:103, 161 Praem 20 Flacc 1

περιπέμπω Conf 116

περιπίπτω (10) Leg 2:77, 84, 86 Deus 73 Abr 37 Ios 154 Mos 1:58 Spec 1:224 QG 1:77 QE 2:6a

περιπλέκω Post 156 Ios 182 QE isf 3

περιπλέω Det 87

περίπλεως Abr 227

περιπληθής Aet 63 Prov 2:17

περιπλοκή Det 41

περιπνέω Leg 3:223

περιπόθητος Spec 3:1

περιποιέω (63) Leg 1:10, 98 Leg 2:71 Leg 3:136, 175 Cher 12, 13, 104, 105, 105 Sacr 84 Det 52, 58, 64, 102, 120, 120 Post 175 Deus 18, 86 Agr 47, 149, 157 Ebr 58, 160 Conf 112 Migr 17, 172 Her 125 Congr 161 Fug 17, 30, 120, 174, 176 Mut 84, 128 Somn 1:162 Ios 188 Mos 1:216, 303, 334 Spec 1:47, 61, 149 Spec 2:95 Spec 3:130 Spec 4:167 Praem 27, 31, 51, 137, 139, 168 Prob 94, 96, 138, 151 Flacc 130, 183 Legat 54 QG 2:11, 4:172

περιπολέω (20) Opif 54 Leg 3:99 Sobr 38 Conf 100, 133, 176 Her 127, 264 Congr 133 Fug 62, 63 Somn 1:34, 85, 119 Abr 71 Decal 57, 104 Spec 2:142 Praem 41 Prov 2:6

περιπόλησις (6) Opif 45 Cher 26 Mos 1:120 Mos 2:102 Spec 1:34 QG 4:51b

περιπταίω Ios 147 Spec 4:198

περιπωμάζω Spec 3:147

περιρραίνω (13) Somn 1:210, 212, 214, 220 Mos 1:216 Mos 2:139, 225 Spec 1:261, 261, 262, 266 Spec 3:89, 205

περιρραντήριον (20) Cher 96 Det 20 Deus 3, 8 Plant 116 Her 82 Fug 81 Somn 1:226 Mos 1:14 Mos 2:138 Decal 45, 158 Spec 1:159, 191, 258, 261 Spec 2:148 Spec 3:63 Virt 137, 146

περιρρέω (7) Leg 1:85 Det 131 Her 72 Mut 91 Spec 1:7 Prob 9, 64

περιρρήγνυμι Ios 16 Mos 1:138

περιρρήσσω Spec 1:115

περίσεμνος Sobr 23 Abr 56 Praem 93

περίσημος Mos 2:72 Spec 3:184 Legat 134, 191

περισκάπτω Spec 2:172 Virt 156

περισκελής Mos 2:143

περισκέπτομαι Leg 3:7 Det 155 Decal 85 Flacc 101 QG 1:93

περίσκεψις Sacr 137 Det 130 Ebr 166 Sobr 27 Legat 259

περισκοπέω Det 11 Gig 62 Ebr 158 QG 3:3

περισπάω Opif 121 Leg 1:14

περισπένδω Legat 356

περισσεύω (10) Leg 3:200 Conf 137 Her 142, 191 Mut 61 Abr 205 Ios 243 Spec 1:80, 305 Prov 1

περισσός (98) Opif 13, 13, 153 Leg 1:34 Leg 2:16 Leg 3:140, 147, 149, 154, 236 Sacr 50 Det 15, 101, 108 Post 4, 161, 170 Gig 34, 41, 50 Deus 163 Agr 39, 43, 43, 58, 59, 135 Plant 101 Ebr 129, 214, 219 Sobr 4 Conf 116 Migr 48 Her 32 Congr 143, 178 Fug 54 Mut 103, 103 Somn 2:64, 132, 215 Abr 163, 199 Ios 4, 61, 107 Mos 1:11, 116, 267 Mos 2:2 Decal 20, 20, 93 Spec

1:9, 52, 167, 254, 292, 339 Spec 2:28, 58, 172, 195 Spec 3:50, 154, 199 Spec 4:5, 146, 184, 205 Virt 156, 192 Praem 99 Prob 103 Contempl 14 Aet 104 Flacc 3, 14, 14 Legat 59, 170, 182, 212, 253, 304 Prov 1, 2:33 QG 2:14, 14, 3:38a, 49a, 49b, 61, 61, 4:88 QE 2:71

περίσσωμα (9) Opif 123 Leg 1:13 Spec 1:74, 148, 216, 268 Contempl 9 QG (Par) 2:6, 2:7

περιστέλλω Leg 2:57 Sacr 30 Somn 1:113

περιστερά (12) Ebr 173 Her 126, 127, 234 Mut 233, 234, 245, 248 Spec 1:162, 162 Spec 4:117 QG 2:38

περιστεφανόω Spec 3:149

περιστήθιον Somn 1:214 Spec 1:94

περιστρέφω Somn 2:80

περιστροφή Abr 151

περίστῳον Prov 2:17

περισυλάω Leg 3:174 Somn 1:107 Somn 2:213 Flacc 57

περισύρω Sacr 79 Plant 110

περισφίγγω Post 5

περισῴζω Legat 196, 230

περιτείνω Post 122 Plant 157

περιτειχίζω Leg 1:87

περιτέμνω (10) Agr 39 Sobr 8 Migr 92 Somn 2:25 Spec 1:6, 7, 305 QG 3:52 QE 2:2, 2

περιτίθημι (16) Leg 1:75 Cher 33 Agr 152 Conf 89 Her 154 Mut 198, 240 Somn 1:235 Somn 2:44 Mos 2:243, 243 Decal 138 Virt 217 Aet 41, 129 QE isf 31

περιτομή (6) Migr 92 Somn 2:25, 25 Spec 1:2, 8, 9

περιτρέπω Leg 3:16, 223 Deus 129 Fug 191

περίτριμμα Legat 203

περιτροπή Mut 150 Mos 1:42 Legat 206

περιτυγχάνω Deus 91

περιυβρίζω Her 109 Fug 153

περιφαίνομαι Ebr 86 Her 305 Virt 162 Praem 114

περιφανής (13) Leg 1:21 Leg 3:69, 75, 77, 186 Agr 22 Ebr 16, 87 Her 308 Mut 6 Mos 1:284 Spec 3:37, 184

περιφεγγής Somn 1:72 Aet 91

περιφέρεια Agr 138 Conf 156 QG (Par) 2:2

περιφερής (8) Ebr 183 Her 210 Mos 2:122, 133 Spec 1:85, 86 Spec 4:109 QG (Par) 2:2

περιφέρω (11) Conf 107 Fug 85 Mut 111, 164 Somn 2:203 Mos 1:59 Spec 4:200 Virt 120 Prob 117 Legat 77 QG 1:70:1

περίφημος Spec 1:241

περιφθείρομαι Hypoth 6:3

περιφλέγω Virt 93 Praem 121

περιφοιτάω Agr 36 Ebr 159

περίφοιτος Her 82

περιφορά (10) Opif 54 Cher 88 Somn 1:53 Mos 2:124 Decal 103 Spec 1:90 Spec 2:57 Aet 4, 52 QG 2:34a

περιφράσσω QG 2:72

περιφρουρέω Her 273 Mos 2:180

περιφύω Ios 71 Virt 76

περιχάρεια Migr 156 Mos 2:257 Spec 2:146

περιχαρής Her 3

περιχέω Ebr 88 Ios 182 Praem 159

περίψυξις Opif 161 Mos 1:119 Decal 77 Spec 2:191 Legat 123

περιψύχω Opif 80 Virt 93 Praem 121

περιωδυνία Mos 1:128

πέρνημι (πιπράσκω) (45) Cher 108, 109, 121, 122 Deus 111, 169 Ebr 122 Her 44 Fug 15 Ios 15, 16, 18, 20, 20, 22, 27, 35, 35, 36, 165, 175, 247, 270 Mos 2:212 Spec 1:103, 280 Spec 2:79, 112, 112, 117 Spec 3:51 Spec 4:3, 4, 5, 17, 19, 152, 193 Virt 115, 124, 182 Prob 37, 121 Flacc 132, 138

Πέρσης (11) Deus 174, 174 Somn 2:117 Ios 133, 136, 136 Spec 3:13, 17, 100 Prob 74, 132

Περσικός Spec 3:13

πεσσεία Ios 136 Legat 1

πεσσεύω Mos 1:31

πέσσω Sacr 62 Her 311 QG (Par) 2:7

πέταλον (13) Opif 41 Sacr 25, 83 Deus 38, 39 Migr 103 Her 131 Mut 162 Mos 2:22, 111, 114, 116, 132

πετεινός Leg 2:9 Deus 51 Her 239

Πετεφρῆ Somn 1:78

πέτομαι Gig 6 Mut 158

πέτρα (16) Opif 63 Leg 2:84, 86 Det 115, 115, 115, 118 Ebr 172 Somn 2:221, 222 Mos 1:192, 210 Decal 16 Prob 26, 66 Prov 2:33

πέτρος Legat 237, 238

Πετρώνιος (14) Legat 207, 209, 213, 222, 225, 226, 228, 230, 239, 243, 255, 259, 261, 333

πεύκη Aet 64

πεῦσις (8) Det 57 Fug 169 Abr 175 Mos 2:188, 192, 221, 233 Legat 361

πευστικός Leg 3:51, 53

πεφροντισμένως Conf 86 Decal 102 Spec 1:21 Spec 4:102

πέψις Opif 159 Ebr 106

πῆ (7) Leg 3:252 Sacr 49, 49 Agr 165 Plant 135 Her 16 Flacc 34

πηγάζω Opif 133 Spec 3:147, 199 Virt 128 QG 1:3

πηγή (204) Opif 21, 31, 38, 47, 52, 80, 97, 107, 131, 133, 168 Leg 1:28, 28, 28, 29, 34 Leg 2:41, 84, 87 Leg 3:13, 185 Cher 86, 123 Sacr 64, 120, 131 Det 40, 40, 44, 82, 83, 92, 92, 117 Post 69, 126, 127, 127, 127, 132, 135, 136, 136, 138, 153, 185 Gig 25 Deus 72, 155 Agr 105 Plant 15, 79, 81, 121 Ebr 12, 32 Sobr 53 Conf 23, 182 Migr 30, 42, 47, 71, 71, 117, 137 Her 31, 116 Congr 33, 53, 120 Fug 1, 1, 97, 177, 177, 178, 179, 181, 182, 182, 183, 183, 186, 187, 188, 188, 189, 189, 192, 194, 195, 196, 196, 197, 197, 198, 198, 198, 202, 202 Mut 6, 58, 69, 133, 165 Somn 1:19, 97, 115 Somn 2:150, 204, 222, 242, 245, 281 Abr 42, 157, 159 Ios 23, 238 Mos 1:48, 52, 59, 65, 84, 99, 115, 117, 182, 185, 186, 188, 189, 192, 211, 211, 212, 228, 255, 255, 255 Mos 2:63, 127, 143, 186 Decal 16, 81, 91, 122, 153, 173 Spec 1:121, 262, 277, 279, 303, 322 Spec 2:20, 40, 143, 156, 172, 199, 202, 204 Spec 3:58, 186 Spec 4:56, 75, 84, 100, 140, 231 Virt 6, 10, 35, 79, 79, 125, 129 Praem 10, 73, 168 Prob 47, 57, 117, 139 Contempl 39 Aet 66 Flacc 9, 157 Legat 9, 22, 85, 101, 149, 223, 348 Prov 1 QG 1:3, 3, 2:29, 64a, 4:191c

πῆγμα Congr 116

πήγνυμι (69) Opif 14, 27, 33, 35, 171 Leg 1:31 Leg 2:54 Leg 3:22, 46, 107, 172, 172 Sacr 80 Det 7, 85 Post 83, 85, 91 Gig 54 Deus 179 Agr 76, 136 Plant 16, 22 Ebr 100 Conf 87, 172, 175 Migr 3, 150 Her 73, 126, 140, 202, 219 Congr 19, 48, 105 Fug 98 Mut 180 Somn 1:21 Somn 2:126 Ios 214, 239 Mos 1:177 Mos 2:42, 127 Decal 103 Spec 1:266, 287 Spec 2:58 Spec 3:47, 194 Virt 128, 144 Praem 21 Contempl 86 Aet 59, 74, 79, 129, 145 Flacc 115 Legat 189, 238, 238, 272 Prov 2:45 QG 4:8b

πηδάλιον Post 142 Decal 14 Legat 129

πηδαλιουχέω (8) Leg 3:223 Ebr 86 Conf 98 Migr 6 Her 301 Praem 51 Aet 83 Legat 50

πηδάω (13) Opif 163 Leg 2:105 Her 126, 239, 239 Mut 72 Somn 1:54 Spec 1:207 Spec 4:114, 115 Aet 128 Flacc 162 Prov 2:17

πηλίκος Deus 106 Decal 31

Πήλιον Conf 4, 4

πηλός (12) Opif 38 Conf 1, 89, 102, 102, 103, 104, 104 Mos 1:38 Legat 201 Prov 2:46, 46

πημαίνω Conf 54

πῆξις (7) Opif 124 Leg 2:55 Leg 3:22, 172 Agr 158, 160 Mos 2:253

πηρός (12) Leg 3:91, 109, 109, 110, 231 Ebr 6 Fug 123, 165 Somn 1:27 Mos 1:124 Spec 2:77 Hypoth 7:6

πηρόω (30) Leg 3:112, 112 Cher 58, 116 Sacr 69 Det 22, 49, 49, 175 Post 8, 21, 112 Deus 93 Ebr 167, 223 Her 76, 77 Fug 121 Somn 1:117 Somn 2:276 Decal 68 Spec 1:117, 341 Spec 3:6, 196 Spec 4:62 Virt 7, 193 Contempl 10 Prov 2:20

πήρωσις (18) Ebr 155, 156, 160 Sobr 4 Conf 16, 20 Her 284 Decal 170 Spec 1:204 Spec 3:168, 181 Spec 4:200 Virt 5, 11 Praem 33, 143 Prob 55 Legat 107

πήσσω Sacr 80 Det 160 Conf 102, 103

πῆχυς (25) Plant 75, 75 Her 144, 144 Mut 190 Mos 1:54 Mos 2:60, 83, 84, 84, 85, 85, 89, 89, 90, 91, 91, 91 Spec 1:158 Spec 2:120 Contempl 33 QG (Par) 2:2, 2:5, 2:5, 2:5

πιαίνω (14) Opif 63 Leg 1:98 Sacr 33 Det 98, 106 Post 120, 122 Congr 159 Somn 1:250 Abr 160 Spec 1:216 Spec 2:91 Prob 121 Prov 2:32

πιέζω (68) Leg 3:152 Cher 2, 78 Sacr 69 Det 16 Post 9, 74 Gig 31 Deus 14 Agr 37 Ebr 104, 122, 214 Sobr 5 Conf 22, 106 Migr 14, 157 Her 272, 288 Somn 1:110 Somn 2:204, 204 Abr 91 Ios 179, 186, 190, 191, 259 Mos 1:5, 39, 88, 128, 210, 231, 233, 271, 286 Decal 4 Spec 1:69, 100 Spec 2:83, 89 Spec 3:114, 193, 195 Spec 4:114, 173, 212, 216 Virt 116, 128, 156 Praem 156 Contempl 15, 45 Aet 65, 129, 129 Flacc 62, 119, 153, 160 Legat 125, 146, 269, 324 Prov 2:23

πιθανός (31) Opif 45, 72 Leg 3:229, 233 Cher 9 Sacr 12, 12, 13 Det 1, 38 Post 52 Conf 39 Migr 76, 171 Her 248, 302, 306 Somn 1:107, 220 Mos 1:174, 196 Mos 2:261 Decal 3 Spec 1:38, 61, 63, 214 Praem 29 Aet 78 Legat 57, 260

πιθανότης (16) Leg 3:36, 41 Agr 16, 96 Plant 165 Ebr 29, 70 Conf 129 Migr 76 Her 304, 305, 308 Congr 18, 29 Somn 2:278 Ios 143

πικραίνω Congr 164 Fug 149 Mos 1:302 Mos 2:261 Legat 262

πικρία (13) Ebr 222, 223 Migr 36, 36 Congr 163, 163 Somn 2:191 Abr 184 Mos 1:172 Prob 90, 120 Legat 89, 169

πικρίς Congr 162

πικρός (37) Cher 70 Post 154, 155, 156, 158 Ebr 122, 190 Conf 26 Her 186, 208 Congr 71, 162, 163 Mut 173 Somn 2:192, 281 Ios 23 Mos 1:182, 186, 211, 247 Mos 2:182, 183 Decal 16 Spec 1:292 Virt 130 Praem 139, 139, 145, 145 Prob 106 Aet 104 Flacc 157 Legat 355 QG 1:41, 4:227, 227

Πιλᾶτος Legat 299, 304

πιλέω Agr 6 Conf 102 Prob 26

πίλησις Mos 1:123

πίλημα Cher 26 Deus 78 Somn 1:22, 145

πίλησις Ebr 185

πῖλος Legat 79

πίμπλημι (πλήθω) (10) Sacr 33 Post 132, 136 Deus 122 Fug 195 Somn 2:62, 167 Mos 2:34 Hypoth 6:1 QG 1:100:2a

πίμπρημι Leg 3:202 Ios 78 Spec 3:62 Prob 99

πινάκιον Cher 104 Fug 153

πίναξ Sobr 36

Πίνδαρος Virt 172 Aet 121 Prov 2:50

πίνω (57) Leg 2:29, 60 Leg 3:142, 157, 202 Sacr 24 Det 113, 157 Post 132, 132, 132, 139, 147 Deus 145, 145, 155, 158, 169, 171 Agr 1 Plant 140, 160 Ebr 127, 138, 138, 138, 143, 149, 221 Her 41, 269 Congr 163, 163 Fug 31 Mut 165 Somn 2:60, 150, 157, 163 Abr 118, 118 Ios 78, 207 Spec 1:98, 249 Spec 3:62 Prob 25, 99, 103 Contempl 37, 40, 43, 45 Aet 63 QG 2:68a, 4:200a QG (Par) 2:7

πιότης (10) Post 120, 120, 122, 123 Deus 178 Migr 101 Mos 1:64 Spec 2:35, 169 Spec 4:125

πιπράσκω πέρνημι

πίπτω (67) Opif 157 Leg 2:94, 99, 100, 100, 101, 103, 103 Leg 3:217 Det 42 Post 170, 175 Agr 74, 75, 76, 77, 94, 109, 122, 122, 170, 170 Ebr 67, 156 Sobr 2 Conf 17, 17, 38, 38 Migr 5, 65, 80, 85, 122, 225 Her 84, 251 Fug 31 Mut 54, 54, 55, 56, 56, 56, 56, 57, 154, 155, 156, 175, 175, 175 Somn 2:280 Abr 269, 269 Ios 122 Mos 1:124, 175, 233 Virt 3, 7 Praem 6, 95, 148 Aet 128 Flacc 61 QG 2:68b

πίσσα Conf 187

πιστεύω (87) Opif 45 Leg 2:88, 88, 89 Leg 3:164, 218, 228, 228, 229, 229, 229 Cher 24, 65 Sacr 70, 93 Det 9, 25, 37 Deus 4 Agr 50, 164 Plant 62, 92 Ebr 169, 198, 205 Conf 57 Migr 18, 43, 44, 68, 122, 132, 138 Her 14, 90, 90, 92, 92, 93, 99, 101, 101, 101, 101, 129, 251, 287 Mut 166, 177, 177, 178, 181, 186, 186, 218 Somn 2:24 Abr 228, 262, 263, 269, 269, 275 Ios 149, 179 Mos 1:83, 196, 225, 284 Mos 2:166, 259 Spec 1:242, 343 Spec 2:45 Spec 4:28, 36 Virt 68, 77, 216, 218 Praem 27, 28, 49 Flacc 86 Legat 367 Prov 2:27 QG 2:13a

πίστις (160) Opif 57, 84, 93, 109, 116, 147 Leg 3:204, 208 Cher 14, 85 Sacr 34 Post 13, 97 Deus 101 Plant 70, 82, 101, 101, 150 Ebr 40, 93, 175, 188, 213 Conf 31, 156, 198 Migr 43, 44, 132, 171 Her 19, 91, 94, 94, 108, 206, 305 Congr 78, 178 Fug 136, 150, 152, 154, 178 Mut 106, 135, 155, 182, 201 Somn 1:12, 68 Somn 2:44, 220 Abr 39, 141, 226, 247, 268, 270, 271, 273, 273 Ios

51, 52, 100, 107, 127, 148, 149, 158, 168, 185, 188, 242, 258 Mos 1:34, 63, 90, 247, 261, 274, 280, 298 Mos 2:12, 40, 142, 177, 288 Decal 15, 59, 172 Spec 1:69, 70, 84, 273, 290, 338 Spec 2:8, 43, 143, 227 Spec 3:114 Spec 4:30, 32, 33, 34, 40, 40, 43, 50, 54, 67, 67, 137, 156, 176 Virt 34, 46, 55, 66, 216 Praem 27, 30, 31, 49 Prob 32, 35, 48, 58, 92, 105, 118 Aet 52, 55, 62, 95, 102, 104, 137 Flacc 35, 96, 116, 140, 150, 170, 191 Legat 37, 37, 138, 154, 316 Prov 2:24, 72 QG 2:11, 3:58, 58 QE 2:16, 45a QE isf 4

πιστός (18) Leg 2:67 Leg 3:103, 204, 204, 228 Sacr 17, 93, 93 Det 65 Post 173 Deus 113 Ebr 80, 82 Her 93 Mut 182 Mos 1:82 Spec 4:61 Aet 16

πιστόω (19) Leg 3:206, 206, 207, 208 Sacr 93 Deus 54 Agr 4 Plant 112, 115 Migr 110 Fug 56, 58 Spec 2:16, 161 Spec 3:52 Prob 1 Aet 121 Legat 311 QE 2:9b

πίων (20) Leg 1:26 Sacr 88, 136 Det 34 Migr 101 Her 270 Somn 2:74 Ios 101, 108 Mos 1:224, 291 Spec 1:145, 216 Spec 4:100, 124 Virt 145 Praem 129, 139, 146 Aet 100

πλαγιάζω Ebr 131 Spec 4:167 Praem 148 Aet 113 Legat 171

πλάγιος (13) Sacr 43 Mos 2:245 Virt 173 Prob 4, 155 Contempl 51 Flacc 32, 40 Legat 164, 335 QG (Par) 2:6, 2:6, 2:6

πλαδάω (7) Sacr 80 Conf 103 Migr 36, 150 Congr 121 Praem 21, 64

πλάζω (15) Abr 85, 128 Ios 140, 147 Mos 1:166, 237, 270 Mos 2:73 Decal 81 Spec 2:213 Spec 3:194 Praem 98 Prob 16 Prov 2:19 QE isf 5

πλανάω (34) Leg 3:108, 180 Cher 21 Det 5, 10, 10, 17, 17, 21, 22, 22, 28, 131 Plant 5, 97 Conf 144 Migr 133 Her 12, 82, 208 Congr 104, 108 Fug 119, 127, 131 Mut 67 Decal 104 Spec 1:15, 16 Virt 96, 117 Praem 29, 117 Legat 2

πλάνη (8) Det 19, 24 Abr 85, 245 Decal 104 Praem 163 Prov 1 QE isf 14

πλάνης (38) Opif 31, 54, 70, 113, 126, 147 Leg 1:8 Cher 22, 22, 23, 116 Plant 12 Conf 106 Migr 19 Her 221, 222, 224, 233 Abr 69, 158 Mos 1:212 Mos 2:103 Decal 102, 103, 104 Spec 1:13, 34, 210 Spec 2:45, 57, 151, 255 Spec 3:187 Praem 41 Contempl 5 Aet 10, 46, 83

πλανήτης Leg 3:99 Decal 53

πλάνος (14) Leg 3:180 Cher 66 Ebr 38 Congr 108 Mos 2:272 Decal 52 Spec 1:15, 16, 60 Spec 2:23, 36 Spec 4:158 Virt 65, 178

πλάξ Migr 85 Her 167, 167, 167

πλάσμα (39) Opif 1, 157, 170 Leg 1:31 Leg 3:64 Cher 91 Det 124, 125 Ebr 36 Her 43, 57 Congr 61, 62 Fug 42 Abr 243 Mos 2:161, 271 Decal 55, 70, 76, 156 Spec 1:51, 309, 319 Spec 4:178 Virt 102, 178 Praem 8 Contempl 63 Aet 58, 90 Flacc 164 Legat 13, 22, 77, 160, 237 Prov 2:66 QG 1:28

πλάσσω (51) Opif 2, 134, 134, 137, 141, 151 Leg 1:16, 31, 31, 32, 43, 47, 53, 53, 88, 88 Leg 2:4, 5, 5, 9, 9, 11, 11, 12, 12, 14, 15, 24 Leg 3:104, 185 Agr 25 Plant 27, 29, 32, 41, 44, 44 Migr 167 Her 58 Ios 80 Mos 1:94 Mos 2:281 Spec 1:315 Spec 3:82 Virt 39 Praem 162 Aet 142 Flacc 108, 139 Legat 57, 59

πλάστης (9) Leg 2:26 Cher 11 Post 141 Ebr 109 Conf 194 Her 169 Mos 2:205 Legat 290 Prov 2:15

πλάστιγξ (11) Sacr 122 Post 100 Deus 85 Migr 148 Her 46, 151 Fug 151 Mos 1:218 Mos 2:228, 248 Prob 61

πλαστικός (11) Opif 141 Leg 2:75 Migr 167 Abr 267 Ios 39 Decal 7, 66, 156 Spec 1:29 Spec 3:109 Virt 203

πλαστός (7) Leg 1:54, 55, 55, 55, 90 Leg 2:4 Somn 2:140

πλάτη Post 142 Plant 152

πλάτος (33) Opif 49, 102 Plant 75 Sobr 61, 62 Her 144, 229 Congr 147, 147 Mut 187 Somn 1:26, 130, 131 Mos 2:78, 86, 89, 90, 96 Decal 25, 25 Spec 1:71 Spec 3:188 Virt 19 Praem 47, 47, 48 QG 3:49a QG (Par) 2:2, 2:2, 2:2, 2:5, 2:5, 2:5

πλατύνω Post 121 Sobr 59 Congr 160 Somn 1:3, 175

πλατύς Cher 67 Post 179 Agr 62

πλατυσμός Somn 2:36

Πλάτων (11) Opif 119, 133 Prob 13 Contempl 57 Aet 13, 14, 16, 27, 38, 52, 141

Πλατώνειος Aet 17

Πλατωνικός Contempl 59

πλέγμα Ebr 101 Somn 1:204, 206 Mos 2:110

πλειάδες Opif 115 Spec 2:57

πλέκω Mut 82 Aet 105

πλεονάζω (22) Agr 6, 32, 94, 108 Conf 90 Her 191, 194, 245 Somn 2:47, 276 Abr 53 Ios 111 Mos 1:207 Mos 2:13, 262 Spec 1:9 Spec 2:163 Spec 3:193 Spec 4:79 Contempl 21 QE isf 24, 25

πλεονασμός Spec 1:80

πλεονεκτέω (9) Post 162 Abr 211, 266 Mos 1:153, 324 Aet 116, 116 Prov 2:66 QG 4:173

πλεονέκτημα (11) Det 9, 136, 158 Post 117, 163 Ebr 75 Sobr 61, 67 Mut 51 Mos 1:132 Spec 3:142

πλεονέκτης Sacr 32 Mos 1:56 QG 4:172

πλεονεξία (50) Leg 3:166 Agr 83 Her 105 Mut 103 Somn 2:66 Abr 126, 216 Ios 30, 216 Mos 1:54 Mos 2:186 Decal 135, 155, 171 Spec 1:173, 204, 270, 278 Spec 2:43, 52, 77, 93, 190 Spec 3:158 Spec 4:5, 20, 54, 129, 149, 158, 213, 215, 218 Virt 100 Praem 15, 85, 91, 121, 154 Prob 78, 79, 126, 159 Contempl 2, 70 Legat 80 QG 4:47b, 172, 211 QE 2:64

πλευρά (25) Opif 94 Leg 2:19, 19, 20, 20, 20, 21, 21, 21, 35 Post 33 Plant 122 Mos 2:80, 85, 91 Spec 2:177 Spec 3:44 Contempl 51 Aet 128 Flacc 92, 189 QG 2:14, 14, 3:61 QG (Par) 2:5

πλέω (17) Opif 147 Post 22 Ebr 158 Fug 191 Somn 2:86, 86 Abr 47, 65 Mos 1:194 Spec 2:19 Spec 4:154 Flacc 154 Legat 180, 250, 251 Prov 2:43, 65

πληγή (43) Opif 63 Leg 3:33, 201 Cher 80, 81 Sacr 134 Det 51 Agr 114 Congr 118 Fug 22 Mos 1:95, 129, 143, 270, 325 Decal 144 Spec 2:28, 28 Spec 3:82, 106, 106, 107, 107, 108, 141, 142, 168, 174, 183 Prob 26, 26, 55, 145 Flacc 66, 75, 80, 84, 188, 189 Legat 31, 368 QE 2:24b QE isf 32

πλῆθος (185) Opif 1, 56, 60, 78, 79, 84 Leg 1:3, 102 Leg 2:20, 85 Leg 3:105, 183, 202, 203, 235 Sacr 23, 33, 122 Det 14, 99, 174 Post 3, 49, 110 Gig 26 Deus 14, 73, 85 Agr 86, 88, 151 Plant 7, 38, 67 Ebr 32, 207, 214 Conf 15, 15, 169 Migr 53, 53, 54, 54, 55, 56, 61, 61, 68, 70, 201 Her 31, 86, 89, 109, 109, 190, 212 Congr 6, 76, 87, 90, 133 Fug 68, 71, 71 Mut 89, 144, 145, 225

Somn 1:222 Somn 2:61, 170 Abr 10, 28, 45, 122, 133, 214, 221, 240, 275 Ios 39, 59, 111, 114, 210, 211, 251 Mos 1:64, 84, 92, 121, 147, 147, 171, 178, 224, 224, 225, 227, 229, 230, 232, 236, 255, 288, 293, 306, 330 Mos 2:91, 159, 163, 166, 167, 169, 233, 277 Decal 4, 8, 29, 39 Spec 1:56, 277, 300, 325, 326, 331 Spec 2:164, 217 Spec 3:84 Spec 4:45, 85, 88, 96, 109, 114, 151, 158, 170, 174, 234 Virt 10, 55, 67 Praem 103, 129 Prob 9, 75, 92 Contempl 2, 49, 53 Aet 97 Flacc 33, 39, 56, 60, 86, 90, 99, 142, 172 Legat 80, 215, 247, 250, 256, 280, 287, 299, 319, 337, 347 Hypoth 6:6 Prov 2:1, 12, 17, 22, 25, 33, 35, 40, 62, 64

πληθυντικός Her 164

πληθύνω (16) Leg 3:200, 200, 203, 203 Sacr 55 Deus 20 Agr 84 Conf 24 Mut 23, 263 Spec 3:40, 171 Spec 4:9 Virt 207 Praem 68 Prov 2:65

πληθύς (43) Cher 75 Det 99, 173 Post 54, 171 Gig 2 Agr 31, 31, 178 Ebr 67, 198 Conf 24, 109 Migr 10, 32, 54, 163, 219 Somn 1:175 Somn 2:124 Abr 234 Ios 158 Mos 1:103, 166, 167, 195, 234, 246, 290, 301 Mos 2:172, 214, 262 Spec 1:79 Spec 2:250 Spec 4:157 Virt 35, 35, 42, 58 Praem 76 Legat 223, 226

πλήθω πίμπλημι

πλημμέλεια Mos 2:230 Spec 1:181, 234, 244

πλημμελέω (29) Opif 155, 169 Leg 2:68 Leg 3:72, 152 Det 146 Deus 63 Agr 77 Conf 11, 153, 175 Somn 2:152 Spec 1:188, 197, 227, 233, 236, 238 Spec 2:11 Spec 3:151, 155 Spec 4:8, 63, 63, 200, 237 Prob 57 Flacc 50, 139

πλημμέλημα QG 1:66

πλημμελής (18) Leg 3:31, 35, 131, 223 Cher 24 Sacr 32, 45 Det 141 Post 98 Agr 34, 74 Plant 141 Conf 114 Her 160 Spec 4:187 Praem 20 Aet 59, 85

πλήμμυρα (πλήμυρα) (13) Opif 58 Leg 1:34 Sacr 66 Somn 2:109, 125, 238 Abr 92 Ios 109 Mos 1:265 Mos 2:195, 255 Virt 201 Flacc 63

πλημμυρέω (πλημύρω) (14) Opif 38, 113 Det 100 Sobr 53 Migr 121, 156 Her 32, 315 Somn 1:97 Mos 1:6, 114, 202 Prob 63 Aet 147

πλημύρω (πλημμυρέω) Post 113 Conf 29 Somn 2:221 Abr 42 Prov 2:39

πλήν (50) Opif 36, 59, 63, 141 Leg 2:86 Leg 3:4, 82, 137, 239, 248 Cher 44, 126, 126, 126, 126 Post 5, 136 Deus 7 Agr 9 Ebr 99, 135 Sobr 62 Migr 6 Her 80 Fug 170 Mut 34 Somn 1:108, 110 Somn 2:75 Abr 204, 204 Mos 2:108 Spec 1:72 Spec 3:171 Virt 55 Praem 25, 58, 61 Prob 80 Contempl 80 Aet 8, 115, 126 Flacc 50 Legat 3, 51 Hypoth 7:13 Prov 2:63 QG 1:74, 100:1b

πλῆξις Leg 3:183 Cher 128 Deus 83 Ebr 116 Migr 47

πλήρης (86) Opif 78 Leg 1:23, 44 Leg 3:7, 46, 81, 226 Sacr 9 Det 7, 54 Post 32, 43 Deus 77, 94, 126, 150, 179 Agr 53 Plant 7, 125, 128, 157 Ebr 94, 135 Migr 35, 73 Her 187, 188, 217, 305, 306 Congr 114, 149 Fug 143, 175 Mut 27, 182, 234, 249, 269 Somn 1:22, 75, 94, 127, 198 Somn 2:71, 74, 183, 218, 218, 223, 245 Abr 2 Ios 93, 93, 182, 212 Mos 1:262, 262 Mos 2:157 Spec 1:72, 183, 268 Spec 2:48, 53, 173, 174, 201, 203, 210 Spec 3:160 Spec 4:144 Virt 95, 98 Praem 142, 157, 161 Prob 97 Contempl 54 Flacc 50 Legat 14, 58, 195 QG 2:12b, 4:30 QE 2:1

πληρόω (82) Leg 1:44 Leg 3:4, 60, 60, 138, 149 Sacr 67 Det 92, 153 Post 14, 30, 130, 136, 137, 147, 148 Gig 8, 47, 55 Deus 57, 59, 137 Agr 34, 35, 101 Ebr 5, 67, 146, 149 Conf 10, 136 Congr 64 Fug 194 Mut 111, 192, 270 Somn 1:62 Somn 2:118, 150, 190, 221, 245, 289 Abr 108, 154, 174 Ios 90, 178, 255 Mos 1:52, 103, 121, 144, 177, 178, 187, 195, 211, 302, 333 Mos 2:238, 260 Decal 149, 152 Spec 1:300 Spec 2:92, 216 Spec 4:72, 129, 141 Virt 49, 164 Praem 83, 104, 112 Contempl 55 Flacc 44, 139 Legat 146 QG (Par) 2:7 QE 2:25a QE isf 1

πλήρωμα (13) Abr 116, 268 Mos 2:62 Spec 1:272 Spec 2:200, 213 Spec 4:186 Praem 65, 109 Prob 41, 128, 142 Legat 11

πλήρωσις (7) Det 113 Her 297 Mut 88 Ios 33 Decal 160 Praem 112 Aet 74

πλησιάζω (14) Cher 57, 109 Post 23 Her 310 Somn 1:178 Mos 2:21 Spec 1:342 Virt 167 Prob 62, 76 Contempl 10 Flacc 36 Legat 7 QG 3:8

πλησίος (77) Leg 3:107, 108, 120, 120 Sacr 8 Post 20, 38, 84, 84, 84, 89 Gig 47 Agr 7 Plant 106 Ebr 67, 70, 71, 100, 124 Conf 1, 1, 38, 160, 189, 195 Migr 78 Her 193 Fug 31, 53, 77, 90, 90, 91, 202 Somn 1:92, 128 Somn 2:79 Abr 40 Ios 102 Mos 1:52, 54, 137, 216, 228, 247, 271 Mos 2:161 Spec 1:24, 216, 216, 236 Spec 3:11, 93, 182, 186 Spec 4:21, 39, 75, 93, 149 Virt 24, 40, 116 Praem 73, 80, 100 Prob 68, 122 Contempl 43 Flacc 122 Legat 42, 52, 132, 134, 186, 351 QG 2:64b

πλησιόχωρος (6) Mos 1:5, 21, 23 Spec 3:17 Legat 200, 257

πλησίστιος Cher 38 Agr 174 Mut 215 Legat 177

πλησιφαής (9) Opif 101, 101 Congr 106 Mos 2:224 Spec 1:178, 178, 189 Spec 2:155 Spec 4:234

πλησμονή (13) Cher 75 Agr 38 Sobr 2 Her 297 Somn 1:122 Mos 2:24, 156 Spec 4:129 Virt 163 Contempl 37 Legat 2 QG 2:64c QE isf 14

πλήσσω (38) Opif 77, 161 Leg 2:34 Leg 3:32, 33, 33, 34, 57, 183 Sacr 134 Post 108, 108 Deus 84 Ebr 137 Her 259 Mut 56, 247 Somn 1:29, 107, 114 Somn 2:137 Abr 62 Ios 22, 102, 179, 261 Mos 1:78, 268 Mos 2:163, 179 Decal 35 Spec 1:147, 266 Prob 58 Contempl 14 Flacc 10, 157 Legat 223

πλινθεύω Conf 1, 84

πλίνθινος Legat 203

πλινθίον Opif 107, 111

πλίνθος (16) Conf 1, 1, 84, 87, 88, 92, 95, 96, 99, 101, 102 Mos 1:38, 38 Prob 96 Legat 201 QG 2:54c

πλινθουργέω Conf 91

πλόϊμος (πλώϊμος) Legat 15

πλοῖον Det 144 Conf 114 Mos 2:251

πλοκή Somn 2:53 Mos 2:109

πλόος (πλοῦς) (22) Det 141 Post 22 Agr 64 Plant 152 Conf 115 Congr 65 Mut 149 Somn 1:44, 180 Somn 2:143, 201 Abr 123 Mos 2:148 Decal 14, 14, 84 Virt 176 Flacc 26, 28, 31 Legat 15, 251

πλουθυγεία Post 114

πλοῦς πλόος

πλούσιος (51) Opif 23 Leg 1:45 Leg 2:12 Leg 3:24, 24, 211 Det 34 Post 109 Agr 31 Plant 69 Sobr 56 Congr 76 Fug 16, 102 Somn 1:155 Abr 209 Ios 72, 133, 258 Decal 178 Spec 1:139 Spec 2:71, 87, 107 Spec 4:74, 172, 172 Virt 81, 94, 97, 148, 170, 174 Praem 36 Prob 8, 72, 77

Contempl 35 Flacc 63, 130 Legat 13, 51, 108, 123, 141, 203 Prov 2:7, 29 QG 3:22 QG isf 5, 11

πλούταρχος Somn 2:76

πλουτέω (9) Leg 3:87 Det 131 Her 189 Somn 2:40 Abr 220 Mos 2:38 Spec 1:277 Spec 2:108 Virt 166

πλουτιστήριος Somn 2:76

πλουτοδότης Post 32

πλοῦτος (122) Leg 1:34, 34 Leg 3:39, 86, 163 Cher 107, 117 Sacr 124 Det 33, 122 Post 112, 139, 144, 151, 174 Deus 147, 150 Agr 54 Plant 65, 66 Ebr 52, 57, 75 Sobr 3, 40, 61 Conf 18, 48, 112 Migr 71, 95, 101, 172 Her 27, 48, 76, 212, 286 Congr 5, 27 Fug 15, 16, 16, 17, 19, 25, 151 Mut 214 Somn 1:126, 179, 179, 248 Somn 2:12, 35, 35, 40 Abr 24, 25, 219, 252, 263, 265 Ios 131, 144, 198, 254, 258 Mos 1:153, 155, 155, 312 Mos 2:53, 234 Decal 71 Spec 1:24, 25, 25, 25, 27, 28, 311 Spec 2:19, 19, 20, 23, 208 Spec 3:1 Spec 4:75, 75, 158, 194 Virt 5, 6, 7, 8, 8, 10, 85, 85, 161, 162 Praem 24, 54, 98, 99, 100, 100, 104, 118, 168 Prob 9 Contempl 13, 17 Flacc 77, 148 Legat 199 Hypoth 11:4 Prov 2:1, 19 QG 4:43 QE 2:99 QE isf 16

πλουτοφόρος Congr 171

πλώϊμος πλόϊμος

Πλούτων Decal 54

πλύνω (7) Leg 3:141, 144, 144, 144, 147, 147 QG 2:54c

πλωτήρ (6) Opif 114 Deus 98 Somn 2:86 Spec 1:91 Spec 4:186 Prov 2:44

πλωτός (6) Opif 131 Plant 12 Mos 1:172 Spec 1:335 Spec 4:155 Aet 141

πνεῦμα (151) Opif 29, 30, 30, 41, 58, 80, 113, 131, 135, 135, 144 Leg 1:33, 33, 33, 33, 37, 37, 42, 42, 42, 91 Leg 3:14, 53, 161, 223 Cher 13, 37, 38, 111 Sacr 97 Det 17, 80, 80, 81, 83, 84 Post 22, 67 Gig 10, 10, 19, 19, 22, 22, 23, 23, 24, 24, 24, 26, 27, 28, 29, 47, 53, 55 Deus 2, 2, 26, 35, 60, 84, 98, 175 Agr 44, 174 Plant 18, 24, 44 Ebr 106 Migr 148, 217 Her 55, 57, 208, 265 Congr 133 Fug 134, 182, 186 Mut 123 Somn 1:30 Somn 2:13, 67, 85, 86, 143, 166, 252 Abr 43, 92, 160 Ios 33, 116 Mos 1:41, 93, 175, 179, 277 Mos 2:40, 104, 265 Decal 33, 175 Spec 1:6, 26, 92, 171, 277, 301, 322, 338 Spec 2:71, 153, 191 Spec 4:27, 49, 123, 123, 123, 217 Virt 58, 135, 217 Praem 41, 144 Prob 26, 97 Aet 11, 111, 128, 139 Flacc 155 Legat 63, 125, 177, 188, 243 Prov 2:43, 45, 47 QG 1:51, 2:28, 28, 59, 59 QG (Par) 2:3, 2:3, 2:3, 2:4 QE 2:55b

πνευματικός (9) Opif 67 Her 242 Abr 113 Praem 48 Aet 86, 125 QG 1:92, 2:12d QG (Par) 2:3

πνεύμων (6) Opif 118 Leg 1:12 Ebr 106 Praem 143 QG (Par) 2:3, 2:3

πνέω (17) Deus 174 Congr 108, 159 Mut 215 Somn 1:107, 147 Somn 2:81 Ios 21 Mos 1:30, 155 Mos 2:240 Spec 3:8 Virt 171 Praem 28 Flacc 124, 152 Legat 48

πνιγή Aet 129

πνῖγος Praem 133 Legat 125

πνοή (10) Opif 134 Leg 1:31, 33, 42, 42 Plant 19 Her 56 Somn 1:34 Spec 4:123 QG 2:59

πόα Somn 1:125 Mos 1:65, 320 Aet 63

ποδαγρικός Congr 46 Praem 145

ποδαπός Cher 99

ποδηγετέω (12) Opif 70 Post 31 Deus 143, 182 Migr 23 Fug 21 Somn 2:102 Mos 2:265 Spec 1:269 Spec 4:70 Virt 215 Praem 84

ποδηγέω Leg 3:109

ποδηγός Leg 3:109

ποδήρης (16) Leg 1:81 Leg 2:56 Her 176 Fug 185 Mut 43 Somn 1:214 Mos 2:117, 118, 120, 121, 133, 143 Spec 1:85, 85, 93, 94

ποδιαῖος Somn 1:53

ποδόνιπτρον Contempl 7

ποδώκεια Post 161 Mut 178 Mos 2:170

ποδώκης Legat 99

ποηφάγος Spec 4:104

ποθεινός Det 129 Abr 65 Praem 135

πόθεν (22) Leg 2:69 Cher 114 Post 5, 136 Agr 5, 35 Conf 14, 120 Migr 213 Her 20 Congr 147 Fug 1, 52, 203, 205 Mos 1:141 Spec 4:77, 84, 163 Virt 92 Aet 38 Flacc 143

ποθέω (42) Leg 2:4 Leg 3:12, 27, 249 Det 25, 176 Post 157 Gig 44 Plant 127 Conf 78 Migr 218 Her 270, 310 Congr 105 Fug 8, 130 Somn 1:49, 71, 139 Somn 2:163, 163, 288 Abr 73 Ios 90, 233 Mos 1:29, 224 Decal 146 Spec 1:41, 59 Spec 2:123, 171 Spec 4:43, 112 Virt 76, 215 Contempl 12, 75 Aet 129 Legat 175, 338 QG 4:172

πόθος (59) Opif 5, 71, 77, 111, 152, 152 Cher 20 Det 129 Post 13, 23 Agr 91, 152 Plant 79 Ebr 21, 50, 84 Migr 132 Her 69, 102 Congr 74, 112, 166 Fug 164 Somn 2:106, 150, 235 Abr 29, 63, 65, 170 Ios 157 Mos 1:159 Mos 2:31 Decal 108, 148 Spec 1:45, 50, 160 Spec 2:139, 230 Spec 3:128, 173 Spec 4:161 Virt 30, 120, 215 Praem 39 Prob 22, 71, 113 Contempl 35, 48, 68 Aet 1, 30 Hypoth 6:1 Prov 2:63 QE 2:28 QE isf 11

ποῖ (9) Cher 114, 114 Det 152 Deus 57 Fug 205 Ios 17 Mos 2:251, 251 Hypoth 7:8

ποιέω (630) Opif 2, 10, 13, 23, 26, 27, 27, 28, 28, 29, 29, 35, 36, 44, 62, 62, 64, 72, 72, 74, 75, 82, 94, 96, 104, 129, 140, 150, 158, 171, 172, 172 Leg 1:2, 5, 5, 6, 6, 16, 16, 16, 18, 18, 20, 21, 21, 24, 48, 49, 51, 51, 51, 51, 53, 55, 65, 65, 70, 81, 82, 88, 88, 88 Leg 2:1, 5, 9, 19, 36, 53, 71, 79, 79, 106 Leg 3:2, 14, 15, 24, 24, 27, 50, 55, 59, 65, 66, 69, 73, 75, 79, 86, 96, 97, 102, 111, 120, 121, 122, 140, 164, 180, 194, 203, 205, 209, 210, 216, 219, 219, 238, 243 Cher 19, 32, 43, 45, 76, 77, 79, 87, 88, 90, 116, 130 Sacr 4, 17, 24, 53, 56, 56, 58, 59, 60, 63, 65, 77, 82, 85, 85, 86, 86, 88 Det 2, 6, 32, 49, 49, 50, 56, 57, 58, 69, 69, 70, 70, 74, 78, 81, 86, 108, 122, 123, 126, 133, 148, 154 Post 7, 19, 31, 64, 64, 65, 81, 121, 130, 141, 169, 173, 179, 179, 179, 184, 185 Gig 42 Deus 8, 20, 20, 32, 33, 41, 41, 49, 51, 51, 70, 72, 72, 96, 99, 116, 126, 132, 134, 182 Agr 12, 12, 64, 74, 80, 147, 158, 170, 170, 172 Plant 9, 13, 13, 21, 27, 31, 31, 48, 68, 79, 79, 86, 87, 89, 102, 130, 132, 141, 150, 153 Ebr 13, 16, 30, 39, 41, 67, 87, 133, 133, 199 Sobr 1, 20, 30, 36, 37, 58, 63, 67 Conf 1, 1, 1, 27, 37, 58, 98, 116, 116, 136, 152, 154, 159, 162, 169, 169, 179, 185, 196 Migr 1, 18, 20, 25, 42, 42, 53, 68, 68, 79, 91, 97, 123, 130, 130, 130, 135, 135, 150, 157, 157, 162, 167, 177, 193, 197, 203, 208, 209, 214, 215, 215, 215, 219 Her 30, 44, 79, 92, 122, 134, 156, 159, 162, 162, 162, 164, 164, 164, 196, 199, 205, 231, 231, 246, 247, 260, 277, 289, 314 Congr 5, 49, 82, 86, 86, 86, 86, 86, 99, 114, 160 Fug 12, 23, 51, 68, 68, 71, 71, 72, 72, 95, 95, 97, 148, 155, 202 Mut 31, 42, 46, 65,

76, 137, 153, 178, 206, 220, 249, 269 Somn 1:3, 40, 68, 74, 74, 74, 76, 95, 128, 136, 165, 189, 195, 216, 226, 227, 243 Somn 2:26, 56, 69, 70, 73, 83, 88, 108, 117, 123, 165, 180, 186, 213, 296, 297 Abr 3, 23, 31, 69, 70, 72, 78, 88, 108, 117, 121, 130, 163, 194, 275 Ios 29, 53, 60, 88, 107, 114, 125, 195, 198, 217, 245, 264 Mos 1:19, 128, 149, 185, 185, 209, 230, 280, 285, 292, 300, 310, 328 Mos 2:49, 51, 55, 75, 78, 99, 100, 101, 102, 130, 133, 153, 166, 176, 178, 183, 186, 208, 248 Decal 29, 30, 31, 39, 52, 58, 61, 72, 101, 112, 172 Spec 1:22, 25, 70, 77, 97, 99, 111, 144, 153, 198, 200, 210, 220, 220, 225, 229, 233, 249, 272, 293, 294, 295, 300, 325 Spec 2:2, 5, 9, 11, 13, 20, 23, 32, 36, 40, 44, 46, 115, 119, 137, 168, 184, 185, 202, 203, 207, 228, 255 Spec 3:20, 54, 78, 103, 121, 132, 143, 148, 167, 169, 171, 205 Spec 4:2, 2, 7, 15, 22, 28, 131, 136, 157, 177, 190, 205, 225 Virt 22, 23, 61, 73, 81, 95, 105, 106, 163, 165, 166, 183 Praem 29, 42, 56, 106, 166 Prob 22, 59, 59, 59, 59, 59, 59, 60, 61, 68, 74, 86, 95, 96, 96, 157 Contempl 20, 29, 48, 80, 80, 84, 84 Aet 18, 19, 26, 27, 100, 129 Flacc 3, 12, 18, 24, 42, 43, 55, 96, 115, 161 Legat 69, 83, 134, 138, 153, 221, 239, 253, 275, 315, 316, 323, 356 Hypoth 0:1, 0:1, 7:6, 7:12, 7:17, 11:5 Prov 2:12, 44, 46, 71 QG 1:93, 2:15a, 62, 4:193 QG isf 3, 3, 10, 12 QG (Par) 2:3, 2:6 QE 2:17 QE isf 9

ποίημα (11) Det 125 Plant 131 Congr 61, 61, 62, 77 Fug 42 Abr 23 Mos 1:3 QG isf 3, 3

ποίησις Plant 154 QG 4:161 QG isf 3

ποιητής (114) Opif 4, 7, 9, 21, 53, 77, 88 Det 86, 99, 124, 155 Post 175 Gig 58 Deus 34, 60, 169 Agr 18, 24 Plant 51, 53, 68, 127, 151, 159 Ebr 61, 103 Conf 4, 144, 170 Her 56, 56, 98, 200, 236 Congr 15, 74, 148 Fug 31, 84, 104, 104, 177, 211 Mut 29, 31, 179 Somn 1:123, 135, 205 Somn 2:52, 275 Abr 9, 10, 10, 58, 88 Mos 1:158 Mos 2:48, 100, 238, 256 Decal 41, 51, 64, 105 Spec 1:20, 30, 34, 74, 209, 294, 343 Spec 2:6, 166, 256 Spec 3:178, 189, 199 Spec 4:180, 230 Virt 34, 64, 77, 180, 213 Praem 1, 10, 23, 24, 32, 41 Prob 42, 98, 141, 143 Contempl 1, 40, 58, 80, 90 Aet 15, 17, 63, 127 Flacc 34 Legat 13, 115, 165, 293 Prov 2:13 QG 1:100:2b, 2:15a, 34c QG isf 10

ποιητικός (43) Opif 133, 157 Leg 2:107 Leg 3:109, 114, 142, 184, 240, 240, 240, 250, 251 Cher 66, 105 Sacr 78 Det 124, 125, 157 Post 20 Agr 41 Plant 143 Conf 144 Migr 156, 195 Her 189 Fug 26, 61, 95, 97, 100, 103 Mut 29, 89 Somn 1:57 Somn 2:249 Abr 121, 121 Ios 2 Mos 2:99, 99 Spec 1:29 Spec 2:164 Aet 132

ποικιλία (17) Opif 165 Sacr 21, 23 Det 157, 173 Post 104 Plant 110, 111 Ebr 175 Migr 85 Abr 148 Mos 2:39 Spec 1:95 Virt 149 Contempl 53 Prov 2:15, 71

ποικίλλω (10) Opif 41, 45 Cher 104 Plant 110 Ebr 46 Migr 102 Ios 33 Mos 2:110 Spec 4:76 Aet 64

ποίκιλμα Sacr 83 Somn 1:207, 225

ποικίλος (67) Leg 2:74, 75, 75, 76, 76, 79, 79, 84, 107 Leg 3:2, 61, 66 Sacr 26 Det 6, 6, 28 Gig 18, 18 Deus 113 Agr 95 Plant 111 Ebr 86, 86, 215, 217, 219 Conf 71 Fug 10, 10 Mut 43 Somn 1:8, 189, 189, 200, 202, 208, 208, 209, 213, 214, 216, 216, 219, 219, 220, 255 Somn 2:19, 53, 57, 155 Ios 32, 32, 93 Mos 2:84, 93 Spec 1:84, 299, 343 Prob 58, 58, 66, 155 Aet 6 Flacc 3 Legat 36, 59, 199

ποικιλτής Somn 1:207

ποικιλτικός Somn 1:203, 204, 207, 207

ποιμαίνω (23) Sacr 46, 50 Det 3, 5, 9, 25, 25 Deus 119, 121 Agr 41, 42, 43, 50, 50, 52, 54 Sobr 14 Mut 110, 115 Ios 10 Mos 1:60 Prob 31, 31

ποιμασία Mut 105, 114

ποιμενικός (13) Agr 27, 42, 55, 59, 60, 64 Abr 213 Ios 2, 2, 3, 54 Mos 1:60, 62

ποιμήν (43) Opif 85, 85 Sacr 11, 45, 48, 49, 51, 51 Post 67, 67, 98 Agr 27, 29, 29, 39, 41, 41, 43, 44, 44, 48, 49, 51, 59, 66, 67, 124 Migr 213 Fug 149 Mut 116, 117 Somn 2:152 Abr 221 Ios 2 Mos 1:53, 61 Spec 3:46 Spec 4:22 Virt 58, 144 Prob 30, 31 Legat 44

ποίμνη (25) Post 67 Agr 41, 44, 51, 52, 64 Sobr 12 Conf 124 Fug 9 Mut 111, 113, 115 Somn 1:198 Abr 220 Ios 257 Mos 1:52, 53, 57, 64, 65 Decal 114 Spec 1:136, 141 Virt 58, 126

ποίμνιον (9) Det 3 Post 66, 66, 68, 69 Agr 45 Somn 2:152 Mos 1:133 Spec 1:163

Ποινή Prob 7 Flacc 175

ποῖος (25) Leg 1:90 Leg 3:4 Cher 53 Post 17, 130 Conf 117 Migr 56 Her 277, 288, 314 Congr 22 Fug 163 Mut 35, 91, 264 Somn 2:246 Mos 2:239, 239, 239 Virt 135 Praem 84 Aet 80, 125 Legat 142, 371

ποιός (24) Leg 1:67, 79, 79 Leg 2:18 Leg 3:36, 206 Cher 51, 114, 114 Deus 62 Congr 175, 178 Fug 13 Mut 72, 121, 121, 122, 122, 122, 196 Decal 30 Aet 48, 49, 51

ποιότης (57) Opif 22, 41, 41, 57, 63, 78, 97, 97, 97, 131, 134, 141 Leg 1:51 Leg 2:19, 80 Leg 3:206 Cher 62, 67 Sacr 31 Det 15, 16 Post 168 Deus 55 Agr 13 Plant 133 Conf 85, 185, 186, 187 Migr 28, 28, 103, 213, 213 Her 247 Fug 13 Somn 1:27 Abr 163 Ios 142 Mos 1:97 Decal 31 Spec 1:29, 47, 90, 327, 328, 329, 329 Spec 3:108 Spec 4:187 Praem 112 Contempl 4 Aet 79, 79, 81, 81 QE isf 3

πολεμαρχέω Ios 3

πολεμέω (29) Leg 1:87 Sacr 130 Det 3 Post 122 Gig 66 Agr 162 Migr 61 Her 14, 275 Mut 60 Somn 1:221, 221 Somn 2:90, 265 Abr 223, 225 Mos 1:111, 172, 306, 318, 331, 333 Decal 87 Spec 4:121 Virt 25 Praem 94, 95 Prob 138 QG 4:206b

πολεμικός (10) Leg 3:130 Ebr 115 Conf 43, 49, 57 Migr 67 Abr 225 Mos 1:60 Spec 2:192 Prov 2:56

πολέμιος (75) Leg 1:68 Leg 2:10, 79 Leg 3:111, 111, 185 Cher 15, 77 Sacr 3, 20 Det 72 Post 172 Ebr 10, 111 Conf 18, 48, 159 Migr 114, 150 Her 242, 243 Congr 91 Somn 1:105, 126 Somn 2:121, 125, 281 Abr 233 Ios 14, 188 Mos 1:180, 280 Mos 2:249, 255 Decal 129 Spec 1:301, 313 Spec 3:87, 152 Spec 4:2, 23, 85, 89, 184, 227 Virt 33, 109, 109, 131, 150, 153, 154, 165, 191 Praem 12, 85, 127, 137, 149 Contempl 15, 47, 86 Flacc 24, 116, 143 Legat 64, 174, 211, 215, 229 Prov 2:49 QG 4:206a, 228 QE isf 23, 32

πολεμιστήριος Leg 3:130 Post 119 Praem 132

πολεμιστής Ebr 114 Conf 55

πολεμοποιέω Legat 132, 208, 301 QG 4:206b

πόλεμος (235) Opif 33, 81, 81, 164 Leg 2:91 Leg 3:14, 14, 46, 46, 81, 117, 134, 184, 186, 187 Cher 32, 37, 86 Sacr 4, 17, 25, 35, 130 Det 2, 2, 174 Post 117, 117, 118, 184, 185 Gig 51 Deus 145, 166, 166 Agr 12, 25, 35, 78, 147, 148, 148, 148, 148, 149, 150, 150, 151, 153, 159 Ebr 62, 75, 76, 96, 97, 98, 99, 99, 100, 104, 104, 105 Conf 41, 42, 46, 47, 57, 132 Migr 56, 62, 63

Her 162, 206, 212, 244, 284, 284, 284, 286, 287, 287, 288 Congr 32, 32, 176 Fug 114, 174 Mut 60, 109, 150, 221, 265 Somn 1:106, 174, 174 Somn 2:14, 36, 129, 144, 147, 147, 166, 229, 253, 253, 265 Abr 1, 27, 29, 105, 179, 215, 240, 242, 245, 261, 272 Ios 34, 56, 57, 115, 115, 204 Mos 1:8, 36, 60, 142, 164, 170, 216, 239, 243, 258, 259, 263, 263, 306, 307, 310, 319, 321, 322, 323, 327 Mos 2:13, 16, 173, 236 Decal 5, 153, 178, 178 Spec 1:159, 313 Spec 2:101, 170, 190, 190, 191, 208, 245 Spec 3:16, 69, 169, 172 Spec 4:28, 85, 121, 166, 202, 220, 221, 223, 225 Virt 2, 22, 22, 24, 25, 29, 38, 44, 47, 61, 153, 153 Praem 3, 87, 91, 93, 97, 118, 132, 148, 157 Prob 9, 32, 34, 37, 64, 78, 133 Contempl 60 Aet 68 Flacc 44, 56, 59, 61, 62 Legat 17, 30, 68, 100, 102, 113, 113, 119, 121, 141, 144, 146, 218, 220, 226, 292, 335 Hypoth 6:6 Prov 2:12, 33 QG 3:7, 4:7* QG isf 17 QE 2:64 QE isf 4, 30

πολεμόω Ebr 77, 196 Virt 154

πολιά Abr 271 Spec 2:238

πολίζω Praem 168

πολιορκέω Leg 1:87

πολιορκία Leg 1:75

πολιός (12) Leg 3:175 Sacr 77, 77, 79 Post 152 Deus 120 Plant 168 Her 49 Somn 1:10 Contempl 67 Legat 1 QG 2:74

πόλις (488) Opif 11, 17, 17, 18, 20, 24, 24, 85, 89, 142, 143, 143 Leg 2:10 Leg 3:1, 1, 2, 3, 43, 43, 44, 83, 98, 99, 115, 191, 224, 225, 225, 228, 229, 244 Cher 20, 120, 121, 126, 127 Sacr 49, 106, 124, 124, 126, 126, 127, 128, 130 Det 99, 134, 141, 141, 174 Post 7, 33, 33, 49, 49, 49, 50, 50, 50, 51, 52, 53, 53, 54, 54, 54, 57, 59, 65, 104, 117, 181, 184, 185 Gig 51 Deus 94, 95, 95, 103, 176, 176 Agr 11, 12, 43, 46, 113, 143 Plant 67 Ebr 14, 14, 14, 28, 34, 36, 64, 79, 91, 101, 101, 101, 103, 193, 195, 215 Conf 1, 1, 1, 15, 15, 46, 83, 91, 107, 107, 108, 111, 122, 128, 134, 142, 142, 144, 155, 158, 170, 196 Migr 18, 90, 120 Her 145, 286, 295 Congr 10, 50, 58, 92 Fug 3, 86, 87, 87, 88, 94, 94, 96, 100, 103, 174, 175, 176, 190 Mut 21, 149, 152, 196 Somn 1:7, 46, 77, 77, 77, 78, 137, 177, 177, 188, 222, 233 Somn 2:12, 78, 82, 147, 166, 170, 246, 246, 246, 248, 248, 250, 250, 253, 257, 257, 286 Abr 23, 40, 65, 71, 85, 85, 86, 91, 136, 139, 141, 141, 145, 166, 169, 184, 227, 267, 272 Ios 2, 3, 29, 31, 38, 38, 38, 55, 56, 67, 77, 110, 111, 120, 134, 136, 157, 159, 218, 221, 225, 230, 256, 268 Mos 1:2, 8, 38, 143, 157, 194, 215, 224, 225, 229, 233, 233, 237, 250, 251, 252, 253, 254, 254, 262, 288, 311 Mos 2:2, 18, 19, 29, 34, 35, 49, 51, 54, 56, 73, 157, 205, 216, 246 Decal 2, 2, 4, 8, 9, 10, 13, 14, 15, 96, 127, 135, 136, 151 Spec 1:13, 33, 33, 52, 69, 78, 121, 142, 158, 158, 159, 160, 165, 268, 268, 315, 323, 335 Spec 2:19, 22, 42, 45, 47, 48, 62, 92, 116, 119, 119, 119, 120, 163, 164, 168, 170, 181, 181, 192, 208, 231 Spec 3:16, 16, 17, 31, 37, 39, 74, 77, 77, 78, 78, 123, 124, 128, 130, 132, 139, 162, 170, 189 Spec 4:9, 20, 21, 27, 126, 153, 156, 184, 186, 212, 213, 223, 223, 226 Virt 61, 105, 107, 119, 132, 153, 162, 201, 221 Praem 7, 25, 34, 41, 66, 85, 107, 107, 114, 114, 114, 133, 141, 147, 150, 153, 172 Prob 6, 9, 45, 63, 76, 90, 137, 143 Contempl 2, 19, 19, 62 Aet 20, 56, 139, 140 Flacc 5, 23, 28, 33, 43, 51, 52, 55, 62, 65, 68, 71, 76, 78, 94, 105, 108, 120, 123, 123, 136, 139, 141, 141, 144, 145, 152, 154, 173, 177 Legat 8, 12, 15, 18. 20, 48, 51, 83, 90, 102, 104, 107, 116, 124, 127, 130, 132, 147, 150, 161, 170, 173, 173, 179, 200, 225, 231, 231, 232, 245, 252, 265, 283, 284, 289, 296, 297, 305, 338, 338, 346, 347, 351, 371, 371 Hypoth 11:1 Prov 2:3, 12, 15, 38, 39, 39, 40, 41, 44, 48, 50, 54, 64, 70 QG 3:8, 4:47b, 47b QE 1:21 QE isf 13

πολιτεία (91) Opif 143, 143, 143 Sacr 50, 78 Det 7, 28 Gig 59, 61, 61 Deus 176 Plant 56 Ebr 36, 86, 92, 109 Conf 2, 108, 196 Migr 88 Her 169 Congr 65 Fug 35 Somn 1:78, 219, 220, 224 Abr 61, 242 Ios 28, 29, 29, 31, 32, 38, 38, 54, 150 Mos 1:241 Mos 2:49, 51, 211 Decal 14, 98, 155 Spec 1:33, 51, 60, 63, 314, 319 Spec 2:73, 123 Spec 3:3, 5, 24, 51, 167, 170, 181 Spec 4:10, 47, 55, 100, 105, 120, 149, 156, 159, 237 Virt 87, 108, 127, 175, 180, 219 Praem 11 Prob 83, 158 Flacc 53, 141 Legat 157, 193, 194, 285, 287, 349, 363 Hypoth 6:10 QG 1:51 QE 1:21

πολίτευμα (6) Opif 143 Agr 81 Conf 109 Ios 69 Spec 2:45 Hypoth 0:1

πολιτεύω (15) Ebr 68 Conf 78, 141 Migr 159 Mut 240 Somn 1:221 Ios 36 Decal 14 Spec 4:226 Virt 161 Praem 4 Prob 47, 76, 128 Flacc 81

πολίτης (22) Opif 143, 165 Leg 3:2 Cher 121, 121, 121 Post 109, 185 Her 145 Somn 1:48, 53, 137 Mos 1:35, 252 Spec 1:97 Spec 2:45 Spec 4:70 Prob 7 Contempl 90 Flacc 47 Legat 211, 265

πολιτικός (43) Leg 3:30, 179 Det 135 Ebr 91 Migr 75, 160, 217 Fug 33, 36, 36, 47, 82, 126, 204, 209 Mut 149, 221 Ios 1, 31, 34, 38, 39, 54, 58, 61, 64, 67, 75, 79, 125, 143, 148, 149, 149 Virt 19 Praem 113, 113 Flacc 53, 80 Legat 8, 371 Prov 2:44 QG 3:8

πολῖτις Conf 151 Congr 22

πολλάκις (195) Opif 147 Leg 1:62 Leg 2:16, 32, 69, 69, 70, 85 Leg 3:16, 63, 92, 92, 125, 126, 156, 173, 173, 211, 223, 226, 234 Cher 14, 53, 53, 81 Sacr 37, 38 Det 43, 76, 99, 136 Gig 20, 25, 35, 36, 56 Deus 27, 88, 91, 93, 98, 131 Agr 75, 125, 169, 179 Plant 56, 80, 162, 167 Ebr 90, 139, 177, 198, 206 Sobr 22 Conf 7, 10, 11, 20, 115, 119, 126, 135, 178, 183 Migr 80, 111, 148, 172 Her 46, 46, 202, 245 Congr 73, 122, 127, 135, 135 Fug 14, 27, 156 Mut 98, 100, 105, 254 Somn 1:43, 43, 71, 107, 110, 110, 152, 201 Somn 2:69, 143, 146, 164 Abr 65, 71, 119, 185, 210, 243, 243 Ios 124, 131, 138, 144, 210 Mos 1:31, 202, 251, 264, 270 Mos 2:13, 219, 252 Decal 71, 113, 147 Spec 1:119, 174, 192, 213, 282, 323 Spec 2:24, 112, 197, 256 Spec 3:5, 9, 23, 98, 104, 107, 154, 166, 177 Spec 4:15, 27, 82, 85, 151, 154, 201 Virt 3, 14, 49, 63, 149 Praem 55 Prob 18, 34, 37, 38, 110, 148 Contempl 9 Aet 42, 65, 100 Flacc 12, 12, 50, 93, 98, 108, 132, 162, 162, 176, 181 Legat 7, 33, 43, 97, 122, 196, 262 Hypoth 7:20 Prov 2:5, 17, 41, 44, 46 QG 1:55a, 55a, 92, 4:211 QG isf 5 QE 2:13a QE isf 8, 26

πολλαπλασιάζω Congr 91

πολλαπλάσιος Somn 1:53 Abr 270 Mos 2:174

πολλαχῇ Post 127 Spec 1:226 Aet 147

πολλαχόθεν Spec 3:17

πολλαχόθι Conf 3 Somn 1:19 Spec 1:67

πολλαχοῦ (20) Cher 87 Det 80 Agr 2, 85 Plant 117, 154 Ebr 2 Sobr 7, 16 Conf 148 Migr 8 Her 251 Fug 2 Mut 19, 32 Mos 2:174 Spec 4:44 Virt 15, 22 Contempl 21

πολλαχῶς Leg 3:51 Fug 177 Somn 1:77 Mos 2:38 Aet 3

πολλοστός Somn 1:204 Abr 232 Praem 128

πόλος Her 147 Aet 30

πολυανδρία Hypoth 6:1

πολύανδρος Fug 114, 153

πολυανθρωπία (10) Gig 1 Mos 1:8 Mos 2:55, 232 Spec 1:141 Praem 66, 172 Flacc 45 Legat 214, 226

πολυάνθρωπος (52) Deus 148, 178 Migr 104 Congr 3 Somn 2:83, 121 Abr 141, 170, 180 Ios 63, 251 Mos 1:149, 222, 233, 240, 263 Mos 2:156, 159, 163, 281 Decal 37, 127, 152 Spec 1:2, 7, 78, 133, 321 Spec 2:170 Spec 3:11, 96, 101, 169 Spec 4:28, 47, 50, 156 Virt 34, 64 Praem 57, 95, 109, 133 Prob 74, 75 Contempl 18 Flacc 136 Legat 83, 132, 200 Hypoth 11:1 Prov 2:41

πολυάργυρος Fug 25 Abr 209

πολυαρχία Spec 1:331 Spec 4:178 Virt 179 Legat 149

πολύβυθος Opif 29

πολυγαμία Fug 153

πολυγονία Spec 1:7

πολύγονος Congr 3 Somn 2:14 Spec 1:7 Virt 142

πολυγώνιος Ebr 183 Congr 146

πολύγωνον Decal 22

πολυδεής Virt 9, 9

πολυειδής Ios 34 Mos 1:299 Decal 83 Contempl 49 Legat 111

πολύεργος Somn 2:48

πολυετής Somn 2:144 Spec 2:207 Spec 4:169 Contempl 67 QG 2:13a

πολυετία (6) Sobr 7, 24 Her 290 Abr 182 Ios 255 Mos 2:223

πολύζῳος Opif 85 Abr 209

πολυήμερος Her 34, 162 Ios 181 Decal 161

πολύηχος Ebr 98, 102

πολυθεία Mut 205

πολύθεος (15) Opif 171 Ebr 110 Conf 42, 144 Migr 69, 69, 69 Her 169 Fug 114 Mut 205 Decal 65 Virt 214, 221 Praem 162 QE 2:2

πολυκέφαλος Somn 2:14 QE 1:19

πολυκληματέω Agr 6

πολύκλινος Contempl 49

πολυκοιρανία Conf 170 Legat 149

Πολυκράτης Prov 2:24

πολύκρεως Prov 2:32

πολυμάθεια Congr 15, 20 Somn 1:205

πολυμαθής Deus 107 Plant 80

πολυμέρεια Her 236

πολυμήχανος Det 65 Somn 2:134

πολυμιγής Plant 44 Fug 114, 129 Somn 2:15 Ios 84

πολυμιγία Conf 144 Migr 24

πολύμορφος (9) Opif 41 Post 47 Deus 2 Ebr 170 Fug 129 Somn 1:202 Somn 2:14 Ios 34 Spec 1:90

Πολυξένη Prob 116

πολυοινία Plant 146 Ebr 22

πολυορκία Decal 92 Spec 2:8

πολυπαιδία Abr 196 Mos 1:240

πολύπαις (7) Ios 187 Virt 207 Praem 60, 61, 110, 158 Hypoth 11:13

πολυπλασιάζω Opif 51, 93, 93 Plant 75 Fug 186

πολυπλάσιος (6) Decal 20, 21 Spec 2:97, 233 QG 1:77, 4:189

πολυπληθέω Leg 3:139 Migr 60, 64

πολύπλοκος (8) Leg 2:74, 75 Det 6 Agr 97, 103 Plant 24 Ebr 189 Somn 2:66

πολύπολις Flacc 163

πολυποσία Somn 2:181

πολύπους Ebr 172 Migr 65, 69 Spec 4:113, 113

πολυπραγμονέω (7) Fug 162, 162 Mut 86 Somn 1:54 Spec 3:77, 171 Aet 138

πολυπράγμων Abr 20 Spec 1:69

πολύς (1198) Opif 1, 5, 7, 7, 8, 17, 33, 43, 45, 52, 53, 54, 55, 66, 71, 72, 77, 80, 80, 82, 86, 87, 88, 96, 103, 111, 113, 116, 124, 128, 136, 141, 144, 145, 161, 168, 170, 171, 171 Leg 1:5, 9, 9, 10, 14, 43, 45, 46, 64, 74, 85, 89, 101, 102, 104 Leg 2:2, 2, 2, 4, 8, 15, 22, 26, 26, 35, 37, 45, 68, 77, 83 Leg 3:2, 30, 47, 61, 62, 83, 105, 128, 130, 134, 135, 149, 162, 163, 164, 165, 167, 180, 210, 210, 212, 213, 234, 234, 241 Cher 12, 16, 26, 27, 32, 38, 43, 49, 53, 54, 58, 58, 59, 69, 70, 82, 87, 89, 89, 89, 91, 118, 125 Sacr 1, 6, 7, 21, 24, 29, 37, 49, 64, 67, 71, 75, 95, 98, 102, 108, 137 Det 2, 2, 67, 85, 94, 101, 104, 104, 106, 107, 114, 116, 117, 122, 131, 152 Post 1, 43, 58, 71, 100, 110, 114, 122, 137, 137, 141, 142, 145, 147, 147, 148, 150, 161, 163, 171, 176, 185 Gig 1, 3, 5, 10, 16, 18, 20, 35, 35, 37, 53, 53, 58 Deus 10, 14, 14, 14, 15, 26, 37, 46, 47, 54, 56, 56, 76, 85, 95, 101, 104, 128, 147, 150, 170, 174, 176, 177, 181 Agr 1, 2, 5, 23, 24, 24, 24, 37, 37, 39, 49, 70, 78, 87, 87, 93, 103, 112, 113, 125, 136, 142, 146, 149, 152, 157, 172, 174, 178 Plant 22, 32, 54, 80, 100, 101, 108, 126, 129, 130, 142, 143, 144, 144, 145, 150, 150, 151, 153, 155, 155, 162, 166, 171, 172, 173, 174, 176 Ebr 4, 6, 11, 25, 26, 36, 38, 45, 51, 65, 74, 75, 87, 95, 115, 116, 146, 147, 157, 158, 160, 167, 168, 171, 184, 185, 186, 192, 195, 200, 206, 218 Sobr 3, 4, 11, 23, 25, 27, 42, 49, 60 Conf 13, 20, 23, 25, 29, 39, 42, 54, 85, 93, 106, 112, 118, 133, 144, 144, 149, 153, 161, 169, 192, 192 Migr 12, 15, 23, 26, 33, 55, 55, 55, 59, 59, 60, 61, 61, 62, 63, 64, 68, 68, 69, 71, 72, 75, 76, 79, 86, 87, 88, 90, 93, 100, 107, 115, 123, 136, 139, 147, 152, 152, 152, 153, 153, 153, 170, 171, 179, 220 Her 2, 7, 12, 12, 25, 28, 31, 31, 42, 71, 92, 95, 101, 102, 125, 133, 143, 144, 145, 180, 191, 194, 217, 219, 221, 261, 272, 284, 288, 291, 291, 303, 309, 310 Congr 4, 4, 18, 21, 27, 34, 34, 35, 35, 53, 60, 84, 94, 105, 111, 119, 128, 140, 160, 162, 162, 165, 174 Fug 11, 25, 25, 30, 32, 36, 38, 87, 106, 106, 136, 159, 159, 176, 182, 198 Mut 78, 83, 93, 95, 116, 117, 118, 138, 143, 144, 145, 146, 151, 152, 154, 158, 161, 179, 180, 183, 183, 184, 185, 186, 192, 196, 203, 207, 214, 218, 229, 231, 243, 247, 251, 266, 268, 268, 269 Somn 1:6, 7, 9, 11, 11, 18, 31, 47, 72, 91, 122, 122, 125, 132, 139, 191, 205, 220, 222, 222, 229 Somn 2:2, 8, 9, 11, 12, 49, 51, 57, 57, 58, 62, 102, 104, 143, 169, 181, 188, 206, 233, 252, 268, 275, 278, 295 Abr 5, 16, 16, 19, 22, 22, 23, 38, 52, 59, 59, 64, 79, 84, 87, 89, 91, 103, 110, 131, 135, 138, 147, 155, 160, 162, 164, 175, 179, 181, 183, 188, 190, 191, 200, 207, 208, 211, 213, 219, 226, 227, 227, 228, 229, 229, 235, 235, 241, 247,

248, 251, 252, 255, 257, 258, 267, 271 Ios 5, 12, 12, 20, 22, 22, 25, 26, 26, 26, 28, 34, 34, 37, 39, 43, 49, 56, 56, 109, 112, 135, 140, 142, 145, 152, 153, 157, 166, 175, 176, 176, 193, 202, 204, 213, 216, 227, 227, 230, 240, 242, 247, 249, 257, 258 Mos 1:2, 3, 8, 9, 10, 11, 11, 13, 16, 22, 27, 28, 30, 49, 49, 50, 58, 62, 65, 65, 67, 72, 89, 93, 100, 105, 118, 125, 134, 141, 142, 149, 155, 162, 169, 191, 192, 200, 203, 207, 209, 210, 211, 214, 221, 225, 228, 241, 259, 259, 264, 266, 267, 272, 287, 287, 290, 291, 293, 301, 302, 312, 315, 316, 316, 319, 321, 333 Mos 2:13, 17, 23, 26, 28, 29, 35, 35, 36, 43, 44, 45, 45, 51, 51, 58, 69, 70, 70, 75, 97, 102, 115, 146, 159, 161, 163, 169, 174, 175, 180, 238, 240, 246, 276, 286 Decal 2, 5, 25, 35, 36, 36, 52, 64, 70, 72, 79, 89, 95, 105, 108, 134, 138, 146, 147, 165, 167, 168, 172, 174 Spec 1:1, 3, 11, 11, 25, 30, 32, 37, 37, 55, 60, 63, 64, 67, 72, 74, 76, 81, 81, 101, 109, 120, 125, 146, 159, 164, 165, 184, 189, 199, 199, 220, 229, 242, 246, 259, 262, 289, 296, 300, 314, 316, 321, 327, 329, 332, 332, 339 Spec 2:11, 14, 14, 20, 26, 37, 50, 55, 71, 75, 76, 83, 86, 102, 132, 135, 137, 139, 140, 145, 164, 164, 168, 168, 171, 175, 193, 194, 199, 199, 214, 215, 226, 250, 259, 259, 261 Spec 3:6, 9, 10, 10, 10, 11, 16, 17, 17, 17, 21, 26, 37, 40, 42, 51, 65, 69, 90, 92, 109, 110, 125, 128, 128, 140, 143, 143, 146, 171, 173, 177, 178, 178, 193 Spec 4:28, 46, 47, 50, 54, 56, 67, 78, 92, 105, 107, 109, 113, 120, 136, 138, 151, 154, 158, 179, 190, 196, 202, 204, 212 Virt 1, 5, 6, 33, 43, 43, 46, 48, 78, 79, 84, 86, 93, 99, 127, 127, 129, 133, 133, 140, 155, 157, 161, 162, 162, 166, 173, 179, 180, 198, 204, 207, 213, 217 Praem 8, 19, 20, 20, 24, 26, 29, 36, 38, 52, 58, 88, 94, 100, 106, 107, 107, 120, 122, 122, 124, 124, 132, 135, 153, 159 Prob 1, 2, 8, 14, 18, 21, 23, 30, 31, 35, 37, 54, 54, 55, 63, 65, 71, 77, 82, 89, 95, 102, 104, 113, 118, 132, 149, 157, 158 Contempl 1, 15, 26, 29, 35, 43, 49, 54, 56, 60, 63, 68, 73, 75, 80, 80, 84 Aet 1, 8, 8, 37, 42, 58, 64, 64, 68, 80, 88, 88, 90, 91, 98, 101, 110, 129, 130, 135, 135, 140, 140, 146, 147, 149 Flacc 1, 4, 10, 11, 25, 46, 51, 55, 56, 62, 67, 68, 70, 75, 92, 92, 93, 96, 101, 101, 108, 126, 128, 133, 137, 144, 162, 163, 166, 168, 175, 185, 190, 190 Legat 3, 7, 10, 14, 28, 36, 38, 39, 39, 48, 59, 63, 65, 65, 69, 73, 77, 108, 115, 116, 122, 130, 131, 132, 134, 137, 138, 139, 147, 155, 163, 163, 166, 185, 190, 199, 200, 202, 214, 216, 216, 219, 224, 228, 243, 244, 246, 251, 261, 269, 273, 278, 281, 281, 281, 286, 289, 294, 297, 300, 310, 310, 322, 337, 337, 338, 350, 362, 369 Hypoth 6:2, 6:9, 6:9, 7:7, 7:10, 7:13, 7:13, 7:15, 7:17, 7:20, 11:1, 11:1 Prov 1, 2:2, 8, 8, 24, 31, 32, 36, 41, 48, 60, 66, 71 QG 1:32, 89, 2:11, 26a, 54a, 71a, 3:11c, 4:52c, 76b, 97:2, 102b, 145, 145 QG isf 8, 10, 15 QG (Par) 2:4, 2:7, 2:7 QE 1:7b, 2:6a, 25a, 28 QE isf 5, 14, 17, 25, 26

πολυσαρκία Mos 2:185 Spec 2:35, 91

πολύστροφος Contempl 80

πολυσχιδής (7) Opif 69, 131 Leg 2:75 Deus 2 Mos 1:117 Spec 1:335 Spec 2:63

πολυτέλεια (21) Opif 164 Mos 1:152, 153, 256 Decal 71 Spec 1:71, 73, 95, 276 Spec 2:19, 20 Spec 4:101 Virt 8 Praem 99 Contempl 48, 53 Flacc 91 Legat 14, 157, 344 Hypoth 11:11

πολυτελής (51) Opif 158 Leg 3:156 Cher 104 Sacr 21, 21, 23 Det 20 Post 142 Deus 146 Plant 65 Ebr 211 Her 158, 158 Congr 19 Fug 31 Somn 1:123, 124, 125, 224 Somn 2:53, 54, 57 Ios 23, 196, 205, 234 Mos 1:275, 317 Mos 2:23, 42, 72, 95, 112, 112 Decal 133 Spec 1:87, 176, 271 Spec 2:193 Virt 39 Prob 66 Contempl 37, 69, 74 Flacc 69 Legat 151, 185, 319, 358 Prov 1, 2:29

πολυτόκος Her 211

πολύτρεπτος QG isf 6

πολύτροπος (33) Post 47 Plant 31, 44 Ebr 36, 86, 113, 170 Migr 152, 154 Her 288 Fug 183 Somn 1:202 Somn 2:14, 134 Ios 32 Mos 1:117 Mos 2:289 Decal 83, 169 Spec 3:93, 121 Virt 5, 134 Praem 11, 142 Contempl 39 Aet 129 Flacc 3, 66 Legat 80, 127, 149 QG 4:69

πολυφαγία Somn 2:205

πολύφημος Ebr 92

πολυφόρος Ebr 26

πολύφωνος Ebr 98

πολυχειρία Flacc 111

πολύχηλος Spec 4:109

πολύχους (7) Leg 1:102 Post 137 Ebr 26 Abr 19 Decal 169 Virt 10 Praem 61

πολυχρηματία Sobr 67 Mut 226 Mos 1:155 Spec 2:23

πολυχρήματος (9) Fug 28 Mut 91 Somn 1:155 Ios 76 Spec 1:151 Virt 170 Flacc 130, 148 Prov 2:21

πολυχρόνιος (12) Sacr 124 Sobr 22 Her 290 Mut 178 Abr 271 Ios 256 Mos 1:5 Spec 2:262 Praem 80, 117 Prob 137 Hypoth 11:7

πολύχρυσος Fug 16, 25 Abr 209 Virt 85

πολυχρώματος Ebr 172

πολυψηφία Legat 149

πολυώνυμος (6) Leg 1:43 Ebr 92 Conf 146 Mut 125 Somn 2:254 Decal 94

πολυωρία Hypoth 7:3

πόμα Post 147 Ebr 95 Somn 2:248, 249

πομπεύω Flacc 173

πομπή (11) Deus 146 Plant 65 Somn 2:57, 208 Ios 141 Decal 78 Spec 1:21 Spec 2:158 Prob 140 Flacc 74 QE 2:24b

πομποστολέω Ios 206

πονέω (52) Leg 1:80, 84 Leg 3:25, 135, 227 Sacr 114, 114 Det 11, 64 Post 95, 141, 158 Deus 12, 100 Agr 4, 125, 157 Ebr 207 Migr 27, 27, 134, 221 Congr 144, 150, 164 Fug 128 Mut 84 Somn 1:179, 255 Somn 2:59, 156 Ios 158 Mos 1:48, 52 Decal 163 Spec 2:64, 97 Spec 3:39 Spec 4:173, 216 Virt 29, 30, 98, 157 Praem 145 Prob 69 Contempl 53 Flacc 125 Legat 178 Hypoth 7:11 Prov 1, 2:21

πονηρεύομαι Spec 2:11 Spec 4:63, 76 Virt 227

πονηρία Ebr 223 Ios 212

πονηρός (84) Opif 154 Leg 1:56, 60, 60, 61, 90, 100, 101 Leg 3:69, 69, 71, 71, 71, 74, 74, 110, 110, 237 Post 71, 94, 94, 94, 95, 95 Gig 17, 17 Deus 18, 20 Plant 36 Ebr 14, 28 Conf 24, 80, 169, 180 Her 5, 296 Mut 112 Somn 2:65, 67, 216 Abr 37, 40 Ios 80, 83, 266 Mos 1:40, 244 Decal 91, 92 Spec 1:11 Spec 3:11, 66, 93, 151, 155, 195 Spec 4:42, 185 Virt 189, 191, 194, 196, 211, 222, 227 Praem 2, 3, 67, 142, 149 Flacc 75, 109 Legat 7, 91, 166, 367 Prov 2:1 QG 1:74, 76a, 2:54a, 3:11c, 4:74 QG isf 8

πόνος (136) Opif 167 Leg 1:80, 83, 84 Leg 3:26, 38, 135, 135, 135, 136, 137, 251 Sacr 23, 35, 35, 36, 37, 37, 39, 40, 40, 40, 41, 41, 41, 41, 112, 112, 112, 113, 113,

114, 115, 120, 120 Det 9, 17, 19, 27, 34, 64 Post 78, 95, 154, 156 Deus 92, 93, 96, 170 Agr 91, 103, 155 Ebr 21, 94 Sobr 38, 65 Conf 92 Migr 30, 31, 144, 164, 167, 214, 220, 221, 223, 223, 224 Her 48, 212 Congr 35, 108, 161, 162, 162, 164, 166, 166, 166 Fug 41, 162, 166, 173, 212 Mut 86, 170, 170, 193, 193, 219 Somn 1:6, 120, 168 Somn 2:57 Abr 5, 192 Ios 34, 223 Mos 1:37, 53, 154, 284, 322 Mos 2:1, 21, 183, 183, 184, 273 Spec 1:32, 125, 298 Spec 2:60, 60, 69, 89, 91, 98, 99, 102, 240, 260 Spec 4:38, 124, 215 Praem 27, 36 Prob 69, 96 Contempl 36 Aet 63 Legat 90, 246 Hypoth 7:17, 7:19 Prov 2:33

πόντος Somn 2:118 Aet 121, 121

Πόντος Deus 174 Legat 281

Πόπλιος Legat 333

πορεία (9) Abr 269 Mos 1:166, 167 Decal 50 Spec 2:202 Praem 121 Prob 111 Hypoth 0:1, 6:2

πορεύω (51) Leg 1:63, 69 Leg 2:105 Leg 3:65, 88, 114, 138, 139, 139, 160, 162, 167 Det 5, 5, 11, 28, 30 Deus 144, 145, 167, 179 Agr 148, 148, 148 Ebr 40 Migr 65, 66, 67, 127, 129, 131, 133, 166 Her 20, 239 Congr 30, 70, 86, 86 Fug 1, 127, 127, 203, 205, 206 Somn 1:3, 4 Somn 2:241 Abr 204 Spec 4:183 QG 4:173

πορθέω (7) Plant 159 Conf 47 Mos 1:69 Decal 49 Prob 38 Flacc 54 Legat 114

πόρθησις (11) Agr 151, 168 Congr 92 Somn 2:124 Mos 1:215 Spec 3:16 Prob 118 Flacc 86, 87 Legat 292, 330

πορθμός Aet 139, 139

πορίζω (25) Leg 1:43 Leg 3:242 Cher 9 Sacr 38 Det 33, 36, 55, 55 Post 141, 181 Agr 23, 25 Ebr 29 Conf 13 Congr 78 Somn 1:86 Somn 2:46 Spec 1:23, 75 Spec 2:247 Spec 3:142 Prob 87, 149 Flacc 57, 143

πορισμός (12) Opif 128, 167 Gig 29 Fug 33 Abr 91 Mos 2:211, 219 Decal 117 Praem 11 Contempl 66 Hypoth 11:9 Prov 2:21

ποριστής (7) Gig 36, 60 Mut 90 Mos 1:63 Flacc 57 Legat 158, 343

ποριστικός Cher 33 Det 55

πορνεία Mos 1:300 Spec 1:282

πορνεύω Fug 153 Spec 1:281 Prov 2:18

πόρνη (πόρνος) (25) Leg 3:8 Sacr 21 Conf 144, 144 Migr 69, 69, 224 Congr 124 Fug 114, 114, 149, 149, 149 Mut 205 Somn 1:88 Ios 43 Mos 1:302 Decal 8 Spec 1:102, 104, 280, 326, 326, 332, 332, 344 Spec 3:51

πόρνος Leg 3:8

πορνότροφος Fug 28

πόρος (14) Sacr 61 Deus 39 Abr 232 Mos 1:174 Spec 1:126, 141, 151 Spec 4:127 Virt 87 Praem 142, 143, 145 QG (Par) 2:6, 2:6

πόρρω (34) Opif 63, 141 Det 54, 85 Post 20 Gig 18 Plant 97 Ebr 100, 124, 183 Migr 216 Congr 57 Fug 62 Somn 1:49, 66 Somn 2:180 Abr 169 Mos 1:54, 59, 114, 248 Mos 2:8 Decal 15, 33 Spec 1:324 Spec 4:19, 80, 94 Virt 190 Contempl 24 Flacc 124 Legat 281 QG 1:69, 2:64b

πόρρωθεν (15) Somn 1:66 Abr 75 Mos 1:131 Spec 3:63, 117 Spec 4:203 Virt 21, 116, 160 Flacc 15, 157, 185 Legat 52 Prov 2:55 QG 2:65

πορφύρα (9) Migr 97 Congr 117, 117 Mut 93 Mos 2:84, 87, 88, 111 Decal 71

πορφυρεύς Opif 147

πόρω Prob 119

Ποσειδῶν Decal 54 Contempl 3

ποσθένη Spec 1:4

ποσθία Spec 1:5, 7

πόσις (18) Opif 38 Deus 158 Sobr 3 Congr 29 Mut 164 Somn 2:155, 155, 215 Abr 148 Ios 152, 154, 206 Mos 1:184 Mos 2:23 Spec 1:150 Spec 2:98 Spec 3:97 Spec 4:97

πόσος (ποσός) (30) Opif 61 Cher 114 Det 142, 173, 173, 173 Post 142 Plant 22 Migr 54 Fug 13 Somn 1:19 Mos 1:293, 293 Mos 2:44 Decal 30 Spec 2:255 Spec 4:15, 186, 234 Contempl 14, 16 Aet 89 Legat 5, 308, 354, 370 Prov 1, 2:27 QG 2:64a QG (Par) 2:7

ποσότης (7) Opif 41 Ebr 184, 185 Decal 31 Spec 4:11 Praem 112 Prov 1

ποτάμιος Somn 2:278, 302 Mos 1:81 Praem 90

ποταμός (139) Opif 38, 58, 78, 80, 113, 133 Leg 1:34, 63, 63, 63, 63, 63, 64, 65, 65, 68, 68, 69, 72, 85, 85, 86, 87 Leg 2:89 Leg 3:16, 18 Det 100, 177 Post 128, 129, 163 Gig 7, 13 Plant 24, 67, 144 Ebr 22 Conf 29, 29, 33, 36, 66 Migr 185 Her 136, 315, 315, 315, 315, 316, 316 Congr 133 Fug 49, 179 Mut 214 Somn 1:17, 97, 135, 147 Somn 2:109, 125, 216, 216, 216, 238, 238, 240, 241, 242, 245, 245, 246, 246, 255, 255, 255, 258, 259, 259, 260, 261, 261, 261, 277, 300, 300, 300, 302 Abr 42, 92, 159 Ios 101, 109, 109 Mos 1:6, 10, 14, 99, 101, 105, 114, 116, 117, 144, 155, 192, 202, 212, 228, 265, 289, 319, 321 Mos 2:54, 63, 195 Spec 1:34, 158, 210, 262, 300, 322 Spec 2:143, 147, 172 Spec 3:114 Virt 6 Praem 41, 90 Prob 115 Contempl 54 Aet 62, 66, 147, 148 Flacc 63, 92 Legat 10, 129, 155

ποταπός Leg 1:91 Legat 370

πότε (ποτέ) (227) Opif 16, 156 Leg 1:20, 43, 72, 99 Leg 2:27 Leg 3:74, 116, 128 Cher 27, 58, 82, 114, 130 Sacr 26, 49, 55, 69, 79, 89, 128 Det 76, 133, 143, 143, 143, 143, 143 Post 13, 82, 163, 164, 178 Gig 12, 13, 13, 21, 33 Deus 134, 173, 174, 177, 177 Agr 27, 27, 88, 90, 110, 147, 176 Plant 5, 89, 89, 146, 177 Ebr 101, 146 Sobr 15 Conf 50, 92, 101, 106, 114, 114, 136, 174, 196 Migr 24, 26, 138, 139, 156, 210, 214, 214, 222, 224 Her 6, 7, 19, 78, 142, 206, 249, 285, 291 Congr 42, 167 Fug 57, 57, 62, 113, 149, 151, 152, 155, 161, 181, 191 Mut 118, 139 Somn 1:124, 140, 143, 143, 164 Somn 2:15, 86, 99, 116, 140, 182, 187, 207, 226, 282, 283, 300 Abr 140, 159, 206, 207 Ios 9, 15, 33, 33, 67, 87, 124, 127, 135, 167, 215, 244, 255, 263 Mos 1:146, 161, 164, 186, 212, 290, 320 Mos 2:60, 61, 203, 229 Decal 2, 32, 40, 58, 75 Spec 1:30, 30, 30, 30, 49, 68, 154, 211, 215, 230, 246, 335 Spec 2:4, 54, 68, 87, 198, 252 Spec 3:1, 21, 29, 90, 121, 166 Spec 4:173, 223 Virt 56, 153 Praem 63, 71, 88, 88, 153 Prob 26, 36, 125 Contempl 75 Aet 53, 53, 66, 71, 72, 95, 115 Flacc 80, 94, 94, 127, 138, 165, 169, 172, 183 Legat 29, 48, 61, 102, 111, 154, 292, 329, 363 Hypoth 6:5, 6:6, 6:8 Prov 2:7, 8, 11, 26, 39 QG 4:52b, 166, 174, 204

πότερον πότερος

πότερος (πότερον) (28) Opif 155 Leg 2:16, 16, 20 Leg 3:13, 168 Post 40 Agr 118, 155 Conf 67 Fug 151 Somn 1:22, 23 Abr 162, 162, 162, 162 Mos 1:27, 78 Decal 90 Spec 3:141, 190 Virt 113 Prob 104 Aet 48 Flacc 159 Hypoth 6:6, 6:8

ποτήριον (6) Deus 77 Somn 2:159, 159, 159, 200, 203

ποτίζω (42) Opif 131 Leg 1:28, 63, 65, 65 Leg 2:86, 86, 86, 87 Leg 3:82 Post 125, 126, 126, 126, 127, 127, 128, 130, 132, 132, 132, 139, 139, 147, 148, 151, 153, 158, 164, 176, 176 Deus 37 Ebr 166 Conf 38 Fug 178, 181, 182, 187, 195 Mut 111 Somn 2:241, 242

πότιμος (28) Opif 131 Leg 2:32 Leg 3:12, 184 Post 125, 129, 147, 155 Deus 96 Ebr 12 Her 136 Fug 200 Mut 113 Somn 1:18, 18 Somn 2:259 Mos 1:101, 144, 186 Decal 15, 16 Spec 1:300, 321 Spec 2:29, 62 Spec 4:56 Prob 13 QG 1:3

ποτισμός Post 10, 124, 126, 170

ποτιστήριον Post 132, 150

ποτνιάομαι (15) Ebr 224 Her 37 Mut 228 Somn 2:140, 149, 299 Abr 6 Ios 171 Mos 1:47 Mos 2:201 Spec 1:42, 97 Spec 2:15 Virt 57, 63

ποτόν (78) Opif 119, 133 Leg 1:83, 86 Leg 2:87 Leg 3:141, 147, 161, 239 Sacr 23, 85 Det 19, 116 Deus 156 Agr 36 Plant 79 Ebr 73, 106, 112, 131, 211, 214 Congr 172 Fug 199, 202 Somn 1:36, 124 Somn 2:48, 60, 157 Ios 152, 155 Mos 1:53, 55, 99, 181, 182, 211, 215, 243, 255, 255, 284 Mos 2:24, 68, 69, 148 Decal 12, 17, 159 Spec 1:126, 127, 148, 303 Spec 2:195, 198, 199, 201, 203 Spec 3:61 Spec 4:81, 82 Virt 6, 30, 86, 104, 130, 130 Contempl 3, 25, 34, 37, 56 Flacc 178 Legat 82 Prov 2:67 QG 4:169 QG (Par) 2:7

πότος Plant 160 Ebr 218 Spec 1:304

ποτός Contempl 46

ποῦ (121) Opif 6 Leg 2:69 Leg 3:49, 51, 51, 51, 52, 53, 54, 122 Cher 51, 114, 114, 114, 114, 114, 114, 114, 117 Sacr 35, 121 Det 5, 25, 25, 57, 59, 61, 153 Gig 35 Deus 42, 74, 103 Agr 24, 28, 36, 51, 111, 176 Plant 54, 90, 108 Ebr 61, 99, 172 Sobr 8 Conf 6, 52 Migr 16, 182, 195, 218 Her 161, 163, 188, 279 Congr 123, 176 Fug 1, 32, 115, 127, 132, 133, 134, 134, 134, 149, 197, 203, 206 Mut 35, 119 Somn 1:6, 32, 184, 192 Somn 2:52 Abr 173, 230, 263 Ios 87, 128, 136, 136, 136 Mos 1:6, 26, 111, 141 Mos 2:115, 263 Spec 1:166, 265 Spec 2:49, 132 Spec 4:83, 136 Virt 30 Praem 111, 132 Prob 66, 143 Contempl 3, 69 Aet 65, 78 Flacc 88, 92, 167 Legat 56, 112, 138, 140, 194, 240, 271, 307 Hypoth 7:9 Prov 2:13 QG 4:64, 204

πούς (92) Opif 86, 163 Leg 1:12 Leg 2:105 Leg 3:105, 139, 141, 142, 143, 144, 144 Cher 81, 100 Sacr 25, 38, 63, 96 Post 24, 80, 151 Deus 75, 127, 182 Agr 22, 75, 101, 115 Plant 16, 111 Ebr 101, 106, 167 Conf 3, 38, 38, 38, 96, 98, 113 Migr 64, 98, 103 Her 70, 151, 151, 239 Congr 28, 55 Mut 101, 256 Somn 1:46, 131 Somn 2:229, 278 Mos 1:15, 128, 270, 271 Mos 2:118, 138, 150, 150 Decal 74 Spec 1:166, 199, 206, 207, 232, 341 Spec 3:106, 184 Spec 4:83, 114, 198, 200 Virt 43 Prob 2, 26, 141 Aet 48, 48, 49, 49, 50, 51 Flacc 70 Legat 267 Prov 2:48, 58 QG (Par) 2:2, 2:5 QE 2:26

πρᾶγμα (437) Opif 66, 114, 127, 129, 150 Leg 1:87 Leg 2:15, 15, 27, 98, 102, 105 Leg 3:3, 12, 15, 33, 45, 50, 90, 91, 108, 109, 120, 205, 230, 251 Cher 1, 30, 35, 36, 56, 56, 56, 56, 69, 129 Sacr 15, 63, 64, 69, 79, 85, 87, 91, 102, 115 Det 11, 12, 22, 68, 87, 129, 165 Post 13, 18, 25, 34, 57, 83, 93, 96, 100, 108, 110, 111, 142, 151, 175, 178 Gig 15, 28, 51 Deus 22, 29, 45, 46, 71, 90, 93, 139, 145, 171, 172, 177, 179 Agr 1, 2, 13, 26, 28, 46, 47, 118, 134, 136, 142, 152, 179 Plant 27, 71, 144, 146, 150 Ebr 6, 62, 98, 160, 167, 189, 199, 204, 205, 220 Sobr 6, 40 Conf 21, 74, 140, 144, 175, 183, 184, 190 Migr 12, 12, 19, 35, 76, 77, 88, 89, 110, 171, 205, 214, 216 Her 1, 13, 63, 66, 72, 114, 130, 143, 161, 180, 213, 235, 240, 242, 246, 279, 307, 312 Congr 44, 125, 129, 135, 138 Fug 35, 36, 49, 62, 121, 122, 122, 143, 153, 161 Mut 8, 9, 13, 37, 56, 60, 80, 148, 150, 151, 173, 179, 201, 205, 210, 249, 252, 266 Somn 1:8, 11, 12, 41, 53, 65, 93, 116, 116, 150, 153, 156, 157, 172, 192, 203, 218, 222, 242 Somn 2:31, 32, 33, 35, 39, 42, 44, 78, 97, 101, 105, 124, 134, 138, 169, 186, 202, 227, 252 Abr 1, 81, 84, 102, 111, 120, 186, 193, 218, 222, 236, 243, 246 Ios 7, 28, 32, 48, 55, 90, 118, 136, 140, 141, 142, 146, 147, 149, 150, 170, 176, 195, 204, 205, 218, 225, 238, 252, 258 Mos 1:11, 62, 73, 119, 196, 197, 222, 274, 274, 302, 329 Mos 2:5, 8, 18, 34, 38, 39, 40, 259, 280 Decal 23, 52, 80, 82, 85, 86, 91, 93, 123, 128, 131, 138, 139, 150, 164, 177 Spec 1:2, 99, 195, 197, 224, 327, 334, 342 Spec 2:6, 10, 12, 42, 52, 58, 67, 123, 130, 195, 231, 249 Spec 3:4, 5, 20, 31, 35, 54, 79, 129, 209 Spec 4:5, 15, 29, 30, 31, 39, 43, 44, 58, 60, 60, 60, 64, 66, 70, 71, 77, 104, 153, 155, 156, 170, 173, 190, 218 Virt 22, 24, 37, 54, 63, 71, 105, 135, 166, 183, 200 Praem 11, 47, 56 Prob 21, 23, 24, 38, 47, 50, 62, 63, 120, 136 Contempl 64 Aet 1, 52, 103, 112 Flacc 4, 6, 10, 16, 38, 41, 79, 95, 102, 103, 120, 121, 126, 128, 133, 135, 165, 165 Legat 44, 66, 67, 70, 72, 143, 187, 200, 202, 247, 300, 304, 313, 323, 359, 370 Prov 2:1, 28, 72 QG 1:64a, 100:1b, 2:54a, 71a, 3:3, 22, 4:47b, 67, 76b, 204 QG isf 5, 7, 15 QE 2:28, 44 QE isf 8, 8, 14

πραγματεία (23) Sacr 120 Gig 29 Deus 97 Ebr 202 Congr 147, 149 Fug 33 Mut 53, 75 Somn 1:102, 120 Abr 30 Mos 2:115, 211, 219 Decal 108 Spec 2:65, 102 Spec 3:105 Praem 142 Contempl 1 Flacc 3 Hypoth 11:6

πραγματεύομαι (31) Leg 1:25, 69, 71 Leg 2:31 Leg 3:236 Sacr 115 Det 88, 119, 122 Agr 13, 22 Ebr 91 Her 179 Congr 144 Mut 71 Somn 1:53 Abr 16 Ios 154 Mos 1:151 Mos 2:2 Spec 1:131, 176 Spec 4:96, 104, 145 Virt 208 Flacc 57 Legat 60, 195 Hypoth 11:5 QG 4:206b

πραγματικός Her 237 Mut 41

πραγματολογέω Fug 54 Somn 1:230

πρακτέος (11) Leg 3:94 Deus 130, 134 Sobr 5 Mos 1:54 Mos 2:4, 4 Spec 2:60 Spec 4:142, 220 Hypoth 7:14

πρακτικός (15) Leg 1:57, 57, 57, 58 Leg 2:89 Fug 36, 37, 37 Mos 1:48 Decal 101 Spec 2:64, 64 Praem 11, 51 Contempl 1

πρανής (πρηνής) (9) Opif 157 Leg 3:14 Post 116 Agr 113 Somn 2:269 Abr 59 Spec 4:45, 112 QG (Par) 2:2

πρᾶξις (173) Opif 3, 75, 81, 156 Leg 1:55, 57, 57, 58, 58, 64, 74, 97 Leg 2:89, 90, 93, 93 Leg 3:24, 43, 44, 45, 45, 80, 181, 205, 247, 247 Cher 62, 101, 103, 105 Sacr 36, 57, 73, 130 Det 14, 35, 69, 97, 111 Post 75, 85, 86, 127 Deus 25, 135, 137, 154 Agr 9, 157 Plant 37, 158, 161 Ebr 12, 65, 144, 202, 224 Sobr 5, 11, 48 Conf 38, 48, 83, 121, 198 Migr 37, 130 Congr 4, 46, 69, 90, 113 Fug 18, 22, 51, 52, 199 Mut 236, 243, 245, 245, 249, 249, 255 Somn 1:91 Somn 2:20, 34, 170, 180 Abr 11, 31, 65, 89, 90, 102, 167, 177, 183, 190, 191, 219, 235 Ios 32, 86, 237 Mos 1:48, 189, 242 Mos 2:34, 48, 66, 130, 130, 138, 151, 166, 173, 212, 274 Decal 100, 173 Spec 1:104, 145, 202, 203, 257, 269 Spec 2:14, 23, 29, 61, 142 Spec 3:85, 92, 169, 209 Spec 4:6, 69, 121, 134, 138, 169, 182 Virt 106, 118, 183, 183, 184, 195, 206 Praem 69, 79, 80, 81, 83, 107 Prob 29, 60, 68, 88

Legat 1, 55, 160, 206 QG 1:41, 4:51b, 130, 174 QE 2:20, 25b QE isf 9, 11, 18

πρᾳοπαθέω πραϋπαθέω

πρᾳοπαθής πραϋπαθής

πρᾶος (19) Opif 34, 81 Leg 1:42, 66 Sacr 121 Det 117, 146 Deus 65 Ebr 218 Migr 101 Abr 153, 257 Mos 1:328, 331 Mos 2:279 Legat 43 Hypoth 7:1 QG 2:29 QE 2:25d

πραότης Opif 103 Sacr 27 Decal 167 Spec 1:145

πρασιά Hypoth 7:6

πράσινος (7) Leg 1:63, 66, 67, 79, 81, 82, 84

πρᾶσις (6) Cher 121, 122 Ios 250 Spec 2:113 Prob 37 Contempl 19

πράσον Her 79, 80

πράσσω (144) Opif 2, 144 Leg 1:89 Leg 2:28 Leg 3:94, 126, 144, 209, 210 Cher 16, 16, 16, 93, 93 Sacr 53 Det 6, 134 Post 86, 87, 184 Deus 17, 71, 100 Agr 176 Plant 161 Ebr 131 Conf 38, 59, 59, 59, 117 Migr 225 Her 6, 121 Congr 67, 68, 85 Fug 3, 78, 79 Mut 42, 193, 195, 197, 200, 238, 238 Somn 1:91, 191, 199 Somn 2:187 Abr 6, 144, 163, 178, 197, 208, 226 Ios 29, 37, 59, 60, 64, 77, 87, 119, 148, 173, 216, 220, 239 Mos 1:29, 51, 172, 220, 243, 266, 334 Mos 2:1, 49, 167, 187, 215, 261 Decal 39, 43, 93, 98, 101 Spec 1:114, 235, 317, 321, 340 Spec 2:9, 93, 146 Spec 3:15, 15, 51, 74, 143, 175 Spec 4:138, 194 Virt 52, 154, 170, 171 Praem 34, 51, 55, 118 Prob 61, 103 Aet 83 Flacc 2, 41, 55, 58, 105, 143 Legat 28, 46, 51, 77, 158, 209, 242, 244, 303, 338, 341, 350 Hypoth 7:2, 11:16 QG 1:41, 66, 68, 4:110a, 228 QG isf 10 QE 2:3b QE isf 27

πραΰνω (11) Leg 3:245 Sacr 16, 104 Conf 165 Migr 211 Mut 173 Somn 2:13, 87, 165 Mos 1:26 Hypoth 6:4

πραϋπάθεια Abr 213

πραϋπαθέω (πρᾳοπαθέω) Fug 6

πραϋπαθής (πρᾳοπαθής) Spec 4:93 Legat 335

πραΰτοκος Fug 208

πρεπόντως Ebr 117 Spec 2:130

πρέπω (38) Opif 31 Leg 1:48 Cher 99, 105 Ebr 194 Conf 175 Her 51, 91, 123, 125, 230 Congr 19 Fug 2 Somn 1:102 Somn 2:6 Abr 107 Ios 259 Mos 1:47, 168 Mos 2:245 Decal 83 Spec 1:194, 255 Spec 2:125, 230, 256 Spec 3:48, 50, 172 Spec 4:103 Virt 146 Contempl 30, 33 Aet 40 Legat 42 QG 3:11a, 4:208 QG (Par) 2:6

πρεπώδης (16) Cher 50, 52, 83 Sacr 13, 51 Deus 47 Agr 79 Ebr 111 Conf 131 Somn 1:55 Mos 2:49, 137 Spec 1:75, 96, 145 Virt 168

πρεσβεία (9) Congr 111 Abr 65 Mos 2:34 Flacc 97 Legat 181, 239, 247, 354 QG 4:144

πρεσβεῖον (28) Sacr 16, 17, 20, 42, 42, 72, 77, 119, 119, 120 Post 63 Deus 31 Sobr 29, 29 Her 49, 49 Mut 195 Somn 1:132 Mos 1:242 Mos 2:175, 222 Spec 1:258 Spec 2:139, 175 Virt 208 Legat 289 QG 1:64c, 4:168

πρεσβευτής (7) Gig 16 Her 205 Abr 115 Prob 74 Flacc 98 Legat 182, 370

πρεσβευτικός Mos 1:258

πρεσβεύω (9) Plant 14 Conf 7 Congr 111 Abr 27 Flacc 105 Legat 192, 240, 242, 302

πρέσβυς (219) Opif 16, 26, 100, 130, 133 Leg 2:3, 6, 73, 97, 97 Leg 3:90, 90, 92, 175, 191, 191, 218 Sacr 11, 11, 14, 17, 42, 77, 77, 77, 77, 88, 131, 134 Det 82, 118 Post 62, 62, 63, 64, 89, 89, 90, 91, 99, 138, 181 Gig 24, 24, 24 Deus 31, 76, 108, 120, 145 Plant 59, 121, 139, 161 Ebr 42, 47, 48, 48, 49, 50, 51, 75, 165, 165 Sobr 7, 13, 13, 15, 16, 17, 17, 18, 18, 18, 19, 19, 19, 20, 20, 22, 22, 26, 27, 28, 47 Conf 27, 55, 63, 124, 124, 146, 147, 180 Migr 6, 116, 159, 159, 181, 198, 199, 201, 205 Her 48, 49, 104, 115, 116, 166, 199, 205, 301 Congr 32, 38, 110 Fug 51, 67, 94, 101, 110, 186, 198 Mut 15, 94, 97, 166, 172, 217 Somn 1:75, 163, 168, 190, 230, 240 Somn 2:135, 141, 221, 223 Abr 6, 83, 121, 123, 170, 218, 218, 219, 270, 271, 271, 274 Ios 1, 13, 16, 127, 173, 176, 176, 188, 203, 217, 223, 242 Mos 1:4, 134, 258, 268, 281 Mos 2:31, 59, 99, 175, 219 Decal 53, 69, 166 Spec 1:31, 331 Spec 2:5, 5, 65, 133, 133, 137, 166, 177, 226, 227, 228, 234 Spec 3:23, 134 Spec 4:96, 230 Virt 34, 62, 65, 199, 212, 213 Praem 40, 75, 91 Prob 81, 87 Contempl 31, 67, 67, 73 Aet 13, 57 Legat 5, 172, 289, 301, 354, 369 QG 1:20, 65, 2:74, 4:184

πρεσβύτης (26) Opif 105, 105, 105 Cher 68 Post 71, 109 Agr 56 Conf 28 Fug 107 Ios 223, 227, 253 Mos 1:147 Decal 42, 94, 165, 167 Spec 2:19, 33, 145, 237, 238 Flacc 74 Legat 142, 227 Hypoth 11:13

πρεσβυτικός Mut 48

πρεσβῦτις Spec 2:33, 237 Legat 227

πρήθω Leg 3:148, 150

πρηνής πρανής

πρίαμαι (18) Ios 38, 45, 58 Mos 1:36 Spec 2:114, 117, 121 Spec 4:18 Prob 37, 38, 40, 100, 101, 102, 124 Flacc 64, 168 Legat 122

Πριηνεύς Prob 153

πρίν (110) Opif 78, 114, 129, 129, 159 Leg 1:22, 22, 23, 26 Leg 3:14, 67, 87, 88, 190, 202, 242, 244, 244 Cher 50 Sacr 31, 58, 135 Det 12, 32, 39, 42 Post 16, 145, 163, 176, 185 Gig 29, 62 Deus 132, 177 Agr 59, 76, 91, 163 Plant 96, 107, 161, 176 Ebr 3, 47, 49, 167 Conf 38, 118, 121, 140 Migr 138, 138, 142 Congr 19, 41 Fug 165, 168 Mut 158 Somn 1:11, 56, 112 Somn 2:146, 182, 221 Abr 5, 182, 226 Ios 78, 126, 130, 200 Mos 1:68, 232, 254, 263, 298 Mos 2:217 Decal 12, 80 Spec 1:276, 311 Spec 2:98, 179, 180 Spec 3:17, 103 Spec 4:7, 99, 160 Virt 142, 157, 165 Praem 5, 62 Prob 25, 99, 115 Contempl 46 Aet 142 Flacc 114, 130 Legat 25, 364 Hypoth 11:6 Prov 1, 2:15 QG 2:68a QG (Par) 2:7 QE 1:7b

πρῖνος Legat 127

πρό (289) Opif 26, 33, 45, 46, 49, 129, 129, 140, 143 Leg 1:21, 21, 24, 24 Leg 2:2, 11, 13, 46, 56 Leg 3:4, 4, 77, 85, 86, 146, 236 Cher 6, 28, 67, 96, 114, 114, 120 Sacr 12, 44, 44, 62, 67, 67, 78, 136 Det 37 Post 32, 38, 59, 60, 67, 89 Gig 35 Deus 50, 50, 58, 76, 102, 131, 174, 174, 182 Agr 43, 43, 48, 167, 168, 171 Plant 123, 163 Ebr 1, 31, 34, 42, 167 Sobr 8, 14 Conf 1, 57, 109, 109, 138, 138, 140, 159 Migr 45, 61, 61, 76, 174, 183, 183, 200 Her 1, 165, 165, 251, 254, 291, 310 Congr 49, 49, 138 Fug 3, 31, 58 Mut 12, 27, 46, 97, 160, 161, 161, 163, 163, 165, 177, 227 Somn 1:1, 65, 70, 77, 81, 92, 95, 101, 112, 117, 117, 166, 211 Somn 2:8, 9, 70, 70, 84, 106, 106, 106, 221 Abr 46, 55, 60, 66, 178, 200, 221, 221, 234, 242, 257, 270 Ios 16, 43, 59, 79, 162, 187, 187, 191, 221, 222, 258, 258, 262 Mos 1:16, 46, 62, 191, 205, 207, 259, 321, 328 Mos 2:154, 172, 194, 214, 227, 258, 263, 271 Decal 1, 4, 47, 66, 118, 124, 141 Spec 1:31, 54, 127, 171, 269, 271 Spec 2:1, 21, 90, 122, 133, 166, 166, 166, 196, 209, 239, 245,

255 Spec 3:29, 30, 115, 152, 180 Spec 4:10, 70, 137, 142, 220 Virt 7, 17, 145, 147, 149, 157, 180, 218 Praem 8, 8, 12, 33, 54, 124, 146, 161, 165, 166, 168, 170, 171 Prob 118, 120 Contempl 7, 34, 44, 52, 66, 81 Aet 31, 68, 145 Flacc 2, 8, 9, 18, 62, 79, 92, 126, 126, 147, 152, 163, 173 Legat 2, 14, 15, 56, 56, 63, 67, 96, 107, 141, 179, 222, 244, 285, 300, 327, 336, 337 Prov 2:24, 25, 27, 56 QG 1:62:1, 79, 2:29, 62, 72, 3:20b, 4:131 QG isf 6 QE isf 8

προαγορεύω Somn 2:2 Spec 1:22

προάγω (19) Leg 3:19, 77 Sacr 8 Det 85, 127 Plant 167 Ebr 152 Conf 147 Her 86 Fug 161 Mut 199 Somn 1:101 Somn 2:292 Ios 12, 46 Mos 1:150, 158 Spec 3:109 Contempl 78

προαγωγεία Spec 3:31

προάγων Sacr 4 Fug 36 Ios 3 Mos 1:133 Spec 4:121

προαγωνίζομαι (11) Deus 38 Agr 78 Mos 1:333 Mos 2:252, 273 Decal 114 Spec 1:55 Spec 3:85 Virt 27, 45 Praem 157

προαγωνιστής (8) Opif 160 Somn 1:103 Abr 232 Spec 3:75, 132 Praem 59 Flacc 170 Legat 144

προαδικέω Mos 1:303 QG 1:77

προαίρεσις (39) Cher 32 Sacr 11 Det 60 Gig 50 Deus 102, 114 Agr 60 Ebr 46 Fug 204 Somn 2:47 Abr 251 Ios 150 Mos 1:161, 287 Mos 2:106, 177 Spec 1:59, 102, 243 Spec 3:86 Spec 4:194, 224 Praem 4 Prob 89 Contempl 2, 17, 29, 32, 67, 79 Flacc 144 Legat 114, 230, 316, 321 Hypoth 11:2 QG 1:60:2, 76b QE 2:50b

προαιρετικός Deus 47, 49 Plant 88 Somn 1:22

προαιρέω (26) Leg 1:87 Leg 2:32, 85 Leg 3:3, 85 Sacr 39 Plant 92 Migr 60 Fug 151 Mut 34 Abr 127 Ios 148, 193 Mos 1:134, 325 Spec 2:37, 132, 137 Spec 3:85 Spec 4:32 Prob 96 Legat 98, 115, 298 QG 4:51b QG isf 8

προαισθάνομαι (6) Spec 3:95, 115, 146, 148 Flacc 110 Legat 258

προακούω Ebr 160 Her 63

προαλγέω Spec 3:160

προαλίσκομαι Flacc 7

προαναιρέω Legat 107

προανακρούομαι Decal 150

προαναλίσκω Mos 1:114

προαναπίπτω Cher 82 Deus 66 Ios 113 Mos 1:38

προανατέμνω QG 2:41

προαναφθέγγομαι Somn 2:160

προανείργω Spec 1:325

προανθέω Mut 161 Spec 4:209

προανίστημι Legat 258

προαπαντάω (11) Leg 3:215, 215 Deus 93 Conf 162 Congr 35, 123 Fug 166 Mos 1:22 Virt 98, 185 Praem 167

προαποθνήσκω (11) Leg 3:227 Abr 182 Ios 129, 189 Decal 114 Spec 2:129 Spec 3:154 Virt 11 Flacc 175 Legat 208, 215

προαποστέλλω Her 66

προαποτάσσομαι Spec 3:161

προασπίζω (6) Somn 2:265 Mos 1:142, 284 Decal 114 Spec 4:199 Praem 124

προασπιστής Somn 1:113

προάστιον προάστειον

προάστειον (προάστιον) Congr 10 Mos 1:214, 240 Spec 1:158 Spec 2:120

προαφαυαίνω Spec 4:209

προβαίνω Sobr 17 Somn 1:198 Spec 3:174 Legat 161

προβάλλω (22) Opif 155 Post 134 Deus 143, 153 Somn 2:104 Abr 22, 104, 137, 210 Mos 1:43, 45, 46 Mos 2:9, 19 Spec 2:44, 60 Spec 3:158 Virt 136, 178, 200 Contempl 45 Flacc 102

πρόβασις Mut 111

προβατεύσιμος Mos 1:65, 320

προβάτιον Prob 121

πρόβατον (54) Opif 85 Leg 3:165, 165 Cher 79 Sacr 11, 45, 46, 48, 50, 51, 55, 88, 89, 112, 112 Det 5 Post 67 Deus 119 Agr 42, 43, 44, 61 Migr 152 Her 20, 193 Congr 95, 106 Fug 132, 132 Mut 110, 111, 233, 233, 245, 245, 246, 247, 250 Somn 1:189, 197, 198, 199 Somn 2:19, 19 Spec 1:135, 163 Spec 2:35 Spec 4:11, 12, 12, 13 Virt 95 Prob 30 Prov 2:13

προβέβουλα (προβούλομαι) Prob 134

προβλαστάνω Mut 161

πρόβλημα Ebr 201 Ios 125 Prob 58

πρόβλητος Ios 219

προβουλεύω Spec 3:92

προβούλομαι προβέβουλα

πρόβουλος Her 243 Spec 1:121

προγαμέω Spec 3:27

προγανόω Leg 3:86 Praem 160

προγελάω Mut 162

προγευστρίς Sacr 44 Mut 164

προγεύω Mut 164

προγήθω Mut 161

προγηράσκω Spec 2:91

προγίγνομαι (7) Leg 2:71 Leg 3:87 Mos 1:183, 197 Mos 2:288 Virt 159 QG 1:89

προγιγνώσκω Somn 1:2

προγνωστικός Somn 2:1 Mos 2:190

προγονικός (10) Mut 171 Mos 1:32, 88 Mos 2:270 Spec 1:53 Virt 191, 193, 226 Praem 170 Flacc 29

προγόνη πρόγονος

πρόγονος (προγόνη) (43) Deus 150 Sobr 17 Mut 189 Abr 31, 265 Ios 172, 216 Mos 1:5, 207, 240 Mos 2:55 Spec 1:101, 137, 317 Spec 2:135, 158, 199, 207 Spec 3:16, 20, 26 Spec 4:178 Virt 187, 190, 204, 204, 206, 211, 224, 225 Praem 168 Prob 10, 148 Flacc 46 Legat 54, 224, 232, 278, 290, 322 Hypoth 6:1, 6:1 QG 3:11a

πρόγραμμα Flacc 54

προγάστωρ QG (Par) 2:2

προγυμνασία Mos 1:60

προγύμνασμα Legat 30

πρόδηλος Gig 39

προδηλόω Decal 45, 50

προδιαπλάσσω Mos 2:76

προδιατίθημι Spec 3:95 Legat 68

προδιατυπόω Opif 20 Leg 3:79

προδιδάσκω (9) Mos 1:60, 81, 90 Mos 2:135 Spec 3:27, 32 Spec 4:121, 141 Contempl 11

προδίδωμι Det 173 Ebr 17, 58 Migr 72 Spec 3:61

προδικάζω Mut 164

προδιομολογέομαι Conf 171

προδιορίζω Migr 43 Somn 1:68

προδοκιμάζω Spec 3:36

προδοσία Agr 152 Plant 101 Mos 1:305 Legat 328

προδότης Leg 2:10 Spec 3:164 Legat 327 Prov 2:39

προδουλόω Spec 3:139

προεγχαράσσω Spec 1:106

προεδρία Conf 79 Mos 1:321 Spec 2:238

πρόεδρος Her 243 Somn 2:187 Contempl 75, 79

προεῖδον (προοράω) (16) Sacr 29, 78 Deus 29 Agr 68 Ebr 160 Conf 12 Abr 266 Mos 1:168 Spec 1:99 Spec 3:97, 200 Contempl 15 Aet 102 Flacc 113 QE 2:24a, 49b

πρόειμι (26) Leg 3:159 Det 14 Deus 162 Agr 171 Ebr 221 Sobr 28 Her 70 Congr 82, 116 Fug 158 Mut 100, 256 Somn 1:150 Mos 1:166, 194, 250 Mos 2:64 Spec 1:160 Prob 63 Aet 58, 71 Flacc 92, 111, 167 Legat 77, 97

προεῖπον (18) Leg 1:24 Cher 53 Sacr 23, 28 Det 67, 81, 139 Sobr 33 Migr 49 Abr 9, 49 Ios 99, 104, 178 Mos 1:265 Decal 83 Spec 4:136 Virt 22

προεκδίδωμι Hypoth 7:18

προεκλογίζομαι Spec 2:46

προεκλύω Mos 2:35

προεκπέμπω Mos 1:185 Decal 145

προεκτρέχω (7) Sacr 14, 53 Agr 93 Congr 122 Abr 153 Mos 1:26, 286

προεκτυπόω Opif 16

προεκφοιτάω Spec 2:175

προεμμελετάω Fug 36

προενέρχομαι Virt 31

προενοικέω Mos 1:327

προεντυγχάνω Post 18 Ebr 42 Fug 6 Mos 2:183 QE 2:26

προεξανίσταμαι Spec 1:3

προεξασθενέω Spec 4:211

προεξέρχομαι Mut 162

προεξετάζω Spec 2:6

προέορτος Spec 2:176 Contempl 65

προεπιδείκνυμι Fug 35 Mos 1:82

προεπιλογίζομαι Aet 24

προεπιτίθεμαι Mos 1:250

προεπιχειρέω Praem 86

προεργάζομαι Cher 60 Post 103

προερέω (21) Opif 111 Leg 2:22 Leg 3:253 Cher 111 Deus 1, 2, 69, 77, 96, 118 Sobr 51 Migr 70 Her 218, 314 Congr 142 Fug 77 Abr 60 Mos 2:101, 111 Decal 31 QG 2:30

προέρχομαι (73) Opif 161 Leg 1:41, 83 Leg 2:63, 100 Cher 54 Sacr 98 Det 17, 17, 32 Post 19, 118, 168, 184 Deus 19, 57 Agr 70, 90 Ebr 15, 185 Sobr 56 Her 68, 78 Mut 173 Somn 2:103, 126, 232 Abr 23, 58 Ios 120, 142 Mos 1:73, 104, 124, 137, 228, 246, 248, 251, 265, 269, 269, 277 Mos 2:214 Decal 37, 48 Spec 1:30, 160 Spec 2:207 Spec 3:41, 105, 106, 107, 132 Spec 4:70 Virt 39, 44, 119, 137 Praem 41, 43 Prob 9, 18, 21 Aet 19 Flacc 64, 89, 120, 166, 169 Legat 189, 365, 366

πρόεσις Opif 123

προετοιμάζω (6) Opif 77 Deus 96 Spec 1:165, 262 Spec 2:70 Virt 145

προευαγγελίζομαι Opif 34 Mut 158 Abr 153

προευτρεπίζω (12) Opif 78, 133 Det 110 Conf 83 Somn 1:51, 236 Spec 1:127 Spec 3:60 Praem 9 Contempl 46 Aet 89 Legat 124

προευφραίνω Leg 3:47 Post 21 Mut 165

προεφοδιάζομαι Mos 1:80

προέχω Leg 1:30 Deus 44

προέψημα QG 4:168

προηγέομαι (21) Opif 28 Leg 3:91, 143, 177, 178 Sacr 82 Migr 161 Fug 99 Mos 2:203 Spec 1:195 Spec 2:178 Spec 4:7 Virt 176 Legat 176, 323 Prov 2:47, 53, 53, 59 QG 1:89 QE isf 9

προήγησις Somn 2:289

προηγητήρ Mos 1:166

προηγουμένως Abr 37, 143, 146 Mos 2:215 QG 1:94

προήκω Sobr 7

προθεμελιόω Abr 53

προθεραπεύω Abr 15

πρόθεσις (10) Congr 168 Fug 185 Mut 8 Mos 2:36, 61, 279 Spec 2:161 QG 2:15a, 4:204 QE isf 5

προθεσμία (16) Post 5 Fug 87, 106, 116 Ios 97 Decal 100 Spec 1:143, 144, 161, 251 Spec 2:142, 220 Spec 4:196, 208 Virt 53, 113

προθεσπίζω Her 267 Abr 115 Mos 1:265 Spec 4:49 Praem 111

προθνήσκω Spec 4:202

προθρηνέω Ios 217

προθυμέομαι Spec 1:39

προθυμία (28) Sacr 59 Agr 91, 147, 169 Migr 25, 218 Her 123 Congr 124 Mut 270 Abr 246 Mos 1:63, 251, 315, 318, 325, 327 Mos 2:137, 170 Decal 146 Spec 1:43, 144, 290 Spec 2:83, 146 Spec 4:111, 222 Virt 88 Contempl 71

πρόθυμος (13) Agr 151 Abr 109 Ios 208 Mos 1:52, 260, 333, 333 Spec 1:49, 77 Spec 4:170 Virt 27, 83, 205

πρόθυρον Virt 89

προΐημι (29) Opif 103, 156, 160, 163 Leg 3:72 Post 94 Agr 96 Mut 242 Somn 1:95 Somn 2:184 Abr 187, 196, 259 Ios 77, 191, 227 Mos 1:141 Decal 32 Spec 1:120 Spec 2:78, 122 Spec 3:32, 97 Virt 37, 84, 90 Aet 97, 100 Flacc 23

προικίδιος Spec 2:126 Virt 223

προικίζω Spec 3:70

προίξ (6) Fug 29 Spec 2:79, 116, 125 Spec 3:70 Spec 4:63

προΐστημι (27) Sacr 130 Agr 29, 51 Ebr 153 Conf 29, 95 Her 214 Abr 116, 213 Ios 154, 189, 242, 250 Mos 1:187, 249, 318 Spec 2:125 Spec 3:77 Spec 4:184 Praem 75, 119 Prob 57 Flacc 93, 103, 160 Legat 244, 300

προκάθημαι Mut 164 Mos 1:215

προκαθίστημι Deus 70

προκαλέω (20) Leg 1:34 Leg 3:50 Det 17, 32 Agr 110 Migr 75 Decal 162 Spec 2:4, 71, 95, 96, 114, 234 Spec 3:91 Spec 4:44, 45, 221 Virt 109 Praem 156 Flacc 30

προκάλυμμα (10) Gig 53 Conf 116 Fug 34 Somn 1:97 Decal 172 Spec 2:11 Spec 3:54 Spec 4:2, 7 Flacc 42

προκάμνω (9) Congr 164 Ios 114 Mos 1:306 Spec 1:38 Spec 2:67, 91 Spec 4:112, 205 QE 2:26

προκαταβάλλω (7) Leg 3:113 Agr 132 Conf 5 Her 134 Mut 211 Somn 2:8 Contempl 34

προκαταγιγνώσκω Congr 153 Ios 222 Spec 3:42 Flacc 106, 126

προκαταδύνω (προκαταδύομαι) Praem 147

προκαταδύομαι προκαταδύνω

προκαταλαμβάνω (13) Det 61 Conf 12 Mos 1:104, 326, 330 Mos 2:177 Spec 4:119 Virt 48 Praem 25, 149 Aet 129, 149 Legat 127

προκαταλύω Post 18

προκαταπίπτω Praem 5 Legat 196

προκαταπλήσσω Abr 260

προκατάρχω Her 104 QE 2:11b

προκατασκευάζω Aet 48

προκατασκευή Somn 1:4, 4

προκατεργάζομαι Spec 1:217

προκατέχω Mos 1:104 Spec 3:92 Spec 4:119 Praem 35 Flacc 115

πρόκειμαι (37) Opif 109 Leg 1:74 Leg 3:4, 167 Deus 53, 61, 62 Agr 63 Sobr 18 Her 1, 256 Congr 10, 10, 159 Mut 48, 82, 88 Somn 1:6, 58 Ios 125, 169 Mos 1:48, 151, 194 Mos 2:35 Spec 1:118, 153, 172, 221 Spec 2:40, 223, 257 Spec 4:195 Praem 13, 31, 140 Hypoth 11:12

προκήδομαι Mos 1:328 Hypoth 11:17

προκηρύσσω (6) Sacr 122 Det 63 Gig 39 Agr 17 Her 273 Spec 2:66

προκινδυνεύω Mos 1:316 Virt 27

προκληρονομέω Spec 2:139 Contempl 13

πρόκλησις Det 1, 37, 45 Mos 1:243 Spec 3:53

προκομίζω Flacc 90

προκοπή (32) Leg 2:81, 93 Leg 3:146, 165, 249, 249 Sacr 112, 112, 113, 113, 114, 114, 120 Det 46, 51 Post 97, 132 Agr 157, 158, 168 Ebr 82, 82 Conf 72 Congr 106, 112 Fug 172, 176, 213 Mut 2, 19 Aet 43 QG 3:48

προκόπτω (27) Leg 3:132, 140, 140, 140, 143, 144, 144, 159, 196 Sacr 7 Det 5, 12 Post 78 Agr 159, 160, 165 Fug 202, 213 Mut 24 Somn 2:234, 235, 236, 237 QG 4:30, 51a QE 1:7b, 2:20

προκόσμημα Cher 101 Spec 1:115 Legat 9, 98

προκρίνω (21) Leg 2:50 Leg 3:17, 52 Cher 46 Sacr 72 Ebr 56 Conf 133 Fug 180, 199 Mut 170 Mos 1:3, 221, 235 Spec 1:221 Spec 2:226 Virt 32, 60 Prob 35 Prov 2:36 QG 3:26, 4:198

προλαμβάνω (15) Opif 16, 45 Cher 15, 78, 118 Sacr 10 Agr 38 Fug 99 Somn 1:2, 60 Mos 1:333 Spec 1:26 Legat 208 Prov 2:56 QG 3:58

προλέγω (6) Somn 1:111 Ios 217 Spec 4:50, 159 Legat 109 Prov 2:47

πρόληψις Conf 140 Spec 2:46

προμαλάσσω Legat 223

προμάμμη Legat 135, 291, 319

προμανθάνω (13) Opif 172 Plant 146 Abr 112 Mos 1:220 Mos 2:141 Spec 1:53 Spec 2:96 Spec 3:48 Virt 160 Legat 109, 208, 245, 310

πρόμαχος Ebr 201

προμετωπίδιος Contempl 51

προμήθεια (19) Leg 1:24 Sacr 27, 121 Post 11, 36, 144 Deus 29 Ebr 143 Conf 159 Migr 31 Fug 162 Mut 56 Abr 18 Spec 4:205 Virt 133 Praem 9 Aet 8 Prov 2:41, 46

προμηθέομαι (12) Opif 171 Leg 1:28 Det 56 Deus 72 Migr 120, 181, 186 Somn 2:11 Mos 1:12 Spec 3:119 Virt 146 Prov 2:6

προμηθής (10) Plant 161 Abr 253 Ios 166 Spec 1:262 Spec 2:205 Spec 3:46 Virt 24, 129 Legat 259 Prov 2:54

προμήκης Plant 16

προμηνύω (7) Mut 158 Abr 153 Ios 107 Mos 1:133 Decal 18 Legat 110 Prov 2:26

πρόναος Mos 2:101 Spec 1:156 Contempl 81

προνεύω Prov 2:27

προνοέω (28) Opif 171, 172 Sacr 41, 121 Plant 102 Ebr 19, 19, 84 Conf 114 Migr 88, 93 Somn 1:99 Ios 115 Decal 91 Spec 1:67, 132 Spec 2:112 Spec 3:48, 91, 111, 189, 196 Virt 153, 216 Legat 3, 109 QG isf 5 QE 2:6a

προνοητικός Her 191 Spec 1:209 Flacc 43 Legat 6, 68

πρόνοια (80) Opif 9, 128 Post 11 Deus 29, 47 Agr 39, 130 Ebr 13, 87, 131, 163, 199 Sobr 63 Conf 20, 115, 178 Her 58, 247 Fug 78, 79, 102 Mut 25, 198 Somn 2:64, 137 Abr 6, 40 Ios 99, 116, 161, 236 Mos 1:67, 162, 203 Mos 2:3, 6, 200 Decal 58, 141 Spec 1:166, 308, 309, 310, 318 Spec 2:155 Spec 3:63, 128, 135, 205 Spec 4:213 Virt 130, 135, 215 Praem 33, 42, 104 Aet 47, 49, 51 Flacc 125, 126, 170 Legat 15, 51, 220, 253, 336 Hypoth 6:1, 7:18 Prov 2:1, 9, 22, 42, 45, 52, 59, 59 QG 2:34a QG (Par) 2:7 QE 2:3a

προνομαία Aet 128

προνομή Virt 110

προνομία (38) Opif 30, 45, 53, 92 Sacr 130 Det 52 Fug 51 Somn 1:196 Abr 37, 150 Mos 2:5, 142, 263 Decal 102, 105 Spec 1:159, 159, 229, 303 Spec 2:124, 156, 157, 176, 238 Spec 3:130, 192 Spec 4:11 Virt 102, 107 Praem 7 Prob 44 Contempl 82 Flacc 35 Legat 167, 183, 183, 288 Hypoth 11:13

προξενέω (9) Opif 166 Cher 93 Post 79 Ebr 49 Congr 72, 111, 113 Virt 55 Contempl 90

προοιμιάζομαι Gig 32

προοίμιον (10) Gig 66 Plant 149 Ebr 11 Congr 11, 11 Somn 1:133 Somn 2:219 Mos 2:51, 258 Spec 4:43

πρόοπτος Ebr 192 Her 209 Somn 1:90

προορατικός Mos 2:269

προοράω προεῖδον

προοράω Conf 118 Somn 1:27 Spec 4:165 Praem 72

προπάθεια QG 1:79

προπαίδευμα (19) Leg 3:167 Cher 8, 10, 101, 104 Sacr 38, 43 Agr 9 Congr 9, 24, 35, 152, 180 Fug 2, 183, 187, 187, 213 Mut 263

προπαιδεύω QG 3:30b

πρόπαππος (10) Conf 149 Abr 31 Spec 4:18 Praem 57 Prob 148 Flacc 46 Legat 240, 305, 309, 311 προπάροιθε Ebr 150

προπάσχω Mos 1:181 Spec 2:80 Spec 4:43, 121

προπάτωρ Opif 145 Mos 2:291 QG 4:153

προπέμπω Leg 3:21 Mos 1:195, 227 Spec 3:111

προπέτεια (8) Sacr 22 Ebr 192 Conf 117 Mut 244 Spec 3:66 Spec 4:9 Legat 262 QG 4:52d

προπετής Deus 163 Somn 2:182 Spec 3:105, 175

προπηδάω Abr 153

προπηλακίζω (9) Mos 1:44, 89 Spec 2:95, 232, 243 Spec 3:159, 174 Prob 104 Flacc 75

προπίνω Ios 213

προπίπτω Virt 116

προπιστεύω (8) Leg 3:65, 66 Ebr 193 Conf 140 Mos 1:174 Virt 57, 153 Flacc 89

προπλάσσω Leg 2:6

προπληρόω Mut 165

προπολεμέω Agr 152 Mos 1:316 Mos 2:274 Praem 96

πρόπολος Decal 66

προπομπεύω Spec 3:40

προπομπός Opif 114 Fug 119 Flacc 157

πρόποσις (6) Ebr 148 Somn 2:183 Ios 206, 213 Mos 1:187 Flacc 113

πρόπους Mos 1:228

προπύλαιος (15) Leg 3:98 Cher 100 Post 50 Somn 2:233 Mos 2:80, 86, 86, 91, 92, 93, 136 Praem 75 Legat 150, 151 Prov 2:19

πρόρρησις Flacc 86 Hypoth 7:9

πρός (3148) Opif 3, 10, 14, 16, 21, 23, 23, 31, 32, 36, 39, 41, 41, 43, 44, 48, 48, 48, 48, 48, 49, 51, 52, 55, 56, 60, 61, 66, 69, 70, 71, 74, 77, 77, 78, 83, 84, 85, 86, 88, 88, 96, 96, 96, 98, 103, 104, 106, 106, 106, 106, 107, 107, 107, 108, 108, 109, 109, 113, 113, 115, 115, 115, 115, 117, 123, 131, 132, 137, 138, 138, 139, 139, 144, 145, 146, 147, 149, 149, 152, 153, 153, 153, 155, 156, 158, 159, 159, 161, 163, 164, 169, 170, 171 Leg 1:7, 8, 16, 28, 29, 29, 30, 34, 36, 38, 62, 68, 75, 82, 85, 93, 93, 98, 103, 103, 104, 104 Leg 2:8, 9, 10, 20, 24, 24, 28, 40, 40, 46, 49, 61, 71, 72, 78, 83, 83, 88, 91, 105, 106, 106 Leg 3:13, 15, 17, 23, 24, 24, 24, 25, 26, 26, 30, 30, 34, 38, 43, 47, 48, 52, 53, 60, 61, 63, 67, 70, 85, 115, 134, 140, 144, 150, 167, 172, 174, 175, 178, 179, 179, 182, 184, 185, 185, 189, 190, 190, 191, 201, 201, 202, 202, 202, 202, 213, 214, 214, 214, 215, 220, 220, 221, 227, 234, 244, 245, 246, 246 Cher 4, 6, 15, 15, 22, 25, 26, 30, 31, 34, 49, 49, 50, 62, 67, 72, 74, 75, 81, 83, 86, 86, 86, 91, 92, 95, 97, 103, 104, 104, 110, 115, 115, 117, 117, 117, 117, 117, 117, 120, 120, 121, 122, 124, 125, 130 Sacr 3, 3, 10, 17, 22, 26, 35, 36, 36, 37, 41, 41, 42, 44, 49, 53, 55, 63, 63, 63, 69, 74, 75, 75, 78, 78, 80, 87, 91, 99, 102, 102, 105, 105, 114, 116, 117, 120, 121, 125, 128, 132, 133, 133, 137, 138 Det 1, 4, 4, 5, 6, 7, 7, 9, 9, 9, 9, 10, 10, 15, 17, 21, 22, 26, 26, 28, 28, 28, 36, 36, 38, 39, 41, 43, 50, 52, 53, 57, 57, 69, 74, 77, 77, 79, 79, 79, 81, 83, 89, 92, 93, 95, 95, 99, 101, 101, 102, 105, 107, 107, 110, 113, 120, 122, 127, 129, 134, 134, 138, 141, 141, 142, 142, 143, 149, 151, 154, 154, 157, 160, 161, 162, 162, 162, 165, 165, 167, 171, 172, 173, 173, 176, 178 Post 4, 12, 13, 19, 22, 22, 25, 27, 30, 30, 31, 32, 41, 41, 42, 45, 49, 50, 52, 52, 59, 60, 80, 81, 81, 83, 88, 91, 95, 100, 101, 104, 106, 106, 108, 110, 112, 116, 119, 121, 125, 125, 131, 134, 135, 135, 135, 137, 137, 140, 140, 141, 141, 141, 141, 142, 143, 143, 145, 147, 147, 148, 152, 152, 152, 156, 157, 157, 160, 161, 161, 161, 162, 164, 165, 166, 167, 171, 172, 172, 173, 174, 177, 180, 181, 181, 181, 181, 184 Gig 5, 9, 10, 12, 12, 13, 15, 16, 16, 21, 24, 25, 26, 28, 29, 30, 32, 33, 33, 33, 34, 35, 37, 37, 37, 38, 41, 43, 45, 52, 53, 53, 65 Deus 1, 2, 7, 9, 15, 15, 17, 30, 31, 38, 38, 38, 47, 49, 54, 56, 56, 57, 57, 57, 60, 60, 63, 66, 68, 69, 69, 76, 77, 77, 85, 96, 97, 98, 98, 98, 100, 100, 102, 109, 116, 121, 121, 128, 129, 132, 138, 138, 142, 146, 147, 148, 150, 162, 169, 170, 170, 172, 173, 174, 180 Agr 3, 5, 5, 5, 6, 12, 13, 34, 36, 37, 38, 41, 43, 47, 49, 53, 67, 69, 71, 75, 81, 83, 84, 85, 88, 95, 95, 101, 102, 103, 104, 111, 116, 116, 120, 125, 125, 126, 129, 131, 131, 133, 134, 135, 142, 146, 147, 152, 156, 160, 161, 164, 174, 176, 177 Plant 3, 4, 10, 14, 15, 17, 18, 19, 20, 21, 21, 21, 22, 22, 22, 23, 24, 24, 25, 26, 33, 34, 37, 37, 37, 39, 39, 40, 42, 45, 45, 55, 55, 65, 66, 71, 81, 87, 88, 92, 92, 95, 96, 104, 104, 105, 110, 115, 126, 131, 135, 135, 139, 152, 152, 160, 162, 164, 165, 167 Ebr 3, 6, 17, 18, 18, 18, 21, 21, 23, 29, 36, 37, 37, 37, 37, 40, 40, 45, 46, 51, 51, 53, 54, 57, 59, 61, 63, 70, 73, 75, 76, 77, 77, 78, 79, 85, 85, 86, 91, 96, 98, 99, 100, 100, 101, 105, 106, 116, 116, 116, 121, 122, 130, 131, 133, 142, 146, 149, 150, 151, 152, 155, 156, 160, 174, 175, 177, 186, 187, 200, 202, 207, 209, 211, 212, 214, 216, 217, 220, 220, 223 Sobr 2, 2, 3, 4, 5, 5, 8, 9, 9, 9, 11, 12, 12, 15, 15, 43, 47, 47, 50, 50, 63, 65, 66, 67, 68 Conf 4, 5, 6, 7, 10, 12, 19, 20, 21, 22, 25, 26, 30, 34, 34, 34, 40, 40, 42, 45, 49, 49, 57, 59, 59, 63, 64, 64, 68, 76, 81, 85, 86, 93, 93, 95, 97, 101, 101, 105, 110, 110, 111, 113, 116, 116, 121, 130, 138, 141, 141, 145, 145, 150, 150, 152, 153, 154, 155, 158, 162, 175, 183, 186, 191, 195, 195 Migr 6, 7, 10, 12, 13, 13, 14, 14, 16, 19, 22, 22, 25, 26, 39, 47, 51, 52, 53, 56, 57, 67, 70, 71, 74, 76, 77, 78, 80, 81, 81, 81, 81, 82, 83, 84, 86, 88, 92, 93, 95, 96, 100, 102, 104, 107, 108, 124, 126, 131, 131, 132, 133, 139, 140, 142, 145, 146, 146, 148, 149, 151, 153, 158, 166, 167, 167, 168, 169, 170, 171, 171, 171, 172, 173, 175, 178, 183, 190, 191, 191, 191, 195, 208, 209, 209, 209, 211, 211, 219, 219, 219, 223, 225 Her 5, 6, 7, 13, 14, 14, 15, 15, 19, 20, 20, 20, 21, 21, 30, 32, 34, 35, 43, 45, 45, 45, 45, 45, 47, 53, 53, 61, 62, 66, 67, 70, 71, 77, 78, 79, 79, 81, 90, 91, 92, 93, 93, 94, 96, 98, 98, 102, 106, 110, 113, 113, 116, 117, 119, 119, 119, 119, 123, 123, 126, 137, 147, 147, 147, 154, 156, 164, 165, 168, 168, 169, 169, 172, 172, 176, 176, 182, 196, 197, 197, 200, 201, 205, 205, 206, 206, 207, 223, 225, 231, 236, 238, 238, 241, 246, 254, 254, 255, 256, 256, 262, 264, 266, 266, 266, 275, 276, 277, 280, 283, 285, 285, 285, 289, 289, 291, 295, 307, 307, 310, 315, 316 Congr 1, 1, 3, 8, 8, 12, 12, 12, 12, 13, 14, 14, 17, 17, 23, 23, 23, 23, 24, 25, 31, 31, 32, 33, 46, 48, 48, 52, 56, 56, 57, 63, 73, 74, 78, 78, 78, 79, 79, 80, 84, 84, 86, 86, 87, 88, 91, 91, 92, 94, 94, 98, 98, 106, 108, 119, 119, 119, 119, 121, 122, 122, 123, 123, 125, 125, 125, 132, 132, 138, 141, 144, 144, 152, 152, 156, 162, 163, 177 Fug 1, 11, 14, 14, 23, 23, 30, 38, 44, 46, 51, 55, 59, 61, 62, 66, 69, 71, 78, 80, 89, 93, 93, 96, 97, 98, 101, 103, 105, 112, 114, 114, 115, 122, 129, 129, 142, 144, 148, 148, 149, 150, 150, 151, 151, 152, 153, 154, 154, 159, 159, 159, 160, 160, 168, 172, 176, 183, 189, 190, 191, 191, 194, 205, 206, 207, 210, 211, 212 Mut 1, 2, 7, 11, 13, 20, 20, 20, 21, 22, 27, 28, 35, 38, 40, 40, 41, 44, 44, 44,

45, 45, 51, 56, 56, 57, 63, 72, 74, 76, 76, 80, 81, 82, 85, 87, 88, 91, 94, 101, 101, 101, 104, 105, 106, 107, 109, 111, 112, 114, 114, 114, 116, 120, 123, 123, 124, 127, 138, 138, 143, 143, 147, 151, 154, 159, 162, 163, 163, 164, 170, 171, 171, 172, 173, 180, 184, 185, 190, 190, 192, 192, 200, 200, 201, 201, 208, 215, 215, 215, 228, 229, 230, 231, 232, 234, 235, 235, 246, 246, 255, 257, 263, 265, 270, 270 Somn 1:4, 11, 17, 18, 21, 21, 27, 29, 31, 44, 44, 44, 45, 46, 53, 60, 60, 63, 66, 68, 71, 73, 79, 84, 86, 88, 92, 93, 102, 104, 106, 107, 114, 115, 115, 120, 120, 121, 122, 123, 124, 125, 125, 129, 131, 134, 139, 143, 150, 158, 164, 165, 166, 167, 168, 170, 170, 171, 175, 175, 177, 177, 179, 179, 180, 182, 186, 188, 190, 191, 192, 193, 195, 198, 199, 209, 210, 215, 226, 235, 235, 236, 236, 237, 237, 238, 245, 250, 251, 255 Somn 2:4, 9, 9, 9, 10, 12, 15, 39, 42, 48, 48, 49, 49, 52, 54, 56, 57, 58, 60, 67, 75, 82, 82, 98, 98, 99, 105, 106, 114, 128, 131, 131, 133, 136, 142, 145, 147, 156, 165, 165, 170, 170, 174, 181, 185, 206, 211, 212, 213, 214, 223, 224, 230, 235, 243, 249, 253, 253, 253, 253, 253, 263, 264, 272, 282, 296, 299 Abr 4, 6, 6, 7, 8, 11, 14, 17, 18, 20, 26, 30, 31, 31, 40, 41, 42, 45, 47, 50, 51, 51, 54, 58, 59, 67, 69, 71, 71, 71, 72, 80, 90, 94, 103, 103, 103, 109, 109, 115, 116, 117, 118, 120, 122, 125, 125, 129, 130, 131, 131, 132, 135, 135, 141, 143, 147, 147, 149, 154, 157, 161, 165, 171, 173, 175, 179, 182, 182, 184, 196, 198, 198, 199, 206, 208, 208, 208, 210, 211, 211, 213, 214, 220, 222, 225, 226, 233, 241, 241, 242, 243, 244, 249, 249, 251, 261, 267, 268, 270, 271, 273 Ios 5, 12, 17, 24, 27, 30, 30, 30, 30, 33, 33, 33, 33, 40, 49, 54, 55, 55, 58, 59, 62, 65, 65, 66, 66, 71, 73, 77, 78, 81, 83, 87, 93, 101, 102, 105, 107, 111, 112, 112, 121, 126, 131, 140, 142, 142, 144, 144, 147, 156, 156, 158, 159, 159, 168, 170, 175, 177, 182, 193, 193, 195, 210, 210, 210, 215, 221, 226, 230, 230, 232, 232, 235, 240, 240, 240, 240, 243, 245, 245, 249, 249, 254, 259, 263, 266, 267, 268, 270 Mos 1:3, 5, 15, 27, 32, 35, 38, 41, 44, 45, 48, 49, 60, 60, 61, 62, 62, 63, 65, 67, 68, 69, 73, 77, 78, 81, 84, 85, 88, 93, 94, 96, 96, 98, 102, 103, 103, 103, 108, 110, 111, 111, 115, 116, 118, 129, 132, 137, 139, 145, 148, 150, 150, 153, 154, 158, 160, 160, 161, 169, 170, 172, 176, 177, 177, 178, 183, 186, 192, 192, 192, 193, 200, 201, 203, 204, 206, 210, 211, 211, 213, 216, 217, 218, 223, 224, 224, 228, 233, 233, 235, 238, 239, 239, 239, 240, 241, 242, 244, 245, 248, 258, 258, 259, 267, 273, 275, 275, 280, 280, 284, 286, 290, 295, 295, 298, 300, 301, 302, 304, 304, 305, 309, 314, 319, 321, 321, 324, 326, 331, 332 Mos 2:2, 6, 9, 14, 17, 18, 22, 22, 22, 27, 27, 31, 32, 35, 36, 44, 45, 48, 48, 51, 55, 58, 60, 61, 63, 64, 67, 68, 69, 74, 76, 81, 81, 82, 82, 84, 85, 88, 89, 90, 92, 94, 96, 100, 104, 110, 113, 116, 133, 134, 135, 136, 136, 136, 139, 139, 140, 140, 140, 141, 144, 146, 148, 148, 148, 148, 148, 154, 158, 158, 161, 161, 163, 165, 165, 165, 167, 168, 168, 171, 176, 177, 181, 184, 184, 186, 189, 189, 193, 197, 198, 200, 212, 214, 217, 236, 237, 243, 244, 244, 246, 248, 250, 256, 260, 261, 262, 265, 267, 270, 271, 271, 279, 283, 287, 291, 291 Decal 1, 2, 2, 2, 3, 6, 9, 14, 16, 17, 17, 17, 17, 21, 21, 22, 22, 22, 22, 24, 30, 31, 31, 31, 31, 32, 33, 34, 36, 36, 41, 41, 43, 43, 44, 44, 44, 45, 45, 45, 50, 55, 57, 57, 67, 68, 71, 72, 73, 73, 75, 76, 76, 81, 88, 90, 91, 91, 94, 98, 98, 99, 99, 100, 100, 101, 106, 107, 107, 109, 109, 110, 110, 110, 112, 113, 113, 113, 113, 115, 119, 121, 123, 127, 132, 137, 139, 141, 146, 152, 153, 153, 161, 174, 174, 175 Spec 1:5, 6, 6, 7, 8, 9, 16, 23, 25, 28, 38, 51, 51, 52, 55, 56, 58, 58, 62, 62, 63, 65, 66, 68, 70, 73, 74, 74, 74, 75, 75, 83, 83, 87, 87, 93, 94, 96, 100, 101, 102, 105, 105, 106, 108, 108, 110, 110, 111, 123, 124, 124, 134, 135, 135, 135, 139, 139, 146, 150, 153, 155, 158, 158, 159, 161, 163, 165, 165, 171, 173, 176, 179, 180, 182, 182, 185, 188, 188, 191, 192, 192, 195, 198, 201, 205, 207, 207, 217, 218, 227, 227, 230, 231, 237, 238, 238, 240, 243, 243, 243, 244, 245, 246, 250, 253, 258, 266, 267, 269, 274, 274, 276, 279, 282, 286, 287, 287, 288, 288, 294, 294, 294, 297, 299, 300, 300, 303, 306, 309, 313, 315, 317, 317, 319, 322, 328, 329, 333, 336, 336, 336, 336, 340, 340, 340, 342, 342, 344, 344 Spec 2:6, 7, 12, 18, 19, 20, 25, 32, 32, 33, 34, 36, 38, 38, 38, 38, 39, 39, 40, 40, 42, 45, 50, 52, 52, 52, 56, 56, 60, 60, 62, 63, 63, 64, 65, 68, 69, 70, 71, 72, 73, 80, 80, 82, 83, 91, 91, 91, 93, 94, 97, 98, 99, 101, 101, 102, 102, 104, 107, 108, 113, 122, 122, 127, 133, 136, 137, 140, 147, 148, 151, 151, 156, 158, 161, 161, 163, 163, 167, 169, 170, 171, 173, 173, 174, 174, 174, 175, 175, 175, 180, 186, 190, 190, 190, 190, 191, 194, 207, 209, 209, 209, 212, 223, 224, 225, 225, 228, 231, 232, 232, 233, 237, 237, 239, 239, 239, 240, 243, 243, 244, 247, 251, 254, 256 Spec 3:3, 8, 19, 22, 24, 25, 25, 26, 28, 29, 29, 30, 31, 39, 52, 58, 58, 58, 61, 67, 67, 67, 67, 68, 69, 70, 71, 76, 77, 80, 80, 90, 93, 103, 105, 113, 115, 115, 119, 121, 122, 126, 129, 138, 143, 147, 148, 151, 152, 155, 155, 155, 155, 157, 159, 164, 164, 173, 173, 178, 178, 186, 188, 188, 192, 199, 202, 202, 202, 202, 203, 207 Spec 4:5, 7, 7, 8, 8, 9, 12, 14, 17, 19, 26, 35, 50, 52, 54, 55, 57, 68, 71, 71, 72, 76, 78, 80, 86, 87, 88, 88, 88, 89, 89, 95, 95, 97, 97, 97, 98, 99, 101, 101, 102, 103, 106, 109, 110, 111, 111, 111, 112, 113, 115, 121, 122, 122, 128, 132, 132, 133, 134, 136, 136, 139, 141, 143, 144, 149, 149, 154, 156, 158, 159, 161, 161, 162, 164, 167, 170, 172, 172, 172, 172, 172, 179, 181, 186, 187, 188, 190, 192, 193, 196, 202, 203, 206, 211, 218, 218, 221, 222, 224, 228, 232, 232, 233, 236 Virt 5, 6, 8, 11, 15, 17, 18, 20, 32, 32, 32, 34, 34, 35, 36, 37, 41, 43, 43, 51, 54, 56, 56, 61, 61, 66, 69, 70, 70, 74, 74, 75, 75, 75, 75, 77, 79, 81, 81, 81, 88, 88, 88, 89, 89, 101, 102, 108, 109, 109, 109, 110, 115, 115, 118, 118, 124, 126, 127, 128, 130, 135, 141, 142, 143, 145, 146, 146, 149, 149, 150, 153, 153, 154, 155, 159, 160, 169, 177, 181, 187, 188, 191, 193, 193, 195, 206, 210, 217, 218, 219, 221, 223, 224 Praem 7, 11, 15, 16, 17, 20, 21, 24, 26, 27, 27, 27, 43, 45, 47, 58, 61, 62, 62, 63, 63, 65, 72, 78, 81, 81, 85, 87, 87, 89, 89, 89, 91, 92, 93, 93, 94, 94, 94, 97, 100, 103, 103, 104, 107, 109, 109, 110, 115, 115, 117, 119, 123, 124, 126, 129, 130, 131, 133, 135, 137, 140, 141, 143, 145, 149, 152, 152, 152, 153, 153, 163, 163, 164, 165, 165, 166, 166, 168, 172 Prob 10, 10, 22, 24, 24, 26, 30, 32, 33, 41, 42, 47, 47, 48, 48, 51, 51, 51, 51, 53, 53, 57, 58, 61, 66, 68, 71, 74, 74, 76, 83, 85, 87, 89, 93, 98, 101, 101, 107, 115, 116, 117, 118, 123, 123, 125, 127, 128, 133, 140, 140, 145, 145, 145, 145, 152, 159, 160 Contempl 1, 3, 4, 7, 9, 11, 16, 22, 24, 24, 25, 35, 38, 38, 48, 48, 49, 52, 53, 55, 55, 60, 61, 61, 61, 62, 64, 71, 72, 72, 75, 86, 88, 89 Aet 1, 3, 4, 5, 5, 11, 13, 15, 15, 20, 20, 21, 22, 26, 27, 28, 30, 30, 31, 31, 33, 33, 33, 36, 40, 40, 42, 43, 43, 43, 44, 52, 54, 54, 56, 58, 60, 63, 63, 66, 67, 74, 76, 80, 83, 83, 91, 92, 92, 94, 97, 99, 99, 101, 102, 109, 113, 113, 113, 114, 118, 119, 122, 122, 124, 125, 132, 135, 135, 135, 136, 136, 136, 137, 137, 138, 144, 144, 147, 147, 148, 150 Flacc 3, 5, 11, 11, 11, 12, 15, 18, 24, 25, 27, 27, 27, 28, 29, 35, 37, 43, 45, 45, 48, 51, 58, 60, 61, 74, 75, 76, 78, 78, 82, 84, 89, 90, 93,

94, 94, 96, 97, 106, 106, 106, 110, 121, 123, 124, 125, 127, 129, 130, 142, 144, 146, 147, 147, 148, 149, 155, 160, 174, 174, 178, 179, 179, 186, 188 Legat 2, 5, 6, 9, 20, 21, 22, 22, 25, 29, 30, 32, 34, 37, 38, 38, 39, 43, 44, 44, 48, 49, 52, 55, 64, 73, 82, 83, 84, 89, 89, 101, 103, 106, 108, 109, 110, 112, 117, 118, 126, 129, 132, 133, 141, 144, 144, 144, 144, 145, 155, 157, 159, 161, 167, 168, 169, 169, 171, 178, 178, 180, 181, 195, 196, 197, 199, 201, 205, 207, 215, 216, 229, 231, 233, 236, 236, 244, 245, 250, 253, 253, 253, 259, 259, 259, 259, 261, 262, 262, 277, 279, 294, 295, 296, 300, 300, 303, 314, 318, 322, 322, 322, 322, 323, 326, 335, 335, 339, 346, 346, 349, 350, 359, 359, 360, 361, 367, 367, 371, 372, 373 Hypoth 0:1, 6:1, 6:2, 6:2, 6:4, 6:4, 6:8, 7:3, 7:3, 7:6, 7:8, 7:8, 7:11, 7:11, 7:13, 7:16, 7:18, 7:20, 7:20, 11:3, 11:17 Prov 1, 1, 2:3, 3, 3, 9, 10, 11, 16, 19, 20, 26, 26, 27, 27, 29, 32, 48, 53, 54, 56, 59, 60, 61, 63, 71, 71, 72 QG 1:1, 21, 21, 27, 29, 55b, 55c, 55c, 66, 70:1, 92, 97, 100:2a, 2:15a, 15b, 29, 29, 39, 54a, 54a, 62, 62, 65, 72, 3:11a, 11c, 21, 21, 26, 29, 30b, 58, 4:33b, 51b, 51b, 51c, 69, 76b, 130, 168, 173, 191c, 7*, 7*, 200b, 202a, 202b, 206a QG isf 3, 5, 5, 8, 8, 12, 12, 15, 15 QG (Par) 2:2, 2:4, 2:4, 2:4, 2:4, 2:6, 2:7, 2:7, 2:7 QE 1:7b, 2:2, 2, 4, 11a, 11b, 12, 13b, 15b, 15b, 18, 19, 20, 21, 26, 38a, 40, 47, 65, 71 QE isf 5, 13, 14, 22, 22, 25, 29, 30, 32

προσαγορεύω (80) Opif 15, 36, 127, 131, 148 Cher 121 Det 4, 37 Post 53, 57, 131 Deus 60 Agr 66 Plant 14, 134, 169 Sobr 12 Conf 106, 145, 146, 146 Migr 165, 205 Her 166 Congr 40, 55 Fug 50, 196 Mut 71, 92, 125 Somn 1:40, 68, 171 Abr 12, 117, 121 Ios 12, 121, 219 Mos 1:32, 61, 163 Mos 2:40, 97, 97, 101, 105, 109, 112, 125, 152, 207, 247 Decal 23, 145, 159 Spec 1:1, 88, 183, 186, 307, 330, 332 Spec 2:56, 59, 188, 204, 216 Spec 3:47, 191 Spec 4:21, 51, 184, 233 Virt 4 Praem 44 Prob 105 Flacc 184 Legat 281

προσάγω (47) Leg 1:50 Leg 2:52 Leg 3:90, 136, 141 Cher 96 Sacr 97, 97, 98, 111, 136 Agr 130 Plant 106 Ebr 114, 117 Conf 9 Her 179 Fug 186 Mut 233 Somn 1:194 Ios 218 Mos 1:53, 287 Mos 2:108, 146, 224 Decal 160 Spec 1:83, 180, 180, 189, 198, 222, 251, 253, 254, 256, 259, 276, 286, 291, 298 Spec 2:162, 179, 183, 215 Spec 4:223

προσαγωγός Sacr 31 Spec 3:37 Spec 4:43

προσαδικέω Spec 3:196

προσαναβαίνω Legat 6 QE 2:45b

προσαναδιδάσκω Mos 1:75

προσαναζωγραφέω Somn 2:195

προσαναιρέω Spec 3:145 Flacc 16

προσανακαίω Conf 157

προσαναλίσκω Agr 5

προσαναμάσσω Aet 59 Flacc 141

προσαναπλάσσω (6) Opif 138 Sacr 96 Post 3 Deus 61 Decal 54, 74

προσαναπληρόω Decal 92 Virt 225 Praem 103

προσαναρρήγνυμι (6) Opif 158 Conf 25 Mos 1:160 Mos 2:23 Spec 4:217 Contempl 56

προσαναρριπίζω Virt 215

προσανατέμνω Mos 1:302

προσανατίθημι Legat 137

προσαναφθέγγομαι Cher 121

προσαναφλέγω Migr 99 Spec 1:192 Spec 4:113 QG 4:172

προσανέρομαι Prob 129

προσάντης Spec 4:44 Aet 110

προσαπάγω Abr 229

προσαποβάλλω Sobr 4 Ios 133, 209

προσαποδίδωμι (6) Agr 131 Plant 75 Ebr 11 Migr 136 Ios 28 Mos 2:66

προσαποκόπτω Spec 3:41

προσαποπλύνω Spec 3:206

προσαποσείω Ebr 177

προσαποτίνω Spec 1:236 Spec 2:74

προσάπτω (37) Leg 2:14, 78 Leg 3:29 Deus 8, 167 Plant 164 Ebr 5, 66, 131, 135 Migr 165 Fug 113 Mut 60 Somn 1:253 Somn 2:69 Mos 2:59, 68, 155, 214 Decal 122 Spec 1:113, 119, 204 Spec 2:197 Spec 3:50, 122, 135, 205, 208 Spec 4:56, 86, 145 Virt 18 Praem 35 Contempl 6 Flacc 42 Legat 159

προσάραξις Prov 2:45

προσαράσσω Agr 75 Mos 1:271

προσάρκτιος Somn 1:175

προσαρμόζω Leg 1:70 Sobr 1 QG 2:54d

προσαρτάω Det 155

προσαύξω Spec 4:16

προσαφαιρέω Hypoth 7:4

προσβάλλω (20) Leg 3:60 Cher 96 Det 98 Deus 78 Ebr 180, 183 Conf 161 Migr 42 Her 142 Congr 8 Fug 113, 141 Mut 5 Abr 157 Ios 237 Spec 2:52 Spec 4:40 Praem 68 Legat 342 QG 1:74

πρόσβασις Spec 1:274

προσβλέπω Opif 152 Abr 76 Ios 47, 47

προσβολή (27) Leg 3:111 Post 52, 169 Deus 93 Agr 13 Conf 99, 161 Migr 222 Congr 136 Fug 147 Mut 3 Ios 214 Mos 1:132, 181 Mos 2:70, 123 Decal 147 Spec 1:27, 37 Spec 2:46, 170 Virt 122 Praem 29, 39, 44 Prob 76 QE isf 21

προσγανόω Praem 50

πρόσγειος Somn 1:138 Mos 1:209

προσγίγνομαι (23) Opif 49 Leg 3:246 Sacr 47, 106, 115 Det 97 Post 148, 157, 157 Gig 36 Agr 125 Plant 12, 52 Sobr 36, 48, 61 Mut 141 Spec 1:238 Spec 4:108 Praem 82, 105 Aet 66 QE 2:21

προσγράφω Legat 334

προσδεής Aet 38

προσδέχομαι Ios 97 Spec 2:218 Virt 135 QE 2:55b

προσδέομαι προσδέω

προσδέω (προσδέομαι) (8) Opif 13, 46, 46 Migr 77, 142 Decal 81, 99 Virt 12

προσδιαστέλλω Somn 2:141

προσδιατάσσω (6) Spec 3:151 Spec 4:53, 149 Virt 142 Legat 158, 358

προσδιαφθείρω QG 1:94

προσδιδάσκω Mos 1:111

προσδιερευνάομαι Spec 3:208

προσδιηγέομαι Legat 299

προσδιορίζω Her 284 Abr 265

προσδοκάω (72) Leg 2:42, 43 Leg 3:87 Cher 106 Sacr 29 Det 120, 140, 140 Deus 66, 92 Ebr 109, 204 Migr 25, 156, 211 Her 31, 100, 270, 279 Mut 163, 171, 222 Abr 8, 128, 202 Ios 123, 137, 139, 172, 209 Mos 1:40, 49, 56, 58, 168, 198, 199, 263, 327 Mos 2:252, 288 Decal 16, 117 Spec 1:278, 283, 284 Spec 2:12, 67, 71, 77 Spec 3:39, 62, 162 Spec 4:121, 223 Virt 29, 166 Praem 71, 148 Aet 139 Flacc 87 Legat 186, 192, 226, 268, 324, 341, 341, 366 Prov 2:32 QG 1:74, 4:43

προσδοκία (13) Leg 2:43 Cher 116 Sacr 124 Det 119, 138, 140 Post 26 Migr 43 Mut 163 Somn 2:210 Abr 14 Praem 160 QG 1:79

προσεγχρίω Prob 58

προσεῖδον (προσοράω) Deus 157 Migr 145 Fug 114 Decal 89 Legat 237

πρόσειμι (83) Opif 127, 151 Leg 3:86, 218 Sacr 28, 100 Post 23, 23, 104, 147 Gig 38 Deus 9, 56, 113 Agr 93, 149, 156, 167 Plant 171, 172 Ebr 107, 129, 138, 183, 191 Conf 134 Migr 57, 87, 94 Her 51 Fug 18, 162 Mut 67, 148 Somn 2:66 Abr 126, 153, 195 Ios 14, 182 Mos 1:31, 75 Mos 2:17, 66, 130, 168, 187, 234, 272 Decal 6 Spec 1:98, 102, 116, 219, 219, 282, 293 Spec 2:89, 154, 164 Spec 3:135, 183, 188 Spec 4:34, 106, 111 Virt 8 Prob 19, 136 Aet 38, 60 Flacc 1, 24, 38, 177 Legat 48, 168, 175, 228, 268 Prov 2:18 QG 1:72 QE 2:9a

προσεῖπον (προσλέγω) (19) Opif 37, 89 Agr 44, 175 Conf 191 Migr 145 Fug 40 Mut 19 Somn 1:186, 193 Abr 7, 11 Ios 200 Mos 1:135 Spec 2:142, 157 Legat 154, 289, 352

προσεισφέρω Legat 343

προσεκκαίω Leg 3:225, 225, 234 Migr 99

προσεκλέγω Legat 343

προσεκτικός Congr 68

προσεμπίμπρημι (προσεμπίπρημι) Leg 3:248 Spec 4:29

προσεμπίπρημι προσεμπίμπρημι

προσεμπίπτω Aet 21

προσεντάσσω Flacc 131

προσεξεργάζομαι Ios 212 Decal 140

προσεξέρχομαι Det 127

προσεξετάζω Det 12 Plant 174 Spec 4:116 Praem 49

προσεξευρίσκω Congr 146 Somn 2:55 Aet 16

προσεξηγέομαι Legat 197

προσέοικα Opif 153

προσεπεξεργαζόμαι Flacc 35

προσεπευφημέω Hypoth 7:13

προσεπιβαίνω Ebr 95

προσεπιβάλλω Hypoth 7:7

προσεπιδαψιλεύομαι Her 287 Ios 178 Spec 2:85

προσεπιδίδωμι Spec 4:159

προσεπιθεσπίζω Mos 2:229

προσεπικοσμέω Abr 35 Spec 3:51

προσεπιλέγω Mut 47

προσεπιλιχμάομαι Spec 3:115

προσεπινοέω Mos 1:21

προσεπιρρώννυμι Flacc 25

προσεπισημαίνω Opif 71

προσεπισκέπτομαι Spec 3:190

προσεπισύρω Somn 2:275 Spec 2:202

προσεπισφίγγω Deus 124

προσεπιτείνω Leg 3:144 Mos 1:120 Spec 3:41

προσεπιτίθημι Somn 2:48 Spec 1:234 Spec 2:36

προσεπιφέρω Plant 160 Legat 266 Hypoth 7:7

προσεπιφοιτάω Ios 183

προσεπιψηφίζομαι Spec 4:157

προσεργάζομαι Praem 136

προσερέω (10) Opif 136 Leg 2:44 Migr 84 Her 78 Mut 83, 150 Somn 1:14, 35 Abr 81 Spec 3:21

προσέρχομαι (64) Opif 144, 156 Leg 2:39, 78 Sacr 12, 21 Det 10, 24, 77 Post 80 Gig 21, 32, 33, 34, 35, 35, 37, 38 Deus 8, 28, 161 Agr 123 Plant 56, 64, 97 Ebr 106, 131, 137, 183 Conf 55 Migr 86 Fug 41 Mut 13 Abr 247, 261 Ios 43, 116, 197, 201, 222, 238, 261 Mos 1:122 Mos 2:122, 169, 226, 273 Decal 88, 148 Spec 1:51, 102, 167 Spec 4:140 Virt 116 Prob 64, 124 Flacc 21 Legat 178, 186, 191, 228 QG isf 3 QG (Par) 2:4, 2:7

προσερῶ Somn 2:189

προσετέον Gig 34

προσέτι (28) Opif 40, 48, 59, 81, 112, 147, 148, 153 Cher 111 Det 13 Post 111 Agr 141 Plant 151 Ios 254 Mos 1:23, 148, 192 Mos 2:1 Decal 147 Spec 1:34, 291 Spec 2:5, 200 Spec 3:39 Spec 4:84 Virt 95 Praem 3 Prov 2:17

προσευκαιρέω Legat 181

προσευκτήριον Mos 2:216

προσευχή (19) Flacc 41, 45, 47, 48, 49, 53, 122 Legat 132, 134, 137, 138, 148, 152, 156, 157, 165, 191, 346, 371

προσεύχομαι Her 258 Somn 2:139 Spec 1:24 Contempl 66

προσεχής (10) Opif 76 Sacr 84 Det 82, 131 Post 140 Agr 141 Conf 85, 192 Fug 104 Mut 148

προσέχω (49) Leg 2:26, 70 Leg 3:186, 231 Cher 15 Det 125 Post 38, 179 Agr 174 Ebr 34, 35, 35, 139, 158 Migr 8, 92, 174 Her 90 Congr 20, 65, 66, 69 Fug 154 Mut 99 Somn 2:239, 263 Abr 77, 111 Ios 60, 252 Mos 1:20 Mos 2:169 Decal 91, 140 Spec 1:62, 315 Spec 2:66 Spec 3:117 Spec 4:50, 60, 60 Virt 108, 158 Prob 143 Contempl 77 Flacc 27, 111, 160 Legat 165

προσέψημα Congr 162

προσηγορία Mut 106 Spec 1:4 Spec 3:198 Legat 163 Hypoth 11:1

προσηγορικός Cher 60

προσηκόντως (33) Opif 100, 157 Sacr 63 Deus 16, 122, 140 Plant 126 Conf 35, 179 Migr 142, 145 Her 43, 104, 119, 184 Fug 20, 88, 174 Somn 1:247 Abr 54, 203 Mos 1:189 Mos 2:121, 128 Spec 1:180, 248, 254, 285, 298 Spec 2:27, 252, 255 Spec 4:199

προσήκω (107) Opif 62, 64, 80, 143, 156 Det 18, 99, 102, 132, 175 Deus 103 Agr 26, 124 Plant 2, 141, 144, 162 Sobr 58 Conf 8, 180 Migr 8, 61, 197 Congr 122 Fug 25 Mut 27, 45, 241 Somn 1:127 Somn 2:164, 201, 267 Abr 41, 65, 183, 275 Ios 10 Mos 1:218, 301 Mos 2:4, 8, 69, 75, 101, 120, 141, 145, 154, 202 Decal 41, 62, 67, 112, 128, 172 Spec 1:3, 25, 113, 134, 160, 196, 216, 221, 258, 295 Spec 2:1, 29, 78, 89, 91, 95, 171, 204, 208, 237 Spec 3:6, 96, 104, 106, 137 Spec 4:27, 71, 153, 170, 188, 229, 237 Virt 105, 203, 222 Praem 109, 134

Prob 81 Contempl 1, 56, 80, 82 Flacc 7, 72 Legat 99, 99, 149, 275, 281 QG 1:27, 4:104 QE isf 25

προσηλόω Post 61 Somn 2:213 Prov 2:24

προσήλυτος (8) Cher 108, 119 Somn 2:273 Spec 1:51, 308 QE 2:2, 2, 2

προσημαίνω Opif 59

προσηνής (10) Leg 2:76 Sacr 29 Agr 142 Congr 115, 157 Somn 2:74 Ios 62 Spec 1:155 Spec 2:159 Spec 4:103

πρόσθεμα Plant 95 Mut 89, 90

πρόσθεν (21) Leg 3:202 Migr 175, 176 Abr 170 Ios 78, 193, 199 Mos 1:281, 282 Mos 2:215, 270 Decal 28 Spec 2:122, 157, 251 Spec 4:142 Prob 14, 25, 99 Hypoth 7:17 Prov 2:50

πρόσθεσις (18) Opif 98 Sacr 1, 8, 9, 98 Her 149 Fug 128 Mut 61, 77 Somn 2:47 Ios 28 Spec 4:143, 146, 147 Aet 113, 113 Prov 1 QG 4:169

προσθήκη (23) Deus 19 Plant 128 Her 158, 187 Congr 178 Fug 72 Mut 61, 89, 206 Somn 2:63 Ios 28, 31, 31, 31 Mos 1:323 Mos 2:231 Spec 2:248 Spec 3:167 Spec 4:144, 225 Flacc 44, 153 QE 2:1

προσίημι (30) Leg 3:140, 141, 149 Cher 122 Sacr 128 Det 19, 95 Deus 156 Ebr 128 Congr 54 Mut 174 Somn 1:218 Abr 181 Ios 40 Mos 2:166 Decal 43, 156 Spec 1:42, 104, 223 Spec 3:46 Spec 4:53, 59, 119 Prob 142 Flacc 91 Legat 40, 274 QE isf 4, 5

προσικετεύω Legat 239

προσίπταμαι Conf 21

προσίστημι Flacc 131

προσκαθιδρύω Legat 98

πρόσκαιρος Spec 2:205 Praem 133

προσκαλέω (9) Leg 2:16, 17, 18, 18 Leg 3:44 Gig 44 Abr 127 Mos 1:73 Virt 178

προσκατασκευάζω Spec 1:127

προσκατατάσσω Opif 131

πρόσκειμαι (15) Leg 2:11, 44 Leg 3:40 Ebr 80 Conf 142 Migr 153 Congr 69 Fug 56 Mut 177 Mos 1:191 Spec 1:31, 345 Spec 2:258 Legat 33, 183

προσκεφάλαιον Somn 1:126

προσκληρόω (36) Opif 65 Leg 1:24 Cher 77, 85 Sacr 6, 7, 119 Post 42, 92 Gig 64 Plant 61 Conf 111 Her 43, 278 Congr 20 Fug 148 Mut 33, 127 Somn 2:8, 227, 228 Abr 198 Mos 2:128 Decal 108 Spec 1:114, 319 Spec 3:178 Spec 4:159, 180 Virt 19, 34 Praem 28, 162 Legat 3, 68, 279

προσκλητικός Aet 76

πρόσκοιτος Somn 1:100

προσκολλάω Leg 2:49, 49 QG 1:29 QE 2:3b

προσκοσμέω Legat 198

προσκρίνω Leg 2:3, 3

πρόσκρουσμα Her 246 Somn 2:168, 286 Spec 3:119

προσκρούω Virt 152

προσκτάομαι Plant 67 Ebr 122 Migr 66

προσκυνέω (37) Opif 83 Gig 54 Conf 49 Congr 103 Somn 2:6, 7, 80, 89, 90, 99, 111, 111, 113, 132, 133, 140 Abr 65 Ios 6, 8, 9, 164 Mos 1:276 Mos 2:23, 40, 165 Decal 4, 64, 72, 76 Spec 1:15, 24 Spec 2:199 Spec 4:17 Contempl 9 Legat 310 Prov 2:19 QG 4:130

προσκύνησις Legat 116

πρόσκωπος Plant 152

προσλαλέω Migr 81, 81

προσλαμβάνω (31) Leg 1:9 Leg 2:23, 73 Leg 3:121 Cher 22 Sacr 119 Deus 66 Plant 64 Sobr 39 Conf 110 Migr 55 Her 193 Congr 140 Ios 7, 82, 82 Mos 1:68, 131 Mos 2:225 Decal 25, 136 Spec 2:93 Spec 3:101 Virt 67, 100, 109 Prob 12, 159 Legat 114, 347 QG (Par) 2:2

προσλέγω προσεῖπον

προσμαρτυρέω Migr 54 QG 4:180

προσνέμω (30) Opif 12, 62, 82 Leg 3:33, 164 Cher 129 Plant 14, 15, 38 Conf 42 Migr 105 Her 36, 56, 118, 180 Fug 9 Somn 1:94 Mos 1:147 Mos 2:155 Decal 130, 161 Spec 1:20 Spec 2:131, 146 Spec 4:132 Virt 179 Legat 229 QG 1:51, 51, 64c

προσνομοθετέω (6) Spec 1:98, 247, 291 Spec 2:66 Spec 3:123 Spec 4:35

προσοδεύω (9) Mos 2:245 Spec 2:78, 107, 222 Spec 4:216 Virt 86, 159 Praem 156 Flacc 4

προσόδιος Contempl 80, 84

πρόσοδος (33) Leg 1:30 Post 27 Gig 37 Agr 153 Plant 56, 57 Migr 58 Congr 65 Mut 89 Mos 1:152 Spec 1:16, 76, 76, 131, 141, 145, 156 Spec 2:88, 106, 120, 213 Spec 4:22, 215 Virt 144 Prob 9, 35, 76 Flacc 133 Legat 9, 157, 192, 227, 317

προσομιλέω (7) Opif 144 Sacr 28 Det 30, 31 Agr 60 Migr 190 Her 13

προσόμοιος Hypoth 7:1

προσομολογέω Aet 47, 105

προσονομάζω (11) Opif 143 Her 166 Congr 21 Abr 57 Spec 1:77, 147 Praem 14, 31 Prob 73 Flacc 136 QG 1:20

προσοράω προσεῖδον

προσορμίζω Agr 64 Somn 2:143

προσοφθαλμιάω Spec 4:5 Legat 105

προσοχή (12) Cher 102 Sacr 27 Her 10, 13, 253 Congr 66 Somn 1:193, 197 Somn 2:37 Spec 2:62, 216 Spec 4:43

προσόψημα (10) Mos 1:209 Decal 16 Spec 1:175 Spec 2:20 Spec 3:144 Contempl 73, 81 Legat 275 Prov 2:70 QG 4:200a

πρόσοψις Opif 83 Cher 11, 20 Mut 168

προσπαθέω Ios 41

προσπαλαίω Somn 1:222

προσπαραλαμβάνω (9) Abr 234 Mos 1:73 Spec 1:29 Spec 2:4, 5 Spec 4:31, 105 Virt 101 Prob 140

προσπαράληψις Her 92

προσπάσχω Leg 3:182

προσπελάζω Cher 94

προσπέμπω Legat 181

προσπεριβάλλω Opif 1 Decal 7

προσπεριεργάζομαι Opif 54 Mos 1:46 Legat 71

προσπεριλαμβάνω Spec 3:168

προσπέτομαι Mos 1:145 Spec 1:26

προσπιέζω Virt 146 Prov 2:17

προσπίπτω (28) Leg 3:56, 61 Cher 78 Ebr 169, 179, 189, 196 Conf 52 Migr 157 Somn 1:122, 221 Somn 2:137 Ios 89, 219 Mos 1:30 Decal 142, 149 Spec 2:112, 207 Spec 4:53 Aet 26 Legat 221, 228, 230, 342 Hypoth 7:3, 7:4 QG 1:55c

προσπλάσσω Leg 2:12

προσποιέω (8) Her 44 Mut 169 Spec 2:75, 99 Flacc 40, 81, 98 Legat 132

προσποίησις Somn 2:40 Legat 344

προσποιητός Det 166 Conf 116 Abr 103, 126

προσπολεμέω Leg 1:68

πρόσπολος Spec 1:242

προσπορεύομαι Ebr 127, 138

πρόσπταισμα QE 2:26

προσπταίω (7) Agr 101 Ebr 167 Conf 14 Somn 2:102 Ios 179 Spec 2:23 QE 2:26

προσπυνθάνομαι Migr 213

πρόσραξις Aet 8

πρόσρησις (45) Opif 15, 149 Det 22 Gig 16, 16, 62 Agr 1, 28 Plant 86, 152 Sobr 20, 28 Conf 62 Her 22, 261 Congr 112 Fug 51 Mut 12, 15, 59, 83, 88, 254 Abr 1, 10, 27, 50, 270 Mos 1:76, 158 Mos 2:171, 205 Decal 51, 53 Spec 1:248, 341 Spec 2:80, 179, 254 Contempl 2 Flacc 59 Legat 180, 353, 355 Prov 2:3

προσριζόω (8) Det 85 Gig 31 Plant 31 Her 239, 268 Congr 21, 84 Somn 1:54

προσσαίνω Gig 35 Somn 2:51 Abr 212 Praem 89 Prob 90

προσσυμβιόω QE 2:3b

προσσυναποβάλλω Spec 2:76

πρόσταγμα (15) Opif 168 Leg 2:59 Sacr 72 Ebr 37 Her 8 Congr 86, 86 Mut 104 Abr 275 Mos 1:15 Decal 132 Praem 79, 98 Prob 3 QE isf 9

προστακτικός Fug 104 Ios 29

πρόσταξις (68) Opif 46 Leg 1:93, 93, 93, 94, 94 Leg 3:144, 144, 243 Sacr 53, 107 Deus 53 Agr 148 Plant 139 Ebr 18, 37, 91, 95, 130, 135 Sobr 22 Conf 17 Migr 7, 128, 143 Congr 87, 94, 120 Fug 100, 105 Somn 2:71 Abr 45, 60 Mos 1:99, 156 Mos 2:4, 46, 47, 51, 60, 70, 224 Decal 176 Spec 1:74, 200, 299 Spec 2:29, 145, 200, 240, 257 Spec 3:8, 47, 110, 166 Spec 4:175, 219 Virt 146 Praem 80 Prob 7 Contempl 71, 86 Legat 70, 218, 256 QG 1:51, 2:48 QG isf 17

προστασία (29) Opif 160 Post 181 Agr 47, 54, 64 Ebr 33 Sobr 40 Migr 212 Her 137 Mut 90, 221 Somn 1:222 Somn 2:123 Abr 70 Ios 67, 157, 248 Mos 1:61, 63 Spec 1:16 Spec 2:30 Spec 3:170 Spec 4:178, 183 Virt 58, 63, 64 Prob 57 Flacc 105

προστάσσω (162) Opif 13, 38, 42, 64, 85 Leg 1:94 Leg 2:79, 80, 92 Leg 3:11, 56, 144, 154 Cher 17 Sacr 53, 63, 84, 103, 107, 110, 136 Post 48 Deus 131, 137 Agr 147 Plant 99 Ebr 2, 16, 18, 102 Conf 91 Migr 14, 130 Her 9, 113, 120, 194, 225 Congr 168 Fug 83, 98, 99 Somn 1:100, 100, 214 Somn 2:74 Abr 60, 62, 171, 172, 176, 192, 232 Ios 98, 105, 153, 186, 203, 208, 211 Mos 1:44, 77, 79, 95, 107, 177, 185, 299, 303, 313, 316 Mos 2:4, 50, 63, 137, 178, 187, 202, 220 Decal 39, 106, 167 Spec 1:53, 77, 80, 84, 100, 110, 134, 137, 139, 145, 147, 151, 153, 181, 184, 188, 189, 223, 225, 228, 273, 296 Spec 2:60, 61, 66, 91, 115, 130, 175, 182, 201, 206, 236, 240 Spec 3:26, 73, 152, 198, 206 Spec 4:13, 66, 138, 191, 194 Virt 55, 63, 91, 116 Praem 55, 55, 155 Prob 25, 47 Flacc 75, 84, 87, 92, 96, 114, 173, 185 Legat 69, 157, 188, 208, 220, 221, 222, 265, 337, 364, 365, 367 Hypoth 7:10, 7:16 Prov 2:29 QG 1:21, 2:16, 16 QE isf 9

προστατέω Leg 3:37

προστάτης (9) Post 68 Mut 89 Somn 2:93 Abr 221 Spec 1:334, 337 Virt 155 Praem 77 Prob 45

προστερατεύομαι Decal 56

προστήκομαι Virt 92

προστίθημι (93) Opif 49, 52, 98, 127 Leg 2:42, 62 Leg 3:58, 150, 160, 194, 238 Cher 40, 67, 78 Sacr 1, 1, 5, 5, 5, 6, 8, 10, 114 Det 105, 112, 112, 114, 119, 123, 132 Post 179 Gig 27 Deus 153 Agr 21 Conf 75 Migr 79 Her 130, 144, 157, 189, 197 Congr 13, 141 Fug 48, 56, 128 Mut 41, 64, 90, 138, 216 Somn 1:89, 166 Somn 2:47, 60, 80, 96 Ios 29, 45, 72 Mos 1:37, 233 Mos 2:34 Spec 1:170, 230 Spec 2:14, 166 Spec 3:90, 125 Spec 4:143, 146, 147 Virt 23 Contempl 1, 90 Aet 42, 114 Flacc 49, 54, 79, 99 Prov 1, 2:24 QG 2:11, 54b, 4:153, 153, 169 QE 1:19, 2:2, 25c, 25c, 25d

προστρέπω Somn 1:256

προστρέχω Post 132 Abr 107 Mos 1:16

προστρίβω Decal 10 Virt 107 Legat 198

προστυγχάνω Prov 2:54

προσυπακούω Migr 49

προσυπερβάλλω (19) Post 95 Deus 24 Conf 91 Migr 66 Her 88 Ios 18 Decal 62, 78 Spec 1:5, 137, 330 Spec 3:151 Virt 106, 140, 150 Prob 38, 43 Aet 16, 147

προσυπογράφω Det 100 Fug 211 Mut 80

προσυποδείκνυμι Opif 52

προσυπομένω Flacc 96

προσυφαίνω Her 266 Congr 122

προσφέρω (97) Opif 163, 165, 165 Leg 2:58, 69 Leg 3:81, 81, 82, 173 Cher 84 Sacr 26, 35, 41, 76, 98, 111, 123 Deus 6, 7 Agr 66, 127 Plant 147, 160, 162 Ebr 2, 69, 118, 123, 151, 161, 221 Conf 124 Migr 142 Her 174, 302 Congr 103, 169 Somn 1:51 Somn 2:50, 71, 77, 114, 295 Ios 33, 40, 47, 51, 91, 199 Mos 1:10, 14, 65, 125, 204, 208 Mos 2:24, 106 Decal 13, 160 Spec 1:47, 119, 179, 185, 215, 215, 220, 249, 289 Spec 2:83, 122, 135, 179, 182, 182, 215 Spec 3:9, 80, 98, 139 Spec 4:64, 123, 219 Virt 105 Prob 91, 96 Contempl 34 Aet 98 Flacc 4 Legat 62, 125, 275, 362 Hypoth 7:7 Prov 2:17 QG 1:60:2, 60:2, 62:1

προσφεύγω Det 62 Abr 116 Legat 328 Hypoth 7:9

προσφιλοκαλέω Her 158

προσφιλοτεχνέω Aet 113

προσφιλοτιμέομαι Migr 98

προσφορά Virt 130

πρόσφορος (8) Leg 1:28 Gig 7 Fug 160 Mut 230 Somn 1:68 Ios 206 Mos 2:76 Prov 2:18

προσφυής (21) Opif 165 Leg 3:111, 132, 161, 233 Post 103 Agr 101 Plant 82 Her 47 Congr 57 Fug 168, 196 Mut 101 Somn 1:103, 141 Ios 61 Spec 1:195, 297 Praem 84, 111 Aet 54

πρόσφυξ (7) Sacr 120 Plant 63 Ebr 94 Her 124 Fug 56 Somn 2:273 Spec 2:118

πρόσφυσις Spec 1:150 Aet 133

προσφύω (7) Mos 2:8 Spec 1:80 Spec 4:132 Virt 26 Prob 66 Contempl 63 Aet 132

προσχάσκω Virt 90 Legat 105

προσχέω Her 182 Spec 1:205, 231 Spec 4:125 QG 1:62:1

πρόσχημα Ios 85 Flacc 20

προσχράομαι (9) Leg 3:96 Sacr 36, 100 Her 216 Abr 159 Decal 18 Spec 1:21 Spec 4:163 Praem 26

προσχωρέω Leg 3:148 Gig 66 Her 310

πρόσω (16) Opif 122 Leg 1:4 Det 89 Deus 149 Agr 122 Plant 80 Ebr 189 Conf 139 Fug 122 Somn 1:26, 248 Mos 1:25, 177, 257 Spec 1:72 Flacc 186

προσωπεῖον Mut 198 Flacc 20 Legat 111

πρόσωπον (115) Opif 131, 134, 139 Leg 1:12, 28, 28, 31, 33, 39, 39, 39 Leg 2:66 Leg 3:1, 12, 161, 169, 217, 251 Cher 12, 49, 54 Sacr 77, 77, 79 Det 4, 80, 150, 150, 156, 156, 163, 163 Post 1, 2, 3, 7, 8, 12, 22, 67, 110, 111, 127, 127, 127, 167, 169 Deus 20, 23, 50, 51, 109 Agr 51, 75, 114 Plant 19, 63 Ebr 84, 174 Conf 1, 1, 1, 168 Migr 174 Her 56, 251, 262, 262, 279 Congr 124 Fug 1, 1, 2, 58, 137, 141, 165, 178, 181, 182, 182, 211 Mut 9, 13, 39, 54, 56, 134, 154, 169 Somn 1:34, 145, 235 Somn 2:221 Ios 32 Mos 2:188, 188 Spec 1:226, 226, 245 Spec 2:49 Spec 3:85 Spec 4:39, 123, 177 Contempl 50, 77 QG 1:3, 2:15a, 15a, 59, 3:29 QE isf 3, 3, 3

πρότασις Plant 143 Her 63, 306 QG 2:54a

προτείνω (46) Opif 165 Leg 3:105, 134 Post 7 Agr 98 Plant 36, 75, 103, 142, 176 Conf 114 Migr 27, 124 Her 103, 185 Fug 7, 39, 66, 106, 166 Mut 59, 173, 218 Somn 1:71, 97, 143, 176 Somn 2:249 Abr 144 Mos 1:244, 268 Mos 2:33, 33 Spec 1:235 Spec 3:56, 62 Virt 178 Praem 52 Contempl 75 Flacc 121 Legat 30, 95, 276 Prov 2:21 QG 4:191d QE isf 32

προτείχισμα Post 50

προτέλεια Deus 148 Congr 5 Abr 89

προτεμένισμα Cher 100 Legat 150

προτεραῖος Mos 2:269 Spec 1:222

προτέρω QG 4:144

προτίθημι (48) Opif 50 Cher 56 Sacr 82 Post 131 Gig 53 Deus 67 Agr 2, 112, 121 Plant 38, 50 Ebr 195 Sobr 26 Conf 48 Migr 153 Her 175 Congr 168 Fug 29, 33, 40 Mut 269 Somn 1:230 Somn 2:11, 66, 250 Ios 43 Mos 1:24, 295, 313 Mos 2:9, 160 Spec 1:132, 172, 320, 323 Spec 3:51, 115 Spec 4:72, 121, 142 Virt 175, 205 Praem 3, 16, 67 Prob 86, 88 Legat 147

προτιμάω (16) Opif 170 Sacr 71 Det 95 Agr 41 Conf 79 Migr 61 Congr 68 Fug 152 Mut 104 Spec 3:47, 51, 153 Spec 4:10 Virt 170 Prob 69 Contempl 16

πρότιμος Spec 3:69

προτρεπτικός (9) Leg 1:83 Det 11 Agr 78, 172 Fug 142, 170 Mut 42, 236 Virt 47

προτρέπω (42) Leg 1:93, 96, 97, 101 Sacr 76 Det 1, 15 Post 102, 122 Gig 32 Sobr 15 Conf 110, 110 Migr 25, 26 Her 11, 123 Fug 97, 171 Abr 4 Ios 217, 251 Mos 1:50, 71, 177, 252, 258 Mos 2:31, 51, 183 Decal 100 Spec 1:3, 316 Spec 2:18, 61, 252 Spec 3:24 Spec 4:134 Virt 83, 175 Prob 126 Flacc 33

προτροπάδην Mos 1:175 Praem 94, 148

προτροπή (8) Leg 1:92 Agr 91 Conf 140 Mos 1:154 Spec 2:163 Spec 4:75 Praem 4 Prob 133

προτυπόω Opif 2 Leg 2:13 Conf 176

προϋπαντάω Fug 141 Somn 1:119 Abr 79 Decal 35 Flacc 107

προϋπαντιάζω Abr 150

προϋπάρχω (8) Opif 130 Leg 1:22 Mut 211 Ios 46 Mos 1:309 Spec 1:283, 284 QE isf 14

προΰπειμι Deus 66

προϋπεργάζομαι Sacr 36 Mos 1:85

προϋποδείκνυμι Leg 3:95 Her 50

προϋπόκειμαι (6) Leg 1:29 Her 116 Mos 1:211 Praem 9 Aet 18, 20

προϋπολαμβάνω Spec 4:159

προϋποτυπόομαι (προϋποτυπόω) Her 146 Congr 83

προφαίνω (20) Opif 58 Sacr 30 Det 31, 154 Post 58 Plant 12, 93 Ebr 182 Conf 84 Mut 15 Somn 1:11, 83, 190 Mos 1:176 Mos 2:78, 83, 90, 144 Flacc 177 Legat 12

προφανής Det 1 Somn 2:246

προφασίζομαι (7) Mos 1:268 Spec 3:158 Flacc 130 Legat 23, 257 Hypoth 11:6 Prov 2:34

πρόφασις (47) Opif 155 Cher 38, 116 Agr 145 Ebr 121 Mut 62, 64 Somn 1:128 Abr 126 Ios 7, 14, 50, 130, 179, 200, 233 Mos 1:17, 88, 135, 330 Mos 2:13, 228, 248 Spec 1:115, 120, 143, 151 Spec 2:13 Spec 3:30, 80, 94, 119, 172 Spec 4:24, 200 Virt 126, 135 Prob 11, 102 Contempl 66 Flacc 4, 139 Legat 58, 260, 265, 301, 340

προφασιστικός Prob 19

προφέρω (45) Leg 1:76 Leg 3:36 Det 58 Post 141, 141 Agr 168 Plant 103 Sobr 6 Migr 121 Her 10, 21 Congr 13, 150 Fug 193, 203 Mut 60 Somn 1:91 Abr 57, 60 Ios 52, 197, 217 Mos 1:79 Mos 2:131, 207 Decal 63, 93 Spec 1:232, 241, 279 Spec 2:141, 181, 187 Spec 4:49, 54, 74 Virt 89, 140, 169 Praem 87 Prob 136 Legat 13, 43, 51, 104

προφητεία (20) Her 259 Congr 112, 132 Mut 126, 203 Abr 98 Mos 2:2, 6, 6, 187, 187, 191, 258, 265 Spec 1:315 Spec 4:48, 51, 52 Praem 53, 55

προφητεύω (16) Migr 114, 169 Her 260, 261 Ios 95 Mos 1:175, 283 Mos 2:37, 69, 291 Spec 1:65, 219 Spec 2:104, 189, 256 Praem 56

προφήτης (94) Leg 2:1 Leg 3:103, 173 Cher 17, 49 Sacr 130 Det 39, 40 Gig 49, 56, 61 Deus 136, 138, 138, 139 Agr 50 Plant 138 Ebr 143 Migr 15, 38, 84, 84, 151, 169 Her 4, 78, 258, 258, 259, 260, 262, 262, 262, 266 Congr 170 Fug 140 Mut 11 Somn 2:172, 277 Abr 113 Mos 1:57, 156, 266 Mos 2:3, 40, 76, 187, 188, 190, 191, 192, 209, 213, 246, 250, 257, 262, 269, 275, 278, 280, 284, 292 Decal 18, 19, 175 Spec 1:65, 65, 315, 315, 345 Spec 3:7, 125 Spec 4:49, 192, 192 Virt 51, 119, 218 Praem 1, 2, 55, 123, 158 Contempl 25, 64, 87 Legat 99 QG 1:24, 28, 2:26b QE 2:16, 46, 49b

προφητικός (18) Leg 3:43 Gig 57 Plant 117 Sobr 68 Conf 44 Migr 84 Her 69, 249, 265, 290 Fug 147, 186, 197 Mut 110, 120, 139, 169 Mos 1:277

προφῆτις Somn 1:254 Contempl 87

προφητοτόκος Somn 1:254

προφορά (19) Leg 1:37 Det 133 Post 36, 100 Gig 52 Deus 72 Ebr 70 Conf 11 Migr 2, 12, 71, 71, 78, 117 Fug 92 Mut 188 Mos 2:127 Spec 1:147 QG 1:32

προφορικός (17) Det 39, 66, 92, 126 Conf 52 Migr 78 Fug 90, 92, 191 Mut 69 Abr 29, 83 Mos 2:127, 129, 129 Spec 4:69, 69

προφυλακή (6) Deus 72 Mos 2:145 Decal 98 Spec 3:166 Spec 4:104, 196

προφυλάσσω Cher 34 Spec 3:103 Virt 157

πρόχειρος (25) Sacr 35, 60 Det 47, 155 Post 1 Deus 96, 133 Agr 3 Plant 53, 70 Ebr 65 Sobr 33 Conf 14, 48, 143, 190 Somn 1:127 Ios 55 Decal 69 Spec 1:225 Aet 95 Flacc 2, 34 Legat 362 Hypoth 7:14

προχέω (11) Opif 63, 123 Sacr 64 Post 139, 151 Somn 1:96 Abr 159 Ios 175 Mos 1:200 QG 1:62:2 QE 2:118

πρόχυσις Opif 123

πρόωρος Spec 3:90

προωφελέω Sacr 115

πρύμνα Opif 88 Spec 4:154 Praem 51 Legat 50

πρυτανεῖον Opif 17

πρυτανεύω (18) Opif 11 Conf 170 Somn 2:291 Abr 25, 78, 78 Ios 152, 270 Mos 1:149 Spec 1:14, 207 Spec 2:45, 231 Spec 3:131 Spec 4:169 Virt 195 Legat 48, 336

πρύτανις Somn 2:187 Decal 178 Flacc 126

πρώην Mut 61 Somn 2:123 Spec 2:19 Spec 3:159 Prob 141

πρωΐ Leg 3:169 Her 174, 199 QE 2:15:1

πρωΐα (10) Opif 34, 34, 35 Somn 2:257 Mos 2:259 Spec 1:256, 296 Praem 151 Contempl 89 Flacc 167

πρῴρα Cher 38

Πρωταγόρας Post 35

πρωτεῖον (20) Leg 3:224 Det 29 Deus 12 Agr 111, 113, 120 Plant 27 Somn 2:114 Abr 40 Ios 131 Mos 2:3, 174 Decal 50, 110 Spec 1:22 Flacc 12, 17, 137 Legat 75, 144

Πρωτεύς Ebr 36 Legat 80

πρώτιστος (6) Leg 2:48, 86 Post 63 Ebr 31 Spec 1:332 Aet 17

πρωτογένειος Cher 114 Contempl 52 Hypoth 11:3

πρωτογενής Her 117, 118 QE isf 22

πρωτογέννημα (10) Sacr 52, 72, 76, 87 Decal 160 Spec 1:183 Spec 2:179, 179, 181 QG 1:60:2

πρωτόγονος (6) Post 63 Agr 51 Conf 63, 146 Fug 208 Somn 1:215

πρωτόπλαστος QG 1:32 QE 2:46

πρῶτος (1140) Opif 6, 13, 14, 15, 15, 17, 19, 26, 27, 27, 29, 35, 36, 37, 40, 41, 41, 42, 45, 46, 47, 49, 49, 51, 65, 66, 68, 68, 78, 79, 79, 83, 83, 88, 95, 95, 96, 101, 102, 102, 102, 103, 104, 108, 109, 109, 109, 110, 110, 131, 133, 134, 136, 136, 138, 140, 140, 142, 145, 148, 148, 148, 151, 154, 156, 157, 159, 159, 161, 161, 165, 167, 168, 170 Leg 1:3, 5, 10, 15, 17, 34, 59, 70, 71, 71, 71, 71, 90, 90, 102 Leg 2:5, 5, 6, 9, 12, 12, 14, 15, 15, 15, 15, 36, 37, 40, 73, 74, 80, 93 Leg 3:18, 49, 54, 55, 77, 79, 80, 92, 94, 94, 94, 95, 97, 102, 118, 120, 121, 123, 128, 140, 146, 151, 163, 179, 190, 191, 192, 192, 194, 205, 207, 207, 244, 248 Cher 1, 3, 4, 27, 36, 50, 53, 54, 55, 64, 68, 72 Sacr 2, 6, 7, 8, 11, 11, 17, 18, 25, 35, 51, 52, 52, 52, 53, 54, 55, 57, 65, 70, 72, 72, 72, 73, 73, 76, 79, 84, 87, 88, 125, 128, 130, 132, 136 Det 11, 36, 39, 66, 70, 79, 80, 81, 96, 96, 96, 122, 124, 138 Post 47, 62, 65, 65, 79, 79, 91, 93, 94, 94, 101, 103, 120, 145, 149, 154, 170, 173, 174, 176, 178, 179, 183 Gig 7, 13, 30 Deus 6, 8, 16, 35, 39, 44, 49, 54, 78, 84, 86, 86, 87, 90, 91, 104, 106, 139, 160, 160 Agr 8, 49, 59, 98, 108, 121, 138, 151, 151, 152, 156, 157, 161, 165, 175, 178, 181 Plant 1, 2, 34, 35, 49, 73, 76, 94, 114, 125, 148, 150, 150, 156, 161, 162, 163, 172, 176 Ebr 11, 11, 15, 15, 19, 34, 35, 35, 42, 48, 48, 48, 49, 50, 61, 82, 150, 150, 152, 153, 163, 171, 201, 205 Sobr 1, 22, 22, 25, 26, 29, 30, 36, 66 Conf 23, 30, 44, 59, 61, 64, 78, 98, 109, 123, 147, 156, 168, 170, 176, 183 Migr 2, 38, 38, 46, 53, 70, 75, 87, 101, 106, 118, 157, 176, 177, 181, 194, 194, 194, 211 Her 10, 71, 102, 103, 115, 118, 134, 161, 166, 168, 169, 207, 226, 226, 250, 267, 294, 295, 299, 299 Congr 9, 14, 19, 20, 29, 30, 40, 53, 73, 74, 90, 98, 144, 161 Fug 2, 6, 8, 36, 36, 38, 38, 66, 71, 73, 74, 88, 91, 94, 99, 130, 148, 148, 153, 169, 199 Mut 26, 66, 70, 71, 78, 78, 83, 106, 116, 120, 145, 175, 177, 192, 194, 215, 218, 233, 251, 257, 270 Somn 1:1, 2, 6, 10, 40, 66, 75, 76, 85, 91, 103, 106, 129, 132, 134, 171, 181, 181, 182, 193, 205, 212, 214, 218, 241 Somn 2:2, 3, 4, 6, 6, 7, 17, 30, 42, 52, 65, 69, 76, 114, 139, 159, 159, 166, 197, 217, 237, 257, 299 Abr 1, 2, 3, 5, 7, 12, 13, 38, 42, 47, 48, 50, 52, 56, 60, 61, 61, 65, 67, 67, 70, 72, 75, 75, 77, 78, 79, 82, 84, 87, 88, 105, 113, 114, 115, 118, 123, 128, 156, 192, 193, 206, 218, 228, 234, 251, 255, 270, 271, 272, 273, 274, 276 Ios 1, 8, 23, 36, 38, 48, 54, 89, 90, 92, 98, 101, 109, 109, 109, 123, 129, 138, 141, 158, 158, 162, 166, 175, 187, 187, 189, 189, 190, 194, 195, 197, 201, 210, 212, 213, 215, 216, 223, 232, 237, 242, 244, 245, 246, 249, 250 Mos 1:7, 17, 19, 19, 26, 34, 42, 49, 55, 57, 58, 73, 75, 76, 79, 86, 90, 92, 98, 98, 110, 114, 119, 123, 130, 134, 135, 135, 141, 142, 162, 164, 169, 181, 185, 195, 200, 205, 211, 211, 215, 230, 230, 231, 238, 240, 250, 251, 255, 258, 259, 261, 269, 275, 279, 281, 287, 293, 294, 301, 304, 330 Mos 2:1, 5, 8, 37, 41, 46, 46, 49, 50, 62, 66, 68, 69, 69, 71, 71, 115, 122, 143, 146, 153, 153, 166, 182, 184, 186, 186, 187, 188, 189, 191, 192, 205, 210, 218, 221, 222, 228, 231, 240, 243, 245, 257, 258, 260, 263, 264, 264, 266, 271, 273 Decal 1, 2, 9, 12, 20, 21, 23, 28, 50, 52, 58, 59, 65, 80, 81, 95, 98, 103, 106, 110, 122, 131, 137, 138, 140, 155, 168, 168, 173 Spec 1:1, 6, 12, 32, 38, 69, 74, 85, 96, 99, 101, 105, 126, 132, 138, 147, 152, 157, 157, 168, 178, 178, 181, 181, 183, 186, 193, 195, 198, 203, 211, 217, 225, 231, 234, 237, 241, 242, 249, 253, 263, 274, 276, 277, 289, 307, 311, 314, 326, 341 Spec 2:2, 17, 21, 37, 40, 40, 40, 41, 41, 86, 88, 111, 123, 132, 133, 133, 133, 135, 137, 140, 142, 150, 150, 152, 152, 153, 153, 153, 154, 154, 157, 157, 157, 162, 166, 168, 171, 176, 179, 179, 181, 181, 195, 199, 212, 224, 224, 228, 233, 239, 242, 250, 251, 261 Spec 3:3, 4, 7, 8, 16, 18, 29, 30, 37, 43, 63, 70, 79, 80, 85, 100, 114, 124, 129, 143, 159, 162, 180, 185, 192, 199, 200 Spec 4:1, 5, 13, 16, 28, 29, 35, 39, 53, 56, 59, 60, 60, 68, 73, 82, 112, 123, 127, 129, 135, 136, 137, 149, 154, 160, 175, 186, 189, 196, 203, 208 Virt 1, 6, 16, 22, 26, 38, 44, 52, 52, 55, 59, 66, 67, 77, 101, 113, 120, 123, 129, 130, 134, 141, 145, 148, 160, 169, 172, 176, 178, 179, 180, 187, 199, 199, 199, 203, 207, 215, 216, 216, 222, 222, 223 Praem 3, 7, 9, 10, 20, 21, 25, 27, 35, 58, 61, 68, 68, 68, 68, 74, 77, 79, 79, 85, 88, 89, 98, 102, 111, 125, 127, 145, 146, 149, 153, 158, 162, 163 Prob 1, 15, 15, 15, 18, 62, 63, 73, 76, 85, 94, 112, 118, 122, 160 Contempl 38, 63, 65, 67, 75, 75, 83 Aet 3, 4, 4, 7, 15, 19, 19, 20, 22, 26, 40, 43, 58, 60, 61, 65, 66, 68, 88, 94, 100, 114, 118, 125, 147, 148, 149 Flacc 3, 8, 10, 15, 24, 28, 32, 54, 55, 64, 76, 79, 85, 87, 89, 104, 149, 158, 182, 187 Legat 5, 13, 20, 30, 31, 32, 32, 54, 60, 66, 73, 78, 87, 94, 114, 115, 119, 138, 143, 149, 166, 167, 176, 180, 181, 198, 199, 203, 208, 210, 213, 219, 223, 224, 227, 231, 232, 232, 258, 261, 269, 270, 286, 288, 289, 289, 307, 309, 311, 340, 350, 354, 356, 357, 364 Hypoth 0:1, 0:1, 7:20, 11:16 Prov 2:10, 35, 54, 59 QG 1:20, 20, 20, 20, 21, 55a, 60:1,

64b, 64b, 66, 76b, 2:11, 11, 12b, 13a, 17c, 17c, 26a, 29, 31, 31, 34a, 39, 54a, 54a, 66, 66, 71a, 3:12, 18, 49a, 61, 4:110a, 130, 174 QG isf 5, 10 QG (Par) 2:2, 2:3, 2:7, 2:7 QE 2:21, 24:1, 25b, 46, 105 QE isf 3, 5, 6, 14

πρωτοστατέω Mos 1:178 Spec 2:124, 134

πρωτοστάτης Mos 1:257

πρωτοτοκεύω Leg 2:48 Sacr 19 Sobr 21

πρωτοτόκια (14) Leg 2:47 Leg 3:190, 191, 192, 195 Sacr 18, 19, 120 Sobr 21, 25, 26 QG 4:173, 173, 174

πρωτότοκος (45) Leg 2:48, 48 Leg 3:74 Cher 54 Sacr 19, 19, 19, 88, 89, 118, 118, 118, 118, 118, 119, 126, 134, 134, 134, 134, 136 Sobr 21, 21, 21, 22 Conf 124 Her 117, 124 Congr 98 Somn 1:202 Somn 2:266 Mos 1:134, 145 Spec 1:135, 138, 139, 248 Spec 2:134 Virt 95 QG 1:60:1, 60:2, 4:206a QE isf 22, 22, 22

πταῖσμα Congr 28 Ios 150 Spec 2:71 Spec 3:27 Prov 2:4

πταίω (8) Leg 3:16, 66, 149 Deus 134 Ios 144 Mos 1:306 Spec 4:18, 70

πτέρνα (10) Leg 2:94, 99 Leg 3:65, 188, 188, 190 Agr 94, 106, 107, 107

πτερνίζω (12) Leg 2:99, 99 Leg 3:190, 190, 190, 191 Sacr 42, 135 Migr 200 Her 252 Somn 1:171 QG 4:163:1

πτερνιστής (10) Leg 1:61 Leg 2:89, 99 Leg 3:15, 93, 180 Mut 81, 81 QG 4:163:1, 163:2

πτερόν (7) Cher 25 Mut 179, 179 Somn 1:139 Spec 1:62 Aet 49 Legat 99

πτεροφορέω QE 2:40

πτεροφυέω QE 2:65

πτερόω Det 152 Plant 22 Her 237 Spec 1:207 Aet 63

πτέρυξ Ebr 182 Spec 4:110

πτερύσσομαι Mut 158 Abr 223 Mos 1:26 Praem 62

πτέρωσις Her 238

πτηνός (56) Opif 63, 66, 68, 70, 147 Leg 2:11, 11 Cher 20, 47, 111 Sacr 66 Det 152 Plant 12, 14, 145 Ebr 136 Conf 6, 24 Her 126, 132, 139, 230, 238, 240, 301 Mut 120, 178, 235, 245, 247, 247, 248, 250 Somn 2:212, 213, 288, 294 Abr 264 Mos 1:130, 192, 218 Mos 2:60, 97, 98 Decal 79, 115 Spec 1:162 Spec 3:8 Spec 4:100, 116, 118 Praem 8, 62, 80 Legat 99, 139

πτῆσις Mos 1:209 Spec 4:128

πτίσσω Prob 109

πτοέω (7) Sacr 32 Somn 2:165 Abr 149 Ios 51 Legat 187, 263 Prov 2:25

πτόησις Her 251

πτοία Det 110 Congr 81 Decal 145 Spec 2:189 Praem 148

Πτολεμαῖος (6) Ios 136 Mos 2:29, 30, 30 Prob 125 Legat 140

πτύω Leg 2:66

πτῶμα (14) Leg 2:101, 101 Deus 130 Agr 110, 171 Ebr 156 Migr 80 Mut 55, 57 Somn 1:49 Somn 2:281 Abr 266 Ios 17 Legat 308

πτῶσις Deus 141

πτωχός Hypoth 7:6

πύγαργος Spec 4:105

πυγμή Cher 80 Spec 2:246

Πυθαγόρειος (7) Opif 100 Leg 1:15 Prob 2 Aet 12 QG 1:17b, 2:12a, 4:8b

Πυθαγορικός QG 3:49a

πυθμήν (9) Somn 2:159, 195, 195, 197, 199, 218 Ios 91, 102, 102

πυθόχρηστος Prob 19, 160

πυκνός (7) Somn 1:22 Mos 1:176 Spec 1:50 Virt 43 Aet 103, 105 Flacc 2

πυκνότης (8) Leg 3:115 Ebr 185 Somn 1:20 Somn 2:58 Mos 1:123 Spec 2:8 Spec 4:212 Prob 26

πυκνόω Conf 102 Her 188 Aet 110

πύκνωσις QG 2:64c

πυκτεύω Agr 113 Congr 46

πύκτης Spec 3:174 Prob 146

πύλη (9) Ebr 14 Somn 1:186, 188, 188, 188 Mos 2:214 Spec 4:142, 142 Flacc 122

πυλών Leg 3:40 Fug 183, 183

πυλωρός Fug 145 Abr 15 Spec 1:31, 156 Praem 74

πυνθάνομαι (81) Leg 2:89 Leg 3:53, 59, 59, 66, 66, 88, 173 Sacr 4, 64 Det 24, 25, 30, 57, 57, 57, 58, 58 Post 90 Gig 33 Deus 60, 92 Agr 57, 59, 179 Plant 127 Ebr 120 Migr 196, 213 Her 2, 15, 15, 18, 28, 33, 65, 100 Fug 133, 135, 138, 203 Mut 91, 116, 119 Somn 1:192, 231 Abr 92, 206, 230 Ios 89, 199, 221, 223, 233, 257 Mos 1:16, 74, 200, 274, 274, 277 Mos 2:190, 192, 217 Spec 3:145, 173 Praem 84 Prob 101, 123 Aet 4, 39 Flacc 112, 140 Legat 31, 217, 225, 233, 271, 310, 311 Prov 2:64

πύξ Spec 3:105

πῦρ (237) Opif 146 Leg 1:5, 91 Leg 3:225, 225, 225, 229, 234, 248, 248, 248, 249 Cher 31 Sacr 80, 80 Det 8, 154 Post 158 Gig 7, 25 Deus 60, 79, 107, 153 Agr 36, 51 Plant 3, 3, 4, 6, 10, 10, 12, 108, 120 Ebr 133, 134, 190 Sobr 43 Conf 1, 84, 156 Migr 91, 99, 99, 120, 165 Her 134, 135, 136, 146, 146, 197, 198, 226, 251, 251, 281, 282, 308, 308, 309, 310, 311, 312 Congr 55, 117 Fug 110, 132, 133 Somn 1:21, 22, 23, 85 Somn 2:50, 125, 212 Abr 1, 138, 140, 157, 171, 173 Ios 78, 160 Mos 1:65, 65, 65, 66, 67, 68, 70, 70, 96, 97, 119, 124, 143 Mos 2:53, 55, 56, 58, 88, 88, 106, 133, 148, 154, 155, 158, 158, 219, 219, 219, 220, 220, 254, 263, 286, 287 Decal 31, 33, 44, 46, 48, 48, 49, 53, 54, 122 Spec 1:97, 199, 223, 245, 254, 262, 267, 285, 286, 290 Spec 2:65, 65, 183, 215, 251, 251, 255 Spec 4:26, 26, 27, 28, 29, 29, 56, 83, 118, 125, 223 Virt 9, 135, 162 Praem 38, 153 Prob 96, 101, 108, 119 Contempl 3, 3 Aet 8, 20, 25, 29, 33, 33, 33, 33, 45, 54, 61, 85, 85, 85, 86, 86, 87, 87, 89, 89, 90, 93, 94, 99, 102, 103, 105, 105, 107, 107, 110, 110, 115, 115, 115, 123, 127, 135, 135, 136, 136, 136, 137, 146, 147, 148, 148 Flacc 67, 67, 68, 84 Legat 125, 125, 126, 126, 130, 130, 132, 132 Hypoth 7:6 Prov 2:40, 49, 49 QG 4:51b, 51c, 172 QE 2:28, 46

πυρά Conf 157 Migr 123 Abr 182, 182

πυραμίς Opif 50 QG (Par) 2:5

πυραμοειδής Opif 50

πύργος (21) Post 53 Conf 1, 1, 1, 5, 83, 107, 113, 115, 128, 130, 133, 134, 142, 142, 155, 155, 158, 196 Somn 2:284 Spec 4:229

πυρεῖον Somn 2:186 Spec 1:72

πυρετός Opif 125 Sobr 45, 45 Praem 143 Legat 125

πυρίγονος Gig 7 Plant 12 Aet 45

πυρκαϊά Leg 3:234

πυρόεις Her 224

πυροπωλέω Ios 178

πυρός (15) Sacr 109 Agr 9 Conf 185 Somn 2:23 Ios 102, 260 Mos 2:223 Spec 1:248 Spec 2:179, 186 Spec 3:32 Spec 4:29, 214 Aet 63, 98

πυροφόρος Mos 1:228 Flacc 63

πυρόω (18) Leg 1:67, 77, 84 Leg 2:67 Sacr 87 Post 158, 159 Ebr 147 Conf 101 Migr 210 Her 64 Fug 134 Somn 1:31 Mos 2:280 Spec 1:58 Spec 3:126 Aet 102 Prov 2:17

πυρπολέω Ebr 27 Decal 63 Legat 197

πυρρίζω Det 16

πυρρός Spec 1:268 QG 4:171

πυρσεία Prov 2:49

πυρφόρος Mos 1:179 Mos 2:157 Spec 4:28

πυρώδης Opif 161 Cher 30 Mos 1:114 Aet 135

πυρωπός Ebr 173 Spec 3:193

πύσμα Leg 3:60 Det 58 Agr 140 Congr 149 Fug 206

πύστις Flacc 120, 154

πω (16) Opif 154 Leg 2:64 Leg 3:15 Congr 6, 9 Mut 252 Ios 158, 165, 167, 193 Mos 1:165, 200 Virt 137 Praem 62 Prob 160 Legat 30

πωλέω (6) Cher 122 Gig 39 Ios 162 Spec 2:199 Prob 100 Hypoth 7:2

πωλητήρ Cher 123

πωλοδάμνης Agr 71

πῶλος Spec 3:47

πῶμα Mos 2:95

πώποτε (15) Sacr 25 Post 118 Congr 152 Somn 1:24 Abr 192 Mos 1:152 Mos 2:29, 192 Spec 3:124 Praem 150 Prob 117 Legat 11, 224, 309 Prov 2:21

πῶς (210) Opif 68, 125 Leg 1:14, 28, 38, 61, 83, 83, 83, 91, 103, 104, 104 Leg 2:5, 7, 7, 7, 7, 7, 7, 17, 19, 25, 26, 69, 69, 79, 89 Leg 3:3, 4, 10, 97, 112, 131, 151, 153, 198, 221, 236 Cher 33, 65, 70 Sacr 89 Det 13, 48, 86, 87, 88, 90, 135, 148, 149, 155, 167 Post 8, 17, 93, 95, 132, 164 Gig 3, 32, 39, 56 Deus 11 Agr 22, 64, 90, 117, 176 Plant 4, 7, 84 Ebr 32, 130, 190, 199 Sobr 6 Conf 5, 40, 41, 53, 65, 183 Migr 46, 75, 80, 84, 137, 137, 137, 140 Her 71, 77, 88, 121, 146, 222, 278, 278 Congr 150 Fug 22, 46, 51, 141 Mut 67, 157, 192, 243 Somn 1:54, 55, 55, 55, 173, 199, 207 Somn 2:220, 268 Abr 116, 116, 150, 152, 195 Ios 11, 63, 111, 171, 199, 215, 226, 227, 232 Mos 1:164 Mos 2:5, 16, 43, 239, 261 Decal 35, 60, 66, 85, 101, 112, 157, 177 Spec 1:33, 90, 90, 252, 263, 273, 281 Spec 2:89, 135, 167, 237 Spec 3:35, 85, 97, 106, 111, 208, 209 Spec 4:6, 162, 204 Virt 24, 32, 56, 64, 138 Praem 21, 36, 44, 71, 146, 146 Prob 6, 8, 36, 63 Contempl 6, 50 Aet 49, 67, 73, 105, 107 Flacc 21, 28, 80 Legat 98, 103, 106, 123, 155, 174, 196, 199, 240, 246, 319, 330, 360 Hypoth 6:8 QG 2:39, 54a, 4:52d, 184

P

ρ QG 2:29, 30

ῥάβδος (26) Leg 2:88, 88, 89, 89, 90, 90, 92 Sacr 63 Det 177 Post 95, 96, 97 Plant 110, 153 Migr 85, 85 Congr 94, 95 Fug 150 Mut 135 Mos 1:77, 103, 120 Mos 2:178, 179 Flacc 38

Ῥαγουήλ Mut 103, 105, 114

ῥᾴδιος (94) Opif 66, 86, 166 Leg 2:39 Leg 3:105, 131 Cher 36, 78 Det 14, 49, 95, 110, 144, 151 Post 2 Gig 47 Deus 93 Agr 76, 86 Plant 123 Ebr 134, 150, 165, 173, 192 Conf 14, 89, 183 Migr 220 Her 92 Congr 152 Fug 50 Mut 119, 212, 218, 241, 251 Somn 1:6, 75, 223 Somn 2:131, 197 Abr 5, 59, 73, 185, 240 Ios 252 Mos 1:128, 147, 230, 250 Mos 2:249 Decal 77, 125 Spec 1:28, 43, 105, 230, 299, 325 Spec 2:3, 25, 87 Spec 3:94, 107, 130 Spec 4:50, 52, 88, 109, 112, 124, 185, 215 Virt 34, 47, 54, 80, 193, 196, 196, 205 Praem 6, 91, 117 Prob 8 Aet 58, 97, 102 Legat 250, 368 Hypoth 7:14, 7:15

ῥᾳδιουργέω Hypoth 7:14

ῥᾳδιουργία Cher 80

ῥᾳδιουργός Sacr 32 Det 165 Post 43 Conf 152 Somn 2:148

ῥᾳθυμέω Migr 133 Spec 1:128 Spec 2:240

ῥᾳθυμία (19) Deus 152, 164 Agr 39, 149 Ebr 21 Fug 122 Somn 1:8 Spec 2:6, 60, 99 Spec 3:147, 167 Praem 12 Prob 71, 103 Aet 11, 16 Prov 2:58 QG isf 3

ῥᾴθυμος (7) Sacr 113 Agr 34, 66 Migr 89 Somn 2:114 Aet 146 Prov 2:60

ῥάκιον Somn 1:96

Ῥαμεσσή Post 54, 56 Somn 1:77

ῥανίς Prov 2:46

ῥαντός (7) Somn 1:189, 200, 209, 213, 216, 219 Somn 2:19

ῥᾳστώνη (10) Sacr 29, 35, 37 Agr 103 Migr 211 Mut 170, 170 Mos 2:21 Spec 2:67 Hypoth 7:17

Ῥαχήλ (21) Leg 2:46, 47, 94 Leg 3:20, 146, 180, 180 Det 3 Post 135, 179, 179 Ebr 54 Sobr 12 Her 51, 175 Congr 25, 26, 31, 32 Mut 96 Somn 2:16

ῥαψῳδέω Migr 111

ῥαψῳδία Contempl 17

Ῥεβέκκα (29) Leg 3:88 Cher 41, 47 Sacr 4 Det 30, 45 Post 62, 132, 133, 136, 137, 146 Plant 169, 169 Migr 208 Congr 37, 129 Fug 23, 24, 44, 45, 49, 51, 194 Somn 1:46 QG 4:97:1, 97:2, 131, 166

ῥεῖα Aet 37

ῥεῖθρον (9) Opif 80, 133 Sacr 66 Abr 43 Mos 1:101, 115, 212 Mos 2:63 Virt 6

ῥεμβεύω QE 2:13a

ῥέπω Opif 155 Migr 13 Mos 2:248 Praem 63

ῥεῦμα (28) Leg 1:28, 64 Sacr 66 Det 117, 174 Post 112, 163, 164 Deus 178, 181 Plant 24, 162 Sobr 3 Conf 23, 33 Her 32 Mut 107 Somn 2:13, 275, 302 Ios 130, 141 Mos 1:121 Praem 73, 145 Aet 147 Prov 2:38 QE 2:13a ῥέω (61) Opif 52, 144 Sacr 61, 82 Det 92 Post 163 Gig 22 Deus 176 Agr 53, 133 Ebr 12, 191 Sobr 53 Conf 29, 103, 103 Congr 159 Fug 25, 137, 190, 191 Mut 138, 214, 239 Somn 2:12, 34, 109, 238, 245, 278 Ios 227, 249, 268 Mos 1:84, 114 Mos 2:56, 127 Decal 25, 46, 150, 153, 173 Spec 1:27, 147, 192 Spec 2:20, 55 Spec 4:27, 84 Virt 10 Praem 38, 73, 168 Prob 139 Contempl 39 Aet 88, 125 Flacc 87 Legat 228, 243 Prov 2:12

Ῥήγιον Aet 139

ῥήγνυμι (21) Cher 35 Sacr 30 Plant 157 Conf 194 Somn 2:118 Ios 42 Mos 1:177, 177 Mos 2:253, 282, 282, 286 Spec 3:78 Virt 136 Contempl 86 Aet 30 Flacc 29 Prov 2:33 QG 2:64a, 4:191b QE 2:118

ῥῆμα (67) Leg 1:10 Leg 3:120, 123, 169, 173, 173, 174, 176, 176, 203, 209, 236 Cher 42 Sacr 8, 65, 70 Post 102, 102, 102, 102 Agr 136 Conf 55, 83 Migr 12, 48, 48, 48, 49, 79, 80, 80, 122 Her 4, 72, 282, 291 Congr 53, 100, 149, 170 Fug 137, 139 Mut 63 Somn 2:96, 97, 111, 141, 238 Abr 112 Mos 1:274 Mos 2:37 Decal 47, 92, 140 Spec 3:174 Praem 23 Aet 134 Legat 6, 206, 223, 313 Hypoth 6:9, 7:2, 7:4 QG 1:17b QE 2:44 QE isf 8

Ῥῆνος Legat 10

ῥῆξις (8) Det 90 Post 116 Mos 1:118, 177 Mos 2:253 Spec 4:207 QG 2:64a, 64a

ῥῆσις (12) Leg 3:51 Det 130 Post 53 Migr 111 Her 66 Mut 169 Somn 2:268 Decal 94 Spec 4:59 Flacc 108, 139 Legat 119

ῥητέον Det 58 Mos 2:8 Spec 2:253

ῥητίνη Conf 187

ῥητορεία Det 38

ῥητορεύω Cher 93 Somn 2:272

ῥητορικός (7) Cher 105 Agr 13, 18 Congr 11, 17, 18 Somn 1:205

ῥητός (63) Opif 126 Leg 1:60 Leg 2:14, 14, 19 Leg 3:103 Det 15, 95, 139, 167 Deus 133 Agr 131, 157 Plant 113 Ebr 130 Sobr 33, 65 Conf 190 Migr 89, 93 Her 258 Congr 126 Fug 106, 136, 136, 153 Mut 15 Somn 1:48, 101, 102, 120, 164 Abr 20, 68, 88, 119, 131, 200, 217, 236 Ios 28, 60, 125 Spec 1:23, 139, 200, 287 Spec 2:29, 147, 220, 257 Spec 3:178 Praem 61, 65 Contempl 28, 78 QG 2:68a, 3:24, 4:168, 172 QG (Par) 2:5 QE 2:21, 38a

ῥήτωρ Contempl 31

ῥῖγος Congr 165 Praem 136, 143 Prov 2:23

ῥίζα (51) Opif 41, 80 Cher 102 Sacr 25, 40 Det 84, 107, 107, 108 Post 129, 163 Deus 67 Agr 6, 7, 17, 30 Plant 2, 5, 48, 120 Ebr 8, 223 Sobr 65 Migr 125 Her 34, 116, 116, 279 Congr 56, 82, 120, 146 Somn 1:144, 169 Somn 2:22, 64 Abr 138 Ios 92 Mos 1:65, 189 Spec 4:227 Virt 154, 157, 158 Praem 71, 152, 172 Prob 68, 69 Aet 96 QG 2:15a

ῥιζόω (9) Leg 1:45, 89 Plant 3, 11, 11, 45, 46, 74 Mos 2:285

ῥικνός Praem 146

ῥινηλατέω Somn 1:49 Abr 266

ῥιπή Agr 17 Somn 2:67, 125 Aet 20

ῥιπίζω Ios 124 Aet 125

ῥιπτέω Ios 12

ῥίπτω (23) Leg 2:88, 88, 102 Cher 94 Agr 82 Ebr 111 Sobr 8 Somn 2:269, 269, 276 Ios 13, 25 Mos 1:77, 91, 92, 124 Mos 2:249 Spec 2:245 Spec 3:105 Prob 115 Flacc 37 Legat 105, 326

ῥίς (11) Plant 160 Ebr 87 Conf 194 Migr 51, 188 Congr 143 Fug 182 Somn 1:27, 55 Somn 2:168 Contempl 40

ῥιψοκίνδυνος Agr 167 Decal 61

ρν QG 2:29

ῥόα ῥοιά

ῥόδον Somn 2:62 Prov 2:71

Ῥόδος Aet 120

ῥοιά (ῥόα) Plant 32

ῥοῖζος Mos 1:131 Aet 128

ῥοΐσκος (9) Mos 2:110, 119, 119, 120, 121, 133 Spec 1:93, 93, 94

ῥομφαία (9) Cher 1, 11, 20, 21, 25, 26, 28, 30, 31

ῥόος (ῥοῦς) Spec 2:241

ῥόπαλον Legat 79

ῥοπή (11) Leg 3:164 Deus 85 Fug 151 Abr 196 Ios 131, 176 Spec 4:115 Virt 86, 124 Prob 24 Flacc 165

Ῥουβήν (12) Leg 1:81 Sacr 119, 120, 120 Ebr 94 Fug 73 Mut 97, 97, 98, 101, 210 Somn 2:33

Ῥουμά Congr 43, 45, 52

ῥοῦς ῥόος

ῥοώδης Somn 2:295 Spec 3:10 Spec 4:111 Praem 121

ῥυθμικός Mos 1:23

ῥυθμός (13) Cher 105 Det 125 Agr 137 Plant 159 Sobr 36 Congr 16 Somn 1:205 Spec 1:28, 342, 343 Spec 2:230 Contempl 29 Aet 56

ῥύμη (40) Leg 3:155, 223 Sacr 49, 65, 85 Det 53, 110, 117 Post 145 Gig 34 Deus 153 Agr 68, 115, 180 Sobr 42 Conf 29, 35 Migr 26, 100 Her 16 Mut 117, 186, 214 Somn 1:107 Somn 2:247 Abr 42, 138 Mos 1:93, 284 Mos 2:154 Spec 2:232 Spec 3:79 Spec 4:45 Prob 63 Legat 65, 225 Prov 2:58 QG 2:29 QE 2:25b QE isf 25

ῥύομαι ἐρύω

ῥυπαίνω Det 20 Spec 2:92

ῥυπάω (6) Det 34 Fug 33, 153 Somn 1:148 Ios 105 Virt 92

ῥύπος Mut 48

ῥύπτω Mut 229

ῥυσιάζω Somn 1:114

ῥύσιον (6) Somn 1:95, 97, 114 Ios 185 Spec 3:204 Virt 89

ῥύσις (11) Opif 49, 49 Conf 104 Fug 188, 190 Somn 2:34, 258 Mos 2:119 Spec 1:27, 93, 118

ῥυτός Contempl 49

ῥῶ Mut 61, 61, 77

Ῥωμαϊκός Legat 116, 153, 157, 285, 287

Ῥωμαῖος (7) Opif 127 Flacc 40 Legat 10, 28, 144, 155, 219

ῥωμαλέος Abr 266 Virt 165

ῥώμη (60) Opif 64 Leg 1:42 Leg 3:87, 202 Det 29, 136, 168 Post 159 Deus 150 Agr 78 Ebr 156 Sobr 61 Conf 19 Migr 74, 85 Her 92, 164, 212, 298 Fug 39 Mut 108, 250 Somn 1:69, 129, 250 Somn 2:9, 58, 146 Abr 30, 216, 223, 228, 263 Ios 26, 41, 138 Mos 1:70, 225, 229, 263, 309 Spec 1:311 Spec 2:60, 99 Spec 3:39 Spec 4:74 Virt 33, 44, 155, 193 Praem 29, 94 Aet 37, 62, 80 Flacc 105 Hypoth 7:16 Prov 2:14, 56 QE 2:21

Ῥώμη (12) Flacc 28, 152, 158 Legat 108, 155, 157, 160, 185, 220, 252, 337, 342

ῥώννυμι (ἐρρωμένος) (18) Leg 1:98 Leg 2:21 Leg 3:186 Cher 15, 82 Sacr 88, 103 Deus 65 Fug 96 Somn 2:95, 153 Abr 256 Ios 110 Mos 1:217 Spec 4:222 Virt 88 Legat 17, 19

ῥώξ Virt 91

ῥῶσις Her 299 Legat 18

Σ

ϛ Opif 127

σάββατον (8) Cher 87 Fug 174 Mut 260 Abr 28 Spec 2:41, 86, 194, 194

Σαβέκ Fug 132

σαγηνεύω Mos 1:93, 299 Mos 2:250 Spec 1:160

σαθρός Virt 58

σαίρω Sacr 21 Legat 353

σάκκος Her 54, 54

σαλεύω (16) Leg 3:38, 53 Sacr 21, 90 Post 22, 22 Migr 22, 150 Congr 60 Mut 81 Somn 1:192, 244 Abr 264 Decal 67 Legat 193, 370

Σαλήμ Leg 3:79, 81

Σαλομών Congr 177

σάλος (19) Leg 2:90 Cher 12, 13, 38 Sacr 13, 90, 90 Post 22, 22, 32 Deus 26 Sobr 44, 45, 48 Conf 32 Congr 60 Somn 2:225 Spec 4:139 Prob 24

Σαλπαάδ Migr 205 Mos 2:234, 239

σάλπιγξ (9) Decal 33, 44, 159 Spec 1:186 Spec 2:188, 189, 190, 192, 193

σαλπίζω Spec 2:188

Σαμουήλ (8) Deus 5, 10, 11 Ebr 143, 144 Migr 196 Somn 1:254, 254

σανίς Legat 129 Prov 2:26

Σαούλ Migr 196

σαπρός Agr 153

σάπφειρος Leg 1:81, 81, 81 Conf 96

Σάρα (18) Leg 3:217, 217 Cher 5, 7 Congr 1, 1, 2, 6, 9, 11, 12 Fug 1, 1, 1 Mut 61, 77, 77, 130

Σαρδαναπάλλοι Spec 4:122

σάρδιον Leg 1:81

σαρκάζω Legat 353

σάρκινος Leg 2:20 Sacr 63

σαρκοβόρος (7) Somn 2:49 Ios 25 Mos 1:43 Spec 1:164 Spec 3:115 Spec 4:104, 116

σαρκοφαγία Spec 4:119

Σαρμάτης Legat 10

σάρξ (98) Opif 124 Leg 1:76, 76 Leg 2:20, 20, 37, 38, 38, 40, 40, 41, 41, 49, 49, 50, 50 Leg 3:152, 158, 202 Det 80, 84, 84 Post 67 Gig 19, 29, 29, 29, 30, 31, 32, 32, 32, 34, 35, 40, 40, 45, 65, 65 Deus 2, 56, 140, 141, 141, 142, 142, 142, 143, 143 Agr 25, 44, 97 Ebr 69, 87 Migr 14, 29 Her 56, 56, 57, 71, 243, 268 Mut 32, 174 Somn 2:67, 216, 216, 232 Abr 155, 164, 164 Ios 78, 96 Mos 1:54, 109, 130 Spec 1:118, 176 Spec 3:115 Spec 4:103, 114, 122 Virt 58, 78, 136 Praem 134 Prob 25, 26, 99 Flacc 71 QG 1:29, 29, 2:22, 22, 59, 59, 59 QG (Par) 2:3

Σάρρα (58) Leg 2:82 Leg 3:85, 85, 217, 217, 218, 218, 244, 245 Cher 3, 7, 9, 10, 41, 45, 50 Sacr 59 Det 28, 59, 123, 124 Post 62, 76, 130, 134 Ebr 59 Migr 126, 126, 140, 140 Her 62, 258 Congr 23, 23, 63, 68, 69, 71, 73, 78, 139, 180 Fug 128 Mut 61, 77, 77, 130, 143, 166, 176, 253, 255 Abr 99, 132, 206 QG 2:26b, 3:18, 58 σατραπεία Mos 1:34 Legat 216, 282

σατράπης Decal 61 Spec 4:177 Legat 292

Σαττίν Somn 1:89

σαφήνεια (14) Leg 3:120, 122, 123, 123, 123, 124, 124, 127, 128, 128, 140 Cher 128 Post 105 Decal 33

σαφηνίζω Leg 3:230

σαφής (122) Opif 93, 96, 147 Leg 3:120, 120, 121, 121, 122, 133 Cher 48, 56 Sacr 112 Det 52, 155 Post 38, 90 Deus 23 Plant 48, 115, 118, 121, 134, 153, 174 Ebr 117, 166, 198, 204 Sobr 56, 62 Conf 57, 140, 141 Migr 19, 35, 51, 136, 137, 166, 185, 190 Her 92, 216, 286 Congr 85, 90 Fug 54, 193, 204 Mut 66, 153 Somn 1:13, 21, 26, 39, 60, 71, 82, 116, 156, 230 Somn 2:3, 97, 171, 220, 228 Abr 39, 75, 114, 141, 204, 226, 247, 253 Ios 145, 158, 188, 235 Mos 1:31, 207, 223, 247, 261, 329 Mos 2:11, 40, 142, 154 Decal 15, 59, 91 Spec 1:39, 64, 69, 84, 164, 202, 290, 338 Spec 2:112, 161 Spec 3:140 Spec 4:173 Virt 34, 55, 210 Praem 79 Prob 21, 54, 91, 92 Aet 49 Flacc 76, 96, 170, 174 Legat 317, 317 Prov 2:5, 25 QG 4:172 QE isf 4

σβέννυμι (35) Leg 1:46 Leg 2:25 Sacr 15 Deus 78 Plant 10 Ebr 27, 73, 168, 168, 212 Sobr 43 Her 89 Fug 61 Somn 1:19, 31 Abr 137, 140 Ios 10 Mos 1:118, 124 Mos 2:271 Spec 1:288 Spec 2:47 Virt 135, 191 Praem 171 Aet 86, 89, 89, 91, 102, 127 Flacc 165 Legat 130 Prov 2:15

σβέσις (8) Abr 157, 258 Spec 3:36 Spec 4:118 Aet 91, 92, 103, 110

σβεστήριος Post 71 Plant 144 Spec 4:26

σεαυτοῦ (89) Leg 1:48, 48, 51, 51, 51 Leg 2:79, 79 Leg 3:17, 27, 36, 47, 74, 101, 193, 194 Cher 68, 69, 70, 71, 71 Sacr 55, 97, 113 Det 10, 10, 12, 78, 152, 152 Post 16, 76, 181 Gig 44 Deus 115 Agr 72, 84 Migr 8, 8, 9, 10, 11, 210, 222 Her 44, 69, 69, 74, 74, 104, 196, 198 Fug 25, 31, 46, 46, 47, 48 Mut 8, 226 Somn 1:54, 54, 56, 57, 58, 245 Somn 2:68, 76, 179 Abr 73 Mos 1:293 Decal 88, 89 Spec 1:41, 42, 44, 294 Spec 2:256 Spec 3:67 Spec 4:157 Virt 96, 117 Legat 69, 89, 90, 168, 271, 272 Hypoth 7:1, 7:2

σεβασμός (13) Opif 127, 127 Mos 2:207, 218 Spec 2:71, 86, 234 Virt 102 Legat 86, 93, 143, 152, 338

Σεβαστεῖον Legat 151, 305

Σεβαστή Legat 305

Σεβαστός (19) Flacc 23, 49, 50, 74, 81, 104, 158 Legat 48, 143, 144, 149, 291, 309, 311, 317, 319, 322, 322, 352

σέβομαι (σέβω) (8) Somn 1:204 Mos 2:198, 198 Decal 78 Spec 2:255 Spec 4:33 Virt 34, 179

σέβω σέβομαι

σειρά Migr 168

σειραῖος Contempl 51

σειρομάστης Leg 3:242 Post 182 Ebr 73 Mut 108

σεισμός (10) Opif 59 Sacr 16 Somn 1:77 Somn 2:125, 129 Mos 2:282 Aet 141 Legat 267 Prov 2:41, 53

σείω (7) Post 56 Somn 2:11, 230 Decal 142 Spec 1:147, 292 Spec 4:137

σελήνη (113) Opif 31, 32, 45, 46, 56, 57, 60, 84, 101, 101, 147, 168 Leg 1:8 Cher 88 Sacr 34 Post 19 Agr 51 Plant 118 Ebr 106, 110 Conf 100, 173 Migr 138, 179, 184 Her 224, 247, 280 Congr 106, 133 Mut 59, 67 Somn 1:23, 53, 116, 145, 239 Somn 2:6, 111, 112, 131, 134 Abr 44, 57, 69, 158, 205 Ios 8, 9, 145 Mos 1:212 Mos 2:14, 64, 102, 108, 118, 121, 122, 122 Decal 53, 54, 66 Spec 1:13, 13, 15, 16, 34, 37, 85, 90, 177, 178, 179, 189, 207, 210, 210, 300, 339 Spec 2:41, 45, 57, 140, 140, 141, 142, 142, 143, 143, 144, 151, 155, 155, 210, 255 Spec 3:1, 187, 188 Spec 4:234 Virt 74 Praem 41 Contempl 5, 8 Aet 10, 19, 46, 83 Prov 2:43, 50, 52 QG 2:34a, 3:7, 4:8b

σεληνιακός Mut 267 Somn 1:134 Somn 2:133 Mos 2:224

σέλινον Prob 113

Σελλά Post 75, 112, 112, 119

Σεμέλης Prob 130

σεμίδαλις (13) Sacr 59 Her 174 Congr 102, 103 Mut 234, 245, 245, 249 Somn 2:71, 71, 73 Spec 1:179, 256

Σεμναί Prob 140

σεμνεῖον Contempl 25, 32, 89

σεμνηγορέω Conf 2 Mos 2:130, 195

σεμνολογέω Cher 73 Fug 22

σεμνομυθέω Cher 67 Post 37 Congr 130

σεμνοποιέω (12) Decal 4, 71 Spec 1:21, 337 Spec 2:164 Spec 4:59 Virt 17 Praem 126 Legat 136, 153, 207 Hypoth 11:18

σεμνοποιία Decal 80

σεμνός (67) Opif 2, 4, 12, 127, 164 Leg 1:14 Sacr 49 Post 182 Agr 41 Ebr 130, 149 Congr 80 Somn 1:234 Somn 2:251 Abr 113, 192 Ios 150, 165, 204 Mos 1:153, 161, 275, 302 Mos 2:15, 23 Decal 133, 136, 138 Spec 1:3, 151, 209, 230, 317 Spec 2:19, 58, 160 Spec 3:100, 130, 166, 202, 202 Spec 4:179, 179 Virt 8, 8, 24, 182, 217 Praem 27, 97, 100 Prob 31, 101 Contempl 25, 29, 88 Aet 77 Flacc 4 Legat 42, 163, 167, 361 Hypoth 7:9, 11:18 QG 4:40, 40 QE 2:105

σεμνότης (21) Opif 111, 127 Plant 167 Mut 209 Ios 65, 257 Mos 1:20 Decal 43 Spec 1:74, 142, 152, 159, 324 Spec 2:7, 148, 149, 253 Praem 97 Contempl 66 Legat 198, 296

σεμνύνω (28) Opif 89 Leg 1:64 Leg 2:66 Leg 3:219 Det 137 Deus 88 Ebr 169 Sobr 13 Conf 150 Migr 20 Her 206 Fug 93 Mut 103 Somn 2:203, 211 Abr 5, 13, 69 Ios 18, 244 Mos 1:293 Mos 2:41, 209 Spec 1:311 Virt 206 Prob 141 Aet 39 Prov 2:14

Σεναάρ Conf 1, 60, 68

σέπτεμ Opif 127

Σεπφώρα Cher 41, 47 Post 77 Her 128 Mut 120

Σεσείν Post 60, 61

Σηγώρ Somn 1:85 QG 4:51a

Σηείρ Deus 99

Σήθ (15) Cher 54 Det 138 Post 10, 40, 40, 42, 45, 48, 124, 124, 170, 172, 173, 174 QG 3:11a

Σηιανός Flacc 1 Legat 37, 159, 160

σηκός Spec 1:163 Legat 20, 124

Σήμ (13) Leg 2:62 Post 173 Sobr 51, 52, 53, 58, 59, 59, 62, 65, 66, 67 Mut 189

σῆμα Opif 104, 104 Leg 1:108 Spec 4:188

σημαίνω (27) Leg 2:15 Leg 3:188 Cher 129 Post 44, 155 Plant 114, 115, 151, 152, 173 Ebr 23 Congr 155, 172

Somn 1:2, 63, 85, 87, 216 Somn 2:3 Ios 238 Mos 1:126 Mos 2:14, 39 Spec 2:140 Aet 3, 4 QG 4:148

σημεῖον (79) Opif 49, 49, 55, 58, 59, 98, 102 Leg 1:21, 58 Leg 2:79 Sacr 80, 120 Det 1, 3, 3, 9, 43, 177, 177, 177, 178 Gig 33 Migr 68, 69 Her 198 Congr 92, 146, 147 Fug 5, 60, 204 Mut 164 Somn 1:187, 197, 197, 213 Somn 2:1 Abr 33, 60 Mos 1:76, 77, 95, 178, 188, 210, 269 Mos 2:18, 115, 263, 264 Decal 24, 25, 26 Spec 1:26, 90, 92, 164 Spec 2:189, 218 Spec 4:6, 106, 106, 137, 138 Praem 31, 72 Prob 39, 89 Aet 2, 23, 33, 122 Hypoth 7:17, 7:19 Prov 2:26 QG 1:63, 2:64b, 4:99 QE isf 26

σημειόω (8) Det 38 Plant 18 Mut 135 Ios 235 Spec 1:92 Spec 2:178 Spec 4:110 Legat 254

σημειώδης Sobr 50 Mos 2:275 Contempl 57

σήμερον τήμερον

σήμερον (13) Leg 3:25, 25 Det 150, 156 Post 102 Ebr 67 Congr 123 Fug 56, 56, 57, 57 Virt 184, 184

σήπω Mos 1:100 Mos 2:260 Aet 125

σής (6) Post 56 Somn 1:77, 77 Abr 11 Spec 4:149 Prob 104

σῆψις Mos 1:204 Spec 1:291 Prov 2:59

Σηών (7) Leg 3:225, 225, 225, 228, 229, 233 Mos 1:258

σθεναρός Fug 49 Spec 2:99 Prob 38, 104

σθένος Ebr 65 Migr 9 Her 105 Spec 2:9 Legat 35

σθένω Abr 95, 238 Mos 1:100 Flacc 160 Legat 366

σιαγών Spec 1:147, 147

σιγάω Her 14 Somn 2:265 Prob 101

σίγλος σίκλος

σιδήρειος Spec 2:247 Legat 87

σιδήρεος (σιδηροῦς) (6) Opif 141 Ios 47 Spec 4:7 Praem 131 Flacc 74, 179

σιδηρῖτις Gig 44

σίδηρος (24) Opif 84 Post 50, 116, 117, 119 Agr 114 Somn 1:31 Abr 193 Mos 1:37, 43 Spec 1:58 Praem 58, 132, 132 Prob 26, 65, 108 Aet 20, 23 Flacc 67, 84 Legat 206, 324 Prov 2:61

σιδηροῦς σιδήρεος

Σιδών Legat 222, 337

Σιδώνιος Aet 76

σίελος Opif 123 Leg 1:13

Σικελία Leg 1:62 Ios 132 Aet 139, 139

Σικελικός Aet 139 Prov 2:26

σίκερα Ebr 127, 138

Σίκιμα Leg 3:23, 25, 26, 26

σίκλος (σίγλος) Migr 202

σίκυς σίκυος

σίκυος (σίκυς) Her 80

Σιλανός Legat 62, 71, 71, 75

Σινά Her 251 QE 2:45a

σίνομαι (6) Leg 2:11 Agr 15 Her 114 Abr 191 Mos 1:108 Decal 150

σιρός Spec 2:206

Σισύφειος Cher 78

σιταρχέω Mut 90 Somn 2:46

σιτάρχης Ios 193

σιταρχία Ios 162 Mos 1:206

σιτέω Opif 158 Leg 2:29, 105 Contempl 37

σιτίον (62) Opif 119, 157, 159 Leg 1:83, 86 Leg 3:62, 141, 147, 155, 161, 239 Sacr 23, 85 Det 116 Post 142 Agr 36 Ebr 73, 106, 131, 211, 214 Her 311 Congr 172 Somn 1:36, 49, 124 Somn 2:48 Ios 113, 152, 155, 156 Mos 1:191, 215 Mos 2:24, 68, 69, 267 Decal 12, 17, 159 Spec 1:126, 127, 148, 338 Spec 2:195, 198, 201, 203 Spec 3:198 Spec 4:82 Virt 30, 86, 104, 130, 130 Contempl 25, 34, 56, 81 Flacc 178 Prov 2:67 QG (Par) 2:7

σιτοποιία Ebr 217

σιτοποιός Det 26 Ebr 215 Conf 95 Prob 31

σιτοπονέω Spec 1:132 Prob 140

σιτοπόνος (13) Opif 158 Leg 3:143, 221 Agr 66 Plant 159 Migr 19 Mut 249 Ios 93 Mos 1:208 Spec 1:174 Spec 4:113 Prob 156 Contempl 53

σῖτος (35) Opif 116 Det 19 Post 96 Migr 204 Somn 1:105 Abr 138 Ios 180, 190, 197, 207, 212, 258 Mos 1:5 Spec 1:134, 141, 179 Spec 2:158, 175, 179, 179, 181, 181, 184, 186, 186 Spec 4:98 Virt 95, 149 Praem 8, 107 Prob 122 Flacc 63 Legat 158, 249 QG 4:169

σιτοφόρος Mos 1:319 Virt 92

σιτώνης Ios 161

σιτωνία (6) Ios 163, 178, 184, 193, 194, 225

σιωπάω (14) Her 10, 11, 11, 13, 14 Mut 242 Somn 1:193 Somn 2:263 Spec 4:90 Contempl 63 Legat 39, 133, 282, 360

σιωπή Hypoth 7:13

σκαιός Abr 224 Spec 3:68 Virt 127, 128 QG 4:200c

σκαιότης Spec 1:306 Spec 2:75, 93 Virt 144

σκαληνός Congr 146

σκαπάνη Post 142

σκάπτω Deus 91 Prob 34

σκάφος (24) Leg 2:104 Leg 3:80 Post 100 Deus 129 Agr 174 Plant 24 Conf 22 Migr 148 Her 301 Mut 149, 215 Somn 2:201 Ios 33 Mos 1:172 Mos 2:247 Decal 67 Spec 1:335 Spec 4:50 Prob 128 Flacc 110 Legat 50, 146, 149 QE 2:55b

σκεδάννυμι (16) Leg 1:46 Leg 2:85 Cher 37 Post 104 Conf 119, 120, 196, 197 Migr 197 Her 60 Somn 2:288 Spec 3:162 Aet 80, 114, 137, 147

σκέδασις Somn 2:211

σκεδασμός Somn 2:211

σκεδαστής Leg 3:236, 243 Sacr 48, 69

σκέλος (10) Opif 163 Leg 2:105 Plant 30 Migr 131 Her 239 Mut 54 Spec 1:340 Spec 2:246 Spec 4:114 Aet 128

σκεπάζω Leg 2:53 Congr 131

σκέπασμα Leg 3:239 Sacr 84 Det 19 Migr 215 Decal 77

σκεπαστήριος Opif 84 Her 203

σκέπη (11) Cher 126 Sacr 25 Ios 112 Mos 2:85 Spec 1:83, 165 Praem 99, 99 Contempl 24, 38 Aet 67

σκεπτικός (7) Leg 3:238 Ebr 98, 202 Her 247, 279 Congr 52 Fug 209

σκέπτομαι (49) Leg 1:91 Leg 2:42, 55, 80 Leg 3:13, 28, 116, 252 Cher 55 Sacr 91, 128 Det 26, 150 Post 22, 40, 49, 124 Deus 1, 133 Agr 26 Plant 5 Sobr 31, 33, 62 Conf 1, 15, 75, 168 Migr 148, 216 Her 227, 277 Fug 129,

131, 157 Mut 35, 37, 86, 202 Somn 1:14, 61, 230 Somn 2:182 Ios 50 Mos 2:32 Spec 1:283 Virt 92 Legat 213 QG (Par) 2:5

σκευάζω (8) Ebr 184 Somn 2:51 Abr 109 Mos 1:204, 209 Spec 1:244 Spec 4:129 Legat 98

σκευή Sacr 29 Spec 4:185 Legat 79, 96 QE isf 26

σκεῦος (15) Leg 3:102 Migr 196, 196 Her 226 Mos 1:317 Mos 2:94, 101, 136, 139, 146 Spec 1:231 Spec 3:206 Spec 4:37, 38 Flacc 69

σκευωρέομαι Spec 3:94

σκευωρέω Legat 159

σκέψις (23) Post 16 Deus 70 Plant 142, 149 Ebr 94, 200, 202 Her 253 Fug 55, 126, 130, 141, 166 Mut 157 Somn 1:58, 182 Abr 162 Ios 34 Spec 1:40 Prob 18 Aet 4 Legat 204, 220

σκηνή (76) Leg 2:54, 54, 55 Leg 3:46, 46, 95, 102 Det 59, 63, 160, 160, 160 Post 98 Gig 54 Deus 102 Agr 35 Ebr 100, 127, 129, 132, 134, 135, 138, 139, 177 Migr 202 Her 112, 113 Congr 62, 89, 116 Fug 186 Mut 43, 190 Abr 107 Mos 1:169, 200, 289, 313, 317 Mos 2:42, 74, 79, 82, 83, 85, 86, 88, 90, 91, 91, 92, 92, 93, 94, 141, 146, 153, 213, 282 Spec 1:189 Spec 2:41, 204, 206, 207, 250, 251 Spec 4:129 Flacc 20, 95, 116 Legat 111, 203 Hypoth 11:15 QE 2:49b QE isf 26

σκηνικός Opif 78 Flacc 85 Legat 45

σκηνοβατέω Legat 204, 351

σκηπτός Det 95 Spec 4:201

σκῆπτρον Congr 118 Mut 128, 135 Spec 4:164 Flacc 37

σκηπτροφορέω Spec 4:164

σκήπτω Spec 1:143 Spec 4:37 Flacc 129

σκηρίπτω (9) Cher 59 Plant 153 Somn 2:102 Abr 84 Spec 2:23 Spec 3:106 Spec 4:165 Virt 7 Aet 127

σκῆψις Hypoth 7:1

σκιά (52) Leg 3:96, 96, 96, 96, 99, 100, 100, 102, 103 Post 112, 112, 112, 112, 114, 119, 119 Deus 177 Agr 17, 42 Plant 27, 27, 27, 27 Conf 69, 71, 190 Migr 12, 12 Her 72, 290 Mut 181, 243, 243 Somn 1:188, 206, 206, 206 Abr 119, 119, 120 Ios 140, 146 Decal 82 Spec 1:26, 28 Spec 2:207 Virt 18, 118, 181 Flacc 165 Legat 320 Prov 2:48

σκιαγραφέω Mut 70

σκιαγραφία Post 119

σκιάζω Mos 1:289

σκιαμαχέω Plant 175

σκιαμαχία Cher 81

σκιαμάχος Det 41

σκίδνημι (7) Sacr 61, 109 Agr 32 Plant 133 Abr 91 Spec 1:7 Spec 4:83

σκίπων Plant 153

σκιρόομαι (σκιρρόομαι) Virt 128

σκιρρόομαι σκιρόομαι

σκιρτάω (7) Opif 86 Agr 32, 34 Her 245 Somn 2:293 Abr 135 Spec 1:304

σκίρτησις Agr 71

σκιρτητικός (6) Leg 2:99, 101 Agr 68, 83, 106 Migr 62

σκληραγωγία Spec 4:102 Contempl 69

σκληραύχην (7) Leg 3:136 Sacr 32 Congr 61 Somn 2:80, 184, 293 QG 2:41

σκληρόγεως Aet 119

σκληροδίαιτος Somn 1:125 Somn 2:9 Mos 2:185 Spec 2:98 Spec 4:74

σκληροκαρδία Spec 1:305

σκληρός (12) Ebr 149, 150 Migr 50 Her 181 Fug 42 Abr 239 Mos 2:183 Spec 1:306 Spec 2:39 Spec 3:34 Spec 4:218 Praem 114

σκληρότης Opif 62 Sacr 116 Plant 133 Spec 1:304

σκνίψ Mos 1:107, 112, 145

σκολιός Sobr 10 Prob 155

σκόλοψ Spec 4:229

σκοπέω (64) Opif 155 Leg 1:62 Leg 3:75, 105, 197 Cher 122 Sacr 85 Post 117, 174 Deus 167 Agr 63, 83 Plant 81, 174 Ebr 165, 187 Conf 21, 159, 171 Migr 220 Her 22, 32, 154, 244, 258 Congr 125, 172 Fug 25, 37, 125 Mut 192 Somn 1:6, 146, 167, 191 Somn 2:48, 110, 115, 187 Ios 8, 117, 217, 232 Mos 2:34, 165 Spec 1:209, 219 Spec 2:129, 261 Spec 3:166, 191, 191, 194 Praem 46, 71 Prob 131 Aet 46, 50, 71, 138 Legat 45, 67 QG 4:206a QE isf 8

σκοπή Somn 2:170 Mos 1:16 Spec 3:48 Virt 151

σκοπιά Abr 171 Mos 1:276 Spec 3:2

σκοπός (59) Opif 12, 21, 31, 41, 72, 79, 132 Sacr 82, 82, 116 Post 131 Plant 76, 152 Ebr 76 Sobr 26 Conf 48, 144 Her 156, 284 Congr 50, 69 Fug 64, 116 Mut 81, 201 Somn 1:35, 151 Abr 11, 36, 99, 130, 134 Ios 32, 256 Mos 1:48, 216, 250, 300 Mos 2:2, 127, 151 Spec 1:48, 263 Spec 2:152 Spec 3:59 Spec 4:60, 73, 110 Praem 9, 140 Prob 59 Aet 27, 63, 106 Prov 2:67 QG 2:5a QG (Par) 2:5 QE 1:19, 2:21

σκορακίζω (11) Leg 1:95 Cher 2 Post 135 Gig 34 Ebr 176 Congr 56 Abr 127 Spec 1:242, 324 Spec 4:176 Virt 108

σκόρδον σκόροδον

σκόροδον (σκόρδον) Her 79, 80

σκορπίζω Leg 2:85, 85, 87

σκορπίος Leg 2:84, 86 Mos 1:192 Spec 3:103 Praem 90

σκορπισμός Leg 2:86

σκορπιώδης Legat 205

σκοταῖος Plant 40, 110 Somn 1:227

σκοτεινός Her 249

σκότιος Somn 2:3

σκοτοδινιάω Opif 71 Ios 142 Spec 1:37

σκότος (102) Opif 29, 30, 32, 33, 33, 34, 34, 35 Leg 1:46 Leg 3:7, 167 Cher 59 Sacr 36 Det 101, 128 Post 58 Gig 3, 41 Deus 3, 123, 130 Agr 162 Ebr 155, 157, 161, 167, 168, 209 Conf 116 Migr 191 Her 87, 146, 163, 163, 163, 208, 250, 265, 290, 302, 302 Fug 136, 136 Somn 1:76, 76, 79, 99, 114, 117, 218 Somn 2:39, 105, 106, 133, 140, 282 Abr 70, 205 Ios 106, 140, 145, 166 Mos 1:123, 124, 125, 126, 145 Mos 2:194 Decal 139 Spec 1:54, 279, 288, 296, 319, 320, 321 Spec 2:155, 204, 210 Spec 3:6 Spec 4:2, 7, 166, 187, 190, 231 Virt 164, 179, 221 Praem 36, 152 Contempl 7, 34, 42 Flacc 167 Legat 103, 103, 122, 326 Prov 2:20 QG 2:14, 4:30

σκύβαλον (8) Sacr 109, 139 Somn 2:22 Virt 145 Prov 2:62 QG (Par) 2:6, 2:7, 2:7

Σκύθης Ebr 174 Somn 2:59 Mos 2:19, 19 Legat 10

σκυθρωπάζω Sobr 6 Fug 33 Mut 154, 156 Legat 15

σκυθρωπός Cher 6 Plant 167 Mut 169 Somn 2:165 Mos 1:20

σκυλακευτικός Det 55

σκυλάκιον Agr 115

σκύλαξ Det 55 Post 161 Somn 1:49 Spec 4:120

Σκύλλα Det 178

σκῦλον Leg 2:35 Cher 74

σκύμνος Mos 1:284, 291

σκώληξ Mos 2:260, 262 Praem 128

σκῶμμα Flacc 34 Legat 42, 44, 171

σκωπτικός Sacr 32

σκώπτω Contempl 58 Legat 168, 204

σμάραγδος (7) Leg 1:81 Her 176 Mos 2:112, 122, 123, 133 Spec 1:86

σμῆνος Praem 96 Hypoth 11:8

σμικρός (μικρός) Prob 141

σμύχω Mos 2:157

σοβάς Sacr 21 Fug 153

σοβέω (6) Leg 3:221 Sacr 26 Post 116 Her 70 Spec 3:40 QG 4:99

σόβησις Praem 125

Σόδομα (12) Leg 3:24, 197, 213 Sacr 122 Ebr 222, 222 Somn 1:85 Somn 2:191, 192, 192 Abr 227 QG 4:51a

Σοδομῖται (6) Conf 27 Fug 144 Mut 228 Abr 133, 145, 226

Σοδομῖτις Congr 109

Σόλων Opif 104, 105 Spec 3:22 Prob 47

σορός Migr 16, 23

σός (65) Leg 1:27 Leg 3:22, 27, 101, 192, 192, 192 Cher 37, 69 Sacr 29 Det 166 Ebr 105, 106 Migr 81 Her 20, 29, 31, 32, 33, 39, 44 Fug 47 Mut 18, 23, 27, 29, 31 Somn 2:176 Abr 250 Ios 9, 23, 50, 66, 96, 117, 224, 225, 229 Mos 1:274, 274, 294 Mos 2:239 Decal 38 Spec 1:45, 45, 45, 260, 294 Spec 2:83, 85, 85, 219 Spec 4:157 Virt 124 Prob 112 Flacc 30, 123 Legat 49, 168, 309, 314, 325, 329, 355 QG 3:58

Σουνιάς Flacc 156

Σούρ Fug 1, 203, 203 QG 3:27, 4:59

σοφία (266) Opif 5, 45, 70, 104, 148, 158 Leg 1:43, 43, 64, 65, 77, 77, 77, 78, 103 Leg 2:49, 81, 82, 86, 86, 87, 87 Leg 3:2, 3, 46, 46, 52, 54, 95, 152, 236, 252 Cher 9, 9, 10, 41, 45, 49 Sacr 18, 44, 64, 78, 79 Det 30, 30, 38, 43, 54, 66, 115, 117, 124 Post 18, 62, 78, 101, 122, 125, 136, 137, 138, 138, 146, 151, 151, 174 Gig 15, 23, 27, 29, 39, 47 Deus 4, 5, 26, 79, 92, 110, 125, 143, 148, 160 Agr 65, 146, 161 Plant 23, 52, 65, 69, 80, 97, 167, 168, 169 Ebr 31, 48, 49, 61, 72, 86, 88, 112, 113, 162, 212, 213, 220 Sobr 9 Conf 27, 49, 101, 159 Migr 28, 39, 40, 41, 46, 57, 76, 85, 101, 125, 149, 171, 197, 218 Her 14, 53, 98, 100, 101, 112, 126, 127, 129, 179, 182, 191, 199, 204, 298, 314, 315 Congr 9, 13, 22, 37, 47, 48, 79, 79, 79, 79, 113, 116, 116, 127, 132, 174 Fug 50, 50, 51, 51, 52, 52, 63, 82, 82, 97, 109, 137, 138, 166, 176, 195, 196, 202 Mut 36, 37, 39, 68, 259, 264, 270 Somn 1:12, 50, 66, 70, 80, 169, 175, 200, 205, 208, 211 Somn 2:13, 71, 171, 221, 242, 242, 242, 242, 245, 270 Abr 100, 164, 220, 224, 258, 271 Ios 59, 106 Mos 1:4, 76 Mos 2:33, 58, 114, 204 Spec 1:50, 173, 175, 204, 269, 269, 288, 330 Spec 2:3, 29, 31, 31, 44, 45, 47, 147 Spec 3:6 Spec 4:75, 107 Virt 4, 8, 62, 79, 188 Praem 8, 81, 81, 104, 115, 122 Prob 4, 13, 71, 94, 107, 117 Contempl 19, 35, 68, 68 Aet 46 Prov 1, 2:69 QG 3:29, 4:74, 81 QE isf 29

σοφίζω Leg 3:64 Det 164 Mut 240 Ios 217 Aet 14

σόφισμα (19) Det 1, 38 Gig 59 Agr 16, 164 Conf 65 Her 125, 302, 305 Congr 18, 29, 52 Somn 2:40 Mos 1:94 Spec 3:77 Virt 37 Praem 25 Flacc 112 Legat 26

σοφιστεία (14) Opif 45 Leg 3:206 Cher 9 Det 38 Ebr 71 Sobr 9 Migr 85 Her 85 Mut 203 Mos 1:277 Spec 3:53 Praem 8 Prob 4 Prov 1

σοφιστεύω Det 35

σοφιστής (43) Leg 3:232, 232 Cher 8, 10 Det 38, 39, 71, 72 Post 35, 86, 131, 150 Agr 136, 143, 144, 159 Ebr 71 Sobr 9, 9 Conf 39 Migr 72, 76, 171 Her 246 Congr 67, 129 Fug 209, 211 Mut 10, 208, 257 Somn 1:102, 220 Somn 2:281 Ios 103, 106 Mos 1:92 Mos 2:212 Praem 58 Contempl 4, 31 Aet 132 QG isf 3

σοφιστικός (14) Opif 157 Leg 1:74 Leg 3:41, 233 Det 41, 42 Post 53, 101 Agr 162 Migr 82, 85 Her 304 Mut 263 QE isf 26

Σοφόκλειος Prob 19

σοφός (301) Opif 127, 148 Leg 1:102 Leg 2:15, 60, 87, 89, 93 Leg 3:1, 1, 9, 25, 26, 45, 45, 46, 67, 131, 140, 141, 144, 147, 189, 193, 195, 207, 210, 217, 244, 249 Cher 7, 9, 10, 15, 31, 106, 121 Sacr 8, 64, 79, 111, 120, 121, 122, 135 Det 49, 59, 75, 124, 137, 138, 162, 169, 171, 173, 176 Post 18, 27, 52, 78, 138, 173 Gig 22, 27, 39, 47, 48, 50 Deus 3, 23, 102 Agr 18, 41, 50, 65, 99, 161 Plant 38, 46, 58, 71, 73, 94, 127, 138, 138, 142, 143, 145, 149, 156, 163, 166, 170, 174, 177, 177, 177 Ebr 1, 24, 37, 69, 86, 91, 92, 100, 105, 106, 143 Sobr 9, 9, 10, 17, 18, 20, 27, 29, 55, 65 Conf 26, 30, 35, 39, 45, 49, 74, 77, 81, 94, 192 Migr 13, 38, 39, 56, 58, 59, 94, 109, 109, 113, 122, 129, 130, 134, 140, 168, 197, 201 Her 2, 19, 19, 21, 83, 88, 91, 258, 259, 280, 313 Congr 44, 48, 92, 109, 111, 114, 119 Fug 47, 55, 82, 110, 112, 128, 157, 165, 166, 200 Mut 19, 32, 36, 37, 51, 64, 69, 70, 71, 104, 128, 139, 140, 152, 155, 168, 262, 270 Somn 1:148, 151, 167, 176, 178, 207, 214 Somn 2:4, 8, 66, 89, 90, 226, 229, 237, 243, 244, 248, 255, 278 Abr 27, 31, 37, 68, 77, 80, 80, 82, 84, 109, 115, 118, 131, 142, 168, 199, 202, 207, 213, 229, 255, 261, 272, 275 Ios 1, 143, 191 Mos 1:130 Mos 2:67, 128 Decal 1, 23 Spec 1:92, 204, 287 Spec 2:55, 200 Spec 4:47, 72, 131, 143 Virt 186, 190, 223, 223 Praem 58, 83, 112, 123 Prob 12, 20, 29, 40, 41, 47, 52, 54, 60, 62, 68, 73, 113, 131, 135, 144, 154 Aet 134 Legat 99, 203 Prov 2:23, 67 QG 1:20, 2:10, 62, 68b, 72, 3:24, 24, 4:33b, 47a, 69, 8* QG isf 16 QE 2:13b, 20, 44 QE isf 29

σπάδων Ebr 210 Mut 173

σπαθάω Fug 28

σπάθη Flacc 78

σπαθηφόρος Flacc 78

σπάνιος (16) Leg 1:102 Sacr 111 Gig 1 Agr 180 Ebr 26, 174 Migr 59, 61, 63, 123 Mut 34, 256 Abr 19 Prob 63, 72, 93

σπάνις (35) Det 13 Post 144 Deus 111 Mut 173 Ios 109, 156 Mos 1:170, 192, 210, 243, 251 Decal 16, 140 Spec

1:42 Spec 2:85, 128 Spec 3:80 Spec 4:127, 211 Virt 127, 128, 162 Praem 127, 134, 138 Prob 34 Contempl 1, 15, 62 Flacc 51, 62 Legat 124, 128, 130 Prov 2:38

σπαράσσω Post 56 Conf 69 Her 245 Contempl 55 Legat 366

σπάργανον (18) Sacr 15 Ebr 51, 198 Sobr 24 Somn 1:151 Somn 2:9 Abr 112 Mos 1:88 Spec 1:313, 332 Spec 2:239 Spec 4:68, 150 Prob 98 Legat 54, 115, 170 QG 2:54d

σπαργάω Agr 36

σπαρτίον Leg 3:24 Ebr 105

Σπαρτοί Aet 57, 68

σπαρτός (32) Opif 38, 43, 116 Ebr 106 Conf 185 Abr 45, 138 Mos 1:192, 224 Mos 2:222 Spec 1:172 Spec 2:105, 143, 172, 181, 184, 186, 205 Spec 4:208, 208, 209, 209, 209 Virt 160 Praem 41, 101, 129 Aet 63, 75 Legat 249 QG 4:51b QE 1:1

σπασμός Cher 69

σπασμώδης Leg 3:160

σπάω (26) Leg 1:9 Leg 3:202 Det 17 Gig 10 Plant 39, 174 Ebr 95, 101, 221 Congr 150 Fug 11, 166 Somn 1:178 Somn 2:204 Abr 176 Ios 84 Mos 1:19, 251, 255 Decal 74 Spec 2:180 Spec 3:4 Praem 122 Prob 117 Contempl 85 Legat 127

σπείρω (103) Opif 14, 41, 80 Leg 1:45, 49, 79, 80 Leg 3:170, 180, 181, 181, 219, 245 Cher 44, 44, 44, 52, 106 Sacr 101 Det 102 Post 90, 91, 158, 158, 162, 163, 164, 171, 181 Gig 4 Deus 40, 166 Agr 8, 9, 9, 25 Plant 60, 84 Ebr 30, 211, 224 Conf 3, 21, 152, 196, 196 Migr 3, 35, 142 Her 172, 309 Congr 58, 138 Fug 52, 153, 170, 170, 171, 171 Mut 134, 137, 138, 166, 173, 268, 269, 269 Somn 1:200 Somn 2:69, 76, 170, 185 Abr 101, 101, 135 Mos 1:201, 226 Mos 2:210 Decal 112, 129, 161, 162 Spec 1:294, 305 Spec 2:30, 56, 133, 181 Spec 3:32 Spec 4:212 Praem 128 Contempl 62, 68 Aet 69, 122 Legat 249, 293, 321 QG 1:27, 2:5b, 5b QG (Par) 2:5, 2:5

σπένδω (6) Leg 2:56 Ebr 152 Her 183 Mos 2:150 Flacc 18 QE 2:14

σπέρμα (121) Opif 44, 67, 67, 68, 103, 123, 132 Leg 1:13 Leg 2:37 Leg 3:40, 65, 65, 68, 150, 170, 185, 185, 185, 186, 188, 203, 225, 227, 233, 242, 249 Cher 46, 49 Sacr 123 Det 60 Post 10, 124, 125, 135, 163, 164, 170, 170, 171, 172, 173, 180 Gig 11 Deus 16, 87, 130, 137 Plant 48 Ebr 30, 211, 212 Sobr 36 Migr 24 Her 2, 8, 8, 34, 37, 65, 86, 121, 267, 313 Congr 7, 16, 95, 123, 130, 131, 146 Mut 134, 150 Somn 1:3, 3, 3 Somn 2:16 Ios 260 Mos 1:279 Mos 2:60, 104, 180, 180, 180, 181 Spec 1:7 Spec 2:65 Spec 3:36 Virt 134 Praem 12, 141, 172 Prob 71, 105 Contempl 62 Aet 69, 94, 94, 94, 95, 95, 96, 97, 97, 98, 98, 98, 99, 100, 101, 101, 103 Legat 54, 108, 141, 166, 293 Hypoth 7:7 QG 1:28, 2:15a, 3:12 QE 2:64

σπερματικός (11) Opif 43 Leg 3:150 Post 163 Her 115, 119 Spec 3:33 Aet 85, 93, 99 Legat 55 Prov 2:59

σπερμολόγος Legat 203

σπεύδω (55) Opif 162 Leg 3:179 Sacr 59 Det 129 Post 132, 132, 140 Her 164 Mut 2 Somn 2:156 Abr 43, 47, 86, 87, 108, 233, 269 Ios 137, 182 Mos 1:10, 35, 55, 71, 168, 274, 326, 326 Mos 2:151, 165, 181, 184, 248, 254, 256, 279 Decal 146, 148 Spec 1:42, 253, 330 Spec 2:102, 146, 159 Spec 4:31 Virt 185 Praem 15, 24, 46 Prob 71 Aet 30 Flacc 82, 178, 186 QG 4:173, 200b

σπήλαιον Post 62 Somn 2:26, 90 QG 4:80, 81

σπινθήρ (8) Migr 123 Her 308, 309 Somn 2:93 Spec 4:27 Prob 71 Flacc 17 Legat 197

σπλάγχνον (14) Opif 118 Leg 1:12 Post 118 Ebr 106 Abr 241 Ios 25 Spec 1:62, 216, 216 Praem 134, 151 Legat 126, 368 QG (Par) 2:3

σπλήν Opif 118 Leg 1:12

σπογγιά Opif 38 Conf 186

σπόγγος Conf 186

σποδοειδής (6) Somn 1:189, 200, 209, 213, 219 Somn 2:19

σποδός Her 30 Somn 1:210, 214

σπονδεῖον Her 226 Somn 2:183 Mos 2:146 Legat 319

σπονδή (27) Leg 3:134 Deus 56 Ebr 152, 208, 220 Conf 26, 43 Migr 16, 18, 18 Her 184 Mos 1:298 Spec 1:70, 83, 179, 205, 205, 316 Spec 3:96 Spec 4:125, 221 Virt 40 Praem 154, 167 Contempl 41 Aet 68 Legat 100

σπονδοφόρος Somn 2:183

σπορά (56) Opif 41, 59, 161 Leg 1:10 Leg 3:180 Det 147 Post 176, 177 Her 38, 171 Mut 96, 255 Somn 1:199 Somn 2:184, 211 Abr 46, 101, 111, 132, 137, 250 Ios 43, 260 Mos 1:28, 302 Mos 2:64, 210, 289 Decal 77, 119, 129 Spec 1:172, 326 Spec 2:70, 133 Spec 3:62, 113, 179 Spec 4:12, 203 Virt 145, 199 Praem 10, 60, 139, 155 Aet 65, 66, 97 Hypoth 11:8 Prov 2:66 QG 2:15b, 17c, 3:18, 4:86b QE 2:19

σποράδην Agr 40 Spec 2:168 Virt 16

σποράς (11) Leg 1:31 Leg 3:37, 38 Agr 49 Congr 58 Fug 148 Mos 2:254 Spec 4:159 Virt 58 Praem 165 Flacc 55

σπόρος (20) Opif 115 Fug 171 Mut 144 Somn 1:202 Abr 92 Spec 1:105, 165, 216, 216 Spec 2:29 Spec 3:32, 33 Spec 4:215, 217 Virt 90, 145 Praem 10, 101, 127, 160

σπουδάζω (99) Opif 86, 144, 158 Leg 2:108 Leg 3:45 Cher 6, 95 Sacr 39, 113 Det 103, 129 Post 72, 140, 168 Deus 93, 171 Agr 33, 90, 110, 111, 174 Plant 106, 142, 159 Ebr 14, 75 Conf 48, 97, 146 Migr 20, 38, 96, 146, 151 Her 9, 252 Congr 35, 58, 76, 105 Fug 8, 62, 81, 144, 158 Somn 1:114, 149, 164 Somn 2:55, 83, 103, 133, 225 Abr 7, 60, 108, 267, 275 Ios 172, 209 Mos 1:3, 49, 150, 159, 161, 218, 259, 295 Mos 2:32, 136, 233 Decal 59 Spec 1:2, 17, 102, 149, 186, 254 Spec 2:46, 64, 196 Spec 4:36, 40 Virt 45, 218, 225 Praem 104, 137, 142 Prob 89 Contempl 68 Aet 16, 35 Flacc 103, 135, 138 Legat 75 QG isf 13 QE 2:25b

σπουδαιολόγος Det 139

σπουδαῖος (141) Opif 73, 74, 79 Leg 1:74, 80, 93, 95 Leg 2:17, 17, 53, 65, 90, 97, 97 Leg 3:3, 48, 67, 67, 68, 75, 189, 189, 200, 203, 217, 246, 246 Cher 7, 27 Sacr 47, 124, 128 Det 105, 109, 124, 132, 133 Post 28, 28, 45, 55, 75, 107, 136, 169, 170 Gig 34, 48, 56, 64, 67 Agr 29 Plant 69, 135, 144, 155, 165 Ebr 120 Sobr 68 Conf 34 Migr 110, 129, 157 Her 129, 303 Fug 177 Mut 31, 40, 79, 168, 201, 256 Somn 2:34, 77, 256, 302 Abr 11, 20, 99, 101, 261, 265 Mos 1:157 Mos 2:33, 130, 147 Spec 1:246, 284, 314 Spec 2:2, 29, 157 Spec 3:22 Spec 4:59, 134 Virt 9, 94, 167 Praem 2, 90, 112, 113, 115, 120, 125 Prob 41, 41, 48, 50, 50, 52, 53, 53, 60, 60, 93, 97, 98, 100, 136, 145 Aet 1, 75 Prov 2:21 QG 1:21,

97, 2:41, 3:11b, 21, 4:166, 167, 169, 172, 174, 189, 198, 208, 228 QE 2:6a QE isf 9, 29

σπουδαρχία Deus 115

σπούδασμα Sacr 50 Deus 177 Ebr 86 Somn 2:68

σπουδή (105) Opif 81, 137, 148 Leg 3:47, 83 Cher 8, 30 Sacr 59, 61, 63, 68, 120 Det 118 Post 13 Deus 116, 144 Agr 25, 60, 62, 151, 166 Plant 158, 167 Ebr 16, 62, 152 Conf 93, 103, 178, 193 Migr 25, 151, 197, 218 Her 201, 255 Congr 112, 124, 173 Fug 131, 149 Mut 62, 86, 213 Somn 1:8, 93, 121, 198, 209 Somn 2:13, 67, 70, 115, 121, 213, 232, 302 Abr 40 Ios 2, 62, 152, 206 Mos 1:58, 91, 139, 169, 190, 212, 216, 230 Mos 2:136, 144, 170 Spec 1:36, 57, 79, 144, 220, 264, 305, 314 Spec 2:23 Spec 3:188 Spec 4:81 Virt 17, 18, 53, 215 Prob 110 Contempl 17, 71 Flacc 100, 120 Legat 39, 60, 99, 135, 201, 212, 242, 245, 245, 338, 365 QG isf 8

σπυρίς Spec 3:160

σταγών Her 197

σταδιεύω Agr 180

στάδιον (8) Opif 78 Det 2 Migr 133 Somn 2:257 Spec 2:246 Prob 26 Contempl 42 Flacc 92

σταθερός (σταθηρός) (13) Leg 3:138 Sacr 26, 80 Post 100 Ebr 98 Migr 58 Fug 45, 47 Abr 27, 175, 175 Spec 2:213 Spec 4:220

σταθερότης Her 291 Legat 303

σταθηρός σταθερός

σταθμάω (11) Opif 23 Sacr 59 Post 145 Mut 232 Somn 2:192, 194 Spec 1:139 Prob 152 Aet 108 Prov 1 QG 2:64a

στάθμη Somn 2:193

στάθμημα Mut 232

στάθμιον (9) Her 162, 162, 162, 162 Somn 2:193, 193, 193 Spec 4:193, 194

σταθμός Her 144, 162 Mos 1:188 Spec 2:207

σταῖς Sacr 62 Spec 2:158

στακτή Her 196, 197, 197, 198, 226

στάμνος Congr 100

στασιάζω (8) Opif 33 Abr 243 Spec 2:190 Spec 3:28 Spec 4:223 Virt 184 Prob 138 Legat 301

στασιάρχης Flacc 20

στασιαστικός Abr 210

στάσιμος Contempl 80, 84

στάσις (54) Opif 120 Leg 2:99 Post 23, 24, 29, 119, 183, 184, 185 Gig 49 Agr 45 Ebr 98 Conf 42 Her 163, 244, 246, 248 Congr 92, 176 Mut 54 Somn 1:242, 242 Somn 2:166, 222, 237, 251, 261 Abr 27, 58, 105, 215, 223, 228, 240 Ios 10, 57 Mos 1:232 Mos 2:174, 235, 283 Decal 152 Spec 1:108, 121 Spec 2:192 Spec 3:17 Flacc 17, 44, 135, 140 Legat 113, 292, 335 QE 1:19, 2:11b

στασιώδης Sacr 32 Spec 4:89

σταυρός Agr 11 Spec 4:229 Flacc 72, 84

σταφυλή (13) Plant 112 Ebr 222, 222 Somn 2:159, 159, 171, 191, 191, 199, 203 Ios 91 Mos 2:180 Spec 1:249

σταχυηφορέω (6) Opif 40 Spec 2:158, 191 Virt 145, 149 Praem 132

σταχυηφόρος Legat 249

στάχυς (11) Leg 3:248, 249 Mut 269 Somn 2:218, 218, 218 Ios 102, 108, 108, 113 Aet 98

στέαρ (19) Sacr 88, 136, 136 Post 122, 123 Conf 187 Her 251 Spec 1:132, 212, 213, 216, 232, 233, 239 Spec 4:123, 124, 125 QE 2:15:1, 15a

στεγανός Spec 2:207 Aet 137

στέγος Praem 120

στέγω (6) Abr 261 Ios 5 Virt 69 Flacc 64 Legat 184 Prov 2:32

στεῖρα (28) Opif 38 Leg 2:47 Leg 3:180 Deus 10, 13 Migr 34 Her 36, 51, 208 Congr 3 Mut 143, 143, 143, 143, 144, 225 Somn 1:11, 37, 106 Abr 247 Mos 2:258 Spec 1:11 Spec 3:34, 35 Praem 108 QG 3:18, 18, 20b

στειρόω (25) Leg 3:131 Agr 7 Plant 97 Ebr 211, 223 Conf 27 Migr 123 Her 36, 50, 51 Congr 3, 109 Fug 124 Mut 133, 143 Somn 2:131, 141 Spec 2:154 Spec 4:81, 229 Praem 130, 141, 159, 168 Aet 61

στείρωσις (7) Ebr 222 Somn 2:192 Spec 3:62 Spec 4:211 Contempl 62 QG 4:23 QE 2:19

στείχω Sobr 48 Mut 179 Mos 2:251 Aet 135

στέλεχος (17) Her 34, 220 Congr 82 Fug 183, 183 Mut 224 Somn 2:171 Abr 138 Ios 91 Mos 1:188, 228 Mos 2:77 Virt 157, 158 Praem 172 Aet 96 Prov 2:68

στελεχόω Opif 41 Somn 2:170 Spec 4:75 Praem 152 Prob 69

στέλλω (88) Opif 79, 135 Leg 3:196 Cher 81 Det 25, 110 Post 22, 46, 110 Deus 127, 146 Agr 6, 6 Plant 167 Ebr 9, 26, 101 Sobr 60 Conf 77, 78 Her 270 Congr 84, 107, 162 Fug 36, 159, 176, 190 Mut 38, 215 Somn 1:42, 131 Somn 2:208, 236 Abr 66, 77, 85 Ios 18, 38, 101 Mos 1:163, 177, 278 Mos 2:96, 133, 139, 246, 288 Decal 14, 135 Spec 1:293 Spec 2:21, 25, 146, 158, 163 Spec 4:96, 178 Virt 77, 100, 102, 113, 165, 219 Praem 80 Prob 140, 159 Contempl 22, 51 Aet 81, 91, 102, 103, 103, 135 Flacc 28, 46, 74, 152, 152, 159 Legat 195, 216, 312 Prov 2:64, 70 QG 1:27 QE 2:24b

στεναγμός Leg 3:200, 211, 211

στενάζω (9) Leg 3:212 Det 93, 94 Deus 115, 138 Migr 15, 15, 155 Praem 170

στενός Praem 145

στενότης Sacr 61

στενοχωρέω QG 4:33a

στένω (24) Leg 3:211, 211, 212, 216 Det 119, 119, 130, 140 Agr 33 Conf 92 Mut 24 Abr 22 Mos 1:10, 14, 137, 182, 248 Mos 2:225 Spec 2:87 Spec 3:4 Praem 72 Flacc 88 Legat 116 QG 1:72

στενωπός Opif 17 Post 50 Mos 1:104 Flacc 71

στέργω (17) Cher 73 Ebr 84 Sobr 15, 22, 23 Mut 50 Somn 2:98 Ios 4, 5, 223 Mos 1:45 Spec 2:3, 139 Spec 3:101 Virt 104, 225 Legat 277

στερέμνιος Somn 1:17

στερεομετρία Opif 98

στερεός (στερρός) (33) Opif 36, 36, 49, 49, 50, 92, 98, 102, 106 Leg 1:3, 3 Leg 2:81 Cher 60 Det 115, 115 Deus 13 Plant 7 Conf 89, 102 Migr 223 Her 218 Congr 146, 147 Mut 211, 212 Abr 192 Mos 2:115 Decal 24, 25, 26 Spec 2:212, 212 Legat 301 στερέω (16) Leg 2:46, 63 Leg 3:38 Fug 17, 18, 18, 19, 80, 107 Mos 2:225 Spec 2:55 Spec 4:178 Virt 123 Aet 29 Legat 152 QG 3:3

στερέωμα Opif 36, 36 Conf 96

στέρησις (8) Opif 167 Deus 101 Fug 89 Mos 1:141 Mos 2:234 Spec 4:23 Flacc 118 Legat 17

στεριφόομαι Mos 1:230

στέριφος Aet 129

στέρνον (23) Opif 118 Leg 1:12, 70, 71, 71 Leg 3:114, 115 Post 3 Migr 66 Ios 23 Mos 1:93 Mos 2:118, 124, 133 Spec 1:87, 146 Spec 4:93 Contempl 30 Flacc 157, 189 QG (Par) 2:2, 2:3, 2:5

στερνοτυπία Legat 227

στέρομαι (25) Leg 1:104 Leg 3:114 Cher 59 Post 125 Ebr 156 Ios 58 Mos 2:231, 232 Spec 1:62 Spec 2:111, 113, 121 Spec 3:143, 179, 201, 207 Spec 4:3 Virt 114 Praem 105, 139 Flacc 56, 77, 123, 176 Hypoth 7:4

στερρός στερεός

στερρότης Deus 22

στεφάνη Agr 170

στεφανηφορέω Ios 18, 138

Στεφανίων Flacc 112

στέφανος (27) Leg 2:108 Leg 3:74 Cher 80 Sacr 17 Agr 114, 117 Migr 27, 133, 134 Mut 44, 82, 88, 93, 109 Somn 1:130, 130 Somn 2:62 Mos 2:114 Decal 4 Praem 11, 27 Contempl 42 Legat 46, 95, 103, 133 QG 4:228

στεφανόω (16) Leg 1:80 Leg 2:108 Sacr 53, 53 Det 29 Deus 147 Agr 112, 112, 171 Her 47 Congr 159 Somn 2:62 Praem 13, 52 Contempl 57 Legat 12

στῆθος (22) Leg 1:68, 68 Leg 3:65, 114, 114, 116, 118, 123, 126, 128, 130, 131, 132, 134, 135, 138, 140, 160 Migr 66 Mos 2:112 Spec 1:145, 146

στηθύνιον (6) Leg 3:129, 133, 136, 137, 147 Migr 67

στήλη (37) Opif 128 Leg 3:225, 230, 230, 230 Ebr 164 Her 167 Fug 121 Somn 1:13, 172, 189, 241, 242, 244, 245, 247, 247, 248, 249, 249, 252, 256 Mos 1:276 Decal 50 Spec 1:31, 280, 328 Spec 3:36 Spec 4:1, 41, 61, 149 Prob 46 Legat 133 QG 4:191a QE 2:17, 17

στηλιτεύω (23) Det 75, 125 Ebr 141 Conf 74, 106 Migr 85 Her 176, 258 Congr 58 Fug 122 Abr 4, 158, 177 Mos 2:108 Decal 65 Spec 1:92 Spec 4:69, 142 Virt 15, 51, 95, 210 Prob 95

στηλογραφέω Her 30

στήριγμα Somn 1:158

στηρίζω (19) Opif 67, 84 Leg 3:45, 45 Agr 75, 160 Ebr 156 Migr 148 Congr 58 Fug 49 Somn 1:3, 133, 144, 157, 241 Somn 2:11, 19 Spec 2:202 Praem 30

στιβάς Somn 2:56 Contempl 69

στιγματίας Prob 10

στιγμή Cher 36

στίζω Somn 2:84

στίλβων Cher 22 Her 224 Decal 54

στῖφος (22) Agr 32, 83, 146, 162 Plant 60 Ebr 64, 198 Conf 19, 52, 110, 144, 193 Migr 63 Her 244 Somn 1:149, 174 Somn 2:121, 153 Virt 43 Prob 63, 74 Legat 132

στιφρός Mos 2:182 Spec 2:20 Hypoth 11:12

στίχος Leg 1:81, 81, 81

στοά (8) Leg 3:98 Cher 100 Post 50 Spec 1:71, 156 Legat 150, 151 Prov 2:48

Στοά Aet 8, 89

στοιχεῖον (89) Opif 38, 52, 84, 126, 127, 131, 131, 146 Leg 1:14 Leg 3:121 Cher 127 Sacr 74 Det 7, 8, 8 Gig 22 Deus 46 Agr 136 Plant 10 Her 134, 140, 152, 190, 197, 209, 210, 226, 226, 226, 227, 282 Congr 117, 150, 150 Mut 61, 61, 77 Somn 1:21, 212 Abr 81, 162 Mos 1:96, 97, 155, 156, 216 Mos 2:53, 65, 88, 121, 121, 148, 154, 251, 267, 286 Decal 31 Spec 1:208, 266, 294, 328 Spec 2:151, 255 Virt 73 Praem 44 Contempl 3, 4 Aet 6, 29, 61, 74, 78, 82, 90, 103, 107, 109, 111, 113, 116, 123, 144 Flacc 55, 125 Legat 80 Prov 2:45, 53 QG 4:8b, 51b

στοιχειώδης (6) Gig 7 Deus 104 Agr 181 Migr 180 Her 102 Spec 2:177

στοιχείωσις Agr 140

στοιχηδόν Ios 160 Spec 4:203 Flacc 92, 156

στοῖχος (8) Opif 141 Somn 2:139 Ios 217 Mos 2:124, 133 Spec 2:1 Spec 3:162 Contempl 66

στολή (9) Ebr 85, 86 Conf 74 Migr 203 Mut 43 Spec 4:69 Prob 101 Legat 296 QG 4:203

στόλισις Mos 2:145

στόλος Mos 2:157 Spec 4:28 Flacc 92 Legat 250

στόμα (101) Opif 119, 123 Leg 1:12, 36, 74, 74 Leg 3:103, 103, 174, 176, 176 Cher 116 Sacr 61 Det 23, 39, 92, 100, 102, 134 Post 55, 85, 182 Deus 84 Agr 21, 53, 133 Plant 133 Ebr 103, 191 Conf 33, 36 Migr 47, 71, 80, 81, 81, 81, 84, 114 Her 14, 25, 25, 110, 266 Congr 30, 170 Fug 31, 86, 182, 197 Mut 56, 91, 107, 139, 177, 178, 237, 238, 240, 243 Somn 1:29, 235 Somn 2:60, 132, 165, 180, 275, 278, 280, 302 Abr 29, 42, 191 Ios 214, 246 Mos 1:84, 84, 93, 115 Mos 2:127, 198, 239 Decal 32, 74, 91, 93 Spec 1:241, 272 Spec 3:78 Virt 183, 183 Praem 80, 118 Prob 68 Legat 66, 125, 162, 191, 280, 360 QG (Par) 2:3

στομαργία Spec 1:53

στόμαργος Her 109 Decal 63

στόμαχος (6) Opif 118 Leg 1:12 Spec 1:217, 217 Praem 143 QG (Par) 2:7

στόμιον (12) Det 40, 100, 103 Post 182 Deus 38, 39 Mut 107 Ios 178, 180, 207 Spec 3:147, 149

στομόω Opif 38 Agr 114 Somn 1:31

στοργή Spec 3:91

στόρνυμι (στρώννυμι) Prov 2:26

στοχάζομαι (41) Opif 10, 58, 132, 150 Leg 3:72 Cher 55, 73, 91, 99 Post 141 Agr 40 Migr 95 Her 224 Fug 181 Mut 153, 231 Ios 89, 116, 162 Mos 1:16 Mos 2:151, 164, 245, 264 Spec 1:140, 194 Spec 2:106 Spec 4:39, 213 Virt 22, 146 Praem 33, 43, 52 Aet 126 Legat 42, 236, 246 Prov 1 QG 4:104 QG (Par) 2:6

στοχασμός (20) Opif 59, 72, 114, 157 Post 80 Ebr 167 Conf 159 Somn 1:23 Ios 7, 104, 143 Mos 1:287 Mos 2:122 Decal 18 Spec 1:38, 334 Spec 4:50 Aet 2, 2 Legat 21

στοχαστής Opif 45 Spec 1:61 Praem 46

στοχαστικός Her 248

στραταρχέω Virt 47 Praem 95

στρατάρχης Mos 2:273 Decal 53 Virt 77 Flacc 111

στραταρχία Mos 1:60 Prov 2:54

στρατεία (17) Leg 3:14 Ebr 75, 76 Mut 221 Abr 261 Mos 1:168, 305, 329 Mos 2:236 Spec 1:165 Spec 3:17, 127, 172 Spec 4:213 Virt 28 Prob 33 Flacc 5

στράτευμα (6) Agr 86, 87 Conf 174 Abr 180, 197 Aet 79

στρατεύω (12) Leg 3:14 Agr 154 Ebr 76 Mos 1:315, 316 Mos 2:1 Virt 30 Prob 32, 118 Flacc 86 Legat 8, 342

στρατηγέω Ios 3

στρατήγημα (6) Spec 4:51 Virt 34, 37 Praem 25 Legat 40 QG 4:228

στρατηγία Ios 3

στρατηγιάω Abr 221

στρατηγικός Agr 87 Mos 1:61, 306 Virt 28 Flacc 40

στρατηγός (18) Sacr 130 Abr 272 Mos 1:216, 306, 313 Decal 178 Spec 1:55, 121 Spec 3:74 Spec 4:186 Virt 25, 32, 186 Prob 132, 139 Prov 2:61 QG 4:206b, 228

στρατία (22) Opif 113 Agr 147, 148 Her 203 Abr 234 Mos 1:175, 252, 282, 285, 289, 304 Decal 53, 152 Spec 1:207 Spec 3:187 Virt 32 Praem 41, 54 Flacc 30 Legat 207, 208, 234

στρατιώτης (13) Leg 3:115 Conf 45 Spec 1:146 Spec 4:93 Virt 32, 186 Flacc 5, 5, 86, 109, 111, 113, 115

στρατιωτικός (13) Spec 3:16 Virt 23, 31, 218 Flacc 5, 89 Legat 8, 58, 222, 252, 252, 256 QE 2:45a

στρατοπεδεία Mos 1:276 Mos 2:73

στρατοπεδεύω Leg 3:151 Post 155 Fug 187 Mos 1:169, 288

στρατόπεδον (37) Leg 3:46 Det 160 Gig 54 Agr 11 Ebr 99, 99, 100, 104, 124, 143 Abr 234 Mos 1:200, 209, 288, 312, 313, 315, 316 Mos 2:163, 167, 213, 260, 273 Decal 104 Spec 1:121 Spec 2:190 Spec 3:17 Spec 4:28, 128, 186, 220 Virt 186 Flacc 92, 120, 120 Legat 259 Prov 2:54

στρατός (15) Sacr 5 Post 119 Agr 79 Conf 174 Somn 2:119 Mos 1:216, 250, 258, 294, 306, 320 Mos 2:248 Spec 4:222 Virt 48 Aet 46

στρέβλη Spec 3:159

στρεβλός Post 28

στρεβλόω Abr 104 Prob 106 Legat 206

στρεπτός Somn 2:219

στρέφω (9) Cher 1, 21, 25 Post 83 Migr 115 Fug 121 Flacc 131 QG isf 13 QE 2:55a

στροβέω Cher 75 Agr 126 Conf 23 QE isf 31

στρόγγυλος Leg 3:57

στροφή Ios 136 Spec 1:91 Contempl 80, 84 QE 2:55b

στρυφνός Somn 1:17 Prob 26, 65

στρωμνή (8) Somn 1:123, 125 Somn 2:57 Spec 2:20 Contempl 49, 69 Flacc 148 Prov 2:17

στρώννυμι στόρνυμι

στυγέω (6) Sobr 22, 23 Somn 2:98, 104 Spec 2:139 Virt 200

στυγητός Decal 131

στῦλος Migr 124 Mos 2:90

στωικός Post 133

Στωικός (7) Aet 4, 8, 18, 54, 76, 78, 102

στωμυλία Cher 105 Mos 1:299 Virt 40

στωμύλος Prob 38 Legat 168

σύ (920) Leg 1:48, 51, 90 Leg 2:27, 27, 27, 34, 46, 51, 59, 59, 78, 84, 84, 84, 84, 88, 88, 88, 91, 92, 106 Leg 3:4, 9, 9, 9, 9, 21, 22, 45, 52, 54, 55, 65, 65, 65, 65, 65, 65, 74, 85, 85, 88, 88, 101, 101, 102, 107, 133, 151, 153, 153, 156, 158, 161, 162, 174, 174, 174, 174, 174, 179, 179, 180, 182, 184, 184, 185, 188, 188, 188, 188, 193, 193, 193, 193, 194, 200, 200, 202, 203, 203, 203, 215, 215, 217, 217, 220, 220, 222, 222, 222, 225, 231, 231, 240, 246, 246, 246, 246, 248, 251, 251, 253 Cher 32, 35, 36, 36, 37, 49, 52, 67, 69, 69, 75, 108, 119, 130 Sacr 4, 4, 8, 9, 23, 24, 28, 29, 33, 42, 55, 55, 55, 56, 56, 57, 57, 66, 67, 69, 69, 77, 87, 87, 87, 89, 89, 89, 89, 89, 90, 97, 97, 104, 107, 114 Det 4, 4, 4, 5, 5, 5, 9, 10, 10, 11, 52, 52, 57, 59, 60, 62, 67, 67, 67, 67, 69, 74, 79, 96, 100, 101, 112, 126, 126, 126, 126, 127, 132, 150, 156, 158, 158, 161, 163, 163, 163, 164, 166, 166, 174 Post 24, 24, 24, 24, 28, 29, 29, 29, 30, 30, 30, 30, 35, 38, 41, 41, 69, 76, 76, 83, 85, 89, 89, 89, 89, 89, 102, 132, 132, 135, 135, 143 Gig 24, 44, 44, 44, 49, 50, 60, 63 Deus 6, 23, 50, 74, 114, 145, 145, 145, 145, 145, 145, 149, 149, 153, 157, 166, 167, 168, 169, 169, 171, 171 Agr 12, 21, 21, 21, 21, 51, 51, 57, 59, 78, 78, 84, 107, 107, 111, 129, 167, 167, 167, 170, 170 Plant 47, 47, 47, 53, 54, 59, 59, 59, 59, 63, 95, 95, 95, 95, 137, 138 Ebr 14, 28, 39, 42, 52, 54, 67, 72, 82, 82, 107, 107, 114, 126, 127, 127, 127, 127, 138, 138, 138, 146 Sobr 19 Conf 3, 29, 31, 55, 74, 74, 74, 79, 79, 81, 123, 138, 145, 145, 166, 166, 197, 197 Migr 1, 1, 1, 1, 1, 1, 1, 1, 1, 1, 8, 10, 27, 27, 27, 27, 29, 30, 43, 44, 46, 47, 47, 48, 53, 60, 60, 60, 62, 62, 62, 62, 68, 68, 70, 78, 78, 79, 79, 81, 81, 81, 81, 81, 84, 84, 84, 86, 101, 101, 109, 109, 115, 118, 122, 122, 126, 126, 131, 132, 168, 168, 171, 174, 174, 174, 174, 174, 183, 186, 186, 201, 208, 208 Her 2, 8, 8, 8, 8, 14, 14, 19, 20, 20, 20, 24, 25, 25, 25, 25, 25, 25, 25, 26, 27, 27, 27, 27, 29, 38, 44, 66, 68, 68, 69, 76, 81, 83, 86, 96, 96, 105, 105, 106, 162, 162, 162, 162, 162, 162, 166, 180, 189, 189, 206, 206, 251, 254, 258, 261, 262, 267, 275, 275, 277, 277, 277, 277, 277, 277, 313 Congr 13, 86, 86, 86, 86, 99, 125, 151, 152, 152, 153, 153, 153, 155, 155, 156, 157, 170, 170, 170, 170, 170, 170, 170, 170, 170, 173, 176, 176 Fug 1, 1, 1, 5, 20, 22, 23, 23, 23, 23, 23, 29, 30, 32, 35, 39, 39, 39, 39, 39, 46, 47, 48, 48, 50, 53, 58, 58, 58, 75, 89, 101, 137, 140, 142, 142, 149, 163, 174, 175, 175, 175, 175, 204, 207, 211, 211 Mut 1, 8, 9, 14, 14, 19, 20, 21, 21, 23, 23, 23, 42, 52, 57, 60, 60, 97, 119, 130, 139, 141, 152, 168, 173, 174, 177, 177, 201, 201, 215, 226, 227, 230, 237, 253, 253, 255, 259, 261, 264, 266, 266 Somn 1:3, 3, 3, 3, 3, 3, 3, 3, 3, 3, 3, 3, 54, 54, 56, 114, 143, 148, 148, 149, 159, 165, 166, 166, 173, 173, 176, 179, 179, 180, 189, 189, 189, 189, 189, 195, 195, 227, 227, 228, 229, 237, 238, 240 Somn 2:7, 7, 23, 70, 75, 75, 77, 80, 96, 111, 111, 111, 127, 175, 175, 175, 176, 180, 193, 193, 193, 221, 221, 223, 224, 224, 227, 229, 244, 248, 248, 254, 265, 265 Abr 74, 74, 131, 131, 131, 132, 132, 206, 224, 261 Ios 9, 45, 46, 66, 78, 92, 92, 94, 96, 104, 107, 144, 150, 166, 168, 168, 169, 184, 185, 185, 188, 213, 215, 223, 224, 224, 228, 230, 238, 241, 263, 266 Mos 1:46, 54, 69, 69, 73, 84, 84, 223, 244, 277, 280, 281, 289, 289, 290, 291, 293, 298, 322, 322, 323, 325, 329, 331, 332 Mos 2:235, 239, 252, 252, 273 Decal 74, 91, 100 Spec 1:41, 42, 42, 42, 42, 44, 45, 45, 47, 48, 266, 277, 294, 294, 299, 300, 306, 311, 318 Spec 2:11, 11, 75, 79, 82, 83, 91, 207, 207, 219,

261 Spec 3:53, 61, 155, 166 Spec 4:39, 59, 149, 214 Virt 59, 60, 60, 117, 124, 127, 127, 127, 132, 133, 165, 166, 184, 184, 195, 195, 195, 197 Praem 111, 128, 128, 131 Prob 25, 48, 68, 68, 68, 96, 99, 101, 101, 112, 115, 124, 124, 125, 144, 144 Flacc 6, 22, 22, 22, 23, 30, 98, 121, 170, 170 Legat 43, 81, 87, 88, 91, 142, 168, 230, 230, 255, 256, 263, 265, 274, 276, 277, 283, 284, 284, 287, 288, 288, 289, 291, 291, 294, 294, 298, 299, 301, 301, 311, 315, 319, 323, 327, 328, 329, 347, 353, 353, 355 Hypoth 6:4, 7:14, 7:20 Prov 2:72 QG 1:51, 55a, 66, 66, 70:1, 2:11, 11, 11, 11, 26b, 26b, 48, 48, 3:11a, 23, 23, 23, 24, 58, 58, 4:52d, 131, 180, 191c, 206a, 228 QE 2:1, 2, 18, 18, 18, 18, 18, 21, 24:1, 28

Συβαρίτης Spec 3:43 Spec 4:102

συβαριτικός Mos 1:3

συγγένεια (93) Opif 74, 77, 106, 145, 146 Leg 2:59 Det 88, 159 Gig 42 Agr 67 Plant 18 Ebr 61, 224 Conf 150 Migr 1, 2, 7, 10, 178 Her 26, 27, 69, 92, 238, 244, 277 Congr 104, 177 Fug 88, 112 Mut 114, 127 Somn 2:26 Abr 31, 41, 62, 154, 170 Ios 45, 172, 185 Mos 1:241, 243, 314 Mos 2:171, 244, 281 Decal 41, 107, 127, 152 Spec 1:111, 112, 317, 317 Spec 2:40, 80, 82, 124, 127, 128, 128, 223, 243 Spec 3:16, 25, 28, 126, 155, 158, 178 Spec 4:122, 159, 159 Virt 79, 146, 192, 196, 218 Praem 24, 57, 57, 109, 133, 163 Prob 79 Contempl 9, 18 Legat 29, 83, 104, 289 Prov 2:3

συγγενής (189) Opif 12, 62, 144, 147, 151, 163 Leg 1:4, 17 Leg 2:20, 85 Leg 3:33, 71, 161, 205, 242 Sacr 15, 39 Det 18, 82, 109, 164, 165 Post 30, 45, 52, 136, 153, 172, 180 Gig 8, 33, 66 Deus 4, 69, 79, 84 Agr 26, 45, 141, 154, 155 Plant 15, 29 Ebr 40, 90 Sobr 61 Conf 6, 30, 76, 90, 183 Migr 3, 10, 52, 60, 160 Her 21, 146, 267, 277 Congr 48, 142 Fug 17, 39, 191 Mut 29, 49, 98, 171, 193 Somn 1:45, 86, 109, 169, 248 Somn 2:82, 83, 205, 266 Abr 55, 63, 65, 106, 116, 245 Ios 77, 142 Mos 1:39, 239, 249, 258, 303, 307, 322 Mos 2:8, 9, 171, 220, 225, 226, 243, 265, 273 Decal 112, 134, 177 Spec 1:52, 68, 160, 200, 247, 253, 294, 297 Spec 2:19, 126, 127, 129, 204, 215 Spec 3:20, 44, 65, 65, 85, 90, 101, 131, 131, 149, 155, 155, 162, 165, 192 Spec 4:14, 19, 69, 88, 133, 135, 141, 159, 178, 210 Virt 51, 60, 64, 103, 116, 134, 140, 144, 165, 173, 176, 179, 195, 227 Praem 17, 36, 92, 162 Prob 1, 9, 21, 35, 71 Contempl 7, 13, 13, 14, 41 Flacc 60, 64, 72, 83 Legat 110, 138, 321 Prov 1, 2:4, 17, 19, 55, 69 QG 1:65, 2:34a QG isf 10

συγγενίδος QG 3:20a

συγγενικός (16) Det 68 Her 12 Congr 70 Mut 180 Somn 2:107 Abr 198 Ios 9 Mos 1:32 Mos 2:230 Spec 1:137 Spec 2:73 Spec 3:27 Virt 53 Prob 148 Legat 74, 235

συγγεννάω Agr 30 Conf 136 Spec 4:68 Praem 62

συγγίγνομαι Leg 3:42 Abr 63 Spec 3:1 Prov 2:14

συγγιγνώσκω (9) Mos 1:173, 184, 197, 273, 311 Mos 2:166 Spec 2:15 Praem 137 QG 3:52

συγγνώμη (16) Deus 134 Fug 84 Mos 1:37 Mos 2:208 Spec 1:42, 67, 235 Spec 2:23, 196 Spec 3:35, 42, 76, 195 Praem 166 Flacc 7 QG 1:68

συγγνώμων Spec 3:121 Spec 4:23 QG 4:193

συγγνωστός Ios 53, 150 Spec 3:121 Virt 127

σύγγραμμα (6) Abr 23 Mos 1:3 Contempl 29 Aet 12, 15 Hypoth 0:1

συγγραφεύς (7) Det 99 Congr 15, 148 Somn 1:52 Mos 2:48 Prob 98 Legat 165

συγγράφω Mos 2:11, 45 Prov 2:26

συγγυμνάζω Congr 141 Legat 175

συγκαθαιρέω Legat 133

συγκαθαίρω Somn 1:177

συγκαθιερόω Migr 98 Spec 1:179

συγκαθίζω Her 243, 247

συγκακουργέω Decal 91

συγκαλέω Leg 3:50 Ebr 98 Legat 213

συγκάμνω Det 168 Somn 2:154 Mos 1:40

συγκαταβαίνω Somn 1:147 Abr 105

συγκατάθεσις Post 175 Mos 2:228

συγκαταθύω Virt 134

συγκατακρημνίζω Conf 20

συγκαταπίμπρημι Abr 139

συγκαταπίνω Agr 68

συγκαταπλέκω Mos 2:111

συγκαταριθμέω Opif 15 Leg 2:94

συγκατατάσσω Conf 86 Somn 2:257 Mos 2:81

συγκατατίθημι Leg 3:246

συγκαταφλέγω Abr 182 Flacc 69

συγκεράννυμι (8) Opif 146 Cher 127 Migr 207 Mut 184 Spec 1:264 Virt 76 Aet 29 QG 2:59

συγκεφαλαιόω QG 1:1

συγκινέω Leg 2:55 Conf 67 Somn 1:2 Somn 2:2 Decal 44

συγκλείω (17) Migr 34 Congr 1, 12, 13 Somn 2:36 Abr 23 Ios 23 Mos 1:167 Spec 1:320 Spec 2:105, 207 Prob 13 Flacc 56, 166, 172 Legat 190, 330

συγκληρονόμος (6) Spec 2:73 Legat 28, 29, 67, 75, 87

σύγκλητος Somn 2:187 Legat 75

σύγκλυς (12) Leg 1:50 Leg 3:187 Ebr 36 Migr 154 Fug 85 Mut 144 Ios 59 Mos 1:147 Decal 10 Spec 3:79 Flacc 4, 135

συγκολάζω Spec 3:165

συγκομιδή (11) Opif 115 Mos 2:269 Decal 161 Spec 2:198 Spec 4:208 Praem 128, 129 Flacc 93 Legat 249, 253, 257

συγκομίζω (30) Opif 80 Leg 3:249 Migr 202 Somn 2:76, 272 Abr 173 Ios 112 Mos 1:38, 203, 205, 205, 254 Mos 2:214, 220, 220, 259, 262 Spec 1:183 Spec 2:70, 153, 197, 205, 213 Spec 4:12, 29 Virt 90 Praem 102, 103, 129 Legat 260

συγκόπτω Ebr 23 Legat 364, 366

συγκραταιόω Her 311

σύγκριμα (22) Leg 1:26 Leg 2:2, 2 Leg 3:191 Sacr 49, 105 Det 52, 84, 103, 126, 139 Post 58, 68 Gig 62 Deus 111, 117, 117 Fug 164 Mut 184 Mos 1:155 Praem 44 Aet 6

συγκρίνω (22) Leg 1:106 Sacr 39, 108 Post 105 Deus 104 Agr 155 Ebr 43, 45 Her 282 Somn 1:211, 212 Spec 1:73 Spec 3:202 Spec 4:179 Praem 134, 143 Contempl 3, 9, 58 Flacc 58, 59, 128

σύγκρισις (27) Opif 97, 138 Sacr 14 Det 151 Gig 41 Deus 82 Plant 68 Ebr 187 Sobr 8 Conf 20 Migr 19 Somn 2:24 Abr 36 Ios 158 Mos 1:83 Mos 2:194, 198 Spec 4:42 Virt

85, 203 Praem 130 Aet 46 Flacc 162, 187 Legat 78, 165 QG 2:54a

σύγκριτος Cher 114, 114 Sacr 48 Mut 3 Virt 203

συγκροτέω (47) Post 52 Gig 60 Agr 35, 88, 146 Plant 139 Conf 46, 101, 162 Her 110 Congr 17 Fug 114 Mut 85 Somn 1:170, 251 Somn 2:263, 274 Abr 29, 105 Ios 1, 2, 81 Mos 1:251, 264, 310 Mos 2:185 Spec 1:206, 259 Spec 2:98 Spec 4:45, 101 Virt 18, 51, 70 Praem 88 Prob 34 Contempl 60 Flacc 5, 135, 162 Legat 39, 96, 119, 171, 178, 255 Prov 2:56

συγκρύπτω (10) Leg 2:53 Leg 3:49, 158 Conf 116 Somn 1:104, 109 Ios 25, 68, 238 QG isf 7

συγκτάομαι Virt 216

συγκυκάω Legat 267

συγχαίρω (7) Leg 2:82, 82 Leg 3:219 Det 123, 124 Post 21 Mut 138

συγχαρητικός Leg 2:82

συγχειρουργέω Abr 97 Flacc 44

συγχέω (55) Opif 38 Leg 3:127 Sacr 82 Det 73, 77 Agr 129, 167 Plant 3 Ebr 77, 103, 143 Sobr 3 Conf 1, 1, 84, 152, 168, 182, 189, 191 Migr 56, 59, 163 Her 246, 294 Congr 129 Mut 72, 189 Somn 2:239, 290, 290 Abr 20, 174, 230 Ios 22, 97, 197, 218 Mos 1:26, 178 Spec 1:30, 62, 106, 326, 328 Spec 2:94 Spec 3:209 Spec 4:77, 208 Virt 24 Flacc 135 Legat 132, 143, 330 QG 2:12c

συγχορεύω Mos 2:7 Spec 1:207

συγχράομαι Post 13 Abr 216

σύγχυσις (38) Opif 33 Leg 3:123, 224 Post 53, 81 Deus 166 Plant 3 Conf 1, 1, 9, 43, 109, 158, 183, 184, 187, 188, 191, 191, 192, 192, 195, 198 Mut 150 Somn 2:152, 286 Mos 2:277 Spec 1:120, 329 Praem 76, 143 Aet 6, 79, 79, 82, 82 Legat 94 Prov 2:1

συγχυτικός Somn 2:286

συγχωρέω QG 4:194

συζάω (συζῶ) (11) Leg 3:77 Det 34 Her 295 Fug 43 Somn 2:141 Abr 20 Ios 83 Spec 2:49 Virt 11 QG 4:74 QE isf 32

συζεύγνυμι (12) Leg 2:4 Sacr 37 Det 15 Post 60, 62 Sobr 60 Migr 17 Her 92 Mos 1:184 Aet 59, 73, 139

συζήτησις Leg 3:131 Det 1

συζυγή Det 15 Post 60 QG 4:72

συζυγία (9) Post 61 Agr 124 Mos 2:7 Spec 4:207, 208 Praem 71 Aet 104, 104, 105

συζῶ συζάω

συκέα συκῆ

συκῆ (συκέα) QG 1:41

σῦκον Plant 112

συκοφαντέω (19) Cher 36 Mut 240 Ios 197, 198, 210, 222, 235, 244, 270 Mos 1:281 Decal 172 Spec 3:62, 80, 82 Spec 4:39, 40 Flacc 95 Legat 169, 356

συκοφάντημα Spec 4:40 Flacc 86, 86, 89

συκοφάντης (8) Cher 35 Plant 72 Somn 2:148 Spec 3:53 Spec 4:40, 42 Virt 141 Legat 355

συκοφαντία Ios 209 Spec 4:84

συλάω (6) Leg 3:20 Conf 47 Decal 133, 136 Spec 3:203 Prov 2:33

Συλεύς Prob 102, 103

σύλη σῦλον

συλλαβή Post 94 Mut 64 Flacc 131

συλλαβομαχέω Congr 53 QE isf 8

συλλαμβάνω (50) Leg 1:30 Leg 3:99 Cher 40, 46, 54, 57, 57 Sacr 4 Post 33, 124 Gig 20 Deus 38 Agr 24, 33 Ebr 14, 101 Migr 223 Her 310 Congr 66, 126, 126 Fug 167, 167 Ios 14, 79 Mos 1:71, 209, 227 Mos 2:214 Decal 146 Spec 4:9, 33, 34, 83, 107, 170 Prob 147 Flacc 40, 74, 96, 140, 140, 186 Legat 128, 219 Prov 2:64 QG 2:65, 3:18, 4:206a, 228

συλλέγω (18) Leg 3:14 Deus 38 Agr 86 Her 191 Mut 84 Somn 2:146 Mos 1:106, 208 Spec 1:268, 325 Spec 2:60, 148, 251 Spec 4:214 Virt 91 Praem 157 Flacc 68 Hypoth 7:19

συλλειτουργέω Spec 1:96

συλλήβδην (8) Migr 9 Abr 49 Mos 2:288 Decal 39 Spec 1:224 Aet 82, 144 Legat 184

σύλληψις (10) Ebr 172 Mut 237 Ios 51 Spec 4:81, 128, 129 Flacc 108, 116, 119, 145

συλλογή Ios 6

συλλογίζομαι Leg 2:99 Leg 3:37, 38 Ios 113

συλλογισμός Spec 2:36

συλλογιστικός Plant 115

σύλλογος (13) Leg 3:81 Post 177 Deus 111 Mut 198 Somn 2:184 Abr 20 Spec 1:321, 325, 344 Spec 2:44 Spec 3:169 Contempl 30 Legat 73

συλλούομαι Legat 175

σῦλον (σύλη) Spec 4:84

συμβαίνω (328) Opif 49, 51, 61, 67, 68, 79, 102, 121, 122, 124, 129, 136, 143, 144, 153, 164 Leg 1:14, 19, 70 Leg 3:115, 117, 122, 168, 172, 244 Cher 4, 22, 34, 35, 37, 38, 66, 80, 80, 86 Sacr 2, 15, 54, 56, 70, 80, 93, 103, 106, 123, 134 Det 40, 82, 178 Post 6, 23, 25, 40, 100, 167 Gig 62 Deus 15, 27, 93, 97, 131 Agr 22, 33, 99, 101, 141, 157, 164 Plant 30, 43, 65, 84, 120, 147, 150, 172, 177 Ebr 51, 104, 114, 115, 152, 169, 182, 211 Conf 6, 9, 10, 32, 43, 98, 119, 136, 149, 174, 177, 196 Migr 2, 34, 137, 140, 171, 180, 181, 188, 201 Her 173, 191, 199, 233, 236, 246, 249, 265, 285, 289, 310 Congr 2, 11, 18, 22, 25, 26, 32, 51, 74 Fug 76, 77, 104, 128 Mut 28, 81, 90, 100, 106, 125, 142, 148, 155, 161, 163, 236, 239, 248, 249 Somn 1:8, 16, 36, 82, 84, 111, 144, 160, 169, 218 Somn 2:20, 152, 194, 268 Abr 4, 11, 27, 35, 50, 74, 115, 119, 141, 204, 240, 257, 257 Ios 12, 20, 26, 85, 100, 104, 150, 189, 217, 218, 236, 241, 248 Mos 1:12, 37, 58, 65, 98, 119, 129, 136, 138, 165, 183, 187, 191, 196, 200, 204, 217, 219, 226, 227, 234, 248, 253, 257, 269, 276, 279, 308, 310 Mos 2:24, 38, 56, 57, 59, 154, 181, 226, 235, 266, 288 Decal 11, 16, 19, 29, 47, 73, 140, 147 Spec 1:36, 49, 66, 67, 78, 140, 148, 183, 202, 216, 219, 221, 222, 232, 246, 314, 323 Spec 2:46, 68, 81, 151, 158, 162, 164, 189, 197, 214, 215, 239, 260 Spec 3:19, 42, 57, 65, 74, 91, 99, 123, 134, 198, 206 Spec 4:10, 13, 25, 57, 91, 123, 133, 143, 162, 200, 209, 233 Virt 8, 26, 30, 55, 138, 157, 186 Praem 1, 23, 32, 34, 59, 61, 98, 170 Prob 31, 55, 85, 113, 151 Aet 63, 87, 99, 100, 104, 113, 133 Flacc 78, 120, 125 Legat 158, 215, 245 Hypoth 6:3, 7:16 Prov 2:58 QG 2:15b, 3:11a, 22, 4:166 QG isf 5 QG (Par) 2:7

συμβάλλω (15) Leg 3:60 Cher 104 Post 5 Ebr 95 Migr 219 Her 104 Congr 79 Somn 1:98 Spec 2:39, 78 Virt 83, 84 Flacc 139 QG 2:29, 4:191a σύμβασις (9) Det 149 Deus 56 Somn 2:108 Ios 156, 237, 240 Spec 3:31 Spec 4:221 Praem 167

συμβατήριος (8) Leg 3:134 Ebr 220 Migr 202 Abr 214 Virt 151, 178 Aet 68 Legat 100

συμβατός Deus 29

συμβιβάζω Ebr 37 Her 25, 25

σύμβιος Post 78 Congr 59

συμβιόω (17) Congr 36, 41 Fug 213 Somn 2:234 Abr 1, 50, 163, 248 Mos 2:162 Spec 2:30 Spec 3:167 Spec 4:150 Praem 23 Contempl 68 QG 3:29, 4:200b QE 2:2

συμβίωσις Congr 5, 32 Spec 3:35

συμβιωτής Abr 23 Spec 2:31 Flacc 158

συμβόλαιον Mut 104 Spec 4:30

συμβολή (8) Ebr 20, 21, 22, 23, 25, 29, 95 Contempl 51

συμβολικός (52) Opif 154, 164 Leg 1:1, 21, 68, 72 Leg 2:27, 72 Leg 3:93, 159 Sacr 47, 57 Det 15, 122, 160 Post 32, 53, 57, 148 Deus 95 Conf 101, 115, 133 Her 106, 112, 127, 177, 296 Fug 77 Mut 110, 237, 253 Somn 1:79, 118, 134, 146 Somn 2:238, 260 Abr 99, 103, 147 Ios 148 Mos 2:82 Spec 1:205, 206, 293, 332 Spec 2:185 Spec 3:179 Praem 47 QG 2:64c QE 2:17

συμβολοκοπέω Ebr 14, 23

σύμβολον (204) Opif 157 Leg 1:26, 58, 80, 97 Leg 2:15, 89 Leg 3:24, 45, 74, 120, 135, 167, 176, 209, 232, 248 Cher 5, 12, 26, 28 Sacr 112, 120 Det 32 Post 97, 100, 112, 137, 163 Deus 96, 103, 128, 137, 154 Agr 108, 109 Plant 38, 43, 77, 82, 122 Ebr 4, 15, 85, 95, 134 Sobr 23, 28 Conf 23, 37, 72 Migr 2, 77, 89, 92, 93, 95, 103, 165, 188, 207, 213, 221 Her 197, 198, 199, 217, 226, 227, 227, 239, 263 Congr 11, 20, 21, 30, 44, 83, 117, 117, 161 Fug 45, 59, 64, 111, 128, 150, 183 Mut 2, 12, 14, 44, 52, 60, 69, 70, 78, 98, 99, 124, 134, 158, 193, 228, 247, 249, 261 Somn 1:6, 38, 74, 89, 90, 92, 102, 127, 144, 160, 198, 217, 242 Somn 2:33, 73, 109, 169 Abr 52, 72, 119, 202 Ios 7, 96, 210 Mos 1:23, 67, 217 Mos 2:96, 98, 101, 103, 105, 115, 119, 120, 121, 122, 130, 138, 150, 183, 186 Decal 48 Spec 1:8, 25, 80, 85, 86, 93, 97, 103, 145, 167, 172, 175, 200, 200, 250, 253, 260, 269, 277, 285, 287, 292, 317 Spec 2:29, 180, 184 Spec 3:56, 57, 58, 178, 179 Spec 4:106, 108, 112, 114, 138 Virt 183, 183 Praem 61 Prob 2, 29, 36, 68, 82, 136 Contempl 28, 46, 78 Aet 68 Legat 98 Prov 2:24 QG 2:38 QE 2:14, 24b

συμβουλευτικός Spec 1:342

συμβουλεύω (11) Leg 3:244 Agr 165 Ios 15 Mos 1:236, 294, 294, 300 Spec 4:173 Flacc 26, 43 Legat 222

συμβουλή Fug 24

συμβουλία Ios 116

σύμβουλος (25) Opif 79 Sacr 10 Agr 95, 97 Migr 136 Congr 61 Fug 6 Mut 104 Somn 1:111, 113, 191 Somn 2:292 Abr 14, 256 Ios 60, 240 Decal 177 Spec 4:175 Virt 1, 118 Flacc 18 Legat 70, 203, 204, 206

Συμεών (11) Leg 1:81 Ebr 94 Migr 224 Fug 73 Mut 97, 97, 99, 101, 200, 200 Somn 2:33

συμμαχία (29) Leg 3:14 Det 166 Ebr 58, 79 Conf 39 Migr 56 Somn 1:147, 227 Somn 2:265 Abr 95, 180, 232, 235 Mos 1:50, 111, 216, 260, 328, 333 Decal 42 Spec 3:16, 172 Spec 4:121, 178, 219, 222 Virt 46, 109 Praem 93

συμμαχικός Somn 2:267 Mos 1:217

σύμμαχος (34) Leg 2:7, 10, 24 Leg 3:31 Cher 39 Sacr 45 Det 33 Gig 67 Agr 63, 86, 151, 151 Ebr 13, 29, 64, 68 Conf 34, 111 Migr 62 Somn 2:50 Abr 231, 242 Mos 1:56, 306, 313, 327, 333 Spec 4:219 Virt 23, 48, 153 Prob 132, 139 QE 2:16

συμμένω Hypoth 6:3

συμμεταβάλλω (8) Deus 22, 28 Plant 87 Abr 151 Ios 33 Spec 3:194, 209 QG isf 5

συμμετρέω Legat 253

συμμετρία (7) Opif 138 Post 142 Agr 168 Congr 75 Mos 2:140 QG 4:102a QG (Par) 2:5

σύμμετρος Mos 2:256

συμμορία Flacc 135

συμπάθεια (8) Opif 113, 117 Migr 178, 180 Somn 1:53 Abr 69 Spec 1:16, 250

συμπαθέω Spec 2:115

συμπαθής Leg 1:8 Mos 2:228 Spec 4:202 Legat 273

συμπαραλαμβάνω Agr 179 Legat 355

συμπαράληψις Opif 75 Leg 3:235

συμπαραχωρέω Hypoth 7:17

συμπάρειμι Legat 171

συμπαρέρχομαι Aet 135

σύμπας (242) Opif 3, 25, 38, 56, 57, 71, 89, 100, 102, 130, 131, 131, 143 Leg 1:44, 57 Leg 2:49 Leg 3:5, 11, 29, 78, 145, 150 Cher 26, 44, 49, 88, 91, 99 Sacr 8, 34, 40, 78 Det 55, 75 Post 19, 114, 144, 155 Deus 19, 21, 57, 73, 79, 106, 107 Agr 18, 77 Plant 69, 116, 125, 126, 127 Ebr 49, 75, 152 Conf 5, 19, 50, 98, 100, 100, 170, 173 Migr 6, 36, 67, 131 Her 55, 130, 140, 156, 197, 206, 245, 247, 283, 301, 314 Congr 11, 120, 133 Fug 46, 97, 103, 109, 182, 198 Mut 30, 53, 54, 55, 135, 140, 224 Somn 1:59, 63, 73, 128 Somn 2:81, 188 Abr 57, 58, 75, 97, 136, 166, 256, 260 Ios 37, 145 Mos 1:7, 23, 99, 112, 112, 155, 160, 189, 200, 201, 234, 318, 320 Mos 2:14, 36, 53, 59, 62, 79, 89, 98, 112, 115, 118, 133, 150, 186, 209, 214, 216, 224, 250, 271, 291 Decal 49, 53, 53, 66, 71, 150 Spec 1:23, 32, 34, 37, 44, 66, 81, 88, 175, 177, 181, 189, 199, 226, 232, 300, 302, 322 Spec 2:5, 92, 97, 113, 130, 145, 162, 165, 167, 170, 171, 171, 224, 230, 255, 260 Spec 3:1, 38, 131 Spec 4:85, 113, 146, 154, 157, 179, 180 Virt 74, 79, 85, 119, 129, 131, 185, 212 Praem 23, 32, 36, 41, 85, 123, 129 Prob 142, 143 Contempl 5, 28 Aet 21, 47, 83, 89, 102, 103, 123 Flacc 1, 11, 92, 123, 141, 188 Legat 6, 19, 39, 68, 108, 144 Hypoth 6:2, 6:4, 7:20 Prov 2:2 QG 2:34a, 64b, 3:3, 4:51b QG isf 1 QE 2:55a

συμπάσχω Spec 3:194 Prov 2:23

συμπείθω Ios 236 Mos 1:59 Legat 59

συμπέμπω Ios 184

συμπεραιόω Spec 4:235

συμπέρασμα Spec 2:41, 142, 211, 212, 213

συμπεριάγω Plant 12

συμπεριπολέω Opif 70 Spec 1:37 Spec 2:45 Spec 3:1 Praem 121

συμπήγνυμι Sacr 85

συμπίπρημι Legat 133

συμπίπτω (7) Cher 36 Sobr 6 Ios 99 Mos 1:118 Spec 3:104 Prob 24 Legat 117 συμπλεκτικός Her 198

συμπλέκω (10) Somn 1:200 Somn 2:146, 276 Abr 229 Mos 1:259, 309 Spec 2:190 Spec 3:87, 108, 172

συμπλέω Prob 128 QG 4:74

συμπληρόω (12) Opif 13, 101, 115 Leg 1:8 Leg 2:38 Plant 6 Somn 2:180 Mos 2:79, 80 Spec 2:177, 177 Legat 7

συμπλήρωμα Somn 2:116

συμπλήρωσις (8) Leg 2:24 Ebr 53 Conf 179 Somn 2:113 Mos 1:97 Spec 4:132 Aet 21 Prov 2:69

συμπληρωτικός Spec 3:118

συμπλοκή Her 198 Spec 3:105

συμπνέω Conf 69 Ios 176 Spec 1:138 QG 2:26a

συμποδίζω Deus 4

συμπολιτεύω QG 4:74

συμπορεύομαι Migr 164, 171, 173

συμποσίαρχος Somn 2:249 Flacc 137

συμπόσιον (27) Opif 78 Ebr 91 Somn 2:167 Abr 117 Decal 41 Spec 1:176, 221 Spec 2:148, 193 Spec 4:91 Contempl 40, 40, 42, 44, 48, 57, 57, 64, 71, 73, 83, 89 Flacc 112, 113, 115 Legat 42 QG 2:68a

συμπότης Ios 204 Contempl 45, 75

συμποτικός Ebr 91 Ios 203 Spec 3:186

σύμπραξις (8) Opif 72, 168 Conf 9, 175 Mut 4, 31, 259 Mos 1:133

συμπράσσω (9) Sacr 117 Mos 1:239 Decal 139, 172 Spec 1:60, 216 Spec 4:42 Virt 2 Legat 372

συμπρόειμι Legat 97

συμπροπέμπω Migr 173 QG 4:20

συμφερόντως (6) Sacr 19 Congr 137 Somn 1:233 Somn 2:153 Decal 132 QG 3:38b

συμφέρω (99) Opif 33 Leg 3:19, 61, 84, 160 Cher 13 Sacr 28, 35, 60, 71 Det 6, 53, 53, 72, 145 Gig 12 Deus 135 Agr 48, 68 Ebr 16, 20, 26, 33, 160, 166, 166, 197 Conf 16, 112 Her 14, 247 Congr 45, 85 Fug 26 Mut 91, 170, 170, 197 Somn 1:111, 142, 191 Somn 2:9, 150 Abr 18, 38, 105, 215, 256 Ios 30, 62, 63, 65, 73, 75, 77, 77, 143 Mos 1:235, 274 Mos 2:38, 58, 272 Decal 95 Spec 1:149, 203, 204, 206, 250, 301, 320, 330 Spec 2:12, 24, 42, 62, 236 Spec 4:45, 55, 85, 161, 174 Virt 3, 19, 69, 177, 181 Praem 33, 52, 55, 113 Contempl 15 Aet 79 Flacc 26 Legat 21, 108, 218, 221, 312 QG 4:206b

συμφεύγω QG 1:77

συμφθείρω (7) Leg 1:78 Det 75, 78 Agr 167 Mut 80 Somn 1:31 Mos 1:119

συμφοίτησις Legat 316

συμφοιτητής Abr 67 Prob 34 Flacc 158

συμφορά (96) Leg 3:121 Det 98, 176 Post 81 Deus 183 Conf 22, 22, 154, 166, 177 Migr 156 Abr 64, 142, 189, 257 Ios 17, 22, 27, 56, 80, 94, 179, 187, 226, 244, 248 Mos 1:11, 47, 69, 72, 90, 104, 135, 170, 173, 179, 183, 198, 216, 325 Mos 2:60 Decal 131, 152 Spec 1:237 Spec 3:16, 44, 93, 101, 115, 126, 140, 158, 195 Spec 4:85, 179, 200, 201 Virt 110, 111, 200 Praem 72, 127, 130, 134 Prob 56, 89, 90 Flacc 10, 53, 67, 72, 77, 104, 117, 124, 153, 160, 179, 180, 189 Legat 61, 91, 100, 121, 127, 192, 227, 234, 293, 325, 336, 340 QG 1:73, 2:54b, 4:52a QG isf 6

συμφορέω (8) Sacr 108 Conf 84, 192 Migr 152 Mut 144 Spec 1:336 Virt 90 Legat 130

συμφόρημα Sacr 108, 108 Deus 113 Somn 1:220

σύμφορος Det 45 Ebr 139 Praem 48

συμφρονέω (10) Conf 22, 55 Mos 1:45 Mos 2:175 Spec 2:48, 232 Spec 3:73 Flacc 128 Legat 8, 215

συμφυής (13) Cher 59 Gig 15 Agr 6, 45, 64 Her 242 Mut 53 Somn 1:122 Mos 2:147 Virt 103 Praem 72, 120, 144

συμφυΐα (8) Leg 3:38 Deus 35, 40 Spec 3:118 Virt 138 Contempl 7 Aet 114 Flacc 71

συμφύρω Migr 154

σύμφυτος (6) Opif 18 Her 272 Somn 1:246 Abr 160 Mos 1:198 Spec 4:16

συμφύω (6) Somn 2:180 Abr 63 Mos 2:254 Decal 87 Virt 197 QG 4:74

συμφωνέω (8) Ebr 202 Conf 26, 195 Abr 136, 211 Mos 1:24 QG 2:26a QE isf 18

συμφωνία (62) Opif 48, 51, 78, 95 Leg 1:72, 72 Cher 110 Sacr 36, 74, 75 Deus 25 Ebr 116, 117 Conf 15, 15, 21, 41, 43, 58, 67, 150, 150, 188, 198 Migr 178 Her 15, 28, 266 Congr 16, 76 Somn 1:28, 202 Somn 2:27, 28, 284 Ios 145, 269 Mos 1:117 Mos 2:48, 115, 119, 140, 256 Decal 22, 23 Spec 1:93, 102, 342 Spec 2:130, 157 Spec 4:102, 134 Virt 35, 73 Praem 145 Contempl 88 Aet 75 QG 1:17b, 2:26b, 34b, 4:174 QE 2:20

σύμφωνος (9) Opif 22 Ebr 116 Her 15 Mut 200 Ios 230 Mos 2:75 Virt 184 Legat 8 QE 2:38a

σύν (125) Opif 26, 41 Leg 2:2, 37, 44, 45, 45, 80 Leg 3:124, 132, 134, 135, 155, 156, 158, 158, 192, 217 Cher 24 Sacr 24, 49, 74 Det 104, 109, 113, 120 Post 30, 87 Deus 152 Agr 41, 70 Ebr 111, 190 Sobr 8 Conf 85, 102, 117, 117, 117, 163 Migr 88 Her 14, 42, 219 Congr 104, 143, 166 Fug 27, 72, 78, 90 Somn 2:30, 38, 71, 74, 96, 154, 188, 257 Abr 18, 64, 170, 245 Ios 107, 169, 259 Mos 1:10, 18, 125, 154, 168, 329 Mos 2:91, 96, 99, 121, 185 Decal 159 Spec 1:55, 56, 209, 268 Spec 2:62, 193, 231, 231, 235 Spec 3:31, 53, 74, 86, 125, 128 Spec 4:47, 48, 120, 156 Virt 32, 84, 95, 144, 158 Praem 57, 151 Prob 57, 124 Contempl 42 Flacc 112, 159, 184 Legat 59, 119, 165, 173, 241, 246, 336, 344, 361 Hypoth 7:12 Prov 2:58 QG 1:76a, 2:12d, 54d, 3:22

συναγορεύω Ebr 14 Ios 215 Mos 1:24 Legat 350

συνάγω (62) Opif 78, 152 Leg 1:37 Leg 2:72 Leg 3:105, 162, 163, 164, 165, 166 Cher 81 Sacr 36 Det 103, 162 Post 96, 104, 110 Deus 95 Plant 9 Ebr 19, 191 Sobr 19, 60 Conf 136, 197 Migr 202 Her 20, 40, 103, 244, 261, 270 Congr 162 Mut 32 Somn 1:12, 70, 205 Somn 2:60, 126, 262 Abr 232 Ios 38, 158 Mos 1:86, 258 Spec 3:65 Spec 4:74, 158 Virt 73, 146, 178 Praem 117 Prob 132 Aet 102 Flacc 27 Legat 26, 72, 156, 157, 315 Hypoth 7:12 QG 2:66

συναγωγή (7) Post 67, 67 Agr 44, 44 Prob 81 QG 2:66 QE 1:19

συναγώγιον Somn 2:127 Legat 311

συναγωγός (6) Leg 2:71 Cher 27 Plant 10 Decal 132 Spec 1:247, 291

συναγωνίζομαι Spec 4:179 Flacc 111 Legat 32

συναγωνιστής Det 58 Ebr 14 Somn 1:111 Spec 4:178 Legat 183

συναδικέω (6) Ebr 25 Conf 9, 10 Decal 123 Spec 3:73, 73

συνᾴδω (29) Opif 3 Det 72 Deus 133 Plant 50, 113, 138 Ebr 48 Sobr 27, 65 Conf 59 Migr 104 Congr 103 Fug 18 Ios 2, 253 Mos 1:287 Mos 2:52, 257, 257 Spec 1:202 Spec 2:130 Spec 4:60 Virt 31, 145 Prob 155 Legat 42 QG 4:174 QE isf 8, 26

συναηδίζομαι Conf 7

συναίνεσις (7) Ebr 165, 165, 198, 203 Conf 121 Somn 1:13 Spec 4:44

συναινέω (27) Opif 2, 156 Sacr 23, 28, 29 Ebr 104, 165, 165, 166 Migr 61 Congr 68, 115, 143 Somn 1:13 Abr 97 Ios 14, 173, 252 Mos 1:85 Spec 3:70, 71 Spec 4:44, 47, 54 Virt 39 Legat 248, 368

συναιρέω (14) Opif 73, 81, 98 Cher 111 Deus 175 Plant 44 Ebr 180 Migr 152 Mut 179, 221 Abr 153 Mos 2:19, 90 Aet 101

συναίρω Abr 235

συναισθάνομαι (11) Congr 151 Ios 48, 197 Spec 1:272 Virt 76 Flacc 41, 112, 186 Legat 18, 120, 267

συναίτιος Her 115 Flacc 35 Legat 219

συνακολουθέω Mos 1:85 Prob 94

συνακροάομαι Contempl 32

συναλγέω (8) Abr 260 Ios 94, 205 Decal 110 Spec 2:76 Flacc 72, 154 Legat 243

συνάμφω Aet 142

συναναβαίνω Migr 152

συναναβλαστάνω Plant 100 Migr 55

συνανάγω Somn 2:119

συναναιρέω (8) Mos 1:304 Spec 1:329 Spec 3:164 Aet 84, 85, 92 Flacc 14 Legat 329

συνανακεράννυμι Spec 1:254 Spec 3:95

συναναλάμπω Mos 2:44

συναναμείγνυμι Mos 1:278

συναναμέλπω Migr 104

συνανασπάω Somn 1:147 Aet 135

συνανατρέπω Somn 2:285

συναναφέρω Congr 102

συναναφλέγω Plant 108 Aet 20

συνάνειμι Migr 163

συνανέλκω Aet 136

συνανέρχομαι Agr 71

συνανίημι Abr 152

συναντάω Leg 3:81 Conf 29 Somn 2:277, 300 Flacc 160

συνάντησις (6) Det 30, 126 Post 132 Deus 145 Migr 79 Somn 1:71

συναπαίρω Spec 3:77, 78

συναπέρχομαι Migr 159

συναποδημέω Congr 48 Ios 217 Prob 94 QG 4:74

συναποθνήσκω Spec 1:108

συναπολαύω Virt 202 Prov 2:54

συναπόλλυμι (7) Leg 3:9, 10 Conf 22 Mut 80 Abr 46 Virt 139 Aet 128

συναπονοέομαι (6) Mos 1:236, 325 Mos 2:169 Spec 3:126 Spec 4:45 Praem 75

συναπορρύπτομαι Leg 3:142

συνάπτω (30) Leg 3:121 Post 104 Agr 137, 141 Plant 18 Ebr 8, 95 Sobr 64 Congr 76 Fug 49 Somn 1:28, 205 Somn 2:28, 28 Abr 42, 54 Mos 2:78, 80 Decal 106 Spec 2:150, 157 Praem 102 Aet 79, 80, 113, 139 Legat 217, 326 QG 3:23 QE 1:1

συναριθμέω (6) Leg 3:165 Her 12, 193 Mos 1:278 Mos 2:86 Spec 4:128

συναριστάω Legat 175

συναρμόζω Leg 2:4 Spec 2:157 Praem 120

συναρπάζω (11) Plant 39 Congr 126 Ios 36 Mos 1:125 Spec 1:29 Praem 73 Flacc 19, 65, 95 Legat 25, 243

συναρτάω Sacr 41 Aet 112

συνάρχω Spec 4:170 Legat 29

συνασεβέω Decal 89

συνασκέω Somn 1:250 Spec 1:206 Praem 4, 64

συνασμενίζω Spec 1:316

συνασμενισμός QE isf 14

συνατιμάζω Decal 119

συναυξάνω (συναύξω) (39) Opif 41, 158 Sacr 15, 123 Det 111 Post 129 Deus 87, 88 Agr 6, 56, 86 Ebr 224 Conf 29, 128, 144 Migr 55, 83, 193 Somn 1:105 Somn 2:170 Abr 63 Ios 159 Mos 2:19, 23, 55, 122 Decal 137 Spec 1:305, 336 Spec 2:99 Spec 3:84 Virt 225 Praem 146 Prob 63 Contempl 25 Aet 103 Flacc 135 Legat 116, 338

συναύξησις (11) Opif 103 Agr 23 Her 116 Somn 1:199 Ios 7 Spec 3:183 Spec 4:26, 234 Virt 157, 201 Prob 92

συναύξω συναυξάνω

συναφανίζομαι Legat 194

συναφηβάω Hypoth 11:7

συνάχθομαι Post 21 Conf 6

συνδειπνέω Flacc 115

σύνδεσμος Agr 136 Her 198 Congr 149

σύνδετος Leg 1:108 Leg 3:72 Det 48 Somn 1:46, 110

συνδέω (6) Somn 2:37 Mos 1:324 Spec 2:240 Aet 13 Flacc 92, 190

συνδιαιτάομαι Opif 144 Migr 214 Mos 1:277 Spec 1:127 Prov 2:63

συνδιαίτησις (7) Somn 2:16 Abr 67, 87 Ios 10 Praem 21, 100 Legat 310

συνδιαιωνίζω Mos 2:108 Spec 1:31, 76 Praem 71

συνδιαπορέω Prov 2:42

συνδιασκοπέω Her 293

συνδιατρίβω (14) Leg 3:84 Deus 27 Congr 127 Fug 43, 52 Somn 1:79 Abr 210 Ios 84 Mos 1:27, 143 Spec 4:37, 37 Legat 264 QG 4:74

συνδιαφέρω Agr 151

συνδιαφθείρω Somn 2:214 QG 1:94

συνδιέπω Prob 42 Legat 219

συνδικάζω Spec 4:170

συνδιοικέω Spec 4:170 Virt 55

συνδράω Cher 79 Aet 83

συνδυασμός Opif 14

συνεγγίζω (10) Opif 147 Cher 18 Post 27 Ebr 124 Migr 58, 59, 59 Somn 2:228 Praem 84 QE isf 10

συνεγγυάω Ios 133

συνεγείρω Virt 116

συνεδρεύω Mos 2:214 Decal 98 Hypoth 7:13

συνέδριον (7) Ebr 165 Conf 86 Somn 1:193 Praem 28 Prob 11 Contempl 27 Legat 213

σύνεδρος Sobr 19 Legat 244, 254, 350, 350

συνείδησις Det 146 Spec 2:49 Virt 124 QE isf 32

συνεῖδον (συνοράω) (14) Somn 1:163 Ios 49 Mos 1:274 Spec 1:193 Spec 3:94, 167 Spec 4:173 Prob 22, 132 Aet 58, 102 Legat 33, 263 QG 3:12

συνειλέω Flacc 119

σύνειμι (27) Opif 167 Deus 11, 103, 130 Plant 160 Ebr 30 Sobr 29 Conf 23 Abr 235 Ios 83, 116 Spec 1:56, 127 Spec 2:52, 235 Spec 3:63 Virt 112 Praem 26 Prob 73, 76 Flacc 15, 30 Legat 156, 295, 310, 313 QG 4:74

συνεῖπον Aet 55

συνείρω (26) Det 7, 130 Plant 89, 176 Migr 111 Congr 64, 178 Mut 61, 198 Ios 49, 205, 214, 246 Decal 94 Spec 1:344 Spec 4:83, 134 Virt 16 Prob 141 Contempl 76 Flacc 6, 34, 108, 139 Legat 177, 365

συνεισβάλλω Legat 173

συνεισέρχομαι Leg 3:126 Plant 98 Mos 2:133 Spec 2:207 Legat 307

συνεισπορεύομαι Leg 3:125

συνεισφέρω Spec 2:233 Legat 313

συνεκδίδωμι Fug 29

συνεκπέμπω Ios 225

συνεκπληρόω Praem 110, 125

συνεκπολεμέω Mos 1:239

συνεκτείνω Abr 152

συνεκτικός (21) Opif 8, 101, 162 Leg 1:59 Leg 3:5, 81, 145, 145 Cher 88, 88 Det 81 Deus 72 Somn 2:256, 284 Abr 222 Ios 154 Spec 1:211 Spec 4:97 Virt 73 Prov 2:54 QG (Par) 2:2

συνεκφέρω Migr 81 Spec 1:44

συνελαύνω Prob 119 Flacc 37, 55 Legat 124, 128

συνεμπίπρημι Prov 2:33

συνεμπίπτω Abr 119

συνεμφαίνω Aet 53

συνεννοέω Spec 3:194

συνεξαιματόω Mos 1:99

συνεξαμαρτάνω Decal 141 Spec 3:165

συνεξέρχομαι Abr 212 Ios 254 Mos 1:147

συνεξετάζω Decal 98 Aet 95

συνεπάγω Ios 195

συνεπαινέω Ios 117

συνεπελαφρίζω Aet 136

συνεπηχέω Agr 139

συνεπιγράφω (13) Ebr 183, 205 Migr 180 Her 303 Somn 1:13 Mos 1:325 Spec 2:26, 252 Spec 3:19, 70 Virt 43 Aet 77 Flacc 24

συνεπικοσμέω Opif 17 Abr 191

συνεπικουφίζω Spec 4:171 Virt 116 Legat 27

συνεπιμαρτυρέω Mos 2:123

συνεπινεύω Conf 54 Abr 110 Mos 2:5 Flacc 98, 124

συνεπισκέπτομαι συνεπισκοπέω

συνεπισκοπέω (συνεπισκέπτομαι) (7) Cher 91 Sacr 24 Post 32 Deus 86 Plant 99 Mos 2:5 Spec 4:1

συνεπισπάω Migr 168 Her 46 Mos 1:145

συνεπιστρέφω Mos 2:20

συνεπιτίθημι Spec 1:175 Flacc 9 Legat 14

συνεπιτροπεύω Prob 42

συνεπιψεύδομαι Spec 4:34

συνεπιωθέω Mos 1:120

συνέπομαι Sacr 27

συνερανίζω (6) Ebr 192, 192 Conf 188 Congr 33 Ios 84 Aet 21

συνεργάτις Prob 76

συνεργέω (22) Opif 61, 72 Leg 1:103 Leg 3:112 Cher 96 Sacr 65 Det 28 Deus 87 Agr 13, 174 Migr 142, 219 Mut 259 Somn 1:158 Spec 2:11 Spec 4:60 Praem 45, 45 Aet 98, 99, 142 Prov 2:60

συνεργία Conf 22

συνεργός (14) Opif 75 Sacr 36 Conf 110, 168 Her 302 Fug 21, 68, 168 Mut 4, 84 Mos 1:110 Spec 1:29 Praem 43 Aet 86

συνέρχομαι (49) Leg 2:72 Cher 43, 125, 126 Post 34, 75 Deus 3, 102 Conf 186, 187 Migr 149, 170, 172 Her 196 Congr 75, 76 Mut 37 Abr 248 Ios 59 Mos 2:64, 282 Spec 1:105 Spec 2:119 Spec 3:12, 24, 34, 80, 96, 113 Virt 33, 40, 111, 199 Praem 95 Contempl 24, 30, 32, 63, 66 Aet 28, 31 Flacc 137, 138 Legat 202, 311 Hypoth 7:13 Prov 2:71 QG 1:17b QE 2:3b

σύνεσις (25) Opif 103, 153, 154 Leg 3:205 Gig 23, 27 Agr 135 Plant 36 Sobr 3, 40 Congr 98, 121 Fug 125 Ios 7, 205, 246, 269 Mos 1:154, 249 Spec 4:57 Virt 217 Prob 54 Legat 33 Hypoth 6:4 Prov 2:6

συνεστιάω Ios 201 Spec 3:186 Contempl 68 Flacc 115

συνέστιος Spec 1:120

συνεταιρίς Det 15

συνετός (11) Post 176 Agr 95 Plant 138 Mut 139, 140, 220 Somn 1:155 Somn 2:260 Ios 114, 117 Prov 2:67

συνευεργετέω Legat 284

συνευνάζω Agr 152 Ebr 203 Migr 19

συνευρύνω Det 90

συνευφημέω Ios 117

συνευφραίνομαι Plant 170 Conf 6

συνευωχέομαι Spec 4:119

συνεφάπτομαι (6) Ios 177 Mos 2:202, 274 Virt 64, 98 Legat 30

συνεφέλκω Ios 142, 176 Spec 1:130 Spec 4:114

συνέφηβος Prob 34

συνέχεια (8) Cher 41 Migr 105 Somn 2:38 Abr 188, 193 Mos 1:123 Prob 58 Hypoth 7:15

συνεχής (151) Opif 63, 125, 167 Leg 3:16, 92, 115, 169, 227 Cher 2, 20, 88 Sacr 16, 23, 37, 85, 86, 127 Det 55, 62, 89, 95, 118, 174 Post 12, 129, 144, 144, 156, 164, 167, 185 Gig 26, 51 Deus 36, 116, 130, 153, 165, 182 Agr 40, 47, 71, 126, 147, 160, 171 Plant 89, 91 Ebr 21, 148, 151, 219 Conf 38, 39, 46, 104 Migr 26, 56, 101, 222 Her 17, 200 Congr 6, 16, 24, 39 Fug 41, 159 Mut 86, 95 Somn 1:22, 115, 249 Somn 2:245, 247, 253 Abr 23, 29, 43, 91, 129, 154, 245 Ios 27, 206 Mos 1:118, 128, 145, 209 Mos 2:27, 54, 60, 163, 263 Decal 57, 96

Spec 1:27, 30, 50, 96, 146, 259, 338 Spec 2:8, 43, 56, 60, 92, 98, 180, 202, 260 Spec 3:140 Spec 4:38, 59, 107, 161, 212 Virt 6, 52, 93 Praem 37, 65, 101, 114, 154 Prob 69, 71, 84, 121 Contempl 23, 36 Aet 64, 109, 112, 119, 119 Flacc 2, 9, 121, 180 Legat 13 Hypoth 7:16, 11:14 Prov 2:12, 26, 26, 56, 68 QG 4:99 QG (Par) 2:7

συνέχω (30) Opif 131, 131, 141 Sacr 40 Agr 76 Plant 4, 157 Ebr 162, 224 Migr 181 Her 23, 246 Fug 112, 197, 201 Mut 140 Abr 74 Mos 2:133, 238 Spec 1:289 Spec 3:190 Contempl 63 Aet 36, 37, 75, 137, 137 Legat 171 Hypoth 7:2 QG (Par) 2:4

συνέψω Virt 144, 144

συνηγορέω Somn 2:278 Contempl 44

συνηγορία Ebr 188 Somn 2:276

συνηγορικός Agr 13

συνήγορος Conf 121

συνήδομαι (9) Conf 7 Abr 235 Ios 250 Decal 110 Virt 179 Prob 157 Contempl 79 Legat 181, 231

συνήθεια (13) Ebr 63, 68, 164 Conf 13 Migr 217 Somn 1:110 Decal 13 Spec 3:35 Spec 4:161 Praem 18 Legat 61, 305 QG 4:52c

συνήθης (41) Opif 50 Leg 1:10 Cher 53, 55 Sacr 22, 28 Deus 124 Plant 65 Migr 34, 63, 75 Fug 122, 167 Mut 219 Somn 1:111, 139 Somn 2:126 Abr 28, 65 Ios 171 Mos 1:106, 139, 213 Decal 46 Spec 1:10, 68, 282 Spec 2:102, 104, 150 Virt 178 Prob 123 Contempl 18, 41, 89 Flacc 18, 57, 57 Legat 268, 361 Hypoth 11:6

συνημερεύω Her 83 Spec 3:5

συνησυχάζω Mos 2:219

συνηχέω (22) Leg 3:22 Cher 110 Gig 64 Deus 84 Plant 10, 167 Ebr 116, 177 Conf 55, 189 Migr 104 Mos 1:29, 136 Mos 2:120, 256 Spec 1:147 Spec 4:134 Contempl 84 Legat 66, 101, 227, 284

συνήχησις Spec 1:93

σύνθεσις (19) Opif 51, 51, 102 Sacr 70 Plant 76, 124 Ebr 185 Her 190, 196, 196, 199, 199, 226 Decal 26 Spec 1:91 Aet 28 Prov 2:60, 71 QG 4:76b

σύνθετος (12) Opif 135 Sacr 52 Post 114 Agr 25 Ebr 23, 101, 144 Her 183 Abr 51 Spec 2:181 Prob 69 Aet 28

συνθέω Flacc 154

συνθήκη Congr 78 Legat 37

σύνθημα (10) Ios 6 Mos 1:133 Mos 2:170 Spec 3:126 Praem 164 Flacc 41, 113, 137 Legat 225, 225

συνθλίβω Aet 110

συνθνήσκω Migr 21 Flacc 11 Legat 71

σύνθρονος Leg 3:247

συνιερουργέω Somn 1:215 Mos 2:232

συνίζω Somn 2:238 Aet 103, 110, 110, 147

συνίημι (19) Opif 50 Det 74 Agr 162 Plant 138 Migr 155 Fug 123 Mut 139 Ios 6 Mos 1:274, 283 Praem 170 Prob 62 Contempl 77 Aet 27 Legat 70, 71, 303, 364 Prov 2:30

συνίστημι (172) Opif 17, 17, 19, 26, 29, 49, 54, 60, 63, 67, 67, 91, 95, 95, 97, 97, 103, 106, 107, 114, 132, 134, 161, 171 Leg 1:2, 3, 4, 30, 45, 55, 59, 79, 86, 87, 107 Leg 2:2, 5, 74 Leg 3:10, 92, 113, 113, 145, 161, 175, 245 Cher 41, 91, 102, 113 Sacr 35, 47, 126 Det 2, 43, 68, 122, 160 Post 5, 10, 48, 52, 117, 140, 167, 173, 185 Gig 10, 51 Agr 161 Plant 6 Ebr 61, 69, 91, 144, 184, 191, 191, 198 Conf 33, 42, 62, 108, 124, 172 Migr 106, 135 Her 42, 58, 75, 152, 152, 280, 281, 282, 311 Fug 38, 168 Mut 28, 88, 111, 184, 237, 256, 257 Somn 1:15, 158, 186, 205 Somn 2:1, 72, 209, 288 Abr 105, 125, 159, 218, 238, 240 Ios 56 Mos 1:113 Mos 2:125, 132, 256 Decal 27, 33 Spec 1:6, 16, 87, 201, 203, 211, 333 Spec 2:23, 64, 149, 177, 214 Spec 3:189 Spec 4:127 Virt 43, 176 Praem 94 Contempl 65, 85, 90 Aet 4, 8, 14, 25, 25, 48, 52, 60, 101, 107, 149 Legat 68 Prov 2:45 QG 1:60:2, 89, 94, 2:5a, 14, 3:61, 4:8b, 184 QG (Par) 2:2, 2:4, 2:5 QE 2:21, 46

συννέμω Ios 101

συννεωτερίζω Hypoth 11:3

σύννοια (16) Cher 37 Plant 167 Her 48 Somn 2:168 Abr 151 Ios 89, 170 Mos 2:166, 226 Decal 144 Spec 2:214 Spec 3:193 Praem 35 Prob 122, 123 Legat 15

σύννομος Cher 58 Decal 132 Praem 89 Legat 20 QG isf 10

συννοσέω Legat 16, 356

σύννους Somn 2:165

συνοδοιπορέω Her 241 Somn 1:71

συνοδοιπόρος Det 29 Deus 61 Migr 173 Somn 1:179

σύνοδος (46) Opif 161 Leg 1:106 Cher 29, 50, 124 Sacr 33 Det 8 Deus 56, 79 Agr 49, 145 Ebr 211 Conf 40, 188 Migr 26, 30, 63 Congr 12, 63 Fug 140 Mut 38 Abr 101, 137 Ios 43 Mos 2:119, 287 Spec 1:109, 178, 178, 178 Spec 2:41, 140, 140, 140 Spec 3:70, 72, 187 Spec 4:234, 234 Virt 114 Contempl 40 Flacc 4, 136, 166 Legat 312, 316

σύνοιδα (37) Opif 128 Det 23 Post 59 Deus 100, 128 Ebr 125 Conf 121 Her 6, 7 Fug 159 Ios 47, 48, 68, 197, 215, 262, 265 Mos 2:11 Decal 91 Spec 1:203, 235 Spec 3:54 Spec 4:6, 40 Virt 206 Praem 84, 163 Prob 99, 124, 149 Flacc 7, 99, 145 Legat 39, 165, 341 QG 4:202b

συνοιδέω Mos 1:127

συνοικέω (27) Cher 41 Sacr 3, 20, 22, 128, 133 Ebr 155 Migr 13, 28 Her 265 Congr 34, 52 Abr 215, 243 Ios 60, 64 Decal 87 Spec 3:27, 71, 78, 82 Prob 85 Flacc 52 Legat 201, 371 QG 2:26b, 3:8

συνοικίζω Somn 2:246 Spec 3:61 Praem 172

συνοικισμός Mos 2:157

συνοικοδομέω Spec 1:274 Spec 2:119 Praem 120, 139 Contempl 33

σύνοικος Sacr 130 Conf 52 Prob 107 QE isf 32

σύνολος (149) Opif 91, 92, 166 Leg 1:1, 31 Leg 2:19, 46, 71 Leg 3:15, 44, 88, 129, 206, 216 Cher 90 Sacr 46, 49, 73, 76, 106, 121 Det 18, 75, 87, 136, 142 Post 14, 80, 85, 96, 109, 117, 134 Gig 2 Deus 52, 157, 171 Agr 78 Plant 43, 71, 83, 112, 116, 146, 177 Sobr 2, 38 Conf 106, 123, 134 Migr 5, 48, 64, 90, 105, 217, 219 Her 118, 210, 246 Congr 34, 46, 65, 172 Fug 57, 134 Mut 45, 50, 63, 91, 104, 219, 240 Somn 1:27, 30, 55, 184, 187 Somn 2:13, 62, 131 Abr 102, 141, 267 Ios 112, 115 Mos 1:26 Mos 2:30, 205 Decal 21, 51, 156, 171 Spec 1:48, 55, 90, 100, 115, 121, 124, 224, 236, 339, 342 Spec 2:44, 46, 73, 180, 224 Spec 3:103, 135, 183, 194 Spec 4:22, 113, 116 Virt 96, 125, 149, 167, 170, 177, 194, 206, 219, 221 Praem 45, 59, 87, 129, 142, 171 Prob 51, 78, 158 Contempl 39, 70 Flacc 117 Legat 38, 38, 103, 107, 136, 158, 262, 341 Prov 2:18 QG 2:12d QE isf 14 συνομαρτέω Sacr 22 Deus 179 Migr 166 Mut 163 Contempl 76

συνομιλία QG 1:28

συνόμνυμι (συνομνύω) Conf 28, 60

συνομνύω συνόμνυμι

συνομολογέω Congr 130, 154

συνοράω συνεῖδον

συνοράω (7) Sacr 76 Somn 1:94 Virt 166 Praem 67 Prob 47, 55 Aet 112

συνορθιάζω Agr 122

συνορχέομαι Legat 42

συνουσία (24) Leg 2:29 Leg 3:155, 156 Cher 57 Det 99, 113, 171, 176 Deus 137 Agr 37, 38 Ebr 220 Sobr 23 Fug 14 Mut 144 Somn 1:200 Ios 203 Spec 1:9, 101 Spec 3:9 Virt 36 Legat 310 Prov 2:32 QG 3:18

συνουσιαστικός Abr 149

συνταγματαρχέω Ios 176

σύνταξις (15) Agr 49 Plant 174 Her 1 Fug 139 Mut 53 Abr 2, 13 Mos 2:1 Decal 1 Spec 1:1 Spec 2:1 Virt 52, 101 Praem 3 Flacc 92

συνταράσσω Mut 189 Legat 120

συντάσσω (23) Opif 126 Leg 2:2 Leg 3:169 Agr 32 Sobr 67 Conf 110 Migr 61, 114 Fug 139 Somn 2:113 Abr 116 Ios 176 Mos 1:330 Mos 2:1, 204 Spec 1:88, 130, 207 Flacc 21 Legat 132, 225, 265 QG 1:76b

συντείνω (43) Cher 119 Det 157 Gig 60 Ebr 3 Her 81, 113 Fug 97 Mut 116 Somn 2:139, 180, 232 Abr 62, 108, 233 Ios 54, 105, 139, 181, 195, 212, 245, 256 Mos 1:54, 59, 63, 151, 168, 269 Mos 2:165 Decal 14, 100 Spec 1:23, 74 Spec 3:7, 22, 58 Virt 121 Praem 97, 165 Flacc 87, 94, 112 Legat 225

συντέλεια Her 17, 17 Spec 2:58

συντελέω (15) Leg 1:1, 2, 3 Ebr 52, 53 Her 122 Mut 270 Somn 2:23, 29, 59, 116 Abr 240 Spec 1:67 QG (Par) 2:5, 2:5

συντέμνω Det 105

συντήκω Contempl 61 Prov 2:33

συντήξις Post 157

συντίθημι (45) Opif 2, 47, 51, 92, 94, 101, 102, 133 Cher 113 Det 7 Plant 75, 123, 125, 131 Ebr 115 Conf 4, 14, 95, 187, 187 Migr 34, 112 Her 190, 197 Congr 149 Fug 186 Somn 2:284 Ios 18, 173 Mos 1:3, 130 Mos 2:91 Spec 1:70 Spec 2:40, 110 Spec 3:29, 94, 98 Praem 74 Aet 28, 38 Flacc 89 Legat 122, 177 QG isf 13

σύντομος Praem 50

συντόμως Flacc 179

σύντονος (27) Leg 2:74 Leg 3:138, 160 Post 13 Agr 55, 85, 150 Ebr 27, 218 Migr 25, 175 Her 201 Mut 84, 84, 116, 215 Somn 2:166, 238 Abr 160 Mos 2:145, 154 Decal 147 Praem 73 Aet 128 Flacc 120 Legat 101, 135

συντρέφω Migr 214, 224 Her 78 Mut 171 Abr 70

συντρέχω (12) Sacr 66 Plant 98 Migr 166 Fug 82 Mos 1:138 Mos 2:39, 40 Spec 3:86 Spec 4:34 Virt 225 Prob 128 Aet 103

συντρίβω (12) Her 201 Fug 197, 201 Praem 93, 124 Legat 366 QE 2:17, 17, 17, 17, 17, 17

συντροφία Abr 67 Legat 29

σύντροφος (16) Cher 69 Sacr 15 Ebr 164 Sobr 26 Her 234 Congr 81 Mut 219 Somn 1:139 Spec 1:53, 282 Spec 2:109 Spec 4:68, 218 Virt 26, 220 Praem 15

συντυγχάνω (7) Post 137 Sobr 29 Conf 76, 187, 192 Migr 118 Virt 218

συντυχία (17) Deus 29 Ebr 111 Somn 1:110, 156, 221 Somn 2:105, 145, 212 Ios 15, 270 Mos 2:229, 233 Spec 1:259 Flacc 25 Legat 200, 237 QG 4:204

συνυπάρχω Aet 91, 105, 130

συνυπογράφω Legat 368

συνυφαίνω (46) Leg 1:81 Cher 60 Sacr 6, 83, 83 Det 6 Post 14, 104 Deus 20, 69, 113 Conf 171 Her 188, 217 Congr 63, 117 Fug 72, 119, 185 Mut 43, 199 Somn 1:205 Mos 1:4, 228 Mos 2:87, 111, 191, 212, 277 Decal 32, 55 Spec 1:165 Spec 2:104 Spec 3:7 Spec 4:2, 39, 76, 207 Virt 16, 76, 107 Praem 1, 24 Prob 93 Legat 169 QG (Par) 2:2

συνυφίστημι Sacr 65

συνῳδός (16) Det 125 Post 88, 108 Deus 133 Plant 156 Migr 102, 165, 176 Spec 2:142, 157 Spec 3:20 Spec 4:39 Virt 18, 121 Legat 77 Prov 2:7

συνωθέω Spec 3:25, 79 Legat 103, 128

συνωνυμέω Agr 28 Plant 154

συνωνυμία Det 118 Plant 150, 150

συνώνυμος (8) Leg 2:10 Leg 3:251 Cher 13 Det 119 Post 102 Plant 150 Her 22 Mut 131

Συρία (29) Leg 3:18 Congr 41 Somn 2:59 Abr 91, 133 Ios 230 Mos 1:163, 237 Mos 2:56, 246 Spec 2:217 Virt 221 Prob 75 Flacc 26, 39 Legat 179, 207, 219, 220, 222, 231, 245, 250, 252, 259, 281, 333 Hypoth 6:1 Prov 2:64

Συριακός Legat 252

συρίζω Legat 368

συρμός (9) Cher 37 Sacr 61 Gig 13 Deus 177 Somn 2:87 Abr 59, 160 Spec 4:112, 113

Σύρος (14) Leg 3:16, 18, 18 Congr 41, 43 Fug 7, 44, 44, 44, 45, 49 Flacc 39, 39 Hypoth 6:6

συρρᾳδιουργέω Decal 91

συρράπτω Spec 1:165

συρράσσω Aet 136

συρρέω Opif 38 Mos 1:91, 211 Flacc 41

σύρρυσις Aet 139

συρρώννυμι Det 168

σύρω Flacc 65, 190

σῦς (9) Agr 144, 145 Somn 2:87, 89 Spec 1:148 Spec 3:36, 113 Spec 4:101 Prov 2:57

συσκιάζω (28) Leg 2:66 Leg 3:27, 158 Sacr 30 Deus 30 Plant 116 Ebr 6, 65 Sobr 6 Somn 1:83, 87, 97, 104, 109 Abr 174 Ios 90, 166 Mos 2:128 Decal 44, 125 Spec 1:75 Spec 2:75 Spec 4:128, 183 Aet 64 Legat 22, 105, 332

συσσίτιον (6) Spec 2:148, 193 Spec 3:96 Prob 86, 91 Hypoth 11:5

σύστασις (19) Opif 151 Leg 1:1, 5, 18, 19, 88 Leg 3:22, 77 Det 154 Post 115 Migr 3, 6 Her 136 Mut 21 Mos 1:59 Mos 2:233 Decal 31 Praem 75 Aet 25

συστατός Aet 26

συστέλλω Leg 2:60 Leg 3:35, 154 Virt 144

σύστημα (14) Opif 48 Leg 1:2 Leg 3:163 Post 164 Deus 113, 157 Migr 104 Congr 141 Mut 150 Somn 1:86 Spec 1:342 Contempl 72 Aet 4 QG 4:145

συστηρίζω Somn 1:158

συστολή Praem 47

συστρατεία Abr 245

συστρατεύω Mos 1:317

συσφαιρίζω Legat 175

συσφίγγω Det 103

Συχέμ (10) Det 5, 5, 9 Migr 216, 221, 221, 223, 224 Mut 193, 194

συχνός Abr 91

σφαγεύς Legat 92

σφαγή (10) Abr 176 Mos 1:227, 314 Spec 2:13 Prob 133 Flacc 178, 189 Legat 75, 208, 233

σφαγιάζω (12) Abr 169, 179, 185, 188, 196, 197, 201 Spec 1:231, 244, 268 Spec 2:148 Virt 137

σφάγιον Spec 1:238 Virt 135 Prob 119

σφαδᾴζω (15) Cher 36 Ebr 121 Migr 156 Abr 257 Mos 1:170 Spec 3:44 Spec 4:81 Virt 30, 128 Praem 140 Prob 39 Flacc 18, 162, 180 Legat 184

σφάζω (6) Her 20 Somn 2:144 Spec 1:212 Spec 3:91 Aet 20 Prov 2:32

σφαῖρα (15) Cher 21, 23 Conf 5, 157 Her 225, 229, 233 Somn 1:21, 134, 203 Decal 57, 102, 104 Spec 2:178 Spec 3:189

σφαιρηδόν Sacr 95

σφαιρικός Post 104 QG (Par) 2:2

σφαιρόω Her 14

σφαιρωτήρ Leg 3:24 Ebr 105

σφακελίζω Praem 143

σφαλερός (9) Fug 27, 27, 43 Somn 1:224 Abr 263, 264 Spec 4:166 Flacc 177 Legat 215

σφάλλω (32) Leg 1:35, 94 Leg 3:90, 105, 106 Sacr 32, 54 Deus 100 Sobr 11 Conf 127 Migr 225 Her 72 Congr 142 Fug 86, 105, 115, 145 Somn 1:44, 112 Somn 2:99 Ios 87 Mos 1:214 Mos 2:269 Decal 147 Spec 1:38 Virt 205, 207 Prov 2:5, 8, 36 QG isf 12 QE isf 5

σφάλμα (13) Leg 3:106 Sacr 47 Agr 173 Conf 53 Fug 76, 102, 117 Mos 1:167 Decal 141 Spec 1:230, 230 Spec 2:166 Spec 4:191

σφεῖς Virt 74 Prob 119

σφενδόνη Flacc 90

σφενδονήτης Mos 1:168

σφετερίζω (12) Post 42 Abr 206 Mos 1:313 Spec 1:236 Spec 2:54 Virt 94 Praem 74 Legat 80, 89, 198, 346 QG 4:172

σφέτερος Agr 6

σφηκία QE 2:24:1

σφηκόω Contempl 50

σφήξ Spec 1:291 Praem 96 QE 2:24a, 24b

σφίγγω (16) Opif 141 Post 104 Deus 38 Plant 9 Ebr 152 Conf 136, 166 Her 23, 188 Fug 112 Somn 2:58 Mos 2:113, 144 Spec 1:146 Aet 30, 137

σφόδρα (147) Leg 2:40 Leg 3:15, 83, 91, 128, 144, 170, 251 Cher 61, 73 Sacr 49, 63, 121, 125 Det 118, 160 Post 43, 66, 84, 86, 100, 132, 137, 155 Gig 40 Deus 14, 16, 80, 122, 170 Agr 1, 19, 54, 66, 114, 115 Plant 102, 105, 113, 136, 161 Ebr 27, 35, 116, 182, 214 Conf 20, 39, 43, 93, 121, 163 Migr 152, 189, 208 Her 2, 22, 54, 92, 202, 251, 312 Congr 140, 158 Fug 138 Mut 237 Somn 1:123 Somn 2:3, 156 Abr 73, 126 Ios 40, 77, 101, 154, 183, 189, 205, 225, 257 Mos 1:43, 58, 192, 211, 292, 301, 328 Mos 2:1, 202, 222, 223 Decal 64, 93, 112, 139, 143, 170 Spec 1:33, 64, 138, 148, 269, 275, 298, 321, 340 Spec 2:72, 169, 246 Spec 3:21, 47, 77, 158, 205 Spec 4:23, 39, 66, 183, 221 Virt 5, 17, 27, 41, 69, 87, 88, 201 Praem 17 Prob 18, 91, 91, 122, 146, 149 Contempl 22, 24, 52 Flacc 108, 119 Legat 36, 73, 259, 344 Hypoth 6:8, 11:13 Prov 2:68 QE isf 10

σφοδρός (32) Opif 128, 167 Leg 2:74 Leg 3:80, 160, 211 Cher 2 Sacr 37, 54, 69 Post 116, 157 Deus 26, 79 Ebr 218 Her 3, 249 Congr 64 Mut 84 Somn 2:7, 13 Ios 89 Mos 1:40 Mos 2:255 Spec 1:314, 314, 343 Spec 2:90 Spec 4:102 Virt 113 Praem 105 Aet 63

σφοδρότης Cher 38 Fug 146

σφοδρύνω Plant 171 Mos 1:120

σφραγίζω (8) Opif 172 Leg 3:105, 106, 106 Agr 169 Somn 2:45 Mos 1:30 Legat 330

σφραγίς (33) Opif 6, 25, 34, 129, 134 Leg 1:22, 100 Det 76 Post 94 Deus 43 Agr 166 Plant 18 Ebr 133, 133, 137 Migr 97, 103, 103 Her 181 Fug 12 Mut 80, 135 Somn 1:202, 219 Somn 2:45 Ios 120 Mos 2:14, 76, 112 Spec 1:47, 106 Spec 2:152 Spec 4:137

σφριγάω (6) Opif 63, 85 Deus 13 Plant 157 Her 125 Mut 33

σφῦρα Decal 72

σφυρηλατέω Post 116

σφυροκόπος Post 116

σφυρόν Mos 2:119, 121 Flacc 70 Legat 131

σχέδην Contempl 77

σχεδόν (112) Opif 17, 96, 126 Leg 1:14, 103, 106 Leg 2:19, 76, 102 Leg 3:113, 122, 124, 138, 145, 235 Sacr 70 Det 34, 43, 99, 131 Post 119 Agr 49, 103, 143 Plant 81, 93, 156, 164 Ebr 51, 57, 119, 126, 171, 186, 193, 198, 220 Sobr 8, 17, 29, 53, 54 Conf 22, 178 Migr 35, 50, 88 Her 33, 151, 152, 154, 173, 177, 207, 247, 284, 291 Congr 64 Mut 104, 143, 164, 196, 229, 236 Somn 1:237 Somn 2:210 Abr 112, 197 Ios 28, 167, 172 Mos 1:39, 66, 114 Mos 2:17, 19, 69, 87, 172, 194, 218 Decal 27, 31 Spec 1:78, 262, 332 Spec 2:220 Spec 3:64 Spec 4:72, 138, 179, 209 Virt 12, 12, 17, 54, 55, 118, 120 Prob 77, 98, 138 Contempl 59 Flacc 92, 130 Legat 138, 167, 173, 179, 182, 310 Hypoth 7:13

σχέσις (32) Opif 117 Leg 3:34, 34, 206 Cher 62 Sacr 26, 73 Gig 48 Agr 35 Ebr 204 Sobr 34, 34, 47, 47 Conf 11, 134 Her 110, 119 Mut 257 Ios 126 Decal 57 Spec 2:230 Spec 4:141 Virt 32, 40, 173, 217 Praem 113 Contempl 77 Legat 55, 112, 270

σχετικός Leg 3:210

σχετλιάζω Gig 50 Mos 1:274 Virt 136

σχετλιασμός Conf 152

σχέτλιος Det 45, 116 Conf 20, 116

σχετλιότης Conf 17

σχῆμα (68) Opif 50, 50, 97, 97, 98, 101, 120, 165 Leg 3:15, 57, 95 Cher 52, 117 Sacr 28, 46 Det 101, 173 Post 104, 110 Deus 15 Plant 121, 133, 159 Ebr 46, 217 Conf

87, 87, 89 Migr 147 Her 245 Congr 146 Fug 26 Mut 111 Somn 1:21, 27, 188 Somn 2:126 Abr 148, 239 Ios 72, 205 Mos 2:128 Spec 1:29, 90, 102, 205, 315, 339 Spec 2:82, 106, 148, 208 Virt 223 Prob 101 Contempl 4, 30, 51, 72 Aet 135 Flacc 126 Legat 83, 359 Prov 2:18 QG 4:8b, 206b QG (Par) 2:2, 2:2, 2:2

σχηματίζω (16) Opif 9 Leg 3:201 Cher 79 Ebr 90 Conf 90 Her 157 Somn 2:45 Mos 1:38, 96, 166 Mos 2:38 Decal 33 Spec 1:48 Praem 2 Legat 201 QG (Par) 2:3

σχηματισμός Leg 1:8 Mut 67 Spec 1:178

σχίζω (7) Opif 117 Cher 23 Post 127 Agr 30 Fug 91 Somn 1:27 Somn 2:243

σχοίνισμα Post 89

σχολάζω (17) Opif 128 Migr 189 Congr 113 Ios 53 Mos 1:125 Mos 2:211 Decal 98 Spec 1:70 Spec 2:60, 101 Spec 3:1 Prob 63 Flacc 33, 36 Legat 128, 175 QG (Par) 2:7

σχολαῖος Contempl 76

σχολή (15) Leg 1:98 Agr 103 Conf 3 Mos 1:89, 89, 322 Mos 2:267 Spec 1:70, 104 Spec 2:196 Spec 3:93 Spec 4:160 Prob 69 Flacc 41 QG 4:47a

σῴζω (55) Opif 145 Leg 2:101 Leg 3:137, 189, 225 Cher 130 Sacr 123, 125 Det 165 Deus 66, 129 Agr 13 Ebr 14, 17, 29, 121, 140 Conf 25 Migr 162 Her 270 Fug 27, 27, 96 Somn 2:126 Abr 145, 146 Ios 76 Mos 1:143, 236 Mos 2:58 Decal 12, 64, 104 Spec 1:59, 222, 239, 253, 253 Spec 3:80, 115, 141 Spec 4:18, 79, 202 Virt 47 Aet 85 Flacc 11 Legat 34, 55, 60, 325 Prov 2:18 QG 2:11, 12d, 34c

Σωκράτης Somn 1:58 Contempl 57 Prov 2:21 QG (Par) 2:3, 2:6

σωληνοειδής Spec 1:217

σῶμα (998) Opif 30, 34, 36, 36, 49, 50, 53, 53, 66, 67, 69, 69, 85, 86, 98, 102, 102, 105, 118, 119, 120, 123, 123, 125, 134, 135, 135, 136, 136, 138, 139, 140, 141, 144, 145, 146, 147, 150, 152, 164, 166 Leg 1:3, 4, 12, 12, 13, 26, 26, 27, 28, 32, 39, 39, 59, 62, 71, 71, 71, 91, 91, 103, 103, 103, 104, 105, 106, 106, 107, 108, 108 Leg 2:2, 2, 6, 6, 22, 51, 55, 59, 71, 77, 80 Leg 3:15, 20, 20, 22, 37, 41, 42, 46, 50, 55, 57, 58, 58, 62, 64, 69, 69, 70, 71, 72, 72, 73, 74, 75, 77, 80, 108, 124, 146, 146, 151, 152, 152, 161, 161, 161, 161, 161, 178, 190, 191, 198, 206, 238, 239, 242, 253 Cher 41, 57, 58, 59, 59, 60, 61, 64, 68, 82, 95, 113, 114, 114, 115, 117, 117, 128 Sacr 9, 26, 33, 39, 46, 48, 49, 59, 72, 73, 97, 98, 106, 108, 115, 126, 130 Det 7, 8, 9, 9, 9, 15, 17, 19, 19, 20, 29, 33, 38, 43, 49, 68, 81, 84, 85, 86, 87, 88, 98, 109, 109, 110, 136, 137, 141, 151, 158, 158, 159, 159, 163, 165, 170 Post 26, 26, 57, 60, 61, 62, 96, 112, 112, 115, 117, 118, 120, 123, 127, 137, 138, 155, 158, 162, 162, 184 Gig 12, 13, 14, 15, 33, 33, 35, 37, 60 Deus 8, 8, 35, 45, 45, 52, 55, 56, 65, 66, 120, 127, 150, 167 Agr 22, 22, 22, 40, 46, 56, 64, 65, 88, 89, 97, 118, 119, 130, 139, 142, 152, 163 Plant 5, 7, 7, 14, 20, 21, 25, 28, 30, 43, 44, 55, 79, 100, 105, 111, 133, 145, 146, 147, 160, 160, 162 Ebr 22, 22, 46, 52, 66, 69, 70, 71, 75, 87, 87, 95, 99, 101, 101, 108, 111, 121, 124, 130, 131, 133, 140, 147, 154, 155, 156, 160, 167, 171, 174, 178, 180, 190, 190, 191, 200, 201, 206, 207, 208, 214 Sobr 2, 2, 3, 4, 5, 11, 12, 13, 16, 38, 45, 45, 60, 61, 67 Conf 11, 16, 17, 18, 21, 23, 36, 38, 49, 52, 62, 67, 78, 80, 81, 82, 88, 95, 100, 105, 106, 125, 136, 149, 172, 177, 185, 190 Migr 2, 2, 3, 7, 9, 12, 12, 14, 16, 18, 21, 22, 50, 51, 51, 51, 51, 64, 77, 87, 88, 93, 93, 97, 137, 141, 157, 160, 180, 188, 190, 192, 193, 193, 195, 197, 200, 203, 216, 217, 219 Her 45, 54, 64, 68, 69, 71, 72, 73, 81, 82, 82, 84, 85, 89, 92, 114, 118, 119, 130, 143, 154, 155, 161, 209, 228, 235, 237, 239, 242, 242, 242, 243, 243, 256, 256, 267, 267, 268, 274, 284, 285, 286, 286, 291, 296, 309, 312, 315, 315 Congr 12, 12, 19, 20, 30, 31, 59, 59, 60, 65, 97, 135, 143, 155, 169 Fug 18, 27, 55, 75, 90, 91, 92, 110, 112, 122, 146, 147, 148, 151, 153, 164, 180, 182 Mut 3, 4, 8, 9, 33, 36, 56, 60, 84, 89, 107, 165, 171, 173, 173, 174, 179, 187, 209, 215, 219, 221, 230 Somn 1:11, 17, 20, 21, 23, 25, 26, 27, 30, 30, 31, 33, 42, 43, 46, 55, 62, 68, 76, 78, 81, 102, 102, 110, 117, 122, 123, 128, 136, 138, 139, 147, 148, 157, 177, 181, 187, 192, 192, 200, 210, 232, 236, 250 Somn 2:9, 11, 12, 13, 46, 52, 58, 83, 101, 106, 109, 128, 134, 168, 219, 232, 237, 255, 256, 256, 256 Abr 23, 26, 66, 74, 76, 93, 96, 100, 101, 118, 136, 147, 168, 172, 175, 182, 201, 236, 241, 241, 251, 258, 258, 263, 266, 271, 272 Ios 25, 43, 50, 53, 71, 71, 82, 106, 130, 138, 160, 162, 179, 264, 269 Mos 1:22, 27, 29, 38, 39, 40, 43, 100, 105, 127, 128, 135, 166, 182, 184, 229, 237, 259, 279, 301, 305, 311, 315, 318, 327 Mos 2:16, 53, 68, 69, 74, 118, 140, 150, 171, 172, 184, 185, 255, 273, 283, 288 Decal 4, 33, 44, 60, 68, 71, 71, 77, 79, 82, 93, 107, 122, 124, 124, 150, 157, 173 Spec 1:3, 5, 5, 40, 49, 58, 62, 80, 81, 82, 90, 99, 99, 100, 102, 103, 107, 113, 117, 137, 165, 166, 173, 174, 211, 216, 218, 219, 222, 222, 224, 232, 239, 250, 254, 257, 257, 258, 261, 264, 266, 269, 269, 288, 289, 289, 291, 298, 298, 311, 339, 340, 341 Spec 2:6, 16, 34, 45, 46, 52, 60, 61, 64, 64, 64, 64, 67, 90, 90, 94, 95, 98, 101, 101, 103, 147, 163, 201, 202, 214, 229, 230, 230, 240, 246, 249, 260, 262 Spec 3:1, 10, 23, 28, 33, 37, 47, 51, 61, 79, 81, 82, 99, 99, 99, 107, 131, 159, 161, 163, 179, 182, 182, 184, 190, 202, 205, 208 Spec 4:11, 74, 82, 83, 89, 100, 114, 122, 123, 157, 170, 188, 200, 237 Virt 3, 8, 9, 11, 12, 13, 15, 19, 25, 26, 27, 30, 31, 31, 32, 32, 37, 40, 45, 46, 68, 72, 74, 76, 88, 103, 103, 118, 138, 143, 173, 176, 181, 182, 187, 188, 193, 208, 217 Praem 6, 11, 16, 21, 30, 31, 33, 33, 95, 114, 118, 120, 121, 122, 125, 136, 139, 146, 156, 166 Prob 12, 17, 17, 17, 33, 40, 96, 96, 106, 107, 110, 111, 133, 134, 146, 146, 149, 158 Contempl 2, 10, 25, 34, 36, 37, 40, 44, 61, 61, 68, 78, 89 Aet 18, 21, 26, 51, 63, 67, 69, 73, 79, 80, 87, 102, 114 Flacc 37, 58, 60, 61, 68, 71, 72, 77, 149, 173, 174, 176, 182, 188, 189, 190 Legat 1, 2, 14, 16, 27, 55, 63, 80, 82, 82, 109, 111, 112, 127, 131, 215, 229, 238, 250, 270, 310, 324 Hypoth 6:3, 6:6, 7:2, 7:16, 11:3, 11:7, 11:7, 11:11 Prov 2:1, 15, 17, 17, 22, 23, 25, 28, 56, 56 QG 1:70:1, 2:12c, 12d, 12d, 3:11a, 11a, 11c, 21, 4:43, 43, 99, 200a QG (Par) 2:1, 2:2, 2:2, 2:2, 2:3, 2:4, 2:5, 2:6 QE 2:46, 46 QE isf 1, 14, 16, 21, 21

σωμασκία Abr 48

σωματικός (85) Opif 16, 18, 36, 55, 66, 92, 92, 132 Leg 1:83 Leg 2:28, 57, 77, 80 Leg 3:21, 26, 41, 47, 146, 149, 151, 151, 151, 172, 212 Cher 96 Sacr 139 Det 27, 27, 158, 160 Post 61, 116, 119, 137, 159, 159, 163, 164, 182 Gig 54 Deus 165 Agr 57 Plant 7 Ebr 104, 124 Sobr 68 Conf 55, 92 Migr 15, 20, 23, 28, 151, 154, 187, 190, 191 Her 84, 283, 316 Congr 96, 155 Fug 124 Mut 21, 33, 90, 209 Somn 1:43 Somn 2:16, 42, 258 Abr 164, 164, 219, 269 Ios 151 Mos 1:97, 279 Mos 2:24 Virt 2 Praem 143 Legat 189, 267 QE 2:4 QE isf 15 σωμάτιον Legat 273

σωματοειδής (9) Opif 36 Leg 1:1 Sacr 6 Ebr 62 Congr 21 Virt 203 Aet 50, 51, 72

σωματοφύλαξ Flacc 30 Prov 2:17

σωματόω Her 73

σωρεύω Prov 2:62

σωρηδόν (9) Conf 17 Mos 1:100, 105, 200 Mos 2:255 Spec 2:8 Prob 119 Flacc 90 Legat 9

σωρός Sacr 40 Conf 185 Her 284 Ios 162 Legat 124

σῶς (22) Agr 157 Plant 114 Mut 109 Somn 2:95 Abr 90, 145, 235, 235 Ios 188, 195, 210 Mos 1:65, 204, 205, 309 Mos 2:266 Decal 122 Spec 1:78 Praem 60 Contempl 44 QG 2:15a QE 2:38a

σῶστρα Sacr 121 Conf 93 Her 44 Spec 1:185 Spec 3:145

σώτειρα Leg 3:17

σωτήρ (39) Opif 169 Leg 2:56 Leg 3:27 Sacr 70, 71 Post 121, 156 Deus 137, 156 Agr 80 Sobr 55 Conf 93 Migr 25, 124 Her 60 Congr 171 Fug 162 Mut 56, 203 Somn 1:75 Abr 137, 176 Ios 195 Spec 1:209, 252, 272 Spec 2:134, 198 Praem 39, 117, 163 Contempl 87 Flacc 74, 126 Legat 22, 196 QG 2:13a QE 2:2 QE isf 10

σωτηρία (85) Opif 88, 125 Leg 2:94, 101, 101, 104 Leg 3:242 Cher 15, 130 Deus 17, 129 Agr 88, 94, 94, 96, 98, 123, 152, 156 Plant 146 Ebr 13, 25, 72, 111, 140 Migr 2, 26, 124, 124 Fug 80 Mut 121 Somn 1:86 Abr 187, 197 Ios 33, 63, 183 Mos 1:10, 104, 146, 210, 317 Mos 2:59, 65, 249 Spec 1:77, 197, 210, 222, 223, 224, 252, 283 Spec 2:195 Spec 3:36, 115, 157 Spec 4:58, 154 Virt 14, 34, 176, 202 Praem 33, 87, 148 Contempl 86 Aet 37, 116 Flacc 11, 60, 75 Legat 18, 19, 329, 355 Hypoth 7:3 Prov 2:60, 63 QG 2:11, 22, 41, 4:51a, 198 QE 2:64

σωτήριος (90) Leg 1:9 Leg 2:105 Leg 3:76, 129, 133, 137 Sacr 132 Det 45, 72, 110 Post 178 Deus 73, 74, 124 Agr 99 Plant 90, 144 Ebr 12, 23, 141, 172, 199 Sobr 50 Conf 98, 171, 181 Migr 36 Her 37, 136, 203, 297 Somn 1:51, 58, 62, 112, 147 Somn 2:149, 154 Abr 70, 102 Ios 13, 55, 73, 110, 149 Mos 1:96, 101, 178 Decal 14, 53, 60, 155, 177 Spec 1:184, 185, 194, 196, 197, 212, 220, 222, 224, 225, 232, 239, 247, 251, 252, 254, 343 Spec 3:97, 99 Spec 4:181 Virt 49, 133 Praem 22, 34, 117, 144, 145, 170 Aet 69 Legat 50, 106, 151, 190 Prov 2:17 QG 2:41 QG isf 13 QE 2:25d

σωφρονέω Cher 69 Det 114 Spec 4:193, 223

σωφρονίζω (34) Leg 2:100 Sacr 56 Det 3, 49 Gig 46 Deus 52, 64, 134 Conf 46 Migr 14 Her 167 Congr 158, 172, 179 Fug 98, 208 Somn 1:237 Ios 73, 187 Mos 1:70, 147 Spec 2:170 Spec 3:48 Virt 94, 115 Praem 19, 133, 148, 152 Prob 143 Flacc 154 Legat 7 Prov 2:55 QG 1:77

σωφρονισμός (8) Leg 3:193 Post 97 Deus 182 Ebr 29 Migr 14 Mut 135 Mos 1:328 Virt 75

σωφρονιστήριον Ios 86

σωφρονιστής (14) Sacr 51 Det 146 Agr 40 Migr 116 Her 77, 109 Congr 161 Abr 213, 243 Ios 254 Spec 2:18, 240 Legat 52 Prov 2:70

σωφρόνως QG 4:204

σωφροσύνη (100) Opif 73, 81 Leg 1:63, 65, 69, 69, 70, 70, 70, 71, 86, 86 Leg 2:79, 79, 79, 79, 81, 81, 81, 82, 83, 87, 93, 93, 96, 98, 99, 105 Leg 3:156 Cher 5 Sacr 27, 84 Det 18, 24, 72, 73, 114, 143 Post 128 Deus 164 Agr 9, 18, 98, 101, 101, 104, 106, 109 Ebr 23 Sobr 61 Her 48, 128, 209 Congr 2, 124, 176 Fug 5, 17, 33, 154 Mut 172, 197, 217, 225 Somn 1:124 Somn 2:182, 211 Abr 103, 219 Ios 40, 57, 87, 153 Mos 1:25, 154 Mos 2:55, 137, 185, 216 Spec 1:138 Spec 2:62, 135 Spec 3:51, 62 Spec 4:96, 135 Virt 14, 39 Praem 15, 52, 160 Prob 67, 70, 145, 159 Aet 2 Legat 204, 312 Prov 2:5 QE isf 24

σώφρων (31) Leg 2:18 Sacr 54 Det 75, 95 Post 175 Plant 49 Sobr 38, 40 Migr 219 Congr 5, 142 Mut 50, 146, 146, 153, 206 Abr 194 Ios 50 Spec 1:102 Spec 3:59 Virt 167, 174, 182, 189, 194 Praem 137, 139 Prob 57 Legat 5, 64 Prov 2:5

T

τ QG (Par) 2:5

ταγηνίζω Spec 1:256

τάγμα Migr 100, 209

ταγματαρχέω Ebr 76

ταινία Agr 112 Fug 187

ταινιόω Spec 2:246

τακτικός Agr 87

ταλαιπωρέω Spec 3:17 Aet 4 Flacc 155

ταλαιπωρία Opif 167 Mut 189, 193 Somn 1:174 Mos 1:322

ταλαίπωρος Congr 174 Mut 189 Legat 274

ταλαντεύω (19) Leg 2:83 Post 22 Gig 28 Deus 85 Plant 7, 25 Conf 141 Congr 164 Fug 151 Mut 185 Somn 2:226 Abr 196 Ios 140 Mos 2:228 Spec 4:156 Praem 62, 63 Prob 24 Aet 136

τάλαντον Her 145

ταλάρος Virt 95

τάλας (8) Conf 128 Somn 2:51, 208 Mos 2:156 Spec 1:174 Spec 4:113 Prob 156 Legat 275

ταλασία Spec 3:174

ταμεῖον (ταμιεῖον) (9) Det 68 Deus 42 Ios 258 Spec 1:78 Spec 2:92 Virt 85 Praem 104, 142 Prob 86

ταμίας (10) Leg 3:163, 189 Det 66 Deus 113 Plant 26 Ebr 80 Conf 79 Somn 2:272 Praem 22 Hypoth 11:10

ταμιεία Migr 89

ταμιεῖον ταμεῖον

ταμιεύω (47) Leg 1:89 Leg 3:36 Cher 48 Sacr 23, 60, 94 Det 128 Post 145, 150 Deus 79 Agr 19, 168 Conf 14, 37, 71, 124 Migr 78, 115 Her 13, 74, 106 Fug 200 Somn 1:46 Somn 2:272 Ios 5, 8, 113, 161, 166, 243 Mos 1:203 Spec 1:325 Spec 2:175, 187, 198 Spec 3:200 Spec 4:38 Virt 5, 145, 152, 152 Praem 169 Aet 91 Flacc 88, 150 Legat 158 QG 2:13a

Τάνις Post 60, 62, 62, 62

ταντάλειος Her 269

Ταντάλειος Decal 149 Spec 4:81

τανῦν (νῦν) Opif 27, 67

ταξιαρχέω Sobr 29 Conf 174 Migr 60 Spec 1:207 Prob 154

ταξιάρχης ταξίαρχος

ταξίαρχος (ταξιάρχης) (10) Agr 87 Ebr 143 Mos 1:317, 318 Decal 38 Spec 1:114, 121 Spec 2:230 Virt 127 Prob 139

τάξις (239) Opif 13, 13, 22, 28, 28, 34, 67, 67, 68, 78, 87, 99, 106, 113 Leg 1:70 Leg 2:24, 73 Leg 3:61 Cher 23, 24, 50, 121, 129 Sacr 11, 52, 72, 73, 82 Det 23, 66, 134, 145 Post 64 Gig 43, 65 Deus 5, 27, 31, 34 Agr 57 Plant 3, 14 Ebr 14, 35, 48, 52, 75, 93, 143, 201 Sobr 25 Conf 133, 151, 174 Migr 23, 60, 196 Her 46, 87, 224, 224, 241 Congr 51, 104, 108, 110, 133 Fug 10, 73, 74, 145, 186 Mut 45, 104, 200 Somn 1:29, 113, 152, 173, 205, 241 Somn 2:152, 232, 247 Abr 17, 19, 47, 61, 69, 101, 124, 150, 219, 232 Ios 85, 92, 145, 176, 177, 187, 199, 203, 222 Mos 1:178, 206, 251, 280, 288 Mos 2:46, 71, 174, 222, 244, 245, 263, 276, 277 Decal 38, 82, 103, 104, 106, 123, 128, 166, 178 Spec 1:5, 19, 51, 54, 94, 109, 114, 120, 124, 156, 157, 168, 296, 345 Spec 2:69, 115, 124, 127, 137, 140, 140, 144, 150, 151, 153, 154, 181, 215, 224, 227, 228, 230 Spec 3:26, 108, 177, 192 Spec 4:1, 9, 28, 50, 63, 92, 117, 168, 187, 206, 210, 210, 235, 237 Virt 43, 77, 127, 137, 176, 209, 211, 211, 218 Praem 7, 41, 42, 59, 74, 111, 130, 152 Prob 24, 30, 81 Contempl 11, 61, 75, 80 Aet 31, 32, 34, 40, 40, 65, 75, 106 Flacc 86, 98, 109, 126, 128, 131 Legat 29, 58, 69, 74, 94, 95, 104, 147, 175, 204, 227, 228, 261, 278, 286, 296, 307, 328 Prov 2:9, 44 QG 1:64a, 64d, 2:16, 34a, 34b

ταπεινός (39) Leg 1:68 Leg 2:89 Leg 3:18, 19, 82, 84, 134 Det 13, 16, 34 Post 47, 48, 74, 79, 109, 149 Deus 167 Agr 61 Ebr 128 Migr 147 Her 29 Congr 175 Mut 222 Ios 144 Mos 1:31 Mos 2:51, 241 Decal 41, 61 Spec 1:308 Spec 2:106 Spec 3:1 Spec 4:176, 176 Prob 24, 24, 101 Prov 2:1 QG isf 5

ταπεινότης Leg 3:214 Post 136 Congr 107

ταπεινόω (9) Sacr 62 Post 46, 48, 74 Fug 1, 207 Mut 194 Ios 150 Spec 4:88

ταπείνωσις (9) Leg 1:68, 68 Post 41, 46, 74 Her 268 Fug 1, 5, 207

τάρανδρος Ebr 174

ταραξίπολις Flacc 20, 137

ταράσσω Conf 69 Flacc 135 Legat 143 QG 2:28

ταραχή (31) Leg 3:123, 160 Post 119 Agr 45, 159 Conf 42 Her 244 Congr 176 Somn 2:147, 152, 166, 251, 286 Abr 27, 202 Ios 10, 143, 145, 211 Mos 1:178 Mos 2:164 Decal 86 Spec 1:121 Praem 76 Contempl 19 Flacc 41 Legat 68, 90, 113, 261 Prov 2:1

ταραχώδης (6) Conf 70 Abr 151, 210, 213 Spec 1:69 Legat 186

ταρσός Plant 152 Mut 158 Mos 1:218 Legat 99

τάρταρος Praem 152

Τάρταρος Legat 49, 103 QE 2:40

τάσις Leg 1:14 Post 116 Somn 1:28, 29

τάσσω (114) Opif 45, 49, 49, 60, 98 Leg 1:19, 19, 87 Leg 2:3, 4 Leg 3:99, 248 Cher 1, 1, 23 Sacr 69, 120 Det 166 Post 42, 144 Gig 43 Deus 5, 5, 11, 182 Agr 87 Plant 10, 57 Ebr 143, 144 Sobr 24, 29, 62 Migr 160, 196 Her 88, 97, 97, 163 Congr 4 Fug 73, 93, 166 Mut 244 Somn 1:1, 113, 254 Somn 2:94, 182, 234 Abr 19, 27, 61, 101, 150, 180, 244, 274 Ios 222 Mos 1:28, 178, 239, 257, 280 Mos 2:103, 125, 241 Decal 24, 38 Spec 1:48, 87, 98, 217, 255, 296, 300, 345 Spec 2:126, 137, 175 Spec 3:159, 177, 181, 187, 199 Spec 4:63, 155, 193 Virt 2, 75, 77, 127, 176, 188, 211, 218 Praem 59, 74, 77, 110 Prob 30, 101 Contempl 72 Aet 3, 20, 32 Flacc 5, 149 Legat 7, 20, 95, 175 QG 2:16 QE 2:19

ταυρόμορφος Mos 2:165

ταῦρος (20) Opif 85 Post 161, 165 Deus 117 Ebr 95 Fug 186 Mut 160 Abr 266 Mos 2:162, 270 Decal 76 Spec 1:79 Spec 3:44, 44, 125, 144 Spec 4:206 Prob 101, 102 Legat 317

ταυρωπός Mut 160

ταυτολογία Congr 73

ταυτότης Opif 22 Decal 104 Spec 4:187

ταφή (10) Sacr 10 Ios 25, 27 Mos 2:283 Spec 2:95 Flacc 61, 65, 83 Legat 131 Hypoth 7:7

τάφος Abr 139 Ios 24 Mos 2:291 Flacc 159

τάφρος (6) Det 106 Agr 6 Spec 2:172 Spec 4:229 Prob 33 Prov 2:26

τάχα (65) Opif 6 Leg 1:35 Leg 2:23 Leg 3:181 Cher 51, 117 Deus 127 Agr 28 Plant 54 Ebr 163, 172 Conf 118 Migr 195 Her 23, 90, 142, 229 Congr 153 Mut 48, 120 Somn 1:98, 151, 233, 255 Somn 2:34 Abr 76, 76, 240 Ios 129, 129, 169, 204 Mos 1:114, 114, 116, 162, 166, 185, 185, 185 Mos 2:115, 263 Spec 1:286 Spec 2:82, 157, 193, 212 Spec 3:29, 91, 107, 138 Spec 4:103, 119, 119, 192 Virt 177 Contempl 3 Aet 54, 78, 140 Legat 68, 140, 218, 240 QG 4:64

τάχος (36) Sacr 59 Det 117 Post 161 Agr 70, 85, 93, 180 Plant 161 Ebr 119 Conf 100 Migr 25, 151, 207 Her 149 Mut 116, 142, 179, 247 Somn 2:238 Abr 233 Ios 141 Mos 1:168 Mos 2:144 Decal 35, 146 Spec 1:83, 243, 316 Spec 2:83, 146, 158 Spec 3:8 Flacc 112, 120 Legat 101, 135

ταχυναυτέω Agr 174 Plant 152 Flacc 26, 110

ταχύς (70) Sacr 64, 64, 64, 76, 125 Det 152 Post 123, 156 Gig 55 Deus 92 Plant 144, 161 Ebr 32, 120, 218 Conf 48 Migr 224 Her 149 Fug 41, 63, 97, 159, 168, 169, 169 Mut 239, 247, 253 Abr 59, 62, 67, 109, 176, 258 Ios 4, 181, 193, 256 Mos 1:18, 77, 177, 183, 184, 237, 292 Mos 2:165 Spec 2:221 Spec 3:101, 105, 114, 162 Spec 4:25 Virt 86 Praem 87, 105 Prob 27, 97 Aet 30, 133 Flacc 66, 66, 178 Legat 105, 118, 183, 220, 220, 241, 260 Hypoth 6:9

ταχυτής Somn 2:38

τέ (2051) Opif 7, 12, 13, 13, 15, 15, 20, 27, 27, 28, 30, 30, 31, 34, 37, 38, 41, 41, 44, 45, 48, 49, 52, 53, 54, 54, 54, 54, 56, 56, 58, 59, 60, 61, 61, 62, 63, 64, 67, 69, 70, 72, 73, 73, 75, 76, 77, 78, 78, 80, 80, 81, 81, 82, 84, 85, 90, 92, 92, 94, 95, 101, 104, 104, 104, 106, 113, 113, 116, 118, 125, 126, 126, 134, 135, 136, 138, 139, 139, 140, 140, 140, 141, 141, 144, 145, 145, 150, 152, 153, 156, 158, 158, 158, 159, 160, 161, 161, 161, 162, 163 Leg 1:4, 7, 8, 10, 12, 13, 14, 14, 15, 17, 17, 18, 18, 19, 19, 21, 22, 28, 29, 34, 39, 41, 56, 59, 61, 67, 68, 70, 72, 79, 79, 79, 84, 86, 89, 91, 103, 106 Leg 2:4, 8, 8, 19, 19, 22, 22, 30, 30, 40, 51, 53, 53, 63, 64, 64, 83, 85 Leg 3:1, 3, 10, 18, 20, 22, 28, 29, 30, 33, 33, 45, 45, 45, 57, 57, 57, 67, 67, 69, 74, 75, 79, 80, 87, 87, 88, 91, 99, 99, 99, 100, 106, 113, 113, 113, 114, 118, 127, 128, 128, 131, 140, 143, 151, 161, 170, 183, 184, 190, 199, 204, 206, 210, 215, 220, 220, 223, 223, 223, 225, 229, 242, 246, 250, 252, 253, 253 Cher 5, 10, 11, 22, 22, 29, 29, 35, 39, 54, 57, 63, 66, 70, 88, 88, 88, 91, 92, 105, 111, 112, 112, 113, 115, 119, 124, 124, 128, 128 Sacr 1, 4, 5, 33, 37, 40, 41, 45, 49, 53, 59, 60, 60, 61, 63, 69, 75, 76, 78, 85, 85, 97, 100, 105, 112, 112, 115, 116, 121, 123, 124, 137, 138 Det 2, 7, 8, 29, 44, 48, 49, 49, 52, 52, 54, 57, 62, 66, 72, 73, 75, 75, 79, 82, 87, 88, 88, 88, 89, 100, 102, 103, 105, 110, 117, 119, 127, 127, 131, 131, 136, 140, 146, 168, 172, 173 Post 3, 4, 5, 10, 12, 28, 28, 29, 32, 37, 37, 38, 43, 44, 46, 53, 68, 71, 71, 83, 88, 91, 91, 92, 95, 102, 106, 108, 109, 110, 122, 124, 125, 126, 130, 133, 138, 142, 151, 155, 155, 163, 167, 168, 174, 177, 179, 182 Gig 8, 11, 29, 32, 42, 42, 49, 60, 60, 62, 62, 62, 64 Deus 7, 30, 37, 38, 38, 39, 39, 45, 48, 48, 49, 57, 69, 69, 79, 79, 83, 95, 95, 100, 107, 109, 110, 113, 113, 119, 120, 142, 142, 145, 147, 161, 164, 164, 166, 167, 169, 173 Agr 3, 8, 15, 16, 17, 17, 24, 26, 30, 34, 35, 36, 36, 39, 39, 47, 47, 48, 51, 51, 59, 62, 63, 67, 75, 80, 83, 83, 86, 86, 89, 89, 91, 91, 102, 108, 109, 111, 112, 124, 124, 128, 130, 133, 136, 137, 137, 138, 140, 141, 141, 141, 145, 147, 151, 152, 153, 157, 161, 162, 165, 168, 176, 176, 178, 180, 181 Plant 1, 2, 3, 10, 13, 14, 14, 14, 26, 27, 30, 30, 34, 37, 42, 45, 57, 62, 69, 81, 93, 105, 108, 115, 115, 118, 118, 118, 120, 120, 121, 126, 131, 133, 134, 136, 139, 146, 147, 151, 151, 154, 158, 159, 161, 162, 162, 172, 172 Ebr 1, 2, 5, 8, 13, 18, 20, 27, 29, 32, 33, 37, 46, 75, 75, 85, 91, 91, 91, 91, 95, 96, 109, 109, 119, 124, 129, 134, 142, 152, 156, 160, 165, 169, 169, 171, 173, 174, 176, 178, 179, 180, 184, 185, 185, 190, 191, 191, 191, 198, 198, 202, 203, 210, 214, 214, 223 Sobr 2, 7, 12, 14, 20, 38, 38, 40, 41, 42, 53, 61, 61 Conf 7, 12, 12, 15, 19, 19, 19, 21, 21, 21, 23, 23, 24, 28, 34, 38, 42, 52, 52, 72, 85, 85, 85, 89, 90, 90, 90, 91, 96, 105, 106, 115, 115, 118, 123, 127, 128, 136, 136, 138, 151, 151, 157, 161, 170, 175, 175, 176, 176, 176, 187, 188, 188, 190, 194, 197, 198 Migr 3, 8, 14, 18, 25, 34, 54, 54, 67, 68, 70, 73, 81, 82, 84, 89, 97, 99, 101, 102, 102, 107, 115, 119, 119, 119, 128, 147, 158, 165, 167, 179, 179, 189, 191, 194, 195, 195, 198, 201, 202, 211, 223, 224 Her 5, 7, 18, 28, 33, 48, 55, 55, 64, 68, 82, 85, 89, 92, 97, 110, 110, 114, 114, 118, 119, 125, 126, 128, 132, 134, 135, 135, 138, 138, 140, 140, 143, 147, 147, 147, 148, 149, 149, 151, 152, 152, 153, 154, 160, 161, 162, 166, 166, 167, 171, 172, 174, 175, 176, 178, 183, 187, 188, 189, 190, 190, 193, 195, 198, 199, 203, 217, 226, 233, 234, 235, 235, 235, 236, 245, 245, 247, 247, 247, 247, 249, 251, 261, 264, 281, 283, 285, 291, 295, 295, 296, 296, 298, 298, 310 Congr 15, 20, 20, 22, 29, 30, 33, 43, 52, 53, 61, 63, 64, 81, 84, 89, 98, 101, 104, 108, 125, 125, 129, 129, 133, 136, 137, 142, 144, 146, 148, 148, 154, 155, 171, 172, 173 Fug 12, 25, 33, 35, 36, 36, 36, 46, 50, 52, 73, 73, 74, 82, 82, 82, 99, 99, 103, 105, 112, 112, 112, 112, 122, 125, 126, 139, 154, 161, 169, 184, 195, 196, 201, 206, 206, 209, 210 Mut 4, 8, 9, 26, 30, 43, 45, 52, 54, 54, 57, 58, 63, 67, 67, 75, 78, 81, 86, 88, 96, 97, 97, 99, 107, 110, 118, 130, 134, 140, 144, 144, 146, 153, 155, 156, 167, 167, 202, 202, 205, 209, 220, 238, 247, 248, 248, 263 Somn 1:1, 2, 8, 18, 20, 20, 23, 27, 35, 37, 52, 53, 57, 57, 73, 76, 77, 80, 102, 105, 110, 113, 115, 118, 121, 124, 145, 159, 163, 168, 175, 177, 177, 194, 197, 199, 205, 205, 205, 205, 205, 216, 217, 221, 233, 235, 249 Somn 2:5, 6, 10, 12, 13, 13, 13, 26, 34, 38, 51, 55, 80, 83, 83, 86, 93, 99, 100, 104, 122, 124, 127, 140, 145, 147, 153, 155, 160, 161, 163, 165, 165, 169, 170, 173, 180, 187, 209, 215, 219, 221, 226, 227, 238, 244, 247, 257, 267, 274, 291, 293, 295, 297 Abr 2, 6, 13, 20, 23, 24, 27, 28, 29, 42, 43, 53, 57, 65, 67, 69, 70, 71, 75, 75, 76, 79, 84, 88, 90, 93, 95, 121, 126, 133, 141, 147, 148, 159, 159, 161, 166, 168, 184, 192, 194, 208, 214, 226, 227, 244, 253, 274 Ios 1, 11, 12, 29, 37, 38, 39, 39, 39, 54, 56, 60, 61, 63, 71, 73, 73, 76, 81, 88, 94, 94, 104, 108, 117, 118, 118, 126, 130, 147, 149, 149, 149, 157, 158, 185, 185, 193, 194, 195, 203, 223, 236, 240, 242, 243, 244, 257, 259, 260, 260, 269 Mos 1:3, 3, 6, 6, 9, 10, 15, 23, 23, 23, 24, 26, 27, 28, 28, 29, 33, 34, 40, 40, 48, 48, 51, 57, 60, 65, 74, 75, 77, 80, 82, 98, 110, 115, 115, 117, 119, 120, 120, 126, 127, 128, 130, 138, 144, 148, 149, 150, 157, 158, 158, 162, 168, 176, 178, 182, 188, 189, 190, 198, 200, 212, 216, 218, 223, 224, 224, 227, 229, 229, 237, 239, 240, 242, 248, 250, 255, 257, 257, 257, 260,

262, 265, 277, 287, 288, 294, 297, 298, 301, 302, 312, 313, 313, 317, 317, 320, 321, 329 Mos 2:1, 1, 2, 3, 5, 7, 12, 14, 15, 21, 25, 31, 38, 40, 40, 40, 40, 41, 43, 49, 50, 51, 51, 53, 54, 56, 57, 59, 60, 63, 64, 66, 66, 67, 69, 87, 92, 95, 98, 99, 103, 113, 115, 117, 121, 121, 122, 122, 126, 127, 127, 128, 128, 128, 128, 129, 132, 133, 134, 139, 140, 141, 141, 143, 146, 151, 153, 158, 158, 159, 162, 162, 167, 167, 174, 180, 185, 189, 191, 196, 209, 215, 215, 216, 216, 223, 224, 225, 238, 255, 256, 272, 278 Decal 20, 21, 21, 21, 22, 23, 24, 28, 45, 54, 56, 57, 60, 65, 66, 66, 66, 67, 72, 74, 78, 82, 98, 101, 103, 109, 126, 126, 147, 148, 149, 149, 150, 153, 157, 157, 158, 159, 162, 163, 164, 168, 173, 174 Spec 1:3, 16, 20, 21, 21, 21, 34, 43, 44, 46, 70, 73, 73, 82, 83, 86, 90, 93, 97, 97, 99, 99, 99, 101, 109, 110, 111, 118, 127, 131, 132, 134, 135, 137, 137, 138, 138, 141, 141, 145, 147, 149, 159, 163, 164, 165, 166, 171, 172, 175, 178, 201, 206, 208, 209, 209, 210, 210, 212, 212, 214, 214, 218, 222, 224, 224, 224, 227, 247, 256, 257, 257, 261, 269, 281, 295, 298, 302, 305, 307, 307, 309, 316, 317, 322, 322, 322, 324, 325, 331, 331, 334, 336, 336, 338, 340, 342, 342, 344, 344 Spec 2:1, 24, 30, 34, 34, 35, 39, 40, 40, 40, 42, 43, 45, 52, 52, 52, 52, 54, 57, 63, 64, 68, 69, 86, 86, 98, 100, 103, 123, 125, 129, 130, 133, 135, 138, 143, 143, 145, 148, 150, 151, 154, 156, 157, 157, 157, 160, 160, 160, 163, 164, 164, 165, 166, 167, 167, 168, 169, 171, 171, 173, 177, 181, 182, 183, 187, 193, 193, 195, 196, 198, 200, 203, 204, 204, 205, 205, 206, 209, 213, 223, 224, 224, 225, 226, 227, 229, 230, 230, 230, 230, 233, 233, 233, 233, 233, 235, 237, 239, 239, 240, 255, 256, 256, 259 Spec 3:1, 7, 8, 14, 14, 16, 16, 20, 23, 27, 27, 31, 33, 37, 39, 49, 49, 50, 51, 71, 71, 73, 74, 80, 90, 101, 116, 117, 117, 118, 119, 134, 135, 139, 142, 143, 151, 152, 174, 186, 188, 189, 191, 191, 201, 201, 209 Spec 4:13, 16, 25, 26, 32, 33, 40, 40, 40, 49, 57, 60, 66, 69, 74, 78, 82, 84, 87, 94, 96, 98, 98, 100, 100, 105, 106, 107, 108, 109, 111, 116, 123, 125, 127, 141, 142, 152, 154, 155, 156, 161, 163, 186, 186, 187, 193, 198, 199, 202, 205, 209, 211, 216, 217, 231, 231, 232, 233, 234, 235, 235, 237 Virt 3, 3, 6, 9, 13, 19, 20, 22, 32, 32, 46, 49, 53, 54, 56, 64, 72, 73, 74, 77, 77, 77, 81, 95, 102, 103, 103, 103, 108, 118, 118, 119, 126, 126, 128, 130, 144, 148, 155, 156, 156, 156, 160, 160, 162, 168, 168, 169, 170, 173, 174, 175, 176, 182, 182, 184, 185, 188, 190, 191, 195, 199, 205, 210, 212, 212, 213, 214, 216, 225 Praem 3, 11, 28, 29, 34, 35, 39, 41, 41, 44, 48, 54, 54, 54, 59, 60, 60, 67, 87, 89, 89, 107, 113, 119, 120, 136, 145, 146, 148, 151, 151, 152, 153, 158, 160, 161, 168, 168 Prob 31, 42, 47, 65, 74, 76, 79, 79, 80, 83, 87, 99, 103, 112, 118, 122, 134, 137, 138, 140, 152, 154, 156 Contempl 2, 2, 3, 5, 6, 9, 17, 17, 22, 23, 23, 24, 33, 37, 37, 37, 38, 39, 48, 49, 50, 51, 53, 54, 56, 57, 57, 58, 61, 61, 66, 68, 81, 83, 84, 87, 89 Aet 1, 5, 5, 6, 7, 7, 11, 12, 13, 19, 21, 22, 25, 29, 35, 36, 37, 37, 38, 43, 52, 57, 61, 63, 63, 63, 73, 74, 74, 74, 75, 79, 80, 83, 86, 98, 98, 102, 119, 120, 121, 122, 132, 132, 135, 140 Flacc 2, 4, 8, 9, 16, 26, 26, 28, 40, 43, 46, 51, 53, 57, 64, 77, 97, 117, 118, 123, 126, 133, 148, 148, 149 Legat 4, 6, 6, 10, 10, 10, 10, 11, 13, 13, 13, 14, 15, 22, 22, 31, 34, 46, 47, 54, 55, 55, 63, 67, 68, 74, 80, 82, 83, 83, 86, 90, 90, 94, 96, 99, 102, 127, 132, 161, 167, 178, 207, 214, 214, 215, 222, 245, 246, 250, 261, 267, 267, 270, 281, 283, 287, 297, 299, 300, 300, 306, 338, 338, 349, 351, 351, 368 Hypoth 6:1, 6:1, 6:2, 6:6, 6:6, 7:9, 7:13, 7:19, 7:20 Prov 2:1, 1, 2, 10, 12, 15, 19, 23, 29, 33, 35, 45, 47, 52, 53, 64 QG 1:1, 20, 68, 77, 2:29, 34a, 34c, 38, 59, 3:18, 49a, 61, 4:33b, 47b, 47b, 47b, 189, 206b, 211 QG (Par) 2:3, 2:7 QE 2:14, 24a, 25c, 55b, 65 QE isf 3, 4, 8, 14, 14

τέγος Spec 3:149 Contempl 33

τέθηπα (21) Opif 83 Ebr 56 Conf 49 Fug 161 Somn 1:142, 203 Somn 2:80 Ios 6, 80 Mos 1:27 Mos 2:23, 40, 70 Decal 4 Spec 1:24, 186 Spec 3:8 Contempl 65 Legat 211 Hypoth 11:18 QG 3:29

τέθριππος (7) Det 141, 141 Conf 114 Mut 93 Legat 134, 135 Prov 2:58

τείνω (66) Leg 1:29, 30, 37 Leg 2:37, 38, 45, 62 Leg 3:185 Sacr 75 Det 84, 106 Post 14, 104, 126 Gig 18 Deus 35, 79 Agr 6, 24, 113 Plant 9, 22, 116 Ebr 106, 106, 152 Conf 136, 181 Her 172, 217 Fug 182 Mut 28 Somn 1:54, 70, 77, 134, 145, 179 Somn 2:8, 283, 294 Abr 58, 125 Mos 1:78, 107 Mos 2:35, 93, 118. 196 Decal 147 Spec 1:85 Spec 2:224 Spec 3:2 Spec 4:48, 236 Virt 9, 30, 81, 88 Contempl 61 Aet 86 Legat 163, 262 Prov 2:9 QG 3:11b QG (Par) 2:4

τειχήρης Agr 24 Flacc 62 Legat 20, 128

τεῖχος (48) Opif 17 Leg 1:75, 86 Det 105 Post 50, 52 Agr 11, 15 Migr 215 Her 68 Fug 203 Mut 74 Somn 1:108, 188 Somn 2:82 Abr 139 Mos 1:38, 115, 177 Mos 2:34, 72, 78, 253, 255 Spec 2:116, 116, 117, 121 Spec 3:74, 87, 132 Spec 4:21, 142, 220, 222 Virt 109, 186 Prob 33, 38, 151 Contempl 20, 86 Aet 129, 140 Flacc 167 Prov 2:57 QG 3:27, 4:59

τειχοφυλακέω Spec 1:301

τεκμαίρομαι (14) Det 1 Post 35 Congr 152 Somn 1:54, 212 Abr 99 Ios 106, 234 Spec 1:72, 141 Spec 2:56 Legat 261, 270 Prov 2:47

τεκμήριον (26) Leg 2:25, 103 Leg 3:57, 74, 111, 175, 195, 204 Cher 18 Det 10, 30, 163 Deus 37, 148, 181 Agr 56 Ebr 13, 117 Migr 150 Somn 1:156 Abr 77 Mos 1:207 Decal 75 Spec 2:8 Legat 212, 311

τεκμηριόω (8) Opif 102, 136 Abr 151 Ios 37 Spec 2:237 Spec 3:193 Aet 91 Prov 2:67

τεκνοκτονία Spec 3:112, 114

τεκνοκτόνος Migr 140 Mos 1:10

τέκνον (107) Opif 167, 171 Leg 2:46 Leg 3:90, 180, 181, 181, 209, 216, 217 Cher 50 Sacr 19, 64, 129 Det 145 Post 109 Deus 10, 14, 14, 19, 92 Plant 146 Ebr 120 Sobr 10, 10, 11, 21, 25 Migr 208, 217 Her 38 Fug 15, 23, 39, 40, 46, 88, 132, 169 Mut 130, 143, 145, 145, 147, 147, 147 Somn 2:83, 128, 178, 184 Abr 175, 187, 196, 248, 250 Ios 23, 74, 182, 187 Mos 1:13, 85, 150 Mos 2:245 Decal 119, 128 Spec 1:114, 130, 139, 139, 313 Spec 2:133, 134, 225, 233 Spec 3:11, 34, 62, 113, 131, 159 Spec 4:142, 203 Virt 53, 112, 132 Praem 148, 148, 159 Prob 119, 151 Contempl 18, 47 Flacc 14, 62, 68, 87 Legat 121, 124, 230, 308 Hypoth 11:17 Prov 2:3 QG 2:26a, 4:145 QG isf 10, 13 QE 2:19

τεκνοποιέω Congr 1, 12, 14

τεκταίνομαι Opif 28, 137 Mos 2:270 Spec 3:198 Aet 26

τεκτονέω Sobr 36

τεκτονικός Leg 1:57 Sobr 36

τέκτων Sobr 35, 36

τελειογονέω (16) Opif 36, 116, 124 Mos 2:66, 104, 222 Spec 1:172 Spec 3:111 Virt 49, 145, 154, 156, 158 Praem 130 Aet 60, 98 τέλειος (τέλεος) (421) Opif 9, 13, 14, 14, 41, 41, 42, 47, 48, 54, 54, 70, 82, 89, 101, 143 Leg 1:3, 15, 18, 19, 34, 61, 94, 94, 94 Leg 2:17, 17, 27, 48, 55, 91 Leg 3:18, 89, 89, 131, 131, 134, 135, 135, 140, 140, 140, 144, 147, 159, 176, 179, 192, 196, 196, 203, 207, 219, 241, 244, 244, 244, 244, 249 Cher 9, 43, 59, 86, 106, 109, 114 Sacr 8, 10, 10, 36, 37, 43, 43, 60, 65, 78, 85, 106, 111, 111, 111, 115, 120, 132 Det 7, 60, 60, 64, 64, 65, 65, 96, 125, 132, 132, 132, 144, 154, 154, 157, 160, 175 Post 26, 48, 88, 95, 96, 103, 130, 148, 152, 171, 172, 173 Gig 5, 45 Deus 4, 23, 73, 81, 92, 96, 117, 118, 132, 142, 154 Agr 9, 9, 50, 53, 80, 83, 100, 127, 140, 140, 145, 157, 160, 165, 168 Plant 2, 2, 4, 6, 6, 6, 31, 37, 49, 64, 76, 91, 93, 128, 128, 131, 135, 161 Ebr 33, 48, 51, 83, 90, 94, 103, 115, 135, 148, 164 Sobr 8, 9, 13, 15, 62 Conf 75, 97, 180 Migr 27, 33, 36, 44, 46, 55, 55, 73, 96, 127, 166, 169, 199, 202, 208, 223 Her 82, 91, 114, 121, 125, 126, 156, 199, 275, 293, 306, 315 Congr 19, 38, 45, 88, 90, 90, 105, 113, 116, 130, 137, 138, 138, 148, 154, 154, 160 Fug 12, 12, 13, 18, 36, 40, 41, 43, 43, 51, 128, 146, 184, 213 Mut 19, 23, 24, 50, 68, 88, 122, 122, 128, 184, 188, 188, 189, 192, 192, 205, 223, 227, 227, 230, 230, 248, 270 Somn 1:36, 37, 39, 59, 162, 177, 198, 199, 200, 205, 213, 213, 213, 216 Somn 2:10, 22, 27, 33, 34, 234, 235, 236, 270 Abr 2, 26, 31, 34, 36, 47, 54, 100, 116, 160, 168, 254, 271 Ios 57, 110, 210 Mos 1:1, 19, 62, 77, 96, 96, 123, 159 Mos 2:5, 5, 50, 84, 111, 134, 150, 180, 187, 196, 267 Decal 28, 33, 158, 175 Spec 1:18, 35, 63, 71, 149, 177, 177, 178, 200, 201, 205, 210, 252, 272, 277, 286, 287 Spec 2:11, 23, 32, 40, 41, 51, 53, 59, 59, 68, 128, 171, 200, 201, 203, 231, 233, 262 Spec 3:119, 134, 169, 200 Spec 4:95, 105, 140, 182, 234 Virt 60, 112, 129, 146, 156, 158, 184, 189, 217 Praem 1, 58, 65, 65, 120, 161 Prob 91, 92 Contempl 5, 7, 11, 21 Aet 15, 15, 26, 26, 26, 41, 50, 57, 59, 60, 73, 73, 75, 103 Flacc 15 Legat 5, 318 Hypoth 7:5, 11:3 Prov 1, 1, 2:43 QG 1:97, 3:52, 61, 4:30, 30, 88, 104 QG isf 2, 16 QG (Par) 2:7 QE 2:1

τελειότης (35) Sacr 120 Det 64, 90 Post 132, 143 Gig 26 Deus 26 Agr 133, 146, 157, 158, 165, 168 Plant 135 Ebr 82, 82, 85 Conf 72 Migr 73 Her 121, 156, 310 Fug 115, 172 Mut 2, 12, 24, 123 Abr 26, 54 Mos 2:58 Spec 1:80 Spec 2:64, 177 Spec 4:69

τελειόω (55) Opif 89 Leg 1:6, 10 Leg 2:61, 91 Leg 3:45, 74, 245 Cher 35 Sacr 7 Det 39 Agr 42, 158, 159, 160, 165, 169 Plant 81, 94 Conf 89, 155, 155, 158, 181 Migr 139, 174, 214 Congr 35 Fug 172 Mut 85, 270 Somn 1:131, 200 Somn 2:45 Abr 53, 62 Mos 1:283 Mos 2:261, 275 Spec 2:39, 158 Spec 4:209 Virt 69, 157 Praem 9, 36, 49, 62, 127, 128, 131 Contempl 25 Aet 71 QG isf 8 QE 1:1

τελείωσις (33) Opif 103 Leg 1:1, 10 Leg 3:129, 130, 213 Post 97, 174 Deus 122 Agr 161, 166 Migr 67 Her 251, 311 Congr 33 Mos 2:141, 149, 152, 288 Decal 99, 161 Spec 2:9, 38, 58, 204 Spec 3:58 Virt 145 Praem 11, 27 Aet 71, 99, 100 QG 3:12

τέλεος (τέλειος) (29) Leg 2:102 Leg 3:35, 100 Sacr 7 Post 173 Deus 25, 106, 118, 183 Agr 18, 52 Plant 66 Migr 98, 106, 220 Her 26, 76 Congr 13 Mut 240 Abr 74, 84 Mos 1:155 Mos 2:218 Decal 81 Spec 2:258 Prob 57 Contempl 46, 55 Aet 1

τελεσιουργέω (13) Opif 130 Leg 2:24 Leg 3:227 Cher 102 Sacr 83 Post 171 Conf 156, 158, 175 Somn 1:207 Abr 147 Spec 3:33 Virt 94

τελεσφορέω (26) Opif 59, 102, 113 Leg 1:76 Sacr 124 Det 60 Post 97 Deus 39, 40 Plant 127, 151 Ebr 126 Congr 138, 162 Fug 170 Mos 1:226 Mos 2:5 Spec 1:16, 172, 179 Spec 2:59, 143, 260 Spec 3:188 Virt 77 Praem 126

τελεσφόρος (14) Opif 102, 103, 106, 107 Deus 5 Agr 173 Ebr 30 Migr 31, 139 Somn 1:115 Somn 2:76, 142, 272 Spec 2:204

τελετή (25) Leg 3:219 Cher 42, 42, 43, 48, 94 Sacr 60, 62 Gig 54 Ebr 129 Mut 107 Somn 1:82 Abr 122 Mos 2:149, 153 Decal 41 Spec 1:56, 319, 319 Spec 3:40 Praem 121 Prob 14 QG 4:8c QE isf 13, 14

τελευταῖος (63) Opif 83, 95, 108, 109, 110, 110 Leg 3:41 Sacr 63 Plant 85 Ebr 15 Congr 109 Fug 166 Somn 1:14, 218 Somn 2:281 Abr 50, 95, 195, 219 Ios 23, 175, 187, 217, 249 Mos 1:134, 195, 311 Mos 2:2, 146, 153, 187, 233 Decal 106, 142 Spec 1:222 Spec 2:157, 186, 204, 211, 243 Spec 3:39 Spec 4:23, 28, 78, 207 Virt 72 Praem 110 Contempl 54 Flacc 61, 72, 115, 156, 175, 187 Legat 15, 135, 239, 267, 274, 290, 302, 308 Prov 2:40

τελευτάω (99) Leg 2:46 Leg 3:45, 212, 212, 212, 253 Sacr 8 Det 75, 94, 94, 95, 151 Post 5, 173, 181 Agr 95, 155 Migr 177 Her 202, 292 Fug 55, 59, 83, 83, 107, 113 Mut 62, 228 Somn 1:10, 26, 31 Abr 245 Ios 216, 261, 264, 268 Mos 1:100, 136, 145 Mos 2:225, 231, 235, 235, 291, 291 Spec 1:105, 108, 129, 161, 250 Spec 2:2, 41, 124, 127, 127, 131, 139, 142 Spec 3:14, 20, 30, 106, 107, 133, 148, 148, 206 Spec 4:36, 169, 202, 202 Prob 112 Contempl 13 Aet 23, 86, 97, 97, 129, 143 Flacc 9, 12, 50, 66, 71, 75, 84 Legat 26, 58, 141, 168, 268, 325 QG 1:70:1, 70:2, 76a, 3:11a, 4:173 QE 2:26 QE isf 19

τελευτή (59) Leg 2:6 Det 178 Deus 75 Agr 25, 156 Ebr 143 Conf 42 Migr 16 Her 31, 126, 209 Fug 171 Somn 1:11, 47 Abr 230, 255 Ios 128, 156, 179, 226, 262 Mos 2:34, 226, 234, 281, 292 Decal 99, 117 Spec 1:102, 112, 159 Spec 2:16, 16, 42, 95 Spec 3:123, 131, 161, 205 Spec 4:119 Virt 52, 67 Prob 110, 113, 133, 135 Aet 20, 60, 74, 111 Flacc 2, 74 Legat 8, 72, 160, 192 Prov 2:25, 50 QG 4:145

τελέω (25) Opif 104, 104 Cher 48 Gig 54 Deus 39 Agr 58 Mut 36, 107 Somn 2:144 Abr 122, 243 Mos 1:62, 303 Mos 2:150 Decal 41 Spec 1:56, 319, 319, 323 Spec 2:78 Spec 3:131, 190 Virt 76 Contempl 25 Legat 56

τέλμα Opif 38

τελματώδης Her 32

τέλος (215) Opif 44, 44, 44, 44, 82, 82, 82, 82, 103, 144, 158, 162 Leg 1:6, 6, 84, 89 Leg 2:73 Leg 3:37, 45, 47, 205, 249, 253 Cher 86, 91 Sacr 42, 113, 115, 115, 125 Det 88, 114 Post 21, 29, 53, 80, 152, 157, 174 Gig 14, 53 Deus 25, 61, 67, 98, 100 Agr 5, 76, 91, 125, 126, 169, 173, 180, 181 Plant 37, 49, 76, 76, 80, 82, 90, 93, 99, 161, 168 Ebr 115, 202, 204, 218 Sobr 60 Conf 144, 144, 144, 145, 153, 155 Migr 56, 103, 128, 131, 133, 134, 134, 139, 139, 143, 153, 225 Her 120, 120, 121, 121, 122, 172, 172, 246, 315 Congr 12, 141 Fug 171, 172 Mut 102, 216 Somn 1:8, 66, 151, 167, 171, 230 Somn 2:11, 29, 107, 141, 142, 250 Abr 46, 46, 49, 93, 130, 172, 177, 230, 235, 260 Ios 1, 43, 98, 122, 246, 250 Mos 1:46, 91, 122, 151, 168, 194, 221, 251, 327, 329 Mos 2:151, 181, 181, 181, 181, 287, 290 Decal 35, 50, 51, 73, 81, 121, 123 Spec 1:143, 188, 188, 266, 317, 333, 336, 344, 345 Spec 2:38, 142, 157, 157, 157, 236 Spec 3:13, 29, 54, 86, 98, 125 Spec 4:12 Virt 15,

75, 182 Praem 23, 24, 28, 28, 142, 162 Prob 127, 160 Contempl 88 Aet 36 Flacc 4, 141, 183 Legat 25, 26, 108, 110, 144, 222, 252, 300, 303 Hypoth 6:6 Prov 2:17 QG 1:96:1, 4:86b, 9*, 9*, 200b QG isf 6 QE 1:1, 1, 7b, 2:26

τεμενίζω Flacc 51

τέμενος (9) Post 50 Her 75 Mos 2:89 Decal 78 Legat 137, 139, 151, 151, 296

τέμνω (73) Opif 159 Leg 1:3 Leg 2:86 Leg 3:170, 226 Cher 15 Sacr 25, 74, 74, 82, 83, 84, 85, 100, 131 Det 90, 107, 110 Deus 66, 166 Agr 133, 134, 136 Plant 100, 104, 114 Conf 8, 85, 89, 90, 176, 191, 192 Migr 48 Her 130, 131, 132, 135, 136, 138, 139, 146, 161, 165, 167, 179, 213, 225, 233, 234, 235 Mut 148, 179 Somn 1:17 Somn 2:171 Ios 76 Mos 1:243 Mos 2:22, 123 Decal 162 Spec 1:194, 211, 217, 226, 331, 333 Spec 2:63 Spec 3:198 Spec 4:229 Virt 135, 150, 154 QG 2:34a

τεναγώδης Opif 63 Mos 2:35

τέρας (9) Agr 96 Mos 1:80, 90, 91, 95 Spec 2:218 Spec 3:45 Aet 2, 121

τεράστιος (11) Plant 4 Congr 173 Abr 118 Mos 1:71, 165 Mos 2:257, 266 Spec 2:188 Spec 4:129 Prob 5 Aet 69

τερατεύομαι Her 97 Decal 76 Praem 8 Aet 48, 68

τερατολογία Her 228

τερατοσκόπος Conf 159 Somn 1:220 Spec 1:60 Spec 4:48

τερατουργία Leg 1:83

τερατουργός Sacr 28

τερατώδης (6) Abr 118 Mos 1:118, 178, 217 Mos 2:154, 268

τερέβινθος Leg 3:23

τερθρεία Cher 42 Det 35 Decal 64 Spec 1:319 Praem 58

τέρμα (6) Deus 79, 143, 143 Sobr 42 Somn 1:159 Mos 1:2

τερπνός Leg 3:237 Somn 2:209

τέρπω (7) Leg 2:75 Det 157 Ebr 176 Congr 66 Spec 1:39 Legat 50, 296

τέρψις (22) Opif 54, 162 Cher 104 Sacr 30 Det 9, 33 Post 122, 155 Agr 91 Conf 85 Migr 19 Her 48 Somn 2:156 Abr 65, 164 Ios 61 Spec 1:74, 322 Spec 2:214 Spec 4:141 Legat 12, 46

τεσσαράκοντα (18) Leg 3:142 Migr 154 Somn 1:36 Mos 1:206 Mos 2:69, 70, 77, 78, 80, 86, 89 Decal 27 Spec 1:158 Spec 2:33, 33, 120, 199 Legat 148

τεσσαρακονταετία Mos 2:258 QE 2:49a

τεσσαρακοντάς Mos 2:84

τεσσαρακοστός Mos 1:238

τέσσαρες (171) Opif 48, 48, 48, 48, 48, 51, 52, 52, 93, 93, 93, 95, 96, 96, 97, 97, 98, 99, 99, 102, 102, 102, 102, 102, 104, 106, 106, 106, 107, 107, 108, 109, 109, 110, 131 Leg 1:63, 63, 63, 63, 64, 66 Leg 2:102, 105 Leg 3:139, 139, 139, 139 Cher 127 Det 8, 119, 154 Post 128, 128, 129 Agr 83, 137 Plant 117, 120, 123, 124, 124, 124, 124, 124, 124 Ebr 15, 35, 93, 105 Her 140, 152, 153, 153, 197, 226, 239, 269, 281, 282, 283 Congr 76, 92, 117, 117 Fug 73, 87 Somn 1:14, 15, 16, 21, 25, 28, 39 Somn 2:241, 243, 243, 257 Abr 145, 162, 164, 226, 236, 236, 237, 242, 244 Ios 112 Mos 2:7, 9, 78, 80, 84, 87, 93, 101, 114, 115, 124, 124, 132, 133, 156, 187, 192 Decal 21, 22, 22, 26, 26, 27, 27, 27, 28, 53 Spec 1:3, 71, 87, 98, 189, 208, 231, 320 Spec 2:177, 177, 200, 224, 261 Spec 3:126 Spec 4:12, 12, 113 Virt 41 Praem 53, 56, 71 Contempl 33 Aet 25, 29, 107, 108, 113, 117 Flacc 55 Legat 300, 351 QG 1:69, 2:5a, 65, 3:61, 4:8b QG (Par) 2:5

τεσσαρεσκαίδεκα Mos 1:287

τεσσαρεσκαιδεκαετής Leg 1:10

τεσσαρεσκαιδέκατος (7) Ios 43 Mos 2:224, 228, 231 Spec 2:149 QG 2:5b QG (Par) 2:5

τεταγμένως Spec 2:57

τεταρταΐζω Conf 151

τέταρτος (85) Opif 45, 102, 103, 104, 106, 106, 121, 131, 141, 141, 171 Leg 1:33, 63, 72, 72, 81 Leg 2:105 Plant 95, 117, 118, 119, 125, 132, 134, 134 Ebr 27 Sobr 48 Migr 86 Her 170, 258, 293, 293, 298, 298, 298, 299 Fug 87, 95, 106, 166, 177 Somn 1:14, 15, 23, 24, 24, 25, 30, 33, 33, 37, 38, 40, 40, 87 Somn 2:237 Abr 12, 13, 170 Ios 1, 15, 113, 189, 222 Mos 2:103, 244 Decal 15, 21, 96, 158, 172 Spec 1:7, 333 Spec 2:41, 142, 145 Spec 4:41 Virt 158 Praem 56 Aet 61, 130 Flacc 85 QG 2:65, 3:12 QG (Par) 2:3

τετραγράμματος Mos 2:115

τετραγωνικός QG (Par) 2:2

τετράγωνος (35) Opif 51, 92, 92, 93, 93, 94, 94, 94, 106, 106, 106, 106, 106 Leg 3:57 Plant 75, 121, 122 Conf 87 Mos 2:113, 128 Decal 22, 28 Spec 1:231 Spec 2:40 QG 2:5a, 14, 3:61, 4:72 QG (Par) 2:2, 2:2, 2:2, 2:2, 2:2, 2:4, 2:5

τετράδιον Flacc 111

τετράδραχμος Det 162, 162 Somn 1:98

τετραίνω Leg 3:32

τετράκις Opif 93, 105 Spec 2:177 Legat 307

τετρακισχίλιοι Opif 94 Mos 1:304

τετρακόσιοι Her 269 Flacc 94 Legat 350

τετραπλάσιος (8) Opif 48, 48, 95, 95 Mos 2:115 Decal 22 Spec 2:200 Spec 4:13

τετράπους (8) Leg 2:11 Gig 31 Agr 83, 92 Ebr 111 Spec 3:49, 49, 49

τετράρχης Flacc 25

τετράς (31) Opif 47, 47, 47, 48, 48, 49, 49, 50, 52, 52, 53, 62, 95, 97, 97, 106, 106 Plant 123, 125, 125, 125, 139 Abr 13 Mos 2:84, 115, 115, 115 Spec 2:40 Virt 158, 159 Aet 113

τετρασκελής Leg 2:99 Spec 4:113, 113

τετράστιχος Leg 1:81

τετραστοιχεί Mos 2:112 Spec 1:87

τετραφάρμακος Conf 187 Aet 79

τετραχῇ Opif 52 Mos 2:124 Spec 4:235

τετρώροφος Mos 2:60

τέττιξ Prob 8 Contempl 35

τεῦχος QG 1:1

τεύχω Migr 195 Somn 1:57

τέφρα (16) Deus 161 Her 29 Somn 1:211, 214, 220 Abr 139 Ios 53 Mos 1:127 Mos 2:56, 157 Spec 1:232, 244, 262, 264, 267, 268

τεφρόω Ebr 223

τεχνάζω (18) Leg 3:24 Ios 213 Mos 1:19 Decal 55 Spec 3:36, 37, 80, 97, 158 Spec 4:52 Virt 34 Prob 105 Contempl 62 Aet 37, 90 Flacc 68, 110 Prov 2:27

τέχνη (224) Opif 67, 69, 78, 81, 82, 168 Leg 1:6, 14, 57, 57, 94 Leg 2:75 Leg 3:15, 30, 61, 64, 92, 98, 99, 178, 232 Cher 68, 71, 100 Sacr 37, 64, 64, 113, 115, 116 Det 17, 18, 20, 35, 37, 38, 42, 43, 43, 88, 104, 105, 109, 110, 111, 145, 154, 166 Post 36, 53, 101, 103, 107, 119, 130, 141, 152 Gig 59, 60 Deus 100 Agr 4, 7, 20, 43, 64, 68, 71, 71, 77, 93, 119, 181 Plant 1, 2, 31, 71, 81, 81, 81, 94, 110 Ebr 88, 88, 88, 89, 90, 215, 218 Sobr 35 Migr 31, 39, 42, 42, 55, 74, 77, 82, 120, 142, 167, 167 Her 115, 116, 156, 159, 160, 169, 172, 199, 210, 210, 252, 266 Congr 3, 36, 46, 65, 78, 126, 138, 140, 140, 141, 142, 142, 143, 144 Fug 27, 69, 82, 168, 170, 170 Mut 80, 122, 150, 219, 220, 249, 260 Somn 1:7, 10, 107, 203, 205, 207, 220, 251 Somn 2:4, 50, 60, 61, 110, 214 Abr 153, 267 Ios 39, 75 Mos 1:23, 92, 94, 287 Mos 2:146, 205, 211, 219, 220 Decal 125 Spec 1:266, 335 Spec 2:65, 99, 159, 159, 161, 172 Spec 3:33, 86, 93, 94, 121 Spec 4:40, 48, 154, 156, 156 Virt 203, 206 Praem 9, 12, 142 Prob 33, 34, 49, 68, 76, 157 Contempl 16, 42 Aet 38, 41, 43, 54, 64, 130, 145, 146, 149, 149 Flacc 1, 52 Legat 46, 47, 89, 199 Hypoth 6:4, 11:9 Prov 1, 2:13, 60 QG 4:69, 76b, 76b, 228

τεχνικός (21) Leg 2:75 Leg 3:36 Det 18, 108, 109 Post 140 Gig 2 Plant 141 Migr 75 Her 119, 157, 158, 160, 216 Fug 47 Mut 220 Mos 2:111 Spec 1:35, 35 Prob 51 Contempl 49

τεχνιτεύω (21) Opif 146 Leg 3:102, 221 Sacr 26 Gig 59 Ebr 109 Congr 136 Mut 29 Somn 2:201, 205, 208 Mos 1:295 Decal 69, 71 Spec 1:174 Spec 3:108 Spec 4:113 Legat 9, 171, 246 Prov 1

τεχνίτης (66) Opif 20, 67, 135 Leg 1:18, 29, 31 Leg 3:36, 80, 98, 99, 102, 178 Cher 32, 53, 57, 128 Det 104 Post 109, 162 Gig 23, 60 Deus 30, 30 Agr 138 Plant 31, 71, 81, 82, 159 Sobr 35, 36 Conf 195 Migr 120 Her 133, 158, 218, 225 Congr 46, 105, 142 Fug 95 Mut 31, 122 Somn 1:123, 136 Somn 2:116 Mos 2:76, 78, 90, 109, 128, 136, 138 Decal 69, 71 Spec 1:41 Prob 51 Contempl 4 Aet 8, 42, 44 Flacc 57 Legat 103 Prov 1, 1, 2:15

τεχνολογέω Leg 2:14

τέως (20) Deus 37, 90, 177 Agr 33 Migr 123 Mut 113 Somn 1:199 Abr 242 Mos 1:106 Mos 2:61, 254 Spec 1:70 Virt 151 Aet 139 Flacc 3, 153 Legat 372 Prov 2:7, 9 QE 1:19

τηθίς Spec 3:26

τηκεδών Praem 143, 151

τήκω (7) Ebr 190 Her 226 Mos 1:118 Mos 2:262, 264 Praem 136 Aet 110

τηλαύγημα Sobr 49

τηλαυγής (38) Leg 1:21 Leg 3:40, 45, 171 Cher 61 Det 48, 118, 128 Post 57, 65 Deus 29 Plant 22, 27, 115 Ebr 44 Migr 39, 79 Congr 135, 140, 143 Mut 7, 82, 162 Somn 1:171, 201, 202 Somn 2:3, 17, 42, 140 Ios 145 Decal 35, 149 Spec 4:52, 52 Legat 326 QG 3:3 QE isf 4

τηλεθάω Aet 132

τηλέφαντος Aet 121

τηλικοῦτος (6) Abr 46 Ios 244 Mos 2:217, 261 Spec 4:234 Flacc 89

τημελέω Leg 1:47 Sacr 47 Prov 2:4

τήμερον (σήμερον) Mut 116 Mos 2:252 Legat 322

τηνικαῦτα (20) Leg 1:26, 82 Leg 3:152 Sacr 71, 134, 139 Deus 135 Migr 138 Her 29, 51 Fug 6 Mut 160 Abr 30 Mos 1:218, 327 Decal 14 Spec 1:157 Prov 2:38, 40 QG 2:41

τηρέω (13) Leg 3:65, 65, 184, 188, 188, 188, 188, 189 Agr 107, 107 Legat 240, 298 QG 3:23

τηρητικός Mos 2:106

Τιβέριος (34) Flacc 2, 8, 9, 9, 10, 12, 14, 22, 28, 105, 112, 128, 158 Legat 8, 14, 23, 24, 26, 29, 33, 35, 38, 58, 141, 159, 166, 167, 298, 299, 301, 303, 303, 309, 329

Τίβερις Legat 155, 181

τίγρις Leg 1:69 Praem 89

Τίγρις Leg 1:63, 69, 85, 86

τιθασεία Post 156 Migr 211 Somn 2:89 Abr 126

τιθασεύω (14) Opif 83 Det 111 Congr 158 Mut 173 Somn 2:51, 87, 92 Mos 1:26 Mos 2:61 Spec 2:82 Spec 4:82 Praem 88 Aet 68 Legat 174

τιθασός (19) Leg 3:140 Sacr 20, 104 Det 6 Post 101 Migr 210 Her 127, 234 Congr 94 Fug 209 Mut 39 Somn 2:135 Spec 1:162, 162 Spec 4:104, 117 Virt 141 Praem 91 Hypoth 7:1

τίθημι (240) Opif 33, 33, 34, 39, 78, 148, 149, 155 Leg 1:43, 47, 47, 53, 53, 55, 55, 65, 88, 89 Leg 2:15, 15, 15, 16, 79 Leg 3:30, 36, 65, 107, 112, 134, 182, 184, 203 Cher 1, 24, 54, 55, 56, 56, 85 Sacr 19, 30, 65, 72, 78, 79 Det 15, 71, 96, 177 Post 34, 70, 116, 120, 142 Deus 56, 139, 158 Agr 13, 104, 116, 119 Plant 3, 16, 32, 41, 42, 45, 86, 111 Ebr 34, 62, 70, 80, 149, 150, 198, 210, 212, 220 Sobr 30, 47 Conf 4, 26, 51, 52, 97, 112, 137, 140, 169 Migr 16, 92, 114, 118, 142, 158, 158, 182, 217 Her 47, 132, 175, 207, 283 Congr 23, 61, 115, 137, 162, 163, 179 Fug 40, 53, 54, 60, 73, 97, 196 Mut 29, 43, 52, 52, 63, 91, 94, 103, 104, 118, 179, 201, 216, 233, 261 Somn 1:4, 69, 74, 81, 120, 132, 201, 225 Somn 2:244, 256, 290 Abr 5, 5, 16, 47, 121, 150, 216 Ios 87, 205, 217 Mos 1:17, 139, 149, 190, 280, 285 Mos 2:39, 47, 80, 81, 99, 104, 115, 154, 235, 236, 243 Decal 2, 23, 123, 129, 162, 172 Spec 1:176, 290, 307, 341, 344, 345 Spec 2:9, 18, 164, 178, 194, 237, 239, 261 Spec 3:23, 26, 69, 103, 191 Spec 4:5, 10, 21, 110, 123, 198, 203 Virt 5, 7, 17, 64, 85, 88, 134, 146, 198, 202, 209 Praem 22, 57, 57, 72, 131, 150, 166 Prob 140 Contempl 3 Aet 16, 109 Flacc 54, 150 Legat 78, 278 Hypoth 0:1, 6:8 Prov 1, 2:44 QG 1:21, 100:1b, 3:20b, 4:43, 194 QE 2:19 QE isf 8

τιθηνέω (6) Opif 41 Sacr 25 Post 181 Agr 18 Spec 2:143 Virt 156

τιθηνοκομέω Sobr 13 Prob 160

τιθηνοκόμος Det 115

τιθηνός (8) Ebr 31, 61 Conf 49 Migr 24 Her 20, 38, 52 Virt 93

τίκτω (132) Opif 43, 132 Leg 1:76, 80 Leg 2:48, 82, 95 Leg 3:85, 85, 131, 146, 180, 181, 181, 216, 216, 216, 217 Cher 40, 40, 43, 45, 46, 46, 53, 54, 57 Sacr 1, 3, 19, 25 Det 101 Post 33, 74, 97, 124 Deus 10, 11, 13, 15, 15, 40 Agr 46, 101 Plant 77, 122, 134, 134, 135, 135 Ebr 214 Sobr 8, 21, 22, 24 Conf 21, 44, 49, 164 Migr 4, 114, 141, 142, 142 Her 20, 49, 51, 137, 162, 175 Congr 1, 1, 5, 6, 6, 7, 7, 7, 9, 9, 12, 13, 13, 43, 54, 59, 129,

131, 135 Fug 1, 167, 167, 167, 168, 204, 210 Mut 96, 108, 137, 143, 143, 143, 143, 144, 176, 188, 225, 253, 255, 261, 264 Somn 1:11, 37, 38, 200 Spec 3:14, 49 Spec 4:100 Virt 133, 142, 143, 157, 157, 162 Praem 158 Contempl 68 Aet 65, 96 QG 3:18, 18, 58 QE isf 22

τίλλω Ios 16 Legat 223

Τιμαῖος Aet 13, 25, 141

τιμαλφής (6) Cher 100 Mos 2:112 Decal 133 Spec 1:86 Prob 66 Contempl 49

τιμάω (168) Opif 128 Leg 1:99, 99, 99 Leg 2:47, 56 Leg 3:9, 10, 167 Sacr 72, 77 Det 4, 32, 33, 34, 52, 52 Post 38, 61, 63, 105, 122, 183, 185 Deus 69, 152, 170 Agr 90, 118 Plant 64 Ebr 17, 17, 56, 77, 81, 87, 95, 107, 117 Sobr 4, 14, 68 Conf 43, 108, 148 Migr 76, 95, 99, 169, 204 Her 52, 169 Congr 49, 105, 108, 133 Mut 40 Somn 1:82, 163, 204 Somn 2:70, 80, 90, 99, 100, 132, 154 Abr 13, 27, 103, 127, 129, 178, 218, 228 Ios 46, 144, 150, 167, 216, 242, 267 Mos 1:198, 298, 328 Mos 2:9, 18, 58, 67, 128, 198, 225 Decal 9, 65, 78, 80, 105 Spec 1:139, 187, 197, 204, 209, 209, 242, 248, 276, 289, 300, 323 Spec 2:3, 21, 34, 36, 71, 86, 132, 142, 144, 145, 160, 164, 164, 170, 175, 204, 234, 235, 235, 246, 255, 256, 259, 260, 261 Spec 3:64, 82, 148, 180 Spec 4:11, 19, 74, 166, 169, 223, 235 Virt 34, 95 Praem 90 Prob 24 Contempl 3 Flacc 23, 40, 48, 51, 81, 81 Legat 98, 173, 272, 277, 291 Prov 2:9, 16, 65 QG 1:60:2, 2:65, 4:194 QE 2:21

τιμή (263) Opif 37, 128 Leg 2:107 Leg 3:86, 126 Cher 117, 122 Sacr 16, 63, 68, 77, 77, 117, 138 Det 33, 52, 53, 54, 54, 122, 157, 169 Post 12, 37, 112, 115, 117, 120, 165, 181 Gig 15, 36 Deus 17, 145, 168, 169, 169, 171 Agr 80, 91, 120, 128, 143, 171, 171 Plant 61, 126, 131, 146 Ebr 37, 57, 65, 75, 75, 109, 110, 110, 194 Sobr 16 Conf 18, 42, 112, 129 Migr 110, 131, 141, 172, 203 Her 170 Congr 65, 80, 98, 119 Fug 26, 35 Somn 1:37, 130, 246, 246 Somn 2:43, 91, 99 Abr 94, 125, 184, 187, 188, 253, 263, 264 Ios 6, 18, 35, 70, 119, 123, 131, 176, 178, 180, 197, 203, 207, 212, 230, 235, 242, 249, 257, 258, 263 Mos 1:23, 61, 154, 243, 245 Mos 2:17, 44, 47, 67, 142, 173, 174, 177, 194, 207, 209, 225, 232, 242, 273 Decal 6, 6, 7, 38, 51, 61, 61, 62, 70, 76, 81, 81, 83, 106, 121, 165 Spec 1:20, 25, 52, 52, 54, 57, 65, 70, 122, 124, 131, 131, 142, 152, 159, 195, 234, 245, 317 Spec 2:7, 32, 33, 36, 36, 113, 114, 115, 132, 146, 149, 156, 165, 223, 224, 226, 233, 245, 246, 260 Spec 3:20, 21, 29, 125, 128, 143, 145, 148, 197 Spec 4:65, 77, 178 Virt 34, 102, 105, 166, 179, 181, 188, 202, 219, 220, 227 Praem 7, 7, 52, 107, 118 Prob 37, 140 Contempl 8 Flacc 30, 35, 40, 41, 49, 49, 52, 80, 97 Legat 7, 46, 75, 80, 86, 92, 133, 137, 140, 141, 149, 149, 153, 154, 165, 172, 191, 240, 293, 299, 301, 305, 316, 347 Hypoth 6:4, 6:8, 11:13, 11:18 Prov 2:1, 23 QG 1:20, 27, 3:23, 4:47b, 130, 202a QE 2:2

τίμημα Her 145

τίμησις Hypoth 7:1

τιμητής Spec 2:37

τιμητικός Deus 7 Mut 226 Legat 211

τίμιος (43) Opif 68 Leg 1:67, 77 Leg 2:81 Leg 3:83, 205 Cher 107 Sacr 18, 26, 30, 83, 134 Det 20, 157 Agr 129 Plant 118 Ebr 86 Sobr 12, 13 Her 159 Congr 113 Abr 123 Ios 213 Decal 6 Spec 1:271, 275, 277 Spec 2:23, 34, 140 Spec 3:198, 207 Spec 4:178, 193 Virt 84, 117, 195 Praem 172 Legat 4, 299 QG 4:51a, 228 QG (Par) 2:4

τιμωρέω (11) Leg 1:96 Abr 137 Ios 79, 249 Mos 1:109 Spec 3:103, 182 Spec 4:23, 127 Flacc 40, 82

τιμωρητής Her 109

τιμωρία (147) Opif 169 Leg 1:107, 107 Cher 78 Det 169, 176 Gig 47 Agr 100, 116 Sobr 48 Conf 25, 25, 116, 119, 119, 161, 182 Her 204, 269 Congr 65, 118 Fug 66, 74, 74, 83, 84, 106 Mut 129, 244 Somn 1:22, 236 Somn 2:290, 295 Abr 64, 96, 97, 128, 137, 144 Ios 79, 86, 104, 169, 220, 221 Mos 1:11, 96, 102, 106, 107, 111, 113, 130, 133, 139, 143, 245, 303, 326 Mos 2:49, 53, 57, 162, 197, 200, 204, 217, 221, 227, 284, 286 Decal 95, 95, 136, 141, 149, 177 Spec 1:54, 55, 284, 316 Spec 2:232, 242, 253, 255, 257 Spec 3:42, 62, 64, 76, 84, 94, 96, 98, 102, 107, 122, 131, 143, 150, 151, 156, 159, 160, 160, 165, 167, 168 Spec 4:8, 40, 57, 77, 81 Virt 200 Praem 52, 69, 70, 162, 166 Flacc 50, 72, 81, 84, 121, 126, 180, 181 Legat 7, 59, 219, 335, 341 Prov 2:32, 33, 34, 34, 37, 55 QG 1:74, 77, 77, 2:54a, 3:52, 52, 4:52d QE 2:6a QE isf 32

τιμωρός (7) Opif 80 Post 12 Conf 121 Spec 4:90 Virt 227 Flacc 104 Hypoth 7:9

τινάσσω (7) Deus 175 Conf 69, 70, 73 Somn 2:129 Mos 2:282 Flacc 176

τίνω (12) Deus 48, 74 Conf 24, 118 Mos 1:47, 245, 278 Mos 2:248 Spec 3:31, 136, 175 Prov 2:40

τίς (1208) Opif 20, 23, 24, 36, 38, 41, 54, 54, 54, 59, 67, 72, 111, 144, 146, 149 Leg 1:2, 9, 24, 33, 33, 33, 33, 34, 37, 37, 40, 42, 43, 48, 48, 53, 60, 70, 79, 82, 85, 87, 90, 91, 91, 91, 105 Leg 2:1, 9, 9, 11, 12, 16, 16, 16, 16, 16, 16, 16, 16, 19, 20, 21, 26, 36, 42, 44, 55, 68, 72, 76, 80, 86, 88, 88, 89, 98, 103, 107 Leg 3:5, 6, 12, 18, 20, 21, 27, 36, 40, 41, 41, 49, 50, 58, 58, 58, 58, 58, 59, 65, 66, 66, 77, 78, 83, 85, 86, 90, 91, 95, 97, 113, 116, 121, 121, 125, 134, 147, 152, 169, 169, 171, 173, 173, 173, 175, 184, 188, 205, 205, 206, 222, 230, 238, 240, 240, 241, 246, 248, 252 Cher 10, 14, 21, 36, 44, 52, 53, 55, 68, 69, 77, 114, 121, 125, 126, 126, 126, 126, 126 Sacr 4, 4, 10, 11, 14, 20, 20, 24, 24, 33, 46, 51, 64, 72, 79, 94, 100, 100, 112, 128 Det 4, 5, 24, 24, 30, 32, 33, 33, 36, 50, 58, 58, 59, 69, 69, 70, 74, 74, 74, 74, 74, 76, 78, 82, 88, 99, 118, 132, 138, 141, 141, 150, 151, 153, 156, 162, 163, 167, 167, 177 Post 2, 5, 9, 15, 29, 33, 34, 35, 37, 49, 50, 73, 80, 86, 87, 92, 92, 109, 109, 109, 110, 112, 133, 143, 161, 161, 162 Gig 1, 9, 10, 10, 20, 23, 25, 28, 36, 50 Deus 1, 7, 7, 22, 33, 38, 44, 57, 57, 59, 60, 60, 66, 70, 79, 86, 89, 92, 104, 104, 108, 108, 119, 122, 147, 150, 152, 157, 167, 174, 174, 174, 175 Agr 3, 7, 9, 15, 36, 57, 59, 87, 94, 115, 134, 148, 148, 148, 149, 150, 154, 175 Plant 5, 33, 34, 43, 54, 64, 85, 91, 99, 101, 138, 138, 147, 160, 163, 170, 172 Ebr 1, 13, 14, 19, 32, 57, 57, 57, 68, 71, 83, 120, 152, 155, 178, 180, 184, 189, 190, 190, 192, 193, 195, 197, 211, 213 Sobr 3, 3, 3, 3, 3, 3, 4, 17, 23, 31, 33, 37, 44, 53, 53, 54, 58, 62, 62 Conf 3, 13, 16, 17, 21, 46, 53, 53, 93, 94, 94, 100, 115, 116, 119, 126, 129, 135, 142, 144, 156, 160, 164, 168, 171, 183, 184 Migr 3, 6, 19, 26, 31, 47, 51, 55, 57, 68, 68, 86, 106, 112, 132, 132, 134, 137, 137, 137, 137, 137, 137, 140, 148, 176, 176, 178, 184, 197, 210, 211, 212, 216, 219, 219, 219, 219, 219, 219, 219, 219, 219, 219, 219, 219, 219, 219, 219, 219, 220 Her 1, 2, 3, 14, 15, 20, 20, 21, 22, 24, 26, 27, 28, 31, 31, 33, 33, 40, 40, 42, 48, 48, 48, 48, 63, 68, 74, 90, 100, 107, 114, 115, 130, 167, 177, 183, 212, 224, 227, 251,

261, 261, 261, 262, 267, 274, 291, 300, 302 Congr 35, 46, 65, 73, 73, 81, 114, 120, 125, 125, 125, 126, 140, 145, 149, 149, 149, 149, 149, 149, 149, 149, 149, 149, 149, 149, 149, 161, 163, 171, 177, 178 Fug 8, 25, 27, 35, 46, 46, 46, 53, 54, 55, 61, 84, 84, 87, 87, 87, 87, 94, 94, 96, 103, 105, 105, 105, 127, 131, 133, 133, 137, 137, 138, 139, 140, 140, 140, 151, 154, 156, 157, 161, 164, 164, 164, 169, 172, 172, 178, 187 Mut 10, 10, 11, 14, 15, 18, 35, 35, 46, 46, 48, 67, 67, 72, 72, 72, 72, 72, 81, 82, 83, 88, 94, 97, 97, 116, 119, 119, 126, 135, 135, 135, 135, 139, 141, 145, 152, 158, 177, 181, 202, 203, 203, 209, 210, 217, 227, 227, 232, 236, 241, 246, 250, 253, 253, 256, 258, 259 Somn 1:4, 5, 5, 5, 5, 5, 5, 12, 14, 21, 21, 22, 23, 26, 30, 30, 31, 41, 41, 53, 53, 53, 53, 54, 54, 54, 54, 54, 54, 55, 55, 55, 55, 55, 55, 55, 55, 55, 61, 61, 61, 91, 92, 93, 95, 97, 99, 100, 101, 108, 109, 110, 135, 163, 163, 167, 179, 182, 186, 189, 194, 196, 209, 211, 224, 229, 238, 255 Somn 2:5, 48, 48, 52, 53, 53, 53, 53, 53, 54, 54, 55, 55, 58, 60, 61, 63, 63, 63, 63, 73, 73, 85, 86, 87, 91, 100, 111, 130, 135, 137, 137, 140, 141, 145, 146, 146, 153, 176, 176, 181, 183, 189, 200, 202, 237, 249, 251, 269, 272, 282, 286, 288, 291, 291, 296, 296, 296, 296, 300 Abr 24, 35, 35, 39, 63, 73, 86, 86, 104, 115, 118, 122, 125, 159, 163, 163, 163, 163, 163, 183, 190, 199, 199, 204, 216, 216, 263, 266, 266, 266, 266, 275 Ios 16, 17, 17, 20, 21, 25, 27, 42, 44, 47, 47, 56, 59, 62, 70, 77, 86, 123, 131, 167, 187, 215, 220, 226, 231, 265 Mos 1:11, 25, 27, 32, 46, 58, 69, 74, 88, 92, 98, 108, 109, 111, 112, 122, 123, 137, 158, 172, 172, 174, 194, 200, 200, 200, 202, 207, 235, 274, 277, 278, 279, 294, 324 Mos 2:3, 21, 23, 38, 108, 124, 137, 165, 198, 199, 216, 217, 217, 219, 230, 239, 240, 272 Decal 2, 6, 6, 13, 29, 41, 47, 79, 88, 89, 112, 128, 133, 143, 151, 157 Spec 1:27, 32, 33, 33, 33, 41, 62, 90, 91, 91, 191, 213, 213, 248, 248, 259, 269, 281, 282, 294, 295, 301, 320, 329, 332 Spec 2:10, 13, 27, 70, 75, 75, 86, 128, 129, 132, 143, 172, 178, 189, 193, 195, 200, 229, 247, 248, 258 Spec 3:14, 25, 25, 25, 34, 34, 78, 78, 95, 108, 113, 116, 144, 156, 158, 165, 165, 184, 190, 190, 191, 191, 193, 198, 203 Spec 4:13, 21, 38, 54, 59, 60, 69, 73, 79, 87, 97, 138, 177, 190, 201, 227, 230, 232, 234 Virt 18, 59, 59, 60, 85, 90, 99, 99, 105, 107, 127, 128, 132, 135, 136, 136, 154, 166, 172, 179, 193, 193, 196, 199, 200, 203, 213, 226 Praem 13, 27, 64, 69, 70, 83, 108, 137 Prob 8, 22, 33, 36, 40, 41, 42, 62, 68, 85, 95, 97, 123, 135, 138, 138, 143, 150 Contempl 3, 15, 29, 56 Aet 5, 21, 37, 39, 52, 61, 63, 68, 68, 75, 78, 83, 84, 85, 90, 92, 99, 107, 114, 125, 126, 127, 132, 137, 146 Flacc 6, 35, 43, 49, 50, 51, 54, 55, 55, 60, 86, 94, 94, 114, 114, 114, 143, 159, 159, 178, 179, 184, 186 Legat 1, 8, 27, 46, 53, 68, 69, 81, 86, 99, 101, 101, 102, 103, 109, 110, 119, 134, 136, 136, 136, 139, 141, 142, 143, 152, 152, 178, 182, 182, 192, 192, 197, 208, 224, 234, 242, 242, 246, 258, 258, 268, 275, 286, 287, 294, 298, 307, 308, 309, 319, 324, 327, 327, 329, 329, 337, 347, 350, 361, 363, 365, 370, 370, 371, 371, 371 Hypoth 6:4, 6:8, 7:12, 7:18 Prov 2:1, 1, 15, 16, 22, 22, 41, 48 QG 1:1, 21, 51, 62:1, 70:1, 72, 74, 74, 94, 2:13a, 15a, 26a, 59, 62, 3:11a, 52, 4:51a, 76b, 88, 144, 145, 166, 173, 173, 180, 189, 191c, 200a, 228 QG (Par) 2:1, 2:2, 2:2, 2:3, 2:3, 2:3, 2:3, 2:4, 2:5, 2:7 QE 2:1, 2, 11a, 12, 49b, 49b QE isf 3, 4, 4, 16

τις (2140) Opif 4, 7, 16,17, 17, 17, 17, 21, 21, 24, 26, 28, 31, 32, 41, 45, 47, 50, 51, 59, 63, 64, 66, 66, 69, 72, 77, 78, 78, 84, 85, 87, 88, 88, 90, 94, 95, 102, 104, 104, 106, 107, 109, 111, 112, 117, 118, 124, 126, 130, 134, 135, 136, 136, 137, 140, 141, 143, 151, 153, 157 Leg 1:15, 15, 15, 20, 22, 22, 25, 33, 35, 37, 42, 42, 48, 50, 51, 59, 62, 62, 75, 82, 85, 87, 87, 87, 91, 93, 94, 98 Leg 2:2, 2, 15, 19, 23, 25, 26, 32, 32, 43, 46, 51, 61, 61, 79, 82, 85, 89 Leg 3:4, 4, 4, 4, 5, 5, 5, 6, 10, 25, 32, 33, 36, 40, 40, 50, 56, 59, 59, 60, 67, 69, 71, 77, 78, 78, 82, 89, 95, 98, 99, 100, 101, 101, 110, 113, 115, 136, 139, 141, 143, 145, 152, 155, 160, 167, 168, 180, 182, 185, 198, 204, 204, 209, 210, 213, 236, 240, 241, 241 Cher 19, 26, 29, 33, 40, 43, 46, 48, 48, 49, 53, 61, 65, 69, 69, 74, 74, 75, 78, 80, 81, 91, 96, 100, 102, 110, 118, 123, 125, 126, 127 Sacr 1, 4, 9, 16, 29, 31, 37, 38, 44, 45, 46, 49, 58, 62, 70, 70, 70, 72, 75, 77, 82, 83, 97, 97, 99, 109, 115, 116, 122, 123, 123, 124, 125, 131 Det 3, 8, 8, 13, 14, 18, 19, 20, 22, 22, 29, 33, 35, 38, 42, 43, 46, 46, 49, 51, 51, 55, 56, 58, 58, 59, 61, 63, 64, 74, 75, 75, 75, 75, 76, 77, 78, 81, 81, 83, 88, 91, 92, 95, 95, 98, 99, 110, 110, 113, 119, 124, 125, 127, 129, 134, 134, 134, 136, 142, 148, 153, 154, 165, 168, 176 Post 6, 6, 7, 9, 34, 35, 38, 44, 44, 49, 50, 58, 61, 65, 68, 71, 75, 80, 81, 88, 90, 100, 108, 108, 108, 115, 115, 117, 120, 126, 127, 131, 136, 137, 141, 147, 154, 163, 168, 170, 176 Gig 16, 18, 26, 30, 32, 33, 35, 36, 41, 42, 43, 44, 45, 51, 51, 58, 62 Deus 1, 8, 11, 17, 18, 19, 20, 21, 22, 24, 27, 38, 39, 42, 43, 50, 52, 52, 55, 67, 70, 71, 84, 88, 89, 90, 91, 91, 93, 97, 99, 100, 100, 105, 106, 111, 112, 122, 127, 127, 134, 134, 135, 135, 141, 146, 146, 150, 157, 158, 170, 170, 171, 172, 172, 177 Agr 4, 5, 10, 11, 19, 22, 26, 33, 46, 51, 51, 53, 62, 64, 66, 67, 68, 76, 83, 85, 91, 95, 109, 110, 110, 113, 117, 117, 122, 126, 126, 128, 130, 132, 134, 157, 168, 169, 175, 175, 180 Plant 7, 8, 14, 19, 22, 24, 33, 39, 48, 50, 51, 52, 65, 65, 69, 70, 76, 77, 80, 113, 114, 116, 123, 127, 131, 136, 138, 142, 147, 147, 157, 159, 159, 165, 167, 167, 171, 176, 177, 177, 177 Ebr 7, 13, 18, 22, 23, 25, 29, 31, 42, 45, 58, 61, 65, 69, 79, 101, 102, 130, 131, 132, 133, 135, 137, 140, 142, 146, 148, 150, 156, 158, 158, 162, 164, 164, 165, 167, 167, 174, 176, 177, 178, 179, 183, 186, 187, 189, 195, 199, 205, 205 Sobr 31, 36, 37, 68 Conf 6, 6, 6, 9, 13, 14, 16, 22, 24, 25, 25, 27, 33, 38, 38, 39, 43, 62, 67, 67, 73, 85, 86, 87, 89, 91, 102, 106, 106, 118, 122, 133, 142, 142, 146, 154, 160, 160, 162, 163, 165, 167, 168, 173, 175, 183, 185, 185, 188, 190, 192 Migr 16, 28, 55, 60, 89, 110, 110, 112, 122, 137, 142, 147, 148, 155, 172, 188, 191, 191, 206, 207, 208, 209, 210, 218, 219, 221, 222, 225 Her 10, 12, 18, 20, 21, 28, 28, 29, 31, 40, 41, 42, 63, 69, 69, 81, 81, 81, 82, 84, 90, 90, 101, 103, 111, 116, 116, 118, 121, 143, 154, 157, 158, 161, 164, 181, 185, 222, 223, 243, 249, 256, 258, 278, 280, 281, 282, 282, 283, 287, 287, 290, 297, 307 Congr 9, 18, 21, 22, 24, 45, 46, 50, 51, 52, 53, 66, 77, 78, 87, 101, 109, 112, 115, 127, 127, 128, 131, 137, 137, 138, 141, 143, 144, 146, 148, 175, 177, 178 Fug 3, 8, 12, 23, 36, 46, 53, 53, 61, 63, 63, 77, 78, 82, 88, 90, 107, 113, 114, 115, 115, 129, 145, 146, 150, 151, 151, 151, 159, 164, 164, 169, 178, 191, 198 Mut 4, 7, 8, 27, 28, 28, 28, 33, 35, 36, 50, 56, 69, 74, 81, 81, 91, 91, 93, 111, 116, 124, 128, 129, 131, 140, 148, 152, 157, 157, 158, 159, 160, 161, 161, 161, 165, 173, 175, 180, 181, 187, 188, 191, 192, 199, 199, 207, 211, 212, 213, 214, 225, 225, 225, 238, 239, 240, 240, 241, 242, 242, 242, 251, 262 Somn 1:2, 10, 10, 12, 21, 22, 22, 24, 25, 27, 39, 40, 41, 42, 42, 42, 44, 46, 46, 52, 58, 59, 68, 82, 91, 91, 95, 96, 98, 98, 99, 101, 101, 105, 110, 111, 111, 115, 119, 120, 124, 125, 128, 143,

145, 150, 154, 156, 158, 163, 177, 177, 183, 184, 184, 184, 185, 188, 188, 188, 192, 192, 203, 230, 230, 236, 237, 245, 248 Somn 2:5, 24, 32, 49, 57, 58, 60, 62, 62, 62, 85, 87, 89, 92, 99, 103, 109, 114, 117, 123, 126, 127, 130, 131, 147, 154, 172, 172, 188, 191, 192, 219, 221, 245, 245, 245, 246, 251, 257, 259, 260, 260, 263, 268, 288, 297, 300, 300, 301, 301 Abr 5, 5, 6, 12, 22, 26, 28, 31, 45, 51, 58, 61, 63, 70, 70, 71, 73, 75, 80, 82, 84, 89, 102, 110, 115, 115, 116, 119, 120, 121, 126, 134, 150, 151, 152, 154, 168, 169, 170, 183, 187, 188, 189, 189, 189, 193, 195, 196, 196, 197, 198, 198, 199, 199, 204, 210, 219, 220, 221, 222, 223, 230, 232, 237, 271, 275 Ios 3, 7, 9, 10, 13, 15, 15, 21, 23, 25, 27, 34, 36, 38, 38, 61, 69, 69, 71, 74, 75, 77, 83, 84, 89, 94, 94, 101, 106, 109, 115, 124, 125, 127, 137, 139, 140, 143, 146, 154, 158, 162, 165, 166, 168, 170, 178, 180, 182, 183, 192, 194, 194, 200, 200, 202, 216, 230, 231, 232, 234, 238, 238, 239, 243, 243, 246, 247, 248, 248, 261, 263, 263 Mos 1:1, 1, 3, 4, 10, 22, 30, 34, 42, 43, 45, 46, 46, 49, 49, 52, 58, 60, 65, 65, 65, 65, 66, 66, 68, 69, 76, 95, 108, 109, 111, 114, 124, 124, 125, 127, 128, 130, 133, 141, 146, 147, 153, 160, 160, 166, 181, 194, 199, 212, 213, 214, 217, 218, 236, 240, 241, 245, 250, 254, 263, 266, 270, 272, 276, 282, 285, 292, 294, 298, 302, 303, 305, 310, 313, 333 Mos 2:2, 7, 10, 10, 13, 13, 16, 27, 30, 34, 44, 48, 51, 52, 62, 80, 98, 118, 121, 122, 122, 126, 127, 132, 135, 139, 142, 154, 167, 167, 168, 168, 191, 193, 196, 198, 199, 201, 206, 212, 213, 214, 214, 217, 234, 238, 239, 239, 239, 249, 251, 251, 254, 263, 264, 266, 269, 275, 281, 289 Decal 1, 4, 15, 24, 30, 31, 31, 31, 31, 33, 36, 38, 39, 43, 48, 52, 58, 61, 61, 69, 72, 74, 76, 76, 77, 85, 88, 91, 92, 93, 93,94, 94, 98, 104, 108, 110, 114, 120, 125, 130, 132, 135, 137, 146, 147, 147, 151, 171, 177, 177 Spec 1:10, 13, 20, 21, 27, 33, 35, 47, 47, 48, 49, 54, 56, 56, 65, 68, 69, 69, 72, 80, 85, 97, 98, 103, 104, 106, 107, 110, 113, 114, 116, 116, 117, 117, 117, 118, 118, 119, 120, 128, 129, 131, 141, 153, 154, 156, 159, 166, 195, 195,199, 203, 219, 223, 233, 235, 238, 239, 241, 248, 248, 249, 254, 254, 255, 262, 264, 271, 275, 277, 277, 277, 282, 284, 289, 297, 302, 311, 315, 316, 317, 327, 333, 340, 340 Spec 2:3, 5, 6, 9, 13, 16, 16, 17, 18, 19, 19, 19, 20, 23, 26, 26, 32, 34, 35, 35, 36, 36, 41, 44, 52, 54, 62, 67, 67, 71, 73, 74, 77, 79, 80, 81, 85, 87, 94, 95, 110, 112, 114, 122, 127, 132, 135, 147, 151, 152, 164, 167, 172, 175, 182, 182, 193, 195, 213, 215, 215, 216, 228, 232, 234, 237, 240, 243, 246, 247, 248, 249, 253, 254, 258, 261 Spec 3:1, 6, 8, 9, 21, 27, 31, 32, 33, 46, 50, 51, 53, 53, 55, 63, 64, 64, 66, 67, 69, 69, 70, 72, 72, 78, 79, 84, 86, 86, 91, 92, 94, 95, 97, 98, 101, 101, 104, 105, 106, 108, 110, 111, 113, 116, 117, 119, 130, 132, 133, 134, 143, 144, 145, 147, 147, 147, 148, 148, 149, 155, 156, 158, 159, 159, 166, 166, 167, 173, 173, 174, 174, 175, 175, 181, 183, 184, 186, 191, 193, 194, 195, 195, 196, 198, 199, 201, 202, 202, 203, 205, 206, 209 Spec 4:1, 7, 7, 10, 11, 16, 20, 21, 22, 26, 28, 29, 31, 34, 37, 39, 47, 48, 52, 53, 57, 60, 60, 60, 61, 63, 64, 67, 72, 73, 74, 79, 82, 95, 99, 101, 103, 120, 121, 123, 125, 126, 131, 133, 136, 140, 144, 146, 146, 147, 152, 153, 156, 156, 157, 160, 172, 179, 180, 182, 188, 188, 194, 202, 203, 217, 218, 230 Virt 2, 4, 7, 12, 14, 19, 22, 26, 27, 28, 29, 31, 33, 34, 43, 51, 57, 61, 62, 63, 63, 69, 74, 74, 76, 83, 88, 88, 89, 90, 90, 96, 98, 105, 108, 115, 115, 117, 124, 125, 126, 128, 129, 135, 136, 140, 142, 142, 144, 144, 152, 156, 157, 160, 171, 180, 184, 188, 194, 197, 201, 202, 203, 205, 208, 227 Praem 5, 20, 27, 34, 40, 41, 42, 43, 43, 44, 44, 45, 45, 46, 56, 60, 61, 67, 68, 69, 70, 71, 72, 74, 80, 84, 84, 87, 94, 99, 102, 108, 110, 117, 117, 119, 121, 131, 138, 138, 149, 165 Prob 1, 7, 21, 22, 25, 27, 27, 34, 36, 37, 37, 38, 41, 41, 45, 47, 50, 52, 52, 53, 54, 60, 62, 62, 64, 66, 69, 75, 78, 82, 86, 92, 97, 101, 105, 108, 112, 113, 114, 116, 117, 124, 125, 126, 127, 130, 131, 136, 136, 138, 141, 144, 144, 148, 152, 157, 157, 157, 157 Contempl 5, 12, 19, 20, 22, 25, 34, 34, 35, 36, 40, 40, 46, 48, 56, 58, 59, 64, 66, 69, 70, 73, 75, 75, 75, 75, 80 Aet 1, 2, 4, 5, 9, 9, 12, 14, 21, 21, 21, 21, 22, 23, 24, 31, 35, 45, 46, 48, 48, 49, 52, 54, 54, 55, 58, 58, 58, 59, 63, 66, 66, 67, 72, 78, 79, 80, 89, 89, 91, 91, 99, 102, 104, 104, 105, 105, 106, 107, 107, 108, 112, 113, 114, 114, 126, 126, 126, 128, 131, 132, 132, 135, 138, 139, 143, 145 Flacc 6, 10, 11, 23, 24, 25, 29, 29, 29, 35, 35, 35, 35, 36, 37, 37, 39, 42, 50, 59, 60, 67, 73, 78, 79, 79, 79, 83, 83, 86, 88, 92, 94, 95, 95, 101, 110, 111, 111, 112, 112, 112, 113, 115, 119, 120, 120, 120, 126, 128, 135, 137, 138, 139, 139, 140, 144, 148, 150, 157, 159, 166, 167, 168, 174, 174, 178, 179, 180, 182 Legat 3, 5, 5, 9, 9, 10, 11, 20, 22, 24, 30, 32, 38, 42, 43, 44, 44, 46, 49, 54, 56, 59, 63, 75, 89, 91, 93, 99, 103, 111, 115, 124, 125, 127, 128, 128, 128, 135, 136, 136, 143, 149, 149, 152, 154, 158, 159, 165, 166, 173, 174, 179, 182, 186, 186, 186, 192, 193, 195, 195, 199, 199, 200, 200, 200, 200, 203, 203, 205, 207, 209, 214, 215, 218, 221, 223, 226, 228, 229, 237, 238, 243, 245, 245, 248, 248, 258, 259, 261, 262, 267, 292, 292, 293, 293, 295, 299, 299, 299, 301, 303, 310, 334, 334, 335, 336, 336, 337, 338, 339, 339, 340, 342, 343, 344, 345, 346, 357, 359, 361, 362, 369 Hypoth 6:1, 6:4, 6:5, 6:8, 7:1, 7:1, 7:3, 7:4, 7:6, 7:7, 7:9, 7:11, 7:11, 7:13, 7:13, 7:16, 7:17, 7:17, 11:13 Prov 1, 1, 1, 1, 2:7, 11, 12, 13, 15, 17, 26, 29, 30, 34, 35, 40, 42, 44, 46, 46, 47, 48, 49, 54, 54, 54, 55, 55, 58, 58, 60, 62, 64, 66, 67 QG 1:17b, 20, 28, 55c, 58, 58, 58, 64d, 65, 79, 85, 2:54d, 62, 64a, 64a, 64b, 66, 68a, 3:3, 30b, 4:51b, 64, 88, 167, 191a, 191c, 191c, 200b, 211, 228 QG isf 6 QG (Par) 2:1, 2:2, 2:3, 2:3, 2:3, 2:5, 2:7, 2:7 QE 2:9a, 12, 17, 28, 118 QE isf 3, 3, 5, 22, 26

τίσις Mos 2:169, 203 Legat 133

τίτθη Sacr 15 Her 295 Spec 2:233 Spec 4:68 Virt 178

τιτρώσκω (30) Leg 2:99 Leg 3:15, 113, 202, 248, 253 Det 46, 49, 49, 51, 99 Deus 99, 100 Ebr 23 Somn 1:89 Somn 2:120, 122 Abr 104 Ios 103 Mos 1:56, 68, 309 Decal 87 Spec 3:103 Praem 140 Legat 127, 171, 206 QG 2:64b QE 2:24a

τλάω Cher 78

τλητικός (14) Sacr 112 Det 9 Deus 66 Congr 165 Mut 86 Somn 2:38 Mos 1:199 Mos 2:184 Spec 2:60 Prob 24, 109, 120, 133, 146

τμῆμα (42) Opif 15, 56, 57, 152 Leg 3:170 Cher 59, 60 Sacr 108, 132, 132 Post 3 Agr 139 Plant 114 Conf 89, 192 Migr 73 Her 64, 132, 134, 141, 141, 142, 143, 164, 207, 213, 214, 242 Somn 1:135, 203 Abr 44 Mos 1:177, 179, 254 Mos 2:27, 253 Spec 3:176 Flacc 37, 151 Legat 132, 144, 147

τμητικός Leg 3:26

τμητός Opif 62

τοι (44) Opif 28 Leg 2:10, 74, 91 Leg 3:180, 183, 221, 228, 230, 236, 246 Sacr 78, 81 Post 163 Agr 104 Plant 163 Ebr 19, 55 Conf 147 Migr 195 Her 3, 116, 142 Congr 12, 110, 140 Fug 61 Mut 19, 177 Somn 1:57, 93

Somn 2:223, 245 Abr 70 Mos 2:61 Spec 2:257 Spec 3:6, 86 Spec 4:93 Praem 161 Prob 44 Aet 27 Legat 119 Prov 2:28

τοιγαροῦν (36) Leg 3:219 Det 148, 149 Plant 26, 159 Conf 79, 105 Migr 85, 113 Fug 41 Mut 80, 136, 203 Somn 2:65, 84, 276, 285 Ios 172, 174 Mos 1:155, 156, 284, 291 Mos 2:67 Spec 2:22 Virt 202, 209 Prob 108, 144 Contempl 44 Aet 49 Flacc 173 Legat 159, 345 Hypoth 7:14 QG 2:26b

τοιγάρτοι (16) Cher 52 Deus 18, 48, 103 Plant 172 Ebr 85 Congr 134 Mut 41 Somn 1:247 Somn 2:66, 89, 212 Mos 1:326 Spec 2:76, 94, 256

τοίνυν (140) Leg 1:20 Leg 2:8, 72 Leg 3:87, 104 Cher 16, 55, 83, 90, 98, 122, 124 Sacr 2, 108 Det 32, 37, 174 Post 41, 52, 112, 170 Deus 1, 45, 80 Agr 7, 8, 27, 37, 52, 66, 68, 72, 111, 119, 158, 176 Plant 2, 7, 21, 28, 73, 75, 86, 93, 142, 174 Ebr 11, 16, 27, 33, 80, 80, 206 Sobr 1, 5, 16, 38, 42 Conf 15, 117 Migr 7, 42, 106, 130, 177 Her 40, 191 Congr 55, 126, 175 Fug 126 Mut 67, 131, 145, 178, 201, 236 Somn 1:6, 37, 41, 102, 120, 134, 159, 173, 201 Somn 2:112, 207, 262, 283 Abr 7, 50, 60, 158, 192, 217, 225 Ios 28 Mos 1:163 Mos 2:46, 66, 187 Decal 50, 136 Spec 1:33 Spec 2:29, 41, 171, 228 Spec 4:153 Virt 22, 82, 85, 105, 141, 149, 168, 189, 226 Praem 28, 70 Prob 17, 45, 48, 59, 85 Aet 4, 24, 35, 53, 75, 88, 100, 104, 106 Flacc 53 Hypoth 11:14 Prov 2:33 QG 1:60:1, 2:28

τοιόσδε (54) Opif 82 Leg 3:54 Sacr 28, 89, 107 Det 168 Post 28 Agr 82, 127 Plant 127 Ebr 197 Conf 62, 81, 108, 166 Migr 27, 86, 168 Her 14 Fug 56, 58, 178 Mut 139 Somn 2:159, 227 Abr 91, 201 Ios 148, 151 Mos 1:8, 77, 208, 306, 329 Mos 2:77, 91, 161, 168 Decal 51 Spec 1:224 Spec 2:217 Spec 3:131, 178 Virt 184, 184 Praem 81 Aet 28, 124, 128 Flacc 108 Legat 229 Prov 2:7, 60 QG 2:54a

τοιοῦτος (459) Opif 132, 140, 170 Leg 1:16, 16, 22, 27, 43, 67, 98, 99 Leg 2:13, 16, 50, 55, 64, 94, 101 Leg 3:7, 40, 53, 61, 61, 78, 79, 80, 85, 110, 135, 139, 170, 184, 188, 206, 219, 225, 233, 243, 252 Cher 9, 18, 37, 69, 84, 86, 94, 104, 106 Sacr 8, 10, 33, 71, 72, 73, 82, 88, 109, 111, 114, 116, 127, 131 Det 1, 21, 29, 33, 56, 57, 58, 58, 119, 119, 130, 134, 135, 149, 167 Post 13, 18, 32, 53, 54, 72, 84, 88, 95, 95, 120, 154, 166 Gig 19, 24, 25, 64 Deus 50, 52, 54, 56, 64, 70, 70, 90, 104, 118, 170 Agr 7, 61, 76, 77, 102, 110, 110, 110, 112, 162, 165 Plant 46, 72, 74, 96, 109, 113, 116, 149, 156, 177, 177 Ebr 40, 47, 68, 77, 104, 131, 142, 213, 223 Sobr 6 Conf 4, 49, 73, 107, 117, 118, 161, 161, 175, 182 Migr 61, 105, 129, 169, 172 Her 2, 20, 63, 81, 187, 246, 251, 290, 300, 306 Congr 3, 32, 114, 117, 155, 167, 178 Fug 35, 38, 40, 60, 66, 81, 123, 126, 133, 154, 162, 168, 181, 188, 213 Mut 12, 13, 20, 42, 44, 44, 58, 65, 76, 91, 115, 140, 145, 172, 175, 197, 198, 203, 203, 226, 254 Somn 1:11, 13, 22, 23, 59, 67, 70, 94, 96, 102, 113, 124, 146, 153, 198, 219, 240 Somn 2:6, 7, 14, 71, 99, 133, 135, 203, 205, 216, 246, 292, 301, 301 Abr 47, 47, 107, 118, 126, 131, 136, 164, 211, 256, 276 Ios 12, 23, 27, 49, 85, 87, 110, 116, 122, 167, 170, 205, 211, 226, 231, 253, 267 Mos 1:29, 29, 30, 36, 42, 47, 58, 81, 92, 105, 113, 126, 138, 170, 184, 190, 193, 196, 273, 300 Mos 2:5, 11, 31, 32, 64, 85, 117, 131, 220, 236, 264, 265, 270, 272, 292, 292 Decal 21, 48, 64, 81, 89, 101, 131 Spec 1:9, 28, 47, 203, 236, 242, 245, 267, 278, 315, 317, 319, 319, 344 Spec 2:11, 55, 76, 79, 81, 246 Spec 3:31, 34, 37, 42, 49, 49, 82, 88, 96, 98, 109, 130, 134, 136, 140, 166 Spec 4:40, 51, 51, 68, 71, 76, 145, 163, 163, 194, 199, 217, 218 Virt 2, 34, 87, 133, 135, 136, 161, 174, 178 Praem 81, 113, 114, 136 Prob 11, 71, 88, 97, 112, 124, 132, 147 Contempl 56, 64, 66, 75 Aet 16, 26, 36, 43, 48, 55, 70, 72, 78, 113 Flacc 15, 25, 33, 83, 94, 126, 135, 160, 166, 180, 184, 191 Legat 23, 26, 45, 52, 58, 60, 60, 67, 73, 76, 111, 136, 142, 151, 152, 153, 154, 200, 217, 223, 224, 225, 232, 235, 262, 279, 287, 319, 321, 363, 368, 372 Hypoth 6:4, 7:9, 7:9, 7:18 Prov 2:23, 23, 30, 32, 50, 53, 63 QG 2:12c, 4:33b, 47b, 167, 228 QG (Par) 2:2, 2:5 QE 2:3b, 17, 28, 49b QE isf 3, 22

τοιουτοσί Det 35

τοιουτότροπος (9) Agr 141 Ebr 218 Mos 1:204 Mos 2:205 Decal 7 Spec 1:92 Spec 2:206 Spec 3:183 Aet 20

τοῖχος (10) Cher 104 Post 22, 100 Agr 89, 153 Migr 148 Somn 2:54 Mos 1:124 Mos 2:87 Contempl 33

τοιχωρυχέω Spec 4:7 Flacc 73

τοιχωρύχος Ios 84 Spec 4:33, 87

τοκεύς (8) Plant 118 Ebr 13, 33 Her 115 Abr 195 Praem 158 Prob 36 Prov 2:4

τοκογλύφος Fug 28 Spec 2:76 Virt 85

τόκος (9) Fug 168 Mut 147 Spec 2:74, 74, 78, 122 Virt 82, 84 Legat 343

τόλμα (8) Conf 116, 161 Migr 170 Her 21 Mos 1:131, 225, 309 Spec 4:111

τολμάω (58) Opif 26, 45, 160, 165 Leg 2:67 Leg 3:179, 198 Cher 63, 67, 70, 96 Conf 133, 152, 158 Migr 83, 136 Her 72 Mut 61 Somn 1:54 Somn 2:83, 119, 122, 130, 182 Abr 231 Ios 197, 216, 225 Mos 1:124, 140 Mos 2:198, 206 Decal 88, 90 Spec 1:56 Spec 2:6, 94, 167, 249 Spec 3:6, 42, 88, 172 Spec 4:14, 146 Virt 94, 202 Prob 10, 104 Contempl 6, 75 Flacc 40, 160 Legat 28, 56, 56, 178 QE 2:1

τόλμημα (11) Deus 151 Conf 8, 116 Her 72 Somn 2:286 Mos 1:140 Mos 2:274 Spec 1:56 Praem 75 Legat 213, 305

τολμηρός Opif 170

τολμητής Ios 222 Praem 86

τομεύς (11) Det 110 Her 130, 131, 140, 165, 166, 179, 180, 215, 225, 314

τομή (26) Sacr 74, 82, 85, 87 Det 82 Agr 6, 13, 129 Ebr 93 Conf 9, 192, 192 Her 133, 136, 139, 207 Mut 192, 252 Somn 1:179 Somn 2:35, 39 Ios 76 Decal 150 Spec 1:209 QG 1:64a, 4:30

τομίας Spec 1:164 Spec 3:198

τονική Leg 1:30 Sacr 68

τόνος (31) Leg 2:28 Leg 3:183, 183, 186, 238 Cher 82 Post 46, 71, 72, 106, 163 Deus 25, 84 Ebr 95, 116, 122 Her 242 Fug 39 Mut 33 Somn 1:88 Ios 61 Decal 122 Spec 1:99 Spec 3:33 Virt 88 Praem 21, 48 Aet 125 Legat 189, 267 QG (Par) 2:3

τονόω Prob 146

τόνωσις Cher 105

τοξεία Mos 2:151

τοξεύω (9) Conf 103 Congr 129, 129 Somn 1:221 Somn 2:95, 120 Prob 151 Legat 104, 174

τόξον (8) Leg 3:26 Plant 152 Flacc 90 Legat 95, 104 QG 2:64b, 64b, 64c τοξότης Sacr 82 Post 131 Conf 144

τοπάζιον Leg 1:81

τοπάζω Ios 11, 197 Mos 1:127 Spec 4:50 Legat 262

τοπικός (7) Leg 1:65, 67 Post 30 Somn 2:243 Mos 1:23, 229 QE 2:45a

τοποκρατέω Virt 48

τόπος (229) Opif 17, 17, 20, 20, 63, 86, 139, 147, 161 Leg 1:44, 45, 67 Leg 2:65, 85 Leg 3:4, 6, 18, 51, 51, 53, 115, 115, 116, 151, 194 Cher 98 Sacr 68 Det 5, 151 Post 14, 14, 17, 17, 17, 30, 81, 111, 182 Deus 35 Plant 3, 11, 12, 38, 78, 162 Ebr 14, 39, 47, 181, 195 Sobr 34, 63 Conf 68, 96, 135, 136 Migr 35, 37, 52, 139, 166, 177, 178, 216, 216, 220, 221, 224 Her 241 Congr 163 Fug 2, 53, 63, 75, 75, 77, 87, 118, 149, 149, 153, 163, 163, 213 Mut 270 Somn 1:4, 4, 4, 5, 53, 61, 61, 62, 62, 62, 63, 64, 64, 64, 64, 64, 65, 66, 67, 67, 67, 68, 68, 70, 71, 71, 72, 72, 116, 117, 117, 118, 120, 120, 127, 181, 182, 183, 184, 184, 185, 187, 189, 227, 228, 228, 229, 238, 238 Somn 2:222, 286 Abr 67, 99, 167, 172, 246 Ios 12, 29, 32, 151 Mos 1:65, 103, 143, 222, 224, 228, 278, 282, 285, 320 Mos 2:34, 36, 63, 70, 72, 101, 120, 180, 180, 192 Decal 30, 31, 44, 94 Spec 1:85, 88, 115, 148, 193, 231, 240, 240, 273, 276, 327 Spec 2:6, 29, 221 Spec 3:74, 77, 77, 125, 128, 130, 184 Spec 4:20, 31, 94, 141 Virt 16, 22, 48 Praem 35 Prob 81, 96, 96, 130, 148, 149, 151, 151 Aet 18, 29, 31, 33, 33, 100, 101, 101, 115, 115, 135, 148 Flacc 49, 140, 190 Legat 31, 174, 318 QG 2:59, 64b QE 1:19 QE isf 1, 8

τορεία Contempl 49

τορευτός Her 216

τορεύω Leg 3:104

τορνεύω Post 104

τοσόσδε Aet 41

τοσοῦτος (300) Opif 16, 30, 53, 57, 61, 85, 85, 99, 101, 111, 140, 148 Leg 1:36, 38, 43, 91 Leg 2:20, 76 Leg 3:110 Sacr 26, 40, 49, 124 Det 13, 62, 74, 90, 100, 150, 152 Post 54, 91, 94, 105, 152 Gig 26, 26, 67 Deus 44, 147 Agr 25, 60, 60, 123, 157 Plant 22, 62, 68 Ebr 67, 152, 161, 161 Sobr 2, 5, 58 Conf 11, 113, 116, 133, 157 Migr 17, 75, 125, 154, 163, 168, 184, 203 Her 19, 86, 89, 221, 275 Congr 66, 156 Fug 96, 166, 184 Mut 72, 72, 78, 179, 255 Somn 1:19, 39, 93, 157, 209 Somn 2:98, 116, 117, 208, 223, 277 Abr 15, 36, 46, 56, 159, 208, 231, 255, 275 Ios 12, 37, 80, 87, 132, 143, 147, 157, 158, 160, 166, 191, 215, 220, 229, 247, 255, 258 Mos 1:32, 100, 103, 108, 112, 121, 143, 169, 195, 206, 211, 223, 233, 242, 284, 306, 309 Mos 2:6, 15, 29, 58, 85, 86, 94, 177, 194, 197, 200, 202, 233, 257, 261, 271, 285 Decal 33, 36, 59, 121, 175 Spec 1:3, 12, 58, 91, 153, 156, 166, 194, 212, 226, 260, 275, 308, 318, 323 Spec 2:4, 6, 52, 55, 71, 85, 94, 107, 121, 121, 161, 167, 168, 176, 177, 223, 234, 250 Spec 3:15, 20, 46, 63, 104, 112, 175, 205 Spec 4:48, 84, 104, 132, 136, 188, 202, 205, 210, 226, 234 Virt 18, 44, 50, 86, 143 Praem 18, 42, 134, 148 Prob 36, 44, 117, 121, 130 Contempl 90 Aet 10, 46, 47, 68, 78, 103, 105, 108, 118, 132 Flacc 28, 78, 118, 130, 133, 143, 159, 163, 179 Legat 19, 27, 33, 34, 38, 43, 71, 73, 91, 93, 108, 124, 135, 142, 148, 153, 153, 182, 215, 227, 237, 242, 250, 257, 264, 268, 278, 284, 290, 308, 318, 321, 344, 346, 347, 347, 360, 361, 367, 368 Hypoth 6:1, 6:4, 6:4, 11:13 Prov 2:1, 7, 22 QG 2:28, 30, 34b QG (Par) 2:4, 2:7 QE 2:4, 45b

τότε (255) Opif 67, 88, 88, 112, 112, 117, 117 Leg 1:32, 72, 99 Leg 2:63 Leg 3:74, 137, 150, 152, 157, 183, 191, 224, 225, 246, 246 Cher 3, 11, 37, 37, 45, 58, 88, 88, 88, 93, 93, 93 Sacr 45, 130, 137, 137 Det 23, 23, 73, 93, 94, 97, 100, 117, 117, 129 Post 22, 91, 110, 110, 145, 145 Gig 25, 39, 39, 39 Deus 30, 30, 38, 44, 44, 103, 126, 139, 139, 140, 158, 158, 161, 174, 175, 175, 182 Agr 89, 106, 112 Plant 61, 144, 144 Ebr 97, 97, 178, 178, 204, 222 Sobr 3 Conf 5, 22, 96 Migr 31, 140, 146, 146, 148, 148, 162, 162, 190, 190, 208, 209 Her 4, 30, 66, 109, 109 Congr 35, 35, 61, 61, 108, 135, 135, 148 Fug 189 Mut 103, 103, 134, 260 Somn 1:41, 41, 60, 99, 130, 150, 150, 150, 150, 172, 172, 195, 238 Somn 2:150, 154, 171, 174, 231, 238, 238, 271 Abr 41, 45, 45, 73, 73, 78, 91, 91, 113, 122, 122, 212, 212, 254, 256 Ios 5, 115, 165, 168 Mos 1:69, 122, 124, 132, 135, 149, 163, 176, 185, 204, 205, 211, 211, 219, 234, 260, 274 Mos 2:42, 56, 217, 264, 264, 286, 288 Decal 4, 4, 14, 77, 77 Spec 1:183, 186, 298 Spec 2:30, 30, 36, 61, 70, 106, 108, 143, 143, 145, 146, 146, 151, 189, 199 Spec 3:2, 2, 17, 17, 76, 76, 171 Virt 24, 59, 199 Praem 89, 90, 106, 106, 147, 147 Prob 142 Contempl 81, 84, 84 Aet 43, 87, 90, 136, 149 Flacc 89, 92, 106, 152, 164 Legat 13, 79, 79, 140, 167, 182, 231, 295, 306, 306 Prov 1, 1 QG 1:24, 2:13b, 64c, 3:21, 21

τουτέστι (εἰμί) (102) Leg 1:24, 29, 65, 74, 92, 98 Leg 2:38, 41, 45, 59, 62, 77, 87, 92, 92, 93, 103 Leg 3:11, 14, 15, 16, 20, 25, 28, 32, 34, 35, 35, 45, 46, 52, 95, 123, 126, 142, 143, 145, 153, 154, 157, 172, 176, 214, 230, 230, 231, 232, 242, 244 Cher 17 Sacr 62, 80, 86, 119 Det 10, 16, 28, 59, 118, 119 Post 14, 53, 150, 162, 168, 182 Gig 53, 54 Deus 49, 167 Agr 162 Plant 42, 116 Ebr 40, 53, 70, 73, 95, 123, 125, 216 Conf 70 Migr 67, 70 Her 289, 304 Congr 49 Fug 49, 59, 135, 192, 201 Somn 1:110, 112 Somn 2:76 Mos 1:158 Spec 1:306 Praem 81 QG 2:54d, 64a, 72 QE 2:16

τραγέλαφος Spec 4:105

τραγικός (12) Leg 3:202 Sacr 28 Ios 78 Prob 116, 134, 152 Aet 5, 30, 49, 144 Legat 234, 234

τράγος (14) Leg 2:52 Post 70, 165 Plant 61 Her 179 Somn 1:189, 197, 198, 199 Somn 2:19 Decal 76 Spec 3:36, 46, 113

τραγῳδέω Decal 43, 153 Praem 136

τραγῳδία Leg 2:75 Post 165 Congr 61 Mut 114 Prob 141

τραγῳδός Ebr 177 Legat 203

τρανής (τρανός) (30) Opif 66, 71 Leg 3:16, 121, 121, 122 Her 72 Congr 135, 136 Mut 108 Somn 2:3, 18, 127 Abr 60, 118 Mos 1:66, 95, 199 Spec 1:273 Spec 2:89 Spec 3:100, 161 Spec 4:86, 203 Virt 215 Prob 47, 74 Flacc 124, 162 Prov 2:9

τρανός τρανής

τρανότης Ios 145 Decal 33 Spec 1:106

τρανόω (11) Opif 122, 127 Mos 2:10, 39 Decal 46, 148 Spec 2:4, 7, 132 Spec 4:233 Flacc 165

τράπεζα (38) Opif 158 Her 175, 226, 226, 227, 227 Congr 167, 168 Fug 31 Somn 1:51 Somn 2:210 Ios 196, 205, 210 Mos 2:23, 94, 104, 146 Spec 1:118, 127, 172, 176, 220, 242 Spec 2:20, 161, 193 Spec 3:96 Spec 4:91, 119 Contempl 41, 54, 73, 81, 81 Hypoth 11:12 QG 4:8* QE isf 14

τραπεζοποιός Somn 2:50

τραῦμα (15) Det 46, 50 Agr 93 Migr 124 Mut 203 Somn 1:112 Somn 2:168 Mos 1:119 Decal 170 Spec 1:103, 204 Spec 2:13 Spec 3:168, 181 Prob 133

τραυματίας Deus 183 Mut 203 Mos 1:284

τραχηλίζω (8) Cher 78 Her 274, 274 Mut 81 Mos 1:297, 322 Praem 153 Prob 159

τράχηλος Leg 1:12 Leg 3:193 Ios 150 Spec 1:306

τραχύς (33) Leg 1:34 Leg 2:7, 39 Leg 3:58, 253 Post 104, 154 Deus 84 Ebr 150, 150 Conf 26 Migr 50 Congr 28 Somn 1:17 Somn 2:124, 259 Abr 152, 239 Ios 21 Mos 1:167, 192 Mos 2:138, 202 Spec 1:106, 301 Spec 4:14, 112 Praem 148 Flacc 186 Prov 2:18, 33 QG 1:41 QE 2:13a

τραχύτης (6) Opif 62 Agr 142 Plant 133 Ebr 185 Migr 208 Flacc 71

Τραχωνῖτις Legat 326

τρεῖς (255) Opif 48, 48, 50, 60, 60, 84, 96, 97, 97, 98, 102, 102, 102, 102, 102, 102, 106, 108, 108, 136 Leg 1:3, 28, 37, 37, 55, 57, 72, 93 Leg 2:42, 65 Leg 3:11, 11, 124, 249 Cher 22, 22 Sacr 47, 59, 60, 136 Det 7 Post 49, 49, 54, 96 Deus 41 Agr 136 Plant 95, 113, 113, 113, 114, 116, 123, 124, 124, 124, 124 Ebr 201, 210, 214, 214 Sobr 60 Conf 4 Migr 2, 105, 154 Her 108, 132, 144, 144, 165, 165, 215, 216, 218, 224, 226 Congr 100, 100, 101, 106, 131, 147 Fug 3, 4, 87, 103, 104, 150 Mut 12, 69, 88, 235, 236, 236, 238, 245 Somn 1:5, 15, 25, 26, 40, 40, 167, 169, 213, 219, 242 Somn 2:9, 159, 180, 195, 195, 207, 208, 210, 210, 257, 281, 283 Abr 47, 49, 51, 53, 54, 54, 54, 60, 107, 108, 110, 122, 122, 124, 131, 131, 142, 149, 169, 208, 232, 241 Ios 1, 1, 54, 91, 92, 92, 93, 96, 96, 97, 152, 152, 193 Mos 1:9, 11, 73, 76, 76, 97, 97, 123, 130, 163, 181, 224, 292 Mos 2:2, 91, 101, 102, 103, 112, 121, 121, 124, 124, 124, 133, 150, 152, 156, 187, 212, 276 Decal 20, 21, 22, 22, 24, 25, 25, 26, 26, 27, 28, 28, 45, 126 Spec 1:87, 87, 147, 158, 163, 168, 188, 194, 197, 197, 212, 232, 240, 247, 251, 253, 253, 268, 320 Spec 2:1, 2, 34, 35, 58, 177, 177 Spec 4:12, 235 Virt 183, 202, 207 Praem 1, 49, 61, 65, 80, 97, 166 Contempl 33, 35 Aet 79, 140 Flacc 76 Legat 74, 74, 141, 148, 298, 351 Prov 2:33 QG 1:55c, 2:59, 65, 4:30

τρέμω (9) Leg 3:54 Det 119, 119, 140 Her 24 Mut 217 Praem 72 Prov 2:25 QG 1:72

τρεπτός Cher 51 QG isf 6

τρέπω (121) Opif 31, 67, 113, 126 Leg 2:31, 32, 33, 33, 34, 61, 63, 86, 87, 89 Leg 3:94, 109, 125, 152, 213 Cher 88, 90 Sacr 127, 130 Det 71, 97, 152 Post 7, 9, 10, 18, 23, 28, 30, 110, 168 Gig 48, 67 Deus 22, 132 Agr 125 Plant 97, 135, 162 Ebr 206 Conf 42 Migr 209 Her 50, 84, 256 Fug 13, 25, 143, 189 Mut 85, 130 Somn 1:20, 79, 80, 107, 123, 133 Somn 2:222, 276 Abr 233 Ios 212 Mos 1:15, 72, 79, 96, 99, 124, 210, 242, 250, 263, 273, 274, 282, 284, 288, 301 Mos 2:27, 45, 55, 251 Decal 50, 75, 76, 98 Spec 1:12, 64, 210, 218, 300 Spec 2:20, 102, 147 Spec 3:80, 80 Spec 4:5, 8, 16, 136, 144, 221, 235 Virt 118 Praem 52, 134, 169 Prob 123 Aet 91 Flacc 27, 53, 56 Legat 18, 52, 119, 367 Hypoth 11:6 QG 1:93

τρέφω (100) Opif 167 Leg 1:97, 98, 99 Leg 3:141, 152, 161, 162, 168, 176, 176, 176, 177, 177, 177, 179, 226 Cher 84 Sacr 85, 86 Det 106, 108 Post 90, 122, 129, 130, 130 Deus 37, 39, 59, 87, 88, 157, 157 Agr 56, 58 Plant 79, 114, 133 Sobr 13, 23 Conf 181, 181 Migr 36, 140 Her 240, 275, 284, 284, 285 Congr 167, 174 Fug 67, 67, 137, 159 Mut 113, 120 Somn 1:7, 36, 198, 253 Somn 2:32, 48, 147, 204, 259 Abr 188 Ios 64, 113 Mos 1:5, 8, 31, 54 Decal 113, 117 Spec 1:126, 127, 319 Spec 2:198, 207, 262 Spec 4:15, 129 Virt 221 Praem 40 Prob 8, 79 Contempl 18, 35 Aet 99 Flacc 46, 158 Legat 30 Prov 2:43, 65, 66 QG (Par) 2:7 QE 2:18, 18

τρέχω (13) Det 154 Post 132 Deus 75 Her 201 Congr 46 Mut 117, 247 Somn 1:171 Somn 2:81 Ios 200 Flacc 45 Legat 145, 231

τρῆμα Post 182

τριακάς Somn 2:257

τριάκοντα (16) Opif 60 Somn 2:112, 257 Ios 121 Mos 1:238 Mos 2:60, 86, 91, 91 Decal 27 Virt 111, 113 Flacc 74 QG 2:5a QG (Par) 2:5, 2:5

τριακονταετία QG 2:5b QG (Par) 2:5

τριακοντάς QG 2:5a QG (Par) 2:5

τριακόσιοι Det 14 Mos 2:60 Legat 138 QG (Par) 2:5

τριακοστός QG (Par) 2:5

τριάς (35) Opif 13, 13, 49, 49, 50, 51, 62, 95, 97, 97, 98, 106, 106 Leg 1:3, 3 Her 215, 216, 219 Congr 8, 91 Abr 48, 56 Mos 2:115 Spec 4:168, 208 Praem 24, 24 Aet 113, 113 QG 2:5a, 3:61, 4:8a, 8b, 30 QG (Par) 2:5

τριβή Sacr 87 Ebr 219

τριβόλιον Leg 3:250

τρίβολος Leg 3:248, 253 Somn 2:161

τρίβος (6) Leg 2:94, 98 Det 24 Agr 94, 102, 102

τρίβω (21) Leg 2:98, 98 Leg 3:33, 33, 253 Sacr 86 Det 49 Agr 102 Migr 154 Congr 52 Somn 2:186 Abr 271 Mos 1:208, 238 Decal 31, 31 Spec 3:37 Spec 4:171, 175 Prob 14 Flacc 128

τρίβων Somn 2:63

τρίγλα τρίγλη

τρίγλη (τρίγλα) Her 154

τριγονία Virt 124 Prob 10

τρίγωνος (9) Opif 50, 97, 97 Leg 3:57 Mos 2:80 Decal 22 Spec 2:177 Contempl 65 QG 4:8b

τρίδυμος Agr 14

τριετηρίς Deus 36 Agr 113 Flacc 93

τριετία Virt 156, 158

τριετίζω Her 126

τριηράρχος Spec 1:121

τριήρης Conf 45 Abr 220 Spec 1:121 Prob 33

τρίκλινος Contempl 49

τρικυμία Ebr 79 Mut 239 Somn 2:279 Mos 1:115, 179

τριμερής (8) Leg 1:70 Leg 3:11, 115 Sacr 47 Plant 114, 116 Conf 21 Her 225

τρίμετρος Prob 22, 48, 141 Contempl 80 Aet 27

τριοδῖτις Sacr 21 Fug 153

τρίοδος Congr 124 Mos 1:100, 105 Prov 2:64

τριπλάσιος Opif 91, 91, 92 Abr 270 Decal 21

τριπλάσιων Opif 93

τριπόθητος (8) Post 12 Her 42 Mut 7, 174 Ios 255 Mos 1:207 Spec 1:40 Aet 138

τρίπρατος Ios 36

Τριπτόλεμος Praem 8

τρίς (6) Opif 105 Mos 1:183 Spec 2:177 Legat 58, 307, 356

τρισευδαίμων Ios 20 Spec 1:31 Spec 3:178 Contempl 6

τρισκαίδεκα Sobr 8 Fug 186 Ios 270

τρισκαιδέκατος Contempl 17

τρισμακάριος Ios 20 Spec 1:31 Spec 4:123 Praem 30

τρισσός (14) Leg 3:250 Sacr 59 Migr 125, 154 Her 45 Somn 2:208 Abr 119, 131 Ios 45 Spec 4:92 Prob 83 Aet 7, 74, 86

τριστάτης Ebr 111

τρισχίλιοι Ebr 67 Mos 2:172, 274

τρισώματος Legat 80

τρίτατος Opif 104

τρίτος (176) Opif 13, 82, 102, 102, 103, 106, 106, 110, 110, 110, 138, 141, 141, 157, 171 Leg 1:3, 10, 33, 63, 69, 69, 70, 71, 71, 71, 71, 71 Leg 2:64, 71, 72, 73 Leg 3:53, 115 Cher 27, 48 Sacr 12, 54 Det 4 Post 17, 145, 173 Gig 22 Agr 67, 121 Plant 165 Ebr 35, 35, 201 Sobr 48 Conf 89 Migr 70, 139 Her 164, 170, 231, 257, 287, 297, 299 Congr 22, 52, 67, 76 Fug 87, 95, 133, 133, 134, 135, 143, 166, 170, 177, 211 Mut 142, 145 Somn 1:5, 61, 63, 68, 85, 104, 112, 168, 209, 216 Somn 2:1, 1, 4, 237 Abr 52, 124, 142, 219 Ios 113, 178, 216, 235 Mos 1:81 Mos 2:29, 66, 190, 191, 210, 244, 268 Decal 14, 21, 21, 40, 135, 140, 157, 171 Spec 1:6, 74, 97, 128, 135, 186, 220, 223, 223, 226, 242, 250, 261, 298, 331 Spec 2:34, 41, 89, 139, 140, 141, 197 Spec 3:162, 197, 205 Spec 4:1, 5, 70, 139, 175, 212 Virt 108, 114 Praem 1, 22, 36, 55, 60, 64, 167 Aet 4, 124, 143 Flacc 25, 54, 85, 125 Legat 62, 74, 187, 356 Hypoth 6:8 QG 1:55c, 55c, 3:12, 4:8b, 52d QG isf 5 QG (Par) 2:2, 2:3, 2:7 QE isf 14

τριχῆ Opif 36, 49 Leg 1:3 Post 85 Somn 1:26

τριχθά QG 4:8a

τριχῶς Leg 2:54 Somn 1:62

τριώροφος Mos 2:60 QG (Par) 2:7, 2:7

τρόμος Legat 267

τροπαιοφορέω Abr 235

τροπαιοφόρος Congr 93

τροπή (107) Opif 22, 45, 113, 151 Leg 1:8, 17, 62, 76 Leg 2:31, 31, 32, 34, 34, 60, 60, 62, 62, 63, 78, 78, 83 Leg 3:49, 94, 211, 212, 234 Cher 88, 89 Sacr 90, 127, 127, 137 Det 87, 122 Post 178, 178 Deus 38, 88, 89, 90, 90, 130, 138 Agr 51, 176, 179 Ebr 91, 96, 121, 172, 178 Migr 148 Her 136, 149, 149, 149, 247 Congr 104 Fug 76, 76, 96, 102, 117, 159 Mut 57, 180, 186, 239, 239, 243, 250 Somn 1:20, 154, 192 Abr 18, 151, 175, 230 Ios 134, 144 Mos 1:114, 118, 144, 200, 212 Mos 2:18, 121, 124, 125, 186, 264 Decal 104 Spec 1:26, 34, 227, 238 Spec 2:143 Spec 3:135, 178, 194 Spec 4:235 Virt 93, 151 Praem 170 Aet 59 Legat 67 Prov 2:23

τροπικός (19) Opif 112, 112 Leg 1:45 Leg 2:14 Cher 41 Det 167 Post 1, 55 Deus 71 Conf 134, 190 Her 50, 147 Ios 125, 151 Virt 57 Praem 80, 125 QE 1:21

τρόπις Leg 2:6

τρόπος (625) Opif 10, 20, 32, 38, 40, 54, 65, 66, 69, 71, 78, 95, 97, 101, 107, 131, 141, 165, 168 Leg 1:17, 17, 28, 28, 29, 59, 82, 98 Leg 2:6, 11, 30, 38, 71, 91, 95, 96, 99, 103 Leg 3:12, 14, 28, 53, 56, 60, 81, 83, 84, 95, 98, 126, 128, 134, 151, 155, 160, 163, 177, 178, 190, 202, 203, 206, 212, 212, 213, 220, 237, 248 Cher 5, 13, 25, 53, 55, 65, 68, 110 Sacr 5, 21, 30, 36, 45, 56, 61, 62, 74, 83, 88, 89, 90, 97, 110, 115, 133 Det 3, 8, 13, 22, 38, 41, 43, 75, 95, 100, 101, 105, 111, 117, 125, 127, 128, 151, 167, 170 Post 10, 11, 27, 50, 61, 86, 98, 100, 107, 110, 111, 131, 137, 139, 155, 159, 163, 170 Gig 22, 22, 32, 32, 35, 50 Deus 5, 6, 15, 45, 68, 88, 92, 112, 153 Agr 15, 22, 24, 29, 34, 67, 69, 77, 89, 95, 114, 120, 158 Plant 15, 28, 40, 60, 63, 64, 81, 134, 136, 163, 177 Ebr 22, 23, 28, 31, 36, 74, 90, 93, 116, 140, 148, 158, 164, 190, 192, 217, 223 Sobr 6, 14, 24 Conf 5, 6, 6, 9, 18, 29, 44, 60, 69, 73, 86, 87, 95, 102, 106, 119, 122, 133, 144, 183, 196 Migr 22, 28, 40, 47, 47, 75, 95, 139, 144, 159, 164, 188, 192, 196, 211, 219, 219, 221 Her 31, 42, 60, 65, 74, 81, 100, 101, 113, 128, 138, 139, 144, 146, 185, 186, 191, 194, 203, 220, 222, 238, 239, 270, 278, 282, 293, 301, 307, 308, 309 Congr 19, 32, 48, 55, 58, 71, 92, 119, 131, 135, 159 Fug 19, 30, 32, 39, 40, 81, 88, 91, 115, 122, 123, 126, 140, 148, 155, 169, 177, 180, 209 Mut 5, 26, 30, 33, 38, 51, 57, 71, 73, 80, 97, 111, 113, 136, 137, 142, 148, 161, 173, 180, 192, 200, 212, 235, 239 Somn 1:25, 42, 45, 49, 58, 62, 69, 84, 107, 115, 119, 128, 129, 162, 169, 178, 194, 202, 214, 236, 247, 254 Somn 2:8, 13, 14, 50, 67, 98, 191, 198, 212, 242, 248, 274, 301 Abr 2, 10, 45, 47, 52, 63, 83, 98, 99, 123, 130, 147, 203, 205, 212, 217, 218, 220, 223, 237, 240, 259 Ios 3, 20, 23, 28, 33, 36, 61, 61, 68, 82, 83, 88, 101, 160, 162, 193, 215, 223, 263 Mos 1:22, 34, 87, 102, 121, 142, 177, 189, 254, 262, 278 Mos 2:23, 30, 39, 39, 59, 89, 93, 118, 121, 133, 135, 141, 143, 153, 160, 217, 231, 252, 267, 273 Decal 1, 12, 14, 32, 33, 44, 49, 61, 69, 81, 124, 138 Spec 1:17, 26, 35, 40, 65, 68, 85, 105, 110, 129, 138, 142, 148, 191, 216, 239, 246, 262, 289, 304, 311, 327, 332, 336 Spec 2:3, 30, 71, 75, 91, 121, 131, 132, 132, 142, 147, 152, 164, 181, 182, 183, 207, 228, 248 Spec 3:5, 33, 36, 39, 78, 79, 103, 113, 130, 171, 187, 189, 194, 208 Spec 4:2, 31, 39, 58, 60, 70, 83, 86, 91, 93, 107, 113, 114, 147, 168, 177, 182, 202, 214, 217, 218, 236 Virt 6, 9, 14, 31, 61, 69, 74, 76, 83, 88, 98, 123, 138, 144, 156, 164, 186, 194, 197, 205 Praem 34, 34, 45, 61, 70, 73, 125, 139, 172 Prob 1, 18, 30, 30, 32, 89, 90 Contempl 29, 33, 40, 47, 55, 72, 83 Aet 14, 19, 20, 31, 58, 73, 79, 80, 83, 85, 86, 97, 109, 113, 114, 115, 126, 128, 132, 134, 144, 149 Flacc 29, 49, 60, 108, 116, 159, 166, 189 Legat 48, 49, 59, 76, 80, 115, 125, 134, 137, 157, 159, 174, 191, 200, 228, 281, 289, 339, 344 Hypoth 7:18 Prov 2:1, 6, 23, 39, 39, 40, 55 QG 2:41, 66, 3:3, 52, 4:198 QG isf 9 QG (Par) 2:3, 2:5 QE 2:2, 118 QE isf 8, 14, 15

τροφεύς Leg 3:177 Migr 24 Congr 171 Spec 3:112

τροφεύω Mos 1:17

τροφή (303) Opif 38, 40, 41, 43, 115, 119, 133, 153, 158, 167, 169 Leg 1:24, 26, 26, 26, 97, 98, 98 Leg 3:60, 81, 152, 161, 161, 162, 169, 173, 178, 179, 183, 251 Sacr 41, 41, 41, 44, 62, 73, 86, 98, 98, 98, 109, 125, 139 Det 25, 85, 106, 108, 115, 116, 116, 120 Post 98, 98, 148, 149, 158 Deus 37, 39, 40, 59, 63, 155 Agr 6, 9, 9, 32, 58, 132, 142 Plant 15, 15, 35, 35 Ebr 22, 171 Sobr 3, 8, 36 Conf 55 Migr 29, 36, 37, 140, 157, 204 Her 79, 79, 137, 191, 226, 247, 253, 311 Congr 6, 19, 19, 29, 33, 100, 171, 173 Fug 137, 176 Mut 90, 165, 223, 230, 258, 259 Somn 1:38, 48, 51, 58, 97, 122 Somn 2:9, 10, 31, 46, 48, 73, 156, 156, 163, 204, 204, 215 Abr 91, 149 Ios 111, 113, 161, 178, 198, 210,

243, 249, 259 Mos 1:5, 8, 11, 15, 17, 20, 34, 65, 125, 153, 184, 195, 202, 204, 205, 208, 209 Mos 2:1, 60, 69, 70, 104, 148, 222, 223, 258, 259, 264, 266, 266, 266, 266, 267, 268, 270 Decal 12, 13, 16, 16, 45, 160 Spec 1:62, 132, 133, 133, 148, 165, 173, 184, 216, 217, 217, 218, 255, 338, 338 Spec 2:83, 150, 158, 159, 160, 161, 175, 179, 180, 181, 184, 186, 191, 197, 199, 201, 202, 205, 229, 233, 247 Spec 3:10, 57, 97, 116, 144, 144, 198, 199, 200, 201, 202, 203 Spec 4:12, 24, 26, 94, 104, 107, 211 Virt 6, 86, 130, 130, 143, 145, 149, 149, 149, 152, 154, 154, 156 Praem 8, 99, 99, 100, 134, 136, 142 Prob 86, 98, 121, 121, 122, 160 Contempl 9, 35, 35, 73 Aet 38, 62, 66, 85, 86, 88, 91, 91, 92, 92, 98, 98, 98, 99, 129 Flacc 64 Legat 252, 273 Hypoth 7:5, 7:5, 7:6, 11:10 Prov 2:11, 11, 45, 59, 66, 66 QG 4:8a, 51b QG (Par) 2:2, 2:7, 2:7, 2:7, 2:7 QE 2:14, 14, 18, 18

τρόφιμος (15) Leg 1:99 Leg 2:105 Det 101 Plant 77, 114 Migr 205 Fug 174, 183, 200 Somn 2:22, 22, 77 Mos 2:104 Spec 3:97 Virt 223

τροφός (10) Sacr 25 Det 115 Plant 14 Ebr 61 Her 38, 52, 163 Somn 2:139 Mos 1:18 QG isf 4

Τροφώνιος Legat 78

τροχάζω Plant 152

τροχίζω Det 176 Spec 4:82 Flacc 72, 85 Legat 206

τροχός Cher 80 Deus 102 Somn 2:44 Decal 146 Prov 2:58

τρυγάω Praem 128

τρυγητής Virt 90

τρύγητος Praem 101, 101

τρυγών (10) Her 126, 127, 234 Mut 233, 234, 245, 248 Spec 1:162, 162 Spec 4:117

τρυπάω Leg 3:199 Cher 72

τρυτάνη Somn 2:226 Spec 4:167 Virt 86

τρυφάω (16) Leg 1:45, 64 Agr 48, 150 Sobr 56 Migr 204 Somn 1:121, 125 Mos 1:54 Decal 117 Spec 1:134 Spec 4:126 Virt 133 Contempl 35, 73 Flacc 184

τρυφερός Somn 2:9

τρυφή (21) Leg 1:45, 96 Leg 3:167 Cher 1, 12, 12 Sacr 21 Post 32 Plant 38 Ebr 21 Somn 1:123 Somn 2:242 Ios 44, 243 Mos 1:89 Mos 2:13 Spec 2:99, 240 Praem 146 Contempl 48 Legat 168

τρύφος Opif 131

Τρύφων Flacc 76

τρύχω Leg 1:84

τρώγλη (6) Migr 188, 188 Fug 45 Somn 1:41, 55 Abr 72

τρώκτης Sacr 32

τυγχάνω (243) Opif 84, 137, 140, 166 Leg 1:60, 84, 88 Leg 2:15, 69 Leg 3:74, 86, 89, 125, 130, 170, 211 Cher 2, 45, 54, 56, 59, 66, 72, 109 Sacr 37, 53, 54, 90, 99, 99 Det 104, 123, 176 Post 9, 13, 83, 112, 147 Gig 61, 62 Deus 48, 98, 104, 171 Agr 6, 34, 44, 49, 50, 98, 114, 148, 161 Plant 7, 53, 160 Ebr 17, 121, 198 Sobr 20 Conf 7, 114, 146, 182 Migr 38, 57, 133, 155 Her 83, 90, 159, 296, 310 Congr 7, 22, 50, 109, 127 Fug 47, 107 Mut 47, 62, 77, 127, 128, 146, 254, 262, 268 Somn 1:163 Somn 2:168, 187 Abr 7, 29, 39, 122, 128, 146, 153, 165 Ios 19, 62, 80, 104, 117, 127, 154, 212 Mos 1:24, 169, 247, 248, 256, 329 Mos 2:6, 57, 65, 172, 291 Decal 6, 92, 105, 127, 146, 151 Spec 1:4, 41, 42, 124, 163, 223, 248, 285 Spec 2:8, 13, 19, 77, 86, 97, 121, 122, 127, 216, 228 Spec 3:27, 30, 59, 67, 71, 75, 79, 100, 106, 108, 123, 143, 145 Spec 4:15, 17, 23, 31, 36, 127, 127, 181, 182, 200 Virt 16, 26, 64, 96, 122, 124, 124, 160, 185, 189, 196, 202, 208, 226 Praem 11, 32, 53, 53, 63, 82, 86, 114, 124, 163, 165 Prob 44, 60, 136, 140, 152 Contempl 72 Aet 13, 128, 129 Flacc 11, 14, 14, 17, 23, 50, 66, 83, 109, 113, 167, 185 Legat 32, 76, 114, 140, 167, 178, 180, 181, 183, 211, 225, 288, 289, 289 Hypoth 6:6, 6:8, 7:2, 7:2, 7:9, 7:10, 11:13 Prov 2:32 QG 2:65, 4:74, 88, 168, 198, 200c, 227 QE 2:17

τυμβεύω Spec 4:122

τύμβος Deus 150 Somn 1:139 QG 1:70:1

τύμπανον Leg 3:21 Fug 22 Spec 2:193

τύπος (83) Opif 18, 19, 34, 71, 129, 145, 157, 166 Leg 1:61, 61, 62, 79, 100 Leg 3:16, 83, 183 Cher 29, 55 Sacr 135, 137 Det 28, 76, 78, 83, 86, 127 Post 93, 94, 99 Gig 9 Deus 43, 121 Plant 125 Ebr 36, 174, 187, 192 Sobr 36 Conf 84, 87, 148 Her 181, 231 Mut 31 Somn 1:129, 173, 216 Somn 2:191 Abr 32, 199 Mos 1:119, 159 Mos 2:34, 76, 76 Decal 11, 101, 168 Spec 1:30, 47, 103, 106, 325 Spec 2:216, 255 Spec 4:78, 107, 160, 218, 218 Virt 19 Prob 15, 75, 95 Aet 2, 49, 79 Flacc 144 Legat 178, 211, 316 QG 2:62, 4:99

τυπόω (47) Opif 6, 14, 65 Leg 1:22, 30, 31, 38, 100 Leg 2:20 Leg 3:60, 230 Cher 51 Sacr 86 Det 76, 87 Post 110 Deus 44, 84 Agr 167, 167 Plant 18, 44 Ebr 90, 137 Migr 103 Her 56, 294 Mut 79, 80, 135, 200 Somn 1:15, 202, 219 Somn 2:15, 45 Spec 1:81, 87 Spec 2:152 Spec 3:83, 207 Spec 4:140 Virt 52, 195, 203 Prob 46, 62

τύπτω (31) Leg 3:38, 108, 201 Cher 79, 80, 81 Det 49, 49, 49 Plant 153 Fug 83 Ios 74, 86 Mos 1:44, 270 Spec 2:28, 94, 232, 243, 244 Spec 3:105, 142, 142, 159 Prob 26, 104, 134 Aet 128 Flacc 77, 78, 80

τυπώδης Praem 67 Legat 55

τύπωσις Leg 1:61 Deus 43

τυραννέω Det 94 Her 270 Prob 45

τυραννικός (6) Ios 66 Mos 2:50 Spec 3:137 Spec 4:89 Prob 120 Flacc 1

τυραννίς (8) Conf 197 Abr 242 Mos 2:13 Decal 136 Flacc 54, 105 Prov 2:28, 37

τυραννοκτονία Prov 2:55

τύραννος (29) Leg 2:91 Leg 3:79, 80, 81 Det 94 Agr 46 Ebr 198 Conf 83, 113, 164 Somn 2:83 Ios 76, 132 Mos 1:9 Mos 2:16 Decal 40 Spec 1:308 Spec 3:138, 164 Spec 4:177 Prob 106 Flacc 96 Legat 350 Prov 2:2, 29, 29, 37, 39, 41

τυρεύω Ios 174

τυρός Somn 2:49 Spec 2:20 Spec 4:12, 12 Virt 144

τυφλός (63) Leg 3:91, 108, 108, 109, 110 Cher 58, 62 Sacr 134 Deus 130 Agr 54, 81 Sobr 40 Conf 27, 191 Migr 18, 38, 123, 222 Her 48, 76, 250 Congr 109 Fug 19, 122, 123, 144 Mut 105, 143 Somn 1:164, 248 Somn 2:102, 161, 192 Abr 25, 65, 84 Ios 258 Mos 1:124, 153 Mos 2:199, 271 Decal 129 Spec 1:25, 54 Spec 2:23, 77 Spec 3:79, 178 Spec 4:5, 70, 189, 198 Virt 5, 7, 172, 179 Praem 54 Contempl 13 Legat 109, 114 Prov 2:12, 20 QG isf 15

τυφλόω (6) Leg 3:231 Ebr 108 Contempl 61 QE isf 4, 6, 31

τυφλοπλαστέω τυφοπλαστέω

τύφλωσις Ebr 222 Somn 2:192 QG 4:23

τυφλώττω (6) Migr 69 Ios 254 Decal 67 Spec 1:332 Contempl 13 Legat 21

τυφοπλαστέω (τυφλοπλαστέω) Congr 15 Somn 1:218 Somn 2:66 Legat 153 Prov 2:18

τυφοπλάστης Spec 4:59

τῦφος (56) Cher 42, 91 Post 165 Gig 50 Agr 43, 43 Ebr 36, 39, 40, 95, 124, 124 Conf 71, 79 Migr 19, 136, 160 Her 291 Fug 90 Mut 103, 103, 114 Somn 2:47, 61, 63, 95, 97, 139, 140 Mos 1:88 Mos 2:169, 270 Decal 4, 5, 6, 80 Spec 1:21, 27, 30, 53, 79, 309 Spec 2:259 Spec 3:125 Virt 17, 178, 195 Praem 24, 25, 27, 58 Prob 66 Contempl 39 Flacc 4 Legat 116 Prov 2:8

τυφόω Det 101 Conf 106 Congr 127, 128 Somn 2:64

τύφω Prob 71 Legat 120

τυφῶν (τυφώς) Deus 89, 89 Plant 24 Somn 2:129

τυφώς τυφῶν

τύχη (56) Leg 3:210 Det 104 Post 109, 142 Deus 173, 176 Agr 151 Conf 164 Fug 16 Mut 242 Somn 1:192 Somn 2:81, 146, 282 Abr 6, 186, 265 Ios 81, 140, 144, 238 Mos 1:31 Mos 2:13 Decal 41 Spec 1:246 Spec 2:23, 34, 46, 52, 231 Spec 3:137, 137 Spec 4:18, 153, 201 Virt 122 Praem 71 Prob 18, 24, 35, 39, 121, 126 Flacc 64, 154 Legat 1, 140, 179, 190, 284, 300, 309, 327 Prov 2:34, 34 QG isf 5

τυχηρός (14) Gig 15 Ebr 201 Sobr 15, 43 Conf 16, 20 Fug 44 Mut 91, 91 Ios 150 Prob 120 Legat 1, 1 QE isf 16

τωθάζω Legat 165

τωθασμός Mos 1:20 Spec 2:193 Legat 169

Υ

ὑακίνθινος Mos 2:110, 118 Spec 1:85, 94

ὑάκινθος (7) Migr 97 Congr 117, 117 Mos 2:84, 87, 88, 111

ὕαλος Legat 364

ὑβρίζω (19) Opif 169 Leg 3:241 Conf 47 Mut 196 Mos 1:3 Spec 2:83, 95, 254 Spec 3:76, 80, 173, 173 Praem 139, 140 Flacc 32, 40 Hypoth 7:2 QG 4:33b, 204

ὕβρις (50) Leg 2:70 Cher 92 Post 98 Agr 32, 113 Conf 117 Fug 30 Abr 228 Ios 74 Mos 1:72, 88, 258 Mos 2:13, 164 Decal 4, 86, 126, 170 Spec 1:204, 281 Spec 2:18, 94, 245 Spec 3:43, 64, 82, 108, 168, 173, 174, 186 Virt 89, 162 Praem 52 Prob 55 Contempl 42 Flacc 40, 58, 59, 77, 79, 91, 95, 104, 117, 136, 173 Legat 64, 302 Hypoth 7:3

ὑβριστής (7) Agr 116 Ios 84 Spec 2:245 Spec 3:78 Praem 100 Prov 2:12 QG 4:204

ὑβριστικός Virt 113

ὑγεῖα ὑγίεια

ὑγιάζω Det 44 Praem 21

ὑγιαίνω (56) Opif 167 Leg 2:70, 97 Cher 16 Sacr 44 Det 5, 12, 12, 13, 95, 95 Post 184 Deus 124, 124, 125, 125, 129 Agr 164 Plant 114, 157 Ebr 179, 223 Conf 22, 25 Migr 87, 87, 119, 124 Her 67, 202 Congr 39 Fug 117, 160 Mut 204, 230 Abr 223, 275 Ios 199 Mos 1:50, 124, 135 Mos 2:34, 167 Decal 142 Spec 1:191 Spec 2:233 Spec 4:134, 182 Virt 3, 13, 32, 226 Aet 70, 96 Legat 107 QG 3:22

ὑγίεια (ὑγεῖα) (63) Leg 2:86 Leg 3:86, 86, 178 Sacr 39, 123 Post 159 Deus 57, 87, 150 Agr 98 Ebr 140, 140, 201 Sobr 61, 67 Conf 19 Migr 87, 162, 162 Her 92, 209, 285, 299 Congr 31, 93, 96 Fug 151, 160 Mut 221 Somn 2:299 Abr 26, 263 Ios 130 Mos 2:185 Spec 1:222, 237, 252, 283 Spec 2:2, 197 Spec 4:237 Virt 13, 14, 176 Praem 33, 64, 119 Prob 12 Aet 37, 116 Legat 14, 106 Hypoth 7:16 Prov 2:1, 19, 71 QG 1:85, 4:43 QE 2:18, 18, 25d QE isf 16

ὑγιεινός (23) Det 16, 34, 72 Gig 34 Ebr 141, 214 Her 286, 297 Congr 25, 101 Mut 230 Abr 267 Ios 62 Mos 1:64 Spec 1:343 Spec 3:107 Praem 122 Contempl 23 Legat 14, 82, 270 QG 2:41 QE 2:25d

ὑγιής (39) Leg 1:23 Leg 2:97 Leg 3:32, 150, 233 Cher 14, 15, 36, 66, 127 Sacr 26 Det 10, 65, 138 Gig 49 Deus 124 Conf 93, 124 Her 290 Congr 61, 141 Somn 1:79 Somn 2:99, 134 Mos 1:268 Spec 1:118, 173, 238, 246 Spec 2:164 Spec 3:55 Spec 4:44, 60 Virt 207 Aet 52, 143 Flacc 136, 170 QG 2:12c

ὑγρός (27) Opif 67, 132, 132, 132 Leg 2:2 Sacr 108 Ebr 186, 190, 191 Conf 89, 184 Her 135, 135, 146, 151, 153, 208, 282 Spec 1:216 Spec 2:19, 240 Spec 4:91, 193 Contempl 47 Aet 98, 100 QG 2:12d

ὑγρότης Opif 132 Conf 102 Her 294 Spec 3:33

ὑδατώδης Her 197 Virt 130

ὕδρα Somn 2:14

ὑδρεία Post 137 Mos 1:228 Prob 32

ὑδρεύω Post 132, 132, 138, 148

ὑδρηρός Conf 38

ὑδρία (12) Post 132, 132, 132, 132, 136, 137, 137, 140, 146, 150 Fug 195 Mos 1:187

ὑδρίον Mos 1:211

ὑδρόβιος QG 2:39

ὑδρορρόα Post 50, 127

ὑδροφορέω Contempl 50

ὕδωρ (279) Opif 29, 38, 38, 39, 63, 64, 80, 84, 131, 131, 136, 146 Leg 1:33 Leg 2:84, 84, 103 Leg 3:5, 81, 82, 99, 101, 141, 142, 144 Cher 38, 62, 89, 111, 111 Sacr 97 Det 62, 151, 152, 154, 170 Post 130, 132, 137, 139, 158, 158, 162, 163, 163, 164 Gig 22, 22, 22 Deus 107, 145, 145, 157, 169, 171 Agr 24, 51 Plant 3, 3, 3, 4, 6, 10, 12, 78, 78, 80, 83, 120, 127 Ebr 106, 106, 110, 182, 218, 223 Sobr 8 Conf 29, 30, 70, 70, 70, 89, 136, 185, 186, 186, 186 Migr 36, 83 Her 134, 135, 136, 146, 146, 197, 198, 208, 226, 247, 281, 282 Congr 104, 117, 163, 163, 163, 166 Fug 1, 110, 176, 177, 183, 183, 187, 197 Mut 59 Somn 1:8, 16, 18, 19, 19, 31, 33, 36, 38, 39, 81, 136, 210, 210, 211, 214, 220 Somn 2:48, 116, 122, 222, 238, 245, 277 Abr 1, 43, 44, 44, 138 Ios 12, 155 Mos 1:17, 17, 55, 81, 96, 97, 98, 98, 99, 101, 103, 107, 113, 117, 143, 144, 200, 202, 210, 211, 212, 243, 255, 256, 289 Mos 2:37, 53, 63, 88, 88, 101, 104, 119, 119, 119, 120, 121, 121, 126, 133, 143, 148, 238, 263 Decal 15, 16, 31, 53, 78 Spec 1:93, 93, 94, 97, 249, 262, 262, 264, 264, 266 Spec 2:255 Spec 3:58, 58, 59, 60, 62, 111, 147, 152 Spec 4:81, 118 Virt 154 Praem 36, 99 Contempl 3, 3, 37, 73 Aet 18, 25, 29, 33, 33, 45, 61, 66, 87, 103, 103, 107, 107, 110, 110, 110, 110, 111, 111, 111, 111, 115, 115, 115, 115, 119, 125, 131, 137, 146, 147, 147, 148, 148 Legat 275, 350 Hypoth 7:6 Prov 2:43, 46, 68 QG 1:3, 2:28, 28, 28, 29, 30, 30, 48, 54c, 64c, 66 QE 2:18, 18, 18, 18

ὑετός (30) Post 144 Deus 87, 156, 157 Ebr 106 Migr 101 Fug 180 Mut 21 Mos 1:6, 117, 118, 145, 200, 200, 202, 202 Mos 2:195, 286 Spec 2:206 Virt 93, 145 Praem 101, 131, 132 Aet 137, 137 Prov 2:23, 43, 45 QG 4:51b

ὑθλέω Prov 1

ὕθλος Post 166

ὑϊιδῆ (ὑϊιδοῦς) Spec 3:26

ὑϊιδοῦς ὑϊιδῆ

υἱός (291) Leg 2:48, 48, 48, 51, 77, 94 Leg 3:15, 85, 90, 133, 133, 181, 203, 212, 214, 225, 232 Cher 8, 9, 54, 67, 67, 69, 69 Sacr 19, 19, 19, 19, 19, 20, 47, 48, 118, 118 Det 13, 14, 49, 94, 138 Post 33, 63, 66, 69, 73, 74, 89, 91, 119, 124, 158, 179 Gig 1, 3, 5 Deus 31, 32, 54, 119, 119, 121, 145 Agr 51 Plant 59, 60, 63, 134, 136 Ebr 14, 14, 30, 67, 67, 72, 84, 93, 127, 131, 138 Sobr 1, 6, 12, 21, 21, 21, 21, 21, 22, 27, 30, 31, 32, 44, 47, 48, 48, 56 Conf 1, 41, 63, 93, 122, 142, 145, 145, 146, 147, 148, 149 Migr 15, 21, 54, 126, 140, 141, 193, 193, 205, 206, 224 Her 2, 8, 39, 40, 49, 52, 59, 113, 117, 124, 195 Congr 42, 43, 54, 58, 86, 175, 177, 177, 177, 177 Fug 1, 89, 208 Mut 92, 92, 93, 94, 97, 97, 98, 131, 189, 206, 206, 207, 217, 226, 227, 227, 253, 255, 261, 261 Somn 1:37, 52, 117, 173, 195, 237, 254 Somn 2:33, 33, 36, 89 Abr 50, 98, 110, 132, 168, 169, 173, 176, 181, 187, 188, 192, 194, 198, 198, 254 Ios 4, 11, 22, 163, 167, 182, 188, 195, 217, 231, 255, 256, 257 Mos 1:19, 135, 150, 283, 301, 304, 328, 330 Mos 2:64, 134, 142, 234, 243, 243, 244 Spec 1:41, 96, 111, 112, 130, 130, 139, 312, 316, 318, 318 Spec 2:124, 127, 129, 130, 136, 138, 227, 247 Spec 3:14, 19, 26, 29, 153, 153, 154, 168, 168 Spec 4:184 Virt 53, 59, 66, 192 Praem 24, 59, 61, 63, 65, 109, 134, 158, 166, 167 Prob 37, 37, 122 Contempl 13, 72 Legat 27, 28, 29, 38, 62, 71, 71, 300 Hypoth 7:5 Prov 2:4 QG 1:55a, 2:26a, 54a, 65, 65, 3:58, 4:88, 88, 180, 180, 198, 202a QE 2:47 QE isf 22, 22

υἱωνός (18) Post 114 Deus 31 Sobr 31, 44, 47 Abr 50 Spec 3:14 Praem 24, 109 Flacc 10, 12, 13, 25 Legat 23, 24, 29, 33, 35

ὑλακτέω Somn 1:108 Somn 2:168, 267

ὑλακτικός Plant 151

ὕλη (177) Opif 40, 42, 62, 136, 137, 142, 146, 153, 171 Leg 1:3, 29, 31, 42, 49, 83, 88 Leg 2:19, 51, 80, 107 Leg 3:114, 152, 240, 243, 252 Cher 80, 100, 125, 126, 127 Det 20, 105, 109, 111, 117 Post 61, 115, 116, 120, 128, 163, 165 Deus 8, 153 Agr 19, 25, 40, 48, 95, 97 Plant 5, 8, 22, 97 Ebr 61, 86, 88, 89, 90, 109, 132, 217 Sobr 36, 39, 43 Conf 83, 107 Migr 97, 120, 204 Her 137, 157, 158, 158, 159, 160, 216, 307 Congr 11, 55, 112, 144 Fug 9, 35, 45, 129, 133, 134, 134, 198 Mut 89, 152, 215 Somn 1:126 Somn 2:93, 181 Abr 220, 223 Mos 1:60, 65, 153, 192, 317 Mos 2:58, 72, 76, 88, 90, 93, 136, 139, 214, 220, 220 Decal 12, 66, 72, 133, 173 Spec 1:21, 22, 22, 25, 47, 71, 74, 86, 104, 248, 254, 273, 276, 328, 329 Spec 3:180, 180 Spec 4:26, 83, 118, 125, 209, 229 Virt 149, 162 Praem 132 Prob 65, 71 Contempl 4, 49, 69 Aet 64, 96, 127, 132 Flacc 68, 148 Legat 9, 129, 130, 132, 170, 201, 222 Prov 1, 1, 1, 1, 1, 2:40, 59 QG 1:58, 2:12b, 12b, 4:172 QE 2:15a, 47, 50b

ὑλικός (8) Det 153 Migr 192 Fug 11, 26 Mos 2:76 QG 3:38a, 49b, 61

ὑλοτομέω Post 50

ὑλοφορέω Mos 1:38

ὑμέτερος (21) Det 74, 74 Conf 116 Migr 184, 186, 192 Mut 120 Somn 1:165 Ios 6, 45, 198 Mos 1:223, 322 Spec 4:220 Virt 38, 68 Flacc 76, 98 Legat 48, 181, 279

ὑμήν Her 217

ὑμνέω (25) Opif 4, 90 Leg 2:82, 102 Det 73 Ebr 111 Conf 149 Her 111, 161 Congr 89 Fug 185, 186 Mut 196 Somn 2:28, 268 Abr 9, 36 Ios 253 Mos 2:239 Spec 4:177, 230 Virt 22, 72, 187 Flacc 121

ὑμνογράφος Gig 17

ὕμνος (52) Leg 2:82 Leg 3:26 Agr 79, 80, 82 Plant 29, 126, 135 Ebr 94, 105, 110, 121 Sobr 13, 58 Conf 39, 52, 108 Migr 113, 157, 157 Her 110 Fug 59 Mut 115 Somn 1:35, 37, 75, 256 Somn 2:34, 38, 242, 245 Mos 1:180, 284 Mos 2:162, 256, 256, 257 Spec 1:193, 224, 272 Spec 2:148, 199 Spec 3:125 Contempl 25, 29, 80, 80, 81, 84, 87 Flacc 122 Legat 96

ὑμνῳδία Agr 50 Plant 39, 135 Virt 73, 75

ὑμνῳδός Deus 74 Plant 129

ὑπάγω (34) Opif 165, 166 Deus 32, 168 Agr 33 Plant 67 Ebr 113 Migr 26 Congr 165 Mut 172 Somn 2:79 Abr 63 Ios 70 Mos 1:36, 234, 263, 307 Spec 1:29, 313 Spec 2:82, 85, 122 Spec 3:29 Spec 4:18, 50, 152, 213 Virt 115 Praem 138, 162 Prob 45, 121 Aet 132 Hypoth 11:14

ὑπαίθριος Spec 2:207

ὕπαιθρος (22) Mos 1:103 Mos 2:42, 80, 82, 94, 106, 146, 152 Spec 1:156, 165, 231, 233, 274, 301 Spec 2:206 Spec 3:17, 160, 169 Aet 4 Legat 123, 151 Prov 2:23

ὑπαινίσσομαι Somn 1:181 Ios 7 Decal 165 Hypoth 11:16

ὑπαίτιος (57) Opif 80, 151, 164 Leg 3:75, 205, 247 Det 97 Post 87 Gig 56 Deus 71, 135, 162 Plant 102, 108 Ebr 28 Sobr 49 Conf 114 Her 295 Fug 73, 78, 93 Mut 241, 244 Somn 2:162, 177, 274 Abr 6 Ios 19, 150, 216 Mos 1:314 Decal 87 Spec 2:14, 14, 31, 74, 137, 255 Spec 3:52, 102, 156, 177 Spec 4:42, 79 Virt 206, 211 Praem 13, 20, 55, 58, 116 Prob 98 Prov 2:6, 55 QG 4:198, 198, 228

ὑπακούω (27) Opif 142 Cher 9 Agr 49 Ebr 14, 19, 198 Conf 54, 55 Migr 8 Her 8 Congr 63, 68, 68, 69 Fug 21 Somn 1:162 Abr 226 Ios 269 Mos 1:88, 156 Spec 2:236 Virt 114 Prob 25, 36, 47, 156 QG 1:70:1

ὑπαλλαγή Opif 58 Abr 81 Spec 3:150 Contempl 19

ὑπαλλάσσω (11) Opif 152 Ios 15 Mos 2:167 Spec 2:35, 35 Virt 196 Flacc 131 Legat 1, 69, 211, 327

ὑπαμφίβολος Abr 212 Spec 3:57

ὑπαναδύομαι Mos 1:266

ὑπαναλίσκω Prob 118

ὑπαναπλέω Sacr 61 Agr 132 Fug 129 Mut 100

ὑπαναχωρέω Mos 1:47

ὑπανίημι (6) Agr 70 Mut 84 Mos 1:40 Spec 1:109 Contempl 69 Aet 62

ὑπανίσταμαι (6) Agr 38, 77 Migr 144 Ios 6 Spec 2:238 Aet 118

ὑπαντάω (21) Cher 3 Det 127, 129, 132, 135 Conf 31, 31, 59 Migr 79 Congr 124 Fug 5 Somn 1:61, 68, 70, 72, 117 Mos 1:85, 263, 275 Spec 3:41 Flacc 167

ὑπαντιάζω (11) Post 138 Deus 79 Conf 29, 31 Somn 2:121, 278 Mos 1:115, 164, 215, 250 Flacc 185

ὑπάργυρος Congr 159

ὑπαρκτός (8) Leg 3:197 Sacr 43, 43 Conf 74, 74 Migr 94 Mut 37, 38

ὕπαρξις (18) Opif 170 Det 160 Post 168, 169 Deus 55, 62, 62 Somn 1:231 Decal 83 Spec 1:35, 330 Spec 2:225 Virt 215 Praem 40, 40, 44, 45 Prob 80

ὑπαρχή (6) Deus 38 Agr 33 Conf 7 Legat 18, 326 QE 1:7b

ὕπαρχος (31) Opif 88, 148 Deus 113 Agr 51 Conf 179 Fug 111 Somn 1:140, 241 Abr 115, 228 Ios 157, 158, 163, 248, 257 Mos 1:166, 216 Decal 54, 61, 178 Spec 1:14, 19 Spec 4:171, 174 Virt 55 Aet 53 Flacc 100, 104 Legat 161, 207, 299

ὑπάρχω (107) Opif 140, 150, 170, 172 Leg 1:59, 62, 62, 79, 100 Leg 2:20, 71, 71, 86, 86 Leg 3:51, 72, 179, 197, 234 Cher 4, 66, 114 Sacr 19, 43, 67 Det 14, 55, 160, 160 Post 20, 117, 168 Deus 76, 81, 143 Plant 17 Ebr 14, 45, 48, 197 Sobr 21, 42 Conf 21, 146, 182 Migr 94, 180 Her 64, 181, 213, 230, 236, 236, 299 Congr 2, 26, 26, 51, 80, 137, 156, 179 Fug 66, 101, 205, 212 Mut 18, 37, 60, 160, 173, 173, 231, 243, 246 Somn 1:91, 169 Somn 2:123, 237 Abr 46 Ios 44, 113, 123, 167 Mos 2:207 Decal 83 Spec 1:41 Spec 2:133, 225, 234 Virt 78, 144 Aet 8, 51, 70, 70, 99, 104, 104 Flacc 164 Legat 86 QG 1:32, 2:12d, 29, 4:43, 148, 200a

ὑπασπίζω Her 223

ὑπασπιστής Somn 2:96

ὑπάτη Leg 3:121

ὑπειδόμην ὑφοράω

ὑπειδόμην Ios 8

ὑπείκω (18) Leg 3:56, 201, 202 Cher 78, 79 Sacr 105 Post 74 Ebr 36, 58, 201 Her 181 Mos 1:156 Decal 64 Spec 1:343 Spec 2:232 Spec 3:8 Spec 4:221 Aet 74

ὑπείλλω Spec 4:77

ὕπειμι Mos 1:50 Mos 2:142 QG 2:54a

ὑπεῖπον (7) Opif 2 Mos 1:85 Spec 1:65, 98, 129, 344 Spec 2:224

ὑπεισέρχομαι Spec 4:191

ὑπεκδύομαι Det 159

ὑπέκκαυμα (6) Her 309 Somn 2:202 Ios 154 Mos 1:25 Virt 117, 197

ὑπεκλύω Ebr 95 QG 1:24

ὑπεναντίος Opif 54 Cher 22 Fug 63 Decal 104

ὑπενδίδωμι Sacr 62 Migr 133, 143 Abr 63

ὑπεξαιρέω (21) Opif 15, 84, 87, 160 Ebr 33 Sobr 46 Migr 3, 50 Congr 12 Ios 46, 212 Decal 12, 150 Spec 1:113, 212, 213 Spec 2:22 Spec 3:17, 173 Flacc 12 QG (Par) 2:2

ὑπεξέρχομαι (13) Det 159 Migr 190 Her 73, 74, 74, 76 Ios 9, 128 Flacc 28 Legat 128, 265, 372 QG 2:48

ὑπεξίστημι (7) Opif 35 Leg 3:41 Sacr 135 Mos 1:55 Praem 25 Legat 36, 236

ὑπέρ (332) Opif 5, 32, 38, 128, 167 Leg 1:2 Leg 2:51 Leg 3:14, 72, 136, 166, 205, 242 Cher 46, 72 Sacr 25, 84, 130 Det 14, 27, 175, 176 Post 65, 94, 99 Deus 91, 132 Agr 5, 119, 151, 152, 152, 154, 156 Plant 153 Ebr 129 Conf 38, 98 Migr 76, 144, 149, 200 Her 6, 9, 14, 174, 174, 174, 174, 224, 224, 226, 226, 226, 230, 231, 234, 236, 238, 293 Congr 24, 96 Fug 57, 89, 116, 146, 210 Mut 14, 53, 62, 125, 129, 222, 265 Somn 1:52, 54, 54, 97, 97, 124 Somn 2:62, 265, 278, 298 Abr 4, 98, 140, 140, 179, 179, 187, 197, 214, 225 Ios 10, 12, 92, 148, 171, 178, 215, 228, 237, 267 Mos 1:52, 118, 128, 141, 141, 147, 149, 149, 151, 159, 166, 175, 232, 280, 292, 303, 307, 307, 307, 317 Mos 2:46, 90, 98, 113, 122, 147, 153, 153, 159, 159, 166, 173, 175, 213, 224, 273, 274 Decal 56, 57, 63, 91, 91, 91, 114, 169, 169 Spec 1:30, 44, 57, 79, 86, 97, 97, 97, 97, 113, 139, 152, 156, 168, 168, 168, 169, 169, 169, 171, 171, 188, 190, 190, 205, 211, 222, 229, 244, 260, 260, 298, 298, 314, 317 Spec 2:3, 33, 36, 54, 69, 93, 95, 95, 122, 131, 135, 142, 146, 157, 162, 167, 167, 167, 173, 175, 178, 182, 183, 184, 203, 209, 233, 244 Spec 3:18, 46, 49, 53, 54, 55, 74, 77, 78, 105, 120, 127, 128, 131, 148, 149, 152, 153, 153, 154, 157, 159, 163, 172, 179 Spec 4:9, 10, 15, 24, 54, 63, 78, 81, 98, 142, 142, 161, 161, 216, 223 Virt 42, 45, 77, 109, 109, 137, 154, 156, 156, 172, 223 Praem 56, 105, 114, 126, 137, 143, 156, 157, 166 Prob 108, 111, 111, 117, 118, 131, 133 Contempl 22, 27, 54 Aet 1, 37, 39, 39, 65 Flacc 61, 94, 146, 150 Legat 38, 39, 60, 60, 117, 135, 136, 137, 139, 148, 160, 162, 178, 190, 192, 201, 211, 232, 242, 242, 279, 299, 334, 355, 355, 357, 361 Hypoth 0:1, 11:5, 11:9 Prov 2:40, 48, 55 QG 2:62, 3:18, 4:102a, 202a, 204 QE 2:49b, 49b

ὑπεραιωρέω Prov 2:29

ὑπέραντλος Agr 89 Somn 2:86 Prob 128 Legat 372

ὑπεράνω (20) Leg 3:175 Det 114 Post 14 Plant 144 Conf 137 Migr 7, 125 Congr 105 Fug 101, 115, 164 Somn 1:157 Mos 2:103, 132 Spec 3:184 Spec 4:114 Praem 114, 125 Prob 96 QG 2:54a ὑπερασπίζω (8) Agr 78 Conf 48 Her 58 Mut 40, 113 Somn 2:267 Mos 1:216 Legat 208

ὑπερασπιστής Ebr 111 Somn 1:173 QE 2:16

ὑπεράϋλος Leg 3:82

ὑπέραυχος (15) Agr 62, 83 Ebr 111 Sobr 57 Migr 62, 147 Congr 41 Fug 194 Spec 1:265, 265, 293 Spec 4:165 Virt 165 Praem 119 Flacc 4

ὑπερβαίνω (31) Opif 2 Leg 3:232 Post 180 Deus 149, 157 Sobr 6 Migr 38 Congr 103 Mut 53, 117 Abr 23, 122 Mos 1:4, 14, 24, 25 Decal 43 Spec 1:20, 163 Spec 2:6 Spec 4:198 Praem 77 Contempl 11, 30 Flacc 166 Legat 93, 183, 204 Prov 2:6, 17 QE isf 24

ὑπερβαλλόντως Opif 30 Plant 126 Migr 58

ὑπερβάλλω (95) Opif 4, 6, 23, 45, 71, 148 Leg 1:58 Leg 3:165, 217 Sacr 28, 121 Det 29 Post 9, 119, 141, 162 Deus 44, 116 Ebr 109, 119 Sobr 54, 58 Conf 17, 50, 58, 93, 138, 162 Migr 25, 106, 113, 167 Her 3, 24, 89 Congr 134 Fug 16 Mut 61, 64, 180, 250 Somn 1:132, 143, 184 Somn 2:270, 279 Abr 40, 154, 167, 194, 252, 267 Ios 82, 172, 246 Mos 1:21, 61, 119, 134, 212 Mos 2:1, 200 Spec 1:263 Spec 2:36, 56, 240, 249 Spec 3:34, 45, 101, 129, 154 Spec 4:24, 54, 84, 212 Virt 99, 192 Praem 42 Prob 109 Aet 107, 108, 145 Flacc 3, 8, 48 Legat 27, 63, 106, 143, 341 Hypoth 6:1, 6:8 Prov 1 QE 2:105

ὑπερβατός Mut 13

ὑπερβλύζον Sacr 61

ὑπερβλύζω Ebr 221 Contempl 45 Aet 147

ὑπερβολαία Leg 3:121

ὑπερβολή (83) Opif 136 Leg 1:34 Leg 3:208 Sacr 55 Det 96 Post 161 Deus 7, 21, 73, 80, 162 Agr 154 Plant 128, 145 Ebr 16, 73 Sobr 54 Conf 165 Migr 146 Her 29, 156 Congr 107 Fug 115 Mut 53, 217 Somn 1:56 Somn 2:116, 198, 223 Abr 39, 50, 115, 185 Ios 252, 258 Mos 1:229 Mos 2:196, 197, 198 Decal 4, 70, 91, 112 Spec 1:58, 73, 131, 248, 294 Spec 2:16, 51, 73, 167 Spec 3:54, 209 Spec 4:48, 102, 168, 191, 202 Virt 86, 134, 136, 203 Praem 134, 136 Prob 8, 36, 56, 129 Aet 119 Flacc 59, 107, 146, 179 Prov 2:20, 32 QG 2:13a, 16, 3:20a, 52 QE 1:6, 6, 2:11a

ὑπεργάζομαι Aet 119

ὑπέργηρως Somn 1:10

ὑπερεγγυάω Spec 3:72

ὑπερεῖδον (ὑπεροράω) (14) Leg 2:48 Sacr 19 Sobr 21 Migr 214 Ios 171 Mos 1:53 Mos 2:163 Decal 41 Spec 1:308 Spec 2:136, 195 Praem 30, 58, 148

ὑπερείδω (6) Ebr 156 Mos 2:77 Spec 3:106 Aet 115 QG isf 1 QE 1:21

ὑπερεκχέω Ebr 32

ὑπερετής QE isf 29

ὑπερέχω (29) Opif 108, 108, 109, 109, 109, 110, 110, 110, 110 Leg 3:88 Det 107 Agr 121, 151 Migr 166, 166 Her 58 Somn 2:265 Mos 1:142 Mos 2:277 Decal 21, 21, 21, 21 Spec 4:199, 231, 231 Contempl 69 Aet 140 Legat 220

ὑπερῆλιξ Abr 111, 248

ὑπερήμερος Mos 2:225

ὑπερηφανία Virt 171

ὑπέρθεσις (10) Abr 3 Ios 263 Mos 1:280 Decal 85 Spec 3:94, 102, 103 Flacc 84, 129 Legat 253

ὑπερθετικός Sacr 32

ὑπέρκειμαι Praem 10 Prob 20

ὑπερκύπτω (22) Opif 70 Leg 3:100, 177 Sacr 60, 94 Det 100 Gig 61 Deus 150 Ebr 62 Migr 90, 106, 184 Congr 105, 134 Fug 164 Somn 2:115 Mos 1:27 Spec 2:166 Praem 30 Prob 3 Legat 5, 75

ὑπερμαχέω Mos 2:273 QE isf 7

ὑπέρμαχος (16) Opif 160 Agr 79 Sobr 13 Conf 48, 55 Mut 108 Somn 2:280 Abr 96, 232 Spec 3:75, 132, 140 Spec 4:178 Prob 44 Flacc 104, 170

ὑπερμεγέθης Leg 3:82 Mos 1:77, 231 Spec 3:47

ὑπέρμεστος Flacc 108

ὑπερμήκης QG (Par) 2:5

ὑπέρογκος (14) Leg 3:18, 82 Conf 17 Somn 2:211 Mos 1:83, 306 Mos 2:29 Spec 2:21 Spec 3:18 Virt 183 Praem 80 Prob 126 Legat 154 QE isf 2

ὑπερόπτης Somn 1:124 Mos 1:31 Spec 4:72, 88

ὑπεροράω ὑπερεῖδον

ὑπεροράω (6) Deus 19 Ebr 65 Mut 39, 46 Praem 162 QE 2:12

ὑπερόριος (15) Post 140 Ebr 10, 109 Congr 53 Mos 1:277 Decal 119 Spec 1:323 Spec 2:141, 245 Spec 3:181 Spec 4:75, 189 Praem 153 Aet 56 Legat 49

ὑπερουράνιος Opif 31

ὑπεροχή Opif 109, 109, 109

ὑπεροψία (10) Cher 35 Mos 1:154 Decal 5, 40 Spec 3:137 Virt 161, 163, 165, 165 Praem 47

ὑπερπέτομαι Sacr 8 Agr 180

ὑπερπηδάω Sacr 58 Aet 147 Legat 218

ὑπέρσεμνος Legat 295

ὑπερτετρακισχίλιοι Prob 75

ὑπερτίθημι (24) Opif 67, 156 Leg 2:7, 14, 14 Sacr 69 Gig 57 Migr 102 Her 125, 221 Somn 2:131 Abr 250 Mos 2:191 Decal 29 Spec 1:114, 243 Spec 2:83, 240 Spec 3:70 Spec 4:195 Aet 56, 125 Flacc 81 Legat 305

ὑπερτιμάω Leg 3:126

ὑπερτρέχω Mut 215

ὑπερτροχάζω Sacr 58

ὑπερφέρω Aet 115

ὑπερφυής (12) Deus 149 Ebr 220 Sobr 23 Migr 114 Her 42 Congr 134 Mut 46 Somn 1:71 Virt 136 Praem 112 Legat 8 Prov 1

ὑπέρχομαι Somn 2:90 Legat 134

ὑπερωκεάνιος Conf 134 Somn 2:130 Legat 10

ὑπερῷον (ὑπερῷος) Legat 358

ὑπερῷος Mos 2:60

ὑπεύθυνος Spec 1:19

ὑπέχω Ebr 111 Conf 120 Mos 2:150 Spec 1:19, 199

ὑπήκοος (127) Opif 72, 75, 148, 165 Leg 3:88 Cher 83, 113 Sacr 9, 44, 59, 68, 112 Det 34 Gig 38, 46 Deus 110, 174 Agr 47, 57 Plant 14, 14, 51, 55, 92 Ebr 84, 131, 195 Sobr 62 Conf 40, 54, 91, 162, 173, 175 Migr 8, 20, 63, 73, 185, 186 Her 205 Congr 18, 176 Fug 69, 69, 98 Somn 2:94, 136, 136, 154 Abr 78, 218, 237, 261 Ios

76, 107, 107, 136, 242 Mos 1:61, 124, 160, 324 Mos 2:5, 235, 277 Decal 38, 66, 165, 166, 167 Spec 1:13, 13, 200 Spec 2:48, 80, 226, 227 Spec 3:139, 177 Spec 4:151, 158, 166, 184, 184, 213, 218 Virt 42, 57, 61, 72, 209, 217 Praem 1, 54, 56, 97, 97 Prob 30, 89, 101, 154 Contempl 9 Aet 1 Flacc 17, 19, 19, 80, 86, 126, 127, 128, 147, 163 Legat 50, 53, 58, 69, 69, 69, 119, 287, 303 Hypoth 7:5, 11:15 Prov 2:17 QG 4:206b

ὑπηρεσία (76) Sacr 63, 98 Det 56, 56, 62, 66, 104 Post 4 Gig 16 Deus 47, 56 Ebr 215 Conf 110, 175 Her 53 Fug 37 Somn 2:30 Abr 109, 143, 158 Ios 45, 166 Mos 1:130 Mos 2:22, 67, 159 Decal 44, 167 Spec 1:83, 113, 123, 135, 158, 217, 255 Spec 2:64, 65, 67, 68, 69, 83, 91, 101, 123, 183 Spec 3:8, 50, 143, 197, 201 Spec 4:98, 195 Virt 55, 88, 122, 123, 145, 188 Praem 119, 139 Prob 23, 32, 36, 140, 142 Contempl 50, 52, 66, 75 Flacc 110, 142, 149 Legat 97 Prov 2:39 QG 1:94 QE isf 9

ὑπηρετέω (56) Cher 115 Det 13, 56, 56 Deus 158 Agr 19 Ebr 35, 64, 102, 107 Sobr 53 Conf 54, 91 Migr 14 Congr 76 Fug 66 Mut 14 Somn 2:123 Abr 45 Ios 34, 158, 166 Mos 1:113, 129, 141, 185, 201, 299, 302 Mos 2:158, 198 Spec 1:9, 151, 174, 204, 276 Spec 2:81, 84, 245 Spec 3:49, 121, 129, 136, 177 Spec 4:17 Virt 55 Prob 7, 33, 34 Contempl 7, 71, 72 Flacc 33, 142 Legat 97 Prov 2:40

ὑπηρέτης (27) Opif 159 Sacr 132, 132, 133 Post 50, 92 Deus 57 Plant 55 Ebr 208, 209, 215, 216 Conf 174 Mut 87 Somn 1:143 Somn 2:21 Ios 241 Decal 119, 119, 178 Spec 1:17, 152, 229 Spec 3:122, 201 Spec 4:163 Prov 2:41

ὑπηρέτις (6) Sacr 44 Gig 12 Congr 143 Mos 2:81 Spec 1:16 QG 2:34a

ὑπηχέω (20) Post 155 Ebr 177 Migr 80, 114 Her 259 Congr 67 Mut 139 Somn 1:164 Somn 2:2, 252 Abr 73, 102 Ios 110 Mos 1:274, 281 Spec 2:80 Praem 50, 55 Prob 123 Legat 245

ὑπισχνέομαι (27) Leg 3:218 Post 148 Plant 93 Ebr 53 Migr 44 Her 90, 290 Congr 119 Mut 166 Abr 110, 111, 132, 273 Ios 219, 227 Mos 1:17, 86, 105, 243, 267, 333 Mos 2:246 Spec 3:101 Flacc 103 Legat 173, 183 Hypoth 7:3

ὕπνος (65) Leg 2:26, 30, 31 Leg 3:183 Cher 62, 92 Sacr 23 Det 172 Deus 39, 97 Ebr 131, 159, 204, 220, 221 Sobr 5 Migr 190, 206, 222 Her 257 Congr 81 Fug 189 Somn 1:1, 80, 121, 165, 189, 196 Somn 2:1, 18, 19, 20, 56, 106, 137, 159, 160, 162, 216, 218 Abr 70, 154, 233 Ios 125, 126, 140, 147, 171 Mos 1:284, 289 Spec 1:98, 219, 298, 298 Spec 2:100, 102, 103 Prob 96 Contempl 26, 45 Flacc 27, 177 Legat 270, 272 QG 1:24

ὑπνόω (6) Leg 2:19, 25, 25, 31 Conf 55 Her 257

ὑπό (975) Opif 2, 9, 11, 41, 41, 54, 71, 77, 84, 85, 99, 99, 99, 102, 108, 109, 110, 114, 117, 127, 128, 128, 131, 141, 153, 156 Leg 1:2, 15, 20, 40, 40, 40, 40, 41, 41, 41, 41, 44, 59, 72, 80, 95, 95, 100 Leg 2:28, 34, 39, 39, 39, 39, 39, 43, 43, 43, 55, 67, 69, 69, 77, 84, 85, 87, 87, 87, 93, 101, 103, 103, 107 Leg 3:7, 23, 33, 36, 40, 45, 45, 46, 51, 54, 57, 58, 72, 73, 80, 91, 102, 102, 104, 109, 109, 120, 123, 127, 127, 127, 137, 150, 151, 156, 164, 173, 177, 180, 181, 187, 199, 213, 213, 221, 232, 235 Cher 2, 2, 9, 75, 79, 121, 125, 125, 125, 126, 127, 128, 128, 129 Sacr 17, 21, 31, 50, 54, 59, 81, 103, 104, 106, 106, 113, 123, 135 Det 20, 34, 47, 48, 53, 55, 68, 77, 99, 131, 142, 145, 145, 164, 164, 164, 165, 173, 173, 173 Post 1, 14, 19, 19, 26, 41, 41, 42, 53, 54, 56, 56, 71, 74, 83, 92, 95, 96, 96, 99, 100, 104, 106, 107, 107, 108, 115, 115, 116, 119, 122, 134, 147, 150, 159, 168, 171, 175, 175, 176, 177, 185 Gig 9, 13, 15, 34, 51 Deus 7, 15, 15, 16, 25, 30, 84, 101, 112, 115, 115, 134, 153, 153, 183 Agr 6, 32, 33, 37, 49, 54, 68, 69, 74, 75, 89, 95, 98, 99, 128, 151, 151, 151, 163, 164, 164, 168 Plant 4, 10, 10, 22, 23, 38, 39, 50, 64, 96, 105, 116, 127, 135, 135, 144, 144, 144, 145, 157, 167, 167 Ebr 14, 58, 62, 63, 79, 81, 81, 88, 93, 95, 122, 123, 130, 131, 133, 137, 146, 146, 147, 167, 168, 177, 183, 195, 195, 207 Sobr 3, 20, 25 Conf 5, 16, 21, 35, 59, 64, 70, 70, 70, 96, 113, 126, 136, 166, 175, 180, 181 Migr 5, 22, 35, 37, 40, 42, 48, 51, 52, 65, 71, 72, 85, 95, 123, 140, 143, 148, 150, 151, 165, 170, 171 Her 38, 46, 46, 53, 56, 70, 81, 105, 106, 109, 109, 109, 166, 167, 203, 219, 220, 220, 227, 228, 228, 229, 244, 259, 274, 286, 295, 297, 297, 302, 305, 306, 309 Congr 78, 94, 95, 114, 114, 138, 140, 141, 164, 177, 178, 179, 179, 180 Fug 1, 12, 39, 42, 47, 54, 57, 68, 69, 75, 118, 119, 122, 139, 153, 156, 161, 207 Mut 7, 16, 19, 24, 24, 24, 24, 66, 87, 89, 91, 118, 126, 133, 140, 143, 148, 150, 151, 156, 162, 198, 203, 206, 214, 217, 243, 255, 264 Somn 1:4, 14, 27, 31, 32, 49, 62, 64, 66, 68, 77, 77, 81, 84, 107, 122, 130, 131, 138, 152, 152, 162, 188, 211, 221, 243, 250 Somn 2:11, 12, 12, 24, 39, 44, 46, 67, 67, 69, 76, 100, 101, 101, 113, 115, 126, 132, 144, 147, 192, 227, 243, 250, 286, 290, 292 Abr 11, 12, 19, 44, 60, 68, 68, 78, 79, 84, 96, 122, 135, 150, 163, 174, 184, 188, 205, 209, 209, 213, 213, 230, 237, 240, 253, 258 Ios 14, 15, 22, 22, 25, 26, 35, 38, 38, 48, 52, 56, 61, 77, 80, 85, 88, 101, 102, 135, 147, 149, 149, 150, 165, 175, 193, 200, 209, 223, 223, 237, 242, 242, 247, 248 Mos 1:2, 12, 22, 33, 37, 39, 48, 50, 64, 69, 73, 80, 91, 95, 100, 115, 119, 124, 125, 135, 143, 175, 176, 178, 181, 183, 189, 196, 197, 227, 245, 246, 249, 255, 262, 268, 270, 272, 273, 278, 301 Mos 2:9, 64, 67, 67, 98, 103, 116, 122, 179, 184, 191, 191, 196, 196, 199, 209, 236, 245, 249, 250, 255, 262, 279, 280, 287, 287, 288 Decal 31, 35, 49, 56, 64, 70, 78, 101, 104, 117, 120, 170, 171 Spec 1:10, 30, 30, 33, 35, 42, 46, 55, 68, 86, 94, 106, 120, 127, 147, 148, 160, 160, 166, 192, 214, 217, 217, 235, 267, 290, 292, 293, 306, 332, 344 Spec 2:3, 8, 16, 18, 24, 34, 34, 36, 50, 85, 97, 125, 129, 146, 183, 191, 191, 200, 217, 220, 232, 232, 233, 253 Spec 3:8, 27, 31, 32, 33, 43, 46, 49, 54, 81, 88, 104, 114, 120, 137, 138, 166, 173, 174, 175, 194 Spec 4:6, 8, 10, 31, 34, 40, 79, 85, 93, 103, 129, 140, 149, 168, 184, 193, 212, 212, 215, 224 Virt 2, 5, 6, 14, 23, 41, 46, 51, 63, 68, 69, 77, 88, 127, 128, 130, 135, 206, 208, 223 Praem 5, 12, 19, 29, 32, 40, 40, 42, 54, 58, 73, 76, 84, 103, 106, 107, 124, 128, 146, 153, 170, 172 Prob 11, 26, 31, 34, 37, 46, 46, 53, 63, 71, 81, 87, 89, 93, 104, 105, 106, 110, 114, 118, 121, 121, 123, 137, 141, 159, 159 Contempl 5, 12, 18, 19, 35, 44, 51, 51, 61, 63, 66, 70, 75, 90 Aet 13, 13, 17, 20, 21, 22, 23, 24, 24, 30, 30, 33, 38, 49, 74, 76, 80, 84, 85, 88, 93, 93, 98, 106, 106, 106, 106, 106, 117, 125, 128, 128, 129, 129, 136, 136, 137, 144, 144 Flacc 13, 22, 29, 40, 48, 63, 65, 66, 71, 78, 87, 92, 92, 101, 109, 111, 114, 115, 115, 118, 123, 127, 127, 136, 143, 147, 163, 172 Legat 1, 20, 25, 31, 36, 41, 41, 50, 56, 68, 70, 106, 107, 114, 115, 121, 125, 132, 155, 163, 173, 189, 193, 197, 206, 206, 215, 216, 218, 222, 223, 237, 243, 243, 266, 267, 268, 269, 297, 297, 314, 320, 345, 366 Hypoth 6:4, 6:9, 7:5, 7:14, 11:3, 11:3, 11:13 Prov 2:8, 12, 14, 18, 19, 24, 24, 24, 26, 31, 31, 32, 33, 34, 37, 43, 49, 58, 58, 64, 72 QG 1:20, 58, 58,

73, 2:22, 62, 3:7, 23, 23, 4:8b, 33a, 33b, 64, 88, 144, 191b, 191d, 9*, 202a QG isf 2 QE 1:7a, 2:3a, 14, 21, 45a, 55b, 118 QE isf 1, 3, 14

ὑποβαίνω Spec 2:175

ὑποβάλλω (48) Leg 3:113, 224 Cher 2, 78, 101 Sacr 71, 114, 127 Det 47, 172 Post 61 Gig 30 Deus 50, 115 Agr 71, 102, 167 Sobr 5, 33, 65 Conf 107, 161 Migr 73, 180 Mut 58 Somn 1:29, 169 Somn 2:3, 94 Ios 110 Mos 1:60, 201, 277, 283 Decal 3 Spec 1:65 Spec 2:34 Spec 4:49, 158 Virt 122 Contempl 4 Aet 74 Legat 125, 190, 227, 259 Prov 1 QE 2:17

ὑποβλέπω (13) Somn 2:168 Abr 126 Ios 170 Mos 2:9 Spec 1:143 Spec 3:136 Spec 4:43 Virt 197 Flacc 180 Legat 33, 115, 186, 262

ὑποβολεύς Migr 80, 80 Mut 85 Mos 2:37 Praem 50

ὑποβολή Mut 270

ὑποβολιμαῖος Plant 71 Mut 147 Mos 1:19

ὑποβρέχω Post 176

ὑποβρύχιος Det 152 Virt 14

ὑπογάμιον Spec 3:72

ὑπογάστριος (6) Opif 158 Agr 38 Somn 2:147 Mos 1:28 Mos 2:23 Spec 2:163

ὑπογραφή Mos 1:69 Prov 2:31

ὑπογράφω (29) Opif 67 Leg 1:21, 56, 63 Leg 2:6, 24 Leg 3:62 Sacr 21 Gig 23, 66 Deus 70, 95 Conf 67, 166, 190 Fug 153 Somn 1:206 Ios 92 Spec 1:65 Spec 3:37 Spec 4:106, 158 Contempl 50 Aet 8 Flacc 124 Legat 55, 348 QG 2:65 QE 2:2

ὑπόγυιος Det 134

ὑπόγυος (ὑπόγυιος) Mos 2:226

ὑπόδειγμα Post 122 Conf 64 Her 256 Somn 2:3

ὑποδείκνυμι Mut 69

ὑποδέχομαι (22) Opif 14 Leg 3:194 Cher 99 Ebr 211 Conf 78 Fug 50 Somn 1:42 Somn 2:184 Abr 101, 101, 209 Mos 1:35 Spec 1:217 Spec 3:130 Virt 105, 109, 145, 216, 218 Aet 69 Flacc 187 QG 1:27

ὑποδέω Legat 99

ὑπόδημα Leg 3:24 Sacr 63 Ebr 105

ὑποδιακονικός Mos 1:84

ὑποδιάκονος (9) Abr 115 Ios 123 Decal 178 Spec 1:17, 31, 66, 116, 204 Spec 3:201

ὑπόδικος (9) Ebr 194 Spec 2:249 Spec 3:121, 142, 145 Spec 4:2, 25, 37 Virt 197

ὑποδοχή (10) Plant 33 Mut 107, 138 Abr 108 Ios 202 Mos 1:275 Spec 3:147 Virt 105, 107 QE 2:4

ὑπόδρομος (15) Opif 63 Sacr 90 Post 156 Deus 98, 156 Plant 152 Her 305 Somn 1:124 Mos 2:251 Spec 1:69, 335 Spec 4:50, 154 Flacc 159 Legat 15

ὑποδύτης Migr 103 Mos 2:109, 110

ὑποδύω (14) Leg 3:182 Gig 17 Agr 66 Spec 1:102, 315 Spec 3:156 Spec 4:43, 52 Virt 122, 196, 226 Flacc 126 QG 4:206b QE isf 7

ὑποεπιμερής Decal 20

ὑποζεύγνυμι (8) Leg 1:73, 73 Leg 3:193 Sacr 49 Post 14 Somn 2:83 Spec 1:14 Praem 124

ὑποζύγιον (22) Opif 88 Cher 35 Agr 102 Somn 2:91, 91 Abr 234 Ios 179, 217, 251 Mos 1:133, 141, 169, 203, 269 Mos 2:21 Spec 3:47 Virt 88, 96, 116, 117 Prob 32 Flacc 92

ὑποζώννυμι Flacc 113

ὑποθάλπω Migr 123

ὑπόθεσις (24) Det 81 Post 2 Deus 28 Agr 56 Conf 163 Congr 11, 11 Fug 191 Somn 2:29, 81 Abr 184 Mos 1:3, 69 Decal 29 Spec 4:171, 172 Praem 2 Legat 3, 181, 186, 195, 350, 352, 370

ὑποθετικός Hypoth 0:1

ὑποθήκη Somn 2:73 Spec 1:299 Spec 3:29 Virt 70

ὑποικουρέω (8) Ios 6, 11, 234 Mos 1:280 Decal 129 Virt 31 Legat 329 Prov 2:42

ὑποκαίω Mos 1:127

ὑποκακόηθης Legat 169

ὑποκατακλίνω Decal 64

ὑποκάτω Sobr 8

ὑπόκειμαι (45) Opif 149 Leg 1:25, 29, 30, 37 Leg 2:24, 36, 72, 76 Leg 3:56, 60, 61, 61, 64 Gig 16 Plant 150, 150, 153, 154 Ebr 191, 199 Sobr 47 Conf 106, 148 Her 14, 23, 72, 116, 119 Congr 143 Mut 56 Somn 1:172 Somn 2:254 Abr 119, 131 Ios 39, 126 Decal 82, 147 Spec 1:61 Aet 49, 50, 51 QG 1:1, 92

ὑποκείρω Agr 174

ὑποκνίζω Mos 1:297

ὑποκράνιον (κράνιον) QG (Par) 2:3

ὑποκρίνω Conf 48

ὑπόκρισις (16) Deus 103 Migr 211 Her 43 Fug 34, 156 Somn 1:205 Somn 2:40 Ios 67, 68 Spec 4:183 Prob 90, 99 Legat 22, 162 Hypoth 11:15 QG 4:69

ὑποκριτής Prob 141 QG 4:69 QE isf 26

ὑποκριτικός Leg 2:75

ὑπολαμβάνω (201) Opif 45, 59, 131, 171 Leg 1:6, 20, 43 Leg 2:68 Leg 3:74 Cher 57, 65, 66, 127 Sacr 46, 57 Det 4, 161, 173 Post 136, 158, 164, 177, 177 Gig 7, 16 Deus 22, 52, 73, 127 Agr 22, 28, 56 Plant 33, 37, 51, 91 Ebr 5, 9, 43, 119, 132, 141, 199 Conf 76, 82, 134 Migr 45, 87, 89, 92, 194 Her 28, 82, 97, 246, 300 Congr 127, 152, 152, 159, 171 Fug 38, 155 Mut 51, 70, 74, 94, 172, 217 Somn 1:9, 39, 91, 94, 157, 183, 232 Somn 2:17, 21, 134, 136, 193, 194, 228, 298, 301 Abr 6, 9, 25, 60, 69, 69, 86, 88, 115, 143, 178, 205, 215, 224 Ios 80, 107, 162, 179 Mos 1:32, 45, 119, 122, 153, 241, 310, 315, 328 Mos 2:3, 50, 51, 171, 202, 204, 244, 260 Decal 58, 59, 80, 121, 177 Spec 1:13, 33, 47, 62, 100, 264, 279, 290 Spec 2:46, 51, 120, 132, 154, 173, 197, 201, 252 Spec 3:27, 69, 72, 84, 113, 124, 178 Spec 4:6, 96, 103, 121, 126, 157, 172 Virt 34, 60, 79, 126, 143, 150, 172, 174, 179, 198, 212 Praem 54, 78, 88, 112 Prob 22, 57, 115, 132, 150 Contempl 46, 69 Aet 66, 73, 113 Flacc 29, 108 Legat 29, 65, 74, 120, 164, 198, 210, 267, 345, 368 Hypoth 11:7, 11:12 Prov 2:28 QG 1:70:1, 4:180, 191d QG isf 6 QE 2:24b

ὑπολείπω (63) Opif 64, 64, 158 Leg 3:186 Sacr 43, 46, 109, 139 Det 154 Deus 67, 130, 178 Agr 17 Ebr 25 Conf 115, 186, 186 Migr 17, 83 Her 253 Somn 2:212 Abr 45, 56, 141, 145 Ios 93, 119, 182 Mos 1:121, 179, 186, 330, 331 Mos 2:55, 60, 65, 85, 157, 259, 262, 283 Spec 1:256, 262 Spec 2:206 Spec 3:16, 99 Virt 90, 90 Praem 128, 129, 133, 172 Aet 25, 26, 74, 87, 89, 90, 99 Flacc 53, 65 Legat 131 Prov 2:35

ὑπόληψις (22) Sacr 77, 84 Migr 90, 95 Mut 54, 65, 153 Somn 1:68 Somn 2:106 Abr 116 Mos 1:161 Decal 67 Spec 1:330, 331 Spec 2:235, 260 Virt 216 Legat 77, 262 QG 1:69 QE 2:45a, 107

ὑπόλοιπος Mos 1:305 Virt 143

ὑπομαραίνομαι Spec 1:268

ὑπομειδιάω Abr 151 Flacc 98 Legat 42

ὑπομενετέος Leg 1:65, 68, 68 Spec 4:145

ὑπομένω (177) Opif 169 Leg 2:41, 83, 104 Leg 3:13, 33, 199 Cher 2, 2, 29, 110 Sacr 10, 40, 46, 69, 84, 90 Det 178, 178 Post 9, 22, 49, 87 Deus 8, 65, 66, 98, 115, 130, 170 Agr 75, 173 Ebr 45, 158, 192 Conf 37, 38 Migr 58 Her 269 Congr 72 Fug 84 Mut 153 Somn 1:46, 47, 173 Somn 2:84, 202 Abr 115, 116, 136, 182, 193, 197 Ios 27, 36, 40, 52, 69, 86, 94, 104, 141, 167, 191, 226, 228, 248 Mos 1:72, 90, 102, 106, 125, 146, 164, 182, 199, 222, 224, 237, 247, 281, 297 Mos 2:53, 163, 184, 206 Decal 41, 42, 86 Spec 1:26, 68, 68, 246, 313 Spec 2:60, 68, 69, 87, 88, 91, 95, 207, 218, 222 Spec 3:39, 54, 82, 84, 90, 98, 146, 164, 182, 182, 197 Spec 4:3, 23, 112, 124, 200, 216 Virt 111, 122, 135, 199, 210 Praem 70, 106, 157, 162 Prob 6, 24, 27, 36, 45, 89, 114, 120, 122, 146 Contempl 19, 42, 43 Aet 20, 22, 23, 129 Flacc 53, 77, 104, 114, 116, 117, 132, 166, 175 Legat 31, 69, 127, 192, 209, 234, 307, 308, 355, 369, 372 Hypoth 6:9, 11:4 QG 1:77, 3:29, 52, 4:52d, 52d, 169 QE 2:11a, 25b

ὑπόμεστος Ios 180

ὑπομιμνήσκω (32) Leg 3:17 Sacr 31 Plant 108 Ebr 1, 154, 169, 208 Conf 3 Her 141, 221 Congr 41, 42 Fug 93 Somn 1:93 Somn 2:261 Abr 229, 247 Ios 92, 98 Mos 1:193 Mos 2:139 Spec 1:193, 264 Spec 2:21, 68, 131, 152, 237 Spec 3:128 Virt 22 Praem 119 Contempl 35

ὑπόμνημα (13) Her 176 Fug 4 Somn 2:268 Abr 5 Mos 1:317 Mos 2:48 Spec 1:150 Spec 2:146, 160 Spec 4:162 Virt 20 Legat 347 QG 2:13b

ὑπομνηματίζομαι Flacc 131

ὑπομνηματικός Legat 165

ὑπόμνησις (22) Leg 3:16 Post 153 Agr 142 Congr 40 Somn 1:214 Ios 27, 112, 189 Mos 2:107 Spec 1:215, 222 Spec 2:146, 158, 188, 203, 207, 256 Spec 4:136 Virt 89, 163 Contempl 78 Flacc 153

ὑπομονή (20) Cher 78 Sacr 4 Det 30, 45, 51 Deus 13 Plant 169, 170 Migr 144, 208, 210 Congr 37 Fug 38, 194 Mut 197 Somn 1:46 Ios 52 Prob 26 QG 4:97:1, 97:2

ὑπομονητικός Leg 3:88

ὑπονοέω (27) Opif 17, 130 Leg 3:148 Deus 104 Congr 44, 180 Mut 15, 64 Mos 2:151 Decal 84 Spec 1:235 Spec 3:53 Aet 15, 32, 43, 46, 46, 53, 54, 72, 73, 82, 84 Legat 133 QG 1:74, 93 QE 2:16

ὑπόνοια (41) Opif 157 Cher 21 Det 155, 167 Agr 28, 97, 131 Plant 113 Migr 92 Her 289 Congr 172 Fug 75, 108, 174, 181 Mut 62 Somn 1:15, 77, 120 Somn 2:246 Abr 88, 119 Ios 28, 193, 210, 261, 262 Mos 2:99 Spec 2:257 Spec 3:52, 53, 55, 117 Spec 4:36 Praem 65 Contempl 28, 78 Flacc 12 Legat 35, 38, 337

ὑπόνομος Mos 1:211 Spec 3:147

ὑπονοστέω (8) Sacr 79 Mos 2:63, 63 Spec 4:112 Aet 118 Legat 6 QE 1:7b, 2:40

ὑπονόστησις QG 4:100

ὑποπαραιτέομαι Virt 25

ὑποπαχύνομαι Virt 130

ὑποπερκάζω Ios 91 Mos 1:230

ὑποπίμπλημι (7) Cher 64 Her 71 Abr 223 Virt 67, 162 Praem 74 Hypoth 11:16

ὑποπίπτω Opif 62 Leg 1:86 Leg 3:202 Decal 174

ὑπόπλεος (7) Ebr 128 Mos 1:182 Mos 2:197 Spec 2:54 Spec 3:126 Virt 5, 172

ὑποπόδιον Conf 98

ὑπόποκος Opif 85

ὑπόπτερος Plant 152 Fug 100 Spec 2:45 Spec 3:5

ὑποπτεύω Mos 1:305 Flacc 94, 183

ὑποπτήσσω Somn 2:266 Mos 1:272 Praem 86

ὕποπτος (9) Sacr 32 Mos 1:94 Mos 2:34 Spec 3:102 Flacc 93, 108, 177 Legat 117 Prov 2:26

ὑπόπτωσις Leg 3:201 Cher 79

ὑπόπυος Mos 1:127 Praem 143

ὑπόρειος Aet 64

ὑπορρέω Sacr 79 Spec 3:101 Spec 4:160, 188 Legat 6

ὑπορρίπτω Cher 81 Ebr 122

ὑποσημαίνω (8) Conf 11 Ios 9, 100, 150, 211 Decal 159 Spec 2:101 Contempl 66

ὑποσιωπάω Mos 2:279 Prov 2:56

ὑποσκελίζω (16) Opif 103, 158 Agr 76 Ebr 156 Fug 30 Mut 55 Somn 1:11, 131 Somn 2:134, 146 Abr 269 Ios 122 Mos 1:50, 325 Spec 1:341 Spec 2:240

ὑποσπανίζομαι Ios 163, 225 Mos 1:164 Aet 149

ὑποσπείρω Abr 83 Spec 2:80 Legat 172

ὑπόσπονδος Flacc 61

ὑπόστασις Somn 1:188 Aet 88, 92

ὑποστέλλω (27) Opif 123 Leg 3:41 Sacr 35 Migr 174 Her 42 Fug 172 Ios 68, 95, 125 Mos 1:83 Decal 157 Spec 1:5 Spec 2:207 Spec 4:1, 77, 132, 132 Praem 54, 162 Contempl 30 Flacc 50, 112 Legat 71, 95, 152, 193 Prov 2:9

ὑποστρέφω (14) Opif 101 Cher 3, 6 Her 255 Fug 207 Somn 1:150, 180 Ios 218 Mos 1:164, 167, 274, 277 Spec 1:163 Spec 2:251

ὑποστροφή Gig 35

ὑποσυγχέω Agr 1, 130 Congr 135 Legat 2

ὑποσύγχυτος Sacr 85 Migr 24

ὑποσυλλέγω Spec 1:5

ὑποσύρω (14) Opif 113 Ios 141 Mos 1:176 Mos 2:281, 286 Spec 2:143 Spec 3:149, 152 Spec 4:85 Praem 124, 152 Contempl 86 Legat 372 QE 2:40

ὑπόσχεσις (26) Opif 99 Leg 3:85, 203 Sacr 26 Gig 39 Deus 149 Agr 2 Migr 43 Her 96, 96, 101 Congr 44, 134 Mut 54, 154 Somn 1:175, 181 Ios 267 Mos 1:193 Mos 2:192 Spec 1:236, 267, 318 Spec 2:150 Flacc 100, 140

ὑποταίνιος Somn 1:175 Mos 2:35 Flacc 45

ὑποτάσσω (9) Opif 84 Leg 3:26, 26 Agr 47 Decal 168, 171 Legat 51, 314 QG 3:30a

ὑποτελέω Abr 240 Contempl 59

ὑποτέμνω (9) Opif 9 Agr 10, 86 Somn 1:105 Mos 1:46 Virt 8 Praem 156, 172 QG 1:51

ὑποτίθημι (13) Leg 1:80, 82 Post 12 Conf 144 Migr 221 Congr 85 Fug 188 Mos 1:294 Mos 2:51 Spec 3:184 Hypoth 6:6 QG 4:8b QE 2:6a

ὑποτίμησις Spec 3:157 Hypoth 7:1

ὑποτοπάζω Ebr 147 Her 281 Contempl 57

ὑποτοπέω (18) Cher 25 Sacr 134 Deus 21 Ebr 183, 205 Conf 162 Migr 179, 182 Somn 1:118, 182 Ios 181, 184 Mos 1:66 Mos 2:234 Decal 109 Spec 1:16 Prob 3 Contempl 41

ὑποτρέχω Conf 70 Spec 2:140

ὑπότρομος Flacc 176

ὑποτροπιάζω Migr 150 Flacc 153, 182

ὑποτυπόω Mut 70 Somn 2:17

ὑποτύπωσις Abr 71

ὑποτυφόομαι Somn 2:46

ὑποτύφω (9) Cher 17 Her 37, 308 Ios 168, 235 Spec 2:47 Spec 3:37 Legat 141, 261

ὕπουλος Fug 79 Spec 4:43 Prob 91 Hypoth 11:16

ὑπουργέω Mos 2:138 Contempl 72

ὑπουργία Mos 2:144 Prob 33 Contempl 72

ὑπουργός Opif 159 Mos 1:38

ὑποφαίνω Ios 106 Mos 2:139 Decal 1 Flacc 4

ὑποφέρω Det 107 Mos 2:282 Spec 4:112 Legat 270, 272

ὑποφεύγω Spec 4:81

ὑποφήτης Plant 127 Mut 18 Somn 1:190

ὑποφυσάω Plant 65

ὑποχείριος Conf 162 Congr 155

ὑποχέω Ios 58

ὕποχος Det 97 Sobr 49 Conf 160

ὑπόχρυσος Congr 159

ὑποχωλαίνω Mut 187

ὑποχωρέω Opif 33 Ebr 86 Somn 2:93 Abr 22

ὑποψία Ios 17 Virt 53 Legat 24, 32

ὕπτιος Agr 34, 75, 113

ὑπώρεια Post 49 Legat 20 QG 4:80

ὑπωρόφιος Prov 2:64

ὕσσωπος Spec 1:262, 268 Contempl 37, 73, 81

ὑστεραῖος (14) Ios 207 Mos 1:30, 200, 204, 268, 276 Mos 2:179, 260 Spec 1:222 Contempl 46 Flacc 141 Legat 158, 269, 305

ὑστερέω (9) Leg 2:100 Agr 50, 52, 85 Her 191 Mut 115 Ios 182 Mos 2:233 Prov 2:44

ὑστερίζω (37) Opif 88 Leg 2:100, 101 Sacr 58, 115 Agr 122, 123, 123 Plant 33, 80 Ebr 164, 167 Sobr 22 Conf 141, 162 Congr 35 Fug 51 Somn 1:131, 184 Ios 147, 190 Mos 1:315, 329 Decal 135 Spec 1:113 Spec 2:36 Spec 4:81 Virt 30, 225 Praem 56, 106 Prob 71 Contempl 76 Aet 74 QG 2:72 QE 2:26, 26

ὕστερος (131) Opif 26, 45, 65, 68, 77, 83, 87, 113, 148 Leg 1:53, 55 Leg 2:6, 13 Cher 89 Det 10, 84 Post 24 Deus 54, 105 Agr 17, 21, 138, 150 Plant 132 Ebr 15, 48 Sobr 22, 22 Conf 149 Her 172 Congr 22, 88, 110, 139 Fug 55, 73, 99, 99, 132 Mut 78, 179 Somn 1:126 Somn 2:7, 166, 197, 296 Abr 47, 67, 81, 82, 133, 184, 195, 245, 254 Ios 8, 127, 196, 261 Mos 1:59, 79, 133, 169, 240, 242, 242, 255, 258 Mos 2:29, 50, 55, 63, 69, 70, 186, 186, 262, 275, 283, 288 Decal 11 Spec 1:80, 258 Spec 2:95, 119, 157, 158, 205, 215 Spec 3:35, 44, 85, 102, 107, 142, 162 Spec 4:10, 52, 112 Virt 179, 222 Praem 9, 102, 125 Contempl 44 Aet 7, 120, 125, 128 Flacc 9, 27, 54, 130, 140, 168 Legat 31, 59, 63, 87, 206, 206, 261, 271, 286, 307 QG 2:54a, 4:88 QE 2:21, 49b QE isf 22, 26

ὕστριξ Prov 2:61

ὑστριχίς Spec 2:94

ὕφαιμος Abr 152 Spec 3:193 Legat 186

ὑφαίνω Somn 2:53 Spec 4:203

ὑφαίρεσις Congr 32 Fug 186 Spec 4:38 Legat 117

ὑφαιρέω (22) Opif 110, 110 Det 112, 114 Her 157 Ios 197, 216 Mos 1:233 Decal 135, 137 Spec 1:127 Spec 4:6, 7, 11, 12, 13, 33, 118 Virt 21 Aet 42 Flacc 79 Hypoth 7:6

ὕφαλμος Contempl 62

ὑφάντης Somn 1:203 Spec 1:33

ὑφαντός Prov 2:13

ὑφαρπάζω QG 4:202a

ὕφασμα (16) Ebr 101 Somn 1:203, 220 Mos 2:84, 85, 88, 93, 101, 109, 143 Spec 1:86, 88, 95 Spec 3:174 Prov 2:15, 17

ὕφεσις Leg 3:183 Sacr 122 QG 1:24

ὑφή Mos 2:84

ὑφηγέομαι (42) Opif 65 Leg 3:144 Sacr 76 Det 86 Post 148 Gig 54 Deus 138 Agr 59, 87 Plant 85 Migr 15, 42, 196 Congr 127 Fug 5, 38, 48 Mut 104, 106, 125 Somn 1:68, 91, 191 Somn 2:252 Mos 1:297 Mos 2:11, 51, 60, 143, 215, 273 Decal 39, 58 Spec 2:62, 236 Spec 3:29 Virt 45 Praem 7, 49 Contempl 74 Aet 2 Legat 31

ὑφήγησις (47) Sacr 7, 7, 79 Post 130, 140, 141 Deus 182 Agr 9 Plant 139 Ebr 95, 120, 132 Sobr 23, 38 Conf 55, 59, 148 Migr 151 Her 67, 102 Congr 134 Mut 204 Somn 1:120 Ios 117 Mos 1:3, 21 Spec 1:45 Spec 2:18, 64, 163, 163, 256 Spec 3:125 Spec 4:140, 218 Virt 15, 80, 141, 142, 161, 178, 183 Praem 4 Prob 160 Contempl 64 Legat 157 QG 2:54a

ὑφηγητής (36) Opif 149 Leg 3:102 Sacr 51 Det 6, 68 Post 16, 38, 152 Her 19 Congr 114 Fug 169, 200 Mut 217, 256 Somn 1:173 Somn 2:187 Mos 2:153 Decal 123 Spec 1:41, 41 Spec 2:96, 227, 228, 234 Spec 3:39, 182 Spec 4:140 Prob 36 Aet 16 Flacc 3, 124 Legat 5, 115, 319 QG 1:21 QE isf 25

ὑφίημι (6) Leg 2:28 Leg 3:183 Post 46 Deus 26 Flacc 9 QG 2:64a

ὑφίστημι (42) Leg 2:42, 96 Leg 3:73, 146, 240 Cher 114 Sacr 45, 67, 76, 113 Det 160, 160 Post 163 Deus 32, 66, 172, 177 Agr 91 Plant 114 Ebr 32 Conf 74, 103, 170, 190 Her 29 Somn 1:184 Mos 1:112, 222 Decal 31, 68, 92 Spec 1:26 Spec 2:11 Spec 4:215 Praem 137 Prob 118 Aet 31, 53, 53, 55, 87 Legat 81

ὑφοράω (ὑπειδόμην) Mos 1:46 Flacc 18

ὕφορμος Sacr 90 Spec 4:154 Flacc 27

ὕφος Mos 2:109

ὑψαυχενέω (10) Leg 3:18 Cher 35, 66 Agr 106 Congr 127 Fug 44 Mut 154 Decal 41 Spec 4:120 Prov 2:14

ὑψαύχην Agr 73

ὑψηγορέω Cher 29 Ebr 58

ὑψηγορία Det 79

ὑψήγορος Her 4

ὑψηλός (29) Leg 3:18, 82, 82 Det 152 Post 110, 146 Deus 167, 180 Agr 169 Plant 52 Ebr 128 Migr 216, 223 Abr 41, 43, 169 Mos 1:31, 104, 228, 278 Mos 2:70 Spec 1:73 Spec 2:21 Spec 4:74 Virt 165, 201 Aet 119, 140 QE 2:24b

ὑψηλοτάπεινος Ios 142

ὕψιστος (13) Leg 3:24, 82, 82, 82 Post 89 Plant 59 Ebr 105 Congr 58 Mut 202 Flacc 46 Legat 157, 278, 317

ὑψόθεν Somn 1:154

ὕψος (57) Opif 41 Leg 3:19 Cher 81 Post 136 Agr 10 Plant 24, 145, 152 Sobr 64 Conf 4, 18, 95, 113 Migr 184 Fug 194 Mut 67 Somn 1:115, 131, 150 Somn 2:245, 284 Abr 42, 199 Ios 102, 149 Mos 1:93, 115, 177, 192, 217, 218, 259, 290 Mos 2:60, 90, 90, 96, 285 Decal 44 Spec 1:293, 300 Spec 4:88, 128 Virt 71 Prob 121, 128 Contempl 3 Aet 64, 118, 119, 135, 147 Prov 2:27 QG 2:29, 3:29, 4:100 QE 2:45b

ὑψόω Leg 3:90 Sacr 55 Prov 2:68 QG 2:30

ὕψωμα Praem 2

ὕω (20) Leg 1:25, 29, 29, 34 Leg 3:162 Post 32 Deus 155 Migr 32 Her 76 Fug 137, 180 Mut 259, 259 Abr 138 Mos 1:205, 207 Mos 2:104, 266 Decal 16 Spec 2:199

φαγεῖν (ἐσθίω) (51) Leg 1:90, 90, 90, 97, 97, 98, 98, 100, 100, 101, 101, 101, 101, 105, 105 Leg 3:56, 59, 59, 60, 60, 65, 142, 157, 161, 169, 173, 222, 222, 222, 246, 246, 247, 251, 251 Sacr 24, 55, 79 Det 157 Plant 95, 132 Migr 64 Her 239, 251, 252, 253 Fug 139 Mut 120, 165, 174 Somn 2:157 QG 2:59

φαέθω Her 224

φαιδρός (9) Cher 37 Plant 162 Mos 2:225 Spec 1:77 Virt 67 Contempl 66 Flacc 167 Legat 12, 180

φαιδρύνω (16) Det 20 Deus 8 Agr 171 Fug 153 Mut 124, 229 Somn 1:148 Somn 2:25, 133 Ios 105 Spec 1:191, 269, 269 Aet 2 Legat 235, 317

φαίνω (139) Opif 45, 84, 136, 141, 154, 154, 166 Leg 1:82 Leg 3:17, 35, 71, 170, 218 Cher 22, 28, 55, 59 Sacr 29, 84 Det 16, 141, 159, 170, 173 Post 47, 125 Gig 1 Deus 42, 44, 74, 125, 128, 148, 149, 153 Agr 42, 49, 134, 168 Plant 39, 44 Ebr 56, 63, 166, 169, 170, 180, 205 Sobr 21 Conf 10, 168, 172, 183 Migr 86, 95, 105, 105, 140, 179, 179, 183 Her 81, 224, 270, 286 Congr 8, 35, 80 Fug 129 Mut 17, 18, 31, 42, 106, 113 Somn 1:2, 19, 41, 72, 92, 197, 204, 204, 213 Somn 2:3, 110, 206, 262 Abr 71, 75, 87, 161, 162, 205 Ios 9, 22, 72, 94, 104, 126 Mos 1:175, 256, 274, 327 Mos 2:2, 287 Spec 1:42, 72 Spec 2:217 Spec 4:154 Praem 42, 92, 111, 114, 143 Prob 108 Contempl 50 Aet 101, 130, 142 Flacc 66, 96, 120, 130, 165, 167 Legat 176, 298 Hypoth 6:4, 6:8, 7:8 Prov 2:65 QG 1:55c, 55c, 3:3, 18, 4:30 QE 2:47, 47

φαλαγγηδόν Migr 62

φαλάγγιον Somn 2:88, 89

φάλαγξ Agr 87, 151 Mos 2:251 Virt 43

φανερός (64) Opif 43, 118, 139 Leg 2:13 Leg 3:43 Cher 16, 16, 38 Gig 66 Plant 20 Ebr 58, 183 Sobr 31 Conf 14, 119 Migr 89 Her 82, 291 Congr 152 Fug 24, 160 Mut 65 Somn 1:6, 224 Abr 131, 133, 140, 147, 200 Mos 1:90, 198 Decal 130, 171 Spec 1:56, 127, 200 Spec 3:80, 87, 158, 178 Spec 4:2, 30, 185 Virt 141 Praem 31, 86 Contempl 78 Flacc 24, 32, 40 Legat 2, 66, 122, 146, 263, 317, 350 Prov 2:33, 35 QG 1:21, 2:11, 4:99 QG isf 2 QE 2:38a

φανερότης Prov 2:31

φανερόω Leg 3:47

φανός Spec 1:219

Φανουήλ Conf 129, 130

φαντάζω Ios 141 Spec 1:26

φαντασία (135) Opif 57, 150, 166 Leg 1:30, 30, 30 Leg 2:23, 56 Leg 3:16, 60, 61 Cher 13, 69 Sacr 35, 59, 69, 85 Det 30, 47, 97, 162 Post 1, 8, 47, 56, 159 Gig 20 Deus 41, 43, 55 Plant 36 Ebr 65, 169, 170, 179, 181, 183, 196, 200 Conf 100, 105, 106, 138 Migr 5, 19, 190, 222 Her 108, 119, 132 Mut 3, 15, 16, 223, 257 Somn 1:1, 4, 4, 70, 133, 136, 188, 192 Somn 2:3, 4, 6, 20, 105, 113, 137, 157 Abr 26, 71, 79, 113, 118, 119, 122, 124, 131, 146, 188, 193, 199 Ios 7, 92, 94, 100, 102, 103, 107, 125, 126, 126, 171, 179 Mos 1:78, 213, 230, 268, 289 Mos 2:123, 236, 252, 261 Decal 3, 143 Spec 1:38, 40, 45, 61, 219 Spec 2:89 Spec 3:100 Spec 4:70, 141 Virt 38, 215 Praem 18, 36, 58, 89, 114, 151

Prob 15 Flacc 124, 162, 167 Legat 111, 181 Prov 2:9 QG 1:55c, 3:29 QE 2:45a, 47

φαντασιάζομαι Migr 183

φαντασιόω (33) Leg 1:62 Leg 3:60, 108 Sacr 4 Det 158 Gig 9 Her 71, 110, 301 Mut 7, 17 Somn 1:144, 150, 159, 189, 232, 240 Somn 2:156, 158, 195, 261 Decal 105 Spec 1:334 Spec 4:139 Praem 41, 46, 62, 63, 84 Contempl 26 Legat 85 QG 4:30 QE isf 5

φάντασμα Fug 129, 143 Somn 2:162

φαραγγώδης Conf 26

φάραγξ (6) Agr 101 Conf 26, 26 Mos 2:63, 255 Spec 4:79

Φαραώ (48) Leg 1:40 Leg 3:12, 12, 13, 14, 236, 236, 243 Sacr 9, 48, 69 Det 95, 161, 161 Ebr 208, 210, 210, 210 Migr 84, 159, 160, 160, 162, 162 Her 20, 59, 60 Fug 124, 147 Mut 19, 19, 20, 125, 171, 207 Somn 1:77 Somn 2:5, 159, 159, 183, 184, 189, 195, 200, 211, 215, 277, 279

φαρμακεία Spec 3:94, 98

φαρμακεύς Det 38

φαρμακευτής (6) Migr 83, 85 Spec 3:93, 94, 102, 104

φαρμακεύω Det 38

φαρμακίς Spec 3:94

φάρμακον (30) Leg 3:129, 226 Sacr 70 Det 110 Agr 98 Plant 147, 147 Ebr 27, 128, 172, 184 Migr 124 Congr 53 Somn 1:112 Somn 2:249, 295 Spec 1:343 Spec 3:95, 161 Spec 4:86, 191 Virt 11 Praem 145, 170 Contempl 74 Legat 106 Prov 2:60, 71 QG 2:41, 4:76b

φαρμάσσω Leg 3:62

Φάρος Mos 2:35, 41 Flacc 27, 110

φάρυγξ Opif 159 Migr 188 Somn 1:36 Spec 4:107 Contempl 55

φάσγανον Ios 78

Φασέκ Leg 3:94

φάσις Aet 143 Prov 2:24

φάσκω (132) Opif 9, 67 Leg 1:61 Leg 2:27, 40 Leg 3:207, 237 Cher 33, 54, 69, 127 Sacr 66, 67, 133 Det 25, 33, 38, 46, 61, 62 Post 38, 42, 64, 128 Gig 23, 29 Deus 145, 170 Agr 64, 128 Plant 1, 39, 69, 70, 102, 112, 166 Ebr 18, 19, 47, 67, 105 Sobr 56 Conf 2, 7, 145, 147 Migr 130, 140 Her 2, 24, 71, 81, 100, 206, 207, 246, 263, 266 Congr 57, 62 Fug 2, 63, 77, 80, 84, 160, 161, 169, 209, 211 Mut 18, 41, 57, 137, 177 Somn 1:93, 184, 189, 229 Somn 2:62, 95, 124, 135, 193, 222, 261, 283, 291 Abr 35, 99, 181, 184 Ios 198, 204, 210 Mos 1:11, 83, 87, 170, 234, 320 Spec 1:305 Spec 2:95 Spec 3:141 Spec 4:138, 203 Virt 142 Praem 63, 113 Prob 114 Aet 48, 112, 144 Flacc 26, 30, 130, 143, 184 Legat 43, 44, 67, 182, 187, 255, 268, 322 Prov 2:34, 61 QG 3:11a QG isf 5 QG (Par) 2:5

φάσμα (10) Agr 96 Plant 7 Somn 2:133 Ios 140, 143 Spec 1:26 Spec 2:218 Prob 5 Flacc 164 Hypoth 6:1

φάσσα Spec 4:117

φάτνη Somn 2:144 Abr 160 Spec 1:148 QE 1:19

φάτνιον Spec 1:164

φαυλίζω Mut 60 QG 4:174

Φάυλλος Prov 2:33, 33

φαῦλος (205) Opif 67, 67, 68, 171 Leg 1:51, 62, 76, 93, 93, 93, 94, 95, 99, 102, 104 Leg 2:12, 17, 17, 53, 60, 65, 97, 107 Leg 3:1, 1, 1, 1, 2, 3, 6, 7, 13, 23, 28, 36, 37, 45, 48, 53, 53, 67, 67, 68, 89, 189, 191, 210, 211, 246, 246, 247, 251 Cher 130 Sacr 18, 81, 121, 128 Det 43, 49, 95, 109, 112, 119, 133, 136, 140, 173, 178 Post 22, 55, 75, 83, 94, 95, 107, 159 Gig 2, 56, 67 Deus 4, 70 Agr 22, 22, 29, 45, 143 Plant 164, 172, 172 Ebr 223 Sobr 67 Conf 30, 45, 68, 69, 73, 83, 103, 109, 120, 167, 178 Migr 20, 61, 61, 72, 114, 144, 145, 152 Her 254, 259, 267, 290, 292, 299 Congr 3, 54, 58, 59, 73 Fug 17, 25, 28, 45, 55, 73, 156, 177, 213 Mut 19, 24, 30, 31, 37, 50, 143, 144, 169, 193 Somn 2:162, 237, 256, 274, 282, 302 Abr 20, 21, 27, 83, 103, 265 Mos 2:262 Spec 1:246, 284 Spec 2:11, 49, 96 Spec 3:99, 101 Spec 4:36 Virt 9, 180, 190, 209 Praem 125 Prob 1, 21, 52, 52, 53, 53, 53, 101, 101, 136 Aet 30 Legat 359 Prov 2:7, 10, 13, 13, 20, 42 QG 1:70:1, 72, 100:1b, 100:2b, 2:12c, 68b, 3:8, 4:47b, 51a, 99, 166, 169, 172, 173, 174, 174, 211 QG isf 11 QE isf 18, 32, 33

φέγγος (59) Opif 31, 57 Leg 1:18 Cher 62 Sacr 78 Post 58 Agr 162 Plant 40 Ebr 44, 106, 168 Conf 60 Migr 40, 47, 76 Her 37, 263, 264, 307 Congr 8, 106 Fug 139, 176 Mut 4, 93 Somn 1:23, 53, 72, 82, 84, 114, 116, 117, 118, 164, 202, 217, 218 Somn 2:67, 133 Abr 70 Ios 146 Mos 1:124, 166 Mos 2:70, 271 Spec 1:37, 40, 279, 288, 296, 297 Spec 2:141, 155 Spec 4:52, 236 Praem 38, 45 Aet 86

Φειδίας Ebr 89

φείδομαι Leg 1:66 Leg 3:203 Prob 14 Contempl 16

φειδώ Spec 4:22, 213, 229

φειδωλία (6) Det 24 Deus 163, 164 Spec 1:221 Praem 52 QE isf 24

φειδωλός Det 18

Φεισών Leg 1:63, 66, 66, 74, 85

φενακίζω (11) Opif 165 Agr 164 Conf 48 Her 302 Mut 108 Decal 141 Spec 3:81 Praem 147 Hypoth 11:15 Prov 2:30 QG 4:202a

φενακισμός Sacr 22 Somn 2:40 Flacc 102

φέναξ Sacr 26 Somn 2:140 Legat 59

φέρω οἰστέος

φέρω οἰστός

φέρω (330) Opif 46, 46, 69, 70, 78, 153, 153, 167, 168 Leg 1:22, 73 Leg 2:57, 82, 95, 104 Leg 3:30, 69, 70, 93, 125, 126, 132, 140, 150, 223, 224, 227 Cher 2, 13, 36, 74, 78, 81, 85, 88, 126 Sacr 16, 17, 37, 45, 52, 66, 72, 85, 87, 88, 88, 89, 99, 100, 105, 119, 120 Det 6, 21, 31, 34, 53, 61, 116, 117, 136, 152 Post 145, 163 Gig 22 Deus 15, 65, 67, 75, 84, 102, 177 Agr 7, 7, 8, 9, 10, 19, 20, 34, 35, 48, 56, 68, 68, 69, 76, 76, 76, 110, 113, 114, 149 Plant 24, 25, 27, 33, 76, 100, 106, 135, 139, 152 Ebr 17, 20, 23, 32, 35, 54 Sobr 3, 8 Conf 26, 33, 110, 112, 114 Migr 12, 81, 115, 125, 140, 161, 167, 199, 205 Her 36, 74, 240, 251, 252 Congr 4, 10, 39, 44, 75, 104 Fug 41, 125, 208 Mut 69, 73, 88, 94, 102, 180, 192, 215, 224, 225, 231, 233, 234, 234, 247, 247, 256, 256, 260 Somn 1:51, 97, 111, 116 Somn 2:43, 75, 116, 124, 132, 150, 212, 238, 247, 262, 262, 275, 279 Abr 26, 40, 92, 135, 140, 157, 177, 192, 237, 245 Ios 16, 123, 129, 131, 141, 141, 148, 149, 166, 194, 222 Mos 1:40, 42, 142, 159, 189, 193, 202, 202, 205, 221, 224, 244, 247, 271, 285, 293, 295, 303, 317, 319, 328 Mos 2:3, 13, 62, 62, 62, 154, 202, 227, 249, 258, 267, 268 Decal 4, 110, 147, 148, 161 Spec 1:9, 22, 26, 40, 121, 183, 216, 229, 246, 272 Spec 2:52, 87, 97, 142, 153, 197, 201, 202, 219 Spec 3:1, 15, 106, 116,

126, 148, 175 Spec 4:2, 12, 45, 56, 75, 85, 99, 181, 211, 228 Virt 6, 38, 113, 143, 154, 157, 176 Praem 20, 90, 90, 101, 132, 133, 140, 148, 152 Prob 28, 69, 69, 130, 135 Contempl 54 Aet 32, 94, 105, 118, 135 Flacc 17, 38, 66, 80, 137, 141, 186 Legat 71, 75, 91, 99, 112, 150, 177, 186, 189, 196, 226, 240, 247, 279, 315, 342, 368 Hypoth 0:1 Prov 2:30 QG 2:13a, 4:51c QG isf 5 QG (Par) 2:7 QE 2:50b QE isf 32

φερώνυμος Agr 4 Somn 1:198

φεύγω (78) Leg 2:55, 88, 90, 103, 103 Leg 3:5, 5, 9, 9, 12, 14, 15, 16, 20, 27, 29, 37, 39, 48, 54, 214, 240, 241, 241 Cher 15, 129 Deus 95, 170 Agr 61 Ebr 169 Sobr 13 Conf 40, 70, 70, 178, 197 Migr 189 Her 178, 270 Fug 6, 43, 53, 63, 75, 76, 77, 88, 94, 106 Mut 213 Somn 1:139 Abr 37 Ios 141 Mos 1:170, 172, 178, 292 Mos 2:184, 184 Spec 1:219 Spec 3:128, 159, 159, 159 Spec 4:9, 80, 156 Virt 135 Praem 17, 94, 117, 148 Contempl 18 Flacc 115, 186 Prov 2:62 QG 3:29 QE 2:25a

φευκτός Deus 163, 163 Prob 61

φήμη (16) Sobr 68 Conf 116 Migr 86, 107 Ios 19, 245, 268 Mos 1:265, 282 Praem 148 Contempl 64 Flacc 45 Legat 15, 18, 231, 288

φημί (λέγω) (1302) Opif 3, 13, 21, 25, 26, 30, 32, 41, 42, 46, 61, 64, 66, 69, 75, 76, 100, 100, 105, 112, 114, 119, 123, 124, 129, 129, 131, 134, 135, 139, 147, 149, 157, 162, 170 Leg 1:1, 4, 6, 10, 17, 18, 24, 25, 31, 32, 35, 35, 45, 47, 48, 51, 51, 53, 53, 58, 60, 65, 72, 76, 77, 80, 81, 81, 90, 98, 100, 101, 104, 106, 108 Leg 2:1, 5, 6, 8, 11, 12, 13, 13, 20, 25, 27, 31, 31, 34, 41, 41, 42, 44, 46, 47, 55, 59, 60, 63, 75, 77, 78, 79, 82, 84, 89, 94, 97, 103 Leg 3:2, 2, 8, 10, 12, 13, 15, 18, 20, 24, 27, 28, 29, 32, 39, 40, 43, 43, 56, 56, 59, 60, 71, 77, 81, 85, 88, 90, 95, 97, 102, 105, 106, 106, 107, 110, 111, 119, 120, 123, 129, 129, 132, 133, 139, 141, 14?, 148, 150, 151, 152, 153, 157, 165, 169, 170, 177, 179, 185, 186, 191, 193, 196, 203, 204, 205, 208, 210, 214, 214, 216, 219, 220, 225, 227, 229, 239, 240, 240, 240, 241, 252 Cher 1, 14, 15, 18, 25, 41, 53, 63, 72, 74, 74, 77, 84, 84, 87, 101, 109, 121, 130 Sacr 1, 4, 6, 8, 9, 12, 18, 22, 46, 51, 54, 55, 56, 68, 77, 77, 87, 88, 89, 104, 112, 114, 118, 127, 127, 134 Det 1, 4, 6, 9, 10, 11, 17, 22, 28, 31, 38, 50, 52, 56, 58, 59, 59, 63, 64, 70, 74, 76, 80, 84, 84, 93, 96, 98, 103, 114, 115, 118, 122, 123, 126, 134, 138, 141, 147, 147, 150, 158, 160, 166, 167, 176 Post 25, 26, 29, 30, 32, 33, 33, 34, 35, 47, 60, 67, 70, 80, 84, 85, 90, 95, 96, 100, 102, 103, 115, 116, 120, 124, 132, 134, 136, 139, 139, 140, 142, 142, 147, 148, 162, 168, 170, 175, 180, 183 Gig 9, 19, 22, 25, 33, 33, 39, 40, 55, 65 Deus 1, 4, 11, 18, 19, 20, 44, 57, 60, 60, 70, 74, 88, 90, 91, 92, 94, 109, 117, 119, 127, 131, 136, 140, 154, 166, 169 Agr 14, 21, 24, 44, 57, 78, 85, 88, 91, 94, 97, 103, 106, 109, 110, 122, 123, 131, 145, 148, 157, 161, 166, 170, 175, 179 Plant 12, 12, 19, 34, 41, 44, 52, 52, 63, 65, 74, 77, 78, 80, 80, 83, 95, 96, 113, 117, 118, 125, 126, 127, 131, 132, 134, 134, 137, 143, 145, 157, 163, 168, 171, 177 Ebr 4, 9, 11, 14, 30, 33, 37, 39, 42, 42, 52, 54, 61, 73, 76, 89, 100, 104, 113, 115, 123, 127, 141, 143, 151, 172, 174, 178, 197, 206, 222 Sobr 6, 8, 10, 12, 15, 17, 21, 22, 23, 33, 43, 51, 52, 59, 62, 66 Conf 4, 9, 15, 20, 24, 25, 28, 29, 31, 36, 41, 57, 59, 59, 60, 65, 72, 74, 75, 82, 84, 88, 92, 98, 99, 111, 116, 118, 130, 132, 141, 142, 155, 158, 159, 160, 162, 169, 173, 185, 189, 192 Migr 3, 3, 4, 21, 22, 25, 30, 37, 44, 53, 54, 61, 62, 64, 65, 78, 78, 79, 81, 84, 85, 86, 94, 95, 101, 105, 107, 109, 114, 115, 118, 130, 130, 131, 132, 142, 149, 164, 164, 176, 184, 197, 203, 205, 210, 213, 215, 223 Her 17, 30, 43, 44, 49, 51, 53, 56, 56, 59, 62, 66, 67, 68, 76, 80, 81, 86, 87, 94, 95, 96, 99, 103, 107, 113, 113, 117, 123, 124, 125, 129, 131, 141, 147, 155, 157, 163, 164, 166, 166, 180, 182, 189, 190, 195, 196, 198, 201, 214, 218, 222, 231, 237, 239, 249, 250, 251, 251, 251, 255, 255, 257, 258, 267, 268, 277, 280, 281, 296, 307, 308, 313 Congr 7, 8, 9, 12, 13, 14, 54, 63, 71, 72, 73, 78, 84, 85, 95, 99, 100, 117, 125, 131, 139, 151, 153, 160, 163, 177, 179 Fug 5, 7, 10, 16, 20, 21, 23, 25, 39, 46, 61, 67, 68, 76, 76, 77, 79, 83, 91, 109, 113, 121, 123, 124, 127, 137, 139, 142, 143, 144, 145, 154, 158, 159, 163, 165, 167, 168, 177, 183, 189, 196, 203, 203, 204, 207, 211, 212 Mut 2, 7, 11, 12, 13, 14, 14, 25, 31, 37, 48, 51, 52, 58, 61, 63, 67, 69, 72, 75, 96, 110, 117, 123, 130, 132, 143, 145, 147, 148, 168, 173, 174, 178, 179, 182, 187, 194, 195, 195, 201, 208, 213, 233, 236, 237, 243, 248, 249, 249, 253, 258, 260, 263, 264, 266, 267 Somn 1:4, 8, 10, 26, 46, 53, 54, 58, 62, 71, 72, 75, 76, 78, 81, 89, 89, 90, 91, 95, 102, 107, 112, 116, 117, 120, 133, 150, 154, 167, 172, 176, 179, 181, 182, 183, 194, 195, 196, 197, 227, 238, 240, 241, 245, 247, 252, 253, 254 Somn 2:14, 17, 31, 33, 52, 75, 111, 112, 129, 130, 139, 142, 163, 174, 175, 176, 180, 189, 191, 192, 199, 200, 207, 207, 209, 216, 219, 223, 229, 231, 234, 238, 238, 241, 248, 252, 255, 257, 257, 267, 271, 275, 296, 300 Abr 5, 13, 14, 31, 34, 51, 71, 105, 108, 112, 115, 123, 131, 142, 167, 173, 175, 179, 206, 223, 236, 247, 253, 266, 269, 273, 275, 276 Ios 6, 7, 9, 35, 50, 64, 78, 90, 90, 93, 104, 107, 115, 126, 145, 168, 183, 185, 185, 188, 191, 193, 215, 220, 222, 238, 255, 262 Mos 1:6, 9, 13, 17, 34, 72, 74, 75, 81, 124, 126, 135, 142, 165, 222, 234, 277, 289, 304, 321, 328, 331 Mos 2:2, 38, 53, 59, 84, 98, 115, 132, 139, 168, 187, 230, 234, 239, 243, 259, 272, 273 Decal 15, 30, 38, 84, 88, 97, 100, 114, 116, 120 Spec 1:25, 26, 27, 43, 45, 46, 52, 64, 74, 81, 117, 126, 129, 131, 140, 177, 188, 198, 223, 230, 235, 237, 253, 259, 262, 266, 285, 289, 299, 304, 306, 311, 318, 327, 334, 337, 341, 345 Spec 2:2, 12, 16, 51, 77, 79, 87, 107, 113, 129, 144, 147, 166, 177, 198, 216, 235, 239, 243, 249 Spec 3:29, 30, 43, 53, 58, 69, 76, 77, 90, 100, 101, 115, 117, 120, 131, 133, 152, 165, 183, 184, 202, 208 Spec 4:10, 39, 59, 60, 60, 62, 64, 66, 73, 105, 113, 123, 131, 137, 139, 157, 169, 176, 180, 186, 199, 213, 220, 227, 237 Virt 4, 11, 28, 35, 47, 57, 59, 67, 89, 96, 98, 106, 107, 110, 117, 123, 124, 127, 129, 162, 165, 166, 168, 171, 174, 183, 212, 218, 223 Praem 8, 16, 43, 44, 58, 63, 72, 79, 93, 95, 96, 98, 106, 106, 108, 111, 119, 123, 125, 126, 127, 131, 138, 158 Prob 8, 11, 15, 40, 42, 47, 48, 53, 68, 94, 99, 103, 105, 112, 116, 118, 121, 122, 124, 127, 144, 144 Contempl 35, 40, 43, 71 Aet 4, 7, 10, 13, 17, 19, 38, 41, 48, 49, 49, 52, 61, 62, 66, 74, 78, 79, 80, 83, 87, 89, 94, 107, 107, 111, 114, 117, 119, 120, 121, 127, 128, 130, 132, 140, 141, 146 Flacc 21, 39, 44, 52, 60, 71, 95, 98, 159, 170, 178, 183 Legat 24, 26, 27, 61, 69, 76, 103, 116, 128, 135, 140, 172, 181, 186, 188, 195, 203, 214, 223, 239, 281, 301, 306, 347, 355, 357, 362, 363 Hypoth 0:1, 6:2, 6:4, 7:4, 7:9, 7:10, 7:18 Prov 2:1, 13, 16, 24, 26, 29, 30, 36, 43, 60, 64, 67 QG 1:1, 3, 3, 3, 28, 29, 29, 55a, 55a, 66, 66, 66, 74, 94, 100:2b, 2:11, 15a, 15c, 26b, 28, 28, 29, 54a, 54d, 59, 62, 64a, 64a, 65, 65, 3:11a, 23, 24, 52, 58, 4:51a, 51b, 52d, 144, 148, 153, 167, 173, 173,

198, 202a, 228 QG isf 5, 13 QG (Par) 2:3, 2:6, 2:7 QE 2:6a, 18, 19, 20, 40, 45a, 47 QE isf 3, 3, 22

φημίζω Legat 289

φθάνω (113) Opif 5, 8, 111, 150 Leg 3:105, 215, 215, 215 Cher 5, 28 Sacr 14, 53, 65, 65, 66, 66, 67, 135 Det 89, 153 Post 17, 18, 19, 163 Deus 29 Agr 23, 85, 93, 123, 163 Ebr 120 Conf 59, 113, 153, 162 Migr 52 Her 35, 66, 217 Congr 3 Fug 98 Mut 142, 178, 179, 232 Somn 1:36, 66, 134, 142, 175, 179 Somn 2:146 Abr 58, 150, 161, 176 Ios 19, 34, 118, 141, 159, 245, 250 Mos 1:2, 11, 21, 32, 145, 185, 265, 304, 315, 326 Mos 2:6, 22, 22, 172 Decal 35, 135, 141 Spec 1:144, 272 Spec 2:72, 83, 189 Spec 3:8, 162 Spec 4:90, 175, 186 Virt 28, 226 Praem 26, 50, 161, 167 Contempl 71, 90 Aet 58 Flacc 1, 3, 93 Legat 2, 6, 25, 99, 107 Prov 1, 2:19, 27 QG 1:89 QG isf 8, 8

φθαρτικός Det 164 Her 136

φθαρτός (87) Opif 82, 82, 119, 119 Leg 1:31, 32, 88, 90 Leg 2:3, 89, 95, 99 Leg 3:36, 162 Cher 5, 5, 7, 48 Sacr 97 Det 49, 85 Post 43, 61, 105, 115, 163, 165 Gig 45 Deus 15, 15 Agr 141 Plant 22, 53 Ebr 37, 73, 132, 142, 208, 209 Sobr 3 Conf 108, 149, 154, 176, 176 Migr 198 Her 160, 246, 311 Congr 112 Mut 78, 79, 181 Somn 1:172 Somn 2:234, 253 Abr 55, 157, 157, 243, 244 Mos 2:121, 171 Decal 34 Spec 2:166, 198 Virt 67, 74, 204 Praem 28 Prob 46 Aet 7, 9, 9, 44, 73, 78, 124, 124, 124, 131, 143 Legat 118 QG (Par) 2:7, 2:7 QE isf 5, 15

φθέγγομαι (17) Leg 3:210 Sacr 29 Migr 80 Her 25 Mut 242 Abr 61 Ios 77, 248 Mos 1:283 Mos 2:200, 206 Decal 93 Spec 1:53 Spec 2:198 Spec 3:174 Prob 108 Legat 264

φθείρω (129) Opif 66 Leg 1:7, 78 Leg 2:6, 25 Leg 3:253 Sacr 122, 122 Post 163, 171 Deus 73, 122, 123, 136, 140, 142, 142, 142, 143 Agr 167, 171 Ebr 95, 140, 212 Sobr 42 Conf 47, 89, 198 Migr 224, 225 Her 234, 242, 246, 246, 312 Fug 161, 162, 189 Mut 34 Somn 1:105 Somn 2:258, 258, 260, 266, 283, 286, 290 Abr 45, 45, 140, 164, 165 Ios 56 Mos 1:67, 96, 205, 207, 230 Mos 2:53, 59, 61, 210 Decal 138, 173 Spec 1:76, 266, 341 Spec 2:191, 225 Spec 3:69, 70, 70, 77, 81 Spec 4:130, 203, 203 Virt 31 Prob 69, 113 Contempl 62 Aet 5, 6, 21, 24, 25, 28, 31, 32, 39, 45, 45, 46, 46, 46, 46, 46, 48, 49, 51, 51, 51, 69, 72, 78, 80, 82, 94, 95, 95, 96, 99, 106, 106, 106, 112, 113, 116, 124, 142, 143, 144, 149 Legat 91 Prov 2:59 QG 2:15a, 54a QE 2:49a, 49b

φθινάς Virt 193 Praem 143 Prov 2:30, 33

φθίνω (φθίω) (7) Deus 37 Her 208 Somn 1:26 Prob 112 Aet 26, 61, 126

φθίσις Aet 38

φθίω φθίνω

φθογγάζομαι Prob 134

φθόγγος (19) Opif 121, 126 Leg 1:14 Cher 110 Sacr 74 Deus 24, 84 Plant 167 Ebr 116 Sobr 36 Conf 55, 150 Migr 104 Her 210 Congr 144 Mut 56, 87 Mos 2:256 Prov 2:20

φθονέω (17) Opif 21, 77 Agr 112, 121 Abr 21, 204 Ios 144 Mos 1:64 Spec 2:73, 141, 173 Spec 4:206 Virt 70 Praem 39 Prob 128 Contempl 75 Hypoth 7:6

φθόνος (45) Cher 33 Post 140, 150 Agr 121 Migr 151, 183 Congr 13, 122 Fug 154 Mut 95, 112, 269 Somn 1:107, 223 Abr 191, 203 Ios 5, 17, 234 Mos 1:2, 246 Mos 2:27, 128 Spec 1:320 Spec 2:91, 109, 249 Spec 3:3 Spec 4:75 Virt 116, 170, 223 Praem 87, 168 Prob 13, 129, 129 Aet 134 Flacc 29, 30 Legat 48, 80 QG 1:55a, 4:191b, 194

φθορά (143) Opif 58 Leg 1:7, 105 Leg 2:33, 77, 102 Leg 3:52, 76 Cher 32, 51, 62, 92 Sacr 134 Det 46, 76, 102, 136, 168, 178 Post 164 Deus 16, 124, 183 Agr 108, 109 Plant 114, 114, 157 Ebr 12, 23, 29, 35, 79, 141 Conf 36, 117, 167, 181, 187, 187, 192, 195, 196 Her 204, 209, 239, 247, 276 Congr 119 Mut 3 Somn 1:86, 151 Somn 2:109, 211, 213, 253, 258, 270 Abr 1, 56, 145, 244 Mos 1:39, 119, 133, 145, 146, 180, 300 Mos 2:107, 194, 210, 255, 255, 260, 262, 263 Decal 58 Spec 1:27, 112, 184, 291, 341 Spec 2:13, 134, 154, 192 Spec 3:16, 16, 28, 33, 65, 72, 178 Spec 4:84, 226 Virt 132 Praem 22, 68, 132, 136 Prob 96 Aet 3, 5, 8, 8, 8, 17, 20, 22, 23, 27, 34, 37, 37, 47, 53, 67, 75, 75, 78, 79, 82, 85, 106, 113, 117, 117, 126, 126, 129, 137, 144, 146 Flacc 187 Hypoth 6:3 Prov 2:1, 50 QG 2:22, 22, 4:8b, 51b QE 2:3b

φθορεύς (7) Leg 3:220, 220 Conf 48 Ios 84 Decal 168 Spec 3:70 Spec 4:89

φθοροποιός (18) Leg 3:76 Sacr 110 Deus 60 Agr 10 Migr 219 Somn 2:88 Mos 1:70, 100, 121 Spec 3:97, 167 Spec 4:29 Praem 131 Prob 76 Aet 78 Legat 107, 108 Prov 2:23

φιάλη (6) Migr 202 Mos 2:146, 150 Spec 1:199 Contempl 49 Legat 319

φιλαγαθία Mos 2:9

φιλάγαθος Mos 2:9

Φιλαδέλφειος Mos 2:29

φιλαδελφία Legat 87

φιλάδελφος Ios 218 Legat 92

Φιλάδελφος Mos 2:29, 30

φίλαθλος Gig 37 Congr 25, 162 Somn 1:251

φιλαλήθης Cher 127 Mos 2:281

φιλάλληλος Virt 69

φιλανδρία Abr 245, 253 Spec 3:173 QG 3:20a

φίλανδρος Praem 139

φιλανθρωπία (55) Cher 99 Sacr 27 Post 147 Plant 92 Migr 217 Mut 225 Somn 1:147 Abr 79, 107, 109 Ios 94, 240 Mos 1:198, 249 Mos 2:9, 242 Decal 164 Spec 1:120, 126, 129, 221, 295, 324 Spec 2:63, 71, 78, 79, 104, 110, 138, 141, 183 Spec 3:152 Spec 4:15, 18, 24, 72, 97 Virt 50, 51, 66, 76, 80, 88, 95, 99, 105, 121, 140, 188 Legat 73, 158 Hypoth 7:19, 11:2 Prov 2:6

φιλάνθρωπος (36) Opif 81 Migr 156 Fug 96 Mut 129 Abr 22, 137, 203, 208, 232 Ios 82, 176, 198, 264 Mos 2:9, 163 Decal 110 Spec 2:75, 96 Spec 3:36, 156 Virt 28, 77, 97, 101, 106, 175, 182 Praem 59 Prob 83, 84 Flacc 61 Legat 67, 352 QG 2:54b, 4:193 QE 2:12

φιλαπεχθήμων (10) Fug 5 Mut 60 Abr 178 Ios 226 Mos 1:248 Spec 1:241 Spec 4:20 Virt 34, 182 Flacc 52

φιλαργυρία (9) Mut 226 Ios 218 Spec 1:24, 281 Spec 2:78 Prob 21 Flacc 60 Prov 2:12 QG 4:33a

φιλάργυρος Post 116 Gig 37

φιλάρετος (64) Opif 81, 128 Leg 2:55, 90, 90 Leg 3:107, 130, 131, 147, 237 Cher 6, 106 Det 9, 34, 48, 71, 120 Post 42, 54, 122, 159 Deus 168 Agr 56, 88 Ebr 59, 70 Sobr 24, 24 Conf 44, 128, 181 Migr 16, 28, 114, 146, 163, 215 Her 267 Congr 28 Fug 17, 157 Mut 113, 132,

133, 205 Somn 1:45, 58, 69, 127, 159 Somn 2:29, 242 Abr 7, 27, 31, 68, 221 Mos 1:148 Decal 87 Virt 175, 218 Prob 83, 84 QG 3:8

φιλαύστηρος Opif 164

φιλαυτέω Legat 84

φιλαυτία (17) Sacr 58 Post 52, 180 Deus 16 Agr 173 Conf 128 Her 106 Congr 130 Ios 118 Decal 72 Spec 1:196, 333, 344 Spec 4:131 Praem 12 Legat 193 QG isf 10

φίλαυτος (21) Leg 1:49 Leg 3:231 Cher 74 Sacr 3, 32, 52 Det 32, 32, 68, 78 Post 21 Fug 81 Mut 221 Somn 2:219 Ios 143 Spec 1:344 Hypoth 11:14 QG 1:60:1, 60:2, 60:2, 62:1

φιλέβδομος Opif 111

φιλεγκλήμων Sacr 32 Agr 64

φιλελεύθερος Prob 143

φιλεπιστήμων Spec 3:6 Spec 4:238

φιλεργία Spec 4:195 Legat 230

φιλέρημος Her 127, 234

φίλερις Agr 162 Ebr 16, 17, 29 Legat 52

φιλεστιάτωρ Ios 206

φιλέω (62) Opif 54, 103 Leg 2:99 Leg 3:251 Post 71 Gig 10 Agr 158 Plant 105, 105, 127 Ebr 147, 179, 214 Conf 7, 115 Migr 211 Her 40, 41, 42, 44, 44, 44, 50, 265, 310 Fug 113, 166, 179 Mut 60, 81, 142, 158 Somn 1:6 Somn 2:145 Abr 210, 228 Ios 179, 182, 247 Mos 1:10, 33, 45, 138, 170, 220, 302 Mos 2:24, 136 Decal 125 Spec 1:119 Spec 3:99, 155 Spec 4:51 Virt 24, 115, 225 Praem 148 Aet 148 Flacc 118 Legat 246 Prov 2:62 QG 1:89

φιληδονία (8) Post 180 Abr 24 Decal 122 Spec 1:281 Spec 3:23, 112 Prob 21 QG 4:33a

φιλήδονος (23) Opif 158 Leg 2:90 Leg 3:38, 114, 139, 143, 159, 212, 212, 237 Sacr 32 Det 12 Post 98, 182 Agr 88 Sobr 24, 24 Migr 224 Mut 172 Somn 2:210 Ios 153 Spec 3:113 Spec 4:112

φιλήκοος Ebr 23, 94 Somn 2:239 Virt 116

φίλημα Her 40, 40, 42, 51, 54

φιλία (52) Leg 2:10 Leg 3:182 Sacr 36 Det 15 Post 157 Agr 164 Plant 90, 104, 106, 106 Conf 48 Her 21, 21, 42, 44, 51 Congr 166 Fug 40, 58 Somn 2:97, 108 Abr 129, 129, 194 Ios 74, 210 Mos 2:171 Decal 89 Spec 1:52, 70, 112, 317 Spec 2:26, 119, 240 Spec 3:155, 158 Spec 4:88, 161 Virt 35, 55, 109, 152, 152, 179 Praem 154 Prob 79 Contempl 90 Flacc 11, 19 QG 1:17b QG isf 7

φιλικός (9) Somn 1:196 Abr 212 Mos 1:242 Virt 178 Prob 44 Contempl 18 Legat 344 QG 1:17b QE 2:11b

φίλιος Conf 13 Somn 2:210

Φίλιππος Flacc 25

φιλογυμναστής Gig 37 Congr 25 Somn 1:251 Spec 4:121

φιλογύναιος Spec 3:9

φιλόδειπνος Ios 206

φιλοδέσποτος (10) Det 56, 62 Her 7, 8, 14 Abr 170 Decal 167 Spec 2:67 Spec 4:31 Praem 89

φιλοδίκαιος Her 163 Abr 225 Mos 2:9

φιλοδοξία Abr 24 Spec 1:281 Prob 21 QG 4:33a

φιλόδοξος Post 116 Gig 37 Abr 104, 221

φιλόδουλος Leg 3:194

φιλόδωρος (25) Leg 1:34 Leg 3:40, 106, 166 Cher 20, 29 Det 138 Post 26, 138, 148 Agr 173 Plant 37, 88, 91 Ebr 82 Conf 182 Migr 30 Her 31 Fug 62, 66 Mut 46 Abr 254 Spec 1:221, 298 Praem 126

φιλοεθνής Virt 69

φιλοζωέω Legat 369

φιλόζωος Sacr 32 Spec 2:205 Spec 3:36

φιλοθεάμων (18) Opif 158 Cher 84 Ebr 124 Conf 77 Migr 76, 164, 165, 191 Her 79 Congr 63 Fug 138, 195 Mut 88, 209 Somn 1:39 Somn 2:251, 271 Spec 3:191

φιλόθεος (48) Leg 2:50, 52, 55, 86 Leg 3:74 Cher 7 Sacr 3 Det 32, 48, 78, 103 Post 15, 21, 129 Agr 51, 79, 88 Her 82, 289 Congr 56 Fug 81 Mut 176 Abr 50 Mos 2:67 Decal 63, 110 Spec 1:11, 42, 51, 55, 79, 191, 207, 246, 248, 271, 300, 314 Virt 184 Prob 42, 83, 84 QG 1:60:1, 60:2, 60:2, 62:1 QG isf 10 QE isf 30

φιλόθηρος Spec 4:121

φιλοίκειος (10) Abr 179 Ios 171, 237, 246 Mos 1:12 Mos 2:142 Spec 2:80 Virt 53, 133 Praem 78

φίλοινος Ebr 220

φιλόκαινος Ios 36 Mos 1:213

φιλόκαισαρ Legat 37, 280

φιλόκαλος (8) Opif 81 Mut 133 Abr 221 Ios 4 Mos 1:47, 148 Spec 3:189 Virt 175

φιλοκίνδυνος Agr 151 Virt 45 Praem 137 Prob 131

φιλόκοσμος Flacc 148 QG isf 10

Φιλόλαος Opif 100

φιλομαθής (32) Leg 3:93 Post 137, 138, 149 Gig 60 Deus 120 Agr 132, 158 Ebr 23, 94, 167 Conf 77 Migr 216, 221 Her 63, 311 Congr 16, 68, 74, 111, 125, 126 Fug 10, 161 Mut 70 Somn 1:11 Somn 2:139 Decal 1 Spec 1:39 Spec 3:189, 191 Prov 2:51

Φιλόμηλος Prov 2:33

φιλομήτωρ Ebr 35, 36

φιλονεικέω Leg 3:56 Abr 40, 215 Spec 4:111 Aet 104

φιλονεικία (18) Opif 33 Leg 3:233 Cher 129 Sacr 20 Det 3 Ebr 15, 99 Her 247 Mut 95 Somn 2:115, 276 Mos 1:139 Spec 1:108 Spec 3:28 Aet 138 Legat 114, 218, 335

φιλόνεικος (13) Leg 3:131, 131 Det 45 Ebr 17 Migr 27, 75 Abr 210, 225 Spec 1:273 Legat 52, 198 Prov 2:34, 72

φιλόξενος Abr 114 Virt 105

φιλοπαθής (23) Leg 2:50, 52, 52, 103 Leg 3:107 Sacr 48, 51 Post 98 Deus 111 Agr 83, 88 Ebr 70, 209 Conf 34 Migr 16, 62, 66, 202, 224 Her 203 Fug 18 Somn 2:213, 277

φιλοπάτωρ Ebr 35

φιλοπευστέω (7) Sacr 79 Post 90 Migr 218 Fug 132 Mut 11 Somn 2:26 Aet 1

φιλοπόνηρος Abr 21, 199

φιλοπονία Post 156 Congr 166 Fug 14

φιλόπονος Her 9 Mut 88 Somn 1:127

φιλοπραγμοσύνη (8) Agr 34 Ebr 79 Fug 162 Somn 2:148, 225 Abr 20 Flacc 41 QG 4:47b

φιλοπράγμων Spec 2:44 Flacc 20

φίλος (216) Opif 77, 82 Leg 2:55, 85 Leg 3:1, 20, 71, 71, 71, 123, 152, 182, 204, 205 Cher 11, 20 Sacr 20, 129, 130 Det 33, 33, 37, 37, 165, 166 Post 7, 25, 30, 39, 68,

91, 172 Gig 33, 35, 35, 43, 66 Deus 27, 55, 79, 98, 133, 167 Agr 25, 88, 95, 99, 155, 159, 168 Plant 25, 36 Ebr 40, 58, 66, 69, 94, 102, 104, 159, 165, 176, 179 Sobr 55, 56 Migr 10, 16, 45, 112, 116, 116, 162, 202, 217 Her 21, 21, 21, 21, 48, 83, 83, 92, 186, 203, 243, 246 Congr 91 Fug 3, 6, 29, 89 Mut 32, 40, 174, 196 Somn 1:110, 111, 191, 193, 218, 232, 232 Somn 2:42, 104, 128, 219, 255, 297 Abr 65, 87, 153, 187, 235, 242, 273 Ios 18, 79 Mos 1:31, 35, 39, 45, 136, 156, 156, 209, 280, 303, 307, 310, 322 Mos 2:42, 171, 172, 273 Decal 66, 89, 90 Spec 1:52, 52, 68, 68, 97, 247, 250, 313, 316, 340 Spec 2:19, 132 Spec 3:11, 61, 85, 90, 126, 126, 155, 155 Spec 4:34, 44, 70, 141, 219, 224 Virt 46, 55, 60, 96, 103, 125, 152, 173, 179, 195, 195, 218 Praem 17, 118, 127, 134 Prob 9, 35, 42, 44, 96 Contempl 13, 14, 41, 44 Flacc 18, 32, 40, 43, 50, 60, 62, 64, 72, 158 Legat 40, 268, 272, 285, 299, 327, 343 Hypoth 7:8 Prov 2:4, 17, 21 QG 1:17b, 2:16, 16, 3:29, 4:52c QG isf 10 QE isf 16

φιλοσοφέω (62) Opif 128, 128, 154 Leg 1:56 Leg 2:15 Leg 3:97, 244 Det 7, 74 Post 34, 119, 137 Gig 14, 62 Deus 22, 170 Agr 104, 139 Plant 12, 14, 24 Conf 1, 97 Migr 128, 195 Her 4, 111, 257, 291 Congr 21, 64 Fug 68, 77, 120 Mut 223 Somn 1:55, 58 Abr 164 Ios 49 Mos 2:2, 211, 212, 215, 216 Decal 58, 98, 100, 121 Spec 1:32 Spec 2:61, 214 Praem 11 Prob 80, 82 Contempl 16, 28, 30, 34 Aet 47, 94, 144 QG isf 15

φιλοσοφία (102) Opif 8, 53, 54, 77 Leg 1:57 Leg 3:167 Cher 4, 85, 93, 129 Sacr 1 Post 101, 102 Gig 39 Agr 14, 15 Ebr 49, 51 Migr 34, 147, 191 Her 214, 248, 297 Congr 53, 74, 77, 78, 79, 79, 79, 79, 79, 80, 114, 142, 144, 145, 146, 147, 148, 150 Mut 36, 74, 75, 76, 220 Somn 1:55, 107, 205, 226 Somn 2:127, 170, 244 Abr 164 Ios 86 Mos 1:23, 29, 48 Mos 2:66, 212, 212, 216 Decal 30, 150 Spec 1:37, 322, 336 Spec 2:165, 230 Spec 3:1, 185, 186, 187, 191 Spec 4:92 Virt 65 Prob 3, 43, 74, 80, 88, 111, 160 Contempl 14, 16, 26, 28, 67, 69, 89 Aet 16, 16, 55 Legat 156, 245, 310, 310 Prov 2:16 QG 2:34a, 41 QE isf 4

φιλόσοφος (52) Opif 100, 131 Leg 3:72, 72, 115 Gig 6 Agr 161 Plant 142, 151, 173 Ebr 1, 198 Conf 5 Her 301 Congr 67, 142, 147 Fug 3, 141 Mut 70, 167, 209 Somn 1:141 Abr 13 Mos 2:2, 2, 36 Spec 1:2, 95, 262, 299, 327, 339, 345 Spec 2:163 Spec 3:191, 191 Prob 24, 48, 96, 96, 121, 130 Contempl 2, 57 Aet 8 Flacc 184 Legat 318 Hypoth 7:20 Prov 2:18, 61 QE isf 7

φιλοστοργία (6) Abr 168 Mos 1:150 Spec 2:240 Virt 128 Legat 36 QG 4:202b

φιλόστοργος (7) Abr 198 Spec 2:240 Spec 3:153, 157 Virt 91, 192 Praem 158

φιλοσύντομος Spec 4:96

φιλοσώματος (12) Leg 1:33 Leg 3:72, 74 Post 61, 116 Deus 111 Conf 70 Migr 16, 22 Somn 1:138 Abr 103 Ios 152

φιλότεκνος Abr 179

φιλοτεχνία Spec 4:132

φιλοτιβέριος Legat 37

φιλοτιμέομαι Somn 2:55 Abr 242 Mos 1:256 Decal 60 Spec 4:74

φιλοτίμημα Legat 299

φιλοτιμία (17) Opif 17, 81 Sacr 37 Agr 62 Somn 1:8, 121 Somn 2:13 Abr 110 Mos 1:275 Mos 2:29, 136 Decal 60 Virt 18 Prob 110 Legat 60, 166 Prov 2:46

φιλότιμος Fug 28 Virt 32 Praem 11 Prob 133 Contempl 72

φιλότυφος Somn 2:98

φιλοφρονέομαι Abr 132 Flacc 113 QG 4:8*

φιλοφροσύνη Cher 29 Ios 206, 257 Mos 1:275 Spec 2:39

φιλοχρηματία Mos 1:141 Spec 4:212, 215

φιλοχρήματος Abr 221 Spec 1:23 Spec 4:65

φιλοχωρέω Mos 1:240 Aet 32

φίλτρον (25) Opif 165 Post 135 Gig 44 Deus 170 Agr 98 Ebr 50 Sobr 23 Congr 77 Somn 1:50 Abr 63, 170, 195 Spec 1:9, 52, 56, 137 Spec 2:80 Spec 3:30, 35, 101 Virt 115 Praem 18 Contempl 69 Legat 61 Hypoth 11:17

Φίλων (7) Hypoth 0:1 QG 1:3, 17a, 3:29, 4:161, 163:2 QE 1:4

φιμός Post 182

φιμόω Virt 145

Φινεές (8) Leg 3:242 Post 182 Conf 57 Mut 108 Mos 1:301, 304, 306, 313

Φλάκκος (37) Flacc 1, 2, 7, 16, 21, 30, 35, 40, 41, 51, 73, 79, 79, 92, 95, 103, 107, 110, 112, 113, 116, 121, 138, 139, 139, 142, 145, 150, 157, 162, 163, 180, 185, 185, 191 Legat 314, 315

φλεγμαίνω Plant 144

φλέγω (10) Opif 58 Leg 3:224 Post 71 Plant 108 Ebr 29, 73, 95 Mos 1:67, 277 Legat 125

φλέψ (16) Opif 38 Fug 182 Somn 1:19 Mos 1:99, 211 Spec 1:216, 218 Spec 2:169 Spec 3:147 Praem 144 Prob 65 Aet 128 Flacc 190 Prov 2:17 QG 1:3 QG (Par) 2:3

φλιά Her 83 Spec 4:142

φλόγινος (9) Cher 1, 11, 20, 21, 25, 26, 28, 30, 31

φλογμός (14) Leg 3:160 Sacr 15 Post 71 Somn 2:131 Mos 1:120, 265 Mos 2:63 Decal 77 Spec 1:218 Spec 2:153 Contempl 24 Aet 36, 67 Legat 364

φλογοειδής Mos 1:166 Decal 33

φλογώδης Deus 79 Spec 1:92 Legat 126

φλόγωσις Mos 1:128 Spec 2:191, 206 Legat 123

φλοιός Mos 2:180

φλοιώδης Mos 2:182

φλόξ (68) Leg 3:160, 224, 225, 227, 229, 235 Cher 26 Deus 78 Agr 17 Ebr 131, 223 Conf 156 Migr 100 Her 307, 307, 307 Congr 117 Fug 81, 158, 176 Somn 2:93, 125, 181, 186 Abr 138, 140 Mos 1:65, 66, 70 Mos 2:56, 58, 154, 158 Decal 46, 49, 173 Spec 1:254, 268, 285 Spec 3:10 Spec 4:27, 125 Virt 135 Aet 33, 86, 86, 86, 86, 88, 88, 88, 90, 90, 91, 91, 91, 92, 92, 92, 92, 92, 102 Legat 356 QE 2:15a, 47, 47, 47, 47

φλυαρέω Somn 2:291 Aet 47 Legat 363

φλύαρημα Aet 69

φλυαρία (7) Somn 1:139 Somn 2:117 Spec 1:176 Prob 104 Contempl 10, 64 QE isf 13

φλύκταινα Mos 1:127

φοβερός (30) Leg 2:84 Leg 3:250 Det 140 Gig 47 Deus 64 Her 23, 24, 275, 287 Congr 165 Mut 173 Somn 1:184 Somn 2:70, 266 Abr 185 Ios 189 Mos 1:67, 183, 225, 263 Spec 3:102 Praem 73, 73, 95 Prob 25, 106, 110, 147 Flacc 125 QG 2:17b

φοβέω (39) Leg 2:27, 92 Leg 3:2, 54, 54, 250 Deus 69, 69 Agr 78 Migr 21, 62, 132, 215 Her 25 Mut 21 Somn 1:3,

159, 173, 173, 184 Somn 2:266 Abr 204 Ios 68, 70, 169 Mos 1:10, 57, 329 Spec 1:300 Spec 2:239 Virt 24 Prob 21 Legat 216, 256, 370 Prov 2:25 QG isf 9, 9 QE 2:21

φόβος (148) Opif 79, 142 Leg 2:8 Leg 3:113, 250 Sacr 15 Det 110, 119, 119, 119, 140 Gig 46 Deus 64, 69, 71 Agr 40 Plant 88, 90 Conf 12, 52, 90 Migr 60, 215, 219 Her 23, 28, 249, 270, 270 Congr 172 Fug 3, 3, 4, 5, 6, 6, 23, 98 Mut 23, 24, 72, 163, 163, 163, 262 Somn 1:10, 110, 173, 237 Somn 2:91, 122 Abr 14, 14, 14, 95, 129, 151, 189, 202, 236, 238 Ios 10, 51, 79, 181, 184, 214, 254, 262 Mos 1:73, 161, 164, 167, 181, 233, 291 Mos 2:139, 169, 172, 251 Decal 145, 177 Spec 1:128 Spec 2:3, 26, 30, 48, 157, 163, 209, 239, 239, 240 Spec 3:62, 175 Spec 4:150, 193, 199, 223 Virt 41, 114, 124, 157, 200 Praem 71, 71, 73, 73, 95, 97, 97, 118, 148, 149, 151 Prob 18, 111, 159 Contempl 2 Aet 11 Flacc 9, 12, 32, 87, 96, 129, 176, 181 Legat 7, 17, 35, 87, 122, 209, 276, 293, 325, 372 Hypoth 6:3 Prov 2:8, 30 QG 1:72, 76a QE 2:21, 21, 21, 21 QE isf 33

φοινίκεος (φοινικοῦς) Leg 3:57 Ebr 173 Mos 2:88

Φοινίκη Mos 1:163 Legat 222, 225, 226, 281

φοινικοῦς φοινίκεος

φοῖνιξ (11) Leg 3:74 Deus 137, 137 Agr 112 Fug 183, 183, 186, 187, 187 Mos 1:188, 189

Φοῖνιξ Mos 1:214 Hypoth 6:6

φοινίσσω Ios 14, 22

φοιτάω (23) Leg 3:8, 229 Cher 49 Det 17 Post 91 Gig 52 Her 234 Congr 122 Fug 55 Mut 172, 204, 257 Somn 1:151, 255 Mos 1:2, 190 Mos 2:27 Decal 40 Spec 1:269 Spec 2:70 Legat 296 Prov 2:26 QG 4:51c

φοιτητής (16) Sacr 79 Gig 25 Ebr 33, 114 Congr 124, 127, 177 Somn 1:129 Abr 6 Ios 74 Spec 1:50, 319, 345 Spec 2:88, 256 Virt 66

φονάω (27) Det 46 Agr 97, 107 Ebr 13 Sobr 46 Migr 162 Fug 39 Ios 44 Mos 1:242 Mos 2:202, 273 Spec 1:160, 316 Spec 2:253 Spec 3:38, 96, 129 Spec 4:116, 225 Virt 131, 208 Praem 92 Contempl 43 Flacc 175 Legat 58, 97 QG 2:12c

φονεύω Det 178 Fug 53, 75 Decal 36

φόνος (35) Leg 3:32, 35 Sacr 128, 130, 130, 132 Det 96 Agr 170, 171 Conf 130, 160, 161 Fug 53, 65, 93, 94, 107 Ios 12 Mos 1:313 Mos 2:214 Decal 51 Spec 1:158 Spec 3:86, 91, 92, 121, 122, 128, 142, 149 Flacc 189 Legat 66, 302 Prov 2:23 QG 3:52

φορά (188) Opif 34, 41, 58, 63, 80, 81, 88, 124, 132, 159 Leg 1:8 Leg 2:103 Leg 3:13, 18, 134, 155, 163, 172, 223 Cher 19, 21, 25, 82, 94 Sacr 32, 47, 49, 66, 106, 121 Det 5, 100, 117, 152, 170 Post 19, 113, 129, 144, 161, 163, 167, 178 Gig 13, 51 Deus 87, 153, 171, 178 Agr 41, 88, 94, 126, 180 Plant 12, 89 Ebr 180, 199 Sobr 34, 42, 49, 49 Conf 23, 25, 30, 70, 100, 102, 105, 157 Migr 26, 32, 148, 194 Her 4, 97, 208, 241, 299 Fug 49, 54, 91, 152, 191 Mut 67, 179, 186, 214, 239, 260 Somn 1:107, 153, 192 Somn 2:125, 151, 245, 278 Abr 1, 40, 42, 43, 44, 59, 268 Ios 200 Mos 1:6, 25, 107, 108, 116, 118, 119, 123, 145, 177, 200, 211, 212, 265 Mos 2:35, 54, 58, 63, 186, 264, 286 Decal 16, 44, 160, 163 Spec 1:34, 62, 67, 92, 192 Spec 2:147, 191, 206, 213, 231 Spec 3:15, 28, 32, 33, 79, 129, 189 Spec 4:46, 85, 88, 111, 156, 160, 170, 212 Virt 6, 14, 157, 201 Praem 72, 93, 101, 145, 156 Prob 15, 63 Aet 62, 137, 137, 140, 146 Flacc 9, 101, 157 Legat 9, 91, 186, 223, 243, 306 Prov 2:12, 38, 43 QG 2:29 QG (Par) 2:7 QE 2:25b QE isf 25, 31

φοράδην Flacc 75 Legat 267

φορεῖον Decal 4

φορέω (33) Leg 2:28, 95 Leg 3:38, 153 Sacr 13, 90 Post 23, 25 Deus 172 Agr 75 Ebr 113, 198 Conf 198 Her 121, 287 Congr 58 Fug 28 Mut 214, 239 Somn 1:147, 202 Somn 2:61, 136, 237 Mos 2:228 Spec 3:3 Spec 4:158 Praem 130 Flacc 135, 172 Legat 103, 120 QG (Par) 2:4

φορητός (6) Det 148 Mos 2:73 Spec 1:165 Contempl 1 Legat 287 QE 2:49b

φορμηδόν Flacc 92

φορολογία Spec 3:163

φόρος (19) Agr 8, 58 Plant 57 Migr 204 Abr 228, 237, 240 Spec 1:142 Spec 2:92, 93, 96, 205 Spec 3:159 Spec 4:212, 214, 218 Legat 199, 287 Hypoth 7:18

φορός Migr 100

φορτηγός Legat 47

φορτικός Sacr 32 Fug 82

φορτίον Deus 98

φορτίς Spec 4:186 Legat 146, 251

φόρτος Post 148 Gig 31 Plant 24 Ios 15 Legat 129

φορυτός Sacr 61, 109 Spec 1:156 Spec 4:29 Prov 2:62

Φουά Her 128, 128

φραγμός (7) Det 105 Agr 11, 14, 19 Conf 33 Somn 2:262 Mos 1:271

φράζω (24) Opif 73, 81, 98 Cher 111 Det 18 Deus 175 Ebr 180 Migr 75 Her 42 Mut 221 Abr 153 Mos 1:149, 155 Mos 2:19, 44 Decal 89, 108 Spec 2:20 Spec 3:69 Spec 4:88 Flacc 101 Legat 65, 152 Hypoth 6:9

φράσις Det 79 Somn 1:205 Aet 56

φράσσω (7) Conf 111 Migr 224 Abr 229 Mos 1:224, 260 Virt 186 Prob 152

φραστήρ Ios 256

φρέαρ (46) Leg 3:12 Post 130, 132, 151, 153, 153, 153 Plant 73, 74, 78, 78, 79, 80, 83 Ebr 112, 112, 113 Fug 200, 212, 212, 213 Somn 1:4, 5, 5, 6, 8, 10, 11, 14, 24, 38, 39, 39, 40, 41, 42, 61, 68, 172 Somn 2:271 Abr 241 Mos 1:99, 255, 255, 256 QG 4:193

φρενοβλάβεια (17) Ebr 123 Conf 5, 22 Fug 14 Mut 62, 203 Somn 2:85, 120, 290 Ios 51 Mos 2:197 Spec 2:15 Spec 3:32, 43, 147 Praem 170 Legat 94

φρενοβλαβής (8) Ebr 95 Conf 115, 162 Fug 199 Mos 1:293 Spec 1:20 Praem 135 Legat 206

φρήν (11) Leg 3:20 Cher 69, 71 Migr 138 Fug 200 Somn 2:46 Mos 1:325 Spec 1:311 Spec 4:129, 200 Virt 179

φρίκη Flacc 176 Legat 267, 357

φρικώδης Somn 2:123 Decal 141 Spec 2:8

φρίσσω Det 140 Somn 1:142 Flacc 115, 167 Legat 211

φρονέω (69) Opif 164 Leg 1:67, 74, 79, 79, 79, 79 Leg 3:20, 20, 21, 134 Sacr 29 Det 13, 73, 74, 114, 166 Post 71, 126 Deus 66 Agr 115 Plant 66 Ebr 128, 142, 183 Conf 93, 118 Migr 102, 112, 134 Her 27, 178 Congr 6, 44 Somn 1:56, 209 Somn 2:85, 104, 134, 174, 180, 182 Abr 192, 228, 266 Ios 59, 68, 138, 166, 216 Mos 1:29, 46, 183 Spec 2:8, 256 Spec 3:1 Spec 4:121 Virt 14 Prob 12 Contempl 58, 72 Flacc 147 Legat 152, 182, 190, 258 Prov 2:13, 15, 46 φρόνημα (47) Opif 17 Cher 64 Post 165 Gig 4 Ebr 128, 198 Sobr 20 Her 269 Fug 207 Mut 176 Somn 1:39, 140 Somn 2:9, 79 Abr 26, 223 Ios 4, 79, 144 Mos 1:40, 51, 149, 259, 266, 309, 325 Spec 1:293 Spec 4:45 Virt 3, 71, 165, 172, 216 Praem 74, 119 Prob 24, 62, 111, 119, 121, 130 Flacc 64 Legat 62, 215 Hypoth 6:1, 11:16 QG isf 5

φρόνησις (195) Opif 73, 154 Leg 1:63, 65, 66, 66, 67, 67, 70, 70, 71, 74, 74, 75, 77, 78, 78, 78, 79, 79, 79, 80, 86, 92 Leg 3:14, 150, 151, 152, 247 Cher 5, 96 Sacr 4, 26, 27, 37, 84, 126 Det 18, 24, 73, 75, 114, 143, 157, 165 Post 86, 93, 128, 135, 136 Deus 3, 79, 90, 164, 166 Agr 9, 18, 61, 73, 77, 104, 158 Plant 40, 98, 137, 144, 144, 168 Ebr 10, 20, 23, 86, 140, 148 Sobr 3, 23, 24, 61 Conf 40, 81, 91, 163 Migr 126, 134, 164, 166, 169, 201, 223, 224 Her 49, 209, 258, 290, 298 Congr 2, 5, 24, 35, 72, 73, 98, 114, 129, 129, 154, 155, 156, 179 Fug 17, 45, 52, 63, 125, 194, 198, 207 Mut 79, 79, 79, 81, 124, 137, 149, 197, 260 Somn 1:48, 49, 59, 80, 82, 177, 179, 199 Somn 2:43, 65, 96, 134, 198, 234 Abr 24, 57, 163, 219, 271 Ios 268 Mos 1:25, 249 Mos 2:185, 216, 236 Spec 1:191, 191, 277, 339 Spec 2:12, 18, 31, 48, 62, 173, 259, 259 Spec 4:93, 134, 135, 170 Virt 5, 11, 32, 129, 180 Praem 51, 52, 66, 81, 81, 160 Prob 14, 28, 67, 70, 107, 150, 159 Contempl 14, 31 Aet 2 Legat 33 Prov 2:1 QG 1:20, 3:11b, 22 QE 2:20 QE isf 24

φρόνιμος (47) Leg 1:67, 74, 74, 79, 79, 86 Leg 2:18, 53, 71, 106 Sacr 54 Det 75 Post 32 Ebr 197 Sobr 38, 40 Migr 219 Congr 142 Mut 50, 91, 91, 146, 146, 153, 220 Ios 114, 117, 143 Mos 1:325 Spec 1:3 Virt 167, 174, 177 Prob 59, 59, 72 Aet 94 Legat 53, 64, 142, 222 Prov 2:47, 67 QG 1:31, 2:72, 3:22, 4:204

φροντίζω (52) Opif 130 Deus 57, 167 Agr 35 Ebr 35, 77 Conf 118 Migr 86, 90 Her 191, 302 Fug 52 Somn 1:99 Abr 67, 86, 94, 152, 180, 198 Ios 63, 71, 76, 153, 203, 260 Mos 1:24, 111 Decal 118 Spec 1:176, 316 Spec 2:118, 199, 236, 250 Spec 4:40, 43, 142, 175 Virt 221 Praem 103 Prob 116, 144 Contempl 53, 75 Legat 28, 157, 186, 191, 260, 274, 330 Prov 1

φροντίς (50) Cher 68 Sacr 38, 39, 104, 113, 114, 121 Deus 93 Agr 5, 105 Plant 56 Sobr 63 Her 48 Congr 6 Fug 199 Somn 1:8 Somn 2:12, 165, 206 Abr 30, 70, 96 Ios 103, 179, 229, 234 Mos 1:14, 22, 168 Mos 2:211 Spec 1:62, 69, 125, 219, 260, 298 Spec 2:101, 213 Spec 3:3, 62, 171 Spec 4:124, 188 Virt 155 Praem 161 Prob 87 Aet 67 Hypoth 11:13 QG 2:54d QE 2:13b

φροντιστήριον Prob 13

φροντιστής Somn 1:134 Somn 2:155

φροῦδος Leg 3:116

φρουρά (7) Agr 15, 86 Migr 215 Somn 1:103 Mos 1:246, 257 Flacc 114

φρουρέω Mos 1:235 Decal 74

φρουρός Det 62, 165 Plant 41 Conf 27

φρύαγμα Leg 3:193

φρυάσσομαι (12) Cher 66 Deus 168 Congr 151 Fug 30, 107 Somn 2:61 Mos 1:298, 302 Decal 41 Spec 3:8 Spec 4:74 Virt 173

φρυγανισμός Mos 2:213 Spec 2:250 Prob 32 Flacc 69

φρύγανον Flacc 68 Legat 130

φρυγανώδης Legat 130

φρύγω Sacr 76, 80, 80, 87

φρῦνος Mos 1:105 Spec 3:123

φυγαδευτήριον Fug 100 Flacc 159

φυγαδεύω (35) Opif 155, 168 Leg 1:61 Leg 3:1, 7, 186 Cher 3, 10, 103 Plant 46, 61 Ebr 10 Sobr 8 Conf 196 Congr 53, 57, 171 Fug 107, 114 Mut 205 Somn 1:117 Somn 2:180 Decal 119 Spec 1:89, 150, 160, 323 Spec 4:189 Aet 56, 112 Flacc 94, 144 Legat 49, 87, 123

φυγάς (31) Opif 165 Leg 1:54 Leg 2:98 Leg 3:1, 1, 3, 28, 116, 232 Cher 121 Sacr 128, 128, 128 Gig 67 Her 26, 179 Fug 2, 87, 87, 88, 89, 89, 116, 119 Somn 2:184 Spec 1:160 Spec 3:133 Prob 6 Flacc 161, 172, 183

φυγή (64) Leg 2:91, 91 Leg 3:17, 172, 178, 242 Cher 2, 4, 9, 30, 74 Sacr 129 Det 143 Post 9 Deus 49 Plant 37, 45 Ebr 8, 171, 224 Her 169, 270 Fug 3, 20, 22, 22, 53, 63, 67, 89 Mut 153, 197 Abr 64, 64, 229, 241 Mos 1:77 Spec 1:161, 187, 196, 284, 340 Spec 2:228, 228 Spec 3:123, 123, 150, 168, 181 Spec 4:23, 108 Virt 205 Praem 117, 138 Prob 7, 55, 83, 145 Flacc 105, 151, 181 Legat 110, 341, 341

φῦκος Spec 3:37

φυλακή (25) Leg 1:55 Det 62, 62, 65, 68 Post 181 Deus 17, 96, 113 Plant 104 Ebr 210 Her 105 Congr 98 Mut 74 Mos 1:108 Mos 2:174 Spec 1:154 Spec 2:14, 125 Spec 3:20 Spec 4:149 Legat 192, 240, 249, 308

φυλακτήριον (8) Agr 15, 19 Plant 3 Ebr 201 Migr 215 Somn 2:82 Spec 1:216, 289

φυλακτικός Leg 3:25 Sacr 136 Det 164 Mos 2:106 Legat 210

φύλαξ (31) Leg 1:54, 55 Leg 3:164, 164, 166, 189 Det 57, 62, 62, 63, 63, 64, 65, 65, 66, 68, 165 Deus 113 Plant 26, 41 Ebr 80 Conf 27, 48 Somn 2:272 Spec 2:207, 253 Spec 4:9 Praem 22 Flacc 111, 155, 157

φυλάρχης (φύλαρχος) Her 175, 176, 177 Fug 73 Ios 1 Mos 1:221 Mos 2:112, 178 Virt 77

φύλαρχος φυλάρχης)

φυλάσσω (114) Opif 148 Leg 1:42, 53, 54, 66, 88, 89, 89, 89 Leg 2:57 Leg 3:25, 26 Cher 1, 48, 51, 81 Sacr 60, 60, 61 Det 63, 64, 66, 67, 68 Post 99 Gig 20 Deus 24, 43 Agr 51 Plant 101, 105 Ebr 48, 84, 84, 84, 213 Conf 151, 182 Migr 88, 93, 150, 174 Her 8, 105, 110, 123, 129, 233 Congr 86, 86, 106, 165, 170 Fug 201 Somn 1:27 Somn 2:90, 175 Ios 17, 111, 264 Mos 1:68, 108, 241, 249, 294 Mos 2:17, 19, 145 Decal 74, 125 Spec 1:76, 124, 250, 288 Spec 2:24, 131, 250, 257, 260 Spec 3:14, 94, 145, 146, 166, 172 Spec 4:29, 33, 41 Virt 21, 138, 139, 153, 205 Praem 72, 79, 101 Prob 86, 147 Aet 112 Flacc 50, 83, 134 Legat 109, 152, 174, 226, 232, 305, 322 Prov 2:58 QG 1:69, 2:15a, 64c QE 2:19

φυλέτης (8) Abr 67 Mos 1:7 Spec 2:82, 126, 129 Spec 4:16 Prob 9 QG isf 10

φυλή (59) Leg 2:94 Plant 63, 63 Sobr 66 Conf 111 Migr 1, 118, 119, 122 Her 124, 175 Congr 98, 131, 132, 133, 168 Fug 74, 87, 90, 93, 185 Mut 2 Somn 1:3, 176, 177 Mos 1:189, 221, 227, 288, 306, 306, 320, 327 Mos 2:160, 170, 175, 178, 186, 234, 273, 288 Spec 1:79, 151, 154 Spec 2:119, 120, 126, 128, 128, 161, 183 Spec 3:123, 124, 126 Virt 42, 77 Praem 57, 57, 65

φυλλάς Aet 63

φυλλοβολέω Legat 297

φύλλον Somn 1:125 Praem 148 Aet 132 QG 1:41

φυλλορροέω (6) Ebr 9 Her 270 Mos 2:186 Spec 2:153 Spec 4:209 Aet 132

φύραμα (7) Opif 38 Sacr 107, 107, 108, 108 Spec 1:132 Spec 2:158

φυράω Sacr 59, 60 Somn 1:210

φυρμός QG 4:47b

φύρω (35) Leg 3:187 Det 77 Deus 8 Agr 129 Ebr 57, 100, 143 Migr 59 Her 15, 64, 109, 234 Fug 47, 85, 153 Mut 50 Somn 1:221, 221 Somn 2:66, 290, 290 Abr 20, 83 Ios 53, 256 Spec 1:329 Spec 2:6, 94 Spec 3:209 Spec 4:77, 208 Virt 137 Legat 162 QG 2:12c, 4:33b

φυσάω (34) Cher 37, 64, 70 Post 115 Ebr 93 Her 71, 269, 296 Congr 107, 127 Fug 44 Mut 215 Somn 1:211 Somn 2:16, 115, 290 Mos 1:30, 195, 250 Mos 2:96, 277 Decal 41 Spec 1:10, 293 Spec 2:18 Virt 163, 173 Praem 47 Legat 69, 86, 154, 255 Prov 2:14 QE 2:14

φύσημα Plant 157 Ebr 128 Somn 2:46

φυσικός (106) Opif 117, 123, 132 Leg 1:25, 37, 39, 39, 57, 59, 100 Leg 2:5, 6, 12 Leg 3:16, 61, 177, 185 Cher 57, 66 Sacr 102 Det 129, 145 Post 7, 60, 85, 130, 135 Deus 11, 77, 80 Agr 14, 15 Plant 120 Ebr 9, 99, 118, 202 Sobr 48 Conf 60 Her 254 Fug 19, 108, 112, 116, 128, 149, 153, 194 Mut 74, 75, 92, 97, 147, 156, 184, 220, 262 Somn 1:221 Somn 2:35 Abr 52, 99, 168, 222, 241, 253 Ios 232, 240 Mos 1:76, 132, 150, 184 Mos 2:96, 103 Decal 152 Spec 1:250, 336 Spec 2:93 Spec 3:97, 110, 117 Spec 4:201, 223 Virt 8, 96, 128 Praem 85 Prob 74, 80 Contempl 40, 65 Aet 27, 33, 135, 146 Legat 238 Prov 2:47 QG 2:5a, 4:30, 100, 200a QG (Par) 2:1, 2:3, 2:4, 2:5 QE 1:7a, 2:3a

φυσιογνωμονέω Somn 1:164

φυσιολογέω Leg 3:61 Mut 62 Aet 75, 94

φυσιολογία (14) Leg 1:60 Cher 4, 87, 121 Agr 16 Ebr 91, 92 Her 98 Mut 73, 76, 220 Somn 1:120, 184 Aet 138

φυσιολόγος Cher 7 Hypoth 7:20

φύσις (1342) Opif 3, 8, 13, 15, 21, 23, 29, 33, 35, 36, 38, 44, 45, 49, 49, 49, 53, 54, 55, 60, 61, 66, 67, 67, 67, 68, 69, 73, 73, 79, 82, 82, 83, 83, 84, 85, 85, 89, 90, 95, 97, 97, 102, 105, 106, 111, 113, 114, 124, 126, 128, 129, 130, 133, 133, 134, 134, 135, 135, 139, 140, 143, 144, 146, 149, 150, 150, 151, 154, 159, 169, 171 Leg 1:1, 2, 8, 16, 18, 18, 28, 38, 50, 52, 77, 92, 107, 107 Leg 2:2, 10, 22, 22, 23, 23, 37, 42, 47, 67, 75, 89, 99, 105 Leg 3:7, 12, 24, 61, 64, 67, 71, 75, 77, 78, 84, 89, 91, 104, 108, 110, 115, 130, 145, 147, 157, 161, 162, 206, 206, 207, 210, 213, 219, 226, 242, 252 Cher 9, 19, 36, 38, 39, 41, 43, 50, 51, 54, 61, 67, 76, 86, 87, 90, 92, 97, 111, 115 Sacr 4, 21, 28, 30, 33, 36, 40, 44, 66, 68, 69, 73, 75, 82, 86, 98, 99, 100, 101, 101, 102, 114, 114, 116, 117, 125, 125, 127 Det 7, 28, 29, 33, 52, 62, 68, 75, 76, 77, 83, 84, 87, 88, 88, 89, 101, 106, 108, 125, 138, 151, 152, 154, 177 Post 4, 5, 13, 16, 20, 26, 28, 31, 32, 52, 62, 66, 71, 81, 83, 93, 99, 100, 103, 104, 106, 109, 109, 115, 118, 127, 130, 133, 134, 150, 150, 154, 160, 162, 173, 182, 185 Gig 4, 25, 30, 43, 59, 62, 65 Deus 13, 24, 25, 32, 35, 37, 38, 41, 45, 45, 46, 55, 56, 61, 63, 72, 77, 93, 104, 108, 112, 151 Agr 1, 8, 24, 30, 30, 31, 37, 38, 43, 46, 51, 56, 59, 62, 66, 133, 134, 142, 164, 168, 171, 180 Plant 3, 9, 13, 18, 24, 25, 27, 41, 44, 49, 49, 68, 75, 79, 91, 110, 110, 114, 118, 127, 130, 132, 135, 135, 157, 159, 171 Ebr 8, 13, 13, 14, 24, 25, 34, 37, 47, 48, 55, 55, 68, 70, 90, 90, 105, 115, 121, 131, 133, 135, 141, 164, 166, 167, 169, 172, 180, 180, 182, 189, 190, 190, 190, 201, 211, 212 Sobr 14, 25, 36, 38, 46, 53, 67 Conf 32, 43, 46, 49, 52, 68, 73, 75, 77, 87, 90, 102, 106, 110, 121, 126, 133, 133, 141, 154, 154, 154, 157, 159, 173, 176, 180, 181 Migr 12, 26, 31, 33, 46, 68, 75, 78, 83, 85, 94, 95, 105, 108, 118, 128, 132, 138, 139, 145, 150, 156, 167, 167, 167, 185, 189, 192, 197, 198, 202, 206, 207, 210, 212, 216, 224 Her 33, 36, 49, 53, 66, 71, 75, 76, 88, 95, 110, 115, 115, 116, 116, 116, 121, 121, 130, 135, 137, 142, 146, 152, 154, 164, 172, 176, 180, 182, 184, 204, 213, 217, 232, 233, 234, 235, 237, 238, 238, 246, 246, 252, 258, 274, 279, 302, 312 Congr 2, 4, 17, 25, 25, 36, 37, 52, 59, 61, 61, 71, 85, 88, 108, 113, 117, 122, 129, 133, 143, 144, 144, 146, 165, 169 Fug 11, 14, 22, 34, 50, 51, 63, 66, 72, 74, 99, 112, 118, 122, 141, 141, 146, 148, 154, 155, 162, 163, 164, 167, 168, 169, 170, 171, 172, 172, 172, 172, 179 Mut 2, 7, 12, 12, 14, 46, 60, 71, 84, 86, 88, 89, 90, 101, 105, 108, 112, 117, 133, 140, 151, 158, 159, 162, 167, 173, 178, 184, 186, 197, 199, 211, 211, 219, 225, 231, 246, 247, 257, 260, 264, 266, 270 Somn 1:6, 11, 18, 19, 20, 21, 27, 31, 33, 34, 49, 53, 53, 59, 94, 97, 102, 103, 106, 109, 111, 114, 123, 126, 129, 131, 136, 137, 138, 145, 150, 157, 157, 160, 162, 167, 168, 169, 171, 172, 176, 206, 210, 232, 236, 241 Somn 2:8, 40, 44, 54, 60, 79, 90, 115, 117, 118, 122, 136, 147, 174, 186, 188, 194, 213, 223, 228, 234, 240, 243, 262, 271, 283 Abr 5, 6, 6, 11, 14, 15, 16, 19, 21, 27, 35, 37, 38, 43, 46, 52, 52, 53, 53, 53, 54, 55, 58, 60, 61, 75, 77, 79, 83, 84, 87, 88, 102, 105, 105, 107, 115, 135, 135, 137, 144, 153, 157, 159, 162, 165, 185, 193, 195, 199, 200, 202, 207, 208, 218, 237, 248, 249, 256, 257, 259, 275 Ios 1, 4, 10, 24, 25, 28, 29, 30, 31, 31, 31, 38, 40, 81, 82, 83, 118, 129, 142, 167, 170, 189, 192, 248, 254, 264 Mos 1:3, 5, 8, 21, 22, 26, 28, 32, 39, 48, 59, 60, 68, 70, 72, 76, 83, 93, 101, 103, 113, 117, 124, 130, 143, 149, 153, 158, 160, 165, 185, 190, 197, 211, 218, 226, 241 Mos 2:5, 7, 9, 14, 22, 27, 37, 48, 52, 58, 61, 63, 65, 66, 68, 81, 84, 88, 100, 118, 127, 128, 128, 135, 139, 154, 161, 180, 181, 191, 207, 209, 211, 211, 216, 222, 222, 236, 240, 245, 249, 251, 263, 281, 288 Decal 3, 6, 8, 24, 25, 30, 41, 43, 51, 59, 64, 75, 76, 81, 84, 87, 98, 99, 100, 101, 102, 103, 104, 107, 110, 111, 112, 115, 117, 132, 132, 136, 137, 142, 150, 163, 175, 177, 177 Spec 1:13, 19, 31, 39, 44, 47, 61, 62, 66, 81, 85, 89, 91, 96, 97, 97, 116, 137, 146, 155, 162, 162, 172, 176, 180, 191, 202, 216, 217, 219, 220, 246, 266, 269, 273, 294, 295, 300, 305, 306, 306, 310, 311, 313, 318, 322, 325, 335 Spec 2:3, 6, 13, 16, 21, 23, 23, 29, 39, 40, 42, 45, 45, 48, 50, 51, 52, 55, 58, 69, 69, 73, 84, 100, 103, 109, 122, 124, 129, 130, 137, 141, 150, 158, 159, 159, 161, 165, 166, 170, 172, 173, 177, 178, 190, 191, 196, 198, 205, 210, 212, 225, 230, 231, 232, 233, 235, 239, 241, 253 Spec 3:9, 21, 23, 28, 28, 32, 33, 33, 36, 37, 38, 39, 45, 46, 47, 48, 51, 52, 97, 99, 100, 103, 108, 109, 111, 112, 118, 121, 125, 129, 136, 137, 137, 151, 156, 158, 163, 173, 176, 176, 178, 180, 184, 189, 198, 205 Spec 4:14, 18, 24, 24, 29, 40, 46, 46, 48, 51, 55, 64, 68, 68, 71, 77, 79, 89, 92, 104, 109, 114, 116, 119, 123, 131, 140, 155, 175, 178, 204, 208, 210, 212, 215, 225, 227, 231, 233, 236 Virt 2, 6, 7, 8, 9, 12, 18, 19, 19, 36, 39, 59, 76, 79, 80, 81, 87, 93, 94, 97, 105, 117, 125, 127, 129, 132, 133, 133, 135, 140, 143, 152, 154, 160, 168, 172, 173, 192, 203, 217, 225 Praem 9, 11, 13, 15, 23, 26, 27, 31, 34, 36, 36, 39, 42, 46, 50, 50, 59, 62, 63, 64, 65, 77, 83, 85, 89, 91, 92, 99, 100, 108, 128, 130, 149, 153, 155, 160, 162, 165 Prob 19, 30,

31, 37, 38, 40, 43, 46, 50, 62, 63, 70, 74, 79, 80, 89, 91, 102, 105, 106, 108, 114, 117, 123, 125, 129, 130, 143, 158, 160 Contempl 2, 9, 9, 17, 28, 33, 37, 54, 59, 64, 70, 90 Aet 12, 19, 21, 28, 28, 29, 30, 31, 31, 32, 33, 34, 34, 35, 35, 37, 37, 44, 47, 53, 57, 58, 59, 59, 63, 66, 68, 68, 69, 75, 75, 75, 75, 94, 103, 105, 112, 115, 115, 119, 130, 130, 132, 133, 136, 144, 147, 148 Flacc 1, 4, 25, 29, 29, 59, 66, 79, 106, 154, 176, 180, 187 Legat 1, 1, 1, 23, 30, 34, 50, 56, 57, 68, 70, 75, 81, 91, 106, 112, 114, 118, 126, 143, 159, 161, 162, 168, 190, 190, 193, 213, 229, 230, 243, 244, 245, 301, 310, 320, 339, 355, 359, 367 Hypoth 6:4, 7:20, 11:13, 11:17 Prov 1, 2:3, 6, 12, 16, 16, 18, 18, 22, 23, 27, 38, 47, 49, 50, 51, 52, 53, 57, 57, 58, 59, 61, 69, 70 QG 1:28, 55b, 74, 76b, 2:34a, 41, 41, 54a, 62, 3:7, 38b, 4:51c, 184, 184, 193, 9* QG isf 2, 10 QG (Par) 2:2, 2:3, 2:4, 2:7 QE 2:1, 1, 1, 3b, 19, 25a, 26, 46 QE isf 3, 3, 4, 5, 31

φυτεία Opif 41, 59 Plant 119 Praem 155

φυτεύω (68) Opif 41, 80, 153 Leg 1:41, 43, 43, 45, 48, 48, 48, 48, 49, 49, 49, 49, 49, 51, 52, 52, 56, 80 Leg 3:227 Det 102, 105 Gig 4 Deus 30, 40, 91, 94 Agr 1, 8, 9, 9, 18, 25, 148 Plant 1, 29, 32, 49, 73, 77, 96, 96, 99, 99, 109, 136, 140 Sobr 36 Conf 61, 106 Migr 37, 223 Her 206 Fug 97 Mut 173, 190 Somn 2:170 Mos 2:207 Spec 1:305 Virt 28, 29, 29 Praem 128 Prob 109 Aet 122 QG isf 3

φυτικός Leg 2:22, 45 Spec 1:254

φυτόν (156) Opif 42, 44, 44, 46, 52, 64, 73, 88, 113, 132, 133, 133, 140, 153, 154, 156 Leg 1:49, 56 Leg 2:22, 22, 71, 75 Leg 3:75, 76, 99, 227, 242 Cher 62, 111 Sacr 25, 25, 97 Det 85, 111 Post 125, 163, 171 Deus 37, 41, 44, 48, 87, 107, 119, 154 Agr 7, 14, 14, 15, 17, 18, 51 Plant 2, 2, 2, 11, 11, 13, 14, 15, 16, 17, 28, 29, 31, 36, 37, 42, 48, 73, 73, 78, 93, 97, 100, 101, 101, 104, 106, 139, 141, 141 Ebr 2, 106, 110, 164, 223 Conf 61 Migr 24, 55, 125, 185 Her 110, 115, 115, 121, 140, 211 Congr 4, 123, 133, 138 Fug 124, 132, 187 Mut 63, 74, 74, 149, 161, 264 Somn 1:203 Somn 2:158, 162, 195, 242 Abr 1, 159 Mos 1:65, 68, 121, 145, 212 Mos 2:22, 126, 179 Spec 1:16, 27, 34, 92, 210, 322, 339 Spec 2:151, 154, 172, 172 Spec 3:191 Spec 4:23, 181, 211, 218, 228 Virt 138, 148, 154, 155 Praem 68 Contempl 3 Aet 4, 95, 95, 96 Legat 80 Prov 2:43, 66

φυτουργέω Leg 1:49 Plant 31

φυτουργία (7) Leg 1:43, 46, 54 Agr 181 Plant 2, 32 Hypoth 11:8

φυτουργός (8) Agr 157, 158 Plant 2, 2, 73, 94 Conf 61, 196

φύω (271) Opif 13, 23, 45, 51, 54, 73, 83, 99, 100, 101, 104, 124, 132, 145, 148, 156, 157, 161, 163 Leg 1:4, 46, 76 Leg 2:43, 45, 74 Leg 3:2, 15, 26, 43, 81, 123, 246, 247, 248, 253 Cher 53, 59, 68, 84, 90, 96 Sacr 29, 34, 46, 77, 80, 80, 105, 131, 134 Det 38, 55, 58, 72, 92, 122, 141, 174 Post 24, 42, 85 Gig 3, 42, 46, 48 Deus 19, 29, 54, 97, 117, 119 Agr 19, 85 Plant 42, 79, 84, 114 Ebr 36, 86, 91, 111, 133, 168, 178, 211 Sobr 29 Conf 32, 131, 132, 186 Migr 16, 36, 40, 51, 87, 106, 108, 108, 175, 216, 219 Her 187, 206, 207, 230, 245, 249, 298 Congr 21, 82, 87, 117, 135 Fug 46, 105, 105, 117, 138, 146, 209 Mut 9, 11, 143, 145, 150, 164 Somn 1:15, 20, 25, 42, 60, 153, 154, 230 Somn 2:10, 14, 22, 95, 154, 232 Abr 23, 56, 72, 87, 101, 106, 131, 264 Ios 5, 17, 204 Mos 1:109, 279 Mos 2:11, 43, 61, 106, 122, 176, 181, 183, 184 Decal 4, 34, 49, 92, 137, 155 Spec 1:6, 18, 25, 30, 33, 47, 51, 100, 222, 223, 266, 338 Spec 2:29, 56, 72, 89, 129, 133, 140, 143, 185, 186 Spec 3:13, 17, 17, 43, 65, 84, 85, 91, 194, 209 Spec 4:20, 60, 204, 212, 235 Virt 5, 8, 54, 55, 56, 82, 93, 162, 186, 187, 191, 197, 199 Praem 20, 21, 52, 105, 131, 136, 136, 145, 152, 172 Prob 5, 22, 48, 48, 60, 70, 109, 149, 155 Contempl 62 Aet 23, 23, 24, 30, 43, 62, 67, 98, 119, 126, 132, 140 Flacc 12, 17, 48, 91 Legat 7, 17, 68, 153, 287, 293 Prov 2:36, 66, 66, 69, 71 QG 1:21, 2:64c, 4:51b, 76b QE 1:7b QE isf 3

φωκίς Prov 2:33

φωλεός (7) Det 17, 103 Migr 188, 190 Her 85, 238 Spec 1:62

φωλεύω (10) Leg 1:71 Leg 3:6, 114 Her 45 Somn 1:42 Spec 1:215 Aet 86 Flacc 166 Legat 48 Prov 2:62

φωνασκέω Flacc 138

φωνέω (9) Opif 126 Leg 3:44 Sacr 74 Det 79, 127 Congr 69 Fug 63 Decal 74 Prob 155

φωνή (218) Opif 62, 121, 126, 139, 156, 160, 163, 165 Leg 1:25 Leg 2:7, 26, 39, 75, 88 Leg 3:22, 44, 44, 54, 56, 57, 57, 58, 120, 188, 195, 220, 222, 235, 245 Cher 35, 57, 116, 117 Sacr 23, 30, 31, 34, 74 Det 48, 69, 70, 79, 91, 92, 101, 125, 128, 128, 173 Post 44, 104, 106 Gig 52, 64 Deus 15, 25, 146 Agr 34, 53, 96, 112, 136 Plant 10, 39, 126, 131, 131, 133, 151, 154, 159 Ebr 14, 14, 19, 94, 96, 96, 96, 96, 96, 98, 98, 101, 102, 104, 104, 105, 123 Sobr 36 Conf 1, 1, 9, 10, 15, 123, 189, 189, 192, 194, 195 Migr 47, 47, 48, 48, 48, 49, 50, 51, 52, 104, 111, 115, 208 Her 8, 17, 31, 66, 67, 67, 111, 119, 232 Congr 63, 68, 69, 69, 70, 150, 172 Fug 15, 23, 191 Mut 21, 110, 111, 139, 162, 242, 251 Somn 1:27, 28, 29, 29, 29, 235, 236 Somn 2:175, 260, 262 Abr 60, 81, 101, 119, 148, 176, 239 Ios 42, 48, 166 Mos 1:66, 84, 274, 286, 331 Mos 2:127, 164, 196, 199, 213, 239, 239 Decal 32, 33, 34, 35, 36, 46, 47, 48 Spec 1:147, 266, 342 Spec 2:7, 132, 132, 189, 198, 256 Spec 3:78 Spec 4:49, 88, 132 Virt 10, 136, 217 Prob 90, 95, 96, 141 Contempl 31, 33 Flacc 55, 144 Legat 6, 66, 264, 304, 323 Prov 2:32 QG 1:32, 70:1, 4:227 QG (Par) 2:3, 2:3 QE 2:16, 38b QE isf 16, 21

φωνήεις (11) Opif 126 Leg 1:14 Sacr 74 Det 91, 91 Agr 136 Plant 10 Her 210 Congr 150 Mut 63, 64

φωνητήριος (22) Opif 117 Leg 1:11, 104 Leg 3:119 Cher 35, 105 Det 38, 68, 102, 127 Post 103 Agr 30 Conf 36, 150 Migr 72 Her 4, 266 Congr 29, 33 Mut 56, 69 Spec 1:272

φώρ Congr 150 Ios 68 Spec 1:127 Spec 4:2, 10

φωράω Ios 44 Spec 3:80

φώριος Spec 4:2, 5, 11 Legat 343

φῶς (184) Opif 29, 30, 30, 31, 33, 33, 35, 53, 53, 54, 55, 58, 71 Leg 1:17, 18, 46 Leg 3:45, 45, 45, 45, 104, 167, 167, 167, 167, 167, 167, 171, 179, 230 Cher 61, 96, 97 Sacr 34, 36, 36, 36 Det 101, 117, 118, 127, 128, 128 Post 57 Gig 41 Deus 3, 45, 58, 58, 58, 78, 96, 96, 123, 135 Plant 118 Ebr 155, 157, 168, 190, 191, 208 Sobr 4 Conf 61, 116 Migr 35, 39, 40, 47, 154 Her 146, 163, 163, 163, 197, 208, 264, 290 Congr 45, 45, 47, 48, 48 Fug 110, 136 Mut 4, 5, 6, 92, 162, 162 Somn 1:72, 75, 75, 75, 75, 75, 76, 76, 79, 91, 99, 113, 116, 117, 176, 202 Somn 2:34, 34, 39, 74, 106, 134, 140, 203 Abr 119, 119, 156, 157, 159, 205 Ios 68, 68, 106, 145, 145 Mos 1:66, 125, 126, 145, 212 Mos 2:194

Decal 49, 138, 143 Spec 1:42, 54, 90, 279, 288, 288, 288, 296, 319, 339, 339 Spec 2:59, 155, 204, 210 Spec 3:6, 109, 119 Spec 4:52, 60, 166, 187, 231 Virt 12, 12, 137, 164, 179, 188 Praem 45, 45, 46, 46, 82 Prob 5 Contempl 7, 27, 34, 78 Legat 103, 326, 364 Prov 2:19 QG 2:14, 34a, 4:30, 51a, 93 QE 2:28

φωσφορέω (6) Opif 55, 168 Her 222, 263 Mos 2:103 Decal 49

φωσφόρος (9) Opif 29, 53 Plant 169 Ebr 44 Her 224 Fug 184 Somn 1:214 Mos 1:120 Mos 2:102

φωτίζω (7) Deus 79 Her 307 Congr 106 Fug 139 Decal 49 Spec 1:178 Spec 2:141

φωτισμός Mut 67 Somn 1:53, 75

φωτοειδής Somn 1:217, 220

X

χαίνω χάσκω

Χαιρέας Prob 125

χαίρω (114) Opif 63, 115, 157, 161, 165 Leg 1:8, 64 Leg 3:86, 87, 189, 217, 219 Cher 86, 107 Sacr 13 Det 94, 124, 125, 126, 129, 130, 131, 135, 135, 136, 137, 138 Post 83, 184, 184 Deus 170 Agr 38, 73 Ebr 144, 179, 211 Conf 32, 43, 88 Migr 19, 75, 79, 88, 155, 155, 158 Her 45 Congr 125 Fug 37, 154, 206, 206, 209 Mut 161, 163, 168, 168, 169, 169, 170, 171, 226, 264 Somn 2:74, 176, 234 Abr 22, 30, 165, 202, 204, 206 Ios 74, 83, 208 Mos 1:49, 117, 149, 155, 247 Mos 2:44, 166 Decal 89, 108, 117 Spec 1:144, 148, 271, 271 Spec 2:20, 35, 48, 54, 85, 185 Spec 3:69, 193 Spec 4:91 Virt 103 Praem 20, 27, 152 Aet 40, 85, 121 Flacc 101 Legat 50, 65, 182, 315 Hypoth 11:6 Prov 2:13 QG 3:38b, 4:52b

χαίτη Agr 69 Ios 105 Mos 1:54

χάλαζα (10) Opif 80 Mut 21 Mos 1:118, 118, 118, 119, 121, 126, 145, 200

χαλάω (43) Opif 141 Leg 2:28 Leg 3:153, 183 Sacr 16, 37 Det 103 Post 71 Deus 79 Ebr 116, 185 Conf 166 Mut 160, 215 Somn 2:13, 58, 165, 233, 238, 294, 299 Abr 152 Ios 61 Mos 1:40, 122 Mos 2:113, 130 Decal 40 Spec 2:60, 98 Spec 3:33, 193 Spec 4:102 Virt 113 Praem 48, 144 Aet 62, 118, 149 Flacc 9 Legat 117, 267 QE 1:19

χαλβάνη Her 196, 197, 197, 198, 226

Χαλδαία Somn 1:52

χαλδαΐζω (7) Migr 184 Her 99 Mut 16 Somn 1:161 Abr 70, 77, 77

Χαλδαϊκός (16) Ebr 94 Migr 177, 184 Her 97, 280, 289 Congr 49 Mut 16 Abr 71, 82 Mos 1:23 Mos 2:26, 31, 38, 40 Praem 58

Χαλδαῖος (22) Gig 62 Migr 178, 187 Her 96, 97, 277 Congr 50 Somn 1:53 Abr 8, 12, 67, 69, 72, 188 Mos 1:5 Mos 2:40, 40 Virt 212 Praem 14, 23, 31 Hypoth 6:1

Χαλδαϊστί Abr 99, 201 Mos 2:224 Praem 44 Legat 4

Χάλεβ Mut 123, 123

χαλεπαίνω Opif 156 Abr 259 Mos 1:301

χαλεπός (132) Opif 164, 167 Leg 1:86 Leg 3:36, 124, 194, 216, 235, 245 Cher 66, 68, 71, 96 Sacr 48, 114 Det 98, 100, 101 Post 8, 47, 74, 154, 184 Gig 1 Deus 48, 122 Agr 155, 155, 177 Ebr 102, 144, 150, 160 Sobr 30 Migr 14, 26, 114 Her 41, 284 Congr 164, 169 Fug 121, 147, 156 Mut 239 Somn 1:11 Somn 2:84, 149 Abr 96, 104, 160, 230 Ios 20, 71, 81, 109, 114, 177, 179, 202, 222, 233, 261 Mos 1:89, 171, 184, 191, 192, 193, 194, 216, 227, 232, 244, 285, 307, 308 Mos 2:55, 280 Decal 68, 138, 142, 142 Spec 1:3, 4, 24, 32, 239 Spec 2:16, 83, 93, 136, 146 Spec 3:28, 28, 84, 99, 112, 126, 160, 175, 197, 199, 203 Spec 4:10, 80, 113 Virt 29, 144, 152, 213 Praem 135, 136 Prob 40, 45 Contempl 2, 40, 42 Aet 23 Flacc 58, 66, 68, 127, 141 Legat 107, 118, 171, 241, 324, 346, 370 Prov 2:30

χαλεπότης Sacr 35

χαλιναγωγέω Opif 86

χαλινός (7) Agr 69, 70, 94 Mut 240 Somn 2:294 Spec 2:135 Spec 4:79

χαλινόω Mos 1:177 Spec 2:163

χάλκεος (χαλκοῦς) (10) Leg 2:80, 87, 93 Mos 2:78, 82, 90, 136 Praem 131 Legat 134, 337

χαλκεύς Post 116 Somn 1:31

χαλκευτικός Leg 1:57

χαλκός (14) Leg 2:81 Cher 81 Post 50, 116, 117, 119 Agr 95, 97 Ebr 89 Mos 2:82 Praem 132, 132 Prob 65 Aet 20

χαλκοτυπεῖον Cher 80

χαλκουργός Aet 68

χαλκοῦς χάλκεος

Χάμ (9) Sobr 32, 44, 44, 47, 47, 48 QG 2:65, 71a, 74

χαμάδις Aet 132

χαμαί Post 170 Agr 74

χαμαίζηλος (12) Leg 3:19, 82 Post 79, 163 Deus 37, 167 Migr 55, 163 Spec 1:62 Spec 3:1 Spec 4:115 Virt 156

χαμαιλέων Ebr 172

χαμαίστρωτος Spec 2:20 Contempl 69 Flacc 37

χαμαιτυπεῖον Her 109 Spec 1:103

χαμαιτύπη Sacr 21 Plant 106 Somn 1:88 Ios 43

χαμευνέω Somn 1:126 Somn 2:56

χαμευνία Det 19 Agr 152

Χαμώς Leg 3:225, 231, 231

Χαναάν (15) Leg 2:62 Sobr 32, 32, 44, 45, 47, 47, 48, 51, 51, 59 Congr 71, 86 QG 2:65, 65

Χαναναῖος (10) Sacr 89, 90 Congr 81, 83, 83, 88, 121 Fug 87 Mos 1:163 QG 2:65

Χανάνης Mos 1:250

Χαναν͂ιτις Congr 85 Abr 133 QG 4:88

χανδόν Fug 31 Spec 4:122

χάος Aet 17, 18

χαρά (84) Leg 1:45 Leg 3:43, 81, 86, 86, 86, 87, 87, 107, 217, 218, 219, 247 Cher 8, 12, 13 Sacr 30 Det 120, 123, 124, 135, 137, 140 Plant 38, 167 Ebr 62, 147 Migr 157 Her 3, 7, 315 Congr 36 Mut 1, 131, 154, 156, 161, 162, 163, 163, 163, 163, 175, 188, 261, 264 Somn 1:71 Somn 2:162, 171, 249, 279 Abr 108, 151, 201, 204, 205, 206 Ios 250, 254 Mos 1:177, 182, 255, 333 Spec 1:176 Spec 2:48, 54, 55, 185 Virt 44, 67 Praem 27, 31, 31, 32, 35, 50, 68, 161, 161 Legat 15, 19 QG 1:63, 79, 79

χαράδρα Mos 1:176 Mos 2:63

χαρακτήρ (53) Opif 6, 18, 69, 151 Leg 1:61, 61 Leg 3:95, 97, 104 Cher 4 Sacr 60, 135 Det 28, 77, 83 Post 110, 165 Deus 43, 55, 121 Agr 16 Plant 18 Ebr 88, 90, 133, 137 Conf 102 Her 38, 181, 294 Congr 20, 22 Fug 7, 211 Mut 65, 70, 83, 208 Somn 1:171, 219 Somn 2:17 Abr 101 Ios 54, 106 Spec 1:104 Spec 2:50 Spec 3:99 Spec 4:110, 146, 163 Virt 52 Flacc 144 QE 2:4

χαρακτηρίζω (6) Leg 1:57 Cher 65 Post 115, 140 Sobr 9 Fug 209

χαράκωμα Spec 4:229

χαράκωσιν Agr 12

χάραξ Agr 11

χαράσσω (13) Opif 172 Leg 1:100 Post 99 Plant 44 Ebr 133 Migr 79 Somn 1:208 Spec 3:7 Spec 4:137 Virt 19 Praem 40 Contempl 29 QG 2:62

χαρίεις Prov 2:54

χαριεντίζομαι Plant 167 Contempl 58 Legat 168

χαριέντισμα Legat 167

χαριεντισμός Prob 123

χαρίζομαι (χαρίζω) (113) Leg 1:34 Leg 3:26, 78, 84, 135, 136, 178, 178, 187, 196 Cher 122 Sacr 10, 17, 42, 43, 57 Det 161 Post 36, 66, 80, 103, 142, 142 Gig 43 Deus 107 Agr 53 Plant 89 Ebr 18, 18, 111, 118, 119, 224 Conf 123 Migr 46, 53, 73, 101, 127 Her 278 Fug 29, 155 Mut 63, 70, 79, 133, 145, 218, 231, 232, 253 Somn 1:98, 162 Somn 2:167, 224 Abr 17, 51, 54, 143, 196 Ios 153, 173, 222, 263 Mos 1:204, 241, 333 Mos 2:242, 278 Decal 61, 62, 112, 159 Spec 1:43, 52, 152, 156 Spec 2:13, 22, 39, 50, 141, 148, 240 Spec 3:21, 184, 198 Spec 4:71, 73, 131, 169, 220 Virt 83, 115, 115, 129, 168, 209 Praem 9 Contempl 16 Flacc 46, 51, 139, 179 Legat 133, 297, 326, 326, 371 Prov 2:5 QG 4:130, 153 QE 2:18

χαρίζω χαρίζομαι

χάρις (345) Opif 21, 23, 23, 44, 55, 163, 168, 168 Leg 1:59 Leg 2:32, 56, 60, 80 Leg 3:6, 10, 10, 14, 14, 27, 32, 40, 50, 77, 77, 78, 78, 78, 78, 81, 163, 164, 197, 214, 215, 242 Cher 11, 32, 84, 106, 106, 122, 122, 123 Sacr 54, 57, 77, 93, 113, 127, 128 Det 37, 49, 105, 108, 132, 160 Post 26, 32, 35, 36, 41, 41, 42, 53, 118, 119, 142, 145, 145 Gig 5, 11, 21, 24, 39, 62, 64 Deus 5, 5, 18, 21, 52, 57, 60, 70, 70, 74, 86, 104, 104, 104, 104, 106, 107, 108, 108, 109, 110, 111, 153, 167 Agr 38, 168 Plant 86, 89, 93, 93, 100, 106, 151, 160 Ebr 32, 107, 145, 145, 146, 149, 209, 211 Sobr 15, 44, 53 Conf 8, 116, 123, 127, 136, 141, 155, 160, 176, 179, 182, 189 Migr 13, 30, 31, 70, 78, 122, 153, 183, 196, 209, 218, 221 Her 26, 31, 36, 39, 78, 104, 104, 303, 309 Congr 38, 38, 96, 151, 162 Fug 7, 29, 66, 72, 141, 167, 193 Mut 40, 41, 52, 53, 56, 58, 58, 74, 118, 141, 143, 155, 236, 248, 268 Somn 1:8, 81, 115, 254 Somn 2:39, 116, 177, 183, 213, 223, 259 Abr 5, 7, 39, 86, 105, 118, 131, 144, 158, 248, 250 Ios 45, 46, 69, 156, 157, 181, 185, 198, 229, 231, 240, 241, 249, 262 Mos 1:47, 58, 58, 157, 314 Mos 2:47, 48, 51, 61, 183, 222, 232, 242 Decal 36, 113, 115, 163, 167 Spec 1:3, 43, 112, 116, 122, 170, 187, 196, 220, 284, 285, 296, 330 Spec 2:72, 78, 81, 82, 84, 85, 95, 97, 126, 132, 138, 180, 180, 198, 219 Spec 3:26, 32, 34, 51, 73, 146, 165, 180 Spec 4:11, 17, 125, 238 Virt 9, 72, 79, 83, 94, 98, 118, 129, 135, 136, 138, 145 Praem 101, 111, 114, 119, 126, 168 Prob 38, 113 Contempl 59 Aet 46, 67, 82 Flacc 3, 61, 64, 106, 171, 188 Legat 60, 88, 95, 105, 147, 158, 165, 187, 253, 285, 287, 293, 296, 325, 325, 334, 337, 345, 361, 370 Hypoth 7:12, 7:15 Prov 2:37, 61, 66 QG 1:64a, 89, 94, 96:1, 96:1, 96:1, 96:1, 4:81, 110a, 191d, 204 QE 1:1, 2:18, 71 QE isf 10

χάρισμα Leg 3:78, 78

χαριστήριος (15) Deus 4 Ebr 106, 129 Congr 93 Mos 1:219, 253 Decal 160 Spec 1:138, 152, 183, 185 Spec 2:134, 146, 187 Virt 159

χαριστικός Leg 3:106 Her 166 Somn 1:162, 163

Χάριτες Abr 54 Mos 2:7

Χαρραῖοι Abr 67, 72

Χαρράν (32) Migr 176, 176, 177, 187, 188, 195, 197, 208, 208, 212, 213, 216 Fug 23, 45 Somn 1:4, 5, 5, 41, 41, 42, 45, 46, 47, 47, 48, 52, 53, 55, 59, 61, 68 Abr 72

χαρτίδιον (6) Abr 11 Spec 1:58 Spec 3:62 Spec 4:149 Prob 46, 104

χαρτός (6) Sacr 136 Mut 167 Spec 3:56 Praem 50, 50 Legat 89

χάρυβδις Somn 2:70 Mos 1:176

χάσκω (χαίνω) Det 100, 103 Agr 21 Plant 160

χάσμα Agr 68, 97 Mos 2:281, 287 Prov 2:27

χαῦνος Sacr 32 Post 136 Her 188, 269 Congr 169

Χεβρών (8) Det 5, 15, 15 Post 60, 60, 60, 62 QG 4:72

χεῖλος (35) Leg 3:203 Agr 133 Conf 1, 1, 1, 15, 29, 33, 33, 36, 39, 150 Somn 2:190, 216, 238, 261, 261, 261, 262, 277, 278, 280, 280, 281, 284, 296, 300, 300, 302 Spec 1:37 Spec 4:92 Virt 99, 188 Legat 195, 310

χειμάζω Prov 2:55

χειμαίνω Opif 58 Post 22 Somn 2:166 Prov 2:44

χειμάρροος (χειμάρρους) (38) Opif 71 Leg 3:163 Cher 94 Post 113 Plant 144 Ebr 22 Conf 23 Her 32 Congr 150 Fug 49, 91 Mut 239 Somn 1:97, 107 Abr 42, 159 Ios 141 Mos 1:6, 192, 212 Mos 2:54 Spec 1:30, 34, 210 Spec 2:147, 172 Spec 3:5, 32 Spec 4:85 Virt 6, 41 Praem 41, 73 Prob 63 Aet 118, 147 Prov 2:38 QE isf 6

χειμάρρους χειμάρροος

χειμερινός (7) Opif 112 Deus 38 Her 147, 149 Mos 1:114, 118, 200

χειμών (50) Opif 45, 52, 58 Cher 112, 112 Post 22 Gig 51, 51 Plant 120 Conf 32 Migr 217 Her 136, 146, 208 Congr 60, 93 Fug 180 Somn 1:20 Somn 2:52, 85, 131, 225, 229 Ios 139 Mos 1:116, 265 Mos 2:124 Spec 1:92, 210, 301 Spec 2:20, 208 Spec 3:17 Spec 4:58, 209, 235 Praem 33, 130 Contempl 38 Aet 11 Flacc 125, 156 Legat 145, 190, 190 Hypoth 11:12 Prov 2:44, 47, 48 QG 4:51b

χείρ (253) Opif 88, 118, 148 Leg 1:12 Leg 2:88, 88, 88, 88, 89, 92, 93, 93 Leg 3:23, 24, 36, 43, 45, 90, 90, 186, 240 Cher 74, 81, 81 Sacr 17, 25, 36, 38, 56, 63, 96, 125, 133, 133 Det 121, 122, 140, 177 Post 3, 85, 151 Deus 15, 57, 60, 65, 73, 77 Agr 21, 22, 74, 75, 85, 95, 114, 118 Plant 30, 47, 50, 103, 145, 160 Ebr 67, 101, 101, 105, 106, 167, 177 Sobr 27 Conf 3, 38, 38, 38, 38, 67, 98 Migr 30, 98 Her 50, 58, 59, 103, 151, 151 Congr 113, 153, 155, 155, 156, 164 Fug 1, 1, 1, 53, 74, 93, 145, 149, 207, 209, 209 Mut 21, 126, 220, 232, 233, 234, 237, 238, 249, 250, 256 Somn 1:195, 235 Somn 2:60, 68, 69, 71, 126, 139, 159, 159, 180, 200, 201, 201, 203, 265, 280, 285 Abr 105, 202, 211, 211, 229, 235 Ios 16, 49, 211 Mos 1:8, 56, 79, 79, 80, 82, 112, 127, 142, 142, 174, 197, 215, 217, 218, 235, 239, 249, 256, 263, 311 Mos 2:36, 138, 150, 150, 154, 291 Decal 72, 74 Spec 1:55, 117, 145, 198, 202, 203, 204, 340, 341 Spec 2:6, 88, 145, 205, 244, 245, 245, 246, 248 Spec 3:17, 85, 86, 93, 105, 120, 129, 174, 175, 177, 177, 178, 179, 180 Spec 4:34, 47, 124, 129, 137, 138, 163, 199, 224 Virt 57, 83, 183, 183, 203, 208 Praem 72, 73, 80, 94, 104, 168 Prob 26, 29, 33, 68, 87, 96 Contempl 30, 46, 66, 77, 89 Aet 42 Flacc 121, 162, 189 Legat 2, 49, 51, 95, 104, 109, 141, 181, 220, 228, 229, 255, 258, 353 Hypoth 6:6 Prov 2:17 QG (Par) 2:2

χειραγωγία Mos 1:299

χειρίζω Legat 208

χειροδοτέω Somn 1:129, 186 Hypoth 11:10

χειρόδοτος QG 4:148

χειροήθης (16) Opif 83 Leg 3:17, 140 Cher 111 Sacr 20, 104, 105 Migr 210 Her 138 Somn 2:88 Spec 1:163 Spec 3:110, 145 Praem 88, 89 Prob 76

χειρόκμητος (21) Post 166 Deus 25 Sobr 36 Somn 1:210 Somn 2:118 Decal 51, 66, 76, 156 Spec 1:22, 58, 67 Spec 2:1, 256, 258 Virt 40, 220 Aet 10 Legat 290, 292, 310

χειροκοπέω Spec 2:247

χειρονομέω Det 41

χειροποίητος (16) Opif 142 Conf 32 Mut 26 Somn 2:125 Mos 1:303, 333 Mos 2:51, 88, 165, 168 Spec 1:184 Spec 3:203 Spec 4:154 Contempl 15 Flacc 62 Legat 107

χειροτέχνης Virt 88

χειροτονέω (33) Sacr 9 Det 66, 145, 161 Post 54 Deus 112 Agr 84, 130 Ebr 66 Migr 22 Congr 110 Fug 73 Somn 2:243 Ios 114, 248 Mos 1:56, 113, 148, 162, 198, 223, 267 Mos 2:142, 160 Spec 1:78 Spec 4:9, 55 Virt 63 Praem 54 Flacc 109, 152 Legat 161, 254

χειροτονητός Spec 4:157

χειροτονία (9) Opif 84 Det 39 Mut 151 Ios 120 Mos 1:83 Spec 2:231 Spec 4:9 Virt 64, 218

χειρουργέω Mut 238 Abr 143 Mos 2:224

χειρουργία Post 142 Congr 53

χειρόω Mos 1:250 Praem 95

χείρων κακός

χελιδών Leg 2:75 Her 154 Prov 2:63

χελώνη Somn 2:57 Spec 2:20 Contempl 49

χέρνιψ Ebr 131

Χερουβίμ (13) Cher 1, 11, 20, 21, 23, 25, 25, 28, 29 Her 166 Fug 100, 101 Mos 2:97

χερσαῖος (53) Opif 64, 65, 66, 68, 84, 147, 147 Cher 89, 111 Det 151, 151, 151, 152 Gig 7, 10, 11 Plant 12, 14, 15, 151 Conf 6, 61 Her 139, 139, 238 Fug 180 Somn 1:135 Somn 2:288 Mos 1:130, 192 Mos 2:60 Decal 78, 115 Spec 1:135, 162, 163 Spec 3:8, 115 Spec 4:100, 101, 110, 116, 118, 155 Praem 87 Contempl 8, 54 Aet 45, 65, 117 Flacc 187 Legat 139 Prov 2:69

χερσεύω Spec 3:39

χέρσος (13) Det 85, 151 Deus 177 Plant 17, 37 Her 238 Somn 1:54, 107 Mos 1:103, 144 Spec 1:335 Spec 2:45 Aet 138

χερσόω Contempl 86

Χέτ Somn 2:89 QG 4:79b

Χεττοῦρα Sacr 43, 43

χέω (38) Leg 2:60, 60, 61 Leg 3:22, 154 Post 43, 104 Gig 3 Deus 38, 127 Agr 6 Conf 102, 116 Migr 36, 123 Her 217, 217 Fug 176, 191 Somn 1:178 Abr 119 Mos 1:107 Mos 2:58, 118, 118 Spec 1:192 Spec 2:191 Spec 3:25 Spec 4:26, 83 Virt 144 Praem 47, 143 Aet 88, 91, 102, 132 Legat 214

χήν Spec 4:117

χήρα (χῆρος) (23) Leg 2:63 Det 147, 147 Deus 136, 136, 138 Congr 178 Fug 114 Somn 2:273 Spec 1:105, 108, 308, 310 Spec 2:25, 108 Spec 3:26, 64 Spec 4:176, 177 Virt 114 QE 2:3a, 3a, 3a χηρεία Ebr 5 Mos 2:240 Decal 42 Aet 56

χηρεύω (21) Det 149, 149 Post 6, 68 Deus 136, 137, 137 Conf 163 Fug 114, 190 Somn 2:273 Spec 1:129 Spec 2:30, 31 Spec 3:12, 27, 30 Prob 14, 63 Aet 56 QE 2:3b

χῆρος (χήρα) Mut 149

χήτος Sacr 21 Fug 153

χθαμαλός Abr 41, 43 Spec 1:73 Contempl 22 Aet 118

χθές Somn 2:123

χθών Aet 121, 121

χῖδρον Sacr 76, 82, 86, 87

χιλίαρχος Congr 110 Mos 1:317 Legat 30

χιλιάς (7) Mos 1:306 Mos 2:276 Decal 27, 27, 27 Spec 3:126 Virt 41

χίλιοι Mos 1:306 Virt 42 Aet 145

χιλός (6) Opif 40 Ios 113 Mos 1:319 Prob 32 Aet 63 Legat 252

χίμαιρα Spec 1:226, 228, 233 Spec 3:46

Χίμαιρα Spec 3:45

χίμαρος (10) Fug 157 Mut 159 Spec 1:135, 188, 188, 190, 226, 228, 233 Spec 4:105

χιονώδης Spec 2:191

χιτών (23) Leg 2:56, 57, 58, 58, 58 Det 6 Somn 1:214, 215, 220, 221, 225 Ios 22, 32 Mos 2:118, 118, 121, 121, 143, 144 Spec 1:83, 83, 85 Contempl 51

χιτωνίσκος Spec 1:83 Contempl 51, 72 Prov 2:17

χιών (8) Opif 80 Leg 1:5 Det 177 Fug 138 Mos 1:79, 200 Spec 4:56 Prov 2:45

χλαῖνα Somn 1:124 Spec 2:20 Contempl 38 Hypoth 11:12 Prov 2:17

χλαμύς Flacc 37 Legat 94

χλευάζω (20) Sacr 70 Ebr 146, 150 Sobr 6 Migr 83 Fug 34 Mut 61 Somn 1:126 Somn 2:122 Abr 89 Mos 1:29 Mos 2:240 Decal 80 Spec 2:250 Spec 3:125 Flacc 34 Legat 165, 211, 359, 368

χλευασμός Det 69

χλευαστικός Legat 44

χλεύη (27) Det 69 Post 142, 179 Agr 34, 62 Ebr 65, 131 Congr 61 Fug 31 Somn 2:138 Mos 1:164, 190 Spec 1:3, 176 Spec 2:18, 164 Spec 3:23 Spec 4:59 Virt 5, 202 Prob 54 Contempl 6 Legat 71, 78, 169 QG 2:71a, 4:43

χλιαίνω Ebr 147, 221 Her 309

χλιδάω Agr 154

χλιδή (7) Opif 164 Cher 92 Sacr 21 Post 182 Plant 39 Spec 2:240 Spec 4:102

χλοάω Opif 129 Plant 107

χλόη Opif 129 Mos 2:186 Spec 1:74 Prov 2:70

χλοηφαγέω Spec 4:25

χλοηφαγία Spec 2:109

χλοηφάγος Spec 1:164

χλοηφορέω (8) Opif 40, 47 Ebr 9 Mut 161 Somn 2:199 Abr 140 Spec 2:151 Spec 4:29

χλοηφόρος Somn 2:170 Aet 63

χλωρίζω Det 16

χλωρός (8) Opif 129 Leg 1:21, 23, 23, 24, 24, 24 Plant 110

Χοδολλαγόμορ Ebr 24

χοῖνιξ Hypoth 7:8

χοίρειος Flacc 96 Legat 361

χολή Ebr 222 Somn 2:191 Spec 1:218 Spec 4:130

χονδρίτης Somn 2:207

χορεία (26) Opif 54, 70, 78, 126 Cher 23 Agr 51 Ebr 33 Migr 181, 184 Her 88, 221 Congr 51 Mut 72 Abr 77 Mos 1:212 Spec 1:34 Spec 2:45, 151 Spec 3:187 Spec 4:155 Virt 76 Praem 102, 121 Contempl 84 Aet 4 QG 4:51b

χορευτής (10) Deus 120 Ebr 80, 124 Migr 104, 156 Fug 10 Somn 2:133 Virt 75 Contempl 88, 88

χορεύω (10) Leg 1:66 Cher 3, 23 Deus 176 Plant 108 Fug 45, 74 Spec 1:205 Prob 62 Aet 55

χορηγέω (36) Opif 124, 168 Leg 2:108 Abr 238, 239, 243 Ios 186 Mos 1:6, 25, 28, 117, 189, 209, 255 Mos 2:266, 286 Decal 71, 178 Spec 1:116, 169 Spec 2:29, 199 Spec 3:111 Virt 8, 48, 145, 149, 161 Praem 19, 73, 100, 130 Prob 9 Contempl 35 Legat 9, 257

χορηγία (32) Opif 77, 113 Det 20 Conf 25 Somn 1:186 Abr 134 Ios 253 Mos 1:164, 206, 225 Mos 2:13, 58, 134 Decal 16 Spec 1:71, 153, 189 Spec 2:19, 20, 139, 187, 193, 203 Spec 4:126 Virt 133 Legat 107, 253 Hypoth 11:4 Prov 2:30, 46 QG 4:43, 76b

χορηγός (13) Post 180 Plant 105 Her 76 Fug 28 Mut 168 Spec 2:180, 199 Spec 4:166 Virt 6, 162 Prov 2:24 QG 4:172 QE isf 9

χορικός Contempl 80

χορός (58) Opif 115 Leg 1:61 Leg 3:7, 242 Sacr 22 Det 33 Agr 79, 80, 82, 139 Plant 118 Ebr 31, 70, 95, 96, 121, 124, 153 Conf 35, 44, 55, 174 Migr 104, 104 Her 241 Fug 62, 74, 124 Mut 263 Somn 2:269 Abr 27 Mos 1:180, 180, 255 Mos 2:162, 239, 256, 257, 270, 271 Spec 1:269 Spec 2:249, 259 Spec 3:125 Spec 4:134 Virt 74, 145 Praem 53 Prob 13 Contempl 83, 85, 85, 87 Aet 79 Legat 42, 75, 96, 166

χόρτος (13) Opif 129, 129, 129 Leg 1:21, 24, 24, 24, 24, 24, 24 Leg 3:251, 251, 251

χοῦς (16) Opif 134, 135, 137 Leg 1:31, 31 Det 106 Post 164 Agr 25 Conf 79, 79 Migr 3 Her 29, 58, 162 Praem 133 QG 4:79a

χράομαι (χράω) (786) Opif 2, 16, 19, 23, 24, 52, 54, 65, 102, 102, 113, 119, 128, 139, 143, 157, 160, 169, 170 Leg 1:36, 101, 102, 104 Leg 2:7, 7, 7, 17, 17, 25, 26, 29, 32, 60, 70, 78, 87 Leg 3:47, 54, 63, 73, 73, 80, 88, 92, 102, 110, 122, 124, 128, 135, 139, 147, 149, 151, 151, 152, 153, 154, 155, 157, 165, 194, 211, 211, 213, 236, 240, 247 Cher 17, 17, 34, 36, 39, 53, 55, 66, 70, 96, 96, 97, 99, 117, 119 Sacr 10, 21, 29, 30, 31, 32, 68, 71, 71, 98, 115, 116, 120, 121, 123, 125, 126 Det 6, 19, 20, 20, 29, 38, 42, 44, 45, 46, 46, 48, 54, 58, 60, 61, 70, 72, 98, 113, 114, 118, 119, 138, 142, 157, 170 Post 22, 22, 32, 35, 50, 67, 71, 80, 80, 81, 87, 101, 106, 139, 159, 160, 165, 176 Gig 12, 22, 33, 34, 47, 48, 48, 64 Deus 5, 8, 26, 26, 29, 33, 34, 47, 49, 49, 52, 57, 57, 58, 60, 61, 63, 68, 72, 75, 76, 77, 91, 93, 111, 119, 129, 138, 139, 164, 170, 175, 180, 181 Agr 2, 5, 13, 13, 40, 45, 63, 66, 78, 80, 87, 91, 101, 106, 130, 142, 147, 149 Plant 12, 14, 15, 35, 44, 45, 49, 55, 58, 60, 62, 62, 106, 108, 110, 115, 139, 143, 145, 152, 171 Ebr 2, 2, 4, 12, 17, 18, 23, 51, 68, 87, 90, 97, 101, 103, 122, 135, 151, 164, 170, 195, 198, 201, 203, 206, 209, 214, 215, 216, 223 Sobr 5, 18, 36, 38, 39, 46, 61,

65, 69 Conf 2, 10, 19, 34, 36, 38, 45, 50, 54, 57, 68, 71, 93, 98, 98, 99, 105, 108, 110, 140, 145, 160, 167, 175, 190, 192, 195, 198 Migr 6, 8, 25, 25, 26, 59, 61, 62, 66, 67, 68, 71, 74, 78, 79, 84, 100, 116, 119, 121, 124, 131, 146, 166, 171, 173, 174, 201, 206, 207, 212, 223 Her 4, 7, 16, 19, 19, 22, 87, 94, 102, 111, 125, 145, 149, 166, 182, 191, 191, 226, 237, 238, 241, 244, 246, 249, 270, 276, 277, 291, 299, 301 Congr 3, 5, 11, 15, 19, 24, 40, 41, 45, 46, 61, 81, 120, 121, 129, 143, 153, 156, 173 Fug 6, 8, 27, 32, 70, 76, 90, 92, 102, 122, 124, 126, 129, 151, 168, 202, 204 Mut 2, 4, 40, 47, 84, 85, 86, 86, 88, 98, 105, 108, 112, 116, 124, 128, 129, 143, 157, 173, 190, 217, 226, 243, 246, 251, 257, 262, 270 Somn 1:48, 51, 53, 79, 82, 91, 91, 96, 103, 105, 115, 119, 121, 122, 123, 126, 136, 141, 142, 143, 150, 156, 168, 177, 193, 197, 199, 202, 218, 234, 236 Somn 2:9, 10, 89, 102, 116, 131, 134, 164, 174, 199, 204, 229, 232, 238, 243, 249, 292 Abr 5, 5, 10, 14, 23, 34, 38, 61, 103, 105, 134, 168, 204, 244, 244, 256, 257, 269 Ios 6, 29, 29, 33, 36, 41, 42, 43, 51, 65, 73, 76, 93, 107, 109, 112, 113, 118, 126, 126, 134, 144, 147, 148, 152, 155, 203, 215, 230, 232, 240, 240, 258 Mos 1:14, 49, 63, 65, 92, 96, 110, 111, 132, 148, 150, 160, 167, 184, 218, 220, 240, 242, 243, 260, 284, 286, 290, 305, 309 Mos 2:8, 11, 15, 27, 36, 48, 66, 116, 122, 134, 138, 167, 199, 212, 226, 229, 231, 235, 284 Decal 14, 41, 59, 80, 87, 163, 168, 177, 178 Spec 1:37, 53, 58, 60, 84, 101, 116, 117, 119, 123, 131, 157, 159, 180, 191, 224, 243, 252, 294, 341 Spec 2:6, 6, 10, 11, 15, 18, 19, 28, 64, 64, 67, 95, 105, 158, 160, 163, 167, 171, 182, 183, 199, 240, 241, 259 Spec 3:9, 50, 56, 63, 69, 92, 101, 106, 122, 135, 137, 137, 138, 167, 178, 179, 195 Spec 4:15, 37, 37, 38, 43, 48, 54, 55, 74, 79, 101, 104, 104, 116, 121, 132, 140, 167, 179, 201, 205, 207, 218 Virt 1, 3, 7, 35, 43, 64, 67, 80, 86, 91, 118, 124, 140, 142, 147, 148, 151, 153, 173, 174, 217 Praem 27, 36, 43, 77, 80, 85, 93, 94, 111, 138, 142, 166 Prob 2, 20, 44, 45, 62, 72, 80, 83, 86, 89, 109, 112, 117, 121, 122 Contempl 16, 29, 42, 52, 57, 76 Aet 22, 43, 55, 67, 70, 71, 72, 74, 78, 84, 97, 104, 113, 124, 133 Flacc 14, 18, 26, 27, 28, 31, 34, 59, 69, 94, 151, 170, 182 Legat 2, 6, 16, 21, 33, 41, 76, 107, 129, 134, 163, 164, 178, 190, 201, 203, 217, 270, 316, 319, 363, 372 Hypoth 7:19 Prov 1, 2:20, 29, 41, 57, 70 QG 1:21, 32, 55a, 70:1, 2:12d, 41, 68a, 3:21, 52, 4:76b, 81, 200a, 204 QG isf 5 QG (Par) 2:5 QE 1:6, 2:3a, 10a QE isf 11, 26

χράω χράομαι

χράω (46) Cher 109 Sacr 9 Det 48, 157, 157 Post 28 Gig 49, 63 Deus 114 Plant 138, 173 Sobr 50 Conf 81 Migr 10, 27, 168 Her 8 Fug 60, 162 Mut 19, 34, 177 Somn 1:64, 148 Somn 2:227, 231 Abr 189, 192 Mos 2:63, 97, 176, 188, 230, 253, 270 Decal 157, 175 Spec 2:146 Spec 3:7 Spec 4:37, 50, 102 Virt 68, 184, 215 QG isf 15

χρεία (88) Opif 56 Leg 1:93, 94, 104 Leg 2:16 Leg 3:151, 160 Post 4, 142 Deus 49, 56, 146 Agr 133 Plant 65 Conf 162 Her 40 Congr 36 Fug 47, 66, 105 Somn 1:141, 205 Somn 2:155, 156 Abr 45, 129 Ios 155, 158, 243 Mos 1:84, 185, 201, 266, 267, 269 Mos 2:136, 158, 267, 282 Decal 99 Spec 1:165, 273, 274, 274, 337, 340 Spec 2:2, 6, 65, 69, 101, 112, 187, 206 Spec 3:117, 185, 199 Spec 4:11, 21, 229 Virt 22, 61, 88, 104, 122, 188 Prob 23, 36, 68, 76, 114, 124 Contempl 7, 9, 25, 71 Aet 102 Legat 101, 234, 277, 336 Hypoth 11:9 Prov 2:44, 47 QG 1:92, 2:26a, 4:167 QG (Par) 2:6

χρεῖος (40) Opif 53, 72 Leg 3:181 Cher 44, 109, 112 Det 7, 56 Post 4, 147 Deus 7, 37 Plant 14, 51, 116 Conf 175 Her 58, 123, 177, 193 Congr 115, 155 Fug 45, 105, 170 Somn 1:162, 179 Somn 2:176 Ios 242 Mos 1:111, 137, 174 Decal 81 Spec 1:277 Spec 2:38, 74, 258 Virt 9 Praem 132 Prob 9

χρειώδης (13) Leg 2:17 Her 136 Abr 157 Mos 1:124, 156 Mos 2:148, 155, 158 Contempl 38 Flacc 149 Hypoth 11:10 QG 1:17b QG (Par) 2:4

χρεμετίζω Agr 72 Somn 1:108

χρεμετιστικός Agr 67

χρέος (6) Post 5 Abr 257, 259 Spec 2:68, 248 Virt 123

χρεωκοπέω Plant 107

χρεωκοπία Decal 171 Spec 2:71 Spec 4:84, 87, 196

χρεών Fug 85 Prob 115

χρεώστης (14) Plant 101 Somn 1:93, 95, 95, 100, 101 Spec 2:39, 72, 78, 122 Spec 3:204 Virt 89, 122 Legat 13

χρή (180) Opif 2, 87, 111, 151, 163 Leg 1:60 Leg 2:28 Leg 3:36, 41, 91, 110, 188, 206, 246 Cher 30, 54, 71, 99, 128 Sacr 65, 79, 80, 85, 108, 131 Det 37, 76, 101, 142 Post 1, 34, 41, 87, 113, 150 Deus 38, 134, 150 Agr 48 Plant 22, 109 Ebr 66, 79, 79, 88, 101, 121, 155, 202 Migr 12, 28, 34, 61, 93, 105, 130 Her 88, 167, 295, 297, 301 Congr 11, 83 Fug 5, 32, 63, 84, 95 Mut 153, 158, 195, 238 Somn 1:191, 199, 227, 229 Somn 2:8, 69, 103, 144, 149 Abr 6, 25, 49, 56, 145 Ios 26, 119, 125, 248 Mos 1:88, 144, 329 Mos 2:4, 4, 12, 49, 73, 128, 153, 165, 201, 215, 217 Decal 93, 101, 115, 154, 157 Spec 1:65, 66, 82, 128, 138, 323 Spec 2:3, 7, 53, 59, 129, 143, 215, 242 Spec 3:14, 32, 64, 67, 87, 145, 148, 155 Spec 4:35, 64, 108, 121, 122, 137, 176, 184 Virt 18, 44, 56, 100, 153, 157, 165, 167, 179, 189 Praem 55, 55 Prob 12, 23, 71, 83, 92, 105 Contempl 60, 72 Aet 2, 67, 69, 108, 127, 132, 142 Flacc 31 Legat 31, 46, 81, 192, 211, 261, 268, 350 QG 2:12d, 3:3, 4:52d QE 2:3b, 105

χρήζω (16) Leg 2:2 Sacr 34 Post 142, 144 Ebr 188 Her 286 Congr 20, 33, 33 Fug 200 Mut 28 Ios 144 Spec 2:24 Legat 26, 249 QE 2:10a

χρῆμα (71) Opif 49, 79 Leg 1:75 Leg 2:17 Det 136 Post 35, 117, 184 Gig 15, 36, 37 Deus 163 Plant 66, 126, 171 Ebr 22, 141 Migr 217 Her 48, 92, 246 Fug 28, 39 Somn 1:124 Somn 2:128 Abr 228 Ios 135 Mos 1:141, 267, 293 Decal 151, 153 Spec 1:78, 78, 104, 143, 342 Spec 2:72, 92 Spec 3:70, 82, 139, 168, 181 Spec 4:10, 33, 82, 87, 159 Virt 82, 182 Praem 104, 142 Prob 55, 65, 145 Contempl 14, 16 Flacc 60 Legat 4, 9, 17, 156, 172, 215, 232, 295, 315 Prov 2:11, 33, 69

χρηματίζω (12) Cher 115 Det 143 Deus 121 Migr 25, 192 Ios 71 Mos 2:184, 238, 238 Virt 192 Praem 61 Legat 346

χρηματισμός Abr 65 Contempl 17

χρηματιστής Fug 35 Praem 11

χρήσιμος (36) Opif 60 Leg 2:17 Leg 3:157, 227 Det 28, 41, 102 Deus 170 Agr 19 Sobr 41 Migr 209 Her 315 Fug 35, 120 Ios 154, 155, 266 Mos 1:116 Mos 2:146 Spec 1:83, 323 Spec 2:70, 91, 172, 239, 247 Spec 3:50, 202, 202 Virt 145 Praem 120 Contempl 37 Aet 3 Flacc 69 Prov 2:11, 39

χρῆσις (103) Opif 42, 78, 115, 153 Leg 1:34, 58, 103 Leg 3:112, 155 Cher 53, 55, 108, 113, 113, 118 Sacr 22

Det 60, 60, 114, 119, 156 Post 181, 185 Gig 60 Deus 24, 147, 156 Agr 11, 24, 108, 157 Plant 34, 42, 52, 88, 132, 136, 155, 162, 163, 174 Ebr 6, 214 Sobr 61 Conf 85, 161 Migr 11, 217 Mut 75, 112, 165 Somn 2:57, 134 Abr 154, 261 Mos 1:23, 204, 208 Mos 2:9 Decal 78, 109 Spec 1:100, 132, 135, 179, 220, 223, 295, 322 Spec 2:19, 150, 161, 175, 175, 179, 184, 199, 222 Spec 3:186 Spec 4:12, 30, 100, 104, 105, 117, 118 Virt 6, 30, 169 Praem 100, 103, 103 Prob 32 Legat 11, 274, 362 Prov 2:63, 64, 70 QG 2:68a, 4:76b, 148, 191c

χρησμολογέω Spec 4:52

χρησμός (143) Opif 8 Leg 3:129, 142, 215, 245 Cher 49, 51, 108, 124 Sacr 57 Det 46, 74, 86, 126, 166 Post 143, 169 Deus 62 Plant 23, 36, 63, 109 Ebr 39, 60, 82 Sobr 1, 17, 66 Conf 94, 143, 190, 197 Migr 14, 29, 47, 60, 66, 85, 108, 115, 144, 153, 174, 183, 224 Her 14, 21, 25, 99, 179, 277 Congr 13, 91, 99, 168 Fug 9, 21, 50, 56, 58, 140, 158, 167, 178, 202 Mut 7, 39, 90, 103, 125, 139, 143, 152, 169, 194, 254 Somn 1:159, 172, 177, 207, 247 Somn 2:3, 142, 220, 297 Abr 50, 54, 56, 166, 256, 262, 270 Mos 1:57, 71, 73, 86, 95, 173, 207, 236, 266, 294, 294, 304 Mos 2:34, 60, 67, 69, 176, 188, 192, 213, 228, 246, 260, 268, 270, 284, 289 Decal 15, 32, 43, 49 Spec 1:256, 315 Spec 2:55, 257 Spec 3:208 Spec 4:39, 134 Virt 63, 70 Praem 75, 95 Prob 3 Aet 2 Legat 109, 347 Prov 2:24 QG 2:48, 48, 4:88, 174

χρησμοσύνη Leg 3:7 Spec 1:208

χρησμῳδέω (12) Sacr 4 Det 40 Her 3 Mut 125 Mos 2:275 Decal 45, 175 Spec 4:78, 132 Virt 55 Praem 2 QG 2:62

χρηστήριον Legat 78

χρηστικός Leg 1:58

χρηστός (78) Leg 3:194, 215 Cher 106 Det 38, 46, 146 Agr 126, 126 Ebr 25 Conf 166 Migr 44, 90, 123 Her 100 Fug 96 Mut 253 Somn 2:94, 294 Abr 8, 16, 51, 203, 268 Ios 81, 82, 93, 144, 162, 176, 198, 210, 264 Mos 1:40, 199, 244 Spec 1:70, 284 Spec 2:45, 67, 71, 75, 82, 96, 104, 158, 187, 196, 235 Spec 3:6, 116, 156, 166 Spec 4:17, 203 Virt 29, 75, 97, 101, 109, 123, 125, 131, 146, 160, 182, 196 Praem 5, 156 Flacc 83, 109, 124, 176 Legat 67, 318, 333, 339 Prov 2:30 QG 2:54b

χρηστότης (9) Leg 3:73 Sacr 27 Agr 47 Migr 122 Mos 1:249 Spec 2:141 Virt 84 Praem 166 Legat 73

χρῖσμα Mos 2:146, 152

χρίω Fug 110 Mos 2:150 Spec 1:231, 233 Spec 3:37

χρόα χροιά

χροιά (χρόα) (16) Opif 104 Leg 1:84 Ebr 172, 174 Migr 83 Abr 170 Mos 1:79, 81 Mos 2:112, 123, 124 Spec 1:80, 87 Virt 217 Prob 103 Legat 266

χρονίζω Sacr 53 Praem 136

χρονικός Migr 126, 139 QG 3:23

χρόνιος Praem 70

χρόνος (409) Opif 13, 26, 26, 26, 26, 27, 35, 41, 55, 56, 57, 59, 60, 60, 60, 148, 156, 161 Leg 1:2, 2, 2, 2, 2, 2, 9, 10, 20 Leg 2:3, 42, 42, 73 Leg 3:11, 25, 25, 27, 70, 106, 106, 175, 191, 211 Cher 22, 58, 114, 120 Sacr 10, 14, 16, 17, 47, 64, 65, 68, 76, 77, 79, 98, 119, 121, 124, 134, 137 Det 14, 49, 89 Post 14, 25, 49, 62, 63, 111, 112, 113, 141 Gig 47, 53, 56 Deus 27, 30, 31, 31, 31, 32, 32, 32, 32, 103, 120, 176 Agr 56, 161, 171, 176, 178 Plant 114, 114, 116, 119, 168, 169 Ebr 8, 48, 120, 207 Sobr 7, 22, 29, 56 Conf 17, 76 Migr 43, 67, 154, 205 Her 35, 49, 49, 118, 148, 150, 165, 165, 293 Congr 4, 4, 66, 82, 88 Fug 57, 106, 167, 169 Mut 116, 142, 151, 155, 179, 185, 267, 267, 267 Somn 1:11, 31, 45, 46, 47, 138, 156, 187 Somn 2:9, 36, 41, 51, 57, 100, 112, 157, 195, 208, 210 Abr 10, 23, 26, 36, 40, 47, 67, 70, 71, 91, 155, 188, 195, 207, 214, 228, 245, 248, 251, 254, 271 Ios 10, 22, 44, 89, 100, 112, 118, 168, 170, 204, 223, 238, 247, 261, 263, 264 Mos 1:13, 18, 21, 51, 59, 69, 115, 141, 142, 143, 165, 173, 175, 178, 184, 191, 192, 203, 211, 230, 238, 240, 241, 262, 264, 287, 315, 315 Mos 2:17, 27, 43, 55, 63, 69, 70, 120, 131, 140, 186, 216, 222, 263, 275, 276, 288 Decal 11, 30, 31, 33, 49, 58, 58, 69, 99, 101 Spec 1:16, 30, 58, 69, 76, 78, 90, 91, 98, 155, 172, 193, 220, 222, 240, 240, 249, 281, 295, 297 Spec 2:38, 42, 49, 77, 84, 86, 100, 109, 115, 119, 122, 140, 140, 141, 145, 148, 153, 157, 157, 175, 187, 188, 206, 207, 218, 221, 247 Spec 3:1, 17, 27, 32, 35, 44, 75, 85, 89, 98, 123, 131, 142, 154, 187, 195 Spec 4:49, 51, 173, 209, 238 Virt 26, 39, 56, 123, 129, 130, 134, 135, 180 Praem 66, 85, 91, 101, 110 Prob 14, 73, 81, 104, 130 Contempl 16, 16, 35 Aet 4, 8, 11, 19, 19, 52, 52, 52, 52, 52, 53, 53, 53, 53, 54, 58, 61, 71, 71, 83, 96, 100, 119, 120, 125, 131, 133, 133, 138, 143 Flacc 3, 9, 75, 79, 103, 105, 114, 116, 128, 129, 133, 182 Legat 1, 24, 63, 120, 198, 202, 246, 246, 248, 264, 298, 310, 338, 342 Hypoth 6:3 Prov 2:61, 64 QG 1:1, 100:1b, 100:2b, 2:74, 3:23, 4:51a QG (Par) 2:7, 2:7

χρυσαυγής Leg 1:67

χρύσεος (χρυσοῦς) (32) Leg 1:51 Post 158 Ebr 95 Migr 103 Her 218, 218 Congr 100, 113, 113, 113, 114, 168 Fug 90 Mut 93 Somn 2:44, 61, 62 Ios 120, 150 Mos 1:317 Mos 2:77, 110, 113, 114, 132, 162, 270 Decal 4 Spec 1:22, 93 Spec 3:125 Legat 319

χρυσίον (18) Leg 1:63, 63, 66, 66, 67, 67, 77, 77, 77, 78, 78 Sacr 55, 83 Deus 169 Her 131, 216 Spec 1:23 Spec 4:158

Χρύσιππος Aet 48, 90, 94

χρυσόπαστος Somn 2:57

χρυσόροφος Somn 2:55

χρυσός (59) Leg 1:66 Leg 2:81, 107 Cher 48, 80, 100, 100 Sacr 21, 26, 80, 83, 130 Det 20, 157 Plant 57 Ebr 85, 86, 89 Sobr 41 Migr 97 Her 217 Congr 112 Fug 26 Mut 89 Abr 220 Ios 243, 258 Mos 1:152, 317 Mos 2:77, 82, 111 Decal 48, 66, 71, 133 Spec 1:21, 22, 25, 274, 275 Spec 2:20 Spec 4:74, 223 Virt 188 Prob 9, 31, 65, 76 Contempl 49 Legat 9, 108, 151, 216 Prov 2:10, 12, 17, 31 QG (Par) 2:4

χρυσοῦς χρύσεος

χρυσόω Mut 43 Mos 2:95

χρῴζω Cher 16

χρῶμα (64) Opif 41, 62, 120, 139, 165 Leg 1:25, 83 Leg 2:56 Leg 3:7, 15, 22, 57, 121 Cher 57, 117 Sacr 23, 26, 31, 36, 36, 46 Det 101, 157, 173 Deus 15, 125, 129 Agr 42 Plant 111, 111, 133, 159 Ebr 46, 173, 173, 190, 191 Sobr 36 Migr 50, 213, 213 Congr 76, 77 Fug 26, 134, 153 Mut 111 Somn 1:27, 28, 217 Abr 148, 239 Ios 48 Mos 2:126, 126, 140 Spec 1:29, 90, 118, 339 Contempl 49 Aet 64 Prov 2:20 QG 2:12c

χρωματικός Leg 3:121 Post 104 Agr 137 Somn 1:205

χρώς Deus 123, 124 Somn 1:106 Prob 116

χυλός (32) Opif 62, 139, 159, 165 Leg 1:25 Leg 2:7, 39, 76 Leg 3:58, 220, 220, 235 Cher 57, 70, 117 Sacr 31 Det

99 Plant 133, 159 Ebr 106, 190, 191 Conf 194 Migr 50, 51, 51, 51 Mut 111 Somn 1:27 Somn 2:51 Abr 239 Ios 142

χυλόω QG (Par) 2:7, 2:7

χύλωσις Spec 1:217

χυμός Leg 3:173 Conf 52 QE isf 21

χύσις (7) Leg 3:99 Plant 166 Sobr 49 Somn 1:125 Praem 47 Aet 18, 102

χυτός Leg 1:66 Spec 1:300

χωλαίνω Conf 87 QE 2:26

χωλεύω Somn 1:131

χωλός Congr 48 Praem 56 Aet 99, 127

χῶμα Somn 2:125

χωνευτός Leg 3:22, 36, 36 Spec 1:25

χωνεύω Mos 2:138

χώρα (290) Opif 20, 32, 89, 114 Leg 1:59, 59, 62, 71, 85, 85 Cher 49, 129 Sacr 9, 49, 138 Det 2, 76, 99, 151 Post 22, 26, 54 Gig 51 Deus 40, 116, 132, 173, 176 Agr 57, 64, 88 Plant 3, 56, 57, 63, 67, 96 Ebr 28, 34, 193, 195, 208 Sobr 49 Conf 12, 15, 15, 46, 136 Migr 14, 20, 29, 45, 77, 120, 151, 154, 176, 197 Her 83, 96, 194, 223, 267, 277, 305, 316 Congr 49, 59, 83, 119 Fug 46, 51, 62, 75, 124, 180 Mut 89, 90, 125, 149, 209 Somn 1:17, 46, 62, 63, 68, 127, 177, 177, 181, 184 Somn 2:42, 59, 76, 170, 234, 255, 277, 287 Abr 40, 44, 67, 72, 85, 101, 133, 134, 141, 142, 164, 184, 193, 215, 226, 260 Ios 38, 56, 97, 100, 107, 134, 151, 159, 165, 178, 184, 190, 196, 204, 210, 218, 232, 254, 255, 259, 267 Mos 1:8, 13, 33, 36, 47, 73, 73, 73, 86, 96, 96, 103, 109, 110, 114, 118, 121, 134, 136, 139, 149, 157, 194, 209, 214, 220, 224, 224, 226, 226, 228, 235, 238, 243, 246, 251, 252, 254, 254, 255, 258, 278, 320, 321, 325, 327, 332 Mos 2:19, 29, 58, 72, 78, 82, 103, 120, 127, 162, 195, 195, 232 Decal 76, 152, 162 Spec 1:131 Spec 2:86, 88, 104, 113, 116, 119, 121, 146, 162, 168, 170, 183, 199, 213, 218 Spec 3:139 Spec 4:158, 213, 215 Virt 61, 97, 107, 119, 150 Praem 7, 10, 90, 93, 107, 114, 153, 153, 153, 155, 157 Prob 7, 89 Contempl 15 Aet 32, 33, 34, 42, 86, 122, 131, 136 Flacc 2, 5, 31, 43, 43, 45, 74, 92, 105, 116, 128, 133, 157, 163 Legat 19, 47, 48, 69, 95, 116, 132, 202, 205, 214, 222, 225, 245, 265, 281, 293, 294, 297, 326, 330, 335, 347 Hypoth 6:5, 6:6, 7:17, 7:18 Prov 2:41, 66 QG 2:15b QE 2:2

χωρέω (104) Opif 20, 151 Leg 1:30 Leg 3:56, 139, 163, 195 Cher 96, 114, 114 Sacr 8, 111 Det 11, 68, 89, 90, 103 Post 62, 137, 143, 144, 170 Deus 76, 77 Agr 68 Plant 10, 43, 80, 83 Ebr 16, 32, 92, 130, 189 Conf 106 Migr 23, 157 Her 33, 154, 194, 241 Congr 42 Mut 15, 42, 150, 183 Somn 1:59, 63, 72, 143, 147 Abr 76, 223 Ios 144, 149, 159 Mos 1:115, 257, 270, 280 Mos 2:163, 232, 252, 257 Decal 23, 44 Spec 1:44, 72, 105, 214, 215 Spec 2:203 Spec 3:31, 65, 185 Spec 4:85 Virt 12, 14, 79, 213 Praem 26, 39, 75 Prob 129 Aet 30, 33, 43, 105 Flacc 45, 72, 186 Legat 23, 24, 88, 219, 227, 288, 371 Prov 2:27 QG 2:64b QG (Par) 2:7 QE isf 9, 21, 25

Χωρήβ Somn 2:221

χωρίζω (9) Opif 33 Leg 1:50, 107 Leg 2:96 Sacr 4, 47, 109 Mut 63 Mos 2:180

χωρίον (116) Opif 88, 147, 161 Leg 1:28, 44, 62, 70 Leg 2:61 Leg 3:40, 138 Cher 5, 10, 94, 98 Det 15, 128, 152, 163 Post 6, 30, 146, 155 Deus 91 Agr 5, 105, 169 Plant 14, 22, 28, 29, 40, 61, 73, 74, 74, 85, 93 Ebr 98, 174 Sobr 40, 63 Conf 23, 26, 68, 75, 139, 177 Migr 2, 187, 212 Her 238, 240, 267 Congr 163 Mut 190, 238 Somn 1:42, 105 Somn 2:281 Abr 267 Ios 86, 110, 111 Mos 1:243, 271, 282, 312 Mos 2:34, 41 Decal 36, 94 Spec 1:75, 103, 146, 232, 268 Spec 2:44, 105, 116, 172, 206, 220 Spec 3:25, 76, 130, 183, 184 Spec 4:21, 25, 69, 83, 130, 141, 212, 216, 238 Virt 30, 48, 97, 98, 133, 189 Praem 117 Prob 150, 150 Contempl 22, 62 Aet 66, 102, 148 Flacc 187 Legat 17, 48, 145 Hypoth 11:4 Prov 2:23

χωρίς (70) Leg 1:83, 83 Leg 2:17 Leg 3:30, 65, 66, 69, 75, 77, 134 Cher 47 Sacr 35, 60, 95, 106 Det 14 Post 34 Deus 62, 75, 92, 96, 97 Agr 35, 45 Plant 33, 122, 131 Ebr 172, 199, 219 Conf 11, 115, 148 Migr 202 Her 92, 186 Congr 138 Mut 6, 157, 157, 259, 270 Somn 1:229 Somn 2:62, 187, 187, 257, 258 Abr 64 Mos 1:46, 318 Mos 2:80, 81, 119 Decal 31 Spec 2:164 Spec 3:103, 142 Virt 124, 144 Praem 51, 77 Contempl 30, 69, 69 Aet 48 Legat 54, 351 QG 1:93, 2:59

χωρισμός Leg 1:105 Leg 2:77 Abr 258

χῶρος (34) Leg 2:98 Leg 3:99, 115, 116, 151 Cher 2, 63 Sacr 4 Det 27, 86, 154 Post 31 Gig 54 Deus 112, 151 Ebr 10, 87 Conf 78 Migr 46 Her 238 Congr 57, 57 Fug 131, 162 Somn 1:151 Somn 2:133 Abr 171 Spec 1:89 Spec 3:152 Spec 4:93 Praem 165 Aet 33 Prov 2:43 QE 2:45b

Ψ

ψαιστός Spec 1:271

ψακάς (ψεκάς) Mos 1:118 Praem 131 Aet 119

ψαλτήριον Post 103, 111

ψάμμος Mos 1:192 Mos 2:42, 254 Aet 42

ψαύω (33) Opif 141, 141 Post 20 Deus 35, 168, 171 Plant 22 Sobr 27 Conf 5, 156 Somn 1:36, 220 Somn 2:70 Abr 76, 176 Mos 1:243, 259 Mos 2:116 Decal 65, 146, 149 Spec 1:98, 118, 150, 329 Spec 3:32, 63 Spec 4:121 Virt 3 Prob 3 Hypoth 7:3 QG (Par) 2:3 QE isf 21

ψέγω (11) Agr 118 Migr 108, 110, 110, 112 Her 161 Abr 187 Spec 2:193 Spec 3:155 Spec 4:88 Flacc 50

ψεκάς ψακάς

ψεκτός (26) Cher 24 Deus 48, 162 Agr 66, 90, 118, 129, 129 Plant 45 Ebr 20, 194 Migr 65, 108, 110 Congr 67 Fug 86 Mut 47, 197 Somn 2:40, 259 Abr 14 Spec 3:128, 186 Spec 4:42 Virt 184 QG 1:64b

ψέλιον Congr 113

ψευδαγγελέω Deus 3

ψευδής (64) Leg 1:51 Leg 3:121, 230 Cher 9, 66, 69, 71, 116 Sacr 84 Det 38 Post 52 Gig 15 Deus 64, 102, 172, 172, 181 Agr 141 Ebr 70, 162, 166, 183 Sobr 15 Conf 106, 141 Her 43, 71, 303, 305 Congr 18, 101 Fug 208 Mut 248, 248 Somn 1:218, 220 Somn 2:106, 162, 194, 298 Abr 20 Ios 147 Decal 86, 86, 91 Spec 1:28, 59, 309 Spec 2:252 Spec 3:82 Spec 4:42, 44, 53, 188 Virt 205, 205, 214 Praem 148 Flacc 139 Legat 57, 111, 160 QG 4:204 QE 2:107

ψευδογραφέω Ebr 47, 183

ψευδοδοξέω (7) Leg 2:46 Sacr 76 Ebr 40 Migr 225 Virt 56 Aet 107 Legat 62

ψευδολογία Sacr 22 Conf 117 Virt 182 Aet 69

ψευδομαρτυρέω Decal 138, 172

ψευδομαρτυρία (7) Cher 124 Agr 116 Conf 126 Her 173 Abr 258 Decal 51, 141

ψευδομάρτυς Decal 138 Spec 4:78

ψευδοπροφήτης Spec 4:51

ψευδορκέω Mut 240 Spec 2:224, 258

ψευδορκία Sacr 22 Conf 117 Decal 92 Spec 2:254 Virt 182

ψεύδορκος Conf 48

ψεῦδος (31) Leg 3:127, 229 Det 58 Conf 48 Migr 110 Her 132, 132, 306 Somn 2:47 Ios 22 Mos 1:24 Mos 2:129, 167 Decal 6 Spec 1:28, 53, 89 Spec 4:48, 52, 68 Virt 195 Contempl 10, 39, 39 Aet 76 Flacc 165 Prov 2:62 QG 4:69, 69 QE 2:9b QE isf 17

ψεύδω (26) Leg 3:124 Cher 15 Det 58 Post 34 Gig 59 Mut 240 Somn 1:245 Abr 101 Mos 2:177 Decal 139 Spec 1:235, 315 Spec 4:32, 36, 39, 40, 189 Virt 135 Praem 5, 29 Aet 16, 94 Flacc 102 Prov 2:7 QG 4:204 QE isf 17

ψευδώνυμος (17) Sacr 70 Post 165 Ebr 45 Conf 144 Mut 175 Abr 25 Mos 2:171, 205 Decal 8, 53 Spec 1:230, 332 Virt 4 Legat 102, 110, 366 QE isf 7

ψεῦσμα Her 305 Praem 24 Aet 56

ψῆγμα Opif 41

ψηλαφάω Her 250 Mut 126

ψηλάφημα Leg 3:231 Mut 126

ψηλαφητός Somn 1:114

ψηφίζω (11) Opif 125 Det 143 Ebr 8, 109, 224 Her 169 Fug 119 Praem 171 Flacc 97 Legat 149, 149

ψηφίς Aet 122

ψήφισμα (6) Mut 93 Flacc 97, 98, 100, 101, 103

ψῆφος (6) Deus 75 Migr 115 Somn 2:104 Decal 140, 141 Spec 4:57

ψιλός (19) Opif 121 Leg 1:14 Leg 3:47, 146 Det 21, 60, 97 Deus 55 Agr 12 Plant 155, 174 Migr 106 Her 40 Congr 46, 166 Somn 1:29 Decal 176 Spec 2:39 Legat 274

ψιμύθιον (ψιμμύθιον) Spec 3:37

ψιμμύθιον ψιμύθιον

ψόγος (17) Det 61 Deus 47 Sobr 37, 37 Conf 2 Migr 110, 118 Her 162, 178 Congr 119 Somn 1:244 Abr 178 Ios 19 Mos 1:154 Spec 1:204 Spec 2:234 Prov 2:69

Ψονθομφανήχ Mut 89, 91

ψοφοδεής Sacr 32

ψόφος Sacr 69 Prov 2:26

ψῦξις Somn 1:31 Aet 21

ψυχαγωγέω Det 125 Sobr 3 Congr 78 Mos 2:48

ψυχή (1814) Opif 6, 18, 20, 30, 53, 54, 65, 66, 66, 67, 69, 78, 79, 81, 117, 119, 125, 128, 134, 135, 136, 137, 139, 140, 141, 144, 145, 150, 151, 154, 154, 155, 155, 164, 172 Leg 1:11, 16, 24, 24, 31, 32, 32, 34, 38, 39, 40, 41, 45, 46, 48, 49, 49, 49, 50, 51, 51, 56, 61, 66, 66, 70, 71, 71, 71, 71, 72, 76, 76, 80, 82, 91, 91, 91, 97, 97, 100, 104, 105, 105, 105, 106, 106, 106, 107, 107, 108, 108 Leg 2:2, 2, 5, 5, 6, 8, 8, 9, 9, 11, 13, 18, 18, 23, 23, 24, 24, 32, 34, 34, 53, 53, 54, 55, 55, 56, 60, 61, 61, 62, 62, 63, 63, 67, 73, 75, 77, 77, 77, 80, 83, 84, 85, 86, 86, 89, 90, 90, 91, 93, 95, 95, 97, 97, 98, 100, 101, 102 Leg 3:8, 8, 8, 11, 12, 18, 19, 19, 20, 21, 22, 27, 27, 28, 31, 36, 37, 38, 40, 40, 43, 43, 44, 44, 52, 52, 53, 62, 69, 69, 70, 71, 72, 72, 72, 72, 74, 75, 76, 80, 81, 82, 84, 86, 87, 87, 88, 89, 91, 93, 95, 95, 106, 107, 107, 110, 113, 115, 117, 120, 124, 124, 128, 128, 129, 130, 131, 136, 137, 140, 141, 148, 148, 149, 150, 150, 151, 152, 158, 160, 161, 161, 161, 161, 162, 162, 163, 165, 166, 167, 167, 168, 169, 172, 173, 173, 173, 174, 176, 176, 178, 179, 180, 186, 187, 190, 191, 191, 193, 200, 203, 212, 212, 213, 215, 215, 219, 224, 234, 235, 235, 236, 238, 238, 239, 239, 242, 243, 246, 247, 247, 247, 248, 249, 251 Cher 4, 9, 12, 13, 17, 17, 27, 32, 48, 50, 51, 52, 57, 59, 60, 63, 68, 69, 69, 70, 71, 72, 74, 75, 77, 78, 82, 84, 93, 95, 96, 98, 100, 101, 103, 104, 106, 113, 114, 117, 128 Sacr 1, 3, 3, 5, 5, 6, 9, 10, 16, 20, 21, 29, 36, 37, 39, 39, 44, 45, 48, 59, 60, 61, 64, 64, 69, 70, 72, 72, 73, 78, 79, 80, 80, 84, 85, 86, 87, 94, 101, 102, 103, 108, 111, 111, 112, 114, 117, 119, 121, 122, 126, 127, 130, 134, 136, 139 Det 3, 4, 5, 7, 8, 9, 9, 15, 16, 19, 21, 22, 23, 24, 29, 30, 33, 33, 34, 35, 42, 43, 44, 48, 50, 58, 59, 65, 74, 74, 77, 80, 80, 80, 80, 81, 82, 83, 84, 84, 86, 86, 88, 90, 91, 91, 95, 95, 97, 103, 105, 109, 110, 111, 115, 120, 121, 123, 132, 137, 139, 141, 141, 147, 149, 159, 168, 169, 170, 170, 176 Post 8, 10, 15, 21, 27, 31, 32, 42, 46, 48, 53, 60, 61, 62, 72, 73, 73, 74, 81, 91, 91, 116, 118, 120, 122, 122, 125, 129, 130, 131, 135, 147, 149, 150, 156, 158, 163, 165, 166, 171, 174, 175, 175, 184, 184 Gig 4, 6, 8, 9, 9, 11, 11, 12, 14, 15,

16, 16, 28, 31, 33, 37, 40, 40, 44, 51, 52, 59, 66 Deus 2, 3, 4, 8, 10, 11, 12, 14, 24, 26, 29, 35, 35, 41, 43, 44, 44, 46, 46, 47, 48, 52, 55, 55, 66, 67, 89, 93, 96, 102, 111, 112, 114, 123, 125, 128, 129, 134, 135, 135, 138, 148, 150, 151, 154, 160, 165, 166, 181, 182 Agr 7, 9, 16, 17, 18, 20, 22, 25, 29, 30, 42, 44, 46, 49, 50, 54, 56, 63, 65, 66, 72, 77, 79, 88, 89, 95, 98, 101, 105, 119, 125, 130, 132, 139, 142, 146, 152, 154, 157, 160, 163, 164, 166, 168, 171, 176 Plant 14, 18, 20, 22, 37, 37, 38, 42, 46, 53, 58, 77, 79, 88, 90, 91, 100, 101, 114, 118, 132, 134, 136, 137, 144, 144, 147, 160, 162, 165, 169 Ebr 6, 10, 12, 15, 22, 22, 23, 26, 27, 33, 37, 44, 46, 52, 55, 56, 58, 69, 70, 70, 75, 86, 87, 87, 95, 98, 100, 101, 106, 110, 111, 112, 113, 116, 122, 123, 130, 138, 139, 140, 146, 147, 149, 149, 152, 154, 155, 157, 157, 158, 160, 161, 164, 171, 177, 178, 180, 198, 200, 201, 210, 211, 223, 223, 224 Sobr 2, 3, 3, 4, 5, 6, 7, 11, 12, 12, 13, 14, 16, 18, 20, 24, 28, 38, 43, 45, 45, 46, 49, 60, 61, 62, 67, 68, 68 Conf 10, 16, 17, 19, 21, 22, 23, 25, 27, 31, 36, 42, 43, 46, 52, 54, 55, 60, 62, 69, 72, 77, 79, 84, 86, 90, 91, 92, 93, 102, 105, 107, 111, 128, 131, 144, 145, 149, 161, 163, 165, 166, 174, 174, 176, 179, 181, 194, 195 Migr 2, 3, 5, 5, 13, 14, 17, 18, 28, 33, 34, 36, 37, 39, 43, 48, 49, 52, 53, 60, 64, 66, 67, 67, 68, 69, 90, 93, 93, 96, 98, 100, 101, 104, 105, 114, 115, 116, 124, 124, 125, 131, 137, 140, 146, 150, 151, 152, 152, 157, 160, 165, 168, 169, 170, 175, 179, 181, 191, 197, 199, 200, 201, 202, 202, 205, 206, 208, 214, 214, 214, 215, 219, 223, 224, 225 Her 11, 14, 30, 36, 38, 38, 40, 44, 44, 51, 51, 53, 55, 55, 55, 55, 56, 56, 60, 61, 64, 67, 69, 79, 80, 81, 82, 82, 83, 83, 84, 88, 89, 98, 106, 107, 108, 109, 110, 111, 123, 125, 129, 132, 133, 138, 154, 155, 167, 181, 184, 186, 191, 192, 193, 201, 225, 225, 232, 233, 239, 242, 243, 243, 245, 247, 254, 264, 268, 269, 273, 276, 280, 283, 283, 284, 285, 286, 291, 293, 294, 295, 295, 296, 298, 298, 299, 311 Congr 6, 16, 18, 19, 21, 21, 21, 26, 28, 31, 37, 41, 44, 47, 54, 56, 57, 59, 59, 60, 66, 81, 90, 92, 106, 107, 108, 109, 112, 114, 129, 134, 135, 135, 137, 137, 143, 144, 150, 155, 162, 164, 167, 169, 176 Fug 5, 9, 14, 17, 22, 24, 52, 67, 69, 69, 70, 80, 81, 85, 90, 91, 91, 96, 110, 112, 113, 113, 115, 117, 117, 118, 119, 128, 131, 137, 139, 142, 146, 148, 148, 153, 155, 158, 158, 167, 174, 176, 180, 182, 187, 190, 192, 194, 195, 198, 198, 201, 202, 203, 205, 210, 211, 212, 213 Mut 3, 4, 6, 10, 17, 18, 30, 33, 33, 44, 49, 53, 65, 68, 72, 81, 82, 82, 88, 94, 96, 98, 111, 124, 128, 131, 133, 138, 141, 143, 147, 154, 161, 164, 168, 171, 173, 174, 183, 189, 192, 199, 203, 205, 206, 209, 212, 215, 221, 223, 223, 225, 228, 232, 239, 239, 255, 257, 260, 265 Somn 1:11, 11, 22, 26, 27, 31, 34, 43, 51, 56, 69, 71, 71, 73, 74, 77, 89, 112, 113, 116, 117, 117, 119, 122, 124, 126, 127, 128, 131, 135, 135, 136, 137, 137, 138, 146, 147, 149, 157, 159, 164, 165, 174, 179, 181, 182, 192, 198, 199, 200, 200, 202, 215, 222, 228, 232, 243, 247, 250, 255 Somn 2:1, 2, 9, 11, 12, 14, 25, 45, 46, 68, 71, 72, 72, 73, 74, 83, 90, 90, 95, 98, 109, 122, 134, 134, 139, 141, 145, 151, 153, 160, 165, 173, 184, 187, 196, 198, 203, 207, 215, 219, 223, 236, 239, 242, 248, 249, 250, 255, 256, 256, 258, 271, 272, 273, 281, 283, 284, 296, 298 Abr 7, 8, 16, 23, 26, 26, 32, 47, 48, 52, 54, 57, 58, 59, 65, 66, 68, 70, 79, 88, 89, 93, 96, 99, 101, 104, 105, 108, 115, 119, 127, 136, 147, 148, 150, 153, 153, 154, 168, 170, 174, 193, 198, 199, 207, 210, 217, 221, 223, 233, 236, 242, 256, 258, 268, 269, 272, 272 Ios 10, 26, 26, 47, 50, 61, 67, 87, 106, 114, 124, 142, 147, 162, 166, 167, 179, 182, 211, 254, 255, 264 Mos 1:15, 20, 22, 26, 29, 38, 39, 40, 48, 50, 78, 85, 86, 88, 94, 128, 149, 159, 160, 182, 185, 233, 237, 255, 277, 279, 279, 279, 280, 289, 301, 305, 309, 315, 318 Mos 2:11, 16, 36, 68, 69, 74, 108, 164, 183, 184, 196, 199, 202, 211, 217, 239, 279, 288 Decal 4, 10, 13, 17, 33, 33, 35, 41, 49, 50, 60, 60, 63, 67, 68, 76, 80, 87, 93, 98, 119, 122, 124, 134, 142, 143, 146, 157, 173 Spec 1:10, 29, 37, 62, 66, 80, 81, 82, 89, 99, 100, 102, 103, 105, 106, 137, 167, 174, 191, 191, 197, 201, 205, 207, 209, 211, 222, 237, 239, 257, 257, 258, 258, 269, 272, 281, 282, 287, 288, 289, 289, 292, 298, 298, 300, 302, 305, 313, 333, 342, 345 Spec 2:6, 21, 29, 31, 42, 45, 49, 52, 61, 64, 64, 64, 80, 83, 90, 96, 98, 141, 147, 157, 163, 163, 163, 185, 198, 202, 214, 229, 230, 239, 240, 256, 256, 260, 262 Spec 3:1, 4, 4, 6, 10, 11, 20, 23, 31, 33, 35, 37, 51, 52, 54, 67, 75, 86, 99, 99, 99, 103, 135, 137, 158, 161, 163, 178, 179, 180, 182, 182, 192, 194, 195, 204, 204, 207, 208 Spec 4:16, 18, 45, 49, 68, 69, 75, 75, 79, 80, 81, 82, 83, 92, 95, 100, 103, 107, 112, 114, 122, 122, 123, 130, 134, 140, 140, 141, 149, 157, 160, 161, 163, 165, 170, 183, 189, 194, 196, 218, 225, 237, 238 Virt 3, 5, 8, 9, 10, 13, 13, 17, 18, 26, 27, 30, 30, 31, 32, 37, 40, 42, 52, 57, 67, 70, 74, 76, 78, 85, 87, 103, 126, 126, 132, 138, 141, 144, 147, 148, 160, 162, 164, 165, 172, 172, 173, 176, 178, 182, 187, 200, 203, 205, 211, 213, 216, 217, 223 Praem 5, 10, 12, 16, 21, 25, 26, 32, 35, 37, 47, 48, 52, 59, 62, 63, 65, 71, 88, 95, 97, 114, 116, 120, 129, 136, 139, 146, 148, 151, 156, 158, 163, 166, 172 Prob 5, 12, 15, 17, 17, 22, 27, 38, 40, 55, 63, 63, 70, 76, 80, 96, 97, 98, 107, 110, 113, 123, 126, 135, 140, 143, 149, 158 Contempl 2, 10, 27, 31, 34, 36, 37, 60, 61, 68, 76, 78, 78, 90 Aet 2, 40, 47, 50, 51, 51, 63, 63, 69, 73, 75, 84, 84, 97, 111, 111, 125, 126 Flacc 4, 48, 126, 164, 167, 173, 176, 180, 186 Legat 1, 5, 14, 27, 55, 56, 73, 82, 89, 111, 112, 119, 166, 196, 206, 210, 213, 215, 218, 224, 245, 280, 310, 324, 341, 366, 368 Hypoth 7:4, 11:7, 11:11 Prov 2:7, 8, 9, 14, 17, 18, 25, 35, 39, 40, 56, 63, 67 QG 1:21, 55c, 70:1, 2:11, 12c, 12d, 22, 34a, 54a, 54c, 59, 59, 59, 59, 59, 59, 59, 59, 59, 62, 74, 3:11a, 11a, 21, 26, 4:99, 100 QG isf 12, 13 QE 1:7b, 2:2, 2, 3b, 3b, 4, 13a, 14, 15b, 15b, 20, 26, 47 QE isf 5, 11, 14, 20, 25, 31, 32

ψυχικός (43) Opif 66 Leg 1:76, 97 Leg 2:22, 45, 56, 59, 81, 85, 91 Leg 3:24, 54, 146, 171 Cher 82, 105 Sacr 20 Det 70, 117 Agr 25 Migr 92, 144 Congr 106 Fug 39, 130, 143 Mut 33 Somn 1:88 Abr 219 Mos 1:153 Mos 2:137, 170 Spec 1:205, 222, 253 Spec 2:17, 54 Spec 4:75 Praem 115 Legat 16, 63 QG 1:51 QE 2:4

ψυχογόνιμος Mos 1:97

ψυχοειδής Opif 66 Abr 113

ψῦχος Her 165 Prov 2:23

ψυχόω (15) Opif 9, 139 Leg 1:36, 39, 40 Gig 7, 11 Her 185 Somn 1:136, 137 Somn 2:260 Mos 1:77 Virt 14 Praem 125 Prov 2:59

ψυχρός (28) Opif 41, 62, 161 Leg 2:2 Leg 3:61 Sacr 108 Deus 79 Plant 3, 4 Ebr 186 Conf 157 Migr 50 Her 135, 135, 146, 153, 208, 282 Somn 1:18, 31 Abr 159, 239 Mos 1:212 Contempl 73 Aet 26, 105 Legat 126 Prov 2:23

ψυχρότης Plant 133

ψύχω Leg 1:5 Cher 88

ψύχωσις Opif 66 Gig 10

ψωμίζω (6) Leg 2:84 Leg 3:174 Det 114 Migr 157 Congr 170, 173

ψωμός Contempl 40

ψώρα Praem 143

Ω

ω Leg 3:121

ὦ Conf 136

ὦ (171) Leg 1:49, 51 Leg 2:1, 46, 91, 106 Leg 3:9, 11, 17, 22, 31, 36, 47, 52, 74, 75, 116, 158, 165, 179, 192, 219 Cher 29, 35, 48, 52, 53, 75 Sacr 20, 22, 32, 55, 64, 64, 70, 101 Det 13, 78, 101, 150, 158 Post 135 Gig 40, 44 Deus 4, 61, 66, 114, 146, 149 Agr 86, 111, 112, 149, 167 Plant 53, 65, 72, 108 Ebr 120, 149 Sobr 50 Conf 41, 44, 49, 116, 116, 162 Migr 9, 84, 138, 169, 173, 184, 222 Her 31, 71, 81, 91, 105 Congr 54, 113, 156 Fug 39, 46, 58, 85, 149, 149, 169, 213 Mut 25, 177, 187, 227, 255, 264 Somn 1:54, 93, 149, 164 Somn 2:68, 76, 176, 179, 181, 252, 253, 296 Abr 71, 175 Ios 9, 24, 64, 104, 166, 183 Mos 1:277, 296, 325 Mos 2:199, 204, 212, 239 Decal 20, 73, 88 Spec 1:210, 223, 223, 259, 271, 299, 320 Spec 2:75, 82, 84, 96, 129, 219, 247 Spec 3:66, 166 Spec 4:10, 59, 200, 227 Virt 59, 127, 133 Prob 1 Aet 54, 121, 132 Flacc 6, 6, 52, 121, 123 Legat 86, 87, 141, 208, 239, 276, 326 Prov 2:7, 37 QG 4:52d, 191c QE 2:28

ὠγύγιος Sacr 78 Post 168 Deus 154

ὧδε (54) Leg 2:88 Leg 3:4, 38, 218 Cher 13, 43, 63, 81, 108 Sacr 19, 67, 68, 90 Det 86 Post 22 Agr 50, 75, 84 Plant 29, 130 Conf 1, 138 Migr 20, 183, 184 Her 134, 272, 287, 293, 298 Fug 149, 162, 188 Somn 1:79, 133 Somn 2:155, 221 Abr 119, 120, 212 Mos 1:270 Mos 2:20, 165, 192 Decal 67 Spec 1:15, 62, 299 Spec 4:158 Aet 27, 50, 86, 130 QE 2:55b

ᾠδή (25) Leg 3:26, 105 Det 114 Post 121, 167 Agr 81 Plant 59 Sobr 10, 58 Mut 182, 220 Somn 1:36 Somn 2:34, 191, 269 Mos 2:257 Spec 1:343 Spec 2:209 Spec 3:125 Virt 72, 74, 95 Contempl 35 Flacc 122 Legat 44

ὠδίνω (19) Opif 43 Leg 1:74, 75, 75, 75 Cher 57 Sacr 3, 102 Det 127 Post 135 Deus 14, 137 Agr 101 Ebr 60 Conf 21 Migr 33 Congr 160 Mos 1:280 QG 2:26b

ὠδίς (16) Opif 167 Leg 1:75, 76, 76 Cher 42 Det 101 Post 74, 176 Deus 5 Ebr 30 Conf 26 Fug 208 Mut 96 Virt 128 Aet 65 Legat 189

ὠθέω ἀνωθέω

ὠθέω (6) Somn 2:121 Mos 1:148, 176 Spec 2:18 Spec 4:111 Aet 136

ὠθισμός Legat 125

ὠκεανός Sobr 53 Legat 10

Ὠκεανός Opif 131

ὠκυδρομέω Migr 151, 154 Fug 97

ὠκύδρομος (7) Cher 26 Sacr 78 Det 89 Post 19 Agr 180 Fug 159 Somn 1:184

ὠκύμορος (9) Her 34 Ios 24 Mos 2:245 Decal 42 Praem 110 Legat 29, 62 QG (Par) 2:7, 2:7

ὠκύς Conf 99 Aet 133 Legat 18, 132

ὠκύτης Det 117 Agr 115 Flacc 186

ὠμίασις Leg 3:25 Migr 221

ὠμοβόρος Somn 2:87

ὠμόθυμος (11) Abr 95 Mos 1:37, 70 Spec 3:158, 203 Spec 4:89 Virt 124 Prob 40, 91, 106 Flacc 180 ὦμος (9) Leg 1:80 Det 9 Agr 75 Sobr 8 Migr 221 Mut 193 Mos 1:203 Mos 2:130 Flacc 38

ὠμός (19) Sacr 62 Det 110 Her 186, 273 Somn 1:98 Somn 2:84 Ios 25 Spec 1:295 Spec 2:96 Spec 3:119, 197 Virt 126 Contempl 20, 40 Flacc 70 Legat 73, 87, 131 Prov 2:39

ὠμότης (27) Agr 114, 154 Sobr 46 Her 60 Ios 18, 20, 81 Mos 1:102, 245 Spec 2:95 Spec 3:114, 137 Spec 4:16, 202 Virt 107, 132, 144 Praem 171 Prob 89, 121 Flacc 59, 66 Legat 302, 341 Prov 2:2, 22 QE 2:2

Ὤν Post 54, 57, 57 Somn 1:77

ὠνέομαι (21) Cher 122, 122 Deus 169 Ebr 122 Abr 187 Ios 36, 58, 190 Spec 2:37, 112, 112, 117 Spec 4:194 Prob 35, 40, 124, 144 Flacc 41, 132 Hypoth 7:8, 11:10

ὠνή Prob 104

ὠνητικός Fug 150 Ios 162 Prob 123, 145 Flacc 138

ὤνιος (7) Gig 39 Plant 107 Mos 1:243 Mos 2:212 Spec 3:51 Spec 4:63, 193

ὦνος Deus 169

ᾠότοκος Her 211

Ὤρ Leg 3:45, 45

ὥρα (93) Opif 52, 55, 58, 59, 59, 85, 103, 105, 113, 153, 158, 168 Cher 88 Det 87 Post 22, 163 Deus 39 Plant 105, 120 Ebr 91 Conf 151 Migr 92, 126, 126 Her 150, 165 Congr 4, 133 Fug 153, 184 Mut 67, 266 Somn 1:20 Somn 2:62, 131, 257, 257 Abr 1, 69 Mos 1:114, 139, 212, 226, 297 Mos 2:124, 125, 148 Decal 151 Spec 1:16, 34, 87, 103, 144, 179, 181, 210, 280, 322, 325 Spec 2:57, 125, 158, 191, 210 Spec 3:38, 51, 94 Spec 4:99, 208, 215, 228, 235, 235, 235 Virt 93, 112, 157 Praem 41, 130, 132 Prob 67 Aet 19, 63, 109, 132 Flacc 27, 85, 175 Legat 132, 203 Prov 2:44, 48 QG 4:51b

ὡραΐζω Somn 1:199 Spec 3:39

ὡραῖος Leg 1:56, 58 Leg 3:177 Sacr 25 Spec 2:220

ὥριος Opif 104

ὠρύομαι Somn 1:108

ὡς (2492) Opif 2, 2, 3, 4, 6, 7, 9, 11, 12, 13, 15, 19, 23, 25, 26, 26, 27, 38, 38, 44, 44, 47, 47, 59, 62, 62, 63, 66, 67, 69, 69, 71, 73, 75, 77, 77, 81, 82, 82, 83, 85, 88, 91, 100, 106, 106, 107, 108, 112, 113, 119, 124, 124, 131, 132, 133, 133, 138, 138, 139, 142, 145, 147, 147, 148, 149, 150, 154, 155, 161, 162, 163, 168, 171, 172 Leg 1:4, 9, 17, 22, 23, 24, 24, 29, 29, 35, 38, 38, 42, 42, 42, 43, 43, 45, 45, 47, 59, 59, 65, 76, 76, 82, 88, 93, 95, 96, 96, 96, 100, 104, 108, 108 Leg 2:3, 6, 6, 8, 8, 9, 10, 10, 11, 17, 17, 17, 17, 17, 18, 23, 25, 35, 44, 60, 63, 68, 77, 82, 90, 99 Leg 3:1, 1, 6, 7, 13, 18, 21, 21, 36, 36, 40, 54, 56, 62, 64, 65, 71, 78, 84, 91, 96, 96, 100, 100, 102, 105, 111, 111, 112, 129, 132, 135, 139, 165, 165, 168, 170, 171, 171, 184, 191, 197, 202, 202, 203, 203, 204, 205, 210, 216, 217, 221, 226, 231, 238, 247, 249 Cher 11, 11, 11, 11, 15, 20, 20, 23, 26, 34, 48, 49, 53, 55, 56, 64, 65, 74, 76, 76, 78, 79, 79, 83, 84, 84, 93, 93, 93, 94, 98, 104, 109, 112, 115, 115, 118, 121, 128, 129, 129, 129, 130 Sacr 1, 1, 2, 2, 6, 8, 11, 12, 25, 28, 30, 30, 37, 38, 46, 46, 61, 65, 66, 68, 70, 76, 77, 77, 77, 79, 80, 85, 86, 89, 91, 94, 98, 101, 101, 107, 112, 122, 123, 124, 127, 129, 130, 135 Det 4, 4, 9, 10, 13, 25, 32, 33, 38, 42, 46, 52, 52, 61, 64, 70, 73, 79, 84, 88, 88, 88, 91, 100, 103, 106, 115, 118, 122, 138, 138, 149, 157, 157, 157, 160, 165, 165, 166, 178 Post 20, 25, 27, 28, 31, 34, 42, 42, 63, 71, 74, 80, 85, 89, 102, 111, 113, 123, 136, 141, 151, 151, 156, 161, 161, 163, 168, 171, 172, 172, 179, 182 Gig 10, 19, 20, 28, 30, 38, 38, 41, 44, 48, 48, 55 Deus 1, 4, 27, 29, 36, 42, 44, 48, 53, 53, 54, 62, 62, 62, 69, 69, 80, 80, 87, 87, 87, 87, 87, 87, 88, 90, 93, 99, 103, 104, 113, 125, 127, 128, 129, 133, 134, 143, 146, 147, 147, 150, 152, 163, 163, 168, 170, 174, 176, 182 Agr 3, 5, 6, 10, 13, 17, 20, 24, 24, 25, 26, 27, 36, 38, 41, 44, 45, 56, 60, 62, 70, 70, 70, 73, 76, 85, 86, 88, 89, 102, 106, 108, 119, 124, 125, 127, 130, 130, 142, 145, 147, 152, 157, 157, 158, 164, 171, 174 Plant 1, 7, 8, 11, 17, 22, 27, 27, 33, 40, 44, 50, 53, 59, 65, 71, 71, 72, 72, 82, 82, 89, 90, 102, 103, 105, 108, 113, 121, 125, 125, 131, 131, 137, 139, 147, 149, 152, 157, 158, 158, 161, 162, 171, 172 Ebr 1, 3, 8, 9, 13, 17, 22, 30, 32, 33, 44, 45, 51, 51, 55, 58, 69, 73, 87, 87, 89, 90, 92, 94, 95, 95, 96, 101, 106, 111, 111, 130, 131, 131, 134, 140, 143, 143, 144, 144, 146, 152, 156, 161, 161, 165, 166, 166, 166, 169, 174, 176, 176, 177, 177, 177, 183, 196, 197, 198, 205, 205, 211, 224 Sobr 9, 16, 16, 20, 33, 45, 47, 48, 52, 58, 63, 63, 68 Conf 2, 2, 6, 6, 8, 9, 9, 9, 12, 12, 13, 13, 13, 18, 20, 28, 38, 43, 50, 52, 55, 69, 76, 76, 81, 81, 82, 83, 84, 86, 91, 92, 92, 96, 98, 98, 99, 99, 100, 101, 103, 106, 106, 108, 108, 108, 111, 113, 114, 114, 114, 114, 114, 116, 118, 121, 123, 129, 129, 133, 134, 135, 139, 144, 146, 155, 156, 160, 164, 164, 167, 167, 168, 169, 169, 175, 181, 183, 185, 187, 189, 192, 197 Migr 5, 7, 8, 8, 10, 19, 26, 35, 42, 45, 51, 51, 53, 54, 56, 66, 73, 74, 79, 80, 80, 82, 83, 85, 85, 85, 86, 88, 91, 95, 99, 101, 101, 106, 106, 110, 116, 120, 121, 122, 122, 124, 129, 130, 131, 133, 133, 136, 140, 141, 144, 144, 150, 150, 157, 161, 164, 167, 171, 177, 179, 183, 183, 183, 184, 186, 186, 189, 190, 191, 193, 202, 203, 204, 204, 213, 213, 214, 216, 217, 220, 221, 222, 224, 225 Her 1, 3, 5, 12, 14, 28, 34, 44, 49, 66, 71, 71, 71, 73, 73, 75, 87, 94, 105, 109, 115, 121, 121, 123, 124, 131, 133, 143, 144, 144, 154, 157, 161, 162, 164, 175, 181, 189, 191, 199, 206, 206, 214, 215, 223, 225, 226, 248, 250, 253, 254, 258, 262, 267, 267, 268, 268, 279, 280, 280, 283, 283, 285, 295, 300, 300, 307, 308, 309, 315 Congr 3, 5, 6, 7, 8, 11, 18, 19, 20, 20, 20, 22, 30, 31, 31, 32, 32, 32, 33, 34, 42, 42, 51, 58, 61, 63, 65, 72, 81, 84, 91, 100, 112, 117, 124, 143, 143, 144, 150, 152, 152, 152, 153, 153, 153, 154, 154, 154, 156, 156, 161, 162, 165, 169, 171, 173 Fug 4, 11, 15, 16, 22, 22, 25, 31, 33, 35, 51, 56, 59, 61, 61, 68, 71, 71, 76, 76, 76, 78, 79, 81, 82, 82, 91, 95, 98, 99, 107, 110, 110, 112, 126, 141, 144, 147, 148, 148, 152, 153, 154, 157, 160, 160, 164, 167, 168, 170, 171, 176, 176, 176, 190, 198, 200, 208, 209, 210, 212 Mut 2, 9, 12, 12, 15, 15, 16, 23, 24, 24, 24, 24, 25, 26, 26, 38, 39, 48, 58, 63, 69, 71, 71, 84, 87, 97, 98, 98, 102, 107, 114, 122, 128, 134, 138, 138, 144, 148, 148, 161, 162, 168, 173, 173, 177, 179, 179, 182, 185, 186, 191, 199, 199, 205, 210, 211, 218, 230, 243, 249, 251, 267, 268 Somn 1:1, 2, 3, 9, 10, 12, 17, 21, 22, 23, 27, 36, 36, 36, 41, 45, 45, 52, 52, 70, 76, 76, 77, 79, 82, 84, 84, 85, 86, 87, 87, 88, 91, 92, 95, 96, 98, 99, 99, 101, 103, 106, 109, 112, 113, 114, 117, 124, 128, 128, 129, 131, 145, 146, 149, 150, 152, 154, 157, 157, 163, 163, 164, 166, 168, 168, 169, 172, 176, 181, 184, 184, 188, 191, 191, 191, 191, 192, 194, 207, 215, 224, 228, 232, 232, 236, 236, 237, 237, 239, 239, 239, 241, 247 Somn 2:1, 12, 16, 25, 31, 32, 36, 39, 41, 42, 44, 52, 57, 66, 70, 74, 74, 86, 93, 93, 98, 100, 101, 104, 107, 108, 110, 115, 116, 119, 119, 121, 122, 122, 124, 128,

133, 133, 134, 144, 150, 161, 162, 162, 163, 164, 166, 178, 182, 189, 202, 204, 212, 218, 223, 223, 226, 226, 230, 234, 236, 245, 245, 246, 248, 259, 260, 260, 279, 281, 282, 288, 293, 294, 298 Abr 2, 3, 3, 5, 8, 10, 14, 14, 17, 17, 19, 21, 28, 30, 33, 34, 35, 40, 42, 43, 44, 45, 46, 47, 54, 63, 64, 79, 79, 82, 84, 88, 88, 96, 103, 103, 107, 107, 114, 118, 119, 119, 121, 123, 126, 131, 131, 132, 134, 137, 142, 153, 165, 168, 170, 176, 178, 181, 183, 183, 185, 185, 188, 192, 193, 195, 199, 202, 217, 223, 229, 230, 235, 235, 246, 250, 252, 253, 257, 258, 258, 260, 266, 267, 269, 272, 273, 273, 276, 276 Ios 6, 8, 11, 14, 14, 17, 22, 22, 25, 25, 30, 37, 37, 38, 46, 46, 46, 47, 51, 52, 52, 55, 64, 67, 68, 78, 79, 80, 85, 87, 90, 91, 93, 97, 104, 109, 109, 110, 122, 126, 126, 126, 135, 137, 139, 140, 140, 141, 145, 149, 149, 153, 156, 156, 164, 167, 167, 171, 175, 177, 178, 179, 182, 184, 184, 185, 191, 193, 193, 197, 198, 200, 205, 205, 210, 210, 213, 214, 215, 217, 219, 220, 226, 230, 233, 235, 236, 242, 243, 247, 248, 249, 249, 250, 257, 258, 262 Mos 1:9, 11, 11, 13, 14, 15, 17, 17, 21, 24, 25, 26, 27, 29, 34, 34, 36, 36, 38, 39, 46, 47, 58, 59, 61, 61, 64, 68, 68, 70, 71, 75, 78, 80, 82, 84, 85, 86, 89, 90, 94, 99, 100, 102, 103, 112, 114, 115, 117, 119, 120, 121, 123, 124, 130, 132, 133, 138, 141, 142, 142, 142, 150, 153, 153, 155, 156, 167, 167, 169, 175, 179, 181, 182, 182, 183, 183, 186, 190, 196, 198, 201, 207, 209, 211, 211, 228, 233, 233, 240, 248, 251, 256, 266, 272, 280, 280, 283, 283, 284, 284, 284, 286, 287, 288, 289, 289, 289, 289, 291, 293, 294, 295, 300, 302, 304, 309, 309, 311, 320, 322, 324, 325, 328, 331, 331, 333, 334 Mos 2:4, 9, 9, 9, 10, 12, 15, 17, 18, 25, 29, 33, 35, 39, 40, 50, 50, 53, 53, 56, 58, 59, 69, 70, 70, 75, 87, 89, 91, 97, 103, 120, 121, 122, 122, 122, 128, 132, 143, 146, 157, 158, 163, 167, 175, 176, 188, 191, 193, 194, 195, 202, 205, 211, 212, 215, 219, 219, 220, 231, 232, 242, 243, 247, 248, 248, 254, 268, 278, 278, 279, 282, 291, 291, 291, 291, 291 Decal 8, 18, 20, 21, 21, 32, 33, 34, 36, 36, 37, 38, 39, 39, 41, 43, 44, 46, 47, 49, 51, 59, 66, 66, 69, 69, 75, 75, 80, 84, 87, 87, 88, 88, 88, 89, 91, 92, 95, 101, 105, 107, 120, 124, 129, 134, 149, 149, 151, 173, 176 Spec 1:3, 4, 7, 10, 10, 14, 15, 21, 21, 23, 24, 26, 27, 30, 34, 35, 37, 41, 41, 42, 49, 53, 54, 58, 64, 67, 72, 72, 74, 77, 78, 84, 99, 113, 114, 125, 127, 131, 133, 140, 142, 143, 149, 157, 167, 171, 180, 180, 187, 187, 188, 188, 195, 197, 201, 203, 208, 210, 218, 220, 222, 229, 233, 243, 243, 244, 245, 245, 250, 256, 259, 261, 264, 269, 271, 273, 278, 289, 290, 290, 291, 300, 300, 306, 313, 313, 314, 316, 318, 321, 326, 328, 330, 330, 340, 343 Spec 2:3, 3, 6, 9, 12, 13, 13, 19, 19, 22, 23, 24, 30, 31, 31, 36, 40, 40, 46, 48, 48, 52, 63, 65, 65, 73, 76, 77, 80, 83, 83, 87, 94, 94, 95, 106, 106, 107, 122, 122, 124, 128, 132, 134, 135, 135, 136, 139, 141, 146, 148, 150, 151, 157, 158, 162, 164, 164, 166, 167, 168, 171, 173, 177, 177, 184, 194, 194, 197, 199, 200, 200, 202, 205, 211, 214, 215, 215, 224, 225, 225, 227, 231, 234, 234, 234, 234, 234, 239, 239, 240, 241, 241, 247, 249, 251, 254, 260 Spec 3:2, 7, 11, 11, 13, 13, 14, 15, 17, 23, 24, 28, 32, 34, 36, 36, 42, 43, 44, 46, 48, 50, 51, 53, 53, 56, 59, 64, 65, 67, 68, 69, 69, 74, 78, 80, 81, 88, 90, 92, 97, 111, 111, 113, 115, 115, 116, 117, 120, 122, 126, 131, 131, 131, 132, 136, 136, 142, 148, 154, 161, 161, 167, 174, 175, 178, 184, 184, 189, 194, 195, 202, 205, 206 Spec 4:1, 13, 14, 18, 23, 31, 32, 33, 37, 38, 41, 43, 47, 50, 50, 52, 52, 52, 54, 56, 60, 61, 68, 69, 77, 80, 82, 83, 88, 89, 92, 95, 95, 96, 102, 102, 102, 105, 108, 111, 113, 116, 119, 119, 120, 123, 125, 125, 126, 126, 129, 130, 133, 138, 143, 144, 146, 149, 152, 157, 159, 170, 175, 184, 184, 200, 201, 206, 219, 224, 227, 231, 233, 235 Virt 21, 29, 30, 30, 35, 37, 43, 51, 57, 61, 74, 74, 76, 79, 82, 86, 88, 88, 90, 91, 93, 94, 103, 103, 103, 103, 104, 108, 108, 110, 111, 112, 115, 120, 121, 141, 143, 146, 151, 152, 153, 153, 160, 161, 162, 162, 162, 167, 167, 167, 171, 173, 173, 173, 173, 173, 174, 175, 178, 181, 183, 186, 187, 208, 210, 210, 216, 216, 217, 218, 218, 225, 226 Praem 1, 1, 9, 11, 12, 12, 13, 13, 14, 18, 21, 21, 26, 30, 31, 31, 32, 40, 43, 44, 48, 51, 53, 56, 61, 63, 64, 72, 72, 76, 80, 84, 86, 87, 89, 89, 91, 92, 94, 95, 98, 100, 102, 105, 109, 112, 113, 127, 140, 148, 151, 169 Prob 1, 11, 14, 21, 22, 22, 28, 39, 40, 43, 54, 59, 61, 61, 63, 69, 71, 73, 76, 79, 79, 80, 80, 87, 94, 100, 101, 101, 101, 105, 116, 117, 117, 119, 123, 124, 132, 133, 133, 137, 146, 148, 150, 154, 157, 157 Contempl 17, 26, 35, 35, 37, 40, 43, 45, 50, 52, 52, 55, 57, 64, 71, 74, 75, 79 Aet 4, 6, 10, 11, 26, 31, 32, 37, 39, 56, 61, 66, 68, 69, 69, 72, 74, 76, 79, 80, 80, 88, 90, 90, 90, 94, 95, 102, 103, 105, 119, 120, 128, 130 Flacc 3, 6, 8, 9, 10, 11, 12, 12, 12, 14, 14, 20, 24, 26, 38, 38, 38, 38, 43, 43, 43, 43, 49, 54, 56, 56, 57, 59, 64, 72, 75, 86, 88, 95, 96, 100, 102, 103, 103, 112, 121, 127, 128, 131, 139, 140, 141, 141, 142, 143, 144, 146, 148, 149, 162, 164, 165, 180, 181, 189 Legat 9, 9, 9, 10, 11, 13, 24, 30, 31, 33, 36, 39, 40, 41, 46, 55, 59, 63, 66, 77, 88, 89, 95, 109, 109, 112, 114, 115, 119, 121, 121, 122, 128, 131, 133, 135, 144, 150, 161, 161, 161, 165, 169, 169, 175, 177, 177, 191, 192, 193, 194, 201, 203, 204, 204, 204, 207, 208, 208, 211, 211, 213, 214, 215, 215, 217, 219, 223, 227, 229, 229, 233, 238, 243, 244, 245, 250, 251, 253, 255, 262, 268, 270, 278, 292, 304, 312, 315, 320, 329, 336, 339, 342, 343, 343, 344, 352, 352, 356, 358, 359, 361, 362, 362, 364, 368, 368 Hypoth 0:1, 6:1, 6:4, 6:4, 6:7, 6:7, 6:8, 7:2, 7:3, 7:5, 7:10, 7:11, 7:19, 11:11, 11:12 Prov 1, 1, 1, 1, 2:5, 7, 9, 13, 20, 23, 24, 26, 28, 40, 42, 43, 59, 59, 60, 61, 61, 62, 65, 66 QG 1:3, 17b, 28, 28, 28, 41, 55a, 55a, 55a, 55a, 58, 58, 58, 65, 65, 66, 66, 68, 96:1, 96:1, 100:1a, 100:1c, 100:2a, 100:2b, 2:11, 12a, 12b, 22, 26b, 29, 54a, 54a, 54a, 54a, 54a, 54a, 54a, 54a, 54a, 54d, 54d, 59, 62, 64a, 65, 65, 68a, 3:29, 38a, 38b, 48, 49b, 52, 52, 4:20, 51b, 51c, 64, 69, 104, 145, 153, 172, 180, 180, 202b, 203, 206a, 227 QG isf 3, 5, 9, 10, 10, 13 QG (Par) 2:1, 2:2, 2:3, 2:3, 2:3, 2:4, 2:5, 2:5 QE 1:6, 2:6a, 6b, 9b, 13a, 17, 17, 18, 21, 25a, 38a, 45a, 45a, 45b, 49b, 107 QE isf 1, 6, 7, 16, 22, 24, 32

ὡσανεί (50) Opif 72 Leg 1:40, 75, 94 Leg 3:28, 96, 136, 145 Plant 77, 149 Ebr 11, 97 Sobr 65 Conf 115, 144, 149, 190 Her 15, 23, 43, 115, 116, 134, 293, 295 Fug 134 Mut 28, 123, 164 Somn 1:128, 146 Somn 2:32, 170, 242 Abr 116 Mos 1:147 Mos 2:82, 92, 95, 106, 113, 114, 182, 191, 243 Decal 23 Aet 50, 50 QG 2:34a QE 2:6a

ὡσαύτως (16) Opif 54 Leg 1:8 Leg 3:99 Cher 23, 51 Gig 50 Plant 49 Conf 106 Her 87, 149 Mut 87 Somn 2:220 Praem 15, 29 Hypoth 7:11, 7:15

ὡσεί (13) Leg 2:94 Leg 3:169, 169, 170, 172 Post 67 Agr 44 Conf 96 Her 20, 251 Somn 2:94 Spec 4:128 QG 2:54c

Ὡσηέ Mut 121, 121

ὥσπερ (580) Opif 18, 43, 55, 71, 73, 73, 73, 76, 77, 132, 140, 168 Leg 1:5, 22, 25, 39, 46, 71, 73, 82, 82, 87, 91, 94, 100 Leg 2:6, 10, 13, 15, 18, 19, 33, 34, 37, 38, 60, 67, 74, 97 Leg 3:10, 33, 40, 62, 75, 77, 80, 86, 94, 96, 98, 99, 102, 105, 107, 113, 115, 115, 140, 155,

158, 160, 168, 177, 182, 183, 198, 201, 201, 203, 213, 223, 239 Cher 61, 62, 68, 70, 73, 79, 94, 120, 122 Sacr 8, 25, 36, 37, 39, 41, 60, 62, 64, 64, 66, 72, 85, 90, 95, 102, 105, 106, 109, 115, 123, 125, 126 Det 15, 18, 33, 44, 52, 58, 75, 123, 126, 129, 144, 151, 162, 177, 178 Post 7, 22, 27, 40, 57, 65, 90, 100, 104, 106, 108, 111, 116, 124, 125, 126, 130, 131, 131, 134, 149, 153, 163, 164, 173, 177, 178 Gig 13, 16, 25, 39, 67 Deus 19, 24, 37, 39, 43, 47, 50, 57, 79, 84, 85, 91, 93, 98, 102, 102, 103, 124, 130, 131, 135, 136, 150, 172, 175, 177 Agr 1, 16, 30, 36, 40, 48, 78, 85, 97, 132, 160, 167, 177 Plant 5, 10, 16, 28, 35, 76, 80, 83, 115, 144, 145, 154, 173 Ebr 8, 12, 23, 29, 44, 69, 79, 79, 94, 94, 95, 95, 101, 139, 147, 166, 222 Sobr 26, 39, 43, 53 Conf 3, 17, 19, 22, 38, 48, 55, 66, 76, 85, 111, 153, 172, 184, 185, 191 Migr 4, 9, 16, 32, 39, 60, 65, 69, 86, 87, 90, 93, 104, 108, 112, 117, 122, 136, 148, 167, 168, 178, 192 Her 12, 41, 46, 67, 69, 109, 109, 120, 136, 180, 229, 244, 246, 269 Congr 10, 53, 53, 54, 79, 79, 90, 101, 113, 124, 127, 143, 150, 164, 176 Fug 146, 182, 183, 189, 192, 192, 193 Mut 69, 114, 143, 157, 163, 170, 193, 198, 237 Somn 1:10, 42, 69, 77, 77, 80, 107, 108, 110, 124, 139, 140, 147, 192 Somn 2:6, 12, 20, 83, 102, 111, 120, 132, 144, 145, 160, 170, 201, 206, 211, 213, 213, 216, 237, 242, 246, 256, 272, 292, 294 Abr 26, 70, 72, 135, 136, 150, 157, 165, 171, 184, 198, 246, 256, 275 Ios 6, 23, 33, 60, 83, 97, 98, 107, 141, 143, 166, 194, 239 Mos 1:22, 25, 30, 42, 95, 106, 110, 115, 119, 148, 150, 187, 189, 191, 194, 217, 222, 255, 270, 277, 283, 285 Mos 2:14, 22, 37, 58, 63, 66, 68, 103, 151, 161, 171, 181, 222, 228, 250, 255, 289 Decal 67, 74, 146, 150, 177 Spec 1:28, 68, 84, 109, 122, 131, 225, 282, 300, 333 Spec 2:20, 29, 110, 119, 129, 152, 231, 237, 259 Spec 3:2, 43, 51, 87, 91, 111, 131, 138, 145, 178, 184, 199 Spec 4:56, 75, 79, 85, 105, 125, 133, 140, 178, 236 Virt 4, 10, 13, 34, 41, 49, 49, 51, 66, 95, 118, 120, 124, 125, 151, 158, 169, 180 Praem 4, 8, 41, 73, 82, 106, 110, 114, 115, 129, 135, 151, 164 Prob 14, 15, 18, 45, 51, 57, 62, 69, 106, 118, 131, 151, 155 Contempl 19, 24, 31, 34, 35, 36, 41, 45, 78 Aet 5, 6, 50, 51, 51, 55, 58, 62, 67, 85, 89, 112 Flacc 1, 19, 72, 127, 138, 157, 159, 160, 169, 175, 180 Legat 9, 20, 52, 79, 101, 108, 110, 111, 117, 122, 143, 206, 223, 225, 226 Hypoth 6:2, 6:4, 7:4, 7:15, 7:18, 11:15 Prov 2:32, 38, 40, 44, 52, 55 QG 1:20, 76b, 2:31, 41, 48, 54d, 72, 4:33b, 76b, 88, 174, 204, 204 QG isf 1, 3 QE 2:26, 47 QE isf 25

ὡσπερεί Conf 162 Spec 1:340

ὥστε (293) Opif 23, 99 Leg 1:2, 7, 17, 29, 36, 40, 53, 62, 79, 90 Leg 2:1, 12, 34, 45, 45, 61, 61, 64, 105 Leg 3:4, 33, 50, 86, 110, 113, 115, 128, 141, 149, 185, 200, 204, 207, 219 Cher 46, 56, 90 Sacr 28, 51, 54, 57, 83, 93, 97, 101, 116, 119, 128, 130, 133 Det 47, 48, 54, 56, 56, 65, 66, 70, 87, 107, 124, 130, 139, 163, 167 Post 3, 4, 13, 19, 23, 30, 36, 54, 65, 70, 88, 94, 95, 102, 122, 156, 176 Gig 23, 35, 47, 53 Deus 6, 15, 28, 31, 32, 49, 54, 108, 142 Agr 41, 50, 68, 71, 99, 112, 146, 167, 173 Plant 6, 19, 62, 69, 72, 76, 96, 122, 132, 141, 154, 166, 172, 174 Ebr 16, 42, 123, 188, 205 Sobr 49 Conf 11, 12, 38, 116, 178, 192, 198 Migr 49, 110, 129, 130, 193, 203, 222 Her 16, 19, 23, 57, 83, 89, 96, 108, 118, 145, 155, 193, 219, 231, 236, 239, 259, 273 Congr 21, 23, 62, 66, 83, 87, 156, 160, 168, 175, 177 Fug 64, 76, 101, 113 Mut 6, 14, 15, 28, 29, 52, 152, 242, 255, 261 Somn 1:24, 135, 144, 170, 203, 238, 251 Somn 2:63, 82, 116, 116, 117, 157, 174, 210, 223, 250, 258 Abr 31 Ios 12, 31, 250, 258 Mos 1:118, 136, 234, 270 Mos 2:51, 79, 266 Decal 44 Spec 1:20, 58, 105, 166, 193, 230, 260 Spec 2:6, 71, 86, 87, 177, 182 Spec 3:20, 46, 63, 77, 86, 100, 118, 209 Spec 4:48, 77, 104, 114, 202, 205, 226 Virt 18, 86, 92, 144 Praem 134 Prob 36, 41, 50, 59, 61, 121, 130, 131 Contempl 29, 37, 37 Aet 28, 41, 43, 47, 52, 65, 69, 71, 93, 99, 107, 116, 131 Flacc 181 Legat 52, 93, 108, 135, 157, 163, 163, 181, 237, 283 Hypoth 11:18 Prov 2:64 QG 1:32, 60:2, 100:2b, 2:12b, 4:184, 228 QE 2:21 QE isf 16, 30

ὠτακουστέω Mos 1:169

ὠφέλεια (119) Opif 56, 61, 135 Leg 3:221 Cher 15 Sacr 31, 70, 71 Det 108, 134 Post 4, 137 Agr 9 Plant 170 Ebr 106, 184 Conf 10, 135, 162, 195 Migr 57, 121, 172, 172 Her 109, 223, 252 Congr 32, 53, 120, 167 Mut 52, 72, 85, 126, 150, 173, 202, 246 Somn 1:111, 165, 176, 191, 238 Somn 2:92, 301 Abr 65, 156 Ios 139, 157, 259 Mos 1:49, 63, 117, 151, 313, 315 Mos 2:7, 148 Decal 167 Spec 1:195, 224, 298, 298, 320, 323, 340, 340, 342, 343 Spec 2:3, 16, 78, 131, 141, 143, 144, 236, 240 Spec 3:103, 157, 185 Spec 4:2, 5, 11, 13, 67, 75, 206 Virt 37, 152, 218 Praem 97, 105, 114 Prob 86, 139 Aet 63 Legat 63, 68, 98, 109, 345 Hypoth 11:4 Prov 2:43, 44, 44, 49, 60, 65 QG 1:74, 2:54a, 4:172, 191b, 204, 227 QE 2:11a, 25c, 25d

ὠφελέω (97) Leg 1:34, 97 Leg 2:8 Leg 3:86 Cher 121 Sacr 69, 92, 92 Det 54, 55, 55, 55, 56, 61, 74, 109, 134, 142 Post 67, 140, 143, 144, 145, 151, 181 Gig 27, 43 Deus 61, 64, 87, 113 Plant 72, 101 Ebr 18, 106, 160 Conf 48, 159 Migr 42, 57, 88, 104, 219 Her 178 Congr 5, 44, 66, 71, 88 Fug 201 Mut 14, 217 Somn 1:91, 162, 191 Somn 2:59, 198, 239, 240 Abr 102 Ios 85, 216 Mos 1:20, 22, 40 Mos 2:36, 128 Decal 114 Spec 1:214, 216, 252, 320, 336 Spec 2:74, 114, 137, 230, 260 Spec 4:65, 93, 186, 228 Virt 118, 210, 226 Prob 76 Contempl 16 Legat 46, 60, 245, 245 Prov 2:71 QG 3:8, 26, 4:69 QE 2:11a, 18

ὠφέλημα Mut 26

ὠφελητικός Opif 64 Leg 3:170 QG 4:172 QE 2:18

ὠφέλιμος (89) Opif 9, 10, 78, 156 Leg 1:14 Leg 3:76, 99, 104, 122 Cher 93 Sacr 78, 98, 109 Det 55, 72, 104, 114 Post 95, 142 Deus 64, 120 Agr 9, 11, 41, 121, 133, 142 Plant 29, 72, 100, 106, 161 Ebr 26, 39, 187 Sobr 2, 23, 28 Conf 13, 164, 182 Migr 31, 147, 164 Her 18 Congr 5, 157, 157, 175 Fug 94 Mut 22, 193 Somn 2:22, 134, 150, 264 Abr 24 Ios 116, 143 Mos 1:146, 222, 227 Decal 77 Spec 1:155, 173, 264, 303 Spec 2:18, 166, 171, 180, 189 Spec 4:43, 112, 181, 228 Virt 25, 154 Praem 8, 27 Contempl 56 Legat 49, 81, 82, 287 Prov 2:37, 51 QG 3:30a QE isf 7

ὠχρός (6) Leg 1:84 Leg 3:57 Det 34 Ebr 173 Mut 33 Legat 266